BAKER'S
BIOGRAPHICAL DICTIONARY OF
MUSICIANS

CREDITS

Laura Kuhn
Classical Editor

Dennis McIntire
Associate Classical Editor

Lewis Porter
Jazz Editor

William Ruhlmann
Pop Editor

Key to Contributors

AB	Andrew Barlett
AG	Andrew Gilbert
BH	Brock Helander
BJH	B. J. Huchtemann
BM	Bill Moody
BP	Bret Primack
BR	Bryan Reesman
BW	Bill Wahl
CH	Chris Hovan
DB	Dan Bindert
DCG	David C. Gross
DD	David Demsey
DDD	Dean D. Dauphinais
DK	Dan Keener
DM	Dennis McIntire
DO	David Okamoto
DPe	Damon Percy
DPr	David Prince
DR	Dennis Rea
ED	Eric Deggans
EH	Ed Hazell
EJL	Eric J. Lawrence
ETA	E. Taylor Atkins
GB	Greg Baise
GBr	Gig Brown
GJ	Gregg Juke
GK	Gregory Kiewiet
GM	Garaud MacTaggart
HB	Hank Bordowitz
JB	Joshua Berrett
JC	John Chilton, *Who's Who of Jazz*
JC-B	John Chilton, *Who's Who of British Jazz*
JE	James Eason
JM	Jeff McMillan
JO	Jim O'Rourke
JTB	John T. Bitter
LK	Laura Kuhn
LP	Lewis Porter
MF	Michael Fitzgerald
MM	*Music Master Jazz and Blues Catalogue*
MS	Matthew Snyder
NAL	Nancy Ann Lee
NC	Norene Cashen
NS	Nicolas Slonimsky
PK	Peter Keepnews
PM	Patricia Myers
PMac	Paul MacArthur
RB	Ralph Burnett
RC	Richard Carlin
RI	Robert Iannapolto
SC	Safford Chamberlain
SH	Steve Holtje
SKB	Susan K. Berlowitz
SP	Sam Prestianni
TP	Ted Panken
TS	Tom Smith
WB	Will Bickart
WF	Walter Faber
WKH	W. Kim Heron
WR	William Ruhlmann

BAKER'S
BIOGRAPHICAL DICTIONARY OF
MUSICIANS

VOLUME 6

STRE - ZYLI

Centennial Edition

NICOLAS SLONIMSKY

Editor Emeritus

LAURA KUHN

Baker's Series Advisory Editor

Schirmer Books

an imprint of the Gale Group

New York • Detroit • San Francisco • London • Boston • Woodbridge, CT

Schirmer Books
1633 Broadway
New York, New York 10019

Gale Group
27500 Drake Road
Farmington Hills, Michigan 48331-3535

Library of Congress Catalog Card Number: 00-046375

Printed in the United States of America

Printing number
1 2 3 4 5 6 7 8 9 10

Library of Congress Cataloging-in-Publication Data

Baker's biographical dictionary of musicians.—Centennial ed. / Nicolas Slonimsky, editor emeritus.
p. cm.
Includes bibliographical references and discographies.
Enl. ed. of: Baker's biographical dictionary of musicians. 8th ed. / rev. by Nicolas Slonimsky.
ISBN 0-02-865525-7 (set : alk. paper) — ISBN 0-02- 865526-5 (vol. 1) — ISBN 0-02-865527-3 (vol. 2) — ISBN 0-02-865528-1 (vol. 3) — ISBN 0-02-865529-X (vol. 4) — ISBN 0-02-865530-3 (vol. 5) — ISBN 0-02-865571-0 (vol. 6)
1. Music—Bio-bibliography—Dictionaries. I. Slonimsky, Nicolas, 1894- II. Slonimsky, Nicolas, 1894- Baker's biographical dictionary of musicians.

ML105.B16 2000
780'.92'2—dc21
[B]

00-046375

ABBREVIATIONS

A.B.	Bachelor of Arts
ABC	American Broadcasting Company
A.M.	Master of Arts
ASCAP	American Society of Composers, Authors, and Publishers
assn./Assn.	association/Association
assoc.	associate
aug.	augmented
b.	born
B.A.	Bachelor of Arts
bar.	baritone
BBC	British Broadcasting Corporation
bjo.	banjo
B.M.	Bachelor of Music
brs.	brass
bs.	bass
CBC	Canadian Broadcasting Corporation
CBS	Columbia Broadcasting System
Coll.	College
cons./Cons.	conservatory/Conservatory
d.	died
dept./Dept.	department/Department
diss.	dissertation
D.M.A.	Doctor of Musical Arts
drm.	drums
ed(s).	edit(ed), editor(s), edition(s)
enl.	enlarged
f.	formed
flt.	flute
gtr.	guitar
har.	harmonica
H.S.	High School
IRCAM	Institut de Recherche et de Coordination Acoustique/Musique
ISCM	International Society for Contemporary Music
inst./Inst.	institute/Institute

kybd.	keyboards
M.A.	Master of Arts
mdln.	mandolin
M.M.	Master of Music
MS(S)	manuscript(s)
Mus.B.	Bachelor of Music
Mus.D.	Doctor of Music
Mus.M.	Master of Music
NAACP	National Association for the Advancement of Colored People
NBC	National Broadcasting Company
n.d.	no date
NEA	National Endowment for the Arts
NHK	Japan Broadcasting Company
no(s).	number(s)
N.Y.	New York
org.	organ
op(p).	opus
orch./Orch.	orchestra/Orchestra
p(p).	page(s)
PBS	Public Broadcasting Service
perc.	percussion
perf.	performance
Ph.D.	Doctor of Philosophy
phil./Phil.	philharmonic/Philharmonic
pno.	piano
posth.	posthumously
prof.	professor
publ.	publish(ed)
RAI	Radiotelevisione Italiana
rds.	reeds
rec.	recorded
rel.	released
rev.	revised
RIAS	Radio in the American Sector
S.	San, Santo, Santa
sax.	saxophone
sop.	soprano
Ss.	Santi, Sante
St(e).	Saint(e)
sym(s).	symphony (-ies)
synth.	synthesizer
tamb.	tamborine
ten.	tenor
tr.	translate(d), translation
trmb.	trombone
trpt.	trumpet
univ./Univ.	university/University
vln.	violin
voc.	vocals
vol(s).	volume(s)
WDR	Westdeutscher Rundfunk (West German Radio)
wdwnd.	woodwinds

S

(CONTINUED)

Street, Tison, American composer; b. Boston, May 20, 1943. He studied violin with Einer Hansen in Boston (1951–59) and composition with Kirchner and Del Tredici at Harvard Univ. (B.A., 1965; M.A., 1971). He was a composer-in-residence at the Marlboro Music Festival (1964, 1965, 1966, 1972) and a visiting lecturer at the Univ. of Calif., Berkeley (1971–72); taught at Harvard Univ. (1979–82). He was the recipient of an award from the National Inst. of the American Academy of Arts and Letters (1973), the Rome Prize Fellowship (1973), and grants from the NEA (1978) and the Guggenheim Foundation (1981).

WORKS: ORCH.: *Adagio in E-flat* for Oboe and Strings (1977); *Montsalvat* for Orch. (1980); *Variations on a Ground* for Organ and Orch. (1981). **CHAMBER:** String Trio (1963); *Variations* for Flute, Guitar, and Cello (1964); String Quartet (1972); String Quintet (1974; rev. 1976); *Piano Phantasy* (1975); *3 Pieces* for consort of Viols and Harpsichord (1977); *John Major's Medley* for Guitar (1977); *Arias* for Violin and Piano (1978). **Piano:** *Romanza* (1989). **VOCAL:** *6 Odds and Ends from "So Much Depends"* for Voices and Diverse Instruments (1964–73). **—NS/LK/DM**

Strehler, Giorgio, Italian opera director; b. Trieste, Aug. 14, 1921; d. Lugano, Dec. 25, 1997. He studied at the Accademia di Filodrammatici in Milan. In 1940 he launched an acting career and in 1943 directed his first theater production. With Paolo Grassi, he founded the Piccolo Teatro in Milan in 1947, the same year he staged his first opera, *La Traviata*. In 1955 he helped organize the Piccola Scala in Milan, where he was regularly engaged as an opera director; also worked at Milan's La Scala. In 1956 he staged a remarkable production of *Die Dreigroschenoper* at the Piccola Scala, winning the praise of Brecht. Strehler first gained wide notice outside Italy with his production of *Die Entführung aus dem Serail* at the Salzburg Festival in 1965. While he continued to work regularly in Milan, he became closely associated with the Théâtre de l'Europe at the Odéon in Paris. Strehler's background as an actor was instrumental in forging his vision of the serious and comic elements of theatrical scores; his productions of Mozart and Verdi were particularly acclaimed. Conversations on his works with the drama critic Ugo Ronfani were publ. as *Io, Strehler* (Milan, 1986).

BIBL.: F. Battistini, *G. S.* (Rome, 1980).**—NS/LK/DM**

Streich, Rita, noted German soprano; b. Barnaul, Russia, Dec. 18, 1920; d. Vienna, March 20, 1987. She studied with Erna Berger, Maria Ivogün, and Willi Domgraf-Fassbänder. She made her operatic debut as Zerbinetta in Aussig in 1943; from 1946 she sang with the Berlin State Opera; in 1951 she joined the Berlin Städtische Oper. She also appeared in Vienna, Bayreuth, Salzburg, and Glyndebourne; made her U.S. debut as Zerbinetta with the San Francisco Opera in 1957. In 1974 she became a prof. at the Folkwang-Hochschule in Essen. She was a leading interpreter of parts in Mozart operas.**—NS/LK/DM**

Streicher, Johann Andreas, German-born Austrian pianist, teacher, piano maker, and composer; b. Stuttgart, Dec. 13, 1761; d. Vienna, May 25, 1833. During a stay in Augsburg in 1793, he married Nannette (Maria Anna) Stein (b. Augsburg, Jan. 2, 1769; d. Vienna, Jan. 16, 1835), daughter of the piano maker Johann Andreas Stein, and then moved the business to Vienna; later it became known as Nannette Streicher geb. Stein und Sohn when their son, Johann Baptist Streicher (b. Vienna, Jan. 3, 1796; d. there, March 28, 1871), entered the business; following his parents' death, he took complete control of the firm. He invented the piano action in which the hammer strikes from above. He was on friendly terms with Beethoven. In 1857 Streicher's son, Emil (1836–1916), became his partner; the business was dissolved when the latter retired. His son, Theodor (b. Vienna, June 7, 1874; d. Wetzelsdorf, near Graz, May 28,

1940), was a composer. He studied elocution with Ferdinand Gregori, counterpoint and composition with Heinrich Schulz-Beuthen, voice with Ferdiana Jager, and piano and instrumentation with Ferdinand Löwe (1895–1900). He attracted wide notice as a song composer with his *30 Lieder aus Des Knaben Wunderhorn* (1903); he wrote numerous other songs in a Romantic vein, but he was unable to sustain his early success; he also composed choral pieces and a String Sextet (1911).

BIBL.: P. Klanert, *Theodore S. in seinen Liedern* (Leipzig, 1911); T. Bolte, *Die Musiker-Familien Stein und S.* (Vienna, 1917); R. Wursten, *Theodor S.: His Life and Music* (diss., Univ. of Wisc., 1977).—**NS/LK/DM**

Streisand, Barbra, b. Brooklyn, N.Y., April 24, 1942. Had she only been an actress or filmmaker, Streisand still would have been one of the most successful entertainers of the past four decades. But it is her singing, her voice, that is most unique and influential. She has recorded everything from classical to show tunes and torch songs to rock and disco, and is the top-selling female recording artist in the world. After graduating early from high school, she won a singing contest at a Manhattan club and soon developed her own nightclub act. Her Broadway career began with 1962's *I Can Get It for You Wholesale*; a year later, she landed a recording contract with Columbia. She eschewed frequent touring in favor of more work on Broadway (including 1964's *Funny Girl,* the 1967 movie adaptation of which earned her an Oscar) and television specials (which in turn spawned albums). Continuing to act in musicals, comedies, and dramas throughout the 1960s and 1970s, her film work eventually included producing (starting with 1977's *A Star Is Born*) and directing (1983's *Yentl* marked her debut). Some 35 years after catching the world's attention with The Voice, and despite frequent accounts of prima donna behavior, Streisand continues to mine success in concert, on record, and on film.

DISC: *I Can Get It for You Wholesale* (Broadway cast recording; 1962); *Pins and Needles* (1962); *The Second Barbra Streisand Album* (1963); *The Barbra Streisand Album* (1963); *The Third Album* (1964); *People* (1964); *Funny Girl* (Broadway cast recording; 1964); *My Name Is Barbra* (1965); *My Name Is Barbra, Two* (1965); *Color Me Barbra* (1966); *Je M'Appelle Barbra* (1966); *Simply Streisand* (1967); *A Christmas Album* (1967); *A Happening in Central Park* (1968); *Funny Girl* (soundtrack; 1968); *What about Today?* (1969); *Hello, Dolly!* (soundtrack; 1969); *Barbra Streisand's Greatest Hits* (1969); *On a Clear Day You Can See Forever* (soundtrack; 1970); *Barbra Joan Streisand* (1971); *Stoney End* (1971); *Live Concert at the Forum* (1972); *Barbra Streisand...and Other Musical Instruments* (1973); *The Way We Were* (1974); *The Way We Were* (soundtrack; 1974); *Butterfly* (1974); *Funny Lady* (soundtrack; 1975); *Lazy Afternoon* (1975); *Classical Barbra* (1976); *A Star Is Born* (soundtrack; 1976); *Streisand Superman* (1977); *Songbird* (1978); *The Main Event—Music from the Original Motion Picture Soundtrack* (1979); *Barbra Streisand's Greatest Hits, Vol. 2* (1978); *Wet* (1979); *Guilty* (1980); *Memories* (1981); *Yentl* (soundtrack; 1983); *Emotion* (1984); *The Broadway Album* (1985); *One Voice* (1987); *Till I Loved You* (1988); *A Collection: Greatest Hits...and More* (1989); *Just for the Record* (1991); *The Prince of Tides* (soundtrack; 1991); *Highlights from Just for the Record* (1992); *Back to Broadway* (1993); *The Concert* (1994); *The Concert—Highlights* (1995); *The Mirror Has Two Faces—Music from the Motion Picture* (1996); *Higher Ground* (1997); *A Love Like Ours* (1999); *Timeless: Live in Concert* (2000).

Strens, Jules, Belgian organist and composer; b. Ixelles, near Brussels, Dec. 5, 1892; d. there, March 19, 1971. He studied with Gilson. In 1925 was one of 8 founders of the Group des Synthétistes (all Gilson pupils), endeavoring to establish a modern style of composition within the formal categories of early music; was active mainly as an organist.

WORKS: DRAMATIC: Opera: *Le Chanteur de Naples* (1937); *La Tragédie d'Agamemnon* (1941). **ORCH.:** *Gil Blas,* symphonic variations (1921); *Les Elfes,* symphonic poem (1923); *Danse funambulesque* (1925); *Rapsodie tzigane* (1927); *Fantaise concertante* for Piano and Orch. (1938); *Symphonie Sylvestre* for Soloists, Chorus, and Orch. (1939); Violin Concerto (1951); Concerto for Organ and Strings (1958). **CHAMBER:** Piano Trio (1920); 4 string quartets (1925, 1929, 1933, 1935); Cello Sonata (1926); String Sextet (1935); Wind Quintet (1943); Quartet for 4 Horns (1950); *Suite* for 4 Horns (1951); Viola Sonata (1954); Trio for Oboe, Clarinet, and Bassoon (1954); Piano Quartet (1955); also piano pieces; organ pieces. **VOCAL:** Songs.—**NS/LK/DM**

Strepponi, Giuseppina (actually, **Clelia Maria Josepha**), prominent Italian soprano, second wife of **Giuseppe Verdi;** b. Lodi, Sept. 8, 1815; d. Sant' Agata, near Busseto, Nov. 14, 1897. She was the daughter of Felician Strepponi (1797–1832), organist at Monza Cathedral and a composer of operas. She studied piano and singing at the Milan Cons. (1830–34), taking first prize for bel canto. After making her operatic debut in *Adria* (Dec. 1834), she scored her first success in Rossini's *Matilda di Shabran* in Trieste (1835); that same year she sang Adalgisa and the heroine in *La Sonnambula* in Vienna, the latter role becoming one of her most celebrated portrayals. She subsequently toured widely with the tenor Napoleone Moriani, who became her lover. In 1839 she made her debut at Milan's La Scala; created Donizetti's Adelia in Rome in 1841; returning to La Scala, she created Verdi's Abigaille on March 9, 1842, but by then her vocal powers were in decline. All the same, she continued to sing in Verdi's operas, having become a favorite of the composer. In 1846 she retired from the opera stage. From 1847 she lived with Verdi, becoming his wife in 1859.

BIBL.: M. Mundula, *La Moglie di Verdi: G. S.* (Milan, 1938); G. Servadio, *Traviata: Vita di G. S.* (Milan, 1994).—**NS/LK/DM**

Stresemann, Wolfgang, German conductor and orchestral Intendant; b. Dresden, July 20, 1904; d. Berlin, Nov. 6, 1998. His father, Gustav Stresemann, was the distinguished chancellor and foreign minister of the Weimar Republic. He was educated in Berlin, Heidelberg, and Erlangen (Dr.Jur., 1928), and also studied music in Berlin. After the Nazis came to power (1933), he left Germany and eventually settled in the U.S. He served as asst. conductor of the National Orch. Assn. in N.Y. (1939–45), and then conducted the Toledo (Ohio) Orch. (1949–55). He returned to Germany and held the post of Intendant of the (West) Berlin Radio Sym. Orch.

(1956–59). In 1959 he assumed the prestigious post of Intendant of the Berlin Phil., with Herbert von Karajan as its artistic director. He retired in 1978, only to be recalled to his post in 1984 during the so-called Karajan affair, when the chief conductor and the musicians of the orch. locked horns in a bitter artistic dispute. After serving as mediator, Stresemann continued as Intendant until retiring for a second time in 1986. He wrote an informative history of the Berlin Phil., *The Berlin Philharmonic from Bülow to Karajan: Home and History of a World-Famous Orchestra* (in Ger. and Eng.; Berlin, 1979), and likewise publ. *Eine Lanze für Felix Mendelssohn* (Berlin, 1984), *Ein seltsamer Mann: Erinnerungen an Herbert von Karajan* (Frankfurt am Main, 1991), and *Zeiten und Klänge: Ein Leben zwischen Musik und Politik* (Frankfurt am Main, 1994). He also composed some orch. music and songs.—**NS/LK/DM**

Strickland, Lily (Teresa), American composer; b. Anderson, S.C., Jan. 28, 1887; d. Hendersonville, N.C., June 6, 1958. She studied at Converse Coll. in Spartanburg, S.C. (1901–4) and then with Albert Mildenberg, William Henry Humiston, Daniel Gregory Mason, and Percy Goetschius at the Inst. of Musical Art in N.Y.; also received private lessons from Alfred John Goodrich. She married J. Courtney Anderson of N.Y. in 1912; traveled in the Orient between 1920 and 1930, and spent several years in India; then returned to the U.S. Among her works were several operettas, including *Jewel of the Desert* (1933) and *Laughing Star of Zuni* (1946), orch. suites, the sacred cantata *St. John the Beloved* (1930), many piano suites, and numerous songs.

Bibl.: A. Howe, *L. S.: Her Contribution to American Music in the Early Twentieth Century* (diss., Catholic Univ. of America, 1968).—**NS/LK/DM**

Strickland, William, American conductor; b. Defiance, Ohio, Jan. 25, 1914; d. Westport, Conn., Nov. 17, 1991. He attended the choir school of the Cathedral of St. John the Divine in N.Y. He was founder-conductor of the National Youth Administration Sinfonietta in N.Y. (1940–41), and then of the Nashville (Tenn.) Sym. Orch. (1946–51). After serving as conductor of the Oratorio Soc. of N.Y. (1955–59), he toured as a guest conductor in the U.S. and abroad as an advocate of American music.—**NS/LK/DM**

Striggio, Alessandro, eminent Italian instrumentalist and composer; b. Mantua, c. 1540; d. there, Feb. 29, 1592. By the 1560s he was the major composer at the court of Cosimo I de' Medici, Duke of Florence; in 1584 he was active at the court of Alfonso II d'Este in Ferrara, but that same year went to Mantua as court composer; all the same, he remained associated with the courts in Ferrara and Florence until his death; also wrote works for the Munich court. His importance rests upon his music for intermedi, stage works, and madrigals, including the 3 musical intermezzi *Psiche ed Amore* (1565). He publ. several books of madrigals and *Il cicalamento delle donne* (1567; descriptive songs in the manner of Janequin); many compositions by Striggio are found in collections of the period. His son, Alessandro, known as Alessandrino (b. Mantua, c. 1573; d. Venice, June 15, 1630), was a librettist, musician, diplomat, and nobleman. He studied law in Mantua and then was a diplomat in the service of the Gonzaga family there; was made secretary to Duke Vincenzo I in 1611 and later was ambassador to Milan; died of the plague while on a diplomatic mission to Venice. He wrote the librettos to Monteverdi's *Orfeo* (Mantua, 1607), *Lamento d'Apollo* (not extant), and probably *Tirsi e Clori* (1615).

Bibl.: R. Tadlock, *The Early Madrigals of A. S.* (diss., Univ. of Rochester, 1958).—**NS/LK/DM**

Stringfield, Lamar (Edwin), American flutist, conductor, and composer; b. Raleigh, N.C., Oct. 10, 1897; d. Asheville, N.C., Jan. 21, 1959. He served in the U.S. Army during World War I; after the Armistice, he studied theory with Goetschius and flute with Barrère at the Inst. of Musical Art in N.Y.; also took lessons in conducting with Chalmers Clifton. In 1930 he organized the Inst. of Folk Music at the Univ. of N.C., and conducted its orch.; was conductor of the Knoxville (Tenn.) Sym. Orch. (1946–47), then of the Charlotte Sym. Orch. (1948–49). The source material of his compositions is largely derived from the folk songs of the U.S. South. He learned the trade of printing and was able to publ. his own works. He wrote *America and Her Music* (Chapel Hill, 1931) and a *Guide for Young Flutists* (MS, c. 1945; included in the Nelson diss. listed in the bibliography below).

Works: DRAMATIC: *The 7th Queue*, ballet (1928); *The Mountain Song*, opera (1929); *Carolina Charcoal*, musical folk comedy (1951–53). ORCH.: *The Desert Wanderer*, overture for Band (1921); *Tango* for Small Orch. (1921); *Valse triste* (1921); *Mountain Suite* for Band (1922); *Indian Legend* (1923); *Asheville Kiwana's March* for Band (1924); *Squaw Dance* (1925); *From the Southern Mountains* (1927); *From a Negro Melody* for Chamber Orch. (1928); *At the Factory*, symphonic fantasy (1929); *Negro Parade* (1931); *The Legend of John henry*, symphonic ballad (1932); *Moods of a Moonshiner* (1934); *From the Blue Ridge*, symphonic sketches (1936); *Peace*, symphonic poem (1942); *Mountain Dawn* for Flute and Strings (1945); *Georgia Buck* for Band (1949). CHAMBER: *Mountain Echoes* for Flute and Harp (1921); *Indian Sketches* for Flute and String Quartet (1922); *Mountain Sketches* for Flute, Cello, and Piano (1923); *Fugue* for String Quartet (1924); *Concert Fugue* for String Quartet (1924); *The Ole Swimmin' Hole* for Flute, Viola, and Cello (1924); Suite for Oboe and Flute (1925); *Elegy* for Cello and Piano (1930); Quintet for Clarinet, Flute, Oboe, Bassoon, and Horn (1932); *A Mountain Episode* for String Quartet (1933); *Dance of the Frogs* for Chamber Ensemble (1939). VOCAL: *Fly Low, Vermillion Dragon* for Voice and Orch. (1925); *The Vagabond's Prayer* for Baritone and String Quartet (1925); *On a Moonbeam* for Voice, Piano, and Flute (1938); *Peace*, cantata for Chorus and Orch. or Organ (1949); *About Dixie* for Chorus and Orch. (1950); songs.

Bibl.: D. Nelson, *The Life and Works of L. S. (1897–1959)* (diss., Univ. of N.C., 1971).—**NS/LK/DM**

Strobel, Heinrich, eminent German musicologist, music critic, and administrator; b. Regensburg, May 31, 1898; d. Baden-Baden, Aug. 18, 1970. He studied musicology with Sandberger and Kroyer and theory with H.K. Schmidt at the Univ. of Munich (Ph.D., 1922, with the diss. *Johann Wilhelm Hässlers Leben und Werke*). He was music critic of the *Thüringer Allgemeine Zeitung* in Erfurt (from 1921) and of the *Börsenkurier* (1927–33) and *Tageblatt* (1934–38) in Berlin; also was the ed. of *Melos* (1933–34) and of the *Neue Musikblatt* (1934–39). In 1939 he went to Paris; in 1946 he returned to Germany and again became ed. of *Melos*; that same year, he also was made director of music at the South West Radio in Baden-Baden; in 1956 he became chairman of the ISCM He devoted himself energetically to the cause of modern music; wrote numerous articles on the subject; promoted programs of avant-garde composers on the radio and at various festivals in Germany.

WRITINGS: *Paul Hindemith* (Mainz, 1928; third ed., enl., 1948); *Claude Debussy* (Zürich, 1940; 5th Ger. ed., 1961; French ed., Paris, 1942); *Igor Stravinsky* (Zürich, 1956; Eng. tr., 1956, as *Stravinsky: Classic Humanist*).—**NS/LK/DM**

Strobel, Valentin, German lutenist and composer; b. Halle (baptized), Oct. 18, 1611; d. Strasbourg, after 1669. He was the son of the German lutenist and composer Valentin Strobel (b. Thuringia, c. 1577; d. Weimar [buried], Oct. 16, 1640). He became a lutenist and theorbo player in the Darmstadt Hofkapelle in 1629. In 1634 he was active at the Stuttgart court. That same year, he entered the service of Margrave Friedrich V of Baden-Durlach, who moved his court to Strasbourg. About 1639 Stroebel was dismissed from the Margrave's service, but in 1640 he was made a citizen of Strasbourg. Some of his distinguished lute pieces, as well as 3 vols. of vocal works, are extant. His son, Johann Valentin Strobel (b. Strasbourg [baptized], Nov. 16, 1643; d. Darmstadt [buried], Aug. 30, 1688), was also a lutenist who was active at the Darmstadt court from 1668.—**LK/DM**

Stroe, Aurel, Romanian composer; b. Bucharest, May 5, 1932. He studied harmony with Negrea, composition with Andricu, and orchestration with Rogalski at the Bucharest Cons. (1951–56); had a course in electronic music in Munich (1966) and attended the annual summer courses in new music given in Darmstadt (1966–69) by Kagel, Ligeti, and Stockhausen. In 1962 he joined the faculty of the Bucharest Cons.; also worked at the Bucharest Computing Center (1966–69). His early music is rooted in folklore, but in his later period he experimented with sonoristic constructions, some of which were put together by computerized calculations.

WORKS: DRAMATIC: Opera: *Ça n'aura pas le Prix Nobel* (*Această piesă nu va primi premiul Nobel*; 1969; Kassel, Nov. 28, 1971); *De Ptolemaeo*, mini-opera for Tape (1970); *Aristophane: La Paix* (1972–73); *Orestia II* (*Purtatoarele de prinoase*), chamber opera (1974–77; Bucharest, Nov. 14, 1978). **Music Theater:** *Agamemnon (Orestia I)* (1979–81; Bucharest, March 1, 1983). **ORCH.:** Concerto for Strings (1956; Bucharest, Dec. 22, 1957); *Uvertură burlescă* (1961); *Arcade* for 11 Instrumental Formations (1962); *Muzică de concert* for Piano, Percussion, and Brass (1964–65; Cluj, April 2, 1966); *Laudes I* for 28 Strings (1966) and *II* for 12 Instrumental Formations (1968); *Canto I* (1967) and *II* (1971) for 12 Instrumental Formations; Clarinet Concerto (1974–75). **CHAMBER:** Trio for Oboe, Clarinet, and Bassoon (1953); 2 piano sonatas (1955, 1984); *Rêver, c'est desengrener les temps superposés II* for Clarinet, Cello, and Harpsichord (1970); String Quartet (1972); *Quintandre*, quintet for Flute, Oboe, Clarinet, Bassoon, and Horn (1984); *Anamorphoses canoniques* for 3 Flutes, Clarinet, Clavichord, Trombone, Cello, and Tape (1984). **VOCAL:** *Chipul păcii*, chamber cantata for Mezzo-soprano, Chorus, and Chamber Orch. (1959); *Monumentum I* for Men's Voices and Orch. (1961) and *II* for Mezzo-soprano, Percussion, Double Bass, and Tape (1982); *Numai prin timp poate fi timpul cucerit* (Only through Time, Time Is Conquered) for Baritone, Organ, 4 Trombones, and 4 Gongs, after T.S. Eliot (1965); *Il giardino delle Strutture + Rime de Michelangelo* for Baritone, Trombone, Violin, Viola, Cello, Harpsichord, and Tape (1975); various solo songs.—**NS/LK/DM**

Strohm, Reinhard, German musicologist; b. Munich, Aug. 4, 1942. He studied with Georgiades at the Univ. of Munich and Dahlhaus at Berlin's Technical Univ. (Ph.D., 1971, with the diss. *Italienische Opernarien des fruhen Settecento [1720–1730]*, 2 vols., Cologne, 1976). He was asst. ed. of the Richard-Wagner-Ausgabe (1970–81), and also lectured on music at King's Coll., Univ. of London (1975–83). Strohm then was prof. of music history at Yale Univ. (from 1983). In 1990 he rejoined the faculty of King's Coll., where he served as director of its Inst. for Advanced Musical Studies from 1991. He publ. several valuable books, among them *Music in Late Medieval Bruges* (1985), *Essays on Handel and Italian Opera* (1985), *Music in Late Medieval Europe* (1987), *The Rise of European Music, 1380–1500* (1993), and *Dramma per musica: Italian Opera Seria in the Eighteenth Century* (1997).—**NS/LK/DM**

Strong, George Templeton, American composer and painter; b. N.Y., May 26, 1856; d. Geneva, June 27, 1948. His father, also named George Templeton Strong, was a lawyer and amateur organist who served as president of the N.Y. Phil. (1870–74) and his mother was a singer. In spite of his father's objections to a career in music, he studied piano, violin, and oboe. In 1879 he entered the Leipzig Cons., where he studied with Richard Hoffman and Salomon Jadassohn. He also learned to play the viola. In 1881 he met Liszt, who encouraged him to pursue a career as a composer. He also was befriended by MacDowell. After teaching at the New England Cons. of Music in Boston in 1891–92, Strong settled in Switzerland. In addition to composing, he also was active as a painter of watercolors. His compositions are the work of a fine craftsman in the Romantic tradition. Among his best known scores are the second Sym., *Sintram*, which was premiered by the N.Y. Phil. under Seidl's direction on March 4, 1893, and the *Chorale on a Theme of Hans Leo Hassler* for String Orch. (1929). Almost all of Strong's works were first performed in Switzerland. He expressed his indignation at the lack of recognition of American composers by his countrymen. Although he lived most of his life in Switzerland, Strong always considered himself an American composer. He donated many of his MSS to the Library of Congress in Washington, D.C.

WORKS: ORCH.: *Ein Totentanz*, symphonic poem (c. 1878); *Undine*, symphonic poem (1883); 3 syms.: No. 1, *In den Bergen* (n.d.), No. 2, *Sintram* (1887–88; N.Y., March 4, 1893), and No. 3, *An der See* (n.d.; not extant); *Le roi Arthur*, symphonic poem (1891–1916); *Die Nacht*, 4 small symphonic poems (Montreux, Nov. 27, 1913); *Elegie* for Cello and Orch. (1917); *Une vie* *d'artiste* for Violin and Orch. (1917; Zürich, June 1920); *Hallali* for Horn and Orch. (1923); *Chorale on a Theme by Hans Leo Hassler* for Strings (1929; St. Pierre-Fusterie, May 13, 1933); *Pollainiani*, 6 pieces for Cello and Orch. (1931); *D'un cahier d'images I-III* (c. 1945); *Ondine*, symphonic poem (c. 1945). **CHAMBER:** String Quartet (1935); many piano pieces. **VOCAL:** *The Haunted Mill*, cantata; numerous songs. **—NS/LK/DM**

Strong, Susan, American soprano; b. Brooklyn, Aug. 3, 1870; d. London, March 11, 1946. She studied with Francis Korbay at the Royal Coll. of Music in London. In 1895 she made her operatic debut as Sieglinde with the Hedmont Co. in London, and then sang at Covent Garden (1895; 1897; 1899–1900; 1902). In 1896 she appeared in N.Y. with the Mapleson Co. Her Metropolitan Opera debut followed there as Elsa in *Lohengrin* on Jan. 27, 1897. She was again on the roster there from 1899 to 1901. Her other roles included Donna Anna, Brünnhilde, Venus, and Aida.**—LK/DM**

Strouse, Charles (Louis), American composer; b. N.Y., June 7, 1928. He studied at the Eastman School of Music in Rochester, N.Y., and later took private lessons in composition with Copland and Boulanger, under whose guidance he wrote some ambitious instrumental music. He was mainly active as a composer for Broadway and films; with the lyricist Lee Adams (b. Mansfield, Ohio, Aug. 14, 1924), he wrote the musicals *Bye Bye Birdie* (N.Y., April 16, 1960) and *Applause* (N.Y., March 30, 1970), both of which won Tony awards. His other musicals include *Golden Boy* (N.Y., Oct. 20, 1964), after a play by Clifford Odets, and *Annie* (N.Y., April 21, 1977). He also composed a Piano Concerto and other orch. pieces and a String Quartet.**—NS/LK/DM**

Strozier, Frank, alto saxophonist with a biting and intense tone and a style that is fiery and spirited; b. Memphis, Tenn., June 13, 1937. Overshadowed by contemporaries such as James Spaulding and Jackie McLean, alto saxophonist Frank Strozier has never really received the attention and acclaim his talent deserves. The early years of his career were spent in Chicago, where he worked with Booker Little, George Coleman, and Harold Mabern. By the end of the 1950s he moved to N.Y. and was a vital member of the group MJT+3, which included Mabern, bassist Bob Cranshaw, and drummer Walter Perkins. That group and Strozier himself led several record dates for the Vee-Jay label that have since become valuable collector's items. Further N.Y. gigs included short stints with Miles Davis and Roy Haynes. Later, he settled on the West Coast where he worked with Don Ellis, Chet Baker, and Shelly Manne. Since the 1970s, he has kept a very low profile, playing infrequently and recording a few albums for various small independent record labels. He has always been a valuable musician; unfortunately, none of his vintage recordings are available on CD, making his continued obscurity all the more frustrating.

DISC.: *Fantastic Frank Strozier—Plus* (1960); *March of the Siamese Children* (1962); *Remember Me* (1976).**—CH**

Strozzi, Barbara, Italian singer and composer, adopted daughter of **Giulio Strozzi;** b. Venice, Aug. 6, 1619; d. probably there, c. 1664. She was adopted about 1628 and received musical training from Cavalli. She played a prominent role at the gatherings of the Accademia degli Unisoni at the Strozzi residence, where she was active as a singer and composer. It is also possible that she was active as a courtesan, but her musical gifts were undeniable and she was highly esteemed as a composer. Her adoptive father wrote the texts for her first book of madrigals (Venice, 1644). In all, she publ. 8 vols. of music, including many fine cantatas, arias, and duets.**—LK/DM**

Strozzi, Giulio, Italian librettist, poet, and dramatist, adoptive father of **Barbara Strozzi;** b. Venice, 1583; d. there, March 31, 1652. He was the illegitimate but later legitimized son of the Venetian banker Roberto Strozzi. After training in Venice, he studied law at the Univ. of Pisa. He was active in Rome as apostolic prothonotary and became a leading figure in the Accademia degli Ordinati. Following sojourns in Padua and Urbino, he returned to Venice in the early 1620s and became a major figure in both literary and musical circles. He was a member of the Accademia degli Incogniti, and also the founder of two academies of his own, the second being the Accademia degli Unisoni (1637), which met in his residence. Strozzi was an important figure in the development of Venetian opera via his role as a librettist. His texts were set by Monteverdi, Manelli, Sacrati, Cavalli et al. He also wrote the texts for his adopted daughter's first book of madrigals. **—LK/DM**

Strozzi, Piero, amateur Italian composer; b. Florence, c. 1550; d. there, after Sept. 1, 1609. He was a nobleman. He was a member of the Bardi circle in Florence, and one of the creators of the "stile rappresentativo," leading to the development of opera. With Caccini, Merulo, and Striggio, he wrote the festival music for the wedding of Francesco de' Medici in 1579. In 1596 he set to music Rinuccini's libretto *La mascherata degli accecati*. Two madrigals by Strozzi are in Luca Bati's *Secondo libro di madrigali* (Venice, 1598).**—NS/LK/DM**

Strube, Gustav, German-American violinist, conductor, music educator, and composer; b. Ballenstedt, March 3, 1867; d. Baltimore, Feb. 2, 1953. He was taught the violin by his father, and later by Brodsky at the Leipzig Cons.; was a member of the Gewandhaus Orch. of Leipzig until 1891, when he emigrated to America. He was a violinist in the Boston Sym. Orch. from 1891 to 1913; also conducted the Boston Pops Orch. (1898; 1900–02; 1905–12); then taught theory and conducting at the Peabody Cons. in Baltimore (from 1913), where he also was its director (1916–46). In 1916 he was appointed conductor of the newly organized Baltimore Sym. Orch., which he led until 1930. He publ. a useful manual, *The Theory and Use of Chords: A Textbook of Harmony* (Boston, 1928).

WORKS: DRAMATIC: Opera: *Ramona* (1916; later renamed *The Captive*). **ORCH.:** Sym., "Lanier," after Sidney Lanier (Washington, D.C., March 17, 1925, composer conducting); *Sinfonietta* (1922); *Symphonic Prologue* (Baltimore, April 24, 1927, composer conducting); 2 violin concertos (1924, 1930); *Americana* (1930); *Harz Mountains*, symphonic poem (1940); *Peace Overture* (1945). **CHAMBER:** 2 string quartets (1923, 1936); 2 violin sonatas (1923); Viola Sonata (1924); Cello Sonata (1925); Piano Trio (1925); Quintet for Wind Instruments (1930). **—NS/LK/DM**

Strungk, Delphin, esteemed German organist and composer, father of **Nicolaus Adam Strungk;** b. 1600 or 1601; d. Braunschweig (buried), Oct. 12, 1694. He was organist at Wolfenbüttel's principal church (1630–32), the Celle court (1632–37), and Braunschweig's Marienkirche (from 1637) and other churches. He wrote vocal works and organ music.**—NS/LK/DM**

Strungk, Nicolaus Adam, prominent German violinist, organist, and composer, son of **Delphin Strungk;** b. Braunschweig (baptized), Nov. 15, 1640; d. Dresden, Sept. 23, 1700. He studied with his father, whose assistant he became at the age of 12 at the Church of St. Magnus in Braunschweig. He also studied violin at Lübeck under Schnittelbach while attending Helmstedt Univ. At 20 he became first violinist in the Wölfenbuttel court chapel; a short time later, he went to the Celle court. After appearing as a violinist at the Vienna court chapel in 1661, he decided to pursue his career there until 1665; then was in the service of the Hannover court chapel. In 1678 Strungk became music director of Hamburg's Cathedral and of the city; wrote and produced operas in German (in keeping with the nationalist trend of the time), among them *Der glücklich-steigende Sejanus* and its sequel, *Der unglücklich-fallende Sejanus* (1678), *Alceste* (1680), *Die Liebreiche, durch Tugend und Schönheit erhöhete Esther* (1680), *Doris, oder der königliche Sklaue* (1680), *Semiramis* (1681), *Theseus* (1681), and *Floretto* (1683). From 1682 to 1686 he was court organist and composer in Hannover; also visited Italy in 1685, meeting Corelli in Rome. In 1688 he became Vice-Kapellmeister and chamber organist in Dresden, succeeding Carlo Pallavicino, whose unfinished opera *L'Antiope* he completed and produced there in 1689. In this post he was beset with difficulties arising from friction with Italian musicians, and only managed to maintain his authority through the intervention of his patron, the Elector Johann Georg III; when Bernhard, Kapellmeister in Dresden, died in 1692, Strungk was appointed to succeed him. In 1693 he organized an opera company in Leipzig; between 1693 and 1700 he wrote 16 operas for it, among them *Alceste* (perf. at the inauguration of the Leipzig opera house, May 18, 1693), *Nero* (1693), *Syrinx* (1694), *Phocas* (1696), *Ixion* (1697), *Scipio und Hannibal* (1698), *Agrippina* (1699), and *Erechtheus* (1700). Financially, the enterprise was a failure, but Strungk continued to receive his salary from Dresden until his retirement on a pension in 1697. He publ. the important manual *Musicalische Übung auf der Violine oder Viola da Gamba in etlichen Sonaten über die Festgesänge, ingleichen etlichen Ciaconen mit 2 Violinen bestehend* (1691). A selection of airs from his operas was publ. in Hamburg under the title *Ein hundert auserlesenen Arien zweyer Hamburgischen Operen, Semiramis und Esther. Mit beigefügten Ritornellen* (1684). Among his instrumental works, a Sonata for 2 Violins and Viola da Gamba and several other sonatas are extant; MS No. 5056 of the Yale Univ. Music Library (Lowell Mason Collection) contains capriccios and ricercari by Strungk, among them the *Ricercar sopra la Morte della mia carissima Madre Catherina Maria Stubenrauen* (Venice, 1685). Six capriccios and a Ricercare by Strungk, included in Denkmäler der Tonkunst in Österreich, 17 (13.ii), are wrongly ascribed to Georg Reutter (Senior).

BIBL.: F. Zelle, *J. Theile und N.A. S.* (Berlin, 1891); F. Berend, *N.A. S., 1640–1700: Sein Leben und seine Werke. Mit Beiträgen zur Geschichte der Musik und des Theater in Celle, Hannover, und Leipzig* (Freiburg im Breisgau, 1915).**—NS/LK/DM**

Strunk, (William) Oliver, distinguished American musicologist; b. Ithaca, N.Y., March 22, 1901; d. Grottaferrata, Italy, Feb. 24, 1980. He studied at Cornell Univ. (1917–19). In 1927 he took a course in musicology with Otto Kinkeldey there, and then entered the Univ. of Berlin to study musicology with J. Wolf (1927–28). Returning to America, he served as a member of the staff of the Music Division at the Library of Congress in Washington, D.C. (1928–34), and then was head of its music division (1934–37). In 1937 he was appointed to the faculty of Princeton Univ.; after retirement in 1966, he lived mostly in Italy. He was a founding member of the American Musicological Soc., serving as the first ed. of its journal (1948) and as its president (1959–60), then was director of Monumenta Musicae Byzantinae (1961–71). He publ. *State and Resources of Musicology in the U.S.* (Washington, D.C., 1932) and the extremely valuable documentary *Source Readings in Music History* (N.Y., 1950; rev. ed., 1998, by L. Treitler). Collections of his writings were publ. as *Essays on Music in the Western World* (N.Y., 1974) and *Essays on Music in the Byzantine World* (N.Y., 1977).

BIBL.: H. Powers, ed., *Studies in Music History: Essays for O. S.* (Princeton, N.J., 1968).**—NS/LK/DM**

Stryker, Dave (actually, **David Michael**), jazz guitarist; b. Omaha, Nebr., March 30, 1957. Stryker grew up in Nebr. and moved to N.Y. in 1980. After studying with Billy Rogers and freelancing, he joined Jack McDuff's group, touring the U.S. and Canada (1984–85). He played with Stanley Turrentine (1986–95), performing at all the major festivals, concert halls, and clubs throughout the world, and with guests Dizzy Gillespie and Freddie Hubbard. Stryker's 1991 album, *Guitar on Top*, reached #13 on the Gavin Radio Chart. He has been awarded three jazz grants from the N.E.A., toured Japan and Europe with Kevin Mahogany, and continues working with his own group. A featured sideman on many releases, Stryker produced *The Guitar Artistry of Billy Rogers* and co-produced *A Tribute to Grant Green*.

DISC.: *First Strike* (1988); *Guitar on Top* (1991); *Full Moon* (1993); *Strike Zone* (1994); *Nomad* (1995); *Blue Degrees* (1995); *Stardust* (1995); *The Greeting* (1996); *Blue to the Bone* (1997).**—LP**

Stubblefield, John(ny IV), jazz tenor, alto, and soprano saxophonist, flutist; b. Little Rock, Ark., Feb. 4, 1945. While studying music, Stubblefield played with

R&B artists, including The Drifters, Little Junior Parker, and Jackie Wilson. In Chicago, he joined the AACM. He studied with Muhal Richard Abrams and George Coleman, and performed and recorded with Joseph Jarman, Anthony Braxton, Maurice McIntyre, and Abrams. After moving to N.Y. in 1971, Stubblefield played with Mary Lou Williams, Charles Mingus, Thad Jones–Mel Lewis, Frank Foster, and George Russell, among others. He toured Europe with Gil Evans and Dollar Brand, and has been prominently featured in McCoy Tyner's big bands, Kenny Barron's quintets, and the Mingus Big Band (1998). He has led his own quartet since 1980. As a jazz eductaor, Stubblefield has taught for the Chicago public schools (1967–70), Jazzmobile (beginning in 1974), Rutgers Univ. (1983–84), and, since the early 1990s, Wesleyan Univ.

DISC.: *Prelude* (1976); *Confessin'* (1984); *Bushman Song* (1986); *Countin' on the Blues* (1987); *Morning Song* (1995).—**LP**

Stuck, Jean-Baptiste, distinguished Italian-born French cellist and composer of German descent; b. probably in Livorno, 1680; d. Paris, Dec. 8, 1755. He began his career as a cellist in Italy, then went to France in the service of the Prince of Carignam. He was in the service of Elector Max Emanuel of Bavaria about 1714. Returning to France, he was ordinaire de la musique du Roy until being pensioned in 1748; also appeared at the Concert Spirituel. In 1733 he became a naturalized French citizen. He won great renown as a cellist; was also a notable composer of cantatas, of which he publ. 4 books (1706, 1708, 1711, 1714). His other works include 3 insignificant operas, *Méléagre* (Paris, May 24, 1709), *Manto la fée* (1709; Paris, Jan. 29, 1711), and *Polidore* (Paris, Feb. 15, 1720), ballets for the Versailles court, and airs in contemporary collections.—**NS/LK/DM**

Stucken, Frank (Valentin) Van der
See **Van der Stucken, Frank (Valentin)**

Stückenschmidt, Hans Heinz, eminent German music critic and writer on music; b. Strasbourg, Nov. 1, 1901; d. Berlin, Aug. 15, 1988. He studied violin, piano, and composition. He was chief music critic of Prague's *Bohemia* (1928–29) and of the *Berliner Zeitung am Mittag* (1929–34); also was active as a lecturer on contemporary music. In 1934 he was forbidden to continue journalism in Germany, and went to Prague, where he wrote music criticism until 1941, when his activities were stopped once more by the occupation authorities; then was drafted into the German army. In 1946 he became director of the dept. for new music of the radio station RIAS in Berlin; also was a lecturer (1948–49), reader (1949–53), and prof. (1953–67) of music history at the Technical Univ. there. With Josef Rufer, he founded and ed. the journal *Stimmen* (Berlin, 1947–49).

WRITINGS: *Arnold Schönberg* (Zürich and Freiburg im Breisgau, 1951; second ed., 1957; Eng. tr., 1960); *Neue Musik zwischen den beiden Kriegen* (Berlin and Frankfurt am Main, 1951); *Strawinsky und sein Jahrhundert* (Berlin, 1957); *Schöpfer der neuen Musik* (Frankfurt am Main, 1958); *Boris Blacher* (Berlin, 1963); *Oper in dieser Zeit* (Velber, 1964); *Johann Nepomuk David* (Wiesbaden, 1965); *Maurice Ravel: Variationen über Person und Werk* (Frankfurt am Main, 1966; Eng. tr., 1968); *Ferruccio Busoni. Zeittafel eines Europaers* (Zürich, 1967; Eng. tr., 1970); *Twentieth Century Music* (London, 1968; Ger. original, 1969); *Twentieth Century Composers* (London, 1970; Ger. original, 1971); *Schönberg: Leben, Umwelt, Werk* (Zürich, 1974; Eng. tr., 1976); *Die Musik eines halben Jahrhunderts: 1925–1975* (Munich, 1976); *Schöfer klassischer Musik: Bildnisse und Revisionen* (Berlin, 1983).

BIBL.: W. Burde, ed., *Aspekte der neuen Musik: Professor H.H. S. zum 65. Geburtstag* (Kassel, 1968).—**NS/LK/DM**

Stückgold, Grete (née Schneidt), German soprano; b. London (of a German father and an English mother), June 6, 1895; d. Falls Village, Conn., Sept. 13, 1977. She studied voice with **Jacques Stückgold**, whom she married (divorced in 1928); later married **Gustav Schützendorf**. She commenced her career as a concert and oratorio singer; made her operatic debut in Nuremberg in 1917; joined the Berlin State Opera in 1922. On Nov. 2, 1927, she made her Metropolitan Opera debut in N.Y. as Eva in *Die Meistersinger von Nürnberg*; she continued to make appearances there until 1939; also sang in San Francisco, Philadelphia, and Chicago. She later taught voice at Bennington (Vt.) Coll.—**NS/LK/DM**

Stückgold, Jacques, Polish singing teacher; b. Warsaw, Jan. 29, 1877; d. N.Y., May 4, 1953. He studied in Venice; taught voice in Germany (1899–1903), where **Grete Stückgold** (née **Schneidt**) became his pupil and wife (divorced, 1928); settled in N.Y. in 1933. He publ. *Der Bankrott der deutschen Gesangskunst* and *Über Stimmbildungskunst*.—**NS/LK/DM**

Stucky, Steven (Edward), American composer, teacher, conductor, and writer on music; b. Hutchinson, Kans., Nov. 7, 1949. He received training in composition from Richard Willis at Baylor Univ. (B.M., 1971) and from Husa, Phillips, and Palmer at Cornell Univ. (M.F.A., 1973; D.M.A., 1978). He also studied conducting with Daniel Sternberg. After serving as a visiting asst. prof. at Lawrence Univ. in Appleton, Wisc. (1978–80), he taught at Cornell Univ. (from 1980), later serving as a prof. and chairman of the music dept. there (1992–97). He also was composer-in-residence of the Los Angeles Phil. (1988–92), and then was its new music advisor. His study *Lutoslawski and His Music* (Cambridge, 1981) won the ASCAP-Deems Taylor Award. He also won the ASCAP-Victor Herbert Prize (1974), first prize of the American Soc. of Univ. Composers (1975), and fellowships from the NEA (1978), the American Council of Learned Societies (1979), the NEH (1979), the Guggenheim Foundation (1986), and the Bogliasco Foundation (1997). Stucky's music is marked by rewarding craftsmanship, technical expertise, and a remarkable command of color and form.

WORKS: ORCH.: *Prelude and Toccata* (1969); 4 syms.: No. 1 (1972), No. 2 (1974), No. 3 (1976), and No. 4, *Kennigar* (1977–78; Terre Haute, Ind., Sept. 25, 1980); *Transparent Things: In Memoriam V. N.* (Appleton, Wisc., May 11, 1980); Double Concerto for Violin, Oboe or Oboe d'Amore, and Chamber Orch. (1982–85; Tallahassee, March 9, 1985; rev. 1989); *Dreamwaltzes* (Minneapolis, July 17, 1986); *Concerto for Orchestra* (1986–87; Philadelphia, Oct. 27, 1988); *Threnos* for Wind Ensemble (1987–88; Ithaca, N.Y., March 6, 1988); *Son et lumière* (Baltimore, May 18, 1988); *Angelus* (1989–90; N.Y., Sept. 27, 1990); *Impromptus* (1989–91; St. Louis, April 26, 1991); *Anniversary Greeting* (Baltimore, May 2, 1991); *Fanfare for Los Angeles* (1993; Los Angeles, March 4, 1994); *Fanfare for Cincinnati* (1993; Cincinnati, March 10, 1995); *Ancora* (1994; Los Angeles, Oct. 6, 1995); *Fanfares and Arias* for Wind Ensemble (1994; Boulder, Colo., Feb. 22, 1995); Concerto for 2 Flutes and Orch. (1994; Los Angeles, Feb. 23, 1995); *Pinturas de Tamayo* (1995; Chicago, March 28, 1996); *Music* for Saxophones and Strings (Lorrach, Germany, May 15, 1996); *Concerto Mediterraneo* for Guitar and Orch. (1997–98; Baltimore, Sept. 17, 1998). **CHAMBER:** *4 Bagatelles* for String Quartet (1969); Duo for Viola and Cello (1969); *Movements* for Cello Quartet (1970); *Divertimento* for Clarinet, Piano, and Percussion (1971); Quartet for Clarinet, Viola, Cello, and Piano (1973); *Notturno* for Alto Saxophone and Piano (Ithaca, N.Y., Sept. 19, 1981); *Varianti* for Flute, Clarinet, and Piano (1982; Ithaca, N.Y., Jan. 30, 1983); *Boston Fancies* for Flute, Clarinet, Percussion, Piano, Violin, Viola, and Cello (Cambridge, Mass., Nov. 15, 1985); *Serenade* for Wind Quintet (1989–90); *Salute* for Flute, Clarinet, Horn, Trombone, Piano, Percussion, Violin, and Cello (Ithaca, N.Y., Nov. 2, 1997); *Ad Parnassum* for Flute, Clarinet, Piano, Percussion, Violin, and Cello (Cambridge, Mass., Oct. 16, 1998); *Nell'ombra, nella luce* for String Quartet (1999–2000; Pittsburgh, Feb. 12, 2000). **VOCAL:** *2 Holy Sonnets of Donne* for Mezzo-soprano, Oboe, and Piano (Waco, Tex., Oct. 14, 1982); *Sappho Fragments* for Mezzo-soprano, Flute, Clarinet, Percussion, Piano, Violin, and Cello (Syracuse, N.Y., Nov. 1, 1982); *Voyages* for Voice and Wind Orch. (1983–84; New Haven, Conn., Dec. 7, 1984); *4 Poems of A.R. Ammons* for Baritone, Flute, Clarinet, Horn, Viola, Cello, and Double Bass (1992; Syracuse, N.Y., March 28, 1993); *Cradle Songs* for Chorus (Los Angeles, Oct. 19, 1997); *American Muse* for Baritone and Orch. (Los Angeles, Oct. 29, 1999). **OTHER:** *Funeral Music for Queen Mary*, transcription and elaboration of music by Purcell for Wind Orch. (Los Angeles, Feb. 6, 1992). **—NS/LK/DM**

Studer, Cheryl, American soprano; b. Midland, Mich., Oct. 24, 1955. She received her training in Ohio, at the Univ. of Tenn., and from Hans Hotter at the Vienna Hochschule für Musik. After appearing in concerts in the U.S., she made her debut at the Bavarian State Opera in Munich as Mařenka in *The Bartered Bride* in 1980. From 1983 to 1985 she sang at the Darmstadt Opera. In 1984 she made her U.S. operatic debut as Micaëla at the Chicago Lyric Opera. From 1985 she sang at the Deutsche Oper in Berlin. She made her Bayreuth Festival debut in 1985 as Elisabeth in *Tannhäuser*. In 1986 she sang Pamina at her debut at the Paris Opéra. In 1987 she made her first appearance at London's Covent Garden as Elisabeth, and also sang at Milan's La Scala. She made her Metropolitan Opera debut in N.Y. in 1988 as Micaëla, and subsequently sang there with success. In 1989 she made her first appearance at the Salzburg Festival as Chrysothemis. In 1990 she sang Elsa at the Vienna State Opera. She appeared as Giuditta at the Vienna Volksoper in 1992. On May 4, 1994, she made her Carnegie Hall recital debut in N.Y. In 1996 she was engaged as Beethoven's Leonore at the Salzburg Festival. She has won particular distinction for such Strauss roles as Salome, the Empress in *Die Frau ohne Schatten*, and Daphne. Among her other admired roles are Donna Anna, Lucia, Aida, and Singlinde.**—NS/LK/DM**

Stumpf, (Friedrich) Carl, eminent German psychologist, acoustician, and musicologist; b. Wiesentheid, Lower Franconia, April 21, 1848; d. Berlin, Dec. 25, 1936. He studied philosophy and theology at the Univ. of Würzburg, and philosophy and natural sciences at the Univ. of Göttingen, where he took his Ph.D. (1870) and completed his Habilitation (1873). He was a prof. of philosophy at the Univs. of Würzburg (1873–79), Prague (1879–84), Halle (1884–89), Munich (1889–93), and Berlin (1893–1928). In 1893 he founded the Psychological Inst. in Berlin; its purpose was a scientific analysis of tonal psychology as it affected musical perception; but, realizing the utterly speculative and arbitrary premises of his theories, he revised them, and proposed the concepts of Konkordanz and Diskordanz to describe the relative euphony of triads and chords of several different notes. With his pupils Hornbostel and Abraham, he founded the Berlin Phonogrammarchiv in 1900. Stumpf publ. *Beiträge zur Akustik und Musikwissenschaft* (1898–1924), which incorporated his evolving theories, and, with Hornbostel, issued the *Sammelbände für vergleichende Musikwissenschaft* (1922–23); also contributed numerous articles to scholarly publications.

WRITINGS: *Tonpsychologie* (2 vols., Leipzig, 1883, 1890; reprint, Hilversum, 1965); *Geschichte des Konsonanzbegriffs* (Munich, 1901); *Die Anfänge der Musik* (Leipzig, 1911); *Die Sprachlaute. Experimentell-phonetische Untersuchungen nebst einem Anhang über Instrumentalklänge* (Berlin, 1926).

BIBL.: *Festscrift für C. S.* (Berlin, 1919); *C. S. zum 75. Geburtstag* (Berlin, 1923); N. Hartmann, *Gedächtnisrede C. S.* (Berlin, 1937).**—NS/LK/DM**

Stuntz, Joseph Hartmann, Swiss conductor and composer of German descent; b. Arlesheim, near Basel, July 23, 1793; d. Munich, June 18, 1859. He studied with Peter von Winter in Munich (1808–12) and with Salieri in Vienna (1813–16), then returned to Munich as conductor of the Italian Opera, where he produced his successful opera *La rappresaglia* (composed 1818–20). In 1825 he was named conductor of the German Opera, but shortly afterward assumed the conductorship of the Court Orch., a position he retained for the rest of his life. He wrote the Singspiel *Heinrich IV zu Givry* (Munich, 1820), the tragic opera *Maria Rosa* (Munich, n.d.), many ballets, cantatas, masses, choruses, and songs.

BIBL.: K. Gross, *J.H. S. als Opernkomponist* (diss., Univ. of Munich, 1934).**—NS/LK/DM**

Sturgeon, Nicholas, English divine and composer; b. place and date unknown; d. between May 31 and June 8, 1454. He was elected a scholar at Winchester Coll. in 1399; held several canonries, including one at St. Paul's Cathedral in London (from 1432), where he was precentor (from 1442); also was a member of the royal household chapel. He was the owner, and possibly the scribe, of the MSS found in Old Hall, near Ware; 7 works by Sturgeon (2 not complete) are part of the Old Hall MS collection, including a curious isorhythmic motet, *Salve mater Domini*, for 3 Voices, which was probably written for the journey of Henry V to France (1416), on which Sturgeon accompanied him. A. Hughes and M. Bent, eds., publ. *The Old Hall Manuscript*, in Corpus Mensurabilis Musicae, XLVI (1969–72).—**NS/LK/DM**

Sturm, George, German-born American music administrator and writer on music; b. Augsburg, March 13, 1930. He settled in the U.S. and became a naturalized American citizen. He was educated at Queens Coll. in N.Y. (B.A., 1952) and at Princeton Univ. (M.F.A., 1955), and then was a student of Luigi Dallapiccola in Florence on a Fulbright grant (1955–57). After working for G. Schirmer/AMP in N.Y. (1958–77), he was vice-president of European American Music (1977–79). In 1980 he became executive director of Music Associates of America, where he was an ed. and a contributor to its publication *MadAminA!*.—**LK/DM**

Stürmer, Bruno, German conductor, teacher, and composer; b. Freiburg im Breisgau, Sept. 9, 1892; d. Bad Homburg, May 19, 1958. He studied piano at the Karlsruhe Cons.; then organ and composition with Wolfrum at the Univ. of Heidelberg, and musicology with Sandberger and Kroyer at the Univ. of Munich. He taught piano in Karlsruhe (1917–22); then was a theater conductor in Remscheid, Essen, and Duisburg (1922–27); in 1927 he founded a music school in Homburg; then was a conductor of choral societies in Kassel and elsewhere (until 1945). He composed in a distinctly modern manner. In addition to numerous vocal works, he wrote concertos and much chamber music. He publ. the book *Frisch fröhlich woll'n wir singen* (Cologne, 1956).—**NS/LK/DM**

Sturzenegger, (Hans) Richard, Swiss cellist, teacher, and composer; b. Zürich, Dec. 18, 1905; d. Bern, Oct. 24, 1976. He studied cello with Fritz Reitz at the Zürich Cons., and then continued his training in Paris (1924–27) with Alexanian and Casals (cello) and Boulanger (harmony and counterpoint). He completed his training in Berlin (1929–35) with Feuermann (cello) and Toch (composition), during which time he served as solo cellist of the Dresden Phil. From 1935 to 1949 he played in the Bern String Quartet, and from 1935 to 1963 he was solo cellist of the Bern Musikgesellschaft. He also taught cello and chamber music at the Bern Cons. From 1954 to 1963 he likewise taught cello in Zürich. In 1963 he became director of the Bern Cons.

Works: DRAMATIC: Opera: *Atalante* (1963–68). **ORCH.:** 4 cello concertos (1933, 1937, 1947, 1974); *Triptychon* (1951); *3 Gesänge Davids* for Violin and Orch. (1963); *Fresco* for Strings (1965). **CHAMBER:** Sonata for Solo Cello (1934); String Trio (1937); 2 string quartets (1940, 1974); Cello Sonata (1950); *Elegie* for Cello, Oboe, Harp, Viola, Cello, and Double Bass (1950); Piano Trio (1964). **VOCAL:** *Chorale Fantasy* for Contralto, Strings, Trumpet, and Drums (1941); *Cantico di San Francesco* for Chorus, Strings, and Harp (1945); *Richardis*, festival music for Chorus, Wind Orch., and Organ (1949).

Bibl.: *R. S., Werkverzeichnis* (Zürich, 1970); E. Hochuli, ed., *Variationen: Festgabe für R. S. zum siebzigsten Geburtstag* (Bern, 1975).—**NS/LK/DM**

Stutschewsky, Joachim, Russian-born Israeli cellist, pedagogue, ethnomusicologist, and composer; b. Romny, Feb. 7, 1892; d. Tel Aviv, Nov. 14, 1982. He received his early education at a music school in Kherson; as a youth, played cello in various orchs. in southern Russia; then studied cello with J. Klengel and orch. playing with H. Sitt at the Leipzig Cons. (1909–12). After playing in the Jena Quartet, he was active as a performer, teacher, and editor in Zürich (1914–24) and Vienna (1924–38), where he entered the circle of Schoenberg, Berg, and Webern. Together with the violinist Rudolf Kolisch, he formed the Wiener Streichquartett (later known as the Kolisch String Quartet). With the usurpation of Austria by the Nazi hordes in 1938, Stutschewsky emigrated to Palestine, and eventually became a naturalized Israeli citizen. From 1939 to 1948 he served as inspector of music in the cultural section of the Jewish National Council. In his early compositions, he followed median modern techniques; then began a study of Jewish folklore in diaspora, and wrote music of profound racial feeling, set in the framework of advanced harmonies. He also contributed to the study of cello techniques and to ethnomusicology.

Writings: *Die Kunst des Cellospiels* (Vols. 1–2, Mainz, 1929; Vols. 3–4, Vienna, 1938); *Mein Weg zur jüdischen Musik* (Vienna, 1935); *Musika yehudit* (Jewish Music; Tel Aviv, 1946); *The Cello and Its Masters: History of Cello Playing* (MS, 1950); *Klezmerim* (Tel Aviv, 1959); *Musical Folklore of Eastern Jewry* (Tel Aviv, 1959); *Korot hayav shel musikai yehudi* (The Life of a Jewish Musician; Tel Aviv, 1975).

Works: ORCH.: Concertino for Clarinet and Strings (1958); *Fantasy* for Oboe, Harp, and Strings (1959); *Safed*, symphonic poem (1960); *Israel*, symphonic suite (1964; Tel Aviv, May 7, 1973). **CHAMBER:** *Dreykut* for Cello and Piano (1924); Duo for Violin and Cello (1940); *Hassidic Suite* for Cello and Piano (1946); *Legend* for Cello and Piano (1952); *Israeli Dances* for Flute, Cello, and Piano (1953); *Verschollene Klänge* for Flute, String Quartet, and Percussion (1955); *Hassidic Fantasy* for Clarinet, Cello, and Piano (1956); Piano Trio (1956); *5 Pieces* for Flute (1956); String Quartet (1956); *Terzetto* for Oboe, Clarinet, and Bassoon (1959); String Trio (1960); Wind Sextet (1960); *Israeli Suite* for Cello and Piano (1962); *Monologue* for Clarinet (1962); *3 Pieces* for Bassoon (1963); *Moods* for Oboe (1963); *Impressions* for Clarinet and Bassoon (1963); *Soliloquy* for Viola (1964); *3 Miniatures* for 2 Flutes (1964); *Kol Kore* (Calling Voice) for Horn (1965); *Fragments* for 2 Clarinets (1966); *4 Movements* for Wind Quintet (1967); *3 for 3*, 3 pieces for 3 Cellos (1967); Woodwind Quintet (1967); *Visions* for Flute (1968); *Thoughts and Feelings* for Violin (1969); *Prelude and Fugue* for 2 Trumpets and 2 Trombones (1969); *Monologue* for Trombone (1970); *Dialogues variés* for 2 Trumpets (1970); *Imaginations* for Flute, Violin, Cello, and Piano (1971); *Kol Nidrei* for Cello and Piano (1972); *The Rabbi's Nigun* for Cello and Piano (1974); *Sine nomine* for Cello (1975); *2 Pieces* for Double Bass (1975). **Piano:** *Palestinian Sketches* (1931); *Israeli Landscapes* (1949); *4 Inattendus* (1967); *Splinters* (1975). **VOCAL:** *Songs of Radiant Sadness*, cantata for Soloists, Chorus, Speaking Chorus, and Orch. (1958); *Jemama baschimscha* (24 Hours in the Looking Glass), chamber cantata for Narrator, 2 Sopranos, and 6 Instruments (1960). **OTHER:** Numerous arrangements for cello of works by Mozart, Tartini, and Boccherini.

Bibl.: *J. S.'s 70th Anniversary: Catalogue of Works* (Tel Aviv, 1971).—**NS/LK/DM**

Stutzmann, Nathalie, French contralto; b. Suresnes, May 6, 1965. She studied at the Nancy Cons. and with Hans Hotter, Christa Ludwig, and Daniel Ferro in Paris. After becoming a laureate at the Brussels vocal competition in 1983, she attracted notice at her operatic debut in *Dido and Aeneas* at the Paris Opéra in 1986. She subsequently concentrated on a career as a soloist with the leading orchs. on both sides of the Atlantic and as a recitalist. Her engagements in opera took her to many of the major French music centers. She was particularly known for her portrayal of Debussy's Geneviève, which she sang not only in France but in Bonn (1991), Venice (1995), and Brussels (1996). **—NS/LK/DM**

Stylistics, The, one of the leading exponents of the lush, mellow sound of Philadelphia soul. **Membership:** Russell Tompkins Jr., lead ten. voc. (b. Philadelphia, Pa., March 21, 1951); Airron Love, ten. voc. (b. Philadelphia, Pa., Aug. 8, 1949); Herbert Murrell, lead bar. voc. (b. Lane, S.C., April 27, 1949); James Dunn, bar. voc. (b. Philadelphia, Pa., Feb. 4, 1950); James Smith, bs. voc. (b. N.Y.C., June 16, 1950).

Under producer Thom Bell, the Stylistics scored a series of pop, R&B, and easy-listening hits in the first half of the 1970s with songs written by Bell and Linda Creed, such as "Betcha By Golly, Wow," "Break Up to Make Up," and "You Make Me Feel Brand New." Sustaining their success under producers Hugo and Luigi for several years after the departure of Bell, the Stylistics continued to score R&B hits through 1986, despite several personnel changes.

The Stylistics formed in 1968 with the merger of two Philadelphia vocal groups, the Percussions and the Monarchs. The group was comprised of Monarchs Russell Tompkins Jr., Airron Love, and James Smith and Percussions James Dunn and Herbert Murrell. They first recorded for Sebring Records in 1969, and their song "You're a Big Girl Now" was later picked up by Avco Embassy (later simply Avco), where it became a smash R&B hit. Teamed with producer Thom Bell and the songwriting team of Bell and Linda Creed, the Stylistics scored a series of smash R&B hits through spring 1974, two of which, "Betcha By Golly, Wow" and "You Make Me Feel Brand New," also became smash pop and easy-listening hits. Burt Bacharach and Hal David's "You'll Never Get to Heaven (If You Break My Heart)" was a smash R&B and easy-listening hit in 1973. Bell-Creed pop and R&B smashes for the Stylistics include "You Are Everything," "I'm Stone in Love with You," and "Break Up to Make Up," all major easy-listening hits. The team's "Stop, Look, Listen (To Your Heart)," "People Make the World Go Round," and "Rockin' Roll Baby" became smash R&B and major pop hits for the Stylistics.

When Thom Bell began working with the Spinners, the Stylistics were placed with the songwriting-production team of Hugo and Luigi under arranger-conductor Van McCoy for 1974's *Let's Put It All Together*. The album's title song was a major pop and easy-listening and smash R&B hit, but the Stylistics never again scored a major pop hit. "Heavy Fallin' Out" and "Thank You Baby" became R&B smashes, but even their popularity in that field began to fade after their switch to H&L Records in 1976. In 1978 James Dunn retired due to ill health and the Stylistics switched to Mercury and then TSOP records for the major R&B hits "First Impressions" and "Hurry Up This Way Again," respectively. James Smith left the group in 1981, and the Stylistics scored their final minor R&B hits on Streetwise Records from 1984 to 1986.

Disc.: *The S.* (1971); *Round 2* (1972); *Rockin' Roll Baby* (1973); *Let's Put It All Together* (1974); *Heavy from the Mountain* (1974); *Best* (1975); *Thank You Baby* (1975); *You Are Beautiful* (1975); *Fabulous* (1976); *Once Upon a Jukebox* (1977); *In Fashion* (1978); *Love Spell* (1979); *Hurry Up This Way Again* (1980); *All-Time Classics* (1986); *Best, Vol. 2* (1986); *Greatest Love Hits* (1986).**—BH**

Styne, Jule (originally, **Stein, Julius Kerwin**), vibrant English-born American composer and theatrical producer; b. London, England, Dec. 31, 1905; d. N.Y., Sept. 20, 1994. Styne reversed the usual pattern for popular composers of his time: Starting his career as a full-time songwriter relatively late, in his mid-thirties, he wrote successfully for the screen, then turned to a lengthier and even more successful stay in the theater. In Hollywood he collaborated frequently with Sammy Cahn and occasionally with Frank Loesser, producing such popular movie songs of the 1940s and 1950s as "I've Heard That Song Before," "I'll Walk Alone," and the Academy Award–winning "Three Coins in the Fountain." On Broadway, working with Cahn, Betty Comden and Adolph Green, Stephen Sondheim, and Bob Merrill, among others, he wrote the music for 16 musicals between 1947 and 1993, including *Funny Girl*, *Gypsy*, and *Bells Are Ringing*. His shows featured such standards as "Diamonds Are a Girl's Best Friend," "Everything's Coming Up Roses," and "People." He was particularly adept at writing for particular performers, such as stars like Frank Sinatra, Doris Day, Ethel Merman, and Barbra Streisand.

Styne's parents were Russian immigrants Isadore and Anna Kertman Stein; in England his father ran a butter-and-egg store, and when the family moved to Chicago in 1912, he became an egg inspector. Styne began piano lessons at six and became a prodigy. At nine he was studying with Esther Harris of the Chicago Coll. of Music, and at nine he performed as soloist with the Chicago, Detroit, and St. Louis symphony orchestras. By his early teens, however, he had turned to popular music and begun to play in local bands. He first tried writing music at 16, and in January 1927 he enjoyed a national hit with "Sunday," recorded by Cliff Edwards among others. (Music and lyrics were credited to Styne, who actually wrote the music, Ned Miller, who wrote the lyrics, Chester Conn, who polished the lyrics, and Benny Krueger, who led the band in which Styne was playing at the time and arranged for the song to be published.) He married Ethel Pauline Rubenstein in September 1927; they had two sons, and Styne later collaborated with the older one, Stanley. The couple divorced in 1952.

Styne organized his own band in the spring of 1932, at which time he was forced to change the spelling of his last name to avoid a conflict with Dr. Julius Stein, head of MCA, his booking agency. In 1934 he moved to N.Y., where he became a vocal coach. Singer Harry Richman hired him as accompanist and conductor in 1936, and in 1937 he went to work at 20th Century–Fox in Hollywood as a vocal coach to such stars as Alice Faye and Shirley Temple. Soon he began contributing occasional songs to films, starting with *Kentucky Moonshine*, released in May 1938. In 1940 he was hired as a songwriter by Republic Pictures, a low-budget studio concerned largely with turning out B movies, mostly Westerns. He quickly amassed numerous film credits. His first movie song to attract attention was "Who Am I?" (lyrics by Walter Bullock) from *Hit Parade of 1941*, released in December 1940 and nominated for an Academy Award.

Styne's music was featured in more than two dozen Republic films released in 1941. Though he did not enjoy any hits from this hastily written material, the period was notable for his first collaborations with Frank Loesser. He moved to the more prestigious Paramount studio, where Loesser worked, and they wrote two songs that became Top Ten hits before being used in the July 1942 release *Sweater Girl*: "I Said No!" recorded by Alvino Rey and His Orch., and "I Don't Want to Walk without You" recorded by Harry James and His Orch. Among Styne's Republic films of the year was *Sleepytime Gal*, which featured "I Don't Want Anybody at All (If I Can't Have You)" (lyrics by Herb Magidson). The song belatedly became a minor hit for Charlie Barnet and His Orch. in December 1944.

Also in 1942, Styne met and began to collaborate with Sammy Cahn. Their first film together was the December 1942 Republic release *Youth on Parade*, which featured "I've Heard That Song Before." In a recording by Harry James, the song became a million-seller and the biggest hit of 1943; it was Styne's second to be nominated for an Academy Award. His third was "A Change of Heart" (lyrics by Harold Adamson), included in *Hit Parade of 1943*, which Republic released in April 1943.

Styne and Cahn had an independently published Top Ten hit in January 1944 when Bing Crosby and The Andrews Sisters took the war-themed "Vict'ry Polka" into the Top Ten. Their next hit also reflected war sentiment. "I'll Walk Alone" was featured in the all-star film *Follow the Boys*, released in April; Dinah Shore, who sang it, recorded it for a #1 hit, and it brought Styne his fourth Oscar nomination.

Styne and Cahn inaugurated their songwriting relationship with Frank Sinatra by writing the songs for his July 1944 film *Step Lively*, but they spent much of the year working on their first stage musical, *Glad to See You* (Philadelphia, Nov. 13, 1944), which closed during tryouts. (In June 1945, Jimmy Dorsey and His Orch. had a Top Ten hit with "Can't You Read between the Lines?" from the score.) They returned to film with the Kay Kyser vehicle *Carolina Blues*, released in December 1944, which generated two hits: "There Goes That Song Again," taken into the Top Ten by Russ Morgan and His Orch., and "Poor Little Rhode Island," recorded by Guy Lombardo and His Royal Canadians and later adopted as R.I.'s state song.

Styne and Cahn led off 1945 with the independently published "Saturday Night (Is the Loneliest Night of the Week)," which Frank Sinatra made into a Top Ten hit. Their next film was *Tonight and Every Night*, starring Rita Hayworth, which was released in March and featured the Oscar-nominated "Anywhere." *Anchors Aweigh*, starring Sinatra and Gene Kelly, came out in July and was one of the top grossing films of the year; its Styne-Cahn score included the hit "What Makes the Sunset?" recorded by Sinatra, and "I Fall in Love Too Easily," which gave the songwriters a second Academy Award nomination for 1945. In November the independent song "It's Been a Long, Long Time" went to #1 for Harry James; Bing Crosby, backed by Les Paul, also topped the charts with it.

In 1946, Styne and Cahn were the primary songwriters for four films, but all their hits for the year came with independent songs. "Let It Snow! Let It Snow! Let It Snow!" topped the charts for Vaughn Monroe and His Orch. in January and went on to become a standard of the holiday season; "Five Minutes More" was a #1 hit for Frank Sinatra in September; and Sinatra took "The Things We Did Last Summer" into the Top Ten in December.

Styne and Cahn wrote the songs Sinatra sang in *It Happened in Brooklyn*, released in March 1947. Sinatra had a Top Ten hit with "I Believe" and a chart entry with "Time after Time." The songwriters then turned to their second stage show, *High Button Shoes*, which became the longest-running musical of the 1947–48 season, playing 727 performances.

Returning to Hollywood, Styne and Cahn signed a three-picture deal at Warner Bros. and wrote the songs for the June 1948 film *Romance on the High Seas*, the movie debut of Doris Day, who had a Top Ten hit with "It's Magic," Styne's seventh Oscar-nominated song. Eddy Howard also had a minor hit with "Put 'Em in a Box, Tie 'Em with a Ribbon (And Throw 'Em in the Deep Blue Sea)" from the film. *Two Guys from Texas*, released in August, featured "Ev'ry Day I Love You (Just a Little Bit More)," a minor hit for Vaughn Monroe. *It's a Great Feeling*, released in August 1949, brought Styne another Academy Award nomination for its title song.

From this point on Styne worked primarily in the Broadway theater, though he still did occasional film work. Sammy Cahn stayed in Hollywood, and Styne teamed with Leo Robin for his next musical, *Gentlemen Prefer Blondes*, starring Carol Channing, which opened in the fall of 1949 for a run of 740 performances. He produced the cast album, which reached the Top Ten and featured "Diamonds Are a Girl's Best Friend."

Styne turned to theatrical production with the unsuccessful musical *Make a Wish* (N.Y., April 18, 1951), with songs by Hugh Martin; he continued to produce stage works through the 1960s, scoring successes with a revival of *Pal Joey* (N.Y., Jan. 3, 1952) and *Mr. Wonderful* (N.Y., March 22, 1956), starring Sammy Davis Jr. His next stage effort as a composer was the revue *Two on the Aisle* (1951), his first collaboration with Betty Comden and Adolph Green, which ran 279 performances.

The release of the Jane Froman film biography *With a Song in My Heart* in April 1952 led to a revival of "I'll

Walk Alone," which Froman sang in the movie and recorded for a chart hit, though the most successful rendition was Don Cornell's Top Ten version. Styne's next musical, *Hazel Flagg* (1953), based on the film *Nothing Sacred* and with lyrics by Bob Hilliard, had an unprofitable run of 190 performances, but Eddie Fisher had a chart hit with "How Do You Speak to an Angel?" The show was adapted into the 1954 film *Living It Up*, starring Dean Martin and Jerry Lewis. The film version of *Gentlemen Prefer Blondes*, meanwhile, was released in July 1953 and was among the most successful movies of the year; starring Marilyn Monroe, it retained only three songs from the stage version, but the soundtrack album was a Top Ten hit.

Styne reunited with Sammy Cahn to write the title song for the May 1954 film *Three Coins in the Fountain*. Frank Sinatra sang the song on the soundtrack, but the Four Aces had the biggest hit with it, topping the charts and selling a million copies; on his ninth try, Styne finally won an Oscar with it. He had another film-related hit in October, when Don, Dick 'n Jimmy scored with "That's What I Like," which he and Bob Hilliard had written for *Living It Up*. That same month he and Comden and Green had half a dozen songs, among them "Never Never Land," in a new musical version of *Peter Pan* (N.Y., Oct. 20, 1954), starring Mary Martin, which had begun with a score by Mark "Moose" Charlap and Carolyn Leigh. Though the show had only a modest initial run on Broadway, it had a successful television broadcast and is revived frequently.

Styne's next full-fledged musical score, again with Comden and Green, was for *Bells Are Ringing* (1956). By the time the curtain opened for the first of the Tony-nominated show's 924 performances in November, Tony Bennett had scored a chart entry with "Just in Time"; Doris Day followed in December with "The Party's Over." The cast album also reached the charts. Styne next worked with Comden and Green on the backstage musical *Say, Darling* (1958), which ran 332 performances and included "Dance Only with Me," a Top 40 hit for Perry Como.

Styne was brought into *Gypsy* (1959), a musical based on the autobiography of stripper Gypsy Rose Lee, after its star, Ethel Merman, objected to having Stephen Sondheim, then an untested composer, do the music. Sondheim, who had previously written lyrics for Leonard Bernstein's music in *West Side Story*, was retained as lyricist. The result was the most critically acclaimed work of Styne's career: the show ran 702 performances and earned a Tony nomination; the cast album stayed in the charts more than two years and tied for the Grammy Award for Best Cast Album; and the score included "Small World," a Top 40 hit for Johnny Mathis and a Grammy nominee for song of the year, "Everything's Coming Up Roses," and "Let Me Entertain You."

Styne and Comden and Green wrote two new songs for the film version of *Bells Are Ringing*, released in June 1960; the resulting LP earned a Grammy nomination for Best Soundtrack Album. Styne next collaborated with George David Weiss on songs for the N.Y. amusement park Freedomland; Johnny Horton had a chart entry with one of them, "Johnny Freedom," in July. Styne's next stage musical, again with Comden and Green, was *Do Re Mi*, a satiric look at the music business. The songwriters demonstrated their expertise on the subject by achieving a chart entry from the score with "Make Someone Happy," recorded by Perry Como, just as the show was opening in December 1960. *Do Re Mi* ran 400 performances and earned a Tony nomination for best musical; the cast LP charted for five months and was nominated for a Grammy for Best Cast Album; "Make Someone Happy" was nominated for a Song of the Year Grammy.

Styne and Comden and Green followed a year later with *Subways Are for Sleeping*. It was a failure, with a run of 205 performances, although the cast album spent a couple of months in the charts. Styne married British model Margaret Ann Bissett Brown on June 4, 1962; the couple had two children. A film version of *Gypsy* was released in November and the soundtrack album became a Top Ten hit. Styne had a rare independent chart entry in November 1963 with the civil rights anthem "Now!" (lyrics by Comden and Green), recorded by Lena Horne.

Funny Girl, a musical based on the life of singer/comedienne Fanny Brice, for which Styne collaborated with Bob Merrill, had a long gestation period, but when it finally opened in 1964 with Barbra Streisand in the lead role, it became the composer's most successful show, running 1,348 performances and earning Tony nominations for Best Musical and Best Score. The cast album hit the Top Ten, went gold, stayed in the charts a year, and won the Grammy Award for Best Cast Recording. Streisand reached the Top Ten with her recording of "People," which earned a Song of the year Grammy nomination. She also charted with an unused title song for the musical.

In May, Styne's first original movie musical in nine years, *What a Way to Go!*, was released. With lyrics and screenplay by Comden and Green and starring Shirley MacLaine, it was among the year's most successful films. The same month, Styne and Comden and Green had another stage musical on Broadway, *Fade In—Fade Out*, starring Carol Burnett; Styne also coproduced. It ran 271 performances and the cast album made the charts. In the fall Styne took on the job of director for the Sammy Fain/Alan and Marilyn Bergman musical *Something More!* (N.Y., Nov. 10, 1964), also writing several songs with the Bergmans, but the show was a flop.

Styne and Merrill's television musical, *The Dangerous Christmas of Little Red Riding Hood* starring Liza Minnelli, was broadcast during the 1965 holiday season. Chris Montez had a Top 40 revival of "Time after Time" in the fall of 1966, and the Styne/Comden and Green television musical *I'm Getting Married* starring Anne Bancroft was broadcast in March 1967. Styne's next stage musical followed in April, when he and Comden and Green mounted *Hallelujah, Baby!* starring Leslie Uggams. It ran 293 performances and won Tony Awards for Best Musical and Best Score; the cast album earned a Grammy nomination for Best Show Recording.

Styne and Bob Merrill wrote a new song called "Funny Girl" for the 1968 movie version of their stage show. When it was released in September it became the highest grossing film of the year, with a million-selling soundtrack LP; the song earned Styne his tenth Academy Award nomination. The Tymes revived "People" for a Top 40 hit, and Diana Ross and the Supremes recorded an entire album of *Funny Girl* songs.

Styne worked on several musicals in the late 1960s and early 1970s, the only successful one being 1972's *Sugar*, written with Bob Merrill and based on the film *Some Like It Hot*. It ran 505 performances and earned a Tony nomination for Best Musical and a Grammy nomination for Best Cast Album.

Styne's subsequent successes came with revivals and remakes. *Lorelei*, a new version of *Gentlemen Prefer Blondes*, starring Carol Channing and with some new songs written with Comden and Green, toured the U.S. in 1973 and ran on Broadway for 320 performances in 1974. A revival of *Gypsy* starring Angela Lansbury ran in London in 1973 and moved to N.Y. in 1974. (There was another Broadway revival starring Tyne Daly in 1990, and a TV version with Bette Midler in 1993.) Also in 1974, Sammy Cahn performed on Broadway in his own revue, *Words and Music*, using many Styne-Cahn compositions. Styne himself performed a nightclub act in 1977. Barry Manilow revived "I Don't Want to Walk without You" for a Top 40 hit in 1980.

Styne taught at N.Y.U. in the 1980s and accompanied Michael Feinstein in the recording of the singer's *Jule Styne Songbook* album in 1991. He also worked on several musicals, notably *Bar Mitzvah Boy* with Don Black, which had a short run in London in 1978 and was produced Off-Broadway as *Song for a Saturday* in 1987, and, with Bob Merrill, *The Red Shoes*, which made it to Broadway for five performances in 1993. He died of heart failure at 88 in 1994.

Works (only for works for which Styne was a primary, credited composer are listed): **FILMS:** *Sing, Dance, Plenty Hot* (1940); *The Girl from Havana* (1940); *Melody and Moonlight* (1940); *Hit Parade of 1941* (1940); *Melody Ranch* (1940); *Ridin' on a Rainbow* (1941); *Sis Hopkins* (1941); *Sheriff of Tombstone* (1941); *Angels with Broken Wings* (1941); *Puddin' Head* (1941); *Nevada City* (1941); *Rags to Riches* (1941); *Ice Capades* (1941); *Sailors on Leave* (1941); *Mountain Moonlight* (1941); *Beyond the Blue Horizon* (1942); *Sweater Girl* (1942); *Priorities on Parade* (1942); *Sleepytime Gal* (1942); *Youth on Parade* (1942); *The Powers Girl* (1943); *Hit Parade of 1943* (aka *Change of Heart*; 1943); *Shantytown* (1943); *Johnny Doughboy* (1943); *Salute for Three* (1943); *Thumbs Up* (1943); *Pistol Packin' Mama* (1943); *Step Lively* (1944); *Carolina Blues* (1944); *Tonight and Every Night* (1945); *Anchors Aweigh* (1945); *Behind City Lights* (1945); *Tars and Spars* (1946); *Cinderella Jones* (1946); *The Kid from Brooklyn* (1946); *Earl Carroll Sketchbook* (1946); *Ladies' Man* (1947); *It Happened in Brooklyn* (1947); *Romance on the High Seas* (1948); *Two Guys from Texas* (1948); *It's a Great Feeling* (1949); *The West Point Story* (1950); *Meet Me after the Show* (1951); *Two Tickets to Broadway* (1951); *Double Dynamite* (1951); *Macao* (1952); *Gentlemen Prefer Blondes* (1953); *Living It Up* (1954); *My Sister Eileen* (1955); *Bells Are Ringing* (1960); *Gypsy* (1962); *What a Way to Go!* (1964); *Funny Girl* (1968). **STAGE** (all dates refer to N.Y. openings unless otherwise noted): *High Button Shoes* (Oct. 9, 1947); *Gentlemen Prefer Blondes* (Dec. 8, 1949); *Two on the Aisle* (July 19, 1951); *Hazel Flagg* (Feb. 11, 1953); *Bells Are Ringing* (Nov. 29, 1956); *Say, Darling* (April 3, 1958); *Gypsy* (May 21, 1959); *Do Re Mi* (Dec. 26, 1960); *Subways Are for Sleeping* (Dec. 27, 1961); *Funny Girl* (March 26, 1964); *Fade Out—Fade In* (May 26, 1964); *Hallelujah, Baby!* (April 26, 1967); *Darling of the Day* (Jan. 27, 1968); *Look to the Lilies* (March 29, 1970); *Sugar* (April 9, 1972); *Lorelei* (Jan. 27, 1974); *Words and Music* (April 16, 1974); *Bar Mitzvah Boy* (London, Oct. 31, 1978); *The Red Shoes* (Dec. 16, 1993). **TELEVISION:** *Ruggles of Red Gap* (Feb. 3, 1957); *Mr. Magoo's Christmas Carol* (1962); *The Dangerous Christmas of Little Red Riding Hood* (Nov. 28, 1965); *I'm Getting Married* (March 16, 1967); *The Night the Animals Talked* (Dec. 6, 1970).

Bibl.: T. Taylor, *J.: The Story of Composer J. S.* (N.Y., 1979).
—**WR**

Styx, late 1970s–early 1980s pop-rockers. **Membership:** Chuck Panozzo, bs. (b. Chicago, Sept. 20, 1947); John Panozzo, drm. (b. Chicago, Sept. 20, 1947; d. there, July 16, 1996); Dennis DeYoung, kybd., voc. (b. Feb. 18, 1947); James Young, gtr., voc. (b. Chicago, Nov. 14, 1949); John Curulewski, gtr.; Tommy Shaw, gtr., voc. (b. Montgomery, Ala., Sept. 11, 1953); Glen Burtnick, gtr., voc.; Todd Sucherman, drm.

A fusion of the classically oriented rock orchestrations of Yes, the pristine studio sheen of REO Speedwagon, and three-part vocal harmonies, Styx became one of the biggest selling acts of the late 1970s and early 1980s. A 1980 Gallup poll named them the most popular band in the U.S. They were the first band in history to have four consecutive triple platinum albums.

The group began in the mid-1960s as a trio of twin brothers John and Chuck Panozzo on drums and bass respectively, with Dennis DeYoung on accordion and vocals. They played cover versions from their teen years as the Tradewinds. They then attended Chicago State Univ. where they became There Were Four (or TW4) with guitarist Tom Nardini, who left the band in the late 1960s. Another Chicago State student, John Curulewski, replaced him. The band augmented itself with another guitarist, James Young, after his band left en masse to become Jehovah's Witnesses.

The five-man TW4 became one of the hottest cover bands in the Midwest. In 1971 they were offered a record contract by RCA-distributed Chicago label Wooden Nickel. They changed their name to one they felt better suited the times, Styx. Their debut single, "Best Thing," charted its first week out, but stalled in the low 80s. The debut album didn't chart at all. For their second album, DeYoung put more effort into writing original songs, including a proto-power ballad love song to his new wife, "Lady." Initially, the single stiffed, as did the album. They discovered that their record company had spent less than $200 to promote the project.

Their two 1984 releases—*The Serpent Is Rising* and *Man of Miracles*—didn't do much to help the band's fortunes. Through the mid-1980s, they were still touring the Midwest, playing basketball courts and bars from Utah to Ark. On a radio promotion swing for *Man of Miracles* in 1985, they paid a visit to powerhouse station WLS. Jim Smits from the station said he wouldn't play anything from the fourth album, but he had been getting a lot of requests for the single "Lady" from the second album, and swore he would keep playing it until it became a hit. And it did, rising to #6 on the pop charts nearly two years after it originally came out! It catapulted the *Styx II* album to #20 and gold. However, the success of the two-year-old record didn't help their current fortunes. None of the singles for *Man of Miracles* charted higher than the high 80s. The band decided that the fault lay not with them but with their record company.

Although other companies made better offers, the band felt they would get a fairer shake at artist-run A&M and signed with them. They led off their 1975 A&M debut *Equinox* with their first Top 40 single since "Lady," a rocker called "Lorelei" with a countrified guitar playing over a sequencer, which hit #27 pop. Their second single off the album, "Mademoiselle," went to #36. The band was back in the big time, sort of.

Just as things were looking up for the band, Curulewski left the group to spend more time with his family. They were about to hit the road in support of *Equinox* and remembered a guitarist they had played with on the road with a band called MS Funk. They called him, auditioned him, and within days, Tommy Shaw had joined Styx. What could have been a disaster turned into one of the best things that had happened in their dozen or so years together. Shaw could hit the high notes, both vocally and on guitar. Beyond that, he added another songwriting voice to the group.

Shaw segued into the group nicely on their next album, 1976's *Crystal Ball*, writing the title track. The group started opening for acts ranging from Seals and Croft to Queen. When they went into the studio again, they were tight, primed, and ready. They cranked out an album that fans regard as a masterpiece, *The Grand Illusion*. Leading off with the single "Come Sail Away," the band broke fast out of the gate. The song hit #8 on the pop charts in 1977. "Fooling Yourself" became a rock radio favorite and crossed over pop to #29. With its blend of crunchy pomp and ersatz science fiction, the album went to #6 and sold triple platinum. The follow-up album, *Pieces of Eight*, a reflection on their hard-won success, also hit #6 and triple platinum, although the singles didn't chart nearly as strongly: "Blue Collar Man," a rumination on their working-class roots hit #21, and "Renegade," with its madrigal-like opening and near martial beat, hit #16. They started to play arenas around the world.

Although their first hit had been the relatively gentle "Lady," the band had drifted into a harder rock sound. DeYoung decided to rein that in a little on their next album, 1979's *Cornerstone*. He wrote a "going on the road" ballad with a singular Fender Rhodes sound. That song, "Babe," went gold and topped the charts for two weeks. Along with the similar "Why Me" at #26, it sent *Cornerstone* to #2 and double platinum.

Their momentum peaked with their next release, 1981's *Paradise Theater*. Loosely a concept album, it dealt with a theater built just before the depression hit, and how it ultimately deteriorates into a parking lot. The deluxe album package included laser etching on the vinyl. With the bombastic "The Best of Times" rising to #3 and the clockwork elegy on unemployment "Too Much Time on My Hands" hitting #9, the album topped the charts for three weeks, going triple platinum, their fourth multi- platinum record in a row.

With that under their belt, Styx attempted an even more ambitious concept with 1983's *Kilroy Was Here*, a futuristic anti-censorship piece, that had a fictitious "warning label" on it. This touch would seem less humorous several years later when these labels were widely attached to pop records. With the gold #3 hit "Mr. Roboto" and the #6 "Don't Let it End," the album still only managed to hit single platinum, rising to #3. Styx tried to turn the concept into a theatrical work during their tour, including a 15-minute film that introduced the show, but it wound up confusing as many fans as it pleased.

In many ways, it was the last straw for the band. After 20 years of non-stop touring, with their success waning and several members of the band suffering substance abuse problems, they decided to go their separate ways. DeYoung released several moderately successful solo albums, and had a Top Ten single with the title track from 1984's *Desert Moon*. Shaw had a minor hit that same year with "Girls with Guns." DeYoung explored the theater, taking roles in *Jesus Christ Superstar*, writing his own musical version of *The Hunchback of Notre Dame*, and recording an album of show tunes. Young worked on several more experimental albums with former Mahavishnu Orch. keyboard player Jan Hammer. From 1990–92, Shaw joined the hard rock supergroup Damn Yankees with Ted Nugent and Night Ranger's Jack Blades, landing the top 3 "High Enough" and the #20 "Where You Going" and a gold and double platinum record.

As Damn Yankees started rising through the charts, Styx started talking again. Everyone but Shaw agreed that it was time to get together again, so they hired studio ace Glen Burtnik to replace him and cut 1990's *Edge of the Century*. While the first single from the album stiffed, the second single "Show Me the Way" rose to #3 on the charts under curious circumstances. A radio edit of the song started making the rounds during the U.S. involvement in the Persian Gulf War, using soundbites from news coverage of the conflict. The song had nothing to do with the war, but it worked.

Shaw rejoined the band for new tracks on a 1995 greatest hits record (including a re-recording of "Lady") and the band came back together and went on a greatest hits tour. However, drummer John Panozzo, whose health was deteriorating thanks to years of hard drinking, did not make the tour. They hired drummer Todd Sucherman to play the drums while Panozzo recovered, but Panozzo died of a stroke while the band was on tour.

After taking some time off, the band signed to CMC records and released the live album *Return to Paradise* in 1997. It became the label's first gold record. In the late 1990s, a number of Styx songs from their back catalog became newly popular. A version of "Come Sail Away" (performed by Isaac Hayes) appeared in the hit cartoon movie *South Park*. "Mr. Roboto" was used in a Volkswagen commercial, doubling sales of the bands greatest hit record the week it came out. Other songs cropped up in other 1970s and 1980s period films. In 1998, the group released their first new studio album since *Kilroy*, 15 years earlier. *Brave New World*, based loosely on the Huxley book, charted briefly. However, key band members were not faring well: DeYoung fell ill with a disease that left him chronically tired and extremely sensitive to bright lights; Chuck Panozzo lost his twin and his mother within the space of a couple of years, and he was not up to the road. Nonetheless, with two fill-in players, the band went on the road.

Disc.: **STYX:** *Styx* (1972); *Styx II* (1973); *The Serpent Is Rising* (1974); *Man of Miracles* (1974); *Equinox* (1975); *Crystal Ball* (1976); *The Grand Illusion* (1977); *Pieces of Eight* (1978); *Cornerstone* (1979); *Paradise Theater* (1981); *Kilroy Was Here* (1983); *Caught in the Act* (1984); *Edge of the Century* (1990); *Return to Paradise* (1997); *Brave New World* (1999). **TOMMY SHAW:** *Girls with Guns* (1984); *What If?* (1985); *Ambition* (1987); *7 Deadly Zens* (1998). **DAMN YANKEES:** *Damn Yankees* (1990); *Don't Tread* (1992). **DENNIS DEYOUNG:** *Desert Moon* (1984); *Back to the World* (1986); *Boomchild* (1988); *10 on Broadway* (1994). **JAMES YOUNG:** *City Slicker* (1986); *Out on a Day Pass* (1994); *Raised by Wolves* (1995). **GLEN BURTNICK:** *Palookaville* (1996).—**HB**

Subirá (Puig), José, eminent Spanish musicologist; b. Barcelona, Aug. 20, 1882; d. Madrid, Jan. 5, 1980. He studied piano and composition at the Madrid Cons. and simultaneously qualified for the practice of law (Dr.Jur., 1923), then held various government posts in Madrid while pursuing musicological research. In 1952 he was elected a member of the Real Academia de Bellas Artes de San Fernando in Madrid. Apart from his scholarly pursuits, he publ. a novel, *Su virginal pureze* (1916), and a historical account, *Los Españoles en la guerra de 1914–1918* (4 vols.).

Writings: *Enrique Granados* (Madrid, 1926); *La música en la Casa de Alba* (Madrid, 1927); *La participación musical en el antiguo teatro español* (Barcelona, 1930); *Tonadillas teatrales inéditas: Libretos y partituras* (Madrid, 1932); *"Celos aun del aire matan": Opera del siglo XVII, texto de Calderón y música de Juan Hidalgo* (Barcelona, 1933); *La tonadilla escénica: Sus obras y sus autores* (Barcelona, 1933); *Historia de la música teatral en España* (Barcelona, 1945); with H. Anglès, *Catálogo musical de la Biblioteca Nacional de Madrid* (Barcelona, 1946–51); *La ópera en los teatros de Barcelona* (Barcelona, 1946); *Historia de la música Salvat* (Barcelona, 1947; third ed., enl., 1958); *Historia y ancedotario del Teatro Real* (Madrid, 1949); *El compositor Iriarte (1750–1791) y el cultivo español del melólogo (melodrama)* (Barcelona, 1949–50); *La música, etapas y aspectos* (Barcelona, 1949); *El teatro del Real palacio (1849–1851), con un bosquejo preliminar sobre la música palatina desde Felipe V hasta Isabel II* (Madrid, 1950); *Historia de la música española e hispanoamericana* (Barcelona, 1958); *Temas musicales madrileños* (Madrid, 1971).—**NS/LK/DM**

Subono, Blacius, popular Indonesian composer and dhalang (shadow puppet master), brother of **Yohanes Subowo;** b. Klaten, Central Java, Feb. 3, 1954. He was born into an artistic family, the seventh of 9 children who all became successful artists. He began his music studies at 6, often accompanying his father, the shadow puppet master Yusuf Kiyatdiharjo; at 12, began to perform alone. While at the high school cons. Konservatori Karawitan (KOKAR), he helped to create a new form of puppet theater, *wayang kancil*, featuring a cast of animal characters and new musical arrangements; at the college cons. Akademi Seni Karawiten Indonesia (A.S.K.I., later Sekolah Tinggi Seni Indonesia [S.T.S.I.]) Surakarta, he was encouraged by its director, S.D. Humardani, to try his hand at musical experimentation. He composed several new works, including another wayang innovation, *wayang sandosa*; in 1983 he attended the national Pekan Komponis Muda (Young Composer's Festival) in Jakarta. He received numerous commissions and invitations to perform the 9-hour *wayang kulit*; performed and lectured in France (1982), Singapore (1982), England and Spain (1984), and Canada and the U.S. (1986); in 1990 he lectured at Simon Fraser Univ. in Vancouver, where he composed his first work with an English text. Subono's output includes popular songs with gamelan accompaniment as well as experimental scores, i.e., 1 for a chamber ensemble made up of only very high-pitched instruments (*griting rasa*), 1 for a wide range of knobbed gongs (*swara pencon*), and several unrealized pieces for very large chorus. His publications concerning musical accompaniment for the new, intensified style of *wayang kulit* called *pakeliran padat* include *Iringan Pakeliran Dewasa Ini* (1981), *Kuliah Letihan Tabuh Iringan Pakeliran Padat di ASKI Surakarta* (1984), and *Evaluasi Garap Iringan Pakeliran Padat* (1987).

Works (all scored for Central Javanese gamelan): **EXPERIMENTAL:** *Swara Pencon I* (1983) and *II* (1986); *Griting Rasa* (1989). **DANCE:** *Komposisi Hitam Putih* (1980); *Rudrah* (1981); *Bisma Gugur* (1982); *Ronggolawe Gugur* (1982); *Kusumo Asih* (1983); *Anila Prahastho* (1985); *Bhagawatgita* (1985); *Gathutkaca Burisrawa* (1985); *Jemparingan* (1985); *Anoman Kataksini* (1986); *Rahwana Gandrung* (1987). **SHADOW PUPPET THEATER (PAKELIRAN PADAT):** *Kangsa Lena* (1983); *Kilat Buana* (1984); *Duryudana Gugur* (1985); *Gandamana Tundhung* (1985). **DANCE OPERA (WAYANG ORANG):** *Seno Kridho* (1984). **MODERN SHADOW PUPPET THEATER (WAYANG SANDOSA):** *Karna Tandhing* (1982); *Dewa Ruci* (1983); *Ciptaning* (1984). **SONGS:** *Pungjir* (1974); *Kidang Kencana* (1980); *Surakarta Lejer Budaya* (1982); *Solo Berseri* (1985); *Gotong Royong* (1985); *Bingung* (1986); *Air Minum* (1987); *Palinglih* (1987); *Sukaharja Papanku* (1987); *Urip Prasaja* (1987); also scripts for puppet theater with animal characters only (*wayang kancil*) and for dance opera (*wayang orang*).—**NS/LK/DM**

Subotnick, Morton, American composer and teacher; b. Los Angeles, April 14, 1933. He studied at the Univ. of Denver (B.A., 1958) and with Milhaud and Kirchner at Mills Coll. in Oakland, Calif. (M.A., 1960); then was a fellow of the Inst. for Advanced Musical Studies at Princeton Univ. (1959–60). He taught at Mills Coll. (1959–66), N.Y.U. (1966–69), and the Calif. Inst. of the Arts (from 1969); also held various visiting professorships and composer-in-residence positions. In 1979 he married **Joan La Barbara**. His compositions run the gamut of avant-garde techniques, often with innovative use of electronics; his *Silver Apples of the Moon* (1967) became a classic. In 1995, working with programmer Mark Coniglio at the Inst. for Studies in the Arts at Ariz. State Univ. in Tempe, he completed *Making Music*, an interactive CD-ROM composition program for children; his *All My Hummingbirds Have Alibis*, an "imaginary ballet" set to a series of Max Ernst's paintings for Flute, Cello, Midi Piano, Midi Mallets, and Electronics (1991), was also later converted into a critically appraised CD-ROM. His interest in the relationship between performers and technology have resulted in the composition of a series of "ghost pieces," 11 chamber works for instruments and interactive electronics in which the "ghost" score (which contains no audible sounds) consists of a digital program that commands electronic modules to modify the instrumental sounds as they are played from a traditionally notated score; in this series are *Axolotl* for Cello and Electronics (1982) and *Tremblings* for Violin, Piano, and Electronics (1983). More recent works utilized computerized sound generation, specially designed software, and intelligent computer controls which allow performers to interact in a complex and musical manner with computer technology. On April 17, 1998 he received the annual SEAMUS Award for significant contributions to the art and craft of electroacoutic music.

Works: DRAMATIC: Opera: *Jacob's Room* (Philadelphia, April 20, 1993). **Incidental Music To:** Genet's *The Balcony* (1960); Shakespeare's *King Lear* (1960); Brecht's *Galileo* (1964) and *The Caucasian Chalk Circle* (1965); Büchner's *Danton's Death* (1966). **ORCH.:** *Play! No. 2* for Orch. and Tape (1964); *Lamination No. 1* for Orch. and Tape (1968) and *No. 2* for Chamber Ensemble and Electronics (1969); *Before the Butterfly* for 7 Solo Instruments and Orch. (1975; Los Angeles, Feb. 26, 1976); *2 Butterflies* for Amplified Orch. (1975); *Place* (1979); *Axolotl* for Cello, Chamber Orch., and Electronics (1982); *Liquid Strata* for Piano, Orch., and Electronics (1982); *The Key to Songs* for Chamber Orch. and Synthesizer (1985); *In Two Worlds*, concerto for Saxophone, Electronic Wind Controller, and Orch. (1987–88); *And the Butterflies Began to Sing* for YCAMS and Chamber Ensemble (1988); *A Desert Flower* (1989). **MIXED MEDIA:** *Mr. and Mrs. Discobolos* for Clarinet, Violin, Cello, Narrator-Mime, and Tape (1958); *Mandolin* for Viola, Tape, and Film (1961–63); *Sound Blocks* for Narrator, Violin, Cello, Xylophone, Marimba, Tape, and Lights (1961); *Play! No. 1* for Wind Quintet, Tape, and Film (1963), *No. 3* for Piano, Tape, and Film (1964), and *No. 4* for 4 Actors, Performers, Piano, Vibraphone, Cello, and 2 Films (1965); *4 Butterflies* for Tape and 3 Films (1973); *The Double Life of Amphibians*, theater piece (1984); *Hungers* (1986). **VOCAL:** *2 Life Histories* for Man's Voice, Clarinet, and Electronics (1977); *Last Dream of the Beast* for Woman's Voice and Electronics (1978); *Jacob's Room* for Voice and String Quartet (1984; San Francisco, Jan. 11, 1985). **INSTRUMENTAL:** *Prelude No. 1 (The Blind Owl)* for Piano and *No. 2 (The Feast)* for Piano (both 1956); Viola Sonata (1959); String Quartet (1960); Sonata for Piano, 4-Hands (1960); *Serenade No. 1* for Flute, Clarinet, Vibraphone, Mandolin, Cello, and Piano (1960) and *No. 2* for Clarinet, Horn, Percussion, and Piano (1962); *10* for 10 Instruments (1963–76); *The Tarot* for Chamber Ensemble (1965); *The Fluttering of Wings* for String Quartet (1982). **INSTRUMENTAL AND ELECTRONICS:** *Preludes Nos. 3 and 4* for Piano and Tape (1962–65); *Serenade No. 3* for Flute, Clarinet, Violin, Piano, and Tape (1963); *Liquid Strata* for Piano and Electronics (1977); *Parallel Lines* for Piccolo, 9 Instruments, and Electronics (1978); *Passages of the Beast* for Clarinet and Electronics (1978); *The Wild Beasts* for Trombone, Piano, and Electronics (1978); *After the Butterfly* for Trumpet, 7 Instruments, and Electronics (1979); *The first Dream of Light* for Tuba, Piano, and Electronics (1979); *Ascent into Air* for 10 Instruments and Electronics (1981); *An Arsenal of Defense* for Viola and Electronics (1982); *Axolotl* for Cello and Electronics (1982); *Tremblings* for Violin, Piano, and Electronics (1983); *All My Hummingbirds Have Alibis* for Flute, Cello, Midi Piano, Midi Mallets, and Electronics (1991). **ELECTRONIC:** *The 5-legged Stool* (1963); *Parades and Changes* (1967); *Silver Apples of the Moon* (1967); *Realty I* and *II* (1968); *The Wild Bull* (1968); *Touch* (1969); *Sidewinder* (1971); *Until Spring* (1975); *Ice Floe* (1978); *A Sky of Cloudless Sulphur* (1978); *Sky with Clouds* (1978); *Return* (1984).—**NS/LK/DM**

Subowo, Yohanes, Indonesian dancer and composer, brother of **Blacius Subono;** b. Klaten, Central Java, Jan. 1, 1960. He was born into an artistic family (his 8 older siblings were professional artists), and although he wanted to join the army, he was persuaded by his father, the shadow puppet master (dhalang) Yusuf Kiyatdiharjo, to pursue a career in the arts. After studying dance and composition at Inst. Seni Indonesia (I.S.I., National Arts Inst.; graduated, 1986), he joined its dance faculty. In 1982 he began experimenting with instruments other than those of the Javanese gamelan; made small instruments from bamboo, tuning them to the gamelan, using cowbells, tin roofing sheets, and whistles made from bamboo and coconut leaves; also transposed music using techniques from Javanese gamelan to such Western instruments as electronic keyboards. In some compositions, he imposes strict limitations on pitch and/or instrumentation and also experiments with such extended vocal techniques as having singers sing into bamboo tubes or bronze pot-gongs. His compositions borrow their structures from jazz, rock, and Western Classical styles, while drawing on African and popular Indonesian music; these include *Orak-Arik, Lesung* (1981), *Gobyog* (1982), *Kentongan, Patmo* (1982), and *Tanggung* (1984), variously scored for Javanese gamelan, found objects, farm tools, and electronic and original instruments. He also experimented with sounds generated by devices attached to a dancer's body. In 1985 he toured England as both a dancer and a musician.—**NS/LK/DM**

Sucher, Josef, Hungarian conductor and composer, husband of **Rosa Sucher** (née **Hasselbeck**); b. Döbör, Nov. 23, 1843; d. Berlin, April 4, 1908. He studied in Vienna with Sechter, and was made a répétiteur (1870) and an asst. conductor (1873) at the Court Opera there, and then was conductor at the city's Komische Theater (1874–76). He was conductor of the Leipzig City Theater (1876–78), where he married Rosa Hasselbeck in 1877; they were at the Hamburg Stadttheater from 1878 to 1888, at which time Sucher became conductor of the Berlin Royal Opera, his wife being engaged there as prima donna. He left the Berlin post in 1899. Sucher was especially distinguished as an interpreter of the Wagnerian repertoire. He composed several vocal works: *Aus alten Märchen* for Women's Voices with Orch., *Waldfräulein* for Soprano, Chorus, and Orch., *Seeschlacht bei Lepanto* for Men's Chorus and Orch., and songs.
—**NS/LK/DM**

Sucher, Rosa (née Hasselbeck), German soprano, wife of **Josef Sucher;** b. Velburg, Feb. 23, 1849; d. Eschweiler, April 16, 1927. She received her early musical training from her father, a chorus master. She sang in provincial operas, then in Leipzig, where she married Josef Sucher in 1877; they subsequently were engaged at the Hamburg Stadttheater (1878–88). In 1882 she made her London debut as Elsa in *Lohengrin;* in 1886 she appeared in Vienna. She made regular visits to the Bayreuth Festivals (1886–96) and was a principal member of the Berlin Royal Opera (1888–98). On June 8, 1892, she made her Covent Garden debut in London as the *Siegfried* Brünnhilde; on Feb. 25, 1895, she made her American debut as Isolde at the Metropolitan Opera in N.Y., under the sponsorship of the Damrosch Opera Co. In 1903 she gave her farewell operatic performance in Berlin as Sieglinde. In 1908 she settled in Vienna as a voice teacher. She publ. her memoirs, *Aus meinem Leben* (Leipzig, 1914). Among her other fine roles were Euryanthe, Elisabeth, and Senta.—**NS/LK/DM**

Suchoff, Benjamin, distinguished American music educator and musicologist; b. N.Y., Jan. 19, 1918. He studied at Cornell Univ. (B.S., 1940), and then took courses in composition with Vittorio Giannini at the Juilliard School of Music in N.Y. (1940–41). After serving in the U.S. Army in Europe and Asia in World War II, he resumed his studies, first at Juilliard (1946–47) and then at N.Y.U. (M.A., 1949; Ed.D., 1956, with the diss. *Guide to Bartók's Mikrokosmos*; publ. in London, 1957; third ed., N.Y., 1982). From 1950 to 1978 he was administrator of music at Hewlett- Woodmere Union Free School on Long Island, where he also taught electronic music. From 1973 to 1984 he was adjunct prof. of arts and letters at the State Univ. of N.Y. at Stony Brook, and also was director of its special collections and of the Center for Contemporary Arts and Letters, where he guided the fortunes of the COMMPUTE Program, a consortium of institutions active in research and development of computer-oriented music studies. In 1953 he became curator of the N.Y. Bartók Archive. From 1968 until the death of Bartók's widow in 1982 he was successor-trustee of the Bartók estate. In 1992 he became adjunct prof. in the dept. of ethnomusicology and systematic musicology at the Univ. of Calif., Los Angeles. He was the ed. of the N.Y. Bartók Archive edition of Bartók's writings in English trs. in its Studies in Musicology series, and also ed. of its edition of Bartók's compositions, known as *The Archive Edition.*

WRITINGS: *A Musician's Guide to Desktop Computing* (N.Y., 1993); *Bartók: The Concerto for Orchestra: Understanding Bartók's World* (N.Y., 1995); ed. *Béla Bartók: Essays* (Lincoln, Nebr., 1997); ed. with E. Antokoletz and V. Fischer, *Bartók Perspectives* (Oxford, 1999).—**NS/LK/DM**

Suchoň, Eugen, significant Slovak composer and pedagogue; b. Pezinok, Sept. 25, 1908; d. Bratislava, Aug. 5, 1993. He studied piano and composition with Kafenda at the Bratislava School of Music (1920–28), then took a course in advanced composition with V. Novák at the Master School of the Prague Cons. (1931–33). He taught composition at the Bratislava Academy of Music (1933–48) and music education at the Univ. of Bratislava (1949–60); was a prof. of theory there from 1959 to 1974; in 1971 he was appointed prof. at the Coll. of Music and Dramatic Art in Bratislava. In 1958 he was named National Artist of the Republic of Czechoslovakia. He was one of the creators of the modern Slovak style of composition, based on authentic folk motifs and couched in appropriately congenial harmonies.

WORKS: DRAMATIC: Opera: *Krútňava* (The Whirlpool; 1941–49; Bratislava, Dec. 10, 1949); *Svätopluk* (1952–59; Bratislava, March 10, 1960). **ORCH.:** *Fantasy and Burlesque* for Violin and Orch. (originally a *Burlesque*, 1933; the *Fantasy* was added in 1948); *Balladic Suite* for Orch. or Piano (1935); *Metamorphoses*, symphonic variations (1951–52); *6 Pieces* for String Ensemble or String Quartet (1955–63); *Sinfonietta rustica* (1956); *Rhapsodic Suite* for Piano and Orch. (1965); *Kaleidoscope*, 6 cycles for Strings, Percussion, and Piano (1967–68); *Symphonic Fantasy on B-A-C-H* for Organ, Strings, and Percussion (1971); Clarinet Concertino (1975); *Prielom Symphony* (1976). **CHAMBER:** Violin Sonata (1930); String Quartet (1931; rev. 1939); *Serenade* for Wind Quintet (1931); Piano Quartet (1932–33); Violin Sonatina (1937); *Poème macabre* for Violin and Piano (1963); piano pieces, including a *Toccata* (1973). **VOCAL:** *Nox et solitudo* for Soprano, and Small Orch. or Piano (1933); *Carpathian Psalm*, cantata (1937–38); *Ad astra*, 5 songs for Soprano and Small Orch. (1961); *Contemplations* for Narrator and Piano (1964).

BIBL.: E. Zavarský, *E. S.* (Bratislava, 1955); J. Kresánek, *Národný umelec E. S.* (National Artist E. S.; Bratislava, 1961). —**NS/LK/DM**

Suchý, František, Czech oboist, pedagogue, and composer; b. Libina u Šumperka, April 9, 1902; d. Brno, July 12, 1977. He studied oboe with Wagner and composition with Kvapil at the Brno Cons. (graduated, 1927), then attended Novák's master classes at the Prague Cons. (until 1937). He was first oboist in the Brno Radio Orch. (1927–47), then a prof. of oboe at the Cons. and a prof. of oboe and theory at the Academy in Brno.

WORKS: DRAMATIC: Opera: *Maryla* (1956). **ORCH.:** Flute Concerto (1939); *Baroque Concerto* for Violin and Orch. (1944); 4 syms. (1946, 1950, 1957, 1962); Oboe Concerto (1948); *Vysočina* (Uplands), symphonic suite (1957). **CHAMBER:** Oboe Sonatina (1927); 2 wind quintets (1928, 1958); Wind Sextet (1960); various sonatas. **VOCAL:** *V. Gethsemanĕ*, oratorio (1933); cantatas; songs.—**NS/LK/DM**

Suckling, Norman, English pianist, teacher, writer on music, and composer; b. London, Oct. 24, 1904. He received his academic education at Queen's Coll., Oxford, specializing in French literature. He was asst. master at Liverpool Collegiate School (1925–43); then was a lecturer in French language and literature at King's Coll., Newcastle upon Tyne, in the Federal Univ. of Durham (1943–70). While thus occupied, he developed sufficient mastery of the piano to give concerts, at which he presented programs of modern French music. He publ. a monograph on Gabriel Fauré (London, 1946) and several books on French literature; also contributed articles on English and French composers to the Listener and other literary publications. His compositions are mostly in small forms; his songs are particularly fine.

WORKS: *Introduction and Scherzo* for String Quartet (1923); *Ode* for Violin and Piano (1925); *A Vision of Avalon*, chamber opera (1928); *A Cycle of Shakespeare Sonnets* for Tenor, Violin, and

Piano (1928); Violin Sonata (1928); *Man in the Beginning*, ballet (1934); *Berceuse élégiaque* for Clarinet and Piano, to commemorate a pet kitten, and written for the composer's first wife (1943); *Pastorale saugrenue* for Flute and Bassoon (1944); *Variations on a Theme of Rameau* for Flute and Piano (1947); many songs to words by English poets.—**NS/LK/DM**

Suda, Stanislav, blind Czech flutist and composer; b. Starý Plzenec, April 30, 1865; d. Plzen, Sept. 2, 1931. He was brought up at the Prague Inst. for the Blind, and developed his innate musical abilities to the point where he could give concerts and compose operas, 3 of which were produced at Plzen: *U Božich Muk* (March 22, 1897), *Lešetińsky Kovář* (April 4, 1903), and *Il divino Boemo* (Dec. 30, 1927). He also wrote an autobiographical symphonic poem, *Život ve tmách* (The Life in Darkness).—**NS/LK/DM**

Sudhalter, Dick (actually, **Richard M.**), jazz cornetist, author; b. Boston, Dec. 28, 1938. Sudhalter was a correspondent for the *New York Post* in the 1950s. In the 1960s, he played with various bands in the U.S. and West Germany, as well as his own bands, Jazz without Walls and Anglo-American Alliance. In the mid-1970s, he was living in London; starting in 1974, he led the New Paul Whiteman Orch. He directed the N.Y. Jazz Repertory Company's Bix Beiderbecke Concert at Carnegie Hall, N.Y. in 1975. During that time, he also led his own sextet, Commodore, which backed up Bobby Hackett. In the mid-1980s, he played in the Classic Jazz Quartet with Dick Wellstood. Since 1989, Sudhalter has performed as a member of the Vineyard Jazz Ensemble with Loren Schoenberg and Joe Muryani. Sudhalter is best-known as a jazz critic and writer; he wrote about jazz for UPI (1964–72) and the *New York Post* (1978–84), and has also written liner notes for various jazz reissues. His most recent book, *Lost Chords*, argued the importance of white musicians in the development of early jazz.

Disc.: *Classic Jazz Quartet* (1984); *After Awhile* (1994); *Anglo–American Alliance: Sweet and Hot* (1968). New Paul Whiteman Orch.: *Runnin' Wild* (1975).

Writings: *Bix: Man and Legend Quartet* (N.Y., 1974); *Lost Chords: White Musicians and Their Contribution to Jazz, 1915–1945* (N.Y., 1999).—**LP**

Sugár, Rezső, Hungarian composer and teacher; b. Budapest, Oct. 9, 1919; d. there, Sept. 22, 1988. He was a pupil of Kodály at the Budapest Academy of Music (1937–42). He taught in Budapest at the Béla Bartók Cons. (1949–68); from 1968 to 1980 he taught at the Academy of Music.

Works: DRAMATIC: Ballet: *Ácisz és Galatea* (Acis and Galatea; 1957; rev. 1961 as *A tenger lánya* [The Daughter of the Sea]). **ORCH.:** *Divertimento* for Strings (1948); *Rondo* for Piano and Strings (1952); *Concerto in Memoriam Béla Bartók* (1962); *Metamorfosi* (1966); *Partita* for Strings (1967); *Variation Symphony* (1970); *Epilogue* (1974); Concertino for Chamber Orch. (1976); *Pastorale e rondo* (1978). **CHAMBER:** *Serenade* for 2 Violins and Viola (1943); Violin Sonata (1946); 3 string quartets (1947, 1950, 1969); *Frammenti musicali*, sextet for Piano and Wind Quintet (1958); *Rhapsody* for Cello and Piano (1959); also *Baroque Sonatina* for Piano (1943–46). **VOCAL: Oratorios:** *Hunyadi: Hősi ének* (Hunyadi: Heroic Song; 1951); *Paraszti háború* (Peasant War; 1976); *Savonarola* (1979). **Cantata:** *Kőmíves Kelemen* (Kelemen, the Mason; 1958). **Other:** Numerous choral pieces; songs.—**NS/LK/DM**

Sugarhill Gang, The, arguably the first hitmaking stars of rap and originators of the phrase "hip-hop". **Membership:** Master G. (real name, Guy O'Brien) (b. N.Y.C., 1963); Wonder Mike (real name, Michael Wright) (b. Englewood, N.J., 1958); Big Bank Hank (real name, Henry Jackson) (b. Bronx, N.Y., 1958).

Owners of several small independent soul labels, Joe and Sylvia Robinson heard rap music at a house party in N.Y.C. and thought it might sell if they recorded it. So they created a track based on the break in Chic's hit "Good Times" and brought in three local rappers. The results, "Rapper's Delight," became the first rap record to reach the pop charts, topping out at #36 (#4 R&B), although the Fatback band had come close earlier in the year with "King Tim (Personality Jock)." With the rappers' boasting rhymes and mildly salacious (especially by today's standards) sexuality, the record was perfect party music. The gang hit the road—the first rap group to do that as well—creating a furor wherever they went. However, their follow-up single, "8th Wonder" topped out at #15 R&B, and their other records didn't chart at all as existing crews like Grandmaster Flash, the Cold Crush Crew, and others started recording. The Gang made a comeback with a children's record released on Rhino in 1999, teaching kids the joys of Dr. Seuss and grammar with rap.

Disc.: *Rapper's Delight: Hip Hop Remix* (1980); *The Sugarhill Gang* (1980); *8th Wonder* (1982); *Jump on It!* (1999).—**HB**

Suggia, Guilhermina, gifted Portuguese cellist; b. Oporto, June 27, 1888; d. there, July 31, 1950. She was a child prodigy, making her first public appearance at age 7, and became first cellist in the Oporto Orch. when she was 12. Under the patronage of the Queen of Portugal, she was sent to Leipzig in 1904 to study with Julius Klengel; in 1905 she joined the Gewandhaus Orch. there. In 1906 she began studies with Casals; they subsequently lived and toured together, although they were never legally married; she appeared in concerts as Mme. Casals-Suggia until they parted company in 1912. Shortly afterward she settled in London, where she continued to appear in concerts until 1949, when she went back to Portugal. She was greatly appreciated for her fine musicianship as well as virtuosity. In 1923 Augustus John painted her portrait, which became famous.

Bibl.: F. Pombo, *G. S. ou o violoncelo luxuriante* (Porto, 1993); idem, *G. S.: A Sonata de sempre* (Porto, 1996).
—**NS/LK/DM**

Suitner, Otmar, Austrian conductor; b. Innsbruck, May 16, 1922. He studied piano at the Innsbruck Cons. and then piano with Ledwinka and conducting with Krauss at the Salzburg Mozarteum (1940–42). In 1945 he conducted at the Innsbruck Landestheater; was then music director in Remscheid (1952–57) and Generalmusikdirektor in Ludwigshafen (1957–60). From 1960 to 1964 he served as Generalmusikdirektor of the Dresden State Opera and Dresden State Orch.; from 1964 to 1971, conducted at the East Berlin State Opera, and from 1974 to 1991 was its Generalmusikdirektor. He also conducted in America; was a guest conductor with the San Francisco Opera.—**NS/LK/DM**

Suk (I), Josef, eminent Czech violinist, pedagogue, and composer, grandfather of **Josef Suk (II);** b. Křečovice, Jan. 4, 1874; d. Benešov, near Prague, May 29, 1935. He received training in piano, violin, and organ from his father, Josef Suk (1827–1913), the Křečovice school- and choirmaster; then took courses in violin with Bennewitz, in theory with Foerster, Knittl, and Stecker, and in chamber music with Wihan at the Prague Cons. (1885–91); after graduating in 1891, he pursued additional training in chamber music with Wihan and in composition with Dvořák at the Cons. (1891–92). In 1898 he married Dvořák's daughter Otilie. He began his career playing second violin in Wihan's string quartet, which became known as the Czech Quartet in 1892; he remained a member of it until his retirement in 1933. He also was a prof. of composition at the Prague Cons. (from 1922), where he was head of its master classes; also served as its rector (1924–26; 1933–35). Suk's early works were greatly influenced by Dvořák; in later years his lyrical Romantic style evolved into an individual style characterized by polytonal writing and harmonic complexity bordering on atonality.

WORKS: DRAMATIC: Incidental Music: *Radúz a Mahulena* for Alto, Tenor, Reciters, Chorus, and Orch., op.13 (Prague, April 6, 1898; rev. 1912); *Pod jabloní* (Beneath the Apple Tree) for Alto, Reciters, Chorus, and Orch., op.20 (1900–1901; rev. 1911, 1915; Prague, Jan. 31, 1934). **ORCH** (all first perf. in Prague unless otherwise given): *Fantasie* for Strings (1888; Jan. 29, 1940); *Smuteční pochod* (Funeral March; 1889; rev. 1934; June 3, 1935); *Dramatická overtura*, op.4 (1891–92; July 9, 1892); *Serenade* for Strings, op.6 (1892; Feb. 25, 1894); *Pohádka zimniho večera* (Tale of a Winter's Evening), overture after Shakespeare, op.9 (1894; April 7, 1895; rev. 1918, 1925); 2 syms.: No. 1 in E major, op.14 (1897–99; Nov. 25, 1899) and No. 2, *Asrael*, op.27 (1905–06; Feb. 3, 1907); *Pohádka* (Fairy Tale), suite from *Radús a Mahulena*, op.16 (1899–1900; Feb. 7, 1901); *Fantasie* for Violin and Orch., op.24 (1902–03; Jan. 9, 1904); *Fantastické scherzo*, op.25 (1903; April 18, 1905); *Praga*, symphonic poem, op.26 (Pilsen, Dec. 18, 1904); *Pohádka léta* (A Summer Fairy Tale), symphonic poem, op.29 (1907–09; Jan. 26, 1909); *Zráni* (The Ripening), symphonic poem, op.34 (1912–17; Oct. 30, 1918); *Meditace na staročeský chorál "Svatý Vaclave"* (Meditation on an Old Czech Chorale "St. Wenceslas") for Strings, op.35a (1914; also for String Quartet); *Legenda o mrtvých vitězich* (Legend of the Dead Victors), op.35b (1919–20; Oct. 24, 1924); *V nozý zivot* (Toward a New Life), march, op.35c (June 27, 1920; also for Piano Duet); *Pod Blanikem* (Beneath Blanik), march (1932; orchestrated by J. Kalaš; Jan. 26, 1934). **CHAMBER:** *Polka* for Violin (1882); String Quartet (1888); *Fantasy* for String Quartet and Piano ad libidum (1888); Piano Quartet, op.1 (1891); Piano Trio, op.2 (1889; rev. 1890–91); *Balada* for String Quartet (1890); *Balada* for Cello and Piano, op.3/1 (1890); *Serenade* for Cello and Piano, op.3/2 (c. 1898); *Balada* for Violin and Piano (1890); *Melodie* for 2 Violins (1893); Piano Quintet, op.8 (1893); String Quartet, op.11 (1896; last movement rev. 1915 and left as an independent work); 4 Pieces for Violin and Piano, op.17 (1900); *Elegie: Pod dojmen Zeyerova Vyšehradu* (Under the Impression of Zeyer's Vyšehrad) for Violin, Cello, String Quartet, Harmonium, and Harp, op.23 (1902; also for Piano Trio); String Quartet, op.31 (1911); *Meditace na staročeský chorál "Svatý Václave"* (Meditation on an Old Czech Chorale "St. Wenceslas") for String Quartet, op.35a (1914; also for String Orch.); *Bagatelle: S kyticí v ruce* (Carrying a Bouquet) for Flute, Violin, and Piano (1917); *Sousedská* for 5 Violins, Double Bass, Cymbals, Triangle, and Large and Small Drums (1935). **Piano:** Sonata (1883); *Overture* (1884–85); *Polonaise* (1886–87); *Jindřichohradecký cyklus* (Jindřichův Hradec Suite; 1886–87); Fugue (1888); *Tři pisně beze slov* (3 Songs without Words; 1891); *Fantaisie-polonaise*, op.5 (1892); 6 pieces, op.7 (1891–93); *Capriccietto* (1893); *Humoreska* (1894); *Lístek do památníku* (Album Leaf; 1895); *Nálady* (Moods), op.10 (1895); 8 pieces, op.12 (1895–96); Sonatina, op.13 (1897; rev. as Suite, op.21, 1900); *Vesnická serenáda* (Village Serenade; 1897); *Jaro* (Spring), op.22a (1902); *Letni dojmy* (Summer Moods), op.22b (1902); *O matince* (About Mother), op.28 (1907); *Psina španělská* (Spanish Joke; 1909); *Životem a snem* (Things Lived and Dreamt), op.30 (1909); *Ukolébavky*, op.33 (1910–12); *O přátelství* (Friendship), op.36 (1920). **VOCAL:** *Křečovická mše* (Křečovice Mass) for Chorus, Strings, and Organ (1888–89); *Epilog* for Soprano, Baritone, Bass, 2 Choruses, and Orch., op.37 (1920–33; Dec. 20, 1933); men's choruses; songs.

BIBL.: J. Kvt, ed., *J. S.: Život a dilo: Studie a vzpomínsky* (J. S.: Life and Works: Studies and Reminiscences; Prague, 1935); idem, *J. S.* (Prague, 1936); J. Šach, ed., *J. S.: Vzpomínková mozaika* (J. S.: A Mosaic of Reminiscences; Prague, 1941); V. Štěpán, *Novák a S.* (Prague, 1945); J. Květ, ed., *Živá slova J.a S.a* (In J. S.'s Own Words; Prague, 1946); O. Filipovský, *Klavirni tvorba J.a S.a* (J. S.'s Piano Works; Plzen, 1947); J. Květ, *J. S.* (Prague, 1947); J. Berkovec, *J. S. (1874–1935): Život a dilo* (J. S. [1874–1935]: Life and Works; Prague, 1956; second ed., 1962; rev. and abr. ed., 1968, as *J. S.*; Eng., Ger., French, and Russian trs., 1968); J. Květ, *J. S. v obrazech* (J. S. in Pictures; Prague, 1964); Z. Sádecký, *Lyrismus v tvorbě J.a S.a* (Lyricism in J. S.'s Works; Prague, 1966); M. Svobodová, *J. S.: Tematický Katalog* (Jinočany, 1993).
—**NS/LK/DM**

Suk (II), Josef, outstanding Czech violinist, grandson of **Josef Suk (I)** and great-grandson of **Antonín (Leopold) Dvořák;** b. Prague, Aug. 8, 1929. He was only a child when he commenced violin lessons with Jaroslav Kocián, who remained his teacher until the latter's death in 1950; Suk also studied at the Prague Cons. (until 1951) and then with M. Hlouňová and A. Plocek at the Prague Academy of Music (1951–53). He made his public debut in 1940; later played in the orch. of the Prague National Theater; also was a member of the Prague Quartet (1951–52). In 1952 he founded the Suk Trio with the pianist Jan Panenka and the cellist Josef Chuchro, and toured widely with it; his interest in chamber music led him to form a duo with Zuzana Růžičkova in 1963; he was also a member of a trio with Julius Katchen and Janos Starker (1967–69). In 1959 he made a grand tour as soloist to 3 continents with the Czech Phil. On Jan. 23, 1964, he made his U.S. debut with the Cleveland Orch., and subsequently appeared as soloist with other American orchs. In 1964 he received a Czech State Prize, in 1970 he was made an Artist of Merit, and in 1977 was named a National Artist of Czechoslovakia.—**NS/LK/DM**

Suk, Váša (Václav; Viacheslav Ivanovich), noted Russian conductor and composer of Czech parentage; b. Kladno, Nov. 16, 1861; d. Moscow, Jan. 12, 1933. He studied violin at the Prague Cons. and composition privately with Fibich. He was concertmaster of the Kiev Opera orch. (1880–82) and a violinist in the Bolshoi Theater orch. in Moscow (1882–87); in 1885 he launched a conducting career, and subsequently appeared throughout Russia; was a conductor of the Bolshoi Theater (1906–32) and principal conductor of the Stanislavsky Opera Theater in Moscow (from 1927). He was appreciated in Russia for his thoroughness in drilling the singers and the orch.; achieved a fine reputation as an operatic conductor. He wrote an opera, *Lord of the Forests*, which he conducted in Kharkov on Feb. 16, 1900, a symphonic poem, *Jan Huss* (Moscow, March 12, 1933); a Serenade for String Orch., piano pieces, and songs.

Bibl.: I. Remezov, *V.I. S.* (Moscow and Leningrad, 1951). **—NS/LK/DM**

Sukegawa, Toshiya, Japanese composer; b. Sapporo, July 15, 1930. He studied with Ikenouchi from 1951; graduated in composition from the Univ. of Arts in Tokyo in 1957.

Works: Dramatic: Television Opera: *Pôra no Hiroba* (1959). **Orch.:** *Passacaglia* (1954); *Partita* (1960); *Legend* (1965). **Chamber:** String Quartet (1956); *Music* for Flute, Clarinet, Violin, Cello, Percussion, and Piano (1958); Wind Quintet (1962); *5 Metamorphoses* for Viola and Piano (1966); *3 Parts* for 5 Flute Players (1967); *3 Scenes* for Jushichigen, 3 Violins, and Viola (1969); *A Projection* for Marimba, Piccolo, Trombone, Piano, and Percussion (1969); *5 Pieces after Paul Klee* for Marimba (1973); *Song of the Wind* for Tape (1980); *Les Jours passants*, trio for Flute, Violin, and Harpsichord (1982); *Eternal Morning* for Tape (1983); *Mirror* for 2 Flutes (1984); *The Berin Strait* for Tape (1986); *Blue Mountain* for Synthesizer and Tape (1987); *La Folia 2 (From the Galaxy Far Away)* for Synthesizer (1988). Piano: Sonata (1958); *Divertimento* for 2 Pianos (1958); *Tapestry* (1966–68); *5 Symbolic Pictures* (1972); *Sequenza* (1985); *Komoriuta* (1986). **Vocal:** *The White World* for Chorus and Piano (1971); *Eika* for Chorus and Japanese Percussion (1972).**—NS/LK/DM**

Sukerta, Pande Made, innovative Indonesian composer, writer on Balinese music, and teacher; b. Tekakula, Singaraja, Bali, 1953. He studied at the high school music cons. in Denpasar, specializing in the rebab (bowed double-stringed fiddle); in 1973 he entered the Akademi Seni Karawitan Indonesia (A.S.K.I.) Surakarta, where he was founding director of various Balinese gamelan groups; also was active as a performer of *eksperimen karawitan baru*, a style of experimental music played on traditional instruments. After graduating in 1979, he joined the faculty at A.S.K.I. (later Sekolah Tinggi Seni Indonesia [S.T.S.I.]), where he led improvisation workshops wherein students explored the sonic potential of both gamelan and "found" instruments. He participated in Jakarta's Young Choreographers' Festival (1978) and at the national Pekan Komponis Muda (Young Composers' Festival; 1979, 1981, 1984); his *Asanawali* for Balinese Gamelan and Chorus was heard at EXPO '86 in Vancouver as part of the first International Gamelan Festival on a program of the Vancouver Sym. Orch., which included works by Debussy and Colin McPhee. In 1989 he was one of 7 composers commissioned to create new works for a recording project of the American Gamelan Inst. in Hanover, N.H. He toured in France, Denmark, Italy, Switzerland, Iran, Australia, Canada, and the U.S. Sukerta's works are variously scored for Balinese and Javanese gamelans and "found" instruments and often include improvisatory aspects; his *Mana 689* (1989) makes use of drums from Java, Sunda, and Sumatra, as well as bottles, marbles, a chanting priest, and screaming children (2 of his own 4). Other works include *Malam, Demung, Gora Suara* (1981), and *Saik 789* (1989). He is also a prolific writer, numbering among his publications an extended essay on the process of composition, an encyclopedia of Balinese instruments, and transcriptions of melodies from the archaic Balinese ensemble Gambuh.

Writings (all publ. in Surakarta): *Gending-gending Semar Pegulingan Saih Pitu* (1977); *Rebaban Karawitan Bali* (1979); *Gending-gending Gong Gede; Gamelan Gong Gede di Desa Batur* (1986; notation and drawings of instruments and cases). **—NS/LK/DM**

Šulek, Stjepan, prominent Croatian violinist, conductor, teacher, and composer; b. Zagreb, Aug. 5, 1914; d. there, Jan. 16, 1986. He studied violin with Huml at the Zagreb Academy of Music; was largely self-taught in composition, although he succeeded in becoming a composer of considerable merit. He was active as a violinist; became best known as a conductor; conducted the Zagreb Radio Chamber Orch. on many tours of Europe; was prof. of composition at the Zagreb Academy of Music (from 1945). His compositions reveal a strong individual profile.

Works: Dramatic: Opera: *Koriolan*, after Shakespeare (Zagreb, Oct. 12, 1958); *Oluja* (The Tempest), after Shakespeare (Zagreb, Nov. 28, 1969). **Orch.:** 6 syms. (1944, 1946, 1948, 1954, 1963, 1966); *Scientiae et arti*, festive prologue (1966); 4 piano concertos (1949, 1951, 1963, 1970); Cello Concerto (1950); Violin Concerto (1951); Bassoon Concerto (1958); Viola Concerto (1959); Clarinet Concerto (1967); Horn Concerto (1972); Organ Concerto (1974). **Other:** *Zadnji Adam* (The Last Adam), cantata (1964); songs; piano pieces.

Bibl.: K. Šipuš, *S. Š.* (Zagreb, 1961).**—NS/LK/DM**

Sullivan, Sir Arthur (Seymour), famous English composer and conductor; b. London, May 13, 1842; d. there, Nov. 22, 1900. His father, Thomas Sullivan, was bandmaster at the Royal Military Coll., Sandhurst, and later prof. of brass instruments at the Royal Military School of Music, Kneller Hall; his musical inclinations were encouraged by his father, and in 1854 he became a chorister in the Chapel Royal, remaining there until 1858 and studying with the Rev. Thomas Helmore. In 1855 his sacred song *O Israel* was publ. In 1856 he received the first Mendelssohn Scholarship to the Royal Academy of Music in London, where he studied with Sterndale Bennett, Arthur O'Leary, and John Goss; then continued his training at the Leipzig Cons. (1858–61), where he received instruction in counterpoint and fugue from Moritz Hauptmann, in composition from Julius Rietz, in piano from Ignaz Moscheles and Louis Plaidy, and in conducting from Ferdinand David. He conducted his overture *Rosenfest* in Leipzig (May 25, 1860), and wrote a String Quartet and music to *The Tempest* (Leipzig, April 6, 1861; rev. version, London, April 5, 1862). His cantata *Kenilworth* (Birmingham Festival, Sept. 8, 1864) stamped him as a composer of high rank. In 1864 he visited Ireland and composed his *Irish Symphony* (London, March 10, 1866). In 1866 he was appointed prof. of composition at the Royal Academy of Music in London. About this time he formed a lifelong friendship with Sir George Grove, whom he accompanied in 1867 on a memorable journey to Vienna in search of Schubert MSS, leading to the discovery of the score of *Rosamunde*. The year 1867 was also notable for the production of the first of those comic operas upon which Sullivan's fame chiefly rests. This was *Cox and Box* (libretto by F.C. Burnand), composed in 2 weeks and performed on May 13, 1867, in London. Less successful were *The Contrabandista* (London, Dec. 18, 1867) and *Thespis* (London, Dec. 26, 1871), but the latter is significant as inaugurating Sullivan's collaboration with Sir W.S. Gilbert, the celebrated humorist, who became the librettist of all Sullivan's most successful comic operas, beginning with *Trial by Jury* (March 25, 1875). This was produced by Richard D'Oyly Carte, who in 1876 formed a company expressly for the production of the "Gilbert and Sullivan" operas. The first big success obtained by the famous team was *H.M.S. Pinafore* (May 25, 1878), which had 700 consecutive performances in London, and enjoyed an enormous vogue in "pirated" productions throughout the U.S. In an endeavor to protect their interests, Gilbert and Sullivan went to N.Y. in 1879 to give an authorized performance of *Pinafore*, and while there they also produced *The Pirates of Penzance* (Dec. 30, 1879). On April 23, 1881, came *Patience*, a satire on exaggerated esthetic poses exemplified by Oscar Wilde, whose American lecture tour was conceived as a "publicity stunt" for this work. On Nov. 25, 1882, *Iolanthe* began a run that lasted more than a year. This was followed by the comparatively unsuccessful *Princess Ida* (Jan. 5, 1884), but then came the universal favorite of all the Gilbert and Sullivan operas, *The Mikado* (March 14, 1885). The list of these popular works is completed by *Ruddigore* (Jan. 22, 1887), *The Yeomen of the Guard* (Oct. 3, 1888), and *The Gondoliers* (Dec. 7, 1889). After a quarrel and a reconciliation, the pair collaborated in 2 further works, of less popularity: *Utopia Limited* (Oct. 7, 1893) and *The Grand Duke* (March 7, 1896).

Sullivan's melodic inspiration and technical resourcefulness, united with the delicious humor of Gilbert's verses, raised the light opera to a new height of artistic achievement, and his works in this field continue to delight countless hearers. Sullivan was also active in other branches of musical life. He conducted numerous series of concerts, most notably those of the London Phil. Soc. (1885–87) and the Leeds Festivals (1880–98). He was principal of, and a prof. of composition at, the National Training School for Music from 1876 to 1881. He received the degree of Mus.Doc. honoris causa from Cambridge (1876) and Oxford (1879); was named Chevalier of the Légion d'honneur (1878); was grand organist to the Freemasons (1887); etc. He was knighted by Queen Victoria in 1883. Parallel with his comic creations, he composed many "serious" works, including the grand opera *Ivanhoe* (Jan. 31, 1891), which enjoyed a momentary vogue. His songs were highly popular in their day, and *The Lost Chord*, to words by Adelaide A. Proctor (publ. 1877), is still a favorite. Among his oratorios, *The Light of the World* (Birmingham Festival, Aug. 27, 1873) may be mentioned. Other stage works (all first perf. in London unless otherwise given) include *The Zoo* (June 5, 1875), *The Sorcerer* (Nov. 17, 1877; rev. version, Oct. 11, 1884), *Haddon Hall* (Sept. 24, 1892), *The Chieftain* (Dec. 12, 1894), *The Martyr of Antioch* (Edinburgh, Feb. 15, 1898; a stage arrangement of the cantata), *The Beauty-Stone* (May 28, 1898), *The Rose of Persia*, romantic opera (Nov. 29, 1899), and *The Emerald Isle* (completed by E. German, April 27, 1901). He also composed 2 ballets: *L'Ile enchante* (May 14, 1864) and *Victoria and Merrie England* (May 25, 1897).

BIBL.: A. Lawrence, *Sir A. S.: Life Story, Letters and Reminiscences* (London, 1899); W. Wells, *Souvenir of Sir A. S., Mus.-Doc., M.V.O.* (London, 1901) B. Findon, *Sir A. S.: His Life and Music* (London, 1904; second ed., rev., 1908, as *Sir A. S. and His Operas*); F. Cellier and C. Bridgeman, *Gilbert, S., and D'Oyly Carte* (London, 1914; second ed., 1927); H. Walbrook, *Gilbert and S. Opera* (London, 1922); A. Godwin, *Gilbert and S.* (London, 1926); H. Wyndham, *A.S. S.* (London, 1926); N. Flower and H. Sullivan, *Sir A. S.: His Life, Letters and Diaries* (London, 1927; second ed., 1950); T. Dunhill, *S.'s Comic Operas: A Critical Appreciation* (London, 1928); I. Goldberg, *The Story of Gilbert and S.* (London, 1929); H. Pearson, *Gilbert and S.* (London, 1935); G. Dunn, *A Gilbert and S. Dictionary* (N.Y., 1936); C. Purdy, *Gilbert and S.: Masters of Mirth and Melody* (N.Y., 1947); W. Darlington, *The World of Gilbert and S.* (N.Y., 1950); A. Jacobs, *Gilbert and S.* (London, 1951); L. Bailey, *The Gilbert and S. Book* (N.Y., 1952; third ed., 1966); A. Williamson, *Gilbert and S. Operas: A New Assessment* (N.Y., 1953); A. Powers-Waters, *The Melody Maker: The Life of Sir A. S.* (N.Y., 1959); M. Green, *Treasury of Gilbert and S.* (London, 1961); N. Wymer, *Gilbert and S.* (London, 1962); C. Bulla, *Stories of Gilbert and S. Operas* (N.Y., 1968); J. Helyar, ed., *Gilbert and S. International Conference: Kansas 1970* (Lawrence, Kans., 1971); P. Young, *Sir A. S.* (London, 1971); L. Ayre, *The Gilbert & S. Companion* (N.Y., 1972); M. Hardwick, *The Osprey Guide to Gilbert and S.* (Reading, 1972); P. Kline, *Gilbert and S. Production* (N.Y., 1972); L. Baily, *Gilbert & S. and Their World* (London, 1973); R. Allen and G. D'Luhy, *Sir A. S.: Composer & Personage* (N.Y., 1975); I. Bradley, ed., *The Annotated Gilbert and S.* (2 vols., London, 1982, 1984); A. Williamson, *Gilbert & S. Opera* (London, 1983); A. Jacobs, *A. S.: A Victorian Musician* (Oxford, 1984; second ed., rev. and enl., 1992); J. Wolfson, *S. and the Scott Russells* (Chichester, 1984); D. Eden, *Gilbert & S.: The Creative Conflict* (Rutherford, N.J., 1986); C. Hayter, *Gilbert and S.* (N.Y., 1987); I. Asimov, ed., *Asimov's Annotated Gilbert & S.* (N.Y., 1988); M. Ffinch, *Gilbert and S.* (London, 1993); M. Saremba, *A. S.: Ein Komponistenleben im viktorischen England* (Wilhelmshaven, 1993); I. Bradley, ed., *The Complete Annotated Gilbert and S.* (N.Y., 1996); P. Dillard, *Sir A. S.: A Resource Book* (Lanham, Md., 1996).—**NS/LK/DM**

Sullivan, Ira (Brevard Jr.), jazz trumpeter, flugelhornist, saxophonist, flutist; b. Washington, D.C., May 1, 1931. He was first associated with the Chicago modern-jazz scene, then moved to Fla. in the mid-1960s and has basically remained there since, performing in the Ft. Lauderdale area. Sullivan toured with Red Rodney in a co-led group in the early and mid-1980s. He is a devout Christian and is astonishingly fluent and impassioned on all his instruments.

DISC.: *Billy Taylor Introduces Ira Sullivan* (1956); *Nicky's Tune* (1958); *Blue Stroll* (1959); *Bird Lives!* (1962); *Horizons* (1967); *Multimedia* (1977); *Ira Sullivan* (1977); *Strings Attached* (1978); *Peace* (1978); *Live at the Village Vanguard* (1980); *Incredible* (1980); *Ira Sullivan Does It All* (1981); *Sprint* (1982). Red Rodney: *Red Rodney Live at the Village Vanguard* (1980).—**LP**

Sullivan, Joe (actually, **Joseph Michael**), jazz pianist, composer; b. Chicago, Nov. 4, 1906; d. San Francisco, Oct. 13, 1971. Sullivan studied for several years at the Chicago Cons. of Music. In the summer of 1923 he led his own quartet in Ind., then worked for 18 months on the vaudeville circuit, beginning with Elmo Mack and His Purple Derbies. He then played mainly in Chicago, working on the radio and making many recordings. Sullivan moved to N.Y. in the late 1920s, and played with Red Nichols's Band there and on tour (1929). Through the early 1930s, he worked with various N.Y. groups, including Roger Wolfe Kahn's Orch. (1930, again spring 1933), Red McKenzie's Mound City Blue Blowers (1931 and early 1932), Ozzie Nelson (mid-1932), and Russ Colombo (late 1932). He moved to Calif. in 1933 and worked regularly in a studio orch. and as Bing Crosby's accompanist (he appeared with Bing in three films). Sullivan moved back to N.Y. in the summer of 1936 and joined Bob Crosby's Band. He remained with Bob Crosby until December 1936; a lung complaint was diagnosed and he spent the next 10 months in a sanatorium recovering. (During 1938 a mammoth benefit concert was held for him in Chicago, featuring Bob Crosby's Band, Roy Eldridge, The Dodds Brothers, and others.) Sullivan subsequently recommenced working as accompanist for Bing Crosby. In the summer of 1939 he briefly rejoined Bob Crosby as featured pianist. He left in September 1939 and a month later began leading his own mixed small band at N.Y.'s Cafe Society; the band continued to work N.Y. clubs until January 1941. From spring 1943 to spring 1945, Sullivan was back in Los Angeles, then worked as a duo with pianist Meade Lux Lewis in Chicago. He played regularly at Eddie Condon's N.Y. club from 1946 to 1947, then returned to the West Coast. During the 1950s Sullivan worked mostly in San Francisco, except for a brief spell with The Louis Armstrong All Stars in early 1952. His health began to fail in the early 1960s due to years of heavy drinking, but he managed to continue to play occasional engagements. He became seriously ill in 1970 and died shortly thereafter.

Sullivan composed many well-known jazz tunes, including "Little Rock Getaway" and "Gin Mill Blues." He appeared in many films in the 1930s; his sextet also recorded the music for the 1940 film *Fight for Life*. In 1955 the original Bob Crosby Band assembled for a television tribute to Sullivan.

DISC.: *Piano* (1944); *New Solos by an Old Master* (1951); *Joe Sullivan Plays Fats Waller* (1954); *Mr. Piano Man* (1955); *Joe Sullivan* (1963).—**JC/LP**

Sullivan, Maxine, jazz singer, valve trombonist, flugelhornist; b. Homestead, Pa., May 13, 1911; d. Bronx, N.Y., April 7, 1987. In the early 1930s, Sullivan did radio work in Pittsburgh and sang locally with The Red Hot Peppers. She was heard by pianist Gladys Mosier, who took her to the Onyx Club where Claude Thornhill (who worked briefly as her musical director) arranged her recording debut. Sullivan worked regularly with John Kirby (to whom she was married from 1938 to 1941) and recorded a big-selling version of "Loch Lomond," arranged by Claude Thornhill. She got national exposure for two years on CBS Radio singing with Kirby; the show *Flow Gently Sweet Rhythm* was the only African American show on the radio network at that time. In the late 1930s Sullivan worked regularly on the West Coast before returning to N.Y. She toured with Benny Carter's Band in the summer of 1941, then temporarily retired to Philadelphia in 1942. In the mid-1940s, she returned to N.Y. and began long residencies at various clubs. She worked in Europe in 1948, then left the music profession for a while and worked as a nurse. Beginning in 1950, Sullivan began a successful comeback that featured her valve trombone playing. She returned to Europe in 1954 before retiring once more that same year. She returned again in 1958 and resumed club work through the 1960s. Sullivan first appeared with The World's Greatest Jazz Band in 1969, and continued to work with them through the decade. She recorded the songs of Harold Arlen, Jules Styne, and Ted Koehler during the 1980s.

DISC.: *Maxine Sullivan and John Kirby* (1940); *Biggest Little Band in the Land* (1940); *Maxine Sullivan* (1955); *Complete Charlie Shavers with Maxine Sullivan* (1956); *Sullivan Shakespeare, Hyman* (1971); *With Ike Isaacs Trio* (1978); *Uptown* (1985); *Together* (1986); *At Vine St. Live* (1986).—**JC/LP**

Sultan, Grete, German-born American pianist; b. Berlin, June 21, 1906. She was reared in a musical family; studied with Kreutzer at the Berlin Hochschule für Musik (1922–25) and later with Fischer, Arrau, and Buhlig. She established herself as a pianist of both Classical and contemporary works in Berlin before going to the U.S. in 1941; she toured widely, giving all-Bach, all-Beethoven, all-Schubert, and all-contemporary programs; made her N.Y. debut in 1947. She became associated with Cowell, with whom she gave performances of works by Schoenberg and Stravinsky; settling in N.Y., she met John Cage, who became a lifelong friend and assoc.; they often appeared in concerts together, and Cage wrote his *Etudes australes*, a chance-determined set of 32 etudes based on star maps, for her; she performed it throughout the U.S. and Europe and in Japan. In 1968–69 she gave a series of programs at N.Y.'s Town Hall under its Jonathan Peterson Lectureship Fund. Sultan's performances, which continue well into her 80s, are always critically acclaimed, her alacrity, sensitivity, and uncompromising directness uniquely enhancing the disparate works she programs; most recently she has championed the works of Ben Weber and Tui St. George Tucker. She was praised by Arrau, who saw her as following "...in the footsteps of the greatest women keyboard masters—Landowska, Haskil, Hess—blessed with musical purity and inwardness, reinforced by mind as well as soul."—**NS/LK/DM**

Sultan, Juma, fusion-jazz bassist, conga player; b. Monrovia, Calif., April 23, 1942. Sultan studied art at UCLA, working as a painter, sculptor, and jewelry maker. He was involved in folk music as a teenager, playing baritone sax, tuba, guitar, and trumpet. He founded the Aboriginal Music Society, an ensemble devoted originally to hand-made and non-Western instruments. In the early 1960s, Sultan moved to N.Y., where he worked with Jimi Hendrix. With James Dubois, he founded the musicians' community center, Studio We. Sultan has also been active in organizing the N.Y. Musicians Festivals, and has worked with Sonny Murray.—**LP**

Sulzer, Julius Salomon, Austrian violinist and conductor, son of **Salomon Sulzer;** b. Vienna, 1834; d. there, Feb. 13, 1891. He served as music director of the Hofburgtheater in Vienna from 1875.—**NS/LK/DM**

Sulzer, Salomon, important Austrian composer, father of **Julius Salomon Sulzer;** b. Hohenems, Vorarlberg, March 30, 1804; d. Vienna, Jan. 17, 1890. He was only 16 when he was appointed cantor at the chief synagogue in his hometown. He studied music with Seyfried in Vienna, and from 1825 to 1881 he was cantor of the new Vienna synagogue. He undertook a bold reform of liturgical music by the introduction of musical form and actual compositions from the Classical period, setting Schubert's songs as a model. By so doing, he succeeded in bringing traditional Jewish cantillation together with Western modes. He brought out an anthology, *Schir Zion* (The Heart of Zion; 2 vols., 1838–40; 1865–66), and *Denkschrift an die hochgeehrte Wiener israelitische Cultus-Gemeinde zum funfzigjährigen Jubiläum des alten Bethauses* (Vienna, 1876).

Bibl.: M. Steiner, *S. S.* (Vienna, 1904); P. Minkowski, *Der S.ismus* (Vienna, 1905); H. Avenary, *Kantor S. S. und seine Zeit: Eine Dokumentation* (Sigmaringen, 1985).—**NS/LK/DM**

Sumac, Yma (real name, **Emperatriz Chavarri),** Peruvian-born American singer of a phenomenal diapason, whose origin is veiled in mystical mist; b. Ichocan, Sept. 10, 1927. She was reared in the Andes; it is credible that she developed her phenomenal voice of 5 octaves in range because her lungs were inflated by the necessity of breathing through oxygen at the high altitude. However that might be, she married Moises Vivanco, who was an arranger for Capitol Records and who launched her on a flamboyant career as a concert singer; with him and their cousin, Cholito Rivero, she toured South America as the Inca Taky Trio (1942–46); then settled in the U.S. and became a naturalized American citizen in 1955. She was billed by unscrupulous promoters as an Inca princess, a direct descendant of Atahualpa, the last emperor of the Incas, a Golden Virgin of the Sun God worshipped by the Quechua Indians. On the other hand, some columnists spread the scurrilous rumor that she was in actuality a Jewish girl from Brooklyn whose real name was Amy (retrograde of Yma) Camus (retrograde of Sumac). But Sumac never spoke with a Brooklyn accent. She exercised a mesmeric appeal to her audiences, from South America to Russia, from Calif. to Central Europe; expressions such as "miraculous" and "amazing" were used by Soviet reviewers during her tour of Russia in 1962; "supersonic vocal skill" was a term applied by an American critic. Her capacity did not diminish with age; during her Calif. appearances in 1984 and again in 1988 she still impressed audiences with the expressive power of her voice.—**NS/LK/DM**

Sumera, Lepo, esteemed Estonian composer and pedagogue; b. Tallinn, May 8, 1950; d. there, June 4, 2000. He received training in conducting and composition at the Tallinn Music H.S. before pursuing his study of composition at the Tallinn State Cons. (1968–73). He later took postgraduate courses at the Moscow Cons. (1979–82). From 1973 to 1978 he was a recording supervisor for the Estonian Radio. In 1976 he became prof. of composition at the Estonian Music Academy, where he was head of the dept. of composition and musicology (1988–89) and director of the electronic music studio (1995–99). From 1990 to 1992 he also served as minister of culture of the Republic of Estonia, and from 1993 he was chairman of the Estonian Composers Union. His works were awarded several Estonian music prizes.

Works: Dramatic: *Anselmi lugu*, ballet (1977–78); *Ja'st'eritsa*, ballet (1986–88); *Saare Piiga laul merest* (The Island Maiden), *Linda matab Kalevit* (Linda Buries Kalev), and *Linda soome Tuuslar* (Linda Becomes Stone), multimedia dance drama for Chamber Chorus, Actors, and Shaman Drum (1988); *Olivia's Master class*, chamber opera (1997); also more than 40 scores for film, television, animation, and theater. **Orch.:** *In Memoriam* (1972); *Music* for Chamber Orchestra (1977–78; Tallinn, June 30, 1979); *Olūpiamuusika* (Olympic Music; 1981); 5 syms.: No. 1 (1980; Tallinn, Oct. 10, 1981), No. 2 (Tallinn, April 4, 1984), No. 3 (Tallinn, Oct. 9, 1988), No. 4, *Serena Borealis* (1992), and No. 5 (1995); *Pikseloits* (Thunder Incantation; 1983); Piano Concerto (1989); *Open(r)ing* (1989); *Music for Glasgow* for Synthesizers and Chamber Orch. (1989); *Musik für Karlsruhe im Barockstil* for Strings and Harp (1989); *Musica Tenera* (1992); *Symphōnē* for Strings and Percussion (1998); Cello Concerto (1999). **Chamber:** *Mäng punkpillidele* for Wind Quintet (1976); *Kaks pala sooloviiulile* for Violin (1977); *Malera Kasuku*, trio for Violin, Cello, and Piano (1977); *Sarvelugu* for Horn (1977); *Pantomiim* for Renaissance Instruments (1980); *Quasi improvisata* for Violin and Piano (1983); 2 capriccios for Clarinet (1984); *Valss* for Violin and Piano (1985); *For Boris Bjōrn Bagger and Friend* for Flute and Guitar (1988); *From 59'22" to 42'49"* for Guitar and Prerecorded Tape (1989); *The Borders* for Acoustic and Amplified Instruments (1990); *To reach yesterday* for Cello and Piano (1993); *Das Spiel für 10 (Canone Terribile, alia Diavolo)* for Chamber Ensemble (1994); String Quartet (1995). **Piano:** *Ostinato-variations* (1967); *Fughetta and Postludium* (1972); *Pianissimo* (1976); *2 Pieces from the Year 1981*: No. 1 and No. 2, *Pardon, Fryderyk!* (1980); *The Butterfly Who Woke Up in Winter* (1982); *The Sad Toreador or The One Who Is Wiser Concedes* (1984). **Vocal:** *Elust ja surmast*, cantata for Chorus and Orch. (1975); *Seenekantaat* (Mushroom Cantata), Part II, *Timor* (Dangerous; 1980; Tallinn, Feb. 7, 1981), Part III, *Carmen autumnus* (Tallinn, April 23, 1982), and Part IV, *Luxuria* (1983); *Laulupea tuli*, cantata (1985); *Kui tume veel kauaks ka sinu maa* for Chorus (1985); *Amore et Igne*, oratorio (1997).—**NS/LK/DM**

Summer, Donna (originally, **Gaines, LaDonna**), the biggest and most enduring female recording star to emerge from the disco scene of the late 1970s; b. Boston, Dec. 31, 1948. Donna Summer scored one of the first disco hits with the erotic "Love to Love You Baby" in late 1975 and became disco's most recognized and popular solo artist. Ably supported by European songwriter-producers Pete Bellotte and Giorgio Moroder, Summer diversified into funk and synthesizer-dominated pop, and blossomed as a songwriter with 1979's *Bad Girl* album, which eventually sold more than six million copies. Switching to Geffen Records in 1980 for several equivocal rock-oriented albums, Summer scored her biggest later success with the 1983 album *She Works Hard for the Money*.

Donna Summer grew up in Dorcester, Mass., and began singing in a church choir as a child. She worked sessions and recorded demonstration records as a teenager, and quit school two months short of high school graduation to join the otherwise all-white group Crow, debuting with them at Boston's Psychedelic Supermarket in 1967. Later in the year she won a role in the Munich, Germany, production of *Hair* and moved to Europe. She performed in the musical for over a year, then joined the Vienna Folk Opera in 1969, performing in productions of *Porgy and Bess* and *Showboat*. In Germany she appeared in *Godspell* and *The Me Nobody Knows* and worked sessions for producer-songwriters Pete Bellotte and Giorgio Moroder. From 1973 to 1975 Summer recorded for the team's Oasis Records, scoring European hits with "Hostage" and "Lady of the Night." In 1975 Moroder brought her recording of "Je T'Aime" to Neil Bogart of Casablanca Records. The song was rerecorded in a 17-minute version with the sound of Summer's simulated orgasms surrounded by electronic keyboards and a disco-style rhythm as "Love to Love You Baby." The song was picked up by N.Y. discos and became a smash American pop and R&B hit in an abbreviated four-minute version.

Summer returned to the United States in late 1975 and toured the country in early 1976 in support of her second album, *Love Trilogy*, which solidified her popularity with the disco crowd. Later in the year she recorded the concept love album *Four Seasons of Love*, which produced major R&B and minor pop hits with "Spring Affair" and "Winter Melody." Scoring a near-smash pop and R&B hit with the synthesizer-dominated "I Feel Love" from *I Remember Yesterday*, Summer appeared in the 1978 disco-comedy movie *Thank God It's Friday* and contributed four songs to the soundtrack album, including the smash crossover hit "Last Dance," essentially her last disco hit.

The two-record set *Live and More* compiled live and studio recordings, including a top pop and near-smash R&B hit version of Jimmy Webb's "MacArthur Park" and the crossover smash "Heaven Knows", recorded with Brooklyn Dreams. The album remained on the album charts for more than a year and expanded Summer's popularity into the pop mainstream. Donna Summer began exploring funk with her masterful *Bad Girls* album in 1979. The album produced the top pop and smash R&B hit "Hot Stuff," the top pop and R&B hit title track, and the pop smash "Dim All the Lights." Before year's end she scored a top pop hit in duet with Barbra Streisand on "No More Tears (Enough Is Enough)," and the anthology set *On the Radio* yielded a crossover smash with the title song.

In 1980 Donna Summer switched to Geffen Records and married Bruce Sudano of Brooklyn Dreams, with whom she wrote Dolly Parton's top country hit "Starting Over Again." Pete Bellotte and Giorgio Moroder produced her debut for the label, *The Wanderer*. The decidedly rock-oriented album yielded a pop smash with the title song and moderate pop hits with "Cold Love" and "Who Do You Think You're Foolin'." The album also revealed her born-again Christianity with songs such as "I Believe in Jesus." However, subsequent albums for Geffen sold progressively less well and all were later deleted by the label. Her next album, *Donna Summer*, produced by Quincy Jones, includes the smash crossover hit "Love Is In Control" and the moderate pop hits "The Woman in Me" and "State of Independence," the latter recorded with an all-star choir that included Michael Jackson, Lionel Richie, Dionne Warwick, and Stevie Wonder.

Summer's social conscious came to the fore with the title song to 1983's *She Works Hard for the Money*, recorded for Mercury Records as part of her legal settlement with Casablanca Records; the song became a smash crossover hit. The album also yielded a near-smash R&B hit with "Unconditional Love." Brenda Russell's "Dinner with Gershwin" became a near-smash R&B hit from 1987's *All Systems Go*, her first album in three years and her final album for Geffen Records. In 1989 Donna Summer moved to Atlantic Records, where she soon had a near-smash pop hit with "This Time I Know It's for Real," but subsequent recordings have fared far less well.

DISC.: *Love to Love You Baby* (1975); *A Love Trilogy* (1976); *Four Seasons of Love* (1976); *I Remember Yesterday* (1977); *The Deep* (soundtrack; 1977); *Once Upon a Time* (1977); *Live and More* (1978); *Bad Girls* (1979); *On the Radio—Greatest Hits, Vols. 1 and 2* (1979); *Greatest Hits, Vol. 1* (1980); *Greatest Hits, Vol. 2* (1980); *Walk Away—Collector's Edition (The Best of 1977–1980)* (1980); *The Dance Collection* (1987); *The Wanderer* (1980); *D. S.* (1982); *Cats without Claws* (1984); *All Systems Go* (1987); *Anthology* (1993); *She Works Hard for the Money* (1983); *The Summer Collection* (1985); *Endless Summer: Donna* (1994); *Another Place and Time* (1989); *Mistaken Identity* (1991).

BIBL.: J. Haskins, *D. S.: An Unauthorized Biography* (Boston, 1983).—**BH**

Summerly, Jeremy, English conductor and musicologist; b. Stoke-on-Trent, Feb. 28, 1961. He was a chorister at Lichfield Cathedral School (1969–74) and Winchester Coll. (1974–78) before pursuing his education at the Univ. of Oxford (B.A., 1982; M.A., 1987) and King's Coll., Univ. of London (M.Mus. in historical musicology, 1989). While at Oxford, he was a choral scholar at New Coll. (1978–82) and was conductor of the New Coll. Chamber Orch. (1980–81) and the Oxford Chamber Choir (1981–82). From 1982 to 1989 he was a studio manager for BBC Radio, and then was a freelance writer/presenter with it from 1990. In 1984 he became founder-conductor of the Oxford Camerata, and in 1992 of the Oxford Camerata Instrumental Ensemble. He was a lecturer (1989–95), head of academic studies (1996–99), and head of undergraduate programs (from 1999) at the Royal Coll. of Music in London. From 1990 to 1996 he was conductor of the Schola Cantorum of Oxford. In 1999 he became director of music at Christ Church, Chelsea, but continued to conduct the Oxford Camerata and Oxford Camerata Instrumental Ensemble. As a conductor, he has toured Europe, the U.S., Japan, South Africa, and other countries. He made his first appearance at the Aldeburgh Festival in 1998 and at the BBC Proms in London in 1999. Summerly has conducted the first performances in modern times of many works from the medieval and Renaissance eras, and has also made many recordings. He has also programmed works by contemporary European composers, most notably György Ligeti, Franco Donatoni, and Arvo Pärt. In 1995 he was honored with the European Cultural Prize of the European Assn. for the Encouragement of the Arts in Basel. He publ. a vol. of medieval songs and carols in 1999.—**LK/DM**

Summers, Jonathan, Australian baritone; b. Melbourne, Oct. 2, 1946. Following training in Melbourne (1964–74), he studied with Otakar Kraus in London (1974–80). In 1975 he made his operatic debut with the Kent Opera as Rigoletto. He sang Falstaff with the Glyndebourne Touring Opera in 1976, and in 1977 he made his first appearance at London's Covent Garden as Kilian in *Der Freischütz*. He also sang with the English National Opera in London, Opera North in Leeds, and the Scottish Opera in Glasgow. In 1981 he sang Germont père with the Australian Opera. He made his Metropolitan Opera debut in N.Y. as Marcello on Jan. 22, 1988. In 1990 he sang Enrico in *Lucia di Lammermoor* at his debut with the Lyric Opera in Chicago, and then returned there in 1994 to sing in *Fedora*. In 1997 he portrayed Mozart's Figaro at the English National Opera. —**NS/LK/DM**

Summers, Patrick, American conductor and musicologist; b. Washington, Ind., Aug. 14, 1963. He received his education at Ind. Univ. From 1989 to 1994 he was music director of the San Francisco Opera Center, where he conducted the U.S. premiere of Reimann's *Die Gespenstersonate* in 1990. He also conducted its touring company, the Western Opera Theater, throughout the U.S. and Canada. He likewise made frequent appearances as a conductor with the San Francisco Opera. In 1994 he made his first appearance with Opera Australia conducting *La Cenerentola*. In 1996 he was engaged to conduct Hoiby's *The Tempest* at the Dallas Opera. He conducted his own realization of Monteverdi's *L'incoronazione di Poppea* at the San Francisco Opera in 1997, the same year he led the English Chamber Orch. on a tour of Europe with Olga Borodina and Dmitri Hvorostovsky as guest soloists. In 1998 he became music director of the Houston Grand Opera, and concurrently served as principal guest conductor of the San Francisco Opera from 2001. He made his Metropolitan Opera debut in N.Y. on Dec. 24, 1998, conducting *Die Fledermaus*. His repertoire is expansive, encompassing scores from the Baroque era to the contemporary period.—**NS/LK/DM**

Sundgrén-Schnéevoigt, Sigrid Ingeborg, Finnish pianist; b. Helsinki, June 17, 1878; d. Stockholm, Sept. 14, 1953. She studied at the Helsinki Cons., and then with Busoni in Berlin (1894–97). In 1907 she married **Georg Schnéevoigt**, with whom she made several tours of Scandinavia and Germany. She also taught at the Helsinki Cons.—**NS/LK/DM**

Sunnegårdh, Thomas, Swedish tenor; b. Stockholm, July 11, 1949. He received vocal instruction in Stockholm. After appearing with the Swedish National Touring Opera, he made his debut as Albert Herring in 1982 at the Royal Opera in Stockholm, where he subsequently sang such roles as Tamino, Fra Diavolo, Ferrando, Lohengrin, and Taverner. In 1983 he created the title role in Nørgard's *Siddharta* in Stockholm. He appeared as Macduff at the Bregenz Festival in 1988, and in 1990 as Lohengrin in Moscow and Stuttgart. In 1991 he made his debut at London's Covent Garden as Erik. He sang Lohengrin in Barcelona in 1992, and in Düsseldorf in 1994. In 1993 he portrayed Walther von Stolzing at the Bavarian State Opera in Munich. In 1996 he was engaged as Paul in Korngold's *Die tote Stadt* in Stockholm.—**NS/LK/DM**

Suñol (y Baulenas), Gregoria María, learned Spanish ecclesiastic and music scholar; b. Barcelona, Sept. 7, 1879; d. Rome, Oct. 26, 1946. He became a Benedictine monk at Montserrat Abbey in 1895; was ordained a priest in 1902, and then served as choirmaster there (1907–28). In 1930 he went to Rome as director of the Istituto Pontifico di Musica Sacra; was made abbot of Ste. Cecilia in Montserrat in 1943. He publ. the valuable books *Método completo de canto gregoriano según la escuela de Solesmes* (8 eds., 1905–43; also in French, Ger., Eng., Italian, and Portuguese) and *Introducció a la paleografía musical gregoriana* (Montserrat, 1925; rev. French ed., Tournai, 1935, with R. Renaudin). —**NS/LK/DM**

Sun Ra (originally, **Blount, Herman "Sonny" Poole**; aka **Bourke, Sonny** and **Le Sony'r Ra**), a unique, influential, and visionary composer, leader, and keyboard player; b. Birmingham, Ala., May 22, 1914; d. there, May 30, 1993. At age 11, Sun Ra began teaching himself piano and became a good sight reader as well. In the summer of 1932, he toured the Carolinas, Va., Wisc., and Ill. in The Society Troubadours, a group financed by his high school music teacher, "Fess" John Tuggle Whatley. In the fall of 1934, Ra went on tour with another group, this time under Whatley's name. In September 1935, he attended Ala. State Agricultural and Mechanical Inst. for Negroes in Huntsville, Ala., where he took a teachers' training course and began his first formal piano lessons with Lula Hopkins Randall. At the end of the school year, around June 1936, he returned to Birmingham and began leading his own bands and composing. From 1936 onward, there are over 150 pieces copyrighted at the Library of Congress, almost all written in Ra's hand. In the fall of 1942, he was drafted into the military, and at a hearing on Oct. 10, he successfully argued to be classified as a conscientious objector. As an alternative, he was assigned to forestry work at a Civilian Public Service camp in Marienville, Pa.; he didn't show up, complaining of pain from his severe hernia, a long-term problem, and was placed under arrest for 39 days, then sent to the camp. When he was observed to be in physical pain as well as psychological distress, he was classified 4-F and sent home on March 22, 1943. Sun Ra made his first recordings with R&B singer Wynonie Harris in Nashville (1946). He moved to Chicago in early 1946 and worked with Fletcher Henderson's Band at Club DeLisa (1946–47). It made a great impact on him and he kept some of Henderson's charts in his book, including "Big John Shuffle." After Henderson left, Ra remained employed at the club as a rehearsal pianist, copyist, and player in the house band. He worked and recorded with bassist Eugene Wright and His Dukes of Swing (late 1948), led his own trio, and played and recorded with Stuff Smith and Coleman Hawkins. He also wrote music for visiting artists at Club DeLisa.

On Oct. 20, 1952, he legally changed his name to Le Sony'r Ra, Sun Ra for short. He later explained that Ra was the sun god in ancient Egypt, and that he was from another planet. When asked if he wished his work were better known, Ra replied that he was evidently well known since everyone yelled Ra Ra Ra at football games. He built the nucleus of a larger ensemble with saxophonists John Gilmore, Charles Davis, Marshall Allen, Pat Patrick, and James Scales; several of these early members remained with him for many years. From around 1954 to 1956, he had two vocal groups with his band, The Cosmic Echoes and The Cosmic Rays; he also coached a third instrumental group at the time. Sun Ra incorporated Saturn Records in 1956 and started recording with the Myth-Science (or Solar) Arkestra. He moved to N.Y. in early 1961, and exercised as strong an influence over young players there as in Chicago. He preferred that his band members live communally and follow a vegetarian diet. Sun Ra pioneered the use of electronic keyboards and free group improvisation, as on *The Magic City*, an album named after his home town. He was an outlandish, self-styled philosopher/mystic/showman who used mixed-media techniques and costumes, dancers, singers, and poetry to produce exciting live performances, unique in jazz. Sun Ra significantly influenced the new jazz styles of the 1960s in parallel with Cecil Taylor and Ornette Coleman. In fall 1968, he settled in Philadelphia with his Arkestra. He played concerts and club dates, traveled to Europe (1970–71), where he developed a following, and Egypt (1971), and recorded continuously. His band played at all major festivals through the 1970s, 1980s, and early 1990s, with varying personnel. Their stage show often involved elaborate costumes and theatrical effects, adding to the band's allure. In early 1993, in poor health, Ra returned to stay with family in Birmingham. He died at Baptist Medical Center–Princeton, where he was in treatment for a series of strokes. His band has continued under the direction of John Gilmore or Marshall Allen.

Sun Ra made many memorable statements, including: "Some call me mystery, but you can call me Mister Ra," "If we have a White House, where is the Black House?" and "It's after the end of the world, don't you know that yet?" Sun Ra's music was powerful enough to attract and hold fine musicians for 20 or 30 years. John Coltrane also respected him and talked with him, and listened closely to his tenor saxophonist John Gilmore. Sun Ra was the subject of the documentary *A Joyful Noise*, the "psychedelic" performance film *Calling Planet Earth*, and the unusual fictional film *Space Is the Place*.

DISC.: *Sound Sun Pleasure* (1953); *Jazz by Sun Ra* (1956); *Sun Song* (1957); *Sound of Joy* (1957); *Jazz in Silhouette* (1958); *Fate in a Pleasant Mood* (1960); *Futuristic Sounds of Sun Ra* (1961); *The Magic City* (1965); *Heliocentric Worlds, Vol. 1, 2* (1965); *Nothing Is* (1966); *Atlantis* (1967); *Solar Myth Approach, Vol. 1, 2* (1970); *It's After the End of the World* (1970); *Fondation Maeght Nights, Vol. 1, 2* (1970); *Space Is the Place* (1972); *Quiet Place in the Universe* (1976); *Live at Montreux* (1976); *St. Louis Blues* (1977); *Solo Piano, Vol. 1, 2* (1977); *John Cage Meets Sun Ra* (1981); *Reflections in Blue* (1986); *Live London 1990* (1990); *At the Village Vanguard* (1991); *Tribute to Stuff Smith* (1992); *At Soundscape* (1994). **C. WILLIAMS:** *Chocolate Avenue* (1933). **W. HARRIS:** "Dig This Boogie" (1946). **J. WILLIAMS:** *Everyday I Have the Blues* (c. 1954).—**LP**

Suolahti, Heikki, Finnish composer; b. Helsinki, Feb. 2, 1920; d. there, Dec. 27, 1936. He studied at the Helsinki Cons. His tragically premature death at the age of 16 moved Sibelius to say that "Finland lost one of her greatest musical talents." Suolahti composed a few fine works, including a Violin Concerto, written at the age of 14, and a *Sinfonia piccola*, which he composed at 15 and which was performed in Helsinki after his death; also left some songs.—**NS/LK/DM**

Supervia, Conchita, famous Spanish mezzo-soprano; b. Barcelona, Dec. 9, 1895; d. London, March 30, 1936. She studied at the Colegio de las Damas Negras in Barcelona. She made her operatic debut with a visiting opera company at the Teatro Colón in Buenos Aires on Oct. 1, 1910, in Stiattesi's opera *Blanca de Beaulieu*. She then sang in the Italian premiere of *Der Rosenkavalier* in Rome in 1911, as Carmen in Bologna in 1912, and as a member of the Chicago Opera (1915–16). She appeared frequently at La Scala in Milan from 1924; also sang in other Italian music centers, and at London's Covent Garden (1934–35). She endeared herself to the Italian public by reviving Rossini's operas *L'Italiana in Algeri* and *La Cenerentola*; she also attracted favorable critical attention by performing the part of Rosina in *Il Barbiere di Siviglia* in its original version as a coloratura contralto. In 1931 she married the British industrialist Sir Ben Rubenstein. She died as a result of complications following the birth of a child.—**NS/LK/DM**

Supičić, Ivo, Yugoslav musicologist; b. Zagreb, July 18, 1928. He studied piano at the Zagreb Academy of Music, graduating in 1953; worked with C.N.R.S. in

Paris (1960–63) while studying musicology at the Sorbonne (Ph.D., 1962, with the diss. *Elementi sociologije muzike*; publ. in an aug. ed., N.Y., 1987, as *Music in Society: A Guide to the Sociology of Music*). He taught at the musicology dept. of the Zagreb Academy of Music (from 1964) and then at Harvard Univ. (1967–68); served on the editorial board of the journals *Acta Musicologica* and *Arti Musices*; also was ed. of the *International Review of the Aesthetics and Sociology of Music*. His numerous publications focus on sociological aspects of music, especially that of the 20th century. In addition to his valuable diss., he also publ. *La Musique expressive* (Paris, 1957). S. Tuksar ed. a Festschrift in his honor (Zagreb, 1993).—**NS/LK/DM**

Suppan, Wolfgang, Austrian musicologist; b. Irdning, Aug. 5, 1933. He studied clarinet, violin, piano, and theory at the Graz Hochschule für Musik and musicology with Federhofer and Marx at the Univ. of Graz (Ph.D., 1959, with the diss. *Heinrich Eduard Joseph von Lannoy [1787–1853]: Leben und Werke*). He worked in Freiburg im Breisgau at the East German Folklore Inst. (1961–63) and as director of the music dept. of the Folk Song Archive (1963–71). He completed his Habilitation at the Univ. of Mainz in 1971. He became a prof. and director of the Ethnomusicological Inst. of the Graz Hochschule für Musik in 1974. His research focuses on European folk music and music education.

WRITINGS: *Hanns Holenia: Eine Würdigung seines Lebens* (Graz, 1960); *Steirisches Musiklexikon* (Graz, 1962–66); *Volkslied: Seine Sammlung und Erforschung* (Stuttgart, 1966; second ed., 1974); *Lexikon des Blasmusikwesens* (Freiburg im Breisgau, 1971; second ed., 1976); ed. *Internationale Gesellschaft zur Erforschung und Förderung der Blasmusik Konferenz* (Tutzing, 1996). —**NS/LK/DM**

Suppé, Franz (von) (real name, **Francesco Ezechiele Ermenegildo, Cavaliere Suppé-Demelli**), famous Austrian composer; b. Spalato, Dalmatia (of Belgian descent), April 18, 1819; d. Vienna, May 21, 1895. At the age of 11 he played the flute, and at 13 wrote a Mass. He was then sent by his father to study law at Padua. On his father's death, he went with his mother to Vienna in 1835, and continued serious study at the Cons. with Sechter and Seyfried. He conducted at theaters in Pressburg and Baden, then at Vienna's Theater an der Wien (1845–62), Kaitheater (1862–65), and Carltheater (1865–82). All the while, he wrote light operas and other theater music of all degrees of levity, obtaining increasing success rivaling that of Offenbach. His music possesses the charm and gaiety of the Viennese genre, but also contains elements of more vigorous popular rhythms. His most celebrated single work is the overture to *Dichter und Bauer*, which still retains a firm place in the light repertoire. His total output comprises about 30 comic operas and operettas and 180 other stage pieces, most of which were brought out in Vienna; of these the following obtained considerable success: *Dichter und Bauer* (Aug. 24, 1846); *Das Mädchen vom Lande* (Aug. 7, 1847); *Dame Valentine, oder Frauenräuber und Wanderbursche* (Jan. 9, 1851); *Paragraph 3* (Jan. 8, 1858); *Das Pensionat* (Nov. 24, 1860); *Die Kartenaufschlägerin* (April 26, 1862); *Zehn Mädchen und kein Mann* (Oct. 25, 1862); *Die flotten Burschen* (April 18, 1863); *Das Corps der Rache* (March 5, 1864); *Franz Schubert* (Sept. 10, 1864); *Die schöne Galatea* (Berlin, June 30, 1865); *Die leichte Kavallerie* (March 24, 1866); *Die Tochter der Puszta* (March 24, 1866); *Die Freigeister* (Oct. 23, 1866); *Banditenstreiche* (April 27, 1867); *Die Frau Meisterin* (Jan. 20, 1868); *Tantalusqualen* (Oct. 3, 1868); *Isabella* (Nov. 5, 1869); *Cannebas* (Nov. 2, 1872); *Fatinitza* (Jan. 5, 1876); *Der Teufel auf Erden* (Jan. 5, 1878); *Boccaccio* (Feb. 1, 1879); *Donna Juanita* (Feb. 21, 1880); *Der Gascogner* (March 21, 1881); *Das Herzblättchen* (Feb. 4, 1882); *Die Afrikareise* (March 17, 1883); *Des Matrosen Heimkehr* (Hamburg, May 4, 1885); *Bellmann* (Feb. 26, 1887); *Die Jagd nach dem Glücke* (Oct. 27, 1888); *Das Modell* (Oct. 4, 1895); *Die Pariserin, oder Das heimlische Bild* (Jan. 26, 1898). Other works include syms., overtures, a Requiem, 3 masses and other sacred works, choruses, dances, string quartets, and songs.

BIBL.: G. Sabalich, *F. S. e l'operetta* (Zara, 1888); O. Keller, *F. v.S.: Der Schöpfer der deutschen Operette* (Leipzig, 1905). —**NS/LK/DM**

Supremes, The, Motown's most successful girl group, led in their heydey by the sweet-voiced Diana Ross. **MEMBERSHIP:** Diana Ross (b. Detroit, Mich., March 26, 1944), Florence Ballard (b. Detroit, Mich., June 30, 1943; d. there, Feb. 22, 1976), Mary Wilson (b. Greenville, Miss., March 6, 1944), and Barbara Martin. Martin left the group in 1962 and Ballard departed in 1967. Ballard was replaced by Cindy Birdsong (b. Camden, N. J., Dec., 15, 1939). Later members included Jean Terrell, Lynda Lawrence, Scherrie Payne, and Susaye Green.

Diana Ross, Florence Ballard, Mary Wilson, and Betty McGlown began singing together while still in high school in 1959 as The Primettes, the companion group to The Primes, whose members Otis Williams and Eddie Kendricks later formed The Temptations. In 1960, Barbara Martin replaced McGlown and the group made their first recording for Lupine Records. They auditioned for Berry Gordy Jr., while still in high school, but he insisted they finish high school. Signed to Tamla Records in January 1961, the group changed their name to The Supremes and recorded two unsuccessful singles for the label before switching to Motown in 1962. Barbara Martin left the group in 1962, and they continued as a trio, working as backup vocalists for other Motown artists until 1964. With Florence Ballard on lead vocals, The Supremes scored their first minor pop hit in 1962 with Smokey Robinson's "Your Heart Belongs to Me" and were subsequently placed with songwriter-producers Brian Holland, Lamont Dozier, and Eddie Holland. After Diana Ross supplanted Ballard as lead vocalist, they finally achieved their first major pop and rhythm-and-blues hit with "When Your Lovelight Starts Shining through His Eyes" in late 1963.

In the summer of 1964, The Supremes' "Where Did Our Love Go" marked their breakthrough and initiated a string of five top pop hits with "Baby Love," "Come See about Me," "Stop! In the Name of Love," and "Back in My Arms Again." Only "Come See about Me" and

"Stop! In the Name of Love" failed to top the rhythm-and-blues charts. In the spring of 1965, they toured Europe, performing at N.Y.'s Copacabana night club in July. Further top pop and R&B hits provided by Holland-Dozier-Holland through the spring of 1967 were "You Can't Hurry Love," "You Keep Me Hangin' On," and "Love Is Here and Now You're Gone." "I Hear a Symphony" and the psychedelic-sounding "The Happening" became top pop and smash rhythm-and-blues hits, and "Nothing but Heartaches," "My World Is Empty without You," and "Love Is Like an Itching in My Heart" were smash pop and rhythm-and-blues hits.

In 1967, Florence Ballard quit or was forced out of The Supremes, to be replaced by Cindy Birdsong, a former member of Patti Labelle and The Blue Belles. Ballard briefly attempted a solo career on ABC Records and eventually died impoverished of cardiac arrest on Feb. 22, 1976, at the age of 32. The group was subsequently billed as Diana Ross and The Supremes, scoring a pop and rhythm-and-blues smash with another pyschedelic soul song, "Reflections." After the near-smash pop and major R&B hit "In and Out of Love," the Holland-Dozier-Holland team left Motown Records. In 1968, Diana Ross and The Supremes scored a top top and smash R&B hit with "Love Child," one of Motown's few attempts at socially conscious lyrics, followed by the crossover smash "I'm Gonna Make You Love Me," recorded with The Temptations. In 1969, "I'm Livin' in Shame" became a crossover smash and "I'll Try Something New," recorded with The Temptations, became a major pop and R&B hit, as did "The Composer." Diana Ross's final single with The Supremes, "Someday We'll Be Together," was a top crossover hit.

At the beginning of 1970, Diana Ross left The Supremes for a solo career. Mary Wilson and Cindy Birdsong persevered with new member Jean Terrell. Over the next two years, they scored major pop and smash rhythm-and-blues hits with "Up the Ladder to the Roof," "River Deep–Mountain High" (with The Four Tops), "Nathan Jones," and "Floy Joy," with the smash pop and top R&B hit "Stoned Love" intervening. Birdsong left the group in 1972 (replaced by Lynda Lawrence), returned in 1974, and left again in 1976. Terrell left in 1973, replaced by Scherrie Payne, sister of Freda Payne (1970's pop smash "Band of Gold"). They scored their last major R&B and moderate pop hit with "I'm Gonna Let My Heart Do the Walking" in the summer of 1976. By late 1976, The Supremes comprised Wilson, Payne, and Susaye Greene. The group essentially disbanded in 1977, although Wilson toured England with two new members in 1978. In 1979, Payne and Greene recorded a duet album and Mary Wilson recorded a solo album for Motown. Wilson subsequently sustained her own career largely in Europe, returning to the American cabaret circuit in the 1990s.

Diana Ross made her solo performing debut in March 1970 and initially worked with songwriter-producers Nicholas Ashford and Valerie Simpson. They provided her with the top pop and rhythm-and-blues hit "Ain't No Mountain High Enough" and the major crossover hits "Reach Out and Touch (Somebody's Hand)," and "Remember Me." Ross's next major pop hit came in 1973 with the top pop and smash R&B hit "Touch Me in the Morning," cowritten by Michael Masser. In the meantime, she had begun regularly appearing on television and made the movie *Lady Sings the Blues*, portraying Billie Holiday. The soundtrack album became a best-seller, remaining on the album charts for more than a year.

In 1973, Diana Ross teamed with Marvin Gaye for *Diana and Marvin*. The album yielded three hits, including the major pop hits "You're a Special Part of Me" (a rhythm-and-blues smash) and "My Mistake (Was to Love You)." In 1975, Ross starred in the film *Mahogany* and the movie's theme (also known as "Do You Know Where You're Going To"), written by Michael Masser and Gerry Goffin, became a top pop and major R&B hit. Her most successful album in years, *Diana Ross*, produced a top pop and R&B hit with the disco-sounding "Love Hangover" and a major pop and R&B hit with "One Love in My Lifetime."

In June 1976, Ross brought her *Evening with Diana Ross* stage show to Broadway, later touring the country with the show and appearing in the first one-woman, prime-time television special in March 1977. After the crossover hit "Gettin' Ready for Love," Ross appeared in the film version of the hit play *The Wiz* with Michael Jackson, Nipsey Russell, and Richard Pryor. Probably the most expensive all-black film ever made ($20 million), the film was visually spectacular, utilizing stunning costuming, elaborate special effects, and massive production numbers, but, despite a $6 million promotional campaign, it proved a relative failure.

Diana Ross was using producers outside the Motown organization by the late 1970s. *The Boss*, produced by Richard Perry, included the major crossover hit title song, written by Nicholas Ashford and Valerie Simpson, and 1980's *Diana*, written and produced by Niles Rodgers and Bernard Edwards of Chic, yielded a top crossover hit with "Upside Down" and a crossover smash with "I'm Coming Out." "It's My Turn," from the movie of the same name, became a major crossover hit and, in 1981, her collaboration with Lionel Richie, "Endless Love" (again from the movie with the same title), became a top pop, easy-listening, *and* rhythm-and-blues hit.

In 1981, Diana Ross switched to RCA Records for a reported $20 million, recording six albums for the label through 1987. Smash rhythm-and-blues and major pop hits through 1985 included a remake of Frankie Lymon and The Teenagers' "Why Do Fools Fall in Love," "Mirror Mirror," "Muscles" (written and produced by Michael Jackson), "Swept Away" (written and produced by Daryl Hall), and "Missing You" (written and produced by Lionel Richie and dedicated to Marvin Gaye). Her final major R&B hits came with "Telephone," "Eaten Alive," and "Dirty Looks." She scored a top British hit in 1986 with "Chain Reaction," written and coproduced by Barry Gibb. In 1989, she conducted a world tour and returned to Motown Records, but Berry Gordy Jr., was by then no longer involved with the company. Neither *Workin' Overtime*, produced by Niles Rodgers, nor *The Force Behind the Power*, largely produced by Peter Asher, sold well. In 1993, Villard Books published Diana Ross's evasive, self-serving autobiography *Secrets of a Sparrow*.

In December 1981, the musical *Dreamgirls*, ostensibly based on the career of The Supremes, began a long run on Broadway and later went into repertoire. Although Diana Ross disavowed the show and refused to see it, Mary Wilson endorsed it. In 1983, The Supremes (Ross, Wilson, and Cindy Birdsong) reunited for the 25th-anniversary Motown television special, but tales of Ross's untoward behavior at the ceremony were confirmed with Wilson's best-selling book *Dreamgirl: My Life as a Supreme*, published by St. Martin's Press in 1986. Having persevered with regular tours of Europe in the 1980s, Wilson experienced a revitalization of her career with the publication of *Dreamgirl*. She later wrote the sequel *Supreme Faith*. From 1986 to 1993, Jean Terrell, Scherrie Payne, and Lynda Lawrence toured as The FLOs (Former Ladies of the Supremes). The Supremes were inducted into the Rock and Roll Hall of Fame in 1988.

Disc.: *Meet The Supremes* (1963); *Where Did Our Love Go* (1965); *A Bit of Liverpool* (1964); *Country, Western and Pop* (1965); *More Hits* (1965); *We Remember Sam Cooke* (1965); *At the Copa* (1965); *Merry Christmas* (1965); *I Hear a Symphony* (1966); *Supremes a Go-Go* (1966); *Sing Holland-Dozier-Holland* (1967); *Sing Rodgers and Hart* (1967). **DIANA ROSS AND THE SUPREMES:** *Reflections* (1968); *Love Child* (1968); *Funny Girl* (1968); *Live at London's Talk of the Town* (1968); *Let the Sunshine In* (1969); *Cream of the Crop* (1969); *Farewell* (1970); *Never-Before-Released Masters* (1987). **THE SUPREMES AND THE TEMPTATIONS:** *The Supremes Join The Temptations* (1968); *T.C.B.* (1968); *Together* (1969); *On Broadway* (1969). **THE SUPREMES AND THE FOUR TOPS:** *The Magnificent Seven* (1970); *The Return of The Magnificent Seven* (1971); *Dynamite* (1971). **THE SUPREMES (WITHOUT DIANA ROSS):** *Right On* (1970); *New Ways, but Love Stays* (1970); *Touch* (1971); *Floy Joy* (1972); *High Energy* (1976); *Mary, Scherrie and Susaye* (1977). **MARY WILSON:** *Mary Wilson* (1979). **SCHERRIE PAYNE AND SUSAYE GREENE:** *Partners* (1979). **DIANA ROSS:** *Diana Ross* (1970); *Diana!* (1971); *Everything Is Everything* (1970); *Surrender* (1971); *Lady Sings the Blues* (1972); *Touch Me in the Morning* (1973); *The Last Time I Saw Him* (1973); *Live at Caesar's Palace* (1974); *Mahogany* (soundtrack; 1975); *Diana Ross* (1976); *An Evening with Diana Ross* (1977); *Baby, It's Me* (1977); *Ross* (1978); *The Boss* (1979); *Diana* (1980); *To Love Again* (1981); *Why Do Fools Fall in Love* (1981); *Silk Electric* (1982/1990); *Ross* (1983); *Swept Away* (1984); *Eaten Alive* (1985); *Red Hot Rhythm and Blues* (1987); *Workin' Overtime* (1989); *The Force behind the Power* (1991); *Endless Love* (1992); *Stolen Moments: The Lady Sings...Jazz and Blues* (1993); *Musical Memoirs, Forever* (1993); *Take Me Higher* (1995). **DIANA ROSS AND MARVIN GAYE:** *Diana and Marvin* (1973). **DIANA ROSS AND OTHERS:** *The Wiz* (soundtrack; 1978).

Bibl.: J. R. Taraborrelli, *Call Her Miss Ross* (Secaucus, N. J., 1989); T. Turner with B. Aria, *All That Glittered: My Life with The S.* (N.Y., 1990); D. Ross, *Secrets of a Sparrow* (N.Y., 1993).—**BH**

Suratno, Nano, prolific Indonesian composer, known as **Nano S.**; b. Pasar Kemis Tarogong, West Java, April 4, 1944. He earned degrees from the Akademi Seni Tari Indonesia (A.S.T.I.) Bandung (1978) and Sekolah Tinggi Seni Indonesia (S.T.S.I.) Surakarta (1989); also studied with Daeng Sutikna (music), Syafei (literature), Tjetje Somantri (choreography and dance), and, especially, Mang Koko (music). He formed his own dance company and then performed with Koko's group, Ganda Mekar. He began composing experimental works for degung, a traditional Sundanese chamber ensemble of tuned gongs, drums, and bamboo flute; in 1979 his *Sangkuriang* was performed at the important national festival Pekan Komponis Muda (Young Composers' Festival); he also began composing highly expressive instrumental music ("karawitan total"), and in 1985 mounted *Umbul-umbul*, involving 75 players in a mixture of over 15 Sundanese styles, on Indonesian TV. Nano S. sees many of his songs as a means of making traditional music more accessible to Sundanese youths; he often recasts classical melodies in forms that conform to popular music styles of the West. Even in his more experimental instrumental works, which he calls "musik total" or "musik murni" (i.e., "absolute" music), he neither borrows from foreign sources nor uses diatonic tuning; while such works have not yet found a place in the standard repertoire of Sunda, audiences abroad have been receptive; in 1989, on a commission from the American Gamelan Inst. in Hanover, N.H., he composed and recorded *Jemplang Polansky*, inspired by his confusion upon listening to the computer music of Larry Polansky, and *Galura* (Emotion; 1988), an instrumental solo piece for kecapi (plucked zither). In 1986 he toured in Canada and the U.S.; after appearing in Japan (1988), he became a guest lecturer and composer at the Univ. of Calif. at Santa Cruz (1989). In 1990 he directed the touring program "Sunda: From Village to City," presented in the U.S. at its Festival of Indonesia. Nano S. is best known in Indonesia as a song composer; his texts are often about young love, cast in the regional language of Sundanese, modern Indonesian, or English. More than 200 audiotapes of his works have been released, several of them distributed by the American Gamelan Inst. Among his publications are a book of songs, *Haleuang Tondang* (Bandung, 1975), and *Mengolah Seni Pertunjukan Sebagai Media Penergangan* (Development of the Performing Arts as an Information Medium; 1989); also some 15 operetta librettos. In 1978 he married the Indonesian singer Dheniarsah; their home in Bandung is a fertile international meeting ground for artists of all disciplines.

Works: *Ki Lagoni*, operetta (1967); *Raja Kecit*, operetta (1974); *Bubat* for Degung (1978); *Sangkuriang* for Gamelan (1979); *Sekar Manis* for 4 Kecapi (1980); *Anjeun* for Degung (1986); *Kalangkang* for Degung (1986); *Kangen* for Degung (1987); *Kalangkang* for Jaipongan (1987; also for Western Band [1987] and Kliningan Wanda Anyar [1988]); *Tibelat* for Pop Sunda (1988); *Cinta* for Pop Degung (1988); *Galura* for Kecapi (1988); *Jemplang Polansky* for Mixed Ensemble (1989); *Love Smir/Parkir* for Gamelan (1990); *Warna* for Gamelan (1990); *Karesman* for Gamelan (1990); many songs.—**NS/LK/DM**

Surdin, Morris, Canadian composer; b. Toronto, May 8, 1914; d. there, Aug. 19, 1979. He learned to play piano, violin, cello, horn, and trombone; studied composition with Gesensway in Philadelphia (1937) and with Brant in N.Y. (1950). He worked as a music arranger for the CBC and CBS. From 1954 he worked in Canada, primarily in scoring for musicals, radio, television, and films.

WORKS: DRAMATIC: *The Remarkable Rocket*, ballet, after Oscar Wilde (1960–61); *Look Ahead*, musical comedy (1962); *Wild Rose*, opera-musical (1967). **ORCH.:** *4 X Strings* for Strings (1947); *Credo* (1950); *Inheritance* for Wind Quartet and Strings (1951); *Concert Ballet* (1955); *Incident I* for Strings (1961); Concerto for Mandolin and Strings (1961–66); *5 Shades of Brass* for Trumpet and Orch. (1961); 2 concertos for Free-bass Accordion: No. 1 (1966; Toronto, Jan. 29, 1967) and No. 2, with Strings, Electric Guitar, and Percussion (1977); *2 Solitudes* for Horn or English Horn and Strings (1967); *Formula I* and *II* for Concert Band (1968–69); *Horizon* for Strings (1968); *Short! No. 1* for Piano and Strings (1969) and *No. 2* for Piano, Wind Quartet, and Strings (1969); *6 Pieces in Search of a Sequence* for Solo Instruments and Strings (1969–78); *Alteration I* for Piccolo and Strings (1970) and *II* for Strings (1970); *Terminus* for Oboe, Bassoon, and Strings (1972); *B'rasheet* (In the Beginning) for Mandolin, Clarinet, and Strings (Toronto, June 15, 1974); *Eine kleine "Hammer-Klapper" Musik* for Chamber Orch. (1976); *Berceuse* for Horn and Chamber Orch. (1977); *A Group of 6* for Strings in first position (1977); *5 for 4* for Strings in first position (1977); *Who's on Bass?* for Strings (1977); Violin Concerto (1978). **CHAMBER:** Suite for Viola and Piano (1954); *Carol Fantasia* for Brass (1955); *Incident II* for Woodwinds, Horns, and Harp (1961); *Elements* for 2 Violins, Double Bass, and Harpsichord (1965); *Matin* for Wind Quartet (1965); *Arioso* for 4 Cellos (1966); String Quartet (1966); Trio for Saxophones (1968); *Piece* for Wind Quintet (1969); *Serious I-XVI* for Accordion (1969–73); *Trinitas in Morte* for 3 Oboes, Bassoon, 3 Horns, Timpani, 8 Cellos, and 2 Double Basses (1973); *Sly'd Trombones I & II* for Trombone and Bass Trombone or Trombone Ensemble (1975); *Heritage I-IV* for Varying Brass Quartets (1975–79); *Landscapes*, sonatina for Harp (1978); *2 fabliaux* for Cello (1979). **Piano:** *Naiveté*, 6 pieces (1962); *Poco Giocoso Variations* (1966); *In Search of Form I* and *II* (1970); *Fragmentations I-III* (1972). **VOCAL:** *A Spanish Tragedy* for Soprano and Orch. (1955); *Suite canadienne* for Chorus and Orch. (1970); *Feast of Thunder* for Soloists, Men's Chorus, and Orch. (1972); *Music Fair* for Soprano, Cello, and Harp (1975); Quartet for Trio for Low Voice, Cello, and Harp (1976); *Pegleg's Fiddle* for Men's Chorus, Solo Violin, Mandolin Orch., Piano, and Percussion (1977); *Leave It Be* for Bass, Chorus, and Orch. (1977; based on the musical comedy *Look Ahead*).—**NS/LK/DM**

Surette, Thomas Whitney, American music educator; b. Concord, Mass., Sept. 7, 1861; d. there, May 19, 1941. He studied piano with Arthur Foote and composition with J.K. Paine at Harvard Univ. (1889–92), but failed to obtain a degree. Deeply interested in making musical education accessible and effective in the U.S., he founded the Concord Summer School of Music in 1915, which continued to operate until 1938; with A.T. Davison, he ed. The Concord Series of educational music, which found a tremendously favorable acceptance on the part of many schools, particularly in New England; the series provided an excellent selection of good music which could be understood by most music teachers and performed by pupils. He was also largely responsible for the vogue of music appreciation courses that swept the country and spilled over into the British Isles. He publ. *The Appreciation of Music* (with D.G. Mason; 5 vols., of which vols. 2 and 5 were by Mason alone; N.Y., 1907; innumerable subsequent printings), and, on a more elevated plane, *Course of Study on the Development of Symphonic Music* (Chicago, 1915) and *Music and Life* (Boston, 1917); he also publ. popular articles on music and musicians, notable for their lack of discrimination and absence of verification of data. He was also a composer of sorts; wrote 2 light operas, *Priscilla, or The Pilgrim's Proxy*, after Longfellow (Concord, March 6, 1889; had more than 1,000 subsequent perfs. in the U.S.), and *The Eve of Saint Agnes* (1897), and a romantic opera, *Cascabel, or The Broken Tryst* (Pittsburgh, May 15, 1899).

BIBL.: C. Heffernan, *T.W. S.: Musician and Teacher* (diss., Univ. of Mich., 1962).—**NS/LK/DM**

Surinach, Carlos, Spanish-born American composer and conductor; b. Barcelona, March 4, 1915. He studied in Barcelona with Morera (1936–39) and later with Max Trapp in Berlin (1939–43). Returning to Spain in 1943, he was active mainly as a conductor. In 1951 he went to the U.S.; became a naturalized American citizen in 1959. Surinach was a visiting prof. of music at Carnegie-Mellon Inst. in Pittsburgh in 1966–67. He won particular success as a composer for the dance.

WORKS: DRAMATIC: Opera: *El Mozo que casó con mujer brava* (Barcelona, Jan. 10, 1948). **Ballet:** *Monte Carlo* (Barcelona, May 2, 1945); *Ritmo jondo* (1953); *Embattled Garden* (1958); *Acrobats of God* (1960); *David and Bathsheba* (1960); *Apasionada* (1962); *Los renegados* (1965); *Venta quemada* (1966); *Agathe's Tale* (1967); *Suite española* (1970); *Chronique* (1974); *The Owl and the Pussycat* (1978); *Blood Wedding* (1979). **ORCH.:** 3 syms.: No. 1, *Passacaglia-Symphony* (Barcelona, April 8, 1945, composer conducting), No. 2 (Paris Radio, Jan. 26, 1950, composer conducting), and No. 3, *Sinfonía chica* (1957); *Sinfonietta flamenca* (1953; Louisville, Jan. 9, 1954); *Feria mágica*, overture (Louisville, March 14, 1956); *Concerto for Orchestra* (1959); *Symphonic Variations* (1962); *Drama Jondo*, overture (1964); *Melorhythmic Dramas* (1966); *Las trompetas de los serafines*, overture (1973); Piano Concerto (1973); Harp Concerto (1978); Concerto for Strings (1978); Violin Concerto (1980); *Symphonic Melismas* (Miami, Oct. 10, 1993). **OTHER:** Chamber music; piano pieces; guitar music; choral works; songs.—**NS/LK/DM**

Surzyński, Józef, Polish theologian, conductor, music scholar, and composer; b. Szrem, near Posen, March 15, 1851; d. Kościan, March 5, 1919. He studied theory with O. Paul in Leipzig (1872–74), where he also took courses at the Cons. and was a violist at the Thomaskirche; studied theology in Rome (doctorate, 1880) and then at the Regensburg school of church music. He was in Posen as Cathedral organist (1881–87), and also conducted its choir; served in Koscian as curate (1894–1919); also was active as a conductor in various Polish cities. He was engaged in the movement to reform church music along Caecilian lines; served as ed. of the journal *Muzyka Kośielna* (Church Music; 1884–1902). His compositions include sacred works and organ music. His publications include *Directorium chori* (Posen, 1885), *Monumenta musices sacrae in Polonia* (Posen, 1885–89), and *Matka Boska w muzyce polskiej* (The Mother of God in Polish Music; Kraków, 1905). He had 2 brothers who were also musicians: Stefan (b. Šroda, Aug. 31, 1855; d. Lwów, April 6, 1919) was an organist, conductor, teacher, and composer; Mieczyslaw (b. Šroda, Dec. 22, 1866; d. Warsaw, Sept. 11, 1924) was an organist, conductor, teacher, and composer.

BIBL.: K. Winowicz, *J. S.* (diss., Univ. of Poznan, 1964). —NS/LK/DM

Susa, Conrad, American composer; b. Springdale, Pa., April 26, 1935. He studied theory with Lopatnikoff, musicology with Dorian, counterpoint with Leich, flute with Goldberg, and cello with Eisner at the Carnegie Inst. of Technology in Pittsburgh (B.F.A., 1957); completed his training in composition with Bergsma and Persichetti at the Juilliard School of Music in N.Y. (M.S., 1961). In 1959 he became composer-in-residence at the Old Globe Theatre in San Diego, where he was active for over 30 years; also was music director of the APA-Phoenix Repertory Co. in N.Y. (1961–68) and the American Shakespeare Festival in Stratford, Conn. (1969–71); also was dramaturge at the Eugene O'Neill Center in Conn. (from 1986).

WORKS: DRAMATIC: Opera: *Transformations* (Minn. Opera, May 5, 1973); *Black River* (Minn. Opera, Nov. 1, 1975); *The Love of Don Perlimplin* (1983); *Dangerous Liaisons* (San Francisco, Sept. 10, 1994). Other Dramatic: Incidental music; television scores. OTHER: *A Sonnet Voyage*, sym. (1963); chamber music; numerous choral works, including *Dawn Greeting* (1976), *The Chanticleer's Carol* (1982), and *Earth Song* (1988); keyboard pieces.—NS/LK/DM

Susato, Johannes de (real name, **Johannes Steinwert von Soest**), German singer and composer; b. Unna, 1448; d. Frankfurt am Main, May 2, 1506. He was a chorister in Cleve. After serving as succentor in Maastricht, he was made music director at the Heidelberg court (1472); also studied medicine there and later at the Univ. of Padua, where he took his M.D. about 1490; became town physician in Worms in 1495 and in Frankfurt am Main in 1500.—NS/LK/DM

Susato, Tylman, German music publisher and composer; b. c. 1500; d. probably in Antwerp, c. 1562. He may have been born in Antwerp, where he pursued his career. He was a calligrapher at the Cathedral (1529–30), becoming a trumpeter there in 1531, and then was a town musician (1532–49). After serving as a partner in a printing venture (1541–43), he set up his own press in 1543 and remained active until at least 1561. His press produced 25 books of chansons, 3 books of masses, 19 books of motets, and 11 Musyck boexken. He was a fine composer of cantus firmus chansons for 2 to 3 Voices (1544; c. 1552).—NS/LK/DM

Susskind (originally, **Süsskind**), **(Jan) Walter,** distinguished Czech-born English conductor; b. Prague, May 1, 1913; d. Berkeley, Calif., March 25, 1980. He studied composition with Suk and Karel Hába and piano with Hoffmeister at the Prague Cons.; also studied conducting with Szell at the German Academy of Music in Prague, where he made his debut as a conductor in 1934 with *La Traviata* at the German Opera; also was pianist with the Czech Trio (1933–38). After the German occupation in 1938, he went to London, where he continued to serve as pianist with the exiled Czech Trio until 1942; became a naturalized British citizen in 1946. He was music director of the Carl Rosa Opera Co. in London (1943–45); then went to Glasgow in that capacity with the Scottish Orch. in 1946, remaining with it after it became the Scottish National Orch. in 1950. After serving as music director of the Victoria Sym. Orch. in Melbourne (1953–55), he was music director of the Toronto Sym. Orch. (1956–65), the Aspen (Colo.) Music Festival (1962–68), the St. Louis Sym. Orch. (1968–75), and the Mississippi River Festival in Edwardsville, Ill. (1969–75); also taught at the Univ. of Southern Ill. (1968–75). His last position was that of music adviser and principal guest conductor of the Cincinnati Sym. Orch. from 1978 until his death. Susskind was a highly accomplished conductor, being a technically secure and polished musician. He also composed; among his works are 4 songs for Voice and String Quartet (Prague, Sept. 2, 1935); *9 Slovak Sketches* for Orch.; *Passacaglia* for Timpani and Chamber Orch. (St. Louis, Feb. 24, 1977).—NS/LK/DM

Süssmayr, Franz Xaver, Austrian composer; b. Schwanenstadt, 1766; d. Vienna, Sept. 17, 1803. He studied composition with Maximilian Piessinger and Georg von Pasterwiz. He went to Vienna in 1788 as a music teacher; about 1790 he was befriended by Mozart, who gave him composition lessons; Mozart utilized his talents, employing him as a composer and collaborator. After Mozart's death, he took lessons in vocal composition from Salieri, then was a harpsichordist and acting Kapellmeister at the National Theater (1792–94). From 1794 until his death he was Kapellmeister of the National Theater's German opera productions. His most successful stage works were the Singspiel *Der Spiegel von Arkadien* (1794) and the ballet *Il noce di Benevento* (1802). After Mozart's death, his widow entrusted the completion of his Requiem to Sussmayr; he was clever in emulating Mozart's style of composition, and his handwriting was so much like Mozart's that it is difficult to distinguish between them. Süssmayr wrote a number of operas and operettas, which he produced in Vienna, among them: *Moses oder Der Auszug aus Ägypten* (May 4, 1792); *L'incanto superato* or *Der besiegte Zauber* (July 8, 1793); *Idris und Zenide* (May 11, 1795); *Die edle Rache* (Aug. 27, 1795); *Die Freiwilligen* (Sept. 27, 1796); *Der Wildfang* (Oct. 4, 1797); *Der Marktschreyer* (July 6, 1799); *Soliman der Zweite, oder Die drei Sultaninnen* (Oct. 1, 1799); *Gülnare oder Die persische Sklavin* (July 5, 1800); *Phasma oder Die Erscheinung im Tempel der Verschwiegenheit* (July 25, 1801). He also wrote secco recitatives for Mozart's opera *La clemenza di Tito* (Prague, Sept. 6, 1791) and composed several numbers for the Vienna production of Grétry's *La Double Épreuve*, given there under the title *Die doppelte Erkenntlichkeit* (Feb. 28, 1796). Other works include 2 clarinet concertos, divertimentos, cassations, some chamber music, sacred works, including a Missa solemnis, 2 German Requiems, and 4 Masses, etc.

BIBL.: G. Sievers, *Mozart und S.* (Mainz, 1829); W. Lehner, *F.X. S. als Opernkomponist* (diss., Univ. of Vienna, 1927); J. Winterberger, *F.X. S.: Leben, Umwelt und Gestalt* (diss., Univ. of Innsbruck, 1946); W. Wlcek, *F.X. S. als Kirchenkomponist* (Tutzing, 1978).—NS/LK/DM

Sutanto, Indonesian composer with radical tendencies; b. Magelang, Central Java, Feb. 5, 1954. He studied with Jack Body at the Akademi Musik Indonesia (A.M.I., a Western music cons. in Yogyakarta), and appeared with him in piano concerts; also studied psychology and literature. He founded a cultural center, Ritus Paguyuban (Inst. of Arts and Cultural Studies), in his native Magelang, and later initiated construction of a center near Candi Mendhut (on the road to Borododur), where he resides. Sutanto calls himself a "social engineer" rather than a composer; arranges day-long conglomerations of performing groups (martial arts, folk music, and trance dance) from neighboring villages and from the more urban Magelang (experimental ensembles). In 1989 he created *Wayang Imaginasi*, a shadow puppet play without shadows or puppets—as the puppet master tells the story and the gamelan plays, a painter stands at intervals and paints characters onto the screen. His works have been played in Indonesia as well as in England, Australia, and New Zealand; his *Sketsa Ide* (1979) was performed at the national festival, Pekan Komponis Muda. He is also active as a journalist and critic.

WORKS: *Proses* (1977); *Apa* (1979); *Sketsa Ide* for Chamber Orch., Percussion, and Pumps (1979); *Musik Opera*, consisting of *Blues in My Shoes* for 2 Guitars, Piano, and Vocalists, *Waras Vs Gila, Pegawai Sinting* (1981), and *Suara Orang-orang Luka dan Lebaran '82* for Tape (musique concrète) and 50 Dancers (July 23, 1982); *Ritus Paguyban* for 9 Ensembles totaling 74 Players; *Senam Flute* (1986); *Wayang Imaginasi* (1989).—**NS/LK/DM**

Suter, Hermann, distinguished Swiss conductor, pedagogue, and composer; b. Kaiserstuhl, April 28, 1870; d. Basel, June 22, 1926. He was a pupil of his father, an organist and precentor in Laufenberg, then studied with Hans Huber and Alfred Glaus in Basel; also took courses at the Stuttgart Cons. with Faisst and at the Leipzig Cons. (1888–91) with Reinecke and Homeyer. From 1892 to 1902 he conducted various Swiss choral groups, then settled in Basel as conductor of the Gesangverein (1902–25), the Liedertafel (1902–25), and the Allgemeine Musikgesellschaft sym. concerts (1902–26). He taught at the Zürich Cons. (1896–1902) and was director of the Basel Cons. (1918–21). He wrote a Sym., a Violin Concerto (1924), an oratorio, *Le Laudi di S. Francesco d'Assisi* (1925), 3 string quartets (1901, 1910, 1921), a String Sextet (1921), songs, piano pieces, and organ music.

BIBL.: W. Merian, *H. S.: Der Dirigent und der Komponist* (Basel, 1936).—**NS/LK/DM**

Suter, Robert, Swiss composer and teacher; b. St. Gallen, Jan. 30, 1919. In 1937 he entered the Basel Cons., where he received instruction in piano from Paul Baumgartner, in theory from Gustav Güldenstein, Walter Müller von Kulm, and Ernst Mohr, and in composition from Walther Geiser; later took private composition lessons with Wladimir Vogel (1956). He taught at the Bern Cons. (1945–50) and at the Basel Academy of Music (1950–84).

WORKS: **DRAMATIC:** *Konrad von Donnerstadt*, musical fairy tale (1950; Basel, May 5, 1954); *Der fremde Baron*, musical comedy (1951; Basel, March 23, 1952). **ORCH.:** *Kleines konzert* for Piano and Chamber Orch. (St. Gallen, Nov. 17, 1948); Suite for Strings (Basel, Sept. 13, 1949); *Petite suite* (1953; Geneva, Dec. 8, 1956); *Impromptu* (1956; Basel, May 11, 1957); *Variationssatz über Schnitter Tod* (1958; Basel, Dec. 2, 1959); *Lyrische Suite* for Chamber Orch. (1959; Lugano, April 29, 1960); *Fantasia* for Clarinet, Harp, and Strings (Zürich, Oct. 6, 1965); *Sonata* (1967; Basel, Feb. 22, 1968); *Epitaffio* for Winds, Strings, and Percussion (Lucerne, Sept. 7, 1968); *Trois nocturnes* for Viola and Orch. (1968–69; Basel, March 19, 1970); *Airs et Ritournelles* for Percussion and Instrumental Group (1973; Basel, April 17, 1974); *Jour de fête* for Winds (Grenchen, Dec. 7, 1975); *Musik* (1975–76; Basel, May 25, 1977); *Sinfonia facile* (Basel, Aug. 26, 1977); *Conversazioni concertanti* for Saxophone, Vibraphone, and Strings (1978; Zürich, March 2, 1979); *L'Art pour l'art* (1979; Basel, June 6, 1980); Concerto Grosso (1984; Lugano, March 7, 1985); *Mouvements* for Winds (1985; Bern, April 3, 1986); *Gruezi* for Winds (Geneva, May 29, 1987); *Capriccio*, concerto for Marimba, Piano, and Orch. (1990–91). **CHAMBER:** 2 string quartets (1952, 1988); Flute Sonata (1954); *Estampida* for Percussion and 7 Instruments (1960); *Serenata* for 7 Instruments (1963–64); Fanfares et Pastorales for 2 Horns, Trumpet, and Trombone (1965); *Pastorale d'hiver* for 5 Instruments (1972); Sonata for Violin, Cello, and Piano (1975); *Jeux à quatre* for Saxophone Quartet (1976); *Music* for Brass (1980–81); *Small Talk* for Flute and Guitar (1984); *Ceremonie* for 6 Percussion (1984); Sextet for 2 Violins, 2 Violas, and 2 Cellos (1987); *Pulsation* for Percussionist (1990); 5 Duos for Violin and Viola (1992); *Musik* for Cello and Piano (1995); *Arie e danze* for Oboe and Cymbal (1996); also piano works. **VOCAL:** *Geisha-Lieder* for Soprano, Chorus, and 6 Instruments (1943); *Musikalisches Tagebuch No. 1* for Alto and 6 Instruments (1946), *No. 2* for Baritone and 7 Instruments (1950), and *No. 3* for Soprano, Tenor, and 10 Instruments (1998); *Ballade von den Seeraeubern* for Men's Chorus and Instruments (1952); *Jedem das Seine* for Women's Chorus (1955); *Heilige Leier, sprich, sei meine Stimme*, chamber cantata for Soprano, Flute, and Guitar (1960); *Ballade von des Cortez Leuten* for Speaker, Chorus, Speaking Chorus, and Chamber Orch. (1960); *Ein Blatt aus Sommerlichen Tagen* for Women's Chorus (1965–66); *Die sollen loben den Namen des Herrn*, motet (1971); *Drei Geistliche Spruche* (1971); *...aber auch lobet den Himmel* for Tenor, Baritone, Bass, Men's Chorus, Children's Chorus, and Instrumental Ensemble (1976); *Der abwesende Gott* for Soprano, Tenor, Speaker, 2 Choruses, Speaking Chorus, and Orch. (1978); *Marcia funèbre* for 3 Sopranos, Tape, and Orch. (1980–81; Zürich, Sept. 1982); *Vergänglichkeit der Schoenheit* for Countertenor, Tenor, Baritone, and 18 Baroque Instruments (1982–83); *Bhalt du mi Allewyyl lieb* for Children's Chorus and Wind Ensemble (1986).

BIBL.: D. Larese and J. Wildberger, *R. S.* (Amriswil, 1967).—**NS/LK/DM**

Sutermeister, Heinrich, distinguished Swiss composer; b. Feuerthalen, Aug. 12, 1910; d. Vaux-sur-Morges, March 16, 1995. He received training in music history from Karl Nef and in piano from Charlotte Schrameck, and also took courses in philology at the univs. of Basel and Paris (1930–31). After further studies with Walter Courvoisier (harmony and counterpoint) and Hugo Röhr (conducting) at the Munich Akademie der Tonkunst (1931–34), he returned to Switzerland and devoted himself principally to composition. He also was president of the Swiss Copyright Soc. (1958–80) and a teacher of composition at the Hannover Hochschule für Musik (1963–75). In 1965 he won the opera prize of the

City of Salzburg, in 1967 the prize of the Swiss Composers Union, and in 1991 the Prix de la Fondation Pierre et Louisa Meylan in Lausanne. In 1977 he was made a member of the Bavarian Akademie der Schönen Künste in Munich. In his music, Sutermeister placed prime importance upon the composer's responsibility to communicate directly with his listeners. While he utilized discordant combinations of sounds as a legitimate means of expression, he rejected what he considered artificial doctrines and opted instead for an effective and melodic style of wide appeal.

WORKS: DRAMATIC: Opera: *Die schwarze Spinne*, radio opera (1935; Bern Radio, Oct. 15, 1936; first stage perf., St. Gallen, March 2, 1949); *Romeo und Julia* (1938–40; Dresden, April 13, 1940; orch. suite, Berlin, April 9, 1941); *Die Zauberinsel* (1941–42; Dresden, Oct. 31, 1942); *Niobe* (1943–45; Zürich, June 22, 1946); *Raskolnikoff* (1945–47; Stockholm, Oct. 14, 1948); *Der rote Stiefel* (1949–51; Stockholm, Nov. 22, 1951); *Titus Feuerfuchs, oder Liebe, Tücke und Perücke*, burlesque opera (1956–58; Basel, April 14, 1958); *Seraphine, oder Die stumme Apothekerin*, opera buffa (Swiss TV, Zürich, June 10, 1959; first stage perf., Munich, Feb. 25, 1960); *Das Gespenst von Canterville*, television opera (1962–63; ZDF, Mainz, Sept. 6, 1964); *Madame Bovary* (1966; Zürich, May 26, 1967); *Der Flaschenteufel*, television opera (1969–70; ZDF, 1971); *Le Roi Bérenger* (1981–83; Munich, July 22, 1985). Ballet: *Das Dorf unter dem Gletscher* (1936; Karlsruhe, May 2, 1937); *Max und Moritz* (Bern Radio, 1951). **ORCH.:** 2 divertimentos: No. 1 for Strings (1936; Basel, May 28, 1937) and No. 2 (1959–60; Lausanne, Nov. 21, 1960); *Lieder und Tänze* for Little String Orch. (1939); Symphonic Suite from the opera *Romeo und Julia* (1940; Winterthur, April 9, 1941); 3 piano concertos: No. 1 (1943; Dresden, April 14, 1944), No. 2 (1953; Hamburg, Oct. 17, 1954), and No. 3 (1961–62; Bern, Dec. 6, 1990); *Die Alpen* for Orch. and Speaker Obbligato (Bern, May 11, 1948); *Marche fantasque* (Bern, Oct. 1950); 2 cello concertos: No. 1 (1954–55; Zürich, June 19, 1956) and No. 2 (1971; Geneva, Nov. 27, 1974); *Poème funèbre: En mémoire de Paul Hindemith* for Strings (Lucerne, Aug. 26, 1965); *Sérénade pour Montreux* for 2 Oboes, 2 Horns, and Strings (Montreux, Sept. 17, 1970); Clarinet Concerto (1975; Geneva, Jan. 19, 1977); *Quadrifoglio*, concerto for Flute, Oboe, Clarinet, Bassoon, and Orch. (1976–77; Bern, Dec. 1, 1977); *Aubade pour Morges* (Morges, April 28, 1979). **CHAMBER:** Concertino for Piano and Wind Quintet (1932; Chicago, March 23, 1994); String Quartet No. 3 (1933); *Capriccio* for Clarinet (1946); 2 serenades: No. 1 for 2 Clarinets, Trumpet, and Bassoon (1949) and No. 2 for Flute, Oboe, Clarinet, Bassoon, Horn, and Trumpet (1961); *Gavottte de Concert* for Trumpet and Piano (1950); *Modeste Mignon* for 10 Wind Instruments (1973; Hannover, Oct. 30, 1975). Piano: *12 zweistimmige Inventionen* (1934); *Bergsommer* (1941); Sonatina (1948); *Hommage à Arthur Honegger* (1955); *Winterferien* (1977). **VOCAL:** *Sieben Liebesbriefe* for Tenor and Orch. (1935); 8 cantatas: No. 1, *Andreas Gryphius*, for Chorus (1935–36; Zürich, March 20, 1938), No. 2 for Alto, Chorus, and 2 Pianos (1944; Zürich, May 18, 1946), No. 3, *Dem Allgegenwärtigen*, for Soprano, Bass-baritone, Chorus, and Orch. (1957–58; Duisburg, June 8, 1958), No. 4, *Das Hohelied*, for Soprano, Baritone, Chorus, and Orch. (1960; Amriswil, June 30, 1962), No. 5, *Der Papagei aus Kuba*, for Chorus and Chamber Orch. (1961; Bern, March 5, 1962), No. 6, *Erkennen und Schaffen*, for Soprano, Baritone, Chorus, and Orch. (1963; Lausanne, April 30, 1964), No. 7, *Sonnenhymne des Echnaton*, for Men's Chorus and Orch. (1965; Lucerne, May 17, 1967), and No. 8, *Omnia ad Unum*, for Baritone, Chorus, and Orch. (1965–66; Hannover, Nov. 18, 1966); *Vier Lieder* for High Voice and Piano (1945); *Der 70. und 86. Psalm* for Alto and Organ (1947); *Missa* for Chorus (1948); *Gloriola* for Chorus, Strings, and Piano (1952); *Max und Moritz* for Vocal Quartet and Piano, 4-Hands (1953); *Zwei Barocklieder* for Vocal Quartet and Chorus (1953); *Missa da Requiem* for Soprano, Baritone, Chorus, and Orch. (RAI, Rome, Dec. 21, 1953); *Vier Lieder* for Baritone, Violin, Flute, Oboe, Bassoon, and Harpsichord (1967; also for Baritone and Piano, 1968); *La Croisade des Enfants* for Soprano, Tenor, Bass, Speaker, Children's Chorus, Mixed Chorus, and Orch. (1968); *Ecclesia* for Soprano, Bass, Chorus, and Orch. (1972–73; Lausanne, Oct. 18, 1975); *Te Deum 1975* for Soprano, Chorus, and Orch. (1974; Zürich, Nov. 25, 1975); *Consolatio philosophiae* for High Voice and Orch. (1977; Geneva, Feb. 21, 1979); *Sechs Liebesbriefe* for Soprano and Orch. (1979; Geneva, Aug. 13, 1980); *Gloria* for Soprano, Chorus, and Orch. (1988; Morges, Nov. 10, 1991); various a cappella choruses.

BIBL.: D. Larese, *H. S.* (Amriswil, 1972).—**NS/LK/DM**

Suthaus, (Heinrich) Ludwig, eminent German tenor; b. Cologne, Dec. 12, 1906; d. Berlin, Sept. 7, 1971. He received his training in Cologne. In 1928 he made his operatic debut as Walther von Stolzing in Aachen. After singing in Essen (1931–33) and Stuttgart (1933–41), he was a member of the Berlin State Opera (1941–49). In 1943 he made his debut at the Bayreuth Festival as Walther von Stolzing, and sang there again in 1944, 1956, and 1957. From 1948 to 1961 he was a member of the Berlin Städtische Oper, and then of its successor, the Deutsche Oper, from 1961 to 1965. In 1949 he appeared as the Emperor in *Die Frau ohne Schatten* at the Teatro Colón in Buenos Aires. He made his U.S. debut as Aegisthus at the San Francisco Opera in 1953, and that same year made his Covent Garden debut in London as Tristan. Suthaus was one of the outstanding Heldentenors of his day. In addition to his Wagnerian roles, he also excelled as Florestan, Tchaikovsky's Hermann, Verdi's Otello, and Janáček's Števa.—**NS/LK/DM**

Sutherland, Dame Joan, celebrated Australian soprano; b. Sydney, Nov. 7, 1926. She first studied piano and voice with her mother; at age 19, she commenced vocal training with John and Aida Dickens in Sydney, making her debut there as Dido in a concert performance of *Dido and Aeneas* in 1947; then made her stage debut there in the title role of Judith in 1951; subsequently continued her vocal studies with Clive Carey at the Royal Coll. of Music in London; also studied at the Opera School there. She made her Covent Garden debut in London as the first Lady in *Die Zauberflöte* in 1952; attracted attention there when she created the role of Jenifer in *The Midsummer Marriage* (1955) and as *Gilda* (1957); also appeared in the title role of Alcina in the Handel Opera Soc. production (1957). In the meantime, she married **Richard Bonynge** (1954), who coached her in the bel canto operatic repertoire. After making her North American debut as Donna Anna in Vancouver (1958), she scored a triumph as Lucia at Covent Garden (Feb. 17, 1959). From then on she pursued a brilliant international career. She made her U.S. debut as Alcina in Dallas in 1960. Her Metropolitan Opera debut in N.Y. as Lucia on Nov. 26, 1961, was greeted by extraordinary acclaim. She continued to sing at the Metropolitan and other major opera houses on both sides of the Atlantic;

also took her own company to Australia in 1965 and 1974; during her husband's music directorship with the Australian Opera in Sydney (1976–86), she made stellar appearances with the company. On Oct. 2, 1990, she made her operatic farewell in *Les Huguenots* in Sydney. Sutherland was universally acknowledged as one of the foremost interpreters of the bel canto repertoire of her time. She particularly excelled in roles from operas by Rossini, Bellini, and Donizetti; was also a fine Handelian. In 1961 she was made a Commander of the Order of the British Empire and in 1979 was named a Dame Commander of the Order of the British Empire. In 1992 she was honored with the Order of Merit. With her husband, she publ. *The Joan Sutherland Album* (N.Y., 1986). Her autobiography appeared in 1997.

BIBL.: R. Braddon, *J. S.* (London, 1962); E. Greenfield, *J. S.* (London, 1972); B. Adams, *La Stupenda: A Biography of J. S.* (London, 1981); Q. Eaton, *S. & Bonynge: An Intimate Biography* (N.Y., 1987); M. Oxenbould, *J. S.: A Tribute* (1991); N. Major, *J. S.: The Authorized Biography* (Boston, 1994).—**NS/LK/DM**

Sutherland, Margaret (Ada), Australian pianist, teacher, and composer; b. Adelaide, Nov. 20, 1897; d. Melbourne, Aug. 12, 1984. She was a student of Edward Goll (piano) and Fritz Hart (composition) at the Marshall Hall Cons. in Melbourne (1914), and then she pursued her training at the Univ. of Melbourne Conservatorium. In 1916 she launched her career as a pianist. In 1923 she went to Europe to study, receiving additional training in Vienna and London. In 1935 she returned to Australia and pursued a pioneering role in new music circles as a pianist, teacher, and composer. In 1970 she was made an Officer of the Order of the British Empire. She was at her best as a composer of chamber music.

WORKS: DRAMATIC: *Dithyramb*, ballet (1937); *A Midsummer Night's Dream*, incidental music to Shakespeare's play (1941); *The Young Kabbarli*, opera (1964). **ORCH.:** *Pavan* (1938); *Prelude and Jig* for Strings (1939); *Suite on a Theme of Purcell* (1939); Piano Concertino (1940); Concerto for Strings (1945); *Homage to J. Sebastian* (1947); *Pastoral* (1947); *Walking Tune* (1947); *4 Symphonic Concepts* (1949); *Bush Ballad* (1950); *The Haunted Hills* (1950); *Open Air Piece* (1953); Violin Concerto (1954); *Concerto Grosso* (1955); *Outdoor Overture* (1958); *3 Temperaments* (1958); *Movement* (1959); Concertante for Oboe, Strings, and Percussion (1961); *Fantasy* for Violin and Orch. (1962). **CHAMBER:** Violin Sonata (1925); Trio for Clarinet, Viola, and Piano (1934); *Fantasy Sonatina* for Saxophone and Piano (1935); *House Quartet* for Clarinet or Violin, Viola, Horn or Cello, and Piano (1936); *Rhapsody* for Violin and Piano (1938); 3 string quartets (1939; *Discussion*, 1954; 1967); *Ballad and Nocturne* for Violin and Piano (1944; later separated); Clarinet Sonata (1944); *Adagio and Allegro Giocoso* for 2 Violins and Piano (1945); Clarinet or Viola Sonata (1949); Trio for Oboe and 2 Violins (1951–56); *Contrasts* for 2 Violins (1953); Quartet for English Horn and String Trio (1955); *6 Bagatelles* for Violin and Viola (1956); Oboe or Violin Sonatina (1957); *Little Suite* for Wind Trio (1957–60); *Divertimento* for String Trio (1958); *Fantasy* for Violin and Piano (1960); Quartet for Clarinet and Strings (1967). **Piano:** *Burlesque* for 2 Pianos (1927); *Holiday Tunes* (1936); 2 suites (1937, 1938); *Miniature Sonata* (1939); *6 Profiles* (1945–46); *Canonical Piece* for 2 Pianos (1957); Sonata (1966); *Extension* (1967); *Chiaroscuro I* and *II* (1968); *Valse Descants* (1968); *Voices I* and *II* (1968). **VOCAL:** Choral pieces; songs; arrangements of old Australian bush ballads.—**NS/LK/DM**

Sutro, Rose Laura (b. Baltimore, Sept. 15, 1870; d. there, Jan. 11, 1957) and **Ottilie** (b. Baltimore, Jan. 4, 1872; d. there, Sept. 12, 1970), American duo-pianists. They were the daughters of Otto Sutro, an art patron and founder of the Baltimore Oratorio Soc. Both began piano lessons with their mother, and in 1889 were sent to Berlin to continue their studies. They made a spectacular debut in London on July 13, 1894; their first American appearance took place in Brooklyn on Nov. 13, 1894, followed by a tour of the U.S. Returning to Europe, they won fresh laurels, and were invited to play before Queen Victoria. Max Bruch wrote his Concerto for 2 Pianos and Orch. expressly for them, and they gave its premiere with the Philadelphia Orch. on Dec. 29, 1916.—**NS/LK/DM**

Suwardi (Soewardi), Aloysius, respected Indonesian composer, performer, teacher, and experimental-instrument maker; b. Sukoharjo, Central Java, June 21, 1951. He studied in Surakarta at the Konservatori Karawitan (KOKAR, high school cons.), then at the Akademi Seni Karawitan Indonesia (A.S.K.I., college cons.), graduating in 1981 with the thesis *The Construction of Suling in Central Java*; subsequently taught classical music there (Sekolah Tinggi Seni Indonesia/ S.T.S.I.). In 1974 he became involved in new music circles and subsequently participated in new music festivals throughout Indonesia. He developed a fine reputation as a player of traditional gamelan music and as a gamelan tuner and restorer; he is often called upon to repair and/or retune Javanese gamelan throughout Indonesia, Europe, and the U.S. In 1986–87 he was a Fulbright visiting scholar to the U.S., teaching at several Midwest univs. As a composer, Suwardi is best known for works that make use of his own experimental instruments; his instrument innovations include placing the bronze keys of the gender on motor-driven resonators, developing a giant-sized gambang (wooden xylophone) inspired by the log xylophones of Africa, and designing and building a kind of water suling wherein the air goes through a tube and into a tin can of water before passing, modified, into a bamboo tube with finger holes. Among his compositions are *Ngalor-Ngidul* (1982; in collaboration with Rustopo and Suparno), *Gender* (1984), *Sebuah Process* (1984), and *Sak-sake* (1988). He is one of the few Indonesian composers to have been invited twice (1984, 1988) to the Pekan Komponis Muda, a national young composers' festival held annually in Jakarta.—**NS/LK/DM**

Suzuki, Shin'ichi, influential Japanese music educator and violin teacher; b. Nagoya, Oct. 18, 1898. He was the son of Masakichi Suzuki (1859–1944), a maker of string instruments and the founder of the Suzuki Violin Seizo Co. He studied violin with Ko Ando in Tokyo and with Karl Klinger in Berlin (1921–28); upon his return to Japan, he formed the Suzuki Quartet with 3 of his brothers; also made appearances as a conductor with his own Tokyo String Orch. He became president of the Teikoku Music School in 1930; subsequently devoted most of his time to education, especially the teaching of children. He maintained that any child, given the right stimuli under proper conditions in a group environment, could achieve a high level of competence as a performer. In 1950 he organized the Saino Kyoiku Kenkyu-kai in Matsumoto, where he taught his method most successfully. In subsequent years, his method was adopted for instruction on other instruments as well. He made many tours of the U.S. and Europe, where he lectured and demonstrated his method. See K. Selden, translator, *Where Love Is Deep: The Writings of Shin- ichi Suzuki* (St. Louis, 1982).

Bibl.: C. Cook, *S. Education in Action* (N.Y., 1970); E. Mills and T. Murthy, eds., *The S. Conception: An Introduction to a Successful Method for Early Music Education* (Berkeley, 1973); C. Barrett, *The Magic of Matsumoto: The S. Method of Education* (Palm Springs, Calif., 1995).—**NS/LK/DM**

Suzuki, Yukikazu, Japanese composer; b. Tokyo, Feb. 11, 1954. He studied with Hara Hoiroshi, Shishido Mutsuo, Matsumura Teizo, and Mayuzumi Toshiro at the Tokyo National Univ. of Fine Arts and Music (degree, 1984). In 1978 he was awarded first prize in the Japan Music Competition, and in 1979 5th prize in the International Contemporary Composer's Conference.

Works: Orch.: *Climat* (1978); *Ode* (1990); *The River of Forest and Stars* for Hichiriki and Orch. (1992); *The Glow in the Dark* for Wind Orch. (1996). **Chamber:** Oboe Sonata (1976); *Kyō-in* for 6 Players (1977); *Symphonic Metamorphoses* for Piano (1980); *Kundarini* for Contrabass (1981); Quintet for Piano, 2 Violins, Viola, and Cello (1987). **Vocal:** *Utsukushi i mono nitsuite*, suite for Chorus (1982); *Sound of Sea*, suite for Chorus (1989).—**NS/LK/DM**

Svanholm, Set (Karl Viktor), celebrated Swedish tenor; b. Vasterås, Sept. 2, 1904; d. Saltsjö-Duvnäs, near Stockholm, Oct. 4, 1964. He was first active as a church organist in Tillberga (1922–24) and Säby (1924–27). After training at the Royal Cons. in Stockholm (1927–29), he was precentor at St. James's Church in Stockholm. He then pursued vocal studies with Forsell at the Royal Cons. Opera School (1929–30). In 1930 he made his operatic debut in the baritone role of Silvio at the Royal Theater in Stockholm. In 1936 he made his debut there as a tenor singing Radames, and subsequently was one of the Royal Theater's most eminent members until 1956. In 1938 he appeared as Walther von Stolzing at the Salzburg Festival, and also sang at the Vienna State Opera that year. In 1941–42 he sang at Milan's La Scala. He made his Bayreuth Festival debut as Siegfried in 1942. He appeared as Tristan in Rio de Janeiro and as Lohengrin in San Francisco in 1946, and continued to sing in the latter city until 1951. On Nov. 15, 1946, he made his Metropolitan Opera debut in N.Y. as Siegfried. During his 10 seasons at the Metropolitan, he appeared in 105 performances and 17 roles. He was acclaimed not only for his Wagnerian heldentenor roles, but also for such roles as Florestan, Herod, Eisenstein, and Aegisth. His farewell to the Metropolitan came on March 4, 1956, when he sang Parsifal. From 1948 to 1957 he also appeared at London's Covent Garden. He served as director of the Royal Theater in Stockholm from 1956 to 1963.—**NS/LK/DM**

Švara, Danilo, Slovenian conductor and composer; b. Ricmanje, near Trieste, April 2, 1902; d. Ljubljana, April 25, 1981. He studied piano with Troste in Vienna (1920–22); pursued training in politics and law at the Univ. of Frankfurt am Main (1922–25) and concurrently took piano lessons from Malata and studied conducting with Scherchen; attended the Frankfurt am Main Hochschule für Musik (1927–30), where he took courses in composition with Sekles, in conducting with von Schmiedel and Rottenberg, and in stage direction with Wallerstein. He began his career as répétiteur and conductor at the Ljubljana Opera in 1925; later conducted there regularly, serving as its director (1957–59); also wrote music criticism and taught conducting at the Ljubljana Academy of Music. His compositions are cast in a modern idiom.

Works: Dramatic: Opera: *Kleopatra* (1937); *Veronika Deseniska* (1943); *Slovo od mladosti* (Farewell to Youth; 1952); *Ocean* (1963). **Ballet:** *Nina* (1962). **Orch.:** 3 syms. (1933, 1935, 1947); *Valse interrompue* (1948); *Sinfonia da camera in modo istriano* (1954); *Concerto grosso dodecafono* (1961); 2 suites (1962); *Dodekafonia*: I, *Duo concertante* for Flute, Harpsichord, and Orch. (1967), II, Violin Concerto (1966), III, Oboe Concerto (1966), IV, *Symposium* for Oboe, Viola, Harp, and Orch. (1968), and V, Clarinet Concerto (1969). **Other:** Chamber music; piano pieces; choral music; songs.—**NS/LK/DM**

Svéd, Sándor, Hungarian baritone; b. Budapest, May 28, 1904; d. Vienna, June 9, 1979. He studied violin at the Budapest Cons., then went to Milan for vocal studies with Sammarco and Stracciari. He made his operatic debut as Count Luna in Budapest in 1930; was a member of the Vienna State Opera (1936–39); also sang at Covent Garden in London and the Salzburg Festival. On Dec. 2, 1940, he made his debut under the name of Alexander Sved at the Metropolitan Opera in N.Y. as Renato in *Un ballo in maschera*; he remained on its roster until 1948, and then returned for the 1949–50 season. He subsequently sang in Rome, in Paris, and at the Bayreuth Festival; also made appearances with the Budapest Opera, and later toured as a concert singer. In 1956 he went to Stuttgart as a vocal teacher.—**NS/LK/DM**

Sveinbjörnsson, Sveinbjörn, Icelandic pianist and composer; b. near Reykjavík, June 28, 1847; d. Copenhagen, Feb. 23, 1927. After theological training, he went to Copenhagen to pursue musical studies with V.C. Ravn (1868–70). Following further studies with Reinecke in Leipzig (1872–73), he settled in Edinburgh, where he taught piano and was active as a concert pianist, making 2 major tours of North America (1911–13; 1919–22). He was an accomplished composer of choral works, songs, and piano pieces; his hymn in celebration of the millennium anniversary of the Norse settlement in Iceland (1874) was adopted as the Icelandic national anthem.

Bibl.: J. Thorarinsson, *S. S.* (Reykjavík, 1969).
—**NS/LK/DM**

Sveinsson, Atli Heimer, Icelandic composer, teacher, conductor, and administrator; b. Reykjavík, Sept. 21, 1938. After studying piano at the Reykjavík Coll. of Music, he took courses in theory and composition with Raphael, Petzold, and Zimmermann at the Cologne Staatliche Hochschule für Musik (1959–62). He also attended composition courses in Darmstadt and Cologne under Stockhausen and Pousseur, and took a course in electronic music in Bilthoven under Koenig. Upon returning to Reykjavík, he played a prominent role in Iceland's musical life. In addition to composing prolifically, he was active as a radio producer, conductor, and organizer. He also taught at the Coll. of Music. From 1972 to 1983 he served as chairman of the Soc. of Icelandic Composers. In 1976 he won the Nordic Council Music Prize for his Flute Concerto. In his music, he has developed a style along Romantic-Expressionistic lines.

WORKS: DRAMATIC: *The Silken Drum*, opera (Reykjavík, June 6, 1982); *Vikivaki*, television opera (1989–90); *Tunglskinseyjan*, chamber opera (1995); *Hertervig*, opera (1997). **ORCH.:** *Hlými* for Chamber Orch. (1963); *Tautophony* (1967); *Tengsl* (1970); *Flower Shower* (1973); *Hreinn: Gallery sum 1974* (1974); Flute Concerto (1975); Bassoon Concerto, *Trobar Clus* (1980); Trombone Concerto, *Jubilus* (1984); *Recitation* for Piano and Chamber Orch. (1984); *Dreamboat*, concerto for Violin, Harpsichord, and Orch. (1987); *A Gledistundu* for Chamber Orch. (1989); *Röckerauschen, Bruit des Robes* for Chamber Orch. (1993); Concerto for Saxophone Quartet and Orch. (1994); *Eldtecken*, piano concerto (1995); *Erjur*, cello concerto (1997); *Íslenskt Rapp V* (1998). **CHAMBER:** *Xanties* for Flute and Piano (1975); Septet (1976); *Plutot Blanche Qu'azurée* for Clarinet, Cello, and Piano (1976); *21 Sounding Minutes* for Flute (1980); *Precious Dances* for Guitar, Flute, Clarinet, Cello, and Piano (1983); *Bicentennial* for String Quartet (1984); Trio for Violin, Cello, and Piano (1985); Quartet for 4 Flutes (1991); *Tanzfiguren* for Accordion and Wind Quintet (1992); *Grand Duo Concertante III* for Flute, Cello, and Tape (1995); *Fantastic Rondos III* for Flute, Oboe, Clarinet, Cello, Piano, and Soprano (1996); piano pieces; organ music. **VOCAL:** *Aria* for Soprano and 5 Instruments (1977); *Autumn Pictures* for Chorus, 2 Violins, Cello, and Accordion (1982); *The Night on Our Shoulders* for Soprano, Alto, Women's Chorus, and Orch. (1986); *Opplaring* for Soprano and Winds (1991); many choral pieces and songs. **OTHER:** *Ode to the Stone* for Piano, Reciter, and Projector (1983).—**NS/LK/DM**

Svenden, Birgitta, Swedish mezzo-soprano; b. Porjus, March 20, 1950. She was educated at the Royal Opera School in Stockholm. After appearing at the Royal Opera in Stockholm, she sang a minor role in the *Ring* cycle at the Bayreuth Festival in 1983. In 1986 she was chosen to create the role of Queen Christina in the premiere of Gefor's *Christina* in Stockholm. She sang Erda at the Metropolitan Opera in N.Y. in 1988. Following an engagement as Wagner's Magdalena in Seattle in 1989, she made her debut at London's Covent Garden as Erda in 1990. She portrayed Octavian at the Théâtre du Châtelet in Paris in 1993. In 1994 she sang at the Bayreuth Festival, where she returned in 1996. In 1995 she was made a Royal Court Singer by the King of Sweden.—**NS/LK/DM**

Svendsen, Johan (Severin), eminent Norwegian composer and conductor; b. Christiania, Sept. 30, 1840; d. Copenhagen, June 14, 1911. His father, a military musician, taught him to play various instruments, and by his early teens he was performing in local dance orchs. and composing dances and marches. After joining the army at age 15, he became solo clarinetist in the regimental band. He then received violin lessons from F. Ursin and played in the Norwegian Theater orch. in Christiania; subsequently studied with Carl Arnold. Receiving a stipend from the King, he pursued his musical training at the Leipzig Cons. (1863–67) with Ferdinand David, Moritz Hauptmann, E.F. Richter, and Carl Reinecke, graduating with a first prize in composition. In 1867 he conducted a concert of his works in Christiania; although an anonymous review written by Grieg was full of praise, the public showed little interest and Svendsen returned to Leipzig. In 1868 he went to Paris, where he became acquainted with young progressive French composers. In 1871 he married the American Sarah Levett in N.Y., and then returned to Leipzig to become concertmaster and second conductor of the Euterpe concerts. He went to Bayreuth in 1872 to play in the special concert of Beethoven's 9th Sym. under Wagner's direction for the laying of the cornerstone of the Festspielhaus. Svendsen subsequently became a close friend to Wagner. In 1872 he returned to Christiania to become co-conductor with Grieg of the Music Soc. concerts; in 1874 he became sole conductor and was granted an annual government composer's salary. After sojourns in Rome (1877–78) and London (1878), he again went to Paris. In 1880 he returned to Christiania and resumed his position as conductor of the Music Soc. concerts. In 1882 he conducted 2 concerts of his own music in Copenhagen, the success of which led to his appointment as principal conductor of the Royal Opera there in 1883, but the loss of his composer's salary from his native country. All the same, he retained his Norwegian citizenship while transforming the musical life of Copenhagen, conducting both operatic and orch. performances of great distinction. He also appeared as a guest conductor in Vienna, St. Petersburg, Moscow, London, Paris, Brussels, and other cities with brilliant success. In 1901 he divorced his first wife and married Juliette (Vilhelmine) Haase, a ballerina. In 1908 he retired from the Royal Opera and was granted an honorary pension by the Danish government; not to be outdone, the Norwegian government restored his annual composer's salary. With Grieg, Svendsen represents the full flowering of the national Romantic movement in Norwegian music. Unlike his famous compatriot, he proved a master of large orch. forms; he was unquestionably the foremost Nordic symphonist of his time, and during the last quarter of the 19th century enjoyed an international reputation equal to that of Grieg.

WORKS: ORCH.: *Caprice* for Violin and Orch. (1863; Leipzig, Dec. 1864); 2 syms.: No. 1, op.4 (1865–67; Christiania, Oct. 12, 1867) and No. 2, op.15 (Christiania, Oct. 14, 1876); Violin Concerto, op.6 (1868–70; Leipzig, Feb. 6, 1872); Cello Concerto, op.7 (1870; Leipzig, March 16, 1871); Symphonic Introduction to Bjørnson's *Sigurd Slembe*, op.8 (Leipzig, Dec. 12, 1871); *Karneval i Paris*, op.9 (Christiania, Oct. 26, 1872); Funeral March for King Carl XV, op.10 (1872); *Zorahayda*, op.11 (Christiania, Oct. 3, 1874; rev. 1879; Christiania, May 11, 1880); *Festival*

Polonaise, op.12 (Christiania, Aug. 6, 1873); Coronation March for Oscar II, op.13 (1873); *Norsk kunstnerkarneval*, op.14 (Christiania, March 17, 1874); *4 Norwegian Rhapsodies*: No. 1, op.17 (1876; Christiania, Sept. 25, 1877), No. 2, op.19 (1876; Munich, 1880), No. 3, op.21 (1876; Paris, Jan. 1879), and No. 4, op.22 (1877; Paris, Feb. 1, 1879); *Romeo og Julie*, fantasy, op.18 (Christiania, Oct. 14, 1876); *Romance* for Violin and Orch., op.26 (Christiania, Oct. 30, 1881); *Polonaise*, op.28 (1882); *Foraaret kommer* (Coming of Spring), ballet, op.33 (Copenhagen, May 26, 1892); *Andante funèbre* (Copenhagen, June 30, 1894); *Prelude* (Copenhagen, Dec. 18, 1898); also several arrangements for String Orch. **CHAMBER:** String Quartet, op.1 (1864; Leipzig, May 21, 1865); String Octet, op.3 (Leipzig, Feb. 24?, 1866); String Quintet, op.5 (Leipzig, May 17, 1867). **Piano:** *Anna*, polka (1854); *Til saeters* (At the Mountain Pasture), waltz (1856). **VOCAL:** 2 partsongs for Men's Voices, op.2 (1865); 5 songs for Voice and Piano, op.23 (1879); 4 songs for Voice and Piano, op.24 (1879); 2 songs, op.25 (1878, 1880); 4 cantatas, op.29 (1881, 1881, 1884, 1892).

BIBL.: B. Kortsen, *J. S.'s Cellokonsert, op. 7. En analyse* (Bergen, 1970); F. Benestad and D. Schjeldrup-Ebbe, *J. S.: Mennesket og kunstneren* (Oslo, 1990; Eng. tr., 1995, as *J. S.: The Man, the Maestro, the Music*).—**NS/LK/DM**

Svetlanov, Evgeny (Feodorovich), prominent Russian conductor and composer; b. Moscow, Sept. 6, 1928. He studied composition with Mikhail Gnessin and piano with Mariya Gurvich at the Gnessin Inst. in Moscow (graduated, 1951); took courses in composition with Shaporin and in conducting with Gauk at the Moscow Cons. (graduated, 1955). In 1953 he made his debut as a conductor with the All-Union Radio orch. in Moscow; was a conductor at the Bolshoi Theater there from 1955, serving as its chief conductor (1962–64). In 1965 he was appointed chief conductor of the State Sym. Orch. of the U.S.S.R.; from 1979 he was a principal guest conductor of the London Sym. Orch. Following the collapse of the Soviet Union in 1991, the U.S.S.R. State Sym. Orch. became the Russian State Sym. Orch. Svetlanov retained his position as its chief conductor, and also served as chief conductor of the Residentie Orch. in The Hague from 1992. He also made appearances as a pianist. In 1968 he was named a People's Artist of the U.S.S.R.; in 1972 he was awarded the Lenin Prize and in 1975 the Glinka Prize. He has won particular distinction for his compelling performances of the Russian repertoire. He wrote a Sym. (1956), *Siberian Fantasy* for Orch. (1953), Piano Concerto (1951), incidental music for plays, and film scores. He is married to **Larissa Avdeyeva**.

BIBL.: L. Krylova, *E. S.* (Moscow, 1986).—**NS/LK/DM**

Sviridov, Georgi (Vasilevich), Russian composer and pianist; b. Fatezh, near Kursk, Dec. 16, 1915; d. Moscow, Jan. 6, 1998. After studies in Kursk (1929–32), he was a student of Yudin (composition) at the Leningrad Central Music Coll. (1932–36) and of Shostakovich (composition and orchestration) at the Leningrad Cons. (graduated, 1941). From 1945 he made appearances as a pianist but devoted much time to composition. In 1970 he was made a People's Artist of the U.S.S.R. His *Oratorio pathétique* (1959) was one of the most successful works by a Soviet composer as per the tenets of socialist realism.

WORKS: DRAMATIC: *Othello*, incidental music to Shakespeare's play (1944); *Twinling Lights*, operetta (1951); film scores. **ORCH.:** Sym. for Strings (1940); *Music* for Chamber Orch. (1964). **CHAMBER:** String Quartet (1945); many piano pieces. **VOCAL:** *The Decembrists*, oratorio (1955); *Oratorio pathétique* (1959); *Poem About Lenin* for Bass, Chorus, and Orch. (1960); *5 Songs About Our Fatherland* for Voices, Chorus, and Orch. (1967); numerous solo songs.

BIBL.: D. Frishman, ed., *G. S.* (Moscow, 1971); A. Sokhor, *G. S.* (Moscow, 1972).—**NS/LK/DM**

Svoboda, Josef, influential Czech opera designer and producer; b. Čáslav, May 10, 1920. He studied architecture in Prague. In 1947 he made his debut in the theater with a production of *Kát'a Kabanová* at the 5th of May Theater in Prague. His *Halka* was seen at the Prague National Theater in 1951, and he subsequently served as its chief designer and technical director until 1956. After working on the premiere of Nono's *Intolleranza 1960* in Venice (1961), his *Cardillac* was seen in Milan in 1964. In 1966 he brought out *Die Frau ohne Schatten* at London's Covent Garden, where he returned with *Pelléas et Mélisande* in 1969, *Nabucco* in 1972, and the *Ring* cycle in 1974–76. In 1969 his *Der fliegende Holländer* was seen at the Bayreuth Festival, his *Die Soldaten* was produced in Munich, and his *Les Vêpres siciliennes* was staged in Hamburg. In 1970 his innovative production of *Die Zauberflöte* was mounted in Munich. He staged *Wozzeck* in Milan in 1971 and *Carmen* at the Metropolitan Opera in N.Y. in 1972. After producing *Les Vêpres siciliennes* in London (1984), *Elektra* in Bonn (1986), and *Salome* in Berlin (1990), he staged *La Sonnambula* at the Macerata Festival in 1992. His *Attila* was mounted at the Macerata Festival in 1996. Svoboda's innovative stage design and production concepts are centered on his creative use of lighting as the crucial element in what he describes as a "psychoplastic" theater experience.—**NS/LK/DM**

Svoboda, Tomáš, Czech-American composer; b. Paris (of Czech parents), Dec. 6, 1939. His father was the renowned mathematician Antonin Svoboda. After the outbreak of World War II, his family went to Boston, where he began piano lessons as a child; in 1946 he went with his family to Prague and studied at the Cons. with Hlobil, Kabeláč, and Dobiáš (1954–62), graduating with degrees in composition, conducting, and percussion; he was only 17 when his first Sym. was premiered by the Prague Sym. Orch. Following further training at the Prague Academy of Music (1962–64), he settled in the U.S. and pursued graduate studies with Dahl and Stevens at the Univ. of Southern Calif. in Los Angeles (1966–69). In 1971 he became a teacher of composition, theory, and percussion at Portland (Ore.) State Univ. His music is marked by broad melodic lines in economically disposed harmonies; there are elements of serialism in chromatic episodes.

WORKS: DRAMATIC: Incidental Music To: D. Seabrook's play *The Clockmaker* (1986). **ORCH.:** *Scherzo* for 2 Euphonias and Orch. (1955; Prague, Sept. 3, 1958); 6 syms.: No. 1, *of Nature* (1956; Prague, Sept. 7, 1957; rev. 1984; Portland,

Ore., March 10, 1985), No. 2 (1964), No. 3 for Organ and Orch. (1965), No. 4, *Apocalyptic* (1975; Portland, Ore., Feb. 19, 1978), No. 5, *in Unison* (1978; Portland, Ore., Nov. 13, 1988), and No. 6 for Clarinet and Orch. (1991; Portland, Ore., April 26, 1992); *In a Linden's Shadow*, symphonic poem for Organ and Orch. (1958); *Dramatic Overture* (Prague Radio, Sept. 18, 1959); *6 Variations* for Violin and String Orch. (1961); *Christmas Concertino* for Harp and Chamber Orch. (1961); Suite for Bassoon, Harpsichord, and Strings (1962; Prague, April 11, 1963); *Étude* for Chamber Orch. (1963); *3 Pieces* (1966; Sacramento, Calif., March 30, 1967); Concertino for Oboe, Brass Choir, and Timpani (1966; Los Angeles, March 21, 1968); *Reflections* (1968; Toronto, March 21, 1972); *Sinfoniette (à la Renaissance)* (Jacksonville, Ore., Aug. 14, 1972); *Labyrinth* for Chamber Orch. (1974); *Prelude and Fugue* for Strings (1974); 2 piano concertos: No. 1 (Portland, Ore., Nov. 17, 1974) and No. 2 (1989); Violin Concerto (1975; Jacksonville, Ore., Aug. 15, 1976); *Overture of the Season* (Bend, Ore., Oct. 6, 1978); *Nocturne (Cosmic Sunset)* (Sunriver, Ore., Aug. 20, 1981); *Eugene Overture (Festive)* (Eugene, Ore., Sept. 24, 1982); *Ex libris* (Louisville, Dec. 3, 1983); *Serenade* (Sarasota, Fla., March 24, 1984); Concerto for Chamber Orch. (1986; Portland, Ore., Sept. 9, 1988); *Dance Suite* (Jacksonville, Ore., Aug. 8, 1987); *3 Cadenzas* for Piano and Orch. (Boston, March 29, 1990); *Swing Dance* (1992; Billings, Mont., Aug. 29, 1993); *Meditation* for Oboe and Strings (1993); Marimba Concerto (1994; Portland, Ore., March 26, 1995). **CHAMBER:** *Evening Negro Songs and Dances* for Piano and 2 Percussionists (1956); 2 string quartets (1960, 1995); *Baroque Quintet* for Flute, Oboe, Clarinet, Cello, and Piano (1962); Trio for Oboe, Bassoon, and Piano (1962); Septet for Bassoon, Harpsichord, and String Quintet (1962); *Divertimento* for 7 Instruments (1967); *Parabola* for Clarinet, Violin, Viola, Cello, and Piano (1971); Trio for Flute, Oboe, and Bassoon (1979); *Passacaglia and Fugue* for Violin, Cello, and Piano (1981); Trio for Electric Guitar, Piano, and Percussion (1982); Trio Sonata for Electric Guitar, Vibraphone, and Piano (1982); Brass Quintet (N.Y., Nov. 22, 1983); Violin Sonata (1984); Trio for Violin, Cello, and Piano (1984); Chorale in E- flat ("homage to Aaron Copland") for Clarinet, Violin, Viola, Double Bass, and Piano (N.Y., May 10, 1985); *Legacy* for Brass Septet (1988); *Military Movements* for Guitar and Harpsichord (1991); *Theme and Variations* for Flute, Clarinet, and Piano (1992); Duo for Xylophone and Marimba (1993); Quartet for 4 Horns (1993); *Arab Dance* for Synthesizer (1994); also piano music, including 2 sonatas (1967, 1985), and organ pieces. **VOCAL:** *44th Sonnet of Michelangelo* for Alto and Instrumental Ensemble (1967); *Separate Solitude* for Chorus and 2 Clarinets (1973; Portland, Ore., March 2, 1976); *Celebration of Life*, cantata for Soprano, Tenor, Chorus, Instrumental Ensemble, and Tape, after Aztec poetry (Portland, Ore., Oct. 31, 1976); *Chorale Without Words* for Chorus and Piano (1984; N.Y., March 16, 1986); *Festival* for Men's Chorus (Portland, Ore., Sept. 9, 1987); *Haleluya* for Men's Chorus (1990); *Summer Fragments* for Soprano and Piano (1992). —**NS/LK/DM**

Swan, Timothy, American composer and tunebook compiler; b. Worcester, Mass., July 23, 1758; d. Northfield, Mass., July 23, 1842. His only musical training consisted of 3 weeks at a singing school, and while serving in the Continental Army he also learned to play the fife. From 1783 he lived in Suffield, Conn., and in 1807 moved to Northfield, Mass. His fuging tunes *Bristol*, *Montague*, and *Rainbow* and his hymn tune *China* were widely known. He publ. a vol. of secular duets as *The Songster's Assistant* (c. 1786) and the tunebook *New England Harmony* (1801).

BIBL.: G. Webb, *T. S.: Yankee Tunesmith* (diss., Univ. of Ill., 1972).—**NS/LK/DM**

Swann, Frederick (Lewis), notable American organist and composer; b. Lewisburg, W.Va., July 30, 1931. He received training in piano and organ in his childhood, and later pursued his education at Northwestern Univ. (Mus.B., 1952) and at the School of Sacred Music at Union Theological Seminary in N.Y. (M. of Sacred Music, 1954). In 1958 he became organist and in 1966 director of music at the Riverside Church in N.Y., positions he retained until 1982. He also was director of music and organist of the Interchurch Center (1960–67) and chairman of the organ dept. at the Manhattan School of Music (1972–82). In 1981 he was chosen to inaugurate the organ at Orchestra Hall in Chicago. Swann became director of music and organist at the Crystal Cathedral in Garden Grove, Calif., in 1983, where his performances via its televised services brought him global recognition. In 1984 he was soloist for the new Ruffatti organ at Davies Symphony Hall in San Francisco. He was a featured recitalist at the American Guild of Organists Centennial Convention in N.Y. in 1996. Upon his retirement from the Crystal Cathedral in 1998, he was made organist emeritus. In 1998 he assumed the position of organist-in-residence at the First Congregational Church in Los Angeles. As a recitalist, he has made numerous tours of North America. In 1998 he made his 12th tour of Europe. Swann has also been active as an organ consultant. As a composer, he has written various choral and organ pieces.—**NS/LK/DM**

Swann, Jeffrey, American pianist; b. Williams, Ariz., Nov. 24, 1951. He was a student of Alexander Uninsky in Dallas (1963–69) before completing his studies at the Juilliard School in N.Y. with Beveridge Webster (B.M., 1972; M.M., 1973) and Adele Marcus (D.M.A., 1980). In 1965 he made his debut as a soloist with the Dallas Sym. Orch. under Donald Johanos's direction. He appeared as a soloist with the Warsaw Phil. conducted by Witold Rowicki in 1971. In 1975 he made his recital debut at Hunter Coll. of the City Univ. of N.Y., and subsequently gave recitals in various U.S. cities and appeared as a soloist with leading orchs. of the country. Following his debut as a soloist with the orch. of La Scala in Milan under Hubert Soudant's direction in 1975, he returned to La Scala in 1976 as a recitalist. In 1981 he made his Paris recital debut at the Théâtre des Champs-Elysées, followed in 1982 by debut recitals at the Tonhalle in Zürich and the Concertgebouw in Amsterdam. He made his debut as a soloist with the Philharmonia Orch. of London under the direction of Jacek Kaspszyk in 1986, and then returned to London in 1987 to make his recital debut at the Queen Elizabeth Hall. He subsequently gave recitals and appeared as a soloist with orchs. in Europe while continuing his active career in the U.S. Swann has particularly distinguished himself as an interpreter of Mozart, Beethoven, Chopin, Liszt, Debussy, and Bartók.—**LK/DM**

Swanson, Howard, black American composer; b. Atlanta, Aug. 18, 1907; d. N.Y., Nov. 12, 1978. He grew up in Cleveland, where he began piano lessons at 9. As a youth, he earned a living by manual labor on the railroad and as a postal clerk. He entered the Cleveland Inst. of Music at the age of 20, enrolling in evening courses with Herbert Elwell (graduated, 1937); obtained a stipend to go to Paris, where he studied composition with Boulanger (1938–40). Returning to the U.S., he took a job with the Internal Revenue Service (1941–45). In 1952 he received a Guggenheim fellowship that enabled him to go back to Paris, where he lived until 1966 before settling permanently in N.Y. Swanson's songs attracted the attention of such notable singers as Marian Anderson and William Warfield, who sang them on tours. He achieved signal success with his *Short Symphony* (Sym. No. 2, 1948), a work of simple melodic inspiration, which received considerable acclaim at its first performance by the N.Y. Phil., conducted by Mitropoulos (Nov. 23, 1950). In 1952 it won the Music Critics' Circle Award.

WORKS: ORCH.: 3 syms.: No. 1 (1945; N.Y., April 28, 1968), No. 2, *Short Symphony* (1948; N.Y., Nov. 23, 1950), and No. 3 (N.Y., March 1, 1970); *Night Music* for Strings and Wind Quintet (1950); *Music* for Strings (1952); *Concerto for Orchestra* (1954; Louisville, Jan. 9, 1957); Piano Concerto (1956); *Fantasy Piece* for Soprano Saxophone or Clarinet and Strings (1969); *Threnody for Martin Luther King Jr.* for Strings (1969). **CHAMBER:** *Nocturne* for Violin and Piano (1948); Suite for Cello and Piano (1949); *Soundpiece* for Brass Quintet (1952); *Vista No. 2* for String Octet (1969; Washington, D.C., Feb. 18, 1986); Cello Sonata (N.Y., May 13, 1973); Trio for Flute, Oboe, and Piano (1975). **Piano:** 3 sonatas (1948; 1970; 1974, unfinished); *2 Nocturnes* (1967). **VOCAL:** *Songs for Patricia* for Soprano and Strings or Piano (1951); *Nightingales* for Men's Voices (1952); *We Delighted, My Friend* for Chorus (1977); 30 songs for Voice and Piano, including *The Negro Speaks of Rivers* (1942), *The Junk Man* (1946), *Ghosts in Love* (1950), and *The Valley* (1951).

BIBL.: E. Ennett, *An Analysis and Comparison of Selected Piano Sonatas by Three Contemporary Black Composers: George Walker, H. S., and Roque Cordero* (diss., N.Y.U., 1973); D. Baker, L. Belt, and H. Hudson, eds., *The Black Composer Speaks* (Metuchen, N.J., 1978).—**NS/LK/DM**

Swarowsky, Hans, noted Austrian conductor and pedagogue; b. Budapest, Sept. 16, 1899; d. Salzburg, Sept. 10, 1975. He studied in Vienna with Schoenberg and Webern, with whom he formed a friendly association; he also was in close relationship with Richard Strauss. He occupied posts as opera conductor in Hamburg (1932), Berlin (1934), and Zürich (1937–40); after conducting the Kraków orch. (1944–45), he was conductor of the Vienna Sym. Orch. (1946–48) and the Graz Opera (1947–50); from 1957 to 1959 he was conductor of the Scottish National Orch. in Glasgow; from 1959, appeared mainly as guest conductor of the Vienna State Opera. He became especially well known as a pedagogue; was head of the conducting class at the Vienna Academy of Music from 1946, where his pupils included Claudio Abbado and Zubin Mehta. As a conductor, he demonstrated notable command of a large symphonic and operatic repertoire, ranging from Haydn to the second Viennese School. He was also a highly competent ed. of music by various composers; also tr. a number of Italian librettos into German. M. Huss ed. his book *Wahrung der Gestalt* (Vienna, 1979).—**NS/LK/DM**

Swarthout, Gladys, American mezzo-soprano; b. Deepwater, Mo., Dec. 25, 1900; d. Florence, July 7, 1969. She received her training at the Bush Cons. in Chicago. In 1924 she made her operatic debut as the Shepherd in *Tosca* with the Chicago Civic Opera. In 1925 she sang Carmen with the Ravinia Opera Co. in Chicago. On Nov. 15, 1929, she made her Metropolitan Opera debut in N.Y. as La Cieca; she sang that role there often until her farewell in 1945. She was particularly admired for her Carmen and Mignon, but she also sang Adalgisa, Maddalena, and Preziosilla with success. She also sang Carmen in Chicago (1939) and San Francisco (1941), and made appearances in films. Swarthout's career was ended by a severe heart attack, and in 1954 she settled in Florence. Her autobiography appeared as *Come Soon, Tomorrow* (N.Y., 1945). Swarthout was admired for the warmth of her vocal technique.—**NS/LK/DM**

Swayne, Giles (Oliver Cairnes), English composer; b. Stevenage, June 30, 1946. He began composing as a teenager, receiving encouragement from his cousin, Elizabeth Maconchy; then pursued training with Leppard and Maw at the Univ. of Cambridge (1963–68); subsequently studied piano with Gordon Green and composition with Birtwistle, Bush, and Maw at the Royal Academy of Music in London (1968–71); later attended Messiaen's classes in composition in Paris (1976–77). In 1982 he visited West Africa to study the music of the Jola people of Senegal and The Gambia. In common with many other British composers of his generation, he resolutely eschewed musical gourmandise in favor of writing music in an avant-garde, yet accessible style.

WORKS: DRAMATIC: *A World Within*, ballet for Tape (Stoke-on-Trent, June 2, 1978); *Le Nozze di Cherubino*, opera (1984; London, Jan. 22, 1985). **ORCH.:** *Orlando's Music* (1974; Liverpool, Feb. 3, 1976); *Charades* for School Orch. (1975); *Pentecost Music* (1977; Manchester, April 8, 1981); Sym. for Small Orch. (London, June 1, 1984); *Naaotwa Lala* (Manchester, Dec. 4, 1984); *The Song of Leviathan* (London, Oct. 10, 1988). **CHAMBER:** *4 Lyrical Pieces* for Cello and Piano (1970; Aldeburgh, June 16, 1971); 3 string quartets: No. 1 (1971), No. 2 (1977; Manchester, Oct. 30, 1978), and No. 3 (1992–93); *Paraphrase on a Theme of Tallis* for Organ (1971); *Canto* for Guitar (1972); *Canto* for Piano (1973); *Canto* for Violin (1973); *Synthesis* for 2 Pianos (1974); *Canto* for Clarinet (1975); *Duo* for Violin and Piano (1975); Suite for Guitar (1976); *Freewheeling* for Viola, Baryton, and Cello (Kuhmo Festival, Finland, July 25, 1980); *Canto* for Cello (1981); *Rhythm-Study I* for 2 Xylophone Players and 2 Marimba Players (1982) and *II* for Percussion Group (1982); *A Song for Haddi* for Flute, Clarinet, Viola, Cello, Double Bass, and Percussion (Bath Festival, June 4, 1983); *into the light* for 7 Players (1986); *PP* for 14 Players (1987); *Tonos* for Flute, Harp, Violin, Viola, and Cello (1987); *Songlines* for Flute and Guitar (1987); *A Memory of Sky* for Brass Quintet (1988). **VOCAL:** *The Good Morrow*, cycle of 5 settings of John Donne for Mezzo-soprano and Piano (1971); *Cry* for 28 Amplified Solo Voices (1979; The Hague, Oct. 22, 1982); *Count-Down* for 16-part

Chorus and 2 Percussion Players (1981; Merton Festival, Yorkshire, May 23, 1982); *Magnificat* for Chorus (1982); *god-song* for Mezzo-soprano, Flute, Trombone, Cello, and Piano (1985–86); *Nunc Dimittis* for Chorus and Organ (1986); *O Magnum Mysterium* for Boy's Voices and Organ (1986); *Veni creator I* and *II* for Chorus and Organ (1987); *No Quiet Place* for Children's Voices, String Trio, and Xylophones (1989); *No Man's Land* for Chorus and Ensemble (1990); *Circle of Silence* for 6 Voices (1991); *The Song of the Tortoise* for Narrator, Children's Voices, Chorus, and Orch. (1992); *The Owl and the Pussycat* for Narrator and 7 Instruments (1993).—**NS/LK/DM**

Sweatman, Wilbur (C.), ragtime-flavored clarinetist, leader, composer; b. Brunswick, Mo., Feb. 7, 1882; d. N.Y., March 9, 1961. Sweatman played three clarinets at once in touring shows from the late 1890s, and continued to perform when he moved to N.Y. in 1913. He led Sweatman's Original Jazz Band from 1918–21, recording for a variety of labels. In 1923, he hired a group of young Washington, D.C.–based musicians—including Duke Ellington—to play with him in N.Y. The job failed to materialize, but Ellington and friends remained in the city and formed the popular Washingtonians group. Beginning in the 1930s, Sweatman concentrated on music publishing and acting as executor for Scott Joplin's estate. He composed "Down Home Rag" and other rag-flavored works.—**JC/LP**

Sweelinck (real name, **Swybbertszoon**), **Jan Pieterszoon,** great Dutch organist, pedagogue, and composer; b. Deventer, May? 1562; d. Amsterdam, Oct. 16, 1621. He was born into a musical family; his father, paternal grandfather, and uncle were all organists. He went as a youth to Amsterdam, which was to be the center of his activities for the rest of his life. Jacob Buyck, pastor of the Oude Kerk, supervised his academic education. He most likely commenced his musical training under his father, then studied with Jan Willemszoon Lossy. He is believed to have begun his career as an organist in 1577, although first mention of him is in 1580, as organist of the Oude Kerk, a position his father held until his death in 1573. Sweelinck became a celebrated master of the keyboard, so excelling in the art of improvisation that he was called the "Orpheus of Amsterdam." He was also greatly renowned as a teacher, numbering among his pupils most of the founders of the so-called north German organ school. His most famous pupils were Jacob Praetorius, Heinrich Scheidemann, Samuel and Gottfried Scheidt, and Paul Siefert. The output of Sweelinck as a composer is now seen as the culmination of the great Dutch school of his time. Among his extant works are about 250 vocal pieces (33 chansons, 19 madrigals, 39 motets, and 153 Psalms) and some 70 keyboard works. Sweelinck was the first to employ the pedal in a real fugal part, and originated the organ fugue built up on one theme with the gradual addition of counter-themes leading to a highly involved and ingenious finale—a form perfected by Bach. In rhythmic and melodic freedom, his vocal compositions show an advance over the earlier polyphonic style, though replete with intricate contrapuntal devices. His son and pupil, Dirck Janszoon Sweelinck (b. Amsterdam [baptized], May 26, 1591; d. there, Sept. 16, 1652), was an organist, music editor, and composer; he was his father's successor as organist at the Oude Kerk (from 1621), where he acquired a notable reputation as an improviser. M. Seiffert ed. a complete edition of his works (12 vols., The Hague and Leipzig, 1894–1901). A new edition of his works, ed. by R. Lagas et al., commenced publication in Amsterdam in 1957.

WORKS: VOCAL: Psalms and Canticles: *50 pseaumes de David, mis en musique* for 4 to 7 Voices (Amsterdam, 1604; second ed., 1624, as *Premier livre des pseaumes de David, mis en musique...seconde edition*); *Rimes françoises et italiennes...* for 2 to 3 Voices, *avec une chanson* for 4 Voices (Leiden, 1612); *Livre second des pseaumes de David, nouvellement mis en musique* for 4 to 8 Voices (Amsterdam, 1613); *Livre troisieme des pseaumes de David, nouvellement mis en musique* for 4 to 8 Voices (Amsterdam, 1614); *Sechs-stimmige Psalmen, auss dem ersten und andern Theil seiner aussgangenen frantzösischen Psalmen* for 6 Voices (Berlin, 1616); *Vierstimmige Psalmen, auss dem ersten, andern und dritten Theil seiner aussgangenen frantzösischen Psalmen* for 4 Voices (Berlin, 1618); *Livre quatriesme et conclusionnal des pseaumes de David, nouvellement mis en musique* for 4 to 8 Voices (Haarlem, 1621). **Motets:** *Canticum in honorem nuptiarum...Iohannis Stoboei...et...Reginae...Davidis Mölleri...relicta vidua* for 8 Voices (Königsberg, 1617); *Cantiones sacrae* for 5 Voices and Basso Continuo (Antwerp, 1619); *Melos fausto quondam thalamo...conjugum Paris dicatum...studio et cura Iohannis Stobaei* for 5 Voices (Danzig, 1638). **Chansons:** *Chansons...de M. Iean Pierre Svvelingh organiste, et Cornille Verdonq nouvellement composées...accomodées tant aux instruments, comme à la voix* for 5 Voices (Antwerp, 1594); *Rimes françoises et italiennes...* for 2 to 3 Voices, *avec une chanson* for 4 Voices (Leiden, 1612). **Madrigals:** *Rimes françoises et italiennes...* for 2 to 3 Voices, *avec une chanson* for 4 Voices (Leiden, 1612). **OTHER:** Many other works, including his keyboard pieces, were preserved in copies made by his pupils and widely circulated.

BIBL.: B. van Sigtenhorst Meyer, *J.P. S. en zijn instrumentale muziek* (The Hague, 1934; second ed., enl., 1946); idem, *J.P. S.* (Amsterdam, 1941); idem, *De vocale muziek van J.P. S.* (The Hague, 1948); A. Voigt, *Die Toccaten J.P. S.s: Ein Beitrag zur frühen Instrumentalmusik* (diss., Univ. of Münster, 1955); G. Gerdes, *Die Choralvariationen in J.P. S.s und seiner Schüler* (diss., Univ. of Freiburg, 1956); R. Tusler, *The Organ Music of J.P. S.* (Bilthoven, 1958); A. Curtis, *S.'s Keyboard Works: A Study of English Elements in Dutch Secular Music of the "Gouden Eeuw"* (diss., Univ. of Ill., 1963); F. Noske, *S.* (Oxford, 1988).—**NS/LK/DM**

Sweet, Sharon, American soprano; b. N.Y., Aug. 16, 1951. She was a student at the Curtis Inst. of Music in Philadelphia and of Marinka Gurewich in N.Y. Following appearances as a recitalist in Philadelphia, she sang Aida in a concert performance in Munich (1985). In 1986 she made her formal operatic debut as Elisabeth in *Tannhäuser* at the Dortmund Opera. In 1987 she joined the Deutsche Oper in Berlin, with which she toured Japan; also appeared as Elisabeth de Valois at the Paris Opéra and the Hamburg State Opera. Other engagements during the 1987–88 season included appearances at the Salzburg Festival and the Vienna State Opera. In 1989 she made her U.S. operatic debut as Aida at the San Francisco Opera, which role she also sang in Dallas in 1992. On Oct. 21, 1993, she sang Lina in the first staging of Verdi's *Stiffelio* by the Metropolitan Opera in N.Y. After appearing as Aida at London's Covent Garden in

1995, she returned there as Turandot in 1997. She sang Aida at the Metropolitan Opera in 1997. She also toured as a concert artist. In 1999 she joined the faculty of Westminster Choir Coll.—**NS/LK/DM**

Swell, Steve, trombonist; b. Newark, N.J., Dec. 6, 1954. Swell was born and raised in N.J., where he studied at Jersey City State Coll. before moving into professional musical life in N.Y.C. in the first part of the 1970s. He played countless gigs prior to 1983, when he toured with Lionel Hampton's band for nearly a year. He then moved on to brief stints with Buddy Rich and pianist Jaki Byard's Apollo Stompers, with whom he first recorded in late 1984. He then traveled headlong into N.Y.'s avant-garde jazz scene, first with composer Makanda Ken McIntyre and then with Jemeel Moondoc, William Parker, Zane Massey, Roy Campbell, Herb Robertson, Joey Baron, Tim Berne, Phillip Johnston, Perry Robinson, Lou Grassi, and others. He currently leads or co-leads several groups: the N.Y.–based quartet ZigZag, a Russian-based free improvisational quintet, a trio with saxophonist Will Connell and drummer Lou Grassi, a large ensemble, the Out and About Quartet with fellow trombonist Roswell Rudd, and a duo with bassist Ken Filiano.

He has picked up the lead in the world of improvising trombone. He's got the vivacious energy and wit of Roswell Rudd, with whom he studied in the mid- 1970s. He also has a fast-moving imagination that liberally doses all his solos and compositions with sly hints of pre-bebop jazz, touches of marching brass swagger, and far-reaching explorations of what his horn can achieve outside the realms of standard tonality, execution, and structure. Most of all, he injects his music with a considerable degree of wholehearted joy and a clear sense that he is having fun while playing. In the late 1990s, as he reaches into his forties, he has perhaps arrived at a point where he can exercise his considerable creativity while maintaining a secure and stable career as a first- call improviser, composer, and bandleader. His recordings with Phillip Johnston's Big Trouble are now matched by powerful showings with saxophonist Michael Marcus, drummer Tom Schmidt, and vocalist Mary LaRose.

Disc.: *The Unknown* (1993); *Observations* (1996); *Out and About* (1996); *Moons of Jupiter* (1997).—**AB**

Swensen, Joseph, American conductor, violinist, and composer; b. N.Y., Aug. 4, 1960. His parents were musicians, and at a very young age he began piano lessons with his mother; at age 5 he took up the violin, and later the viola, clarinet, and tuba. When he was 7 he entered the Juilliard School in N.Y. on a piano scholarship, but at 10 enrolled in the violin class of DeLay, remaining her student until 1982. He also received instruction in conducting from Berglund, Foster, Mester, and Mueller, and in composition from Diamond and Persichetti. After completing his studies with DeLay, he pursued a career as a violin virtuoso, appearing as a soloist with leading orchs. in North America and Europe. He also appeared as a recitalist and chamber music player. Although he first appeared as a conductor at age 15, it was not until much later that he pursued conducting as a career. In 1991 he abandoned his violin career to devote himself fully to conducting. In 1996 he became principal conductor of the Scottish Chamber Orch. in Glasgow, which he led on its first tour of the U.S. in 1999. His most important composition is *Ghazal* for Cello, 5 Women's Voices, and Orch. (1992); he also orchestrated Mahler's Piano Quartet.—**NS/LK/DM**

Swenson, Ruth Ann, American soprano; b. Bronxville, N.Y., Aug. 25, 1959. She studied at the Academy of Vocal Arts in Philadelphia. In 1981 and 1982 she won the San Francisco Opera Auditions, which led to her professional opera debut with the company in 1983 as Despina. In subsequent seasons, she appeared there as Gounod's Juliette, Handel's Dorinda, Meyerbeer's Ines, Verdi's Nannetta and Gilda, and Donizetti's Adina. In 1988 she made her first appearance at the Lyric Opera in Chicago as Nannetta. She made her debut at the Opéra de la Bastille in Paris as Mozart's Susanna in 1990. On Jan. 27, 1991, she sang in the gala concert commemorating the 200th anniversary of Mozart's death with Raymond Leppard conducting the N.Y. Phil. in a program telecast live to the nation over PBS. She sang Mozart's Constanze at her debuts at the Munich and Schwetzingen festivals, and at the Cologne Opera in 1991. On Sept. 24, 1991, she made her Metropolitan Opera debut in N.Y. as Mozart's Zerlina; returned there as Gilda in 1992, as Adina and Zerbinetta in the 1992–93 season, and as Rosina and Susanne in the 1993–94 season. In 1993 she won the Richard Tucker Music Foundation Award and made her debut at the Berlin State Opera as Gilda. During the 1994–95 season, she returned to the Lyric Opera in Chicago as Anne Trulove. In 1997 she was engaged as Gilda at the San Francisco Opera. After portraying Adina at the Metropolitan Opera in 1998, she returned there in 1999 as Lucia. As a concert artist, she sang in principal North American and European music centers. Among her other operatic roles are Cleopatra in Handel's *Giulio Cesare*, Lucia, Martha, and Massenet's Manon.
—**NS/LK/DM**

Swert, Jules de, eminent Belgian cellist, pedagogue, and composer; b. Louvain, Aug. 15, 1843; d. Ostend, Feb. 24, 1891. He commenced his musical training with his father, the Louvain Cathedral choirmaster, and by the time he was 10 he was performing in public; then pursued studies with Servais at the Brussels Cons., where he graduated with the premier prix in 1858. After touring as a virtuoso, he became Konzertmeister in Düsseldorf in 1865, appearing there in trio recitals with Clara Schumann and Auer; then went to Weimar as soloist in the Hofkapelle in 1868, and subsequently was royal Kapellmeister in Berlin, where he taught at the Hochschule für Musik (1869–73). He was active in Wiesbaden (1873–76), and also made occasional tours; made his London debut with notable acclaim in 1875. In 1876 Wagner called him to Bayreuth to engage the musicians for his new orch. During the next few years, he devoted much time to composition; in 1881 he went to Leipzig. He settled in Ostend in 1888 as director of its music school; also was a prof. at the conservatories in Ghent and Bruges. He wrote 2 operas, *Die Albigenser* (Wiesbaden, Oct. 1, 1878) and *Graf Hammerstein* (Mainz, 1884), a Sym., *Nordseefahrt*, 3 cello concertos, romances, fantasias, duos, and solo pieces for cello. His brother, Isidore (Jean Gaspar) de Swert (b. Louvain, Jan. 6, 1830; d. Brussels, Sept. 1896), was a cellist and teacher; he studied with François de Munck at the Brussels Cons., where he graduated with the premier prix in 1846; went to Bruges in 1850 as a teacher at its music school and solo cellist at the theater; then became solo cellist at the Théâtre Royal de la Monnaie in Brussels in 1856; was named a teacher at the Louvain Cons. in 1866, and that same year joined the faculty of the Brussels Cons.—**NS/LK/DM**

Swieten, Gottfried (Bernhard), Baron van, Dutch-born Austrian diplomat, music patron, librettist, and composer; b. Leiden, Oct. 29, 1733; d. Vienna, March 29, 1803. His father was appointed personal physician to Empress Maria Theresa in 1745 and settled in Vienna. After attending the Theresianum Jesuit school, Gottfried entered the Austrian civil service; subsequently was active in the foreign diplomatic service from 1755 to 1777, serving as ambassador to Berlin from 1770 to 1777. Upon his return to Vienna, he was made Prefect of the Imperial Library. In his early years he wrote some opéras-comiques and at least 10 syms., 3 of which were printed under Haydn's name. Van Swieten's significance rests upon his activities as a music patron; he did much to promote the music of J.S. Bach, C.P.E. Bach and Handel. He founded a group of aristocratic patrons, the Associierte, which supported private performances of oratorios. This group commissioned Mozart to prepare his arrangements of Handel oratorios and also sponsored Haydn's *7 Last Words* (choral version, 1796), *The Creation* (1798), and *The Seasons* (1801), the latter 2 works utilizing librettos by van Swieten. Beethoven also found a patron in van Swieten and dedicated his first Sym. to him.

BIBL.: D. Olleson, *G., Baron v.S. and His Influence on Haydn and Mozart* (diss., Univ. of Oxford, 1967).—**NS/LK/DM**

Swift, Richard, American composer, teacher, and writer on music; b. Middlepoint, Ohio, Sept. 24, 1927. He studied with Grosvenor Cooper, Leonard Meyer, and Leland Smith at the Univ. of Chicago (M.A., 1956). In 1956 he joined the faculty of the Univ. of Calif. at Davis, retiring as prof. of music emeritus in 1991; also was chairman of the music dept. (1963–71); in 1977 he was a visiting prof. at Princeton Univ. He held editorial positions with the journal *19th Century Music* (from 1981); also contributed articles to various other journals and to reference works. In his compositions, he applies a variety of functional serial techniques, including electronic and aleatory devices.

WORKS: DRAMATIC: Opera: *The Trial of Tender O'Shea* (Davis, Calif., Aug. 12, 1964). **Other:** Incidental music to various plays. **ORCH.:** *A Coronal* (1954; Louisville, Ky., April 14, 1956); 2 concertos for Piano and Chamber Ensemble (1961, 1980); *Extravaganza* (1961); Concerto for Violin and Chamber Orch. (Oakland, Calif., May 28, 1968); *Tristia* (1967; Oakland, Calif., April 20, 1968); Sym. (1970); *Prime* for Alto Saxophone and Chamber Ensemble (1973); *Some Trees* (1982). **CHAMBER:** String Trio (1954–55); *Study* for Cello (1955); 6 string quartets (1955; 1958; 1964; 1973; 1981–82; 1991–92); *Serenade concertante I* for Piano and Wind Quintet (1956) and *II* for Clarinet, Violin, Cello, and Piano (1985); *Stravaganza I-X* for various instrumentations (1956–85); Clarinet Sonata (1957); Trio for Clarinet, Cello, and Piano (1957); Sonata for Solo Violin (1957); *Music for a While I* for Violin, Viola, and Harpsichord (1965), *II* for 3 Instruments (1969), *III* for Violin and Harpsichord (1975), *IV* for String Quartet (1991), and *V* for Viola and Piano (1993–94); *Thrones* for Alto Flute and Contrabass (1966); Trio for Violin, Cello, and Piano (1976); *Some Versions of Paraphrase* for Violin, Clarinet, and Piano (1987); *In the Country of the Blue*, piano trio No. 2 for Violin, Cello, and Piano (1988); *A Stitch in Time* for Guitar (1989); *In Arcadia* for Clarinet and String Trio (1994); piano pieces. **VOCAL:** Many works.—**NS/LK/DM**

Syberg, Franz (Adolf), Danish organist and composer; b. Kerteminde, July 5, 1904; d. there, Dec. 11, 1955. His father was the painter Fritz Syberg. He took courses with Karg-Elert in Leipzig (1923–28) and studied organ with Peter Thomson in Copenhagen (organists' examination, 1932); then returned to Kerteminde as an organist. His small but finely crafted output was influenced by Nielsen.

WORKS: DRAMATIC: Incidental music. **ORCH.:** Concertino for Oboe and Strings (1932); Sinfonietta (1934); *Adagio* for Strings (1938); Sym. (1939). **CHAMBER:** String Quartet (1930–31); Quintet for Flute, Clarinet, and String Trio (1931); String Trio (1933); Wind Quintet (1940); organ pieces. —**NS/LK/DM**

Sychra, Antonín, Czech aesthetician; b. Boskovice, June 9, 1918; d. Prague, Oct. 21, 1969. He studied musicology with Helfert at the Univ. of Brno; then continued his training at the Univ. of Prague (Ph.D., 1946); subsequently completed his Habilitation (1952) and received his D.Sc. (1959) there. After lecturing at the Education Research Inst. in Prague, he was made a lecturer (1948), dean (1950), and prof. (1951) at the Prague Academy of Music; also lectured on aesthetics and music history at the Univ. of Prague (from 1952), where he was director of the aesthetics dept. (from 1959). His work, which reveals his preoccupation with a Marxist approach to music and aesthetics, was productive for its contribution to musical semantics. Among his publications are *Stranická hudební kritika: Spolutvůrce nove hudby* (Party Music Criticism: A Co-creator of New Music; Prague, 1951; Ger. tr., 1953), *O hudbu zítřka* (The Music of Tomorrow; Prague, 1952), *Oestetické vychově* (Aesthetic Education; with O. Chlup; Prague, 1956), and *Hudba a slovo z experimentálního hlediska* (Music and Word—an Experimental Approach; with K. Sedláček; Prague, 1962).—**NS/LK/DM**

Sydeman, William (Jay), American composer; b. N.Y., May 8, 1928. He studied at the Mannes Coll. of Music in N.Y. with Salzer and Travis (B.S., 1955) and with Franchetti at the Hartt School of Music in Hartford, Conn. (M.M., 1958); also had sessions with Sessions and Petrassi. He taught at the Mannes Coll. of Music

(1959–70) and at Rudolph Steiner Coll. in Fair Oaks, Calif. (1980–82). His early style of composition tended toward atonal Expressionism invigorated by spasmodic percussive rhythms in asymmetrically arranged meters. In his later works, he moved toward tonal scores with elements of folk, pop, and jazz infusions.

Works: **Dramatic:** Opera: *Aria da capo* (1982). Incidental Music: *Encounters* (1967); *Anti-Christ* (1981); *A Winter's Tale* (1982). **Orch.:** *Orchestral Abstractions* (1958; N.Y., Jan. 10, 1962); *Study* No. 1 (1959), No. 2 (1963), and No. 3 (1965); *Oecumenicus*, concerto (1964); Concerto for Piano, 4-Hands, and Orch. (1967); *5 Movements* for Winds (1973). **Chamber:** Woodwind Quintet (1959–61); Quartet for Flute, Clarinet, Piano, and Violin (1963); Duo for Trumpet and Percussion (1965); *Trio montagnana* for Clarinet, Cello, and Piano (1972); *Fugue* for String Quartet or Ensemble, with Optional Soprano (1975); 18 duos for 2 Violins (1976); *Long Life Prayer* for Violin and Speaker (1978); many other works. **Vocal:** *Lament of Elektra* for Alto, Chorus, and Chamber Orch. (1964); *In memoriam: J.F. Kennedy* for Narrator and Orch. (1966); *Full Circle* for 3 Solo Voices, Clarinet, Trombone, Percussion, Organ, and Cello (1971); *Love Songs Based on Japanese Poems* for Soprano, Flute, and Violin (1978); *Calendar of the Soul* for Multi-chorus (1982).—**NS/LK/DM**

Symonds, Norman, Canadian clarinetist, saxophonist, and composer; b. near Nelson, British Columbia, Dec. 23, 1920; d. Toronto, Aug. 21, 1998. He took up the clarinet as a teenager and played in a dixieland band. After training in clarinet, piano, theory, and harmony at the Toronto Cons. (1945–48), he studied composition with Delamont. Between 1949 and 1966 he was active as a clarinetist, alto and baritone saxophonist, and as an arranger with Toronto dance bands. He also led his own jazz octet from 1953 to 1957. Symonds was one of Canada's early champions of the "third stream" idiom. In addition to scores composed in this manner, he also wrote works in an Expressionist vein.

Works: **Dramatic:** *Age of Anxiety*, radio play (1959); *Opera for 6 Voices*, radio opera (1962); *Tensions*, ballet (1966); *Man, Inc.*, mixed media piece (1970); *"Charnisay Versus LaTour"* or *The Spirit of Fundy*, opera (1972); *Laura and the Lieutenant*, musical play for children (1974); *The Canterville Ghost*, music theater (1975); *Lady of the Night*, opera (1977); *Episode at Big Quill*, radio theater (1979); *The Fall of the Leaf*, oratorical music drama (1982); *Sylvia*, music theater (1990). **Orch.:** Concerto Grosso for Jazz Quintet and Orch. (1957); *The Age of Anxiety Suite*for Jazz Orch. (1958); *Autumn Nocturne* for Tenor Saxophone and Strings (1960); *Elegy* for Strings (1962); *Pastel Blue* for Strings (1963); *The Nameless Hour* for Improvising Soloist and Strings (1966); *The Democratic Concerto* for Jazz Quartet and Orch. (Winnipeg, Dec. 14, 1967); *Impulse* (Toronto, March 18, 1969); *3 Atmospheres* (1970); *Maya* (1973); *Big Lonely* (1975; rev. 1978); *Forest and Sky* (1977); *The Gift of Thanksgiving* (1980); *Spaces I: The River* for Strings (1980); *Sylvia*, "adult fairy tale" for Jazz Soloists and Jazz Ensemble (1982); *On an Emerald Sea* (1983); *The Eyes of Bidesuk* for Amplified Accordion and Jazz Orch. (1987); *From the Eye of the Wind* (1987; Toronto, Jan. 1, 1988). **Chamber:** *Fugue* for Reeds and Brass (1952); 2 concertos for Jazz Octet (1955, 1956); *Fugue for Shearing* for Piano and Jazz Ensemble (1957); *A 6 Movement Suite for 10 Jazz Musicians plus 4 Songs and Incidental Music* for Voice and Jazz Tentet (1959); *Fair Wind* for Jazz Ensemble (1965); *A Diversion* for Brass Quintet (1972); *Bluebeard Lives* for String Quintet and Tape (1975); Quintet for Clarinet and Synthesizers (1977); *Elegance* for Percussion (1982); *Salt Wind White Bird* for 4 Flutes (1984). **Vocal:** *Deep Ground, Long Waters* for Medium Voice, Flute, and Piano (1972); *At the Shore: A Sea Image* for Chorus and Percussion (1976); *4 Images of Nature* for Chorus, Bass, and Percussion (1976); *Harvest Choral* for Chorus (1979); *Lullaby* for Chorus (1979); *Pity the Children* for Chorus (1979); *Lady Elegance* for Medium Voice and Piano (1986).—**NS/LK/DM**

Syms, Sylvia, jazz-pop singer; b. Brooklyn, N.Y., Dec. 2, 1917; d. N.Y., May 10, 1992. Syms was originally inspired to sing after hearing Billie Holiday perform on N.Y.'s 52nd St. Holiday took Syms under her wing, and Syms began performing in N.Y. clubs in 1941. Mae West heard her perform in 1948, which led to Syms's first stage role. She had a long career on the Broadway stage, and was much admired by other singers. Frank Sinatra called her "The best saloon singer in the world," and produced her 1982 album, *Syms by Sinatra*. Less active in the 1970s, Syms made a comeback on the cabaret scene in the 1980s. In 1987, while performing at N.Y.'s Algonquin Hotel, she died of a heart attack.

Disc.: *Songs by Sylvia Syms* (1952); *Fabulous Sylvia Syms* (1964); *Syms by Sinatra* (1982); *Jazz Portrait of Johnny Mercer* (1984); *You Must Believe in Spring* (1991).—**LP**

Synowiec, Ewa (Krystyna), Polish composer, teacher, and pianist; b. Kraków, April 12, 1942. She received training in piano from Ludwik Stefański (honors degree, 1967) and in composition from Bogusław Schaeffer (graduated, 1973) at the State Higher School of Music in Kraków. In 1967–68 she held a French government scholarship in Paris, where she completed her piano training with Susanne Roche and Vlado Perlemutter. From 1966 to 1975 she taught piano at the State Higher School of Music in Kraków, and then piano and composition at the Gdańsk Academy of Music, where she became a prof. in 1991.

Works: **Orch.:** *Szkice* (Sketches) for Chamber Orch. (1971); *Schizofonia* (1971); *72* (1972); *Fantazja in B* (Fantasy in B) for Trumpet and Orch. (1973; also for Trumpet and Piano); *Syntonia* for Strings (1976); Concerto for Strings (1978); *Spiegelspiel* (1980–81); Concertino for 3 Soloists and Strings (1980); *Temat z wariacjami* (Theme with Variations) for Strings (1982; also for String Quartet); *Trivium* for Flute or Marimba and Orch. (1983); *Sezon w piekle (Une saison en enfer)* (1983); *Apokalipsa* for Organ and Brass Ensemble (1985–86). **Chamber:** *Dwugłos* (Two Parts) for Flute and Piano (1966); 4 Duets for Winds (1966); *3 X 4* for Flute, Alto, Saxophone, and Bassoon (1966); 3 string quartets: No. 1 (1966), No. 2, *ósemkowy* (quaver-note quartet; 1971), and No. 3, *Resume* (1977; Gdańsk, May 16, 1978); *Mały kwintet* (Little Quintet) for Winds (1967); String Trio (1967); Composition No. 2 for Flute (1968); *I + II* for Cello and Saxophones (1968); *Quartettino d'archi* for Strings (1969); *Gra* (Play) for 2, 3, 4, 5, or 6 Trumpeters (1972); *Serial dla Ryszarda* for Recorder (1973); *Plus ça change—plus c'est la même chose* for String Sextet (1973); *Fantazja in B* (Fantasy in B) for Trumpet and Piano (1973; also for Trumpet and Orch.); *Martwa natura* (Still Life) *I* for Flute, Trumpet, Violin, Viola, and Vibraphone (1974), *II* for 9 Instruments (1974), *III, UDMSW* for 6 Instruments (1975), and *IV* for Flute, Trumpet, and Vibraphone (1976); *Solo* for Percussionist (1975); *TV-Poker* for Any 4 Winds and Tape (1975); *Kompozycja jednostronna* (One-Sided Composition) for

Violin (1976); *Wersja nr 3* (Version No. 3) for Violin (1976); *Fantazja* (Fantasy) for Violin (1976); *Da camera* for Flute, Violin, and Cello (1977; Gdańsk, March 5, 1978); *Postscriptum* for Piano and Percussion (1977; Poznań, April 17, 1978); *Pory roku* (Seasons) for Flute, Violin, Viola, and Cello (1978); Sonata for Solo Violin (1980); *Temat z wariacjami* (Theme with Variations) for String Quartet (1982; also for String Orch.); *ABRA...* for Oboe and English Horn (1985; Wrocław, Feb. 20, 1988). **KEYBOARD: Piano:** Piece for 2 Pianos (1966); Sonata in Open Form (1966); *Sonata minima* (1967); 2 numbered sonatas (1969, 1980); *Change* for 2 Pianists (1972); *Alternative I* for Piano or 2 Pianos (1978) and *II* for Piano or 2 Pianos (1978). **Harpsichord:** *Alternative II* for Harpsichord or 2 Harpsichords (1979; also for Piano or 2 Pianos); *Quasimodo* (1986). **VOCAL:** *Psalm XXII* for Alto, Flute, Violin, and Celesta (1967); *Psalmodia* for Alto and Chorus (1968); *Tytus* for Voice, Flute, and Cello (1973); *Fragmenty do Tekstów Safony* (Fragments to Sappho's Poems) for Voice and 2 Flutes (1974); *Dedykacja* (Dedication) for Chorus (1983). **GRAPHIC:** *Sinfonietta da camera* for Any 10 to 15 Players (1980); *Muzyka i mozg* (Music and the Brain) for Freely-Selected Players (1982; Katowice, Dec. 16, 1984); *Glosy ze ściany* (Voices from the Wall) for Orch. (1982–83); *NDSL-nulla dies sine linea* for Freely Selected Players (1983); *DO-DU czyli DOwolny DUet* (DO-DU or Free Duet) for Any 2 Players (Katowice, Dec. 12, 1984); *aFiMeRaL* for Any 4 to 7 Players (1984); *Diabolus in musica* (1984); *Pejzaże z lotu ptaka* (Bird's-Eye View; 1985); *Bajka japońska* (A Japanese Fairytale; 1987); *Obietnica poranka* (The Promise of Dawn; 1988); *Szkoda tej czarownicy na stos* (The Lady's Not for Burning; 1989); *** (1994).
—NS/LK/DM

Syukur, Slamet Abdul, important Indonesian composer, performer, and teacher; b. Surabaya, East Java, June 30, 1935. He studied piano (1944–52), then attended the Sekolah Musik Indonesia (S.M.I.) Yogyakarta (1952–56). He was a founding member (1957–61) and president (1961–62) of Pertemuan Musik Surabaya, the first music society formed by the Indonesians after the liquidation of the former Dutch Muziek-Kunstkring; then went to Paris and studied organology with Chambure and analysis with Messiaen at the Cons. (1962–63); also earned degrees in piano (1965) and composition (1967) at the École Normale de Musique; in 1967–68, took part in Schaffer's Group de Recherches Musicales de l'ORTF. Syukur is among the many Indonesian composers who, after training in Europe, returned to play an important role in the development of contemporary music in Indonesia while remaining internationally active. From 1976 to 1987 he was a lecturer at the Institut Kesenian Jakarta (I.K.J., Jakarta Arts Inst.), where he also served as head of its music dept. (1981–83); from 1977 to 1981 he was head of the music committee of the Jakarta Arts Council, for which he organized a Festival of Contemporary French Music, the first such series given in Southeast Asia. In 1987 he joined the faculty at the Institut Seni Indonesia (I.S.I., National Arts Inst.); also lectured throughout Java, and from 1975 participated in workshops organized by the Eduard van Beinum Stichting and the Gaudeamus Foundation on the problems of geographic and historical musical acculturation. In 1989 he received a grant from the French government to conduct research on the influence of the Javanese gamelan on the aesthetic of Debussy. Syukur lives in Jakarta, where he founded in 1990 the Forum Musik Jakarta, an Indonesian Soc. for Contemporary Music that also serves as an information and educational center.

WORKS: *Point-Contre* for Vocalizing Trumpet, Percussion, and Harp (1969); *Parenthesis I-II* for Dancer, Prepared Piano, Suspended Chair, and Lighting, *IV* for 2 Electric Guitars, Percussion, Organ, Prepared Piano, 2 Dancers, Painter, Flute, Violin, and Cello (1973), and *VI* for 2 Guitars, Percussion, Children's Toys, Flute, Comedian (with a deep voice), Choreography, and Dancer's Voice; *Laticrak*, electroacoustic music for Dancers (1974); *Angklung* for Voices and Angklung (1975); *Kangen* for 3 Shakuhachi, Kokyu, and Traditional Japanese Percussion (1986); *Cucuku-Cu* for Guitar (1989); *Ji-Lala-Ji* for Flute and Percussion (1989); *Suara* for Piano (1990).
—NS/LK/DM

Szabados, Béla Antal, Hungarian pedagogue and composer; b. Pest, June 3, 1867; d. there (Budapest), Sept. 15, 1936. He studied with Erkel and Volkmann. He became an accompanist and coach at the Academy of Music and Dramatic Art (1888); in 1893 he was made a piano teacher and coach at the reorganized Academy of Music, where he was promoted to prof. of singing in 1920; in 1922 he became director of the dept. for the training of profs. of singing; served as head of the National Cons. from 1927. He wrote 2 operas: *Maria* (Budapest, Feb. 28, 1905; in collaboration with Arpád Szendy) and *Fanny* (Budapest, Feb. 16, 1927); 11 musical comedies; 4 string quartets; a Psalm; several song cycles; also publ. several vocal manuals. His brother, Karóly Szabados (b. Pest, Jan. 28, 1860; d. there [Budapest], Jan. 25, 1892), was a pianist, conductor, and composer who studied with Liszt, Erkel, and Volkmann; became conductor at the Klausenburg National Theater (1880) and then asst. conductor at the Royal Hungarian Opera in Budapest. His most successful score was the ballet *Vióra* (1891).**—NS/LK/DM**

Szabelski, Boleslaw, Polish organist, teacher, and composer; b. Radoryż, near Lublin, Dec. 3, 1896; d. Katowice, Aug. 27, 1979. After studies with Lysakowski in Kiev (1915), he took courses in organ with Surzyński and in composition with Szymanowski and Statkowski at the Warsaw Cons. He made tours as an organist; also was prof. of organ and composition at the Kraków Cons. (1929–39; 1954–57). He wrote in a traditional style until turning to serial techniques in 1958.

WORKS: ORCH.: 5 syms. (1926; 1934, with soprano and chorus; 1951; 1956; 1968, with chorus and organ); Suite (1938); Sinfonietta for Strings and Percussion (1946); *Solemn Overture* (1953); *Concerto grosso* (1954); Piano Concertino (1955); *3 Sonnets* (1958); *Verses* for Piano and Orch. (1961); *Preludes* for Chamber Orch. (1963); Flute Concerto (1964); Piano Concerto (1978). **CHAMBER:** 2 string quartets (1935, 1956); Organ Sonata (1943); *Aphorisms "9"* for Chamber Ensemble (1962). **VOCAL:** *Heroic Poem* for Chorus and Orch. (1952); *Improvisations* for Chorus and Chamber Orch. (1959); *Nicolaus Copernicus*, oratorio (Poznań, April 2, 1976); *The Wola Redoubt* for 3 Soloists and Orch. (Warsaw, Nov. 5, 1976).**—NS/LK/DM**

Szabó, Ferenc, distinguished Hungarian composer and teacher; b. Budapest, Dec. 27, 1902; d. there, Nov. 4,

1969. He studied with Kodály, Siklós, and Leo Weiner at the Budapest Academy of Music (1922–26). In 1926 he became aligned with the labor movement in Hungary and joined the outlawed Communist party in 1927; in 1932 he went to Russia, where he became closely associated with the ideological work of the Union of Soviet Composers. In 1944 he returned to Hungary as an officer in the Red Army; then was prof. of composition (1945–67) and director (1958–67) of the Budapest Academy of Music. He was awarded the Kossuth Prize in 1951 and 1954, and in 1962 was named an Eminent Artist of the Hungarian People's Republic. His music initially followed the trends of Central European modernism, with strong undertones of Hungarian melorhythms, but later he wrote music in the manner of socialist realism; his choruses are permeated with the militant spirit of the revolutionary movement.

WORKS: DRAMATIC: *Lúdas Matyi*, ballet (Budapest, May 16, 1960); *Légy jó mindhalálig* (Be Faithful until Death), opera (1968–69; completed by A. Borgulya; Dec. 5, 1975). **ORCH.:** *Suite* for Chamber Orch. (1926; rev. as *Sérénade oubliée*, 1964); *Class Struggle*, symphonic poem (Moscow, April 27, 1933); *Sinfonietta* for Russian National Instruments (1935); *Lyrical Suite* for Strings (1936); *Moldavian Rhapsody* (1940); *Hazatérés* (Homecoming), concerto (1948); *Számadás* (Summary), symphonic poem (1949); *Emlékeztetö* (Memento), sym. (1952). **CHAMBER:** 2 string quartets (1926, 1962); Trio for 2 Violins and Viola (1927); Sonata for Solo Cello (1929); 2 sonatas for Solo Violin (1930); *Sonata alla rapsodia* for Clarinet and Piano (1964). **Piano:** *Toccata* (1928); *8 Easy Piano Pieces* (1933); 3 sonatas (1940; 1947; 1957–61); *Felszabadult melódiák* (Melodies of Liberation), cycle of pieces (1949). **VOCAL:** *Meghalt Lenin* (Lenin is Dead), cantata (1933); *Föltámadott a tenger* (In Fury Rose the Ocean), oratorio (Budapest, June 15, 1955); *Vallomás* (Declaration) for Chorus, Brass, and Percussion (1967); choruses.

BIBL.: A. Pernye, *S. F.* (Budapest, 1965); J. Maróthy, *S. F. indulása* (Budapest, 1970).—**NS/LK/DM**

Szabolcsi, Bence, eminent Hungarian music scholar; b. Budapest, Aug. 2, 1899; d. there, Jan. 21, 1973. He studied jurisprudence at the Univ. of Budapest; concurrently was a student of Kodály, Weiner, and Siklós at the Budapest Academy of Music (1917–21) and of Abert at the Univ. of Leipzig, where he received his Ph.D. in 1923 with the diss. *Benedetti und Saracini: Beiträge zur Geschichte der Monodie*. He was a prof. of music history at the Budapest Academy of Music from 1945 until his death. He was ed. of the Hungarian music periodical *Zenei Szemle* (with D. Bartha) from 1926 to 1929. With A. Toth, he brought out a music dictionary in the Hungarian language (1930–31); publ. a history of music (Budapest, 1940; 5th ed., 1974), a monograph on Beethoven (Budapest, 1944; 5th ed., 1976), and a number of valuable papers in various European magazines. His greatest contribution as a scholar is found in his valuable study *A melódia története* (A History of Melody; Budapest, 1950; second ed., 1957; Eng. tr., 1965); also made valuable contributions to research on the life and works of Béla Bartók. On his 70th birthday he was presented with a Festschrift, ed. by Bartha, *Studia musicologica Bence Szabolcsi septuagenario* (Budapest, 1969). Of his writings on Bartók, the most important are *Bartók: Sa vie et son oeuvre* (Budapest, 1956; second ed., 1968), *Béla Bartók* (Leipzig, 1968), and *Béla Bartók, Musiksprachen* (Leipzig, 1972). Two of his books were publ. in Eng.: *The Twilight of Ferenc Liszt* (Budapest, 1959) and *A Concise History of Hungarian Music* (Budapest, 1964).
—**NS/LK/DM**

Szalonek, Witold (Jósef), Polish composer and pedagogue; b. Czechowice-Dziedzice, March 2, 1927. He was a student of Wanda Chmielowska (piano) and of Bolesław Woytowicz (composition) at the State Higher School of Music in Katowice (1949–56), and later pursued his training with Nadia Boulanger in Paris (1962–63). In 1970–71 he was in Berlin on a Deutscher Akademischer Austauschdienst scholarship. In 1967 he became a teacher of composition at the State Higher School of Music in Katowice, where he served as chairman of theory and composition from 1970 to 1974. In 1973 he became a prof. at the Berlin Hochschule der Künste. In 1964 he received the music award of the City of Katowice, in 1967 the Minister of Culture and Arts Award, and in 1994 the prize of the Polish Composer's Union.

WORKS: ORCH.: *Pastorale* for Oboe and Orch. (1951–65; also for Oboe and Piano, 1952); *Toccata polyphonica* for Strings (1954); *Suita polifoniczna* (Polyphonic Suite) for Strings (1955); *Satyra symfoniczna* (Symphonic Satire; 1956); Concertino for Flute and Chamber Orch. (1962; Warsaw, Sept. 22, 1963); *Les Sons* (Warsaw, Sept. 30, 1965); *Mutazioni* for Chamber Orch. (1966; Hamburg, June 25, 1969); Concerto for Strings (1971–75); *Musica concertante* for Double Bass and Orch. (Warsaw, Sept. 20, 1977); *Mała symfonia B-A-C-H* (Little B-A- C-H Symphony) for Piano and Orch. (1979–81; Poznań, March 28, 1985); *Dyptyk II* for 16 Saxophones (1993; Berlin, Jan. 1996). **CHAMBER:** *Pastorale* for Oboe and Piano (1952; also for Oboe and Orch., 1952–65); Trio for Flute, Clarinet, and Bassoon (1952); Cello Sonata (1958); *Arabeski* (Arabesques) for Violin and Piano (1964); *Quattro monologhi* for Oboe (1966); *Proporzioni I* for Flute, Viola, and Harp (1967; Warsaw, Sept. 26, 1969), *II* for Flute, Cello, and Piano (1967–70), and *III* for Violin, Cello, and Piano (1977); *Improvisations sonoristiques* for Clarinet, Trombone, Cello, and Piano (London, Feb. 22, 1968); *1+1+1+1* for 1 to 4 String Instruments (1969; version for String Quartet, Warsaw, Sept. 22, 1975); *Aarhus music* for Wind Quintet (1970; Katowice, March 2, 1971); *Trzy szkice* (Three Sketches) for Harp (1972; Berlin, Jan. 15, 1973); *Connections* for Chamber Ensemble (Bergisch Gladbach, Sept. 23, 1972); *Piernikiana* for Tuba (1977; Brussels, Jan. 6, 1978); Trio for Oboe, Clarinet, and Bassoon (1978); *Take the Game...* for 6 Percussionists (1981); *Alice's Unknown Adventures in the Fairy Land of Percussion* for Percussionist (1981); *D. P.'s Five Ghoulish Dreams* for Alto Saxophone (1985; Warsaw, Sept. 27, 1986); *Inside?—Outside?* for Bass Clarinet and String Quartet (1987; Viitasaari, July 25, 1988); *Elegia na śmierć przyjaciela* (Elegy on the Friend's Death) for Clarinet and Piano (Katowice, Nov. 7, 1989); *Głowa Meduzy I* (Medusa's Head I) for 1 to 3 Recorders (1992; Berlin, Feb. 9, 1993) and *II* for 1 to 3 Flutes (1993; Berlin, Sept. 24, 1994); *Invocationi* for 2 Guitars (1992; Espoo, Nov. 7, 1993); *Sept épigrammes modernes* for Saxophone Quartet (Katowice, Nov. 1994); *Meduzy sen o Pegazie I* (Medusa's Dream of Pegasus I) for Horn and Recorder (1997) and *II* for Horn and Flute (1997). **KEYBOARD: Piano:** *Mutanza* (1968); *Toccata e corale* (1990; Berlin, Oct. 1992; also for Organ, Berlin, Nov. 16, 1988). **Organ:** *Toccata e corale* (Berlin, Nov. 16, 1988; also for Piano, 1990; Berlin, Oct. 1992). **VOCAL:** *Nokturn* for Baritone, String Orch., and Harp (1953; Warsaw, Sept. 23, 1980); *Suita* *kurpiowska* (Suite from Kurpie) for Alto and 9 Instruments (1955); *Wyznania* (Confessions) for Reciter, Chorus, and Chamber Orch. (Warsaw, Sept. 17, 1959); *Ziemio mila...* (Oh, Pleasant Earth...), cantata for Voice and Orch. (1969; Katowice, Sept. 18, 1970); *Dyptyk I* for Chorus (Berlin, June 19, 1993).—**NS/LK/DM**

Szalowski, Antoni, Polish-born French composer; b. Warsaw, April 21, 1907; d. Paris, March 21, 1973. He studied composition (with K. Sikorski) and piano and conducting at the Warsaw Cons., graduating in 1930; continued his studies with Boulanger in Paris (1931–36), where he then lived until his death, becoming a naturalized French citizen in 1968. His finely crafted works follow in the neo-Classical tradition with a diverting infusion of French elegance.

WORKS: DRAMATIC: Ballet: *Zaczarowana oberza* (The Enchanted Inn; 1943–46; Warsaw, Feb. 7, 1962); *La Femme têtue* (1958). **ORCH.:** *Symphonic Variations* (1928); Piano Concerto (1930); Overture (1936); Sym. (1939); Sinfonietta (1940); Concerto for Strings (1942); Violin Concerto (1949–54); *Tryptyk* (1950); Concertino for Flute and Strings (1951); Suite (1952); *Partita* for Strings (1954); *La Danse* (1957); *Moto perpetuo* (1958); Concerto for Oboe, Clarinet, Bassoon, and Orch. (1958); *The Resurrection of Lazarus,* symphonic poem (1960); *Intermezzo* (1961); *Allegretto* for Bassoon and Orch. (1962); *Berceuse pour Clemantine* (1964); *Music* for Strings (1970); *6 Sketches* (1972). **CHAMBER:** 4 string quartets (1928, 1934, 1936, 1956); Clarinet Sonatina (1936); Oboe Sonatina (1946); Wind Quintet (1954); *Divertimento* for Oboe, Clarinet, and Bassoon (1955); *2 Pieces* for Ondes Martenot (1967); piano pieces, including a Sonata (1933). **VOCAL:** Songs.—**NS/LK/DM**

Szamotul, Waclaw z, significant Polish composer; b. Szamotuly, near Poznan, c. 1524; d. probably in Pińczów, near Kielce, c. 1560. He studied at Poznan's Collegium Lubranscianum and at the Univ. of Kraków. Aafter serving as secretary to Hieronim Chodkiewicz, governor of Troki in Lithuania (1545–47), he became a composer at the court of King Sigismund II August; about 1550 he espoused the Protestant cause, and from 1555 until his death he was active at the Lithuanian court of Duke Mikolaj Radziwill. He composed several outstanding a cappella sacred works.—**NS/LK/DM**

Szántó, Theodor, Hungarian pianist and composer; b. Vienna, June 3, 1877; d. Budapest, Jan. 7, 1934. He studied with Dachs (piano) and Fuchs (composition) at the Vienna Cons., and later with Busoni in Berlin (1898–1901). He wrote an opera on a Japanese story, *Typhoon* (Mannheim, Nov. 29, 1924), *Japanese Suite* for Orch. (1926), other orch. works, chamber music, and piano pieces.—**NS/LK/DM**

Szász, Tibor, Hungarian-born American pianist and teacher; b. Cluj, Romania, June 9, 1948. He began formal study at 13 with Elisa Ciolan and made his public orch. debut at 16; a laureate of the Georges Enesco International Piano Competition (1967), he subsequently appeared with leading orchs. throughout Romania. He was sentenced to prison during the Ceausescu regime but was granted refugee status; emigrated to the U.S. in 1970, obtaining citizenship in 1980. He made his N.Y. solo debut at Carnegie Recital Hall in 1977; subsequently studied with Leon Fleisher and Theodore Lettvin at the Univ. of Mich. (D.M.A., 1983). He taught at the Univ. of Dayton (1984–87), and in 1987 became pianist-in-residence at Duke Univ. in Durham, N.C. A musician of extraordinary sensitivity and intelligence, Szász has appeared as a recitalist, chamber artist, and soloist with orchs. throughout the U.S. and Europe in a repertoire ranging from Couperin to Messiaen; he has also lectured widely, given master classes, and publ. articles on Liszt and Beethoven.—**NS/LK/DM**

Sze, Yi-Kwei, Chinese bass-baritone; b. Shanghai, June 1, 1919. He received his musical training at the Shanghai Cons., then emigrated to the U.S., where he studied with Alexander Kipnis. He toured widely in Europe, South America, and Asia.—**NS/LK/DM**

Székely, Endre, Hungarian composer; b. Budapest, April 6, 1912; d. there, April 14, 1989. He studied with Siklós at the Budapest Academy of Music (1933–37), then joined the outlawed Communist party, and was active as a conductor and composer with various workers' choral groups; ed. the periodicals *Éneklö Munkás* (The Singing Worker) and *Éneklö Nép* (The People Sing). In 1960 he was appointed to the faculty of the Budapest Training Coll. for Teachers.

WORKS: DRAMATIC: Opera: *Vizirózsa* (Water Rose; 1959; Budapest Radio, 1962); *Kőzene* (Stone Music; 1981). **Operetta:** *Aranycsillag* (The Golden Star; Budapest, 1951). **ORCH.:** 3 suites: No. 1 for Small Orch. (1947), No. 2 for Strings (1961), and No. 3 for Full Orch. (1965); Sym. (1956); *Rhapsody* for Violin and Orch. (1956); *Partita* for Strings (1957); Concerto for Piano, Percussion, and Strings (1958); *Sinfonia concertante* for Violin, Piano, and Chamber Orch. (1960–61); Concerto for 8 Solo Instruments and Orch. (1964); *Partita* (1965); *Fantasma* (1969); Trumpet Concerto (1971); *Riflessioni,* concerto for Cello and Orch. (1973); *Humanisation* for Chamber Ensemble and Tape (1974); *Concerto in memoriam Webern* for Horn and Orch. (1976); Violin Concerto (1979; rev. 1987); *Rapsodia* for Piano and Orch. (1985); *Wave Motions* (1987); Concerto Grosso for Harpsichord and Strings (1987). **CHAMBER:** String Trio (1943); 3 wind quintets (1952, 1961, 1966); 5 string quartets (1953, 1958, 1962, 1972, 1981); *Rhapsody* for Viola and Piano (1956); 2 wind trios (1958, 1959); *Capriccio* for Flute and Piano (1961); *Chamber Music for 8* (1963); *Chamber Music for 3* (1965); *Musica notturna* for Piano, Wind Quintet, and String Quintet (1967); Trio for Percussion, Piano, and Cello (1968–69); *Musica da camera* for Double Bass, Flute, Percussion, and Piano (1978); Horn Sonata (1980); *HaBem Music* for Saxophone and Percussion (1983); Clarinet Sonata (1984); *Quartetto per tromboni* (1988); also 4 piano sonatas (1952, 1962, 1972, 1988). **VOCAL:** 3 oratorios: *Dózsa György* (1959; rev. 1974), *Nenia* (1968–69), and *Justice in Jerusalem* (1986); *Meditations* for Tenor and Orch. (1961–62); *Maqamat* for Soprano and Chamber Ensemble (1970); choruses; songs.—**NS/LK/DM**

Székely, Mihály, noted Hungarian bass; b. Jászberény, May 8, 1901; d. Budapest, March 6, 1963. He studied in Budapest. He made his operatic debut as Weber's Hermit at the Budapest Municipal Theater in 1923; that same year, he made his first appearance at the Budapest Opera as Ferrando in *Il Trovatore,* remaining on its roster until his death; also made guest appearances throughout Europe. On Jan. 17, 1947, he sang the role of Hunding in *Die Walküre* at his Metropolitan Opera debut in N.Y.; continued on the roster until 1948, and then returned for the 1949–50 season. He subsequently sang in Europe, appearing at the Glyndebourne Festival, the Holland Festival, the Bavarian State Opera in Munich, and other music centers. He was renowned for such roles as Sarastro, Osmin, King Marke, Boris Godunov, Rocco, and Bluebeard.

BIBL.: P. Várnai, *S. M.* (Budapest, 1967).—**NS/LK/DM**

Szekelyhidy, Ferenc, Hungarian tenor; b. Tövis, April 4, 1885; d. Budapest, June 27, 1954. He received vocal training in Klausenburg. In 1909 he became a member of the Budapest Opera, where he sang both lyric and dramatic roles with success. He also toured widely as an oratorio and recital artist.—**NS/LK/DM**

Szelényi, István, Hungarian composer and musicologist; b. Zólyom, Aug. 8, 1904; d. Budapest, Jan. 31, 1972. He studied at the Budapest Academy of Music with Kodály. He toured as a concert pianist (1928–30); returning to Budapest, he taught at the Cons. (from 1945), later serving as its director; also taught at the Academy of Music (1956–72); ed. the journal *Új Zenei Szemle* (1951–56). In 1969 he was awarded the Erkel Prize.

WRITINGS (all publ. in Budapest): *Rendszeres modulációtan* (Methodical Theory of Modulation; 1927; second ed., 1960); *A zenetörténet és bölcselettörténet kapcsolatai* (The Interrelations of the History of Music and That of Philosophy; 1944); *Liszt élete képekben* (Liszt's Life in Pictures; 1956); *A romantikus zene harmóniavilága* (The Harmonic Realm of Romantic Music; 1959); *A magyar zene története* (The History of Hungarian Music; 1965); *A népdalharmónizálás alapelvei* (Principles of Folk-Song Harmonization; 1967).

WORKS: **DRAMATIC:** **Pantomimes:** *A tékozlo fiú* (The Prodigal Son; 1931); *Babiloni vásár* (The Fair at Babylon; 1931). **Operetta:** *Hidavatás* (1936). **ORCH.:** Sym. No. 1 (1926); Violin Concerto (1930); *Ouverture activiste* (1931); Triple Concerto for Violin, Cello, Piano, and Wind Orch. (1933); *Géptánc—Munkatánc* (Machine Dance—Work Dance; 1942); *Az ösök nyomában* (In the Footsteps of the Ancestors), sym. for Strings (1946); *Egy gyár szimfóniája* (Symphony for a Factory; 1946–47); *Hommage à Bartók* (1947); Violin Concertino (1947–48); Suite for Strings (1952); *Summa vitae* for Piano and Orch. (1956); *Concerto da camera* (1963); *Dance Suite* for Strings (1964); Piano Concertino (1964); *Variations concertants* for Piano and Orch. (1965); Piano Concerto (1969). **CHAMBER:** 2 sonatas for Solo Violin (1925, 1934); Flute Sonata (1926); 4 string quartets (1927, 1928, 1929, 1964); 2 piano trios (1934, 1962); Sonata for 4 Violins (1946); Sonatina for 2 Violins (1963); *Sinfonietta a tre* for 3 Violins (1964); *3 Dialogues* for Violin and Cello (1965); *Chamber Music* for 2 Trumpets, 2 Horns, and 2 Trombones (1966). **Piano:** 7 sonatas (1924–69); Sonatina (1960); *Toccata* (1964); *Musical Picture Book* (1967). **VOCAL:** Oratorios, including *Virata* (1935), *Spartacus* (1960), *10 Days That Shook the World* (1964), and *Pro Pace* (1968); choral works; songs.—**NS/LK/DM**

Szeligowski, Tadeusz, notable Polish composer and pedagogue; b. Lemberg, Sept. 12, 1896; d. Poznań, Jan. 10, 1963. He studied piano with Kurz in Lemberg (1910–14) and composition with Wallek-Walewski in Kraków, where he also took a doctorate in law at the Univ.; after further studies with Boulanger in Paris (1929–31), he taught in Poznań (1932–39; 1947–62) and in Warsaw (1951–62). From 1951 to 1954 he served as president of the Polish Composers' Union.

WORKS: **DRAMATIC:** **Opera:** *Bunt Żaków* (Rebellion of Clerks; Wroclaw, July 14, 1951); *Krakatuk*, after E.T.A. Hoffmann (1955; Gdansk, Dec. 30, 1956); *Theodor gentleman* (1960; Wroclaw, 1963). **Ballet:** *Paw i dziewczyna* (The Peacock and the Maiden; 1948; Wroclaw, Aug. 2, 1949); *Mazeppa* (1957; Warsaw, 1959). **ORCH.:** *Kaziuki*, suite (1928); *Concerto for Orchestra* (1932); Clarinet Concerto (1932); *Epitaph for Karol Szymanowski* for Strings (1937); Piano Concerto (1941; Kraków, May 17, 1946); *Suita lubelska* for Small Orch. (1945); *Nocturne* (1947); *Burlesque Overture* (1952). **CHAMBER:** 2 string quartets (1929, 1934); *Nocturne* for Cello and Piano (1945); *Orientale* for Cello and Piano (1945); Wind Quintet (1950); Flute Sonata (1953); *Air grave et air gai* for English Horn and Piano (1954); Piano Trio (1956). **Piano:** Sonatina (1940); Sonata (1949). **VOCAL:** *Triptych* for Soprano and Orch. (1946); *Kantata o sporcie* for Voice, Chorus, and Orch. (1947); *Wesele lubelskie* (Lublin Wedding), suite for Soprano, Chorus, and Small Orch. (1948); *Rapsod* for Soprano and Orch. (1949); *Panicz i dziewczyna* (The Young Squire and the Country Girl), musical dialogue for Soprano, Baritone, Chorus, and Orch. (1949); *Karta serc* (The Charter of Hearts), cantata (1952); *Renegade*, ballad for Bass and Orch. (1953); songs.

BIBL.: *T. S.: W 10 rocznice śmierci* (T. S.: On the 10th Anniversary of His Death; Gdańsk, 1973).—**NS/LK/DM**

Szell, George (actually, György), greatly distinguished Hungarian-born American conductor; b. Budapest, June 7, 1897; d. Cleveland, July 30, 1970. His family moved to Vienna when he was a small child. He studied piano with Richard Robert and composition with Mandyczewski; also composition in Prague with J.B. Foerster. He played a Mozart piano concerto with the Vienna Sym. Orch. when he was 10 years old, and the orch. also performed an overture of his composition. At the age of 17, he led the Berlin Phil. in an ambitious program that included a symphonic work of his own. In 1915 he was engaged as an asst. conductor at the Royal Opera of Berlin; then conducted opera in Strasbourg (1917–18), Prague (1919–21), Darmstadt (1921–22), and Düsseldorf (1922–24). He held the position of first conductor at the Berlin State Opera (1924–29); then conducted in Prague and Vienna. He made his U.S. debut as guest conductor of the St. Louis Sym. Orch. in 1930. In 1937 he was appointed conductor of the Scottish Orch. in Glasgow; he was also a regular conductor with the Residentie Orkest in The Hague (1937–39). He then conducted in Australia. At the outbreak of war in Europe in 1939 he was in America, which was to become his adoptive country by naturalization in 1946. His American conducting engagements included appearances with the Los Angeles Phil., NBC Sym. Orch., Chicago Sym. Orch., Detroit Sym. Orch., and Boston Sym. Orch. In 1942 he was appointed a conductor of the Metropolitan Opera in N.Y., where he received high praise for his interpretation of Wagner's music dramas; remained on its roster until 1946. He also conducted performances with the N.Y. Phil. in 1944–45. In 1946 he was appointed conductor of the Cleveland Orch., a post he held for 24 years; he was also music adviser and senior guest conductor of the N.Y. Phil. from 1969 until his death. He was a stern disciplinarian, demanding the utmost exertions from his musicians to achieve tonal perfection, but he was also willing to labor tirelessly at his task. Under his guidance, the Cleveland Orch. rose to the heights of symphonic excellence, taking its place in the foremost rank of world orchs. Szell was particularly renowned for his authoritative and exemplary performances of the Viennese classics, but he also was capable of outstanding interpretations of 20th-century masterworks.

Bibl.: R. Marsh, *The Cleveland Orchestra* (Cleveland and N.Y., 1967).—**NS/LK/DM**

Szeluto, Apolinary, fecund Russian-Polish composer; b. St. Petersburg, July 23, 1884; d. Chodziez, Aug. 22, 1966. He studied with Exner at the Saratov Cons. and with Statkowski and Noskowski at the Warsaw Cons. (1902–05); then received instruction in piano from Godowsky in Berlin (1905–08); also took courses in law in Warsaw and Dorpat. He was active as a pianist (1909–31), then devoted himself to composition. In association with Szymanowski, Fitelberg, and Rózycki, he formed a progressive musical group, Young Poland. He wrote a number of syms. in piano score; only 10 were orchestrated. His music is ultra-Romantic in its essence; most of his works bear descriptive titles. Several of them are inspired by contemporary political and military events.

Works: **ORCH.:** 28 syms., of which 18 exist without complete orchestration: No. 1, *Academic* (1920), No. 2, *Spontaneous* (1938), No. 3, *Impressionistic* (1942), No. 4, *Romantic* (1942), No. 5, *Majestic Room* (1942), No. 6, *Birth of Stalingrad* (1943), No. 7, *Revolutionary* (1943), No. 8, *Resurrection* (1942), No. 9, *Elegiac* (1943), No. 10, *Oriental* (1944), No. 11, *Iberian* (1944), No. 12, *Nordic* (1944), No. 13, *Samurai* (1943–46), No. 14, *Neapolitan* (1943), No. 15, *Los Angeles American* (1944), No. 16, *Fate* (1946), No. 17, *Kujawska Region* (1946), No. 18, *Litewska*, No. 19, *Slaska*, No. 20, *Kupiowska*, No. 21, *Podhalanska*, No. 22, *To the Building of a Communist People's Union*, Nos. 23–28 without titles; 5 piano concertos (1937, 1939, 1940, 1943, 1948); Violin Concerto (1942–48); Cello Concerto (1942); some 32 other orch. works. **OTHER:** 9 ballets; 14 chamber music pieces; 18 choral works; (purportedly) 78 operas; conservatively counting, 205 piano pieces; maybe 165 songs.—**NS/LK/DM**

Szendrei, Aladár, Hungarian-American conductor, musicologist, and composer who Americanized his name to **Alfred Sendrey**; b. Budapest, Feb. 29, 1884; d. Los Angeles, March 3, 1976. He studied with Koessler at the Budapest Academy of Music (1901–05) and later took courses in musicology at the Univ. of Leipzig (Ph.D., 1932). After serving as a theater conductor in Germany, he went to the U.S., where he conducted opera in Philadelphia and Chicago (1911–12); appeared with N.Y.'s Century Co. (1913–14). He returned to Europe in 1914; served in the Austrian army during World War I; after the Armistice, conducted opera in Leipzig (1918–24) and sym. concerts there (1924–32). In 1933 he left Germany and went to Paris, where he conducted at Radiodiffusion Française; he also taught conducting; Charles Munch took private lessons in conducting with him (1933–40); after the fall of Paris, Szendrei emigrated to the U.S. and settled in Los Angeles. He was prof. of Jewish music at the Univ. of Judaism in Los Angeles (1962–73).

Works: **DRAMATIC:** **Opera:** *Der türkisenblaue Garten* (Leipzig, Feb. 7, 1920). **Ballet:** *Danse d'odalisque*. **ORCH.:** *Hungarian Overture* (1904); Sym. (1923). **CHAMBER:** Piano Quintet (1925). **VOCAL:** *Stabat Mater* for 8 Solo Voices and Chorus (1905).

Writings: *Rundfunk und Musikpflege* (Leipzig, 1931); *Dirigierkunde* (Leipzig, 1932; third ed., 1956); *Bibliography of Jewish Music* (N.Y., 1951); *David's Harp: A Popular History of the Music in Biblical Times* (N.Y., 1964); *Music in Ancient Israel* (N.Y., 1969); *The Music of the Jews in the Diaspora (up to 1800)* (N.Y., 1969); *Music in the Social and Religious Life of Antiquity* (Canbury, N.J., 1974).—**NS/LK/DM**

Szendy, Árpád, Hungarian pianist, pedagogue, and composer; b. Szarvas, Aug. 11, 1863; d. Budapest, Sept. 10, 1922. He studied in Budapest at the Cons. and the Academy of Music, then became a student of Liszt (1881). In 1890 he was appointed to the faculty of the Academy of Music, where he was prof. of the piano master classes from 1911; enjoyed great esteem in Hungary as a piano teacher. He publ. numerous eds. of piano classics. His works include an opera, *Mária* (with Béla Szabados; Budapest, Feb. 28, 1905), a String Quartet, much piano music, and songs.—**NS/LK/DM**

Szenkar, Eugen (actually, **Jenő**), Hungarian conductor; b. Budapest, April 9, 1891; d. Düsseldorf, March 28, 1977. He studied music with his father, a prominent organist; later attended classes at the Academy of Music in Budapest. He conducted at the German Theater in Prague (1911–13), the Budapest Volksoper (1913–15), the Salzburg Mozarteum (1915–16), in Altenburg (1916–20), the Frankfurt am Main Opera (1920–23), the Berlin Volksoper (1923–24), and the Cologne Opera (1924–33). With the advent of the Nazi regime, as a Jew he was forced to leave Germany in 1933; lived in Russia until 1937; subsequently conducted the Brazilian Sym. Orch. in Rio de Janeiro (from 1944). He returned to Germany in 1950; was Generalmusikdirektor in Düsseldorf from 1952 to 1960.—**NS/LK/DM**

Szervánszky, Endre, Hungarian composer and teacher; b. Kistétény, Dec. 27, 1911; d. Budapest, June 25, 1977. He received training in clarinet as a child, and then was a student of F. Förster (clarinet; 1922–27) and Siklós (composition; 1931–36) at the Budapest Academy of Music. After teaching at the National Cons. in Budapest (1942–48), he taught at the Academy of Music (from 1948). In 1951 and 1955 he received the Kossuth Prize, in 1953 and 1954 he was awarded the Erkel Prize, and in 1972 he was made a Merited Artist by the Hungarian government. His works followed in the path marked out by Kodály and Bartók.

Works: **DRAMATIC:** *Napkeleti mese* (Oriental Tale), dance play (1948–49); incidental music; film scores. **ORCH.:** *Divertimento I* for Strings (1939), *II* for Small Orch. (1942), and *III* for Strings (1942–43); 2 suites (1944–45; 1948); Sym. (1946–48);

Serenade for Strings (1947–48); *Rhapsody* (1950); *Serenade* for Clarinet and Orch. (1950–51); Flute Concerto (1953); *Variations* (1964); Clarinet Concerto (1965). **CHAMBER:** 2 string quartets (1936–37; 1956–57); *20 Little Duets* for 2 Violins (1942); Violin Sonata (1945); *25 Duos* for 2 Violins (1946); Clarinet Quintet (1948); Trio for Oboe, Clarinet, and Bassoon (1950); Trio for Flute, Violin, and Viola (1951); Flute Sonatina (1951); 2 wind quintets (1953, 1957); *5 Concert Études* for Flute (1956); Suite for 2 Flutes (1956); *2 Duos* for 2 Flutes (1972). **Piano:** Sonatina (1940); Sonatina for Piano Duet (1950). **VOCAL:** *Requiem* for Chorus and Orch. (1963); cantatas; choruses; songs. **—NS/LK/DM**

Szeryng, Henryk, celebrated Polish-born Mexican violinist and pedagogue; b. Zelazowa Wola, Sept. 22, 1918; d. Kassel, March 3, 1988. He commenced piano and harmony training with his mother when he was 5, and at age 7 turned to the violin, receiving instruction from Maurice Frenkel; after further studies with Flesch in Berlin (1929–32), he went to Paris to continue his training with Thibaud at the Cons., graduating with a premier prix in 1937. On Jan. 6, 1933, he made his formal debut as soloist in the Brahms Concerto with the Warsaw Phil. With the outbreak of World War II in 1939, he became official translator of the Polish prime minister Wladyslaw Sikorski's government-in- exile in London; later was made personal government liaison officer. In 1941 he accompanied the prime minister to Latin America to find a home for some 4,000 Polish refugees; the refugees were taken in by Mexico, and Szeryng, in gratitude, settled there himself, becoming a naturalized citizen in 1946. Throughout World War II, he appeared in some 300 concerts for the Allies. After the war, he pursued a brilliant international career; was also active as a teacher. In 1970 he was made Mexico's special adviser to UNESCO in Paris. He celebrated the 50th anniversary of his debut with a grand tour of Europe and the U.S. in 1983. A cosmopolitan fluent in 7 languages, a humanitarian, and a violinist of extraordinary gifts, Szeryng became renowned as a musician's musician by combining a virtuoso technique with a probing discernment of the highest order.**—NS/LK/DM**

Szidon, Roberto, Brazilian pianist of Hungarian descent; b. Porto Alegre, Sept. 21, 1941. He gave a concert in his native city at the age of 9; later studied in N.Y. with Arrau. He then toured in the U.S., South America, and Europe as soloist with the leading orchs. and in recitals. Szidon was especially successful as a champion of the Romantic repertoire.**—NS/LK/DM**

Szigeti, Joseph, eminent Hungarian-born American violinist and teacher; b. Budapest, Sept. 5, 1892; d. Lucerne, Feb. 19, 1973. He began his studies at a local music school; while still a child, he was placed in the advanced class of Hubay at the Budapest Academy of Music; then made his debut in Berlin at age 13. He made his first appearance in London when he was 15; subsequently toured England in concerts with Busoni; then settled in Switzerland in 1913; was a prof. at the Geneva Cons. (1917–25). He made an auspicious U.S. debut playing the Beethoven Concerto with Stokowski and the Philadelphia Orch. at N.Y.'s Carnegie Hall (Dec. 15, 1925); thereafter he toured the U.S. regularly while continuing to appear in Europe. With the outbreak of World War II, he went to the U.S. (1940), becoming a naturalized American citizen in 1951. After the end of the war, he resumed his international career; settled again in Switzerland in 1960, and gave master classes. Szigeti was an artist of rare intellect and integrity; he eschewed the role of the virtuoso, placing himself totally at the service of the music. In addition to the standard repertoire, he championed the music of many 20th-century composers, including Stravinsky, Bartók, Ravel, Prokofiev, Honegger, Bloch, and Martin. He wrote the books *With Strings Attached* (N.Y., 1947), *A Violinist's Notebook* (London, 1965), and *Szigeti on the Violin: Improvisations on a Violinist's Themes* (N.Y., 1969). **—NS/LK/DM**

Szokolay, Sándor, Hungarian composer and teacher; b. Kunágota, March 30, 1931. He studied with Szabó (1950–52) and Farkas (1952–56) at the Budapest Academy of Music (graduated, 1957), concurrently teaching at the Municipal Music School (1952–55); then was music reader and producer for the Hungarian Radio (1955–59) and a teacher (1959–66) and prof. (from 1966) at the Budapest Academy of Music. He received the Erkel Prize (1960, 1965) and the Kossuth Prize (1966); in 1976 he was made a Merited Artist and in 1986 an Outstanding Artist by the Hungarian government. In 1987 he received the Bartók-Pásztory Award.

WORKS: DRAMATIC: Opera: *Vérnász* (Blood Wedding; Budapest, Oct. 30, 1964); *Hamlet* (1965–68; Budapest, Oct. 19, 1968); *Sámson* (Budapest, Oct. 23, 1973); *Ecce homo*, passion opera (1984); *Szávitri* (1987–89); also 2 children's operas. **Ballet:** *Orbán és as ördög* (Urban and the Devil; 1958); *Az iszonyat balladája* (The Ballad of Terror; 1960); *Tetemrehívás* (Ordeal of the Bier; 1961–71); *Az áldozat* (The Victim; 1971). **ORCH.:** *Concert Rondo* for Piano and Strings (1955); Violin Concerto (1956–57); Piano Concerto (1958); *Ballata sinfonica* (1967–68); Trumpet Concerto (1968); *Archaikus nyitány* (Archaic Overture; 1977); *Rapszódia* for Chamber Orch. (1978); Concertino for Alto Flute, Flute, Piccolo, Strings, and Harpsichord (1981); *Concerto for Orchestra* (1982). **CHAMBER:** *Gyermek-kvartett* (Quartet for Children) for 2 Violins, Cello, and Piano (1954); Sonata for Solo Violin (1956); 2 string quartets (1972, 1982); *Sirató és kultikus tánc* (Lament and Ritual Dance) for Cimbalom, Celesta, Piano, and Harp (1974); *Miniature per ottoni* for Brass Sextet (1976); *Alliterációk* (Alliterations) for Brass Quintet (1977); *Játek a hangközökkel* (Playing with Intervals) for 5 Cimbalom Duos (1978); Sonata for Solo Cello (1979); *Polimorfia* (Polymorphy) for Violin, Cello, and Harpsichord or Piano (1980); *Hommage à Bartók*, divertimento for Brass Quintet (1981); *Gregorián változatok* (Gregorian Variations), 5 miniatures for Brass Quintet (1983); *Variáció egy sirató-dallamra* (Variations on a Lament Melody) for 6 Percussionists (1986). **VOCAL:** *Vizimesék* (Water Tales), children's cantata for Soprano, Children's Chorus, and Chamber Orch. (1957); *Világok vetélkedése* (Rivalry of Worlds), cantata for Soprano, Alto, Baritone, Chorus, and Orch. (1959); *Istár pokoljárása* (Isthar's Descent to Hell), oratorio for Soprano, Alto, Baritone, Bass, Chorus, and Orch. (1960–61); *Néger kantáta* (Negro Cantata) for Alto, Chorus, and Orch. (1962); *Deploration: Concerto da requiem* for Piano, Chorus, and Orch. in memory of Francis Poulenc (1964); *Vitézi ének* (Song of Heroes), cantata for Alto, Bass, Men's Chorus, and Orch. (1970); *Ódon ének* (Ancient

Song), cantata for Chorus, Woodwind, Horns, Kettledrum, Harp, and Strings (1972); *Kantáta a gályarabok emlékére* (Cantata in Memory of Galley Slaves) for Narrator, Baritone, Chorus, Organ, and Orch. (1975); *Libellus ungaricus*, cantata for Soprano, Alto, Tenor, Baritone, Bass, Chorus, Organ, and Orch. (1979); *Confessio Augustana*, cantata for Baritone, Chorus, Organ, and Orch. (1980); *Luther-Kantate* for Baritone, Chorus, Chamber Orch., and Organ (1983); *Aeternitas temporis*, cantata for Soprano and String Quartet (1988).—**NS/LK/DM**

Szőllősy, András, Hungarian composer and musicologist; b. Szászváros, Transylvania, Feb. 27, 1921. He studied with Kodály and Viski at the Budapest Academy of Music (1939–44) and took courses in musicology at the Univ. of Budapest (Ph.D., 1943); completed his training in composition with Petrassi at the Accademia di Santa Cecilia in Rome (1947–48). He was a prof. of music history and theory at the Budapest Academy of Music (from 1950). In 1971 he received the Erkel Prize, in 1985 the Kossuth Prize, and in 1986 the Bartók-Pásztory Award. He was made an Artist of Merit (1972) and an Outstanding Artist (1982) of the Hungarian People's Republic; in 1987 the French government made him a Commandeur de l'Ordre des Arts et Lettres. His music draws upon modern resources cast along traditional lines. He publ. a study on Honegger (Budapest, 1960) and ed. the writings of Bartók.

WORKS: DRAMATIC: Ballet: *Oly korban éltem* (Improvisations on Fear; 1963); *Pantomime* (1965; based on *Tre pezzi* for Flute and Piano, 1964); *Diminuendo* (1977; based on *Transfigurazione* for Orch., 1972); *A t&ubdlac;z fiai* (Sons of Fire; 1977). **ORCH.:** 5 concertos: No. 1 for Strings, Brass, Piano, and Percussion (1959), No. 2 (destroyed), No. 3 for 16 Strings (1968; Vienna, Nov. 23, 1969), No. 4 for Small Orch. (Gyor, April 13, 1970), and No. 5, *Lehellet* (1975; Budapest, May 27, 1976); *Musica per orchestra (In memoriam Zoltán Kodály)* (1972; Vienna, Sept. 22, 1973); *Transfigurazioni* (Budapest, July 1, 1972); *Musica concertante* for Chamber Orch. (Zagreb, May 18, 1973); *Preludio, Adagio e Fuga* (1973); *Sonoritá* (1974; Budapest, Sept. 29, 1975); Concerto for Harpsichord and 16 Strings (1978); *Pro somno Igoris Stravinsky quieto* for Chamber Orch. (Budapest, Nov. 17, 1978); *Tristia (Maros Lament)* for 16 Strings (1983); *Canto d'autunno* (1986; Swansea, Jan. 16, 1987); Violin Concerto (1994–95). **CHAMBER:** *Tre pezzi* for Flute and Piano (Darmstadt, July 18, 1964); *Musiche per ottoni*, 20 pieces for 3 Trumpets, 3 Trombones, and Tuba (1975); *A Hundred Bars for Tom Everett* for Bass Trombone and 3 Bongos (1980; Cambridge, Mass. Jan. 17, 1982); *Suoni di tromba* for Trumpet and Piano (1983; London, May 28, 1984); Trombone Quartet (1986); String Quartet (1988; Orlando, July 30, 1989); *4 Little Pieces* for Recorder and Piano (1991); *Elegia* for Wind Quintet and String Quintet (1993; Berlin, May 30, 1994). **Piano:** *Old Hungarian Dance* for Piano Duet (1956); *Paessaggio con morti* (1987; Orkney Islands, June 18, 1988). **VOCAL:** *Night in Kolozsvár*, elegy for Voice and Wind Quintet (1955); *Restless Autumn*, cantata for Baritone and Piano (1955); *Fabula Phaedri* for Vocal Sextet (Budapest, Nov. 23, 1982); *In Pharisaeos* for Chorus and Trumpet (1982); *Planctus Mariae* for Women's Chorus (1982); *Miserere* for Vocal Sextet (1984; Brighton, May 10, 1985); *Fragments* for Mezzo-soprano, Flute, and Viola (Budapest, April 26, 1985).—**NS/LK/DM**

Szönyi, Erzsébet, Hungarian composer and music educator; b. Budapest, April 25, 1924. She studied piano and composition at the Budapest Academy of Music, graduating in 1947; then went to Paris, where she took courses at the Cons. with Aubin and Messiaen; also took private lessons in composition with Boulanger. Returning to Budapest, she taught at the Academy of Music from 1948 to 1981. In 1959 she was awarded the Erkel Prize. She played a major role in promoting Kodály's educational methods in Hungary and elsewhere. Her writings include *A zenei írás-olvasás módszertana* (Methods of Musical Reading and Writing; 4 vols., Budapest, 1953–65; Eng. tr., 1972) and a study on Kodály's teaching methods (Budapest, 1973; numerous trs.).

WORKS: DRAMATIC: Opera: *Dalma* (1952); *The Stubborn Princess* (1955); *Firenzei tragédie* (1957); *The Little Bee with the Golden Wing* (1974); *A Gay Lament* (1979); *The Truth-telling Shepherd* (1979); *Break of Transmission* (1980); *Elfrida* (1985). **ORCH.:** 2 divertimentos (1948, 1951); Organ Concerto (1958); *Musica festiva* (1964); *3 Ideas in 4 Movements* for Piano and Orch. (1980). **CHAMBER:** Trio for Oboe, Clarinet, and Bassoon (1958); Trio Sonata for Violin, Cello, and Piano (1965); Double Bass Sonata (1982); *Evocatio* for Piano and Organ (1985). **Piano:** 2 sonatinas (1944, 1946); Sonata (1953). **VOCAL:** Oratorios; cantatas; choruses.—**NS/LK/DM**

Sztompka, Henryk, Polish pianist and pedagogue; b. Boguslawce, April 4, 1901; d. Kraków, June 21, 1964. He studied with Turczyński at the Warsaw Cons. (diploma, 1926) and with Paderewski in Morges, Switzerland (1928–32); he also took courses in philosophy at the Univ. of Warsaw. After making his formal debut in Paris in 1932, he made tours of Europe and South America. From 1945 he taught at the Kraków State Coll. of Music. He was the author of a monograph on Arthur Rubinstein (Kraków, 1966). Sztompka became best known as an interpreter of Chopin.—**NS/LK/DM**

Szulc, Józef Zygmunt, Polish pianist and composer; b. Warsaw, April 4, 1875; d. Paris, April 10, 1956. He studied at the Warsaw Cons. with Noskowski; then took piano lessons in Paris with Moszkowski. He remained in Paris as a piano teacher; then turned to composition of light operas. His first work in this genre, *Flup* (Brussels, Dec. 19, 1913), was successful and had numerous performances in Europe; he continued to produce operettas at regular intervals; the last one was *Pantoufle* (Paris, Feb. 24, 1945). He also wrote a ballet, *Une Nuit d'Ispahan* (Brussels, Nov. 19, 1909), overtures, chamber music, and piano pieces.—**NS/LK/DM**

Szumowska, Antoinette, Polish-American pianist and teacher; b. Lublin, Feb. 22, 1868; d. Rumson, N.J., Aug. 18, 1938. She studied at the Warsaw Cons. with Michalowski, and later took lessons with Paderewski in Paris (1890–95). In 1895 she emigrated to the U.S., settling in Boston, where she taught at the New England Cons. of Music. In 1896 she married **Josef Adamowski**, and with him and his brother Timothée, a violinist, formed the Adamowski Trio, which presented numerous concerts in New England.—**NS/LK/DM**

Szweykowski, Zygmunt M(arian), eminent Polish musicologist; b. Kraków, May 12, 1929. He was a pupil of Chybiński at the Univ. of Poznań (graduated, 1951) and of Chomiński at the Univ. of Kraków (Ph.D., 1964, with the diss. *Technika koncertujaca w polskiej muzyce wokalnmo-instrumentalnej okresu baroku* [Concerto Technique in Polish Vocal-Instrumental Music of the Baroque]; Eng. tr. in *Studia Hieronymo Feicht septuagenario dedicata*, Kraków, 1967, and in Polish Musicological Studies, I, 1977); completed his Habilitation at the latter in 1976 with his *Musica moderna w ujęciu Marka Scacchiego* (Musica Moderna as Conceived by Marco Scacchi; publ. in Kraków, 1977, with Eng. summary). After serving as Chybiński's assistant at the Univ. of Poznań (1950–53), he went to Kraków as ed. of Polskie Wydawnictwo Muzyczne (1954–61); also taught at the Univ. (from 1954), becoming head of its musicological dept. (1971–74; from 1979); was made a prof. in 1988. Szweykowski is a respected scholar of the Baroque era in Polish music history. He founded Żróda do Historii Muzyki Polskiej in 1960 and ed. various works in Wydawnictwo Dawnej Muzyki Polskiej; also contributed valuable articles to Polish and foreign journals and other publications.

WRITINGS: *Kultura wokalna XVI-wiecznej Polski* (The Vocal Culture of XVI-century Poland; Kraków, 1957); ed. *Z dziejów polskiej kultury muzycznej* (From the History of Polish Musical Culture; Kraków, 1958); *Katalog tematyczny rekopísmiennych zabytków dawnej muzyki w Polsce* (Thematic Catalog of Early Music Manuscripts in Poland; Kraków, 1969).—**NS/LK/DM**

Szymanowska, Maria Agate (née Wolowska),

prominent Polish pianist and composer; b. Warsaw, Dec. 14, 1789; d. St. Petersburg, July 24, 1831. She studied piano with local teachers in Warsaw, and began to play in public as a child. In 1810 she married a Polish landowner, Theophilus Joseph Szymanowski (divorced, 1820). In 1822 she toured in Russia, and was appointed court pianist; in 1823, played in Germany; in 1824, in France; then in England, the Netherlands, and Italy (1824–25), returning to Warsaw in 1826. In 1828 she settled in St. Petersburg as a pianist and teacher, and remained there until her death (of cholera). Goethe held her in high esteem and wrote his *Aussöhnung* for her; she also won the admiration of Glinka and Pushkin. She distinguished herself as a composer for the piano, presaging the genius of Chopin in her studies, nocturnes, and dances. Among her finest works for piano are *20 exercices et préludes* (Leipzig, 1820), *18 Danses* (Leipzig, 1820), *Nocturne: Le Murmure* (Paris, 1825), and *24 Mazurkas* (Leipzig, 1826). She also wrote some chamber music and vocal pieces.

BIBL.: I. Boelza, *M. S.* (Moscow, 1956); M. Iwanejko, *M. S.* (Kraków, 1959).—**NS/LK/DM**

Szymanowski, Karol (Maciej),

eminent Polish composer; b. Timoshovka, Ukraine, Oct. 6, 1882; d. Lausanne, March 28, 1937. The son of a cultured landowner, he grew up in a musical environment. He began to play the piano and compose very early in life. His first teacher was Gustav Neuhaus in Elizavetgrad; in 1901 he went to Warsaw, where he studied harmony with Zawirski and counterpoint and composition with Noskowski until 1904. With Fitelberg, Rózycki, and Szeluto, he founded the Young Polish Composer's Publishing Co. in Berlin, which was patronized by Prince Wladyslaw Lubomirski; the composers also became known as Young Poland in Music, publishing new works and sponsoring performances for some 6 years. Among the works the group publ. was Szymanowski's op.1, 9 Piano Preludes (1906). He was greatly influenced by German Romanticism, and his first major orch. works reveal the impact of Wagner and Strauss. His first Sym. was premiered in Warsaw on March 26, 1909; however, he was dissatisfied with the score, and withdrew it from further performance. In 1911 he completed his second Sym., which demonstrated a stylistic change from German dominance to Russian influences, paralleling the harmonic evolution of Scriabin; it was played for the first time in Warsaw on April 7, 1911. After a Viennese sojourn (1911–12) and a trip to North Africa (1914), he lived from 1914 to 1917 in Timoshovka, where he wrote his third Sym.; he appeared in concert with the violinist Paul Kochański in Moscow and St. Petersburg, giving first performances of his violin works; it was for Kochański that he composed his violin triptych, *Mythes (La Fontaine d'Aréthuse* in this cycle is one of his best-known compositions). About this time, his music underwent a new change in style, veering toward French Impressionism. During the Russian Revolution of 1917, the family estate at Timoshovka was ruined, and Szymanowski lost most of his possessions. From 1917 to 1919 he lived in Elizavetgrad, where he continued to compose industriously, despite the turmoil of the Civil War. After a brief stay in Bydgoszcz, he went to Warsaw in 1920. In 1920–21 he toured the U.S. in concerts with Kochański and Rubinstein. Returning to Warsaw, he gradually established himself as one of Poland's most important composers. His international renown also was considerable; his works were often performed in Europe, and figured at festivals of the ISCM. He was director of the Warsaw Cons. (1927–29) and reorganized the system of teaching along more liberal lines; was rector of its successor, the Warsaw Academy of Music (1930–32). His *Stabat Mater* (1925–26) produced a profound impression, and his ballet-pantomime *Harnasie* (1923–31), based on the life and music of the Tatra mountain dwellers, demonstrated his ability to treat national subjects in an original and highly effective manner. In 1932 he appeared as soloist in the first performance of his fourth Sym., *Symphonie concertante* for Piano and Orch., at Poznań, and repeated his performances in Paris, London, and Brussels. In April 1936, greatly weakened in health by chronic tuberculosis, he attended a performance of his *Harnasie* at the Paris Opéra. He spent his last days in a sanatorium in Lausanne. Szymanowski developed into a national composer whose music acquired universal significance.

WORKS: DRAMATIC: *Loteria na mezós* (The Lottery for Men), operetta (1908–09; not perf.); *Hagith*, op.25, opera (1913; Warsaw, May 13, 1922); *Mandragora*, op.43, pantomime (Warsaw, June 15, 1920); *Król Roger* (King Roger), op.46, opera (1918–24; Warsaw, June 19, 1926); *Kniaź Patiomkin* (Prince Potemkin), op.51, incidental music to T. Micínski's play (Warsaw, March 6, 1925); *Harnasie*, op.55, ballet-pantomime

(1923–31; Prague, May 11, 1935). **ORCH.:** *Salome* for Soprano and Orch., op.6 (c. 1907; reorchestrated 1912); *Concert Overture*, op.12 (1904–05; Warsaw, Feb. 6, 1906; reorchestrated 1912–13); 4 syms.: No. 1, op.15 (1906–07; Warsaw, March 26, 1909), No. 2, op.19 (1909–10; Warsaw, April 7, 1911; reorchestrated with the collaboration of G. Fitelberg, 1936; rev. version by S. Skrowaczewski, Minneapolis, Oct. 14, 1967), No. 3, *Pieśń o nocy* (Song of the Night) for Tenor, Soprano, Chorus, and Orch., op.27 (1914–16; London, Nov. 24, 1921), and No. 4, *Symphonie concertante* for Piano and Orch., op.60 (Poznań, Oct. 9, 1932, composer soloist); *Penthesilea* for Soprano and Orch., op.18 (1908; Warsaw, March 18, 1910; reorchestrated 1912); *Pieśni milosne Hafiza* (Love Songs of Hafiz) for Voice and Orch., op.26 (1914; Paris, June 23, 1925; arranged from op.24, 1911); *Pieśni księźnicki z baśni* (Songs of a Fairy-Tale Princess) for Voice and Orch., op.31 (Warsaw, April 7, 1933; arranged from the songs of 1915); 2 violin concertos: No. 1, op.35 (1916; Warsaw, Nov. 1, 1922) and No. 2, op.61 (Warsaw, Oct. 6, 1933); *Demeter* for Alto, Women's Chorus, and Orch., op.37b (1917; reorchestrated 1924; Warsaw, April 17, 1931); *Agave* for Alto, Women's Chorus, and Orch., op.39 (1917); *Pieśni muezina szalonego* (Songs of the Infatuated Muezzin) for Voice and Orch., op.42 (1934; arranged from the songs of 1918); *Slopiewnie* for Voice and Orch., op.46b (1928; arranged from the version for Voice and Piano of 1921); *Stabat Mater* for Soprano, Alto, Baritone, Chorus, and Orch., op.53 (1925–26; Warsaw, Jan. 11, 1929); *Veni Creator* for Soprano, Chorus, Orch., and Organ, op.57 (Warsaw, Nov. 7, 1930); *Litania do Marii Panny* (Litany to the Virgin Mary) for Soprano, Women's Chorus, and Orch., op.59 (1930–33; Warsaw, Oct. 13, 1933). **CHAMBER:** Violin Sonata, op.9 (1904; Warsaw, April 19, 1909); Piano Trio, op.16 (1907; destroyed); *Romance* for Violin and Piano, op.23 (1910; Warsaw, April 8, 1913); *Nocturne and Tarantella* for Violin and Piano, op.28 (1915); *Mity* (Myths) for Violin and Piano, op.30 (1915); 2 string quartets: No. 1, op.37 (1917; Warsaw, April 1924) and No. 2, op.56 (1927; Paris, 1929); *3 Paganini Caprices* for Violin and Piano, op.40 (Elizavetgrad, April 25, 1918); *Kolysanka* (Lullaby): *La Berceuse d'Aïtacho Enia* for Violin and Piano, op.52 (1925). **Piano:** *9 Preludes*, op.1 (1900); *Variations*, op.3 (1903); *4 Studies*, op.4 (1902); 3 sonatas: No. 1, op.8 (1904; Warsaw, April 19, 1907), No. 2, op.21 (Berlin, Dec. 1, 1911), and No. 3, op.36 (1917); *Wariacje na polski temat ludowy* (Variations on a Polish Theme), op.10 (1904; Warsaw, Feb. 6, 1906); *Fantasy*, op.14 (1905; Warsaw, Feb. 9, 1906); *Prelude and Fugue* (1905–09); *Metopy* (Metopes), op.29 (1915); *12 Studies*, op.33 (1916); *Maski* (Masques), op.34 (St. Petersburg, Oct. 12, 1916); *20 Mazurkas*, op.50 (1924–25); *Valse romantique* (1925); *4 Polish Dances* (1926); *2 Mazurkas*, op.62 (1933–34; London, Nov. 1934). **VOCAL:** About 100 songs.

WRITINGS: *Wychowawcza rola kultury muzycznej w spoleczenstwie* (The Educational Role of Musical Culture in Society; Warsaw, 1931); T. Bronowicz-Chylińska, ed., *Z pism* (From the Writings; Kraków, 1958; selected essays).

BIBL.: Z. Jachimecki, *K. S.: Zarys dotychczasowej twórczości* (K. S.: An Outline of His Output; Kraków, 1927); S. Golachowski, *K. S.* (Warsaw, 1948; second ed., 1956); S. Lobaczewska, *K. S.: Zycie i twórczośc (1882–1937)* (K. S.: Life and Work [1882–1937]; Kraków, 1950); T. Bronowicz- Chylińska, ed., *S. K.: Z listow* (S. K.: From the Letters; Kraków, 1957); J. Chomiński, *Studia nad twórczóscia K.a S.ego* (Kraków, 1969); A. Wightman, *The Music of K. S.* (diss., Univ. of York, 1972); J. Samson, *The Music of S.* (London, 1980); C. Palmer, *S.* (London, 1983); M. Bristiger et al., eds., *K. S. in seiner Zeit* (Munich, 1984); Z. Sierpiński, ed., and E. Harris, tr., *K. S.: An Anthology* (Warsaw, 1986); T. Chylińska, *K. Z.: His Life and Works* (Los Angeles, 1993); S. Downes, *S. as Post-Wagnerian: The Love Songs of Hafiz, op.24* (N.Y., 1994); T. Zieliński, *S.: Liryka i ekstaza* (Kraków, 1997); A. Wightman, *K. S.: His Life and Work* (Brookfield, Vt., 1999). **—NS/LK/DM**

Szymánski, Paweł, Polish composer; b. Warsaw, March 28, 1954. He studied composition with Włodzimierz Kotoński (1974–78) and Tadeusz Baird (1978) at the State Higher School of Music in Warsaw, from which he graduated with honors. After attending the summer courses in new music in Darmstadt (1978, 1980, 1982), he pursued training in Vienna with Roman Haubenstock-Ramati (1984–85). In 1987–88 he worked at the electronic studio of the Technical Univ. in Berlin under the auspices of the Deutscher Akademischer Austauschdienst. In 1979 he won first prize in the Young Composers' Competition of the Polish Composers' Union, in 1988 he was co-winner in the Benjamin Britten Composers' Competition in Aldeburgh, in 1993 he received the Polish Composers' Union Award, and in 1995 he was awarded the principal prize of the International Polish Music Foundation competition.

WORKS: *Epitafium* (Epitaph) for 2 Pianos (Warsaw, April 19, 1974); String Quartet (Warsaw, May 10, 1975); *Limeryki* (Limericks) *I* for Violin and Harpsichord (1975; Warsaw, May 10, 1976) and *II* for Flute, Violin, and Cello (1979; Darmstadt, Aug. 2, 1980); *Partita I* for Orch. (1976), *II* for Orch. (1977–78; Opole, Feb. 15, 1981), *III* for Amplified Harpsichord and Orch. (1985–86; Warsaw, Sept. 28, 1986), and *IV* for Orch. (1986; Belfast, April 24, 1987); *Kyrie* for Boy's Chorus and Orch. (1977; Warsaw, Feb. 17, 1978); *Intermezzo* for 2 Flutes, Percussion, 4 Violins, 3 Violas, 2 Cellos, and Double Bass (1977; Warsaw, Jan. 22, 1979); *10 Pieces* for String Trio (Baranów Sandomierski, Sept. 6, 1979); *Gloria* for Women's Chorus and Instrumental Ensemble (Warsaw, Sept. 16, 1979); *La folia* for Tape (1979); *...under the plane tree* for Tape (1980); *4 Liturgical Pieces* for Soprano and Orch. (1981–82; Poznań, April 11, 1986); *Villanelle* for Countertenor, 2 Violas, and Harpsichord (1981; Lusławice, Sept. 12, 1983); Sonata for Strings and Percussion (Warsaw, Dec. 15, 1982); *2 Pieces* for String Quartet (1982; Zakopane, Oct. 1, 1983); *Appendix* for Piccolo and Chamber Ensemble (1983); *Dwie konstrukcje iluzoryczne* (Two Illusory Constructions) for Clarinet, Cello, and Piano (Lerchenborg, July 28, 1984); *Lux aeterna* for Voices and Instruments (1984; Warsaw, Sept. 26, 1985); *Trop* (Trope) for Piano (1986; Lerchenborg, Aug. 5, 1990); *2 Studies* for Piano (1986; Warsaw, Sept. 15, 1990); *Through the Looking Glass...I* for Chamber Orch. (1987), *II* for Tape (1988), and *III* for Harpsichord (1994; Paris, Jan. 11, 1995; also for Harpsichord and String Quartet, 1994); *A Study of Shade* for Small Orch. (Aldeburgh, June 12, 1989; also for Orch., 1992; Warsaw, Sept. 15, 1994); *A Kaleidoscope for M.C.E.* for Cello (1989; Wrocław, Feb. 24, 1990; also for Violin 1994; Warsaw, Sept. 22, 1997); *Fuga* for Piano (Lerchenborg, Aug. 3, 1990); *quasi una sinfonietta* for Chamber Orch. (London, Nov. 6, 1990); *Sixty- Odd Pages* for Chamber Orch. (Warsaw, Sept. 22, 1991); *A due* for 2 Violins (1992); *2 Studies* for Orch. (1992); *5 Pieces* for String Quartet (1992; Warsaw, Sept. 24, 1993); *Miserere* for Voices and Instruments (Warsaw, March 28, 1993); *3 Pieces* for 3 Recorders and Metronome (Basel, Sept. 18, 1993); *2 Preludes* for Piano (1994); Piano Concerto (1994; Paris, Feb. 12, 1995); *Muzyka filmowa* (Film Music) for Orch. (1994–96); *SONAT(IN)A* for Piano (Warsaw, May 12, 1995); *In Paradisum* for Men's Chorus (Sendai, Aug. 12, 1995); *2 Melodies* for Piano (Budapest, Oct. 1, 1995);

Bagatelle für A. W. for Violin, Clarinet, Tenor Saxophone, and Piano (Bratislava, Nov. 15, 1995); *Recalling a Serenade* for Clarinet, 2 Violins, Viola, and Cello (Kuhmo, July 24, 1996). **—LK/DM**

T

Tabachnik, Michel, Swiss conductor and composer; b. Geneva, Nov. 10, 1942. He received training in piano, composition, and conducting at the Geneva Cons. After attending the summer courses in new music given by Pousseur, Stockhausen, and Boulez in Darmstadt (1964), he served as assistant to Boulez in Basel. He was conductor of the Gulbenkian Foundation Orch. in Lisbon (1973–75), the Lorraine Phil. in Metz (1975–81), and the Ensemble Européen de Musique Contemporaine in Paris (1976–77). As a guest conductor, he appeared with principal orchs. of the world. He became particularly known for his interpretations of contemporary music. His compositions followed along advanced lines.

WORKS: DRAMATIC: Opera: *La Légende de Haïsha* (Paris, Nov. 1989). **ORCH.:** *Supernova* for 16 Instruments (1967); *Fresque* for 33 Instruments (1969); *Invention à 16 voix* for 12 Instruments (1972); *Mondes* for 2 Orchs. (1972); *Sillages* for Strings (1972); *Movimenti* (1973); *Les Imaginaires* (1974); *Les Perseides* (1975); *Cosmogonie pour une rose* (1979–81); Piano Concerto (1989); *Le Cri de Mohim* (1990); *Evocation* (1992). **CHAMBER:** *D'autres Sillages* for 8 Percussion and Tape (1972); *Argile* for 4 Percussion (1974). **VOCAL:** *l'arch* for Soprano and Chamber Orch. (1982); *Le Pacte des Onze* for Soloists, Choruses, Orch., and Tape (1983).—**NS/LK/DM**

Tabnik, Richard, jazz alto saxophone; b. Manhattan, N.Y., April 6, 1952. He grew up in Great Neck, N.Y., and had his first jazz gigs in Providence, R.I., under the tutelage of guitarist Tom Brown. He studied with Hall Overton in 1970, and with Lee Konitz from 1970 to 1972, and attended Berklee for the fall semester of 1972. He also performed in various contexts in Houston, Tex. and Atlanta, Ga. Between 1975 and 1979, he lived in Buffalo, N.Y., working toward a degree through the Empire State Coll. program of SUNY. He appeared on radio and television, and in concert with his own groups. He played lead alto in Frank Foster's Big Band at the State Univ. of N.Y. at Buffalo, and was a featured soloist at the historic Colored Musicians Club. He spent two and a half years with the federally funded Buffalo Jazz Ensemble under the direction of Allen Tinney, formerly of Monroe's Uptown House. He also studied privately with Robert Dick, Ray Ricker, and John Sedola. He moved to N.Y.C. in 1979, studied with Joe Allard from September 1979 to June 1983, began studying with Connie Crothers in January 1980, and was presented in concert at Crother's studio. He then played in duets with Peter Scattaretico on drums and Crothers on piano, and as a soloist at the Greenwich House in 1991. Tabnik gigged around N.Y.C. with a quartet during 1993–94. In the later 1990s, he led his own trio and also worked as a member of pianist Connie Crothers's quartet. He has also worked as a jazz journalist.

DISC.: *Solo Journey* (solo saxophone, 1990); *In the Moment* (1992); *Life at the Core* (1995). Connie Crothers: *Duo Dimension* (1988).—**LP**

Tabourot, Jehan
See **Arbeau, Thoinot**

Tabuteau, Marcel, outstanding French oboist and pedagogue; b. Compiegne, July 2, 1887; d. Nice, Jan. 4, 1966. He studied oboe with Georges Gillet at the Paris Cons., winning a premier prix at the age of 17. In 1905 he went to the U.S., where he played in the N.Y. Sym. Orch. until 1914; also was a member of the orch. of the Metropolitan Opera (from 1908). In 1915 Stokowski engaged him as 1st oboist in the Philadelphia Orch., where he remained until 1954. He was also on the faculty of the Curtis Inst. of Music in Philadelphia (from 1924).—**NS/LK/DM**

Tacchinardi, Nicola, famous Italian tenor and singing teacher; b. Livorno, Sept. 3, 1772; d. Florence, March 14, 1859. He played cello in the orch. of Florence's Teatro della Pergola (1789–97). After vocal studies, he began his operatic career with appearances in Livorno, Pisa, Florence, and Venice in 1804. In 1805 he sang at Milan's La Scala, where he participated in the coronation performances for Napoleon as King of Italy. He scored a triumph in Zingarelli's *La distruzione di Gerusalemme* at the Paris Odéon on May 4, 1811; until 1814 he sang at the Théâtre-Italien, where his performances in Paisiello's *La bella molinara* were particularly acclaimed. After appearances in Spain (1815–17) and Vienna (1816), he returned to Italy; was made primo cantante of the Florence Grand Ducal Chapel in 1822, while continuing his appearances in Italian opera houses; he also revisited Vienna in 1823. He retired in 1831 and devoted himself to teaching; one of his students was his daughter, **Fanny Persiani** (née **Tacchinardi**). His most celebrated role was that of Othello in Rossini's *Otello*. He composed vocal exercises and publ. *Dell'opera in musica sul teatro italiano e de' suoi difetti* (Florence, 2nd ed., 1833). His son, Guido Tacchinardi (b. Florence, March 10, 1840; d. there, Dec. 6, 1917), was a conductor, music critic, and composer; was director of the Florence Istituto Musicale (1891–1917).—**NS/LK/DM**

Tacchino, Gabriel, French pianist and teacher; b. Cannes, Aug. 4, 1934. He was a student of Jean Batalla, Jacques Févier, Marguerite Long, and Francis Poulenc at the Paris Cons. (1947–53), graduating with a premier prix in 1953. He took 1st prize in the Viotti competition in Vercelli (1953), 2nd prize in the Busoni competition in Bolzano (1954), co–2nd prize with Malcolm Frager in the Geneva competition (1955), 1st prize in the Casella competition in Naples (1956), and 4th prize in the Long-Thibaud competition in Paris (1957). Thereafter he pursued an international career as a soloist with orchs. and as a recitalist. In 1975 he became a prof. at the Paris Cons. He distinguished himself as an interpreter of the Classical and Romantic repertoire, but won particular notice for his championship of the music of Poulenc. **—NS/LK/DM**

Tachezi, Herbert, Austrian organist, harpsichordist, and teacher; b. Wiener Neustadt, Feb. 12, 1930. He studied organ with Alois Forer, composition with Alfred Uhl, and musicology with Otto Siegl at the Vienna Academy of Music; also attended the Univ. of Vienna. In 1958 he joined the faculty of the Vienna Academy of Music, where he taught organ and composition; in 1972 he was made a prof. there (it became the Hochschule für Musik in 1970). He appeared regularly as an organist and harpsichordist with the Concentus Musicus in Vienna from 1964; was named organist of Vienna's Hofmusikkapelle in 1974. He toured widely as a recitalist in Europe and the U.S.—**NS/LK/DM**

Tacuchian, Ricardo, Brazilian composer, conductor, and teacher; b. Rio de Janeiro, Nov. 18, 1939. He was the son of Armenian immigrants, and studied music as a child. He later earned both undergraduate and graduate degrees in piano, composition, and conducting from the Federal Univ. of Rio de Janeiro (1961, B.M. in piano; 1965, B.M. in composition), where he studied composition with José Siqueira, Francisco Mignone, and Claudio Santoro; also engaged in graduate studies there in composition and conducting in 1967–68 and studied with Stephen Hartke on a Fulbright scholarship at the Univ. of Southern Calif. (D.M.A., 1990). After giving recitals and lecturing in the U.S., he returned to Brazil and attained a reputation as a first-rate composer, conductor, and scholar. He received numerous honors; was named a Fellow of the Academia Brasileira de Música, founded by Villa-Lobos, and from 1993 to 1997 served as its 5th president. In 1998 he returned to the U.S. as a Fulbright scholar-in-residence at the State Univ. of N.Y. at Albany, where he taught courses in composition and in Brazilian music, and in 2000 he was in residence at the Bellagio Center in Italy. In the 1960s Tacuchian's works were tonal in essence, and characterized by a Brazilian folk ambience, but in the 1970s he exercised a more formal and experimental approach, including the use of aleatoric procedures. From the 1980s he has assumed a post-modern aesthetic, wherein values such as texture, density, timbre, and dynamics are set within a contrasting context of precipitous rhythms, lyric expression, and a cosmopolitan, urban flavor. In the late 1980s he brought forth the *T-System*, a form of pitch control delivered in a "nonatonic" scale, in a serial setting, and in a pitch-class set. He defended this system in a thesis in 1995, whereupon he was granted the title of full. prof. at the Federal Univ. of Rio de Janeiro.

WORKS: ORCH.: *Dia de Chuva* (1963); *Imagem Carioca* (1967); *Concertino para Flauta e Orquestra de Cordas* (1968); *Estruturas Sinfônicas* (1976); *Concertino para Piano e Orquestra de Cordas* (1977); *Núcleos* (1983); *Sinfonieta para Fátima* for Strings (1986); *Hayastan* (1990); *Terra Aberta* (1997). **CHAMBER:** 3 string quartets: No. 1, *Juvenil* (1963), No. 2, *Brasília* (1979), and No. 3 (2000); *Quinteto de Sopros* for Flute, Oboe, Clarinet, Horn, and Bassoon (1969); *Estruturas Sincréticas* for Piccolo, Clarinet, Bass Clarinet, 2 Horns, 2 Trumpets, Trombone, 4 Timpani, and 4 Groups of Percussion (1970); *Estruturas Simbólicas* for Clarinet, Trumpet, Percussion, Piano, and Viola (1973); *Estruturas Obstinadas* for Trumpet, Horn, and Trombone (1974); *Estruturas Primitivas* for Flute, Oboe, Horn, Piano, Viola, and Cello (1975); *Estruturas Verdes* for Violin, Cello, and Piano (1976); *Estruturas Divergentes* for Flute, Oboe, and Piano (1977); *Cáceres* for Percussion Ensemble (4 musicians) (1979); *Texturas* for 2 Harps (1987); *Transparências* for Vibraphone and Piano (1987); *Delaware Park Suite* for Alto Saxophone and Piano (1988); *Rio/L.A.* for English Horn, Trumpet, Horn, Trombone, Tuba, Marimba, Percussion Group, Piano, and Electric Bass Guitar (1988); *Light and Shadows* for Vibraphone, Percussion, Harp, Bass Clarinet, and Double Bass (1989); *Giga Byte* for 14 Winds and Piano Obbligato (1994); *Evocação a Lorenzo Fernandez* for Guitar and Flute (1997); *Omaggio a Mignone* for Wind Quintet and Piano (1997); *Toccata Urbana* for Woodwind Quartet, Piano, and String Quintet (1999); also numerous pieces for Solo Instruments. **Piano:** 2 sonatas (both 1966); *Estruturas Gêmeas* for Piano, 4-Hands (1978); *Capoeira* (1997); *Avenida Paulista* (1999). **VOCAL: Cantatas:** *Cantata dos Mortos* for Baritone, Narrator, Chorus, Oboe, Bassoon, Piano, Timpani, and Percussion (1965); *O Canto do Poeta* for Soprano, Violin, Flute, and Piano (1969); *Cantata de Natal* for Soprano, Baritone, Narrator, Chorus, and Orch. (1978); *Ciclo Lorca* for Baritone, Clarinet, and Strings (1979). **Other:** About 30 works for Chorus; 6 song cycles; songs for Voice and Piano. **COMPUTER:** *Prisma* (1989). **—LK/DM**

Tacuma, Jamaaladeen, bassist of diverse genres, from classical to pop; b. Hempstead, N.Y., June 11, 1956. Tacuma (McDaniel before he converted to Islam) sang doo-wop as a teenager in Philadelphia and started to play the bass at age 13, gigging in R&B bands and making his professional debut in organist Charles Earland's band while still a teenager. When he was 19, guitarist Reggie Lucas introduced him to Ornette Coleman and he was included in Ornette's groundbreaking Prime Time band from its inception, appearing on the seminal Prime Time albums *Dancing in Your Head*, *Of Human Feelings*, and *Body Meta*. His virtuosic and highly melodic style on his trademark Steinberger (headless) bass was a good fit in Coleman's democratically organized Harmolodic music, and has also made him a popular session player with everyone from Jeff Beck, Joe Cocker, Stevie Wonder, Todd Rundgren, and Nile Rodgers to James Blood Ulmer, Olu Dara, Vernon Reid, Julius Hemphill, and David Murray. The bassist even had a pop music fling of his own in the first half of the 1980s, leading the quintet Cosmetic, which released one album and a few rare singles.

Disc.: *Showstopper* (1983); *Renaissance Man* (1984); *So Tranquilizin'* (1984); *Music World* (1986); *Jukebox* (1987); *Gemini* (1987); *Boss of the Bass* (1991); *Sound Symphony* (1992); *The Night of Chamber Music* (1993); *House of Bass: The Best of Jamaaladeen Tacuma* (1994); *Dreamscape* (1996).—**DCG/SH**

Taddei, Giuseppe, noted Italian baritone; b. Genoa, June 26, 1916. He studied in Rome, where he made his debut at the Teatro Reale dell'Opera as the Herald in *Lohengrin* in 1936; sang there until he was drafted into the Italian army in 1942. After World War II, he appeared at the Vienna State Opera (1946–48); made his London debut at the Cambridge Theatre in 1947 and his Salzburg Festival debut in 1948. He sang at Milan's La Scala (1948–51; 1955–61) and at London's Covent Garden (1960–67); also appeared in San Francisco, Chicago, and other music centers. On Sept. 25, 1985, at the age of 69, he made his long-awaited debut at the Metropolitan Opera in N.Y. as Falstaff. In 1986 he appeared as Scarpia at the Vienna State Opera. He sang Falstaff in Stuttgart in 1990. He excelled in both lyrico-dramatic and buffo roles.—**NS/LK/DM**

Tadolini, Eugenia (née Savonari), noted Italian soprano; b. Forlì, 1809; d. Naples, after 1851. She received vocal training from her husband, **Giovanni Tadolini**. After making her operatic debut in Florence in 1828, she made her first appearance outside her homeland at the Paris Théâtre-Italien in Rossini's *Ricciardo e Zoraide* on Oct. 23, 1830; continued to sing in Paris until 1833. On Oct. 1, 1833, she made her debut at Milan's La Scala in Donizetti's *Il furioso all'isola di San Domingo*, and in 1834 she sang as his Adina in Vienna, returning there as his Antonina in 1836. Donizetti chose her to sing in the premiere of his *Linda di Chamounix* there on May 19, 1842, and she returned to create the title role in his *Maria di Rohan* on June 5, 1843. She was an early champion of Verdi, creating the title role in his *Alzira* in Naples (Aug. 12, 1845); returned there to sing Lady Macbeth in 1848. Verdi found her voice beautiful but was dubious about her dramatic talent. On May 20, 1848, she made her London debut in *Linda di Chamounix* at Her Majesty's Theatre. She retired from the operatic stage in 1851.—**NS/LK/DM**

Tadolini, Giovanni, Italian composer and singing teacher; b. Bologna, Oct. 18, 1785; d. there, Nov. 29, 1872. He studied composition with Mattei and singing with Babini. From 1811 to 1814 he was on the staff of the Théâtre-Italien in Paris, then returned to Italy, where he produced a succession of operas: *La fata Alcina* (Venice, 1815), *Le Bestie in uomini* (Venice, 1815), *La principessa di Navarra ossia Il Gianni di Parigi* (Bologna, 1816), *Il credulo deluso* (Rome, 1817), *Tamerlano* (Bologna, 1818), *Moctar, Gran Visir di Adrianopoli* (Bologna, 1824), *Mitridate* (Venice, 1826), and *Almanzor* (Trieste, 1827). He also composed 2 sinfonie, Concertone for Oboe, Horn, and Orch., chamber music, many sacred vocal works, and songs. From 1829 to 1839 he was again at his post at the Théâtre-Italien. He settled in Bologna in 1848 and founded his own singing school. His wife was **Eugenia Tadolini** (née **Savonari**).—**NS/LK/DM**

Taffanel, (Claude-) Paul, eminent French flutist, conductor, and pedagogue; b. Bordeaux, Sept. 16, 1844; d. Paris, Nov. 22, 1908. He was a pupil of Dorus (flute) and Reber (composition). From 1864 to 1890 he was a flutist in the Paris Opéra orch., and from 1867 to 1890, flutist of the Cons. concerts in Paris, which he conducted from 1890 to 1903. From 1892 until his death he was one of the "chefs d'orchestre" at the Paris Opéra; in 1893 he succeeded Altes as prof. of flute at the Cons. In 1879 he founded the Société des Instruments à Vent in Paris, which was active until 1892. Taffanel is considered as the father of the modern French school of flute playing. With Gaubert, he wrote *Méthode complète de flûte*. He also composed some fine chamber music for wind instruments and prepared effective arrangements for flute and piano.—**NS/LK/DM**

Tag, Christian Gotthilf, German organist and composer; b. Beierfeld, April 2, 1735; d. Niederzwönitz, near Zwönitz, June 19, 1811. From 1749 to 1755 he studied at the Kreuzschule in Dresden, and from 1755 to 1808 he was cantor at Hohenstein-Ernstthal. He wrote a large body of Kantorenmusik, winning especial esteem for his lieder and keyboard pieces.

Works: 6 chorale preludes for Organ (1783); 12 preludes and a Sym. for Organ (1794); songs (1783, 1785, 1793, 1798); 70 variations for Piano on an Andantino (1784); *Der Glaube*, melody with Organ (1793); *Urians Reise um die Welt and Urians Nachricht von der Aufklärung* (1797); *Naumann, ein Todtenopfer* (1803; Voice with Piano); *Melodie zum Vaterunser und den Einsetzungsworten* (1803; with Organ); *Wörlitz*, an ode (1803; Voice with Piano); many sacred and instrumental works in MS.

Bibl.: H. Vieweg, *C.G. T. (1735–1811) als Meister der nachbachischen Kantate* (Leipzig, 1933).—**NS/LK/DM**

Tagliabue, Carlo, noted Italian baritone; b. Mariano Comense, Jan. 12, 1898; d. Monza, April 5, 1978. He studied with Gennai and Guidotti. He made his debut as Amonasro in 1922 in Lodi. After singing in Italian provincial opera houses, he joined La Scala in Milan in 1930; continued to appear there regularly until 1943, and again from 1946 to 1953; also sang in Florence and Rome, at the Teatro Colón in Buenos Aires, and at Covent Garden in London (1938, 1946). On Dec. 2, 1937, he made his Metropolitan Opera debut in N.Y. as Amonasro; continued on its roster until 1939. He retired in 1960. He was a distinguished interpreter of Verdi and a fine Wagnerian.—**NS/LK/DM**

Tagliaferro, Magda, French pianist and pedagogue; b. Petropolis, Jan. 19, 1893; d. Rio de Janeiro, Sept. 9, 1986. She studied at the São Paulo Cons. before going to Paris to continue her training at the Cons. there (graduated with a premier prix, 1907); also received private lessons from Cortot. In 1908 she launched her concert career and also was active as a teacher; after teaching a master class at the Paris Cons. (1937–39), she pursued her career in the Americas; from 1949 she was again active in Paris. Her concert career lasted for over 75 years; she made numerous appearances in recitals in the U.S., the last one in 1980; gave a London recital in 1983 at the age of 90. In her prime, she was known for her sensitive readings of the French repertoire; she also gave the premiere of Villa-Lobos's *Momoprecoce* for Piano and Orch. (1929).—**NS/LK/DM**

Tagliafico, (Dieudonné) Joseph, distinguished French bass-baritone; b. Toulon, Jan. 1, 1821; d. Nice, Jan. 27, 1900. He studied with Piermarini and Lablache in Paris, making his debut there in 1844 at the Théâtre-Italien. In 1847 he joined the new Royal Italian Opera company at Covent Garden in London, remaining on its roster until 1876; then was its stage manager until 1882. He appeared as a guest artist in France, Russia, and the U.S. He was best known for his French and Italian roles. —**NS/LK/DM**

Tagliapietra, Gino, Italian pianist, teacher, and composer; b. Ljubljana, May 30, 1887; d. Venice, Aug. 8, 1954. He studied piano with Julius Epstein in Vienna and with Busoni in Berlin. In 1906 he was appointed to the faculty of the Liceo Benedetto Marcello in Venice; retired in 1940. His compositions include a fiaba musicale, *La bella addormentata* (Venice, March 11, 1926), Piano Concerto (1913), *Variazioni a fantasia* for Piano and Strings (1930), *Requiem* (1923), and various choral works, Violin Sonata (1937), songs, many piano pieces, and various didactic works. He ed. *Antologia di musica antica e moderna per il pianoforte* (Milan, 1931–32) and *Raccolta di composizioni dei secoli XVI e XVII* (Milan, 1937).

BIBL.: F. Vadala, *G. T.* (diss., Univ. of Messina, 1976). —**NS/LK/DM**

Tagliapietra, Giovanni, Italian baritone; b. Venice, Dec. 24, 1846; d. N.Y., April 11, 1921. He studied naval architecture and graduated from the Univ. of Padua. After a study of singing with Giovanni Corsi, he appeared in various Italian opera houses. He made a tour of South America, and in 1874 was engaged as member of Max Strakosch's company and sang in the U.S. In 1876 he married **(Maria) Teresa Carreño**, but they divorced.—**NS/LK/DM**

Tagliavini, Ferruccio, prominent Italian tenor; b. Reggio Emilia, Aug. 14, 1913; d. there, Jan. 28, 1995. He received his training from Brancucci in Parma and Bassi in Florence. In 1938 he won 1st prize for voice at the Maggio Musicale in Florence, where he made his operatic debut as Rodolfo in Oct. of that year. He then sang in various Italian opera houses. In 1942 he became a member of Milan's La Scala, where he sang with distinction until 1953. In 1946 he toured South America and made his U.S. operatic debut as Rodolfo in Chicago. He made his Metropolitan Opera debut in N.Y. on Jan. 10, 1947, again as Rodolfo, and remained on its roster until 1954. In 1961–62 he was again on the roster of the Metropolitan Opera. Among the roles he sang there were Count Almaviva, Edgardo, the Duke of Mantua, Alfredo, Cavaradossi, and Nemorino. In 1948–49 and again in 1952 he appeared at the San Francisco Opera. In 1950 he sang Nemorino with the visiting La Scala company at London's Covent Garden, and returned there in 1955–56. After retiring from the operatic stage as Werther in Venice in 1965, he made some appearances as a concert artist. In 1941 he married **Pia Tassinari.**

BIBL.: U. Bonafini, *F. T.: L'uomo, la voce* (Reggio Emilia, 1993); P. Pellizzari, ed., *Musicus perfectus: Studi in onore di L.F. T.: Prattico e specolativo nella ricorrenza del 65. compleanno* (Bologna, 1995).—**NS/LK/DM**

Tagliavini, Luigi Ferdinando, distinguished Italian organist, harpsichordist, and musicologist; b. Bologna, Oct. 7, 1929. He studied organ at the Bologna Cons. and with Marcel Dupré at the Paris Cons. (1947–52); also studied at the Univ. of Padua, receiving his Ph.D. there in 1951 with the diss. *Studi sui testi delle cantate sacre J.S. Bach* (publ. in Padua, 1956). He taught organ at the G.B. Martini Cons. in Bologna (1952–54); also was head of its library (1953–60); concurrently he served as a prof. of organ at the Monteverdi Cons. in Bolzano (1954–64); from 1964 he was on the faculty of the Parma Cons. In 1959 he joined the staff of the Univ. of Bologna; from 1965 he taught music history at the Univ. of Fribourg. With R. Lunelli, he founded the journal *L'organo* in 1960; also served as ed. of Monumenti di Musica Italiana. He is an authority on organ restoration. With O. Mischiati, he ed. *Un anonimo trattato francese di arte organaria del sec. XVIII* (Bologna, 1974). —**NS/LK/DM**

Täglichsbeck, Thomas, German violinist and composer; b. Ansbach, Dec. 31, 1799; d. Baden-Baden, Oct. 5, 1867. He became a violinist in the Isarthortheater orch. in 1817, and in 1819 its music director. In 1822 he was made solo violinist to the Munich court; also toured in Switzerland and Italy. He was named Kapellmeister to Prince Hohenlohe-Hechingen in 1827, and continued to serve his successor Prince Constantine (1838–48); when the latter reorganized his Court Orch. in Lowenberg in 1852, Täglichsbeck resumed his duties, retiring in 1857. He then taught at the Dresden Cons. until 1859.

WORKS: DRAMATIC: Opera: *Webers Bild* (Munich, Aug. 24, 1823); *König Enzio* (Karlsruhe, May 14, 1843); *Guido oder Das Jägerhaus im Walde Sila* (not perf.). **ORCH:** 2 syms.; 2 concertinos for Violin and Orch.; Fantasia for Violin and Orch. **CHAMBER:** Quintet for Clarinet and Strings; 3 string quartets; Piano Trio; 3 sonatas for Violin and Piano; Concert Piece for Viola and Piano; 5 duets for 2 Violins. **VOCAL:** Mass for Solo Voices, Chorus, Orch., and Organ; songs.

BIBL.: E. Burmester, *T. T. und seine Instrumental- Kompositionen* (diss., Univ. of Munich, 1936).—**NS/LK/DM**

Taglietti, Giulio, Italian violinist, teacher, and composer; b. Brescia, c. 1660; d. there, 1718. He may have been the brother of Luigi Taglietti. He pursued his career in Brscia, where he taught at the Jesuit Collegio dei Nobili from about 1702. Taglietti was a notable composer of concertos and sonatas. He publ. 13 vols. of instrumental music (1695–1715), of which 6 are extant. —**LK/DM**

Taglietti, Luigi, Italian trumpet marine player, teacher, and composer; b. 1668; d. probably in Brescia, 1715. He may have been the brother of Giulio Taglietti. From about 1697 he was active at the Jesuit Collegio dei Nobili in Brescia. He played a significant role in the development of the concerto and sonata. He publ. 6 vols. of instrumental music (1697–1709), of which 2 are extant.—**LK/DM**

Tagore, Sir Surindro Mohun (actually, **Rajah Saurindramohana Thakura**), Hindu musicologist; b. Calcutta, 1840; d. there, June 5, 1914. At the age of 17 he began to study Hindu music under Luchmi Prasad Misra and Kshetra Mohun Goswami, and European music under two European mentors. He founded and endowed from his personal fortune the Bengal Music School (1871) and the Bengal Academy of Music (1882), continuing to preside over both until his death. A connoisseur of Eastern instrumentation, he was at various times commissioned by the principal museums of Europe to procure for them instruments of Asiatic nations. He wrote nearly 60 books on an amazing variety of subjects; those concerning music (publ. in Calcutta, in Bengali, and some in Eng.) include *Yantra Kosha, or A Treasury of the Musical Instruments of Ancient and Modern India* (1875), *Hindu Music, from Various Authors* (1875; 2nd ed., in 2 vols., 1882), *Six Principal Ragas, with a Brief View of Hindu Music* (1876; 3rd ed., 1884), *Short Notices of Hindu Musical Instruments* (1877), *The 8 Principal Ragas of the Hindus* (1880), *The Five Principal Musicians of the Hindus, or A Brief Exposition of the Essential Elements of Hindu Music* (1881), *The Musical Scales of the Hindus with Remarks on the Applicability of Harmony to Hindu Music* (1884), *The 22 Musical Srutis of the Hindus* (1886), and *Universal History of Music, together with Various Original Notes on Hindu Music* (1896).

BIBL.: *Visvapati Caudhur: Songs and Addresses in Memory of the Late Raja Sir Saurindramohana Thakura* (Calcutta, 1919). —**NS/LK/DM**

Tailleferre (real name, **Taillefesse**), **(Marcelle) Germaine,** fine French composer; b. Parc-St.-Maur, near Paris, April 19, 1892; d. Paris, Nov. 7, 1983. She studied harmony and solfège with H. Dallier (premier prix, 1913), counterpoint with G. Caussade (premier prix, 1914), and accompaniment with Estyle at the Paris Cons., and also had some informal lessons with Ravel. She received recognition as the only female member of the group of French composers known as Les Six (the other members were Honegger, Milhaud, Poulenc, Auric, and Durey). Her style of composition was pleasingly, teasingly modernistic and feministic (Jean Cocteau invoked a comparison with a young French woman painter, Marie Laurencin, saying that Tailleferre's music was to the ear what the painter's pastels were to the eye). Indeed, most of her works possess a fragile charm of unaffected *joie de jouer la musique*. She was married to an American author, Ralph Barton, in 1926, but soon divorced him and married a French lawyer, Jean Lageat. She visited the U.S. in 1927 and again in 1942. In 1974 she publ. an autobiographical book, *Mémoires dè l'emporte piece*.

WORKS: DRAMATIC: *Le Marchand d'oiseaux*, ballet (Paris, May 25, 1923); *Paris-Magie*, ballet (Paris, June 3, 1949); *Dolorès*, operetta (1950); *Il était un petit navire*, lyric satire (Paris, March 1951); *Parfums*, musical comedy (1951); *Parisiana*, opéra-comique (1955); *Monsieur Petit Pois achète un château*, opéra bouffe (1955); *Le Bel ambitieux*, opéra bouffe (1955); *La Pauvre Eugénie*, opéra bouffe (1955); *La Fille d'opéra*, opéra bouffe (1955); *La Petite Sirène*, chamber opera (1957); *Mémoires d'une bergère*, opéra bouffe (1959); *Le Maître*, chamber opera (1959). **ORCH.:** Piano Concerto (1919); Harp Concertino (1926; Cambridge, Mass., March 3, 1927); *Overture* (Paris, Dec. 25, 1932); Concertino for Flute, Piano, and Orch. (1952); *La Guirlande de Campra* (1952). **CHAMBER:** *Image* for Piano, Flute, Clarinet, String Quartet, and Celesta (1918); *Jeux de plein air* for 2 Pianos (1918); String Quartet (1918); 2 violin sonatas (1921, 1951); *Pastorale* for Violin and Piano (1921); *Pastorale* for Flute and Piano (1939); Harp Sonata (1954); *Partita* for 2 Pianos and Percussion (1964); *4 Pièces* for Flute, Oboe, Clarinet, Trumpet, and Piano (1973). **VOCAL:** *Chansons françaises* for Voice and Instruments (Liège, Sept. 2, 1930); Concerto for 2 Pianos, Voice, and Orch. (Paris, May 3, 1934); *Cantate du Narcisse* for Voice and Orch. (1937); Concertino for Soprano and Orch. (1953); *Concerto des vaines paroles* for Baritone and Orch. (1956).

BIBL.: J. Roy, *Le groupe des six: Poulenc, Milhaud, Honegger, Auric, T., Durey* (Paris, 1994); R. Shapiro, *G. T.: A Bio-Bibliography* (Westport, Conn., 1994); G. Hacquard, *G. T.: La dame des six* (Paris, 1999).—**NS/LK/DM**

Tajćević, Marko, Serbian choral conductor, music critic, teacher, and composer; b. Osijek, Jan. 29, 1900; d. Belgrade, July 19, 1984. He studied in Zagreb, Prague, and Vienna. In 1945 he was appointed a prof. at the Belgrade Academy of Music, retiring in 1966. He was primarily a folklore composer and was at his best in his sacred and secular choral works derived from regional folk songs. He also wrote songs and piano pieces, including *7 Balkan Dances* for Piano (1927), a set of brilliant stylizations of Serbian melorhythms.

BIBL.: D. Despić, *M. T.* (Belgrade, 1972).—**NS/LK/DM**

Tajo, Italo, Italian bass and teacher; b. Pinerolo, April 25, 1915; d. Cincinnati, March 29, 1993. He studied at the Turin Cons. He made his operatic debut as Fafner at the Teatro Regio in Turin in 1935; then was a member of the Rome Opera (1939–48) and of La Scala in Milan (1940–41; 1946–56). He made his U.S. debut in Chicago in 1946. On Dec. 28, 1948, he appeared at the Metropolitan Opera in N.Y. as Don Basilio in *Il Barbiere di Siviglia;* remained on its roster until 1950; also sang with the San Francisco Opera (1948–50; 1952–53; 1956); then appeared on Broadway and in films. In 1966 he was appointed prof. at the Univ. of Cincinnati Coll.-Cons. of Music. He returned to the Metropolitan Opera after an absence of 30 years in 1980, and delighted audiences in buffo roles; made his operatic farewell there as the Sacristan in *Tosca* on April 20, 1991. He was equally adept in dramatic and buffo roles from the standard repertory, and also proved himself an intelligent interpreter in contemporary operas by Milhaud, Malipiero, Pizzetti, and Nono.—**NS/LK/DM**

Takács, Jenő, Hungarian pianist, ethnomusicologist, teacher, and composer; b. Siegendorf, Sept. 25, 1902. He studied composition with Marx and Gál at the Vienna Cons. He taught at the Cairo Cons. (1927–32) and at the Univ. of the Philippines (1932–34), and pursued ethnological research in the Philippines before again teaching in Cairo (1934–36). From 1940 to 1942 he taught at the Music School at Szombathely. He then was director of the Pécs Cons. (1942–48). After teaching piano at the Univ. of Cincinnati Coll.-Cons. of Music (1952–71), he retired to his birthplace. In 1962 he was awarded the Austrian State Prize. Reflecting his background of travel and residence in many different countries, his music contains elements of Hungarian, oriental, American, and cosmopolitan idioms.

WORKS: DRAMATIC: Ballet: *Nile Legend* (1937–39; Budapest, May 8, 1940); *Narcissus* (1939); *The Songs of Silence* (1967). **ORCH.:** 2 piano concertos (1932, 1937); *Philippine Suite* (1934); *Tarantella* for Piano and Orch. (1937); *Antiqua Hungarica* (1941); *Partita* for Guitar and Orch. (1950). **CHAMBER:** *Gumbri,* oriental rhapsody for Violin and Piano (1930); Trombone Sonata (1957); Wind Quintet (1961–62); *Homage to Pan* for 4 Pianos (1968); *Essays in Sound* for Clarinet (1968); *2 Fantastics* for Alto Saxophone and Piano (1969); *Musica reservata* for Double Bass and Piano (1969); *Tagebuch-Fragmente* for 2 Pianos (1973); Octet (1974–75).—**NS/LK/DM**

Takahashi, Aki, innovative Japanese pianist, sister of **Yuji Takahashi;** b. Kakamura, Sept. 6, 1944. She studied first with her mother, then with Yutaka Ito, (Miss) Ray Lev, and George Vásárhelyi at the Tokyo Univ. of the Arts (M.A., 1969). She made her public debut in Tokyo in 1970; her European debut followed in 1972. While acknowledged for her classical musicianship, she is particularly lauded for her imaginative interpretations of contemporary music; among the composers who have written works for her are Cage, Rzewski, Yuasa, Feldman, and Satoh. Her recording career is also distinguished; her *Aki Takahashi Piano Space* (20 works, including those by Berio, Boulez, Cage, Stockhausen, Webern et al.) earned her the Merit Prize at the Japan Art Festival in 1973. Her series of Satie concerts performed in Tokyo (1975–77) heralded the so-called "Satie Boom" in Japan and resulted in her editing and recording the composer's complete piano works; other noteworthy recordings include *Triadic Memories* (Feldman), *Planetary Folklore* (Mamoru Fujieda), *Eonta* (Xenakis), and *L'Histoire de Babar* (Poulenc). Her *Hyper Beatles* (1990–) features arrangements of Beatles songs by internationally recognized composers. In addition to performing throughout Europe, Japan, and the U.S., Takahashi also devoted time to teaching; she was artist-in-residence at the State Univ. of N.Y. at Buffalo (1980–81) and a guest prof. at the Calif. Inst. of the Arts in Valencia (1984). She received the 1st Kenzo Nakajima prize (1982) and the 1st Kyoto Music Award (1986). In 1983 she became director of the "New Ears" concert series in Yokohama.—**NS/LK/DM**

Takahashi, Yuji, Japanese composer and pianist, brother of **Aki Takahashi;** b. Tokyo, Sept. 21, 1938. He studied composition with Shibata and Ogura at the Toho School of Music in Tokyo (1954–58), then went to Berlin and trained in electronics as a student of Xenakis (1963–65); also studied computer music in N.Y. and attended the summer courses at the Berkshire Music Center at Tanglewood (1966–68). He was a member of the Center for Creative and Performing Arts at the State Univ. of N.Y. in Buffalo (1968–69). In his music, he follows the stochastic procedures as practiced by Xenakis. He also has acquired considerable renown as a pianist in programs of avant-garde music.

WORKS: *Phonogène* for 2 Instruments and Tape (1962); *Chromamorphe I* for Violin, Double Bass, Flute, Trumpet, Horn, Trombone, and Vibraphone (1963) and *II* for Piano (1964); *6 Stoicheia (Elements in Succession)* for 4 Violins (1965); *Bridges I* for Electric Harpsichord or Piano, Amplified Cello, Bass Drum, and Castanets (1967) and *II* for 2 Oboes, 2 Clarinets, 2 Trumpets, and 3 Violas (1968); *Rosace I* for Amplified Violin (1967) and *II* for Piano (1967); *Operation Euler* for 2 or 3 Oboes (1967); *Metathèse* for Piano (1968); *Prajna Paramita* for 4 Voices, each in one of 4 Instrumental Ensembles (1969); *Orphika* for Orch. (Tokyo, May 28, 1969); *Yé Guèn* for Tape (1969); *Nikité* for Oboe, Clarinet, Trumpet, Trombone, Cello, and Double Bass (1971); *Kagahi* for Piano and 30 Instruments (Ojai, Calif., May 30, 1971); *Michi-Yuki* for Chorus, 2 Percussionists, and Electric Cello (1971); *Corona Borealis* for Piccolo, Oboe, Clarinet, Bassoon, and Horn (1971); *Tadori* for Tape (1972).—**NS/LK/DM**

Takase, Aki, pianist who draws from the broadest palette to include elements from the Japanese musical tradition as well as from European Classical music; b. Osaka, Japan, Jan. 26, 1948. Aki Takase received her earliest piano training from her mother, a piano teacher, who gave her daughter classical lessons from the age of three. She also played acoustic bass in an all-woman band in high school, and after graduation studied piano at Tohogakuen Univ. of Tokyo. Inspired by recordings of Charles Mingus, Ornette Coleman, and John Coltrane, she began learning on her own how to improvise. She got her first professional gigs in 1971 and by age 25 was leading her own groups. She recorded with saxophonist Dave Liebman in the early 1980s, and appeared with her trio at the Berlin festival. She has worked with artists such as Cecil McBee, Sheila Jordan, and Bob Moses, and a solo piano concert at the East-West Festival in Nuremberg brought her critical acclaim. She played regularly in a duo with Maria Joao from 1988–94, and maintained a busy touring schedule. During the mid-1990s, she toured with Rashed Ali and Reggie Workman (a trio which yielded the recording *Clapping Music*), formed a septet, and recorded with the Toki String Quartet, as well as working as a solo performer. She also plays the koto, a traditional Japanese 17-string, zither-like instrument, but it is her unmatched, multifarious piano performances and her skills as composer-arranger that rank her as a top innovator among her contemporaries.

DISC.: *Perdido* (1982); *Shima Shoka* (1990); *Close Up of Japan* (1993); *Looking for Love* (1993); *Blue Monk* (1994); *Clapping Music* (1995); *Oriental Express* (1996).—**NAL**

Takata, Saburô, Japanese composer and teacher; b. Nagoya, Dec. 18, 1913. He studied with Nobutkoki and Pringsheim at the Tokyo Music School (graduated, 1939). He was a prof. at the Kunitachi Music Coll. in Tokyo (from 1953), and also served as president of the Japanese Society for Contemporary Music (1963–68).

WORKS: DRAMATIC: Opera: *Aoki-ōkami* (The Dark Blue Wolf; 1970–72; Tokyo, Oct. 15, 1972). **ORCH.:** *Ballade Based on a Folk Song from Yamagata (Fantasy and Fugue)* (Tokyo, Nov. 15, 1941; rev. 1965); Seasons, suite (1942); *Ballade* for Violin and Orch. (1943; Tokyo, Jan. 13, 1945); *The New Earth and Man* (1944); *2 Rhapsodies* (both 1945). **CHAMBER:** Octet for Clarinet, Bassoon, Horn, Trumpet, and String Quartet (1939); *Prelude and Fugue* for String Quartet (1940); Violin Sonata (1948–49); Cello Sonatina (1949–50); Suite for Flute, Oboe, 2 Clarinets, and Bassoon (1951); *Marionette*, suite for String Quartet (1954); *Fantasy* for String Quartet (1968). **KEYBOARD: Piano:** 2 sonatas (1935, 1941); *5 Preludes* (1947). **Organ:** Various pieces. **VOCAL:** *Wordless Tears*, cantata for Narrator, Soprano, Baritone, Chorus, and Orch. (Tokyo, March 27, 1964); choruses; songs.—**NS/LK/DM**

Takeda, Yoshimi, Japanese conductor; b. Yokohama, Feb. 3, 1933. He was educated at the Tokyo Univ. of the Arts (graduated, 1958); then went to the U.S. on a fellowship to work with George Szell and the Cleveland Orch. (1962–64). In 1964 he became assoc. conductor of the Honolulu Sym. Orch.; in 1970 he was appointed music director of the Albuquerque (later N.Mex.) Sym. Orch., a position he held until 1985; in addition, he was music director of the Kalamazoo Sym. Orch. (from 1974). He also appeared as a guest conductor with major orchs. in North America, Europe, and Japan.
—**NS/LK/DM**

Takemitsu, Tōru, outstanding Japanese composer; b. Tokyo, Oct. 8, 1930; d. there, Feb. 20, 1996. He received training in composition from Yasuji Kiyosi in Tokyo (1948), but was principally autodidact as a composer. In 1951 he helped to found the Jikken-Kb (Experimental Workshop), a group of composers, painters, performers, and poets, with which he remained active until it was disbanded in 1957. Takemitsu's *Requiem* for Strings, first performed in Tokyo on June 20, 1957, revealed him to be a composer of great promise. In 1958 he was awarded the Prix Italia for his *Tableau Noir* for Speaker and Chamber Orch. He received the prize of the International Rostrum of Composers of UNESCO in Paris in 1965 for his *Textures* for Piano and Orch. A Rockefeller Foundation grant enabled him to visit North America in 1967, during which sojourn his *November Steps* for Biwa, Shakuhachi, and Orch. was premiered in N.Y. (Nov. 9, 1967). Takemitsu served as artistic director of the Space Theater of the Steel Pavilion at Expo '70 in Osaka in 1970. In 1971 he was composer-in-residence at the Marlboro (Vt.) Music School and Festival. He was a visiting prof. at Harvard Univ. in 1973, and then at Yale Univ. in 1975. From 1973 to 1992 he was artistic director of the "Music Tody" festival in Tokyo. Takemitsu was composer-in-residence at the Aldeburgh Festival in 1984, at the Leeds Festival in 1990, at the Berlin Festival in 1993, and at many other festivals around the world. His works were also featured in various venues at home and abroad. In 1995 he was named artistic director of the Tokyo Opera City Cultural Foundation.

Takemitsu was the recipient of numerous honors. In 1979 he was made an honorary member of the Akademie der Künste in East Berlin, in 1985 he was awarded the Ordre des Arts et des Lettres by the French government, in 1986 he was named an honorary member of the Academie des Beaux-Arts of France, and in 1994 he was made an honorary member of the Royal Academy of Music in London. In 1990 he was awarded the Prix International Maurice Ravel, as well as honorary doctorates from the univs. of Leeds and Durham. He received the Grawemeyer Award of the Univ. of Louisville in 1994 for his *Fantasma/Cantos* for Clarinet and Orch. In Feb. 1996, just days before his lamented death, he was honored with the Glenn Gould Prize of Canada. A book of his selected writings was tr. by Y. Kakudo and G. Glasow as *Confronting Silence* (Berkeley, 1995). In his music, Takemitsu demonstrated a mastery in combining the refined craftsmanship of oriental music with the innovative usages of Western avant-garde music.

WORKS: DRAMATIC: *Blue Aurora for Toshi Ichiyanagi*, "event musical" (1964); *Wavelength* for 2 Percussion Players and 2 Dancers with Video Installation (Tokyo, June 1984); over 90 film scores, including *Woman in the Dunes* (1964). **ORCH.:** *Requiem* for Strings (1957; Tokyo, June 20, 1958); *Solitude sonore* (NHK, Nov. 2, 1958); *Scene* for Cello and Strings (NHK, Dec. 1959); *Ki No Kyoku* (Music of Trees; 1961); *Arc I* (1963) and *II* (1964–66) for Piano and Orch.; *Arc* for Strings (1963; from the 3rd movement of *Arc I*); *Textures* for Piano and Orch. (1964; 1st movement of *Arc II*); *The Dorain Horizon* for 17 Strings (1966; San Francisco, Feb. 1967); *November Steps* for Biwa, Shakuhachi, and Orch. (N.Y., Nov. 9, 1967); *Green* (*November Steps II*) (Tokyo, Nov. 3, 1967); *Asterism* for Piano and Orch. (1968; Toronto, Jan. 14, 1969); *Eucalypts I* for Flute, Oboe, Harp, and Strings (Tokyo, Nov. 16, 1970); *Winter* (Paris, Oct. 29, 1971); *Corona* for 22 Strings (1971); *Cassiopeia* for Solo Percussion and Orch. (Chicago, July 8, 1971); *Gémeaux* for Oboe, Trombone, and 2 Orchs. with separate conductors (1971–86; Tokyo, Oct. 15, 1986); *Autumn* for Biwa, Shakuhachi, and Orch. (1973); *Gitimalya* (Bouquet of Songs) for Marimba and Orch. (Rotterdam, Nov. 1975); *Quatrain* for Violin, Cello, Clarinet, Piano, and Orch. (Tokyo, Sept. 1, 1975); *Marginalia* (Tokyo, Oct. 20, 1976); *A Flock Descends into the Pentagonal Garden* (San Francisco, Nov. 30, 1977); *In an Autumn Garden* for Gagaku Orch. (Tokyo, Sept. 28, 1979); *Far calls: Coming, far!* for Violin and Orch. (Tokyo, May 24, 1980); *Dreamtime* (1981; Sapporo, June 27, 1982; ballet version, The Hague, May 5, 1983); *Toward the Sea II* for Alto Flute, Harp, and Strings (1981;

Sapporo, June 27, 1982); *A Way a Lone II* for Strings (1981; Sapporo, June 27, 1982); *Star Isle* (Tokyo, Oct. 21, 1982); *Rain Coming* for Chamber Orch. (London, Oct. 26, 1982); *To the Edge of Dream* for Guitar and Orch. (Liège, March 12, 1983); *Orion and Pleiades* for Cello and Orch. (Paris, May 27, 1984); *Vers, l'arc-en-ciel, Palma* for Guitar, Oboe d'amore, Guitar, and Orch. (Birmingham, England, Oct. 2, 1984); *riverrun* for Piano and Orch. (1984; Los Angeles, Jan. 10, 1985); *Dream/Window* (Kyoto, Sept. 9, 1985); *I Hear the Water Dreaming* for Flute and Orch. (Indianapolis, April 3, 1987); *Nostalgia—In Memory of Andrei Tarkovsky* for Violin and Strings (Edinburgh, Aug. 11, 1987); *Twill by Twilight—In Memory of Morton Feldman* (Tokyo, March 8, 1988); *Tree Line* for Chamber Orch. (London, May 20, 1988); A *String Around Autumn* for Viola and Orch. (Paris, Nov. 29, 1989); *From me flows what you call Time* for Percussion Quintet and Orch. (N.Y., Oct. 19, 1990); *Visions* (Chicago, March 8, 1990); *Fantasma/Cantos I* for Clarinet and Orch. (Cardiff, Sept. 14, 1991) and *II* for Trombone and Orch. (St. Paul, June 3, 1994); *Quotation of Dream* for 2 Pianos and Orch. (London, Oct. 13, 1991); *How slow the Wind* (Glasgow, Nov. 6, 1991); *Ceremonial* for Shō and Orch. (Matsumoto, Sept. 5, 1992); *Archipelago S.* (Aldeburgh, June 18, 1993); *Spirit Garden* (Tokyo, July 14, 1994); *Spectral Canticle* for Violin, Guitar, and Orch. (Kiel, June 27, 1995). **CHAMBER:** *Distance de Fée* for Violin and Piano (Tokyo, Nov. 1951; rev. 1989); *Le Son Calligraphié I-III* for Double String Quartet (1958, 1958, 1963); *Masque* for 2 Flutes (1959); *Landscape* for String Quartet (1960); *Ring* for Flute, Terz-guitar, and Lute (1961); *Sacrifice* for Alto Flute, Lute, and Vibraphone (1962); *Valeria* for Violin, Cello, Guitar, Electric Organ, and 2 Piccolos obbligato (1962; Tokyo, Nov. 1965); *Hika* for Violin and Piano (1966); *Eclipse* for Biwa and Shakuhachi (1966); *Cross Talk* for 2 Bandoneons and Tape (1968); *Stanza II* for Harp and Tape (1971) and *III* for Harp (1970); *Seasons* for 1 or 4 Percussionists (1970); *Voice* for Flute (1971); *Munari by Munari* for Percussion (1972); *Distance* for Oboe or Oboe and Shō (1972); *Voyage* for 3 Biwa (1973); *Folios* for Guitar (1974); *Garden Rain* for 4 Trumpets, 3 Trombones, Bass Trombone, Horn, and Tuba (1974); *Waves* for Clarinet, Horn, 2 Trumpets, and Percussion (1976); *Bryce* for Flute, 2 Harps, Marimba, and Percussion (1976); *Quatrain II* for Clarinet, Violin, Cello, and Piano (1976); *Waterways* for Piano, Clarinet, Violin, Cello, 2 Harps, and 2 Vibraphones (1978); *A Way a Lone* for String Quartet (1980; N.Y., Feb. 23, 1981); *Toward the Sea* for Alto Flute and Guitar (Tokyo, May 31, 1981); *Rain Tree* for 3 Percussionists or 3 Keyboard Players (Tokyo, May 31, 1981); *Rain Spell* for Flute, Clarinet, Harp, Piano, and Vibraphone (1982; Yokohama, Jan. 19, 1983); *Rocking Mirror Daybreak* for Violin Duo (N.Y., Nov. 17, 1983); *From far Beyond Chrysanthemums and November Fog* for Violin and Piano (Tokyo, Dec. 1983); *Orion* for Cello and Piano (Vienna, March 21, 1984); *Entre-temps* for Oboe and String Quartet (Tokyo, May 12, 1986); *All in Twilight* for Guitar (1987; N.Y., Oct. 9, 1988); *Signals from Heaven*, 2 antiphonal fanfares for Chamber Ensemble: *I: Day Signal* (Tokyo, July 25, 1987) and *II: Night Signal* (Glasgow, Sept. 14, 1987); *Itinerant* for Flute (N.Y., Feb. 7, 1989); *And then I knew 'twas Wind* for Flute, Viola, and Harp (Mito, May 19, 1992); *Between Tides* for Violin, Cello, and Piano (Berlin, Sept. 20, 1993); *Equinox* for Guitar (1993; Tokyo, April 4, 1994); *Paths—In Memoriam Witold Lutosławski* for Trumpet (Warsaw, Sept. 21, 1994); *A Bird came down the Walk* for Viola and Piano (1994; Vienna, Oct. 29, 1995); *In the Woods* for Guitar (1995; Tokyo, Oct. 15, 1996); *Air* for Flute (1995; Oberwil, Jan. 28, 1996). **KEYBOARD: Piano:** *Lento in Due Movimenti* (1950); *Uninterrupted Rest* (1952–59); *Piano Distance* (1961); *Corona* for Pianist(s) (1962); *For Away* (1973); *Les Yeux clos I* (1979) and *II* (1988; N.Y., Nov. 11, 1989); *Rain Tree Sketch I* (1981; Tokyo, Jan. 14, 1983) and *II: In memoriam Olivier Messiaen* (Orléans, Oct. 24, 1992); *Litany, in memory of Michael Vyner* (1989; London, May 6, 1990). **Harpsichord:** *Rain Dreaming* (Washington, D.C., June 12, 1986). **VOCAL:** *Tableau noir* for Narrator and Orch. (NHK, July 1958); *Wind Horse* for Chorus (1961–66; Tokyo, Oct. 14, 1966); *Coral Island* for Soprano and Orch. (1962); *Stanza I* for Guitar, Harp, Piano, Vibraphone, and Woman's Voice (1968); *Crossing* for 12 Women's Voices, Guitar, Harp, Piano, Vibraphone, and 2 Orchs. (1969); *Grass* for Men's Chorus (Tokyo, Dec. 1982); *Uta* for Chorus (1983); *Handmade Proverbs–4 pop songs* for 6 Men's Voices (Tokyo, Jan. 23, 1987); *My Way of Life* for Baritone, Chorus, and Orch. (Leeds, June 30, 1990); *Family Tree* for Narrator and Orch. (1992; N.Y., April 20, 1995). **TAPE:** *Sky, Horse and Death* (1958; San Francisco, Jan. 1960); *Static Relief* (1955; Tokyo, Feb. 1956); *Vocalism A–1* (1956); *Water Music* (1960); *Quiet Design* (1960); *Kwaidan* (1966; rev. of music from the film); *Toward* (1970); *A Minneapolis Garden* (Minneapolis, March 1986); *The Sea is Still* (San Diego, May 7, 1986).

BIBL.: N. Ohtake, *Creative Sources for the Music of T. T.* (Aldershot, 1993).—**NS/LK/DM**

Taktakishvili, Otar (Vasilievich), Russian composer and teacher; b. Tiflis, July 27, 1924; d. there (Tbilisi), Feb. 22, 1989. He studied at the Tbilisi Cons., graduating in 1947. He then was on its faculty as a teacher of choral literature (from 1947) and of counterpoint and instrumentation (from 1959), serving as its rector (1962–65); was a prof. (from 1966). In 1974 he was made a People's Artist of the U.S.S.R. In 1982 he was awarded the Lenin Prize. His music is imbued with the characteristic melorhythms of the Caucasus; he had a natural knack for instrumental color.

WORKS: DRAMATIC: Opera: *Mindia* (Tbilisi, July 23, 1961); *Sami novela* (3 Stories; 1967); *Chikor* (1972); *Mtvaris Motatseba* (The Abduction of the Moon; 1976). **Film:** Various works. **ORCH.:** Cello Concerto (1947); 2 syms. (1949, 1953); 3 overtures (1950, 1951, 1955); 2 symphonic poems: *Samgori* (1950) and *Mtsyri* (1956); 2 piano concertos: No. 1 (Tbilisi, Nov. 15, 1951) and No. 2 (1973); Trumpet Concerto (1954); *Humoresque* for Chamber Orch. (1963). **OTHER:** Oratorios; cantatas; choruses; songs; piano pieces.

BIBL.: L. Polyakova, *O. T.* (Moscow, 1956); L.V. Polyakova, *O. T.* (Moscow, 1979).—**NS/LK/DM**

Taktakishvili, Shalva (Mikhailovich), Russian conductor, teacher, and composer; b. Kvemo-Khviti, Aug. 27, 1900; d. Tbilisi, July 18, 1965. He studied at the Tiflis Cons. He then taught theory at the Batumi Music School, of which he was a co-founder; then served as conductor at Tbilisi Radio. From 1952 to his death he conducted the Georgian State Orch.

WORKS: DRAMATIC: Opera: *Rassvet* (Sunrise; 1923); *Deputat* (The Delegate; 1939); *Otarova vdnova* (1942). **ORCH.:** *The Year 1905*, symphonic poem (1931); Cello Concerto (1932); 2 overtures (1944, 1949). **CHAMBER:** 2 string quartets (1930, 1933); Violin Sonata (1952); numerous piano pieces. **VOCAL:** Choruses; songs.

BIBL.: P. Hukua, *S. T.* (Tbilisi, 1962).—**NS/LK/DM**

Tal, Josef (real name, **Joseph Gruenthal**), prominent German-born Israeli composer, pianist, conductor, and pedagogue; b. Pinne, near Posen, Sept. 18,

1910. He took courses with Tiessen, Hindemith, Sachs, Trapp, and others at the Berlin Staatliche Hochschule für Musik (1928–30). In 1934 he emigrated to Palestine, settling in Jerusalem as a teacher of piano and composition at the Cons. in 1936; when it became the Israel Academy of Music in 1948, he served as its director (until 1952). Tal also lectured at the Hebrew Univ. (from 1950), where he was head of the musicology dept. (1965–70) and a prof. (from 1971). He likewise was director of the Israel Center of Electronic Music (from 1961). He appeared as a pianist and conductor with the Israel Phil. and with orchs. in Europe. In 1971 he was awarded the State of Israel Prize and was made an honorary member of the West Berlin Academy of Arts, in 1975 he received the Arts Prize of the City of Berlin, and in 1982 he became a fellow of its Inst. for Advanced Studies. His autobiography was publ. as *Der Sohn des Rabbiners: Ein Weg von Berlin nach Jerusalem* (Berlin, 1985). A true musical intellectual, Tal applies in his music a variety of techniques, being free of doctrinal introversion and open to novel potentialities without fear of public revulsion. Patriotic Hebrew themes often appear in his productions.

WORKS: DRAMATIC: *Saul at Ein Dor*, opera concertante (1957); *Amnon and Tamar*, opera (1961); *Ashmedai*, opera (1968; Hamburg, Nov. 9, 1971); *Massada 967*, opera (1972; Jerusalem, June 17, 1973); *Die Versuchung*, opera (1975; Munich, July 26, 1976); *Else-Hommage*, chamber scene for Mezzo-soprano, Narrator, and 4 Instruments (1975); Scene from Kafka's diaries for Soprano or Tenor Solo (1978); *Der Turm*, opera (1983; Berlin, Sept. 19, 1987); *Der Garten*, chamber opera (1987; Hamburg, May 29, 1988); *Die Hand*, dramatic scene for Soprano and Cello (1987); *Josef*, opera (1993–95; Tel Aviv, June 27, 1995). **ORCH.:** 3 piano concertos: No. 1 (1944), No. 2 (1953), and No. 3 for Tenor and Orch. (1956); *Reflections* for Strings (1950); 6 syms.: No. 1 (1953), No. 2 (1960), No. 3 (Tel Aviv, July 3, 1978), No. 4, *Hayovel* (Jubilee), for the 50th anniversary of the Israel Phil. (1985; Tel Aviv, Jan. 3, 1987); No. 5 (1990–91; Berlin, Feb. 29, 1992), and No. 6 (1991; Eschede, June 19, 1992); Viola Concerto (1954); *Hizayon Hagigi* (Festive Vision; 1959); Concerto for Cello and Strings (1961); Double Concerto for Violin, Cello, and Chamber Orch. (1970); *Dmut* (Shape) for Chamber Orch. (1975); Concerto for Flute and Chamber Orch. (1977); Concerto for 2 Pianos and Orch. (1980); Concerto for Clarinet and Chamber Orch. (1980); *Dance of the Events* (1981; rev. 1986); *Imago* for Chamber Orch. (1982); *Symphonic Fanfares* (1986). **CHAMBER:** *Kina* (Lament) for Cello and Harp (1950); Violin Sonata (1952); Oboe Sonata (1952); 3 string quartets (1959, 1964, 1976); Viola Sonata (1960); Woodwind Quintet (1966); *Fanfare* for 3 Trombones and 3 Trumpets (1968); Trio for Violin, Cello, and Piano (1974); Piano Quartet (1982); *Chamber Music* for Soprano Recorder, Marimba, and Harpsichord (1982); Duo for Oboe and English Horn (1992); Quartet for Tenor Saxophone, Violin, Viola, and Cello (1994); *Perspective* for Viola (1996). **KEYBOARD: Piano:** Sonata (1950); *5 Inventions* (1956); *5 Densities* (1975); *Essay I–IV* (1986–97). **Organ:** Various pieces. **VOCAL:** *Yetsi'at Mitsrayim* (Exodus), choreographic poem for Baritone and Orch. (1946); *The Mother Rejoices*, symphonic cantata for Chorus, Piano, and Orch. (1949); *Succoth Cantata* for Soloists, Chorus, and Chamber Orch. (1955); *Mot Moshe* (The Death of Moses), Requiem for Soloists, Chorus, Orch., and Tape (1967); *Misdar hanoflim* (Parade of the Fallen), cantata for Soprano, Baritone, Chorus, and Orch. (1968); *Song* for Baritone or Alto, Flute, Horn, 2 Tom-toms, and Piano (1971); *Sus Ha'ets* (The Wooden Horse) for Soloists, Chorus, and Electronics (1976); *Bechol nafshecha* (With All Thy Soul), cantata for 3 Sopranos, Baritone, Boy's Chorus, Mixed Chorus, Brass, and Strings (1978); *Halom ha'igulim* (Dream of the Circles) for Baritone, Chorus, and 4 Instruments (1985); *Laga'at makom* (Touch a Place) for Voice and Chorus (1987); *Bitter Line* for Baritone and Chamber Ensemble (1992); *Wars Swept Through Here* for Baritone and 12 Players (1991); *Psalms* for Narrator, Chorus, and Orch. (1992); songs. **TAPE:** *Exodus II*, ballet (1954); Piano Concertos Nos. 4 to 6 for Piano and Tape (1962, 1964, 1970); *Ranges of Energy*, ballet (1963); *From the Depth of the Soul*, ballet (1964); Concerto for Harpsichord and Tape (1964; rev. 1977); *Ashmedai*, overture to the opera (1970); *Variations*, choreographic piece (1970); Concerto for Harp and Tape (1971; rev. 1980); *Min Hametsar Karati Yah* (I Called Upon the Lord in My Distress; 1971); *Frequencies 440–462: Hommage à Boris Blacher* (1972); *Backyard*, choreographic piece (1977).

BIBL.: W. Elias, *J. T.* (Tel Aviv, 1987).—**NS/LK/DM**

Talbert, Thomas, jazz composer, leader, pianist; b. Minneapolis, Minn., Aug. 4, 1924. With no formal music instruction, Talbert worked for a year as chief arranger for an army dance band. He was discharged at Fort Ord, Calif., in summer of 1945, and then worked with several bands. After meeting Johnny Richards in Boston, he moved to L.A. in early 1946; Richards also came to L.A. and encouraged Talbert to start a band. With his brother Jack Cascales as manager, Talbert formed a band that included Babe Russin; they began recording that spring. The band rehearsed and occasionally performed through 1950. In mid-1949, Art Pepper, Wes Hensel, and Jack Montrose joined the band, and when Talbert broke his arm in a fall from a horse, Claude Williamson took over on piano (Williamson had seen the band's rehearsals during his tenure with Charlie Barnet). This group recorded audition "demo" discs in August and November 1949. In early 1950 Talbert disbanded his orchestra and moved to N.Y. to write for Stan Kenton's Innovations Orch. (Pepper was also a member), Talbert continued to work as an arranger through the 1950s and 1960s, doing work for such artists as Claude Thornhill, Boyd Raeburn, Buddy Rich, Oscar Pettiford, and Charlie Ventura. In 1975, Talbert returned to Los Angeles and began a long career scoring television programs. He returned to the big band jazz world in the 1990s; he also formed a foundation to give money to young jazz musicians.

DISC.: Dodo Marmarosa and Lucky Thompson: *Flight of the Vout Bug* (1946). Art Pepper: *Over the Rainbow* (1949), *Bix Fats Duke* (1956); *Louisiana Suite* (1977); *Things As They Are* (1987); *Warm Cafe* (1991); *Duke's Domain* (1993); *Tom Talbert Jazz Orchestra 1946* (1995).—**LP**

Talbot (real name, **Munkittrick**), **Howard,** English conductor and composer; b. Yonkers, N.Y., March 9, 1865; d. Reigate, Sept. 12, 1928. He was taken to England at the age of 4, and studied at the Royal Coll. of Music in London under Parry, Bridge, and Gladstone. From 1900 he was active as a conductor in various London theaters. He was a prolific composer of light operas. His greatest success was *A Chinese Honeymoon* (Hanley, Oct. 16, 1899), and his last work was *The*

Daughter of the Gods (1929). Other operettas included *Monte Carlo* (London, Aug. 27, 1896), *3 Little Maids* (London, May 20, 1902), *The Blue Moon* (Northampton, Feb. 29, 1905), *The White Chrysanthemum* (London, Aug. 31, 1905), *The Girl behind the Counter* (London, April 21, 1906), *The 3 Kisses* (London, Aug. 21, 1907), *The Belle of Brittany* (London, Oct. 24, 1908), *The Arcadians* (London, April 28, 1909), *A Narrow Squeak* (London, June 6, 1913), *The Pearl Girl* (London, Sept. 25, 1913), *A Lucky Miss* (London, July 13, 1914), and *The Light Blues* (Birmingham, Sept. 13, 1915).—**NS/LK/DM**

Talbot, Michael (Owen), English musicologist; b. Luton, Jan. 4, 1943. He was educated at the Royal Coll. of Music in London and at Clare Coll., Cambridge (Mus.B., 1963; Ph.D., 1968). In 1968 he joined the faculty of the Univ. of Liverpool as a lecturer in music, subsequently serving there as senior lecturer (1979–83), reader (1983–86), and the James and Constance Alsop Prof. of Music (from 1986). His articles have appeared in various journals. He also publ. the studies *Vivaldi* (1978; 4th ed., rev., 1993), *Albinoni: Leben und Werk* (1980), *Tomaso Albinoni: The Venetian Composer and His World* (1990), *Benedetto Vinaccesi: A Musician in Brescia and Venice in the Age of Corelli* (1994), *The Sacred Vocal Music of Antonio Vivaldi* (1995), and *Venetian Music in the Age of Vivaldi* (1999).—**NS/LK/DM**

Talich, Václav, eminent Czech conductor; b. Kroměříž, May 28, 1883; d. Beroun, March 16, 1961. He received his early musical training from his father, Jan Talich (1851–1915), a choirmaster and music teacher, then studied violin with Mařák and Ševčik and chamber music with Kàan at the Prague Cons. (1897–1903). He was concertmaster of the Berlin Phil. (1903–04) and of the orch. of the Odessa Opera (1904–05), and then taught violin in Tiflis (1905–06). He conducted the Slovenian Phil. in Ljubljana (1908–12); also took courses in composition with Reger and Sitt and in conducting with Nikisch at the Leipzig Cons.; also studied with Vigna in Milan. He was then opera conductor at Pilsen (1912–15). Talich held the post of 2nd conductor (1918–19) of the Czech Phil. in Prague, and subsequently served as its chief conductor from 1919 to 1931; in 1931–33 he was conductor of the Konsertforeningen in Stockholm; then in 1933 returned as chief conductor of the Czech Phil. (until 1941), which he brought to a high degree of excellence. He was director and conductor of the National Theater in Prague from 1935 to 1944, when the theater was closed by the Nazis; with the defeat of the Nazis, he resumed his activities there but was dismissed in 1945 after disagreements with the state authorities; he was recalled in 1947, but was dismissed once more in 1948 after conflicts with the new Communist regime. He then moved to Bratislava, where he conducted the Slovak Phil. (1949–52); returned as guest conductor of the Czech Phil. (1952–54); retired from concert appearances in 1954. He also taught conducting in Prague and Bratislava; among his pupils were Ančerl and Mackerras. He was renowned for his idiomatic performances of the Czech repertory. He was made a National Artist in 1957.

Bibl.: O. Šourek, ed., *V. T.* (Prague, 1943); V. Pospíšil, *V. T.: Několik kapitol o dile a životě českého umělce* (V. T.: Some Chapters on the Life and Work of a Czech Artist; Prague, 1961); H. Masaryk, ed., *V. T.: Dokument života a dila* (V. T.: A Document of His Life and Work; Prague, 1967); M. Kuna, *V. T.* (Prague, 1980).
—**NS/LK/DM**

Talking Heads, one of the first important bands to emerge from the mid-1970s N.Y.C. punk and New Wave scenes. **Membership:** David Byrne, voc., gtr. (b. Dumbarton, Scotland, May 14, 1952); Jerry Harrison, kybd., gtr. (b. Milwaukee, Wisc., Feb. 21, 1949); Tina Weymouth, bs., synth. (b. Coronado, Calif., Nov. 22, 1950); Chris Frantz, drm. (b. Fort Campbell, Ky., May 8, 1951).

Talking Heads initially featured minimalist instrumentation on leader David Byrne's neurotic yet intelligent and often surreal dance songs of alienation and estrangement. Finding favor with the college audience as well as the New Wave crowd, Talking Heads eventually left behind their minimalist roots to develop a layered, highly percussive, and funk-based sound. The group broke through commercially with *Speaking in Tongues* and its near-smash hit "Burning Down the House," as well as the hit art-house film *Stop Making Sense*. Always open to side projects, Talking Heads officially disbanded in late 1991. David Byrne remained the most conspicuous and productive of the former members, ultimately returning to the basic rock band format for 1994's *David Byrne*.

David Byrne grew up in Baltimore and later attended the R.I. School of Design, where he met Chris Frantz and Tina Weymouth. Byrne and Frantz played with a quintet variously known as the Artistics and the Autistics, and the three moved to N.Y. in early 1975 and formed Talking Heads as a trio. Frantz and Weymouth married, and the three rehearsed for five months, debuting at CBGB's in June 1975. Harvard graduate Jerry Harrison, a member of Jonathan Richman's Modern Lovers until 1974, joined the group in 1976, and the quartet toured Europe with the Ramones. Signed by Sire Records, Talking Heads' debut album won quick acclaim for its stark instrumentation and Byrne's unique vocal and songwriting style. The album included the favorite "Don't Worry About the Government" and produced a minor hit with the bizarre "Psycho Killer."

Talking Heads subsequently toured Europe and America regularly to establish themselves as a live band, and enlisted producer Brian Eno for their next three albums. The first, *More Songs About Buildings and Food*, yielded a major hit with a cover of Syl Johnson's "Take Me to the River" while including "Big Country" and "Found a Job." The rather dense and ominous *Fear of Music* included the African-sounding "I Zimbra," "Heaven," "Memories Can't Wait," and the paranoid anthem minor hit "Life During Wartime."

Talking Heads put their minimalist sound behind them for *Remain in Light*, Brian Eno's final production for the band. Recorded with guitarist Adrian Belew (who had played with Frank Zappa and David Bowie), synthesizer player Bernie Worrell (from Parliament-Funkadelic), and percussionist Steve Scales, the album fused funk and African rhythms, the electronic and synthesizer sound favored by Eno and Worrell, and layered vocals and solos to produce a demanding and intricate series of song constructions. It includes "Crosseyed and Painless" and "Houses in Motion" and yielded a minor hit with "Once in a Lifetime." The group toured the world with an expanded band that included the additional musicians used on the record, with live recordings from this tour eventually released in 1982.

However, Talking Heads were not to record another studio album for almost three years, as the members pursued a variety of outside projects. David Byrne collaborated with Brian Eno on the instrumental album *My Life in the Bush of Ghosts*, which featured the rhythms of Africa and the Middle East; he also composed the score for the Twyla Tharp ballet *The Catherine Wheel*. He later produced The B–52s' *Mesopotamia* EP and Fun Boy Three's *Waiting*. Jerry Harrison recorded a solo album, and Chris Frantz and Tina Weymouth assembled The Tom Tom Club with Tina's sisters Loric, Lani, and Laura, guitarists Adrian Belew and Monte Brown, and keyboardist-producer Steven Stanley. The album produced a British smash with the rap-style "Wordy Rappinghood" and a moderate American hit with "Genius of Love."

With Brian Eno's departure as producer, Talking Heads returned to their basic sound for 1983's *Speaking in Tongues*. The album remained on the charts for nearly a year and contained the near-smash hit "Burning Down the House," the minor hit "This Must Be the Place (Naive Melody)," plus "Girlfriend Is Better" and "Swamp." In December 1983 Talking Heads, as part of their American tour, performed four nights at the Pantages Theater in Los Angeles. The songs were performed in approximate chronologic order, thus providing a historic persepective, and built from Byrne's solo performance (accompanied by a percussion part prerecorded and played on a boom box) of "Psycho Killer" as additional members joined him on stage. Weymouth entered to play "Heaven," then Frantz came on for "Thank You for Sending Me an Angel." By the sixth song the entire entourage, including percussionist Steve Scales, keyboardist Bernie Worrell, and guitarist Alex Weir, was on stage. Filmed under the direction of Jonathan Demme, the performances were assembled into the film *Stop Making Sense*, acclaimed as one of the finest rock concert documentaries ever made upon its release in 1984. The soundtrack album remained on the charts for more than two years and later yielded a minor hit with the new version of "Once in a Lifetime."

In 1984 David Byrne scored and recorded the music for avant-garde artist Robert Wilson's *The Knee Plays*, derived from Wilson's ambitious opera the *CIVIL warS*. Talking Heads recorded the rather accessible *Little Creatures* album, which contained "Road to Nowhere" and "Stay Up Late," yielded a minor hit with "And She Was," and became a best-seller. In 1985 Byrne cowrote, directed, and starred in the movie *True Stories*, an oddly entertaining and droll satire on American life set in the fictional town of Virgil, Tex. Talking Heads' recording of the album's music was remarkably diverse, incorporating country, Tex-Mex, and zydeco musics, while producing a major hit with "Wild Wild Life."

Over the next few years the members of Talking Heads pursued a variety of outside projects. Jerry Harrison played sessions for the Violent Femmes and the BoDeans, among others, while Tina Weymouth and Chris Frantz produced Ziggy Marley's breakthrough album *Conscious Party*. David Byrne collaborated with Ryuichi Sakamoto and Cong Su on the award-winning soundtrack to the film *The Last Emperor*. In 1988 Talking Heads reunited to record *Naked*, which featured "Blind," "Mr. Jones," and "(Nothing But) Flowers," but the group members soon went their separate ways, coming back together only in late 1991 to record four uncompleted tracks for the anthology set *Sand in the Vaseline*.

In 1988 David Byrne established his own record company, Luaka Bop, for various world music recordings. In 1989 he recorded *Rei Momo* with Latin and Brazilian musicians and released two albums of Brazilian music, *Beleza Tropical* and *O Samba*, on Luaka Bop. He toured with a large band of Brazilian musicians in support of *Rei Momo*, and later recorded orchestral music for *The Forest*, a theatrical piece by Robert Wilson. Jerry Harrison assembled the large band the Casual Gods for recordings on Sire Records, and Chris Frantz and Tina Weymouth reassembled The Tom Tom Club, with Weymouth as lead vocalist, for recordings and a 1989 tour. With the demise of Talking Heads in 1991, Byrne utilized many of the musicians from *Rei Momo* to record *Uh-Oh*, but then returned to a basic rock band setup for 1994's *David Byrne*. However, he failed to achieve any hits as a solo artist.

DISC.: **TALKING HEADS:** *T. H.:77* (1977); *More Songs About Buildings and Food* (1978); *Fear of Music* (1979); *Remain in Light* (1980); *The Name of the Band Is T. H.* (1982); *Speaking in Tongues* (1983); *Stop Making Sense* (soundtrack; 1984); *Little Creatures* (1985); *True Stories* (1986); *Naked* (1988); *Popular Favorites, 1976–1991/Sand in the Vaseline* (1992). **DAVID BYRNE AND BRIAN ENO:** *My Life in the Bush of Ghosts* (1981). **DAVID BYRNE:** *The Catherine Wheel* (1981); *Music for "The Knee Plays"* (1985); *Rei Momo* (1989); *The Forest* (1991); *Uh-Oh* (1992); *David Byrne* (1994); *Feelings* (1997); *In Spite of Wishing and Wanting* (1999). **DAVID BYRNE/RYUICHI SAKAMOTO/ CONG SU:** *The Last Emperor* (soundtrack; 1988). **TOM TOM CLUB:** *Tom Tom Club* (1981); *Close to the Bone* (1983); *Boom Boom Chi Boom Boom* (1989); *Dark Sneak Love Action* (1992). **JERRY HARRISON:** *The Red and the Black* (1981). **JERRY HARRISON AND THE CASUAL GODS:** *Casual Gods* (1988); *Walk on Water* (1990).

BIBL.: K. Reese, *The Name of the Band Is T. H.* (London, 1983); D. Gans, *T. H.—The Band and Their Music* (London, 1986).
—BH

Tallat-Kelpša, Juozas, Lithuanian conductor, teacher, and composer; b. Kalnujai, Jan. 1, 1889; d. Vilnius, Feb. 5, 1949. He studied cello at the Vilnius Music School before completing his music education at the St. Petersburg Cons. (1907–16). In 1920 he settled in Kaunas and founded its Opera, which he conducted until 1941 and again from 1944 to 1948. He also taught at the music school (1920–33) and at the Cons. (from

1933). In 1948 he was awarded the Stalin Prize. He wrote instrumental works, piano pieces, and choral songs, and also prepared folk song arrangements. **—NS/LK/DM**

Talley, Marion, American soprano; b. Nevada, Mo., Dec. 20, 1906; d. Los Angeles, Jan. 3, 1983. She sang in churches in Kansas City, Mo., and at 16 appeared in *Mignon* there. Following training from Frank La Forge in N.Y., she completed her studies in Europe. On Feb. 17, 1926, she made her Metropolitan Opera debut in N.Y. as Gilda and created a stir as an American find. However, her success was short-lived. She sang at the Metropolitan for only 3 seasons and then made sporadic opera and recital appearances. In 1936 she sang on the radio and then returned to opera in 1940, but her career soon waned.**—NS/LK/DM**

Tallis (Tallys, Talys, Talles), Thomas, eminent English organist and composer; b. c. 1505; d. Greenwich, Nov. 23, 1585. He was organist at the Benedictine Priory in Dover (1532); was in the employ of London's church of St. Mary-at-Hill (1537–38), most likely as organist. He served as organist at Walthem Abbey (c. 1538–40), and then was a lay clerk at Canterbury Cathedral (1541–42). From about 1543, he served as Gentleman of the Chapel Royal during the reigns of Henry VIII, Edward VI, Mary, and Elizabeth I, and as joint organist with Byrd. With Byrd, he obtained in 1575 letters patent for the exclusive privilege of printing music and ruled music paper, the first work issued by them being 34 *Cantiones quae ab argumento sacrae vocantur, 5 et 6 partium,* in 1575 (includes 17 pieces by each). Tallis's most famous work is *Spem in alium non habui,* a "song of 40 parts" for 8 5-part choirs. A composer of great contrapuntal skill, he was among the first to set English words to music for the rites of the Church of England. Surviving are 3 masses, 2 Magnificats, 2 Lamentations, 52 motets and other pieces with Latin text, over 20 Eng. anthems, 9 psalm tunes, etc., as well as some keyboard music. Modern editions of his music are included in D. Stevens, ed., *T. Tallis: Complete Keyboard Works* (London, 1953) and L. Ellinwood, ed., *T. Tallis: English Sacred Music,* I, *Anthems;* II, *Service Music,* in the Early English Church Music series, XII and XIII (rev. by P. Doe, 1974).**—NS/LK/DM**

Talma, Louise (Juliette), American composer and teacher; b. Arcachon, France, Oct. 31, 1906. She studied at the Inst. of Musical Art in N.Y. (1922–30) and took courses at N.Y.U. (B.M., 1931) and at Columbia Univ. (B.Mus., 1933); took piano lessons with Philipp and composition with Boulanger in Fontainebleau (summers, 1926–39). She taught at Hunter Coll. (1928–79); was the first American to teach at the Fontainebleau School of Music (summers, 1936–39; 1978; 1981–82). She received 2 Guggenheim fellowships (1946, 1947); was the first woman composer to be elected to the National Inst. of Arts and Letters in 1974. In her music, she adopts a strongly impressionistic style. She publ. *Harmony for the College Student* (1966) and *Functional Harmony* (with J. Harrison and R. Levin, 1970).

WORKS: DRAMATIC: Opera: *The Alcestiad* (1955–58; Frankfurt am Main, March 1, 1962). **ORCH.:** *Toccata* (1944; Baltimore, Dec. 20, 1945); *Dialogues* for Piano and Orch. (1963–64; Buffalo, Dec. 12, 1965). **CHAMBER:** String Quartet (1954); Violin Sonata (1962); *Summer Sounds* for Clarinet, 2 Violins, Viola, and Cello (1969–73); *The Ambient Air* for Flute, Violin, Cello, and Piano (1980–83); *Studies in Spacing* for Clarinet and Piano (1982). **Piano:** 2 sonatas (1943; 1944–55); *Passacaglia and Fugue* (1955–62); *Textures* (1977). **VOCAL: Choral:** *The Divine Flame,* oratorio (1946–48); *La corona,* 7 sonnets (1954–55); *A Time to Remember* for Chorus and Orch. (1966–67); *Voices of Peace* for Chorus and Strings (1973); *Mass for the Sundays of the Year* (1984). **With Solo Voice:** *Terre de France,* song cycle for Soprano and Piano (1943–45); *All the Days of My Life,* cantata for Tenor, Clarinet, Cello, Piano, and Percussion (1963–65); *The Tolling Bell* for Baritone and Orch. (1967–69); *Diadem,* song cycle for Tenor and Piano or 5 Instruments (1978–79); *Variations on 13 Ways of Looking at a Blackbird* for Soprano or Tenor and Flute or Oboe or Violin and Piano (1979).**—NS/LK/DM**

Talmi, Yoav, Israeli conductor; b. Kibbutz Merhavia, April 28, 1943. He studied at the Rubin Academy of Music in Tel Aviv (diploma, 1965) and at the Juilliard School of Music in N.Y. (1965–68). He also studied conducting with Susskind at the Aspen (Colo.) School of Music (summer, 1966), Maderna in Salzburg (summer, 1967), Fournet in Hilversum (summer, 1968), and Leinsdorf at the Berkshire Music Center at Tanglewood (summer, 1969), where he won the Koussevitzky Memorial Conducting Prize. He was assoc. conductor of the Louisville Orch. (1968–70), music director of the Ky. Chamber Orch. (1969–71), and co-conductor of the Israel Chamber Orch. (1970–72). After serving as artistic director of Arnhem's Het Gelders Orch. (1974–80) and as principal guest conductor of the Munich Phil. (1979–80), he returned to the Israel Chamber Orch. as its music director in 1984. He was music director-designate (1989–90) and music director (1990–96) of the San Diego Sym. Orch. In 1994 he served as artistic advisor of the Waterloo (N.J.) Festival. He was music director of the Orchestre Symphonique de Québec (from 1998) and of the Hamburg Sym. Orch. (from 2000).**—NS/LK/DM**

Taltabull, Cristòfor, Catalan composer and pedagogue; b. Barcelona, July 28, 1888; d. there, May 1, 1964. He studied piano with Granados and composition with Pedrell. In 1908 he went to Germany, where he took lessons with Reger. In 1912 he went to Paris, where he was an accompanist to singers, a proofreader for the publisher Durand, and a music copyist; he also composed popular songs for vaudeville and wrote film music. After the outbreak of World War II in 1939, he returned to Barcelona, where he became a teacher of composition. Many important Spanish composers of the younger generation were his pupils. As a composer, he was particularly successful in songs to French and Catalan texts. His style of composition is impressionistic, mainly derived from Debussy; he had a delicate sense of color and rhythm; thematically, most of his music retains Spanish, or Catalan, melorhythmic characteristics.**—NS/LK/DM**

Talvela, Martti (Olavi), remarkable Finnish bass; b. Hiitola, Feb. 4, 1935; d. Juva, July 22, 1989. He received training at the Lahti Academy of Music (1958–60). After winning the Finnish lieder competition in 1960, he studied voice with Carl Martin Ohmann in Stockholm. He made his operatic debut there at the Royal Theater as Sparafucile in *Rigoletto* in 1961. He made his first appearance at the Bayreuth Festival in 1962 as Titurel; that same year, joined the Deutsche Oper in Berlin, where he sang leading bass roles. In 1968 he made his U.S. debut in a recital at Hunter Coll. in N.Y. He made his Metropolitan Opera debut in N.Y. as the Grand Inquisitor in *Don Carlos* on Oct. 7, 1968; appeared there in succeeding years with increasing success, being especially acclaimed for his dramatic portrayal of Boris Godunov. From 1972 to 1980 he served as artistic director of the Savonlinna Festival. He was to have assumed the post of artistic director of the Finnish National Opera in Helsinki in 1992, but death intervened. In 1973 he received the Pro Finlandia Award and the Finnish State Prize. A man of towering dimensions (6′7″), his command of the great bass roles was awesome. Among his outstanding portrayals, in addition to Boris Godunov, were Hagen, Hunding, Gurnemanz, the Commendatore, and Sarastro. He also was effective in contemporary roles.—**NS/LK/DM**

Tamagno, Francesco, famous Italian tenor; b. Turin, Dec. 28, 1850; d. Varese, near Turin, Aug. 31, 1905. He studied with Pedrotti in Turin and Vannuccini in Milan, making his debut in Palermo in 1869. After appearances in Turin, he scored a major success with his portrayal of Riccardo in *Un ballo in maschera* in Palermo in 1874. He made his debut at Milan's La Scala as Vasco da Gamba in *L'Africaine* in 1877, establishing himself as its leading tenor; created the role of Azaele in Ponchielli's *Il Figliuol prodigo* (1880), appeared as Gabriele Adorno in the revised version of Verdi's *Simone Boccanegra* (1881), and was the 1st Didier in Ponchielli's *Marion Demore* (1885). He then won international acclaim when Verdi chose him to create the title role in *Otello* (1887), a role he sang in London in 1889 and in Chicago and N.Y. in 1890; also chose it for his Covent Garden debut in London on May 13, 1895. He made his Metropolitan Opera debut in N.Y. as Arnold in Rossini's *Guillaume Tell* on Nov. 21, 1894, remaining on the company's roster for a season. In 1901 he returned to Covent Garden and also sang at La Scala. He made his final stage appearance at Milan's Teatro dal Verme in 1904; his last appearance as a singer took place in Ostend that same year. Tamagno was one of the greatest tenors in the history of opera; in addition to his Othello, he was celebrated for his portrayals of Don Carlos, Radamès, Alfredo, Manrico, Don José, John of Leyden, Faust, Ernani, and Samson.

BIBL.: E. de Amicis, *F. T.* (Palermo, 1902); M. Corsi, *T.* (Milan, 1927).—**NS/LK/DM**

Tamberg, Eino, oustanding Estonian composer and pedagogue; b. Tallinn, May 27, 1930. He was a composition student of Eugen Kapp at the Tallinn Cons., graduating in 1953. From 1953 to 1959 he was a sound engineer for the Estonian Radio. He served as artistic consultant to the Estonian Composers Union from 1960 to 1969. In 1968 he became a teacher of composition at the Estonian Academy of Music, where he was made chairman of the composition dept. in 1978. In 1999 he was honored with the Estonian State Cultural Award in recognition of his eminence as a composer and as an influential teacher. Tamberg's most important contribution to Estonian music is found in his dramatic and symphonic scores. His music is notable for its mastery of form, and for its inventive use of extended tonality and free atonality.

WORKS: DRAMATIC: Opera: *The House of Iron* (Tallinn, July 15, 1965); *Cyrano de Bergerac* (1974; Tallinn, July 2, 1976); *Flight* (1982; Tallinn, Dec. 30, 1983); *Creatures*, chamber opera (1992). **Ballet:** *Ballet-Symphony* (1959; Schwerin, March 10, 1960); *The Boy and the Butterfly* (Tallinn, Nov. 30, 1963); *Joanna tentata* (1970; Tallinn, Jan. 23, 1971). **ORCH.:** Concerto Grosso (1956; Moscow, July 10, 1957); *Symphonic Dances* (Riga, Dec. 22, 1957); *Toccata* (1967); Trumpet Concerto (Tallinn, Nov. 21, 1972); 4 syms.: No. 1 (1978; Tallinn, Jan. 27, 1979), No. 2 (Tallinn, Oct. 23, 1986), No. 3 (Tallinn, Nov. 12, 1989), No. 4 (1998); Violin Concerto (Tallinn, Oct. 17, 1981); Alto Saxophone Concerto (1987; Tallinn, May 6, 1988); *Journey* for Strings (1990; Toronto, May 15, 1991); *Prelude* (Tallinn, May 15, 1993); *Nocturne* (1994); *Music* for Percussion and Orch. (1994; Tallinn, March 23, 1995); Clarinet Concerto (1996); *Sensitive Journey* for Clarinet and Chamber Orch. (1996). **CHAMBER:** String Quartet (1958); *5 Pieces* for Oboe and Piano (1970); 2 wind quintets (1975, 1984); *Waiting* for Alto Flute, Clarinet, Percussion, Violin, and Cello (1991); *Musica triste* for Flute, Vibraphone, and Strings (1991); *Music for 5* for 5 Instruments (1992); *A Play for 5 in 4 Acts* for Saxophone Quartet and Percussion (1994); piano pieces. **VOCAL:** *Moonlight Oratorio* for 2 Narrators, Soprano, Baritone, Chorus, and Orch. (1962; Tartu, Feb. 17, 1963); *Fanfares of Victory*, cantata for Bass, Chorus, and Orch. (1975); *Amores*, oratorio for Vocal Soloists, Chorus, and Orch. (1981; Tallinn, March 27, 1983); Concerto for Mezzo-soprano and Orch. (1985; Tallinn, Sept. 15, 1986); *Night Songs* for Mezzo-soprano, Flute, Violin, and Guitar (1992); other songs. —**NS/LK/DM**

Tamberlik, Enrico, celebrated Italian tenor; b. Rome, March 16, 1820; d. Paris, March 13, 1889. He studied singing with Zirilli in Rome and with Guglielmi in Naples, where he made his stage debut in 1841 as Tybalt in *I Capuleti e i Montecchi*. On April 4, 1850, he made his first London appearance, as Masaniello in Auber's *La Muette de Portici*, at the Royal Italian Opera, Covent Garden, and sang annually in London until 1864, with the exception of 1857, when he undertook an extensive European tour, including Spain and Russia. In 1860 he settled in Paris, and lived there most of his life. Verdi admired him, and wrote the part of Don Alvaro in *La forza del destino* for him; Tamberlik sang in its premiere in St. Petersburg on Nov. 10, 1862, and this role became one of his most famous interpretations. He appeared at the Academy of Music in N.Y. on Sept. 18, 1873, but his American season was a brief one; later toured the U.S. with Maretzek's company. He excelled in many Italian, French, and German roles, being especially renowned as Florestan, John of Leyden, Manrico, Arnold, and Rossini's Otello.—**NS/LK/DM**

Tamburini, Antonio, esteemed Italian baritone; b. Faenza, March 28, 1800; d. Nice, Nov. 8, 1876. He was a pupil of A. Rossi and B. Asioli, making his operatic debut in Generali's *La Contessa di colle* in Cento in 1818. In 1822 he first sang at Milan's La Scala in Rossini's *Matilde di Shabran*, returning there that same year to take part in the premiere of Donizetti's *Chicara e Serafin*. Following engagements in Trieste and Vienna, he went to Rome and sang in the first performance of Donizetti's *L'ajo nell'imbarazzo* (1824). After singing in Naples and Venice, he appeared in Palermo, where he sang in the premiere of Donizetti's *Alahor di Granata* (1826). Returning to La Scala, he created Ernesto in Bellini's *Il Pirata* (Oct. 27, 1827); after appearing in the first performance of Donizetti's *Alina, regina di Golconda* in Genoa (1828), he went to Naples and sang in the premieres of Donizetti's *Gianni di Calais* (1828), *Imelda de' Lammbertazzi* (1830), *Francesca di Foix* (1831), *La Romanziera* (1831), and *Fausta* (1832). On Feb. 14, 1829, at La Scala, he created Valdeburgo in Bellini's *La Straniera*, a role he repeated at the King's Theatre in London on June 23, 1832; that same year he made his first appearance at the Théâtre-Italien in Paris, and subsequently appeared regularly in London and Paris during the next 11 years. On Jan. 24, 1835, he created the role of Sir Richard Forth in Bellini's *I Puritani* at the Théâtre-Italien; returned there to create Israele in Donizetti's *Marino Failiero* (March 12, 1835) and Malatesta in his *Don Pasquale* (Jan. 3, 1843). After singing in St. Petersburg, he returned to London to appear as Assur in *Semiramide* in the first production mounted by the Royal Italian Opera at Covent Garden. In 1855 he retired from the operatic stage; however, in 1860 he sang Rossini's Figaro in Nice. In 1822 he married the mezzo-soprano Marietta Goja (1801–66).

BIBL.: J. de Biez, *T. et la musique italienne* (Paris, 1877); H. Gelli-Ferraris, *A. T. nel ricordo d'una nipote* (Livorno, 1934). **—NS/LK/DM**

Tan, Margaret Leng, significant Singaporean-American pianist; b. Penang, Malaysia, Dec. 12, 1945. She was educated in Singapore. At 16, she went to N.Y., where she studied with Adele Marcus at the Juilliard School, becoming the first woman to graduate with the D.Mus. degree (1971). Tan specializes in new Asian and American music, evolving a highly individual approach to performance wherein sound, choreography, and theater assume equal significance; she has worked closely with such composers as John Cage, Alvin Lucier, William Duckworth, Lois V Vierk, Somei Satoh et al. in defining her role as the world's premiere string piano virtuoso. She became particularly known for her interpretive command of the works of Cage, giving performances throughout Europe, the U.S., and Asia; also appeared in PBS American Masters documentaries on Cage (1990) and Jasper Johns (1989). During the 1990–91 season, she presented retrospective performances of Cage's music in conjunction with retrospective exhibitions of Johns' paintings at the Walker Art Center in Minneapolis, the Whitney Museum of American Art in N.Y., the Hayward Gallery in London, and the Center for Fine Arts in Miami; she also performed for Cage exhibitions at the Neue Pinakothek (Munich 1991), "Il Suono rapido delle Cose (Cage & Company)" at the 45th Venice Biennale (1993), and at the Guggenheim Museum's "Rolywholyover A Circus" and related "Citycircus" events (1994). In 1984 she received an NEA Arts Solo Recitalist award (1984) and in 1988 an Asian Cultural Council grant for contemporary music research in Japan. In 1987 she appeared with the Brooklyn Phil., and in 1991 made her debut with the N.Y. Phil. Among her critically acclaimed recordings are *Litania: Margaret Leng Tan Plays Somei Satoh* (1988), *Sonic Encounters: The New Piano* (1989; with works by Cage, Hovhaness, Crumb, Satoh, and Ge Gan-ru), and *Daughters of the Lonesome Isle* (1994). From 1993 she developed a repertory for the toy piano through commissions and transcriptions. Tan also is a regular contributor to *Piano Today*. She currently resides in Brooklyn, N.Y., with 2 dogs, 3 Steinways, and 9 toy pianos.**—NS/LK/DM**

Tan, Melvyn, talented Singaporean fortepianist and harpsichordist; b. Singapore, Oct. 13, 1956. He went to England, where he entered the Yehudi Menuhin School in Surrey when he was 12; later pursued training at the Royal Coll. of Music in London. His principal mentors were Perlemuter and Boulanger. After commencing his career as a pianist, he took up the fortepiano and harpsichord in 1980; he subsequently appeared in the major British music centers, and in 1985 made his first tour of the U.S. In 1987 he won critical accolades as soloist in a series of Beethoven concerts, with Roger Norrington conducting the London Classical Players. In 1990 he toured in France, Germany, Japan, and Australia, and also played at N.Y.'s Carnegie Hall.**—NS/LK/DM**

Tana, Akira, jazz drummer; b. San Jose, Calif., March 14, 1952. He took a degree in East Asian Studies from Harvard Univ. (1974) and a degree in percussion from the New England Cons. (1979). He played in local Boston jazz clubs with other young players, including Ricky Ford and James Williams. Since moving to N.Y. in the late 1970s, Tana has freelanced with Sonny Rollins, Sonny Stitt, Zoot Sims, Hubert Laws, Milt Jackson, Jim Hall, Art Farmer, The Paul Winter Consort, Paquito D'Rivera, James Moody, J.J. Johnson, Lena Horne, and The Manhattan Transfer. He has performed at the Tanglewood Festival under the direction of Leonard Bernstein, Seiji Ozawa, and Gunther Schuller and has accompanied Charles Aznavour, Maurice Hines, and Van Dyke Parks, among others, on over 100 recordings. Tana has given workshops and clinics at various colleges, and was on a concert-clinic tour of South America with the Heath Brothers sponsored by the U.S. State Department. He has taught at Jersey City State Coll., Queens Coll., and N.Y.U. In 1991 he began co-leading a quintet with Rufus Reid called TanaReid. In 1999, he relocated to Belmont, Calif.

DISC.: *Yours and Mine* (1991); *Blue Motion* (1992); *Passing Thoughts* (1992).**—LP**

Tanabe, Hisao, Japanese musicologist and composer; b. Tokyo, Aug. 16, 1883; d. there, March 5, 1984. His mother played and taught Japanese instruments; he began learning the violin at the Tokyo Music School in 1903. While studying physics at the Univ. of Tokyo

(1904–07), he took courses in composition with Noël Peri; also had postgraduate studies in acoustics (1907–10) and studied Japanese music and dance with Shōhei Tanaka. He taught acoustics, music history, and theory at the Toyo Music School (1907–35) and the Imperial Music Bureau (1919–23); also taught Japanese music history at Kokugakuin Univ. (1923), the Univ. of Tokyo (1930), Waseda Univ. (1947), and Musashino Coll. of Music (1949). In 1936 Tanabe founded and served as the first president of the Soc. for Research in Asiatic Music; his field studies included collections of music from Korea (1921), Formosa and the Ryuku Islands (1922), northern China (1923), and the Pacific Islands (1934). He was a pioneer among modern Japanese musicologists; his writings and lectures on European music were important for its introduction into Japan in the early 20th century. He publ. nearly 50 books on a variety of musical subjects, especially oriental music and acoustics. He also performed widely, both European and Japanese music, and composed a number of works. He publ. his autobiography as *Tanabe Hisao jijoden* (2 vols., 1981, 1982). After his death, the Soc. for Research in Asiatic Music instituted the Tanabe Hisao Prize.

WRITINGS: *Nippon ongaku kōwa* (Lectures on Japanese Music; 1919); *Toyô ongakushi* (History of Oriental Music; 1930); *Ongaku riron* (Theories of Music; 1929; rev. 1956); *Ongaku onkyogaku* (Acoustics of Music; 1951); also ed. *Nihon ongakushû* (Collection of Japanese Music in Staff Notation; 1931) and *Kinsei Nihon ongakushû* (Collection of Modern Japanese Music in Staff Notation; 1931).—**NS/LK/DM**

Tanaka, Karen, Japanese composer; b. Tokyo, April 7, 1961. She began formal composition studies at the age of 10. Following training with Miyoshi at the Toho Gakuen School of Music in Tokyo (1982–86), she studied with Murail in Paris at IRCAM (1986–88). She then had advanced instruction at the Banff Centre for the Arts in Alberta, Canada (1989), and was a pupil of Berio in Florence (1990–91). From 1991 to 1993 she worked at IRCAM.

WORKS: ORCH.: *Prismes* (Tokyo, Oct. 16, 1984); *Anamorphose* for Piano and Orch. (1986; Hilversum, Sept. 13, 1987); *Hommage en cristal* for Piano and Strings (Oslo, Oct. 22, 1991); *Initium* (1992; Tokyo, June 23, 1993); *Wave Mechanics I* (Tokyo, Aug. 23, 1994); *Echo Canyon* (Nagoya, Nov. 26, 1995); *Frozen Horizon* (Bergen, May 22, 1998). **CHAMBER:** *Tristesse* for Flute, Violin, and Piano (Tokyo, Oct. 12, 1983); *Lilas* for Cello (Amsterdam, Sept. 10, 1988); *Wave Mechanics II* for Violin and Computer (Kobe, Nov. 26, 1994); *Polarization* for 2 Percussionists (1994; Radio France, Paris, Feb. 11, 1995); *Metallic Crystal* for Percussionist, Computer, and Live Electronics (1994–95; Paris, June 26, 1995); *Night Bird* for Tenor Saxophone (1996); *Invisible Curve* for Flute, Violin, Viola, Cello, and Piano (Yokohama, June 30, 1996); *The Song of Songs* for Cello and Computer (Mito, Nov. 10, 1996); *Metal Strings* for String Quartet (Tokyo, Nov. 27, 1996); *At the Grave of Beethoven* for String Quartet (1999); *Water and Stone* for 8 Players (1999; Paris, March 4, 2000). **KEYBOARD: Piano:** *Crystalline I* (Tokyo, Sept. 7, 1988) and *II* (1995–96; Yokohama, Jan. 19, 1996); *The Zoo in the Sky* (1994–95). **Harpsichord:** *Jardin des herbes* (Tokyo, March 3, 1988). **TAPE:** *Inuit Voices* (1997); *Questions of Nature* (1998).—**NS/LK/DM**

Tanaka, Toshimitsu, Japanese composer and teacher; b. Aomori, July 17, 1930. He was a student at the Kunitani Music Coll. (graduated, 1951), and then taught there.

WORKS: ORCH.: *Gunzo* (1979); *Pathos* (1981); *Sadlo Concerto* for Marimba and Orch. (1990); *Festival Overture* (1991); *Maze* (1992). **CHAMBER:** Violin Sonata (1957); 2 string quartets (1962, 1988); *Tamanna* for 2 Pianos and Percussion (1967); Suite for Marimba, 7 Strings, and 2 Percussionists (1971); *Earthen Vessel* for Percussion Ensemble (1982); *Locus* for Percussion (1983); *Blue Ladder* for Synthesizer (1984); *Aoi Kizahashi* for Synthesizer (1984); *Persona* for Marimba and Percussion Ensemble (1990); piano pieces. **VOCAL:** *Magic Festival in the Mountain Crease* for Chorus, Ryûteki, and Various Types of Wadaiko (1968); *Epic "Wolf Boy"* for Soprano, Shamisen, Shakuhachi, Wadaiko, and Strings (Tokyo, Nov. 27, 1968); *The Grave*, requiem for Chorus and Orch. (Tokyo Radio, Nov. 5, 1972); *Kodai Sanka* for Chorus and Percussion Ensemble (1987); choruses; songs.—**NS/LK/DM**

Tan Dun, significant Chinese composer; b. Si Mao, central Hunan Province, Aug. 18, 1957. While working among peasants during the Chinese Cultural Revolution, he began collecting folk songs. After playing viola in the Beijing Opera orch. (1976–77), he entered the recently reopened Central Cons. in Beijing in 1978 to study composition (B.A.; M.A.). In the 1980s he attended guest lectures given by Goehr, Henze, Crumb et al. In 1983 his String Quartet won a prize in Dresden, the first international music prize won by a Chinese composer since 1949. His Western compositional leanings led to a 6-month ban on performances or broadcasts of his music soon thereafter. In 1986 he settled in N.Y., where he accepted a fellowship at Columbia Univ. and studied with Chou Wen-Chung, Mario Davidovsky, and George Edwards. His early works are romantic and florid; after 1982, they reveal a progressing advancement of dissonance and sophistication, while retaining Chinese contexts. Many of his compositions require instrumentalists to vocalize in performance.

WORKS: DRAMATIC: *9 Songs*, ritual opera for 20 Singers/Performers (N.Y., May 12, 1989); *Marco Polo*, opera (1993–94). **ORCH.:** *Li Sao*, sym. (1979–80); Piano Concerto (1983); *Symphony in 2 Movements* (1985); *On Taoism* (1985; Hong Kong, June 28, 1986); *Out of Beijing Opera* for Violin and Orch. (1987); *Orchestral Theatre I: Xun* (1990), *II: Re* (1992), and *III: Red* (1994); *Death and Fire: Dialogue with Paul Klee* (1991–92; Glasgow, March 27, 1993); *Yi*, cello concerto (1993–94). **CHAMBER:** *Feng Ya Song*, string quartet (1982); *8 Colors* for String Quartet (1986–88); *In Distance* for Piccolo, Harp, and Bass Drum (1987); *Elegy: Snow in June*, concerto for Cello and 4 Percussionists (1991); *Circle with 4 Trios, Conductor, and Audience* (1992); *Lament: Autumn Wind* for Any 6 Instruments, Any Voice, and Conductor (1993). **Piano:** *5 Pieces in Human Accent* (1978); *Traces* (1989; rev. 1992); *R;Beatles* (1990); *CAGE* (1993). **VOCAL:** *Fu* for 2 Sopranos, Bass, and Ensemble (1982); *Silk Road* for Soprano and Percussion (1989).—**NS/LK/DM**

Tanev, Alexander, Bulgarian composer and teacher; b. Budapest (of Bulgarian parents), Oct. 23, 1928; d. 1996. He studied law at the Univ. of Sofia (1946–50) and composition with Veselin Stoyanov at the Bulgarian State Cons. in Sofia (graduated, 1957). He was a teacher of composition at the latter institution (from 1970), and dean of the faculty of composition and conductor (from 1986). He also served as secretary of the Union of Bulgarian Composers (1972–76).

WORKS: DRAMATIC: *Prasnik v Tsaravets* (Festival of Tsaravets), ballet (1968); *Gramada*, music drama (1977). **ORCH.:** *Sinfonietta* (1959); *Youth Concerto* for Violin and Strings (1969); *Rondo concertante* for Trombone and Orch. (1971); Concerto for Brass and Percussion (1972); *Builder's Music* for 2 Pianos and Orch. or Percussion (1974); *Divertimento concertante* for Piano and Orch. (1976); *Capriccio* for Symphonic and Wind Orchs. (1986); Concerto for Strings (1988). **VOCAL:** 3 oratorios: *Annals of Freedom* for Soloists, Chorus, and Orch. (1975–76), *Testament* for Bass, Reader, Chorus, Children's Chorus, and Orch. (1977–78), and *Native Land* for Bass, Reader, Chorus, Children's Chorus, and Orch. (1984–85); *The Way Is Fearful but Glorious*, symphonic poem for Bass-baritone and Orch. (1979); 3 cantatas: *In Praise of the Song about Damiancho* for Women's Chorus and 2 Pianos (1981), *In Praise of the Rila Monastery* for Bass, Men's Chorus, and Orch. (1982), and *The Song of Songs* for Tenor, Bass, and Orch. (1983); song cycles. **OTHER:** Chamber music; piano pieces.—**NS/LK/DM**

Taneyev, Alexander (Sergeievich), Russian composer; b. St. Petersburg, Jan. 17, 1850; d. there (Petrograd), Feb. 7, 1918. He was educated at the Univ. of St. Petersburg, and also studied composition with F. Reichel in Dresden; upon his return to St. Petersburg, he took lessons with Rimsky-Korsakov. Music was his avocation; he followed a government career, advancing to the post of head of the Imperial Chancellery. The style of his music is Romantic, lapsing into sentimentalism; the main influence is that of Tchaikovsky.

WORKS: DRAMATIC: Opera: *Cupid's Revenge* (concert perf., St. Petersburg, May 19, 1899); *The Snowstorm* (Petrograd, Feb. 11, 1916). **ORCH.:** 3 syms. (1890, 1903, 1908); 2 suites; *Alyosha Popovich*, ballade; *Festival March*; 2 mazurkas; *Reverie* for Violin and Orch.; *Hamlet*, overture. **CHAMBER:** *Bagatelle and Serenade* for Cello and Piano; *Arabesque* for Clarinet and Piano; 3 string quartets; *Feuillet d'album* for Viola and Piano; piano pieces. **VOCAL:** Songs.—**NS/LK/DM**

Taneyev, Sergei (Ivanovich), greatly significant Russian composer and pedagogue; b. Vladimir district, Nov. 25, 1856; d. Dyudkovo, Zvenigorodsk district, June 19, 1915. He began taking piano lessons at the age of 5, and when he was only 9 when he entered the Moscow Cons.; after academic training for a year, he re-entered the Cons. in 1869 as a piano pupil of Eduard Langer; also received instruction in theory from Nikolai Hubert and in composition from Tchaikovsky, who became his lifelong friend; in 1871 Nikolai Rubinstein became his piano mentor. On Jan. 29, 1875, he made his formal debut as a pianist as soloist in the Brahms D-minor Concerto in Moscow; on Dec. 3, 1875, he was soloist in the Moscow premiere of the Tchaikovsky 1st Concerto, and subsequently was soloist in all of Tchaikovsky's works for piano and orch. He graduated from the Cons. in 1875 as the first student to win the gold medal in both performance and composition. In 1876 he toured his homeland with Leopold Auer. In 1878 he succeeded Tchaikovsky as prof. of harmony and orchestration at the Moscow Cons.; after the death of N. Rubinstein in 1881, he took over the latter's piano classes there; in 1883 he succeeded Hubert as prof. of composition; after serving as its director (1885–89), he taught counterpoint (1889–1905). Taneyev was a first-class pianist, and Tchaikovsky regarded him as one of the finest interpreters of his music. His position as a composer is anomalous: he is one of the most respected figures of Russian music history, and there is a growing literature about him; his correspondence and all documents, however trivial, concerning his life are treasured as part of the Russian cultural heritage; yet outside Russia his works are rarely heard. He wrote a treatise on counterpoint, *Podvizhnoi kontrapunkt strogavo pisma* (1909; Eng. tr, Boston, 1962, as *Convertible Counterpoint in the Strict Style*). The style of his compositions presents a compromise between Russian melos and Germanic contrapuntal writing; the mastery revealed in his 4 syms. (1873–1897) and 5 string quartets (1890–1903) is unquestionable. His most ambitious work was the trilogy *Oresteia*, after Aeschylus, in 3 divisions: *Agamemnon, Choëphorai, and Eumenides*, first performed in St. Petersburg on Oct. 29, 1895. After his death, an almost-completed treatise *Ucheniye o kanone* (The Study of Canon) was found and was ed. for publ. by V. Velaiev (Moscow, 1929).

WORKS: DRAMATIC: Musical Trilogy: *Oresteya* (The Oresteia; 1887–94; St. Petersburg, Oct. 29, 1895). **ORCH.:** *Quadrille* for Small Orch. (1972–73); 4 syms.: No. 1 (1873–74), No. 2 (1877–78), No. 3 (1884; Moscow, Jan. 1885), and No. 4 (1896–97; St. Petersburg, April 2, 1898); Piano Concerto (1876); Sym. for Children's Instruments (c. 1897); *Suite de concert* for Violin and Orch. (1909). **CHAMBER:** 5 unnumbered string quartets (1874–76; 1880; 1882–83; 1883; 1911); 5 numbered string quartets (1890; 1895; 1886, rev. 1896; 1899; 1903); *March* for 10 Instruments (1877); 2 string trios (1879–80; n.d.); 2 string quintets (1901, rev. 1903; 1904); Piano Quartet (1906); Trio for Violin, Viola, and Tenor Viola (1910); Piano Quintet (1911); Violin Sonata (1911); other chamber works; various piano pieces. **VOCAL:** Choral works; songs.

BIBL.: K. Kuznetzov, ed., *S.I. T.* (Moscow and Leningrad, 1925); V. Yakovlev, *S.I. T.: Evo muzikalnaya zhizn* (S.I. T.: His Musical Life; Moscow, 1927); V. Protopopov, ed., *Pamyati S.I. T.a 1856–1946: Sbornik statey i materialov k 90-letiyu so dnya rozhdeniya* (In Memory of S.I. T.: A Collection of Articles and Materials for the 90th Anniversary of His Birth; Moscow and Leningrad, 1947); G. Bernandt, *S.I. T.* (Moscow and Leningrad, 1950); V. Kiselyov et al., eds., *S.I. T.: Materiali i dokumenti* (Moscow, 1952); T. Khoprova, *S.I. T.* (Leningrad, 1968); N. Bazhanov, *T.* (Moscow, 1971); L. Korabelnikova, *S.I. T. v Moskovskoy konservatorri* (S.I. T. at the Moscow Cons.; Moscow, 1974).
—**NS/LK/DM**

Tangeman, Nell, American mezzo-soprano; b. Columbus, Ohio, Dec. 23, 1917; d. Washington, D.C., Feb. 15, 1965. She studied violin at Ohio State Univ. (M.A., 1937) and received vocal instruction at the Cleveland Inst. of Music and from Fritz Lehmann, Schorr, and Matzenauer in N.Y. In 1945 she made her debut as a soloist in *Das Lied von der Erde* with Goossens and the Cincinnati Sym. Orch. In 1948 she made her N.Y. recital debut, and then spent a year studying in Italy on a Fulbright scholarship. She created the role of Mother

Goose in Stravinsky's *The Rake's Progress* in Venice in 1951. In subsequent years, she sang throughout the U.S. and Europe in a repertoire extending from the 16th century to the contemporary era.—**NS/LK/DM**

Tango, Egisto, Italian conductor; b. Rome, Nov. 13, 1873; d. Copenhagen, Oct. 5, 1951. He studied engineering before pursuing musical training at the Naples Cons. He made his debut as an opera conductor in Venice (1893), then conducted at La Scala in Milan (1895) and at Berlin (1903–08). He conducted at the Metropolitan Opera in N.Y. (1909–10), in Italy (1911–12), and in Budapest (1913–19), where he gave the earliest performances of stage works by Bartók. From 1920 to 1926 he was active in Germany and Austria. In 1927 he settled in Copenhagen. He was distinguished for the technical precision and interpretative clarity of his performances.—**NS/LK/DM**

Tannenberg, David, German-American organ builder; b. Berthelsdorf, Upper Lusatia, March 21, 1728; d. York, Pa., May 19, 1804. He went with a group of Moravian church colonists to Bethlehem, Pa., in 1749. He was assistant to the organ builder Johann Gottlob Klemm (1757–62), and then active as an organ builder on his own, moving to Lititz, Pa., in 1765, where most of his organs were built; also made some clavichords and virginals.—**NS/LK/DM**

Tannhäuser, Der, German Minnesinger; b. c. 1205; d. c. 1270. He was of noble lineage. He was active in the 5th Crusade to the Holy Land (1228–33) and the Cypriot war, and later was at the court of Friedrich II "der Streitfare" in Vienna and at the court of Otto II of Bavaria in Landshut, among others. His name became legendary through the tale of the Venusberg, pagan intimacy with Venus, penitence, pilgrimage to Rome, and the miracle of the flowering of his pilgrim's staff. Wagner's *Tannhäuser* is based on this legend, which is unconnected with the life of the real Tannhäuser. A complete ed. of his works has been edited by H. Lomnitzer and U. Müller, *Tannhäuser* (Göppingen, 1973).

BIBL.: F. Zander, *Die T.sage und der Minnesinger T.* (1858); J. Siebert, *Der Dichter T.: Leben-Gedichte-Sage* (Hall, 1934). —**NS/LK/DM**

Tansman, Alexandre, Polish-born French pianist, conductor, and composer; b.Łódź, June 12, 1897; d. Paris, Nov. 15, 1986. He studied at theŁódź Cons. (1902–14), and then pursued training in law and philosophy at the Univ. of Warsaw; also received instruction in counterpoint, form, and composition from Rytel in Warsaw. In 1919 he went to Paris, where he appeared as a soloist in his own works (Feb. 17, 1920). In 1927 he appeared as a soloist with the Boston Sym. Orch., and then played throughout Europe, Canada, and Palestine. He later took up conducting; made a tour of the Far East (1932–33). After the occupation of Paris by the Germans in 1940, he made his way to the U.S.; lived in Hollywood, where he wrote music for films; returned to Paris in 1946. His music is distinguished by a considerable melodic gift and a vivacious rhythm; his harmony is often bitonal; there are some impressionistic traits that reflect his Parisian tastes.

WORKS: DRAMATIC: Opera: *La Nuit kurde* (1925–27; Paris Radio, 1927); *La toisson d'or*, opéra bouffe (1938); *Sabbataï Zevi, le faux Messie*, lyric fresco (1953; Paris, 1961); *Le serment* (1954; Brussels, March 11, 1955); *L'usignolo di Boboli* (1962); *Georges Dandin*, opéra comique (1974). **Ballet:** *Sextuor* (Paris, May 17, 1924); *La Grande Ville* (1932); *Bric-à-Brac* (1937); *Train de nuit* (London, 1950); *Les Habits neufs du roi* (Venice, 1959); *Resurrection* (Nice, 1962). **ORCH.:** *Danse de la sorcière* (Brussels, May 5, 1924); 7 syms.: No. 1 (1925; Boston, March 18, 1927), No. 2 (1926), No. 3, *Symphonie concertante* (1931), No. 4 (1939), No. 5 (1942; Baltimore, Feb. 2, 1943), No. 6, *In memoriam* (1943), and No. 7 (1944; St. Louis, Oct. 24, 1947); 2 sinfoniettas: No. 1 (Paris, March 23, 1925) and No. 2 (1978); *Ouverture symphonique* (1926; Paris, Feb. 3, 1927); 2 piano concertos: No. 1 (Paris, May 27, 1926, composer soloist) and No. 2 (Boston, Dec. 28, 1927, composer soloist); Suite for 2 Pianos and Orch. (Paris, Nov. 16, 1930); Viola Concerto (1936); Violin Concerto (1937); *Fantaisie* for Violin and Orch. (1937); *Fantaisie* for Cello and Orch. (1937); *Rapsodie polonaise* (St. Louis, Nov. 14, 1941); *Études symphoniques* (1943); Guitar Concertino (1945); *Ricercari* (St. Louis, Dec. 22, 1949); Concerto (1954); Capriccio (Louisville, March 6, 1955); Clarinet Concerto (1958); Cello Concerto (1963); *Dyptique* for Chamber Orch. (1969); *Stèle: In memoriam Igor Stravinski* (1972); *Elégie (à la mémoire de Darius Milhaud)* (1976); *Les Dix Commandements* (1979). **CHAMBER:** 8 string quartets (1917–56); Violin Sonata (1919); *Danse de la sorcière* for Woodwind Quintet and Piano (1925; a version of the ballet); Flute Sonata (1925); Cello Sonata (1930); String Sextet (1940); *Divertimento* for Oboe, Clarinet, Trumpet, Cello, and Piano (1944); *Suite baroque* (1958); *Symphonie de chambre* (1960); *Musique à six* for Clarinet, String Quartet, and Piano (1977); *Musique* for Clarinet and String Quartet (1983). **Piano:** *20 pièces faciles polonaises* (1924); 5 sonatas; mazurkas, and other Polish dances; *Sonatine transatlantique* (1930; also for Orch., Paris, Feb. 28, 1931; used by Kurt Jooss for his ballet *Impressions of a Big City*, Cologne, Nov. 21, 1932); *Pour les enfants*, 4 albums. **VOCAL:** *Ponctuation française* for Voice and Small Orch. (1946); *Psaumes 118, 119, and 120* for Tenor, Chorus, and Orch. (1961); *Apostrophe à Zion*, cantata for Chorus and Orch. (1977); *8 Stèles de Victor Segalen* for Voice and Chamber Orch. (1979).

WRITINGS: *Stravinsky* (Paris, 1948; Eng. tr., 1949, as *Igor Stravinsky: The Man and His Music*).

BIBL.: I. Schwerke, *A. T., compositeur polonais* (Paris, 1931). —**NS/LK/DM**

Tans'ur (real name, **Tanzer**), **William,** English organist, composer, and writer on music; b. Dunchurch, 1700 (baptized, Nov. 6, 1706); d. St. Neots, Oct. 7, 1783. He was a church organist and taught music in various provincial towns in England.

WORKS AND WRITINGS (all publ. in London unless otherwise given): *The Compleat Melody: or, The Harmony of Sion* (1734); *Heaven on Earth, or the Beauty of Holiness* (1738); *Sacred Mirth, or the Pious Soul's Daily Delight* (1739); *A New Musical Grammar: or, The Harmonical Spectator, with Philosophical Demonstrations on the Nature of Sound* (1746; various subsequent eds.); *The Royal Psalmodist: or, the New Universal Harmony* (1748); *The Royal Melody Compleat: or, the New Harmony of Sion* (1754–55; 3rd ed., 3 parts, 1764–66; later ed. as *The American Harmony*, Newburyport, 1771); *The Psalm-Singer's Jewell: or, Useful Com-*

panion to the Singing-psalms (1760); *The Life of Holy David* (Cambridge, 1770); *Melodia sacra: or, The Devout Psalmist's New Musical Companion* (3rd ed., 1772); *The Beauties of Poetry* (Cambridge, 1776).—**NS/LK/DM**

Tapper, Thomas, American music educator; b. Canton, Mass., Jan. 28, 1864; d. White Plains, N.Y., Feb. 24, 1958. He studied in the U.S. and Europe. He ed. the *Music Record and Review* (1901–07) and the *Musician* (1905–07), then taught at N.Y.U. (1908–12). He was lecturer at the Inst. of Musical Art (1905–24), and also filled other editorial and educational positions. He publ. *The Music Life* (1891), *The Education of the Music Teacher* (1914), *Essentials in Music History* (1914; with Percy Goetschius), *The Melodic Music Course* (28 vols.; with F.H. Ripley), *Harmonic Music Course* (7 vols.), *The Modern Graded Piano Course* (19 vols.), *Music Theory and Composition* (6 vols.), and *From Palestrina to Grieg* (Boston, 1929; 2nd ed., 1946). His wife, Bertha Feiring Tapper (b. Christiania, Norway, Jan. 25, 1859; d. N.Y., Sept. 2, 1915), was a good pianist. She studied with Agathe Backer-Gröndahl in Norway and with Leschetizky in Vienna, then went to America in 1881 where she later taught piano at the New England Cons. in Boston (1889–97) and at the Inst. of Musical Art in N.Y. (1905–10). She ed. 2 vols. of Grieg's piano works, and also publ. piano pieces and songs. She married Tapper on Sept. 22, 1895.—**NS/LK/DM**

Tappy, Eric, Swiss tenor; b. Lausanne, May 19, 1931. He studied with Fernando Carpi at the Geneva Cons. (1951–58), Ernst Reichert at the Salzburg Mozarteum, Eva Liebenberg in Hilversum, and Boulanger in Paris. In 1959 he made his concert debut as the Evangelist in Bach's *St. Matthew Passion* in Strasbourg. His operatic stage debut followed in 1964 as Rameau's Zoroastre at the Paris Opéra-Comique. After singing in Geneva (1966) and Hannover (1967), he made his debut at London's Covent Garden as Mozart's Tito in 1974. He made his U.S. debut in 1974 as Don Ottavio at the San Francisco Opera, where he returned to sing Poppea and Idomeneo in 1977–78. In 1980 he appeared as Tito in Rome. He retired in 1982. Tappy was esteemed for the extraordinary range of his concert and operatic repertoire, which ranged from early music to the avant-garde.—**NS/LK/DM**

Taranov, Gleb (Pavlovich), Ukrainian composer and teacher; b. Kiev, June 15, 1904; d. there, Jan. 25, 1989. He studied composition with Mikhail Chernov at the Petrograd Cons. (1917–19) and composition with Glière and Liatoshinsky and conducting with Blumenfield and Malko at the Kiev Cons. (1920–25). He served on the faculty of the Kiev Cons. (1925–41; 1944–74). In 1957 he was named Honored National Artist of the Ukraine. His works were cast in the accepted Soviet mold, with emphasis on the celebration of historical events.

WORKS: DRAMATIC: Opera: *The Battle on the Ice*, depicting the victory of Alexander Nevsky over the Teutonic Knights at Lake Peipus on April 5, 1242 (1943; rev. 1979). **ORCH.:** Concerto Grosso (1936; rev. 1976); 9 syms. (1943; 1947; 1949, for Orch. of Native Instruments; 1957; *Antifascism*, 1963; "In Memory of Prokofiev" for Strings, 1964; *Heroic*, 1967; *Shushenskaya*, 1969; *The Banner of Victory*, 1974); 5 suites (1950, 1955, 1961, 1964, 1965); 2 symphonic poems: *David Guramishvili* (1953) and *Fire in the Hangar* (1958); *The 1st in Outer Space*, scherzo-poem (1961); *Overture to Memory* (1965); *New Express* (1977). **CHAMBER:** 2 string quartets (1929, 1945); *Enthusiastic Sextet* for Piano and Strings (1945); Woodwind Quintet (1959); works for Solo Instruments. **VOCAL:** Choruses; songs.

BIBL.: M. Mikhailov, *G.P. T.* (Kiev, 1963); S. Miroshnichenko, *G. T.* (Kiev, 1976).—**NS/LK/DM**

Tăranu, Cornel, Romanian composer and teacher; b. Cluj, June 20, 1934. He was a student of Toduţă and Muresianu at the Cluj Cons. (1951–57), and he then joined its faculty. He also studied with Boulanger and Messiaen in Paris (1966–67) and attended the summer courses in music given by Ligeti and Maderna in Darmstadt (1968, 1969, 1972). His music is austerely formal, with atonal sound structures related through continuous variation with permissible aleatory interludes.

WORKS: DRAMATIC: Opera: *Secretul lui Don Giovanni* (The Secret of Don Giovanni; Cluj, July 8, 1970). **ORCH.:** Sym. for Strings (1957); 4 numbered syms.: No. 1, *Sinfonia brevis* (Cluj, Nov. 17, 1962), No. 2, *Aulodica* (1975–76; Cluj, April 8, 1976), No. 3, *Signes* (Cluj, Sept. 25, 1984), and No. 4, *Ritornele* (Cluj, Oct. 9, 1987); *Secvenţe* (Sequences) for Strings (1960); *Simetrii* (Symmetries; 1964; Cluj, Jan. 15, 1966); *Incantaţii* (Incantations; 1965; Cluj, Jan. 15, 1966); Piano Concerto (1966; Cluj, May 29, 1967); *Intercalări* (Intercalations) for Piano and Orch. (1967–69; Cluj, Dec. 13, 1969); *Sinfonietta giocasa* for Strings (1968); *Alternanţe* (Alternations; 1968; Bucharest, May 29, 1969); *Racorduri* (Transitions) for Chamber Orch. (1971); *Cîntec lung* for Clarinet, Piano, and Strings (1974; Bern, April 18, 1975); *Ghirlande* (Garlands; 1979; also for Chamber Ensemble); *Prolegomene II* for Strings and Piano (1982); *Sonata rubato II* for Oboe, Piano, and Strings (1988); *Miroirs* for Saxophone and Chamber Orch. (1990; Cluj, Nov. 15, 1991). **CHAMBER:** String Trio (1952); *Poem-Sonata* for Clarinet and Piano (1954); Cello Sonata (1960); Flute Sonata (1961); Oboe Sonata (1963); *3 Pieces* for Clarinet and Piano (1964); *Dialogues for 6* for Flute, Clarinet, Trumpet, Vibraphone, Percussion, and Piano (1966); *Resonances I* for Guitar (1977) and *II* for Guitar and String Quartet (1978); *Offrande* (Gifts) *I* for Flute and 2 Percussion Groups (1978), *II* for Flute, 2 Percussion Groups, String Quintet, and Piano (1978), and *III* for 4 Flutes, Piano, and Percussion (1988); *Prolegomene I* for String Quartet and Piano (1981); Sonata for Clarinet and Percussion (1985); Sonata for Solo Double Bass (1986); *Sonata rubato I* for Oboe (1986); *Sempre ostinato I* for Soprano Saxophone or Clarinet (1986) and *II* for Saxophone or Clarinet and 7 Instruments (1986–88); Sonata for Solo Viola (1990); Sonata for Solo Cello (1992); *Mosaiques* for Saxophone or Clarinet and Ensemble (1992). **Piano:** *Sonata Ostinato* (1961); *Contrastes I* (1962) and *II* (1963); *Dialogues II* (1967). **VOCAL:** *Ebauche* for Voice, Clarinet, Violin, Viola, Cello, and Piano (1966–68); *Le Lit de Procruste* (The Bed of Procustes) for Baritone, Clarinet, Viola, and Piano (1968–70); *Orfeu* (Orpheus) for Baritone and Chamber Ensemble (1985); *Chansons sans réponse* for Baritone, Narrator, Clarinet, Piano, and Strings (1986–88); *Hommage à Paul Célan* for Mezzo-soprano, Bass, and Chamber Ensemble (1989); *Dedications* for Bass, Narrator, Small Chorus, and Ensemble (1991); cantatas.—**NS/LK/DM**

Tarchi, Angelo, Italian composer; b. Naples, c. 1755; d. Paris, Aug. 19, 1814. He studied at the Cons. dei Turchini in Naples with Fago and Sala. He was music director and composer at the King's Theatre in London in 1787–88 and again in 1789, and then was active in Italy until settling in Paris in 1797. He wrote about 45 operas in Italian, and 6 in French; of these the following were produced at La Scala in Milan: *Ademira* (Dec. 27, 1783), *Ariarte* (Jan. 1786), *Il Conte di Saldagna* (June 10, 1787), *Adrasto rè d'Egitto* (Feb. 4?, 1792), *Le Danaidi* (Dec. 26, 1794), and *L'impostura poco dura* (Oct. 10, 1795). In Paris he produced the French version of *Il Conte di Saldagna* as *Bouffons de la foire St. Germain* (1790), *D'Auberge en auberge* (Opéra-Comique, April 26, 1800), etc. He acquired a certain notoriety by his attempt to rewrite the 3rd and 4th acts of Mozart's *Le nozze di Figaro* (1787); regarding this episode, see A. Einstein, "Mozart e Tarchi," *Rassegna Musicale* (July 1935); also C. Sartori, "Lo Zeffiretto di Angelo Tarchi," *Rivista Musicale Italiana* (July 1954).—**NS/LK/DM**

Tarditi, Paolo, Italian organist and composer; b. place and date unknown; d. after 1649. He was active in Rome, where he was organist at S. Giovanni dei Fiorentini. He later served as maestro di cappella at SS. Giacomo e Ildefonso degli Spagnuoli (c. 1619), S. Maria Maggiore (1629–40), and at the church of the Madonna dei Monti (from 1649). With G.F. Anerio, he was the first composer in Rome to adopt the concertato style with instrumental accompaniment. Among his extant works are Magnificat settings, Psalms, motets, and hymns. —**LK/DM**

Tardos, Béla, Hungarian composer; b. Budapest, June 21, 1910; d. there, Nov. 18, 1966. He studied with Kodály at the Budapest Academy of Music (1932–37). Upon graduation, he was active as a concert manager and music publisher. He composed much choral music for mass singing employing the modalities of Hungarian folk songs.

Works: DRAMATIC: Comic Opera: *Laura* (1958, rev. 1964; Debrecen, Dec. 11, 1966). **ORCH.:** Overture (1949); Suite (1950); Piano Concerto (1954); *Overture to a Fairy Tale* (1955); Sym., in memory of the victims of fascism (1960); *Fantasy* for Piano and Orch. (1961); Violin Concerto (1962); *Evocatio* (1964). **CHAMBER:** Wind Octet (1935); Piano Quartet (1941); 3 string quartets (1947, 1949, 1963); *Improvisations* for Clarinet and Piano (1960); *Prelude and Rondo* for Flute and Piano (1962); *Quartettino-Divertimento* for 4 Wind Instruments (1963); *Cassazione* for Harp Trio (1963); Violin Sonata (1965); piano pieces. **VOCAL: Cantatas:** *A varos peremen* (At the Outskirts of the City; 1944; 2nd version, 1958); *Rolad susog a lomb* (The Leaves Whisper About You; 1949); *Majusi kantata* (May Cantata; 1950); *A beke napja alatt* (Under the Sun of Peace; 1953); *Hajnali dal* (Morning Song; 1953); *Dozsa feje* (Dozsa's Head; 1958); *Szabadsag szuletett* (Liberty Has Been Born; 1960); *Az uj Isten* (The New Gold, 1966). **Other:** Choruses; songs.

Bibl.: P. Várnai, *T. B.* (Budapest, 1966).—**NS/LK/DM**

Tariol-Baugé, Anne, French singer; b. Clermont-Ferrand, Aug. 28, 1872; d. Asnières, near Paris, Dec. 1, 1944. She made her operatic debut in Bordeaux, then went to Russia. Returning to France, she sang in Toulouse and Nantes, then settled in Paris, where she appeared mainly in light opera. She sang the title role at the premiere of Messager's opera *Véronique* at the Bouffes-Parisiens (Dec. 10, 1898); distinguished herself especially in Offenbach's operettas. She was married to the baritone Alphonse Baugé.—**NS/LK/DM**

Tarisio, Luigi, Italian violin maker and trader; b. Fontanetto, near Milan, c. 1795; d. Milan, Oct. 1854. He was a carpenter by trade, and in his leisure hours acquired sufficient skill to play the violin at country fairs. He also began collecting old violins, which he repaired and sold at a profit. In 1827 he made his first trip to Paris, and in 1851 visited London; soon he became known as a reliable trader, and obtained many rich clients. He left a collection of about 200 violins, which were later purchased by Vuillaume in Paris. —**NS/LK/DM**

Tarp, Svend Erik, Danish composer; b. Thisted, Jutland, Aug. 6, 1908; d. Copenhagen, Oct. 19, 1994. He studied theory with Jeppesen and music history with Simonson at the Copenhagen Cons. (1929–31), then was on its faculty (1936–42). He concurrently lectured at the Univ. of Copenhagen (1939–47) and the Royal Theater Opera School (1936–40), and subsequently was an administrator with Edition Dania (1941–60).

Works: DRAMATIC: Opera: *Princessen i det Fjerne* (The Princess at a Distance, 1952; Copenhagen, May 18, 1953); *9,90*, burlesque television opera (Copenhagen, Aug. 12, 1962). **Ballet:** *Skyggen* (The Shadow, after Hans Christian Andersen, 1941–44; Copenhagen, April 1, 1960); *Den detroniserede dyretoemmer* (The Dethroned Tamer; Copenhagen, Feb. 5, 1944). Also film scores. **ORCH.:** *Sinfonietta* for Chamber Orch. (1931); Violin Concertino (1931); Flute Concertino (1937); *Orania*, suite (1937); *Mosaique*, miniature suite (1937); *Comedy Overture No. 1* (1939) and *No. 2* (1950); Piano Concerto (1943); 10 syms.: No. 1, *Sinfonia devertente* (1945), No. 2 (1948), No. 3, *Sinfonia quasi una fantasia* (1958), No. 4 (1975), No. 5 (1975), No. 6 (1976), No. 7 (1977), No. 8 for Girl's Chorus and Orch. (1989), No. 9 (1991), and No. 10 (1992); *Pro defunctis*, overture (1945); *Partita* (1947); *The Battle of Jericho*, symphonic poem (1949); *Preludio patetico* (1952); *Divertimento* (1954); *Scandinavian Design* (1955); *Lyrical Suite* (1956); *Little Dance Suite* (1964); *Little Festival Overture* (1969). **CHAMBER:** *Serenade* for Flute, Clarinet, and String Trio (1930); *Serenade* for Flute and String Trio (1936); Duet for Flute and Viola (1941); String Quartet (1973). **Piano:** Sonata (1950); other pieces. **VOCAL:** *Te Deum* for Chorus and Orch. (1938); *Christmas Cantata* for Narrator, Baritone, Chorus, Organ, and Orch. (1946); songs.—**NS/LK/DM**

Tarr, Edward H(ankins), distinguished American trumpeter, teacher, and musicologist; b. Norwich, Conn., June 15, 1936. He studied the trumpet in Boston with Voisin (1953) and in Chicago with Herseth (1958–59); then studied musicology with Schrade in Basel (1959–64). He subsequently was active both as a trumpet virtuoso and a musicologist; in 1967 he organized the Edward H. Tarr Brass Ensemble, with which he performed Renaissance and Baroque music on original instruments and on modern replicas. From 1968 to

1970 he taught at the Rheinische Musikschule in Cologne; in 1972 he was appointed to the faculty of the Schola Cantorum Basiliensis in Basel as a teacher of cornett and natural trumpet; also taught trumpet at the Basel Cons. (from 1974) and served as conservator of the Trumpet Museum in Bad Sackingen (from 1985). He contributed numerous articles on trumpet playing to various publications, and publ. the book *Die Trompete* (Bern, 1977; 2nd ed., 1978; Eng. tr., 1988). He also ed. a number of trumpet works, including a complete edition of the trumpet music of Torelli.—**NS/LK/DM**

Tárrega (y Eixea), Francisco, celebrated Spanish guitarist, pedagogue, and composer; b. Villarreal, Castellón, Nov. 21, 1852; d. Barcelona, Dec. 15, 1909. He began piano studies in childhood, and in 1862 commenced classical guitar training with Julian Arcas. He then pursued courses in theory, harmony, and piano at the Madrid Cons. (1874–77), and subsequently taught music while establishing himself as a guitar virtuoso. His recital appearances in Paris and London in 1880 secured his reputation outside his homeland; he was acclaimed as the "Sarasate of the guitar." He performed throughout Spain (1885–1903), then toured Italy (1903). His remarkable career was cut short by paralysis of his right arm in 1906. He composed about 80 pieces, and prepared some 120 transcriptions for solo guitar and 21 for 2 guitars.—**NS/LK/DM**

Tartini, Giuseppe, famous Italian violinist, teacher, music theorist, and composer; b. Pirano, Istria, April 8, 1692; d. Padua, Feb. 26, 1770. His parents prepared him for a monastic life by entrusting his education to clerics in Pirano and Capodistria, where he received some violin instruction. In 1708 he renounced the cloister but remained a nominal candidate for the priesthood. In 1709 he enrolled at the Univ. of Padua as a law student, and at the age of 19 contracted a secret marriage to the 21-year-old Elisabetta Premazore, a protegée of the powerful Cardinal Cornaro, who vengefully brought a charge of abduction against him. Tartini had to take refuge from prosecution at the monastery of the Friars Minor Conventual in Assisi, where he joined the opera orch. He was pardoned by the Paduan authorities in 1715, after which he lived in Venice and Padua, being made primo violino e capo di concerto at the basilica of S. Antonio in Padua in 1721. He also was allowed to travel as a virtuoso, and soon acquired a distinguished reputation. From 1723 to 1726 he served as chamber musician to Count Kinsky in Prague, then resumed his residence in Padua, where he organized a music school in 1728; among his students there were Nardini and Pugnani. He subsequently developed a brilliant career as a violinist, making numerous concert tours in Italy. He retained his post at S. Antonio until 1765, and also remained active at his school until at least 1767. In 1768 he suffered a mild stroke that effectively ended his career. His style of playing, and in particular his bowing, became a model for other concert violinists. Tartini was a prolific composer of violin music, including concertos, sonatas, and chamber combinations. An ed. of his collected works was initiated in Milan in 1971 under the editorship of E. Farina and C. Scimone as *Le opere di Giuseppe Tartini.*

Although Tartini lacked scientific training, he made several acoustical discoveries, the most important of which were the summation and differential tones. He observed these effects in 1714 and summarized his findings in his *Trattato di musica secondo la vera scienza dell'armonia* (Padua, 1754); the differential tone became known also as Tartini's tone, or "terzo suono." Tartini's tones were actually described in an earlier German publ., *Vorgemach der musicalischen Composition* by G. Sorge (1745–47). These tones were also known, rather misleadingly, as "beat tones." They are in fact produced by the interference of frequencies of higher overtones. The "wolf tones" of string instruments are different in origin, and are produced by vibrations of the body of the instrument. Violinists are usually aware of interferences from differential tones and also from the less audible summation tones resulting from added frequencies; they correct them experimentally by a slight alteration of tuning. Among Tartini's compositions the most famous is his violin sonata known under the sobriquet *Trillo del Diavolo,* supposedly inspired by Tartini's dream in which the Devil played it for him; the eponymous diabolical trill appears in the last movement of the sonata. A complete ed. of his works commenced publication in Milan in 1971.

WORKS: INSTRUMENTAL: About 135 violin concertos, as well as concertos for several other instruments; a Sinfonie; 4 sonatas a 4 for String Quartet and Basso Continuo; some 40 trio sonatas for 2 Violins and Basso Continuo; about 135 sonatas for Violin and Basso Continuo; some 30 sonatas for Solo Violin or with Basso Continuo ad libitum. The following instrumental works were publ. during his lifetime although some are now considered dubious (all publ. in Amsterdam unless otherwise given): *Sei concerti a 5,* op. 1, lib.1 (1728); *Sei concerti a 5 del...Tartini a G. Visconti,* op. 1, lib.3 (c. 1728); *Sei concerti a 5,* op. 1, lib.2 (1730); *VI sonate* for Violin and Basso Continuo, op. 1 (1732); (12) *Sonate e una pastorale,* op. 1 (1734); *VI concerti a 8,* op. 2 (c. 1734); *VI concerti...d'alcuni famosi maestri,* lib.2 (c. 1740); *VI Sonate* for Violin and Basso Continuo, op. 2 (1743); (12) *Sonate* for Violin and Basso Continuo, op. 2 (Rome, 1745; also publ. as op. 3, Paris, c. 1747); *Nouvelle étude...par Mr. Pétronio Pinelli* (Paris, c. 1747); (6) *Sonates,* op. 4 (Paris, 1747); (6) *Sonates,* op. 5 (Paris, c. 1747); *Sei sonate,* op. 6 (Paris, c. 1748); (6) *Sonate,* op. 7 (Paris, 1748); *Sei sonate a tre,* op. 8 (Paris, 1749); *XII Sonatas* for 2 Violins and Bass (London, 1750); *VI sonate* for 2 Violins and Basso Continuo (c. 1755; also publ. as op. 3, London, 1756); *L'arte del arco* (Paris, 1758); *Sei sonate,* op. 9 (Paris, c. 1763). His famous *Le trille du diable* was first publ. in J. Cartier's *L'art du violon* (Paris, 1798). **SACRED VOCAL:** *Canzoncine sacre* for 1 to 3 Voices; *Stabat mater* for 3 Voices; 2 Tantum ergo for 3 Voices; 3 Miserere for 3, 4, and 5 Voices; Salve regina for 4 Voices; *Pange lingua* for 3 Voices.

WRITINGS: *Regole per arrivare a saper ben suonar il violino* (ed. by E. Jacobi, *Musical Quarterly,* XLVII, 1961; various other versions); *Trattato di musica secondo la vera sienza dell'armonia* (Padua, 1754; reprint, 1966 and 1973); *De' principi dell'armonia musicale contenuta nel diatonico genere* (Padua, 1767; reprint, 1970); *Risposta di Giuseppe Tartini alla critica del di lui trattato di musica di Mons. Le Serre di Ginevra* (Venice, 1767).

BIBL.: F. Fanzago, *Orazione...delle lodi di G. T.* (Padua, 1770; 2nd ed., enl., 1792); F. Fayolle, *Notices sur Corelli, T., Gaviniés,*

Pugnani et Viotti (Paris, 1810); M. Dounias, *Die Violinkonzerte G. T.s* (Wolfenbüttel, 1935; 2nd ed., 1966); H. Schökel, *G. T.* (Berlin, 1936); A. Capri, *G. T.* (Milan, 1945); M. Elmer, *T.'s Improvised Ornamentation* (diss., Univ. of Calif., Berkeley, 1962); P. Petrobelli, *G. T.: le fonti biografiche* (Vienna, Milan, and London, 1968); P. Brainard, *Le sonate per violino di G. T.: catalogo tematico* (Milan, 1975); P. Petrobelli, *T., le sue idee e il suo tempo* (Lucca, 1992); A. Bombi and M. Massaro, eds., *T.: Il tempo e le opere* (Bologna, 1994).—**NS/LK/DM**

Taruskin, Richard, influential American musicologist and music critic; b. N.Y., April 2, 1945. He was educated at Columbia Univ., where he took his Ph.D. in historical musicology (1975); also held a Fulbright-Hayes traveling fellowship, which enabled him to conduct research in Moscow (1971–72). In 1975 he became an asst. prof. at Columbia Univ.; then was assoc. prof. there (1981–87). In 1985 he was a visting prof. at the Univ. of Pa. and in 1987 he was the Hanes-Willis visiting prof. at the Univ. of N.C. at Chapel Hill. In 1986 he was made an assoc. prof. at the Univ. of Calif. at Berkeley, subsequently becoming a prof. there in 1989. He held a Guggenheim fellowship in 1986. In 1987 he was awarded the Dent Medal of England. In 1989 he received the ASCAP-Deems Taylor Award. He contributed many valuable articles on Russian music and composers to *The New Grove Dictionary of Opera* (1992); also contributed articles and/or reviews to the *Journal of Musicology*, the *Journal of the American Musicological Society, Notes, 19th Century Music*, the *N.Y. Times*, the *New Republic*, and other publications. In addition to his ed. and commentary of Busnoys's *The Latin-Texted Works* (2 vols., N.Y., 1990), he publ. the books *Opera and Drama in Russia* (Ann Arbor, 1981; new ed., 1994), *Musorgsky: Eight Essays and an Epilogue* (Princeton, N.J., 1993), *Stravinsky and the Russian Traditions: A Biography of the Works Through Mavra* (2 vols, Berkeley and Los Angeles, 1995), and *Text and Act: Essays on Music and Performance* (N.Y., 1995).—**NS/LK/DM**

Taskin, (Emile-) Alexandre, French baritone; b. Paris, March 8, 1853; d. there, Oct. 5, 1897. His grandfather was the French organist and composer Henri-Joseph Taskin (b. Versailles, Aug. 24, 1779; d. Paris, May 4, 1852). He was a pupil of Ponchard and Bussine at the Paris Cons., making his debut at Amiens in 1875. He sang in Lille and Geneva, then returned to Paris in 1878, where he was engaged at the Opéra-Comique in 1879, and created important parts in many new operas. He retired in 1894, and from then until his death was prof. of lyrical declamation at the Cons. On the night of the terrible catastrophe of the burning of the Opéra-Comique (May 25, 1887) he was singing in *Mignon*; through his calmness and bravery many lives were saved, and the government decorated him with a medal.—**NS/LK/DM**

Taskin, Pascal (-Joseph), French manufacturer of keyboard instruments; b. Theux, near Liège, 1723; d. Paris, Feb. 9, 1793. He went to Paris at an early age and entered Blanchet's atelier, later marrying Blanchet's widow and succeeding to the business in 1766; was named court instrument maker and keeper of the king's instruments in 1774. He became highly celebrated as an instrument maker; invented the leather plectra for the harpsichord (1768), replacing the crow quills previously in use. He built his first piano in 1776. His nephew Pascal-Joseph Taskin (b. Theux, Nov. 20, 1750; d. Versailles, Feb. 5, 1829) was Keeper of the King's Instruments from 1772 until the Revolution. His son Henri-Joseph Taskin (b. Versailles, Aug. 24, 1779; d. Paris, May 4, 1852) was an organist and composer.—**NS/LK/DM**

Tassinari, Pia, Italian soprano and mezzo-soprano; b. Modigliana, Sept. 15, 1903; d. Faenza, May 15, 1996. She received her musical training in Bologna and Milan. She made her operatic debut as Mimi at Castel Monferrato in 1929; then sang at La Scala in Milan (1931–37; 1945–46) and at the Rome Opera (1933–44; 1951–52). She made her American debut at the Metropolitan Opera in N.Y. on Dec. 26, 1947, as Tosca. Although she began her career as a soprano, in later years she preferred to sing mezzo-soprano parts. Her repertoire included both soprano and mezzo-soprano roles, e.g., Mimi, Tosca, Manon, and Marguerite, and also Amneris and Carmen. She was married to **Ferruccio Tagliavini**.—**NS/LK/DM**

Tate, Buddy (George Holmes), jazz tenor saxophonist, clarinetist; b. Sherman, Tex., Feb. 22, 1915. About 1927, two years after his saxophonist brother gave him an alto sax, he began gigging with territory bands. The first was led by his cousin, trumpeter Roy McCloud. In 1929, Tate was with Troy Floyd and Gene Coy, and then with Terrence Holder's 12 Clouds of Joy from 1930–33. Tate first joined Count Basie's in Little Rock, Ark. (c. July 1934), then played with Andy Kirk from late 1934 until early summer 1935. Tate spent a few years with Nat Towles before rejoining Basie in spring 1939. He remained with Basie until September 1948, returned briefly in early 1949, then worked with Hot Lips Page, Lucky Millinder, and Jimmy Rushing (1950–52). Tate formed his own band in 1953. From about 1953–73, he played regularly at the Celebrity Club, Harlem, until the club switched to a rock music format. Tate had accasional reunions with Count Basie, and went to Europe with Buck Clayton's All-Stars in 1959 and 1961. He visited Europe several times in the 1960s, including a tour with own band in late 1968 and a return in 1969. He toured the Orient with Kai Cowens (late 1970), and went to Europe (summer 1971). Tate continued to lead his own group through the mid-1980s. Illness slowed him down in the early 1990s, although he continued to perform occasionally; Branford Marsalis listed him in his liner notes as "the late," then, in apology, performed with him at the West End Cafe in N.Y. in January 1990.

Disc.: *Swinging Like Tate* (1958); *Tate's Date* (1959); *Tate-A-Tate* (1960); *Featuring Milt Buckner* (1967); *And His Buddies* (1973); *Buddy Tate and His Buddies* (1973); *Count's Men* (1973); *Texas Twister* (1975); *Kansas City Joys* (1976); *Meets Dollar Brand* (1977); *Live at Sandy's* (1978); *Muse All-Stars* (1978); *Great Buddy Tate* (1981); *Scott's Buddy* (1981); *Quartet* (1983); *Just Jazz* (1984); *Long Tall Tenor* (1985). Tate/Simkins/Person: *Just Friends* (1990); *Tenors of* (1992).—**JC/LP**

Tate, Erskine, leader, violinist, multi-instrumentalist; b. Memphis, Dec. 19, 1895; d. Chicago, Dec. 17, 1978. While Tate was in his teens, his family relocated to Chicago. He studied violin there at the American Cons. of Music, making his first performance on the instrument in 1912. From 1919 until 1928, he directed the band at the Vendome Theatre, Chicago (Louis Armstrong recorded with him in 1926), then at other theaters including the Cotton Club (of Chicago) before opening a music studio in 1945. At his studio, Tate concentrated on teaching violin, saxophone, trumpet, guitar, piano, and drums. Among his other 1920s-era sidemen were Earl Hines, Freddie Keppard, Buster Bailey, and in the 1930s, Milt Hinton.—**JC/LP**

Tate, Jeffrey, talented English conductor; b. Salisbury, April 28, 1943. Although a victim of spina bifida, he pursued studies at the Univ. of Cambridge and at St. Thomas's Medical School; then attended the London Opera Centre (1970–71). He was a member of the music staff at the Royal Opera, Covent Garden, London (1971–77). He also served as an asst. conductor at the Bayreuth Festivals (1976–80). In 1978 he made his formal conducting debut with Carmen at the Göteborg Opera. On Dec. 26, 1980, he made his first appearance at the Metropolitan Opera in N.Y. conducting Berg's *Lulu*; his debut at Covent Garden followed with *La clemenza di Tito* on June 8, 1982. He appeared as a guest conductor at the Cologne Opera (1981), the Geneva Opera (1983), the Paris Opéra (1983), the Hamburg State Opera (1984), the San Francisco Opera (1984), the Salzburg Festival (1985), and the Vienna State Opera (1986). In 1983 he made his first appearance with the English Chamber Orch., being named its principal conductor in 1985; led it on tours abroad, including one to the U.S. in 1988. In 1986 he also became principal conductor at Covent Garden. In 1990 he was made a Commander of the Order of the British Empire. He was chief conductor of the Rotterdam Phil. from 1991 to 1994. In 1997 he became principal conductor of the Minn. Orch. Viennese Sommerfest. In 1998 he conducted the first complete *Ring* cycle in German in Australia at the State Opera of South Australia in Adelaide, which brought him great acclaim. His extensive operatic and concert repertoire encompasses works from the Classical to the contemporary era.—**NS/LK/DM**

Tate, Phyllis (Margaret Duncan), English composer; b. Gerrards Cross, Buckinghamshire, April 6, 1911; d. London, May 27, 1987. She was a student of Harry Farjeon at the Royal Academy of Music in London (1928–32), and then devoted herself fully to composition. In 1935 she married **Alan Frank.** She was a composer of fine craftsmanship, excelling in works for voices and small ensembles.

WORKS: DRAMATIC: *The Lodger*, opera (1959–60; London, July 14, 1960); *Dark Pilgrimage*, television opera (1963); *Scarecrow*, operetta (1982). **ORCH.:** Cello Concerto (1933); *Valse lointaine* for Small Orch. (1941); *Prelude, Interlude, and Postlude* for Chamber Orch. (1942); Saxophone Concerto (1944); *Occasional Overture* (1955); *Illustrations* for Brass Band (1969); *Panorama* for Strings (1977). **CHAMBER:** Sonata for Clarinet and Cello (1947; Salzburg, June 23, 1951); String Quartet (1952; rev. 1982); *Air and Variations* for Violin, Clarinet, and Piano (1958); *Variegations* for Viola (1970); *The Rainbow and the Cuckoo* for Oboe, Violin, Viola, and Cello (1974); *Sonatina pastorale* for Harmonica and Harpsichord (1974); *Seasonal Sequence* for Viola and Piano (1977); *3 Pieces* for Clarinet (1979); *Prelude, Aria, Interlude, Finale* for Clarinet and Piano (1981). **Piano:** *Explorations Around a Troubadour Song* (1973); *Lyric Suite* for 2 Pianos (1973). **VOCAL:** *Nocturne* for Soloists, String Quartet, Double Bass, Bass Clarinet, and Celesta (1946); *Choral Scene from the Bacchae* for Chorus and Optional Organ (1953); *The Lady of Shalott* for Tenor and Chamber Ensemble (1956); *Witches and Spells* for Chorus (1959); *A Victorian Garland* for Soprano, Contralto, Horn, and Piano (1965); *7 Lincolnshire Folk Songs* for Chorus and Ensemble (1966); *Gravestones* for Voice (1966); *A Secular Requiem* for Chorus, Organ, and Orch. (1967); *Apparitions* for Tenor, Harmonica, and Piano Quintet (1968); *Coastal Ballads* for Baritone and Instruments (1969); *To Words by Joseph Beaumont* for Women's Chorus (1970); *Serenade to Christmas* for Mezzo-soprano, Chorus, and Orch. (1972); *Creatures Great and Small* for Mezzo-soprano, Guitar, Double Bass, and Percussion (1973); *2 Ballads* for Mezzo-soprano and Guitar (1974); *Songs of Sundrie Kinds* for Tenor and Lute (1975); *St. Martha and the Dragon* for Narrator, Soloists, Chorus, and Orch. (1976); *Scenes from Kipling* for Baritone and Piano (1976); *All the World's a Stage* for Chorus and Orch. (1977); *Compassion* for Chorus and Orch. or Organ (1978); *Scenes from Tyneside* for Mezzo-soprano, Clarinet, and Piano (1978); *The Ballad of Reading Gaol* for Baritone, Organ, and Cello (1980).—**NS/LK/DM**

Tattermuschová, Helena, Czech soprano; b. Prague, Jan. 28, 1933. She was a pupil of Vlasta Linhartová at the Prague Cons. In 1955 she made her operatic debut as Musetta in Ostrava. In 1959 she became a member of the Prague National Theater, where she won esteem for her portrayals of roles in operas by Mozart, Smetana, Janáček, Puccini, and Strauss. She also toured with the company abroad and made guest appearances in various European opera houses. She also pursued a concert career.—**NS/LK/DM**

Tatum, Art(hur, Jr.), innovative and highly influential jazz pianist of astonishing capabilities; b. Toledo, Ohio, Oct. 13, 1909; d. Los Angeles, Nov. 5, 1956. His father, Art Sr. (b. Statesville, S.C., c. 1881; d. 1951), was a mechanic, and died from injuries sustained in an industrial accident; his mother, Mildred Hoskins (b. Martinsville, W.Va., prob. 1890; d. Toledo, July 1958), worked as a maid. She is reported to have played church music on the piano (and perhaps a little violin); his father played the guitar and possibly also piano. Art was born with "milk" cataracts on his eyes. After undergoing several operations during his childhood, he gained partial vision, but in his early 20s, was struck by a mugger, leaving him blind in his left eye and with partial vision in his right. He had started playing piano during early childhood, and attended the Cousino School for the Blind, in Columbus, Ohio, where he learned to read Braille music notation. He also studied guitar and violin and regularly doubled on accordion during his early teens. After studying for two years at the Toledo School of Music under Overton G. Ramey, he formed his own small band, which worked in and around Toledo (c. 1926). He spent a few weeks subbing for Herman Berry in Speed Webb's Band and later replaced Berry. However, after three months with the band, Tatum was replaced by Fitz Weston. Tatum began working at clubs in Toledo including a residency at Chicken Charlie's (c. 1928). (A report that Tatum visited N.Y. around 1928 to guest on a Paul Whiteman concert or radio broadcast appears to be false.) In summer of 1929 he started a two-year residency on the local radio station WSPD, continued working at local clubs, and occasionally did short residencies in Cleveland. He worked with Milton Senior's Band at Chateau La France until mid-1931, did short tours with his own band, and then continued playing at local clubs.

In 1932, Tatum was heard by pianist Joe Turner, who recommended him for a job as Adelaide Hall's accompanist; later that year he moved to N.Y. to join Hall, but first played in a duo with pianist Francis Carter. He then worked with Adelaide Hall for about 18 months, making his first recordings with her (and with Carter as a second pianist) on Aug. 5, 1932. On that date he also recorded a "demo" of his solo showpiece, a fast version of "Tiger Rag," but it was not issued until many years later and at first was erroneously credited to Jimmy Lord (a wind player). Also during this time, Tatum filled in by playing at N.Y. night spots; in 1933, he subbed for two weeks in McKinney's Cotton Pickers (pianist Todd Rhodes was ill). From 1934 to mid-1935, he worked mainly in Cleveland, and then had a long residency at the Three Deuces, Chicago (1935–36). In late 1936, he moved to Hollywood, and mainly worked there through 1937; however, he but also played a second residency at the Three Deuces in Chicago. He moved to N.Y. in late 1937 and played at the Famous Door before sailing to Europe in March 1938; this was his only trip abroad. In Europe, he performed not in concerts but on the vaudeville circuit. From 1939 to mid-1940, he worked mainly on the West Coast, then had residencies in N.Y. He continued working as a soloist until 1943, and then performed as part of a as trio (with original members Tiny Grimes and Slam Stewart), playing residencies in N.Y. from 1943–44. In 1945, he began playing annual concert tours, and continued to appear regularly in clubs until 1954. In these later years, he did prolific recordings for impressario Norman Grant. During the last 18 months of his life, he did mainly concert work; his last big concert appearance was before almost 19,000 people at the Hollywood Bowl on Aug. 15, 1956. Always a heavy drinker, he was by this time seriously ill with uremia. He commenced a national concert tour, but illness forced him to return to Los Angeles; he entered Queen of Angels Hospital late on Nov. 4th and died early the next morning.

Tatum's astonishing technique was admired by many in the worlds of jazz and classical music, including Vladimir Horowitz. Tatum played solo or in small groups with material that was highly arranged, leading to criticism that he was not truly an improviser. However, there is ample evidence of his improvisatory gifts in unrestrained and informal settings. It was also said that he couldn't play the blues, but his "Aunt Hagar's Blues" and "Trio Blues" are moving, profound, and highly expressive compositions. Evidently inspired by Fats Waller (whom he acknowledged) and Early Hines (whom he did not), Tatum's work reflected the stride technique and lush touch of the former and the wild runs and chordal daring of the latter. Like most of his generation, he soloed more in chords than single-note lines; however, on occasion, when he was with a rhythm section, such as on "Mop Mop," he produced daring long lines suggesting bitonality. His most enduring contributions were the smooth and sophisticated chord voicings that incorporated ninths, elevenths, and thirteenths. Charlie Parker and other boppers listened closely to these, as did pianists Nat "King" Cole, Bud Powell, Bill Evans, and many others.

Disc.: *Standard Transcriptions* (1935); *Keystone Sessions* (1938); *God Is in the House* (1940); *Solos* (1940); *Art Tatum Solos and Trios* (1944); *Footnotes to Jazz, Vol. 3* (includes trio rehearsal; 1944); *Gene Norman Concert* (1949); *At Shrine Auditorium* (1949); *Complete Capitol Recordings* (1949); *Art Tatum, Vol. 1–10* (1953); *Complete Pablo Solo Masterpieces* (1953); *Genius of Art Tatum, Vol. 1–10* (1953); *Complete Pablo Group Masterpieces* (1954–56); *Genius of Art Tatum, Vol. 9, 11* (1954); *Tatum-Carter-Bellson* (1954); *Art Tatum–Roy Eldridge–Alvin Stoller* (1955); *Art Tatum–Ben Webster Quartet* (1956); *Art Tatum Trio* (1956).

Bibl.: Jorgen Grunnet Jepsen, *Discography of Art Tatum/Bud Powell* (Brande, Denmark, 1961); J. Howard, *The Improvisational Techniques of A. T.* (diss., Case Western Reserve Univ., 1978); J. Distler, *A. T.* (N.Y., 1981); A. Laubich and R. Spencer, *A. T.: A Guide to His Recorded Music* (Metuchen, N.J., 1982); F. Howlett, *An Introduction to A. T.'s Performance Approaches: Composition, Improvisation, and Melodic Variation* (diss., Cornell Univ., 1983); J. Lester, *Too Marvelous for Words: The Life and Genius of Art Tatum* (N.Y., 1994).—**JC/LP**

Taub, Robert (David), American pianist; b. New Brunswick, N.J., Dec. 25, 1955. He studied composition with Babbitt at Princeton Univ. (B.A., 1977) and piano with Lateiner at the Juilliard School in N.Y. (M.M., 1978; D.M.A., 1981). On Oct. 29, 1981, he made his N.Y. recital debut at Alice Tully Hall. Thereafter he toured North and South America, Europe, and the Far East. In 1994 he became artist-in-residence of the Inst. for Advanced Study in Princeton. In addition to the piano literature of the early, Classical, and Romantic eras, he has explored the music of Scriabin, Persichetti, and Babbitt with success.—**NS/LK/DM**

Taube, Michael, Polish-born Israeli conductor, teacher, and composer; b. Łódź, March 13, 1890; d. Tel Aviv, Feb. 23, 1972. He studied at the Leipzig Cons. and with Neitzel (piano), Strässer (composition), and Abendroth (conducting) in Cologne. In 1918 he founded the Bad Godesberg Concert Soc. In 1924 he became a conductor at the Berlin Städtische Oper, and also was founder-conductor of the his own chamber orch. and choir (from 1926). In 1935 he emigrated to Palestine. After appearing as a conductor with the Palestine Sym. Orch., he founded the Ramat Gan Chamber Orch., which he took on tours abroad. He also appeared as a guest conductor in Europe and was active as a teacher of voice and conducting. Taube composed orch. pieces and chamber music.—**NS/LK/DM**

Tauber, Richard, eminent Austrian-born English tenor; b. Linz, May 16, 1891; d. London, Jan. 8, 1948. He was the illegitimate son of the actor Richard Anton Tauber; his mother was a soubrette singer. He was christened Richard Denemy after his mother's maiden name, but he sometimes used the last name Seiffert, his mother's married name. He took courses at the Hoch Cons. in Frankfurt am Main and studied voice with Carl Beines in Freiburg im Breisgau. He made his operatic debut at Chemnitz as Tamino in *Die Zauberflöte* (March 2, 1913) with such success that he was engaged in the same year at the Dresden Court Opera; made his first appearance at the Berlin Royal Opera as Strauss's Bacchus in 1915, and later won particular success in Munich and Salzburg for his roles in Mozart's operas. About 1925 he turned to lighter roles, and won remarkable success in the operettas of Lehár. He made his U.S. debut on Oct. 28, 1931, in a N.Y. recital. In 1938 he settled in England, where he appeared as Tamino and Belmonte at London's Covent Garden. In 1940 he became a naturalized British subject. He wrote an operetta, *Old Chelsea*, taking the leading role at its premiere (London, Feb. 17, 1943). He made his last American appearance at Carnegie Hall in N.Y. on March 30, 1947.

BIBL.: H. Ludwigg, ed., *R. T.* (Berlin, 1928); D. Napier-Tauber (his 2nd wife), *R. T.* (Glasgow, 1949); W. Korb, *R. T.* (Vienna, 1966); C. Castle and D. Napier-Tauber, *This Was R. T.* (London, 1971).—**NS/LK/DM**

Taubert, (Carl Gottfried) Wilhelm, German pianist, conductor, teacher, and composer; b. Berlin, March 23, 1811; d. there, Jan. 7, 1891. He was a piano pupil of Neithardt, later of L. Berger, and for composition, of Bernhard Klein. He appeared early as a concert player, and also taught music in Berlin. He became asst. conductor of the court orch. in 1831, then was Generalmusikdirektor of the Royal Opera, Berlin, from 1845 to 1848; also court Kapellmeister from 1845 to 1869; continued to conduct the court orch. until 1883. He conducted his 1st Sym. in Berlin at the age of 20 (March 31, 1831).

WORKS: DRAMATIC: Opera (all 1st perf. in Berlin): *Die Kirmes* (Jan. 23, 1832); *Marquis und Dieb* (Feb. 1, 1842); *Der Zigeuner* (Sept. 19, 1834); *Joggeli* (Oct. 9, 1853); *Macbeth* (Nov. 16, 1857); *Cesario*, after Shakespeare's *Twelfth Night* (Nov. 13, 1874). **OTHER:** Incidental music to 8 plays. **ORCH.:** 4 syms.; 3 overtures; 2 piano concertos; Cello Concerto; Concertino for Violin. **CHAMBER:** 4 string quartets; 2 piano trios; violin sonatas; piano pieces, including *Minnelieder*, op. 16. **VOCAL:** Choral music; some 300 songs, including the successful *Kinderlieder*, opp. 145, 160.

BIBL.: W. Neumann, *W. T. und Ferdinand Hiller* (Kassel, 1857).—**NS/LK/DM**

Taubman, Howard, American music and drama critic; b. N. Y., July 4, 1907; d. Sarasota, Fla., Jan. 8, 1996. He studied at Cornell Univ. (A.B., 1929). He joined the staff of the *N.Y. Times* in 1929, where he was its music ed. (1935–55), music critic (1955–60), drama critic (1960–66), and critic-at-large (1966–72).

WRITINGS: *Opera: Front and Back* (N.Y., 1938); *Music as a Profession* (N.Y., 1939); *Music on My Beat* (N.Y., 1943); *The Maestro: The Life of Arturo Toscanini* (N.Y., 1951); *How to Build a Record Library* (N.Y., 1953; new ed., 1955); *How to Bring Up Your Child to Enjoy Music* (Garden City, N.Y., 1958); *The Making of the American Theater* (N.Y., 1965; rev. in *Musical Comedy*, XII, 1967); *The New York Times Guide to Listening Pleasure* (N.Y., 1968); *The Pleasure of their Company: A Reminiscence* (Portland, Ore., 1994).

BIBL.: L. Weldy, *Music Criticism of Olin Downes and H. T. in "The New York Times," Sunday Edition, 1924–29 and 1955–60* (diss., Univ. of Southern Calif., 1965).—**NS/LK/DM**

Taubmann, Otto, German conductor, music critic, and composer; b. Hamburg, March 8, 1859; d. Berlin, July 4, 1929. After graduation from school, he followed a commercial career for 3 years; then studied music under Wüllner, Rischbieter, Nicodé, and Blassmann at the Dresden Cons.; traveled a year for further study. He began his career as a theater conductor, and from 1886 to 1889 was director of the Wiesbaden Cons. In 1891–92 he was theater conductor in St. Petersburg, and from 1892 to 1895 conductor of the Cäcilienverein in Ludwigshafen. He then settled in Berlin, where from 1898 he was music critic of the *Börsen-Courier*; also taught at the Hochschule für Musik (1920–25).

WORKS: *Porzia*, opera (Frankfurt am Main, 1916); Sym.; String Quartet; *Eine deutsche Messe* for Soloists, Double Chorus, Organ, and Orch. (1896); *Sängerweihe*, choral drama (1904); *Kampf und Friede*, cantata (1915).—**NS/LK/DM**

Taucher, Curt, German tenor; b. Nuremberg, Oct. 25, 1885; d. Munich, Aug. 7, 1954. He studied with Heinrich Hermann in Munich. He made his operatic debut as Faust in Augsburg in 1908; then sang in Chemnitz (1911–14) and Hannover (1915–20). In 1920 he joined the Dresden State Opera, remaining there until 1934; during his tenure there, he created the role of Menelaus in Strauss's opera *Die Ägyptische Helena*. On Nov. 23, 1922, he sang the role of Siegmund in *Die Walküre* at his Metropolitan Opera debut in N.Y.; continued on its roster until 1927. He made guest appearances at Covent Garden in London (1932), at the Berlin State Opera, and at the Bavarian State Opera in Munich. He was noted for his roles in Wagner's operas.
—**NS/LK/DM**

Tauriello, Antonio, Argentine composer and conductor; b. Buenos Aires, March 20, 1931. He studied piano with Paul Spivak and Walter Gieseking, and composition with Alberto Ginastera. While still a youth, he was engaged to conduct opera and ballet at the Teatro Colón in Buenos Aires. He often appeared in the U.S. as an opera rehearsal coach, working at the Lyric Opera in Chicago, the Opera Soc. in Washington, D.C., and the N.Y.C. Opera in the 1960s. In the 1970s he led Verdi opera festivals in San Diego. His early works, several of which were suppressed, were in a neo-Classical mold. His works composed after 1962 embrace the foundations of the international avant- garde.

WORKS: DRAMATIC: Opera: *Les Guerres Picrocholines* (1969–70). **ORCH.:** *Obertura Sinfonica* (1951); *Serenade* (1957); *Música I* for Trumpet and Strings (1958), *II* for Clarinet and Instruments (1961), and *III* for Piano and Orch. (1966); *Ricercari 1 à 6* (1963); 2 serenatas (1964, 1966); *Transparencias* for 6 Instrumental Groups (1964; Washington, D.C., May 12, 1965); *Canti* for Violin and Orch. (1967); *Ilinx* for Clarinet and Orch.

(1968); Piano Concerto (Washington, D.C., June 29, 1968); *Mansión de Tlaloc* (1969). **CHAMBER:** 4 piano sonatinas (1954); *Plany* for Organ (1968); *Suavissimo* for 2 Pianos (1969); *Al Aire Libre* for Trombone and Percussion (1969); *Signos de los Tiempos* for Quintet or Sextet (1969); *Aria* for Flute and Instruments (1970).—**NS/LK/DM**

Tausch, Franz (Wilhelm), celebrated German clarinetist, basset-horn player, and composer; b. Heidelberg, Dec. 26, 1762; d. Berlin, Feb. 9, 1817. He studied with his father, a member of the Mannheim Court Orch. He joined that orch. when he was only 8, then played in the Munich Court Orch. (1777–89), establishing himself as an outstanding virtuoso. In 1789 he went to Berlin as a member of the Court Orch. There he founded a school for wind players in 1805, and among his pupils were Heinrich Barmann and Bernhard Crusell. He wrote several clarinet concertos, 3 concertantes for 2 Clarinets, *Andante and Polonaise* for Clarinet, clarinet duos, trios for 2 Clarinets with Bassoon, 6 quartets for 2 Basset Horns and 2 Bassoons (with 2 Horns ad libitum), 6 military marches, etc.—**NS/LK/DM**

Tausig, Carl (actually, **Karol**), celebrated Polish pianist and composer; b. Warsaw, Nov. 4, 1841; d. Leipzig, July 17, 1871. He began his training with his father, Aloys Tausig (b. Prague, 1820; d. Warsaw, March 14, 1885), who was a pupil of Thalberg and wrote brilliant piano music. Carl was 14 when his father took him to Liszt in Weimar, where he became Liszt's premier pupil; he received instruction in piano, counterpoint, composition, and instrumentation from him, and also accompanied him on his concert tours. He made his debut in 1858, at an orch. concert conducted by Hans von Bülow at Berlin. During the next 2 years he gave concerts in German cities, making Dresden his headquarters; then went to Vienna in 1862, giving orch. concerts with "advanced" programs similar to Bülow's at Berlin. He settled in Berlin in 1865, and opened the Schule des Höheren Klavierspiels. He gave concerts in the principal towns of Germany, and at St. Petersburg and other Russian centers. He died of typhoid fever at the age of 29. Although his career was lamentably brief, he acquired a brilliant reputation for his technical mastery. His works for piano included 2 études de concert, *Ungarische Zigeunerweisen*, *Nouvelles soirées de Vienna*, *Valses-Caprices* on themes from Strauss, and *Tägliche Studien* (transposing chromatic exercises; ed. by Ehrlich), as well as transcriptions and arrangements. —**NS/LK/DM**

Tausinger, Jan, Romanian-born Czech conductor, teacher, and composer; b. Piatra Neamt, Nov. 1, 1921; d. Prague, July 29, 1980. He studied composition with Cuclin, Jora, and Mendelsohn at the Bucharest Cons., graduating in 1947; then went to Prague, where he had lessons in conducting with Ančerl; concurrently took courses in advanced harmony with Alois Hába and Bořkovec at the Prague Academy of Music (1948–52). He was active as a conductor of radio orchs. in Bucharest, Ostrava, and Plzeň; also taught at the Ostrava Cons., where he was director (1952–58); after working for the Czech Radio in Prague (1969–70), he served as director of the Prague Cons. His music was greatly diversified in style, idiom, and technique, ranging from neo-Classical modalities to integral dodecaphony; he made use of optical representational notation when justified by the structure of a particular piece.

WORKS: DRAMATIC: *Dlouhá noc* (The Long Night), ballet (1966); *Ugly Nature*, opera, after Dostoyevsky (1971). **ORCH.:** *Suite in the Old Style* (1946–47); Sym. No. 1, *Liberation* (1952); Violin Concerto (1962–63); *Confrontazione I* and *II* (1964); *Concertino meditazione* for Viola and Chamber Ensemble (1965); *Praeludium, Sarabande and Postludium* for Winds, Harp, Piano, and Percussion (1967); *Musica evolutiva* for Chamber Orch. (1967; Zagreb, Nov. 24, 1971); *Improvisations*, in honor of Bach, for Piano and Orch. (1970); *Sinfonia slovacca* (1979). **CHAMBER:** Violin Sonata (1954); *Partita* for Viola and Piano (1957–58); 2 string trios (1960, 1965); 4 string quartets (1961; 1966; 1970; *Structures*, 1972); *Colloquium* for 4 Wind Instruments (1964); Trio for Violin, Viola, and Guitar (1965); *Le avventure* for Flute and Harp (1965); *Canto di speranza* for Piano Quartet (1965); *Happening* for Piano Trio, based on proclamation of J. Shweik (1966); *De rebus musicalibus* for Flute, Bass Clarinet, Vibraphone, Piano, and Percussion (1967); *Sonatina emancipata* for Trumpet and Piano (1967); Brass Quintet (1968); *Hommage à Ladislav Černý* for Viola and Piano (1971); *"On revient toujours...,"* suite for Violin and Piano (1974); *"Comme il faut,"* sonatina for Oboe and Piano (1974); *Hukvaldy Nonet* (1974); *"Au dernier amour...,"* suite-sonata for Cello and Piano (1974–75); *Non-isosceles* for Flute, Cello, and Piano (1975); Clarinet Sonata (1975); *4 Evocations* for Flute, Viola, Cello, and Piano (1976); *Sketches*, 2nd nonet (1976); *Reminiscences*, 3rd nonet (1976); Sextet for Wind Quintet and Piano (1976); *7 Microchromophonies* for Clarinet, Viola, and Piano (1977); *4 Nuances* for Flute, Harp, Violin, Viola, and Cello (1978). **Piano:** Sonata (1948–50); *10 Dodecaphonic Studies* (1972). **VOCAL:** *A Prayer* for Soprano and Chamber Orch. (1965); *Čmáranice po nebi* (Scrawling in the Sky) for Soprano, Flute, Bass Clarinet, Piano, and Percussion, after Khlebnikov, an early Russian futurist (1967); *Noc* (The Night), musical collage for Soprano, Chorus, Orch., and Guitar, after Pushkin (1967); *Správná věc* (The Right Thing), symphonic picture for Tenor, Baritone, Chorus, and Orch., after Mayakovsky (1967); *Duetti compatibili: Zerot Point* for Soprano and Viola (1971) and *Starting Point* for Soprano and 2 Violins (1979–80); *Ave Maria* for Narrator, Soprano, and Orch. (Prague, Oct. 17, 1972); *Sinfonia bohemica* for Bass, Men's Chorus, Trumpet, Harpsichord, and Orch. (1973–75); choruses.—**NS/LK/DM**

Tavener, John (Kenneth), remarkable English composer; b. London, Jan. 28, 1944. He took up the piano at an early age, and soon began to improvise and write for the instrument. A music scholarship to Highgate School led him to pursue studies in piano, organ, and composition. He also composed pieces for St. Andrew's Presybterian Church in Frognall, Hampstead, where his father was organist. From 1962 to 1966 he studied at the Royal Academy of Music in London, his principal mentors being Lennox Berkeley and David Lumsdaine. While still a student there, he was soloist in the premiere of his Piano Concerto (London, Dec. 6, 1963). With the premiere of his dramatic cantata *Cain and Abel* (London, Oct. 22, 1966), Tavener won wide recognition as well as the Prince Rainier III of Monaco Prize. He secured his reputation as a composer with *The Whale* (London, Jan. 24, 1968), a score for Soloists,

Chorus, and Orch. It was followed by the fine *Il Alium* for Soprano and Orch., which was first performed at a London Promenade Concert on Aug. 12, 1968. His *Celtic Requiem* for Soprano, Children's Chorus, Mixed Chorus, and Orch. (London, July 16, 1969) was highly esteemed. In 1969 he joined the faculty of London's Trinity Coll. of Music. On June 30, 1974, Tavener's *Ultimos Ritos* for Soloists, Chorus, and Orch. was premiered at the Holland Festival, which brought him even wider recognition outside of his homeland. His religious upbringing and his search for spiritual enlightenment led him to embrace the Russian Orthodox Church, to which he was converted in 1977. In subsequent years, his works reflected a profound sense of spiritual renewal. His scores, both sacred and secular, were nobly wrought and reflected his choice of simplification and asceticism. Among his subsequent works, particularly outstanding were his *Akhmatova Requiem* for Soloists and Orch. (Edinburgh, Aug. 20, 1981), *The Protecting Veil* for Cello and String Orch. (London, Sept. 4, 1989), the oratorio *Resurrection* for Soloists, Actors, Chorus, and Orch. (Glasgow, April 17, 1990), the dramatic score *Mary of Egypt* (Aldeburgh, June 19, 1992), *The Apocalypse* for Soloists, Chorus, and Orch. (London, Aug. 14, 1994), and *Fall and Resurrection* for Soloists, Chorus, and Orch. (London, Jan. 4, 2000).

WORKS: DRAMATIC: *The Cappemakers*, dramatic cantata (Sussex Festival, June 14, 1964; rev. 1965); *Cain and Abel*, dramatic cantata (1965; London, Oct. 22, 1966); *Thérèse*, opera (1973; London, Oct. 1, 1979); *A Gentle Spirit*, chamber opera (Bath, June 6, 1977); *Eis Thanaton*, ritual (1986; Cheltenham, July 5, 1987); *Mary of Egypt*, ikon in music and dance (1991; Aldeburgh, June 19, 1992). **ORCH.:** Piano Concerto (1962–63; London, Dec. 6, 1963); Chamber Concerto (1964; rev. version, London, June 12, 1968); *Grandma's Footsteps* (1967–68; London, March 14, 1968); *Variations on "Three Blind Mice"* (1972; BBC-TV, London, Feb. 1, 1973); *Palintropos* for Piano and Orch. (1978; Birmingham, March 1, 1979); *Towards the Son: Ritual Procession* (Cheltenham, July 12, 1982); *The Protecting Veil* for Cello and Strings (1987; London, Sept. 4, 1989); *The Repentant Thief* for Clarinet and Orch. (1990; London, Sept. 19, 1991); *Eternal Memory* for Cello and Strings (1991; Wellington, New Zealand, Nov. 24, 1992); *Theophany* (1993; Basingstoke, May 3, 1994); *Tears of the Angels* for Violin and Strings (1995; London, June 26, 1996); *Petra* for Strings (1996; Aldeburgh, June 21, 1997); *Wake Up...And Die* for Solo Cello and Orchestral Cello Section (1996; Beauvais Festival, May 5, 1998). **CHAMBER:** *In Memoriam Igor Stravinsky* for 2 Alto Flutes, Organ, and Handbells (1971); *Greek Interlude* for Flute and Piano (Missenden, Oct. 10, 1979); *Trisagion* for Brass Quintet (1981; Huddersfield, Nov. 25, 1985); *Chant* for Guitar (London, May 17, 1984); *Little Missenden Calm* for Oboe, Clarinet, Bassoon, and Horn (Missenden, Oct. 13, 1984); *Song for Ileana* for Flute (1988); *The Hidden Treasure* for String Quartet (1989; Keele, Feb. 18, 1991); *Thrinos* for Cello (Edinburgh, Aug. 24, 1990); *The Last Sleep of the Virgin* for String Quartet and Handbells (1991; Cheltenham, July 15, 1992); *Chant* for Cello (Crickade, Oct. 1, 1995); String Quartet No. 3, *Diódia* (1995; West Cork, July 1, 1997); *Out of the Night* for Viola (1996); *My Gaze is ever upon You* for Violin and Tape (1997; London, Nov. 30, 1998). **KEYBOARD: Piano:** *Palin* (1977; London, Nov. 24, 1980); *My Grandfather's Waltz* for Piano Duet (Missenden, Oct. 10, 1980); *Mandoodles* (1982); *In Memory of Cats* (1986; London, Jan. 31, 1988); *Ypakoë* (1997; London, July 5, 1999). **Organ:** *Mandelion* (1981; Dublin, June 27, 1982). **VOCAL:** *Credo* for Tenor, Chorus, and 9 Instruments (1960; Hampstead, Nov. 1961); *Genesis* for Tenor, Chorus, Narrator, and Orch. (1962); *3 Holy Sonnets* for Baritone and Orch. (1962; London, July 20, 1964); *3 Sections from T.S. Eliot's "The Four Quartets"* for High Voice and Piano (1963–64; London, Nov. 11, 1965); *The Whale* for Mezzo-soprano, Baritone, Children's Chorus, Mixed Chorus, Speakers, 6 Male Actors, Orch., and Tape (1965–66; London, Jan. 24, 1968); *Introit for March 27th, the Feast of St. John Damascene*for Soprano, Alto, Chorus, and Orch. (1967–68; London, March 26, 1968); *3 Surrealist Songs* for Mezzo-soprano, Tape, and Piano Doubling Bongos (1967–68); *In Alium* for Soprano and Orch. (London, Aug. 12, 1968); *Celtic Requiem* for Soprano, Children's Chorus, Mixed Chorus, and Orch. (London, July 16, 1969); *Coplas* for 4 Soloists, Chorus, and Tape (Cheltenham, July 9, 1970); *Nomine Jesu* for Mezzo-soprano, Chorus, 2 Players, and 5 Male Speakers (Dartington, Aug. 14, 1970); *Responsorium in Memory of Annon Lee Silver* for 2 Mezzo-soprano, Chorus, and 2 Flutes ad libitum (Birmingham, Sept. 20, 1971); *Ma fin est mon commencement* for Men's Chorus and Instruments (London, April 23, 1972); *Canciones Españolas* for 2 Countertenors or 2 Sopranos and Instruments (London, June 8, 1972); *Little Requiem for Father Malachy Lynch* for Chorus and Orch. (Winchester, July 29, 1972); *Ultimos Ritos* for Soprano, Alto, Tenor, Bass, Chorus, and Orch. (1972; Holland Festival, June 30, 1974); *Requiem for Father Malachy* for 2 Countertenors, Tenor, 2 Baritones, and Orch. (London, June 10, 1973; rev. version, London, Dec. 1, 1979); *Canticle of the Mother of God* for Soprano and Chorus (1976; Rye, April 22, 1977); *Liturgy of St. John Chrysostom* for Chorus (1977); *6 Russian Folksongs* for Soprano and Instruments (1977; London, Jan. 15, 1978); *Kyklike Kinesis* for Soprano, Cello, Chorus, and Orch. (1977; London, March 8, 1978); *Lamentation, Last Prayer and Exaltation* for Soprano and Handbells or Piano (1977; Rye, April 28, 1978); *The Immurement of Antigone* for Soprano and Orch. (1978; London, March 30, 1979); *6 Abbasid Songs* for Tenor, 3 Flutes, and Percussion (1979; Aldeburgh, June 18, 1980); *Akhmatova Requiem* for Soprano, Baritone, and Orch. (1979–80; Edinburgh, Aug. 20, 1981); *Sappho: Lyrical Fragments* for 2 Sopranos and String Orch. (1980; London, April 25, 1981); *The Great Canon of St. Andrew of Crete* for Chorus (1981); *Prayer for the World* for Chorus (London, Oct. 11, 1981); *Risen!* for Chorus and Orch. (Bedford, Oct. 19, 1981); *Funeral Ikos* for Chorus (1981; London, Sept. 12, 1982); *Doxa* for Chorus (London, Sept. 12, 1982); *The Lord's Prayer* for Chorus (London, Sept. 12, 1982); *The Lamb* for Chorus (Winchester, Dec. 22, 1982); *He Hath Entered the Heaven* for 9 Treble Voices and Optional Handbells (1982; Oxford, Jan. 16, 1983); *To a Child Dancing in the Wind* for Soprano, Flute, Harp, and Viola (Missenden, Oct. 16, 1983); *16 Haiku of Seferis* for Soprano, Tenor, and Orch. (Cardiff, May 18, 1984); *Ikon of Light* for Chorus and String Trio (Cheltenham, July 8, 1984); *Orthodox Vigil Service* for Chorus and Handbells (1984; Oxford, May 17, 1985); *A Mini Song Cycle for Gina* for Soprano and Piano (1984; London, April 3, 1986); *Love Bade Me Welcome* for Chorus (Winchester, June 28, 1985); *Angels* for Chorus and Organ (Basingstoke, Nov. 3, 1985); *2 Hymns to the Mother of God* for Chorus (Winchester, Dec. 14, 1985); *Panikhida* for Chorus (London, June 21, 1986); *Ikon of St. Cuthbert of Lindisfarne* for Chorus (1986; Durham, March 20, 1987); *Magnificat and Nunc Dimittis (Collegium Regale)* for Chorus (1986; Cambridge, April 24, 1987); *Meditation on the Light* for Countertenor, Guitar, and Handbells (1986; Spitalfields, June 24, 1991); *Akathist of Thanksgiving* for Soloists, Chorus, and Orch. (1986–87; London, Nov. 21, 1988); *Wedding Prayer* for Chorus (London, April 1987); *Many Years* for Chorus (Frintonon-Sea, Aug. 22, 1987); *Prayer (for Szymanowski)* for Bass and Piano (Warsaw, Sept. 1987); *Acclamation* for Chorus (Canterbury, Dec. 8, 1987); *God Is With Us* for Tenor or Baritone, Chorus, and Organ (Winchester, Dec. 22, 1987); *Hymn to the Holy Spirit* for Chorus (1987; London, June 30, 1988); *The Tyger* for Chorus (1987; Windsor, Sept. 24, 1989); *Apolytikion for St. Nicholas* for Chorus (1988); *Ikon of St. Seraphim* for Soloists, Chorus, Violin, and Orch. (North Cornwall, Aug. 7, 1988); *The Call* for Chorus (Northampton, Sept. 23, 1988); *Let Not the Prince be Silent (A Hymn to Christ the Saviour)* for 2 Antiphonal Choruses (1988; Sherbourne Abbey, May 1989); *The Uncreated Eros* for Chorus (1988; London, May 18, 1990); *Lament of the Mother of God* for Soprano and Chorus (Norwich, June 28, 1989); *Today the Virgin* for Chorus (London, Dec. 27, 1989); *Resurrection* for Soloists, Actors, Mixed Chorus, Men's Chorus, and Orch. (1989; Glasgow, April 17, 1990); *Eonia* for Chorus (1989; Cork, May 6, 1990); *Psalm 121* for Chorus (1989; London, July 8, 1990); *Ikon of the Trinity* for Soloists and Chorus (1990; London, June 6, 1991); *Thunder Entered Her (A Divine Allegory)* for Chorus, Men's Chorus, Organ, and Handbells (1990; St. Albans, June 15, 1991); *A Christmas Round* for Chorus (1990; London, June 6, 1992); *O, Do Not Move* for Chorus (1990; London, June 6, 1992); *Ikon of the Nativity* for Chorus (1991); *The Child Lived* for Soprano and Cello (London, June 7, 1992); *We Shall See Him As He Is* for Soprano, 2 Tenors, Chorus, and Orch. (Chester, July 18, 1992); *A Village Wedding* for Solo Voices (Penarth, Aug. 28, 1992); *Annunciation* for Soloists and Chorus (London, Nov. 25, 1992); *Hymns of Paradise* for Bass, Women's Chorus, and 6 Violins (1992; London, May 27, 1993); *The Lord's Prayer* for Chorus (Bury St. Edmunds, July 25, 1993); *Akhmatova Songs* for Soprano and Cello (Cricklade, Sept. 28, 1993); *Song for Athene* for Chorus (1993; London, March 28, 1994); *The World Is Burning* for Chorus (1993; London, March 28, 1994); *The Apocalypse* for Soloists, Chorus, and Orch. (1993; London, Aug. 14, 1994); *The Myrrh-Bearer* for Viola, Chorus, and Percussion (1993; London, Oct. 9, 1994); *Innocence* for Soprano, Tenor, Chorus, Cello, and Organ (1994; London, Oct. 10, 1995); *Agraphon* for Soprano, String Orch., and Timpani (1994; Athens, Oct. 29, 1995); *Sayati* for Cello and Chorus (Cricklade, Oct. 1, 1995); *Let's Begin Again* for Chorus and Orch. (Norwich, Oct. 7, 1995); *Feast of Feasts* for Soloists, Chorus, and Orch. (1995; Balamand Abbey, Lebanon, March 22, 1996); *Funeral Canticle* for Chorus and Optional Strings (1996); *Vlepondas* for Soprano, Baritone, and Cello (Delphi, Aug. 10, 1996); *The Hidden Face* for Countertenor, Oboe, 8 Violins, and 8 Violas (London, Oct. 13, 1996); *Hymn of the Unwaning Light* for Chorus (1996; Sherbourne Abbey, May 17, 1997); *Apolytikion of St. Martin* for Chorus (London, Nov. 11, 1997); *The Last Discourse* for Soprano, Bass, Chorus, and Amplified Double Bass (1997; London, March 4, 1998); *Lament for Constantinople* for Baritone and Alto Flute (1997; London, March 6, 1998); *...depart in peace...* for Soprano and Orch. (1997; London, June 25, 1998); *Eternity's Sunrise* for Soprano and Orch. (1997; London, July 1, 1998); *The World* for Soprano and String Quartet (1997; West Cork, July 2, 1999; also for Soprano and String Orch., Belfast, Aug. 27, 1999); *Fall and Resurrection* for Soprano, Countertenor, Baritone, Chorus, and Orch. (1997; London, Jan. 4, 2000); *Apolytikion of the Incarnation* for Chorus (Truro Cathedral, Aug. 5, 1998); *In the Month of Athyr* for Narrator and Chorus (London, Nov. 3, 1998); *Nipson* for Countertenor and Viol Consort (1998; Norwich, Oct. 4, 1999).

Bibl.: G. Haydon, *J. T.: Glimpses of Paradise* (London, 1995). **—NS/LK/DM**

Taverner, John, important English composer; b. South Lincolnshire, c. 1490; d. Boston, Lincolnshire, Oct. 18, 1545. He was a lay clerk of the choir at the collegiate church of Tattershall (1524–25). In 1526 he was appointed master of the choristers at Cardinals' Coll. in Oxford. In 1530 he became lay clerk of the choir of the parish church of St. Botolph, in Boston, Lincolnshire, where he served until 1537. In the latter year he was elected a member of the Guild of Corpus Christi there, serving as one of its 2 treasurers from 1541 to 1543. In 1545 he was appointed a town alderman, but died soon afterward. The widely circulated stories of his imprisonment for heresy and of his serving as an agent for Cromwell are totally unfounded. Taverner was a prolific composer of church music; among his works are 8 masses, 9 mass sections, 3 Magnificats, about 25 motets, 4 part-songs, and 2 instrumental pieces. His church music is found in Vols. I and III of *Tudor Church Music* (1923–24) and in H. Benham, ed., *John Taverner: The Six-part Masses*, Early English Church Music, XX (1978).

Bibl.: H. Benham, *The Music of J. T.: A Study and Assessment* (diss., Univ. of Southampton, 1970); C. Hand, *J. T.: His Life and Music* (London, 1978); D. Josephson, *J. T., Tudor Composer* (Ann Arbor, Mich., 1979).**—NS/LK/DM**

Tavrizian, Mikhail (Arsenievich), Armenian conductor; b. Baku, May 27, 1907; d. Yerevan, Oct. 17, 1957. He studied viola (diploma, 1932) and conducting with Gauk (diploma, 1934) at the Leningrad Cons. After playing viola in the Maly Opera orch. in Leningrad (1928–35), he pursued a conducting career. From 1938 he was principal conductor of the Yerevan Opera and Ballet Theater, where he conducted the premieres of many Armenian works. He also was active as a sym. conductor. In 1956 he was made a People's Artist of the U.S.S.R.**—NS/LK/DM**

Tawaststjerna, Erik (Werner), eminent Finnish musicologist; b. Mikkeli, Oct. 10, 1916; d. Helsinki, Jan. 22, 1993. He studied piano with Hannikainen and Bernhard at the Helsinki Cons. (1934–44), with Leygraf in Stockholm, with Neuhaus in Moscow (1946), and with Cortot and Gentil in Paris (1947); later pursued musicological studies at the Univ. of Helsinki (Mag-.Phil., 1958; Ph.D., 1960). After a brief career as a concert pianist, he devoted himself to musicology; was a prof. at the Univ. of Helsinki (1960–83).

Writings (all publ. in Helsinki unless otherwise given): *Sibeliuksen pianosävellykset ja muita esseitä* (Sibelius's Piano Works; 1955; Eng. tr., 1957); *Sergei Prokofjevin ooppera Sota ja rauha* (Sergei Prokofiev's War and Peace; 1960); *Jean Sibelius* (5 vols., 1965–88; Eng. tr. by R. Layton, 1976–); *Esseitä ja arvosteluja* (Essays and Criticism; 1976); *Voces intimae: Minnesbilder från barndomen* (1990); *Scenes historiques: Kirjoituksia vuosilta 1945–58* (Helsingissä, 1992); *Jean Sibelius: Aren 1865–1893* (1992).

Bibl.: E. Salmenhaara, ed., *Juhlakirja E. T.lle* (Helsinki, 1976).**—NS/LK/DM**

Taylor, Art(hur S., Jr.), jazz drummer; b. N.Y., April 6, 1929; d. there, Feb. 6, 1995. He began playing in N.Y. in the late 1940s and first worked professionally with Howard McGhee. Taylor worked with Coleman

Hawkins in the 1950s, making his first recording session with him. Later, Taylor toured with Buddy DeFranco, then worked twice with Bud Powell's trio and, during the mid- and late-1950s, with George Wallington's trio and quintet; during that decade, Taylor also had stints with Miles Davis and the Donald Byrd/Gigi Gryce group. After touring Europe with Thelonious Monk in 1959, Taylor moved there permanently in 1963. He continued to work, mainly with fellow expatriate Americans, and began interviewing them; eventually, the transcripts were published as a book, *Notes and Tones*. He moved back to N.Y. in 1980 and re-emerged as a performer. He organized and played at the "Tribute to Bud Powell" (in 1980), which he later repeated in 1985 at the Kool Jazz Festival to critical acclaim. He led Taylor's Wailers from 1991; among its members were Jacky Terrason and Ravi Coltrane.

Disc.: *Amazing Bud Powell, Vol. 2* (1953); *Taylor's Wailers* (1956); *Taylor's Tenors* (1959); *A.T.'s Delight* (1960); *Mr. A. T.* (1991); *Wailin' at the Vanguard* (1992); *C. Parker Plays Cole Porter* (1954). John Coltrane: *Giant Steps* (1959).—**MM/LP**

Taylor, Billy (actually, **William Edward Jr.**), jazz pianist, educator, composer; b. Greenville, N.C., July 21, 1921. He was born into a musical family in which everyone played piano and sang. When Taylor was a youngster, the family relocated to Washington, D.C. He took classical piano lessons with Henry Grant and experimented with saxophone, drums, and guitar. This prepared him for his first professional appearance on keyboard at age 13 (he earned $1.00). At Va. State Univ., as a sociology major, he was advised by composer Undine Moore that his future lay in music; thereafter Taylor increased his musical study. Shortly after graduation in 1942, he moved to N.Y. In less than a day, he sat in at Minton's with Ben Webster, who hired him two days later. That same night, Taylor met Art Tatum, who soon became his mentor. He became a regular on the N.Y. scene, working with Stuff Smith (1943) and Tiny Grimes (in a group that included Dizzy Gillespie and Cozy Cole) for Billy Rose's Broadway revue *The Seven Lively Arts*. In the late 1940s, Taylor played at Well's, a bar in Harlem, probably—on occasion—opposite an organist named Charlie Stewart. Taylor went on an eight- month tour of Europe with the Don Redman orchestra in 1946. He returned to N.Y. in 1948 to form a duo with organist Bob Wyatt and to play with Billie Holiday in a Broadway revue called *Holiday on Broadway*. In 1949, he published his first book, an instructional manual for bebop piano, a harbinger of his later pre-eminence as an educator. By that time, he had also begun to publish the first of what would become a body of nearly 300 songs.

In 1951, Taylor was hired as the house pianist at Birdland. Earl May was his bassist and remained with him through 1960. He and May also worked with Lester Young at the Audubon. In 1952, Taylor and May added Charlie Smith on drums to form a trio. The group became popular both on their own and working as accompanists in many posh N.Y. clubs. In 1954, they recorded an album live at Town Hall that featured, among other things, Taylor's incandescent rendering of "Theodora," a ballad for his wife. He had a special interest in Latin music and around this time worked and recorded with Candido, whom he had met through Dizzie Gillespie. He also began a lifelong association with violinist Joe Kennedy.

In 1957, Taylor wrote a scathing article about the lack of support for jazz within the black community, "Negroes Don't Know Anything About Jazz." Around the same time, he embarked on a mission to educate the public—not only black audiences—about jazz music. In the late 1950s, he attended a Yale Univ. conference that explored ways to improve musical instruction in public schools. In 1958, he hosted the 13-part series "The Subject is Jazz" for educational television; guests included Duke Ellington, Lee Konitz, Warne Marsh, Langston Hughes, Aaron Copeland, Cannonball Adderley, and Bill Evans. Taylor also began writing on jazz for various journals. Beginning in 1959, he hosted a weekly radio show on WLIB, then moved to WNEW in 1962; he returned to WLIB in 1966 as program director, remaining there until 1969. In 1964, he co-founded the Jazzmobile, a touring stage that presents free concerts in the streets. Grady Tate began working with Taylor, doing jingles and record dates. When Taylor reformed his trio in the mid-1960s, he used Tate and Ben Tucker. They worked at N.Y.'s Hickory House six nights a week for six or seven years and gave concerts. From 1969–72, Taylor was musical director of the band for David Frost's talk show, the first African American to hold such a position. During the 1970s, he also produced the *Billy Taylor Show* and served as musical director for Tony Brown's *Black Journal Tonight* In 1979, he became host of National Public Radio's *Jazz Alive* and the 13-week series, *Taylor Made Piano*; both won Peabody Awards. Since 1981, he has been a contributing correspondent for the CBS *Sunday Morning* television program, and has profiled many jazz musicians. Since the mid-1990s, he has hosted a radio series for National Public Radio of live broadcasts from the Kennedy Center.

From the late 1970s, Taylor became increasingly active as an educator, serving as a visiting faculty at Howard Univ., the Manhattan School of Music, U.C. Irvine, N.C. Central Coll., Shaw Univ., and many other colleges and universities, as well as an adjunct faculty member at C.W. Post. He held the Wilber D. Barrett Chair in Music at the Univ. of Mass., Amherst, through the 1990s, and hosted a regular summer jazz program there. In October 1997, he began a Distance and Learning program originating in Prince William County, Va., that allowed students nationwide to participate through an online hook-up.

During this period, Taylor began composing extended compositions that melded classical forms with jazz. Among the more successful of these works is *Peaceful Warrior*, commissioned by the Atlanta Symphony, a choral work in memory of Dr. Martin Luther King Jr., and *Make a Joyful Noise*, a suite commissioned by Tufts Univ. Taylor has received numerous honorary degrees and awards. Most notably, he was only the third jazz musician to receive the National Medal of Arts, an award he won in 1992. (The other two jazz musicians to receive this award were Dizzy Gillespie and Ella

Fitzgerald.) Taylor continues to lead a trio, and worked in the 1990s with bassist Chip Jackson and drummer Steve Johns.

Taylor is a fine jazz pianist who has become better known as a broadcaster and educator, and as an international leader and spokesperson in the field. He appears to have influenced Herbie Hancock, among many others. Though his ubiquitous presence has drawn skepticism from some, he has proved honest and sincere. He is courageous in handling difficult issues and his ample musicianship lends support to his words.

DISC.: *Billy Taylor Piano* (1945); *Billy Taylor Trio, Vols. 1, 2* (1952); *Mambo Jazz* (1953); *Billy Taylor Mambos* (1953); *Cross Section* (1953); *Billy Taylor Trio in Concert at Town Hall* (inc. "Theodora"; 1954); *Live! at Town Hall* (1954); *With Candido* (1954); *Billy Taylor Presents Ira Sullivan* (1956); *With Four Flutes* (1959); *Billy Taylor Trio Uptown* (1960); *Warming Up* (1960); *Wish I Knew How It Would Feel to Be Free* (1967); *Today* (1969); *OK Billy!* (1970); *Live at Storyville* (1977); *Solo* (1988); *Jazzmobile All-Stars* (1989); *Homage* (1994); *Music Keeps Us Young* (1996); *Ten Fingers, One Voice* (solo; rel. 1998).—**JC/LP**

Taylor, Cecil (Percival), African American jazz pianist and composer; b. N.Y., March 15, 1933. He began piano lessons at age 5; was improvising and composing by the age of 8; later studied percussion. He studied harmony and composition at the N.Y. Coll. of Music; subsequently studied composition at the New England Cons. of Music in Boston; also immersed himself in the Boston jazz scene. He then worked with his own combos in N.Y.; first appeared at the Newport Jazz Festival (1957); gained a name for himself as a performer in the Off-Broadway production of Jack Gelber's The Connection (1959). He made his first tour of Europe in 1962, and then played in many jazz centers on both sides of the Atlantic; performed at N.Y.'s Carnegie Hall in 1977. He made a number of remarkable recordings, including *Into the Hot* (1961), *Unit Structures* (1966), *Silent Tongues* (1975), *The Cecil Taylor Unit* (1978), and *3 Phasis* (1978). His digitally agile piano style and penchant for extended improvisation made him an important figure in avant-garde jazz circles in his time. —**NS/LK/DM**

Taylor, Clifford, American composer and teacher; b. Avalon, Pa., Oct. 20, 1923; d. Abington, Pa., Sept. 19, 1987. He studied composition with Lopatnikoff at the Carnegie-Mellon Univ. in Pittsburgh, and with Fine, Hindemith, Piston, and Thompson at Harvard Univ. (M.A., 1950). He taught at Chatham Coll. in Pittsburgh (1950–63), and in 1963 joined the faculty of Temple Univ. in Philadelphia.

WORKS: DRAMATIC: Opera: *The Freak Show* (1975). **ORCH.:** *Theme and Variations* (1951); *Concerto Grosso* for Strings (1957); 3 syms.: No. 1 (1958), No. 2 (1965; Philadelphia, Dec. 16, 1970), and No. 3 (1978); Concerto for Organ and Chamber Orch. (1963); *Sinfonia Seria* for Concert Band, Flute, and Baritone Horn (1965); Piano Concerto (1974). **CHAMBER:** Violin Sonata (1952); String Quartet for Amateurs (1959); Trio for Clarinet, Cello, and Piano (1959–60); 2 string quartets (1960, 1978); *Concert Duo* for Violin and Cello (1961); Duo for Saxophone and Trombone (1965); *Movement* for 3 for Violin, Cello, and Piano (1967); *Serenade* for Percussion Ensemble (1967); *5 Poems* for Oboe and 5 Brasses (1971). **Piano:** 2 sonatas (1952, 1978); *Fantasia and Fugue* (1959); *30 Ideas* (1972); *36 More Ideas* (1976). **VOCAL:** Numerous a cappella choruses, including choral settings of Western Pennsylvania folk songs (1958) and *A Pageant of Characters from William Shakespeare* for Chorus and Soloists (1964); songs.—**NS/LK/DM**

Taylor, James, prominent artist of the 1970s singer-songwriter movement; b. Boston, March 12, 1948. James Taylor established himself in the forefront of the 1970s singer-songwriter movement with the desperately personal "Fire and Rain" single and *Sweet Baby James* album. Finding an audience with both pop and easy-listening fans, Taylor continued to be a best-selling album artist through the 1970s, as his songs came to reflect less personal anguish and more gentle compassion. Married to Carly Simon from 1972 to 1983, Taylor continued to record albums of substantial popularity into the 1990s.

James Taylor and his siblings Alex, Kate, and Livingston were raised in affluence and moved with their parents to Chapel Hill, N.C., after Livingston's birth in 1950. They spent summers on exclusive Martha's Vineyard beginning in 1953. From an early age, Alex studied violin, Livingston and Kate learned piano, and James took cello lessons. After meeting guitarist Danny "Kootch" Kortchmar on Martha's Vineyard in 1963, James formed the Fabulous Corsairs with brother Alex and three friends in N.C. in 1964. While later attending boarding school near Boston, James began to suffer bouts of depression, which led him to commit himself voluntarily to a psychiatric hospital in 1965, where he began writing songs. After discharging himself nine months later, he went to N.Y. in summer 1966 and formed the Flying Machine with Kortchmar, bassist Zach Weisner, and drummer Joel O'Brien. The group debuted at the Cafe Bizarre that fall and later moved up to the Night Owl, where they played regularly for seven months. Before disintegrating in spring 1967, they made some recordings that were later issued after the success of *Sweet Baby James*.

James Taylor next moved to London, where he made a demonstration tape that so impressed Paul McCartney and Apple A&R chief Peter Asher that he was signed to the Beatles' record label. His debut solo album, which contained odd orchestral segues between songs, included the ominous "The Blues Is Just a Bad Dream," "Knocking 'Round the Zoo," "Something in the Way She Moves" (which provided an opening line for George Harrison's "Something"), and the excellent "Carolina on My Mind" and "Rainy Day Man." However, the album went generally unnoticed, and with affairs in disarray at Apple, Peter Asher negotiated a contract for Taylor with Warner Bros. Records.

After debuting at Los Angeles's Troubadour Club in summer 1969, James Taylor recorded his next album in Calif. with Peter Asher, now his manager, producing. *Sweet Baby James* established him in the vanguard of the emerging singer-songwriter movement with its anguished smash hit single "Fire and Rain." Recorded with Danny Kortchmar, Carole King, and drummer

Russ Kunkel, among others, the album also featured the moderate hit "Country Road" and the gentle "Sunny Skies" and "Blossom." Taylor next recorded *Mud Slide Slim and the Blue Horizon* with Kortchmar, King, Kunkel, and bassist Leland Sklar under producer Asher. The album yielded a top pop and easy-listening hit with King's "You've Got a Friend" and a moderate hit with "Long Ago and Far Away," while including "Love Has Brought Me Around," "You Can Close Your Eyes," and the classic "Hey Mister, That's Me Up on the Jukebox." Taylor's then-girlfriend, Joni Mitchell, provided backing vocals on the record.

In the wake of James Taylor's enormous success, siblings Livingston, Kate, and Alex launched their own recording careers. Livingston's modest-selling debut for Atco produced a minor hit with "Carolina Day," but subsequent albums for Capricorn sold poorly. He later recorded for Epic, Critique, and Vanguard. Kate recorded her first album with James, Carole King, and Linda Ronstadt, and the album sold moderately without yielding a hit single. In the late 1970s she recorded two albums for Columbia. Alex fared the least well of the three, and he died of a heart attack in Sanford, Fla., on March 12, 1993, at age 47.

In 1972 Danny Kortchmar, already a veteran of the band Jo Mama, formed the Section with keyboardist Craig Doerge, bassist Leland Sklar, and drummer Russ Kunkel to back James Taylor on tour and record independently. Kortchmar also recorded a solo album, and the Section later served as Peter Asher's "house band" and toured with Jackson Browne on his Running on Empty tour.

On Nov. 3, 1972, James Taylor married songstress Carly Simon, shortly before the release of *One Man Dog*. Recorded with Simon, Carole King, Linda Ronstadt, and the Section, the album produced a major hit with "Don't Let Me Be Lonely Tonight" and a minor hit with "One Man Parade." In 1973 Taylor costarred with Beach Boy Dennis Wilson in the miserable film *Two-Lane Blacktop*, and scored a smash hit with Carly Simon on a deplorable off-key version of "Mockingbird." Taylor's next album, *Walking Man*, the first not produced by Peter Asher, failed to produce a hit single, but 1975's *Gorilla* yielded a smash pop and top easy-listening hit with Holland-Dozier-Holland's "How Sweet It Is (To Be Loved by You)" and a moderate hit with "Mexico." Taylor toured again in 1975, and his final album for Warner Bros., *In the Pocket*, includes the major pop and top easy-listening hit "Shower the People."

Switching to Columbia Records, James Taylor's debut for the label, *JT*, reunited him with producer Peter Asher and furnished a smash hit with a remake of Jimmy Jones's "Handy Man," a major hit with "Your Smiling Face," and a minor country hit with "Bartender's Blues," a smash country hit for George Jones in 1978. Early that year Taylor had a major pop and top easy-listening hit with Sam Cooke's "Wonderful World," recorded with Paul Simon and Art Garfunkel for Garfunkel's album *Watermark*. After scoring a major hit with Carole King and Gerry Goffin's "Up on the Roof" from *Flag*, Taylor scored his last major pop hit in 1981 with "Her Town Too," recorded with J. D. Souther.

Taylor had a minor hit in 1985 with a cover of Buddy Holly's "Everyday," and another with 1988's "Never Die Young." His 1991 album, *New Moon Shine*, presented him with a more country-style accompaniment, although it failed to perform well in either country or pop markets. Success returned, however, with 1997's *Hourglass*, which charted in the Top Ten and earned him a Grammy Award for Best Pop Album.

DISC.: *J. T. and the Original Flying Machine 1967* (1971); *J. T.* (1968); *Sweet Baby James* (1970); *Mud Slide Slim* (1971); *One Man Dog* (1972); *Walking Man* (1974); *Gorilla* (1975); *In the Pocket* (1976). *Greatest Hits* (1976); *JT* (1977); *Flag* (1979); *Dad Lives His Work* (1981); *That's Why I'm Here* (1985); *Never Die Young* (1988); *New Moon Shine* (1991); *Live* (1993); *Best Live* (1994); *Hourglass* (1997); *Greatest Hits, Vol. 2* (2000). **LIVINGSTON TAYLOR:** *Livingston Taylor* (1970); *Liv* (1971); *Over the Rainbow* (1973); *3-Way Mirror* (1994); *Life Is Good* (1988); *Our Turn to Dance* (1993). **KATE TAYLOR:** *Sister Kate* (1971); *Kate Taylor* (1978); *It's in There and It's Got to Come Out* (1979). **ALEX TAYLOR:** *With Friends and Neighbors* (1971); *Dinnertime* (1972); *The Third Time's for Music* (1974); *Dancing with the Devil* (1991).—**BH**

Taylor, Janis (actually, **Janice Kathleen** née **Schuster**), American-born Canadian mezzo-soprano; b. Westfield, N.Y., March 10, 1946. She studied piano and clarinet before going to Montreal in 1967. In 1972 she became a naturalized Canadian citizen. Following vocal studies with Bernard Diamant, she studied with Lina and Antonio Narducci, Stevenson Barrett, Gérard Souzay, and Danielle Valin. In 1971 she made her recital debut in Montreal. Her orch. debut followed in 1973 as a soloist in *Messiah* with the Toronto Sym. She made her operatic debut as the Queen in Somer's *The Fool* at the Stratford (Ontario) Festival in 1975, and thereafter appeared with various Canadian and American opera houses. In 1979 she made her U.S. orch. debut as a soloist in *Messiah* with the National Sym. Orch. in Washington, D.C. Her European operatic stage debut came that same year when she appeared in Shostakovich's *Lady Macbeth of the District of Mtzensk* at the Spoleto Festival. In 1980 she made her first appearance as an orch. soloist in Europe in *Messiah* with the RAI Orch. in Milan. She sang Handel's Alessandro in a concert performance in N.Y.'s Carnegie Hall in 1985. In 1989 she made her London debut as a soloist in Verdi's Requiem with the London Sym. Orch. In 1990 she was the center of attention when she starred in Schoenberg's *Erwartung* at the Holland Festival in Amsterdam. Taylor has won particular distinction for her varied concert repertoire, being especially admired for her performances of the music of Mahler.—**NS/LK/DM**

Taylor, (Joseph) Deems, greatly popular American composer and writer on music; b. N. Y., Dec. 22, 1885; d. there, July 3, 1966. He graduated from N.Y.U. (B.A., 1906); studied harmony and counterpoint with Oscar Coon (1908–11). After doing editorial work for various publishers and serving as war correspondent for the N.Y. Tribune in France (1916–17), he was music critic for the *N.Y. World* (1921–25), ed. of *Musical America* (1927–29), and music critic for the *N.Y. American* (1931–32). He was an opera commentator for NBC (from

1931); was intermission commentator for the N.Y. Phil. national broadcasts (1936–43); also served as director (1933–66) and president (1942–48) of ASCAP. In 1924 he was elected a member of the National Inst. of Arts and Letters and in 1935 of the American Academy of Arts and Letters. In 1967 the ASCAP-Deems Taylor Award was created in his memory for honoring outstanding writings on music. Following the success of his orch. suite *Through the Looking-Glass*, after Lewis Carroll's tale (1923), he was commissioned by Walter Damrosch to compose a symphonic poem, *Jurgen* (1925). Meanwhile, 2 widely performed cantatas, *The Chambered Nautilus* and *The Highwayman*, had added to his growing reputation, which received a strong impetus when his opera *The King's Henchman*, to a libretto by Edna St. Vincent Millay and commissioned by the Metropolitan Opera, was premiered in that house on Feb. 17, 1927. Receiving 14 performances in 3 seasons, it established a record for American opera at the Metropolitan Opera, but it was surpassed by Taylor's next opera, *Peter Ibbetson* (Feb. 7, 1931); this attained 16 performances in 4 seasons. These successes, however, proved ephemeral, and the operas were allowed to lapse into unmerited desuetude.

WORKS: DRAMATIC: Opera: *The King's Henchman* (1926; N.Y., Feb. 17, 1927); *Peter Ibbetson* (1929–30; N.Y., Feb. 7, 1931); *Ramuntcho* (Philadelphia, Feb. 10, 1942); *The Dragon* (N.Y., Feb. 6, 1958). **Other:** *Cap'n Kidd & Co.*, comic opera (1908); *The Echo*, musical play (1909); *The Breath of Scandal*, operetta (1916); incidental music. **ORCH.:** *The Siren Song*, symphonic poem (1912; N.Y., July 18, 1922); *Through the Looking- Glass* for Chamber Orch. (1917–19; N.Y., Feb. 18, 1919; for Full Orch., 1921–22; N.Y., March 10, 1923); *Jurgen*, symphonic poem (N.Y., Nov. 19, 1925; rev. 1926 and 1929); *Circus Day* for Jazz Orch. (1925; orchestrated by F. Grofé for Full Orch., 1933); *Marco Takes a Walk* (N.Y., Nov. 14, 1942); *A Christmas Overture* (N.Y., Dec. 23, 1943); *Elegy* (1944; Los Angeles, Jan. 4, 1945); *Restoration Suite* (Indianapolis, Nov. 18, 1950). **CHAMBER:** *The Portrait of a Lady*, rhapsody for 10 Instruments (1919); piano pieces. **VOCAL:** *The Chambered Nautilus*, cantata for Chorus and Orch. (1914); *The Highwayman*, cantata for Baritone, Mixed Voices, and Orch. (1914); song cycles; solo songs.

WRITINGS (all publ. in N.Y.): *Of Men and Music* (1937); *The Well Tempered Listener* (1940); *Walt Disney's Fantasia* (1940); ed., *A Treasury of Gilbert and Sullivan* (1941); *Music to My Ears* (1949); *Some Enchanted Evenings: The Story of Rodgers and Hammerstein* (1953).

BIBL.: J. Howard, *D. T.* (N.Y., 1927; 2nd ed., 1940). **—NS/LK/DM**

Taylor, Raynor, English-American singer, organist, teacher, and composer; b. London, 1747; d. Philadelphia, Aug. 17, 1825. He received his early training as a chorister in the Chapel Royal, and in 1765 became organist of a church in Chelmsford; that same year, he was also appointed music director at Marylebone Gardens and at Sadler's Wells Theatre, London. In 1792 he emigrated to the U.S. He presented musical entertainments in Richmond, Va., Baltimore, and Annapolis, where he was organist at St. Anne's Church. Moving to Philadelphia in 1793, he was organist of St. Peter's Church (1795–1813); in 1820 he was one of the founders of the Musical Fund Soc. A gifted singer, he gave humorous musical entertainments which he called "olios," and in 1796 conducted an orch. concert that included several of his own compositions. In collaboration with A. Reinagle, who had been his pupil in London, he composed a monody on the death of Washington (Philadelphia, Dec. 23, 1799), and a ballad opera, *Pizarro, or the Spaniards in* Peru (1800). Some of his song MSS are in the N.Y. Public Library.

BIBL.: J. Cuthbert, *R. T. and Anglo-American Musical Life* (diss., W.Va. Univ., 1980).**—NS/LK/DM**

Tchaikovsky, Boris (Alexandrovich), Russian composer; b. Moscow, Sept. 10, 1925. He studied at the Moscow Cons. with Shostakovich, Shebalin, and Miaskovsky (1941–49). His later works make use of expanded tonality.

WORKS: DRAMATIC: Opera: *The Star* (1949; unfinished). **Other:** Much music for films, radio, and plays. **ORCH.:** *Procession* (1946); 3 syms.: No. 1 (1947; Moscow, Feb. 7, 1962), No. 2 (Moscow, Oct. 17, 1967), and No. 3, Sevastopol (1980; Moscow, Jan. 25, 1981); *Slavonic Rhapsody* (1951); *Sinfonietta* for Strings (1953); *Fantasia on Russian Folk Themes* (1954); *Capriccio on English Themes* (1954); Clarinet Concerto (1957); Overture (1957); Cello Concerto (1964); Chamber Sym. (Moscow, Oct. 27, 1967); Violin Concerto (1969; Moscow, April 25, 1970); Concerto for Piano, 2 Horns, Side Drum, Bass Drum, and Strings (Kaunas, Oct. 17, 1971); *Theme and 8 Variations* (1973; Dresden, Jan. 23, 1974); *6 Studies* for Strings and Organ (1976; Leningrad, Jan. 30, 1979). **CHAMBER:** Piano Trio (1953); 6 string quartets (1954, 1961, 1967, 1972, 1974, 1976); String Trio (1955); Cello Sonata (1957); Violin Sonata (1959); Suite for Cello (1960); Piano Quintet (1962); *Partita* for Cello and Chamber Ensemble (1966). **Piano:** 2 sonatas (1944, 1952); Sonatina (1946); Sonata for 2 Pianos (1973). **VOCAL:** *Signs of the Zodiac*, cantata for Soprano, Harpsichord, and Strings (1974; Leningrad, Jan. 29, 1976); *The Last Spring*, song cycle for Mezzo-soprano, Flute, Clarinet, and Piano (1980); songs.**—NS/LK/DM**

Tchaikovsky, Modest, Russian playwright and librettist, brother of **Piotr Ilyich Tchaikovsky;** b. Alapaevsk, Perm district, May 13, 1850; d. Moscow, Jan. 15, 1916. He was the closest intimate of Tchaikovsky, and the author of the basic biography. His plays had only a passing success, but he was an excellent librettist; he wrote the librettos of Tchaikovsky's last 2 operas, *The Queen of Spades* and *Iolanthe*.**—NS/LK/DM**

Tchaikovsky, Piotr Ilyich, famous Russian composer, brother of **Modest Tchaikovsky;** b. Votkinsk, May 7, 1840; d. St. Petersburg, Nov. 6, 1893. The son of a mining inspector at a plant in the Urals, he was given a good education; had a French governess and a music teacher. When he was 10, the family moved to St. Petersburg and he was sent to a school of jurisprudence, from which he graduated at 19, becoming a government clerk; while at school he studied music with Lomakin, but did not display conspicuous talent as either a pianist or composer. At the age of 21 he was accepted in a musical inst., newly established by Anton Rubinstein, which was to become the St. Petersburg Cons. He studied with Zaremba (harmony and counterpoint) and Rubinstein (composition), graduating in 1865, winning a silver medal for his cantata to Schiller's *Hymn to Joy*. In

1866 he became prof. of harmony at the Moscow Cons. As if to compensate for a late beginning in his profession, he began to compose with great application. His early works reveal little individuality. With his symphonic poem *Fatum* (1868) came the first formulation of his style, highly subjective, preferring minor modes, permeated with nostalgic longing and alive with keen rhythms. In 1869 he undertook the composition of his overture-fantasy *Romeo and Juliet*; not content with what he had written, he profited by the advice of Balakirev, whom he met in St. Petersburg, and revised the work in 1870; but this version proved equally unsatisfactory; Tchaikovsky laid the composition aside, and did not complete it until 1880; in its final form it became one of his most successful works. The Belgian soprano, Désirée Artôt, a member of an opera troupe visiting St. Petersburg in 1868, took great interest in Tchaikovsky, and he was moved by her attentions; for a few months he seriously contemplated marriage, and so notified his father (his mother had died of cholera when he was 14 years old). But this proved to be a passing infatuation on her part, for soon she married the Spanish singer Padilla; Tchaikovsky reacted to this event with a casual philosophical remark about the inconstancy of human attachments. Throughout his career Tchaikovsky never allowed his psychological turmoil to interfere with his work. Besides teaching and composing, he contributed music criticism to Moscow newspapers for several years (1868–74), made altogether 26 trips abroad (to Paris, Berlin, Vienna, N.Y.), and visited the first Bayreuth Festival in 1876, reporting his impressions for the Moscow daily *Russkyie Vedomosti*. His closest friends were members of his own family, his brothers (particularly Modest, his future biographer), and his married sister Alexandra Davidov, at whose estate, Kamenka, he spent most of his summers. The correspondence with them, all of which was preserved and eventually publ., throws a true light on Tchaikovsky's character and his life. His other close friends were his publisher, Jurgenson, Nikolai Rubinstein, and several other musicians. The most extraordinary of his friendships was the epistolary association with Nadezhda von Meck, a wealthy widow whom he never met but who was to play an important role in his life. Through the violinist Kotek she learned about Tchaikovsky's financial difficulties, and commissioned him to write some compositions, at large fees; then arranged to pay him an annuity of 6,000 rubles. For more than 13 years they corresponded voluminously, even when they lived in the same city (Moscow, Florence); on several occasions she hinted that she would not be averse to a personal meeting, but Tchaikovsky invariably declined such a suggestion, under the pretext that one should not see one's guardian angel in the flesh. On Tchaikovsky's part, this correspondence had to remain within the circumscribed domain of art, personal philosophy, and reporting of daily events, without touching on the basic problems of his existence. On July 18, 1877, he contracted marriage with a conservatory student, Antonina Milyukova, who had declared her love for him. This was an act of defiance of his own nature; Tchaikovsky was a homosexual, and made no secret of it in the correspondence with his brother Modest, who was also a homosexual. He thought that by flaunting a wife he could prevent the already rife rumors about his sexual preference from spreading further. The result was disastrous, and Tchaikovsky fled from his wife in horror. He attempted suicide by walking into the Moskva River in order to catch pneumonia, but suffered nothing more severe than simple discomfort. He then went to St. Petersburg to seek the advice of his brother Anatol, a lawyer, who made suitable arrangements with Tchaikovsky's wife for a separation. (They were never divorced; she died in an insane asylum in 1917.) Von Meck, to whom Tchaikovsky wrote candidly of the hopeless failure of his marriage (without revealing the true cause of that failure), made at once an offer of further financial assistance, which he gratefully accepted. He spent several months during 1877–78 in Italy, Switzerland, Paris, and Vienna. During these months he completed one of his greatest works, the 4th Sym., dedicated to von Meck. It was performed for the first time in Moscow on Feb. 22, 1878, but Tchaikovsky did not cut short his sojourn abroad to attend the performance. He resigned from the Moscow Cons. in the autumn of 1878, and from that time dedicated himself entirely to composition. The continued subsidy from von Meck allowed him to forget money matters. Early in 1878 he completed his most successful opera, *Evgeny Onegin* ("lyric scenes," after Pushkin); it was first produced in Moscow by a cons. ensemble, on March 29, 1879, and gained success only gradually; the first performance at the Imperial Opera in St. Petersburg did not take place until Oct. 31, 1884. A morbid depression was still Tchaikovsky's natural state of mind, but every new work sustained his faith in his destiny as a composer, despite many disheartening reversals. His Piano Concerto No. 1, rejected by Nikolai Rubinstein as unplayable, was given its premiere (somewhat incongruously) in Boston, on Oct. 25, 1875, played by Bülow, and afterward was performed all over the world by famous pianists, including Nikolai Rubinstein. The Violin Concerto, criticized by Leopold Auer (to whom the score was originally dedicated) and attacked by Hanslick with sarcasm and virulence at its premiere by Brodsky in Vienna (1881), survived all its detractors to become one of the most celebrated pieces in the violin repertoire. The 5th Sym. (1888) was successful from the very first. Early in 1890 Tchaikovsky wrote his 2nd important opera, *The Queen of Spades*, which was produced at the Imperial Opera in St. Petersburg in that year. His ballets *Swan Lake* (1876) and *The Sleeping Beauty* (1889) became famous on Russian stages. But at the peak of his career, Tchaikovsky suffered a severe psychological blow; von Meck notified him of the discontinuance of her subsidy, and with this announcement she abruptly terminated their correspondence. He could now well afford the loss of the money, but his pride was deeply hurt by the manner in which von Meck had acted. It is indicative of Tchaikovsky's inner strength that even this desertion of one whom he regarded as his staunchest friend did not affect his ability to work. In 1891 he undertook his only voyage to America. He was received with honors as a celebrated composer; he led 4 concerts of his works in N.Y. and one each in Baltimore and Philadelphia. He did not linger in the U.S., however, and returned to St.

Petersburg in a few weeks. Early in 1892 he made a concert tour as a conductor in Russia, and then proceeded to Warsaw and Germany. In the meantime he had purchased a house in the town of Klin, not far from Moscow, where he wrote his last sym., the *Pathétique*. Despite the perfection of his technique, he did not arrive at the desired form and substance of this work at once, and discarded his original sketch. The title *Pathétique* was suggested to him by his brother Modest, and the score was dedicated to his nephew, Vladimir Davidov. Its music is the final testament of Tchaikovsky's life, and an epitome of his philosophy of fatalism. In the first movement, the trombones are given the theme of the Russian service for the dead. Remarkably, the score of one of his gayest works, the ballet *The Nutcracker*, was composed simultaneously with the early sketches for the *Pathétique*. Tchaikovsky was in good spirits when he went to St. Petersburg to conduct the premiere of the *Pathétique*, on Oct. 28, 1893 (which was but moderately successful). A cholera epidemic was then raging in St. Petersburg, and the population was specifically warned against drinking unboiled water, but apparently he carelessly did exactly that. He showed the symptoms of cholera soon afterward, and nothing could be done to save him. The melodramatic hypothesis that the fatal drink of water was a defiance of death, in perfect knowledge of the danger, since he must have remembered his mother's death of the same dread infection, is untenable in the light of publ. private letters between the attendant physician and Modest Tchaikovsky at the time. Tchaikovsky's fatalism alone would amply account for his lack of precaution. Almost immediately after his death a rumor spread that he had committed suicide, and reports to that effect were publ. in respectable European newspapers (but not in Russian publications), and repeated even in some biographical dictionaries (particularly in Britain). After the grim fantasy seemed definitely refuted, a ludicrous paper by an emigre Russian woman was publ., claiming private knowledge of a homosexual scandal involving a Russian nobleman's nephew (in another version a member of the Romanov imperial family) which led to a "trial" of Tchaikovsky by a jury of his former school classmates, who offered Tchaikovsky a choice between honorable suicide or disgrace and possible exile to Siberia; a family council, with Tchaikovsky's own participation, advised the former solution, and Tchaikovsky was supplied with arsenic; the family doctor was supposed to be a part of the conspiracy, as were Tchaikovsky's own brothers. Amazingly enough, this outrageous fabrication was accepted as historical fact by some biographers, and even found its way into the pages of *The New Grove Dictionary of Music and Musicians* (1980). In Russia, the truth of Tchaikovsky's homosexuality was totally suppressed, and any references to it in his diary and letters were expunged.

As a composer, Tchaikovsky stands apart from the militant national movement of the "Mighty Five." The Russian element is, of course, very strong in his music, and upon occasion he made use of Russian folk songs in his works, but this national spirit is instinctive rather than consciously cultivated. His personal relationship with the St. Petersburg group of nationalists was friendly without being close; his correspondence with Rimsky-Korsakov, Balakirev, and others was mostly concerned with professional matters. Tchaikovsky's music was frankly sentimental; his supreme gift of melody, which none of his Russian contemporaries could match, secured for him a lasting popularity among performers and audiences. His influence was profound on the Moscow group of musicians, of whom Arensky and Rachmaninoff were the most talented. He wrote in every genre, and was successful in each; besides his stage works, syms., chamber music, and piano compositions, he composed a great number of lyric songs that are the most poignant creations of his genius. By a historical paradox, Tchaikovsky became the most popular Russian composer under the Soviet regime. His subjectivism, his fatalism, his emphasis on melancholy moods, even his reactionary political views (which included a brand of amateurish anti-Semitism), failed to detract from his stature in the new society. In fact, official spokesmen of Soviet Russia repeatedly urged Soviet composers to follow in the path of Tchaikovsky's aesthetics. His popularity is also very strong in Anglo-Saxon countries, particularly in America; much less so in France and Italy; in Germany his influence is insignificant.

WORKS: DRAMATIC: Opera: *Voyevoda*, op. 3 (1867–68; Moscow, Feb. 11, 1869; destroyed by Tchaikovsky; reconstructed by Pavel Lamm); *Undine* (destroyed by Tchaikovsky; only fragments extant); *Oprichnik* (1870–72; St. Petersburg, April 24, 1874); *Kuznets Vakula* (Vakula the Smith; 1874; St. Petersburg, Dec. 6, 1876); *Evgeny Onegin* (1877–78; Moscow, March, 29, 1879); *Orleanskaya deva* (The Maid of Orleans; 1878–79; St. Petersburg, Feb. 25, 1881; rev. 1882); *Mazepa* (1881–83; Moscow, Feb. 15, 1884); *Cherevichki* (The Little Shoes; 1885; Moscow, Jan. 31, 1887; rev. version of *Kuznets Vakula*); *Charodeyka* (The Sorceress; 1885–87; St. Petersburg, Nov. 1, 1887); *Pikovaya dama* (The Queen of Spades), op. 68 (St. Petersburg, Dec. 19, 1890); *Iolanta*, op. 69 (1891; St. Petersburg, Dec. 18, 1892). **Ballet:** *Lebedinoye ozero* (Swan Lake), op. 20 (1875–76; Moscow, March 4, 1877); *Spyashchaya krasavitsa* (The Sleeping Beauty), op. 66 (1888–89; St. Petersburg, Jan. 15, 1890); *Shchelkunchik* (The Nutcracker), op. 71 (1891–92; St. Petersburg, Dec. 18, 1892). **ORCH.:** 6 numbered syms.: No. 1, op. 13, *Winter Dreams* (1st and 2nd versions, 1866; 2nd version, Moscow, Feb. 15, 1868; 3rd version, 1874; Moscow, Dec. 1, 1883), No. 2, op. 17, *Little Russian* or *Ukrainian* (1st version, 1872; Moscow, Feb. 7, 1873; 2nd version, 1879–80; St. Petersburg, Feb. 12, 1881), No. 3, op. 29, *Polish* (Moscow, Nov. 19, 1875), No. 4, op. 36 (1877–78; Moscow, Feb. 22, 1878), No. 5, op. 64 (St. Petersburg, Nov. 17, 1888), and No. 6, op. 74, *Pathétique* (St. Petersburg, Oct. 28, 1893); also *Manfred Symphony*, op. 58 (1885; Moscow, March 23, 1886) and Sym. in E- flat Major (1892; unfinished; sketches utilized in Piano Concerto No. 3, op. 75, and in *Andante and Finale* for Piano and Orch., op. 79; sym. reconstructed and finished in 1957 by S. Bogatyrev, and publ. as Sym. No. 7); *Allegro ma non tanto* for Strings (1863–64); *Little Allegro* for 2 Flutes and Strings (1863–64); *Andante ma non troppo* for Small Orch. (1863–64); *Agitato and Allegro* for Small Orch. (1863–64); *Allegro vivo* (1863–64); *The Romans in the Coliseum* (1863–64; not extant); *Groza* (The Storm), overture to Ostrovsky's play, op. 76 (1864; St. Petersburg, March 7, 1896); Overture (1st version for Small Orch., 1865; St. Petersburg, Nov. 26, 1865; 2nd version for Large Orch., 1866; Moscow, March 16, 1866); Concerto Overture

(1865–66; Voronezh, 1931); *Festival Overture* on the Danish national anthem, op. 15 (1866; Moscow, Feb. 11, 1867); *Fatum*, symphonic poem, op. 77 (1868; Moscow, Feb. 27, 1869; destroyed by Tchaikovsky; reconstructed, 1896); *Romeo and Juliet*, fantasy overture (1st version, 1869; Moscow, March 16, 1870; 2nd version, 1870; St. Petersburg, Feb. 17, 1872; 3rd version, 1880; Tiflis, May 1, 1886); *Serenade for Nikolai Rubinstein's Name Day* for Small Orch. (Moscow, Dec. 18, 1872); *Burya* (The Tempest), symphonic fantasia, op. 18 (Moscow, Dec. 19, 1873); 3 piano concertos: No. 1, op. 23 (Boston, Oct. 25, 1875), No. 2, op.44 (1879–80; N.Y., Nov. 11 [public rehearsal], Nov. 12 [official premiere], 1881), and No. 3, op. 75 (1893; St. Petersburg, Jan. 19, 1895); *Sérénade mélancolique* for Violin with Orch., op. 26 (1875; Moscow, Jan. 28, 1876); *Slavonic March*, op. 31 (Moscow, Nov. 17, 1876); *Francesca da Rimini*, symphonic fantasia, op. 32, after Dante (1876; Moscow, March 9, 1877); *Variations on a Rococo Theme* for Cello and Orch., op. 33 (1876; Moscow, Nov. 30, 1877); *Valse-Scherzo* for Violin and Orch., op. 34 (1877; Paris, Sept. 20, 1878); Violin Concerto, op. 35 (1878; Vienna, Dec. 4, 1881); 4 suites: No. 1, op. 43 (Moscow, Nov. 23, 1879), No. 2, op. 53 (1883; Moscow, Feb. 16, 1884), No. 3, op. 55 (1884; St. Petersburg, Jan. 28, 1885), and No. 4, op. 61, *Mozartiana* (Moscow, Nov. 26, 1887); *Italian Capriccio*, op. 45 (Moscow, Dec. 18, 1880); *Serenade* for Strings, op. 48 (1880; St. Petersburg, Oct. 30, 1881); *1812 Overture*, op. 49 (1880; Moscow, Aug. 20, 1882); *Festival Coronation March* (Moscow, June 4, 1883); *Concert Fantasia* for Piano and Orch., op. 56 (1884; Moscow, March 6, 1885); *Elegy* for Strings (Moscow, Dec. 28, 1884); *Jurists' March* (1885); *Pezzo capriccioso* for Cello with Orch., op. 62 (1887; Moscow, Dec. 7, 1889); *Hamlet*, fantasy overture, op. 67 (St. Petersburg, Nov. 24, 1888); *Voyevoda*, symphonic ballad, op. 78 (Moscow, Nov. 18, 1891); *Shchelkunchik* (The Nutcracker), suite from the ballet, op. 71a (St. Petersburg, March 19, 1892); *Andante and Finale* for Piano and Orch., op. 79 (1893; unfinished; finished and orchestrated by Taneyev; St. Petersburg, Feb. 20, 1896). **CHAMBER:** 3 string quartets: No. 1, op. 11 (1871), No. 2, op. 22 (1874), and No. 3, op. 30 (1876); Piano Trio, op. 50 (Moscow, Oct. 30, 1882); *Adagio* for 4 Horns (1863–64); *Adagio* for 2 Flutes, 2 Oboes, 2 Clarinets, English Horn, and Bass Clarinet (1863–64); *Adagio molto* for String Quartet and Harp (1863–64); *Allegretto* for String Quartet (1863–64); *Allegretto molto* for String Trio (1863–64); *Allegro* for Piano Sextet (1863–64); *Allegro vivace* for String Quartet (1863–64); *Andante ma non troppo*, prelude for String Quartet (1863–64); *Andante molto* for String Quartet (1863–64); String Quartet (1865; 1 movement only); *Souvenir d'un lieu cher* for Violin and Piano, op. 42 (1878); *Souvenir de Florence* for String Sextet, op. 70 (1890; rev. 1891–92; St. Petersburg, Dec. 7, 1892). **Piano:** *Allegro* (1863–64; unfinished); *Theme and Variations* (1863–64); Sonata, op. 80 (1865); 2 pieces, op. 1 (1867); *Souvenir de Hapsal*, op. 2 (1867); *Valse caprice*, op. 4 (1868); *Romance*, op. 5 (1868); *Valse-Scherzo*, op. 7 (1870); *Capriccio*, op. 8 (1870); *Trois morceaux*, op. 9 (1870); *Deux morceaux*, op. 10 (1871); *6 morceaux*, op. 19 (1873); *6 morceaux, composés sur un seul thème*, op. 21 (1873); *Les Quatre Saisons*, 12 characteristic pieces for each month of the year (1875–76); *March for the Volunteer Fleet* (1878); *Album pour enfants: 24 pièces faciles (à la Schumann)*, op. 39 (1878); *Douze morceaux (difficulté moyenne)*, op. 40 (1878); Sonata, op. 37 (1878); *6 morceaux*, op. 51 (1882); *Impromptu-Caprice* (1884); *Dumka: Russian Rustic Scene*, op. 59 (1886); *Valse-Scherzo* (1889); *Impromptu* (1889); *Aveu passioni* (c. 1892); Military march (1893); *Dix-huit morceaux*, op. 72 (1893); *Impromptu (Momento lirico)* (c. 1893; unfinished; finished by Taneyev). **VOCAL: Choral:** *K radosti* (Ode to Joy), cantata for Soloists, Chorus, and Orch. (1865; St. Petersburg, Jan. 10, 1866); Cantata for the bicentenary of the birth of Peter the Great for Tenor, Chorus, and Orch. (Moscow, June 12, 1872); Cantata for Tenor, Chorus, and Orch. (1875; St. Petersburg, May 6, 1876); *Liturgy of St. John Chrysostom* for Chorus, op. 41 (1878); Vesper Service for Chorus, op. 52 (1881–82); *Moskva* (Moscow), coronation cantata for Soloists, Chorus, and Orch. (Moscow, May 27, 1883); 9 sacred pieces for Chorus (1884–85); Hymn in honor of Saints Cyril and Methodius for Chorus (Moscow, April 18, 1885); *Legenda* for Chorus, op. 54/5 (1889); etc. **Other:** About 100 songs, among them such favorites as *Nur wer die Sehnsucht kennt* (after Goethe) and *Berceuse*.

BIBL.: COLLECTED WORKS, SOURCE MATERIAL: An exhaustive ed. of his compositions was publ. in Moscow and Leningrad (1940–71). His diaries for the years 1873–91 were publ. in Moscow and Petrograd (1923; Eng. tr., 1945). He wrote a treatise which was publ. in an Eng. tr. as *Guide to the Practical Study of Harmony* (Leipzig, 1900). A complete ed. of his literary works and correspondence commenced publ. in Moscow in 1953. The *New Edition of the Complete Works* began publ. in Moscow and Mainz in 1993. **BIOGRAPHICAL, ANALYTICAL, AND CRITICAL:** H. Laroche, *Na pamyat o P.I. T.* (In Memory of P.I. T.; St. Petersburg, 1894); idem, *Pamyati T.* (Memories of T.; St. Petersburg, 1894); V. Baskin, *P.I. T.* (St. Petersburg, 1895); R. Newmarch, *T.: His Life and Works* (London, 1900); M. Tchaikovsky, *Zhizn P.I. T.* (The Life of P.I. T.; 3 vols., Moscow, 1900–2; abr. Eng. tr. by R. Newmarch as *The Life and Letters of P.I. T.*, London, 1906); E. Evans, *T.* (London, 1906; 2nd ed., rev., 1935); I. Glebov, *P.I. T.: evo zhizn i tvorchestvo* (P.I. T.: Life and Works; Petrograd, 1922); idem, *Instrumentalnoye tvorchestvo T.* (The Instrumental Works of T.; Petrograd, 1922); idem, *T.: opit kharakteristiki* (T: An Attempt at a Characterization; Petrograd, 1923); E. Blom, *T.: Orchestral Works* (London, 1927); N. Findeisen, *Kamernaya muzika T.* (T.'s Chamber Music; Moscow, 1930); G. Abraham, ed., *T.: A Symposium* (London, 1945); H. Weinstock, *T.* (N.Y., 1946); D. Shostakovich et al., *Russian Symphony: Thoughts About T.* (N.Y., 1947); B. Yarustovsky, *Opernaya dramaturgiya T.* (T.'s Operatic Dramatury; Moscow and Leningrad, 1947); E. Orlova, *Romansi T.* (T.'s Songs; Moscow and Leningrad, 1948); A. Nikolayev, *Fortepiaovye naslediye T.* (T.'s Piano Legacy; Moscow and Leningrad, 1949; 2nd ed., 1958); D. Zhitmorsky, *Baleti P. T.* (P. T.'s Ballets; Moscow and Leningrad, 1950; 2nd ed., 1958); A. Nikolayev, *Fortepiannoye proizvedeniya P.I. T.* (P.I. T.'s Piano Works; Moscow, 1957); V. Protopopov and N. Tumanina, *Opernoye tvorchestvo T.* (T.'s Operas; Moscow, 1957); N. Nikolayeva, *Simfonii P.I. T.* (P.I. T.'s Symphonies; Moscow, 1958); L. Raaben, *Skripichniye i violonchel niye proizvedeniya P.I. T.* (P.I. T.'s Violin and Cello Works; Moscow, 1958); A. Alshvang, *P.I. T.* (Moscow, 1959); A. Dolzhansky, *Simfonicheskaya muzika T.* (T.'s Symphonic Music; Moscow, 1961; 2nd ed., 1965); G. Krauklis, *Skripichniye proizvedeniya P.I. T.* (P.I. T.'s Violin Works; Moscow, 1961); N. Tumanina, *T.* (Moscow, 1962–68); A. Alshvang, *P.I. T.* (Moscow, 1967); J. Warrack, *T.: Symphonies and Concertos* (London, 1969); E. Garden, *T.* (London, 1973; 2nd ed., rev., 1984); J. Warrack, *T.* (London, 1973); V. Volkoff, *T.* (Boston and London, 1974); D. Brown, *T.: A Biographical and Critical Study*: Vol. I: *The Early Years (1840–1874)* (London, 1978), Vol. II: *The Crisis Years (1874–1878)* (London, 1982), and Vol. III: *The Years of Wandering (1878–1885)* (London, 1986); J. Warrack, *T. Ballet Music* (London, 1979); W. Strutte, *T.* (Sydney, 1983); R. Wiley, *T.'s Ballets* (Oxford, 1985); E. Yoffe, *T. in America: The Composer's Visit to Celebrate the Opening of Carnegie Hall in New York City* (N.Y., 1986); H. Zajaczkowski, *T.'s Musical Style* (Ann Arbor, 1987); N. John, ed., *T.: Eugene Onegin* (London, 1988); A. Kendall, *T.: A Biography* (London,

1988); A. Orlova, *T. Day by Day: A Biography in Documents* (ed. by M. Brown and tr. by F. Jonas; Ann Arbor, 1988); idem, *T.: A Self- Portrait* (Oxford, 1990); A. Poznansky, *T.: The Quest for the Inner Man* (N.Y., 1991); J. Brenner, *T., ou, La nuit d'octobre: 1840–1893* (Monaco, 1993); C. Casini and M. Delogu, *T.: La vita tutte le composizioni* (Milan, 1993); E. Garden and N. Gotteri, eds., and G. von Meck, tr., *"To my Best Friend: " Correspondence Between T. and Nadezha von Meck, 1876–1878* (Oxford, 1993); A. Lischke, *P.I. T.* (Paris, 1993); A. Poznansky, *T.'s Last Days: A Documentary Study* (Oxford, 1996); N. Berberova, *T.* (St. Petersburg, 1997); L. Kearney, ed., *T. and His World* (Princeton, 1998); L. Sidelnikov, *T.* (Rostov-na- Donu, 1998).—**NS/LK/DM**

Tchaikowsky, André, Polish pianist and composer; b. Warsaw, Nov. 1, 1935; d. Oxford, June 26, 1982. Most of his family fell victim to the Nazis, but he and his grandmother were hidden by a Catholic family in Warsaw (1942–45). After the liberation, he studied piano at the Łódź State Music School (1945–47) and with Emma Tekla Altberg at the Warsaw Cons. (1947–48); then took an advanced piano course with Lazare Lévy at the Paris Cons. (premier prix, 1950); subsequently studied piano with Stanislaw Szpinalski and composition with Kazimierz Sikorski at the Warsaw Cons. (1950–55); made his debut as a pianist in 1955. He went to Paris to study composition with Boulanger (1957), and then to England to continue his studies with Musgrave and later with Hans Keller. Although he continued to make appearances as a pianist, he gave increasing attention to his work as a composer from 1960. An eccentric to the end, he bequeathed his skull to the Royal Shakespeare Co. for use in the graveside scene in *Hamlet* ("Alas, poor André, A fellow of infinite jest"); it made its debut in 1984.

WORKS: DRAMATIC: Opera: *The Merchant of Venice* (1960–82). **ORCH.:** Violin Concerto (1950); Flute Concerto (1950); 2 piano concertos (1953, 1971); Clarinet Concerto (1953); Sym. (1958). **CHAMBER:** Sonata for Viola and Clarinet (1954); *Concerto classico* for Violin (1957); Clarinet Sonata (1959); Octet (1961); 2 string quartets (1967, 1975); *Trio notturno* (1978); piano pieces. **OTHER:** Vocal music.—**NS/LK/DM**

Tchakarov, Emil, Bulgarian conductor; b. Burgas, June 29, 1948; d. Paris, Aug. 4, 1991. He received his training at the Bulgarian State Cons. in Sofia, where he conducted its youth orch. (1965–72). From 1968 to 1970 he also was conductor of the Bulgarian TV Chamber Orch. After capturing 3rd prize in the Karajan Competition (1971), he pursued training in conducting with Ferrara (1972) and Jochum (1974). In 1974 he became conductor of the Plovdiv State Phil. On Sept. 27, 1979, he made his Metropolitan Opera debut in N.Y. conducting *Eugene Onegin*, and remained on its roster until 1983. In 1985–86 he was chief conductor of the Flanders Phil. in Antwerp. As a guest conductor, he appeared in many music centers around the globe.—**NS/LK/DM**

Tcherepnin, Alexander (Nikolaievich), distinguished Russian-born American pianist, conductor, and composer, son of **Nikolai (Nikolaievich) Tcherepnin** and father of **Serge (Alexandrovich) Tcherepnin** and **Ivan (Alexandrovich) Tcherepnin;** b. St. Petersburg, Jan. 20, 1899; d. Paris, Sept. 29, 1977. He studied piano as a child with his mother, and was encouraged by his father in his first steps in composition, although he did not take formal lessons with him. He composed a short comic opera when he was 12, and a ballet when he was 13, and then produced a number of piano works, composing 14 sonatas before he was 19. In 1917 he entered the Petrograd Cons., where he studied theory with Sokolov, and piano with Kobiliansky, but remained there only one school year. He then joined his parents in a difficult journey to Tiflis during the Civil War, where he took lessons in composition with Thomas de Hartmann. In 1921 the family went to Paris, where he continued his studies, taking lessons in piano with Philipp and in composition with Vidal. In 1922 he played a concert of his own music in London; in 1923 he was commissioned by Anna Pavlova to write a ballet, *Ajanta's Frescoes*, which she produced in London with her troupe. Tcherepnin progressed rapidly in his career as a pianist and a composer; he played in Germany and Austria; made his first American tour in 1926. Between 1934 and 1937 he made two journeys to the Far East; gave concerts in China and Japan; numerous Chinese and Japanese composers studied with him; he organized a publishing enterprise in Tokyo for the publication of serious works by young Japanese and Chinese composers. He married a Chinese pianist, Lee Hsien-Ming. Despite his wide travels, he maintained his principal residence in Paris, and remained there during World War II. He resumed his concert career in 1947; toured the U.S. in 1948. In 1949 he and his wife joined the faculty of De Paul Univ. in Chicago, and taught there for 15 years. In the meantime, his music became well known; he appeared as a soloist in his piano concertos with orchs. in the U.S. and Europe. He became a naturalized American citizen in 1958. In 1967 he made his first visit to Russia after nearly a half century abroad. He was elected a member of the National Inst. of Arts and Letters in 1974. In his early works, he followed the traditions of Russian Romantic music; characteristically, his Piano Sonata No. 13, which he wrote as a youth, is entitled *Sonatine romantique*. But as he progressed in his career, he evolved a musical language all his own; he derived his melodic patterns from a symmetrically formed scale of 9 degrees, subdivided into 3 equal sections (e.g. C, D, E-flat, E, F-sharp, G, G-sharp, A-sharp, B, C); the harmonic idiom follows a similar intertonal formation; his consistent use of such thematic groupings anticipated the serial method of composition. Furthermore, he developed a type of rhythmic polyphony, based on thematic rhythmic units, which he termed "interpunctus." However, he did not limit himself to these melodic and rhythmic constructions; he also explored the latent resources of folk music, both oriental and European; he was particularly sensitive to the melorhythms of Russian national songs. A composer of remarkable inventive power, he understood the necessity of creating a communicative musical language, and was primary concerned with enhancing the lyric and dramatic qualities of his music. At the same time, he showed great interest in new musical resources, including electronic sound.

WORKS: DRAMATIC: Opera: *Ol-Ol* (1925; Weimar, Jan. 31, 1928; rev. 1930); *Die Hochzeit der Sobeide* (1930; Vienna, March 17, 1933); *The Farmer and the Nymph* (Aspen, Colo., Aug. 13, 1952). **Ballet:** *Ajanta's Frescoes* (London, Sept. 10, 1923); *Training* (Vienna, June 19, 1935); *Der fahrende Schüler mit dem Teufelsbannen* (1937; score lost during World War II; reconstructed, 1965); *Trepak* (Richmond, Va., Oct. 10, 1938); *La Légende de Razine* (1941); *Le Déjeuner sur l'herbe* (Paris, Oct. 14, 1945); *L'Homme à la peau de léopard* (Monte Carlo, May 5, 1946; in collaboration with A. Honegger and T. Harsányi); *La Colline des fantômes* (1946); *Jardin persan* (1946); *Nuit kurde* (Paris, 1946); *La Femme et son ombre* (Paris, June 14, 1948); *Aux temps des tartares* (Buenos Aires, 1949); *Le gouffre* (1953). **ORCH.:** 6 piano concertos: No. 1 (1919–20; Monte Carlo, 1923), No. 2 (1923; Paris, Jan. 26, 1924), No. 3 (1931–32; Paris, Feb. 5, 1933), No. 4 (1947; retitled *Fantasia*), No. 5 (Berlin, Oct. 13, 1963), and No. 6 (1965; Lucerne, Sept. 5, 1972); Overture (1921); *Rhapsodie georgienne* for Cello and Orch. (1922); *Concerto da camera* for Flute, Violin, and Chamber Orch. (1924); 4 syms.: No. 1 (Paris, Oct. 29, 1927), No. 2 (1947–51; Chicago, March 20, 1952), No. 3 (1952; Indianapolis, Jan. 15, 1955), and No. 4 (1957; Boston, Dec. 5, 1958); *Mystère* for Cello and Chamber Orch. (Monte Carlo, Dec. 8, 1926); *Magna mater* (1926–27; Munich, Oct. 30, 1930); Concertino for Violin, Cello, Piano, and Strings (1931); *Russian Dances* (Omaha, Feb. 15, 1934); *Suite georgienne* for Piano and Strings (1938; Paris, April 17, 1940); *Evocation* (1948); Harmonica Concerto (1953; Venice, Sept. 11, 1956); Suite (1953; Louisville, May 1, 1954); *Divertimento* (Chicago, Nov. 14, 1957); *Symphony-Prayer* (1959; Chicago, Aug. 19, 1960); *Serenade* for Strings (1964); *Russian Sketches* (1971); *Musica sacra* for Strings (Lourdes, April 28, 1973). **CHAMBER:** *Ode* for Cello and Piano (1919); 2 string quartets (1922, 1926); Violin Sonata (1922); 3 cello sonatas (1924, 1925, 1926); Piano Trio (1925); Piano Quintet (1927); *Elegy* for Violin and Piano (1927); *Le Violoncelle bien temperé*, 12 preludes for Cello with Piano, 2 with Drum (Berlin, March 23, 1927); *Mouvement perpetuel* for Violin and Piano (1935); Kettledrum Sonatina (1939); *Sonatine sportive* for Bassoon or Saxophone and Piano (1939); *Andante* for Tuba and Piano (1939): Trio for Flutes (1939); Quartet for Flutes (1939); *Marche* for 3 Trumpets (1939); Suite for Cello (1946); *Sonata da chiesa* for Viola da Gamba and Organ (1966); Quintet for 2 Trumpets, Horn, Trombone, and Tuba (1972); Woodwind Quintet (1976); Duo for 2 Flutes (1977). **KEYBOARD: Piano:** *10 bagatelles* (1913–18); *Scherzo* (1917); *Sonatine romantique* (1918); 2 sonatas (1918, 1961); *Feuilles libres* (1920–24); *Toccata* (1921); *5 arabesques* (1921); *9 inventions* (1921); *2 novelettes* (1922); *4 préludes nostalgiques* (1922); *6 études de travail* (1923); *Message* (1926); *Entretiens* (1930); *Études de piano sur la gamme pentatonique* (1935); *Autour des montagnes russes* (1937); *Badinage* (1942); *Le Monde en vitrine* (1946); 12 Preludes (1952); 8 Pieces (1954). **Harpsichord:** Suite (1966). **VOCAL: Cantatas:** *Vivre d'amour* (1942); *Pan Kéou* (Paris, Oct. 9, 1945); *Le Jeu de la Nativité* (Paris, Dec. 30, 1945); *Les Douze* for Narrator, Strings, Harp, Piano, and Percussion (Paris, Nov. 9, 1947); *Vom Spass und Ernst*, folksong cantata for Voice and Strings (1964); *The Story of Ivan the Fool*, with Narrator (London, Dec. 24, 1968); *Baptism Cantata* for Chorus and Orch. (1972). **Other:** *Lost Flute*, 7 songs on poems translated from the Chinese, for Narrator and Piano (1954); several albums of songs to poems in Russian, French, and Chinese.

BIBL.: W. Reich, *A. Tscherepnine* (Bonn, 1959; 2nd ed., rev., 1970); C.-J. Chang, *A. T., His Influence on Modern Chinese Music* (diss., Columbia Univ. Teachers Coll., 1983); E. Arias, *A. T.: A Bio-Bibliography* (Westport, Conn., 1988).—**NS/LK/DM**

Tcherepnin, Ivan (Alexandrovich), French-born American composer of Russian descent, son of **Alexander (Nikolaievich) Tcherepnin** and brother of **Serge (Alexandrovich) Tcherepnin;** b. Issy-les-Moulineaux, near Paris, Feb. 5, 1943; d. Boston, April 11, 1998. He studied composition with his father at home and at the Académie Internationale de Musique in Nice, and also had piano lessons with his mother. He went to the U.S. and became a naturalized American citizen (1960), where he continued his studies with Thompson and Kirchner at Harvard Univ. (B.A., 1964; M.A., 1969). He received the John Knowles Paine Travelling Fellowship to pursue training in electronic music with Stockhausen and Pousseur in Cologne and in conducting with Boulez (1965). He likewise studied electronic techniques in Toronto (1966). He taught at the San Francisco Cons. and at Stanford Univ. (1969–72), where he served as co-director, with Chowning, of its new-music ensemble, Alea II. He then was assoc. prof. and director of the electronic music studio at Harvard Univ. (from 1972). In 1989 he traveled to China, where he performed and gave lectures in Shanghai and Beijing. In 1996 he won the Grawemeyer Award at the Univ. of Louisville for his Double Concerto. From 1984 his work was evenly divided between electronic and instrumental pieces; his Rhythmantics series used digital sampling techniques and temporal displacement to explore areas of rhythmic pattern formation. His instrumental works, generally more referential, drew on musical resources ranging from gagaku and gamelan to Western tonal structures.

WORKS: ORCH.: *Le Va et le vient* (1978); Concerto for Oboe and Orch. or Wind Orch. (1980; rev. 1988); *New Consonance* for Strings (1983); *Solstice* for Chamber Orch. (1983); *Status* for Wind Orch. (1986); *Constitution* for Narrator and Wind Orch. (1987); *Concerto for 2 Continents* for Synthesizer and Wind Orch. (1989); *Carillona* for Wind Orch. (1993); *Dialogue Between the Moon and Venus as Overheard by an Earthling* for Wind Orch. (1994); Double Concerto for Violin, Cello, and Orch. (Cambridge, Mass., June 3, 1995); Triple Concertino for English Horn, Trombone, Contrabass Clarinet, and Wind Orch. (1996). **CHAMBER:** *Suite progressive* for Flute, Cello, and Timpani (1959); *Deux entourages pour un thème russe* for Horn or Ondes Martenot, Piano, and Percussion (1961); *Suite Mozartienne* for Flute, Clarinet, and Bassoon (1962); *Cadenzas in Transition* for Clarinet, Flute, and Piano (1963); *Sombres lumières* for Flute, Guitar, and Cello (1965); *Wheelwinds* for 9 Wind Instruments (1966); *Explorations* for Flute, Clarinet, String Trio, Piano, and Optional Live Electronics (1985); *Trio Fantasia* for Violin, Cello, and Piano (1985); *Fanfare for Otto Hall* for 3 Trumpets and 4 Horns (1991); *7 Fanfares* for 3 Trumpets (1995). **Piano:** *4 Pieces from Before* (1959–62); *Beginnings* (1963); *2 Reminiscences* (1968); *Silent Night Mix* for 2 Pianos (1969); *3 Pieces* for 2 Pianos (1970–72); *12 Variations on Happy Birthday* (1970–80); *Fêtes* (1975); *Valse éternelle: "The 45 R.P.M."* (1977); *Summer Nights* (1980). **WITH ELECTRONICS:** *AC-DC (Alternating Currents)* for 8 Percussionists and Tape (1967); *Rings* for String Quartet and Ring Modulators (1969); *Light Music* for 4 Instrumental Groups, 4 Sound-activated Strobe Lights, Photocells, Electronics, and Tape (1970); *Les Adieux* for Tenor, Alto, 14 Instruments, Electronics, Tape, and Colored Lights (1971); *Globose Floccose* for Brass Quintet, String Quartet, Electronics, and Tape (1973); *Set, Hold, Clear, and Squelch* for Oboe, Frequency

Follower, Electronics, and Tape (1976); *Santur Opera* for Santur, Electronics, Actors, and Projections (1977; rev. 1994 as *Santur Opera II, the Sequel*); *Flores musicales* for Oboe, Violin, Cello, Psalter, and Electronics (1979); *5 Songs* for Contralto, Flute, and Electronics (1979); *Cantilenas/Hybrids* for Violin and Electronics (1983); *New Rhythmantics* for String Quartet and Electronics (1985); *Explorations* for Flute, Clarinet, String Trio, Piano, and Optional Electronics (1985); *New Rhythmantics IV* for String Quartet, Trumpet, and Electronics (1987); *The Creative Act* for 4 Performers and Live Electronics (1990); *Pictures at an Exhibition I: "Untitled" by Jasper Johns* for Samplers (1992); also solo pieces for Tape. **VOCAL:** *And So It Came to Pass*, cantata for Soprano, Tenor, Chorus, and Orch. (1991).—**NS/LK/DM**

Tcherepnin, Nikolai (Nikolaievich), noted Russian conductor, pedagogue, and composer, father of **Alexander (Nikolaievich) Tcherepnin;** b. St. Petersburg, May 15, 1873; d. Issy-les-Moulineaux, near Paris, June 26, 1945. He was a student of Rimsky-Korsakov at the St. Petersburg Cons. (1895–98), and in 1905 he was appointed to its faculty, teaching orchestration and conducting; Prokofiev was among his students. In 1908 he became a conductor at the Marinsky Theater and the Imperial Opera in St. Petersburg; was conductor of the initial season of the Ballets Russes in Paris in 1909. After the Russian Revolution in 1917, he served as director of the Tiflis Cons. (1918–21); then settled in Paris, where he was director of the Russian Cons. (1925–29; 1938–45). His music embodies the best elements of the Russian national school; it is melodious and harmonious; lyrical and gently dynamic; in some of his works, there is a coloristic quality suggesting French impressionistic influence.

WORKS: DRAMATIC: Opera: *Svat* (1930); *Vanka* (1932; Belgrade, 1935). **Ballet:** *Le pavillon d'Armide* (St. Petersburg, Nov. 25, 1907); *Narcisse et Echo* (Monte Carlo, April 26, 1911); *Le Masque de la Mort Rouge* (Petrograd, Jan. 29, 1916); *Dionysus* (1922); *Russian Fairy Tale* (1923); *Romance of the Mummy* (1924). **ORCH.:** *Prelude* to Rostand's play *La Princesse lointaine* (1897); *Fantaisie dramatique* (1903); *Le Royaume enchanté*, symphonic tableau (1904); Piano Concerto (1907). **CHAMBER:** *Poème lyrique; Cadence fantastique; Un Air ancien* for Flute and Piano; *Pièce calme* for Oboe and Piano; *Pièce insouciante* for Clarinet and Piano; *Variations simples* for Bassoon and Piano; *Fanfare* for Trumpet and Piano; String Quartet; Quartet for Horns; *Divertissement* for Flute, Oboe, and Bassoon. **Piano:** *14 esquisses sur les images d'un alphabet russe* (orch. version of 8, Boston, Nov. 27, 1931); *Primitifs; Pièces de bonne humeur; Pièces sentimentals.* **VOCAL:** Liturgical music of the Russian Orthodox rite, including masses a cappella; *Pilgrimage and Passions of the Virgin Mary* (Paris, Feb. 12, 1938); over 200 songs; realization and completion of Mussorgsky's opera *The Fair at Sorochinsk* (Monte Carlo, March 17, 1923).—**NS/LK/DM**

Tcherepnin, Serge (Alexandrovich), French-born American composer and electronic musical instrument inventor of Russian descent, son of **Alexander (Nikolaievich) Tcherepnin** and brother of **Ivan (Alexandrovich) Tcherepnin;** b. Issy-les-Moulineaux, near Paris, Feb. 2, 1941. He studied violin as a child; was taken to the U.S. in 1949 and became a naturalized American citizen in 1950. He studied theory with his father and received instruction in harmony from Boulanger, then took courses with Billy Jim Layton and Kirchner at Harvard Univ. (B.A., 1965), attended Princeton Univ. (1963–64), and completed his training with Eimert, Stockhausen, Nono, Earle Brown, and Boulez in Europe. He was director of the electronic music studio at N.Y.U. (1968–70), and was a teacher of composition at the Valencia (Calif.) School of Music (from 1970) and at Dartington Hall in England (summers, 1979–80). He invented the Serge, a modular synthesizer, which was manufactured by his own company (from 1974).

WORKS: *Inventions* for Piano (1960); String Trio (1961); *Kaddish* for Narrator, Flute, Oboe, Clarinet, Piano, 2 Percussion, and Violin (1962); *Figures-grounds* for 7 to 77 Instruments (1964); *2 Tapes: Giuseppe's Background Music I-II* for 4-track Tape (1966); *2 More Tapes: Addition and Subtraction* for 2-track Tape (1966); *Morning After Piece* for Saxophone and Piano (1966); *Quiet Day at Bach* for Instrument and Tape (1967); *Piece of Wood* for Performers, Actor, and Composer (1967); *Piece of Wood with Weeping Woman* for Musicians, Women, Stagehand, and Tape (1967); *Film* for Mixed Media (1967); *"Hat" for Joseph Beuys* for Actor and Tape (1968); *For Ilona Kabos* for Piano (1968); *Definitive Death Music* for Amplified Saxophone and Instrumental Ensemble (1968); *Paysages électroniques*, film score (1977); *Samba in Aviary*, film score (1978).—**NS/LK/DM**

Tchicai, John (Martin), avant-garde jazz saxophonist, leader; b. Copenhagen, April 28, 1936. The son of a Danish mother and a Congolese father, he began studying violin at the age of 10, and took up alto saxophone and clarinet at age 16. He studied saxophone privately and at the Aarhus Academy of Music and the Academy of Music, Copenhagen, for three years. He made his recording debut in 1962, playing in Warsaw with local musicians; the same year he met Archie Shepp and Bill Dixon at the Helsinki Festival. On their advice, he moved to N.Y.C. in 1963. He played with Don Cherry; formed the New York Contemporary Five with Shepp, Dixon, Don Moore, and J. C. Moses; and toured Europe with this group, though Cherry replaced Dixon. He also worked in N.Y.C. with Roswell Rudd, Milford Graves, Steve Swallow, or Eddie Gomez as the N.Y. Art Quartet in 1964 and 1965. He joined the Jazz Composers Guild and played with Carla Bley. Returning to Denmark in 1966, he co-founded and led the workshop ensemble Cadentia Nova Danica from 1967 to 1971 and performed with them in London in 1968. This was, at one time, a 40-piece ensemble that recorded "Afrodisiaca." In approximately 1969, a group of university students in Cambridge, England, who were interested in free jazz and spontaneous improvisation put on a concert under the name "Natural Music" that featured Tchicai, Yoko Ono, and numerous others. Tchicai recorded with Ono and John Lennon in 1969.

During the late 1960s and early 1970s, Tchicai began to play bamboo flutes, bass clarinet, soprano saxophone, and some percussion; in 1972 he began working on hatha yoga and meditation. He performed less often during this period, but taught full-time in elementary schools, composed, and led workshops. He resumed active playing in 1977, when he was the first jazz-musician to receive a three-year composing stipend from the Danish Ministry of Culture. The same year, he joined Pierre Dorge's New Jungle Orch. Since the early

1980s, the tenor saxophone has been his main instrument; he also uses keyboards and sequencers as tools for composing. He began touring Europe, India, Japan, and Africa. as both the leader of his own groups and as a sideperson. He also played with Johnny Dyani, Abdullah Ibrahin, Misha Mengelberg, Lee Konitz, Cecil Taylor, and Gunter Hampel. The Danish Ministry of Culture awarded him a lifetime grant in 1990. Based in Davis, Calif., since 1991, he founded John Tchicai and the Archetypes, a seven-piece band that fuses afro-jazz with blues-rock. Tchicai teaches at Univ. Calif., Davis, and conducts workshops in schools and prisons. He also composes and works on various new projects, as a Calif. Artist-in-Residence (for composition,1996–97) and as a Calif. Arts Council roster-artist. He often incorporates poetry and audience participation into his performances and has collaborated with Amiri Baraka, John Stewart, and David Gitin as well as with painters, actors, and dancers. He has composed for film, theater, plays, and video projects. His compositions for classical ensembles include *Disturbances on the Fish Scale*, 1989; *Forwards and Backwards*, 1990; *United Spirits of America*, 1992; *Movement for Symphony Orchestra*, 1989; *Bohe*, for six percussionists, 1987.

Disc.: *Archie Shepp in Europe Vols. 1 & 2* (1963). New York Contemporary Five: *Consequences* (1963). John Tchicai–Archie Shepp: *Rufus* (1963). Archie Shepp: *Four for Trane* (1964); *New York Art Quartet & Imamu Amiri Baraka* (1964); *New York Eye and Ear Control* (1964). The Jazz Composers Orchestra: *Communication* (1964). New York Art Quartet: *Mohawk* (1965). John Coltrane: *Ascension* (1965). New York Art Quartet: *Roswell Rudd* (1965); *John Tchicai and Cadentia Nova Danica* (1968). Instant Composers Pool: *Instant Composers Pool* (1968). John Tchicai and Cadentia Nova Danica: *Afrodisiaca* (1969). John Lennon and Yoko Ono: *Unfinished Music No. 2: Life with the Lions* (1969); *Instant Composers Pool* (1970). The John Tchicai/ Irene Schweizer Group: *Willie the Pig* (1975); *John Tchicai and the Strange Brothers* (1977); *John Tchicai/Andre Goudbeek: Duets* (1977); *John Tchicai/Andre Goudbeek: Barefoot Dance* (1978). The Berlin Jazz Workshop Orchestra: *Who Is Who?* (1978). Johnny Dyani: with John Tchicai and Dudu Pukwana: *Witchdoctor's Son* (1978). John Tchicai/Hartmut Geerken: *Continent* (1980). John Tchicai solo: *John Tchicai Live in Athens* (1980). John Tchicai/Pierre Dorge: *Ball at Louisiana* (1981). John Tchicai Orchestra: *Merlin Vibrations* (1983). Cecil Taylor: *Winged Serpent* (1984). Moye, Tchicai, Geerken: *The African Tapes Vols. I and II* (1985). John Tchicai & Clinch: *Tchicai/Clinch* (1988). John Tchicai & Vitold Rek: *Satisfaction* (1992). John Tchicai Quartet w. Misha Mengelberg: *Grandpa's Spells* (1993). John Tchicai & the Archetypes: *Love Is Touching* (1995).—**LP**

Teagarden, Charlie (actually, **Charles**; aka **Little T**), jazz trumpeter, brother of **Jack Teagarden;** b. Vernon, Tex., July 19, 1913; d. Las Vegas, Dec. 10, 1984. He was a sterling player overshadowed by his brother Jack, with whom he worked in 1936 and at various times from 1940 through 1951. Beginning in 1929, he worked with Ben Pollack, Red Nichols, Paul Whiteman (most of the period 1933–40), Jimmy Dorsey (on and off from 1948 until 1950), and Bob Crosby (regularly 1954–58). Teagarden did studio work in Hollywood during the 1950s, then freelanced and led his own bands in Las Vegas from about 1960 on. He retired from playing to become an executive in the musicians' union there in the mid-1960s.

Disc.: *Big Horn of Little "T"* (1962).—**JC/LP**

Teagarden, Jack (**Weldon Leo**; aka **Big T**), jazz trombonist, singer, brother of **Charlie Teagarden;** b. Vernon, Tex., Aug. 29, 1905; d. New Orleans, Jan. 15, 1964. His mother Helen played piano and his father Charles was an amateur trumpeter. His brothers Charlie and Cub and his sister Norma were all musicians. Teagarden started playing piano at age five, and his father bought him a baritone horn two years later. By the age of 10, Teagarden was playing trombone. In 1918, he moved with his family to Chappell, Nebr.; there, he played briefly in local theatres accompanied by his mother on piano. After living in Oklahoma City, Teagarden moved to San Angelo to live with his uncle. He began gigging with local bands and then played in a quartet led by drummer Cotton Bailey at Horn Palace Inn, near San Antonio, from late 1920 until September 1921, except for a short summer season in Shreveport. It was Bailey who named him Jack. From September 1921 until spring 1923 he played with pianist Peck Kelley's Bad Boys; he would rejoin Kelley briefly in 1924. He primarily worked with Doc Ross's band, making his first trip to the West Coast and N.Y. with this outfit. He moved to N.Y. in late 1927, and worked with Ben Pollack from late June 1928, remaining with him, except for brief spells, until leaving for Chicago in May of 1933. During this period, he led his own recording orchestra and took part in many studio recordings with Benny Goodman, Red Nichols, Louis Armstrong, Eddie Condon, and others. In October 1928, Teagarden cut "Makin' Friends" with Eddie Condon. He made history by using a water glass as a substitute for a mute, removing the bell of the trombone and holding the glass over the open end of the tubing to produce a unique sound.

He worked with various Chicago-based bands from June–December 1933, then joined the Paul Whiteman Orch., remaining with Whiteman until December 1938, except for a one-month engagement in N.Y. in December 1936 with the Three T's (Jack and Charlie Teagarden and Frankie Trumbauer). He left Whiteman at Christmas 1938, and shortly afterwards began rehearsing with his own band, which made its debut in N.Y. (February 1939). From then until November 1946, Teagarden led his own big bands, which were successful musically rather than financially. Kitty Kallen and David Allyn sang with Teagarden's band. He did many freelance recordings and was also featured at the Esquire Jazz Concert in January 1944. He led his own sextet from late 1946 until he appeared as a guest at Louis Armstrong's Town Hall concert in spring 1947 (they sang a classic duet on "Old Rockin' Chair's Got Me"). Teagarden then joined Louis Armstrong All Stars from July 1947 until August 1951. He then left to form his own All Stars, which he continued to lead until playing with Ben Pollack for several months in 1956. He then reformed his own All Stars, and co-led (with Earl Hines) a sextet which visited Britain and Europe in autumn of 1957 to acclaim. Led his own All Stars on tour of Asia (September 1958 to January 1959), a group that he continued to lead until the time of his death. He played his last engagement at The Dream Room in New Orleans while suffering from bronchial pneumonia. Teagarden returned to his motel after the gig; the next morning, a maid found him dead on the floor, clad in his dress shirt and shorts.

Songs associated with Teagarden include "I Ain't Lazy, I'm Just Dreaming," "I Gotta Right to Sing the Blues," "Meet Me Where They Play the Blues," "A Hundred Years from Today," "Basin Street Blues" (he originated the introductory phrase "Won't you come along with me"), and many others. An incessant tinkerer with things mechanical, he made his own water valve on his trombone. It is also said he made mouthpieces. He appeared in a number of films: *Thanks a Million* (1935), as a member of the Paul Whiteman Orch.; *Birth of the Blues* (1941); *Twilight on the Prairie* (1944); *The Strip* (1951), with Louis Armstrong; *Glory Alley* (1952), in which Teagarden plays himself, and which includes an appearance by Armstrong; *The Glass Wall* (1953), with Teagarden as himself and music by Shorty Rogers; *Jazz on a Summer's Day* (1959); as well as "soundie" shorts and others.

DISC.: "I Gotta Right to Sing the Blues" (1929); "100 Years from Today" (1931); "On The Air" (1936); *Jack Teagarden's Big Eight* (1938); "Rompin' and Stompin'" (1939); *Big "T" & The Condon Gang* (1944); *With His Sextet and Eddie Condon* (1947); *Meet Me Where They Play the Blues* (1954); *Jack Teagarden in Concert* (1958); *On Okinawa* (1959); *Jazz Maverick* (1960); *Portrait of Mr. T* (1961); *Sextet in Person* (1963); *The Mosaic Complete Capitol Recordings* (rec. 1950s); *Live at the Monterey Jazz Festival* (1963; with family and friends). Louis Armstrong: *Knockin' a Jug*; with Eddie Condon: *Makin' Friends* (1928); *That's a Serious Thing* (1928). Johnny Johnson and His Statler Pennsylvanians: "Thou Swell"/"My One and Only" (1927).

BIBL.: Jay D. Smith and Len Gutteridge, *Jack Teagarden: The Story of a Jazz Maverick* (England, 1960); Howard J. Water Jr., *Jack Teagarden's Music: His Career and Recordings* (Stanhope, N.J., 1960).—**JC/LP/MM**

Tear, Robert, distinguished Welsh tenor and conductor; b. Barry, Glamorgan, March 8, 1939. He was a choral scholar at King's Coll., Cambridge, where he graduated in English (1957–61); received vocal instruction from Julian Kimbell. He became a lay vicar at St. Paul's Cathedral in London in 1960; also was active with the Ambrosian Singers. In 1963 he made his operatic debut as Quint in Britten's *The Turn of the Screw* with the English Opera Group in London, where he made regular appearances until 1971; also sang at London's Covent Garden, where he created the role of Dov in Tippett's *The Knot Garden* in 1970; was chosen to sing the role of the Painter in the first complete performance of Berg's *Lulu* in Paris in 1979; in 1984 he appeared in the premiere of Tippett's *The Mask of Time* in Boston; in 1991 he sang the title role in Penderecki's *Ubu rex* in Munich. He made guest appearances with various opera houses at home and abroad; also won particular renown as a concert artist; after making his debut as a conductor in Minneapolis in 1985, he appeared as a guest conductor with many orchs. In 1986 he was appointed to the International Chair of Vocal Studies at the Royal Academy of Music in London. From 1992 to 1994 he was artistic director of the vocal faculty of the London Royal Schools of Music. In 1984 he was made a Commander of the Order of the British Empire. His autobiography was publ. as *Tear Here* (London, 1990).—**NS/LK/DM**

Tebaldi, Renata, celebrated Italian soprano; b. Pesaro, Feb. 1, 1922. Her mother, a nurse, took her to Langhirano after the breakup of her marriage to a philandering cellist. Renata was stricken with poliomyelitis when she was 3. After initial vocal training from Giuseppina Passani, she studied with Ettore Campogaliani at the Parma Cons. (1937–40) and with Carmen Melis at the Pesaro Cons. (1940–43). She made her operatic debut in Rovigo as Elena in Boito's *Mefistofele* in 1944. In 1946 Toscanini chose her as one of his artists for the reopening concert at La Scala in Milan, and she subsequently became one of its leading sopranos. She made her first appearance in England in 1950 with the visiting La Scala company at London's Covent Garden as Desdemona; also in 1950 she sang Aida with the San Francisco Opera. On Jan. 31, 1955, she made her Metropolitan Opera debut in N.Y. as Desdemona in Verdi's *Otello*; she continued to appear regularly there until 1973. She toured Russia in 1975 and 1976. Her repertoire was almost exclusively Italian; she excelled in both lyric and dramatic roles; was particularly successful as Violetta, Tosca, Mimi, and Madame Butterfly. She also sang the role of Eva in *Die Meistersinger von Nürnberg*. On Nov. 3, 1958, she was the subject of a cover story in *Time* magazine.

BIBL.: K. Harris, *R. T.: An Authorized Biography* (N.Y., 1974); C. Casanova, *R. T.: The Voice of an Angel* (Dallas, 1995). —**NS/LK/DM**

Tebaldini, Giovanni, Italian conductor, music scholar, and composer; b. Brescia, Sept. 7, 1864; d. San Benedetto del Tronto, May 11, 1952. He studied with Ponchielli, Panzini, and Amelli at the Milan Cons. (1883–85) and with Haller and Haberl at the Regensburg School for Church Music (1888). He served as maestro of the Schola Cantorum at San Marco in Venice (1889–93), maestro di cappella at the Basilica of S. Antonio in Padua (1894–97), and director of the Parma Cons. (1897–1902). After teaching at the Cons. di San Pietro a Majella in Naples (1925–30), he went to Genoa, where he was appointed director of the Ateneo Musicale (1931). His specialty was Italian sacred music, but he gained sensational prominence when he publ. an article provocatively entitled "Telepatia musicale" (*Rivista Musicale Italiana*, March 1909), in which he cited thematic similarities between the opera *Cassandra* (1905) by the relatively obscure Italian composer Vittorio Gnecchi and *Elektra* by Richard Strauss, written considerably later, implying a "telepathic" plagiarism on the part of Strauss. However, the juxtaposition of musical examples from both operas proved specious and failed to support Tebaldini's contention.

WRITINGS: *La musica sacra in Italia* (Milan, 1894); *Gasparo Spontini* (Recanati, 1924); *Ildebrando Pizzetti* (Parma, 1931). —**NS/LK/DM**

Tedesco, Ignaz (Amadeus), Bohemian pianist and composer, called the "Hannibal of octaves"; b.

Prague, 1817; d. Odessa, Nov. 13, 1882. He studied with Triebensee and Tomaschek. He made successful concert tours, especially in southern Russia; settled in Odessa. He composed for piano in a salon style and also produced transcriptions.—**NS/LK/DM**

Teed, Roy (Norman), English pianist, organist, teacher, and composer; b. Herne Bay, Kent, May 18, 1928. He studied composition with Lennox Berkeley, piano with Virginia McLean, and harmony and counterpoint with Paul Steinitz at the Royal Academy of Music in London (1949–53). From 1966 to 1992 he was on its faculty, and from 1966 to 1979 he also taught at the Colchester Inst. Music School.

Works: Dramatic: Opera: *The Overcoat* (1988–93). **Orch.:** Piano Concerto (1952); *Festival Suite* for Cello and String Orch. (1958); *Around the Town,* comedy march (1962); *Music for a Ballet,* suite (1975); *A Celebration Overture,* for Sir Lennox Berkeley's 80th birthday (1983); Concertino for Treble Recorder and Strings (1984); Overture (1989). **Chamber:** *Introduction and Scherzo* for Flute, Oboe, and Piano (1960); Quartet for Flute and Strings (1961); *Serenade* for 10 Winds (1982); Trio for Violin, Cello, and Piano (1985); *Sextet Variations* for Clarinet, Bassoon, Horn, Violin, Viola, and Cello (1987); *Elegy, Scherzo, and Trio* for Trumpet and Piano (1988); *Rondo with Variations* for Violin and Piano (1991); *Concert Piece* for Oboe and Piano (1994); Violin Sonata (1994); organ works. **Vocal:** *5 Funny Songs* for Medium Voice and Clarinet or Piano or Orch. (1954); *So Blest a Day,* Christmas cantata (1960); *The Pied Piper* for Soloists, Chorus, and Orch. (1961); *The Jackdaw of Rheims,* narrative cantata (1964); *The Pardoner's Tale* for Baritone, Chorus, and Orch. (1966); 2 sets of *5 Epitaphs,* humorous song cycles (1969, 1978); *Music of the Seasons* for Baritone, Chorus, and Orch. (1980); *Music Fills the Air* for Chorus (1984); *A Trip to the Zoo,* 23 songs for Very Young Singers and Piano or Orch. (1987); *Psalm 89* for Chorus and Organ (1993); *6 Poems* for Medium Voice and Piano or Strings (1994); *5 Love Poems* for Tenor and Piano or Piano Quintet (1995); other choral pieces and songs; carols. —**NS/LK/DM**

Teichmüller, Robert, German pianist and teacher; b. Braunschweig, May 4, 1863; d. Leipzig, May 6, 1939. He studied piano with his father and with Reinecke at the Leipzig Cons., where from 1897 until his death he taught piano; was made a prof. in 1908. With K. Hermann, he publ. *Internationale moderne Klaviermusik* (Leipzig, 1927).

Bibl.: A. Baresel, *R. T. als Mensch und Künstler* (Leipzig, 1922); idem, *R. T. und die Leipziger Klaviertradition* (Leipzig, 1934).—**NS/LK/DM**

Teitelbaum, Richard (Lowe), innovative American composer and performer; b. N.Y., May 19, 1939. He began classical piano studies at the age of 6, and was later educated at Haverford Coll. in Pa. (B.A., 1960) and Yale Univ. (M.Mus., 1964), studying at the latter with Allen Forte and Mel Powell; also studied with Stockhausen, Ligeti, and Babbitt in Darmstadt (1964), and with Luigi Nono and Goffredo Petrassi on a Fulbright fellowship in Rome (1964–66). In 1966 he returned to Europe with the first Moog synthesizer to appear in Europe. He gave numerous concerts, and in 1967 helped to found the now-legendary live electronic music group Musica Elettronica Viva (MEV), with Frederic Rzewski and Alvin Curran. In 1970 he created the equally pioneering intercultural world music group World Band at Wesleyan Univ., where he conducted special research in ethnomusicology, with emphasis on shakuhachi, Javenese gamelan, and West African drumming. In 1976–77 a Senior Fulbright grant enabled him to travel to Japan, where he studied Gagaku with Masataro Togi and shakuhachi with Katsuya Yokoyama. In 1999 he held residencies at the Bellagio Center (Rockefeller Foundation) and the Liguria Study Center (Bogliasco Foundation). Teitelbaum taught at the Calif. Inst. for the Arts in Valencia, Calif. (1971); he also established the Electronic Music Studio at the Art Inst. of Chicago (1972–73), and from 1973 to 1976 taught at York Univ. in Toronto. In 1984–85 he was a visiting artist in Berlin on a Deutscher Akademischer Austauschdienst grant, and in 1986 an Asian Cultural Council Grant permitted him six weeks in Japan to realize the vocal composition *Iro wa Niedo* for 20 Japanese Shingon Buddhist Monks. In 1988 he was in residence at the Mass. Inst. of Technology, then joined the faculty of Bard Coll. in Annandale-on-Hudson, N.Y., where he currently directs its Electronic Music Studios. Teitelbaum has been an acknowledged pioneer in electronic music and multimedia for nearly three decades, combining in his works electronics with classical forms, jazz improvisation, and world music. He has also performed with artists from diverse cultures, including an American tour with Noh flute virtuoso Meisho Tosha, concerts with Indonesian and Thai musicians at the first International Festival of New Arts in Bangkok, and an all-night benefit concert for earthquake victims in Kobe, Japan. In the U.S., he has performed extensively as a soloist and with such artists as saxophonists Anthony Braxton, Steve Lacy, and Lee Konitz, violinist Mark Feldman, guitarists Fred Frith and Derek Bailey, cellist Tom Cora, and pianist Yuji Takahashi; he also collaborated with Nam June Paik on his *Video Opera* (1993). Among his awards are NEA grants (1976, 1979, 1988, 1997) and grants from the N.Y. State Council on the Arts (1984, 1987, 1995), and his commissions have ranged from the Venice Biennale (1983) and Cologne's WDR (1985, 1990) to Berlin's Hebbel Theater/Inventionen Festival (1992) and the Woodstock Chamber Orch. (2000).

Works: *Intersections* for Piano (1963); *Music for Flute Alone* (1963); *The Rose* for Voice and Piano (1963); *Concerto da Camera* for 14 Instruments (1965); *Tutto e Perduto* for Voice and Instruments (1965); *In Tune* for Amplified Brainwaves, Heartbeats, Breath, and Moog Synthesizer (1967); *High Culture Imports* for World Band (1970–71); *La Mattina Presto* for Tape (1970–71); *Tuning* for Wind Instruments and Keyboards (1970–71) and *Tuning II* for Wind Instruments, Piano, Synthesizer, Trumpet, and Percussion (1973); *Border Region* for Optigan, Voice, Film, Slides, and Tape (1972); *A Space* for Indeterminate Instrumentation (1974); *Hi Kaeshi Hachi Mi Fu* for Shakuhachi (1974); *Tai Chi Alpha Tala* for Tai Chi Performer, Biomedical Telemetry System, Synthesizer, Mrdangam, and Video Synthesizer (1974); *Threshold Music* for Soft Instruments and Environmental Sounds (1974); *Ghosts* for Tape and Bells (1975); *Kei-San* for Percussion and Synthesizer (1975); Trio for Winds, Piano, and Synthesizer (1975); *Valley* for Percussion and Tape (1975);

Behemoth Dreams for Contrabass Clarinet and Synthesizers (1976; in collaboration with A. Braxton); *Crossing* for Synthesizers and Winds (1976; in collaboration with A. Braxton); *Ranbyoshi* for Violin and Synthesizers (1976); *Blends* for Shakuhachi and 2 Synthesizers (1977); *In Memoriam* for Synthesizers, Soprano Saxophone, Piano, Trombone, and Trumpet (1977); *In Memoriam: H.M.* for Piano, Flute, Saxophone, Percussion, and Synthesizers (1977); *King William's Town* for Piano, Flute, Saxophone, and Synthesizers (1977); *Via Della Luce* for Synthesizer, Vibraphone, Melodica, Soprano Saxophone, Trumpet, Trombone, and Piano (1977); *Asparagus*, film soundtrack for Synthesizers, Trombone, and Saxophones (1978); *Shrine* for Synthesizers (1979); *Solo* for Synthesizers (1979); *Is This The Boid?* for Film, Vocoder, and Synthesizers (1980); *Mirror on the Wall*, environmental music for Tape and Outdoor Muzak System (1980); *Ode* for Voice and Harmonizer (1980); *BLT* for Synthesizers and Computers (1981; in collaboration with D. Behrman and G. Lewis); *Colourless Green Ideas Sleep Furiously* for Solo Performers, Synthesizers, and Microcomputer (1981); *Duets* for Synthesizers and Winds (1981; in collaboration with A. Braxton); *Interlude in Prolog* for Digital Piano System (1982); *In the Accumulate Mode* for Digital Piano System (1982); *Solo for Pianos* for Digital Piano System (1982); *Solo for 3 Pianos* for Digital Piano System (1982); *Digital Piano Music* for Digital Piano System (1983); *Dramland* for Digital Piano System (1983); *Frankfurt Cakewalk* for Digital Piano System (1983); *Reverse Polish Notation* for Digital Piano System (1983); *Run Some By You* for Digital Piano System (1983); *Short Shift* for Digital Piano System (1983); *Digital Music and Jazz Live* for Synthesizers and Winds (1984; in collaboration with A. Braxton): *Improvisations* for 2 Synthesizers and 2 Violins (1984); *Concerto Grosso* for Winds, Brass, Digital Pianos, and Synthesizers (1985) and *Concerto Grosso No. 2* for Piano, Robotic Piano, Trombone, Synthesizers, and Interactive Computer Music Systems (1988; in collaboration with R. Rowe); *Digital Keyboard Music* for Digital Pianos and Synthesizers (1985); *Interlace* for Digital Pianos, Trombone, and Synthesizer (1985; in collaboration with G. Lewis); *Duet* for 2 Pianos and 2 Synthesizers (1986; in collaboration with H. Miyake); *Iro Wa Nioedo* for 20 Japanese Shingon Buddhist Monks (1986); Trio for Synthesizers, Wind Instruments, and Trombone (1986; in collaboration with A. Braxton and G. Lewis); *Agora Nada* for Violin, Synthesizers, and Computers (1987; in collaboration with C. Zingaro); *Golem I* for Synthesizers, Digital Sampler, Computers, and Musicians (1987); *Golem Sketches* for Violin, Synthesizers, and Computers (1987; in collaboration with C. Zingaro); *Golem Studies* for Synthesizers, Digital Sampler, Computers, and Musicians (1987); *Man Made Ears* for Synthesizers, Violin, and Shamisen (1987); *The Sea Between* for Violin, Synthesizers, and Computers (1987; in collaboration with C. Zingaro); *Golemics* for Robotic Piano, Amplified Zither, Synthesizers, and Musicians (1988); *Golem*, interactive opera for Voices, Trombone, Violin, Percussion, Robotic Pianos, and Interactive Video System (1989–94); *Melog Xram*, radio soundpiece (1990); *Intera* for Yokobue (Japanese bamboo flute), Western Reeds, and Interactive Computer Music System (1992); *The Emperor Walks* for Disklavier with synthesizer obbligato (1993); *Mountain Dreams, City Scenes* for Shakuhachi and Sampler/Synthesizer (1994); *Kyotaku/Denshi* for Shakuhachi, Sampler/Synthesizer, Computer, Bass, and Drums (1995); *Dal Niente* for MIDI Piano, Sampler, and Computer (1997); *Reibo Universe* for Shakuhachi, Computer, and Visual Projections (1998); *Seq Transit Parammers* for 2 Disklaviers and Interactive Computer System (1998); Concertino for Piano and Chamber Orch. (2000).—**LK/DM**

Te Kanawa, Dame Kiri, brilliant New Zealand soprano; b. Gisborne, March 6, 1944. Her father was an indigenous Maori who traced his ancestry to the legendary warrior Te Kanawa; her mother was Irish. She attended Catholic schools in Auckland, and was coached in singing by a nun. She was sent to Melbourne to compete in a radio show; won 1st prize in the Melbourne Sun contest. In 1966 she received a grant for study in London with Vera Rozsa. She made her operatic debut at the Camden Festival in 1969 in Rossini's *La Donna del Lago*; first appeared at London's Covent Garden in a minor role that same year, and then as the Countess in *Le nozze di Figaro* in 1971. She made her U.S. debut in the same role with the Santa Fe Opera in 1971; it became one of her most remarkable interpretations. She sang it again with the San Francisco Opera in 1972. A proverbial coup de théâtre in her career came on Feb. 9, 1974, when she was called upon to substitute at a few hours' notice for the ailing Teresa Stratas in the part of Desdemona in Verdi's *Otello* at the Metropolitan Opera in N.Y.; it was a triumphant achievement, winning for her unanimous praise. She also sang in the film version of *Le nozze di Figaro*. In 1977 she appeared as Pamina in *Die Zauberflöte* at the Paris Opéra. On Dec. 31, 1977, she took the role of Rosalinde in a Covent Garden production of *Die Fledermaus*, which was televised to the U.S. In 1990 she sang Strauss's Countess at the San Francisco Opera. She was a soloist in the premiere of Paul McCartney's *Liverpool Oratorio* in 1991. After singing Mozart's Countess at the Metropolitan Opera in 1992, she returned there in that role in 1997. In 1998 she sang Strauss's Countess at the Glyndebourne Festival.

Te Kanawa excelled equally as a subtle and artistic interpreter of lyric roles in Mozart's operas and in dramatic representations of Verdi's operas. Among her other distinguished roles were the Marschallin and Arabella. She also won renown as a concert artist. In later years she expanded her repertoire to include popular fare, including songs by Cole Porter and Leonard Bernstein's *West Side Story*. Hailed as a prima donna assoluta, she pursued one of the most successful international operatic and concert careers of her day. In 1981 she sang at the royal wedding of Prince Charles and Lady Diana Spencer in London, a performance televised around the globe. In 1973 she was made an Officer of the Order of the British Empire; in 1982 she was named a Dame Commander of the Order of the British Empire.

BIBL.: D. Fingleton, *K. T.K.* (N.Y., 1983).—**NS/LK/DM**

Telemann, Georg Michael, German composer and writer on music, grandson of **Georg Philipp Telemann;** b. Plon, April 20, 1748; d. Riga, March 4, 1831. He was reared and trained in music by his grandfather in Hamburg, and matriculated at the Univ. of Kiel (1768). He was a teacher at the Nicolaischule in Hamburg before settling in Riga as Kantor and teacher at the cathedral school (1773–1828), where he oversaw performances of many of his grandfather's works in his own eds.

WORKS: *Beytrag zur Kirchenmusik*, 10 choral anthems for 2 to 4 Voices, Oboes, 2 Trumpets, Horn, Timpani, Strings, and

Basso Continuo, and 10 chorale preludes and 2 fugues for Organ (Königsberg and Leipzig, 1785); *Sammlung alter und neuer Choralmelodien für das seit 1810 in...Riga eingeführte Neue Gesangbuch* (Mitau, 1811–12); a few occasional choral works, including the cantata *Deutschlands Pflegerin* for the installation of C.P.E. Bach as Hamburg Kantor (1768).

WRITINGS: *Unterricht im Generalbass-Spielen, auf der Orgel oder sonst einem Clavier-Instrumente* (Hamburg, 1773); *Beurteilung der im 23. Bande der Allgemeinen deutschen Bibliothek befindlichen Recension seines Unterrichts* (Riga, 1775); *Über die Wahl der Melodie eines Kirchenliedes* (Riga, 1821).—**NS/LK/DM**

Telemann, Georg Philipp, greatly significant German composer; b. Magdeburg, March 14, 1681; d. Hamburg, June 25, 1767. He received his academic training at a local school, and also learned to play keyboard instruments and the violin; he acquired knowledge of music theory from the cantor Benedikt Christiani. He subsequently attended the Gymnasium Andreanum in Hildesheim, where he became active in student performances of German cantatas. In 1701 he entered the Univ. of Leipzig as a student of jurisprudence; in 1702 he organized a collegium musicum there; later was appointed music director of the Leipzig Opera, where he used the services of his student singers and instrumentalists. In 1705 he went to Sorau as Kapellmeister to the court of Count Erdmann II of Promnitz. In 1708 he was appointed Konzertmeister to the court orch. in Eisenach; later he was named Kapellmeister there. In 1709 he married Louise Eberlin, a musician's daughter, but she died in 1711 in childbirth. In 1712 Telemann was appointed music director of the city of Frankfurt am Main; there he wrote a quantity of sacred music as well as secular works for the public concerts given by the Frauenstein Society, of which he served as director. In 1714 he married Maria Katharina Textor, the daughter of a local town clerk. They had 8 sons and 2 daughters, of whom only a few survived infancy. His wife later abandoned him for a Swedish army officer. In 1721 he received the post of music director of 5 churches in Hamburg, which became the center of his important activities as composer and music administrator. In 1722 Telemann was appointed music director of the Hamburg Opera, a post he held until 1738. During his tenure he wrote a number of operas for production there, and also staged several works by Handel and Keiser. In 1737–38 he visited France. His eyesight began to fail as he grew older; his great contemporaries Bach and Handel suffered from the same infirmity. An extraordinarily prolific composer, Telemann mastered both the German and the Italian styles of composition prevalent in his day. While he never approached the greatness of genius of Bach and Handel, he nevertheless became an exemplar of the German Baroque at its grandest development. According to Telemann's own account, he composed about 20 operas for Leipzig, 4 for Weissenfels, 2 for Bayreuth, and 3 operettas for Eisenach. He lists 35 operas for Hamburg, but included in this list are preludes, intermezzi, and postludes. His grandson, Georg Michael Telemann (b. Plon, April 20, 1748; d. Riga, March 4, 1831), was also a composer and writer on music. A complete ed. of his works, *Georg Philipp Telemann: Musikalische Werke*, began publication in Kassel and Basel in 1950.

WORKS: DRAMATIC: Opera (all 1st perf. in Hamburg): *Der gedultige Socrates* (Jan. 28, 1721); *Ulysses* (1721; in collaboration with Vogler); *Sieg der Schönheit* (1722; later performed as *Gensericus*); *Belsazar* (July 19, 1723; 2nd version, Sept. 30, 1723); *Der Beschluss des Carnevals* (1724; in collaboration with Campara and Conti); *Omphale* (1724); *Der neu-modische Liebhaber Damon* (June 1724); *Cimbriens allgemeines Frolocken* (Feb. 17, 1725); *Pimpinone oder Die ungleiche Heyrath*, intermezzo (Sept. 27, 1725); *La Capricciosa e il Credula*, intermezzo (1725); *Adelheid* (Feb. 17, 1727); *Buffonet und Alga*, intermezzo (May 14, 1727); *Calypso* (1727); *Sancio* (1727); *Die verkehrte Welt* (1728); *Miriways* (May 26, 1728); *Emma und Eginhard* (1728); *Aesopus* (Feb. 28, 1729); *Flavius Bertaridus, König der Langobarden* (Nov. 23, 1729); *Margaretha, Königin in Castilien* (Aug. 10, 1730); *Die Flucht des Aeneas* (Nov. 19, 1731); *Judith, Gemahlin Kayser Ludewig des Frommen* (Nov. 27, 1732; in collaboration with Chelleri); *Orasia oder Die rachgierige Liebe* (Oct. 1736). **Oratorios:** *Der königliche Prophete David als ein Fürbild unseres Heilands Jesu* (1718; not extant); *Freundschaft geget über Liebe* (1720; not extant); *Donnerode* (1756–60); *Sing, unsterbliche Seele, an Mirjam und deine Wehmut*, after Klopstock's *Der Messias* (1759); *Das befreite Israel* (1759); *Die Hirten bei der Krippe zu Bethlehem* (1759); *Die Auferstehung und Himmelfahrt Jesu* (1760); *Der Tag des Gerichts* (1762). **INSTRUMENTAL:** One of his most important collections was his *Musique de table* (Hamburg, 1733); it contained 3 orch. suites, 3 concertos, 3 quartets, 3 trios, and 3 sonatas. His orch. output was prodigious, comprising numerous overtures, concertos, sonatas, quartets, quintets, etc.

BIBL.: Telemann's autobiography of 1718 was publ. in J. Mattheson, *Grosse Generalbassschule* (Hamburg, 1731); his autobiography of 1739 was publ. in J. Mattheson, *Grundlage einer Ehren-Pforte* (Hamburg, 1740; new ed. by M. Schneider, Berlin, 1910); both of these, plus his autobiographical letter to Walther of 1729, have been republ. in W. Kahl, *Selbstbiographien deutscher Musiker des XVIII. Jahrhunderts* (Cologne, 1948). See also the following: B. Schmid, ed., *Herr G.P. T.: Lebenslauf* (Nuremberg, c. 1745; in Ger. and Fr.); M. Frey, *G.P. T.s Singe-, Spiel- und Generalbass-Übungen* (Zürich, 1922); H. Graeser, *G.P. T.s Instrumental-Kammermusik* (diss., Univ. of Munich, 1924); E. Valentin, *G.P. T.* (Burg, 1931; 3rd ed., 1952); H. Hörner, *G.P. T.s Passionsmusiken* (Leipzig, 1933); K. Schäfer-Schmuck, *G.P. T. als Klavierkomponist* (diss., Univ. of Kiel, 1934); H. Büttner, *Das Konzert in den Orchestersuiten G.P. T.s* (Wolfenbüttel and Berlin, 1935); W. Menke, *Das Vokalwerk G.P. T.s* (Kassel, 1942); F. Funk, *The Trio Sonatas of G.P. T.* (diss., George Peabody Coll. for Teachers, 1954); C. Rhea, *The Sacred Oratorios of G.P. T.* (diss., Fla. State Univ., 1958); E. Valentin, *T. in seiner Zeit* (Hamburg, 1960); R. Petzoldt, *T. und seine Zeitgenossen* (Magdeburg, 1966); C. Gilbertson, *The Methodical Sonatas of G.P. T.* (diss., Univ. of Ky., 1967); R. Petzoldt, *G.P. T.: Leben und Werk* (Leipzig, 1967; in Eng., 1974); K. Zauft, *T.s Liedschaffen und seine Bedeutung für die Entwicklung des deutschen Liedes in der 1. Hälfte des 18. Jahrhunderts* (Magdeburg, 1967); *G.P. T., Leben und Werk: Beiträge zur gleichnamigen Ausstellung* (Magdeburg, 1967); A. Hoffmann, *Die Orchestersuiten G. P. T.s* (Wolfenbüttel and Zürich, 1969); S. Kross, *Das Instrumentalkonzert bei G.P. T.* (Tutzing, 1969); M. Peckham, *The Operas of G.P. T.* (diss., Columbia Univ., 1969); K. Grebe, *G.P. T. in Selbstzeugnissen und Bilddokumenten* (Reinbeck bei Hamburg, 1970); I. Allihn, *G.P. T. und J.J. Quantz* (Magdeburg, 1971); H. Grosse and H. Jung, eds., *G.P. T., Briefwechsel* (Leipzig, 1972); *T.- Renaissance: Werk- und Wiedergabe* (Magdeburg, 1973); W. Maertens, *T. Kapitänsmusiken* (diss., Univ. of Halle, 1975); *G.P. T.: Leben—Werk—Wirkung* (Berlin, 1980); E. Klessmann, *T. in Hamburg* (Hamburg, 1980); M. Ruhnke, ed.,

G.P. T.: Thematisch-systematisches Verzeichnis seiner Werke: Instrumentalwerke, Vol. I (Kassel, 1984); B. Stewart, *G.P. T. in Hamburg: Social and Cultural Background and Its Musical Expression* (diss., Stanford Univ., 1985); W. Hirschmann, *Studien zum Konzertschaffen von G.P. T.* (Kassel and N.Y., 1986); W. Menke, *G.P. T.: Leben, Werk und Umwelt in Bilddokumenten* (Wilhelmshaven, 1987); D. Gutknecht, H. Krones, and F. Zschoch, eds., *T.iana et alia musicologica: Feschrift für Günter Fleischhauer zum 65. Geburtstag* (Oschersleben, 1995); W. Hobohm, C. Lange, and B. Reipsch, eds., *T.s Auftrags- und Geiegenheitswerke: Funktion, Wert und Bedeutung* (Oschersleben, 1997); C. Klein, *Dokumente zur T.-Rezeption 1767 bis 1907* (Oschersleben, 1998).—**NS/LK/DM**

Tellefsen, Thomas (Dyke Acland), Norwegian pianist and composer; b. Trondheim, Nov. 26, 1823; d. Paris, Oct. 6, 1874. He began his training in Trondheim with his father, Johan Christian Tellefsen, an organist, and with O. Lindeman, making his debut there at age 18. He then went to Paris in 1842, where he continued his studies with Charlotte Thygeson, and also received some lessons from Kalkbrenner; in 1844 he became a pupil of Chopin, and accompanied him to England and Scotland in 1848. In later years he gave frequent concerts in Paris, London, and Scandinavia; about 1861 ill health compelled him to concentrate his energies on teaching and composing. His early works were greatly influenced by Chopin; he wrote 2 piano concertos (1852, 1854), a Piano Trio (1861), 2 violin sonatas (1856), a Sonata for 2 Pianos (1870), 16 mazurkas, and a number of Norwegian dances. He also made use of Norwegian folk songs in many of his works, and thus became an early proponent of national music in Norway.—**NS/LK/DM**

Telmányi, Emil, Hungarian-Danish violinist, conductor, and pedagogue; b. Arad, June 22, 1892; d. Holte, June 12, 1988. He took courses in violin, conducting, and composition at the Royal Academy of Music in Budapest. In 1911 he made his Berlin debut as a violinist, and subsequently made tours of Europe and North America. He first played in Copenhagen in 1912, and soon settled in Denmark. In 1919 he made his debut as a conductor in Copenhagen; he taught at the Århus Cons. (1940–69) and toured with his own Telmányi Quintet (from 1959). In 1970 he settled in Holte as a conductor and teacher. He supervised the construction of a curved bow for playing Bach's violin works, which became known as the Vega bow (1954). In 1918 he married Anne Marie Nielsen, a daughter of Carl Nielsen; in 1936 he married the pianist Annette Schiøler.—**NS/LK/DM**

Telva (real name, **Toucke**), **Marian,** American contralto; b. St. Louis, Dec. 26, 1897; d. Norwalk, Conn., Oct. 23, 1962. She changed her name to Telva for the sake of euphony. She sang in church in her hometown, then went to N.Y. for further study, and soon was engaged at the Metropolitan Opera, where she sang minor roles between 1920 and 1933 (1931–32 season excepted). In the meantime she married a wealthy banker and afterward made only sporadic appearances as a concert singer.—**NS/LK/DM**

Temianka, Henri, distinguished Polish-born American violinist, conductor, and pedagogue; b. Greenock, Scotland (of Polish parents), Nov. 19, 1906; d. Los Angeles, Nov. 7, 1992. He studied violin with Blitz in Rotterdam (1915–23), W. Hess at the Berlin Hochschule für Musik (1923–24), and Boucherit in Paris (1924–26); completed his training with Flesch (violin) and Rodzinski (conducting) at the Curtis Inst. of Music in Philadelphia (graduated, 1930). In 1932 he made his N.Y. recital debut at Town Hall, and then gave recitals in Paris and London; was concertmaster of the Scottish Orch. in Glasgow (1937–38) and of the Pittsburgh Sym. Orch. (1941–42). In 1945 he became a naturalized American citizen. In 1946 he founded the Paganini String Quartet, which he served as 1st violinist until it disbanded in 1966; in 1961 he founded the Calif. Chamber Sym. Orch., with which he toured extensively; in 1982 he organized the Baroque Virtuosi from its ranks. He served as a prof. at the Univ. of Calif. at Santa Barbara (1960–64) and at Calif. State Univ. at Long Beach (1964–76); also gave master classes. In addition to articles on violin technique, he publ. a book of reminiscences as *Facing the Music* (N.Y., 1973). He was equally esteemed as a violin soloist and chamber player, conductor, and teacher. —**NS/LK/DM**

Temirkanov, Yuri, outstanding Russian conductor; b. Nalchik, Dec. 10, 1938. He received his training at the Leningrad Cons., where he graduated as a violinist in 1962 and as a conductor in 1965. In 1965 he made his first appearance as a conductor at the Leningrad Opera. After capturing 1st prize in the All-Union Conductors' Competition in 1966, he appeared as a guest conductor with many Russian orchs. and opera houses. From 1968 to 1976 he was music director of the Leningrad Sym. Orch. He also appeared as a guest conductor abroad, making his Salzburg Festival debut in 1971 with the Vienna Phil. In 1977 he made his London debut as a guest conductor with the Royal Phil., and subsequently appeared with the major British orchs. From 1977 to 1988 he was artistic director of the Kirov Opera and Ballet, which he also led on tours. In 1978 he made a tour of the U.S. In 1979 he was named principal guest conductor of the Royal Phil. In 1988 he became chief conductor of the Leningrad (later St. Petersburg) Phil. In 1992 he was made principal conductor of the Royal Phil. while retaining his position in St. Petersburg. During the 1992–93 season, he conducted the St. Petersburg Phil. on a tour of Europe and Japan and the Royal Phil. on a tour of the U.S. and Germany. Temirkanov has won particular renown for his brilliant and idiomatic performances of works from the Russian repertoire. —**NS/LK/DM**

Temperley, Nicholas, distinguished English-born American musicologist; b. Beaconsfield, Aug. 7, 1932. He was educated at Eton Coll. (1945–51), the Royal Coll. of Music in London (1951–52), and King's Coll., Cambridge (B.A., 1955; B.Mus., 1956; Ph.D., 1959, with the diss. *Instrumental Music in England, 1800–1850*). From 1959 to 1961 he was a postdoctoral fellow at the Univ. of Ill. He was an asst. lecturer in music at the Univ. of Cambridge from 1961 to 1966, and also a fellow and director of studies in music (1961–66) and a visiting fellow (1970–71) at Clare Coll., Cambridge. In 1966–67 he was an asst. prof. at Yale Univ. From 1967 to 1972 he was an assoc. prof., from 1972 to 1996 a prof., and from 1996 prof. emeritus at the Univ. of Ill., where he also served as chairman of its musicology dept. from 1972 to 1975 and from 1992 to 1996. In 1975–76 he held an NEH fellowship. He became a naturalized American citizen in 1977. From 1978 to 1980 he was ed. of the *Journal of the American Musicological Society*. In 1980 he was honored with the Otto Kindeldey Award of the American Musicological Soc. In 1986 he became general ed. of the Oxford Studies in British Church Music series. In addition to his books and editions, Temperley has also contributed articles to learned journals.

WRITINGS: *Jonathan Gray and Church Music in York, 1770–1840* (York, 1977); *The Music of the English Parish Church* (2 vols., Cambridge, 1979); ed. *The Romantic Age, 1800–1914*, Vol. 5 of *The Athlone History of Music in Britain* (London, 1981); with C. Manns, *Fuging Tunes in the Eighteenth Century* (Detroit, 1983); ed. *The Lost Chord: Essays in Victorian Music* (Bloomington, Ind., 1989); *Haydn: The Creation* (Cambridge, 1991); with C. Manns and J. Herl, *The Hymn Tune Index: A Census of English-Language Tunes in Printed Sources from 1535 to 1820* (4 vols., Oxford, 1998). **—NS/LK/DM**

Templeton, Alec (Andrew), blind Welsh-born American pianist and composer; b. Cardiff, July 4, 1909; d. Greenwich, Conn., March 28, 1963. He studied at Worcester Coll. and in London at the Royal Coll. of Music and at the Royal Academy of Music. He was only 12 when he began to appear on the BBC, remaining with it until 1935. He went to the U.S. in 1935 as a member of Jack Hylton's jazz band; became a naturalized American citizen in 1941. He was extremely successful as a radio pianist, especially with his humorous musical sketches, parodies, etc., such as *Bach Goes to Town, Mozart Matriculates*, etc. He also wrote some more ambitious works, including *Concertino lirico* (1942) and *Gothic Concerto* for Piano and Orch (N.Y., Dec. 19, 1954, composer soloist). With R. Baumel, he publ. *A. T.'s Music Boxes* (N.Y., 1958). **—NS/LK/DM**

Templeton, John, Scottish tenor; b. Riccarton, near Kilmarnock, July 30, 1802; d. New Hampton, near London, July 2, 1886. He sang in various churches in Edinburgh, then went to London, where he took lessons in singing with Welch, De Pinna, and Tom Cooke. On Oct. 13, 1831, he made his London debut at Drury Lane as Belville in Sheild's *Rosina*; subsequently was a regular member there. Maria Malibran selected him as tenor for her operatic appearances in London (1833–35). In 1842 he was in Paris; during the season of 1845–46, he made an American tour announced as "Templeton Entertainment," singing folk songs of Great Britain. His commentaries and reminiscences were publ. as *A Musical Entertainment* (Boston, 1845). He retired in 1852.

BIBL.: W. Husk, ed., *T. and Malibran: Reminiscences* (London, 1880).**—NS/LK/DM**

Temptations, The, Motown's most popular and most enduring male vocal group. **MEMBERSHIP:** Eddie Kendricks, ten. (b. Birmingham, Ala., Dec. 17, 1939; d. there, Oct. 5, 1992); Otis Williams (real name, Otis Miles), bar. (b. Texarkana, Tex., Oct. 30, 1941); Melvin Franklin (real name, David English), bs. (b. Montgomery, Ala., Oct. 12, 1942; d. Los Angeles, Feb. 23, 1995); Paul Williams, bar. (b. Birmingham, Ala., July 2, 1939; d. Detroit, Mich., Aug. 17, 1973); Eldridge Bryant. Bryant left in late 1963, to be replaced by David Ruffin, bar. (b. Meridian, Miss., Jan. 18, 1941; d. Philadelphia, June 1, 1991). David Ruffin left the group in 1968, to be replaced by Dennis Edwards (b. Birmingham, Ala., Feb. 3, 1943). David Ruffin's brother Jimmy Ruffin (b. Collinsville, Miss., May 7, 1939) was a solo artist for Motown. Eddie Kendricks and Paul Williams left The Temptations in 1971, to be replaced by Richard Street (b. Detroit, Mich., Oct. 5, 1942) and Damon Harris (b. Baltimore, Md., July 3, 1950). Later members included Glenn Leonard, Louis Price, Ali Ollie Woodson, Ron Tyson, Theo Peoples, and Ray Davis.

The evolution of The Temptations began during the late 1950s with two Detroit-based groups, The Primes and The Distants. The Distants, with Otis Williams, Melvin Franklin, Richard Street, and Eldridge Bryant, had been formed by members of The Questions and The Elegants. The Primes (whose companion group The Primettes later became The Supremes) had formed in Birmingham, Ala., and included Eddie Kendricks and Paul Williams. In 1960, Kendricks and Paul Williams joined Bryant, Franklin, and Otis Williams to become The Elgins, signing with Berry Gordy's Miracle label. They changed their name to The Temptations in 1961 and switched to the Gordy label in 1962, scoring their first R&B hit with "Dream Come Home." In 1963, choreographer Cholly Atkins started teaching the group intricate synchronized dance routines that became their performance trademark. Late that year, Bryant quit the group and was replaced by David Ruffin.

In early 1964, The Temptations achieved their first major pop hit with "The Way You Do the Things You Do," cowritten and produced by William "Smokey" Robinson and featuring the lead vocals of Eddie Kendricks. After the major pop hit "Girl (Why You Wanna Make Me Blue)," written by Eddie Holland and Norman Whitfield, the group scored a top pop and R&B hit with the classic "My Girl," cowritten (with Ronald White) and produced by Robinson, with Ruffin on lead vocals. Subsequent major pop and smash R&B hits for The Temptations produced by Robinson included "It's Growing," "Since I Lost My Baby," and "My Baby" (cowritten by Robinson and Warren Moore) and Robinson's "Get Ready."

The Temptations next recorded primarily under songwriter-producer Norman Whitfield, who produced (and coauthored with Eddie Holland) the top R&B and smash pop hits "Ain't Too Proud to Beg," "Beauty Is Only Skin Deep," and "(I Know) I'm Losing You." Frank Wilson coauthored and produced the crossover smash "All I Need," and Whitfield produced and coauthored the crossover smashes "You're My Everything," "(Loneliness Made Me Realize) It's You That I Need," the classic "I Wish It Would Rain," and "I Could Never Love Another (After Loving You)." In July 1968, David Ruffin left the group for a solo career and was replaced by Dennis Edwards of The Contours. By then, former

Distant and Monitor member, Richard Street, began filling in for an ailing Paul Williams.

David Ruffin's brother Jimmy had been recording for Berry Gordy's Soul label since 1964. He scored a near-smash pop and R&B hit with "What Becomes of the Brokenhearted" in 1966 and subsequent major crossover hits with "I've Passed This Way Before" and "Gonna Give Her All the Love I've Got." David Ruffin managed a smash pop and R&B hit with "My Whole World Ended (The Moment You Left Me)" in 1969, followed by the major R&B hits "I've Lost Everything I Ever Loved" and "I'm So Glad I Fell for You." A 1970 duet album yielded a major R&B hit with "Stand by Me," but by 1972, Jimmy Ruffin had left the Motown organization. David Ruffin stayed on, eventually scoring a top R&B and near-smash pop hit with "Walk Away from Love" and near-smash R&B hits with "Heavy Love" and "Everything's Coming up Love" in 1975 and 1976. In 1980, Jimmy Ruffin scored a near-smash pop hit with "Hold on to My Love," cowritten and produced by Bee Gee Robin Gibb.

The reconstituted Temptations were teamed with The Supremes in 1968 and 1969. They scored a smash crossover hit with a remake of Dee Dee Warwick's late 1966 hit "I'm Gonna Make You Love Me" and a major crossover hit with "I'll Try Something New." Beginning in late 1968, Norman Whitfield began experimenting with psychedelic soul and social consciousness for The Temptations. With this new style, The Temptations scored a top pop and R&B hit with the classic "I Can't Get Next to You" and smash R&B and pop hits with "Cloud Nine," "Run Away Child, Running Wild," "Psychedelic Shack," and "Ball of Confusion," all cowritten by Whitfield and Barrett Strong.

The Temptations returned to their mellow ballad style in 1971 for the top pop and R&B hit classic "Just My Imagination (Running Away with Me)" with Eddie Kendricks on lead vocals. That summer, Kendricks left the group for a solo career and was permanently replaced by Damon Harris. Around the same time, Paul Williams retired from touring due to illness and was replaced by stand-in Richard Street. On Aug. 17, 1973, Paul Williams was found dead in his car in Detroit, an apparent suicide at the age of 34.

In 1973, Eddie Kendricks's solo career took off. The disco-style songs "Keep on Truckin' (Part 1)" and "Boogie Down" became top R&B and pop hits and were followed by seven R&B smashes, including the major pop hits "Son of Sagittarius" and "Shoeshine Boy." In 1978, he switched to Arista Records, where he managed one major R&B hit, "Ain't No Smoke without Fire."

From late 1971 to 1974, The Temptations scored numerous smash R&B hits for Motown. Of these, "Superstar (Remember How You Got Where You Are)" and "Let Your Hair Down" became major pop hits, the classic "Papa Was a Rolling Stone" was a top pop hit, and "Masterpiece" proved a near-smash pop hit. After Norman Whitfield left the Motown organization, The Temptations achieved top R&B hits with "Happy People" (cowritten by Lionel Richie) and "Shakey Ground" (their last major pop hit) and the R&B smash "Keep Holding On" in 1975 and 1976. In 1975, Glenn Leonard replaced Damon Harris, who returned to his former group (which later became Impact) before attempting a solo career in late 1978. Dennis Edwards left the group from 1977 to 1979, replaced by Louis Price.

The Temptations switched to Atlantic Records in May 1977, but were back at Gordy by 1980, by which time Edwards had returned to replace Price. In 1982, The Temptations reunited with David Ruffin and Eddie Kendricks for one album and tour. The reunion album yielded a R&B smash with "Standing on the Top—Part 1," featuring Rick James. Ron Tyson replaced Glenn Leonard in 1983, the year The Temptations toured internationally with The Four Tops. In 1983, Ali Ollie Woodson replaced Edwards and the group managed another R& B smash with "Treat Her Like a Lady." However, they would not achieve another major pop hit until 1991. Between 1986 and 1987, The Temptations had smash R&B hits with "Lady Soul, " "I Wonder Who She's Seeing Now," and "Look What You Started."

In May 1985, David Ruffin and Eddie Kendrick (he had shortened his name) joined white soul singers Daryl Hall and John Oates for the reopening of the Apollo Theater in Harlem. The four scored a major pop hit with "The Apollo Medley," which comprised "The Way You Do the Things You Do" and "My Girl." Ruffin and Kendrick subsequently toured together and later recorded a duet album that yielded a major R&B hit with "I Couldn't Believe It." On June 1, 1991, David Ruffin died in Philadelphia of a drug overdose at the age of 50. On Oct. 5, 1992, Eddie Kendricks died in Birmingham, Ala., of lung cancer at the age of 52.

In 1989, The Temptations scored a smash R&B hit with "Special," and, in 1991, they accompanied Rod Stewart on the near- smash pop hit "The Motown Song" from his *Vagabond Heart* album. By 1992, The Temptations were regularly touring with The Four Tops. The group continued to record for Motown in the 1990s, but, on Feb. 23, 1995, Melvin Franklin died in Los Angeles of heart failure at the age of 52. By the late 1998 broadcast of the NBC-TV miniseries "The Temptations" and the release of *Phoenix Rising*, The Temptations were anchored by Ron Tyson and original member Otis Williams.

Disc.: **THE TEMPTATIONS:** *Meet The Temptations* (1964); *The Temptations Sing Smokey* (1965); *Temptin' Temptations* (1965); *Gettin' Ready* (1966); *Live!* (1967); *With a Lot O' Soul* (1967); *In a Mellow Mood* (1967); *I Wish It Would Rain* (1968); *Live at the Copa* (1968); *Cloud Nine* (1969); *The Temptations Show* (TV; 1969); *Puzzle People* (1969); *Christmas Card* (1969); *Psychedelic Shack* (1970); *At London's Talk of the Town* (1970); *Sky's the Limit* (1971); *Solid Rock* (1972); *All Directions* (1972); *Masterpiece* (1973); *The Temptations* (1974); *A Song for You* (1975); *House Party* (1975); *Wings of Love* (1976); *Hear to Tempt You* (1977); *Bare Back* (1978); *Power* (1980); *Give Love at Christmas* (1980); *The Temptations* (1981); *Reunion* (1982); *Surface Thrills* (1983); *Back to Basics* (1983); *Truly for You* (1984); *Touch Me* (1986); *To Be Continued* (1986); *Together Again* (1987); *Special* (1989); *Milestone* (1991); *For Lovers Only* (1995). The Supremes: *The Supremes Join The Temptations* (1968); *T.C.B.* (1968); *Together* (1969). **JIMMY RUFFIN:** *Top Ten* (1967); *Ruff 'n Ready* (1969); *Groove Governor* (1970); *Sunrise* (1980). **DAVID AND JIMMY RUFFIN:** *I Am My Brother's Keeper* (1970). **DAVID RUFFIN:** *My Whole World Ended* (1969); *Doin' His Thing—Feelin' Good* (1969); *David Ruffin*

(1973); *Me 'n Rock 'n Roll Are Here to Stay* (1974); *Who I Am* (1975); *Everything's Coming Up Love* (1976); *In My Stride* (1977); *So Soon We Change* (1979); *Gentleman Ruffin* (1980). **DARYL HALL AND JOHN OATES WITH DAVID RUFFIN AND EDDIE KENDRICK:** *Live at the Apollo* (1985). **DAVID RUFFIN AND EDDIE KENDRICK:** *Family* (1987). **EDDIE KENDRICKS:** *All By Myself* (1971); *People... Hold On* (1972); *Eddie Kendricks* (1973); *Boogie Down* (1974); *For You* (1974); *The Hit Man* (1975); *He's a Friend* (1975); *Goin' Up in Smoke* (1976); *Slick* (1977); *Vintage '78* (1978); *Something More* (1979); *Love Keys* (1981). **MONITORS (WITH RICHARD STREET):** *Greetings! We're The Monitors* (1969). **TRUE REFLECTION (WITH GLENN LEONARD):** *Where I'm Coming From* (1973). **IMPACT (WITH DAMON HARRIS):** *Impact* (1976); *The 'Pac Is Back* (1977). **DAMON HARRIS:** *Damon* (1978). Dennis Edwards: *Don't Look Any Further* (1984); *Coolin' Out* (1985).

BIBL.: T. Turner, with B. Aria, *Deliver Us from Temptation: The Tragic and Shocking Story of The Temptations and Motown* (N.Y., 1992); O. Williams, with P. Romanowski. *Temptations* (N.Y., 1988).—**BH**

Tenaglia, Antonio Francesco, Italian keyboard player, lutenist, and composer; b. Florence, c. 1615; d. Rome, after 1661. He was in Rome by 1644 as a musician in the service of Donna Olimpia Aldobrandini, wife of Camillo Pamphili. That same year, he entered the service of Cardinal Antonio Barberini. Following a sojourn abroad (1648–54), he returned to Rome and was active as a keyboard player and lutenist. He composed the operas *Il giudizio de Paride* (Rome, Carnival 1656) and *Il Clearco* (1661), but distinguished himself as a composer of cantatas.—**LK/DM**

10cc, popular British band of the 1970s. **MEMBERSHIP:** Eric Stewart, gtr., voc. (b. Manchester, England, Jan. 20, 1945); Graham Gouldman, bs., voc. (b. Manchester, England, May 10, 1946); Lawrence "Lol" Creme, gtr., kybd., voc. (b. Manchester, England, Sept. 19, 1947); Kevin Godley, drm. (b. Manchester, England, Oct. 7, 1945). Kevin Godley and Lol Creme left in 1977. Godley was replaced by Rick Fenn, voc., gtr., and Tony O'Malley, kybd.; Creme was replaced first by Paul Burgess, then Stuart Tosh. The group disbanded in 1980, with Eric Stewart and Graham Gouldmam leading various revived versions of the band into the 1990s.

Formed by highly experienced English musicians, 10cc was one of the most popular British bands of the 1970s, managing American smash hits with "I'm Not in Love" and "The Things We Do for Love." With its roots in the pop-rock group Wayne Fontana and the Mindbenders and the short-lived rock outfit Hotlegs, the group developed into one of the leading purveyors of British pop.

Formed in Manchester, England, in 1963, Wayne Fontana and the Mindbenders included lead vocalist Wayne Fontana (b. Glynn Ellis, Oct. 28, 1945, Manchester, England) and lead guitarist Eric Stewart. The group scored a British-only hit with "Um Um Um Um Um Um" in 1964 and a top American and smash British hit with "Game of Love" in 1965. After "It's Just a Little Bit Too Late," Fontana left the group in October 1965 for a solo career that produced British-only hits with "Come On Home" and "Pamela Pamela." The Mindbenders persevered, scoring a smash British and American hit with "A Groovy Kind of Love" and a British-only hit with "Ashes to Ashes" in 1966. The group added bassist Graham Gouldman in 1968 but soon disintegrated. By then, Gouldman had written a number of pop-style hits for several different English groups, including "For Your Love" and "Heart Full of Soul" for the Yardbirds; "Look Through Any Window," "Bus Stop," and "Stop Stop Stop" for the Hollies; and "Listen People" and "No Milk Today" for Herman's Hermits. Gouldman also recorded a solo album for RCA in 1968.

With the demise of the Mindbenders, Graham Gouldman joined the Kasenetz-Katz organization as a songwriter, while Eric Stewart set up Strawberry Studios in Stockport, where he rehearsed with guitarist-keyboardist Lol Creme and drummer Kevin Godley. The three scored a smash British hit with "Neanderthal Man" in 1970 and quickly formed Hotlegs to tour in support of the hit. Later adding Gouldman, the group backed Neil Sedaka on his comeback British-only albums *Solitaire* and *The Tra La La Days Are Over* in 1971 and 1972.

In 1972 Creme, Godley, Stewart, and Gouldman took their recording of Creme and Godley's 1950s parody "Donna" to producer Jonathon King, who issued it as a single on his newly formed U.K. label as performed by 10cc. It became a smash British-only hit and was followed by the top British hit "Rubber Bullets" and the major British hits "The Dean and I," "Wall Street Shuffle," and "Silly Love" through 1974. Debuting in August 1973, 10cc made their first American tour the following February. Switching to Phonogram Records (Mercury in the United States) in February 1975, they soon achieved a smash British and American hit with the aurally layered Gouldman-Stewart composition "I'm Not in Love." However, subsequent American hits eluded them, as they scored major British hits with "Art for Art's Sake," "Life Is a Minestrone," and "I'm Mandy Fly Me."

In October 1976 Lol Creme and Kevin Godley announced their departure from 10cc. The group's first album produced by Eric Stewart and Graham Gouldman, 1977's *Deceptive Bends,* yielded a smash British and American hit with "The Things We Do for Love" and a smash British hit with "Good Morning Judge." 10cc managed their last British hit with "Dreadlock Holiday" in 1978 and their last (minor) American hit with "For You and Me" in 1979. Gouldman and Stewart persevered with 10cc into the 1980s. Later member Rick Fenn recorded a mostly instrumental album with Nick Mason of Pink Floyd in 1985. Eric Stewart cowrote six of the ten songs on Paul McCartney's 1986 album *Press to Play,* and Gouldman formed Wax (later Wax U.K.) with American studio musician Andrew Gold, scoring a moderate hit with "Right Between the Eyes" in 1986.

In 1977 Lol Creme and Kevin Godley recorded *Consequences* to showcase their own invention, the Gizmo, a guitar attachment that enabled the instrument to create synthesizer effects. Neither the Gizmo nor the album proved successful, yet Creme and Godley continued to record into the late 1980s, scoring a major hit with "Cry" in 1985. Beginning in 1980, Creme and Godley diversified their careers, producing videos for Asia ("In the Heat of the Moment"), The Police ("Wrapped Around Your Finger" and "Every Breath You Take"), Sting ("Set Them Free"), Duran Duran ("A View to a Kill"), Wang Chung ("Everybody Have Fun Tonight"), and Huey Lewis and the News ("Hip to Be Square"). Lol Creme directed the 1992 Jamaican comedy movie *The Lunatic*. Graham Gouldman and Eric Stewart reunited as 10cc for 1995's *Mirror Mirror*, recorded with the assistance of Paul McCartney.

DISC.: **WAYNE FONTANA AND THE MINDBENDERS:** *Game of Love* (1965); *Best* (1994). **THE MINDBENDERS:** *A Groovy Kind of Love* (1966). **WAYNE FONTANA:** *Wayne Fontana* (1967). **GRAHAM GOULDMAN:** *The Graham Gouldman Thing* (1968); *Animalympics* (1980). **HOTLEGS** *Thinks School Stinks* (1971). **10CC:** *10cc* (1973); *Sheet Music* (1974); *Two Classic Albums by 10cc: 10cc and Sheet Music* (1990); *100 cc* (1975); *The Original Soundtrack* (1975); *How Dare You!* (1976); *Deceptive Bends* (1977); *Live and Let Live* (1977); *Bloody Tourists* (1978); *Greatest Hits, 1972–1978* (1979); *Look, Hear?* (1980); *Ten Out of Ten* (1982); *Mirror Mirror* (1995). **KEVIN GODLEY AND LOL CREME:** *Consequences* (1977); *L* (1978); *Freeze Frame* (1980); *The History Mix, Vol. 1* (1985); *Goodbye Blue Sky* (1988). **RICK FENN AND NICK MASON:** *Profiles* (1985). **WAX U.K.** *Magnetic Heaven* (1986); *American English* (1988).

BIBL.: G. Tremlett, *The 10cc Story* (London, 1976).—**BH**

Tenducci, Giusto Ferdinando, celebrated Italian castrato soprano, nicknamed "Triorchis" (triple-testicled); b. Siena, c. 1735; d. Genoa, Jan. 25, 1790. He made appearances in Venice and Naples before going to London in 1758, where he sang at the King's Theatre until 1760; after a stay in a debtor's prison, he resumed his career and secured a notable success as Arbaces in the premiere of Arne's *Artaxerxes* in 1762; was again active at the King's Theatre (1763–66). He then went to Ireland, where he contracted a marriage with his 16-year-old pupil Dora Maunsell in Cork; outraged members of her family had him jailed and his new bride spirited away; shortly afterward, however, the 2 were reunited and allegedly produced 2 children. After a sojourn in Edinburgh, he returned to England in 1770 and sang at the Worcester Three Choirs Festival; then was a featured artist in the Bach-Abel Concerts in London. By 1778 he was in Paris; sang again in London in 1785. He adapted 4 operas for the Dublin stage, and also wrote English, French, and Italian songs. His wife is reputed to have been the author of the book *A True Genuine Narrative of Mr and Mrs Tenducci* (1768). —**NS/LK/DM**

Tenney, James (Carl), highly influential American pianist, conductor, teacher, and composer; b. Silver City, N.Mex., Aug. 10, 1934. He studied engineering at the Univ. of Denver (1952–54) before devoting himself to music; received instruction in piano from Steuermann at the Juilliard School of Music in N.Y. (1954–55), took courses in piano and composition at Bennington (Vt.) Coll. (B.A., 1958), and worked with Gaburo, Hiller, and Partch at the Univ. of Ill. (M.Mus., 1961); was also associated with Chou Wen-chung, Ruggles, and Varèse (1955–65). He was co-founder of the Tone Roads Chamber Ensemble in N.Y. (1963–70) and was active as a performer with the Steve Reich and Philip Glass ensembles; concurrently conducted research at the Bell Laboratories (with Max Matthews; 1961–64), Yale Univ. (1964–66), and the Polytechnic Inst. of Brooklyn (1966–70). He taught at the Calif. Inst. of the Arts (1970–75), the Univ. of Calif. at Santa Cruz (1975–76), and York Univ. in Toronto (from 1976). As both a performer and a scholar, he is a prominent advocate of contemporary music; is also a notable authority on Ives and Nancarrow. A pioneer in the field of computer music, he is currently engaged in computer-assisted research on various aspects of musical perception. He publ. *A History of Consonance and Dissonance* (N.Y., 1988).

WORKS: **ORCH.:** *Essay* for Chamber Orch. (1957); *Quiet Fan for Erik Satie* (1970); *Clang* (Los Angeles, June 1, 1972); *Chorales* (Valencia, Calif., May 4, 1974). **CHAMBER:** *Seeds* for Flute, Clarinet, Bassoon, Horn, Violin, and Cello (Bennington, Vt., Aug. 25, 1956; rev. 1962); Sonata for 10 Wind Instruments (1958; rev. 1983); *Monody* for Clarinet (1959); *Stochastic* [String] *Quartet* (Los Angeles, Feb. 1, 1963); *String Complement* for Strings (1964); *Quintext I-V: Five Textures* for String Quartet and Double Bass (1972; Valencia, Calif., May 27, 1973); *In the Aeolian Mode* for Prepared Piano and Variable Ensemble (1973); *3 Pieces* for Drum Quartet (1974–75; Santa Cruz, Calif., Aug. 19, 1976); *Harmonia* Nos. 1 to 6 for Various Ensembles (1976–81); *Saxony* for 1 or More Saxophones and Tape Delay (Toronto, April 30, 1978); *Three Rags* for Strings (1978; also for Piano, 1969); *3 Indigenous Songs* for 2 Piccolos, Alto Flute, Tuba or Bassoon, and 2 Percussion (Toronto, Feb. 2, 1979); Septet for 6 Electric Guitars and Double Bass (1981); *Glissade* for Viola, Cello, Double Bass, and Tape Delay (Toronto, April 30, 1982); *Koan* for String Quartet (1984; Aspen, Aug. 20, 1985); *Water on the mountain... Fire in heaven* for 6 Electric Guitars (1985); *Changes: 64 Studies* for 6 Harps (Toronto, Dec. 15, 1985); *Critical Band* for Variable Ensemble (Miami, Dec. 8, 1988); *Rune* for Percussion Quintet (Toronto, Nov. 26, 1988); *Tableaux Vivants* for Soprano, Violin, Clarinet/Bass Clarinet, Bassoon, Saxophone/Baritone Saxophone, Piano, and Percussion (Montreal, Nov. 6, 1990); *Cognate Canons* for String Quartet and 2 Percussionists (1995). **KEYBOARD:** *Music* for Player- Piano (1964); *Three Rags* for Pianoforte (1969; also for Strings, 1978); *Spectral CANON for CONLON Nancarrow* for Player Piano (1974); *Bridge* for 2 Microtonal Pianos, 8-Hands (Hartford, Conn., May 7, 1984); *The Road to Ubud* for Gamelan and Prepared Piano (1986; Toronto, April 5, 1987). **COMPUTER, TAPE, ELECTROACOUSTIC:** *Collage #1: Blue Suede* for Tape (1961); *Analog #1: Noise Study* for Computer (1961); *Stochastic Quartet*: String Quartet for Computer or Strings (1963); *Dialogue* for Computer (1963); *Ergodos I* (1963) and *II* (1964) for Computer; *Phases* for Computer (1963); *Fabric for Che* for Computer (1967); *For Ann (rising)* for Computer (N.Y., May 23, 1969). **VOCAL:** *13 Ways of Looking at a Blackbird* for Bass, Alto, Flute, Oboe, Viola, Cello, and Double Bass, after Wallace Stevens (1958; rev. 1971); *Voice(s)* for Women's Voice(s), Instrumental Ensemble, and Multiple Tape Delay (1982). **OTHER:** Theater works.—**NS/LK/DM**

Tennstedt, Klaus, brilliant German conductor; b. Merseburg, June 6, 1926.; d. Kiel, Jan. 11, 1998. He studied piano, violin, and theory at the Leipzig Cons. In 1948 he became concertmaster in Halle an der Saale, beginning his career as a conductor there in 1953. After serving as a conductor at the Dresden State Opera (1958–62), he was conductor in Schwerin (1962–71); also appeared as a guest conductor throughout East Germany, Eastern Europe, and the Soviet Union. In 1971 he settled in the West; after guest engagements in Sweden, he served as Generalmusikdirektor of the Kiel Opera (1972–76). In 1974 he made a remarkable North American debut as a guest conductor with the Toronto Sym. Orch., and also appeared with the Boston Sym. Orch., which led to numerous engagements with other major U.S. orchs. In 1976 he made his British debut as a guest conductor of the London Sym. Orch. He was chief conductor of the North German Radio Sym. Orch. in Hamburg (1979–81); was also principal guest conductor of the Minn. Orch. in Minneapolis (1979–83). From 1980 to 1983 he was principal guest conductor of the London Phil., and then served as its principal conductor from 1983 until a diagnosis of throat cancer compelled him to give up his duties in 1987. He continued to make guest appearances in subsequent seasons. On Dec. 14, 1983, he made his Metropolitan Opera debut in N.Y. conducting *Fidelio*. In 1994 his worsening health compelled him to announce that he would no longer conduct in public. His appearances around the globe elicited exceptional critical acclaim; he was ranked among the foremost interpreters of the Austro-German repertoire of his day. **—NS/LK/DM**

Tenschert, Roland, Austrian musicologist; b. Podersam, Bohemia, April 5, 1894; d. Vienna, April 3, 1970. He studied at the Leipzig Cons. (1913–15) and received instruction in musicology from Adler at the Univ. of Vienna (Ph.D., 1921); also studied composition with Schoenberg and conducting with L. Kaiser. He was librarian at the Salzburg Mozarteum (1926–31) and prof. of music history at the Vienna Academy of Music (from 1945).

WRITINGS: *Mozart: Ein Künstlerleben in Bildern und Dokumenten* (Leipzig, 1931); *Mozart* (Leipzig, 1931); *Joseph Haydn* (Berlin, 1932); *Musikerbrevier* (Vienna, 1940); *Mozart: Ein Leben für die Oper* (Vienna, 1941); *Dreimal sieben Variationen über das Thema Richard Strauss* (Vienna, 1944; 2nd ed., 1945); *Frauen um Haydn* (Vienna, 1946); *Salzburg und seine Festspiele* (Vienna, 1947); *Vater Hellmesberger: ein Kapitel Wiener Musikerhumor* (Vienna, 1947); *Richard Strauss und Wien, Eine Wahlverwandtschaft* (Vienna, 1949); *Wolfgang Amadeus Mozart* (Salzburg, 1951; Eng. tr., 1952); *Christoph Willibald Gluck: der grosse Reformer der Oper* (Olten and Freiburg im Breisgau, 1951).

BIBL.: E. Tenschert, *Musik als Lebensinhalt* (Vienna, 1971; contains a list of writings).**—NS/LK/DM**

Teodorini, Elena, Romanian soprano; b. Craiova, March 25, 1857; d. Bucharest, Feb. 27, 1926. She studied piano with Fumagalli and voice with Sangiovanni at the Milan Cons.; also received vocal instruction from G. Stephănescu at the Bucharest Cons. In 1877 she commenced her career with appearances in Italian provincial theaters as a contralto, but her voice gradually changed to a mezzo-soprano of wide range. She made her debut at Milan's La Scala as Gounod's Marguerite on March 20, 1880; subsequently sang in various South American music centers; was particularly associated with the Italian Opera and the National Opera in Bucharest. In 1904 she retired from the operatic stage and became a teacher in Paris; after teaching in Buenos Aires (1909–16) and Rio de Janeiro (1916–23), she settled in Bucharest. Her most notable pupil was Bidú Sayão. Among her prominent roles were Rosina, Donna Anna, Amelia, Lucrezia Borgia, Amneris, and Gioconda. In 1964 the Romanian government issued a postage stamp in her honor bearing her stage portrait.

BIBL.: V. Cosma, *Cîtăreata E. T.* (Bucharest, 1962). **—NS/LK/DM**

Terentieva, Nina (Nikolaievna), Russian mezzo-soprano; b. Kusa, Jan. 9, 1946. She received vocal training at the Leningrad Cons. From 1971 to 1977 she was a member of the Kirov Opera in Leningrad, and then appeared with the Bolshoi Theater in Moscow from 1979. She appeared at the Vienna State Opera from 1987. In 1990 she sang Eboli in Los Angeles, a role she reprised at her Metropolitan Opera debut in N.Y. on March 19, 1992, and at the San Francisco Opera that same year. In 1995 she was engaged as Amneris at London's Covent Garden, a role she sang in San Francisco in 1997. She also was a guest artist of opera houses in Milan, Berlin, Hamburg, Munich, Bordeaux, and Buenos Aires. Among her other roles were Marta, Lubasha, Lubava, Marina, Azucena, Dalila, and Santuzza.**—NS/LK/DM**

Terényi, Ede, Romanian composer and teacher of Hungarian descent; b. Tîrgu-Mureş, March 12, 1935. He studied at the Tîrgu-Mureş Music Coll. (1942–52) and with Jodál and Demian at the Cluj Cons. (1952–58), and was on the latter's faculty from 1960. In his compositions, he applies a variety of modernistic resources.

WORKS: ORCH.: Concertino for Strings, Organ, and Electronics (1958; rev. 1969); *Pasărea măiastră* (The Wonderful Bird), symphonic variations (1965; Cluj, June 11, 1967); 5 syms.: No. 1, *Brâncusiană* (1965; rev. 1986), No. 2 for Strings, *In memoriam Bakfark* (1978), No. 3 for 2 Percussionists (1978), No. 4, *Hofgreff* (1982; rev. 1986), and No. 5 for Strings and Timpani (1984); Piano Concerto (1969); *Muzică în Do*, concerto grosso (Cluj, Dec. 11, 1979); 6 neo-Baroque concertos: No. 1 for Flute and Chamber Orch., *Vivaldiana* (Cluj, May 27, 1983), No. 2 for Oboe and Chamber Orch., *Suită franceză* (1984), No. 3 for Trumpet and Chamber Orch., clarino concerto (1984), No. 4 for Cello and Chamber Orch., *Rapsodi barocă* (1984; Cluj, March 20, 1985), No. 5 for Harp and Chamber Orch., *Capriccio grazioso* (Cluj, Oct. 10, 1985), and No. 6 for Viola and Chamber Orch., *Rapsodisme händeliene* (1985). **CHAMBER:** 2 preludes for Flute (1962, 1966); 2 string quartets (1974, 1984); *Sonatina burletta* for Cello and Piano (1975); *Dansuri galante*, suite for Flute, Oboe, Harpsichord, and Cello (1977); 2 violin sonatas (1980, 1985); Sonata for 2 Percussionists (1980); Sonata for Solo Violin (1985); 2 percussion quartets (*Swinging Music*, 1985; *Hommage à Coltrane*, 1986); piano pieces; organ music. **VOCAL:** Cantata No. 1: *In memoriam* for Tenor or Soprano and Piano (1964; rev. and orchestrated as *In memoriam József Attila*, Cluj, May 19, 1968); *Terzine de Dante*, scenic cantata for Baritone, Trombone, and Piano (1971–72); *Micropantomimes* for Mezzo-soprano and Piano (1981).**—NS/LK/DM**

Terfel, Bryn (in full, **Bryn Terfel Jones**), outstanding Welsh bass-baritone; b. Pantglas, Nov. 9, 1965. He was a student of Arthur Reckless and Rudolf Piernay at the Guildhall School of Music and Drama in London (1984–89), winning the Kathleen Ferrier Memorial Scholarship (1988) and the Gold Medal (1989). After winning the Lieder Prize at the Cardiff Singer of the World Competition in 1989, he made his operatic debut as Guglielmo with the Welsh National Opera in Cardiff in 1990. In 1991 he sang Mozart's Figaro at his first appearance with the English National Opera in London, which role he also sang that same year at his U.S. debut in Santa Fe. In 1992 he appeared for the first time at the Salzburg Easter Festival as the Spirit Messenger in *Die Frau ohne Schatten*; that same year, he also made his Salzburg Festival debut as Jochanaan and his first appearance at London's Covent Garden as Massetto. In 1993 he made his debut with the Lyric Opera of Chicago as Donner and at the Vienna State Opera as Mozart's Figaro; also appeared as Verdi's Ford with the Welsh National Opera. In 1994 he returned to the Vienna State Opera as Offenbach's 4 villains, at Covent Garden as Mozart's Figaro, and at the Salzburg Festival as Leporello. In 1994 he made an impressive appearance in the closing night gala concert of the 100th annivesary season of the London Promenade Concerts as soloist with Andrew Davis and the BBC Sym. Orch. His highly acclaimed Metropolitan Opera debut in N.Y. followed on Oct. 19, 1994, as Mozart's Figaro. On Oct. 24, 1994, he made his N.Y. recital debut at Alice Tully Hall. In 1995 he returned to the Lyric Opera of Chicago and at the Metropolitan Opera as Leporello. He portrayed Nick Shadow at the Welsh National Opera in 1996. In 1997 he was engaged as Mozart's Figaro at Milan's La Scala and the San Francisco Opera, and as Jochanaan at Covent Garden. He appeared as Mozart's Figaro at the Metropolitan Opera and as Scarpia at the Netherlands Opera in Amsterdam in 1998. In 1999 he portrayed Don Giovanni in Paris and made his Australian debut as Falstaff in Sydney. In addition to his operatic repertoire, Terfel has won a wide following for his concert engagements, in a repertoire extending from Bach to Walton. **—NS/LK/DM**

Ternina, Milka, outstanding Croatian soprano; b. Doljnji, Moslavina, Dec. 19, 1863; d. Zagreb, May 18, 1941. She studied with Ida Winterberg in Zagreb and then with Gansbacher at the Vienna Cons. (1880–82). She made her operatic debut as Amelia in *Un ballo in maschera* in Zagreb (1882); then sang in Leipzig (1883–84), Graz (1884–86), and Bremen (1886–89). In 1889 she appeared as a guest artist at the Hamburg Opera, joining its roster in 1890; also was a member of the Munich Court Opera (1890–99), where she distinguished herself as a Wagnerian singer. She was engaged by Walter Damrosch for his German Opera Co. in N.Y., and made her American debut as Elsa in *Lohengrin* in Boston on March 4, 1896; also appeared at Covent Garden, London, as Isolde (June 3, 1898); after a series of successes at the Bayreuth Festivals (1899), she made her Metropolitan Opera debut in N.Y. as Elisabeth on Jan. 27, 1900, and sang there until 1904 (1902–03 season excepted); she sang Tosca at the American premiere (Feb. 4, 1901) and Kundry in *Parsifal* (Dec. 24, 1903). She made her farewell stage appearance as Sieglinde in Munich on Aug. 19, 1906. In subsequent years, she was active as a teacher, giving instruction at the Inst. of Musical Art in N.Y. and later in Zagreb, where she was the mentor of Zinka Milanov. She was renowned for her portrayals of Isolde and Beethoven's Leonore. **—NS/LK/DM**

Terrabugio, Giuseppe, Italian composer; b. Fiera di Primiero, May 13, 1842; d. there, Jan. 8, 1933. He studied in Padua, and then in Munich under Rheinberger. In 1883 he settled in Milan, where, as ed. of *Musica Sacra*, he exerted a strong influence in reforming Italian church music. His publ. works (about 100 opus numbers) are almost exclusively for the church and include 12 masses, a Requiem, litanies, motets, etc. He also publ. *L'organista pratico* (3 vols.).**—NS/LK/DM**

Terradellas, Domingo (Miguel Bernabe), distinguished Spanish composer who became best known via his Italianized name of Domenico Terradeglias; b. Barcelona (baptized), Feb. 13, 1713; d. Rome, May 20, 1751. He began his musical training in Barcelona, then studied at the Cons. dei Poveri di Gesù Cristo in Naples (1732–38); while still a student, he produced his first significant score, the oratorio *Giuseppe riconosciuto* (1736). He gained an outstanding success with his opera *Merope* (Rome, Jan. 3, 1743). From 1743 to 1745 he was active at the Spanish church of Santiago y S. Ildefonso in Rome, and devoted much time to writing sacred music. During the 1746–47 season, he composed 2 operas for the King's Theatre in London; then returned to the Continent; was again in Italy by 1750. His last opera, *Sesostri re d'Egitto*, scored a major success at its premiere in Rome (Carnival 1751).

WORKS: DRAMATIC: Opera: *Astarto* (Rome, Carnival 1739); *Gli intrighi delle cantarine* (Naples, 1740); *Issipile* (Florence, 1741 or 1742); *Merope* (Rome, Jan. 3, 1743); *Artaserse* (Venice, Carnival 1744); *Semiramide riconosciuta* (Florence, Carnival 1746); *Mitridate* (London, Dec. 2, 1746); *Bellerofonte* (London, March 24, 1747); *Didone abbandonata* (Turin, Carnival 1750); *Imeneo in Atene* (Venice, May 6, 1750); *Sesostri re d'Egitto* (Rome, Carnival 1751). **SACRED VOCAL:** 2 oratorios (Naples, 1736 and 1739); Missa Solemnia; masses; Te Deum, etc.**—NS/LK/DM**

Terrasse, Claude (Antoine), French composer; b. L'Arbresle, Rhône, Jan. 27, 1867; d. Paris, June 30, 1923. He studied at the Lyons Cons. and at the École Niedermeyer in Paris. From 1888 to 1895 he was church organist in Arcachon, and then in Paris until 1899, when he began to write for the stage, producing a series of successful operettas. The best known are *Les Travaux d'Hercule* (March 7, 1901), *Le Sire de Vergy* (April 16, 1903), *Monsieur de la Palisse* (Nov. 2, 1904), *La Marquise et le marmiton* (Dec. 11, 1907), *Le Coq d'Inde* (April 6, 1909), *Le Mariage de Télémaque* (May 4, 1910), *Les Transatlantiques* (May 20, 1911), and *Cartouche* (March 9, 1912). His other works include the ballet *Les lucioles* (Dec. 28, 1910), 2 masses, a motet, songs, and piano pieces.**—NS/LK/DM**

Terrell, Tammi (Thomasina Montgomery), singing partner to Marvin Gaye who died far too young; b. Philadelphia, April 29, 1945; d. Cleveland, Ohio,

March 16, 1970. Terrell's uncle was boxer Bob Montgomery, her mother an actress. By her 15th birthday, Tommi Montgomery started singing on records for Wand. She was produced by James Brown during this period, toured with his Revue, and was allegedly his abused girlfriend. She also changed her name to "Tammi" at this time. At age 20, she signed with Motown and entered into another allegedly abusive relationship with David Ruffin of the Temptations. She hooked up with Marvin Gaye—musically but not romantically—two years later. During 1967 they cut such classic Ashford and Simpson written tracks as "Ain't No Mountain High Enough" (#19 pop) and "Your Precious Love" (#5 pop). However, late in the year, Terrell collapsed on stage. In the hospital, she was diagnosed as having a brain tumor. She continued to sing, releasing duets with Gaye including "If I Could Build My Whole World Around You" (#10, 1968), the classic "Ain't Nothing Like the Real Thing" (#8 pop, #1 R&B, 1968), and "You're All I Need to Get By" (#7 pop, #1 R&B—five weeks—1968). By the time "Keep On Lovin' Me Honey" and "Good Lovin' Ain't Easy to Come By" came out, Terrell's parts were actually being performed by Valerie Simpson, because Terrell was too weak to sing. Her passing in the late winter of 1970 threw Gaye into a tailspin that kept him from recording for two years and performing until 1972. It also precluded her having any kind of solo career on Motown.

DISC.: *Irresistible* (1968); *United* (1968); *You're All I Need* (1968).—**HB**

Terry, Brett, American composer and classical guitarist; b. N.Y., Feb. 20, 1968. His parents founded the Renaissance Revival in 1977, a choral group, in which he sang. He studied at Wesleyan Univ. with Neely Bruce and Alvin Lucier (B.A. 1990), then at the Univ. of Ill. with Scott Wyatt, Bill Brooks, and Erik Lund (M.Mus. 1994, M.S. in computer science, 1995). In addition to composing, he has authored several music software programs, including Caspar aural skills. His choral and chamber works exhibit a strong lyrical sense, blending Renaissance and late Romantic chromatic harmony within a framework of polyrythmic counterpoint. His electroacoustic works utilize spatiality as an integral contrapuntal element.

WORKS: *O Magnum Mysterium* for Mixed Voices (1989); *Estuans Interius* for Women's Chorus (1990); *Burnt Finnegan* for 4-channel Tape (1991); *Mosaic* for 4-channel Tape (1994); *Nisi Dominus* for Women's Chorus (1995); Sextet No. 1 for Strings and Woodwinds (1995); *Clotho* for 4-channel Tape and Women's Chorus (1996); *Mycelis Muralis Decussate* for 8-channel Tape and Cello (2000).—**LK/DM**

Terry, Charles Sanford, eminent English music scholar; b. Newport Pagnell, Buckinghamshire, Oct. 24, 1864; d. Westerton of Pitfodels, near Aberdeen, Nov. 5, 1936. He studied history at Clare Coll., Cambridge (1883–86) and in 1890 became a lecturer in history at Durham Coll. of Science, Newcastle upon Tyne. He joined the faculty of the Univ. of Aberdeen in 1898, and from 1903 to 1930 held the Burnett-Fletcher chair of history there, occupying himself with historical research; at the same time, he devoted much of his energy to the study of Bach and his period. His biography of Bach (London, 1928; 2nd ed., rev., 1933; 6th ed., 1967) places Bach's life within historical perspective with a fine discernment; it has become a standard in the literature on Bach in English. Other books and eds. dealing with Bach include *Bach's Chorals* (Cambridge, 1915–21), *Joh. Seb. Bach: Cantata Texts, sacred and secular, with a Reconstruction of the Leipzig Liturgy of his Period* (London, 1926), *The Origin of the Family of Bach Musicians* (London, 1929), *Bach: The Historical Approach* (1930), *Bach's Orchestra* (1932; 4th ed., 1966), and *The Music of Bach: An Introduction* (1933). To the Musical Pilgrim series he contributed analyses of the B-minor Mass (1924), the cantatas and oratorios (1925), the Passions (1926), and the Magnificat, Lutheran masses, and motets (1929). He also ed. *Coffee and Cupid (The Coffee Cantata): An Operetta by Johann Sebastian Bach* (London, 1924) and *The Four-part Chorals of J.S. Bach* (London, 1929; 2nd ed., 1964). He also wrote a biography of Johann Christian Bach (1929; 2nd ed., rev., 1967 by H.C. Robbins Landon). —**NS/LK/DM**

Terry, Clark (Mumbles), influential jazz trumpeter, flugelhornist, singer; b. St. Louis, Dec. 14, 1920. His oldest sister Ada was married to the tuba player Cy McField, who played with Dewey Jackson's Musical Ambassadors. On occcasion, Terry would hear them rehearsing at his sister's home and, after befriending one of the trumpeters, he was drawn to the instrument. In high school, he played a few gigs at a bar and began singing there as well. He credits his style to the soft "felt-muted" sound prevalent in the area. While in the Navy (1942–45), he was sent to one of the training camps for black seamen near Waukegan, Ill., just north of Chicago. From these camps, bands were sent out to bases around the country. At the camp near Waukegan, Terry met and worked with Willie Smith. Terry spent a brief period with Lionel Hampton; in 1946 he joined Charlie Barnet's band. In 1947, he played a Town Hall concert with Doc Severinsen as a bandmate, then was back in St. Louis with George Hudson's band and in and out of N.Y. There, in 1948, Teagarden was hired by Count Basie, who was rehearsing at Nola's Studios on Broadway. After Basie's Big Band broke up, Terry toured and appeared on film with Basie's small group. In 1951, Ellington made him an offer, and he joined the group that November. Terry says he contributed to the ending of Ellington's "Newport Suite" (1957). While with Ellington he began doubling on the flugelhorn for the softer "St. Louis" type of sound. Later, he worked with Keith Eckert, technical advisor for Selmer Brass, to develop the first fluegelhorn that Selmer issued in America.

Terry left Ellington's band in Paris in 1959 to join Quincy Jones's band, which was signed to play in the Harold Arlen musical *Free and Easy.* When the show unexpectedly closed in early February 1960, Terry accepted an offer to join the NBC *Tonight Show* Orch. in N.Y. During the day the band members worked playing music for commercials; the Tonight Show was taped early in the evening, ending at 8 pm, after which Terry would play gigs. In 1961, he worked with Gerry Mulligan's band, and in 1964–67 he co-led a celebrated quintet with Bob Brookmeyer at the Half Note. In 1964, he had a solo hit with the song "Mumbles," accompanied by the Oscar Peterson trio. This scat-singing masterwork gained him his nickname. The trumpeters for the *Tonight Show*, Severinsen, Jimmy Maxwell, Bernie Glow, and Terry, would occasionally be asked by local schools to talk to students; this started his work as a teacher. He started the Harlem Youth Band, bought instruments for some of the students and taught them how to read music. Gene Ghee, head of the jazz program at Boys High in Brooklyn, was one of the students. Terry chose to remain in N.Y. when The *Tonight Show* moved to Burbank, Calif. in 1972, though he did appear as a guest on occasion when in the area. Since then, he has continued to lead small groups, such as his Big B-A-D Band, which plays occasionally, and numerous clinics. Wynton and Branford Marsalis and Danny House played in Europe with his youth band in 1980. The Clark Terry International Inst. of Jazz Studies in Le Mars, Iowa, founded in 1995, coordinates his educational work. He received an honorary doctorate from Manhattan School and from NEC (T. Monk Ins.), both in May 1997.

Known for his smooth, sweet tone and great facility, Terry was also capable in his early years of creating hair-raising brassy excitement (e.g., on "Move" and "Scrapple from the Apple," 1950). He was a pioneering jazz flugelhornist and a major influence on the young Miles Davis. Through his generosity as a teacher he has inspired many musicians. He is a witty singer whose "mumbles" blues are both hilarious and musical.

DISC.: Wardell Grey: "Move" and "Scrapple from the Apple" (1950); *Introducing Clark Terry* (1955); *Duke with a Difference* (1957); *Serenade to a Bus Seat* (1957); *In Orbit* (1958; w. Monk); *Color Changes* (1960); *Eddie Costa Memorial* (1962); *Clark Terry Tonight* (1964); *Oscar Peterson Trio with C.T.* (1964); *Power of Positive Swinging* (1964); *Tonight* (1964); *Gingerbread Men* (1966); *Mumbles* (1966); *Clark Terry's Big B-A-D-Band Live* (1974); *Live at the Wichita Jazz Festival* (1974); *Mother...! Mother...!* (1979); *Clark Terry Spacemen* (1989); *Live from the Village Gate* (1990); *Second Set* (1990); *Shades of Blues* (1994).—**LP**

Terry, Sir R(ichard) R(unciman), noted English organist, choirmaster, and music scholar; b. Ellington, Northumberland, Jan. 3, 1865; d. London, April 18, 1938. In 1890 he was appointed organist and music master at Elstow School, and from 1892 to 1896 he was organist and choirmaster at St. John's Cathedral, Antigua, West Indies. From 1896 to 1901 he was at Downside Abbey, where he attracted attention by his revival of the Catholic church music of early English masters (Byrd, Tallis, Tye, Morley, Mundy, White, Fayrfax, etc.); from 1901 to 1924, he was organist and director of music at Westminster Cathedral. He was chairman of the committee appointed to prepare the Eng. supplement of the Vatican Antiphonary, and music ed. of the Westminster Hymnal (London, 1912; 3rd ed., rev., 1916; 7th ed., 1937), the official Roman Catholic hymnal for England. He was knighted in 1922. Besides masses, motets, and other church music, he composed *48 Old Rhymes with New Tunes* (1934). He ed. *The Shanty Book* (2 vols.; 1921; 1926), *Old Christmas Carols* (1923), *Hymns of Western Europe* (with Davies and Hadow; 1927), *Salt Sea Ballads* (1931), *A Medieval Carol Book* (1932), *200 Folk Carols* (1933), and *Calvin's First Psalter [1539], harmonized* (1932), and also the collections of 16th-century music *Downside Masses and Downside Motets, Motets Ancient and Modern*, and many separate works by early Eng. composers. He wrote the books *Catholic Church Music* (1907), *On Music's Borders* (1927), *A Forgotten Psalter and Other Essays* (1929), *The Music of the Roman Rite* (1931), and *Voodooism in Music and Other Essays* (1934).

BIBL.: H. Andrews, *Westminster Retrospect: A Memoir of Sir R. T.* (London, 1948).—**NS/LK/DM**

Terteryan, Avet, Azerbaijani composer and teacher; b. Baku, July 29, 1929; d. Yekaterinburg, Dec. 11, 1994. He received training in composition from Mirzoyan at the Yerevan Cons. (1952–57). In 1970 he joined its faculty as an instructor, and in 1983 he became a prof. Terteryan's music is made forceful with ancient sonorities, employing a dramatic character that verges on barely controlled chaos. His influences range from Armenian pagan rites to Western 12-tone dodecaphony. The backbone of his relatively small output, his syms., explore paths that were daring in the Soviet Union of the 1970s, often given solo roles to folk instruments such as the duduk, zurna, and kemancha.

WORKS: DRAMATIC: *The Ring of Fire*, opera (1967; rev. 1977); *Monologue Richard III*, ballet (1977–79); *The Earthquake in Chile*, after Kleist (1986). **ORCH.:** 9 syms: No. 1 for Brass, Percussion, Piano, Organ, and Bass Guitar (1969), No. 2 for Men's Chorus, Mixed Chorus, and Orch. (1972), No. 3 for Duduk, Zurna, and Orch. (1975), No. 4 for Orch. and Tape (1976), No. 5 for Zuran, Kyamancha, Burvar, and Orch. (1978), No. 6 (1981), No. 7 (1987), No. 8 (1989), and No. 9 (1994; unfinished). **CHAMBER:** Cello Sonata (1955); 2 string quartets (1962, 1991); *Poem* for Cello and Piano (1964).—**LK/DM**

Tertis, Lionel, eminent English violist and teacher; b. West Hartlepool, Dec. 29, 1876; d. London, Feb. 22, 1975. He studied violin at the Leipzig Cons. and at the Royal Academy of Music in London. He took up the viola at 19 and became active as a chamber music artist; served as principal violist in the Queen's Hall Orch. (1900–1904), and in Beecham's orch. (1909); eventually became one of the most renowned violists in Europe. In 1901 he became prof. of viola at the Royal Academy of Music, where he was director of its ensemble class (1924–29). In 1936 he retired from his concert career, but in later years made occasional appearances; his farewell performance was given at the age of 87. In 1950 he was made a Commander of the Order of the British Empire. He prepared many transcriptions for his instrument and also commissioned various works from noted English composers. He wrote *Beauty of Tone in String Playing* (London, 1938) and the autobiographical *Cinderella No More* (London, 1953; 2nd ed., rev. and enl., 1974, as *My Viola and I: A Complete Autobiography*). He designed the Tertis viola (16 3/49), which is described in *Music & Letters* (July 1947).—**NS/LK/DM**

Tervani, Irma, Finnish mezzo-soprano; b. Helsinki, June 4, 1887; d. Berlin, Oct. 29, 1936. She received her primary training with her mother, the soprano Emmy Strömer-Ackté, then studied voice in Paris and Dresden. She made her operatic debut with the Dresden Court Opera in 1908 as Dalila, remaining on its roster until 1932. She gained renown through her appearance in the role of Carmen opposite Caruso in Frankfurt am Main in 1910.—**NS/LK/DM**

Terzakis, Dimitri, Greek composer and teacher; b. Athens, March 12, 1938. He studied composition with Iannis Papaioannou at the Hellenic Cons. in Athens (1957–64), then pursued studies with Bernd Alois Zimmermann at the Cologne Hochschule für Musik (diploma, 1970); also studied Byzantine music and at Mount Athos. He was co-founder of the Greek Soc. for Contemporary Music (1966). He lectured on Byzantine music and instrumentation at the Robert Schumann Inst. in Düsseldorf (from 1974), where he taught composition at the Hochschule für Musik (1987–93). From 1990 he taught composition at the Bern Hochschule für Musik and from 1994 he was prof. of composition at the Leipzig Hochschule für Musik. In 1980 he founded the International Inst. of Research on the Relations Between Occidental and Southeast-European Music in Nauplia, Greece. Terzaki's music steers a resolute course in the cosmopolitan avant-garde, leaving no tonal stone unturned; ancestral Grecian ethos is present, however, both in the titles and in the modalities of his output. In 1994 he began to compose monophonic scores.

WORKS: DRAMATIC: Opera: *Torquemada* (1974–76); *Circus Universal*, chamber opera (1975); *Hermes* (1983–84). **ORCH.:** *Ikona* for Strings (1963); Oboe Concerto (1968); *Chroai* (1970); *Transcriptions télégraphiques* (1971); *Kosmogramm* (1974); *Tropi* (1975); *Prooimion in Ethods C* for Chamber Orch. (1979); *Lachesis* (1984–85); Violin Concerto (1985–86); *Per aspera ad Astra* (1989–90); *Ikaros-Daidalos* for Saxophone Quartet and Brass Orch. (1990); Alto Saxophone Concerto (1994–95). **CHAMBER:** Septet for 7 Flutes (1965–66); Trio for Guitar, Cello, and Percussion (1966); 4 string quartets (1969; 1976; 1981–82; 1990); *Stixis II* for Clarinet (1973); Brass Quintet (1983); Saxophone Quartet (1986); Octet (1988); *Trias*, piano trio (1989); *Rabasso* for Saxophone Quartet, Viola, Cello, and Double Bass (1991–92); *Der Hölle Nachklang I* for Alto Saxophone and Piano (1992); *Jeux* for Recorder and Guitar (1993); Trio for Flute, Bass Clarinet, and Piano (1993); *Sonetto* for Viola and Piano (1993). **VOCAL:** *Okeaniden* for Chorus and Orch. (1967); *Ikos* for Chorus (1968); *Nuances* for Soprano and Tape (1970); *X* for Baritone and Ensemble (1971); *Karawassia* for 6 Singers (1971–72); *Ethos B* for Soprano and 3 Instruments (1972); *Stichiron* for Chorus and Brass (1972); *Passionen*, oratorio (1978–79); *Erotikon* for Soprano and 3 Instruments (1979); *6 Monologe* for Soprano and Orch. (1985); *Das sechste Siegel* for Chorus and Ensemble (1987); *Apokryphen* for Narrator, Soprano, and Chamber Ensemble (1988–89); *Der Hölle Nachklang II* for Soprano and Organ (1992–93); *Daphnis und Chloe* for Soprano and Viola (1994); *Lieder ohne Worte* for Soprano (1994). **ELECTRONIC:** *Ichochronos I* (1967).—**NS/LK/DM**

Terziani, Eugenio, Italian conductor, teacher, and composer; b. Rome, July 29, 1824; d. there, June 30, 1889. He studied with Mercadante at the Naples Cons. and later with Baini in Rome. At the age of 19 he produced an oratorio, *La caduta di Gerico* (Rome, March 31, 1844), followed by the operas *Giovanna regina di Napoli* (Ferrara, 1844) and *Alfredo* (Rome, Feb. 21, 1852). He was conductor in Rome at the Teatro Apollo (1847–69), at La Scala in Milan (1867–71), and again in Rome (1871–75), where he then taught composition and singing at the Liceo Musicale di S. Cecilia (from 1875). He also wrote the opera *L'assedio di Firenze* (Rome, Feb. 24, 1883), 2 ballets, including *Una Silfide a Pechino* (Rome, Dec. 26, 1859), an *Inno sinfonico* (1882), and much sacred music. —**NS/LK/DM**

Teschemacher, Frank (aka Tesch), early jazz clarinetist, alto saxophonist, violinist, arranger; b. Kansas City, Mo., March 13, 1906; d. Chicago, March 1, 1932. He was raised in Chicago, attended Austin H.S., and began gigging with classmates Jimmy McPartland, Bud Freeman, and Jim Lanigan in The Blue Friars. In 1924, he worked at Merry Gardens Ballroom with Wingy Manone and played alto with the Red Dragons, which was essentially The Blue Friars under Husk O' Hare. The title also served as the group's name while they were house band for WHT Radio. During the following year, while playing a season at Lost Lake, Wisc., he took up clarinet and received some instruction from Bud Jacobson. He worked in a band opposite Sig Meyers in White City, Chicago, then played briefly in Fla. with Charlie Straight. From 1926–28, he worked mostly with Floyd Town's Band, but also played with Charlie Straight and Art Kassel and did various recording sessions. Teschemacher arranged the four tracks on the McKenzie-Condon Chicagoans recording date in 1927. In June 1928, he went to N.Y. with the Chicagoans (later called the Chicago Gang), worked for a week accompanying a variety act, and then gigged around N.Y. He deputized for Gil Rodin in Ben Pollack's Band (August 1928); recorded with Ted Lewis, Red Nichols, and Miff Mole, and played tenor sax on the first recording session led by the Dorsey Brothers. He went to Atlantic City as a member of Sam Lanin's society band, then played there with Nichols for a month before returning to Chicago in September 1928. In Chicago, he played for various bandleaders, including Joe Kayser, Charlie Straight, Floyd Town, and with Jess Stacy's Aces, and possibly Eddie Neibauer, Eddie Valzos, and Benny Meroff. During the last two years of his life. Teschemacher worked mainly on alto and violin. He toured with Jan Garber in autumn 1931, but left the tour and returned to Chicago, where he continued gigging. He then served as musical director of Bill Davison's Big Band. Davison could not read music in 1932, so Teschemacher essentially co-led the group, which performed Reginald Forsythe's sophisticated arrangements.

Teschemacher's death is shrouded in myth and legend. He was killed in a head-on automobile collision early in the morning hours of March 1, 1932. Davison was driving the car, which was struck head on by a taxicab driver. It is said that the passenger in the taxi was a bouncer who had a beef with Teschemacher; although he didn't intend to kill the musician, he hoped to at least ruffle his feathers. Additionally, Davison and Teschemacher probably had been drinking prior to getting into the car. The bouncer was said to have mob connections, which helped to cover up the true cause of the accident.

Disc.: McKenzie-Condon Chicagoans: "Sugar," "China Boy" (both 1927); "Nobody's Sweetheart," "Liza" (1927). Jungle Kings: "Friars Point Shuffle," "Darktown Strutters Ball" (1928). **—TS/JC**

Teschemacher, Margarete, German soprano; b. Cologne, March 3, 1903; d. Bad Wiesse, May 19, 1959. She was trained in Cologne. After making her operatic debut in Cologne as Micaëla (1924), she sang in Aachen (1925–27), Dortmund (1927–28), Mannheim (1928–31), and Stuttgart (1931–34). From 1935 to 1946 she was a member of the Dresden State Opera, where Strauss chose her to create his Daphne in 1938. She also made appearances at London's Covent Garden (debut as Pamina, 1931) and at Buenos Aires's Teatro Colón (1934). From 1947 to 1952 she sang in Düsseldorf. Among her other roles were Donna Elvira, Countess Almaviva, Sieglinde, Senta, Jenůfa, and Arabella. **—NS/LK/DM**

Tesi-Tramontini, Vittoria, famous Italian contralto, known as **La Moretta**; b. Florence, Feb. 13, 1700; d. Vienna, May 9, 1775. She received her instruction in Florence and Bologna, appearing on the stage at the age of 16 in Parma in Dafni; then was engaged in Venice (1718–19). She sang in Italy every year, and also appeared in Madrid (1739). In 1748 she sang the title role in Gluck's *Semiramide riconosciuta* in Vienna, where she continued to appear until 1751; then devoted herself to teaching. She was married to one Tramontini, a barber by trade, and adopted the professional name Tesi-Tramontini. She was remarkably free in her morals, and many stories, in which it is impossible to separate truth from invention, were circulated about her life. Her letters to a priest were publ. by Benedetto Croce in his book *Un Prelato e una cantante del secolo XVIII* (Bari, 1946).**—NS/LK/DM**

Tess (real name, **Tesscorolo**), **Giulia,** noted Italian mezzo-soprano, later soprano; b. Verona, Feb. 9, 1889; d. Milan, March 17, 1976. She studied with Bottagisio in Verona. She made her operatic debut as a mezzo-soprano in 1904 in Prato; later sang soprano roles after being encouraged by Battistini. In 1922 she was invited by Toscanini to sing at La Scala in Milan, where she created the role of Jaele in Pizzetti's *Debora e Jaele*. She continued to sing there with great distinction until 1936; then was director of stage craft at the Florence Centro di Avviamento al Teatro Lirico (1940–42), at the Bologna Cons. (1941–46), and at the La Scala opera school (from 1946). Her students included Tagliavini and Barbieri; she also produced opera at La Scala and other Italian opera houses. She was married to the conductor Giacomo Armani (1868–1954). In addition to the Italian repertoire, she gained distinction as an interpreter of roles by Richard Strauss, excelling as Salome and Elektra.**—NS/LK/DM**

Tessarini, Carlo, Italian violinist and composer; b. Rimini, c. 1690; d. probably in Amsterdam, after 1766. He was a follower, if not actually a pupil, of Corelli. By 1720 he was a violinist at San Marco in Venice, and later was concertmaster of the concerts of the Cons. Ss. Giovanni e Paolo (from 1729); was active at the chapel of Urbino Cathedral (from c. 1733). After a sojourn at the court of Cardinal Wolfgang Schrattenbach in Brunn (c. 1735–38), he was again active at Urbino Cathedral until 1744; also made tours as a concert artist in 1739; appeared in the Netherlands in 1747. He was once more active at Urbino Cathedral (1750–57) although he continued to pursue his concert career; subsequently settled in Holland. His violin sonatas, generally in 3 movements, contributed to the establishment of a 3-movement sonata as a norm. He publ. many trio sonatas, duets, concertinos, and concerti grossi, as well as the interesting treatise, *Gramatica di musica: insegna il modo facile e breve per bene imparare di sonae il violino su la parte* (Rome, 1741; Eng. tr., 1765).**—NS/LK/DM**

Tessier, André, French musicologist; b. Paris, March 8, 1886; d. there, July 2, 1931. He studied law, history of art, and other subjects, and then devoted himself to musicology, taking his diploma at the École du Louvre, 1921. He was archivist in the Ministry of Fine Arts, and also ed. of the *Revue de Musicologie*. He ed. the complete works of Chambonnières (with P. Brunold; 1925), and Denis Gaultier's *Rhétorique des Dieux* (facsimile, 1932; transcription, 1933). He was the author of a book on Couperin (Paris, 1926); prepared materials for the complete ed. of Couperin's works, but died before his work was finished. A complete list of his writings was publ. by A. Schaeffner in *Revue de Musicologie* (Dec. 1953).**—NS/LK/DM**

Tessier, Charles, French lutenist and composer who flourished in the late 16th and early 17th centuries. He was chamber musician to Henri IV. His book *Premier livre de chansons et airs de cour tant en français qu'en italien et en gascon à 4 et 4 parties* was publ. in London (1597), and dedicated to Lady Penelope Riche (Sir Philip Sidney's "Stella"). His *Airs et villanelles français, espagnols, suices et turcqs...à 3, 4, et 5 parties* was publ. in Paris (1604; 2nd ed., 1610).

Bibl.: N. McBride, *The Chansons of C. T.: A Transcription and Commentary* (diss., Queen's Univ., Belfast, 1977).**—NS/LK/DM**

Testore, Carlo Giuseppe, Italian instrument maker; b. Novara, c. 1660; d. c. 1720. He was a pupil of Grancino and worked in Milan (1690–1715). He made mostly cellos and double basses, and only a few violins. His son, Paolo Antonio (1690–1760), made violins on the model of Guarneri.**—NS/LK/DM**

Testori, Carlo Giovanni, Italian music theorist, violin pedagogue, and composer; b. Vercelli, March 24, 1714; d. there, May 20, 1782. He studied violin and composition in Milan, then taught violin in Vercelli. He publ. *La musica raggionata* (Vercelli, 1767), a theoretical treatise based on the system of Rameau; it was followed by 3 supplements (1771, 1773, 1782).**—NS/LK/DM**

Tetrazzini, Eva, Italian soprano, sister of **Luisa Tetrazzini**; b. Milan, March, 1862; d. Salsomaggiore,

Oct. 27, 1938. She studied with Ceccherini in Florence, where she made her operatic debut in 1882 as Marguerite in *Faust*. She sang Desdemona in Verdi's *Otello* at its first American production (N.Y., April 16, 1888). On May 15, 1887, she married **Cleofonte Campanini**. She sang with the Manhattan Opera in N.Y. in 1908, and then returned to Italy.—**NS/LK/DM**

Tetrazzini, Luisa (actually, **Luigia**), celebrated Italian soprano, sister of **Eva Tetrazzini;** b. Florence, June 28, 1871; d. Milan, April 28, 1940. She learned the words and music of several operas by listening to her sister; then studied at the Liceo Musicale in Florence with Ceccherini. She made her operatic debut as Inez in *L'Africaine* in Florence (1890); then sang in Europe and traveled with various opera companies in South America. In 1904 she made her U.S. debut at the Tivoli Opera House in San Francisco. She made her London debut at Covent Garden as Violetta on Nov. 2, 1907. She was then engaged by Hammerstein to sing with his Manhattan Opera House in N.Y., where she sang Violetta on Jan. 15, 1908; she remained with the company until it closed in 1910; subsequently appeared for a single season at the Metropolitan Opera (1911–12), making her debut there on Dec. 27, 1911, as Lucia. After singing at the Chicago Grand Opera (1911–13), she toured as a concert artist. She made the first broadcast on the British radio in 1925; her last American appearance was in N.Y. in 1931. She then taught in Milan. Her fame was worldwide, and her name became a household word, glorified even in food, as in Turkey Tetrazzini. She publ. *My Life of Song* (London, 1921) and *How to Sing* (N.Y., 1923). She acquired a great fortune, but died in poverty.

BIBL.: C. Gattey, *L. T.: The Florentine Nightingale* (Portland, Ore., 1995).—**NS/LK/DM**

Tetzlaff, Christian, German violinist; b. Hamburg, April 29, 1966. He began violin lessons at age 6 with Maren Tanke, and then pursued training with Evelyn Distler at the Hamburg Hochschule für Musik. At 14, he made his debut as soloist in the Brahms Violin Concerto in Hamburg. He then studied with Uwe-Martin Haiberg at the Lübeck Hochschule für Musik, where he also received training in theory and composition. In 1984 he took 2nd prize at the Munich Competition; then held a scholarship for further study with Walter Levin at the Univ. of Cincinnati-Coll. Cons. of Music (1985–86). In 1988 he won particular notice as soloist in the Schoenberg Violin Concerto with Celibidache and the Munich Phil. at the Berlin Festival, and then made his U.S. orch. debut in the same work with Dohnányi and the Cleveland Orch.; thereafter he was engaged as a soloist with the foremost orchs. of the world and also toured extensively as a recitalist and chamber music artist, appearing throughout Europe (1992–93) and then widely in North America (1994–95). Tetzlaff has won merited praise for his fine musicianship in which he displays a remarkable balance between virtuosity and refinement of expression. In addition to his performances of the standard literature, he frequently performs works by such 20th-century masters as Schoenberg, Stravinsky, Janáček, Ravel, Bartók, and Hartmann.—**NS/LK/DM**

Texier, Henri, contemporary jazz bassist, multi-instrumentalist, composer; b. Paris, Jan. 27, 1945. He began on the piano at age eight and played in an amateur Dixieland band at 14. He became interested in modern jazz in 1960 and took up bass the following year. Soon he was playing with Jef Gilson and at the Chat Qui Peche and Blue Note clubs with Americans such as Chet Baker, Bud Powell, and Johnny Griffin. In 1965, he began to play festivals with his own quintets, one of which briefly included Enrico Rava, Michel Portal, and Aldo Romano. That same year, he played with Don Cherry, Steve Lacy, Mal Waldron, Barney Wilen. In 1966, Texier played with Lee Konitz, Rene Thomas, and Dexter Gordon. After military service in 1967, Texier played with Hampton Hawes, Dave Pike, Slide Hampton, and Art Farmer before joining Phil Woods on tour through 1970. During the early 1970s, he formed a folk-rock group, Total Issue; worked with Jean-Luc Ponty and George Gruntz, and in 1976 began giving solo concerts. He then worked in a trio with Didier Lockwood and cellist Jean-Charles Capon, and in 1979–80 with François Jeanneau and Daniel Humair. Since then he has mostly led his own groups; these groups often include special guests such as Kenny Wheeler and Dewey Redman in 1987–88 (with Joe Lovano added in 1988), and Aldo Romano, with whom he continues to work. In the 1990s, Texier formed the quartet Azu with Glenn Ferris and was active in founding the jazz musicians union in France.

DISC.: *A Cordes et a Cris* (1979); *La Companera* (1983); *Paris-Batignolles* (1986); *Colonel Skopje* (1988). Jef Gilson: *Blue-Bizz* (1962). P. Woods: *The Day When the World* (1970).—**LP**

Teyber, family of Austrian musicians:

(1) Matthäus Teyber, violinist; b. Weinzettel, c. 1711; d. Vienna, Sept. 6, 1785. He settled in Vienna, where he entered the Kapelle of the Empress Elisabeth Christine in 1741; was a court musician from 1757. His family, who became friendly with the Mozart family, included 4 children who distinguished themselves as musicians:

(2) Elisabeth Teyber, soprano; b. Vienna (baptized), Sept. 16, 1744; d. there, May 9, 1816. She was a pupil of Haase and Tesi, appearing in Haase's *Partenope* in Vienna in 1767; then was successful in Naples, Bologna, Milan, Turin, and other Italian opera centers; also sang in Russia.

(3) Anton Teyber, pianist, organist, cellist, and composer; b. Vienna, Sept. 8, 1754; d. there, Nov. 18, 1822. He studied in Vienna and with Padre Martini in Bologna. After touring with his sister in Italy, and appearing in Spain and Portugal, he returned to Vienna about 1781. He was 1st organist at the Dresden Hofkapelle (1787–91), then went again to Vienna as Weigl's deputy at the National-Hoftheater, a position that was soon abolished; however, he petitioned the emperor and was named court composer and keyboard teacher to the imperial children in 1793. His compositions include a melodrama, *Zermes (Zerbes) und Mirabelle* (Vienna, July 15, 1779), 36 syms., 6 violin concertos, 4 keyboard concertos, 2 horn concertos, a Double Concerto for Violin and Keyboard, 3 octets for 4 Strings, 2 Oboes, and 2 Horns, 2 sextets for 4 Strings and 2 Oboes, 29 string quartets, 2 oratorios, *Gioas, rè di Giuda* (1786) and *La Passione di Gesù Cristo* (c. 1790), 11 masses, graduals, antiphons, and motets.

(4) Franz Teyber, organist, conductor, cellist, bass singer, and composer; b. Vienna, Nov. 15, 1756; d. there, Oct. 22, 1810. He studied with his father and with Wagenseil. After touring in Swabia, Switzerland, and Baden, he became a conductor and composer with Schikaneder's itinerant opera troupe in 1786. After pursuing his career in Karlsruhe (1788–89), in Cologne (1791–93), and in Regensburg, Augsburg, and Bern (1796–98), he returned to Vienna. He wrote the successful opera *Alexander* for the opening of the Theater an der Wien (June 13, 1801), where he was active until 1805; composed for the Leopoldstadt Theater (1807–10); was made organist at St. Stephen's Cathedral in 1809 and court organist in 1810.

WORKS: DRAMATIC (all 1st perf. in Vienna unless otherwise given): *Laura Rosetti*, opera (Pressburg, Aug. 1785); *Die Dorfdeputierten*, comic opera (Dec. 18, 1785); *Abelheid von Veltheim*, Singspiel (Karlsruhe, 1788); *Fernando und Jariko oder Die Indianer*, Singspiel (Sept. 5, 1789); *Alexander*, grand opera (June 13, 1801); *Der Schlaftrunk*, Singspiel (Nov. 12, 1801); *Der Neuigkeitskrämer oder Der Telegraph*, Singspiel (May 12, 1802); *Pfändung und Personalarrest*, Singspiel (Dec. 7, 1803); *Der Zerstreute*, comic opera (Jan. 29, 1805); *Andrassek und Jurassek*, pantomime (Feb. 20, 1807); *Ruthards Abenteuer oder Die beiden Sänger*, comic opera (July 26, 1808); *Pumphia und Kulikan*, caricature opera (Oct. 8, 1808); *Der bezauberte Blumenstrauss*, pantomime (Aug. 29, 1809); *Der lebendige Postillonstiefel oder Die Luftreise des Arlequin und der Columbina*, pantomime (July 7, 1810). **OTHER:** Sacred vocal works; 6 string quartets; 3 quartets for Keyboard and Strings; Sonata for Piano, Violin, and Cello; 3 piano sonatas; organ music; etc.

(5) Therese Teyber, soprano; b. Vienna (baptized), Oct. 15, 1760; d. there, April 15, 1830. She studied with Bonno and Tesi, making her operatic debut as Fiametta in Ulbrich's *Frühling und Liebe* at the Vienna Court Theater (Sept. 8, 1778). She continued to sing there regularly and also in concerts of the Tonkünstler-Sozietät, creating the role of Blondchen in *Die Entführung aus dem Serail* (July 16, 1782); retired in 1791. Her husband was the tenor Ferdinand Arnold.
—NS/LK/DM

Teyte (real name, **Tate**), **Dame Maggie,**

distinguished English soprano; b. Wolverhampton, April 17, 1888; d. London, May 26, 1976. She studied in London; then was a pupil of Jean de Reszke in Paris (1903–07). In 1906 she made her debut at a Mozart Festival in France under her real name. In order to ensure correct pronunciation of her name in France, she changed the original spelling Tate to Teyte. She made her operatic debut as Tyrcis in Offenbach's *Myriame et Daphne* in Monte Carlo in 1907; was very successful as a concert singer in Paris, and appeared with Debussy at the piano; Debussy also selected her as successor to Mary Garden in the role of Mélisande (1908). She sang at the Paris Opéra-Comique (1908–10), with Beecham's Opera Co. in London (1910–11), with the Chicago Opera Co. (1911–14), and with the Boston Grand Opera Co. (1914–17). She made appearances at London's Covent Garden (1922–23; 1930; 1936–38); then sang in operetta and musical comedies in London; later devoted herself mainly to French song recitals there. In 1951 she made her farewell appearance in opera as Purcell's Belinda in London; gave her last concert there in 1955. She was made a Chevalier of the French Légion d'honneur in 1957 and a Dame Commander of the Order of the British Empire in 1958. In addition to her famous portrayal of Mélisande, she won notable distinction for such roles as Cherubino, Blondchen, Marguerite, Nedda, Madama Butterfly, and Mimi; she also created the Princess in Holst's *The Perfect Fool*. She had 2 indifferent husbands and 2 prominent lovers: Sir Thomas Beecham in London and Georges Enesco in Paris. She publ. a book of memoirs, *Star on the Door* (London, 1958).

BIBL.: G. O'Connor, *The Pursuit of Perfection: A Life of M. T.* (N.Y., 1979).**—NS/LK/DM**

Thalben-Ball, Sir George (Thomas),

Australian-born English organist, choirmaster, teacher, and composer; b. Sydney, June 18, 1896; d. London, Jan. 18, 1987. He was a student of Parry, Stanford, and Davies at the Royal Coll. of Music in London. At the age of 16, he was made a Fellow of the Royal Coll. of Organists in London. He served as acting organist (1919–23) and as organist and choirmaster (1928–81) at the Temple Church in London, and also was a teacher at the Royal Coll. of Music. From 1949 to 1983 he likewise served as city and Univ. organist in Birmingham. In 1967 he was made a Commander of the Order of the British Empire and in 1982 he was knighted. Among his compositions were choral works and organ music.

BIBL.: J. Rennert, *G. T.-B.* (Newton Abbot and London, 1979).**—NS/LK/DM**

Thalberg, Sigismond (Fortuné François),

celebrated Swiss-born pianist and composer; b. Pâquis, near Geneva, Jan. 8, 1812; d. Posillipo, near Naples, April 27, 1871. His parents were Joseph Thalberg of Frankfurt am Main and Fortunée Stein, also of Frankfurt am Main, but resident in Geneva. Thalberg, however, pretended to be the natural son of Count Moritz Dietrichstein and Baroness von Wetzlar, who took charge of his education. At age 10 he was sent to Vienna to prepare himself for a career as a diplomat; however, he also received instruction in music from Mittag, 1st bassoonist in the orch. of the Court Opera; he subsequently studied piano with Hummel and theory with Sechter. He played as a precocious pianist in the aristocratic salons of Vienna, and began to compose. In 1830 he made a successful concert tour of England and Germany. After further training with J. Pixis and F. Kalkbrenner in Paris and with Moscheles in London, he returned to Paris in 1836 and set himself up as a serious rival to Liszt; the 2 eventually became friends, and Thalberg went on to pursue a brilliant career as a virtuoso, performing mostly his own works. In 1843 he married the widow of the painter Boucher. In 1855 he set out on a concert tour through Brazil and then visited the U.S. (1856); made a 2nd Brazilian tour in 1863, and in 1864 retired to Naples. Thalberg was unexcelled as a performer of fashionable salon music and virtuoso studies. He possessed a wonderful legato, eliciting from Liszt the remark, "Thalberg is the only artist who can play the violin on the keyboard." His technical specialty was to play a central melody with the thumb of either hand, surrounding it with brilliant arpeggios and arabesques. To present this technique graphically in notation, he made use of the method initiated by Francesco Pollini of writing piano music on 3 staves. He wrote 2 operas, *Florinda* (London, July 3, 1851) and *Cristina di Suezia* (Vienna, June 3, 1855), which were not successful, but his brilliant piano pieces were the rage of his day, easily eclipsing in popular favor those of Chopin, his close contemporary. Among them are a group of nocturnes, several *Caprices, 2 Romances sans paroles, Grandes valses brillantes, Le Départ, varié en forme d'étude, Marche funèbre variée, Barcarole, Valse mélodique, Les Capricieuses, Tarentelle, Souvenir de Pest, La Cadence* (very popular), *Les Soirées de Pausilippe* (6 albums), *Célèbre Ballade, La Napolitaine,* several sonatas, many pianistic studies, and fantasies on operas by Rossini, Bellini, Meyerbeer, Weber, Verdi, and others.

Bibl.: R. Lott, *The American Concert Tours of Leopold de Meyer, Henri Herz, and S. T.* (diss., City Univ. of N.Y., 1986). **—NS/LK/DM**

Tharpe, Sister Rosetta (originally, **Nubin, Rosetta**), gospel/jazzsinger, guitarist; b. Cotton Plant, Ark., March 20, 1915; d. Oct. 9, 1973. Her mother, Katie Bell Nubin, was a gospel singer known as "Mother Bell." She began singing gospel in church. She signed to Decca records in 1938 and scored gospel hits with "This Train" (which became her signature song), as well as more risque material such as "I Want a Tally Skinny Papa." During the 1930s and 1940s, she appeared at Cotton Club revues and worked with Cab Calloway. In addition, she recorded with gospel stars, Marie Knight, and her mother. She crossed over from the gospel market to jazz with ease, while simultaneously introducing elements of blues to her recordings and dynamic live shows. She continued to perform and record through the late 1960s.

Disc.: *Sacred & Secular* (1941); *Sister Rosetta Tharpe/The Sam Price Trio* (1958); *Gospel Train, Vol. 2* (1960); *Live in 1960* (1960); *Sister on Tour* (1962); *Live in Paris: 1964* (1964); *Live at the Hot Club de France* (1966); *Gospel Train* (1989); *Sincerely, Sister Rosetta Tharpe* (1992); *Completed Recorded Works, Vol. 1 (1938–41)* (1996); *Complete Recorded Works, Vol. 2 (1942–44)* (1996); *Complete Recorded Works, Vol. 3* (1998); *Above My Head* (1999).**—MM/LP**

Thayer, Alexander Wheelock, eminent American music scholar; b. South Natick, Mass., Oct. 22, 1817; d. Trieste, July 15, 1897. He was educated at Harvard Univ. (B.A., 1843; M.A., 1846; LL.B., 1848), and an assistant at the Harvard Coll. library (1845–47), where he pursued valuable research in American psalmody that resulted in his World of Music (1846–47); also contributed to the *Philharmonic Journal, Boston Musical Gazette,* and *Musical Times* (1848–52). He went to Germany in 1849 to study German; wrote a detailed and trustworthy biography of Beethoven. In 1852 he returned to the U.S. and became a leading contributor to *Dwight's Journal*; also was on the staff of the *N.Y. Tribune* (1852–54). He was again in Europe to pursue Beethoven research (1854–56), and after cataloguing the Lowell Mason private library in Boston (1856–57), he settled there. In 1862 he was attached to the American embassy in Vienna, then was the American consul in Trieste (1866–82). He publ. a *Chronologisches Verzeichniss der Werke Ludwig van Beethoven* (Berlin, 1865); in 1866, Vol. I of his lifework, *Ludwig van Beethovens Leben*, appeared in German, tr. from the Eng. MS by Deiters; Vol. II was publ. in 1872, and Vol. III in 1879. Deiters completed vols. IV and V from Thayer's material, but died before their publication. Riemann then took charge of the project, bringing out revised versions of Deiters's vols. IV (1907) and V (1908); he then revised and enlarged vols. II (1910) and III (1911), completing his task by reediting vol. I (1917). Krehbiel ed. the Eng. version (3 vols., 1921). A redaction, titled *Thayer's Life of Beethoven*, prepared by Elliot Forbes, was publ. in 1964 (2nd ed., rev., 1967). Thayer also publ. *Ein kritischer Beitrag zur Beethoven-Literatur* (Berlin, 1877; Eng. version in *Dwight's Journal of Music*, XXXVII, 1877–78).**—NS/LK/DM**

Thebom, Blanche, American mezzo-soprano; b. Monessen, Pa., Sept. 19, 1918. She studied singing with Margaret Matzenauer and Edyth Walker in N.Y. She made her concert debut there in 1941 and her operatic debut, with the Metropolitan Opera, as Fricka on Dec. 14, 1944; remained on its roster until 1959, and sang there again from 1960 to 1967; also sang in various opera houses in America and Europe, with increasing success. In 1967 she was appointed head of the Southern Regional Opera Co. in Atlanta; it folded in 1968; in 1980 she was appointed director of the opera workshop of San Francisco State Univ. Among her best roles were Ortrud, Azucena, Amneris, Laura in *La Gioconda*, and Carmen.**—NS/LK/DM**

Theil, Johann, distinguished German composer, teacher, and music theorist; b. Naumburg, July 29, 1646; d. there (buried), June 24, 1724. He began his musical training with Johann Scheffler, Kantor in Magdeburg, then pursued the study of law at the Univ. of Leipzig; also received musical instruction from Schütz. In 1673 he was appointed Kapellmeister to Duke Christian Albrecht in Gottorf; after the Duke lost his position in 1675, Theile followed him to Hamburg, where he was chosen to compose the inaugural opera for the new opera house in the Gänsemarkt in 1678. He was Kapellmeister in Wölfenbuttel (1685–91), where he also acquired a fine reputation as a teacher; then held that position at the court of Duke Christian I in Merseburg (1691–94), where he continued to be active as a teacher. About 1718 he settled with his son in Naumburg. Theil was a notable composer of sacred music, known by his contemporaries as "the father of contrapuntists." His theoretical works are also of value.

WORKS (all 1st perf. in Hamburg): **DRAMATIC:** *Adam und Eva, oder Der erschaffene, gefallene und auffgerichtete Mensch* (Jan. 2, 1678); *Orontes* (1678); *Die Geburth Christi* (1681). **VOCAL: Sacred:** *Pars prima* [6] *missarum* for 4 Voices and Basso Continuo (Wismar, 1673); *Passio nach dem Heiligen Evangelisten Matthäo* for 4 Voices, 4 Viols, and Basso Continuo (Lübeck, 1673; ed. in Denkmäler Deutscher Tonkunst, XVII, 1904); other masses; 7 Psalms; various motets. **Secular:** *Weltlicher Arien und Canzonetten erstes, anderes und drittes Zehen* for 1, 2, and 4 Voices, 4 Viols, and Basso Continuo (Leipzig, 1667); Sonata for 2 Violins, Trombone, Bassoon, and Basso Continuo; Sonata for Violin, 2 Viols, Violone, and Basso Continuo.

WRITINGS (all in MS): *Musikalisches Kunst-Buch; Curieuser Unterricht von den gedoppelten Contrapuncten; Contrapuncta praecepta; Von den dreifachten Contrapuncten; Gründlicher Unterricht von den gedoppelten Contrapuncten; Von dem vierfachen Contrapunct alla octava.*

BIBL.: F. Zelle, *J. T. und N.A. Trungk* (Berlin, 1891); W. Maxton, *J. T.* (diss., Univ. of Tübingen, 1926); J. Mackey, *The Sacred Music of J. T.* (diss., Univ. of Mich., 1968).—**NS/LK/DM**

Theodorakis, Mikis (actually, **Michael George**), prominent Greek composer; b. Chios, July 29, 1925. He studied at the Athens Cons. During the German occupation of his homeland, he was active in the resistance. After the liberation, he joined the Left but was arrested and deported during the civil war. In 1953 he went to Paris and studied with Messiaen, and soon after he began to compose. After returning to Greece in 1961, he resumed his political activities and served as a member of Parliament in 1963. Having joined the Communist Party, he was arrested after the military coup in 1967 and incarcerated. During this period, he wrote the music for the film *Z*, dealing with the police murder of the Socialist politician Gregory Lambrakis in Salonika in 1963. The film and the music were greatly acclaimed in Europe and the U.S., and the fate of Theodorakis became a cause célèbre. Yielding to pressure from international public opinion, the military Greek government freed Theodorakis in 1970. In 1972 he quit the Communist Party and was active in the United Left; returning to the Communist Party, he served in Parliament in 1981 and again in 1985–86 before quitting it once more. In 1989 he became an ambassador of conservatism in Greece, going so far as to enter the race for the legislature on the New Democracy ticket; with 416 like-minded painters, writers, musicians, singers, and actors, Theodorakis signed his name to a manifesto (Nov. 3, 1989) condemning the divisive policies of the former Socialist government of Andreas Papandreou; he also ended 4 years of musical silence by appearing on an Athens stage before a crowd of 70,000 people, singing songs of protest and love in the name of national unity. From 1990 to 1992 he served in the Greek government as a Minister without Portfolio. In 1993 he became general director of the orch. and chorus of the Greek State Radio in Athens. His 4-vol. autobiography was publ. in Athens (1986–88).

WORKS: DRAMATIC: Opera: *Kostas Kariotakis* (1985); *Zorbas*, ballet-opera (1988); *Medea* (1990); *Elektra* (1993); *Antigone* (Athens, Oct. 7, 1999). **Ballet:** *Carnaval* (1953; rev. as *Le Feu aux Poudres*, 1958); *Les Amants de Teruel* (1958); *Antigone* (1958); *Antigone II* (1971); *Elektra* (1976); *Mythologie* (1976); *Zorba* (1976); *7 danses grecques* (1982). Also incidental music to various dramas; film scores, including *Zorba the Greek* (1962) and *Z* (1973). **ORCH.:** *Assi-Gonia* (1945–50); *Oedipus Tyrannus* (1946; also for Strings, 1955); 8 syms., including No. 1 (1948–50), No. 2 for Piano, Children's Chorus, and Orch. (1958), No. 3 for Soprano, Chorus, and Orch. (1980), No. 4 for 2 Soloists, Chorus, and Orch. (1986), No. 7 for 4 Soloists, Chorus, and Orch. (1983), and No. 8, *Canto Olympico* (1991); 3 suites: No. 1 for Piano and Orch. (1954), No. 2 for Chorus and Orch. (1956), and No. 3 for Soprano, Chorus, and Orch. (1956); Piano Concerto (1957). **CHAMBER:** Trio for Violin, Cello, and Piano (1947); Flute Sextet (1948); 2 violin sonatinas (1955, 1958); various piano pieces. **VOCAL:** *L'Amour et la mort* for Mezzo-soprano and String Orch. (1948); *Axion Esti* for 2 Baritones, Speaker, Chorus, and Orch. (1960); *Épiphanie Averof* for Soloist, Chorus, and Piano (1968); *Canto General*, oratorio for 2 Soloists, Chorus, and Orch. (1971–74); *Sadoukeon Passion*, cantata for Tenor, Baritone, Bass, Speaker, Chorus, and Orch. (1982); *Phaedra*, 12 songs for 2 Soloists, Chorus, and Orch. (1983); *Requiem* for 4 Soloists, Chorus, and Children's Chorus (1984); *Dionysos*, religious drama for Voice, Chorus, and Chamber Ensemble (1984); also choruses and songs.

BIBL.: J. Coubard, *M. T.* (Paris, 1969); G. Giannaris, *M. T.: Music and Social Change* (London, 1973); G. Host, *T.: Myth and Politics in Modern Greek Music* (Amsterdam, 1981).—**NS/LK/DM**

Theremin (real name, **Termen,** Leon), (pronounced in Russian with the accent on the last syllable; Gallicized as Thérémin; Anglicized as Theremin, with the accent on the first syllable), Russian inventor of the space-controlled electronic instrument that bears his name; b. St. Petersburg, Aug. 15, 1896; d. Moscow, Nov. 3, 1993. He studied physics and astronomy at the Univ. of St. Petersburg; also cello and theory. He continued his studies in physics at the Petrograd Physico-Technical Inst.; in 1919 he became director of its Laboratory of Electrical Oscillators. On Aug. 5, 1920, he gave a demonstration there of his Aetherophone, which was the prototype of the Thereminovox; also gave a special demonstration of it for Lenin, who at the time was convinced that the electrification of Russia would ensure the success of communism. In 1927 he demonstrated his new instruments in Germany, France, and the U.S., where, on Feb. 28, 1928, he obtained a patent for the Thereminovox. On April 29, 1930, at Carnegie Hall in N.Y., he presented a concert with an ensemble of 10 of his instruments, also introducing a space-controlled synthesis of color and music. On April 1, 1932, in the same hall, he introduced the first electrical sym. orch., conducted by Stoessel and including Theremin fingerboard and keyboard instruments. He also invented the Rhythmicon, for playing different rhythms simultaneously or separately (introduced by Henry Cowell), and an automatic musical instrument for playing directly from specially written musical scores (constructed for Percy Grainger). With the theorist Joseph Schillinger, Theremin established an acoustical laboratory in N.Y.; also formed numerous scientific and artistic associations, among them Albert Einstein, who was himself an amateur violinist. Einstein was fascinated by the relationships between music, color, and geometric and stereometric figures; Theremin provided him a work space to study these geometries, but he himself took no further interest in these correlations, seeing himself "not as a theorist, but as an inventor." More to Theremin's point were experiments made by Stokowski, who tried to effect an increase in sonority among certain instrumental groups in the Philadelphia Orch., particularly in the double basses. These experiments had to be abandoned, however, when the players complained of deleterious effects upon their abdominal muscles, which they attributed to the electronic sound waves produced by the Thereminovox. In 1938 Theremin decided to return to Russia. He soon had difficulties with the Soviet government, which was suspicious of his foreign contacts. He was convicted of anti-Soviet propaganda and was imprisoned for 7 years in Magadan, Siberia. During his imprisonment, he did research for the Soviet government. His invention of a miniature electronic eavesdropping instrument led to a secret award of the Stalin Prize and his release. In subsequent years, he was active in research for the KGB. In 1964 he became a prof. of acoustics at the Moscow Cons. After Harold C. Schonberg wrote an article on him for the *N.Y. Times* in 1967, Theremin lost his professorship due to the unwanted publicity. He later worked in an electronics institute in Moscow. With the advent of new liberal policies in the U.S.S.R., he was able to travel abroad, appearing in Paris and in Stockholm in 1989. Among his American students from the 1930s, he especially commended Clara Rockmore, a well-known Thereminist. His career was surveyed in Steven M. Martin's British television documentary "The Electronic Odyssey of Leon Theremin" (1993). —**NS/LK/DM**

Thern, Károly, Hungarian composer of German birth; b. Iglau, Aug. 13, 1817; d. Vienna, April 13, 1886. After studies at the Univ. of Pest, he worked as asst. conductor at the National Theater (1841). He taught at the National Cons. (1853–64), and later settled in Vienna. He wrote the operas *Giyul* (1841), *Tihany ostroma* (The Siege of Tihany; 1845), and *A képzelt beteg* (The Imaginary Invalid; 1855), as well as a Sym. (1871), chamber music, songs, and piano pieces. His sons, Vilmos (1847–1911) and Lajos (1848–1920), studied with Reinecke and Moscheles at the Leipzig Cons., and later with Liszt; after winning distinction as a duo-piano team in Europe, they settled in Vienna as teachers. —**NS/LK/DM**

Thévenard, Gabriel-Vincent, esteemed French singer; b. Orléans or Paris, Aug. 10, 1669; d. Paris, Aug. 24, 1741. He settled in Paris in 1690. Following training from Destouches, he was a principal singer with the Académie Royale de Musique from 1698 until 1729. He created roles in many operas, including those by Destouches, Campra, Marais, and Desmarets. —**NS/LK/DM**

Thibaud, Jacques, celebrated French violinist; b. Bordeaux, Sept. 27, 1880; d. in an airplane crash near Mt. Cemet, in the French Alps, en route to French Indochina, Sept. 1, 1953. He began his training with his father and made his debut at age 8 in Bordeaux; at 13, he entered the Paris Cons. as a pupil of Martin Marsick, graduating with the premier prix in 1896. Obliged to earn his living, he played the violin at the Café Rouge in Paris, where he was heard by the conductor Colonne, who offered him a position in his orch.; in 1898 he made his debut as a soloist (with Colonne) with such success that he was engaged for 54 concerts in Paris in the same season. Subsequently he appeared in all the musical centers of Europe, and from 1903 visited America numerous times. With his 2 brothers, a pianist and a cellist, he formed a trio, which had some success; but this was discontinued when he joined Alfred Cortot and Pablo Casals in a famous trio (1930–35). With Marguerite Long, he founded the renowned Long-Thibaud competition in 1943. His playing was notable for its warmth of expressive tone and fine dynamics; his interpretations of Beethoven ranked very high, but he was particularly authoritative in French music.

BIBL.: J.-P. Dorian, ed., *Un Violon parle: Souvenirs de J. T.* (Paris, 1947).—**NS/LK/DM**

Thibaudet, Jean-Yves, talented French pianist; b. Lyons, Sept. 7, 1961. When he was 5, he entered the Lyons Cons., where he was a pupil of Herrenschmidt and Bossard; after winning its gold medal in 1974, he pursued training with Descaves, Gianoli, Hubeau, and Ciccolini at the Paris Cons. (1974–81), taking premiers prix in piano and chamber music (1977). In 1978 he won the silver medal at the Busoni Competition in Bolzano; then took 2nd prize at the Casadesus Competition in Cleveland (1979) and at the Tokyo Competition (1980); in 1981 he won the Young Concert Artists International Auditions in N.Y., and subsequently pursued a fine international career. In 1989 he gave a recital at N.Y.'s Lincoln Center. His brilliance as a technician is complemented by his Gallic sensitivity; in addition to his notable interpretations of the French repertoire, he has won accolades for his performances of the masterworks of the 19th and 20th centuries.—**NS/LK/DM**

Thibault, Geneviève (La Comtesse Hubert de Chambure), French musicologist; b. Neuilly-sur-Seine, May 20, 1902; d. Strasbourg, Aug. 31, 1975. She went to Paris and studied piano with L. Lévy (1919–20), harmony and counterpoint with Eugene Cools (1915–20), and fugue and organ with Boulanger (1917–23). She also took courses at the Sorbonne (diplôme d'Études Supérieurs, 1920), and later completed her musicological training with Pirro at the École des Hautes Études (diploma, 1952). She became engaged in business, but continued her great interest in musical research; assembled a fine private library, containing rare eds. of Renaissance music, which she opened to research scholars; initiated the Société de Musique d'Autrefois in 1925, for the purpose of presenting concerts of early music performed on early instruments; from 1955 she lectured at the Sorbonne. Her contributions to musicology include: with L. Perceau, *Bibliographie des poésies de P. de Ronsard mises en musique au XVIe siècle* (Paris, 1941); with F. Lesure, *Bibliographie des éditions d'Adrien Le Roy et Robert Ballard (1551–1598)*

(Paris, 1955; supplement in *Revue de Musicologie*, XL, 1957); with A. Berner and J. van der Meer, *Preservation and Restoration of Musical Instruments* (London, 1967). **—NS/LK/DM**

Thibaut IV, Count of Champagne and Brie and King of Navarre, famous French trouvère; b. Troyes, May 30, 1201; d. Pamplona, July 7, 1253. He became king of Navarre in 1234, and led the crusade of 1239–40. Some 47 of his works, along with 14 others of joint authorship, have been identified. See H. Anglès, ed., *Las canciones del Rey Teobaldo* (Pamplona, 1973), and K. Brahney, translator, *The Poetry of Thibaut de Champagne* (N.Y., 1988).

BIBL.: A. Wallenskold, *Les Chansons de T. de Champagne, roi de Navarre* (Paris, 1925).**—NS/LK/DM**

Thielemann, Christian, German conductor; b. Berlin, April 1, 1959. He received training in Berlin. In 1979 he became an assistant to Karajan in Berlin and Salzburg. After working in opera houses in Gelsenkirchen, Karlsruhe, Hannover, and Düsseldorf (1982–85), he served as Generalmusikdirektor in Nuremburg (1988–92). In 1991 he conducted at the San Francisco Opera and at the Deutsche Oper in Berlin. He conducted at the Hamburg State Opera in 1992, the same year he made his Metropolitan Opera debut in N.Y. conducting *Der Rosenkavalier*. In 1995 he appeared as a guest conductor with the N.Y. Phil. From 1997 to 2001 he was Generalmusikdirektor of the Deutsche Oper in Berlin.**—NS/LK/DM**

Thielemans, Toots, an innovative guitarist, and largely responsible for introducing the chromatic harmonica as a jazz instrument; b. Brussels, Belgium, April 29, 1922. Inspired after hearing the pop harmonica sounds of Larry Adler in the movies, he started playing the harmonica at age 17 while in college. But after he contracted a lung infection, he taught himself to play guitar by listening to Django Reinhardt recordings, and was soon playing in clubs all over Brussels. He did take up harmonica again and after World War II, and performed in American GI clubs in Europe. He emigrated to the U.S. in 1948, shared the bill with saxophonist Charlie Parker at the Paris International Jazz Festival in May 1949, and toured with the Benny Goodman Sextet in 1950. From 1953 to 1959, he played guitar (and some harmonica) with the George Shearing Quintet. He subsequently formed his own group, but he continued to freelance with other leaders and do studio work. His whistling while he played guitar caught the ear of arranger-producer Quincy Jones who used him on a number of successful recordings. During the 1960s, he began regular tours of Europe where he recorded his most popular composition, "Bluesette," in 1962, which featured him on guitar and whistling. This worldwide hit made him an in-demand player in the U.S. and he has continued playing harmonica and whistling on various studio dates, for film soundtracks such as the *Midnight Cowboy* theme song, for TV themes, and on pop and jazz recordings.

He is a bop-oriented player, but is able to play a variety of jazz styles, which are evident on his many recordings as leader and sideman since the 1960s. In 1981, he had a major stroke, but he has mostly recovered and continues to play. He began incorporating Brazilian rhythms in his music and gathered Brazil's best musicians to perform on his "Brasil Project" albums in the early 1990s.

DISC.: *The Sound* (1955); *Man Bites Harmonica* (1958); *Time Out for Toots* (1958); *Soul of Toots Thielemans* (1959); *The Whistler and His Guitar* (1962); *Toots and Svend* (1972); *Live* (1974); *Live., Vol. 2* (1975); *Apple Dimple* (1979); *Live in the Netherlands* (1980); *Autumn Leaves* (1984); *Just Friends* (1986); *Only Trust Your Heart* (1988); *Do Not Leave Me* (1989); *In Tokyo* (1989); *Footprints* (1991); *For My Lady* (1991); *Brasil Project* (1992); *East Coast West Coast* (1992); *Brasil Project II* (1993); *Two Generations* (1996); *Chez Toots* (1998).**—NAL**

Thienen, Marcel van, French composer and sculptor; b. Paris, Oct. 3, 1922. He studied in Paris, receiving instruction in violin at the École Normale de Musique and at the Cons. (graduated, 1940); also studied composition at the Cons. Russe. After serving as director of the Haiti Cons. (1954–57), he returned to Paris and founded an electronic music studio. In the mid-1960s he turned to sculpture.

WORKS: *Le Ferroviaire*, opera-farce (1951); *Petite symphonie sur le temps* (1944); *Petite suite digestive* (1951); several pieces for various instruments under the generic title *Amusette*; *Le Damne* for Soprano, Baritone, Men's Chorus, Electronic Music, and Orch. (1962); songs with orch. accompaniment.**—NS/LK/DM**

Thill, Georges, distinguished French tenor; b. Paris, Dec. 14, 1897; d. Draguignan, Oct. 17, 1984. He studied at the Paris Cons. and with Fernando De Lucia in Naples. Returning to Paris, he sang at the Opéra-Comique; made his first appearance at the Opéra as Nicias in *Thaïs* (Feb. 4, 1924), and continued to sing there regularly until 1940. He appeared at London's Covent Garden (1928, 1937); made his Metropolitan Opera debut in N.Y. as Romeo (March 20, 1931), remaining on the company's roster until 1932. His farewell appearance was as Canio at the Opéra-Comique in 1953. His outstanding roles included Don José, Romeo, Julien in *Louise*, Aeneas, and Samson; he was also a fine singer of Italian and German roles.

BIBL.: R. Mancini, *G. T.* (Paris, 1966); A. Segond, *Album G. T.* (Aix-en-Provence, 1991).**—NS/LK/DM**

Thilman, Johannes Paul, German composer and pedagogue; b. Dresden, Jan. 11, 1906; d. there, Jan. 29, 1973. He was a pupil of Hindemith, Grabner, and Scherchen, and also studied at the Dresden Technical Univ. During the Nazi era (1933–45) he was declared an unacceptable composer, and it was only after the fall of the 3rd Reich that he was permitted to pursue his career in earnest. He was founder-director of the "New Music in Dresden" concert series (1947–51); he also taught at the Univ. of Dresden, and later was prof. of composition at the Dresden Hochschule für Musik (from 1965). He publ. *Probleme der neuen Polyphonie* (1949), *Neue Musik: Polemische Beiträge* (1950), and *Musikalische Formenlehre* (1952). Among his compositions are 7 syms. and other orch. works, much chamber music, choral works, piano pieces, and numerous works for school and domestic use.**—NS/LK/DM**

Thiriet, Maurice, French composer; b. Meulan, May 2, 1906; d. Puys, near Dieppe, Sept. 28, 1972. He began his training at the Paris Cons. with Charles Silver, and later studied with Koechlin (counterpoint and fugue) and Roland-Manuel (composition and orchestration). He was a composer of much dramatic music.

Works: Dramatic: *Le Bourgeois de Falaise,* opéra-bouffe (1933; Paris, June 21, 1937); *La Véridique Histoire du docteur* (1937); *La Locandiera,* opéra-comique (1959); 16 ballets; film scores; radio music. **Orch.:** *Le Livre pour Jean* (1927–29); *Poème* for Chamber Orch. (1935); *Rapsodie sur des thèmes incas* (Lyons, Jan. 20, 1936); *Introduction, chanson et ronde* for Harp and Orch. (1936); *Les Visiteurs du soir,* suite (1947); *Afriques* (1949); *Danceries françaises* for Strings (1957); Concerto for Flute and Strings (1959). **Chamber:** *4 Pièces* for Violin and Piano (1943); *Lai et virelais* for String Trio (1956); *Suite en trio* for Flute, Viola, and Harp (1956); piano pieces. **Vocal:** *Oedipe-Roi,* oratorio for Men's Chorus and Orch. (1940–41); *6 Poèmes lyriques du vieux Japon* for Soprano and Orch. (1968); choruses; songs.—**NS/LK/DM**

Thomán, István, Hungarian pianist and pedagogue; b. Homonna, Nov. 4, 1862; d. Budapest, Sept. 22, 1940. He studied with Erkel and Volkmann in Budapest (1882–85); then was a pupil of Liszt there and in Weimar and Rome. He taught at the Royal Academy of Music in Budapest (1888–1906). He was greatly esteemed as a teacher; among his students were Dohnányi and Bartók. He publ. a collection of technical piano studies in 6 vols., and also composed songs and piano pieces. His wife, Valerie Thomán (b. Budapest, Aug. 16, 1878; d. there, Sept. 8, 1948), was a renowned concert singer, who gave early performances of works by Kodály and Bartók; their daughter Mária Thomán (b. Budapest, July 12, 1899; d. there, Feb. 25, 1948), a pupil of Hubay, Vecsey, and Flesch, was a fine violinist who toured throughout Europe.—**NS/LK/DM**

Thomas, Arthur Goring, English composer; b. Ratton Park, Sussex, Nov. 20, 1850; d. (suicide) London, March 20, 1892. He was a pupil of Emile Durand in Paris (1873–75), and of Arthur Sullivan and Ebenezer Prout at the Royal Academy of Music in London (1877–80), and later studied orchestration in Berlin with Max Bruch. He was mainly interested in creating English operas in the best German tradition. His operas were performed in England and Germany, and he had many important supporters for his art in England, but his music totally lacked vitality, and became of only antiquarian interest after his death. In the last year of his life he suffered from a mental illness.

Works: Dramatic: Opera: *The Light of the Harem* (partial perf., Lon don, Nov. 7, 1879); *Esmeralda* (London, March 26, 1883; rev. version, London, July 12, 1890); *Nadezhda* (London, April 16, 1885); *The Golden Web* (Liverpool, Feb. 15, 1893). **Other:** *The Sun-worshippers,* choral ode (Norwich Festival, 1881); *The Swan and the Skylark,* cantata (completed and orchestrated by C. Stanford; Birmingham Festival, 1894); chamber music; songs.—**NS/LK/DM**

Thomas, Augusta Read, American composer; b. Glen Grove, N.Y., April 24, 1964. She was a student of Karlins and Stout at Northwestern Univ. (1983–87) and of Druckman at Yale Univ. (M.M., 1988) before completing postgraduate studies at the Royal Academy of Music in London (1988–89). She received numerous awards and honors, among them ASCAP prizes (1987–91), NEA fellowships (1988, 1992), a Guggenheim fellowship (1989), the International Orpheus Prize for Opera of Spoleto, Italy (1994), the Charles Ives Fellowship (1994), and the Siemens Foundation Prize (2000). In addition to composing, she taught at the Eastman School of Music in Rochester, N.Y. In 1994 she married **Bernard Rands**. From 1997 to 2000 she served as composer-in-residence of the Chicago Sym. Orch.

Works: Dramatic: *Ligeia,* chamber opera (1991–94; Evian, May 19, 1994); *Conquering the Fury of Oblivion,* theatrical oratorio (1994–95); *Passions,* ballet (1997; St. Paul, Oct. 2, 1998). **Orch.:** *Glow in the Light of Darkness* for Chamber Orch. (1983); *Tunnel at the End of Light* for Piano and Orch. (1984); *Sonnet from the Daybreak Moon* (1986); *Moon and Light* for Trumpet and Orch. (1987); *Under the Sun* (1987); *Glass Moon* (1988; Philadelphia, Dec. 14, 1990); *Sunset of Empire* (1988); *Crystal Planet* (1989); *...to the light unseen...* for Flute and Strings (1989); *Wind Dance* (1989; N.Y., July 27, 1990); *Haiku* for Violin, Cello, and Chamber Orch. (1990; N.Y., April 28, 1991); *Vigil* for Cello and Chamber Orch. (Cleveland, Nov. 4, 1990); *Overture Concertante* (1990); *Air and Angels* (Washington, D.C., Sept. 10, 1992); *Cathedral Summer* for Violin and Orch. (1992); *Sinfonia Concertante* for Soprano Saxophone and Orch. (1992); *Ancient Chimes* (1993); *Night's Midsummer Blaze,* triple concerto for Flute, Viola, Harp, and Orch. (Louisville, Nov. 18, 1993); *Fantasy* for Piano and Chamber Orch. (1993–94); *Echo Echo* for Trombone Quartet and Chamber Orch. (1994–95); *Meditation* for Trombone and Chamber Orch. (1995); *Words of the Sea* (1995–96; Chicago, Dec. 12, 1996); *Eclipse Musings* for Flute, Guitar, and Chamber Orch. (1996); *Spirit Musings* for Violin and Chamber Orch. (1997); *Enchanted Orbits* for Flute and Chamber Orch. (1997); *Chanson* for Cello and Chamber Orch. (1997); *Brass Axis* for Saxophone Quartet and Orch. (1997; N.Y., Jan. 11, 1998); *Concertino for Orchestra* (1997–98; Rochester, May 21, 1998); *Orbital Beacons* (Chicago, Nov. 27, 1998); *Ritual Incantations* for Cello and Chamber Orch. (1998; Aspen, July 16, 1999); *Ceremonial* (1999; Chicago, Jan. 6, 2000); *Aurora,* piano concerto (1999–2000). **Chamber:** *Fantasy on 2 Klee Studies* for Cello (1988); Sonata for Solo Trumpet (1989); *Karumi* for Flute (1990); *Chant* for Cello and Piano (1990–91); *Angel Chant* for Piano Trio (1991; rev. 1994); *Nocturne* for String Quartet and Mezzo-soprano (1993–94); *Spring Song* for Cello (1995); *Incantation* for Violin (1995); *Manifesto* for 12 Brasses and Timpani (1995); *Fire Song* for Soprano Saxophone and Sympathetically Vibrating Instrument (1997); *Invocations* for String Quartet (1999); *Passion Prayers* for Cello and 6 Instruments (1999); *Angel Musings* for Clarinet, Violin, Viola, Cello, and Piano (1999). **Piano:** *Whites* (1988). **Vocal:** *Ring Out Wild Bells to the Wild Sky* for Soprano, Chorus, and Orch. (1999–2000; Washington, D.C., Feb. 15, 2000); *Silver Litanies* for 6 Women's Voices, 3 Clarinets, Vibraphone, and String Quartet (2000).—**NS/LK/DM**

Thomas, (Charles Louis) Ambroise, noted French composer and teacher; b. Metz, Aug. 5, 1811; d. Paris, Feb. 12, 1896. He entered the Paris Cons. in 1828, where his teachers were Zimmerman (piano) and Dourlen (harmony and accompaniment); he also studied privately with Kalkbrenner (piano) and Barbereau (harmony), and subsequently studied composition with Le

Sueur at the Cons., where he won the Grand Prix de Rome with his cantata *Hermann et Ketty* (1832). After 3 years in Italy, and a visit to Vienna, he returned to Paris and applied himself with great energy to the composition of operas. In 1851 he was elected to the Académie, and in 1856 became a prof. of composition at the Paris Cons.; in 1871 he became director there. As a composer of melodious operas in the French style, he was second only to Gounod; his masterpiece was *Mignon*, based on Goethe's *Wilhelm Meister* (Paris, Nov. 17, 1866), which became a mainstay of the repertoire all over the world; it had nearly 2,000 performances in less then 100 years at the Opéra-Comique alone. Equally successful was his Shakespearean opera *Hamlet* (Paris, March 9, 1868). In 1845 he was made a Chevalier of the Légion d'honneur, being the first composer to receive its Grand Croix in 1894.

WORKS (all 1st perf. in Paris): **DRAMATIC** (all opéras-comiques unless otherwise given): *La double échelle* (Aug. 23, 1837); *Le perruquier de la régence* (March 30, 1838); *Le panier fleuri* (May 6, 1839); *Carline* (Feb. 24, 1840); *Le comte de Carmagnola* (April 19, 1841); *Le guerillero* (June 22, 1842); *Angélique et Médor* (May 10, 1843); *Mina, ou Le Ménage à trois* (Oct. 10, 1843); *Le caïd* (Jan. 3, 1849); *Le songe d'une nuit d'été* (April 20, 1850); *Raymond, ou Le secret de la reine* (June 5, 1851); *La Tonelli* (March 30, 1853); *La cour de Célimène* (April 11, 1855); *Psyché* (Jan. 26, 1857); *Le carnaval de Venise* (Dec. 9, 1857); *Le roman d'Elvire* (Feb. 4, 1860); *Mignon* (Nov. 17, 1866); *Hamlet*, opera (March 9, 1868); *Gille et Gillotin*, opera (April 22, 1874); *Françoise de Rimini*, opera (April 14, 1882). **Ballet:** *La gipsy* (Jan. 28, 1839; in collaboration with F. Benoist and M. Marliani); *Betty* (July 10, 1846); *La tempête* (June 26, 1889). **ORCH.:** *Fantaisie brillante* for Piano and Orch. (n.d.; also for Piano and String Quartet); *Marche religieuse* (March 25, 1865); *Chant de psaume laudate* for Violin and Orch. (n.d.). **CHAMBER:** String Quartet (1833); Piano Trio (c. 1835); String Quintet (1835); piano pieces; organ music. **VOCAL:** Sacred works, including *Requiem Mass* for Chorus and Orch. (c. 1840) and *Messe solennelle* for Chorus and Orch. (Nov. 22, 1857); secular vocal works.

BIBL.: H. Delaborde, *Notice sur la vie et les œuvres de M.A. T.* (Paris, 1896); H. de Curzon, *A. T.* (Paris, 1921).—**NS/LK/DM**

Thomas, Christian Gottfried, German horn player, music publisher, impresario, writer on music, and composer; b. Wehrsdorf, near Bautzen, Feb. 2, 1748; d. Leipzig, Sept. 12, 1806. He studied law at the Univ. of Leipzig (1770–71) before devoting himself to music. In 1771 he was made 1st horn player of the Leipzig Grosses Konzert. In 1776 he organized a music copying and MS storehouse enterprise in Leipzig, where he became an influential impresario; also toured as a horn player. Among his works, most of which are lost, were syms., 2 double concertos for Waldhorn, *Gloria* for 3 Choirs and 24 Instruments (Hamburg, Aug. 18, 1789), *Psalm CXLIX* for Double Choir (1789–94), Cantata for 2 Choirs and 24 Instruments (Prague, Aug. 13, 1792), (2) *Gedichte* for Soprano, Tenor, and 18 Instruments (1792), *Schlachtgesang* for 2 Choirs and 30 Instruments (1795), (4) *Volksgesänge* for Choir and 20 Instruments (1797), and *Psalm CXVII* for 7 Choirs and Orch. His writings include *Praktische Beyträge zur Geschichte der Musik, musikalischen Litteratur und gemeinen Besten* (Leipzig, 1778), *Kurzgefasster Entwurf des Plan's des zuerrichtenden öffentlichen Musik-Conservatoriums und Musikalienhandlung zu N.N. (nach der neuesten vorsunehmende Einrichtung)* (Leipzig, 1781), *Unpartheiische Kritik* (Leipzig, 1798–1800?; continued as *Musikalische kritische Zeitschrift*, 1800?–1806), *Nachtricht an ein verehrungswürdiges Publikum: Die Herausgabe einer kritischen musicalischen Zeitschrift in Vergleichung mit einem andren ähnlichen Unternehmen betreffend* (Leipzig, July 11, 1798), and *Musikalisch-litterarische Anzeige* (Leipzig, Aug. 15, 1798).—**NS/LK/DM**

Thomas, David (Lionel Mercer), English bass; b. Orpington, Kent, Feb. 26, 1943. He was educated at St. Paul's Cathedral Choir School, King's School, Canterbury, and King's Coll., Cambridge. He first gained recognition as a soloist with Rooley's Consort of Musicke, Hogwood's Academy of Music, and other early music groups in England; subsequently appeared throughout Europe. In 1982 he made his U.S. debut at the Hollywood Bowl. In later years, he pursued an international career, specializing in the Baroque and Classical concert and operatic repertoires. He won particular distinction for his performances of works by Monteverdi, Purcell, Bach, Handel, and Mozart. —**NS/LK/DM**

Thomas, Gary (Daniel), jazz tenor saxophonist, flutist; b. Baltimore, June 10, 1961. At 12 he asked for the easiest instrument and was advised to begin classical flute. He later took up the tenor and played in dance and rock bands. In 1986, he toured with DeJohnette, then Miles Davis, then returned to DeJohnette and began recording regularly as a sideperson for Michele Rosewoman, Steve Coleman, Cassandra Wilson, guitarist Christy Doran, among others. He also recorded as a leader.

DISC.: *Seventh Quadrant* (1987); *Code Violations* (1988); *By Any Means Necessary* (1989); *While the Gate Is Open* (1990); *Kold Kage* (1991); *Till We Have Faces* (1992); *Exile's Gate* (1993).—**LP**

Thomas, (Georg Hugo) Kurt, prominent German choral conductor, pedagogue, and composer; b. Tönning, May 25, 1904; d. Bad Oeynhausen, March 31, 1973. He studied organ with Straube, piano with Teichmüller, and composition with Grabner at the Leipzig Cons., and composition with A. Mendelssohn in Darmstadt. He taught theory and composition at the Leipzig Cons. (1925–34), and was conductor of the choir at the Inst. of Church Music in Leipzig (1928–34); then was a prof. at the Berlin Hochschule für Musik (1934–39). He went to Frankfurt am Main as director of the Musisches Gymnasium (1939–45) and as Kantor of the Dreikönigskirche (1945–56); also was a prof. at the North West German Music Academy in Detmold (1947–55). After serving as director of the Leipzig Thomaskantorei and of the Thomasschule (1955–61), he resumed his post with the Frankfurt am Main Dreikönigskirche and also became conductor of the Cologne Bach Soc.; taught choral conducting at the Lübeck Academy of Music (from 1969). He publ. the important manual *Lehrbuch der Chorleitung* (3 vols., Leipzig, 1935–48; Eng. tr., 1971, as *The Choral Conductor*). Among his compositions were many choral works, including a Mass (1925), *Passions-*

musik nach den Evangelisten Markus, Weihnachts-Oratorium, Auferstehungs-Oratorium, cantatas, Psalms, and motets; several orch. works, including a Piano Concerto; chamber music, organ pieces, and songs.

BIBL.: M. Kluge, ed., *Choreziehung und neue Musik: Für K. T. zum 65. Geburtstag* (Wiesbaden, 1969); N. Bethke, *K. T.: Studien zu Leben und Werk* (Kassel, 1989).—**NS/LK/DM**

Thomas, Jess (Floyd), American tenor; b. Hot Springs, S.Dak., Aug. 4, 1927; d. San Francisco, Oct. 11, 1993. After studying psychology at the Univ. of Nebr. and at Stanford Univ., he turned to singing; had formal study with Otto Schulman. He made his formal operatic debut as Malcolm at the San Francisco Opera in 1957, then continued his training with Emmy Seiberlich in Germany. He was a member of the Karlsruhe Opera (1958–61); sang Parsifal at the Bayreuth Festival (1961) and appeared in other German music centers. On Dec. 11, 1962, he made his Metropolitan Opera debut in N.Y. as Walther von Stolzing. In 1963 he joined the Bavarian State Opera in Munich, and was honored with the title of Kammersänger; also made guest appearances in Salzburg, Vienna, London's Covent Garden, and other major opera centers.—**NS/LK/DM**

Thomas, John, celebrated Welsh harpist and composer; b. Ogmore, Glamorgan, March 1, 1826; d. London, March 19, 1913. He received instruction in harp from his father, and in 1840 entered the Royal Academy of Music in London and studied harp with Chatterton. In 1871 he was made Harpist to the Queen. He gave in London a series of annual concerts of Welsh music; the first took place at St. James's Hall, July 4, 1862, with a chorus of 400, and 20 harps. He was also a leader of the Eisteddfod festivals. He wrote a Sym., 2 harp concertos, the cantatas *Llewelyn* (Aberdare, 1863) and *The Bride of Neath Valley* (1863), and pieces for Solo Harp, and various transcriptions for his instrument. He also ed. *Welsh Melodies* (1862–74). His brother, Thomas Thomas (1829–1913), was also a harpist.—**NS/LK/DM**

Thomas, John Charles, American baritone; b. Meyersdale, Pa., Sept. 6, 1891; d. Apple Valley, Calif., Dec. 13, 1960. He studied at the Peabody Cons. of Music in Baltimore. From 1913 he sang in musical comedy in N.Y. He made his operatic debut as Amonasro in Washington, D.C. (March 3, 1924). In 1925 he made his European operatic debut as King Herod in Massenet's *Hérodiade* at the Théâtre Royal de la Monnaie in Brussels, where he sang until 1928; made his Covent Garden debut in London as Valentin in *Faust* (June 28, 1928). He then sang opera in Philadelphia (1928), San Francisco (1930, 1943), and Chicago (1930–32; 1934–36; 1939–42); made his Metropolitan Opera debut in N.Y. as the elder Germont on Feb. 2, 1934, and remained on the company's roster until 1943. Throughout these years, he toured widely in the U.S. as a concert artist; also appeared regularly on the "Bell Telephone Hour" radio program. Among his other roles were Rossini's Figaro, Scarpia, and Strauss's Jochanaan.—**NS/LK/DM**

Thomas, Leon (actually, **Amos Leone, Jr.**), jazz singer; b. East St. Louis, Ill., Oct. 4, 1937; d. N.Y., May 8, 1999. He began studying music in high school and continued his musical studies at Tenn. State Univ. He first did theater tours in the late 1950s, working with Art Blakey and Mary Lou Williams. In 1961, he replaced "Big" Joe Williams in Count Basie's band, working with him through most of the decade. He then worked with Pharoah Sanders (1969–72) and Santana (1973), before going out on his own. He attracted attention with his yodeling, which some say was modelled after traditional African Pgymy vocalizations. During the 1980s and 1990s he was a regular on the N.Y. club scene.

DISC.: *Spirits Known and Unknown* (1969); *In Berlin* (1970); *Leon Thomas Album* (1970); *Gold Sunrise on Magic Mountain* (1971); *Blues and the Soulful Truth* (1972); *Facets* (1972); *Full Circle* (1973); *Precious Energy* (1987); *Blues Band* (1988); *Leon Thomas Blues Band* (1988).—**LP**

Thomas, Michael Tilson, greatly talented American conductor; b. Los Angeles, Dec. 21, 1944. A grandson of Boris and Bessie Thomashefsky, founders of the Yiddish Theater in N.Y., he was brought up in a cultural atmosphere. He studied at the Univ. of Southern Calif. in Los Angeles, where he received instruction in composition with Dahl; he also studied with the pianist John Crown and the harpsichordist Alice Ehlers; concurrently took courses in chemistry. He acquired his conductorial skill by practical work with the Young Musicians Foundation Debut Orch., which he led from 1963 to 1967. He served as pianist in the master classes of Heifetz and Piatigorsky at the Univ. of Southern Calif. in Los Angeles; also conducted at the Monday Evening Concerts, where he presented first performances of works by Stravinsky, Copland, Boulez, and Stockhausen. In 1966 he attended master classes at the Bayreuth Festival; in 1967 he was asst. conductor to Boulez at the Ojai Festival; he conducted there also in 1968, 1969, and 1973. As a conducting fellow at the Berkshire Music Center at Tanglewood in the summer of 1968, he won the Koussevitzky Prize. The turning point in his career was his appointment in 1969 as asst. conductor of the Boston Sym. Orch.; he was the youngest to receive such a distinction with that great ensemble. He was spectacularly catapulted into public notice on Oct. 22, 1969, when he was called upon to conduct the 2nd part of the N.Y. concert of the Boston Sym. Orch., substituting for its music director, William Steinberg, who was taken suddenly ill. In 1970 he was appointed assoc. conductor of the Boston Sym. Orch., and then was a principal guest conductor there with Colin Davis from 1972 to 1974. From 1971 to 1979 he was music director of the Buffalo Phil.; served as music director of the N.Y. Phil. Young People's Concerts (1971–76). He was a principal guest conductor of the Los Angeles Phil. (1981–85). From 1986 to 1989 he was music director of the Great Woods Performing Arts Center in Mansfield, Mass., the summer home of the Pittsburgh Sym. Orch. He served as artistic advisor of the New World Sym. in Miami (from 1987). In 1988 he became principal conductor of the London Sym. Orch. In 1993 he was named music director designate of the San Francisco Sym., and in 1995 he stepped down from his position with the London Sym. Orch. to take up his duties there. From 1995 he also held the title of principal guest conductor of the London Sym. Orch. In 1993 he received the Alice M. Ditson Award for his services to American music. From 1994 he served as music director of the Ojai (Calif.) Festival. He has also appeared widely as a guest conductor throughout North America and Europe. His repertoire is exhaustive, ranging from the earliest masters to the avant-garde. He is also an excellent pianist. Above all, he is a modern musician, energetic, pragmatically proficient, and able to extract the maximum value of the music on hand.

Bibl.: E. Seckerson, *M.T. T., Viva Voce: Conversations with Edward Seckerson* (London, 1994).—**NS/LK/DM**

Thomas, Rene, guitarist; b. Liege, Belgium, Feb. 25, 1927; d. of a heart attack, Santander, Spain, Jan. 3, 1975. He was a self-taught guitarist, influenced by Django Reinhardt, who gained experience playing with visiting American musicians in the jazz clubs of Paris. He emigrated to N.Y. in 1958, where he played with Toshiko Akiyoshi and then Sonny Rollins, who praised Thomas's playing. In late 1959 he was playing in Canada with Paul Bley. He returned to Europe in 1961 and finally settled back in Paris in 1963, where he played with Kenny Clarke and later the Stan Getz Quartet.

Disc.: *Guitar Groove* (1960); *Meeting Mr. Thomas* (1963); *Blue Note* (1964); *Eddy Louiss–Kenny Clarke–Rene Thomas* (1974). **—MM/LP**

Thomas, Theodore (Christian Friedrich), renowned German-American conductor; b. Esens, East Friesland, Oct. 11, 1835; d. Chicago, Jan. 4, 1905. Taught by his father, a violinist, he played in public at the age of 6. In 1845 the family went to N.Y., where Thomas soon began to play for dances, weddings, and in theaters, helping to support the family; in 1851 he made a concert tour as a soloist, and in 1853 he joined Jullien's orch. on its visit to N.Y., later touring the country with Jenny Lind, Grisi, Sontag, Mario, et al. He became a member of the N.Y. Phil. Society in 1854. With the pianist William Mason, he founded a series of monthly matinee chamber concerts at N.Y.'s Dodworth Hall in 1855, which remained a vital force until it was disbanded in 1869. He first gained notice as a conductor when he led a performance of *La favorite* at the N.Y. Academy of Music on April 29, 1859. In 1862 he led his first orch. concerts at N.Y.'s Irving Hall, which became known as Symphonic Soirées in 1864; they were continued at Steinway Hall (1872–78); in 1865 he began a series of summer concerts in Terrace Garden, relocating these in 1868 to Central Park Garden. The influence of these enterprises on musical culture in N.Y. was enormous, and Thomas's programs attained European celebrity. The first concert tour with the Theodore Thomas orch. was made in 1869, and in subsequent years he led it on many tours of the U.S. and Canada. In 1873 he established the famous Cincinnati Biennial May Festival, which he conducted until his death. He also founded the Cincinnati Coll. of Music, of which he was president and director from 1878 to 1880, having given up his own orch. in N.Y. and the conductorship of the N.Y. Phil. Society (1877–78) to accept this post. After his resignation, he returned to N.Y., where he immediately reorganized his own orch. and was reelected conductor of the Phil. Society Orch. and the Brooklyn Phil. Orch. (having been conductor of the latter in 1862–63, 1866–68, and 1873–78). Besides conducting these orch. bodies, he was at different times director of several choruses; from 1885 to 1887 he was conductor and artistic director of the American Opera Co. In 1891 he settled permanently in Chicago as conductor of the Chicago Orch. In recognition of Thomas's distinguished services, a permanent home, Orch. Hall, was built by popular subscription, and formally opened in Dec. 1904, with a series of festival concerts, which were the last directed by him. After his death, the name of the orch. was changed to the Theodore Thomas Orch. in 1906; it became the Chicago Sym. Orch. in 1912.

The influence of Thomas upon the musical development of the U.S. has been strong and lasting. An ardent apostle of Wagner, Liszt, and Brahms, he also played for the first time in America works of Tchaikovsky, Dvořák, Rubinstein, Bruckner, Goldmark, Saint-Saëns, Cowen, Stanford, Raff, and Richard Strauss. He likewise programmed many works by American composers.

Bibl.: G. Upton, ed., *T. T.: A Musical Autobiography* (2 vols.; Chicago, 1905); R. Thomas (his 2nd wife), *Memoirs of T. T.* (N.Y., 1911); C. Russell, *The American Orchestra and T. T.* (N.Y., 1927); T. Russell, *T. T.: His Role in the Development of Musical Culture in the United States, 1835–1905* (diss., Univ. of Minn., 1969); E. Schabas, *T. T.: America's Conductor and Builder of Orchestras, 1835–1905* (Champaign- Urbana, 1989).—**NS/LK/DM**

Thomas Aquinas, Saint, famous Italian theologian, philosopher, and poet; b. Roccasecca, near Aquino, 1224 or 1225; d. Fossanova, March 7, 1274. In 1263 Pope Urban IV commissioned him to compose a communion service, which contains the memorable numbers *Lauda Sion* (Corpus Christi sequence) and *Pange lingua, Sacra solemnis, Verbum supernum,* and *Adoro te* (hymns). An extended chapter on music is contained in his *Summa Theologica* (II, *quaestio XLI*).

Bibl.: G. Amelli, *S. Tomaso e la musica* (1876); *D. Thomas Aquinatis de arte musica nunc primum ex codice bibl. univ. Ticinensis ed. illustr. Sac. Guarinus Amelli* (1880); C. Bellet, *St. Th. d'Aquin* (Paris, 1902); J. Callahan, *A Theory of Esthetics According to the Principles of St. Th. Aquinas* (diss., Catholic Univ., Washington, D.C., 1927).—**NS/LK/DM**

Thomas (Sabater), Juan María, Spanish organist and composer; b. Palma, Majorca, Dec. 7, 1896; d. there, May 4, 1966. He studied with Daniel, Mas y Serracant, and Huré. He was organist at the Palma Cathedral (from 1914). He founded the Capella Classica (1932), with which he toured worldwide. He publ. the study *Don Manuel de Falla en la isla* (Palma, 1947), and composed choral works, songs, organ music, and piano pieces.—**NS/LK/DM**

Thomas-San-Galli, Wolfgang Alexander, German violist and writer on music; b. Badenweiler, Sept. 18, 1874; d. Baden-Baden, June 14, 1918. He studied philosophy, history, and law in Freiburg, Bonn, Munich, and Marburg (Dr. Jur., 1898). From 1899 to 1908 he was the violist of the Suddeutsches Streich-Quartett in Freiburg, and from 1908 to 1911, ed. of the *Rheinische Musikund Theaterzeitung* in Cologne; then lived in Berlin as a writer. In 1898 he married the pianist Helene San-Galli. He ed. *Beethovens Briefe* (1910; selection with commentary) and *Beethovens Briefe an geliebte Frauen* (1913).

WRITINGS: *Sein oder Nichtsein? Aphorismen über Ethisches und Ästhetisches* (1905); *Johannes Brahms. Eine musikpsychologische Studie* (1905); *Musik und Kultur* (1908); *Musikalische Essays* (1908); *Die "unsterbliche Geliebte" Beethovens, Amalie Sebald* (1909); *Beethoven und die unsterbliche Geliebte. Amalie Sebald, Goethe, Therese Brunswick, und Anderes* (1910); *Mozart-Schatzkästlein* (1911); *Johannes Brahms* (1912; 5th ed., 1922); *Ludwig van Beethoven* (1913).—**NS/LK/DM**

Thomé, Francis (baptized **François Luc Joseph**), French composer and teacher; b. Port Louis, Mauritius, Oct. 18, 1850; d. Paris, Nov. 16, 1909. He went to Paris as a youth, and studied at the Cons. with Marmontel (piano), Duprato (harmony), and A. Thomas (composition), winning a premier prix for counterpoint and fugue (1870); then was active as a composer and teacher. He wrote the operas *Le Caprice de la Reine* (Cannes, April 1892) and *Le Château de Königsberg* (Paris, April 22, 1896), the ballets *Djemmah* (1886), *La Folie parisienne* (1900), etc., the religious mystery play *L'Enfant Jésus* (1891), 2 symphonic odes, *Hymne à la nuit* and *Vénus et Adonis*, Piano Trio (1893), Violin Sonata (1901), numerous songs, and much piano music. —**NS/LK/DM**

Thommessen, Olav Anton, imaginative Norwegian composer and teacher; b. Oslo, May 16, 1946. He studied composition with Bernhard Heiden at the Ind. Univ. School of Music in Bloomington (B.M., 1969), where he also attended the lectures of Xenakis; continued his training in Warsaw, and then pursued studies in electronic music with Werner Kaegi and Otto Laske at the Instituut voor Sonologie at the Univ. of Utrecht. In 1973 he joined the faculty of the Norwegian State Academy of Music in Oslo. In his compositions, he utilizes Western and non-Western elements in a contemporary style mainly within the tonal tradition.

WORKS: DRAMATIC: *Hermaphroditen* (The Hermaphrodite), chamber opera comprising the following 6 works: *Det Hemmelige Evangeliet* (The Secret Gospel; Bergen, May 24, 1976), *Hermaphroditen* (1975; Vadstena, Sweden, July 28, 1976), *Et Konsert-Kammer* (A Concert- Chamber; 1971; Warsaw, Feb. 6, 1972), *Ekko av et ekko* (Echo of an Echo; Malmö, Oct. 26, 1980), *Gjensidig* (Mutually; 1973; Luleå, Sweden, July 4, 1974), and *Overtonen* (The Overtone; Bergen, May 31, 1977); *Melologer og Monodramaer* (Wordless Chamber Opera; Vadstena, July 20, 1982); *Hertuginnen dr* (The Duchess Dies), chamber opera (1987); incidental music. **ORCH.:** *Vårlosning* (Thaw; Bloomington, Ind., May 8, 1969); *Opp-Ned* (Up-Down; 1972–73; Oslo, March 23, 1973); *Stabsarabesk* (1974; orchestrated by A. Bukkvoll as *Barbaresk*, 1974–77; Trondheim, March 24, 1977); *Et Glassperlespill* (A Glass Bead Game), comprising the following 6 works: *Pedagogisk Ouverture* (Pedagogical Overture) for Narrator and Strings (1979–80; Oslo, Feb. 13, 1981), *Makrofantasi over Griegs a-moll Konsert* (Macrofantasy on Grieg's A-minor Concerto; 1980; Bergen, Jan. 14, 1982), *Hinsides neon* (Beyond Neon), post-commercial sound sculptures for Horn and Orch. (1981; Minneapolis, Sept. 22, 1982), *Korsymfoni over Beethoven Åttende* for Chorus and Orch. (1980), *Gjennom prisme* (Through a Prism), double concerto for Cello, Organ, and Orch. (1984; Norwegian Radio, Jan. 1989), and *Ekstranummer over Verdis Dies Irae: Apotheose* (Encore on Verdi's Dies Irae: Apotheosis) for Chorus and Orch. (1979–80); *Fra Oven* (From Above), concerto for Synthesizer and Orch. (1986; Stavanger, Sept. 16, 1987); *Trusselen mot lyset* (The Threat Toward the Light; 1986); *The Great Attractor*, "cadenza accompagnata" for Violin and Orch. (Oslo, Aug. 4, 1988); *The 2nd Creation*, orch. drama for Trumpet and Orch. (Oslo, Sept. 15, 1988); *Music for a Futurist Feature* for Symphonic Band (1990); *2 Instrumental Madrigals*, sinfonietta (1990–91); *Cassation 1*, sinfonietta (1994); *A Film Scene* (1997–98); *Bulls Eye: A Symphonic Wrapping for Ole Bull* (1998); *Through Reflection—Thought Through* (1999). **CHAMBER:** Violin Sonata (1966); Duo Sonata for Cello and Piano (1968); 2 string quartets (1969, 1970); *Kvadratspill I* (1972) and *II* (1974) for 4 Percussionists; *Stanza* for Clarinet (1975); *S 15* for Vihuela, Renaissance Lute or Guitar, Alto Guitar, and Small Percussion (1976); *Nok en til* (Yet Another) for Woodwind Quintet (1977); *Vennligst godta min hrsel* (Please Accept My Ears) for Violin and Piano (1981); *Blokkfuglen* (The Block-bird) for Alto or Tenor Recorder (1981); *Scherzofonia/Scherzofrenia* for Violin, Cello, and Piano (Bergen, March 6, 1982); *Gratias Agimus* for Trumpet and Piano (1983); *Minia-Teks-Tur* for Tuba and Percussion (1985); *Rhapsodia improvizata* for 2 Cellos (1985); *Smaragd tavlen* (The Emerald Tablet) for 2 Pianos and 2 Percussion (1985); *L'Éclat approchant* for Piano, Harpsichord, and Synthesizer (1986); *Tibil* for Organ and Synthesizer (1986); Piano Sonata (1986); *Bellow-Canto* for 2 Accordions (1989); *The Phantom of Light* for Cello and 2 Woodwind Quintets (1990); *Étude-Cadenza* for Cello (1994); *Cassation 2* for Saxophone (1995); *The Uncovering of Slowness: A Paragraph on a Texture* for Chamber Ensemble (1996–97); *Sarabanda Smorzata* for Violin and Cello (1999). **VOCAL:** *Maldoror/Hunhaien* for 2 Vocal Actors and 4 Percussionists (1974); *Stabat Mater speciosa* for Chorus (1977); *Elfuglen* (The Electric Bird) for Soprano and Electronics (1980); *Sjelen, Lyttende—En gnostisk kantate* (The Ears of the Mind—A Gnostic Cantata) for Soprano, Reciter, 2 Cellos, Double Bass, Organ, and 2 Percussion (1984); *Gratias agimus* for Soprano and Piano (1988); *Woven in Stems*, symphonic song for Soprano and Strings (1991); *Near the Comet Head*, orch. drama for Viola, Alto, Women's Chorus, and Orch. (1993–94).—**NS/LK/DM**

Thompson, Danny (actually, **Daniel Henry Edward**; aka **Harnzah**), pop-jazz double bassist, trombonist, composer; b. Teignmouth, Devon, England, April 4, 1939. Lived in London from age of five. Made early efforts on tenor sax, drums, trumpet, and mandolin, then played tea-chest bass in a skiffle group. At age 16, began playing professionally in clubs, then did two years in the Army, and played trombone in Army bands. After his discharge, he returned to London where he worked with various bands and led his own trio (featuring John McLaughlin and Tony Roberts). He then played with blues-revivalist Alexis Korner (1964–67), and was a founding member of the folk-jazz group Pentangle (1968–73). During the 1970s worked often in Stan Tracey's Open Circle, and (from 1974) with singer/songwriter John Martyn, while continuing to do freelance session work. His freelance work grew greatly in the 1980s and 1990s when he worked with pop acts like Talk Talk, Kate Bush, and Rod Stewart. He formed the group Whatever to play an eclectic mix of jazz and other music in the late 1980s. Since the early 1990s, he has often accompanied guitarist/songwriter Richard Thompson (no relation) on both duo and band tours; the two collaborated on an album on the decline of industrial Britain in 1996.

Disc.: *Whatever* (1988); *Whatever Next* (1989); *Elemental* (1990). Richard Thompson: *Industry* (1996).—**JC-B/LP**

Thompson, Hank (Henry William), American country music singer and songwriter; b. Waco, Tex., Sept. 3, 1925. Thompson effected a transition between the Western Swing style of country music and the more hard-edged honky-tonk style, especially in the late 1940s and early 1950s, when he scored such hits as "The Wild Side of Life," "Rub-a-Dub-Dub," and "Wake Up, Irene."

Thompson took up the harmonica as a child and switched to guitar after receiving one for Christmas when he was ten. As a teenager he had his own radio show on a local Waco station. After graduating from high school in January 1943 he enlisted in the navy and served during World War II in the Pacific theater of operations. Discharged in 1945, he used the G.I. Bill to attend Princeton Univ., Southern Methodist Univ. in Dallas, and the Univ. of Tex. at Austin. In 1946 he returned to his radio show, formed a band, The Brazos Valley Boys, and began recording for small record labels.

Thompson signed to Capitol Records in 1947; his first single for the label, the self-penned "Humpty Dumpty Heart," peaked in the country Top Ten in March 1948. He scored four more country Top Tens through 1949, the most successful being a remake of his composition "Whoa Sailor," which he had first cut three years earlier. But his real breakthrough came in 1952, when he released the honky tonk anthem "The Wild Side of Life" (music and lyrics by Arlie Carter and William Warren), which topped the charts in May and became the biggest hit of the year.

Thompson had two more country Top Tens in 1952 and four in 1953, among them the chart-toppers "Rub-a-Dub-Dub" (music and lyrics by Hank Thompson) and "Wake Up, Irene" (music and lyrics by Weldon Allard and John Hathcock), the latter an answer record to "Goodnight, Irene." The most successful of the five country Top Ten hits he scored in 1954 was a remake of his 1948 record "Green Light," "The New Green Light" (music and lyrics by Hank Thompson); among his four 1955 country Top Tens was an instrumental recording of "Wildwood Flower" (music and lyrics by A. P. Carter and Hank Thompson) that featured Merle Travis.

Thompson's record sales diminished in the second half of the 1950s, although he scored five more country Top Ten hits through 1961, the most successful of which was 1958's "Squaws Along the Yukon" (music and lyrics by Cam Smith). His sales picked up when he moved to Warner Bros. Records in 1966 and again when he joined Dot Records in 1968, the latter association quickly bringing him two new country Top Ten hits, "On Tap, in the Can, or in the Bottle" and "Smoky the Bar." Though he had at least one single in the country charts every year through 1983, his last two Top Tens came in 1974 with "The Older the Violin, the Sweeter the Music" and "Who Left the Door to Heaven Open?" Meanwhile, he and his band toured regularly, playing hundreds of dates each year well into the 1990s.

Disc.: *Live at the Golden Nugget* (1958); *The Best of Hank Thompson* (rec. 1966–78; rel. 1996).—**WR**

Thompson, Malachi, veteran of Chicago's Association for the Advancement of Creative Musicians (AACM), this trumpeter is an iconoclastic, enterprising musician; b. Chicago, Ill., Aug. 21, 1949. Malachi Thompson leads several ensembles, including his regular Freebop Band (documented on his first Delmark album in 1989) and his Africa Brass big band (formed in 1991). He has recorded six albums as leader for the Delmark label, and has recorded as sideman for a variety of labels. A devoted historian, he is involved in spearheading the revival of the Sutherland Hotel on Chicago's South side.

He received his first trumpet at age 11, began classical studies with a musician in his church band, and took weekly lessons at a music instrument company. His interest in jazz was sparked when his mother (an avid music fan who shared her jazz record collection with her son) took him to see Count Basie perform. He began to learn the language of jazz by combining what he heard on recordings with what he learned through his associations with musicians. An Art Blakey record featuring trumpeter Bill Hardman inspired him to play bebop. In the meantime, he was developing his classical chops, and by seventh grade, beat out the competition for lead trumpet in the concert band.

During the 1960s, Chicago's music scene was flourishing with active players such as John Stubblefield, Eddie Harris, Gene Ammons, and others. After a dispute with his parents over his playing club gigs, he moved out into his own apartment. Throughout his teens, he had been gigging a few nights a week and, by his high school graduation in 1967, was performing with R&B bands, big bands, and was backing touring R&B artists. He began to tour, playing "bread-and-butter" R&B gigs with a variety of musicians.

He performed his first jazz gig with the AACM, fulfilling a requirement that young musicians produce a concert of original music. He began playing with the AACM big band, learning the principles and the AACM philosophy of integrity and experimentation. As he shifted from playing stock charts to challenging, experimental music by Henry Threadgill and Muhal Richard Abrams, he was enthralled and encouraged. He recorded his debut album, *The Seventh Son*, in 1972. Before he left Chicago for N.Y. in 1974, he had met saxophonist Carter Jefferson, with whom he would eventually form a quintet and begin a 20-year association that lasted until Jefferson's death on Dec. 9, 1993. The last time he saw Jefferson, they recorded a tribute tune Thompson wrote, "CJ's Blues," which appears on his *47th Street* album.

At the coaxing of Jefferson, he moved in 1974 to N.Y.C., where he had been playing gigs on tour since he was 18. He remained in N.Y. for nine years, freelancing most of the time, playing with small groups led by

Jackie McLean and Joe Henderson, and with the Sam Rivers big band. From 1975 to 1980, he and Norman Spiller co-led Brass Proud, the forerunner of Lester Bowie's Brass Fantasy and a band featuring seven trumpets and a rhythm section. Olu Dara, Tommy Terrentine, Victor Lewis, and others were in the band and they worked around N.Y. and along the East Coast. He was also still leading his Freebop band. It was back during N.Y.C.'s "loft" days, and he absorbed all that he could until he burned out and moved to Washington D.C. after his marriage ended in divorce. While D.C. was a hotbed of activity, he remained a road musician, working mostly with the short-lived N.Y. Hot Trumpet Repertory Company, featuring trumpeters Lester Bowie, Olu Dara, Wynton Marsalis, and Stanton Davis. He left D.C. and lived in Vienna, Austria, for a few years. He had been working frequently in Europe with the Freebop band, and after moving there, he participated in special projects with David Murray, Oliver Lake, Stan Davis, and Philip Wilson, and performed in large ensembles and with all-star big bands. He was doing well until 1989 when he was diagnosed with a rare form of lymphoma. He returned to Chicago for treatment and spiritual renewal, and today is cancer-free.

He is a member of the Sutherland Community Arts Initiative, a community-based organization that seeks to restore music to the Sutherland Hotel and Ballroom located at 47th and Drexel (his old neighborhood) on Chicago's South side. It was there during the 1960s that jazz artists such as Dizzy Gillespie, Miles Davis, John Coltrane, Nancy Wilson, Gene Ammons, Sonny Stitt, James Moody, and others performed.

He also teaches music through the Urban Gateways arts education program. In 1995, he was recognized for his lifelong achievements as a recipient of the Arts Midwest Jazz Master Award. He was selected as 1996 *Chicago Tribune* Chicagoan of the Year, and was a 1997 Chicago Endowments for the Arts honoree for his support of the arts and his community involvement through arts residencies. On Sept. 18, 1997, his stage production, *The Sutherland*, opened at the Victory Gardens Theater. Highly autobiographical, it is a musical about a young musician who grows up in the shadow of the Sutherland Hotel, leaves the U.S. to go on a European tour, and returns to discover that the tight-knit neighborhood he knew has deteriorated. Some of the music is performed on his 1997 Delmark CD, *47th Street*.

Disc.: *Spirit* (1989); *The Jaz Life* (1992); *Lift Every Voice* (1993); *New Standards* (1994); *Buddy Bolden's Rag* (1995); *47th Street* (1997).—**NAL**

Thompson, Oscar, American music critic and editor; b. Crawfordsville, Ind., Oct. 10, 1887; d. N.Y., July 3, 1945. He was educated at the Univ. of Wash., Seattle, and also studied music with G. Campanari and others. He took up journalism and in 1919 joined the staff of *Musical America*, later becoming assoc. ed. and finally ed. (1936–43). He was music critic for the *N.Y. Evening Post* (1928–34); from 1937 to his death he was music critic for the *N.Y. Sun*. In 1928 he established the first class in music criticism in the U.S. at the Curtis Inst. of Music in Philadelphia; he also gave courses at Columbia Univ. and the N.Y. Coll. of Music. In 1939 he brought out *The International Cyclopedia of Music and Musicians* in one vol. of more than 2,000 pages, with feature articles by eminent authorities; it went through 11 eds. and reprints. He wrote the books *Practical Musical Criticism* (1934), *How to Understand Music* (1935; 2nd ed., enl., 1958), *Tabulated Biographical History of Music* (1936), *The American Singer* (1937), and *Debussy, Man and Artist* (1937). He also ed. *Plots of the Operas* (1940) and *Great Modern Composers* (1941), both vols. being extracts from the *Cyclopedia*.—**NS/LK/DM**

Thompson, Randall, eminent American composer and pedagogue; b. N.Y., April 21, 1899; d. Boston, July 9, 1984. He was a member of an intellectual New England family. He studied at Lawrenceville School in N.J., where his father was an English teacher, and began taking singing lessons and received his rudimentary music training from the organist Francis Cuyler Van Dyck. When he died, Thompson took over his organ duties in the school. Upon graduation, he went to Harvard Univ., where he studied with Walter Spalding, Edward Burlingame Hill, and Archibald T. Davison (B.A., 1920; M.A., 1922). In 1920–21 he had some private lessons in N.Y. with Bloch. In 1922 he submitted his orch. prelude *Pierrot and Cothurnus*, inspired by the poetical drama *Aria da Capo* by Edna St. Vincent Millay, for the American Prix de Rome, and received a grant for residence in Rome; he conducted it there at the Accademia di Santa Cecilia on May 17, 1923. Encouraged by its reception, he proceeded to compose industriously, for piano, for voices, and for orch. He returned to the U.S. in 1925. From 1927 to 1929 he taught at Wellesley Coll., and again from 1936 to 1937; in 1929 he was appointed a lecturer in music at Harvard Univ.; in 1929–30 he held a Guggenheim fellowship. On Feb. 20, 1930, his 1st Sym. had its premiere in Rochester, N.Y., with Howard Hanson conducting, and on March 24, 1932, Hanson conducted in Rochester the first performance of Thompson's 2nd Sym., which was destined to become one of the most successful symphonic works by an American composer; it enjoyed repeated performances in the U.S. and also in Europe. Audiences found the work distinctly American in substance; the unusual element was the inclusion of jazz rhythms in the score. Equally American and equally appealing, although for entirely different reasons, was his choral work *Americana*, to texts from Mencken's satirical column in his journal, the *American Mercury*. There followed another piece of Americana, the nostalgic choral work *The Peaceable Kingdom*, written in 1936, and inspired by the painting of that name by the naturalistic fantasist Edward Hicks; for it, Thompson used biblical texts from the Prophets. Another piece for chorus, deeply religious in its nature, was *Alleluia* (1940), which became a perennial favorite in the choral literature; it was first performed at Tanglewood, Mass., at the inaugural session of the Berkshire Music Center, on July 8, 1940. In 1942 Thompson composed his most celebrated piece of choral writing, *The Testament of Freedom*, to words of Thomas Jefferson; it was first performed with piano accompaniment at the Univ. of Va. on April 13, 1943. A version with orch. was presented by the Boston Sym. Orch. on April 6, 1945. With this work Thompson firmly established his reputation as one of the finest composers of choral music in America. But he did not limit himself to choral music. His 1st String Quartet in D minor (1941) was praised, as was his opera, *Solomon and Balkis*, after Kipling's *The Butterfly That Stamped*, a parody on Baroque usages, broadcast over CBS on March 29, 1942. In 1949 Thompson wrote his 3rd Sym., which was presented at the Festival of Contemporary American Music at Columbia Univ. in N.Y. on May 15, 1949. Thompson's subsequent works were an orch. piece, *A Trip to Nahant* (1954), a *Requiem* (1958), an opera, *The Nativity According to St. Luke* (1961), *The Passion According to St. Luke* (1965), the cantata *The Place of the Blest* (1969), and *A Concord Cantata* (1975). During all this time, he did not neglect his educational activities; he taught at the Univ. of Calif. at Berkeley (1937–39); the Curtis Inst. of Music in Philadelphia, where he served as director from 1939 to 1941; the School of Fine Arts at the Univ. of Va. (1941–46); Princeton Univ. (1946–48); and Harvard Univ. (1948–65), where he retired as prof. emeritus in 1965. He also publ. a book, *College Music* (N.Y., 1935). In 1938 he was elected a member of the National Inst. of Arts and Letters; in 1959 he was named "Cavaliere ufficiale al merito della Repubblica Italiana." In his compositions, Thompson preserved and cultivated the melodious poetry of American speech, set in crystalline tonal harmonies judiciously seasoned with euphonious discords, while keeping resolutely clear of any modernistic abstractions.

WORKS: DRAMATIC: Opera: *Solomon and Balkis*, after Kipling's *The Butterfly That Stamped* (CBS, N.Y., March 29, 1942; 1st stage perf., Cambridge, Mass., April 14, 1942); *The Nativity According to St. Luke* (Cambridge, Mass., Dec. 13, 1961). **Ballet:** *Jabberwocky* (1951). **Incidental Music To:** *Torches* (1920); *Grand Street Follies* (N.Y., June 25, 1926; not extant); *The Straw Hat* (N.Y., Oct. 14, 1926); *The Battle of Dunster Street* (1953). **ORCH.:** *Pierrot and Cothurnus* (1922; Rome, May 17, 1923); *The Piper at the Gates of Dawn*, symphonic prelude (Rome, May 27, 1924); *Jazz Poem* for Piano and Orch. (Rochester, N.Y., Nov. 27, 1928); 3 syms.: No. 1 (1929; Rochester, N.Y., Feb. 20, 1930), No. 2 (1931; Rochester, N.Y., March 24, 1932), and No. 3 (1947–49; N.Y., May 15, 1949); *A Trip to Nahant*, symphonic fantasy (1953–54; Philadelphia, March 18, 1955). **CHAMBER:** *All on a Summer's Eve: Song* for Violin or Cello and Piano (1917); Septet for Flute, Clarinet, String Quartet, and Piano (1917); Quintet for Flute, Clarinet, Viola, Cello, and Piano (1920); *Scherzino* for Piccolo, Violin, and Viola (1920); *The Wind in the Willows* for String Quartet (1924); Suite for Oboe, Violin, and Viola (1940); 2 string quartets (1941, 1967); Trio for 3 Double Basses, a dinner-piece in honor of Koussevitzky (1949); *Katie's Dance* for Instrument (1969); *Wedding Music: A Wedding in Rome* for String Quartet and Double Bass ad libitum (1971); *Fuga a tre* for Instrument (1977). **Piano:** *Allegro* (1918); *Indianola Variations*, 7 variations for 2 Pianos (1918; Nos. 2, 4, and 5 by L. Mannes). 2 scherzos (1921, 1921); *Varied Air* (1921–22); 2 sonatas (1922; 1922–23); Suite (1924); *The Boats were Talking* (1925); *Mazurka* (1926); *Song after Sundown* (1935); *Little Prelude* (1935); also *20 Chorale Preludes, 4 Inventions, and a Fugue* for Keyboard Instrument (1947–59). **VOCAL:** *The Last Invocation* for Chorus (1922); *5 Odes of Horace* for Chorus and Piano or Orch. (1924; Lauro, Italy, May 16, 1925); *2 Amens* for Chorus (Montclair, N.J., Feb. 26, 1927); *Pueri hebraeorum* for Women's Chorus (Wellesley, Mass., Feb. 5, 1928); *Rosemary* for Women's Chorus (1929; N.Y., Dec. 18, 1930); *Americana* for Chorus and Piano or Orch., after Mencken's journal, the *American Mercury* (N.Y., April 3, 1932); *The Peaceable Kingdom* for Chorus, inspired by a painting of Edmund Hicks (Cambridge, Mass., March 3, 1936); *Tarantella: Do you Remember an Inn, Miranda?* for Men's Chorus (New Haven, Conn., Nov. 12, 1937); *The Lark in the Morn* for Chorus (Berkeley, Calif., Dec. 2, 1938); *Alleluia* for Chorus (Lenox, Mass., July 8, 1940); *The Testament of Freedom* for Men's Chorus and Piano or Orch., after Thomas Jefferson (Charlottesville, Va., April 13, 1943; with orch., Boston, April 6, 1945); *Noel* for Chorus (1947); *Now I Lay me down to Sleep* for Women's Chorus (1947); *The Last Words of David* for Chorus and Piano or Orch. (with orch., Lenox, Mass., Aug. 12, 1949); *Felices ter: Horace Ode for A.T. Davison* for Chorus (1953); *Mass of the Holy Spirit* for Chorus (1955–56; Cambridge, Mass., March 22, 1957); *Ode to the Virginian Voyage* for Chorus and Piano or Orch. (1956–57; Williamsburg, Va., April 1, 1957); *Requiem* for Double Chorus (1957–58; Berkeley, Calif., May 22, 1958); *Glory to God in the Highest* for Chorus (1958); *The Gate of Heaven* for Women's Chorus (Hollins Coll., Va., Feb. 22, 1959; also for Mixed Chorus and for Men's Chorus); *Frostiana* for Chorus and Piano, after Robert Frost (Amherst, Mass., Oct. 18, 1959; also with orch., Cambridge, Mass., April 23, 1965); *The Lord is my Shepherd* for Women's Chorus and Piano, Organ, or Harp (1962; N.Y., May 1964); *The Best of Rooms* for Chorus (Evanston, Ill., April 7, 1963); *A Feast of Praise*, cantata for Chorus, Brass Choir, and Harp or Piano (Stanford, Calif., Aug. 11, 1963); *Hymn: Thy Book Falls Open* for Chorus and Organ or Band (1964); *The Passion According to St. Luke*, oratorio for Soloists, Chorus, and Orch. (1964–65; Boston, March 28, 1965); *A Psalm of Thanksgiving*, cantata for Chorus, Children's Chorus, and Orch., Piano, or Organ (Boston, Nov. 15, 1967); *The Eternal Dove* for Chorus (1968; Cambridge, Mass., May 18, 1970); *The Place of the Blest*, cantata for Women's Chorus and Piano or Chamber Orch. (N.Y., March 2, 1969); *2 Herbert Songs* for Chorus (N.Y., Oct. 25, 1970); *The Mirror of St. Anne* for Chorus (1972); *Farewell* for Chorus (Merrick, N.Y., March 4, 1973); *A Hymn for Scholars and Pupils* for Women's Chorus, Chamber Orch., and Organ (Washington, Conn., June 8, 1973; also for Chorus, Flute, 2 Trumpets, Trombone, Tuba, Organ, and Strings, Raleigh, N.C., Nov. 11, 1973); *A Concord Cantata* for Chorus and Orch., for the bicentennial of Concord, Mass. (Concord, Mass., May 2, 1975); various songs.

BIBL.: B. McGilvray, *The Choral Music of R. T., an American Eclectic* (diss., Univ. of Mo., Kansas City, 1979); C. Benser and D. Urrows, *R. T.: A Bio-Bibliography* (Westport, Conn., 1986).
—NS/LK/DM

Thompson, "Sir" Charles, jazz pianist, organist, composer; b. Springfield, Ohio, March 21, 1918. He started on violin but switched to piano as a young teenager. From the mid-1930s he freelanced with Lloyd Hunter (1936), Nat Towles (1937), Lionel Hampton (1940), Lee and Lester Young's Band at Café Society, Manhattan (1942), Coleman Hawkins in Calif. (1944–45), and Illinois Jacquet (1947–48). He composed "Robbin's Nest," which was a major hit for Jacquet. He also did arranging for Count Basie, Jimmy Dorsey, Lionel Hampton, and Fletcher Henderson. He lived briefly in Cleveland from 1948–49, then returned to N.Y., where he worked as an organist through the 1950s, both leading various groups of "All-Stars" and on his own as a soloist. He first toured Europe in 1959, and continued to work abroad on various occasions through the mid-1960s. He was less active from 1964–74, but then returned to performing in 1975. In the early 1990s, he married a Japanese native, and the couple moved to Japan in 1992 where he continued to work in clubs. Lester Young reputedly "knighted" him Sir.

DISC.: "Takin' Off" (1945); *Sir Charles Thompson and His All Stars* (1951); *Bop This* (1953); *Sir Charles Thompson Sextet* (1953); *Sir Charles Thompson Quartet* (1954); *With Coleman Hawkins* (1954); *Sir Charles Thompson Trio* (1955); *Rockin' Rhythm* (1961); *Hey, There!* (1974); *Midnight Shows, Vol. 8* (1977); *For the Ears* (1980).—**LP**

Thompson, Will L(amartine), American music publisher and composer; b. Beaver County, Pa., Nov. 7, 1847; d. N.Y., Sept. 20, 1909. He studied at the Boston School of Music, the Boston Cons. of Music, and the Leipzig Cons. (1870–75), and then settled in East Liverpool, Ohio, where he founded his own music publishing firm. He wrote some 100 songs, both sacred and secular, perhaps his best-known song being the hymn *Softly and Tenderly Jesus Is Calling*. He ed. and publ. *Thompson's Popular Anthems* (1894), *The New Century Hymnal* (1904), and *Enduring Hymns* (1908).—**NS/LK/DM**

Thomson, Bryden, Scottish conductor; b. Ayr, July 16, 1928; d. Dublin, Nov. 14, 1991. He studied at the Royal Scottish Academy of Music in Glasgow and at the Hochschule für Musik in Hamburg, his principal mentors being Schmidt-Isserstedt and Markevitch. He was asst. conductor of the BBC Scottish Orch. (1958–62) and assoc. conductor of the Scottish National Orch. (1966–68) in Glasgow. From 1968 to 1973 he was principal conductor of the BBC Northern Sym. Orch. in Manchester; then was music director of the Ulster Orch. in Belfast (1977–85); also was principal conductor of the BBC Welsh Sym. Orch. in Cardiff (1978–82) and the R(adio) T(elefis) E(ireann) Sym. Orch. in Dublin (1984–87). In 1988 he returned to the Scottish National Orch. as its principal conductor, becoming well known for his championship of British music.—**NS/LK/DM**

Thomson, César, eminent Belgian violinist and teacher; b. Liège, March 17, 1857; d. Bissone, near Lugano, Aug. 21, 1931. He entered the Liège Cons. at the age of 7, where he began his training with Dupuis. He won the Gold Medal at 11, and subsequently studied with Vieuxtemps, Léonard, Wieniawski, and Massart. In 1873 he entered the service of Baron Paul von Derwies in Lugano, and in 1879 he became concertmaster of Bilse's orch. in Berlin. In 1882 he became prof. of violin at the Liège Cons., then in 1898 at the Brussels Cons., where he founded a celebrated string quartet (with Lamoureux, Vanhout, and Jacobs). In 1914 he settled in Paris as a prof. at the Cons. In 1924 he visited America; taught at the Cons. of Ithaca, N.Y., and at the Juilliard School of Music, N.Y., returning to Europe in 1927. He was a famous violin teacher, emphasizing perfection of technical and expressive performance, rather than bravura. He made arrangements for the violin of various works by early Italian composers.

BIBL.: H. Timerman, *How to Produce a Beautiful Tone on the Violin...in Accordance with the Principles of C. T.* (N.Y., 1923).—**NS/LK/DM**

Thomson, George, Scottish collector of folk songs; b. Limekilns, Dunfermline, March 4, 1757; d. Leith, Feb. 18, 1851. For 59 years (1780–1839) he was secretary to the Board of Trustees for the Encouragement of Arts and Manufactures in Scotland; from 1780, was active as a violinist in the orch. and as a singer in the choir of the Edinburgh Musical Society. An ardent collector of Scotch, Welsh, and Irish melodies, he issued a series of vols. containing authentic melodies, with piano accompaniments and instrumental arrangements by the most celebrated musicians of his time, including Beethoven, Haydn, Pleyel, and Koželuh. Each song had, in accordance with his plan, a prelude, coda, and ad libitum parts throughout (for violin, or flute, or cello). The collections are *A Select Collection of Original Scottish Airs* (6 vols., London; Vol. I, 1793; Vol. II, 1798; Vol. III, 1799; Vol. IV, 1802; Vol. V, 1818–26; Vol. VI, 1841), *Collection of the Songs of R. Burns, Sir W. Scott, etc.* (6 vols., London, 1822), *Select Collection of Original Welsh Airs* (3 vols., London, 1809), *Select Collection of Original Irish Airs* (2 vols., London, 1814–16), and *20 Scottish Melodies* (Edinburgh, 1839).

BIBL.: J. Hadden, *G. T., the Friend of Burns. His Life and Correspondence* (London, 1898).—**NS/LK/DM**

Thomson, John, Scottish composer and writer on music; b. Sprouston, Roxburgh, Oct. 28, 1805; d. Edinburgh, May 6, 1841. He studied in Leipzig with Schnyder von Wartensee, and became a friend of Mendelssohn, Schumann, and Moscheles. In 1839 he was appointed the 1st Reid Prof. of Music at the Univ. of Edinburgh. At the 3rd concert given by the Edinburgh Professional Society (Feb. 1837), an analytical program was issued by Thomson, then conductor; this is the first recorded instance of the use of such programs. He composed the opera *Hermann, or The Broken Spear* (London, Oct. 27, 1834), the drama *The House of Aspen* (Edinburgh, Dec. 19, 1829), and the musical play *The Shadow on the Wall* (London, April 20, 1835); also orch. works, including Overture in C minor (1830) and *Allegro maestroso and allegro grazioso* for Flute and Orch. (c. 1830), *Benedictus and Osanna* for Voices and Instruments (1829), chamber music, piano pieces, and songs.—**NS/LK/DM**

Thomson, Virgil (Garnett), many-faceted American composer of great originality and a music critic of singular brilliance; b. Kansas City, Mo., Nov. 25, 1896; d. N.Y., Sept. 30, 1989. He began piano lessons at age 12 with local teachers, and also received instruction in organ (1909–17; 1919) and played in local churches. He took courses at a local junior college (1915–17; 1919), then entered Harvard Univ., where he studied orchestration with E.B. Hill and became assistant and accompanist to A.T. Davison, conductor of its Glee Club; also studied piano with Heinrich Gebhard and organ with Wallace Goodrich in Boston. In 1921 he went with the Harvard Glee Club to Europe, where he remained on a John Knowles Paine Traveling Fellowship to study organ with Boulanger at the Paris École Normale de Musique; also received private instruction in counterpoint from her. Returning to Harvard in 1922, he was made organist and choirmaster at King's Coll.; after graduating in 1923, he went to N.Y. to study conducting with Clifton and counterpoint with Scalero at the Juilliard Graduate School. In 1925 he returned to Paris, which remained his base until 1940. He established friendly contacts with cosmopolitan groups of musicians, writers, and painters; his association with Gertrude Stein was particularly significant in the development of his aesthetic ideas. In his music, he refused to follow any set of modernistic doctrines; rather, he embraced the notion of popular universality, which allowed him to use the techniques of all ages and all degrees of simplicity or complexity, from simple triadic harmonies to dodecaphonic intricacies; in so doing he achieved an eclectic illumination of astonishing power of direct communication, expressed in his dictum "jamais de banalité, toujours le lieu commun." Beneath the characteristic Parisian persiflage in some of his music there is a profoundly earnest intent. His most famous composition is the opera *Four Saints in Three Acts*, to the libretto by Gertrude Stein, in which the deliberate confusion wrought by the author of the play (there are actually 4 acts and more than a dozen saints, some of them in duplicate) and the composer's almost solemn, hymn-like treatment, create a hilarious modern opera-buffa. It was first introduced at Hartford, Conn., on Feb. 8, 1934, characteristically announced as being under the auspices of the "Society of Friends and Enemies of Modern Music," of which Thomson was director (1934–37); the work became an American classic, with constant revivals staged in America and Europe. In 1940 Thomson was appointed music critic of the *N.Y. Herald-Tribune*; he received the Pulitzer Prize in Music in 1948 for his score to the film *Louisiana Story*. Far from being routine journalism, Thomson's music reviews are minor masterpieces of literary brilliance and critical acumen. He resigned in 1954 to devote himself to composition and conducting. He received the Légion d'honneur in 1947; was elected to membership in the National Inst. of Arts and Letters in 1948 and in the American Academy of Arts and Letters in 1959. In 1982 he received an honorary degree of D.Mus. from Harvard Univ. In 1983 he was awarded the Kennedy Center Honor for lifetime achievement. He received the Medal of Arts in 1988.

WORKS: DRAMATIC: Opera: *Four Saints in Three Acts* (1927–28; orchestrated 1933; Hartford, Conn., Feb. 8, 1934); *The Mother of Us All*, to a libretto by Gertrude Stein on the life of the American suffragist Susan B. Anthony (N.Y., May 7, 1947); *Lord Byron* (1961–68; N.Y., April 13, 1972). **Ballet:** *Filling Station* (1937; N.Y., Feb. 18, 1938); *The Harvest According* (N.Y., Oct. 1, 1952; based on the *Symphony on a Hymn Tune*, the Cello Concerto, and the Suite from *The Mother of Us All*); *Parson Weems and the Cherry Tree* (Amherst, Mass., Nov. 1, 1975). **Film:** *The Plow that Broke the Plains* (N.Y., May 25, 1936; orch. suite, Philadelphia, Jan. 2, 1943); *The River* (New Orleans, Oct. 29, 1937; orch. suite, N.Y., Jan. 12, 1943); *The Spanish Earth* (1937; in collaboration with M. Blitzstein); *Tuesday in November* (1945); *Louisiana Story* (Edinburgh, Aug. 22, 1948; orch. suite as *Acadian Songs and Dances*, Philadelphia, Jan. 11, 1951); *The Goddess* (1957; Brussels, June 1958); *Power among Men* (1958; N.Y., March 5, 1959; orch. suite as *Fugues and Cantilenas*, Ann Arbor, May 2, 1959); *Journey to America* (N.Y., July 1964; orch. suite as *Pilgrims and Pioneers*, N.Y., Feb. 27, 1971). **ORCH.:** 3 syms.: No. 1, *Symphony on a Hymn Tune* (1928; N.Y., Feb. 22, 1945), No. 2 (1931; rev. version, Seattle, Nov. 17, 1941), and No. 3 (1972; N.Y., Dec. 26, 1976); *The John Moser Waltzes* (1935; orchestrated 1937); *The Plow that Broke the Plains*, suite from the film score (1936; Philadelphia, Jan. 2, 1943); *The River*, suite from the film score (1937; N.Y., Jan. 12, 1943); *Filling Station*, suite from the ballet (1937; WNYC Radio, N.Y., Feb. 2, 1941); *Canons for Dorothy Thompson* (N.Y., July 23, 1942); *The Major LaGuardia Waltzes* (Cincinnati, May 14, 1942); *Bugles and Birds: Portrait of Pablo Picasso* (1940; orchestrated 1944; Philadelphia, Nov. 17, 1944); *Cantabile for Strings: Portrait of Nicolas de Chatelain* (1940; orchestrated 1944; Philadelphia, Nov. 17, 1944); *Fanfare for France: Portrait of Max Kahn* (1940; Cincinnati, Jan. 15, 1943); *Fugue: Portrait of Alexander Smallens* (1940; orchestrated 1944; Philadelphia, Nov. 17, 1944); *Meditation: Portrait of Jere Abbott* (1935; orchestrated 1944; Vancouver, Nov. 21, 1948); *Aaron Copland: Persistently Pastoral* (1942; orchestrated as Pastorale, 1944; N.Y., March 15, 1945); *Percussion Piece: Portrait of Jessie K. Lasell* (1941; orchestrated 1944; Philadelphia, Nov. 17, 1944); *Tango Lullaby: Portrait of Mlle Alvarex de Toledo* (1940; orchestrated 1944; Philadelphia, Nov. 17, 1944); *Fugue and Chorale on Yankee Doodle*, suite from the film score *Tuesday in November* (1945; Atlanta, April 16, 1969); *The Seine at Night* (1947; Kansas City, Mo., Feb. 24, 1948); *Acadian Songs and Dances* from the film score *Louisiana Story* (1948; Philadelphia, Jan. 11, 1951); *Louisiana Story*, suite from the film score (Philadelphia, Nov. 26, 1948); *Wheat Field at Noon* (Louisville, Dec. 7, 1948); *At the Beach*, concert waltz for Trumpet and Band (1949; N.Y., July 21, 1950; based on *Le bains-bar* for Violin and Piano, 1929); *The Mother of Us All*, suite from the opera (1949; Knoxville, Tenn., Jan. 17, 1950); *A Solemn Music* for Band (N.Y., June 17, 1949; also for orch., 1961; N.Y., Feb. 15, 1962); Cello Concerto (Philadelphia, March 24, 1950); *Sea Piece with Birds* (Dallas, Dec. 10, 1952); *Concerto: Portrait of Roger Baker* for Flute, Harp, Strings, and Percussion (Venice, Sept. 14, 1954; also for Flute and Piano); *Eleven Chorale Preludes* (1956; New Orleans, March 25, 1957; arr. from Brahms's op. 122); *The Lively Arts Fugue* (1957); *Fugues and Cantilenas* from the film score *Power among Men* (Ann Arbor, May 2, 1959); *A Joyful Fugue* (1962; N.Y., Feb. 1, 1963; also for Band); *Autum*, concertino for Harp, Strings, and Percussion (Madrid, Oct. 19, 1964; based on the *Homage to Marya Freund* and the Harp and the Piano Sonata No. 2); *Pilgrims and Pioneers* from the film score *Journey to America* (1964; N.Y., Feb. 27, 1971; also for Band); *Ode to the Wonders of Nature* for Brass and Percussion (Washington, D.C., Sept. 16, 1965); *Fantasy in Homage to an Earlier England* (Kansas City, Mo., May 27, 1966); *Edges: Portrait of Robert Indiana* (1966; also for Band, 1969); *Study Piece: Portrait of a Lady* for Band (1969; originally *Insistences: Portrait of Louise Crane*, 1941); *Metropolitan Museum Fanfare: Portrait of an American Artist* for Brass and Percussion (N.Y., Oct. 16, 1969; originally *Parades: Portrait of Florine Stettheimer*, 1941); *Thoughts for Strings* for Strings (1981); *A Love Scene* (1982; originally *Dead Pan: Mrs. Betty Freeman*); *Intensely Two: Karen Brown Waltuck* (1981; orchestrated 1982); *Loyal, Steady, and Persistent: Noah Creshevsky* (1981; orchestrated 1982); *Something of a Beauty: Ann-Marie Soullière* (1981; orchestrated 1982); *David Dubal in Flight* (1982). **CHAMBER:** *Sonata da chiesa* for Clarinet, Trumpet, Horn, Trombone, and Viola (Paris, May 5, 1926; rev. 1973); (8) *Portraits for Violin Alone* (1928–40); *Five Portraits for Four Clarinets* for 2 Clarinets, Alto Clarinet, and Bass Clarinet (1929); *Le bains-bar* for Violin and Piano (1929; arr. as *At the Beach*, concert waltz for Trumpet and Band, 1949; N.Y., July 21, 1950); *Portraits* for Violin and Piano (1930–40); Violin Sonata (1930; Paris, Jan. 24, 1931);

Serenade for Flute and Violin (1931); 2 string quartets: No. 1 (Paris, June 15, 1931; rev. 1957) and No. 2 (1932; Hartford, Conn., April 14, 1933; rev. 1957); *Sonata for Flute Alone* (1943); *Barcarolle for Woodwinds: A Portrait of Georges Hugnet* for Flute, Oboe, English Horn, Clarinet, Bass Clarinet, and Bassoon (1944; Pittsburgh, Nov. 29, 1946; based on a piano piece); *Lamentations: Étude for Accordion* (1959); *Variations* for Koto (1961); *Étude for Cello and Piano: Portrait of Frederic James* (1966); *Family Portrait* for 2 Trumpets, Horn, and 2 Trombones (1974; N.Y., March 24, 1975); *For Lou Harrison and his Jolly Games of 16 Measures (count 'em)*, theme without instrumentation (1981); *A Short Fanfare* for 2 Trumpets or 3 Trumpets or 3 Trumpets and 2 Drums (1981); *Bell Piece* for 2 or 4 Players (1983); *Cynthia Kemper: A Fanfare* (1983); *Lili Hasings* for Violin and Piano (1983); *A Portrait of Two* (1984); *Jay Rosen: Portrait and Fugue* for Bass Tuba and Piano (1984–85); *Stockton Fanfare* for 3 Trumpets and 2 Drums (1985); also numerous solo piano pieces. **VOCAL:** Choral pieces; solo vocal works.

WRITINGS (all publ. in N.Y.): *The State Of Music* (1939; 2nd ed., rev., 1961); *The Musical Scene* (1945); *The Art of Judging Music* (1948); *Music Right and Left* (1951); *Virgil Thomson* (1966); *Music Reviewed, 1940–1954* (1967); *American Music Since 1910* (1971); *A Virgil Thomson Reader* (1981); *Music with Words: A Composer's View* (1989).

BIBL.: K. Hoover and J. Cage, *V. T.: His Life and Music* (N.Y., 1959); K. Ward, *An Analysis of the Relationship between Text and Musical Shape and an Investigation of the Relationship between Text and Surface Rhythmic Detail in "Four Saints in Three Acts" by V. T.* (diss., Univ. of Tex., Austin, 1978); M. Meckna, *The Rise of the American Composer-critic: Aaron Copland, Roger Sessions, V. T., and Elliott Carter in the Periodical Modern Music, 1924–1946* (diss., Univ. of Calif., Santa Barbara, 1984); A. Tommasini, *The Musical Portraits of V. T.* (N.Y., 1985); M. Meckna, *V. T.: A Biography* (Westport, Conn., 1986); T. and V. Page, eds., *Selected Letters of V. T.* (N.Y., 1988); A. Tommasini, *V. T.: Composer on the Aisle* (N.Y., 1997).—**NS/LK/DM**

Thórarinsson, Leifur, Icelandic composer; b. Reykjavík, Aug. 13, 1934; d. there, April 24, 1998. He was a student of Jón Thoórarinsson at the Reykjavík Coll. of Music, of Jelinek in Vienna (1954), and of Riegger and Schuller in N.Y. In addition to composing, he was active as a music critic.

WORKS: ORCH.: *Epitaph (Wallingford Riegger in Memoriam)* (1961); 2 syms. (1963, 1997); Violin Concerto (1969); *Jó* (1975); *Rent* for Strings (1976); Oboe Concerto (1982); *Haustspil* (1983); Flute Concerto (1984); *Styr* for Piano and orch. (1988); *För* (1988); *Mót* (1990); *Hnit* (1991); *Vor*, chamber concerto (1993). **CHAMBER:** 3 string quartets (1969, n.d., 1993); *Per Voi* for Flute and Piano (1975); *Sumarmál* for Flute and Harpsichord (1978); *Áfangar* for Clarinet, Violin, and Piano (1979); *Capriccio* for Horn and Harpsichord (1982); *Fimma X*, quintet for Flute, 2 Percussion, Cello, and Harpsichord (1994). **KEYBOARD:** Piano Pieces, including a Sonata (1957); organ music. **VOCAL:** *Angelus domini* for Mezzo-soprano and Chamber Ensemble (1975); Cantata for Soloists, Chorus, and Organ (1979); *Blom vorsins*, Requiem (1988); *Maríamúsík* for Chorus (1992); songs. —**NS/LK/DM**

Thorborg, Kerstin, noted Swedish contralto; b. Venjan, May 19, 1896; d. Falun, Dalarna, April 12, 1970. She studied at the Royal Cons. in Stockholm. She made her operatic debut there as Ortrud at the Royal Theater in 1924, remaining on its roster until 1930; sang in Prague (1932–33), at the Berlin Städtische Oper (1933–35), at the Salzburg Festivals (1935–37), at the Vienna State Opera (1935–38), and at London's Covent Garden (1936–39). On Dec. 21, 1936, she made her Metropolitan Opera debut in N.Y. as Fricka, remaining on the company's roster until 1946; sang there again from 1947 to 1950; also appeared in concerts. In 1944 she was made a Swedish court singer; taught voice in Stockholm from 1950. She was particularly esteemed as a Wagnerian; also excelled as Gluck's Orfeo, Saint-Saëns's Delilah, and Strauss's Herodias and Clytemnestra.—**NS/LK/DM**

Thoresen, Lasse, Norwegian composer and teacher; b. Oslo, Oct. 18, 1949. He was a student of Mortensen at the Oslo Cons. (graduated, 1972) and then of Kaegi at the Inst. of Sonology at the Univ. of Utrecht. In 1975 he joined the faculty of the Norwegian State Academy of Music in Oslo. His *Stages of the Inner Dialogue* for Piano was named the Norwegian composition of the year in 1981, an honor he received again in 1993 with his *Ab Uno* for Flute, Clarinet, String Quartet, Percussion, and Synthesizer. His music reflects the influence of French spectral music, Harry Partch's microtonal system, and Norwegian folk music. He was the first composer in Norway to incorporate the non-tempered intervals of folk music into concert music. His Bahai faith is reflected in his choice of titles for many of his scores.

WORKS: DRAMATIC: *Skapelser*, television ballet (1977); *Vidunderlampen* (The Wonder Lamp), children's operetta (1984). **ORCH.:** *Rettferdighetens Sol* (The Sun of Justice), symphonic poem (Bergen, Dec. 2, 1982); *Transition* for Strings (1983); Symphonic Concerto for Violin and Orch. (1984–86); *Illuminations*, concerto for 2 Cellos and Orch. (1986–90); *Hymnisk Dans* (1987); *Carmel Eulogies*, symphonic poem for the 75th anniversary of the Oslo Phil. (Oslo, Nov. 9, 1994); *Emergence*, symphonic poem (1997). **CHAMBER:** *Etter-Kvart* for 2 Violins, Viola, and Cello (1971); *With an Open Hand or a Clenched Fist?* for Flute (1976); *Origins* for 3 Instruments (1980); *Interplay* for Flute and Piano (1981); *Bird of the Heart*, piano trio (1982); *Les Trois Régénérations* for 2 Cellos, Harp, 2 Percussion, Tape, and Electronics (Paris, Oct. 29, 1985); *Miranda's Flourish* for Recorder (1985); *Qudrat* for 3 Percussionists and 3 Synthesizers (1987); *Narrative* for 4 Saxophones (1988); *Thus* for Flute, Clarinet, 3 Percussion, and Synthesizer (1990); *Yr* for Violin (1991); *Ab Uno* for Flute, Clarinet, String Quartet, Percussion, and Synthesizer (1992); *Aion* for String Quartet (1996). **Piano:** *4 Inventions: To the Memory of Fartein Valen* (1967–68); *Stages of the Inner Dialogue* (1980); *Arise!* (1980); *Solspill* (1983–86). **VOCAL:** *Magnificetur nomen tuum* for 4 Voices and Chorus (1974); *Aeterne rerum conditor* for 2 Voices, Women's Voices, and 3 Percussion (1975); *The Garden* for Voice, Violin, Cello, 2 Percussion, and Piano (1976); *Helligkvad* for Voice (1979–93); *Tidings of Light* for 4 Voices and Chorus (1981); *The Song of Khadijih-Bagum* for Voice(s) and Piano (1984–99); *Banners of Peace*, cantata for 2 Voices, Cello, and 2 Percussion (1986); *Say: God is the Lord* for 2 Choruses (1986); *Bicinium nuptiale* for 2 Voices (1989); *Cantio PM CL* for 4 Voices (1989); *The Tablet of the Holy Mariner* for Chorus (1995); *Fire and Light*, "cantata and transformation" for 2 Women Folk Singers, Chorus, and Instrumental Ensemble (1998). **ELECTRONIC:** *Marm* (1973); *Utstrømning* (1976). —**NS/LK/DM**

Thorne, Francis, American composer and music patron; b. Bay Shore, Long Island, N.Y., June 23, 1922. Of a cultural heritage (his maternal grandfather was **Gustav Kobbé**), he absorbed musical impressions crouching under the grand piano while his father, a banker, played ragtime. He received instruction in composition from Donovan and Hindemith at Yale Univ. (B.A., 1942). After working in banking and stock brokerage (1946–54), he was active as a jazz pianist in the U.S. and Italy (1955–61). He also studied with Diamond in Florence. Impressed, depressed, and distressed by the inhumanly impecunious condition of middle-aged atonal composers, he established the eleemosynary Thorne Music Fund (1965–75), drawing on the hereditary wealth of his family, and disbursed munificent grants to those who qualified, among them Wolpe, Weber, Harrison, Trimble, Cage, and Diamond. He served as executive director of the Lenox Arts Center (1972–76) and of the American Composers' Alliance (1975–85). In 1976 he co-founded the American Composers Orch. in N.Y., subsequently serving as its president. In 1988 he was elected to membership in the American Academy and Inst. of Arts and Letters. In 1994 he was composer-in-residence at the American Academy in Rome. Thorne's music shares with that of his beneficiaries the venturesome spirit of the cosmopolitan avant-garde, with a prudently dissonant technique serving the conceptual abstractions and titular paronomasia of many modern compositions.

WORKS: DRAMATIC: *Fortuna*, operetta (N.Y., Dec. 20, 1961); *Opera buffa for Opera Buffs* (1965); *After the Teacups*, ballet (N.Y., July 31, 1974); *Echoes of Spoon River*, ballet (N.Y., June 20, 1976); *Mario and the Magician*, opera (1991–93; N.Y., March 12, 1994). **ORCH.:** 7 syms. (1961, 1964, 1969, 1977, 1984, 1992, 1996); *Elegy* (1963); *Burlesque Overture* (1964); *Rhapsodic Variations* for Piano and Orch. (1964); 3 piano concertos (1965, 1974, 1990); Double Concerto for Viola, Double Bass, and Orch. (1967–68); *Sonar Plexus* for Electric Guitar and Orch. (1968); *Liebesrock* for 3 Electric Guitars and Orch. (1969); *Fanfare, Fugue and Funk* for 3 Trumpets and Orch. (1972); Violin Concerto (1976); *Pop Partita* for Piano and Chamber Orch. (1976); *Divertimento No. 1* for Flute and Strings (1979) and *No. 2* for Bassoon and Strings (1980); *Humoresque*, overture (1985); *Concerto Concertante* for Flute, Clarinet, Violin, Cello, and Orch. (1985); *Rhapsodic Variations No. 3* for Oboe and Strings (1986); Cello Concerto No. 2 (1996); Clarinet Concerto (1997); *Flash Dances* (1998); Oboe Concerto (2000). **CHAMBER:** 4 string quartets (1960, 1967, 1975, 1983); *Music for a Circus* for 7 Instruments (1963); *Lyric Variations No. 2* for Woodwind and Percussion (1972), *No. 3* for Piano, Violin, and Cello (1972), and *No. 8* for Flute, Celesta, and Cello (1999); Piano Sonata (1972); *Evensongs* for Flute, Harp, Guitar, Celesta, and Percussion (1972); *Prufrock Ballet Music* for 7 Instruments (1974); Chamber Concerto for Cello and 10 Instruments (1975); *5 Set Pieces* for Saxophone Quartet (1977); *Grand Duo* for Oboe and Harpsichord (1977); *Eine Kleine Meyermusik* for Clarinet and Cello (1980); *Burlesk Pit Music* for Clarinet and Cello (1983); *Divertimento No. 3* for Woodwind Quintet (1983); *Rhapsodic Variations No. 2* for Clarinet, Violin, and Cello (1985), *No. 3* for Oboe and String Quartet (1986), *No. 5* for Viola and Piano (1988), and *No. 7* for Piano (1998); *2 Environments* for Brass Quintet (1990); Partita No. 2 for Chamber Ensemble (1991); *Electrified Elan* for Guitar (1992); *How Wild the Rose* for Flute, Clarinet, Violin, and Cello (1996); *Quiet Night Song* for Cello and Piano (1997). **VOCAL:** *De profundis* for Soprano, Chorus, and Organ (1959); *Nocturnes* for Voice and Piano or String Quartet (1962); *Song of the Carolina Low Country* for Chorus and Orch. (1968); *A Mad Wriggle*, madrigal (1970); *Cantata Sauce* for Mezzo-soprano, Baritone, and 8 Players (1973); *Love's Variations* for Flute, Soprano, and Piano (1977); *La Luce Eterna* for High Voice and Orch. (1978); *Praise and Thanksgiving* for Chorus and Orch. (1983); *The Affirming Flame* for Soprano and Small Ensemble (1987); *Money Matters* for Tenor and Ensemble (1988); *Echo* for Soprano and Chorus (1995).—**NS/LK/DM**

Thornhill, Claude, American pianist, bandleader, and composer; b. Terre Haute, Ind., Aug. 10, 1909; d. Caldwell, N.J., July 1, 1965. He studied piano and composition at the Cincinnati Cons. and at the Curtis Inst. of Music in Philadelphia. He was an arranger for Benny Goodman and others, and in 1940 organized a band of his own. Because of his uncommon musical literacy, he was able to make use of plausible novelties in his arrangements.—**NS/LK/DM**

Thorpe Davie, Cedric, Scottish composer and teacher; b. London, May 30, 1913; d. Kirkcudbrightshire, Jan. 18, 1983. He began his training at the Royal Scottish Academy of Music in Glasgow, then studied in London with Craxton, Thiman, and A. Brain at the Royal Academy of Music and with R.O. Morris, Vaughan Williams, and G. Jacob at the Royal Coll. of Music, where he won the Cobbett and Sullivan prizes in composition (1935); subsequently received instruction in piano from Petri, and also in composition from Kodály in Budapest and from Kilpinen in Helsinki. He taught theory and composition at the Royal Scottish Academy of Music (1936–45), then was master (1945–73) and prof. (1973–78) of music at St. Andrews Univ. In 1955 he was awarded the Order of the British Empire. He publ. *Musical Structure and Design* (London, 1953) and ed. the *Oxford Scottish Song Book* (London, 1968).

WORKS: DRAMATIC: *Gammer Gurton's Needle*, opera (1936); comic operas; operettas; music for theater, films, and broadcasting. **ORCH.:** *Elegy* (1932); *Concert Overture* (1934); Concerto for Piano and Strings (1943); Sym. (1945); *The Beggar's Benison* (1949); *Festival Overture* (1950); *Royal Mile*, march (1952); *Diversions on a Tune by Dr. Arne* (1964); *New Town*, suite (1966). **CHAMBER:** Piano Trio (1932); *Fantasy-Quartet* for Strings (1935); Violin Sonata (1939). **VOCAL:** *Dirge for Cuthullin* for Chorus and Orch. (1935); 3 anthems for Chorus and Organ (1937); *Ode for St. Andrew's Night* for Tenor and Orch. (1950); part songs; solo songs; arrangements.

BIBL.: C. *T.D.: Catalogue of Works* (Fife, 1988).—**NS/LK/DM**

Thow, John H(olland), American composer; b. Los Angeles, Oct. 6, 1949. He studied composition with Adolph Weiss while in high school, and later at the Univ. of Southern Calif. with Anthony Vazzana and Ramiro Cortes (B.Mus., 1971) and at Harvard Univ. with Leon Kirchner and Oliver Strunk (Ph.D., 1977). He also studied with Luciano Berio on a Fulbright fellowship in Rome (1973–74) and with Franco Donatoni at the Accademia Musicale Chigiana in Siena (1973–74), and later again in Rome with Berio upon receipt of a Rome Prize

Fellowship (1977–78). He was an asst. prof. at Boston Univ. (1978–80), and in 1981 joined the faculty of the Univ. of Calif. at Berkeley as an asst. prof., becoming an assoc. prof. in 1986 and a full prof. in 1990. serving as dept. head and as director of the Berkeley Contemporary Music Players. Thow's works are cast in a variety of genres in an eclectic post-tonal style. He often incorporates quoted or paraphrased music from sources as diverse as plain chant, Native American music, and European music of the 19th century. He received a Guggenheim fellowship (1986–87) and both the Goddard Lieberson Fellowship (1983) and the Academy Award in Music Composition (1994) from the American Academy of Arts and Letters. He also residencies at both the Yaddo (1976, 1980) and Djerassi (1986, 1987) Foundations.

WORKS: DRAMATIC: Opera: *Serpentina* for 8 Soloists, Chorus, and Chamber Orch., after E.T.A. Hoffmann (1998–99). **ORCH.:** *Trigon* (1974); *Astraeus* (1975); *Canto del Quetzal* for Chamber Orch. (1978); *Resonance* (1986); *Into the Twilight* (1988); Trombone Concerto (1990; rev. 1993); *Lene Tawi* (Hope Rain Song) for Chamber Orch. (1996). **CHAMBER:** *Divergences* for Flute, Clarinet, Viola, and Cello (1974); *Phoenix Music* for Flute, 9 Strings, Piano, and Percussion (1981); *All Hallows* for Flute, Clarinet, Violin, Viola, Cello, Piano, and Percussion (1982); *Live Oak* for 10 Players (1983); *Rounds* for Percussion Quartet (1986); *Madrone* for 14 Players (1987); *Trilce* for Flute/Piccolo, Oboe/English Horn, Cello, and Piano (1991); *Breath of the Sun* for 3 Flutes and Alto Flute (1993); Sextet for Flute/Piccolo, Clarinet/Bass Clarinet, Violin, Viola, Cello, and Piano (1993); Quartet for Clarinet, Violin, Cello, and Piano (1995); *The Wood is Singing* for 4 Cellos (1995); *To Invoke the Clouds* for Baroque (transverse) Flute (solo or duo) or Modern Flute (solo or duo), with or without Interactive Electronics (1995); *Musica d'amore* for Oboe d'amore, Viola d'amore, and Harp (1996); *Al Cabrero* for Guitar (1997); *A Return to Roslin Castle* for 8-key Flute and Guitar (1997); *Chumash Songs (Kapumi Xucu)* for Violin, Clarinet, Piano, and Percussion (2000). **Piano:** *Three Elements* for 2 Pianos (1986); *Remembering Op. 109* (1994). **VOCAL: Chorus:** *Night* for Women's Chorus and Strings (1975); *Cantico* for Soloists, Chorus, and Chamber Orch. (1997–98). **Solo Voice with Instrument(s):** *Siempre* for Soprano and Orch., after Pablo Neruda (1978); *Seven Charms for a New Day* for Soprano and Piano (1982); *When You Were Born* for Soprano, Flute, Cello, and Harp (1987); *A Water Cycle* for Baritone and Chamber Ensemble (1991); *Songs for the Earth* for Mezzo-soprano, Flute, Clarinet, Violin, Cello, Piano, and Percussion (1994).—**LK/DM**

Thrane, Waldemar, Norwegian violinist, conductor, and composer; b. Christiania, Oct. 8, 1790; d. there, Dec. 30, 1828. He studied violin with Henrik Groth in Christiania, and then with Claus Schall in Copenhagen (1814–15); then went to Paris, where he was a pupil of Baillot (violin) and of Reicha and Habeneck (composition). Returning to Christiania in 1818, he was made conductor of the orchs. of the Dramatical Society and of the Musical Lyceum; also toured as a violinist throughout his homeland and made appearances in Stockholm. He is historically important as the composer of the first Norwegian opera, *Fjeldeventyret* (A Mountain Adventure; 1824; Christiania, Feb. 9, 1825). Other works include a Concert Overture (1818), a Finale for Orch. (1818; not extant), a Cantata (1827; not extant), and some piano music.

BIBL.: F. Benestad, *W. T.: En pioner i norsk musikk* (Oslo, 1961).—**NS/LK/DM**

Threadgill, Henry (Luther), talented avant-garde jazz alto saxophonist, flutist, composer; b. Chicago, Feb. 15, 1944. He studied at the American Cons. of Music, Governor's State Univ; played with marching bands, theatre bands, and gospel and blues bands; and was in the army stationed in Kans. He played with Eugene Hunter, Richard Davis, and the Phil Cohran Heritage Ensemble. In 1963, he became active in education as a music instructor and choir director. He joined Muhal Richard Abrams's sextet in the early 1960s and was a founding member of the AACM. In the early 1970s, along with Fred Hopkins and Steve McCall, he founded the trio Air; the trio traveled extensively and recorded in Venezuela and Trinidad. Air moved to N.Y. in 1975 and continued until McCall left in 1983; the group then continued as New Air from 1983 to 1986. Threadgill then formed his Sextet (six pieces plus himself). His groups often included Deidre Murray on cello, Frank Lacy on trombone, Rasul Sadik on trumpet, Fred Hopkins on bass, Pheeron akLaff, and Reggie Nicholson on drums. Hopkins and akLaff also play in New Air; Threadgill and they also played in Oliver Lake's combo as well. In the early 1990s, Threadgill took his Very Very Circus band on a bus and toured across the country, stopping in small towns and performing free sets of music in town squares and parks. In the later 1990s, his band, now called Make a Move, included Brandon Ross on electric and classical guitars, Tony Cedras on accordion and harmonium, Stomu Takeishi on five-string fretless bass, and new member Toby Williams on drums. Around this time he also assembled a 21-piece "dance band" for some performances in Europe.

An eccentric personality, Threadgill has no telephone, and communicates with the outside world through faxes he sends from a local copy center. He maintains a residence in N.Y., but around 1994 began living in India for half of the year with his wife and young child.

DISC.: *X–75, Vol. 1* (1979); *When Was That?* (1982); *You Know the Number* (1986); *Live at Koncepts* (1991); *Song out of My Trees* (1993); *Too Much Sugar for a Dime* (1993); *Carry The Day* (1994); *Makin' a Move* (1995); *Where's Your Cup?* (1997); *Flute Force Four* (with co-leader James Newton; 1990). Air: *Air* (1971); *Air Song* (1975); *Air Raid* (1976); *Live Air* (1976); *Air Time* (1977); *Live at Montreux 1978* (1978); *Open Air Suite* (1978); *Air Lore* (1979); *Air Mail* (1980); *80 Degrees Below '82* (1982); *New Air: Live at the Montreux I* (1983); *Air Show No. 1* (1986).—**LP**

Thuille, Ludwig (Wilhelm Andreas Maria), renowned Austrian composer and pedagogue; b. Bozen, Tirol, Nov. 30, 1861; d. Munich, Feb. 5, 1907. He studied theory, piano, and organ with Joseph Pembaur in Innsbruck, then went to Munich, where he was a pupil of Karl Bärmann (piano) and Joseph Rheinberger (composition) at the Königliche Musikschule, graduating with honors in 1882; in 1883 he joined its faculty and was promoted to prof. in 1890. Encouraged by Alexander Ritter, he began to compose music in the grand Wagnerian manner. He wrote 3 operas and other works, but he made his mark chiefly as a fine pedagogue. With Rudolf Louis, he publ. the well-known manual *Harmonielehre* (1907; abr. ed. as *Grundriss der Harmonielehre*, 1908; 10th ed., rev., 1933 by W. Courvoisier and others).

WORKS: DRAMATIC: Opera: *Theuerdank* (1893–95; Munich, Feb. 12, 1897), *Lobetanz* (1896; Karlsruhe, Feb. 6, 1898); *Gugeline* (1898–1900; Bremen, March 4, 1901). **Melodrama:** *Die Tanzhexe* (1899–1900). **ORCH.:** Sym. (1886); *Romantische Ouverture*, overture to *Theuerdank* (1896). **CHAMBER:** Sextet for Flute, Oboe, Clarinet, Bassoon, Horn, and Piano (1886–88); Piano Quintet (1897–1901); Cello Sonata (1901–02); Violin Sonata (1903–04); piano pieces. **VOCAL:** Choral works; 78 songs.

BIBL.: F. Munter, *L. T.* (Munich, 1923).—**NS/LK/DM**

Thursby, Emma (Cecilia), prominent American soprano; b. Williamsburg, N.Y., Feb. 21, 1845; d. N.Y., July 4, 1931. She was trained in the U.S. and Italy, her principal mentors being Julius Meyer, Achille Errani, Francesco Lamperti, Sangiovanni, and Erminie Rudersdorff. After beginning her career with solo appearances in churches in Brooklyn and N.Y., she sang with Theodore Thomas and his orch., with Patrick Gilmore and his band, and in Leopold Damrosch's oratorio concerts. She won extraordinary success touring as a concert singer in Europe (1878–82), then gave concerts and recitals in the U.S. until her farewell in Chicago in 1895. She subsequently was active as a teacher, serving as a prof. at the Inst. of Musical Art in N.Y. (1905–11). Her most celebrated pupil was Geraldine Farrar. Although she declined to appear in operatic productions, she included numerous arias in her concert repertoire, winning acclaim for her coloratura gifts.

BIBL.: R. Gipson, *The Life of E. T., 1845–1931* (N.Y., 1940). —**NS/LK/DM**

Thursfield, Anne (née **Reman**), English mezzo-soprano; b. N.Y., March 28, 1885; d. London, June 5, 1945. She received her training principally in Berlin, and then developed a fine concert career in England. Thursfield's interpretations of the song literature were particularly admired for their insight in and handling of both German and French texts, as well as those in her native English tongue.—**NS/LK/DM**

Thurston, Frederick (John), English clarinetist and pedagogue; b. Lichfield, Sept. 21, 1901; d. London, Dec. 12, 1953. After initial training from his father, he was a student of Charles Draper in London. He played in several orchs. before serving as principal clarinetist in the BBC Sym. Orch. in London from 1930 to 1946. Thereafter he pursued a distinguished career as a soloist with orchs. and as a chamber music player. From 1930 he taught at the Royal Coll. of Music in London. Among his students was **Thea King**, who became his wife. With A. Frank he publ. *The Clarinet* (London, 1939). He was also the author of *Clarinet Technique* (London, 1956). In 1952 he was made a Commander of the Order of the British Empire. Thurston gave premiere performances of works by such composers as Bax, Bliss, Howells, Finzi, Ireland, and Rawsthorne.—**NS/LK/DM**

Thybo, Leif, Danish organist, teacher, and composer; b. Holstebro, June 12, 1922. He studied in Copenhagen at the Cons. (1940–45) and the Univ. (1945–48). He taught harmony and counterpoint at the Univ. of Copenhagen (1949–65); taught theory (from 1952) and organ (from 1960) at the Copenhagen Cons.; was also active as a church organist.

WORKS: CHAMBER Opera: *Den odödliga berättelsen* (The Immortal Story; Vadstena, Sweden, July 8, 1971). **ORCH.:** Concerto for Chamber Orch. (1947); 2 organ concertos (1954, 1956); Concerto for Strings (1957); *Philharmonic Variations* (1958); Cello Concerto (1961); Piano Concerto (1961–63); Concerto for Flute and Chamber Orch. (1966); Violin Concerto (1969); Viola Concerto (1972). **CHAMBER:** Cello Sonata (1950); 2 violin sonatas (1953, 1960); Sonata for Violin and Organ (1955); Trio for Clarinet, Cello, and Piano (1963); 2 string quartets (1963, 1990); Flute Quintet (1965); *Concerto breve* for Piano, Flute, Violin, Viola, and Cello (1966); *Hommage à Benjamin Britten* for Flute Quartet (1968); Trio for Oboe, Horn, and Bassoon (1970); *Engels nachtegaltje* for Recorder, Flute, and Organ (1974); Concertino for 2 Trumpets and Organ (1976); 2 piano trios (1976, 1985). **KEYBOARD:** Solo piano works, including 2 sonatas (1947, 1956); organ pieces. **VOCAL:** Concertino for Organ, Chamber Orch., and Mezzo-soprano (Copenhagen, Oct. 19, 1960); *Markus-passionen* (Passion According to St. Mark) for Soloists, Chorus, and Orch. (Copenhagen, March 19, 1964); *Te Deum* for Chorus and Winds (Copenhagen, Nov. 18, 1965); *Prophetia* for Soprano, Bass, Chorus, and Orch. (Copenhagen, Feb. 28, 1965); *In dieser Zeit* for Solo Voice, Vocal Quartet, and Instruments (1967); *Dialogue* for Soloists, Chorus, and Instruments (Copenhagen, May 27, 1968); *The Ecstacy* for Soprano, Narrator, Recorder, Oboe, Viola da Gamba, and Spinet (1972); songs.—**NS/LK/DM**

Tibaldi, Giuseppe (Luigi), Italian tenor; b. Bologna, Jan. 22, 1729; d. c. 1790. He studied voice with Domenico Zanardi and composition with Padre Martini in Bologna, where he joined its Accademia Filarmonica as a singer (1747) and as a composer (1750), later serving as its principe (1759, 1777, 1783). In 1751 he became maestro di cappella at S. Giovanni in Monte in Bologna, a post he gave up a few years later to pursue a distinguished career as a singer. Tibaldi sang in the premieres of Gluck's *Alceste* (Vienna, Dec. 16, 1767) and Mozart's *Ascanio in Alba* (Milan, Oct. 17, 1771). His son, Ferdinando Tibaldi (b. c. 1750; d. 1785), was a singer and composer.—**NS/LK/DM**

Tibbett (real name, **Tibbet**), **Lawrence,** outstanding American baritone; b. Bakersfield, Calif., Nov. 16, 1896; d. N.Y., July 15, 1960. His real name was accidentally misspelled when he appeared in opera, and he retained the final extra letter. His ancestry was connected with the Calif. Gold Rush of 1849; his great-uncle was reputed to be a pioneer in the navel orange industry; Tibbett's father was a sheriff of Bakersfield who was shot dead by one of the outlaws he had hunted. His mother ran a hotel in Long Beach. Tibbett led a typical cowboy life, but dreamed of a stage career; he played parts in Shakespearian productions. During World War I, he served in the U.S. Navy; after the Armistice, he earned a living by singing at weddings and funerals in a male quartet. He also took vocal lessons with Joseph Dupuy, Basil Ruysdael, Frank La Forge, and Ignaz Zitomirsky. He made his operatic debut in N.Y. with the Metropolitan Opera on Nov. 24, 1923, in the minor role of Lovitsky in *Boris Godunov;* then sang Valentin in *Faust* (Nov. 30, 1923); achieved a striking success as Ford in Verdi's *Falstaff* (Jan. 2, 1925), and thereafter was one of the leading members on its roster. Among his roles were Tonio in *Pagliacci*, Wolfram in *Tannhäuser*, Telramund in *Lohengrin*, Marcello in *La Bohème*, Scarpia in *Tosca*, Iago in *Otello*, and the title roles in *Rigoletto* and *Falstaff*. He also sang important parts in modern American operas, such as Colonel Ibbetson in Taylor's *Peter Ibbetson*, Brutus Jones in Gruenberg's *The Emperor Jones*, and Wrestling Bradford in Hanson's *Merry Mount*. During his first European tour in 1937, he sang the title role in the premiere of *Don Juan de Mañara* by Eugene Goossens (Covent Garden, London, June 24, 1937); he also sang in Paris, Vienna, and Stockholm. A sincere believer in musical democracy, he did not disdain the lower arts; he often appeared on the radio and in films, among them *The Rogue Song*, *The Southerner*, and *Cuban Love Song*. During World War II, he sang in army camps. He made his farewell appearance at the Metropolitan Opera as Ivan in *Khovanshchina* on March 24, 1950. His last stage appearance was in the musical comedy *Fanny* in 1956. He publ. an autobiography, *The Glory Road* (Brattleboro, Vt., 1933; reprint, 1977, with discography by W. Moran).

Bibl.: A. Farkas, ed., *L. T.: Singing Actor* (Portland, Maine, 1989); H. Weinstat and B. Wechsler, *Dear Rogue: A Biography of the American Baritone L. T.* (Portland, Ore., 1996).—**NS/LK/DM**

Tibbits, George (Richard), Australian composer and architect; b. Boulder, Nov. 7, 1933. He studied architecture and urban planning at the Univ. of Melbourne; music was his avocation, which he plied off and on at leisure hours. His compositions often follow pictorial and literary images; a number of his instrumental pieces bear titles related to passages from the writings of James Joyce; their technical idiom oscillates quaquaversally from a Dorian columnar manner to lapidary dodecaphony. In 1968 he was appointed lecturer in architectural history at the Univ. of Melbourne.

Works: Orch.: *Neuronis Nephronicus and His Lowly Queen* (1968); *Fanfare for the Great Hall* (1968); *I thought you were all glittering with the noblest of carriage*, after James Joyce (1969); *Serenade* (1969); *Beside the rivering waters of*, after James Joyce (1970); *Where oranges have been laid to rest upon the green*, after James Joyce (1971); *Antediluvia* for Strings (1971); *The Rose Garden of the Queen of Navarre* (1975); Violin Concerto (1975). **Chamber:** *Silop* for Flute and Celesta (1963); Quintet for Flute, Clarinet, Viola, Cello, and Piano (1964); String Sextet (1964); Trio for Flute, Viola, and Harpsichord (1964); *Ziz, King of Birds* for Flute, Clarinet, English Horn, French Horn, Violin, and Piano (1966); *Quashq* for Flute, Clarinet, Horn, and Piano (1966); *Pili* for 13 Instruments (1966); String Quartet (1968); *Macrame* for Flute, Bassoon, and Guitar (1974); *Gâteau* for Wind Quintet (1975). **Keyboard: Piano:** *Variations* for Piano, 4-Hands (1969); *Stasis*, 12 pieces (1970). **Organ:** *Fantasy on the ABC* (1975). **Vocal:** *5 Songs for* Contralto and Piano (1969); *Golden Builders* for Soprano, Small Chorus, and Chamber Ensemble (1972); *5 Bells* for Soprano and String Quartet, after Kenneth Slesson (1972); *Shadows* for Soprano, Harpsichord, and Small String Orch., after Kenneth Slesson (1974); *The Ice Fisherman—Lake Erie* for Soprano and Orch. (1974).
—**NS/LK/DM**

Tiberi, Frank, jazz tenor saxophonist, clarinetist, flutist, bassoonist; b. Camden, N.J., Dec. 4, 1928. He began club work at as a young teenager. He did performance tours with Bob Chester in 1948, and in the early 1950s with Benny Goodman, Urbie Green, Dizzy Gillespie, and others. For many years he has been in the Woody Herman band, first joining it under Herman in 1969 and then as its leader since 1987. He is a fascinating theoretician inspired by John Coltrane and has a legendary collection of unissued tapes of Coltrane performing in clubs.—**LP**

Tiby, Ottavio, Italian musicologist; b. Palermo, May 19, 1891; d. there, Dec. 4, 1955. He studied at the Palermo Cons., graduating in composition in 1921; later studied in Rome. Returning to Palermo, he devoted himself to collecting Sicilian songs. He was also an authority on Byzantine music.

Writings: *Acustica musicale e organologia degli strumenti musicali* (Palermo, 1933); *Antichi musicisti siciliani* (Palermo, 1933); *La musica bizantina: Teoria e storia* (Milan, 1938); *Vincenzo Bellini* (Turin, 1938); *Carl Maria von Weber* (Turin, 1941); *Claudio Monteverdi* (Turin, 1942); *La musica in Grecia e a Roma* (Florence, 1942); *I polifonisti siciliani del XVI e XVII secolo* (Palermo, 1969).
—**NS/LK/DM**

Tichatschek, Joseph (real name, **Josef Aloys Ticháček**), noted Bohemian tenor; b. Ober-Weckelsdorf, July 11, 1807; d. Blasewitz, Jan. 18, 1886. He was the son of a poor weaver. In 1827 he went to Vienna as a medical student, but then joined the chorus at the Kärnthnertortheater, and had vocal instruction from Ciccimara. He was engaged at Graz in 1837, then sang in Vienna (1837). His career received a new impetus after his highly successful appearance as Auber's Gustavus III in Dresden (Aug. 11, 1837); in 1838 he joined the Dresden Court Opera, where he remained one of its leading members until he was pensioned in 1861; continued to make appearances there until 1870. He created the roles of Rienzi (Oct. 20, 1842) and Tannhäuser (Oct. 19, 1845) in Wagner's operas. Wagner mentions him often and with great praise in his autobiography.

Bibl.: M. Fürstenau, *J. T.* (Dresden, 1868).—**NS/LK/DM**

Tiensuu, Jukka, prominent Finnish harpsichordist, pianist, conductor, teacher, and composer; b. Helsinki, Aug. 30, 1948. He was a pupil of Heininen at the Sibelius Academy in Helsinki (1967–72), where he received diplomas in piano and composition (1972); after attending the Juilliard School in N.Y. (1972–73), he pursued studies in harpsichord and Baroque chamber music at the Freiburg im Breisgau Staatliche Hochschule für Musik (diplomas, 1976). He then was active as a researcher and composer at IRCAM in Paris (1978–82); pursued computer music research at the Univ. of Calif. at San Diego and at the Mass. Inst. of Technology (1989).

He toured widely as a performer in Europe, North America, and Asia; served as director of the Helsinki Biennale in 1981 and 1983; was founder-director of the International Festival and Summer Academy of Contemporary Music in Viitasaari (1982); taught at the Sibelius Academy and gave master classes on Baroque and avant-garde music. In 1988 his *Tokko* was awarded 1st prize at the UNESCO International Composers Rostrum in Paris. As a performing musician, Tiensuu has won accolades for his insightful interpretations of both contemporary and Baroque scores. His own compositions utilize various avant-garde techniques.

WORKS: ORCH.: *Largo* for Strings (1971); *Flato* for Wind Orch. (Helsinki, Nov. 22, 1974); *Mxpzkl* (1977; Helsinki, March 13, 1985); *M* for Amplified Harpsichord, Percussion, and Strings (1980; Hilversum, Sept. 13, 1981); *Puro* for Clarinet and Orch. (Helsinki, April 26, 1989); *Lume* for Orch. and Tape (Helsinki, March 14, 1991); *Halo* (Kuopio, Nov. 19, 1994); *Plus V* for Accordion and Strings (Tampere, April 8, 1994); *Alma* for Orch. and Tape (Helsinki, Aug. 23, 1995); *Vento* for Clarinet Choir (1995). **CHAMBER:** *Cadenza* for Flute (Helsinki, Oct. 1, 1972); *Concerto da camera* for Cello, Flute, English Horn, Clarinet, and Bassoon (1972; Helsinki, March 24, 1973); *Ouverture* for Flute and Harpsichord (Helsinki, Oct. 1, 1972); *4 Etudes* for Flute (1974; No. 1, Helsinki, Feb. 22, 1978; Nos. 2 and 3, Helsinki, March 5, 1979; No. 4, Viitasaari, June 22, 1982); *PreLUDI, LUDI, postLUDI* for Guitar (1974; Helsinki, Nov. 8, 1983); *Aspro* for Clarinet, Trombone, Cello, and Piano (1975; Amsterdam, Sept. 1976); *Rubato* for Any Ensemble (1975; Helsinki, May 11, 1977); *Aufschwung* for Accordion (Lahti, Nov. 3, 1977); *Dolce amoroso* for Guitar (1978); *Sinistro* for Accordion and Guitar (Helsinki, Oct. 17, 1977); *Yang I* (Helsinki, Nov. 17, 1978) and *II* (1979; Helsinki, Nov. 8, 1983) for Ensemble; *Narcissus* for Oboe and Tape (Hameenlinna, July 3, 1979); *Le Tombeau de Beethoven* for Oboe, Cello, Piano, and Tape (Helsinki, Sept. 23, 1980); *Prélude mesuré* for Harpsichord and Optional Live Electronics (Viitasaari, July 26, 1983); *Fantango* for Any Keyboard Instrument (1984; with harpsichord, Viitasaari, Aug. 11, 1985); *Tango lunaire* for Oboe or Flute, Clarinet, Violin, Cello, and Any Keyboard Instrument (1985; Tampere, Feb. 15, 1986); *mutta* for 3 Accordions (1985–87; Helsinki, Nov. 2, 1985; rev. version, Viitasaari, July 27, 1987); *Manaus (Ghost Sonata)* for Concert Kantele (1988; Viitasaari, July 23, 1989); *Le Tombeau de Mozart* for Violin, Clarinet, and Piano (Turku, Aug. 18, 1990); *Arsenic and Old Lace* for Micro-tonally Tuned Harpsichord and String Quartet (Helsinki, Sept. 4, 1990); *Plus I* for Clarinet and Accordion (Helsinki, May 9, 1992), *II* for Clarinet and Cello (Helsinki, March 8, 1992), *III* for Cello and Accordion (Karkkila, Feb. 19, 1992), and *IV* for Clarinet, Accordion, and Cello (1992; Toronto, March 28, 1993); *oddjob* for Viola or Violin or Cello and Electronics (Helsinki, March 11, 1995). **Piano:** *Solo* for Piano and Live Electronics (Darmstadt, July 24, 1976); *Prélude non-mesuré* (Helsinki, June 15, 1976); */L* for Amplified Piano, 4-Hands (1981; Joensuu, Sept. 29, 1982); *...kahdenkesken* for Piano, 4-Hands (Helsinki, May 14, 1983); *Ground* (Helsinki, Feb. 15, 1990). **VOCAL:** *Tanka* for High Voice and Small Orch. (1973; Helsinki, April 23, 1976); *Passage* for Soprano, Chamber Ensemble, and Live Electronics (Paris, Feb. 25, 1980); *P=Pinocchio?* for Soprano, Flute, Bass Clarinet, Harpsichord, Violin, Cello, Tapes, and Computer (Paris, Dec. 3, 1982); *Tokko* for Men's Chorus and Computer-generated Tape (1987; Helsinki, May 14, 1988). **TAPE:** *Interludes I-IV* for Tape and Optional Harpsichord (Helsinki, March 11, 1987); *Prologi* (Helsinki, March 11, 1993); *Logos I-II* (Helsinki, March 11, 1993); *Epilogi* (Helsinki, March 11, 1993); *Sound of Life* (Helsinki, Nov. 27, 1993); *Ai* (Helsinki, Nov. 11, 1994). **—NS/LK/DM**

Tierney, Vivian, English soprano; b. London, Nov. 26, 1957. She studied with Rita Crosby, Eduardo Asquez, and Jeffrey Neilson-Taylor. At age 17, she joined the chorus of the D'Oyly Carte Co., and soon sang principal roles with it at home and abroad. After appearances with the Kent Opera and Opera 80, she made her debut with the English National Opera in London in *Orpheus in the Underworld* in 1986. In 1989 she created the role of Regan in the British premiere of Reimann's *Lear* in London. From 1989 to 1991 she was a member of the Freiburg im Breisgau Opera, where her roles included the Marschallin, Katerina Ismailova, Iduna in Burkhard's *Das Feuerwerk*, and Renata in *The Fiery Angel*. In 1990 she created the title role in Holloway's *Clarissa* in London. She portrayed Rosalinde at the English National Opera in 1991, and then sang Ellen Orford at the Glyndebourne Festival in 1992. In 1993 she was engaged as Berg's Marie with Opera North in Leeds. During the 1994–95 season, she sang the Dyer's Wife in *Die Frau ohne Schatten* in Basel. She appeared as Gutrune at London's Covent Garden in 1995. After appearing as Mrs. Coyle in *Owen Wingrave* at the Glyndebourne Festival in 1997, she returned to London to sing Tatiana in 1998 and Salome in 1999.**—NS/LK/DM**

Tiersot, (Jean-Baptiste-Elisée-) Julien, French musicologist; b. Bourg-en-Bresse, July 5, 1857; d. Paris, Aug. 10, 1936. He was a pupil of Savard, Massenet, and Franck at the Paris Cons. In 1883 he was appointed asst. librarian at the Cons., and in 1909, chief librarian, retiring in 1921. He was also a prof. at the École des Hautes Etudes Sociales and president of the Société Française de Musicologie. His compositions include a Mass on the tercentenary of the death of Roland de Lassus (1894), *Danses populaires françaises* for Orch. (1900), *Hellas* for Chorus and Orch., after Shelley, etc.

WRITINGS: (all publ. in Paris): *Histoire de la chanson populaire en France* (1889); *Musiques pittoresques: promenades musicales à l'Exposition de 1889* (1889); *Rouget de Lisle, Son oeuvre, sa vie* (1892); *Le messe Douce mémoire de Roland de Lassus* (1894); *Les Types mélodiques dans la chanson populaire française* (1894); *Étude sur les Maîtres-Chanteurs de Nuremberg de Richard Wagner* (1899); *Hector Berlioz et la société de son temps* (1904); *Les Fêtes et les chants de la Révolution française* (1908); *Gluck* (1910); *Beethoven, musicien de la Révolution* (1910); *Jean-Jacques Rousseau* (1912; 2nd ed., 1920); *Histoire de la Marseillaise* (1915); *Un Demi-siècle de musique française: entre deux guerres 1870–1917* (1918; 2nd ed., 1924); *La Musique dans la comédie de Molière* (1921); *La Damnation de Faust de Berlioz* (1924); *Les Couperin* (1926; 2nd ed., 1933); *Smetana* (1926); *La Musique aux temps romantiques* (1930); *La Chanson populaire et les écrivains romantiques* (1931); *Don Juan de Mozart* (1933); *J.-S. Bach* (1934). **FOLKSONG EDITIONS:** *Mélodies populaires des provinces de France* (1888–1928); *Noëls français* (1901); *Chansons populaires recueillies dans les Alpes françaises* (1903); *Chants populaires, pour les écoles* (1896–1902); *44 French Folksongs and Variants from Canada, Normandy, and Brittany*

(1910); *60 Folksongs of France* (1915); *Chansons populaires françaises* (1921); *Chansons nègres* (1933).

Bibl.: L. de La Laurencie, *Un musicien bressan: J. T.* (Bourg-en-Bresse, 1932).—**NS/LK/DM**

Tiessen, (Richard Gustav) Heinz, German conductor, music critic, teacher, and composer; b. Königsberg, April 10, 1887; d. Berlin, Nov. 29, 1971. He studied music with Rüfer and Klatte in Berlin. He was music critic of the *Allgemeine Musikzeitung* (1911–17); led Der Jungen Chor for children of workers (1922–32). In 1925 he was appointed to the faculty of the Hochschule für Musik in Berlin; from 1946 to 1949, was director of the Berlin Cons., returning in 1949 to the Hochschule. He left the Hochschule in 1955 to become director of the music division at the West Berlin Academy of the Arts. He publ. an autobiography, *Wege eines Komponisten* (Berlin, 1962). He composed in both traditional and modern idioms; birdcalls played a prominent role in a number of his works. His compositions include 2 syms. (1911, 1912), *Totentanz-Suite* for Violin and Orch. (1918; rev. as *Visionen*, 1954), *Konzertante Variationen über eine eigene Tanzmelodie* for Piano and Orch. (1962); *Amsel-Septett* for Flute, Clarinet, Horn, and String Quartet (1915; rev. 1957), String Quintet (1919–22), piano pieces, including a Sonata (1910), choruses, musical plays, and songs.—**NS/LK/DM**

Tietjen, Heinz, noted German conductor and opera producer; b. Tangier, June 24, 1881; d. Baden-Baden, Nov. 30, 1967. He studied conducting with Nikisch. He was then active as an opera producer in Trier (1904–22); later was administrator of the Berlin City Opera (1925–27); from 1931 to 1944, was artistic director of the Bayreuth Festivals, where he also conducted. He was again administrator of the Berlin City Opera (1948–55) and then of the Hamburg State Opera (1956–59). —**NS/LK/DM**

Tietjens, Therese (Carolina Johanna Alexandra), famous German soprano; b. Hamburg, July 17, 1831; d. London, Oct. 3, 1877. She was trained in Hamburg and Vienna, and in 1849 made her operatic debut in Altona as Donizetti's Lucrezia Borgia, which became her most celebrated role. After singing in Frankfurt am Main (1850–51), Brünn, and Vienna, she made her London debut as Valentine in *Les Huguenots* at Her Majesty's Theatre on April 13, 1858; subsequently appeared in London every season until her death, making her Covent Garden debut as Lucrezia Borgia on Oct. 24, 1868. She also sang opera in Paris (1863), at the Teatro San Carlo in Naples (1862–63; 1868–69), and in the U.S. (1874, 1876); also became well known as an oratorio singer in England. Stricken with cancer, she made her farewell appearance at Covent Garden as Lucrezia Borgia on May 19, 1877, collapsing on the stage at the close of the performance. Among her other outstanding roles were Mozart's Countess, Pamina, and Donna Anna, Cherubini's Medea, Beethoven's Leonore, Bellini's Norma, Verdi's Leonora, and Wagner's Ortrud. —**NS/LK/DM**

Tiffany (Renee Darwish), pop singer who became the first teenaged girl and the first person born in the 1970s to have a #1 record; b. Oct. 2, 1971. Tiffany Darwish made her first public appearance as a musician at the age of nine at a honky-tonk. After they passed the hat around for her, she went home with over $200. She performed in country venues around Los Angeles in the late 1970s. Mae Axton saw her at the Palomino one night and took the little 10- year-old to Nashville, where she made some demos and television appearances. By 1982, she was opening for artists including Jerry Lee Lewis and George Jones. In 1984 a songwriter asked her into the studio to sing on a demo of his songs. The studio owner, George Tobin, heard her and signed her to a management and production contract. Several singles came out without much success. Tiffany appeared on the syndicated TV show *Star Search* in 1985, losing to another teen singer. After a couple of years of plugging, Tobin finally got her signed to MCA.

MCA released her eponymous debut in 1987. At first, sales were slow. To promote her music to adolescent girls, they came up with "The Beautiful You: Celebrating the Good Life Shopping Mall Tour." Sending the young singer to 10 malls, it brought the music to her peers. After the Mall tour, she joined labelmates the Jets on a tour of high schools. Her cover of Tommy James's "I Think We're Alone Now" started to get heavy requests on the radio and MCA put it out as a single. It wound up displacing Michael Jackson atop the charts for two weeks. The follow-up single "Could've Been," hit #1 pop and adult contemporary as well. Another cover, "I Saw Him Standing There," rose to #7. In a matter of months, the album that had languished in the warehouses for months was #1 and quadruple platinum.

In 1988 Tiffany went on the road with New Kids on the Block as her opening act. In anticipation of her second album, her forthcoming single "All This Time" was played on the season premier of the popular sitcom "Growing Pains." The album *Hold an Old Friend's Hand* came out in November 1988, followed early in December by the single, "All This Time," which peaked at #6. However, the follow-up, "Radio Romance," stalled at #35. The album only went to #17 and single platinum. In 1989 Tiffany dubbed the voice of Judy Jetson and performed three songs on *The Jetsons* soundtrack, but the movie and the album both stiffed. Several more singles failed to chart.

With her next album, 1990's *New Inside*, Tiffany switched to a harder R&B sound, but the album didn't chart, despite several television guest appearances. Tiffany's career quickly collapsed. By 1993, she was playing lounges in Las Vegas and her *Dreams Never Die* album came out only in Japan. For the next few years, she gave herself over to her home and child. In 1997 she signed on with former Garth Brooks and Trisha Yearwood manager Pam Lewis to try and revive her country career. That fell by the wayside after about a year. She recorded a song for the movie *The Thin Pink Line* in 1998 and fronted the industrial band Front Line Assembly on a cover of U2's "New Year's Day" on a tribute album. Early in 2000 she signed a four-album deal with Modern Records, but as of this writing, nothing has been released.

DISC.: *Tiffany* (1987); *Hold an Old Friend's Hand* (1988); *New Inside* (1990).—**HB**

Tigranian, Armen (Tigran), Armenian composer and teacher; b. Alexandropol, Dec. 26, 1879; d. Tbilisi, Feb. 10, 1950. He studied flute and theory in Tiflis. He returned to Alexandropol in 1902 and organized a choral society, specializing in Armenian music; in 1913 he settled in Tiflis, where he became an esteemed music pedagogue; received the Order of Lenin in 1939. He composed the operas *Anush* (1908–12; Alexandropol, Aug. 17, 1912) and *David-bek* (1949; Yerevan, Dec. 3, 1950), *Dance Suite* for Orch. (1946), *The Bloody Night*, cantata (1936), *Suite of Armenian Dances* for Piano (1938) and numerous other piano pieces, songs, and theater music.

BIBL.: K. Melik-Wrtanessian, *A. T.* (Moscow, 1939); R. Atanian and M. Muradian, *A. T.* (Moscow, 1966).—**NS/LK/DM**

Tijardović, Ivo, Croatian composer; b. Split, Sept. 18, 1895; d. Zagreb, March 19, 1976. He studied in Zagreb. He began his professional career by conducting theater orchs. He wrote operettas of the Viennese type; of these, *Little Floramy* (1924) became successful in Yugoslavia. His opera *Dimnjiaci uz Jadran* (The Chimneys of the Adriatic Coast; Zagreb, Jan. 20, 1951) depicts the patriotic uprising of Yugoslav partisans during World War II; he also wrote the opera *Marco Polo* (Zagreb, Dec. 3, 1960).

BIBL.: I. Plamenac, *I. T.* (Split, 1954).—**NS/LK/DM**

Tikka, Kari (Juhani), Finnish conductor and composer; b. Siilinjärvi, April 13, 1946. He received training in oboe (diploma, 1968), in conducting from Panula (diploma, 1979), and in composition from Englund, Kokkonen, and Rautavaara at the Sibelius Academy in Helsinki; also studied conducting with Arvid Jansons in Leningrad and with Luigi Ricci in Rome. He played oboe in the Helsinki Phil. (1965–67) and the Finnish National Opera Orch. in Helsinki (1967–68). In 1968 he made his conducting debut in Helsinki; subsequently conducted at the Finnish National Opera there (1970–72), then was a conductor of the Finnish Radio Sym. Orch. (1972–76) and director of the Ensemble for Modern Music of the Finnish Radio. From 1975 to 1977 he was a conductor of the Royal Opera in Stockholm; then again was a conductor at the Finnish National Opera (from 1979); also appeared as a guest conductor throughout Europe. His works include a Cello Concerto (1984) and other orch. pieces, *The Prodigal Son*, oratorio for 3 Soloists, Chorus, and Orch. (1985), cantatas, accompanied and unaccompanied choral works, chamber music, and solo songs.—**NS/LK/DM**

Tikotsky, Evgeni (Karlovich), Russian composer of Polish descent; b. St. Petersburg, Dec. 25, 1893; d. Minsk, Nov. 24, 1970. He studied composition with Volkova-Bonch-Bruievich in St. Petersburg (1912–14) before pursuing the study of physics and mathematics at the Univ. there (1914–15). He taught in a music school in Bobruysk (1927–34); then settled in Minsk, where he taught at the music school (1934–41); was artistic director of the Belorussian State Phil. (1944–45; 1953–57). In 1944 he received the Order of Lenin and in 1955 was made a People's Artist of the U.S.S.R.

WORKS: DRAMATIC: Opera: *Mihas Podhorny* (Minsk, March 10, 1939); *Alesya* (Minsk, Dec. 24, 1944; rev. 1952–53). **OTHER:** Incidental music; film scores. **ORCH.:** 5 syms. (1927; 1941; 1948–59; 1958; 1963); Trombone Concerto (1934); Concerto for Piano and Belorussian Folk Orch. (1953; also for Piano and Sym. Orch., 1954); *Slava* (Glory), overture (1961). **OTHER:** Chamber works; choruses; folk song arrangements.

BIBL.: I. Gusin, *E.K. T.* (Moscow and Leningrad, 1965).—**NS/LK/DM**

Tilles, Nurit, accomplished American pianist; b. N.Y., May 29, 1952. She studied at the preparatory division of the Juilliard School of Music in N.Y. (1961–68) and at the Oberlin (Ohio) Coll. Cons. of Music (B.Mus., 1973); after taking courses in tabla and gamelan at the Center for World Music (1974), she attended the State Univ. of N.Y. at Stony Brook (M.Mus., 1976), where she studied piano with Gilbert Kalish and chamber music with Arthur Weisberg. She performed and recorded with Steve Reich and Musicians (from 1975), Laura Dean Dancers & Musicians (1980–82), the Mother Mallard Band, a.k.a. the David Borden Music Co. (1980–87), and the Meredith Monk Ensemble (from 1984); collaborated with Monk on Fayum Music for Voice and Hammered Dulcimer and frequently toured with her. In 1978 she formed the piano duo Double Edge with Edmund Niemann, giving premiere performances in the U.S. and Europe of works specially composed for them by Borden, John Cage, "Blue" Gene Tyranny et al. Her solo recording *Ragtime: Here and Now* received high critical praise.—**NS/LK/DM**

Tillyard, H(enry) J(ulius) W(etenhall), English musicologist; b. Cambridge, Nov. 18, 1881; d. Saffron Walden, Jan. 2, 1968. He studied at Gonville and Caius Coll., Cambridge (1900–04), then studied Greek church music with J. Sakellarides in Athens (1904–07). After teaching Greek at the Univ. of Edinburgh (1908–17), he was a prof. of classics at the Univ. of Johannesburg, South Africa (1919–21), prof. of Russian at the Univ. of Birmingham (1921–26), and prof. of Greek at the Univ. of Cardiff (1926–44); he then was a lecturer in classics at Rhodes Univ. in Grahamstown, South Africa (1946–49). Tillyard was an authority on Byzantine chant. He publ. *Byzantine Music and Hymnography* (London, 1923) and *Handbook of the Middle Byzantine Notation* in Monumenta Musicae Byzantinae, *Subsidia*, I (1935).—**NS/LK/DM**

Tilmant, Théophile (Alexandre), noted French violinist and conductor; b. Valenciennes, July 8, 1799; d. Asnières, near Paris, May 7, 1878. He studied violin with Rodolphe Kreutzer at the Paris Cons. (premier prix, 1819), then was a member of the orchs. at the Théâtre-Italien (from 1819) and of the Opéra (from 1825). He was deputy conductor of the Société des Concerts du Conservatoire (1818–60), and then its chief conductor (1860–63); also was deputy conductor (1834–38) and chief conductor (1838–49) of the Théâtre-Italien, as well as conductor of the Opéra-Comique (1849–68). With his brother, the cellist Alexandre Tilmant (b. Valenciennes, Oct. 14, 1808; d. Paris, June 13, 1880), he was active in a chamber music society. —NS/LK/DM

Tilmouth, Michael, English musicologist; b. Grimsby, Lincolnshire, Nov. 30, 1930; d. Edinburgh, Nov. 12, 1987. He was a student of Dart, John Stevens, and Orr at Christ's Coll., Cambridge (B.A., 1954; Ph.D., 1960, with the diss. *Chamber Music in England, 1675–1720*). He was asst. lecturer (1959–62), lecturer (1962–71), and Tovey Prof. of Music (from 1971) at the Univ. of Edinburgh. From 1968 to 1976 he was ed. of the *RMA Research Chronicle*. He also was general series ed. of Musica Britannica, for which he compiled the chamber music of Matthew Locke, XXXI-XXXII (1971–72). —NS/LK/DM

Tilney, Colin, English harpsichordist; b. London, Oct. 31, 1933. He studied modern languages and music at King's Coll., Cambridge, then took lessons in harpsichord with Mary Potts and with Gustav Leonhardt in Amsterdam. He subsequently became engaged as a soloist and ensemble player in England and on the Continent, making his first tour of the U.S. in 1971. His extensive repertoire covers the harpsichord literature of the 16th, 17th, and 18th centuries; it is his preference to use historical instruments or modern replicas of harpsichords, clavichords, and fortepianos in his concerts. —NS/LK/DM

Timmermans, Ferdinand, Dutch organist and carillonneur; b. Rotterdam, Sept. 7, 1891; d. Oostenrijk, July 8, 1967. He studied organ with J.H. Besselaar and H. de Vries. In 1924 he became the municipal carillonneur at Rotterdam, and in 1926, at Schiedam. He subsequently gave exhibitions in Belgium, France, and England; soon he won the reputation of being one of the world's greatest carillonneurs. On May 5, 1954, he gave a concert in Washington, D.C., playing on the 50-bell carillon presented to the U.S. by the people of the Netherlands. He publ. *Luidklokken en beiaarden in Nederland* (Amsterdam, 1944).—NS/LK/DM

Tinctoris, Johannes, renowned Franco-Flemish music theorist and lexicographer; b. Braine l'Alleud, near Nivelles, c. 1435; d. before Oct. 12, 1511. He matriculated at the German Nation of Orleans Univ. (April 1, 1463). About 1472 he became tutor to the daughter of King Ferdinand I of Naples. In 1487 Ferdinand dispatched him to the courts of Charles VIII of France and Maximilian of Rome to recruit singers for his chapel. At the time of his death, Tinctoris was a canon and prebendary in Nivelles. About 1472 he compiled a dictionary of musical terms, *Terminorum musicae diffinitorium* (Treviso, 1495), which was the first of its kind. The only other work known to have been publ. in his lifetime was *De inventione et usu musicae* (Naples, c. 1487). Tinctoris also wrote poetry, and served as a cleric. For editions of his writings, see C.E.H. de Coussemaker, ed., *Johannes Tinctoris tractatus de musica* (Lille, 1875) and A. Seay, *Johannes Tinctoris: Opera theoretica*, in Corpus scriptorum de musica, XXII (1975). For a modern edition of his musical works, see W. Melin, ed., *Johannes Tinctoris: Opera omnia*, in Corpus Mensurabilis musicae, XVIII (1976).

WRITINGS: *Terminorum musicae diffinitorium* (Treviso, 1495; Ger. tr. in *Jahrbuch für Musikwissenschaft*, I, 1863; French tr., Paris, 1951; Eng. tr., London, 1964); *Complexus effectuum musices* (written c. 1473–74; It. tr., Bologna, 1979); *Proportionale musices* (written c. 1473–74: Eng. tr. in *Journal of Music Theory*, I, 1957); *Liber imperfectionum notarum musicalium* (written c. 1474–75); *Tractatus de regulari valore notarum* (written c. 1474–75); *Tractatus de notis et pausis* (written c. 1474–75); *Liber de natura et proprietate tonorum* (dated Nov. 6, 1476; Eng. tr., Colorado Springs, 1967; 2nd ed., rev., 1976); *Liber de arte contrapuncti* (dated Oct. 11, 1477; Eng. tr. in *Musicological Studies and Documents*, V, 1961); *Tractatus alterationum* (written after 1477); *Scriptum super punctis musicalibus* (written after 1477); *Expositio manus* (written after 1477); *De inventione et usu musicae* (Naples, c. 1487).

WORKS: VOCAL: Sacred: *Missa "Cunctorum plasmator summus"* for 4 Voices; *Missa "Nos amis"* for 3 Voices; *Missa sine nomine* (2 for 3 Voices; one for 4 Voices); *Alleluia* for 2 Voices; *Fecit potentiam* for 2 Voices; *Lamentationes Jeremie* for 4 Voices; *O virgo miserere mei* for 3 Voices; *Virgo Dei throno digna* for 3 Voices. **Secular:** Various chansons.

BIBL.: G. Pannain, *La teoria musicale di Giovanni T.* (Naples, 1913); K. Weinmann, *J. T. und sein unbekannter Traktat "De inventione et usu musicae"* (Regensburg, 1917); L. Balmer, *Tonsystem und Kirchentöne bei J. T.* (diss., Univ. of Bern, 1935); E. Krenek, *A Discussion of the Treatment of Dissonances in Ockeghem's Masses as Compared with the Contrapuntal Theory of J. T.* (St. Paul, Minn., 1947); W. Melin, *The Music of J. T. (c. 1435–1511): A Comparative Study of Theory and Practice* (diss., Ohio State Univ., 1973); G. Gerritzen, *Untersuchungen zur Kontrapunktlehre des J. T.* (diss., Univ. of Cologne, 1974).—NS/LK/DM

Tinel, Edgar (Pierre Joseph), Belgian pianist, pedagogue, and composer; b. Sinaii, East Flanders, March 27, 1854; d. Brussels, Oct. 28, 1912. He was taught at first by his father, a schoolmaster and organist, then entered the Brussels Cons. in 1863 as a pupil of Brassin, Dupont, Gevaert, Kufferath, and Mailly; in 1873 he took 1st prize for piano playing and in 1877 won the Belgian Prix de Rome with the cantata *De Klokke Roeland*. In 1881 he became director of the Malines Inst. of Religious Music; was appointed to the staff of the Brussels Cons. in 1896, and in 1908 became its director. He publ. *Le Chant grégorien: Théorie sommaire de son exécution* (Mechelen, 1890). Among his works were the operas *Godelieve* (Brussels, July 22, 1897) and *Katharina* (Brussels, Feb. 27, 1909) and the oratorio *Franciscu* (Mechelen, 1888).

BIBL.: A. van der Elst, *E. T.* (Ghent, 1901); P. Tinel, *E. T.: Le récit de sa vie et l'exégèse de son œuvre de 1854 à 1886* (Brussels, 1922); idem, *E. T.* (Brussels, 1946).—NS/LK/DM

Tinsley, Pauline (Cecilia), English soprano; b. Wigan, March 27, 1928. She studied at the Northern School of Music in Manchester, then with Joan Cross at the National School of Opera in London. She made her operatic debut in London in 1951 as Desdemona in

Rossini's *Otello;* sang with the Welsh National Opera in Cardiff (from 1962) and the Handel Opera Soc. She joined the Sadler's Wells Opera in London in 1963; sang at London's Covent Garden from 1965. In 1969 she made her U.S. debut as Anna Bolena at the Santa Fe Opera, and later sang with other U.S. opera companies. Among her prominent roles were Mozart's Countess and Fiordiligi, Aida, Lady Macbeth, Elektra, and Turandot.—**NS/LK/DM**

Tintner, Georg (Bernhard), Austrian-born New Zealand conductor; b. Vienna, May 22, 1917; d. (suicide) Halifax, Oct. 2, 1999. He sang in the Vienna Boys' Choir (1926–30), with which he gained experience as a youthful conductor. He studied composition with Marx (diploma, 1936) and conducting with Weingartner (diploma, 1937) at the Vienna Academy of Music. In 1937 he became an asst. conductor at the Vienna Volksoper, but the Anschluss in 1938 compelled him to flee the Nazis. He settled in New Zealand and became a naturalized New Zealand citizen. He conducted the Auckland Choral Soc. (1946–54) and the Auckland String Players (1947–54), and then was resident conductor of the National Opera of Australia (1954–56) and the Elizabethan Trust Opera Co. (later the Australian Opera; 1956–63; 1965–67). From 1964 to 1968 he was music director of the New Zealand Opera in Wellington. He conducted the Cape Town Municipal Orch. (1966–67) and at the Sadler's Wells Opera in London (1967–70). From 1970 to 1973 he was music director of the West Australian Opera Co. He conducted at the Australian Opera from 1973 to 1976. From 1977 to 1987 he was music director of the Queensland Theatre Orch. in Brisbane. He was music director of Sym. Nova Scotia in Canada from 1987 to 1994, thereafter serving as its conductor laureate.—**NS/LK/DM**

Tiny Tim (originally, **Khaury, Herbert Buckingham),** oddball pop phenomenon of the late 1960s; b. N.Y., April 12, 1933; d. Minneapolis, Minn., Nov. 30, 1996. When Tiny Tim appeared on *Rowan & Martin's Laugh-In* in 1968, no one was quite sure what to make of him. Here's this guy with a massive, hooked nose, powdered face, and long, scraggly, dyed hair, wearing baggy clothes, singing one of the greatest hits of 1929 (12 weeks at #1 in 1929 for Nick Lucas), "Tiptoe Through the Tulips" in a vibrato-laden falsetto, strumming a ukulele.

As it turned out, the answer to both questions was yes. Herbert Khaury was born to a Lebanese father and Jewish mother, both working in the garment industry. As a young man, he didn't fit in. He spent hours poring through the sheet music collections at the N.Y. Public Library, learning songs on his ukulele. By the late 1950s, he was playing the songs of Rudy Vallee on the ukulele as "Larry Love the Singing Canary," performing at Hubert's Museum in Times Square as a freak attraction. By the early 1960s, he'd moved up in the world, playing places like Café Bizarre in Greenwich Village. By 1964, he had taken the Dickensian moniker of Tiny Tim for keeps and often played at a club called the Scene, one of the places Jimi Hendrix would frequent only a few years later. Tim earned some notoriety for singing both parts of romantic duets, singing the woman's part in a warbly falsetto and the man's in his natural baritone. He was booked on TV shows like Merv Griffin and earned a part in Peter Yarrow's film *You Are What You Eat*. Yarrow, of Peter, Paul, and Mary, brought Tim to the attention of the president of his record company, who signed the unlikely performer. His first album, 1968's *God Bless Tiny Tim*, which included "Tiptoe through the Tulips," went to #7 while the single hit #17. Thus began Tim's 15 minutes of fame.

Tim became a regular on the *Tonight Show*, leading to his Dec. 17, 1969 wedding to 17-year-old "Miss Vicki" Budinger on the show. For several decades, this episode of the show was the highest-rated late night show ever! However, Tim's second album didn't do nearly as well, and by the time he put out *For All My Little Friends* in 1969, he had lost his novelty appeal. There just weren't that many people who enjoyed the sheer musicology of what Tim did. By 1977, his marriage to Budinger had gone the way of his musical career. Tim performed club dates when he could through the late 1970s and 1980s, occasionally recording material that ranged from minstrel show songs from the turn of the century to AC/DC.

In the mid-1990s, Tim attracted the attention of a new generation of musical experimenters. In 1996 he recorded *Girl* with Tex.-bred polkamaniacs Brave Combo, featuring his underground hit cover of "Hey Jude." He also appeared on TV shows like *Roseanne*. In the midst of this renewed activity, he suffered a heart attack, collapsing on stage at a ukulele convention in Mass. He died shortly afterwards in his new hometown of Minneapolis, where he'd moved after his third marriage.

Disc.: *God Bless Tiny Tim* (1968); *Tiny Tim's Second Album* (1969); *For All My Little Friends* (1969); *Tiptoe through the Tulips: Resurrection* (1987); *Live in Chicago* (1995); *I Love Me* (1995); *Prisoner of Love* (1996); *Girl* (1996); *Christmas Album* (1996); *Rock* (2000).—**HB**

Tio, Lorenzo, Jr., early jazz clarinetist, tenor saxophonist, arranger, oboist; b. New Orleans, April 21, 1893 (from his draft registration); d. N.Y., Dec. 24, 1933. His father, Lorenzo Sr. (1866–c. 1920), and his uncle, Luis "Papa" (1863–1927), were renowned clarinetists and teachers. From c. 1910 he played with the Onward Brass Band and began regular teaching, some of his pupils included: Barney Bigard (who was also said to have studied with his uncle), Albert Burbank, Johnny Dodds, Albert Nicholas, Jimmie Noone. He played with Papa Celestin from c. 1913, and then worked in Chicago with Manuel Perez in 1916. A year later he returned to New Orleans, rejoined Papa Celestin, and from 1918–28 worked mainly with Armand Piron (including N.Y. residencies). He worked in New Orleans with the Tuxedo Brass Band, then returned to N.Y., where he freelanced and played for a period on the Albany, N.Y., steamboats. He returned to New Orleans again and worked regularly with Armand Piron. During the last few months of his life he played at the Nest Club in N.Y. After his death, his body was taken back to New Orleans for burial.

DISC.: **JELLY ROLL MORTON:** *1929–30* (1996); *New York: 1928–30: Great Original Performances* (2000).

BIBL.: Charles Kinzer, *The Tio Family: Four Generations of New Orleans Musicians, 1814–1933* (LSU, 1993).—**JC/LP**

Tiomkin, Dimitri, Ukrainian-born American composer of film music; b. Poltava, May 10, 1894; d. London, Nov. 11, 1979. He studied composition with Glazunov and piano with Blumenfeld and Vengerova at the St. Petersburg Cons., and in 1921 went to Berlin, where he studied with Busoni, Petri, and Zadora. He was soloist in Liszt's 1st Piano Concerto with the Berlin Phil. (June 15, 1924), and that same year gave several concerts with Michael Khariton in Paris. He appeared in vaudeville in the U.S. in 1925. In 1937 he became a naturalized American citizen. He made his conducting debut with the Los Angeles Phil. (Aug. 16, 1938), and later conducted his music with various U.S. orchs. Tiomkin married Albertina Rasch, a ballerina, for whose troupe he wrote music. From 1930 to 1970 he wrote over 150 film scores, including several for the U.S. War Dept. Among his most notable scores were *Alice in Wonderland* (1933), *Mr. Smith Goes to Washington* (1939), *The Corsican Brothers* (1942), *The Moon and Sixpence* (1943), *The Bridge of San Luis Rey* (1944), *Duel in the Sun* (1946), *Champion* (1949), *High Noon* (1952; Academy Award), *Dial M for Murder* (1954), *The High and the Mighty* (1954; Academy Award), *Giant* (1956), *The Old Man and the Sea* (1958; Academy Award), *The Alamo* (1960), *The Guns of Navarone* (1961), *55 Days at Peking* (1963), *The Fall of the Roman Empire* (1964), and *Tchaikovsky* (1970). His film music betrayed his strong Russian Romantic background, tempered with American jazz. He received an honorary LL.D. from St. Mary's Univ., San Antonio, Tex.; was made a Chevalier and an Officer of the French Légion d'honneur; also received awards of merit, scrolls of appreciation, plaques of recognition, and a Golden Globe. With P. Buranelli, he publ. the autobiography *Please Don't Hate Me* (N.Y., 1959).

BIBL.: C. Palmer, *D. T.: A Portrait* (London, 1984).
—**NS/LK/DM**

Tipo, Maria (Luisa), Italian pianist and pedagogue; b. Naples, Dec. 23, 1931. She studied in Naples before completing her training with Casella and Agosti. In 1948 she won 2nd prize (no 1st prize was given) at the Geneva International Competition, and returned in 1949 to capture its 1st prize; after winning 3rd prize at the Queen Elisabeth of Belgium Competition in Brussels in 1952, she toured in Europe and abroad; in 1955 she made her N.Y. debut; she eventually devoted much time to teaching, giving courses at the Bolzano Cons. and in Florence and Geneva. After an absence of 32 years, she returned to N.Y. in 1991 as a recitalist at the Metropolitan Museum of Art. She championed the cause of traditional Italian keyboard music, most notably the works of Scarlatti and Clementi.—**NS/LK/DM**

Tippett, Sir Michael (Kemp), greatly renowned English composer; b. London, Jan. 2, 1905. His family was of Cornish descent, and Tippett never refrained from proclaiming his pride of Celtic ancestry. He was equally emphatic in the liberal beliefs of his family. His father was a free thinker, which did not prevent him from running a successful hotel business. His mother was a suffragette who once served a prison term. Her last name was Kemp, which Tippett eventually accepted as his own middle name. He took piano lessons as a child and sang in his school chorus but showed no exceptional merit as a performer. He studied in London at the Royal Coll. of Music (1923–28), where his teachers in composition were Charles Wood and C.H. Kitson; took piano lessons there with Aubin Raymar and attended courses in conducting with Boult and Sargent; studied counterpoint and fugue with R.O. Morris (1930–32). He subsequently held several positions as a teacher and conductor; from 1933 to 1940 he led the South London Orch. at Morley Coll.; then served as director of music there (1940–51). Socially Tippett had difficulties even early in life. He openly proclaimed his extremely liberal political views, his overt atheism, and his strenuous pacifism. His oratorio *A Child of Our Time* was inspired by the case of Henschel Grynsban, a Jewish boy who assassinated a member of the German embassy in Paris in 1938. As a conscientious objector during World War II, he refused to serve even in a non-combatant capacity in the British military forces; for this intransigent attitude he was sentenced to prison for 3 months; he served his term in a Surrey County gaol with the suggestive name Wormwood Scrubs (June 21-Aug. 21, 1943). He regained the respect of the community after the end of the war. In 1951 he initiated a series of broadcasts for the BBC; from 1969 to 1974 he directed the Bath Festival. He received high honors from the British government; in 1959 he was named a Commander of the Order of the British Empire; in 1966 he was knighted; in 1979 he was made a Companion of Honour; in 1983 he received the Order of Merit. He visited the U.S. in 1965, and thereafter was a frequent guest in America; his symphonic works were often performed by major American orchs. Tippett's works have a grandeur of Romantic inspiration that sets them apart from the prevalent type of contemporary music; they are infused with rhapsodic eloquence and further enhanced by a pervading lyric sentiment free from facile sentimentality. He excelled in large-scale vocal and instrumental forms; he was a consummate master of the modern idioms, attaining heights of dissonant counterpoint without losing the teleological sense of inherent tonality. Yet he did not shun special effects; 3 times in his 4th Sym. he injects episodes of heavy glottal aspiration, suggested to him by viewing a film depicting the dissection of fetuses of pigs. A man of great general culture, Tippett possesses a fine literary gift; he writes his own librettos for his operas and oratorios. He publ. *Moving into Aquarius* (London, 1958; 2nd ed., 1974). M. Bowen ed. *Music of the Angels: Essays and Sketchbooks of Michael Tippett* (London, 1980). Tippett's autobiography was publ. as *Those Twentieth-Century Blues* (London, 1991). M. Bowen ed. the vol. *Tippett on Music* (Oxford, 1995).

WORKS: **DRAMATIC:** *Don Juan*, incidental music to Flecker's play (Oxted, Feb. 1930); *Robin Hood*, folk song opera (1934); *Robert of Sicily*, children's opera (1938); *The Midsummer Marriage*, opera (1946–52; London, Jan. 27, 1955); *King Priam*, opera (1958–61; Coventry, May 29, 1962); *The Tempest*, incidental music to Shakespeare's play (London, May 29, 1962); *The Knot Garden*, opera (1966–69; London, Dec. 2, 1970); *The Ice Break*, opera (1973–76; London, July 7, 1977); *New Year*, opera (1986–88; Houston, Oct. 27, 1989). **ORCH.:** 1 unnumbered sym. (1933; rev. 1934); 4 numbered syms.: No. 1 (1944–45; Liverpool, Nov. 10, 1945), No. 2 (1956–57; London, Feb. 5, 1958), No. 3 for Soprano and Orch. (1970–72; London, June 22, 1972), and No. 4 (1976–77; Chicago, Oct. 6, 1977); Concerto for Double String Orch. (1938–39; London, April 21, 1940, composer conducting); *Fantasia on a Theme by Handel* for Piano and Orch. (1939–41; London, March 7, 1942); *Little Music* for Strings (London, Nov. 9, 1946); *Ritual Dances from The Midsummer Marriage* (1947–52; Basel, Feb. 13, 1953); *Suite in D for the Birthday of Prince Charles* (BBC, London, Nov. 15, 1948); *Fantasia Concertante on a Theme by Corelli* for Strings (London, Aug. 29, 1953, composer conducting); *Divertimento on Sellinger's Round* (1953–54; Zürich, Nov. 5, 1954); Piano Concerto (1953–55; Birmingham, Oct. 30, 1956); *Concerto for Orchestra* (1962–63; Edinburgh, Aug. 28, 1963); *Braint* (1966; Swansea, Jan. 11, 1967); Triple Concerto for Violin, Viola, Cello, and Orch. (1978–79; London, Aug. 22, 1980); *Water Out of Sunlight* for Strings (London, June 15, 1988; arr. from the String Quartet No. 4 by M. Bowen); *New Year Suite* (1989); *The Rose Lake* (1991–93). **Band:** *Festal Brass with Blues* (1983; Hong Kong, Feb. 6, 1984); *Triumph* (1992). **CHAMBER:** String Trio (1932; London, Jan. 13, 1965); 5 string quartets: No. 1 (1934–35; London, Dec. 9, 1935; rev. 1943), No. 2 (1941–42; London, March 27, 1943), No. 3 (1945–46; London, March 27, 1946), No. 4 (1977–78; Bath, May 20, 1979), and No. 5 (1990–91); 5 fanfares for Brass: No. 1 (Northampton, Sept. 21, 1943), No. 2 (St. Ives, June 6, 1953), No. 3 (St. Ives, June 6, 1953), No. 4, *Wolf Trap* (Vienna, Va., June 29, 1980), and No. 5 (1987); *4 Inventions* for Descant and Treble Recorders (London, Aug. 1, 1954); Sonata for 4 Horns (London, Dec. 20, 1955); *Praeludium* for Brass, Bells, and Percussion (London, Nov. 14, 1962); *In memoriam magistri* for Flute, Clarinet, and String Quartet (1971; London, June 17, 1972); *The Blue Guitar* for Guitar (1982–83; Pasadena, Calif., Nov. 9, 1983); *Prelude: Autumn* for Oboe and Piano (1991). **KEYBOARD: Piano:** *Jockey to the Fair* (1929–30; Oxted, April 5, 1930); 4 sonatas: No. 1 (1936–38; London, Nov. 11, 1938; rev. 1942 and 1954), No. 2 (Edinburgh, Sept. 3, 1962), No. 3 (1972–73; Bath, May 26, 1973), and No. 4 (1984; Los Angeles, Jan. 14, 1985). **Organ:** *Preludio al Vespro di Monteverdi* (London, July 5, 1946). **VOCAL:** *A Child of Our Time*, oratorio for Soprano, Alto, Tenor, Bass, Chorus, and Orch., to a text by the composer about a Jewish boy (Henschel Grynsban) who, in 1938, assassinated a Nazi member of the German embassy in Paris (1939–41; London, March 19, 1944); *The Source* for Chorus (1942; London, July 17, 1943); *The Windhover* for Chorus (1942; London, July 17, 1943); *Boyhood's End*, cantata for Tenor and Piano, after W.H. Hudson (London, June 5, 1943); *Plebs angelica* for Double Chorus (1943–44; Canterbury, Sept. 16, 1944); *The Weeping Babe* for Soprano and Chorus (London, Dec. 24, 1944); *The Heart's Assurance*, song cycle for Voice and Piano, after Sidney Keyes and Alun Lewis (1950–51; London, May 7, 1951; arr. for Voice and Orch. by M. Bowen, 1990); *Dance, Clarion Air*, madrigal for 5 Voices, after Christopher Fry (1952; London, June 1, 1953); *Bonny at Morn* for Unison Voices and 3 Recorders (Trogen, Switzerland, April 1956); *4 Songs from the British Isles* for Chorus (1956; Royaumont, France, July 6, 1958); *Crown of the Year*, cantata for Chorus and Chamber Ensemble, after Christopher Fry (Bristol, July 25, 1958); *Lullaby* for Alto and Chorus (1959; London, Jan. 31, 1960); *Music* for Voices, Strings, and Piano (Tunbridge Wells, April 26, 1960; also for Voices and Piano); *Music for Words, Perhaps* for Narrator and Chamber Ensemble, after W.B. Yeats (London, June 8, 1960); *Magnificat and Nunc Dimittis* for Chorus and Organ (1961; Cambridge, March 13, 1962); *Songs for Achilles* for Tenor and Guitar (Aldeburgh, July 7, 1961); *Songs for Ariel* for Voice and Piano or Harpsichord or Chamber Ensemble (1962; London, Sept. 21, 1963); *The Vision of Saint Augustine* for Baritone, Chorus, and Orch. (1963–65; London, Jan. 19, 1966, Dietrich Fischer-Dieskau soloist, composer conducting); *The Shires Suite* for Chorus and Orch. (1965–70; Cheltenham, July 8, 1970, composer conducting); *Songs for Dov* for Tenor and Small Orch. (1969–70; Cardiff, Oct. 12, 1970); *The Mask of Time* for Soprano, Mezzo-soprano, Tenor, Baritone, Chorus, and Orch. (1980–82; Boston, April 5, 1984); *Byzantium* for Soprano and Orch. (1989–90; Chicago, April 11, 1991).

BIBL.: I. Kemp, ed., *M. T.: A Symposium on His 60th Birthday* (London, 1965); M. Hurd, *T.* (London, 1978); E. White, *T. and His Operas* (London, 1979); D. Matthews, *M. T.: An Introductory Study* (London, 1980); M. Bowen, *M. T.* (London, 1982); A. Whittall, *The Music of Britten and T.: Studies in Themes and Techniques* (Cambridge, 1982; 2nd ed., 1990); I. Kemp, *T.: the Composer and his Music* (London, 1984); N. John, ed., *Operas of M. T.* (London, 1985); G. Lewis, ed., *M. T. O. M.: A Celebration* (Tunbridge Wells, 1985); G. Theil, *M. T.: a Bio-Bibliography* (Westport, Conn., 1989); M. Scheppach, *Dramatic Parallels in M. T.'s Operas: Analytical Essays on the Musico-Dramatic Techniques* (Lewiston, N.Y., 1990); R. Jones, *The Early Operas of M. T.: A Study of The Midsummer Marriage, King Priam, and The Knot Garden* (Lewiston, N.Y., 1996); M. Bowen, *M. T.* (N.Y., 1998); D. Clarke, *T. Studies* (Cambridge, 1998).—**NS/LK/DM**

Tischhauser, Franz, Swiss composer; b. Bern, March 28, 1921. He studied counterpoint and composition with Paul Müller and piano with Walter Lang and Rudolf Wittelsbach at the Zürich Cons. In 1951 he joined the staff of the Zürich Radio, and later served as director of its music dept. (1971–83).

WORKS: ORCH.: *Der Geburtstag der Infantin* (1941); Concertino for Piano and Small Orch. (1945); *Feierabendmusik* for Strings (1946); *Landpartie* for 2 Horns and Strings (1948); *Seldwyliana* for Orch. and Percussion (1960–61); *Omaggi a Mälzel* for 12 Strings (1963); *Mattinata* for 23 Winds (1965); *Konzertänze* for 2 Orchs. (1967–68); *The Beggar's Concerto*, concerto for Clarinet and Strings (1975–76); *Dr. Bircher und Rossini* for Harpsichord and Strings (1978–79). **CHAMBER:** *Kassation* for 9 Instruments (1951); Octet for Clarinet, Horn, Bassoon, 2 Violins, Viola, Cello, and Double Bass (1953); *Die Bremer Stadtmusikanten* for Bassoon, Clarinet, Oboe, Flute, and Piano (1982–83); *Das Vierklaklavier* for 4 Clarinets (1984); *Beschallung der Stadt Kalau* for Horn Quartet and Wind Octet (1989); piano music. **VOCAL:** *Klein Irmchen*, 6 songs for Soprano and Piano (1937); *Duo Catulli carmina* for Tenor and Guitar (1949); *Das Nasobem* for Chorus (1950); *Amores* for Tenor, Trumpet, Percussion, and Stringed Instrument (1955–56); *Punctus contra punctum* for Tenor, Bass, and Small Orch. (1962); *Antiphonarium profanum* for 2 Men's Choruses (1966–67); *Eve's Meditation on Love* for Soprano, Tuba, and String Orch. (1970–71); *Die Hampeloper oder Joggeli söll ga Birli schüttle!* for 11 Vocalists, 3 Choral Groups, and Small Orch. (1985–86).—**NS/LK/DM**

Tischler, Hans, distinguished Austrian-American musicologist; b. Vienna, Jan. 18, 1915. He studied piano with Paul Wittgenstein and Bertha Jahn-Beer, composition with Richard Stohr and Franz Schmidt, and musicology with Robert Lach, Robert Haas, and Egon Wellesz at the Univ. of Vienna (Ph.D., 1937, with the diss. *Die Harmonik in den Werken Gustav Mahlers*). He left Austria in 1938, and continued his musicological studies with Leo Schrade at Yale Univ. (Ph.D., 1942, with the diss. *The Motet in 13th-Century France*). He taught music history at W. Va. Wesleyan Coll. (1945–47) and at Roosevelt Univ. in Chicago (1947–65). In 1965 he was appointed prof. of musicology at Ind. Univ. in Bloomington, where he remained until his retirement in 1985.

WRITINGS: *The Perceptive Music Listener* (N.Y., 1955); *Practical Harmony* (Boston, 1964); *A Structural Analysis of Mozart's Piano Concertos* (Brooklyn, N.Y., 1966); the Eng. ed. of Willi Apel's *History of Keyboard Music to 1700* (Bloomington, Ind., 1973); *A Medieval Motet Book* (N.Y., 1973); *The Montpellier Codex* (3 vols., Madison, Wisc., 1978); with S. Rosenberg, *Chanter m'estuet: Songs of the Trouvères* (Bloomington, 1981); *The Earliest Motets: A Complete Comparative Edition* (New Haven, Conn., 1982); *The Earliest Motets: Their Style and Evolution* (Henryville, Pa., 1985); *The Parisian Two-Part Organa: A Complete Comparative Edition* (N.Y., 1987); *The Monophonic Songs in the Roman de Fauvel* (Toronto, 1988); *Trouvère Lyrics with Melodies: Complete Comparative Edition* (Stuttgart-Neuhausen, 1997).—**NS/LK/DM**

Tishchenko, Boris (Ivanovich), Russian composer and teacher; b. Leningrad, March 23, 1939. He was a student of Salmanov, Voloshinov, and Evlakhov at the Leningrad Cons. (graduated, 1962), and then of Shostakovich (1962–65). In 1965 he joined the faculty of the Leningrad Cons., where he was made an assoc. prof. in 1980 and a full prof. in 1986. In 1978 he was awarded the Glinka Prize and in 1987 was made a People's Artist of the U.S.S.R. Tishchenko's music is crafted in a masterly fashion in an advanced idiom without overstepping the bounds of tonality.

WORKS: **DRAMATIC:** *The 12*, ballet (1963); *Fly-bee*, ballet (1968); *The Stolen Sun*, opera (1968); *A Cockroach*, musical comedy (1968); *The Eclipse*, ballet (1974); incidental music. **ORCH.:** 2 violin concertos: No. 1, op.9/29 (1958; rev. as op.29, 1964) and No. 2, op.84 (1981); 7 syms.: No. 1 (1960), No. 2, *Marina*, for Chorus and Orch. (1964), No. 3 for Chamber Orch. (1966), No. 4 for Narrator and Orch. (1974), No. 5 (1976), No. 6 for Soprano, Contralto, and Orch. (1988), and No. 7 (1993); *The French Symphony*, op.12/116 (1958; rev. as op.116, 1993); Piano Concerto (1962); 2 cello concertos: No. 1 for Cello, 17 Winds, Percussion, and Harmonium (1963) and No. 2 for Cello, 48 Cellos, 12 Double Basses, and Percussion (1969; also for Cello and Orch., 1979); *Sinfonia Robusta* (1970); Concerto for Flute, Piano, and Strings (1972); Harp Concerto (1977); *The Siege Chronicles*, sym. (1984); *Pushkin Symphony*, op.38/125 (1998; rev. version of the incidental music to *Death of Pushkin*, op.38, 1967). **CHAMBER:** 5 string quartets (1957, 1959, 1969, 1980, 1984); 2 sonatas for Solo Violin (1957, 1976); 2 sonatas for Solo Cello (1960, 1979); *Capriccio* for Violin and Piano (1965); Piano Quintet (1985); 4 Pieces for Tuba (1985); *The Dog's Heart*, "novels" for Chamber Ensemble (1988); *Concerto alla marcia* for 16 Soloists (1989); Concerto for Clarinet and Piano Trio (1990); *Fantasy* for Violin and Piano (1994); Sonata for 5 Recorders (1 Player) and Organ (1999). **KEYBOARD:** **Piano:** 2 suites (1957, 1957); 10 sonatas (1957, rev. 1995; 1960; 1965; 1972; 1973; 1976; 1982, with bells; 1986; 1992; 1997, a revision of Suite No. 1); *8 Portraits* for Piano, 4-Hands (1996). **Organ:** *12 Inventions* (1964); *12 Portraits* (1992). **VOCAL:** *Lenin is Alive*, cantata (1959); *Suzdal*, suite for Soprano, Tenor, and Chamber Orch. (1964); *Requiem* for Soprano, Tenor, and Orch. (1966); *To My Brother* for Soprano, Flute, and Harp (1986); *The Will* for Soprano, Harp, and Organ (1986); *The Garden of Music*, cantata (1987); *The Chelom Wise Men* for Soprano, Bass, Violin, and Piano (1991).—**NS/LK/DM**

Tisné, Antoine, French composer; b. Lourdes, Nov. 29, 1932; d. Paris, Feb. 14, 1998. He studied at the Paris Cons. with Hugon, N. Gallon, Dufourcq, Milhaud, and Rivier, taking premiers prix in harmony, counterpoint, fugue, and composition. In 1962 he won the 2nd Grand Prix de Rome and the Lili Boulanger Prize. From 1967 to 1992 he served as an inspector of music for the French Ministry of Culture. He also was a prof. of composition and orchestration at the Univ. of Paris. In 1992 he became inspector of music for the municipal conservatoires of the City of Paris. Among his honors were the Grand Prix musical of the City of Paris (1979) and the prize for composers of the Soc. of Authors, Composers, and Editors of Music (1988). In his music, Tisné adopted various contemporary techniques.

WORKS: **DRAMATIC:** *La Ramasseuse de sarments*, music theater (1980); *Point fixe*, ballet (1982); *Les Enfants du Ciel*, children's musical spectacle (1984); *Instant*, ballet (1985); *Le Chemin des bulles*, children's opera (1988); *Pour l'amour d'Alban*, opera (1993). **ORCH.:** 4 piano concertos (1959, 1961, 1962, 1992); 3 syms. (1959, 1963, 1994); *Chant d'amour et de mort* (1962); *A une ombre* (1962); *Mouvements symphoniques* (1963); Cello Concerto (1965); Concerto for Flute and Strings (1965); *Étude d'après Goya* (1966); *Cosmogonies* for 3 Orchs. (1967); *Séquences pour un rituel* for Strings (1968); Violin Concerto (1969); *Arches de lumière* (1972); *Ondes flamboyantes* for Strings (1973); *Stratégies* for 4 Brass Groups (1973); *Impacts* for Ondes Martenot and 2 String Orchs. (1973); *Dolmen II* for Percussion Ensemble (1978); *Reliefs irradiants de N.Y.* (1979); *Orbes de feu* (1981); *Temps spectral* for Piano, 2 Wind Ensembles, and Percussion (1982); *Mouvement concertant* for Piano, Brass, and Strings (1985); *La Tour* for Harmony Orch. (1987); *Hymne pour notre temps* for 15 Saxophones (1989); *Les Voiles de la nuit* (1991); *De la nuit à l'aurore* for Oboe and Strings (1991); *Célébration II* for Strings (1991). **CHAMBER:** 4 string quartets (1956, 1979, 1979, 1988); Cello Sonata (1960); Wind Quintet (1961); Violin Sonata (1963); *Visions des temps immémoriaux* for Ondes Martenot, Piano, and Percussion (1964); Flute Sonata (1964); Viola Sonata (1966); *Musique en trio* for Piano, Violin, and Cello (1967); *Strates colorées* for Oboe, Trumpet, Trombone, and Viola (1970); *Profils d'ombres* for Violin and Piano (1972); *Héraldiques* for Trumpet and Piano (1975); *Les Muses inquiétantes* for Wind Septet and Percussion (1975); *Isomorphies* for String Sextet (1975); *Musique en quatuor* for Flute, Clarinet, Violin, and Cello (1976); *Profils éclatés* for Organ and 5 Brass (1976); *Reflets d'un songe* for Flute, Viola, and Harp (1977); *Cyclades* for Ondes Martenot and Piano (1978); *Espaces irradiés* for Alto Saxophone and Piano (1978); *3 Études* for String Quartet (1978); *Iles de temps* for Ondes Martenot Sextet (1980); *Épisodes new-yorkais* for Flute, Clarinet, Violin, Cello, Piano, and Reciter ad libitum (1985); *Sérénade de la nuit* for Flute, Violin, and Viola (1990); *Les Voix de l'ombre* for Flute and String Trio (1991); *3 Études d'apres des toiles de Maurice Denis* for Flute and String Trio (1994). **KEYBOARD:** **Piano:** Sonata (1964); *Soleils noirs* (1967); *Solars Vortices* (1970); *Bocéphal* for 2 Pianos (1982). **Organ:** *Luminescenes* (1974); *Alatamira* (1975); *Préludes* (1989); *Processional* (1993). **VOCAL:** *Cantique du printemps* for Soprano, Tenor, and Orch. (1960); *Chants d'espace I* and *II* for Children's Chorus (1974); *Célébration I* for 3 Choruses and

3 Orchs. (1975); *Ragas* for Reciter and Ondes Martenot Trio (1978); *Passage* for Soprano and Strings (1985); *L'Heure des hommes*, oratorio for Soprano, Men's Chorus, and Harmony Orch. (1985); *Le Fond du temps* for 12 Voices (1986); *Le Chant des yeux*, oratorio for Soprano, Chorus, and Orch. (1986); *Antienne pour l'au-delà* for Baritone and Strings (1987); *Psaume 138* and *57* for Vocal Ensemble, Chorus, and Organ (1989); *Maryam*, oratorio for Soloists, Chorus, and Orch. (1990); *Dans la lumière d'Orcival* for Chorus (1992); *Invocation* for Baritone and Orch. (1993).

Bibl.: D. Niemann, *A. T., ou composer c'est exister* (Paris, 1991).—**NS/LK/DM**

Titelouze, Jean or **Jehan,** eminent French organist and composer; b. St. Omer, c. 1562; d. Rouen, Oct. 24, 1633. He is believed to have received his academic and musical training in St. Omer, where he was a priest and substitute organist at the Cathedral by 1585; that same year he settled in Rouen as organist at St. Jean. He served as organist at Rouen Cathedral from 1588 until his death, and also was made canon by the cathedral chapter there in 1610. He was the pioneering figure of the French organ school. He publ. 2 major collections, *Hymnes de l'Église pour toucher sur l'orgue, avec les fugues et recherches sur leur plain-chant* (Paris, 1623) and *Le Magnificat, ou Cantique de la Vierge pour toucher sur l'orgue, suivant les huit tons de l'Église* (Paris, 1626), versets based on plainsong. His vocal music is lost. He was also a poet and won awards from the Académie des Palinods (1613, 1630) as well as the title of Prince des Palinods in 1630. For his extant music, see A. Guilmant and A. Pirro, *J. Titelouze: OEuvres complètes d'orgue*, Archives des Maîtres de l'Orgue, vol. I (Paris, 1898), and N. Dufourcq, ed., *J. Titelouze: OEuvres complètes d'orgue* (Paris, 1965–67).

Bibl.: A. Pirro, *Les Organistes français du XVIIe siècle: Jean T.* (Paris, 1898); N. Dufourcq, *La Musique d'orgue française de Jehan T. à Jehan Alain* (Paris, 1941; 2nd ed., 1949).—**NS/LK/DM**

Titov, Alexei Nikolaievich, Russian violinist and composer, brother of **Sergei Nikolaievich Titov** and father of **Nikolai Alexeievich Titov;** b. St. Petersburg, June 24, 1769; d. there, Nov. 20, 1827. He served in the cavalry, reaching the rank of major general at his retirement. He was an amateur violinist, and wrote operas in the traditional Italian style; of these, the following were produced in St. Petersburg: *Andromeda and Perseus* (1802); *The Judgment of Solomon* (1803); *Nurzadakh* (June 7, 1807); *The Wedding of Filatka* (April 25, 1808); *Errant Moment* (July 10, 1812); *Emmerich Tekkely* (Dec. 13, 1812); *Intrigue in the Basket* (May 12, 1817); *Valor of the People of Kiev, or These Are the Russians* (May 12, 1817); *The Feast of the Mogul* (Sept. 15, 1823); also *The Brewer, or The Hidden Ghost of Evil* (Moscow, 1788). A ballet-pantomime, *Le Nouveau Werther*, was first given in St. Petersburg, on Jan. 30, 1799.—**NS/LK/DM**

Titov, Nikolai Alexeievich, Russian composer, son of **Alexei Nikolaievich Titov;** b. St. Petersburg, May 10, 1800; d. there, Dec. 22, 1875. He received a military upbringing, and, like his father, reached the rank of major general before retiring in 1867. He had no formal musical education, but took some singing lessons, and studied a manual of thoroughbass. He was a typical dilettante, but possessed a gift of melodic invention; he knew Glinka and Dargomyzhsky, who helped him to develop his ability. He wrote about 60 songs, which were extremely popular in his time; his early song *Sosna* (The Pine) was erroneously believed to be the first Russian art song, but it had precursors. Other of his songs that were popular include *Sharf goluboy* (The Blue Scarf; 1830) and *Kovarniy drug* (Treacherous Friend; 1831). He wrote a curious *Quadrille* for Piano, 3-Hands, the treble part to be played by a beginner. Another interesting project was a "musical romance in 12 waltzes" (under the general title *When I Was Young*), which remained incomplete.—**NS/LK/DM**

Titov, Sergei Nikolaievich, Russian violinist, cellist, and composer, brother of **Alexei Nikolaievich Titov;** b. St. Petersburg, 1770; d. 1825. He rose to major general in the army. His best known works were the opera *Krestyane, ili Vstrecha nezvanikh* (The Peasants, or the Party for the Uninvited; 1814) and the ballet *Noviy Verter* (The New Werther). His son, Nikolai Sergeievich Titov (b. probably in St. Petersburg, 1798; d. 1843), also pursued a military career; also was a fine composer of songs, which included the popular *Talisman* (1829). —**NS/LK/DM**

Titus, Alan (Wilkowski), American baritone; b. N.Y., Oct. 28, 1945. He was a student of Aksel Schiøtz at the Univ. of Colo. and of Hans Heinz at the Juilliard School of Music in N.Y., where he sang as Rossini's Figaro. In 1969 he made his formal operatic debut as Marcello in Washington, D.C. He first gained wide recognition when he created the role of the Celebrant in Bernstein's *Mass* at the inauguration of the Kennedy Center in Washington, D.C., on Sept. 8, 1971. After appearing with the N.Y.C. Opera and the San Francisco Spring Opera in 1972, he made his European debut as Pelléas in Amsterdam in 1973. On March 20, 1976, he made his Metropolitan Opera debut in N.Y. as Harlekin in *Ariadne auf Naxos*. He made his first appearance at the Glyndebourne Festival in 1979 as Guglielmo. In 1984 he sang Don Giovanni at the Deutsche Oper am Rhein in Düsseldorf. In 1985 he appeared as Storch in *Intermezzo* in Santa Fe. In 1987 he sang Oliviero in *Capriccio* at the Maggio Musicale in Florence. He appeared as Creonte in Haydn's *Orfeo ed Euridice* at the Salzburg Festival in 1990, and that same year sang Storch in the Italian premiere of *Intermezzo* in Bologna. In 1992 he sang Donizetti's Duca d'Alba at the Spoleto Festival. In 1995 he appeared in the title role of Hindemith's *Mathis der Maler* at London's Covent Garden. He portrayed Pizzaro in Rome in 1996.—**NS/LK/DM**

Titus, Hiram, American pianist and composer; b. Minneapolis, Jan. 28, 1947. He studied with Emil Dananberg (piano) and Richard Hoffman (composition) at Oberlin (Ohio) Coll. (B.A., 1958), with Guy Duckworth (piano) and Dominick Argento (composition) (1957–63), and with Walter Hartley in Interlochen, Mich. (summers, 1963–64). In addition to concert and stage works, he composed a number of scores for television and theater productions, winning DramaLogue awards for music (1979, 1980). Among his compositions are *Bach Abashed* for Chamber Ensemble (1968), the opera *Rosina* (Minneapolis, 1980), Guitar Concerto (1984), and *The Sand Hills*, oratorio for Soloists, Men's Chorus, Tape, and Ensemble (Los Angeles, 1987).—**NS/LK/DM**

Tizol, Juan (Vincente Martinez), jazz valve trombonist, long associated with Duke Ellington, composer; b. San Juan, P.R., Jan. 22, 1900; d. Inglewood, Calif., April 23, 1984. He came to the U.S.A. in 1920 with the Marie Lucas Orch., and eventually joined Duke Ellington from August 1929 until April 1944 (except for absences through illness), then Harry James from April 1944 until March 1951 when he rejoined Ellington. Left in late 1953 and worked with Harry James throughout remainder of 1950s, temporary return to Duke Ellington in spring of 1960. Lived in Los Angeles before moving to Las Vegas. After 1961, he retired from performing, although remained active in the musicians' union. Several of his famous compositions (including "Perdido" and "Caravan") were recorded originally by Duke Ellington.

Disc.: IVIE ANDERSON AND DUKE ELLINGTON: *Ivie Anderson with Duke Ellington & His Famous Orchestra* (1991); *Raisin' the Rent* (2000). **COUNT BASIE:** *This Is Jazz, Vol. 11* (1996). **LOUIS BELLSON:** *Just Jazz All Stars* (1952). **BARNEY BIGARD:** *Barney Bigard: 1928–48* (1996). **LAWRENCE BROWN:** *Lawrence Brown 1929–44* (1997). **BENNY CARTER:** *New Jazz Sounds: The Urbane Sessions* (1952). **JUNE CHRISTY:** *Day Dreams* (1947). **NAT KING COLE** *Complete After Midnight Sessions* (1956); *Piano Style of Nat King Cole* (1956). **BING CROSBY:** *That's Jazz* (1991). **DORIS DAY:** *It's Magic* (1994). **PATTI DUNHAM:** *Repertoire* (1992). **DUKE ELLINGTON:** *Early Ellington: The Complete Brunswick Recordings (1926–31)* (1926); *Jungle Nights in Harlem* (1927); *Okeh Ellington* (1927); *Rockin' in Rhythm* (1927); *Jubilee Stomp* (1928); *Jazz Cocktail* (1928); *Jungle Band: Brunswick Era, Vol. 2* (1929); *Duke Ellington & His Orchestra: 1929–30* (1930); *Duke Ellington & His Orchestra: 1930* (1930); *Duke Ellington & His Orchestra: 1930–31* (1931); *Duke Ellington & His Orchestra: 1931–32* (1932); *Duke Ellington & His Orchestra: 1932–33* (1933); *Great Original Performances 1927–34* (1934); *Duke's Men: The Small Groups, Vol. 1* (1938); *Blanton-Webster Band* (1939); *Through the Roof* (1939); *In Boston 1939–40* (1940); *In a Mellotone* (1940); *Fargo 1940, Vol. 1* (1940); *Sophisticated Lady* (1940); *Duke Ellington & His Orchestra, Vol. 3: 1943* (1943); *Carnegie Hall Concerts (January 1943)* (1943); *Uptown* (1951); *Two Great Concerts* (1952); *1952 Seattle Concert* (1952); *At Birdland 1952* (1952); *Jazz Profile* (1953); *Pasadena Concert (1953)* (1953); *Happy Birthday, Duke! The Birthday Sessions, Vols. 1–5* (1954); *Three Suites* (1960). **ELLA FITZGERALD:** *Get Happy* (1957); *Complete Elle Fitzgerald Song Books* (1964). **JOHNNY HODGES:** *Caravan: With the Duke Ellington All-Stars and the Billy Strayhorn All-Stars* (1951); *Classic Solos (1928–42)* (1994); *Jeep's Blues* (1996); *His Best Recordings* (1996). **BILLIE HOLIDAY:** *Billie Holiday: The Legacy Box 1933–58* (1958). **HARRY JAMES:** *Stompin' at the Savoy* (1948); *Harry James and His Great Vocalists* (1953); *More Harry James in Hi-Fi* (1955); *Best of the Big Bands [Harry James]* (1995); *Big John Special '49* (1998); *Trumpet Blues: The Best of Harry James* (1999); *You Turned the Tables on Me* (1999); *Meadowbrook Memories* (2000). **THE MILLS BROTHERS:** *Four Boys and a Guitar* (1931). **FRANK SINATRA:** *Complete Capitol Singles* (1953). **BEN WEBSTER:** *Best of Ben Webster 1930–44* (1995); *Evolution* (1995); *Cotton Tail* (1997).—**JC/LP**

Tjader, Cal(len Radcliffe, Jr.), Latin drummer; b. St. Louis, Mo., July 16, 1925; d. Manila, May 5, 1982. Diehard Latin-music fans decry his cool jazz tendencies and hard-core jazzers lament his Latin daliances, but his dedication to the music helped to popularize and promote Latin jazz to the average jazz fan. He was an important conduit between the two styles, and his contributions served as a prelude to the Latin-rock fusion of Santana.

He got started in show business at an early age. At age four he joined his parents' vaudeville act. At age seven he was dancing with Bill "Bojangles" Robinson in the movie *The White of the Dark Cloud of Joy.* A few years later, the family moved to northern Calif. and Cal's interests turned to the drums. After a three-year hitch as a Navy medic during World War II, he returned to Calif. and continued to study music at San Francisco State. In 1948, he joined Dave Brubeck's octet as the drummer. He then joined the George Shearing Quintet in 1953, giving him important national exposure and igniting his interest in Latin music. He formed his own group, including Armando Peraza (from Shearing's group), Willy Bobo, and Mongo Santamaria. His timing was excellent: the country was caught in a mambo craze, and his music was a perfect fit. In 1965, he had a hit with a reworked version of Dizzy Gillespie's "Guachi Guaro," renamed "Soul Sauce." The following year he toured with Eddie Palmieri and recorded the outstanding *El Sonido Nuevo*, a groundbreaking mix of the Palmieri's hot salsa and his cool jazz. This was a marked departure from previous Latin-jazz ventures like those by Stan Getz, who mixed cool jazz with cool samba to make bossa nova. He stayed on the West Coast and continued to perform and record throughout the 1970s and 1980s with a wide range of musicians, including Clare Fischer, Herbie Hancock (under the psuedonym Dawili Gonga), and Pancho Sanchez. He died suddenly while on tour in Manila.

Disc.: *Good Vibes* (1951); *Mambo with Tjader* (1954); *Tjader Plays Mambo* (1954); *Black Orchid* (1956); *Latin Kick* (1956); *Los Ritmos Calientes* (1957); *Latin Concert* (1958); *Stan Getz/Cal Tjader Sextet* (1958); *Jazz at the Blackhawk* (1959); *Monterey Concerts* (1959); *Latino!* (1960); *Cal Tjader Plays/Mary Stallings Sings* (1961); *Sona Libre* (1963); *Cal Tjader's Greatest Hits* (1965); *Soul Sauce* (1965); *El Sonido Nuevo* (1966); *The Best of Cal Tjader* (1968); *Plugs In* (1969); *Primo* (1970); *Descarga* (1971); *Tambu* (1973); *Amazonas* (1975); *Here and There* (1976); *Huracan* (1978); *La Onda Va Bien* (1979); *Gozame! Pero Ya* (1980); *Fuego Vivo* (1981); *Shining Sea* (1981); *Heat Wave* (1982); *Sentimental Moods* (1996).—**JE**

Tjeknavorian, Loris, Iranian-born American conductor and composer of Armenian descent; b. Boroujerd, Oct. 13, 1937. He studied at the Tehran Cons. (1950), the Vienna Academy of Music (composition diploma, 1961), with Carl Orff (1963–64), and at the Univ. of Mich. (D.M.A., 1966). After serving as a prof. of theory at the Tehran Cons. (1961–63), he was composer-in-residence at Concordia Coll. (1966–67), Moorhead State Univ. (1967–70), and with the Iranian Ministry of

Culture and Fine Arts (1970–73). From 1970 to 1975 he was principal conductor of the Tehran Opera and Ballet. In 1974 he appeared as a guest conductor of the Hallé Orch. in Manchester, and returned to England in 1975 as a guest conductor of the Philharmonia Orch. in London and the London Sym. Orch. He subsequently was a guest conductor with various orchs., among them the London Phil., the Royal Phil. in London, the Royal Liverpool Phil., the Danish National Radio Sym. Orch. in Copenhagen, the American Sym. Orch. in N.Y., the Mexico State Sym. Orch., the Helsinki Phil., the Yomiuri Nippon Sym. Orch. in Tokyo, the English Chamber Orch., and the St. Paul (Minn.) Chamber Orch. In 1976 he founded the Inst. of Armenian Music in London, which he served as chairman until 1980. In 1980–81 he was founder- program advisor of Armenian music studies of the School of the Performing Arts at the Univ. of Southern Calif. at Los Angeles. He became a naturalized American citizen in 1987. In 1989 he became director and principal conductor of the Armenian Phil. in Yerevan, which he conducted in its U.S. debut on Dec. 7 of that year at N.Y.'s Carnegie Hall. In addition to the standard repertoire, Tjeknavorian has programmed works by many Armenian composers, and has also conducted several of his own compositions. Among his works are 2 operas, the ballet *Othello*, 5 syms., concertos, the oratorio *Book of Revelation*, and chamber music. **—LK/DM**

TLC, three-woman vocal group that encapsulated the gestalt of turn of the millennium R&B. **Membership:** Tionne Tenese "T-Boz" Watkins, voc. (b. Des Moines, Iowa, April 26, 1970); Lisa "Left Eye" Lopes, rapper (b. Philadelphia, Pa., May 27, 1971); Rozanda "Chilli" Thomas, voc. (b. Atlanta, Ga., Feb. 27, 1971).

With a unique fusion of funk, rap, and new jack swing, along with a liberated sexiness, TLC became one of the most successful and acclaimed groups of the 1990s and into the new millennium. With four Grammy Awards over the course of two albums, they have the respect of their fans, pop radio, and their peers. They have surpassed The Supremes in terms of sales, and are the most successful female group of all time.

Initially recording artist Peri "Pebbles" Reid managed and mentored the group, signing them to her husband's (LA Reid's) label, LaFace. Their first single, "Ain't Too Proud to Beg," with its combination of rap, chant, and harmonies over an interesting blend of hip-hop beats and samples rose to #5 and went platinum in 1992. With a more Minneapolis funk, balladic sound "Baby, Baby, Baby" topped the R&B charts, spent six weeks at #2 on the pop charts, and went platinum. The funkier "What About Your Friends" rose to #7 and gold, while "Hat 2 Da Back" topped out at #30. The debut album, *Ooooooohhh...On the TLC Tip* got to #14 and eventually sold quadruple platinum. The group didn't hurt sales with some of their more outrageous behavior, like dressing in condoms to advocate safe sex.

Many of their songs deal with lovers gone bad. The group's rapper, Lisa "Left Eye" Lopes, practiced what she preached when she was arrested for destroying the cars and setting fire to the home of her boyfriend, professional football player Andre Rison. That stunt landed her in rehab, although she got a suspended sentence from the courts.

While their debut was huge, it was nothing compared to their 1994 release *CrazySexyCool*. A more cohesive, more mature effort, it was launched with the single "Creep," a mid-tempo tune with a signature trumpet sample, lots of scratching and ensemble singing, but not much in the way of actual rapping. The single topped the R&B charts for nine weeks, the pop charts for four, and went platinum. The bluesy, overtly sexy "Red Light Special" spent three weeks at #2 and went gold. Another slow jam full of lots of jazzy samples and a steaming rap, "Waterfalls" topped the pop charts for seven weeks, going platinum. Yet another slow jam, "Diggin' on You," rose to #5 and went gold. They also did the theme songs for the Nickelodeon show *All That* and contributed a song to the *Poetic Justice* soundtrack.

However, in the midst of all this success, the group declared bankruptcy. Lopes little stunt made her liable for the damages on Rison's house, and she owed the insurance company well over a million dollars. They were also squeezed by the estrangement between the head of their record company, LA Reid, and his wife, their manager. As the separation between the Reids became more nasty, TLC found themselves caught in the middle of a dispute, with Peri Reid claiming the band owed her half a million dollars. The group was able to settle all these claims when they won the Best R&B Performance By a Duo or Group with Vocal Grammy for "Creep" and the Best R&B album award for the *CrazySexyCool* album in 1995. With this added impetus, the album achieved diamond (10 million sales) status, and suddenly TLC found it much easier to live up to their financial obligations.

They took some time off to do some musical and extramusical activities between albums. Thomas had a baby and did some acting. Watkins also did some acting, and wrote a book of poetry and prose called *Thoughts*, in which she detailed her struggle with sickle cell anemia. Lopes hosted a show on MTV and started her own production company.

They got back together and cut the even slicker, more honest, and maturer *Fanmail*, released in 1998. Led off by a single guaranteed to grab their fans, "No Scrubs" topped the charts, going gold. A masterpiece of pop, and a breakaway from the group's sassy confidence, the startlingly honest "Unpretty" followed into the top slot and gold. At the 1999 Grammys, "No Scrubs" won Best R&B duo or group with Vocal and Best R&B Song, and the album took Best R&B Album honors. *Fanmail* topped the album charts for four weeks, and by the beginning of 2000, had gone quintuple platinum.

Like most great groups, however, there was a certain amount of tension within the group. Lopes gave interviews when the album was released stating her unhappiness with the group and its music. Nonetheless, she participated in the tour to support the album. At the beginning of 2000, Lopes challenged the other members of the band to a solo album competition, with the winner—the record that charted highest—taking $1.5 million! Rumors of the group's break-up continue to circulate.

DISC.: *Ooooooohhh...On the TLC Tip* (1992); *CrazySexyCool* (1994); *Fanmail* (1999).—**HB**

Tobias, Rudolf, Estonian organist and composer; b. Kaina, May 29, 1873; d. Berlin, Oct. 29, 1918. He studied organ with L. Homilius and composition with Rimsky-Korsakov at the St. Petersburg Cons., graduating in 1897. He was an organist in St. Petersburg (1898–1904) and Tartu (1905–8); in 1910, settled in Berlin. In several of his compositions, he made use of national Estonian subjects.

WORKS: *Des Jonah Sendung*, oratorio (1909); *Black Raven, Harbinger of War* for Voices and Orch. (1909); *The Virgin of Light*, after an Estonian epic, for Soprano and Orch. (1911); 2 melodramas for Narrator and Orch.: *Kalevipoeg's Dream* (1906) and *Kalevipoeg at the Gate of the Kingdom of Death* (1912); choruses; chamber music; songs.

BIBL.: *R. T.* (Tallinn, 1973).—**NS/LK/DM**

Tocchi, Gian Luca, Italian composer; b. Perugia, Jan. 10, 1901; d. Rome, Sept. 14, 1992. He studied with Respighi (composition) and Molinari (conducting) at the Cons. di Santa Cecilia in Rome, and in 1930 he won the composition prize of the Governatorato di Roma. After appearances as a conductor (1935–45), he was active as a composer, writer, and producer with the Italian radio (from 1952); he also taught composition at the Accademia di Santa Cecilia in Rome (1959–71).

WORKS: **ORCH.:** *Danza sull'aia* (1927); *Il destino*, symphonic poem (1930); *Rapsodia romantica* (1931); *Record* (1935); Concerto for 3 Saxophones, 2 Pianos, and Orch. (1935); *Film* (1936); *Luna Park* (1937); *3 Pieces* (1938); *Divertimento con antiche musiche* (1939); *Quadro sonore* (1941); *Omaggi* for Harpsichord and Strings (1961). **CHAMBER:** *Arlecchino* for 6 Instruments (1937); Quartet; *Arie e danze tedesche* for Harp, Flute, and Viola; *Canzone, notturno, e ballo* for Harp, Flute, and Viola (1945); 12 studies for Harp; piano pieces. **OTHER:** Incidental music to plays; film scores; choral works; songs.—**NS/LK/DM**

Tocco, James, American pianist and teacher; b. Detroit, Sept. 21, 1943. He began piano lessons when he was 6 and made his debut as soloist in Beethoven's 2nd Piano Concerto at age 12. Following training at the Salzburg Mozarteum and in Paris with Tagliaferro, he completed his studies in N.Y. with Arrau. In 1973 he won 1st prize in the ARD Competition in Munich. In 1975 he won critical accolades when he played Tchaikovsky's 1st Piano Concerto at the Vienna Festival. In subsequent years, he toured internationally as a soloist with orchs., as a recitalist, and as a chamber music artist. In 1977 he joined the faculty of the Ind. Univ. School of Music in Bloomington. In 1991 he became eminent scholar and artist-in-residence at the Univ. of Cincinnati Coll.-Cons. of Music, and he also served as prof. of piano at the Lübeck Hochschule für Musik. Tocco maintains an extraordinarily diversified repertoire, ranging from Bach and Handel to Berg and Bernstein. He also performs rarely heard scores from the past and present, including transcriptions.—**NS/LK/DM**

Toch, Ernst, eminent Austrian-born American composer and teacher; b. Vienna, Dec. 7, 1887; d. Los Angeles, Oct. 1, 1964. His father was a Jewish dealer in unprocessed leather, and there was no musical strain in the family; Toch began playing piano without a teacher in his grandmother's pawnshop; he learned musical notation from a local violinist, and then copied Mozart's string quartets for practice; using them as a model, he began to compose string quartets and other pieces of chamber music; at the age of 17, he had one of them, his 6th String Quartet, op. 12 (1905), performed by the famous Rosé Quartet in Vienna. From 1906 to 1909 he studied medicine at the Univ. of Vienna. In 1909 he won the prestigious Mozart Prize and a scholarship to study at the Frankfurt am Main Cons., where he studied piano with Willy Rehberg and composition with Iwan Knorr. In 1910 he was awarded the Mendelssohn Prize; also won 4 times in succession the Austrian State Prize. In 1913 he was appointed instructor in piano at Zuschneid's Hochschule für Musik in Mannheim. From 1914 to 1918 he served in the Austrian army during World War I. After the Armistice he returned to Mannheim, resumed his musical career, and became active in the modern movement, soon attaining, along with Hindemith, Krenek, and others, a prominent position in the new German school of composition. He also completed his education at the Univ. of Heidelberg (Ph.D., 1921, with the diss. *Beiträge zur Stilkunde der Melodie*; publ. in Berlin, 1923, as *Melodielehre*). In 1929 he went to Berlin, where he established himself as a pianist, composer, and teacher of composition. In 1932 he made an American tour as a pianist playing his own works; he returned to Berlin, but with the advent of the Nazi regime was forced to leave Germany in 1933. He went to Paris, then to London, and in 1935 emigrated to the U.S.; gave lectures on music at the New School for Social Research in N.Y.; in 1936, moved to Hollywood, where he wrote music for films. He became a naturalized American citizen on July 26, 1940. In 1940–41 he taught composition at the Univ. of Southern Calif. in Los Angeles; subsequently taught privately; among his students were many, who, like Andre Previn, became well-known composers in their own right. From 1950 until his death, Toch traveled frequently and lived in Vienna, Zürich, the MacDowell Colony in N.H., and Santa Monica, Calif.

Toch's music is rooted in the tradition of the German and Austrian Romantic movement of the 19th century, but his study of the classics made him aware of the paramount importance of formal logic in the development of thematic ideas. His early works consist mostly of chamber music and pieces for piano solo; following the zeitgeist during his German period, he wrote several pieces for the stage in the light manner of sophisticated entertainment; he also composed effective piano works of a virtuoso quality, which enjoyed considerable popularity among pianists of the time. Toch possessed a fine wit and a sense of exploration; his *Geographical Fugue* for speaking chorus, articulating in syllabic counterpoint the names of exotic places on earth, became a classic of its genre. It was not until 1950 that Toch wrote his first full-fledged sym., but from that time on, until he died of stomach cancer, he composed fully 7 syms., plus sinfoniettas for Wind and String Orch. He was greatly interested in new techniques; the theme of his last String

Quartet (No. 13, 1953) is based on a 12-tone row. In the score of his 3rd Sym. he introduced an optional instrument, the Hisser, a tank of carbon dioxide that produced a hissing sound through a valve.

Among the several honors Toch received were the Pulitzer Prize in Music for his 3rd Sym. (1956), membership in the National Inst. of Arts and Letters (1957), and the Cross of Honor for Sciences and Art from the Austrian government (1963). An Ernst Toch Archive was founded at the Univ. of Calif., Los Angeles, in 1966, serving as a depository for his MSS. His grandson is the noted American writer Lawrence Weschler.

WORKS: DRAMATIC: Opera: *Wegwende* (1925; unfinished; sketches destroyed); *Die Prinzessin auf der Erbse* (Baden-Baden, July 17, 1927); *Der Facher* (Königsberg, June 8, 1930); *The Last Tale* (1960–62). **Film:** *Peter Ibbetson* (1935); *Outcast* (1937); *The Cat and the Canary* (1939); *Dr. Cyclops* (1940); *The Ghost Breakers* (1940); *Ladies in Retirement* (1941); *First Comes Courage* (1943); *None Shall Escape* (1944); *Address Unknown* (1944); *The Unseen* (1945). **Other:** Incidental music for stage and radio plays. **ORCH.:** *Scherzo* (1904); Piano Concerto (1904; not extant); *Phantastische Nachtmusik* (1920; Mannheim, March 22, 1921); *Tanz-Suite* for Chamber Orch. (1923); *5 Pieces* for Chamber Orch. (1924); Concerto for Cello and Small Orch. (1924; Kiel, June 17, 1925); Piano Concerto (Düsseldorf, Oct. 8, 1926; Gieseking, soloist); *Spiel für Blasorchester* (Donaueschingen, July 24, 1926); *Narziss* (1927; not extant); *Gewitter* (1927; not extant); *Komödie für Orchester* (Berlin, Nov. 13, 1927); *Vorspiel zu einem Märchen* (for the opera *Die Prinzessin auf der Erbse*; 1927); *Fanal* for Organ and Orch. (1928); *Bunte Suite* (1928; Frankfurt am Main, Feb. 22, 1929); *Kleine Theater-Suite* (1930; Berlin, Feb. 9, 1931); *Tragische Musik* (1931; not extant); *2 kultische Stücke* (1931; not extant); Sym. for Piano and Orch. (Piano Concerto No. 2, 1932; London, Aug. 20, 1934); *Miniature Overture* for Winds (1932); *Variations on Mozart's Unser dummer Pöbel meint* (1933); *Big Ben*, variation fantasy on the Westminster Chimes (Cambridge, Mass., Dec. 20, 1934; rev. 1955); *Pinocchio*, "a merry overture" (1935; Los Angeles, Dec. 10, 1936); *Musical Short Story* (1936; not extant); *Orchids* (1936; not extant); *The Idle Stroller*, suite (1938); "The Covenant," 6th movement of 7-movement, collaborative *Genesis Suite* (Los Angeles, Nov. 18, 1945; not extant); *Hyperion*, dramatic prelude after Keats (1947; Cleveland, Jan. 8, 1948); 7 syms.: No. 1 (1949–50; Vienna, Dec. 20, 1950), No. 2, dedicated to Albert Schweitzer (1950–51; Vienna, Jan. 11, 1952), No. 3 (Pittsburgh, Dec. 2, 1955), No. 4 (Minneapolis, Nov. 22, 1957), No. 5, *Jephta, Rhapsodic Poem* (1961–62; Boston, March 13, 1964), No. 6 (1963; Zürich Radio, Jan. 22, 1967), and No. 7 (1964; Bavarian Radio, 1967); *Circus Overture* (1953; Chicago, July 8, 1954); *Notturno* (1953; Louisville, Jan. 2, 1954); *Peter Pan*, fairy tale (Seattle, Feb. 13, 1956); *Epilogue* (1959); *Intermezzo* (1959); *Short Story* (1961); *Capriccio* (1963); *Puppetshow* (1963); *The Enamoured Harlequin* (1963); Sinfonietta for Strings (1964; Philadelphia, Feb. 13, 1967); Theme with Variations "Muss i denn zum Stadle hinaus" (1964). **CHAMBER:** 13 string quartets: Nos. 1–5 (1902–03; not extant), No. 6 (1905), No. 7 (1908), No. 8 (1910), No. 9 (1919), No. 10, on "BASS" (1921), No. 11 (1924), No. 12 (1946), and No. 13 (1953); *Kammersymphonie* (1906); Duos for Violins (1909; for open strings only in the pupil's part); *Serenade* for 3 Violins (1911); 2 violin sonatas (1913, 1928); *"Spitzweg" Serenade* for 2 Violins and Viola (1916): *Tanz Suite* for Flute, Clarinet, Violin, Viola, Bass, and Percussion (1923; excerpts choreographed as *Der Wald*, Mannheim, Nov. 19, 1923; Münster, Oct. 29, 1924); *2 Divertimenti* for String Duos (1926); *Studie* for Mechanical Organ (1927); Cello Sonata (1929); *2 Études* for Cello (1930); String Trio (1936); Piano Quintet (1938); *Dedication* for String Quartet or String Orch. (1948); *Adagio elegiaco* for Clarinet and Piano (1950); *5 Pieces* for Flute, Oboe, Clarinet, Bassoon, 2 Horns, and Percussion (1959); *Sonatinetta* for Flute, Clarinet, and Bassoon (1959); *3 Impromptus* for Solo Violin, Solo Viola, and Solo Cello (1963); Sinfonietta for Winds and Percussion (1964; Zürich Radio, Nov. 11, 1967); Quartet for Oboe, Clarinet, Bassoon, and Viola (1964). **Piano:** *Melodische Skizzen* (1903); *3 Preludes* (1903); *Impromptu* (1904; not extant); *Capriccio* (1905; not extant); 3 sonatas (1905, not extant; 1905, not extant; 1928); *Stammbuchverse* (1905); *Begegnung* (1908); *Reminiszenzen* (1909); *4 Klavierstücke* (1914; not extant); *Canon* (1914); *3 Burlesken* (1923; includes the popular *Der Jongleur*, publ. separately); *3 Klavierstücke* (1924); *5 Capriccetti* (1925); *3 Originalstücke für das Welte-Mignon Klavier* (1926); *Tanz- und Spielstücke* (1926?); *Kleinstadtbilder* (1929); *Fünfmal Zehn Etüden*, 50 études (1931); *Profiles* (1946); *Ideas* (1946); *Diversions* (1956); *Sonatinetta* (1956); *3 Little Dances* (1961); *Reflections*, 5 pieces (1961); Sonata for Piano, 4-Hands (1962). **VOCAL:** *An mein Vaterland*, sym. for Soprano, Mixed and Boy's Choruses, Orch., and Organ (1913); *Die chinesische Flöte*, chamber sym. for Soprano and 14 Solo Instruments (1921; Frankfurt am Main, June 24, 1923; rev. 1949); 9 songs for Soprano and Piano (1926); *Der Tierkreis* for Chorus (1930); *Das Wasser*, cantata for Tenor, Baritone, Narrator, Flute, Trumpet, Percussion, and Strings (Berlin, June 18, 1930); *Gesprochene Musik* for Speaking Chorus (Berlin, June 17, 1930; includes the famous *Fuge aus der Geographie*, publ. separately in Eng. and Ger. eds.); *Music for Orchestra and Baritone Solo on Poems by Rilke* (1931); *Cantata of the Bitter Herbs* for Soloists, Narrator, and Chorus (1938); *Poems to Martha* for Voice and String Quintet (1942); *The Inner Circle*, 6 choruses (1947–53); *There Is a Season for Everything* for Soprano, Flute, Clarinet, Violin, and Cello, after Ecclesiastes (1953); *Vanity of Vanities, All Is Vanity* for Soprano, Tenor, Flute, Clarinet, Violin, and Cello, after Ecclesiastes (1954); *Phantoms* for Solo Voices and Chorus (1958); *Lange schon haben meine Freunde versucht* for Soprano and Baritone (1958); *Song of Myself* for Chorus, after Whitman (1961); *Valse* for Speaking Chorus (1961; in separate Eng. and Ger. eds.); folk song arrangements.

WRITINGS: *The Shaping Forces in Music* (N.Y., 1948; new ed. by L. Weschler, 1977); M. Hood, ed., *Placed as a Link in this Chain: A Medley of Observations by Ernst Toch* (Los Angeles, 1971).

BIBL.: C. Johnson, *The Unpublished Works of E. T.* (diss., Univ. of Calif., Los Angeles, 1973); L. Weschler, *E. T., 1887–1964: A Biographical Essay Ten Years after His Passing* (Los Angeles, 1974); J. Diane, *The Musical Migration and E. T.* (Ames, Iowa, 1989).—**NS/LK/DM**

Toczyska, Stefania, Polish mezzo-soprano; b. Gdańsk, Feb. 19, 1943. She was a pupil of Barbara Iglikovska at the Gdańsk Cons. She took prizes in competitions in Toulouse (1972), Paris (1973), and 's-Hertogenbosch (1974). In 1973 she made her operatic debut as Carmen at the Gdańsk Opera, and then sang throughout Poland. In 1977 she made her Western European operatic debut as Amneris with the Basel Opera. Later that year she made her first appearance at the Vienna State Opera as Ulrica, and returned there to sing Carmen, Azucena, Eboli, and Preziosilla. In 1979 she sang Eboli at the Bavarian State Opera in Munich and at the Hamburg State Opera, and then appeared as Laura in *La Gioconda* at the San Francisco Opera. She made her Covent Garden debut in London in 1983 as Azucena and in 1986 made her first appearance at the Chicago Lyric Opera as Giovanna Seymour in *Anna Bolena*. In 1987 she sang Adalgisa at the Houston Grand Opera and Venus in *Tannhäuser* at the Barcelona Opera. She made her Metropolitan Opera debut in N.Y. as Laura in *La Gioconda* in 1989. In 1990 she sang at the Caracalla Festival in Rome. In 1992 she appeared as Massenet's Dulcinée in Toulouse. She was engaged as Amneris at the Metropolitan Opera in 1997. In addition to her active operatic career, she has also toured widely as a concert artist.—**NS/LK/DM**

Toda, Kunio (actually, **Morikuni**), Japanese composer and teacher; b. Tokyo, Aug. 11, 1915. He studied at the Univ. of Heidelberg (1938–39); following diplomatic service in Moscow (1939–41), he returned to Tokyo to study with Saburo Moroi. He was sent to Indochina in 1944; when World War II ended in 1945, he was detained until 1948. Upon his return to Tokyo, he became active in contemporary-music circles; introduced 12-note serialism to his homeland. He remained active as a diplomat until 1964; taught at the Toho Gakuen School of Music (from 1955), remaining on its faculty as a prof. when it became a college in 1961; also was director and a prof. at the Senzolku Gakuen Academy of Music (from 1975); he retired in 1988 from the latter, but continued as a guest prof. until 1991.

WORKS: DRAMATIC: Opera: *Akemi* (Tokyo, 1956); *Kyara monogatari* (History of the City of Kyara; Tokyo, 1973). **Monodrama:** *Anna la Bonne*, after Cocteau (1998). **Ballet:** *Atorie no Salome* (Salome in Studio; Tokyo, Nov. 23, 1951); *Akai tenmaku* or *Le Cirque rouge* (Tokyo, Nov. 4, 1953); *Dokutsu* (The Cave; Tokyo, Nov. 7, 1954); *Miranda* (Tokyo, Oct. 26, 1968). **Scenic-Oratorio Mystery:** *Shito Paolo* (St. Paul; 1961–64; concert perf., Tokyo, Feb. 15, 1973). **ORCH.:** *Overture* (1943); *Densetsu* (Legend), symphonic fantasy (1944); 2 piano concertos (1944, 1955); *Passacaglia and Fugue* (1949); *Overtura buffa* (1950); Sym. (1956); *Concerto grosso* for 6 Solo Instruments and Orch. (Tokyo, Jan. 25, 1968). **CHAMBER:** Piano Trio (1947); *Amoroso* for Violin and Piano (1951); Violin Sonata (1957; rev. 1959); *Music* for 2 Koto (1959); Bassoon Sonata (1966); *Introduzione-Movimento-Rapido* for String Quartet, Quintet, or Ensemble (1994). **KEYBOARD: Piano:** *3 intermezzi* (1942); *Koto no ne ni yoru gensōkyoku* (Fantasy on the Sound of the Koto; 1965); Sonatina (1966); *Yottsu no yuganda kyoku* or *4 pezzi deformati* (1968). **Electronic Organ:** *Passacaglia and Fugue* (Tokyo, Aug. 5, 1994). **VOCAL:** *Jochu no Anna* (Anna la Bonne), monodrama for Soprano, 2 Violas, and Tape (Tokyo, Nov. 17, 1978); *Kesa to Morito* (Kesa and Morito), dramatic cantata for Soprano, Baritone, and String Quintet (Tokyo, Nov. 16, 1979); *Toraware no O'Shichi* (O'Shichi, the Prisoner), mono-cantata for Soprano, Flute, and Marimba (Tokyo, Sept. 16, 1981); *Ô-kawa no Uta* (Song of River) for Mezzo-soprano, Baritone, and Orch. (Tokyo, March 6, 1989); choruses; songs.—**NS/LK/DM**

Todi, Luisa (actually, **Luiza Rosa** née **d'Aguiar**), famous Portuguese mezzo-soprano; b. Setubal, Jan. 9, 1753; d. Lisbon, Oct. 1, 1833. She made her debut as a comic actress at age 14 in Lisbon, and married the violinist Francesco Saverio Todi, concertmaster of the theater orch., when she was 16. She studied with David Perez, making her opera debut in 1770 in Scolari's *Il Viaggiatore ridicolo* in Lisbon; during the 1777–78 season, she sang comic opera at the King's Theatre in London, then established herself as a serious artist with her debut at the Paris Concert Spirituel (Nov. 1, 1778). After appearances in Germany, Austria, and Italy, she returned to Paris in 1783 and became a rival of Gertrud Elisabeth Mara at the Concert Spirituel; 2 hostile factions squared off, the Todistes and the Maratistes. After singing at Berlin's Royal Opera, she went to St. Petersburg in 1784, winning great acclaim for her appearances in Sarti's *Armida e Rinaldo* (Jan. 1786) and *Castore e Polluce* (Sept. 22, 1786). After singing in Moscow in Pollinia (April 23, 1787), she returned to Berlin (1788–89); also sang in Mainz, Hannover, and Venice (1790–91). After further engagements in Italy and in Prague (1791), she appeared at the Madrid Opera (1792–93; 1794–95); then sang at the Teatro San Carlo in Naples (1797–99). In 1803 she retired to Lisbon, where she spent her final years in total blindness.

BIBL.: J. Ribeiro Guimarães, *Biographia de Luiza de Aguiar T.* (Lisbon, 1872); J. de Vasconcellos, *Luiza T.: Estudo critico* (Oporto, 1873; 2nd ed., 1929); M. de Sampayo Ribeiro, *Luisa de Aguiar T.* (Lisbon, 1934).—**NS/LK/DM**

Toduţă, Sigismund, Romanian composer and teacher; b. Simeria, May 30, 1908; d. Cluj, July 3, 1991. He studied with Negrea at the Cluj Cons. (1931–33), and later at the Accademia di Santa Cecilia in Rome (1936–38) with Pizzetti (composition) and Casella (piano); also took courses in musicology at the Pontificio Istituto di Musica Sacra in Rome (Ph.D., 1938, with a diss. on G.F. Anerio). In 1946 he was appointed to the faculty of the Cluj Cons. (he was its director from 1962 to 1964); in 1971 he became managing director of the Cluj State Phil. His music was distinguished by a flowing Romantic melody in large rhapsodic sonorities.

WORKS: DRAMATIC: Opera: *Meşterul Manole* (Master-builder Manole; 1943–47; as an opera-oratorio, 1977–82; Cluj, Oct. 1, 1985). **ORCH.:** *Egloga* (1933); *Symphonic Variations* (1940); Piano Concerto (1943); 4 concertos for Strings (1951; 1972–73; 1974; 1980); *Divertisement* for Strings (1951); 5 syms.: No. 1 (1954), No. 2, "in memoria lui George Enesco" (1954–56), No. 3, *Ovidiu* (1957), No. 4 (1961), and No. 5 (1963–76; Cluj, Feb. 7, 1976); *Uvertură festivă* (1959); *Simfonieta* (1966; Cluj, Jan. 21, 1977); Concerto for Winds and Percussion (1975–76; Cluj, Sept. 4, 1976); Concerto for Flute and Strings (Sibiu, April 3, 1984); *Simfonia B—A—C—H* (1984); Concerto for Oboe and Strings (1986). **CHAMBER:** Cello Sonata (1952); Flute Sonata (1952); Violin Sonata (1953); Oboe Sonata (1956); *Ioko*, 4 pieces for Harp (1975); *6 Pieces* for Oboe (1981); piano pieces, including *Passacaglia* (1943), Sonatina (1950), *Preludiu, Coral, Toccata* (1973–75), and *3 Pieces* (1980). **VOCAL:** 3 oratorios: *Mioriţa* (1958–68; Bucharest, Oct. 7, 1968), *Balada steagului* (1961), and *Pe urmele lui Horea* (1976–78; Cluj, Dec. 2, 1978); choruses; songs. —**NS/LK/DM**

Toebosch, Louis, Dutch organist, conductor, teacher, and composer; b. Maastricht, March 18, 1916. He studied at the School of Church Music in Utrecht, the Music Lyceum in Maastricht, and then the Royal Cons. in Liège (1934–39). He was active as a church organist in Breda (1940–65), conducted the Tilburg Sym. Orch.

(1946–52), and then was founder-conductor of the Orlando di Lasso Choir (from 1953). He taught at the conservatories of Tilburg and Maastricht (1944–65); was director of the Brabant Cons. (1965–74). His music combines the polyphonic style of the Renaissance with modern techniques; he applies the 12-tone method of compostion in both secular and sacred music.

WORKS: ORCH.: 2 suites (1939, 1948); *Allegro* for Organ and Orch. (1941); *Tema con variazioni* (1945); *Het Lied van Hertog Jan* (1949); *Carnavalsige Ouverture* (1955); *Concertante Ouverture* (1956); *Variaties* (1957); *Feestelijke Ouverture* (1960); *Sinfonietta No. 2* (1961); *Agena* (1966); *Changements* for Organ and Orch. (1968); Organ Concerto (1983). **CHAMBER:** *Sarabande en allegro* for Wind Quintet (1959); *The King's Quartet* for String Quartet (1968); *Toccata, aria e finale* for Viola (1969); *Bilingua* for Recorder and Harpsichord (1977); *Muziek voor 3 barokinstrumenten* for Recorder, Viola da Gamba, and Harpsichord (1980); Trio for Violin, Viola, and Cello (1991); *Trois conversations* for Viola (1996); *Kassel '97: Documenta X* for Clarinet, Alto Saxophone, Trombone, Accordion, and Piano (1997). **KEYBOARD: Piano:** Sonata (1947); *Suite polyphonica* for 2 Pianos (1962); *Pasticcio di Rofena* for Piano, 4-Hands (1973); *Zes speelstukken* for 3 Pianos (1983); *Trois positions* (1991); *Hamerslag* (1995). **Organ:** *Tryptique* (1939; rev. 1980); *Praeludium et Fuga super Te Deum laudamus* (1954); *2 postludia* (1964); *Toccana* (1973); *Orgelspiegel* (1975); *3 Movements* (1986); *Suite Gregorienne* (1994); *Dominica pentecostes* (1994); *Autres pensées* (1997); *Meditazione communio Pascha nostrum* (1998). **VOCAL:** *Cantatorium carnevale* for Tenor, Baritone, and Orch. (1957); *Philippica-moderata* for Solo Voices, Chorus, and Orch. (1963); *De vier seizoenen*, cantata-oratorio for Chorus and Orch. (1981); *Cantata alfabetica* for Chorus and Organ (1982); *De twaalf maanden* for Chorus and String Quartet (1990); *Victimae Paschali* for Women's Chorus and Organ (1993); *Canticum europaeum* for Soprano, Baritone, Chorus, and Orch. (1994).—**NS/LK/DM**

Toeschi, family of prominent German musicians of Italian descent, originally named **Toesca**:

(1) Alessandro Toeschi, violinist and composer; b. probably in Rome, before 1700; d. Mannheim (buried), Oct. 15, 1758. He was descended from a family of the nobility. After touring in England and Germany, he served as court musician to the Landgrave Ernst Ludwig of Hesse in Darmstadt (1719–24); then was 2nd maître des concerts at the Württemberg court in Stuttgart (1725–37). He subsequently settled in Mannheim as Konzertmeister about 1742, and was director of instrumental church music at the Palatine court there from about 1750. His extant works consist of a Concerto for 2 Violins, Strings, and Continuo, and a Sonata for Violin and Continuo. He had 2 sons who became musicians:

(2) Carl Joseph Toeschi, violinist and composer, the most outstanding member of the family; b. Ludwigsburg (baptized), Nov. 11, 1731; d. Munich, April 12, 1788. He studied with Johann Stamitz and Anton Filtz, and in 1752 he became a violinist in the Mannheim Court Orch.; was made its Konzertmeister in 1759, and in 1774 was named music director of the electoral cabinet; followed the court to Munich in 1778. He was one of the leading composers of the Mannheim school. Among his output were over 66 syms., some 30 ballets, and much chamber music.

(3) Johann (Baptist) (Maria) Christoph Toeschi, violinist and composer, known as **Toesca de Castellamonte**; b. Stuttgart (baptized), Oct. 1, 1735; d. Munich, March 3, 1800. He studied with Johann Stamitz and Christian Cannabich; in 1755 became a violinist in the Mannheim Court Orch., and was also director of the Court Ballet there (from 1758); was named Konzertmeister in 1774. In 1778 he followed the court to Munich, where he was music director (from 1793); also was director of the court chapel in 1798; that same year his family was granted hereditary Italian nobility and the right to use the title "de Castellamonte." He wrote a melodrama, *Dirmel und Laura* (Munich, 1784), and at least 4 ballets, but his only extant compositions are 6 trio sonatas (Paris, 1768), a Sonata for Viola d'Amore and Continuo (ed. by D. Newlin and K. Stumpf, Vienna, 1963), and 3 viola d'amore pieces. His son, Karl Theodor Toeschi (b. Mannheim, April 17, 1768; d. Munich, Oct. 10, 1843), was also a composer; was active at the Munich court (1780–89); was named Bavarian chamber composer in 1801. He wrote an opera, a ballet, syms., overtures, a Violin Concerto, and other works, most of which are lost.

BIBL.: R. Münster, *Die Sinfoien T.s* (diss., Univ. of Munich, 1956).—**NS/LK/DM**

Tofft, Alfred, Danish organist, music critic, and composer; b. Copenhagen, Jan. 2, 1865; d. there, Jan. 30, 1931. He studied with J. Nebelong (organ) and G. Bohlmann (theory). He was music critic for the *Berlinske Tidende* in Copenhagen, and president of the Danish Composers' Society. He was a fine organist and a talented composer of songs (op.2, *Heine-Album*; op.4, *Jacobsen-Album*; etc.). Two operas were produced in Copenhagen: *Vifandaka* (Jan. 1, 1898) and *Anathema* (May 10, 1928).—**NS/LK/DM**

Tofts, Catherine, English soprano; b. c. 1685; d. Venice, 1756. She first gained notice as a singer when she appeared in a series of London concerts (1703–04). In 1704 she sang at London's Drury Lane, where she soon became a leading rival of Margherita de L'Epine. From 1705 until she was stricken with insanity in 1709 she was a member of the company. She apparently recovered sufficiently to marry Joseph Smith, who served as English consul in Venice.—**NS/LK/DM**

Togi, Suenobu, Japanese performer and ethnomusicologist; b. Tokyo, Jan. 1, 1932. He attended the Imperial Court Music School in Tokyo (1943–52), where he learned Japanese court music and dance as well as Western music (cello and violin); also studied Western music at the Tokyo Univ. of Fine Arts (1950–52). He taught and performed in the Imperial Court Music Dept. in both the Japanese Court Orch. (gagaku and bugaku) and the Imperial Court Orch. (Western music) from 1952 to 1961; then went to the U.S., where he taught Japanese court music and dance at the Univ. of Calif., Los Angeles (1961). He returned to Tokyo in 1964; in 1968, joined the faculty at the Univ. of Calif., Los Angeles; also gave concerts and lectures throughout the U.S. Togi is the only former court musician teaching gagaku outside of Japan. He employs the strictest court tradition (which determines gagaku practice throughout Japan); revisited Tokyo in 1973 and 1985 to remain current with changes in Imperial practice.—**NS/LK/DM**

Togni, Camillo, Italian composer; b. Brescia, Oct. 18, 1922; d. there, Nov. 27, 1993. He received training from Casella in Siena and Rome (1939–42), attended the Parma Cons. (diploma, 1946), and studied philosophy at the Univ. of Padua (graduated, 1948). After composing in a neo-Classical vein, Togni embraced the 12-tone method.

WORKS: ORCH.: *Variations* for Piano and Orch. (1946); *Fantasia concertante* for Flute and Strings (1957; Cologne Radio, March 25, 1958); *Some Other Where* (RAI, Naples, June 16, 1977). **CHAMBER:** *Aubade* for 6 Instruments (Rome, April 22, 1965); *Cinque pezzi* for Flute and Guitar (1975–76; RAI, Naples, June 16, 1976); *Für Herbert* for 2 Violins, Viola, and Harpsichord (Milan, Nov. 21, 1976); Trio for Violin, Viola, and Cello (Naples, June 15, 1978); *Quasi una serenata* for Guitar (Spoleto, July 8, 1979); *Due preludi* for Piccolo (Perugia, Aug. 20, 1980); *Du bleicher Geselle* for Chamber Group (1989); *Per Maila* for Piano or Flute and Piano (1992); *Fantasia* for Harp (1993); many piano pieces. **VOCAL:** *Psalmus CXXVII* for Solo Voices, Violin, Viola, and Cello (Brussels, June 24, 1950); *Ricercar* for Baritone and 5 Instruments (1953); *Helian di Trakl* for Voice and Piano (1955; also for Soprano and Chamber Orch., Palermo, May 24, 1961); *Gesang zur Nacht* for Soprano and Chamber Orch. (Venice, April 11, 1962); *Rondeaux per 10* for Soprano and 9 Instruments (1963; Madrid, June 24, 1965); *Preludes et rondeaux* for Soprano and Harpsichord (1963–64; Florence, April 17, 1964); *Sei notturni* for Contralto, Clarinet, Violin, and 2 Pianos (1965; Rome, March 4, 1966); *Tre pezzi* for Chorus and Orch. (Venice, Sept. 17, 1972); *Tre duetti* for Soprano and Flute (1977–80); *La Guirlande de Blois* for Soprano and Piano (Naples, June 15, 1978); *Les Feuilles Ameres* for Soprano (RAI, Milan, Sept. 30, 1989). **ELECTRONIC:** *Recitativo* (Venice, April 15, 1962).—**NS/LK/DM**

Tokatyan, Armand, Bulgarian tenor of Armenian descent; b. Plovdiv, Feb. 12, 1896; d. Pasadena, Calif., June 12, 1960. He was educated in Alexandria, Egypt; then studied voice with Cairone in Milan and Wolf in Vienna. He made his operatic debut in Milan in 1921; then went to the U.S., where he toured with the Scotti Opera Co. He made his debut at the Metropolitan Opera in N.Y. on Nov. 19, 1922, as Turiddu in a concert performance of Cavalleria rusticana, and remained a member of the company, with interruptions, until 1946. He also made appearances in London, Berlin, and Vienna.—**NS/LK/DM**

Tolbecque, family of Belgian-French musicians:

(1) Jean-Baptiste-Joseph Tolbecque, violinist, conductor, and composer; b. Hanzinne, Namur, April 17, 1797; d. Paris, Oct. 23, 1869. He studied violin with Kreutzer and counterpoint and fugue with Reicha at the Paris Cons. He was a violinist in the orch. of the Opéra Italien (1820–25), and then conductor of the Tivoli gardens orch. in Paris; subsequently oversaw the court dances for Louis Philippe I and helped to organize the Société des Concerts du Conservatoire, where he was a violist. With Gilbert and Guiraud, he wrote the opéra-comique *Charles V et Duguesclin* (1827), and with Deldevez, the ballet *Vert-Vert* (Paris, 1851), but he became best known as a composer of waltzes, galops, quadrilles, polkas, and other popular dances. Three of his brothers were also musicians:

(2) Isidore-Joseph Tolbecque, conductor and composer; b. Hanzinne, April 17, 1794; d. Vichy, Allier, May 10, 1871. He pursued a career as a conductor and composer of dance music.

(3) August-Joseph Tolbecque, violinist; b. Hanzinne, Feb. 28, 1801; d. Paris, May 27, 1869. He was a pupil of Kreutzer at the Paris Cons., where he won the premier prix (1821). He was a member of the Opera orch. (1824–31); also played in the Société des Concerts du Conservatoire and subsequently performed at Her Majesty's Theatre in London.

(4) Charles-Joseph Tolbecque, violinist, conductor, and composer; b. Paris, May 27, 1806; d. there, Dec. 29, 1835. He studied with Kreutzer at the Paris Cons., taking the premier prix in violin (1823). After playing in the Société des Concerts du Conservatoire, he became conductor at the Théâtre des Variétées (1830). He wrote incidental music for theater productions and songs.

(5) Auguste Tolbecque, cellist, instrument maker, and composer, son of **Auguste-Joseph Tolbecque;** b. Paris, March 30, 1830; d. Niort, Deux Sèvres, March 8, 1919. He studied cello (premier prix, 1849) with Vaslin and harmony with Reber at the Paris Cons. After playing in the orch. of the Grand Théâtre and teaching at the Cons. in Marseilles (1865–71), he returned to Paris and played with the Société des Concerts du Conservatoire, the Lamoureux Quartet, and the Maurin Quartet. He received instruction in instrument making from Victor Rambaux and then settled in Niort, where he devoted himself to restoring early instruments and making copies of same. He ed. *Monde Musical* and publ. the exercise vol. *La Gymnastique du violoncelle* (Paris, 1875). His works include the opéra-comique *Après la valse* (Niort, 1894) and many cello works. His son, Jean Tolbecque (b. Niort, Oct. 7, 1857; d. probably in Paris, 1890), was also a cellist; was a pupil of Alexandre Chevillard at the Paris Cons. (premier prix, 1873), and then was a member of the Opéra-Comique orch.

WRITINGS: *Quelques considérations sur la lutherie* (Paris, 1890); *Souvenirs d'un musicien en province* (Niort, 1896); *Notice historique sur les instruments à cordes et à archet* (Paris and Niort, 1898); *L'Art du luthier* (Niort, 1903).—**NS/LK/DM**

Toldrá, Eduardo, Catalan violinist, conductor, and composer; b. Villanueva y Geltru, Catalonia, April 7, 1895; d. Barcelona, May 31, 1962. He studied violin and composition at Barcelona's municipal music school. He made his debut as a soloist at the Barcelona Ateneo (1912), then was founder–1st violinist of the Quartet Renaixement (1912–21). In 1921 he became a prof. of violin at Barcelona's municipal music school; in 1944, was appointed conductor of the Municipal Orch. He composed the comic opera *El giravolt de Maig* (Barcelona, 1928), orch. pieces, chamber music, and songs.

BIBL.: M. Capdevila, *E. T.* (Barcelona, 1995).—**NS/LK/DM**

Tolonen, Jouko (Paavo Kalervo), Finnish musicologist and composer; b. Porvoo, Nov. 2, 1912; d.

Turku, July 23, 1986. He studied piano with Linko, composition with Krohn, Madetoja, and Fougestedt, and conducting in Helsinki, then pursued training in musicology at the Univ. there (Ph.D., 1969). He was director of the music dept. of the Finnish Broadcasting Co. (1946–55) and general director of the Finnish National Opera (1956–60); taught at the Sibelius Academy in Helsinki (1960–66) and at the Univ. of Turku (from 1965), where he was prof. of musicology (1972–77). He composed *Andante and Rondo alla burla* for Orch. (1948), *Andante* for Piano and Strings (1950), Sym. (1952), *3 Arabesques* for Orch. (1953), *Les Fanfares* for Brass (1970), incidental music for plays and films, and vocal pieces. **—NS/LK/DM**

Tolstoy, Dmitri, Russian composer; b. Berlin, Jan. 20, 1923. He was the son of the writer Alexei Tolstoy, with whom he went to Russia after the latter's temporary emigration. He studied at the Leningrad Cons., graduating in 1947, and also took courses in composition with Shebalin in Moscow and Shostakovich in Leningrad.

WORKS: 2 operas: *Masquerade* (1955; Moscow, Jan. 17, 1956) and *Mariuta* (Perm, Dec. 30, 1960); *Poem about Leningrad* for Orch. (1953); piano pieces; cantatas; songs.**—NS/LK/DM**

Tomadini, Jacopo, Italian composer; b. Cividale del Friuli, Aug. 24, 1820; d. there, Jan. 21, 1883. He studied with G.B. Candotti at the local church school. In 1846 he took holy orders, and later succeeded Candotti as organist and maestro di cappella at the Cividale del Fiuli Cathedral. In 1874 he organized the Associazione Ceciliana Italiana in Venice. With G. Amelli et al., he founded the journal *Musica sacra* in 1877. Tomadini was a leading figure in the reform movement of Roman Catholic church music.**—LK/DM**

Tomaschek, Wenzel Johann (actually, **Václav Jan Křtitel Tomášek),** important Bohemian composer and pedagogue; b. Skutsch, April 17, 1774; d. Prague, April 3, 1850. He was the youngest of 13 children. He learned the rudiments of singing and violin playing from P.J. Wolf and studied organ with Donat Schuberth. In 1787 he became an alto chorister at the Minorite monastery in Iglau; in 1790 he went to Prague, supporting himself by playing piano in public places; also took law courses at the Univ. of Prague. From 1806 to 1822 he was attached to the family of Count Georg Bucquoy de Longeval as music tutor. In 1824 he established his own music school in Prague. Among his many pupils were J.H. Woržischek (Voříšek), Dreyschock, Hanslick, and Schulhoff. Tomaschek was the first to use the instrumental form of the rhapsody systematically in a number of his piano pieces, although it was anticipated by W.R. Gallenberg in a single composition a few years earlier; he also adopted the ancient Greek terms "eclogue" and "dithyramb" for short character pieces. He wrote an autobiography, publ. in installments in the Prague journal *Libussa* (1845–50); a modern ed. was prepared by Z. Nmec (Prague, 1941), excerpts of which appeared in the *Musical Quarterly* (April 1946).

WORKS: DRAMATIC: Opera: *Seraphine, oder Grossmut und Liebe* (Prague, Dec. 15, 1811); *Alvaro* (unfinished). **ORCH.:** 3 syms. (1801, 1805, 1807); 2 piano concertos (1805, 1806). **CHAMBER:** 3 string quartets (1792–93); Piano Trio (1800); Piano Quartet (1805). **Piano:** 7 sonatas (1800–06); 42 eclogues (1807–23); 15 rhapsodies (1810); 6 *allegri capricciosi* (1815, 1818); 6 dithyrambs (1818–23). **CHORAL:** Requiem (1820); *Krönungsmesse* (1836); Te Deum.

BIBL.: M. Tarantová, *Václav Jan Tomášek* (Prague, 1946). **—NS/LK/DM**

Tomášek, Jaroslav, Czech composer; b. Koryčany, Moravia, April 10, 1896; d. Prague, Nov. 26, 1970. He studied music with Novák, and also attended a course in musicology at the Univ. of Prague. He composed mostly in small forms. Among his works were 2 song cycles, *To Woman* for High Voice (1919–20; with Orch., 1944–46) and *Grief* for Tenor, Soprano, Bass, and Orch. (1958–59), *Rondo* for Piano, left hand (1924), Piano Sonata for left hand (1925), 2 string quartets, *Symphonic Rondo* for Piano and Orch. (1962), and songs. His wife, Jaromíra Tomášková-Nováková (b. Jaroměř, May 23, 1892; d. Prague, April 25, 1957), was a soprano who taught singing at the Prague Cons. (from 1920). **—NS/LK/DM**

Tomasi, Biagio, Italian organist and composer; b. Comacchio, near Ferrara, c. 1585; d. Massafiscaglia, near Ferrara, 1640. He was a student of Girolamo Belli in Argenta. In 1609 he became cathedral organist in Comacchio. He also pursued the study of theology and took holy orders. He later served as a canon and director of music at the collegiate church in Massafiscaglia. Tomasi publ. 5 vols. of sacred and secular music (Venice, 1611–35).**—LK/DM**

Tomasi, Henri (Frédien), French composer; b. Marseilles, Aug. 17, 1901; d. Paris, Jan. 13, 1971. He studied with Paul Vidal at the Paris Cons., winning the 2nd Grand Prix de Rome for his cantata *Coriolan* (1927). He served in the French army (1939–40). Tomasi was awarded the Grand Prix de Musique Française in 1952. His music is marked by impressionistic colors; he was particularly attracted to exotic subjects, depicting in fine instrumental colors scenes in Corsica, Cambodia, Laos, Sahara, Tahiti, etc. He also wrote music inspired by Gregorian chant and medieval religious songs. During his last period he was motivated in his music by political events, and wrote pieces in homage to the Third World and Vietnam.

WORKS: DRAMATIC: Opera: *Miguel de Manâra* (1942; Munich, March 29, 1956); *L'Altantide* (1952; Mulhouse, Feb. 26, 1954); *La triomphe de Jeanne* (1955; Rouen, 1956); *Sampiero Corso* (Bordeaux, May 1956); *Il Poverello* (1957); *Le silence de la mer* (1959); *Ulysse* (1961); *L'élixir du révérend père Gaucher* (1962). **Ballet:** *La Grisi* (Paris, Oct. 7, 1935); *La Rosière de village* (Paris, May 26, 1936); *Les Santons* (Paris, Nov. 18, 1938); *La Féerie cambodgienne* (Marseilles, Jan. 31, 1952); *Les Folies mazarguaises* (Marseilles, Oct. 5, 1953); *Noces de cendre* (Strasbourg, Jan. 19, 1954); *Les Barbaresques* (Nice, 1960); *Nana*, after Émile Zola (1962). **Choreographic Poem:** *Dassine, sultane du Hoggar* for 2 Speakers, Chorus, and Orch. (1959). **ORCH.:** *Chants de Cyrnos*, symphonic poem (Paris, Nov. 30, 1929); *Mélodies corses* (1931); *Vocero*, symphonic poem

(Paris, Feb. 5, 1933); *Scènes municipales* (1933); *Tam-Tam*, symphonic poem (Paris, June 13, 1933); *Chants laotiens* (1934); *2 danses cambodgiennes* (1934); *Chant des geishas* (1936); *Impressions sahariennes* (1938); Sym. (Paris, May 4, 1943); *Concert asiatique* for Percussion and Orch. (1939); Flute Concerto (1947); Trumpet Concerto (1949); Viola Concerto (1951); Saxophone Concerto (1951); Horn Concerto (1955); Clarinet Concerto (1956); Trombone Concerto (1956); Bassoon Concerto (1958); Oboe Concerto (1958); *Jabadao*, symphonic poem (Paris, Jan. 10, 1960); Violin Concerto (1962); *Taïtienne de Gauguin* (1963); *Symphonie du tiers monde* (Paris, Feb. 18, 1968); *Chant pour le Vietnam*, symphonic poem for Wind Band and Percussion (Paris, Dec. 7, 1969); Cello Concerto (1970). **CHAMBER:** *Concerto champêtre* for Oboe, Clarinet, and Bassoon (1939); String Trio (1943); *Divertimento Corsica* for Woodwind Trio (1952); Wind Quintet (1952); *Danseuses de Degas* for Harp and String Quartet (1964); *Concerto de printemps* for Flute, Strings, and Percussion (1965); *La Moresca* for 8 Wind Instruments (1965); *Sonatine attique* for Clarinet (1966); many piano pieces. **VOCAL:** Song cycles.
—NS/LK/DM

Tomasini, Alois Luigi, Italian violinist and composer; b. Pesaro, June 22, 1741; d. Eisenstadt, April 25, 1808. In 1757 he became a manservant to Prince Paul Anton Esterházy, who sent him to Venice to complete his musical instruction in 1759. By 1761 he was back in the Esterházy service as 1st violinist in the Hofkapelle, where he became a friend of Haydn; later served as its Konzertmeister until his death (1790–94 excepted) and also as director of the Esterházy chamber music (from 1802). He wrote at least 2 syms. (both lost), 3 violin concertos (1 lost), and much chamber music, of which the 3 String Quartets, op. 8 (Vienna, 1807?), are particularly noteworthy; in all, he composed 30 string quartets (6 lost), 24 divertimentos (Nos. 1–6 and 13–24 for Baryton, Violin, and Cello, and Nos. 7–12 for Baryton, Viola, and Cello), 9 duo concertants for 2 Violins, 6 sonatas for Violin and Bass, and other works. See E. Schenck, ed., *Luigi Tomasini: Ausgewählte Instrumentalwerke*, Denkmäler der Tonkunst in Österreich, CXXIV (1972). He had 2 sons who became musicians: Anton (Edmund) Tomasini (b. Eisenstadt, Feb. 17, 1775; d. there, June 12, 1824) was a violinist and violist; studied with his father; in 1796 joined the Esterházy Kapelle, where he was made deputy director (1805) and then director (1818) of the orch. Alois (Basil Nikolaus) (Luigi) Tomasini (b. Esteraz, July 10, 1779; d. Neustrelitz, Feb. 19, 1858) was a violinist and composer; received his music training from his father; about 1793 he entered the Esterházy Kapelle as a violinist, winning the high commendation of Haydn; after marrying the singer Sophie Croll (1785–1847) in 1808, he went with her to Neustrelitz, where he later served as Konzertmeister. He was succeeded by his son, Carlo Tomasini (1813–80). Their daughter, Friederike (1810–86), a singer, studied in Munich and then appeared at the Neustrelitz Court Theater.

BIBL.: E. Fruchtman, *The Baryton Trios of T., Burgksteinner, and Neumann* (diss., Univ. of N.C., 1960).**—NS/LK/DM**

Tómasson, Jónas, Icelandic composer, teacher, and conductor; b. Ísafjördur, Nov. 21, 1946. He studied with J. Thorárinsson (theory) and T. Sigurbjörnsson (counterpoint and composition) at the Reykjavík Coll. of Music (graduated, 1967), and with Ton de Leeuw and Jos Kunst (composition) and Leon Ortel (orchestration) in Amsterdam (1969–72). He was active in Ísafjördur as a composer, teacher, and conductor.

WORKS: ORCH.: 2 syms. (1969, 1973); 1.41 (1970); *Leikleikur* (1972); *Ellefu Hugleidingar um Landnám* (1974); Violin Concerto (1974); *Orgia* (1975); *Notturno IV* (1982); *Skerpla II* (1983); *Midi* for 2 Pianos and Orch. (1985); *Í Raudum Gördum* (1991); Piano Concerto, *Kraków* (1998). **OTHER:** 22 sonatas for various instruments; piano pieces; organ music; vocal music, including 4 cantatas (1972, 1973, 1979, 1981), a *Missa Brevis* (1975), choruses, and songs.**—NS/LK/DM**

Tombelle, (Antoine Louis Joseph Gueyrand) Fernand (Fouant) de la
See **La Tombelle, (Antoine Louis Joseph Gueyrand) Fernand (Fouant) de**

Tomkins, family of English musicians:

(1) Thomas Tomkins, organist and composer; b. St. Davids, Pembrokeshire, 1572; d. Martin Hussingtree, Worcester (buried), June 9, 1656. He was the son of Thomas Tomkins, vicar choral of the Cathedral of St. Davids and later master of the choristers and organist there. He was a pupil of William Byrd; in 1596 he became instructor choristarum at Worcester Cathedral. He was made a member of the Chapel Royal, becoming a Gentleman in Ordinary by 1620; was one of its organists (from 1621), becoming senior organist about 1625; continued to be active at Worcester Cathedral until parliamentary forces took the city in 1646. He was allowed to live in the cathedral precincts, where he remained until settling at his son Nathaniel's home in Martin Hussingtree in 1654. Tomkins was the last representative of the followers of William Byrd. He wrote 29 madrigals, 28 of which were publ. in Songs of *3. 4. 5. & 6. parts* (London, 1622; ed. by E. Fellowes in *The English Madrigalists*, 2nd ed., rev., 1960, by T. Dart); one other madrigal has been ed. in *The English Madrigalists*, 2nd ed., 1962. While his importance as a madrigalist remains in dispute among contemporary scholars, his sacred works are generally admired; these include 5 services, about 120 anthems, and other works, most of which were publ. in *Musica Deo sacra et ecclesiae anglicanae* (London, 1668; ed. by B. Rose in *Early English Church Music*, V, 1965, IX, 1968, and XIV, 1973). He was a fine composer of keyboard music, his consort music being of very high quality; see S. Tuttle, ed., *Thomas Tomkins: Keyboard Music*, Musica Britannica, V (1955; 2nd ed., 1964). His son, Nathaniel Tomkins (b. Worcester, 1599; d. Martin Hussingtree, Oct. 20, 1681), was a musician; was educated at Balliol Coll., Oxford (B.D., 1629); served as a canon at Worcester Cathedral (from 1629).

BIBL.: S. de B. Taylor, *T. T.* (London, 1933); R. Cavanaugh, *The Anthems in "Musica Deo Sacra" by T. T.* (diss., Univ. of Mich., 1953); D. Stevens, *T. T.* (London, 1957; 2nd ed., 1967).

(2) John Tomkins, organist and composer, half-brother of **Thomas Tomkins;** b. St. Davids, 1586; d. London, Sept. 27, 1638. He was a scholar at King's Coll., Cambridge, where he became organist in 1606 and took the Mus.B. degree in 1608. He settled in London in 1619 as organist at St. Paul's Cathedral, becoming a Gentleman Extraordinary (1625) and a Gentleman in Ordinary (1627) of the Chapel Royal. A few of his sacred works are extant. Two of his brothers were also musicians:

(3) Giles Tomkins, organist and composer; b. St. Davids, after 1587; d. Salisbury, before Nov. 30, 1688. He was named organist of King's Coll., Cambridge, in 1624 and of Salisbury Cathedral in 1629. In 1630 he was made Musician for the Virginals in the King's Musick, a post he held until Cromwell's rise to power; was again in the royal service after the Restoration. Two of his verse anthems are extant.

(4) Robert Tomkins, instrumentalist and composer who flourished in the last half of the 17th century. He was active as a court musician from 1633. Only a handful of his anthems are extant.—**NS/LK/DM**

Tomlinson, John (Rowland), distinguished English bass; b. Oswaldtwistle, Lancashire, Sept. 22, 1946. He took a B.Sc. degree in civil engineering at the Univ. of Manchester, and also received vocal training at the Royal Northern Coll. of Music in Manchester and from Otakar Kraus in London. In 1970 he became a member of the Glyndebourne Festival Chorus; his first operatic role of consequence was as the 2nd Armed Man in *Die Zauberflöte* with the Glyndebourne Touring Opera Co. in 1970, which led to his first major role with the company in 1972 as Colline; he also appeared as Leporello that year with the Kent Opera. After an engagement with the New Opera Co. in London (1972–74), he sang regularly with the English National Opera in London (1975–80), where he distinguished himself as Masetto, King Marke, Rossini's Moses, Méphistophélès, Baron Ochs, and Bartók's Bluebeard. He made his debut at London's Covent Garden in 1979 as Colline, and returned there successfully in such roles as Mozart's Figaro, Leporello, the Commendatore, and Don Basilio. In 1988 he made his first appearance at the Bayreuth Festival as Wotan, a role he sang there regularly for 5 seasons; he also appeared as the Wanderer there (from 1989). In 1992 he sang Gurnemanz at the Berlin State Opera, and in 1993 returned to Covent Garden as Hans Sachs. In 1994 he again appeared as Wotan at the Bayreuth Festival, a role he reprised at the Berlin State Opera in 1996. In 1997 he was engaged as Baron Ochs and as Hans Sachs at Covent Garden. He portrayed Schoenberg's Moses at his Metropolitan Opera debut in N.Y. on Feb. 8, 1999. Tomlinson's commanding vocal technique and histrionic abilities have rendered him as one of the leading bassos of his generation. Among his other notable roles are Hunding, Philip II, Boris Godunov, Attila, and John Claggart.—**NS/LK/DM**

Tommasini, Vincenzo, Italian composer; b. Rome, Sept. 17, 1878; d. there, Dec. 23, 1950. He studied violin with Pinelli, and later theory with Falchi at the Liceo di Santa Cecilia in Rome; then went to Berlin, where he took lessons with Bruch; after sojourns in Paris, London, and N.Y., he returned to Rome. He wrote music in the poetic tradition of Italian Romanticism; his operas, symphonic works, and chamber music obtained immediate performances and favorable receptions; however, his most successful piece, *Le Donne di buon umore*, was not an original work but a comedy-ballet written on music from sonatas by Domenico Scarlatti, arranged in a series of tableaux and brilliantly orchestrated; this was a commission for the Ballets Russes of Diaghilev, who staged it at Rome in April 1917, and kept it in the repertoire during his tours all over the world. He publ. *La luce invisible* (1929) and *Saggio d'estetica sperimentale* (1942).

WORKS: DRAMATIC: Opera: *Medea* (1902–04; Trieste, April 8, 1906); *Amore di terra lontana* (1907–08); *Uguale fortuna* (1911; Rome, 1913); *Dielja* (c. 1935); *Il tenore sconfitto, ovvero La presunzione punita* (Rome, 1950). **Ballet:** *Le donne di buon umore* (1916; Rome, April 1917; suite, 1920; based on sonatas by D. Scarlatti); *Le diable s'amuse* (1936; N.Y., 1937); *Tiepolesco* (Naples, 1945). **ORCH.:** *La vita e un sogno* (1901); *Poema erotico* (1908–09); *Inno alla belta* (1911); *Ciari di luna* (1914–15; Rome, 1916); *Il beato regno* (1919–20; Rome, 1922); *Paesaggi toscani* (1922; Rome, 1923); *Il carnevale di Venezia* (1928; N.Y., Oct. 10, 1929); *Napule* (1929–30; Freiburg im Breisgau, Dec. 7, 1931); Concerto for Violin and Small Orch. (1932); *4 pezzi* (1931–34); Concerto for String Quartet and Orch. (1939); *La tempesta* (1941); Concerto for Orch. and Cello Obbligato (1943); *Duo concertante* for Piano and Orch. (1948). **CHAMBER:** 4 string quartets (1898; 1908–09; 1926; 1943); Violin Sonata (1916–17); 2 piano trios (1929, 1946); Harp Sonata (1938); piano pieces. **VOCAL:** *Messa da requiem* for Chorus and Organ (1944); choruses; songs.—**NS/LK/DM**

Tomotani, Kōji, Japanese composer; b. Hiroshima, Sept. 26, 1947. He studied at the Kunitachi Music Coll. in 1974, then went to France, where he had lessons with M. Bitsch and Messiaen (1974–76) and also studied at the École Normale de Musique de Paris (degree, 1975). His *Cosmic Landscape* trilogy is rooted in the concept of "eternal return," the "wheel of time symbolizing an intimate link between boundless space (the cosmos) and boundless time (eternity); each of the three works variously contrasts the elements of 'sound-space,' represented by tone-clusters and time relationships, and 'spaces,' which punctuate the elements comprising the 'sound-space.'"

WORKS: Concerto for Biwa and Orch. (1977); *Gyō* for Fué and Biwa (1978); *Livre de Shura* for Percussion Ensemble (1980); *Kâla-Cakra I* for Flute and Piano (1981) and *II* for Shakuhachi and Percussion (1983); *Torana* for Soprano, Oboe d'Amore, and Piano (1982); *Cosmic Landscape I* for Flute and Harpsichord (1985), *II* for Orch. (1987), and *III* for Clarinet (1990); *Spectrum I* for Flute and Piano (1988) and *II* for Piano (1989).—**NS/LK/DM**

Tomowa-Sintow, Anna, admired Bulgarian soprano; b. Stara Zagora, Sept. 22, 1941. She studied at the Bulgarian State Cons. in Sofia with Zlatew-Tscherkin and Zpiridonowa. In 1965 she made her operatic debut as Tatiana in Stara Zagora. She made her first appearance at the Leipzig Opera as Abigaille in 1967, and subsequently sang Arabella, Cio-Cio-San, Desdemona, and Violetta there. After winning the Sofia (1970) and Rio de Janeiro (1971) competitions, she made her debut at the Berlin State Opera as Mozart's Countess in 1972. Her career was assured when Karajan chose her to create the role of Sibyl in the premiere of Orff's *De temporum fine comoedia* at the Salzburg Festival in 1973.

She continued to sing there with much success in subsequent years, and also appeared at Karajan's Salzburg Easter Festivals. In 1974 she sang Donna Anna at the Bavarian State Opera in Munich, and made her U.S. debut that same year at the San Francisco Opera in the same role. In 1975 she appeared for the first time at London's Covent Garden as Fiordiligi. She made her debut at the Vienna State Opera in 1977 as Mozart's Countess. Her subsequent successes there led to her being made an Austrian Kammersängerin in 1988. On April 3, 1978, she made her Metropolitan Opera debut in N.Y. as Donna Anna. She appeared as Wagner's Elisabeth at the Paris Opéra in 1984. In 1990 she sang Yaroslavna in *Prince Igor* at Covent Garden. In 1992 she appeared as Tosca in Helsinki. She was engaged as Ariadne in Lisbon in 1996. She also sang extensively as a concert artist. Among her other notable roles were Verdi's Amelia and Aida, Wagner's Elsa, and Strauss's Marschallin.—**NS/LK/DM**

Tom Petty and the Heartbreakers, one of the most consistently successful American rock bands of the 1980s. **Membership:** Tom Petty, lead voc., 6- and 12-string gtr. (b. Gainesville, Fla., Oct. 20, 1953); Benmont Tench, kybd. (b. Gainesville, Fla., Sept. 7, 1954); Mike Campbell, lead gtr. (b. Gainesville, Fla., Feb. 1, 1954); Ron Blair, bs. (b. Macon, Ga., Sept. 16, 1952); Stan Lynch, drm. (b. Gainesville, Fla., May 21, 1955). Howard (Howie) Epstein (b. July 21, 1955) replaced Ron Blair in 1982 and Steve Ferrone (b. Brighton, England, April 25, 1950) replaced Stan Lynch in 1994.

Tom Petty and the Heartbreakers played engaging, unpretentious ensemble rock characterized by Petty's chiming guitar and accessible, perceptive songwriting. Achieving their first recognition in Great Britain, Tom Petty and the Heartbreakers were able to appeal to the New Wave crowd as well as mainstream rock fans. Since their breakthrough 1979 hit, "Refugee," the group has rarely been off the charts. Petty meanwhile has taken several sabbaticals from the group, first to perform with the supergroup the Traveling Wilburys, then to record two solo albums.

Taking up guitar at an early age, Tom Petty played around Gainesville, Fla., in various bands, including the Epics and Mudcrutch, between ages 14 and 17. He quit high school at 17 to tour with Mudcrutch, which included Mike Campbell and Benmont Tench. The three ended up in Los Angeles in the early 1970s and recorded a demonstration tape that led to a recording contract with Shelter Records. The group ultimately stabilized around Petty, Campbell, Tench, and two other Gainesville-based musicians, Ron Blair and Stan Lynch. Their eponymous debut album, recorded in 1976, contained "Fooled Again (I Don't Like It)," the British hit "American Girl," and the moderate American hit "Breakdown." By the release of *You're Gonna Get It!*, Tom Petty and the Heartbreakers were well established as a club band in Los Angeles. The album included "Restless" and produced two minor hits with "I Need to Know" and "Listen to Her Heart."

Tom Petty and the Heartbreakers subsequently became embroiled in legal disputes when Shelter Records was taken over by ABC Records and ABC was sold to MCA. As the group pursued a new contract independent of MCA, they were enjoined from recording. Ultimately MCA agreed to create a new label, Backstreet, headed by Petty's friend Danny Bramson, for the group's recordings. Their debut for the label, *Damn the Torpedoes*, set the precedent for the group's subsequent success: midtempo ensemble rock songs with catchy melodies and hooks and accessible lyrics. The album contained "What Are You Doin' in My Life?" and "Here Comes My Girl" and yielded two major hits, "Don't Do Me Like That" and "Refugee."

Graduating from medium-size-hall to arena tours by 1981, Tom Petty and the Heartbreakers backed Stevie Nicks of Fleetwood Mac on her debut solo album, *Bella Donna*, which yielded the smash hit the Petty-Nicks duet "Stop Draggin' My Heart Around." Nicks reciprocated by recording "The Insider" for the group's *Hard Promises*, which produced a major hit with "The Waiting" and a minor hit with "A Woman in Love (It's Not Me)." In 1981 Petty was one of several contemporary artists to encourage Del Shannon to return to recording, producing his comeback album, *Drop Down and Get It*. During 1982 Howie Epstein replaced Ron Blair in the group, and their next album, *Long After Dark*, included the caustic "Same Old You" and yielded major hits with "You Got Lucky" and "Change of Heart."

After their lengthy tour of 1983, the members of Tom Petty and the Heartbreakers worked on outside projects. Stan Lynch toured with T-Bone Burnett, while Benmont Tench did shows with Stevie Nicks, and Howie Epstein backed John Hiatt on some dates. Mike Campbell later cowrote the smash hit "The Boys of Summer" with Don Henley. While completing work on the group's next album, Petty broke his left hand in a fit of pique in October 1984. Released in 1985 on MCA Records, *Southern Accents* was rather disjointed, with some songs revolving around Southern themes and some songs written with Dave Stewart of the Eurythmics, including the major hit "Don't Come Around Here No More."

During 1985 Tom Petty and the Heartbreakers resumed touring, appearing at both the Live Aid and Farm Aid benefits. Recordings from the tour were compiled for *Pack Up the Plantation*, which included cover versions of concert favorites such as "Shout," "Needles and Pins," and "So You Want to Be a Rock and Roll Star." The band backed Dylan at Farm Aid and later conducted a brief tour of Japan and Australia with Dylan. In 1986 Dylan, with Petty and the Heartbreakers as his supporting band, mounted a full-scale tour of America, his first in six years. With Petty and the Heartbreakers performing brief sets of their own between sets by Dylan, the tour introduced both acts to new audiences. The band also appeared on Dylan's *Knocked Out Loaded* album, which included "Got My Mind Made Up," cowritten by Petty and Dylan.

Tom Petty and the Heartbreakers' *Let Me Up (I've Had Enough)* includes "My Life"/"Your World" and produced hits with "Jammin' Me," cowritten by Petty and Dylan. In 1988 Petty joined George Harrison, Dylan, Roy Orbison, and Jeff Lynne in the supergroup the

Traveling Wilburys, and their acoustic-based album *Volume One* yielded a moderate hit with "Handle with Care." Orbison's near-smash hit from *Mystery Girl*, "You Got It," was cowritten by Orbison, Lynne, and Petty. Petty's association with Lynne continued with *Full Moon Fever*, released as a solo Tom Petty album. Coproduced by Jeff Lynne and Mike Campbell, the album was recorded with Lynne, Harrison, and all the members of the Heartbreakers except Stan Lynch. It yielded a major hit with "I Won't Back Down," "Runnin' Down a Dream," and a near-smash with "Free Fallin'." In 1990 Petty rejoined Lynne, Harrison, and Dylan for a second album as the Traveling Wilburys, *Volume 3*.

Tom Petty and the Heartbreakers reassembled to record *Into the Great Wide Open* with Jeff Lynne as coproducer. The album, hailed as Petty's finest in years, included a number of songs cowritten with Lynne and yielded a major hit with "Learning to Fly." At the end of 1993 the group scored a major hit with "Mary Jane's Last Dance," one of two songs specifically created for Petty's Disney Channel cable-television special in January 1994. In October Stan Lynch left the group to work as an independent writer and producer. Switching to Warner Bros., Tom Petty recorded a second solo album, *Wildflowers*, which yielded a major hit with "You Don't Know How It Feels," then toured with the Heartbreakers in 1995.

DISC.: TOM PETTY AND THE HEARTBREAKERS: *T. P. and the H.* (1976); *You're Gonna Get It!* (1978); *Damn the Torpedoes* (1979); *Hard Promises* (1981); *Long After Dark* (1982); *Southern Accents* (1985); *Pack Up the Plantation-Live!* (1985); *Let Me Up (I've Had Enough)* (1987); *Into the Great Wide Open* (1991); *Greatest Hits* (1993); *Playback* (1995); *Echo* (1999). **THE TRAVELING WILBURYS:** *Volume One* (1988); *Volume 3* (1990). **TOM PETTY:** *Full Moon Fever* (1989); *Wildflowers* (1994).—**BH**

Tone, Yasunao, Japanese multimedia artist and experimental composer; b. Tokyo, March 31, 1935. He graduated with a degree in literature from the Japanese National Univ. in Chiba (1957), then studied at the Tokyo Univ. of Arts, where he co-founded the group Ongaku, dedicated to "event music." In 1962 he joined the American modern movement FLUXUS, which presented his first works in a Tokyo program under the title "One Man Show by a Composer"; also joined other modernistic groups that encompassed experimental happenings. His tape pieces *Days*, *Number*, and *Clapping Piece* won special prizes in the 1964 Nova Consonanza Festival in Rome. He further wrote works for theater and dance scenarios, among them 4 for the Merce Cunningham Dance Co., of which *Geography* and *Music* became one of the company's most popular productions under the title *Roadrunners* (1979). He publ. a book of collected essays, *Gendai Bijutsu no Iso* (Can Art Be Thought; 1970), and pursued his multiplicity of artistic interests as an ed. for the leading Japanese art magazine, the *Bijutsu Shihyo*. In 1972 he settled in N.Y. while continuing to travel widely as a guest of several New Wave music events. Beginning in 1976, Tone produced musical compositions as compounds of cultural studies, using visual materials compiled in combination with ancient oriental texts and electronic sounds. He contributed numerous works to ultramodern media groups, among them *Dinner Happening* (1962), *Miniature Restaurant* (1963), *Metropolitan Scavening Movement* (1964), *Dance Concert with 2 Titles* (1966), *Intermedia Art Festival* (1969), *Multi Performance* (1972), *Voice and Phenomenon* (1976), *The Wall and the Books* (1982), and *Word of Mouth* (1988). From 1979 he received a steady stream of commissions for multimedia works; received a N.Y. Foundation for the Arts Fellowship (1987; performance art/emergent forms). He has been a regular participant in festivals of avant-garde art, including the Annual Avant-Garde Festival (1973–77; 1980), FLUXUS festivals (1975, 1979, 1984, 1987), Dharma Music Festival (1985), Pioneer Performance Artists (1985), Japon des Avant-gardes (1986), Miami New Wave Media Festival (1988), Venice Biennale (1990), and the 2nd Acoustic International Festival (1990).

WORKS: DRAMATIC: *Anti-Dance and Anti-Music* (1961); *Ki* and *Waranin* (for Kaoru Kawana; 1962); *Kimigayo Electronic* and *Dictionary Music* (for Yoshie Aotsu and Mika Suzuki; 1963); *Theater Piece for Computer* (1966); *Kin no Sai Sarushima Dairi*, electronic music for a Kabuki play (1968); *Clockwork Video* (for the Merce Cunningham Dance Co. as Events #82 and #83; 1973); *Theatrum Philosophicum* (for the Merce Cunningham Dance Co. as Events #151 and #152; 1975); *Genealogy, Music* (for the Merce Cunningham Dance Co. as Event #201; 1978); *Geography and Music* (for the Merce Cunningham Dance Co. as *Roadrunners*; 1979); *Blind Dates* (for Blondel Cummings and Senga Nengudi; 1982); *Personal Documents* (for Susana Heyman-Chaffey; 1984); *Caught in the Fringe* (for Nancy Zendora; 1985); *Econologos* (with Nancy Zendora and Barbara Held; 1986); *Techno Eden* (for Kay Nishikawa; 1986); *Setsubun, Day of Chance* (1990; in collaboration with A. Knowles); *Spectaclum Lyrictronica*, "anarchic flight in paramedia space" (1990; in collaboration with B. Held). **INSTRUMENTAL:** *Improvisation and Object Sonore* (Ongaku collaboration; 1961); *Piano sound with magnetic tape* (1962); *Tone Work* (1963); *Mono Tone* (1963); *Ready-made Prohibition* (1965); *Kinegraphia* (1967); *815 Catch passage* (1968); *A 2nd Music* (1972); *One day Wittgenstein...* (1973); *Communication with Mr.* (1974); *Geodesy* for Harpsichord (1975); *Harpsichord* for 50 Fingers (1975); *Voice and phenomenon* (1976); *Fruits for towers* (1977); *Trio for a flute player* (1985); *Piano for Taoists* (1985); *Aletheia* (1987); *Lyrictron* for Flute (1988); *What is left from a Rembrandt...* (1989), **OTHER:** Tape pieces, including *T.V. is a chewing gum for eyes* (1969), *This is not a condom* (for Vernita Nemec; 1984), and *Music for 2 C.D. Players* (1986; rev. 1989); graphic scores, including *Music for Reed Organ* (1962); film scores, including *An event for film projector* (for Taka Imura; 1962) and *Gingakei...Galaxy* (for Masao Adachi; 1967). —**NS/LK/DM**

Tony Orlando and Dawn, multi-ethnic popsters of the 1970s. **MEMBERSHIP:** Tony Orlando (real name, Michael Anthony Orlando Cassavitis), (b. N.Y., April 3, 1944); Telma Hopkins (b. Louisville, Ky., Oct. 28, 1948); and Joyce Vincent (b. Detroit, Dec. 14, 1946).

Tony Orlando preferred singing doo-wop to attending high school. He and his group, the Five Gents, spent their days during the early 1960s singing in the halls of the Brill Building, home to much of the music business at the time. Eventually, the group got discouraged, but Orlando persevered. Finally, Don Kirshner hired him for $50 a week to sing on songwriter demos—the versions of songs sent to famous singers in hopes they would record the tune. One tape, Carole King's "Halfway to Heaven," was deemed good enough to be released by Epic Records in 1961, and the song eked its way into the Top 40 at #39. A couple of months later, Orlando took Neil Diamond's "Bless You" and rode it up to #15. Trimming away some 60 pounds of baby fat, the 16-year-old singer became a minor-league teen idol for part of 1961. Then his star faded.

Orlando was able to parlay his brief stardom and experience with Kirshner into a publishing career, first with Screen Gems, which had bought Kirshner's company, then as head of April Blackwood music, one of the publishing arms of Columbia Records. He continued to occasionally record, scoring a #28 hit fronting the studio group Wind on "Make Believe" in 1969. In 1970, he was approached by a producer from the tiny Bell label to add a male vocal to a track that had already been recorded by a pair of female vocalists named Telma Hopkins and Joyce Vincent. They had done many sessions, singing backgrounds on hits like Freda Payne's "Band of Gold," Marvin Gaye's "Heard It Through The Grapevine," and The Four Tops' "Reach Out, I'll Be There." Orlando didn't see any harm. The record wouldn't even have his name on it; Bell was releasing it as Dawn. Besides which, as he told *Newsweek* years later, "I couldn't believe the corniness of their song. I kept wondering who would listen to that crap."

Apparently, a lot of people listened. The record, "Candida," rose to #3 on the charts and went gold. Orlando was approached to appear on the followup, "Knock Three Times"; it spent three weeks at #1 and also went gold. Suddenly, Tony Orlando was making hit records again. He signed with the label and went on tour with Vincent and Hopkins as "Dawn, featuring Tony Orlando." What followed were a couple of years of relatively minor hits, like "I Play and Sing" (#25, 1971), "Summer Sand" (#33, 1971), and "What Are You Doing Sunday" (#39, 1971). The cold streak didn't end until they recorded a song based on a Pete Hamill story that appeared in *Reader's Digest*. With its hokey, carnival music, "Tie a Yellow Ribbon Round the Ole Oak Tree" topped the adult- contemporary charts in 1973 for two weeks and the pop charts for four, taking both the single and the *Tuneweaving* album to gold. They followed this with another gold single, "Hey Has Anybody Seen My Sweet Gypsy Rose," which topped the adult-contemporary charts for three weeks, hitting #3 pop, and going gold. Yet another song with an impossibly long title, "Who's in the Strawberry Patch with Sally," finished off the year at #27.

During the summer of 1974, CBS hired Tony Orlando and Dawn as a summer replacement for its highly rated Sonny and Cher Show. Despite the almost painful hokey-ness of the show, it got huge ratings and ran for two more years. During that time the group continued to record, landing a #7 hit with "Stepping Out (Gonna Boogie Tonight)" as the show took off in the summer of 1974. The group started off 1975 with the #11 "Look in My Eyes Pretty Woman," topping the pop and adult-contemporary charts once more that spring with "He Don't Love You (Like I Love You)," its first (and only major) hit for Elektra. Dawn followed this with the #14 "Mornin' Beautiful" and the #34 "You're All I Need to Get By" that summer. In 1976, after a #22 hit, "Cupid," but the group started slipping in popularity. Orlando, troubled by the deaths of his sister, grandfather, and friend Freddie Prinze, as well as his own drug dependencies, walked off stage in the middle of a concert in Mass. in July 1977, temporarily retiring from show business. Dawn forged on without him, but, without hits, it finally broke up: Vincent retired to raise a family; Hopkins became an in-demand comedic actress, with regular roles in such sitcoms as *Gimme a Break*, *Bosom Buddies*, *Family Matters*, and *Cosby*.

After about four months of "retirement," Orlando returned to the stage as a solo act in Las Vegas. He recorded, but nothing sold well. He became a staple on the lounge circuit. In 1980, he filled in while the star of *Barnum* on Broadway took a vacation. He briefly reunited with Dawn in 1988, also on the lounge circuit. When Branson, Mo., became a hotbed for has- been performers in the mid-1980s, Orlando opened the Tie a Yellow Ribbon Theater. When that hit financial difficulty, he went into business with Wayne Newton, calling the theater TOWN (for their initials). At the turn of the millennium, Newton and Orlando were embroiled in lawsuits over the theater.

DISC.: *Candida* (1970); *Dawn Featuring Tony Orlando* (1971); *Tuneweaving* (1973); *Dawn's New Ragtime Follies featuring Tony Orlando* (1973); *Prime Time* (1974); *He Don't Love You (Like I Love You)* (1975); *Skybird* (1975); *To Be with You* (1976). **TONY ORLANDO:** *I Got Rhythm* (1979).—**HB**

Töpfer, Johann Gottlob, famous German organist, teacher, and writer on organ building; b. Niederrossla, Dec. 4, 1791; d. Weimar, June 8, 1870. He studied with the cantor Schlomilch, then at Weimar with Destouches and A.E. Müller. He also attended the Weimar Seminary, where he became a teacher of music in 1817; from 1830 he was town organist of Weimar. An expert on organ construction, he wrote *Die Orgelbaukunst* (Weimar, 1833–34), *Die Scheibler'sche Stimm-Methode* (Erfurt, 1842), *Theoretisch-praktische Orgelschule* (Erfurt, 1845), and *Lehrbuch der Orgelbaukunst* (4 vols., Weimar, 1855; 2nd ed., rev., 1888 by M. Allihn as *Die Theorie und Praxis des Orgelbaus*; 3rd ed., rev., 1936 by P. Smets). He composed *Orgelweihe* for Organ, Chorus, and Tenor, various preludes, fugues, chorale preludes, and choral fantasias for Organ, a Piano Trio, and a Piano Sonata.

BIBL.: A. Gottschalg, *J.G. T.* (Berlin, 1870).—**NS/LK/DM**

Töpper, Hertha, Austrian mezzo-soprano; b. Graz, April 19, 1924. She received her musical training in Graz, studying violin with her father at the Cons. and voice with Franz Mixa at the opera school. She made her operatic debut in 1945 as Ulrica at the Graz Landestheater, where she sang until 1952. In 1951 she appeared at the Bayreuth Festival; after singing as a guest artist at the Bavarian State Opera in Munich in 1951–52, she joined its roster; was made a Bavarian Kammersängerin in 1955. In 1953 she made her first appearance at London's Covent Garden as Clairon with the visiting Bavarian State Opera, and later returned for guest appearances. She made her U.S. debut at the San

Francisco Opera in 1960 as Octavian, a role she repeated for her Metropolitan Opera debut in N.Y. on Nov. 19, 1962. From 1971 to 1981 she was a prof. at the Munich Hochschule für Musik. In 1980 she retired from the operatic stage. Her operatic repertoire included many roles by Wagner, Verdi, and Strauss; as a concert artist, she was particularly noted for her performances of the music of Bach.—**NS/LK/DM**

Toradze, Alexander (David), Russian-American pianist and teacher, son of **David (Alexandrovich) Toradze;** b. Tbilisi, May 30, 1952. He was a pupil at the Central Music School (1958–69) and Cons. (1969–71) in Tbilisi, and later studied at the Moscow Cons. with Yakov Zak, Boris Zemlyansky, and Lev Naumov. He began his career at the age of 9 with an appearance with the Tbilisi Sym. Orch., and subsequently toured widely in his homeland; he attracted wide notice in the West when he won the Silver Medal at the Van Cliburn Competition in 1977, which led to engagements in the U.S. In 1983 he settled in the U.S. but continued to pursue an international career in his many tours. In 1992 he became prof. of piano at Ind. Univ. in South Bend. —**NS/LK/DM**

Toradze, David (Alexandrovich), noted Russian composer, father of **Alexander (David) Toradze;** b. Tiflis, April 14, 1922; d. there (Tbilisi), Nov. 7, 1983. He studied composition with Barkhudarian and piano with Virsaladze at the Tbilisi Cons.; after pursuing composition studies with Glière at the Moscow Cons., he completed postgraduate work at the Tbilisi Cons. (1948–51). Then in 1952 he joined its faculty, being made a reader in 1966 and a prof. in 1973. He received various honors, including the State Prize (1951), People's Artist of the Georgian S.S.R. (1961), and the Order of Lenin.

WORKS: DRAMATIC: Opera: *The Sumarmi Fortress* (1942); *The Call of the Mountains* (Tbilisi, Nov. 20, 1947); *The Bride of the North* (Tbilisi, 1958). **Ballet:** *Gorda* (Tbilisi, 1949); *For Peace* (Tbilisi, June 17, 1953; rev. as *The Unsubdued*, 1970). **Musical Comedies:** *Natel* (1948); *The Avengers* (1952). **Other:** Film scores. **ORCH.:** *Festival*, overture (1944); 2 syms. (1946, 1968); *Afrikanskiye eskizi*, symphonic poem for Soloists, Chorus, and Orch. (1962); *Georgian Folk Refrains*, choral sym. (1972). **OTHER:** Chamber music; songs. —**NS/LK/DM**

Torchi, Luigi, eminent Italian musicologist; b. Mondano, near Bologna, Nov. 7, 1858; d. Bologna, Sept. 18, 1920. He studied composition at the Accademia Filarmonica in Bologna, with Serrao at the Naples Cons., with Jadassohn and Reinecke at the Leipzig Cons., and in France. He was prof. of music history and librarian at the Liceo Musicale Rossini in Pesaro (1885–91), and from 1895 to 1916 he held similar positions at the Bologna Cons., also teaching composition there. From its foundation (1894) until 1904 he was ed. of the *Rivista Musicale Italiana*, for which he wrote many valuable essays. In 1890 he publ. *Riccardo Wagner: Studio critico* (2nd ed., 1913). Besides a collection of *Eleganti canzoni ed arie italiane of the 17th century* (Milan, 1894) and *A Collection of Pieces for the Violin Composed by Italian Masters of the 17th and 18th Centuries* (London; both with piano accompaniment by Torchi), from 1897 to 1907 he publ. the important anthology *L'arte musicale in Italia.*

BIBL.: C. Criscione, *L. T.: Un musicologo italiano tra Otto e Novecento* (Imola, 1997).—**NS/LK/DM**

Torelli, Gasparo, Italian composer and poet; b. Borgo S. Sepolcro, near Lucca, date unknown; d. probably in Padua, c. 1613. He entered the clergy, and by 1593 was active in Padua, where he was associated with the Accademia degli Avveduti (from 1601). He set a number of his own texts to music. Among his works are a favola pastorale for 4 Voices, *I fidi amanti* (Venice, 1600; ed. by B. Somma and L. Bianchi in Capolavori Polifonici del Secolo XVI, Vol. VII, 1967), as well as *Canzonette* for 3 Voices (Venice, 1593), *Il secondo libro delle canzonette* for 3 to 4 Voices (Venice, 1598), *Brevi concetti d'amore: Il primo libro de madrigali* for 5 Voices (Venice, 1598), and *Amorose faville: Il quarto libro delle canzonette* for 3 Voices (Venice, 1608).—**NS/LK/DM**

Torelli, Giuseppe, famous Italian violinist, pedagogue, and composer; b. Verona, April 22, 1658; d. Bologna, Feb. 8, 1709. He was the brother of the noted painter Felice Torelli. After going to Bologna about 1682, he was made a member of the Accademia Filarmonica as suonatore di violino in 1684. He received instruction in composition from G.A. Perti, and in 1686 he entered the cappella musicale at S. Petronio as a viola player; later played tenor viol there (1689–96) and also toured as a violinist. After further travels as a violinist, he served as maestro di concerto to the Margrave of Brandenburg in Ansbach (1698–99). From 1699 until at least 1700 he was active in Vienna. By 1701 he was again in Bologna, where he became a violinist in the cappella musicale at S. Petronio. He had many pupils, most notably Francesco Manfredini. Torelli was an important figure in the development of the instrumental concerto, excelling in concerto grosso and solo concerto writing.

WORKS: (10) *Sonate a 3*, with Basso Continuo, op. 1 (Bologna, 1686); (12) *Concerto da camera* for 2 Violins and Basso Continuo, op. 2 (Bologna, 1686); (12) *Sinfonie* for 2 to 4 Instruments, op. 3 (Bologna, 1687); (12) *Concertino per camera* for Violin and Cello, op. 4 (Bologna, 1688); (6) *Sinfonie a 3 e* [6] *concerti a 4*, op. 5 (Bologna, 1692); (12) *Concerti musicali*, op. 6 (Augsburg, 1698; no. 1 ed. by G. Piccioli, Rome, 1952, and by W. Kolneder, Mainz, 1958; no. 10 ed. in Nagels Musikarchiv, LXX, 1931); op. 7 (unknown; not extant); (12) *Concerti grossi con una pastorale per il Ss. Natale*, op. 8 (Bologna, 1709; nos. 1, 3, 7, and 9 ed. by P. Santi, Milan, 1959; no. 6 ed. by D. Stevens, London, 1957; no. 8 ed. by E. Praetorius, London, 1950); other instrumental works in contemporary collections; also a few vocal works, including the oratorio *Adam auss dem irrdischen Paradiess verstossen* (music not extant), other sacred pieces, and arias.

BIBL.: F. Giegling, *G. T., Ein Beitrag zur Entwicklungsgeschichte des italienischen Konzerts* (Kassel, 1949); R. Norton, *The Chamber Music of G. T.* (diss., Northwestern Univ., 1967); E. Enrico, *G. T.'s Music for Instrumental Ensemble with Trumpet* (diss., Univ. of Mich., 1970).—**NS/LK/DM**

Torff, Brian (Quade), bassist; b. Hinsdale, Ill., March 16, 1954. His father sang on an amateur basis.

Torff studied at the Berklee Coll. of Music (1973) and the Manhattan School of Music (1974). His first professional work was accompanying Cleo Laine (1974). Through the 1970s, he worked with several older artists, including pianists Mary Lou Williams (1975) and Marian McPartland (1978, 1979) and violinist Stephane Grappelli (with whom he recorded at Carnegie Hall in 1978 and also toured the Far East). He worked with pianist George Shearing in 1979–82, and also worked as an accompanist for husband-and-wife team Jackie (Cain) and Roy (Kral) from 1979–80. In 1986, he formed the fusion-jazz group Etosha. In 1989, he was named director of jazz studies at the Fairfield (Conn.) Univ., a position he continues to hold; he directs the university's jazz band and, since 1995, codirects its world music ensemble. In the early 1990s, he worked with Jimmy Cobb (1989–91) and Red Rodney (1991), among others. In the mid- to late 1990s, he worked in a trio with vibist Dave Samuels and guitarist Joe Beck, as well as the fusion group, Thunderstick.

Disc.: *Blues Alley & Jazz* (with George Shearing, 1979); *Manhattan Hoe Down* (1983); *Hitchiker of Karoo* (1985); *Workin' on a Bassline* (with Thunderstick, 1997); *Union* (with Hobgood and Wertico, 1997).—**JC-B/LP**

Torkanowsky, Werner, German-born American conductor, violinist, and composer; b. Berlin, March 30, 1926; d. Bar Harbor, Maine, Oct. 20, 1992. He was taken to Palestine in 1933. After obtaining a violin diploma at the Palestine Cons. in Tel Aviv (1947), he emigrated to the U.S. in 1948 and pursued his studies with Rafael Bronstein. In 1952 he became a naturalized American citizen and a violinist in the Pittsburgh Sym. Orch. Following studies in conducting with Pierre Monteux (1954–59), he won the Naumburg Award for conducting in N.Y. in 1961. From 1963 to 1977 he was music director of the New Orleans Phil., and then of the Bangor Sym. Orch. from 1981. He also was active as a violinist, mainly as a chamber musician. Among his works were orch. pieces, chamber music, and songs.—**NS/LK/DM**

Torke, Michael, American composer and pianist; b. Milwaukee, Sept. 21, 1961. He began piano lessons at 5 and commenced composing while still a youth. After studying composition with Rouse and Schwantner and piano with Burge at the Eastman School of Music in Rochester, N.Y. (graduated, 1984), he pursued graduate studies with Druckman and Bresnick at Yale Univ. (1984–85). He won the Prix de Rome and held a residency at the American Academy in Rome in 1986. His output reveals an effective blend of serious and pop music genres.

Works: DRAMATIC: *Estatic Orange*, ballet (N.Y., May 10, 1985; includes *Verdant*, later renamed *Green*, for Orch., Milwaukee, Nov. 20, 1986, and the ballet *Purple*, N.Y., June 11, 1987); *The Directions*, chamber opera (Iraklion, Crete, Aug. 6, 1986); *Black and White*, ballet (N.Y., May 7, 1988); *Slate*, ballet (N.Y., June 15, 1989); *King of Hearts*, television opera (1993; Channel 4, England, Jan. 1995); *Central Park*, opera (Glimmerglass, N.Y., July 24, 1999; in collaboration with R. Beaser and D. Drattell). **ORCH.:** *Vanada* for Chamber Ensemble (1984; Amsterdam, Oct. 11, 1985); *Bright Blue Music* (N.Y., Nov. 23, 1985; also as *The Harlequins Are Looking at You* for Piano Trio); *Adjustable Wrench* for Chamber Ensemble (Huddersfield, Nov. 24, 1987); *Copper* for Brass Quintet and Orch. (Midland, Mich., June 3, 1988); *Ash* for Chamber Orch. (St. Paul, Minn., Feb. 3, 1989; also for Orch.); *Rust* for Piano and Wind Ensemble (Huddersfield, Nov. 21, 1989); *Bronze* for Piano and Orch. (1990; N.Y., Jan. 6, 1991, composer soloist); *Red* (1991); *Music on the Floor* for Chamber Ensemble (Milwaukee, April 10, 1992); *Monday and Tuesday* for Chamber Ensemble (London, Dec. 8, 1992); *Run* (1992; N.Y., April 29, 1993); Piano Concerto (1993; Troy, N.Y., Jan. 14, 1994, composer soloist); Saxophone Concerto (1993; Troy, N.Y., Jan. 14, 1994); *Bone* for Chamber Ensemble and Wordless Woman's Voice (Rensselaer, N.Y., April 15, 1994); *Javelin* (Atlanta, Sept. 8, 1994); *Nylon* for Guitar and Chamber Orch. (Derby, England, Nov. 9, 1994); *December* for Strings (Des Moines, April 1, 1995); *Flint* for Chamber Ensemble (Palermo, Oct. 27, 1995); *Overnight Mail* for Chamber Ensemble (Amsterdam, Sept. 29, 1997); *Brick Symphony* (1997; San Francisco, Jan. 16, 1998); *Four Seasons*, sym. for Soloists, Chorus, Boys' Chorus, and Orch. (N.Y., Oct. 8, 1999). **CHAMBER:** *Ceremony of Innocence* for Flute, Clarinet, Violin, Cello, and Piano (Tanglewood, July 30, 1983); *The Yellow Pages* for Flute, Clarinet, Violin, Cello, and Piano (New Haven, Conn., April 8, 1985); *The Harlequins Are Looking at You* for Piano Trio (N.Y., Nov. 22, 1985; also for Orch.); *Chalk* for String Quartet (Manchester, England, Oct. 1, 1992); *Chrome* for Flute and Piano (1993); *July* for Saxophone Quartet (Cardiff, Aug. 16, 1995); *The Blue Pages* for Flute, Clarinet, Violin, Cello, and Piano (Milwaukee, Sept. 9, 1995); *The White Pages* for Flute, Clarinet, Violin, Cello, and Piano (Milwaukee, Sept. 9, 1995); *Sprite* for Flute and Piano (N.Y., Feb. 14, 1996); *July 19* for String Quartet (Utrecht, May 12, 1996). **Piano:** *Laetus* (1981). **VOCAL:** *Mass* for Baritone, Chorus, and Chamber Orch. (N.Y., June 27, 1990); *4 Proverbs* for Woman's Voice and Chamber Ensemble (Milwaukee, May 28, 1993); *Book of Proverbs* for Soprano, Baritone, Chorus, and Orch. (Utrecht, Sept. 15, 1996); *Pentecost* for Soprano, Organ, and String Orch. (1997; Elm Grove, Wisc., Oct. 18, 1998). **—NS/LK/DM**

Tormé (Torme), Mel(vin Howard), versatile American singer, songwriter, and actor; b. Sept. 13, 1925; d. Los Angeles, June 5, 1999. In a career that lasted 67 years, Tormé achieved his greatest recognition as a jazz-oriented singer of classic pop songs. But he also dabbled successfully in a wide range of activities in entertainment. He wrote hundreds of songs, among them the seasonal standard "The Christmas Song (Merry Christmas to You)" and worked as a drummer, pianist, and musical arranger. He acted in films and on television and also wrote, produced, and hosted TV shows. He wrote articles and books ranging from fiction to biography. But he spent most of his career in nightclubs and concert halls, singing with a burnished baritone, his phrasing exceptionally flexible, his repertoire ranging from the songs of Rodgers and Hart to those of Steely Dan's Donald Fagen. Though he never achieved widespread popularity as a recording artist, by the 1970s he was recognized as one of the most outstanding jazz singers of his time.

Tormé's father, William Torma, a retail merchant, had his name rendered as "Torme" when he passed through Ellis Island as a Russian immigrant; Tormé added the accent as a teenager. His mother, Sarah Sopkin Torme, was a song demonstrator. When he was four his parents took him to a nightclub in Chicago to see the Coon-Sanders Orch., and Carlton Coon invited him onstage to sing. He continued to sing with the band weekly for six months, then had other singing engagements. He began to study the drums at age seven, and by 1934 he was appearing as a child actor on local radio. In August 1942, Harry James and His Orch. with Dick Haymes on vocals scored a Top Ten hit with his composition "Lament to Love."

In August 1942, Tormé joined a big band led by Chico Marx of the Marx Brothers as a singer, vocal arranger, and eventually, drummer; he stayed with the band until it broke up the following year. Spotted by a talent scout for RKO Pictures, he made his film debut in the movie musical *Higher and Higher*, released in December 1943, next appearing in the films *Pardon My Rhythm* and *Ghost Catchers*, both released in May 1944. He took over a vocal group he named the Mel-Tones and became their lead singer and vocal arranger. He served briefly in the military in 1944 before being discharged for having flat feet.

In 1945, Tormé appeared in two more films, *Let's Go Steady*, released in March, and *Junior Miss*, released in June. His song "Stranger in Town" was recorded by Martha Tilton and made the Top Ten in July. Meanwhile, he was getting work with the Mel-Tones, accompanying Bing Crosby on the March 1946 chart entry "Day By Day" (music by Paul Weston and Axel Stordahl, lyrics by Sammy Cahn) and Artie Shaw and His Orch. on "I Got the Sun in the Morning" (music and lyrics by Irving Berlin), which was in the charts in July 1946. He also appeared in the film *Janie Gets Married*, released in June. But his most memorable effort of 1946 was "The Christmas Song (Merry Christmas to You)" (music by Mel Tormé, lyrics by Robert Wells), the million-selling Top Ten hit recorded by Nat "King" Cole's King Cole Trio.

Signed to the MGM film studio, Tormé appeared in the movie musical *Good News*, released in December 1947, as well as sang "Blue Moon" (music by Richard Rodgers, lyrics by Lorenz Hart) in the Rodgers and Hart film biography *Words and Music*, released in December 1948. But although he worked on two more films in this period, lending his voice to the Disney animated feature *So Dear to My Heart*, released in January 1949, and appearing in *Duchess of Idaho*, released in July 1950, he did not become a movie star. Instead, signed to Capitol Records, he had a series of successful recordings, scoring five Top Ten hits in a little over a year during 1949–50, starting with "Careless Hands" (music by Carl Sigman, lyrics by Bob Hilliard), which hit #1 in April 1949, and followed by "Again" (music by Lionel Newman, lyrics by Dorcas Cochran), "The Four Winds and the Seven Seas" (music by Don Rodney, lyrics by Hal David), "The Old Master Painter" (a duet with Peggy Lee; music by Beasley Smith, lyrics by Haven Gillespie), and "Bewitched" (music by Richard Rodgers, lyrics by Lorenz Hart).

By the 1950s, Tormé had launched a successful career as a nightclub singer, with regular forays into recording and television and film work. He was a regular on the summer TV series *TV's Top Tunes* (1951) and *Summertime U.S.A.* (1953) and had his own daytime talk show for a time, also making dramatic appearances on such programs as *Playhouse 90*. He returned to filmmaking in the late 1950s and appeared in minor roles in a series of films: *The Fearmakers* (1958), *The Big Operator* (1959), *Girls Town* (1959), *Walk Like a Dragon* (1960), *The Private Lives of Adam and Eve* (1960), *The Patsy* (1964), and *A Man Called Adam* (1966). His recordings became increasingly jazz-oriented, featuring top jazz musicians as sidemen and frequently employing arranger/conductor Marty Paich. His recording of "Mountain Greenery" (music by Richard Rodgers, lyrics by Lorenz Hart) was a Top Ten hit in the U.K. in 1956; "Comin' Home Baby" (music by Bob Tucker, lyrics by Bob Dorough) made the American Top 40 in 1962 and earned him his first Grammy nominations, for Best Solo Vocal Performance, Male, and Best Rhythm & Blues Recording; and "Lover's Roulette" was in the Top Ten of the easy-listening charts in 1967.

Tormé wrote and produced for television as well. Notably, he wrote arrangements and special material for *The Judy Garland Show* (1963–64), an experience he describes in his first book, *The Other Side of the Rainbow* (1970). He hosted the 1971 documentary series *It Was a Very Good Year*.

Since the 1970s he began to gain greater recognition as a musician and jazz performer, exemplified by a series of Grammy nominations. He was nominated for Best Arrangement Accompanying Vocalist(s) for "Gershwin Medley" from his 1974 album *Live at the Maisonette*, but most of the nods came in the Best Jazz Vocal Performance category in 1978 for his album with Buddy Rich, *Together Again, for the First Time*; in 1980 for *Tormé/A New Album;* and in 1981 for *Mel Tormé and Friends Recorded Live at Marty's New York*.

After a career of jumping from label to label, Tormé finally found a recording home with the independent Concord Jazz imprint in 1982, where he did some of his best work. *An Evening with George Shearing and Mel Tormé* won him his first Grammy for Best Jazz Vocal Performance, Male, in 1982, though he protested that pianist Shearing deserved to share the award, and he repeated in the same category with *Top Drawer* in 1983. Further nominations came with *An Evening at Charlie's* (1984), *An Elegant Evening* (1986), *A Vintage Year* (1988), and "Ellington Medley" from *Mel and George Do World War II* (1991).

In 1996, Tormé suffered a stroke that ended his career; he died of complications related to it three years later. He was married four times and had five children.

Writings: *The Other Side of the Rainbow: Behind the Scenes on the Judy Garland Television Series* (N.Y., 1970); *Wynner: A Novel* (N.Y., 1978); *It Wasn't All Velvet: An Autobiography* (N.Y., 1988); *Traps the Drum Wonder: The Life of Buddy Rich* (N.Y., 1991); *My Singing Teachers: Reflections on Singing Popular Music* (N.Y., 1994).

Disc.: *Collection* (rec. 1942–85; rel. 1996); *It's a Blue World* (1955); *Swings Schubert Alley* (1960); *Encore at Marty's* (1982); *With Rob McConnell and the Boss Brass* (1986); *Mel Torme and the Marty Paich Dek-tette* (1988); *Night at the Concord Pavillion* (1990); *Fujitsu: Concord Jazz Festival in Japan* (1990); *Mel & George "Do" World War II* (1991); *Sing, Sing, Sing* (1993); *Velvet and Brass* (1995); *A&E An Evening with Mel Torme* (1996); *That's All* (1997).
—WR

Tormis, Veljo, Estonian composer; b. Harjamaa, Aug. 7, 1930. His musical studies led him to pursue an interest in Estonian folk music. This initial interest prompted him to explore the rich musical heritage of the Baltic-Finnish peoples, which served as an inspiration for his creative work. Tormis has composed many choral works that approach the stature of symphonic scores. Particularly outstanding is his large choral cycle *Forgotten Peoples* (1970–89). His works have been performed widely abroad, and many have been recorded. **—LK/DM**

Törne, Bengt (Axel) von, Finnish composer; b. Helsinki, Nov. 22, 1891; d. Turku, May 4, 1967. He studied composition with Furuhjelm at the Helsinki Inst. of Music (1910–16) and orchestration with Sibelius (1916–17). He wrote 6 syms. (1935–66), 3 sinfoniettas, *Sinfonia da camera* for Strings (1951), Piano Concerto, Piano Quintet, 2 string quartets, 2 violin sonatas, and a Piano Trio. He publ. a monograph on Sibelius (London, 1937; in Italian, Florence, 1943; in Finnish, Helsinki, 1945; in Swedish, Stockholm, 1945) and an autobiography (Borga, 1945).**—NS/LK/DM**

Torrefranca, Fausto (Acanfora Sansone dei duchi di Porta e), eminent Italian musicologist; b. Monteleone Calabro, Feb. 1, 1883; d. Rome, Nov. 26, 1955. Trained as an engineer, he took up music under E. Lena in Turin (harmony and counterpoint) and also studied by himself. It was through his initiative that the first chair of musicology was established in Italy. In 1913 he became a lecturer at the Univ. of Rome; from 1914 to 1924, was a prof. of music history at the Cons. di S. Pietro in Naples, and from 1915, also librarian there; from 1924 to 1938, was librarian of the Milan Cons. From 1907 he was ed. of the *Rivista Musicale Italiana*. In 1941 he was appointed a prof. of music history at the Univ. of Florence.

WRITINGS: *La vita musicale dello spirito: La musica, le arti, il dramma* (Turin, 1910); *Giacomo Puccini e l'opera internazionale* (Turin, 1912); *Le origine italiane del romanticismo musicale: I primitivi della sonata moderna* (Turin, 1930); *Il segreto del quattrocento: Musiche ariose e poesia popularesca* (Milan, 1939). **—NS/LK/DM**

Torres-Santos, Raymond, Puerto Rican composer, conductor, keyboardist, and music educator; b. San Juan, June 19, 1958. He grew up in a musical family; one of his grandfathers was a violinist, and the other played the German accordion. He was educated in P.R. at the Univ. (B.A. in humanities, 1980) and the Cons. of Music (B.A. in music, 1980); also had lessons with Ginastera (summers, 1977–78); continued his studies at the Univ. of Calif. at Los Angeles (M.A., 1982; Ph.D., 1986), where his mentors were Henri Lazarof, Paule Reale, and David Raksin; also attended new music courses in Darmstadt (1982). He was a visiting composer at the Center for Computer Research in Music and Acoustics at Stanford Univ. (1984) and the Centro di Sonologia Computazionale at the Univ. of Padua (1988). From 1986 to 1991 he was a prof. at Calif. State Univ. in San Bernardino, where he also was director of the electronic and commercial music programs. After serving as chairman of the music dept. at the Univ. of P.R. (1991–93), he was chancellor of the P.R. Cons. of Music (from 1994). His compositional style is eclectic and inclusive, and his craftsmanship applicable to virtually any genre; in some of his works, he makes effective use of indigenous Puerto Rican instruments. His more than 60 popular songs and over 300 arrangements have been performed by singers and orchs. throughout Latin America and in Los Angeles.

WORKS: ORCH.: *Sinfonia Concertante* (1980); *Exploraciones* for Strings (1980); *Areytos: a Symphonic Picture* (1985); *El pais de los cuatro pisos* (1988); *La cancion de las Antillas* (San Juan, Sept. 8, 1990). **CHAMBER:** Flute Sonata (1975); Violin Sonata (1977); *Un jibarito en N.Y.* for String Quartet (1977); *Music* for Brass and Percussion (1977); String Quartet (1978); *Cordillera central* for Clarinet and Cuatro (Puerto Rican stringed instrument; 1980); *La guaracha del macho camacho* for Acoustic Piano and Electronically Modified Electric Piano (1983); Brass Quintet (1985); *Epitafio* for 6 Horns (1988); *Descarga* for Percussion Ensemble (1988); *Danzas tropicales* for Chamber Ensemble (1988). **VOCAL:** *Esta es mi vida: A Cantata* for Chorus and Orch. (1979); *Elegia de Reyes: A Christmas Cantata* for Narrator, Soprano, Chorus, Symphonic Band, and "Rondalla" (an ensemble of Spanish Guitars, Mandolins, Cuatros, etc.; 1981); *Gwakia Baba* for Chorus (1988). **OTHER:** Numerous solo pieces; electronic and computer music; dance pieces; film scores; commercials; arrangements and orchestrations; popular songs; stage works.**—NS/LK/DM**

Torri, Pietro, Italian composer; b. Peschiera, c. 1650; d. Munich, July 6, 1737. He served as court organist and later Kapellmeister at the court in Bayreuth (until 1684), and in 1689 he became organist at the court of Max Emanuel II, Elector of Bavaria, in Munich. When the elector became governor of the Spanish Netherlands in 1692, he took Torri with him to Brussels as his maître de chapelle. In 1696 he was conductor for the carnival season at Hannover; in 1701 he was appointed court chamber music director at Munich, following the Elector to Brussels upon the latter's exile in 1704; he fled Brussels with the Elector (1706). In Brussels he produced the oratorio *La vanitá del mondo* (March 5, 1706); from 1715 he was again in Munich, where he was made Hofkapell-Direktor; later he was named Hofkapellmeister (1732). He composed about 20 operas, 2 of which were produced at the Munich court: *Lucio Vero* (Oct. 12, 1720) and *Griselda* (Oct. 12, 1723), as well as some chamber duets, but he became best known in his lifetime for his vocal chamber pieces.

BIBL.: K. Kremer, *P. T. und seine kammermusiaklische Werke* (diss., Univ. of Munich, 1956).**—NS/LK/DM**

Tortelier, Paul, noted French cellist, pedagogue, composer, and political idealist, father of **Yan Pascal Tortelier;** b. Paris, March 21, 1914; d. Villarceaux, Yvelines, Dec. 18, 1990. He studied cello with Gérard Hekking at the Paris Cons., winning 1st prize at the age of 16. He made his debut with the Lamoureux Orch. at the age of 17; from 1935 to 1937 he was 1st cellist of the orch. in Monte Carlo; from 1937 to 1939 he was a member of the Boston Sym. Orch. He was subsequently 1st cellist of the Paris Cons. Orch. in Paris (1946–47). In

1947 he was a soloist at the Festival of Richard Strauss in London. Tortelier inherited his progressive ideals from his father, a cabinetmaker by profession and a Marxist by political persuasion. He participated in a number of organizations destined to create a better world-at-large; he was quite serious in his work to prevent aggression or injustices to countries governed by repressive rules. Although not a Jew, he saw great hope in the formation of individual communes in Israel and spent a year there working in a kibbutz (1955–56). He then resumed his career as a professional musician; also was a prof. at the Paris Cons. (1957–59) and at the Nice Cons. (1978–80). He made some appearances as a conductor. His wife, Maud Martin Tortelier, was also a cellist, and his daughter, Maria de la Pau, was a pianist; both appeared in performances of Tortelier's works, which included *Israel Symphony*, several cello concertos, a Cello Sonata, and a *Suite* for Solo Cello. He publ. *How I Play, How I Teach* (London, 1975) and *Paul Tortelier, Self-Portrait* (with D. Blum; London, 1984).—**NS/LK/DM**

Tortelier, Yan Pascal, French conductor, son of **Paul Tortelier;** b. Paris, April 19, 1947. At the age of 12, he began studying harmony and counterpoint with Boulanger; after winning the premier prix for violin at the Paris Cons. when he was 14, he made his debut as a soloist in the Brahms Double Concerto in London (1962). Following conducting studies with Ferrara at the Accademia Musicale Chigiana in Siena (1973), he served as assoc. conductor of the Orchestre du Capitole in Toulouse (1974–83); also conducted opera there and appeared as a guest conductor in other French cities. In 1978 he made his British debut as a guest conductor with the Royal Phil. of London. In 1985 he made his U.S. debut as a guest conductor with the Seattle Sym. Orch., and subsequently appeared with other North American orchs. In 1989 he became principal conductor and artistic director of the Ulster Orch. in Belfast. In 1992 he became principal conductor of the BBC Phil. in Manchester.—**NS/LK/DM**

Tosatti, Vieri, Italian composer, writer, and teacher; b. Rome, Nov. 2, 1920; d. there, March 23, 1999. He was a student of Dobici, Ferdinandi, Jachino, and Petrassi at the Rome Cons. (diploma, 1942) and of Pizzetti (1942–45). He taught at the Pontificio Istituto di Musica Sacra (1966–86) and the Cons. di Santa Cecilia (1973–80) in Rome. His compositions followed along conservative lines in an eclectic style.

WORKS: DRAMATIC: Opera: *Dionisio* (1945–46); *Il sistema della dolcezza* (Bergamo, Oct. 25, 1951); *Il giudizio universale* (Milan, April 2, 1955); *L'isola del tesoro* (concert perf., Rome, June 22, 1958; stage perf., Bologna, Nov. 20, 1958); *La fiera della meraviglie* (1959–61; Rome, Jan. 30, 1963); *Il paradiso e il poeta* (1964–65; concert perf., Turin, Dec. 3, 1971). **ORCH.:** Piano Concerto (1945); Viola Concerto (1966); *Concerto iperciclico* for Clarinet and Orch. (1970). **CHAMBER:** Concerto for Wind Quintet and Piano (1945); *Introduzione fiabesca* for Piano Trio (1943); *Piccola sonata* for Violin and Piano (1945); a variety of whimsical piano pieces. **VOCAL:** *Sinfonia corale* for Chorus and Orch. (1944); *Il concerto della demenza* for Narrator, 2 Pianos, and Chamber Orch. (1946); *Requiem* (1963); *2 coretti* for 3 Women's Voices (1970); songs.—**NS/LK/DM**

Toscanini, Arturo, great Italian conductor; b. Parma, March 25, 1867; d. N.Y., Jan. 16, 1957. He entered the Parma Cons. at the age of 9, studying the cello with Carini and composition with Dacci; graduated in 1885 as winner of the 1st prize for cello; received the Barbacini Prize as the outstanding graduate of his class. In 1886 he was engaged as cellist for the Italian opera in Rio de Janeiro; on the evening of June 30, 1886, he was unexpectedly called upon to substitute for the regular conductor, when the latter left the podium at the end of the introduction after the public hissed him; the opera was *Aida*, and Toscanini led it without difficulty; he was rewarded by an ovation and was engaged to lead the rest of the season. Returning to Italy, he was engaged to conduct the opera at the Teatro Carignano in Turin, making his debut there on Nov. 4, 1886, and later conducted the Municipal Orch. there. Although still very young, he quickly established a fine reputation. From 1887 to 1896 he conducted opera in the major Italian theaters. On May 21, 1892, he led the premiere of *Pagliacci* in Milan, and on Feb. 1, 1896, the premiere of *La Bohème* in Turin. He also conducted the first performance by an Italian opera company, sung in Italian, of *Götterdämmerung* (Turin, Dec. 22, 1895) and *Siegfried* (Milan, 1899); he made his debut as a sym. conductor on March 20, 1896, with the orch. of the Teatro Regio in Turin. In 1898 the impresario Gatti-Casazza engaged him as chief conductor for La Scala, Milan, where he remained until 1903, and again from 1906 to 1908. In the interim, he conducted opera in Buenos Aires (1903–4; 1906). When Gatti-Casazza became general manager of the Metropolitan Opera (1908), he invited Toscanini to be principal conductor; Toscanini's debut in N.Y. was in *Aida* (Nov. 16, 1908). While at the Metropolitan, Toscanini conducted Verdi's *Requiem* (Feb. 21, 1909), as well as 2 world premieres, Puccini's *The Girl of the Golden West* (Dec. 10, 1910) and Giordano's *Madame Sans-Gêne* (Jan. 25, 1915); he also brought out for the first time in America Gluck's *Armide* (Nov. 14, 1910), Wolf-Ferrari's *Le Donne curiose* (Jan. 3, 1912), and Mussorgsky's *Boris Godunov* (March 19, 1913). On April 13, 1913, he gave his first concert in N.Y. as a sym. conductor, leading Beethoven's 9th Sym. In 1915 he returned to Italy; during the season of 1920–21, he took the La Scala Orch. on a tour of the U.S. and Canada. From 1921 to 1929 he was artistic director of La Scala; there he conducted the posthumous premiere of Boito's opera *Nerone*, which he completed for performance (May 1, 1924). In 1926–27 he was a guest conductor of the N.Y. Phil., returning in this capacity through the 1928–29 season; then was its assoc. conductor with Mengelberg in 1929–30; subsequently was its conductor from 1930 to 1936; took it on a tour of Europe in the spring of 1930. He conducted in Bayreuth in 1930 and 1931. Deeply touched by the plight of the Jews in Germany, he acceded to the request of the violinist Huberman, founder of the Palestine Sym. Orch., to conduct the inaugural concert of that orch. at Tel Aviv (Dec. 26, 1936). During this period, he also filled summer engagements at the Salzburg Festivals (1934–37), and conducted in London (1935; 1937–39). He became music director of the NBC Sym. Orch. in N.Y. in 1937, a radio orch. that had been organized especially for him; he conducted his first broadcast on Dec. 25,

1937, in N.Y. He took it on a tour of South America in 1940, and on a major tour of the U.S. in 1950. He continued to lead the NBC Sym. Orch. until the end of his active career; he conducted his last concert from Carnegie Hall, N.Y., on April 4, 1954 (10 days after his 87th birthday).

Toscanini was one of the most celebrated masters of the baton in the history of conducting; undemonstrative in his handling of the orch., he possessed an amazing energy and power of command. He demanded absolute perfection, and he erupted in violence when he could not obtain from the orch. what he wanted (a lawsuit was brought against him in Milan when he accidentally injured the concertmaster with a broken violin bow). Despite the vituperation he at times poured on his musicians, he was affectionately known to them as "The Maestro" who could do no wrong. His ability to communicate his desires to singers and players was extraordinary, and even the most celebrated opera stars or instrumental soloists never dared to question his authority. Owing to extreme nearsightedness, Toscanini committed all scores to memory; his repertoire embraced virtually the entire field of Classical and Romantic music; his performances of Italian operas, of Wagner's music dramas, of Beethoven's syms., and of modern Italian works were especially inspiring. Among the moderns, he conducted works by Richard Strauss, Debussy, Ravel, Prokofiev, and Stravinsky, and among Americans, Samuel Barber, whose *Adagio for Strings* he made famous; he also had his favorite Italian composers (Catalani, Martucci), whose music he fondly fostered. In his social philosophy, he was intransigently democratic; he refused to conduct in Germany under the Nazi regime. He militantly opposed Fascism in Italy, but never abandoned his Italian citizenship, despite his long years of residence in America. In 1987 his family presented his valuable private archive to the N.Y. Public Library.

BIBL.: G. Ciampelli, *A. T.* (Milan, 1923); E. Cozzani, *A. T.* (Milan, 1927); T. Nicotra, *A. T.* (tr. from the Italian, N.Y., 1929); D. Bonardi, *T.* (Milan, 1929); P. Stefan, *A. T.* (Vienna, 1936; Eng. tr., N.Y., 1936); L. Gilman, *T. and Great Music* (N.Y., 1938); S. Hoeller, *A. T.* (N.Y., 1943); G. Ciampelli, *T.* (Milan, 1946); A. Della Corte, *T.* (Vicenza, 1946); D. Nives, *A. T.* (Milan, 1946); F. Sacchi, *T.* (Milan, 1951; Eng. tr. as *The Magic Baton: T.'s Life for Music*, N.Y., 1957); H. Taubman, *The Maestro: The Life of A. T.* (N.Y., 1951); S. Chotzinoff, *T.: An Intimate Portrait* (N.Y., 1956); R. Marsh, *T. and the Art of Orchestral Performance* (Philadelphia, 1956); B. Haggin, *Conversations with T.* (N.Y., 1959; 2nd ed., enl., 1979); S. Hughes, *The T. Legacy: A Critical Study of A. T.'s Performances of Beethoven, Verdi, and Other Composers* (London, 1959); L. Frassati, *Il Maestro A. T. e il suo mondo* (Turin, 1967); H. Schonberg, *The Great Conductors* (N.Y., 1967); A. Armani, ed., *T. e La Scala* (Milan, 1972); G. Marek, *T.* (N.Y., 1975); H. Sachs, *T.* (Philadelphia, 1978; new ed., 1995); D. Matthews, *A. T.* (Tunbridge Wells and N.Y., 1982); J. Freeman and W. Toscanini, *T.* (N.Y., 1987); J. Horowitz, *Understanding T.: How He Became an American Culture-God and Helped to Create a New Audience for Old Music* (N.Y., 1987); H. Sachs, *A. T. dal 1915 al 1946: l'arte all'ombra della politica: omaggio al maestro nel 30 anniversario della scomparsa* (Turin, 1987); idem, *Reflections on T.* (N.Y., 1991); G. Marchesi, *A. T.* (Turin, 1993).—**NS/LK/DM**

Toselli, Enrico, Italian pianist, teacher, and composer; b. Florence, March 13, 1883; d. there, Jan. 15, 1926. He studied with Sgambati and Martucci, and gave concerts in Italy as a pianist. He wrote the operettas *La cattiva Francesca* (1912) and *La principessa bizzarra* (1913), the symphonic poem *Il fuoco*, and various salon pieces for Voice and Piano, the most celebrated being *Serenata* (1900). In 1907 he married the former Crown Princess Luise of Saxony, creating an international furor; following their separation in 1912, he recounted this affair in his book *Mari d'altessee: 4 ans de mariage avec Louise de Toscane, ex-princesse de Saxe* (Paris, 1913; Eng. tr., 1913).

BIBL.: L. Previero, *E. T.: Il musicista della serenata* (Florence, 1997).—**NS/LK/DM**

Toshiko

See **Akiyoshi, Toshiko**

Tosi, Pier Francesco, prominent Italian castrato contralto, teacher, diplomat, and composer; b. Cesena, c. 1653; d. Faenza, April 1732. He studied with his father, then sang successfully in Italy and throughout Europe; in 1692, settled in London, where he gave regular concerts, and was highly esteemed as a vocal teacher. He was a composer at the Viennese court (1705–11), while concurrently serving as an emissary to Count Johann Wilhelm of the Palatinate. About 1723 he returned to London, where he remained until 1727; later returned to Italy and took holy orders in Bologna in 1730; finally settled in Faenza. He wrote the valuable treatise *Opinioni de' cantori antichi e moderni, o sieno Osservazioni sopra il canto figurato* (Bologna, 1723; in Eng. as *Observations on the Florid Song*, 1742; in Ger. as *Anleitung zur Singkunst*, 1757; in Fr. as *L'Art du chant*, 1774). He composed some chamber cantatas. —**NS/LK/DM**

Tosti, Sir (Francesco) Paolo, Italian-born English singing teacher and composer; b. Ortano sul Mare, April 9, 1846; d. Rome, Dec. 2, 1916. He was a pupil, from 1858, of the Collegio di S. Pietro a Majella, Naples, and was appointed sub-teacher (maestrino) by Mercadante (until 1869). He visited London in 1875, where he had great success in concerts and settled as a teacher, becoming singing master to the royal family in 1880, and prof. of singing at the Royal Academy of Music in 1894. He became a British subject in 1906 and was knighted in 1908; retired to Rome in 1912. Besides many original songs, in both English and Italian, he publ. a collection of *Canti popolari abruzzesi*. His songs were highly popular; some of the best known are *Goodbye Forever and Forever*, *Mattinata*, and *Vorrei morire*.

BIBL.: E. Mario, *F.P. T.* (Siena, 1947); A. Piovano, *Ommagio a F.P. T.* (Ortona, 1972); J. Little, *Romantic Italian Song in the Works of F.P. T. and some of his Contemporaries* (diss., Univ. of Ill., 1977); F. Sanvitale and A. Manzo, *Il canto di una vita: F.P. T.* (Turin, 1996).—**NS/LK/DM**

Totenberg, Roman, Polish-born American violinist and pedagogue; b. Łódź, Jan. 1, 1911. He studied violin with Mieczyslaw Michalowicz in Warsaw, Flesch in Berlin, and Enesco in Paris. In 1932 he won the Mendelssohn Prize in Berlin. In 1935–36 he toured Europe with Karol Szymanowski, giving violin-piano recitals; then emigrated to the U.S.; became a naturalized American citizen in 1943. In 1943–44 he taught at the Peabody Cons. of Music in Baltimore. In 1947 he was made chairman of the string dept. at the Music Academy of the West in Santa Barbara. He was head of the violin dept. at the Aspen (Colo.) School of Music (1950–60) and a teacher at the Mannes Coll. of Music in N.Y. (1951–57) before serving as prof. of music and chairman of the string dept. at Boston Univ. (1961–78). He then was director of the Longy School of Music (1978–85).**—NS/LK/DM**

Tóth, Aladár, eminent Hungarian writer on music and opera administrator; b. Székesfehérvár, Feb. 4, 1898; d. Budapest, Oct. 18, 1968. He received training in piano and composition in his native city, then studied at the Scientific Univ. of Budapest (Ph.D., 1925, with the diss. *Adatok Mozart zenedrámáinak esztétikájához*; Contribution to the Aesthetics of Mozart's Dramatic Music). He was a music critic for the newspapers *Új nemzedék* (1920–23) and *Pesti napló* (1923–39), and also for the literary journal *Nyugat* (1923–40). After living in Switzerland during World War II, he returned to Budapest to serve as director of the Hungarian State Opera (1946–56). In 1952 he was awarded the Kossuth Prize. He married the distinguished Hungarian pianist Annie Fischer (b. Budapest, July 5, 1914) in 1937.

WRITINGS (all publ. in Budapest unless otherwise given): *Mozart: Figaro lakodalma* (Mozart: Marriage of Figaro; 1928); ed. with B. Szabolcsi, *Zenei lexikon* (1930–31; 2nd ed., rev., 1965); *Zoltán Kodály* (Vienna, 1932); *Liszt Ferenc a magyar zene útján* (Franz Liszt on the Trail of Hungarian Music; 1940); with B. Szabolcsi, *Mozart* (1941); *Verdi művészi hitvallása* (Verdi's Artistic Confession; 1941); F. Bónis, ed., *Tóth Aladár válogatott zenekritikái* (Aladár Tóth's Selected Criticisms of Music; 1968). **—NS/LK/DM**

Toto, the band that helped invent studio-slick pop rock. **MEMBERSHIP:** David Paich, kybd., voc. (b. Los Angeles, June 21, 1954); Steve Lukather, gtr., voc. (b. Los Angeles, Oct. 21, 1957); Bobby Kimball, voc. (b. Vinton, La., March 29, 1947); Steve Porcaro, kybd. (b. Hartford, Conn., Sept. 27, 1957); Jeff Porcaro, drm. (b. Hartford, Conn., April 1, 1954; d. Hidden Hills, Calif., Aug. 5, 1992); David Hungate, bs.; Mike Porcaro, bs. (b. Hartford, Conn., May 29, 1955); Dennis Frederiksen, voc. (b. Wyoming, Mich., May 15, 1951); Joseph Williams, voc. (b. Santa Monica, Calif.); Simon Phillips, drm. (b. June 2, 1957).

A second-generation group of studio musicians, the Porcaro brothers are the sons of session percussionist Joe Porcaro, who worked with David Paich on an Eric Carmen record and did sessions with Tom Waits, among many, many others. Paich's father was arranger Marty Paich. Paich (the Junior), bassist David Hungate, guitarist Steve Lukather, and the younger Porcaros all attended the same high school and started playing sessions very young. Paich, Hungate and Jeff Porcaro were all featured on Boz Scaggs's quintuple platinum slick pop R&B breakthrough *Silk Degrees*. Paich co-wrote the hits "Lowdown" and "The Lido Shuffle." While Toto slowed down their studio work, all the members of Toto remain first-call session musicians, playing with Bruce Springsteen and writing hits for bands like the Tubes.

In the wake of Scaggs's success, they put together their own band and signed to his label, Columbia. Their eponymous debut album went double platinum and hit #9, largely on the strength of the gold #5 single "Hold the Line." The tune mixed pristine studio chops with a crunchy guitar riff and high harmonies that became a staple of late 1970s–early 1980s rock. Ironically, although they mentored this sound, their next two albums, *Hydra* and *Turn Back*, did not fare nearly as well: Hydra went gold and hit #37, with the minor smooth rock ballad "99" going to #8; *Turn Back* topped out at #41.

The group's real breakthrough was *Toto IV*. Written about Steve Lukather's girlfriend at the time, actress Rosanna Arquette, "Rosanna," a jittery ballad punctuated by blasts of keyboard "horns" spent five weeks at #2, going gold. While the sophomore single "Make Believe" only rose to #30, the group topped the charts with the atmospheric "Africa," which also went gold. "Won't Hold You Back" hit #10, helping to propel the album to #4 and triple platinum. At the Grammys, the group took home six awards: Record of the Year, Best Instrumental Arrangement Accompanying a Vocal and Best Vocal Arrangement for Two or More Voices (all for "Rosanna") and Album of the Year, Producer of the Year, Best Engineered Recording for the album.

However, they couldn't maintain the momentum. For one thing, both Hungate and Kimball left the band before they could go into the studio for their fifth album. On *Isolation*, they were replaced by Dennis Fredericksen on vocals and a third Porcaro brother, Steven, on bass. The album barely went into the Top 50, and the single "Stranger in Town" stalled at #30. They created songs for David Lynch's ponderous film version of *Dune*. Fredericksen left the band, replaced by another legacy musician, composer John William's son Joseph. *Fahrenheit* rose as high as #40, with the single "I'll Be Over You" topping the adult contemporary charts for two weeks, but only reaching #11 pop and "Without You Love" scraping into the Top 40 at #38.

Before recording *The Seventh One*, Steve Porcaro left the band. Shortly afterwards, Williams left as well. The single "Pamela" rose to #22, but the album didn't fare too well. After trying to replace him for one song, Lukather took over the vocals. After the group finished *Kingdoms of Desire*, Jeff Porcaro died of an allegedly cocaine-induced heart attack. Veteran English drummer Simon Phillips replaced him on *Tambu*, another album that didn't sell very well. The group reunited with Kimball leading the *Toto IV* line-up (minus Jeff Porcaro) on 1999's *Mindfields* and its live companion album. Lukather produced a record for Jeff Beck and Paich produced Boz Scaggs. While American audiences have become indifferent to the group's brand of studio-honed chops, they remain a popular attraction in Europe and Japan.

Disc.: *Toto* (1978); *Hydra* (1979); *Turn Back* (1981); *Toto IV* (1982); *Isolation* (1984); *Dune* (1984); *Fahrenheit* (1986); *The Seventh One* (1988); *Past to Present: 1977–1990* (1990); *Kingdom of Desire* (1993); *Absolutely Live* (1993); *Tambu* (1995); *Toto XX: 1977–1997* (1998); *Mindfields* (1999); *Livefields* (1999).—**BH**

Tough, Dave (actually, **David Jarvis**), well-known big band era drummer; b. Oak Park, Ill., April 26, 1908; d. Newark, N.J., Dec. 6, 1948. Although he didn't attend Chicago's Austin High, he began playing with the jazz musicians from there in the early 1920s. He also played at summer resorts (1923–24) and for various bandleaders in Chicago from 1925, before taking two trips to Europe from the summer of 1927 through c. May 1929, including work in Belgium, France, Germany (including a recording in Berlin) and Paris. He struggled with alcoholism all his professional life, which led to several extended periods of inactivity. After working with Benny Goodman and touring in autumn 1929 with Red Nichols, he spent his first extended period in recovery, living in Chicago but performing very little until 1935. He enjoyed his longest period of activity in the mid-1930s and early 1940s, where he worked with several bands, including Tommy Dorsey (February 1936–Jan. 1, 1938; again early summer 1939), Benny Goodman (March–July 1938), and Jack Teagarden (August and September 1939). He spent January–May 1940 recovering from another alcoholic breakdown, then worked with various leaders, most notably Goodman (February–April 1941) and Artie Shaw (starting August 1941). Joined U.S. Navy and served as a member of Artie Shaw's Naval Band, after a tour of the Pacific area returned to the U.S.A. and was medically discharged in February 1944. After his service, he worked sporadically with Woody Herman from April 1944–September 1945, with several absences due to his drinking. After that, he again freelanced around N.Y., playing many dates at Eddie Condon's new club, including on its opening night in December 1945. He was back in the hospital in mid-1947 but then returned to playing briefly in N.Y. before going to Chicago to play with Muggsy Spanier at the newly opened Blue Note Club (November 1947–January 1948). He then returned to N.Y., but was soon back in the hospital. Late in 1948, during the time that he was an out-patient, he incurred fatal head injuries after falling down in a Newark street. His body was taken back to Oak Park, Ill., for burial.

Tough's "swishing" drum work was much admired, particularly during his stints with Artie Shaw and Woody Herman, and influenced other big band drummers.

Disc.: *The Happy Monster* (while at Barbarrina Cabaret, Berlin, 1928). Chubby Jackson: "Cool'N Blue" (1944); "Small Herd" (1945). Woody Herman: "The Thundering Herds" (1945). —**JC/LP**

Touma, Habib Hassan, Arab composer and ethnomusicologist; b. Nazareth, Dec. 12, 1934. He studied at the Haifa Cons. and the Rubin Academy of Music in Tel Aviv (1956–62); then went to the Free Univ. of Berlin, where he received a Ph.D. with a diss. on Arab music theory (1968). He went on to teach there, and to work at the Internationale Institut für Vergleichende Musikstudien und Dokumentation. His studies of Arab music theory and history greatly influenced his compositions, which include *Oriental Rhapsody* for 2 Flutes and Percussion (1958), *Reflexus I* for 23 Strings (1965), and *Maqam for Natalie* for Piano (1974). He publ. *Die Musik der Araber* (Wilhelmshaven, 1975).—**NS/LK/DM**

Tourangeau, (Marie Jeannine) Huguette, Canadian mezzo-soprano; b. Montreal, Aug. 12, 1940. She studied voice at the Montreal Cons. with Ruzena Herlinger, repertoire with Otto-Werner Mueller, and declamation with Roy Royal. In 1962 she made her debut in Monteverdi's *Vespro della Beata Virgine* at the Montreal Festival; her operatic debut followed as Mercedes in *Carmen* in Montreal in 1964. She toured in the U.S. as a member of the Metropolitan Opera National Co. (1964–65); then appeared in Seattle, London, San Francisco, and Hamburg. On Nov. 28, 1973, she made her formal Metropolitan Opera debut in N.Y. as Nicklausse in *Les Contes d'Hoffmann*, and returned in later seasons as a guest artist. In 1974 she sang at the Sydney Opera and made her debut at London's Covent Garden as Elisabetta in *Maria Stuarda* in 1977. Her repertory included roles from French, German, and Italian operas. —**NS/LK/DM**

Tourel (real name, **Davidovich**), **Jennie,** prominent Russian-born American mezzo-soprano; b. Vitebsk, June 22, 1900; d. N.Y., Nov. 23, 1973. She played flute; then studied piano. After the Revolution, her family left Russia and settled temporarily near Danzig; they later moved to Paris, where she continued to study piano and contemplated a concert career; she then began to take voice lessons with Anna El-Tour, and decided to devote herself to professional singing; she changed her last name to Tourel by transposing the syllables of her teacher's name. She made her operatic debut at the Opéra Russe in Paris in 1931; then her debut at the Metropolitan Opera in N.Y. on May 15, 1937, as Mignon. In 1940, just before the occupation of Paris by Nazi troops, she went to Lisbon, and eventually emigrated to the U.S.; appeared on the Metropolitan Opera roster in 1943–45 and 1946–47. She became a naturalized American citizen in 1946. In 1951 she created the role of Baba the Turk in Stravinsky's *The Rake's Progress* in Venice. In later years, she devoted herself to recitals and orch. engagements, excelling particularly in the French repertoire. She also taught at the Juilliard School of Music in N.Y. and at the Aspen (Colo.) School of Music.—**NS/LK/DM**

Tourjée, Eben, American music educator; b. Warwick, R.I., June 1, 1834; d. Boston, April 12, 1891. While working in a cotton factory in Harrisville, R.I., he played the organ in church; then studied with Carl August Haupt in Berlin. Returning to America, he settled in Boston, and in 1867 founded (with R. Goldbeck) the New England Cons. of Music, which he directed until his death; also was dean of the college of music at Boston Univ. (from 1873). He was the first president of the Music Teachers National Assoc. (1876).

BIBL.: E. Nason, *The Lives of the Eminent American Evangelists...also a Sketch of the Lives of Philip P. Bliss and E. T.* (Boston, 1877); L. Tourjée, *For God and Music: The Life Story of E. T.* (Los Angeles, 1960).—**NS/LK/DM**

Tournemire, Charles (Arnould), distinguished French organist and composer; b. Bordeaux, Jan. 22, 1870; d. Arachon, Nov. 3, 1939. He began his training as a child in Bordeaux; was only 11 when he became organist at St. Pierre, and later was organist at St. Seurin; then went to Paris, where he studied piano with Bériot, harmony with Taudou, and organ (premier prix, 1891) with Widor and Franck at the Cons.; also studied composition with d'Indy at the Schola Cantorum. He was organist at Ste. Clotilde (from 1898) and a prof. at the Cons. (from 1919); also toured Europe. His major achievement as a composer was *L'Orgue mystique*, comprising 51 Offices for the Roman Catholic liturgy.

WORKS: DRAMATIC: Opera: *Nittetis* (1905–07); *Les Dieux sont morts* (1910–12; Paris, March 19, 1924); *La Légende de Tristan* (1925–26); *Il Poverello di Assisi* (1936–38). **ORCH.:** 8 syms.: No. 1, *Romantique* (1900), No. 2, *Ouessant* (Paris, April 4, 1909), No. 3, *Moscou* (Amsterdam, Oct. 19, 1913), No. 4, *Pages symphoniques* (1912–13; Paris, 1914), No. 5, *Dans les Alpes* (1913–14; The Hague, March 10, 1920), No. 6 for Soloist, Chorus, Organ, and Orch. (1915–18), No. 7, *Les Danses de la vie* (1918–22), and No. 8, *La Symphonie du triomphe de la mort* (1920–24); *Poème* for Organ and Orch. (1909–10). **CHAMBER:** Violin Sonata (1892–93); 3 pièces for Oboe and Piano (1894); Cello Sonata (1895); *Andante* for Horn and Piano (1896); Suite for Viola and Piano (1897); Piano Quartet (1897–98); Piano Trio (1901); *Poème* for Cello and Piano (1908); *Pour une épigramme de Théocrite* for 3 Flutes, 2 Clarinets, and Harp (1910); *Musique orante* for String Quartet (1933); *Sonate-poème* for Violin and Piano (1935). **KEYBOARD: Piano:** *Sérénade* (1896); Sonata (1899); *Sarabande* (1901); *Rhapsodie* (1904); *Poème mystique* (1908); (12) *Préludes-poèmes* (1932); *Cloches de Châteauneuf-du-Faou* (1933); *Études de chaque jour* (1936). **Organ:** *Andantino* (1894); *Sortie* (1894); *Offertoire* (1894–95); *Pièce symphonique* (1899); *Suite de morceaux I* (1901) and *II* (1902); *Triple choral* (1901); *L'Orgue mystique* (1927–32); *3 poèmes* (1932); *6 Fioretti* (1932); *Fantaisie symphonique* (1933–34); *Petites fleurs musicales* (1933–34); *7 chorals-poèmes* (1935); *Postludes libres* (1935); *Symphonie-choral* (1935); *Symphonie sacrée* (1936); *Suite évocatrice* (1938); *2 fresques symphoniques sacrées* (1938–39). **VOCAL:** *Le Sang de la sirène* for Soloists, Chorus, and Orch. (1902–03; Paris, Nov. 17, 1904); *Psalm LVII* for Chorus and Orch. (1908–09); *Psalm XLVI* for Chorus and Orch. (1913); *Trilogie: Faust-Don Quichotte-St. François d'Assise* for Soloists, Chorus, and Orch. (1916–29); *La Queste du Saint-Graal* for Soloists, Chorus, and Orch. (1926–27; Lyons, Jan. 1930); *Apocalypse de St. Jean* for Soloists, Chorus, Organ, and Orch. (1932–35); *La Douloureuse Passion du Christ* for Soloists, Chorus, and Organ (1936–37); songs.

WRITINGS: *César Franck* (Paris, 1931); *Précis d'exécution, de registration et d'improvisation à l'orgue* (Paris, 1936); *Petite méthode d'orgue* (Paris, 1949).

BIBL.: J.-M. Fauquet, *Catalogue de l'oeuvre de C. T.* (Geneva, 1979).—**NS/LK/DM**

Touront, Johannes, significant composer who flourished from about 1450 to 1480. He was active in Bohemia. Touront excelled as a composer of sacred music, his Mass Ordinaries being particularly outstanding. Some of his works are found in Denkmäler der Tonkunst in Österreich, XIV-XV, Jg. VII/1–2 (1900) and in L. Gottlieb, *The Cyclic Masses of Trent Codex 89* (diss., Univ. of Calif., Berkeley, 1958).—**LK/DM**

Tours, Berthold, Dutch-born English organist, violinist, and composer, father of **Frank E(dward) Tours;** b. Rotterdam, Dec. 17, 1838; d. London, March 11, 1897. He received his initial musical training from his father, the organist Barthelemy Tours (1797–1864), and from Verhulst. He went to London in 1861, and in 1878 became musical adviser and ed. for Novello & Co. He was an accomplished composer of Anglican hymn tunes, anthems, and services; also had success as a composer of instrumental pieces and songs.—**NS/LK/DM**

Tours, Frank E(dward), English-American composer, son of **Berthold Tours;** b. London, Sept. 1, 1877; d. Santa Monica, Calif., Feb. 2, 1963. He studied with Stanford, Parratt, and Bridge at the Royal Coll. of Music in London, then went to N.Y. in 1904 and conducted light opera productions. Later he entered the motion picture field. He wrote many successful songs, among them *Mother o' Mine, Beyond the Sunset, Red Rose,* and *In Flanders Fields.*—**NS/LK/DM**

Tourte, François (Xavier), celebrated French bow maker; b. Paris, 1747; d. there, April 26, 1835. He was born into a family of bow makers. After being apprenticed to a clockmaker in childhood, he took up the family profession. About 1785 he perfected the Tourte bow, which has since remained the standard. His mastery of workmanship led him to be hailed as the "Stradivari of the bow."—**NS/LK/DM**

Tovey, Sir Donald (Francis), eminent English music scholar, pianist, and composer; b. Eton, July 17, 1875; d. Edinburgh, July 10, 1940. He studied privately with Sophie Weisse (piano), Parratt (counterpoint), and James Higgs and Parry (composition) until 1894, when he won the Nettleship scholarship at Balliol Coll., Oxford. He graduated with Classical Honors (B.A., 1898). In 1894 he appeared as a pianist with Joachim, and subsequently performed regularly with his quartet. In 1900–01 he gave a series of chamber music concerts in London, at which he performed several of his own works. In 1901–02 he gave similar concerts in Berlin and Vienna, and then was an active participant in the concerts of the Chelsea Town Hall and of the Classical Concert Soc. In 1914 he succeeded Niecks as Reid Prof. of music at the Univ. of Edinburgh. He founded the Reid Orch. in 1917. He made his U.S. debut as a pianist in 1925; presented a series of concerts with renowned guest artists in Edinburgh in 1927–28. In 1935 he was knighted. Though highly esteemed as a composer, he was most widely known as a writer and lecturer on music, his analytical essays being models of their kind. Besides much chamber music and several piano pieces (a sonata, *Balliol Dances* for 4-Hands, etc.), he composed an opera, *The Bride of Dionysus* (1907–18; Edinburgh, April 23, 1929), Piano Concerto (1903), Sym. (1913), Cello Concerto (Edinburgh, Nov. 22, 1934, Casals soloist, composer conducting); etc.

WRITINGS (all publ. in London): *A Companion to the Art of the Fugue* (1931); *Essays in Musical Analysis* (6 vols., 1935–39); with G. Parratt, *Walter Parratt: Master of Music* (1941); *A Musician Talks* (1941); H. Foss, ed., *Essays in Musical Analysis: Chamber Music* (1944); idem, ed., *Musical Articles from the Encyclopaedia Britannica* (1944); idem, ed., *Beethoven* (1944); *A Companion to Beethoven's Piano Sonatas* (1948); H. Foss, ed., *Essays and Lectures on Music* (1949).

BIBL.: M. Grierson, *D.F. T.* (London, 1952).—**NS/LK/DM**

Tower, Joan (Peabody), American composer, pianist, and teacher; b. New Rochelle, N.Y., Sept. 6, 1938. She took courses in composition with Brant and Calabro and studied piano at Bennington (Vt.) Coll. (B.A., 1961); completed her training with Luening, Beeson, Ussachevsky, and others at Columbia Univ. (M.A., 1964; D.M.A., 1978). In N.Y. in 1969 she co-founded the Da Capo Chamber Players, which became known for its promotion of contemporary music; she served as its pianist until 1984. She taught at Bard Coll. in Annandale-on-Hudson (from 1972) and was composer-in-residence of the St. Louis Sym. Orch. (1985–87). In 1976 she held a Guggenheim fellowship; held NEA fellowships in 1974, 1975, 1980, and 1984; received a Koussevitzky Foundation grant in 1982, and an American Academy and Inst. of Arts and Letters award in 1983. In 1990 she received the Grawemeyer Award of the Univ. of Louisville for her *Silver Ladders* for Orch. Her music is marked by an innovative handling of structural forms, sweeping energy, and a deft handling of coloristic writing.

WORKS: DRAMATIC: Ballet: *Stepping Stones* (1993). **ORCH.:** *Composition* (1967); *Amazon II* (Poughkeepsie, N.Y., Nov. 10, 1979; orchestrated from the work for Flute, Clarinet, Viola, Cello, and Piano, 1977) and *III* for Chamber Orch. (1982); *Sequoia* (N.Y., May 18, 1981); *Music* for Cello and Orch. (N.Y., Sept. 29, 1984); *Island Rhythms* (Tampa, June 29, 1985); Piano Concerto, *Homage to Beethoven* (1985; Annandale-on-Hudson, Jan. 31, 1986); *Silver Ladders* (1986; St. Louis, Jan. 9, 1987); Clarinet Concerto (N.Y., April 10, 1988); *Island Prelude* for Oboe and Strings (St. Louis, May 4, 1989; also for Chamber Ensemble); Flute Concerto (1989; N.Y., Jan. 28, 1990); *Concerto for Orchestra* (St. Louis, May 16, 1991); Violin Concerto (Salt Lake City, April 24, 1992); Concerto for Chamber Orch. (1994; Los Angeles, Jan. 23, 1995); *Tambor* (1998); *Last Dance* (1999; N.Y., Feb. 24, 2000). **CHAMBER:** *Pillars* for 2 Pianos and Percussion (1961); *Study* for 2 Strings and 2 Winds (1963); Percussion Quartet (Bennington, Vt., Aug. 17, 1963; rev. 1969); *Brimset* for 2 Flutes and Percussion (1965); *Opa eboni* for Oboe and Piano (1968); *Movements* for Flute and Piano (1968); *Prelude* for 5 Players (1970); *Hexachords* for Flute (1972); *Breakfast Rhythms I* and *II* for Clarinet, Flute, Violin, Cello, Piano, and Percussion (1974–75); *Black Topaz* for Piano, Flute, Clarinet, Trumpet, Trombone, and 2 Percussion (1976); *Platinum Spirals* for Violin (1976); *Amazon I* for Flute, Clarinet, Violin, Cello, and Piano (1977; orchestrated as *Amazon II*, 1979); *Petroushskates* for Flute, Clarinet, Violin, Cello, and Piano (1980); *Wings* for Flute (1981); *Noon Dance* for Flute, Clarinet, Violin, Cello, Piano, and Percussion (1982); *Fantasy...Harbor Lights* for Clarinet and Piano (1983); *Snow Dreams* for Flute and Guitar (1983); *Clocks* for Guitar (1985); *Fanfare for the Uncommon Woman Nos. 1–5* for Instrumental Ensemble (1986–93); *Island Premiere* for Wind Quintet (1989; also for Oboe and String Quintet and for Oboe and String Orch.); *Elegy* for Trombone and String Quartet (1993); *Night Fields* for String Quartet (1994); *Tres Lent* for Cello and Piano (1994); Clarinet Quintet (1995); piano pieces. —**NS/LK/DM**

Towles, Nat, early jazz band leader, bassist; b. New Orleans, Oct. 10, 1905; d. Berkeley, Calif., Nov. 1962. He gigged in the early 1920s with Buddie Petit, Henry "Red" Allen, and others before touring the South and Southwest with his own bands intermittently from 1923–33. In 1934 he briefly led his own band in Dallas; in 1935 took over the Wiley Coll. Students' Band in Austin, Tex., and resumed leading in Dallas; the following year the band took up residency at the Dreamland Ballroom, Omaha, Nebr. Throughout the late 1930s and 1940s this band toured regularly; in 1943 they played several residencies in and around N.Y. including bookings at the Apollo Theatre in December 1943. Towles continued to lead his own band until moving to Calif. in 1959; he ran his own tavern until suffering a fatal heart attack.—**JC/LP**

Townsend, Douglas, American composer and musicologist; b. N.Y., Nov. 8, 1921. He studied at the H.S. of Music and Art in N.Y., then received lessons in composition from Serly, Wolpe, Copland, Luening, Greissle et al. He taught at Brooklyn Coll. of the City Univ. of N.Y. (1958–69), Lehman Coll. of the City Univ. of N.Y. (1970–71), the Univ. of Bridgeport, Conn. (1973–75), and the State Univ. of N.Y. in Purchase (1973–76). He served as ed. of the *Musical Heritage Review* (1977–80).

WORKS: DRAMATIC: 3 4-minute operas (1947); 3 folk operettas (1947); *Lima Beans*, chamber opera (1954; N.Y., Jan. 7, 1956); *The Infinite*, ballet (1951; N.Y., Feb. 13, 1952); film and television scores. **ORCH.:** *Divertimento* for Strings and Winds (1949); *Fantasy* for Chamber Orch. (1951); *Adagio* for Strings (1956); 2 chamber syms. (1958, 1961); 2 syms. for Strings: No. 1 (N.Y., Nov. 29, 1958) and No. 2 (1984); 3 chamber concertos: No. 1 for Violin and Strings (1959), No. 2 for Trombone and Strings (1962), and No. 3 for Flute, Horns, Piano, and Strings (1971); 2 suites for Strings (1970, 1974); *Fantasy on Motives of Burt Bacharach* (1979); *Gentlewoman's Polka* for Band (1985); *Ridgefield Rag* for Band (1985). **CHAMBER:** Septet for Brass (1945); *Ballet Suite* for 3 Clarinets (1953); Duo for 2 Violas (1957); *Tower Music* for Brass Quintet (1959); *Dr. Jolly's Quickstep* for Brass Quintet (1974); piano pieces. **VOCAL:** Choral works; folk song arrangements.—**NS/LK/DM**

Toyama, Yuzo, Japanese composer; b. Tokyo, May 10, 1931. He received his training at the Tokyo Academy of Music (graduated, 1951) and in Vienna (1958–60).

WORKS: DRAMATIC: *Yugen*, ballet (1965); *Gion Festival*, musical (1966); *Such a Long Absence*, opera (Osaka, April 3, 1972). **ORCH.:** 5 syms.: *Little Symphony* (1953), *Homeward* (1966), *Song of Flame* for Chorus and Orch. (1970), *Nagoya* for 2 Percussionists and Strings (1984), and *Sinfonia per Archi* (1990); *Rhapsody on an Okinawan Melody* (1961); *Divertimento* (1961); 2 piano concertos (1962, 1963); 2 violin concertos (1963, 1966); *Fantasy* for Clarinet and Strings (1963); *War Cry 1* (1965) and *2* (1966); Cello Concerto (1967); *Kaleidoscope* (1968); *Fantasy* for Violin and Orch. (1983); *Kyoto*, fantasia for Percussion and Strings (1983); Concerto for Piano, Percussion, and Strings

(1984); *Midorino Honō* (1985); Concerto for Flute, Glockenspiel, Fūrin, and Strings (1986); *Fantasy* for Flute and Orch. (1989); *Maruyama-gawa*, symphonic poem (1990); *Ishikawa* (1992); Harp Concerto (1992). **CHAMBER:** Trio for Flute, Cello, and Piano (1958); Chamber Concerto for Wind Quintet, Piano, Double Bass, Vibraphone, and Percussion (1958); Violin Sonata (1964); *Guzai* for String Quartet (1965); Sonata for Solo Flute (1983); *Quartettuba* for 4 Tubas (1987); Bassoon Sonata (1987); *Passa Tempo* for 6 Horns (1989); Sonata for Solo Violin (1991). **VOCAL:** *Ofukuro* for Chorus and Strings (1968); *Response* for Chorus and Strings (1968–69); *Kyoto*, cantata for Soprano, Chorus, Harp, and Orch. (1970); *If We Shall...*, cantata for Chorus, Percussion, and String Ensemble (1984); *Kono Hachigatsu ni* for Chorus and Orch. (1988); *Dream Time* for Chorus and Orch. (1992).—**NS/LK/DM**

Tozzi, Giorgio (actually, **George**), gifted American bass; b. Chicago, Jan. 8, 1923. He commenced vocal training when he was 13, and later studied biology at De Paul Univ. while pursuing his vocal studies with Rosa Raisa, Giacomo Rimini, and John Daggett Howell in Chicago. On Dec. 29, 1948, he made his professional debut under the name George Tozzi as Tarquinius in Britten's *The Rape of Lucretia* in N.Y. After singing in the musical comedy *Tough at the Top* in London in 1949, he received further vocal instruction from Giulio Lorandi in Milan. In 1950 he made his debut as Rodolfo in *La sonnambula* at Milan's Teatro Nuovo. He sang for the first time at Milan's La Scala in 1953 as Stromminger in *La Wally*. On March 9, 1955, he made his Metropolitan Opera debut in N.Y. as Alvise. He remained on its roster until 1975, becoming well known for such roles as Rossini's Basilio, Mozart's Figaro, Pimen, Boris Godunov, Sparafucile, Ramfis, Hans Sachs, and Pogner; he also created the role of the Doctor in Barber's *Vanessa* there in 1958. His career took him to such operatic centers as San Francisco, Hamburg, Salzburg, Florence, and Munich. In 1977 he appeared in the U.S. premiere of Glinka's *Ruslan and Ludmilla* in Boston. A remarkably versatile artist, he was successful not only in opera and concert settings but also in films, television, and musical comedy. His fine vocal technique was complemented by his assured dramatic gifts. From 1991 he taught at the Ind. Univ. School of Music in Bloomington.—**NS/LK/DM**

Trabaci, Giovanni Maria, eminent Italian organist and composer; b. Monte Pelusio, c. 1575; d. Naples, Dec. 31, 1647. He settled in Naples, where he was made a tenor at the church of the Annunziata in 1594, and later was organist at the Oratorio dei Filippini. He was named organist of the royal chapel of the Spanish viceroys in 1601, and then was maestro di cappella there from 1614 until the end of his life. During the rebellion of the Neapolitan populace against the fruit tax of 1647, Trabaci fled to the monastery of the Trinita degli Spagnuoli, where he died. He is known to have composed 169 sacred vocal works, 60 secular vocal compositions, and 165 keyboard pieces. His greatest contribution was to the keyboard genre; among his works were *Ricercate, canzone francese, capricci, canti fermi, gagliarde, patite diverse, toccate, durezze e ligature, et un madrigale passagiato nel fine* (Naples, 1603; 12 ed. in Monumenti di Musica Italiana, I/3, 1964) and *Il secondo libro de ricercate & altri varij capricci* (Naples, 1615). His canzonas include examples of rhythmic variants of a single theme ("variation canzonas"), anticipating Frescobaldi in this respect.

BIBL.: R. Jackson, *The Keyboard Music of G.M. T.* (diss., Univ. of Calif., Berkeley, 1964).—**NS/LK/DM**

Tracy, Hugh (Travers), South African ethnomusicologist; b. Willand, Devon, Jan. 29, 1903; d. Krugersdorp, Transvaal, Oct. 23, 1977. He emigrated to Southern Rhodesia in 1921, and in 1929 began to record indigenous songs. From 1930, on advice from Holst and Vaughan Williams, he devoted himself to recording folk music from sub-Saharan Africa; also began a career as a broadcaster. He was regional director for Natal of the South African Broadcasting Corp. (1935–47); was co-founder of the African Music Soc. (1947), serving as its secretary and ed. of its newsletter (1948–53); also ed. the journal *African Music* (1955–71). He established the International Library of African Music in Roodepoort (1953); under his direction, it acquired an important collection of instruments and recordings, largely through his own fieldwork; he also ed. a series of more than 200 commercial recordings from its holdings. Tracey lectured at more than 50 univs. in Africa, Britain, and the U.S., and was awarded an honorary doctorate by the Univ. of Cape Town (1965). His publications and broadcasts were largely concerned with the role of African music in African education, and in the growth and understanding of modern African society.

WRITINGS: *Nyoma: An Introduction to Music for Southern Africans* (London, 1941); *Chopi Musicians: Their Music, Poetry, and Instruments* (London, 1948; 2nd ed., 1970); *African Dances of the Witwatersrand Gold Mines* (Johannesburg, 1952); *The Lion on the Path* (London, 1967).—**NS/LK/DM**

Traetta, Filippo, Italian-American teacher and composer, son of **Tommaso (Michele Francesco Saverio) Traetta;** b. Venice, Jan. 8, 1777; d. Philadelphia, Jan. 9, 1854. He was a pupil of Fenaroli and Perillo at Venice, later of Piccinni at Naples. Becoming a soldier in the patriot ranks, he was captured and cast into prison; he escaped 6 months afterward, and sailed to Boston, arriving there in 1799. With Mallet and Graupner, he founded Boston's American Conservatorio in 1801. Shortly after he went to Charleston, S.C., where he was active in N.Y. as a performer and teacher (1808–17). He settled in Philadelphia in 1822 and founded the American Cons. Among his compositions were an opera, *The Venetian Maskers* (n.d.), and 3 oratorios, *Peace* (N.Y., Feb. 21, 1815), *Jerusalem in Affliction* (1828), and *The Daughters of Zion* (1829); also cantatas, piano pieces, and songs.

WRITINGS (all publ. in Philadelphia): *An Introduction to the Art and Science of Music (n.d.); Rudiments of the Art of Singing, written and composed ... A. D. 1800* (1841–43); *Trajetta's Preludes for the Piano Forte ... Introductory to His System of Thorough Bass* (1857).—**NS/LK/DM**

Traetta, Tommaso (Michele Francesco Saverio), esteemed Italian composer, father of **Filippo Traetta;** b. Bitonto, near Bari, March 30, 1727; d.

Venice, April 6, 1779. He entered the Cons. di S. Maria di Loreto in Naples at the age of 11, where he studied with Porpora and Durante. After leaving the Cons. in 1748, he wrote his first known opera, *Il Farnace*, which was produced at the Teatro San Carlo with fine success, on Nov. 4, 1751; there followed several more operas in Naples, and later in other Italian cities. In 1758 he was appointed maestro di cappella to the Duke of Parma. His *Armida* was staged in Vienna (Jan. 3, 1761) with excellent success, and he was commissioned to write another opera for Vienna, *Ifigenia in Tauride*, which was produced there on Oct. 4, 1763. He settled in Venice in 1765, and was director of the Cons. dell'Ospedaletto S. Giovanni for 3 years. In 1768 he was engaged for the court of Catherine the Great as successor to Galuppi, and arrived in St. Petersburg in the autumn of that year. He staged several of his operas there (mostly versions of works previously performed in Italy); also arranged music for various occasions (anniversary of the coronation of Catherine the Great, celebration of a victory over the Turkish fleet, etc.). He left Russia in 1775 and went to London, where he produced the opera *Germondo* (Jan. 21, 1776), without much success. By 1777 he had returned to Venice, where he produced his last 2 operas, *La disfatta di Dario* (Feb. 1778) and *Gli eroi dei campi Elisi* (Carnival 1779). In many respects, Traetta was an admirable composer, possessing a sense of drama and a fine melodic gift. In musical realism, he adopted certain procedures that Gluck was to employ successfully later on; he was highly regarded by his contemporaries. Besides operas, he wrote an oratorio, *Rex Salomone* (Venice, 1766), a Stabat Mater and other church music, 3 sinfonie, an overture, etc.

BIBL.: V. Capruzzi, *T. e la musica* (Naples, 1873); A. Nuovo, *T. T.* (Rome, 1922); F. Schlitzer, ed., *T. T., Leonardo Leo, Vincenzo Bellini: Notizie e documenti, Chigiana*, IX (1952); E. Saracino, *T. T.: Cenni biografico-artistici* (Bitonto, 1954); F. Casavola, *T. T. di Bitonto (1727–1779): La vita e le opere* (Bari, 1957); D. Binetti, *T. Te F. Trajetta nella vita e nell'arte* (1972); J. Riedlbauer, *Die Opern von T. T.* (Hildesheim, 1994).—**NS/LK/DM**

Trampler, Walter, eminent German-American violist and pedagogue; b. Munich, Aug. 25, 1915; d. Port Joli, Nova Scotia, Sept. 27, 1997. He received his early musical training from his father, and then was a student at the Munich Academy of Music (until 1934). In 1933 he made his debut as a violinist as soloist in the Beethoven Concerto in Munich, and in 1935 he made his first appearance as a violist in Mozart's Sinfonia Concertante in Berlin. From 1935 to 1938 he held the position of 1st solo violist with the Deutschlandsender orch. In 1939 he emigrated to the U.S., where he played in the Boston Sym. Orch. (1942–44) and the in the sym. and opera orch. at N.Y.'s City Center (1946–48). In 1947 he helped to found the New Music String Quartet, of which remained a member until 1956. He also made appearances with the Budapest, Juilliard, and Guarneri string quartets and with the Beaux Arts Trio. From 1969 to 1994 he was a member of the Chamber Music Soc. of Lincoln Center in N.Y. As a soloist, he appeared with major orchs. in the U.S. and abroad. He taught at the Juilliard School of Music in N.Y. (1962–72), the Peabody Cons. of Music in Baltimore (1968–70), the Yale Univ. School of Music (1970–72), Boston Univ. (1972–82), the New England Cons. of Music in Boston (1982–95), and the Mannes Coll. of Music in N.Y. (1993–97). Trampler was a master of his instrument who did much to create an audience for the viola. In addition to his performances of the standard works for his instrument, he showcased many contemporary scores. He also commissioned works by Berio and Bainbridge.—**NS/LK/DM**

Trần, Van Khê, Vietnamese ethnomusicologist; b. Binh Hoa Dong, July 24, 1921. He studied medicine in Hanoi (1941–43), then went to Paris to attend the Institut d'Études Politiques (1949–51). He studied organology with Schaeffner and musicology with Chailley of the Faculté des Lettres (1952–58), and historical research with Gaspardone at the Collège de France (1954–57); received his doctorate with the diss. *La Musique vietnamienne traditionelle* (1958; publ. in Paris, 1962). In 1960 he joined the CNRS, where he became director of research in 1973. In 1964 he became director of the Centre d'Études de Musique Orientale, where he taught Vietnamese instrumental performance. He began teaching at the Institut de Musicologie of the Univ. of Paris in 1968. His research focuses on the systematic and comparative study of Asian musical languages. He publ. *Viêt-Nam: Les Traditions musicales* (Paris, 1967). —**NS/LK/DM**

Tranchell, Peter (Andrew), English composer and teacher; b. Cuddalore, India, July 14, 1922. He studied at King's Coll., Univ. of Cambridge (B.A., 1946; Mus.B., 1949; M.A., 1950). He taught at the Univ. from 1950 to 1989; was made a Fellow and director of music at Gonville and Caius Coll., Cambridge, in 1960.

WORKS: DRAMATIC: Opera: *The Mayor of Casterbridge* (Cambridge, July 30, 1951); *Zuleika* (1954); *Bacchae* (1956); *Troades* (1957); *Antigone* (1959). **Ballet:** *Falstaff* (1950); *Fate's Revenge* (1951); *Euridice* (1952); *Spring Legend* (1957); *Images of Love* (1964). **Concert Entertainments:** *Daisy Simpkins* for Solo Voices, Chorus, and 2 Pianos (1954); *Murder at the Towers* for Solo Voices, Chorus, and 2 Pianos (1955; rev. 1986); *Aye, aye, Lucian!* for Men's Voices, Men's Chorus, and Piano (1960); *The Mating Season* for Solo Voices, Men's Chorus, and Piano (1962; rev. 1969); *His 1st Mayweek* for Solo Voices, Men's Chorus, and 2 Pianos (1963); *The Robot Emperor* for Men's Voices, Men's Chorus, and Orch. (1965). **ORCH.:** *Decalogue* for Brass, Percussion, and Organ (1956); *Scherzetto* (1960); *Eclogue* (1962); *Festive Overture* (1966); Concerto Grosso (1972). **CHAMBER:** Organ Sonata (1958); Organ Sonatina (1968); *Movements* for Flute, Viola, Bassoon, Harpsichord, and Piano (1987); piano pieces. **VOCAL:** *The Joyous Year* for Chorus and Orch. (1961); *3 Poems of Po Chü-i* for Baritone, Men's Chorus, and Orch. (1964); *Saul's Successor*, cantata for Soloists, Men's Voices, Organ, Percussion, and Timpani (1969); *Te Deum* for Chorus, 2 Violins, Piano, and Organ (1975); choral songs; anthems and carols; Psalms.—**NS/LK/DM**

Trapp, (Hermann Emil Alfred) Max, German composer and teacher; b. Berlin, Nov. 1, 1887; d. there, May 29, 1971. He studied piano with Dohnányi and composition with Juon at the Berlin Hochschule für Musik (1905–11), where he later was on its piano faculty

(1920–34); also gave a master class in composition at the Dortmund Cons. (1924–30); in 1929, became a member of the Prussian Academy of Arts in Berlin, where he taught a master class in composition (1934–45); from 1951 to 1953 he taught at the Berlin Cons. In 1955 he was elected to membership in the Berlin Academy of Arts. His style was neo-Classical with a strong polyphonic texture, in the tradition of Max Reger. He was also active as a landscape painter.

WORKS: ORCH.: 7 syms., including No. 1, *Sinfonia giocosa* (1915), No. 2 (1918), No. 3 (1924), No. 4 (1931), No. 5 (1936), and No. 6 (1946); Violin Concerto (1922); Piano Concerto (1930); 3 concertos for Orch. (1934, 1940, 1946); Cello Concerto (1935); *Allegro deciso* (1942); *Kleine Spielmusik* for Chamber Orch. (1944); *Symphonischer Prolog* (1944). **CHAMBER:** 2 piano quintets; 3 piano quartets; String Quartet (1935); Violin Sonata; piano pieces. **VOCAL:** Choral works, including *Vom ewigen Licht* for Soprano, Baritone, Chorus, and Orch. (1942); songs. **—NS/LK/DM**

Traubel, Helen (Francesca), noted American soprano; b. St. Louis, June 20, 1899; d. Santa Monica, Calif., July 28, 1972. She studied with Vetta Karst. She made her concert debut as soloist in Mahler's 4th Sym. with the St. Louis Sym. Orch. on Dec. 13, 1923. On May 12, 1937, she made her Metropolitan Opera debut in N.Y. as Mary Rutledge in Damrosch's *The Man without a Country*; her first major role there was Sieglinde on Dec. 28, 1939; subsequently became the leading American Wagnerian soprano on its roster, excelling especially as Isolde, Elisabeth, Brünnhilde, Elsa, and Kundry. In 1953 she made appearances in N.Y. nightclubs; this prompted objections from the Metropolitan Opera management, and as a result she resigned from the Metropolitan. She also appeared on Broadway in *Pipe Dream* (1955), in films, and on television. She publ. the mystery novels *The Ptomaine Canary* and *The Metropolitan Opera Murders* (N.Y., 1951), and an autobiography, *St. Louis Woman* (N.Y., 1959).**—NS/LK/DM**

Trautwein, Friedrich (Adolf), German electrical engineer; b. Würzburg, Aug. 11, 1888; d. Düsseldorf, Dec. 20, 1956. He was trained in electrical engineering, then was active in radio work. He became a lecturer (1930) and a prof. of musical acoustics (1935) at the Berlin Hochschule für Musik; founded his own composition school in Düsseldorf after World War II, which was made part of the Robert Schumann Cons. in 1950. In 1930 he constructed an electronic musical instrument which became known, after the first syllable of his name, as the Trautonium. Hindemith wrote a concerto for it. Trautwein publ. a Trautonium method as *Trautoniumlehre* (1936); also wrote numerous articles on acoustics and electronic music.**—NS/LK/DM**

Travers, John, English organist and composer; b. probably in Windsor, c. 1703; d. London, June 1758. He was probably a chorister of St. George's Chapel, Windsor. He was apprenticed to Maurice Greene in 1719, and also a pupil of J.C. Pepusch; was an organist at the Royal Chapel (1737–58). He publ. *The Whole Book of Psalms* for 1 to 5 Voices and Harpsichord (London, c. 1746–50) and *18 Canzonets* for 2 to 3 Voices and Harpsichord (London, 1746); also various other sacred and secular works and *12 Voluntaries* for Organ or Harpsichord (London, c. 1769).**—NS/LK/DM**

Travis, Roy (Elihu), American composer and teacher; b. N.Y., June 24, 1922. He studied with William J. Mitchell and Luening at Columbia Univ. (B.A., 1947; M.A., 1951); also studied privately with Salzer (1947–50), with Wagenaar at the Juilliard School of Music in N.Y. (B.S., 1949; M.S., 1950), and with Milhaud on a Fulbright scholarship in Paris (1951–52). He taught at Columbia Univ. (1952–53), the Mannes Coll. of Music (1952–57), and at the Univ. of Calif. at Los Angeles (from 1957), where he was a prof. (from 1968). In 1972–73 he held a Guggenheim fellowship.

WORKS: DRAMATIC: Opera: *The Passion of Oedipus* (1965; Los Angeles, Nov. 8, 1968); *The Black Bacchants* (1982). **ORCH.:** *Symphonic Allegro* (1951); *Collage* (1967–68); Piano Concerto (1969). **CHAMBER:** String Quartet (1958); *Duo concertante* for Violin and Piano (1967); *Barma*, septet for Flute or Piccolo, Piano, Clarinet, Violin, Cello, Double Bass, and Percussion (1968); *Switched-on Ashanti* for Flute or Piccolo and Tape (1973); piano pieces, including 2 sonatas (1954; *African*, 1966). **VOCAL:** Songs.**—NS/LK/DM**

Traxel, Josef, German tenor; b. Mainz, Sept. 29, 1916; d. Stuttgart, Oct. 8, 1975. He studied at the Hochschule für Musik in Darmstadt. He made his operatic debut as Don Ottavio in Mainz in 1942. In 1946 he joined the Nuremberg Opera, and from 1952 he was a member of the Württemberg State Theater in Stuttgart; later taught at the Hochschule für Musik there. He also sang at Salzburg, Bayreuth, Berlin, Vienna, and Munich; toured North America as well. His operatic repertoire ranged from Mozart to Wagner; he was also a concert singer.**—NS/LK/DM**

Treadwell, George (McKinley), jazz trumpeter; b. New Rochelle, N.Y., Dec. 21, 1919; d. N.Y., May 14, 1967. He worked in house band at Monroe's Uptown House in N.Y. during the early 1940s, then toured with Benny Carter (1942–43), Cootie Williams (late 1943–early 1946), and J. C. Heard (1946–47). During this period married Sarah Vaughan and toured with her in the U.S. and overseas as musical director. They were subsequently divorced but Treadwell carried on with managerial duties during the 1950s. When that arrangement ended he became an A&R man in the record business, and also had some success as a songwriter. **—JC/LP**

Trebelli, Zélia (real name, **Gloria Caroline Gillebert**), noted French mezzo-soprano; b. Paris, 1838; d. Étretat, Aug. 18, 1892. She took up the study of voice at 16 with Wartel, and in 1859 made her operatic debut as Rosina in *Il Barbiere di Siviglia* in Madrid; sang at the Berlin Royal Opera in 1860 and at the Théâtre-Italien in Paris in 1861. On May 6, 1862, she made her first appearance in London in *Lucrezia Borgia* at Her Majesty's Theatre, remaining a London favorite for a quarter of a century. She sang Siebel in *Faust* (June 11,

1863), Taven in *Mireille* (July 5, 1864), and Preziosilla in *La forza del destino* (June 22, 1867) at their London premieres; appeared at Drury Lane (1868–70), where she sang Frederick in the London premiere of *Mignon* (July 5, 1870); sang at Covent Garden (1868–71; 1881–82; 1888). She toured the U.S. with Mapleson's company in 1878; on Oct. 26, 1883, she made her Metropolitan Opera debut in N.Y. as Azucena, remaining on the company's roster until 1884. She retired from the operatic stage in 1888. Her husband was the tenor Alessandro Bettini.

BIBL.: M. de Mensiaux, *T.: A Biographical Sketch* (London, 1890).—**NS/LK/DM**

Treger, Charles, American violinist, teacher, and administrator; b. Detroit, May 13, 1935. He studied with William Engels (1944–52), Szymon Goldberg, Ivan Galamian, and William Kroll. He made his debut as a soloist in the Wieniawski 2nd Violin Concerto when he was 11. After winning the Wieniawski Competition in Warsaw in 1962, he toured Europe as soloist with the Pittsburgh Sym. Orch. (1964); in 1969 he was a founding member of the Chamber Music Soc. of Lincoln Center, with which he remained active until 1973; from 1978 he toured widely with Andre Watts. He became a visiting prof. at the Hartt School of Music in Hartford, Conn., in 1972, and also gave master classes; in 1984 he was named president and director of the Meadowmount School in Westport, Conn. Treger has won accolades for his championship of neglected works from the violin repertoire.—**NS/LK/DM**

Tregian, Francis, English musician; b. 1574; d. London, 1619. He was a recusant, and fled England to escape persecution. He was attached to Catholic dignitaries in Douai and in Rome. Returning to England to settle his father's estate, he was convicted in 1609, remaining in prison until his death. His significance for English music lies in the fact that he was the scribe of the *Fitzwilliam Virginal Book* (ed. by J. Fuller Maitland and W. Squire, London and Leipzig, 1894–99) and of 2 MSS containing more than 2,000 motets, madrigals, etc., some of them of his own composition.—**NS/LK/DM**

Treigle, Norman, remarkable American bass-baritone; b. New Orleans, March 6, 1927; d. there, Feb. 16, 1975. He sang in a church choir as a child, and upon graduation from high school in 1943, he served in the navy. After two years in service, he returned to New Orleans and studied voice with Elizabeth Wood. He made his operatic debut in 1947 with the New Orleans Opera as Lodovico in Verdi's *Otello*. He then joined the N.Y.C. Opera, making his debut there on March 28, 1953, as Colline in *La Bohème*; he remained with the company for 20 years, establishing himself as a favorite with the public. Among his most successful roles were Figaro in Mozart's *Le nozze di Figaro*, Don Giovanni, Méphistophélès, and Boris Godunov; he also sang in modern operas, including leading roles in the premieres of 3 operas by Carlisle Floyd: *The Passion of Jonathan Wade* (N.Y., Oct. 11, 1962), *The Sojourner and Mollie Sinclair* (Raleigh, N.C., Dec. 2, 1963), and *Markheim* (New Orleans, March 31, 1966). Treigle's other parts in contemporary operas were the title role in Dallapiccola's *The Prisoner* and that of the grandfather in Copland's *The Tender Land*. His untimely death, from an overdose of sleeping pills, deprived the American musical theater of one of its finest talents.—**NS/LK/DM**

Treitler, Leo, learned German-born American musicologist; b. Dortmund, Jan. 26, 1931. He emigrated to the U.S. and became a naturalized American citizen in 1946. He studied at the Univ. of Chicago (B.A., 1950; M.A., 1957), pursued training in composition with Blacher at the Berlin Hochschule für Musik (1957–58), and completed his education at Princeton Univ. (M.F.A., 1960; Ph.D., 1966, with the diss. *The Aquitanian Repertories of Sacred Monody in the 11th and 1 2th Centuries*). After teaching at Princeton Univ. (1960–61), the Univ. of Chicago (1962–66), and Brandeis Univ. (1966–75), he became a prof. at the State Univ. of N.Y. at Stony Brook in 1974. In 1987 he was made a Distinguished Prof. at the Graduate Center of the City Univ. of N.Y. In 1996 he was made an honorary member of the American Musicological Soc. and in 1997 a fellow of the American Academy of Arts and Sciences. His valuable articles on the music of the Middle Ages and early Renaissance, as well as on the philosophy and historiography of music, have appeared in many scholarly journals. He publ. *Music and the Historical Imagination* (1989) and the rev. edition of Strunk's *Source Readings in Music History* (1998).—**NS/LK/DM**

Tremblay, George (Amedée), Canadian-born American pianist, teacher, and composer; b. Ottawa, Jan. 14, 1911; d. Tijuana, Mexico, July 14, 1982. He studied music with his father, a church organist. In 1919 he was taken to the U.S.; eventually settled in Los Angeles, where he met Schoenberg (1936) and became his ardent disciple and friend. In 1939 he became a naturalized American citizen. He adopted the method of composition with 12- tones, which he diversified considerably, expounding his theoretical ideas in a book, *The Definitive Cycle of the 12-Tone Row and its Application in all Fields of Composition, including the Computer* (1974). He became an esteemed teacher; among his students were André Previn, Quincy Jones, and Johnny Mandel, as well as numerous successful composers for television and films.

WORKS: ORCH.: 2 unnumbered syms.: *Chaparral Symphony* (1938) and *The Phoenix: A Dance Symphony* (1982); 3 numbered syms. (1949, 1952, 1973); *Prelude, Aria, Fugue and Postlude* for Symphonic Band (1967). **CHAMBER:** 4 string quartets (1936–63); 2 wind quintets (1940, 1950); Piano Trio (1959); Quartet for Oboe, Clarinet, Bassoon, and Viola (1964); String Trio (1964); Duo for Viola and Piano (1966); Double Bass Sonata (1967); Wind Sextet (1968); piano pieces, including 3 sonatas.—**NS/LK/DM**

Tremblay, Gilles (Léonce), Canadian composer, teacher, and pianist; b. Arvida, Quebec, Sept. 6, 1932. He studied privately with Jocelyne Binet (counterpoint), Isabelle Delorme (solfège), Papineau- Couture (acoustics), and Edmond Trudel (piano) before pursuing his training at the Montreal Cons. (1949–54), where he was a student of Champagne (composition and theory) and Germaine Malépart (piano; premier prix, 1953). After attending the Marlboro (Vt.) Music School (summers, 1950–51; 1953) and studying music history with Vallerand at the Univ. of Montreal (1952–53), he went to Paris and pursued his training with Loriod (theory and piano, 1954–57) and, at the Cons., with Messiaen (analysis, 1954–57; premier prix, 1957), and Martenot (Ondes Martenot, 1956–58; première médaille, 1958). He also studied with Stockhausen at the summer courses in new music in Darmstadt and was a student of Vaurabourg-Honegger at the École Normale Superieure de Musique in Paris (counterpoint; licence en musique, 1958). From 1959 to 1961 he worked with the Groupe de recherches musicales at the ORTF in Paris, and he returned to Darmstadt to attend the courses given by Boulez and Pousseur in 1960. Returning to Canada, he taught at the Quebec Cons. (1961–66). From 1982 to 1988 he was president of the Société de musique contemporaine du Quèbec in Montreal, serving also as its artistic director from 1986 to 1988. In 1968 he was awarded the Prix de musique Calixa-Lavallée. He was made an Officer of the Ordre national du Quèbec in 1991 and Chevalier of the Ordre des Arts et des Lettres of France in 1992. In his music, Tremblay is ever cognizant of the many- faceted elements of sonority. His compositions are particularly notable for their coloristic writing.

WORKS: DRAMATIC: *Un 9* for Mime, 2 Trumpets, and 2 Percussion (Montreal, April 9, 1987). **ORCH.:** *Cantique de durées* (1960; Paris, March 24, 1963); *Jeux de solstices* (Ottawa, April 23, 1974); *Fleuves* (1976; Montreal, May 3, 1977); *Vers le soleil* (Paris, March 11, 1978); *Katadrone (Contrecri)* (Montreal, Oct. 19, 1988); *Musique du feu* for Piano and Wind Orch. (1991); *Avec: Wampum symphonique* for Soprano, Bass, Narrator, Chorus, and Orch. (1992); *Traversée*, flute concerto (1994); *Les Pierres crieront* (1998). **CHAMBER:** *Mobile* for Violin and Piano (1962); *Champs I* for Piano and 2 Percussion (1965; rev. 1969), *II: Souffles* for 2 Flutes, Oboe, Clarinet, Horn, 2 Trumpets, 2 Trombones, 2 Percussion, Double Bass, and Piano (Montreal, March 21, 1968), and *III: Vers* for 2 Flutes, Clarinet, Trumpet, Horn, 3 Violins, Double Bass, and 3 Percussion (Stratford, Ontario, Aug. 2, 1969); *...le sifflement des vents porteurs de l'amour...* for Flute, Percussion, and Microphones (Ottawa, March 1, 1971); *Solstices (ou Les Jours et les saisons tournent)* for 1, 2, 3, or 4 Groups of 6 Instruments (1971; Montreal, May 17, 1972); *Compostelle I* for 18 Instruments (Paris, Nov. 30, 1978); *Le Signe du lion* for Horn and Tam- tam (Montreal, Oct. 8, 1981); *Envoi, conarto vol* for Piano and 15 Instruments (Montreal, Feb. 17, 1983); *Envol* for Flute (1984); *Triojubilus* for Flute, Harp, and Cowbells (1985); *Cedres en voiles* for Cello (1989); *Aubes*, trio for Bass Flute, Double Bass, and Percussion (1990); *D'une goutte* for Microtonal Membranophone (1994); *L'arbre de borobudur* for Sundanese Gamelan and 8 Western Instruments (1995). **KEYBOARD: Piano:** *Deux Pièces pour piano: Phases* and *Réseaux* (1956–58); *Traçantes* (1976). **Organ:** *Vers une étoile* (1993). **VOCAL:** *Kékoba* for Soprano, Mezzo-soprano, Tenor, Percussion, and Ondes Martenot (1965; Montreal, Feb. 25, 1966; rev. 1967); *Oralléluiants* for Soprano, Flute, Bass Clarinet, Horn, 3 Double Basses, 2 Percussion, and Microphones (Toronto, Feb. 8, 1975); *DZEI (Voies de feu)* for Soprano, Flute, Bass Clarinet, Piano, and Percussion (Vancouver, April 12, 1981); *Les Vêpres de la Vierge* for Soprano, Chorus, and 13 Instruments (Abbey of Notre-Dame de Sylvanès, France, July 20, 1986); *L'espace du coeur, Miron-Machaut* for Chorus and Percussion (1995); *A Quelle heure commence le temps* for Bass-baritone, Piano, and 15 Instruments, after Bernard Levy (1999). **ELECTROACOUSTIC:** *Exercise I* (1959) and *II* (1960); *Centre-elan* (1967); *Sonorisation de Pavillion du Québec* (1967).—**NS/LK/DM**

Trent, Alphonso (also **Alphonse**), jazz band leader, pianist; b. Fort Smith, Ark., Aug. 24, 1905; d. there, Oct. 14, 1959. The six titles recorded by his band in 1933 support the oral testimony of many musicians to the energy, creativity and fine soloists (notably Stuff Smith and Peanuts Holland) of his group. He studied at Shorter Coll. in Little Rock, Ark. (1923–24), worked with Eugene Crook's Synco Six, was later appointed leader and this became his band (c. 1924). Gained long residency at Adolphus Hotel, Dallas, Tex., with radio broadcasts, regular touring during the late 1920s including dates at the Savoy Ballroom, N.Y. until 1934 when he temporarily retired from music. Led own small band regularly from 1938, later returned to his home town, where he did part-time playing.

DISC.: *Richmond Rarities: The Complete Recordings of Alex Johnson, Red Perkins, Alphonso Trent, and Zack Whyte* (1998). —**JC/LP**

Trento, Vittorio, Italian composer; b. Venice, 1761; d. probably in Lisbon, 1833. He was a pupil of Bertoni at the Cons. dei Mendicanti in Venice. He produced several ballets at Venice, followed by a number of cantatas, farces, and comic operas; returned to Venice to serve as maestro al cembalo at the Teatro La Fenice. He served as maestro concertatore of the Italian Opera in Amsterdam (from 1806), then took up a similar post in Lisbon in 1809. His most popular stage work was the opera buffa *Quanti casi in un sol giorno, ossia Gli assassini* (Venice, 1801), which was also given in London, as *Roberto l'assassino* (Feb. 3, 1807). Other operas include *Teresa vedova* (Venice, Jan. 13, 1802), *Ines de Castro* (Livorno, Nov. 9, 1803), *Ifigenia in Aulide* (Naples, Nov. 4, 1804), *Andromeda* (Naples, May 30, 1805), and *Le Gelosie villane* (Florence, Nov. 2, 1825). He also wrote 6 cantatas, some sacred vocal pieces, 6 string quartets, and 2 duets for 2 Violins.—**NS/LK/DM**

Treptow, Günther (Otto Walther), German tenor; b. Berlin, Oct. 22, 1907; d. there, March 28, 1981. He studied at the Berlin Hochschule für Musik. He made his operatic debut in 1936 at the Deutsches Opernhaus in Berlin as the Italian Tenor in *Der Rosenkavalier*. Although placed on the forbidden list of non-Aryans by the Nazis, he continued to sing in Berlin until 1942, when he joined the Bavarian State Opera in Munich. After the Nazi collapse, he again sang in Berlin at the Städtische Oper (1945–50) and at the Vienna State Opera (1947–55); appeared as Siegmund in 1951 and 1952 at the Bayreuth Festival and as Siegfried at London's Covent Garden in 1953. He made his Metropolitan Opera debut in N.Y. as Siegmund in *Die Walküre* on Feb. 1, 1951; remained on its roster until the close of that season; continued to sing in Europe until his retirement in 1961. In 1971 he was made a Kammersänger. —**NS/LK/DM**

Tretyakov, Viktor (Viktorovich), noted Russian violinist; b. Krasnoyarsk, Oct. 17, 1946. He studied at the Irkutsk Music School as a child, stoutly braving the Siberian cold; then moved to a more temperate climate in Moscow, where he studied at the Central Music School with Yury Yankelevich (from 1959), continuing with him at the Cons. (graduated, 1970) and as a postgraduate student. In 1966 he won the Tchaikovsky Competition, which automatically lifted him to the upper layers of the violinistic firmament, with applause-rich tours in Russia and later the enviable European and American engagements. A typical product of the Russian school of violin playing, Tretyakov combines the expected virtuosity in technical resources with a diffuse lyricism touched with melancholy in the Romantic repertoire.—**NS/LK/DM**

Treu, Daniel Gottlob, German composer; b. Stuttgart, 1695; d. Breslau, Aug. 7, 1749. He learned to sing and to play the violin and keyboard as a child, and also received training in composition from Johann Kusser; about 1716 he went to Venice to pursue training with Vivaldi and Biffi. In 1725 he became Kapellmeister to an Italian opera troupe in Breslau, where he brought out 4 of his own operas: *Astaro* (1725), *Caio Martio Coriolano* (1726), *Ulisse e Telemacco* (1726), and *Don Chisciotte* (1727). In 1727 he went to Prague, where he served several families of the nobility as Kapellmeister, instrumentalist, and composer; also was active at the Viennese and Silesian courts, and in Breslau. In 1740 he was made Kapellmeister to the court of Karl Schaffgotsch of Hirschberg in Silesia; he eventually settled in Breslau. Among his other works were violin concertos, serenatas, wind partitas, sonatas, sacred music, and arias, most of which are lost.—**NS/LK/DM**

Tréville, Yvonne de (real name, **Edyth La Gierse**), American soprano; b. Galveston, Tex. (of a French father and an American mother), Aug. 25, 1881; d. N.Y., Jan. 25, 1954. She made her debut in N.Y. as Marguerite (1898), then went to Paris, where she studied with Madame Marchesi. She appeared at the Opéra-Comique as Lakmé (June 20, 1902); sang in Madrid, Brussels, Vienna, Budapest, Cairo, and in Russia; from 1913, gave concert tours in the U.S. and sang in light operas. Her voice had a compass of 3 full octaves, reaching high G.—**NS/LK/DM**

T. Rex, English glam-rock innovators, and one of the biggest bands in England during the 1970s. **Membership:** Marc Bolan (b. Mark Feld), voc., gtr. (b. London, England, Sept. 30, 1947; d. there, Sept. 16, 1977); Steve Peregrine Took (born Steve Turner), perc., voc. (b. England, July 28, 1949; d. Oct. 27, 1980); Mickey Finn, perc., voc. (b. June 3, 1947); Steve Currie, bs. (b. May 21, 1947; d. 1981); Bill Legend, drm. (b. Bill Fyfield, Essex, England, May 6, 1944); Jack Green, gtr. (b. Glasgow, Scotland, March 12, 1951); Gloria Lynn, voc. (b. Long View, Tex., Sept. 12, 1938); Pat Hall, voc.; Dino Dines, kybd.

Marc Bolan's parents were working-class Londoners: his mom worked at a fruit stand, his father held a number of odd jobs. By all accounts, his parents doted on their son. They spent a month's salary to buy him his first guitar, filled his closets with clothes that he would change three or four times a day during the mod movement, and encouraged his dreams of becoming just like pop singer Cliff Richard some day. In many ways he did. While Bolan only earned one American pop hit, and charted but two albums in the Top 40, in early 1970s England he ruled the charts. He and his band became so popular, the British tabloids dubbed the period "T-Rextasy." His influence on everything from glam to punk to 1980s "hair metal" cannot be overstated.

In his youth, Bolan's friends included the likes of Keith Reid (of Procul Harum), Cat Stevens, and David Jones (a.k.a. David Bowie). In his early teens, Bolan was in a skiffle band with Helen Shapiro, who beat him to the charts by about five years, becoming an English teen sensation. Bolan became a mod, his wardrobe impressing a journalist from the *Evening Standard* to do a photo feature on him that led to modeling jobs. However, by the time he was 17, Bolan was back playing music, doing his best English Bob Dylan impression under the name of "Toby Tyler." He cut a few demos (released in the 1990s), but nothing much came of these recordings. Bolan did some TV extra work before going to France for a couple of months. There, he allegedly met a magician who turned him on to Celtic mysticism as epitomized by the work of J. R. R. Tolkien. On his return to England in 1965, Bolan took to writing songs reflecting this new infatuation, landing a singles deal with Decca to release "The Wizard." When he got the test pressings, Decca had changed his name to Marc Boland. He asked them to shorten it to Marc Bolan, and he kept that as his professional name for the rest of his career, although that single and several that followed didn't reach an audience.

Bolan hooked up with manager/producer Simon Napier-Bell, auditioning in person in Bell's office for over two hours. They worked on a couple of solo singles that went nowhere. Bell had Bolan join another group he managed, John's Children, who already had a recording contract and had attracted a great deal of press thanks to their naked publicity photos. They recorded a Bolan tune called "Desdemona" that was banned by the BBC for lyrics they deemed offensive. Bolan lasted six months in the group.

Being in a band led Bolan to the conclusion that he had to be in charge. He met a percussionist named Steve Turner, who demonstrated an uncanny knack for harmonizing with Bolan's voice. He convinced Turner to change his name to Steve Peregrine Took after one of the hobbits in *Lord of the Rings*. They started playing shows around London as Tyrannosaurus Rex, with Bolan on acoustic guitar and Took on bongos. They came to the attention of former pirate radio operator John Peel, who was booking a Covent Garden club. He hired them as the house band. Before long, Peel became a personality on Radio One and had the band play live in the studio.

After a show at the UFO club, producer Tony Visconti, who worked with TRO/Essex music, approached them. He signed them as the company's token underground group, got a $1,000 budget, and took them into a small, eight-track studio to cut an album's worth of songs and a single. The album was released in 1968 as *My People Were Fair and Had Sky in Their Hair...But Now They're Content to Wear Stars on Their Brows.* The album rose to #15 on the English charts, and the single "Deborah" hit #34. They started playing better venues and earning about five times the fee they previously charged for an evening. Later in 1968, they released *Prophets, Seers and Sages, The Angels of the Ages.* The album did okay and the single "One Inch Rock" hit #28.

Up to this point in their careers, Tyrannosaurus Rex was an acoustic band, appealing to the folkie/hippie audience that didn't buy many records. For their next album, *Unicorn,* Bolan started moving away from the more mystical themes. With better sound than their previous albums, it rose to #12, in the U.K. It came out in the U.S. as well, but failed to reach an audience. By this point, Bolan had started playing electric guitars. This blatantly commercial move repelled radical hippie Took, who left the band during a disastrous American tour in 1969. Bolan found another percussionist, Mickey Finn, who joined the band. Together, they cut *A Beard of Stars,* even more pop than the previous records, but oddly not as successful. After four albums, Bolan was still more or less a cult artist.

The next album was such a radical departure—with a decided electric/pop slant—that it required a new identity. The group became T. Rex. The "new" group's first single, the bluesy, chiming "Ride a White Swan," rose to #2 in 1971. Then, before an appearance on *Top of the Pops,* Bolan started playing with makeup, adding glitter to his look. His appearance caused a sensation and marked the beginning of glitter or glam rock. The new electric sound demanded more of a band than just pick-up musicians, so Bolan added Steve Currie on bass and Bill Legend on drums. The second single, "Hot Love," became the first T. Rex chart topper. The band and Visconti went into the studio while on tour in the U.S. and recorded "Get It On (Bang a Gong)." It again topped the U.K. charts, and became the group's only chart single in the U.S., hitting #10 in the winter of 1972. They followed "Get It On" with "Jeepster," another bit of skiffle-boogie that went to #2 in the U.K. The more experimental "Telegram Sam," with its modified strings, went to #1, the group's third chart topper of the year.

Bolan next worked with Ringo Starr on the tracks "Have You Seen My Baby" and "Back Off Boogaloo," which actually went to #9, in the U.S. Starr, in turn, filmed a documentary about Bolan and the band called *Born to Boogie.* In the film, he recorded a version of "Children of the Revolution" with Starr and pianist Elton John. He recorded the next T. Rex album at John's favorite studio in France. Presaged by the group's fourth U.K. #1, 1972's *The Slider* topped the album charts in England and rose to #17 in the U.S. A remake of "Children of the Revolution" went to #2, as did the follow-up "Solid Gold Easy Action." The next single, the distorted, hard rocking "Twentieth-Century Boy" hit #3. Ironically, it was followed shortly by the next T. Rex album, *Tanx,* that was somewhat mellower than *Slider* and the first since the name change not to find an audience. A non-LP single "The Groover" hit #4 in the U.K., but didn't stay on the charts very long.

In 1974 Bolan added two female vocalists, Pat Hall and Gloria "Tainted Love" Jones, to the band as well as guitarist Jack Green. Jones eventually became Bolan's lover. Bolan released the next album, *Zinc Alloy & the Hidden Riders of Tomorrow,* without even including the T. Rex name on the record's first pressing. Although the single, a string-laden 1950s pastiche "Whatever Happened to the Teenage Dream" did fairly well, the album tanked. Bolan, who had rarely even indulged in a glass of wine with dinner, began to abuse cocaine and alcohol. He and Visconti parted company and Bolan moved to Calif. to avoid the high English taxes in 1975. He released a few singles and the album *Bolan's Zip Gun* that were among his worst. During this period, Mickey Finn left the band and opened an antique shop.

When Bolan seemed to reach rock bottom, Jones became pregnant. This seemed to energize him. They moved back to England, quit drugs, and reformed the band with Currie and others. He cut a tune called "New York City" that made use of some of the new synthesizers hitting the market. It went to #15, a reasonable comeback. While Bolan was doing the talk show circuit, Thames TV was impressed enough to hire him to do his own show. In 1976 he cut the *Futuristic Dragon* album and the single "I Love to Boogie" went to #13. He toured with the Damned, at once embracing punk and claiming to have innovated it. In 1977 *Dandy in the Underworld* was released, which didn't do as well as peak T. Rex, but sold reasonably well. Bolan also began writing a monthly column for the magazine *The Record.* On the cusp of this rebound, he and Jones were in an automobile accident that killed Bolan instantly. Took choked on a cocktail cherry pit in 1980, and Currie was in a fatal car accident in Portugal in 1981.

Bolan's influence on rock continued after his death. In the late 1970s, rockabilly revivalists the Polecats had a minor hit with "Jeepster." Hanoi Rocks brought the T. Rex sensibility to hair metal, covering several Bolan tunes. The Power Station took "Bang a Gong" to #9 in the U.S. some 13 years after Bolan rode it to #10.

Disc.: *My People Were Fair* (1968); *Prophets, Seers & Sages* (1968); *Unicorn* (1969); *A Beard of Stars* (1970); *T. Rex* (1970); *Electric Warrior* (1971); *The Slider* (1972); *Tanx* (1973); *Light of Love* (1974); *Zinc Alloy & the Hidden Riders of Tomorrow* (1974); *Bolan's Zip Gun* (1975); *Futuristic Dragon* (1976); *Dandy in the Underworld* (1977); *Precious Star* (1996); *Live 1977* (1997).—**HB**

Trial, family of French musicians and actors:

(1) Jean-Claude Trial, violinist and composer; b. Avignon, Dec. 13, 1732; d. Paris, June 23, 1771. A child prodigy, he began playing violin and composing for the instrument at an early age. He settled in Paris as 1st violinist in the Opéra-Comique orch. After serving as 2nd violinist in the private orch. of Prince Conti, he was made its director; was co-director (with Pierre Berton) of the Paris Opéra (1767–69).

Works: Dramatic: *Renaud d'Ast,* opéra-comique (Fontainebleau, Oct. 12, 1765; in collaboration with P. Vachon); *Silvie,* opéra-ballet (Fontainebleau, Oct. 17, 1765; in collaboration with P. Berton); *Escope à Cythère*, comédie (Paris, Dec. 15, 1766; in collaboration with P. Vachon); *Thénois, ou Le Toucher*, pastorale héroïque (Fontainebleau, Oct. 11, 1767; in collaboration with P. Berton and L. Granier); *La Fête de Flore*, pastorale héroïque (Fontainebleau, Nov. 15, 1770); *La Chercheuse d'esprit*, comédie (1771); *Linus*, opera (unfinished; in collaboration with P. Berton and A. Dauvergne). **OTHER:** Overtures, divertissements, violin pieces, cantatas, and ariettes.

(2) Antoine Trial, tenor and actor, brother of the preceding; b. Avignon, 1737; d. (suicide) Paris, Feb. 5, 1795. He received his education at the maîtrise at Avignon Cathedral. He went to Paris and became a member of the Prince of Conti's theater troupe, making his public debut in Paris as Bastien in Philidor's *Le Sorcier* at the Comédie-Italienne (July 4, 1764); became well known for his portrayal of peasants and simpletons. He was a champion of Robespierre and played a prominent role in the period of the Reign of Terror; after Robespierre's downfall in 1794, he lost his following on the stage and took his own life by poison. His wife was the soprano and actress Marie-Jeanne (née Milon) Trial (b. Paris, Aug. 1, 1746; d. Versailles, Feb. 13, 1818); after vocal training, she made her debut at the Théâtre-Italien in Paris under the name Félicité Mandeville in 1766; following her first husband's death, she married Trial and became a popular favorite on the Parisian stage; poor health led to her retirement in 1786. She was particularly esteemed for her performances in works by Grétry and Monsigny. Their son, Armand-Emmanuel Trial (*fils*) (b. Paris, March 1, 1771; d. there, Sept. 9, 1803), was a pianist and composer; he began composing for the Comédie-Italienne when he was 17; was director of singing at the Théâtre-Lyrique (from 1797); his dissolute ways led to an early demise. His works, all first performed in Paris, included *Julien et Colette, ou La Milice*, comédie (March 3, 1788), *Adélaide et Mirval, ou La Vengeance paternelle* (June 6, 1791), *Les Deux Petits aveugles*, opéra-comique (July 28, 1792), *Cécile et Julien, ou Le Siège de Lille*, comédie (Nov. 21, 1792), *Le Congrés des rois*, opera (Feb. 26, 1793; in collaboration with others), and *La Cause et les effets, ou Le Reveil du peuple*, opéra-comique (Aug. 17, 1793).—**NS/LK/DM**

Tricarico, Giuseppe, Italian composer; b. Callipoli, near Lecce, June 25, 1623; d. there, Nov. 14, 1697. He received training in Naples. In 1654 he became maestro di cappella at the Accademia dello Spirito Santo in Ferrara. By 1659 he was active in Vienna, where he composed several operas. He also served as maestro di cappella to the Dowager Empress Elonora (1660?–63) before settling in Gallipoli as a teacher. His extant works comprise the opera *L'Oronie* (Venice, Feb. 1660), the oratorios *La gara della Misericordia e Giustizia di Dio* (Vienna, 1661) and *Adamo ed Eva* (Naples?, 1663), *Concentus ecclesiastici, liber quartus* for 2 to 4 Voices (Rome, 1649), a Mass for 8 Voices, and several motets, madrigals, and cantatas.—**LK/DM**

Trier, Johann, German organist and composer; b. Themar, Sept. 2, 1716; d. Zittau (buried), Jan. 6, 1790. He matriculated at the Univ. of Leipzig (1741). After serving as director of the Leipzig collegium musicum (1746–47), he was organist at St. John's Church in Zittau (from 1754). He was highly respected as an organist. Among his compositions are 2 cantata cycles for the church year and various pieces for organ and clavier.—**LK/DM**

Trifunović, Vitomir, Serbian composer; b. Bukovica, Nov. 4, 1916. He studied composition with Slavenski and Živković at the Belgrade Academy of Music. He became an ed. for new music at Radio Belgrade in 1959. His early music is Romantic, but later he acquired a thoroughly modern sound.

WORKS: ORCH.: *Šumadija*, suite for Chamber Orch. (1960); *Lamentoso* for Strings (1961); *Heroic Overture* (1962); *Toccata* (1963); *Simfonijska slika* (Symphonic Picture; 1964); *Folklorni triptih* (Folklore Triptychon; 1961); *Symphonic Dance* (1968); *Synthesen 4* (1969); *Antinomije* (1972); *Asocijacije* (Associations; 1973). **CHAMBER:** Piano Sonatina (1956); Violin Sonata (1958); 2 string quartets (1959, 1973). **VOCAL:** *Vidici* (The Horizons), cantata (1971); arrangements of folk music. —**NS/LK/DM**

Trimble, Lester (Albert), American music critic, teacher, and composer; b. Bangor, Wisc., Aug. 29, 1920; d. N.Y., Dec. 31, 1986. He began violin studies in Milwaukee when he was 9; later studied with Lopatnikoff and Dorian at the Carnegie Inst. of Technology in Pittsburgh (B.F.A., 1948; M.F.A.); also studied with Milhaud and Copland at the Berkshire Music Center at Tanglewood, and then with Boulanger, Milhaud, and Honegger in Paris (1950–52). He began writing music criticism for the *Pittsburgh Post-Gazette* while in school; then was a music critic for the *N.Y. Herald-Tribune* (1952–62), the *Nation* (1957–62), the *Washington Evening Star* (1963–68), and *Stereo Review* (1968–74); also was managing ed. of *Musical America* (1960–61). He was composer-in- residence of the N.Y. Phil. (1967–68) and at the Wolf Trap Farm Park (1973). He was prof. of composition at the Univ. of Md. (1963–68) and taught at N.Y.'s Juilliard School (from 1971).

WORKS: DRAMATIC: *Little Clay Cart*, incidental music (1953); *The Tragical History of Dr. Faustus*, incidental music (1954); *Boccaccio's Nightingale*, opera (1958–62; rev. 1983); film scores. **ORCH.:** 3 syms.: No. 1 (1951), No. 2 (1968), and No. 3, *The Tricentennial* (1984–85; Troy, N.Y., Sept. 26, 1986); Concerto for Wind and Strings (1954); *Closing Piece* (1957; rev. as *Sonic Landscape*, 1967); *5 Episodes* (1961–62; also for Piano); *Notturno* for Strings (1967; arranged from the String Quartet No. 2); *Duo Concertante* for 2 Violins and Orch. (1968); *Panels I* for 11 Instruments (1969–70), *II* for 13 Instruments (1971–72), and *IV* for 16 Instruments (1973–74; orig. a ballet); *Panels for Orchestra* (1976; rev. 1983); Violin Concerto (1976–81); band music. **CHAMBER:** 2 string quartets (1949, 1955); *Woodwind Serenade* (1952); Double Concerto for Instrumental Ensemble (1964); *Panels V* for String Quartet (1974–75), *VI: Quadraphonics* for Percussion Quartet (1974–75), and *VII: Serenade* for Oboe, Clarinet, Horn, Harpsichord, Violin, Viola, Cello, and Percussion (1975). **OTHER:** Choruses; song cycles; solo songs; electronic pieces.—**NS/LK/DM**

Trimpin, (Gerhard), German-born inventor, practitioner, and builder of soundsculpture and computerized acoustical instruments; b. Istein bei Lörrach, Basel,

Nov. 26, 1951. Professionally he is known by only his surname. He had an ordinary musical training, with an emphasis on playing wind instruments, but recurrent lip infections forced him to abandon such labial practices; he then studied electro-mechanic engineering (1966–73). In 1979 he received a degree from the Univ. of Berlin in social pedagogy; later was an instructor at the Sweelinck Cons. in Amsterdam (1985–87), where he also conducted research in music and acoustic sound technologies. From 1976 to 1979 he also was active with Berlin's Theater Zentrifuge; also produced set designs for San Quentin Drama Workshop. Trimpin designed 4 Bowed Cymbals for Ton de Leeuw's *Resonances* (1987). He also designed a percussive installation of 96 suspended Dutch wooden shoes for the 1986 New Music Festival in Middelburg; in 1987 he designed a similar installation, *Floating Klompen*, at the Jan van Eyck Art Academy in Maastricht, which was subsequently seen at the San Francisco Exploratorium in 1990. From 1988 he collaborated with Conlon Nancarrow in Mexico City. Trimpin originated his own composition entitled *Circumference* for specially adapted instruments, first seen at the New Music America Festival in N.Y. in 1989, and subsequently in Seattle, Minneapolis, and Vancouver. Other works include *Three Ply* (Seattle, 1984), *The Cocktail Party Effect* (Banff, 1990), *Messing Around* (Seattle, 1990; Valencia, Calif., 1992; Mexico City, 1993), *Contraption 1PP71512* (San Francisco, 1991; Newfoundland, 1992; Los Angeles, 1992; Seattle, 1993; Montreal, 1994), *D.R.A.M.A.ohno* (Seattle, 1993; Minneapolis, 1993; Iowa City, 1993), *Ringo* (Amsterdam, 1985; Madrid, 1994), *Liquid Percussion* (N.Y. and San Francisco, 1991), and *PHFFFT* (N.Y., 1991; Portland, Ore., 1992; Tacoma, 1993; Ghent and Donaueschingen, 1994). In 1979 he settled in Seattle, where he resides in a Faustian workshop-laboratory, filled with synchronously and anachronously activated sound objects. In 1989 he participated in the "Composer-to-Composer" symposium in Telluride, Colo., and in 1990 was artist-in-residence at the Banff Art Center. Among his awards are grants from the Seattle Arts Commission (1990), the NEA (1992), Meet the Composer (1993), the Foundation for Contemporary Performance Arts (1994), and the Lila Wallace-Reader's Digent "Artist in Giverny, France" program. In 1995 he received a commission from the Merce Cunningham Dance Foundation. In 1995 he also designed a lavish installation of sounding fabrics, entitled *Singing Textiles*, for Switzerland's Museum Technorama. When not engaged in musical endeavors, Trimpin periodically engages in one of his other specialties, salmon fishing. **—NS/LK/DM**

Tristano, Lennie (actually, **Leonard Joseph**), influential third-stream/cool jazz pianist, composer, educator; b. Chicago, March 19, 1919; d. N.Y., Nov. 18, 1978. Born during an epidemic of measles, he was totally blind by the age of nine. He had begun playing piano at age four. He spent almost ten years in a state institution for the blind in Ill., and while there learned to play saxophone, clarinet, and cello. At 19, he led his first band. He later studied at the American Cons. in Chicago and earned a Bachelor's of Music degree. During the early 1940s he gigged in Chicago on piano and tenor saxophone and became seriously involved in teaching; among his first students were Lee Konitz and Bill Russo. He moved to N.Y. in August 1946, played gigs there and in Calif. in late 1946 and then settled on Long Island. He formed a trio with students Billy Bauer and Arnold Fishkind, with whom he made his first commercially released records. Championed by critic Barry Ulanov, Tristano enjoyed some fame in 1948–50, he lead a sextet with Konitz and another student, Warne Marsh; he recorded with and arranged for the Metronome All Stars; and broadcast with Charlie Parker and Dizzy Gillespie. On ballads his groups played a free counterpoint that would sometimes take a piece far from its origins. At a sextet session in early 1949, two tracks were the first "free jazz" ever documented; the group had practiced improvising in a contrapuntal texture, one entering at a time, but in free atonality; their record label, Capitol Records, was outraged with the results and refused to pay for the dates. Disk jockey Symphony Sid played the yet unissued titles on his program helping to convince Capitol to finally release them.

During the late 1940s, Tristano worked with Charlie Ventura, but was mainly active leading his own trio at the Three Deuces, N.Y., his own quintet at The Royal Roost, and his own sextet at The Clique. In June 1951 he opened his own studio and instructed Konitz, Marsh, Bauer, and Sal Mosca, among others. For a 1955 recording on Atlantic he used techniques he had been practicing at his home studio; overdubbing himself on piano, playing over pre-recorded bass and drum parts, and speeding up his own piano part. Although his virtuosity was unmistakeable, several critics accused him of tampering with the music and of not being capable of playing without tape manipulation. This experience also contributed to his ceasing to record commercially, but not before responding to his critics in 1962 with an all-solo piano album that clearly stated on its sleeve: "no overdubbing." His "C Minor Complex" is spellbinding and dazzling. He was later associated with Peter Ind, Lenny Popkin, and Connie Crothers. During the 1960s and 1970s he was mainly active as a teacher, but played dates with Lee Konitz and Warne Marsh in the late 1950s and in the 1960s (Half Note in 1964 was broadcast on radio and on TV); he also played solo dates in Canada, and in Europe in 1965 and 1968.

Tristano was a remarkable musician whose earliest recordings from the mid-1940s feature dense dissonance and polytonality; his mid-1950s recordings feature him improvising long, intense, brilliant melodic lines with an even eighth-note feel. He had a direct impact on the large circle of disciples that grew around him and an indirect impact on many others including Martial Solal, Bill Evans (who credited Konitz and whose private recordings from around 1950 bear an unmistakeable Tristano influence), probably Cecil Taylor, and possibly Herbie Hancock (judging from his work on Davis's *E.S.P.* and *Miles Smiles*). Yet his reputation has suffered. He required a cultish dedication of students; was an outspoken critic whose verbal pronouncements appeared in print and on radio; his compositions occasionally expressed a somewhat classical esthetic and his music was unfairly dogged by a recurrent charge of emotional coldness; he played less and less in public and even stopped making studio recordings after 1962. His teaching stressed perfect tempo (not rushing) and a proficiency on the solos of Lester Young, Parker, and others so that one could not hear the soloist when playing along with the recording. He required that students learn to associate scales and altered scales with chords. For the most part he and his disciples improvised over the chords of standards, composing fantastic heads that often threatened to turn the beat around. He insisted that drummers play quietly and not rush, but steadiness of tempo seems to have been more important than volume, as he had no trouble playing with Buddy Rich, Ray Haynes, and Art Taylor.

DISC.: *Live at Birdland* (1945); *Lost Session* (1945); *Holiday in Piano* (1946); *Rarest Trio / Quartet Sessions* (1946); *Crosscurrents* (1949); *Lennie Tristano Quintet* (EP; 1949); *First Sessions* (1949–50); *Wow* (1950); *Descent into the Maelstrom* (1952); *Lennie Tristano Memorial Concert* (1952); *Live in Toronto* (1952); *Lennie Tristano Quartet* (1955); *N.Y. Improvisations* (1955); *Requiem* (1955); *Continuity* (1958); *New Tristano* (1960); *Note to Note* (1964); *Lennie Tristano Memorial Concert* (1979); *Complete Lennie Tristano on Keynote* (rec. 1940s–60s).

BIBL.: François Billard, *Lennie Tristano* (Montpellier, France,1989); John Francis McKinney, *The Pedagogy of Lennie Tristano* (diss., Fairleigh Dickinson Univ., 1978).—**LP/JC**

Tritonius, Petrus (real name, **Peter Treybenreif**), esteemed Austrian composer; b. Bozen, c. 1465; d. probably in Hall, Tirol, c. 1525. After studies at the Univ. of Vienna (1486), he matriculated at the Univ. of Ingolstadt (1497); it was about this time that he took the name Petrus Tritonius and became associated with the humanist Conradus Celtis. He then was active as a Latin teacher in the Tirol. After taking a doctorate at the Univ. of Padua (1502), he went to Vienna as a teacher. He then served as director of the Lateinschule in Bozen (1508–12), and later was active in Halle and Schwaz am Inn. He composed a distinguished set of Horatian odes, *Melopoiae sive harmoniae tetracenticae super XXII genera carminum Heroicorum Elegiacorum Lyricorum et ecclesiasticorum hymnorum* (Augsburg, 1507; 2nd ed., 1507; 3rd ed., 1532; 4th ed., 1551), which exercised influence on German composers in the 16th century.—**NS/LK/DM**

Tritto, Giacomo (Domenico Mario Antonio Pasquale Giuseppe), Italian composer and teacher; b. Altamura, April 2, 1733; d. Naples, Sept. 16, 1824. He studied with Cafaro at the Cons. della Pietà de' Turchini in Naples, becoming maestrino there and Cafaro's assistant; was made maestro straordinario in 1785, secondo maestro in 1793, and primo maestro in 1799. In 1804 he was appointed maestro of the royal chamber. Bellini, Spontini, Mercadante, Meyerbeer, and Conti were his pupils. He wrote over 50 operas, both comic and serious; many were produced in various Neapolitan theaters, and others in Rome, Madrid, Vienna, and Venice; however, they were generally undistinguished. He also composed much sacred music. He publ. *Partimenti e regole generali per conoscere qual numerica dar si deve ai vari movimenti del basso* (Milan, 1821) and *Scuola di contrappunto, ossia Teoria musicale* (Milan, 1823).

BIBL.: F. Florimo, *La scuola musicale di Napoli ed i suoi conservatorii*, III (Naples, 1882); G. de Napoli, *La triade melodrammatica altamurana: G. T., Vincenzo Lavigna, Saverio Mercandante* (Milan, 1931).—**NS/LK/DM**

Trneček, Hanuš, Bohemian harpist, pianist, pedagogue, and composer; b. Prague, May 16, 1858; d. there, March 28, 1914. He studied at the Prague Cons. He was harpist in the Schwerin Court Orch. (1882–88), and then taught harp and piano at the Prague Cons. He wrote some fine works for solo harp and didactic piano pieces which were widely known.

WORKS: DRAMATIC: Opera: *Der Geigenmacher von Cremona* (Schwerin, April 16, 1886); *Amaranta* (1884–89; Prague, Nov. 16, 1890); *Andrea Crini* (1898; Prague, Feb. 2, 1900). **ORCH.:** 3 syms.; 2 suites; 2 violin concertos; Piano Concerto; Clarinet Concerto; Flute Concerto. **CHAMBER:** 2 piano quintets; Piano Quartet; pieces for Violin, Cello, and Harp; Violin Sonata; solo harp pieces; much piano music, including over 50 etudes.—**NS/LK/DM**

Trojahn, Manfred, German composer and teacher; b. Cremlingen, near Braunschweig, Oct. 22, 1949. He received training in orch. music at the Niedersächsische Musikschule in Braunschweig (1966–70; diploma, 1970) and composition with Diether de la Motte at the Staatlichen Hochschule für Musik in Hamburg. In 1975 he won the Bach Prize in Hamburg. In 1979–80 he was in residence at the Villa Massimo in Rome. He was awarded the Niedersächsisches Künstlerstipendium in 1984. In 1991 he became a teacher of composition at the Robert-Schumann-Hochschule in Düsseldorf. Trojahn utilizes various contemporary modes of expression with a subsuming individuality.

WORKS: DRAMATIC: *Enrico*, dramatic comedy (1989–91; Schwetzingen, April 11, 1991); *Das wüste Land*, opera (1994). **ORCH.:** 4 syms.: No. 1 (1973), No. 2 (Donaueschingen, Oct. 22, 1978), No. 3 (1984; Berlin, April 19, 1985), and No. 4 for Tenor and Orch. (Hamburg, Aug. 16, 1992); *Notturni trasognati* for Alto Flute and Chamber Orch. (London, June 13, 1977); *Abschied...* (Düsseldorf, Oct. 18, 1978); *Conduct* for Strings and Percussion (1978; Gelsenkirchen, May 14, 1979; also for Organ); *Erstes See-Bild* (1979–80; Berlin, Nov. 9, 1980; 1st part of *Fünf See-Bilder* for Mezzo-soprano and Orch., 1981–83); *Berceuse* (Stuttgart, Oct. 4, 1980); Flute Concerto (1981–83; Berlin, Sept. 14, 1983); *L'Autunno* (1986–90; Berlin, June 23, 1990); *Cinq Epigraphes* (Berlin, Sept. 12, 1987); *Variationen* (Cleveland, Sept. 24, 1987); *Transir* (Freiburg im Breisgau, May 24, 1988); *Notturno* for Winds, Strings, Celesta, and Harp (Hamburg, Sept. 3, 1989); Oboe Concerto (1990–91; Munich, June 7, 1991); *Quattro pezzi* (1992; Kiel, Sept. 1993); *Divertissement* for Oboe and Chamber Orch. (1992–93; Munich, May 7, 1993); *Cornisches Nachtlied* (1994). **CHAMBER:** *Deux pièces brèves* for String Quartet (Aurillac, France, Aug. 29, 1973); 3 string quartets: No. 1 (1976), No. 2 with Clarinet and Mezzo-soprano (1979–80; Frankfurt am Main, Sept. 9, 1981), and No. 3 (Hamburg, Nov. 4, 1983); *Fantasia* for Guitar (Stuttgart, Oct. 10, 1979); *...une campaagne noire de soleil*, 7 ballet scenes for Chamber Ensemble: *I: Déplorations* (Berlin, Dec. 14, 1982), *II: Silences* (1982; Cambridge, Mass., April 2, 1983), *III: Chimèrès* (Nuremberg, Nov. 19, 1983), *IV: Cigales* (1992), *V: Chants noirs* (Cologne, Oct. 10, 1986), *VI: Exaltations* (1992–92), and *VII: Processions* (1986; Ludwigshafen,

Jan. 12, 1987); *Berceuse* for 5 Strings (1983; Bavarian Radio, Munich, May 26, 1984); Violin Sonata (Mannheim, Oct. 11, 1983); Cello Sonata (1983; Hamburg, Feb. 11, 1984); *Soleares*, 2 pieces for Piano and String Quartet (1st piece, Braunschweig, Oct. 20, 1985; 2nd piece, 1988; Cologne, Nov. 14, 1990); *Épitaphe* for 4 Flutes (Berlin, Aug. 27, 1986); *Fragmente für Antigone*, 6 pieces for String Quartet (Barcelona, Oct. 11, 1988); *Fünf Intermezzi* for Guitar and Chamber Ensemble (1988–89); *Poème abandonné* for Saxophone Quartet, Viola, Cello, and Double Bass (1989; Łwów, April 17, 1990). KEYBOARD: Piano: *Berceuse* (1980; Hannover, Jan. 26, 1981); *La folia* for 2 Pianos (Berlin, Sept. 16, 1982). Organ: *Conduct* for 2 Organists (Kassel, Sept. 22, 1977; also for Strings and Percussion). VOCAL: *Madrigal* for Chorus (1975); *...stiller Gefährt der Nacht* for Soprano, Flute, Cello, Percussionist, and Celesta (Karlsruhe, June 6, 1978); *Fünf See-Bilder* for Mezzo-soprano and Orch. (1979–83; 1st complete perf., Hamburg, Feb. 12, 1984); *Elegía del tiempo final* for Tenor and 7 Instruments (1981–82); *Quattro Madrigali* for Chorus, 4 Violins, and 4 Cellos (1983; Stuttgart, Feb. 28, 1984); *Trakl-Fragmente* for Mezzo-soprano and Piano (1983–84; Hamburg, Feb. 10, 1984); *Nachtwandlung* for Mezzo-soprano and 14 Instruments (1983–84; Paris, Feb. 17, 1986); *Requiem* for Soprano, Mezzo-soprano, Baritone, Chorus, and Chamber Orch. (1983–85; Braunschweig, Nov. 10, 1985); *Die Nachtigall* for 2 Sopranos, Mezzo-soprano, and 3 Clarinets (Hannover, Nov. 17, 1984); *Zwei Motetten* for Chorus (1984; Hannover, May 23, 1985); *Aubade* for 2 Sopranos (1987; Leningrad, April 18, 1990); *Spätrot* for Mezzo-soprano and Piano (1987); *Lieder auf der Flucht* for Baritone, Guitar, and 13 Instruments (1988–89; Frankfurt am Main, Sept. 2, 1989); *Ave Maria* for Chorus (1991; Braunschweig, May 27, 1992); *Grodek* for Baritone and 8 Instruments (Berlin, Sept. 29, 1991).—**NS/LK/DM**

Trojan, Václav, Czech composer and teacher; b. Pilsen, April 24, 1907; d. Prague, July 5, 1983. He was a student of Wiedermann (organ) and of Ostrčil and Dědeček (conducting) at the Prague Cons. (1923–27) He also attended the master classes in composition given by Suk and Novák (1927–29), and received instruction in quarter tone and 6th tone music in A. Hába's class there. From 1937 to 1945 he was music manager of the Prague Radio, and then lectured on theater and film music at the Prague Academy of Music from 1949. In 1982 he was made a National Artist by the Czech government.

WORKS: DRAMATIC: *Kolotoč* (The Merry-Go-Round), children's opera (1936–39); *Zlatá brána* (Golden Gate), scenic poem (1971–73); *Sen noci svatojánské* (A Midsummer Night's Dream), ballet-pantomime (1982); music for puppet films. ORCH.: *Tarantella* (1940); *Pohádka* (Fairy Tale; 1946); *Průvod starobylou Prahou* (Procession Through Old Prague; 1956–57); *Tarantella di Taranto* (1957); *Pohádky* (Fairy Tales) for Accordion and Orch. (1959); *Sinfonietta armoniosa* for Chamber Orch. (1970); *Čtyři karikatury (s jednou navíc)* [4 Caricatures (and 1 Extra)] for Wind Orch., Percussion Instruments, and Piano (1974); Concertino for Trumpet and Small Orch. (1977). CHAMBER: String Quartet (1927); 2 string quartets (1929, 1945); 2 wind quintets (1937, 1953); *Princ Bajaja* (Bajaja the Prince), fairy suite for Violin, Guitar, and Accordion (1967); *Divertimento* for Wind Quintet (1977); *Noneto Favoloso* for Flute, Oboe, Clarinet, Horn, Violin, Viola, Cello, and Double Bass (1977). VOCAL: Cantatas; choruses; songs.—**NS/LK/DM**

Trombetti (real name, Cavallari), Girolamo, Italian singer, trombonist, and composer, brother of **Ascanio Trombetti;** b. Bologna (baptized), Dec. 7, 1557; d. there, 1624. He was a singer at the Santa Casa in Loreto from 1566 to 1575. From 1582 he was a civic trombonist. In 1591 he succeeded his brother as maestro di cappella at S. Giovanni in Monte, a position he retained until his death. He publ. a vol. of madrigals (Venice, 1590).—**LK/DM**

Trombly, Preston (Andrew), American composer; b. Hartford, Conn., Dec. 30, 1945. He studied composition with Whittenberg at the Univ. of Conn. (B.M., 1968), with Arel and Davidovsky at Yale Univ. (M.M.A., 1972), and with Crumb at the Berkshire Music Center at Tanglewood; also had some instruction in conducting from Bernstein and Barzin. He then devoted himself to teaching and composing.

WORKS: ORCH.: *Set* for Jazz Orch. (1968); *Doubles* (1970); *Music for the Theatre* (1972); Chamber Concerto for Piano and 11 Instruments (1975). CHAMBER: Woodwind Quintet (1968); *Opera/Septima* for Flute, Oboe, Bass Clarinet, Trumpet, Violin, Viola, and Cello (1969–70); *Music* for Violin, Viola, and Cello (1970); *In memoriam: Igor Stravinsky* for Woodwind Quartet, Viola, and Double Bass (1972); Trio in 3 Movements for Flute, Double Bass, and Percussion (1973); *Trio da camera* for Flute, Cello, and Piano (1975); *The Windmills of Paris* for Flute, Clarinet, Violin, Cello, and Piano (1976); *The Bridge: 3 Pieces after Hart Crane* for Clarinet, Saxophone, Cello, and Piano (1979); String Quartet (1979); *Time of the Supple Iris* for Viola, Double Bass, Oboe or English Horn, Bass Clarinet, and Percussion (1980); *Aurora Quartet* for Oboe, Violin, Cello, and Harpsichord (1983–84). With Tape: *Kinetics III* for Flute (1971); *G.H-.M.T.S.* for Flute, Clarinet, Double Bass, and Vibraphone (1971–72); *Fantasy* for Cello (1974); *Toccata* for Trombone (1974); *The Trumpets of Solitude* for Flute, Clarinet, Violin, Cello, and Piano (1982).—**NS/LK/DM**

Tromboncino, Bartolomeo, important Italian composer; b. in or near Verona, c. 1470; d. in or near Venice, c. 1535. He was active in Mantua until 1489, when he went to Florence; in 1494 he returned to Mantua, where he was active at the court; also traveled to other courts. His association with the Mantuan court was a stormy one, even though he was held in high esteem there; he fled the court in 1495 and went to Venice, but returned that same year. When he discovered his wife entertaining a lover in 1499, he murdered her; he appears, however, to have been pardoned at his trial. In 1501 he left Mantua again and made his way to Ferrara, where he was in the service of Lucrezia Borgia until 1508. He remained in Ferrara until at least 1513; in 1521 he went to Venice. Tromboncino was one of the leading composers of secular music of his era, producing over 150 frottolas. He also wrote some sacred music, including Lamentations and laude.—**NS/LK/DM**

Tromlitz, Johann Georg, German flutist, teacher, instrument designer, and composer; b. Reinsdorf über Artern, Nov. 8, 1725; d. Leipzig, Feb. 4, 1805. He began his training in Gera before settling in Leipzig, where he took courses in law at the Univ. and earned the title of Imperial Public Notary. He was 1st flutist in Hiller's Grosses Konzert (from 1754), and also toured as a virtuoso. About 1775 he gave up public appearances and devoted himself to teaching and working to improve the flute. Tromlitz's extant compositions comprise 3 concerts for Flute and String Quartet, and several sonatas for Keyboard, Cello, and Flute or Violin.

WRITINGS: *Kurze Abhandlung vom Flötenspielen* (Leipzig, 1786); *Ausführlicher und gründlicher Unterricht die Flöte zu spielen* (Leipzig, 1791; Eng. tr., 1991, by A. Powell as *The Virtuoso Flute-Player*); *Über die Flöten mit mehrern Klappen* (Leipzig, 1800; Eng. tr., 1996, by A. Powell as *The Keyed Flute*); the 2 preceding were later publ. as *Flötenschule*.

BIBL.: F. Demmler, *J.G. T.* (diss., Free Univ. of Berlin, 1961). **—NS/LK/DM**

Trotter, Thomas (Andrew), English organist; b. Birkenhead, April 4, 1957. He studied at the Royal Coll. of Music in London, the Univ. of Cambridge (M.A., 1979), and the Cons. Rueil-Malmaison (1979–81). In 1979 he won both 1st Prize and the Bach Prize at the St. Alban's International Organ Competition. He made his first appearance at London's Royal Festival Hall in 1980. In 1982 he became organist at St. Margaret's Church, Westminster, and in 1983 of the City of Birmingham. He made his debut at the London Promenade Concerts in 1986. As a recitalist, Trotter has toured extensively in Europe, North America, Australia, and Japan. His repertoire embraces a broad spectrum of the organ literature, ranging from Bach and Soler to Jehan Alain and Messiaen.**—LK/DM**

Troup, Bobby, pop-jazz songwriter, pianist, and vocalist; b. Oct. 18, 1918, Harrisburg, Pa.; d. Sherman Oaks, Calif., Feb. 7, 1999. He was a staff songwriter with Tommy Dorsey; wrote, produced, and directed service musicals during World War II; wrote the hits "(Get Your Kicks On) Route 66!" and "Baby, Baby All The Time" for the Nat Cole Trio in 1946, and then settled in Hollywood. He was married to Julie London and produced her albums; his many film songs included "The Girl Can't Help It," the title track to the delightful rock 'n' roll movie of 1956. He is certainly the only songwriter who co-wrote with Johnny Mercer ("I'm with You") and also wrote a hit for Little Richard. His television show "Stars of Jazz" in 1956–58 featured Max Roach with Booker Little, etc. He also worked as an actor, portraying Arthur Schutt in the film *The Five Pennies* (1959) and Tommy Dorsey in *The Gene Krupa Story* (1960), as well as playing Dr. Joe Early on the television drama *Emergency*.

DISC.: *Bobby* (1953); *Bobby Troup* (1955); *Bobby Troup Sings Johnny Mercer* (1955); *Bobby Troup and His Trio* (1955); *Bobby Troup and His Jazz All-Stars* (1958); *Stars of Jazz* (1958); *Cool* (1959).**—MM/LP**

Trowell, Brian (Lewis), English musicologist; b. Wokingham, Berkshire, Feb. 21, 1931. He was educated at Christ's Hospital and Gonville and Caius Coll., Cambridge (B.A., 1953; Mus.B., 1956; Ph.D., 1960, with the diss. *Music Under the Later Plantagenets*). He taught at the Univ. of Birmingham (1957–62) and at King's Coll., London (1964–65). From 1967 to 1970 he was head of radio opera for the BBC in London. In 1970 he was Regents' Prof. at the Univ. of Calif. at Berkeley. He rejoined the faculty of King's Coll. as a reader in music in 1970, and then was King Edward VII Prof. of Music there from 1974 to 1988. In 1988 he became Heather Prof. of Music at the Univ. of Oxford, retiring in 1996. He was president of the Royal Musical Assn. from 1983 to 1988. From 1983 to 1993 he was chairman of the editorial committee of Musica Britannica, and from 1987 to 1998 he was founding chairman of the Handel Inst. Trust and Council. Trowell is an authority on English music of the 15th century, on Elgar, and on opera in all eras. He has contributed valuable articles to various journals, reference works, and other publications. With M. and I. Bent, he edited the 2nd edition, rev., of Dunstable's complete works in Musica Britannica, VIII (1970).**—NS/LK/DM**

Troyanos, Tatiana, brilliant American mezzo-soprano; b. N.Y., Sept. 12, 1938; d. there, Aug. 21, 1993. She studied at the Juilliard School of Music in N.Y. (graduated, 1963) and with Hans Heinz. On April 25, 1963, she made her operatic debut as Hippolyta in *A Midsummer Night's Dream* at the N.Y.C. Opera, where she then appeared as Marina, Cherubino, and Jocasta. In 1965 she made her first appearance at the Hamburg State Opera as Preziosilla. She remained on its roster until 1975, winning distinction for such roles as Elisetta, Dorabella, and Baba. She also created the role of Jeanne in *The Devil's of Loudun* there in 1969. In 1966 she sang for the first time at the Aix-en-Provence Festival as Strauss' Composer. In 1969 she made her debut at London's Covent Garden and at the Salzburg Festival as Octavian. In 1971 she sang Ariodante in the first operatic production given at the Kennedy Center in Washington, D.C.; that same year she also made her debut at the Chicago Lyric Opera as Charlotte. In 1975 she sang Bellini's Romeo in Boston. On March 8, 1976, she made a memorable debut at the Metropolitan Opera in N.Y. as Octavian. In subsequent years, Troyanos was one of the leading members of the Metropolitan Opera, excelling in such roles as Amneris, Brangäne, Eboli, the Composer, Kundry, Didon, Santuzza, Orlovsky, Adalgisa, and Geschwitz. In 1992 she created the role of Queen Isabella in Glass's *The Voyage* there. Her death from cancer deprived the Metropolitan Opera of the extraordinary gifts of one of America's finest singers. **—NS/LK/DM**

Truax, Barry (Douglas), Canadian composer and teacher; b. Chatham, Ontario, May 10, 1947. He studied physics and mathematics at Queen's Univ. in Kingston (B.S., 1969), and then pursued music studies with Hultberg at the Univ. of British Columbia (M.M., 1971), and with Laske and Koenig at the Inst. of Sonology at the Univ. of Utrecht (1971–73). In 1973 he became associated with R. Murray Schafer through the World Soundscape Project in Vancouver. After serving as director of the Sonic Research Studio and asst. prof. in the dept. of communication at Simon Fraser Univ. (1976–83), he was prof. in the School of Communication and the School for the Contemporary Arts there. He publ. the vols. *Handbook for Acoustic Ecology* (1978) and

Acoustic Communication (1985). Truax is one of Canada's leading composers of electroacoustic music.

WORKS: DRAMATIC: *The Little Prince* for Narrator, Singers, and Tape, after Saint-Exupery (1971); *Gilgamesh* for Narrator, Singers, Dancers, Sopranino Recorder, Oboe, and 4 Soundtracks (1972–74); *Powers of Two,* electroacoustic music opera for 6 Singers, 2 Dancers, Video Tape, and 8 Soundtracks (1995–99); *Adrogyne, Mon Amour,* music theater piece for Amplified Male Double Bass Player and 2 Soundtracks, after Tennessee Williams (1996–97). **Mixed Media with Tape:** *Divan* for Computer Graphic Slides and 2 Soundtracks (1985); *The Wings of Nike* for Computer Graphic Slides and 2 Soundtracks (1987); *Beauty and the Beast* for Narrator (Oboe d'Amore and English Horn), Computer Images, and 2 Soundtracks (1989); *Pacific Dragon* for Computer Graphic Slides and 4 Soundtracks (1991); *Night of the Conjurer* for Video Tape and Optional Cello (1992); *Song of Songs* for Oboe d'Amore, English Horn, 2 Soundtracks, and Computer Graphic Images (1992); *Threshing (On the Mechanics of Nostalgia)* for Video (1993). **INSTRUMENTS AND/OR VOICE AND TAPE:** *She, a Solo* for Mezzo-soprano and Tape (1973); *Trigon* for Mezzo-soprano, Alto Flute, Piano, and Tape (1974–75); *Nautilus* for Percussion and 4 Soundtracks (1976); *Sonic Landscape No. 4* for Organ and 4 Soundtracks (1977); *Aerial* for Horn and 4 Soundtracks (1979); *Love Songs* for Woman's Voice and 4 Soundtracks (1979); *East Wind* for Amplified Recorder and 4 Soundtracks (1981); *Nightwatch* for Marimba and 4 Soundtracks (1982); *Etude* for Cello and 2 Soundtracks (1983–84); *Tongues of Angels* for Oboe d'Amore, English Horn, and 4 Soundtracks (1988); *Pacific Fog,* soundscape with English Horn (1990); *Dominion* for Chamber Ensemble and 2 Soundtracks (1991); *Bamboo, Silk and Stone* for Asian Instruments and 2 Soundtracks (1994; in collaboration with Randy Raine- Reusch); *Inside* for Bass Oboe and 2 Soundtracks (1995); *Patterns* for Woman Speaker and 2 Soundtracks (1996); *Wings of Fire* for Woman Cellist and 2 Soundtracks (1996); *Twin Souls* for Chorus and 2 Soundtracks (1997). **OTHER:** *Tapes from Gilgamesh* for 12 4-Channel Tapes (1972–73); *Sonic Landscape No. 3,* spatial environment for 4 Computer- synthesized Soundtracks (1975; rev. 1977); *Androgyny* for 4 Computer- synthesized Soundtracks (1978); *Ascendance* for Stereo Electronic Tape (1979); *The Blind Man* for 2-Channel Tape (1979); *Arras* for 4 Computer-synthesized Soundtracks (1980); *Wave Edge* for 4 Computer-synthesized Soundtracks (1983); *Solar Ellipse* for 4 Computer-synthesized Soundtracks (1984–85); *Riverrun* for 4 Computer-synthesized Soundtracks (1986); *Pacific* for 4 Digital Soundtracks (1990); *Basilica* for 2 Digital Soundtracks (1992); *Sequence of Later Heaven* for 4 Digital Soundtracks (1993); *Pacific Fanfare* for 2 Digital Soundtracks (1996); *Pendlerdrøm* for 2 Digital Soundtracks (1997); *Sequence of Earlier Heaven* for 8 Digital Soundtracks (1998).—**NS/LK/DM**

Trube, Adolph, German organist, pianist, choral conductor, teacher, and composer; b. Waldenburg, Jan. 16, 1815; d. Glauchau, March 17, 1857. He was the son of the German organist and teacher Johann Adolph Trube (b. Grosserkmannsdorf, 1789; d. Waldenburg, Feb. 8, 1839). He studied with Fincke at the Plauen seminary, where he then was Präzeptor and organist. After teaching in Schneeberg, he settled in Glauchau as Kantor, music director, and singing teacher in 1840. He later was active as a pianist, choral conductor, and concert organizer. His output includes instrumental pieces, sacred music, men's choruses, and songs.—**LK/DM**

Trumbauer, Frankie (also **Trombar, Frank**), influential early jazz Alto and C-melody saxophonist, multi-instrumentalist, singer; b. Carbondale, Ill., May 30, 1901; d. Kansas City, Mo., June 11, 1956. His mother was a concert pianist, his son, Bill, became a professional trumpet player and music teacher. Raised in St. Louis, during early teens played piano, trombone, flute, and violin before concentrating on "C" melody sax (later in his career Trumbauer also recorded on cornet, alto sax, and bassoon; on some of his most famous sides, possibly including "Singin' the Blues," he played alto and not C-Melody, says researcher Carl Woideck.) At 17 formed own band in St. Louis then, after service in U.S. Navy, returned to St. Louis to join Max Goldman's Orch., Subsequently with Ted Jansen's Band and Earl Fuller, Joined Gene Rodemich's Band and with them made recording debut, worked with Joe Kayser's Orch. (1921), then joined Benson Orch. in Chicago before playing with Ray Miller's Orch. during 1923–24. Subsequently became a musical director for the Jean Goldkette band and led a band at the Arcadia Ballroom which featured Bix Beiderbecke. Together with Bix played for Goldkette until 1927, during this time these two musicians made many small band recordings together. They both worked in Adrian Rollini's short-lived big band (September–October 1927) and with Paul Whiteman's Orch.; Trumbauer remained with Whiteman until the spring of 1932. Organized own band and did extensive touring before rejoining Whiteman in late 1933. Co-led the Three T's in late 1936 (with Jack and Charlie Teagarden), then left Whiteman and moved to West Coast, co-led band with Manny Klein, then worked with George Stoll (early 1938) before organizing own big band (March 1938), using the name "Trombar." Left full-time music in March 1939 to become an inspector for the Civil Aeronautics Authority in Kansas City. Led own band again in 1940. Worked as a test pilot throughout World War II, in late 1945. returned to music and worked with Russ Case's Studio group and with Raymond Paige's NBC Orch. in N.Y. Moved to Santa Monica in 1947, retired from full-time music. Again worked for Civil Aeronautical Authority in Kansas City, but continued to play occasionally and guested at Dixieland Jubilee Bix tribute in October 1952. Died of a heart attack in 1956.

Trumbauer was an important early saxophonist who influenced Lester Young, Benny Carter, Buddy Tate, Budd Johnson, and many others.

DISC.: MILDRED BAILEY: *L'Art Vocal, Vol. 9: 1931–39* (1997); *Mildred Bailey: 1929–32* (1999). **BIX BEIDERBECKE:** *And the Chicago Cornets* (1924); *Indispensable* (1924); *Bix Beiderbecke, Vol. 1: Singin' the Blues* (1927); *Bix Beiderbecke, Vol. 2: At the Jazz Band Ball* (1927); *Bix Beiderbecke: 1924–30* (1986); *At the Jazz Band Ball* (1991); *Felix the Cat* (1993); *Bix Beiderbecke: Vol. 4 (1927–28)* (1994); *Bix Beiderbecke 1928–29, Vol. 7* (1994); *Wa Da Da* (1994); *Bix Beiderbecke: 1927, Vol 3* (1995); *Bix Beiderbecke: 1928, Vol. 5* (1995); *Bix Beiderbecke: 1929–30, Vol 8* (1996); *His Best Recordings* (1996); *Great Original Performances: 1924–30* (1997). **HOAGY CARMICHAEL:** *Classic Hoagy Carmichael* (1927). **BING CROSBY:** *Classic Crosby: 1931 to 1938* (1994); *Bing Crosby: 1928–45* (1997). **DUKE ELLINGTON:** *Complete Edition, Vol. 1 (1924–26)* (1996). **COLE PORTER:** *Stars of the 30's* (1991); *From This Moment On: The Songs of Cole Porter* (1992).

JACK TEAGARDEN *Indispensable* (1928); *I Gotta Right to Sing the Blues* (1929); *Jack Teagarden & His Orchestra (1934–39)* (1939); *Big T* (1994). **JOE VENUTI:** *Violin Jazz 1927–34* (1934). **JOE VENUTI & EDDIE LANG** *Joe Venuti and Eddie Lang (1926–33)* (1933); *Stringing the Blues* (2000). **PAUL WHITEMAN:** *King of Jazz* (1920); *Paul Whiteman and His Orchestra* (1996); *Say It with Music* (2000).—**JC/LP**

Trutovsky, Vasili (Fyodorovich), Russian composer and folk-song collector; b. Ivanovskaya Sloboda, c. 1740; d. St. Petersburg, 1810. He was the son of an Orthodox priest. He was a court singer and player on the gusli during the reigns of Elizabeth, Peter III, and Catherine II. His historic achievement was the compilation of the first comprehensive collection of Russian folk songs, in 4 fascicles (1776, 1778, 1779, 1795). He also was the first in Russia to publ. piano pieces; the earlier publications of Russian piano music were anonymous. His *Chanson russe variée* for Harpsichord or Piano (St. Petersburg, 1780) was ed. by A. Drozdov and T. Trofimov (Moscow, 1946).—**NS/LK/DM**

Trythall, (Harry) Gil(bert), American composer and teacher, brother of **Richard Trythall;** b. Knoxville, Tenn., Oct. 28, 1930. He studied theory and composition with David Van Vactor at the Univ. of Tenn. (B.A., 1951), composition with Riegger at Northwestern Univ. (M.Mus., 1952), and composition with Palmer and musicology with Grout at Cornell Univ. (D.M.A., 1960). He was asst. prof. at Knox Coll. in Galesburg, Ill. (1960–64); after serving as prof. of theory and composition (1964–75) and chairman of the music school (1973–75) at George Peabody Coll. for Teachers in Nashville, he was prof. of music (from 1975) and dean of the creative arts center (1975–81) at W.Va. Univ. in Morgantown. He publ. *Principles and Practices of Electronic Music* (N.Y., 1974), *Eighteenth Century Counterpoint* (Dubuque, Iowa, 1993), and *Sixteenth Century Counterpoint* (Dubuque, Iowa, 1994).

WORKS: DRAMATIC: Opera: *The Music Lesson*, opera buffa (1960); *The Terminal Opera* (1982; rev. 1987). **ORCH.:** *A Solemn Chant* for Strings (1955); Sym. No. 1 (1958; rev. 1963); Harp Concerto (1963); *Dionysia* (1964); *Chroma I* (1970); *Cindy the Synthe (Minnie the Moog)* for Synthesizer and Strings (1975); Sinfonia Concertante 1989). **CHAMBER:** Flute Sonata (1964); *A Vacuum Soprano* for Brass Quintet and Tape (1966); *Entropy* for Brass, Harp, Celesta, Piano, and Tape (1967); *Parallax* for 4 to 40 Brass, Tape, Audience, and Slide Projection (1968); *Echospace* for Brass and Tape (1973); piano pieces; organ works. **VOCAL:** *In the Presence* for Chorus and Tape (1969); *Spanish Songs* for Soprano and Synthesizer (1986–87); Mass in English and Spanish for Congregation, Organ, and Descant (1988); *From the Egyptian Book of the Dead* for Soprano, Saxophone or Wind Controller, and Synthesizer (1990); *9:01 Hard Start Variations* for Jazz Soprano, Wind Controller, Synthesizer, and Sequencer (1991); *The Pastimes of Lord Chaitanya* for Jazz Soprano and Synthesizer (1993); *Intermission* for Soprano and Synthesizer (1994). **OTHER:** Electronic pieces; mixed media works; film scores.—**NS/LK/DM**

Trythall, Richard, American pianist and composer, brother of **(Harry) Gil(bert) Trythall;** b. Knoxville, Tenn., July 25, 1939. He studied with David Van Vactor at the Univ. of Tenn. (B.M., 1961) and with Sessions, Kim, and Cone at Princeton Univ. (M.F.A., 1963), then continued his training at the Berlin Hochschule für Musik on a Fulbright fellowship (1963–64); held a Guggenheim fellowship (1967–68). He settled in Rome, where he became a teacher at St. Stephen's School in 1966 and music liaison at the American Academy in 1975. As a pianist, Trythall is a determined champion of modern music and has performed scores ranging from Ives to Stockhausen.

WORKS: ORCH.: Sym. (1961); *Composition* for Piano and Orch. (1965); *Penelope's Monologue* for Soprano and Orch. (1966); *Costruzione* (1967); *Continuums* (1968). **CHAMBER:** Duets for Treble Instruments (1958); Suite for Harpsichord and Tape (1973); *Variations on a Theme by Haydn* for Woodwind Quintet and Tape (1976); *Salute to the '50s* for Percussionist and Tape (1977); *Bolero* for 4 Percussion (1979); piano pieces. **OTHER:** Vocal works, including *4 Songs* for Soprano and Piano (1962); tape pieces, including *Study No. 1* (1967) and *Omaggio a Jerry Lee Lewis* (1975).—**NS/LK/DM**

Tsontakis, George, American composer; b. N.Y., Oct. 24, 1951. He studied with Sessions (1974–79), at the Juilliard School in N.Y. (1978–86), and with Stockhausen in Rome (1981). He was an assistant to the electronic faculty at the Juilliard School (1978) and an asst. prof. at the Brooklyn Coll. Cons. of Music (1986–87). In 1987 he received the Koussevitzky Foundation orchestral commission.

WORKS: ORCH.: *5 Sighs and a Fantasy* (N.Y., Oct. 20, 1984); *Fantasia Habanera* (Baltimore, May 28, 1986); *Overture Vera* (1988); *To the Sowers of the Seed* (Aspen, Colo., Aug. 18, 1989). **CHAMBER:** 4 string quartets: No. 1, *The Mother's Hymn*, with Mezzo-soprano (1980), No. 2, *Emerson* (N.Y., April 29, 1984), No. 3, *Coraggio* (Aspen, Colo., July 26, 1986), and No. 4, *Beneath the Tenderness of Thy Heart* (N.Y., Jan. 17, 1989); *3 Sighs*, 3 variations for Violin (Haywood, Calif., Sept. 25, 1981); *Preludio ed Fantasia* for Cello, Brass Quintet, Piano, and Timpani (N.Y., May 22, 1983); *Birdwind Quintet* for Wind Quintet (Aspen, Colo., July 10, 1983); Brass Quintet (N.Y., April 18, 1984); *The Past, The Passion* for 14 to 15 Players (N.Y., March 4, 1987); *Mercurial Etudes* for Flute (N.Y., Dec. 7, 1988); *3 Mood Sketches* for Wind Quintet (Leningrad, Nov. 22, 1989); *Heartsounds*, quintet for Piano and Strings (Cambridge, Mass., April 20, 1990). **VOCAL: Sacred:** *Scenes from the Apocalypse* for Vocal Soloists, Actor, Chorus, and Orch. (1978); *The Epistle of James, Chapter 1* for Reader, Chorus, and Orch. (1980); *5 Choral Sketches on "Is Aghios" (One, Holy)* for Chorus and Clarinet obbligato (N.Y., May 22, 1984); *Saviors* for Soprano, Chorus, and Orch. (N.Y., May 11, 1985); *Byzantium Kanon* for Chorus and Brass Quintet (N.Y., June 1, 1986); *3 Byzantine Hymns* for Chorus and Brass Quintet (1988); *Stabat Mater* for Soprano, Chorus, and Orch. (N.Y., May 19, 1990). **Secular:** *Erotokritos*, oratorio for Chorus and Orch. (N.Y., May 15, 1982); *Galway Kinnell Songs* for Mezzo-soprano, Piano, and String Quartet (N.Y., Feb. 4, 1987).—**NS/LK/DM**

Tsoupaki, Calliope, Greek pianist and composer; b. Piraeus, May 27, 1963. She studied piano and theory at the Hellinicon Cons. in Athens, then entered the composition class of Yannis Ionnithis at the Nikos Skalkottas Cons. (1985). In 1988 she settled in The

Hague, where she continued her studies with Louis Andriessen and with Gilus van Bergeyk and Dick Raaijmakers (electronic composition) at the Royal Cons. of Music; also attended summer courses with Xenakis (1985), Messiaen (1987), and Boulez (1988) at Darmstadt. In 1991 and 1993 her music was performed at the Gaudeamus International Music Week in Amsterdam; in 1993 she was a composer-in-residence at Budapest's Pepiniéres for Young Artists Foundation. In 1995 she was a featured composer at the "Other Minds" Festival in San Francisco.

WORKS: DRAMATIC: Music Theater: *Nadere kenmismaking* (1995). **ORCH.:** *Eclipse* (1986). **CHAMBER:** *Earinon* for 8 Horns and Percussion (1986); *Krystallina Ymenea* for Chamber Ensemble (1986); *Orfikon* for Viola (1986); *Revealing Moment* for Alto Flute (1987); *Touch of a Silent Echo* for Oboe, Viola, Cello, Percussion, and Piano (1987); *Silver Moments* for 2 Pianos and 2 Percussion Players (1987); *Mania* for Amplified Violin (1988); *Nocturnal Sounds...and the Ivy Leafs Are Trembling* for Cello and Piano (1988); *Music for Saxophones* for Saxophone Quartet (1989); *Visions of the Night* for Amplified Chamber Ensemble (1989); *When I Was 27* for Amplified Viola and Double Bass (1990); *Kentavros* for Wind Ensemble, Double Bass, and Piano (1991); *Episode* for Chamber Ensemble (1991); *Song for Four* for String Quartet (1991); *Dance* for 16 Oboes (1991); *Echoing Purple* for Violin and Chamber Ensemble (1992); *Eros and Psyche* for Wind Octet and Double Bass (1992); *Orphic Fields* for Flute, 2 Harps, and 2 Pianos (1993); *Compulsive Caress* for Guitar (1993); *Phantom* for Tuba (1994); *Her Voice* for Harp (1994); *Sweet if you Like* for Electric Guitar, Tuba, Double Bass, and Percussion (1994); *Charavgi* for Alto ("Ganassi") Recorder (1994); *Ethra* for Flute, Violin, Viola, Cello, and Harp (1995); *Blue* for Oboe (1995); *Pas de deux* for Harp (1995); *Ketting* for 3 Ensembles (1995; in collaboration with others). **KEYBOARD:** Piano: *Echoes of a Deep Sea*, children's piece (1988); *Moments I* and *II* (1988); *Greek Dance* (1990); *Ananda* (1991). Harpsichord: *Common Passion* (1993). **VOCAL:** *For Always* for Women's Voice, Tape, and Lights (1989); *Your Thought* for Voice, Tape, and Lighting (1989); *Paraklitikon* for Vocal Ensemble (1990); *Sappho's Tears* for Violin, Tenor Recorder, and Woman's Voice (1990); *Melos Hidiston* for Woman's Voice, Tenor Recorder, Viola, Cello, Double Bass, and Piano (1991); *Offerande* and *Untitled Love* for Woman's Voice and Fortepiano (1993); *Epigramma* for Chorus and Orch. (1995); *Lineos* for Chorus and Ensemble (1995).—**NS/LK/DM**

Tsouyopoulos, Georges, Greek composer; b. Athens, Oct. 11, 1930. He received his early training in Athens and Milan, then went to Zürich to study with Hindemith. In 1962 he settled in Munich. His early compositions are neo-Classical in style; later he adopted serial methods, determinedly pursuing the goal of structural indeterminacy.

WORKS: *Sinfonietta da camera* for 8 Instruments (1955); *Serenata* for Soprano, Flute, Guitar, and Viola (1957); *2 madrigali* for Soprano and Orch. (1957); *3 frammenti* for Chorus and Orch. (1958); 3 toccatas for Piano (1958, 1959, 1965); *Music for Percussion* (1959); 2 string quartets; vocal pieces.—**NS/LK/DM**

Tsuji, Shōichi, Japanese musicologist; b. Gifu, Dec. 20, 1895; d. Tokyo, April 21, 1987. He took a degree in psychology at the Univ. of Tokyo (1920), and also studied composition and conducting with Ryūtarō Hirota, violin with Shin Kusakawa, and gagaku with Yoshiisa Oku. He taught at St. Paul's Univ., Tokyo (1922–65), and also lectured at the Univ. of Tokyo, the Tokyo National Univ. of Fine Arts and Music, and Kyūshū Univ. In 1968 he became a prof. at Kunitachi Music Coll. Tsuji, the first important Japanese scholar to specialize in Western music, introduced musicology to Japan. He specialized in J.S. Bach and Protestant church music, and wrote biographies of Bach, Mozart, and Schubert. He was one of the founders of the Japanese Musicological Soc.; served as its president (1964–70). After his death, St. Paul's Univ. instituted the annual Shōichi Tsuji Award for achievement in the enhancement of Christian music studies and/or performance. —**NS/LK/DM**

Tsukatani, Akihirô, Japanese composer and pedagogue; b. Tokyo, March 16, 1919; d. 1995. He studied law at the Univ. of Tokyo (graduated, 1941) and received training in theory from Saburo Moroi. He taught economic history at the Univ. of Tokyo before serving on its music faculty.

WORKS: DRAMATIC: Opera: *Pongo* (1965); *Ajatasatru* (1966); *Kakitsubata* (Tokyo, May 24, 1967). Musical: *Fairy's Cap* (Tokyo, Dec. 9, 1968). Ballet: *Mythology of Today* (1956). **ORCH.:** *Festival*, symphonic suite (1950); Suite for Percussion and Strings (1960); Piano Concerto (1961); *Japan Festival Dance Music* for Chamber Orch. (1969); *Musashino*, symphonic poem (1989); *Music* for Violin and Chamber Orch. (1991). **CHAMBER:** Sonata for Flute, Cello, and Piano (1949); Clarinet Sonata (1952); Suite for Horn, Trumpet, Trombone, and Timpani (1959); *Fu 1* and *2* for Flute (1970); *3 Worlds* for Flute (1971–72); *2 Movements* for Cello (1972); *Fantasia* for Violin, Piano, and Tam-tam (1973); *Oracle* for Nonet (1983); *Composition* for Oboe and Piano (1984); *Images* for Ondes Martenot, Flute, Oboe, and String Quartet (1987); *2 Compositions* for Oboe (1988); *3 Movements* for Guitar (1990); *Chimata no Uta 1* for Oboe (1993) and *2* for Oboe and Cymbal (1994). **VOCAL:** Choruses; songs. —**NS/LK/DM**

Tsvetanov, Tsvetan, Bulgarian composer and teacher; b. Sofia, Nov. 6, 1931; d. Paris, April 4, 1982. He studied composition with Hadzhiev and Vladigerov at the Bulgarian State Cons. in Sofia (graduated, 1956); in 1958 he joined its faculty, becoming a prof. in composition and harmony in 1976; also was its rector (1976–80). He served as secretary of the Union of Bulgarian Composers (1969–75; 1976–80).

WORKS: DRAMATIC: *Orpheus and Rodopa*, ballet (1960; also an orch. suite); incidental music for plays; film scores. **ORCH.:** *Sinfonietta* (1956); 4 syms.: No. 1 (1965), No. 2 (1968), No. 3, 1923 (1972), and No. 4 for Chamber Orch. (1975); *Overture* (1968); Concertino for Piano and Chamber Orch. (1970); *Overture of Joy* (1971); *Festive Concerto* (1974); *Symphonic Variations* (1976). **CHAMBER:** *Variations* for String Quartet (1953); Violin Sonata (1955); Piano Sonata (1961); Cello Sonata (1973). **VOCAL:** *The Great Beginning*, symphonic poem for Narrator and Orch. (1961–63); *The Staircase*, ballad for Alto, Men's Chorus, and Orch. (1966); *Ballad of Botev's Kiss*, poem for Chorus and Orch. (1973); *Back to the Feat*, symphonic poem for Narrator and String Orch. (1977); *Immortality*, oratorio (1981); songs; vocal pieces for amateurs; folk song transcriptions. —**NS/LK/DM**

Tua, Teresina (actually, **Maria Felicità**), Italian violinist; b. Turin, May 22, 1867; d. Rome, Oct. 29, 1955. She studied with Massart at the Paris Cons., where she took the 1st prize in 1880. She toured the Continent with brilliant success; made her English debut at the Crystal Palace in London, May 5, 1883; appeared in America (1887). In 1889 she married Count Franchi-Verney della Valetta, and withdrew from the concert stage until the autumn of 1895, when she set out on a successful European tour, including Russia, where her accompanist and joint artist was Rachmaninoff. Franchi died in 1911; in 1913 she married Emilio Quadrio. She taught at the Milan Cons. from 1915 to 1924, and then at the Accademia di Santa Cecilia in Rome; subsequently abandoned her career, and entered the Convento dell'Adorazione in Rome as Sister Maria di Gesù. **—NS/LK/DM**

Tubb, Carrie (actually, **Caroline Elizabeth**), English soprano; b. London, May 17, 1876; d. there, Sept. 20, 1976. She studied at the Guildhall School of Music in London. She began her career singing in a vocal quartet during her student days; after winning notice as an oratorio singer, she appeared at Covent Garden and at His Majesty's Theatre in London (1910); however, she soon abandoned opera and pursued a career as a concert artist until her retirement in 1930; in the latter year, she became a prof. at the Guildhall School of Music, where she taught for almost 30 years. She excelled both in Mozart arias and in concert excerpts from Wagner and Verdi.**—NS/LK/DM**

Tubb, Ernest (Dale), American country music singer, songwriter, and guitarist; b. Crisp, Tex., Feb. 9, 1914; d. Nashville, Tenn., Sept. 6, 1984. One of the most popular country music performers of the 1940s and 1950s, Tubb deliberately evolved the style of Jimmie Rodgers into a more modern sound, fostering the development of what had been called "hillbilly" music into "country and western." Introducing the electric guitar into country, he performed in a hard-edged honky-tonk style that influenced such successors as Johnny Cash, Merle Haggard, and Waylon Jennings. He had more than 90 records on the country charts between 1944 and 1979, the biggest hits including "Walking the Floor Over You," "Soldier's Last Letter," and "It's Been So Long Darling."

Tubb's father, Calvin Robert Tubb, was a sharecropper; his mother, Sarah Ellen Baker Tubb, played piano and organ. The family moved around Tex. when Tubb was a child. His schooling was minimal. During his teens he worked at menial jobs while living with his mother or his father, who had divorced, or with other family members. He developed an attachment to the music of Jimmie Rodgers and began to sing and play guitar in imitation of his hero. He made his radio debut in San Antonio, probably in late 1933. On May 26, 1934, he married Lois Elaine Cook. They had three children, the oldest of whom, Justin Tubb, became a successful country singer. They were divorced in 1948.

Tubb contacted Rodgers's widow, Carrie Rodgers, who encouraged him and became his sponsor. She arranged for his first recording session on Oct. 27, 1936, for RCA Victor, Rodgers's label, at which he recorded such songs as "The Passing of Jimmie Rodgers" and "The Last Thoughts of Jimmie Rodgers," both of which were written by Elsie McWilliams, Carrie Rodgers's sister. But these and subsequent recordings were unsuccessful, and Tubb struggled to achieve recognition over the next few years, performing on various radio stations in Tex. while supporting himself with jobs outside music.

Tubb got another chance to record, this time for Decca, beginning with a session on April 4, 1940. That fall he found steady, sponsored work on KGKO in Fort Worth. On April 26, 1941, he recorded his breakthrough hit, "Walking the Floor Over You," which he had written himself. Released during the summer, it reportedly sold over a million copies, enabling him to begin to tour beyond Tex. He went to Hollywood in July 1942 for a part in his first motion picture, *Fighting Buckaroo*, released in early 1943, and returned in November for a second film, *Riding West*, not released until May 1944. In January 1943 he first performed on the *Grand Ole Opry* radio show, and he joined the program as a regular the following month, moving to Tenn. He also performed on other shows on station WSM, which broadcasts the *Opry*.

Tubb reached the pop charts and the Top Ten of the country charts in January 1944 with the self-written "Try Me One More Time." He made another film that month, *Jamboree*, which was released in March. Both sides of his next single, "Soldier's Last Letter" (music and lyrics by Henry "Redd" Stewart) and "Yesterday's Tears" (music and lyrics by Ernest Tubb), hit the Top Ten of the country charts and crossed over to the pop charts in the spring and summer; "Soldier's Last Letter" hit #1 on the country charts in September. In 1945 he placed four songs in the Top Ten of the country charts, including "It's Been So Long Darling" (music and lyrics by Ernest Tubb), which hit #1 in December. "Rainbow at Midnight" (music and lyrics by Arthur Q. Smith [real name, James Arthur Pritchett], though credited to Lost John Miller) became his third country chart-topper in January 1947, one of three Top Ten hits he released in 1946. He had three more Top Ten hits in 1947, the most successful of which was the self-penned "Don't Look Now (But Your Broken Heart Is Showing)." That year he opened the Ernest Tubb Record Shop adjacent to the Ryman Auditorium, from where the *Grand Ole Opry* was broadcast, and began a post-*Opry* Saturday night radio series, *Midnite Jamboree*. He also made his final film appearance, a starring role in *Hollywood Barn Dance*, shot in March and released in July 1947.

Tubb had six songs in the country charts during 1948, the most notable of which were the Top Ten hits "Forever Is Ending Today" (music and lyrics by Ernest Tubb, Cyrus Whitfield "Johnny" Bond, and Ike Cargill), which crossed over to the pop charts, and a revival of the 1933 song "Have You Ever Been Lonely? (Have You Ever Been Blue)" (music by Peter DeRose, lyrics by Billy Hill). He had a remarkable 12 Top Ten country hits in release in 1949, the most successful of which were the chart-toppers "Slipping Around" (music and lyrics by

Floyd Tillman) and "Blue Christmas" (music and lyrics by Billy Hayes and Jay Johnson), which also made the pop charts. Two records made with other artists also hit the top: "I'm Biting My Fingernails and Thinking of You" (music and lyrics by Ernest Tubb, Roy West, Ernest Benedict, and Lenny Sanders) with the Andrews Sisters (another crossover to the pop charts), and "Tennessee Border No. 2" (music by Jimmy Work, lyrics by Henry D. "Homer" Haynes and Kenneth C. "Jethro" Burns) with Red Foley.

On June 3, 1949, Tubb married Olene Adams Carter. They had five children and their marriage lasted 26 years, ending in a legal separation in 1975, though they never formally divorced.

Tubb charted another 12 country Top Ten hits in 1950, the most successful of which were his #1 duet with Red Foley, "Goodnight Irene" (music and lyrics by Lead Belly), which crossed over to the Top Ten of the pop charts; "Letters Have No Arms" (music and lyrics by Archie Gibson and Ernest Tubb); and "I Love You Because" (music and lyrics by Leon Payne). His commercial success on records fell off gradually during the rest of the 1950s, although he managed to score another 16 Top Ten country hits through the end of the decade, notably "Too Old to Cut the Mustard" (music and lyrics by Bill Carlisle), another duet with Red Foley, "Missing in Action" (music and lyrics by Helen Kaye and Arthur Q. Smith), and "Fortunes in Memories" (music and lyrics by Charlie Walker and Lou Wayne), all released in 1952. He and his son Justin, who had joined the *Grand Ole Opry*, appeared as regulars on monthly broadcasts of a television version of the show from October 1955 to September 1956.

Tubb continued to tour extensively and to perform regularly on the *Grand Ole Opry* until 1982. From 1965 to 1968 he had a syndicated television series, *The Ernest Tubb Show*. He returned to the Top Ten of the country charts with the single "Thanks a Lot" (music and lyrics by Don Sessions and Eddie Miller) in 1963 and a *Thanks a Lot* LP in 1964. He had two country Top Ten albums in 1967, *Another Story* and *Singin' Again*, the latter a duet LP with Loretta Lynn. He left MCA Records, which had acquired Decca, after 1975, but he returned to the country Top Ten in 1979 with the album *Ernest Tubb: The Legend and the Legacy, Vol. One*, on Cachet Records, a disc featuring rerecordings of his hits with such guest stars as Willie Nelson, George Jones, Loretta Lynn, Johnny Cash, Marty Robbins, Merle Haggard, and Conway Twitty. He appeared as himself in the 1980 film biography of Loretta Lynn, *Coal Miner's Daughter*.

In declining health, Tubb gave his last concert on Nov. 13, 1982. His final recording was as a guest vocalist on Hank Williams Jr.'s Top Ten country hit "Leave Them Boys Alone" (music and lyrics by Dean Dillon, Hank Williams Jr., Gary Stewart, and Tanya Tucker) in 1983. He died of emphysema at 70 in 1984.

DISC.: *Country Music Hall of Fame* (rec. 1940–60s; rel. 1991); *Live 1965* (rel. 1989); *Guests* (rec. 1978–79; rel. 1989).

BIBL.: N. Barthel, *E. T. Discography, 1936–1969* (Roland, Okla., 1970); N. Barthel, *E. T.: The Original E. T.* (Roland, Okla., 1984); R. Pugh, *E. T.: The Texas Troubadour* (Durham, N.C., 1996).
—**WR**

Tubin, Eduard, Estonian-born Swedish composer and conductor; b. Kallaste, near Tartu, June 18, 1905; d. Stockholm, Nov. 17, 1982. He studied with A. Kapp at the Tartu Cons. and later with Kodály in Budapest. From 1931 to 1944 he conducted the Vanemuine Theater Orch. in Tartu. In 1944 he settled in Stockholm and in 1961 became a naturalized Swedish citizen. In 1982 he was elected to the Royal Swedish Academy of Music. He was at work on his 11th Sym. at the time of his death.

WORKS: DRAMATIC: Opera: *Barbara von Tisenhusen* (Tallinn, Dec. 4, 1969); *Prosten fran Reigi* (The Priest from Reigi; 1971). **Ballet:** *Skratten* (Laughter; 1939–41). **ORCH.:** 10 syms.: No. 1 (1934), No. 2, *Legendary* (1937), No. 3 (1942; Tallinn, Feb. 26, 1943), No. 4, *Lyrical* (1943; Tallinn, April 16, 1944; rev. 1978; Bergen, Nov. 5, 1981), No. 5 (1946), No. 6 (1954), No. 7 (1958), No. 8 (1966), No. 9, *Sinfonia semplice* (1969; Stockholm, Nov. 20, 1971), and No. 10 (1973); *Estonian Dance Suite* (1938); 2 violin concertos (1942, 1945); Piano Concertino (1944–46); Double Bass Concerto (1948); Balalaika Concerto (1964). **CHAMBER:** 2 violin sonatas (1936, 1949); Saxophone Sonata (1951); Sonata for Solo Violin (1962); Viola Sonata (1965); *Capriccio* for Violin and Piano (1971); Flute Sonata (1979); *Suite on Estonian Dance Tunes* for Violin (1979); *Quartet on Estonian Motifs* for String Quartet (1979). **Piano:** *10 preludes* (1928–76). **VOCAL:** *Ylermi*, ballad for Baritone and Orch. (1935; rev. 1977); *5 Kosjalaulud* for Baritone and Orch. (1975); *Requiem for Fallen Soldiers* for Alto, Men's Chorus, Trumpet, Percussion, and Organ (1979).

BIBL.: M. Pärtlas, *E. T.s sumfooniad: Teemastik ja vorm* (Tallinn, 1995).—**NS/LK/DM**

Tucci, Gabriella, Italian soprano; b. Rome, Aug. 4, 1929. She studied at the Accademia di Santa Cecilia in Rome, and then with Leonardo Filoni, who became her husband. In 1951 she made her operatic debut in Lucca. After winning the Spoleto competition that year, she sang Leonora in *La forza del destino* at the Spoleto Festival. In 1953 she appeared as Cherubini's Médée in Florence. She made a tour of Australia in 1955. In 1959 she made her first appearance at Milan's La Scala as Mimi. On Sept. 25, 1959, she made her U.S. debut as Giordano's Madeleine at the San Francisco Opera. From 1959 to 1969 she sang regularly at the Verona Arena. She made her Metropolitan Opera debut in N.Y. as Cio-Cio-San on Oct. 29, 1960, and remained on its roster until 1973. Among her most successful roles there were Euridice, Marguerite, both Verdi Leonoras, Aida, Violetta, Alice Ford, and Mimi. She also sang Tosca at her Covent Garden debut in London in 1960. As a guest artist, she sang at the Vienna State Opera, the Deutsche Oper in Berlin, the Bavarian State Opera in Munich, the Bolshoi Theater in Moscow, and the Teatro Colón in Buenos Aires. She later taught at the Ind. Univ. School of Music in Bloomington (1983–86).—**NS/LK/DM**

Tucker, Mickey, one of many to suffer from a lack of name recognition and critical acclaim, this pianist is a supremely talented mainstream player who also happens to be an accomplished composer and organ player; b. Durham, N.C., April 28, 1941. Mickey Tucker's highly developed harmonic sense and crystal-clear tone put him on par with just about any other pianist of his generation. Since taking up the piano while in his teens, he has worked as a school teacher, an arranger for the R&B group Little Anthony and the Imperials, and appeared with a lengthy list of jazz artists, including Roland Kirk, Willis Jackson, Art Blakey, Eric Kloss, and Sonny Fortune. During the 1970s, he toured Africa and Europe with Art Blakey's Jazz Messengers and recorded several times for the Xanadu and Muse labels (sadly, all of these are currently unavailable). The next decade found him working with the newly revived Farmer/Golson Jazztet before taking up residence in Australia. Not as often recorded as he should be, he has lately been leading sessions for SteepleChase Records that rank among the finest work of his career.

Disc.: *Blues in Five Dimensions* (1989); *Hang in There* (1991); *Sweet Lotus Lips* (1993).—**CH**

Tucker, Richard (real name, **Reuben Ticker**), brilliant American tenor; b. N.Y., Aug. 28, 1913; d. Kalamazoo, Mich., Jan. 8, 1975. He sang in a synagogue choir in N.Y. as a child; studied voice with Paul Althouse; subsequently sang on the radio. His first public appearance in opera was as Alfredo in *La Traviata* in 1943 with the Salmaggi Co. in N.Y. On Jan. 25, 1945, he made his Metropolitan Opera debut in N.Y. as Enzo in *La Gioconda*; he remained on its roster until his death, specializing in the Italian repertoire. In 1947 he made his European debut at the Verona Arena as Enzo (Maria Callas made her Italian debut as Gioconda in the same performance); he also sang at Covent Garden in London (debut as Cavaradossi, 1958), at La Scala in Milan (1969), in Vienna, and in other major music centers abroad. He died while on a concert tour. He was the brother-in-law of **Jan Peerce**.

Bibl.: J. Drake, *R. T.: A Biography* (N.Y., 1984).
—**NS/LK/DM**

Tuckey, William, English-American singer, singing teacher, and composer; b. Somerset, 1708; d. Philadelphia, Sept. 14, 1781. He claimed to have been a vicar-choral at Bristol Cathedral before going to N.Y. in 1753, where he was active as a singer and singing teacher until 1773; also conducted what was probably the first American performance of Handel's *Messiah* (Jan. 16, 1770; overture and 16 numbers). About 1773 he settled in Philadelphia, where he was made clerk at St. Peter's Church in 1778. He wrote several hymn tunes. —**NS/LK/DM**

Tuckwell, Barry (Emmanuel), noted Australian-born American horn player and conductor; b. Melbourne, March 5, 1931. He studied horn with Alan Mann in Sydney. After playing in the Sydney Sym. Orch. (1947–50), he played in the Hallé Orch. in Manchester (1951–53) and the Scottish National Orch. in Glasgow (1953–54). In 1954–55 he was 1st horn in the Bournemouth Sym. Orch., and then held that position with the London Sym. Orch. from 1955 to 1968. He subsequently pursued a solo career, achieving recognition as one of the finest horn virtuosos of the day. From 1963 to 1974 to he was prof. of horn at the Royal Academy of Music in London. In addition to the standard horn literature, Tuckwell also plays works composed especially for him, including scores by Thea Musgrave, Richard Rodney Bennett, Iain Hamilton, Alun Hoddinott, and Don Banks. In later years, he became active as a conductor and appeared as a guest conductor with orchs. in Australia, Europe, and the U.S. From 1980 to 1983 he was conductor of the Tasmanian Sym. Orch. In 1982 he became music director of the newly founded Md. Sym. Orch. in Hagerstown, a position he retained until 1998. He 1965 he was made an Officer of the Order of the British Empire. In 1996 he became a naturalized American citizen.—**NS/LK/DM**

Tudor, David (Eugene), significant American pianist and composer; b. Philadelphia, Jan. 20, 1926; d. Tomkins Cove, N.Y., Aug. 13, 1996. He studied piano with Josef Martin and Irma Wolpe, organ and theory with H. William Hawke, and composition and analysis with Stefan Wolpe. At the age of 11, he encountered one of Messiaen's organ compositions, an occasion marking the beginning of his devotion to the music of his time. Although for many years he performed a wide variety of earlier music in his capacity as accompanist for such dancers as Katherine Litz and Jean Erdman and the saxophonist Sigurd Rascher, Tudor's role as a pioneer in the performance of new music was established as early as 1950, when he gave the U.S. premiere of Boulez's 2nd Piano Sonata (N.Y., Dec. 17, 1950). At that time, he also began a close association with John Cage, whose works he propagated with eloquence in the U.S., Europe, and Japan. From 1950 to 1965 he was a touchstone and at times even a catalyst for the composition of a body of music of often extreme radicalism, giving first or early performances of works by Brown, Bussotti, Feldman, Stockhausen, Wolff, Wolpe, and Young, many written expressly for him.

Tudor was affiliated with the Merce Cunningham Dance Co. since its inception in 1953, creating an array of works including *Rainforest* (1968; for *Rainforest*), *Toneburst* (1975; for *Sounddance*), *Forest Speech* (1976; for "Event"), *Weatherings* (1978; for *Exchange*), *Phonemes* (1981; for *Channels/Inserts*), *Sextet for Seven* (1982; for *Sextet*), *Virtual Focus* (1990; for *Polarity*), and *Soundings: Ocean Diary* (1994; for *Ocean*). Upon Cage's death in 1992, he was named music director, a position he retained until his death, being succeeded by Takahisa Kosugi. Tudor was a member of the summer faculty of Black Mountain Coll. from 1951 to 1953, and he also taught courses in piano and the performance of new music in Darmstadt (1956, 1958, 1959, and 1961). He gave seminars in live electronic music at the State Univ. of N.Y. at Buffalo (1965–66), the Univ. of Calif. at Davis (1967), Mills Coll. in Oakland, Calif. (1967–68), and the National Inst. of Design in Ahmedabad, India (1969). In 1968 he was selected as one of the four Core Artists for the design and construction of the Pepsico Pavilion at Expo 70 in Osaka.

Recent research into Tudor's work as a performer during the critical period of 1950 to 1965, in particular by John Holzaepfel, has shown two common assumptions to be false. First, Tudor did not work under the supervision of the American avant-garde composers whose music he played but rather prepared his performances of their works privately and independently. Second, in music in which some degree of indeterminacy is a compositional principle, Tudor did not limit himself to improvising from the score. Rather, it was his practice in numerous cases to undertake a rigorous series of preparatory steps, including measurements, calculations, computations, and conversation tables, translating the results into a more conventional notation for use in performance. Nevertheless, it may have been inevitable that the freedoms entrusted him by composers, combined with Tudor's own extensions of the use of sonic materials in his realizations and his sense of a decrease in the challenge he saw as essential to the composer-performer relationship, gradually led him away from piano playing and into the performance of live electronic music, an area in which he was also a pioneer, with a series of works to which he signed his own name. As a composer, Tudor was experimental and radical, drawing upon technological resources both flexible and complex. He was a pioneer in this respect, and an inspiration to a new generation of composers and performers, designing his own sources of sound production, using conventional sound- transmitters as sound-generators, programming feedback as a component of his compositions, and mixing both output and input matrices. His works were often collaborative; in addition to works for dances by Cunningham, he created works for laser productions by Lowell Cross, visual installations by Jacqueline Matisse Monnier, as well as collaborative works for television, theater, and film. Some of his pieces took the form of electroacoustic environments in which sounds might be activated by audience movements. The *Neural Synthesis* series (1992–94) used a neural-network chip to process both analog and digital signals.

Tudor's considerable library of manuscripts, electronic equipment and modular devices, and audio tapes was acquired after his death by the Getty Research Inst. for the History of Art and the Humanities in Los Angeles.

WORKS: *Fluorescent Sound* (Stockholm, Sept. 13, 1964); *Bandoneon!* for Factorial Bandoneon (N.Y., Oct. 14 and 18, 1966); *Assemblage* (1968; in collaboration with J. Cage and G. Mumma); *Rainforest* (Buffalo, N.Y., March 9, 1968); *Reunion* (Toronto, March 5, 1968; in collaboration with D. Behrman, J. Cage, L. Cross, M. and T. Duchamp, and G. Mumma); *Video III* (San Diego, May 10, 1968; in collaboration with L. Cross); *Video/Laser I* (Oakland, Calif., May 9, 1969; in collaboration with L. Cross) and *II* (1970; in collaboration with L. Cross and C. Jeffries); *Pepsibird, Microphone, Pepscillator*, and *Anima Pepsi* (1970); *First week of June* (Paris, June 5, 1970; in collaboration with J. Cage and G. Mumma); *Melodics for Amplified Bandoneon* (1972); *Monobird* (Munich, Aug. 30, 1972; for J. Cage's Birdcage); *Rainforest 3* (Radio Bremen, May 5, 1972; for J. Cage's *Mureau*); *Untitled* (Radio Bremen, May 8, 1972; for J. Cage's *Mesostics re Merce Cunningham*); *Free Spectral Range I* (Oberlin, Ohio, Feb. 16, 1973; in collaboration with L. Cross), *II* (1973; in collaboration with L. Cross), *III* (1976; in collaboration with L. Cross), and *IV* (1977; in collaboration with L. Cross); *Microphone (1 to 9)* (1973); *Laser Bird* and *Laser Rock* (Iowa City, June 12–14, 1973); *Rainforest IV* (1973; in collaboration with others); *Photocell Action* (1974; in collaboration [light composition] with A. Martin); *Toneburst* (Detroit, March 8, 1975); *Forest Speech* (1976) and *Forest Speech 2* (1978; in collaboration with others); *Pulsers* (1976) and *Pulsars 2* (1978); *Video Pulsers* (1977; in collaboration with V. Farber and R. Rauschenberg); *Weatherings* (N.Y., Sept. 27, 1978); *Audio Laser* (1979; in collaboration with L. Cross); *Laser Concert* (1979; in collaboration with L. Cross); *Phonemes* (1981); *Likeness to Voices/Dialects* (1982); *Sextet for Seven* (Paris, Oct. 27, 1982); *Sea Tails* (1983; in collaboration [film] with M. Davies and [underwater kites] J. Monnier; also *Sea Tails [sound totem version]*, 1986); *Dialects* (Oakland, Calif., Oct. 5, 1984); *Fragments* (Angers, Dec. 7, 1984); *Hedgehog* (Boston, Sept. 28 and 29, 1985); *Web, for John Cage* (1985) and *Web, for John Cage II* (Munich, Oct. 17, 1987); *Electronics With Talking Shrimp* (N.Y., April 25, 1986); *Line & Cluster* (Munich, Nov. 17, 1986); *9 Lines, Reflected* (N.Y., Sept. 17, 1986; in collaboration with J. Monnier); *Webwork* (N.Y., March 4, 1987); *Five Stone* (Berlin, June 16, 1988); *Virtual Focus* (N.Y., March 20, 1990); *Coefficient I* (1991) and *Coefficient: frictional percussion and electronics* (N.Y., Feb. 26, 1991); *Neural Network Plus* (1992) and *Neural Syntheses Nos. 1–9* (1992–94); *Untitled (1975/1994)* (1994); *Soundings: Ocean Diary* (Brussels, May 17, 1994); *Toneburst: Maps and Fragments* (1996; in collaboration with S. Ogielska).

BIBL.: J. Holzaepfel, *D. T. and the Performance of American Experimental Music 1950–1959* (diss., City Univ. of N.Y., 1993).
—NS/LK/DM

Tudoran, Ionel, Romanian tenor; b. Baragtii de Vede, June 24, 1913. He studied at the Iaşi Cons. He made his operatic debut as Roland in Ziehrer's *Landstreicher* in 1936 in Iaşi, then sang with the Cluj Opera (1937–48) and the Bucharest Opera (1948–63); also made guest appearances in Prague, Leipzig, Berlin, Dresden, Moscow, and other music centers. He retired in 1963 and taught voice at the Bucharest Cons. until 1972. His finest roles were Don José, Faust, and Cavaradossi. **—NS/LK/DM**

Tudway, Thomas, English organist, music transcriber, and composer; b. c. 1650; d. Cambridge, Nov. 23, 1726. He was a chorister at the Chapel Royal. He served as organist at King's Coll., Cambridge (1670–1706; 1707–26), where he also was master of the choristers (1670–80) and still later Univ. organist and organist at Pembroke Coll. In 1681 he took the Mus. B. degree at Cambridge; in 1705 the Univ. resuscitated the title of prof. of music for him and granted him the Mus.D. degree. He composed services, motets, and anthems. His *Collection of Services and Anthems used in the Church of England from the Reformation to the Restoration of King Charles II*, in 6 MS vols., is in the British Museum. **—NS/LK/DM**

Tufts, John, American minister and pioneer compiler of church music; b. Medford, Mass., Feb. 26, 1689; d. Amesbury, Mass., Aug. 17, 1750. He graduated from Harvard Univ. in 1708. He was ordained a minister at Newbury, Mass., in 1714, where he then served at the Second Church until 1738; then settled in Amesbury as a shopkeeper. In 1721 he publ. in Boston *A Very Plain and Easy Introduction to the Art of Singing Psalm Tunes*; in this book, letters instead of notes were used on the staff; it was very popular (at least 11 eds. publ. up to 1774; reprint of the 5th ed. of 1726, Philadelphia, 1954). **—NS/LK/DM**

Tuksar, Stanislav, Croatian musicologist; b. Gornji Kraljevec, July 27, 1945. He studied philosophy and English at the Univ. of Zagreb, then cello with R. Matz and musicology with I. Supicić at the Zagreb Cons.; subsequently studied with E. Weber in Paris (1974–76). He was a researcher at the Zagreb Inst. of Musicology and taught at the Cons.; received the Humboldt scholarship from the Institut für Musikforschung in Berlin (1986). He wrote numerous articles about aesthetics, philosophy, and terminology of music of the 16th to 18th centuries and about the musical archives in Croatia. He publ. a book on Croatian music theorists of the Renaissance, *Hrvatski renesansni teoreticari glazbe* (Zagreb, 1978; Eng. tr., 1980). Among the books he ed. were *Glazba, ideje i društvo: Svečani zbornik za Evana Supičića/Music, Ideas, and Society: Essays in Honor of Ivan Supičić* (Zagreb, 1993) and *The Musical Baroque, Western Slavs, and the Spirit of the European Cultural Communion/Glazbeni barok i zapadni Slaveni u kontekstu europskog kulturnog zajedništva* (Zagreb, 1993). He also wrote music criticism and tr. several books by Zofia Lissa and Erich Fromm into Croatian.—**NS/LK/DM**

Tulindberg, Erik (Eriksson), Finnish composer; b. Lillkyro, Feb. 22, 1761; d. Åbo, Sept. 1, 1814. He studied academic disciplines at the Åbo Academy, obtaining the degree of Magister Philosophiae in 1782. He subsequently was a municipal functionary, music being his avocation. He learned to play the violin, and owned a large library, including works of Mozart, Haydn, and Boccherini. In 1797 he was elected a member of the Royal Swedish Academy of Music. He wrote a Violin Concerto and 6 string quartets in the traditional style of the Viennese School.—**NS/LK/DM**

Tully, Alice, American mezzo-soprano, soprano, and music patroness; b. Corning, N.Y., Sept. 11, 1902; d. N.Y., Dec. 10, 1993. A scion of a family of wealth, she studied voice in Paris with Jean Périer and Miguel Fontecha, where she made her concert debut with the Pasdeloup Orch. in 1927. Returning to the U.S., she gave a song recital in N.Y. in 1936, and received critical praise for her interpretation of French songs. She eventually gave up her artistic ambition and devoted herself to various philanthropic endeavors. Her major gift was to Lincoln Center in N.Y. for the construction of a chamber music hall; it was dedicated as Alice Tully Hall in 1969. She also helped to organize the Chamber Music Soc. of Lincoln Center. She received the National Medal of Arts in 1985. Her 90th birthday was celebrated in a N.Y. gala on Sept. 14, 1992, at Lincoln Center.—**NS/LK/DM**

Tulou, Jean-Louis, prominent French flutist, pedagogue, and composer; b. Paris, Sept. 12, 1786; d. Nantes, July 23, 1865. He was only 10 when he entered the Paris Cons., receiving the 2nd prix in 1799 and the premier prix in 1801. He launched his career in 1804; joined the orch. of the Paris Opéra in 1813, resigning in 1822, but resumed the position in 1826 (with the title of "première flûte solo"). In 1829 he was appointed prof. of flute at the Cons., then retired from both positions in 1856. He performed on the old-fashioned flute, and obstinately opposed the introduction of Böhm's improved instrument into the Cons. With J. Nonon, he pursued a partnership as a flute manufacturer from 1831 to 1853; then continued to make flutes under his own name. He wrote 5 flute concertos, *airs variés* for flute with orch., a Trio for 3 Flutes, flute duos, and many solo pieces for flute. He also publ. *Méthode de flute* (Mainz, c. 1835; modern ed., Kassel, 1965).—**NS/LK/DM**

Tuma, Franz (actually, **František Ignác Antonin Tůma**), Czech viola da gambist, theorbist, and composer; b. Kostelec, Oct. 2, 1704; d. Vienna, Jan. 30, 1774. He began music studies with his father, a Kostelec organist. After serving as a chorister at the Minorite church of St. James in Prague under B. Cernohorsky, he went to Vienna. By 1722 he was a vice-Kapellmeister; by 1731 he was Compositor und Capellen-Meister to Count Franz Ferdinand Kinsky, the High Chancellor of Bohemia, who made it possible for him to receive counterpoint lessons from Fux. He was Kapellmeister to the dowager Empress Elisabeth (1741–50), and thereafter remained active at the court as a viola da gambist, theorbist, and composer. About 1768 he went to the Premonstratensian monastery in Geras, but returned to Vienna shortly before his death. He was praised as both an instrumentalist and a composer by his contemporaries. Among his works are some 60 masses, 3 Magnificats, a Te Deum, 29 vespers and Psalms, 25 motets, offertories, and graduals, 20 litanies, 13 Marian antiphons, 8 hymns, 13 sinfonias, 18 partitas for Strings, 16 sonatas, and a Fugue for Organ. Several of his instrumental works have been ed. in Musica Antiqua Bohemica, LXVII (1965) and LXIX (1967).

Bibl.: O. Ball, *Franz Tuma* (diss., Univ. of Vienna, 1901); A. Peschek, *Die Messen von Franz Tuma* (diss., Univ. of Vienna, 1956; includes thematic catalogue and list of MS sources).
—**NS/LK/DM**

Tunder, Franz, celebrated German organist and composer; b. Bannesdorf, near Burg, Fehmarn, 1614; d. Lubeck, Nov. 5, 1667. From 1632 to 1641 he was court organist at Gottorp, where he studied with J. Heckelauer, a pupil of Frescobaldi; in 1641 he became organist of the Marienkirche in Lübeck, being succeeded at his death by his son-in-law, **Dietrich Buxtehude**. In addition to his regular duties as organist there, he founded a series of evening concerts (Abendmusiken) for the performance of organ works by himself and other German composers and vocal pieces by Italian composers. His extant works comprise 17 vocal pieces, 14 organ works, and a Sinfonia. See M. Seiffert, ed., *Franz Tunder: Kantaten und Chorwerke*, Denkmäler Deutscher Tonkunst, III (1900), idem, ed., *Franz Tunder: Vier Praeludien*, Organum, IV/6 (Leipzig, 1925), R. Walter, ed., *Franz Tunder: Sämtliche Choralbearbeitungen* (Mainz, 1959), J. Golos and A. Sutkowski, eds., *Keyboard Music from Polish Manuscripts: Organ Chorales by Heinrich Scheidemann and Franz Tunder*, Corpus of Early Keyboard Music, X (1967), and K. Beckmann, ed., *Franz Tunder: Sämtliche Orgelwerke* (Wiesbaden, 1974).—**NS/LK/DM**

Tunley, David (Evatt), respected Australian musicologist and composer; b. Sydney, May 5, 1930. He was educated at the New South Wales State Conservatorium of Music in Sydney (diploma, 1950), Trinity Coll., London (diploma, 1950), the Univ. of Durham (B.Mus., 1958; M.Mus., 1963), with Nadia Boulanger in Paris on a French government scholarship (1964–65), and the Univ. of Western Australia (D.Litt., 1970, with the diss. *The 18th Century Secular French Cantata*; publ. in London, 1974; 2nd ed., 1997). In 1958 he joined the faculty of the Univ. of Western Australia, where he was a prof. from 1979 until being named prof. emeritus in 1994, and where he also was head of the music dept. from 1985 to 1991. In 1980–81 he was national president of the Musicological Soc. of Australia, of which he was made an honorary life member. He was chairperson of the Music Board of the Australia Council in 1984–85. From 1991 to 1994 he was national chairperson of the Australian Music Examinations Board. In 1980 he was made a fellow of the Australian Academy of the Humanities, in 1983 a Chevalier dans l'Ordre des Palmes Académiques of France, and in 1987 a member of the Order of Australia. In addition to his contributions to various reference works and scholarly journals, he has prepared modern performing editions of French vocal music of the 17th to 19th centuries.

WRITINGS: Ed. with F. Callaway, *Australian Composition in the 20th Century* (Melbourne, 1980); *Couperin* (London, 1982); *Harmony in Action* (London, 1984); ed. *The 18th Century French Cantata in Facsimile* (17 vols., N.Y., 1990–91); ed. *Romantic French Song 1830–1870 in Facsimile* (6 vols., N.Y., 1994); *The Bel Canto Violin: The Life and Times of Alfredo Campoli 1906–1991* (London, 1999).

WORKS: *2 Carols* for Chorus, after Gerard Manley Hopkins (1955); *A Wedding Masque* for Soloists, Women's Chorus, and Small Orch. (1961; rev. 1970): *2 Preludes* for Piano (1962); Suite for 2 Violins (1965); Concerto for Clarinet and Strings (1966; rev. 1999); *Inflorescence* for Chorus, Clarinet, and Timpani (1978); *Elegy—in memoriam Salek Mine* for Chamber Ensemble (1986); *Immortal Fire* for Chorus and Children's Voices (1999). **—NS/LK/DM**

Tupkov, Dimiter, Bulgarian composer; b. Sofia, July 12, 1929. He studied with Goleminov at the Bulgarian State Cons. in Sofia, graduating in 1956; then joined its faculty.

WORKS: ORCH.: Flute Concerto (1955); *The Story of Belassitsa Mountain*, overture (1956); *3 Children's Sinfoniettas* (1961, 1968, 1975); *Concerto for Orchestra* (1969); *Rhapsodic Divertimento* (1970); Harp Concerto (1971); *6 Bagatelles* (1972); *September Overture* (1974). **CHAMBER:** 2 string quartets (1956, 1958). **VOCAL:** *Peace Cantata* (1975); choral songs; folk song arrangements.**—NS/LK/DM**

Turchi, Guido, Italian composer and teacher; b. Rome, Nov. 10, 1916. He studied piano and composition with Dobici, Ferdinandi, and Bustini at the Rome Cons. (diplomas, 1940) and pursued graduate training with Pizzetti at the Accademia di Santa Cecilia in Rome (diploma, 1945). He taught at the Rome Cons. (1941–67; again from 1972); was artistic director of the Accademia Filarmonica in Rome (1963–66); served as director of the Parma and Florence cons. (1967–72); was artistic director of the Teatro Comunale in Bologna (1968–70) and at the Accademia di Santa Cecilia in Rome (from 1970). In his early music, Turchi followed Pizzetti's style of Italian Baroque, with Romantic and impressionistic extensions; he then changed his idiom toward a more robust and accentuated type of music-making, influenced mainly by a study of the works of Béla Bartók. Turchi's Concerto for String Orch. is dedicated to Bartók's memory.

WORKS: DRAMATIC: *Il buon soldato Svejk*, opera (Milan, April 6, 1962); *Dedalo*, ballet (Florence, 1972); incidental music to plays; film scores. **ORCH.:** Concerto for Strings (Venice, Sept. 8, 1948); *Piccolo concerto notturno* (1950); *3 metamorfosi* (1970). **CHAMBER:** Trio for Flute, Clarinet, and Viola (1945); *Dedica* for Flute (1972). **VOCAL:** *Invettiva* for Small Chorus and 2 Pianos (1946); choral works; songs.**—NS/LK/DM**

Tureck, Rosalyn, eminent American pianist, harpsichordist, and clavichordist; b. Chicago, Dec. 14, 1914. She studied piano in Chicago with Sophia Brilliant-Liven (1925–29), Jan Chiapusso (1929–31), and Gavin Williamson (1931–32), then went to N.Y., where she studied with Olga Samaroff at the Juilliard School of Music, graduating in 1935. In her concert career she dedicated herself mainly to Bach. In 1947 she made her first European tour; subsequently gave concerts in South America, South Africa, and Israel. She made some appearances as a conductor from 1956; however, she concentrated her activities on the keyboard, making appearances as a harpsichordist and a clavichordist (from 1960) as well as a pianist. In 1971 she made a world tour. She held teaching posts at the Philadelphia Cons. of Music (1935–42), Juilliard School of Music (1943–55), and Univ. of Calif., San Diego (1966–72). In 1966 she founded the International Bach Inst. and in 1981 the Tureck Bach Inst. She received honorary doctorates from Roosevelt Univ. in 1968 and the Univ. of Oxford in 1977. In order to demonstrate the universal applicability of Bach's keyboard techniques, she played Bach on the Moog synthesizer; in 1971 she gave a concert announced as "Bach and Rock." She publ. *An Introduction to the Performance of Bach* (3 vols., London, 1959–60; also publ. in Japanese, 1966, and Spanish, 1972).**—NS/LK/DM**

Turetzky, Bertram (Jay), American double bass player and composer; b. Norwich, Conn., Feb. 14, 1933. He was a pupil of Joseph Iadone and Josef Marx at the Hartt School of Music in Hartford, Conn. (graduated, 1955), and also studied privately with David Walter. He studied musicology with Sachs at N.Y.U. and took courses in music history at the Univ. of Hartford (M.M., 1965). On Oct. 19, 1964, he made his N.Y. recital debut in a program featuring specially commissioned works for the double bass. In subsequent years, he toured widely as a virtuoso double bass player in programs largely devoted to avant- garde scores. He publ. *The Contemporary Contrabass* (1974). Among his compositions were pieces for double bass.**—NS/LK/DM**

Turini, Gregorio, prominent Italian singer and instrumentalist; b. Brescia, c. 1560; d. Prague, c. 1600. He was a pupil of Giovanni Contino in Brescia. He entered the service of Emperor Rudolf II in Prague as a singer and cornett player in 1582, and was held in great esteem there; later was active as a trumpeter and drummer as well. He publ. *Cantiones admondum devotae cum aliquot psalmis Davidicis* for 4 Equal Voices (Venice, 1589; 15 ed. in K. Proske, Musica Divina, II and III, Regensburg, 1854–59), *Neue liebliche teutsche Lieder, nach Art der welschen Villanellen* for 4 Voices (Nuremberg, 1590), and *Il primo libro de canzonette* for 4 Voices (Nuremberg, 1597). His son, Francesco Turini (b. Prague, c. 1589; d. Brescia, 1656), was an esteemed organist, teacher, and composer; studied with his father. He was only 12 when he was made court organist. Emperor Rudolf made it possible for him to pursue training in organ, singing, and composition in Venice and Rome; after returning to Prague, he resumed his court post. He went to Italy about 1612, and was organist at Brescia Cathedral (1620–56).—**NS/LK/DM**

Turini, Ronald, Canadian pianist and teacher; b. Montreal, Sept. 30, 1934. He received piano lessons as a child and was a student of Frank Hanson at the McGill Cons. in Montreal. At 9, he entered the Montreal Cons., where he continued his training with Yvonne Hubert, Germaine Malépart, and Isidor Philipp. In 1950 he received the premier prix there, and also won the Prix Archambault. In 1953 he became a student of Isabelle Vengerova and Olga Stroumillo at the Mannes Coll. of Music in N.Y., and then studied for 5 years with Vladimir Horowitz. From 1956 he made regular tours. In 1958 he captured 2nd prize in the Busoni competition in Bolzano and in the Geneva competition, and in 1960 won 2nd prize in the Queen of Elisabeth of Belgium competition in Brussels. In 1961 he made his Carnegie Hall debut in N.Y., and played there again in 1964 and 1967. He was a soloist with the Montreal Sym. Orch. on its tour of Europe in 1962, and again in 1976. In 1971 he was soloist with the Melbourne Sym. Orch. on its North American tour. In 1975 he became a founding member of Quartet Canada. From 1977 he also taught at the Univ. of Western Ontario.—**NS/LK/DM**

Türk, Daniel Gottlob, eminent German organist, pedagogue, music theorist, and composer; b. Claussnitz, near Chemnitz, Aug. 10, 1750; d. Halle, Aug. 26, 1813. He was the son of Daniel Türcke, an instrumentalist in the service of Count Schönburg. He received music lessons from his father and studied wind instruments with his father's fellow musicians, then received instruction in harmony and counterpoint from G.A. Homilius at the Dresden Kreuzschule. He subsequently entered the Univ. of Leipzig in 1772, but also pursued music training with J.A. Hiller, in whose "popular concerts" he served as 1st violinist; also studied clavichord with J.W. Hässler. In 1774 he settled in Halle, where he became Kantor at the Ulrichskirche and a teacher at the Lutheran Gymnasium; in 1779 he was named director of music at the Univ., where he taught theory and composition; left his Gymnasium post in 1787 to become organist and music director of the city's principal church, the Marktkirche (Liebfrauenkirche). He was given an honorary doctorate at the Univ. in 1808, and that same year was promoted to prof. of music there. As the leading Halle musician of his day, he played an energetic role in its concert life as both a performer and an organizer. He was held in the highest esteem by his contemporaries. Among his compositions are various vocal works and keyboard pieces. R. Haggh tr. with notes Türk's *School of Clavier Playing: Instructions in Playing the Clavier for Teachers and Students* (Lincoln, Nebr., 1982).

BIBL.: J. Lippert, *Verzeichniss der musikalischen und andern Bücher, so wie auch der gedruckten und geschriebenen Musikalien des seligen Professor der Musik und Universitäts-Musikdirektor Dr. T., welche...versteigert werden sollen* (Halle, 1816); G. Hedler, *D.G. T. (1750–1813)* (diss., Univ. of Leipzig, 1936); B. Grahmann, ed., *D.G. T.: der Begründer der hallischen Händeltradition* (Wolfenbüttel and Berlin, 1938).—**NS/LK/DM**

Turnage, Mark-Anthony, English composer; b. Grays, Essex, June 10, 1960. He was a student of Knussen in the junior dept. of the Royal Coll. of Music in London (1974–78), where he continued his training as a senior student of John Lambert (diploma, 1982); he then studied with Schuller and Henze at the Berkshire Music Center in Tanglewood (summer, 1983). From 1989 to 1993 he served as composer-in-association with the City of Birmingham Sym. Orch., and from 1995 to 1998 of the English National Opera in London. In his music, Turnage has pursued an eclectic course in an accessible style which has found inspiration in various contemporary modes of expression, including rock and jazz.

WORKS: DRAMATIC: Opera: *Greek* (1986–88; Munich, June 17, 1988); *Killing Time*, television opera (1991); *The Country of the Blind*, chamber opera (1996–97; Aldeburgh, June 13, 1997); *The Silver Tassie* (1999; London, Feb. 16, 2000). **ORCH.:** *Let Us Sleep Now* for Chamber Orch. (1979–82; Shape, June 14, 1983); *Night Dances* (1981–82; London, Feb. 1, 1982); *Kind of Blue: In Memoriam, Thelonious Monk* (1981–82; London, March 21, 1982); *Ekaya: Elegy in Memory of Marvin Gaye* (1984; Greenwich, March 29, 1985); *Gross Intrusion* for Amplified String Quartet and String Orch. (Glasgow, Sept. 19, 1987); *3 Screaming Popes* (Birmingham, Oct. 5, 1989); *Momentum* (1990–91; Birmingham, June 12, 1991); *Drowned Out* (1992–93; Nottingham, Oct. 20, 1993); *Your Rockaby* for Soprano Saxophone and Orch. (1992–93; London, Feb. 23, 1994); *Blood on the Floor* for 3 Jazz Soloists and Large Ensemble (1993–96; London, May 30, 1996); *Dispelling the Fears* for 2 Trumpets and Orch. (1994–95; Bedford, Oct. 29, 1995); *Four-Horned Fandango* for 4 Horns and Orch. (1995–96; Birmingham, July 5, 1997); *Tune for Toru* for Jazz Ensemble (1996; also for Piano, Yokohama, April 10, 1996). **CHAMBER:** *And Still a Softer Morning* for Flute, Vibraphone, Harp, and Cello (1978; rev. 1983; Montepulciano, July 31, 1984); *After Dark* for Wind Quintet and String Quintet (1982–83; London, April 13, 1983); *On All Fours* for Chamber Ensemble (1985; London, Feb. 4, 1986); *Sarabande* for Soprano Saxophone and Piano (1985; London, Jan. 10, 1986); *Release* for 8 Players (1987; BBC Radio, Dec. 4, 1988); *Kai* for Cello and Ensemble (1989–90; Birmingham, Dec. 18, 1990); *3 Farewells* for Flute, Clarinet, Harp, and String Quartet (London, July 8, 1990); *Are You Sure?* for String Quartet (1990; rev. 1991); *Forty Bob Fanfare* for 10 Players (1992); *Sleep on*, 3 lullabies for Cello and Piano (King's Lynn, July 31, 1992); *This Silence* for Clarinet, Horn, Bassoon, and String Quartet (1992; Cologne, Sept. 13, 1993); *Set to* for Brass Ensemble (1992–93; Aldeburgh, Aug. 24, 1993); *A Deviant Fantasy* for 4 Clarinets (London, Oct. 31, 1993); *2 Elegies Framing a Shout* for Soprano Saxophone and Piano (1994; Bristol, Jan. 12, 1995); *Barries Deviant Fantasy* for String

Quartet and Referee's Whistles (London, July 3, 1995). **Piano:** *Entranced* (Huddersfield, Nov. 25, 1982); *Tune for Toru* (Yokohama, April 10, 1996; also for Jazz Ensemble). **VOCAL:** *Lament for a Hanging Man* for Soprano and Ensemble (1983; Durham, Feb. 4, 1984); *1 Hand in Brooklyn Heights* for 16 Voices and Percussion (Bath, June 3, 1986); *Beating About the Bush* for Mezzo-soprano and 6 Instruments (London, June 14, 1987); *Greek Suite* for Mezzo-soprano, Tenor, and Chamber Ensemble (Frankfurt am Main, March 20, 1989); *Some Days* for Mezzo-soprano and Orch. (1989; London, July 21, 1991); *Leaving* for Soprano, Tenor, Chorus, and Ensemble (1990; rev. version, Birmingham, May 9, 1992); *Her Anxiety* for Soprano and Ensemble (1991; London, Sept. 15, 1992); *Twice Through the Heart* for Mezzo-soprano and 16 Players (1994–96; Aldeburgh, June 13, 1997).—**NS/LK/DM**

Turner, (Big) Joe (actually, **Joseph Vernon Turner Jr.**), American blues and R&B singer; b. Kansas City, Mo., May 18, 1911; d. Inglewood, Calif., Nov. 24, 1985. Blues shouter Joe Turner (sometimes called "Big Joe" to distinguish him from jazz pianist Joe Turner) was the leading voice of the rhythmic boogie-woogie music of the late 1930s and early 1940s. He then became one of the major R&B singers of the 1950s, with such hits as "Honey Hush," "Chains of Love," and "Shake, Rattle and Roll," which influenced early rock 'n' roll musicians.

The son of Joseph Turner Sr. and Georgie Harrington Turner, Joe Turner sang on the streets of Kansas City as a child. After his father died when he was 15, he helped support his family by selling newspapers and selling drugs, then worked as a waiter and bartender in local clubs. By the age of 21 he was singing, and he formed a partnership with pianist Pete Johnson. The two worked briefly in N.Y. in 1936 and were brought back to the city by talent scout John Hammond, who featured them in his From Spirituals to Swing concert at Carnegie Hall in December 1938. Staying in N.Y., Turner signed to Vocalion Records and began appearing with Johnson and pianists Albert Ammons and Mead Lux Lewis at the two Café Society nightclubs. He also toured nationally and appeared during the summer of 1941 in Duke Ellington's *Jump for Joy* revue in Los Angeles. By then he had moved to Decca Records, where he recorded with such jazz musicians as Benny Carter and Art Tatum.

Turner was based on the West Coast during the second half of the 1940s. Recording for National Records, he reached the Top Ten of the R&B chart with "S.K. Blues—Part I" (music and lyrics by Saunders King) in March 1945 and with "My Gal's a Jockey" in August 1946. He married Luella "Lou Willie" Brown in 1945, and she became his manager; the marriage ended around 1965. Also in 1945, he and Johnson opened the Blue Room Club in Los Angeles. From 1947 he had brief associations with several record companies, and he returned to the R&B Top Ten with "Still in the Dark" on Freedom Records in March 1950.

Turner signed to Atlantic Records in 1951, and at his first session in April cut "Chains of Love" (music by Harry "Van" Walls, lyrics by Atlantic Records president Ahmet Ertegun), which neared the top of the R&B charts and reportedly sold a million copies. He followed it with a string of Top Ten R&B hits over the next five years: "The Chill Is On" (music and lyrics by Joe Turner; December 1951); "Sweet Sixteen" (music and lyrics by Ahmet Ertegun; April 1952); "Don't You Cry" (music and lyrics by Doc Pomus; August 1952); "Honey Hush" (music and lyrics by Joe Turner, though credited to Lou Willie Turner), which went to #1 in December 1953 and reportedly sold a million copies; "TV Mama" (music and lyrics by Joe Turner, though credited to Lou Willie Turner; January 1954); "Shake, Rattle and Roll" (music and lyrics by Jesse Stone under the pseudonym Charles Calhoun), which went to #1 in June 1954; "Well All Right" (November 1954); "Flip Flop and Fly" (music and lyrics by Jesse Stone under the pseudonym Charles Calhoun and Joe Turner, though credited to Lou Willie Turner; March 1955); "The Chicken and the Hawk (Up, Up and Away)" and "Morning, Noon and Night" (music and lyrics by Jesse Stone under the pseudonym Charles Calhoun; January 1956); "Corrine Corrina" (traditional, adapted music and lyrics by J. Mayo Williams and Bo Chatman, new lyrics by Mitchell Parish), which also reached the pop charts in May 1956; and "Lipstick, Powder and Paint" (music and lyrics by Jesse Stone; September 1956).

Turner appeared in the motion pictures *Rhythm-and-Blues Revue* (1955) and *Shake, Rattle and Rock!* (1956). His recordings continued to reach the charts until 1960. He toured extensively, appearing in Europe in 1958, 1965, and 1971 and becoming a fixture at major jazz festivals such as those held in Newport, R.I., and Monterey, Calif. In 1969 he married Pat Sims. In the early 1970s, based in Los Angeles, he recorded for the jazz label Pablo with Count Basie and others. In March 1974 he participated in the documentary *The Last of the Blue Devils*, about the Kansas City jazz scene.

Despite declining health, Turner continued to record and perform in the early 1980s. *Blues Train*, an album he made with the group Roomful of Blues, earned a 1983 Grammy Award nomination for Best Traditional Blues Recording. He earned two Grammy Award nominations for Best Traditional Blues Recording in 1985, for the albums *Big Joe Turner with Knocky Parker and His House-rockers* and *Patcha, Patcha, All Night Long*, a duet with Jimmy Witherspoon, but these accolades were made posthumously; he died in 1985 at 74 of a heart attack.

DISC.: JOE TURNER *Have No Fear, Big Joe Turner is Here* (1945); *Kansas City Jazz* (1953); *Joe Turner and Pete Johnson* (1955); *Joe Turner* (1957); *Joe Turner and the Blues* (1958); *Rockin' the Blues* (1958); *Big Joe Is Here* (1959); *Big Joe Rides Again* (1959); *Jumpin' the Blues* (1962); *Best* (1963); *Careless Love* (1963); *Singing the Blues* (1967); *Texas Style* (1971); *Roll 'Em* (1973); *Nobody in Mind* (1976); *In the Evening* (1976); *Things That I Used to Do* (1977); *Great R&B Oldies* (1981); *Have No Fear, Joe Turner Is Here* (rec. 1945–47; 1982); *Kansas City Here I Come* (1982); *Roll Me Baby* (1982); *Life Ain't Easy* (1983); *Rock This Joint* (1984); *Blues'll Make You Happy* (1985); *The Rhythm and Blues Years* (1986); *Greatest Hits* (1987); *Memorial Album* (1987); *Steppin' Out* (1988); *Midnight Special* (1987); *I've Been to Kansas City Vol. 1* (1990); *Stormy Monday* (1991); *Tell Me Pretty Baby* (1992); *Every Day in the Week* (1993); *Jumpin' with Joe—The Complete Aladdin and Imperial Recordings* (rec. late 1940s–early 1950s; rel. 1994); *Shake, Rattle and Roll* (1994); *Early Big Joe*; *Turns On the Blues*; *Still The Boss of the Blues*; *The Very Best of Joe Turner—Live* (2000); *The Blues Boss—Live*

(2000). Pete Johnson: *Boss of the Blues* (1956). Dizzy Gillespie, Roy Eldridge, and others: *Trumpet Kings Meet Joe Turner* (rec. 1974; rel. 1975). Pee Wee Clayton: *Everyday I Have the Blues* (rec. 1975; rel. 1976). Knocky Parker and The Houserockers: *Joe Turner* (1984). **BIG JOE TURNER AND COUNT BASIE:** *Flip, Flop and Fly* (rec. 1972; rel. 1975); *The Bosses* (1975). **BIG JOE TURNER AND ROOMFUL OF BLUES:** *Blues Train* (1983). **BIG JOE TURNER AND JIMMY WITHERSPOON:** *Patcha, Patcha, All Night Long* (1986). **BIG JOE TURNER AND T-BONE WALKER:** *Bosses of the Blues, Vol. 1* (1989).—**WR**

Turner, Dame Eva, distinguished English soprano; b. Oldham, March 10, 1892; d. London, June 16, 1990. She was a pupil of Dan Roothan in Bristol; Giglia Levy, Edgardo Levy, and Mary Wilson at the Royal Academy of Music in London; and Albert Richards Broad. In 1916 she made her operatic debut as a Page in *Tannhäuser* with the Carl Rosa Opera Co., with which she sang until 1924; sang with the company at London's Covent Garden in 1920. In 1924 she made her first appearance at Milan's La Scala as Freia in *Das Rheingold*; then toured Germany with an Italian opera company in 1925. She sang Turandot in Brescia in 1926; appeared at Covent Garden (1928–30; 1933; 1935–39; 1947–48); was a guest artist in other European music centers, in Chicago, and in South America. She taught at the Univ. of Okla. (1950–59) and then at the Royal Academy of Music. In 1962 she was made a Dame Commander of the Order of the British Empire. Her other esteemed roles included Agatha, Amelia, Santuzza, Aida, Isolde, Sieglinde, and Cio-Cio-San.—**NS/LK/DM**

Turner, Ike and Tina, R&B bandleader/producer (Ike) and hip-shakin', powerful shouter (Tina) together formed one of the most dynamic groups of the 1960s and early 1970s; later Tina enjoyed a solo career on her own. Ike Turner (real name, Izear Turner), pno., gtr., voc. (b. Clarksdale, Miss., Nov. 5, 1931) and Tina Turner (real name, Anna Mae Bullock), voc. (b. Brownsville, Tenn., Nov. 26, 1939).

Bandleader, songwriter, arranger, producer, and multi-instrumentalist Ike Turner achieved his first success in 1951 with his Kings of Rhythm behind Jackie Brenston's top R&B hit "Rocket 88," often regarded as the first "rock 'n' roll" record. He later worked as a talent scout for Modern Records, ostensibly producing B. B. King, Howlin' Wolf, and Elmore James. Devising a revue format for his Kings of Rhythm in St. Louis, Turner added vocalist and wife-to-be Tina in 1957. Touring the so-called "chitlin" circuit for a decade, Ike and Tina Turner developed a gutsy and ribald stage act, with Tina, the show's focal point, performing in an overtly sexual manner, complete with feigned orgasms and provocative verbal exchanges with Ike. One of the most exciting musical acts of its time, The Ike and Tina Turner Revue was rivaled by only James Brown and The Fabulous Flames in terms of musical spectacle. Perhaps on the strength of their smash British hit, "River Deep-Mountain High," produced by the legendary Phil Spector, Ike and Tina Turner became far more popular in Great Britain than in the United States. They eventually attained the first massive exposure of their stage act on The Rolling Stones' 1969 American tour and subsequently looked to the world of rock music for material and an expanded audience, which they achieved with their smash crossover hit, "Proud Mary," in 1971. Ike and Tina Turner were inducted into the Rock and Roll Hall of Fame in 1991.

Ike Turner started playing piano at the age of five and initiated his musical career at age 11 as piano accompanist to Sonny Boy Williamson (Aleck Ford) and Robert Nighthawk. By 1945, he was working as a disc jockey at WROX in Clarksdale, Miss., forming The Rhythm Kings in the late 1940s, with Ike on piano. Mastering guitar, Turner was hired as a songwriter and talent scout by Modern Records, ostensibly "discovering" B. B. King and Howlin' Wolf and playing sessions for King, Wolf, Elmore James, and Johnny Ace. Around 1954, he moved to East St. Louis, Mo., where he became a rhythm-and- blues star with The Rhythm Kings.

Tina Turner grew up in Knoxville, Tenn., and sang in a local church choir as a child. She moved to St. Louis around 1954 and met Ike Turner at the age of 17. She eventually succeeded in joining Ike Turner's revue in 1957. The couple soon married and Ike developed an exciting stage act billed as "The Ike and Tina Turner Revue" in 1960 based around Tina as lead vocalist, accompanied by his Kings of Rhythm and a female backing vocal trio dubbed The Ikettes. Recording for the Midwestern rhythm-and-blues label Sue, Ike and Tina Turner scored a series of R&B smashes in the early 1960s with "A Fool in Love" (a major pop hit), "I Idolize You," "It's Gonna Work Out Fine" (another major pop hit), "Poor Fool," and "Tra La La La La."

In 1962, The Ikettes had a smash R&B and major pop hit with "I'm Blue (The Gong-Gong Song)" on Atco Records. In 1965, The Ikettes, with Vanetta Fields, Jessie Smith, and Robbie Montgomery, scored a moderate pop and R&B hit with "Peaches 'n' Cream" and a major R&B hit with "I'm So Thankful" on Modern Records. By 1968, this edition of The Ikettes had left the Turners, recording as The Mirettes and achieving a major R&B hit with "In the Midnight Hour" on Revue Records. Later lineups of The Ikettes included P. P. Arnold, Claudia Lennear, and Bonnie Bramlett (later of Delaney and Bonnie).

Relocating to Los Angeles in 1962, The Ike and Tina Turner Revue toured the "chitlin" circuit of rhythm-and-blues clubs with their raunchy stage act and recorded for a variety of labels, including Warner Brothers, Loma, Pompeii, Blue Thumb, and Minit. They met songwriter-producer Phil Spector while working on the film *The T 'n' T Show* and he coauthored and produced their "River Deep-Mountain High" single, regarded as one of the finest singles of all time, in 1966. Although the song became a smash hit in Great Britain, it fared dismally in the United States and led to Spector's withdrawal from the music business.

The Ike and Tina Turner Revue toured Great Britain with The Rolling Stones in 1966 and received their first widespread American exposure in support of The Rolling Stones' 1969 tour of North America. They soon began recording contemporary material such as The

Beatles' "Come Together," The Rolling Stones' "Honky Tonk Women," and Sly Stone's "I Want to Take You Higher." They finally broke through with the mainstream audience with a dynamic reworking of Creedence Clearwater Revival's "Proud Mary," a smash pop and R&B hit from *Workin' Together*, the best-selling album of their career, on Liberty Records. They conducted a hugely successful European tour in 1971, recording the live set *What You Hear Is What You Get* for United Artists, which had absorbed Liberty Records. They scored another major pop hit in 1973 with Tina's autobiographical "Nutbush City Limits." Ike and Tina Turner were inducted into the Rock and Roll Hall of Fame in 1991.

Tina Turner launched her solo recording career on United Artists Records in 1974. She appeared in the equivocal film *Tommy* as the Acid Queen in 1975, singing The Who song of the same name. In July 1976, in the face of contractual obligations for albums and tours, Tina Turner walked out on her abusive husband Ike. Over the next eight years, she struggled to survive and establish herself in a solo career. She divorced Ike and developed a slick but ribald lounge act for Las Vegas casinos and later the Fairmont hotel chain. She recorded the last of three solo albums for United Artists in 1978. Ike Turner recorded an album for Fantasy Records in 1980 and later became mired in legal and drug-related problems that led to his incarceration for 18 months in 1990 and 1991.

In 1979, Tina Turner met Australian promoter Roger Davies, who became her manager the next year. She moved away from easy-listening material and toured the United States with The Rolling Stones in 1981. She began a concerted comeback effort in 1982 at London's Hammersmith Odeon and later performed showcase dates at the Ritz Hotel in N.Y.C. In 1983, she signed with Capitol Records, recording her debut for the label, *Private Dancer*, in Great Britain.

Private Dancer launched Tina Turner into international prominence. It produced five hits, including a smash R&B and major pop hit with her version of Al Green's "Let's Stay Together," the top pop and smash R&B hit "What's Love Got to Do with It," and the pop and R&B smashes "Better Be Good to Me" and "Private Dancer," the latter written by Mark Knopfler. The album stayed on the charts for more than two years and sold ten million copies worldwide (five million in the United States). She conducted a world tour of more than 100 cities in 1985, as the third *Mad Max* film, *Beyond Thunderdome*, costarring Turner, became one of the year's hit movies. The soundtrack album included her crossover smash "We Don't Need Another Hero" and the major pop hit "One of the Living." During the year, she also helped record USA for Africa's "We Are the World" and performed at Live Aid, duetting with Mick Jagger.

In 1986, Tina Turner recorded the best-selling *Break Every Rule* album and William Morrow published her autobiography, *I, Tina*. Although not as consistent as *Private Dancer*, *Break Every Rule* yielded four hits, including the crossover smash "Typical Male" and the major pop hit "What You Get Is What You See." Tina Turner conducted a world tour from March 1987 to March 1988 and her *Live in Europe* album included Robert Palmer's "Addicted to Love" and her own "Nutbush City Limits." *Foreign Affair* produced a major pop hit with "The Best." She again toured the United States in 1993 as the movie *What's Love Got to Do with It*, based on her autobiography, became one of the year's most highly acclaimed hits. As well as serving as a dynamic musical movie and yielding the near-smash hit "I Don't Wanna Fight," the film celebrated Tina's ability to survive and reestablish herself with pride and dignity in the face of domestic violence. Tina Turner performed the title song to the James Bond film *Goldeneye* in 1995 and recorded her first entirely new studio album in seven years, *Wildest Dreams*, featuring a remake of John Waite's top 1984 hit "Missing You," for Virgin Records in 1996. She toured North America again in 1997. In early 2000, she began a new tour of North America and Europe to support her album, *Twenty Four Seven*.

WRITINGS: With K. Loder, *I, Tina* (N.Y., 1986).

DISC.: **IKE TURNER:** *Rocks the Blues Crown* (1963); *A Black Man's Soul* (1969); *Blues Roots* (1972); *Confined to Soul* (1973); *Bad Dreams* (1973); *The Edge* (1980). **IKE AND TINA TURNER:** *The Soul of Ike and Tina Turner* (1960); *The Sound of Ike and Tina Turner* (1961); *Dance with Ike and Tina Turner* (1962); *Festival of Live Performances* (1962); *Dynamite* (1963); *Don't Play Me Cheap* (1963); *It's Gonna Work Out Fine* (1963); *Please, Please, Please* (1964); *The Ike and Tina Show Live* (1965); *River Deep–Mountain High* (1966); *Live* (1967); *In Person* (1968); *So Fine* (1968); *Cussin', Cryin' and Carryin' On* (1969); *Outta Season* (1969); *The Hunter* (1969); *Her Man...His Woman* (1970); *Come Together* (1970); *Workin' Together* (1970); *What You Hear Is What You Get* (1971); *'Nuff Said* (1971); *Feel Good* (1972); *Let Me Touch Your Mind* (1972); *The World of Ike and Tina Turner* (1973); *Nutbush City Limits* (1973); *The Gospel According to Ike and Tina Turner* (1974); *Revue Live* (1975); *Airwaves* (1978); *Get Back* (1985); *Workin' Together* (1986); *The Ike and Tina Sessions* (1987); *What You Hear Is What You Get: Live at Carnegie Hall* (1996). **THE IKETTES:** *Soul Hits* (1965). **TINA TURNER:** *Turns the Country On* (1974); *Acid Queen* (1975); *Rough* (1978); *Private Dancer* (1984); *Break Every Rule* (1986); *Tina Live in Europe* (1988); *Foreign Affair* (1989); *Simply the Best* (1991); *What's Love Got to Do* (1993); *Wildest Dreams* (1996); *Twenty Four Seven* (2000).

BIBL.: L. Fissinger, *Tina Turner* (N.Y., 1985); B. Mills, *Tina* (N.Y., 1985); R. Wynn, *Tina: The Tina Turner Story* (N.Y., 1985).
—BH

Turner, Joe (actually, **Joseph H.**), stride pianist; b. Baltimore, Nov. 3, 1907; d. Montreuil-sous-Bois hospital, Paris, July 21, 1990. He went to N.Y.C. around 1925 and played with Hilton Jefferson, Benny Carter (1929), Louis Armstrong (1930) and others; he accompanied Adelaide Hall in the 1930s and toured to Europe with her; he stayed on to play solo dates in Czechoslovakia (1936), Hungary, France, etc, in August 1939 was on his way to Turkey (via Switzerland), immediately returned from Turkey to France on outbreak of World War II and returned to the U.S.A. in October 1939. Worked as a single before service in U.S. Army, in 1944–45 worked in all-star service band directed by Sy Oliver. Returned to Europe in 1948, worked in Hungary, Switzerland (1949), then was based in Paris for the rest of his life, though touring all over Europe. Temporarily returned to United States in 1976 for a series of successful engagements. He died of a heart attack in 1990.

DISC.: *Stride by Stride* (1960); *Another Epoch: Stride Piano* (1976); *Effervescent* (1976); *Swing Time Shooters, Vol. 1* (1995). **LOUIS ARMSTRONG:** *Louis Armstrong and the Big Bands (1928–30)* (1930); *Louis Armstrong Collection, Vol. 6: St. Louis Blues* (1930); *Louis Armstrong (1928–31)* (1931); *Louis Armstrong & His Orchestra: 1930–31* (1931); *Portrait of the Artist as a Young Man* (1934). **ADELAIDE HALL:** *As Time Goes By* (1996). **—JC/LP**

Turner, Mark, tenor saxophonist; b. Fairborn, Ohio, Nov. 10, 1965. He was raised in Southern Calif. He studied alto sax in high school, but entered college in Long Beach to study to be an illustrator in 1987; soon he moved to Boston to study tenor sax at the Berklee School (B.M., 1990). While there, he jammed with fellow students including Joshua Redman and Geoff Keezer. He moved to N.Y. after graduation, and replaced Dan Faulk in TanaReid (Akira Tana and Rufus Reid) and gradually gained a reputation for originality. He also gigged around town with various other leaders, including Charlie Haden, Slide Hampton and Brad Mehldau. He began leading his own quartet, and was signed by Warner Brothers in the mid-1990s as a leader/solo act. Combining the influences of Warne Marsh and Coltrane, Turner has a unique style. He performed at the IAJE Convention in N.Y., early January 1998.

DISC.: *Yam Yam* (1995).**—LP**

Turner, Robert (Comrie), Canadian composer and teacher; b. Montreal, June 6, 1920. He was a student of Douglas Clarke and Claude Champagne at McGill Univ. in Montreal (B.Mus., 1943; D.Mus., 1953), of Howells and Jacob at the Royal Coll. of Music in London (1947–48), of Roy Harris at the George Peabody Coll. for Teachers in Nashville, Tenn. (M.Mus., 1950), and of Messiaen at the Berkshire Music Center in Tanglewood (summer, 1949). From 1952 to 1968 he was senior music producer for the CBC in Vancouver. He taught at the Univ. of British Columbia in Vancouver (1955–57), Acadia Univ. in Wolfville, Nova Scotia (1968–69), and the Univ. of Manitoba (1969–85), where he subsequently was prof. emeritus. In 1982 he held a Manitoba Arts Council grant. In 1987 he was a fellow at the MacDowell Colony. In 1990–91 he held a Canada Council Artists grant. He was awarded a commemorative medal marking the 125th anniversary of Canadian confederation in 1992. His compositions are couched in an eclectic style that is both simple and complex, traditional and nontraditional, tonal and atonal, and lyrical and ironic.

WORKS: DRAMATIC: *The Brideship*, lyric drama (1966–67; Vancouver, Dec. 12, 1967); *Vile Shadows*, opera (1982–83; rev. 1986); music for radio and television. **ORCH.:** *Opening Night*, theater overture (1955; Vancouver, Feb. 5, 1956); *Lyric Interlude* (1956); *Nocturne* (1956–65; Vancouver, Feb. 7, 1968); *A Children's Overture* (1958); *The Pemberton Valley*, suite (1958; rev. 1988; Winnipeg, Jan. 18, 1991); *Robbins' Round*, concertino for Jazz Band (1959); 3 syms.: Sym. for Strings (1960; Montreal, March 27, 1961), *Symphony in 1 Movement: Gift from the Sea* (1983; Winnipeg, Dec. 5, 1986), and Sym. No. 3 (Winnipeg, Sept. 21, 1990); *3 Episodes* (1963; Toronto, Feb. 27, 1966); Concerto for 2 Pianos and Orch. (1971; Winnipeg, Jan. 22, 1972); *Eidolons*, 12 images for Chamber Orch. (Vancouver, Sept. 12, 1972); Chamber Concerto for Bassoon and 17 Instruments (Vancouver, Sept. 15, 1973); *Variations on The Prairie Settler's Song* (1974); *Capriccio Concertante* for Cello, Piano, and Orch. (1975; Vancouver, May 5, 1976); *From a Different Country: Homage to Gabrieli* (1976); *Encounters I-IX* for Various Soloists and Orch. (Winnipeg, July 12, 1985); *Playhouse Music* (1986); Viola Concerto (1987; Montreal, May 24, 1988); *Shades of Autumn* (1987; Edmonton, Sept. 21, 1990); *Manitoba Memoir* for Strings (1989; Manitoba, Feb. 26, 1991); *House of Shadows* (1994); *Festival Dance* (1997; Winnipeg, Jan. 30, 1998); *Diverti- memento* (1997; Winnipeg, Dec. 8, 1999). **CHAMBER:** 3 string quartets (1949, 1954, 1975); *Lament* for Flute, Oboe, Clarinet, Bassoon, and Piano (1951); Violin Sonata (1956); *Little Suite* for Harp (1957); *Vignette* for Clarinet and String Quartet (1958; rev. 1988); *Variations and Toccata* for Woodwind Quintet and String Quintet (1959); *Serenade* for Woodwind Quintet (1960); *4 Fragments* for Brass Quintet (1961); *Fantasia* for Organ, Brass Quintet, and Timpani (1962); *Diversities* for Violin, Piano, and Bassoon (1967); Trio for Violin, Cello, and Piano (1969); *Fantasy and Festivity* for Harp (1970); *Nostalgia* for Soprano Saxophone and Piano (1972); *Shadow Pieces* for Flute, Bassoon, Violin, Cello, and Piano (1981). **KEYBOARD: Piano:** *Sonata Lyrica* (1955; rev. 1963); *Dance of the Disenchanted* (1959; rev. 1988); *A Merry-Mournful Mood* (1973); *Vestiges* (1987). **Organ:** *6 Voluntaries* (1959). **VOCAL:** 2 Choral Pieces (1952); 4 Songs for High Voice and Piano (1959); *Mobile* for Chorus and 7 Percussion (1960); *Prophetic Song* for Women's Chorus (1961); *The 3rd Day* for Soloists, Chorus, and Orch. (Vancouver, April 25, 1962); *The House of Christmas* for Chorus (1963); *The Phoenix and the Turtle* for Mezzo-soprano and 8 Instruments (1964); *Suite: In Homage to Melville* for Soprano, Contralto, Viola, and Piano (1966); *Johann's Gift to Christmas* for Narrator and Orch. (1972); *5 Canadian Folksongs* for Chorus (1973); *10 Canadian Folksongs* for High and Medium Voice and Piano (1973; orchestrated 1980; Vancouver, March 25, 1987); *Amoroso Canto* for Chorus (1978); *Lament for Linos* for Reciter, Flute, Clarinet, and Piano (1978); *Time for 3* for Mezzo-soprano, Viola, and Piano (1985); *A Group of 7* for Reciter, Viola, and Orch. (1991; Ottawa, Oct. 28, 1992); *The River of Time* for Chorus and Orch. (1994; Winnipeg, Sept. 15, 1995); *4 Last Songs* for Mezzo-soprano, Violin, and Piano (Winnipeg, Oct. 15, 1995).**—NS/LK/DM**

Turner, William, English singer and composer; b. Oxford, 1651; d. London, Jan. 13, 1740. He received training in music as a chorister under Edward Lowe at Christ Church, Oxford, then was a chorister at the Chapel Royal, where he collaborated with Blow and Humfrey on "The Club Anthem" I will always give thanks; in 1666 he was placed in charge of Henry Cooke. He was master of the choristers at Lincoln Cathedral (1667–69), and in 1669 he became a Gentleman of the Chapel Royal, where he remained until his death. In 1672 he became a member of the King's Private Musick; in 1683 he was made a vicar-choral at St. Paul's Cathedral; in 1699 he became a lay vicar in the choir at Westminster Abbey. In 1696 he received the Mus.D. degree from the Univ. of Cambridge. He was buried in Westminster Abbey. Turner particularly distinguished himself as a composer for the church, producing more than 40 anthems, 3 services, a motet, hymns, and chants. Among his secular works are 2 odes, a cantata, many songs, a few pieces for theater productions, and 3 keyboard works.—**NS/LK/DM**

Turnhout, Gérard de (van), Flemish composer; b. Turnhout, c. 1520; d. Madrid, Sept. 15, 1580. He began his career at Antwerp Cathedral and at the church of St. Gommaire of Lierre, where he was made maître de chapelle in 1559. He took Holy Orders, and was made music master of the Confrérie de la Vierge at Antwerp Cathedral in 1562, and then maître de chant there in 1563; in 1571 he was named maestro de capilla to the court of Philip II of Spain in Madrid. He publ. *Sacrarum ac aliarum cantionum trium vocum* (Louvain, 1569); his *Missa O Maria vernans rosa* for 5 Voices was included in *Praestantissimorum divinae musices auctorum missae decem* (Louvain, 1570), 3 Latin works and 10 chansons in *Liber musicus* (Louvain, 1571), 4 Dutch songs in *Een duytsch Musyck Boeck* (Louvain, 1572; ed. by F. Van Duyse, Vereeniging voor Nederlandsche Muziekgeschiedenis, XXVI, 1903), 4 French sacred works and other pieces in *Premier livre du meslange des pseaumes et cantiques* (Geneva, 1577), and a French sacred work and other pieces in *Second livre du meslange des pseaumes et catiques* (Geneva, 1577). See L. Wagner, ed., *Gérard de Turnhout, Sacred and Secular Songs for Three Voices* (Madison, Wisc., 1970). His brother, Jan-Jacob van (Jean-Jacque de) Turnhout (b. probably in Brussels, c. 1545; d. probably there, after 1618), was also a composer. He was maître de chapelle at St. Rombaut in Mechelen (1577–80?), and maître de chapelle to Alexander Farnese, governor general of the Low Countries, by 1586. In 1611 he served with Géry Ghersem as maître de chapelle for the funeral of Archduchess Margaret of Austria. He publ. *Il primo libro de madrigali* for 6 Voices (Antwerp, 1589) and *Sacrarum cantionum* for 5 to 6 and 8 Voices *...liber primus* (Douai, 1594).—**NS/LK/DM**

Turnovský, Martin, Czech conductor; b. Prague, Sept. 29, 1928. He studied at the Prague Academy of Music (1948–52), his principal mentors being Robert Brock (piano) and Ančerl (conducting); later he pursued private instruction in conducting with Szell (1956). In 1952 he made his debut as a conductor with the Prague Sym. Orch. From 1955 to 1960 he conducted the Czech Army Sym. Orch. In 1958 he captured 1st prize in the Besançon competition. He was music director of the Brno State Phil. (1959–63) and the Plzeň Radio Sym. Orch. (1963–66). In 1966 he became Generalmusikdirektor of the Dresden State Opera and Orch. However, he resigned his position in 1968 when East German troops participated in the Soviet invasion of his homeland. After making his U.S. debut as a guest conductor with the Cleveland Orch. in 1968, Turnovsky appeared as a conductor with various orchs. and opera houses. From 1975 to 1980 he was music director of the Norwegian Opera in Oslo. He was music director of the Bonn City Theater from 1979 to 1983. During this time, he also served as co-chief conductor (with Jan Krenz) of the Beethovenhalle Orch. in Bonn. In 1992 he became music director of the Prague Sym. Orch.—**NS/LK/DM**

Turok, Paul (Harris), American composer and music critic; b. N.Y., Dec. 3, 1929. He studied composition at Queens Coll. with Rathaus (B.A., 1950), and then at the Univ. of Calif., Berkeley, with Sessions (M.A., 1951) and at the Juilliard School of Music with Wagenaar (1951–53). He later studied at Baruch Coll. (M.S., 1986). He was a lecturer on music at the City Coll. of N.Y. (1960–63) and was a visiting prof. at Williams Coll. in Williamstown, Mass. (1963–64). Turok then wrote music criticism for the *N.Y. Herald-Tribune* (1964–65), the *Music Journal* (1964–80), *Ovation* (1980–89), and *Fanfare* (from 1980). From 1989 he was ed. of his own review journal *Turok's Choice*. As a composer, Turok follows the principle of stylistic freedom and technical precision, without doctrinaire adherence to any circumscribed modernistic modus operandi.

WORKS: DRAMATIC: Opera: *Scene: Domestic*, chamber opera (1955; Aspen, Colo., Aug. 2, 1973); *Richard III* (1975); *A Secular Masque* (1979). **Ballet:** *Youngest Brother* (N.Y., Jan. 23, 1953). **ORCH.:** Violin Concerto (1953); *Symphony in 2 Movements* (1955); *Lyric Variations* for Oboe and Strings (1971; Louisville, March 9, 1973); *A Scott Joplin Overture* (Cleveland, June 19, 1973); *A Sousa Overture* (1975; Philadelphia, May 13, 1976); *Ragtime Caprice* for Piano and Orch. (1976); *Threnody* for Strings (1979); *Canzona concertante No. 1* for English Horn and Orch. (1980) and *No. 2* for Trombone and Orch. (1982); *Ultima Thule* (1981). **CHAMBER:** *Variations on a Theme by Schoenberg* for String Quartet (1952); String Trio (1954); 3 string quartets (1955, 1969, 1980); Wind Quintet (1960); Brass Quintet (1971); Clarinet Trio (1974); Quintet for English Horn and String Quartet (1981); piano pieces. **VOCAL:** Choruses; songs.—**NS/LK/DM**

Turovsky, Yuli, Russian-born Canadian cellist, conductor, and teacher; b. Moscow, June 7, 1939. He began training in cello at the age of 7, and after studies at the Moscow Central Music School (1946–57), he pursued training with Galina Kozolupova at the Moscow Cons. (diploma, 1962; Ph.D., 1969). He was principal cellist in the Moscow Chamber Orch., conductor of a chamber orch. at the Gnesin Coll. of Music in Moscow, and a teacher at the Moscow Central Music School. In 1969 he won the U.S.S.R. Cello Competition and in 1970 took 2nd prize in the Prague Spring Competition. In 1976 he organized the Borodin Trio, with which he toured widely. In 1977 he settled in Canada and in 1980 became a naturalized Canadian citizen. In 1983 he became founder and artistic director of I Musici de Montréal, a string orch. he conducted in a vast repertoire at home and abroad. He also taught at the Montreal Cons. (1977–85) and the Univ. of Montreal (from 1981). His wife, Eleonora Turovsky (b. Moscow, Sept. 23, 1939), is a violinist and teacher. She was educated at the Moscow Central Music School (1956–58) and the Moscow Cons. (diploma, 1963; Ph.D., 1966). In 1977 she went to Canada with her husband and became a naturalized Canadian citizen in 1980. From 1978 to 1990 she played in the Montreal Sym. Orch. She was also founding concertmaster of I Musici de Montréal from 1983. —**NS/LK/DM**

Turré, Steve, jazz trombonist, conch shell player, composer, arranger; b. Omaha, Nebr., Sept. 12, 1948. His parents, of Mexican ancestry, met at a Count Basie dance and are both big band fans. His mother is a pianist and flamenco dancer. originally wanted to play violin but his father suggested a wind instrument. At about nine or ten, he began playing trombone in the school band. Two or three years later he joined a local band for which his older brother played saxophone. Kid Ory was his first big influence—he used to play "Muskrat Ramble" and "When the Saints Go Marching In." Then in high school, he received a J.J. Johnson record, and Johnson became his idol. Later on, he was influenced by Coltrane, Ellington, McCoy Tyner, Woody Shaw, Dizzy Gillespie, Lester Bowie, and Rahsaan Roland Kirk. In 1970 Kirk asked him to sit in during a stint at San Francisco's Jazz Workshop. In the years that followed, he played with Kirk in local appearances, and inspired Turré to take it up the conch shell. He also worked with the Escovedo Brothers, Van Morrison, and Charles Moffett. In 1972, he went on a European tour with Ray Charles (his younger brother, Pete, was Charles's drummer in the late 1990s). The following year Art Blakey asked him to play with his band. He then worked with Cedar Walton, Thad Jones/Mel Lewis Orch., and Elvin Jones. In 1980, he began an association with Woody Shaw that through 1987 would yield 12 recordings and gain Turré credibility as a composer. He subsequently worked with Lester Bowie's Brass Fantasy (1983–on), Manny O' Quendo, and his idols Gillespie and Tyner. He was also a member of the band for the television show *Saturday Night Live* from 1988–94. Since 1986 he has led the Shell Choir (a ten-member aggregation of trombone/shell players, percussionists and a keyboardist) and various quartets, quintets, and sextets, at festivals from Monterey to Montreal and Hawaii (August 1995) and club residencies from Sweet Basil in N.Y. (including August 1997) to Yoshi's in Berkeley. He has composed music for TV commercials and movies, including a film, *Anna Oz*, by French filmmaker, Eric Rochant. His wife, cellist Akua Dixon, occasionally works with him and is the leader of Quartet Indigo with Regina Carter.

Disc.: *Viewpoint* (1987); *Fire and Ice* (1988); *Right There* (1991); *Sanctified Shells* (1992); *Rhythm Within* (1995); *Steve Turre* (1997).—**LP**

Turrentine, Stanley (William), jazz-fusion tenor saxophonist; b. Pittsburgh, April 5, 1934; d. N.Y., Sept. 12, 2000. He played with Lowell Fulson, Earl Bostic, and others, then made his first records while with Max Roach in 1958. He formed his own group and married organist Shirley Scott, working with her through the 1960s; made solo LPs on Blue Note, as well as recording with Jimmy Smith, Ike Quebec, and others. He and Scott separated in 1971. One of the first key artists to join the record label CTI in 1970, he established himself as a top-selling artist with that albums for that label (*Sugar*, *Salt Song*), Fantasy Records (*Pieces of Dreams*) from 1974–78, and later with Elektra; some of his jazz albums reached the Top 200 in the U.S. Many find his work since the 1970s overly commercial, although at his best he maintained a hard-driving funky sound that lesser artists never achieved. In the later 1990s, he returned to playing more straight-ahead jazz.

His brother, Tommy (Thomas Walter Jr.; b. Pittsburgh, April 22, 1928; d. N.Y., May 13, 1957) was a trumpeter who is said to have worked with Coltrane in Gay Crosse's band in early 1952. He struggled with drug addiction throughout his career. Active from the 1960s as a freelancer in N.Y., he enjoyed a long association with saxophonist Clarence "C" Sharpe playing in small N.Y. clubs through the 1970s and 1980s. He also composed and arranged for various leaders, including Stanley. Another brother, Marvin, plays drums.

Disc.: *Stan the Man Turrentine* (1959); *Blue Hour* (1960); *Up at Minton's, Vol. 1, 2* (1961); *Never Let Me Go* (1963); *Joyride* (1965); *Spoiler* (1966); *Sugar* (1970); *In Concert* (1973); *Nightwings* (1977); *Mr. Natural* (1981); *Straight Ahead* (1984); *Ballads* (1993); *If I Could* (1993); *Three of a Kind Meet Mr. T* (1995); *Time* (1995). **—MM/LP**

Türrschmidt, Carl, German cor basse player and composer; b. Wallerstein, Feb. 24, 1753; d. Berlin, Nov. 1, 1797. He was a pupil of his father, Johann Türrschmidt (b. Leschgau, June 24, 1725; d. Wallerstein, 1800), a horn player in the Prince of Oettingen-Wallerstein's orch. In 1770 he went to Paris, where he appeared in duos with Johann Palsa. They also played in the Prince of Monaco's private orch. before entering the Landgrave of Hessen-Kassel's orch. in 1783. In 1786 they performed in London, the same year they were called to the Berlin court. Palsa died in 1792 but Türrschmidt continued to perform in Berlin, and also made tours as a virtuoso. With Palsa, he composed a set of 50 horn duos (publ. in Berlin, 1795). His son, Carl Nicholaus Türrschmidt (b. Paris, Oct. 20, 1776; d. Berlin, Sept. 18, 1862), was a horn player and teacher in Berlin.—**LK/DM**

Turski, Zbigniew, Polish composer; b. Konstancin, near Warsaw, July 28, 1908; d. Warsaw, Jan. 7, 1979. He was a student of Rytel (composition) and Bierdiajew (conducting) at the Warsaw Cons. From 1936 to 1939 he was music producer of the Polish Radio in Warsaw. In 1945–46 he was conductor of the Baltic Phil. in Gdańsk. His compositions were in an advanced harmonic idiom.

Works: Dramatic: *Rozmowki* (Chats), micro-opera (1966); *Tytania i osiol* (Titania and the Donkey), ballet (1966); incidental music for the theater, films, and radio. **Orch.:** 3 syms. (*Sinfonia da camera*, 1947; *Sinfonia Olimpica*, 1948; 1953); 2 violin concertos (1951, 1959); *Little Overture* (1955). **Chamber:** 2 string quartets (n.d., 1951); piano pieces. **Vocal:** *L'Ombre* for Tenor, Chorus, and Percussion (1967); *Canti de nativitate patriae* for Tenor, Bass, Chorus, and Orch. (1969); *Regno Ejukori* for Bass and Orch. (Wroclaw, Sept. 2, 1974); cantatas; songs.—**NS/LK/DM**

Turtles, The, 1960s popsters turned into 1970s and 1980s-era cult band led by the amazing "Flo and Eddie." **Membership:** Mark Volman, gtr., sax., lead voc. (b. Los Angeles, April 19, 1944); Howard Kaylan (real name, Howard Kaplan), kybd., sax., backing and harmony voc. (b. N.Y., June 22, 1945); Al Nichol, kybd., gtr., bs., voc. (b. Winston-Salem, N.C., March 31, 1946); Jim Tucker, gtr. (b. Los Angeles, Oct. 17, 1946); Charles "Chuck" Portz, bs. (b. Santa Monica, Calif., March 28, 1945); Don Murray drm. (b. Los Angeles, Nov. 8, 1945).

Later members included drummers John Barbata (b. N.J., April 1, 1946) and John Seiter (b. St. Louis, Miss., Aug. 17, 1944), and bassist Jim Pons (b. Santa Monica, March 14, 1943).

Mark Volman and Howard Kaylan met at Westchester H.S. in Los Angeles in 1961, the year Kaylan formed the surf group The Nightriders with Al Nichol, Chuck Portz, and Don Murray. Adding Volman on saxophone in 1963, the group became The Crossfires, releasing two local singles. In 1965, they signed with White Whale Records and changed their name to The Turtles, adding second guitarist Jim Tucker. Capitalizing on the burgeoning folk-rock movement, The Turtles' debut album included "Eve of Destruction" and three Bob Dylan songs, including the near-smash hit "It Ain't Me, Babe." They next scored major hits with P. F. Sloan's "Let Me Be" and Sloan and Steve Barri's "You Baby." In mid-1966, Murray and Portz departed, to be replaced by John Barbata and Jim Pons, a founding member of The Leaves ("Hey Joe").

The Turtles subsequently achieved their most successful year in 1967 with the top pop hit "Happy Together" (backed by Warren Zevon's "Like The Seasons"), the smash hit "She'd Rather Be with Me," and the major hits "You Know What I Mean" and "She's My Girl," all written by Gary Bonner and Alan Gordon. In mid-1968, The Turtles scored a moderate hit with Harry Nilsson's "The Story of Rock and Roll," next recording *The Turtles Present the Battle of the Bands*. The album yielded smash hits with the group's "Elenore" and "You Showed Me," written by Gene Clark and Jim McGuinn of The Byrds. For the album, the group recorded under a variety of different names in different styles, showcasing a developing satirical bent with songs such as "Surfer Dan," "I'm Chief Kamanananalea (We're the Royal Macadamia Nuts)," and "Chicken Little Was Right." After *Turtle Soup*, produced by The Kinks' Ray Davies, The Turtles disbanded in mid-1970. John Barbata joined Crosby, Stills and Nash for a time, later joining The Jefferson Airplane in 1972.

Mark Volman and Howard Kaylan (and later Jim Pons) subsequently joined Frank Zappa's Mothers of Invention as the Phlorescent Leech and Eddie. Touring Europe and America extensively with Zappa, Mark "Flo" Volman and Howard "Eddie" Kaylan performed their own feature spot in concert and recorded two live albums with the group. They also helped record *Chunga's Revenge* and the soundtrack to the movie *200 Motels*, in which they appeared. Volman and Kaylan also recorded as background vocalists for Marc Bolan/T. Rex in 1971 and 1972 (including the major hit "Bang a Gong"). With the dissolution of the current edition of The Mothers of Invention at the end of 1971, Flo and Eddie recorded two outstanding yet neglected albums of rock satire for Reprise Records and toured in support of Alice Cooper's "Billion Dollar Babies" tour in 1973.

Howard Kaylan and Mark Volman later wrote the screenplay to the X-rated animated movie *Cheap*, wrote satirical articles for the American rock press, and hosted their own successful syndicated radio show originating from Los Angeles's KROQ. Signed to Columbia Records in 1975, the duo recorded two more excellent yet overlooked albums of rock parody and satire before moving into sessions and television work. They recorded a silly reggae album in 1981, wrote radio and television commercials (including all of the commercials for David Bowie's RCA albums), and wrote and recorded music for the children's cartoons *Strawberry Shortcake* and *The Care Bears*. In 1984 and 1985, with a reconstituted Turtles, they headlined two "Happy Together Tours" with other 1960s groups, subsequently touring independently as The Turtles.

DISC.: THE CROSSFIRES: *Out of Control* (1981). THE TURTLES: *It Ain't Me Babe* (1965); *You Baby* (1966); *Happy Together* (1967); *The Turtles Present the Battle of the Bands* (1968); *Turtle Soup* (1969); *Wooden Head* (1970); *Chalon Road* (1987); *Shell Shock* (1987); *Captured Live* (1992). FLO AND EDDIE WITH FRANK ZAPPA AND THE MOTHERS OF INVENTION: *Chunga's Revenge* (1970); *Fillmore East, June 1971* (1971); *Just Another Band from L.A.* (1972); *Playground Psychotics* (1992). FLO AND EDDIE: *The Phlorescent Leech and Eddie* (1972); *Flo and Eddie* (1973); *Illegal, Immoral and Fattening* (1975); *Moving Targets* (1976); *Rock Steady with Flo and Eddie* (1981).—**BH**

Tusler, Robert Leon, American musicologist; b. Stoughton, Wisc., April 1, 1920. He studied piano and organ at Friends' Univ., Wichita, Kans. (B.M., 1947) and musicology at the Univ. of Calif., Los Angeles (M.A., 1952) and then at the Univ. of Utrecht, the Netherlands (1956–58). In 1958 he joined the music faculty of the Univ. of Calif., Los Angeles; retired in 1983. He wrote *The Style of J.S. Bach's Chorale Preludes* (Berkeley, Calif., 1956) and *The Organ Music of Jan Pieterszoon Sweelinck* (Bilthoven, 1958).—**NS/LK/DM**

Tutev, Georgi, Bulgarian conductor and composer; b. Sofia, Aug. 23, 1924; d. there, Sept. 13, 1994. He studied law in Sofia while pursuing private instruction in composition from Pipkov. His formal studies in composition followed with Bely and Shaporin at the Moscow Cons. (1946–50). About the time of his graduation, his father was the victim of a politically staged trial in Bulgaria on charges of revisionism. For the next 17 years, Tutev was not allowed to use his last name, opting for the pseudonym "Ivanov." He was finally able to again use his last name upon the rehabilitation of his father in 1967. From 1954 to 1958 he was secretary of the Bulgarian Composers Union, and then was chief music ed. of the Bulgarian National Radio from 1958 to 1961. He subsequently served as music director and principal conductor of the Orch. of the National Youth Theater from 1961 to 1987. In 1990 he founded the Soc. of Contemporary Music of Bulgaria, and was its president until his death. His early works were in a romantic Soviet style, but in the late 1960s he adopted more advanced techniques, eventually embracing serialism.

WORKS: *Legend of the Lopian Forest*, symphonic poem (1950–51; Sofia, Feb. 15, 1951); *The Mutiny on the S. S. Nadezhda*, symphonic poem (1955); 2 syms.: No. 1 (1959; Sofia, June 22, 1960) and No. 2, *Variations* (1969–72); *Divertimento* for Clarinet, Violin, Harpsichord, and Chamber Orch. (1962); *Overtura da Requiem* for Orch. (1963); *Metamorphoses* for 13 Strings (1966); *Tempi Rithmizati* for Strings, Piano, and Percussion (1968); *Musica Concertante* for Strings, Flute, Harpsichord, and Percussion (1968); *Soli per tre* for Wind Trio (1974); *Yearning for the Lost Harmony* for Strings, Keyboards, and Percussion (1969–82); *Calvinomusica* for Cello and Chamber Ensemble (1987); *J.S.B. Meditations* for Chamber Ensemble (1992).—**LK/DM**

Tuthill, Burnet Corwin, American composer and conductor; b. N.Y., Nov. 16, 1888; d. Knoxville, Tenn., Jan. 18, 1982. His father, William Burnet Tuthill, was the architect of Carnegie Hall in N.Y. He studied at Columbia Univ. (B.A., 1909; M.A., 1910) and the Cincinnati Coll. of Music (M.M., 1935). He conducted the Columbia Univ. Orch. (1909–13). In 1919 he organized the Soc. for Publication of American Music, which continued to function for nearly half a century, and which publ. about 85 works by American composers; also was executive secretary of the National Assn. of Schools of Music in Cincinnati (1924–59). After serving as general manager of the Cincinnati Coll. of Music (1922–30), he was head of the music dept. at Southwestern Univ. in Memphis (1935–59); also was conductor of the Memphis Sym. Orch. (1938–46) and head of the fine arts dept. of Shrivenham American Univ. in England (1945). He began to compose rather late in life, but compensated for this delay by increasing productivity in subsequent years. His autobiography was publ. as *Recollections of a Musical Life, 1900–74* (Memphis, 1974).

Works: **ORCH.:** *Bethlehem*, pastorale (Interlochen, Mich., July 22, 1934); *Laurentia*, symphonic poem (Rochester, N.Y., Oct. 30, 1936); *Come 7*, rhapsody (1935; St. Louis, Feb. 19, 1944); Sym. (1940); Concertos for clarinet (1949), double bass (1962), saxophone (1965), trombone (1967), and tuba (1975). **OTHER:** Numerous pieces with a multiplicity of clarinets; Flute Sonata; Oboe Sonata; Trumpet Sonata; Saxophone Sonata; a plethora of sacred choruses.

Bibl.: J. Raines, *B.C. T.: His Life and Music* (diss., Mich. State Univ., 1979).—**NS/LK/DM**

Tuukkanen, Kalervo, Finnish conductor and composer; b. Mikkeli, Oct. 14, 1909; d. Helsinki, July 12, 1979. He studied composition with Leevi Madetoja and theory with Krohn in Helsinki. He subsequently conducted local orchs. and choirs; from 1967 to 1969 he was a visiting prof. of music at the Chinese Univ. of Hong Kong. He wrote 2 violin concertos (1943, 1956), 6 syms. (1944, 1949, 1952, 1958, 1961, 1978), Cello Concerto (1946), *Sinfonietta* (1948), *Man and the Elements* for Soprano, Chorus, and Orch. (1949), *Indumati*, opera (1962), *Youth Cantata* (1963), and *A Chorale Echo* for Flute and Piano (1967). He also publ. a monograph on the life and works of Leevi Madetoja (Helsinki, 1947).—**NS/LK/DM**

Tüür, Erkki-Sven, Estonian composer; b. Kärdla, Oct. 16, 1959. He first studied flute at the Music School (graduated, 1980), and then composition with Jaan Rääts at the Cons. (graduated, 1984) in Tallinn. He pursued private instruction in composition from Lepo Sumera, and also studied electronic music in Darmstadt. Tüür began his career with the rock group In Spe, with which he appeared as a singer. His diverse musical background, ranging from formal training in art music to freewheeling rock, has led him to follow an eclectic but innovative path as a composer. His *Requiem* (1994) won the UNESCO International Rostrum of Composers Competition in Paris.

Works: **ORCH.:** 3 syms. (1984, 1987, 1997); *Insula deserta* for Chamber Orch. (1989); *Searching for Roots: Hommage à Sibelius* for Chamber Orch. (1990); *Zeitraum* (1992); *Illusion* for Chamber Orch. (1993); *Passion* for Chamber Orch. (1993); Cello Concerto (1996); *Lighthouse* (1997); Violin Concerto (1999–2000). **CHAMBER:** *Architectonics I-VII* for Various Chamber Groups (1984–94); Piano Sonata (1985); *Drama* for Flute, Violin, and Guitar (1994); *Crystallisatio* for Chamber Group (1995). **VOCAL:** *Dona nobis pacem*, cantata (1982); *Ante finem saeculi*, oratorio (1985); *Lumen et canius*, mass (1988); *Requiem* (1994). —**LK/DM**

Tuxen, Erik (Oluf), Danish conductor; b. Mannheim (of Danish parents), July 4, 1902; d. Copenhagen, Aug. 28, 1957. After training in architecture, medicine, and philosophy, he pursued studies in music in Copenhagen, Paris, Vienna, and Berlin. He conducted at the Lübeck Opera (1927–29), and then at the Royal Theater in Copenhagen. In 1936 he became conductor of the Danish Radio Sym. Orch. in Copenhagen. During World War II (1939–45), he lived in Sweden. Returning to Copenhagen in 1945, he was again conductor of the Danish Radio Sym. Orch. until his death. He conducted it at the Edinburgh Festival in 1950 in an acclaimed performance of Nielsen's 5th Sym. In 1950–51 he conducted in the U.S. and in 1954 in South America. Tuxen was a particularly persuasive interpreter of Nielsen. —**NS/LK/DM**

Tveitt, (Nils) Geirr, Norwegian composer, teacher, and pianist; b. Kvam, Oct. 19, 1908; d. Oslo, Feb. 1, 1981. He learned to play the piano and violin in childhood. Following studies with Grabner and Weninger in Leipzig (1928–32), he pursued his training in Vienna with Wellesz and in Paris with Honegger and Villa-Lobos (1932–35). Returning to Norway, he devoted himself mainly to composition, producing over 300 works. He also made some tours abroad as a pianist. In 1941 the Norwegian government granted him an annual income. However, his activities during the German occupation of Norway led to his loss of the Norwegian government grant after the liberation in 1945. It was finally restored in 1958. In his study *Tonalitätstheorie des parallelen Leittonssystems* (Oslo, 1937), Tveitt attempted to formulate the foundation of his own compositional style by claiming that the modal scales are in actuality old Norse keys. Many of his works employ modal scales.

Works: **DRAMATIC:** **Opera:** *Nordvest—Sud—Nordaust—Nord* (1939); *Dragaredokko* (1940); *Roald Amundsen* (n.d.); *Stevleik*, chamber opera (n.d.); *Jeppe* (1964; Bergen, June 10, 1966; rev. 1968). **Ballet:** *Baldurs draumar* (1935); *Birgingu* (1939); *Husguden* (1956). **Incidental Music:** *Jonsoknatt* (1936). **ORCH.:** 6 piano concertos (1930, 1933, 1947, 1947, 1954, 1960); Concerto for String Quartet and Orch. (1933); *Variations* for 2 Pianos and Orch. (1937); Violin Concerto (1939); 2 Hardanger fiddle concertos (1956); 3 syms.; 5 Hardanger suites (based on a set of piano pieces). **CHAMBER:** Quartet for 4 Violins; 2 string quartets; 3 string sextets. **Piano:** 29 sonatas; *100 Folk Tunes from Hardanger*. **VOCAL:** Various pieces.

BIBL.: R. Storass, *Tonediktaren G. T.: Songjen i fossaduren* (Oslo, 1990).—**NS/LK/DM**

Twain, Shania (originally, **Eileen Evans**), Canadian-born songstress who broke the country mold (b. Windsor, Ontario, Canada, Aug. 28, 1965). Shania Twain has emerged as one of the best-selling artists in popular music in the late 1990s. Her two albums *The Woman in Me* (1995) and *Come on Over* (1997) have each sold over 10 million copies worldwide, a first for any female artist. Although nominally a "country" artist, Twain's music is mainstream pop at its most professional, packaged with a high sheen by her producer/ husband Robert John "Mutt" Lange.

Twain's parents were divorced when she was young, and her mother remarried a Native-American from the Obijway tribe named Jerry Twain. (Later, when Shania first hit Nashville, there was a "scandal" involving her supposed exaggeration of her Native-American heritage. Although not her blood father, Twain did raise the young woman, although his connections with Indian culture were slight, at best.)

As a teenager, Twain began performing on local television, and in bars and clubs. She also began writing her own songs. Her mother encouraged her to perform. Twain's family life took a tragic turn when her mother and stepfather were killed in an automobile accident when she was 21. She soon landed a job at a Canadian resort singing in a Vegas-flavored floorshow as a means of supporting her younger siblings.

In the early 1990s, Twain headed to Nashville in search of a record deal. In 1992, she landed one, but her label was less-than-enthusiastic about allowing her to record her own material. Instead, she was forced to work with Nashville songwriters and producers, and the result—while competent—showed little originality. The label also asked her to change her name, and she chose "Shania," the Obijway word for "on my way" (according to her publicity).

Nonetheless, the video for the second single from the album—"Dance with the One That Brought You," directed by Hollywood bad-boy actor Sean Penn—caught the eye of the Australian-born, mainstream pop producer John Robert "Mutt" Lange. Lange had previously brought success to heavy metal stars Def Leppard and AC/DC, and pop balladeers including Michael Bolton and Bryan Adams. He phoned Twain, and they began a six-month collaboration which ended in their marriage.

Lange produced Twain's breakthrough second album, 1995's *The Woman in Me*. The duo cowrote most of the songs, which projected a sassy, take-no-guff woman's viewpoint towards relationships. Twain scored big right out of the box with the single "Whose Bed Have Your Boots Been Under?," the most country-flavored item on the album. The video emphasized Twain's considerable personal charms, raising eyebrows among the more conservative Nashville crowd who were shocked by her flirtatious dress.

The album produced a string of hits, each cleverly playing on age-old country themes but polishing them up for the 1990s. Just as Loretta Lynn scolded her heavy-drinking husband in the 1960s, Twain warns her boyfriend that "(If You're Not in It for Love) I'm Out of Here." Unlike other country stars, Twain initially did not tour, making her success that much more remarkable.

Although undeniably sexy, Twain projected a wholesome, girl-next-door image that made her acceptable to a wide range of fans. For women, her fashion-plate wardrobe and self-assured attitude was very appealing; and men had plenty of eye candy to keep them happy. Twain's music was also cleverly packaged: the lyrics were kept simple and direct; the hook-soaked melodies emphasized the song's title; and the simple rock beats were easy to follow. There was just enough fiddles and steel guitars to make the music "country," but not so much as to turn off more mainstream listeners (who could enjoy the electric guitar solos and heavy drum beat).

Given their pop proclivities, it was not surprising that Lange-Twain's next collaboration, the 1997 album *Come on Over*, crossed over to pop success big time. The lead single, "Still the One," became a major pop hit. It was followed by a big-throated ballad that would have made Celine Dion proud, "From This Moment," written in memory of Twain's parents. Both videos got heavy airplay on VH–1, and neither emphasized a "country" look for the star, who was dressed more like a fashion model than a cowgirl. Twain also began to tour heavily, and proved as attractive a performer on stage as she was on video.

The hits kept coming in 1998–99. Twain signed an endorsement deal with Revlon, who heavily promoted her anthemic hit "Feel Like a Woman." She also starred in her own live television program, including a special appearance by Elton John, giving his own middle-of-the-road blessings to her. And, after years of being snubbed by the country establishment, she was given a special award at the 1999 Country Music Association's award show, for popularizing the music around the world, as well as garnering an Entertainer of the Year trophy.

DISC.: *Shania Twain* (1993); *The Woman in Me* (1995); *Come on Over* (1997).—**RC**

Twardowski, Romuald, Polish composer and teacher; b. Vilnius, June 17, 1930. He was a student of Julius Juzeliunas (piano and composition) at the Vilnius State Cons. (1952–57), of Bolesław Woytowicz (composition) at the State Higher School of Music in Warsaw (1957–60), and of Nadia Boulanger (Gregorian chant and medieval polyphony) in Paris (1963, 1966). In 1971 he became a prof. at the State Higher School of Music in Warsaw. He won 1st prize in the International Competition for Composers in Prague in 1965, 1st prizes in the Prince Rainier III International Competition for Composers in Monaco in 1965 and 1973, and the awards of the West European Assn. of Choral Societies and of the Polish Composer's Union in 1994.

WORKS: DRAMATIC: *Nagi książę* (The Naked Prince), ballet-pantomime (1960; Warsaw, Sept. 19, 1964); *Cyrano de Bergerac*, opera (1962; Bytom, July 6, 1963); *Posągi czarnoksiężnika (Rzeźby mistrza Piotra)* (The Sorcerer's Statues [Sculptures of Master Peter]), ballet- pantomime (1963); *Parabola* (Parable), pantomime (1964); *Tragedyja albo Rzecz o Janie i Herodzie* (Tragedy or Story of John and Herod), opera- morality (1965; Łódź, April 26, 1969); *Upadek ojca Suryna* (The Fall of Father Suryn), radio musical drama (1969); *Lord Jim*, musical drama (1970–73); *Maria Stuart*, musical drama (1978); *Historya o sw. Katarzynie* (History of St. Catherine), musical morality (1981; Warsaw, Dec. 14, 1985). **ORCH.:** *Suita w dawnym stylu* (Suite in the Old Style; 1957); *Mała symfonia* (Little Sym.) for Piano, Strings, and Percussion (1959; Wrocław, Nov. 25, 1964); *Antifone* for 3 Orch. Groups (1961; Warsaw, Sept. 16, 1962); *Nomopedia* (1962); *Oda* (Ode) *64* (1964); *Preludium, toccata i choral* (1973; Białystok, Nov. 28, 1974); *Tryptyk Miriacki* (Triptych of the Virgin Mary) for Strings (Toruń, Sept. 10, 1973); *Studium in a* (1974; Warsaw, Sept. 21, 1976); *Dwa pejzaże* (Two Landscapes; 1975; Szczecin, Jan. 16, 1976); *Capriccio in blue* for Violin and Orch. or Piano (1979); Piano Concerto (1984; Gdańsk, Sept. 13, 1985); *Fantazja hiszpańska* (Spanish Fantasia) for Violin and Orch. (1985; Zielona Góra, April 11, 1986; also for Violin and Piano); *Trzy freski* (Three Frescoes; 1986; Bydgoszcz, Sept. 1988); *Wariacje symfoniczne na temat George's Gershwina* (Symphonic Variations on a Theme by George Gershwin) for Percussion Solo and Orch. (1986; Kraków, Jan. 13, 1987); *Koncert staropolski* (Old Polish Concerto) for Strings (1987); *Album włoski* (Italian Album; 1989); *Niggunim* for Violin and Orch. (Kraków, June 5, 1991; also for Violin and Piano); Cello Concerto (1995); *Concerto breve* for Strings (1998; Warsaw, May 8, 1999). **CHAMBER:** *Oberek* for Violin and Piano (1955); *Mała suita* (Little Suite) for Violin and Piano (1962); *Na czterech strunach* (On Four Strings) for Violin and Piano (1980); *Mały tryptyk* (Little Triptych) for Wind Quintet (1986; Warsaw, Sept. 27, 1987); Trio for Violin, Cello, and Piano (1987); *Wariacje litewskie* (Lithuanian Variations) for Flute, Oboe, Clarinet, Horn, and Bassoon (1988; Poznań, April 2, 1989); *Espressioni* for Violin and Piano (1990; Warsaw, Dec. 9, 1991); *Plejady* (Pleiades) for Violin and Piano (Warsaw, Oct. 25, 1993); *Trio młodziezoe* (Youngster Trio) for Violin, Cello, and Piano (1993); *Inwokacja i capriccio* (Invocation and Capriccio) for 2 Cellos (1996). **Piano:** *Trzy miniatury* (Three Miniatures; 1957); *Mała sonata* (Little Sonata; 1958); *Capricci* (1968); *Improvvisazione e toccata* for 2 Pianos (1974; Poznań, April 25, 1977); *Musica concertante* (1980); *Symfonie dzwonów* (Bell Symphonies) *I-III* (1988–91; Warsaw, Oct. 26, 1992). **VOCAL:** *Pieśń o białym domu* (Song About a White House), cantata for Chorus, 2 Pianos, and Percussion (1959); *Cantus antiqui* for Soprano, Harpsichord, Piano, and Percussion (1962); *Psalmus 149* for Chorus (1962; Warsaw, Feb. 23, 1974); *Mała liturgia prawosławna* (Little Orthodox Liturgy) for Vocal Ensemble and 3 Instrumental Ensembles (1968); *Oda do młodości* (Ode to Youth) for Reciter, Chorus, and Orch. (1969); *Trzy sonety pożegnalne* (Three Farewell Sonnets) for Bass-baritone and Chamber Orch. (Bydgoszcz, Sept. 14, 1971; also for Bass-baritone and Piano); *Laudate Dominum* for 2 Choruses (1976); *Sequentia de ss. Patronis Polonis* for Baritone, Chorus, and Instrumental Ensemble (1977); *Joannes Rex*, cantata for Baritone, Chorus, and Orch. (1983); *Sonety Michala Aniola* (Michelangelo's Sonnets) for Baritone and Piano (1988; Warsaw, April 17, 1989); *Trzy sonety do Don Kichota* (Three Sonnets to Don Quixote) for Bass-baritone and Piano (1990; Warsaw, Oct. 26, 1991); *Tu es Petrus* for Baritone, Chorus, and Orch. (Kraków, May 1991); *Pieśni Maryjne* (Songs for the Virgin Mary) for Soprano and Orch. (1993; Częstochowa, May 5, 1994); *Canticum Canticorum* for Soprano, Flute, Clarinet, and Strings (1994; Częstochowa, May 1995); numerous choruses and many songs.—**NS/LK/DM**

Tweedy, Donald (Nichols), American composer and teacher; b. Danbury, Conn., April 23, 1890; d. there, July 21, 1948. He was educated at Harvard Univ. (B.A., 1912; M.A., 1917), where his teachers were William Heilman, E.B. Hill, and Walter Spalding; later studied in Europe and with Goetschius in N.Y. He taught at Vassar Coll. (1914–16), the Eastman School of Music (1923–27), Hamilton Coll. (1937–38), and Tex. Christian Univ. (1945–46). He publ. a *Manual of Harmonic Technic Based on the Practice of J.S. Bach* (1928).

WORKS: DRAMATIC: Ballet: *Alice in Wonderland* (1935). **ORCH.:** *L'Allegro*, symphonic study (Rochester, N.Y., May 1, 1925); *3 Dances* (1925); *Williamsburg*, suite (1941). **CHAMBER:** Viola Sonata (1916); Violin Sonata (1920); Cello Sonata (1930); piano pieces.—**NS/LK/DM**

Tye, Christopher, English organist and composer; b. c. 1505; d. c. 1572. In 1536 he received his Mus.B. from Cambridge, and in 1537 was made lay clerk at King's Coll. there. In 1543 he became Magister choristarum at Ely Cathedral, and in 1545 he received the D.Mus. degree from the Univ. of Cambridge. After becoming a deacon and a priest in 1560, he left his position at Ely Cathedral in 1561; held livings at Doddington-cum-Marche in the Isle of Ely (from 1561), and at Wilbraham Parva (1564–67) and Newton-cum-capella (1564–70). His son-in-law was **Robert White** or **Whyte**. He described himself as a gentleman of the King's Chapel on the title page of his only publ. work, *The Actes of the Apostles*, translated into *Englyshe metre to synge and also to play upon the Lute* (London, 1553; it includes the first 14 chapters of the Acts). The hymn tunes *Windsor* and *Winchester Old* are adaptations from this collection. Tye was an important composer of English church music; he left masses, services, motets, and anthems. The following eds. of his works have been publ.: R. Weidner, *Christopher Tye: The Instrumental Music* (New Haven, Conn., 1967), J. Satterfield, *Christopher Tye: The Latin Church Music* (Madison, Wisc., 1972), and J. Morehen, *Christopher Tye: The English Sacred Music* in Early English Church Music, XIX (1977).—**NS/LK/DM**

Tyes, John, English organist and composer who flourished in the early 15th century. A Gloria for 2 Voices and One Instrument and a Sanctus for 4 Voices are among the works included in the *Old Hall Manuscripts*. —**NS/LK/DM**

Tyler, Charles (Lacy), avant-garde jazz baritone and alto saxophonist; b. Cadiz, Ky., July 20, 1941; d. June 27, 1992. He started on piano then took up clarinet in college. He also studied the alto sax before playing the baritone in an army band. He moved to Cleveland in 1960, where he played with Albert Ayler. He later moved to N.Y. and played with Ayler's group (1965–66). He led his own group, and worked with others. In the late 1960s, he moved to Calif., and taught music for four years at Merritt Coll. and worked with Arthur Blythe, David Murray, and Bobby Bradford. When he returned to N.Y. in 1976, he began leading his own quartet, sextet, and big band. Through the later 1970s, he worked with Dave Baker, Dewey Redman, Frank Lowe, Steve Reid, and Cecil Taylor, and recorded and played with the Billy Bang Ensemble in 1981 and 1982. He then toured

Europe with Sun Ra, settling in Denmark in 1984; he moved to France a year later. He continued to work through the late 1980s in Europe, returning to N.Y. in the early 1990s shortly before his death.

DISC.: *Charles Tyler Ensemble* (1966); *Eastern Man Alone* (1967); *Charles Tyler Live in Europe* (1978); *Saga of the Outlaws* (1980); *Folk and Mystery Stories* (c. 1980); *Sixty Minute Man* (1981); *Autumn in Paris* (1988); *Mid Western Drifter* (1992). Ayler: *Bells; Spirits Rejoice.* Played C-melody sax on a bootleg album with Ayler and Ornette Coleman on trumpet.—**LP**

Tyler, James (Henry), American lutenist, guitarist, and viol player; b. Hartford, Conn., Aug. 3, 1940. He attended the Univ. of Conn. and studied lute with Joseph Iadone. In 1961 he made his concert debut as a lutenist with the Consort Players, with whom he performed in "An Elizabethan Evening at the White House" in Washington, D.C., in 1963. He also made his recording debut in 1963 with the N.Y. Pro Musica. In 1967 he went to Germany and recorded with the Studio der frühen Musik and, in 1969, to England, where he performed with Musica Reservata. In the same year, he joined the Early Music Consort of London, with whom he toured and recorded until director David Munrow's death in 1976. From 1974 to 1990 he also was a member of the Julian Bream Consort. In 1976 he founded the London Early Music Group, an ensemble specializing in music of the Renaissance and early Baroque eras. It made its debut in 1977 at the Queen Elizabeth Hall in London, and then performed in chamber music series and festivals throughout Europe, North America, and Australia, and made various recordings. He also recorded as a Baroque mandolin soloist with the English Concert and the Academy of St. Martin-in-the-Fields. A versatile musician, Tyler played tenor banjo and was a member of the Original Rag Quartet with Max Morath (1961–67) and with his own ensemble, the New Excelsior Talking Machine, which he founded in 1974. In 1986 he joined the faculty of the Univ. of Southern Calif. Thornton School of Music in Los Angeles, where he is prof. of music and director of the early music performance program. In addition to numerous articles in *The New Grove Dictionary of Music and Musicians* (1980; rev. ed., 2000), *The New Grove Dictionary of Musical Instruments* (1984), and *Early Music*, he publ. *The Early Guitar* (Oxford, 1980) and, with P. Sparks, *The Early Mandolin* (Oxford, 1989). He has composed and arranged the music for several BBC-TV productions, most notably *Romeo and Juliet, Measure for Measure, Henry VIII*, and *Hamlet* ("The Play Within a Play").—**NS/LK/DM**

Tyner, (Alfred) McCoy, influential jazz pianist, composer; b. Philadelphia, Dec. 11, 1938. Both his parents were from Murfreesboro, N.C.; his mother's family moved to Philadelphia, and later his father's family did so as well. He also has relatives in Ahoskie, N.C., and as a teenager he went to N.C. to work on tobacco farms. At his mother's encouragement, he began playing piano around age 12; he studied some at the West Philadelphia Music School and the Granoff School. He also played conga drums for a period. When he was a teenager, Bud Powell lived around the corner from him for three or four months; Powell even played Tyner's piano; he and his friends used to follow Powell around asking him to play. In addition to Powell, Thelonius Monk was a strong influence, and Tyner was sometimes called "Bud Monk"! He also listened to Bud's pianist brother, Richie. Lee Morgan was a childhood friend and he and Tyner used to have jam sessions in North and West Philadelphia, where Tyner lived, as well as in Tyner's mother's beauty shop. He and Morgan played Atlantic city several summers; the two also played fraternity dances. He played some gigs with Gillespie, and worked with Cal Massey in the mid-1950s.

In May 1957, Tyner was in Massey's group with Albert Heath, Jimmy Garrison, and saxophonist Clarence Sharpe at the Red Rooster, where, the following week, the same rhythm section accompanied Coltrane. Coltrane said "[I] promised myself to call him if I formed my own group one day." From November 1959 Tyner was touring with the Jazztet of Benny Golson and Art Farmer, and when Coltrane asked him to join his new quartet he could not at first get free, but in late May 1960 he joined Coltrane at the Jazz Gallery in Manhattan. He and Coltrane influenced each other and Tyner's powerful sound and solid sense of time became an important element in many of Coltrane's most famous recordings and performances. When Coltrane began working with two drummers and with free rhythm (without a walking bass line), Tyner left near the end of 1965. In early 1966, he was working with Tony Scott and rehearsing to lead his own group. By April 1966 the McCoy Tyner group—a quartet—was performing at Slug's on East Third Street in Manhattan. He worked with Art Blakey for about six months. In the late 1960s he taught in the Bronx in a program sponsored by the State of N.Y. that was organized by Bill Lee. He continued to lead his own groups, featuring, Freddie Waits on drums for two or three years, Calvin Hill on bass, and for a time Gary Bartz. Around 1969 this group was playing to small audiences—as were many acoustic groups of the day—but soon Tyner's record sales and audiences began growing. In 1974 his new group with Sonny Fortune and Alphonse Mouzon thrilled audiences at the Berkeley, Calif., jazz festival and elsewhere. Other former group members include Eric Gravatt, Azar Lawrence, and Marvin Peterson. He stabilized his group in the early 1980s by hiring Avery Sharpe. Aaron Scot has been his drummer since the late 1980s. In the late 1980s he began leading a big band for occasional tours and recordings. He taught in the mid-1990s at Rubin academy in Israel and Stanford Univ. He won Grammy awards for his recordings *The Turning Point* and *Journey*. For a time he was a practicing Muslim (though not Nation of Islam) with the name Sulaimon Saud, but he no longer considers himself a Muslim.

Tyner's dramatic style and technical brilliance have made him one of the most influential jazz musicians of the past 40 years. In his earliest recordings he displayed an ability to get deep inside chord progressions with lyricism, subtle chromatic detail, and virtuosity. During the mid-1970s, working with producer Orrin Keepnews, Tyner recorded a series of albums that showed a constant maturation and exploration, without succumbing to the "jazz-fusion" fever of the day.

DISC.: *Inception* (1962); *Live at Newport* (1963); *McCoy Tyner Live at Newport* (1963); *Nights of Ballads and Blues* (1963); *Reaching Fourth* (1963); *Today and Tomorrow* (1963); *McCoy Tyner Plays Ellington* (1964); *Real McCoy* (1967); *Expansions* (1968); *Time for Tyner* (1968); *Extensions* (1970); *Echoes of a Friend* (1972); *Sahara* (1972); *Song of the New World* (1973); *Trident* (1975); *Fly with the Wind* (1976); *Supertrio* (1977); *Passion Dance* (1978); *Together* (1978); *4 X 4* (1980); *Double Trios* (1986); *Live at Musicians Exchange Cafe* (1987); *Live at Sweet Basil, Vols. 1 & 2* (1989); *N.Y. Reunion* (1991); *Remembering John* (1991); *Soliloquy* (1991); *Turning Point* (1991); *Infinity* (1995); *Prelude and Sonata* (1995); *What The World Needs Now: The Music of Burt Bacharach*.—**LP**

Typp, W., English singer and composer who flourished in the early 15th century. An Agnus Dei, 2 Credos, and 4 Sanctus settings by him are found among the *Old Hall Manuscripts*.—**NS/LK/DM**

Tyranny, Blue Gene (real name, **Robert Nathan Sheff**), American keyboardist and composer; b. San Antonio, Jan. 1, 1945. He studied piano and composition privately (1957–62), winning a BMI Student Composers award for his *Piano Sonata on Expanding Thoughts* (1961). He was active in the ONCE Group in Ann Arbor (1962–68), helping to establish its reputation for mixed media and cross-cultural performance; also taught keyboard and jazz composition at Mills Coll. in Oakland, Calif. (1971–81). He made numerous recordings, and performed with Laurie Anderson and Peter Gordon; collaborated on Robert Ashley's *Perfect Lives (Private Parts)* (1976–83); also wrote scores for dance, theater, film, and video. A 1975 fire destroyed about half of his early scores, many of which he is reconstructing. Tyranny is an important proponent of integrating jazz and rock elements into concert music; the range of imagination and genre evidenced by his catalog is remarkable.

WORKS: PROCEDURAL SCORES: *The Interior Distance* (1960; realized for 7 Instruments or Voices, 1990); *How to Make Music from the Sounds of Your Daily Life* (1967; realized on Tape as *Country Boy Country Dog*); *How to Do It* (1973; intentionally incomplete); *Archaeo-Acoustics (The Shining Net)* (1977); *PALS/Action at a Distance* (1977); *The Telekinesis Tape* (1977); *Taking Out the Garbage* (1977); *The Intermediary* (1981; realized for Piano, Tape, and Computer); *The More He Sings, The More He Cries, The Better He Feels...Tango* (1984; realized for Tape and Piano; orchestrated, 1985); *A Letter from Home* (1986; orig. for Voice and Electronics, 1976); *Somewhere in Arizona, 1970* (1987); *Extreme Realizations Just Before Sunset (Mobile)* (1987; realized for Tape and Piano). **OTHER:** *Music for 3 Begins* for Tapes and Audio Engineer (1958); *4 Chorales* for Keyboard and Electronic Sampling (1958); *How Things That Can't Exist May Exist*, 20-odd theater and street pieces (1958–76); *Ballad/The Road and Other Lines* for 1 to 40 Instruments or Voices (1960); *Meditation/The Reference Moves, The Form Remains*, graphic score (1962; orchestrated, 1963); *Diotima*, graphic score with Tape (1963); *Home Movie* for Film, Tape, and Rock Band (1963); *Just Walk On In*, theater work (1965); *Closed Transmission* for Tape (1966); *The Bust* for Any Kind of Band (1967); *The CBCD Transforms*, electronic codes for acoustic performance (1968–71); *Live and Let Live* for Video and Live Electronics (1972); *Remembering* for Voice and Electronics (1974); *A Letter from Home* for Voice and Electronics (1976; recomposed as procedural score, 1986); *No Job, No Warm, No Nothing*, songs with Electronics (1976); *David Kopay (Portrait)* for Instruments (1976); *Harvey Milk (Portrait)* for Tape (1978); *The White Night Riot* for Tape and Movement (1979); *The Country Boy Country Dog Concert* for Improvisors and Electronics (1980; arranged as *The Country Boy Country Dog Variations* for Soloist[s] and Orch.); *The World's Greatest Piano Player* for Electric Keyboard (1981); *The Song of the Street of the Singing Chicken* for Keyboard (1981); *A Rendition of Stardust* for Tape (1982); *Choral Ode 3* for Voice and Electronics (1987); *The Forecaster* for Orch. and Electronics (1988–89); *Nocturne with and without Memory* for 1 to 3 Pianos (1988–89); *The Great Seal (Transmigration)* for Piano Duo (1990); *My Language Is Me (Millennium)* for Voice and Electronics (1990); *Vocal Responses during Transformation* for Voices and Live Electronics (1990); songs.—**NS/LK/DM**

Tyrrell, John, distinguished English musicologist and lexicographer; b. Salisbury, Southern Rhodesia, Aug. 17, 1942. He was educated at the univs. of Cape Town (1960–63; B.Mus., 1963), Oxford (1964–68; Ph.D., 1969, with the diss. *Janáček's Stylistic Development as an Operatic Composer as Evidenced in his Revisions of the First Five Operas*), and Brno (1966–67). He taught at the univs. of Cape Town (1969), Stellenbosch (1970), and Brimingham (1975–76), and was assoc. ed. of *The Musical Times* (1972–76) and a member of the editorial staff of *The New Grove Dictionary of Music and Musicians* (1973–76). He was a lecturer (1976–89), reader in opera studies (1989–95), and prof. of music (1995–97) at the Univ. of Nottingham. From 1992 to 1994 he also was a British Academy research reader in the humanities. In 1996 he became deputy ed. and in 1997 executive ed. of the rev. edition of *The New Grove Dictionary of Music and Musicians* (2000). Tyrrell is the leading authority on the life and music of Janáček, and has made invaluable contributions to the study of that Czech master.

WRITINGS: With R. Wise, *A Guide to International Congress Reports in Music 1900–1975* (London, 1979); *Leoš Janáček: Kát'a Kabanová* (Cambridge, 1982); *Czech Opera* (Cambridge, 1988); *Janáček's Operas: A Documentary Account* (London, 1992); ed. and tr. *Intimate Letters: Leoš Janáček to Kamila Stösslová* (London, 1994); with N. Simeone and A. Němcová, *Janáček's Works: A Catalogue of the Music and Writings of Leoš Janáček* (Oxford, 1997); ed. and tr. *Zdenka Janáčková: My Life with Janáček* (London, 1998). —**LK/DM**

Tyrwhitt-Wilson, Sir Gerald Hugh, Baronet
See **Berners, Lord**

Tyson, Alan (Walker), esteemed Scottish musicologist; b. Glasgow, Oct. 27, 1926. He was educated at Magdalen Coll., Oxford, where he studied litterae humaniores (1947–51); in 1952 he was elected a fellow of All Souls Coll., Oxford; later pursued training in psychoanalysis and medicine (qualified, 1965). In 1971 he became a senior research fellow at All Souls Coll., a position he retained until 1994. He also was a visiting prof. of music at Columbia Univ. (1969), the Lyell Reader in Bibliography at the Univ. of Oxford (1973–74), the Ernest Bloch Prof. of Music at the Univ. of Calif., Berkeley (1977–78), a member of the Inst. for Advanced

Study at Princeton Univ. (1983–84), and a visiting prof. at the Graduate Center of the City Univ. of N.Y. (1985). In 1989 he was made a Commander of the Order of the British Empire. In 1991 he was made a corresponding member of the American Musicological Soc. He has made extensive textual and bibliographical studies of the period 1770–1850; particularly noteworthy are his contributions to the study of Beethoven.

WRITINGS: *The Authentic English Editions of Beethoven* (London, 1963); with O. Neighbour, *English Music Publishers' Plate Numbers in the First Half of the Nineteenth Century* (London, 1965); *Thematic Catalogue of the Works of Muzio Clementi* (Tutzing, 1967); ed., *Beethoven Studies* (N.Y., 1974), *Beethoven Studies 2* (London, 1977), *Beethoven Studies 3* (London, 1982); *Mozart: Studies of the Autograph Scores* (Cambridge, Mass., 1987); ed. with A. Rosenthal, *Mozart's Thematic Catalogue: A Facsimile* (1990); *Watermarks in Mozart's Autographs* in the *Neue Mozart-Ausgabe* (X/33/Abteilung, 2, 1992).

BIBL.: S. Brandenburg, ed., *Haydn, Mozart, and Beethoven: Studies in the Music of the Classical Period: Essays in Honour of A. T.* (Oxford, 1995).**—NS/LK/DM**

Tzipine, Georges, French conductor; b. Paris, June 22, 1907; d. there, Dec. 8, 1987. He studied violin at the Paris Cons., winning a premier prix. He made his debut as a violinist with the Paris Radio (1926), then pursued training in harmony, counterpoint, and conducting. In 1931 he began his career as a conductor with the Paris Radio; after further studies with Marc de Rance and Reynaldo Hahn, he appeared as a guest conductor with various Paris orchs. and toured France as a ballet conductor. He was music director of the Cannes Casino (1945–49); then toured Europe and North and South America as a guest conductor. After serving as music director of the Melbourne Sym. Orch. (1961–65), he taught conducting at the Paris Cons. (from 1966).**—NS/LK/DM**

U

U2, Irish rock band, called everything from "pompous and self-righteous social crusaders" to "sincere and involved political activists," formed Dublin, Ireland, 1976. **Membership:** Bono (actually Bono Vox; originally Paul Hewson), voc. (b. Dublin, May 10, 1960); Adam Clayton, bs. (b. Dublin, March 13, 1960); The Edge (originally David Evans), gtr. (b. Wales, Aug. 8, 1961); Larry Mullen Jr., drms. (b. Oct. 31, 1961). Dick "Dik" Evans, gtr., left the group in 1976.

U2 started off humbly enough as a Dublin, Ireland, school boy band formed in response to an ad placed on the Mount Temple H.S. notice board by Larry Mullen Jr. in 1976. Of the several students who came to his house to audition for the rock band, Mullen noted that, although some could play, technical merit wasn't the decisive factor. Mullen told Jay Cocks of *Time* that the original band consisted of one fellow who "meant to play the guitar, but he couldn't play very well, so he started to sing. He couldn't do that either. But, he was such a charismatic character that he was in the band as soon as he arrived." That fellow was Paul Hewson, who later adopted the name Bono Vox (Latin for "good voice," which Hewson appropriated from a billboard advertisement for a hearing aid retailer). David "The Edge" Evans, a guitarist who *could* play; Adam Clayton, a bassist who "just looked great and used all the right words, like gig"; Larry Mullen Jr. on drums; and second guitarist Dick (Dik) Evans, The Edge's older brother, made up the rest of the band.

U2 began their musical odyssey as Feedback. After playing mainly cover tunes for a few shows in small local venues, Dik Evans left the band to form The Virgin Prunes, and the band changed its name to the Hype. Clayton, acting as band manager, sought advice from all the music industry sources he knew, including Steve Rapid, a singer for the local band The Radiators, who suggested that they change their name. Clayton wanted something ambiguous; Rapid suggested U2 because there was a U2 spy plane, a U2 submarine, a U2 battery made by Eveready, as well as the obvious "you, too" and "you two." The remaining members were skeptical at first but eventually accepted it.

In March of 1978, U2 entered a talent competition sponsored by Guinness at the Limerick Civic Week. They won a cash prize and the opportunity to audition for CBS Ireland, after which they secured supporting spots on tours with The Stranglers and The Greedy Bastards. In September, they recorded additional demos at Dublin's Windmill Lane Studios with Chas de Whalley, which subsequently lead to their signing by CBS Ireland. After building a considerable following in Ireland, they released their first EP, *U2:3,* which featured the tracks "Out of Control," "Stories," and "Boy-Girl." It was available only in Ireland, where it topped the charts. It was in December of the next year that U2 played their first U.K. dates—to a cool reception. They were even mis-billed as "V2" at the Hope & Anchor pub in London, where a mere nine people showed up to see them perform.

Although they played to sold-out shows in their homeland, U2 had yet to conquer the U.K. charts. In February of 1980, "Another Day" hit #1 in Ireland and the band took another try at playing the U.K. This time around the reception was better and talent recruiter Bill Stewart signed them to U.K.'s Island Records (although they remained on CBS in Ireland). In May, their debut Island single, "11 o'Clock Tick Tock," was released but it failed to break into the U.K. charts. The band embarked on another U.K. tour and appeared at the Dalmount Festival in Dublin with The Police and Squeeze. Their debut album, *Boy,* was preceded by the singles "A Day without Me" and "I Will Follow," both of which failed to chart in either the U.K. or the U.S. However, in conjunction with the release of *Boy,* U2 was given the opportunity to embark on their first U.S. campaign: a three-week club tour of the East Coast. When they returned to the U.K. in December, they supported The Talking Heads on a U.K. tour.

In 1981, U2 embarked on their first major U.S. tour, pushing *Boy* onto the U.S. charts. In July, U2 finally broke into the U.K. charts at #35 with "Fire," which was then followed by *Boy,* belatedly breaking in at #52. By the end of the year, after an 18-date U.K. tour and the release of the album *October,* U2 readied themselves for a new series of U.S. dates. By mid- 1982, after playing to an Irish audience for the first time in over a year and to sold-out crowds in the U.K., U2 retired to the studio to record new music. It was that October, during a concert in Belfast, that they introduced "Sunday, Bloody Sunday" to their fans. That song carried a message of peace in Northern Ireland that would later become the focal point of the band, seemingly fusing their lyrics and politics. In February of 1983, the band that had played to only nine people in a London pub just four years earlier, opened a sold-out, 27-date U.K. tour with the single "New Year's Day." The song topped the U.K. charts at #10, and their album *War* reached #12 in the U.S. By March, their album took the #1 spot on the U.K. charts. It looked as though U2 had finally arrived. The band spent the next few months touring arenas in the U.S., including participating in the three-day US Festival in San Bernardino, Calif. In November, as a bid to meet the growing demand for new work, U2 released *Under a Blood Red Sky,* their first live album. It became the most successful live album of the time, but it didn't end the circulation of bootleg U2 recordings, which was rampant.

Their next studio album, 1984's *The Unforgettable Fire,* reached #1 in the U.K. Later that year, the band's humanitarian side resurfaced when they participated in the Band Aid recording of "Do They Know It's Christmas?" for Ethiopian famine relief, with Bono contributing a lead vocal and Clayton playing bass. 1985 found the band headlining at Madison Square Garden; *Rolling Stone* touted them as "The Band of the Eighties." Once again giving in to their charitable tendencies, U2 performed at Live Aid in July, and in November, Bono appeared in the Little Steven–organized Artists Against Apartheid single and video "Sun City." U2 also released a U.S. EP, *Wide Awake in America.* In 1986 they resumed their world touring, which included performing on Amnesty International's 25th anniversary tour with artists like Peter Gabriel and Sting. Also lending a hand at home, U2 helped to raise funds for the unemployed in Ireland by playing Self Aid with other Irish rock acts.

Although it seemed that U2 were the social crusaders of their generation, Bono assured *Time*'s Cocks that he "would hate to think everybody was into U2 for 'deep' and 'meaningful' reasons. We're a noisy rock 'n' roll band. If we got on stage, and instead of going 'Yeow!' the audience all went 'Ummmm' or started saying the rosary, it would be awful." Regardless of how Bono saw it, the band's social consciousness is one of the main reasons, according to Christopher Connelly of *Rolling Stone,* U2 "has become one of the handful of artists in rock (and) roll history...that people are eager to identify themselves with."

In 1987 U2 embarked on a 110-date world tour. Their new album, *The Joshua Tree,* entering the U.K. charts at #1 and the album went platinum in 48 hours, making it, at the time, the fastest-selling album in U.K. history. In mid-April, *The Joshua Tree* reached the top of the U.S. charts where it remained for nine weeks. Shortly thereafter, the band appeared on the cover of *Time* with the headline: "U2: Rock's Hottest Ticket" and everyone seemed to want a piece of them. The Edge released a soundtrack for the political kidnapping film *Captive.* Favorably reviewed, the soundtrack will always be remembered for featuring the album debut of yet another Irish act, Sinead O'Connor, who sings "Heroine (Theme from Captive)." In November, Eamon Dunphy's book *Unforgettable Fire: The Story of U2* was released. It became a bestseller in the U.K. although the band retracted their support of the volume after they could not get parts of the text changed that they maintained were inaccurate. They received the MTV viewer's choice award for the video of "With or Without You," and in December, contributed "Christmas (Baby Please Come Home)" to noted producer Jimmy Iovine's charity album *Special Christmas.*

In 1988 U2 received the award for best international group at the British Record Industry Awards, which was followed by their first Grammy awards—for best rock performance by a group and album of the year for *The Joshua Tree.* That same year, the Iovine-produced double album *Rattle and Hum,* featuring live recordings from the previous two years as well as studio tracks, was released and topped the charts in both the U.S. and the U.K. U2 also released the live documentary film *Rattle and Hum,* directed by Philip Joanou. As if these achievements hadn't raised their profile high enough, the band also appeared on the live television show *Smile Jamaica* for Jamaican Hurricane relief, where they were joined onstage by Keith Richards and Ziggy Marley.

The year 1989 brought the group the British Record Industry Award for best international group for the second year in a row. Grammy awards for best rock performance for "Desire," best performance music video for "Where the Streets Have No Name," and an MTV Music Video award for their collaboration with B. B. King on "When Love Comes to Town," followed. The rest of the year, the band spent working tirelessly, touring Australia, New Zealand, Japan, and then finally returning home to Dublin, where the tour culminated with a New Year's Eve show that was broadcast live on the radio. The BBC and RTE, which collaborated to transmit the show throughout Europe and the former U.S.S.R., estimated the listening audience at more than 500 million.

Although they had not released an album since 1988, U2 discovered new diversions in 1990. In February, the Royal Shakespeare Co. produced *A Clockwork Orange 2004,* which featured music by The Edge. In June, drummer Mullen wrote the official Eire World Cup Soccer team's song. But as always, busy as they were, U2 found time for good works. This time they contributed to an anthology of Cole Porter songs that was released as *Red Hot + Blue* and benefitted AIDS education. They also traveled to Berlin to film a video featured in a TV special airing on International AIDS Day.

In November of 1991, U2's next, long-awaited album finally surfaced—but without the media blitz that seemed to accompany all the other year-end major releases. U2 had decided that the album would sell itself to their fans just fine without the fanfare. They were right, as initial shipments of *Achtung Baby* totalled upwards of 1.4 million units. They were also the first major act to request that their CD be distributed in the shrink-wrapped jewel box only, or the non-disposable DigiTrak (longbox size) packaging, which folds into a jewel box-sized case.

In February of the next year, U2 began their "Zoo TV" tour. They took the radio transmission concept inaugurated on New Year's Eve 1989 one step further by incorporating a satellite dish into the show. A short European tour followed, during which a contest winner had the show beamed live by satellite to his home in Nottinghamshire from Stockholm, courtesy of MTV. The tour concluded with a Greenpeace concert in Manchester to protest a second nuclear processing plant being opened at Sellafield in Cumbria. In spite of (but not in breach of) a court injunction preventing a protest at the plant, U2 participated in a "by sea on the beach" protest with Greenpeace, during which they delivered barrels of contaminated sand from the beaches of England, Ireland, Scotland, and Wales back to the plant. In August, they went back on the tour circuit, taking "Zoo TV" to the stadiums of the U.S. with their outside broadcast tour. When the tour ended in mid-November in Mexico City, U2 had played to an estimated 2.5 million people.

During a break in the "Zoo TV" tour, U2 took the time to record an EP. That EP eventually became the ten-song *Zooropa* album, winner of the 1993 Grammy Award for alternative album of the year. For the first time in his career, The Edge took on producing duties with Flood and Brian Eno, as well as doing a lead vocal on the album's first single, "Numb." On May 9th the "Zoo TV" tour, which had since mutated into the "Zooropa '93" tour, started an ambitious schedule of visiting 18 countries in four months. Closing the trip back in Dublin on Aug. 28th, the boys were glad that they were finally home.

When asked what they're all about, Bassist Adam Clayton explained it best in an interview with Robert Hilburn of the *Los Angeles Times* when he said, "I feel we made a decision then (going into the 1990s) that if we are going to be the righteous men of rock 'n' roll, we are going to be very miserable. I think we realized that issues are more complicated than we once thought, and we don't want to be continually earnest about what we do. We are not a religious cult...we are not a political theory. We are a rock 'n' roll band."

DISC.: *U2:3* (EP; 1979); *Boy* (1980); *October* (1981); *War* (1983); *Under a Blood Red Sky* (live; 1983); *Unforgettable Fire* (1984); *Wide Awake in America* (EP; 1985); *The Joshua Tree* (1987); *Rattle and Hum* (1988); *Achtung Baby* (1991); *Zooropa* (1993); *Pop* (1997); *The Best of 1980–1990* (1998); *All That You Can't Leave Behind* (2000).

BIBL.: Eamon Dunphy, *Unforgettable Fire: The Story of U2* (1987); Sam Goodman, *U2: Burning Desire: The Complete U2 Story* (1993); Bill Graham, *The Complete Guide to the Music of U2* (1995); Bill Flanagan, *U2 at the End of the World* (1996); Alan Carter, *U2: The Road to Pop* (1997); Niall Stokes, *Into the Heart: The Stories behind Every U2 Song* (1998); Susan Black and Dave Thompson, *Bono: In His Own Words* (1998); Dianne Ebertt Beeaff and Michelle Perez, *A Grand Madness: Ten Years on the Road with U2* (1999).

UB40, one of the most successful reggae bands ever. **MEMBERSHIP:** Ali Campbell, voc., gtr. (b. Birmingham, England, Feb. 15, 1959); Robin Campbell, gtr. (b. Birmingham, England, Dec. 25, 1954); Earl Falconer, bs. (b. Birmingham, England, Jan. 23, 1957); Mickey Virtue, kybd. (b. Birmingham, England, Jan. 19, 1957); Brian Travers, sax. (b. Birmingham, England, Feb. 7, 1959); Jim Brown, drm. (b. Nov. 21, 1957); Norman Hassan, perc. (b. Birmingham, England, Jan. 26, 1958); Astro (real name, Terence Wilson), "toastemaster," (b. Birmingham, England, June 24, 1957).

The product of England's industrial melting pot, UB40 were a multiracial band like the two-tone ska bands that were peaking in popularity at the time. There were several crucial differences, though. Rather than playing the hyped-up ska that the two-tone bands favored, UB40 opted for a slower, more contemporary rock-steady sound. They also tended, at least in their early years, to take a far more political stance than the ska revivalists did. For them, "Stand Down Margaret" was a starting point for some ferocious anti-Thatcher music.

Legend has it, the members of UB40 met on the unemployment line; their name derives from the form used to get jobless benefits in England. The core of the band, Robin and Ali Campbell came from a musical family (their parents are Ian and Lorna Campbell, notables in the British folk scene). They bought instruments with money Ali received in the settlement of a bar brawl. Most of them had just a marginal idea of how to play. They spent six months in a basement, learning to play songs by artists like Gregory Isaacs. By February 1979, they began playing out. A demo tape started getting played on the radio and BBC deejay John Peel liked it enough that he brought them in for one of his infamous Radio One sessions. Chrissie Hynde brought them aboard as the opening act for the Pretender's first tour of the U.K.

With all this exposure, the group signed a "one of" deal with independent Graduate Records, releasing the single "Food for Thought," decrying third world poverty. The B-side, "King," a tribute to slain American civil rights leader Martin Luther King Jr., was a long-time favorite with live audiences. The single rose to #4 on the U.K. charts. Their debut album, *Signing Off*, featured several other singles as well. The album package looked like the form from which the band took their name, with the title rubber-stamped on it. The band announced, with their musical success, that they could sign off the dole.

Despite the hit record, they didn't get rich. As radical thinkers, they decided to control the means of production and formed their own DEP International Records for the release of their next album, *Present Arms*. The album included one of the finest pieces of political pop ever recorded, the single "One in Ten," the title referring to England's prevailing 10 percent unemployment rate at the time. It went to the English Top Ten. The band then took a cue from Jamaican artists, who nearly always released vocal-less versions of records remixed with lots of echo and effects. Called "dub" records, they took the music to a different place. A dub version of *Present Arms* also sold extremely well, the first dub record to make the U.K. charts.

The packaging on their third album, *UB44*, was also distinctive. It was one of the first albums to use a hologram on the cover. However, the technology at the time was so primitive that many couldn't read it, so after the limited first pressing of the album, they gave it a more conventional cover.

The band really broke out with its fourth album, a project members had been itching to do since they came together. Called *Labour of Love*, it covered some of their favorite reggae singles, including a Jamaican hit by an artist named Tony Tribe. Although the band didn't realize that it was a Neil Diamond cover, the song "Red, Red Wine" rose to the top of the U.K. charts, and hit #34 in the U.S. This catapulted the album to #39 in the U.S. as well. They had a string of other English hits from the album, including versions of Jimmy Cliff's "Many Rivers to Cross" and "Please Don't Make Me Cry." When their follow-up album, *Geffrey Morgan*, came out, the single "If It Happens Again" entered the U.K. charts at #9.

Their next album, *Baggariddim*, marked several collaborations. They reunited with Chrissie Hynde. She and Ali Campbell took a reggaefied version of Sonny and Cher's "I Got You Babe" to the top of the U.K. charts, hitting #28 in the U.S. The album hit #40 in the U.S. Many of the tracks also featured the work of reggae DJs for England. The tune "Don't Break My Heart" hit #3 in the U.K. as well. They followed this with the *Rat in the Kitchen* album, which spawned the #5 U.K. hit "Sing Our Own Song," featuring a trumpet solo by the head of their American record company, Herb Alpert. The tour for the album included dates in the USSR.

Their eponymous 1988 album featured another duet with Chrissie Hynde on the song "Breakfast in Bed." The year-long tour that followed the release included the Nelson Mandela Homecoming show, broadcast around the world. Their version of "Red Red Wine" at the show sparked new interest in the record in the U.S., where a new version with a toast by Astro reached #1 and went gold. This sent the original *Labour of Love* album to #14 and platinum, just in time for the second edition, *Labour of Love II*, to come out. A duet with Robert Palmer on Bob Dylan's "I'll Be Your Baby Tonight" did well in the U.K., as did a cover of the Chi Lights "Homely Girl," which rose to #6. A version of the Temptations' "The Way You Do the Things You Do" went gold and rose to #6 in the U.S., and a cover of Al Green's "Here I Am (Come and Take Me)" hit #7, propelling the album to 30 and platinum in the States.

Following a period of road work and rest, UB40 released *Promises and Lies*. A cover of Elvis's "I Can't Help Falling in Love with You," featured in the Sharon Stone film *Sliver*, topped both the U.K. and U.S. charts, going platinum after seven weeks at #1. The album hit #1 in the U.K., rising to #6 and platinum in the U.S. However, the group became embroiled in a lawsuit claiming that a young woman named Debbie Banks had actually written the lyrics to "Don't Break My Heart." She won the suit, earning considerable back royalties. In the meantime, the band only cut the instrumental backing to a children's record featuring Denzel Washington telling folk tales, *Anansi the Spider*.

The group came back with *Guns in the Ghetto*, which spawned a couple of minor hits, including "Tell Me Is It True," featured on the soundtrack to the film *Speed II*. They furthered their commitment to the state of the art in Jamaican music with *The Dancehall Album*, a recording that featured a variety of Jamaican toasters, including Beenie Man, Mad Cobra, and Lady Saw. They followed this with a successful third edition of *Labour of Love*. After nearly a quarter century, the group remained on top of their game.

Disc.: *Signing Off* (1980); *Present Arms* (1981); *Present Arms in Dub* (1981); *UB44* (1982); *Labour of Love* (1983); *Live* (1983); *Geffery Morgan* (1984); *Little Baggariddim* (1985); *Baggariddim* (1985); *Rat in the Kitchen* (1986); *UB40 CCCP: Live in Moscow* (1987); *UB40* (1988); *Labour of Love II* (1989); *Promises and Lies* (1993); *Anansi* (1995); *Guns in the Ghetto* (1997); *Presents the Dancehall Album* (1998); *Labour of Love III* (1998).—**BH**

Uber, family of German musicians:

(1) Christian Benjamin Uber, lawyer, glass-harmonica player, and composer; b. Breslau, Sept. 20, 1746; d. there, 1812. He was educated in Halle and Breslau, becoming a civil servant in the latter city in 1772; although an amateur musician, he excelled as a performer on the glass harmonica at concerts he gave in his own home. He wrote a comic opera, *Clarissa oder Das unbekannte Dienstmädchen* (1772), two cantatas and other vocal pieces, and much chamber music. He had two sons who became professional musicians:

(2) Christian Friedrich Hermann Uber, violinist, conductor, and composer; b. Breslau, April 22, 1781; d. Dresden, March 2, 1822. After training with his father, he engaged in law studies in Halle; receiving encouragement from D.G. Türk, he decided to pursue a career in music. In 1804 he accompanied Prince Radziwill to Berlin, where he entered the service of Prince Louis Ferdinand; then was a violinist in Braunschweig. He was director of the Kassel Opera (1808–14); after conducting in Mainz (1814–16), he went to Dresden as director of the Seconda company; after a sojourn in Leipzig as a teacher, lecturer, and writer on music, he returned to Dresden in 1818 to serve as Kantor at the Kreuzschule and music director of the Kreuzkirche. He composed two operas, *Der frohe Tag* (Mainz, 1815) and *Les Marins*, a melodrama, *Der Taucher*, an intermezzo, *Der falsche Werber* (Kassel, 1808), and incidental music to plays; also the oratorio *Die letzten Worte des Erlösers* (1822), some cantatas, violin concertos, and songs.

(3) Alexander Uber, cellist and composer; b. Breslau, 1783; d. Carolath, Silesia, 1824. He received initial training from his father in Breslau, where he later studied violin with J. Janetzek, cello with J. Jäger, and theory with J.I. Schnabel; following tours as a virtuoso, he settled as Kapellmeister to the Prince of Schönaich-Carolath. He wrote several overtures, a Cello Concerto,

(2) *Air varié* for Flute and Orch., Variations for Cello and Orch., 16 Variations for Cello and Orch., choruses and other vocal pieces, and various chamber works. —**NS/LK/DM**

Uberti (real name, **Hubert**), **Antonio,** celebrated Italian castrato soprano, known as "Il Porporino," after his teacher Porpora; b. Verona (of German parents), 1697; d. Berlin, Jan. 20, 1783. He was Porpora's favorite pupil. In 1741 he entered the service of Friedrich II the Great in Berlin. He was greatly renowned in Germany for his singing of Italian operas. He was the teacher of Gertrud Mara.—**NS/LK/DM**

Uccellini, Marco, significant Italian composer; b. c. 1603; d. Forlimpopoli, near Forli, Sept. 10, 1680. He was educated in Assisi, then went to Modena, where he became head of instrumental music at the Este court in 1641 and maestro di cappella at the Cathedral in 1647; subsequently was maestro di cappella at the Farnese court in Parma (1665–80). Most of his works for the stage are not extant, but his concertos are preserved and give evidence of excellent knowledge of technique in writing for the violin and other string instruments.

Works: Dramatic: Opera: *Gli eventi di Filandro ad Edessa* (Parma, 1675). **Ballet:** *Le navi d'Enea* (Parma, 1673); *Il Giove d'Elide fulminato* (Parma, 1677). **Other** (all publ. in Venice unless otherwise given): *Sonate, sinfonie et correnti, a 2–4,* with Basso Continuo, *libro II* (1639); *Sonate, arie et correnti, a 2, 3,* with Basso Continuo (1642); *Sonate, correnti et arie, a 1–3,* with Basso Continuo, op.4 (1645; 2 sonatas, 3 correnti, and 3 arias ed. by L. Torchi in *L'arte musicale in Italia,* VII, Milan, 1907); *Sonate, over canzoni* for Violin and Basso Continuo, op.5 (1649); *Salmi* for 1 and 3 to 5 Voices and Basso Continuo, *concertante parte con instrumenti e parte senza, con Letanie della beata virgine* for 5 Voices and Basso Continuo, op.6 (1654); *Ozio regio: Compositioni armoniche sopra il violino e diversi altri strumenti* for 1 to 6 Voices and Basso Continuo, *libro VII* (abr. ed., 1660; not extant; 2nd ed. as *Sonate sopra il violini,* Antwerp, 1668); *Sinfonici concerti brevi e facili, a 1–4,* op.9 (1667); *Sinfonie boscareccie* for Violin, Basso Continuo, and 2 Violins ad libitum, op.8 (Antwerp, 1669).—**NS/LK/DM**

Uchida, Mitsuko, talented Japanese pianist; b. Tokyo, Dec. 20, 1948. She began training in childhood in her native city, and at the age of 12 became a pupil of Richard Hauser at the Vienna Academy of Music. In 1968 she won the Beethoven Competition, and in 1970 received 2nd prize at the Chopin Competition in Warsaw. In 1982 she won particular notice in London and Tokyo for her performances of the complete piano sonatas of Mozart. During the 1985–86 season, she appeared as soloist-conductor in all the piano concertos of Mozart with the English Chamber Orch. in London. On Feb. 15, 1987, she made her N.Y. recital debut. In 1989 she was soloist in Mozart's Piano Concerto, K.271, in Salzburg. In subsequent years, she toured all over the world, appearing as a soloist with leading orchs. and as a recitalist. Her repertoire includes, in addition to the classics, works by Debussy, Schoenberg, and Bartók. —**NS/LK/DM**

Udbye, Martin Andreas, distinguished Norwegian organist and composer; b. Trondheim, June 18, 1820; d. there, Jan. 10, 1889. He studied organ with Carl Becker and composition with Hauptmann at the Leipzig Cons. (1851–52); pursued further studies in Berlin, Leipzig, Dresden, Vienna, and London (1858–59). From 1844 to 1869 he served as organist at the Hospitalskirken in Trondheim, and after 1869 was organist at the church of Our Lady there. He was regarded as one of the finest Norwegian composers of his era; he wrote the first Norwegian opera, *Fredkulla* (The Peacemaker; 1858). His other works include the operettas *Hr. Perrichons reise* (1861), *Hjemve* (Homesickness; 1862; Christiania, April 8, 1864), and *Junkeren og flubergrosen* (The Squire and the Rose of Fluberg; 1867; Christiania, Jan. 7, 1872), the orch. sketch *Lumpasivag-abundus* (1861), Fantasy for Violin and Orch. (1866), the cantatas *Sonatorrek* (The Loss of a Son; 1872) and *Islaendinger i Norge* (1873), choral pieces, three string quartets (1851–55), 20 piano trios, and 100 organ preludes.—**NS/LK/DM**

Ugalde, Delphine (née **Beaucé**), French soprano; b. Paris, Dec. 3, 1829; d. there, July 19, 1910. She received her first instruction in singing from her mother, an actress, then subsequently studied with Moreau-Sainti, making her debut in Paris in 1848 as Angèle in Auber's *Domino noir*. In 1866 she assumed the management of the Bouffes-Parisiens, taking leading roles in Offenbach's operettas; in 1867 she appeared in her own operetta, *La Halte au moulin*. She retired in 1871, and became a successful vocal teacher.—**NS/LK/DM**

Ugarte, Floro M(anuel), Argentine composer and teacher; b. Buenos Aires, Sept. 15, 1884; d. there, June 11, 1975. He studied in Buenos Aires, and at the Paris Cons. under Pessard, Lavignac, and Fourdrain, with whom he collaborated in writing the ballet *Sigolene*. He returned to Argentina in 1913, and in 1924 became a prof. at the National Cons. in Buenos Aires. He was general director of the Teatro Colón, founder-president of the National Music Soc., prof. at the Escuela Superior de Bellas Artes at La Plata Univ., and director of the Buenos Aires Municipal Cons.

Works: Dramatic: Operatic Fairy Tale: *Saika* (1918; Buenos Aires, July 21, 1920). **Orch.:** *Entre las montanas,* symphonic suite (1922); *De mi tierra,* 2 symphonic suites (1923, 1934); *La rebelión del agua,* symphonic poem (1931; Buenos Aires, Oct. 16, 1935); *Piri,* choreographic poem (1944); Sym. (1946; Buenos Aires, May 13, 1952); *Vidala* (1948); *Preludio* (1949); *Tango* (Buenos Aires, Sept. 5, 1951); Violin Concerto (1963). **Chamber:** Piano Quartet (1921); Sonata for Violin or Cello and Piano (1928); String Quartet (1935); piano pieces. **Vocal:** Songs.—**NS/LK/DM**

Ughi, Uto, talented Italian violinist; b. Busto Arsizio, near Milan, Jan. 21, 1944. A child prodigy, he commenced musical training when he was four and made his formal debut at seven in a recital at Milan's Teatro Lirico; pursued studies at the Conservatorio di Santa Cecilia in Rome, and also received lessons from Enesco (1954). In 1959 he made an extensive tour of Europe; after performing in Australia (1963), he made his U.S. debut in N.Y. on Feb. 27, 1967; subsequently toured worldwide. In 1977 he was made a member of the

Accademia di Santa Cecilia in Rome. In 1979 he organized the "Hommage to Venice" festival to raise funds for restoring the city's art treasures. His instrument is the "Van Houten-Kreutzer" Stradivarius, which dates from 1701. His repertoire includes, besides the classics, a wide selection of modern concertos for the violin. **—NS/LK/DM**

Ugolina da Orvieto (Ugolino di Francesco Urbevetano), Italian music theorist and composer; b. probably in Orvieto, c. 1380; d. Ferrara, 1457. He was active in the chapter at Forlì Cathedral by 1411, where he was made a canon in 1415 and archdeacon in 1425 at S. Croce, as well as rector at S. Antonio di Rivaldini. As a leading figure in the Guelph faction, he was compelled to leave Forlì in the wake of the success of the Ghibelline faction in 1430. He settled in Ferrara, where he was archpresbyter at the Cathedral from about 1437 until 1448. He wrote the treatise *Declaratio musice discipline* (modern critical ed. by A. Seay, three vols., Corpus Scriptorum Musicae, 1959–62.**—NS/LK/DM**

Ugolini, Vincenzo, Italian composer; b. Perugia, c. 1580; d. Rome, May 6, 1638. He was a pupil of G.B. Nanino from 1592 to 1594 at the choir school of S. Luigi dei Francesi, Rome, where he was a bass from 1600 and from 1603 to 1609 maestro di cappella at S. Maria Maggiore. From 1610 to 1614 he was at Benevento Cathedral. Returning to Rome, he was director of music to Cardinal Arrigoni (from 1614); from 1616 to 1620, was maestro di cappella at S. Luigi dei Francesi, and from 1620 to 1626 at the Cappella Giulia at St. Peter's. In 1631 he resumed his former post at S. Luigi dei Francesi, retaining it until his death. He was the teacher of Benevoli. A notable representative of Palestrina's school, he publ. four books of motets for one to four Voices (1616–19), one book of Psalms for eight Voices and Basso Continuo (1628), one book of Psalms and motets for two Voices and Basso Continuo (1630), two books of madrigals for five Voices (1630), etc.; also other works in contemporary collections.

BIBL.: V. Raeli, *Da V. U. ad Orazio Benevoli nella cappella della Basilica Liberiana (1603–1646)* (Rome, 1920).**—NS/LK/DM**

Uhde, Hermann, noted German bass-baritone; b. Bremen, July 20, 1914; d. during a performance in Copenhagen, Oct. 10, 1965. He studied at Philipp Kraus's opera school in Bremen, making his operatic debut there as Titurel in *Parsifal* in 1936; appeared in Freiburg im Breisgau and then sang with the Bavarian State Opera in Munich (1940–43) and with the German Opera at The Hague (1943–44). He subsequently was engaged at Hannover (1947–48), Hamburg (1948–50), Vienna (1950–51), Munich (1951–56), Stuttgart (1956–57), and again in Vienna (1957–61). He made his American debut at the Metropolitan Opera in N.Y. as Telramund in *Lohengrin* on Nov. 18, 1955, remaining on its roster until 1957, then again from 1958 to 1961 and in 1963–64. He was particularly acclaimed for his performances in Wagnerian roles.**—NS/LK/DM**

Uhl, Alfred, Austrian composer and pedagogue; b. Vienna, June 5, 1909; d. there, June 8, 1992. He studied composition with Franz Schmidt at the Vienna Academy of Music (diploma, 1932); then in 1940–41, during World War II, was in the Austrian army, where he was severely wounded. In 1943 he became a composition teacher at the Vienna Academy of Music; also served as president of the Austrian copyright society (1970–75). In 1980 he was awarded the Austrian Badge of Honor for Science and Arts. His music was patterned after Classical forms, with emphasis on contrapuntal clarity.

WORKS: DRAMATIC: *Katzenmusik*, ballet-opera (1957); *Der Mysteriöse Herr X*, opera (1962–65; Vienna, June 8, 1966). **ORCH.:** *Wiener Waltz* (1938); *Sinfonischer Marsch* (1942); *Konzertante Sinfonie* for Clarinet and Orch. (1943; Vienna, Nov. 5, 1944); *4 Capricen* (1944–45); *Introduktion und Variationen über eine Melodie aus dem 16. Jahrhundert* for Strings (1947); *Sonata graziosa* (1947); *Rondeau* (1948); Concertino for Violin and 22 Winds (1949; also for Violin and Orch., 1964); *Concerto a ballo* (1966; N.Y., Oct. 9, 1967); Sinfonietta (1978; Vienna, May 31, 1979); *3 Sketches* (1980); Concerto for 2 Oboes, 2 Horns, and Strings (Murcia, Spain, April 21, 1984). **CHAMBER:** Trio for Violin, Viola, and Guitar (1928; rev. 1981); *Kleines Konzert* for Clarinet, Viola, and Piano (1936; rev. for Violin, Cello, and Piano, 1972); *Divertimento* for 3 Clarinets and Bass Clarinet (1943); *Eine vergnugliche Musik* for 8 Winds (1944); 2 string quartets (1945–46, rev. 1969; *Jubilaumsquartett*, 1961); 15 études for Bassoon (1972); 20 études for Viola (1974); *Commedia Musicale* for Clarinet, Viola, and Piano (1982); *3 Stücke* for Flute and Guitar (1982). **VOCAL:** *Gilgamesh*, oratorio (1954–56; rev. 1967–68; Vienna, June 13, 1969); *Wer einsam ist, der hat es gut*, cantata (1960; rev. 1963; Linz, Jan. 27, 1964); *Festlicher Auftrakt* for Chorus, Organ, and Orch. (1970); choruses; songs.

BIBL.: A. Witeschnik, *A. U.: Eine biographische Studie* (Vienna, 1966).**—NS/LK/DM**

Uhl, Fritz, Austrian tenor; b. Matzleinsdorf, near Vienna, April 2, 1928. He studied at the Vienna Academy of Music (1947–52). In 1952 he made his operatic debut in Graz. In 1957 he made his first appearance at the Bayreuth Festival as Vogelsang, and continued to sing there until 1964. In 1958 he became a member of the Bavarian State Opera in Munich, where he was made a Kammersänger in 1962. From 1961 he also sang at the Vienna State Opera. He made his debut at London's Covent Garden as Walther von Stolzing in 1963. In 1968 he sang for the first time at the Salzburg Festival as Florestan, and continued to appear there until 1972. In 1981 he became a prof. at the Vienna Cons. Uhl was particularly known for his Wagnerian portrayals. **—NS/LK/DM**

Ujfalussy, József, eminent Hungarian musicologist; b. Debrecen, Feb. 13, 1920. He received training in piano and composition at the Debrecen Music School, and in the classics at the Univ. of Debrecen (Ph.D., 1944, with a diss. on Homer's epics); then studied composition with Veress, conducting with Ferencsik, musicology with Szabolcsi and Bartha, and folk music with Kodály at the Budapest Academy of Music (1946–49). He became a member (1948) and served as head of the music dept. (1951–55) of the Ministry of Culture; then was prof. of aesthetics and theory at the Budapest Academy of Music (from 1955). In 1961 he became associated with the Bartók Archives (the Inst. of Musicology from 1969) of the Hungarian Academy of Sciences; in 1973 he was made a corresponding member of the latter, where he was president of the musicological commission and director of the Inst. of Musicology (from 1973). In 1961 he received the Erkel Prize and in 1966 the Kossuth Prize.

WRITINGS: Ed. *Bartók-breviárium* (Bartók Breviary; Budapest, 1958; 2nd ed., rev., 1974; letters, writings, and documents); *Achille-Claude Debussy* (Budapest, 1959); *A valóság zenei képe* (The Musical Image of Reality; Budapest, 1962); *Bartók Béla* (Budapest, 1965; 2nd ed., enl., 1970; Eng. tr., 1971); *Az esztétika alapjai és a zene* (The Bases of Aesthetics and Music; Budapest, 1968); *Farkas Ferenc* (Budapest, 1969); ed. *A Liszt Ferenc zeneműveszeti föiskola 100 eve* (100 Years of the Franz Liszt Academy of Music; Budapest, 1977).—**NS/LK/DM**

Ujj, Béla, Hungarian composer of operettas; b. Vienna, July 2, 1873; d. there, Feb. 1, 1942. He lost his sight in childhood, but studied music and composed a number of successful operettas that were premiered in Vienna: *Der Herr Professor* (Dec. 4, 1903), *Kaisermanöver* (March 4, 1905), *Die kleine Prinzessin* (May 5, 1907), *Drei Stunden Leben* (Nov. 1, 1909), *Chanteclee* (Oct. 25, 1910), *Der Turmer von St. Stephan* (Sept. 13, 1912), *Teresita* (June 27, 1914), and *Der Müller und sein Kind* (Oct. 30, 1917). —**NS/LK/DM**

Ulanowsky, Paul, Austrian-born American pianist and teacher; b. Vienna, March 4, 1908; d. N.Y., Aug. 4, 1968. He studied theory and composition with Marx and piano with Eisenberger at the Vienna Academy of Music, taking diplomas in conducting and composition (1930). He also received private instruction in violin and viola, and took courses in musicology at the Univ. of Vienna (1926–30) with Adler, Fischer, and Ficker. After performing in Vienna, he went to the U.S. as accompanist to Enid Szantho in 1935. He decided to settle there and became a naturalized American citizen in 1943. From 1937 to 1951 he toured as accompanist to Lotte Lehmann and other celebrated artists. From 1960 he served as the pianist of the Bach Aria Group. He taught at the Berkshire Music Center in Tanglewood (summers, 1950–56) and at Boston Univ. (1951–55). In 1952–53 he was a visiting artist at the Univ. of Ill., where he became a prof. in 1960.—**NS/LK/DM**

Ulfrstad, Marius Moaritz, Norwegian composer; b. Borgund, Sept. 11, 1890; d. Oslo, Oct. 29, 1968. He studied piano and composition at the Christiania Cons. (graduated, 1910), and continued his training in Berlin, with Pizzetti in Florence, Respighi in Rome, and Ravel in Paris. He settled in Christiania, where he founded his own music school (1921). He was music critic of the *Morgenposten* (1922–40) and the *Aftenposten* (1945–47).

WORKS: DRAMATIC: Incidental music. **ORCH.:** 5 syms. (1921–44); 2 violin concertos (1923, 1935); Piano Concerto (1935); several suites, most inspired by the geography of Norway, Iceland, and Greenland (Stavern og Sorlands, Islandia, Arctic, Norvegia, Gronlandia, Svalbardia, More og Romsdal, Oslo, Norwegian Middleage, etc.). **OTHER:** Chamber music; cantatas; about 250 choral pieces; nearly 1,000 songs, including folk song arrangements.—**NS/LK/DM**

Ulfung, Ragnar (Sigurd), Norwegian tenor and opera director; b. Oslo, Feb. 28, 1927. He studied at the Oslo Cons. and in Milan. In 1949 he launched his career singing in concerts. In 1952 he made his stage debut as Magadoff in Menotti's *The Consul* in Stockholm, and then sang in Bergen and Göteborg. In 1958 he became a member of the Royal Opera in Stockholm, where he created the role of the Deaf Mute in Blomdahl's *Aniara* in 1959. In 1959 he also made his British debut as Verdi's Gustavus III with the visiting Royal Opera of Stockholm at the Edinburgh Festival, and returned with it in 1960 in the same role at London's Covent Garden. In 1963 he returned to Covent Garden as Don Carlos. He made his U.S. debut in Santa Fe in 1966, and then appeared at the San Francisco Opera in 1967. In 1969 he sang at the Hamburg State Opera. In 1971 he appeared at the Chicago Lyric Opera. He created the title role in Maxwell Davies's *Taverner* at Covent Garden in 1972, and also made his first appearance at Milan's La Scala. On Dec. 12, 1972, he made his Metropolitan Opera debut in N.Y. as Mime in *Siegfried*, and then returned there for occasional appearances in subsequent years in such roles as Mime, Loge, Herod, Berg's Captain, and Weill's Fatty. In 1973 he made his bow as an opera director with *La Bohème* in Santa Fe, and thereafter directed works there and in Stockholm and Seattle. During the 1974–76 seasons, he sang Mime in the *Ring* cycle at Covent Garden. In 1986 he appeared as Herod in San Francisco. He created the role of Jadidja in *Die schwarze Maske* at its U.S. premiere in Santa Fe in 1988. In 1989 he sang Strauss's Aegisthus in London. In 1990 he appeared as Puccini's Goro in Lyons.—**NS/LK/DM**

Ullmann, Viktor, Austrian composer, pianist, conductor, and music critic; b. Teschen, Jan. 1, 1898; d. in the concentration camp in Auschwitz, on or about Oct. 15, 1944. After initial training in Teschen, he went to Vienna in 1914, where he later was a student of Schoenberg (1918–19). From 1920 to 1927 he was an assistant to Zemlinsky at the New German Theater in Prague. In 1927–28 he served as director of the Ústí nad Labem Opera. He was active in Germany until the Nazi takeover of 1933 compelled him to return to Prague. He was associated with the Czech Radio, wrote music and book reviews, and taught privately. From 1935 to 1937 he attended A. Hába's classes in quarter tone music at the Cons. With the Nazi dismemberment of Czechoslovakia in 1939, Ullmann's life became precarious. In 1942 the Nazis deported him to the Theresienstadt ghetto. In spite of the hardships there, he played an active role in the artistic endeavors of the ghetto. He composed the opera *Der Kaiser von Atlantis* during this time, a work depicting a tyrannical monarch who outlaws death only to beg for its return in order to relieve humanity from the horrors of life. The opera reached its dress rehearsal in 1944, but when the Nazi guards realized that the monarch was a satirical characterization of Hitler, Ullmann was sent to the Auschwitz concentration camp and put to death in the gas chamber. While a number of his works have been lost, several of his surviving scores have been revived. In his early music, Ullmann was influenced by Schoenberg. His later works were classical in form with polytonal textures. His fine songs reveal the influence of Mahler.

WORKS: DRAMATIC: Opera: *Peer Gynt* (1928); *Der Sturz des Antichrist* (1935; Bielefeld, Jan. 7, 1995); *Der zerbrochene Krug* (1941); *Der Kaiser von Atlantis oder der Tod dankt ab* (1943; Amsterdam, Dec. 16, 1975). **ORCH.:** *Variations and Double Fugue on a Theme of Arnold Schoenberg* (1929–34; based on the piano piece, 1925–29); Piano Concerto (1939); *Slavonic Rhapsody* for Alto Saxophone and Orch. (1940); 2 syms.: No. 1, *Vom meiner Jugen* (1943; partial reconstruction by B. Wulff; Philadelphia, Jan. 26, 1995) and No. 2 (1944; partial reconstruction by B. Wulff; Stuttgart, Oct. 18, 1989); *Don Quixote tanzt Fandango*, overture (1944; partial reconstruction by B. Wulff; Lucerne, Sept. 2, 1995). **CHAMBER:** 3 string quartets (n.d., n.d., 1943); Octet for Piano, Winds, and Strings; Sonata for Quarter Tone Clarinet and Piano; Violin Sonata. **Piano:** *Variations and Double Fugue on a Theme of Arnold Schoenberg* (1925–29; also for Orch., 1929–34); 7 sonatas (1936; 1938–39; 1940; 1941; n.d.; n.d.; 1944). **VOCAL:** *Sechs Lieder nach Gedichten von Albert Steffen* for Soprano and Piano (1937); *Fünf Liebeslieder von Ricarda Huch* for Soprano and Piano (1938–39); *Drei Sonette aus dem Portugiesischen* by Elizabeth Barrett Browning for Voice and Piano (1939–40); *Geistliche Lieder* for High Voice and Piano (1940); *Liederbuch des Hafis* for Bass and Piano (1940); *Six Sonnets de Louize Labé* for Voice and Piano (1941); *Die Weise von Liebe und Tod des Cornets Christoph Rilke* for Speaker and Orch. (1944; partial reconstruction by H. Brauel; Prague, May 27, 1995).

BIBL.: H.-G. Klein, ed., *V. U., Materialien* (Hamburg, 1992); idem, ed., *"...es wird der Tod zum Dichter: " Die Referate des Kolloquiums zur Oper "Der Kaiser von Atlantis" von V. U. in Berlin am 4./5.11.1995* (Hamburg, 1997).—**NS/LK/DM**

Um Kalthoum (actually, **Fatma el-Zahraa Ibrahim**), Egyptian singer; b. Tamay az-Zahirah, 1898; d. Cairo, Feb. 3, 1975. During a career of more than 50 years, she was one of the most famous singers in the Arab world, being particularly renowned for her renditions of nationalistic, religious, and sentimental songs, which resulted in her being dubbed the "Star of the East" and the "Nightingale of the Nile." Her death precipitated widespread mourning in Egypt and other Arab countries.—**NS/LK/DM**

Umlauf, Carl Ignaz Franz, noted Austrian zither player, teacher, and composer; b. Baden, near Vienna, Sept. 19, 1824; d. Vienna, Feb. 25, 1902. He studied violin with Jansa and theory with Sechter, then made regular tours of Europe as a virtuoso (from 1844). He held the title of Hofmusikus at the Austrian court. With the zither manufacturer Anton Kiendl, he developed the Viennese zither. He publ. the standard method, *Neue vollständige theoretisch-praktische Zitherschule* (Vienna, 1859), and also brought out *Salon-Album für Zitherspieler* (18 vols.), which includes his own works and transcriptions.—**NS/LK/DM**

Umlauf, Ignaz, Austrian violist, conductor, and composer, father of **Michael Umlauf;** b. Vienna, 1746; d. Meidling, near Vienna, June 8, 1796. By 1772 he was 4th violist in the Vienna court orch., and by 1775 he was principal violist in the German Theater orch. there, where he was made Kapellmeister in 1778. By 1782 he was deputy court Kapellmeister under Salieri. He was a highly popular composer of Singspiels. He inaugurated the season of the German Singspiels at the Burg Theater (Feb. 17, 1778) with his piece *Die Bergknappen* (ed. by R. Haas in Denkmäler der Tonkunst in Österreich, XXXVI, Jg. XVIII/1, 1911). His other Singspiels, all first performed in Vienna, were *Die Insul der Liebe* (1772?), *Die Apotheke* (June 20, 1778), *Die schöne Schusterin oder Die pücefarbenen Schuhe* (June 22, 1779), *Das Irrlicht oder Endlich fand er sie* (Jan. 17, 1782), *Welche ist die beste Nation?* (Dec. 13, 1782), *Die glücklichen Jäger* (Feb. 17, 1786), and *Der Ring der Liebe oder Zemirens und Azors Ehestand* (Dec. 3, 1786). "Zu Steffan sprach im Traume," an aria from *Das Irrlicht*, enjoyed great popularity; Eberl wrote a set of variations on it that was misattributed to Mozart. He also wrote a Piano Concerto, a Concerto for two Pianos, some chamber music, and sacred vocal pieces.—**NS/LK/DM**

Umlauf, Michael, Austrian violinist, conductor, and composer, son of **Ignaz Umlauf;** b. Vienna, Aug. 9, 1781; d. Baden, near Vienna, June 20, 1842. He joined the Vienna court orch. as a violinist at an early age, and conducted at court theaters from about 1809 to 1825; from 1840 he served as music director of the two court theaters. He assisted Beethoven in conducting the 9th Sym. and other works (actually led the performances, with Beethoven indicating the initial tempos). Umlauf had some success as a composer of ballets, the most successful being *Paul und Rosette oder Die Winzer* (Vienna, March 5, 1806). Other works include the Singspiel *Der Grenadier* (July 8, 1812), and the ballets *Amors Rache* (Oct. 18, 1804) and *Das eigensinnige Landmädchen* (April 9, 1810); he also composed a few sacred vocal works and piano pieces.—**NS/LK/DM**

Underwood, James, American composer; b. Richmond, Calif., March 4, 1951. He played the trumpet as a youth, then studied composition with Robert Basart at Calif. State Univ. in Hayward (1969–75; M.A., 1975) and with Frederick Fox at Ind. Univ. (1978–82; D.A., 1982). His music is prudently modernistic, with atonal and polytonal divagations from modal harmonic structures within a general Baroque framework; there is an element of neo- Handelian humor in some of his compositions.

WORKS: ORCH.: *Variations on B-A-C-H* (Hayward, Calif., June 8, 1973); *The Orchestral Noises of October Nights* (1980–81; Bloomington, Ind., March 31, 1982); *Joyyoku* (1984; Indianapolis, Sept. 24, 1985); *Sonorous Regions* for Chamber Orch. (1986); *Bachanlia for a Lot of Cellos* (1986; perf. by 40 cellos, Bloomington, Ind., Feb. 3, 1987); *Glider* (Bloomington, Ind., April 24, 1990); *Kyrie* (1991); *Grendel* (Bloomington, Ind., Oct. 25, 1992); *Grendel's Mother* (Bloomington, Ind., Oct. 24, 1993); *Back Home? Again??* (1995). **CHAMBER:** *Lament* for Clarinet (1970); *Textures I* for 5 Instruments (1971), *II* for Flute (1979), and *III* for 2 Cellos (1972); *Loomings* for Double String Quartet and Bass (1979); *4 Jurassic Scenes* for Trombone, Bass Trombone, and 3 Percussionists (1980); *Nightwork* for 8 Instruments (1981); *Brave New Zoos* for String Quartet (1982); *Reactions* for Piccolo (1982); *Green County Purple* for Bassoon (1983); *Cadenzas* for Alto Trombone, String Quartet, Piano, and Percussion (1983); *Deluge* for Brass Quintet (1983); *3 Phantasms* for Violin and Piano (1987); *Intro and Weird Boogaloo* for 4 Horns (1994). **VOCAL:** *The Road* for Chorus and Orch. (Richmond, Calif., June 11, 1969); *Requiem* for Man's Voice and Orch. (1970); *Dynamisms* for

Soprano and Orch. (Hayward, Calif., May 2, 1975); *Arms and the Boy* for Soprano, Narrator, Flute, Bass Clarinet, Trumpet, 2 Violins, Viola, Piano, and 5 Percussionists (1979); *To Eros* for Soprano, Violin, Viola, Piano, and Percussion (1980); *After Dinner with Al Capone* for Soprano and Trumpet (1981); *Remembrance* for Soprano and 6 Instruments (1982); *Dulce et Decorum est* for Soprano and Chamber Orch. (1987; Bloomington, Ind., Dec. 1, 1988); *Friends* for Soprano and 5 Instruments (1991). **—NS/LK/DM**

Ung, Chinary, Cambodian-born American composer; b. Prey Lovea, Nov. 24, 1942. He left his homeland in 1964 and settled in the U.S. He studied clarinet at the Manhattan School of Music in N.Y.; then composition with Chou Wen-Chung at Columbia Univ. in N.Y. (D.M.A., 1974). He then devoted himself to composing and teaching; from 1987 to 1995 he was Regents Prof. at Ariz. State Univ. in Tempe, and in 1995 he assumed the position of prof. of music at the Univ. of Calif. at San Diego. He received awards from the American Academy of Arts and Letters, NEA grants, and a Guggenheim fellowship; also a Kennedy Center Friedheim Award (1992) and a Koussevitsky Foundation commission (1993). In 1990 he was awarded the Cultural Preservation Award for commitment to traditional music from the United Cambodian Community Circle of Friends in Long Beach, Calif., and in 1989 he became the first and youngest American composer to receive the prestigious Grawemeyer Award for his *Inner Voices* for Chamber Orch. (1986). Ung's compositions reveal a strong sense of commitment to tradition, as well as to ingenuity, technique, and imagination.

WORKS: ORCH.: *Anicca* for Chamber Orch. (1970); *Inner Voices* for Chamber Orch. (1986); *Grand Spiral ("Desert Flowers Bloom")* (1990; Sendai, Japan, June 1, 1992; also for Band); *Triple Concerto: A Sonorous Path* for Solo Cello, Percussion, Piano, and Orch. (1993); *Water Rings* for Chamber Orch. (1993); *Antiphonal Spirals* (1995). **Band:** *Grand Spiral ("Desert Flowers Bloom")* (1990; also for Orch.). **CHAMBER:** *Khse Buon* for Cello (1979); *Child Song I* for Flute, Violin, Cello, and Piano, and *II* for Alto Flute, Viola, Cello, and Piano (both 1985); *Spiral I* for Cello, Piano, and Percussion (1986), *II* for High Voice, Tuba, and Piano (1987), *III* for String Quartet (1988), *VI* for Clarinet, Violin, Cello, and Piano (1988), and *VII* for Alto Flute, English Horn, Bass Clarinet, Horn, and Bassoon (1989); *"...Still Life after Death"* for High Voice, Flute, Clarinet, Violin, Cello, Piano, and Percussion (1995). **VOCAL:** *Tall Wind* for Soprano, Flute, Oboe, Guitar, and Cello, after e.e. cummings (1969; requiring 5 scores for performance); *Mohori* for Mezzo-soprano, Flute, Oboe, 2 Percussion, Piano, Guitar, Harp, Cello, and Strings (1974). **—NS/LK/DM**

Unger, Caroline, famous Hungarian contralto; b. Stuhlweissenburg, Oct. 28, 1803; d. near Florence, March 23, 1877. She studied piano as a child, and then received singing lessons from Joseph Mazotti and Ugo Bassi; then studied voice with Aloysia Weber, J.M. Vogl, and in Milan with D. Roncini. In 1824 she made her operatic debut in Vienna as Dorabella in *Così fan tutte*. Beethoven chose her to sing the contralto part in the first performance of his 9th Sym. (May 7, 1824); long afterward, she recounted that she turned Beethoven around that he might see the applause, which he could no longer hear. She went to Italy, where she changed the spelling of her name to Ungher, to secure proper pronunciation in Italian. Several Italian composers (Donizetti, Bellini, Mercadante) wrote operas especially for her. In 1833 she appeared in Paris. In 1839 she was engaged to be married to the poet Lenau, but the engagement soon was broken; in 1841 she married the French writer François Sabatier (1818–91) and retired from the stage. She publ. an album of 46 songs, *Lieder, Mélodies et Stornelli*.

BIBL.: *Trionfi melodrammatici di Carolina U. in Vienna* (Vienna, 1839); F. Margit Polgar, *U.-Sabatier* (Budapest, 1941). **—NS/LK/DM**

Unger, (Ernst) Max, German musicologist, conductor, and painter; b. Taura, Saxony, May 28, 1883; d. Zürich, Dec. 1, 1959. He studied at the Leipzig Cons., and also attended Riemann's lectures at the Univ. of Leipzig (Ph.D., 1911, with the diss. *Muzio Clementis Leben*; publ. in Langensalza, 1914). He was conductor of the Vereinigte Leipziger Schauspielhauser in 1906; then was conductor of the Leipzig Madrigal Soc. (1912–14) and ed. of the *Neue Zeitschrift für Musik* (1919–20); after living in Zürich (1932–40), he went to Italy; returned to Germany after World War II. He devoted his research mainly to Beethoven, and publ. about 150 papers dealing with various aspects of Beethoven's life and works. Among his books are *Mendelssohn-Bartholdys Beziehungen zu England* (Langensalza, 1909), *Auf Spuren von Beethovens unsterblicher Geliebten* (Langensalza, 1911), *Beethoven über eine Gesamtausgabe seiner Werke* (Bonn, 1920), *Ludwig van Beethoven und seine Verleger S.A. Steiner und Tobias Haslinger in Wien, Ad. Mart. Schlesinger in Berlin* (Berlin and Vienna, 1921), *Beethovens Handschrift* (Bonn, 1926), and *Ein Faustopernplan Beethovens und Goethes* (Regensburg, 1952). He also ed. the catalogue of the Bodmer Beethoven collection in Zürich, under the title *Eine schweizer Beethovensammlung: Katalog* (Zürich, 1939).**—NS/LK/DM**

Unger, Georg, famous German tenor; b. Leipzig, March 6, 1837; d. there, Feb. 2, 1887. He was originally a student of theology, making his operatic debut in Leipzig at the age of 30. Hans Richter heard him in Mannheim and recommended him to Wagner for the role of Siegfried, which he created at the Bayreuth Festival (1876). After appearing in London in a series of Wagner concerts in 1877, he went that year to Leipzig, where he sang with the Opera until 1881. He was the first Wagnerian Heldentenor.**—NS/LK/DM**

Unger, Gerhard, German tenor; b. Bad Salzungen, Nov. 26, 1916. He received training in Eisenach and at the Berlin Hochschule für Musik. After beginning his career as a concert artist, he joined the Weimar Opera in 1947. From 1949 to 1961 he was a member of the (East) Berlin State Opera. He also appeared as David at the Bayreuth Festivals (1951–52). From 1961 to 1963 he sang in Stuttgart, and in 1962 appeared as Pedrillo at the Salzburg Festival. He then was a member of the Hamburg State Opera (1963–66) and the Vienna State Opera (1966–70). In later years, he became particularly esteemed for his character roles. His last major appearance was as Mime in Stuttgart in 1987. As a concert artist, his repertoire ranged from the Baroque era to contemporary scores.—**NS/LK/DM**

Uppman, Theodor, American baritone and teacher; b. San Jose, Calif., Jan. 12, 1920. He received training at the Curtis Inst. of Music in Philadelphia (1939–41) before attending opera workshops at Stanford Univ. (1941–42) and the Univ. of Southern Calif. in Los Angeles (1948–50). In 1941 he made his professional debut with the Northern Calif. Sym. Orch. He first gained notice when he sang Debussy's Pelléas in a concert version with the San Francisco Sym. Orch. in 1947. In 1948 he chose that same role for his debut with the N.Y.C. Opera. On Dec. 1, 1951, he created the title role in Britten's *Billy Budd* at London's Covent Garden. He made his Metropolitan Opera debut in N.Y. as Pelléas on Nov. 27, 1953, and then was on its roster from 1955 to 1978, appearing in such roles as Papageno, Marcello, Eisenstein, Guglielmo, Paquillo, Sharpless et al. He also was a guest artist with other U.S. opera companies and toured as a concert artist. In 1962 he created Floyd's Jonathan Wade at the N.Y.C. Opera and in 1983 Bernstein's Bill in *A Quiet Place* at the Houston Grand Opera. He taught at the Manhattan School of Music, the Mannes Coll. of Music in N.Y., and the Britten-Pears School for Advanced Musical Studies in Aldeburgh.—**NS/LK/DM**

Upshaw, Dawn, greatly admired American soprano; b. Nashville, Tenn., July 17, 1960. She studied at Ill. Wesleyan Univ. (B.A., 1982) and then pursued vocal training with Ellen Faull at the Manhattan School of Music in N.Y. (M.A., 1984); she also attended courses given by Jan DeGaetani at the Aspen (Colo.) Music School. In 1984 she won the Young Concert Artists auditions and entered the Metropolitan Opera's young artists development program. She was co-winner of the Naumburg Competition in N.Y. (1985). After appearing in minor roles at the Metropolitan Opera in N.Y., she displayed her vocal gifts in such major roles as Donizetti's Adina and Mozart's Despina in 1988. In 1990 she sang Pamina in a concert performance of *Die Zauberflöte* at the London Promenade Concerts. In 1992 she appeared as the Angel in Messiaen's *St. François d'Assise* at the Salzburg Festival. In 1995 she portrayed Strauss's Sophie in Houston. In 1996 she was engaged as Handel's Theodora at the Glyndebourne Festival. She sang Mozart's Cherubino and Stravinsky's Anne Trulove at the Metropolitan Opera in 1997. She also pursued a notably successful career as a soloist with major orchs. and as a recitalist. Her remarkable concert repertoire ranges from early music to the most intimidating of avant-garde scores.—**NS/LK/DM**

Upton, George P(utnam), American writer on music; b. Roxbury, Mass., Oct. 25, 1834; d. Chicago, May 19, 1919. He studied at Brown Univ., graduating in 1854. He then was music critic of the *Chicago Tribune* (1863–81), where he was its assoc. ed. (1872–1905).

WRITINGS: (all publ. in Chicago unless otherwise given): *Woman in Music* (Boston, 1880; 2nd ed., rev. and enl., 1886); *The Standard Operas* (1886; rev. and enl. by F. Borowski, 1928); *The Standard Oratorios* (1887; 12th ed., 1909); *The Standard Cantatas* (1888; 7th ed., 1899); *The Standard Symphonies* (1889); *Musical Pastels* (1902); *The Standard Light Operas* (1902); ed. *Theodore Thomas: A Musical Autobiography* (1905); with G. Kelley, *Edouard Remenyi: Musician, Litterateur and Man* (1906); *Musical Memories: My Recollections of Celebrities of the Half Century, 1850–1900* (1908); *The Standard Concert Guide* (1908; 3rd ed., rev. and enl. by F. Borowski, 1930); *Standard Concert Repertory* (1909); *Standard Musical Biographies* (1910); *The Song* (1915); *In Music's Land* (1920).

BIBL.: M. Feldman, *G.P. U.: Journalist, Music Critic and Mentor in Early Chicago* (diss., Univ. of Minn., 1983).
—**NS/LK/DM**

Urban, Heinrich, German violinist, pedagogue, and composer; b. Berlin, Aug. 27, 1837; d. there, Nov. 24, 1901. He studied with Ries (violin), Laub, and others in Berlin, and was a professional violinist. He wrote much symphonic and chamber music. In 1881 he became a prof. at Kullak's Academy in Berlin. He acquired fame as a theory teacher, numbering among his pupils Paderewski. His works include a concert overture, *Scheherazade*, a sym., *Frühling*, Violin Concerto, many violin pieces, and songs. His brother, Friedrich Julius Urban (b. Berlin, Dec. 23, 1838; d. there, July 17, 1918), was a singing teacher and composer.—**NS/LK/DM**

Urbaniak, Michal, avant-garde jazz violinist, tenor saxophonist, bandleader; b. Warsaw, Poland, Jan. 22, 1943. He began to play violin at age six and studied at the Academy of Music in Warsaw, where he also took up alto saxophone. In the early 1960s he worked in a number of Polish jazz bands, initially Dixieland style troupes, before moving on to bop bands with Zbignew Namyslowski, AndrzejTrzaskowski, and Krzysztof Komeda. In August of 1962 with Namyzlowski, Urbaniak made his first trip to the U.S. In 1965 he moved to Scandinavia with Ursula Dudziak, who later became his wife. They toured throughout Europe for several years and returned to Poland in 1969. He formed Constellation with Dudziak, Adam Makowicz, Czeslaw Bartkowski, and Pawel Jarzebski (later Roman Dylag). When Urbaniak won a scholarship to Berklee Coll. of Music in Boston in the early 1970s, he moved to the States. Settling in N.Y. in 1974, he founded Fusion, a band that incorporated elements of Polish folk music, the melodies and rhythms informed by his classical training, and his knowledge of avant-garde jazz composition. Fusion signed to Columbia Records and toured steadily throughout the States and occasionally Europe. They performed and recorded until 1977, and made some compelling albums that blended Dudziak's singing and vocal effects, Polish folk melodies, and irregular meters. He worked and recorded with Larry Coryell and Dudziak in the 1980s, and led his own bands. He also did sessions with Archie Shepp and performed at the first Kuwait jazz festival in 1998.

Urbaniak won the Grand Prix for Best Soloist at the Montreux Jazz Festival in 1971, among other honors. He plays a customized five-string violin, violin synthesizer and violectra (an electronic bowed string instrument an octave lower than a violin), and most famously the lyricon, an electronic saxophone-like instrument which is linked to a synthesizer. He has been a leader in introducing electronics into jazz music.

Disc.: *Constellation in Concert* (1973) *Super Constellation* (1973); *Fusion* (1975); *Fusion III* (1975); *Tribute to Komeda* (1976); *Heritage* (1977); *Urbaniak* (1977); *Music for Violin and Jazz Quartet* (1980). Folk Songs: *Children's Melodies* (1981); *Cinemode* (1988); *Songbird* (1990); *Manhattan Man* (1992).**—MM/LP**

Urbanner, Erich, Austrian composer, teacher, and conductor; b. Innsbruck, March 26, 1936. He was a student of Schiske and Jelinek (composition), Grete Hinterhofer (piano), and Swarowsky (conducting) at the Vienna Academy of Music (1955–61). He also attended the composition courses of Fortner, Stockhausen, and Maderna in Darmstadt. In 1961 he became an instructor at the Vienna Academy of Music. From 1968 he was also active as a conductor. In 1969 he was named a prof. of composition and harmony at the Vienna Hochschule für Musik. Among his honors were Vienna's Förderungspreis (1962), the City of Innsbruck prize (1980), the Würdigungspreis of the Austrian Ministry of Education and Art (1982), the City of Vienna prize (1984), and the Tiroler Landespreis for the arts (1993). Urbanner's music is strikingly modern without adhering to any particular school.

Works: DRAMATIC: *Der Gluckerich, oder Tugend und Tadel der Nützlichkeit*, musical burlesque (1963; Vienna, May 26, 1965); *Ninive, oder Das leben geth weiter*, opera (1987; Innsbruck, Sept. 24, 1988); *Johannes Stein, oder Der Rock des Kaisers*, monodrama (1990–91; Vienna, March 31, 1992); *Die Tochter des Kerensteiners*, musical scenes (1994). **ORCH.:** *Prolog* (1957; Innsbruck, May 11, 1958); *Intrada* for Chamber Orch. (1957; Vienna, June 1958); 2 piano concertos: No. 1 (1958; Innsbruck, June 1959) and No. 2 (1976; Innsbruck, May 11, 1977); Flute Concerto (1959; Innsbruck, June 4, 1964); Concertino for Organ and Strings (Innsbruck, May 1961); *Symphony in 1 Movement* (1963; Vienna, April 5, 1964); *Dialoge* for Piano and Orch. (1965; Vienna, April 2, 1967); Concerto for Oboe and Chamber Orch. (1966; Innsbruck, June 9, 1968); *Rondeau* (1967; Vienna, Jan. 15, 1971); *Thema, 19 Variationen und ein Nachspiel* (1968); *Kontraste II* (1970; Innsbruck, April 27, 1971); Violin Concerto (1971; Innsbruck, Oct. 19, 1972); *Concerto "Wolfgang Amadeus"* for 3 Trombones, Celesta, and 2 Orchs. (1972; Salzburg, Jan. 20, 1973); Double Bass Concerto (1973; Innsbruck, Nov. 26, 1974); *Retrospektiven* (1974–75; rev. version, Graz, Oct. 13, 1979); Concerto for Alto Saxophone and 12 Players (1978–79; Graz, Nov. 4, 1982); *Sinfonietta 79* for Chamber Orch. (1979; Innsbruck, April 30, 1980); *Sonata brevis* for Chamber Orch. (1980; Vienna, March 7, 1981); Cello Concerto (1981; Innsbruck, May 2, 1982); *Sinfonia Concertante* for Chamber Orch. (1982; Vienna, March 12, 1983); Double Concerto for Flute, Clarinet, and Orch. (Salzburg, Aug. 8, 1984). **CHAMBER:** 4 string quartets: No. 1 (1956; Vienna, March 1958), No. 2 (1957), No. 3 (1972; Vienna, May 8, 1973), and No. 4 (1991–92; Vevey, Jan. 31, 1993); *5 Pieces* for Violin and Piano (1961); *Étude* for Wind Quintet (1965; Vienna, Feb. 16, 1966); *Acht Aphorismen* for Flute, Clarinet, and Bassoon (Vienna, May 26, 1966); *4 Pieces* for Viola (1967); *5 Pieces* for Flute (1967); *Improvisation III* for Chamber Ensemble (1969; Vienna, Jan. 23, 1970) and *IV* for Wind Quintet (1969; Vienna, March 30, 1979); *Lyrica* for Chamber Ensemble (1971; Vienna, Jan. 13, 1974); *Solo* for Violin (Solbad Hall, April 2, 1971); *Burleske* for Flute and Organ (1973; Düsseldorf, Sept. 18, 1974); *Pastorale* for Chamber Ensemble (1975; Innsbruck, March 24, 1976); *Takes* for Piano Trio (1977; Vienna, May 2, 1978); *Quartetto Concertato* for String Quartet and 6 String Duos (Innsbruck, April 5, 1978); *Nachtstück* for Recorder Ensemble (1978; Ossiach, Aug. 9, 1980); *Arioso-Furioso* for Cello and Piano (Vienna, Oct. 21, 1980); *Sechs Phan-Tasten und zwei Schlagzeuger* for 7 Instrumentalists (1980; Innsbruck, Feb. 24, 1981); *Nonett 1981* (Utrecht, Sept. 7, 1981); *Ballade* for Guitar (1982; Alpbach, Aug. 28, 1983); *Emotionen* for Saxophone Quartet (1984; Washington, D.C., Feb. 10, 1985); *Trio Mobile* for Flute, Viola, and Cello (Brussels, Dec. 8, 1987); *...In Bewegung...*, trio for Violin, Cello, and Piano (1990; Vienna, April 9, 1991); Duo for Accordion and Double Bass (1992; Linz, March 16, 1993); *quasi una fantasia*, 6 concertante pieces for 15 Instruments (1993). **KEYBOARD: Piano:** 2 sonatinas (1956, 1957); *Variation* (1958); *5 Pieces* (1959); *Adagio* (1966); *Variation* (1981); *13 Charakterstücke* (1988–89; Innsbruck, June 20, 1989). **Organ:** *Improvisation I* (1961; Innsbruck, Aug. 30, 1974); *Zyklus* (1992; Vienna, March 5, 1993). **VOCAL:** *Missa benedicite gentes* for Chorus and Organ (Innsbruck, May 15, 1958); 5 Songs for Mezzo-soprano and Small Ensemble (1961); *Das Ahnenbild* for Soprano and Piano (1961); *Requiem* for Soloists, Chorus, and Orch. (1982–83; Innsbruck, Feb. 20, 1985); *Acht Ächte Tyroller Lieder* for Soprano, Tenor, and Chamber Ensemble (1985; Innsbruck, April 5, 1986).**—NS/LK/DM**

Urfey, Thomas d', English playwright and poet; b. Exeter, 1653; d. London, Feb. 26, 1723. He produced about 30 plays, the songs in some of which were set to music by Purcell (e.g. *The Comical History of Don Quixote*, in 3 parts, 1694–96). He ingratiated himself into the circle of Charles II by his talent for singing his poems, adapted to popular airs of his time. Between 1683 and 1710 he publ. several collections of airs with music, and in 1719 he ed. *Songs Compleat, Pleasant and Divertive* (5 vols., his own songs assembled in Vols. 1 and 2). This was reissued the same year under the better-known title *Wit and Mirth: or Pills to Purge Melancholy* (a 6th vol. was added in 1720), and the whole was reprinted and ed. by C. Day (N.Y., 1959).

Bibl.: C. Day, *The Songs of T. D'U.* (Cambridge, Mass., 1933).**—NS/LK/DM**

Urhan, Chrétien, French violist, violinist, organist, and composer of German descent; b. Montjoie, near Aachen, Feb. 16, 1790; d. Paris, Nov. 2, 1845. He taught himself to play various instruments, then settled in Paris, where he studied composition with Le Sueur. He became a member of the Opéra orch. in 1814, where he was made 1st violinist in 1823 and soloist in 1836 and also appeared as a violist with it. In 1827 he became organist at St. Vincent and in 1828 concertmaster of the Société des Concerts du Conservatoire; also played in chamber-music concerts. In the Cons. Concerts he employed a 5-stringed violin (*violon-alto*, with the tuning *c-g-d*^{1}*-a*^{1}*-e*^{2}), producing charming effects. He composed a cantata, *Les champs de repos*, 2 string quintets, piano pieces, and songs.**—NS/LK/DM**

Uribe-Holguín, Guillermo, eminent Colombian composer and pedagogue; b. Bogotá, March 17, 1880; d. there, June 26, 1971. He studied violin with

Figueroa at the Bogotá Academy of Music (1890) and with Narciso Garay; taught at the Academy (1905–07). In 1907 he went to Paris, where he studied with d'Indy at the Schola Cantorum, and then took violin lessons with César Thomson and Emile Chaumont in Brussels. He returned to Colombia in 1910 and became director of the newly reorganized National Cons. in Bogotá; resigned in 1935 and devoted his time to the family coffee plantation. He continued to compose and was active as a conductor; was again director of the Cons. from 1942 to 1947. In 1910 he married the pianist Lucia Gutiérrez. His music bears the imprint of the modern French style, but his thematic material is related to native musical resources; particularly remarkable are his *Trozos en el sentimiento popular* for Piano, of which he wrote about 350; they are stylizations of Colombian melorhythms in a brilliant pianistic setting. He publ. an autobiography, *Vida de un músico colombiano* (Bogotá, 1941).

WORKS: DRAMATIC: Opera: *Furatena.* **ORCH:** (all 1st perf. in Bogotá): 11syms. (1910–50); *Sinfcnia del terruño* (Oct. 20, 1924); *3 danzas* (May 27, 1927); *Marcha festiva* (Aug. 20, 1928); *Serenata* (Oct. 29, 1928); *Carnavalesca* (July 8, 1929); *Cantares* (Sept. 2, 1929); *Villanesca* (Sept. 1, 1930); *Bajo su ventana* (Oct. 20, 1930); *Suite típica* (Nov. 21, 1932); *Concierto a la manera antigua* for Piano and Orch. (Oct. 15, 1939); *Bochica* (April 12, 1940); *Conquistadores* (April 3, 1959); 2 violin concertos; Viola Concerto. **CHAMBER:** 10 string quartets; 2 piano trios; 7 violin sonatas; Cello Sonata; Viola Sonata; Piano Quartet; 2 piano quintets. **VOCAL:** Choruses; song cycles.—**NS/LK/DM**

Urio, Francesco Antonio, Italian composer; b. Milan, c. 1631; d. there, c. 1719. He became a Franciscan friar. He served as maestro di cappella at Spoleto Cathedral (1679), in Urbino (1681–83), in Assisi, in Genoa, at the Basilica de' Santi Dodici Apostoli in Rome (1690), at I Frari in Venice (1697), and at S. Francesco in Milan (1715–19). He publ. *Motetti di concerto a 2, 3, e 4 voci con violini e senza*, op.1 (Rome, 1690) and *Salmi concertati a 3 voci con violini*, op.2 (Bologna, 1697), and also composed several oratorios and a Te Deum, from which Handel "borrowed" numerous themes, chiefly for his *Dettingen Te Deum*, and also for his *Saul and Israel in Egypt*. Urio's Te Deum was publ. by Chrysander in Denkmäler der Tonkunst (Vol. V, Bergedorf, near Hamburg, 1871; later publ. as Supplement 2 of Handel's complete works).—**NS/LK/DM**

Urlus, Jacques (Jacobus), noted Dutch tenor; b. Hergenrath, near Aachen, Jan. 9, 1867; d. Noordwijk, June 6, 1935. When he was 10, his parents moved to Tilburg, the Netherlands, where he received instruction from an uncle who was a choral conductor; he later studied singing with Anton Averkamp, Hugo Nolthenius, and Cornelie van Zanten. He was a member of the Dutch National Opera (1894–99) and of the Leipzig Opera (1900–14), where he excelled as a Wagnerian. In 1910 he made his London debut at Covent Garden as Tristan, a role he repeated for his U.S. debut in Boston on Feb. 12, 1912, and for his Metropolitan Opera debut in N.Y. on Feb. 8, 1913. He remained on the roster of the Metropolitan Opera until 1917, and in subsequent years toured in Europe and the U.S. His other distinguished roles included Parsifal, Tamino, Otello, and Don José. He publ. *Mijn Loopbaan* (My Career; Amsterdam, 1930).

BIBL.: O. Spengler, *J. U.* (N.Y., 1917).—**NS/LK/DM**

Urner, Catherine Murphy, American singer, teacher, and composer; b. Mitchell, Ind., March 23, 1891; d. San Diego, April 30, 1942. She studied at the Univ. of Calif. at Berkeley and with Koechlin in Paris (1920–21). After serving as director of vocal music at Mills Coll. in Oakland, Calif. (1921–24), she devoted much time to performing, teaching and composing. She made tours of the U.S., France, and Italy. Urner studied Amerian Indian tribal melodies, which she utilized in a number of compositions. She also collaborated with Koechlin on several scores.

WORKS: ORCH.: *Esquisses normandes*, suite (1929; rev. and orchestrated by Koechlin, 1945); *3 Movements* for Chamber Orch. (1938); Flute Concerto (1940). **CHAMBER:** *Petite Suite* for Flute, Violin, Viola, and Cello (1930); *Jubilee Suite* for Flute and Piano (1931); Violin Sonata (1942); piano pieces; organ works. **VOCAL:** Over 100 songs.—**NS/LK/DM**

Urreda, Johannes, eminent composer who flourished in the 2nd half of the 15th century. He may have been of Flemish birth; whatever the case, he pursued his career in Spain. In 1476 he became a singer in the chapel of Garcia Alvarez de Toledo, the 1st Duke of Alva; by 1477 he was in the service of King Ferdinand V as master of the court chapel. His works were widely disseminated in Spain, Italy, and France. Among the most celebrated were the hymn *Pange lingua* for four Voices and the cancion *Nunca fue pena mayor* for three Voices, both of which were borrowed by subsequent composers. A few other sacred and secular vocal works are extant.—**NS/LK/DM**

Urrutia-Blondel, Jorge, Chilean composer, teacher, and writer on music; b. La Serena, Sept. 17, 1903; d. Santiago, July 5, 1981. He studied with Pedro Humberto Allende and Domingo Santa Cruz, and in 1928 traveled to Europe, where he took lessons with Koechlin, Dukas, and Boulanger in Paris, and with Hindemith and Mersmann in Berlin. Returning to Chile, he was appointed prof. of harmony at the Cons. in Santiago (1931). His early works followed along nationalist lines but he later turned to post-impressionism and neo-classicism. He wrote many articles on contemporary music and folk music in his homeland, and, with S. Claro, he publ. the study *Historia de la música en Chile* (Santiago, 1973).

WORKS: DRAMATIC: Ballet: *La guitarra del diablo* (Santiago, Nov. 27, 1942; 2 sym. suites., 1942). **ORCH.:** *Música para un Cuento de Antano* (1948); Piano Concerto (1950). **CHAMBER:** Piano Trio (1933); Concertino for Harp and Guitar (1943); String Quartet (1944); Violin Sonata (1954); piano pieces. **VOCAL:** Choruses; song cycles on Chilean motifs. —**NS/LK/DM**

Urso, Camilla, esteemed French-American violinist; b. Nantes, June 13, 1842; d. N.Y., Jan. 20, 1902. Her father was an Italian musician and her mother a Portuguese singer. A child prodigy, she entered the Paris Cons. when she was seven, becoming the first girl ever accorded that distinction; she was a pupil there of Lambert Massart, winning 1st prizes in all subjects. On Oct. 29, 1852, she made her U.S. debut in N.Y. She appeared with Marietta Alboni, toured widely with the Germania Musical Soc., and gave concerts with Henriette Sontag. After withdrawing from public life (1855–63), she resumed her career with major tours of the U.S. and Europe; also toured Australia (1879, 1894) and South Africa (1895). In 1895 she retired and settled in N.Y. as a teacher.

BIBL.: C. Barnard, *C.: A Tale of a Violin, Being the Artist Life of C. U.* (Boston, 1874).—**NS/LK/DM**

Ursprung, Otto, learned German musicologist; b. Günzlhofen, Jan. 16, 1879; d. Schöndorf-am-Ammersee, Sept. 14, 1960. He studied philosophy and theology at the Univ. of Munich (1899–1904) and was ordained as a Catholic priest. He then returned to the Univ. of Munich (Ph.D., 1911, with the diss. *Jacobus de Kerle: sein Leben und seine Werke (1531/32–91)*; publ. in Munich, 1913), holding the title of honorary prof. of music history there (1932–49). He was an authority on Catholic church music and the musical history of Munich.

WRITINGS: *Restauration und Palestrina-Renaissance in der katholischen Kirchenmusik der letzten zwei Jahrhunderte* (Augsburg, 1924); *Münchens musikalische Vergangenheit* (Munich, 1927); *Die katholische Kirchenmusik* (Potsdam, 1931).
—**NS/LK/DM**

Ursuleac, Viorica, noted Romanian soprano; b. Cernăuţi, March 26, 1894; d. Ehrwald, Tirol, Oct. 22, 1985. She studied in Vienna with Franz Steiner and Philip Forstén and in Berlin with Lilli Lehmann. She made her operatic debut as Charlotte in Massenet's *Werther* in Agram in 1922; then sang in Cernăuţi (1923–24) and with the Vienna Volksoper (1924–26). In 1926 she joined the Frankfurt am Main Opera, and then pursued a distinguished career as a member of the Vienna State Opera (1930–34), the Berlin State Opera (1935–37), and the Bavarian State Opera in Munich (1937–44). Richard Strauss held her in the highest esteem; in his operas she created the roles of Arabella (Dresden, July 1, 1933), Maria in *Der Friedenstag* (Munich, July 24, 1938), the Countess in *Capriccio* (Munich, Oct. 28, 1942), and Danae in *Die Liebe der Danae* (public dress rehearsal, Salzburg, Aug. 16, 1944). She was also highly successful in the operas of Mozart, Wagner, and Verdi. She was married to **Clemens Krauss**, with whom she often appeared in concert. After his death in 1954, she settled in Ehrwald. With R. Schlötterer, she wrote *Singen für Richard Strauss: Erinnerungen und Dokumente* (Vienna, 1986).—**NS/LK/DM**

Usandizaga, José Maria, Basque composer; b. San Sebastián, March 31, 1887; d. there, Oct. 5, 1915. Encouraged by Planté and d'Indy, he entered the Paris Schola Cantorum when he was 14, where he studied piano with Grovlez and counterpoint with Tricon. In 1906 he returned to his native city and associated himself with the Basque musical movement, to which he gave a great impetus with the production of his stage work *Mendi mendiyan* (High in the Mountains; 1909–10; San Sebastián, 1911); then followed his drama lírico *Las golondrinas* (The Swallows; 1913; Madrid, Feb. 5, 1914; rev. as an opera by his brother, R. Usandizaga, Barcelona, 1929), which obtained excellent success; his last stage work was the drama lirico *La llama* (The Flame; 1915; completed by R. Usandizaga, San Sebastián, 1918). He also wrote several orch. works, including a Suite (1904), a symphonic poem, *Dans la mer* (1904), *Ouverture symphonique sur un theme de plain-chant* (1904–05), and band pieces; choral music; songs; folksong arrangements; a String Quartet; works for violin or cello and piano; piano pieces; organ music. His death from tuberculosis at the age of 28 was deeply lamented by Spanish musicians.

BIBL.: L. Villalba Muñoz, *Últimos músicos españoles: J.M. U.* (Madrid, 1918); J. de Arozamena, *J.M. U. y la bella época donostiarra* (San Sebastian, 1969).—**NS/LK/DM**

Usmanbaş, Ilhan, Turkish composer and teacher; b. Constantinople, Sept. 28, 1921. He was a student of Cemal Reşit Rey at the Constantinople Cons. (1941–42), and then studied with Hasan Ferit Alnar (piano) and Ulvi Cemal Erkin (composition) at the Ankara State Cons. (1942–48); he subsequently received additional training from Dallapiccola at the Berkshire Music Center in Tanglewood (summer, 1952). From 1948 he taught at the Ankara State Cons. His early works followed the ethnic patterns of Turkish folk songs, but he later adopted serial techniques, with occasional aleatory episodes.

WORKS: ORCH.: Violin Concerto (1946); 2 syms.: No. 1 (1948) and No. 2 for Strings (Ankara, April 20, 1950); *On 3 Paintings of Salvador Dali* for Strings (1953); *Gölgeler* (Shadows; 1964); *Bursting Sinfonietta* (1968); *Music for a Ballet* (1969); *Symphonic Movement* (1972); *Little Night Music* (1972). **CHAMBER:** 2 string quartets (1947, 1970); Clarinet Quintet (1949); Oboe Sonata (1949); Trumpet Sonata (1949); *A Jump into Space* for Violin and 4 Instruments (1966); piano pieces. **VOCAL:** *Music* for Strings, Percussion, Piano, and Narrator (1950); *Mortuary* for Narrator, Chorus, and Orch. (1952–53); *Japanese Music* for Women's Chorus and Orch. (1956); *Music with a Poem* for Mezzo-soprano, Flute, Clarinet, Bassoon, and 2 Violins (1958); *Un coup de des* for Chorus and Orch. (1959).
—**NS/LK/DM**

Ussachevsky, Vladimir (Alexis), innovative Russian-born American composer; b. Hailar, Manchuria, Nov. 3, 1911; d. N.Y., Jan. 2, 1990. His parents settled in Manchuria shortly after the Russo-Japanese War of 1905, at the time when Russian culture was still a powerful social factor there. His father was an officer of the Russian army, and his mother was a professional pianist. In 1930 he went to Calif., where he took private piano lessons with Clarence Mader; from 1931 to 1933 he attended Pasadena Jr. Coll.; in 1933 he received a scholarship to study at Pomona Coll. (B.A., 1935). He then enrolled in the Eastman School of Music in Rochester in N.Y. in the classes of Hanson, Rogers, and Royce in composition (M.M., 1936; Ph.D., 1939); he also had some instruction with Burrill Phillips. In 1942, as a naturalized American citizen, Ussachevsky was drafted into the U.S. Army; thanks to his fluency in Russian, his knowledge of English and French, and a certain ability to communicate in rudimentary Chinese, he was engaged in the Intelligence Division; subsequently he served as a research analyst at the War Dept. in Washington, D.C. He then pursued postdoctoral work with Luening at Columbia Univ., joining its faculty in 1947; was prof. of music (1964–80). At various times he taught at other institutions, including several years as composer-in-residence at the Univ. of Utah (from 1970) and was a faculty member there (1980–85). His early works were influenced by Russian church music, in the tradition of Tchaikovsky and Rachmaninoff. A distinct change in his career as a composer came in 1951, when he became interested in the resources of electronic music; to this period belong his works *Transposition, Reverberation, Experiment, Composition* and *Underwater Valse*, which make use of electronic sound. On Oct. 28, 1952, Stokowski conducted in N.Y. the first performance of Ussachevsky's *Sonic Contours*, in which a piano part was metamorphosed with the aid of various sonorific devices, superimposed on each other. About that time, he began a fruitful partnership with Luening; with him he composed *Incantation for Tape Recorder*, which was broadcast in 1953. Luening and Ussachevsky then conceived the idea of combining electronic tape sounds with conventional instruments played by human musicians; the result was *Rhapsodic Variations*, first performed in N.Y. on March 20, 1954. The work anticipated by a few months the composition of the important score *Déserts* by Varèse, which effectively combined electronic sound with other instruments. The next work by Ussachevsky and Luening was *A Poem in Cycles and Bells* for Tape Recorder and Orch., first performed by the Los Angeles Phil. on Nov. 22, 1954. On March 31, 1960, Leonard Bernstein conducted the N.Y. Phil. in the commissioned work by Ussachevsky and Luening entitled *Concerted Piece for Tape Recorder and Orchestra*. On Jan. 12, 1956, Ussachevsky and Luening provided taped background for Shakespeare's *King Lear*, produced by Orson Welles, at the N.Y.C. Center, and for Margaret Webster's production of *Back to Methuselah* for the N.Y. Theater Guild in 1958. They also provided the electronic score for the documentary *The Incredible Voyage*, broadcast over the CBS-TV network on Oct. 13, 1965. Among works that Ussachevsky wrote for electronic sound without partnership were *A Piece for Tape Recorder* (1956), *Studies in Sound, Plus* (1959), and *The Creation* (1960). In 1968 Ussachevsky began experimenting with the synthesizer, with the aid of a computer. One of the works resulting from these experiments was *Conflict* (1971), intended to represent the mystical struggle between two ancient deities. In 1959 Ussachevsky was one of the founders of the Columbia-Princeton Electronic Music Center; was active as a lecturer at various exhibitions of electronic sounds; traveled also to Russia and to China to present his music. He held two Guggenheim fellowships (1957, 1960). In 1973 Ussachevsky was elected to membership in the National Inst. of Arts and Letters.

WORKS: TAPE: *Transposition, Reverberation, Experiment, Composition* (1951–52); *Sonic Contours* (N.Y., Oct. 28, 1952); *Underwater Valse* (1952); *Piece for Tape Recorder* (1956); *Metamorphoses* (1957); *Improvisation on 4711* (1958); *Linear Contrasts* (1958); *Studies in Sound, Plus* (1959); *Wireless Fantasy: De Forrest Murmurs* (1960); *Of Wood and Brass* (1964–65); *Suite from Music for Films* (1967); *Piece for Computer* (1968); *2 Sketches for Computer Piece No. 2* (1971); *Conflict*, electronic scene from *Creation* (1973–75). **WITH TAPE:** *3 Scenes from Creation: Prologue "Enumu Elish"* for 2 Choruses and Tape, *Interlude* for Soprano, Mezzo-soprano, and Tape (1960; rev. 1973), and *Epilogue: "Spell of Creation"* for Soprano and Chorus (1971); *Creation Prologue* for 4 Choruses and Tape (1960–61); *Scenes from No Exit* for Speaker and Tape (1963); *Colloquy* for Solo Instruments, Orch. and Tape (Salt Lake City, Feb. 20, 1976); *Two Experiments* for Electronic Valve Instrument and Tape (1979; in collaboration with N. Steiner); *Celebration 1980* for Electronic Valve Instrument, String Orch., and Tape (N.Y., April 1980); *Pentagram* for Oboe and Tape (BBC, London, Nov. 1980); *Celebration 1981* for Electronic Valve Instrument, 6 Winds, Strings, and Tape (N.Y., Oct. 30, 1981; rev. as *Divertimento* for Electronic Valve Instrument, 3 Winds, 3 Brass, Strings, Percussion, and Tape, 1980–81); *Dialogues and Contrasts* for Brass Quintet and Tape (N.Y., Feb. 12, 1984). **INCIDENTAL MUSIC FOR TAPE:** *To Catch a Thief* (sound effects for the film; 1954); *Mathematics* (television score; 1957); *The Boy who Saw Through* (film; 1959); *No Exit* (film; 1962); *Line of Apogee* (film; 1967); *Mourning Becomes Electra* (sound effects for the opera by M. Levy; 1967); *The Cannibals* (play; 1969); *2 Images for the Computer Piece* (film; 1969); *Duck, Duck* (film; 1970); *We* (radio play; 1970). **Film:** *Circle of Fire* (1940). **ORCH.:** *Theme and Variations* (1936); *Piece* for Flute and Chamber Orch. (1947); *Miniatures for a Curious Child* (1950); *Intermezzo* for Piano and Orch. (1952); *Dances and Fanfares for a Festive Occasion* (1980). **CHAMBER:** *2 Dances* for Flute and Piano (1948); *4 Studies* for Clarinet and Electronic Valve Instrument (1979); *Suite* for Trombone Choir (1980); *Triskelion* for Oboe and Piano (1982); *Nouvelette pour Bourges* for Electronic Valve Instrument and Piano (1983); piano pieces. **VOCAL:** *Jubilee Cantata* for Baritone, Reader, Chorus, and Orch. (1937–38); *Psalm XXIV* for Chorus and Organ, or for Organ and 5 Brass, or for 7 Brass (1948); *2 Autumn Songs on Rilke's Text* for Soprano and Piano (1952); *Missa Brevis* for Soprano, Chorus, and Brass (1972). **WITH OTTO LUENING:** *Incantation* for Tape (1953); *Rhapsodic Variations* for Orch. and Tape (1953–54; N.Y., March 20, 1954); *A Poem in Cycles and Bells* for Orch. and Tape (Los Angeles, Nov. 22, 1954); *Of Identity*, ballet for Tape (1954); *Carlsbad Caverns*, television score for Tape (1955); *King Lear*, incidental music (3 versions, 1956); *Back to Methuselah*, incidental music for Tape (1958); *Concerted Piece* for Orch. and Tape (N.Y., March 31, 1960); *Incredible Voyage*, television score for Tape (1968; also with Shields and Smiley).—**NS/LK/DM**

Ustvolskaya, Galina (Ivanovna), significant Russian composer and pedagogue; b. Petrograd, June 17, 1919. She studied at the arts college affiliated with the Leningrad Cons. (1937–39) and composition with Shostakovich and Steinberg at the Leningrad Cons. (1940–41; 1945–47), where she pursued postgraduate training with G. Rimsky-Korsakov (1947–50). From 1948 to 1977 she taught composition there. In 1992 she was awarded the Artist's Prize of Heidelberg. During the Stalin era, her music was rarely performed; although never officially condemned by the Soviet state, her compositions were accused of being difficult to understand, "narrow- minded," and "obstinate." Shostakovich defended her against such accusations and held her in such esteem that he sent MSS of his own scores to her for comment. He quoted from the finale of her Clarinet Trio (1949) in his String Quartet No. 5 and in his *Suite on Verses of Michelangelo*. Ustvolskaya's early music was marked by a Romantic Russian manner, but she later developed greater melodic diversity and harmonic complexity, with occasional usages of serial techniques. Some of her works are of vast dimensions. The spiritual qualities of many of her scores are a welcome complement to their startling dissonances and rhythmic drive.

WORKS (all 1st perf. in Leningrad unless otherwise given): **ORCH.:** Concerto for Piano, Strings, and Timpani (1946); 5 syms.: No. 1 for 2 Boy's Voices and Orch. (1955), No. 2, *True and Eternal Bliss*, for Voice and Orch. (1979; Oct. 8, 1980), No. 3, *Jesus, Messiah, Save Us!* (1983; Amsterdam, Jan. 18, 1995), and Nos. 4 and 5 (see **CHAMBER**). **CHAMBER:** String Quartet (1945); Trio for Clarinet, Violin, and Piano (1949; Jan. 11, 1968); Octet for 2 Oboes, 4 Violins, Timpani, and Piano (1949–50; Nov. 17, 1970); Violin Sonata (1953; March 5, 1961); *Grand Duet* for Cello and Piano (1959; Dec. 14, 1977); Duet for Violin and Piano (1964; May 23, 1968); *Composition No. 1: Dona nobis pacem* for Piccolo, Tuba, and Piano (1970–71; Feb. 19, 1975), *No. 2: Dies irae* for 8 Double Basses, Percussion, and Piano (1972–73; Feb. 14, 1977), and *No. 3: Benedictus, Qui Venit* for 4 Flutes, 4 Bassoons, and Piano (1974–75; Dec. 14, 1977); Sym. No. 4, *Prayer*, for Contralto, Trumpet, Tam-tam, and Piano (1985–87; Heidelberg, June 24, 1988); Sym. No. 5, *Amen*, for Male Speaker, Oboe, Trumpet, Tuba, Violin, and Percussion (1989–90). **Piano:** 6 sonatas: No. 1 (1947; Feb. 20, 1974), No. 2 (1949; Dec. 14, 1977), No. 3 (1952; Feb. 16, 1972), No. 4 (1957; April 4, 1973), No. 5 (1986), and No. 6 (1988); *12 Preludes* (1953; March 20, 1968). **—NS/LK/DM**

Utendal, Alexander,

Utendal, Alexander, Netherlandish composer; b. c. 1535; d. Innsbruck, May 7, 1581. He entered the service of the Habsburgs at an early age. He became an alto in the court choir of the emperor's son, Archduke Ferdinand, in Prague in 1564. He followed his patron to Innsbruck when the latter became governor of the Tirol in 1566. From about 1572 until his death he was deputy Kapellmeister in the court chapel.

WORKS (all publ. in Nuremberg): *7 psalmi poenitentiales* (1570); *Sacrarum cantionum* for 5 Voices (1571); *Sacrae cantiones* for 6 and More Voices (1573); *3 missae* for 5 to 6 Voices (1573); *Fröliche neue teutsche und frantzösiche Lieder* for 4 to 5 and More Voices (1574); *Liber 3 sacrarum cantionum* for 5 to 6 Voices (1577); *Responsoria* (1586); other works in contemporary collections and MSS.

BIBL.: J. Lechthaler, *Die kirchenmusikalischen Werke von A. U.* (diss., Univ. of Vienna, 1919).**—NS/LK/DM**

Uttal, Jai, American singer and musician; b. N.Y. He studied classical piano as a child before also learning to play banjo, harmonica, and electric guitar. His diverse musical abilities were reflected in his learning a wide range of styles and absorbing everything from Jimi Hendrix to John Coltrane to modern classical music. By age 19, he became entranced by the music of world famous Indian musician Ali Akbar Khan and was compelled to move to Calif. to study voice and the 25-string sarod under Khan's guidance. He was later able to apply his Indian classical training to the other forms of music he played during the 1970s and 1980s, including reggae, punk, Motown, and blues. During the 1970s, he made many pilgrimages to India while also studying music in Calif. under various tutors. One of those Indian treks was incredibly influential—he lived and played amongst Bengalese street musicians named the Bauls, communicating with them entirely through music, and the lessons learned there would permanently alter his musical course. Uttal has been categorized both as a world and jazz musician, but his music blends those elements with pop and fusion to form a signature sound that is full of warmth and romanticism. The musician originally began his recording career with his 1990 debut *Footprints*, an album that found him taking his inspirational journeys to India (particularly his time spent with the Bauls) and applying it to his Western heritage.

As his work has progressed, he has moved away from works that center more on him and work in a group setting (including occasional songwriting collaborations), one which includes guitar, trombone, violin, bass, and percussion. The electronic influences of his debut soon were stripped away and replaced by more pop-based sounds, which later lead to fusion and even a few reggae influences. His main instrument is the dotar, which sonically resembles a sitar but possesses a crisper sound with less twang. It dominates his first two albums, but as his music has matured, he has let the sounds of the Pagan Love Orch. become stronger and more independent. No matter what album you listen to, though, the sound of Uttal and his orchestra is very distinct. He has also performed on albums by the Hieroglyphics Ensemble, Tulku, the Peter Apfelbaum Sextet, and Gabrielle Roth & the Mirrors, and has produced two albums for Ali Akbar Khan.

DISC.: *Footprints* (1990); *Monkey* (1992); *Beggars and Saints* (1995); *Shiva Station* (1997); *Spirit Room: A Retrospective* (2000). **—BR**

Uttini, Francesco Antonio Baldassare, Italian composer and conductor; b. Bologna, 1723; d. Stockholm, Oct. 25, 1795. He studied with Padre Martini, Perti, and Sandoni. In 1743 he became a member of the Accademia dei Filarmonici in Bologna. He first appeared as a singer and conductor with Mingotti's operatic touring group (c. 1752); in 1755, went to Stockholm as conductor of an Italian opera company; was named Master of the King's Music in 1767, and also was principal conductor at the Royal Opera until his retirement in 1788. Historically he is important as the composer of the earliest operas on Swedish texts; the first, *Thetis och Pelée*, was written for the inauguration of the new Royal Opera in Stockholm (Jan. 18, 1773); another opera to a Swedish libretto, tr. from the French, was *Aline, Drotning uti Golconda* (Aline, Queen of Golconda), produced at the Royal Opera on Jan. 11, 1776. Of Uttini's Italian operas, the best is *Il Re pastore* (Stockholm, July 24, 1755). A great admirer of Gluck, he brought out many of that composer's works in Stockholm. He also wrote three sinfonie, the oratorios *La Giuditta* (Bologna, 1742) and *La passione di Gesù* (Stockholm, 1776), several cantatas, six sonatas for Harpsichord (Stockholm, 1756), and six Sonatas for two Violins and Bass (London, 1768). **—NS/LK/DM**

Utyosov, Leonid (Osipovich), composer, singer, leader; b. Odessa, Ukraine, March 21, 1895; d. Moscow, Russia, March 10, 1982. He played violin as a child; after the Revolution, he performed as an actor and entertainer in various cabarets, often incorporating different elements, including acrobatics. In 1920 Utyosov organized the first Soviet jazz group Tea Jazz, the name alluding to the song "Tea for Two" by Youmans, which was immensely popular in Russia at the time; subsequently he created various musical comedies such as *Jazz on the Turning Point* (1930). He also performed numerous popular Russian songs and revived old army and navy ballads.

BIBL.: L. Utyosov, *Thanks, Heart* (Moscow, 1976).—**NS/LP**

V

Vaccai, Nicola, Italian composer and singing teacher; b. Tolentino, March 15, 1790; d. Pesaro, Aug. 5, 1848. He went to Rome as a youth and took lessons in counterpoint with Jannaconi, then studied with Paisiello in Naples (from 1812). He was a singing teacher in Venice (1818–21), Trieste (1821–23), and in Frohsdorf, near Wiener Neustadt (1822). He taught in Paris (1830) and in England (1830–33) before returning to Italy; later became vice censore at the Milan Cons., assuming the post of censore in 1838; in 1844 he retired to Pesaro. Although he found little success as a composer for the theater, he won distinction as a singing teacher; his *Metodo pratico di canto italiano per camera diviso in 15 lezioni, ossiano Solfeggi progressivi ed elementari sopra parole di Metastasio* (London, 1832) became a standard work in its field. Among his operas were *Pietro il Grande, ossia Un geloso all tortura* (Parma, Jan. 17, 1824), *La Pastorella feudataria* (Turin, Sept. 18, 1824), and *Giulietta e Romeo*, after Shakespeare (Milan, Oct. 31, 1825), the last scene of which was often used in performances of Bellini's *I Capuletti e i Montecchi*. He also composed much vocal music, including sacred works, cantatas, and over 100 chamber pieces.

BIBL.: G. Vaccai, *La vita di N. V. scritta dal figlio Giulio con prefazione del professore A. Biaggi* (Bologna, 1882).—**NS/LK/DM**

Vacek, Miloš, Czech composer; b. Horní Roveň, June 20, 1928. He studied organ at the Prague Cons. (1943–47), then took a course in composition with Řídký and Pícha at the Prague Academy of Arts and Music (1947–51). From 1954 he devoted himself totally to composition.

WORKS: DRAMATIC: Opera: *Jan Želivský* (1953–56; rev. 1974; Olomouc, April 15, 1984); *Bratr Žak* (Brother Jacques; 1976–78; Ostrava, June 12, 1982); *Romance pro křídlovku* (Romance for Bugle Horn; 1980–81; Czech Radio, Plzeň, Oct. 26, 1983; 1st stage perf., České Budějovice, Dec. 12, 1987); *Kocour Mikeš* (Mikeš the Tom Cat; 1981–82; Brno, March 28, 1986). **Ballet:** *Komediantská pohádka* (The Comedian's Fairytale; 1957–58); *Vitr ve vlasech* (Wind in the Hair; 1960–61); *Posledni pampeliška* (The Last Dandelion; 1963–64); *Milá sedmi loupežníků* (The Mistress of Seven Robbers; 1966); *Meteor* (1966); *Štastná sedma* (Lucky Sevens; 1966). **Musicals:** *Noc je můj den* (The Night Is My Day), blues drama about the life of Bessie Smith (1962; Frankfurt am Main, March 15, 1964); *Cisařovy nové šaty* (The Emperor's New Clothes; 1962); *Madame Sans Gêne* (1968); *Vitr z Alabamy* (Wind from Alabama; 1970). **ORCH.:** *Sinfonietta* (1951); *Jarní suita* (Spring Suite) for Flute, Clarinet, Horn or English Horn, and Strings (1963); *Serenáda* for Strings (1965); *Symfonie Májová* (May Sym.; 1974); *Olympijský oheň* (Olympic Flame), symphonic poem (1975); *Mé Kamenici nad Lipou* (To My Kamenici nad Lipou), suite (1979); *Svědomí světa* (World's Conscience), symphonic poem to commemorate the 40th anniversary of the razing of Lidice and Ležáky (1981). **CHAMBER:** Suite for Cello and Piano (1947); Violin Sonatina (1949); String Quartet (1949); *Divertimento* for Violin, Cello, Guitar, and Bass Clarinet (1965); *Šumavské metamorfózy* (Šumava Metamorphoses), quintet for Flute, Oboe, Violin, Viola, and Cello (1971); *Lovecká suita* (Hunting Suite) for 4 Horns (1973); *Bukolická suita* (Bucolic Suite) for 4 Trombones (1977); *Dialogue* for Oboe and Piano (1977); also works for Piano, including *Sonata drammatica* (1972) and *Zatoulané listy z milostného deníčku* (Sheets from a Love Diary Gone Astray; 1972; also for Chamber Orch.). **VOCAL:** *Poéma o padlých hrdinech* (Poem of Fallen Heroes) for Alto and Orch. (1974); cantatas; choruses; songs. —**NS/LK/DM**

Vache, Warren (Webster Jr.), jazz cornetist, flugelhornist; b. Rahway, N.J., Feb. 21, 1951. He grew up with jazz; his father was a bassist in a Dixie-style band and a committed jazz chronicler. His father's band included Pee Wee Erwin, who gave Vache Jr. lessons when he took up the cornet. He also studied with Jim Fitzpatrick and was influenced by Bobby Hackett and Ruby Braff. After taking a degree in music, he frequently played with his father's band and then with Benny Goodman, where his reputation flourished. He soon became a regular at Eddie Condon's club in N.Y. with Vic Dickenson and Bob Wilber and became a fixture in the N.Y. Jazz Repertory Orch. (c. 1972–74). Around this time he met Scott Hamilton, and the two men began a collaboration that lasts until today. In the late 1970s Vache made a series of solo albums, each becoming more successful, while continuing to make recordings with Hamilton. The duo created albums that solidified their reputations as kings of the mainstream. Throughout the 1980s Vache toured the world extensively and cemented his position as a major talent. His records, from solo efforts to the duet affairs with Hamilton and, recently, his *Warm Evenings* album with the Beaux Arts String Quartet, continue to sell in massive quantities. In 1984 he suffered an accident which severed the tendons in his right hand; fortunately it had no lasting effect on his playing, and later that year he appeared at the Edinburgh Festival to a standing ovation.

Disc.: *Jersey Jazz at Midnight* (1975); *First Time Out* (1976); *Blues Walk* (1977); *In N.Y. City* (1978); *Jillian* (1978); *Polished Brass* (1979); *Iridescence* (1981); *Midtown Jazz* (1982); *Easy Going* (1986); *Warm Evenings* (1989); *Horn of Plenty* (1993); *Swingin' & Singin'* (1994); *Syncopatin Seven* (1994); *Talk to Me Baby* (1995); *Stardust* (1995); *Celebrate the Music of Isham Jones* (1996); *Live at the Vineyard* (1996); *Shine* (1997); *Warren Plays Warren* (1997); *Plays Harry Warren: An Affair to Remember* (1998); *Recorded Live in Hamburg* (1999); *Mrs. Vache's Boys* (1999); *What Is There to Say?* (2000); *Swingtime!* (2000).—**MM/LP**

Vachon, Pierre, French violinist and composer; b. Arles, June 1731; d. Berlin, Oct. 7, 1803. He studied with Chiabrano in Paris from 1751, first appearing at the Concert Spirituel on Dec. 24, 1756, as soloist in his own concerto. From 1761 he was 1st violinist in the orch. of the Prince de Conti. In 1772 he gave concerts in London and then returned to Paris; by 1775 he was again in London, where he remained for some 10 years. He then went to Germany, and became concertmaster of the royal orch. in Berlin in 1788; was pensioned in 1798.

Works: DRAMATIC: *Renaud d'Ast*, comédie (Fontainebleau, Oct. 12, 1765; in collaboration with J.-C. Trial); *Ésope à Cythère*, comédie (Paris, Dec. 15, 1766; in collaboration with J.-C. Trial); *Les Femmes et le secret*, comédie (Paris, Nov. 9, 1767); *Hippomène et Atalante*, ballet-héroïque (Paris, Aug. 8, 1769); *Sara, ou La Fermière écossaise*, comédie (Paris, May 8, 1773). **ORCH.:** *6 symphonies á 4 parties* with Horns ad libitum (Paris, 1761); other syms.; at least 2 violin concertos. **CHAMBER:** String quartets: 6 as op.6 (Paris, c. 1773), 6 as op.7, book 2 (Paris, 1773; also publ. as *6 Quartettos*, London, c. 1776), 6 as op.9, book 3 (Paris, 1774), 6 as op.5 (London, c. 1775), 6 as op.6 (London, 1776), *6 quatuors concertans*, op.11 (Paris, 1782), and *3 Quartettos* (London, n.d.); 6 sonates for Violin and Bass, op.1 (Paris, 1760); 6 sonates for Violin and Bass, op.3 (Paris, 1769; also publ. as *6 soli*, London, c. 1769); 6 trios for 2 Violins and Bass, op.4 (Paris, c. 1772); 6 trios for 2 Violins and Cello, op.5 (Paris, c. 1772); 6 trios for 2 Violins and Basso Continuo, op.4 (London, c. 1775); *6 Easy Duettos* for 2 Violins, op.5 (London, c. 1775); other pieces in contemporary collections.—**NS/LK/DM**

Vačkář, family of Czech composers:

(1) Václav Vačkář; b. Prague, Aug. 12, 1881; d. there, Feb. 4, 1954. He received training in military music in Przemyśl, Poland (1895–98), then was active as a conductor and orch. player in various locales before playing in the Czech Phil. (1913–19), the Vinohrad Opera Orch. (1919–20), and the Šak Phil. (1920–21); after composition studies with Říhovský and Křička (1920–22), he devoted himself to composing, writing on music, and administrative work. He was awarded the Smetana Prize of Prague in 1952. He wrote *Lidová nauka o harmonii* (Popular Treatise on Harmony; Prague, 1942) and with D. Vačkář, *Instrumentace symfonického orchestru a hudby dechové* (Instrumentation for the Symphony Orchestra and Wind Music; Prague, 1954). Of his more than 300 works, about half are in a popular or light vein, including numerous marches and waltzes. He also wrote several symphonic poems, a clarinet concertino, four string quartets, choral pieces, and songs.

(2) Dalibor Cyril Vačkář, son of the preceding; b. Korčula, Sept. 19, 1906; d. Prague, Oct. 21, 1984. He studied violin with Reissig and composition with Šín at the Prague Cons. (1923–29); also attended master classes of Hoffmann and Suk (1929–31). From 1934 to 1945 he played violin in the Prague Radio Orch.; after working as a film dramatist (1945–47), he devoted himself mainly to composition; also wrote music criticism, poetry, and plays. He used the pseudonyms Pip Faltys, Peter Filip, Tomáš Martin, and Karel Raymond for his light music. With his father, he wrote *Instrumentace symfonického orchestru a hudby dechové* (Instrumentation for the Symphony Orchestra and Wind Music; Prague, 1954).

Works: DRAMATIC: Ballet: *Švanda dudák* (Svanda the Bagpiper; 1950–53; Prague Radio, April 7, 1954); *Sen noci svatojanské* (A Midsummer Night's Dream), after Shakespeare (1955–57). **ORCH.:** *Overture* (1929); two violin concertos (1931, 1958); five syms.: No. 1, *Optimistická* (Optimistic; 1941), No. 2, *Země vyvolená* (The Chosen Land), for Contralto, Chorus, and Orch. (1947), No. 3, *Smoking Symphony* (1947–48; orchestration of his *Smoking Sonata* for Piano; the curious subtitle, symbolizing fire and smoke in the lives of men from antiquity to the present, is in Eng. only), No. 4, *O míru* (Of Peace; 1949–50), and No. 5, *Pro juventute* (1978–82); *Symphonic Scherzo* (1945); two sinfoniettas (1947; *Jubilee*, 1984); *Czech Concerto* for Piano and Orch. (1952); *Prelude and Metamorphoses* (1953); *Furiant-Fantasie* for Chamber Orch. (1960); *Concerto da camera* for Bassoon and Chamber String Orch. (1962); *Charakteristikon*, trombone concerto (1965); *Legenda o člověku* (Legend of Men), concerto for Harpsichord, Winds, and Percussion (1966); Clarinet Concerto (1966); *Prelude* for Chamber String Orch. (1966); *Concerto grosso* for Soprano Saxophone, Accordion, Guitar, and Orch. (1967); *In fide, spe et caritate*, concerto for Organ, Winds, and Percussion (1969); *Appellatio* for Women's Chorus and Orch. (1970; Prague, Oct. 20, 1977); *Příběh o pěti kapitolách* (5-Chapter Story) for Clarinet, Strings, and Percussion (1971); *Musica concertante* (1973). **CHAMBER:** *Trio giocoso* for Piano Trio (1929); 2 violin sonatas (1930; *Dedication*, 1961, with each movement dedicated to Vačkář's teachers: Reissig, Šín, Hoffmann, and Suk); String Quartet (1931–32); *Jaro 38*, piano trio (1938); *Monolog* for Violin (1940); Quartet for Piano, Oboe, Clarinet, and Bassoon (1948); *Quintetto giocoso* for Wind Instruments (1950; music from the ballet *Švanda dudák*); *Suite giocoso* for Piano Trio (1960); *Dialogue* for Violin (1961); *3 Studies* for Harpsichord (1961); Concerto for String Quartet (1962); Concerto for Trumpet, Piano, and Percussion (1963); *Pianoforte cantante*, 5 lyric reminiscences for Piano, Double Bass, and Percussion (1968); *Partita* for Trumpet (1968); *Milieu d'enfant* for 5 Percussion Groups (1970); *Intimní hudba* (Private Music) for Violin and Piano (1972); *Furiant-fantasie* for Piano Trio (1974); *Verses* for Flute and Guitar (1975); *Symposium* for Brass Quintet (1976); Oboe concertante for Oboe, Clarinet, Bass Clarinet,

Horn, String Quartet, Percussion, and Piano (1977); *Monograms*, 4 poems for String Quartet (1979; transcribed from the piano work); *Portraits* for Wind Quintet (1980; transcribed from the piano work); *Juniores*, 4 movements for String Quartet (1981; transcribed from the piano work); *Extempore*, piano quartet (1983). **Piano:** *Smoking Sonata* (1936); *Extempore*, 6 pieces (1937); *Piano Fantasy*, on a theme from Schubert's *The Arch* (1962); *Perspektivy* (1971); *3 Etudes* (1977); *Monograms* (1978); *Portraits* (1980); *Juniores* (1981).

(3) Tomas Vačkář, son of the preceding; b. Prague, July 31, 1945; d. (suicide) there, May 2, 1963. He was a gifted composer, but chose to end his life shortly after his graduation from the Prague Cons. at the age of 18. His works, all written between July 1960 and April 1963, include *Sonatina furore* for Piano, *Concerto recitativo* for Flute, String Orch., and Piano, *Tři dopisy divkam* (Three Letters to a Girl), after a poem by an anonymous Czech student, for Voice and Piano or Winds and Percussion, *Teen-agers*, piano sonata, *Metamorfózy na tema japonske ukolebavky* (Metamorphoses on the Theme of a Japanese Lullaby) for Orch., *Scherzo melancolico* for Orch., and *Skicář Tomáše Vačkáře* (Tomáš Vačkář's Sketchbook), 10 pieces for Piano; a *Requiem* remained unfinished. **—NS/LK/DM**

Vadé, Jean-Joseph, French poet, dramatist, and composer; b. Ham, Picardy, Jan. 17, 1719; d. Paris, July 4, 1757. He was taken to Paris by his family when he was five. He was made contrôleur du vingtième arrondissement (a tax-collecting position) in Soissons in 1739; after serving in this capacity in Laon and Rouen, he was made secretary to the Duke of Agenois in Paris in 1743. He began writing for the Comédie-Française in Paris in 1749, achieving success with his first opéra-comique, *La Fileuse* (1752); subsequently brought out other works there. He was awarded a pension by Louis XV (1751). His importance rests upon his creation of the genre poissard, or fish-market style, which permeates his opéras-comiques and chansons.

WORKS: DRAMATIC: Opéras-comiques: (all 1st perf. in Paris): *La Fileuse* (March 8, 1752); *Le Poirier* (Aug. 7, 1752); *Le Bouquet du roi* (Aug. 24, 1752; in collaboration with J. Fleury and Lattaignant); *Le Suffisant, ou Le Petit Maître dupé* (March 12, 1753); *Le Rien* (April 10, 1753); *Le Trompeur trompé, ou La Rencontre imprévue* (Feb. 18, 1754); *Il était temps* (June 28, 1754); *La Fontaine de jouvence* (Sept. 17, 1754; in collaboration with Noverre); *La Nouvelle Bastienne* (Sept. 17, 1754; in collaboration with L. Anseaume); *Compliment de clôture* (Oct. 6, 1754); *Les Troyennes en Champagne* (Feb. 1, 1755); *Jérôme et Fanchonette, ou La Pastorale de la grenouillère* (Feb. 18, 1755); *Compliment de clôture* (April 6, 1755); *Le Confidant heureux* (July 31, 1755); *Folette, ou L'Enfant gâté* (Sept. 6, 1755); *Nicaise* (Feb. 7, 1756); *Les Raccoleurs* (March 11, 1756); *L'Impromptu du coeur* (Feb. 8, 1757); *Compliment pour la clôture de l'Opéra-Comique* (April 3, 1757); *Le Mauvais plaisant, ou Le Drôle de corps* (Aug. 17, 1757); also *La Folle raisonnable* (not perf.).**—NS/LK/DM**

Vaduva, Leontina, Romanian soprano; b. Rosiile, Dec. 1, 1960. She studied at the Bucharest Cons. After winning the Concours de Chant in Toulouse in 1986, she made her operatic debut as Manon in Toulouse and won the 's-Hertogenbosch Competition in the Netherlands in 1987. In 1988 she sang Ninetta in *La gazza ladra* at the Théâtre des Champs-Elysées in Paris and made her debut as Manon at London's Covent Garden. Her subsequent engagements at Covent Garden included Juliette in 1994 and Micaëla in 1996. She also sang in Bordeaux, Avignon, Bonn, Monte Carlo, and other European cities.**—NS/LK/DM**

Vaet, Jacobus, Flemish composer; b. Courtrai or Harelbeke, c. 1529; d. Vienna, Jan. 8, 1567. He was a choirboy in the Church of Notre Dame at Courtrai (1543–46). After his voice changed, he received a scholarship from the church, and entered the Univ. of Louvain in 1547. In 1550 he was a tenor in the Flemish Chapel of Charles V, and by Jan. 1, 1554, he was listed as Kapellmeister of the chapel of Maximilian, then the nominal King of Bohemia. His position was enhanced when his patron became Emperor Maximilian II. Vaet's music exhibits a great variety of techniques, ranging in style from those of Josquin des Prez to those of Lassus. The formative influence, however, is mainly that of Nicolas Gombert, with a characteristic florid imitation in contrapuntal parts. See M. Steinhardt, ed., *Jacobus Vaet: Sämtliche Werke*, Denkmäler der Tonkunst in Österreich, XCVIII (1961), C (1962), CIII-CIV (1963), CVIII-CIX (1964), CXIII-CXIV (1965), CXVI (1967), and CXVIII (1968).

WORKS: 9 masses; 8 Magnificats; motets: *Modulationes, liber I* for 5 Voices (Venice, 1562); *Modulationes, liber II* for 5 to 6 Voices (Venice, 1562); *Qui operatus est Petro* for 6 Voices (Venice, 1560); other motets publ. in contemporary collections; 8 Salve Reginas; 8 hymns; several other pieces, including 3 chansons.

BIBL.: M. Steinhardt, *J. V. and His Motets* (East Lansing, Mich., 1951).**—NS/LK/DM**

Vainberg, Moisei, Polish-born Russian composer; b. Warsaw, Dec. 8, 1919. He studied piano with Turczynski at the Warsaw Cons., graduating in 1939, then studied composition with Zolotarev at the Minsk Cons. In 1943 he settled in Moscow. In his music he follows the precepts of socialist realism in its ethnic aspects; according to the subject, he makes use of Jewish, Polish, Moldavian, or Armenian folk melos, in tasteful harmonic arrangements devoid of abrasive dissonances.

WORKS: DRAMATIC: Opera: *The Sword of Uzbekistan* (1942); *The Woman Passenger* (1968); *Love of D'Artagnan*, after Alexandre Dumas (1972). **Ballet:** *Battle for the Fatherland* (1942); *The Golden Key* (1955); *The White Chrysanthemum* (1958); *Requiem* (1967). **ORCH.:** 16 syms.: No. 1 (1942), No. 2 for Strings (1946), No. 3 (1949), No. 4 (1957), No. 5 (1962), No. 6 for Boy's Chorus and Orch. (1963), No. 7 for Strings and Harpsichord (1964), No. 8, *The Flowers of Poland*, for Tenor, Chorus, and Orch. (1964), No. 9, *Surviving Pages*, for Reader, Chorus, and Orch. (1967), No. 10 for Strings (1968), No. 11, *Triumphant Symphony*, for Chorus and Orch., dedicated to Lenin's centennial (1969), No. 12 (1976; Moscow, Oct. 13, 1979), No. 13 (1976), No. 14 (1977; Moscow, Oct. 8, 1980), No. 15, "I have faith in this earth," for Chorus and Orch. (1977; Moscow, April 12, 1979), and No. 16 (1981; Moscow, Oct. 19, 1982); 2 sinfoniettas (1948, 1960); *Moldavian Rhapsody* (Moscow, Nov. 30, 1949); *Slavic Rhapsody* (1950); Cello Concerto (1956); Violin Concerto (1960); Flute Concerto (1961); Trumpet Concerto (1967); Clarinet Concerto (1970). **CHAMBER:** 12 string quartets (1937–70); Piano Quintet (1944); Piano Trio (1945); String

Trio (1951); 20 sonatas and 2 sonatinas for Various Instruments, with Piano; 24 preludes for Cello Solo; 23 preludes for Piano. **VOCAL:** 3 cantatas: *The Diary of Love* (1965), *Hiroshima Haikus* (1966), *On This Day Lenin Was Born* for Chorus and Orch. (1970); songs.—**NS/LK/DM**

Vajda, János, Hungarian composer; b. Miskolc, Oct. 8, 1949. He received training in choral conducting from István Párkai and in composition from Emil Petrovics at the Budapest Academy of Music (graduated, 1975); after serving as répétiteur with the Hungarian Radio and Television Choir (1974–79), he completed his composition studies at the Sweelinck Cons. in Amsterdam (1979–80). From 1981 he taught at the Budapest Academy of Music. He won the Erkel Prize in 1981.

WORKS: DRAMATIC: Opera: *Barabbás* (1976–77); *Mario és a varázsló* (Mario and the Magician; 1983–85). **Ballet:** *Az igazság pillanata* (The Moment of Truth; 1981); *Don Juan árnyéka rajtunk* (Don Juan's Shadow Is Cast on Us; 1981); *Izzó planéták* (Glowing Planets; 1983); *Jön a cirkusz* (Circus Is Coming; 1984). **ORCH.:** *Holland anziksz* (Picture Postcard from Holland) for Chamber Ensemble (1979); *Búcsú* (Farewell; 1978–80); *Pentaton, in memoriam R.M.* for Chamber Ensemble (1983). **CHAMBER:** *Gregorián ének* (Gregorian Chant) for Cimbalom (1974); *De angelis* for Wind Quintet and Tape (1978); *All That Music* for 2 Cimbaloms (1981); *Just for You No. 1* for Cello (1984) and *No. 2* for Violin (1987); *Mozi-zene* (Movie Music) for Piano and String Trio (1986); *Változatok* (Variations) for Piano (1987). **VOCAL:** *Tenebrae factae sunt* for Chorus (1972); *Két teszt* (2 Tests) for Mezzo-soprano, Flute, Clarinet, and Bassoon (1975); *Fekete gloria* (Black Halo) for Chorus (1977); *Stabat Mater* for 2 Women's Voices, Women's Chorus, and Chamber Ensemble (1978); *Ave Maris Stella* for Chorus (1979); Cantata for Chamber Chorus, Wind Quintet, String Quintet, and Celesta (1981); *Tristis est anima mea* for Chorus (1982); *Via crucis* for Chorus, 8 Winds, and Organ (1983); *Alleluja* for Chorus (1983); *Kolinda* for Chorus (1984); *Karácsonyi kantáta* (Christmas Cantata) for 2 Child Soloists, Chorus, Children's Chorus, and Orch. (1984–86); *Rapszódia* for Chorus (1987–88).—**NS/LK/DM**

Valcárcel, Edgar, Peruvian composer and teacher, nephew of **Teodoro Valcárcel;** b. Puno, Dec. 4, 1932. He studied composition with Andrés Sas at the Lima Cons., then went to N.Y., where he studied with Donald Lybbert at Hunter Coll.; subsequently traveled to Buenos Aires, where he took composition lessons with Ginastera; also had sessions with Messiaen in Paris, and with Malipiero, Maderna, and Dallapiccola in Italy; furthermore, he joined the Columbia-Princeton Electronic Music Center and worked with Ussachevsky. He held 2 Guggenheim fellowships (1966, 1968). He was prof. of composition at the Lima Cons. (from 1965). In his compositions, he adopted an extremely advanced idiom that combined serial and aleatory principles, leaving to the performer the choice to use or not to use given thematic materials.

WORKS: ORCH.: Concerto for Clarinet and Strings (1965; Lima, March 6, 1966); *Quenua* (Lima, Aug. 18, 1965); *Aleaciones* (Lima, May 5, 1967); Piano Concerto (Lima, Aug. 8, 1968); *Checán II* (Lima, June 5, 1970); *Ma'karabotasaq hachana* (1971); *Sajra* (1974); *Anti Memoria II* (Washington, D.C., April 25, 1980). **CHAMBER:** 2 string quartets (1962, 1963); *Espectros I* for Flute, Viola, and Piano (1964), *II* for Horn, Cello, and Piano (1968), and *III* for Oboe, Violin, and Piano (1974); *Dicotomías III* for 12 Instruments (Mexico City, Nov. 20, 1966); *Fisiones* for 10 Instruments (1967); *Hiwana uru* for 11 Instruments (1967); Trio for Amplified Violin, Trombone, and Clarinet (1968); *Poema* for Amplified Violin, Voice, Piano, and Percussion (1969); *Checán I* for 6 Instruments (1969), *III* for 19 Instruments (1971), and *V* for Strings (1974); *Montage 59* for String Quartet, Clarinet, Piano, and Lights (1971). **Piano:** 2 sonatas (1963, 1972); *Dicotomías I* and *II* (1966). **OTHER:** Choral pieces; multimedia works; electronic music, including *Antaras* for Flute, Percussion, and Electronics (1968).—**NS/LK/DM**

Valcárcel, Teodoro, Peruvian composer, uncle of **Edgar Valcárcel;** b. Puno, Oct. 17, 1900; d. Lima, March 20, 1942. He studied at the Milan Cons. (1914–16) and with Felipe Pedrell in Barcelona. In 1928 he won the National Prize for Peruvian composers, and was awarded a gold medal from the municipality of Lima for his studies in Peruvian folk music. In 1929 he went to Europe once more; presented a concert of his works in Paris (April 12, 1930). In 1931 he settled in Lima. He was of pure Indian origin; as a native of the highlands, he was able to collect Indian songs unpolluted by urban influences. He publ. *30 cantos de alma vernacular; 4 canciones incaicas; 25 romances de costa y sierra peruana; 180 melodias del folklore*. Among his original works are the ballets (with singing) *Suray-Surita* and *Ckori Kancha*; 2 symphonic suites (both 1939); *En las ruinas del Templo del Sol*, tone poem (1940); *Concierto indio* for Violin and Orch. (1940); *3 ensayos* for an ensemble of Native Instruments; *Fiestas andinas* for Piano; *Suite autóctona* for Violin and Piano; songs. A catalogue of his works was publ. by R. Holzmann in *Boletín Bibliográfico de la Universidad nacional mayor de San Marcos*, XII (1942).—**NS/LK/DM**

Valdengo, Giuseppe, Italian baritone; b. Turin, May 24, 1914. He studied cello at the Turin Cons., and also played the oboe; then decided to cultivate his voice, and took singing lessons with Michele Accoriutti. In 1936 he made his operatic debut as Figaro in *Il Barbiere di Siviglia* in Parma; in 1939, was engaged to sing at La Scala in Milan. On Sept. 19, 1946, he made his N.Y.C. Opera debut as Sharpless, remaining on its roster until 1948. On Dec. 19, 1947, he made his Metropolitan Opera debut in N.Y. as Tonio; continued on the company's roster until 1954; was also chosen by Toscanini to sing the roles of Amonasro, Renato, Iago, and Falstaff with the NBC Sym. Orch. He made guest appearances in London, Paris, Vienna, and South America. He also acted the part of Antonio Scotti in the film *The Great Caruso*. His association with Toscanini is related in his *Ho cantato con Toscanini* (Como, 1962).—**NS/LK/DM**

Valderrábano, Enrique Enriquez de *See* **Enriquez de Valderrábano, Enrique**

Valdes, Maximiano, Chilean conductor; b. Santiago, June 17, 1949. He studied piano, violin, and music history at the Santaigo Cons. After taking courses in composition and conducting at the Santa Cecilia Cons. in Rome, he continued conducting studies with Ferrara in Bologna, Siena, and Venice. He also attended conducting courses given by Bernstein and Ozawa at the Berkshire Music Center in Tanglewood (summer, 1977). From 1976 to 1980 he was an asst. conductor at the Teatro La Fenice in Venice. After winning 1st prize in the Malko conducting competition in Copenhagen in 1980, he appeared as a guest conductor throughout Europe. In 1984 he became principal guest conductor of the Orquesta Nacional de España in Madrid. In 1986–87 he conducted the Orquesta Sinfónica de Euskadi in San Sebastian. He was music director of the Buffalo Phil. from 1989 to 1998.—**NS/LK/DM**

Válek, Jiří, notable Czech composer, writer, and teacher; b. Prague, May 28, 1923. He was a composition student of Řídký at the Prague Cons., graduating from its master school in 1947. He also received private training in philosophy, aesthetics, music history, and theory. After graduating from the Prague Coll. of Higher Education in 1950, he took his Ph.D. at the Charles Univ. in Prague in 1952. From 1949 to 1952 he held the position of creative secretary of the Union of Czech Composers. He was a senior staff member of the state publishing firm Panton from 1959 to 1973. In 1966 he became a prof. at the Prague Cons. He was also artistic director of the state recording firm Supraphon (1974–79) and an assoc. prof. of composition at the Prague Academy of Musical Arts (from 1979). Among his writings are literary works and monographs. In his 17 syms., Válek has traversed an extensive ideological and artistic landscape, embracing both historical and contemporary events. Several of his stage pieces are rich in topical and satirical expression.

WORKS: DRAMATIC: *Shakespearean Variations*, music drama for 9 Actors, Commentator, and Nonet (1967); *Hour of Truth*, opera (1980); *Sonata on Auxiliary Life* for Moderator, Violin, Piano, and Percussion (1983); *Hamlet, our Contemporary*, satirical opera (1985); *Don't let us stone pygmies*, satirical opera (1991). **ORCH.:** Sinfonietta (1945); 17 syms.: No. 1, *Year 1948*, for Trumpet, Piano, and Orch. (1948), No. 2, *Classical*, for Chamber Orch. (1957; also for 2 Flutes, 2 Oboes, and Chamber String Orch.), No. 3, *Romantic*, for Soprano, Tenor Saxophone, and Orch. (1957–63), No. 4, *Dialogues with an Inner Voice*, for Mezzo-soprano, Baritone, Wind Orch., Piano, and Percussion, after Shakespeare (1964–65), No. 5, *Guernica*, after the Picasso painting (1968), No. 6, *Ekpyrosis*, for Flute, Piano, Percussion Ensemble, and Chamber Orch. (1969), No. 7, *Pompeian Frescoes*, for Chamber Orch., Piano, and Percussion Ensemble (1970), No. 8, *Hic sunt homines*, for Soprano and Orch., after a novella by Stefan Zweig (1971), No. 9, *Renaissance*, sym.- triple concerto for Violin, Viola, Cello, and Orch. (1971), No. 10, *Baroque*, for Violin, Piano, and Orch. (1973), No. 11, *Revolutionary*, for Violin, Viola, Piano, Wind Quintet, and Orch. (1974), No. 12, *Shakespearean*, sym.-concerto for Violin, Viola, and Orch. (1975; also for Violin, Viola, String Orch., Piano, and Percussion), No. 13, *Gothic*, for Chorus and Orch., to commemorate the 600th anniversary of the death of the Czech King Charles IV (1978), No. 14, *Trionfale*, for 2 Pianos and Orch. (1983), No. 14, *Sarcastic*, sym.-oratorio for Baritone, Bass, Women's Chorus, and Orch., after Karel Borovský (1986), No. 16, *Neter*, for Bass-baritone and Orch. (1987), and No. 17, *Station of Hradčany*, sym.-opera for Soprano, Mezzos-soprano, Tenor, Baritone, Bass-baritone, Chorus, and Orch. (1992); *The Dam*, symphonic poem (1959); *3 Nocturnes* for Viola and Chamber String Orch. (1960); *Beyond the Bounds of Tomorrow*, ceremonial march (1972); *Concerto drammatico* for Double Bass, Chamber Orch., and Percussion (1974); Violin Concerto, *Hymn of the Sun* (1975); Concerto for 2 Flutes and Chamber Orch. (1975); Marimba Concerto, *Festivo* (1975); *Ceremonial Overture* (1976); Piano Concerto, *Eroico* (1977); Viola Concerto, *Lirico* (1977); Concerto for Flute, Marimba, Harp, and Orch., *Giocoso* (1978); *Ceremonial fresco* (1979); *Cathedral* for Viola and Chamber String Orch. (1979); Cello Concerto, *Maestoso* (1981); *Concerto burlesco* for Horn and Chamber Orch. (1986). **CHAMBER:** 4 string quartets (1943; 1945; 1960; *Quattrocento*, 1972–73); 2 violin sonatas (1944, 1960); Suite for Flute, Clarinet, and Piano (1946); 2 viola sonatas (1948; *Tragic*, 1961); Concertino for 9 Winds and Piano (1960); Trumpet Sonata, *Eroica* (1960; also for Clarinet and Piano or String Orch.); *Concerto notturno* for Violin, Viola, and Cello (1967); *Suite drammatica* for Double Bass and Piano (1967); Flute Sonata (1969); 2 concertos for Flute, Oboe, Violin, Viola, Cello, and Harpsichord (1970; *Discovering the Day*, 1979); *Villa dei Misteri* for Violin and Piano (1971); *3 Sentences in Memory of A. Einstein* for Violin, Cello, and Piano (1973); *Cinque canzoni da sonar* for Oboe, Flute, Clarinet, and Bassoon (1974); *Revolutionary Quartet* for Violin, Viola, Clarinet, and Piano (1974); *5 Meditations on Themes from Czech Folk Songs* for Bass Clarinet and Piano (1974); *Tre sorrisi in onore W.A. Mozart* for Flute, Oboe, Violin, Viola, Cello, and Harpsichord (1975); *Fireworks and Fountains* for Marimba and Piano (1976); *4 Sculptures* for Renaissance Instruments (1977); Wind Quintet, *Gaiaemente e degnamente* (1977); Trio for Flute, Violin, and Piano (1978); *Clouds* for Violin and Piano (1979); *Dramas* for Cello and Guitar (1979); *4 Profiles after Shakespeare* for Oboe and Bassoon (1979); *Rectangular Circle*, grotesque for 5 Flutes (1979); *Concertant meditation* for Clarinet, Violin, Viola, and Cello (1980); *Dramatic Fresco* for Viola (1980); *5 capricci concerti* for Flute, Guitar, and Marimbaphone (1981); *Burlesque* for Flute and Piano (1986); *To be or not to be* for 8 Winds and 3 Timpani (1990). **Piano:** 3 sonatas (*The Year 1942*, 1942; 1965; 1970); *To have or to be*, concerto drammatico "in memory of Alexander Dubček" (1993). **VOCAL:** *The Glory of Nameless People*, cantata for Solo Voices, Chorus, and Piano (1958); *7 Monologues About Love* for Soprano and Piano (1959); *5 Variations on the Theme VERITAS* for Soprano and Piano (1970–76; also for Soprano, Men's Chorus, Wind Quintet, and Percussion, or Soprano, Men's Chorus, and Chamber Orch.); *La partenza della primavera* for Soprano and Orch. (1971; also for Soprano and Piano); *7 Musical Fables* for Low Voice and Piano (1972; also for Children's Chorus, Reciter, Children's Games, Flute, 2 Clarinets, Bassoon, and Percussion); *Life*, 5 sonnets for Men's Chorus (1975); *Sonatine of the Universe* for Children's Chorus, Vibraphone, and Piano (1976); *Virelais festivo in onore G. de Machaut et imperatore Bohemiae Carolus IV* for Soprano and Gothic Instruments (1978); *5 Shadows and Epilogue* for Bass Baritone, Piano, and Percussion (1978); *Song of Praise* for Soprano, Alto, Tenor, Bass, and Piano (1981); *Satirikon* for 1 or 2 Low Voices and Piano (1989); *The Young Gypsy Played*, song cycle for Woman's Voice, Man's Voice, and Instrumental Ensemble (1998).—**NS/LK/DM**

Valen, (Olav) Fartein, noted Norwegian composer; b. Stavanger, Aug. 25, 1887; d. Haugesund, Dec. 14, 1952. His father was a missionary in Madagascar, and Valen spent his early childhood there. When he was 6 the family returned to Stavanger, and he received piano lessons from Jeannette Mohr and others; taught himself theory. In 1906 he entered the Univ. of Christiania as a student of language and literature; he soon devoted himself entirely to music, pursuing his training in theory with Elling at the Christiania Cons., graduating as an organist in 1909; then received instruction in composition from Bruch, in theory and composition from Karl Leopold Wolf, and in piano from Heschberg at the Berlin Hochschule für Musik (1909–11). From 1916 to 1924 he lived on his family's farm in Valevåg; he then was active in Oslo, where he held the post of inspector of the Norwegian Music Collection at the library of the Univ. (1927–36). In 1935 he received the Norwegian State Salary of Art (a government life pension). His early music reflects the influence of Brahms, but later he developed a sui generis method of composition which he termed "atonal polyphony," completely free from traditional tonal relationships but strongly cohesive in contrapuntal fabric and greatly varied in rhythm; his first work in which he made use of this technique was a Piano Trio written in 1924. He never adopted an explicit 12-tone method of composition, but a parallelism with Schoenberg's music is observable. Valen stood apart from all nationalist developments in Oslo, yet his music attracted attention in modern circles; a Valen Soc. was formed in Norway in 1949, and in England in 1952, shortly before his death.

Works: Orch.: *Pastorale* (1929–30); *Sonetto di Michelangelo* (1932); *Nenia* (1932); *Cantico di ringraziamento* (1932–33); *An die Hoffnung* (1933); *Epithalamion* (1933); *Le Cimetiere marin* (1933–34); *La isla de las calmas* (1934); 5 syms.: No. 1 (1937–39; Bergen, Feb. 2, 1956), No. 2 (1941–44; Oslo, March 28, 1957), No. 3 (1944–46; Oslo, April 13, 1951), No. 4 (1947–49; Malmö, Oct. 16, 1956), and No. 5 (1951–52; unfinished); *Ode til Ensomheten* (Ode to Silence; 1939); Violin Concerto (1940; Oslo, Oct. 24, 1947); Concerto for Piano and Chamber Orch. (1949–51; Oslo, Jan. 15, 1953). **Chamber:** Violin Sonata (1916); Piano Trio (1917–24); 2 string quartets (1928–29; 1930–31); *Serenade* for Wind Quintet (1946–47). **Keyboard: Piano:** *Legend* (1907); 2 sonatas (1912; *The Hound of Heaven*, 1940–41); *4 Pieces* (1934–35); *Variations* (1935–36); *Gavotte and Musette* (1936); *Prelude and Fugue* (1937); *2 Preludes* (1937); *Intermezzo* (1939–40). **Organ:** *Prelude and Fugue* (1939); *Pastoral* (1939). **Vocal:** *Ave Maria* for Soprano and Orch. (1917–21); *Mignon*, 2 songs for Soprano and Orch., after Goethe (1920–27); *Dearest Thou Now, O Soul* for Soprano and Orch., after Whitman (1920–28); *3 Gedichte von Goethe* for Soprano and Orch. (1925–27); *2 chinesische Gedichte* for Soprano and Orch. (1925–27); *La noche oscura del alma* for Soprano and Orch., after St. John of the Cross (1939); motets.

Bibl.: O. Gurvin, *F. V., En banebryter i nyere norsk musikk* (F. V., a Pioneer in Norwegian Music; Oslo, 1962); B. Kortsen, *Studies of Form in F. V.'s Music* (Oslo, 1962); idem, *Melodic Structure and Thematic Unity in F. V.'s Music* (2 vols., Glasgow, 1963); idem, *F. V., Life and Music* (3 vols., Oslo, 1965); Anonymous, *Komponisten F. V. 1887–1952* (Oslo, 1976); P. Rapoport, *Opus Est: Six Composers from Northern Europe* (London, 1978). **—NS/LK/DM**

Valens, Ritchie (originally, Valenzuela, Richard),

Latino rock star whose career was cut tragically short; b. Pacoima, Calif., May 13, 1941; d. near Clear Lake, Iowa, Feb. 3, 1959. Of Mexican-American and Native-American descent, Richard Valenzuela grew up in poverty in Pacoima, Calif. He took up acoustic guitar at age nine and manufactured his first electric guitar at 11. While attending Pacoima J.H.S., he joined the mixed-race band The Silhouettes and quickly became the group's frontman. In the spring of 1958, he auditioned for Bob Keene, owner of the Hollywood-based label Del-Fi Records. Keene signed him to the label, shortening his name to Ritchie Valens, and his first recording session yielded "Come On, Let's Go," a major R&B and moderate pop hit. In August he made his first U.S. tour with Eddie Cochran and appeared on Dick Clark's *American Bandstand*. He returned to Los Angeles to record his own ballad "Donna" and a rocked-up version of the traditional Mexican folk song "La Bamba." He later performed at his old junior high school and filmed a segment for the film *Go, Johnny, Go.*

In November "Donna" became a smash hit, quickly followed by the major flip-side pop hit "La Bamba." He again appeared on *American Bandstand* and subsequently joined "The Winter Dance Party" tour with Buddy Holly, J. P. "The Big Bopper" Richardson, and Dion and The Belmonts. Following a concert at Clear Lake, Iowa, Ritchie Valens, then 17, Buddy Holly, and The Big Bopper died when their chartered plane crashed shortly after takeoff. Released posthumously in April, Ritchie Valens's debut album contained the three hits plus "That's My Little Suzie," a minor pop hit. Within a year, Del-Fi had assembled two more albums.

Beginning in the early 1980s, Ritchie Valens's recordings were reissued by Rhino. In 1987, at the behest of the Valenzuela family, the Chicano rock band Los Lobos recorded eight songs, including versions of Valens's first three hits for the film musical biography of Valens, *La Bamba*, starring Lou Diamond Phillips. Los Lobos scored hits with "La Bamba" and with "Come On, Let's Go." Unreleased tapes by Ritchie Valens discovered in 1990 were issued by Ace Records as *The Lost Tapes*.

Disc.: *Ritchie Valens* (1959); *Ritchie* (1959); *Ritchie Valens/Ritchie in Concert at Pacoima Jr. High* (1960); *The Original Ritchie Valens* (1963); *The Original "La Bamba"* (1963); *The History of Ritchie Valens* (1981); *The Ritchie Valens Story* (1993); *The Lost Tapes* (1992).

Bibl.: Beverly Mendheim, *Ritchie Valens: The First Latino Rocker* (Tempe, Ariz., 1987); Larry Lehmer, *The Day the Music Died: The Last Tour of Buddy Holly, the Big Bopper, and Richie Valens* (N.Y., 1997).**—BH**

Valente, Antonio,

blind Italian organist and composer who flourished in the 2nd half of the 16th century, known as "il Cieco" ("the blind man"). He became blind as a child. He was organist at Sant'Angelo a Nido in Naples (1565–80). His first publication, *Intavolatura de cimbalo: Recercate, fantasie et canzoni francese desminuite con alcuni tenori balli et varie sorti de contraponti...* (Naples, 1575), is in Spanish keyboard tablature and contains early keyboard fantasias, written out in detail. His second book, *Versi spirituali sopra tutte le note, con diversi canoni spartiti per suonar negli organi, messe, vespere et altri offici divini* (Naples, 1580), represents an early type of keyboard partitura. I. Fuser ed. *Antonio Valente: Versi spirituali per organo* (Padua, 1958).

Bibl.: J. Burns, *Neapolitan Keyboard Music from V. to Frescobaldi* (diss., Harvard Univ., 1953; includes an ed. of the *Intavolatura de cimbalo*).**—NS/LK/DM**

Valente, Benita, distinguished American soprano; b. Delano, Calif., Oct. 19, 1934. She began serious musical training with Chester Hayden at Delano H.S. At 16, she became a private pupil of Lotte Lehmann, and at 17 received a scholarship to continue her studies with Lehmann at the Music Academy of the West in Santa Barbara; in 1955 she won a scholarship to the Curtis Inst. of Music in Philadelphia, where she studied with Singher. Upon graduation in 1960, she made her formal debut in a Marlboro (Vt.) Festival concert. On Oct. 8, 1960, she made her N.Y. concert debut at the New School for Social Research. After winning the Metropolitan Opera Auditions in 1960, she pursued further studies with Margaret Harshaw. She then sang with the Freiburg im Breisgau Opera, making her debut there as Pamina in 1962; after appearances with the Nuremberg Opera (1966), she returned to the U.S. and established herself as a versatile recitalist, soloist with orchs., and opera singer. Her interpretation of Pamina was especially well received, and it was in that role that she made her long-awaited Metropolitan Opera debut in N.Y. on Sept. 22, 1973. She won praise for her performances in operas by Monteverdi, Handel, Verdi, Puccini, and Britten. Her extensive recital and concert repertoire ranges from Schubert to Ginastera. **—NS/LK/DM**

Valente, Vincenzo, Italian composer; b. Corigliano Calabro, Feb. 21, 1855; d. Naples, Sept. 6, 1921. At the age of 15 he wrote a song, *Ntuniella*, which became popular. He continued writing Neapolitan songs of great appeal (*Basta ca po', Comme te voglio amà!, Canzone cafona, Mugliera comme fa, Ninuccia, Tiempe felice, L'acqua,* etc.), about 400 in all. He also brought out operettas: *I Granatieri* (Turin, Oct. 26, 1889), *La Sposa di Charolles* (Rome, March 3, 1894), *Rolandino* (Turin, Oct. 15, 1897), *L'usignuolo* (Naples, May 10, 1899), *Lena* (Foggia, Jan. 1, 1918), *L'Avvocato Trafichetti* (Naples, May 24, 1919), and *Nèmesi* (posthumous, Naples, July 23, 1923). His son, Nicola Valente (b. Naples, Aug. 28, 1881; d. there, Sept. 16, 1946), was also a composer of Neapolitan songs and light operas.**—NS/LK/DM**

Valenti, Fernando, noted American harpsichordist and teacher; b. N.Y., Dec. 4, 1926; d. Red Bank, N.J., Sept. 6, 1990. He studied piano with José Iturbi, then attended Yale Univ., where he took instruction in harpsichord with Ralph Kirkpatrick. He made his N.Y. recital debut in 1950. In 1951 he was appointed prof. of harpsichord at the Juilliard School of Music in N.Y.; also taught at various other academic institutions. He publ. the book *The Harpsichord: A Dialogue for Beginners* (1982). His performances of the music of Domenico Scarlatti were highly praised.**—NS/LK/DM**

Valentin, Erich, distinguished German musicologist; b. Strasbourg, Nov. 27, 1906; d. Bad Aibling, March 16, 1993. He studied music with Courvoisier and Rohr in Munich, then took courses in musicology with Sandberger at the Univ. of Munich, where he received his Ph.D. in 1928 with the diss. *Die Entwicklung der Tokkata im 17. und 18. Jahrhundert* (publ. in Munich, 1930). From 1929 to 1935 he taught at the Staatliches Privatmusiklehrer-Seminar in Magdeburg, and from 1939 to 1945 he was director of the Zentralinstitut für Mozartforschung. He taught at the Hochschule für Musik in Munich from 1953, where he was a prof. from 1955 and its director (1964–72). From 1950 to 1955 he was ed.-in-chief of the *Zeitschrift für Musik*, and from 1955 to 1959 he was co-ed. of the *Neue Zeitschrift für Musik*. He became ed.-in-chief of *Acta Mozartiana* in 1954. In addition to his many articles for music journals, he also prepared eds. of works by Mozart, Telemann, and others.

WRITINGS: *Georg Philipp Telemann* (Burg, 1931; 3rd ed., 1952); *Richard Wagner* (Regensburg, 1937); *Dichtung und Oper: Eine Untersuchung zum Stilproblem der Oper* (Leipzig, 1938); *Hans Pfitzner* (Regensburg, 1939); *Wege zu Mozart* (Regensburg, 1941; 4th ed., 1950); *Beethoven* (Salzburg, 1942; Eng. ed., N.Y., 1958); *W.A. Mozart: Wesen und Wandlung* (Hamelin, 1948); *Kleine Bilder grosser Meister* (Mainz, 1952); *Handbuch der Chormusik* (Regensburg, 1953–74); *Handbuch der Instrumentenkunde* (Regensburg, 1954; 6th ed., 1974); *Der früheste Mozart* (Munich, 1956); *Beethoven* (pictorial bibliography; Munich, 1957); *Die Tokkata*, in *Das Musikwerk*, XVII (1958); *Mozart* (pictorial bibliography; Munich, 1959); *Musica domestica: Über Wesen und Geschichte der Hausmusik* (Trossingen, 1959); *Telemann in seiner Zeit* (Hamburg, 1960); *Handbuch der Schulmusik* (Regensburg, 1962); *Die goldene Spur: Mozart in der Dichtung Hermann Hesses* (Augsburg, 1965); with F. Hofmann, *Die evangelische Kirchenmusik* (Regensburg, 1967); with W. Gebhardt and W. Vetter, *Handbuch des Musikunterrichts* (Regensburg, 1970); *Die schönsten Beethoven-Briefe* (Munich, 1973); *Lübbes Mozart-Lexikon* (Bergisch-Gladbach, 1983); *Don-Juan-Reflexionen: Eine Auswahl literarischer Zeugnisse* (Augsburg, 1988).

BIBL.: G. Weiss, ed., *E. V. zum 70. Geburtstag* (Regensburg, 1976).**—NS/LK/DM**

Valentini, Giovanni, Italian composer; b. Venice, 1582; d. Vienna, April 29, 1649. He was a pupil of Giovanni Gabrieli. He was organist to King Sigismund III at the Polish court. From 1614 he was chamber organist to the Archduke Ferdinand at Graz, becoming court organist at Vienna when Ferdinand ascended the throne in 1619; by 1626 he was Imperial Kapellmeister.

WORKS (all publ. in Venice unless otherwise given): *Canzoni, libro primo* for 3, 5 to 6, and 8 Voices (1609); *Motetti* for 4 to 6 Voices (1611); *Secondo libro de madrigali* for 4 to 5 and 8 to 11 Voices and Basso Continuo (1616); *Missae concertatae* for 4, 6, and 8 Voices and Basso Continuo (1617); *Salmi, hinni, Magnificat, antifone, falsibordone et motetti* for 1 to 4 Voices and Basso Continuo (1618); *Musiche concertate* for 6 to 10 Voices and Basso Continuo (1619); *Musica di camera, libro quarto* for 1 to 6 Voices and Basso Continuo (1621); *Missae quatuor* for 8 to 12 Voices with Basso Continuo ad libitum (1621); *Messa, Magnificat et Jubilate Deo*, 7 choruses with Trumpet (Vienna, 1621); *Musiche* for 2 Voices (1622); *Il quinto libro de madrigali* for 3 to 6 Voices and Basso Continuo (1625); *Sacri concerti* for 2 to 5 Voices and Basso Continuo (1625); various other works in contemporary collections.**—NS/LK/DM**

Valentini, Giuseppe, Italian violinist and composer; b. Florence, c. 1680; d. after 1759. He was at Rome in 1700. He was in the service of Prince Francesco Maria Ruspoli as a violinist, c. 1708–13, and may then have been at Bologna in the service of the Prince di Caserta. From 1735 he was at the grand-ducal court of Florence. His violin technique was highly developed (some compositions call for the 6th position).

WORKS: DRAMATIC: Opera: *La finta rapita* (Cisterna, 1714; in collaboration with N. Romaldi and G. Cesarini); *La costanza in amore* (Cisterna, 1715). **Oratorios and Cantatas:** *La superbia punita in Absalone* (Rome, 1705); *Oratorio per l'assunzione della beata vergine* (Rome, 1730); *Cantata da recitarsi nel palazzo apostolico la notte del santissimo natale* (Rome, 1733); *Cantata per la nativita della beata vergine* (Rome, 1746); *Nell'amoroso foco,* cantata for Soprano, 2 Violins, and Basso Continuo. **INSTRUMENTAL** (all publ. in Rome unless otherwise given): (12) *Sinfonie* for 2 Violins, Cello, and Bass (1701); (7) *Bizzarrie per camera* for 2 Violins and Violone or Harpsichord (1703); (12) *Fantasie musicali* for 2 Violins and Violone or Harpsichord (1706); (7) *Idee per camera* for Violin and Violone or Harpsichord (1706–07); (12) *Villeggiature armoniche* for 2 Violins and Cello or Basso Continuo (1707); *Rime varie* (not extant); (12) *Concerti grossi* for 2 or 4 Violins, Viola, and Cello Concertino or 2 Violins and Bass (Bologna, 1710); (12) *Allettamenti per camera* for Violin and Cello or Harpsichord (1714); *X concerti* for 2 Violins and Bass Concertino and 2 Violins, Viola, and Bass (Amsterdam, 1724); several concertos in contemporary collections.—**NS/LK/DM**

Valentini, Pier (Pietro) Francesco,

Italian music theorist, poet, and composer; b. Rome, c. 1570; d. there, 1654. He was a pupil of G. B. Nanino. Although he called himself an amateur musician, he especially distinguished himself as a music theorist.

WORKS (all publ. in Rome): **VOCAL: Sacred:** *Canone sopra le parole del Salve Regina, "Illos tuos misericordes oculos ad nos converte," con le resolutioni a 2, 3, 4 e 5 voci* (1629; a canon with over 2,000 possible resolutions; the theme is in Kircher's *Musurgia,* I); *In animas purgatorii: canon 4 compositus subjectis* for 20 Voices (1645); *Motetti, libro primo* for Voice, Instruments, and Basso Continuo (1654); *Motetti, libro secondo* for Voice, Instruments, and Basso Continuo (1654); *Motetti e concerti, libro primo* for 2 to 4 Voices and Basso Continuo (1654); *Letanie e concerti* for 2 to 4 Voices, Violin, Cornetto, Theorbo or Lute, and Basso Continuo (1654); *Motetti per le processioni del Corpus Domini, della beata vergine, e della settimana santa, libro primo* for 4 to 5 Voices (1655); *Motetti per processioni diversi, libro secondo* (1655); other works in MS. **Secular:** *Madrigali, musica e parole del Signor...Valentini...libro primo* for 5 Voices and Basso Continuo ad libitum (1654); *Madrigali...libro secondo* for 5 Voices and Basso Continuo ad libitum (1654); *Canzonette et arie, musica e parole del Signor...Valentini...libro primo* for 1 to 2 Voices and Basso Continuo (1657); *Canzonette et arie...libro secondo* for 1 to 2 Voices and Basso Continuo (1657); other works in MS.

BIBL.: L. Kurz, *Die Tonartenlehre des römischen Theoretikers und Komponisten P.F. V.* (diss., Univ. of Kassel, 1937).
—**NS/LK/DM**

Valentini-Terrani, Lucia,

Italian mezzo-soprano; b. Padua, Aug. 28, 1948; d. Seattle, June 11, 1998. She received training in Padua. In 1969 she made her operatic debut in the title role of Rossini's *La Cenerentola* in Brescia, and then appeared in various Italian operatic centers. From 1973 she sang at Milan's La Scala. On Nov. 16, 1974, she made her Metropolitan Opera debut in N.Y. as Rossini's Isabella. In 1979 she appeared as a soloist in the Verdi Requiem with Giulini and the Los Angeles Phil., returning to Los Angeles in 1982 to sing Mistress Quickly under Giulini's direction. From 1984 she sang at the Pesaro Festivals. In 1987 she appeared as Rossini's Rosina at London's Covent Garden. She sang Gluck's Orféo in Naples in 1990. In 1992 she appeared as Rossini's Isabella in Turin. Her guest engagements also took her to the Vienna State Opera, the Paris Opéra, the Bolshoi Theater in Moscow, and the Lyric Opera in Chicago. She was particularly known for her roles in operas by Rossini and Verdi.—**NS/LK/DM**

Valerius, Adrianus (Adriaan, Adriaen),

Dutch lawyer, historian, poet, and musician; b. probably in Middelburg, c. 1575; d. Veere, Zeeland, Jan. 27, 1625. He settled in Veere as a notary in 1606, and later became sheriff and served as dean of the chamber of rhetoric. He wrote *Neder-landtsche gedenck-clanck* (Haarlem, 1626), a history of the Dutch and Spanish wars from 1555 to 1625; it includes 76 popular songs with accompaniments in French tablature for 1 or more 7-stringed lutes and 4-stringed citterns. P. J. Meertens, N. B. Tenhaeff, and A. Komter-Kuipers edited a complete ed. of the text with melodies but without the tablatures (Amsterdam, 1942). K. Bernet Kampers and C. Lelij ed. the song texts and tunes as *De liederen uit Valerius' Nederlandtsche gedenck-clanck* (Rotterdam, 1941).—**NS/LK/DM**

Valesi, Giovanni (real name, Johann Evangelist Walleshauser),

German tenor and singing teacher; b. Unterhattenhofen, Upper Bavaria, April 28, 1735; d. Munich, Jan. 10, 1816. He was a student of Placius von Camerloher. After briefly singing as a bass, he became a tenor and was a court singer to the Prince-Bishop Johann Theodor of Freising and Liège (1754–56) and subsequently to Duke Clemens in Munich. From 1770 to 1798 he was a leading member of the Munich Court Opera. He also sang in Amsterdam and Brussels (1755), Italy (from 1758), where he adopted the name Giovanni Valesi, and Prague, Dresden, and Berlin (1777–78). Valesi was chosen to create the role of the High Priest of Neptune in Mozart's *Idomeneo* in Munich on Jan. 29, 1781. Among his numerous pupils were five of his own children, as well as such notable musicians as Carl Maria von Weber and Valentin Adamberger.
—**NS/LK/DM**

Valkare, Gunnar,

Swedish organist, teacher, and composer; b. Norrköping, April 25, 1943. He studied piano with Stina Sundell, organ with Alf Linder, and composition with Ingvar Lidholm at the Stockholm Musikhögskolan (1963–69). He was active as an organist and teacher (1964–79), and served as resident composer in Gislaved (1973) and Kalmar (1977–78). His music is militantly aggressive in its tonal, atonal, and polytonal assault on the most cherished notions of harmonious sweetness.

WORKS: *4 Cardiograms* for Solo Singers, Chorus, and Instruments in varying combinations (1965–66); *A Study in the Story of Human Stupidity* for Orch. (Århus, Feb. 5, 1968); *Nomo* for 7 Narrators, 6 Winds, and Tape (1967); *Eld för ett altare* (Fire from an Altar), church drama (1968); *Kanske en pastoral om det får* *tina upp* (Perhaps a Pastorale If It Will Thaw) for Percussion, Piano, and Strings (1968); *A Play about the Medieval Värend and the Dacke Feud,* musical-dramatic dance for Winds, Violin, Nickelharp, and Xylophone (1971); *Från mitt rosa badkar* (From My Rosy Bathtub) for Orch., Pop Group, and Chorus (1971); *Det ringer i mitt öra* (There Is a Ringing in My Ears) for Voices and Instruments (1972); *Tahuantisuyos ekonomi* for Chorus, Winds, and Strings (1974); *Mellan berg och hav, mellan himmel och jard* (Between the Mountains and the Ocean, Between the Sky and the Earth), play for Singer, Actor, and Instrumental Ensemble (1975); *Stages* for 6 Musicians (1976); *Variationer och tema* for 4 Clarinets (1978); *Gesellen* for Chorus and Organ (1979); *Blöpark* for Wind Orch. and Percussion (1982); Concerto for Treble Recorder and Chamber Orch. (1983); *Flight of the Mechanical Heart* for Flute, Guitar, and Harpsichord (1984); Sym. (1986; Norrköping, Nov. 12, 1987); *Kinema* for Orch. (1988); *Örnen och ugglan: En inidansk saga* for Voices and Instrumental Accompaniment (1988); *Second Flight of the Mechanical Heart* for Chamber Orch. (1990); *Intermedium I* for Chamber Orch. and Tape (1991) and *II* for Chamber Orch. (1991); *Concerto d'incontro,* theater piece (1992); *Passage I-V* for Solo Instrument (1993); *Refrains* for 6 Instruments (1994); *Viaggio,* concerto for Accordion and String Orch. (1996); *Scapes* for String Orch. (1997); *Réflexion: Hommage à Bo Nilsson* for Chamber Ensemble (1998); *Stockholm City Serenade,* stage music for Chorus and Orch. (1998–99); *Bhairava* for Sitar and Orch. (1999).—**NS/LK/DM**

Vallas, Léon, distinguished French musicologist; b. Roanne, Loire, May 17, 1879; d. Lyons, May 9, 1956. After studying medicine in Lyons, he pursued his musicological training at the Univ. there (Ph.D., 1908). In 1902 he became music critic of *Tout Lyon*; in 1903, founded the *Revue Musicale de Lyon*, which became the *Revue Française de Musique* in 1912 and the *Nouvelle Revue Musicale* in 1920; also wrote for the *Progrès de Lyon* (1919–54). With G. Witkowski, he founded a schola cantorum in Lyons in 1902; taught theory at the Univ. (1908–11) and the Cons. (1912) there, and later at the Sorbonne in Paris (1928–30). He was president of the Société Française de Musicologie (1937–43) and artistic director of Radiodiffusion de Lyon (1938–41).

WRITINGS: *Georges Migot* (Paris, n.d.); *Debussy, 1862–1918* (Paris, 1926); *Les Idées de Claude Debussy, musicien français* (Paris, 1927; 2nd ed., 1932; Eng. tr., 1929, as *The Theories of Claude Debussy*); *Claude Debussy et son temps* (Paris, 1932; 2nd ed., 1958; Eng. tr., 1933, as *Claude Debussy: His Life and Works*); *Achille-Claude Debussy* (Paris, 1944); *Vincent d'Indy* (2 vols., Paris, 1946, 1949); *César Franck* (London, 1951; in French, 1955, as *La Véritable Histoire de César Franck*).—**NS/LK/DM**

Vallée, Rudy (Hubert Prior), American singer, songwriter, bandleader, and actor; b. Island Pond, Vt., July 28, 1901; d. Los Angeles, Calif., July 3, 1986. Vallée was one of the most successful singers of the 1930s. One of the earliest crooners, he used the properties of the microphone to achieve an intimate singing style. His biggest hits were "Honey" (1929), "Stein Song (Univ. of Maine)" (1930), and "As Time Goes By" (recorded in 1931, popular in 1943). He hosted variety shows on radio for the better part of two decades and appeared in dozens of movies, gradually turning into an accomplished comic actor and good-naturedly sending up the breezy, collegiate image he had cultivated at his popular peak.

Vallée was the son of Charles Alphonse and Katherine Agnes Lynch Vallée. His father was a pharmacist. When he was a child the family moved to Westbrook, Maine, where he grew up. His first instrument was the drums, followed by the clarinet. He made his first professional appearance as a singer in 1914. In 1919 he began playing the saxophone, and his interest in saxophonist Rudy Wiedoeft led to the adoption of his nickname. He made his first professional appearance as a saxophonist in a movie theater in Portland.

Vallée attended the Univ. of Maine during the 1921–22 school year, then transferred to Yale, paying for his studies by working as a musician. He cut down a megaphone and used it to amplify his voice when he sang; it later became an important stage prop. He took a year off from college to play saxophone in the Havana Band at the Hotel Savoy in London from September 1924 to June 1925.

Vallée returned to Yale in the fall of 1925 and graduated in June 1927. He toured with his college group during the summer and had brief stints as a saxophonist with the bands of Vincent Lopez and Ben Bernie. Then he accepted an offer to organize a group to play in the newly opened Heigh-Ho Club in N.Y., and the Yale Collegians (later renamed the Connecticut Yankees) opened there on Jan. 8, 1928. Vallée had not intended to sing, but the club owner required him to do so. On Feb. 8 a local radio station began broadcasts from the club that soon were picked up by a string of stations, and Vallée's lighthearted style made him a sensation. (That spring he wed heiress Leonie Cauchois, but the marriage was quickly annulled.) Later, the band moved to the Versailles club, which was renamed the Villa Vallée.

Vallée and the Connecticut Yankees made their first stage appearance in February 1929 at Keith's 81st Street Theater, a N.Y. vaudeville house, where they were greeted with the kind of frenzy later seen at early appearances by Frank Sinatra, Elvis Presley, and the Beatles. By April the band was appearing at the Palace, vaudeville's top venue.

A few of Vallée's recordings for a small label had become popular by this time, and he signed to Victor Records, quickly achieving a flurry of major hits that included "Marie" (music and lyrics by Irving Berlin), "Weary River" (music by Louis Silvers, lyrics by Grant Clarke), and "Deep Night" (music by Charlie Henderson, lyrics by Vallée), though his most popular recording of the period was "Honey" (music by Richard A. Whiting, lyrics by Seymour Simons and Haven Gillespie), which was a best-seller from April to June 1929. Other notable recordings were "My Time Is Your Time" (music by R. S. Hooper, lyrics by H. M. Tennant), a hit in June that later became Vallée's radio theme song, and "I'm Just a Vagabond Lover" (music and lyrics by Vallée and Leon Zimmerman), a hit in July that became a signature song for him and that he sang in two movies released toward the end of the year, *The Vagabond Lover* and *Glorifying the American Girl*.

On Oct. 24, 1929, Vallée became the host of a weekly national radio show named for its sponsor, Fleischmann's Yeast. He scored a major hit in November with "Lonely Troubadour" (music and lyrics by John Klenner), and had the biggest hit of his career with "Stein Song (Univ. of Maine)" (music by Emil Fenstad and lyrics by Lincoln Colcord, based on one of Brahms's "Hungarian Dances"), a college drinking song that became a best-seller in March 1930 and was the most popular record of the year. Vallée's collegiate image was also burnished by "Betty Co-Ed" (music and lyrics by J. Paul Fogarty and Vallée), with which both he and Bob Haring and His Orch. enjoyed hits in August 1930.

Vallée was married for the second time to actress Fay Webb on July 6, 1931; they were divorced on May 20, 1936. He performed in the Broadway revue *George White's Scandals* (N.Y., 1931), which ran 204 performances, and he scored hits with three songs from the show, "Life Is Just a Bowl of Cherries," "The Thrill Is Gone," and "My Song" (all three: music by Ray Henderson, lyrics by Lew Brown). But his biggest hit of 1931 was "When Yuba Plays the Rhumba on the Tuba" (music and lyrics by Herman Hupfeld), from the revue *The Third Little Show*.

Vallée made changes in his career in 1932. The format of his radio show was altered to present a mixture of comic and dramatic sketches along with the music and to bring in more guest stars and introduce new talent. He altered his style with more substantial material, notably in his biggest hit of the year, the Depression anthem "Brother, Can You Spare a Dime?" (music by Jay Gorney, lyrics by E. Y. Harburg) from the revue *Americana*, which became a best-seller in December. His other big hits of the year included such romantic fare as "I Guess I'll Have to Change My Plan (The Blue Pajama Song)" (music by Arthur Schwartz, lyrics by Howard Dietz) and "Let's Put Out the Lights and Go to Sleep" (music and lyrics by Hupfeld) from *George White's Music Hall Follies*.

Vallée devoted the bulk of his time to his radio program in the mid-1930s, though he made the occasional film appearance and returned to the stage in *George White's Scandals of 1936* (N.Y., 1935), which ran 110 performances. His record sales diminished, although he had hits with "There's Always a Happy Ending" in May 1936, "Vieni, Vieni" (music by Vincent Scotto, Italian and French lyrics by George Koger and Henri Varna, English lyrics by Vallée) in November 1937, and "Oh, Ma-Ma" (based on "Luna Merro Mare," music and lyrics by Paolo Citorello, English lyrics by Lew Brown and Vallée) in the summer of 1938.

Vallée began to take more film roles in the late 1930s, but it was not until his appearance as the wealthy J. D. Hackensacker III in Preston Sturges's screwball comedy *The Palm Beach Story*, released in December 1942, that he found his feet as a comic character actor. He played another millionaire in the musical comedy *Happy Go Lucky*, released in March 1943. In April, as a result of the popularity of the film *Casablanca* and the ongoing recording ban, he scored a surprise Top Ten hit with a reissue of his 1931 recording of "As Time Goes By" (music and lyrics by Hupfeld).

When the U.S. entered World War II, Vallée enlisted in the Coast Guard and led a service band; he continued to host his radio program until July 1, 1943, when he gave it up to devote all his time to the war effort. On Dec. 2, 1943, he married actress Jane Greer; they were divorced July 27, 1944. After World War II, Vallée picked up his career on radio, hosting shows through 1948, and made frequent film appearances as a comic actor, notably in the Preston Sturges films *The Sin of Harold Diddlebock* (1947; reedited and released as *Mad Wednesday* in 1950), *Unfaithfully Yours* (1948), and *The Beautiful Blonde from Bashful Bend* (1949).

Vallée developed a nightclub act in the late 1940s with which he toured through the 1950s. He married Eleanor Kathleen Norris on Sept. 4, 1949, and they remained married until his death. He returned to radio as a disc jockey in 1951 and hosted the *Kraft Music Hall* radio series from February to August 1955. He appeared as a guest star on television and was in a musical version of *Hansel and Gretel* broadcast on NBC on April 27, 1958.

Vallée made his debut in a book musical on Broadway with *How to Succeed in Business Without Really Trying* (N.Y., 1961). The show ran 1,417 performances, and Vallée was in it for three years; he also appeared in the 1967 film version and in several regional productions. He was the host of *On Broadway Tonight*, a variety series on television that ran during the summer of 1964 and from January to March 1965. He continued to make occasional appearances in films and on television into the 1970s. He toured in an autobiographical one-man show called *Something Different* until shortly before his death at age 84 due to complications from an operation for throat cancer.

DISC.: *The Young R. V.* (1961); *Stein Songs* (1962); *The Funny Side of R. V.* (1964); *Ho Ho, Everybody* (1966).

WRITINGS: *Vagabond Dreams Come True* (N.Y., 1930); with Gil McKean, *My Time Is Your Time: The R. V. Story* (N.Y., 1962); *Let the Chips Fall...* (Harrisburg, Pa., 1975).

BIBL.: L. Kiner, *The R. V. Discography* (Westport, Conn., 1985); E. Vallée (his widow) with J. Amadio, *My Vagabond Lover: An Intimate Biography of R. V.* (Dallas, Tex., 1996).—**WR**

Vallerand, Jean (d'Auray), Canadian composer, music critic, teacher, and administrator; b. Montreal, Dec. 24, 1915; d. there, June 24, 1994. He received violin lessons from Lucien Sicotte (1921–36), and also studied at the Collège Ste.-Marie de Montréal (B.A., 1935), and was a composition pupil of Claude Champagne (1935–42). He also obtained a diploma in journalism (1938) and a licence ès lettres (1939) from the Univ. of Montreal. He ed. *Quartier Latin* (1937–39); then wrote music criticism for *Le Canada* (1941–46), *Montréal-Matin* (1948–49), *Le Devoir* (1952–61), *Nouveau Journal* (1961–62), and *La Presse* (1962–66). From 1942 to 1963 he was secretary general of the Montreal Cons., where he also taught orchestration. He also taught orchestration and music history at the Univ. of Montreal from 1950 to 1966. After serving as head of radio music for the CBC in Montreal (1963–66), he was cultural attaché for the Quebec government in Paris (1966–70). In 1971 he was named director of music education for the Ministry of Cultural Affairs of Quebec. Following its reorganization that year, he was its director of performing arts until 1975. From 1971 to 1978 he also was director of the

Cons. de musique et d'art dramatique du Québec. In 1967 he was awarded the Centenary Medal of Canada, and in 1975 received an honorary doctorate from the Univ. of Ottawa. In 1991 he was made a Chevalier of the Ordre national du Québec. In addition to his many reviews and articles in journals, he publ. the books *Introduction a la musique* (Montreal, 1949) and *La Musique et les tout-petits* (Montreal, 1950). He wrote music in a neo-Romantic manner; in his later compositions, he experimented with serial techniques.

WORKS: DRAMATIC: Opera: *Le Magicien* (Orford, Quebec, Sept. 2, 1961, with piano; Montreal, May 30, 1962, with orch.). **ORCH.:** *Le Diable dans le beffroi*, symphonic poem (1939; Montreal, April 24, 1942); *Nocturne* (1944); *Prélude* (1946); *Réverbérations contradictoires* (1960; Montreal, Feb. 26, 1961); *Cordes en mouvement* for Strings (Montreal, March 27, 1961); *Étude concertante* for Violin and Orch. (1968; Montreal, June 1969). **CHAMBER:** Violin Sonata (Montreal, Nov. 9, 1950; also for Violin and Orch., 1951); String Quartet (Radio Canada, Feb. 28, 1955). **VOCAL:** *Les Roses a la mer* for Voice and Piano (1939; also for Voice and String Orch.); *Notre-Dame de la Couronne* and *Notre-Dame du Pain*, cantatas for Tenor, Chorus, and Orch. (1946); *Quatre mélodies sur des poèmes de St. Denys Garneau* for Voice and Piano (1954).

BIBL.: M.-T. Lefebvre, *J. V. et la vie musicale du Québec, 1915–1994* (Montreal, 1996).—**NS/LK/DM**

Valleria (real name, **Schoening**), **Alwina,** noted American soprano; b. Baltimore, Oct. 12, 1848; d. Nice, Feb. 17, 1925. She went to London and entered the Royal Academy of Music in 1867, where she studied piano with W. H. Holmes and voice with Wallworth; after further studies with Arditi, she made her formal debut in a London concert on June 2, 1871. On Oct. 23, 1871, she made her operatic debut with the Italian Opera in St. Petersburg in *Linda di Chamounix*; after appearances in Germany and Italy, she returned to London and sang at the Drury Lane Theatre (1873–75), Her Majesty's Theatre (1877–78), and Covent Garden (1879–82). On Oct. 22, 1879, she made her U.S. debut as Marguerite in N.Y. with Mapleson's company; after appearances with the Carl Rosa company in England (1882–83), she returned to the U.S. and made her Metropolitan Opera debut in N.Y. as Leonora in *Il Trovatore* on Oct. 26, 1883, remaining on its roster for the season; then pursued her career in England until retiring in 1886.—**NS/LK/DM**

Vallet or **Valet, Nicolas,** eminent French-born Netherlandish lutenist and composer; b. probably in Corbény, Ile-de-France, c. 1583; d. probably in Amsterdam, after 1642. He apparently received his musical training in his homeland, and was in Amsterdam by 1614. He was greatly esteemed as a performer and composer, and also active as a teacher. A. Souris edited *OEuvres de Nicolas Vallet pour luth seul: Le Secret des Muses, livres I, II* (1970).

WORKS (all publ. in Amsterdam): *21 Psalmen Davids* for Voice and Lute (1615; 2nd ed., 1619, as *XXI pseaumes de David*); *Secretum musarum* for Lute (1615; 2nd ed., 1618, as *Le Secret des Muses: Paradisus musicus testudinis*); *Het tweede boeck van de* (30) *luyt-tablatuer* for 1 and 4 Lutes (1616; 2nd ed., 1619, as *Le Second Livre de tablature de luth, intitulé Le Secret des Muses*); *Bruylofts-gesang* for 5 Voices (1619); *Regia pietas, hoc est* (150) *Psalmi Davidici* for Lute (1620); *Apollinis susse Leyr, das ist ... Pavannen, Galliarden, Balletten, Bransles, Couranten...fransösiche Stuck...engelsche Stück* for Viola and Basso Continuo (1642); *Le Mont Parnasse...contenant plusiers pavannes, galliardes, ballets, bransles, courantes, fantasies, et batailles, a 5, 6* (c. 1644); several lute pieces in MS collections.—**NS/LK/DM**

Valletti, Cesare, notable Italian tenor; b. Rome, Dec. 18, 1922; d. Genoa, May 13, 2000. He was a student of Tito Schipa. In 1947 he made his operatic debut as Alfredo in Bari. After singing in Rome (1947–48), he appeared as Count Almaviva in Palermo and as Elvino in *La sonnambula* in Naples in 1949. In 1950 he sang Don Narciso in *Il Turco in Italia* at the Eliseo in Rome. Following his London debut as Fenton with the visiting La Scala company of Milan in 1950, he appeared with the company in Milan in such roles as Lindoro in *L'Italiana in Algeri*, Nemorino, and Vladimir in *Prince Igor*. In 1951 he sang Alfredo in Mexico City opposite Callas. He made his U.S. debut as Werther at the San Francisco Opera in 1953. On Dec. 10, 1953, he made his Metropolitan Opera debut in N.Y. as Don Ottavio, where he remained on the roster until 1960 singing such admired roles as Tamino, Ferrando, Count Almaviva, Alfredo, Massenet's Des Grieux, and Alfred in *Die Fledermaus*. In 1958 he sang Alfredo opposite Callas at London's Covent Garden, and appeared as Giacomo in *Donna del lago* at the Florence Maggio Musicale Fiorentino. In 1960 he sang Don Ottavio at the Salzburg Festival. In 1968 he appeared as Nero in *L'incoronazione di Poppea* at the Caramoor Festival in Katonah, N.Y. He retired from the operatic stage that same year. Valletti's admired vocal gifts placed him in the forefront of the bel canto revival of his day.—**NS/LK/DM**

Vallin, Ninon, French soprano; b. Montalieu-Vercieu, Sept. 8, 1886; d. Lyons, Nov. 22, 1961. She studied at the Lyons Cons. and with Meyriane Heglon in Paris. After appearing in concerts, she attracted the notice of Debussy, who chose her to sing in the premiere of his *Le martyre de Saint Sébastien* in 1911. He later accompanied her in recitals. In 1912 she made her operatic debut as Micaëla at the Paris Opéra-Comique, where she sang until 1916. In 1916 she made her first appearance at the Teatro Colón in Buenos Aires, continuing to sing there until 1936. She appeared at Milan's La Scala in 1916 and in Rome in 1917. In 1920 she made her debut at the Paris Opéra as Thaïs. In 1934 she sang at the San Francisco Opera. Thereafter she toured as a concert artist. After teaching at the Montevideo Cons. (1953–59), she settled in Lyons. Among her finest roles were Zerlina, Alceste, Charlotte, Mignon, Juliette, and Mélisande. As a concert singer, she excelled in works by French and Spanish composers.

BIBL.: R. de Fragny, *N. V.: Princesse du chant* (Lyons, 1963).—**NS/LK/DM**

Vallotti, Francesco Antonio, Italian music theorist and composer; b. Vercelli, June 11, 1697; d. Padua, Jan. 10, 1780. A Franciscan monk, he was a pupil of Donati in Milan and in Padua, where he settled. He became 3rd organist at the basilica of S. Antonio in 1723, where he subsequently was its maestro di cappella from 1730 until his death. As a composer, he greatly distinguished himself as a contrapuntist. He composed much sacred vocal music, including masses, Psalms, hymns, antiphons, and other pieces; also wrote 30 fugues for various instruments. He wrote various treatises, which remain in MS. Also publ. *Della scienza teorica e pratica della moderna musica,* book 1 (Padua, 1779; books 2–4 ed. by G. Zanon and B. Rizzi as *Trattato della moderna musica,* Padua, 1950).

Bibl.: L. Sabbatini, *Notizie sopra la vita e le opere del rev. P. F. A. V.* (Padua, 1780).—**NS/LK/DM**

Valls, Francisco, Spanish composer; b. Barcelona, 1665; d. there, Feb. 2, 1747. He was maestro de capilla at Mataró parish church, at Gerona Cathedral (1688–96), and at S. María del Mar in Barcelona (1696). In 1696 he became assistant to the maestro de capilla at the Barcelona Cathedral, where he later served as interim maestro (1706–09) and titular maestro (1709–40). Valls won distinction as a composer of sacred music, which included 12 masses, 16 Magnificats, 22 responsories, 12 Psalms, some 35 motets, and about 120 villancicos. He also engendered great controversy with his use of an unprepared dissonance (9th chord) in his *Missa Scala Aretina* (1702), a practice he defended in his treatise *Mapa armónico práctico* (MS).—**LK/DM**

Valvasensi, Lazaro, Italian organist and composer; b. Valvasone, near Udine (baptized), June 20, 1585; d. there, June 26, 1661. In 1622 he was an organist at Murano Cathedral (Venice), in 1626, choirmaster at Tolmezzo Cathedral (Udine), and from 1634 to 1640, an organist at Valvasone. Later he was apostolic protonotary and canon in Caorle.

Works (all publ. in Venice): *Brevi concerti ecclesiastici alla romana* for Voice and Harpsichord (1620); *Letanie della B. V.* for 5 Voices (1622); *Compieta concertata* for 4 Voices and Basso Continuo (1626); *Secondo giardino d'amorosi fiori* for Voice and Basso Continuo (1634); *Messe concertate* for 2 to 4 Voices and Basso Continuo (1636); *Salmi concertati* for 2 Voices and Basso Continuo (1640).—**NS/LK/DM**

Valverde, Joaquín, Spanish composer; b. Badajoz, Feb. 27, 1846; d. Madrid, March 17, 1910. He played the flute in bands from the age of 13, then studied at the Madrid Cons. His sym., *Batylo,* won a prize of the Sociedad Fomento de las Artes (1871). He wrote some 30 zarzuelas, some in collaboration with others; his most celebrated was *La gran vía* (Madrid, July 2, 1886; in collaboration with Chueca); it contains the march *Cádiz,* which became immensely popular. He publ. the book *La flauta: Su historia su estudio* (Madrid, 1886). His son, Quinto (Joaquín) Valverde Sanjuán (b. Madrid, Jan. 2, 1875; d. Mexico City, Nov. 4, 1918), was also a composer; he studied with his father and with Irache; wrote some 250 light pieces for the theater; his zarzuela *El gran capitán* was especially successful. He died during a tour which he undertook as conductor of a light opera company.—**NS/LK/DM**

Van Allan, Richard (real name, **Alan Philip Jones**), English bass; b. Clipstone, Nottinghamshire, May 28, 1935. He studied at the Worcester Coll. of Education and received vocal training from David Franklin at the Birmingham School of Music; he also had private vocal lessons with J. Strasser. In 1964 he became a member of the Glyndebourne Festival Chorus. In 1966 he made his operatic debut at the Glyndebourne Opera in a minor role in *Die Zauberflöte.* In 1969 he joined the Sadler's Wells Opera in London, and later sang there after it became the English National Opera in 1974. In 1970 he created the role of Jowler in Maw's *The Ring of the Moon* at Glyndebourne. He made his debut at London's Covent Garden as the Mandarin in *Turandot* in 1971. In 1976 he sang Baron Ochs at the San Diego Opera. In 1986 he became director of the National Opera Studio. However, he continued to pursue his stage career. In 1990 he sang Don Alfonso at the Metropolitan Opera in N.Y. In 1992 he created the role of Jerome in the stage premiere of Gerhard's *The Duenna* in Madrid. He appeared as Massenet's Don Quichotte at the Victoria State Opera in Melbourne in 1995. Among his other roles are Osmin, Don Giovanni, Leporello, Mozart's Figaro, the Grand Inquisitor, Philip II, and Verdi's Banquo.—**NS/LK/DM**

van Appledorn, Mary Jeanne, American composer, pianist, and teacher; b. Holland, Mich., Oct. 2, 1927. She studied piano with Cecile Staub Genhart (B.Mus., 1948), theory (M.Mus., 1950), and composition with Bernard Rogers and Alan Hovhaness at the Eastman School of Music in Rochester, N.Y., where she received her Ph.D. in 1966 with the diss. *A Stylistic Study of Claude Debussy's Opera, Pelléas et Mélisande.* She pursued postdoctoral studies at the Mass. Inst. of Technology (1982). From 1950 to 1987 she was prof. and chairman of the theory and composition dept. in the music school of Tex. Tech. Univ. in Lubbock, and then was the Paul Whitfield Horn Prof. of Music from 1989 to 2000. She received the ASCAP Standard Panel Awards (1980–99).

Works: Dramatic: Ballet: *Set of 7* (N.Y., May 10, 1988). **Orch.:** *Concerto Brevis* for Piano and Orch. (1954); *A Choreographic Overture* for Concert Band (1957); Concerto for Trumpet and Band (1960); *Passacaglia and Chorale* (1973); *Cacophony* for Wind Ensemble, Percussion, and Toys (1980); *Lux: Legend of Sankta Lucia* for Symphonic Band, Percussion Ensemble, and Handbells (1981); *Ayre* for Strings, Viola da Gamba Consort, and Clarinet or Saxophone Choir (1989); *Terrestial Music,* double concerto for Violin, Piano, and Strings (Nagano, Japan, Aug. 8, 1992); *Cycles of Moons and Tides* for Symphonic Band (1995); *Rhapsody* for Violin and Orch. (1997); *Meliora,* fanfare for Orch. or Symphonic Band (1999). **Chamber:** *Cellano Rhapsody* for Cello and Piano (1948); *Burlesca* for Piano, Brass, and Percussion (1951); *Matrices* for Saxophone and Piano (1979); *Liquid Gold* for Saxophone and Piano (1982); *4 Duos* for Alto Saxophones (1985); *4 Duos* for Viola and Cello (1986); *Sonic Mutation* for Harp (1986); Clarinet Sonatine (N.Y., Oct. 17, 1988); *Cornucopia* for Trumpet (1988); *Windsongs* for Brass Quintet (1991); *Incantations* for Trumpet and Piano (1992); *Atmospheres* for Trombone Ensemble (1993); *Reeds Afire,* duos for Clarinet and Bassoon (1994); *Passages* for Trombone and Piano (1996); *A Native American Mosaic* for Native American Flute (1997); *Incan-*

tations for Oboe and Piano (1998); *Galilean Galaxies* for Flute, Bassoon, and Piano (1998); *Gestures* for Clarinet Quartet (1999); various piano pieces. **VOCAL:** *Peter Quince at the Clavier* for Women's Chorus, Narrator, Flute, Oboe, Horn, and Piano (1958); *Darest Thou Now, O Soul* for Women's Chorus and Organ (1975); *West Texas Suite* for Chorus, Symphonic Band, and Percussion Ensemble (1976); *Rising Night After Night*, cantata for 3 Soloists, Narrator, Choruses, and Orch. (1978; Lubbock, Tex., Jan. 27, 1979); *Danza Impresión de España* for Vocal Octet and Ballet (1979); *Missa Brevis* for Voice and Organ or Trumpet and Organ (1988); *Les Hommes Vidés* for Chorus (1994); *5 Psalms* for Tenor, Trumpet, and Piano (1998); *Songs Without Words* for 2 Sopranos and Piano (1999).—**NS/LK/DM**

Van Asperen, Bob, Dutch harpsichordist and teacher; b. Amsterdam, Oct. 8, 1947. He was a student of Gustav Leonhardt at the Amsterdam Cons. His career as a virtuoso commenced in 1971, and he subsequently appeared as a recitalist, chamber music player, and soloist with various early music ensembles. He also taught at the Royal Cons. of Music at The Hague (1973–88) and at the Berlin Hochschule für Musik (from 1987). Van Asperen has particularly distinguished himself in the harpsichord repertoire of the 16th to 18th centuries.—**LK/DM**

Van Bree, Jean Bernard
See **Bree, Jean Bernard van**

Vancea, Zeno (Octavian), outstanding Romanian composer and musicologist; b. Bocşa-Vasiova, Oct. 21, 1900. He studied at the Cluj Cons. (1919–21) and with Kanitz (composition) at the Vienna Cons. (1921–26; 1930–31). He taught at conservatories in Tîrgu- Mureş (1926–40; director, 1946–48), Timişoara (1940–45), and Bucharest (1949–73). He was the ed. of the important Romanian monthly *Muzica* (1953–64). Vancea belongs to the national school of Romanian composers; in his music he makes use of folk-song patterns without direct quotations. Harmonically, he adopts many procedures of cosmopolitan modern music while cautiously avoiding abrasive sonorities.

WRITINGS: *Istoria muzicii românesti* (Bucharest, 1953); *Creaţia muzicală românească, secolele XIX-XX* (Romanian Musical Compositions of the XIX-XX Centuries; Bucharest, 1968); *Studii şi eseuri muzicale* (Musical Studies and Essays; Bucharest, 1974).

WORKS: DRAMATIC: Ballet-pantomime: *Priculiciul* (The Werewolf; 1933; Bucharest, April 30, 1943; rev. 1957). **ORCH.:** *Rapsodia bănăteană No. 1* (1926); *Scoarte*, suite for Chamber Orch. (1928); *2 Grotesque Dances* (1937); *Simfonieta I* (1948); *O zi de vară* (On a Summer Day), suite (Bucharest, Sept. 23, 1951); *Triptic simfonic: Preambul, Intermezzo, Marş* (1958; Bucharest, May 10, 1959); *Burlesca* (1959); *Concerto for Orchestra* (1961; Bucharest, May 10, 1962); *5 Piese* (Pieces) for Strings (1964; Romanian TV, Feb. 4, 1965); *Prolog simfonic* (Bucharest, March 9, 1974); *Elegie* for Strings (Tîrgu- Mureş, June 10, 1977). **CHAMBER:** *Cvartet bizantin* (Byzantine Quartet; 1931); 8 string quartets (1934, 1953, 1957, 1965, 1970, 1970, 1978, 1980); String Trio (1981). **VOCAL:** *Requiem* for Soprano, Alto, Tenor, Bass, Chorus, and Orch. (1941); *Cîntecul păcii* (Song of Peace) for Soprano, Chorus, and Orch. (1961); 5 songs for Tenor and Orch. (Tîrgu-Mureş, Sept. 25, 1977); choruses; solo songs with piano. —**NS/LK/DM**

Van Dam, José (real name, Joseph Van Damme), outstanding Belgian bass-baritone; b. Brussels, Aug. 25, 1940. He began to study piano and solfège at 11. He commenced vocal studies at 13, and then entered the Brussels Cons. at 17, graduating with 1st prizes in voice and opera performance at 18. He subsequently captured 1st prizes in vocal competitions in Liège, Paris, Toulouse, and Geneva. After making his operatic debut as Don Basilio in *Il Barbiere di Siviglia* in Liège, he gained experience as a member of the Opéra and the Opéra-Comique in Paris (1961–65) and of the Geneva Opera (1965–67). In 1967 he joined the Berlin Deutsche Oper, where he established himself as one of its principal artists via such roles as Figaro, Leporello, Don Alfonso, Caspar, and Escamillo. While continuing to sing in Berlin, he pursued a notable international career. In 1973 he made his first appearance at London's Covent Garden as Escamillo, a role he also chose for his Metropolitan Opera debut in N.Y. on Nov. 21, 1975. He was chosen to create the title role in Messiaen's opera *Saint François d'Assise* at the Paris Opéra on Nov. 28, 1983, thereby adding further luster to his reputation. During the 1985–86 season, he appeared as Hans Sachs at the Chicago Lyric Opera. He sang Saint François at the Salzburg Festival in 1992. On Feb. 25, 1994, he made his Carnegie Hall recital debut in N.Y. In 1996 he appeared as Philip II in London and Paris. After singing the Dutchman in Rome in 1997, he portrayed Boris Godunov in Toulouse in 1998. He sang Leporello in Paris in 1999. Among his other esteemed roles are Don Giovanni, Verdi's Attila, Golaud, and Wozzeck. He has also won renown as a concert artist, making appearances with the foremost orchs. of Europe and the U.S. —**NS/LK/DM**

Van Delden, Lex
See **Delden, Lex van**

Van de Moortel, Arie, Belgian composer and violist; b. Laeken, July 17, 1918; d. Brussels, May 1, 1976. He studied at the Royal Cons. in Brussels and in Ghent, making his debut as a violist in 1938 in the "Trio of the Court of Belgium." He taught chamber music at the Brussels Cons. (1946–76), and was director of the music academy at Anderlecht (1957–76).

WORKS: *Silly Symphony*; Trio for Oboe, Clarinet, and Bassoon (1939; rev. 1954); Concerto for Orch.; *Toccata* for Piano; Viola Sonata; *Nocturne* for Clarinet, Saxophone, Cello, and Piano; Sonata for Solo Harp (1955); *Capriccio* for Carillon (1957); *Danse d'Espagne* for Harp; *Improvisation on a Choral Theme* for Flute and Piano (1967); Sonata for Flute Solo (1968); Violin Sonatina (1969); *Rondo-pastorale*, in memoriam E. Ysaÿe, for Violin and Piano (1970); *Sonata ostinato* for Violin and Organ (1974).—**NS/LK/DM**

Van den Boorn-Coclet, Henriette, Belgian composer; b. Liège, Jan. 15, 1866; d. there, March 6, 1945. She studied with Radoux and Dupuis at the Liège Cons., where she subsequently taught harmony. Her compositions attracted considerable attention, and included a Sym., a symphonic poem, *Le Renouveau*, *Sérénade* for Cello and Piano, various piano pieces (*Mazurka*, *Caprice*, etc.), and songs.—**NS/LK/DM**

Van den Borren, Charles (-Jean-Eugène), eminent Belgian musicologist; b. Ixelles, near Brussels, Nov. 17, 1874; d. Brussels, Jan. 14, 1966. He received training in music history from Kufferath and in harmony, counterpoint, and fugue from E. Closson. He was a barrister in the court of appeals until 1905; was music critic of *L'Indépendance Belge* (1909–14); then taught at the Brussels Institut des Hautes Études Musicales et Dramatiques and at the Free Univ., where he later was prof. of music history (1926–45); also was librarian at the Royal Cons. in Brussels (1919–40) and a lecturer in musicology at the Univ. of Liège (1927–44). He served as first chairman of the Société de Musicologie Belge (1946); in 1939, was elected a member of the Academie Royale de Belgique, Classe des Beaux-Arts, serving as its president in 1953.

WRITINGS: *L'Oeuvre dramatique de César Franck, Hulda et Ghiselle* (Brussels, 1907); *Les Origines de la musique de clavecin en Angleterre* (Brussels, 1912; Eng. tr., 1914, as *The Sources of Keyboard Music in England*); *Les Musiciens belges en Angleterre à l'époque de la Renaissance* (Brussels, 1913); *Les Débuts de la musique à Venise* (Brussels, 1914); *Origine et développement de l'art polyphonique vocal du XVIe siècle* (Brussels, 1920); *Orlando de Lassus* (Paris, 1920); *Le Manuscrit musical M.222 C.22 de la Bibliothèque de Strasbourg* (Antwerp, 1924); *Guillaume Dufay: Son importance dans l'évolution de la musique au XVe siècle* (Brussels, 1926); *Études sur le quinzième siècle musical* (Antwerp, 1941); *Peter Benoît* (Brussels, 1942); *Roland de Lassus* (Brussels, 1943); *Geschiedenis van de muziek in de Nederlanden* (2 vols., Amsterdam, 1948, 1951); *César Franck* (Brussels, 1949); with E. Closson, *La musique en Belgique du Moyen-Âge à nos jours* (Brussels, 1950). **EDITIONS:** With G. van Doorslaer, *Philippe de Monte: Opera omnia* (Bruges and Düsseldorf, 1927–39); *Polyphonia sacra: A Continental Miscellany of the Fifteenth Century* (Burnham, Buckinghamshire, 1932; 2nd ed., rev., 1962).

BIBL.: *Hommage à C. V.d. B. à l'occasion du centenaire de sa naissance* (Brussels, 1974).—**NS/LK/DM**

Van den Eeden, Jean-Baptiste
See **Eeden, Jean-Baptiste van den**

Van der Horst, Anthon
See **Horst, Anthon van der**

Vandermaesbrugge, Max, Belgian composer; b. Couillet, June 14, 1933. He studied with Moulaert, Souris, Stehman, Louel, and Absil at the Royal Cons. of Music in Brussels (1951–60). He taught piano and solfeggio at the music academies in Anderlecht (1955–62), Josse-ten-Noode (1958–62), and de Forest (1959–62), and at Etterbeck (1963–66). In 1966 he was appointed to the faculty of the Royal Cons. of Music in Brussels and in 1972 he succeeded Defossez as inspector of Belgian music schools.

WORKS: *Drum Follies,* variations for 10 Percussionists (1961); *Caprice* for Violin and Piano (1961); *4 fables de Florian* for Soprano, Contralto, and Baritone (1961); *Miniature Variations* for Guitar (1962); *Duo* for Flute and Viola (1962); *En petits caractères* for 2 Trumpets and Piano obbligato (1963); Quartet for 4 Clarinets (1965); *Tema e Variazioni* for Carillon (1967); *Divertimento* for Flute and Strings (1969); *Hiver,* symphonic poem (1970); *4 instantanés* for Flute and Guitar (1972); *Sinfonia* for Strings (1972); *Saxofolies* for Saxophone Septet (1974); *Intrada e Scherzando* for Trumpet and Piano (1978).—**NS/LK/DM**

Vandernoot, André, Belgian conductor; b. Brussels, June 2, 1927; d. there, Nov. 6, 1991. He received training at the Royal Cons. of Music in Brussels and at the Vienna Academy of Music. In 1951 he was a laureate in the Besançon conducting competition. From 1954 he appeared regularly as a conductor with the Orchestre National de Belgique in Brussels. In 1958 he was named to the post of 1st conductor of the Royal Flemish Opera in Antwerp. He was music director of the Théâtre Royal de la Monnaie in Brussels from 1959 to 1973. In 1974–75 he was music director of the Orchestre National de Belgique. From 1976 to 1983 he held the title of 1st guest conductor of the Antwerp Phil. He also was music director of the Noordhollands Phil. in Haarlem in 1978–79. From 1979 to 1989 he was music director of the Brabants Orch. From 1987 he also was chief conductor of the Orchestre Symphonique de la RTBF in Brussels. —**NS/LK/DM**

Van der Slice, John, American composer, ethnomusicologist, and teacher; b. Ann Arbor, Feb. 19, 1940. He studied at the Univ. of Calif., Berkeley (B.A., 1964), with Russell, McKay, and Dahl at the Univ. of Hawaii (M.A. in ethnomusicology; M.M., 1973), and at the Univ. of Ill., Urbana (Ph.D., 1980, with a diss. on Ligeti's *Atmosphères*). He taught at the Univ. of Hawaii at Hilo and served in an administrative position at the Univ. of Hawaii at Honolulu; then joined the faculty of the Univ. of Miami. His musical tastes range from the medieval period to the contemporary era, and also include jazz and non-Western musics; he studied performance traditions of the Japanese koto, the Korean kayakeum, and the bonang panerus member of the Javanese gamelan. His compositional language involves both pitch set permutation and a subtle implication of tonal hierarchy.

WORKS: ORCH.: *Jo-ha-kyu* (1977–79); *Fantasia* (1988). **CHAMBER:** *Pulse/Impulse* for Percussion (1983); Trio for Clarinet, Viola, and Marimba (1984); *Doodle Music* for Piccolo and Percussion (1985); Piano Trio (1986); *Animistic Study* for Double Bass (1986); *Time Shadows* for 11 Instruments (1987). —**NS/LK/DM**

Van der Straeten, Edmond, Belgian music historian; b. Audenarde, Dec. 3, 1826; d. there, Nov. 26, 1895. He studied philosophy in Ghent, then went to Brussels in 1857 as secretary to Fétis, with whom he studied counterpoint. He held a lifelong position at the Royal Library, and rarely left Belgium. He was active as a music critic (1859–72), and also wrote an opera, *Le Proscrit.* His reputation rests upon his scholarly publications, dealing with music in the Low Countries. He publ. a monumental work of reference, *La Musique au Pays-Bas avant le XIXe siècle* (8 vols., 1867–88); other writings are *Coup d'oeil sur la musique actuelle à Audenarde* (1851), *Notice sur Charles-Félix de Hollande* (1854), *Notice sur les carillons d'Audenarde* (1855), *Recherches sur la musique à Audenarde avant le XIXe siècle* (1856), *Examen des chants populaires des Flamands de France, publiés par E. de Coussemaker* (1858), *J.-F.-J. Janssens* (1866), *Wagner: Verslag aan den heer minister van binnenlandsche Zaaken* (1871), *Le Théâtre villageois en Flandre* (2 vols., 1874, 1880), *Les Musiciens belges en Italie* (1875), *Voltaire musicien*

(1878), *Les Ballets des rois en Flandre; Xylographie, musique, coutumes, etc.* (1892), *Charles V musicien* (1894), and *Les Willems, luthiers gantois du XVIIe siècle* (1896; with C. Snoeck).—**NS/LK/DM**

Van der Stucken, Frank (Valentin), American conductor and composer; b. Fredericksburg, Tex., Oct. 15, 1858; d. Hamburg, Aug. 16, 1929. In 1866 he was taken by his parents to Antwerp, where he studied with Peter Benoit at the Cons.; then with Reinecke in Leipzig (1877–79). In 1881 he became conductor at the Breslau Stadttheater. In 1884 he became Leopold Damrosch's successor as conductor of the Arion Soc., a men's chorus in N.Y., and soon acquired a reputation as an advocate of American music. He conducted MacDowell's Piano Concerto with the composer as soloist, as well as works by Chadwick, Foote, and Paine at the Paris Exposition (July 12, 1889). After serving as conductor of the North American Sangerbund in Newark (1891) and N.Y. (1894), he was the first permanent conductor of the Cincinnati Sym. Orch. (1895–1907). He was also dean of the Cincinnati Coll. of Music (1896–1901), and served as music director of the Cincinnati May Festival (1906–12), returning there in 1923 and once again serving as its music director in 1925 and 1927. He lived mostly in Europe from 1907. In 1898 he was elected to the National Inst. of Arts and Letters and in 1929 to the American Academy of Arts and Letters. He composed a few orch. works, choral music, numerous songs, and piano pieces.—**NS/LK/DM**

Van der Velden, Renier, Belgian composer; b. Antwerp, Jan. 14, 1910; d. there, Jan. 19, 1993. He received training from Jan Broeckx, Karel Candael, and Joseph Jongen in Brussels. In 1945 he was became program director of the French services of the Belgian Radio in Antwerp. In 1970 he was made a member of the Royal Flemish Academy of Arts, Letters, and Sciences.

WORKS: DRAMATIC: Ballet: *Indruk aan Zee* (1930); *Provinciestad 1900* (1937); *L'Enlèvement de Proserpine* (1947); *De zakdoekjes* (1947); *Les Amours de torero* (1948); *Dulle Griet* (1949; rev. 1967); *Les Ancêtres* (1949); *Arlequinade* (1950); *Judith* (1951); *De Triomf van de dood* (1963); *Oostendse maskers* (1965); *Ballet Music* (1972). **ORCH.:** *Impression maritime* for Small Orch. (1930); *Divertimento* for Strings (1938); *Hommage à Ravel* (1938); Trumpet Concerto (1940); Oboe Concerto (1941); 2 sinfoniettas (1942, 1969); 2 suites (1945, 1955); 4 concertinos: No. 1 for Clarinet, Bassoon, Piano, and Strings (1949), No. 2 for Viola and Chamber Orch. (1964), No. 3 for Flute and Strings (1965), and No. 4 for Piano and Strings (1971); *Beweging* (Movement; 1968); *Hulde aan Janáček* for Flute, Oboe, and Strings (1973); *Landschappen* for Chamber Orch. (1976); *Nocturne voor beeldhouwer Mark Macken* for Strings (1979). **CHAMBER:** 2 concertos for Wind Quintet (1939, 1955); *Adagio and Finale* for String Trio (1940); Trio for Oboe, Clarinet, and Bassoon (1943); Sextet for Wind Quintet and Piano (1948); *Divertimento* for Oboe, Clarinet, and Bassoon (1957); Concertino for Brass Quintet and 2 Pianos (1965); *Fantaisie* for 4 Clarinets (1967); *2 Dialogues* for Clarinet and Piano (1971); *Nocturne* for Flute, Guitar, and Cello (1980). **Piano:** 2 suites (1937, 1944); *Beweging* (Movement) for 2 Pianos (1965). **VOCAL:** Songs, including *8 poèmes de Karel van de Woestijne* for High Voice and Piano (1946; orchestrated 1951).—**NS/LK/DM**

Van de Vate, Nancy, American composer and record producer; b. Plainfield, N.J., Dec. 30, 1930. She studied piano at the Eastman School of Music in Rochester, N.Y., Wellesley Coll. (A.B., 1952), and with Bruce Simonds at Yale Univ., and then concentrated on composition at the Univ. of Miss. (M.M., 1958) and Fla. State Univ. (D.M., 1968). She taught at Memphis State Univ. (1964–66), the Univ. of Tenn. (1967), Knoxville Coll. (1968–69; 1971–72), Maryville Coll. (1973–74), the Univ. of Hawaii (1975–76), and Hawaii Loa Coll. (1977–80). In 1975 she founded the International League of Women Composers, and served as its chairperson until 1982. In 1985 she settled in Vienna. In 1990 she and her husband, Clyde Smith, founded Vienna Modern Masters, a CD company dedicated primarily to recording new music for orchestra. She continued to oversee the company after her husband's death. By 2000, VMM had 49 CDs of orchestral and orchestral-choral music in its catalog, and 33 CDs of unusual new music for solo instruments and chamber ensembles. Van de Vate's music—highly charged and dissonantly colored by way of influences as varied as Prokofiev, Shostakovich, Penderecki, Crumb, and Varèse—has won international awards.

WORKS: DRAMATIC: Opera: *The Death of the Hired Man*, after Robert Frost (1958; Tupelo, Miss., Feb. 8, 1960; rev. 1998; Oxford, Miss., Nov. 19, 1999); *In the Shadow of the Glen*, after Synge (1994; Cambridge, Mass., March 12, 1999); *Der Herrscher und das Mädchen*, children's opera (Vienna, June 21, 1995); *Nemo: Jenseits von Vulkania* (1995); *All Quiet on the Western Front*, after Remarque (1999). **Music Theater:** *A Night in the Royal Ontario Museum* (1983; College Park, Md., April 13, 1984); *Cocaine Lil* (1986; Bremen, April 22, 1988). **ORCH.:** *Adagio* (1957; Tuscaloosa, Ala., April 18, 1958); *Variations* for Chamber Orch. (1958; Hattiesburg, Miss., March 13, 1963); Piano Concerto (1968; Tuscaloosa, Ala., April 26, 1969; rev. version, Koszalin, Poland, Nov. 26, 1993); *Concertpiece* for Cello and Small Orch. (1978; Boston, April 29, 1979); *Dark Nebulai* (1981; Columbus, Ohio, June 29, 1983); *Gema Jawa (Echoes of Java)* (1984; Jakarta, Jan. 30, 1985); *Journeys* (1984; Eugene, Ore., Feb. 25, 1985); *Distant Worlds* (1985; Kraków, June 20, 1987); 2 violin concertos: No. 1 (Pittsburg, Kans., Nov. 15, 1987) and No. 2 (Ruse, Bulgaria, June 21, 1996); *Pura Besakih (Besakih Temple, Bali)* (1987; San Francisco, Feb. 6, 1988); *Chernobyl* (1987); *Kraków Concerto* for Percussion and Orch. (1988; Kraków, Nov. 28, 1989); Viola Concerto (1990; Kraków, Sept. 14, 1993); *Adagio and Rondo* for Violin and Strings (Lancut, Poland, July 25, 1994); *Suite from Nemo* (Ruse, Bulgaria, June 27, 1996); Harp Concerto (1996; Olomouc, June 21, 1998); *A Peacock Southeast Flew*, concerto for Pipa and Orch. (1997); *Western Front* (1997; Olomouc, June 21, 1998). **CHAMBER:** *Short Suite* for Brass Quartet (1960); Woodwind Quartet (1964); String Quartet No. 1 (1969); Oboe Sonata (1969); *6 Etudes* for Viola (1969; N.Y., Dec. 24, 1974); Clarinet Sonata (1970); *3 Sound Pieces* for Brass and Percussion (1973; Atlanta, Feb. 23, 1974); Brass Quintet (1974; Jacksonville, Fla., Feb. 23, 1975; rev. 1979); String Trio (1974; Stowe, Vt., Aug. 1975); Quintet for Flute, Violin, Clarinet, Cello, and Piano (1975; Honolulu, Jan. 12, 1976); Suite for Violin (1975; N.Y., Dec. 3, 1976); *Music* for Viola, Percussion, and Piano (1976; Honolulu, Feb. 27, 1977); Trio for Bassoon, Percussion, and Piano (Honolulu, Dec. 7, 1980); Trio for Violin, Cello, and Piano (1983; Mexico City, March 24, 1984); *Music for MW2* for Flute, Cello, Piano, 4-Hands, and Percussion (1985; N.Y., Feb. 10, 1989); *Teufelstanz* for 6 Percussion (1988; Munich, Feb. 24, 1989); 7

Pieces for Violin and Piano (1989; Vienna, July 19, 1991); *4 Fantasy Pieces* for Flute and Piano (Vienna, Nov. 15, 1993); *Divertimento* for Harp and String Quintet (1996). **KEYBOARD: Piano:** 2 sonatas: No. 1 (1978) and No. 2 (1983; Mexico City, March 23, 1984); *9 Preludes* (1978; Los Angeles, April 2, 1982); *Contrasts* for 2 Pianos, 6-Hands (Jakarta, May 23, 1984); *12 Pieces* for Piano on 1 to 12 Notes (1986; Vienna, Sept. 19, 1990); *Fantasy Pieces* (1995; Utrecht, March 5, 1996); *Night Journey* (1996; Eisenstadt, April 19, 1997). **Harpsichord:** *Fantasy* (1982; Ann Arbor, May 6, 1983); Sonata (1982; Davis, Calif., Nov. 12, 1983). **VOCAL:** *4 Somber Songs* for Soprano or Mezzo-soprano and Piano (1970; Oak Ridge, Tenn., Oct. 21, 1973; also for Mezzo-soprano and Orch., 1992); *An American Essay* for Soprano, Chorus, Piano, and Percussion (Knoxville, Tenn., May 16, 1972; also for Soprano, Chorus, and Orch., Koszalin, Poland, June 29, 1994); *Letter to a Friend's Loneliness* for Mezzo-soprano and String Quartet (Johnson City, Tenn., Nov. 8, 1976); Cantata for Women's Voices and 7 Players (1979; Los Angeles, April 1, 1982; also as *Voices of Women* for Soprano, Mezzo-soprano, Chorus, and Orch., 1993); *Songs for the Four Parts of Night* for Soprano and Piano (Paris, Oct. 25, 1984); *Katyn* for Chorus and Orch. (Kraków, Nov. 28, 1989); *Choral Suite from Nemo* for Chorus and Orch. (1997).—**NS/LK/DM**

Van de Woestijne, David, Belgian composer; b. Llanidloes, Wales, Feb. 18, 1915; d. Brussels, May 18, 1979. He was the son of the painter Gustav van de Woestijne and the nephew of the Flemish poet Karel van de Woestijne. After studies in harmony and counterpoint with Defauw and Gilson, he took lessons with Espla. Van de Woestijne's music reflects the trends of cosmopolitan modernism.

WORKS: DRAMATIC: Opera: *Le Débat de la folie et de l'amour*, opera-ballet (1959); *De zoemende musikant*, television opera (1967); *Graal 68 ou L'Impromptu de Gand* (Ghent, 1968). **ORCH.:** Double Concerto for Piano, Cello, and Orch. (1935); *Fantasia* for Oboe and Orch. (1936); Piano Concerto (1938); *Ballade* for Piano and Orch. (1940); Concerto for Violin and 12 Solo Instruments (1945); *Sérénades* for Piano, 12 Wind Instruments, Double Bass, and Percussion (1946; Copenhagen, June 2, 1947); Sym. (1958); Sym. in 1 Movement (1965); *Concertino da camera* for Flute, Oboe, and Strings (1967); Concerto for 2 Pianos and Orch. (1972); Concerto for String Quartet, 14 Wind Instruments, and Double Bass (1974); *Hommage à Purcell* for Harpsichord and Strings (1974); *Eénentwintig* for Piano, 19 Winds, and Double Bass (1976). **CHAMBER:** *Divertimento* for Oboe, Clarinet, and Bassoon (1942); Quintet for Flute, Oboe, Violin, Viola, and Cello (1953); Violin Sonata (1956); *Variations* for 7 Instruments (1965); *Sarabande* for 2 Guitars (1965); *Devant une sculpture* for 12 Instruments (1969); String Quartet (1970); *Notturno* for Flute and Piano (1976); *Music* for Tuba or Saxhorn and Piano (1976); *Minuetto capriccioso* for Trumpet and Piano (1976). **Piano:** *Toccata* (1935); Sonatina (1945); Sonata for 2 Pianos (1955). **VOCAL:** 2 cantatas: La *Belle Cordière* for Soprano and Orch. (1954) and *Les Aéronautes* for Soloists, Chorus, Speaking Chorus, and Orch. (1963); *Aswoendag* (Ash Wednesday) for Narrator, Soloists, Chorus, and Orch. (1971); songs.
—**NS/LK/DM**

Van Dieren, Bernard
See **Dieren, Bernard van**

Van Doorslaer, Georges, Belgian musicologist; b. Mechelen, Sept. 27, 1864; d. there, Jan. 16, 1940. He was a physician by profession, but studied music as an avocation. He wrote the valuable treatises *Herry Bredemers, 1472–1522* (Antwerp, 1915), *De Toonkunstenaars der familie Vredeman* (Antwerp, 1920), *La Vie et les oeuvres de Philippe de Monte* (Brussels, 1921), and *Rinaldo del Mel* (Antwerp, 1922), and also ed. eight vols. in the collected edition of works by Philippe de Monte.—**NS/LK/DM**

Vandross, Luther, African-American session singer turned R&B star turned pop star; b. N.Y., April 20, 1951. One of the most popular and successful singers of the last quarter of the 20th century, Luther Vandross manages to neatly balance art and commerce. On the commerce side, nearly every album Vandross has made has gone at least platinum. On the art side, Vandross possesses one of the finest vocal instruments to grace a pop record, with a range that goes from a growling baritone to a yearning tenor, with raw, affecting emotion in it.

Raised on the Lower East Side of Manhattan, his family was immersed in both sacred and secular music. His older sister performed with the doo-wop group the Crests. He began to learn piano before he started kindergarten and by his early 20s had worked with musical theater workshops at the Apollo Theater and had a song, "Everybody Rejoice (A Brand New Day)" in the Broadway musical *The Wiz*. He also did sessions, mostly jingles for clients ranging from Burger King to the Army, until his friend Carlos Alomar landed in David Bowie's band and introduced Vandross to Bowie as he went in to record *Young Americans*. Vandross wound up both arranging and singing the background vocals on the album and tour, contributing the song "Fascination."

Suddenly his career took off and he became a first-call backing vocalist, working with artists ranging from Ringo Starr to Chic (he was featured on the one-time best-selling single of all time, "Dance, Dance, Dance"). His success with the studio dance group Change on the hit "Glow of Love" led to two solo records that failed to establish him as a star in his own right, partially because he had limited input into the production. He went back to the studios and to backing artists in concert. While he was working with Roberta Flack, she fired him so he could give a solo career another shot. He recorded his own song, "Never Enough," and a cover of "A House Is Not a Home." On the basis of these songs, he got a contract with Epic that gave him creative control. The album, with those demos unchanged except for some added strings, went to #19 pop and platinum, topping the R&B charts, as did the title track "Never Too Much," although it only hit #33 pop.

This would be a recurring theme in Vandross's career throughout the 1980s, when he became massively popular in R&B but a marginally popular pop artist. Top Ten R&B hits like "Bad Boy/Having a Party," "I'll Let You Slide," "Superstar/Until You Come Back to Me (That's What I'm Going to Do)," "It's Over Now," "Give Me the Reason," "I Really Didn't Mean It," "For Your Love," and even R&B chart toppers like "Any Love" and his duet with Gregory Hines "There's Nothing Better than Love" all failed to make the pop chart during the 1980s.

During his first decade as a solo artist, only the R&B chart topper "Stop to Love," the R&B #3 "She Won't Talk to Me," and the R&B #4 "'Til My Baby Comes Home" made any real impression on the pop charts, hitting #15 in 1986, #30 in 1989, and #29 in 1985, respectively. His only other pop hit, a duet with Dionne Warwick on "How Many Times Can We Say Goodbye," rose to #27 in 1983. However, during this same period, he had seven platinum albums, including two that went double platinum. Only 1988's *Any Love*, however, broke the pop album Top Ten, hitting #9. Most of his albums followed a similar formula: a couple of upbeat numbers, a few ballads, at least one of which teeters on the brink of being overwrought, and one well-chosen, exquisitely performed cover.

In addition to producing his own records, he became a successful producer of other artists. His production of Aretha Franklin's *Jump to It* took both the album and the title track to the top of the R&B charts and gave her her first Top 40 pop hit in six years, starting her revival. He also worked with Teddy Pendergrass and Whitney Houston, among many others.

His fortunes in the pop market started to change at the turn of the decade with the release of his first greatest hits collection, *The Best of Love*. The album included one new track, "Here and Now." Although it didn't give him the chart topper he'd hoped for, it hit #6 pop, spent two weeks on top of the R&B charts, and went gold. The track won him a Grammy Award for Best R&B Vocal Performance, Male.

He rode this momentum with another well-crafted album of new material, *Power of Love*. The single "Power of Love/Love Power" featured Darlene Love and Cissy Houston, and although it topped the R&B charts yet again, it also hit a respectable #4 pop. He followed this with the #9 "Don't Want to Be a Fool," which again made it to #4 R&B. "The Rush" hit #6 R&B, but didn't cross over pop. The album hit #7 and went double platinum.

He once again topped the R&B charts dueting with Janet Jackson on "The Best Things in Life Are Free" from the 1992 movie *Mo' Money*. The tune hit #10 pop. It took a year before his own album came out. While *Never Let Me Go* went platinum and charted at #6 pop, once again he was playing to the R&B audience. "Sometimes It's Only Love" and the title track didn't cross over pop, going to #9 and #31 R&B. The #10 R&B tune "Little Miracles (Happen Every Day)" and the #24 R&B hit "Heaven Knows" didn't break the pop Top 40, peaking at #62 and #94, respectively. Vandross seemed to have lost the ground he created.

After taking a stab at the movies, playing a hitman in Robert Townsend's movie *Meteor Man*, Vandross regained his pop momentum, expanding one element of nearly every album—the covers—to the whole thing. *Songs* featured material ranging from McFadden and Whitehead's disco anthem "Ain't No Stoppin' Us Now" to show tunes like "The Impossible Dream." He had a gold duet with rising star Mariah Carey on the Diana Ross/Lionel Richie chart topper "Endless Love." They took it to #2 on the pop charts and gold status. The album hit #5 and platinum.

After a successful holiday album, Vandross put out *Your Secret Love*. In addition to the usual formula, he invited Spinderella from Salt-N-Pepa to add some hip-hop to one of the tracks. A year later, he left Epic after nearly two decades, signing with Virgin for *I Know*. This album expanded his palette, with two hip-hop tracks with a Salt-N-Pepa sound-alike named Precise on one end of the spectrum and "I'm Only Human," a duet with jazz star Cassandra Wilson featuring keyboard by pop jazz icon Bob James. It showed Vandross as a performer who continues to evolve but ever so slowly. This might account, along with his mighty talent, for his longevity.

DISC.: *Never Too Much* (1981); *Forever, for Always, for Love* (1982); *Busy Body* (1983); *The Night I Fell in Love* (1985); *Give Me the Reason* (1986); *Any Love* (1988); *Power of Love* (1991); *Never Let Me Go* (1993); *Songs* (1994); *This Is Christmas* (1995); *Your Secret Love* (1996); *I Know* (1998).—**BH**

Van Durme, Jef, Belgian composer; b. Kemzeke-Waas, May 7, 1907; d. Brussels, Jan. 28, 1965. He was a pupil of Alpaerts at the Royal Flemish Cons. of Music in Antwerp and of Berg in Vienna (1931).

WORKS: DRAMATIC: Opera: *Remous*, after Weterings (1936); *The Death of a Salesman*, after Arthur Miller (1954–55); *King Lear* (1955–57); *Anthony and Cleopatra* (1957–59); *Richard III* (1960–61). **Ballet**: *De dageraad* (1932–33); *Orestes* (1934–35; orch. suite, 1936–40). **ORCH.**: 2 symphonic poems (*Hamlet*, 1929; *Beatrice*, 1930); *2 Elegies* (1933, 1938); 6 numbered syms.: (1934; 1938–39; 1945–46; 1950–51; 1952; 1953); 1 unnumbered sym.: *Breughel* (1935–42); *Poème héroïque* (1935); *2 Sinfonie da camera* (1937, 1949); *3 Ballads* (*In memoriam Alban Berg*, 1938; 1947–48; 1961); 2 piano concertos (1943, 1946); *Symphonic Prologue* (1944–45); Violin Concerto (1946–47); 4 suites (1947; 1948–60; *Van Gogh*, 1954; 1962); Sinfonietta for Strings (1962). **CHAMBER**: 3 violin sonatas (1928, 1938, 1947); 4 piano trios (1928, 1929, 1942, 1949); Sextet for Piano and Wind Quintet (1930); 5 string quartets (1932–33; 1937; 1945–48; 1948–53; 1953); Piano Quartet (1934); Wind Quintet (1951–52); Cello Sonata (1952). **Piano**: 2 sonatas (1946; 1952–53). **VOCAL**: *De 14 stonden*, oratorio (1931); songs.—**NS/LK/DM**

Van Dyck, Ernest (Marie Hubert), distinguished Belgian tenor; b. Antwerp, April 2, 1861; d. Berlaer-lez-Lierre, Aug. 31, 1923. He studied law, and was a journalist in Paris, where he studied voice with Saint-Yves Bax. He sang at the Lamoureux concerts (from 1883); made his operatic debut in Lohengrin (May 3, 1887). After further training with Julius Kniese, he appeared at the Bayreuth Festival as Parsifal in 1888, a role he sang there regularly until 1912; also appeared as Lohengrin there in 1894. From 1888 to 1900 he was a member of the Vienna Court Opera; on May 19, 1891, he made his London debut at Covent Garden, returning there in 1897, 1898, and 1901; made his first appearance at the Paris Opéra as Lohengrin on Sept. 16, 1891, which role he also sang at his debut at the Théâtre Royal de la Monnaie in Brussels on April 28, 1894. He made his U.S. debut as Tannhäuser in Chicago (Nov. 9, 1898); made his first appearance at the Metropolitan Opera in N.Y. in the same role (Nov. 29, 1898), and remained with the company until 1902. In 1907 he served as manager of the German Opera season at Covent Garden, where he also sang Tristan and Siegmund; in 1908 he sang Siegfried in *Götterdämmerung* and in 1914 Parsifal at the Paris Opéra. He taught voice in Paris and later in Brussels. He was equally at home in Wagnerian roles and the French repertoire.—**NS/LK/DM**

Van Eps, George (Abel), noted jazz guitarist, son of Fred van Eps; b. Plainfield, N.J., Aug. 7, 1913; d. Newport Beach, Calif., Nov. 29, 1998. He had three brothers who were professional musicians: Bobby (piano), Freddy (trumpet), and John (tenor sax); their father, Fred van Eps, who recorded extensively in the 1910s and 1920s, was a noted ragtime banjoist; their mother played piano. George began doing gigs at 13, playing banjo in a band led by his brother, Fred; he did his first solo broadcast at 14 and was teaching at 15. He studied watch-making, but began touring with Harry Reser's Junior Artists and then worked with the Dutch Master Minstrels before joining Smith Ballew from 1929–31. Van Eps spent six months working with his idol, guitarist Eddie Lang; then, after a two-year spell with Freddy Martin, he worked with Benny Goodman in 1934 and 1935; he left in summer 1935 to work with Ray Noble's Orch., working with him for a year. He then moved to Hollywood for freelance studio work, remaining there until late 1939. He designed a seven-string guitar (featuring an extra bass string) and wrote a text on guitar playing. Van Eps worked again with Ray Noble from autumn of 1940 until spring of 1941, spent two years in his father's sound laboratory, and then moved to the West Coast to recommence prolific studio work. He participated in the film *Pete Kelly's Blues* and in the television series of the same name in the middle and late 1950s. He played various festivals in the 1960s and 1970s. Illness restricted his activities during the early 1970s, however, and from then until his death he performed only occasionally. He worked with Peanuts Hucko in 1986. Van Eps was the seventh recipient of the American Federation of Jazz Societies Benny Carter Award (1997).

DISC.: *Mellow Guitar* (1956); *My Guitar* (1965); *George Van Eps's Seven-String Guitar* (1967); *Soliloquy* (1968); *Hand-Crafted Swing* (1991); *Seven & Seven* (1992).—**JC/LP**

Vaness, Carol (Theresa), talented American soprano; b. San Diego, July 27, 1952. She grew up in Pomona, where she took piano lessons; while attending a parochial girls' school, she sang in its choir, then studied English and piano at Calif. State Polytechnic Coll. before concentrating on music at Calif. State Univ. in Northridge (M.A., 1976), where her vocal instructor was David Scott. After serving an apprenticeship at the San Francisco Opera, she made her N.Y.C. Opera debut as Vitellia in *La clemenza di Tito* on Oct. 25, 1979, and continued to appear there until 1983, when she scored a major success as Handel's Alcina. On Jan. 9, 1981, she made her European debut as Vitellia in Bordeaux. She made her first appearance at the Glyndebourne Festival in 1982 as Donna Anna in *Don Giovanni*, a role she subsequently sang to much acclaim throughout Europe. In 1982 she also made her debut at London's Covent Garden as Mimi. On Feb. 14, 1984, she made her Metropolitan Opera debut in N.Y. as Armida in Handel's *Rinaldo*, and continued to sing there in later seasons; also appeared with other U.S. opera houses and toured as a concert artist. In 1988 she made her first appearance at the Salzburg Festival as Vitellia. In 1990 she sang Mozart's Elettra at Milan's La Scala. On Dec. 19, 1991, she made her N.Y. Phil. debut singing excerpts from Strauss's *Daphne* under Leinsdorf's direction. In 1992 she appeared as Rossini's Mathilde in San Francisco. In 1994 she appeared as Desdemona at the Metropolitan Opera, where she returned as Fiordiligi in 1996. She also sang Norma at the Houston Grand Opera in the latter year. In 1997 she portrayed Tosca at the San Francisco Opera. She returned to the Metropolitan Opera as Rosalinde in 1999. Her other roles include Dalila in Handel's *Samson*, Elettra in *Idomeneo*, the Countess in *Le nozze di Figaro*, Rosina, Violetta, Gilda, Nedda, and Mimi.—**NS/LK/DM**

Van Gilse, Jan
See **Gilse, Jan van**

Van Hagen, Peter Albrecht, Sr., Dutch-American musician; b. in the Netherlands, 1755; d. Boston, Aug. 20, 1803. After marrying Elizabeth Joanetta Catherine van Hagen (b. probably in Amsterdam, 1750; d. Suffolk County, Mass., c. 1809), he went with her to Charleston, S.C., in 1774. By 1789 they were in N.Y., where they were active as performers, teachers, and concert managers, and also promoted their own "Old City Concerts" series. They settled in Boston in 1796, taking the name Von Hagen. He was active as a music dealer and publisher, also directed a theater orch., and served as organist at King's Chapel (1798–1803). His son, Peter Albrecht Von Hagen Jr. (b. probably in Charleston, S.C., c. 1779; d. Boston, Sept. 12, 1837), was a violinist, organist, violist, and composer. In 1810 he was made organist at Trinity Church in Boston, and he later conducted bands in South Boston and in Fort Eustis, Va.; his later years were plagued by alcoholism. All the members of the family composed, and the authorship of many of the works of the father and son is in dispute. Their output includes overtures, marches for piano, and songs. Elizabeth composed two piano concertos, a Piano Sonata, and *The Country Maid*, a set of keyboard variations.—**NS/LK/DM**

Vanhal (also **van Hal, Vanhall, Wanhal, etc.**), **Johan Baptist** (actually, **Jan Křtitel**), noted Czech composer and teacher; b. Nové Nechanice, Bohemia, May 12, 1739; d. Vienna, Aug. 20, 1813. He was born into a bonded peasant family. He began his musical training as a teacher and organist in Maršov, and then studied organ with the cantor A. Erban in Nové Nechanice. In 1757 he became organist in Opocno; in 1759 he was named choirmaster in Hnevceves. After he won the favor of Countess Schaffgotsch, his patron took him to Vienna about 1761, and he was able to further his training under Dittersdorf. He obtained his release from bondage, and then traveled in Italy (1769–71) before returning to Vienna. Although stricken with mental illness, he recovered and devoted his energies to teaching and composing. He was a prolific composer; some 700 works are extant, of which his 73 syms. (c. 1767–85) in the early Classical style were most notable. His keyboard sonatas are also notable. His output includes works for both professional and amateur performers. He publ. the pedagogical vol. *Anfangsgründe des Generalbasses* (Vienna, 1817).

WORKS: DRAMATIC: Opera: *Il Demofoonte* (Rome, 1770); *Il trionfo di Clelia* (Rome, 1770). **ORCH.:** About 73 syms. (c. 1767–85); several concertos for Harpsichord or Piano; other concertos for Violin, Cello, Viola, Flute, Bassoon, Clarinet, and Double Bass; marches, dances, etc. **CHAMBER:** 6 string quintets; over 75 string quartets; more than 100 string trios; many other chamber pieces, including keyboard trios, string duos, keyboard duos, and solo keyboard works of various descriptions. **VOCAL:** About 60 masses; more than 60 motets; Stabat Mater, Te Deum, Passion oratorio, and other sacred works; many secular songs.

BIBL.: J. Bušek, *Jansa, Kalivoda, V.* (Prague, 1926); P. Bryan, *The Symphonies of J. V.* (diss., Univ. of Mich., 1955); N. Dlouhá-Mikotová, *Klavirni koncerty J.K. V.a* (J.K. V.'s Keyboard Concertos; diss., Univ. of Prague, 1958); A. Borková, *Stylová charakteristika klavírnich sonát J.K. V.a* (Stylistic Characteristics of J.K. V.'s Keyboard Sonatas; diss., Univ. of Brno, 1967); P. Bryan, *J. W., Viennese Symphonist: His Life and His Musical Environment* (Stuyvesant, N.Y., 1997).—**NS/LK/DM**

Van Halen, mainstays of heavy-metal music since the late 1970s. **MEMBERSHIP:** David Lee Roth, lead voc., gtr. (b. Bloomington, Ind., Oct. 10, 1955); Edward Van Halen, lead gtr. (b. Nijmegen, Netherlands, Jan. 26, 1957); Michael Anthony, bs., voc. (b. Chicago, June 20, 1955); Alex Van Halen, drm. (b. Nijmegen, Netherlands, May 8, 1955). David Lee Roth left in 1985, to be replaced by Sammy Hagar (b. Monterey, Calif., Oct. 13, 1947), who left in 1996 and was eventually replaced by Gary Cherone (b. July 26, 1961.)

Garnering a huge following among American male youth for their live shows, Van Halen was propelled by the inventive, rapid-fire playing of lead guitarist Eddie Van Halen, often regarded as the most influential guitarist since Jimmy Page. The band featured the bombastic, narcissistic, debauched personality of vocalist David Lee Roth until 1985. Van Halen continued their hit-making and best-selling ways after Roth's departure with new vocalist Sammy Hagar, who brought a mellower and more commercial sound to the group with his songwriting. Maintaining a low profile after 1988's Monsters of Rock tour, one of the most successful tours of the year and one of the most expensive ever mounted, Van Halen were challenged in the heavy-metal field by upstarts Metallica and Guns N' Roses by the late 1980s. Nonetheless, their success continued unabated as Roth struggled to establish himself in a solo career.

Edward and Alex Van Halen took classical piano lessons as children, moving with their family to the United States in 1965 and settling in Pasadena, Calif., in 1968. Eddie took up guitar at age 12, and the brothers formed Broken Crumbs with bassist Michael Anthony in the early 1970s. They later recruited vocalist David Lee Roth, a onetime student of Pasadena City Coll., from the Red Ball Jets for the group Mammoth. Spotted by Gene Simmons of Kiss, who produced a demonstration tape for the band, Mammoth changed their name to Van Halen in 1974 and began several years of playing the Southern Calif. bar circuit. The band eventually signed with Warner Bros. Records, with Ted Templeman producing all their albums through 1993.

Van Halen's debut album remained on the album charts for more than three years, yielded a moderate hit with a remake of the Kinks's "You Really Got Me," and eventually sold more than six million copies. The group quickly became established as a hugely popular live act in the United States, particularly among male white youth. David Lee Roth's sex, drugs, and alcohol party-persona and Eddie Van Halen's outstanding guitar playing, characterized by extended solos and his unique technique of hammering on the guitar strings with both hands, were major draws. Their second album became an instant best-seller and produced their first major hit, "Dance the Night Away." Despite scoring only one more major hit through 1983—1982's cover version of Roy Orbison's "Oh, Pretty Woman"—Van Halen's albums sold in the millions, save 1981's *Fair Warning*. They reaffirmed their position as the leading purveyor of pop-style heavy-metal music with *1984*, which yielded the top hit "Jump" and major hits "I'll Wait" and "Panama."

By early 1985 David Lee Roth had recorded a mini-album that produced a smash hit with a remake of the Beach Boys' "California Girls" and a major hit with his copy of Louis Prima's rendition of the medley "Just a Gigolo/I Ain't Got Nobody." Buoyed by the success, Roth left Van Halen for a solo career. Recruiting guitarist Steve Vai and bassist Billy Sheehan, Roth toured in support of the best-selling *Eat 'Em and Smile* (1986) and *Skyscraper* (1988) albums. The first album yielded the major hit "Yankee Rose" and the second produced the smash "Just Like Paradise," but Roth never scored another major hit. In the 1990s Roth retired his boisterous and self-serving persona, eventually reemerging for a club tour in support of the eclectic *Your Filthy Little Mouth*, which included a duet with Travis Tritt on "Cheatin' Heart Cafe."

Despite dire predictions that Van Halen would never be the same without David Lee Roth, the band not only survived but maintained their astounding level of popularity with new vocalist Sammy Hagar, a veteran of Montrose and a successful solo recording artist (1982–1983's "Your Love Is Driving Me Crazy" and 1984's "I Can't Drive 55"). Hagar favored harmony vocals, perhaps to cover his limited vocal range, and brought a pop sensibility to the band's basic heavy-metal sound. His debut with Van Halen, *5150*, sold more than four million copies and yielded a smash hit with the ballad "Why Can't This Be Love" and the major hits "Dreams" and "Love Walks In." In 1987 Sammy Hagar recorded a solo album that yielded a major hit with "Give to Live."

In 1988 Van Halen recorded the formulaic *OU812*, which produced the smash hit "When It's Love" and major hit "Finish What Ya Started." They toured with Metallica and the Scorpions, among others, on the heavily attended Monsters of Rock tour. Overshadowed by Metallica on tour and challenged in the heavy-metal field by Metallica and Guns N' Roses, Van Halen withdrew for several years, reemerging in 1991 with *For Unlawful Carnal Knowledge*, its major hit "Top of the World," and a new round of touring. Their 1993 tour yielded the live set *Right Here, Right Now*. In 1994 Van Halen recorded their first album without producer Ted Templeman, *Balance*, touring once again in 1995. *Unboxed*, issued in 1994, compiled Sammy Hagar's greatest hits of the 1980s, along with two newly recorded songs.

Tensions between Eddie Van Halen and Sammy Hagar led to an acrimonious split in 1996, and David Lee Roth was brought in to the studio to record two new songs for a 1996 compilation album. However, the reunion didn't last, and former Extreme singer Gary Cherone was chosen as the band's new vocalist, recording Van Halen's 1998 album; Cherone has since left the band.

DISC.: *V. H.* (1978); *V. H. II* (1979); *Women and Children First* (1980); *Fair Warning* (1981); *Diver Down* (1982); *1984 (MCMLXXXIV)* (1984); *5150* (1986); *OU812* (1988); *For Unlawful Carnal Knowledge* (1991); *V. H. Live: Right Here, Right Now* (1993); *Balance* (1995); *Best of Van Halen, Vol. 1* (1996); *Van Halen 3* (1998). **DAVID LEE ROTH:** *Crazy from the Heat* (mini; 1985); *Eat 'Em and Smile* (1986); *Skyscraper* (1988); *A Little Ain't Enough* (1991); *Your Filthy Little Mouth* (1994). **SAMMY HAGAR:** *Sammy Hagar (reissued as "I Never Said Goodbye")* (1987); *Unboxed* (1994).—**BH**

Van Heusen, James "Jimmy" (originally, **Babcock, Edward Chester**), American composer; b. Syracuse, N.Y., Jan. 26, 1913; d. Rancho Mirage, Calif., Feb. 7, 1990. Working primarily with lyricists Johnny Burke and Sammy Cahn, Van Heusen wrote the music for songs used in at least 68 motion pictures released between 1940 and 1974. These efforts brought him 14 Academy Award nominations for Best Song—the most for any composer—and four awards, for "Swinging on a Star," "All the Way," "High Hopes," and "Call Me Irresponsible." He was a favorite songwriter of Bing Crosby, writing songs used in 22 of the singer's films, and of Frank Sinatra, who recorded far more Van Heusen tunes than those of any other composer. Among his most successful songs with Burke were "Imagination," "Sunday, Monday or Always," and "Personality"; with Cahn he wrote such hits as "Love and Marriage," "(Love Is) The Tender Trap," and "The Second Time Around."

Van Heusen was the son of Arthur Edward Babcock, a building contractor and amateur musician, and Ida Mae Williams Babcock, through whom he was said to be related to Stephen Foster. Van Heusen showed an early interest in music and took piano lessons as a child. In his teens he worked as an announcer and program host on local radio stations, which led to the adoption of his pseudonym. From 1930 to 1932 he attended Syracuse Univ., studying piano and composition; he also studied singing with Howard Lyman. He collaborated with a fellow student, Jerry Arlen, younger brother of Harold Arlen, through whose auspices they placed two songs, "Harlem Hospitality" and "There's a House in Harlem for Sale," in the 23rd edition of the *Cotton Club Parade* in 1933. This brought Van Heusen to N.Y., where he worked as a pianist for song publishers for several years until he collaborated with Jimmy Dorsey on "It's the Dreamer in Me" (music and lyrics by Van Heusen and Dorsey). This song was recorded by Dorsey, Paul Whiteman, Harry James, and Bing Crosby and reportedly sold almost 100,000 copies of sheet music, leading Van Heusen's employer, Remick's, to sign him to a two-year contract as a staff composer.

Van Heusen formed a songwriting partnership with bandleader, singer, and lyricist Eddie De Lange, and the two wrote "So Help Me," which was recorded by Mildred Bailey and spent 12 weeks in the hit parade starting in September 1938. Their next song, "Deep in a Dream," did even better; recorded by Artie Shaw and His Orch., it spent 14 weeks in the hit parade starting in December.

Van Heusen's career took off in 1939. "Good for Nothin' but Love" (lyrics by De Lange), recorded by Fats Waller, had a week in the hit parade in March; "Heaven Can Wait" (lyrics by De Lange), recorded by Glen Gray and the Casa Loma Orch., hit #1 in April; and "All I Remember Is You" (lyrics by De Lange), recorded by Tommy Dorsey and His Orch., had a week in the chart in July. His next hit, "Oh, You Crazy Moon," marked his first collaboration with Johnny Burke; recorded by Tommy Dorsey, it spent six weeks in the hit parade starting in September.

With De Lange, Van Heusen wrote the songs for a swing musicalization of Shakespeare's play *A Midsummer Night's Dream. Swingin' the Dream*, which featured such performers as Louis Armstrong and Benny Goodman, ran only 13 performances after opening at Radio City Music Hall in November But "Darn That Dream" from the score was recorded by Goodman with Mildred Bailey on vocals and topped the hit parade in March 1940. By then Van Heusen had already placed two more songs in the chart: "Can I Help It?" (lyrics by De Lange), recorded by Bob Crosby and His Orch., and "Speaking of Heaven" (lyrics by Mack Gordon), recorded by Glenn Miller and His Orch., had each spent two weeks in the hit parade in December 1939.

Van Heusen again collaborated with Burke on "Imagination," recorded by Glenn Miller, which topped the hit parade in June 1940. This was enough to convince Paramount Pictures, Burke's employer, that Van Heusen would make a good replacement for Burke's departing songwriting partner James V. Monaco. The studio signed the composer, who moved permanently to Calif. to write for the movies. Meanwhile, two final efforts written with De Lange: "Shake Down the Stars," recorded by Glenn Miller, and a promotional title song written for the motion picture *All This and Heaven Too*, recorded by Tommy Dorsey with Frank Sinatra on vocals, made the charts during the summer.

Van Heusen and Burke began their partnership at Paramount with the Jack Benny–Fred Allen comedy *Love Thy Neighbor*, released in December 1940. They then wrote songs for *Road to Zanzibar*, the second of the series of "road" movies starring Bing Crosby and Bob Hope, released in April 1941. Although the radio ban on ASCAP material prevented any of the songs from becoming hits at the time, "It's Always You," recorded by Tommy Dorsey with Frank Sinatra on vocals, became a Top Ten hit upon reissue in July 1943. Van Heusen and Burke next wrote songs for two Kay Kyser vehicles, *Playmates* (December 1941) and *My Favorite Spy* (May 1942), then for the third "road" movie, *Road to Morocco* (November 1942), from which Crosby recorded the chart entry "Constantly" and the Top Ten hit "Moonlight Becomes You"; Harry James and His Orch. had a million-selling version of the latter.

Van Heusen toured army camps as Crosby's accompanist during the summer of 1942. Under his real name he also took a job as a test pilot for the Lockheed airplane manufacturing company, maintaining the risky occupation throughout the war without telling Paramount.

Van Heusen and Burke's next movie with Crosby was *Dixie* (June 1943), a film biography of songwriter Daniel Emmett. From it, Crosby (recording a cappella due to the musicians' union recording ban) scored a million-selling #1 hit with "Sunday, Monday or Always" and a chart entry with "If You Please."

The team had songs in four movies released in 1944, enough to dominate the charts and the box office for the year. "Suddenly It's Spring" was cut to only an instrumental accompaniment to Ginger Roger's dancing in *Lady in the Dark*, released in February, but Glen Gray took a version into the charts in May. That month Paramount released *Going My Way*, in which Bing Crosby played a priest who sang, among other songs, the million-selling, Academy Award–winning #1 hit "Swinging on a Star" and the charting title song. The movie was the top-grossing hit of 1944, and Crosby's studio album of the songs hit #1 in October 1945. *And The Angels Sing*, released in July 1944, starred Dorothy Lamour and Betty Hutton. The score generated two Top Ten hits, "His Rocking Horse Ran Away," recorded by Hutton, and "It Could Happen to You," recorded by Jo Stafford. *Belle of the Yukon*, released toward the end of the year, gave a Top Ten hit to Dinah Shore, who sang the Oscar-nominated "Sleigh Ride in July" in the picture, and a chart entry to Crosby with "Like Someone in Love."

Van Heusen and Burke had songs in three features released in 1945, but their first hit for the year was the novelty duet "Yah-Ta-Ta Yah-Ta-Ta (Talk, Talk, Talk)," which hit the Top Ten for Bing Crosby and Judy Garland in June. In July, the film *The Great John L* featured "A Friend of Yours," taken into the Top Ten by Tommy Dorsey. *Duffy's Tavern*, released in September, did not add to the songwriters' hit total, but *The Bells of St. Mary's*, the sequel to *Going My Way*, released in December, featured "Aren't You Glad You're You?" which earned an Academy Award nomination and which Crosby took into the Top Ten; the film was the top box office hit of 1946. Van Heusen's last hit of 1945 was another special song, "Nancy (With the Laughing Face)," written for Frank Sinatra's baby daughter. With lyrics credited to actor-comedian Phil Silvers (reportedly with assistance from Burke and Sammy Cahn), the song was recorded by Sinatra for a Top Ten hit in December.

The long-delayed fourth "road" movie, *Road to Utopia*, finally released in early 1946, gave Van Heusen and Burke a #1 hit with "Personality" recorded by Johnny Mercer. At the same time the songwriters mounted their first Broadway musical together, *Nellie Bly*; it was a flop, running only 16 performances, but "Harmony" from the score became a belated hit in November 1947 after it was used in the film *Variety Girl* and recorded by Johnny Mercer and the King Cole Trio. Returning to their regular job with Crosby, Van Heusen and Burke wrote the songs for his August 1947 release, *Welcome Stranger*, which became the most successful film of the year, then for the fifth "road" movie, *Road to Rio*, which topped the box office rankings for 1948 and featured "But Beautiful," a chart hit for Frank Sinatra in April 1948.

A second recording ban kept them from scoring hits for the rest of the year, but their score for the Bing Crosby film *A Connecticut Yankee in King Arthur's Court*, released in April 1949, contained the chart singles "Once and for Always" (recorded by Jo Stafford) and "If You Stub Your Toe on the Moon" (recorded by Tony Martin), and Crosby's *A Connecticut Yankee* album was a Top Ten hit. Crosby also recorded a Top Ten album of the Van Heusen and Burke songs from his December 1950 film *Mr. Music*.

Van Heusen and Burke wrote songs for *The Golden Circle*, an unproduced Paramount feature, in 1951, and they contributed songs to the sixth "road" movie, *Road to Bali*, released in November 1952, and to the Crosby film *Little Boy Lost*, released in September 1953. Their main efforts during the early 1950s, however, were directed to their second Broadway musical, *Carnival in Flanders*, which also opened in September 1953. It was another failure, running only six performances, and it marked the end of the songwriting team, as Burke became ill and was unable to work.

Van Heusen began trying out other lyricists. With Carl Sigman, he wrote "I Could Have Told You," which Frank Sinatra recorded in December 1953 and released as a B-side single the following spring. "You, My Love," written with Mack Gordon, was used in the Sinatra film *Young at Heart*, released in December 1954. Van Heusen he wrote the title song for the June 1955 box office hit *Not as a Stranger* with Buddy Kaye, but he didn't find a permanent partner until he teamed with Sammy Cahn. They wrote songs for a television musical adaptation of Thornton Wilder's play *Our Town* featuring Sinatra. Among these songs was "Love and Marriage," which Sinatra recorded for a Top Ten hit in December 1955. The song won a 1955 Emmy Award for Best Musical Contribution.

Hollywood was less interested in producing original movie musicals by the mid-1950s, but opportunities remained to write title songs for nonmusical motion pictures. Van Heusen and Cahn specialized in this field, starting with "(Love Is) The Tender Trap," the theme for the Sinatra-starring film *The Tender Trap*, released in November 1955. Sinatra's recording of the song hit the Top Ten, and it was nominated for an Academy Award. Their theme from *The Man with the Golden Arm*, Sinatra's December 1955 release, was not used in the film, but several orchestras recorded instrumental treatments that made the charts. The most successful of these was Richard Maltby's, which hit the Top 40. Van Heusen also reached the charts in 1956 with non-movie songs: "My Dream Sonata" (lyrics by Mack David) was a minor hit for Nat "King" Cole in July, and "It's Better in the Dark" (lyrics by Sammy Cahn) scored modestly for Tony Martin in September.

Van Heusen and Cahn contributed "All the Way" to Frank Sinatra's September 1957 film biography of comedian Joe E. Lewis, *The Joker Is Wild*; it became a Top Ten hit and won the Academy Award. Continuing their work with the singer in 1958, they wrote title songs for his albums *Come Fly with Me* and *Frank Sinatra Sings for Only the Lonely*, both of which topped the charts; *Only the Lonely* went gold. They also wrote "To Love and Be Loved," the theme from the Sinatra film *Some Came Running*, securing another Academy Award nomination. Among the other eight films to which they contributed songs in 1959, the most successful was "High Hopes," featured in the Sinatra film *A Hole in the Head* in July and recorded by him for a Top 40 hit; it then earned a Grammy Award nomination for Song of the Year and won the Academy Award for Best Song. Again during the year, they wrote title songs for two Sinatra LPs as well: the January release *Come Dance with Me!*, which hit the Top Ten and went gold, and *No One Cares*, released in August, which hit the Top Ten.

Van Heusen and Cahn wrote songs used in seven films released in 1960, the most notable among them being the title song for the April release *Wake Me When It's Over*, which was recorded for a chart entry by Andy Williams, and "The Second Time Around," from the Bing Crosby vehicle *High Time*, released in September, which earned Best Song Oscar and Song of the Year Grammy nominations and, in February 1961, became a chart entry for Frank Sinatra, who released it as his first single for his newly founded Reprise Records label. Sinatra's first Reprise LP, the Top Ten *Ring-a-Ding Ding!*, released in April 1961, featured a Van Heusen and Cahn title song, and the singer also recorded their Oscar-nominated title song from the December 1961 film *Pocketful of Miracles* for a Top 40 hit. Their next chart entry came with "The Boys' Night Out," Patti Page's recording of the near-title song for the June 1962 film *Boys' Night Out*.

Years earlier, Van Heusen and Cahn had written songs for a proposed film version of *Papa's Delicate Condition*, which was to star Fred Astaire. The songs were shelved when the project was dropped, but in 1963 it was retooled for Jackie Gleason, and one song was reinstated, "Call Me Irresponsible." Upon the film's release in March, the song became a chart entry for Jack Jones, and it went on to win the Academy Award and earn a Grammy Award nomination for Song of the Year.

The last year in which Van Heusen and Cahn were occupied writing for the movies on a full-time basis was 1964. They contributed scores to three films and wrote title songs for two more released during the year. The soundtrack for *Robin and the Seven Hoods*, which featured Frank Sinatra, Dean Martin, Sammy Davis Jr., and Bing Crosby, was released more than a month before the film opened in August and spent three months in the charts. It earned a Grammy nomination for Best Original Score Written for a Motion Picture or TV Show, and "My Kind of Town" from the score was nominated for an Academy Award. The songwriters earned a second Oscar nomination the same year for their title song from *Where Love Has Gone*, with which Jack Jones scored a chart entry two and a half months in advance of the film's November release. Also in 1964, Van Heusen and Cahn completed a score for a sequel to *The Wizard of Oz*, *Journey Back to Oz*, and it was recorded by a cast that included Liza Minnelli and Ethel Merman. The animated children's feature was not released for a decade, however.

Van Heusen and Cahn wrote "The September of My Years" for Frank Sinatra's August 1965 LP *September of My Years*. The album reached the Top Ten and went gold, and the song was nominated for a Grammy Award for Song of the Year. In November the songwriters mounted their first Broadway musical together, *Skyscraper*. Though it did not turn a profit, it ran 248 performances, making it Van Heusen's most successful stage work—the cast album spent two months in the charts. On Aug. 20, 1966, at age 53, Van Heusen married singer Josephine Perlberg, a former member of the Brox Sisters singing group. In November, Van Heusen and Cahn had another Broadway musical, *Walking Happy*. It ran 161 performances, and the title song (another tune written ten years before for the unproduced Fred Astaire version of *Papa's Delicate Condition*) became a hit on the easy-listening charts for Peggy Lee.

Van Heusen and Cahn were less active after 1966. In 1967 they wrote the songs for a musical version of *Jack and the Beanstalk* that was broadcast on television in February. They contributed two songs to the Julie Andrews box office hit *Thoroughly Modern Millie*, released in March, including the title song, which was nominated for an Academy Award; the soundtrack album spent nearly a year in the charts. They wrote the title song for the Julie Andrews box office flop *Star!*, released in October 1968, and it earned them their final Oscar nomination. The last film for which they wrote songs was the June 1969 release *The Great Bank Robbery*. Van Heusen then retired, though he collaborated with Johnny Mercer on "Empty Tables," recorded by Frank Sinatra in 1973 and later released on a single. In 1990 he died at 77 after a long illness. In 1995, *Swinging on a Star*, a musical using many of his songs with Johnny Burke, played on Broadway.

WORKS (only works for which Van Heusen was the primary, credited composer are listed): **MUSICALS/REVUES** (dates refer to N.Y. openings): *Swingin' the Dream* (1939); *Nellie Bly* (1946); *Carnival in Flanders* (1953); *Skyscraper* (1965); *Walking Happy* (1966); *Swinging on a Star* (1995). **FILMS:** *Love Thy Neighbor* (1940); *Road to Zanzibar* (1941); *Playmates* (1941); *My Favorite Spy* (1942); *Road to Morocco* (1942); *Dixie* (1943); *Going My Way* (1944); *And the Angels Sing* (1944); *Belle of the Yukon* (1944); *Road to Utopia* (1946); *Cross My Heart* (1946); *My Heart Goes Crazy* (aka *London Town*; 1946); *Welcome Stranger* (1947); *Road to Rio* (1947); *Mystery in Mexico* (1948); *A Connecticut Yankee in King Arthur's Court* (1949); *Top o' the Morning* (1949); *Riding High* (1950); *Mr. Music* (1950); *Road to Bali* (1952); *Little Boy Lost* (1953); *Pardners* (1956); *The Joker Is Wild* (1957); *Paris Holiday* (1958); *Say One for Me* (1959); *A Hole in the Head* (1959); *Journey* *to the Center of the Earth* (1959); *Ocean's Eleven* (1960); *Let's Make Love* (1960); *High Time* (1960); *Boys' Night Out* (1962); *The Road to Hong Kong* (1962); *Papa's Delicate Condition* (1963); *Come Blow Your Horn* (1963); *Honeymoon Hotel* (1964); *Robin and the Seven Hoods* (1964); *The Pleasure Seekers* (1964); *Thoroughly Modern Millie* (1967); *The Great Bank Robbery* (1969); *Journey Back to Oz* (1974). **TELEVISION:** *Our Town* (1955); *Jack and the Beanstalk* (1967).—**WR**

Van Hoogstraten, Willem
See **Hoogstraten, Willem van**

Van Immerseel, Jos, Belgian harpsichordist, pianist, conductor, and pedagogue; b. Antwerp, Nov. 9, 1945. He received training at the Antwerp Cons. His principal mentors were Flor Peeters and Kenneth Gilbert. He pursued an active career as a recitalist in Europe, becoming known as an interpreter of early keyboard music. In 1972 he became a prof. at the Antwerp Cons. He founded Anima Eterna in Brussels in 1985, an orch. devoted to performing music on period instruments. Among his notable recordings is a complete set of Mozart's piano concertos with that ensemble with van Immerseel conducting from the keyboard (1990–91). In 1992 he became a prof. at the Paris Cons. —**LK/DM**

Van Katwijk, Paul
See **Katwijk, Paul van**

Van Lier, Bertus, Dutch composer, conductor, music critic, and teacher; b. Utrecht, Sept. 10, 1906; d. Roden, Feb. 14, 1972. He was a student of Pijper (composition) in Amsterdam and of Scherchen (conducting) in Strasbourg. After a period as a conductor, music critic, and composer in Utrecht, he taught at the Rotterdam Cons. (1945–60) and then was active in the art history dept. at the Univ. of Groningen. He publ. the vols. *Buiten de maastreep* (Beyond the Bar Line; Amsterdam, 1948) and *Rhythme en metrum* (Groningen, 1967). Van Lier's early compositions were modeled on Pijper's "germ-cell" theory, to which he imparted a literary symbolism.

WORKS: DRAMATIC: Ballet: *Katharsis* (1945; concert version, Utrecht, Nov. 29, 1950). **Incidental Music To:** Sophocles's *Ajax* (1932) and *Antigone* (1952). **ORCH.:** 3 syms. (1928; 1930–31, rev. 1946; 1938–39); Concertino for Cello and Chamber Orch. (1933); Bassoon Concerto (1950); *Symfonia* for 2 String Orchs., Double Wind Quintet, and Timpani (1954); *Divertimento facile* (1957); *Concertante Music* for Violin, Oboe, and Orch. (1959); *Intrada reale e Sinfonia festiva* (1964); *Variaties en thema* (1967; Bergen, Jan. 17, 1968). **CHAMBER:** String Quartet (1929); Sonata for Solo Violin (1931); *Small Suite* for Violin and Piano (1935); piano pieces. **VOCAL:** *De dijk* (The Dike) for Narrator and Chamber Orch. (1937); *Canticum* for Women's Chorus, 2 Flutes, Piano, 4-Hands, and Strings (1939); *O Netherlands, Pay Attention*, cantata for Chorus, Timpani, and Strings (1945); *Het Hooglied* (The Song of Songs) for Soloists, Chorus, and Small Orch. (1949); *Cantate voor Kerstmis* (Christmas Cantata) for Chorus and Orch. (1955); *3 Old Persian Quatrains* for Soprano, Bass Flute, Oboe d'Amore, and Piano (1956); *5 Mei: Zij* (5th of May: They), oratorio (Radio Hilversum, May 5, 1963); choruses.—**NS/LK/DM**

Van Lier, Jacques, Dutch cellist; b. The Hague, April 24, 1875; d. Worthing, England, Feb. 25, 1951. He studied cello with Hartog in The Hague and with Eberle in Rotterdam. He joined the Berlin Phil. in 1897; from 1899 to 1915 he was a cello instructor at the Klindworth-Scharwenka Cons. in Berlin. He was cellist in the Hollandisches Trio with J. van Veen (violin) and Coenraad Bos (piano); the trio enjoyed a European reputation (1900–07); in 1915 he settled in The Hague; went to England in 1939. He publ. *Violoncellbogentechnik and Moderne Violoncelltechnik der linken und der rechten Hand*; also ed. about 400 classical pieces for cello.—**NS/LK/DM**

Van Maldeghem, Robert Julien
See **Maldeghem, Robert Julien van**

Van Maldere, Pierre
See **Maldere, Pierre van**

Van Nes, Jard, Dutch mezzo-soprano; b. Zwollerkarspel, June 15, 1948. Following vocal studies in her homeland, she was active mainly as a concert artist, winning critical acclaim as a soloist in Mahler's 2nd Sym. in 1983 with Haitink and the Concertgebouw Orch. in Amsterdam; in subsequent years, became a great favorite with the orch. and toured with it abroad. She made her operatic stage debut also in 1983 as Bertarido in Handel's *Rodelinda* with the Netherlands Opera in Amsterdam, where she returned to sing such successful roles as Handel's Orlando and Wagner's Magdalena; also sang at the Holland Festivals. During the 1987–88 season, she toured North America as soloist with Edo de Waart and the Minn. Orch. She made her N.Y. recital debut at the Frick Collection during the 1994–95 season. In 1997 she sang in the premiere of the revised version of Ligeti's *Le Grand Macabre* at the Salzburg Festival. Her concert repertoire ranges from Bach to Berio, but she has won greatest acclaim as an interpreter of Mahler. —**NS/LK/DM**

Van Nevel, Paul, Belgian conductor, teacher, and music scholar; b. Hasselt, Feb. 4, 1946. After his academic and musical training, he joined the faculty of the Schola Cantorum Basiliensis in Basel. He later founded and became conductor of the Huelgas Ensemble, a vocal group which attained notable distinction for the performance of medieval and Renaissance polyphony. He also pursued intensive research in various European libraries studying and making transcriptions of early music MSS. In addition to his concerts and recordings with the Huelgas Ensemble, Van Nevel has appeared as a guest conductor of early music groups in Europe. He also teaches at the Sweelinck Cons. in Amsterdam. Among his writings are many articles for journals and a monograph on Ciconia. Van Nevel and the Huelgas Ensemble have won numerous awards, including an Edison Award (1990), Cecilia Prizes (1990, 1993, 1995), Diapason d'Or Awards (1991 et seq.), and the ECHO-Deutscher Schallplattenpreis (1997).—**LK/DM**

Vanni-Marcoux
See **Marcoux, Vanni (Jean Émile Diogène)**

Vannuccini, Luigi, noted Italian singing master; b. Fojano, Dec. 4, 1828; d. Montecatini, Aug. 14, 1911. He studied at the Florence Cons. He became an opera conductor (1848), then turned to the study of the piano, and appeared as a concert pianist with excellent success. He finally settled in Florence, devoted himself exclusively to vocal training, and acquired fame as a singing master. He publ. some songs and piano pieces. **—NS/LK/DM**

Van Otterloo, (Jan) Willem
See **Otterloo, (Jan) Willem van**

Van Raalte, Albert
See **Raalte, Albert van**

Van Rooy, Anton(ius Maria Josephus), celebrated Dutch bass-baritone; b. Rotterdam, Jan. 1, 1870; d. Munich, Nov. 28, 1932. He studied voice with Julius Stockhausen in Frankfurt am Main. In 1897 he made his first appearance at the Bayreuth Festival as Wotan, a role he sang there each season until 1902; also appeared there as Hans Sachs in 1899 and as the Dutchman in 1901 and 1902. From 1898 to 1913 he sang at London's Covent Garden. On Dec. 14, 1898, he made his U.S. debut as Wotan in *Die Walküre* at the Metropolitan Opera in N.Y., remaining on its roster until 1908, except for 1900–01. In 1908 he was engaged as a regular member of the Frankfurt am Main Opera, retiring in 1913. He was particularly distinguished in Wagnerian roles, but also was noted for his interpretations of Escamillo, Valentin, and Don Fernando in *Fidelio*. He also distinguished himself as a lieder artist.**—NS/LK/DM**

Van Slyck, Nicholas, American pianist, conductor, music educator, and composer; b. Philadelphia, Oct. 25, 1922; d. Boston, July 3, 1983. He studied piano with George Reeves, conducting with Henry Swoboda, and composition with Piston at Harvard Univ., where he obtained his M.A. He was founder and conductor of the Dedham (Mass.) Chorus in 1954 and also led the Quincy (Mass.) Orch. (1962–67); served as director of the South End Music Center of Boston (1950–62) and of the Longy School of Music (1962–76). In 1976 he organized the New School of Music in Cambridge, Mass. His music is pragmatic in its form and destination, while the technical structure is catholic, ranging from triadic to dodecaphonic. He compiled a piano anthology, *Looking Forward* (1981).

WORKS: ORCH.: *Variations* for Piano and Orch. (1947); 2 divertimenti for Chamber Orch. (1947, 1948); Sonatina for Clarinet and Strings (1948); *Concert Music* for Piano and Orch. (1954); Piano Concerto No. 2 (1957); *2 Symphonic Paraphrases* (1960, 1966); *Legend of Sleepy Hollow* for Chamber Orch. (1963). **CHAMBER:** 2 clarinet sonatas (1947, 1958); 2 cello sonatas (1954, 1968); 4 violin sonatas (1956–65); Flute Sonata (1957); Quartet for Clarinet, Violin, Cello, and Piano (1959); Octet for Flute, Clarinet, Horn, Violin, Viola, Cello, Timpani, and Piano (1962). **Piano:** 6 sonatas (1947–59); 6 sonatinas (1956–68). **VOCAL:** Songs.**—NS/LK/DM**

Van't Hof, Jasper, jazz keyboardist; b. Enschede, Netherlands, June 30, 1947. He was raised in a musical environment; his father was a jazz trumpeter; his mother a classical singer. He was given classical piano lessons for six years before studying briefly at the Jazzklinik with Wolfgang Dauner. He formed a quartet with the guitarist Toto Blanke that won second prize at the jazz competition in Loosdrecht, near Hilversum, in 1970. He played in Association PC (1970–72), led by Pierre Courbois, and with Chris Hinze (1973, recording in 1974); the group Piano Conclave (1974) and with Archie Shepp (1974). In the mid-1970s he led the group Pork Pie with Charlie Mariano and Philip Catherine, other members included Jean-Luc Ponty (1975–77) and Manfred Schoof (recording in 1976–77, performing in 1977). During this period he also played with Zbigniew Seifert. Later he recorded several times as a leader (from 1973), as an unaccompanied soloist (1977, 1981), in a duo with Shepp (1982), and in the trio Total Music with Chris Hinze and Sigi Schwab (1982). He continued working with Charlie Mariano into the 191980s and in 1987 recorded again with Shepp. He has collaborated with Stu Martin and others, while forming several groups of his own including Eyeball and Didi-Didi (who incorporate elements of African music and computer generated sound in their compositions). Van't Hof has embraced electronic innovation and aimed to utilize new technologies in both his composing and recording.

DISC.: *Jazzbuhne Berlin '80* (1980); *Eyeball* (1980); *My World of Music* (1981); *Balloons* (1982); *Pilipili* (1984); *Solo Piano* (1987); *At The Concertgebouw-Solo* (1993).**—MM/LP**

Van Tieghem, David, highly successful American composer, percussionist, and actor; b. Washington, D.C., April 21, 1955. He studied in N.Y. with Justin DiCioccio at the H.S. of Music and Art, and also attended the Manhattan School of Music (1973–76), where he studied with Paul Price. In 1977 he created a solo percussion theater piece using found objects and sophisticated technology; he then performed variations on this work throughout the U.S. and Europe as *Message Received...Proceed Accordingly* or *A Man and His Toys*. He performed with Steve Reich and Musicians (1975–80), and recorded with Laurie Anderson, Robert Ashley, and Brian Eno, among others; also created scores for films, performance works, and dance pieces, including for Twyla Tharpe's *Fait Accompli* (1983), later released on recording as *These Things Happen* (1984). In 1989 he wrote the music for and performed the lead role in the theater piece *The Ghost Writer* at N.Y.'s Dance Theater Workshop. His interesting variations on dance and percussion textures have led to his widespread popularity in the N.Y. commercial and avant-garde music communities. Throughout the 1990s he composed scores for numerous theater works on Broadway, including Chekhov's *Uncle Vanya*, James Lapine's *The Moment When*, Pirandello's *Naked*, Ibsen's *Hedda Gabler*, and Tim Blake Nelson's *The Grey Zone*, for which he received a 1996 Drama Desk Award, the same year he was awarded an Obie for Sustained Excellence of Music. In 1997–98 he was resident sound designer for The Long Wharf Theatre in New Haven, Conn., and designed their productions of *She Stoops to Conquer, A Question of Mercy, Mystery School*, and Margaret Edson's Pulitzer Prize-winning *Wit*. He also received a 1997 Theatre

Crafts International Design Award. Other awards have come from the NEA, Meet The Composer, the Foundation for Contemporary Performance Arts, Art Matters, Inc., the Jerome Foundation, and the N.Y. State Council on the Arts; in 1986 he received N.Y.'s Bessie Award for Music. His other recordings include *Safety in Numbers* (1987) and *Strange Cargo* (1989), as well as *Galaxy* (1987), a popular music video utilizing sophisticated digital video technology and computer animation.—**NS/LK/DM**

Van Vactor, David, American flutist, conductor, teacher, and composer; b. Plymouth, Ind., May 8, 1906; d. Los Angeles, March 24, 1994. He enrolled in the premedical classes at Northwestern Univ. (1924–27), then changed to the music school there, studying flute with Arthur Kitti and theory with Arne Oldberg, Felix Borowski, and Albert Noelte (B.M., 1928; M.M., 1935); also studied flute with Josef Niedermayr and composition with Franz Schmidt at the Vienna Academy of Music (1928–29), and then flute with Marcel Moyse at the Paris Cons. and composition with Dukas at the École Normale de Musique in Paris. Returning to the U.S., he was engaged as a flutist in the Chicago Sym. Orch. (1931–43); also was an asst. conductor of the Chicago Civic Orch. (1933–34) and a teacher of theory at Northwestern Univ., where he was conductor of its sym. and chamber orchs. (1935–39). From 1943 to 1945 he was asst. conductor of the Kansas City Phil., where he also was a flutist; was founder-conductor of the Kansas City Allied Arts Orch. (1945–47); concurrently was head of the theory and composition dept. at the Kansas City Cons. From 1947 to 1972 he was conductor of the Knoxville Sym. Orch.; in 1947 he organized the fine arts dept. at the Univ. of Tenn., where he was a prof. until 1976. In 1941 he toured as a flutist with the North American Woodwind Quintet and in 1945, 1946, and 1964 as a conductor in South America under the auspices of the U.S. State Dept. He held Fulbright and Guggenheim fellowships in 1957–58. In 1976 he was honored with the title of Composer Laureate of the State of Tenn. He publ. *Every Child May Hear* (1960). As a composer, Van Vactor adhered mainly to basic tonalities, but he enhanced them with ingeniously contrived melodic gargoyles, creating a simulation of atonality. The rhythmic vivacity of his inventive writing created a cheerful, hedonistic atmosphere.

WORKS: ORCH.: *Chaconne* for Strings (Rochester, N.Y., May 17, 1928); *5 Small Pieces for Large Orchestra* (Ravinia Park, Ill., July 5, 1931); *The Masque of the Red Death*, after Edgar Allan Poe (1932); Flute Concerto (Chicago, Feb. 26, 1933); *Passacaglia and Fugue* (Chicago, Jan. 28, 1934); *Concerto grosso* for 3 Flutes, Harp, and Orch. (Chicago, April 4, 1935); 8 syms.: No. 1 (1936–37; N.Y., Jan. 19, 1939, composer conducting), No. 2, *Music for the Marines* (Indianapolis, March 27, 1943; programmed as a suite, not a sym.), No. 3 (1958; Pittsburgh, April 3, 1959; perf. and recorded as No. 2), No. 4, *Walden*, for Chorus and Orch., after Thoreau (1970–71; 1st complete perf., Maryville, Tenn., May 9, 1971; listed as Sym. No. 3 at its premiere), No. 5 (Knoxville, Tenn., March 11, 1976), No. 6 for Orch. or Band (1980; for Orch., Knoxville, Nov. 19, 1981; for Band, Muncie, Ind., April 13, 1983), No. 7 (1983), and No. 8 (1984); *Overture to a Comedy No. 1* (Chicago, June 20, 1937) and *No. 2* (Indianapolis, March 14, 1941); *5 Bagatelles* for Strings (Chicago, Feb. 7, 1938); *Symphonic Suite* (Ravinia Park, Ill., July 21, 1938); Viola Concerto (Ravinia Park, July 13, 1940); *Variazioni Solenne* (1941; 1st perf. as *Gothic Impressions*, Chicago, Feb. 26, 1942); *Pastorale and Dance* for Flute and Strings (1947); Violin Concerto (Knoxville, April 10, 1951); *Fantasia, Chaconne and Allegro* (Louisville, Feb. 20, 1957); Suite for Trumpet and Small Orch. (1962); *Suite on Chilean Folk Tunes* (1963); *Passacaglia, Chorale and Scamper* for Band (1964); *Sinfonia breve* (1964; Santiago, Chile, Sept. 3, 1965); *Sarabande and Variations* for Brass Quintet and Strings (1968; Knoxville, May 4, 1969); *Requiescat* for Strings (Knoxville, Oct. 17, 1970); *Andante and Allegro* for Saxophone and Strings (1972); *Set of 5* for Winds and Percussion (1973); *Nostalgia* for Band (1975); *Prelude and Fugue* for Strings (1975); *Fanfare and Chorale* for Band (1977); *The Elements* for Band (Knoxville, May 22, 1979). **CHAMBER:** Quintet for 2 Violins, Viola, Cello, and Flute (1932); *Suite* for 2 Flutes (1934); *Divertimento* for Wind Quintet (1936); 2 string quartets (1940, 1949); Piano Trio (1942); Flute Sonatina (1949); *Duettino* for Violin and Cello (1952); Wind Quintet (1959); *Children of the Stars*, 6 pieces for Violin and Piano (1960); *5 Etudes* for Trumpet (1963); Octet for Brass (1963); *Economy Band No. 1* for Trumpet, Trombone, and Percussion (1966) and *No. 2* for Horn, Tuba, and Percussion (1969); *Music* for Woodwinds (1966–67); *4 Etudes* for Wind Instruments and Percussion (1968); Tuba Quartet (1971); Suite for 12 Solo Trombones (1972); *5 Songs* for Flute and Guitar (1974). **VOCAL:** *Credo* for Chorus and Orch (1941); Cantata for 3 Treble Voices and Orch. (1947); *The New Light*, Christmas cantata (1954); *Christmas Songs for Young People* for Chorus and Orch. (1961); *A Song of Mankind*, 1st part of a 7-part cantata (Indianapolis, Sept. 26, 1971); *Processional "Veni Immanuel"* for Chorus and Orch. (1974); *Brethren We Have Met to Worship* for Chorus and Orch. (1975); *Episodes—Jesus Christ* for Chorus and Orch. (Knoxville, May 2, 1977); *Processional* for Chorus, Wind Instruments, and Percussion (Knoxville, Dec. 1, 1979).—**NS/LK/DM**

Van Vleck, Jacob, Moravian minister, violinist, and organist; b. N.Y., 1751; d. Bethlehem, Pa., July 3, 1831. He was director of the Young Ladies' Seminary at Bethlehem from 1790 to 1800. He was consecrated a bishop in 1815. Van Vleck was the first American-born Moravian to be active as a composer.—**NS/LK/DM**

Van Westerhout, Nicola, Italian pianist and composer of Dutch descent; b. Mola di Bari, Dec. 17, 1857; d. Naples, Aug. 21, 1898. He was a pupil of Nicola d'Arienzo, De Giosa, and Lauro Rossi at the Naples Cons. and of Antonio Tari at the Univ. of Naples, then pursued a fine career as a pianist. He taught harmony at the Naples Cons. (1897–98).

WORKS: DRAMATIC: Opera: *Una notte a Venezia* (rev. as *Cimbelino*, Rome, April 7, 1892); *Fortunio* (Milan, May 16, 1895); *Dona Flor* (Mola di Bari, April 18, 1896, on the opening of the Teatro Van Westerhout, named after him); *Colomba* (Naples, March 27, 1923); *Tilde* (not perf.). **ORCH.:** 3 syms., No. 3 unfinished; *Serenata*; *Overture* to Shakespeare's *Julius Caesar*; Violin Concerto. **OTHER:** Chamber music; many piano pieces of considerable merit; songs.—**NS/LK/DM**

Van Wyk, Arnold(us Christian Vlok) *See* **Wyk, Arnold(us Christian Vlok) van**

Van Zandt, Marie, American soprano; b. N.Y., Oct. 8, 1858; d. Cannes, Dec. 31, 1919. She studied with her mother, the well-known American soprano Jennie van Zandt, and with Lamperti, making her operatic debut as Zerlina in Turin (Jan. 1879). Her first appearance in London followed later that year as Amina at Her Majesty's Theatre; she then sang with notable success at the Paris Opéra-Comique (1880–85). She made her U.S. debut as Amina in Chicago on Nov. 13, 1891, which role she sang at her Metropolitan Opera debut in N.Y. on Dec. 21, 1891, where she sang for one season. She continued to tour as a guest artist until her marriage in 1898. Delibes wrote the role of Lakmé for her, which she created at the Opéra-Comique on April 14, 1883. Among her other roles were Cherubino, Dinorah, and Mignon. **—NS/LK/DM**

Van Zanten, Cornelie, famous Dutch soprano and pedagogue; b. Dordrecht, Aug. 2, 1855; d. The Hague, Jan. 10, 1946. She studied with K. Schneider at the Cologne Cons., and in Milan with Lamperti, who developed her original contralto into a coloratura soprano voice. She made her operatic debut in Turin in 1875 as Leonora in *La Favorite;* sang in Breslau (1880–82) and Kassel (1882–83), then in Amsterdam (from 1884); also toured in the U.S. in 1886–87 as a member of the National Opera Co. under the directorship of Theodore Thomas. She then appeared in special performances of *Der Ring des Nibelungen* in Russia. She taught at the Amsterdam Cons. (1895–1903); subsequently lived in Berlin, where she became highly esteemed as a singing teacher. She eventually settled in The Hague. Her most distinguished roles were Orfeo, Fidès, Ortrud, Azucena, and Amneris. She publ. songs to German and Dutch texts; with C. Poser, brought out *Leitfaden zum Kunstgesang* (Berlin, 1903).**—NS/LK/DM**

Varady, Julia, Hungarian-born German soprano; b. Nagyvárad, Sept. 1, 1941. She received training at the Cluj Cons. and the Bucharest Cons. In 1962 she made her operatic debut as Fiordiligi at the Cluj Opera, where she sang until 1970. From 1970 to 1972 she was a member of the Frankfurt am Main Opera. In 1972 she joined the Bavarian State Opera in Munich. In 1974 she made her British debut as Gluck's Alcestis with Glasgow's Scottis Opera during its visits to the Edinburgh Festival. She made her first appearance at the Salzburg Festival in 1976 as Mozart's Elettra. On March 10, 1978, she made her Metropolitan Opera debut in N.Y. as Mozart's Donna Elvira. On July 9, 1978, she created the role of Cordelia in Reimann's *Lear* in Munich. While continuing to sing in Munich, she also appeared as a guest artist in Hamburg, Vienna, Berlin, Paris, and other operatic centers. In 1984 she was engaged as Idomeneo at Milan's La Scala. She portrayed Senta at London's Covent Garden in 1992. In 1997 she sang Aida at the Munich Festival. Among her other roles are Countess Almaviva, Elisabeth de Valois, Tatiana, Desdemona, and Lady Macbeth. Her concert repertoire embraces works from Mozart to Reimann. In 1977 she married **Dietrich Fischer-Dieskau**.**—NS/LK/DM**

Varcoe, Stephen, esteemed English baritone; b. Lostwithiel, May 19, 1949. He studied at King's Coll., Cambridge (B.A. in mathematics and land economy, 1970) before pursuing vocal training in London with Arthur Reckless at the Guildhall School of Music (1970–71) and privately with Helga Mott (1972–85) and Audrey Langford (1985–90). In 1970 he made his debut as a soloist at the Wooburn Festival under Richard Hickox's direction. His operatic debut took place in 1971 in Springhead as Purcell's Aeneas. In 1975 he made his first appearance in recital at London's Wigmore Hall, where he frequently returned in subsequent years. He sang in Handel's *Solomon* under Gardiner's direction at the Göttingen Festival in 1983, and then in the *St. John Passion* under that conductor's direction in London in 1985. In the latter year, he portrayed Apollo in Rameau's *Les Borèades* in Aix-en-Provence and Lyons. He sang Zoroastro in Handel's *Orlando* in Glasgow in 1986. In 1991 he was engaged as a soloist in Bach's Mass in B Minor at London's Royal Albert Hall under Hickox's direction, and also sang Nanni in Haydn's *L'infedeltà delusa* in Antwerp. After appearing as Zossina in Tavener's *Mary of Egypt* at Snape Maltings in 1992, he portrayed the title role in Britten's *Noye's Fludde* in Blackheath in 1993. In 1994 he was engaged to sing in Purcell's *King Arthur* with the Monteverdi Orch. under Gardiner's direction in Paris, Vienna, and London. Following an engagement as Death in Holst's *Sāvitri* in Cambridge in 1997, he appeared as Demetrio in Britten's *A Midsummer Night's Dream* in London in 1998. In 1999 he portrayed Salieri in Rimsky-Korsakov's *Mozart and Salieri* in London.**—NS/LK/DM**

Vardi, Emanuel, outstanding Israeli-American violist; b. Jerusalem, April 21, 1917. He began to study the viola in his youth, and also studied painting at the Florence Academy of Fine Arts. In 1940 he went to the U.S., and soon established himself as an outstanding virtuoso in the limited field of viola literature. He arranged works by Bach, Frescobaldi, Tartini, Paganini, and Chopin for viola; also commissioned works for the viola from Michael Colgrass, Alan Hovhaness, Alan Shulman, and others. For variety's sake, he made an incursion into the conducting arena; was music director of the South Dakota Sym. Orch. (1978–82). In his leisure time, he painted. In 1951 he won the International Prize of Rapallo, and had one-man exhibits in N.Y., South Dakota, and Italy.**—NS/LK/DM**

Varèse, Edgard (Victor Achille Charles), remarkable French-born American composer, who introduced a totally original principle of organizing the materials and forms of sound, profoundly influencing the direction of new music; b. Paris, Dec. 22, 1883; d. N.Y., Nov. 6, 1965. The original spelling of his first Christian name was Edgard, but most of his works were first publ. under the name **Edgar**; about 1940 he chose to return to the legal spelling. He spent his early childhood in Paris and in Burgundy, and began to compose early in life. In 1892 his parents went to Turin; his paternal grandfather was Italian; his other grandparents were French. He took private lessons in composition with Giovanni Bolzoni, who taught him gratis. Varese gained some performing experience by playing percussion in the school orch. He stayed there until 1903; then went to Paris. In 1904 he entered the Schola Cantorum, where he studied composition, counterpoint, and fugue with Roussel, preclassical music with Bordes, and conducting with d'Indy; then entered the composition class of Widor at the Cons. in 1905. In 1907 he received the "bourse artistique" offered by the City of Paris; at that time, he founded and conducted the chorus of the Université Populaire and organized concerts at the Château du Peuple. He became associated with musicians and artists of the avant-garde; also met Debussy, who showed interest in his career. In 1907 he married a young actress, Suzanne Bing; they had a daughter. Together they went to Berlin, at that time the center of new music that offered opportunities to Varèse. The marriage was not successful, and they separated in 1913. Romain Rolland gave Varèse a letter of recommendation for Richard Strauss, who in turn showed interest in Varese's music. He was also instrumental in arranging a performance of Varèse's symphonic poem *Bourgogne*, which was performed in Berlin on Dec. 15, 1910. But the greatest experience for Varèse in Berlin was his meeting and friendship with Busoni. Varèse greatly admired Busoni's book on new music aesthetics, and was profoundly influenced by Busoni's views. He composed industriously, mostly for orch.; the most ambitious of these works was a symphonic poem, *Gargantua*, but it was never completed. Other works were *Souvenirs, Prélude à la fin d'un jour, Cycles du Nord*, and an incomplete opera, *Oedipus und die Sphinx*, to a text by Hofmannsthal. All these works, in manuscript, were lost under somewhat mysterious circumstances, and Varèse himself destroyed the score of *Bourgogne* later in life. A hostile reception that he encountered from Berlin critics for *Bourgogne* upset Varèse, who expressed his unhappiness in a letter to Debussy. However, Debussy responded with a friendly letter of encouragement, advising Varèse not to pay too much attention to critics.

As early as 1913, Varèse began an earnest quest for new musical resources; upon his return to Paris, he worked on related problems with the Italian musical futurist Luigi Russolo, although he disapproved of the attempt to find a way to new music through the medium of instrumental noises. He was briefly called to the French army at the outbreak of the First World War, but was discharged because of a chronic lung ailment. In 1915 he went to N.Y. There he met the young American writer Louise Norton, with whom he set up household; in 1921, when she obtained her own divorce from a previous marriage, they were married. As in Paris and Berlin, Varèse had chronic financial difficulties in America; the royalties from his few publ. works were minimal; in order to supplement his earnings he accepted a job as a piano salesman, which was repulsive to him. He also appeared in a minor role in a John Barrymore silent film in 1918. Some welcome aid came from the wealthy artist Gertrude Vanderbilt, who sent him monthly allowances for a certain length of time. Varèse also had an opportunity to appear as a conductor. As the U.S. neared the entrance into war against Germany, there was a demand for French conductors to replace the German music directors who had held the monopoly on American orchs. On April 1, 1917, Varèse conducted in N.Y. the *Requiem Mass* of Berlioz. On March 17, 1918, he conducted a concert of the Cincinnati Sym. Orch. in a program of French and Russian music; he also included an excerpt from *Lohengrin*, thus defying the general ban on German music. However, he apparently lacked that indefinable quality that makes a conductor, and he was forced to cancel further concerts with the Cincinnati Sym. Orch.

Eager to promote the cause of modern music, he organized a sym. orch. in N.Y. with the specific purpose of giving performances of new and unusual music; it presented its first concert on April 11, 1919. In 1922 he organized with Carlos Salzedo the International Composers' Guild, which gave its inaugural concert in N.Y. on Dec. 17, 1922. In 1926 he founded, in association with a few progressive musicians, the Pan American Soc., dedicated to the promotion of music of the Americas. He intensified his study of the nature of sound, working with the acoustician Harvey Fletcher (1926–36), and with the Russian electrical engineer Leon Theremin, then resident in the U.S. These studies led him to the formulation of the concept of "organized sound," in which the sonorous elements in themselves determined the progress of composition; this process eliminated conventional thematic development; yet the firm cohesion of musical ideas made Varèse's music all the more solid, while the distinction between consonances and dissonances became no longer of basic validity. The resulting product was unique in modern music; characteristically, Varèse attached to his works titles from the field of mathematics or physics, such as *Intégrales*, *Hyperprism* (a projection of a prism into the 4th dimension), *Ionisation*, *Density 21.5* (the specific weight of platinum), etc., while the score of his large orch. work *Arcana* derived its inspiration from the cosmology of Paracelsus. An important development was Varèse's application of electronic music in his *Deserts* and, much more extensively, in his *Poème électronique*, commissioned for the Brussels World Exposition in 1958. He wrote relatively few works in small forms, and none for piano solo. The unfamiliarity of Varèse's idiom and the tremendous difficulty of his orch. works militated against frequent performances. Among conductors, only Leopold Stokowski was bold enough to put Varèse's formidable scores *Amériques* and *Arcana* on his programs with the Philadelphia Orch.; they evoked yelps of derision and outbursts of righteous indignation from the public and the press. Ironically, it was left to a mere beginner, Nicolas Slonimsky, to be the first to perform and record Varèse's unique masterpiece, *Ionisation*.

An extraordinary reversal of attitudes toward Varèse's music, owing perhaps to the general advance of musical intelligence and the emergence of young music critics, took place within Varèse's lifetime, resulting in a spectacular increase of interest in his works and the number of their performances; also, musicians themselves learned to overcome the rhythmic difficulties presented in Varèse's scores. Thus Varèse lived to witness this long-delayed recognition of his music as a major stimulus of modern art; his name joined those of Stravinsky, Ives, Schoenberg, and Webern among the great masters of 20th-century music. Recognition came also from an unexpected field when scientists working on the atom bomb at Oak Ridge in 1940 played Slonimsky's recording of *Ionisation* for relaxation and stimulation in their work. In 1955 he was elected to membership in the National Inst. of Arts and Letters and in 1962 in the Royal Swedish Academy. He became a naturalized American citizen in 1926. Like Schoenberg, Varèse refused to regard himself as a revolutionary in music; indeed, he professed great admiration for his remote predecessors, particularly those of the Notre Dame school, representing the flowering of the Ars Antiqua. On the centennial of his birth in 1983, festivals of his music were staged in Strasbourg, Paris, Rome, Washington, D.C., N.Y., and Los Angeles. In 1981, Frank Zappa, the leader of the modern school of rock music and a sincere admirer of Varèse's music, staged a concert of Varèse's works in N.Y. at his own expense; he presented a similar concert in San Francisco in 1982. Upon Varèse's death, his former student Chou Wen-chung became musical executor of his estate. He reconstructed and edited several of Varèse's scores left in various states of unreadiness.

WORKS: *Un Grand Sommeil noir* for Voice and Piano (1906; orchestrated by Antony Beaumont; Amsterdam, Aug. 24, 1998); *Amériques* for Orch. (1918–21; Philadelphia, April 9, 1926, Stokowski conducting; rev. 1927; Paris, May 30, 1929, Poulet conducting); *Dedications*, later renamed *Offrandes*, for Soprano and Chamber Orch. (1921; N.Y., April 23, 1922, Koshetz soloist, Salzedo conducting); *Hyperprism* for 9 Wind Instruments and 18 Percussion Devices (N.Y., March 4, 1923, composer conducting); *Octandre* for Flute, Oboe, Clarinet, Bassoon, Horn, Trombone, and Double Bass (1923; N.Y., Jan. 13, 1924, Schmitz conducting); *Intégrales* for 11 Instruments and 4 Percussion (N.Y., March 1, 1925, Stokowski conducting); *Arcana* for Orch. (1925–27; Philadelphia, April 8, 1927, Stokowski conducting; rev. 1960); *Ionisation* for 13 Percussionists (using instruments of indefinite pitch), Piano, and 2 Sirens (1929–31; N.Y., March 6, 1933, Slonimsky conducting); *Ecuatorial* for Bass, 4 Trumpets, 4 Trombones, Piano, Organ, Percussion, and Thereminovox (1932–34; N.Y., April 15, 1934, Baromeo soloist, Slonimsky conducting; also for Men's Chorus, 2 Ondes Martenot, and Orch.); *Density 21.5* for Flute (N.Y., Feb. 16, 1936; Barrère, soloist, on his platinum flute of specific gravity 21.5); *Étude pour Espace* for Chorus, 2 Pianos, and Percussion (N.Y., Feb. 23, 1947, composer conducting); *Tuning Up* for Orch. (1947; developed by Chou Wen-chung from fragments "suggesting the sound of an orch. tuning up" for a score to the film *Carnegie Hall*; Amsterdam, Aug. 24, 1998); *Dance for Burgess* for Chamber Ensemble (1949; reconstructed in 1998 from an abandoned short dance piece for an unsuccessful Bugess Meredith musical *Happy as Larry*); *Déserts* for Wind Instruments, Percussion, and 3 Interpolations of Electronic Sound (1950–54; Paris, Dec. 2, 1954, Scherchen conducting); *La Procession de Vergès*, tape for the film *Around and About Joan Mirò* (1955); *Poème électronique* for More Than 400 Spatially Distributed Loudspeakers (1957–58; Brussels Exposition, May 2, 1958); *Nocturnal* for Soprano, Bass Chorus, and Chamber Orch. (N.Y., May 1, 1961, R. Craft conducting; unfinished; completed from notes and sketches by Chou Wen-Chung).

WRITINGS: L. Hirbour, ed., *Écrits* (Paris, 1983).

BIBL.: J. Klaren, *E. V., Pioneer of New Music in America* (Boston, 1928); F. Ouellette, *E. V.* (Paris, 1966; rev. and aug. ed., 1989; Eng. tr., 1968); L. Varèse, *V.: A Looking Glass Diary* (N.Y., 1972); O. Vivier, *V.* (Paris, 1973); J.-J. Nattiez, *Essai d'analyse distributionelle de 'Densité 21.5' de V.* (Montreal, 1975; Eng. tr. by A. Barry in *Music Analysis*, I, 1982); G. Wehmeyer, *E. V.* (Regensburg, 1977); S. Van Solkema, ed., *The New Worlds of E. V.: Symposium* (Brooklyn, 1979); A. Carpentier, *V. vivant* (Paris, 1982); M. Bredel, *E. V.* (Paris, 1984); J. Bernard, *The Music of E. V.* (New Haven, Conn., 1987); H. de la Motte-Haber and K. Angermann, eds., *E. V., 1883–1965: Dokumente zu leben und Werk* (Frankfurt am Main, 1990); H. de la Motte-Haber, ed., *Die Befreiung des Klangs: Symposium E. V. Hamburg 1991* (Hofheim, 1992); H. De la Motte-Haber, *Die Musik von E. V.: Studien zu seinen nach 1918 entstandenen Werken* (Hofheim, 1993); K. Angermann, *Work in Progress: V.s Amériques* (Munich, 1996). **—NS/LK/DM**

Varesi, Felice, noted French-Italian baritone; b. Calais, 1813; d. Milan, March 13, 1889. He made his debut in Donizetti's *Furioso all'isola di San Domingo* in Varese in 1834, then sang throughout Italy; made guest appearances at Vienna's Kärnthnertortheater (1842–47), where he created the role of Antonio in Donizetti's *Linda di Chamounix* (May 19, 1842). He was chosen to create the title roles in Verdi's *Macbeth* (Florence, March 14, 1847) and *Rigoletto* (Venice, March 11, 1851), and Germont père in *La Traviata* (Venice, March 6, 1853). On April 19, 1864, he made his London debut as Rigoletto at Her Majesty's Theatre. His wife was the soprano Cecilia Boccabadati (b. c. 1825; d. Florence, 1906); their daughter, Elena Boccabadati-Varesi (b. Florence, c. 1854; d. Chicago, June 15, 1920), was also a soprano; made her London debut as Gilda at Drury Lane (April 17, 1875); after appearing throughout Europe, she settled in Chicago, where she taught voice from 1888; her finest role was Lucia; was also admired for her portrayals of Zerlina and Amina.**—NS/LK/DM**

Varga, Gilbert (Anthony), English conductor of Hungarian descent, son of **Tibor Varga;** b. London, Jan. 17, 1952. He received training from Ferrara, Celibidache, and Bruck. In 1974 he commenced his conducting career. After serving as music director of the Hofer Sym. Orch. (1980–85) and the Philharmonia Hungarica in Marl Kreis Recklinghausen (1985–90), he was principal guest conductor of the Stuttgart Chamber Orch. (from 1992). He was principal guest conductor of the Malmö Sym. Orch. (1997–99). From 1998 to 2001 he was music director of the Orquesta Sinfónica de Euskadi in San Sebastián.**—NS/LK/DM**

Varga, Ovidiu, Romanian composer and teacher; b. Pascani, Oct. 5, 1913; d. Bucharest, July 15, 1993. He received training in violin and composition in Iaşi, and later taught at the Bucharest Cons. He composed much vocal music, including *Scînteia Eliberării*, oratorio for Soloists, Chorus, and Orch. (1954), the *Cantata bucuriei* for Soloists, Chorus, and Orch. (Bucharest, July 1960), mass songs, and solo songs. Among his other works were a String Quartet, *Primăvara vieţii* (1953), and a Concerto for Strings and Percussion (1957).**—NS/LK/DM**

Varga, Tibor, respected Hungarian-born English violinist, conductor, and pedagogue, father of **Gilbert (Anthony) Varga;** b. Györ, July 4, 1921. He was a pupil of Hubay at the Budapest Academy of Music and of Flesch at the Berlin Hochschule für Musik, and also studied philosophy at the Univ. of Budapest. He made his debut at 10 and, following World War II, pursued an international career as a violin virtuoso. In 1949 he became a prof. of violin at the North West German Music Academy in Detmold, where he founded the Tibor Varga Chamber Orch. in 1954. In 1955 he settled in Switzerland and in 1964 he organized the Tibor Varga Festival in Sion, where he oversaw his own music academy and international violin competition; he also taught master classes at the Salzburg Mozarteum. He continued to conduct his chamber orch. until 1988, and then was music director of l'Orchestre des Pays de Savoie à Annecy from 1989. While he was admired for his performances of the standard violin repertoire, he won special distinction for his championship of such modern masters as Nielsen, Schoenberg, Stravinsky, Berg, Bartók, and Blacher.—**NS/LK/DM**

Vargas, António Pinho, Portuguese composer and pianist; b. Vila Nova de Gaia, near Oporto, Aug. 15, 1951. He studied piano at the Porto Cons. (degree 1988), then received a scholarship from the Gulbenkian Foundation which enabled him to study composition with Klaas de Vries at the Rotterdam Cons. In 1974 he developed an interest in jazz and began performing with various international artists and also touring with his own ensemble throughout Europe and the U.S.; also recorded six albums, including *Outros Lugares* (1983), *Cores e Aromas* (1985), and *A Luz e a Escurido* (1996). From 1991 he taught composition at the Escola Superior de Musica in Lisbon.

WORKS: DRAMATIC: *Édipo—Tragédia do Saber*, chamber opera (1995–96); *Os Dias Levantados*, opera (1998); also incidental music for plays, music for dance, and film scores. **ORCH.:** *Geometral* (1988); *Explicit Drama* for Orch. and Jazz Trio (1992); *Mechanical String Toys* (1992); *Acting-Out* for Percussion and Orch. (1998); *A Impaciência de Mahler* (2000). **CHAMBER:** *Estudo/Figura* for 8 Instruments (1990); *Poetica dell'Estinsione* for Flute and String Quartet (1991); *Monodia— Quasi un Requiem* for String Quartet (1993); *Três Quadros para Almada* for 10 Instruments (1994); *Nocturno/Diurno* for String Sextet (1994); *Três Versos de Caeiro* for 12 Instruments (1997); also numerous keyboard works, including *Mirrors* for Piano (1989). **VOCAL:** *Nove Canções de António Ramos Rosa* for Voice and Piano (1995). —**LK/DM**

Vargas, Ramón (Arturo), Mexican tenor; b. Mexico City, Sept. 11, 1960. He received vocal training in Mexico City, where he gained experience singing such roles as Fenton, Nemorino, Don Ottavio, and Count Almaviva. In 1987 he appeared at the Vienna State Opera, the Salzburg Festival, and in Pesaro. Following an engagement as Tamino in Mexico City in 1988, he sang in Lucerne (1989–90). In 1991 he appeared as Aménophis in Rossini's *Moïse* in Bologna and as that composer's Leicester in Naples. He sang Count Almaviva in Rome and Rodrigo in *La donna del lago* in Amsterdam in 1992, and on Dec. 18 of that year he made his Metropolitan Opera debut in N.Y. as Edgardo. After singing Fenton at Milan's La Scala in 1993, he portrayed Elvino in San Diego in 1994, where he returned as Edgardo in 1995. He sang Fernand in *La Favorite* at the Teatro Colón in Buenos Aires in the latter year. In 1996 he appeared as Alfredo at London's Covent Garden, as Nemorino in Los Angeles, and as the Duke of Mantua in Paris. He returned to Covent Garden in the latter role in 1997, and to Los Angeles as Werther in 1998. In 1999 he sang the Duke of Mantua at the Metropolitan Opera. —**NS/LK/DM**

Varkonyi, Béla, Hungarian-American composer and teacher; b. Budapest, July 5, 1878; d. N.Y., Jan. 25, 1947. He studied with Koessler and Thomán at the Royal Academy of Music in Budapest (Ph.D. in law and M.M. in music, 1902). After winning the Robert Volkmann Competition twice and receiving the Hungarian national scholarship, he studied in London and Paris. He returned in 1907 to Budapest, where he taught at the Royal Academy of Music. At the outbreak of World War I in 1914, he joined the Hungarian army, was captured by the Russians, and spent three years as a prisoner of war; he continued to compose, but his MSS were destroyed when the Danish Consulate was burned. After the war, he emigrated to the U.S. (1923); taught at Breneau Coll., Ga. (until 1928) and at Centenary Coll. in Tenn. (1928–30); then settled in N.Y., where he was active as a teacher and composer. Varkonyi is reported to have had a fantastic memory; he was able to recount more than 40 years of his life by day and date; S. Rath devotes a chapter to it in his book *Hungarian Curiosities* (1955).

WORKS: DRAMATIC: Melodramas: *Captive Woman* (1911); *Spring Night* (1912). **ORCH.:** Piano Concerto (1902); Overture (1902); *Dobozy*, symphonic poem (1903); *Symphonic Ballad* (1907); Sym. (1913); *Fantastic Scenes* (n.d.). **CHAMBER:** Piano Trio (N.Y., Nov. 24, 1918); Scherzo for String Quartet (N.Y., Nov. 24, 1918); many piano pieces. **VOCAL:** *Hungarian Chorus Rhapsody*; about 100 songs. —**NS/LK/DM**

Varlamov, Alexander Egorovich, Russian composer of Moldavian descent; b. Moscow, Nov. 27, 1801; d. St. Petersburg, Oct. 27, 1848. At the age of ten he entered the Imperial Chapel at St. Petersburg, where his fine voice attracted the attention of Bortiansky, the director, who then became his teacher; after Varlamov's voice broke in 1818, he left the choir and went to The Hague in 1819 as director of the choir at the Russian ambassadorial chapel. In 1823 he returned to St. Petersburg as singing teacher at the Drama School, which post he held until 1826. After teaching the young solo singers in the court chapel choir (1829–31), he served as Kapellmeister of the Moscow imperial theaters (1832–43); he returned in 1845 to St. Petersburg, where he gave private singing lessons. He composed two ballets, incidental music to 17 plays, and piano pieces, but became best known as a song composer. In addition to the songs he wrote for plays, he wrote 138 solo songs, 31 songs for vocal ensembles, and arrangements of over 50 folk melodies. A complete edition of his works was ed. by F. Stellovsky as *Polnoye sobraniye sochineniy* (12 vols., St. Petersburg, 1861–64). He publ. *Polnaya shkola peniya* (Complete School of Singing; Moscow, 1840; 2nd ed., 1953).

BIBL.: N. Listova, *A. V.* (Moscow, 1968).—**NS/LK/DM**

Várnai, Péter P(ál), Hungarian writer on music; b. Budapest, July 10, 1922; d. there, Jan. 31, 1992. He studied composition with Szervánszky and conducting with Ferencsik at the Budapest Cons. He worked for the Hungarian Radio (1945–50) and was active as a conductor (1951–54). He then devoted himself to music research and criticism and was an ed. of Editio Musica in Budapest (1956–82). In addition to his writings on contemporary Hungarian music and musicians, he wrote authoritatively on Verdi.

WRITINGS (all publ. in Budapest): *Goldmark Károly* (1956); *A lengyel zene története* (History of Polish Music; 1959); *Heinrich Schütz* (1959); *Tardos Béla* (1966); *Maros Rudolf* (1967); *Székely Mihály* (1967); *Rösler Endre* (1969); *Oratóriumok könyve* (Book of Oratorios; 1972); *Operalexikon* (1975); *Verdi Magyarországon* (Verdi in Hungary; 1975); *Verdi-operakalauz* (Verdi's Operas; 1978); *Beszélgetések Ligeti György-gyel* (In Conversation with György Ligeti; 1979; Eng. tr., 1983).—**NS/LK/DM**

Varnay, Astrid (Ibolyka Maria), noted Swedish-born American soprano and mezzo-soprano; b. Stockholm (of Austro-Hungarian parents), April 25, 1918. Her parents were professional singers. She was taken to the U.S. in 1920, and began vocal studies with her mother; then studied with Paul Althouse, and with the conductor Hermann Weigert (1890–1955), whom she married in 1944. She made her debut as Sieglinde at the Metropolitan Opera in N.Y. (Dec. 6, 1941), substituting for Lotte Lehmann without rehearsal; appeared at the Metropolitan until 1956, and again from 1974 to 1976; her last performance there was in 1979. From 1962 she sang mezzo-soprano roles, appearing as Strauss's Herodias and Clytemnestra and as Begbick in Weill's *Aufstieg und Fall der Stadt Mahagonny*; however, she was best known for such Wagnerian roles as Isolde, Kundry, Senta, and Brünnhilde.

BIBL.: B. Wessling, *A. V.* (Bremen, 1965).—**NS/LK/DM**

Varner, Tom, jazz French hornist, composer; b. Morris Plains, N.J., June 17, 1957. He took a degree from the New England Cons. (B.Mus. 1979), studying with Peter Gordon, Thomas Newell, Jaki Byard, George Russell, and Ran Blake. He also studied privately with Julius Watkins and Dave Liebman, and received an NEA Study Grant in 1981. He came to N.Y. in 1979 and has led groups there, featuring Lee Konitz, Bobby Previte, and Mark Feldman, among others. He has worked as a sideperson with the ensembles of Steve Lacy, John Zorn, David Liebman, Bobby Watson, LaMonte Young, Bobby Previte, Bob Mover, George Gruntz, Urs Blochlinger, Thomas Chapin, Mel Lewis Big Band, Jane Ira Bloom, Mark Dresser, and others, taking him on 25 European tours, two North American tours, and single tours of South America, USSR, and the Far East. He performed in the orchestra supporting Miles Davis directed by Quincy Jones at Montreux 1991. Varner received an NEA Performance Grant (1993), was a *Down Beat* Poll Winner (1983), and a Jazz Times Poll Winner (1990, 1993); he has lectured and performed at the Netherlands Horn Society (1983), Berklee Coll. of Music (1985), International Horn Society Annual Workshop at Towson State (1985), East Tenn. State (1987), SUNY Potsdam (1988), New England Brass Conference (1993), and W.Va. Univ. (1995). A highly original composer, Varner has also written music for numerous recording projects, including the soundtrack for the Paul Mones feature film *Saints and Sinners* (released spring 1995).

DISC.: *Tom Varner Quartet* (1980); *Motion / Stillness* (1982); *Jazz French Horn* (1985); *Long Night Big Day* (1985); *Covert Action* (1987); *Mystery of Compassion* (1993); *Martian Heartache* (1997). —**LP**

Varney, Louis, French composer and conductor, son of **Pierre Joseph Alphonse Varney;** b. New Orleans, La., May 30, 1844; d. Paris, Aug. 20, 1908. He was taken to Paris at the age of 7. He studied with his father, then began his career as a conductor at the Théâtre de l'Athénée, where he also brought out several stage works. From 1880 to 1905 he produced some 40 operettas, the best known of which is *Les Mousquetaires au couvent* (Paris, March 16, 1880). Other operettas include *La Femme de Narcisse* (April 14, 1892), *La Fiancée de Thylda* (Jan. 26, 1900), and *Mademoiselle George* (Dec. 2, 1900), all first performed in Paris.—**NS/LK/DM**

Varney, Pierre Joseph Alphonse, French composer and conductor, father of **Louis Varney;** b. Paris, Dec. 1, 1811; d. there, Feb. 7, 1879. He studied with Reicha at the Paris Cons., then was active as a theater conductor in Belgium, the Netherlands, and France. From 1840 to 1850 he was director of the French Opera Co. in New Orleans, where he married Jeanne Aimée Andry. The family returned to Paris in 1851. Varney set to music a poem by Rouget de Lisle, *Mourir pour la patrie,* which became popular during the Paris revolution of 1848.—**NS/LK/DM**

Varviso, Silvio, Swiss conductor; b. Zürich, Feb. 26, 1924. He studied piano at the Zürich Cons. and conducting in Vienna with Clemens Krauss. In 1944 he made his debut at St. Gallen, conducting *Die Zauberflöte,* and remained at the theater there until 1950. He then conducted at the Basel Stadttheater, where he later served as its music director (1956–62). He also made guest appearances in Berlin and Paris in 1958, and then made his U.S. debut with the San Francisco Opera in 1959. On Nov. 26, 1961, he made his Metropolitan Opera debut in N.Y., conducting *Lucia di Lammermoor;* he remained on its roster until 1966 and returned there in 1968–69 and in 1982–83. In 1962 he made his British debut at the Glyndebourne Festival; later that year he made his first appearance at London's Covent Garden. In 1969 he made his Bayreuth Festival debut with *Der fliegende Holländer*. From 1965 to 1972 he was chief conductor of the Royal Theater in Stockholm; after serving as Generalmusikdirektor at the Württemberg State Theater in Stuttgart (1972–80), he was chief conductor of the Paris Opéra (1980–86).—**NS/LK/DM**

Varvoglis, Mario, Greek composer and teacher; b. Brussels, Dec. 22, 1885; d. Athens, July 30, 1967. He studied in Paris at the Cons. with Leroux and G. Caussade and at the Schola Cantorum with d'Indy. Returning to Athens, he taught at the Cons. (1920–24) and at the Hellenic Cons. (from 1924), where he was co-director in 1947; served as president of the League of Greek Composers (from 1957). His output was strongly influenced by d'Indy, Fauré, and Ravel.

WORKS: DRAMATIC: Opera: *Aya Varvara* (1912; only fragments extant); *Tó apóyeme tís agápis* (The Afternoon of Love; 1935; Athens, June 10, 1944). OTHER: Incidental music to 6 Greek dramas. ORCH.: *Tó panigyri*, tone poem (1906–09); *Suite pastorale* for Strings (1912; also for String Quartet); *Sainte-Barbara*, symphonic prelude (1912); *Caprice grec* for Cello and Orch. (1914; also for Cello and Piano); Sym. (c. 1919; destroyed); *Dáphnes ke kyparíssia* (Laurels and Cypresses), symphonic study (1950). CHAMBER: *Hommage à César Franck* for Violin and Piano (1922); *Meditation of Areti* for String Quartet (1929); *Stochasmós* (Meditation) for String Quartet (1932; rev. for String Orch., 1936); *Laikó poíma* (Folk Poem) for Piano Trio (1943); piano pieces, including 14 for children. VOCAL: Choruses; songs.—**NS/LK/DM**

Vásáry, Tamás, noted Hungarian-born Swiss pianist and conductor; b. Debrecen, Aug. 11, 1933. He studied piano at the Franz Liszt Academy of Music in Budapest. In 1947 he won 1st prize in the Liszt Competition, and later garnered several more prizes. He made his London debut in 1961, and played in N.Y. in 1962. In 1971 he became a naturalized Swiss citizen. He made his conducting debut at the Merton Festival in 1971, and subsequently appeared as a guest conductor throughout Europe and the U.S. With Iván Fischer, he served as co-conductor of the Northern Sinfonia in Newcastle upon Tyne (1979–82). From 1989 to 1991 he was principal conductor of the Bournemouth Sinfonietta. In 1993 he became music director of the Budapest Sym. Orch. —**NS/LK/DM**

Vasconcelos, Jorge Croner de, Portuguese composer and teacher; b. Lisbon, April 11, 1910; d. there, Dec. 9, 1974. He studied in Lisbon with Aroldo Silva (piano; 1927–31) and at the Cons. with Freitas Branco (composition; 1927–34), then completed his training with Dukas, Boulanger, and Roger-Ducasse in Paris (1934–37). From 1939 he taught composition at the Lisbon Cons.

WORKS: *Melodias sobre antigos textos portugueses* for Voice, Flute, and String Quartet (1937); Piano Quartet (1938); 2 ballets: *A Faina do mar* (1940) and *Coimbra* (1959); *Partita* for Piano (1961); *A vela vermelha* for Orch. (1962); *Vilancico para a Festa de Santa Cecilia* for Chorus and Orch. (1967).

BIBL.: G. Miranda, *J.C.d. V., 1910–1974: Vida e obra musical* (Lisbon, 1992).—**NS/LK/DM**

Vasilenko, Sergei (Nikiforovich), noted Russian conductor, pedagogue, and composer; b. Moscow, March 30, 1872; d. there, March 11, 1956. He studied jurisprudence at the Univ. of Moscow, graduating in 1895, and also took private music lessons with Gretchaninoff and G. Conus. In 1895 he entered the Moscow Cons. in the classes of Taneyev, Ippolitov-Ivanov, and Safonov, graduating in 1901. He also studied ancient Russian chants under the direction of Smolensky. In 1906 he joined the faculty of the Moscow Cons.; subsequently was prof. there (1907–41; 1943–56). From 1907 to 1917 he conducted in Moscow a series of popular sym. concerts in programs of music arranged in a historical sequence. In 1938 he went to Tashkent to help native musicians develop a national school of composition. His music is inspired primarily by the pattern of Russian folk song, but he was also attracted by exotic subjects, particularly those of the East; in his harmonic settings, there is a distinct influence of French Impressionism.

WORKS: DRAMATIC: Opera: *Skazaniye o grade velikom Kitezhe i tikhom ozere Svetoyare* (The Legend of the Great City of Kitezh and the Calm Lake Svetoyar), dramatic cantata (Moscow, March 1, 1902; operatic version, Moscow, March 3, 1903); *Sin solntsa* (Son of the Sun; Moscow, May 23, 1929); *Khristofor Kolumb* (Christopher Columbus; 1933); *Buran* (The Snowstorm; 1938; Tashkent, June 12, 1939; in collaboration with M. Ashrafi); *Suvorov* (1941; Moscow, Feb. 23, 1942). Ballet: *Noyya*, ballet-pantomime (1923); *Iosif prekrasniy* (Joseph the Handsome; Moscow, March 3, 1925); *V solnechnikh luchakh* (In the Rays of the Sun; 1926); *Lola* (1926; rev. version, Moscow, June 25, 1943); *Treugolka* (The Tricorn; 1935); *Tsigani* (The Gypsies; 1936; Leningrad, Nov. 18, 1937); *Akbilyak* (1942; Tashkent, Nov. 7, 1943); *Mirandolina* (1946; Moscow, Jan. 16, 1949). ORCH.: *3 Combats*, symphonic poem (1900); *Poème épique*, symphonic poem (Moscow, March 14, 1903); 5 syms.: No. 1 (1904; Moscow, Feb. 17, 1907), No. 2 (Moscow, Jan. 7, 1913), No. 3, *Italian*, for Wind Instruments and Russian Folk Instruments (1925), No. 4, *Arctic* (Moscow, April 5, 1933), and No. 5 (1938); *Sad smerti* (The Garden of Death; Moscow, May 4, 1908); *Hircus nocturnus* (Moscow, Feb. 3, 1909); Violin Concerto (1910–13); *Au Soleil*, suite (Moscow, 1911); *Valse fantastique* (Moscow, Jan. 16, 1915); *Zodiac*, suite on old French melodies (1914); *Chinese Suite* (Leningrad, Oct. 30, 1927); *Hindu Suite* (Moscow, 1927); *Turkmenian Suite* (Moscow, 1931); Balalaika Concerto (1931); *Soviet East* (1932); *Uzbek Suite* (1942); Cello Concerto (1944); *Ukraine* (1945); Trumpet Concerto (1945). CHAMBER: 3 string quartets; Piano Trio; Viola Sonata; *Serenade* for Cello and Piano; Oriental Dance for Clarinet and Piano (1923); *Japanese Suite* for Wind Instruments, Xylophone, and Piano (1938); *Chinese Sketches* for Woodwind Instruments (1938); Woodwind Quartet on American themes (1938); Suite for Balalaika and Accordion (1945). VOCAL: *Vir* for Bass and Orch. (Kislovodsk, July 6, 1896); *A Maiden Sang in a Church Choir*, song (1908); *Incantation* for Voice and Orch. (1910); *Exotic Suite* for Tenor and 12 Instruments (1916); *10 Russian Folk Songs* for Voice, Oboe, Balalaika, Accordion, and Piano (1929).

WRITINGS: *Stranitsi vospominaniy* (Pages of Reminiscences; Moscow and Leningrad, 1948); *Instrumentovka dlya simfonicheskovo orkestra* (Vol. I, Moscow, 1952; ed. with a supplement by Y. Fortunatov, Moscow, 1959); T. Livanova, ed., *Vospominaniya* (Memoirs; Moscow, 1979).

BIBL.: V. Belaiev, *S.N. V.* (Moscow, 1927); G. Polianovsky, *S.N. V.* (Moscow, 1947); idem, *S.N. V.: Zhizn i tvorchestvo* (S.N.V.: Life and Work; Moscow, 1964).—**NS/LK/DM**

Vasks, Pēteris, Latvian composer and teacher; b. Aizpute, April 16, 1946. He attended the Riga Academy of Music before completing a diploma in double bass at the Lithuanian State Cons. in Vilnius in 1970. He then studied composition with Utkins at the Latvian Cons. (1973–78). Vasks played double bass in the Lithuanian

Phil. (1966–69), the Latvian Phil. Chamber Orch. (1969–70), and the Latvian Radio and TV Sym. Orch. (1971–74). From 1980 he taught composition in Riga. In 1993 he received the Lithuanian Grand Music Award, in 1996 the Herder Prize of the Univ. of Vienna, and in 1997 the Latvian Grand Music Award. Vasks's compositions reveal several influences; some, such as his Cello Concerto, are indebted to Shostakovoch, while others blend elements of minimalism with archaic Latvian folk music into an evocation of ecology and praise for the mysteries of nature.

WORKS: ORCH.: *Rush Hour* (1978); *Cantabile* for Strings (1979); *Vestijums Botschaft* for Strings, Percussion, and 2 Pianos (1982); *Musica dolorosa* for Strings (1983); *Lauda* (1986); English Horn Concerto (1989); 2 syms.: No. 1, *Balsis* (Voices) for Strings (1990–91; Kokkola, Finland, Sept. 8, 1991) and No. 2 (1998–99; Bournemouth, July 30, 1999); Cello Concerto (1993–94; Berlin, Nov. 26, 1994); *Musica adventus* for Strings (1995–96; orchestration of the 3rd String Quartet); *Tâlâ gaisma* (Distant Light), concerto for Violin and String Orch. (1996–97; Salzburg, Aug. 10, 1997). **CHAMBER:** *3 Pieces* for Clarinet and Piano (1973); *Partita* for Cello and Piano (1974); *Chamber Music* for Winds and Percussion (1975); *Moments musicaux* for Clarinet (1977); 2 wind quintets: No. 1, *Muzika aizlidojusajiem putniem* (Music for Flying Birds; 1977) and No. 2, *Musika aizgajusam draugam* (In Memory of a Friend; 1982); 3 string quartets (1977; *Summer Tunes*, 1984; 1995); *The Book* for Cello (1978); Concerto for Timpani and Percussion (1979–86); *Ainava ar putneim* (Landscape with Birds) for Flute (1980); *Touches* for Oboe (1982); *Little Summer Music* for Violin and Piano (1985); *Episodi e Canto perpetuo* for Piano Trio (1985); Sonata for Solo Double Bass (1986); *Pavasara sonate* (Spring Sonata) for String Sextet (1987); *Musique de soir* for Horn and Organ (1988); *Sonata of Loneliness* for Guitar (1990); Sonata for Solo Flute (1992). **KEYBOARD: Piano:** *Music* for 2 Pianos (1974); *In Memoriam* for 2 or 4 Pianos (1977); *A Little Night Music* (1978); *White Scenery* (1980); *Autumn Music* (1981); *Izdegusas zemes ainavas* (Landscapes of the Burned-Out Earth; 1992); *Spring Music, "quasi una sonata"* (1995). **Organ:** *Cantus ad pacem* (1984); *Musica seria* (1988); *Te Deum* (1991). **VOCAL:** *Concerto vocale* for Chorus (1978); *Latvija*, chamber cantata (1987); *Dona nobis pacem* for Chorus and String Orch. or Organ (1996); other choral pieces and songs.—**LK/DM**

Vasquez (Vázquez), Juan, eminent Spanish composer; b. Badajoz, c. 1510; d. probably in Seville, c. 1560. He was a singer at Badajoz Cathedral by 1530, becoming sochantre in 1535; became a singer at Palencia Cathedral in 1539. After serving as maestro de capilla at the provincial cathedral in Badajoz (1545–50), he went to Seville and entered the service of Don Antonio de Zuñiga, a nobleman, in 1551. He was greatly admired as a composer of secular music, but also distinguished himself as a composer of sacred works. Vihuela intabulations of several of his secular works were publ. by Valderrábano in 1547 and by Pisador in 1552.

WORKS: VOCAL: Secular: (26) *Villancicos i canciones* for 3 to 5 Voices (Osuna, 1551); *Recopilación de* (67) *sonetos y villancicos* for 4 to 5 Voices (Seville, 1560; ed. in Monumentos de la Música Española, IV, 1946). **Sacred:** *Agenda defunctorum* for 4 Voices (Seville, 1556; ed. by S. Rubio, Madrid, 1975).

BIBL.: E. Russell, *Villancicos and Other Secular Polyphonic Music of J. V.: A Courtly Tradition in Spain's Siglo del Oro* (diss., Univ. of Southern Calif., 1970); F. Pedraja Munoz, ed., *J. V., polifonista pacense del siglo XVI* (Badajoz, 1974).—**NS/LK/DM**

Vasseur, Léon (Félix Augustin Joseph), French organist, conductor, and composer; b. Bapaume, Pas-de-Calais, May 28, 1844; d. Paris, July 25, 1917. He studied at the École Niedermeyer in Paris, and in 1870 became organist of the Versailles Cathedral. After a few years, he turned to composing light music and also conducting theater orchs. He wrote about 30 operettas, but his most successful was *La Timbale d'argent* (Paris, April 9, 1872). Other operettas include *Le Voyage de Suzette* (Paris, 1890), *Au premier hussard* (Paris, Aug. 6, 1896), and *La Souris blanche* (Paris, Nov. 9, 1897; in collaboration with de Thuisy). He also publ. sacred music, including *L'Office divin* (a collection of masses, offertories, antiphons, etc.), *20 motets des grands maîtres*, a method for organ or harmonium (Paris, 1867), and transcriptions for harmonium and piano.—**NS/LK/DM**

Vaughan, Denis (Edward), Australian conductor and music scholar; b. Melbourne, June 6, 1926. He studied at Wesley Coll., Melbourne (1939–42), and at the Univ. of Melbourne (Mus.B., 1947), then went to London, where he studied organ with G. Thalben-Ball and double bass with E. Cruft at the Royal Coll. of Music (1947–50); also studied organ with A. Marchal in Paris. He played double bass in the Royal Phil. in London (1950–54); in 1953 he made his debut as a conductor in London; served as Beecham's assistant (1954–57), and was founder-conductor of the Beecham Choral Soc.; also toured in Europe as an organist, harpsichordist, and clavichordist. He made a special study of the autograph scores versus the printed eds. of the operas of Verdi and Puccini, discovering myriad discrepancies in the latter; proceeded to agitate for published corrected eds. of these works. From 1981 to 1984 he was music director of the State Opera of South Australia.—**NS/LK/DM**

Vaughan, Elizabeth, Welsh soprano, later mezzo-soprano; b. Llanfyellin, Montgomeryshire, March 12, 1937. She studied with Olive Groves at the Royal Academy of Music in London (1955–58), where she took the gold and silver medals, and also won the Kathleen Ferrier Scholarship (1959); she also studied privately with Eva Turner. In 1960 she sang Abigail in *Nabucco* with the Welsh National Opera in Cardiff. In 1962 she made her debut at London's Covent Garden as Gilda. She made her Metropolitan Opera debut in N.Y. as Donna Elvira on Sept. 23, 1972. She also appeared with other English opera companies and was a guest artist in Vienna, Berlin, Paris, Hamburg, Munich, Prague, and other European opera centers. In 1984 she toured the U.S. with the English National Opera of London. After singing such roles as Violetta, Liù, Mimi, Tatiana, Tosca, and Cio-Cio-San, she turned to mezzo-soprano roles. In 1990 she appeared as Herodias at Glasgow's Scottish Opera, returning there as Kabanicha in 1993. She also was a prof. of voice at the Guildhall School of Music and Drama in London.—**NS/LK/DM**

Vaughan, Sarah (Lois), legendary and extremely talented jazz singer, pianist; b. Newark, N.J., March 27, 1924; d. Los Angeles, April 3, 1990. She began to study music as a child and sang and played piano in church in her native Newark. On a dare she entered the famous Apollo Theater Amateur Hour contest and won, singing "Body and Soul." Billy Eckstine heard her and recommended her to his boss, Earl Hines. This was in 1943, when Charlie Parker and Dizzy Gillespie were in the Hines band; Vaughan followed them into Eckstine's new and revolutionary big band in late 1944, remaining with the group through 1945. She worked with John Kirby (1945–46) and subsequently pursued a successful solo career as a jazz and pop singer, appearing on radio, television, and recordings, often dueting with Eckstine. From the 1950s she toured usually with a trio. Vaughan enjoyed a long relationship with Mercury Records between 1954–63, often using jazz musicians associated with the label's EmArcy jazz division, including Clifford Brown and Count Basie, as her sidemen. Her career went into somewhat of a slump in the mid-1960s, and she did not return to recording until 1971. Although Vaughan recorded prolifically in the last two decades of her life and often focused on jazz material, she also turned to recording a wider variety of pop material. She often sang with symphony orchestras in the 1980s and also sang in the London studio recording of *South Pacific '86* on CBS, with Kiri Te Kanawa and Jose Carreras in leading roles. One of Vaughan's most unusual projects was recording songs based on poems by Pope John Paul II at a live concert in Dusseldorf in 1985—The Planet Is Alive...Let It Live. She had the Pope's poems adapted in English by lyricist Gene Lees and put to music by Italian composers. Vaughan continued performing until six months before her death from lung cancer in 1990.

With her effortless swing, wide vocal range (said to have been three octaves or more), exciting scatting (though she rarely did it except on an occasional blues), perfect pitch, and vocal color, Vaughan was hailed as one of the century's great singers.

Disc.: *Time After Time* (1944); *Lover Man* (1945); *The Man I Love* (1945); *The Divine Sarah* (1946); *It's You or No One* (1946); *Tenderly* (1946); *Time and Again* (1946); *One Night Stand: The Town Hall Concert* (1947); *In Hi Fi* (1949); *I'll Be Seeing You* (1949); *Hot Jazz* (1953); *Swingin' Easy* (1954); *The Divine Sarah Sings* (1954); *Sarah Vaughan with Clifford Brown* (1954); *The Gershwin Songbook* (1954); *The Rodgers & Hart Songbook* (1954); *Tops in Pops* (1955); *In the Land of Hi-Fi* (1955); *Sassy* (1956); *Linger Awhile* (1956); *At Mister Kelly's* (1957); *The Irving Berlin Songbook* (1957); *Misty* (1958); *No Count Sarah* (1958); *Great Songs from Hit Shows, Vol. 1, 2* (1959); *Dreamy* (1960); *After Hours* (1961); *Star Eyes* (1962); *You're Mine You* (1962); *Sarah Sings Soulfully* (1963); *Sassy Swings the Tivoli* (1963); *Vaughan with Voices* (1964); *Viva! Vaughan* (1965); *Sarah Vaughan Sings the Mancini Songbook* (1965); *Sassy Swings Again* (1967); *With Michel Legrand* (1972); *Live in Japan, Vol. 1, 2* (1973); *I Love Brazil* (1977); *How Long Has This Been Going On?* (1978); *The Duke Ellington Songbook, Vol. 1, 2* (1979); *Crazy and Mixed Up* (1982); *Billy and Sarah* (1985); *Sarah Vaughan at the Blue Note* (1985); *Brazilian Romance* (1987).

Bibl.: R. Leydi, *S. V.* (Milan, 1961).—**MM/LP/NS**

Vaughan Brothers, The, blues guitarists. Jimmie Vaughan (b. Dallas, March 20, 1951); Stevie Ray Vaughan (b. Dallas, Oct. 3, 1954; d. East Troy, Wisc., Aug. 27, 1990). **THE FABULOUS THUNDERBIRDS,** R&B group. **Membership:** Jimmie Vaughan, gtr.; Kim Wilson, voc., har. (b. Detroit, Jan. 6, 1951); Keith Ferguson, bs. (b. Houston, Tex., July 23, 1946; d. Austin, Tex., April 29, 1997); Mike Buck, drm. (b. June 17, 1952). Mike Buck left in 1980, to be replaced by Fran Christina (b. Westerly, R.I., Feb. 1, 1951). In 1984 Keith Ferguson departed and was replaced by Preston Hubbard (b. Providence, R.I., March 15, 1953). Group reorganized in 1991 with Wilson, Christina, Hubbard, and guitarists Duke Robillard (b. Woonsocket, R.I., Oct. 4, 1948) and Kid Bangham. **STEVIE RAY VAUGHAN AND DOUBLE TROUBLE,** blues group. **Membership:** Stevie Ray Vaughan, gtr.; Tommy Shannon, bs.; Chris Layton, drm. Reese Wynans joined as keyboardist in 1985.

As lead guitarists with the Fabulous Thunderbirds and Double Trouble, respectively, Jimmie and Stevie Ray Vaughan helped foster the blues revival of the 1980s, along with artists such as George Thorogood and Robert Cray. While the Fabulous Thunderbirds favored a more R&B style, scoring their biggest hit with 1986's "Tuff Enuff," Stevie Ray Vaughan and Double Trouble played under the influence of Tex. and Chicago blues guitarists, as well as Jimi Hendrix. Jimmie Vaughan left the Fabulous Thunderbirds in 1990 and recorded *Family Style* with his brother, but on Aug. 27, 1990, Stevie Ray was killed in a helicopter crash in East Troy, Wisc. Jimmie Vaughan has since recorded a solo album, while the Fabulous Thunderbirds continue to tour with new guitarist Duke Robillard. The remaining members of Double Trouble have recorded an album with two new guitarists as Arc Angel.

Stevie Ray Vaughan began playing guitar in 1963, by which time his brother Jimmie was playing with such Dallas groups as the Swinging Pendulums. Stevie Ray began playing Dallas clubs at 14 with such bands as Blackbird and Cracker Jack. Jimmie moved to Austin in 1970, where he formed Storm with guitarist Denny Freeman. After a brief stay in Calif., Jimmie returned to Austin, forming Jimmie Vaughan and the Fabulous Thunderbirds with vocalist Lou Ann Barton and drummer Otis Lewis. Barton and Lewis left in late 1974, and Keith Ferguson, a veteran of both Storm and the Nightcrawlers (with Stevie Ray), joined, as did Kim Wilson, who became the group's chief songwriter and musical director as well as lead singer and harmonica player.

With the addition of drummer Mike Buck, the Fabulous Thunderbirds became the house band at the recently opened Austin club Antone's; they subsequently won a reputation as one of the most engaging blues bands in the state. Their first recognition outside Tex. came at the 1978 San Francisco Blues Festival, and they signed with Takoma Records. In 1980 Fran Christina replaced Mike Buck during the recording of *What's the Word* on Takoma's parent label Chrysalis. The Fabulous Thunderbirds played up to three hundred engagements a year, yet their albums failed to sell and they were dropped by Chrysalis in 1982.

Stevie Ray Vaughan followed his brother to Austin in 1973, where he played with the Nightcrawlers and the Cobras. Around 1977 he formed Triple Threat with Lou

Ann Barton and guitarist W. C. Clark. By 1978 Barton had left and the band evolved into Double Trouble, with Vaughan, bassist Tommy Shannon from Blackbird and Cracker Jack, and drummer Chris Layton. In April 1982 the band auditioned in N.Y.C. for the Rolling Stones, and in July Atlantic Records producer Jerry Wexler convinced the promoters of Switzerland's Montreux Jazz Festival to book Vaughan and the band. Among those in the audience were Jackson Browne and David Bowie. Vaughan subsequently played guitar on six songs for Bowie's *Let's Dance* album, including the hits "Let's Dance," "China Girl," and "Modern Love."

Jackson Browne offered the group free studio time at his studio in Los Angeles, and John Hammond Jr., the blues-playing son of Columbia executive John Hammond, submitted a tape recording of the group's performance at Montreux to his father. Signed to the Columbia subsidiary Epic, Stevie Ray Vaughan and Double Trouble used the studio time to record their debut album, 1983's *Texas Flood*, generally considered the group's finest album. The follow-up *Couldn't Stand the Weather* featured Vaughan's stunning rendition of Jimi Hendrix's "Voodoo Chile (Slight Return)," and 1985's *Soul to Soul* saw the permanent addition of keyboardist Reese Wynans.

The Fabulous Thunderbirds continued to tour arduously following the expiration of their Chrysalis contract. Keith Ferguson left in 1984 and was replaced by Preston Hubbard. They then recorded *Tuff Enuff* in London in 1985 with Dave Edmunds producing, and the album became a best-seller when released on CBS Associated, producing a major hit with the title song and a moderate hit with "Wrap It Up." The band began playing concert halls rather than clubs, but subsequent albums sold progressively less well. Jimmie Vaughan left the group in 1990 and recorded *Family Style* with his brother Stevie Ray. However, before the album's release, Stevie Ray Vaughan was killed in a helicopter crash on Aug. 27, 1990, in East Troy, Wisc., after performing at a concert with his brother, Eric Clapton, Robert Cray, and Buddy Guy.

With Kim Wilson and Fran Christina as mainstays, the Fabulous Thunderbirds regrouped with guitarists Duke Robillard and Kid Bangham, and, later, pianist Gene Taylor, but by 1993 the band was again without a recording contract. Double Trouble musicians Tommy Shannon and Chris Layton formed Arc Angels with guitarists Charlie Sexton and Doyle Bramhall II, recording an album for DGC Records in 1992. Jimmie Vaughan recorded his solo debut album in 1994.

DISC.: **THE FABULOUS THUNDERBIRDS:** *The Fabulous Thunderbirds* (1979); *What's the Word* (1980); *Butt Rockin'* (1981); *T-Bird Rhythm* (1982); *The Essential Fabulous Thunderbirds* (1991); *Tuff Enuff* (1986); *Hot Number* (1987); *Powerful Stuff* (1989); *Walk That Walk, Talk* (1991); *Hot Stuff: The Greatest* (1992); *Roll of the Dice* (1995). **STEVIE RAY VAUGHAN AND DOUBLE TROUBLE:** *In the Beginning* (1992); *Texas Flood* (1983); *Couldn't Stand the Weather* (1984); *Soul to Soul* (1985); *Live Alive* (1986); *In Step* (1989); *The Sky Is Crying* (1991). **THE VAUGHAN BROTHERS:** *Family Style* (1990). **JIMMIE VAUGHAN:** *Strange Pleasure* (1994). **ARC ANGELS:** *Arc Angels* (1992).—**BH**

Vaughan Thomas, David, Welsh organist, teacher, and composer; b. Ystelyfera, March 15, 1873; d. Johannesburg, Sept. 15, 1934. He won the solo harmonium competition at the National Eisteddfod in 1883. After training from Joseph Parry in Swansea, he attended Llandovery Coll. and then took courses in music and mathematics at Exeter Coll., Oxford (B.A., 1895; B.Mus., 1907; D.Mus., 1909). He pursued a career as a church organist, recitalist, and teacher. He was an accomplished composer of choral music and songs. Among his other works were orch. pieces, chamber music, and piano pieces.

BIBL.: E. Cleaver, *D. V.T.* (Llandybie, 1964).—**NS/LK/DM**

Vaughan Williams, Ralph, great English composer who created a gloriously self-consistent English style of composition, deeply rooted in native folk songs, yet unmistakably participant of modern ways in harmony, counterpoint, and instrumentation; b. Down Ampney, Gloucestershire, Oct. 12, 1872; d. London, Aug. 26, 1958. His father, a clergyman, died when Vaughan Williams was a child; the family then moved to the residence of his maternal grandfather at Leith Hill Place, Surrey, where he began to study piano and violin. In 1887 he entered Charterhouse School in London and played violin and viola in the school orch. From 1890 to 1892 he studied harmony with F. E. Gladstone, theory of composition with Parry, and organ with Parratt at the Royal Coll. of Music in London. He then enrolled at Trinity Coll., Cambridge, where he took courses in composition with Charles Wood and in organ with Alan Gray, obtaining his Mus.B. in 1894 and his B.A. in 1895; he subsequently returned to the Royal Coll. of Music, studying with Stanford. In 1897 he went to Berlin for further instruction with Max Bruch; in 1901 he took his Mus.D. at Cambridge. Dissatisfied with his academic studies, he decided in 1908 to seek advice in Paris from Ravel in order to acquire the technique of modern orchestration that emphasized color. In the meantime, Vaughan Williams became active as a collector of English folk songs; in 1904 he joined the Folk Song Soc. In 1905 he became conductor of the Leith Hill Festival in Dorking, a position that he held, off and on, until his old age. In 1906 he composed his *3 Norfolk Rhapsodies*, which reveal the ultimate techniques and manners of his national style; he discarded the 2nd and 3rd of the set as not satisfactory in reflecting the subject. In 1903 he began work on a choral sym. inspired by Walt Whitman's poetry and entitled *A Sea Symphony*; he completed it in 1909. There followed in 1910 *Fantasia on a Theme of Thomas Tallis*, scored for string quartet and double string orch.; in it Vaughan Williams evoked the song style of an early English composer. After this brief work, he engaged in a grandiose score, entitled *A London Symphony* and intended as a musical glorification of the great capital city. However, he emphatically denied that the score was to be a representation of London life. He even suggested that it might be more aptly entitled *Symphony by a Londoner*, which would explain the immediately recognizable quotations of the street song *Sweet Lavender* and of the Westminster chimes in the score; indeed, Vaughan Williams declared that the work must be judged as a piece of absolute or abstract music. Yet prosaically minded commentators insisted that *A London Symphony* realistically depicted in its four movements the scenes of London at twilight, the hubbub of Bloomsbury, a Saturday-evening reverie, and, in conclusion, the serene flow of the Thames River. Concurrently with *A London Symphony*, he wrote the ballad opera *Hugh the Drover*, set in England in the year 1812 and reflecting the solitary struggle of the English against Napoleon.

At the outbreak of World War I in 1914, Vaughan Williams enlisted in the British army and served in Salonika and in France as an officer in the artillery. After the Armistice, from 1919 to 1939, he was a prof. of composition at the Royal Coll. of Music in London; from 1920 to 1928 he also conducted the London Bach Choir. In 1921 he completed *A Pastoral Symphony*, the music of which reflects the contemplative aspect of his inspiration; an interesting innovation in this score is the use of a wordless vocal solo in the last movement. In 1922 he visited the U.S. and conducted *A Pastoral Symphony* at the Norfolk (Conn.) Festival; in 1932 he returned to the U.S. to lecture at Bryn Mawr Coll. In 1930 he was awarded the Gold Medal of the Royal Phil. Soc. of London; in 1935 he received the Order of Merit from King George V. In 1930 he wrote a masque, *Job*, based on Blake's *Illustrations of the Book of Job*, which was first performed in a concert version in 1930 and was then presented on the stage in London on July 5, 1931.

His 4th Sym., in F minor, written between 1931 and 1935 and first performed by the BBC Sym. Orch. in London on April 10, 1935, presents an extraordinary deviation from his accustomed solid style of composition. Here he experimented with dissonant harmonies in conflicting tonalities, bristling with angular rhythms. A peripheral work was *Fantasia on Greensleeves*, arranged for harp, strings, and optional flutes. This was the composer's tribute to his fascination with English folk songs; he had used it in his opera *Sir John in Love*, after Shakespeare's *The Merry Wives of Windsor*, performed in London in 1929. He always professed great admiration for Sibelius; indeed, there was a harmonious kinship between the two great contemporary nationalist composers; there was also the peculiar circumstance that in his 4th Sym. Sibelius ventured into the domain of modernism, as did Vaughan Williams in his own 4th Sym., and both were taken to task by astounded critics for such musical philandering. Vaughan Williams dedicated his 5th Sym., in D major, composed between 1938 and 1943, to Sibelius as a token of his admiration. In the 6th Sym., in E minor, written during the years 1944 to 1947, Vaughan Williams returned to the erstwhile serenity of his inspiration, but the sym. has its turbulent moments and an episode of folksy dancing exhilaration.

Vaughan Williams was 80 years old when he completed his challenging *Sinfonia antartica*, scored for soprano, women's chorus, and orch.; the music was an expansion of the background score he wrote for a film on the expedition of Sir Robert Scott to the South Pole in 1912. Here the music is almost geographic in its literal representation of the regions that Scott had explored; it may well be compared in its realism with the *Alpine Symphony* of Richard Strauss. In *Sinfonia antartica* Vaughan Williams inserted, in addition to a large orch., several keyboard instruments and a wind machine. To make the reference clear, he used in the epilogue of the work the actual quotations from Scott's journal. Numerically, *Sinfonia antartica* was his 7th; it was first performed in Manchester on Jan. 14, 1953. In the 8th Sym. he once more returned to the ideal of absolute music; the work is conceived in the form of a neo-Classical suite, but, faithful to the spirit of the times, he included in the score the modern instruments, such as vibraphone and xylophone, as well as the sempiternal gongs and bells. His last sym. bore the fateful number 9, which had for many composers the sense of the ultimate, since it was the numeral of Beethoven's last sym. In this work Vaughan Williams, at the age of 85, still asserted himself as a composer of the modern age; for the first time, he used a trio of saxophones, with a pointed caveat that they should not behave "like demented cats," but rather remain their romantic selves. Anticipating the inevitable, he added after the last bar of the score the Italian word "niente." The 9th Sym. was first performed in London on April 2, 1958; Vaughan Williams died later in the same year. It should be mentioned as a testimony to his extraordinary vitality that after the death of his first wife, he married the poet and writer Ursula Wood on Feb. 7, 1953 (at the age of 80), and in the following year he once more paid a visit to the U.S. on a lecture tour to several American univs.

Summarizing the aesthetic and technical aspects of the style of composition of Vaughan Williams, there is a distinctly modern treatment of harmonic writing, with massive agglomeration of chordal sonorities; parallel triadic progressions are especially favored. There seems to be no intention of adopting any particular method of composition; rather, there is a great variety of procedures integrated into a distinctively personal and thoroughly English style, nationalistic but not isolationist. Vaughan Williams was particularly adept at exploring the modern ways of modal counterpoint, with tonality freely shifting between major and minor triadic entities, a procedure that astutely evokes sweetly archaic usages in modern applications; thus Vaughan Williams combines the modalities of the Tudor era with the sparkling polytonalities of the modern age.

WORKS: DRAMATIC: Opera: *Hugh the Drover*, ballad opera (1911–14; London, July 14, 1924); *The Shepherds of the Delectable Mountains*, "pastoral episode" after Bunyan's *The Pilgrim's Progress* (1921–22; London, July 11, 1922); *Sir John in Love*, after Shakespeare's *The Merry Wives of Windsor* (1925–29; London, March 21, 1929); *Riders to the Sea*, after the drama by John Millington Synge (1925–32; London, Dec. 1, 1937); *The Poisoned Kiss*, "romantic extravaganza" (1927–29; Cambridge, May 12, 1936; rev. 1934–37 and 1956–57); *The Pilgrim's Progress*, "morality" (includes material from the earlier opera *The Shepherds of the Delectable Mountains*; 1925–36, 1944–51; London, April 26, 1951). **Ballet:** *Old King Cole* (Cambridge, June 5, 1923); *On Christmas Night*, masque (1925–26; Chicago, Dec. 26, 1926); *Job, a Masque for Dancing* (1927–30; concert perf., Norwich, Oct. 23, 1930; stage perf., London, July 5, 1931). **Incidental Music To:** Ben Jonson's *Pan's Anniversary* (Stratford-upon-Avon, April 24, 1905); Aristophanes's *The Wasps* (Cambridge, Nov. 26, 1909). **Film:** *49th Parallel* (1940–41); *The People's Land* (1941–42); *Coastal Command* (1942);

The Story of a Flemish Farm (1943; suite for Orch., London, July 31, 1945); *Stricken Peninsula* (1944); *The Loves of Joanna Godden* (1946); *Scott of the Antarctic* (1947–48; material taken from it incorporated in the *Sinfonia antartica*); *Dim Little Island* (1949); *Bitter Springs* (1950); *The England of Elizabeth* (1955); *The Vision of William Blake* (1957). **Other:** *The Mayor of Casterbridge*, music for a radio serial after Thomas Hardy (1950). **ORCH.:** *Serenade* for Small Orch. (1898); *Bucolic Suite* (Bournemouth, March 10, 1902); *2 Impressions: Harnham Down* and *Boldrewood* (1902; London, Nov. 12, 1907); 9 syms.: No. 1, *A Sea Symphony*, for Soprano, Baritone, Chorus, and Orch., after Walt Whitman (1906–09; Leeds Festival, Oct. 12, 1910, composer conducting), No. 2, *A London Symphony* (1911–14; London, March 27, 1914; rev. version, London, May 4, 1920), No. 3, *A Pastoral Symphony* (1916–21; London, Jan. 26, 1922), No. 4, in F minor (1931–35; London, April 10, 1935, Boult conducting), No. 5, in D major (1938–43; London, June 24, 1943, composer conducting), No. 6, in E minor (1944–47; London, April 21, 1948, Boult conducting), No. 7, *Sinfonia antartica* (1949–52; Manchester, Jan. 14, 1953, Barbirolli conducting), No. 8, in D minor (1953–55; Manchester, May 2, 1956, Barbirolli conducting), and No. 9, in E minor (1956–58; London, April 2, 1958, Sargent conducting); *3 Norfolk Rhapsodies* (1906; No. 1, in E minor, London, Aug. 23, 1906, No. 2, Cardiff Festival, Sept. 27, 1907, and No. 3, not perf.; Nos. 2 and 3 withdrawn by the composer); *In the Fen Country*, symphonic impression (1904 and subsequent revs.; London, Feb. 22, 1909, Beecham conducting); *The Wasps*, Aristophanic suite (1909; London, July 23, 1912, composer conducting); *Fantasia on a Theme by Thomas Tallis* for String Quartet and Double String Orch. (Gloucester Festival, Sept. 6, 1910, composer conducting; rev. 1923); *The Lark Ascending*, romance for Violin and Orch. (1914–20; London, June 14, 1921); Concerto in D minor for Violin and Strings, *Concerto accademico* (1924–25; London, Nov. 6, 1925); Piano Concerto in C major (1926–31; London, Feb. 1, 1933; also rev. for 2 Pianos and Orch., 1946); *Fantasia on Sussex Folk-Tunes* for Cello and Orch. (London, March 13, 1930, Casals, soloist, Barbirolli conducting); Prelude and Fugue in C minor (Hereford, Sept. 12, 1930); Suite for Viola and Small Orch. (London, Nov. 12, 1934); *Fantasia on Greensleeves* (arr. from the opera *Sir John in Love* by Greaves, 1934); *5 Variants of "Dives and Lazarus"* for String Orch. and Harp, commissioned by the British Council for the N.Y. World's Fair (N.Y., June 10, 1939); *Serenade to Music* (orch. version of 1938 original, 1940; London, Feb. 10, 1940); Concerto in A minor for Oboe and Strings (1943–44; Liverpool, Sept. 30, 1944); *Partita* for Double String Orch. (orch. version of Double Trio for String Sextet, 1946–48; BBC, London, March 20, 1948); Concerto Grosso for Strings (London, Nov. 18, 1950, Boult conducting); *Romance* in D-flat major for Harmonica, Strings, and Piano (1951; N.Y., May 3, 1952); Concerto in F minor for Tuba and Orch. (London, June 14, 1954); *Flourish for Glorious John* [for] (Manchester, Oct. 16, 1957, Barbirolli conducting). **CHAMBER:** 1 unnumbered string quartet, in C minor (1898; June 30, 1904); 2 numbered string quartets: No. 1, in G minor (London, Nov. 8, 1909) and No. 2, in A minor (1942–44; London, Oct. 12, 1944); Quintet in D major for Clarinet, Horn, Violin, Cello, and Piano (June 5, 1900); Piano Quintet in C minor for Piano, Violin, Viola, Cello, and Double Bass (London, Dec. 14, 1905); *Phantasy Quintet* for 2 Violins, 2 Violas, and Cello (1912; London, March 23, 1914); 6 studies in English folk song for Cello and Piano (London, June 4, 1926); Double Trio for String Sextet (London, Jan. 21, 1939); Violin Sonata in A minor (BBC, London, Oct. 12, 1954); also some short piano pieces; Introduction and Fugue for 2 Pianos (1946); organ pieces. **VOCAL:** *Willow Wood* for Baritone, Women's Chorus, and Orch., after Dante Gabriel Rossetti (1903; Liverpool Festival, Sept. 25, 1909); *Songs of Travel* for Voice and Piano, after Robert Louis Stevenson (London, Dec. 2, 1904); *Toward the Unknown Region* for Chorus and Orch., after Walt Whitman (1905–07; Leeds Festival, Oct. 10, 1907; rev. 1918); *On Wenlock Edge*, song cycle for Tenor, Piano, and String Quartet ad libitum, after A. E. Housman's *A Shropshire Lad* (London, Nov. 15, 1909); *5 Mystical Songs* for Baritone, Optional Chorus, and Orch. (Worcester Cathedral, Sept. 14, 1911); *Fantasia on Christmas Carols* for Baritone, Chorus, and Orch. (Hereford Festival, Sept. 12, 1912); *4 Hymns* for Tenor and Piano, with Viola obbligato (1914; Cardiff, May 26, 1920); *Mass* in G minor (1920–21; Birmingham, Dec. 6, 1922); *Sancta civitas* for Tenor, Baritone, Chorus, and Orch. (1923–25; Oxford, May 7, 1926); *Flos Campi*, suite for Viola, Wordless Mixed Chorus, and Small Orch. (London, Oct. 19, 1925); *Te Deum* for Chorus and Organ (Canterbury Cathedral, Dec. 4, 1928); *Benedicite* for Soprano, Chorus, and Orch. (1929; Dorking, May 2, 1930); *The Hundredth Psalm* for Chorus and Orch. (1929; Dorking, April 29, 1930); *3 Choral Hymns* for Baritone, Chorus, and Orch. (Dorking, April 30, 1930); *In Windsor Forest*, cantata for Chorus and Orch., adapted from the opera *Sir John in Love* (Windsor, Nov. 9, 1931); *Magnificat* for Contralto, Women's Chorus, and Orch. (Worcester Cathedral, Sept. 8, 1932); *5 Tudor Portraits* for Mezzo-soprano, Baritone, Chorus, and Orch. (1935; Norwich Festival, Sept. 25, 1936); *Dona nobis pacem* for Soprano, Baritone, Chorus, and Orch. (Huddersfield, Oct. 2, 1936); *Festival Te Deum* (1937); *Flourish for a Coronation* (London, April 1, 1937); *Serenade to Music* for 16 Solo Voices and Orch. (London, Oct. 5, 1938); *The Bridal Day*, masque after Edmund Spenser's *Epithalamion* (1938–39; rev. 1952–53; BBC television, London, June 5, 1953, in celebration of the coronation of Elizabeth II; rev. as the cantata *Epithalamion*, London, Sept. 30, 1957); *Thanksgiving for Victory* for Soprano, Speaker, Chorus, and Orch. (1944; BBC broadcast, London, May 13, 1945); *An Oxford Elegy* for Speaker, Chorus, and Orch., after Matthew Arnold (Dorking, Nov. 20, 1949); *Folk Songs of the 4 Seasons*, cantata on traditional folk songs, for Women's Voices and Orch. (1949; London, June 15, 1950); *The Sons of Light* for Children's Chorus (London, May 6, 1951); *Hodie (This Day)*, Christmas cantata for Soprano, Tenor, Baritone, Chorus, and Orch. (1953–54; Worcester, Sept. 8, 1954); *A Vision of Aeroplanes*, motet for Chorus and Organ, after Ezekiel, Chapter 1 (1955; St. Michael's, Cornhill, London, June 4, 1956); *10 Blake Songs* for Tenor and Oboe (BBC, London, Oct. 8, 1958); other songs to words by English poets; arrangements of English folk songs; hymn tunes; carols.

WRITINGS: *The English Hymnal* (1906; 2nd ed., 1933); *Songs of Praise* (with M. Shaw; 1925; 2nd ed., 1931); *The Oxford Book of Carols* (with P. Dearmer and M. Shaw; 1928); lectures and articles, reprinted in *National Music and Other Essays* (London, 1963); R. Palmer ed. *Folk Songs Collected by Ralph Vaughan Williams* (London, 1983).

BIBL.: A. Dickinson, *An Introduction to the Music of R. V. W.* (London, 1928); H. Foss, *R. V. W.* (London, 1950); E. Payne, *The Folksong Element in the Music of V. W.* (diss., Univ. of Liverpool, 1953); P. Young, *V. W.* (London, 1953); F. Howes, *The Music of R. V. W.* (London, 1954); J. Bergsagel, *The National Aspects of the Music of R. V. W.* (diss., Cornell Univ., 1957); S. Pakenham, *R. V. W.: A Discovery of His Music* (London, 1957); J. Day, *V. W.* (London, 1961; 2nd ed., rev., 1975); A. Dickinson, *V. W.* (London, 1963); M. Kennedy, *The Works of R. V. W.* (London, 1964; rev. 1980; 2nd ed., rev., 1996, as *A Catalogue of the Works of R.V. W.*); E. Schwartz, *The Symphonies of R. V. W.* (Amherst, 1964); U.

Vaughan Williams, *R. V. W.: A Biography* (London, 1964); H. Ottaway, *V. W.* (London, 1966); P. Starbuck, *R. V. W., O.M., 1872–1958: A Bibliography of His Literary Writings and Criticism of His Musical Works* (diss., Library Assn., 1967); M. Hurd, *V. W.* (London, 1970); J. Lunn and U. Vaughan Williams, *R. V. W.: A Pictorial Biography* (London, 1971); R. Douglas, *Working with R. V. W.* (London, 1972); H. Ottaway, *V. W. Symphonies* (London, 1972; rev. ed., 1988); U. Vaughan Williams, *R. V. W.: A Biography of R. V. W.* (Oxford, 1988); N. Butterworth, *R. V. W.: A Guide to Research* (N.Y., 1989); W. Mellers, *V. W. and the Vision of Albion* (1989); J. Northrop Moore, *V. W.: A Life in Photographs* (Oxford, 1992); A. Frogley, ed., *V. S. Studies* (N.Y., 1996); P. Holmes, *V. W.: His Life and Times* (London, 1997); J. Day, *V. W.* (Oxford, 1998).
—NS/LK/DM

Vaughn, Billy, American bandleader, arranger, and vocalist; b. Glasgow, Ky., April 12, 1919; d. Escondido, Calif. Sept. 26, 1991. Vaughn had three distinct yet overlapping careers as a popular musician from the 1950s to the 1970s: as the baritone singer in the male vocal quartet the Hilltoppers he shared in their 20 chart singles between 1952 and 1957, including the million-seller "P.S. I Love You"; as musical director of Dot Records, he arranged successful recordings by such artists as Pat Boone, The Fontane Sisters, and Gale Storm; and as the leader of his own studio orchestra he made a series of largely instrumental recordings, many employing a "twin sax" sound, reaching the singles charts 35 times and the albums charts 41 times between 1954 and 1970, with among others the chart-topping single "Melody of Love" and the #1 LP *Theme from "A Summer Place"*.

Vaughn attended Western Ky. State Coll. in Bowling Green and went to a barbers school in Louisville. He served in the army during World War II. He was the pianist in Ace Dinning's band in Bowling Green when he met Jimmy Sacca, a student at Western Ky. State who sang barbershop harmonies with his fellow students Seymour Spiegelman and Don McGuire. Vaughn wrote "Trying" and recorded it with them, adding his own voice to create a quartet, The Hilltoppers. The recording was picked up by Dot Records and released in May 1952. It entered the charts in August and reached the Top Ten in October.

The Hilltoppers returned to the Top Ten in October 1953 with a million-selling revival of the 1934 song "P.S. I Love You" (music by Gordon Jenkins, lyrics by Johnny Mercer), which was backed by another Top Ten hit, Vaughn's composition "I'd Rather Die Young (Than Grow Old Without You)." In November both sides of their next single, "To Be Alone"/"Love Walked In" (music by George Gershwin, lyrics by Ira Gershwin), peaked in the Top Ten, and they scored two more Top Ten hits in 1954, "Till Then" (music and lyrics by Eddie Seiler, Sol Marcus, and Guy Wood) in February and "From the Vine Came the Grape" (music by Leonard Whitcup, lyrics by Paul Cunningham) in March.

Vaughn reduced his involvement with the Hilltoppers during 1954, hiring a replacement to tour while still continuing to record with them, and he began arranging and conducting other recording sessions at Dot Records. In February 1955 he scored back-to-back million-selling #1 singles, first with the Fontane Sisters' recording of "Hearts of Stone" (music by Rudy Jackson, lyrics by Eddy Ray) and then with his own instrumental "Melody of Love" (music by H. Engelmann, new lyrics by Tom Glazer). Before the end of the year he had participated in six more Top Ten hits, often by writing and conducting middle-of-the-road arrangements of recent R&B and rock 'n' roll songs: "Only You (And You Alone)" (music and lyrics by Buck Ram and Andre Rand) by the Hilltoppers; "Seventeen" (music and lyrics by John Young Jr., Chuck Gorman, and Boyd Bennett) by the Fontane Sisters; the million-selling #1 "Ain't That a Shame" (music and lyrics by Fats Domino and Dave Bartholomew) and "At My Front Door (Crazy Little Mama)" (music and lyrics by John C. Moore and Ewart G. Abner Jr.) by Pat Boone; "I Hear You Knocking" (music and lyrics by Dave Bartholomew and Pearl King) by Gale Storm; and his own version of the novelty song "The Shifting Whispering Sands" (music by Mary M. Hadler, lyrics by V. C. Gilbert), with a spoken narration by Ken Nordine.

Another nine Top Ten singles were conducted and arranged by Vaughn in 1956, five of them by Pat Boone, including the million-sellers "I'll Be Home" (music and lyrics by Stan Lewis and Ferdinand Washington), "I Almost Lost My Mind" (music and lyrics by Ivory Joe Hunter), and "Friendly Persuasion (Thee I Love)" (music by Dmitri Tiomkin, lyrics by Paul Francis Webster); the others were by Gale Storm and the Fontane Sisters. In August, Vaughn released his first album under his own name, *The Golden Instrumentals*; it eventually went gold.

There were another nine Vaughn-related Top Ten hits in 1957, including Boone's five million-sellers "Don't Forbid Me" (music and lyrics by Charles Singleton), "Why Baby Why" (music and lyrics by Luther Dixon and Larry Harrison), "Love Letters in the Sand" (music by J. Fred Coots, lyrics by Nick Kenny and Charles Kenny), "Remember You're Mine" (music and lyrics by Kal Mann and Bernie Lowe), and "April Love" (music by Sammy Fain, lyrics by Paul Francis Webster), and Vaughn's own million-selling, double-sided instrumental single "Sail Along Silvery Moon" (music by Percy Wenrich, lyrics by Harry Tobias)/"Raunchy" (music by William E. Justis Jr., and Sidney Manker).

Pat Boone scored another four Vaughn-arranged Top Ten hits in 1958, including the million-seller "A Wonderful Time Up There," but as the singer's career faded, Vaughn turned increasingly to his own instrumental albums, and he charted with three during the year, notably the gold-selling, Top Ten LP *Sail Along Silv'ry Moon*, released in March. Prominently employing two saxophones pitched a third of an octave apart to play the melody, he turned out albums largely devoted to his own arrangements of recent hits. There were three more chart albums in 1959, including the gold-selling, Top Ten hit *Blue Hawaii*, released in May.

Vaughn reached his commercial peak in 1960, when he released five albums, three of which, *Theme from "A Summer Place"*, *Look for a Star*, and *Theme from "The Sundowners"*, made the Top Ten, with *Theme from "A Summer Place"* topping the charts in May and going gold. Three more albums reached the charts in 1961, among them *Orange Blossom Special* and *Wheels*, which reached the Top Ten. Vaughn also arranged and conducted another major hit for Pat Boone, "Moody River" (music and lyrics by Gary D. Bruce), which topped the charts in June. He scored three new chart albums in 1962, including the Top Ten *A Swingin' Safari*, and two of his three 1963 chart albums, *1962's Greatest Hits* and *Sukiyaki and 11 Hawaiian Hits*, also reached the Top Ten.

After 1963, Vaughn's record sales fell off, although he charted four albums in 1964, two in 1965, three in 1966, six in 1967 (including two by the Billy Vaughan Singers and a hits compilation), two in 1968, and one each in 1969 and 1970. He continued to record until his death of cancer at 72 in 1991.—**WR**

Vautor, Thomas, English composer; b. c. 1590; d. place and date unknown. He was in the service of the Villiers family, and was admitted B.Mus. of Oxford through Lincoln Coll. (1616). He publ. *The First Set, beeing Songs of Divers Ayres and Natures, of Five and Sixe Parts, Apt for Vyols and Voyces* (London, 1619–20; ed. in The English Madrigalists, XXXIV, 1958).—**NS/LK/DM**

Vázsonyi, Bálint, distinguished Hungarian-born American pianist, writer, and lecturer; b. Budapest, March 7, 1936. He entered the Franz Liszt Academy of Music in Budapest as a youth. At age 12, he made his professional debut. In the wake of the abortive Hungarian Revolution in 1956, he fled his homeland and pursued training at the Vienna Academy of Music (1957–58) and with Dohnányi at Fla. State Univ. (1960). In 1964 he became a naturalized American citizen. His performance of all of Beethoven's 32 piano sonatas presented in chronological order in N.Y. on Oct. 31 and Nov. 1, 1976, brought him wide recognition. In 1977 he made a transcontinental tour of the U.S. From 1978 to 1984 he was a prof. at the Ind. Univ. School of Music in Bloomington. In 1983 he founded Telemusic, Inc., in Bloomington, which he served as chief executive officer until 1998. In 1991 he was the Republican candidate for mayor of Bloomington, but was defeated by his Democratic opponent. In 1993 he became a senior fellow of the Potomac Foundation in McLean, Va., where he was made director of its Center for the American Founding in 1996. He has appeared on various radio and television programs as a defender of Conservative ideals. As a pianist, Vázsonyi's playing is marked by a transcendental virtuosity of technique coupled with the mellow lyricism typical of the traditional Hungarian school of pianism. His writings include the standard biography of Dohnányi (Budapest, 1971), as well as the political tomes *The Battle for America's Soul* (1995) and *America's 30 Years War: Who Is Winning?* (1998).—**NS/LK/DM**

Vazzana, Anthony, American composer and educator; b. Troy, N.Y., Nov. 4, 1922. He was of a musical family; his father played the mandolin. He studied piano with George H. Pickering, and attended the State Univ. of N.Y. Coll. at Potsdam. In 1943 he was inducted into the U.S. Air Force, where he arranged and conducted suitable music in concert bands. He resumed his musical studies after his discharge, and in 1946 enrolled at the Berkshire Music Center at Tanglewood, where his instructors were Fine, Shaw, Chapple, Bernstein, and Ross. In 1948 he enrolled at the Univ. of Southern Calif. in Los Angeles in the classes of Stevens, Dahl, and Kanitz; Vazzana received his M.M. in 1948. Subsequently he divided his time between composing and teaching; he was successively on the faculty of Calif. State Univ. at Long Beach and at Los Angeles, Champlain Coll., and Danbury (Conn.) State Coll. In 1959 he received the degree of doctor in composition at the Univ. of Southern Calif. and joined the faculty of its School of Music. In his teaching, Vazzana resolutely promoted advanced techniques in composition; he wrote a set of books on theory, *Projects in Musicianship* (4 vols., 1965–68). In his compositions, he pursued a logical evolutionary line, beginning with neo-Classical formations and continuing with progressive harmonic and contrapuntal complications, in which dissonances are ultimately emancipated and rhythms become increasingly asymmetrical; all of this is aided and abetted by eloquent pregnant pauses separating brief melodic ejaculations. Special effects, such as striking the bodies of musical instruments with taps and kicks, soundlessly blowing through the embouchure of a wind instrument, such as a horn, and the like, add to the quaquaversal quality of sonorism in his works.

WORKS: ORCH.: *Andante and Allegro* (1949); *Symphonic Allegro* (1958); *Harlequin Suite* (1959); *Suite* for Strings (1963); Sym. No. 1 (1963); *Spectra* for Band (1965); *Partite sopra victimae paschali laudes* for Wind Orch. (1976); *Trinakie* (1977); *Varianti* (1982); *Odissea* (1989); *Metamorphoses* for Wind Orch. (1989); *Concerto Sapporo* for Euphonium and Orch. (Sapporo, Aug. 10, 1990); *Sinfonia Tejana* for Symphonic Band (1992). **CHAMBER:** Sonata for Clarinet, Horn, and Piano (1947); String Quartet (1948); Woodwind Quintet (1948); Suite for Viola and Piano (1948); Quartet for Violin, Viola, Cello, and Piano (1949); Violin Sonata (1958); *Music* for 2 Flutes (1962); *Fantasia concertante* for Cello and Piano (1970); *Incontri* for Violin and Piano (1971); *Tre monodie* for Trombone (1976); *Cambi* for Tuba and Percussion (1977); *Montaggi* for 4 Tubas (1978); *Studi* for Saxophone (1979); *Buccina* for Horn and Piano (1979); *Partita* for Euphonium, Piano, and Percussion (1980); *Concerto a tre* for Clarinet, Double Bass, and Instrumental Ensemble (1981); *Corivolano* for Viola and Horn (1982); *Lamentazione* for Viola (1985); *Fantasia Concertante* for Cello and Piano (1985); *Introduzione e Danza* for Bass Clarinet and Piano (1986); *Capriccio* for Clarinet and Piano (1987); *Saggi Musicali* for Soprano Saxophone and Piano (1988); *Disegni II* for Cello, Piano, and Percussion (1989); *Linea* for Horn (1990); *Chamber Concertino* for Piano and Chamber Ensemble (1991–93); *Gesti* for Bassoon (1992). **KEYBOARD: Piano:** Sonata (1962); *Disegni I* (1978). **Organ:** *Meditation* (1994). **VOCAL:** *Songs of Life and Nature* for Voice and Piano (1962). —**NS/LK/DM**

Veasey, Josephine, English mezzo-soprano and teacher; b. Peckham, July 10, 1930. She studied with Audrey Langford in London. In 1949 she joined the chorus at London's Covent Garden; she made her Covent Garden debut as the Shepherd Boy in *Tannhäuser* in 1955 and later appeared there as Waltraute, Fricka, Brangäne, Berlioz's Dido, Dorabella et al. Veasey also created the role of the Emperor in Henze's *We Come to* *the River* there (1976). From 1957 to 1969 she appeared at the Glynebourne Festivals. On Nov. 22, 1968, she made her Metropolitan Opera debut in N.Y. as Fricka, remaining on the roster until 1969; she also made guest appearances throughout Europe and in South America and sang in concerts. In 1982 Veasey retired from the operatic stage and became active as a teacher; she taught at the Royal Academy of Music (1983–84) and was a voice consultant to the English National Opera (from 1985) in London. In 1970 Veasey was made a Commander of the Order of the British Empire. **—NS/LK/DM**

Vecchi, Horatio (actually, **Orazio Tiberio**), significant Italian composer; b. Modena (baptized), Dec. 6, 1550; d. there, Feb. 19, 1605. He received ecclesiastical training from the Benedictines of S. Pietro in Modena, and also studied music in Modena with the Servite monk Salvatore Essenga; he later took Holy Orders. He was maestro di cappella at Salò Cathedral (1581–84); in 1584 he became maestro di cappella at Modena Cathedral, where he adopted the rendering of Horatio for his first name. Within a short time he accepted the post of maestro di cappella in Reggio Emilia and then became canon at Correggio Cathedral in 1586; he was made archdeacon in 1591. In 1593 Vecchi returned to Modena Cathedral as maestro di cappella, and he was elevated to mansionario in 1596; he also served in the brotherhood of the Annunciation at the churches of S. Maria and S. Pietro. In 1598 he was named maestro di corte by Duke Cesare d'Este. In 1604 Vecchi was dismissed from his duties at the Cathedral for disregarding the bishop's admonition to cease directing music at the Cathedral convent. He was greatly admired in his day for his six books of Canzonette. His lasting fame is due above all to his "commedia harmonica" *L'Amfiparnasso*, performed at Modena in 1594 and printed at Venice in 1597; this is a kind of musical farce written not in the monodic style of Peri's *Dafne* but in madrigal style, with all the text sung by several voices (i.e., a chorus of four or five); it has been called a "madrigal opera," but it was not intended for the theater and stood entirely apart from the path that opera was to take. It was ed. in *Publikationen Älterer Praktischer und Theoretischer Musikwerke*, XXVI, 1902, in *Capolavori Polifonici del Secolo* XVI, V (Rome, 1953), and in *Early Musical Masterworks* (Chapel Hill, 1977). Another important secular work was his *Dialoghi da cantarsi et concertarsi con ogni sorte di stromenti* for Seven to Eight Voices (1608); other works appeared in contemporary collections, and some of his works were later included in 19th- and 20th-century collections. He also publ. in Venice a number of sacred works, including *Lamentationes cum 4 paribus vocibus* (1587) and *Hymni qui per totum annum in Ecclesia Romana concinuntur* for Four Voices (1604).

Bibl.: A. Catellani, *Della vita e delle opere di O. V.* (Milan, 1858); J. Hol, *H. V. als weltlicher Komponist* (diss., Univ. of Basel, 1917); idem, *H. V.s weltliche Werke* (Strasbourg, 1934); W. Martin, *The Convito musicale of O. V.* (diss., Univ. of Oxford, 1964); R. Rüegge, *O. V.s geistliche Werke* (Bern, 1967); R. Dalmonte and M. Privitera, *Gitene, canzonette: Studio e trascrizione delle Canzonette a sei voci d'H. V. (1587)* (Florence, 1996).**—NS/LK/DM**

Vecchi, Orfeo, distinguished Italian composer; b. probably in Milan, c. 1550; d. there before April 1604. He became a priest and was maestro di cappella of the royal and ducal church of S. Maria della Scala in Milan from about 1590 until his death. He was an outstanding polyphonist.

Works (all publ. in Milan unless otherwise given): *Missarum liber primus* for 5 Voices (1588); *Missa, psalmi ad Vesperas dominicales, Magnificat et psalmorum modulationes* (1590); *Psalmi integri in totius anni solemnitatibus, 2 Magnificat, 4 antiphonae ad B.V.M.* for 5 Voices and Basso Continuo (1596); *Missarum liber primus* for 4 Voices and Basso Continuo (1597); *Missarum liber secundus, Missa pro defunctis, sacrae cantiones* for 5 Voices (1598); *Motectorum liber secundus* for 5 Voices and Basso Continuo (1598); *Motectorum liber tertius* for 6 Voices (1598); *Falsi bordoni figurati sopra gli otto toni ecclesiastici, Magnificat, Te Deum laudamus, hinni, antifone, Letanie* for 3 to 5 and 8 Voices (1600); *Hymni totius anni...cum antiphonis et Litaniis B.V.M.* for 5 Voices (1600); *In septem Regii Prophetae psalmos, liber quartus* for 6 Voices (1601); *Psalmi in totius anni solemnitatibus, 2 Magnificat* for 5 Voices (1601); *Missarum liber tertius* for 5 Voices (1602); *La donna vestita di sole...21 madrigali* (1602); *Magnificat liber primus* for 5 Voices (1603); *Motectorum liber primus* for 4 Voices (1603); *Cantiones sacrae* for 6 Voices (Antwerp, 1608); other works in contemporary collections.**—NS/LK/DM**

Vécsey, Jenö, Hungarian musicologist and composer; b. Felsöcéce, July 19, 1909; d. Budapest, Sept. 18, 1966. He studied composition with Kodály at the Budapest Academy of Music (diploma, 1935), took courses in chemistry and biology at the Univ. of Budapest (graduated, 1941), and completed his musical training in Vienna (1941–42). He joined the staff of the National Széchényi Library in Budapest in 1942, where he was head of its music dept. from 1945 until his death. He made valuable contributions to the historical and bibliographical music literature preserved there, initiated and directed editorial work on the Musica Rinata series (1963–66), and did preparatory work on the new Haydn Collected Edition. He publ. *Joseph Haydn művei az Országos Széchényi könyvtár zenei gyűjteményében* (Joseph Haydn's Compositions in the Music Collection of the National Széchényi Library; Budapest, 1959; Eng. tr., 1960).

Works: Dramatic: Ballet: *Kele diák* (Scholar Kele; 1943). **Orch.:** *Divertimento* (1939–40); *Rhapsody* (1940–41); *Intermezzi* for Strings (1942); *2 Symphonic Dances* (1945; from *Kele diák*); *Boldogkő vara* (Boldogkő Castle), symphonic poem (1951; rev. as *Praeludium, notturno és scherzo*, 1958); Piano Concertino (1953); Double Bass Concertino (1954); *Szimfonikus concerto Krúdy Gyula emlékeré* (Symphonic Concerto in Memory of Gyula Krúdy; 1958). **Chamber:** String Quartet (1942); String Sextet (1956); *Bagatelles* for 2 Pianos (1962). **Vocal:** Songs.**—NS/LK/DM**

Vedernikov, Alexander, Russian bass; b. Mokino, Dec. 23, 1927. He studied voice at the Moscow Cons., graduating in 1955. He won 1st prize at the International Schumann Competition in Berlin in 1956 and, in the same year, 1st prize at the Soviet competition for his performance of songs by Soviet composers. In 1957 he made his debut at the Bolshoi Theater in Moscow as Susanin. In 1961 he entered the La Scala

Opera School of Milan as an aspirant and subsequently toured as a concert singer in France, Italy, England, Austria, and Canada. He also sang with the Bolshoi Theater, with which he made tours abroad. He was particularly noted for his performances of the Russian repertoire; his portrayal of Boris Godunov in Mussorgsky's opera approached Chaliapin's in its grandeur. He also distinguished himself in Italian buffo roles. **—NS/LK/DM**

Veerhoff, Carlos, Argentine-German composer; b. Buenos Aires, June 3, 1926. He was a student of Grabner at the Berlin Hochschule für Musik (1943–44). After teaching at the National Univ. in Tucuman (1948–51), he returned to Berlin as an assistant to Fricsay (1951–52). After completing his training with Blacher at the Hochschule für Musik (1952) and privately with Thomas and Scherchen, he chose to remain in Germany.

WORKS: DRAMATIC: *Pavane royale*, ballet (1953); *Targusis*, chamber opera (1958); *El porquerizo del ray*, ballet (1963); *Die goldene Maske*, opera (1968; rev. 1978); *Es gibt doch Zebrastreifen*, mini-opera (1971; Ulm, Jan. 20, 1972); *Der Grüne*, chamber opera (1972); *Dualis*, ballet (1978). **ORCH.:** *Prólogo sinfónico* (1951); *Symphonic Movement* (1952); 5 syms.: No. 1, *Panta rhei* (Everything Flows; 1953), No. 2 (1956), No. 3, *Spirales* (1966; rev. 1969), No. 4 (1974), and No. 5 for Strings (1977); *Mirages* (1961); *Akroasis* for 24 Winds and Percussion (1966); *Textur* for Strings (1969; rev. 1971); *Sinotrauc* (1972; Munich, Jan. 19, 1973); *Torso* (1973; Lübeck, Jan. 14, 1974); *Dorefamie* (1975); Violin Concerto (1975–76); 2 piano concertos (1978–79; 1990); *Concertino da camera* (1979); Concerto for 2 Violins and Orch. (1985); Concerto for Cello, Double Bass, and Orch. (1989); Percussion Concerto (1993–94; Munich, Oct. 28, 1994). **CHAMBER:** 2 string quartets (1951, 1974); Sonata for Solo Violin (1954); 2 wind quintets (1958, 1969); *Dialogue I* for Saxophone and Piano (1967) and *II* for Viola and Percussion (1987); String Trio (1986); Horn Trio (1994). **VOCAL:** *Gesänge auf dem Wege* for Baritone and Orch. (1964); *Ut omnes unum sint*, chamber cantata (1967); *Gesänge für Sangsâra* for Mezzo-soprano, Voices, Orch., and Tape (1976); *Pater noster in Form einer Messe "en miniature"* for Chorus and Orch. (1988).**—NS/LK/DM**

Vega, Aurelio de la, Cuban-born American composer, teacher, and writer on music; b. Havana, Nov. 28, 1925. He studied in Havana at De La Salle Coll. (B.A. in humanities, 1944), with Fritz Kramer (1943–46), at the Univ. (M.A. in diplomacy, 1946), and at the Ada Iglesias Music Inst. (M.A. in musicology, 1956); he also studied with Toch in Calif. (1947–48). During the Cuban years of his career, he was president of the Cuban section of the ISCM (1952–54), worked as a music critic (1952–57), and served as prof. of music and chairman of the music dept. at the Univ. of Oriente in Santiago de Cuba (1953–59). In 1959 he settled in Los Angeles and in 1966 became a naturalized American citizen. In the summer of 1959 he was a visiting prof. of music at the Univ. of Southern Calif. In 1959 he joined the faculty of San Fernando Valley State Coll. (later Calif. State Univ. at Northridge), where he subsequently was a distinguished prof. of music, director of the electronic music studio, and composer-in-residence. In 1992 he retired as distinguished prof. emeritus. In 1978 and 1984 he received Kennedy Center Friedheim awards. He held a Fulbright Research Award in 1985. His numerous articles and essays, as well as paintings, have appeared in various publications. In his compositions, he experimented with various avant-garde means of expression without proscribing the use of Cuban nationalist elements.

WORKS: ORCH.: *Obertura a una Farsa Seria* (1950; Havana, April 28, 1951); *Introducción y Episodio* (1952; Havana, April 3, 1953); *Elegía* for Strings (London, Nov. 16, 1954); *Divertimento* for Piano, Violin, Cello, and Strings (1956; Redlands, Calif., Jan. 28, 1958); *Symphony in 4 Parts* (1960; Washington, D.C., April 30, 1961); *Intrata* (Los Angeles, May 12, 1972); *Adiós* (1977; Los Angeles, April 20, 1978, Mehta conducting). **CHAMBER:** *La Muerte de Pan* for Violin and Piano (Redlands, Calif., March 16, 1948); Trio for Violin, Cello, and Piano (1949; Havana, April 27, 1952); *Soliloquio* for Viola and Piano (1950; Havana, April 1, 1951); *Levenda del Ariel Criollo* for Cello and Piano (1953; Havana, March 25, 1954); String Quartet, "In Memoriam Alban Berg" (1957; Washington, D.C., April 20, 1958); Woodwind Quintet (1959; Los Angeles, Jan. 30, 1961); Trio for Flute, Oboe, and Clarinet (1960; Northridge, Calif., March 19, 1961); *Structures* for Piano and String Quartet (1962; Washington, D.C., May 8, 1964); *Segmentos* for Violin and Piano (Berkeley, Calif., Oct. 2, 1964); *Exametron* for Flute, Cello, and 4 Percussionists (Los Angeles, Oct. 11, 1965); *Interpolation* for Clarinet with or without Pre-recorded Sounds (1965; Los Angeles, April 23, 1966); *Exospheres* for Oboe and Piano (1966; Los Angeles, Nov. 25, 1968); *Labdanum* for Flute, Vibraphone, and Viola (Los Angeles, Nov. 30, 1970); *Tangents* for Violin and Pre-recorded Sounds (1973; Los Angeles, Oct. 21, 1974); *Para-Tangents* for Trumpet and Pre-recorded Sounds (1973; Los Angeles, Dec. 14, 1974); *Septicilium* for Clarinet and 6 Instrumentalists (1974; Los Angeles, April 12, 1975); *Olep ed Arudamot* for Any Number of Instruments and/or Voices (1974; Tujunga, Calif., March 14, 1976); *The Infinite Square* for Any Number of Instruments and/or Voices (1975; Northridge, Calif., Nov. 12, 1976); *Andamar-Ramadna* for Any Number of Instruments and/or Voices (1975; Mexico City, May 22, 1977); *Sound Clouds* for Guitar (1975; Los Angeles, Feb. 11, 1978); *Astralis* for Any Number of Instruments and/or Voices (1977; Buenos Aires, July 27, 1979); *Nones* for Any Number of Instruments and/or Voices (1977; San Francisco, Feb. 20, 1979); *Undici Colori* for Bassoon with or without Projected Color Transparencies (1981; Los Angeles, Jan. 25, 1982); *Galandiacoa* for Clarinet and Guitar (1982; Los Angeles, Jan. 10, 1983); *Tropimapal* for 9 Instruments (Los Angeles, April 18, 1983); piano pieces. **VOCAL:** *La Fuente Infinata*, song cycle for Soprano and Piano (1944; Havana, Dec. 18, 1945); Cantata for 2 Sopranos, Contralto, and 21 Instruments (1958; Washington, D.C., Nov. 1, 1964); *Inflorescenia* for Soprano, Bass Clarinet, and Pre-recorded Sounds (Los Angeles, Oct. 25, 1976); *Asonante* for Soprano, Female Dancer, 7 Instruments, and Tape (1985; Los Angeles, March 4, 1987); *Adramante* for Soprano and Piano (La Jolla, Calif., Dec. 7, 1985); *Magias e Invenciones*, song cycle for Soprano and Piano (1986; Mexico City, April 27, 1988); *Testimonial* for Mezzo-soprano and 5 Instruments (Buenos Aires, July 5, 1990); *Madrigales de Entonces* for Chorus (1991; Mexico City, May 28, 1993). **ELECTRONIC:** *Vectors* (1963; Ojai, Calif., May 30, 1964); *Extrapolation* (Los Angeles, Dec. 5, 1981).**—NS/LK/DM**

Vega, Ray, Latin-jazz trumpeter, percussionist, composer, arranger; b. April 3, 1961. He was raised in the South Bronx and grew up immersed in salsa and jazz. He began playing trumpet in junior high and continued his studies at N.Y.'s H.S. of Music and Art. He won a music scholarship to Long Island Univ., but left after two years to work at as a banker. Two years later, he returned to music and soon was gigging extensively on the salsa scene. He worked with Mongo Santamaria for four and a half years (1982–86), then briefly with Mario Bauza's Afro-Cuban Jazz Orch. After touring Europe with Bauza, he joined Ray Barretto and New World Spirit (1988); shortly thereafter, he was invited to join Tito Puente's Latin Jazz group. After two years of playing for both bands, Vega devoted himself to playing with Puente, working as lead trumpeter. In the mid-1990s, he was signed to Concord Jazz to record as a leader on his own.

DISC.: *Ray Vega* (1996).—**LP**

Vega, Suzanne, American songwriter , singer, and guitarist; b. Santa Monica, Calif., July 11, 1960. She was reared in N.Y., where she attended the H.S. of Music and Art and later received a degree in English literature from Barnard Coll. In the early 1980s she joined the Greenwich Village folk-music scene, becoming a devotee of Nichiren Buddhism. Her first album, *Suzanne Vega* (1985), attracted notice for its cool, sophisticated lyrics and hypnotically repetitive melodies. Other albums include *Live in London* (1986), *Solitude Standing* (1987), *Days of Open Hand* (1990), *99.9°* (1992), and *Nine Objects of Desire* (1996); also a music video, *Live at the Royal Albert Hall* (1987).—**NS/LK/DM**

Végh, Sándor (Alexandre), Hungarian-born French violinist, conductor, and pedagogue; b. Klausenburg, May 17, 1912. He was a pupil of Zsolt, Waldbauer, and Weiner at the Budapest Academy of Music, then studied violin with Hubay and composition with Kodály. He was a member of the Hungarian Trio (1931–33) and the Hungarian Quartet (1934–40); also made appearances as a soloist (from 1934). In 1940 he founded the Végh Quartet, which remained active until 1980. From 1941 to 1946 he was a prof. at the Budapest Academy of Music; he subsequently emigrated to France, becoming a naturalized French citizen in 1953. From 1953 to 1969 he was active at the Prades Festivals; also taught master classes in various European locales. From 1968 to 1971 he conducted the Orchestre du Chambre Sándor Végh; he taught at the Salzburg Mozarteum (from 1971), where he was conductor of its Camerata Academica (from 1978).—**NS/LK/DM**

Veinus, Abraham, American musicologist; b. N.Y., Feb. 12, 1916. He was educated at the City Coll. of N.Y. (B.A., 1936), Cornell Univ. (M.A., 1937), and Columbia Univ. (1946–48). From 1948 until his retirement in 1982 he was prof. of musicology and fine arts at Syracuse Univ. In addition to his articles and reviews on various aspects of music and art, he publ. the books *The Concerto* (1944; 2nd ed., rev., 1964), *The Victor Book of Concertos* (1948), *The Pocket Book of Great Operas* (with H. Simon, 1949), and *Understanding Music: Style, Structure and History* (with W. Fleming, 1958).—**NS/LK/DM**

Veit, Wenzel Heinrich (actually, **Václav Jindřich**), Bohemian composer; b. Řepnice, near Leitmeritz, Jan. 19, 1806; d. Leitmeritz, Feb. 15, 1864. He studied organ and piano and took courses in law and philosophy at the Univ. of Prague; hewas active as a private music teacher while pursuing a legal career. He was briefly music director in Aachen (1841) but then decided to devote himself fully to composition. He helped to advance the cause of the Romantic movement in music in his homeland.

WORKS: ORCH.: Overture (1842); Violin Concertino (1844); Sym. in E minor (1859). **CHAMBER:** 3 quintets for 2 Violins, Viola, and 2 Cellos (1835); 2 quintets for 2 Violins, 2 Violas, and Cello (1837, 1851); 4 string quartets (1836, 1838, 1839, 1840); Piano Trio (1860); Les Adieux for Cello and Piano (c. 1845); piano pieces. **VOCAL:** *Hymnus* (1840); Mass in D major (1858); Te Deum (1863); *Böhmens bester Bergsegen*, cantata (1845); part-songs for men's voices; solo songs.—**NS/LK/DM**

Vejvanovský, Pavel Josef, distinguished Moravian trumpeter and composer; b. Hukvaldy or Hlucin, c. 1633; d. Kroměříž (buried), Sept. 24, 1693. He was educated at the Opava Jesuit Coll., and entered the service of E. Castelle, an administrator at the court of the Prince-Bishop of Olmötz, Leopold Wilhelm, as a trumpeter in 1661. He then was made principal trumpeter and Kapellmeister to the new Prince-Bishop, Karl Liechtenstein-Kastelkorn, in 1664, and later served as his Hof- und Feldtrompeter. His masterful writing for the trumpet and the cornett is found in both his instrumental and his vocal works. Among his output are 14 masses, offertories, motets, vespers, litanies, antiphons, a number of sonatas in which the trumpet is prominent, balletti, Intrada, and Serenadas. See J. Pohanska, ed., *Pavel Josef Vejvanovský: Serenate e sonate per orchestra*, Musica Antiqua Bohemica, XXXVI (1950), and *Pavel Josef Vejvanovský: Composizioni per orchestra*, ibid., XLVII-XLIX (1960–61).—**NS/LK/DM**

Velimirović, Miloš, eminent Serbian- American music scholar; b. Belgrade, Dec. 10, 1922. He studied violin and piano at the Belgrade Academy of Music with Stojanović. In 1943 he was sent to a forced labor camp by the German occupation authorities. After the liberation, he studied Byzantine art at the Univ. of Belgrade, graduating in 1951; simultaneously took composition lessons with Mihovil Logar at the Belgrade Academy of Music. In 1952 he emigrated to the U.S.; studied at Harvard Univ., obtaining his M.A. in 1953 and his Ph.D. in 1957 with the diss. *Byzantine Elements in Early Slavic Chant* (publ. in an enl. ed., 1960, in Monumenta Musicae Byzantinae, *Subsidiae*, IV, 1960); also took a course in Byzantine music with Wellesz at Dumbarton Oaks in Washington, D.C. (1954). He was on the faculty of Yale Univ. (1957–69) and the Univ. of Wisc. (1969–73); in 1973, was appointed a prof. of music at the Univ. of Va. in Charlottesville; served as chairman of the music dept. there (1974–77). A linguist, he has contributed a number of scholarly articles to various publications, mainly on subjects connected with liturgical music in Byzantium and in the Slavic countries. He was general ed. of Collegium Musicum (1958–73) and assoc. ed. (jointly with E. Wellesz) of *Studies in Eastern Chant* (4 vols., London, 1966–78); wrote articles on Russian and Slavic church music for *The New Grove Dictionary of Music and Musicians* (1980).—**NS/LK/DM**

Velluti, Giovanni Battista, famous Italian castrato soprano; b. Montolmo, Ancona, Jan. 28, 1781; d. Sambruson di Dolo, Venice, Jan. 22, 1861. He studied with Mattei in Bologna and with Calpi in Ravenna, making his debut in 1801 in Forlì. He then sang in Naples in the premieres of Guglielmi's *Asteria e Teseo* and Andreozzi's *Pirano e Tisbe*. From 1805 to 1808 he was in Rome, where he appeared in the premiere of Nicolini's *Traiano in Dacio*; his La Scala debut in Milan followed in that composer's *Coriolano* (Dec. 26, 1808). After appearances in Venice (1810) and Turin (1811), he sang in Vienna (1812); also appeared in Munich, where he was named Bavarian court singer. He sang in the premiere of Rossini's *Aureliano in Palmira* in Milan (Dec. 26, 1813), and then toured throughout Italy; also made appearances in Germany and Russia. On March 7, 1824, he created the role of Armando in Meyerbeer's *Il Crociato in Egitto* in Venice; chose that same role for his London debut on June 3, 1825, at the King's Theatre, where he continued to sing until 1826, making his farewell to London in 1829. Velluti was the last great castrato of the age.—**NS/LK/DM**

Veltri, Michelangelo, Argentine conductor; b. Buenos Aires, Aug. 16, 1940; d. there, Dec. 18, 1997. He studied at the Buenos Aires Cons. and with Panizza and Votto in Italy. After conducting in South America, he became music director of the Teatro Liceu in Barcelona in 1966. In 1969 he made his first appearance at Milan's La Scala conducting *Don Carlos*. On Nov. 10, 1971, he made his Metropolitan Opera debut in N.Y. conducting *Rigoletto*, returning there regularly in performances of the Italian repertory until 1983. From 1972 to 1977 he was artistic director of the Caracas Festival, and thereafter conducted at the opera houses in Santiago and Rio de Janeiro. He was artistic director of the Avignon Opera from 1983 to 1987. In 1986 he conducted *Lucia di Lammermoor* at London's Covent Garden. From 1996 until his death he served as artistic director of the Teatro Colón in Buenos Aires. As a guest conductor, he appeared in Vienna, Berlin, Salzburg, Amsterdam, Paris, Marseilles, Monte Carlo, Turin, Philadelphia, and Washington, D.C.—**NS/LK/DM**

Velvet Underground, The, seminal late 1960s band whose influence far outstripped their meager record sales; leader Lou Reed later had a long solo career garnering critical respect if not smash-hit status. **Membership:** Lou Reed (actually, Louis Firbank), voc., kybd., gtr. (b. Freeport, Long Island, N.Y., March 2, 1943); John Cale, voc., viola, kybd., bs. (b. Crynant, Wales, Dec. 5, 1940); Sterling Morrison, gtr., bs. (b. East Meadow, Long Island, N.Y., Aug. 29, 1942; d. Poughkeepsie, N.Y., Aug. 30, 1995); Nico (Christa Paffgen), voc. (b. Cologne, West Germany, Oct. 16, 1938; d. Ibiza, Spain, July 18, 1988); Maureen "Mo" Tucker, drm. (b. N.J., 1945). Nico left after the first album and John Cale after the second. He was replaced by Doug Yule.

Lou Reed first played professionally while in his early teens with Long Island bands such as Pasha and The Prophets and The Jades. Studying journalism and creative writing at Syracuse Univ., he worked as a journalist and as a songwriter for Pickwick Records; he met John Cale in 1964. Cale had studied classical viola and piano in London, and his compositions had been broadcast by the BBC when he was eight years old. Cale came to the U.S. in 1963 on a Leonard Bernstein fellowship but abandoned his classical studies to pursue his interest in avant-garde music, joining LaMonte Young's experimental group The Dream Syndicate on electric viola. Reed teamed with Cale and classically trained guitarist Sterling Morrison in bands such as The Ostriches and The Primitives, adding female drummer Maureen Tucker in 1965. Becoming The Velvet Underground—named after a book of the same name—the group enjoyed a residency at Cafe Bizarre in Greenwich Village in the winter of 1966 and immediately sparked controversy for their unorthodox music and stage demeanor.

The Velvet Underground came to the attention of artist Andy Warhol, who was looking for a rock group to add to his multimedia outfit, The Factory. Among the members of The Factory was Nico, who had been a European model since the age of 16. She had moved to N.Y. in 1959 and studied acting with Lee Strasberg before appearing in Warhol's 1966 film *Chelsea Girls*. Augmented by Nico, The Velvet Underground joined Warhol's "total environment" show, The Exploding Plastic Inevitable, which opened in N.Y. and subsequently toured Canada and the U.S.

Signed to MGM/Verve Records, The Velvet Underground recorded their debut album with Andy Warhol as nominal producer. Packaged in a jacket that featured Warhol's famous peelable banana cover, *The Velvet Underground and Nico* comprised music and lyrics the likes of which had not yet appeared in rock music. Propelled by John Cale's innovative musical experimentation and Lou Reed's disarmingly realistic and sinister lyrics, the album included the startling "Heroin," with its screeching, electronic drugged-out crescendo, the sadomasochistic "Venus in Furs," the gritty "I'm Waiting for the Man," "There She Goes Again," and the gentle "Sunday Morning" and "I'll Be Your Mirror," the latter sung by Nico. Garnering virtually no radio airplay, the album failed to sell, yet it was eventually recognized as one of the most influential albums of the 1960s.

Nico subsequently left The Velvet Underground to pursue a solo career and, with the attendant loss of interest by Warhol and the press, the group's *White Light/White Heat* was largely ignored by the public, yet it contained the lurid 17-minute classic "Sister Ray." The group toured to diminishing audiences and Cale left in March 1968. He was replaced by multi-instrumentalist Doug Yule for the subtle *The Velvet Underground* album, which featured the ballad "Pale Blue Eyes." Recordings made for a fourth (unreleased) MGM/Verve album surfaced in 1985 on *VU*. The group switched to Cotillion Records for their final studio album, *Loaded*, which included "Rock and Roll" and "Sweet Jane." Following a summer's residency at Max's Kansas City in N.Y., Reed left The Velvet Underground in August 1970. Morrison left in March 1971, soon followed by Tucker, after which the group was maintained with new members through 1973.

Nico was the first former member of The Velvet Underground to record a solo album, but *Chelsea Girl* failed to sell despite the inclusion of Jackson Browne's "These Days" and Bob Dylan's "I'll Keep It with Mine." *The Marble Index*, for Elektra, featured her own morose songwriting and harmonium playing, and her two subsequent albums, *Desertshore* and *The End*, were produced by John Cale. By the mid-1970s, her career had fallen into disarray, although she continued to record until her death on July 18, 1988, of a cerebral hemorrhage incurred in a bicycle accident on the Spanish island of Ibiza.

In the meantime, John Cale had produced The Stooges' debut album, launched his own recording career on Columbia with *Vintage Violence*, and recorded *Church of Anthrax* with minimalist saxophonist-keyboardist Terry Riley. Cale switched to Reprise for *The Academy in Peril* and the critically acclaimed *Paris 1919*, recorded with Lowell George and Ritchie Hayward of Little Feat. However, by 1974, Cale had returned to England.

By 1972, Lou Reed had signed a solo contract with RCA Records, recording his self-titled debut album in London. His second, *Transformer*, produced in London by David Bowie and Mick Ronson, yielded a major hit with "Walk on the Wild Side" and served as his breakthrough album. However, the *Berlin* album sold poorly, so Reed assembled a touring band to record *Rock 'n' Roll Animal* at N.Y.'s Academy of Music. The album became the best-seller of his career and included "Heroin," "Sweet Jane," and the classic "Rock 'n' Roll." *Sally Can't Dance* also sold quite well despite its air of parody. Reed's career reached its nadir with 1975's *Metal Machine Music*, which consisted of little more than feedback, electronic beeps, and tape hiss.

In 1974, Nico and John Cale performed a concert at London's Rainbow Theatre with synthesizer player Brian Eno (of Roxy Music) and bassist Kevin Ayers and percussionist Robert Wyatt (of Soft Machine) that produced the live album *June 1, 1974*. Cale recorded *Fear* (regarded as one of his finest solo albums) and *Slow Dazzle* with Eno and guitarist Phil Manzanera, another veteran of Roxy Music, and toured Europe in the spring of 1975. He produced Patti Smith's stunning debut *Horses* and The Modern Lovers' debut album; he then switched to A&M Records for *Sabotage Live*.

Following the sedate *Coney Island Baby*, Lou Reed switched to Arista Records for a number of poor-selling mediocre albums, save perhaps *Street Hassle*, through 1980. That year he appeared in a cameo role in Paul Simon's movie *One Trick Pony*. Returning to RCA Records, he recorded more accessible and mature albums for the label beginning with 1982's acclaimed *The Blue Mask*. He helped record the "Sun City" single, toured with the first Amnesty International tour, and performed a number of benefits for the homeless. Reed returned to his anxious style of songwriting with the politicized *New York* album on Sire Records, hailed as his most vital album in 15 years. In 1990, Reed joined John Cale for the first time in 20 years to compose and perform the tribute album to the late Andy Warhol, *Songs for Drella*.

John Cale recorded several albums in the 1980s, most notably *Music for a New Society*, assisting Brian Eno in the recording of 1990's *Wrong Way Up*. Maureen Tucker reemerged with 1981's *Playin' Possum* and later recorded for the independent label 50 Skidillion Watts. Reed recorded the moving yet demanding *Magic and Loss*, inspired by the deaths of two friends, one of whom was songwriter Doc Pomus. In January 1993, Lou Reed performed at President Bill Clinton's inaugural ball, later joining Sterling Morrison, Maureen Tucker, and John Cale as The Velvet Underground for a European tour and *Live MCMXCIII*, recorded at L'Olympia Theatre in Paris. On Aug. 30, 1995, Sterling Morrison died of non-Hodgkins lymphoma in Poughkeepsie, N.Y., at the age of 53. By 1996, the year The Velvet Underground was inducted into the Rock and Roll Hall of Fame, Reed had switched to Warner Brothers for *Set the Twilight Reeling*, recorded entirely in his home studio. Cale recorded the music for the film *I Shot Andy Warhol* and the album *Walking on Locusts* for Hannibal/Rykodisc in 1996, the year Maureen Tucker joined songwriter-guitarist Mark Goodman in Magnet.

DISC.: *The Velvet Underground and Nico* (1967); *White Light/White Heat* (1968); *The Velvet Underground* (1969); *Loaded* (1970); *1969 Live* (1974); *Live at Max's Kansas City* (rec. Aug. 1970; rel. 1972); *The Velvet Underground* (1971); *Archetype* (1974); *Lou Reed with The Velvet Underground* (1973); *VU* (1985); *Another View* (1986); *The Best of the Velvet Underground: Words and Music of Lou Reed* (1989); *Live MCMXCIII* (1993); *Peel Slowly and See* (1995). **NICO:** *Chelsea Girl* (1967); *The Marble Index* (1968); *Desertshore* (1970); *The End* (1974); *Icon* (1996); *Drama of Exile* (1983); *Chelsea Girl Live* (1995); *Do or Die* (1982); *Live Heroes* (1986); *Hanging Gardens* (1988). **JOHN CALE:** *Vintage Violence* (1970); *The Academy in Peril* (1972); *Paris 1919* (1973); *Fear* (1975); *Slow Dazzle* (1975); *Guts* (1977); *Sabotage Live* (1979); *Honi Soit* (1981); *Music for a New Society* (1982); *Caribbean Sunset* (1984); *John Cale Comes Alive* (1984); *Words for the Dying* (1989); *Even Cowgirls Get the Blues* (1991); *Fragments of a Rainy Season* (1992); *Walking on Locusts* (1996); *Eat/Kiss* (1997); *I Shot Andy Warhol* (music from soundtrack; 1996). **JOHN CALE AND TERRY RILEY:** *Church of Anthrax* (1971). **JOHN CALE, KEVIN AYERS, BRIAN ENO AND NICO:** *June 1, 1974* (1974). **JOHN CALE AND BRIAN ENO:** *Wrong Way Up* (1990). **JOHN CALE AND BOB NEUWIRTH:** *Last Day on Earth* (1994). **LOU REED:** *Lou Reed* (1972); *Transformer* (1972); *Berlin* (1973); *Rock 'n' Roll Animal* (1974); *Sally Can't Dance* (1974); *Live* (1975); *Metal Music Machine: The Amine Beta Ring* (1975); *Coney Island Baby* (1976); *Rock and Roll Heart* (1976); *Street Hassle* (1978); *Live...Take No Prisoners* (1978); *The Bells* (1979); *Growing Up in Public* (1980); *Rock 'n' Roll Diary, 1967–80* (1980); *The Blue Mask* (1982); *Legendary Hearts* (1983); *New Sensations* (1984); *Mistrial* (1986); *New York* (1989); *Magic and Loss* (1991); *Set the Twilight Reeling* (1996); *Perfect Night* (1998); *Ecstasy* (2000). **LOU REED AND JOHN CALE:** *Songs for Drella* (1990). **MAUREEN TUCKER:** *Playin' Possum* (1981); *Life in Exile After Abdication* (1989); *I Spent a Week There the Other Night* (1991); *Dogs Under Stress* (1993). **MAGNET:** *Don't Be a Penguin* (1997).

BIBL.: Victor Bockris, Gerard Melanga. *Up-tight: The Velvet Underground Story* (N.Y., 1983); V. Bockris, *Transformer: The Lou Reed Story* (N.Y., 1994); James Young, *Nico: The End* (Woodstock, N.Y., 1993).—**BH**

Venegas de Henestrosa, Luis, Spanish organist and composer; b. Henestrosa, Burgon, c. 1510; d. Toledo, c. 1557. He was in the service of Cardinal Juan Tavera in Toledo (c. 1534–45), and also a priest in Hontova (1543). He publ. the oldest known Spanish book of organ music, *Libro de cifra nueva para tecla, harpa y vihuela* (Alcalá de Henares, 1557; ed. by H. Anglès, Monumentos de la Música Espanola, II, 1944), which contains organ pieces by Palero, P. Vila, Soto, Venegas himself, et al., pieces for vihuela, transcriptions of sacred works by Morales, Josquin, Soto, et al., and solo songs with instrumental accompaniment. The book is written in Spanish organ tablature.—**NS/LK/DM**

Vengerov, Maxim, accomplished Russian violinist; b. Novosibirsk, Aug. 15, 1974. He was a student of Zakhar Bron. After making his formal debut in a recital in Moscow in 1985, he played throughout Russia; soon began to tour abroad in Western Europe. After winning the Flesch competition in London in 1990, he made his U.S. debut as soloist with the N.Y. Phil.; in subsequent years, appeared as a soloist with the principal orchs. of the globe and as a recitalist in the leading music centers. His playing is marked by an extraordinary virtuoso technique.—**NS/LK/DM**

Vengerova, Isabelle (actually, **Isabella Afanasievna**), distinguished Russian-born American pianist and pedagogue; b. Minsk, March 1, 1877; d. N.Y., Feb. 7, 1956. She studied at the Vienna Cons. with Joseph Dachs, and privately with Leschetizky, then with Essipova in St. Petersburg. In 1906 she was appointed an instructor at the St. Petersburg Cons., and in 1910 became a prof. there, remaining on its faculty until 1920. She made tours in Russia and Europe (1920–23); then went to the U.S. in 1923; made her American debut with the Detroit Sym. Orch. (Feb. 8, 1925) in Schumann's Piano Concerto. She became a prof. at the Curtis Inst. of Music in Philadelphia when it was founded in 1924; in 1950 she received an honorary doctor's degree there. Among her piano pupils at the Curtis Inst. were Bernstein, Barber, and Foss. She also taught privately in N.Y. Her nephew was **Nicolas Slonimsky**.

Bibl.: R. Schick, *The V. System of Piano Playing* (University Park, Pa., 1982); J. Rezits, *Beloved Tyranna: The Legend and Legacy of I. V.* (Bloomington, Ind., 1995).—**NS/LK/DM**

Vento, Ivo de, organist and composer; b. 1544; d. Munich, 1575. He was a choirboy at the Bavarian Hofkapelle in Munich (1556–59), then studied organ with Claudio Merulo in Venice (1560); within a few years, he returned to Munich to serve as 3rd organist at the Hofkapelle. After holding the post of choirmaster at the Landshut court (1568–69), he resumed his duties in Munich, where he sometimes served as sole organist. He became best known for his lieder, which influenced such composers as Lechner and Hassler.

Works (all publ. in Munich): **VOCAL:** **Sacred:** *Latinae cantiones, quas vulgo moteta vocant* for 4 Voices (1569); *Latinae cantiones, quas vulgo moteta vocant* for 5 Voices (1570); *Liber motetorum* for 4 Voices (1571); *Mutetae aliquot sacrae* for 4 Voices (1571); also 3 masses for 4 to 6 Voices in MS. **Secular:** *Neue teutsche Liedlein* for 5 Voices (1569); *Neue teutsche Lieder* for 4 to 6 Voices (1570); *Neue teutsche Lieder* for 4 Voices, *samt zweien Dialogen* (1570); *Neue teutsche Lieder* for 3 Voices (1572); *Schöne auserlesene neue teutsche* Lieder for 4 Voices (1572); *Teutsche Lieder* for 5 Voices, *samt einem Dialogo* for 8 Voices (1573); *5 motetae, 2 madrigalia, (2) gallicae cantiones...et 4 germanicae* for 5 and 8 to 9 Voices (1575); other madrigals in contemporary collections.

Bibl.: K. Huber, *I. d.V. (ca. 1540–1575)* (Lindenberg im Allgäu, 1918).—**NS/LK/DM**

Ventures, The, enormously successful instrumental group. **Membership:** Bob Bogle, gtr., bs. (b. Wagoner, Okla., Jan. 16, 1936); Don Wilson, gtr. (b. Tacoma, Wash., Feb. 10, 1933); Noke Edwards, bs. (b. Noel Floyd Edwards, Lahoma, Okla., May 9, 1939); Skip Moore, drm.; Howie Johnson, drm. (b. 1938; d. 1988); Gerry McGee, gtr. (b. Eunice, La., Nov. 17); Mel Taylor, drm. (b. Brooklyn, N.Y., Sept. 24, 1933; d. Aug. 11, 1996); Leon Taylor, drm. (b. Johnson City, Tenn., Sept. 23, 1955).

Don Wilson sold a used car to Bob Bogle, who was in construction. Wilson asked Bogle for a job, and the two started working construction jobs together. As they got to know each other better, they both evinced a love of the guitar. They bought a couple of pawned acoustics and started playing together, eventually graduating to pawned electric guitars and the odd gig around the Tacoma area. They played as The Impacts and The Versatones with various rhythm sections before hooking up with Nokie Edwards and Skip Moore, at which point they changed their name to The Ventures. Their first, self-released single was "Cookies and Coke."

One of the pieces in their repertoire was a cover of "Walk, Don't Run," based on a version from a Chet Atkins record. Their take was twangy, with a heavy beat. Initially released on their own label, one of the local news shows started using it for theme music. Dolton Records picked up the single and it rose to #2 in the summer of 1960, presaging surf music. They followed that up with "Perfida," another rocked-out version of a jazz tune that they rode to #15 that fall.

As well as the singles did, The Ventures debut album rose to #11. While they would have half a dozen Top 40 singles through the 1960s (their final being the theme from "Hawaii Five–0," which rose to #4 in the spring of 1969), during the same period they charted 17 albums, three of which went gold. They manage to balance their distinctive sound and their versatility in genres from "The Twist" to disco, from country to reggae. This has kept them a popular live attraction to this day and allows them to maintain an impressive recording career in Europe and especially in Japan, mostly because instrumentals don't require translation. Although they group has gone through numerous personnel changes, the core of Wilson and Bogle continues to power the quartet.

Disc.: *The Ventures* (1961), *Another Smash!!!* (1961); *The Colorful Ventures* (1961); *Dance! (Twist with the Ventures)* (1962); *Dance with the Ventures (The Ventures Twist...)* (1962); *The Ventures' Beach Party (Mashed Potatoes...)* (1962); *Going to the Ventures' Dance Party!* (1962); *The Ventures Play Telstar, The Lonely Bull* (1962); *Surfing* (1963); *Bobby Vee Meets the Ventures* (1963); *I Walk the Line (Ventures Play the Country...)* (1963); *Let's Go!*

(1963); *Ventures in Space* (1963); *The Fabulous Ventures* (1964); *Walk Don't Run, Vol. 2* (1964); *The Ventures Knock Me Out!* (1965); *Play Guitar with the Ventures, Vols. 2–4* (1965); *The Ventures in Japan, Vols. 1–2* (live; 1965); *The Ventures on Stage* (live; 1965); *Ventures a Go-Go* (1965); *The Ventures' Christmas Album* (1965); *Where the Action Is!* (1966); *All About the Ventures* (1966); *"Batman" Theme (The Ventures)* (1966); *Go with the Ventures!* (1966); *Wild Things!* (1966); *Guitar Freakout* (1967); *The Ventures on Stage Encore* (live; 1967); *Pops in Japan* (1967); *Super Psychedelics (Changing Times)* (1967); *$1,000,000 Weekend* (1967); *Flights of Fantasy* (1968); *The Ventures Live Again* (1968); *Pops in Japan, Vol. 2* (1968); *The Horse (The Ventures on the Scene)* (1968); *The Ventures in Tokyo '68* (live; 1968); *Underground Fire* (1968); *Hawaii Five-O* (1969); *Swamp Rock* (1969); *The Ventures' 10th Anniversary Album One Way* (1970); *Live! The Ventures* (1970); *Golden Pops* (1970); *New Testament* (1971); *Theme from "Shaft"* (1971); *Pops in Japan '71* (live; 1971); *The Ventures* (1971); *The Ventures on Stage '71* [live; 1971); *Joy! The Ventures Play the Classics* (1972); *Rock & Roll Forever* (1972); *The Ventures on Stage '72* (live; 1972); *Pops in Japan '73* (live; 1973); *The Ventures on Stage '73* (live; 1973); *Only Hits One Way* (1973); *The Jim Croce Songbook* (1974); *The Ventures on Stage '74* (live; 1974); *The Ventures Special '74 on Japanese Tour* (live; 1974); *The Ventures on Stage '75* (live; 1975); *Rocky Road* (1976); *Hollywood* (1976); *Sunflower '76* (1976); *The Ventures on Stage '76* (live; 1976); *TV Themes* (1977); *Live in Japan '77* (1977); *Latin Album* (1979); *The Ventures Original Four* (1980); *Super Live '80* (1980); *Chameleon* (1980); *60's Pops* (1981); *Pops in Japan '81* (1981); *St. Louis Memory* (1982); *The Last Album on Liberty* (1982); *The Ventures Today* (1983); *Live in Japan '65* (1995); *Wild Again* (1997); *New Depths* (1998).—**BH**

Venuti, Joe (Giuseppe), influential and highly talented jazz violinist; b. Philadelphia, Pa., Sept. 16, 1903 (or Lecco, near Milan Italy, April 4, 1898); d. Seattle, Wash., Aug. 14, 1978. He was cagey about his date and place of birth. Raised in Philadelphia, he received a thorough classical training on the violin, but after meeting guitarist Eddie Lang, he turned to popular music. Together they began working in Bert Estlow's Quintet in Atlantic City (1921); subsequently they played in the Hotel Knickerbocker Hotel Orch. Venuti played briefly with Red Nichols, then began directing the Book-Cadillac Hotel Orch. for Jean Goldkette (late 1924). Moved to N.Y. and took part in countless recording sessions with various leaders and waxed many sides in small groups with Eddie Lang, beginning in 1926. He toured with Jean Goldkette, with Roger Wolfe Kahn (October 1925 until June 1926); played for many Broadway shows; worked in the short-lived Adrian Rollini Big Band (September 1927). Throughout the 1920s regularly co-led band with Ed Lang in N.Y. and other East coast clubs. Joined Paul Whiteman in May 1929, made remarkable recovery from injuries sustained in car crash (summer 1929), returned to Whiteman from October 1929 until May 1930. Briefly with Smith Ballew in autumn of 1930, then freelance studio and session work in N.Y., again with Roger Wolfe Kahn in spring of 1932.

When Lang died suddenly in 1933, Venuti was at first inconsolable, but soon found his form again. He brought his own small group to Britain in the summer of 1934, and during this visit recorded in London on violin and guitar. From 1935 regularly led own band, continued touring and residencies until the early 1940s. However, with World War II breaking out, most of Venuti's band members were drafted, and he had to end the band in 1943. He moved to Calif. and early in 1944 became an MGM studio musician. He led his own band on the West Coast during the late 1940s, then recommenced widespread touring, occasionally working as a soloist. In the 1950s and 1960s, Venuti continued to work around the country in small groups, often playing an amplified violin; however, he was less active in the early to mid-1960s due to problems with alcoholism. He made a triumphant appearance at the 1968 Newport Jazz Festival leading to a return to active recording and performing through the 1970s. Although he was seriously ill in April 1970, he soon recovered and toured extensively in the U.S. and Europe, recording with Marian McPartland, Zoot Sims, Earl Hines, and many others. He was honored by the Newport Hall of Fame at the 1975 Newport Jazz Festival. He continued to perform nearly up to his death, despite the fact that he was suffering from cancer through the second half of the 1970s.

Second only to Stephane Grappelli (whom Venuti inspired), Venuti was the greatest jazz violinist of his day. His recordings with Eddie Lang inspired Django Reinhardt and Stephane Grappelli to form their quintet in the mid-1930s. Venuti had a bluesier tone than Grappelli and was more comfortable with high-speed pyrotechnics than with the kind of ballads the French player preferred. He also employed many vaudeville "tricks" in his performances, including loosening the bow and placing the violin between the hair and the stick, playing behind his head, etc. Venuti was also a notorious practical joker, his jokes having an element of nastiness to them: among his famous exploits were pushing a piano out of a hotel window, pouring jelly into Bix Beiderbecke's bathwater, putting flour in the tub during the filming of Paul Whiteman's *King of Jazz*, playing a horse's member with his bow, and inviting dozens of bassists to meet on a street corner for a gig that didn't exist.

DISC.: *Stringin' the Blues* (1927); *Fiddlesticks* (1931); *Pretty Trix* (1934); *Mad Fiddler from Philly* (1952); *Joe Venuti and Eddie Lang* (1955); *With Tommy Dorsey, Jimmy Dorsey* (1955); *Dutch Swing College Band Meets* (1971); *Joe Venuti in Milan* (1971); *Joe and Zoot* (1973); *Blue Four* (1974); *Joe Venuti and Zoot Sims* (1975); *'S Wonderful: 4 Giants of Swing* (1976); *Venuti-Barnes Live* (1976); *Joe in Chicago* (1978). Earl Hines: *Hot Sonatas* (1975).
—JC/MM/NS

Veprik, Alexander (Moiseievich), Russian composer and musicologist; b. Balta, near Odessa, June 23, 1899; d. Moscow, Oct. 13, 1958. While still a young boy he went to Leipzig, where he took piano lessons with Karl Wendling; then pursued training in composition with Zhitomirsky at the Petrograd Cons. (1918–21) and with Miaskovsky at the Moscow Cons. (1921–23), where he subsequently taught orchestration (1923–43). He was associated with the Jewish cultural movement in Russia, and composed several works in the traditional ethnic manner of Jewish cantillations. In his harmonic and formal treatment, he followed the "orientalistic" tradition of the Russian national school.

WORKS: DRAMATIC: Opera: *Toktogul*, on Kirghiz

motifs (1938–39; Frunze, 1940); *Toktogul* (1949; in collaboration with A. Maldibaiev). **Other**: Film music. **ORCH.**: 2 syms. (1931, 1938); *Traurnaya pesnya* (Sad Song; 1932); *Pesnya likovaniya* (Peace Song; 1935); *Pastorale* (1946; rev. 1958); *2 poems* (1957); *Improvizatsiya* (1958). **CHAMBER**: *Rhapsody* for Viola and Piano (1926); piano pieces, including 3 sonatas (1922, 1924, 1928). **VOCAL**: 2 cantatas: *Proklyatiye fashizmu* (Fascism Be Cursed; 1944) and *Narod-geroy* (The People-The Hero; 1955); songs.

WRITINGS: *O metodakh prepodavaniya instrumentovki: K voprosu o klassovoy obuslovlennosti orkestrovovo pisma* (Methods of Instrument Teaching: On the Question of the Classification of Orchestral Writing; Moscow, 1931); *Traktovka instrumenov orkestra* (The Treatment of Orchestral Instruments; Moscow, 1948; 2nd ed., 1961).

BIBL.: V. Bogdanov-Berezovsky, *A.M. V.* (Moscow and Leningrad, 1964).—**NS/LK/DM**

Veracini, Antonio, esteemed Italian violinist, teacher, and composer, uncle of **Francesco Maria Veracini;** b. Florence, Jan. 17, 1659; d. there, Oct. 26, 1733. His father, Francesco di Niccolo, was a gifted violinist, and he most likely received his initial training from him and appeared with him as a youth. Antonio Veracini was in the service of Grand Duchess Vittoria of Tuscany (1682–94). From 1700 he served as maestro di cappella at the church of S. Michele and also was active at other Florentine churches; in 1708 he took over his father's music school, where he was mentor to his nephew. His extant works are (10) *Sonate a tre* for 2 Violins, Violone or Archlute, and Basso Continuo, op.1 (Florence, 1692), (10) *Sonate da camera* for Violin, op.2 (Modena, c. 1694), and (10) *Sonate da camera a due* for Violin, Violone or Archlute, and Basso Continuo, op.3 (Modena, 1696). —**NS/LK/DM**

Veracini, Francesco Maria, noted Italian violinist and composer, nephew of **Antonio Veracini;** b. Florence, Feb. 1, 1690; d. there, Oct. 31, 1768. He studied violin with his uncle, with whom he appeared in concerts in Florence, and also received instruction from Giovanni Maria Casini and Francesco Feroci, and from G.A. Bernabei in Germany (1715). In 1711 he went to Venice, where he appeared as a soloist at the Christmas masses at San Marco; in 1714 he gave a series of benefit concerts in London, and in 1716 entered the private service of the Elector of Saxony; in 1717 he went to Dresden and entered the court service. In 1723 he returned to Florence, where he was active as a performer and composer of sacred works; he also gave private concerts. In 1733 he returned to London, where he played for the Opera of the Nobility, a rival to Handel's opera company; he also composed operas during his London years. In 1745 he returned to Italy, where from 1755 until his death he was maestro di cappella for the Vallambrosian fathers at the church of S. Pancrazio in Florence; he also held that position for the Teatini fathers at the church of S. Michele agl'Antinori there (from 1758). He acquired a reputation as an eccentric, and some considered him mad. Nonetheless he was esteemed as a violinist and composer.

WORKS: DRAMATIC: Opera (all 1st perf. in London): *Adriano in Siria* (Nov. 26, 1735); *La clemenza di Tito* (April 12, 1737); *Partenio* (March 14, 1738); *Rosalinda* (Jan. 31, 1744). **INSTRUMENTAL:** (12) *Sonate* for Violin or Recorder and Basso Continuo (1716; ed. by W. Kolneder, Leipzig, 1959–61); (12) *Sonate* for Violin and Basso Continuo, op.1 (Dresden, 1721; ed. by W. Kolneder, Leipzig, 1958–59); (12) *Sonate accademiche* for Violin and Basso Continuo, op.2 (London and Florence, 1744; ed. by F. Bar, Kassel, 1959–); (12) *Dissertazioni...sopra l'opera quinta del Corelli* (n.d.; ed. by W. Kolneder, Mainz, 1961); 15 sonatas in MS; 3 concertos in contemporary collections; 2 concertos and an overture in MS. **VOCAL:** 8 oratorios, all lost; a few sacred works, all of which are lost; some cantatas and songs.

BIBL.: H. Smith, *F.M. V.'s Il trionfo della pratica musicale* (diss., Ind. Univ., 1963); M. Clarke, *The Violin Sonatas of F.M. V.: Some Aspects of Italian Late Baroque Instrumental Style Exemplified* (diss., Univ. of N.C., 1967); J. Hill, *The Life and Works of F.M. V.* (diss., Harvard Univ., 1972; rev., Ann Arbor, 1979). —**NS/LK/DM**

Verbesselt, August, Belgian flutist and composer; b. Klein-Willebroek, Oct. 22, 1919. He studied at the Antwerp Cons. From 1942 he was flutist in the orch. of the Antwerp Royal Flemish Opera.

WORKS: ORCH.: Flute Concerto (1952); *Diagrams* for Chamber Orch. (1972); *Universum* for 2 Orchs. and Tape (1975); *Strukturen* (1981); Clarinet Concerto (1983); Piano Concerto (1986); Oboe Concerto (1986); Concerto for Clarinet Quartet and Chamber Orch. (1986); *Pax* for Chamber Orch. (1986); *Sluierdans* for Harmony Orch. (1988); *Oase* for Chamber Orch. (1988); Chamber Concerto for Bass Clarinet and Strings (1988); ballet music. **CHAMBER:** *Hexatone-Synthese* for Flute, Oboe, Clarinet, Cello, and Harp (1964); *3 Monologhi* for Flute (1981); *Tre movimenti* for Clarinet (1982); *Conversazione* for Oboe and Piano (1982); *Introduzione ed Allegro* for Saxophone and Piano (1982); *Iberia* for Flute and Guitar (1982); *12 Concert Studies* for Flute (1984); *Due dialoghi* for Bassoon and Piano (1984); *Iskato*, trio for Oboe, Clarinet, and Bassoon (1985); 2 clarinet quartets (both 1985); *Per flauto* for Flute (1986); *Per violino* for Violin (1987); *Metropolis* for Flute and Piano (1987). **VOCAL:** Various pieces. —**NS/LK/DM**

Vercoe, Barry, New Zealand-born American composer and computer-music specialist; b. Wellington, July 24, 1937. He was educated at the Univ. of Auckland (Mus.B. in composition, 1959; B.A. in mathematics, 1962) and the Univ. of Mich. (A.Mus.D., 1968). After completing postdoctoral research at Princeton Univ. (1968–70), he served as U.S. adviser to the UNESCO Joint European Studies Committee on Technology and Arts (1977–78); he also was resident composer/researcher at IRCAM (1983–84), where he developed "cpmusic," a system for synchronizing computer-processed sound with live instruments by computer tracking of performers in real time. He was a visiting lecturer at the Yale Univ. School of Music (1970–71) then joined the faculty at the Mass. Inst. of Technology, first as an assoc. prof. in its dept. of humanities (1971–85) and then as a prof. in its dept. of media arts and sciences (from 1985). His work in psychoacoustic and computer music research has been supported by sizable grants from the National Science Foundation (1976, 1987–89), the NEA (1978–82), and the John D. and Catherine T. MacArthur Foundation (1981), among others. He held a

Guggenheim fellowship (1982–83). His developments in the field of computer audio systems include "Music–11" (1976; in 1984, rewritten to "Csound"), for fast digital processing of audio on PDP–11 minicomputers, and "MUSIC 360" (1969), a programming language used for processing sound on large IBM machines. He is married to **Elizabeth Vercoe**.

WORKS: *Digressions* for Band, 2 Choruses, Computer, and Orch. (1968); *Synthesism* for Computer (1970); *Synapse I* for Viola and Computer (1976) and *II* for Flute and 4X Processor (1984). **—NS/LK/DM**

Vercoe, Elizabeth, American composer; b. Washington, D.C., April 23, 1941. She was educated at Wellesley Coll. (B.A., 1962), the Univ. of Mich. (M.M., 1963), and Boston Univ. (D.M.A., 1978). She taught at Westminster Choir Coll. in Princeton, N.J. (1969–71), and Framingham (Mass.) State Coll. (1973–74). She was composer-in-residence at the Cite Internationale des Arts in Paris and the Charles Ives Center for American Music; in 1988 she participated in the U.S./U.S.S.R. Young Composers' Exchange. She wrote a variety of articles actively promoting the cause of women's music; was a founding member of the Mass. Chapter of American Women Composers (1984) and a board member of the International League of Women Composers; co-directed the Women's Music Festival/85 in Boston. She is married to **Barry Vercoe**.

WORKS: *Children's Caprice* for Orch. (1963); *Herstory I* for Soprano, Piano, and Vibraphone, after American women poets (1975), *II: 13 Japanese Lyrics* for Soprano, Piano, and Percussion, after medieval Japanese women poets (1979), and *III: Jehanne de Lorraine*, staged monodrama for Voice and Piano, after Villon, Shaw, Twain et al. (1986); Violin Concerto (1977); *Irreveries from Sappho* for Women's Chorus and Piano (1981); *Fantavia* for Flute and Percussion (1982); *Suite française* for Violin (1983); *Despite our Differences No. 1* for Violin, Cello, and Piano (1984) and *No. 2* for Piano and Chamber Orch. (1988); *9 Epigrams from Poor Richard* for Voice and Tape (1986).**—NS/LK/DM**

Verdelot, Philippe, noted French composer; b. Verdelot, Les Loges, Seine-et-Marne, c. 1470–80; d. before 1552. He made his way to northern Italy, and by 1522 he was in Florence, where he served as maestro di cappella at the Baptisterium S. Giovanni (1523–25) and at the Cathedral (1523–27); he also was in Rome (1523–24). With the siege of Florence (1529–30), Verdelot disappeared from the pages of history. His extant works include two masses, one known as *Philomena*, a *Magnificat sexti toni*, some 58 motets, numerous madrigals, including some publ. in *Madrigali a cinque, libro primo* (Venice, c. 1535), and four chansons. His madrigals and motets were widely disseminated in the 16th century. A number of works attributed to him are of doubtful authenticity. The *Opera omnia*, ed. by A.-M. Bragard in Corpus Mensurabilis Musicae, began publication in 1966.

BIBL.: D. Hersh, *P. V. and the Early Madrigal* (diss., Univ. of Calif., Berkeley, 1963); A.-M. Bragard, *Étude bio-bibliographique sur P. V., musicien français de la Renaissance* (Brussels, 1964); N. Böker-Heil, *Die Motetten von P. V.* (Cologne, 1967).**—NS/LK/DM**

Verdi, Giuseppe (Fortunino Francesco), great Italian opera composer whose genius for dramatic, lyric, and tragic stage music has made him the perennial favorite of a multitude of opera enthusiasts; b. Le Roncole, near Busseto, Duchy of Parma, Oct. 9, 1813; d. Milan, Jan. 27, 1901. His father kept a tavern, and street singing gave Verdi his early appreciation of music produced by natural means. Pietro Baistrocchi, a magister parvulorum and a church organist, noticed his love of musical sound and took him on as a pupil. When Baistrocchi died, Verdi, still a small child, took over some of his duties at the keyboard. His father sent him to Busseto for further musical training; there he began his academic studies and also took music lessons with Ferdinando Provesi, the director of the municipal music school.

At the age of 18 Verdi became a resident in the home of Antonio Barezzi, a local merchant and patron of music; Barezzi supplied him with enough funds so that he could go to Milan for serious study. Surprisingly enough, in view of Verdi's future greatness, he failed to pass an entrance examination to the Milan Cons.; the registrar, Francesco Basili, reported that Verdi's piano technique was inadequate and that in composition he lacked technical knowledge. Verdi then turned to Vincenzo Lavigna, an excellent musician, for private lessons, and worked industriously to master counterpoint, canon, and fugue. In 1834 he applied for the post of maestro di musica in Busseto, and after passing his examination received the desired appointment. On May 4, 1836, he married a daughter of his patron Barezzi; it was a love marriage, but tragedy intervened when their two infant children died, and his wife succumbed on June 18, 1840. Verdi deeply mourned, but he found solace in music.

In 1838 Verdi completed his first opera, *Oberto, conte di San Bonifacio*. In 1839 he moved to Milan. He submitted the score of *Oberto* to the directorship of La Scala; it was accepted for a performance, which took place on Nov. 17, 1839, with satisfactory success. He was now under contract to write more operas for that renowned theater. His comic opera *Un giorno di regno* was performed at La Scala in 1840, but it did not succeed at pleasing the public. Somewhat downhearted at this reverse, Verdi began composition of an opera, *Nabucodonosor*, on the biblical subject (the title was later abbreviated to *Nabucco*). It was staged at La Scala on March 9, 1842, scoring considerable success. Giuseppina Strepponi created the leading female role of Abigaille. *Nabucco* was followed by another successful opera on a historic subject, *I Lombardi alla prima Crociata*, produced at La Scala on Feb. 11, 1843. The next opera was *Ernani*, after Victor Hugo's drama on the life of a revolutionary outlaw; the subject suited the rise of national spirit, and its production in Venice on March 9, 1844, won great acclaim. Not so popular were Verdi's succeeding operas, *I due Foscari* (1844), *Giovanna d'Arco* (1845), *Alzira* (1845), and *Attila* (1846). On March 14, 1847, Verdi produced his first Shakespearean opera, *Macbeth*, in Florence. In the same year he received a commission to write an opera for London; the result was *I Masnadieri*, based on Schiller's drama *Die Räuber*. It was produced at Her Majesty's Theatre in London on July 22, 1847, with

Jenny Lind taking the leading female role. A commission from Paris followed; for it Verdi revised his opera *I Lombardi alla prima Crociata* in a French version, renamed *Jérusalem*; it was produced at the Paris Opéra on Nov. 26, 1847; the Italian production followed at La Scala on Dec. 26, 1850. This was one of the several operas by him and other Italian composers where mistaken identity was the chief dramatic device propelling the action.

During his stay in Paris for the performance of *Jérusalem*, Verdi renewed his acquaintance with Giuseppina Strepponi; after several years of cohabitation, their union was legalized in a private ceremony in Savoy on Aug. 29, 1859. In 1848 he produced his opera *Il Corsaro*, after Byron's poem *The Corsair*. There followed *La battaglia di Legnano*, celebrating the defeat of the armies of Barbarossa by the Lombards in 1176. Its premiere took place in Rome on Jan. 27, 1849, but Verdi was forced to change names and places so as not to offend the central European powers that dominated Italy. The subsequent operas *Luisa Miller* (1849), after Schiller's drama *Kabale und Liebe*, and *Stiffelio* (1850) were not successful.

Verdi's great triumph came in 1851 with the production of *Rigoletto*, fashioned after Victor Hugo's drama *Le Roi s'amuse*; it was performed for the first time at the Teatro La Fenice in Venice on March 11, 1851, and brought Verdi lasting fame; it entered the repertoire of every opera house around the globe. The aria of the libidinous Duke, *La donna è mobile*, became one of the most popular operatic tunes sung, or ground on the barrel organ, throughout Europe. This success was followed by an even greater acclaim with the production in 1853 of *Il Trovatore* (Rome, Jan. 19, 1853) and *La Traviata* (Venice, March 6, 1853); both captivated world audiences without diminution of their melodramatic effect on succeeding generations in Europe and America, and this despite the absurdity of the action represented on the stage. *Il Trovatore* resorts to the common device of unrecognized identities of close relatives, while *La Traviata* strains credulity when the eponymous soprano sings enchantingly and long despite her struggle with terminal consumption. The character of Traviata was based on the story of a real person, as depicted in the drama *La Dame aux camélias* by Alexandre Dumas fils. The Italian title is untranslatable, *Traviata* being the feminine passive voice of the verb meaning "to lead astray," and it would have to be rendered, in English, by the construction "a woman who has been led astray."

Another commission coming from Paris resulted in Verdi's first French opera, *Les Vêpres siciliennes*, after a libretto by Scribe to Donizetti's unfinished opera *Le Duc d'Albe*; the action deals with the medieval slaughter of the French occupation army in Sicily by local patriots. Despite the offensiveness of the subject to French patriots, the opera was given successfully in Paris on June 13, 1855. His next opera, *Simone Boccanegra*, was produced at the Teatro La Fenice in Venice on March 12, 1857. This was followed by *Un ballo in maschera*, which made history. The original libretto was written by Scribe for Auber's opera *Gustave III*, dealing with the assassination of King Gustave III of Sweden in 1792. But the censors would not have regicide shown on the stage, and Verdi was compelled to transfer the scene of action from Sweden to Mass. Ridiculous as it was, Gustave III became Governor Riccardo of Boston; the opera was produced in this politically sterilized version in Rome on Feb. 17, 1859. Attempts were made later to restore the original libretto and to return the action to Sweden, but audiences resented the change of the familiar version.

Unexpectedly, Verdi became a factor in the political struggle for the independence of Italy; the symbol of the nationalist movement was the name of Vittorio Emanuele, the future king of Italy. Demonstrators painted the name of Verdi in capital letters, separated by punctuation, on fences and walls of Italian towns (V.E.R.D.I., the initials of Vittorio Emanuele, Re D'Italia), and the cry "Viva Verdi!" became "Viva Vittorio Emanuele Re D'Italia!"

In 1861 he received a commission to write an opera for the Imperial Opera of St. Petersburg, Russia; he selected the mystic subject *La forza del destino*. The premiere took place in St. Petersburg on Nov. 10, 1862, and Verdi made a special trip to attend. He then wrote an opera to a French text, *Don Carlos*, after Schiller's famous drama. It was first heard at the Paris Opéra on March 11, 1867, with numerous cuts; they were not restored in the score until a century had elapsed after the initial production. In June 1870 he received a contract to write a new work for the opera in Cairo, Egypt, where *Rigoletto* had already been performed a year before. The terms were most advantageous, with a guarantee of 150,000 francs for the Egyptian rights alone. The opera, based on life in ancient Egypt, was *Aida*; the original libretto was in French; Antonio Ghislanzoni prepared the Italian text. It had its premiere in Cairo on Christmas Eve of 1871, with great éclat. A special boat was equipped to carry officials and journalists from Italy to Cairo for the occasion, but Verdi stubbornly refused to join the caravan despite persuasion by a number of influential Italian musicians and statesmen; he declared that a composer's job was to supply the music, not to attend performances. The success of *Aida* exceeded all expectations; the production was hailed as a world event, and the work itself became one of the most famous in opera history.

After Rossini's death, in 1868, Verdi conceived the idea of honoring his memory by a collective composition of a Requiem, to which several Italian composers would contribute a movement each, Verdi reserving the last section, *Libera me*, for himself. He completed the score in 1869, but it was never performed in its original form. The death of the famous Italian poet Alessandro Manzoni in 1873 led him to write his great *Messa da Requiem*, which became known simply as the "Manzoni" Requiem, and he incorporated in it the section originally composed for Rossini. The *Messa da Requiem* received its premiere on the first anniversary of Manzoni's death, on May 22, 1874, in Milan. There was some criticism of the Requiem as being too operatic for a religious work, but it remained in musical annals as a masterpiece. After a lapse of some 13 years of rural retirement, Verdi turned once more to Shakespeare; the result this time was *Otello*; the libretto was by Arrigo

Boito, a master poet who rendered Shakespeare's lines into Italian with extraordinary felicity. It received its premiere at La Scala on Feb. 5, 1887. Verdi was 79 years old when he wrote yet another Shakespearean opera, *Falstaff*, also to a libretto by Boito; in his libretto Boito used materials from *The Merry Wives of Windsor* and *Henry IV. Falstaff* was performed for the first time at La Scala on Feb. 9, 1893. The score reveals Verdi's genius for subtle comedy coupled with melodic invention of the highest order. His last composition was a group of sacred choruses, an *Ave Maria, Laudi alla Vergine Maria, Stabat Mater*, and *Te Deum*, publ. in 1898 as *4 pezzi sacri;* in the *Ave Maria*, Verdi made use of the so-called scala enigmatica (C, D, E, F, G, A, B, and C).

Innumerable honors were bestowed upon Verdi. In 1864 he was elected to membership in the Académie des Beaux Arts in Paris, where he filled the vacancy made by the death of Meyerbeer. In 1875 he was nominated a senator to the Italian Parliament. Following the premiere of *Falstaff*, the King of Italy wished to make him "Marchese di Busseto," but he declined the honor. After the death of his 2nd wife, on Nov. 14, 1897, he founded in Milan the Casa di Riposo per Musicisti, a home for aged musicians; for its maintenance, he set aside 2,500,000 lire. On Jan. 21, 1901, Verdi suffered an apoplectic attack; he died six days later at the age of 87.

Historic evaluation of Verdi's music changed several times after his death. The musical atmosphere was heavily Wagnerian; admiration for Wagner produced a denigration of Verdi as a purveyor of "barrel-organ" music. Then the winds of musical opinion reversed their direction; sophisticated modern composers, music historians, and academic theoreticians discovered unexpected attractions in the flowing Verdian melodies, easily modulating harmonies, and stimulating symmetric rhythms; a theory was even advanced that the appeal of Verdi's music lies in its adaptability to modernistic elaboration and contrapuntal variegations. By natural transvaluation of opposites, Wagnerianism went into eclipse after it reached the limit of complexity. The slogan "Viva Verdi!" assumed, paradoxically, an aesthetic meaning. Scholarly research into Verdi's biography greatly increased. The Istituto di Studi Verdiani was founded in Parma in 1959. An American Inst. for Verdi Studies was founded in 1976 with its archive at N.Y.U.

WORKS: DRAMATIC: Opera: In the literature on Verdi, mention is sometimes made of two early operatic attempts, *Lord Hamilton* and *Rocester*; however, nothing definitive has ever been established concerning these two works. The accepted list of his operas is as follows: *Oberto, conte di San Bonifacio* (1837–38; La Scala, Milan, Nov. 17, 1839; libretto rev. by Graffigna and given as *I Bonifazi ed i Salinguerra* in Venice in 1842); *Un giorno di regno* (later known as *Il finto Stanislao*), melodramma giocoso (La Scala, Milan, Sept. 5, 1840); *Nabucodonosor* (later known as *Nabucco*), dramma lirico (1841; La Scala, Milan, March 9, 1842); *I Lombardi alla prima Crociata*, dramma lirico (1842; La Scala, Milan, Feb. 11, 1843; rev. version, with a French libretto by Royer and Vaëz, given as *Jérusalem* at the Paris Opéra, Nov. 26, 1847); *Ernani*, dramma lirico (1843; Teatro La Fenice, Venice, March 9, 1844); *I due Foscari*, tragedia lirica (Teatro Argentina, Rome, Nov. 3, 1844); *Giovanna d'Arco*, dramma lirico (1844; La Scala, Milan, Feb. 15, 1845); *Alzira*, tragedia lirica (Teatro San Carlo, Naples, Aug. 12, 1845); *Attila*, dramma lirico (1845–46; Teatro La Fenice, Venice, March 17, 1846); *Macbeth* (1846–47; Teatro alla Pergola, Florence, March 14, 1847; rev. version, with a French tr. by Nuittier and Beaumont of the Italian libretto, Théâtre-Lyrique, Paris, April 21, 1865); *I Masnadieri* (1846–47; Her Majesty's Theatre, London, July 22, 1847); *Il Corsaro* (1847–48; Teatro Grande, Trieste, Oct. 25, 1848); *La battaglia di Legnano*, tragedia lirica (1848; Teatro Argentina, Rome, Jan. 27, 1849); *Luisa Miller*, melodramma tragico (Teatro San Carlo, Naples, Dec. 8, 1849); *Stiffelio* (Teatro Grande, Trieste, Nov. 16, 1850; later rev. as *Aroldo*); *Rigoletto*, melodramma (1850–51; Teatro La Fenice, Venice, March 11, 1851); *Il Trovatore*, dramma (1851–52; Teatro Apollo, Rome, Jan. 19, 1853; rev. 1857); *La Traviata* (Teatro La Fenice, Venice, March 6, 1853); *Les Vêpres siciliennes* (1854; Opéra, Paris, June 13, 1855); *Simone Boccanegra* (1856–57; Teatro La Fenice, Venice, March 12, 1857; rev. 1880–81; La Scala, Milan, March 24, 1881); *Aroldo* (revision of *Stiffelio;* 1856–57; Teatro Nuovo, Rimini, Aug. 16, 1857); *Un ballo in maschera*, melodramma (1857–58; Teatro Apollo, Rome, Feb. 17, 1859); *La forza del destino* (1861; Imperial Theater, St. Petersburg, Nov. 10, 1862; rev. version, La Scala, Milan, Feb. 27, 1869); *Don Carlos* (1866; Opéra, Paris, March 11, 1867; rev. version, 1883–84, with Italian libretto by Lauzières and Zanardini, La Scala, Milan, Jan. 10, 1884); *Aida* (1870–71; Opera House, Cairo, Dec. 24, 1871); *Otello*, dramma lirico (1884–86; La Scala, Milan, Feb. 5, 1887); *Falstaff*, commedia lirica (1889–93; La Scala, Milan, Feb. 9, 1893). **OTHER:** *Inno popolare* for Men's Voices and Piano (1848); *Inno delle Nazioni* for Solo Voice, Chorus, and Orch. (London, May 24, 1862; composed for the London Exhibition); *Libera me* for Soprano, Chorus, and Orch. (1868–69; composed for the *Rossini Requiem*, and later incorporated in the *Messa da Requiem*); String Quartet in E minor (1873); *Messa da Requiem* for Soprano, Alto, Tenor, Bass, Chorus, and Orch., the "Manzoni" Requiem (1873–74; San Marco, Milan, May 22, 1874); *Ave Maria* for Soprano and Strings (1880); *Pater noster* for 5-part Chorus (1880); *4 pezzi sacri: Ave Maria* for Chorus (1888–89), *Stabat Mater* for Chorus and Orch. (1895–97), *Laudi alla Vergine Maria* for Women's Chorus (1888–89), and *Te Deum* for Soprano, Double Chorus, and Orch. (1895–97). **SONGS:** *6 romanze* (1838; *Non t'accostare all'urna; More, Elisa, lo stanco poeta; In solitaria stanza; Nell'orro di notte oscura; Perduta ho la pace; Deh, pietoso, oh Addolorata*); *Notturno* for Soprano, Tenor, Bass, and Piano, with Flute obbligato (1839); *L'Esule* (1839); *La seduzione* (1839); *Chi i bei di m'adduce ancora* (1842); *6 romanze* (1845; *Il tramonto* [2 versions]; *La Zingara; Ad una stella; Lo Spazzacamino; Il mistero; Brindisi*); *Il Poveretto* (1847); *Suona la tromba* (1848); *L'Abandonnée* (1849); *Barcarola* (1850); *La preghiera del poeta* (1858); *Il brigidino* (1863); *Tu dici che non m'ami* (1869); *Cupo e il sepolcro mutolo* (1873); *Pieta, Signor* (1894). Also a *Tantum ergo* for Tenor and Orch. (1836?); *Romanza senza parole* for Piano (1865); Waltz for Piano.

BIBL.: COLLECTED WORKS, SOURCE MATERIAL: There is still no complete critical ed. of Verdi's works, but Ricordi and the Univ. of Chicago Press are preparing a definitive ed. Important sources include the following: C. Vanbianchi, *Nel I centenario di G. V., 1813–1913: Saggio di bibliografia verdiana* (Milan, 1913); C. Hopkinson, *A Bibliography of the Works of G. V., 1813–1901* (2 vols., N.Y., 1973, 1978); M. Chusid, *A Catalog of V.'s Operas* (Hackensack, N.J., 1974); M. Mila, *La giovinezza di V.* (Turin, 1974); D. Rosen and A. Porter, eds., *V.'s Macbeth: A Sourcebook* (Cambridge, 1984); G. Harwood, *G. V.: A Guide to Research* (N.Y., 1998). **BIOGRAPHICAL:** G. Monaldi, *V. e le sue opere* (Florence, 1878); L. Parodi, *G. V.* (Genoa, 1895); Prince de Valori, *V. et son oeuvre* (Paris, 1895); F. Crowest, *V.: Man and Musician* (London, 1897); G. Cavarretta, *V.:*

Il genio, la vita, le opere (Palermo, 1899); G. Monaldi, *V.* (Turin, 1899; Ger. tr. as *G. V. und seine Werke*, Stuttgart, 1898, publ. before the Italian original; 4th Italian ed., 1951); C. Perinello, *G. V.* (Berlin, 1900); M. Basso, *G. V.: La sua vita, le sue opere, la sua morte* (Milan, 1901); O. Boni, *V.: L'Uomo, le opere, l'artista* (Parma, 1901; 2nd ed., 1913); E. Checchi, *G. V.* (Florence, 1901); N. Marini, *G. V.* (Rome, 1901); E. Colonna, *G. V. nella vita e nelle opere* (Palermo, 1902); F. Garibaldi, *G. V. nella vita e nell'arte* (Florence, 1904); L. Sorge, *G. V.: Uomo, artista, patriota* (Lanciano, 1904); P. Voss, *G. V.: Ein Lebensbild* (Diessen, 1904); G. Bragagnolo and E. Bettazzi, *La vita di G. V. narrata al popolo* (Milan, 1905); A. Visetti, *V.* (London, 1905); A. d'Angeli, *G. V.* (Bologna, 1910; 2nd ed., 1912); C. Bellaigue, *V.: Biographie critique* (Paris, 1912; Italian tr., Milan, 1913); M. Chop, *V.* (Leipzig, 1913); M. Lottici, *Bio-bibliografia di G. V.* (Parma, 1913); A. Mackenzie, *V.* (N.Y., 1913); A. Neisser, *G. V.* (Leipzig, 1914); G. Roncaglia, *G. V.* (Naples, 1914); A. Weissmann, *V.* (Berlin, 1922); A. Bonaventura, *G. V.* (Paris, 1923); E. Gasco Contell, *V.: Su vida y sus obras* (Paris, 1927); F. Ridella, *V.* (Genoa, 1928); F. Bonavia, *V.* (London, 1930; 2nd ed., 1947); C. Gatti, *V.* (Milan, 1931; 2nd ed., 1951; Eng. tr. as *V.: The Man and His Music*, N.Y., 1955); F. Toye, *G. V.: His Life and Works* (London, 1931); H. Gerigk, *G. V.* (Potsdam, 1932); R. Manganella, *V.* (Milan, 1936); L. d'Ambra, *G. V.* (Milan, 1937); D. Hussey, *V.* (London, 1940; 5th ed., 1973); F. Botti, *G. V.* (Rome, 1941); G. Roncaglia, *G. V.* (Florence, 1941); K. Holl, *V.* (Vienna, 1942); U. Zoppi, Angelo Mariani, *G. V. e Teresa Stolz* (Milan, 1947); D. Humphreys, *V., Force of Destiny* (N.Y., 1948); F. Törnblom, *V.* (Stockholm, 1948); G. Cenzato, *Itinerari verdiani* (Parma, 1949; 2nd ed., Milan, 1955); A. Cherbuliez, *G. V.* (Zürich, 1949); A. Oberdorfer, *G. V.* (Verona, 1949); L. Orsini, *G. V.* (Turin, 1949); F. Abbiati, ed., *G. V.* (Milan, 1951); L. Gianoli, *V.* (Brescia, 1951); G. Monaldi, *V., La vita, le opere* (Milan, 1951); E. Radius, *V. vivo* (Milan, 1951); G. Stefani, *V. e Trieste* (Trieste, 1951); idem, *G. V.* (Siena, 1951); F. Botti, *V. e l'ospedale di Villanova d'Arda* (Parma, 1952); G. Mondini, *Nel cinquantennio della morte di G. V.* (Cremona, 1952); T. Ybarra, *V., Miracle Man of Opera* (N.Y., 1955); M. Mila, *G. V.* (Bari, 1958); P. Petit, *V.* (Paris, 1958); V. Sheean, *Orpheus at Eighty* (N.Y., 1958); F. Abbiati, *G. V.* (4 vols., Milan, 1959); F. Walker, *The Man V.* (N.Y., 1962); G. Martin, *V.: His Music, Life and Times* (N.Y., 1963; 3rd ed., rev., 1983); J. Wechsberg, *V.* (N.Y., 1974); W. Weaver, ed., *V.: A Documentary Study* (N.Y. and London, 1977); G. Marchesi, *G. V., l'uomo, il genio, l'artista* (Rozzano, 1982); G. Tintori, *Invito all'ascolto di G. V.* (Milan, 1983); M. Conati, ed., and R. Stokes, tr., *Interviews and Encounters with V.* (London, 1984); J. Budden, *V.* (London, 1985; rev. ed., 1993); C. Osborne, *V.: A Life in the Theatre* (N.Y., 1987); M. Phillips-Matz, *V.: A Biography* (Oxford, 1993); F. Cafasi, *G. V.: Fattore di Sant'Agata* (Parma, 1994); M. Chusid, *V.'s Middle Period* (Chicago, 1997). **CRITICAL, ANALYTICAL:** A. Basevi, *Studio sulle opere di G. V.* (Florence, 1859); G. Bertrand, *Les Nationalités musicales étudiées dans le drame lyrique: V.sme et Wagnérisme* (Paris, 1872); B. Roosevelt, *V., Milan and Otello* (Milan, 1887); V. Maurel, *A propos de la mise-en- scène du drame lyrique "Otello"* (Rome, 1888); E. Destranges, *L'Evolution musicale chez V.: Aïda, Otello, Falstaff* (Paris, 1895); C. Abate, *Wagner e V. Studio critico-musicale* (Mistretta, 1896); P. Bellezza, *Manzoni e V., i due grandi* (Rome, 1901); A. Soffredini, *Le opere di G. V.: Studio critico-analitico* (Milan, 1901); G. Tebaldini, *Da Rossini a V.* (Naples, 1901); J. Hadden, *The Operas of V.* (London, 1910); K. Regensburger, *Über den "Trovador" des García Gutiérrez, die Quelle von V.s "Il Trovatore"* (Berlin, 1911); C. Vanbianchi, *Saggio di bibliografia v.iana* (Milan, 1913); G. Roncaglia, *G. V.: L'ascensione dell'arte sua* (Naples, 1914); P. Berl, *Die Opern V.s in ihrer Instrumentation* (diss., Univ. of Vienna, 1931); G. Menghini, *G. V. e il melodramma italiano* (Rimini, 1931); M. Mila, *Il melodramma di V.* (Bari, 1933); A. Parente, *Il problema della critica v.ana* (Turin, 1933); L. Unterholzner, *G. V.s Operntypus* (Hannover, 1933); R. Gallusser, *V.s Frauengestalten* (diss., Univ. of Zürich, 1936); G. Engler, *V.s Anschauung vom Wesen der Oper* (diss., Univ. of Breslau, 1938); J. Loschelder, *Das Todesproblem in V.s Opernschaffen* (Cologne, 1938); G. Roncaglia, *L'ascensione creatrice di G. V.* (Florence, 1940); G. Mule and G. Nataletti, *V.: Studi e memorie* (Rome, 1941); M. Rinaldi, *V. critico* (Rome, 1951); C. Gatti, *Revisioni e rivalutazioni v.ane* (Turin, 1952); G. Roncaglia, *Galleria v.ana: Studi e figure* (Milan, 1959); M. Mila, *Il melodramma di V.* (Milan, 1960); W. Herrmann Jr., *Religion in the Operas of G. V.* (diss., Columbia Univ., 1963); P. Pingagli, *Romanticismo di V.* (Florence, 1967); S. Hughes, *Famous V. Operas* (London, 1968); C. Osborne, *The Complete Operas of V.* (London, 1969); G. Baldini, *Abitare la battaglia: La storia di G. V.* (Milan, 1970); J. Budden, *The Operas of V.* (3 vols., London, 1973–81); A. Geck, *"Aïda," die Oper: Schriftenreiche über musikalische Bühnenwerke* (Berlin, 1973); D. Lawton, *Tonality and Drama in V.'s Early Operas* (diss., Univ. of Calif., Berkeley, 1973); V. Godefroy, *The Dramatic Genius of V.: Studies of Selected Operas* (2 vols., London, 1975, 1977); F. Noske, *The Signifier and the Signified: Studies in the Operas of Mozart and V.* (The Hague, 1977); H. Busch, *V.'s Aida: The History of an Opera in Letters and Documents* (Minneapolis, 1978); W. Weaver and M. Chusid, eds., *The V. Companion* (N.Y., 1979; 2nd ed., rev., 1988); D. Kimbell, *V. in the Age of Italian Romanticism* (Cambridge, 1981); R. Parker, *Studies in Early V. (1832–1844): New Information and Perspectives on the Milanese Musical Milieu and the Operas from Oberto to Ernani* (diss., King's Coll., London, 1981); H. Gál, *G. V. und die Oper* (Frankfurt am Main, 1982); A. Duault, *V., la musique et la drame* (Paris, 1986); S. Corse, *Opera and the Uses of Language: Mozart, V., and Britten* (London and Toronto, 1987); J. Hepokoski, *G. V.: Otello* (Cambridge, 1987); J.-F. Labie, *Le cas V.* (Paris, 1987); H. Busch, *V.'s Otello and Simon Boccanegra in Letters and Documents* (Oxford, 1988); M. Engelhardt, *Die Chöre in der frühen Opern G. V.s* (Tutzing, 1988); A. Sopart, *G. V.s "Simon Boccanegra" (1857 and 1881): Eine musikalisch-dramaturgische Analyse* (Laaber, 1988); G. Martin, *Aspects of V.* (London, 1989); G. Marchesi, *V.: Anni, opere* (Parma, 1991); S. Einsfelder, *Zur musikalische Dramaturgie von G. V.s Otello* (Kassel, 1994); R. Petrobelli, *Music in the Theater: Essays on V. and Other Composers* (Princeton, 1994); V. Prosperi, *La Messa da Requiem di G. V.* (Cortona, 1994); K. Jürgensen, *The V. Ballets* (Parma, 1995); D. Rosen, *V.: Requiem* (Cambridge, 1995); F. Wedell, *Annäherung an V.: Zur Melodik des jungen V. und ihren musiktheoretischen und asthetischen Voraussetzungen* (Kassel, 1995); U. Bermbach, ed., *V.-Theater* (Stuttgart, 1997); H. Busch, ed. and tr., *V.'s Falstaff in Letters and Contemporary Reviews* (Bloomington, Ind., 1997); P. Mioli, *Il teatro di V.: La vita, le opere, gli interpreti* (Milan, 1997); R. Parker, *Leonora's Last Act: Essays in V.an Discourse* (Princeton, 1997); P. Crippa, *G. V.: Il melodrama italiano e la sua estetica nell'800* (San Marino, 1998); T. Klier, *Der. V.-Klang: Die Orchesterkonzeption in den Opern von G. V.* (Tutzing, 1998); G. de Van, *V.'s Theater: Creating Drama Through Music* (Chicago, 1998). **CORRESPONDENCE, ICONOGRAPHY:** I. Pizzi, *Ricordi verdiani inediti* (Turin, 1901); T. Costantini, *Sei lettere di V. a Giovanni Bottesini* (Trieste, 1908); G. Cesari and A. Luzio, *G. V.: I copialettere pubblicati e illustrati* (Leipzig, 1913; Eng. tr. in an abr. ed. by C. Osborne as *Letters of G. V.*, 1971); G. Monaldi, *Saggio di iconografia verdiana* (Bergamo, 1913); A. Martinelli, *G. V.: Raggi e Penombre. Le ultime lettere* (Trieste, 1926); F. Werfel and P. Stefan, *Das Bildnis G. V.s* (Vienna, 1926); G. Morazzoni, *Lettere inedite di G. V.* (Milan, 1929); A. Alberti, *V. intimo: Carteggio di G. V. con il conte Opprandino Arrivabene (1861–1866)* (Verona, 1931); L.

Garibaldi, *G. V. nelle lettere di Emanuele Muzio ad Antonio Barezzi* (Milan, 1931); A. Luzio, *Carteggi verdiani* (Rome; Vols. I-II, 1935; Vols. III-IV, 1947); H. Schultz, *G. V., 1813–1901: Sein Leben in Bildern* (Leipzig, 1938); C. Gatti, *V. nelle immagini* (Milan, 1941); C. Graziani, *G. V.: Autobiografia dalle lettere* (censored ed., Milan, 1941; complete ed., 1951, under Graziani's real name, Aldo Oberdorfer); E. Downes, *V.: The Man in His Letters* (N.Y., 1942); H. Kuehner, *G. V. in Selbstzeugnissen und Bilddokumenten* (Reinbek bei Hamburg, 1961); R. Petzoldt, *G. V., 1813–1901: Sein Leben in Bildern* (Leipzig, 1961).—**NS/LK/DM**

Verdonck, Cornelis, Flemish composer; b. Turnhout, 1563; d. Antwerp, July 5, 1625. He was a chorister in the court chapel of Philip II in Madrid before studying with Séverin Cornet in Antwerp. After singing in the royal chapel in Madrid (1584–98), he pursued his career in his homeland. He was a skilled composer of chansons and madrigals. He also wrote some sacred music, including a Magnificat and motets.

BIBL.: P. Bergmans, *La biographie du compositeur C. V.* (Brussels, 1919).—**LK/DM**

Vere (real name, **Wood de Vere**), **Clémentine Duchene de,** French soprano; b. Paris, Dec. 12, 1864; d. Mount Vernon, N.Y., Jan. 19, 1954. Her father was a Belgian nobleman, and her mother, an English lady. Her musical education was completed under the instruction of Mme. Albertini-Baucardé in Florence, where she made her debut at the age of 16 as Marguerite de Valois in *Les Huguenots*. On Feb. 2, 1896, she made her American debut at the Metropolitan Opera, N.Y., as Marguerite in Gounod's *Faust*; she remained on its roster until 1897; was again at the Metropolitan from 1898 to 1900; her other roles with it were Violetta, Gilda, and Lucia. In 1892 she married the conductor Romualdo Sapio; taught voice from 1914. Her voice was a brilliant high soprano, and she excelled in coloratura. —**NS/LK/DM**

Vered, Ilana, Israeli pianist; b. Tel Aviv, Dec. 6, 1939. Her mother was a concert pianist and her father was a violinist, and she took piano lessons as a child with her mother. At 13, won an Israeli government grant to continue her studies at the Paris Cons., and subsequently took lessons with Rosina Lhévinne and Nadia Reisenberg at the Juilliard School of Music in N.Y. In 1969 she received a grant from the Martha Baird Rockefeller Foundation for a major tour of Europe; subsequently made regular tours there and in the U.S. —**NS/LK/DM**

Veremans, Renaat, Belgian composer, opera administrator, and teacher; b. Lierre, March 2, 1894; d. Antwerp, June 5, 1969. He received training at the Lemmens Inst. in Mechelen and from De Boeck at the Antwerp Cons., winning the premier prix in organ and piano (1914). From 1921 to 1944 he was director of the Flemish Opera in Antwerp. He also taught at the Antwerp Cons. As a composer, Veremans remained faithful to the Romantic tradition.

WORKS: DRAMATIC: Opera: *Beatrijs* (1928); *Anna-Marie* (Antwerp, Feb. 22, 1938); *Bietje* (1954); *Lanceloot en Sanderien* (Antwerp, Sept. 13, 1968). **Operetta:** Various pieces. **ORCH.:** 3 syms. (1959, 1961, 1968); Trumpet Concerto (1960); Concerto for Flute and Chamber Orch. (1962); Concerto for Oboe and Small Orch. (1964); Horn Concerto (1965); symphonic poems. **OTHER:** Chamber music; choruses; many songs.—**NS/LK/DM**

Veress, Sándor, eminent Hungarian-born Swiss composer and pedagogue; b. Kolozsvár, Feb. 1, 1907; d. Bern, March 6, 1992. He studied piano with his mother, and also received instruction in piano from Bartók and in composition from Kodály at the Royal Academy of Music in Budapest (1923–27). He obtained his teacher's diploma (1932), and also took lessons with Lajtha at the Hungarian Ethnographical Museum (1929–33). He worked with Bartók on the folklore collection at the Academy of Sciences in Budapest (1937–40); subsequently taught at the Academy of Music in Budapest (1943–48). In 1949 he went to Switzerland, where he received an appointment as guest prof. on folk music at the Univ. of Bern; then taught at the Bern Cons. from 1950 to 1977; also was active as a guest lecturer in the U.S. and elsewhere. He taught musicology at the Univ. of Bern (1968–77). In 1975 he became a naturalized Swiss citizen.

WORKS: DRAMATIC: Children's Opera: *Hangjegyek lázadása* (Revolt of the Musical Notes; 1931). **Ballet:** *Csodafurulya* (The Miraculous Pipe; 1937; Rome, 1941); *Térszili Katicza* (Katica from Térszil; 1942–43; Stockholm, Feb. 16, 1949). **ORCH.:** *Divertimento* for Small Orch. (1935); *Partita* for Small Orch. (1936); Violin Concerto (1937–39; Zürich, Jan. 9, 1951); *Csürdöngölő* (Hungarian Barn Dance; 1938); 2 syms: No. 1 (1940) and No. 2, *Sinfonia minneapolitana* (1952; Minneapolis, March 12, 1954); *4 danze transilvane* for Strings (1944–49); *Sirató ének* [Threnody] *in memoriam Béla Bartók* (1945); *Előjáték egy tragédiahoz* (Prelude to a Tragedy; 1947); *Drámai változatok* (Dramatic Variations; 1947); *Respublica*, overture (1948); *Hommage à Paul Klee*, fantasia for 2 Pianos and Strings (1951; Bern, Jan. 22, 1952); Concerto for Piano, Strings, and Percussion (1952; Baden-Baden, Jan. 19, 1954); Sonata (Brussels, July 8, 1952); Concerto for String Quartet and Orch. (1960–61; Basel, Jan. 25, 1962); *Passacaglia concertante* for Oboe and Strings (Lucerne, Aug. 31, 1961); *Variations on a Theme by Zoltán Kodály* (1962); *Expovare* for Flute, Oboe, and Strings (1964); *Musica concertante* for 12 Strings (1965–66); Clarinet Concerto (1981–82); *Orbis tonorum* for Chamber Orch. (1986); *Concerto Tilinko* for Flute and Orch. (1988–89); Concerto for 2 Trombones and Orch. (1989). **CHAMBER:** 2 string quartets (1931; 1936–37); Sonata for Solo Violin (1935); 2nd Violin Sonata (1939); Trio for Violin, Viola, and Cello (1954); Trio for Piano, Violin, and Cello (1963); Sonata for Solo Cello (1967); Wind Quintet (1968); *Introduzione e Coda* for Clarinet, Violin, and Cello (1972); Trio for Baryton, Viola, and Cello (1985); *Stories and Fairy Tales* for 2 Percussionists (1987); piano pieces, including *Fingerlarks*, 88 pieces (1946). **VOCAL:** *Elegie* for Baritone, String Orch., and Harp (1964); choral works; songs.

WRITINGS: With L. Lajtha, *Népdal, népzenegyűtjés* (Folk Song, Folk Music Collecting; Budapest, 1936); *Béla Bartók, the Man and the Artist* (London, 1948); *La raccolta della musica popolare ungherese* (Rome, 1949).

BIBL.: A. Traub, *S. V.: Festschrift zum 80. Geburtstag* (Berlin, 1986); A. Traub, ed., *Aufsätze, Vorträge, Briefe: S. V.* (Ger. and Eng.; Hofheim, 1998).—**NS/LK/DM**

Veretti, Antonio, Italian composer and music educator; b. Verona, Feb. 20, 1900; d. Rome, July 13, 1978. After initial training in Verona, he studied with Mattioli and Alfano at the Bologna Liceo Musicale (graduated, 1921). He then founded his own Cons. Musicale della Gioventù Italiana in Rome, which he directed until 1943; subsequently was director of the Pesaro Cons. (1950–52), the Cagliari Cons. (1953–55), and the Florence Cons. (1956–70). While his music generally followed Italian modernist traditions, he later experimented with serial techniques.

WORKS: DRAMATIC: *Il Medico volante*, opera (1928); *Il Favorito del re*, opera (1931; Milan, March 17, 1932; rev. as the opera-ballet, *Burlesca*, Rome, Jan. 29, 1955); *Il galante tiratore*, ballet (1932; San Remo, Feb. 11, 1933); *Un favola di Andersen*, ballet (Venice, Sept. 15, 1934); *I sette peccati*, choreographic musical mystery (Milan, April 24, 1956); film music. **ORCH.:** *Sinfonia italiana* (Liège, Sept. 4, 1930); Suite (1934); *Sinfonia epica* (1938); Piano Concerto (Venice, Sept. 9, 1950); *Ouverture della campana* (RAI, Nov. 10, 1951); *Fantasie* for Clarinet and Orch. or Piano (1959); Concertino for Flute and Chamber Orch. or Piano (1959). **CHAMBER:** *Duo strumentale* for Violin and Piano (1925); Cello Sonata (1926); Piano Trio (1927); *Divertimento* for Harpsichord and 6 Instruments (1939); Violin Sonata (1952). **VOCAL:** *Il Cantico dei Cantici*, oratorio (1922); *Morte e deificazione di Dafni* for Voice and 11 Instruments (Venice, Sept. 8, 1937); *Il Figliuol prodigo*, oratorio (Rome, Nov. 21, 1942); *Sinfonia sacra* for Men's Voices and Orch. (1946; Rome, April 1947); *4 poesie di Giorgio Vigolo* for Voice and Orch. (1950; Turin, Feb. 17, 1956; also for Voice and Piano); *Elegie in Friulano* for Voice, Violin, Clarinet, and Guitar (1963).—**NS/LK/DM**

Vergnet, Edmond-Alphonse-Jean, French tenor; b. Montpellier, July 4, 1850; d. Nice, Feb. 25, 1904. He first played violin in the orch. of the Théâtre-Lyrique in Paris, then studied voice in Paris. He made his debut at the Paris Opéra in 1874, continuing as a member there until 1893; also made guest appearances at La Scala in Milan, Covent Garden in London (1881–82), and in the U.S. (1885–86). Among the roles he created were Jean in Massenet's *Hérodiade* and Admeto in Catalani's *Dejanice*; his other roles were Faust, Radamès, and Lohengrin. —**NS/LK/DM**

Verhulst, Johannes (actually, **Josephus Hermanus**), Dutch conductor and composer; b. The Hague, March 19, 1816; d. there, Jan. 17, 1891. He studied in The Hague and Cologne, and in 1838 went to Leipzig, where he became friendly with Schumann. He was engaged as conductor of the Euterpe concerts (until 1842), and then returned to The Hague. He was conductor of the renowned Diligentia concerts at The Hague from 1860 until 1886, and also conducted in Amsterdam and Rotterdam. He wrote a Sym. (1841), four overtures, much choral music, two string quartets, piano pieces, and songs.

BIBL.: J. van Riemsdijk, *J.J.H. V.* (Haarlem, 1886). —**NS/LK/DM**

Verikovsky, Mikhail (Ivanovich), Ukrainian conductor, teacher, and composer; b. Kremenetz, Nov. 20, 1896; d. Kiev, June 14, 1962. He was a pupil of Yavorsky at the Kiev Cons. He was conductor of the operas in Kiev (1926–28) and Kharkov (1928–35), and also director of the opera studio of the Kharkov Inst. of Music and Drama (1934–35). In 1946 he became a prof. at the Kiev Cons. He composed the first Ukrainian ballet, *Pan Kanyovsky* (1930).

WORKS: DRAMATIC: Opera: *Dela nebesniye* (Heavenly Things; 1932); *Sotnik* (The Ensign; 1938); *Naymichka* (For Purchase; 1943); *Batrachka* (The Maid; 1946); *Basnya o chertopolokhe i roze* (The Fable of the Thistle and the Rose; 1948); *Begletsi* (Fugitives; 1948); *Slava* (Glory; 1961). **Musical Comedy:** *Viy* (1946). **Ballet:** *Pan Kanyovsky* (1930). **OTHER:** Orch. music; chamber music; piano pieces; oratorios and cantatas on political themes; choruses; songs.

BIBL.: N. Herasimova-Persidska, *M.I. V.* (Kiev, 1959); N. Shurova, *M. V.* (Kiev, 1972).—**NS/LK/DM**

Vermeulen, Matthijs, remarkable Dutch composer and music critic; b. Helmond, Feb. 8, 1888; d. Laren, July 26, 1967. Principally self-taught, he traveled in 1905 to Amsterdam, where he received musical guidance from Daniël le Lange and Alphons Diepenbrock. In 1907 he began to write music criticism for Dutch and French publications, and continued his journalistic activities until 1956. In 1921 Vermeulen went to France; returned to the Netherlands in 1947, when he became music ed. of *De Groene Amsterdammer*. He entertained a strong belief in the mystical powers of music; in order to enhance the universality of melodic, rhythmic, and contrapuntal elements, he introduced in his compositions a unifying set of cantus firmi against a diversified network of interdependent melodies of an atonal character; it was not until the last years of his life that his works began to attract serious attention for their originality and purely musical qualities.

WORKS: ORCH.: 7 syms.: No. 1, *Symphonia Carminum* (1912–14; Arnhem, March 12, 1919; 1st professional perf., Amsterdam, May 5, 1964), No. 2, *Prélude à la nouvelle journée* (1919–20; 1st perf. as an identified work, Amsterdam, July 5, 1956; had won 5th prize at the Queen Elisabeth Composition Competition in Brussels in 1953, and was performed anonymously on Dec. 9), No. 3, *Thrène et Péan* (1921–22; Amsterdam, May 24, 1939), No. 4, *Les Victoires* (1940–41; Rotterdam, Sept. 30, 1949), No. 5, *Les Lendemains Chantants* (1941–45; Amsterdam, Oct. 12, 1949), No. 6, *Les Minutes heureuses* (1956–58; Utrecht, Nov. 25, 1959), and No. 7, *Dithyrambes pour les temps à venir* (1963–65; Amsterdam, April 2, 1967); *Passacaille et Cortège* (1930; concert fragments from his music for the open-air play *The Flying Dutchman*); *Symphonic Prolog* (1930). **CHAMBER:** 2 cellos sonatas (1918; 1938); String Trio (1924); Violin Sonata (1925); String Quartet (1960–61). **VOCAL:** Songs.

WRITINGS: *De twee muzieken* (The Two Musics; 2 vols., Leyden, 1918); "Klankbord" (Sound Board) and "De eene grondtoon" (The One Key Note) in *De vrije bladen* (Amsterdam, 1929 and 1932); *Het avontuur van den geest* (The Adventure of the Spirit; Amsterdam, 1947); *Principen der Europese Muziek* (Principles of European Music; Amsterdam, 1948); *De Muziek, Dat Wonder* (Music, A Miracle; The Hague, 1958).

BIBL.: P. Rapoport, *Opus Est: Six Composers from Northern Europe* (London, 1978).—**NS/LK/DM**

Verne (real name, **Wurm**), family of English pianists, all sisters. They adopted the name Verne in 1893.

(1) Mathilde Verne, b. Southampton, May 25, 1865; d. London, June 4, 1936. She studied with her parents, and then became a pupil of Clara Schumann in Frankfurt am Main. She was very successful in England, and from 1907 to 1936 gave concerts of chamber music in London. She was a renowned teacher.

(2) Alice Verne Bredt, b. Southampton, Aug. 9, 1868; d. London, April 12, 1958. She was best known as a piano teacher, but she also composed pedagogical works.

(3) Adela Verne, b. Southampton, Feb. 27, 1877; d. London, Feb. 5, 1952. She studied with her sisters, and later took lessons from Paderewski in Switzerland. Returning to London, she developed a successful career, and became extremely popular as a concert player in England; also made tours in the U.S.

BIBL.: M. Verne, *Chords of Remembrance* (London, 1936). **—NS/LK/DM**

Vernon, Ashley
See **Manschinger, Kurt**

Verrall, John (Weedon), American composer and teacher; b. Britt, Iowa, June 17, 1908. He studied piano and composition with Donald Ferguson, then attended classes at the Royal Coll. of Music in London with R. O. Morris, and took lessons with Kodály in Budapest. Returning to the U.S., he studied at the Minneapolis Coll. of Music and Hamline Univ. (B.A., 1932); received further training at the Berkshire Music Center at Tanglewood, with Roy Harris, and with Frederick Jacobi; and held a Guggenheim fellowship (1947). He held teaching positions at Hamline Univ. (1934–42), at Mount Holyoke Coll. (1942–46), and at the Univ. of Wash. in Seattle (1948–73).

WORKS: DRAMATIC: Opera: *The Cowherd and the Sky Maiden,* after a Chinese legend (1951; Seattle, Jan. 17, 1952); *The Wedding Knell,* after Hawthorne (Seattle, Dec. 5, 1952); *3 Blind Mice* (Seattle, May 22, 1955). **ORCH.:** 3 syms: No. 1 (1939; Minneapolis, Jan. 16, 1940), No. 2 (1948), and No. 3 (1968); Violin Concerto (1946); *Symphony for Young Orchestras* (1948); *The Dark Night of St. John* for Chamber Orch. (1949); *Sinfonia festiva* for Band (1954); Piano Concerto (1960); Viola Concerto (1968); *Radiant Bridge* (1976); *Rhapsody* for Horn and Strings (1979). **CHAMBER:** 2 viola sonatas (1939, 1963); 7 string quartets (1941, 1942, 1948, 1949, 1952, 1956, 1961); 2 serenades for Wind Quintet (1944, 1950); Piano Quintet (1953); *Nocturne* for Bass Clarinet and Piano (1956); Septet for Winds (1966); Nonet for Wind Quintet and String Quartet (1966); Flute Sonata (1972); *Eusebius Remembered* for Horn and Piano (1976); *Invocation to Eos* for Horn and Piano (1983); Sonata for 2 Pianos (1984). **VOCAL:** Choruses; songs.

WRITINGS: *Elements of Harmony* (n.p., 1937); with S. Moseley, *Form and Meaning in the Arts* (N.Y., 1958); *Fugue and Invention in Theory and Practice* (Palo Alto, Calif., 1966); *Basic Theory of Scales, Modes and Intervals* (Palo Alto, Calif., 1969). **—NS/LK/DM**

Verrett, Shirley, noted African-American mezzo-soprano, later soprano; b. New Orleans, May 31, 1931. Her father, a choirmaster at the Seventh-Day Adventist church in New Orleans, gave her rudimentary instruction in singing. Later she moved to Calif. and took voice lessons with John Charles Thomas and Lotte Lehmann. In 1955 she won the Marian Anderson Award and a scholarship to the Juilliard School of Music in N.Y., where she became a student of Marion Székely-Freschl; while still a student, she appeared as soloist in Falla's *El amor brujo* under Stokowski (1960) and made her operatic debut as Britten's Lucretia in Yellow Springs, Ohio (1957). In 1962 she scored a major success as Carmen at the Festival of Two Worlds at Spoleto, Italy. In 1963 she made a tour of the Soviet Union and sang Carmen at the Bolshoi Theater in Moscow. In 1966 she made her debut at Milan's La Scala and at London's Covent Garden. On Sept. 21, 1968, she made her debut at the Metropolitan Opera in N.Y., again as Carmen. On Oct. 22, 1973, she undertook two parts, those of Dido and Cassandra, in *Les Troyens* of Berlioz, produced at the Metropolitan. As a guest artist, she also appeared in San Francisco, Boston, Paris, Vienna, and other operatic centers. In 1990 she sang Dido at the opening performance of the new Opéra de la Bastille in Paris. She won distinction in mezzo-soprano roles, and later as a soprano; thus she sang the title role in Bellini's *Norma,* a soprano, and also the role of mezzo-soprano Adalgisa in the same opera. Her other roles included Tosca, Azucena, Amneris, and Dalila. She also showed her ability to cope with the difficult parts in modern operas, such as Bartók's *Bluebeard's Castle.* Her voice is of a remarkably flexible quality, encompassing lyric and dramatic parts with equal expressiveness and technical proficiency. Her concert repertory ranges from Schubert to Rorem, and also includes spirituals.**—NS/LK/DM**

Verstovsky, Alexei (Nikolaievich), important Russian composer; b. Seliverstovo, March 1, 1799; d. Moscow, Nov. 17, 1862. He was taken as a child to Ufa, and at the age of 17 he was sent to St. Petersburg, where he entered the Inst. of Transport Engineers. He took piano lessons with Johann Heinrich Miller, Daniel Steibelt, and John Field, studied violin with Ludwig Maurer, and studied voice with Tarquini. Verstovsky became a member of the flourishing literary and artistic milieu in St. Petersburg; among his friends was Pushkin. In 1823 he went to Moscow; in 1825 he was named inspector of its theater, then was director of all of its theaters (1842–60). Almost all of his compositions for the stage followed the French model, with long scenes of speech accompanied on the keyboard. His first effort was couplets for the vaudeville, *Les perroquets de la mère Philippe* (1819); he also composed popular songs and couplets for various other vaudevilles and stage pieces. He contributed a great deal to the progress of operatic art in Russia, but his music lacked distinction and inventive power. With the advent of Glinka and Dargomyzhsky on the Russian operatic scene, Verstovsky's productions receded into insignificance.

WORKS: DRAMATIC: Opera (all 1st perf. in Moscow) *Pan Twardowski* (June 5, 1828); *Vadim, ili Probuzhdeniye dvendtsati spyashchikh dev* (Vadim, or The Awakening of the Twelve Sleeping Maidens; Dec. 7, 1832); *Askoldova nogila* (Askold's Grave; Sept. 27, 1835); *Tosko po rodine* (Longing for the Homeland; Sept. 2, 1839); *Churova Dolina, ili Son nayavu* (Chur

Valley, or The Waking Dream; Aug. 28, 1841); *Gromoboy* (Feb. 5, 1858). **OTHER:** Incidental music; songs for dramas; couplets, and romances for vaudevilles; choruses; solo songs; orch. music; piano pieces.

BIBL.: B. Dobrohotov, *A.N. V.* (Moscow, 1949). **—NS/LK/DM**

Vesque von Püttlingen, Johann, Austrian composer; b. Opole, Poland, July 23, 1803; d. Vienna, Oct. 29, 1883. He studied law in Vienna, and became a councillor of state. At the same time he studied with Moscheles (piano) and Sechter (theory), and made his mark as a composer of operas, under the pseudonym J. Hoyen. He also publ. a book on musical copyright, *Das musikalische Autorrecht* (Vienna, 1864).

WORKS: DRAMATIC: Opera (all 1st perf. in Vienna unless otherwise given) *Turandot* (Oct. 3, 1838); *Johanna d'Arc* (Dec. 30, 1840); *Liebeszauber* (1845); *Ein Abenteuer Carls des Zweiten* (Jan. 12, 1850); *Der lustige Rat* (Weimar, April 12, 1852). **OTHER:** Orch. music; 2 masses; 3 string quartets; some 300 songs; piano pieces.

BIBL.: H. Schultz, *J.V. v.P.* (Regensburg, 1930); H. Ibl, *Studien zu J.v. v.P.s Leben und Opernschaffen* (diss., Univ. of Vienna, 1950).**—NS/LK/DM**

Vetter, Michael, German composer and performer; b. Obertsdorf, Allgau, Sept. 18, 1943. He studied philosophy and theology (1964–69), then became known as a recorder player, specializing in early and contemporary works. He was associated with Stockhausen's circle, and performed in *Alphabet pour Liège* (1972). His notated compositions are almost exclusively graphic. His recordings of the 1980s include *Overtones, Tambura Preludes*, and *Pro-Vocationes*, all scored for voice and tambura; the voice uses a multiphonic technique similar to Buddhist chant, supported by the dense overtones of the tambura in an improvisational structure. He publ. a textbook, *Il flauto dolce e acerbo* (Celle, 1964–69).

WORKS: *Figurationen III* for Any Instrument (1965); *Orzismus* for Audience, Players, and Projections (1969); *Sonnenuntergang* for Electric Guitar, Electric Recorder, Trumpet, and Percussion (1971).**—NS/LK/DM**

Vetter, Walther, distinguished German musicologist; b. Berlin, May 10, 1891; d. there, April 1, 1967. He studied at the Leipzig Cons., and subsequently took a course in musicology with Hermann Abert at the Univ. of Halle, where he received his Ph.D. in 1920 with the diss. *Die Arie bei Gluck*; he completed his Habilitation at the Univ. of Breslau with his *Das frühdeutsche Lied* in 1927 (publ. in Munster, 1928). He taught at the univs. of Halle, Hamburg, Breslau, and Greifswald before joining the Univ. of Poznań in 1941; from 1946 to 1958 he was a prof. at Humboldt Univ. in Berlin, and also served as director of its Inst. of Musicology. From 1948 to 1961 he was co-ed. of *Die Musikforschung*, and from 1956 to 1966 he was ed. of the *Deutsches Jahrbuch für Musikwissenschaft*.

WRITINGS: *Der humanistische Bildungsgedanke in Musik und Musikwissenschaft* (Langensalza, 1928); *Franz Schubert* (Potsdam, 1934); *Antike Musik* (Munich, 1935); *J.S. Bach: Leben und Werk* (Leipzig, 1938); *Beethoven und die militär-politischen Ereignisse seiner Zeit* (Poznań, 1943); *Der Kapellmeister Bach: Versuch einer Deutung Bachs auf Grund seines Wirkens als Kapellmeister in Köthen* (Potsdam, 1950); *Der Klassiker Schubert* (2 vols., Leipzig, 1953); *Mythos—Melos—Musica: Ausgewählte Aufsätze zur Musikgeschichte* (a collection of articles; 2 vols., Leipzig, 1957 and 1961); *Christoph Willibald Gluck* (Leipzig, 1964).

BIBL.: *Musa—mens—musici: Im Gedenken an W. V.* (Leipzig, 1969).**—NS/LK/DM**

Veyron-Lacroix, Robert, noted French harpsichordist, pianist, and teacher; b. Paris, Dec. 13, 1922; d. Garches, Hauts-de-Seine, April 3, 1991. He studied with Samuel-Rousseau and Nat at the Paris Cons., where he won premiers prix in piano, harpsichord, and theory. After making his formal debut in a concert broadcast on the French Radio in 1949, he pursued a career as a soloist and chamber music artist. He became closely associated with Jean-Pierre Rampal, with whom he gave numerous concerts. He taught at the Schola Cantorum in Paris (1956) and at the Nice International Academy (1959) before becoming a prof. at the Paris Cons. (1967). He was the author of *Recherches de musique ancienne* (Paris, 1955). While he was particularly known for his interpretations of early music, he frequently programmed modern pieces, including those by Falla, Poulenc, Milhaud, Jolivet, Ohana, and Françaix. **—NS/LK/DM**

Viadana (real name, **Grossi**), **Lodovico,** esteemed Italian composer and teacher; b. Viadana, near Parma, c. 1560; d. Gualtieri, near Parma, May 2, 1627. He adopted the name Viadana when he entered the order of the Minor Observants; was maestro di cappella at Mantua Cathedral (c. 1594–97). After a sojourn in Rome, he was maestro di cappella at the convent of S. Luca in Cremona in 1602. He then held that post at Concordia Cathedral (1608–09) and at Fano Cathedral (1610–12), and served as diffinitor of his order for Bologna province (1614–17). After a sojourn in Busseto, he settled in the convent of S. Andrea in Gualtieri. He was formerly accredited with the invention of the basso continuo (thoroughbass), but Peri's *Euridice* (publ. 1600) has a figured bass in certain numbers, as does Banchieri's *Concerti ecclesiastici* (publ. 1595), whereas Viadana's *Cento concerti con il basso continuo* did not appear until 1602 (Venice). However, he was the first to write church concertos with so few parts that the organ continuo was employed as a necessary harmonic support. A prolific composer, he publ. numerous masses, Psalms, Magnificats, Lamentations, motets, etc. C. Gallico brought out *Opere di Lodovico Viadana* in Monumenti Musicali Mantovani (Kassel, 1964 et seq.).

BIBL.: A. Parazzi, *Della vita e delle opere musicali di L. Grossi-V. inventore del basso continuo nel secolo XVI* (Milan, 1877). **—NS/LK/DM**

Vianna, Fructuoso (de Lima), Brazilian pianist, teacher, and composer; b. Itajubá, Oct. 6, 1896; d. Rio de Janeiro, April 22, 1976. He studied music with his father, a municipal judge, who composed polkas and waltzes. In 1917 he entered the Rio de Janeiro Cons., and

studied piano with Oswald and harmony with Gouveia and França; in 1923 he went to Europe, where he pursued piano training with Hanschild in Berlin, De Greef in Brussels, and Selva in Paris, where he also studied the Dalcroze method of eurhythmics. Returning to Brazil, he was active as a teacher; was prof. of piano at the Belo Horizonte Cons. (1929–30) and the São Paulo Cons. (1930–38), and prof. of choral singing at the National Technical School in Rio de Janeiro (from 1942); also was prof. of piano at Bennet Coll. His works are based on native Brazilian melorhythms pleasurably seasoned with acrid dissonances, achieving a certain *trompe-l'oreille* euphony. His musical output consists mainly of piano pieces and songs of such nature; among them are numerous "valsas" (European waltzes in a Brazilian dressing), "toadas" (melodious romances), and "tanguinhos" (little tangos à la *brésilienne*). They are all perfumed with impressionistic overtones.
—NS/LK/DM

Vianna da Motta, José, esteemed Portuguese pianist and pedagogue; b. Isle St. Thomas, Portuguese Africa, April 22, 1868; d. Lisbon, May 31, 1948. His family returned to Lisbon when he was a year old, and he studied with local teachers. He gave his first concert at the age of 13, then studied piano in Berlin with X. Scharwenka and composition with P. Scharwenka. In 1885 he went to Weimar, where he became a pupil of Liszt; also took lessons with Hans von Bülow in Frankfurt am Main (1887). He then undertook a series of concert tours throughout Europe (1887–88), the U.S. (1892–93; 1899), and South America (1902). He was in Berlin until 1915, then became director of the Geneva Cons. In 1919 he was appointed director of the Lisbon Cons., retiring in 1938. At the height of his career, he was greatly esteemed as a fine interpreter of Bach and Beethoven. He was also the author of many articles in German, French, and Portuguese; wrote *Studien bei Bülow* (1896), *Betrachtungen über Franz Liszt* (1898), *Die Entwicklung des Klavierkonzerts* (as a program book to Busoni's concerts), essays on Alkan, critical articles in the *Kunstwart, Klavierlehrer, Bayreuther Blätter*, etc. He was a prolific composer; among his works are *Die Lusiaden* for Orch. and Chorus; Sym.; String Quartet; many piano pieces, in some of which (e.g., the *5 Portuguese Rhapsodies* and the Portuguese dance *Vito*) he employs folk themes with striking effect. In 1951 the Vianna da Motta International Piano Competition was founded in Lisbon in his memory.

BIBL.: F. Lopes Graça, *V. d.M.: Subsidios para una biographia* (Lisbon, 1949).**—NS/LK/DM**

Viardo, Vladimir, esteemed Russian pianist and pedagogue; b. Krasnaja Poliana, Nov. 14, 1949. After lessons from Zinovi Neiman in Ukraine (1955–58), he went to Moscow and pursued his studies with Ikina Naumov at the Gnessin Coll. of Music (1965–69) and with Lev Naumov at the Cons. (1969–77; D. Mus.). In 1971 he won 3rd prize and the Prix du Prince Rainier at the Long-Thibaud Competition in Paris. After capturing 1st prize in the Van Cliburn Competition in 1973, he toured widely. In 1975 he was appointed an asst. prof. of piano at the Moscow Cons., but shortly thereafter the Soviet government revoked his visa. He continued to teach at the Moscow Cons. and finally began to tour internationally again when his visa was restored in 1988. In the same year he was appointed artist-in-residence and prof. of piano at the Univ. of North Tex. in Denton. In 1990 he resigned his position with the Moscow Cons., but in 1998 he agreed to return as a Distinguished Prof. while retaining his positions at the Univ. of North Tex. Viardo has appeared as a soloist with the world's leading orchs. and has played at major festivals. His recital engagements have taken him to principal music centers, and he also has been active as a chamber music player. His repertoire ranges from Bach, Haydn, Mozart, Beethoven, and Schubert to Rachmaninoff, Prokofiev, Messiaen, Lutosławski, and Penderecki. He also plays various Liszt transcriptions for piano of works by Bach and Schubert, and Harold Bauer's transcription of works by Franck. Viardo has also prepared and recorded his own transcription of Franck's 2nd and 3rd chorales (1995). He has likewise prepared and performed his own brilliant transcription of Stravinsky's *Le Sacre du printemps*.**—LK/DM**

Viardot-García, (Michelle Fedinande) Pauline, celebrated French mezzo-soprano and pedagogue of Spanish descent, daughter of **Manuel del Popolo García** and sister of **Maria Malibran;** b. Paris, July 18, 1821; d. there, May 18, 1910. She commenced vocal training with her mother, then received lessons in piano from Meysenberg and Liszt and in composition from Reicha. Her concert debut was in Brussels in 1837; her stage debut was in London, May 9, 1839, as Desdemona in Rossini's *Otello*. She was then engaged by Louis Viardot, director of the Théâtre-Italien in Paris, where she scored a notable success in her debut as Desdemona on Oct. 8, 1839; she sang there until her marriage to Viardot in 1840, who then accompanied her on long tours throughout Europe. In 1843 she made her first appearances in Russia, where she won distinction singing in both Italian and Russian; in subsequent years she championed the cause of Russian music. She created the role of Fidès in Meyerbeer's *Le Prophète* at the Paris Opéra in 1849, and that of Sapho in Gounod's opera in 1851; after another succession of tours, she took the role of Orphée in Berlioz's revival of Gluck's opera at the Théâtre-Lyrique in Paris (1859), singing the part for 150 nights to crowded houses. She retired in 1863. Her *École classique de chant* was publ. in Paris in 1861. In 1871 she settled in Paris, and devoted herself to teaching and composing. Through her efforts, the music of Gounod, Massenet, and Fauré was given wide hearing. She was one of the great dramatic singers of her era, excelling particularly in the works of Gluck, Meyerbeer, and Halévy. Among her compositions are some operettas. Two of her children were musicians: Louise (Pauline Marie) Héritte (b. Paris, Dec. 14, 1841; d. Heidelberg, Jan. 17, 1918) was a contralto, teacher, and composer who devoted herself mainly to teaching in St. Petersburg, Frankfurt am Main, Berlin, and Heidelberg, publ. *Memories and Adventures* (London, 1913), and composed a comic opera, *Lindoro* (Weimar, 1879). Paul (Louis Joachim) (b. Courtavenel, July 20, 1857; d. Algiers, Dec. 11, 1941) was a violinist, conductor, and composer who studied with Léonard, conducted at the Paris Opéra, wrote the books *Histoire de la musique* (Paris, 1905), *Rapport officiel (mission artistique de 1907) sur la musique en Scandinavie* (Paris, 1908), and *Souvenirs d'un artiste* (Paris, 1910).

BIBL.: La Mara, *P. V.-G.* (Leipzig, 1882); L. Torrigi, *P. V.-G.: Sa biographie, ses compositions, son enseignement* (Geneva, 1901); C. Kaminski, *Lettres à Mlle. V. d'Ivan Tourgéneff* (Paris, 1907); L. Héritte-Viardot, *Memories and Adventures* (London, 1913; tr. from original Ger. MS; Fr. tr., Paris, 1923); A. Rachmanowa (pseud.), *Die Liebe eines Lebens: Iwan Turgenjew und P. V.* (Frauenfeld, 1952); A. FitzLyon, *The Price of Genius: A Life of P. V.* (London, 1964).—**NS/LK/DM**

Vibert, Nicolas, French violinist and composer; b. c. 1710; d. Paris, Aug. 16, 1772. He pursued his career in Paris. In 1752 he joined the 24 Violons du Roi. After playing in the orch. of the Opéra-Comique (from 1753), he became a supernumerary violinist in the Opéra orch. (1757). He also was 1st violinist in the orch. of the Concert Spirituel (1760–63). Vibert was a composer of several fine sonatas.—**LK/DM**

Vicentino, Nicola, noted Italian music theorist and composer; b. Vicenza, 1511; d. Rome, 1575 or 1576. He was a pupil of Willaert in Venice, then became maestro and music master to Cardinal Ippolito d'Este in Ferrara and in Rome. In 1563–64 he was maestro di cappella at Vicenza Cathedral, and by 1570 he was in Milan as rector of St. Thomas; he died during the plague of 1575–76. His book of madrigals for five voices (Venice, 1546), an attempt to revive the chromatic and enharmonic genera of the Greeks, led to an academic controversy with the learned Portuguese musician Lusitano. Defeated, Vicentino publ. a theoretical treatise, *L'antica musica ridotta alla moderna prattica* (Rome, 1555; 2nd ed., 1557), which contains a description of his invention, an instrument called the archicembalo (having six keyboards, with separate strings and keys for distinguishing the ancient genera-diatonic, chromatic, and enharmonic). It was followed by his treatise *Descrizione dell'arciorgano* (Venice, 1561; annotated Eng. tr. by H. Kaufmann, *Journal of Music Theory*, V, 1961). He also invented and described (1561) an "archiorgano." In chromatic composition he was followed by Cipriano de Rore and Gesualdo. His work paved the way for the monodic style, and the eventual disuse of the church modes. H. Kaufmann brought out the modern ed. *Nicola Vicentino: Opera omnia* in Corpus Mensurabilis Musicae, XXVI (1963).

WORKS: *Madrigali* for 5 Voices, *libro primo* (Venice, 1546); *Moteta* for 5 Voices, *liber quartus* (Milan, 1571); *Madrigali* for 5 Voices, *libro quinto* (Milan, 1572); pieces in contemporary collections.—**NS/LK/DM**

Vick, Graham, English opera producer; b. Liverpool, Dec. 30, 1953. He was educated at the Royal Northern Coll. of Music in Manchester. After gaining experience at Glyndebourne and with the English Music Theatre, he produced *Madama Butterfly* at the English National Opera in London in 1984. From 1984 to 1987 he was director of productions at the Scottish Opera in Glasgow. In 1986 he staged *Die Entführung aus dem Serail* in St. Louis. He became artistic director of the City of Birmingham Touring Opera in 1987. In 1989 he produced the British premiere of Berio's *Un re in ascolto* at London's Covent Garden, returning there to stage *Mitridate* in 1992, *Die Meistersinger von Nürnberg* in 1993, *King Arthur* in 1995, and *The Midsummer Marriage* in 1996. In 1992 he produced *The Queen of Spades* at the Glyndebourne Festival, and in 1994 he was made its director of productions, a position he retained until 2000. His first staging at the Metropolitan Opera came in 1994 when he produced *Lady Macbeth of the District of Mtsensk*. In 1997 he produced *Parsifal* at the Opéra de la Bastille in Paris. In 1999 he staged Schoenberg's *Moses und Aron* at the Metropolitan Opera. His productions are both innovative and tasteful.—**NS/LK/DM**

Vickers, Jon(athan Stewart), renowned Canadian tenor; b. Prince Albert, Saskatchewan, Oct. 29, 1926. He began singing as a child. After his voice developed into the tenor range, he acquired experience singing in Baptist church choirs in Prince Albert and Flin Flon. While accepting various singing engagements, he worked in chain stores to make ends meet. After singing major roles in Gilbert and Sullivan and Victor Herbert operettas, he won a scholarship to the Royal Cons. of Music of Toronto in 1950 to study with George Lambert. During this time, he continued to sing in concerts. In 1954 he sang the Duke of Mantua with the Canadian Opera Co. in Toronto, and returned there in such roles as Alfredo in *La Traviata* (1955) and Don José (1956); in the latter year, he appeared in a concert performance of *Medea* in N.Y. In Jan. 1957 he made his first appearance with the Royal Opera of Covent Garden, London, on tour. It was as Siegmund in *Die Walküre* at the Bayreuth Festival in 1958 that Vickers first won notable acclaim. In 1959 he sang Jason in *Medea* in Dallas and Radamès in San Francisco. On Jan. 17, 1960, he made his Metropolitan Opera debut in N.Y. as Canio, where he continued to sing with success in subsequent years. He sang Florestan at Milan's La Scala and Siegmund at the Chicago Lyric Opera in 1961. In 1966, 1967, and 1968 he appeared at Karajan's Easter Festivals. He sang Otello at Expo 67 in Montreal in 1967. In 1975 he appeared as Tristan with the Opéra du Québec. In 1985 Vickers sang Handel's Samson at Covent Garden in a production marking the 300th anniversary of the composer's birth. Throughout the years, he continued to make occasional appearances as a soloist with orchs. and as a recitalist. His remarkable career came to a close with his retirement in 1988. In 1968 he was made a Companion of the Order of Canada. Vickers was acknowledged as one of the principal dramatic and Heldentenors of his era. In addition to roles already noted, he also excelled as Berlioz's Aneas, Don Alvaro, Don Carlos, Parsifal, and Peter Grimes.—**NS/LK/DM**

Victoria, Tomás Luis de, great Spanish organist and composer; b. Avila, 1548; d. Madrid, Aug. 20, 1611. He was a choirboy at Avila Cathedral. In 1565 he went to Rome and entered the Jesuit Collegium Germanicum to prepare himself for the priesthood; his teacher may have been Palestrina, who from 1566 to 1571 was music master at the Roman Seminary, at this time amalgamated with the Collegium Germanicum. Victoria was about the same age as Palestrina's two sons, Rodolfo and Angelo, who were students at the Roman Seminary; the Italian master is known to have befriended his young Spanish colleague, and when Palestrina left the Seminary in 1571, it was Victoria who succeeded him as maestro there. In 1569 Victoria had left the Collegium Germanicum to become singer and organist in the Church of Sta. Maria di Montserrato, posts he held until 1564; from this time on he also officiated frequently at musical ceremonies in the Church of S. Giaccomo degli Spagnuoli. He taught music at the Collegium Germanicum from 1571, becoming its maestro di cappella in 1573; it moved to the Palazzo di S. Apollinaire in 1574 and to the adjoining church in 1576, where he remained as maestro di cappella until 1577. In Aug. 1575 he was ordained a priest. In Jan. of that year he had received a benefice at Leon from the Pope, and in 1579 he was granted another benefice at Zamora, neither requiring residence. In 1577 he joined the Congregazione dei Preti dell'Oratorio; served as chaplain at the Church of S. Girolamo della Carità from 1578 until 1585; this was the church where St. Philip Neri held his famous religious meetings, which led to the founding of the Congregation of the Oratory in 1575. Though Victoria was not a member of the Oratory, he must have taken some part in its important musical activities, living as he did for five years under the same roof with its founder (St. Philip left S. Girolamo in 1583); Victoria is known to have been on terms of the closest friendship with Juvenal Ancina, a priest of the Oratory who wrote texts for many of the "Laudi spirituali" sung at the meetings of the Congregation. Victoria served as chaplain to the King's sister, the Dowager Empress Maria, at the Monasterio de las Descalzas in Madrid from at least 1587 until her death in 1603; also was maestro of its convent choir until 1604, and then was its organist until his death. His last work, a Requiem Mass for the Empress Maria, regarded as his masterpiece, was publ. in 1605.

Beginning with a vol. of motets in 1572, dedicated to his chief patron, Cardinal Otto Truchsess, Bishop of Augsburg, most of Victoria's works were printed in Italy, in sumptuous eds., showing that he had the backing of wealthy patrons. A vol. of masses, Magnificats, motets, and other church music publ. at Madrid in 1600 is of special interest because it makes provision for an organ accompaniment.

A man of deep religious sentiment, Victoria expresses in his music all the ardor and exaltation of Spanish mysticism. He is generally regarded as a leading representative of the Roman School, but it should be remembered that, before the appearance of Palestrina, this school was already profoundly marked by Hispanic influences through the work of Morales, Guerrero, Escobedo, and other Spanish composers resident in Rome. Thus Victoria inherited at least as much from his own countrymen as from Palestrina, and in its dramatic intensity, its rhythmic variety, its tragic grandeur and spiritual fervor, his music is thoroughly personal and thoroughly Spanish. See F. Pedrell, ed., *Tomas Luis de Victoria: Opera omnia* (eight vols., Leipzig, 1902–13) and H. Anglès, ed., *Tomas Luis de Victoria: Opera omnia*, Monumentos de la Música Española, XXV, XXVI, XXX, and XXXI (1965–68).

WORKS (all publ. in Rome unless otherwise given): (33) *Motecta* for 4 to 6 and 8 Voices (Venice, 1572); *Liber primus: qui missas, psalmos, Magnificat...aliaque complectitur* for 4 to 6 and 8 Voices (Venice, 1576); *Cantica beatae virginis vulgo Magnificat, una cum 4 antiphonis beatae virginis per annum* for 4 to 5 and 8 Voices (1581); (32) *Hymni totius anni secundum sanctae romanae ecclesiae consuetudinem* for 4 Voices, *una cum 4 psalmis, pro praecipuis festivitatibus* for 8 Voices (1581; 2nd ed., 1600); (9) *Missarum libri duo* for 4 to 6 Voices (1583); (53) *Motecta* for 4 to 6, 8, and 12 Voices (1583; 2nd ed., 1589; 3rd ed., rev. 1603); (37) *Motecta festorum totius anni cum communi sanctorum* for 4 to 6 and 8 Voices (1585); (37) *Officium Hebdomadae Sanctae* for 3 to 8 Voices (1585); (7) *Missae, una cum antiphonis Asperrges, et Vidi aquam totius anni: liber secundus* for 4 to 6 and 8 Voices (1592); (32) *Missae, Magnificat, motecta, psalmi et alia quam plurima* for 3 to 4, 8 to 9, and 12 Voices (Madrid, 1600); *Officium defunctorum: in obitu et obsequiis sacrae imperatricis* for 6 Voices (Madrid, 1605).

BIBL.: H. Collet, *V.* (Paris, 1914); F. Pedrell, *T.L. d.V. Abulense* (Valencia, 1918); W. Hirschl, *The Styles of V. and Palestrina: A Comparative Study, with Special Reference to Dissonance Treatment* (diss., Univ. of Calif., Berkeley, 1933); E. Young, *The Contrapuntal Practices of V.* (diss., Univ. of Rochester, N.Y., 1942); H. von May, *Die Kompositions-Technik T.L. d.V.s* (Bern, 1943); N. Saxton, *The Masses of V.* (diss., Westminster Choir Coll., Princeton, N.J., 1951); T. Rive, *An Investigation into Harmonic and Cadential Procedures in the Works of T.L. d.V., 1548–1611* (diss., Univ. of Auckland, 1963); J. Kriewald, *The Contrapuntal and Harmonic Style of T.L. d.V.* (diss., Univ. of Wisc., 1968); J. Soler, *V.* (Barcelona, 1983); E. Cramer, *T.L. d. V.: A Guide to Research* (Levittown, N.Y., 1998).—**NS/LK/DM**

Victory, Gerard (real name, Alan Loraine),

Irish composer, conductor, and broadcasting administrator; b. Dublin, Dec. 24, 1921; d. there, March 14, 1995. He was educated at Belvedere Coll., Dublin, the Univ. of Ireland (B.A.), and Trinity Coll., Univ. of Dublin (B.Mus.). From 1948 to 1953 he was active with the Irish Radio Service. He was a radio (1953–61) and television (1961–62) producer with Radio Telefis Eireann. After serving as its deputy director of music (1962–67), he was its director of music (1967–82). From 1981 to 1983 he was president of UNESCO's International Rostrum of Composers. In 1972 he was awarded an honorary Mus.D. degree from Trinity Coll. In 1975 he received the Chevalier de l'Ordre des Arts et des Lettres of France and the Order of Merit of the Federal Republic of Germany. Victory created an extensive body of music in various genres and styles. His works were always handsomely crafted and couched in a generally accessible idiom.

WORKS: DRAMATIC: Opera: *An Fear a phós Balbhán* (The Silent Wife; 1952; Dublin, April 6, 1953); *Iomrall Aithne* (1955–56); *The Stranger* (1958); *The Music Hath Mischief* (1960); *Chatterton* (1967); *Eloise and Abelard* (1970–72); *Circe 1991*, radio opera (1971); *An Evening for Three* (1975); *The Rendezvous* (1988–89; Dublin, Nov. 2, 1989); *The Wooing of Etain*, children's opera (1994). **Operetta:** *Nita* (1944); *Once Upon a Moon* (1949); *The 2 Violins* (1955). **Musical Plays:** *Eldorado* (1953); *The Martinique Story* (1960–61). **Other:** Incidental music for plays; film music. **ORCH.:** *The Enchanted Garden* (1950–51); *Elegy* (1951); *Marche Pittoresque* (1951); 2 piano concertos (1954, 1972); *Charade*, overture (1955); *Patrician Theme*

(1956); *The Rapparee*, overture (1959); 4 syms.: No. 1, *Short Symphony* (1961), No. 2, *Il Ricorso* (1977), No. 3, *Refrains* (1984; Dublin, July 19, 1985), and No. 4 (1990; Dublin, Dec. 7, 1991); *Ballade* (1963); *5 Mantras* for Strings (1963); *Pariah Music* (1965); *La Montana* (1965); *Treasure Island*, overture (1966); *Favola di Notte* (1966; Dublin, Feb. 26, 1967); *Spook Galop* (1966); *Homage to Petrarch* for Strings (1967); *4 Tableaux* (1968); Accordion Concerto (1968; RTE, Dublin, May 22, 1970); *Miroirs* (1969); *Jonathan Swift-A Symphonic Portrait* (1970); *Praeludium* (1970); *Cyrano de Bergerac Overture* (1970; Dublin, March 14, 1972); *The Spirit of Molière*, suite (1971); Harp Concerto (1971); *Tetragon* for Oboe and Orch. (1971); *From Renoir's Workshop* (1973; RTE, Dublin, Aug. 20, 1974); *Canto* (1973); *Capriccio* for Violin and Orch. (1975); *Olympic Festival Overture* (RTE, Dublin, Sept. 1, 1975); *Barocco Suite* (1978); Cello Concerto (1978); *9 Variations on the Cravate* (1978); *Fabula Mystica Graeca* for Strings (1980); *3 Irish Pictures* (1979–80); *6 Epiphanies on the Author (In Memory of James Joyce)* (1981; Dublin, Feb. 5, 1982); *5 Inventions* for Violins and Strings (Galway, May 1, 1982); *The Broad and the Narrow Ways*, suite (1984; Dublin, June 1985); *Tableaux Sportifs* (1984; Radio France, June 1985; also for Chamber Ensemble); *Monte Cristo*, concert overture (1987; also for Concert Band); *Concertino à la Grecque* for Trombone and Orch. (1987; Dublin, Feb. 23, 1995); *Salute to the President* or *Ómós don Uachtarán*, concert overture (Dublin, Oct. 10, 1990); *Eblana: A Symphonic Portrait of Dublin* (1990–91; Belfast, June 20, 1993); *Ave Scientia*, concert overture (1994; Galway, Oct. 1995); also pieces for Brass and Concert Bands. **CHAMBER:** Wind Quintet (1957); *Esquisse* for Oboe and Piano (1960); *Canzona* for Violin and Piano (1962); String Quartet (1963); *Rodomontade* for Woodwind Quintet (1964); *Semantiques* for Flute and Piano (1967); *3 Legends* for Piano, Violin, Clarinet, and Cello (1969); Piano Quintet (1970); *Trois contes de fee* for Clarinet and Piano (1970); Trio for Accordion, Guitar, and Percussion (1970); Alto Saxophone Sonatine (1975); *Adest Hora* for Violin, Clarinet, Cello, Piano, and Percussion (1977); *5 Exotic Dances* for Brass Sextet (1979); String Trio (1982; Dublin, Jan. 30, 1984); *Commedia* for Brass Quintet (1985; Dublin, Jan. 1986); Trio for Violin, Horn, and Piano (1986); *Runic Variations* for Flute and Clarinet (1988); *Moresca* for Violin, Cello, and Harp (1989; Dublin, Feb. 6, 1990); *Denkmal* for String Trio (1993). **Piano:** Sonata (1958); *Prélude and Toccata* (1962); *3 Masks* (1965); *Cinque Correlazioni* (1966; Dublin, Jan. 10, 1971); *Verona Préludes* (1979; Dublin, Jan. 5, 1980). **VOCAL:** *Quartetto* for Soloists, Narrator, and Chorus (1965); *The Island People*, cantata for Children's Chorus, Narrator, and Instruments (1967); *Civitas Nova* for Soloists, Chorus, and Organ (1968); *The Magic Trumpet* for Speaker, Chorus, and Orch. (1970; rev. 1983); *Mass for Christmas Day* for Baritone, Chorus, and Organ (1973); *Processus*, cantata for Chorus, Instruments, and Tape (1973–75; RTE, Dublin, June 28, 1976); *Sailing to Byzantium* for Alto and Orch. (1975); *Mass of the Resurrection* for Chorus and Organ (1977); *7 Songs of Experience* for Soloists and Chorus (1977–78); *Ultima Rerum*, symphonic Requiem for Soloists, Chorus, and Orch. (1979–81; Dublin, March 3, 1984); *King Sweeney*, cantata for Speaker, Tenor, Chorus, and Chamber Ensemble (1983); *Songs from Lyonnesse*, cantata for Chorus and Piano (1983); *Children of the Last Music*, dramatic cantata for Narrator, Soloists, Chorus, Piano, and 2 Percussion (1990); *Seasons of Eros* for Baritone and Piano or Orch. (1990); *Responsibilities* for Chorus (1991); *The Everlasting Voices*, cantata for Chorus and Organ (Belfast, Aug. 27, 1993); *A Musical Instrument* for Soprano and Chorus (1993); many other choral works, song cycles, and solo songs.—**NS/LK/DM**

Vidal, Paul (Antonin), noted French conductor, pedagogue, and composer; b. Toulouse, June 16, 1863; d. Paris, April 9, 1931. He studied at the Paris Cons., and in 1883 won the Prix de Rome with his cantata *Le Gladiateur*. In 1889 he joined the staff of the Paris Opéra as asst. choral director; later became chief conductor there (1906). He taught elementary courses at the Paris Cons. from 1894 until 1909, when he was appointed a prof. of composition. He was music director of the Opéra-Comique from 1914 to 1919. His brother, Joseph Bernard Vidal (b. Toulouse, Nov. 15, 1859; d. Paris, Dec. 18, 1924), was a conductor and composer; made a name for himself as a composer of operettas.

WORKS: DRAMATIC: *Eros*, fantaisie lyrique (Paris, April 22, 1892); *L'Amour dans les enfers* (1892); *La Maladetta*, ballet (Paris, Feb. 24, 1893); *Fête russe*, ballet (Paris, Oct. 24, 1893); *Guernica*, drame lyrique (Paris, June 7, 1895); *La Burgonde*, opera (Paris, Dec. 23, 1898); *Ramsès*, drame (Paris, June 27, 1900); *L'Impératrice*, ballet (1903); *Zino-Zina* (1908); *Ballet de Terpsichore* (1909); also pantomimes, incidental music to plays. **OTHER:** Orch. pieces; choral works; chamber music; songs; piano pieces.—**NS/LK/DM**

Viderø, Finn, noted Danish organist, pedagogue, and composer; b. Fuglebjerg, Aug. 15, 1906; d. Copenhagen, March 13, 1987. He went to Copenhagen and studied at the Cons. (graduated, 1926), then pursued musicological training at the Univ. (M.A., 1929). He was active as a church organist there, holding appointments at the German-French Reformed (1928), Jaegersborg (1940), Trinitas (1947), and St. Andreas (1971) churches; also toured as a recitalist. He taught theory (1935–45) and organ and harpsichord (1949–74) at the Univ. of Copenhagen; was a visiting prof. at Yale Univ. (1959–60) and North Tex. State Univ. (1967–68); also gave master classes. He wrote valuable articles on 16th- and 17th-century performance practice and ed. vols. of organ music, hymn tunes, choral pieces, and folk songs; also publ. *Orgelskole* (with O. Ring; 1933; 2nd ed., 1963). He composed choral works, organ music, piano pieces, and songs.—**NS/LK/DM**

Vierdanck, Johann, German organist and composer; b. c. 1605; d. (buried) Stralsund, April 1, 1646. He was a chorister at the Dresden Hofkapelle, where he received training in composition, violin, and cornet. He was sent to Vienna in 1628 for further study, after which he was organist at the Marienkirche in Stralsund (1635–46). Among his works are *Erster Theil geistlicher Concerten* for two to four (Greifswald, 1641) and *Erster Theil newer Pavanen Gagliarden, Balletten und Correnten* for two Violins and Basso Continuo (Greifswald, 1637).

BIBL.: G. Weiss, *J. V. (ca. 1605–1646): Sein Leben und sein Werk* (diss., Univ. of Marburg, 1956).—**NS/LK/DM**

Vierk, Lois V, American composer; b. Hammond, Ind., Aug. 4, 1951. (The middle V is without punctuation; it is derived from Von Viereck, the old version of her family name, traditionally abbreviated without a period.) She studied composition privately with Stein and at the Calif. Inst. of the Arts with Powell and Subotnick (M.F.A., 1978); also studied gagaku with

Suenobu Togi in Los Angeles (1971–78), and ryuteki (a transverse flute) in Tokyo with Sukeyasu Shiba (1982–84). She produced radio programs of world music for KPFK-FM in Los Angeles and collaborated with choreographer Anita Feldman to create a unified approach to tap dance and sound. In 1989 she formed LVV, an ensemble devoted to the performance of her music, which was featured on the "Lois V Vierk Special" on WNYC-FM in N.Y. Her minimalistic music is often microtonal and monochromatic, involving numerous similar instruments live or on tape; they typically reach an intense, gradual climax consisting of sensually overlapping textures. Her most frequently played work, *Go Guitars* for five Electric Guitars (1981), makes use in its title of the Japanese character for "five," transcribed as "go."

WORKS: *Go Guitars* for 5 Electric Guitars (1981); *Tusk* for 18 Trombones (1981); *Hyaku Man No Kyu* (One Million Spheres) for 8 Ryuteki Flutes (1983); *Crane With 1,000 Wings* for 8 Violins (1984); *Dark Bourn* for 4 Bassoons and 4 Cellos (1985); *Manhattan Cascade* for 4 Accordions (1985); *Simoom* for 8 Cellos (1986); *Cirus* for 6 Trumpets (1987); *Attack Cat Polka* for Accordion, Voice, and Chamber Ensemble (1988); *Hexa* for 3 Tap Dancers on Tap Dance Instrument (patented), Percussion, and Electronic Processing (1988); *Red Shift* for Cello, Electric Guitar, Synthesizer, and Percussion (1989), *2* for 2 Cello, Synthesizer, and Percussion (1990), *3* for Trumpet, Cello, Electric Guitar, Synthesizer, and Percussion (1991), and *4* for Cello, Trumpet, Electric Guitar, Piano/Synthesizer, and Percussion (1991); *Jagged Mesa* for 2 Trumpets, 2 Trombones, 2 Bass Trombones or Larger Brass Ensemble (1990); *Yeah Yeah Yeah* for Piano (1990); *Timberline* for Flute, Clarinet, Bassoon, Viola, String Bass, Piano/Synthesizer, and Percussion (1991); *Devil's Punchbowl* for Orch. (1993); *River Beneath the River* for String Quartet (1993); *Twister* for Cello, Marimba, and 2 Tap Dancers on Tap Dance Instrument (patented) (1993; in collaboration with A. Feldman); *Into the Brightening Air* for String Quartet (1994); *Swash* for 2 Tap Dancers and 2 Singers (1994; in collaboration with A. Feldman); *To Stare Astonished at the Sea* for String Piano (1994); *Spin 2* for 2 Pianos (1995); *Blue Jets Red Sprites* for Accordion (1996); *Demon Star* for Cello and Marimba (1996); *Silversword* for Gagaku Orch. (1996); *Europa* for Brass Quintet (1997); *Io* for Amplified Flute, Amplified Marimba, and Electric Guitar (1998); *Shoo* for Percussion and 2 Tap Dancers on Tap Dance Instrument (patented) (1998; in collaboration with A. Feldman).—**NS/LK/DM**

Vierne, Louis, eminent French organist, pedagogue, and composer; b. Poitiers, Oct. 8, 1870; d. while playing his 1,750th recital at Notre-Dame Paris, June 2, 1937. He was born blind but gained limited sight through an operation in 1877. He showed musical talent at an early age and studied at the Institution Nationale des Jeunes Aveugles in Paris (1881–88). He received organ lessons from Franck, then was a pupil of Widor at the Paris Cons. (1890–93), winning a premier prix in organ (1894). In 1892 he became Widor's assistant at St.-Sulpice in Paris and in 1900 was appointed organist at Notre-Dame in Paris, where he remained until his death. He taught organ in Paris at the Cons. (1894–1911) and at the Schola Cantorum (from 1911); among his pupils were Nadia Boulanger and Marcel Dupré. In 1927 he made a four-month North American concert tour. His six organ syms. are principal works of the genre.

WORKS: **ORCH.:** Sym. (1907–08; Paris, Jan. 26, 1919); *Les djinns*, symphonic poem (1919); *Marche triomphale pour le centenaire de Napoléon* for Brass, Timpani, and Organ (1921); *Poème* for Piano and Orch. (1926); *Symphonic Piece* for Organ and Orch. (1926; arranged from the 1st 3 organ syms.). **CHAMBER:** String Quartet (n.d.); Violin Sonata (1906); Cello Sonata (1910); Piano Quintet (1917); *Soirs étrangers* for Cello and Piano (1928). **KEYBOARD:** **Organ:** *Allegretto* (1894); 6 syms. (1898–99; 1902–3; 1911; 1914; 1923–24; 1930); *Messe basse* (1912); *24 pièces en style libre* (1913–14); *Pièces de fantaisie* (4 books, 1926–27); *Triptyche* (1929–31); *Messe basse pour les défunts* (1934). **Piano:** Several pieces. **VOCAL:** *Messe solonnelle* for 4 Voices and 2 Organs (1900); *Praxinoé*, symphonic legend for Soloists, Chorus, and Orch. (1903–06); *Psyché* for Voice and Orch. (1914); *Les Angélus* for Voice and Organ or Orch. (1930); *Ballade du désespéré* for Tenor and Piano or Orch. (1931); songs.

BIBL.: *In Memoriam L. V.* (Paris, 1939); B. Gavoty, *L. V., La Vie et l'oeuvre* (Paris, 1943).—**NS/LK/DM**

Vieru, Anatol, distinguished Romanian composer and musicologist; b. Iaşi, June 8, 1926; d. Bucharest, Oct. 8, 1998. He was a student of Klepper (composition), Constantinescu (harmony), and Silvestri (conducting) at the Bucharest Cons. (1946–51) before pursuing training with Khachaturian (composition) at the Moscow Cons. (1951–54). He later attended the summer courses in new music at Darmstadt (1967) and subsequently took his Ph.D. in musicology at the Cluj Cons. (1978) with the diss. *De la moduri, spre un model al gîndirii muzicale intervalice* (From Modes Towards a Model of Intervallic Musical Thought; publ. as *Cartea Modurilor* [Book of Modes], Bucharest, 1980; 2nd ed., 1993). From 1955 he taught composition at the Bucharest Cons. He was founder-director of the Musiques parallèles concerts (1970–84), at which he presented the first Romanian performances of works by such modern masters as Schoenberg, Varèse, and Ives. In 1973 he was in Berlin under the auspices of the Deutscher Akademischer Austauschdienst. In 1984, 1992, and 1994 he gave courses in Darmstadt and in 1992–93 he was composer-in-residence at N.Y.U. Among his honors were the Reine Marie José prize of Geneva (1962), a Koussevitzky Foundation grant (1966), the prize of the Romanian Academy (1967), and the Gottfried von Herder Prize of the Univ. of Vienna (1986). He contributed articles to various journals and publ. the vol. *Cuvinte despre sunete* (Words About Sounds; Bucharest, 1993). Beginning with neo-modal models, Vieru developed a highly personal compositional style in which microstructures served as the foundation upon which to build scores notable for their inventive handling of modal, tonal, and serial elements.

WORKS (all 1st perf. in Bucharest unless otherwise given): **DRAMATIC:** **Opera:** *Jonah* (1972–75; concert perf., Oct. 30, 1976); *The Feast of the Cadgers* (1978–81; concert perf., June 24, 1984; 1st stage perf., Berlin, Nov. 10, 1990); 3 "pocket" operas (1982–83): *Telegrams* (Nov. 8, 1983), *Theme and Variations* (Nov. 8, 1983), and *A Pedagogue of the New School* (April 7, 1987); *The Last Days, the Last Hours* (1990–95); film and television scores. **ORCH.:** *Suite in Ancient Style* for Strings (1945; May 21, 1966); *Concerto for Orchestra* (1954–55; Feb. 2, 1956); Concerto for Strings (1958; transcription of String Quartet No. 1, 1955); 2 flute concertos: No. 1 (1958–59; Dec. 7, 1961) and No. 2 (1996);

2 cello concertos: No. 1 (1962; Geneva, March 27, 1963) and No. 2 (1992)); *Jeux* for Piano and Orch. (1963; Iaşi, March 18, 1966); Violin Concerto (1964; Cluj, Oct. 14, 1967); 6 syms.: No. 1, *Ode to Silence* (1966–67; March 28, 1968), No. 2 (1973; Berlin, Jan. 26, 1974), No. 3, *An Earthquake Symphony* (1977–78; March 1, 1979), No. 4 (1979–83; Cluj, May 5, 1983), No. 5 for Chorus and Orch. (1984; Jan. 30, 1986), and No. 6, *Exodus* (1988–89); *Museum Music* for Harpsichord and 12 Strings (1968; Paris, July 2, 1970); *Clepsydra I* (1968–69; Donaueschingen, Oct. 10, 1969); *Screen* (1970; Royan, April 4, 1971); Clarinet Concerto (1974–75; Iaşi, Feb. 3, 1978); Concerto for Violin, Cello, and Orch. (June 3, 1980); *Shell* for 15 Strings (1981; Timişoara, Nov. 6, 1982); *Narration II* for Saxophone(s) and Orch. (1985; Nice, Feb. 9, 1986); Sinfonia Concertante for Cello and Orch. (Feb. 2, 1989); *Taragot* for 2 Instrumentalists and Orch. (May 24, 1992); *Kaleidoscope* for Piano and Orch. (1993); *Music* for Organ and Strings (1996); Guitar Concerto (1996). **CHAMBER:** 2 Pieces for Trumpet and Piano (1953); 8 string quartets: No. 1 (1955; Moscow, Dec. 12, 1957), No. 2 (1956; June 7, 1957), No. 3, with Woman's Voice (1973; Sept. 8, 1977), No. 4 (1980; Nov. 6, 1981), No. 5 (1981–82; June 16, 1984), No. 6 (1986; April 7, 1987), No. 7 (1987; Turin, Sept. 29, 1988), and No. 8 (1991); Clarinet Quintet (1957); Sonata for Solo Cello (1962; May 16, 1968; also with Percussion, 1975); *Steps of Silence* for String Quartet and Percussionist (1967; Washington, D.C., Jan. 12, 1968); *The Eratosthenes Sieve* for Clarinet, Violin, Viola, Cello, and Piano (Mainz, Oct. 8, 1969); *Mosaics* for 3 Percussionists (1972; Zagreb, May 13, 1977); *Inscriptio* for 2 Flutes, 2 Trombones, Electric Guitar, and Bass Guitar (June 20, 1978); *Over the Treetops* for 8 Instrumentalists (1979); *Joseph and His Brothers* for 11 Instrumentalists and Tape (Metz, Nov. 16, 1979); *Double Duos* for Alto Saxophone, Vibraphone, and Piano (1983; Darmstadt, July 15, 1990; also for Alto Saxophone and Vibraphone, Sept. 15, 1986); *Soroc I* for 6 or 7 Instrumentalists (July 16, 1984) and *II* for Wind Quintet, Viola, and 2 Percussionists (Darmstadt, July 29, 1984); Sonata for Violin and Cello (1985; April 7, 1987); *Millefolium* for 4 Flutists Playing 12 Flutes (1986; Amsterdam, Nov. 11, 1987); *Trinta* for Saxophone(s) and Percussion (1987); *Diaphonie* for Cello and Double Bass (1987; Cologne, June 28, 1988); *Dar I* for Flute (1988) and *II* for Cello (1989); *Multigen* for Alto Flute, Oboe, Alto Saxophone, Percussion, and Piano (1988); *Giusto* for Alto Saxophone, Synthesizer, Electric Guitar, and Bass Guitar (1988; Berlin, Jan. 29, 1990); *Versete* for Violin and Piano (1989); *4 Sax* for Saxophone Quartet (1990; Berlin, Nov. 17, 1991); Cello Sonata (Radio classique, Paris, Dec. 15, 1992); *Eclisse* for Violin, Viola, Cello, Double Bass, and Piano (May 30, 1992); *Ricercar for NYU* for Chamber Ensemble (N.Y., Dec. 7, 1992); *Tabor* for 7 Instrumentalists (1992; Feb. 2, 1993); Trio for Bassoon, Guitar, and Double Bass (1992; N.Y., May 13, 1994); *Cracium*, violin sonata (1994); *Couple* for Clarinet and Viola (1995); *Leggero* for Flute(s) and Percussion (1995). **KEYBOARD: Piano:** *Die Kinderwelt*, 20 miniatures (1958); *Nautilos* for Piano and Tape (Dec. 10, 1968); 2 sonatas: No. 1 (Oct. 30, 1976) and No. 2 (1994). **Organ:** *Narration* (1975; Berlin, March 6, 1977). **VOCAL:** *Mioritsa*, oratorio for Tenor, Baritone, Chorus, Children's Chorus, and Orch. (1956–57; Feb. 27, 1958); *Music for Bacovia and Labis* for Voices and Instruments (1959–63; Oct. 4, 1982); *Cantata of the Light Years* for Chorus and Orch. (June 18, 1960); Sym. for Mezzo-soprano and 15 Instrumentalists (1963; Cluj, Dec. 11, 1965); *Clepsydra II* for Chorus and Orch. (1971; Nov. 20, 1972); *Quatre angles pour regarder Florence* for Soprano, Piano or Harpsichord, and Percussion (1973; Champigny, April 19, 1974); *The Treasure in the Currant* for Children's Chorus and Orch. (Braşov, July 3, 1982); *Psalm 91* for Baritone, Organ, Cello, and Double Bass (1983; Berlin, Jan. 15, 1984); *Archaic Love Songs* for Various Vocalists and Instrumental Combinations (1985–89); *Life Sentence* for Mezzo-soprano, Clarinet, and Percussionist (1992; Nov. 25, 1993); *Archipelagus* for Baritone and Percussion (1994). **MULTIMEDIA AND TAPE:** Quartet for Dancer, Clarinet, Horn, and Percussion (1967; April 20, 1970); *Clocks* for Tape, Instruments, Dancer, and Reciter (April 20, 1970); *Stone Land* for Tape (1972); *Antiphony to Stone Land* for Trombone, Organ, and Tape (1984); *Die Waage* for Tape, Violin, Cello, Clarinet, Bassoon, Guitar, Piano, and Reciter (Nov. 25, 1986); *Pelinarium* for Synthesizer and Tape (1986).—**NS/LK/DM**

Vieuxtemps, Henri, celebrated Belgian violinist and composer; b. Verviers, Feb. 17, 1820; d. Mustapha, Algiers, June 6, 1881. His first teacher was his father, an amateur musician. He then continued his training with Lecloux-Dejonc. At age six he made his debut in Verviers. After performing in Liège in 1827, he gave several concerts in Brussels in 1828, where he attracted the notice of Bériot, who accepted him as a pupil; Vieuxtemps studied with Bériot until 1831. In 1833 his father took him on a concert tour of Germany. He continued his studies in Vienna, where he received lessons in counterpoint from Sechter. On March 16, 1834, he performed as soloist in the Beethoven Violin Concerto in Vienna, scoring a notable success. On June 2, 1834, he made his British debut with the Phil. Society of London. After training in composition from Reicha in Paris (1835–36), he set out on his first tour of Europe (1837). During his constant travels, he composed violin concertos and other violin works which became part of the standard repertoire, and which he performed in Europe to the greatest acclaim. He made his first American tour in 1843–44. In 1846 he was engaged as a prof. at the St. Petersburg Cons., and remained in Russia for five seasons; his influence on Russian concert life and violin composition was considerable. In 1853 he recommenced his concert tours in Europe. Vieuxtemps paid two more visits to America, in 1857–58 (with Thalberg) and in 1870–71 (with Christine Nilsson). He was a prof. of violin at the Brussels Cons. (1871–73). A stroke of paralysis, affecting his left side, forced him to end all his concert activities, but he continued to teach privately. He went to Algiers for rest, and died there; one of his most prominent pupils, Jenö Hubay, was with him at his death. In 1844 Vieuxtemps married the pianist Josephine Eder (b. Vienna, Dec. 15, 1815; d. Celle-St. Cloud, June 29, 1868). His great-grandson was **Marcel Landowski**. With Bériot, Vieuxtemps stood at the head of the French school of violin playing; contemporary accounts speak of the extraordinary precision of his technique and of his perfect ability to sustain a flowing melody; the expression "le roi du violon" was often applied to him in the press. He had two brothers who were musicians: (Jean-Joseph-) Lucien Vieuxtemps (b. Verviers, July 5, 1828; d. Brussels, Jan. 1901), was a pianist and teacher who studied with Edouard Wolff in Paris, made his debut at a concert given by his elder brother in Brussels (March 19, 1845), devoted himself mainly to teaching there, and also wrote a few piano pieces. (Jules-Joseph-) Ernest Vieuxtemps (b. Brussels, March 18, 1832; d. Belfast, March 20, 1896), was a cellist. He appeared with his elder brother in London (1855).

He was solo cellist in the Italian Opera Orch. there before going to Manchester as principal cellist of the Hallé Orch. (1858).

WORKS: ORCH.: 7 violin concertos: No. 1 in E major, op.10 (1840); No. 2 in F-sharp minor, op.19 (1836); No. 3 in A minor, op.25 (1844); No. 4 in D minor, op.31 (c. 1850); No. 5 in A minor, op.37, *Grétry* (1861); No. 6 in G major, op.47 (Paris, 1883); No. 7 in A minor, op.49 (Paris, 1883). **Violin and Orch. or Piano:** *Hommage à Paganini*, op.9 (Leipzig, c. 1845); *Fantaisie-caprice*, op.11 (Mainz, 1845); *Norma*, fantasia on the G string, op.18 (Leipzig, c. 1845); *Fantasia appassionata*, op.35 (Leipzig, c. 1860); *Ballade and Polonaise*, op.38 (Leipzig, c. 1860); 2 cello concertos (Paris, 1877, c. 1883); *Duo brillant* for Violin, Cello, and Orch., op.39 (Paris, c. 1864); Overture and Belgian national anthem for Chorus and Orch., op.41 (Mainz, 1863). **CHAMBER:** 3 string quartets (1871, 1884, 1884); Piano Trio on themes from Meyerbeer's *L'Africaine* (Paris, n.d.); *Elégie* for Viola or Cello and Piano, op.30 (c. 1854); Viola Sonata, op.36 (1863); Allegro and Scherzo for Viola and Piano, op.60 (1884); numerous works for Violin and Piano.

BIBL.: M. Kufferath, *H. V.* (Brussels, 1882); J. Radoux, *V., Sa vie, ses oeuvres* (Liège, 1891; Eng. tr., 1983); P. Bergmans, *H. V.* (Turnhout, 1920).—**NS/LK/DM**

Viganò, Salvatore, Italian composer and choreographer, nephew of **Luigi (Ridolfo) Boccherini;** b. Naples, March 25, 1769; d. Milan, Aug. 10, 1821. He was the son and pupil of a dancer. He studied music with his uncle then began his career as a dancer at Rome in 1783, where he also produced an opera buffa, *La Vedova scoperta.* In 1789 he went to Madrid, where he married the celebrated ballerina María Medina; they subsequently toured as dancers, winning particular distinction in Vienna in 1793. After separating from his wife, he served as ballet-master in Vienna (1799–1803). Beethoven wrote the music for Viganò's "heroic ballet" *Die Geschöpfe des Prometheus* (Vienna, March 28, 1801), in which Vigaò danced the leading male role. After producing ballets in several Italian cities, he was active at Milan's La Scala (1811–21)

BIBL.: C. von Ayrenhoff, *Über die theatratischen Tänze und die Ballettmeister Noverre, Muzzarelli, und V.* (Vienna, 1794); C. Ritorni, *Commentarii della vita e delle opere coreodrammatiche di S. V.* (Milan, 1838); A. Levinson, *Meister des Balletts: Stendhal und V.: Eine Seite aus der Geschichte der Romantik* (Potsdam, 1923). —**NS/LK/DM**

Viglione-Borghese, Domenico, Italian baritone; b. Mondovi, July 3, 1877; d. Milan, Oct. 26, 1957. He studied in Milan and Pesaro. He made his operatic debut as the Herald in *Lohengrin* in Lodi in 1899 and continued to sing in provincial Italian opera companies. In 1901 he gave up singing and went to the U.S., where he earned his living as a railroad worker in San Francisco. There he met Caruso, who recommended him to the impresario Scognamillo, who engaged him for a South American tour (1905–06); Viglione-Borghese subsequently pursued his career in Italy, retiring in 1940. He sang some 40 roles, the best known being Jack Rance in Puccini's *La Fanciulla del West*, which he first sang in Brescia in 1911 and for the last time in Rome in 1940. —**NS/LK/DM**

Vignas, Francisco, noted Spanish tenor; b. Moya, near Barcelona, March 27, 1863; d. Barcelona, July 14, 1933. He studied at the Barcelona Cons. and later in Paris. He made his debut in Barcelona in 1888 as Lohengrin and later sang in Italian opera houses. He made his first appearance in London in 1893 at the Shaftesbury Theatre. On Nov. 29, 1893, he made his Metropolitan Opera debut in N.Y. as Turiddu; after only one season there, he returned to Europe.—**NS/LK/DM**

Vignola, Frank, jazz guitarist and banjoist; b. Islip, N.Y., Dec. 30, 1965. He grew up in a musical environment. His father played banjo in a group with other banjoists, and Frank started playing guitar when he was five. His father bought him records by Django Reinhardt, Joe Pass, and Bucky Pizzarelli. For the next seven years he got Joe Pass records for Christmas. These were the only records he listened to until age 12, when he took up the banjo, playing it so well that at 14 he won the Grand National Banjo Championship in Canada and recorded an album. As a teenager he heard and played rock and roll, but continued to explore jazz. He also studied during this period at the Cultural Art Center of Long Island, which broadened his outlook. He has played on the *Tonight Show* (with Johnny Carson), on PBS with ragtime pianist Max Morath, at the Blue Note and Michael's Pub in N.Y., at jazz festivals in the U.S. and Europe, and on recordings and gigs with Leon Redbone, Milt Hinton, Billy Mitchell, and Ringo Starr. He performed and recorded as leader of his own Hot Club, a group dedicated to Django Reinhardt. He has been a guest lecturer and teacher at Boston Univ., and the Univ. of Pittsburgh, among others. Vignola also heads the Jazz Guitar department at Ariz. State Univ.; co- leads a group with Sam Pilafian, Travelin' Light, and joined with Howard Alden and Jimmy Bruno to form the Concord Jazz Guitar Collective.

DISC.: *Appel Direct* (1993); *Let It Happen* (1994); *Look Right, Jog Left* (1995); *Deja Vu* (1999).—**LP**

Vila, Pedro Alberto, Spanish organist and composer; b. 1517; d. Barcelona, Nov. 15, 1582. He was organist and canon at Barcelona Cathedral, and one of the few Spanish composers who cultivated the madrigal. He publ. *Odarum quas vulgo Madrigales appellamus* (Barcelona, 1561), with texts in Spanish, Catalan, Italian, and French. Some of his organ works are found in the tablature book of Venegas de Henestrosa. His nephew Luis Ferrán Vila succeeded him as organist at Barcelona Cathedral.—**NS/LK/DM**

Villalba Muñoz, Padre Luis, Spanish musicologist and composer; b. Valladolid, Sept. 22, 1872; d. Madrid, Jan. 8, 1921. He entered the Augustinian order at the age of 14, and was maestro de capilla at the monastery of the Escorial (1898–1916); he also taught history and other subjects, He ed. the review *La Ciudad de Dios* (1898–1916), to which he contributed valuable essays on Spanish music, and founded the *Biblioteca sacro* (1911). He then was organist at S. Sebastian in Madrid and ed. of the *Ilustración Española y Americana.* He publ. the valuable *Antologia de organistas clásicos* *españoles* (Madrid, 1914; 2nd ed., 1971, by S. Rubio) and *Dies canciones españolas de los siglos XV y XVI, traducidas y transcritas para piano y canto* (Madrid, n.d.). He wrote monographs on Pedrell, Granados, and Usandizaga, and *Ultimos músicos españoles del siglo XIX* (Madrid, 1914). Among his compositions were organ works, sacred choruses, and chamber music.—**NS/LK/DM**

Villa-Lobos, Heitor, remarkable Brazilian composer of great originality and unique ability to recreate native melodic and rhythmic elements in large instrumental and choral forms; b. Rio de Janeiro, March 5, 1887; d. there, Nov. 17, 1959. He studied music with his father, a writer and amateur cello player; after his father's death in 1899, Villa-Lobos earned a living by playing the cello in cafés and restaurants; he valso studied cello with Benno Niederberger. From 1905 to 1912 Villa-Lobos traveled in Brazil in order to collect authentic folk songs. In 1907 he entered the National Inst. of Music in Rio de Janeiro, where he studied with Frederico Nascimento, Angelo França, and Francisco Braga. In 1912 he undertook an expedition into the interior of Brazil, where he gathered a rich collection of Indian songs. On Nov. 13, 1915, he presented a concert of his compositions in Rio de Janeiro, creating a sensation by the exuberance of his music and the radical character of his technical idiom. He met Artur Rubinstein, who became his ardent admirer; for him Villa-Lobos composed a transcendentally difficult *Rudepoema*. In 1923 Villa-Lobos went to Paris on a Brazilian government grant; upon returning to Brazil in 1930, he was active in São Paulo and then in Rio de Janeiro in music education, founding a Cons. under the sponsorship of the Ministry of Education in 1942. He introduced bold innovations into the national program of music education, with an emphasis on the cultural resources of Brazil. He also compiled a *Guia pratico*, containing choral arrangements of folk songs of Brazil and other nations and organized the "orpheonic concentrations" of schoolchildren, whom he trained to sing according to his own cheironomic method of solfeggio. In 1944 he made his first tour of the U.S., and conducted his works in Los Angeles, Boston, and N.Y. In 1945 he established the Brazilian Academy of Music in Rio de Janeiro, serving as its president from 1947 until his death. He made frequent visits to the U.S. and France during the last 15 years of his life.

Villa-Lobos was one of the most original composers of the 20th century. He lacked formal academic training, but far from hampering his development, this deficiency liberated him from pedantic restrictions, so that he evolved an idiosyncratic technique of composition, curiously eclectic, but all the better suited to his musical aesthetics. An ardent Brazilian nationalist, he resolved from his earliest attempts in composition to use authentic Brazilian song materials as the source of his inspiration, yet he avoided using actual quotations from popular songs; rather, he wrote melodies which are authentic in their melodic and rhythmic content. In his desire to relate Brazilian folk resources to universal values, he composed a series of extraordinary works, *Bachianas brasileiras*, in which Brazilian melorhythms are treated in Bachian counterpoint. He also composed a number of works under the generic title *Chôros*, a popular Brazilian dance form marked by incisive rhythm and a ballad-like melody. An experimenter by nature, Villa-Lobos devised a graphic method of composition, using geometrical contours of drawings and photographs as outlines for the melody; in this manner he wrote *The New York Skyline*, using a photograph for guidance. Villa-Lobos wrote operas, ballets, syms., chamber music, choruses, piano pieces, and songs, the total number of his compositions being in excess of 2,000.

WORKS: DRAMATIC: Opera: *Izaht* (1912–14; rev. 1932; concert premiere, Rio de Janeiro, April 6, 1940; stage premiere, Rio de Janeiro, Dec. 13, 1958); *Magdalena* (1947; Los Angeles, July 26, 1948); *Yerma* (1953–56; Santa Fe, Aug. 12, 1971); *A menina das nuvens* (1957–58; Rio de Janeiro, Nov. 29, 1960); others left unfinished. **Ballet** (many converted from symphonic poems): *Uirapuru* (1917; Buenos Aires, May 25, 1935; rev. 1948); *Possessão* (1929); *Pedra Bonita* (1933); *Dança da terra* (1939; Rio de Janeiro, Sept. 7, 1943); *Rudá* (1951); *Gênesis* (1954; as a symphonic poem, 1969); *Emperor Jones* (1955; Ellenville, N.Y., July 12, 1956). **9 BACHIANAS BRASILEIRAS:** No. 1 for 8 Cellos (Rio de Janeiro, Sept. 12, 1932), No. 2 for Chamber Orch. (1933), No. 3 for Piano and Orch. (1934), No. 4 for Piano (1930–40; orchestrated, N.Y., June 6, 1942), No. 5 for Voice and 8 Cellos (1938; Rio de Janeiro, March 25, 1939), No. 6 for Flute and Bassoon (1938), No. 7 for Orch. (1942; Rio de Janeiro, March 13, 1944), No. 8 for Orch. (1944; Rome, Aug. 6, 1947), and No. 9 for Chorus or String Orch. (1944) **15 CHÔROS:** No. 1 for Guitar (1920), No. 2 for Flute and Clarinet (1921), No. 3 for Men's Chorus and 7 Wind Instruments (1925), No. 4 for 3 Horns and Trombone (1926), No. 5, *Alma brasileira*, for Piano (1926), No. 6 for Orch. (1926; Rio de Janeiro, July 15, 1942), No. 7 for Flute, Oboe, Clarinet, Saxophone, Bassoon, Violin, and Cello (1924), No. 8 for Large Orch. and 2 Pianos (1925; Paris, Oct. 24, 1927), No. 9 for Orch. (1929; Rio de Janeiro, July 15, 1942), No. 10, *Rasga o Coração*, for Chorus and Orch. (1925; Rio de Janeiro, Dec. 15, 1926), No. 11 for Piano and Orch. (1928; Rio de Janeiro, July 15, 1942), No. 12 for Orch. (1929; Cambridge, Mass., Feb. 21, 1945), No. 13 for 2 Orchs. and Band (1929), No. 14 for Orch., Band, and Chorus (1928), and No. 15, a supernumerary *Chôros bis* for Violin and Cello (1928). **OTHER ORCH.:** *Dansas africanas* (1914; Paris, April 5, 1928); 2 cello concertos: No. 1, *Grand Concerto* (1915), and No. 2 (1953; N.Y., Feb. 5, 1955); 12 syms.: No. 1, *Imprevisto* (1916; Rio de Janeiro, Aug. 30, 1920), No. 2, *Ascenção* (1917), No. 3, *Guerra* (Rio de Janeiro, July 30, 1919), No. 4, *Vitória* (1920), No. 5, *Paz* (1921), No. 6, *Montanhas do Brasil* (1944), No. 7, *Odisséia da paz* (1945; London, March 27, 1949), No. 8 (1950; Philadelphia, Jan. 14, 1955), No. 9 (1951; Caracas, May 16, 1966), No. 10, *Sume Pater Patrium*, for Soloists, Chorus, and Orch. (1952; Paris, April 4, 1957), No. 11 (1955; Boston, March 2, 1956), and No. 12 (1957; Washington, D.C., April 20, 1958); 2 sinfoniettas (1916, 1947); *Amazonas* (1917; Paris, May 30, 1929); *Fantasy of Mixed Movements* for Violin and Orch. (Rio de Janeiro, Dec. 15, 1922); *Momoprecoce* for Piano and Orch. (Amsterdam, 1929); *Caixinha de Boãs Festas* (Rio de Janeiro, Dec. 8, 1932); *Ciranda das sete notes* for Bassoon and Strings (1933); 3 of 4 suites titled *Descobrimento do Brasil* (1937; No. 4 is an oratorio); *The New York Skyline* (1939); *Rudepoema* (orch. version of the piano work of that name; Rio de Janeiro, July 15, 1942); *Madona*, tone poem (1945; Rio de Janeiro, Oct. 8, 1946); 5 piano concertos (1945; 1948; 1952–57; 1952; 1954); *Fantasia* for Cello and Orch. (1945); *Fantasia* for Soprano Saxophone, Strings, and 2 Horns (1948); *Erosion, or The Origin of the Amazon River* (Louisville, Nov. 7, 1951); Guitar Concerto (1951);

Harp Concerto (1953; Philadelphia, Jan. 14, 1955); *Odyssey of a Race*, symphonic poem written for Israel (1953; Haifa, May 30, 1954); *Dawn in a Tropical Forest* (1953; Louisville, Jan. 23, 1954); Harmonica Concerto (1955; Jerusalem, Oct. 27, 1959); *Izi*, symphonic poem (1957). **OTHER CHAMBER:** 3 piano trios (1911, 1916, 1918); *Quinteto duplo de cordas* (1912); 4 *Sonatas-Fantasia* for Violin and Piano (1912, 1914, 1915, 1918); 17 string quartets (1915, 1915, 1916, 1917, 1931, 1938, 1942, 1944, 1945, 1946, 1948, 1950, 1952, 1953, 1954, 1955, 1958); 2 cello sonatas (1915, 1916); Piano Quintet (1916); *Mystic Sextet* for Flute, Clarinet, Saxophone, Celesta, Harp, and Guitar (1917); Trio for Oboe, Clarinet, and Bassoon (1921); Woodwind Quartet (1928); *Quintet in the Form of a Chôros* for Flute, Oboe, Clarinet, Bassoon, and English Horn (1928; rev. 1953, replacing English Horn with French Horn); String Trio (1946); *Duo* for Violin and Viola (1946); *Fantasia concertante* for Piano, Clarinet, and Bassoon (1953); *Duo* for Oboe and Bassoon (1957); Quintet for Flute, Harp, Violin, Viola, and Cello (1957); *Fantasia concertante* for Cello Ensemble (N.Y., Dec. 10, 1958). **VOCAL:** *Crianças* for Chorus (1908); *Vidapura*, oratorio for Chorus, Orch., and Organ (1918; Rio de Janeiro, Nov. 11, 1922); *Hinos aos artistas* for Chorus and Orch. (1919); Quartet for Harp, Celesta, Flute, Saxophone, and Women's Voices (1921); Nonetto for Flute, Oboe, Clarinet, Saxophone, Bassoon, Harp, Celesta, Percussion, and Chorus (1923); *Cantiga da Roda* for Women's Chorus and Orch. (1925); *Na Bah a tem* for Chorus (1925); *Canção da Terra* for Chorus (1925); *Missa São Sebastião* for Chorus (1937); Suite No. 4 of *Descobrimento do Brasil* for Orch. and Chorus (1937); *Mandu-Carará*, cantata profana for Chorus and Orch. (1940; N.Y., Jan. 23, 1948; also a ballet); *Bendita sabedoria* (Blessed Wisdom) for Chorus (1958); *Magnificat-Alleluia* for Boy Contralto, Chorus, Organ, and Orch. (Rio de Janeiro, Nov. 8, 1958; by request of Pope Pius XII); etc. **Songs:** *Confidencia* (1908); *Noite de Luar* (1912); *Mal secreto* (1913); *Fleur fanée* (1913); *Il nome di Maria* (1915); *Sertão no Estio* (1919); *Canções típicas brasileiras* (10 numbers; 1919); *Historiettes* (6 numbers; 1920); *Epigrammes ironiques et sentimentales* (8 numbers; 1921); *Suite* for Voice and Violin (1923); *Poème de l'Enfant et de sa Mère* for Voice, Flute, Clarinet, and Cello (1923); *Serestas* (suite of 14 numbers; 1925); *3 poemas indígenas* (1926); *Suite sugestiva* for Voice and Orch. (1929); *Modinhas e canções* (2 albums; 1933, 1943); *Poem of Itabira* for Alto and Orch. (1941; Rio de Janeiro, Dec. 30, 1946); *Canção das aguas claras* for Voice and Orch. (1956). **PIANO:** *Valsa romantica* (1908); *Brinquedo de Roda* (6 pieces; 1912); *Primeira suite infantil* (5 pieces; 1912); *Segunda suite infantil* (4 pieces; 1913); *Fábulas características* (3 pieces; 1914–18); *Danças africanas* (1915); *Prole do Bebé*, Suite No. 1 (8 pieces, including the popular *Polichinello*; 1918), No. 2 (9 pieces; 1921), and No. 3 (9 pieces; 1929); *Historia da Carochinha* (4 pieces; 1919); *Carnaval das crianças brasileiras* (8 pieces; 1919); *Lenda do Caboclo* (1920); *Dança infernal* (1920); *Sul América* (1925); *Cirandinhas* (12 pieces; 1925); *Rudepoema* (1921–26); *Cirandas* (16 pieces; 1926); *Alma brasileira* (*Chôros* No. 5; 1926); *Lembrança do Sertão* (1930); *Caixinha de música quebrada* (1931); *Ciclo brasileiro* (4 pieces; 1936); *As Três Marías* (3 pieces; 1939); *Poema singelo* (1942); *Homenagem a Chopin* (1949).

BIBL.: V. Mariz, *H. V.-L.* (Rio de Janeiro, 1949; 11th ed., 1990); C. de Paula Barros, *O Romance de V.-L.* (Rio de Janeiro, 1951); *Homenagem a V.-L.* (Rio de Janeiro, 1960); M. Beaufils, *V.-L., Musicien et poete du Brésil* (Rio de Janeiro, 1967); E. Nogueria França, *V.-L.: Síntese critica e biográfica* (Rio de Janeiro, 1970; 2nd ed., 1973); L. Guimarães, *V.-L. visto da plateia e na intimidade (1912–1935)* (Rio de Janeiro, 1972); L. Peppercorn, *H. V.-L.: Leben und Werk des Brasilianischen Komponisten* (Zürich, 1972); F. Pereira da Silva, *V.-L.* (Rio de Janeiro, 1974); T. Santos, *H. V.-L. and the Guitar* (Bank, County Cork, 1985); P. Carvalho, *V.-L.: Do crépusculo à alvorada* (Rio de Janeiro, 1987); M. Claret, ed., *O Pensamento vivo de H. V.-L.* (São Paulo, 1987); M. Machado, *H. V.-L.: Tradição e renovacão na música brasileira* (Rio de Janeiro, 1987); A. Schic, *V.-L.: Souvenirs de l'indien blanc* (Arles and Paris, 1987); E. Stornio, *V.-L.* (Madrid, 1987); D. Appleby, *H. V.-L.: A Bio-bibliography* (N.Y., 1988); L. Peppercorn, *V.-L.: Collected Studies* (Aldershot, 1992); S. Wright, *V.-L.* (Oxford, 1992); G. Behague, *H. V.-L.: The Search for Brazil's Musical Soul* (Austin, Tex., 1994); L. Peppercorn, *The World of V.-L. in Pictures and Documents* (Aldershot, 1995); E. Tarasti, *H. V.-L.: The Life and Works, 1887–1959* (Jefferson, N.C., 1995).—**NS/LK/DM**

Villoing, Alexander, notable Russian pianist and teacher, uncle of **Vasili Villoing;** b. Moscow, March 12, 1804; d. there, Sept. 2, 1878. He was born of a French emigre family. He studied piano with John Field in Moscow, where he taught piano (1830–62), enjoying a reputation as one of the best pedagogues in Russia. Anton and Nikolai Rubinstein were among his pupils; he traveled with them in Europe. His *École pratique du piano* (St. Petersburg, 1863) was accepted by the St. Petersburg Cons. as a teaching guide. He publ. a book of piano exercises, which he called *Exercises for the Rubinstein Brothers*.—**NS/LK/DM**

Villoing, Vasili, Russian pianist, violinist, conductor, teacher, and composer, nephew of **Alexander Villoing;** b. Moscow, Oct. 28, 1850; d. Nizhny-Novgorod, Sept. 15, 1922. He studied piano with his uncle and violin with Ferdinand Laub at the Moscow Cons. He then moved to Nizhny-Novgorod, where he organized a music school and conducted a local orch. founded by him. Among his piano students were Dobrowen and Liapunov. He composed three operas, four string quartets, and a number of piano pieces and songs.
—**NS/LK/DM**

Vinacessi, Benedetto, Italian composer and organist; b. Brescia, c. 1670; d. Venice, c. 1719. After studies with Pietro Pelli, he was in the service of Prince Ferdinand Gonzaga of Catiglione delle Stiviere, near Mantua, and of Count Alemano Gabara of Brescia. In 1704 he was made a Cavaliere and 2nd organist at San Marco in Venice. His successful dramatic works for Venice included *L'innocenza giustificata* (Dec. 1698), *Gli amanti generosi* (Carnival 1703), and *Gli sponsali di giubilo* (1705). Among his other works were two books of trio sonatas (1687, 1692), a Mass, four oratorios, two cantatas, and a book of motets (1714).

BIBL.: M. Talbot, *B. V.: A Musician in Brescia and Venice in the Age of Corelli* (Oxford, 1994).—**NS/LK/DM**

Viñao, Ezequiel, Argentine composer; b. Buenos Aires, July 21, 1960. As a child he studied in Buenos Aires with Jacobo Ficher, and then later attended the Dept. of Acoustic Musical Studies. Encouraged by the legendary American pianist Earl Wild and through the auspices of the United Nations, he then moved to N.Y., where he studied at the Juilliard School, his mentors including György Sandor, Adele Marcus, and Milton

Babbitt; also studied with Messiaen in France (1987).

WORKS: DRAMATIC: Opera: *Merlin*, after Caleb Carr (1998–2000). **ORCH.:** *El Sueño de Cristobal* (1992; Boston, May 16, 1993; rev. 1998; N.Y., March 8, 1999). **CHAMBER:** *La Noche de las Noches* for String Quartet and Tape (1987–89; N.Y., Nov. 13, 1990); *El Simurgh, Book I, The Conference of the Birds* for Piano and Tape (1991; London, March 2, 1993) and *Book II, The Seven Valleys* for Violin and Tape (1992; Austin, Tex., March 29, 1993); Trio for Piano, Violin, and Cello (1995; N.Y., Feb. 29, 1996). **Piano:** *Études, Book I* (1993; Washington, D.C., Oct. 29, 1995); *Fantaisie* (1998; N.Y., Jan. 20, 1999). **VOCAL:** *Arcanum* for Soprano, Oboe/Horn, Trombone, String Quintet, and Percussion (1996; N.Y., May 13, 1997); *Viviane of Avalon* for Dramatic Coloratura Soprano and Orch., arr. from the opera *Merlin* (1998; Paris, Feb. 5, 1999). **TAPE:** *Sinfonia, The Voices of Silence* for FM Sounds (1986–87; Helsinki, Dec. 8, 1987).—**LK/DM**

Vinay, Ramón, Chilean baritone, later tenor; b. Chillán (of French and Italian parents), Aug. 31, 1912; d. Puebla, near Mexico City, Jan. 4, 1996. He was a pupil of José Pierson in Mexico City, where he made his operatic debut as Alfonso in *La Favorite* (1931); after appearances in baritone roles, he pursued further training and turned to the tenor repertory, making his 2nd debut as Don José in Mexico City in 1943; he chose that same role for his N.Y. debut in 1945. On Feb. 22, 1946, Vinay made his Metropolitan Opera debut in N.Y. as Don José; he remained on its roster until 1958, and sang there again from 1959 to 1962 and in 1965–66. He also appeared in Europe, opening the 1947–48 season at Milan's La Scala in his most famous role, Otello; he sang at the Bayreuth Festivals (1952–57) and regularly at London's Covent Garden (1953–60). From 1969 to 1971 he was artistic director of the Santiago Opera. Among his other roles were Bartolo, Iago, Falstaff, Scarpia, Telramund, Parsifal, Tristan, Siegfried, and Tannhäuser.—**NS/LK/DM**

Vincent, Gene (originally, **Craddock, Vincent Eugene**), early rockabilly star who had a larger impact in England than he did at home; b. Norfolk, Va. Feb. 11, 1935; d. Newhall, Calif., Oct. 12, 1971.

Gene Vincent quit school to join the Navy. While in the service, he suffered severe injuries to his left leg in a motorcycle crash that left him permanently disabled. While convalescing after his discharge in May 1955, he took up singing and, by March 1956, he was sitting in with the house band at Norfolk's WCMS radio. He was noticed by local disc jockey "Sheriff" Tex Davis, who arranged for Vincent to record a demonstration tape with a backing group, subsequently dubbed The Blue Caps. Davis forwarded the tape, which included "Be-Bop-A-Lula," to Ken Nelson of Capitol Records, which was seeking an answer to RCA's Elvis Presley.

Gene Vincent signed with Capitol and he and The Blue Caps (lead guitarist Cliff Gallup, rhythm guitarist Willie Williams, stand-up bassist Jack Neal, and drummer Dickie Harrell) traveled to Nashville in May 1956, where they recorded four songs. "Be-Bop-A-Lula" became a near-smash pop, country and R&B hit, but the flip side, "Woman Love," was banned by some radio stations as too risque. Touring extensively, the group returned to Nashville in June to complete recordings for their first album, which included "Who Slapped John" and the neglected rockabilly classic "Blue Jean Bop." By Sept. Paul Peek had replaced Willie Williams, and the group soon appeared in the film *The Girl Can't Help It* with Little Richard, Eddie Cochran, and Fats Domino. Scoring a minor hit with "Race with the Devil," the group recorded their second album in October, but Gallup left in December, to be replaced by lead guitarist Johnny Meeks. Vincent was re-hospitalized in early 1957 and later that year the group achieved major pop and near-smash R&B hits with "Lotta Lovin'" and "Dance to the Bop." By June the band included only one original member, Dickie Harrell. In early 1958 Vincent and The Blue Caps appeared in the film *Hot Rod Gang*, performing four songs.

Plagued by reports of hotel wrecking and involvement with underage females, Gene Vincent began suffering from limited airplay. His unruly and ribald stage act and rowdy lower-class image were attracting less attention than boy-next-door types like Buddy Holly and Ricky Nelson. Vincent began drinking heavily and, by the end of 1958, he had abandoned The Blue Caps. At the end of 1959 he moved to Great Britain, where he toured regularly, adopting black leather stage attire, and became one of the country's biggest-drawing attractions. His hits continued in England through the summer with "Wild Cat," "My Heart," "Pistol Packin' Mama" and "She She Little Sheila." However, on the night of April 16, 1960, Vincent was badly injured in the car crash that killed Eddie Cochran. His physical and psychological state subsequently deteriorated through neglect and alcohol and drug abuse. His Capitol contract expired in 1963 and, in 1964, he recorded a British-only album for Columbia Records.

Gene Vincent returned to America in 1966 and enjoyed some renewed popularity with the rock 'n' roll revival of the late 1960s. However, his attempts at a comeback on Dandelion and Kama Sutra Records fared dismally. Gene Vincent died in obscurity of cardiac failure attributed to a bleeding ulcer at the age of 36. He has yet to be inducted into the Rock and Roll Hall of Fame. In 1993 Jeff Beck recorded an entire album of Vincent's songs, *Crazy Legs*.

DISC.: GENE VINCENT AND THE BLUE CAPS: *Blue Jean Bop* (1956); *Gene Vincent and His Blue Caps* (1957); *Gene Vincent Rocks and The Blue Caps Roll* (1958); *Hot Rod Gang* (soundtrack; 1958); *A Gene Vincent Record Date* (1958); *Sounds Like Gene Vincent* (1959); *The Bop That Just Won't Stop* (1974); *Gene Vincent* (1990). **GENE VINCENT:** *Crazy Times* (1960); *I'm Back and I'm Proud* (1969); *Gene Vincent–If You Could See Me Now* (1970); *The Day the World Turned Blue* (1971); *Forever* (1982); *Rockabilly Fever* (1982); *Ain't That Too Much* (1993); *Bird Doggin'* (1996).

BIBL.: Britt Hagarty. *The Day the World Turned Blue* (Vancouver, B.C., 1983).—**BH**

Vincent, John, American composer and teacher; b. Birmingham, Ala., May 17, 1902; d. Santa Monica, Calif., Jan. 21, 1977. He studied flute with Georges Laurent at the New England Cons. of Music in Boston (1922–26), and composition there with Converse and Chadwick (1926–27), then took courses at the George Peabody

Coll. in Nashville, Tenn. (M.A., 1933) and at Harvard Univ., where his principal teacher was Piston (1933–35). He then went to Paris, where he studied at the École Normale de Musique (1935–37), and took private lessons with Boulanger; received his Ph.D. from Cornell Univ. in 1942. He was in charge of music in the El Paso (Tex.) public schools (1927–30); taught at George Peabody Coll. in Nashville (1930–33), at Western Ky. Teachers Coll. (1937–46), and at the Univ. of Calif., Los Angeles (1946–69). After his death, the John Vincent Archive was established at UCLA. In his music, he evolved a tonal idiom which he termed "paratonality"; fugal elements are particularly strong in his instrumental compositions. He publ. the books *Music for Sight Reading* (N.Y., 1940); *More Music for Sight Reading* (N.Y., 1941); *The Diatonic Modes in Modern Music* (N.Y., 1951; 2nd ed., rev., 1974).

WORKS: DRAMATIC: *3 Jacks*, ballet (1942; rev. 1954; rev. as an orch. suite, 1954; rev. as *The House That Jack Built* for Narrator and Orch., 1957); *The Hallow'd Time*, incidental music (1954); *Primeval Void*, opera (1969). **ORCH.:** Suite (1929); *A Folk Symphony* (1931; not extant); *Nude Descending a Staircase* for Strings (1948; also for Xylophone and Piano or Strings, 1974); *Symphonic Poem after Descartes*, with the motto of Descartes, "Cogito ergo sum," suggested by the thematic rhythm on the kettledrums (1958; Philadelphia, March 20, 1959); *La Jolla Concerto* for Chamber Orch. (La Jolla, Calif., July 19, 1959; rev. 1966 and 1973); *Overture to Lord Arling* (1959); *Benjamin Franklin Suite* for Glass Harmonica and Orch. (Philadelphia, March 24, 1963); *Rondo Rhapsody* (Washington, D.C., May 9, 1965); *The Phoenix, Fabulous Bird*, symphonic poem (Phoenix, Ariz., Feb. 21, 1966). **CHAMBER:** *Nacre, Mother of Pearl* for Flute and Piano (1925; rev. 1973; also for Band, 1973); *Suite: Prelude, Canon, and Fugue* for Flute, Oboe, and Bassoon (1936); 2 string quartets (1936, rev. as *Recitative and Dance* for Cello Obbligato and Strings, 1948; 1967, rev. 1969); *Consort* for Piano and String Quartet (1960; also for Piano and String Orch.; also as Sym. No. 2 for Strings, 1976); *Victory Salute* for 12 Brass (1968); Suite for 6 Percussion (1973); piano pieces. **VOCAL:** *3 Grecian Songs* for Chorus (1935); *How Shall we Sing* for Voices and Piano (1944; rev. 1951); *Sing Hollyloo* for Mezzo-soprano or Baritone and Piano (1951; also for Men's Voices and Piano); *Stabat Mater* for Soprano, Men's Voices, and Piano or Organ (1969; also for Soprano, Men's Voices, and Orch., 1970); *A Christmas Psalm* for Voice and Piano (1969; rev. as *Prayer for Peace* for Soprano, Alto, Chorus, and Organ or Piano, 1971).—**NS/LK/DM**

Vinci, Leonardo, noted Italian composer; b. Strongoli, c. 1690; d. Naples, May 27, 1730. He studied at the Cons. dei Poveri di Gesù Cristo in Naples, where he was a pupil of Gaetano Greco. In 1719 he served as maestro di cappella to the Prince of Sansevero; was provicemaestro at the Royal Chapel in Naples from 1725 until his death; in 1728 he was also maestro di cappella at the Cons. dei Poveri di Gesù Cristo. He was highly esteemed by his contemporaries as a composer for the theater. He produced a number of opera series, including *Silla dittatore* (Naples, Oct. 19, 1723), *L'Astianatte* (Naples, 1725), *La caduta dei Decemviri* (Naples, Oct. 1, 1727), and *Artaserse* (Rome, Feb. 4, 1730); he also produced many commedie musicali, an oratorio, *Le glorie del Ss. Rosario*, 6 chamber cantatas, etc.

BIBL.: G. Silvestri Silva, *Illustri musici calabresi: L. V.* (Genoa, 1935).—**NS/LK/DM**

Vinci, Pietro, distinguished Italian composer and teacher; b. Nicosia, Sicily, c. 1535; d. there or in Piazza Armerina, c.June 15, 1584. After living in various areas of Italy, he served as maestro di cappella at the Basilica of S. Maria Maggiore in Bergamo (1568–80); then returned to Sicily in 1581. He was distinguished as a madrigalist. Among his pupils were Paolo Caracciolo and Antonio Il Verso. He composed masses, other sacred works, 12 books of madrigals (1561–84), and ricercares. A complete ed. of his works was publ. in Musiche Rinascimentali Siciliane (1971 et seq.).

BIBL.: F. Mompellio, *P. V. madrigalista siciliano* (Milan, 1937).—**NS/LK/DM**

Vinco, Ivo, Italian bass; b. Verona, Nov. 8, 1927. He studied at the Verona Liceo Musicale and with Ettore Campogalliani in Milan. After making his operatic debut as Ramfis in Verona in 1954, he sang there regularly in succeeding years; also appeared in virtually all Italian opera centers. On March 19, 1970, he made his Metropolitan Opera debut in N.Y. as Oroveso, remaining on its roster until 1973, and returning for the 1976–78 seasons. Among his prominent roles were the Grand Inquisitor, Mozart's Dr. Bartolo, Alvise, Ferrando, Donizetti's Raimondo, and Sparafucile. In 1958 he married **Fiorenza Cossotto**.—**NS/LK/DM**

Vincze, Imre, Hungarian composer and teacher; b. Kocs, Sept. 26, 1926; d. Budapest, May 3, 1969. He studied with Szabó at the Budapest Academy of Music (graduated, 1951); after serving as Szabó's assistant there, he was a prof. until 1968. In 1952 and 1956 he won the Erkel Prize.

WORKS: DRAMATIC: Film music. **ORCH.:** 3 syms. (1951, 1953, 1967); *Greeting*, overture (1954); *Movimento sinfonico* (1957); *Aforismo* for Strings (1959); *Cantata senza parole* (1960); Concertino (1961); *Rapsodia concertante* for Piano and Orch. (1966). **CHAMBER:** 4 string quartets (1954, 1958, 1961, 1965); Violin Sonata (1956); *Divertimento* for Wind Quintet (1962); Bassoon Sonata (1964). **Organ:** *Fantasy and Fugue* (1960). **VOCAL:** *Szerelem, szerelem* (Love, Love) for Chorus (1955); *Perzsa dalok* (Persian Songs) for Voice and Piano (1967). —**NS/LK/DM**

Vine, Carl, Australian composer and pianist; b. Perth, Oct. 8, 1954. He was a student at the Univ. of Western Australia in Nedlands of Stephen Dornan (piano) and John Exton (composition). After serving as pianist of the West Australian Sym. Orch. in Perth (1973–75), he was a pianist with various organizations, including the Sydney Dance Co. (1975–78), where he was also resident composer (1978). In 1979 he was guest resident composer of the London Contemporary Dance Theatre. From 1979 to 1989 he was co-director, pianist, and conductor of the contemporary music ensemble Flederman. He lectured on electronic music at the Queensland Conservatorium of Music in Brisbane (1980–82), and then was resident composer of the New South Wales State Conservatorium of Music in Sydney (1985), the Australian Chamber Orch. (1987), and Western Australian Univ. (1989). From 1992 to 1995 he was deputy chairman of the Australia Council. In 1993 he was honored with the Australian Screen Composers Guild Award for his music to the film *Bedevil*. Vine has composed in various genres, ranging from dance, film, and theater scores to orch., chamber, and electronic pieces. He has demonstrated a deft handling of tonal writing, notable for its harmonic refinement and lyricism.

WORKS: DRAMATIC: Theater: Music for: Shakespeare's *The Tempest* (1975), Andrew Simon's *The Dreamers* (1975), Judith Anderson's *New Sky* (1981), Patrick White's *Singal Driver* (1982), *Shepherd on the Rocks* (1987), and *Ham Funeral* (1989); Ibsen's *Master Builder* (1991). **Dance:** *961 Ways to Nirvana* (1977); *Incident at Bull Creek* (1977); *Everymans Troth* (1978); *Poppy* (1978); *Knips Suite* (1979); *Kisses Remembered* (1979); *Scene Shift* (1979); *Return* (1980); *Missing Film* (1980); *Colonial Sketches* (1981); *Donna Maria Blues* (1981); *Hate* (1982); *Daisy Bates* (1982); *A Christmas Carol* (1983); *Porologue+Canzona* (1986); *Legend* (1988); *On the Edge* (1988); Piano Sonata (1990); *The Tempest* (1991); *Beauty and the Beast* (1993). **Film:** *You Can't Push the River* (1992); *Bedevil* (1993). **ORCH.:** *Curios* (Sydney, Feb. 5, 1980); *Canzona* for Strings (1985); 6 syms.: No. 1, *MicroSymphony* (Sydney, Aug. 17, 1986), No. 2 (Melbourne, April 23, 1987), No. 3 (Adelaide, March 5, 1990), No. 4 (Sydney, May 23, 1993), No. 5, *Percussion Symphony* (1994; Sydney, March 17, 1995), and No. 6, *Choral Symphony* (1995); Concerto for Percussion and Orch. or Tape (1987); *Legend Suite* (Perth, July 8, 1988); Concerto grosso for Chamber Orch. (1989; Sydney, June 16, 1991); *Celebrare Celeberrime* (1993; Dayton, Ohio, Jan. 10, 1994); *Gaijin* for Koto, Strings, and Tape (Adelaide, March 11, 1994). **CHAMBER:** *Miniature I* for Viola (1973), *II* for 2 Violas (1974), *III* for Flute, Trombone or Cello, Piano, and Percussion (1983), and *IV* for Flute, Clarinet, Violin, Viola, Cello, and Piano (1988); *Tergiversative Blues* for Lute (1977); *Free Game* for Trombone and Electronics (1979); *Occasional Poetry* for Trombone and Piano (1979); *Images* for Flute, Trombone, Cello, Piano, Harpsichord, and Percussion (1981); Sinfonia for Flute, Clarinet, Violin, Cello, Piano, and Percussion (1982); 3 string quartets, including No. 2 (1984) and No. 3 (1994); *Cafe Concertino* for Flute, Clarinet, Violin, Viola, Cello, and Piano (1984); *Elegy* for Flute, Cello, Trombone, Piano 4-Hands, and Percussion (1985); *Love Song* for Trombone and Tape (1986); *Defying Gravity* for Percussion Quartet (1987); Flute Sonata (1992); *Harmony in Concord* for Trombone, Marimba or Vibraphone, Percussion, and Tape (1992); *Inner World* for Cello and Tape (1994). **VOCAL:** *Aria* for Soprano, Flute, Cello, Piano, Celesta, and Percussion (1984); *After Campion* for Chorus and 2 Pianos (1989). **OTHER:** *Tape Piano Piece* for Tape (1976); *Heavy Metal* for Tape and Improvisation (1980); *Kondallila Mix* for Tape and Improvisation (1980); *Intimations of Mortality* for Computer Tape (1985).—**NS/LK/DM**

Viñes, Ricardo, Spanish pianist; b. Lérida, Feb. 5, 1875; d. Barcelona, April 29, 1943. He studied in Barcelona with Juan Pujol, then settled in Paris in 1887, where he studied piano with Beriot (premier prix, 1894), composition with Godard, and harmony with Lavignac at the Cons. In 1895 he gave his first concert in Paris. He established himself in later years as an ardent propagandist of new French and Spanish music; he possessed particular affinity with the composers of the modern French school, and performed their works in a colorful and imaginative manner. He gave concerts in London, Berlin, and other music centers, but lived most of his life in Paris. He contributed articles on Spanish music to publications in France and Spain.—**NS/LK/DM**

Vinnegar, Leroy, American bassist; b. Indianapolis, Ind., July 13, 1928. He made his reputation in the early 1950s playing in the house rhythm section of Chicago's Beehive club, accompanying traveling musicians such as Charlie Parker, Sonny Stitt, Lester Young, Howard McGhee, and Johnny Griffin. He moved to Los Angeles in 1954 as Art Tatum's substitute bassist and soon became the city's first-call bassman. He recorded with most of L.A.'s leading musicians, including tenor saxophonists Stan Getz, Teddy Edwards, and Harold Land, trumpeter Shorty Rogers, guitarist Barney Kessel, and pianists Andre Previn and Les McCann. He also recorded important sessions with Sonny Rollins, Kenny Dorham, and Phineas Newborn Jr. Television, movie, and studio work preoccupied him for much of the 1960s, though he continued to play jazz. Health problems sidelined him in the 1980s and he moved to Portland, where he has become an important part of the Pacific Northwest jazz scene.

DISC.: *Leroy Walks!* (1957); *Leroy Walks Again!* (1962–63); *Swiss Movement* (1969); *Walkin' the Basses* (1993).—**AG**

Vinson, Eddie "Cleanhead", R&B/jazz alto saxophonist, singer, bandleader; b. Houston, Tex., Dec. 18, 1917; d. Los Angeles, July 2, 1988. His nickname comes from his bald head, which he once said was shaved as a result of botched attempts to straighten his hair. He learned to play the alto saxophone in his youth, first worked in Chester Boone's Band in late 1932, then was with Milt Larkin's Band during the 1930s. From 1940–41 he was with Floyd Ray's Orch. and in early 1942 he went to N.Y., where he played in Cootie Williams's band (1942–45); his vocals with Williams's band achieved great commercial success. Vinson's biggest hit with the blues was the honkin' "Cherry Red Blues," which would become his signature song. After briefly serving in the Army in early 1945, he rejoined Cootie Williams from spring until September 1945, then formed his own band, which gained popularity through blues performances. He led several small groups through the late 1940s, including one legendary group that featured saxophonist John Coltrane (November 1948–May 1949). With this group, he expanded into more jazz-oriented compositions, including two pieces, "Tune Up" and "Four," that Miles Davis would later take credit for but that were actually composed by Vinson. Late in the 1940s Vinson led his own short-lived 16-piece band; he worked as a single during the early 1950s and rejoined Cootie Williams briefly in 1954. He reformed his own band, playing residencies in Chicago, then co-led with Arnett Cobb in Houston. During the early 1960s Vinson worked mainly in Kansas City, Mo. He toured Europe with Jay McShann in 1969 then led his own band in Calif., and also played with Johnny Otis. He made his home in Los Angeles, but frequently appeared in U.S. and European jazz and blues centers. He starred at Montreux Festival (June 1971). Vinson recorded with Cannonball Adderley, Arnett Cobb, Jay McShann, Johnny Otis, and others. He was hospitalized in mid-June 1988, and subsequently suffered a heart attack and died.—**LP/JC/NS**

Vinton, Bobby (actually, **Stanley Robert**), popular singer of romantic songs from the 1960s; b. Canonsburg, Pa., April 14, 1935. His father led a band, and Bobby Vinton had visions of working with a big band even as the genre faded into nostalgia. He earned a degree at Duquesne in musical composition while supporting himself in various bands. By the end of his matriculation, he could play piano, clarinet, saxophone, trumpet, drums, and oboe. An appearance by his band on Guy Lombardo's TV show earned him a four-week run on the program, which in turn got him a contract with Epic Records.

Vinton's earliest records featured big band versions of contemporary hits. Not needing an instrumental act, Epic asked Vinton to sing. His first single, "Roses Are Red," proved him a palatable and profitable vocalist. It topped the pop and adult contemporary charts for four weeks in the summer of 1962, going gold. He followed this with the #12 "Rain Rain Go Away." Several minor Top 40 hits followed this, but just about a year after his first chart topper, he went to #3 with "Blue on Blue." This was followed by one of his most enduring hits, "Blue Velvet," which topped the pop charts for three weeks and spent eight on the top of the adult contemporary charts during the summer of 1963. His next big hit, "There, I've Said It Again," also topped the charts for four weeks, topping the adult contemporary charts for five. Tellingly, it was knocked out of the #1 position by the Beatles's "I Want to Hold Your Hand."

Vinton's jejune love songs continued to succeed, however, long after the other "boy singers" faded before the British Invasion. In the spring of 1964, he was all over the airwaves with "My Heart Belongs to Only You," which went to #9. He followed this with the #13 "Tell Me Why." The success of these songs might have, in their own way, reflected the rise of rock. The four aforementioned hits covered previous hits from the late 1940s and early 1950s. The Beatles spoke to "the kids." Vinton's string-heavy pledges of puppy love played for romantic adults.

The late fall of 1964 found Vinton atop the charts again with "Mr. Lonely," his fourth Top 40 hit (and second Top Ten) of the year. With this, he became the male vocalist with the most #1 hits during the first ten years of the rock era. Although only the follow-up "Long Lonely Nights" broke the Top 20, Vinton landed another four Top 40 hits in 1965, totaling 17 Top 40 records in three years. This streak slowed down for a bit in the mid-1960s, although he did make the Top Ten with "Please Love Me Forever." He hit a stride again in 1968, landing yet another four Top 40 hits including "Take Good Care of My Baby" and the gold #9 "I Love How You Love Me." By the summer of 1972, when he hit #19 with his version of "Sealed with a Kiss," Vinton had put a remarkable 28 songs into the Top 40.

While still a popular performer at casinos and cabarets, Vinton started his second decade as a star by failing to chart for the first year since "Roses Are Red." He staged a brief comeback in 1974 with the polka- flavored "My Melody of Love." He sang one verse of the song in Polish, endearing him to people of his ancestry. He became known as the Polish Prince (which became the title of his autobiography). The song rose to #3 and went gold. He followed it with a version of the "Beer Barrel Polka" that provided his final Top 40 hit in 1975. However, he remains a major attraction on the casino and cabaret circuit, with the occasional oldies tour as well. In the late 1970s, he had his own CBS-TV variety show. He tried to launch another one in syndication during the mid-1980s. "Blue Velvet" rose back onto the pop culture radar when filmmaker David Lynch used it as the theme to his film of the same name. When Branson, Mo., began to become an entertainment destination, he opened the Blue Velvet Theater, which continues as a thriving enterprise.

Disc.: *Dancing at the Hop* (1961); *Young Man with a Big Band* (1961); *Bobby Vinton Sings the Big Ones* (1962); *Roses Are Red* (1962); *Live at the Copa* (1962); *Blue Velvet* (1963); *Mr. Lonely* (1964); *Tell Me Why* (1964); *There! I've Said It Again* (1964); *Bobby Vinton Sings for Lonely Nights* (1965); *Drive- In Movie Time* (1965); *Country Boy* (1966); *Satin Pillows and Careless* (1966); *Please Love Me Forever* (1967); *I Love How You Love Me* (1968); *Take Good Care of Her* (1968); *Vinton* (1969); *My Elusive Dreams* (1970); *Ev'ry Day of My Life* (1972); *Sealed with a Kiss* (1972); *With Love* (1974); *Melodies of Love* (1974); *Heart of Hearts* (1975); *The Bobby Vinton Show* (1975); *The Name Is Love* (1977); *Great Songs of Christmas* (1990); *A Very Merry Christmas* (1994); *Kissin' Christmas: The Bobby Vinton* (1995); *Branson City Limits* (live; 1998).—**BH**

Viola, Alfonso dalla
See **Dalla Viola, Alfonso**

Viola, Francesco dalla
See **Dalla Viola, Francesco**

Viola, P. Anselm, Catalan composer; b. Teruel, July 1738; d. Montserrat, Jan. 25, 1798. He was a monk at Montserrat. He wrote much instrumental music of surprising excellence in a fine Baroque style. His Concerto for 2 Oboes, 2 Horns, Violins, and Cellos obbligato is included in D. Pujol, ed., *Música instrumental* (Vol. II, Montserrat, 1936).—**NS/LK/DM**

Viole, Rudolf, German pianist and composer; b. Schochwitz, Mansfeld, May 10, 1825; d. Berlin, Dec. 7, 1867. He was a pupil of R. Hentschel in Weissenfels and of Liszt, who recommended his compositions and ed. his 100 études. He was active in Berlin as a piano teacher and writer on music. Viole wrote mostly for piano, including 11 sonatas, a *Caprice héroïque*, a Ballade, a Polonaise, etc.—**NS/LK/DM**

Viotti, Giovanni Battista, famous Italian violinist and composer; b. Fontanetto da Po, May 12, 1755; d. London, March 3, 1824. His father, a blacksmith, was an amateur musician who taught his son music and also bought a small violin for him to practice on. At the age of 11, Viotti was sent to Turin, where he gained the favor of Alfonso del Pozzo, Prince della Cisterna, who oversaw his education. After lessons with Antonio Celoniat, Viotti became a pupil of Pugnani in 1770. In 1775 he became a member of the last desk of 1st violins in the orch. of the Royal Chapel in Naples. In 1780 he and Pugnani launched a major concert tour, performing in Switzerland, Dresden, Berlin, Warsaw, and St. Petersburg. By 1782 Viotti was in Paris on his own, where he first appeared at the Concert Spirituel (March 17). He immediately established himself as the premier violin virtuoso of the day, and gave regular concerts there until 1783. In 1784 he entered the service of Marie Antoinette in Versailles; he also acted as concertmaster of the orch. of Prince Rohan-Guéménée. Thanks to the patronage of the Court of Provence, he opened the Théâtre de Monsieur in Paris in 1788, which became the Théâtre Feydeau in 1791. During his tenure there, he staged major works from the Italian and French repertories, including those of his close friend Cherubini. In 1792 he fled the revolution-wracked city of Paris for London, where he made his debut at Salomon's Hanover Square Concert on Feb. 7, 1793. He was the featured violinist of Salomon's concerts until 1795, and also acting manager of the Italian opera at the King's Theatre (1794–95). He became music director of the new Opera Concerts in 1795 and, in 1797, concertmaster and director of the orch. at the King's Theatre. In 1798 he was ordered by the British government to leave England on suspicion of Jacobin sympathies. After living in Schenfeldt, near Hamburg (1798–99), he was back in London by 1801, where he was engaged mainly in a wine business, although he later helped to found the Phil. Society and appeared in some of its chamber-music programs. In 1818 his wine business failed, and he returned to Paris, where he became director of the Opéra in 1819. He resigned in 1821, serving as its nominal director until 1822, but then abandoned music altogether and returned to London in 1823.

Viotti's role in the history of instrumental music, in both performance and composition, was very important. He elevated performing standards from mere entertainment to artistic presentation, and he may be regarded as one of the chief creators of modern violin playing. He was the first to write violin concertos in a consciously formulated sonata form, with the solo part and the orch. accompaniment utilizing the full resources of instrumental sonority more abundantly than ever before in violin concertos. He publ. 29 violin concertos (of which No. 22, in A minor, is a great favorite), 10 piano concertos (some of which are transcriptions of violin concertos), 2 symphonies concertantes for 2 Violins, Strings, Oboes, and Horns, 21 string quartets, 21 string trios, various duos for 2 Violins, 6 serenades for 2 Violins, several duos for 2 Cellos, 3 divertissements for Violin Unaccompanied, 12 sonatas for Violin and Piano, etc. His song known as "La polacca de Viotti" (used in Paisiello's *La Serva padrona*, 1794) acquired great popularity. For the rectification of Viotti's birth date (heretofore given as May 23, 1753), see Stampa di Torino of Sept. 29, 1935, which publ. for the first time the text of his birth certificate; an infant brother of Viotti was born in 1753; their Christian names were identical (the brother having died before the birth of the future musician), which led to confusion. The bicentennial of Viotti was widely celebrated in the wrong year (1953). C. White ed. a thematic catalogue of his works (N.Y., 1985).

Bibl.: A. d'Eymar, *Anecdotes sur V., précédées de quelques réflexions sur l'expression en musique* (Paris, 1792); F. Fayolle, *Notices sur Corelli et V.* (Paris, 1810); P. Baillot, *Notice sur J.B. V.* (Paris, 1825); E. Miel, *Notice historique sur J.B. V.* (Paris, 1827); R. Giazotto, *G.B. V.* (Milan, 1956); C. White, *G.B. V. and his Violin Concertos* (diss., Princeton Univ., 1957); V. Milton, *An Analysis of Selected Violin Concertos of G.B. V. Within the Context of the Violin Concerto in France of the Late Eighteenth and Early Nineteenth Centuries* (diss., American Cons. of Music, 1986).—**NS/LK/DM**

Viotti, Marcello, Italian conductor; b. Vallorbe, June 29, 1954. He received training at the Lausanne Cons. In 1981 he took 1st prize in the Gino Martinuzzi Competition in San Remo. He was permanent guest conductor of the Teatro Regio in Turin from 1985 to 1987. From 1987 to 1990 he was artistic director of the Lucerne Opera. He was Generalmusikdirektor in Bremen from 1990 to 1993. In 1991 he became chief conductor of the Saarland Radio Sym. Orch. in Saarbrücken and was named to the post of 1st guest conductor of the Vienna State Opera. He concurrently served as 1st guest conductor of the Deutsche Oper in Berlin and permanent guest conductor of the Bavarian State Opera in Munich from 1993. In 1998 he became music director of the Munich Radio Orch.—**NS/LK/DM**

Virchi, Paolo, Italian instrumentalist and composer; b. Brescia, c. 1550; d. Mantua, May 1610. He was the son of the Italian instrument maker Girolamo di Virchi (b. Brescia, c. 1523; d. after 1754). By 1574 he was an organist in Brescia. In 1579 he entered the service of the Este court in Ferrara as an organist, instrumentalist, and teacher. From 1598 he was organist at the church of S. Barbara in Mantua. Virchi publ. four distinguished vols. of madrigals (Venice, 1574–91).—**LK/DM**

Virdung, Sebastian, German music theorist and composer; b. Amberg, Jan. 19 or 20, c. 1465; d. place and date unknown. He was educated at the Univ. of Heidelberg, and also studied with Johannes von Soest at the chapel of the Palatine court in Heidelberg, where he was an alto and Kapellmeister. After being ordained, he also served as chaplain. He was a singer at the Wurttemberg court chapel in Stuttgart (1506–7), then was one of the nine succentors at Konstanz Cathedral (1507–8). He wrote a work of importance for the history of musical instruments, *Musica getutscht und auszgezogen durch Sebastianum Virdung, Priesters von Amberg, und alles Gesang ausz den Noten in die Tabulaturen diser benannten dryer Instrumenten, der Orgeln, der Lauten und der Flöten transferieren zu lernen kurtzlich gemacht* (Basel, 1511; facsimile reprint in Eitner's *Publikationen Alterer Praktischer und Theoretischer Musikwerke,* vol. 11, 1882; also by L. Schrade, Kassel, 1931, and by K. Niemoller, Kassel, 1970; Eng. tr. by B. Bullard, Cambridge, 1993). Virdung's method was violently attacked by Arnolt Schlick in his *Tabulatur etlicher Lobgesänge* (1512). Four of Virdung's songs are in Schöffer's *Teutsche Lieder mit 4 Stimmen* (1513).—**NS/LK/DM**

Virizlay, Mihály, Hungarian-born American cellist, teacher, and composer; b. Budapest, Nov. 2, 1931. He began violin studies at an early age with his father. After receiving instruction in cello from Janos Starker, he studied with Miklós Zsambolski and Edi Banda (cello) and Pál Járdanyi and Kodály (composition) at the Budapest Academy of Music (graduated, 1955). In 1957 he emigrated to the U.S., and became a naturalized American citizen (1962). After playing in the Dallas Sym. Orch., he was asst. principal cellist of the Pittsburgh Sym. Orch. (1960–62) and then principal cellist of the Baltimore Sym. Orch. (from 1962); also pursued a career as an orch. soloist, recitalist, and chamber music artist, making appearances on both sides of the Atlantic. He taught at the Peabody Cons. of Music in Baltimore (from 1963), and also held master classes throughout the U.S. He was distinguished for his performances of contemporary music.

WORKS: ORCH.: *The Emperor's New Clothes*, suite (1964); Trombone Concerto (Baltimore, Nov. 2, 1985); Cello Concerto (1985; Baltimore, Feb. 12, 1987). **CHAMBER:** *Ének* (Song) for Cello and Piano (1955); Sonata for Solo Cello (1972); *Rhapsody* for Cello and Piano (1973); Piano Sonata (1981); *Grand Duo* for 2 Flutes (1985).—**NS/LK/DM**

Visconti (di Modrone), Count Luchino, prominent Italian film, theater, and opera director; b. Milan, Nov. 2, 1906; d. Rome, March 17, 1976. After World War II, he assumed a leading position among film directors, producing films notable for their realism. In 1954 he enlarged the scope of his work to include opera, his first production being Spontini's *Le vestale* at Milan's La Scala with Maria Callas; his first production outside his homeland was *Don Carlos* at London's Covent Garden in 1958; that same year, his *Macbeth* opened the Spoleto Festival, where he maintained a close association in subsequent seasons. His opera productions were impressive, particularly for his ability to complement the dramatic qualities of the music with the action on stage to effect a total theatrical experience.

BIBL.: M. Esteve, ed., *L. V.: L'Histoire et l'esthétique* (Paris, 1963); G. Smith, *L. V.* (London, 1967).—**NS/LK/DM**

Visée, Robert de, French guitarist, theorbo and viol player, singer, and composer; b. c. 1650; d. c. 1725. About 1680 he became a chamber musician to Louis XIV. He was guitar teacher to the King from 1695, a position he held officially from 1719; he also sang in the royal chapel from 1709. His guitar works have been ed. by R. Strizich (Paris, 1971).

WORKS: *Livre de guittarre dédié au roy* (Paris, 1682); *Livre de pièces pour la guittarre* (Paris, 1686); *Pièces de théorbe et de luth mises en partition dessus et basse* (Paris, 1732); other works in contemporary collections.—**NS/LK/DM**

Vishnevskaya, Galina (Pavlovna), prominent Russian soprano; b. Leningrad, Oct. 25, 1926. After vocal studies with Vera Garina in Leningrad, she sang in operetta. In 1952 she joined the operatic staff of the Bolshoi Theater in Moscow, where her roles were Violetta, Tosca, Madama Butterfly, and an entire repertoire of soprano parts in Russian operas. In 1955 she married **Mstislav Rostropovich**, with whom she frequently appeared in concert. She made her debut at the Metropolitan Opera in N.Y. on Nov. 6, 1961, as Aida. Owing to the recurrent differences that developed between Rostropovich and the cultural authorities of the Soviet Union (Rostropovich had sheltered the dissident writer Solzhenitsyn in his summer house), they left Russia in 1974 and settled in the U.S. when Rostropovich was appointed music director of the National Sym. Orch. in Washington, D.C., in 1977. In March 1978, both he and Vishnevskaya, as "ideological renegades," were stripped of their Soviet citizenship by a decree of the Soviet government. Her autobiography was publ. as *Galina: A Russian Story* (N.Y., 1984). After Gorbachev's rise to power in her homeland, her Soviet citizenship was restored in 1990.

BIBL.: C. Samuel, *Mstislav Rostropovich and G. V.: Russia, Music, and Liberty: Conversations with Claude Samuel* (Portland, Ore., 1995).—**NS/LK/DM**

Viski, János, Hungarian composer and teacher; b. Kolozsvár, June 10, 1906; d. Budapest, Jan. 16, 1961. He was a student of Kodály at the Budapest Academy of Music (1927–32). In 1940 he became a prof. at the Budapest National Cons. After serving as director of the Cluj Cons. (1941–42), he was a prof. of composition at the Budapest Academy of Music from 1942 until his death. In 1954 he won the Erkel Prize, in 1955 he was made a Merited Artist by the Hungarian government, and in 1956 he received the Kossuth Prize. His music was permeated by Hungarian melorhythms set in classical forms.

WORKS: ORCH.: *Symphonic Suite* (1935); *2 Hungarian Dances* (1938); *Enigma* (1939); Violin Concerto (1947); Piano Concerto (1953); Cello Concerto (1955). **CHAMBER:** String Trio (1930; not extant); *5 Little Piano Pieces* (1948); *Epitaph for Anton Webern* for Piano (1960). **VOCAL:** *Az irisórai szarvas* (The Heart of Irisora), ballad for Baritone and Orch. (1958); choruses; solo songs.—**NS/LK/DM**

Visse, Dominique, French countertenor; b. Lisieux, Aug. 30, 1955. He was a chorister at Notre Dame Cathedral in Paris, pursued studies in organ and flute at the Versailles Cons., and received training in voice from Alfred Deller, René Jacobs, and Nigel Rogers (1976–78). He founded the Ensemble Clément Janequin, with which he gave performances of works from the medieval and Renaissance periods. In 1982 he made his operatic debut in Monteverdi's *L'incoronazione di Poppea* in Tourcoing. After singing Flora in Vivaldi's *L'incoronazione di Dario* in Grasse in 1984, he portrayed Charpentier's Actéon at the Edinburgh Festival in 1985. In 1987 he sang Nirenus in Handel's *Giulio Cesare* at the Paris Opéra, and then Delfa in Cavalli's *Giasone* in Innsbruck in 1988. He created the role of Geronimo in Claude Prey's *Le Rouge et Noir* in Aix-en-Provence in 1989. In 1991 he sang Annio in Gluck's *La clemenza di Tito* in Lausanne. He portrayed the role of the Nurse in *L'incoronazione di Poppea* in Buenos Airea in 1996. —**NS/LK/DM**

Vitale, Edoardo, Italian conductor; b. Naples, Nov. 29, 1872; d. Rome, Dec. 12, 1937. He studied composition with Terziani at the Accademia di Santa Cecilia in Rome, where he then taught harmony (1893–97). He was only 14 when he began conducting operettas at Rome's Teatro Metastasio. From 1897 he conducted throughout Italy. After conducting at Milan's La Scala (1908–10), he was chief conductor of the Rome Opera (1913–26). He conducted the first Italian performances of *Elektra* (1904) and *Boris Godunov* (1909). He also led many premieres, including Mascagni's *Parisina* and Zandonai's *Francesca da Rimini*, and revived many works. In 1897 he married the soprano Lina Pasini. —**NS/LK/DM**

Vitali, Filippo, Italian composer; b. Florence, c. 1590; d. probably there, after April 1, 1653. In 1631 he became a singer in the Pontifical Choir in Rome; also was a priest in the service of Cardinal Francesco Barberini and Cardinal Antonio Barberini. In 1642 he returned to Florence as maestro di cappella of the grand ducal chapel of S. Lorenzo, and in 1648–49 he was also maestro di cappella at S. Maria Maggiore in Bergamo. His "favola in musica" *L'Aretusa*, performed on Feb. 8, 1620, at the home of Monsignor Corsini, is regarded as the first attempt at opera in Rome (publ. there, 1620). In 1622 he composed six intermedi for the comedy *La finta mora* by J. Cicognini, performed at the palace of Cardinal de' Medici in Florence (publ. there, 1623). He was highly esteemed by his contemporaries for his mastery of polyphony; his most significant works are the cycle of 34 hymns set to Latin texts and publ. in the *Brevarium romanum* (1632). He also composed other sacred and secular works.

BIBL.: J. Pruett, *The Works of F. V.* (diss., Univ. of N.C., 1962).—**NS/LK/DM**

Vitali, Giovanni Battista, significant Italian composer; b. Bologna, Feb. 18, 1632; d. there, Oct. 12, 1692. He became a singer and violoncino player (cellist) at S. Petronio in Bologna, where he was a pupil of Cazzati, its maestro di cappella; was a member of the Accademia Filarmonica of Bologna by 1666. After serving as maestro di cappella at S. Rosario in Bologna (1673–74), he was made one of the two vicemaestri di cappella to Duke Francesco II at the Este court in Modena; was his maestro di cappella from 1684 to 1686 before reverting to vicemaestro in 1686. Vitali was a leading figure in the development of the Baroque sonata, most particularly of the trio sonata. He publ. the influential pedagogical work *Artificii musicali*, op.13 (Modena, 1689).

WORKS: INSTRUMENTAL: *Correnti, e balletti da camera* for 2 Violins and Basso Continuo, op.1 (Bologna, 1666); *Sonate* for 2 Violins and Basso Continuo (organ), op.2 (Bologna, 1667); *Salmi concerti* for 2 to 5 Instruments, op.6 (Bologna, 1677); *Balletti, correnti alla francese, gagliarde, e brando per ballare* for 4 Instruments, op.3 (Bologna, 1679); *Balletti, correnti, gighe, allemande, e sarabande* for Violin, Violone or Spinet, and 2 Violins ad libitum, op.4 (Bologna, 1668); *Sonate* for 2 to 5 Instruments, op.5 (Bologna, 1669); *Varie partite del passemezo, ciaccona, capricii, e passagalii* for 2 Violins and Violone or Spinet, op.7 (Modena, 1682); *Balletti, correnti, e capricci per camera* for 2 Violins and Basso Continuo, op.9 (Venice, 1684); *Varie sonate alla francese, e all'itagliana* for 6 Instruments, op.11 (Modena, 1684); *Balli in stile francese* for 5 Instruments, op.12 (Modena, 1685); *Artificii musicali ne qualli se contengono canoni in diverse maniere, contrapunti dopii, inventioni curiose, capritii, e sonate*, op.13 (Modena, 1689; ed. by L. Rood and G. Smith, Smith Coll. Music Archives, XIV, 1959); T. Vitali, ed., *Sonate da camera* for 2 Violins and Violone, op.14 (Modena, 1692). **VOCAL:** 6 oratorios, including *L'ambitione debellata overo La caduta di Monmuth* (Modena, 1686) and *Il Giono* (Modena, 1689); 10 cantatas; *Hinni sacri per tutto l'anno* for Voice and 5 Instruments, op.10 (Modena, 1684).

BIBL.: J. Suess, *G.B. V. and the "Sonata da chiesa"* (diss., Yale Univ., 1963).—**NS/LK/DM**

Vitalini, Alberico, Italian conductor and composer; b. Rome, July 18, 1921. He studied at the Santa Cecilia Cons. in Rome, obtaining diplomas in violin (1940), viola (1942), composition (1944), and conducting (1945). He subsequently became active mainly as a conductor; in 1950, was appointed director of musical programs of Radio Vaticana; in 1973, was nominated a member of the Accademia Internazionale de Propaganda Culturale. He specialized in sacred choral music.

WORKS: *Fantasia* for Piano and Orch. (1949); *Assisi* for Chorus and Orch. (1949); *Le sette parole di Cristo* for Baritone and String Orch. (1952); *Magnificat* for Soprano, Chorus, and Orch. (1954); *Tiberiade* for Small Orch. (1955); *Canti in italiano*, for a new liturgy in the Italian language (1965–71).—**NS/LK/DM**

Vitalis, George, Greek composer and conductor; b. Athens, Jan. 9, 1895; d. there, April 27, 1959. He studied with Armani in Milan. He conducted light opera in Athens (1923–36), then went to the U.S. in 1945 and settled in N.Y. He composed the operas *Perseus and Andromeda, The Return of the Gods*, and *Golfo* (concert perf., N.Y., Jan. 1, 1949), as well as *Greek Fantasy* for Orch. (Athens, Nov. 11, 1945) and light orch. pieces under the pseudonym Giorgio Valente.—**NS/LK/DM**

Vitro, Roseanna, singer; b. Hot Springs, Ark., Feb. 28, 1951. She has a musical background of gospel singing, blues, rock, classical, and show music, but fell in love with jazz. Her jazz career began in Houston, Tex. in 1973, under the guidance of Ray Sullenger (vocalist and wind player from Ted Weems band) and Arnett Cobb. Cobb featured her on gigs and in his summer jazz workshops educating children from poor families (as she herself was). In Houston, she ran her own group for a few years, and had a radio program where she performed and featured other artists, including Oscar Peterson (and sat in with him). Relocating to N.Y. in 1980, she studied with Ken Werner, Fred Hersch, Anne Marie Moss, Joe Lovano, Bobby McFerrin, David Leonhart; she also studied classical voice with Cabore Carelli at the Manhattan School of Music. She started the vocal jazz program in September 1996 at Jersey City State Coll. The *Down Beat* Critics poll voted her Talent Deserving Wider recognition in 1994 and 1995.

DISC.: Kenny Barron, Steve Allen, Marian McPartland: *Listen Here* (1982). Fred Hersch: *Quiet Place* (1988). George Coleman: *Reaching for the Moon* (1991); *Softly* (1993). Elvin Jones, Gary Bartz: *Passion Dance* (1995). David Fathead Newman: *Catchin' Some Rays* (1997).—**LP**

Vitry, Philippe de, famous French music theorist, composer, poet, and churchman, also known as **Philip-**

pus de Vitriaco; b. Vitry, Champagne, Oct. 31, 1291; d. Meaux, June 9, 1361. There are six towns in Champagne named Vitry, and it is not known in which of these Vitry was born. He was educated at the Sorbonne in Paris, where he later was magister artium. He was ordained a deacon early in life, and from 1323 he held several benefices; he also served as canon of Soissons and archbishop of Brie. He became a clerk of the royal household in Paris and about 1346 was made counselor of the court of requests ("maître des requêtes"). From 1346 to 1350 he was also in the service of Duke Jean of Normandy (heir to the throne), with whom he took part in the siege of Aiguillon (1346). When Duke Jean became king in 1350, he sent Vitry to Avignon on a mission to Pope Clement VI, who appointed him bishop of Meaux on Jan. 3, 1351. Vitry was known as a poet and a composer, but his enduring fame rests on his *Ars nova*, a treatise expounding a new theory of mensural notation, particularly important for its development of the principle of binary rhythm; it also gives the most complete account of the various uses to which colored notes were put. Of the four treatises attributed to Vitry in Coussemaker's *Scriptores*, III, only the last 10 of the 24 chapters of *Ars nova* (publ., with corrections, in *Musica Disciplina*, 1956) are now considered authentic. Most of Vitry's works are lost. L. Schrade ed. 12 of his motets as *The Works of Philippe de Vitry*, Polyphonic Music of the Fourteenth Century, I (Monaco, 1956); another motet, with tenor only, is also extant.—**NS/LK/DM**

Vittadini, Franco, Italian composer; b. Pavia, April 9, 1884; d. there, Nov. 30, 1948. He studied at the Milan Cons. After serving as organist and maestro di cappella in Varese, he returned to Pavia, where he was founder-director of the Istituto Musicale (1924–48).

WORKS: DRAMATIC: Opera: *Il mare di Tiberiade* (c. 1912–14); *Anima allegra* (1918–19; Rome, April 15, 1921); *Nazareth* (Pavia, May 28, 1925); *La Sagredo* (Milan, April 26, 1930); *Caracciolo* (Rome, Feb. 7, 1938); *Fiammetta e l'avvaro* (1942). **Pastoral Triptych:** *Il natale di Gesù* (Bari, Dec. 20, 1933). **Ballet:** *Vecchia Milano* (1928); *Fiordisole* (Milan, Feb. 14, 1935); *La Taglioni* (1945). **Other:** Film music. **ORCH.:** *Armonie della notte* (1923); *Scherzo* (1931); *Poemetto romantico* for Strings (1938). **OTHER:** Chamber music; piano pieces; organ music; masses; motets; songs.

BIBL.: A. Baratti, *Vita del musicista F. V.* (Milan, 1955). —**NS/LK/DM**

Vittori, Loreto, prominent Italian castrato soprano and composer; b. Spoleto (baptized), Sept. 5, 1600; d. Rome, April 23, 1670. After serving as a chorister at Spoleto Cathedral (1614–17), he went to Rome to pursue his musical training; about 1618 he proceeded to Florence, where he continued his studies and began his operatic career in 1619. Returning to Rome, he was in the service of Cardinal Lodovico Ludovisi (1621–32); also sang in the papal choir (1622–47), where he was camerlengo (1642–44); likewise was in the service of Cardinal Antonio Barberini (1637–42). About 1623 he was created Cavaliere della Milizia di Gesù Cristo by Pope Urban VIII; in 1643 he entered the priesthood. He composed both sacred and secular dramatic works, but the music to most of these is lost; his fine pastoral opera, *La Galatea* (Rome, 1639), is extant. He was also a poet; publ. *Dialoghi sacri, e morali* (Rome, 1652) and *La Troja rapita* (Macerata, 1662).

BIBL.: C. Rau, *L. V.: Beiträge zur historisch-kritischen Würdigung seines Lebens, Wirkens und Schaffens* (Munich, 1916). —**NS/LK/DM**

Vivaldi, Antonio (Lucio), greatly renowned Italian composer; b. Venice, March 4, 1678; d. Vienna, July 28, 1741. He was the son of Giovanni Battista Vivaldi (b. Brescia, c. 1655; d. Venice, May 14, 1736), a violinist who entered the orch. at San Marco in Venice in 1685 under the surname of Rossi, remaining there until 1729, and was also director of instrumental music at the Mendicanti (1689–93). The younger Vivaldi was trained for the priesthood at S. Geminiano and at S. Giovanni in Oleo, taking the tonsure on Sept. 18, 1693, and Holy Orders on March 23, 1703. Because of his red hair he was called "il prete rosso" ("the red priest"). In 1703 he became maestro di violino at the Pio Ospedale della Pietà, where he remained until 1709. During this period, his first publ. works appeared. In 1711 he resumed his duties at the Pietà, and was named its maestro de' concerti in 1716. In 1711 his set of 12 concerti known as *L'estro armonico*, op.3, appeared in print in Amsterdam; it proved to be the most important music publication of the first half of the 18th century. His first known opera, *Ottone in Villa*, was given in Vicenza in May 1713, and soon thereafter he became active as a composer and impresario in Venice. From 1718 to 1720 he was active in Mantua, where the Habsburg governor Prince Philipp of Hessen-Darmstadt made him maestro di cappella da (or di) camera, a title he retained even after leaving Mantua. In subsequent years he traveled widely in Italy, bringing out his operas in various music centers. However, he retained his association with the Pietà. About 1725 he became associated with the contralto Anna Giraud (or Giro), one of his voice students; her sister, Paolina, also became a constant companion of the composer, leading to speculation by his contemporaries that the two sisters were his mistresses, a contention he denied. His *La cetra*, op.9 (2 books, Amsterdam, 1727), was dedicated to the Austrian Emperor Charles VI. From 1735 to 1738 he once more served as maestro di cappella at the Pietà. He also was named maestro di cappella to Francis Stephen, Duke of Lorraine (later the Emperor Francis I), in 1735. In 1738 he visited Amsterdam, where he took charge of the musical performances for the centennial celebration of the Schouwburg theater. Returning to Venice, he found little favor with the theatergoing public; as a result, he set out for Austria in 1740, arriving in Vienna in June 1741, but dying a month later. Although he had received large sums of money in his day, he died in poverty and was given a pauper's burial at the Spettaler Gottesacher (Hospital Burial Ground).

Vivaldi's greatness lies mainly in his superb instrumental works, most notably some 500 concertos, in which he displayed an extraordinary mastery of ritornello form and of orchestration. More than 230 of his concertos are for solo violin and strings, and another 120 or so are for other solo instrument and strings. In some

60 concerti ripieni (string concertos sans solo instrument), he honed a style akin to operatic sinfonias. He also wrote about 90 sonatas. Only 21 of his operas are extant, some missing one or more acts. He also composed various sacred vocal works.

WORKS: DRAMATIC: Opera: *Ottone in Villa* (Vicenza, May 1713); *Orlando finto pazzo* (Venice, 1714); *Nerone fatto Cesare* (Venice, Carnival 1715); *La costanza trionfante degl'amori e de gl'odii* (Venice, Carnival 1716); *Arsilda Regina di Ponto* (Venice, 1716); *L'incoronazione di Dario* (Venice, Carnival 1717); *Tieteberga* (Venice, 1717); *Scanderbeg* (Florence, June 22, 1718); *Armida al campo d'Egitto* (Venice, Carnival 1718); *Teuzzone* (Mantua, Carnival 1719); *Tito Manlio* (Mantua, Carnival 1719); *La Candace o siano Li veri amici* (Mantua, Carnival 1720); *La verità in cimento* (Venice, 1720); *Tito Manlio*, pasticcio (Rome, 1720; in collaboration with G. Boni and C. Giorgio); *Filippo Re di Macedonia* (Venice, Carnival 1721; in collaboration with G. Boneveni); *La Silvia* (Milan, Aug. 26, 1721); *Ercole su'l Termodonte* (Rome, Jan. 23, 1723); *Giustino* (Rome, Carnival 1724); *La virtù trionfante dell'amore e dell'odio overo Il Tigrane* (Rome, Carnival 1724; in collaboration with B. Micheli and N. Romaldi); *L'inganno trionfante in amore* (Venice, 1725); *Cunegonda* (Venice, Carnival 1726); *La Fede tradita e vendicata* (Venice, Carnival 1726); *Dorilla in Tempe* (Venice, 1726); *Ipermestra* (Florence, Carnival 1727); *Siroe, Re di Persia* (Reggio, May 1727); *Farnace* (Venice, 1727); *Orlando (furioso)* (Venice, 1727); *Rosilena ed Oronta* (Venice, Jan. 17, 1728); *L'Atenaide o sia Gli affetti generosi* (Florence, Dec. 29, 1728); *Argippo* (Prague, 1730); *Alvilda, Regina de' Goti* (Prague, 1731); *La fida ninfa* (Verona, Jan. 6, 1732; rev. as *Il giorno felice*); *Semiramide* (Mantua, Carnival 1732); *Motezuma* (Venice, 1733); *L'Olimpiade* (Venice, Carnival 1734); *Griselda* (Venice, May 1735); *Aristide* (Venice, May 1735); *Bajazet* or *Tamerlano* (Venice, Carnival 1735; based on music by other composers); *Ginerva, Principessa di Scozia* (Florence, Jan. 1736); *Didone* (London, April 1737); *Catone in Utica* (Verona, May 1737); *Il giorno felice* (Vienna, 1737); *Rosmira (fedele)* (Venice, Carnival 1738; based on music by other composers); *L'oracolo in Messenia* (Venice, Carnival 1738); *Feraspe* (Venice, 1739). **Serenatas:** *Le gare del dovere* for 5 Voices (Rovigo, 1708); *Dall'eccelsa mia Reggia* (1725); *Questa, Eurilla gentil* for 4 Voices (Mantua, July 31, 1726); *L'unione della Pace e di Marte* for 3 Voices (Venice, 1727); *La Sena festeggiante* for 3 Voices (1726); *Il Mopso* (Venice, c. 1738); *Le gare della Giustizia e della Pace; Mio cor povero cor* for 3 Voices; 31 solo cantatas with Basso Continuo; 9 solo cantatas with Instrument(s) and Basso Continuo. **Oratorios:** *La vittoria navale* (Vicenza, 1713); *Moyses Deus Pharaonis* (Venice, 1714); *Juditha triumphans devicta Holofernes barbarie* (Venice, 1716); *L'adorazione delli tre re magi* (Milan, 1722); other sacred vocal works include 7 masses or Mass sections, Psalms, hymns, antiphons, motets, etc. **CONCERTOS AND SINFONIAS** (all publ. in Amsterdam): *L'estro armonico*, op.3 (2 books, 1711); *La stravaganza*, op.4 (2 books, c. 1714); *VI concerti a 5 stromenti*, op.6 (1716–17); *Concerti a 5 stromenti*, op.7 (2 books, c. 1716–17); *Il cimento dell'armonia e dell'inventione*, op.8 (2 books, 1725); *La cetra*, op.9 (2 books, 1727); *VI concerti*, op.10 (c. 1728); *6 concerti*, op.11 (1729); *6 concerti*, op.12 (1729). **SONATAS:** *Suonate da camera a 3* for 2 Violins and Violone or Harpsichord, op.1 (Venice, 1705); *Sonate* for Violin and Harpsichord (Venice, 1709; publ. as op.2, Amsterdam, 1712–13); *VI sonate* for Violin or 2 Violins and Basso Continuo, op.5 (Amsterdam, 1716); *VI sonates* for Cello and Basso Continuo (Paris, 1740).

BIBL.: COLLECTED EDITIONS, SOURCE MATERIAL: G.F. Malipiero et al., eds., *Le opere di A. V.* (Rome, 1947–72). A new critical ed. commenced publication in Milan in 1982 under the auspices of the Istituto Italiano Antonio Vivaldi. P. Ryom ed. *Verzeichnis der Werke A. V.s: Kleine Ausgabe* (Leipzig, 1974; 2nd ed., 1979) and Repertoire des oeuvres d'A. V. (Vol. I, Copenhagen, 1986). See also M. Rinaldi, *Catalogo numerico tematico delle composizioni di A. V.* (Rome, 1945); M. Pincherle, *Inventaire thématique* (Paris, 1948; Vol. II of *A. V. et la musique instrumentale*); A. Fanna, *A. V.: Catalogo numerico-tematico delle opere strumentali* (Milan, 1968; rev. ed., 1986); K. Heller, *Die deutsche Überlieferung der Instrumentalwerke V.s* (Leipzig, 1971); N. Ohmura, *A Reference Concordance Table of V.'s Instrumental Works* (Tokyo, 1972); P. Ryom, *A. V.: Table de concordances des oeuvres* (Copenhagen, 1973); idem, *Les Manuscrits de V.* (Copenhagen, 1977); M. Talbot, *A. V.: A Guide to Research* (N.Y., 1988). **BIOGRAPHICAL, ANALYTICAL:** *A. V.: Note e documenti sulla vita e sulle opere,* Chigiana, I (1939); M. Abbado, *A. V.* (Turin, 1942); M. Rinaldi, *A. V.* (Milan, 1943); M. Pincherle, *A. V. et la musique instrumentale* (Paris, 1948); W. Kolneder, *Aufführungspraxis bei V.* (Leipzig, 1955; 2nd ed., 1973); M. Pincherle, *V.* (Paris, 1955; Eng. tr., 1958); R. Eller, *V.s Konzertform* (diss., Univ. of Leipzig, 1956); G. Malipiero, *A. V., il prete rosso* (Milan, 1958); H. Rarig, *The Instrumental Sonatas of A. V.* (diss., Univ. of Mich., 1958); L. Rowell, *4 Operas of A. V.* (diss., Univ. of Rochester, 1958); W. Kolneder, *Die Solokonzertform bei V.* (Strasbourg and Baden-Baden, 1961); R. Giazotto, *V.* (Milan, 1965); W. Kolneder, *A. V.: Leben und Werk* (Wiesbaden, 1965; Eng. tr., 1970); R. de Cande, *V.* (Paris, 1967); M. Dunham, *The Secular Cantatas of A. V. in the Foa Collection* (diss., Univ. of Mich., 1969); *V.ana* (Brussels, 1969); R. Giazotto, *A. V.* (Turin, 1973); W. Kolneder, *Melodietypen bei V.* (Berg am Irchel and Zürich, 1973); F. Degrada and M. Muraro, eds., *A. V. da Venezia all'Europa* (Milan, 1978); M. Talbot, *V.* (London, 1978; 4th ed., rev., 1993); W. Kolneder, *A. V.: Dokumente seines Lebens und Schaffens* (Wilhelmshaven, 1979); E. Cross, *The Late Operas of A. V., 1727–1738* (Ann Arbor, 1980); A. Bellini, B. Brizi, and M. Pensa, *I libretti V.ana: Recensione e collazione dei testimoni a stampa* (Florence, 1982); K. Heller, *Concerto ripieno und Sinfonia bei V.* (diss., Univ. of Rostock, 1982); R.-C. Travers, *La Maladie de V.* (Poitiers, 1982); M. Collins and E. Kirk, eds., *Opera and V.* (Austin, Tex., 1984); H. Keller, *A. V.* (Leipzig, 1991); A. Fanna and M. Talbot, eds., *V., vero e falso: Problemi di attribuzione* (Florence, 1992); A. Hermes-Neumann, *Die Flötenkonzerte von A. V.* (Egelsbach, 1993); H.C. Robbins Landon, *V.: Voice of the Baroque* (London, 1993); M. Talbot, *The Sacred Vocal Music of A. V.* (Florence, 1995); P. Everett, *V.: The Four Seasons and Other Concertos, op.8* (Cambridge, 1996); U. Dannemann, *Befreiung aus der Bedrängnis: A. V.s 37. Konzerte für Fagott* (Holzkirchen, 1997); F. Fanna and M. Talbot, eds., *Cinquantíanni di produzioni e consumi della musica dell'età di V., 1947–1997* (Florence, 1998); C. Fertonani, *La musica strumentale di A. V.* (Florence, 1998); M. Talbot, *Venetian Music in the Age of V.* (Aldershot, 1999).—**NS/LK/DM**

Vives, Amadeo, Spanish composer; b. Collbato, near Barcelona, Nov. 18, 1871; d. Madrid, Dec. 1, 1932. He was a pupil of Ribera and then of Felipe Pedrell in Barcelona, and with L. Millet he founded the famous choral society Orfeó Català (1891). In his first opera, *Artus* (Barcelona, 1895), he made use of Catalonian folk songs. Subsequently he moved to Madrid, where he produced his comic opera *Don Lucas del Cigarral* (Feb. 18, 1899); his opera *Euda d'Uriach*, originally to a Catalan libretto, was brought out in Italian at Barcelona (Oct. 24, 1900). Then followed his most popular opera, *Maruxa* (Madrid, May 28, 1914); other operas are *Balada de Carnaval* (Madrid, July 5, 1919) and *Doña Francisquita*

(Madrid, Oct. 17, 1923). The style of his stage productions shared qualities of the French light opera and the Spanish zarzuela; he wrote nearly 100 of these, and also composed songs and piano pieces. He publ. a book of essays, *Sofia* (Madrid, 1923).

BIBL.: A. Sagardia, *A. V.: Vida y obra* (Madrid, 1971). **—NS/LK/DM**

Vivier, Claude, Canadian composer; b. Montreal, April 14, 1948; d. (murdered) Paris, March 7, 1983. He studied with Tremblay (composition) and Heller (piano) at the Montreal Cons. (1967–71). From 1971 he lived in Europe on a Canada Council grant, where he studied with Koenig at the Inst. of Sonology at the Univ. of Utrecht, with Stockhausen and Humpert in Germany, and with Méfano in France. His love for the music of the Orient prompted him to tour that region in 1977, where he spent much time on the island of Bali. In 1981 the Canada Music Council named him its composer of the year. In 1982 he went to Paris on another Council grant, where he was brutally murdered by a chance acquaintance. In 1983 Les Amis de Claude Vivier was organized in Montreal to champion his compositions and writings. Vivier developed a thoroughly individual compositional style in which simplicity became its hallmark. In some of his vocal works, he created texts based on his own invented language.

WORKS: DRAMATIC: *Love Songs*, ballet (1977); *Nanti malam*, ballet (1977); *Kopernicus*, opera (Montreal, May 8, 1980). **ORCH.:** *Siddhartha* (1976); *Orion* (1979); *Zipangu* for Strings (1980). **CHAMBER:** String Quartet (1968); *Prolifération* for Ondes Martenot, Piano, and Percussion (1968; rev. 1976); *Deva et Asura* for Chamber Ensemble (1972); *Désintégration* for 2 Pianos, 4 Violins, and 2 Violas (1972); *Improvisation* for Bassoon and Piano (1975); *Pièce* for Flute and Piano (1975); *Pièce* for Cello and Piano (1975); *Pièce* for Violin and Piano (1975); *Pour guitare* (1975); *Pour Violin et Clarinet* (1975); *Learning* for 4 Violins and Percussion (1976); *Pulau Dewata* for Percussion Ensemble or Instrumental Ensemble (1977); *Paramirabo* for Flute, Violin, Cello, and Piano (1978); *Cinq Chansons* for Percussion (1980); *Et je reverrai cette ville étrange* for Trumpet, Viola, Cello, Double Bass, Piano, and Percussion (1981); *Samarkind* for Wind Quintet (1981). **KEYBOARD: Piano:** *Pianoforte* (1975); *Shiraz* (1977). **Organ:** *Les Communiantes* (1977). **VOCAL:** *Ojikawa* for Soprano, Clarinet, and Percussion (1968); *Hiérophanie* for Soprano, 2 Percussion, and Winds (1971); *Musik für das Ende* for 20 Voices and Percussion (1971); *Chants* for 7 Women's Voices (1973); *O! Kosmos* for Chorus (1974); *Jesus erbarme Dich* for Chorus (1974); *Lettura di Dante* for Soprano, Oboe, Clarinet, Bassoon, Trumpet, Trombone, Viola, and Percussion (1974); *Hymnen an die Nacht* for Soprano and Piano (1975); *Liebesgedichte* for Vocal Quartet and Winds (1976); *Journal* for 4 Voices, Chorus, and Percussion (1977); *Lonely Child* for Soprano and Orch. (1980); *Prologue pour un Marco Polo* for 5 Voices, Speaker, Percussion, 6 Clarinets, and Strings (1981); *Bouchara* for Soprano, Wind Quintet, String Quintet, and Percussion (1981); *Wo bist du Licht!* for Mezzo-soprano, Percussion, 20 Strings, and Tape (1981); *Trois airs pour un opéra imaginaire* for Soprano, Bass, Piccolo, 2 Clarinets, Horn, Strings, and Percussion (1982); *Crois-tu en l'immortalité de l'âme* for Chorus, 3 Synthesizers, and 2 Percussion (1983).**—NS/LK/DM**

Vlad, Roman, prominent Romanian-born Italian composer, administrator, teacher, pianist, and writer on music; b. Cernăuti, Dec. 29, 1919. After training at the Cernăuti Cons., he went to Rome and studied engineering at the Univ. and attended Casella's master classes at the Accademia di Santa Cecilia (graduated, 1942). He began his career as a pianist and lecturer. In 1951 he became a naturalized Italian citizen. From 1955 to 1958 he was artistic director of the Accademia Filarmonica in Rome. He was president of the Italian section of the ISCM from 1960 to 1963. In 1964 he was artistic director of the Maggio Musicale Fiorentino in Florence, and returned to that city in that capacity with the Teatro Comunale from 1968 to 1973. He also was prof. of composition at the Turin Cons. from 1968. From 1976 to 1980 he was artistic director of the RAI orch. in Turin. From 1982 to 1984 he was president of the International Confederation of the Soc. of Authors and Composers. In 1987 he became president of the Società Italiana Autori ed Composers. In 1995 he was made artistic director of Milan's La Scala. He was ed. of the journals *Musica e Dossier* and *Lo Spettatore*, and co-ed. of the journal *Nuova Rivista Musicale*. His scholarly articles appeared in various Italian and foreign publications. He also publ. several books. In his music, Vlad developed a non-dogmatic serial technique that respected the role of tradition in the compositional process. In some of his works, he utilized quarter tones and electronics.

WORKS: DRAMATIC: Opera: *Storia di una mamma* (Venice, Oct. 5, 1951); *Il dottore di vetro*, radio opera (RAI, Turin, Feb. 23, 1959); *La fantarca*, television opera (1967); *Il Sogno* (Bergamo, Oct. 3, 1973). **Ballet:** *La strada sul caffé* (1942–43); *La dama delle camelie* (Rome, Nov. 20, 1945; rev. 1956); *Masques ostendais* (Spoleto, June 12, 1959; rev. 1960); *Die Wiederkehr* (1962; rev. 1968 as *Ricercare*); *Il Gabbiano* (Siena, Sept. 5, 1968). **Other:** Incidental music for plays and film scores. **ORCH.:** *Sinfonietta* (1941); Suite (1941); *Sinfonia all'antica* (1947–48; Venice, Sept. 8, 1948); *Variazioni concertanti su una serie di 12 note dal Don Giovanni di Mozart* for Piano and Orch. (Venice, Sept. 18, 1955); *Musica per archi* (1955–57); *Musica concertata* for Harp and Orch. (Turin, April 24, 1958); *Ode super Chrysaea Phorminx* for Guitar and Orch. (1964); *Divertimento sinfonico* (1965–67; RAI, Naples, March 29, 1968). **CHAMBER:** Flute Sonatina (1945); *Divertimento* for 11 Instruments (1948); String Quartet (1955–57); *Serenata* for 12 Instruments (1959); *Improvvisazione su di una melodia* for Clarinet and Piano (Spoleto, July 8, 1970); *Il magico flauto di Severino* for Flute and Piano (1971); *Meditazioni sopra un antico canto russo, ricordando Igor Strawinsky* for Clarinet and 7 Instrumentalists (L'Aquila, Oct. 30, 1982); *Musica per archi N. 2 sempre di nuovo "Immer Wieder"* for 11 Strings (1987–88; L'Aquila, July 28, 1988). **KEYBOARD: Piano:** *Studi dodecafonici* (1943; rev. 1957); *Variazioni intorno all'ultima mazurka di Chopin* (1964); *Sognando il sogno* (1971; Rome, March 10, 1974). **Harpsichord:** *Giochi con Bach sul clavicembalo* (Rome, March 23, 1979). **VOCAL:** *Poemi della luce* for Voice and Piano (1939); 3 cantatas: No. 1, *Dove sei, Elohim?*, for Chorus and Orch. (1940–42), No. 2, *De profundis*, for Chorus and Orch. (1942–46), and No. 3, *Le ciel est vide*, for Chorus and Orch. (1952–53); 3 *invocazioni* for Voice and Orch. or Piano (1948–49); *5 elegie* for Voice and Strings or Piano (1952); *Colinde trasilvane* for Chorus (1957); *Lettura di Michelangelo* for Chorus (1964; Cork, Ireland, May 6, 1966; rev. version as *Cadenze michelangiolesche* for Soprano or Tenor and Orch., Venice, Sept. 13, 1967); *Immer wieder* for Soprano and 8 Instruments (1965); *Piccolo divertimento corale* for Chorus (1968); *"Ego autem" in memoria di Alfredo Casella* for

Baritone and Organ (Rome, March 12, 1972); *Lettura di Lorenzo il Magnifico* for Chorus (Cork, Ireland, April 26, 1974); *Due letture* for Chorus and 13 Instruments (Rome, Oct. 25, 1976); *3 Poesie di Montale* for Baritone and Piano (Siena, Aug. 28, 1978; rev. version for Baritone and Orch., 1980); *Preludio, recitativo e rilettura di Michelangelo* for Bass and Piano (Lille, Oct. 24, 1981); *3 Poesie di Alberto Bevilacqua* for Soprano and Piano (L'Aquila, May 26, 1984); *1 Poesia di Valerio Magrelli* for Baritone and Piano (1987; Turin, March 5, 1990); *Temura* for Baritone and Piano (Turin, March 5, 1990). **OTHER:** Tape music; transcriptions.

WRITINGS: *Modernita e tradizione nella musica contemporanea* (Turin, 1955); with A. Piovesan and R. Craft, *Le musiche religiose di Igor Strawinsky* (Venice, 1956); *Luigi Dallapiccola* (Milan, 1957); *Storia della dodecafonia* (Milan, 1958); *Strawinsky* (Turin, 1958; Eng. tr., 1960; 3rd ed., rev., 1979); co-ed., *Enciclopedia dello spettacolo* (1958–62).—**NS/LK/DM**

Vladigerov, Alexander, Bulgarian conductor and composer, son of **Pantcho Vladigerov;** b. Sofia, Aug. 4, 1933. He studied composition with his father and conducting with Simeonov at the Bulgarian State Cons. in Sofia, graduating in 1956; also took conducting courses in Kiev with Rakhlin. He was conductor of the orch. in Ruse, and then engaged as conductor for Bulgarian Radio and Television.

WORKS: **DRAMATIC:** **Children's Operetta:** *Little Red Riding Hood* (1969). **Musicals:** *The Jolly Town Musicians* (1971); *The Wolf and the 7 Kids* (1973). **ORCH:** *Youth March* (1948); *Rondo concertante* for Violin and Orch. (1955); *Rumanian Dance* (1960). **Piano:** Various pieces. —**NS/LK/DM**

Vladigerov, Pantcho, prominent Bulgarian composer, father of **Alexander Vladigerov;** b. Zürich, March 13, 1899, in a geminal parturition; d. Sofia, Sept. 8, 1978. Distrustful of Bulgarian puerperal skill, his mother sped from Shumen to Zürich as soon as she learned that she was going to have a plural birth. Pantcho's non-identical twin brother, Luben, a violinist, was born 16 hours earlier than Pantcho, on the previous day, March 12, 1899. Vladigerov studied piano and theory with local teachers in Sofia (1910–12); then went to Berlin, where he took lessons in composition with Paul Juon and Georg Schumann, and piano with Leonid Kreutzer at the Akademie der Künste. He then served as conductor and composer of the Max Reinhardt Theater (1921–32); subsequently was a reader (1932–38) and a prof. of piano and composition (1938–72) at the Bulgarian State Cons. of Music in Sofia. His music was rooted in Bulgarian folk songs, artfully combining the peculiar melodic and rhythmic patterns of native material with stark modern harmonies; the method was similar to that of Bartók.

WORKS: **DRAMATIC:** *Tsar Kaloyan*, opera (1935–36; Sofia, April 20, 1936); *Legenda za ezeroto* (Legend of the Lake), ballet (1946; Sofia, Nov. 11, 1962). **ORCH.:** 5 piano concertos (1918, 1930, 1937, 1953, 1963); *Legend* (1919); *3 Impressions* (1920; orchestration of 3 of his *10 Impressions* for Piano); 2 violin concertos (1921, 1968); *Burlesk Suite* for Violin and Orch. (1922); *Scandinavian Suite* (1924); *Bulgarian Suite* (1927); *Vardar*, Bulgarian rhapsody (1927; orchestration of his earlier violin and piano piece); *7 Bulgarian Symphonic Dances* (1931); 2 overtures: *Zemja* (1933) and *The 9th of September* (1949); 2 syms.: No. 1 (1939) and No. 2, *Majska* (May) for Strings (1949); *Concert Fantasy* for Cello and Orch. (1941); *4 Rumanian Symphonic Dances* (1942); *Improvisation and Toccata* (1942; orchestration of the final 2 pieces of his piano cycle *Episodes*); *2 Rumanian Symphonic Sketches* (1943); 2 suites (1947, 1953); *Prelude and Balkan Dance* (1950); *Evreyska poema* (Jewish Poem) (1951); *Song of Peace*, dramatic poem (1956); *7 Pieces* for Strings (1969–70; orchestration of pieces taken from 3 different piano cycles). **CHAMBER:** Violin Sonata (1914); Piano Trio (1916); 5 works for Violin and Piano: *2 Improvisations* (1919), *4 Pieces* (1920), *Vardar* (1922), *2 Bulgarian Paraphrases* (1925), and *2 Pieces* (1926); String Quartet (1940); several piano cycles, many of which are also scored for chamber orch.: *4 Pieces* (1915); *11 Variations* (1916); *10 Impressions* (1920); *4 Pieces* (1920); *3 Pieces* (1922); *6 Exotic Preludes* (1924); *Classical and Romantic*, 7 pieces (1931); *Bulgarian Songs and Dances* (1932); *Sonatina concertante* (1934); *Shumen*, 6 miniatures (1934); *5 Episodes* (1941); *Aquarelles* (1942); *3 Pictures* (1950); *Suite*, 5 pieces (1954); *3 Pieces* (1957); *3 Concert Pieces* (1959); *5 Novelettes* (1965); *5 Pieces* (1965). **OTHER:** Orchestration of Dinicu's *Hora staccato*.

BIBL.: E. Pavlov, *P. V.: A Monograph* (Sofia, 1961); S. Dimitrov, *Slovoto na P. V.* (Sofia, 1988).—**NS/LK/DM**

Vlasov, Vladimir (Alexandrovich), Russian conductor, ethnomusicologist, and composer; b. Moscow, Jan. 7, 1903; d. there, Sept. 7, 1986. He studied violin at the Moscow Cons., then was active as a teacher. In 1936 he traveled to Frunze, Kirghizia, where he diligently went about collecting authentic songs of the natives. In collaboration with Vladimir Fere, similarly intentioned, he wrote a number of operas based on Kirghiz national melorhythms supplied by local musicians. These included: *Altin kiz* (The Golden Girl; Frunze, May 1, 1937); *Aychurek* (Moon Beauty; Frunze, May 1, 1942); *Za schastye naroda* (For the People's Happiness; Frunze, May 1, 1941); *Sin naroda* (A Son of His People; Frunze, Nov. 8, 1947); *Na beregakh Issikh-kulya* (On the Shores of Lake Issik; Frunze, Feb. 1, 1951); *Vedma* (The Witch; 1961); etc. He also composed two operettas and several ballets, two cello concertos, three string quartets, a Suite for Folk Instruments (1955), and more than 1,000 songs.

BIBL.: V. Vinogradov, *A. Maldibayev, V. V., Vladimir Fere* (Moscow, 1958).—**NS/LK/DM**

Vlijmen, Jan van, Dutch composer, music educator, and administrator; b. Rotterdam, Oct. 11, 1935. He received training in piano and organ at the Utrecht Cons., where he later studied composition with Kees van Baaren. From 1961 to 1965 he was director of the Amersfoort Music School, and then was a lecturer in theory at the Utrecht Cons. from 1965 to 1967. In 1967 he became deputy director and in 1971 director of the Royal Cons. of Music at The Hague. From 1985 to 1988 he was general manager of the Netherlands Opera in Amsterdam. In 1991 he was director of the Holland Festival.

WORKS: **DRAMATIC:** **Opera:** *Reconstructie* (Amsterdam, June 29, 1969; in collaboration with L. Andriessen, R. de Leeuw, M. Mengelberg, and P. Schat); *Axel* (1975–77; Scheveningen, June 10, 1977; in collaboration with R. de Leeuw); *A Wretch Clad in Black* (Amsterdam, Nov. 16, 1990). **ORCH.:** *Gruppi* (1961–62; rev. 1980); *Spostamenti* (1963); *Serenata II* for Flute and 4 Instrumental Groups (Amsterdam, Sept. 10, 1965);

Sonata for Piano and 3 Instrumental Groups (1966); *Per diciasette* for Wind Orch. (1967); *Interpolations* for Orch. and Electronics (Rotterdam, Nov. 24, 1968; rev. 1981); *Ommagio a Gesualdo* for Violin and 6 Instrumental Groups (Amsterdam, April 9, 1971); *Quaterni* (1979); Piano Concerto (1991). **CHAMBER:** String Quartet (1955); 2 wind quintets (1958, 1972); *Construzione* for 2 Pianos (1959); *Serie* for 6 Instruments (1960); *Serenata I* for 12 Instruments and Percussion (1963–64; rev. 1967); *Dialogue* for Clarinet and Piano (1966); *Trimurti, trittico* for String Quartet (1980); *Faithful* for Viola (1984); Nonet (1985); *Solo II* for Clarinet (1986); *Tombeau* for Cello (1991); *Against That Time* for Alto Flute (1995); String Quartet (1996); *Sei pezzi* for Violin and Piano (1998). **VOCAL:** *Morgensternlieder* for Mezzo- soprano and Piano (1958); *Mythos* for Mezzo-soprano and 9 Instruments (1962); *4 Songs* for Mezzo-soprano and Orch. (1975); *Inferno*, cantata for Chorus and Instrumental Ensemble (1991–93); *Monumentum* for Mezzo-soprano and Orch. (1998).
—NS/LK/DM

Vodušek, Valens, Slovenian ethnomusicologist and conductor; b. Ljubljana, Jan. 29, 1912. He studied at the Univ. of Ljubljana (L.L.D., 1938) and took courses in piano and conducting at the Ljubljana State Cons. (1930–36); was self-taught in musicology and ethnomusicology. He was head of the music section at the Ministry of Culture in Slovenia (1946–51), then joined the Inst. for Ethnomusicology in Ljubljana. He was director of the Ljubljana Opera (1951–55), returning to the Inst. as director until 1972, when it combined with the Inst. of Ethnology of the Slovene Academy of Sciences and Arts; at that time he became head of its ethnomusicology dept. He conducted the Ljubljana Radio Choir (1946–51; renamed the Slovene Phil. Choir in 1948), and was artistic director of the Slovene Octet (1956–72). Vodušek instigated systematic fieldwork and classification in Slovene ethnic music.**—NS/LK/DM**

Vogel, Charles Louis Adolphe, French violinist and composer, grandson of **Johann Christoph Vogel;** b. Lille, May 17, 1808; d. Paris, Sept. 11, 1892. He studied in Lille and then at the Paris Cons. with A. Kreutzer (violin) and Reicha (theory). After winning popularity with his song *Les Trois Couleurs* during the July Revolution (1830), he brought out a series of successful operas: *Le Podestat* (Paris, Dec. 16, 1831), *Le Siège de Leyde* (The Hague, March 14, 1847), *La Moissonneuse* (Paris, Sept. 3, 1853), *Rompons* (Paris, Sept. 21, 1857), *Le Nid de Cigognes* (Baden-Baden, Sept. 1858), *Gredin de Pigoche* (Paris, Oct. 19, 1866), and *La Filleule du roi* (Brussels, April 1875). He also wrote syms., chamber music, sacred works, songs, and piano pieces.**—NS/LK/DM**

Vogel, Jaroslav, Czech conductor and composer; b. Pilsen, Jan. 11, 1894; d. Prague, Feb. 2, 1970. He studied violin with Ševčik and composition with Novák in Prague; after taking courses in Munich (1910–12) and at the Paris Schola Cantorum with d'Indy (1912–13), he completed his training with Novák at the Prague Cons. (graduated, 1919). He was a conductor at the Pilsen Opera (1914–15) and in Ostrava (1919–23); after conducting in Prague (1923–27), he was chief conductor of the Ostrava Opera (1927–43); then conducted at the Prague National Theater (1949–58), and was chief conductor of the Brno State Phil. (1959–62). In 1964 he was made an Artist of Merit by the Czech government. As a conductor, he championed the music of Smetana, Janáček, and Novák. He publ. (in German) the useful study *Leoš Janáček: Sein Leben und Werk* (Prague, 1958; abr. Eng. tr., 1962; Czech original, 1963). He composed the operas *Maréja* (Olomouc, 1923), *Meister Georg or Mistr Jíra* (Prague, 1926), *Jovana* (Ostrava, 1939), and *Hiawatha* (Ostrava, 1974), orch. pieces, and chamber music.
—NS/LK/DM

Vogel, Johann Christoph, German composer, grandfather of **Charles Louis Adolphe Vogel;** b. Nuremberg (baptized), March 18, 1756; d. Paris, June 27, 1788. He was a pupil of Riepel at Regensburg. He went to Paris in 1776 and was in the service of the Duke of Montmorency, and later was in the service of the Count of Valentinois. He wrote two operas in Gluck's style, *La Toison d'or* (Paris, Sept. 5, 1786) and *Démophon*, which he completed shortly before his untimely death at the age of 32, and which was produced posthumously (Paris, Sept. 22, 1789). He also composed an oratorio, *Jepthe* (1781), three syms., several simphonies concertantes, a Violin Concerto (1782), three flute concertos, two oboe concertos, some six clarinet concertos, a Bassoon Concerto (1782), and much chamber music.

BIBL.: A. Bickel, *J.C. V.: Der grosse Nürnberger Komponist zwischen Gluck und Mozart (1756–1788)* (Nuremberg, 1956).
—NS/LK/DM

Vogel, Wladimir (Rudolfovich), significant German-Russian-born Swiss composer; b. Moscow (of a German father and a Russian mother), Feb. 29, 1896; d. Zürich, June 19, 1984. He began composing in his youth. At the outbreak of World War I (1914), he was interned in Russia as an enemy alien; after the Armistice in 1918, he went to Berlin, where he studied with Tiessen (1919–21) and Busoni (1921–24). He was greatly influenced by both Busoni and Schoenberg. From 1929 to 1933 Vogel taught at the Klindworth-Scharwenka Cons. in Berlin; with the advent to power of the Nazi government, Vogel, although not a Jew, chose to leave Germany. He worked in Strasbourg and Brussels with Scherchen on various problems of musical techniques; then went to Switzerland, and in 1954 became a naturalized Swiss citizen. Vogel's idiom of composition underwent several changes throughout the years. A convinced believer in the mystical power of music, he felt great affinity with Scriabin's mystical ideas and techniques; he built his melodies along the upper overtones of the harmonic series, and his harmonies on a massive superimposition of perfect fourths and tritones. Gradually he approached the method of composition in 12 tones as promulgated by Schoenberg, while Busoni's precepts of neo-Classical structures governed Vogel's own works as far as formal design was concerned; many of his polyphonic compositions adhered to the Classical harmonic structures in four parts, which he maintained even in choral pieces using the Sprechstimme. Serialist procedures were adumbrated in Vogel's music through the astute organization of melodic and rhythmic elements.

Works: Orch.: *Sinfonia fugata* (1924); *4 Studies: Ritmica funèbre, Ritmica scherzosa, Ostinato perpetuo,* and *Ritmica ostinata* (1930–32); *Rallye* (1932); *Tripartita* (1934; Geneva, Nov. 21, 1935); Violin Concerto (1937); *Passacaglia* (1946); *Sept aspects d'une série de douze sons* (1949–50); *Spiegelungen* (1952; Frankfurt am Main, June 26, 1953); Cello Concerto (1954; Zürich, Nov. 27, 1956); *Interludio lirico* (1954); *Preludio, Interludio lirico, Postludio* (1954); *Hörformen I* (1967) and *II* (1967–69); *Cantique en forme d'un canon à quatre voix* (1969); *Abschied* for Strings (1973); *Meloformen* for Strings (1974); *Hommage* for Strings (1974). **Chamber:** *La Ticinella* for Flute, Oboe, Clarinet, Saxophone, and Bassoon (1941); *12 variétudes* for Flute, Clarinet, Violin, and Cello (1942); *Inspiré par Jean Arp* for Violin, Flute, Clarinet, and Cello (1965); *Analogien,* "Hörformen" for String Quartet (1973); *Monophonie* for Violin (1974); *Für Flöte, Oboe, Klarinette, und Fagott* (1974); *Poème* for Cello (1974); *Terzett* for Flute, Clarinet, and Bassoon (1975). **Piano:** *Nature vivante,* 6 expressionistic pieces (1917–21); *Einsames Getröpfel und Gewuchsel* (1921; rev. 1968); *Dai tempi più remoti,* 3 pieces (1922–31; rev. 1968); *Etude-Toccata* (1926); *Epitaffio per Alban Berg* (1936); *Klavier-eigene Interpretationsstudie einer varierten Zwölftonfolge* (1972); *4 Versionen einer Zwölftonfolge* (1972); *Musik* for Wind Quartet and Strings (1975). **Vocal:** *Wagadus Untergang durch die Eitelkeit,* cantata for 3 Soloists, Mixed Chorus, Speaking Chorus, and 5 Saxophones (1930); *Thyl Claes* (Till Eulenspiegel), oratorio in 2 parts: *Oppression* (1938) and *Liberation* (1943–45; orch. suite, Palermo, April 26, 1949); *An die Jugend der Welt* for Chorus and Chamber Orch. (1954); *Goethe- Aphorismen* for Soprano and Strings (Venice, Sept. 1955); *Eine Gotthardkantate* for Baritone and Strings (1956); *Jona ging doch nach Ninive* for Baritone, Speaking Soloists and Chorus, Mixed Chorus, and Orch. (1958); *Meditazione su Amadeo Modigliani* for 4 Soloists, Narrator, Chorus, and Orch. (Lugano, March 31, 1962); *Die Flucht,* dramatic oratorio (1963–64; Zürich, Nov. 8, 1966); *Schritte* for Alto and Orch. (1968); *Gli Spaziali* for Speakers, Vocalists, and Orch., after the writings of Leonardo da Vinci, *Autour de la lune* by Jules Verne, and utterances of the American astronauts (1969–71).

Bibl.: H. Oesch, *W. V.: Sein Weg zu einer neuen musikalischen Wirklichkeit* (Bern, 1967); W. Labhart, *W. V.: Konturen eines Mitbegrundes der Neuen Musik* (Zürich, 1982); F. Geiger, *Die Dramma-Oratorien von M. V., 1896–1984* (Hamburg, 1998). **—NS/LK/DM**

Vogelweide, Walther von der, famous German Minnesinger and poet; b. c. 1170; d. probably in Würzburg, c. 1230. He learned his craft as a singer and poet in Austria, and from about 1190 to 1198 he was active in Vienna, where he was associated with the court. He led a wandering life, and visited various European courts, finally entering the service of Friedrich of Sicily (later Emperor Friedrich II), who gave him a fief in Würzburg about 1220. Many of his poems are extant; however, only one complete original melody by him is preserved, the so-called *Palästinalied.* For text eds. of his works, see K. Lachmann, *Die Gedichte Walthers von der Vogelweide* (Berlin, 1827; 10th ed., rev., 1936, by C. von Kraus; 13th ed., 1965, by H. Kuhn), W. Wilmanns, ed., *Walther von der Vogelweide* (Halle, 1869; 4th ed., rev., 1916–24, by V. Michels), H. Paul, ed., *Walther von der Vogelweide: Gedichte* (Halle, 1882; 6th ed., rev., 1943, by A. Leitzmann; 9th ed., 1959, by H. Kuhn), and F. Maurer, ed., *Die Lieder Walthers von der Vogelweide, unter Beifügung erhältener und erschlossener Melodien,* Altdeutsche Textbibliothek, XLIII (Tübingen, 1956; 2nd ed., rev., 1965). For his music, see E. Jammers, ed., *Ausgewählte Melodien des Minnesangs* (Tübingen, 1963), H. Moser and J. Müller-Blattau, eds., *Deutsche Lieder des Mittelalters* (Stuttgart, 1968), and R. Taylor, ed., *The Art of the Minnesinger* (Cardiff, 1968).

Bibl.: C. von Kraus, *W. v.d.V.: Untersuchungen* (Berlin, 1935); J. Huisman, *Neue Wege zur dichterischen und musikalischen Technik W.s v.d.V.* (Utrecht, 1950); K. Klein, *Zur Spruchdichtung und Heimatfrage W.s v.d.V.* (Innsbruck, 1952); D. Kralik, *Die Elegie W.s v.d.V.* (Vienna, 1952); K. Halbach, *W. v.d.V.* (Stuttgart, 1965; 2nd ed., rev., 1968); F. Scheibe, *W. v.d.V., Troubadour of the Middle Ages: His Life and Reputation in the English-Speaking Countries* (N.Y., 1969); M. Scholz, *Bibliographie zu W. v.d.V.* (Berlin, 1969). **—NS/LK/DM**

Vogl, Adolf, German writer on music and composer; b. Munich, Dec. 18, 1873; d. there, Feb. 2, 1961. He was a pupil of Hermann Levi. After a brief career as a conductor in Trier, Saarbrücken, St. Gallen, and Bern, he returned to Munich and devoted his energies to writing and composing. During the Nazi era, he was imprisoned but resumed his activities after the demise of the Third Reich. Among his insightful books were *Tristan und Isolde: Briefe an eine deutsche Künstlerin* (Munich, 1913; 3rd ed., 1922) and *Parsifal: Tiefe Schau in die Mysterien des Bühnenweihfestspiels* (Munich, 1914). He composed the operas *Maja* (1908) and *Die Verdammten* (1934), various choral pieces, and songs.**—NS/LK/DM**

Vogl, Heinrich, famous German tenor; b. Au, near Munich, Jan. 15, 1845; d. Munich, April 21, 1900. He studied music with Franz Lachner, making a successful debut as Max in *Der Freischütz* at the Munich Court Opera (Nov. 5, 1865), and remained on its roster until his death. He succeeded Schnorr von Carolsfeld as the model Tristan in Wagner's opera, and was for years considered the greatest interpreter of that role. He created the roles of Loge in *Das Rheingold* (Sept. 22, 1869) and of Siegmund in *Die Walküre* (June 26, 1870) and sang Loge in the first complete *Ring* cycle at the Bayreuth Festival (1876). He also appeared as Siegfried in the first Munich mountings of *Siegfried* and *Götterdämmerung* (1878), Loge and Siegmund in the first Berlin *Ring* cycle (1881), and Loge and Siegfried in the first London *Ring* cycle (1882). In 1882 he toured in Europe with Angelo Neumann's Wagner Co.; in 1886 he sang Tristan and Parsifal in Bayreuth. On Jan. 1, 1890, he made his debut at the Metropolitan Opera in N.Y. as Lohengrin, where he appeared later in the season as Tannhäuser, Loge, both Siegfrieds, and Siegmund. On April 17, 1900, just four days before his death, he appeared as Canio in his last role in Munich. He was also a composer, numbering among his works an opera, *Der Fremdling,* in which he sang the leading role (Munich, May 7, 1899). In 1868 he married the German soprano Therese Thoma (b. Tutzing, Nov. 12, 1845; d. Munich, Sept. 29, 1921), who was a member of the Munich Court Opera (1866–92), where she appeared as Isolde opposite her husband's Tristan (1869), Wellgunde in the premiere of *Das Rheingold* (1869), and Sieglinde in the premiere of *Die Walküre* (June 26, 1870). She also appeared as Brünnhilde in the first complete *Ring* cycles in Munich (1878) and London

(1882); she gave her farewell appearance as Isolde in Munich (Oct. 9, 1892).

BIBL.: H. von der Pfordten, *H. V.: Zur Erinnerung und zum Vermächtnis* (Munich, 1900); R. Wünnenberg, *Das Sangerehepaar H. und T. V.: Ein Beitrag zur Operngeschichte des 19. Jahrhunderts* (Tutzing, 1982).—**NS/LK/DM**

Vogl, Johann Michael, Austrian baritone and composer; b. Ennsdorf, near Steyr, Aug. 10, 1768; d. Vienna, Nov. 19, 1840. He was orphaned at an early age; his vocal gifts were admired by the parish church choirmaster, who gave him his first music lessons. While studying languages and philosophy at the Kremsmünster Gymnasium, he was befriended by his fellow pupil, Franz Xaver Süssmayr; in 1786 he went to Vienna to study law at the Univ. After briefly practicing law, he joined Süssmayr's German opera company, making his debut at the Hofoper on May 1, 1795; hewas chosen to sing the role of Pizarro in the revised version of Beethoven's *Fidelio* in 1814. In 1817 he met Schubert, who became his close friend and whose lieder he subsequently championed; he also created the leading role in Schubert's opera *Die Zwillingsbrüder* (1820).

BIBL.: A. Weiss, *Der Schubertsänger J.M. V.* (Vienna, 1915); A. Liess, *J.M. V.: Hofoperist und Schubertsänger* (Graz and Cologne, 1954).—**NS/LK/DM**

Vogler, Carl, Swiss organist, conductor, pedagogue, and composer; b. Oberrohrdorf, Feb. 26, 1874; d. Zürich, June 17, 1951. He was a pupil of Breitenbach at the Lucern Organistenschule (1891–93), of Hegar and Kempter at the Zürich Music School (1893–95), and of Rheinberger at the Munich Cons. (1895–97). From 1897 to 1919 he was an organist and music teacher in Baden in Aargau, and also was founder-director of the Gemischter Chor and the Musikkollegium. He taught counterpoint at the Zürich Cons. from 1915, where he was co-director (1919–39) and director (1939–45). From 1907 to 1932 he was president of the Musikpädagogischer Verband, and also of the Schweizerischer Tonkünstlerverein from 1931 to 1941. In 1924 he founded the Gesellschaft für Aufführungsrechte, serving as its president until his death. He ed. the book *Der Schweizerische Tonkünstlerverein* (Zürich, 1925) and publ. the study *Der Schweizer Musiker und seine Berufsbildung* (Zürich, 1942). His music, which included *Mutter Sybille*, Singspiel (1906), *Rübezsahl*, Märchenspiel (1917), *Friedelhänschen*, Märchenspiel (1924), choral music, songs, and organ pieces, followed mainly the precepts of late Romanticism.—**NS/LK/DM**

Vogler, Georg Joseph, noted German pianist, organist, pedagogue, music theorist, and composer, known as **Abbé** or **Abt Vogler**; b. Pleichach, near Würzburg, June 15, 1749; d. Darmstadt, May 6, 1814. His father was a violinist and instrument maker at the court of the Prince-Bishop of Würzburg. After studying humanities at the Univ. of Würzburg (magisterium, 1766), he received training in law there (1766–67) and in theology in Bamberg (1767–70). In 1771 he went to Mannheim as almoner at the court of Carl Theodor, the Elector Palatine; by 1772 he was court chaplain there. With the assistance of the elector, he pursued his musical training in Italy (1773–75); was active in Bologna, Padua, Venice, and Rome, his principal mentors being Padres Martini and Francesco Antonio Vallotti; while in Rome, Pope Pius VI made him a chamberlain, a prothonotary, and a Knight of the Order of the Golden Spur. In 1775 he returned to Mannheim as spiritual counselor and Vice-Kapellmeister to his patron. He founded the Mannheimer Tonschule for teaching his own method of composition. In 1780 he was in Paris, where he submitted a paper to the Académie Royale des Sciences, *Essai de diriger le goût des amateurs de musique*, an explanation of his system of teaching (publ. in Paris, 1782); in Paris he also produced his opera *La Kermesse* (1783), which was a fiasco; that same year he visited London, where his method won the approbation of the Royal Soc. After serving as 1st Kapellmeister at the Electoral Court in Munich (1784–86), he became Kapellmeister and teacher to the Crown Prince at the Swedish court in Stockholm in 1786; also traveled extensively in Europe, and in 1792–93 visited North Africa. Following the conclusion of his contract in Stockholm in 1794, he once again traveled in Europe, during which time he was active as both a performer and a teacher. In 1807 he was made Hofkapellmeister and privy councillor for ecclesiastical affairs at the Hessen-Darmstadt court; founded a Tonschule there, where Weber and Meyerbeer were his pupils. Vogler established himself as a leading keyboard virtuoso, teacher, and music theorist. He was a distinguished master of keyboard improvisation. While in Amsterdam in 1789, he completed construction of a portable organ, the "orchestrion," which he promoted in succeeding years during his various concert tours. His writings proved influential, but his compositions, which included stage works, syms., piano concertos, and chamber works, failed to make an impact and are now completely forgotten.

WRITINGS: *Tonwissenschaft und Tonsetzkunst* (Mannheim, 1776); *Stimmbildungskunst* (Mannheim, 1776); *Kuhrpfälzische Tonschule* (Mannheim, 1778); *Betrachtungen der Mannheimer Tonschule*, I-III (Mannheim, 1778–81); *Entwurf eines neuen Wörterbuchs für die Tonschule* (Frankfurt am Main, 1780); *Essai propre à diriger le goût de ceux qui ne sont pas musiciens* (Paris, 1782); *Verbesserung der Forkel'schen Veränderungen über das englische Volkslied God Save the King* (Frankfurt am Main, 1793); *Erste musikalische Preisausteilung für das Jahr 1791 nebst 40 Kupfertafeln* (Frankfurt am Main, 1794); *Inledning til harmoniens kännedom* (Stockholm, 1794); *Clavér-schola med 44 graverade tabeller* (Stockholm, 1798); *Organist-schola med 8 graverade tabeller* (Stockholm, 1798–99); *Lection til choral eleven* (Stockholm, 1799–1800); *Choral-System* (Copenhagen, 1800); *Data zur Akustik* (Leipzig, 1801); *Handbuch zur Harmonielehre und für den Generalbass* (Prague, 1802); *Zergliederung der 32 Orgelpräludien* (Munich, 1806); *Über die harmonische Akustik* (Offenbach, 1807); *Zergliederung der musikalischen Bearbeitung der Busspsalmen* (Munich, 1807); *Grundliche Anleitung zum Clavirstimmen* (Stuttgart, 1807); *Utile dulci: Belehrende musikalische Herausgaben*, I (Munich, 1808); *Über Sprach- und Gesangsautomaten* (Frankfurt am Main, 1810); *System für den Fugenbau* (Offenbach, c. 1818); *Über Choral- und Kirchengesange* (Munich, 1813).

BIBL.: J. Fröhlich, *Biographie des grossen Tonkünstlers Abt G.J. V.* (Würzburg, 1845); H. Künzel, *Abt V.* (Darmstadt, 1867); E. Pasqué, *Abt V. als Tonkünstler, Lehrer und Priester* (Darmstadt,

1884); K. von Schafhäutl, *Abt G.J. V., Sein Leben, sein Charakter und musikalisches System* (Augsburg, 1888); J. Simon, *Abt V.s kompositorisches Wirken* (Berlin, 1904); E. Rupp, *Abbé V. als Mensch, Musiker, und Orgelbautheoretiker* (Ludwigsburg, 1922); P. Vretland, *Abbé V. in Stockholm* (Wurzburg, 1924); idem, *Abbé V.* (1933); H. Schweiger, *Abbé G.J. V.s Orgellehre* (diss., Univ. of Vienna, 1938); H. Kreitz, *Abbé G.J. V. als Musiktheoretiker* (diss., Univ. of Saarbrücken, 1957); D. Britton, *Abbé G.J. V.: His Life and His Theories on Organ Design* (diss., Univ. of Rochester, 1973); F. and M. Grave, *In Praise of Harmony: The Teachings of Abbé G.J. V.* (Lincoln, Nebr., 1987).—**NS/LK/DM**

Vogt, Gustave, noted French oboist, pedagogue, and composer; b. Strasbourg, March 18, 1781; d. Paris, May 30, 1870. He was taken to Paris at an early age, and enrolled in 1798 at the Cons., where he was a pupil of A. Sallantin (premier prix, 1799) and then of Rey. In 1798 he became 2nd oboist in the orch. of the Théâtre Montansier; in 1801 he joined the orch. of the Théâtre de l'Ambigu-Comique, and shortly afterward was made 1st oboist in the orch. of the Théâtre-Italien. He served as 1st oboist in Napoleon's private orch. (1804–14), the orch. of the Opéra (1812–34), the orch. at the Théâtre Feydeau (1814), and Louis XVIII's orch. (1814; 1819–30). In 1828 he became a founding member and 1st oboist of the Société des Concerts du Conservatoire, where he played until 1844. He was a prof. at the Cons. (1816–53). He publ. *Solfège à l'usage des écoles primaires* (Kolmar, 1862); also wrote a *Méthode de hautbois*. Among his compositions are five oboe concertos, four oboe concertinos, various other virtuoso works for oboe and orch., an English Horn Concerto, serenades for wind band, marches, some chamber music, including several works utilizing oboe, various solo oboe pieces, piano music, and a few vocal scores.—**NS/LK/DM**

Vogt, Hans, German composer and pedagogue; b. Danzig, May 14, 1911; d. Metternich, May 19, 1992. He studied with Georg Schumann (master class in composition, 1929–34) at the Prussian Academy of Arts and received training in piano, cello, conducting, and music education at the Akademie für Kirchen- und Schulmusik (1930–34) in Berlin. In 1933 he won the Mendelssohn Prize in Berlin. From 1935 to 1938 he was chief conductor of the Detmold Opera, and then was music director in Stralsund from 1938 to 1944. In 1951 he became a teacher of composition at the Mannheim Hochschule für Musik, where he was a prof. from 1971 to 1978. From 1963 to 1984 he was also chairman of the Gesellschaft für Neue Musik in Mannheim. In 1961 and 1969 he won the Prix Reine Elisabeth of Belgium. He won the Prix Rainer III Prince de Monaco in 1961. He received the Premio Città di Trieste in 1968. In 1978–79 he was in residence at the Villa Massimo in Rome. He was a contributor to *Neue Musik seit 1945* (Stuttgart, 1972; 3rd ed., 1982) and author of *Johann Sebastien Bachs Kammermusik* (Stuttgart, 1981).

WORKS: DRAMATIC: *Die Stadt hinter dem Strom*, oratorio-opera (1953); *Athenerkomödie (The Metropolitans)*, comic opera (1962; rev. 1987). **ORCH.:** 2 concertos for Orch. (1950, 1960); *Rhythmische Suite* for Strings (1952); Piano Concerto (1955); *Monologue*, 4 pieces (1964); Cello Concerto (1968); *Konzertante Divertimenti* for Piano and Small Orch. (1968; rev. 1982); *Azioni sinfoniche* (1971); *Arco trionfale* (1979); Violin Concerto (1981); *Symphony in 1 Movement, Dona nobis pacem* (1984); *Tim Finnigan's Wake* for Oboe and Strings (1987); *Aprèslude* for Orch. and Mezzo-soprano ad libitum (1988); *Gestalten-Szenen-Schatten* for Strings (1988). **CHAMBER:** Trio for Flute, Viola, and Harp (1951; rev. 1989); Quintet for Flute, Oboe, Violin, Bassoon, and Harpsichord (1958); Flute Sonata (1958); *Konzertante Sonata* for Chamber Ensemble (1959); 4 string quartets (1960; 1975; 1977; 1984, rev. 1991); *Dialog* for Piano, Violin, and Cello (1960); String Quintet (1967); String Trio (1969); *Elemente zu einer Sonate* for Cello and Piano (1973); *Giuoco degli flauti* for 5 Flutes and Percussionist (1974); *Antiphonen* for Oboe and Organ (1976); Sonatina for Violin and Double Bass (1976); *Preludio, Presto 3 Pezzo variato* for Cello (1977); *Rondo sereno* for Cello and Contrabass (1980; also for Violin and Viola, 1987); *Sonata lirica* for Violin and Piano (1983); *Movimenti*, duo for Violin and Cello (1985); String Octet (1988); *Sonata per quattro archi* for Violin, Viola, Cello, and Double Bass (1989); String Sextet, *Ballata Notturna* (1990); *Fantasie über das Magnificat* for Violin (1990); *La Danza* for Contrabass (1991). **Piano:** *Sonata alla toccata* (1957); Sonata for Piano, 4-Hands (1959); *Musik* for 2 Pianos (1967). **VOCAL:** *De profundis clamavi ad te, Domine* for Chorus (1951); *Historie der Verkündigung*, chamber oratorio for 3 Women Soloists, Chorus, and 13 Instruments (1955); *Masken* for Soprano, String Orch., and 3 Percussionists (1956); *Vier englische Lieder* for Soprano, Oboe, Clarinet, Violin, Cello, and Harp (1957); *Fabeln des Äsop* for Chorus, Clarinet, Double Bass, and Percussionist (1959); *Poems from Herman Moon's London Hourbook* for Vocal Quartet and Piano (1960); *Ihr Töchter von Jerusalem, weinet nicht über mich* for Tenor, Chorus, and 2 Percussionists (1963); *Sine nomine* for Tenor, Chorus, and Orch. (1964); *Magnificat* for Soprano, Chorus, and Orch. (1966); *Requiem* for Soprano, Bass, Chorus, and 2 Percussionists (1969); *Drei Madrigale nach Gedichten von W.H. Auden* for Chorus (1973); *Strophen* for Baritone and Orch. (1975); *Canticum Simeonis* for Chorus and Flute (1976); *Historie vom Propheten Jona*, chamber oratorio for Alto, Tenor, Chorus, and 6 Instruments (1979); *Drei geistliche Gesänge nach barocken Dichtungen* for Baritone and Organ (1981–83); *Drei deutsche Madrigale* for Chorus and Percussionist (1983–89).—**NS/LK/DM**

Voicu, Ion, Romanian violinist and conductor; b. Bucharest, Oct. 8, 1925. He enrolled at the Bucharest Cons. at 13 as a violin pupil of George Enacovici. After making his debut on the Bucharest Radio in 1940, he continued his training with Enesco (1945); then studied with Yampolsky and Oistrakh at the Moscow Cons. (1955–57). In 1969 he founded a chamber orch. in Bucharest; toured widely with this ensemble in succeeding years. From 1971 to 1982 he was music director of the Georges Enesco Phil. in Bucharest.—**NS/LK/DM**

Voigt, Deborah, outstanding American soprano; b. Chicago, Aug. 4, 1960. She studied on a vocal scholarship at the Crystal Cathedral in Garden Grove, Calif., attended Calif. State Univ. at Fullerton, and graduated from the San Francisco Opera Merola Program. In 1988 she won the Pavarotti Competition and appeared as a soloist in the Verdi Requiem at N.Y.'s Carnegie Hall. In 1989 she won the Verdi Competition in Bussetto, and in 1990 she took 1st prize in the Tchaikovsky Competition in Moscow. Her engagement as Ariadne at the Boston Lyric Opera in 1991 won her critical accolades, which was followed on Oct. 17th of that year by her Metropolitan Opera debut in N.Y. as Amelia. She returned to the Metropolitan Opera in 1992 and scored a major success as Chrysothemis. That same year, she was honored with the Richard Tucker Award. In 1993 she sang Chrysothemis at the London Promenade Concerts. She made her debut at London's Covent Garden as Amelia and appeared as Senta at the Vienna State Opera in 1995. In 1996 she sang Sieglinde at the Metropolitan Opera, and returned there in 1997 as Ariadne. Her Elsa was portrayed at both the Metropolitan Opera and Covent Garden in 1998, and that same year she won further success as soloist in Strauss's *Vier letzte Lieder* with Masur and the N.Y. Phil. On Dec. 31, 1998, she was a soloist with Masur and the N.Y. Phil. in a New Year's Eve Gala Concert televised live to the nation by PBS. In 1999 she sang Chrysothemis at the Metropolitan Opera and Sieglinde in the *Ring* cycle at the San Francisco Opera. In addition to her compelling interpretations of Wagner and Strauss, Voigt has also won notable distinction for her roles in operas by Rossini, Weber, Berlioz, and Verdi. Her concert appearances have also been acclaimed.—**NS/LK/DM**

Voisin, Roger (Louis), distinguished French-born American trumpeter and teacher; b. Angers, June 26, 1918. He was taken to Boston as a child by his family, and became a naturalized American citizen in 1932. He studied initially with his father, a member of the Boston Sym. Orch., then with Georges Mager (1933) and Marcel LaFosse (1934). In 1935 he became 3rd trumpeter in the Boston Sym. Orch.; after serving as its 1st trumpeter (1949–67), he was again 3rd trumpeter from 1967 until his retirement in 1973. He taught at the Berkshire Music Center in Tanglewood, the New England Cons. of Music in Boston, and Boston Univ.—**NS/LK/DM**

Volans, Kevin, gifted South African-born Irish composer; b. Pietermaritzburg, July 26, 1949. He studied at the univs. of the Witwatersrand in Johannesburg and Aberdeen before pursuing training in composition with Stockhausen, A. Kontarsky, and Kagel in Cologne (1973–81). After serving as a teacher at Natal Univ. in Durban (1982–84) and as composer-in-residence at the Queen's Univ. in Belfast (1986–89), he settled in Dublin and became a naturalized Irish citizen. In 1992 he was composer-in-residence at Princeton Univ. Volans developed the so-called "new simplicity" style of composition in the early 1970s. In the mid-1970s he created a synthesis of Western and African music as he was influenced by field trips he made in Africa to record traditional music of Zululand and Lesotho.

WORKS: DRAMATIC: *The Man with Footsoles of Wind,* chamber opera (1988–93; London, July 2, 1993); *Correspondances,* dance opera (London, Oct. 16, 1990; also as String Quartet No. 4, *The Ramanugan Notebooks,* London, Dec. 16, 1990; rev. 1994); *Plane-Song,* television piece (1994; BBC2, London, April 11, 1995; rev. as String Quartet No. 5, *Dancers on a Plane,* 1994); *Duetti,* dance piece (1995; Ghent, May 7, 1996; in collaboration with Matteo Fargion); *5.4,* dance piece (1996; Frankfurt am Main, Jan. 31, 1997); *Things I Don't Know,* dance piece (1997–98; London, April 29, 1998); *Wild Air,* dance piece (1998; Oxford, May 7, 1999). **ORCH.:** *One Hundred Frames* (Belfast, Dec. 6, 1991); Concerto for Piano and Winds (Rotterdam, Oct. 18, 1995); Cello Concerto (Munich, Dec. 12, 1997); Double Violin Concerto (Belfast, May 4, 1999). **CHAMBER:** *Matepe* for 2 Harpsichords and Rattles (1980); *Mbira* for 2 Harpsichords and Rattles (1980); *White Man Sleeps* for 2 Harpsichords, Viola da Gamba, and Percussion (1982; also as String Quartet No. 1, London, July 13, 1986); *Walking Song* for Flute, Harpsichord/Virginal or Piano, and 4 Handclappers/Finger Clickers (1984; also for Organ, 1986); *She Who Sleeps With a Small Blanket* for Percussion (Salzburg, Oct. 22, 1985); 5 string quartets: No. 1, *White Man Sleeps* (London, July 13, 1986; also for 2 Harpsichords, Viola da Gamba, and Percussion, 1982), No. 2, *Hunting: Gathering* (San Francisco, Dec. 11, 1987), No. 3, *The Songlines* (N.Y., Nov. 26, 1988; rev. 1993), No. 4, *The Ramanugan Notebooks* (London, Dec. 16, 1990; rev. 1994; also as the dance opera *Correspondances,* London, Oct. 16, 1990), and No. 5, *Dancers on a Plane* (1994; rev. from the television piece *Plane-Song,* 1994; BBC2, London, April 11, 1995); *Into Darkness* for Piano, Clarinet, Trumpet, Violin, Cello, and Percussion (London, Jan. 28, 1987; rev. 1989); *Movement* for String Quartet (Durban, April 8, 1987); *Chevron* for Chamber Ensemble (Brighton, May 24, 1990); *Wanting to Tell Stories* for Piano, Clarinet, Viola, and Double Bass (Brighton, May 13, 1993); *Leaping Dance* for Wind Ensemble (1995; also for 2 Pianos, 1984; London, Aug. 25, 1985); *Asanga* for Percussion (1997; Berlin, June 12, 1998); *Akrodha* for Percussion (1997–98; Southampton, March 18, 1999). **KEYBOARD: Piano:** *Nine Beginnings* for 2 Pianos (1976; Cologne, June 1, 1979; rev. 1985); *Newer Music* (1981); *Leaping Dance* for 2 Pianos (1984; London, Aug. 25, 1985; also for Wind Ensemble, 1995); *Kneeling Dance* for 2 Pianos (London, Aug. 25, 1985; also for 6 Pianos, Southampton, Nov. 13, 1992); *Cicada* for 2 Pianos (Los Angeles, April 25, 1994); *March* (1996; Dublin, May 1997). **Organ:** *Walking Song* (1986; also for Flute, Harpsichord/Virginal or Piano, and 4 Handclappers/Finger Clickers, 1984). **ELECTRONIC:** *Studies in Zulu History* (1977–79); *Kwazulu Summer Landscape* (1979); *Cover Him with Grass* (1982).—**LK/DM**

Volbach, Fritz, German choral conductor, music scholar, and composer; b. Wipperfürth, near Cologne, Dec. 17, 1861; d. Wiesbaden, Nov. 30, 1940. He studied at the Cologne Cons. with Hiller, Jensen, and Seiss, and in Berlin with Taubert and Löschhorn; completed his education at the Univ. of Bonn (Ph.D., 1899, with the diss. *Die Praxis der Händel-Aufführung*). In 1892 he was appointed conductor of the Liedertafel and the Damengesangverein in Mainz; after serving as music director at the Univ. of Tübingen (1907–18), he went to Munster as prof. at the Univ. and as conductor of the city orch.; retired to Wiesbaden in 1930. A versatile musician, he had command of almost every orch. instrument.

WORKS: DRAMATIC: Opera: *Die Kunst zu lieben* (1910). **ORCH.:** 3 symphonic poems: *Ostern* (1895), *Es waren zwei Königskinder* (1901), and *Alt-Heidelberg, du feine* (1904); Sym. (1909). **OTHER:** Chamber music, including a Piano Quitet (1912) and piano pieces; numerous choral works; lieder.

WRITINGS: *Lehrbuch der Begleitung des gregorianischen Gesangs* (Berlin, 1888); *G.F. Händel* (Berlin, 1898; 2nd ed., 1907); *Beethoven: Die Zeit des Klassizismus* (Munich, 1905; 2nd ed., 1929); *Die deutsche Musik im 19. Jahrhundert* (Kempten, 1909); *Das moderne Orchester in seiner Entwicklung* (Leipzig, 1910; 2nd ed., 1919); *Die Instrumente des Orchesters* (Leipzig, 1913; 2nd ed., 1921); *Erläuterwungen zu den Klavier-Sonaten Beethovens* (Cologne, 1919; 3rd ed., 1924); *Handbuch der Musikwissenschaften* (2 vols., Münster, 1926, 1930); *Die Kunst der Sprache* (Mainz, 1929);

Der Chormeister (Mainz, 1931); *Erlebtes und Erstrebtes* (autobiography; Mainz, 1956).

BIBL.: J. Hagemann, *F. V., Monographien Moderner Musiker*, III (Leipzig, 1909); G. Schwake, *F. V.s Werke* (Münster, 1921); K. Hortschansky, ed., *F. V., 1861–1940: Komponist, Dirigent und Musikwissenschaftler* (Hagen, 1987).—**NS/LK/DM**

Volckmar, Wilhelm (Adam Valentin), German organist, teacher, and composer; b. Hersfeld, Dec. 26, 1812; d. Homberg, near Kassel, Aug. 27, 1887. He received his training from his father. In 1835 he settled at Homberg, where he taught music and played organ; toured extensively as an organ virtuoso. In 1846 he received an honorary doctorate; was made a prof. in 1868. He publ. an *Orgelschule* (Leipzig, 1863) and other books, and also ed. various organ works. His own compositions total nearly 700 works, including organ syms., concertos, 36 sonatas, and liturgical pieces, as well as many orch. and vocal works.

BIBL.: Bibl.: *H. Gehrig, W. V.* (Homberg, 1888). —**NS/LK/DM**

Volek, Jaroslav, prominent Czech musicologist and aesthetician; b. Trenčín, July 15, 1923; d. Prague, Feb. 22, 1989. He studied composition at the Prague Cons. (1941–46) and then attended the master classes of Šín, Hába, and Řídký there (1946–48). He took courses in musicology and aesthetics at the Univ. of Bratislava (Ph.D., 1952, with the diss. *Teoretické základy harmonie z hladiska vedeckej filozófie* [The Theoretical Bases of Harmony from the Viewpoint of Scientific Philosophy]; publ. in Bratislava, 1954) and at the Univ. of Prague (C.Sc., 1958, with the diss. *O specifičnosti předmětu uměleckého odrazu skutečnosti* [Specific Quality in the Artistic Reflection of Reality]; publ. in L. Tondl et al., *Otázky teorie poznáni*, Prague, 1957; D.Sc., 1968, with the diss. *Základy obecné teorie umění* [The Bases of General Art Theory]; publ. in Prague, 1968). He was a lecturer (1952–57), reader (1957–68), and prof. (from 1968) at the Univ. of Prague, and he was also active as a music critic and served as ed. of the journal *Estetika* (1969–71). He played a significant role in the development of Marxist music criticism.

WRITINGS (all publ. in Prague): *Novodobé harmonické systémy* (Contemporary Harmonic Systems; 1961); *Kotázkám předmětu a metod estetiky a obecné teori uměni* (The Subject and Methods of Aesthetics and the General Theory of Art; 1963); *Die Frage der Zahl der Funktion in der traditionellen Harmonik* (1968); *Kapitoly z dějin estetiky* (Chapters from the History of Aesthetics; 1969); *K antropologické problematice estetiky a obecné teorie uměni* (Anthropological Problems in the Aesthetics and General History of Art; 1970).—**NS/LK/DM**

Völker, Franz, gifted German tenor; b. Neu-Isenburg, March 31, 1899; d. Darmstadt, Dec. 5, 1965. He studied in Frankfurt am Main. He made his operatic debut at the Frankfurt am Main Opera as Florestan in 1926, and he continued on its roster until 1935. Völker also sang at the Vienna State Opera (1931–36; 1939–40; 1949–50), the Berlin State Opera (1933–43), and the Bavarian State Opera in Munich (1936–37; 1945–52); he also made guest appearances at London's Covent Garden and in Salzburg and Bayreuth. After his retirement in 1952, he taught voice in Neu-Isenburg, and he was a prof. at the Stuttgart Hochschule für Musik from 1958. Among his finest roles were Parsifal, Lohengrin, Siegmund, Florestan, the Emperor in *Die Frau ohne Schatten*, Otello, and Max in *Der Freischütz*.—**NS/LK/DM**

Volkert, Franz (Joseph), Austrian organist, conductor, and composer, b. Heimersdorf, Bohemia, Feb. 2, 1767; d. Vienna, March 22, 1845. He was active as an organist in Vienna, and from c. 1814 until 1824 was deputy Kapellmeister at the Leopoldstadt Theater. He produced over 100 comic operas, Singspiels, melodramas, farces, etc., many of which were popular. He also composed church music, chamber music, and organ pieces.—**NS/LK/DM**

Volkmann, (Friedrich) Robert, significant German composer; b. Lommatzsch, April 6, 1815; d. Budapest, Oct. 29, 1883. He studied organ and piano with his father, a cantor, and at 17 entered the Freiberg Gymnasium and studied music with Anacker. In 1836 Volkmann went to Leipzig as a student of C. F. Becker, and he was greatly encouraged by Schumann. After teaching music in Prague (1839–41) he settled in Budapest, where he spent the rest of his life, except for four years (1854–58) in Vienna. In 1875 Volkmann was appointed a prof. at the National Academy of Music in Budapest. His music was regarded very highly in his lifetime, but after his death it faded into oblivion.

WORKS: ORCH.: 2 syms.; 3 serenades for Strings; 4 overtures; Cello Concerto; *Konzertstück* for Piano and Orch. **CHAMBER:** 6 string quartets; 2 piano trios; *Chant du Troubadour* for Violin and Piano; *Allegretto capriccioso* for Violin and Piano; 2 violin sonatas; *Romanze* for Cello and Piano; *Capriccio* for Cello and Piano; *Schlummerlied* for Harp, Clarinet, and Horn (also arranged for Piano, Viola, and Cello; his last completed work). **Piano:** Many solo works, including *Phantasiebilder, Dithyrambe und Toccate, Souvenir de Maróth, Nocturne*, Sonata in C minor, *Buch der Lieder, Deutsche Tanzweisen, Cavatine und Barcarole, Visegrád*, 4 marches, *Wanderskizzen, Fantasie, Intermezzo, Variations* on a theme of Handel, *Lieder der Grossmutter*, 3 *Improvisations, Am Grab des Grafen Széchenyi, Ballade und Scherzetto*, and transcriptions of songs by Mozart and Schubert; also works for Piano, 4-Hands, including *Musikalisches Bilderbuch, Ungarische Skizzen, Die Tageszeiten*, 3 marches, *Rondino und Marsch-Caprice*, and transcriptions of his other works. **VOCAL:** Several works, including 2 masses for Men's Chorus, 5 sacred songs for Mixed Chorus, offertories, Christmas carol of the 12th century, old German hymn for Double Men's Chorus, 6 duets on old German poems, *An die Nacht* for Alto Solo with Orch., *Sappho*, dramatic scene for Soprano and Orch., *Kirchenarie* for Bass, Flute, and Strings, *Weihnacht* for Women's Chorus, and *Im Wiesengrun* for Mixed Chorus.

BIBL.: B. Vogel, *R. V.* (Leipzig, 1875); H. Volkmann, *R. V. Sein Leben und seine Werke* (Leipzig, 1903; abr. ed., 1915; 2nd ed., rev., 1922); C. Preiss, *R. V. Kritische Beitrage zu seinem Schaffen* (Graz, 1912); H. Volkmann, ed., *Briefe von R. V.* (Leipzig, 1917); idem, *Thematisches Verzeichnis der Werke von R. V.* (Dresden, 1937); T. Brawley, *The Instrumental Works of R. V.* (diss., Northwestern Univ., 1975).—**NS/LK/DM**

Volkonsky, Andrei (Mikhailovich), Russian harpsichordist, conductor, and composer; b. Geneva (of

Russian parents of princely nobility), Feb. 14, 1933. He was 11 when he began piano studies with Auber at the Geneva Cons. He then received training in composition from Boulanger in Paris (1945–47) and also continued his piano study with Lipatti, after which he went to Russia and pursued training at the Tambov Music School. Volkonsky completed his training in composition with Shaporin at the Moscow Cons. (1950–54). In 1955 he was a co-founder, with Barshai, of the Moscow Chamber Orch. He then devoted himself to harpsichord playing, and in 1964 Volkonsky organized in Moscow the concert group Madrigal, with which he gave annual series of highly successful concerts in the Soviet Union, East Germany, and Czechoslovakia. His early works were set in evocative impressionistic colors, in the manner of the French modern school, but soon he deployed a serial technique of composition analogous to Schoenberg's method of composition with 12 tones outside traditional tonality. He was outspoken in his criticism of the direction that Soviet music was taking, and he entirely rejected the official tenets of socialist realism. This attitude, and the nature of his own music, resulted in the cancellation of performances of his works; he was expelled from the Union of Soviet Composers, and could no longer give concerts. In 1973 he returned to Switzerland.

WORKS: DRAMATIC: Music for plays. **ORCH.:** *Concerto for Orchestra* (Moscow, June 10, 1954); *Capriccio*; *Serenade to an Insect* for Chamber Orch. (1959); *Replique* for Small Orch. (1969). **CHAMBER:** Piano Quintet (1954); String Quartet (1955); Piano Sonata (1956); *Musica stricta* for Piano (1956); *Music* for 12 Instruments (1957); Viola Sonata (1960); *Jeux à trois* for Flute, Violin, and Harpsichord (1962); *Les Mailles du temps* for 3 Instrumental Groups (1969). **VOCAL:** 2 cantatas: *Rus* (Russia), after Gogol (1952) and *The Image of the World* (Moscow, May 8, 1953); *2 Japanese Songs* for Chorus, Electronic Sound, and Percussion (1957); *Suite des miroirs* for Soprano, Organ, Guitar, Violin, Flute, and Percussion (1960); *The Lament of Shaza* for Soprano and Small Orch. (1961; Moscow, May 12, 1965); *Concerto itinerant* for Soprano, Violin, Percussion, and 26 Instruments (1967).—**NS/LK/DM**

Vollenweider, Andreas, popular Swiss composer and instrumentalist; b. Zürich, Oct. 4, 1953. His father was the organist Hans Vollenweider, and the family home was often frequented by artists and musicians. He studied guitar, flute, and other instruments before settling on the harp, which he modified and amplified in developing his own technique. Vollenweider played concerts and made recordings with the ensemble Poetry and Music; his first solo recording was *Eine art Suite* (1979), and it was followed by the debut concert of Andreas Vollenweider and Friends at the 1981 Montreux Jazz Festival. His ensuing recordings were highly successful, marketed under jazz, pop, and classical categories, and considered among the most engaging of New Age recordings. His first U.S. tour was in 1984; that same year he directed the video *Pace verde*. In 1989 he produced another video, *Pearls and Tears*. His titles reflect his mystical roots; the music itself involves a delicate mix of electric and acoustic timbres in lively, syncopated textures. Other noteworthy recordings include *...Behind the Gardens—Behind the Wall—Under the Tree...* (1981), *Caverna Magica (...Under the Tree—In the Cave...)* (1983), *White Winds* (1985), *Down to the Moon* (1986), and *Dancing with the Lion* (1989).—**NS/LK/DM**

Vomáčka, Boleslav, Czech composer; b. Mladá Boleslav, June 28, 1887; d. Prague, March 1, 1965. He studied law at the Charles Univ. in Prague (LL.D., 1913) and studied organ (1906–09), composition (with Novák; 1909–10), and singing (with Krummer) at the Prague Cons. He was in the service of the Labor Ministry in Prague (1919–50); wrote music criticism in several newspapers there; was ed. of *Listy Hudební Matice* (1922–35). In 1955 he was made an Artist of Merit by the Czech government. He publ. *Josef Suk* (Prague, 1922), *Stanislav Suda* (Prague, 1933), and *Sukova sborová tvorba* (Suk's Choral Works; Prague, 1935). He began to compose early in life, developing a strong national style.

WORKS: DRAMATIC: Opera: *Vodník* (The Water Spirit; 1934–37; Prague, Dec. 17, 1937); *Čekanky* (Waiting for a Husband; 1939; 1956–57); *Boleslav I* (1953–55; Prague, March 8, 1957). **ORCH.:** *Ciaconna* (1910); Sym. (1945); *Dukla*, overture (1948); *Fanfary miru* (Fanfares of Peace) for Trumpet and Orch. (1960). **CHAMBER:** Violin Sonata (1912); Duo for Violin and Cello (1925–27); Sonatina for 2 Violins (1936; also for Violin and Viola and as *Kvartetino* for String Quartet, 1941); Nonet for Wind Instruments (1957); String Quartet (1959). **Piano:** 2 sonatas (1917; *Sonata quasi fantasia*, 1942); other pieces. **VOCAL: Cantatas:** *Romance Svatojiršká* (Romance of St. George; 1920, 1943); *Živí mrtvým* (To the Dead; 1927–28; Prague, Feb. 24, 1929); *Strážce majáku* (The Keeper of the Lighthouse; 1931–33); *Prapor míru nad Duklou* (The Banner of Peace Over Duklou; 1951); *Bojka partyzánka* (The Partisan Struggle; 1952). **Other:** Many choral works; sets of songs.

BIBL.: H. Doležil, *B. V.* (Prague, 1941).—**NS/LK/DM**

Vonk, Hans, prominent Dutch conductor; b. Amsterdam, June 18, 1942. He studied law at the Univ. of Amsterdam, took courses in piano, conducting, and composition at the Amsterdam Cons., then studied conducting with Scherchen and Ferrara. From 1966 to 1973 he was conductor of the Netherlands National Ballet; he was also asst. conductor of the Concertgebouw Orch. in Amsterdam. In 1974 Vonk made his U.S. debut as a guest conductor with the San Francisco Sym. Orch. He was conductor of the Netherlands Radio Phil. in Hilversum (1973–79) and assoc. conductor of the Royal Phil. in London (1976–79). He served as chief conductor of the Netherlands Opera in Amsterdam (1976–85) and of the Residentie Orch. in The Hague (1980–85). He appeared regularly as a guest conductor with the Dresden State Orch. and Opera from 1980; and he was permanent conductor (1984–85) and chief conductor (1985–91) of the Dresden State Opera, and also chief conductor of the Dresden State Orch. (1985–91). From 1991 to 1997 Vonk was chief conductor of the Cologne Radio Sym. Orch. In 1996 he became music director of the St. Louis Sym. Orch.—**NS/LK/DM**

Von Stade, Frederica, remarkable American mezzo-soprano; b. Somerville, N.J., June 1, 1945. She was educated at the Norton Academy in Conn., and after an apprenticeship at the Long Wharf Theater in New Haven, she studied with Sebastian Engelberg, Paul Berl, and Otto Guth at the Mannes Coll. of Music in N.Y. Although she reached only the semi-finals of the Metropolitan Opera Auditions in 1969, she attracted the attention of Rudolf Bing, its general manager, who arranged for her debut with the company in N.Y. as the 3rd boy in *Die Zauberflöte* on Jan. 11, 1970; she gradually took on more important roles there before going to Europe, where she gave an arresting portrayal of Cherubino at the opera house at the palace of Versailles in 1973. In 1974 she sang Nina in the premiere of Pasatieri's *The Seagull* at the Houston Grand Opera. In 1975 she made her debut at London's Covent Garden as Rosina; subsequently attained extraordinary success in lyric mezzo-soprano roles with the world's major opera houses and also pursued an extensive concert career, appearing regularly with the Chamber Music Soc. of Lincoln Center in N.Y. In 1988 she sang the role of Tina in the premiere of Argento's *The Aspern Papers* at the Dallas Opera, and in 1990 appeared in recital in N.Y.'s Carnegie Hall. She celebrated the 25th anniversary of her Metropolitan Opera debut in 1995 as Debussy's Mélisande, a role she reprised at the San Francisco Opera in 1997. In 1999 she appeared in Sondheim's *A Little Night Music* in Houston. Her memorable roles include Dorabella, Idamante, Adalgisa in *Norma*, Charlotte in *Werther*, Mélisande, Octavian, and Malcolm in *La Donna del lago*. She has also proved successful as a crossover artist, especially in Broadway musical recordings.—**NS/LK/DM**

Voorhees, Donald, American conductor; b. Guthville, Pa., July 26, 1903; d. Cape May Court House, N.J., Jan. 10, 1989. He joined the Lyric Theatre orch. in Allentown, Pa., as a pianist at age 12, becoming its conductor when he was 15; at 17, he made his first appearance as a conductor on Broadway with the musical revue *Broadway Brevities* of 1920. Voorhees subsequently conducted various Broadway shows. He also was active as a conductor on radio from 1925, and in 1940 he became music director of the highly successful network radio show the *Bell Telephone Hour*, for which he composed its signature theme, the *Bell Waltz*. After the show moved to television in 1959, he remained as its music director until its last telecast in 1968.—**NS/LK/DM**

Voormolen, Alexander (Nicolas), Dutch composer; b. Rotterdam, March 3, 1895; d. The Hague, Nov. 12, 1980. He was a scion of a family of municipal functionaries in the Netherlands, and on his mother's side was a descendant of Claude Rameau, a brother of Jean-Philippe Rameau. He entered the Utrecht School of Music, where he studied with Johan Wagenaar and Willam Petri. Voormolen began to compose as a very young man; from his earliest steps he experienced a strong influence of French Impressionism. He went to Paris in 1916, where he was befriended by Ravel, whose influence became decisive. In 1923 he settled in The Hague; after serving as a music critic of the *Nieuwe Rotterdamsche Courant*, he was librarian of the Royal Cons. of Music of The Hague (1938–55). In his early idiom, Voormolen affected richly extended harmonies and followed Ravel's example in writing works in neo-Baroque forms, marked by gentle symmetric melodies. His compositions later followed along neo-Classical lines. His works were initially successful in his homeland, but eventually fell into desuetude.

WORKS: DRAMATIC: Ballet: *Le Roi Grenouille* (1916; withdrawn); *Baron Hop* (2 suites, 1923–24; 1931); *Diana* (1935–36); *Spiegel-Suite*, after Langendijk's play (1943). **ORCH.:** *De drei ruitertjes* (The 3 Little Horsemen), variations on a Dutch song (1927); *Een Zomerlied* (1928); Oboe Concerto (1938); *Sinfonia* (1939); *Kleine Haagsche Suite* for Small Orch. (1939); *Pastorale* for Oboe and Strings (1940); Cello Concerto (1941); *Arethuza*, symphonic myth, after L. Couperus (1947; Amsterdam, Nov. 11, 1948); *La Sirène* for Saxophone and Orch. (1949); Concerto for 2 Harpsichords or Pianos and Orch. (1950); *Sinfonia concertante* for Clarinet, Horn, and Strings (1951); *Eline*, nocturne (1957; orchestrated and enl. version of the 1951 piano piece); *Chaconne en Fuga* (1958). **CHAMBER:** 2 violin sonatas (1917, 1934); Suite for Cello and Piano (1917); Piano Trio (1918); Suite for Harpsichord (1921); *Divertissement* for Cello and Piano (1922); 2 string quartets (1939, 1942); Viola Sonata (1935). **Piano:** *Valse triste* (1914); Suite No. 1 (1914–16); *Falbalas* (1915); *Elephants* (1919); *Tableaux des Pays Bas*, in 2 series (1919–20, 1924); *Scène et danse érotique* (1920); *Le Souper clandestin* (1921); *Sonnet* (1922); *Livre des enfants* (2 series, 1923, 1925); *Berceuse* (1924); Sonata (1944); *Eline*, nocturne (1951). **VOCAL:** *Beatrijs*, melodrama for Narrator and Piano (1921); *3 Gedichten* for Voice and Orch. (1932); *Een nieuwe Lente op Holland's erf* for Voice and Orch. (1936); *Herinneringen aan Holland* (Memories of Holland) for Baritone, Bass Clarinet, and Strings (1966); *Stanzas of Charles II* for Baritone, Flute, English Horn, Celesta, Percussion, and Strings (1966); *Amsterdam*, cantata (1967); *From: The Recollection* for Medium Voice, String Orch., and Celesta (1970); *Ex minimis patet ipse Deus*, hymn for Middle Voice, Strings, and Celesta (1971; many alternate versions); *Ave Maria* for Chorus, Harp, and String Orch. (1973; many alternate versions); choruses. —**NS/LK/DM**

Voorn, Joop, Dutch composer and teacher; b. The Hague, Oct. 16, 1932. He received training at the Brabant Cons., where he subsequently taught (from 1969).

WORKS: ORCH.: *Immobile: Music for Tutankhamun* (1973; Brabant, Dec. 2, 1975); *Petit concert* for Flute and Chamber Orch. (1975; Brabant, April 25, 1976); Sym. (1981); *Symphony for Gemet* for Winds (1981); *Petit concert d'automne* for Alto Saxophone and Orch. (1989); *The Sun Dances* (1990). **CHAMBER:** 2 string quartets (n.d.; 1970, rev. 1980); *Nakupenda*, trio for Flute, Violin, and Viola (1971); *Sucevita chorals* for 2 Oboes, 2 Clarinets, Bass Clarinet, and Bassoon (1972; rev. 1974); *Soft Music for Angela* for Flute (1973); Trio for Oboe, Clarinet, and Bassoon (1975); *Preludium en fuga*, quintet for Oboe, Clarinet, Bassoon, Horn, and Piano (1976); *Divertimento* for 3 Flutes (1978); *3 Pieces* for English Horn (1979); Clarinet Quintet (1983); Saxophone Sonata (1984); *Vjif schetsen* for 2 Guitars (1984); Piano Trio (1985); *Schrijdende* for Oboe, Clarinet, Bassoon, Horn, and Organ (1985); *Serenade* for Bassoon and Piano (1986); piano pieces; organ music. **VOCAL:** *Psalm CXIV—In Exitu* for Soprano, Children's Chorus, and Orch. (1968); *Speaking of Siva* for Chorus and Chamber Orch. (1977); *Song of Enitharmon* for Chorus and Orch. (1980); *Perceval et Blanchefleur* for Tenor and Orch. (1982); 7 Lieder for Soprano and Alto Lyre or Piano, after Christian Morgenstern (1990); *Lofsang van Braband* for Chorus and Wind Quintet (1996).—**NS/LK/DM**

Vopelius, Gottfried, German composer; b. Herwigsdorf, near Zittau, Jan. 28, 1635; d. Leipzig, Feb. 3, 1715. He studied at the Univ. of Leipzig, and was made collaborator ultimus at the St. Nikolai school in Leipzig in 1671; was made Kantor there and at the Nikolaikirche in 1676. He publ. the valuable collection *Neu Leipziger Gesangbuch, von den schönsten und besten Liedern verfasset...mit 4. 5. bis 6. stimmen, deren Melodeyen Theils aus Johann Herman Scheins Cantional, und Andern guten Autoribus zusammen getragen, theils aber selbsten componiret* (Leipzig, 1682), which includes over 400 works, among them 3 by Vopelius.—**NS/LK/DM**

Vorlová, Sláva (actually, **Miroslava Johnova**), Czech composer; b. Náchod, March 15, 1894; d. Prague, Aug. 24, 1973. She studied piano with her mother, then received training in voice at the Vienna Academy of Music; took private lessons in composition with Novák and in piano with Štěpán in Prague. After passing her state examinations in piano and singing (1918), she continued her piano studies with Maxián and her composition studies with Řídký, completing her training with the latter at the Prague Cons. master classes (graduated, 1948). She became interested in writing music for instruments rarely used for solo performances and wrote one of the few concertos for bass clarinet. Her music is tinted with impressionistic colors.

WORKS: DRAMATIC: Opera: *Zlaté ptáče* (The Golden Birds; 1949–50); *Rozmarýnka* (Rosemary; 1952; Kladno, 1955); *Náchodská kasace* (The Náchod Cassation; 1955); *Dva světy* (2 Worlds; 1958). **ORCH.:** *Fantasy* for Cello and Orch. (1940); *Symphony JM*, dedicated to Jan Masaryk (1947–48); *Božena Němcová*, suite (1950–51); Oboe Concerto (1952); *3 Bohemian Dances* (1952–53); Trumpet Concerto (1953); Viola Concerto (1954); Clarinet Concerto (1957); *Memento* (1957); *Thuringian Dances* (1957); Flute Concerto (1959); Concerto for Bass Clarinet and Strings (1961); *Kybernetic Studies* (1962); Concerto for Oboe, Harp, and Orch. (1963); *Dedications* (1965); *Bhukhar* (Fever Birds; 1965); Concerto for Double Bass and Strings (1968); *Correlations* for Bass Clarinet, Piano, and Strings (1968); *Polarization* for Harp, Wind Orch., and Percussion (1970); *Emergence* for Violin and Orch. (1973; Prague, March 24, 1974). **CHAMBER:** String Quartet (1939); Nonet (1944); *Melodious Variations* for String Quartet (1950); *Puzzles* for 2 Pianos (1953); *Miniatures* for Bass Clarinet and Piano (1962); *Dessins tetraharpes* for 4 Harps (1963); *Variations on a Theme by Handel* for Bass Clarinet and Piano (1965); *6 pro 5* for Brass Quintet (1967); *Immanence* for Bass Clarinet, Piano, and Percussion (1970). **VOCAL:** *Songs of Gondwana*, symphonic epos for Soloists, Chorus, and Orch. (1948–49); *2 African Fables* for Narrator, Alto Flute, and Percussion (1964); *Brief Considerations* for Soprano, Alto, and Piano (1971); songs.—**NS/LK/DM**

Voss, Charles, German pianist and composer; b. Schmarsow, Sept. 20, 1815; d. Verona, Aug. 29, 1882. He studied in Berlin, but made his career in Paris, where he went in 1846. Voss enjoyed great success in Paris society as a pianist and composer. He publ. a great number of salon pieces, transcriptions, paraphrases, etc., and also wrote piano concertos and etudes. His first Piano Concerto, in F minor, was praised by Mendelssohn. —**NS/LK/DM**

Voss, Friedrich, German composer, b. Halberstadt, Dec. 12, 1930. He studied composition and piano at the (West) Berlin Hochschule für Musik (1949–54), then devoted himself to composition, winning the Munich Chamber Orch. competition (1955), the Stuttgart Music Prize (1960), the (West) Berlin Art Prize (1961), the Düsseldorf Robert Schumann Prize (1962), the Villa Massimo Award (1964, 1977), and the Mannheim Johann Wenzel Stamitz Prize (1985).

WORKS: DRAMATIC: Ballet: *Die Nachtigall und die Rose*, after Oscar Wilde (1961; Oberhausen, Jan. 5, 1962). **ORCH.:** *Concerto da camera* for Strings (1953); Symphonic Suite (1954; Berlin, July 9, 1958); 4 syms.: No. 1 (1958–59; Berlin, March 23, 1960), No. 2 (1962–63; Bonn, March 7, 1966), No. 3 (1966–67; Berlin, Nov. 12, 1969), and No. 4 (1972–76); 2 violin concertos: No. 1 (1962; Brussels, May 28, 1966) and No. 2 (1985–87); *Hamlet Overture* (1968–69); *Dithryrambus über ein Motiv von Beethoven* (1969); *Metamorphosis* (1978–79; Tokyo, June 10, 1980). **OTHER:** Chamber music, including 3 string quartets; choral pieces.—**NS/LK/DM**

Vossius, Isaac, Netherlands scholar; b. Leiden, 1618; d. Windsor, England, Feb. 21, 1689. He was educated at the Univ. of Leiden. After traveling in England, France, and Italy (1641–46), he taught at the court of Queen Christina of Sweden (1649–54). He was active in The Hague from 1655 before settling in England in 1670. That same year he was made a doctor of civil law by Oxford Univ. He became canon of St. George's Chapel, Windsor, in 1673. In addition to his writings on non-musical subjects, he wrote the important treatise *De poematum cantus et viribus rythmi* (London, 1673), which influenced such composers as Bach, Kuhnau, and Mattheson.—**NS/LK/DM**

Vostřák, Zbyněk, Czech composer and conductor; b. Prague, June 10, 1920; d. Strakonice, Aug. 4, 1985. He studied composition privately with Rudolf Karel (1938–43) and attended the conducting classes of Pavel Dědeček at the Prague Cons. In 1963 he became conductor of the Prague chamber ensemble Musica Viva Pragensis. He also worked in an electronic music studio in Prague. His music evolved from the Central European type of modernism; later he annexed serial techniques, electronic sound, and aleatory practices.

WORKS: DRAMATIC: Opera: *Rohovín čtverrohý* (The 4-horned Rohovin; 1947–48; Olomouc, 1949); *Kutnohorští havíři* (The King's Master of the Mint; 1951–53; Prague, 1955); *Pražské nokturno* (A Prague Nocturne; 1957–58; Ustí-on-the-Elbe, 1960); *Rozbitý džbán* (The Broken Jug; 1960–61; Prague, 1963). **Ballet:** *The Primrose* (1944–45); *Filosofská historie* (A Story of Students of Philosophy; 1949); *Viktorka* (Little Victoria; 1950); *Sněhurka* (Snow White; 1955); *Veselí vodníci* (Jolly Water Sprites; 1978–79). **ORCH.:** *Prague Overture* (1941); *Zrození měsíce* (The Birth of the Moon) for Chamber Orch. (1966; Prague, March 8, 1967); *Kyvadlo času* (The Pendulum of Time) for Cello, 4 Instrumental Groups, and Electric Organ (1966–67; Donaueschingen, Oct. 19, 1968); *Metahudba* (Metamusic) (1968; Prague, March 2, 1970); *Tajemství elipsy* (The Secret of Ellipsis) (1970; Prague, March 5, 1971); *Parable* for Orch. and Tape (1976–77); *Kapesní vesmír* (The Pocket Universe) for Flute, Dulcimer, and Strings (1980–81); *The Cathedral* (1982); *The Crystals* for English Horn, Strings, and Percussion (1983); Piano

Concerto (1984). **CHAMBER:** *Elements* for String Quartet (1964); *Synchronia* for 6 Instruments (1965); *Trigonum* for Violin, Oboe, and Piano (1965); *Kosmogonia* for String Quartet (1968); *Sextant* for Wind Quintet (1969); *Fair Play* for Harpsichord and 6 Instruments (1978); String Quartet No. 4 (1979); *The Secret of the Rose* for Organ, Brass Quintet, and Percussion (1985); piano works. **OTHER:** Tape pieces.—**NS/LK/DM**

Votapek, Ralph, American pianist and teacher; b. Milwaukee, March 20, 1939. He studied at Northwestern Univ. (B.A., 1960), with Gui Mombaerts and Robert Goldsand at the Manhattan School of Music in N.Y. (M.M., 1961), and with Rosina Lhévinne at the Juilliard School of Music in N.Y. (1961–62). He won the Van Cliburn Competition in 1962, and then embarked on a concert career. He taught at Mich. State Univ. in East Lansing (from 1968).—**NS/LK/DM**

Votto, Antonino, Italian conductor; b. Piacenza, Oct. 30, 1896; d. Milan, Sept. 9, 1985. He studied piano with Longo and composition with De Nardis at the Cons. di Musica S. Pietro a Majella in Naples. He made his debut as a concert pianist in Trieste in 1919. From 1919 to 1921 he taught piano at the Cons. di Musica G. Verdi in Trieste. In 1921 he became a conductor at the Teatro Colón in Buenos Aires; in 1923 he made his first appearance at Milan's La Scala conducting *Manon Lescaut*; then was a répétiteur and asst. conductor there under Toscanini until 1929. He subsequently made guest conducting appearances throughout Italy, Europe, and South America. From 1948 to 1970 he was a regular conductor at La Scala, during which period he led performances in major productions with Callas and other famous singers; also conducted at the Chicago Lyric Opera (1960–61; 1970). He was on the faculty of the Milan Cons. (1941–67).—**NS/LK/DM**

Vranken, Jaap, Dutch organist, teacher, and composer; b. Utrecht, April 16, 1897; d. The Hague, April 20, 1956. He was the son of the organist Joseph Vranken (1870–1948), with whom he studied organ and theory. From 1916 to 1918 he was in the U.S., studying with Percy Goetschius. He returned to the Netherlands in 1920, and was appointed organist at the church of St. Anthonius in The Hague. Vranken acquired a fine reputation as a teacher. He composed mostly sacred music, and he also wrote instrumental music in Classical style and publ. a manual on counterpoint (1948). —**NS/LK/DM**

Vrebalov, Aleksandra, promising Yugoslav composer; b. Novi Sad, Sept. 22, 1970. She studied composition with Miroslav Slatkic at the Novi Sad Univ. (B.M., 1992), with Zoran Erich at Belgrade Univ. (1993–94), with Elinor Armer at the San Francisco cons. (M.M., 1996), and with Ivana Loudova at the Prague Academy of Music (1997). She held residencies at the MacDowell Colony (1998) and at Tanglewood (1999), and in 2000 was a fellow at the Rockefeller Bellagio Center in Italy. Her works have been widely performed throughout the U.S., her *Times* for Orch. (1995) winning both the Highsmith Composition Competition of the SFCM (1996) and the Vienna Modern Masters Recording Award (1997).

WORKS: ORCH.: *Times* (1995); Piano Concerto (1999). **CHAMBER:** *Duo Uran* for Clarinet and Viola (1996); 2 string quartets: No. 1 (1995), and No. 2, *Sketches on pendulums, autism, loss, nine places* (1997); *Air and Fugue* for Harpsichord, Percussion, and Harp (1996); *Vladimir Trio* for Flute, Violin, and Viola (1997); *Pannonia Boundless* for String Quartet (1998); *Transparent Walls* for 11 Winds, Percussion, and Piano (2000). **VOCAL:** *Elegy for NN* for Soprano and Chamber Ensemble (1996); *Op. 29* for Soprano and String Quartet (2000).—**LK/DM**

Vredenburg, Max, Dutch composer; b. Brussels (of Dutch parents), Jan. 16, 1904; d. Laren, the Netherlands, Aug. 9, 1976. He was taken to the Netherlands as a child and received an elementary musical education there. In 1926 he went to Paris and studied at the École Normale de Musique with Dukas; was a music correspondent for the *Nieuwe Rotterdamsche courant* (1936–40). He fled the Nazis and went to Java in 1941, where he was interned by the Japanese (1942–45) but was allowed to organize concerts with his fellow internee, Szymond Goldberg. After his liberation, Vredenburg settled in Amsterdam, where he was director of the Dutch section of the Federation Internationale des Jeunesses Musicales (1953–69) and also founder- director of the National Youth Orch. (1957–76). He wrote the book *Langs de vijf Lijnen* (1947).

WORKS: *Au pays des vendanges*, wind quintet (1951); Oboe Concerto (1951); *Akiba* for Mezzo-soprano and Chamber Orch. (1951); *Du printemps* for Mezzo-soprano and Chamber Orch. (1952); *Lamento* for Viola and Piano (1953); *Suite dansante* for Youth Orch. (1956); *Horizons hollandaises* for Orch. (1959); Trio for Oboe, Clarinet, and Bassoon (1965); piano pieces; many songs.—**NS/LK/DM**

Vreuls, Victor (Jean Léonard), Belgian composer and music educator; b. Verviers, Feb. 4, 1876; d. Brussels, July 27, 1944. He studied at the Verviers Cons., with Dupuis (harmony) and Radoux (counterpoint) at the Liège Cons., and with d'Indy in Paris. After serving as a prof. of harmony at the Schola Cantorum in Paris (1901–06), he was director of the Luxembourg Cons. (1906–26). In 1925 he was elected a member of the Belgian Royal Academy in Brussels. His major works were written in an expansive Romantic style.

WORKS: DRAMATIC: Opera: *Olivier le simple* (1909–11; Brussels, March 9, 1922); *Un Songe d'une nuit d'été*, after Shakespeare (1923–24; Brussels, Dec. 17, 1925). **Ballet:** *Le Loup-garou* (1935). **ORCH.:** 3 symphonic poems: *Cortège heroïque* (1894), *Jour de fête* (1904), and *Werther* (1907); Sym. (1899); 2 poèmes for Cello and Orch. (1900, 1930); *Elégie* for Flute and Chamber Orch. (1917); *Morceau de concert* for Trumpet and Orch. (1917); *Fantaisie* for Horn and Orch. (1918); *Romance* for Violin and Chamber Orch. (1924); *Caprice* for Violin and Chamber Orch. (1924); *Suite de danses* (1939); *Ouverture pour un drame* (1940). **CHAMBER:** Piano Quartet (1894); Piano Trio (1896); 2 violin sonatas (1899, 1919); String Quartet (1918); Cello Sonata (1922). **VOCAL:** Choruses; songs.—**NS/LK/DM**

Vriend, Jan, Dutch composer and conductor; b. Sijbekarspel, Nov. 10, 1938. He studied with Ton de

Leeuw at the Amsterdam Cons. (1960–67), with Koenig at the Inst. of Sonology at the Univ. of Utrecht (1965–67), and with Xenakis at the Paris Schola Cantorum (1967–68). While in Paris, he also was active with the Groupe de Recherches Musicales of the ORTF. Returning to the Netherlands, he was active as a conductor and as a lecturer. He later was active in England and was conductor of the New Stroud Orch. (1989–94). Having taught himself mathematics, he became interested in its applications to music. His works reflect advanced compositional modes of expression.

WORKS: ORCH.: *Diamant*, "sym. for the Earth" (1964–67); *Mater-Muziek* for Orch. and Electronics (1966); *Huantan* for Organ and Wind Orch. (1967–68); *Bau* (1970); *Elements of Logic* for Wind Orch. (1972; Scheveningen, Feb. 25, 1973; in collaboration with J. Kunst); *Hallelujah II: Ouverture à la Nouvelle alliance* (1988) and *I: A Symphony of the North* for Bass Clarinet and Orch. (1990; rev. 1997); *...de origen volcánico*, overture (1992). **CHAMBER:** *Pour le flûte* (1961); String Quartet (1962–63); *Paroesie* for 10 Instruments (1963); *Eclipse I: Heterostase* for Flute, Bass Clarinet, and Piano (1981), *II: Athema Keramitis* for Flute and Clarinet (1985), and *III: Aura (Interlude)* for Piano (1994); *Toque por la tierra vacía* for 2 Guitars (1981; rev. 1983); *Vectorial*, "a monument for J.S. Bach" for Oboe, Clarinet, Bass Clarinet, Bassoon, 2 Trumpets, and Piano (1983; rev. 1987); *Gravity's Dance* for Piano (1984; rev. 1986); *Wu Li* for Cello (1986; rev. 1987); *Symbiosis* for 9 Instruments (1993); Piano Quintet (1999); piano pieces; organ music. **VOCAL:** *Transformation (on the way to Halleluja)* for Chorus and Orch. (1965–67); *Introitus (Hommage to Ton de Leeuw)* for Chorus, 6 Clarinets, 2 Bass Clarinets, and 4 Trombones (1969); *3 Songs* for Mezzo-soprano and Orch. (1991); *Du-Dich-Dir* for Chorus (1998).—**NS/LK/DM**

Vrieslander, Otto, German composer and writer on music; b. Münster, July 18, 1880; d. Tegna, Switzerland, Dec. 16, 1950. He was a student of Stemhauer and Buths in Düsseldorf (1891–1900), of Van de Sandt and Klauwell at the Cologne Cons. (1901–02), and of Schenker in Vienna (1911–12). In 1929 he settled in Switzerland. He publ. *Carl Philipp Emanuel Bach* (Munich, 1923), and also wrote articles on and prepared eds. of C. P. E. Bach's music. Vrieslander was an accomplished lieder composer.—**NS/LK/DM**

Vronsky, Vitya, Russian-born American pianist; b. Evpatoria, Crimea, Aug. 22, 1909; d. Cleveland, June 28, 1992. She received training at the Kiev Cons., from Petri and Schnabel in Berlin, and from Cortot in Paris. From 1930 she performed in Europe. In 1933 she married **Victor Babin**, with whom she regularly performed in a piano duo. In 1937 they emigrated to the U.S. and established themselves as the leading piano duo of the day. From 1945 their tours took them to principal music centers of the world. Their repertoire extended from Bach to Babin.—**NS/LK/DM**

Vroons, Frans (actually, **Franciscus**), Dutch tenor; b. Amsterdam, April 28, 1911; d. 's-Hertogenbosch, June 1, 1983. He studied in Amsterdam and Paris. He made his operatic debut as Pelléas in 1937, and in 1945 he became the principal tenor at the Netherlands Opera in Amsterdam, where he sang for two decades; he was also its co-director (1956–71). In 1948 Vroons made his first appearance at London's Covent Garden as Don José and in 1951 he appeared in San Francisco as Massenet's Des Grieux. He taught voice in Amsterdam (from 1971). His other roles included Florestan, Tamino, Hoffmann, and Peter Grimes.—**NS/LK/DM**

Vuataz, Roger, distinguished Swiss organist, conductor, broadcasting administrator, and composer; b. Geneva, Jan. 4, 1898; d. Chêne-Bougeries, Aug. 2, 1988. He studied at the Collège Calvin and pursued musical training at the Academy of Music and at the Cons. in Geneva, his principal mentors being Delaye, Mottu, and O. Barblan. He later studied Ondes Martenot in Paris (diploma, 1931) and attended the Institut Jaques-Dalcroze in Geneva (rhythm dipoloma, 1936). Vuataz's career was centered on Geneva, where he served as an organist of the Protestant Reformed Church from 1917 to 1978. He was founder-director of the Cathedral Choir (1940–60). From 1944 to 1964 he was head of the music dept. of Radio Geneva. From 1961 to 1971 he taught at the Geneva Cons. He was president of the International Music Competition from 1962 to 1969, and also of the Viñes singing competition in Barcelona from 1963 to 1978. In 1967 he was awarded the music prize of the City of Geneva. In 1975 the Assn. of Swiss Musicians gave him its composer's prize. Vuataz's music was well crafted and displayed the influence of the Protestant Reformed tradition in his sacred scores.

WORKS: DRAMATIC: *Le Rhône*, ballet (1929); *Poème méditerranéen pour un ballet* (1938–50); *Monsieur Jabot*, opera-buffa (1957; Geneva, Nov. 28, 1958); *Solitude*, ballet (1962); *L'Esprit du Mal*, lyric drama (1967); *Cora, Amour et Mort*, lyric tragedy (1978–80); radiophonic pieces; film music. **ORCH.:** *Triptyque* (1929–42); *Petit Concert* for Small Orch. (1932); *Deuxième Suite sur des Thèmes populaires* for Strings (1937); *Images de Grèce*, sym. (1938); *Nocturne heroïque* for Trumpet and Orch. (1940; also for Trumpet and Piano); *Impromptu* for Saxophone and Orch. (1941; also for Saxophone and Piano); *Promenade et Poursuite* for Bassoon and Orch. (1943; also for Bassoon and Piano); *Epopée antique*, 2 suites (1947, 1951); Violin Concerto (1948); *Cinq Estampes genevoises* (1959); *Ouverture pour Phèdre* (1959); Piano Concerto (1963–64); Harp Concerto, *Fantaisies I-III* (1972); *Les Tragiques*, sym. for Reciter and Orch. (1974–75); Cello Concerto, *Images poétiques et pathétiques* (1977). **CHAMBER:** Cello Sonata (1928); 2 suites for Ondes Martenot (1930); Violin Sonatina (1933–34); *Musique* for Wind Quintet (1935–65); *Nocturne et Danse* for Alto Saxophone and Piano (1940: *Nocturne heroïque* for Trumpet and Piano (1940; also for Trumpet and Orch.); *Impromptu* for Saxophone and Piano (1941; also for Saxophone and Orch.); *Promenade et poursuite* for Bassoon and Piano (1943; also for Bassoon and Orch.); *Frivolités* for Sextet (1952); *Incantation* for Alto Saxophone and Piano (1953); Flute Sonata (1954–57); *Destin* for Saxophone, Harp, and Percussion (1954–79); *Thrène* for Horn and Piano (1960); *Ballade* for Viola and Piano (1960); String Quartet (1966–70); *Quatre Conversations avec Bach* for Flute, Oboe, Bassoon, and Clarinet (1966–83); *Plaintes et Ramages* for Oboe and Piano (1971); *Nocturnes I-III* for Cello (1974); *Elegie et Danse* for Flute (1978); *Méditation sur BACH* for Violin (1985). **Piano:** 2 sonatas (*Sonate française*, 1937; *Variations- Sonate*, 1956–59, rev. 1978); *Rhapsodie sur trois thèmes grecs* for 2 Pianos (1937–59); *Trois Sonatines* (1962–63). **VOCAL:** *Huit Poèmes d'Orient* for Soprano and Orch. or Piano (1922–66); *La Flûte de Roseau*, motet for Children's, Women's, and Men's Choruses (1937); *Genève ouverte au ciel* for Tenor, Narrator, Children's, Men's, and Women's Choruses, and Orch. (1940–41); *Grande Liturgie* for Men's Chorus (1943); *Quatre Rondeaux de Charles d'Orleans* for Soprano and Orch. or Piano (1944–61); *Le Temps de vivre* for Mezzo-soprano and Piano (1944–66); *Jésus*, oratorio for Vocal Quintet, Narrator, Double Men's Chorus, and Orch. (1949–50); *Cantate de Psaumes* for Men's Chorus and 21 Instruments (1954); *Motet poétique* for Men's Chorus (1974); *Huit Villanelles* for Soprano, Baritone, and Piano (1982); *Sechs Lieder* for Mezzo-soprano and Piano (1983). **—NS/LK/DM**

Vučković, Vojislav, Serbian conductor, musicologist, and composer; b. Pirot, Oct. 18, 1910; d. (murdered by the German police) Belgrade, Dec. 25, 1942. He went to Prague and studied composition with Karel and conducting with Malko at the Cons., becoming a pupil in Suk's master class in composition there in 1943. Vučković also took courses in musicology at the Univ. of Prague (Ph.D., 1934). He then returned to Belgrade, where he was active as a conductor, lecturer, broadcaster, and writer on music; he also taught at the Stanković Music School. He publ. pamphlets on the materialistic interpretation of music in the light of Marxist dialectics. He was in the resistance movement during the German occupation of his homeland but was hunted down and murdered. His collected essays were publ. as *Studije, eseji, kritike* (Belgrade, 1968). After a period of composition in the expressionistic manner (including the application of quarter- tones), he abruptly changed his style out of ideological considerations and embraced programmatic realism.

WORKS: DRAMATIC: Ballet: *Čovek koji je ukrao sunce* (The Man Who Stole the Sun; 1940). **ORCH.:** Overture for Chamber Orch. (1933); 3 syms.: No. 1 (1933), No. 2 (1942; unfinished; orchestrated by P. Osghian), and No. 3, *Heroic Oratorio* for Soloists, Chorus, and Orch. (1942; unfinished; orchestrated by A. Obradović; Cetinje, Sept. 5, 1951); *Zaveštanje Modesta Musorgskog* (Modest Mussorgsky's Legacy; 1940); *Ozareni put* (The Radiant Road), symphonic poem (1940); *Vesnik bure* (The Harbinger of the Storm), symphonic poem (1941); *Burevesnik* (Stormy Petrel), symphonic poem (1942; Belgrade, Dec. 25, 1944). **OTHER:** Chamber music; choral works; songs.

BIBL.: *V. V.: Umetnik i borac* (Belgrade, 1968).**—NS/LK/DM**

Vuillaume, Jean-Baptiste, celebrated French violin maker; b. Mirecourt, Oct. 7, 1798; d. Paris, March 19, 1875. He came from a family of violin makers, and learned the trade from his father, Claude Vuillaume (1772–1834). At 19 he went to Paris and worked with Chanot until 1821, and from 1821 to 1825 for Lété, with whom he then entered into partnership. After Lété's retirement in 1828, Vuillaume worked alone and put his own name on several instruments which he had constructed with the greatest care and fine craftsmanship. Vuillaume, however, was unable to overcome the general distrust of the native product and began manufacturing imitations of Italian instruments. After long and patient labor he placed a "Stradivarius" violin on the market for 300 francs; it bore the master's label and possessed a full, sonorous tone; he also built a cello priced at 500 francs. The sight of a Duiffoprugcar viola da gamba inspired him with the idea of further imitations, hence the hundreds of "Duiffoprugcar" violins and cellos with their quaint shape, carved scrolls, inlays, and the motto "viva fui in sylvis, etc." By dint of indefatigable research and experiments, Vuillaume carried the construction of these various instruments to the highest perfection. His own inventions were numerous: in 1849 the huge "Octobasse," a double bass four meters in length, three-stringed (CC-GG-C), with a special lever-mechanism to aid the left hand (an "octobasse" is in the Museum of the Paris Cons.); in 1855 a viola, which he called the "contre-alto," with greater strength of tone, but clumsy to play; in 1867 a kind of mute, the "pédale sourdine"; also a machine for manufacturing gut strings of perfectly equal thickness. He also formulated the laws governing the tapering of the stick of the Tourte bow. His brother, Nicolas-François Vuillaume (b. May 21, 1802; d. Jan. 16, 1876), was also a violin maker. After receiving his training from Jean-Baptiste, he was active in Brussels (1842–76). A nephew, Sébastien Vuillaume (b. June 18, 1835; d. Nov. 17, 1875), was also a violin maker.

BIBL.: R. Millant, *J.-B. V., Sa vie et son oeuvre* (London, 1972; in Fr., Eng., and Ger.).**—NS/LK/DM**

Vuillermoz, Jean, French composer; b. Monte Carlo, Dec. 29, 1906; d. (killed while on patrol duty in the last hours before the Franco-German armistice), Lobsonn, Alsace, June 21, 1940. He studied with Büsser and Rabaud at the Paris Cons., receiving the 2nd Prix de Rome for his cantata *Le Pardon* (1932).

WORKS: DRAMATIC: Ballet: *Veglione* (1937). **ORCH.:** *Triptique* (Paris, May 31, 1932); Horn Concerto (Paris, March 11, 1934); Cello Concerto; *Promenade zoologique* for Chamber Orch. **CHAMBER:** Piano Trio; String Trio.**—NS/LK/DM**

Vukdragović, Mihailo, Serbian conductor, pedagogue, and composer; b. Okučani, Nov. 8, 1900; d. Belgrade, March 14, 1986. He was a pupil in composition of Milojević at the Belgrade School of Music, then studied composition with Jirák and Novák and conducting with Talich at the Prague Cons. (graduated, 1927). He subsequently was active as a choral, operatic, and sym. conductor in Zagreb and Belgrade. He was prof. and director of the Stanković School of Music, prof. of conducting (1940–73) and rector (1947–52) of the Belgrade Academy of Music, and also of the Belgrade Academy of the Arts (1957–59). Vukdragović was made a corresponding member (1950) and a full member (1961) of the Serbian Academy. He wrote several works in an impressionistic style before embracing the aesthetics of socialist realism.

WORKS: DRAMATIC: Theater music; film scores. **ORCH.:** *Simfonijska meditacija* (1938); *Put u pobedu* (Road to Victory), symphonic poem (1944; Belgrade, Oct. 19, 1945); *Besmirtna mladost* (Immortal Youth), symphonic suite (1948). **CHAMBER:** 2 string quartets (1925, 1944). **VOCAL:** *Vezilja slobode* (The Embroidress of Freedom), cantata (1947; Belgrade, Jan. 5, 1948); *Svetli groboiv* (Illustrious Tombs), cantata (1954); *Vokalna lirika* for Voice and Orch. (1955); *Srbija* (Serbia), cantata (Nis, July 6, 1961); choruses; folk song arrangements. **—NS/LK/DM**

Vulpius (real name, **Fuchs**), **Melchior,** German composer, writer on music, and schoolmaster; b.

Wasungen, near Meiningen, c. 1570; d. Weimar (buried), Aug. 7, 1615. He studied with Johann Steuerlein at the Wasungen Lateinschule. In 1589 he became a supernumerary teacher of Latin at the Schleusingen Lateinschule, finally attaining a permanent teaching post in 1592; then was municipal Kantor and a teacher at the Weimar Lateinschule (1596–1615). He was a prolific composer of sacred music, his Protestant hymn tunes becoming widely known in Germany during his lifetime. He wrote the theoretical vol. *Musicae compendium latino germanicum M. Heinrici Fabri...aliquantulum variatum ac dispositum, cum facili brevique de modis tractatu* (1608).

WORKS: SACRED VOCAL (all publ. in Jena unless otherwise given): *Pars prima cantionum sacrarum* for 6 to 8 and More Voices (1602; ed. by M. Ehrhorn, Kassel, 1968); *Pars secunda selectissimarium cantionum sacrarum* for 6 to 8 and More Voices (1603); *Kirchen Gesend und geistliche Lieder...mehrerntheils auff zwey oder dreyerley art...contrapunctsweise* for 4 to 5 Voices (Leipzig, 1604; 2nd ed., enl., 1609 as *Ein schön geistlich Gesangbuch*); *Canticum Beatissimae Virginis Mariae* for 4 to 6 and More Voices (1605); *Opusculum novum selectissimarum cantionum sacrarum* for 4 to 8 Voices (Erfurt, 1610); *Erster Theil deutscher sontäglicher evangelischer Sprüche von Advent bis auff Trinitatis* for 4 Voices (1612; ed. by H. Nitsche and H. Stern, Stuttgart, 1960); *Das Leiden und Sterben...Jesu Christi, aus dem heiligen Evangelisten Matthäo* for 4 and More Voices (Erfurt, 1613; ed. by K. Ziebler, Kassel, 1934); *Der ander Theil deutscher sontäglicher evangelischer Sprüche von Trinitatis bis auff Advent* for 4 and More Voices (1614; ed. by H. Nitsche and H. Stern, Stuttgart, 1960); some other vols. are not extant.

BIBL.: H. Eggebrecht, *M. V.* (diss., Univ. of Jena, 1949). —**NS/LK/DM**

Vycpálek, Ladislav, eminent Czech composer; b. Prague, Feb. 23, 1882; d. there, Jan. 9, 1969. He received training in voice, violin, and piano in his youth, studied Czech and German at the Univ. of Prague (Ph.D., 1906, with a diss. on legends in Czech literature concerning the youth of Mary and Jesus), and took composition lessons with Novák (1908–12). In 1907 he joined the staff of the Univ. of Prague library, where he later was founder-director of its music section (1922–42); Vycpálek was also active as a violinist in the amateur quartet led by Josef Pick (1909–39); in 1936 he served as artistic director of the National Theater. In 1924 he became a member of the Czech Academy; he later served as chairman of its music section (1950–51). In 1957 Vycpálek was made an Artist of Merit and in 1967 a National Artist by the Czech government. He greatly distinguished himself as a composer of vocal music, numbering among his finest scores the *Kantáta o posledních věcech člověka* (Cantata on the Last Things of Man; 1920–22).

WORKS: ORCH.: *Vzůhru srdce* (Lift Up Your Hearts), 2 variation fantasias on hymns from Hus's day (1950). **CHAMBER:** String Quartet (1909); Sonata "Chvála housli" (Praise to the Violin) for Violin, Mezzo-soprano, and Piano (1927–28); Suite for Viola (1929); Suite for Violin (1930); Violin Sonatina (1947); solo piano pieces, including *Cestou* (On the Way), 5 pieces (1911–14), and *Doma* (Home), suite (1959). **VOCAL:** *Kantáta o posledních věcech cloveka* (Cantata on the Last Things of Man) for Soprano, Baritone, Chorus, and Orch. (1920–22); *Blashoslavený ten člověk* (Blessed Is This Man), cantata for Soprano, Baritone, Chorus, and Orch. (1933); *České requiem "Smrt a spaseni"* (Czech Requiem "Death and Redemption") for Soprano, Alto, Baritone, Chorus, and Orch. (1940); choruses; songs; folk song arrangements.

BIBL.: J. Smolka, *L. V.: Tvůrči vývoj* (L. V.: Creative Evolution; Prague, 1960); M. Svobodova and H. Krupka, *Národní umělec L. V.* (Prague, 1973).—**NS/LK/DM**

Vysloužil, Jiří, distinguished Czech musicologist; b. Košice, May 11, 1924. He studied musicology with Jan Racek and Bohumír Štědroň, philosophy with Arnošt Bláha and Mirko Novák, and history with Josef Macůrek at the Univ. of Brno (Ph.D, 1949, with the diss. *Problémy a metody hudebního lidopisu* [Problems and Methods of Music Ethnography]. Vysloužil also received a C.Sc., 1959, with the diss. *Leoš Janáček a lidova piseň* [Leos Janáček and Folk Song] and a D.Sc., 1974, with the diss. *Alois Hába*; publ. in Prague, 1974). He worked at the Dept. for Ethnography and Folklore in Brno until 1952; after serving as a lecturer and vice-dean at the Brno Academy (1952–61), in 1961 he joined the faculty of the Univ. of Brno, where he became a prof. in 1973. He served as head of the editorial board of the complete critical ed. of the works of Janáček, which commenced publication in Prague in 1978. He publ. *Hudobníci 20. storočia* (Musicians of the 20th Century; Bratislava, 1964; 2nd ed., 1981), *Leoš Janáček* (Brno, 1978), and *Leoš Janáček: Für Sie porträtiert von Jiří Vysloužil* (Leipzig, 1981).—**NS/LK/DM**

Vyvyan, Jennifer (Brigit), English soprano; b. Broadstairs, Kent, March 13, 1925; d. London, April 5, 1974. She studied piano and voice at the Royal Academy of Music in London (1941–43) then voice with Roy Henderson. She made her operatic debut as Jenny Diver in *The Beggar's Opera* with the English Opera Group (1947). After further vocal training with Fernando Carpi in Switzerland (1950), she won 1st prize in the Geneva international competition (1951). Vyvyan gained success with her portrayal of Constanze at London's Sadler's Wells Opera Co. (1952) then created the role of Penelope Rich in Britten's *Gloriana* at London's Covent Garden (1953). She made guest appearances at the Glyndebourne Festivals and in Milan, Rome, Vienna, and Paris. She appeared in many contemporary operas and was closely associated with those of Britten; she created the Governess in his *Turn of the Screw* (1954), Tytania in *A Midsummer Night's Dream* (1960), and Miss Julian in *Owen Wingrave* (1971).—**NS/LK/DM**

W

Waart, Edo (actually, **Eduard**) **de,** noted Dutch conductor; b. Amsterdam, June 1, 1941. He began piano lessons as a child and at 13 began to study the oboe. He pursued training at the Amsterdam Muziek-lyceum as an oboe and cello student (1957–62; graduated, 1962), and also studied conducting with Dean Dixon in Salzburg (summer, 1960). In 1962–63 he was an oboist in the Amsterdam Phil., and then played in the Concertgebouw Orch. in Amsterdam. He also studied conducting with Franco Ferrara in Hilversum, where he made his debut as a conductor with the Netherlands Radio Phil. in 1964. That same year, he was a co-winner in the Mitropoulos Competition in N.Y. and then served as an asst. conductor of the N.Y. Phil. (1965–66). In 1966 he became asst. conductor of the Concertgebouw Orch., which he accompanied on its 1967 tour of the U.S. He first attracted notice with his Netherlands Wind Ensemble, with which he toured and recorded. In 1967 he became a guest conductor of the Rotterdam Phil. In 1969 he made his British debut as a guest conductor with the Royal Phil. of London in Folkestone. In 1971 he toured the U.S. with the Rotterdam Phil. and also made his first appearance as an opera conductor in the U.S. in Santa Fe. In 1974 he was a guest conductor with the San Francisco Sym., and in 1975 he was named its principal guest conductor. He made his debut at London's Covent Garden in 1976 conducting *Ariadne auf Naxos.* In 1977 he became music director of the San Francisco Sym., which he conducted in a gala concert at the opening of its new Louise M. Davies Symphony Hall in 1980. In 1979 he made his first appearance at the Bayreuth Festival. He resigned as music director of the San Francisco Sym. in 1986 and served in that capacity with the Minn. Orch. in Minneapolis until 1995. From 1988 he also was artistic director of the Dutch Radio Orch. in Hilversum. He likewise served as chief conductor of the Sydney Sym. Orch. from 1993. De Waart's objective approach to interpretation, combined with his regard for stylistic propriety and avoidance of ostentatious conductorial display, makes his performances of the traditional and contemporary repertoire particularly appealing.
—NS/LK/DM

Wachsmann, Klaus P(hilipp), noted German ethnomusicologist; b. Berlin, March 8, 1907; d. Tisbury, Wiltshire, July 17, 1984. He received training in musicology with Blume and Schering and in comparative musicology with Hornbostel and Sachs at the Univ. of Berlin (1930–32); after further studies with Fellerer at the Univ. of Fribourg in Switzerland (Ph.D., 1935, with the diss. *Untersuchungen zum vorgregorianischen Gesang;* publ. in Regensburg, 1935), he pursued linguistic studies at the London School of Oriental and African Studies. He then was active in Uganda, where he was made curator of the Uganda Museum in Kampala in 1948; after serving as scientific officer in charge of ethnological collections at the Wellcome Foundation in London (1958–63), he taught in the music dept. and Inst. of Ethnomusicology at the Univ. of Calif. at Los Angeles (1963–68), then was prof. in the school of music and dept. of linguistics at Northwestern Univ. in Evanston, Ill. (from 1968). He was an authority on African music, specializing in organology and tribal music of Uganda. His years spent outside of academic circles made him an independent and imaginative thinker about music in its relation to culture and philosophy. C. Seeger ed. *Essays for a Humanist: An Offering to Klaus Wachsmann* (N.Y., 1977).

WRITINGS: *Folk Musicians in Uganda* (Kampala, 1956); ed. *An International Catalogue of Published Records of Folk Music* (London, 1960); ed. *A Select Bibliography of Music in Africa* (London, 1965); ed. *Essays on Music and History in Africa* (Evanston, Ill., 1971).**—NS/LK/DM**

Wachtel, Theodor, famous German tenor; b. Hamburg, March 10, 1823; d. Frankfurt am Main, Nov. 14, 1893. The son of a livery-stable keeper, he carried on the business from the age of 17, after his father's death. When his voice was discovered, he was sent to Hamburg for study, and soon appeared in opera. He made his operatic debut in Hamburg (March 12, 1849); made his debut at London's Covent Garden as Edgardo (June 7, 1862), and sang at the Berlin Royal Opera (1862–79); he also toured the U.S. (1871–72; 1875–76). His voice was a powerful and brilliant lyric tenor; the role in which he made himself famous was that of the postilion in Adam's *Le Postillon de Longjumeau*, which he sang more than 1,000 times; he also was successful as Manrico, John of Leyden, and Pollione.—**NS/LK/DM**

Wade, Joseph Augustine, Irish composer; b. Dublin, 1796; d. London, July 15, 1845. He went to London in 1821 and established himself as a highly successful composer of popular ballads. His song "Meet Me by Moonlight Alone" (1826) enjoyed great vogue, as did his vocal duet "I've Wandered in Dreams." He also wrote the comic operas *The Two Houses of Granada* (London, Oct. 31, 1826) and *The Convent Belles* (London, July 8, 1833; in collaboration with W. Hawes), and an operetta, *The Pupil of Da Vinci* (London, Nov. 30, 1839). —**NS/LK/DM**

Wadsworth, Charles (William), American pianist and harpsichordist; b. Barnesville, Ga., May 21, 1929. He studied piano with Tureck and conducting with Morel at the Juilliard School of Music in N.Y. (B.S., 1951; M.S., 1952); he also studied the French song repertoire with Bernac in Paris and German lieder with Zallinger in Munich. In 1960 Menotti invited him to organize the Chamber Music Concerts at the Festival of Two Worlds in Spoleto, Italy; he was its director and pianist for 20 years. In 1969 he helped to found the Chamber Music Society of Lincoln Center in N.Y., and was its artistic director until 1989; in 1977 he also created the chamber music series for the Charleston, S.C., Spoleto Festival U.S.A. In addition to numerous appearances as a pianist and harpsichordist with various ensembles, he appeared in performances with many noted artists of the day, including Dietrich Fischer-Dieskau, Beverly Sills, Hermann Prey, and Shirley Verrett.—**NS/LK/DM**

Wadsworth, Stephen, American opera producer, librettist, and translator; b. Mount Kisco, N.Y., April 3, 1953. Afer working as a journalist, he turned to opera production. He served as artistic director of the Skylight Opera in Milwaukee, where he oversaw his first production, *L'incoronazione di Poppea*, in 1982. His subsequent stagings there included *Orfeo* and *Il ritorno d'Ulisse in patria*. He wrote the libretto for Bernstein's *A Quiet Place* (1983), which he staged in Milan and Vienna. He then produced *Alcina* in St. Louis (1987), *Partenope* in Omaha (1988), *Der fliegende Holländer* in Seattle (1989), and *Die Entführung aus dem Serail* in San Francisco (1990). In 1991 he produced *Fidelio* and *La clemenza di Tito* at the Scottish Opera in Glasgow, and in 1992 he staged *Alcina* at London's Covent Garden. In 1996 his staging of *Xerxes* was seen in Boston, Los Angeles, and Santa Fe, and in 1999 his *La clemenza di Tito* was mounted in N.Y. His translations include operas by Monteverdi and Handel.—**NS/LK/DM**

Waechter, Eberhard, Austrian baritone and opera administrator; b. Vienna, July 9, 1929; d. there, March 29, 1992. He studied at the Univ. of Vienna, the Vienna Academy of Music (1950–53), and with Elisabeth Rado. In 1953 he made his operatic debut as Silvio at the Vienna Volksoper. From 1954 he was a member of the Vienna State Opera, and in 1963 he was named an Austrian Kammersänger. He made his debut at London's Covent Garden as Count Almaviva and his first appearance at the Salzburg Festival as Arbace in *Idomeneo* in 1956. In 1958 he made his debut at the Bayreuth Festival as Amfortas. He sang for the first time at the Paris Opéra as Wolfram in 1959. In 1960 he sang Count Almaviva at his debuts at Milan's La Scala and Chicago's Lyric Opera. On Jan. 25, 1961, he made his Metropolitan Opera debut in N.Y. as Wolfram. In subsequent years, he continued to appear regularly in Vienna, where he created the role of Joseph in Einem's *Jesu Hochzeit* in 1980. In 1987 he became director of the Vienna Volksoper, and from 1991 he was also co-director of the Vienna State Opera.—**NS/LK/DM**

Waelput, Hendrik, Belgian conductor and composer; b. Ghent, Oct. 26, 1845; d. there, July 8, 1885. He studied at the Brussels Cons., winning the Prix de Rome for his cantata *Het woud* (The Forest; 1867). He was asst. director of the Bruges music school (1869–71); and conducted theater orchs. at The Hague, Dijon, Douai, Fécamp, and Lille (1872–76). From 1876 to 1879 he was conductor of the Ghent Theater; in 1879, he was appointed prof. of harmony at the Antwerp Cons. He became director of the Ghent Opera in 1884. He wrote three operas, *La Ferme du diable* (Ghent, 1865), *Berken de diamantslijper* (1868), and *Stella* (Brussels, March 14, 1881), as well as 5 syms., 4 overtures, Flute Concerto, several cantatas, including *Her woud* (1867), *Memlingcantate* (1871), and *De pacificatier van Gent* (1876), partsongs, solo songs, chamber music, and piano pieces.

BIBL.: E. Callaert, *Levensschets van H. W.* (Ghent, 1886); E. De Vynck, *Henry W.* (diss., Univ. of Brussels, 1935).
—**NS/LK/DM**

Waelrant, Hubert, Flemish singer, teacher, music editor, and composer; b. between Nov. 20, 1516, and Nov. 19, 1517; d. Antwerp, Nov. 19, 1595. He was active mainly in Antwerp, where he began his career as a tenor soloist at the Cathedral (1544–45); taught music in a school operated by his landlord, Gregorius de Coninck (1553–56). From 1554 to about 1566 he served as music ed. for the printer Jean de Laet. He was a fine composer of motets. He has been credited with abandoning the old system of solmization by hexachords and introducing a new system of the 7 tone-names, *bo ce di ga lo ma ni* (hence called "bocedization"; also "voces Belgicae").

WORKS (all publ. in Antwerp unless otherwise given): (15) *Sacrarum cantionum...liber sextus* for 5 to 6 Voices (1556?); several other motets in contemporary collections; metrical Psalms: 9 in various contemporary collections; chansons: *Il primo libro de madrigali et* [11] *canzoni francezi* for 5 Voices (1558); other chansons in contemporary collections; madrigals: *Il primo libro de* [9] *madrigali et canzoni francezi* for 5 Voices (1558); other madrigals in contemporary collections; napolitane: *Le* [30] *canzoni napolitane* for 4 Voices (Venice, 1565); other napolitane in contemporary collections.

Bibl.: G. Becker, *H. W. et ses psaumes: Notice biographique et bibliographique* (Paris, 1881); R. Weaver, *The Motets of H. W. (c. 1517–1595)* (diss., Syracuse Univ., 1971).—**NS/LK/DM**

Waesberghe, Jos(eph Maria Antonius Franciscus) Smits van

See **Smits van Waesberghe, Jos(eph Maria Antonius Franciscus)**

Wagemans, Peter-Jan, Dutch composer; b. The Hague, Sept. 7, 1952. He studied organ, composition (with Vlijmen), and theory.

Works: ORCH.: Overture for Wind Orch. (1972); Sym. (1972); *Muziek I* for Wind Orch. (1974), *II* for Orch. (1977), *III* for Wind Orch. (1985; rev. 1987), and *IV* for Ensemble (1988); *Alla marcia* (1977); *Romance* for Violin and Orch. (1981; rev. 1983); *Irato* (1983; rev. 1990); *Klang* (1986); *Dreams* (1991; rev. 1995); *Requiem* for Strings and Percussion (1992; rev. 1994); *Panthalassa* (1994); *De stad en de engel* (1996; rev. 1997). **CHAMBER:** 2 wind quintets (1973; 1992–93, rev. 1997); Saxophone Quartet (1975); *3 Small Pieces* for 4 Recorders and 2 Xylophones (1979); 2 string quartets (1980, rev. 1986; 1997, rev. 1998); Octet for 2 Clarinets, 2 Bassoons, 2 Violins, Viola, and Cello (1980); *Great Expectations* for Violin and Piano (1986); Quartet for 4 Recorders (1993). **Piano:** *2 Pieces* (1972); *Ira* for 2 Pianos, 8-Hands (1983–84). **VOCAL:** *De regenboogbrug* for Chorus and Orch. (1996).—**NS/LK/DM**

Wagenaar, Bernard, Dutch-born American composer and teacher, son of **Johan Wagenaar;** b. Arnhem, July 18, 1894; d. York, Maine, May 19, 1971. He was a student of Gerard Veerman (violin), Lucie Veerman-Becker (piano), and his father (composition) in Utrecht. After conducting and teaching in the Netherlands (1914–20), he settled in the U.S. and became a naturalized American citizen in 1927. He was a violinist in the N.Y. Phil. (1921–23). From 1925 to 1946 he taught fugue, orchestration, and composition at the Inst. of Musical Art in N.Y., and then at its successor, the Juilliard School of Music, from 1946 to 1968. He was made an Officer of the Order of Oranje-Nassau of the Netherlands. His output followed along neo-Classical lines.

Works: DRAMATIC: Chamber Opera: *Pieces of Eight* (1943; N.Y., May 9, 1944). **ORCH.:** 4 syms.: No. 1 (1926; N.Y., Oct. 7, 1928), No. 2 (1930; N.Y., Nov. 10, 1932), No. 3 (1936; N.Y., Jan. 23, 1937), and No. 4 (1946; Boston, Dec. 16, 1949); 2 divertimentos: No. 1 (1927; Detroit, Nov. 28, 1929) and No. 2 (1952); Sinfonietta (1929; N.Y., Jan. 16, 1930); Triple Concerto for Flute, Harp, Cello, and Orch. (1935; N.Y., May 20, 1941); *Fantasietta on British-American Ballads* for Chamber Orch. (1939); Violin Concerto (1940); *Fanfare for Airmen* (1942); *Feuilleton* (1942); *Song of Mourning* (1944); Concert Overture for Small Orch. (1952); *5 Tableaux* for Cello and Orch. (1952); *Preamble* (1956). **CHAMBER:** Violin Sonata (1925); 4 string quartets (1926, 1932, 1936, 1960); Cello Sonatina (1934); Concertino for 8 Instruments (1942); *4 Vignettes* for Harp (1965). **KEYBOARD: Piano:** Sonata (1928); *Ciacona* (1942). **Organ:** *Eclogue* (1940). **VOCAL:** *3 Songs from the Chinese* for Soprano, Flute, Harp, and Piano (1921); *From a Very Little Sphinx* for Voice and Piano (1925); *El trillo* for Chorus, 2 Guitars, and Percussion (1942); *No quiero tus avellanas* for Alto, Women's Chorus, Flute, English Horn, 2 Guitars, and Percussion (1942).—**NS/LK/DM**

Wagenaar, Johan, distinguished Dutch organist, choral conductor, pedagogue, and composer, father of **Bernard Wagenaar;** b. Utrecht, Nov. 1, 1862; d. The Hague, June 17, 1941. He studied with Richard Hol in Utrecht (1875–85) and with H. von Herzogenberg in Berlin (1889). From 1887 to 1904 he was director of the Utrecht Music School; he also was organist at the Cathedral (1887–1919). From 1919 to 1936 he was director of the Royal Cons. in The Hague.

Works: DRAMATIC: Opera: *De Doge van Venetie* (1901; Utrecht, 1904); *De Cid* (1915; Utrecht, 1916); *Jupiter Amans*, burlesque opera (Scheveningen, 1925). **ORCH.:** 3 symphonic poems: *Levenszomer* (1901), *Saul en David* (1906), and *Elverhoi* (1939); 5 overtures: *Koning Jan* (1889), *Cyrano de Bergerac* (1905), *De getemde feeks* (1906), *Driekoningenavond* (1927), and *De philosofische prinses* (1931). **OTHER:** Numerous choral works; songs; organ pieces.—**NS/LK/DM**

Wagenseil, Georg Christoph, Austrian composer and music theorist; b. Vienna, Jan. 29, 1715; d. there, March 1, 1777. He studied with J. J. Fux, and served as the music teacher of the Empress Maria Theresa and her children. In 1739 he was appointed court composer, remaining in the Imperial service until his death. He wrote many operas in Italian. Additionally, he publ. the following: *Suavis, artificiose elaboratus concentus musicus, continens: 6 selectas parthias ad clavicembalum compositas* (1740), *18 Divertimenti di cembalo*, opp. 1–3, Divertimento for 2 Harpsichords, 2 divertimentos for Harpsichord, 2 Violins, and Cello, op.5, 10 syms. for Harpsichord, 2 Violins, and Cello, opp. 4, 7, 8, and 6 violin sonatas with Harpsichord, op.6. Two syms. and a Trio Sonata are in Denkmäler der Tonkunst in Österreich, 31 (15.ii); a Divertimento was ed. by Blume.

Works: DRAMATIC: OPERA (all 1st perf. in Vienna): *La generosità trionfante* (1745); *Ariodante* (May 14, 1746); *La clemenza di Tito* (Oct. 15, 1746); *Alexander der Grosse in Indien* (July 7, 1748); *Il Siroe* (Oct. 4, 1748); *L'Olimpiade* (May 13, 1749); *Andromeda* (March 30, 1750); *Antigone* (May 13, 1750); *Armida placato* (Aug. 28, 1750); *Euridice* (July 26, 1750); *Le Cacciatrici amanti* (Laxenburg, June 1755); *Demetrio* (1760). **OTHER:** 3 oratorios; 30 syms.; 27 harpsichord concertos; organ works.

Bibl.: K. Horwitz, *W. als Symphoniker* (diss., Univ. of Vienna, 1906); J. Pelikant, *Die Klavier-Werke W.s* (Vienna, 1926); J. Kucaba, *The Symphonies of G.C. W.* (diss., Boston Univ., 1967); H. Scholz- Michelitsch, *G.C. W. als Klavierkomponist: Eine Studie zu seinen zyklischen Soloklavierwerken* (diss., Univ. of Vienna, 1967).—**NS/LK/DM**

Wagenseil, Johann Christoph, German scholar; b. Nuremberg, Nov. 26, 1633; d. Altdorf, Oct. 9, 1708. He traveled throughout Europe in the capacity of a Hofmeister (traveling companion to young patricians). He was made prof. of public and canon law, history, and oriental languages at the Civic Univ. of Nuremberg in Altdorf in 1649, where he later served as rector, dean of law, and librarian; he received a doctor of laws degree from the Univ. of Orléans. He publ. an important book, *De Sacri Rom. Imperii Libera Civitate Noribergensi Commentatio* (Altdorf, 1697), with a 140-page supplement (in German), *Buch von der Meister-Singer holdseligen Kunst: Anfang, Fortübung, Nutzbarkeiten und Lehr-Sätz*, containing poems and melodies by Frauenlob, Mügling, Marner, and Regenbogen; this section was the main literary source that Wagner used in *Die Meistersinger von Nürnberg*.—**NS/LK/DM**

Wagner, (Adolf) Wieland (Gottfried), German opera producer and stage designer, son of **Siegfried (Helferich Richard) Wagner** and brother of **Wolfgang (Manfred Martin) Wagner;** b. Bayreuth, Jan. 5, 1917; d. Munich, Oct. 16, 1966. He received his general education in Munich, and devoted himself to the problem of modernizing the productions of Wagner's operas. With his brother, Wolfgang Wagner, he served as co-director of the Bayreuth Festivals from 1951 to 1966. Abandoning the luxuriant scenery of 19th-century opera, he emphasized the symbolic meaning of Wagner's music dramas, eschewing realistic effects, such as machinery propelling the Rhine maidens through the wavy gauze of the river, or the bright paper flames of the burning Valhalla. He even introduced Freudian sexual overtones, as in his production of *Tristan und Isolde*, where a phallic pillar was conspicuously placed on the stage.

BIBL.: W. Panofsky, *W. W.* (Bremen, 1964); C. Lust, *W. W. et la survie du théâtre lyrique* (Lausanne, 1969); W. Schäfer, *W. W.: Persönlichkeit und Leistung* (Tübingen, 1970); G. Skelton, *W. W.: The Positive Sceptic* (London, 1971); B. Wessling, *W. W., der Enkel: Eine Biographie* (Cologne, 1997); C. Cheyrezy, *Essai sur la représentation du drame musical: W. W. in memoriam* (Paris, 1998). —**NS/LK/DM**

Wagner, Cosima, wife of **Richard Wagner**, daughter of **Franz Liszt** and the Countess Marie d'Agoult; b. Bellagio, on Lake Como, Dec. 24, 1837; d. Bayreuth, April 1, 1930. She received an excellent education in Paris and married **Hans von Bülow** on Aug. 18, 1857. There were 2 daughters from this marriage, Blandine and Daniela; the third daughter, Isolde, was Richard Wagner's child, as was the fourth, Eva, and the son, Siegfried. A divorce followed on July 18, 1870; the marriage to Wagner took place in a few weeks, on Aug. 25, 1870. A woman of high intelligence, practical sense, and imperious character, Cosima Wagner emerged after Wagner's death as a powerful personage in all affairs regarding the continuance of the Bayreuth Festivals, as well as the complex matters pertaining to the rights of performance of Wagner's works all over the world. She publ. her reminiscences of Liszt: *Franz Liszt, Ein Gedenkblatt von seiner Tochter* (Munich, 2nd ed., 1911). Her diaries were ed. by M. Gregor-Dellin and D. Mack as *Cosima Wagner: Die Tagebücher, 1869–1877* (2 vols., Munich, 1976–77; Eng. tr. by G. Skelton as *Cosima Wagner's Diaries*, 2 vols., N.Y., 1977 and 1980).

BIBL.: M. Strauss, *Wie ich Frau C. W. sehe* (Magdeburg, 1912); W. Siegfried, *Frau C. W.* (Stuttgart, 1930); M. von Waldberg, *C. W.s Briefe an ihre Tochter Daniela von Bülow, 1866–85* (Stuttgart, 1933); P. Pretzsch, *C. W. und H.S. Chamberlain im Briefwechsel, 1888–1908* (Leipzig, 1934); L. Scalero, *C. W.* (Zürich, 1934); M. von Millenkovich (M. Morold), *C. W.: Ein Lebensbild* (Leipzig, 1937); E. Thierbach, ed., *Die Briefe C. W.s an Friedrich Nietzsche* (Weimar, 1938–40); A. Sojoloff, *C. W., Extraordinary Daughter of Franz Liszt* (N.Y., 1969); D. Mack, ed., *C. W.: Das zweite Leben: Briefe und Aufzeichnungen, 1883–1930* (Munich, 1980); G. Marek, *C. W.* (N.Y., 1981); G. Skelton, *Richard and C. Wagner: Biography of a Marriage* (London, 1982).—**NS/LK/DM**

Wagner, Georg Gottfried, German violinist and composer; b. Mühlberg, April 5, 1698; d. Plauen, March 23, 1756. He studied with Kuhnau at the Thomasschule in Leipzig (1712–18) and also studied at the Univ. of Leipzig (1718–26). He was a violinist in Bach's orch. and was recommended by Bach for the post of cantor at Plauen, which he held from 1726 to his death. He wrote numerous sacred works and instrumental compositions; his motet *Lob und Ehre* was misattributed to Bach by Breitkopf & Härtel (publ. 1819 as BWV anh.162).—**NS/LK/DM**

Wagner, Johanna, German soprano; b. Lohnde, near Hannover, Oct. 13, 1826; d. Würzburg, Oct. 16, 1894. She was a natural daughter of Lieutenant Bock von Wülfingen of Hannover and was adopted by Richard Wagner's brother, Albert; she was thus regarded as Wagner's niece. Of a precocious talent, she acted on the stage as a small child; through Wagner she obtained a position at the Dresden Opera when she was 17, producing an excellent impression as Agathe in *Der Freischütz*, and was engaged as a regular member. She studied the part of Elisabeth in *Tannhäuser* with Wagner and sang it at the premiere of the opera on Oct. 19, 1845, when she was barely 19 years old. In 1846 she went to Paris for further study with Pauline Viardot-García (1846–48), then was engaged at the Hamburg Opera (1849) and finally at the Court Opera in Berlin (1850–61). In 1856 she made her London debut at Her Majesty's Theatre. In 1859 she married the district judge Alfred Jachmann. After 1862 she acted mainly on the dramatic stage, reappearing in opera at the Bayreuth Festival in 1876 in the parts of Schwertleite and the 1st Norn in the first complete mounting of the *Ring* cycle. She taught at the Royal Music School in Munich (1882–84), then privately.

BIBL.: J. Kapp and H. Jachmann, *Richard Wagner und seine erste "Elisabeth," J. J.-W.* (Berlin, 1927; Eng. tr. as *Wagner and His First Elisabeth*, London, 1944).—**NS/LK/DM**

Wagner, Joseph (Frederick), American conductor, composer, and teacher; b. Springfield, Mass., Jan. 9, 1900; d. Los Angeles, Oct. 12, 1974. He was a student of Converse (composition) at the New England Cons. of Music in Boston (diploma, 1923). After further training from Casella in Boston (1927), he studied at Boston Univ. (B.M., 1932). In 1934–35 he completed his studies with Boulanger (composition) and Monteux (conducting) in Paris, as well as with Weingartner (conducting) in Basel. From 1923 to 1944 he was asst. director of music in the Boston public schools. He also was founder-conductor of the Boston Civic Sym. Orch. (1925–44) and a teacher at Boston Univ. (1929–40). He taught at Brooklyn Coll. (1945–47) and at Hunter Coll. (1945–56) in N.Y., and was conductor of the Duluth Sym. Orch. (1947–50) and the Orquesta Sinfónica Nacional de Costa Rica in San José (1950–54). In 1961 he became a prof. at Pepperdine Coll. in Los Angeles. He publ. the useful books *Orchestration: A Practical Handbook* (N.Y., 1958) and *Band Scoring* (N.Y., 1960). His music was distinguished by excellent craftsmanship, and was set in a fairly advanced idiom, with bitonality as a frequent recourse in his later works.

WORKS: OPERA: *New England Sampler* (1964; Los Angeles, Feb. 26, 1965). **BALLET:** *The Birthday of the Infanta* (1935); *Dance Divertissement* (1937); *Hudson River Legend* (1941; Boston, March 1, 1944). **ORCH.:** 2 violin concertos (1919–30; 1955–56); *Miniature Concerto* for Piano and Orch. (1919; Providence, R.I., June 11, 1920; rev. version, New Brunswick, N.J., Aug. 3, 1930); *Rhapsody* for Piano, Clarinet, and Strings (1925); 4 syms.: No. 1 (Rochester, N.Y., Oct. 19, 1944), No. 2 (1945; Wilmington, March 1, 1960), No. 3 (1951), and No. 4, *Tribute to America*, for Narrator, Soprano, Chorus, and Orch. (1974); Sinfonietta No. 1 (1931) and No. 2 for Strings (1941); *Pastoral Costarricense* (1958); *Merlin and Sir Boss* for Concert Band, after Mark Twain's *A Connecticut Yankee* (1963); Concerto for Organ, Brass, and Percussion (1963); Harp Concerto (1964). **CHAMBER:** Quintet for Flute, Clarinet, Viola, Cello, and Piano (1933); String Quartet (1940); Violin Sonata (1941); Cello Sonata (1943); *Introduction and Scherzo* for Bassoon and Piano (1951); *Patterns of Contrast* for Wind Quartet (1959); *Fantasy Sonata* for Harp (1963); *Preludes and Toccata* for Harp, Violin, and Cello (1964); *Fantasy and Fugue* for Woodwind Quartet (1968). **KEYBOARD: Piano:** *Radio City Snapshots* (1945); Sonata (1946); Sonata for 2 Pianos (1963). **Organ:** *12 Concert Preludes* (1974). **VOCAL:** *David Jazz* for Men's Chorus and Piano (1934); *Under Freedom's Flag* for Chorus (1940); *Ballad of Brotherhood* for Chorus (1947); *Missa sacra* for Mezzo-soprano, Chorus, and Orch. (1952); *American Ballad* for Chorus (1963).

BIBL.: L. Bowling, ed., *J. W.: A Retrospective of a Composer-Conductor* (Lomita, Calif., 1976).—**NS/LK/DM**

Wagner, Karl Jakob, German oboist, conductor, and composer; b. Darmstadt, Feb. 22, 1772; d. there, Nov. 24, 1822. He was apprenticed to the Darmstadt Hofkapelle when he was 16, becoming a member of its orch. as violinist and horn player at 18; he studied theory with Abbé Vogler. In 1800 he was named master of military music; after touring as a concert artist, he was active in Paris (1805–11), then returned to Darmstadt as Hofkapellmeister (1811–20). He wrote 4 operas for Darmstadt, *Der Zahnarzt* (1803), *Pygmalion* (1809), *Siuph und Nitetis* (1811), and *Chimene* (1821), as well as incidental music to plays, orch. pieces, chamber music, vocal works, and piano pieces.—**NS/LK/DM**

Wagner, Peter (Joseph), eminent German musicologist; b. Kurenz, near Trier, Aug. 19, 1865; d. Fribourg, Switzerland, Oct. 17, 1931. He studied at the Univ. of Strasbourg, receiving his Ph.D. in 1890 with the diss. *Palestrina als weltlicher Komponist* (publ. as "Das Madrigal und Palestrina," *Vierteljahrsschrift für Musikwissenschaft*, VIII, 1892); he studied further in Berlin under Bellermann and Spitta. In 1893 he was appointed an instructor at the Univ. of Fribourg in Switzerland; subsequently he was a prof. (1902–21) and rector (1920–21). In 1901 he established its Académie Grégorienne for theoretical and practical study of plainsong, a field in which he was an eminent authority. He was a member of the Papal Commission for the Editio Vaticana of the Roman Gradual (1904) and was made a Papal Chamberlain.

WRITINGS: *Einführung in die gregorianischen Melodien: Ein Handbuch der Choralwissenschaft* (vol. I, Fribourg, 1895; 3rd ed., 1911; Eng. tr., 1907; vol. II, Leipzig, 1905; 2nd ed., 1912; vol. III, Leipzig, 1921); *Elemente des gregorianischen Gesanges zur Einführung in die vatikanische Choralausgabe* (Regensburg, 1909); *Geschichte der Messe I: bis 1600* (Leipzig, 1913); *Einführung in die katholische Kirchenmusik: Vorträge gehalten an der Universität Freiburg in der Schweiz für Theologen und andere Freunde kirchlicher Musik* (Düsseldorf, 1919).

BIBL.: K. Weinmann, ed., *Festschrift P. W. zum 60. Geburtstag* (Leipzig, 1926).—**NS/LK/DM**

Wagner, Roger (Francis), French-born American choral conductor; b. Le Puy, Jan. 16, 1914; d. Dijon, Sept. 17, 1992. He was taken to the U.S. as a child. After studying for the priesthood in Santa Barbara, Calif., he returned to France to study organ with Dupré. He settled in Los Angeles in 1937 and became organist and choirmaster at St. Joseph's; he also took courses in philosophy and French literature at the Univ. of Calif. and the Univ. of Southern Calif. He studied conducting with Klemperer and Walter and orchestration with Caillet. In 1946 he founded the Roger Wagner Chorale and toured extensively with it in the U.S., Canada, and Latin America. He was also founder-conductor of the Los Angeles Master Chorale and Sinfonia Orch. (1965–85). He was head of the dept. of music at Marymount Coll. in Los Angeles (1951–66); he also taught at the Univ. of Calif. from 1959 to 1981. He was knighted by Pope Paul VI in 1966.

BIBL.: W. Belan, ed., *Choral Essays: A Tribute to R. W.* (San Carlos, Calif., 1993).—**NS/LK/DM**

Wagner, Siegfried (Helferich Richard), German conductor and composer, son of **(Wilhelm) Richard Wagner** and **Cosima Wagner** and father of **(Adolf) Wieland (Gottfried) Wagner;** b. Triebschen, June 6, 1869; d. Bayreuth, Aug. 4, 1930. His parents were married on Aug. 25, 1870, and thus Siegfried was legitimated. Richard Wagner named the *Siegfried Idyll* for him, and it was performed in Wagner's house in Triebschen on Christmas Day, 1870. He studied with Humperdinck in Frankfurt am Main and then pursued training as an architect in Berlin and Karlsruhe; during his tenure as an assistant in Bayreuth (1892–96), he studied with his mother, Hans Richter, and Julius Kniese. From 1896 he was a regular conductor in Bayreuth, where he was general director of the Festival productions from 1906. On Sept. 21, 1915, he married Winifred Williams, an adopted daughter of Karl Klindworth. In 1923–24 he visited the U.S. in order to raise funds for the reopening of the Bayreuth Festspielhaus, which had been closed during the course of World War I. He conducted from memory, and left-handed. In his career as a composer, he was greatly handicapped by inevitable comparisons with his father. His memoirs were publ. in Stuttgart in 1923.

WORKS: DRAMATIC: Opera: *Der Bärenhäuter* (1898; Munich, Jan. 22, 1899); *Herzog Wildfang* (Munich, March 14, 1901); *Der Kobold* (1903; Hamburg, Jan. 29, 1904); *Bruder Lustig* (Hamburg, Oct. 13, 1905); *Sternengebot* (1907; Hamburg, Jan. 21, 1908); *Banadietrich* (1909; Karlsruhe, Jan. 23, 1910); *Schwarzschwanenreich* (1911; Karlsruhe, Dec. 6, 1917); *Sonnenflammen* (1914; Darmstadt, Oct. 30, 1918); *Der Heidenkönig* (1914; Cologne, Dec. 16, 1933); *Der Friedensengel* (1915; Karlsruhe, March 4, 1926); *An allem ist Hütchen Schuld* (1916; Stuttgart, Dec. 6, 1917); *Der Schmied von Marienburg* (1920; Rostock, Dec. 16, 1923); *Wahnopfer* (1928; unfinished). **ORCH.:** *Sehnsucht*, symphonic poem (1895); *Konzertstück* for Flute and Orch. (1914); Violin Concerto (1915); *Und wenn die Welt voll Teufel wär!*, scherzo (1923); *Glück*, symphonic poem (1924); Sym. in C major (1925). **VOCAL:** *Das Märchen von dicken fetten Pfannkucken* for Baritone and Orch. (1913); *Der Fahnenschwur* for Men's Chorus, Orch., and Organ (1915); *Wer liebt uns* for Men's Chorus and Woodwinds (1924). **OTHER:** Chamber music.

BIBL.: L. Karpeth, *S. W. als Mensch und Künstler* (Leipzig, 1902); C. Glasenapp, *S. W.* (Berlin, 1906); idem, *S. W. und seine Kunst* (Leipzig, 1911; essays on the operas; new series, 1913, as *Schwarzschwanenreich*; 2nd new series, ed. by P. Pretzsch, 1919, as *Sonnenflammen*); P. Pretzsch, *Die Kunst S. W.s* (Leipzig, 1919); O. Daube, *S. W. und sein Werk* (Bayreuth, 1925); *Festschrift zu S. W.s 60. Geburtstag* (Bayreuth, 1929); H. Rebois, *Lettres de S. W.* (Paris, 1933); O. Daube, *S. W. und die Märchenoper* (Leipzig, 1936); F. Starsen, *Erinnerungen an S. W.* (Detmold, 1942); Z. von Kraft, *Der Sohn: S. W.s Leben und Umwelt* (Graz, 1963); P. Pachl, *S. W.s musikdramatisches Schaffen* (Tutzing, 1979); idem, *Weltbild in S. W.s Opern* (Karlsruhe, 1998).—**NS/LK/DM**

Wagner, Sieglinde, Austrian mezzo-soprano; b. Linz, April 21, 1921. She studied at the Linz Cons. and with Luise Willer and Carl Hartmann in Munich. In 1942 she made her operatic debut as Erda in Linz. From 1947 to 1952 she sang at the Vienna Volksoper. In 1949 she made her first appearance at the Salzburg Festival as the 2nd Lady in *Die Zauberflöte*, and returned there to create the roles of Lady Capulet in Blacher's *Romeo und Julia* (1950), Leda in Strauss's *Die Liebe der Danae* (official premiere, Aug. 14, 1952), and Frau Jensen in Wagner-Régeny's *Das Bergwerk zu Falun* (1961). In 1952 she became a member of the Berlin Städtische Oper. After it became the Deutsche Oper in 1961, she continued as a member until 1986. In 1962 she made her debut as Flosshelde at the Bayreuth Festival, where she made regular appearances until 1973. She also pursued an active career as a concert artist.—**NS/LK/DM**

Wagner, (Wilhelm) Richard, great German composer whose operas, written to his own librettos, have radically transformed the concept of stage music, postulating the inherent equality of dramatic and symphonic writing and establishing the uninterrupted continuity of the action; b. Leipzig, May 22, 1813; d. Venice, Feb. 13, 1883. The antecedents of his family, and his own origin, are open to controversy. His father was a police registrar in Leipzig who died when Wagner was only 6 months old. His mother, Johanna (Rosine), née Pätz, was the daughter of a baker in Weissenfels; it is possible also that she was an illegitimate offspring of Prince Friedrich Ferdinand Constantin of Weimar. Eight months after her husband's death, Johanna Wagner married the actor Ludwig Geyer on Aug. 28, 1814. This hasty marriage generated speculation that Geyer may have been Wagner's real father; Wagner himself entertained this possibility, pointing out the similarity of his and Geyer's prominent noses; in the end he abandoned this surmise. The problem of Wagner's origin arose with renewed force after the triumph of the Nazi party in Germany, as Hitler's adoration of Wagner was put in jeopardy by suspicions that Geyer might have been Jewish; if Wagner was indeed his natural son, then he himself was tainted by Semitic blood. The phantom of Wagner's possible contamination with Jewish hemoglobin struck horror into the hearts of good Nazi biologists and archivists; they delved anxiously into Geyer's own and, much to the relief of Goebbels and other Nazi intellectuals, it was found that Geyer, like Wagner's nominal father, was the purest of Aryans; Wagner's possible illegitimate birth was of no concern to the racial tenets of the Nazi Weltanschauung.

Geyer was a member of the Court Theater in Dresden, and the family moved there in 1814. Geyer died on Sept. 30, 1821; in 1822 Wagner entered the Dresden Kreuzschule, where he remained a pupil until 1827. Carl Maria von Weber often visited the Geyer home; these visits exercised a beneficial influence on Wagner in his formative years. In 1825 he began to take piano lessons from a local musician named Humann and also studied violin with Robert Sipp. Wagner showed strong literary inclinations and, under the spell of Shakespeare, wrote a tragedy, *Leubald*. In 1827 he moved with his mother back to Leipzig, where his uncle Adolf Wagner gave him guidance in his classical reading. In 1828 he was enrolled in the Nikolaischule; while in school, he had lessons in harmony with Christian Gottlieb Müller, a violinist in the theater orch. In June 1830 Wagner entered the Thomasschule, where he began to compose; he wrote a String Quartet and some piano music. His *Overture* in B-flat major was performed at the Leipzig Theater on Dec. 24, 1830, under the direction of Heinrich Dorn. Now determined to dedicate himself entirely to music, he became a student of Theodor Weinlig, cantor of the Thomaskirche, from whom he received a thorough training in counterpoint and composition. His first publ. work was a Piano Sonata in B-flat major, to which he assigned the opus number 1; it was brought out by the prestigious publishing house of Breitkopf & Härtel in 1832. He then wrote an overture to *König Enzio*, which was performed at the Leipzig Theater on Feb. 17, 1832; it was followed by an Overture in C major, which was presented at a Gewandhaus concert on April 30, 1832. Wagner's first major orch. work, a Sym. in C major, was performed at a Prague Cons. concert in Nov. 1832; on Jan. 10, 1833, it was played by the Gewandhaus Orch. in Leipzig. He was 19 years old at the time. In 1832 he wrote an opera, *Die Hochzeit*, after J. G. Büsching's *Ritterzeit und Ritterwesen*; an introduction, a septet, and a chorus from this work are extant. Early in 1833 he began work on *Die Feen*, to a libretto after Carlo Gozzi's *La Donna serpente*. Upon completion of *Die Feen* in Jan. 1834, he offered the score to the Leipzig Theater, but it was rejected. In June 1834 he began to sketch out a new opera, *Das Liebesverbot*, after Shakespeare's play *Measure for Measure*. In July 1834 he obtained the position of music director of Heinrich Bethmann's theater company, based in Magdeburg; he made his debut in Bad Lauschstadt, conducting Mozart's *Don Giovanni.* On March 29, 1836, in Magdeburg he led the premiere of his opera *Das Liebesverbot*, presented under the title *Die Novize von Palermo*. Bethmann's company soon went out of business; Wagner, who was by that time deeply involved with Christine Wilhelmine ("Minna") Planer, an actress with the company, followed her to Königsberg, where they were married on Nov. 24, 1836. In Königsberg he composed the overture *Rule Britannia*; on April 1, 1837, he was appointed music director of the Königsberg town theater. His marital affairs suffered a setback when Minna left him for a rich businessman by the name of Dietrich. In Aug. 1837 he went to Riga as music director of the theater there; coincidentally, Minna's sister was engaged as a singer at the same theater; Minna soon joined her, and became reconciled with Wagner. In Riga Wagner worked on his new opera, *Rienzi, der letzte der Tribunen*, after a popular novel by Bulwer-Lytton.

In March 1839 he lost his position in Riga, and he and Minna, burdened by debts, left town to seek their fortune elsewhere. In their passage by sea from Pillau they encountered a fierce storm, and the ship was forced to drop anchor in the Norwegian fjord of Sandwike. They made their way to London, and then set out for Boulogne; there Wagner met Meyerbeer, who gave him a letter of recommendation to the director of the Paris Opéra. He arrived in Paris with Minna in Sept. 1839, and remained there until 1842. He was forced to eke out a meager subsistence by making piano arrangements of operas and writing occasional articles for the *Gazette Musicale*. In Jan. 1840 he completed his *Overture to Faust* (later rev. as *Eine Faust-Ouvertüre*). Soon he found himself in dire financial straits; he owed money that he could not repay, and on Oct. 28, 1840, he was confined in debtors' prison; he was released on Nov. 17, 1840. The conditions of his containment were light, and he was able to leave prison on certain days. In the meantime he had completed the libretto for *Der fliegende Holländer*; he submitted it to the director of the Paris Opéra, but the director had already asked Paul Foucher to prepare a libretto on the same subject. The director was willing, however, to buy Wagner's scenario for 500 French francs. Wagner accepted the offer (July 2, 1841). Louis Dietsch brought out his treatment of the subject in his opera *Le Vaisseau fantôme* (Paris Opéra, Nov. 9, 1842).

In 1842 Wagner received the welcome news from Dresden that his opera *Rienzi* had been accepted for production; it was staged there on Oct. 20, 1842, with considerable success. *Der fliegende Holländer* was also accepted by Dresden, and Wagner conducted its first performance there on Jan. 2, 1843. On Feb. 2 of that year, he was named 2nd Hofkapellmeister in Dresden, where he conducted a large repertoire of Classical operas, among them *Don Giovanni, Le nozze di Figaro, Die Zauberflöte, Fidelio,* and *Der Freischütz*. In 1846 he conducted a memorable performance in Dresden of Beethoven's 9th Sym. In Dresden he led the prestigious choral society Liedertafel, for which he wrote several works, including the "biblical scene" *Das Liebesmahl der Apostel*. He was also preoccupied during those years in working on the score and music for *Tannhäuser*, completing it on April 13, 1845. He conducted its first performance in Dresden on Oct. 19, 1845. He subsequently revised the score, which was staged to better advantage there on Aug. 1, 1847. Concurrently, he began work on *Lohengrin*, which he completed on April 28, 1848. Wagner's efforts to have his works publ. failed, leaving him again in debt. Without waiting for further performances of his operas that had already been presented to the public, he drew up the first prose outline of *Der Nibelungen-Mythus als Entwurf zu einem Drama*, the prototype of the epic *Ring* cycle; in Nov. 1848 he began work on the poem for *Siegfrieds Tod*. At that time he joined the revolutionary Vaterlandsverein, and was drawn into active participation in the movement, culminating in an open uprising in May 1849. An order was issued for his arrest, and he had to leave Dresden; he made his way to Weimar, where he found a cordial reception from Liszt; he then proceeded to Vienna, where a Prof. Widmann lent him his own passport so that Wagner could cross the border of Saxony on his way to Zürich. There, he made his home in July 1849; Minna joined him there a few months later. Shortly before leaving Dresden he had sketched 2 dramas, *Jesus von Nazareth* and *Achilleus*; both remained unfinished. In Zürich he wrote a number of essays expounding his philosophy of art: *Die Kunst und die Revolution* (1849), *Das Kunstwerk der Zukunft* (1849), *Kunst und Klima* (1850), *Oper und Drama* (1851; rev. 1868), and *Eine Mitteilung an meine Freunde* (1851). The ideas expressed in *Das Kunstwerk der Zukunft* gave rise to the description of Wagner's operas as "music of the future" by his opponents; they were also described as Gesamtkunstwerk, "total artwork," by his admirers. He rejected both descriptions as distortions of his real views. He was equally opposed to the term "music drama," which nevertheless became an accepted definition for all of his operas.

In Feb. 1850 Wagner was again in Paris; there he fell in love with Jessie Laussot, the wife of a wine merchant; however, she eventually left Wagner, and he returned to Minna in Zürich. On Aug. 28, 1850, Liszt conducted the successful premiere of *Lohengrin* in Weimar. In 1851 he wrote the verse text of *Der junge Siegfried*, and prose sketches for *Das Rheingold* and *Die Walküre*. In June 1852 he finished the text of *Die Walküre* and of *Das Rheingold*; he completed the entire libretto of *Der Ring des Nibelungen* on Dec. 15, 1852, and it was privately printed in 1853. In Nov. 1853 he began composition of the music for *Das Rheingold*, completing the full score on Sept. 26, 1854. In June 1854 he commenced work on the music of *Die Walküre*, which he finished on March 20, 1856. In 1854 he became friendly with a wealthy Zürich merchant, Otto Wesendonck, and his wife, Mathilde. Wesendonck was willing to give Wagner a substantial loan, to be repaid out of his performance rights. The situation became complicated when Wagner developed an affection for Mathilde, which in all probability remained platonic. However, he set to music 5 lyric poems written by Mathilde herself; the album was publ. as the *Wesendonk-Lieder* in 1857. In 1855 he conducted a series of 8 concerts with the Phil. Soc. of London (March 12-June 25). His performances were greatly praised by

English musicians, and he had the honor of meeting Queen Victoria, who invited him to her loge at the intermission of his seventh concert. In June 1856 he made substantial revisions in the last dramas of *Der Ring des Nibelungen*, changing their titles to *Siegfried* and *Götterdämmerung*. Throughout these years he was preoccupied with writing a new opera, *Tristan und Isolde*, permeated with the dual feelings of love and death. In April 1857 he prepared the first sketch of *Parzival* (later titled *Parsifal*). In 1858 he moved to Venice, where he completed the full score of the second act of *Tristan und Isolde*. The Dresden authorities, acting through their Austrian confederates and still determined to bring Wagner to trial as a revolutionary, pressured Venice to expel him from its territory. Once more Wagner took refuge in Switzerland. He decided to stay in Lucerne; while there he completed the score of *Tristan und Isolde*, on Aug. 6, 1859.

In Sept. 1859 he moved to Paris, where Minna joined him. In 1860 he conducted 3 concerts of his music at the Théâtre-Italien. Napoleon III became interested in his work, and in March 1860 ordered the director of the Paris Opera to produce Wagner's opera *Tannhäuser*; after considerable work, revisions, and a tr. into French, it was given at the Opéra on March 13, 1861. It proved to be a fiasco, and Wagner withdrew the opera after 3 performances. For some reason the Jockey Club of Paris led a vehement protest against him; the critics also joined in this opposition, mainly because the French audiences were not accustomed to the mystically romantic, heavily Germanic operatic music. Invectives hurled against him by the Paris press make extraordinary reading; the comparison of Wagner's music with the sound produced by a domestic cat walking down the keyboard of the piano was one of the favorite critical devices. The French caricaturists exercised their wit by picturing him in the act of hammering a poor listener's ear. A Wagner "Schimpflexikon" was compiled by Wilhelm Tappert and publ. in 1877 in the hope of putting Wagner's detractors to shame, but they would not be pacified; the amount of black bile poured on him even after he had attained the stature of celebrity is incredible for its grossness and vulgarity. Hanslick used his great literary gift and a flair for a striking simile to damn him as a purveyor of cacophony. Oscar Wilde added his measure of wit. "I like Wagner's music better than anybody's," he remarked in *The Picture of Dorian Gray*. "It is so loud that one can talk the whole time without people hearing what one says." In an amazing turnabout, Nietzsche, a worshipful admirer of Wagner, publ. a venomous denunciation of his erstwhile idol in *Der Fall Wagner*, in which he vesuviated in a sulfuric eruption of righteous wrath; Wagner made music itself sick, he proclaimed; but at the time Nietzsche himself was already on the borderline of madness.

Politically, Wagner's prospects began to improve; on July 22, 1860, he was informed of a partial amnesty by the Saxon authorities. In Aug. 1860 he visited Baden-Baden, in his first visit to Germany in 11 years. Finally, on March 18, 1862, he was granted a total amnesty, which allowed him access to Saxony. In Nov. 1861 Wesendonck had invited Wagner to Venice; free from political persecution, he could now go there without fear. While in Venice he returned to a scenario he had prepared in Marienbad in 1845 for a comic opera, *Die Meistersinger von Nürnberg*. In Feb. 1862 he moved to Biebrich, where he began composing the score for *Die Meistersinger*. After a brief period of reconciliation with Wagner, Minna left him, settling in Dresden, where she died in 1866. In order to repair his financial situation, he accepted a number of concert appearances, traveling as an orch. conductor to Vienna, Prague, St. Petersburg, Moscow, and other cities (1862–63). In 1862 he gave a private reading of *Die Meistersinger* in Vienna. It is said that Hanslick was angered when he found out that Wagner had caricatured him in the part of Beckmesser in *Die Meistersinger* (the original name of the character was Hans Lick), and he let out his discomfiture in further attacks on Wagner.

Wagner's fortunes changed spectacularly in 1864 when young King Ludwig II of Bavaria ascended the throne and invited him to Munich with the promise of unlimited help in carrying out his various projects. In return, Wagner composed the *Huldigungsmarsch*, which he dedicated to his royal patron. The publ. correspondence between Wagner and the King is extraordinary in its display of mutual admiration, gratitude, and affection; still, difficulties soon developed when the Bavarian Cabinet told Ludwig that his lavish support of Wagner's projects threatened the Bavarian economy. Ludwig was forced to advise him to leave Munich. Wagner took this advice as an order, and late in 1865 he went to Switzerland. A very serious difficulty also arose in Wagner's emotional life, when he became intimately involved with Liszt's daughter Cosima, wife of Hans von Bülow, the famous conductor and an impassioned proponent of Wagner's music. On April 10, 1865, Cosima Bülow gave birth to Wagner's daughter, whom he named Isolde after the heroine of his opera that Bülow was preparing for performance in Munich. Its premiere took place with great acclaim on June 10, 1865, 2 months after the birth of Isolde, with Bülow conducting. During the summer of 1865 he prepared the prose sketch of *Parzival*, and began to dictate his autobiography, *Mein Leben*, to Cosima. In Jan. 1866 he resumed the composition of *Die Meistersinger*; he settled in a villa in Tribschen, on Lake Lucerne, where Cosima joined him permanently in Nov. 1868. He completed the full score of *Die Meistersinger* on Oct. 24, 1867. On June 21, 1868, Bülow conducted its premiere in Munich in the presence of King Ludwig, who sat in the royal box with Wagner. A son, significantly named Siegfried, was born to Cosima and Wagner on June 6, 1869. On Sept. 22, 1869, *Das Rheingold* was produced in Munich. On June 26, 1870, *Die Walküre* was staged there. On July 18, 1870, Cosima and Bülow were divorced, and on Aug. 25, 1870, Wagner and Cosima were married in Lucerne. In Dec. 1870 Wagner wrote the *Siegfried Idyll*, based on the themes from his opera; it was performed in their villa in Bayreuth on Christmas morning, the day after Cosima's birthday, as a surprise for her. In 1871 he wrote the *Kaisermarsch* to mark the victorious conclusion of the Franco-German War; he conducted it in the presence of Kaiser Wilhelm I at a concert in the Royal Opera House in Berlin on May 5, 1871.

On May 12 of that year, while in Leipzig, Wagner made public his plans for realizing his cherished dream of building his own theater in Bayreuth for the production of the entire cycle of *Der Ring des Nibelungen*. In Dec. 1871 the Bayreuth town council offered him a site for a proposed Festspielhaus; on May 22, 1872, the cornerstone was laid; Wagner commemorated the event by conducting a performance of Beethoven's 9th Sym. (this was his 59th birthday). In 1873 Wagner began to build his own home in Bayreuth, which he called "Wahnfried," i.e., "Free from Delusion." In order to complete the building of the Festspielhaus, he appealed to King Ludwig for additional funds. Ludwig gave him 100,000 talers for this purpose. Now the dream of Wagner's life was realized. Between June and Aug. 1876 *Der Ring des Nibelungen* went through 3 rehearsals; King Ludwig attended the final dress rehearsals; the official premiere of the cycle took place on Aug. 13, 14, 16, and 17, 1876, under the direction of Hans Richter. Kaiser Wilhelm I made a special journey from Berlin to attend the performances of *Das Rheingold* and *Die Walküre*. In all, 3 complete productions of the *Ring* cycle were given between Aug. 13 and Aug. 30, 1876. Ludwig was faithful to the end to Wagner, whom he called "my divine friend." In his castle Neuschwanstein he installed architectural representations of scenes from Wagner's operas. Soon Ludwig's mental deterioration became obvious to everyone, and he was committed to an asylum. There, on June 13, 1883, he overpowered the psychiatrist escorting him on a walk and dragged him to his death in the Starnberg Lake, drowning himself as well. Ludwig survived Wagner by 4 months.

The spectacles in Bayreuth attracted music-lovers and notables from all over the world. Even those who were not partial to Wagner's ideas or appreciative of his music went to Bayreuth out of curiosity. Tchaikovsky was one such skeptical visitor. Despite world success and fame, Wagner still labored under financial difficulties. He even addressed a letter to an American dentist practicing in Dresden (who also treated Wagner's teeth) in which he tried to interest him in arranging Wagner's permanent transfer to the U.S. He voiced disillusionment in his future prospects in Germany, and said he would be willing to settle in America provided a sum of $1 million would be guaranteed to him by American bankers, and a comfortable estate for him and his family could be found in a climatically clement part of the country. Nothing came of this particular proposal. He did establish an American connection when he wrote, for a fee of $5,000, a *Grosser Festmarsch* for the observance of the U.S. centennial in 1876, dedicated to the "beautiful young ladies of America." In the middle of all this, Wagner became infatuated with Judith Gautier; their affair lasted for about 2 years (1876–78). He completed the full score of *Parsifal* (as it was now called) on Jan. 13, 1882, in Palermo. It was performed for the first time at the Bayreuth Festival on July 26, 1882, followed by 15 subsequent performances. At the final performance, on Aug. 29, 1882, Wagner stepped to the podium in the last act and conducted the work to its close; this was his last appearance as a conductor. He went to Venice in Sept. 1882 for a period of rest (he had angina pectoris). Early in the afternoon of Feb. 13, 1883, he suffered a massive heart attack, and died in Cosima's presence. His body was interred in a vault in the garden of his Wahnfried villa in Bayreuth.

Wagner's role in music history is immense. Not only did he create works of great beauty and tremendous brilliance, but he generated an entirely new concept of the art of music, exercising an influence on generations of composers all over the globe. Richard Strauss extended Wagner's grandiose vision to symphonic music, fashioning the form of a tone poem that uses leading motifs and vivid programmatic description of the scenes portrayed in his music. Even Rimsky-Korsakov, far as he stood from Wagner's ideas of musical composition, reflected the spirit of *Parsifal* in his own religious opera, *The Legend of the City of Kitezh*. Schoenberg's first significant work, *Verklärte Nacht*, is Wagnerian in its color. Lesser composers, unable to escape Wagner's magic domination, attempted to follow him literally by writing trilogies and tetralogies on a parallel plan with his *Ring*; a pathetic example is the career of August Bungert, who wrote 2 operatic cycles using Homer's epics as the source of his libretti. Wagner's reform of opera was incomparably more far-reaching in aim, import, and effect than that of Gluck, whose main purpose was to counteract the arbitrary predominance of the singers; this goal Wagner accomplished through insistence upon the dramatic truth of his music. When he rejected traditional opera, he did so in the conviction that such an artificial form could not serve as a basis for true dramatic expression. In its place he gave the world a new form and new techniques. So revolutionary was Wagner's art that conductors and singers had to undergo special training in the new style of interpretation in order to perform his works. Thus he became the founder of interpretative conducting and of a new school of dramatic singing, so that such terms as "Wagnerian tenor" and "Wagnerian soprano" became a part of the musical vocabulary.

In his many essays and declarations Wagner condemns the illogical plan of Italian opera and French grand opera. To quote his own words, "The mistake in the art-form of the opera consists in this, that a means of expression (music) was made the end, and the end to be expressed (the drama) was made a means." The choice of subjects assumes utmost importance in Wagner's aesthetics. He wrote: "The subject treated by the word-tone poet [*Worttondichter*] is entirely human, freed from all convention and from everything historically formal." The new artwork creates its own artistic form; continuous thematic development of basic motifs becomes a fundamental procedure for the logical cohesion of the drama; these highly individualized generating motifs, appearing singly, in bold relief, or subtly varied and intertwined with other motifs, present the ever-changing soul states of the characters of the drama, and form the connecting links for the dramatic situations of the total artwork, in a form of musical declamation that Wagner described as "Sprechsingen." Characters in Wagner's stage works themselves become symbols of such soul states, so that even mythical gods, magic-workers, heroic horses, and speaking birds become expressions of eternal verities, illuminating the human behavior. It is for this reason that in most of his operas

Wagner selected figures that reflect philosophical ideas. Yet, this very solemnity of Wagner's great images on the stage bore the seeds of their own destruction in a world governed by different aesthetic principles. Thus it came to pass that the Wagnerian domination of the musical stage suddenly lost its power with changes in human society and aesthetic codes. Spectators and listeners were no longer interested in solving artistic puzzles on the stage. A demand for human simplicity arose against Wagnerian heroic complexity. The public at large found greater enjoyment in the realistic drama of Verdi's romantic operas than in the unreality of symbolic truth in Wagner's operas. By the second quarter of the 20th century, few if any composers tried to imitate Wagner; all at once his grandeur and animation became an unnatural and asphyxiating constraint.

In the domain of melody, harmony, and orchestration, Wagner's art was as revolutionary as was his total artwork on the stage. He introduced the idea of an endless melody, a continuous flow of diatonic and chromatic tones; the tonality became fluid and uncertain, producing an impression of unattainability, so that the listener accustomed to Classical modulatory schemes could not easily feel the direction toward the tonic; the *Prelude* to *Tristan und Isolde* is a classic example of such fluidity of harmonic elements. The use of long unresolved dominant-ninth-chords and the dramatic tremolos of diminished-seventh-chords contributed to this state of musical uncertainty, which disturbed the critics and the audiences alike. Wagnerian harmony also became the foundation of the new method of composition that adopted a free flow of modulatory progressions. Without Wagner the chromatic idioms of the 20th century could not exist. In orchestration, too, Wagner introduced great innovations; he created new instruments, such as the so-called "Wagner tuba," and he increased his demands on the virtuosity of individual orch. players. The vertiginous flight of the bassoon to the high E in the *Overture* to *Tannhäuser* could not have been attempted before the advent of Wagner.

Wagner became the target of political contention during World War I when audiences in the Allied countries associated his sonorous works with German imperialism. An even greater obstacle to further performances of Wagner's music arose with the rise of Hitler. Hitler ordered the slaughter of millions of Jews; he was an enthusiastic admirer of Wagner, who himself entertained anti- Semitic notions; ergo, Wagner was guilty by association of mass murder. Can art be separated from politics, particularly when politics become murderous? Jewish musicians in Tel Aviv refused to play the *Prelude* to *Tristan und Isolde* when it was put on the program of a sym. concert under Zubin Mehta, and booed him for his intention to inflict Wagner on Wagner's philosophical victims.

Several periodicals dealing with Wagner were publ. in Germany and elsewhere; Wagner himself began issuing *Bayreuther Blätter* in 1878 as an aid to understanding his operas; this journal continued publication until 1938. Remarkably enough, a French periodical, *Revue Wagnérienne*, began appearing in 1885, at a time when French composers realized the tremendous power of Wagnerian aesthetics; it was publ. sporadically for a number of years. From 1888 to 1895, a Wagner Soc. in London publ. a quarterly journal entitled, significantly, *The Meister*.

WORKS: DRAMATIC: Opera and Music Drama: *Die Hochzeit* (1832–33; partly destroyed; introduction, septet, and chorus perf. at the Neues Theater, Leipzig, Feb. 13, 1938); *Die Feen*, romantische Oper (1833–34; Königliches Hof- und Nationaltheater, Munich, June 29, 1888, Fischer conducting); *Das Liebesverbot, oder Die Novize von Palermo*, grosse komische Oper (1834–35; Magdeburg, March 29, 1836, composer conducting); *Rienzi, der Letzte der Tribunen*, grosse tragische Oper (1837–40; Königliches Hoftheater, Dresden, Oct. 20, 1842, Reissiger conducting; rev. 1843); *Der fliegende Holländer*, romantische Oper (1841; Königliches Hoftheater, Dresden, Jan. 2, 1843, composer conducting; reorchestrated in 1846, then rev. in 1852 and 1860); *Tannhäuser und der Sängerkrieg auf Wartburg*, grosse romantische Oper (first titled *Der Venusberg*; "Dresden" version, 1842–45; Königliches Hoftheater, Dresden, Oct. 19, 1845, composer conducting; rev. 1845–47; "Paris" version, a rev. version with additions and a French tr., 1860–61; Opéra, Paris, March 13, 1861, Dietsch conducting; final version, with a German tr. of the French revision and additions, 1865; Königliches Hof- und Nationaltheater, Munich, March 5, 1865); *Lohengrin*, romantische Oper (1845–48; Hoftheater, Weimar, Aug. 28, 1850, Liszt conducting); *Tristan und Isolde* (1856–59; Königliches Hof- und Nationaltheater, Munich, June 10, 1865, Bülow conducting); *Die Meistersinger von Nürnberg* (1st sketch, 1845; 1861–67; Königliches Hof- und Nationaltheater, Munich, June 21, 1868, Bülow conducting); *Der Ring des Nibelungen*, Bühnenfestspiel für drei Tage und einen Vorabend (1st prose outline as *Der Nibelungen- Mythus als Entwurf zu einem Drama*, 1848; Vorabend: *Das Rheingold*, 1851–54; Königliches Hof- und Nationaltheater, Munich, Sept. 22, 1869, Wüllner conducting; erster Tag: *Die Walküre*, 1851–56; Königliches Hof- und Nationaltheater, Munich, June 26, 1870, Wüllner conducting; zweiter Tag: *Siegfried*, first titled *Der junge Siegfried*; 1851–52, 1857, 1864–65, and 1869; Festspielhaus, Bayreuth, Aug. 16, 1876, Richter conducting; dritter Tag: *Götterdämmerung*, first titled *Siegfrieds Tod*; 1848–52 and 1869–74; Festspielhaus, Bayreuth, Aug. 17, 1876, Richter conducting; 1st complete perf. of the *Ring* cycle, Festspielhaus, Bayreuth, Aug. 13, 14, 16, and 17, 1876, Richter conducting); *Parsifal*, Bühnenweihfestspiel (first titled *Parzival*; first sketch, 1857; 1865 and 1877–82; Festspielhaus, Bayreuth, July 26, 1882, Levi conducting). **ORCH.:** Overture in B-flat major, the *Paukenschlag-Ouverture* (Leipzig, Dec. 24, 1830; not extant); Overture to Schiller's *Die Braut von Messina* (1830; not extant); Overture in C major (1830; not extant); Overture in D minor (Leipzig, Dec. 25, 1831); Overture in E-flat major (1831; not extant); Overture to Raupach's *König Enzio*, in E minor (Leipzig, Feb. 17, 1832); Overture in C major (Leipzig, April 30, 1832); Sym. in C major (Prague, Nov. 1832); Sym. in E major (1834; fragment); Overture to Apel's *Columbus*, in E-flat major (Magdeburg, Feb. 16, 1835); Overture *Polonia*, in C major (begun 1832, finished 1836); Overture *Rule Britannia*, in D major (1837); music for Singer's *Die letzte Heidenverschwörung in Preussen* (1837; fragment); Overture to Goethe's *Faust* (1840; reorchestrated 1843–44; Dresden, July 22, 1844; rev. and reorchestrated as *Eine Faust-Ouvertüre*, 1855; Zürich, Jan. 23, 1855); *Trauermusik* for Wind Instruments, after motifs from Weber's *Euryanthe* (Dresden, Dec. 14, 1844, for the reburial ceremony of Weber's remains); *Träume* for Violin and Small Orch. (Zürich, Dec. 23, 1857); *Huldigungsmarsch* (1st version, for Military Band, Munich, Oct. 5, 1864; 2nd version, for Large Orch., completed by

Raff); *Siegfried Idyll* for Small Orch. (Tribschen, Dec. 25, 1870); *Kaisermarsch* (Berlin, May 5, 1871); *Grosser Festmarsch zur Eröffnung der hundertjährigen Gedenkfeier der Unabhängigkeitserklärung der vereinigten Staaten von Nord-Amerika* (also known as *The American Centennial March*; Philadelphia, May 10, 1876). Also a projected orch. work in E minor (1830?; fragment); a scene for a pastoral play after Goethe's *Laune der Verliebten* (1830?); *Entreacte tragique No. 1*, in D major (1832?; fragment) and *No. 2*, in C minor (1832?; sketch). **Piano:** Sonata in D minor (1829; not extant); Sonata in F minor (1829; not extant); *Doppelfuge* (1831?; 103 bars, with corrections in Weinlig's hand); Sonata in B-flat major, for 4-Hands (1831; not extant); Sonata in B-flat major, op.1 (1831); *Fantasie* in F-sharp minor, op.3 (1831); *Polonaise* in D major (1831–32); *Polonaise* in D major, for 4- Hands, op.2 (1832?); Sonata in A major, op.4 (1832); *Albumblatt (Lied ohne Worte)* in E major (1840); Polka in G major (1853); *Eine Sonate für das Album von Frau M*[athilde].*W*[esendonck]. in A-flat major (1853); *Züricher Vielliebschen: Walzer, Polka oder sonst was* in E-flat major (1854); *Albumblatt, In das Album der Fürstin M*[etternich]. in C major (1861); *Ankunft bei den schwarzen Schwänen* (Albumblatt for Countess Pourtalès) in A-flat major (1861); *Albumblatt für Frau Betty Schott* in E-flat major (1875). **VOCAL: Choral:** *Neujahrs-Kantate* for Chorus and Orch. (Magdeburg, Dec. 31, 1834; arranged with a new text by Peter Cornelius as *Künstlerweihe*, and perf. at Bayreuth on Wagner's 60th birthday, May 22, 1873); *Nicolai Volkshymne* for Tenor or Soprano, Chorus, and Orch. (Riga, Nov. 21, 1837); *Descendons, descendons* for Chorus, for *La Descente de la courtille* (1840); *Weihegruss zur feierlichen Enthüllung des Denkmals Königs Friedrich August I ("des Gerechten") von Sachsen (Der Tag erscheint)* for Men's Chorus (1843; as *Gesang zur Enthüllung des Denkmals Sr. Mag. des hochseligen Königs Friedrich August des Gerechten am 7. Juni 1843* for Men's Chorus and Brass; for the unveiling of the statue of King Friedrich August of Saxony, Dresden, June 7, 1843); *Das Liebesmahl der Apostel*, biblical scene for Men's Chorus and Orch. (Dresden, July 6, 1843); *Gruss seiner Treuen an Friedrich August den Geliebten (Im treuen Sachsenland)* for Men's Chorus (Dresden, Aug. 12, 1843; for the return from England of King Friedrich August of Saxony); *Hebt an den Sang (An Webers Grabe)* for Men's Chorus (Dresden, Dec. 15, 1844; for the reburial ceremony of Weber's remains); *Wahlspruch für die deutsche Feuerwehr (Treue sei unsre Zier)* (1869); *Kinderkatechismus zu Kosels Geburtstag* for 4 High Voices (1873; orchestrated 1874). Also a scene and aria for Soprano and Orch. (1832; not extant); "Doch jetzt wohin ich blicke," aria for Tenor and Orch. for Marschner's opera *Der Vampyr* (1833); aria for Bass and Orch. for Weigl's opera *Die Schweizerfamilie* (1837; not extant); "Sanfte Wehmut will sich regen," aria for Bass and Orch. for Blum's Singspiel *Marie, Max und Michel* (Riga, Sept. 1, 1837); "Norma il prédesse," aria for Bass, Men's Chorus, and Orch. for Bellini's opera *Norma* (1839). **Songs:** *Sieben Kompositionen zu Goethes Faust*, op.5: 1, *Lied der Soldaten (Burgen mit hohen Mauern)*; 2, *Bauern unter der Linde (Der Schäfter putzte sich zum Tanz)*; 3, *Branders Lied (Es war eine Ratt im Kellernest)*; 4, *Lied des Mephistopheles (Es war einmal ein König)*; 5, *Lied des Mephistopheles (Was machst du mir vor Liebchens Tür)*; 6, *Gretchen am Spinnrade (Meine Ruh ist hin)*; 7, *Melodram Gretchens (Ach neige, du Schmerzenreiche)* (1831; rev. 1832); *Glockentöne* (1832; not extant); *Carnevalslied from Das Liebesverbot* (1835–36); *Der Tannenbaum* (1838); *Tout n'est qu'images fugitives* (1839); *3 mélodies:* 1, *Dors, mon enfant*; 2, *Mignonne*; 3, *L'Attente* (1839); *Adieux de Marie Stuart* (1840); *Les Deux Grenadiers*, to the poem by Heine (1840); *Gruss seiner Treuen an Friedrich August den Geliebten (Im treuen Sachsenland)* (a version for Baritone; 1844); *5 Gedichte für eine Frauenstimme* (Wesendonk-Lieder): 1, *Der Engel* (1857); 2, *Stehe still* (1858); 3, *Im Treibhaus* (1858); 4, *Schmerzen* (1857); 5, *Träume* (1857); *Scherzlied für Louis Kraft* (1871); also *Extase* (1839; fragment) and *La Tombe dit à la rose* (1839; fragment). **ARRANGEMENTS AND EDITIONS:** Piano score of Beethoven's 9th Sym. (1830; unpubl.); Piano score of J. Haydn's Sym. No. 103, in E-flat major (1831–32; not extant); Aria from Bellini's *Il Pirata*, as orchestrated from the piano score for use in *La Straniera* (1833); arrangement of vocal score for Donizetti's *La Favorite* (1840) and *L'elisir d'amore* (1840); arrangement of vocal score for Halévy's *La Reine de Chypre* (1841) and *Le Guitarrero* (1841); new tr. and new close to the overture of Gluck's *Iphigénie en Aulide* (1846–47; Dresden, Feb. 22, 1847); Palestrina's *Stabat Mater*, with indications for performance (Dresden, March 8, 1848); Mozart's *Don Giovanni*, version of dialogues and recitatives and, in parts, new tr. (Zürich, Nov. 8, 1850; not extant).

WRITINGS: Wagner devoted a large amount of his enormous productive activity to writing. Besides the dramatic works he set to music, he also wrote the following: *Leubald. Ein Trauerspiel* (1826–28); *Die hohe Braut, oder Bianca und Giuseppe*, 4-act tragic opera (prose scenario, 1836 and 1842; music composed by Johann Kittl and perf. as *Bianca und Giuseppe, oder Die Franzosen vor Nizza* in Prague, 1848); *Männerlist grösser als Frauenlist, oder Die glückliche Bärenfamilie*, 2-act comic opera (libretto, 1837; some music completed); *Eine Pilgerfahrt zu Beethoven*, novella (1840); *Ein Ende in Paris*, novella (1841); *Ein glücklicher Abend*, novella (1841); *Die Sarazenin*, 3-act opera (prose scenario, 1841–42; verse text, 1843); *Die Bergwerke zu Falun*, 3-act opera (prose scenario for an unwritten libretto, 1841–42); *Friedrich I.*, play (prose scenario, 1846 and 1848); *Alexander der Grosse*, sketch for a play (184?; not extant); *Jesus von Nazareth*, play (prose scenario, 1849); *Achilleus*, sketch for a play (1849–50; fragments only); *Wieland der Schmied*, 3-act opera (prose scenario, 1850); *Die Sieger*, opera (prose sketch, 1856); *Luther* or *Luthers Hochzeit*, sketch for a play (1868); *Lustspiel in 1 Akt* (draft, 1868); *Eine Kapitulation: Lustspiel in antiker Manier*, poem (1870). Wagner expounded his theories on music, politics, philosophy, religion, etc., in numerous essays; among the most important are *Über deutsches Musikwesen* (1840); *Die Kunst und die Revolution* (1849); *Das Kunstwerk der Zukunft* (1849); *Kunst und Klima* (1850); *Oper und Drama* (1851; rev. 1868); *Eine Mitteilung an meine Freunde* (1851); *Über Staat und Religion* (1864); *Über das Dirigieren* (1869); *Beethoven* (1870); *Über die Anwendung der Musik auf das Drama* (1879); and *Religion und Kunst* (1880). The first ed. of his collected writings, *R. Wagner: Gesammelte Schriften und Dichtungen* (9 vols., Leipzig, 1871–73; vol. 10, 1883), was prepared by Wagner himself; W.A. Ellis ed. and tr. it into Eng. as *Richard Wagner's Prose Works* (8 vols., London, 1892–99). H. von Wolzogen and R. Sternfeld ed. the 5th ed. of the German original as *Samtliche Schriften und Dichtungen*, adding Vols. XI and XII (Leipzig, 1911); they also prepared the 6th ed., adding Vols. XIII-XVI (Leipzig, 1914). Wagner's important autobiography, *Mein Leben*, in 4 parts, was privately publ.; parts 1–3, bringing the narrative down to Aug. 1861, were publ. between 1870 and 1875; part 4, covering the years from 1861 to 1864, was publ. in 1881; these were limited eds., being distributed only among his friends; the entire work was finally publ. in an abridged ed. in Munich in 1911 (Eng. tr. as *My Life*, London and N.Y., 1911); the suppressed passages were first publ. in *Die Musik*, XXII (1929–30), and then were tr. into Eng. in E. Newman's *Fact and Fiction about Wagner* (London, 1931); a definitive ed., based on the original MS, was publ. in Munich in 1963, ed. by M. Gregor-Dellin. Another important source is Wagner's diary-notebook, the so-called *Brown Book*, in which he made entries between 1865 and 1882; it was ed. by J. Bergfeld as *Richard Wagner: Das Braune Buch: Tagebuchaufzeichnungen, 1865–1882* (Zürich, 1975; Eng. tr. by G. Bird as *The Diary of Richard Wagner, 1865–1882; The Brown Book*, London, 1980). See also the diaries of Cosima Wagner; they have been ed. by M. Gregor-Dellin and D. Mack as *Cosima Wagner: Die Tagebücher, 1869–1877* (2 vols., Munich, 1976–77; Eng. tr. by G. Skelton as *Cosima Wagner's Diaries*, 2 vols., N.Y., 1977, 1980).

BIBL.: COLLECTED EDITIONS, SOURCE MATERIAL: The first collected ed. of his works, *R. W.s Werke*, was ed. by M. Balling (10 vols., Leipzig, 1912–29); the Bayerische Akademie der Schönen Künste of Munich is publ. a new critical ed., the *Gesamtausgabe der Werke R. W.s*, under the editorship of C. Dahlhaus et al. (Mainz, 1970 et seq.). E. Kastner prepared a *W.-Catalog: Chronologisches Verzeichniss der von und über R. W. erschienenen Schriften, Musikwerke* (Offenbach, 1878). J. Deathridge, M. Geck, and E. Voss ed. an exhaustive *Verzeichnis der musikalischen Werke R. W.s und ihrer Quellen* (Mainz, 1983). Other sources include: N. Oesterlein, *Katalog einer R. W.-Bibliothek: Nach den vorliegenden Originalien zu einem authentischen Nachschlagebuch durch die gesammte insbesondere deutsche W.-Litteratur bearbeitet und veröffentlicht* (4 vols., Leipzig, 1882, 1886, 1891, 1895); C. Glasenapp and H. von Stein, *W.- Lexikon: Hauptbegriffe der Kunst und Weltanschauung W.s in wörtlichen Ausführungen aus seinen Schriften zusammengestellt* (Stuttgart, 1883); C. Glasenapp, *W.-Enzyklopädie: Haupterscheinungen der Kunst- und Kulturgeschichte im Lichte der Anschauung W.s in wörtlichen Ausführungen aus seinen Schriften dargestellt* (2 vols., Leipzig, 1891); E. Kastner, *Verzeichnis der ersten Aufführungen von R. W.s dramatischen Werken* (Vienna, 1896; 2nd ed., Leipzig, 1899); H. Silège, *Bibliographie w.ienne française* (Paris, 1902); P. Pabst, *Verzeichnis von R. W.s Werken, Schriften und Dichtungen, deren hauptsächlichsten Bearbeitungen, sowie von besonders interessanter Litteratur, Abbildungen, Büsten und Kunstblättern, den Meister und seine Schöpfungen betreffend* (Leipzig, 1905); M. Burrell, *Catalogue of the Burrell Collection of W. Documents, Letters and Other Biographical Material* (London, 1929); O. Strobel, *Genie am Werk: R. W.s Schaffen und Wirken im Spiegel eigenhandschriftlicher Urkunden: Führer durch die einmalige Ausstellung einer umfassenden Auswahl von Schätzen aus dem Archiv des Hauses Wahnfried* (Bayreuth, 1933; rev. ed., 1934); E. Terry, *A R. W. Dictionary* (N.Y., 1939); C. von Westernhagen, *R. W.s Dresdener Bibliothek, 1842–1849: Neue Dokumente zur Geschichte seines Schaffens* (Wiesbaden, 1966); H. Kirchmeyer, *Das zeitgenössische W.-Bild* (3 vols., Regensburg; Vol. I, *W. in Dresden*, publ. 1972; Vol. II, *Dokumente, 1842–45*, publ. 1967; Vol. III, *Dokumente, 1846–50*, publ. 1968); H.-M. Plesske, *R. W. in der Dichtung: Bibliographie deutschsprachiger Veröffentlichungen* (Bayreuth, 1971); W. Schuler, *Der Bayreuther Kreis von seiner Entstehung bis zum Ausgang der wilhelminischen Ära: W.kult und Kulturreform im Geiste völkischer Weltanschauung* (Münster, 1971); H. Klein, *Erst- und Frühdrucke der Textbücher von R. W.: Bibliographie* (Tutzing, 1979); H. Klein, *Erstdrucke der musikalischen Werke von R. W.* (Tutzing, 1983); U. Müller, ed., *R.-W.-Handbuch* (Stuttgart, 1986; Eng. tr. as *W. Handbook*, Cambridge, 1992); H.-J. Bauer, *R. W. Lexikon* (Bergisch Gladbach, 1988); B. Millington, ed., *The W. Compendium: A Guide to W.'s Life and Music* (N.Y., 1992); W. Brieg, M. Dürrer, and A. Mielke, *W.- Briefe-Verzeichnis: Chronologisches Verzeichnis der Briefe von R. W.* (Wiesbaden, 1998). **YEARBOOKS AND OTHER PUBLICATIONS:** *Bayreuther Blätter* (founded by Wagner; Chemnitz, later Bayreuth, 1878–1938); *La Revue Wagnérienne* (Paris, 1885–88); *R.-W.-Jahrbuch* (Stuttgart, 1886); *The Meister* (quarterly journal of the British Wagner Soc., London, 1888–95); *Bayreuth: Handbuch für Festspielbesucher* (Bayreuth, 1894–1930); *Bayreuther Festspielführer* (also issued under other titles; Bayreuth, 1901–39); L. Frankenstein, ed., *R.-W.-Jahrbuch* (5 vols., Berlin, 1906, 1907, 1908, 1912, 1913); O. Strobel, ed., *Neue W.-Forschungen: Veröffentlichungen der R.-W.-Forschungsstatte Bayreuth* (Karlsruhe, 1943); *Das Bayreuther Festspielbuch* (Bayreuth, 1950–51); *"Bayreuth"-Jahreshefte* (Bayreuth, 1954 et seq.); *Tribschener Blätter* (publ. by the Zeitschrift der Schweizerischen Richard-Wagner-Gesellschaft of Lucerne, 1956 et seq.); *W.* (publ. by the Wagner Soc. of London, 1971 et seq.). **CORRESPONDENCE:** Almost all of the collections of his letters to 1912 were republ. by Breitkopf & Härtel as *R. W.s Briefe in Originalausgaben* (17 vols., Leipzig, 1912); a number of the letters appear in mutilated form (portions expressing political and religious views being suppressed); an early attempt to bring out an unmutilated ed. was begun by J. Kapp and E. Kastner, *R. W.s Gesammelte Briefe* (1830–50) (2 vols., Leipzig, 1914); however, this ed. was never completed; see also the following: E. Kloss, *Briefe an Hans von Bülow* (Jena, 1916); S. von Hausegger, ed., *R. W.s Briefe an Frau Julie Ritter* (Munich, 1920); L. Karpath, ed., *R. W.: Briefe an Hans Richter* (Berlin, 1924); W. Altmann, *R. W.s Briefe, ausgewählt und erläutert* (2 vols., Leipzig, 1925; Eng. tr., London, 1927); W. Lippert, *R. W.s Verbannung und Rückkehr, 1849–62* (Dresden, 1927; Eng. tr. as *W. in Exile*, London, 1930); R. Sternfeld, *R. W. Aufsätze und Briefe des Meisters aus Paris* (Grossenwörden, 1927); H. Scholz, ed., *R. W. an Mathilde Maier (1862–1878)* (Leipzig, 1930); E. Lenrow, ed. and tr., *The Letters of R. W. to Anton Pusinelli* (N.Y., 1932); J. Tiersot, *Lettres françaises de R. W.* (Paris, 1935); W. Schuh, ed. and tr., *Die Briefe R. W.s an Judith Gautier* (Zürich, 1936; enl. ed., with French original, as *R. et Cosima W.: Lettres à Judith Gautier*, ed. by L. Guichard, 1964); O. Strobel, ed., *König Ludwig II. und R. W.: Briefwechsel, mit vielen anderen Urkunden* (5 vols., Karlsruhe, 1936–39); J. Burk, ed., *Letters of R. W. The Burrell Collection* (N.Y., 1950; Ger. ed., Frankfurt am Main, 1953); G. Strobel and W. Wolf, eds., *R. W.: Sämtliche Briefe* (Leipzig, 1967 et seq.); S. Spencer and B. Millington, trs. and eds., *Selected Letters of R. W.* (London, 1987). **BIOGRAPHICAL:** C. Cabrol, *R. W.* (Paris, 1861); A. de Gasperini, *La Nouvelle Allemagne musicale: R. W.* (Paris, 1866); F. Hueffer, *R. W.* (London, 1872; 3rd ed., 1912); F. Filippi, *R. W.* (Leipzig, 1876); C. Glasenapp, *R. W.s Leben und Wirken* (2 vols., Leipzig, 1876–77; 3rd ed., rev. and enl., as *Das Leben R. W.s*, 6 vols., Leipzig, 1894–1911; Eng. tr. by W. Ellis as *Life of R. W.*, 6 vols., London, 1900–08; Vols. I-III based on Glasenapp; reprinted N.Y., 1977, with new introduction by G. Buelow; 5th Ger. ed., rev., 1910–23); P. Lindau, *R. W.* (Paris, 1885); A. Jullien, *R. W.: Sa vie et ses oeuvres* (Paris, 1886; Eng. tr., Boston, 1892); G. Kobbé, *W.'s Life and Works* (2 vols., N.Y., 1890); H. Finck, *W. and His Works* (2 vols., N.Y., 1893; 5th ed., 1898); H. Chamberlain, *R. W.* (Munich, 1896; Eng. tr., London, 1897; 9th Ger. ed., 1936); M. Burrell, compiler, *R. W.: Life and Works from 1813 to 1834* (London, 1898); W.J. Henderson, *R. W., His Life and His Dramas* (N.Y., 1901; rev. ed., 1923); R. Bürkner, *R. W.: Sein Leben und seine Werke* (Jena, 1906; 6th ed., 1911); M. Koch, *R. W.* (3 vols., Berlin, 1907, 1913, and 1918); J. Kapp, *R. W.* (Berlin, 1910); F. Pfohl, *R. W.: Sein Leben und Schaffen* (Berlin, 1911; 4th ed., Bielefeld, 1924); E. Newman, *W. as Man and Artist* (London, 1914; 2nd ed., rev., 1924); L. Barthou, *La Vie amoureuse de R. W.* (Paris, 1925; Eng. tr. as *The Prodigious Lover*, N.Y., 1927); H. Lichtenberger, *W.* (Paris, 1925); W. Wallace, *W. as He Lived* (London, 1925; new ed., 1933); V. d'Indy, *R. W. et son influence sur l'art musical français* (Paris, 1930); M. Morold (pen name of Max von Millenkovitch), *W.s Kampf und Sieg, dargestellt in seinen Beziehungen zu Wien* (Zürich, 1930; 2nd ed., 1950); H. Reisiger, *Unruhiges Gestirn: Die Jugend R. W.s* (Leipzig, 1930; in Eng. as *Restless Star*, N.Y., 1932); G. de

Pourtalès, *W.: Histoire d'un artiste* (Paris, 1932; Eng. tr., N.Y., 1932; 2nd French ed., enl., 1942); P. Lalo, *R. W.* (Paris, 1933); E. Newman, *The Life of R. W.* (4 vols., N.Y., 1933, 1937, 1941, 1946); A. Spring, *R. W.s Weg und Wirken* (Stuttgart, 1933); W. Turner, *W.* (London, 1933); M. Fehr, *R. W.s Schweizer Zeit* (2 vols., Aarau, 1934, 1953); W. Hadow, *R. W.* (London, 1934); R. Jacobs, *W.* (London, 1935; 3rd ed., 1947); H. Malherbe, *R. W. Révolutionnaire* (Paris, 1938); E. Kretzschmar, *R. W.: Sein Leben in Selbstzeugnissen, Briefen und Berichten* (Berlin, 1939); O. Strobel, *Neue Urkunden zur Lebensgeschichte R. W.s, 1864–1882* (a suppl. to his ed. of *König Ludwig II. und R. W.: Briefwechsel*; Karlsruhe, 1939); M. von Millenkovitch, *Dreigestirn: W., Liszt, Bülow* (Leipzig, 1941); W. Reich, *R. W.: Leben, Fühlen, Schaffen* (Olten, 1948); K. Ipser, *R. W. in Italien* (Salzburg, 1951); L. Strecker, *R. W. als Verlagsgefährte: Eine Darstellung mit Briefen und Dokumenten* (Mainz, 1951); T. Adorno, *Versuch über W.* (Berlin, 1952); P. Loos, *R. W., Vollendung und Tragik der deutschen Romantik* (Munich, 1952); O. Strobel, *R. W.: Leben und Schaffen: Eine Zeittafel* (Bayreuth, 1952); Z. von Kraft, *R. W.: Ein dramatisches Leben* (Munich, 1953); R. Dumesnil, *R. W.* (Paris, 1954); H. Mayer, *R. W.s geistige Entwicklung* (Düsseldorf and Hamburg, 1954); C. von Westernhagen, *R. W.: Sein Werk, sein Wesen, seine Welt* (Zürich, 1956); H. Mayer, *R. W. in Selbstzeugnissen und Bilddokumenten* (Reinbek bei Hamburg, 1959; Eng. tr., 1972); R. Gutman, *R. W.: The Man, His Mind and His Music* (London, 1968); C. von Westernhagen, *W.* (2 vols., Zürich, 1968; 2nd ed., rev. and enl., 1978; Eng. tr., Cambridge, 1978); M. Gregor-Martin, *W.-Chronik: Daten zu Leben* (Munich, 1972; 2nd rev. ed., 1983); H. Barth, D. Mack, and E. Voss, eds., *W.: Sein Leben und seine Welt in zeitgenössischen Bildern und Texten* (Vienna, 1975; Eng. tr. as *W.: A Documentary Study*, London, 1975); R. Taylor, *R. W.: His Life, Art and Thought* (London, 1979); D. Watson, *R. W.: A Biography* (N.Y. and London, 1979); M. Gregor-Dellin, *R. W.: Sein Leben, sein Werk, sein Jahrhundert* (Munich, 1980; Eng. tr. as *R. W.: His Life, His Work, His Century*, London, 1983); D. Watson, *R. W.* (N.Y., 1981); G. Skelton, *R. and Cosima W.: A Biography of a Marriage* (London, 1982); M. van Amerongen, *W.: A Case History* (London, 1983); M. Kahane and N. Wild, *W. et la France* (Paris, 1983); E. Voss, ed., *R. W.: Dokumentarbiographie* (Munich and Mainz, 1983); B. Millington, *W.* (London, 1984; rev. ed., 1992); J. Katz, *The Darker Side of Genius: R. W.'s Anti-Semitism* (Hanover, N.H. and London, 1986); R. Sabor, *The Real W.* (London, 1987); W. Beck, *R. W.: Neue Dokumente zur Biographie: Die Spiritualität im Drama seines Lebens* (Tutzing, 1988); A. Aberbach, *R. W.: A Mystic in the Making* (Wakefield, N.H., 1991); H.-J. Bauer, *R. W.: Sein Leben und Wirken oder die Gefühlwerdung der Vernunft* (Berlin, 1995); M. Schneider, *W.* (Paris, 1995); W. Tanner, *W.* (Princeton, 1996); H. Mayer, *R. W.* (Frankfurt am Main, 1998). **PERSONAL REMINISCENCES:** H. von Wolzogen, *Erinnerungen an R. W.* (Leipzig, 1883; Eng. tr., Bayreuth, 1894); A. Schilling, *Aus R. W.s Jugendzeit* (Berlin, 1898; reminiscences of Wagner's stepsister Cäcilie Avenarius); E. Schuré, *Souvenirs sur R. W.* (Paris, 1900; Ger. tr., Leipzig, 1900); E. von Possart, *Die Separat-Vorstellungen vor König Ludwig II. Erinnerungen* (Munich, 1901); L. Schemann, *Meine Erinnerungen an R. W.* (Stuttgart, 1902); G. Kietz, *R. W. in den Jahren 1842–49 und 1873–75* (Dresden, 1905); A. Kohut, *Der Meister von Bayreuth* (Berlin, 1905); E. Michotte, *Souvenirs: La Visite de R. W. à Rossini (Paris, 1860): Détails inédites et commentaires* (Paris, 1906; Eng. tr. by H. Weinstock, Chicago, 1968); A. Gobineau, *Ein Erinnerungsbild aus Wahnfried* (Stuttgart, 1907); A. Neumann, *Erinnerungen an R. W.* (Leipzig, 1907; Eng. tr., N.Y., 1908); H. Schmidt and U. Hartmann, *R. W. in Bayreuth. Erinnerungen* (Leipzig, 1910); S. Wagner, *Erinnerungen* (Stuttgart, 1923; extended ed., privately printed, 1935); J. Gautier, *Auprès de R. W.: Souvenirs (1861–1883)* (Paris, 1943). **RELATIONS WITH CONTEMPORARIES:** J. Craemer, *König Ludwig II. und R. W.* (Munich, 1901); F. Gerard, *Romance of King Ludwig II of Bavaria: His Relation with R. W.* (London, 1901); S. Röckel, *Ludwig II. und R. W. in den Jahren 1864–65* (Munich, 1903; 2nd ed., 1913); J. Kapp, *R. W. und Franz Liszt: Eine Freundschaft* (Berlin, 1908); H. Bélart, *Friedrich Nietzsches Freundschaftstragödie mit R. W.* (Dresden, 1912) and *R. W.s Liebestragödie mit Mathilde Wesendonck* (Dresden, 1912); J. Kapp, *R. W. und die Frauen* (Berlin, 1912; new rev. ed., 1951; Eng. tr., 1931, as *The Women in W.'s Life*); E. Förster-Nietzsche, *W. und Nietzsche zur Zeit ihrer Freundschaft* (Munich, 1915; Eng. tr., 1921, as *The Nietzsche-W. Correspondence*); C. Sarti, *W. and Nietzsche* (N.Y., 1915); E. Schuré, *Femmes inspiratrices* (Paris, 1930); M. Herwegh, *Au banquet des dieux: F. Liszt, R. W. et ses amis* (Paris, 1931) P.G. Dippel, *Nietzsche und W.* (Berne, 1934); D. Fischer-Dieskau, *W. und Nietzsche* (Stuttgart, 1974; Eng. tr., 1976); C. and P. Jost, *R. W. und sein Verleger Ernst Wilhelm Fritzsch* (Tutzing, 1997). **CRITICAL, ANALYTICAL:** Liszt's essays on *Tannhäuser* (1849), *Lohengrin* (1850), *Der fliegende Holländer* (1854), and *Das Rheingold* (1855) are in Vol. III, 2, of his *Gesammelte Schriften* (Leipzig, 1899); F. Hinrichs, *R. W. und die neuere Musik: Eine kritische Skizze* (Halle, 1854); F. Müller, *R. W. und das Musik-Drama* (Leipzig, 1861); L. Nohl, *Gluck und W. über die Entwicklung des Musikdramas* (Munich, 1870); F. Nietzsche, *Die Geburt der Tragödie aus dem Geiste der Musik* (Leipzig, 1872; Eng. tr. by W. Kaufmann as *The Birth of Tragedy out of the Spirit of Music* in *The Basic Writings of Nietzsche*, N.Y., 1968); E. Dannreuther, *R. W.: His Tendencies and Theories* (London, 1873); F. Hueffer, *R. W. and the Music of the Future* (London, 1874); E. Schuré, *Le Drame musical: I. La Musique et la poésie dans leur développement historique, II. W. Son oeuvre et son idée* (Paris, 1875; 3rd ed., aug., 1894); G. Kobbé, *R. W.s "Tristan und Isolde"* (N.Y., 1886); W. Ellis, *R. W. as Poet, Musician and Mystic* (London, 1887); F. Nietzsche, *Der Fall W.* (Leipzig, 1888; Eng. tr. by W. Kaufmann as *The Case of W.* in *The Basic Writings of Nietzsche*, N.Y., 1968); idem, *Nietzsche contra W.* (Leipzig, 1888; Eng. tr. by W. Kaufmann in *The Portable Nietzsche*, N.Y., 1954); H. von Wolzogen, *W.iana: Gesammelte Aufsätze über R. W.s Werke vom Ring bis zum Gral* (Bayreuth, 1888); M. Kufferath, *Parsifal de R. W.: Légende, drame, partition* (Paris, 1890; Eng. tr., 1904); L. Torchi, *Riccardo W.: Studio critico* (Bologna, 1890); H. Krehbiel, *Studies in the W.ian Drama* (N.Y., 1891); M. Kufferath, *Le Théâtre de W. de Tannhäuser à Parsifal: Essais de critique littéraire, esthétique et musicale* (6 vols., Paris, 1891–98); A. Smolian, *The Themes of "Tannhäuser"* (London, 1891); H. Chamberlain, *Das Drama R. W.s: Eine Anregung* (Leipzig, 1892; 5th ed., 1913; Eng. tr., London, 1915); M. Kufferath, *Guide thématique et analyse de Tristan et Iseult* (Paris, 1894); A. Lavignac, *Le Voyage artistique à Bayreuth* (Paris, 1897; Eng. tr. as *The Music-Dramas of R. W.*, N.Y., 1898; new ed., 1932); G. Servières, *R. W. jugé en France* (Paris, 1897); G.B. Shaw, *The Perfect W.ite* (London, 1898; 4th ed., 1923; also in Vol. 17 of the complete works, 1932); J. Tiersot, *Études sur les Maîtres-Chanteurs de Nuremberg, de R. W.* (Paris, 1899); A. Smolian, *R. W.'s Bühnenfestspiel Der Ring des Nibelungen: Ein Vademecum* (Berlin, 1901); A. Seidl, *W.iana* (2 vols., Berlin, 1901, 1902); G. Kobbé, *W.'s Music Dramas Analyzed* (N.Y., 1904); W. Dry, *Erläuterungen zur R. W.s Tondramen* (2 vols., Leipzig, 1906, 1907); W. Golther, *Tristan und Isolde in den Dichtungen des Mittelalters und der neuen Zeit* (Leipzig, 1907); S. Hamer, *The Story of "The Ring"* (N.Y., 1907); M. Burckhardt, *Führer durch R. W.s Musikdramen* (Berlin, 1909); E. Istel, *Das Kunstwerk R. W.s* (Leipzig, 1910; 2nd ed., 1919); E. Kloss, *R. W. über die "Meistersinger von Nürnberg": Aussprüche des Meisters über sein Werk* (Leipzig,

1910); W. Krienetz, *R. W.s "Feen"* (Munich, 1910); E. Lindner, *R. W. über "Parsifal": Aussprüche des Meisters über sein Werk* (Leipzig, 1913); idem., *R. W. über "Tannhäuser": Aussprüche des Meisters über sein Werk* (Leipzig, 1914); A. Seidl, *Neue W.iana: Gesammelte Aufsätze und Studien* (Regensburg, 1914); H. von Wolzogen, *R. W. über den "Fliegenden Holländer": Die Entstehung, Gestaltung und Darstellung des Werkes aus den Schriften und Briefen des Meisters zusammengestellt* (Leipzig, 1914); E. Kurth, *Romantische Harmonik und ihre Krise in W.s "Tristan"* (Berlin, 1920; 2nd ed., 1923); F. Zademack, *Die Meistersinger von Nürnberg: R. W.s Dichtung und ihre Quellen* (Berlin, 1921); W. Wilmshurst, *Parsifal* (London, 1922); P. Bekker, *R. W.: Das Leben im Werke* (Stuttgart, 1924; Eng. tr., London, 1931); A. Coeuroy, *La Walkyrie de R. W.* (Paris, 1924); O. Strobel, *R. W. über sein Schaffen: Ein Beitrag zur "Künstlerästhetik"* (Munich, 1924); H. Wiessner, *Der Stabreimvers in R. W.s "Ring des Nibelungen"* (Berlin, 1924); A. Himonet, *Lohengrin de R. W.* (Paris, 1925); L. Leroy, *W.'s Music Drama of the Ring* (London, 1925); C. Winn, *The Mastersingers of W.* (London, 1925); A. Dickinson, *The Musical Design of "The Ring"* (London, 1926); W. Hapke, *Die musikalische Darstellung der Gebärde in R. W.s Ring des Nibelungen* (Leipzig, 1927); A. Buesst, *R. W.: The Nibelung's Ring* (London, 1932; 2nd ed., 1952); W. Engelsmann, *W.s klingendes Universum* (Potsdam, 1933); J. Kapp, *Das Liebesverbot, Entstehung und Schicksale des Werkes von R. W.* (Berlin, 1933); idem, *W. und die Berliner Oper* (Berlin, 1933); R. Grisson, *Beiträge zur Auslegung von R. W.'s "Ring des Nibelungen"* (Leipzig, 1934); H. Nathan, *Das Rezitativ der Frühopern R. W.s: Ein Beitrag zur Stilistik des Opernrezitativs in der ersten Hälfte des 19. Jahrhunderts* (diss., Univ. of Berlin, 1934); A. Bahr-Mildenburg, *Tristan und Isolde: Darstellung der Werke R. W.s aus dem Geiste der Dichtung und Musik: Vollständige Regiebearbeitung sämtlicher Partien mit Notenbeispielen* (Leipzig, 1936); L. Gilman, *W.'s Operas* (N.Y., 1937); V. d'Indy, *Introduction à l'étude de Parsifal de W.* (Paris, 1937); R. Schuster, *R. W. und die Welt der Oper* (Munich, 1937); E. Borrelli, *Estetica w.iana* (Florence, 1940); E. Hutcheson, *A Musical Guide to the R. W. Ring of the Nibelung* (N.Y., 1940); J. Barzun, *Darwin, Marx, W.: Critique of a Heritage* (Boston, 1941; rev. ed., 1958); S. Luciani, *Il Tristano e Isolda di R. W.* (Florence, 1942); G. Gavazzeni, *Il Siegfried di R. W.* (Florence, 1944); M. Doisy, *L'Œuvre de R. W. du Vaisseau fantôme à Parsifal* (Brussels, 1945); M. Beaufils, *W. et le w.isme* (Paris, 1947); K. Overhoff, *R. W.s Tristan Partitur: Eine musikalisch-philosophische Deutung* (Bayreuth, 1948); E. Newman, *W. Nights* (London, 1949; American ed. as *The W. Operas*, N.Y., 1949); K. Overhoff, *R. W.s Parsifal* (Lindau im Bodensee, 1951); T. Adorno, *Versuch über W.* (Berlin and Frankfurt am Main, 1952); P. Jacob, *Taten der Musik: R. W. und sein Werk* (Regensburg, 1952); P. Loos, *R. W.: Vollendung und Tragik der deutschen Romantik* (Bern and Munich, 1952); V. Levi, *Tristano e Isotta di Riccardo W.* (Venice, 1958); J. Stein, *R. W. and the Synthesis of the Arts* (Detroit, 1960); H. von Stein, *Dichtung und Musik im Werk R. W.s* (Berlin, 1962); M. Vogel, *Der Tristan-Akkord und die Krise der modernen Harmonie-Lehre* (Düsseldorf, 1962); C. von Westernhagen, *Vom Holländer zum Parsifal: Neue W. Studien* (Freiburg im Breisgau, 1962); J. Bergfeld, *W.s Werk und unsere Zeit* (Berlin and Wunsiedel, 1963); R. Donington, *W.s "Ring" and Its Symbols: The Music and the Myth* (London, 1963; 3rd ed., rev. and enl., 1974); H. Gál, *R. W.: Versuch einer Würdigung* (Frankfurt am Main, 1963; Eng. tr., 1976); H. Scharschuch, *Gesamtanalyse der Harmonik von R. W.s Musikdrama "Tristan und Isolde": Unter spezifischer Berücksichtigung der Sequenztechnik des Tristanstiles* (Regensburg, 1963); E. Zuckerman, *The First Hundred Years of W.'s "Tristan"* (N.Y. and London, 1964); H. Mayer, *Anmerkungen zu W.* (Frankfurt am Main, 1966); W. White, *An Introduction to the Life and Works of R. W.* (Englewood Cliffs, N.J., 1967); K. Overhoff, *Die Musikdramen R. W.s: Eine thematisch-musikalische Interpretation* (Salzburg, 1968); R. Raphael, *R. W.* (N.Y., 1969); C. Dahlhaus, ed., *Das Drama R. W.s als musikalisches Kunstwerk* (Regensburg, 1970); idem, *Die Bedeutung des Gestischen in W.s Musikdramen* (Munich, 1970); E. Voss, *Studien zur Instrumentation R. W.s* (Regensburg, 1970); C. Dahlhaus, *Die Musikdramen R. W.s* (Velber, 1971; Eng. tr. as *R. W.'s Music Dramas*, Cambridge, 1979); idem, *W.s Konzeption des musikalischen Dramas* (Regensburg, 1971); A. Sommer, *Die Komplikationen des musikalischen Rhythmus in den Bühnenwerken R. W.s* (Giebing, 1971); C. von Westernhagen, *Die Entstehung des "Ring," dargestellt an den Kompositionsskizzen R. W.s* (Zürich, 1973; Eng. tr. as *The Forging of the "Ring,"* Cambridge, 1976); K. Kropfinger, *W. und Beethoven: Untersuchungen zur Beethoven-Rezeption R. W.s* (Regensburg, 1975); J. Culshaw, *Reflections on W.'s Ring* (N.Y., 1976); H.-J. Bauer, *W.s Parsifal: Kriterien der Kompositionstechnik* (Munich, 1977); J. Deathridge, *W.'s Rienzi: A Reappraisal Based on a Study of the Sketches and Drafts* (Oxford, 1977); J. Di Gaetani, *Penetrating W.'s Ring: An Anthology* (Cranbury, N.J., 1978); F. Oberkogler, *R. W.: Vom Ring zum Gral: Wiedergewinnung seines Werkes aus Musik und Mythos* (Stuttgart, 1978); P. Wapnewski, *Der traurige Gott: R. W. in seinen Helden* (Munich, 1978); P. Burbridge and R. Sutton, eds., *The W. Companion* (N.Y., 1979); D. Cooke, *I Saw the World End: A Study of W.'s Ring* (London, 1979); L. Rather, *The Dream of Self-Destruction: W.'s Ring and the Modern World* (Baton Rouge, La., 1979); A. Blyth, *W.'s Ring: An Introduction* (London, 1980); L. Beckett, *R. W.: Parsifal* (Cambridge, 1981); D. Borchmeyer, *Das Theater R. W.s* (Stuttgart, 1982; Eng. tr. as *R. W.: Theory and Theatre*, Oxford, 1991); M. Ewans, *W. and Aeschylus: The Ring and the Oresteia* (London, 1982); N. Benvenga, *Kingdom on the Rhine: History, Myth and Legend on W.'s Ring* (Harwich, 1983); A. Aberbach, *The Ideas of R. W.* (Lanham, 1984); S. Fay and R. Wood, *The Ring: An Anatomy of an Opera* (London, 1984); A. Ingenhoff, *Drama oder Epos?: R. W.s Gattungstheorie des musikalischen Dramas* (Tübingen, 1987); H.-M. Palm, *R. W.s 'Lohengrin': Studien zur Sprachbehandlung* (Munich, 1987); L. Shaw, N. Cirillo, and M. Miller, eds., *W. in Retrospect: A Centennial Reappraisal* (Amsterdam, 1987); D. White, *The Turning Wheel: A Study of Contracts and Oaths in W.'s 'Ring'* (Selinsgrove, N.Y., 1988); W. Cord, *The Teutonic Mythology of R. W.'s "The Ring of the Nibelung"* (3 vols., Lewiston, N.Y., 1989–91); P. Buck, *R. W.s Meistersinger: Eine Führung durch das Werk* (Frankfurt am Main, 1990); E. Magee, *R. W. and the Nibelungs* (Oxford, 1990); A. Mork, *R. W. als politischer Schriftsteller: Weltanschauung und Wirkungsgeschichte* (Frankfurt am Main, 1990); J. Nattiez, *W. androgyne: Essai sur l'interprétation* (Paris, 1990); C. Osborne, *The Complete Operas of R. W.* (London, 1990); P. Peil, *Die Krise des neuzeitlichen Menschen im Werk R. W.s* (Cologne, 1990); H. Brown, *Leitmotiv and Drama: W., Brecht, and the Limits of "Epic" Theatre* (Oxford, 1991); H. Kesting, *Das schlechte Gewissen an der Musik: Aufsätze zu R. W.* (Stuttgart, 1991); H. Richardson, ed., *New Studies in R. W.s The Ring of the Nibelung* (Lewiston, N.Y., 1991); P. Urban, *Liebesdämmerung: Ein psychoanalytischer Versuch über R. W.s "Tristan und Isolde"* (Eschborn, 1991); M. Cicora, *From History to Myth: W.'s Tannhäuser and Its Literary Sources* (Bern and N.Y., 1992); B. Millington and S. Spencer, eds., *W. in Performance* (New Haven, 1992); P. Rose, *W.: Race and Revolution* (New Haven, 1992); G. Skelton, *W. in Thought and Practice* (Portland, Ore., 1992); W. Darcy, *W.'s Das Rheingold* (Oxford, 1993); H. Hubert, *Götternot: R. W.s grose Dichtungen* (Asendorf, 1993); K. Richter, *R. W.: Visionen* (Vilsbiburg, 1993); B. Benz, *Zeitstrukturen in R. W.s 'Ring'- Tetralogie* (Frankfurt am Main, 1994); B. Heldt, *R. W.: Tristan und Isolde: Das Werk und seine*

Inszenierung (Laaber, 1994); J. Warrack, *R. W.: Die Meistersinger von Nürnberg* (Cambridge, 1994); C. Weismüller, *Das Drama der Notation: Ein philosophischer Versuch zu R. W.s Ring des Nibelungen* (Vienna, 1994); T. Grey, *W.'s Musical Prose: Texts and Contexts* (Cambridge, 1995); E. Roch, *Psychodrama: R. W. im Symbol: Mit 34 Abbildungen* (Stuttgart, 1995); M. Weiner, *R. W. and the Anti-Semitic Imagination* (Lincoln, Nebr., 1995); P.-H. Wilberg, *R. W.s mythische Welt: Versuche wider den Historismus* (Freiburg im Breisgau, 1996); M. Bless, *R. W.s Opera "Tannhäuser" im Spiegel seiner geistigen Entwicklung* (Eisenbach, 1997); D. Schneller, *R. W.s "Parsifal" und die Erncuerung des Mysteriendramas in Bayreuth: Die Vision des Gesamtkunstwerks als Universalkultur der Zukunft* (Bern, 1997); D. Scholz, *Ein deutsches Missverständnis: R. W. zwischen Barrikade und Walhalla* (Berlin, 1997); M. Cicora, *Mythology as Metaphor: Romantic Irony, Critical Theory, and W.'s Ring* (Westport, Conn., 1998); J. McGlathery, *W.'s Operas and Desire* (N.Y., 1998); M. Cicora, *W.'s Ring and German Drama: Comparative Studies in Mythology and History in Drama* (Westport, Conn., 1999). **WAGNER'S ART IN RELATION TO AESTHETICS, PHILOSOPHY, AND RELIGION:** F. von Hausegger, *R. W. und Schopenhauer* (Leipzig, 1878; 2nd ed., 1897); J. Freson, *Essais de philosophie et de l'art: L'Esthétique de R. W.* (2 vols., Paris, 1893); M. Hébert, *Le Sentiment religieux dans l'oeuvre de R. W.* (Paris, 1894); R. Louis, *Die Weltanschauung R. W.s* (Leipzig, 1898); D. Irvine, *Parsifal and W.'s Christianity* (London, 1899); M. Kufferath, *Musiciens et philosophes: Tolstoy, Schopenhauer, Nietzsche, W.* (Paris, 1899); P. Moos, *R. W. als Ästhetiker* (Berlin, 1906); R. Richter, *Kunst und Philosophie bei R. W.* (Leipzig, 1906); H. Bélart, *F. Nietzsche und R. W.: Ihre persönlichen Beziehungen, Kunst- und Weltanschauungen* (Berlin, 1907); G. Robert, *Philosophie et drame: Essai d'une explication des drames wagnériens* (Paris, 1907); O. Schmiedel, *R. W.s religiöse Weltan schauung* (Tubingen, 1907); W. Vollert, *R. W.s Stellung zur christlichen Religion* (Wismar, 1907); L. Dauriac, *Le Musicien-poète R. W.: Étude de psychologie musicale* (Paris, 1908); G. Braschowanoff, *Von Olympia nach Bayreuth* (2 vols., Leipzig, 1911–12); F. Gross, *Die Wiedergeburt des Sehers* (Zürich, 1927); A. Drews, *Ideengehalt von W.s dramatischen Dichtungen* (Leipzig, 1931); G. Wooley, *R. W. et le symbolisme français* (Paris, 1931); F. Gross, *Der Mythos W.s* (Vienna, 1932); G. Frommel, *Der Geist der Antike bei R. W.* (Berlin, 1933); I. Wyzewska, *La Revue Wagnérienne: Essai sur l'interprétation esthétique de W. en France* (Paris, 1934); K. Karzer, *R. W. der Revolutionär gegen das 19. Jahrhundert* (1934); W. Engelsmann, *Erlösung dem Erlöser: R. W.s religiöse Weltgestalt* (Leipzig, 1936); M. Boucher, *Les Idées politiques de R. W.* (Paris, 1948; Eng. tr., N.Y., 1950); K. Overhoff, *R. W.s germanisch-christlicher Mythos* (Dinkelsbühl, 1955); B. Magee, *Aspects of W.* (London, 1968; rev. ed., 1972); M. Gregor-Dellin, *R. W.: Die Revolution als Oper* (Munich, 1973); R. Hollinrake, *Nietzsche, W. and the Philosophy of Pessimism* (London, 1982); A. Aberbach, *R. W.'s Religious Ideas: A Spiritual Journey* (Lewiston, N.Y., 1996); S. Friedrich, *Das auratische Kunstwerg: Zur ésthetik von R. W.s Musiktheater-Utopie* (Tübingen, 1996). **WAGNER AND BAYREUTH:** F. Nietzsche, *W. in Bayreuth* (Chemnitz, 1876; in Vol. I of *Nietzsches Werke*, Leipzig, 1895; new ed., 1931; Eng. tr in complete works, Edinburgh, 1910–14); H. von Wolzogen, *Grundlage und Aufgabe des Allgem. Patronalvereins zur Pflege und Erhaltung der Bühnenfestspiele in Bayreuth* (Chemnitz, 1877); K. Heckel, *Die Bühnenfestspiele in Bayreuth* (Leipzig, 1891); H. Porges, *Die Bühnenproben zu den Festspielen des Jahren 1876* (Leipzig, 1896); F. Weingartner, *Bayreuth, 1876–96* (Berlin, 1896; 2nd ed., 1904); H. Chamberlain, *Die ersten 20 Jahre der Bayreuther Bühnenfestspiele* (Bayreuth, 1896); E. Kloss, *Zwanzig Jahre Bayreuth* (Berlin, 1896; Eng. tr., London, 1896); A. Prüfer, *Die Bühnenfestspiele in Bayreuth* (Leipzig, 1899; 2nd ed., 1909, as *Das Werk von Bayreuth*; new ed., 1930, as *Tannhäuser und der Sängerkrieg auf der Wartburg*); F. Hofmann, *Bayreuth und seine Kunstdenkmale* (Munich, 1902); W. Golther, *Bayreuth* (Berlin, 1904); R. Sternfeld, *R. W. und die Bayreuth Bühnenfestspiele* (2 vols., Berlin, 1906; new ed., 1927); M. Conrad, *W.s Geist und Kunst in Bayreuth* (Munich, 1906); K. Glazenapp, *Bayreuther Briefe von R. W.* (Berlin, 1907; abr. Eng. tr. as *The Story of Bayreuth as Told in the Bayreuth Letters of R. W.*, Boston, 1912); A. Prüfer, *R. W. in Bayreuth* (Leipzig, 1910); H. von Wolzogen, *Heinrich von Steins Briefwechsel mit H. von Wolzogen: Ein Beitrag zur Geschichte des Bayreuther Gedankens* (Leipzig, 1910); H. Bahr and A. Bahr-Mildenburg, *Bayreuth und das W.-Theater* (Leipzig, 1910; 2nd ed., 1912; Eng. tr., London, 1921); R. Du Moulin-Eckart, *Wahnfried* (Leipzig, 1925); P. Bülow, *R. W. und sein Werk von Bayreuth* (Frankfurt am Main, 1927); F. Klose, *Bayreuth: Eindrücke und Erlebnisse* (Regensburg, 1929); O. Bie, *R. W. und Bayreuth* (Leipzig, 1931); J. Kneise, *Der Kampf zweier Welten um das Bayreuther Erbe* (Kassel, 1931); L. Reichwein, *Bayreuth* (Bielefeld and Leipzig, 1934); H. Brand, *Aus R. W.s Leben in Bayreuth* (Munich, 1935); S. Rützow, *R. W. und Bayreuth* (Munich, 1943; 2nd ed., 1953); J. Bertram, *Der Seher von Bayreuth* (Berlin, 1943); E. Ebermayer, *Magisches Bayreuth, Legende und Wirklichkeit* (Stuttgart, 1951); W. Wagner, ed., *R. W. und das neue Bayreuth* (Munich, 1962); G. Skelton, *W. at Bayreuth: Experiment and Tradition* (London, 1965; rev. ed., 1976); P. Turing, *New Bayreuth* (London, 1969; rev. ed., 1971); H. Barth, ed., *Der Festspielhügel: 100 Jahre Bayreuther Festspiele in einer repräsentativen Dokumentation* (Bayreuth, 1973; 2nd ed., 1976); L. Lucas, *Die Festspiel-Idee R. W.s* (Regensburg, 1973); M. Karbaum, *Studien zur Geschichte der Bayreuther Festspiele: 1876–1976* (Regensburg, 1976); R. Hartford, ed., *Bayreuth: The Early Years* (London, 1980); B. Wessling, ed., *Bayreuth im Dritten Reich: R. W.s politische Erben: Eine Dokumentation* (Weinheim, 1983); F. Spotts, *A History of the W. Festival* (New Haven, 1994). **WAGNER AS WRITER:** H. von Wolzogen, *Die Sprache in R. W.s Dichtungen* (Leipzig, 1878); J. Gautier, *R. W. et son oeuvre poétique* (Paris, 1882); B. Vogel, *W. als Dichter: Ein Überblick seines poetischen Schaffens* (Leipzig, 1889); A. Ernst, *L'Art de W.: L'OEuvre poétique* (Paris, 1893); H. Lichtenberger, *R. W., poète et penseur* (Paris, 1898; new ed., 1931; Ger. tr., Dresden, 1899 [aug. ed., 1913]); O. Lüning, *R. W. als Dichter und Denker* (Zürich, 1900); W. Golther, *R. W. als Dichter* (Berlin, 1904; Eng. tr., London, 1905); R. Weltrich, *R. W.s "Tristan und Isolde" als Dichtung: Nebst einigen allgemeinen Bemerkungen über W.s Kunst* (Berlin, 1904); E. Meinck, *Fr. Hebbels und R. W.s Nibelungen-Trilogien* (Leipzig, 1905); J. Schuler, *The Language of R. W.'s "Ring des Nibelungen"* (Lancaster, Pa., 1910); K. Reichelt, *R. W. und die englische Literatur* (Leipzig, 1912); E. von Schrenck, *R. W. als Dichter* (Munich, 1913); P. Bülow, *Die Jugendschriften R. W.s* (Leipzig, 1917); W. Ramann, *Der dichterische Stil R. W.s* (Leipzig, 1929); O. Strobel, *Skizzen und Entwürfe zur Ring-Dichtung* (Munich, 1930); H. Galli, *W. und die deutsche Klassik* (Berne, 1936); H. Garten, *W. the Dramatist* (London, 1977) **ICONOGRAPHY:** J. Grand-Carteret, *R. W. en caricatures* (Paris, 1892); E. Fuchs and E. Kreowski, *R. W. in der Karikatur* (Berlin, 1907; 6th ed., 1913); A. Vanselow, *R. W.s photographische Bildnisse* (Munich, 1908); E. Engel, *R. W.s Leben und Werke im Bilde* (2 vols., Vienna, 1913; new ed., Leipzig, 1922); J. Kapp, *R. W. Sein Leben, sein Werk, seine Welt in 260 Bildern* (Berlin, 1933); P. Bülow, *R. W.: Sein Leben in Bildern* (Leipzig, 1936); R. Bory, *R. W.: Sein Leben und sein Werk in Bildern* (Leipzig, 1938); M. Geck, *Die Bildnisse R. W.s* (Munich, 1970); W.-S. Wagner, *Die Geschichte unserer Familie in Bildern* (Munich, 1976; Eng. tr. as *The W. Family*

Albums, London, 1976); S. Weber, *Das Bild R. W.s: Ikonographische Bestandsaufnahme eines Künstlerkults* (Mainz, 1993). **MISCELLANEOUS:** C. Baudelaire, *R. W. et Tannhäuser à Paris* (Paris, 1861); W. Tappert, *W.- Lexikon: Wörterbuch der Unhöflichkeit* (Leipzig, 1877; new aug. ed. as *R. W. im Spiegel der Kritik*, 1903); *Über Schicksale und Bestimmung des W.-Museums* (Leipzig, 1892); E. Kloss, *Das W.-Museum in Eisenach, in Ein W.-Lesebuch* (Leipzig, 1904); K. Grunsky, *R. W. und die Juden* (Munich, 1921); W. Lange, *R. W. und seine Vaterstadt, Leipzig* (Leipzig, 1921); J. Marnold, *Le Cas W.: La Musique pendant la guerre* (Paris, 1920); P. Stefan, *Die Feindschaft gegen W.* (Regensburg, 1918); E. Newman, *Fact and Fiction about W.* (N.Y., 1931); E. Stemplinger, *W. in Munich* (Munich, 1933); W. Golther, *R. W.: Leben und Werke in urkundlichen Zeugnissen, Briefen, Schriften, Berichten* (Ebenhausen, near Munich, 1936); W. Lange, *R. W.s Sippe* (Leipzig, 1938); L. Weinhold, *Handschriften von R. W. in Leipzig* (Leipzig, 1938); O. Daube, *Humor bei R. W.* (Gütersloh, 1944); L. Stein, *The Racial Thinking of R. W.* (N.Y., 1950); L. Strecker, *R. W. als Verlagsgefährte* (Mainz, 1951); R. Holloway, *Debussy and W.* (London, 1979); F. Glass, *The Fertilizing Seed: W.'s Concept of the Poetic Intent* (Ann Arbor, 1983); P. Hodson, *Who's Who in W.: An A-to-Z Look at his Life and Work* (N.Y., 1984); D. Large and W. Weber, eds., *W.ism in European Culture and Politics* (N.Y., 1984); D. Scholz, *R. W.s Antisemitismus* (Würzburg, 1993); E. Voss, *W. und sein Ende: Betrachtungen und Studien* (Zürich, 1996); F. Gabriel, *R. W.: Le chant de l'inconscient* (Paris, 1998). **—NS/LK/DM**

Wagner, Wolfgang (Manfred Martin), German opera producer, son of **Siegfried (Helferich Richard) Wagner** and brother of **(Adolf) Wieland (Gottfried) Wagner;** b. Bayreuth, Aug. 30, 1919. He studied music privately in Bayreuth, then worked in various capacities at the Bayreuth Festivals and the Berlin State Opera. With his brother, Wieland Wagner, he was co-director of the Bayreuth Festivals from 1951 to 1966; after his brother's death in 1966, he was its sole director. Like his brother, he departed radically from the traditional staging of the Wagner operas, and introduced a psychoanalytic and surrealist mise en scène, often with suggestive phallic and other sexual symbols in the decor. His autobiography was publ. in both Ger. and Eng. in 1994.

BIBL.: M. Linhart, *Mit ihm, Musiktheatergeschichte: W. W. zum 75. Geburtstag: eine Ausstellung* (Tutzing, 1994). **—NS/LK/DM**

Wagner-Régeny, Rudolf, Romanian-born German composer, pedagogue, pianist, and clavichordist; b. Szász-Régen, Transylvania, Aug. 28, 1903; d. Berlin, Sept. 18, 1969. He entered the Leipzig Cons. as a piano pupil of Robert Teichmüller in 1919, and in 1920 enrolled at the Berlin Hochschule für Musik as a student in conducting of Rudolf Krasselt and Siegfried Ochs, in orchestration of Emil Rezniček, and in theory and composition of Friedrich Koch and Franz Schreker. He first gained notice as a composer with his theater pieces for Essen; in 1930 he became a naturalized German citizen, and with the rise of the Nazis was promoted by a faction of the party as a composer of the future; however, the success of his opera *Der Günstling* (Dresden, Feb. 20, 1935) was followed by his supporters' doubts regarding his subsequent output, ending in a scandal with his opera *Johanna Balk* at the Vienna State Opera (April 4, 1941). In 1942 he was drafted into the German army; after the close of World War II, he settled in East Germany; was director of the Rostock Hochschule für Musik (1947–50); then was a prof. of composition at the (East) Berlin Hochschule für Musik and at the Academy of Arts. After composing works along traditional lines, he adopted his own 12-note serial technique in 1950.

WORKS: DRAMATIC: Opera: *Sganarelle oder Der Schein trügt* (1923; Essen, March 1929); *Moschopulos* (Gera, Dec. 1, 1928); *Der nackte König* (1928; Gera, Dec. 1, 1930); *Der Günstling oder Die letzten Tage des grossen Herrn Fabiano* (1932–34; Dresden, Feb. 20, 1935); *Die Bürger von Calais* (1936–38; Berlin, Jan. 28, 1939); *Johanna Balk* (1938–40; Vienna, April 4, 1941); *Das Bergwerk zu Falun* (1958–60; Salzburg, Aug. 16, 1961). **Ballet:** *Moritat* (1928; Essen, March 1929); *Der zerbrochene Krug* (Berlin, 1937). **Other Dramatic:** *Esau und Jacob*, biblical scene for 4 Soloists, Speaker, and String Orch. (1929; Gera, 1930); *La Sainte Courtisane* for 4 Speakers and Chamber Orch. (Dessau, 1930); *Die Fabel vom seligen Schlachtermeister* (1931–32; Dresden, May 23, 1964); *Persische Episode* (1940–50; Rostock, March 27, 1963); *Prometheus*, scenic oratorio (1957–58; Kassel, Sept. 12, 1959); incidental music to 7 plays.

BIBL.: A. Burgartz, *R. W.-R.* (Berlin, 1935); T. Müller-Medek, ed., *R. W.-R.: Begegnungen, biographische Aufzeichnungen, Tagebücher und sein Briefwechsel mit Caspar Neher* (Berlin, 1968). **—NS/LK/DM**

Wagoner, Porter (Wayne), American country singer, guitarist, and songwriter; b. near West Plains, Mo., Aug. 12, 1927. Wagoner was a reliable source of country hits from the mid-1950s to the mid-1960s, many of them in the maudlin, melodramatic style of his best-known recording, "Green, Green Grass of Home." This was one of his biggest hits of the period, along with "A Satisfied Mind," "Eat, Drink, and Be Merry (Tomorrow You'll Cry)," "Misery Loves Company," "Skid Row Joe," and "The Cold Hard Facts of Life." For 20 years he hosted a syndicated television show that brought Dolly Parton to prominence. He duetted with her on 21 chart hits between 1967 and 1980, including "If Teardrops Were Pennies," "Please Don't Stop Loving Me," and "Making Plans," while also scoring such solo hits as "The Carroll County Accident" and "Big Wind."

The son of Charles and Bertha Wagoner grew up on a farm and was forced to take on much of the work early in his life when his father was stricken with arthritis. He picked up the guitar at ten. In 1943 the family lost the farm and moved into West Plains, Mo., where he held a series of menial jobs. On April 29, 1944, he married Velma Johnson, a marriage that lasted only a short time, although it apparently was never officially dissolved. On Jan. 25, 1946, he married Ruth Olive Williams, with whom he had three children; they separated in 1966 and divorced in 1986.

In 1950, Wagoner's employer, a butcher, bought time on the local radio station and had him sing and do advertisements for the store. He became a full-time entertainer when he was hired away by a station in Springfield, Mo., in September 1951. He signed to RCA Victor Records in August 1952 but was initially unable to score on the country charts, though one of his compositions, "Trademark" (music and lyrics by Porter Wagoner and Gary Walker), became a hit for Carl Smith in July 1953. Then, in October 1954, Wagoner himself entered the country charts with "Company's Comin'," which peaked in the Top Ten in January 1955. His next single, "A Satisfied Mind" (music and lyrics by Red Hayes and Jack Rhodes), hit #1 in July, and "Eat, Drink, and Be Merry (Tomorrow You'll Cry)," entered the charts in December, peaking in the Top Ten in January 1956.

Starting in 1954, Wagoner had been appearing as a regular on the Springfield-based *Ozark Jubilee* television show hosted by Red Foley. In January 1955 the show was picked up for national network broadcast, affording Wagoner much greater exposure; he stayed with it through 1956. That year, he had three country chart entries, including the Top Ten hit "What Would You Do? (If Jesus Came to Your House)." On Feb. 23, 1957, he joined the *Grand Ole Opry* radio show in Nashville. He had relatively few country chart entries in the late 1950s but bounced back in 1960 after he was hired to host a syndicated television series, *The Porter Wagoner Show*. He returned to the Top Ten in March 1961 with "Your Old Love Letters" (music and lyrics by Johnny Bond). It was the first of four consecutive country Top Ten hits through the end of 1962, the most successful of which was the chart-topping "Misery Loves Company" (music and lyrics by Jerry Reed) in March 1962.

Wagoner gained his first recognition from NARAS in 1963 when his album *The Porter Wagoner Show* was nominated for the Grammy for Best Country & Western Recording. Thereafter, he was cited primarily for his inspirational efforts on which he was accompanied by the Blackwood Brothers: they won the Grammy for Best Sacred Recording, Musical, for *Grand Old Gospel* in 1966, for Best Gospel Performance for *More Grand Old Gospel* in 1967, and again in the gospel category for *In Gospel Country* in 1969.

Wagoner scored a few more country Top Ten hits in the mid- 1960s—"Sorrow on the Rocks" (music and lyrics by Tony Moon) in 1964; "Green, Green Grass of Home" (music and lyrics by Curly Putnam) in 1965; "Skid Row Joe" (music and lyrics by Freddie Hart) in 1966; and "The Cold Hard Facts of Life" (music and lyrics by Bill Anderson) in 1967 (the last earning him Grammy nominations for Best Country & Western Recording and Best Country & Western Solo Vocal Performance, Male)—but his career really took off in September 1967 when Dolly Parton replaced Norma Jean as the female singer on his TV show and on his tours. Their duet recording, "The Last Thing on My Mind" (music and lyrics by Tom Paxton), peaked in the country Top Ten in February 1968, and they had three more country chart entries during the year, two of which made the Top Ten.

On his own, Wagoner returned to the country Top Ten at the end of 1968 with "The Carroll County Accident" (music and lyrics by Bob Ferguson), which earned him another Grammy nomination for Best Country Solo Vocal Performance, Male. He had five more songs in the country charts during 1969, three in the Top Ten—"Yours Love" and "Just Someone I Used to Know" (music and lyrics by Jack Clement) with Parton and "Big Wind" (music and lyrics by George McCormick, Wayne Walker, and Alex Zanetis) solo—which was enough to make him the most successful recording artist in country music that year.

The Wagoner-Parton partnership lasted another five years, and they scored six country Top Ten hits together, the most successful of which was "Please Don't Stop Loving Me" (music and lyrics by Dolly Parton and Porter Wagoner), which hit #1 in October 1974. "Daddy Was an Old Time Preacher Man" (1970), "Better Move It on Home" (1971), and "If Teardrops Were Pennies" (music and lyrics by Carl Butler), each of which reached the country Top Ten, earned Grammy nominations for Best Country Vocal Performance, Duo or Group. During this period Wagoner scored one major hit on his own, "What Ain't to Be, Just Might Happen" (music and lyrics by Porter Wagoner), which peaked in the country Top Ten in April 1972. Meanwhile, his television show was being broadcast by upwards of a hundred stations.

Parton left Wagoner in 1974, although the partnership produced three more Top Ten country hits, "Say Forever You'll Be Mine" (music and lyrics by Dolly Parton) and "Is Forever Longer Than Always" (music and lyrics by Porter Wagoner and F. Dycus) in 1975 and, after a financial settlement, "Making Plans" (music and lyrics by Voni Morrison and Johnny Russell) in 1980.

Wagoner performed less frequently after the mid-1970s but continued to reach the country charts through 1980, when he left RCA. In 1981 his television series came to an end after 20 years. He signed to Warner Bros. Records, for whom he recorded a couple of more country chart entries, and appeared in the 1982 film *Honky Tonk Man*. He was less active in the 1980s, but by the early 1990s he had become a fixture at the *Grand Ole Opry*, at the theme park Opryland, and on the country-music cable-TV network TNN, cohosting the show *Opry Backstage* with Bill Anderson.

DISC.: *The Thin Man from West Plains* (rec. 1951–60s); *Essential* (rec. 1950s–70s; rel. 1997).

BIBL.: S. Eng, *A Satisfied Mind: The Country Music Life of P. W.* (Nashville, 1992).—**WR**

Wahlberg, Rune, Swedish conductor, pianist, and composer; b. Gävle, March 15, 1910; d. there, Jan. 26, 1999. He received training in piano, conducting, and composition at the Stockholm Musikhögskolan (1928–35) and in conducting at the Leipzig Cons. (1936–37; diploma, 1937). He made tours as a pianist. After serving as music director of the Göteborg City Theater (1943–51), he was municipal music director in Kramfors (1953–57), Hofors (1957–64), Härnösand (1964–69), and Hudiksvall (1969–75). His music generally followed along romantic lines with expressionistic infusions.

WORKS: DRAMATIC: Opera: *En Saga* (1952). **ORCH.:** Piano Concerto (1938); 7 syms.: No. 1 (1941), No. 2 (1945), No. 3 (1951; Toronto, March 6, 1961), No. 4 (1959; Hofors, March 13, 1960), No. 5, *Havet*, for Men's Chorus and Orch. (1979), No. 6, *Episoder* (1980), and No. 7, *Jordesång* (1981); *Meditation* for Violin and Orch. (1941); *Nordic Suite* (1943); *Afrodite*, suite (1944); *Preludium, Larghetto and Fugue* (1952);

Oriental Dance (1953); Violin Concerto (1958); *Concerto barocco* for Violin and Strings (1960); Cello Concerto (1961); Bass Clarinet Concerto (1961); *Concert Suite* for Strings (1961); *Concert Fantasy* for Piano and Orch. (1967); *Lantlig Suite* for Strings (1977); *Canzone* for Violin and Orch. (1980); *Jubileumsspel* (1980); *Ett vårepos* (1981); 3 symphonic poems (1982); *Introduction and rondo giocoso* for Piano and Strings (1983); *Fantasia concertante* for 2 Violas and Orch. (1985); *Ödesmarschen* (1986); *Amoroso* for Chamber Orch. (1988–91). **CHAMBER:** *Preludium and Fugue* for String Trio (1937); Violin Sonata (1959); *Prisma* for String Quartet (1961); *Helgdagsvisa* for 4 Violins (1971); String Quartet (1972); *Lyric Fantasy* for Violin and Piano (1975); *Preludium and Largo* for Violin (1981); Trio for Violin, Cello, and Piano (1977); *Serïos dans* for Piano Trio (1981); *Två lyriska poem* for Piano Trio (1982); Cello Sonata (1983); *Preludium and Fugue* for String Quartet (1985); *Preludium and Finale* for String Quartet (1987); *Notturno* for Flute or Violin and Piano (1988); *Dance-Poem* for Clarinet and Piano (1992); many piano pieces. **VOCAL:** *Nordland* for Men's Chorus and Orch. (1957); *Florez och blanzeflor* for Men's Chorus and Orch. (1963); *Det signade landet* for Chorus, Men's Chorus, and Wind Band (1966); *Havsfuren* for Men's Chorus and Orch. (1971); *Ottesång* for Women's Chorus and String Orch. (1976); *En vårfantasi* for Chorus, Piano, and String Orch. (1993); *Sång bortom asarna* for Voice, String Quartet, and Piano (1995); *Sång bortom asarna* for Voice, String Quartet, and Piano (1995).—**NS/LK/DM**

Waissel (Waisselius), Matthäus, German lutenist and intabulator; b. Bartenstein, East Prussia, c. 1537; d. probably in Königsberg, 1602. He matriculated at the Univ. of Königsberg (1561), and received lute training during tours in Germany and Italy (1565–70). He was Rektor of the school in Schippenbeil, East Prussia (1573–74), then parish priest in Langheim, near Rastenburg (1574–87).

WORKS (all publ. in Frankfurt an der Oder): *Tablatura continens insignes et selectissimas quasque cantiones, testudini aptatas* for Lute (1573); *Tabulatura allerley künstlicher Preammbulen, auserlesener deudtscher und polnischer Tentze* for Lute (1591); *Lautenbuch, darinnen von der Tabulatur und Application der Lauten gründlicher und voller Unterricht* for Lute (1592); *Tabulatura guter gemeiner deudtscher Tentze* for 1 to 2 Lutes (1592).—**NS/LK/DM**

Waits, Tom, idiosyncatic and effective American songwriter and performer; b. Pomona, Calif., Dec. 7, 1949. Waits began his career playing in Los Angeles clubs as a singer, pianist, and guitarist, sometimes with his group, Nocturnal Emissions. After being signed by Frank Zappa's manager in 1972, he produced his first record album, *Closing Time*, in 1973. He slowly rose from cultdom to stardom through such songs as "Ol'55," "Shiver Me Timbers," "Diamonds on My Windshield," and "The Piano Has Been Drinking." Other noteworthy albums of this period include *Nighthawks at the Diner* (1975) and *Heartattack & Vine* (1980). He made a number of recordings for the Asylum label, then switched to Island. With the album *Swordfishtrombones* (1983), he expanded his accompaniment to include a broad spectrum of exotic instruments. Waits wrote the score for Francis Ford Coppola's film *One from the Heart* in 1982, and later made the concert movie *Big Time* (1987). He also collaborated with his wife, Kathleen Brennan, on the stage show *Frank's Wild Years* in 1987, which includes the pastiches "Temptation" and "Innocent When You Dream." In 1993 he created a performance work, *The Black Rider*, in collaboration with Robert Wilson and William S. Burroughs. Among artists who have performed his music are Bette Midler, Crystal Gayle, Bruce Springsteen, The Eagles, and The Manhattan Transfer. He also made frequent appearances as a film and stage actor. Waits is a jazz songwriter who regards the beatniks of the 1950s as his primary inspiration. His imaginative lyrics are full of slang and focus on the sad characters who populate cheap bars and motels. He accompanies his gravelly voice and delivery with rough instrumentation, but always with sensitive musicianship and ironic pathos.

DISC.: *Closing Time* (1973); *The Heart of Saturday Night* (1974); *Nighthawks at the Diner* (1975); *Small Change* (1976); *Foreign Affairs* (1977); *Blue Valentine* (1978); *Heartattack and Vine* (1980); *One from the Heart* (soundtrack; 1982); *Swordfishtrombones* (1983); *Raindogs* (1985); *Anthology of Tom Waits* (1985); *Franks Wild Years* (1987); *Big Time* (1988); *The Early Years* (1991); *Night on Earth* (soundtrack; 1992); *Bone Machine* (1992); *The Early Years, Vol. 2* (1993); *The Black Rider* (1993); *Beautiful Maladies: The Best of the Island Years* (1998); *Mule Variations* (1999).—**NS/LK/DM**

Wakasugi, Hiroshi, Japanese conductor; b. Tokyo, May 31, 1935. He studied conducting with Hideo Saito and Nobori Kaneko; in 1967 he was awarded a prize by the Japanese Ministry of Culture. In 1975 he became conductor of the Kyoto Sym. Orch. From 1977 to 1983 he was chief conductor of the Cologne Radio Sym. Orch.; also was Generalmusikdirektor of the Deutsche Oper am Rhein in Düsseldorf (1982–87). In 1981 he made his U.S. debut as a guest conductor of the Boston Sym. Orch. He was chief conductor of the Tonhalle Orch. in Zürich (1985–91) and the Tokyo Metropolitan Sym. Orch. (from 1987).—**NS/LK/DM**

Walaciński, Adam, Polish composer and teacher; b. Kraków, Sept. 18, 1928. He received private instruction in violin from Wacław Niemczyk (1945–46), and then studied violin with Eugenia Uminska (1947–52) and composition with Artur Malawski (1952) at the State Higher School of Music in Kraków. He then studied composition privately with Stefan Kisielewski, and later completed his training with Bogusław Schaeffer at the State Higher School of Music in Kraków (honors degree, 1974). In 1972 he joined its faculty, where he was a prof. (from 1991) and vice-rector (1993–96). In 1966 he received the State Award, 1st Class, in 1976 the City of Kraków Award, and in 1981 the Minister of Culture and Arts Award.

WORKS: ORCH.: *Composizione "Alfa"* for Strings (1958); *Horyzonty* (Horizons) for Chamber Orch. (1962); *Sequenze* (1963); *Concerto da camera* for Violin and Strings (1964; rev. 1967); *Epigramy* (Epigrams) for Chamber Orch. (1967; Kraków, April 17, 1969); *Refrains et réflexions* (1969); *Notturno 70* for 24 Strings, 3 Flutes, and Percussion (1970); *Torso* (1971; Kraków, Jan. 21, 1972); *Drama e burla* (Warsaw, Oct. 21, 1988). **CHAMBER:** String Quartet (1959); *Modyfikacje* (Modifications) for Viola and Piano (1960; Kraków, Jan. 22, 1975); *Intrada* for 7 Players (1962); *Canto tricolore* for Flute, Violin, and Vibraphone (1962); *Fogli Volanti* for String Trio (1965); *Canzona* for Viola, Prepared Piano, and Tape (1966); *Dichromia* for Flute and Piano (1967; Kraków,

June 5, 1969); *On peut écouter...* for Oboe, Clarinet, and Bassoon (1971; rev. 1997; Kraków, June 1, 1998); *Divertimento interrotto* for 13 Players (1974; Warsaw, Sept. 27, 1975); *Ballada* for Flute and Piano (1986; Kraków, March 26, 1987); *Mała muzyka jesienna* (Little Autumn Music) for Oboe and String Trio (Kraków, Oct. 27, 1986); *Pastorale* for Violin, Flute, and Oboe (Kraków, June 1992); *Fantasia sopra "Ave Maris Stella"* for Cello (Kraków, May 18, 1997); *La Vida es sueño* for Flute, Guitar, and Viola (Warsaw, Sept. 18, 1998); Duo for Viola and Cello (Kraków, May 24, 1999); *Serenata* for Oboe and String Trio (Kraków, May 24, 1999); *Girlanda* (Garland) for 8 Flutes (Kraków, April 17, 1999). **Piano:** *Rotazione* (1961); *Allaloa* for Electronically transformed Piano (1970; Bydgoszcz, Oct. 16, 1971; also with tape, Wrocław, Feb. 23, 1972); *Moments musicaux* for 2 Pianos (Kraków, March 20, 1987). **VOCAL:** *Liryka sprzed zaśnięcia* (A Lyric Before Falling Asleep) for Soprano, Flute, and 2 Pianos (Warsaw, Dec. 1963); *Microphonies* for Soprano, Actor, Clarinet, Viola, Cello, Harp, and Percussion (1974).—**NS/LK/DM**

Walcha, (Arthur Emil) Helmut, renowned German organist and pedagogue; b. Leipzig, Oct. 27, 1907; d. Frankfurt am Main, Aug. 11, 1991. Although stricken with blindness at age 16, he courageously pursued organ studies with Ramin at the Leipzig Cons. (1922–27). At 17, he made his debut in Leipzig, where he then served as asst. organist at the Thomaskirche (1926–29). In 1929 he settled in Frankfurt am Main as organist of the Friedenskirche. In 1944 he became organist at the Dreikönigskirche. In 1933 he became a teacher at the Hoch Cons. From 1938 to 1972 he was a prof. at the Hochschule für Musik. After World War II, Walcha became internationally known via his recital tours and recordings. His performances of the complete organ works of Bach were distinguished by their insightful interpretations and virtuoso execution. He also championed Bach's music on period instruments and made appearances as a harpsichordist. Walcha ed. the organ concertos of Handel and composed 25 organ chorales of his own invention.

BIBL.: W. Dehnhard and G. Ritter, eds., *Bachstunden* (Frankfurt am Main, 1978; Festschrift for W.'s 70th birthday). —**NS/LK/DM**

Walcker, Eberhard Friedrich, German organ builder; b. Cannstadt, near Stuttgart, July 3, 1794; d. Ludwigsburg, Oct. 2, 1872. Trained in the workshops of his father, Johann Eberhard Walcker (1756–1843), a skilled organ builder, he set up for himself in Ludwigsburg in 1820 and won great renown by his excellent work and numerous inventions. After his death, the business passed to his 5 sons: Heinrich (b. Oct. 10, 1828; d. Kirchheim, Nov. 24, 1903), Friedrich (b. Sept. 17, 1829; d. Dec. 6, 1895), Karl (b. March 6, 1845; d. Stuttgart, May 19, 1908), Paul (b. May 31, 1846; d. 1928), and Eberhard (b. April 8, 1850; d. 1927). In 1916, Friedrich's son Oscar Walcker (b. Ludwigsburg, Jan. 1, 1869; d. there, Nov. 4, 1948) became head of the firm; it was merged with W. Sauer of Frankfurt am Main in 1910, and then with Ziegler of Steinsfurt in 1932. His reminiscences, *Erinnerungen eines Orgelbaumeisters*, were publ. in Kassel in 1948. In 1948 his grandson, Werner Walcker-Mayer (b. Ludwigsburg, Feb. 1, 1923), took charge of the firm; its headquarters were moved to Murrhardt in 1975. Among the firm's finest instruments are those in Ulm Cathedral (1841–56; 3 manuals, 100 stops), Festival Hall, Boston (1863; 4 manuals, 89 stops), St. Stephen's, Mulhouse (1865; 3 manuals, 61 stops), Riga Cathedral (1881; 4 manuals, 122 stops), the Petrikirche, Hamburg (1884; 3 manuals, 60 stops), the old Gewandhaus, Leipzig (1884; 3 manuals, 54 stops), St. Stephen's Cathedral, Vienna (1886; 3 manuals, 90 stops), St. Michaelis, Hamburg (1909–12; 15 manuals, 163 stops), City Hall, Stockholm (1924–25; 4 manuals, 115 stops), Kongresshalle, Nuremberg (1936; 5 manuals, 220 stops), Stuttgart Radio (1951; 4 manuals, 72 stops), and the Stiftskirche, Stuttgart (1958; 4 manuals, 84 stops).

BIBL.: H. Walcker, *Das Geschlecht der W. in sechs Jahrhunderten* (Belser, 1925; 2nd ed., 1940); J. Fischer, *Das Orgelbauergeschlecht W. in Ludwigsburg* (Kassel, 1966).—**NS/LK/DM**

Waldman, Frederic, Austrian-born American conductor and teacher; b. Vienna, April 17, 1903; d. N.Y., Dec. 1, 1995. He studied piano with Richard Robert, orchestration and conducting with Szell, and composition with Weigl. After serving as music director of the Ballet Joos of the Netherlands, he was active in England from 1935 In 1941 he settled in N.Y. and was active as a piano accompanist. After teaching at the Mannes Coll. of Music, he taught at the Juilliard School of Music (1947–67), where, as music director of its Opera Theater, he conducted the American premieres of Strauss' *Capriccio* (1954) and Kodály's *Háry János* (1960). In 1961 he founded the Musica Aeterna Orch. and Chorus, which he conducted in enterprising programs of rarely heard music of the past and present eras, ranging from Monteverdi to Rieti.—**NS/LK/DM**

Waldmann, Maria, Austrian mezzo-soprano; b. Vienna, 1842; d. Ferrara, Nov. 6, 1920. She studied in Vienna with Passy-Cornet and in Milan with Lamperti, making her debut as Pierotto in *Linda di Chamounix* in Pressburg in 1865. She then sang in Wiesbaden, Amsterdam, Trieste, and Moscow (with the Italian Opera, 1869–70), at La Scala in Milan (1871–72), and in Cairo (1873–76). She retired in 1876. Verdi admired her singing, and chose her for the premiere of his Requiem. —**NS/LK/DM**

Waldrop, Gideon W(illiam), American music educator, conductor, and composer; b. Haskell County, Tex., Sept. 2, 1919; d. N.Y., May 19, 2000. He studied at Baylor Univ. (B.M., 1940) and took courses in composition with Rogers and Hanson at the Eastman School of Music in Rochester, N.Y. (M.M., 1941; Ph.D., 1952). He was conductor of the Waco-Baylor Sym. Orch. (1939–51); also was assoc. prof. at Baylor Univ. (1946–51). He served as ed. of the *Musical Courier* (1953–58) and as music consultant to the Ford Foundation (1958–61). He was assistant to the president (1961–63) and then dean (1963–85) of the Juilliard School in N.Y.; then was president of the Manhattan School of Music (1986–88).

WORKS: ORCH.: *From the Southwest,* suite (1948); Sym. No. 1 (1951); *Pressures* for Strings (1955); *Prelude and Fugue* (1962). **VOCAL:** *Songs of the Southwest* for Baritone and Chamber Orch. (1982); choral pieces; other songs. **OTHER:** Chamber music.—**NS/LK/DM**

Waldstein, Ferdinand Ernst Joseph Gabriel, Count von Waldstein und Wartenberg zu Dux, German-Bohemian amateur musician; b. Duchov, Bohemia, March 24, 1762; d. Vienna, Aug. 29, 1823. In 1787 he began his novitiate in the Teutonic Order in Ellingen, transferring to the electoral court in Bonn in 1788, where he received his order. He became acquainted with Beethoven, and on several occasions aided him materially, pretending that the sums were extra allowances from the Elector; after Beethoven's departure for Vienna, Waldstein introduced him in the circles of the aristocracy there. From 1795 he traveled widely, first in the military and later in diplomatic service. By 1812 his relations with Beethoven had cooled. In 1816 he declared bankruptcy and eventually died in poverty. Beethoven wrote a set of variations in C for Piano, 4-Hands, on a theme of Waldstein (publ. 1794), and later (1805) dedicated to him the great Sonata in C, op.53. Waldstein also planned the *Ritter-Ballet* (1791), to which Beethoven wrote the music (score publ. 1872). Waldstein composed a Sym. in D major (ed. in Denkmäler Rheinischer Musik, I, Düsseldorf, 1951).

BIBL.: J. Heer, *Der Graf von W. und sein Verhältnis zu Beethoven* (Leipzig, 1933).—**NS/LK/DM**

Waldteufel (original family surname, Lévy), (Charles-) Emile, famous French conductor and composer of light music; b. Strasbourg, Dec. 9, 1837; d. Paris, Feb. 12, 1915. His father, Louis (1801–84), and his brother, Leon (1832–84), were violinists and dance composers, and his mother was a pianist. In 1842 the family went to Paris, where he studied piano with his mother and then with Joseph Heyberger; subsequently, Waldteufal was an auditor in L.-A. Marmontel's class at the Paris Cons., where he became a pupil of A. Laurent in 1853, but left before completing his courses. He became a piano tester for the manufacturer Scholtus and also taught piano and played in soirées; when he had time, Waldteufal composed dance music for Paris salons. In 1865 he became court pianist to the Empress Eugénie and in 1866 conductor of the state balls. His first waltz, "Joies et peines," which he publ. at his own expense in 1859, was an immediate success, and he became known in Paris high society. In 1867 he publ. another successful waltz, with the German title "Vergissmeinnicht." Then followed a series of waltzes that established his fame as a French counterpart to Johann Strauss Jr.: "Manola" (1873), "Mon Rêve" (1877), "Pomone" (1877), "Toujours ou jamais" (1877), "Les Sirènes" (1878), "Très jolie" (1878), "Pluie de diamants" (1879), "Dolorès" (1880), and the most famous of them, "Les Patineurs" (1882). His dance music symbolized the "gai Paris" of his time as fittingly as the music of Johann Strauss reflected the gaiety of old Vienna. Waldteufel lived most of his life in Paris, but he also filled conducting engagements abroad, visiting London in 1885 and Berlin in 1889.

BIBL.: A. Lamb, *E. W. (1837–1915): The Parisian Waltz King* (Littlehampton, 1979); J.- P. Zeder, *Les W. et la valse française* (Strasbourg, 1980); A. Lamb, *Skaters' Waltz: The Story of the W.s* (Croydon, 1994).—**NS/LK/DM**

Walker, Alan, English musicologist; b. Scunthorpe, April 6, 1930. He was educated at the Guildhall School of Music in London (ARCM, 1949) and at the Univ. of Durham (B.Mus., 1956; D.Mus., 1965); also studied with Hans Keller (1958–60). He was prof. of harmony and counterpoint at the Guildhall School of Music (1958–60). After serving as a producer for the BBC music division (1961–71), he was chairman of the music dept. and a prof. at McMaster Univ. in Hamilton, Ontario (from 1971).

WRITINGS (all publ. in London unless otherwise given): *A Study in Musical Analysis* (1962); *An Anatomy of Musical Criticism* (1966); ed., *Frederic Chopin: Profiles of the Man and the Musician* (1966; 2nd ed., rev. and enl., 1978); ed., *Franz Liszt: The Man and His Music* (1970; 2nd ed., rev., 1976); Liszt (1971); ed., *Robert Schumann: The Man and His Music* (1972; 2nd ed., rev., 1976); *Schumann* (1976); *Franz Liszt: Vol. I, The Virtuoso Years, 1811–1847* (1983; rev. 1987); *Franz Liszt: Vol. II, The Weimar Years, 1848–1861* (1989); with G. Erasmi, *Liszt, Carolyne, and the Vatican: The Story of a Thwarted Marriage* (Stuyvesant, N.Y., 1991).

BIBL.: M. Saffle and J. Deaville, eds., *New Light on Liszt and His Music: Essays in Honor of A. W.s 65th Birthday* (Stuyvesant, N.Y., 1997).—**NS/LK/DM**

Walker, Edyth, American mezzo-soprano; b. Hopewell, N.Y., March 27, 1867; d. N.Y., Feb. 19, 1950. She studied singing with Aglaja Orgeni at the Dresden Cons. She made her debut as Fidès in *Le Prophète* at the Berlin Royal Opera on Nov. 11, 1894. She was a member of the Vienna Court Opera (1895–1903) and made her debut at London's Covent Garden as Amneris in 1900. She made her U.S. debut at the Metropolitan Opera in N.Y. (Nov. 30, 1903), remaining on its roster until 1906, singing soprano as well as mezzo-soprano roles; also sang both mezzo-soprano and soprano roles at the Hamburg Opera (1903–12); was the first London Electra (1910). After singing at the Bayreuth and Munich Festivals (1912–17), she turned to private teaching and was on the faculty of the American Cons. in Fontainebleau (1933–36) before settling in N.Y.—**NS/LK/DM**

Walker, George (Theophilus), esteemed African American composer, pianist, and teacher; b. Washington, D.C., June 27, 1922. After piano lessons with local teachers, he pursued his musical training at the Oberlin (Ohio) Coll. Cons. of Music (Mus.B., 1941). He then studied at the Curtis Inst. of Music in Philadelphia with Serkin (piano) and Scalero (composition), taking his artist diploma in both in 1945. His other mentors there included Horszowski, Primrose, Menotti, and Piatigorsky. In 1945 he won critical accolades when he made his debut as a pianist at N.Y.'s Town Hall. That same year, he became the first black instrumentalist to win the Philadelphia Orch. auditions, which resulted in his appearance as soloist in Rachmaninoff's 3rd Piano Concerto under Ormandy's direction. Further study with Casadesus earned him an artist diploma at the American Academy in Fontainebleau in 1947. He later studied at the Eastman School of Music in Rochester, N.Y., where he became the first black to earn the D.M.A. degree in 1956. In 1957 he went to France to study composition with Boulanger, and returned there in 1959 as the 1st John Hay Whitney composition fellow. He taught at Dillard Univ. in New Orleans (1953–54), the Dalcroze School of Music and the New School for Social

Research in N.Y. (1960–61), and at Smith Coll. (1961–68). After serving as a visiting prof. at the Univ. of Colo. in Boulder (1968–69), he joined the faculty of Rutgers Univ. in 1969, where he was a Distinguished Prof. and chairman of the music dept. from 1976 until his retirement in 1992. He also held the first Minority Distinguished Chair at the Univ. of Del. (1975–76) and was a teacher of piano and composition at the Peabody Inst. in Baltimore (1975–78). Among his numerous honors are 2 Guggenheim fellowships (1969, 1988), Rockefeller Foundation grants (1971, 1974), NEA grants (1971, 1975, 1978, 1984), 2 Koussevitzky Foundation grants (1988), the Pulitzer Prize in Music (1996), an American Music Center citation (1998), the Lancaster Sym. Orch. Composer's Award (1998), and membership in the American Academy of Arts and Letters (1999), as well as many commissions. In his music, Walker has utilized several compositional techniques, including serialism. In a few of his scores he has also demonstrated a deft handling of jazz infusions.

WORKS: ORCH.: *Lyric* for Strings (1946; rev. 1990; based on String Quartet No. 1); Trombone Concerto (1957; also for Trombone and Wind Ensemble, 1995); *Address* (1959; rev. 1991 and 1995); *Antifonys* (1968; also for Strings); *Variations* (1971); *Spirituals*, later renamed *Folksongs* (1974); Piano Concerto (1975); Violin Concerto (1975; rev. as *Poème* for Violin and Orch., 1991); *Dialogus* for Cello and Orch. (1975; Cleveland, April 22, 1976); *In Praise of Folly*, overture (1980); Cello Concerto (1981; N.Y., Jan. 14, 1982); *An Eastman Overture* (1983); *Serenata* for Chamber Orch. (1983); 2 sinfonias (1984, 1990); *Orpheus* for Chamber Orch. (1994; Cleveland, March 12, 1995); *Tangents* for Chamber Orch. (1999). **CHAMBER:** 2 string quartets (1946, 1968); 2 violin sonatas (1957, 1979); Cello Sonata (1957); *Perimeters* for Clarinet and Piano (1966); *Music for 3* for Violin, Cello, and Piano (1970); *5 Fancies* for Clarinet and Piano, 4-Hands (1975); *Music for Brass, Sacred and Profane* for Brass Quintet (1975); Viola Sonata (1989); *Modus* for Chamber Ensemble (1998); *Windset* for Woodwind Quintet (1999). **KEYBOARD: Piano:** *Caprice* (1940); *Prélude* (1945); 4 sonatas (1953, 1957, 1975, 1984); *Variations on a Kentucky Folksong* (1953); *Spatials* (1961); *Spektra* (1971); Sonata for 2 Pianos (1975; based on Piano Sonata No. 2); *Bauble* (1981). **Organ:** *3 Pieces* (publ. 1985); 2 *Pieces* (1996); *Spires* (1997). **VOCAL:** Mass for Soprano, Contralto, Tenor, Baritone, Chorus, and Orch. (1977; Baltimore, April 13, 1979); Cantata for Soprano, Tenor, Boy's Chorus, and Orch. (1982); *Poem* for Soprano and Chamber Ensemble (1986); *Lilacs* for Voice and Orch. (1996); choruses; songs; arrangements of spirituals.—**NS/LK/DM**

Walker, Jerry Jeff (originally, **Crosby, Ronald Clyde**); b. Oneonta, N.Y., March 14, 1942. In a diverse 1960s career, Jerry Jeff Walker started as a folk-style artist, manned a rock band called Circus Maximus, and recorded several neglected solo albums before scoring his most conspicuous success as the author of the classic "Mr. Bojangles," a near-smash hit for the Nitty Gritty Dirt Band in late 1970. Moving to Austin, Tex., in 1971, Walker became intimately involved with the area's burgeoning country- music scene, later labeled the outlaw movement. Although he never attained the success of fellow outlaws Waylon Jennings and Willie Nelson, Walker regularly recorded the compositions of Tex. songwriters such as Guy Clark and Rodney Crowell.

Jerry Jeff Walker obtained his first guitar at 13 and left home at 16 to drift around the country, eventually playing coffeehouses in the early 1960s. In 1966 he helped form Circus Maximus, which Vanguard Records promoted as a psychedelic group. Their debut album included the underground favorite "Wind" and Walker's "Fading Lady." After their second album, Walker left the group and recorded a solo album for Vanguard that was released after the modest success of his classic "Mr. Bojangles" on Atco in the summer of 1968. Popularized by N.Y.'s underground FM radio station WBAI, the song was written about a street dancer whom Walker met in a New Orleans jail. "Mr. Bojangles" ultimately became a hit for the Nitty Gritty Dirt band in 1970 and has since been recorded by dozens of other artists.

With the profits from "Mr. Bojangles," Jerry Jeff Walker retreated to Austin, Tex., in 1971. Signed to MCA Records and given artistic control over his recordings, Walker recorded his debut for the label largely in Austin, employing musicians who became the Lost Gonzo Band, his touring band until 1977. The album included his own "Hairy Ass Hillbillies" and"David and Me" and Guy Clark's "That Old Time Feeling" and "L.A. Freeway," the latter a minor hit. Becoming an integral part of the developing Austin music scene, Walker recorded *Viva Teralingua* live in 1973 in an abandoned saloon in the near-ghost town of Luckenback (immortalized by Waylon Jennings in 1977). The best-selling album of his career, it contained his own "Gettin' By" and "Sangria Wine," plus Ray Wylie Hubbard's barroom classic "Up Against the Wall, Red Neck," Guy Clark's "Desperados," and Lost Gonzo Band leader Gary P. Nunn's "London Homesick Blues," later used as the theme for the public-television music show *Austin City Limits*. After *Collectibles* (with "I Like to Sleep Late in the Morning") and *Ridin' High* (with Willie Nelson's "Pick Up the Tempo"), Walker recorded the excellent *It's a Good Night for Singin'*, which featured Tom Waits's "(Lookin' for) The Heart of Saturday Night," Billy Joe Shaver's "Old Five and Dimers," "Couldn't Do Nothin' Right" (coauthored by Walker and Nunn), and "Some Day I'll Get Out of These Bars."

Beginning in 1975, the Lost Gonzo Band attempted their own recording career, as Jerry Jeff Walker continued to record for MCA until 1978. Featuring Rodney Crowell's "Song for the Life," Rusty Wier's "Don't It Make You Wanna Dance," and "Railroad Lady," cowritten by Walker and Jimmy Buffett, Walker's *A Man Must Carry On* sold quite well. However, subsequent albums sold progressively less well, and by 1978 Walker had switched to Elektra Records, only to return to MCA in 1981.

By the late 1980s Jerry Jeff Walker was touring as a solo act. In 1986 he formed the record label Tried and True Music, with manufacture and distribution handled by Rykodisc. Walker scored three minor country hits in 1989 with "I Feel Like Hank Williams Tonight," "The Pickup Truck Song," and "Trashy Women" and enjoyed a revitalization of his career with *Live at Gruene Hall*. He played the inaugurals of Tex. Governor Ann Richards in 1991 and President Bill Clinton in 1993, and in the early

1990s hosted the music show *Texas Connection* on the Nashville cable network (TNN). In 1993 Jerry Jeff Walker recorded the sequel to *Viva Teralingua, Viva Luckenback!*

DISC.: **CIRCUS MAXIMUS:** *Circus Maximus* (1967); *Neverland Revisited* (1968). **JERRY JEFF WALKER:** *Driftin' Way of Life* (1969); *Mr. Bojangles* (1968); *Five Years Gone* (1969); *Bein' Free* (1970); *J. J. W.* (1973); *Viva Teralingua* (1973); *Walker's Collectibles* (1974); *Ridin' High* (1975); *It's a Good Night for Singin'* (1976); *A Man Must Carry On* (1977); *Contrary to Ordinary* (1978); *Best* (1980); *Jerry Jeff* (1978); *Too Old to Change* (1979); *Reunion* (1981); *Cowjazz* (1982); *Great Gonzos* (1991); *Mr. Bojangles* (1982); *Gypsy Songman* (1988); *Live at Gruene Hall* (1989); *Navajo Rug* (1991); *Hill Country Rain* (1992); *Viva Luckenback!* (1993). **THE LOST GONZO BAND:** *The Lost Gonzo Band* (1975); *Thrills* (1976); *Signs of Life* (1978); *Rendezvous* (1992).—**BH**

Walker, Penelope, English mezzo-soprano; b. Manchester, Oct. 12, 1956. She studied at the Guildhall School of Music and Drama in London (1974–78) and the National Opera Studio (1978–80), and received vocal instruction in Munich from Fassbaender and in Paris from Souzay. In 1976 she made her concert debut at London's Royal Albert Hall. After winning the Kathleen Ferrier Prize in 1980, she made her operatic debut at the Paris Opéra-Comique in 1982. Her London operatic debut followed in 1983 as Pacini's Maria Tudor with Opera Rara. In 1985 she sang Sosostris in *The Midsummer Marriage* at the English National Opera in London. She portrayed Fricka in the *Ring* cycle at the Welsh National Opera in Cardiff in 1986. In 1989 she made her first appearance at the London Promenade Concerts singing Grimgerde in *Die Walküre*. In 1991 she was engaged at the Zürich Opera. She appeared as Grimgerde at the Théâtre du Châtelet in Paris in 1994, and also sang at Milan's La Scala and at London's Covent Garden. In 1996 she portrayed Handel's Riccardo Primo at the Göttingen Festival. Her concert engagements have taken her to many European music centers. She married **Phillip Joll**.—**NS/LK/DM**

Walker, Robert (Ernest), English composer; b. Northampton, March 18, 1946. He was a chorister at St. Matthew's Church in Northampton and a choral and then organ scholar at Jesus Coll., Cambridge (1965–68; M.A., 1968). After serving as an organist and schoolmaster in Lincolnshire, he devoted himself to composing, teaching, and broadcasting.

WORKS: **ORCH.:** *Pavan* for Violin and Orch. (Eltham Palace, June 26, 1975); *At Bignor Hill* (Lisbon, April 9, 1979); Chamber Sym. No. 1 (1981; Greenwich, June 15, 1982); *Variations on a Theme of Elgar* (Chichester, July 13, 1982); *Charms and Exultations of Trumpets* (1985; Salisbury, April 2, 1986); Sym. No. 1 (Exeter, May 26, 1987). **CHAMBER:** String Quartet No. 1 (1982); *Gonfalons* for 4 Trumpets, 4 Trombones, Organ, and Optional Unison Chorus (1983); Piano Quintet (1984); *Serenade* for Flute, Harp, Violin, Viola, and Cello (1987). **Piano:** *Five Capriccios*, Set 1 (1982) and Set 2 (1985); *Passacaglia* for 2 Pianos (1984). **VOCAL:** *Requiem* for Tenor, Chorus, and Orch. (1976); *Canticle of the Rose* for Soprano, Baritone, Chorus, and Orch. (1980); *The Sun Used to Shine* for Tenor, Harp, and String Orch. (1983); *Magnificat and Nunc Dimittis* for Chorus and Organ (1985); *Missa Brevis* for Chorus and Organ (1985); *Singer by the Yellow River* for Soprano, Flute, and Harp (1985); *Jubilate* for Chorus and Brass Quintet (1987); *English Parody Mass* for Chorus and Organ (1988); *Journey into Light*, choral sym. (1992); also various unaccompanied vocal pieces.—**NS/LK/DM**

Walker, Sarah, English mezzo-soprano; b. Cheltenham, March 11, 1943. She studied violin with A. Brosa, cello with H. Philips, and voice with R. Packer and V. Rozsa at the Royal Coll. of Music in London (1961–65). In 1969 she made her operatic debut as Monteverdi's Ottavia with the Kent Opera, and then sang Diana and Jove in Cavalli's *Calisto* at the Glyndebourne Festival in 1970. In 1972 she became a member of the Sadler's Wells Opera in London, and continued to appear there after it became the English National Opera in 1974. She appeared as Magdalene in *Die Meistersinger von Nürnberg* in Chicago in 1977. In 1979 she made her debut at London's Covent Garden as Charlotte. In 1981 she sang Berlioz's Dido in Vienna. On Feb. 3, 1986, she made her Metropolitan Opera debut in N.Y. as Micah in Handel's *Samson*. In 1987 she created the role of Caroline in the British premiere of Sallinen's *The King Goes Forth to War* at Covent Garden. As a concert artist, she appeared throughout Europe and North America. In 1991 she was made a Commander of the Order of the British Empire. —**NS/LK/DM**

Wallace, John, Scottish trumpeter; b. Fife, April 14, 1949. He studied at King's Coll., Cambridge, the Royal Academy of Music in London, and the Univ. of York. In 1976 he became principal trumpet in the Philharmonia Orch. in London, a position he held until 1995. During this period, he also garnered wide recognition via solo appearances with it and many other orchs. of the world. In 1986 he founded the Wallace Collection, an ensemble devoted to the performance of the vast brass repertoire. He toured widely with it, making his first visit to the U.S. in 1993. In addition to the standard literature for his instrument, Wallace has introduced various modern scores, including concertos by Sir Malcolm Arnold (1981), Sir Peter Maxwell Davies (1988), and Tim Souster (1988).—**NS/LK/DM**

Wallace, Lucille, American-born English harpsichordist and pianist; b. Chicago, Feb. 22, 1898; d. London, March 21, 1977. She studied at the Bush Cons. in Chicago (B.Mus.), attended Vassar Coll., took courses in music history with Adler at the Univ. of Vienna (1923–24), and was a student of Boulanger and Landowska in Paris, and of Schnabel in Berlin. She became principally known as an accomplished harpsichordist, winning esteem as an interpreter of Domenico Scarlatti and Couperin. In 1931 she married **Clifford Curzon**.—**NS/LK/DM**

Wallace, Stewart (Farrell), prominent American composer; b. Philadelphia, Nov. 21, 1960. He studied literature and philosophy at the Univ. of Tex. at Austin (B.A. with special honors, 1982), and composed his first opera as his thesis. However, he was autodidact in composition. He received various awards and fellowships, and also a MacDowell Colony residency, a Yaddo residency, and a Rockefeller Foundation residency in Bellagio, Italy. In 1998 he was one of the principal figures at the new Inst. on the Arts and Civic Dialogue at Harvard Univ. Wallace has demonstrated a particular flair for dramatic composition. His theater scores reveal an imaginative eclecticism that draws upon elements ranging from high art to pop culture. He first attracted widespread notice with his zany opera *Where's Dick?* (Houston, May 24, 1989), which was later transformed into the first feature-length animated opera. It was followed by his opera *Kabbalah* (N.Y., Nov. 14, 1989), the subject of which is Jewish mysticism. His *Harvey Milk* (Houston, Jan. 21, 1995), an operatic treatment of the murders of San Francisco mayor George Moscone and city supervisor Harvey Milk by disgruntled ex-city supervisor Dan White, earned Wallace critical encomiums in the U.S. and abroad. He followed this opera with *Hopper's Wife* (Long Beach, Calif., June 14, 1997), a sexually charged treatment of the American painter Edward Hopper. His subsequent scores include *Yiddisher Teddy Bears* (1999), a "punk-klezmer" opera, and *High Noon* (2000), a "gun" opera. Among his other scores are *Gorilla in a Cage* for Percussion and Orch. (1997), *Kaddish for Harvey Milk* for 3 Soloists, Chorus, and Orch. (1997), *The Cheese and the Worms* for Percussion and Piano (1999), and the film score *Afraid of Everything* (1999).—**NS/LK/DM**

Wallace, William, Scottish composer, physician, classical scholar, writer, teacher, and painter; b. Greenock, July 3, 1860; d. Malmesbury, Wiltshire, Dec. 16, 1940. He studied medicine at the Univ. of Glasgow (M.B. and M.Ch., 1885), and then pursued training in ophthalmology in Vienna, Paris, and Moorfields before returning to Glasgow to take his M.D. (1888). His interest in music led him to enter the Royal Academy of Music in London in 1889, where he remained for only two terms. He thus was mainly autodidact in composition. With Bantock, he was active with the *New Quarterly Musical Review* (1893–96) but also devoted much time to composition. From 1911 to 1913 he was honorary secretary of the Phil. Soc. of London. During World War I (1914–18), he served in the Royal Army Medical Corps, from which he retired with the rank of Captain in 1919. In later years he was a prof. of harmony and composition at the Royal Academy of Music. Wallace was married to the sculptress Ottilie Helen McLaren, daughter of Lord McLaren. His symphonic poem *The Passing of Beatrice* (1892) is generally acknowledged as the first such work in the genre written by a British composer. He also wrote 5 other symphonic poems, as well as a remarkable *Creation Symphony*. His output, while not large, reflects a lively imagination and a craftsmanship in writing for the orch.

WORKS: DRAMATIC: Opera: *Brassolis*. **ORCH.:** *The Lady from the Sea*, after Ibsen (1892); 6 symphonic poems: *The Passing of Beatrice*, after Dante (1892), *Amboss oder Hammer*, after Goethe (1896), *Sister Helen*, after D.G. Rossetti (1899), *To the New Century* (1901), *Sir William Wallace*, after Robert Burns (London, Sept. 19, 1905), and *Villon* (London, March 1909); *Prelude to the Eumenides of Aeschylus* (London, Oct. 21, 1893); *Creation Symphony* (1896–99); *Pelléas et Mélisande*, after Maeterlinck (Brighton, Aug. 19, 1900). **OTHER:** *Koheleth*, choral sym.; *The Massacre of the MacPhersons*, choral ballad; cantatas; songs; chamber music; *A Suite in the Olden Style* for Piano.

WRITINGS: *The Threshold of Music: An Inquiry into the Development of the Musical Sense* (1908); *The Musical Faculty: Its Origins and Processes* (1914); *Richard Wagner as He Lived* (1925); *Liszt, Wagner and the Princess* (1927).—**NS/LK/DM**

Wallace, (William) Vincent, Irish violinist, organist, and composer; b. Waterford, March 11, 1812; d. Château de Bagen, Haute- Garonne, France, Oct. 12, 1865. The son of a bandmaster, Wallace was brought up in a musical atmosphere. He was 13 when the family moved to Dublin. He soon entered a professional career, playing violin in theater orchs. and organ in churches. One of his earliest compositions was *The Harp in the Air*, which later became famous when he incorporated it into his opera *Maritana*. In 1831 he married Isabella Kelly. He applied himself to the study of violin, and subsequently was able to give successful concerts. With his wife he traveled in Australia, South America, Mexico, and the U.S. Returning to Europe in 1844, he toured Germany; in 1845 he was in London, where he produced his opera *Maritana* (Drury Lane, Nov. 15, 1845), which obtained excellent success; it was followed by another opera, *Matilda of Hungary* (Drury Lane, Feb. 2, 1847), which was a failure. About 1850 he "married" the American pianist Hélène Stoepel, declaring his first marriage invalid; she made appearances as Mrs. Wallace from 1851. From 1850 to 1853 he visited South and North America. His other operas include *Lurline* (1847; Covent Garden, Feb. 23, 1860), *The Maid of Zürich* (unpubl.), *The Amber Witch* (Haymarket, Feb. 28, 1861), *Love's Triumph* (Covent Garden, Nov. 3, 1862), and *The Desert Flower* (Covent Garden, Oct. 12, 1863); he also wrote the opera *Estrella* (unfinished) and the operettas *Gulnare* and *Olga*. Other works include the cantata *Maypole*, a Violin Concerto, and numerous piano pieces.

BIBL.: A. Pougin, *W.V. W.: Étude biographique et critique* (Paris, 1866); W. Flood, *W.V. W.: A Memoir* (Waterford, 1912); R. Phelan, *W.V. W.: A Vagabond Composer* (Waterford, Ireland, 1994).—**NS/LK/DM**

Wallat, Hans, German conductor; b. Berlin, Oct. 18, 1929. He was educated at the Schwerin Cons. and then conducted in several provincial German music centers. He was music director in Cottbus (1956–58) and 1st conductor of the Leipzig Opera (1958–61); he then conducted in Stuttgart (1961–64) and at the Deutsche Oper in West Berlin (1964–65). He was Generalmusikdirektor at the Bremen Opera (1965–70). Wallat made appearances as a guest conductor with various opera houses and orchs. in Europe. On Oct. 7, 1971, he made his Metropolitan Opera debut in N.Y. conducting *Fidelio*. He was Generalmusikdirektor in Mannheim (1970–80), in Dortmund (1980–85), and of the Deutsche Oper am Rhein in Düsseldorf (1987–97).—**NS/LK/DM**

Wallberg, Heinz, German conductor; b. Herringen-Hamm, March 16, 1923. He studied at the Dortmund Cons. and the Cologne Hochschule für Musik. After pursuing a career as a trumpeter and violinist, he turned to conducting; was Generalmusikdirektor in

Wiesbaden (1961–74) and chief conductor of the Vienna Niederösterreichisches Tonkünstler-Orch. (1964–75). Subsequently, he was music director of the Munich Radio Orch. (1975–82) and of the Essen Phil. (1975–91). In 1991 he made his U.S. debut as a guest conductor with the National Sym. Orch. in Washington, D.C.

Bibl.: J. Glauber and W. Mämpel, *H. W.* (Düsseldorf, 1997). **—NS/LK/DM**

Wallek-Walewski, Boleslaw, Polish conductor, pedagogue, and composer; b. Lemberg, Jan. 23, 1885; d. Kraków, April 9, 1944. He studied theory and composition with Soltys and Niewiadomski and piano with Maliszowa and Zelinger in Lemberg; he then continued his training with Żeleński and Szopski at the Kraków Cons. and completed his studies with Riemann and Prüfer in Leipzig. He became a prof. (1910) and director (1913) of the Kraków Cons. He was founder-conductor of his own choral society, and also appeared as an operatic and sym. conductor. His compositions followed along Romantic lines.

Works: **Dramatic:** **Opera:** *Pan Twardowski* (1911; Kraków, 1915); *Dola* (Lot; Kraków, 1919); *Pomsta Jontkowa* (1926); *Legenda o królewnie Wandzie* (The Legend of the King's Daughter Wanda; 1936). **Orch.:** 2 symphonic poems: *Pawel i Gawel* (1908) and *Zygmunt August i Barbara* (1912). **Vocal:** Oratorios; cantatas; songs.**—NS/LK/DM**

Wallen, Errollyn, versatile English composer and formidable pianist; b. Belize City, Belize, April 10, 1958. After studies at Goldsmiths' and King's Coll., Univ. of London, where she took her masters degree, Wallen worked as a performer and composer in pop, jazz, and classical settings. She also set up her own recording studio and wrote for film, television, and radio. She wrote and presented *The Music Machine,* a youth program for BBC Radio 3 (April 1994), and also contributed to *Backtracks,* a series for London's Channel 4 about music composition for film. She formed Ensemble X, comprised of players from pop, jazz, and classical worlds, to perform her music. Her music has been recorded and broadcast throughout Europe, Africa, and Australia. Wallen has worked with a variety of artists across genres, including Courtney Pine, Juliet Roberts, Peter Gabriel, and Claudia Brucken. Her output ranges from large orchestral works to choral compositions and string quartets, from ballets and operas to pop songs. Among her remarkably eclectic compositions are *In our Lifetime* (1992), a ballet in celebration of Nelson Mandela's release from prison, choreographed by Christopher Bruce for London's Contemporary Dance Theatre, *Waiting,* a ballet (1993), *Concerto for Percussion and Orchestra* (1994, a BBC commission), *LOOK! NO HANDS!,* opera (1996), to a libretto by Cindy Owens, presented at the Nottingham Concert Series in a program devoted entirely to her work, *Hunger* (1997), a large-scale instrumental work, and *Meet Me at Harold Moore's* (1998), her first impeccably produced solo album. Other works include *Music for Alien Tribes* for Voice, Violin, Electric Keyboard, and Tape (1996; in collaboration with Gerald Simpson), *Never Ending* for Voice and Piano (1997); *One Week Short of a Valentine* for Mezzo-soprano, Flute, Cello, Piano, and Double Bass (1997); *The Devil and the Doctor* for Voice, Strings, and Piano (1997); *Benediction* for Women's Chorus (1998); *Oil* for Voice, Electronics, and Electric Bass (1998); *The Warm and The Cold* for Baritone and Piano, after Ted Hughes (1998); and *Courtly Love* for Mezzo-soprano and Piano (1998).**—LK/DM**

Wallenstein, Alfred, American cellist and conductor; b. Chicago, Oct. 7, 1898; d. N.Y., Feb. 8, 1983. His parents were of German and Austrian extraction, and Wallenstein believed that he was a direct descendant of Albrecht von Wallenstein, the illustrious leader of the Thirty Years' War. The family moved to Los Angeles in 1905, where Wallenstein took cello lessons with the mother of Ferde Grofé. As a young boy, Wallenstein played in hotels and movie theaters; he also gave public recitals advertised as "the wonder-boy cellist." He played with the San Francisco Sym. Orch. (1916–17), and subsequently toured in South America with the troupe of Anna Pavlova, being featured as cello soloist to accompany her famous portrayal of the dying swan. In 1919 he became a member of the Los Angeles Phil. In 1920 he studied cello with Julius Klengel in Leipzig. He was a cellist in the Chicago Sym. Orch. (1922–29) and also appeared with it as a soloist; from 1927 to 1929 he was head of the cello dept. of the Chicago Musical Coll. In 1929 Toscanini engaged him as 1st cellist with the N.Y. Phil.; it was Toscanini who urged Wallenstein to try his hand at conducting. Wallenstein began his conducting career by leading classical programs over the radio. In 1933 he formed the Wallenstein Sinfonietta, giving regular Sunday broadcasts; an important feature was a series of performances of Bach's cantatas. He also programmed numerous premieres of works by contemporary composers. After Toscanini resigned as music director of the N.Y. Phil. in 1936, Wallenstein also left his job as first cellist of the orch. and devoted himself exclusively to radio performances and guest conducting. In 1943 he was named conductor of the Los Angeles Phil.; he was also director of the Hollywood Bowl (1952–56). In 1956 he made a tour of the Orient with the Los Angeles Phil. under the auspices of the State Dept.; after this tour he resigned as its conductor and subsequently made appearances as a guest conductor. In 1968 he joined the faculty of the Juilliard School of Music in N.Y. as instructor in conducting. In 1979, at the age of 81, he made his last public appearance as a conductor, leading the Juilliard School Orch. in N.Y. Wallenstein never pretended to be a glamorous virtuoso of the baton, but he was a master builder of orch. organizations. More in praise than in dispraise, he was described as a "vertical" conductor who offered dispassionate rather than impassionate interpretations, but no one doubted his selfless devotion to music and musicians. **—NS/LK/DM**

Waller, Fats (Thomas Wright), comical African American keyboard player, composer, and singer; b. N.Y., May 21, 1904; d. Kansas City, Dec. 15, 1943. Waller emerged from the stride-piano-playing tradition to achieve success in several musical forms. He was a widely respected jazz instrumentalist on piano and organ; he composed music for three Broadway shows and many hit songs, among them "Ain't Misbehavin'," "Honeysuckle Rose," and "Black and Blue"; he was among the most successful recording artists of the 1930s, scoring 23 Top Ten hits between 1934 and 1940, including "A Little Bit Independent," "All My Life," "Two Sleepy People," and "I'm Gonna Sit Right Down and Write Myself a Letter"; and his engaging, humorous personality was displayed onstage, on film, and in concerts.

Waller's parents were Edward Martin and Adeline Lockett Waller. His father was a preacher; his mother was a keyboard player, and he learned piano, harmonium, and organ at a young age. He left high school in the spring of 1918 and was hired as the organist at the Lincoln Theatre. In 1919 he wrote his first tune, "Boston Blues," which became "Squeeze Me" when Clarence Williams added lyrics to it several years later.

When Waller's mother died in November 1920, he moved in with the family of the pianist Russell Brooks, who introduced him to famed stride pianist James P. Johnson. He studied with Johnson and also later claimed to have taken lessons from pianist Leopold Godowsky and to have studied composition with Carl Bohm of the Juilliard School of Music. Around this time he married Edith Hatchett, and the couple had a son, Thomas Waller Jr. However, Waller and Hatchett separated and divorced within a few years. Waller married Anita Rutherford in 1926, and they had two sons, Maurice and Ronald. Each of Waller's sons became a musician.

Waller made his first solo recordings, "Muscle Shoals Blues" and "Birmingham Blues," on Oct. 21, 1922. By the mid-1920s he was recording and performing onstage and on the radio while writing songs and contributing to revues in Harlem. *Keep Shufflin'* (N.Y., Feb. 27, 1928) was an all-black revue that ran on Broadway for 104 performances; Waller and James P. Johnson wrote the music and played piano in the pit orchestra.

Waller broke through to success as a composer in 1929, primarily with his tunes from the all-black Broadway revue *Hot Chocolates* (N.Y., June 20, 1929), which ran for 228 performances and introduced his most popular songs. "Ain't Misbehavin'" (music also by Harry Brooks, lyrics by Andy Razaf) earned many recordings, the most successful of which was the one by Leo Reisman and His Orch., though Waller's own instrumental treatment was popular and later was inducted into the Grammy Hall of Fame. The score also contained "Black and Blue" (music also by Harry Brooks, lyrics by Andy Razaf) and "Honeysuckle Rose" (lyrics by Andy Razaf), both of which became standards. In August 1929, Gene Austin scored a hit with Waller's "I've Got a Feeling I'm Falling" (music also by Harry Link, lyrics by Billy Rose); Waller played piano on the recording. The song became his first to be featured in a motion picture when Helen Morgan sang it in *Applause*, released in October.

During the Depression years of the early 1930s, Waller continued to enjoy occasional success as a songwriter. "Rollin' Down the River" (lyrics by Stanley Adams), written for a revue at the nightclub Connie's Inn in Harlem, became a hit for Guy Lombardo and His Royal Canadians in July 1930; "Keepin' Out of Mischief Now" (lyrics by Andy Razaf), a song patterned after "Ain't Misbehavin'," was a hit for Louis Armstrong in June 1932; and "Honeysuckle Rose" was revived by Fletcher Henderson for a hit in February 1933. Meanwhile, Waller's primary outlet as a performer was radio, as he appeared regularly on such shows as *Paramount on Parade* (1930–31); *Radio Roundup* (1931–32); and, from station WLW in Cincinnati, *Fats Waller's Rhythm Club* (1932–34).

In May 1934, Waller began a series of recordings for RCA Victor backed by a quintet under the name Fats Waller and His Rhythm. It was with these recordings, along with frequent appearances on the CBS radio network, that he established himself as a singer and personality, while his composing and instrumental skills were less emphasized. The approach led to a string of hits. In 1934 he scored in June with "I Wish I Were Twins" (music by Joseph Meyer, lyrics by Frank Loesser and Eddie DeLange); in September with "Then I'll Be Tired of You" (music by Arthur Schwartz, lyrics by E. Y. Harburg); and in October with "Don't Let It Bother You" (music by Harry Revel, lyrics by Mack Gordon) and "Sweetie Pie" (music and lyrics by John Jacob Loeb). Also in October, he had a minor hit with his own composition "How Can You Face Me?" [lyrics by Andy Razaf].

In 1935, Waller continued to score frequent hits, including "Believe It, Beloved" (music by J. C. Johnson, lyrics by George Whiting and Nat Schwartz) in January; "I Believe in Miracles" (music by George W. Meyer and Pete Wendling, lyrics by Sam M. Lewis) in February; "Lulu's Back in Town" (music by Harry Warren, lyrics by Al Dubin) in July; "Truckin'" (music by Rube Bloom, lyrics by Ted Koehler) in August; and "Rhythm and Romance" (music by J. C. Johnson, lyrics by George Whiting and Nat Burton) in September. His most successful recording of the year was "A Little Bit Independent" (music by Joe Burke, lyrics by Edgar Leslie), which reached the top of the hit parade in December. Waller appeared in two 1935 films, *Hooray for Love*, released in July, and *King of Burlesque*, which opened in December.

Waller's hot streak extended through the middle of 1936, including such Top Ten hit parade entries as "I'm Gonna Sit Right Down and Write Myself a Letter" (music by Fred E. Ahlert, lyrics by Joe Young) in February; "West Wind" (music and lyrics by Milton Ager, Charles Newman, and Murray Mencher) in March; "All My Life" (music by Sam H. Stept, lyrics by Sidney Mitchell) in April; "It's a Sin to Tell a Lie" (music and lyrics by Billy Mayhew) in May; "Let's Sing Again" (music by Jimmy McHugh, lyrics by Gus Kahn) and "Cross Patch" (music by Vee Lawnhurst, lyrics by Tot Seymour) in July; and "You're Not the Kind" (music and lyrics by Will Hudson and Irving Mills) and "Bye, Bye, Baby" (music by Lou Handman, lyrics by Walter Hirsch) in August.

With the onset of the Swing Era in the second half of the 1930s, Waller's music became less fashionable, but he still was able to reach the hit parade at least once a year through the end of the decade, with "You're Laughing at Me" (music and lyrics by Irving Berlin) in March 1937; "I Love to Whistle" (music by Jimmy McHugh, lyrics by Harold Adamson) in April 1938; "Two Sleepy People" (music by Hoagy Carmichael, lyrics by Frank Loesser) in November 1938; "Good for Nothing" (music by Jimmy Van Heusen, lyrics by Eddie DeLange) in March 1939; and "Little Curly in a High Chair" (music by Nat Simon, lyrics by Charles Tobias) in June 1940.

Waller continued to tour during this period, performing in Europe from July to October 1938 and from March to June 1939. For a time in the early 1940s he acceded to current trends and led a big band. He scored his final hit as a recording artist in November 1942 with his own organ instrumental "The Jitterbug Waltz," which reached the Top Ten on the R&B charts.

Waller wrote the music for the Broadway musical *Early to Bed* (June 17, 1943), which, with a run of 380 performances, was his most successful show during his lifetime. He appeared in the all-black movie musical *Stormy Weather*, released in July 1943, performing his signature song, "Ain't Misbehavin'." He was on a train returning from Los Angeles to N.Y. after a club engagement in Hollywood when he succumbed to pneumonia in December at the age of 39.

"Ain't Misbehavin'," Waller's most popular song, was heard frequently in the years immediately after his death. It turned up in the August 1944 film *Atlantic City* and again in the film *You Were Meant for Me* in January 1948. In March 1948, Dinah Washington scored a Top Ten R&B hit with a revival of the song, which was also used in the films *Rainbow 'round My Shoulder* (1952), *Gentlemen Marry Brunettes* (1955), and, of course, *Ain't Misbehavin'* (1955).

A major Waller revival in the 1970s kicked off with Waller's co-scoring credit for the avant-garde film *Eraserhead* (1976). The Broadway revue *Bubbling Brown Sugar* (N.Y., March 2, 1976) used some Waller music, and a second revue, *Ain't Misbehavin'* (N.Y., May 8, 1978), was devoted to his songs; it ran 1,604 performances and that spawned a charted cast album. Waller was taken up by country musicians in the 1980s: Willie Nelson starred in a movie called *Honeysuckle Rose* in 1981 (though he did not perform the song on the soundtrack), and in 1986 Hank Williams Jr. revived "Ain't Misbehavin'" for a #1 country hit. Waller returned to Broadway with selections from another long-running all-black revue, *Black and Blue* (N.Y., Jan. 26, 1989).

BIBL.: J. Davies, *The Music of T "F." W.* (London, 1950; rev. ed., 1953); C. Fox, *F. W.* (London, 1960); W. Kirkeby (his last manager), D. Schiedt, and S. Traill, *Ain't Misbehavin': The Story of F. W.* (N.Y., 1966); J. Vance, *F. W.: His Life & Times* (Chicago, 1977); M. Waller (his son) and A. Calabrese, *F. W.* (N.Y., 1977); H. Sill, *Misbehavin' with F.: A Toby Bradley Adventure* (1978); W. Balliett, *Jelly Roll, Jabbo and F.* (N.Y., 1983); P. Machlin, *Stride: The Music of F. W.* (Boston, 1985); A. Shipton, *F. W.: His Life & Times* (N.Y., 1989); L. Wright, *"F." in Fact* (1992).—**WR**

Wallfisch, Raphael, English cellist and teacher; b. London, June 15, 1953. He commenced cello playing at age 8, and later studied with Amaryllis Fleming in London (1966–69), Amadeo Baldovino in Rome (1969), Derek Simpson at the Royal Academy of Music in London (1969–72), and with Gregor Piatigorsky in Los Angeles (1972–74); won 1st prize in the Gaspar Cassadó competition in Florence in 1977. He made his formal debut as soloist in the Schumann Cello Concerto with the English Chamber Orch. in London in 1974; subsequently appeared as a soloist with major orchs. on both sides of the Atlantic, and also gave recitals and played in chamber music settings. In 1980 he became a prof. at the Guildhall School of Music in London. His repertoire includes some 60 concertos, ranging from early scores to contemporary works, as well as numerous solo and chamber music pieces.—**NS/LK/DM**

Wallington, George, Italian pianist; b. Palermo, Sicily, Italy, Oct. 27, 1924, d. N.Y., Feb. 15, 1993. He was the son of an opera singer and immigrated to the United States with his family just prior to his first birthday. His earliest work of considerable merit was as part of the Dizzy Gillespie group, the first bebop combo to play on N.Y.'s famed 52nd Street. Through the mid-1950s, he worked with an impressive number of jazz luminaries, including Charlie Parker, Red Rodney, Zoot Sims, Gerry Mulligan, Serge Chaloff, Kai Winding, and Terry Gibbs. He would also form and lead his own quintet that featured up-and-comers of the time trumpeter Donald Byrd and altoist Phil Woods, making several consummate albums for the Prestige label prior to the end of the decade. Any one of these recordings will reveal the great fluidity and technical expertise that marked his archetypal playing. A cerebral musician in some ways, he nonetheless played with a great deal of swing and joyful exuberance. A sad loss for jazz fans, he left the music scene in 1960 to labor in his family's business, only returning briefly in the mid-1980s to record three albums. His death in 1993 cut short any chances of further musical activity and possible rediscovery by a new generation of jazz listeners and followers.

DISC.: *The George Wallington Trios* (1949); *Live at the Cafe Bohemia* (1955); *Jazz for the Carriage Trade* (1956); *The New York Scene* (1957); *Jazz at Hotchkiss* (1957); *Pleasure of a Jazz Inspiration* (1985).—**CH**

Walliser, Christoph Thomas, important Alsatian composer; b. Strasbourg, April 17, 1568; d. there, April 26, 1648. After attending the Protestant Gymnasium in Strasbourg, he pursued his training in the liberal arts and sciences in Bohemia, Hungary, Italy, Switzerland, and Germany. Upon his return to Strasbourg in 1598, he was made musicus ordinarius at the Gymnasium; he also was active at the Thomaskirche (from 1600). With the coming of the Thirty Years' War, he lost his post at the Gymnasium (1634) and spent his last years in poverty. He was the foremost Alsatian composer of his time, excelling particularly in music for the church.

WORKS (all publ. in Strasbourg unless otherwise given): *Teutsche Psalmen* for 5 Voices (Nuremberg, 1602); *Hexastichon* for 6 Voices (Liegnitz, 1610); *Choris musici...in Andromeda Tragoedia* for 3 to 6 Voices (1612); *In festum nativitatis Domini* for 5 Voices

(1613); *Ecclesiodiae* for 4 to 6 Voices (1614); *Te Deum laudamus* for 6 Voices (1617); *Ecclesiodiae novae* for 4 to 7 Voices (1625); *Herrn Wilhelmus Salusten von Bartas Triumph des Glaubens* for 5 Voices (1627); *Chorus musicus...D. Leopoldo Austria Archduci* for 3 Voices (1628); *Fons Israelis* for 8 Voices (1641); also motets in contemporary collections, and madrigals.

BIBL.: U. Klein, *C.T. W. (1568–1648): Ein Beitrag zur Musikgeschichte Strassburgs* (diss., Univ. of Tex., 1964). **—NS/LK/DM**

Walmisley, Thomas Attwood, English organist, teacher, and composer, son of **Thomas Forbes Walmisley;** b. London, Jan. 21, 1814; d. Hastings, Jan. 17, 1856. He studied composition with his godfather, Thomas Attwood, and at 16 became organist at Croydon Parish Church. In 1833 he received the combined organistships of Trinity and St. John's Colleges, Cambridge, obtaining his Mus.B. from the former that same year. He matriculated at Corpus Christi Coll. (1834). While still an undergraduate, he was appointed prof. of music in 1836. He received the B.A. degree and became a full member of Trinity Coll. in 1838; he took his M.A. in 1841 and his Mus.D. in 1848. Walmisley distinguished himself as an organist and teacher. As a composer, he is best known for his Evening Service in D minor (c. 1855). His other works include anthems, part-songs, solo songs, some orch. works, and several chamber music pieces. His father ed. *T. A. Walmisley: Cathedral Music, a Collection of Services and Anthems* (London, 1875).**—NS/LK/DM**

Walmisley, Thomas Forbes, English organist, teacher, and composer, father of **Thomas Attwood Walmisley;** b. London, May 22, 1783; d. there, July 23, 1866. He was a chorister at Westminster Abbey, and studied with John Spencer and Thomas Attwood. He was active as a teacher of piano and singing (from 1803), and later organist at the Female Orphan Asylum (1810–14) and at St. Martin-in-the-Fields (1814–54). He was a popular composer of glees, and publ. 3 sets containing 6 glees each. He also publ. *A Collection of Glees, Trios, Rounds and Canons* (1826) and several single glees and songs, and ed. *T.A. Walmisley: Cathedral Music, a Collection of Services and Anthems* (London, 1875). **—NS/LK/DM**

Walsh, Joe, one of the finest lead guitarists in rock; b. Wichita, Kans., Nov. 20, 1947. **The James Gang,** Ohio-based hard-rock group. **MEMBERSHIP:** Original lineup, 1967: Jim Fox, drms.; Tom Kriss, bs.; Glen Schwartz, gtr. Glen Schwartz left in 1969 and was replaced by Joe Walsh; Tom Kriss left and was replaced by Dale Peters. Walsh left in 1971 and was replaced by guitarist Dominic Troiano and vocalist Roy Kenner. Troiano left in 1973 and was replaced by guitarist Tommy Bolin (b. Sioux City, Iowa, 1951; d. Miami, Fla., Dec. 4, 1976). The group disbanded in 1974 and reformed in 1975 with Fox, Peters, guitarist Richard Shack, and guitarist-vocalist Bubba Keith; it ended again in 1976.

Acknowledged as one of the foremost lead guitarists in rock, Joe Walsh manned the James Gang during their greatest hit-making period. He then formed his own band, scoring a major hit with "Rocky Mountain Way" from his best-selling 1973 album, *The Smoker You Drink, the Player You Get*. Walsh was a member of The Eagles from 1975 to 1982, and he continued to record solo albums during his tenure with the group and after the group's breakup. He rejoined The Eagles for their reunion album and tour in 1994.

Joe Walsh was raised in N.J., took up clarinet and oboe in junior high school, and later switched to rhythm guitar with the duo The G-Clefs. After playing bass for The Nomads during his senior year of high school, he enrolled at Kent State Univ. in Ohio in fall 1965, later playing lead guitar for the Measles for three years. Recruited for the hard-rock Ohio-based group the James Gang in April 1969, Walsh sang and played lead guitar with the power trio through their most successful period. Authoring their hit "Walk Away" and coauthoring "Funk #49,"Walsh recorded four albums with the group before leaving in November 1971. Walsh was replaced by Dominic Troiano, who in turn left in 1973 to join the Guess Who and was replaced by Tommy Bolin, but the group never again achieved their previous popularity.

After moving to Boulder, Colo., Walsh formed Barnstorm with bassist Kenny Passarelli and drummer Joe Vitale. Their second album, *The Smoker You Drink, the Player You Get*, yielded a major hit with "Rocky Mountain Way" and remained on the album charts for more than a year. Walsh next recorded 1974's *So What* with the assistance of Eagles Glenn Frey, Don Henley, and Randy Meisner, retaining Henley and Frey for *You Can't Argue with a Sick Mind* from a year later, and the best-selling *But Seriously Folks*, released in 1978, which produced a major hit about his sardonic view of stardom, "Life's Been Good."

Meanwhile, at the end of 1975 Walsh joined The Eagles as Bernie Leadon's replacement, adding a much-needed instrumental punch to the group's mellow sound, as evidenced by 1977's "Life in the Fast Lane," which he cowrote. Walsh scored a major hit on his own with "All Night Long" from the soundtrack to the movie *Urban Cowboy*. His 1980s solo outings were less successful, and by the early 1990s he was touring with Ringo Starr's All-Starr Band as well as a reunited James Gang. Walsh rejoined The Eagles for their 1994 *Hell Freezes Over* album and tour.

DISC.: THE JAMES GANG (WITH JOE WALSH): *Yer Album* (1969); *The James Gang Rides Again* (1970); *Thirds* (1971); *Live in Concert* (1971); *Best* (1973); *16 Greatest Hits* (1974). **JOE WALSH:** *Barnstorm* (1972); *The Smoker You Drink, the Player You Get* (1973); *So What* (1974); *You Can't Argue with a Sick Mind* (1976); *Best* (1978); *Look What I Did: The J. W. Anthology* (1995); *But Seriously Folks* (1978); *There Goes the Neighborhood* (1981); *You Bought It, You Name It* (1983); *The Confessor* (1985); *Got Any Gum?* (1987); *Ordinary Average Guy* (1991); *Songs for a Dying Planet* (1992).

Walsh, John, English music seller, publisher, and instrument maker; b. c. 1666; d. London, March 13, 1736. From about 1690 he had his business at the sign of the "Golden Harp and Hoboy" in the Strand in London, and in 1692 he was appointed "musical instrument maker in ordinary to His Majesty." He developed a flourishing trade and achieved great renown; in England he was unquestionably the foremost publisher of music in his time. In 1711 he publ. Handel's *Rinaldo*, and the firm became Handel's principal publisher. In about 1730, he was succeeded by his son, also named John Walsh (b. London, Dec. 23, 1709; d. there, Jan. 15, 1766), who maintained the firm's high standards; he was also made instrument maker to the King in 1731.

Bibl.: W. Smith, *A Bibliography of the Musical Works published by J. W. during the Years 1695–1720* (London, 1948); J. Walsh, *A Catalogue of Music Published by J. W. and his Successors* (London, 1953); W. Smith and C. Humphries, *A Bibliography of the Musical Works published by the Firm of J. W., 1721–1766* (London, 1968).—**NS/LK/DM**

Walter or **Walther** (real name, **Blanckenmüller**), **Johann(es),** German composer and poet; b. Kahla, Thuringia, 1496; d. Torgau, March 25, 1570. He was adopted by a townsman in Kahla and pursued his career under the name Johann Walter. He studied at the Univ. of Leipzig from 1521 to 1525, during which time he entered the chapel of the Elector Friedrich the Wise of Saxony as a bass (the Elector divided his residence between Altenburg, Torgau, and Weimar). In 1524, at Wittenberg, he publ. the *Geystliches gesangk Buchleyn* for 3 to 5 Voices, the first Protestant singing book. In 1525 he was summoned to Wittenburg by Luther to assist in the composition and regulation of the German Mass. Shortly after the death of the Elector Friedrich (1525), his chapel was disbanded, and Walter became cantor of the Municipal Latin-School in Torgau and director of the Stadtkantorei (community choir) there (1526–48). In 1548 he was called upon by the new Elector of Saxony, Moritz, to organize the court chapel in Dresden, and remained there as Kapellmeister until 1554, when he retired to Torgau on a pension. See O. Schröder, ed., *Johann Walter: Sämtliche Werke* (6 vols., Kassel, 1953–73).

Works: *Cantio septem vocum in laudem Dei omnipotentis et Evangelii ejus* (Wittenberg, 1544); *Ein schöner geistlicher und Christlicher Berckreyen...Herzlich tut mich erfrewen* (Wittenberg, 1552); *Magnificat octo tonorum* for 4 to 6 Voices (Jena, 1557); *Ein newes Christliches Lied* for 4 Voices (Wittenberg, 1561); *Das Christlich Kinderlied D. Martini Lutheri Erhalt uns Herr* for 6 Voices (Wittenberg, 1566); various other works, including Magnificat settings, passion music, motets, and fugues.

Writings: *Lob und Preis der löblichen Kunst Musica* (Wittenberg, 1538; ed. by W. Gurlitt, Kassel, 1938); *Lob und Preis der himmlischen Kunst Musica* (Wittenberg, 1564).

Bibl.: O. Michaelis, *Johann Walter (1496–1570), der Musiker-Dichter in Luthers Gefolgschaft* (Leipzig and Hamburg, 1939); C. Gerhardt, *Die Torgauer Walter-Handschriften; Eine Studie zur Quellenkunde der Musikgeschichte der deutschen Reformationszeit* (Kassel, 1949); J. Stalmann, *Johann Walters Cantiones latinae* (diss., Univ. of Tübingen, 1960); W. Blankenburg, *J. W.: Leben und Werk* (Tutzing, 1991).—**NS/LK/DM**

Walter, Arnold (Maria), prominent Moravian-born Canadian music educator, administrator, musicologist, and composer; b. Hannsdorf, Aug. 30, 1902; d. Toronto, Oct. 6, 1973. He studied harmony and composition with Bruno Weigl in Brno. After taking a doctorate in jurisprudence at the Univ. of Prague (1926), he studied musicology with Abert, Sachs, and Wolf at the Univ. of Berlin. He concurrently pursued training in piano with Breithaupt and Lamond, and in composition with Schreker. When the Nazis came to power in Germany in 1933, Walter went to Majorca. In 1936 he went to England. He settled in Toronto in 1937 and taught at the Upper Canada Coll. until 1943. In 1945 he founded the Senior School as the graduate dept. of the Toronto Cons. of Music, where he also founded its opera school. From 1952 to 1968 he was director of the music faculty of the Univ. of Toronto. Walter served as president of the International Soc. for Music Education (1953–55), the Canadian Music Centre (1959, 1970), the Canadian Music Council (1965–66), the Canadian Assn. of Univ. Schools of Music (1965–67), and the Inter-American Music Council (1969–72). From 1956 to 1962 he was chairman of the editorial board of the *Canadian Music Journal*. In 1945 Walter was awarded the Christian Culture Medal of Assumption Coll. in Windsor, Ontario. He was made an Officer of the Order of Canada in 1972. In 1974 the concert hall of the Edward Johnson Building at the Univ. of Toronto was dedicated in his memory. He contributed articles to several journals, publ. the study *Music and the Common Understanding* (Saskatoon, 1966), and ed. the vol. *Aspects of Music in Canada* (Toronto, 1969). In his compositions, he remained faithful to traditional forms and modes of expression.

Works: **Dramatic:** Music for radio plays. **Orch.:** Sym. (1942; Toronto, Feb. 1, 1944); *Concerto for Orchestra* (1958). **Chamber:** Cello Sonatina (1940); Trio for Violin, Cello, and Piano (1940); Violin Sonata (1940). **Piano:** Suite (1945); *Toccata* (1947); Sonata (1950); *Legend* (1962). **Vocal:** *Sacred Songs* for Soprano and String Trio (1941); *For the Fallen* for Soprano, Chorus, and Orch. (1949). **Tape:** *Summer Idyll* (1960; in collaboration with M. Schaeffer and H. Olnick).

Bibl.: E. Seiffert, *A. W.: His Contribution to Music Education in Canada 1946–68* (thesis, Univ. of Western Ontario, 1980). —**NS/LK/DM**

Walter, Bruno (full name, **Bruno Walter Schlesinger**), eminent German-born American conductor; b. Berlin, Sept. 15, 1876; d. Beverly Hills, Feb. 17, 1962. He entered the Stern Cons. in Berlin at age 8, where he studied with H. Ehrlich, L. Bussler, and R. Radecke. At age 9, he performed in public as a pianist but at 13 decided to pursue his interest in conducting. In 1893 he became a coach at the Cologne Opera, where he made his conducting debut with Lortzing's *Waffenschmied*. In the following year he was engaged as asst. conductor at the Hamburg Stadttheater, under Gustav Mahler; this contact was decisive in his career, and in subsequent years he became an ardent champion of Mahler's music. Walter conducted the premieres of the posthumous Sym. No. 9 and *Das Lied von der Erde*. During the 1896–97 season, Walter was engaged as second conductor at the Stadttheater in Breslau; then became principal conductor in Pressburg, and in 1898 at Riga, where he conducted for 2 seasons. In 1900 he received the important engagement of conductor at the Berlin Royal Opera under a 5-year contract; however, he left this post in 1901 when he received an offer from Mahler to become his assistant at the Vienna Court

Opera. He established himself as an efficient opera conductor, and also conducted in England (first appearance, March 3, 1909, with the Royal Phil. Soc. in London). He remained at the Vienna Court Opera after the death of Mahler. On Jan. 1, 1913, he became Royal Bavarian Generalmusikdirektor in Munich; under his guidance, the Munich Opera enjoyed brilliant performances, particularly of Mozart's works. Seeking greater freedom for his artistic activities, he left Munich in 1922, and gave numerous performances as a guest conductor with European orchs. He conducted the series "Bruno Walter Concerts" with the Berlin Phil. from 1921 to 1933. Beginning in 1925, he also conducted summer concerts of the Salzburg Festival; his performances of Mozart's music there set a standard. He also appeared as pianist in Mozart's chamber works. On Feb. 15, 1923, he made his American debut with the N.Y. Sym. Soc., and appeared with it again in 1924 and 1925. From 1925 to 1929 he was conductor of the Städtische Oper in Berlin-Charlottenburg; in 1929 he succeeded Furtwängler as conductor of the Gewandhaus Orch. in Leipzig, but continued to give special concerts in Berlin. On Jan. 14, 1932, he was guest conductor of the N.Y. Phil., acting also as soloist in a Mozart piano concerto; he was reengaged during the next 3 seasons as assoc. conductor with Toscanini. He was also a guest conductor in Philadelphia, Washington, D.C., and Baltimore. With the advent of the Nazi regime in Germany in 1933, his engagement with the Gewandhaus Orch. was canceled, and he was also prevented from continuing his orch. concerts in Berlin. He filled several engagements with the Concertgebouw Orch. in Amsterdam and also conducted in Salzburg. In 1936 he was engaged as music director of the Vienna State Opera; this was terminated with the Nazi annexation of Austria in 1938. With his family, Walter, then went to France, where he was granted French citizenship. After the outbreak of World War II in 1939, he sailed for America, establishing his residence in Calif., and eventually became a naturalized American citizen. He was guest conductor with the NBC Sym. Orch. in N.Y. (1939); he also conducted many performances of the Metropolitan Opera in N.Y. (debut in *Fidelio* on Feb. 14, 1941). From 1947 to 1949 he was conductor and musical adviser of the N.Y. Phil.; he returned regularly as guest conductor until 1960. He also conducted in Europe (1949–60), giving his farewell performance in Vienna with the Vienna Phil. in 1960.

Walter achieved the reputation of a perfect classicist among 20th-century conductors; his interpretations of the masterpieces of the Vienna School were particularly notable. He is acknowledged to have been a foremost conductor of Mahler's syms. His own compositions include 2 syms.; *Siegesfahrt* for Solo Voices, Chorus, and Orch.; String Quartet; Piano Quintet; Piano Trio; several albums of songs. He publ. the books *Von den moralischen Kräften der Musik* (Vienna, 1935); *Gustav Mahler* (Vienna, 1936; 2nd ed., 1957; Eng. tr., 1927; 2nd ed., 1941); *Theme and Variations: An Autobiography* (N.Y., 1946; Ger. original, 1947); *Von der Musik und vom Musizieren* (Frankfurt am Main, 1957; Eng. tr., 1961); L. Walter-Lindt, ed., *Briefe 1894–1962* (Frankfurt am Main, 1970).

Bibl.: M. Komorn-Rebhan, *Was wir von B. W. lernten* (Vienna, 1913); P. Stefan, *B. W.* (Vienna, 1936); B. Gavoty, *B. W.* (Geneva, 1956).—**NS/LK/DM**

Walter, David Edgar, American bass-baritone and composer; b. Boston, Feb. 2, 1953. He studied voice with John Powell at Rutgers Univ. (1970–75), Oren Brown, Lois Bove, and Shirley Meier at Trenton (N.J.) State Coll. (M.A., 1978), and Janet Wheeler at the New England Cons. of Music in Boston. He also studied with Diamond, Luening, and Persichetti at the Juilliard School in N.Y. (B.M. in composition, 1975), Edward Richter and Calvin Hampton (1976–78), and Del Tredici, Mekeel, and John Thow at Boston Univ. (1978–81). Walter subsequently was active as a singer in Boston and N.Y. churches. As a composer, he writes in an accessible style. Among his works are dramatic pieces, sacred scores, chamber music, piano pieces, organ music, and choruses.—**NS/LK/DM**

Walter, Georg A., German tenor, pedagogue, and composer; b. Hoboken, N.J., Nov. 13, 1875; d. Berlin, Sept. 13, 1952. He studied singing in Milan, Dresden, Berlin, and London, and composition with Wilhelm Berger in Berlin. He made a career as a singer, particularly distinguishing himself in the works of Bach and Handel. He was a prof. at the Stuttgart Hochschule für Musik (1925–34), then settled in Berlin as a vocal teacher; his most celebrated student was Dietrich Fischer-Dieskau. He brought out new eds. of works by the sons of Bach, Schütz et al.—**NS/LK/DM**

Walter, Thomas, American clergyman and tune-book compiler; b. Roxbury, Mass., Dec. 13, 1696; d. there, Jan. 10, 1725. He was the son of a clergyman, and a nephew of Cotton Mather. He was educated at Harvard Coll. (M.A., 1713), and on Oct. 29, 1718 was ordained at the First Church of Roxbury; was asst. pastor to his father at Roxbury. With the aim of correcting what he described as "an horrid medley of confused and disorderly sounds" prevailing in the singing in New England churches, he publ. *The Grounds and Rules of Musick Explained; or, an Introduction to the Art of Singing by Note; Fitted to the Meanest Capacities* (Boston, 1721; 8 eds. up to 1764). It was the second singing book to be publ. in America, following that of John Tufts. He also publ. *The Sweet Psalmist of Israel* (1722).—**NS/LK/DM**

Waltershausen, H(ermann) W(olfgang Sartorius), Freiherr von, German composer, writer on music, and teacher; b. Göttingen, Oct. 12, 1882; d. Munich, Aug. 13, 1954. He began his music studies with M. J. Erb in Strasbourg, and although he lost his right arm and leg in an accident when he was 10, he learned to play the piano and conduct with his left hand. He settled in Munich in 1901, where he studied composition with Thuille and piano with Schmid-Lindner; Waltershausen also studied music history with Sandberger at the Univ. of Munich. In 1917 he established there a seminar for operatic dramaturgy, the Praktisches Seminar für Fortgeschrittene Musikstudierende. He was a prof. and asst. director of the Munich

Akademie der Tonkunst (1920–22), then director (1922–33); later, he founded his own Seminar für Privatmusiklehrer, which became the Waltershausen-Seminar in 1948. In his music he adopted a neo-Romantic style, rather advanced in harmonic treatment.

WORKS: DRAMATIC: 2 operas: *Else Klapperzehen* (Dresden, May 15, 1909) and *Oberst Chabert* (Frankfurt am Main, Jan. 18, 1912); *Richardis*, dramatic mystery (Karlsruhe, Nov. 14, 1915); *Die Rauensteiner Hochzeit* (Karlsruhe, 1919); *Die Gräfin von Tolosa* (1934; Bavarian Radio, Munich, 1958). **ORCH.:** *Apokalyptische Symphonie* (1924); *Hero und Leander*, symphonic poem (1925); *Krippenmusik* for Chamber Orch. and Harpsichord Obbligato (1926); *Orchesterpartita über 3 Kirchenlieder* (1928). **CHAMBER:** String Quartet (1910); piano pieces, including studies and transcriptions for left hand alone. **VOCAL:** Songs.

WRITINGS (all publ. in Munich unless otherwise given): *Der Freischütz: Ein Versuch über die musikalische Romantik* (1920); *Das Siegfried-Idyll oder die Rückkehr zur Natur* (1920); *Die Zauberflöte: Eine operndramaturgische Studie* (1920); *Richard Strauss: Ein Versuch* (1921); *Orpheus und Euridike: Eine operndramaturgische Studie* (1923); *Musik, Dramaturgie, Erziehung* (collected essays; 1926); *Dirigentenerziehung* (Leipzig, 1929); *Die Kunst des Dirigierens* (Berlin, 1942; 2nd ed., 1954); *Dramaturgie der Oper* (in manuscript).

BIBL.: K.-R. Danler and R. Mader, *H.W. v.W.* (Tutzing, 1984).—**NS/LK/DM**

Walther, Johann Gottfried, eminent German organist, music scholar, pedagogue, and composer; b. Erfurt, Sept. 18, 1684; d. Weimar, March 23, 1748. He studied organ in Erfurt with Johann Bernhard Bach and Johann Andreas Kretschmar. He became organist of the Thomaskirche there in 1702 and concurrently studied philosophy and law briefly at the Univ. of Erfurt. He studied composition with Johann Heinrich Buttstett; after travel in Germany, he continued his studies with Wilhelm Hieronymus Pachelbel in Nuremberg (1706), then became organist of the church of St. Peter and St. Paul in Weimar (1707), a post he held for the rest of his life. He also served as music master at the ducal court and was made Hofmusicus of the ducal Court Orch. in 1721. Walther assembled a valuable library of music and books on music, which prompted him to pursue diligent musical research. This culminated in his great *Musicalisches Lexicon* (1732), the first music dictionary to encompass biographies of musicians of the past and present, musical terms, and bibliographies. He also left in MS the important treatise *Praecepta der musicalischen Composition* (1708), which was not publ. until the 20th century. He composed much sacred vocal music, but only one work, *Kyrie, Christe, Kyrie eleison über Wo Gott zum Haus nicht giebt sein Gunst*, has survived. However, over 100 chorale preludes for organ are extant. These place him next to J. S. Bach—his distant relation and lifelong friend—as a master of the genre. He also prepared valuable MS copies of works by other composers, many of which remain the only known sources. For his organ music, see M. Seiffert, ed., *J. G. Walther: Gesammelte Werke für Orgel*, in Denkmäler Deutscher Tonkunst, XXVI-XXVII (1906; this ed. includes some works now known not to be by Walther); other works for keyboard are also extant.

WRITINGS: *Praecepta der musicalischen Composition* (1708; ed. by P. Benary, Leipzig, 1960); *Alte und neue musicalische Bibliothek* (Weimar and Erfurt, 1728; only entries under the letter A publ. as a preliminary to the following); *Musicalisches Lexicon, oder Musicalische Bibliothec* (Leipzig, 1732; facsimile, with bibliographical notes, ed. by R. Schaal, Kassel, 1953).

BIBL.: H. Egel, *J. G. W.s Leben und Werke* (diss., Univ. of Leipzig, 1904); O. Brodde, *J. G. W.: Leben und Werk* (Kassel, 1937); K. Beckmann and H.-J. Schulze, eds., *J. G. W.: Briefe* (Leipzig, 1987).—**NS/LK/DM**

Walther, Johann Jacob, noted German violinist and composer; b. Witterda, near Erfurt, c. 1650; d. Mainz, Nov. 2, 1717. After a period in Florence (c. 1670–73), he returned to Germany to accept the appointment of primo violinista da camera at the Electoral Court of Saxony in Dresden (from Jan. 1, 1574). He remained there until at least 1681, when he became clerk and Italian secretary in charge of the correspondence with Rome at the Electoral Court in Mainz. He was designated a Doctor in 1693.

WORKS: *Scherzi da violini solo con il basso continuo per l'organo o cembalo accompagnabile anche con una viola o leuto* (Frankfurt am Main and Leipzig, 1676; 2nd ed., 1687; reprinted in Das Erbe Deutscher Musik, 1st series, XVII, 1941); *Hortulus chelicus uni violino duabus, tribus et quatuor subinde chordis simul sonantibus harmonice modulanti* (Mainz, 1688; 2nd ed., 1694, as *Wohlgepflanzter Violinischer Lustgarten*; 3 works ed. in the Saslav diss. listed below).

BIBL.: I. Saslav, *Three Works from J.J. W.'s "Hortulus chelicus"* (diss., Ind. Univ., 1969).—**NS/LK/DM**

Walther von der Vogelweide
See **Vogelweide, Walther von der**

Walthew, Richard Henry, English composer, conductor, and pedagogue; b. London, Nov. 4, 1872; d. East Preston, Sussex, Nov. 14, 1951. He studied with Parry at the Royal Coll. of Music in London (1890–94). After a directorship of the Passmore Edwards Settlement Place (1900–1904), he was appointed instructor of the opera class at the Guildhall School of Music in London; in 1907 he became a prof. of music at Queen's Coll.; also conducted provincial orchs. His works included 2 operettas, *The Enchanted Island* (London, May 8, 1900) and *The Gardeners* (London, Feb. 12, 1906), 2 cantatas, *Ode to a Nightingale* and *The Pied Piper of Hamelin*, Piano Concerto, Piano Quintet, Piano Quartet, 2 piano trios, Violin Sonata, vocal quartets, with piano, and songs. He was the author of *The Development of Chamber Music* (1909).—**NS/LK/DM**

Walton, Sir William (Turner), eminent English composer; b. Oldham, Lancashire, March 29, 1902; d. Ischia, Italy, March 8, 1983. Both his parents were professional singers, and Walton himself had a fine singing voice as a youth; he entered the Cathedral Choir School at Christ Church, Oxford, and began to compose choral pieces for performance. Sir Hugh Allen, organist of New Coll., advised him to develop his interest in composition, and sponsored his admission to Christ

Church at an early age; however, he never graduated, and instead began to write unconventional music in the manner that was fashionable in the 1920s. His talent manifested itself in a string quartet he wrote at the age of 17, which was accepted for performance for the first festival of the ISCM in 1923. In London he formed a congenial association with the Sitwell family of quintessential cognoscenti and literati, who combined a patrician sense of artistic superiority with a benign attitude toward the social plebs; they also provided Walton with residence at their manor in Chelsea, where he lived off and on for some 15 years. Fascinated by Edith Sitwell's oxymoronic verse, Walton set it to music bristling with novel jazzy effects in brisk, irregular rhythms and modern harmonies; Walton was only 19 when he wrote it. Under the title *Facade*, it was first performed in London in 1923, with Edith Sitwell herself delivering her doggerel with a megaphone; as expected, the show provoked an outburst of feigned indignation in the press and undisguised delight among the young in spirit. However, Walton did not pursue the path of facile hedonism so fashionable at the time; he soon demonstrated his ability to write music in a Classical manner in his fetching concert overture *Portsmouth Point*, first performed in Zürich in 1926, and later in the comedy- overture *Scapino*. His biblical oratorio *Belshazzar's Feast*, written in 1931, reveals a deep emotional stream and nobility of design that places Walton directly in line among English masters from Handel and Elgar. His symphonic works show him as an inheritor of the grand Romantic tradition; his concertos for violin, for viola, and for cello demonstrate an adroitness in effective instrumental writing. Walton was a modernist in his acceptance of the new musical resources, but he never deviated from fundamental tonality and formal clarity of design. Above all, his music was profoundly national, unmistakably British in its inspiration and content. Quite appropriately, he was asked to contribute to two royal occasions: he wrote *Crown Imperial March* for the coronation of King George VI in 1937 and *Orb and Sceptre* for that of Queen Elizabeth II in 1953. He received an honorary doctorate from the Univ. of Oxford in 1942. King George VI knighted him in 1951. He spent the last years of his life on the island of Ischia off Naples with his Argentine-born wife, Susana Gil Passo. In 1984 the William Walton Trust was formed, with its offices in Stratford-upon-Avon, as was the Italian Fondazione William Walton, situated in Ischia, where the house and gardens of Walton's estate are maintained for public viewing and where master classes for young musicians are conducted. D. Lloyd-Jones served as general ed. of the William Walton Edition of his complete works (23 vols., Oxford, 1999 et seq.).

WORKS: DRAMATIC: Opera: *Troilus and Cressida*, after Chaucer (1947–54; London, Dec. 3, 1954; rev. 1963 and 1972–76; London, Nov. 12, 1976); *The Bear*, after Chekhov (1965–67; Aldeburgh, June 3, 1967). **Ballet:** *The First Shoot* (1935); *The Wise Virgins*, after J.S. Bach (1939–40; London, April 24, 1940); *The Quest* (1943). **Entertainment:** *Façade* for Reciter and Instrumental Ensemble, after Edith Sitwell (1921; 1st perf. privately at the Sitwell home in London, Jan. 24, 1922; 1st public perf., London, June 12, 1923; rev. 1926, 1928, 1942, and 1951; rev. as *Façade 2*, 1978; arranged as a ballet, 1929, with subsequent changes). **Incidental Music For the Theater and Radio:** *A Son of Heaven* (1924–25); *The Boy David* (1935); *Macbeth* (1941–42); *Christopher Columbus* (1942). **Film:** *Escape Me Never* (1934); *As You Like It* (1936); *Dreaming Lips* (1937); *Stolen Life* (1938); *Major Barbara* (1940); *Next of Kin* (1941); *The Foreman Went to France* (1941–42); *The First of the Few* (1942); *Went the Day Well?* (1942); *Henry V* (1943–44); *Hamlet* (1947); *Richard III* (1955); *The Battle of Britain* (1969); *Three Sisters* (1969). **ORCH.:** *Portsmouth Point*, overture (1924–25; Zürich, June 22, 1926); *Siesta* (1926); *Façade*, 2 suites after the entertainment: No. 1 (1926; Siena, Sept. 14, 1928) and No. 2 (N.Y., March 30, 1938); *Sinfonia concertante* for Piano and Orch. (1926–27; London, Jan. 5, 1928; rev. 1943); Viola Concerto (1928–29; London, Oct. 3, 1929, Paul Hindemith soloist; rev. 1936 and 1961; London, Jan. 18, 1962); 2 syms.: No. 1 (1931–35; London, Nov. 6, 1935) and No. 2 (1957–60; Edinburgh, Sept. 2, 1960); *Crown Imperial*, coronation march for King George VI (Westminster Abbey, London, May 12, 1937; rev. 1963); Violin Concerto (1938–39; Cleveland, Dec. 7, 1939, Jascha Heifetz soloist; rev. 1943); *The Wise Virgins*, suite from the ballet (1940); *Music for Children* (1940; orchestrtion of *Duets for Children* for Piano); *Scapino*, comedy overture (1940; Chicago, April 3, 1941; rev. 1950); *Spitfire Prelude and Fugue* (1942); *2 Pieces* for Strings from the film score to *Henry V* (1943–44); *Orb and Sceptre*, coronation march for Queen Elizabeth II (1952–53; Westminster Abbey, London, June 2, 1953); Finale for *Sellinger's Round, Variations on an Elizabethan Theme* for Strings (1953; in collaboration with others); Cello Concerto (1955–56; Boston, Jan. 25, 1957, Piatigorsky soloist); *Johannesburg Festival Overture* (Johannesburg, Sept. 25, 1956); *Partita* (1957; Cleveland, Jan. 30, 1958); *Variations on a Theme by Hindemith* (1962–63; London, March 8, 1963); *Capriccio Burlesco* (N.Y., Dec. 7, 1968); *Improvisations on an Impromptu of Benjamin Britten* (1968–69; San Francisco, Jan. 14, 1970); *Sonata* for Strings (1971; orchestration of the String Quartet, 1945–47); *Varii Capricci* (1975–76; London, May 4, 1976; orchestration of the *5 Bagatelles* for Guitar); *Prologo e Fantasia* (1981–82; London, Feb. 20, 1982). **CHAMBER:** Piano Quartet (1918–21; rev. 1974–75); 2 string quartets (1919, rev. 1921–22; London, July 5, 1923; 1945–47; orchestrated as *Sonata* for Strings, 1971); *Toccata* for Violin and Piano (1922–23); Violin Sonata (1947–48; rev. 1949–50); *2 Pieces* for Violin and Piano (1948–50); *5 Bagatelles* for Guitar (1970–71; orchestrated as *Varii Capricci*, 1975–76); *Passacaglia* for Cello (1979–80); *Duettino* for Oboe and Violin (1982). **KEYBOARD: Piano:** *Duets for Children* (1940; orchestrated as *Music for Children*). **Organ:** *3 Pieces* from the film score to *Richard III* (1955). **VOCAL:** *Belshazzar's Feast*, oratorio for Baritone, Chorus, and Orch. (1930–31; Leeds, Oct. 8, 1931; rev. 1948 and 1957); *In Honour of the City of London* for Chorus and Orch. (1937); *Coronation Te Deum* for 2 Choruses, 2 Semi Choruses, Boy's Chorus, Organ, Orch., and Military Brass, for the coronation of Queen Elizabeth II (1952–53; London, June 2, 1953); *Anon in Love*, 6 songs for Tenor and Guitar (1959; also for Tenor and Small Orch., 1971); *Gloria* for Contralto, Tenor, Bass, Chorus, and Orch. (1960; Liverpool, Nov. 24, 1961); *A Song for the Lord Mayor's Table*, 6 songs for Soprano and Piano (London, July 18, 1962; also for Soprano and Orch., 1970); *The Twelve* for Chorus and Organ (1964–65; Oxford, May 16, 1965); *Missa Brevis* for Double Chorus and Organ (1965–66; Coventry, April 10, 1966); *Jubilate Deo* for Chorus and Organ (1972); *Magnificat and Nunc Dimittis* for Chorus and Organ (1974; rev. 1975); *Antiphon* for Chorus and Organ (1977); other vocal pieces, including choruses and songs.

BIBL.: F. Howes, *The Music of W. W.* (2 vols.; London, 1942 and 1943; new amplified ed., 1965); S. Craggs, *W. W.: A Thematic Catalogue of His Musical Works* (London, 1977; rev. ed., 1990); A. Poulton, *Sir W. W.: A Discography* (London, 1980); N. Tierney, *W. W.: His Life and Music* (London, 1984); S. Walton, *W. W.: Behind the Facade* (Oxford, 1988); M. Kennedy, *Portrait of W.* (Oxford, 1989); S. Craggs, *W. W.: A Source Book* (Aldershot, 1993); idem, ed., *W. W.: Music and Literature* (Aldershot, 1999).—**NS/LK/DM**

Waltz, Gustavus, German bass; b. place and date unknown; d. London, c. 1759. His first recorded appearance was at the Little Haymarket Theatre in London in Lampe's Amelia (March 13, 1732). He then sang in the pirated ed. of Handel's *Acis and Galatea* there (May 17, 1732), and subsequently appeared in various London theaters. After accompanying Handel to Oxford in 1733, where he appeared in several of his works, he returned to London as a member of Handel's company until 1736. He created the roles of Minos in *Arianna in Creta* (Jan. 26, 1734), Mars in *Il Parnasso in festa* (April 13, 1734), the King of Scotland in *Ariodante* (Jan. 8, 1735), Melisso in *Alcina* (April 16, 1736), and Nicandro in *Atalanta* (May 12, 1736); he also sang in various oratorio performances. He was subsequently active as a singer in light English theater pieces; however, he continued to make some concert appearances, and sang in performances of Handel's *Messiah* at the Foundling Hospital (1754, 1758, 1759). He is mentioned in the reported acrid comment of Handel on Gluck: "He knows no more of counterpoint than my cook, Waltz."—**NS/LK/DM**

Wand, Günter, eminent German conductor; b. Elberfeld, Jan. 7, 1912. He received training in Wuppertal before going to Cologne, where he was a student at the Univ. and of Philipp Jarnach (composition) and Paul Baumgartner (piano) at the Cons. He pursued training in conducting with Franz von Hoesslin at the Munich Academy of Music. After conducting in Detmold, he conducted at the Cologne Opera from 1939 to 1944. In 1944–45 he conducted the Salzburg Mozarteum Orch. In 1946 he became Generalmusikdirektor of Cologne. He became conductor of the Gürzenich Orch. there in 1947, a position he retained until 1974. During his tenure there, he returned the orch. to its pre- World War II high standard and programmed many classical and contemporary scores previously unperformed by the orch. From 1948 he was also prof. of conducting at the Cologne Hochschule für Musik. In 1951 he made his first appearance in the British capital as a guest conductor with the London Sym. Orch. He also appeared as a guest conductor throughout Europe and in Japan. From 1974 to 1982 he conducted the Bern Sym. Orch. In 1982 he became chief conductor of the North German Radio Sym. Orch. in Hamburg, a position he held with great distinction until his retirement as conductor laureate in 1991. It was during his Hamburg tenure that Wand acquired international renown via a series of notable recordings. On Jan. 19, 1989, he made his belated U.S. debut at the age of 77 as a guest conductor with the Chicago Sym. Orch. In his last years, Wand attained a revered and honored place among the world's podium figures as one of the last exponents of the hallowed Austro-German art of conducting. His interpretations of such masters as Mozart, Beethoven, Brahms, and most especially Bruckner, were acclaimed.

BIBL.: F. Berger, *G. W.: Gürzenichkapellmeiser 1947–1974* (Cologne, 1974); W. Seifert, *G. W.: So und nicht anders: Gedanken und Erinnerungen* (Hamburg, 1998).—**NS/LK/DM**

Wangenheim, Volker, German conductor, teacher, and composer; b. Berlin, July 1, 1928. He studied piano, oboe, violin, composition, and conducting at the Hochschule für Musik in Berlin. He began his career as an oboist with several Berlin ensembles. He was founder-principal conductor of the Berlin Mozart Orch. (1950–59); also conducted at the Mecklenburg State Theater in Schwerin (1951–52) and with the Berlin Academic Orch. (1954–57). He was music director (1957–63) and then Generalmusikdirektor (1963–78) in Bonn, where he served as principal conductor of the Beethovenhalle Orch., the Phil. Choir, and the Bonn Beethoven Festivals; also was co-founder and artistic director of the German National Youth Orch. (1969–84). He appeared as a guest conductor in Germany and abroad from 1954. In 1972 he became a prof. at the Cologne Hochschule für Musik.

WORKS: ORCH.: *Sinfonietta concertante* (1963); Concerto for Strings (1964); *Sinfonia notturna* (1965); *Symphony 1966* (1968); *Klangspiel I* for Strings (1971) and *II* for Chamber Ensemble (1973). **VOCAL:** *Psalm 123* for Chorus (1973); *Nicodemus Iesum nocte visitat: Canticum secundum Ioannem* for Chorus (1980); various folksongs for chorus.—**NS/LK/DM**

Wangermée, Robert, distinguished Belgian musicologist; b. Lodelinsart, Sept. 21, 1920. He received training in music from J. Absil, and pursued musicological studies at the Free Univ. of Brussels (Ph.D., 1946, with the diss. *Le Goût musical en France au XIX*e *siècle*); then was on its faculty as a lecturer (1948–62), reader (1962–65), and prof. (from 1975). He also was active with the Belgian Radio and Television (from 1946), serving as its director of music (1953–60) and as director-general of its French-language broadcasts (1960–84).

WRITINGS (all publ. in Brussels): *Jean-Sébastien Bach* (1944); *Ludwig van Beethoven* (1945); *Les Maîtres de chant des XVII*e *et XVIII*e *siècles à la collégiale des SS. Michel et Gudale, à Bruxelles* (1950); *François-Joseph Fétis, musicologue et compositeur* (1951); *La Musique belge contemporaine* (1959); *La Musique flamande dans la société des XV*e *et XVI*e *siècles* (1965; Eng. tr., 1965); *La Musique en Wallonie et à Bruxelles* (2 vols., 1980–82); ed. *Paul Collaer: Correspondance avec des amis musiciens* (Brussels, 1996).

BIBL.: H. Vanhulst and M. Haine, eds., *Musique et Société: Hommages à R. W.* (Brussels, 1988).—**NS/LK/DM**

Wanless, John, English organist and composer; b. place and date unknown; d. York (buried), Feb. 2, 1712. He was organist at the Lincoln Cathedral between 1616 and 1625. Only a few of his church works are extant, among them an anthem, *Plead Thou My Cause*. His son, Thomas Wanless (d. 1721), was organist of York Minster from 1691 to 1695. He publ. a psalter, *The Metre Psalmtunes*, in 4 parts (London, 1702) and composed *York Litany*.—**NS/LK/DM**

Wannenmacher (Latinized as **Vannius**), **Johannes,** important German composer; b. probably in Neuenburg am Rhein, c. 1485; d. Bern, 1551. He was choirmaster at the Vincentius-Stift in Bern (1510–13), then went to Fribourg as choirmaster at St. Nikolaus in 1513, where he he became choirmaster at the new college foundation in 1515. He later was removed from his post, arrested, tried, and finally exiled. He served as magistrate's clerk in Interlaken from 1531. He was one of the leading composers in Switzerland in his era. His extant works number 26, including both sacred and secular vocal pieces. Several of his works appeared in contemporary collections.

BIBL.: A. Geering, *Die Vokalmusik in der Schweiz zur Zeit der Reformation: Leben und Werke von Bartholomäus Frank, J. W., Cosmas Alder* (Aarau, 1933).—**NS/LK/DM**

War, a Southern Calif. band of more than twenty years experience with varying personnel. **MEMBERSHIP:** Howard Scott, gtr., perc. (b. San Pedro, Calif., March 15, 1946); Leroy "Lonnie" Jordan, kybd. (b. San Diego, Calif., Nov. 21, 1948); Charles Miller, rds. (b. Olathe, Kans., June 2, 1939; d. Los Angeles, 1980); Morris "B.B." Dickerson, bs., perc. (b. Torrance, Calif., Aug. 3, 1949); Lee Oskar (Oskar Hansen), har. (b. Copenhagen, Denmark, March 24, 1948); Thomas Sylvester "Papa Dee" Allen, perc. (b. Wilmington, Del., July 18, 1931); Harold Brown, drm. (b. Long Beach, Calif., March 17, 1946).

War took their name and stabilized their membership with the addition of Danish-born white harmonica player Lee Oskar under former Animals vocalist Eric Burdon. Scoring a pop smash with Burdon on "Spill the Wine," War left Burdon and initiated their own career in 1971 and became popular with white AM radio listeners while retaining an avid black following. Achieving crossover smashes with "The World Is a Ghetto," "The Cisco Kid," "Why Can't We Be Friends," and "Low Rider," War was alternately mellow and percussive in their sound, distinctly fusing elements of jazz and funk with harmonious singing on catchy, melodic tunes. Overwhelmed by the rise of disco in the late 1970s, War served as an inspiration to rap acts of the 1980s and 1990s and returned to recording in 1994.

Ostensibly started as a group by Howard Scott, Charles Miller, and Harold Brown around 1959, the three were joined by B. B. Dickerson and Lonnie Jordan in the formation of the Creators during the early 1960s. Enduring frequent personnel changes, the group persevered on the Southern Calif. club circuit under a variety of names. Around 1966, Brown, Miller, and Scott got together with Jordan, Dickerson, and "Papa Dee" Allen as Night Shift. Introduced to former Animals vocalist Eric Burdon and his harmonica-playing friend Lee Oskar, Night Shift began working with the two as War.

Eric Burdon and War recorded two albums for MGM and scored a smash pop hit with "Spill the Wine" in 1970. The band toured with, then without, Burdon, and signed with United Artists Records as an act in their own right. Their debut album was largely overlooked, but their second, *All Day Music*, yielded a moderate hit with the title song and a major pop and R&B hit with "Slippin' into Darkness." War was established with both black and white audiences with their late 1972 album, *The World Is a Ghetto*, which stayed on the album charts for more than a year. It yielded crossover smashes with the title song and "Cisco Kid." After *Deliver the Word*, which produced the crossover smash "Gypsy Man" and the major crossover hit "Me and Baby Brother," War became entangled in legal disputes with United Artists for two years, returning with the new studio album *Why Can't We Be Friends?* in 1975. The album produced R&B and pop smash hits with the title song and "Low Rider" and was soon followed by the crossover smash "Summer."

After *Platinum Jazz* on United Artists's Blue Note label, War switched to MCA Records, while Lee Oskar recorded several solo albums. However, the group never scored another major pop hit, as personnel changes began to affect the group. War managed major R&B hits with "Youngblood (Livin' in the Streets)" on United Artists and "Good, Good Feelin'" on MCA, eventually moving to RCA in the early 1980s for the R&B hits "You Got the Power" and "Outlaw." The group continued to record into the late 1980s, with Howard Scott and Lonnie Jordan as mainstays. In 1992 Avenue Records issued *Rap Declares War*, recorded by artists such as De La Soul, Ice-T, and the Beastie Boys in homage to the group's work. The following year, War re-formed with Jordan, Scott, Lee Oskar, and latter-day drummer Ronnie Hammon. Joined by Harold Brown, who had set up a recording studio in New Orleans, War recorded a new album for Avenue Records, who have reissued many of their earlier recordings.

DISC.: **ERIC BURDON AND WAR:** *Eric Burdon Declares "War"* (1970); *(reissued as) Spill the Wine* (1981); *Black Man's Burdon* (1970); *Love Is All Around* (1976); *Best* (rec. 1969–1971; rel. 1995). **WAR:** *W.* (1971); *All Day Music* (1971); *The World Is a Ghetto* (1972); *Deliver the Word* (1973); *W. Live* (1974); *Why Can't We Be Friends?* (1975); *Greatest Hits* (1976); *Youngblood* (soundtrack; 1978); *Platinum Jazz* (1977); *Galaxy* (1977); *The Music Band* (1979); *The Music Band—2* (1979); *The Music Band Live* (1980); *Best of the Music Band* (1982); *Music Band Jazz* (1983); *Outlaw* (1982); *Life (Is So Strange)* (1983); *Best of W. ... and More* (1987); *W.* (1994); *Anthology (1970–1994)* (1994). **LEE OSKAR:** *Lee Oskar* (1976); *Before the Rain* (1978); *My Road Our Road* (1981). **LONNIE JORDAN:** *Different Moods of Me* (1978). **TRIBUTE ALBUM:** *Rap Declares War* (1992).—**BH**

Ward, David, esteemed Scottish bass; b. Dumbarton, July 3, 1922; d. Dunedin, New Zealand, July 16, 1983. He was a student of Clive Carey at the Royal Coll. of Music in London and of Hans Hotter in Munich. In 1952 he joined the chorus of the Sadler's Wells Opera in London, where he made his operatic debut as the Old Bard in Boughton's *The Immortal Hour* in 1953. He continued to sing there until 1958. In 1960 he made his debut at London's Covent Garden as Pogner, and returned there as Arkel and Rocco. He also created the role of Morosus in the first British staging of Strauss' *Die Schweigsame Frau* there in 1961. In 1960 he appeared as Titurel at the Bayreuth Festival, where he sang again in 1961 and 1962. In 1964 he sang Wotan at Covent Garden and in 1967 at the Teatro Colón in Buenos Aires. On Jan. 3, 1964, he made his Metropolitan Opera debut in N.Y. as Sarastro, where he remained on the roster until 1966;

he was again on its roster from 1973 to 1975 and from 1978 to 1980. Ward also pursued a highly distinguished concert career. In 1972 he was made a Commander of the Order of the British Empire. Among his other roles were Hunding, Fasolt, King Marke, Philip II, and Boris Godunov.—**NS/LK/DM**

Ward, Helen, jazz singer best remembered for her association with Benny Goodman; b. N.Y., Sept. 19, 1916; d. Arlington, Va., April 21, 1998. She studied piano as a child and began singing in her teens. After performing on radio station WOR in N.Y. (1933), she became a staff musician at NBC and sang with Benny Goodman on his radio show "Let's Dance." She toured and made recordings with Goodman from 1934–36; her signature song was the perky "Goody Goody." Between 1937 and 1942 she sang exclusively on recordings, accompanied by various musicians. She continued to tour and record through the 1940s and 1950s, including three reunions (1953, 1957, 1958) with Goodman. After a long period of inactivity, in 1979 she resumed performing and recording sporadically through the mid-1990s.

DISC.: **B. GOODMAN:** "Goody Goody" (1936); *It's Been So Long* (1954); *The Helen Ward Song Book* (1981).—**JC/LP**

Ward, John, English composer; b. Canterbury (baptized), Sept. 8, 1571; d. before Aug. 31, 1638. He settled in London and entered the employ of the office of the Remembrancer of the Exchequer, where he eventually attained the rank of Attorney; also served as household musician to Sir Henry Fanshawe and his family. He dedicated *The First Set of [25] English Madrigals to 3, 4, 5 and 6 Parts apt both for Viols and Voyces, with a Mourning Song in Memory of Prince Henry* (London, 1613; ed. in The English Madrigalists, XIX, 2nd ed., 1968) to Fanshawe. His other works include 2 sacred services, 22 verse anthems (ed. in Early English Church Music, XI, 1970), and various instrumental pieces, including 42 fantasias for viols.

BIBL.: M. Strover, *The Fantasias and In Nomines of J. W.* (diss., Oxford Univ., 1957); M. Forster, *The Sacred Music of J. W.* (diss., Univ. of Durham, 1971).—**NS/LK/DM**

Ward, John M(ilton), American musicologist; b. Oakland, Calif., July 6, 1917. He studied at San Francisco State Coll. (B.A., 1941), the Univ. of Wash. (M.M., 1942), with Milhaud (composition, 1943–44), and at N.Y.U. (Ph.D., 1953, with the diss. *The Vihuela de Mano and Its Music (1536–1576)*. He taught at Mich. State Univ. (1947–53), the Univ. of Ill. (1953–55), and at Harvard Univ. (1955–85). He ed. *The Dublin Virginal Manuscript, Wellesley Edition*, III (1954; 2nd ed., rev. and aug., 1964; new ed., 1983) and *Music for Elizabethan Lutes* (2 vols., Oxford, 1992), and also contributed numerous essays and specialized articles to various scholarly music magazines.

BIBL.: A. Shapiro, ed., *Music and Context: Essays for J.M. W.* (1985).—**NS/LK/DM**

Ward, Robert (Eugene), American composer and teacher; b. Cleveland, Sept. 13, 1917. He studied with Rogers, Royce, and Hanson at the Eastman School of Music in Rochester, N.Y. (B.Mus., 1939) and with Jacobi at the Juilliard Graduate School in N.Y. (certificate, 1946); he also studied conducting with Stoessel and Schenkman and received some training in composition from Copland. He taught at Columbia Univ. (1946–48) and at the Juilliard School of Music (1946–56). He also was music director of the 3rd Street Music Settlement (1952–55), then was vice-president and managing ed. of the Galaxy Music Corp. (1956–67). After serving as president of the N.C. School of the Arts in Winston-Salem (1967–74), where he continued as a teacher of composition until 1979, he held the chair of Mary Duke Biddle Prof. of Music at Duke Univ. (1979–87). In 1950, 1952, and 1966 he held Guggenheim fellowships; in 1962 he won the Pulitzer Prize in Music and the N.Y. Music Critics' Circle Award for his opera *The Crucible*. In 1972 he was elected a member of the National Inst. of Arts and Letters. He evolved an effective idiom, modern but not aggressively so; composed a number of dramatic and compact stage works on American subjects.

WORKS: **DRAMATIC:** **Opera:** *He Who Gets Slapped* (1955; N.Y., May 17, 1956; rev. 1973); *The Crucible* (N.Y., Oct. 26, 1961); *The Lady from Colorado* (Central City, Colo., July 3, 1961; rev. as *Lady Kate*, 1981; Wooster, Ohio, June 8, 1994); *Claudia Legare* (1973; Minneapolis, April 14, 1978); *Minutes till Midnight* (1978–82; Miami, June 4, 1982); *Abelard and Heloise* (1981); *Roman Fever* (1993). **Ballet:** *The Scarlet Letter* (1990). **ORCH.:** *Slow Music* (1938); *Ode* (1939); 6 syms.: No. 1 (N.Y., May 10, 1941), No. 2 (1947; Washington, D.C., Jan. 25, 1948), No. 3 (Washington, D.C., March 31, 1950), No. 4 (1958), No. 5, *Canticles of America*, for Soprano, Baritone, Narrator, Chorus, and Orch., after Whitman and Longfellow (1976), and No. 6 (1989); *Jubilation Overture* (Los Angeles, Nov. 21, 1946); *Concert Piece* (1947–48); *Concert Music* (1948); *Night Music* for Small Orch. (1949); *Fantasia* for Brass Choir and Timpani (1953); *Euphony* (1954); *Divertimento* (1960); *Night Fantasy* for Band (1962); *Invocation and Toccata* (1963); *Antiphony* for Winds for Woodwinds and Percussion (1968); Piano Concerto (1968); *Sonic Structure* (1981); *Dialogues* for Violin, Cello, and Orch. (1983; arr. for Piano Trio, 1984); Tenor Saxophone Concerto (1984; rev. 1987); *Byways of Memories* (1991). **CHAMBER:** 2 violin sonatas (1950, 1990); String Quartet (1966); *Raleigh Divertimento* for Wind Quintet (1986); *Appalachian Ditties and Dances* for Violin and Piano (1989); piano pieces. **VOCAL:** *Fatal Interview* for Soprano and Orch. (1937); *Jonathan and the Gingery Snare* for Narrator, Small Orch., and Percussion (N.Y., Feb. 4, 1950); *Sacred Songs for Pantheists* for Soprano and Orch. (1951); *Earth Shall Be Fair*, cantata for Soprano, Chorus, Children's Chorus, Organ, and Orch. (1960); *Let the Word Go Forth* for Chorus and Instruments (1965); *Sweet Freedom Songs*, cantata for Bass, Narrator, Chorus, and Orch. (1965); *Images of God* for Chorus (1989); songs.

BIBL.: K. Kreitner, *R. W.: A Bio-Bibliography* (Westport, Conn., 1988).—**NS/LK/DM**

Ward, Samuel Augustus, American composer and dealer in musical instruments; b. Newark, N.J., Dec. 28, 1848; d. there, Sept. 28, 1903. He was the author of the famous hymn *Materna*, first publ. in the Parish Choir (Boston, 1888) to the words of "O Mother dear, Jerusalem." Eventually, his hymn tune was combined with the words of the poem *America, the Beautiful*, written by Katherine Lee Bates in 1893, and became one of the most widely sung patriotic American anthems.—**NS/LK/DM**

Ward-Steinman, David, American composer, teacher, and pianist; b. Alexandria, La., Nov. 6, 1936. He studied at Fla. State Univ. (B.Mus., 1957), and also received training from Riegger (1954), Milhaud at the Aspen (Colo.) Music School (1956), and Babbitt and Copland at the Berkshire Music Center, Tanglewood (summer, 1957); after further studies at the Univ. of Ill. (M.M., 1958), he pursued private training with Boulanger in Paris (1958–59); then returned to the Univ. of Ill. to complete his education (D.M.A., 1961). In 1961 he became a faculty member and composer-in-residence at San Diego State Univ., where he served as prof. of music (from 1968); also was the Ford Foundation composer-in-residence of the Tampa Bay area in Fla. (1970–72) and the Fulbright Senior Scholar at Victorian Coll. of the Arts and La Trobe Univ. in Melbourne, Australia (1989–90). In 1995 he was a participant at the Académie d'été at IRCAM in Paris. With S. Ward- Steinman, he publ. *Comparative Anthology of Musical Forms* (2 vols., Belmont, Calif., 1976); also publ. *Toward a Comparative Structural Theory of the Arts* (San Diego, 1989).

WORKS: DRAMATIC: *Western Orpheus*, ballet (1964; San Diego, Feb. 26, 1965; rev. version, El Cajon, Calif., April 17, 1987); *These Three*, ballet (N.Y., Sept. 13, 1966); *Tamar*, music drama (1970–77); *Rituals* for Dancers and Musicians (Channel 13 TV, Tampa, Dec. 5, 1971). **ORCH.:** Concert Overture (1957; Urbana, Ill., May 6, 1958); Sym. (1959; San Diego, Dec. 4, 1962); Concerto Grosso for Combo and Chamber Orch. (1960; N.Y., Nov. 8, 1964); Concerto No. 2 for Chamber Orch. (1960–62; La Jolla, Calif., March 3, 1963); *Prélude and Toccata* (1962; Albuquerque, March 21, 1963); Cello Concerto (1963–65; Tokyo, June 13, 1967); *Antares* for Orch., Synthesizer or Tape, and Gospel Choir ad libitum (Tampa, April 22, 1971); *Arcturus* for Orch. and Synthesizer (Chicago, June 15, 1972); *Season's Greetings* (1981; San Diego, Dec. 15, 1983); *Olympics Overture* (San Diego, June 10, 1984); *Chroma*, concerto for Multiple Keyboards, Percussion, and Chamber Orch. (Scottsdale, Ariz., May 7, 1985); *Elegy for Astronauts* (San Diego, Dec. 7, 1986); *Winging It* for Chamber Orch. (Las Cruces, N.Mex., Nov. 22, 1986); *Cinnabar Concerto* for Viola and Chamber Orch. (1991–93; San Diego, April 16, 1994); Double Concerto for 2 Violins and Orch. (1994–95). **Band or Wind Ensemble:** *Jazz Tangents* (Grand Forks, N.Dak., April 23, 1967); *Gasparilla Day* (1970); *Rāga* (Atlanta, March 10, 1972); *Scorpio* (Tucson, April 10, 1976); *Bishop's Gambit* (1979; Alexandria, Va., March 22, 1980); *Quintessence* (1985; Anaheim, April 11, 1986). **CHAMBER:** *3 Songs* for Clarinet and Piano (1957); *Quiet Dance* for Flute, Clarinet, Guitar, and Cello (1958); 2 brass quintets: No. 1 (1958–59; Urbana, Ill., April 5, 1960) and No. 2, *Brancusi's Brass Beds* (1976; Bowling Green, Ky., Jan. 22, 1978); Duo for Cello and Piano (1964–65; San Diego, April 16, 1970); *Child's Play* for Bassoon and Piano (1968); 2 woodwind quintets: No. 1, *Montage* (San Diego, June 6, 1968) and No. 2, *Night Winds* (San Diego, Nov. 4, 1993); *Putney 3* for Woodwind Quintet, Prepared Piano, and Putney Synthesizer or Tape (1970; Tampa, Nov. 9, 1971); *The Tracker* for Clarinet, Fortified Piano, and Tape (Fullerton, Calif., Nov. 13, 1976); *Toccata* for Synthesizer and Slide Projectors (Tempe, Ariz., Nov. 2, 1978); *Golden Apples* for Alto Saxophone and Piano (San Diego, Dec. 4, 1981); *Epithalamion* for Flute and Cello (1981); *Intersections I* for Fortified Piano and Tape (1982) and *II: Borobudur* for Fortified Piano and Percussion (1989; Canberra, March 5, 1990); *Moiré* for Piano and Chamber Ensemble (1983; Redlands, Calif., April 27, 1984); *Summer Suite* for Oboe and Piano (1987); *Étude on the Name of Barney Childs* for Clarinet (1990); *Cinnabar* for Viola and Piano (Ithaca, N.Y., June 15, 1991). **Piano:** Sonata (1956–57); *Improvisations on a Theme of Darius Milhaud* (1960); *3 Lyric Preludes* (1961–65); *Latter-Day Lullabies* (1961–66); *3 Miniatures* (1964); *Improvisations on Children's Songs* (1966); *Elegy for Martin Luther King* (San Diego, April 7, 1968); Sonata for Fortified Piano (Tampa, June 23, 1972); *What's Left* for Piano, Left-Hand (1987); *Under Capricorn* (1989). **VOCAL:** *Psalms of Rejoicing* for Chorus (1960); *Fragments from Sappho* for Soprano, Flute, Clarinet, and Piano (1962–65; La Jolla, Calif., April 29, 1966); *The Song of Moses* for Narrator, Soloists, Double Chorus, and Orch. (1963–64; San Diego, May 31, 1964); *The Tale of Issoumbochi* for Narrator, Soprano, Flute, Clarinet, Percussion, Piano, and Cello (San Diego, April 18, 1968); *Grant Park* for Baritone and Chamber Ensemble (1969; Cedar Falls, Iowa, March 16, 1970); *Season* for Soprano and Fortified Piano (1970); *God's Rock* for Soprano, Chorus, Piano or Organ, and Optional Double Bass and Percussion (1973); *And in These Times*, Christmas cantata for Narrator, Soloists, Chorus, Cello, and Ensemble (1979–81; San Diego, Dec. 12, 1982); *Of Wind and Water* for Chorus, Piano, and 2 Percussion (Bloomington, Ill., March 4, 1982); *...And Waken Green*, 7 poems for Medium Voice or Voices and Piano (1983); *Children's Corner Revisited*, 4 songs for Medium Voice and Piano (1985); *Voices from the Gallery* for Soprano, Tenor, Baritone, and Piano (1990; San Diego, Feb. 13, 1994); *Seasons Fantastic* for Chorus and Harp (1991–92; San Diego, June 25, 1992). —**NS/LK/DM**

Warfield, Sandra, American mezzo-soprano; b. Kansas City, Mo., Aug. 6, 1929. After training at the Kansas City Cons., she began her career singing in operettas. She then pursued her studies in N.Y. with Fritz Lehmann. In 1953 she won the Metropolitan Opera Auditions of the Air and made her debut with the company in N.Y. as a peasant girl in *Le nozze di Figaro* on Nov. 20, 1953. By 1955 she was singing major roles there, most notably Ulrica. When her husband, **James McCracken**, left the Metropolitan Opera in 1957, Warfield did likewise and made her debut at the Vienna State Opera as Ulrica. In 1961 she created the role of Katerina in Martinů's *Greek Passion* at the Zürich Opera. She sang Dalila at the San Francisco Opera in 1963. She was again on the roster of the Metropolitan Opera in 1965–66, 1967–68, and 1971–72. As a guest artist, she sang with various American and European opera houses. She also toured extensively as a concert artist, frequently appearing with her husband. Warfield was especially admired for her dramatic vocal gifts. Among her best roles were Dalila, Amneris, Carmen, Ulrica, Marcellina, and Fricka. With her husband, she publ. the autobiographical vol. *A Star in the Family* (N.Y., 1971).—**NS/LK/DM**

Warfield, William (Caesar), African American baritone and teacher; b. West Helena, Ark., Jan. 22, 1920. He studied at the Eastman School of Music in Rochester, N.Y. (B.Mus., 1942). Following service in the U.S. Army, he returned to Eastman in 1946 to pursue graduate training. After further studies with Otto Herz and Yves Tinayre, he completed his training with Rosa Ponselle

(1958–65). From 1947 he appeared in N.Y. theaters. On March 19, 1950, he made his recital debut at N.Y.'s Town Hall. After a concert tour of Australia in 1950, he sang Joe in *Showboat* in N.Y. in 1951. In 1952–53 he toured Europe as Porgy in *Porgy and Bess*. He continued to sing in musicals and operas in the U.S. and abroad, and also made concert tours of Africa and the Middle East (1956), Europe (with the Philadelphia Orch., 1956), and Asia (1958). In 1974 he became a teacher at the Univ. of Ill. In 1984 he was elected president of the National Assn. of Negro Musicians. He married **Leontyne Price** in 1952, but they were divorced in 1974. With A. Miller, he publ. *William Warfield: My Music & My Life* (Champaign, Ill., 1991).—**NS/LK/DM**

Waring, Fred(eric Malcolm), famous American conductor of popular music and inventor of sundry kitchen appliances; b. Tyrone, Pa., June 9, 1900; d. Danville, Pa., July 29, 1984. He learned music at his mother's knee, and a sense of moral rectitude was inculcated in him by his father, a banker who gave speeches at spiritual revivals and temperance meetings. He took up the banjo at 16, and organized a quartet that he called The Banjazzatra. He studied engineering and architecture at Pa. State Univ.; he retained his love for gadgets throughout his musical career and, in 1937, patented the Waring Blender, for whipping food or drinks to a foam; another invention was a traveling iron. He acquired fame with his own band, the Pennsylvanians, which played on national tours at concert halls, hotels, and college campuses; the group was particularly successful on radio programs sponsored by tobacco companies and the Ford Motor Co. His repertoire consisted of wholesome American songs, many composed by himself. Among his soloists on special programs were Bing Crosby, Hoagy Carmichael, Irving Berlin, and Frank Sinatra. Waring had a natural streak for publicity; he once bet that he could lead a bull into a Fifth Avenue china shop, and succeeded, without breaking a single piece of crockery. He was a friend of President Dwight Eisenhower. In 1983 President Ronald Reagan awarded him the Congressional Gold Medal. He continued to lead youth choral groups, giving a concert at Pa. State Univ. a day before he suffered a stroke, and 2 days before his death.—**NS/LK/DM**

Warland, Dale, eminent American conductor and composer; b. Fort Dodge, Iowa, April 14, 1932. He was educated at St. Olaf Coll. (B.A., 1954), at the Univ. of Minn. (M.A. in theory and composition, 1960), and at the Univ. of Southern Calif. in Los Angeles (D.M.A. in choral conducting, 1965). After serving as director of choral music at Humboldt State Coll. in Arcata, Calif., and at Keuka Coll. in Keuka Park, N.Y., he was prof. of music and director of choral activities at Macalester Coll. in St. Paul, Minn. (1967–85). In 1972 he established the Dale Warland Singers, a professional mixed chorus, which he led with notable distinction. While his expansive repertoire ranges from the 16th century to the present era, his primary emphasis has been on music of the 20th century, including the commissioning of new works.—**NS/LK/DM**

Warlich, Reinhold von, German baritone; b. St. Petersburg, May 24, 1877; d. N.Y., Nov. 10, 1939. His father was an opera conductor active in St. Petersburg; studied at the Hamburg Cons., in Florence, and in Cologne. He toured in Europe as a singer of German lieder, and was especially distinguished as an interpreter of Schubert, whose song cycles he gave in their entirety. He lived for some time in Canada; later, he was a singing teacher in Paris and London. He made concert tours in the U.S. from 1909, eventually settling in N.Y. —**NS/LK/DM**

Warlock, Peter
See **Heseltine, Philip (Arnold)**

Warrack, Guy (Douglas Hamilton), Scottish conductor and composer, father of **John (Hamilton) Warrack;** b. Edinburgh, Feb. 8, 1900; d. Englefield Green, Feb. 12, 1986. He studied at the Univ. of Oxford and received training in conducting from Boult and in composition from Vaughan Williams at the Royal Coll. of Music in London, where he subsequently taught (1925–35); in 1925 he made his conducting debut in London. After conducting the BBC Scottish Orch. in Glasgow (1936–45), he returned to London to serve as music director of the Sadler's Wells Royal Ballet (1948–51). He publ. the book *Sherlock Holmes and Music* (1947) and wrote articles for many journals. Among his compositions are a Sym. and a number of documentary film scores, including the official coronation film for Queen Elizabeth II, *A Queen Is Crowned* (1953). —**NS/LK/DM**

Warrack, John (Hamilton), English writer on music, son of **Guy (Douglas Hamilton) Warrack;** b. London, Feb. 9, 1928. He studied at Winchester Coll., then took up oboe and composition at the Royal Coll. of Music in London. Subsequently he played oboe in several ensembles. In 1953 he became music ed. of the Oxford Univ. Press. In 1954 he joined the staff of the *Daily Telegraph*, where he was a music critic; he then was chief music critic of the *Sunday Telegraph* (1961–72). After serving as director of the Leeds Festival (1977–83), he was a lecturer in music and a fellow at St. Hughes Coll., Oxford (1984–93). He contributed numerous articles and reviews to *Opera* and *Gramophone*. His biography of Weber is the standard modern source.

WRITINGS: *Six Great Composers* (London, 1958); co-ed. with H. Rosenthal, *The Concise Oxford Dictionary of Opera* (London, 1964; 2nd ed., rev., 1979); *Carl Maria von Weber* (London, 1968; also in Ger., 1972; 2nd ed., rev., London, 1976); *Tchaikovsky Symphonies and Concertos* (London, 1969; 2nd ed., rev., 1974); *Tchaikovsky* (London, 1973); *Tchaikovsky Ballet Music* (London, 1978); ed. *Carl Maria von Weber: Writings on Music* (Cambridge, 1982); co.-ed. with E. West, *The Oxford Dictionary of Opera* (Oxford, 1992).—**NS/LK/DM**

Warren, Diane, a one-woman music industry, and one of the most successful songwriters and publishers ever, b. Van Nuys, Calif., Sept. 11, 1956. Songwriting has obsessed Diane Warren ever since her father brought home a guitar in her preteen years. She worked over the same melody for hours. By the time she was 11, Warren fell in love with the idea of writing songs. By the time she was 14, Warren was writing three songs a day and sending them out to publishers. She developed a thick skin against rejection. By her 18th birthday, she had her first song published, although it remained unrecorded. Barbara Mandrell and Patti Austin did record early Warren compositions, but they weren't hits.

Another non-hit from this time was a tune called "If You Loved Me," which appeared on Laura Branigan's 1982 debut album. On the strength of Branigan's gold record hit "Gloria," (which stayed at #2 in *Billboard* for three weeks) the album went gold as well. Warren wrote a song for Branigan's second album, 1983's *Branigan 2*. That song, "Solitaire," went to #7 on *Billboard*, bringing the album along for her second gold LP.

If people didn't exactly sit up and take notice of Diane Warren yet, with a Top Ten hit under her belt she could at least persuade more of them to listen. Occasionally, projects came to her. Motown was making a film called *The Last Dragon* and needed a tune for one of their rising bands, DeBarge. She came up with a song called "Rhythm of the Night," which rose to #3. Since then, Warren has contributed songs to over 50 films. Hit songs like "Nothing's Going to Stop Us Now" earned forgettable films like *Mannequin* nominations for Oscars, Golden Globes and a Grammys solely on the strength of Warren's songs.

As Diane's songwriting career started ascending, she started having problems with her publisher that ended in court. Her publisher wouldn't publish her songs and no other publisher would, either, since that would make them party to the lawsuit. Warren's solution was to form her own publishing company, Realsongs, a ploy usually used by songwriters far further along in their careers. Contacting artists and managers of her acquaintance only when she had the right song, she started placing her tunes regularly. As a publishing company, Realsongs represents only one songwriter, Diane Warren. However, in 1990 *Billboard* named the company Singles Publisher of the Year. At one point she had a record-breaking seven hits on the singles chart at the same time.

Since then, Warren has won three ASCAP Writer of the Year awards, the only woman ever to earn so many. Along with Gloria Estefan, she wrote "Reach," the theme song for the 1996 Olympics. In addition to the phenomenal success that she had with Celine Dion and "Because You Loved Me," she had another mega-hit with Toni Braxton's version of "Unbreak My Heart." Heartfelt and full of pop-craft, like many Warren compositions, it rode the top of the *Billboard* Hot 100 Singles chart for 11 weeks.

Many of her most recent successes came out of the movies. Warren finally came home with a 1996 Grammy for Best Song Written Specifically for a Motion Picture of Television for the chart-topping, "Because You Loved Me." She also won her third Oscar for "How Do I Live." The song was on the charts simultaneously by two artists, performed in the movie by Leanne Rimes and also recorded by Trisha Yearwood. "I Don't Want to Miss a Thing," recorded by Aerosmith, topped the pop charts, while a version by country star Mark Chesnutt topped the country charts.

Over her entire songwriting career, Diane Warren has demonstrated a canny sense of what makes a pop song successful. Beyond that, she displays an uncanny knack for reaching people where they live.—**HB**

Warren, Elinor Remick, American pianist and composer; b. Los Angeles, Feb. 23, 1900; d. there, April 27, 1991. She studied piano as a small child with Kathryn Cocke, taking up composition studies at 14; her first works were publ. while she was still in high school. After attending Mills Coll. in Oakland, Calif., she studied with Olga Steeb, Paolo Gallico, Frank La Forge, and Clarence Dickinson in N.Y.; much later, she received training from Boulanger in Paris (1959). She was mainly active as a piano accompanist to such singers as Bori and Tibbett.

WORKS: ORCH.: *The Fountain* (1942); Suite (1955; rev. 1958); *The Crystal Lake* (1958); *Along the Western Shore: Dark Hills, Nocturne, Sea Rhapsody* (1963); *Intermezzo* (1970); Sym. in 1 Movement (1971). **CHAMBER:** Woodwind Quintet; various piano pieces. **VOCAL:** Sacred and secular choral pieces; numerous songs.

BIBL.: V. Bortin, *E.R. W.: Her Life and her Music* (Metuchen, N.J., 1987); idem, *E.R. W.: A Bio-Bibliography* (Westport, Conn., 1993).—**NS/LK/DM**

Warren, Harry (originally, **Guaragna, Salvatore**), productive American film-song composer; b. N.Y., Dec. 24, 1893; d. Los Angeles, Sept. 22, 1981. Warren was the first major American song composer to write primarily for film. Immediate predecessors such as Jerome Kern worked extensively on Broadway before turning to motion pictures. Fifty-six feature films released between 1933 and 1961 carry Warren' credit as songwriter; add all the Hollywood movies in which newly written or existing Warren songs were used between 1929 and 1975, and that number swells to an astonishing 135. Nominated for the Academy Award for Best Song 11 times, he won three Oscars: for "Lullaby of Broadway" (lyrics by Dubin), "You'll Never Know" (lyrics by Gordon), and "On the Atchison, Topeka and the Santa Fe" (lyrics by Mercer). His other major hits included "I Found a Million-Dollar Baby (In a Five-and-Ten-Cent Store)" (lyrics by Mort Dixon and Billy Rose), "I Only Have Eyes for You" (lyrics by Dubin), "You Must Have Been a Beautiful Baby" (lyrics by Mercer), "Jeepers Creepers" (lyrics by Mercer), "Chattanooga Choo Choo" (lyrics by Gordon), and "(I've Got a Gal in) Kalamazoo" (lyrics by Gordon).

Warren was the son of Italian immigrants Antonio and Rachel Deluca Guaragna, who settled in Brooklyn. His father, a bootmaker, legally changed the family name to Warren when he was a child. Warren showed an early interest in music, but his parents could not afford lessons. Though he went without formal training, he taught himself to play his father's accordion, sang in the church choir, and, by the age of 14, had also begun to earn money as a drummer. He dropped out of high school to play drums in a band led by his godfather, Pasquale Pucci, in the Keene and Shippey traveling carnival. Back in Brooklyn, he taught himself to play piano and worked as a fruit seller and as a stagehand at local theaters before finding employment at the Vitagraph Motion Picture Studios, where he did everything from acting and assistant directing to piano playing; he also worked as a pianist in cafés and silent-movie houses. On Dec. 19, 1917, he married Josephine Wensler; they had a son and a daughter. In 1918 he joined the navy and was stationed on Long Island.

Warren began to write songs while in the service, "I Learned to Love You When I Learned My ABCs" (lyrics by Warren), though it wasn't published, earned him a job as a song plugger with Stark and Cowan, a music-publishing company, in 1920. His first published song, "Rose of the Rio Grande" (music also by Ross Gorman; lyrics by Edgar Leslie), became a record hit for Marion Harris in April 1923. He and Leslie tried another song with a river theme, "By the River Sainte Marie," but it was rejected by publishers until Guy Lombardo and His Royal Canadians had a best-selling record with it in March 1931. Warren and Leslie's "Back Home in Pasadena" was published by Shapiro, Bernstein and Company in 1924, and the firm took Warren on as staff composer. (In 1961 the Temperance Seven revived "Pasadena" for a U.K. Top Ten hit.)

Working with lyricist Bud Green, he wrote two hits for Gene Austin, "The Only, Only One for Me" (music also by James V. Monaco) in July 1925 and "Ya Gotta Know How to Love" in September 1926, and one for Fred Waring's Pennsylvanians, "I Love My Baby" in May 1926. Warren worked with Al Dubin for the first time in 1926 and wrote "Too Many Kisses" (lyrics also by Billy Rose), though their partnership would not flourish until four years later. Teaming with Mortimer Weinberg and Charley Marks, he then wrote another hit for Waring, "Where Do You Work-a, John?" in March 1927. "One Sweet Letter from You," a hit for Ted Lewis and His Band, among others, in July 1927, was a collaboration with lyricists Lew Brown and Sidney Clare.

Warren moved to the Remick publishing company in 1928 and there found a regular collaborator in Mort Dixon starting with another Ted Lewis hit, "Hello, Montreal!" (lyrics also by Rose) in July 1928; their "Old Man Sunshine, Little Boy Bluebird" became a hit for George Olsen and His Orch. in September and "Nagasaki" scored for the Ipana Troudadors in October. Warren wrote a few songs with Gus Kahn, notably "Where the Shy Little Violets Grow," which became a hit for Lombardo in February 1929, though his most significant work with Kahn would not take place for another decade.

Warren's first song to be written for a motion picture was "Mi Amado" (lyrics by Sam M. Lewis and Joe Young), which was used in Paramount's *The Wolf Song* (1929). After Warner Bros. acquired Remick in 1929 and thus became his employer, Warren went to Hollywood to work on the screen adaptation of Richard Rodgers and Lorenz Hart's *Spring Is Here* (1930), writing six songs with Sam M. Lewis and Joe Young, including "Have a Little Faith in Me," a hit for Lombardo in January 1930, and "Cryin' for the Carolines," a hit for Waring among others in February. Also written for the film was "Absence Makes the Heart Grow Fonder (For Someone Else)," a hit for Bernie Cummins and His Orch. in June. The same month, Nick Lucas had a hit with "Telling It to the Daisies," which Warren wrote with Joe Young.

Despite the success of the songs from *Spring Is Here*, Warren did not enjoy his sojourn in Calif., and the studios lost interest in movie musicals with the advent of the Depression. Consequently, he returned to N.Y. to write songs for Billy Rose's Broadway revue *Sweet and Low* (N.Y., Nov. 17, 1930); he wrote "Cheerful Little Earful" (lyrics by Ira Gershwin and Rose), a hit for Tom Gerun and His Orch. in December, and "Would You Like to Take a Walk?" (lyrics by Dixon and Rose), a hit for Rudy Vallée in March 1931.

Warren was the primary composer of a Broadway show for the first time with *Billy Rose's Crazy Quilt*, which ran for only 67 performances but featured a best-selling hit in "I Found a Million-Dollar Baby (In a Five-and-Ten-Cent Store)"; Waring had the most popular recording in July, with Bing Crosby and the Boswell Sisters close behind. Even more successful was *The Laugh Parade*, produced by, directed by, and starring comedian Ed Wynn, which ran 243 performances and spun off a double-sided hit record for the Arden-Ohman Orch. of "You're My Everything" and "Ooh! That Kiss" (both lyrics by Dixon and Joe Young) in the fall.

Warren and Dubin had their first major hit with "Too Many Tears," which became a best-seller for Lombardo in March 1932. Given the success of his songs in the hands of Vallée and Crosby, Warren must have seemed a perfect choice to write for the Warner film *Crooner* (1932), a satire on such singers. "Three's a Crowd" (lyrics by Dubin and Irving Kahal) was used in the picture and became a hit for Gerun in September 1932. By that time Warren had accepted another assignment from Warner Bros. to return to Hollywood and collaborate with Dubin on an original movie musical, *42nd Street*. A box office smash, the film was the turning point in his career, and it restored the studios' faith in musicals. Of the five songs the team wrote for it, four became hits: "You're Getting to Be a Habit with Me," a best-seller for Crosby backed by Lombardo's band; the title song, a best-seller for Don Bestor and His Orch.; "Shuffle Off to Buffalo," which was equally successful for Bestor and for Hal Kemp and His Orch.; and "Young and Healthy," also for Crosby and Lombardo.

The success of *42nd Street* caused Warner to go into production with another musical, *Gold Diggers of 1933*, once again with five songs by Warren and Dubin. This time the hits were the best-seller "The Shadow Waltz" and "I've Got to Sing a Torch Song," both for Crosby, and "We're in the Money" (or "The Gold Diggers' Song") for Ted Lewis, among others. After this film too became a hit, Warner signed Warren to the first of a series of renewable one- year contracts. He and Dubin next contributed two songs to *Footlight Parade*, one of which was "Honeymoon Hotel," which became a hit for Leo Reisman and His Orch. in December 1933. The team was allowed to write the songs for Eddie Cantor's movie musical *Roman Scandals* though it was an independent production released through United Artists; their score included "Keep Young and Beautiful," a hit for Abe Lyman and His Calif. Orch. in February 1934.

Warren and Dubin's next picture was also released by United Artists when Warner loaned the team out for *Moulin Rouge*. All three of the songs they wrote were hits, also in February 1934: "The Boulevard of Broken Dreams" for Jan Garber and His Orch.; "Coffee in the Morning (Kisses in the Night)" for the Boswell Sisters, who appeared in the film; and "Song of Surrender" for Wayne King and His Orch.

Back at Warner the pair had three more musicals in release during 1934. *Wonder Bar*, an adaptation of the Al Jolson stage show with Jolson starring featured the title song, which scored for Emil Coleman and His Orch. in March, and the April hit for Eddy Duchin and His Orch., "Why Do I Dream Those Dreams?" Among the four songs Warren and Dubin wrote for *Twenty Million Sweethearts* were the hits "I'll String Along with You," a best-seller for Ted Fiorito and His Orch., and "Fair and Warmer," a hit for Dick Powell, who was in the film; both of these songs were hits in May. *Dames* produced a hit for Duchin in its title track, but it is best remembered for "I Only Have Eyes for You," initially a hit in July 1934 for Ben Selvin and His Orch., among others; it subsequently became a standard.

The busiest year in Warren's career was 1935; he and Dubin were the primary songwriters on five films and contributed to another eight. The result was a series of hits that began in March when Victor Young and His Orch. had a successful recording of the title song from *Sweet Music*. Among the three songs in *Gold Diggers of 1935* was "Lullaby of Broadway," which topped the hit parade in May, becoming one of the biggest hits of the year in a recording by the Dorsey Brothers Orch. and winning the Academy Award. *Go into Your Dance*, a vehicle for Jolson and his wife, Ruby Keeler, who had become a film star in *42nd Street*, brought "She's a Latin from Manhattan" into the hit parade for Victor Young, while Ozzie Nelson and His Orch. scored with "About a Quarter to Nine." Russ Morgan and His Orch. had a hit with "The Rose in Her Hair" from *Broadway Gondolier*, which also featured "Lulu's Back in Town," a hit for Fats Waller.

As a navy veteran Warren had a special feeling for the subject of *Shipmates Forever*, and "Don't Give Up the Ship" not only became a hit for Tommy Dorsey and His Orch., it was also adopted by the U.S. Naval Academy as its official song. Hal Kemp had the hit recording of the title song from *Page Miss Glory*, and at the end of the year *Stars Over Broadway* produced a hit in Little Jack Little's recording of "Where Am I?"

Warren and Dubin had primary responsibility for four films released during 1936 while contributing to four more. Their major hits were "I'll Sing You a Thousand Love Songs" from *Cain and Mabel*, which topped the hit parade in December for Eddy Duchin, and "With Plenty of Money and You" from *Gold Diggers of 1937*, on top in February 1937 for Henry Busse and His Orch.

The next year found Warren and Dubin writing songs for six Warner features. "September in the Rain" from *Melody for Two* was recorded by Lombardo and topped the hit parade in May and June, becoming the biggest hit of the year. Lombardo also took "I Know Now" from *The Singing Marine* into the hit parade, and the film gave a hit to Kay Kyser and His Orch. with "'Cause My Baby Says It's So." Anson Weeks and His Orch. had a hit with "How Could You?" from *San Quentin*, and Bing Crosby topped the hit parade in November with "Remember Me?" from *Mr. Dodd Takes the Air*, a Best Song Oscar nominee.

Although Warren was the primary song composer for four Warner films in 1938 and contributed songs to two more, earning his usual number of hits, the year marked the end of a number of associations for him. Personally, he lost his teenage son Harry Warren Jr. to pneumonia on April 2. Professionally, his partnership with Al Dubin gave way as the lyricist became unreliable and was replaced by Johnny Mercer. Though Warren coped with the changes at first, he opted not to renew his Warner contract after 1939. Nevertheless, there were hits, all of them written with Mercer: "Day Dreaming" from *Gold Diggers in Paris* for Vallée, who starred; and "You Must Have Been a Beautiful Baby" from *Hard to Get*, at the top of the hit parade in December and January 1939 for Crosby; and "Jeepers Creepers" from *Going Places*, which topped the hit parade in January and February 1939 for Al Donohue and His Orch. and was nominated for an Academy Award.

In 1939, Warren's final two films for Warner, *Naughty but Nice* and *Wings of the Navy*, were released, and he was loaned out to MGM to work with Gus Kahn on *Honolulu*. However, his only song in the hit parade during the year was "Tears from My Inkwell" (lyrics by Dixon) for Glen Gray and the Casa Loma Orch. in May. In 1940 he signed to 20th Century–Fox, headed by Darryl Zanuck, who had brought him to Warner Bros. eight years before. With lyricist Mack Gordon he wrote a new series of musicals, most of them starring Alice Faye and/or Betty Grable and nominally set in exotic locations, many featuring the leading swing bands of the day. In anticipation of those efforts, Glenn Miller and His Orch. scored a minor hit in June 1940 with "Devil May Care," an independent song on which Warren collaborated with Johnny Burke. Warren's most successful work of the year came on his second Fox feature, *Down Argentine Way*, which produced the near-title song "Down Argentina Way," an Oscar nominee most successfully recorded by Bob Crosby and His Orch., with many competing versions, and "Two Dreams Met," recorded by Tommy Dorsey among others.

Warren and Gordon wrote songs for five Fox films in 1941, their biggest success coming with *Sun Valley Serenade*, which featured Miller, who performed one of the year's biggest hits, the million-selling, Oscar- nominated "Chattanooga Choo Choo," as well as the hits "I Know Why (And So Do You)" and "It Happened in Sun Valley." Miller also starred in *Orchestra Wives* the following year, and from that film he recorded the Warren-Gordon hits "At Last," "Serenade in Blue," and the chart-topping gold record "(I've Got a Gal in) Kalamazoo," which was nominated for an Academy Award.

Harry James and His Orch. were featured in *Springtime in the Rockies* and scored their own gold chart topper with "I Had the Craziest Dream." Sammy Kaye and His Orch. were featured in *Iceland*; their Warren-Gordon hit was "There Will Never Be Another You."

The onset of the recording ban by the musicians' union in 1942 made it more difficult to score newly recorded hits, but Dick Haymes recorded a cappella for a gold #1 hit with Warren and Gordon's "You'll Never Know" from *Hello, Frisco, Hello* in July 1943; the dreamy ballad won the Academy Award and became Warren's all-time best-seller in sheet music. After Decca Records settled with the union in September, Glen Gray topped the charts in January 1944 with "My Heart Tells Me (Should I Believe My Heart?)" from *Sweet Rosie O'Grady. The Gang's All Here*, which found Warren teaming with lyricist Leo Robin, featured Benny Goodman and His Orch. but brought chart records to Judy Garland, with "A Journey to a Star" and Ella Mae Morse with the war-themed "No Love, No Nothin' (Until My Baby Comes Home)."

Warren moved from Fox to MGM in 1944 after completing work on a final film, *Billy Rose's Diamond Horseshoe*, which produced two Top Ten hits for its star, Dick Haymes, in "I Wish I Knew" and "The More I See You" (both lyrics by Gordon). Warren then wrote songs with Arthur Freed for MGM's all-star *Ziegfeld Follies* and the Fred Astaire film *Yolanda and the Thief*. But his first major success at MGM came with *The Harvey Girls*, which marked a reunion with Johnny Mercer. The two wrote seven songs for the Judy Garland musical, among them "On the Atchison, Topeka and the Santa Fe," which Mercer and the Pied Pipers recorded well in advance of the film's release, resulting in a chart-topping hit in the summer of 1945; the song went on to win the 1946 Academy Award.

The late 1940s saw a slowing in Warren's remarkable output as MGM made fewer musicals. "This Is Always" (lyrics by Gordon) was a holdover from his days at Fox; after being used instrumentally in the studio's September 1946 release *Three Little Girls in Blue*, it became a Top Ten hit for Harry James. Warren's next MGM effort, in collaboration with Ralph Blane, was *Summer Holiday* (1948), an adaptation of Eugene O'Neill's play *Ah! Wilderness* starring Mickey Rooney. Jo Stafford had a minor hit with "The Stanley Steamer" from the score. Warren and Blane wrote five new songs for a remake of *Twenty Million Sweethearts* retitled *My Dream Is Yours* (1949) at Warner Bros., then Warren teamed with Ira Gershwin back at MGM for *The Barkleys of Broadway* (1949), the final Fred Astaire–Ginger Rogers film.

The final Judy Garland film at MGM was *Summer Stock* (1950), on which Warren collaborated with Gordon and with Saul Chaplin and Jack Brooks; the same year he again teamed with Arthur Freed for the Esther Williams musical *Pagan Love Song*, and 1951 saw him writing for another Esther Williams vehicle, *Texas Carnival*, with lyricist Dorothy Fields. None of these efforts produced song hits for Warren, but he did return to the charts in the May 1951 with the independent song "Rose, Rose, I Love You" (lyrics by Brooks), a Top Ten hit for Frankie Laine, and in February 1952 Ray Anthony and His Orch. had a Top Ten revival of "At Last."

Warren later complained that MGM was lax in promoting his songs. After two more musicals, such as the Fred Astaire film *The Belle of New York*, with lyrics by Mercer and Esther Williams's *Skirts Ahoy!* with lyrics by Blane, Warren left the studio and went to Paramount at the request of Bing Crosby to work on *Just for You*, which resulted in the hit "Zing a Little Zong" (lyrics by Leo Robin). In 1953 Rosemary Clooney and Harry James revived "You'll Never Know" for a hit while Warren and Brooks wrote songs for the Dean Martin–Jerry Lewis comedy *The Caddy*, among them "That's Amore," which became a gold-selling hit for Martin and brought Warren his tenth Oscar nomination. Warren, Brooks, and Martin tried for another Italian-flavored hit with "Innamorata" from the 1955 Martin and Lewis comedy *Artists and Models* and didn't do quite as well, though Martin's recording did get into the Top 40 in April 1956.

By the mid-1950s, Hollywood had lost interest in original movie musicals of the kind it had made in the 1930s and 1940s, and Warren found time to write his first stage musical in 25 years in 1956. *Shangri-La* was a flop, running only 21 performances, but Warren was back in the pop charts in the fall when The Platters revived "You'll Never Know" yet again for a Top 40 hit. Back at Paramount, Warren was called upon largely to write title songs and incidental music for essentially nonmusical films. In 1957 he collaborated with Harold Adamson and director Leo McCarey on several songs for the Cary Grant–Deborah Kerr romance *An Affair to Remember*, including the title song, which became a Top 40 hit for Vic Damone (who sang it over the film's credits) in August; it earned him his 11th Academy Award nomination.

After the breakup of Martin and Lewis, Warren continued to write songs for Jerry Lewis's Paramount comedies, *Rock-a-Bye Baby* (with Sammy Cahn; 1958), *Cinderfella* (with Brooks; 1960), and *The Ladies' Man* (with Brooks; 1961) before leaving the studio to work freelance in 1961. He wrote several title songs in the 1960s, the last of which was for the Rosalind Russell film *Rosie!* in 1967 with Mercer. (He also finished a non film project in 1962, composing the music for a Catholic Mass with a Latin text, although it was not performed in public until 1980 when it was premiered by the Loyola-Marymount Coll. Mixed Chorus in Los Angeles.)

Meanwhile, his songs came in for frequent revival. The Flamingos had the biggest hit of their career with their Top Ten rendition of "I Only Have Eyes for You" in 1959. Bobby Darin had a Top Ten hit with "You Must Have Been a Beautiful Baby" in 1961, the same year that Dinah Washington hit the Top 40 with "September in the Rain." Floyd Cramer had a Top 40 instrumental recording of "Chattanooga Choo Choo" in 1962, and Chris Montez reached the Top 40 with two Warren songs, "The More I See You" and "There Will Never Be Another You" in 1966. The Dave Clark Five were in the Top 40 with their version of "You Must Have Been a Beautiful Baby" in 1967. Art Garfunkel's revival of "I Only Have Eyes for You" made the U.S. Top 40 and topped the U.K. charts in 1975, and Tuxedo Junction had a disco-flavored Top 40 hit with "Chattanooga Choo Choo" in 1978.

The late 1970s brought a resurgence of theatrical interest in Warren's music. A series of musical revues was mounted, including *Harry's Back in Town* in Toronto in 1976, *Mr. Warren's Profession* in London in 1977, and *Lullaby of Broadway* Off-Broadway in 1979. Finally, in 1980, impresario David Merrick produced a stage adaptation of *42nd Street* on Broadway; it used the film's score plus other Warren songs and ran 3,486 performances, making it one of the most successful musicals in Broadway history. Warren was too ill to attend the opening. At the time of his death he was working on *Manhattan Melody*, an original movie musical to be directed by James Bridges at 20th Century–Fox.

Works (only works for which Warren was the primary, credited song composer are listed): **MUSICALS/REVUES:** *Billy Rose's Crazy Quilt* (N.Y., May 19, 1931); *The Laugh Parade* (N.Y., Nov. 2, 1931); *Shangri-La* (N.Y., June 13, 1956); *42nd Street* (N.Y., Aug. 25, 1980). **FILMS:** *42nd Street* (1933); *Gold Diggers of 1933* (1933); *Roman Scandals* (1933); *Moulin Rouge* (1934); *Wonder Bar* (1934); *Twenty Million Sweethearts* (1934); *Dames* (1934); *Gold Diggers of 1935* (1935); *Go into Your Dance* (1935); *Broadway Gondolier* (1935); *Shipmates Forever* (1935); *Stars over Broadway* (1935); *I Found Stella Parrish* (1935); *Colleen* (1936); *Hearts Divided* (1936); *Cain and Mabel* (1936); *Sing Me a Love Song* (1936); *The Singing Marine* (1937); *Mr. Dodd Takes the Air* (1937); *Gold Diggers in Paris* (1938); *Garden of the Moon* (1938); *Hard to Get* (1938); *Going Places* (1938); *Naughty but Nice* (1939); *Honolulu* (1939); *Young People* (1940); *Down Argentine Way* (1940); *That Night in Rio* (1941); *The Great American Broadcast* (1941); *Sun Valley Serenade* (1941); *Weekend in Havana* (1941); *Charlie Chan in Rio* (1941); *Orchestra Wives* (1942); *Iceland* (1942); *Springtime in the Rockies* (1942); *Sweet Rosie O'Grady* (1943); *The Gang's All Here* (1943); *Billy Rose's Diamond Horseshoe* (1945); *Yolanda and the Thief* (1945); *The Harvey Girls* (1946); *Summer Holiday* (1948); *My Dream Is Yours* (1949); *The Barkleys of Broadway* (1949); *Summer Stock* (1950); *Pagan Love Song* (1950); *Texas Carnival* (1951); *The Belle of N.Y.* (1952); *Skirts Ahoy!* (1952); *Just for You* (1952); *The Caddy* (1953); *Artists and Models* (1955); *The Birds and the Bees* (1956); *An Affair to Remember* (1957); *Rock-a-Bye Baby* (1958); *Cinderfella* (1960); *The Ladies' Man* (1961).

Bibl.: T. Thomas, *H. W. and the Hollywood Musical* (Secaucus, N.Y., 1975).—**WR**

Warren, Leonard, outstanding American baritone; b. N.Y., April 21, 1911; d. there, on the stage of the Metropolitan Opera House while singing the role of Don Carlo during a performance of *La forza del destino*, March 4, 1960. The original family name was Warenoff; it was Americanized as Warren when his Russian father settled in the U.S. Warren was first employed in his father's fur business in N.Y. In 1935 he joined the chorus of Radio City Music Hall; he also studied voice with Sidney Dietch and Giuseppe De Luca. In 1938 Warren won the Metropolitan Opera Auditions of the Air and was granted a stipend to study in Italy, where he took voice lessons with Pais and Piccozi. Returning to America, Warren made his debut at the Metropolitan Opera in excerpts from *La Traviata* and *Pagliacci* during a concert in N.Y. on Nov. 27, 1938; his formal operatic debut took place there on Jan. 13, 1939, when he sang Paolo in *Simon Boccanegra*. He quickly advanced in public favor, eventually assuming a leading place among the noted baritones of his time. He also sang in San Francisco, Chicago, Canada, and South America. He appeared at La Scala in Milan in 1953; in 1958 he made a highly successful tour of the Soviet Union. His last complete performance at the Metropolitan Opera was as Simon Boccanegra on March 1, 1960, 3 days before his tragic death. He was particularly acclaimed as one of the foremost interpreters of the great Verdi baritone roles; he also sang the parts of Tonio in *Pagliacci*, Escamillo in *Carmen*, and Scarpia in *Tosca*. He collapsed while singing the aria "Urna fatale dal mio destino," underlining the tragic irony of the words, and died of a cerebral hemorrhage backstage. He was reputed to be a person of an intractable character, who always tried to impose his will on stage designers, managers, and even conductors in matters of production, direction, and tempi. He caused pain, a colleague said, but he had a great voice.—**NS/LK/DM**

Warren, Raymond (Henry Charles), English composer and teacher; b. Weston-super-Mare, Nov. 7, 1928. He studied with Robin Orr at Corpus Christi Coll., Cambridge (1949–52; M.A., 1952), continuing his education at the Univ. of Cambridge (M.A., 1955; Mus.D., 1967); he also was a student of Tippett (1952–54) and Berkeley (1958). In 1955 he became a teacher at Queen's Univ. in Belfast, where he was a prof. from 1966 to 1972. From 1972 to 1994 he was a prof. at the Univ. of Bristol. He publ. *Opera Workshops: Studies in Understanding and Interpretation* (Brookfield, 1995).

Works: DRAMATIC: *The Lady of Ephesus*, chamber opera (1958; Belfast, Feb. 16, 1959); *Finn and the Black Hag*, children's opera (Belfast, Dec. 11, 1959); *Graduation Ode*, comic opera (Belfast, Nov. 20, 1963); 3 children's church operas: *Let My People Go* (Liverpool, March 22, 1972), *St. Patrick* (Liverpool, May 3, 1979), and *In the Beginning* (Clifton, July 22, 1982); incidental music for plays. **ORCH.:** *Nocturne* (1964); 2 syms. (1965, 1969); Violin Concerto (1966); *Seaside Sketches* (1968); *Wexford Bells* (1970). **CHAMBER:** 3 string quartets (1965, 1975, 1977); Duo Concertante for Cello and Piano (1972); *Burnt Norton Sketches* for Piano Trio (1985); *Exchanges* for Oboe and Piano (1986); Violin Sonata (1993). **Piano:** 2 sonatas (1952, 1977). **VOCAL:** 2 oratorios: *The Passion* (Belfast, Dec. 11, 1959) and *Continuing Cities* (Bristol, April 22, 1989); choral pieces; song cycles; solo songs.—**NS/LK/DM**

Wartel, Pierre-François, noted French tenor and teacher; b. Versailles, April 3, 1806; d. Paris, Aug. 3, 1882. In 1825 he entered the Paris Cons. as a pupil of Halévy, but soon thereafter began studies with Choron at the Institut de la Musique Religieuse; in 1828 he returned to the Paris Cons. to pursue vocal training with Davide Banderali and Adolphe Nourrit (premier prix in singing, 1829). He was a member of the Paris Opéra (1831–46), and also made successful concert tours to Berlin, Prague, and Vienna. With Nourrit, he helped create an appreciation of Schubert's lieder in France via his song recitals. He was mainly active as a singing teacher from 1842; his most prominent pupils were Christine Nilsson and Zelia Trebelli. His wife, Atale Thérèse Annette (née Adrien) Wartel (b. Paris, July 2,

1814; d. there, Nov. 6, 1865), was a talented pianist; studied at the Paris Cons.; after serving as an accompanist there, she was a prof. of piano (1831–38). She composed piano studies and other pieces.—**NS/LK/DM**

Warwick, Dionne (originally, **Warrick, Marie Dionne**), smooth-voiced vocalist long associated with the songwriting team of Burt Bacharach and Hal David; b. East Orange, N.J., Dec. 12, 1940. Dionne Warwick was born into a family of gospel singers and began singing in the New Hope Baptist Church choir in Newark, N.J., at the age of six. She played piano with the gospel group The Drinkard Singers and later was a member of The Gospelaires with sister Dee Dee and aunt Cissy Houston (Whitney's mother). Dionne graduated from Hart Music Coll. in Conn. In the late 1950s, the Warwick sisters, Cissy Houston, and Doris Troy began singing together at recording sessions in N.Y. During the session for The Drifters' "Mexican Divorce" in 1961, Dionne met songwriter-producer-arranger Burt Bacharach, who helped secure her sessions work and a recording contract with Scepter Records.

With Bacharach and lyricist Hal David producing and writing the songs, Dionne Warwick scored her first major pop and smash rhythm-and-blues hit with her debut single, "Don't Make Me Over," at the end of 1962. Subsequent successes for the team through 1966 included the smash pop, rhythm-and-blues, and easy-listening hits "Anyone Who Had a Heart," "Walk on By," and "Message to Michael," and the major pop and R&B hits "Reach Out for Me," "Trains and Boats and Planes," and "I Just Don't Know What to Do with Myself."

By 1964, sister Dee Dee Warwick was pursuing her own solo career, recording "You're No Good" for Jubilee Records. She signed with the Blue Rock subsidiary of Mercury Records, scoring a major rhythm-and-blues hit "We're Doing Fine," in 1965. Moving to the parent label in 1966, she achieved major rhythm-and-blues hits with "I Want to Be with You" (the tune that crossed over onto the pop chart), "I'm Gonna Make You Love Me" (another crossover hit for The Supremes and The Temptations in 1968 and 1969), and "Foolish Fool" through 1969. She subsequently recorded for Atco Records, managing a near-smash rhythm-and-blues hit with "She Didn't Know (She Kept on Talking)" in 1970. She continued to record into the 1980s for Private Stock and RCA.

Debuting on the cabaret circuit by 1967 and fully established as an international recording artist, Dionne Warwick began recording less dynamic Bacharach-David songs as the team began working on movie scores and stage musicals. Through 1968, she scored a smash crossover hits with "I Say a Little Prayer" and "(Theme from) The Valley of the Dolls," and major crossover hits with "Alfie," "Do You Know the Way to San Jose," and "Promises, Promises." "This Girl's in Love with You" became a pop and R&B smash in 1969 and "I'll Never Fall in Love Again" became a pop smash in 1970. The rest of her smash hits through 1971, including "Who Is Gonna Love Me," "Let Me Go to Him," "Make It Easy on Yourself," and "Who Gets the Guy," came in the easy-listening field.

By 1971, Dionne Warwick had switched to Warner Bros. Records, but after a single album with Burt Bacharach and Hal David, the duo and the singer parted company. She used the last name Warwicke from late 1971 to 1975, achieving her only major pop hit until 1979 with 1974's "Then Came You." Recorded in Philadelphia with The Spinners and produced by Thom Bell, the song became a top pop and smash rhythm and blues and easy-listening hit. Bell produced her *Track of the Cat* album, which yielded a rhythm-and-blues smash with "Once You Hit the Road," and she next toured and recorded the live *A Man and a Woman* with Isaac Hayes.

In 1979, Dionne Warwick switched to Arista Records, where here debut, simply *Dionne*, was produced by Barry Manilow. It yielded three hits, including the smash pop hit "I'll Never Love This Way Again" and the major pop hit "Deja Vu," and became the best-selling album of her career. "No Night So Long" became another top easy-listening and major pop/R&B hit in 1980, and Bee Gee Barry Gibb produced her *Heartbreaker* album, which yielded a top easy-listening and major pop/R&B hit with the title tune. Luther Vandross produced Warwick's *How Many Times Can We Say Goodbye*, and the title song, sung as a duet, became a smash rhythm-and-blues and pop hit.

In 1980 and 1981 and again in 1985 and 1986, Dionne Warwick hosted the syndicated variety television series *Solid Gold*. She reunited with Burt Bacharach for 1984's *Finder of Lost Loves*. In 1985, she took part in the recording of USA for Africa's "We Are the World," scoring a top pop, rhythm-and-blues, and easy-listening hit with "That's What Friends Are For" late in the year. Written by Bacharach and his wife Carole Bayer Sager, the song was recorded with "Friends" Elton John, Gladys Knight, and Stevie Wonder, and, at the request of Elizabeth Taylor, profits from the song were donated to the cause of AIDS research. Frequently appearing at benefit and tribute concerts throughout the 1980s and 1990s, Warwick managed her last major pop/R&B (and top easy-listening) hit with "Love Power," a duet with Jeffrey Osborne, in 1987.

Dionne Warwick toured with Burt Bacharach in 1992 and reunited with Bacharach *and* Hal David for *Friends Can Be Lovers*. In 1994, she recorded a collection of Brazilian songs, *Aquarela Do Brasil*, for Arista, and *Celebration in Vienna* with opera singer Placido Domingo, for Sony Classical. She subsequently became perhaps better known for her "infomercials" for the *Psychic Friends Network*.

Disc.: *Presenting Dionne Warwick* (1963); *Anyone Who Had a Heart* (1964); *Make Way for Dionne Warwick* (1964); *The Sensitive Sound of Dionne Warwick* (1965); *Here I Am* (1965); *In Paris* (1966); *Here, Where There Is Love* (1966); *On Stage and at the Movies* (1967); *The Windows of the World* (1967); *Magic of Believing* (1968); *Valley of the Dolls* (1968); *Promises, Promises* (1968); *Soulful* (1969); *I'll Never Fall in Love Again* (1970); *Very Dionne* (1970); *Dionne* (1971); *From Within* (1972); *Just Being Myself* (1973); *Then Came You* (1975); *Track of the Cat* (1975); *Love at First Sight* (1977); *Dionne* (1979); *No Night So Long* (1980); *Hot! Live and Otherwise* (1981); *Friends to Love* (1982); *Heartbreaker* (1982); *How Many Times Can We Say Goodbye* (1983); *Finder of Lost Loves* (1984); *Dionne Warwick and Friends* (1985); *Reservations for Two* (1987); *Sings Cole Porter* (1990); *Friends Can Be Lovers* (1992); *Aquarela Do*

Brasil (1994). **DIONNE WARWICK AND ISAAC HAYES:** *A Man and a Woman* (1977). **DIONNE WARWICK AND PLACIDO DOMINGO:** *Celebration in Vienna* (1994). **—BH**

Washburn, Robert, American composer and music educator; b. Bouckville, N.Y., July 11, 1928. He received training in music education at the Crane School of Music at the State Univ. of N.Y. Coll. at Potsdam (B.S., 1949; M.S., 1955) and in composition at the Eastman School of Music in Rochester, N.Y. (Ph.D., 1960), with Milhaud at the Aspen (Colo.) Music School (summer, 1963), and with Boulanger in Paris (1964). From 1954 to 1985 he taught at the Crane School of Music, where he also was its dean (1982–85). Thereafter he held the titles of dean emeritus and senior fellow in music. He made tours throughout North America and overseas as a guest composer-conductor. His articles on music education appeared in various journals. Among his honors were a Ford Foundation fellowship (1959–60), a MacDowell Colony fellowship (1963), an NEA grant (1981), a Fulbright fellowship (1986), and Meet the Composer grants (1991, 1993). Washburn has been especially effective in composing works for college and high school groups. He favors a tonal mode of expression along neo-Classical lines. He has also utilized non-Western elements in some of his scores.

WORKS: ORCH.: 3 Pieces (1959); Suite for Strings (1959); Sym. No. 1 (1959; 1st movement publ. as *Festive Overture*); *Synthesis* (1959); *St. Lawrence Overture* (1962); *Passacaglia and Fugue* for Strings (1963); *Sinfonietta* for Strings (1963); *Serenade* for Strings (1966); *Song and Dance* for Strings (1967); *North Country Sketch* (1969); *Prologue and Dance* (1970); *Excursion* (1970); *Elegy* (1974); *Mid-America*, overture (1976); *5 Adirondack Sketches* for Small Orch. (1989); *Saraswati Suite* for Strings and Tabla (1990); *New England Holiday* (1992); *Queen Noor Suite* for Strings (1992); *Scottish Fantasy* (1993); *Knightsbridge Suite* for Strings (1993); *Caravelle Overture* (1994); *It's the Pizz.!* for Strings (1994). **Band:** *March and Chorale* (1955); *Ode* (1955); *Burlesk* (1956); *Pageantry* (1962); Sym. (1963); *Partita* (1964); Suite (1967); *Ceremonial Music* (1968); *Intrada, Chorale, and Toccata* (1970); *Prelude and Paragrams* (1972); *Epigon IV* (1974); *Trigon* (1975); *3 Diversions* (1978); *Impressions of Cairo* (1978); *Olympic March* (1979); *Kilimanjaro* (1981); *Equinox* (1983); *Pageant Royale* (1988); *Tower Bridge* (1992); *Temple on the Nile* (1992); *Hoosier Holiday* (1994); *Tidewater Festival Overture* (1994); *Far East Fantasy* (1995); *Song of Krishna* (1995). **CHAMBER:** Suite for Wind Quintet (1960); String Quartet (1963); Concertino for Brass and Wind Quintets (1964); Woodwind Quintet (1967); Brass Quintet (1970); *Prayer and Alleluia* for Organ, 2 Trumpets, Trombone, and Timpani (1972); *Pent- agons* for Percussion (1973); *Festive Fanfare* for Brass and Percussion (1975); *French Suite* for Oboe, Clarinet, and Bassoon (1980); Trio for Piano and Strings (1984); *Hornography* for Horn Quartet (1990). **VOCAL:** *3 Shakespearean Love Songs* for Men's Chorus, Piano, and Optional Horn (1963); *Spring Cantata* for Chorus (1973); *We Hold These Truths* for Narrator, Chorus, and Band or Orch. (1974); *3 Thoughts from Thoreau* for Voices and Piano (1976).**—NS/LK/DM**

Washington, Dinah (originally, **Jones, Ruth Lee**), American singer; b. Tuscaloosa, Ala., Aug. 29, 1924; d. Detroit, Mich., Dec. 14, 1963. Though Washington was embraced with varying degrees of enthusiasm by fans of gospel, jazz, and blues music, she found her greatest success as an R&B singer, reaching the R&B singles charts with 46 recordings between 1944 and 1961, among them "Baby Get Lost" and her duets with Brook Benton, "Baby (You've Got What It Takes)" and "A Rockin' Good Way (To Mess Around and Fall in Love)." Toward the end of her career she successfully crossed over to pop music, scoring 21 entries in the pop singles chart between 1959 and 1963, starting with "What a Diff'rence a Day Makes."

Washington was the daughter of Ollie Jones and Alice Williams Jones; her father was a gambler, and her mother, a domestic, was also a music teacher who played piano and led the church choir. The family moved to Chicago in 1927, and Washington learned to sing and play the piano in church. She began to perform in nightclubs as a teenager, but also toured with a gospel group. In 1943 she was hired by Lionel Hampton and sang with his orchestra through 1946. She made her recording debut on Dec. 29, 1943, in a session organized by jazz critic Leonard Feather for Keynote Records that produced two Top Ten R&B hits, "Salty Papa Blues" and "Evil Gal Blues" (both music and lyrics by Leonard Feather). Her only popular recording with Hampton, the R&B Top Ten hit "Blow-Top Blues," reached the charts in May 1947, after she had left the band to go solo.

Washington recorded briefly for Apollo Records in December 1945, then began a 15-year association with Mercury Records in January 1946. She scored four Top Ten hits on the R&B charts in 1948, among them the chart-topper "Am I Asking Too Much?" This success continued through the first half of the 1950s: she had four R&B Top Ten hits in 1949, including the #1 "Baby Get Lost"; five in 1950; four in 1951, including a version of Hank Williams's "Cold, Cold Heart"; four in 1952; two in 1953; three in 1954; and one in 1955. At the same time, she made more jazz-oriented recordings on Mercury's EmArcy label.

After a relative commercial lull of a few years, Washington made a comeback in 1959 with "What a Diff'rence a Day Makes," which made the Top Ten of both the pop and R&B charts and won her a Grammy for Best Rhythm & Blues Performance. In 1960 her duets with Brook Benton, the million-selling "Baby (You've Got What It Takes)" and "A Rockin' Good Way (To Mess Around and Fall in Love)," and the solo recording "This Bitter Earth" all topped the R&B charts, and the Benton duets also made the pop Top Ten.

Washington scored a final Top Ten R&B hit with "September in the Rain" in 1961, after which she switched from Mercury to Roulette Records and quickly recorded a series of LPs for the new label. She died of an accidental overdose of liquor and sleeping or diet pills in 1963 at the age of 39. At the time, she was married to professional athlete Richard "Night Train" Lane. Her other husbands, legal and common-law, included John Young, drummer George Jenkins (with whom she had a son), Robert Grayson (with whom she had another son), bassist Walter Buchanan, saxophonist Eddie Chamblee, cab-driver Horatio Maillard, actor Rafael Campos, and Jackie Hayes.

DISC.: *Dinah Washington Songs* (1950); *Dynamic Dinah* (1951); *Blazing Ballads* (1951); *After Hours with Miss D* (1954); *Dinah Jams* (1954); *For Those in Love* (1955); *Dinah* (1956); *In the Land of Hi-Fi* (1956); *The Swingin' Miss D* (1956); *Sings Fats Waller* (1957); *The Jazz Sides* (1976); *Music for a First Love* (1957); *Music for Late Hours* (1957); *The Best in Blues* (1957); *Sings Bessie Smith* (1958); *Newport '58* (1958); *The Queen* (1959); *What a Diff'rence a Day Makes* (1959); *Newport '58* (1959); *Sings Fats Waller* (1959); *Unforgettable* (1960); *I Concentrate on You* (1961); *For Lonely Lovers* (1961); *September in the Rain* (1961); *Tears and Laughter* (1962); *I Wanna Be Loved* (1962); *Dinah '62* (1962); *In Love* (1962); *Drinking Again* (1962); *Back to the Blues* (1962); *Dinah '63* (1963); *In Tribute* (1963); *The Good Old Days* (1963); *This Is My Story, Vol. 1* (1963); *This Is My Story, Vol. 2* (1963); *Stranger on Earth* (1964); *Dinah Washington* (1964); *Best* (1965); *The Queen and Quincy (with Quincy Jones)* (1965); *Dinah Discovered* (1967); *A Slick Chick (On the Mellow Side)* (1981); *Golden Hits, Vol. 1* (1985); *The Complete Dinah Washington on Mercury, Vol. 1 (1946–1949)* (1987); *The Complete Dinah Washington on Mercury, Vol. 2 (1950–1952)* (1987); *Dinah Washington* (1987); *Sings the Blues* (1988); *The Complete Dinah Washington on Mercury, Vol. 3 (1952–1954)* (1988); *The Complete Dinah Washington on Mercury, Vol. 4 (1954–1956)* (1988); *The Complete Dinah Washington on Mercury, Vol. 5 (1956–1958)* (1989); *The Complete Dinah Washington Washington on Mercury, Vol. 6 (1958–1960)* (1989); *The Complete Dinah Washington on Mercury, Vol. 7 (1961)* (1989); *The Great Songs* (1992); *Mellow Mama* (1992); *The Best of Dinah Washington: The Roulette Years* (1993); *Jazz 'Round Midnight* (1993); *The Dinah Washington Story* (1993); *Verve Jazz Masters 19: Dinah Washington* (1994); *Verve Jazz Masters 40: Dinah Washington Sings Standards* (1994); *Teach Me Tonight* (1995); *All of Me* (1996); *How to Do It* (1997); *The Classic Dinah* (1985); *Golden Classics* (1990). **BROOK BENTON AND DINAH WASHINGTON:** *The Two of Us* (1960).

BIBL.: J. Haskins, *Queen of the Blues: A Biography of D. W.* (N.Y., 1987).—**WR**

Washington, Grover Jr., pop-jazz tenor, alto, soprano saxophonist; b. Buffalo, N.Y., Dec. 12, 1943; d. N.Y., Dec. 17, 1999. Washington's father was a tenor saxophonist and his mother sang in the church choir. Washington began saxophone when he was ten, and then left school when he was 16 to tour with the R&B group The Four Clefs (originally from Columbus, Ohio). He remained with the group until they disbanded in 1963, and then worked briefly with organist Keith McAllister before enlisting in the Army. He played in the Fort Dix (N.J.) 19th Army Band, while continuing to moonlight as a jazz player. After discharge from the Army, he returned to playing funk-jazz with Don Gardener's Sonotones (1967–68) and then jazz-funk organists Charles Earland and Johnny Hammond. In 1971, he scored a huge pop hit when he recorded "Inner City Blues" for Creed Taylor's CTI label. Through the mid-1970s and early 1980s, he produced a string of soft-jazz hits. Signed to Motown, he released the hit LP *Mister Magic* (1975) and the self-produced *Reed Seed* in 1978, but despite the relative success of the record, he was unhappy at the label. Although still contractually obliged to issue alternate releases through Motown, he signed to Elektra and realized even greater commercial success. His album *Winelight* (1981), a mixture of soul, jazz, and pop, sold over two million copies and won two Grammys. It included the single "Just the Two of Us," featuring Bill Withers on vocals, which shot to #2 on the U.S. chart. However, Washington was unable to equal this enormous success, and during the later 1980s and 1990s mixed his work in pop- funk-jazz with returns to more mainstream playing. Washington lived in Philadelphia from the mid-1960s until his death in 1999, and was active on the local scene. He died of an apparent heart attack after taping some songs for an early morning television appearance.

DISC.: *Inner City Blues* (1971); *Feels So Good* (1975); *Mister Magic* (1975); *Winelight* (1981); *Baddest* (1981); *In Concert* (Video) (1981); *Then and Now* (1988); *Time Out of Mind* (1989); "Love Like This" (1992); *All My Tomorrows* (1994).—**MM/LP**

Wasielewski, Wilhelm Joseph von, eminent German violinist, conductor, and music scholar; b. Gross-Leesen, near Danzig, June 17, 1822; d. Sondershausen, Dec. 13, 1896. He studied with Mendelssohn, Hauptmann, and David at the Leipzig Cons. (1843–46). He played in the Gewandhaus Orch. (until 1850), then went to Düsseldorf, where he was concertmaster under Schumann (1850–52). After serving as choral conductor in Bonn (1852–55), he settled in Dresden as a writer, in which capacity he greatly distinguished himself. In 1869 he became town music director in Bonn, remaining in that position until 1884, when he went to Sondershausen, where he settled as a teacher of music history at the Cons.

WRITINGS: *Robert Schumann* (Dresden, 1858; 2nd ed., rev. and aug., 1906 by Waldemar von Wasielewski; Eng. tr., 1871); *Die Violine und ihre Meister* (Leipzig, 1869; 3rd ed., aug., 1893; 5th ed., rev., 1910 by Waldemar von Wasielewski; 8th ed., 1927); *Die Violine im XVII. Jahrhundert und die Anfange der Instrumentalkomposition* (Bonn, 1874); *Geschichte der Instrumental-Musik im XVI. Jahrhundert* (Berlin, 1878); *Schumanniana* (Bonn, 1883); *Ludwig van Beethoven* (Berlin, 1888); *Das Violoncell und seine Geschichte* (Leipzig, 1889; 3rd ed., rev. and aug., 1925, by Waldemar von Wasielewski; Eng. tr., 1894); *Carl Reinecke* (Leipzig, 1892); *Aus 70 Jahren: Lebenserinnerungen* (Stuttgart, 1897).

BIBL.: R. Federhofer-Königs, *W.J. v.W. (1822–1896) im Spiegel seiner Korrespondenz* (Tutzing, 1975).—**NS/LK/DM**

Wasitodiningrat, K. R. T. (Kanjeng Raden Tumengung, a title of honorary royal status**),** important Indonesian composer and performer; b. Yogyakarta, Java, March 17, 1909. (His former names are Wasitolodoro, Tjokrowasito, and Wasitodipuro; he is frequently known as Ki Wasitodiningrat, Ki being an honorific for artistic achievement.) He was born in the Pakualaman Palace, one of 3 principal courts of central Java, where his father was director of musical activities. Wasitodiningrat studied dance from the age of 6, graduating from the SMA National H.S. in 1922. He became music director of the Yogyakarta radio station MAVRO in 1934, and remained there through the Japanese occupation, when the station was called Jogja Hosokjoku. In 1945 the station became RRI (Radio Republic Indonesia); he served as director there again in 1951. Between 1951 and 1970 he taught dance at the Konservatori Tari and the Academy Tari, both in Yogyakarta, and music at the Academy Karawitan in Surakarta; he also founded and directed the Wasitodipuro Center for Vocal Studies in Yogyakarta. In 1953 he toured Asia,

North America, and Europe. In 1961 he became associated with the new dance/theater form *sendratari*, later becoming music director for P.L.T. Bagong Kussudiardjo's troupe. He succeeded his father as director of the Pakualaman gamelan in 1962. In 1971 he joined the faculty of the Calif. Inst. of the Arts as master of Javanese gamelan; taught workshops at both the Los Angeles and Berkeley campuses of the Univ. of Calif. Wasitodiningrat is a leading performer and composer of central Javanese music; the Pakualaman gamelan's recordings are considered exemplary; one is included in the 40 minutes of music installed in the spacecraft *Voyager*, intended to represent our planet's music to outsiders. His numerous awards include a gold medal from the Indonesian government honoring his devotion to Javanese music. He frequently performs with his daughter, Nanik, and her Balinese husband, **Nyoman Wenten**.—**NS/LK/DM**

Wassenaer, Count Unico Wilhelm van, Dutch government official and talented amateur composer; b. Twickel, Nov. 2, 1692; d. The Hague, Nov. 9, 1766. He received his education in Leiden and assumed control of the family estate in 1717; later held government posts and served as the United Provinces ambassador abroad. His *6 Concerti armonici*, publ. anonymously in 1740, were attributed to Pergolesi and then to Ricciotti before being confirmed as the work of Wassenaer.

Bibl.: A. Dunning, *Count U.W. v.W. (1692–1766); A Master Unmasked; or, The Pergolesi-Ricciotti Puzzle Solved* (Buren, 1980); R. Rasch and K. Vlaardingerbroek, eds., *U.W. v. W., 1692–1766: Componist en staatsman* (Hilversum, 1993).—**NS/LK/DM**

Watanabe, Akeo, Japanese conductor; b. Tokyo, June 5, 1919; d. there, June 22, 1990. He studied piano and violin as a youth, then received training in conducting from Joseph Rosenstock at the Tokyo Academy of Music and from Jean Morel at the Juilliard School of Music in N.Y. In 1945 he made his conducting debut with the Tokyo Sym. Orch. He was conductor of the Tokyo Phil. (1948–54), served as founder-conductor of the Japan Phil. in Tokyo (1956–68), and was conductor of the Tokyo Metropolitan Sym. Orch. (1972–78); also appeared as guest conductor in the U.S. and Europe. He served again as conductor of the Japan Phil. (1978–83), then was music director of the Hiroshima Sym. Orch. (from 1988).—**NS/LK/DM**

Watanabe, Sadao, Japanese jazz alto and soprano saxophonist, flutist, teacher; b. Utsunomiya, Japan, Feb. 1, 1933. He did not begin playing music until he was 15, when he was inspired to take up the clarinet after seeing the film *Birth of the Blues*. He became proficient enough on the instrument to join a professional dance band in Tokyo after graduating high school in 1951. In 1953 he was asked to fill the saxophone chair in the nationally popular Cosy Quartet by its pianist-leader Toshiko Akiyoshi. Over the next two years, Sadao developed greater proficiency on the saxophone as well as a keen love for Charlie Parker. When Parker died in March, 1955, Watanabe was asked to perform a tribute to Charlie Parker that was aired on Japanese radio. He emigrated to Boston in 1962 to attend the Berklee Coll. of Music, leading the double life of a musical theory/technique student by day and sideman for Mingus, Gary McFarland, and Chico Hamilton by night. After three years he returned to Japan establishing a jazz music school and his own performing unit. Between 1965 and 1968, he recorded 13 albums, firmly establishing himself as Japan's most prolific and well-known jazz artist. In 1968 he made his first appearance at the Newport Jazz Festival and recorded his *Sadao Meets Brazilian Friends*, which was Japan's first formal introduction to Brazilian music. After his appearance at the Montreux Jazz Festival in 1970, he began playing a fusion of samba, pop, and straight-ahead jazz, earning him an audience outside of Japan. During the 1980s, he became a U.S.-touring staple, and his 1984 album *Rendezvous* reached #2 on the U.S. *Billboard* jazz charts. Through the rest of the decade he received increasing international acclaim and displayed an ongoing fascination with Brazilian pop/jazz music. He continued to record and tour extensively in the 1990s, including a 1995 tour of the U.S. backed by American musicians.

Disc.: *Bossa Nova Concert* (1967); *Iberian Waltz* (1967); *Nabasada and Charlie* (1967); *Sadao Meets Brazilian Friends* (1968); *Dedicated to Charlie Parker* (1969). **CHICK COREA:** *Round Trip* (1974); *I'm Old Fashioned* (1976); *Bird of Paradise* (1977); *California Shower* (1978); *Morning Island* (1979); *Rendezvous* (1983); *Sweet Deal* (1983); *Maisha* (1985); *Parker's Mood* (1985); *Jazz and Bossa* (1986); *Elis* (1988); *Made in Coracao* (1988); *Earth Step* (1994); *In Tempo* (1995).—**LP**

Waters, Ethel, African American singer and actress; b. Chester, Pa., Oct. 31, 1896; d. Chatsworth, Calif., Sept. 1, 1977. In the course of 60 years, Waters pursued successive careers as a blues singer, a jazz singer, a musical comedy star, a dramatic actress, and a gospel singer. As an African American and a female, she was responsible for a number of firsts: she was the first black woman to sing on the radio and to appear on television, and she was the first black woman to star at the Palace Theater in N.Y. (the peak of success in vaudeville), in a network radio series, in an integrated Broadway show, and in a straight play on Broadway. Her career parallels the struggle for racial equality in the U.S. during the first three-quarters of the 20th century and stands as an example of its success. As an actress she was usually cast as a domestic servant, but she earned awards and nominations for her performances. As a singer she scored numerous hits, including "Am I Blue?" and "Stormy Weather." Her combination of soulful interpretation and precise diction made her a profound influence on later singers both black and white.

Waters was the illegitimate child of 12-year-old Louise Tar Anderson, who was raped by John Wesley Waters. Raised largely by her grandmother, Sarah Harris Anderson, she was singing in church by the age of five. When she was 11, she began to win dance contests at Pop Grey's Dance Hall in Chester. In 1910, at the age of 13, she married Merritt Purnsley and dropped out of school after the sixth grade to work at a series of menial jobs. The couple separated within a year.

On Oct. 31, 1917, the day she turned 21, Waters sang at a Halloween Party at Jack's Rathskeller, a saloon in Philadelphia, where she was seen by the vaudeville team of Braxton and Nugent, who offered her a job with their troupe. Billed as Sweet Mama Stringbean, she made her first professional appearance with them shortly afterward at the Lincoln Theatre in Baltimore, then went on tour as part of the Hill Sisters into 1918. Returning to Philadelphia, she appeared at Barney Gordon's saloon, moving on to N.Y. by 1919, where she debuted at another Lincoln Theatre, then performed at Edmond's Cellar, a nightclub in Harlem. Later in the year, she appeared in the musical *Hello, 1919!* at Harlem's Lafayette Theater and on tour. She made her first recordings, "The New York Glide" and "At the New Jump Steady Ball," backed by Albury's Blue and Jazz Seven, for Cardinal Records in 1921. That same year she was signed to Black Swan Records, the first black-owned record company, and scored her first hit, "Down Home Blues," in September.

Waters toured extensively in the early 1920s, both on her own and with various revues. She gradually crossed over from exclusively black to both white and black audiences. In 1925 she introduced "Dinah" (music by Harry Akst, lyrics by Sam M. Lewis and Joe Young) at the Plantation Club in N.Y.; she recorded it in October and it became a major hit in January 1926, after which she was sufficiently well known to tour in her own revues under such titles as *Ethel Waters Floor Show* and *Ethel Waters Vanities*.

Waters made her Broadway debut in the all-black revue *Africana* (N.Y., July 11, 1927); she sang "I'm Coming, Virginia" (music by Donald Heywood, lyrics by Heywood and Will Marion Cook), which she had already recorded for a hit. The show ran 77 performances. Before it went on tour, Waters starred at the Palace for the first time.

Waters toured with *Africana* and with her own revue in 1928. Around this time she married her second husband, Clyde Edward Matthews; this marriage lasted until about 1933.

Waters made her film debut in *On with the Show* in May 1929. The two songs she sang, "Am I Blue?" and "Birmingham Bertha" (both music by Harry Akst, lyrics by Grant Clarke), appeared on either side of a Columbia Records single that became a best-seller in October. She spent most of the year in Europe.

Waters returned to Broadway in another all-black revue, *Lew Leslie's Blackbirds* (N.Y., Oct. 22, 1930), which ran 61 performances. The same month she was seen as part of Duke Ellington's orchestra in the film *Check and Double Check*, and she recorded "Three Little Words" (music by Harry Ruby, lyrics by Bert Kalmar) from the score for a hit in January 1931. Producer Lew Leslie had yet another all-black revue ready by the spring, and Waters appeared in *Rhapsody in Black* (May 4, 1931), which ran 80 performances and from which she recorded "You Can't Stop Me from Loving You" (music by Alberta Nichols, lyrics by Mann Holiner) for a hit in July. She toured with *Rhapsody in Black* and with other revues into 1933.

Waters's fame was increased by her appearance in the revue *Cotton Club Parade* (N.Y., April 6, 1933) at the Cotton Club in Harlem with Duke Ellington. The performances were frequently broadcast on radio, and Waters introduced "Stormy Weather" (music by Harold Arlen, lyrics by Ted Koehler), which she recorded for the biggest hit of her career. The effect of this success was to permanently expand her appeal beyond exclusively black productions: before the year was out she had recorded with Benny Goodman's orchestra, become the host of her own network radio show, *American Revue*, and returned to Broadway in an integrated revue, Irving Berlin's *As Thousands Cheer* (N.Y., Sept. 30, 1933), which had a run of 390 performances and in which she sang "Supper Time," a song about the lynching of Southern blacks, and "Heat Wave," which she recorded for a hit in October.

Waters returned to N.Y. after the national tour for *As Thousands Cheer* in 1935 and went into another revue, *At Home Abroad* (N.Y., Sept. 19, 1935), which had songs by Arthur Schwartz and Howard Dietz and ran 198 performances. Around this time she was with her third (apparently common-law) husband, trumpeter and bandleader Eddie Mallory, whose band backed her during her extensive tours in the second half of the 1930s.

Waters starred in Dorothy and Du Bose Heyard's drama *Mamba's Daughters* (N.Y., Jan. 3, 1939), which ran 162 performances and marked her transition from singing to serious acting, though she did sing one song in the play, Jerome Kern and Du Bose Heyward's "Lonesome Walls."

Waters next starred in the all-black musical *Cabin in the Sky* (N.Y., Oct. 25, 1940), with a score by Vernon Duke and John Latouche; it ran 156 performances. After the U.S. entry into World War II, she toured military bases for the USO, but she also found time for several film roles, appearing in *Tales of Manhattan* and *Cairo* in 1942 and in *Cabin in the Sky* and *Stage Door Canteen* in 1943. She returned to Broadway in the revues *Laugh Time* (N.Y., Sept. 8, 1943), which ran 126 performances in N.Y. after a national tour that began in Los Angeles, and *Blue Holiday* (N.Y., May 21, 1945), which was a flop.

After the war Waters returned to touring in nightclubs and theaters throughout the country. Her next film role, in *Pinky* (1949), earned her an Academy Award nomination for Best Supporting Actress. Her performance in the straight play *The Member of the Wedding* (N.Y., Jan. 5, 1950) ran 501 performances and brought her the N.Y. Drama Critics Award for Best Actress; when she repeated her role in the 1952 film version she got another Oscar nomination. Beginning Oct. 3, 1950, she starred in the television comedy series *Beulah*, continuing through April 1952. She published her first autobiography, *His Eye Is on the Sparrow*, in 1951; it became a best- seller.

Starting in 1953, Waters performed in her own stage production, *At Home with Ethel Waters* (later *An Evening with Ethel Waters*), touring North America into the 1960s. She also acted in many regional revivals of *The Member of the Wedding*. She made a few more film appearances, in *Carib Gold* (1955), *The Heart Is a Rebel* (1956), and *The*

Sound and the Fury (1959), and appeared as a guest star on several television series, including an episode of *Route 66* in 1961 that brought her an Emmy nomination. But her primary activity during the last two decades of her life was performing as part of the religious crusades of evangelist Billy Graham. She published her second autobiography, *To Me It's Wonderful*, in 1972. She died at age 80 of kidney failure and cancer.

WRITINGS: With Charles Samuels, *His Eye Is on the Sparrow* (Garden City, N.Y., 1951); *To Me It's Wonderful* (N.Y., 1972).

BIBL.: J. DeKorte, *E. W.: Finally Home* (Old Tappan, N.J., 1978); T. Knaack, *E. W.: I Touched a Sparrow* (Waco, Tex., 1978). —WR

Waters, Muddy (originally, **Morganfield, McKinley**), premier blues-music singer, guitarist, and songwriter; b. near Rolling Fork, Miss., April 4, 1915; d. Westmont, Ill., April 30, 1983. Waters effected the transition between the rural, acoustic folk blues he inherited from such influences as Robert Johnson and Son House while living in the Mississippi River Delta and the urban, electrified blues he developed after moving to Chicago that went on to influence generations of rock 'n' roll musicians starting with The Rolling Stones, who named their band after one of his songs. His career had two distinct phases: in the 1940s and 1950s he dominated the Chicago blues scene and recorded a string of R&B hits that included such boastful songs as "I'm Your Hoochie Coochie Man," "Just Make Love to Me" (aka "I Just Want to Make Love to You"), and "I'm Ready" and, from the 1960s to the 1980s, as his music was discovered by rock 'n' roll fans, he became increasingly successful as a national and international touring act while making a series of albums that either attempted to update his style or to re-create his earlier work.

Waters was the son of Ollie Morganfield, a farmer who also sang and played guitar. His mother, Berta Jones, died when he was three, after which he was raised by his maternal grandmother, Della Jones, a sharecropper, on a plantation near Clarksdale, Miss. He had a few years of grade school but was doing farm work by about the age of ten. He began playing the harmonica at seven, and he took up the guitar around the age of 17. On Nov. 20, 1932, he married Mabel Berry, but he fathered a child by another woman two years later; they separated in 1940 when he began to live with Sally Ann Adams, whom he married on Dec. 23, 1942. For the rest of the 1930s and into the 1940s he worked as a sharecropper, augmenting his income by playing music.

In August 1941 folklorist Alan Lomax, doing field recordings for the Library of Congress, was in Miss. looking for Robert Johnson, who had died three years earlier. Instead he was directed to Waters and recorded the singer/guitarist then and on a second trip in July 1942. In May 1943, Waters moved to Chicago, where he worked at menial jobs while building up his reputation as a musician. In 1947 he made his first recordings to be commercially released under his name, the original songs "Gypsy Woman" and "Little Anna Mae," issued as a single that spring on the Aristocrat label. In April 1948, at a second Aristocrat recording session, he recorded his compositions "I Can't Be Satisfied" and "I Feel Like Going Home." These too were released as a single, and in September "I Feel Like Going Home" reached the national R&B charts. In the late 1940s he married Geneva Wade; they remained married until her death in May 1973, although Waters had liaisons with many women and he acknowledged fathering three more illegitimate children.

In June 1950, Aristocrat became Chess Records. In January 1951, Waters scored the first of 14 R&B Top Ten hits with "Louisiana Blues," his first record made with a full band. This was followed by "Long Distance Call" (April 1951); "Honey Bee" (July 1951); "Still a Fool" (November 1951); "She Moves Me" (February 1952); "Mad Love" (November 1953); "I'm Your Hoochie Coochie Man" (music and lyrics by Willie Dixon; March 1954); "Just Make Love to Me" (music and lyrics by Dixon; June 1954); "I'm Ready" (music and lyrics by Dixon; October 1954); "Mannish Boy" (music and lyrics by Waters, Mel London, and Ellas McDaniel [Bo Diddley]; July 1955); "Trouble No More" (January 1956); "Forty Days & Forty Nights" (music and lyrics by Bernard Roth; May 1956); "Don't Go No Farther" (music and lyrics by Dixon; September 1956); and "Close to You" (music and lyrics by Dixon; October 1958). (Music and lyrics are credited to Waters unless otherwise noted.)

With his recording success, by the mid-1950s Waters was touring nationally, albeit still in clubs. By the late 1950s his opportunities to play had expanded further: in October 1958 he performed in England; in April 1959 he was part of a folk music concert at Carnegie Hall in N.Y.; and in July 1960 he appeared at the Newport Jazz Festival. The last resulted in an album, *Muddy Waters at Newport 1960*, from which "Got My Mojo Working" (music and lyrics by Preston Foster) was nominated for the 1960 Grammy Award for Best Rhythm & Blues Performance.

Waters returned to Europe in 1962, 1963, and 1964 as part of package tours of U.S. blues performers, helping to fuel a blues revival that led to the formation of such groups as The Rolling Stones, who in turn brought his music back to the U.S.: their version of "I Just Want to Make Love to You" appeared on their debut album in 1964. Meanwhile, Chess Records attempted to position Waters to take advantage of the folk music revival, and he returned to playing the acoustic guitar for the album *Folk Singer*, released in January 1964. With the onset of The Beatles-led British Invasion, however, he began to perform more frequently at rock 'n' roll concerts attended by young white fans than at blues venues attended by older black fans.

In 1968, Chess released *Electric Mud*, an album on which Waters rerecorded many of his songs in a psychedelic style heavily influenced by guitar virtuosos like Jimi Hendrix. Blues fans were dismayed but the album spent several months in the charts. A better compromise with contemporary styles was achieved on 1969's *Fathers and Sons*, which found Waters accompanied by such disciples as Paul Butterfield and Mike Bloomfield and which also spent months in the charts.

On Oct. 27, 1969, Waters was involved in an automobile accident that sidelined him for several months. In 1970 he earned a Grammy Award nomination for Best Ethnic or Traditional Recording for his album *Sail On*, a resequenced reissue of his first album, the compilation *The Best of Muddy Waters*, originally released in 1958 and consisting of recordings made between 1948 and 1954. For the next ten years he was nominated for the same award nearly every year and frequently won. His first victory came in 1971 for the album *They Call Me Muddy Waters*, which contained recordings made between 1951 and 1967. He won a second time in 1972 for the newly recorded *The London Muddy Waters Sessions*, on which he was accompanied by such British musicians as Steve Winwood and drummer Mitch Mitchell, formerly of The Jimi Hendrix Experience, and was nominated for his 1973 album *Can't Get No Grindin'* as well as for the 1974 album *London Revisited*, which also featured recordings by Howlin' Wolf. He won for the third time for the 1975 album *The Muddy Waters Woodstock Album*, featuring members of The Band, which also reached the charts and was his final album for Chess before the company ceased to be an active label.

In 1976, Waters signed to Blue Sky, a label run by Johnny Winter's manager and distributed by CBS Records. Winter oversaw his Blue Sky recordings, starting with *Hard Again*, which reached the charts in 1977 and earned his fourth Grammy Award. *I'm Ready* (1978) repeated this success, as did 1979's *Muddy "Mississippi" Waters Live*. Waters married Marva Jean Brooks on June 5, 1979. His fourth and final Blue Sky album, *King Bee*, reached the charts in May 1981. He earned another Grammy nomination for Best Ethnic or Traditional Recording in 1981 as part of the various artists album *Blues Deluxe*. He gave his final performance as a guest of Eric Clapton at a concert in Miami on June 30, 1982. After suffering from cancer in his final year, he died of a heart attack at 68 in 1983.

DISC.: **MUDDY WATERS:** *Best (recorded 1948–1954)* (1958); *Sings Big Bill Broonzy* (1961); *At Newport 1960* (1961); *Folk Singer* (1964); *Muddy, Brass and the Blues* (1966); *More Real Folk Blues* (1967); *Electric Mud* (1968); *After the Rain* (1969); *Down at Stovall's Plantation* (1969); *They Call Me Muddy Waters* (1971); *AKA McKinley Morganfield* (1971); *Live at Mr. Kelly's* (1971); *London Muddy Waters Sessions* (1972); *Can't Get No Grindin'* (1973); *Mud in Your Ear* (1973); *"Unk" in Funk* (1974); *At Woodstock* (1975); *Muddy Waters* (1977); *Rolling Stone* (1982); *Rare and Unissued* (1984); *Trouble No More: Singles (1955–1959)* (1989); *The Chess Box* (1989); *Live in Switzerland 1976* (1991); *Unreleased in the West* (1992); *Unreleased in the West* (1992); *Muddy Waters Chicago Blues Band: Live in Switzerland 1976, Vol. 2* (1993); *The Complete Plantation* (1993); *Goin' Home Live in Paris 1970* (1993); *One More Mile: Chess Collectibles, Vol. 1 (recorded 1948–1972)* (1994); *Goodbye Newport Blues* (1995); *Blues Straight Ahead* (1995); *Baby Please Don't Go* (1996); *Live at Newport (with B.B. King and Big Mama Thornton)* (1993); *Sweet Home Chicago* (1980); *The Complete Plantation Recordings/The Historic 1941–1942 Library of Congress Field Recordings* (1993); *Chicago Blues: The Beginning* (1966); *His Best, 1947 to 1955* (1997); *The Warsaw Session* (1976); *The Warsaw Sessions, Vol. 2*. **MUDDY WATERS, BO DIDDLEY, AND LITTLE WALTER:** *Super Blues* (1967). **MUDDY WATERS, HOWLIN' WOLF, AND BO DIDDLEY:** *The Super Super Blues Band* (1968). **MUDDY WATERS, OTIS SPANN, AND OTHERS:** *Fathers and Sons* (1969). **MUDDY WATERS AND OTIS SPANN:** *Collaboration* (1995). **MUDDY WATERS AND HOWLIN' WOLF:** *London Revisited* (1974). **MUDDY WATERS AND MEMPHIS SLIM:** *Chicago Blues Master, Vol. 1* (1995).

BIBL.: A. Maass, *M. W.* (c. 1951); P. Oliver, *M. W.* (Bexhill-on-Sea, 1964); J. Rooney, *Bossmen: Bill Monroe & M. W.* (N.Y., 1971); S. Tooze, *M. W.: The Mojo Man* (Toronto, 1997).—**WR**

Watkins, Julius, jazz French horn player, composer; b. Detroit, Oct. 10, 1921; d. Short Hills, N.J., April 4, 1977. A pioneering musician, his solos had a brilliance that would have shown on any instrument, but were especially suited to his chosen one. He took up the horn in school at age eight and later studied with Francis Hellstein of the Detroit Symphony. He wanted to be a soloist and decided he would have more opportunities in jazz than in classical music. He played trumpet with the Erne Fields band 1943–46, recorded with Babs Gonzales on Jan. 20, 1949, and played trumpet and horn with Milt Buckner around 1949. In 1950, he settled in N.Y. where he studied theory and composition for three years at the Manhattan School of Music and studied horn with Robert Schultze of the N.Y. Philharmonic. In 1953 he recorded with Monk, toured with Pete Rugolo, and soon worked live or on record with Johnny Griffin, Kenny Clarke, Milt Jackson, and Oscar Pettiford. In 1955 he formed the Jazz Modes with Charlie Rouse, a colleague from Pettiford's sextet; they first recorded in 1956 and disbanded for lack of work in 1959, which led Watkins to join George Shearing. He was in the Quincy Jones big band which was stranded when the show *Free and Easy* failed in Europe in early 1960. From that point on he mostly supported himself playing in Broadway shows and recording sessions, including numerous big band dates with Jones and with Gil Evans (1958–64 and 1969), and specific sessions with Coltrane (1961), Tadd Dameron (1962), Freddie Hubbard (1963), and Jazz Composer's Orch. (1969). He worked with Charles Mingus at the Monterey festival in 1965 and in 1972 was a co-leader of the Jazz Contemporaries, which recorded live at the Village Vanguard with George Coleman, Clifford Jordan, and Harold Mabern. In 1994, an annual Jazz French Horn Festival was begun in N.Y. named in his honor.

DISC.: **BABS GONZALES:** *Capitolizing, Professor Bop* (1949); *New Faces-New Sounds: Julius Watkins Sextet* (1954); *Julius Watkins Sextet, Vol. 2* (1955); *Jazzville* (1956); *Jazz Modes* (1958); *French Horns for My Lady* (1961).—**LP**

Watkinson, Carolyn, English mezzo-soprano; b. Preston, March 19, 1949. She received her training at the Royal Manchester Coll. of Music and in The Hague. She first established herself as a fine concert singer, especially excelling in Baroque music. In 1978 she sang Rameau's Phèdre at the English Bach Festival at London's Covent Garden. In 1979 she appeared as Monteverdi's Nero with the Netherlands Opera in Amsterdam. In 1981 she made her debut at Milan's La Scala as Ariodante and sang Rossini's Rosina in Stuttgart. She appeared as Gluck's Orfeo with the Glyndebourne Touring Opera in 1982, and then made her formal debut at the Glyndebourne Opera as Cherubino in 1984. In 1987 she made a tour of Australia. She was a soloist in Bach's *St. John Passion* at Gloucester Cathedral in a performance shown on BBC-TV on Good Friday in 1989. In 1990 she appeared as Purcell's Dido at the Salerno Cathedral and sang Nero at the Innsbruck Festival. She also continued to sing regularly as a concert artist in a repertoire ranging from early music to the contemporary period.—**NS/LK/DM**

Watley, Jody, former *Soul Train* dancer who went on to singing success in Shalamar and as a solo artist; b. Chicago, Ill., Jan. 30, 1959. Her godfather is the late Jackie Wilson. Her father was a radio evangelist who hosted a gospel music show as well. However, the thing Jody Watley wanted more than anything else as a teen was to dance on *Soul Train*. When her family relocated from Chicago to Calif., she got her chance and took it. She and her partner Jeffrey Daniels became the most popular pair on the show, known for starting the trend of matching costumes and using props like rollerskates and balloons. The show's host and producer, Don Cornelius, invited the pair to become part of Shalimar, a new group he was putting together with Dick Griffey. Between 1977 and 1984, the group landed a spate of R&B hits including "A Night to Remember," "Take That to the Bank," and the R&B chart topping (#8 pop), gold "Second Time Around."

Watley, however, disliked the lack of creative input the group allowed her and left in 1982. She moved to England for a while, doing some modeling and singing on records by Musical Youth, the Art of Noise, and Band Aid, where she was one of the few Americans participating. In the mid-1980s, she moved back to Los Angeles, where she hooked up with former Prince bassist Andre Cymone. They collaborated on a number of songs that became Watley's eponymous debut in 1987.

With her dancing and modeling background, Watley was perfect for MTV. That Cymone's Minneapolis funk was very similar to the Minneapolis funk with which Terry Lewis and Jimmy Jam were scorching the charts on Janet Jackson records didn't hurt, either. Chock-full of dance rhythms, the album rose to #10 and went platinum on the strength of slick, soulful songs like the R&B chart topping (#2 pop) "Looking for a New Love," the #6 pop "Don't You Want Me," and the #10 "Some Kind of Lover." She took home the 1987 Grammy for Best New Artist.

Although that Grammy has frequently been the kiss of death, Watley came back strong with *Larger Than Life*. The first single, "Real Love," went gold, hitting #2 pop and topping the R&B charts. A duet with rappers Eric B and Rakim, "Friends" rose to #9. She followed this with the ballad "Everything," which hit #4. The album rose to #16 and went gold. She followed this with a dance remix compilation of songs from the previous two albums.

In an effort to continue the change of artistic gears (and to support the cause of AIDS research) Watley participated in the fund-raising Cole Porter tribute *Red, Hot and Blue*, covering "After You, Who" with a torch-like intensity. This carried over to her *Affairs of the Heart* album, which included more ballads and less dance music. While critics loved it, although it only spawned one minor hit, the #19 "I'm the One You Need." Her next album, *Intimacy*, again wowed fans and critics, but didn't reach her old dance audience or make too many new fans. MCA let her go, and in 1995 Watley started her own label, Avitone, recording *Affection*, for which she also wrote, produced, and even directed the videos. Unfortunately, the record got little in the way of radio play and didn't sell very well.

With poor sales of the previous two records, Watley was put in the position of making a comeback. Signing with Atlantic, she released *Flower*, recorded with a spate of the more successful contemporary soul producers to update her sound. While the album worked on an artistic level, it failed to find an audience.

Disc.: *Jody Watley* (1987); *Larger than Life* (1989); *You Wanna Dance with Me?* (1990); *Affairs of the Heart* (1991); *Intimacy* (1993); *Affection* (1995); *Flower* (1998).—**BH**

Watson (real name, McLamore), Claire, American soprano; b. N.Y., Feb. 3, 1924; d. Utting, Germany, July 16, 1986. She studied voice in N.Y. with Elisabeth Schumann and Sergius Kagen, then received further training in Vienna. She made her operatic debut as Desdemona in Graz in 1951, then was a member of the Frankfurt am Main Opera (1956–58) and the Bavarian State Opera in Munich from 1958 until her farewell as the Marschallin in 1976. As a guest artist, she appeared at London's Covent Garden (1958–63; 1964; 1970; 1972), the Glyndebourne Festival (1959), and the Salzburg Festival (1966–68). She also sang in Vienna, Milan, Rome, Chicago, Buenos Aires, and San Francisco. Among her other roles were Donna Elvira, Elisabeth de Valois, Eva, Sieglinde, Ariadne, and Tatiana.
—**NS/LK/DM**

Watson, Doc (Arthel Lane), American guitarist, singer, and banjo player; b. near Deep Gap, N.C., March 3, 1923. Watson gained renown as a flat-picking guitarist during the folk boom of the early 1960s, due to his virtuosity and extensive knowledge of traditional folk songs and old-time country music. Usually accompanied by his son Merle from the mid-1960s to the mid-1980s, he toured and recorded extensively, keeping a rural musical tradition alive and influencing a generation of upcoming country and bluegrass musicians.

Watson was the son of General Dixon Watson, a farmer, and Annie Greene Watson. He lost his sight during infancy. Most of the members of his family were musical, and several of them eventually recorded with him, including his mother, who taught him hymns and traditional songs. His father sang and played the banjo, and he built a banjo for Watson when the boy was 11. At 13 he bought his first guitar. He first played in public at a fiddler's convention in Boone, N.C., when he was 17, and at 18 he was part of a group that played on a local radio station. Around 1947 he married Rosa Lee Carlton, the daughter of fiddler Gaither W. Carlton, from whom he learned many traditional songs. He and his wife had two children, the first of whom was his son Eddy Merle Watson, known as Merle, born Feb. 8, 1949.

In the late 1940s and early 1950s, Watson earned his living tuning pianos. Around 1953 he met pianist Jack Williams, who hired him to play electric guitar in a band that performed contemporary country and popular music around western N.C. and Tenn.; he stayed with this band for the rest of the 1950s. In the summer of 1960, folklorists Ralph Rinzler and Eugene Earle came to N.C. to record Watson's neighbor, Clarence Ashley, and in so doing discovered Watson, who played in Ashley's string band. The session led to the Folkways Records album *Old-Time Music at Clarence Ashley's*, released in 1961, and to a concert appearance at Town Hall in N.Y. in March 1961. The group recorded a second volume of music for Folkways and in May 1962 traveled to Los Angeles to appear at the Ash Grove folk club. In December 1962, Watson debuted as a solo performer at Gerde's Folk City in N.Y. He made several recordings for Folkways and appeared at the Newport Folk Festival in July 1963.

Watson signed to Vanguard Records in 1964 and released his debut album for the label, *Doc Watson*, in September. Meanwhile, his teenage son Merle had taken up the guitar, and he became his father's backup musician and aide, enabling the blind musician to tour extensively. His next album, released in June 1965, was called *Doc Watson and Son*, and Merle Watson played with him on record and in concert for the next 20 years. They recorded an average of one album a year for Vanguard through 1971. In 1967, Watson accompanied Lester Flatt and Earl Scruggs on their Columbia Records album *Strictly Instrumental*, which reached the country charts in June. Doc and Merle Watson toured Africa under the auspices of the State Department in 1968.

At the conclusion of his Vanguard contract, Watson signed to the Poppy Records division of United Artists Records and released *Elementary, Doctor Watson!*, which became his first country chart album in June 1972. Along with other notable traditional performers, he accompanied the Nitty Gritty Dirt Band on their album *Will the Circle Be Unbroken*, released in October 1972, which hit the country Top Ten, went gold, and earned the participants a Grammy nomination for Best Country Vocal Performance by a Duo or Group.

Watson again reached the country charts with his next Poppy album, *Then and Now*, in May 1973, and with the single "Bottle of Wine" (music and lyrics by Tom Paxton) in July; the album won him a Grammy for Best Ethnic or Traditional Recording. He and his son won the same award the following year for their 1974 album *Two Days in November*. In 1975, Watson switched from Poppy to the main United Artists label and released the two-LP set *Memories*, produced by his son. The album reached both the pop and country charts in August. Its follow-up, *Doc and the Boys*, was in the country charts in August 1976.

Watson remained with United Artists through the end of the decade, releasing three more albums: *Lonesome Road* (1977); *Look Away!* (1978), featuring the country chart single "Don't Think Twice, It's All Right" (music and lyrics by Bob Dylan); and *Live and Pickin'* (1979), featuring the track "Big Sandy/Leather Britches," which won a Grammy for Best Country Instrumental Performance, a category in which he was nominated repeatedly in subsequent years. Leaving United Artists, he recorded a duo album with Chet Atkins, *Reflections*, which made the country charts and earned a Grammy nomination.

Watson moved to the independent folk label Flying Fish in 1981, releasing *Red Rocking Chair*, which earned him and his son another Grammy nomination for the track "Below Freezing." The two also were nominated for their 1983 album *Doc & Merle Watson's Guitar Album*, for the track "Twin Sisters" from *Down South* (1984), which marked their move to the independent N.C.-based label Sugar Hill, and for the track "Windy and Warm" from their final Flying Fish album, *Pickin' the Blues* (1985).

On Oct. 23, 1985, Merle Watson was killed in a tractor accident. After his death, Watson cut back on his touring, though he still performed regularly, adding Jack Lawrence as second guitarist. His next album, *Riding the Midnight Train*, won the 1986 Grammy for Best Traditional Folk Recording. He ceased recording for a time in the late 1980s, finally returning to the recording studio for two 1990 albums, the gospel collection *On Praying Ground*, which won the Grammy for Best Traditional Folk Recording; and *Doc Watson Sings for Little Pickers*, which was nominated for the Grammy for Best Recording for Children. His 1991 album, *My Dear Old Southern Home*, earned a Grammy nomination for Best Traditional Folk Album, but he again refrained from recording until 1995's rockabilly collection *Docabilly*, a Grammy nominee for Best Country Instrumental Performance for the track "Thunder Road/Sugarfoot Rag." He maintained a regular performance schedule into the late 1990s.

DISC.: *Old Time Music at Clarence Ashley's Vol. 1* (1961); *Old Time Music at Clarence Ashley's Vol. 2* (1963); *The Watson Family* (1963); *Jean Ritchie and Doc Watson at Folk City* (1963); *Doc Watson* (1964); *And Son* (1965); *Southbound* (1966); *Home Again!* (1966); *Ballads from Deep Gap* (1967); *Strictly Instrumental* (with Lester Flatt and Earl Scruggs; 1967); *Good Deal: Doc Watson in Nashville* (1968); *On Stage* (1970); *Elementary Doc Watson* (1972); *Then and Now* (1973); *Two Days in November* (1974); *Memories* (1975); *The Doc Watson Family* (rec. 1962–63; rel. 1977); *Reflections* (with Chet Atkins, 1980); *Red Rockin' Chair* (1982); *Pickin' the Blues* (1983); *Guitar Album* (1983); *Down South* (1984); *Riding the Midnight Train* (1986); *Portrait* (1987); *On Praying Ground* (1990); *Sings Songs for Little Pickers* (1990); *Doc Watson & Family* (rec. 1963–65; rel. 1991); *Remembering Merle* (1992); *My Dear Old Southern Home* (1992); *Live Duet Recordings* (with Bill Monroe, rec. 1963–80; rel. 1993); *Vanguard Years* (rec. 1963–68; rel. 1995); *Docabilly* (1995).—**WR**

Watson, Lillian, English soprano; b. London, Dec. 4, 1947. She studied at the Guildhall School of Music and Drama in London and at the London Opera Centre, and received private vocal instruction from Vera Rozsa and Jessica Cash. In 1970 she made her formal operatic debut as Cis in *Albert Herring* at the Wexford Festival.

She sang Papagena at her first appearance at the Welsh National Opera in Cardiff in 1971, and continued to sing there until 1975. In 1971 she made her debut at London's Covent Gaden as Rossini's Barbarina, where her subsequent roles included Blondchen, Tatiana, Janáček's Vixen, and Tippett's Bella. In 1975 she appeared as Despina with the Glyndebourne Touring Opera, and in 1976 she sang Susanna at the Glyndebourne Festival, a role she also chose for her debut at the English National Opera in London in 1978. In 1982 she made her first appearance at the Salzburg Festival as Marzelline, and then sang Blondchen in Vienna in 1983. She was engaged at the Théâtre des Champs-Elysées in Paris in 1989 as Strauss's Sophie. In 1993 she portrayed the Fairy Godmother in the first British performance of *Cendrillon* at the Welsh National Opera.—**NS/LK/DM**

Watters, Lu(cious), jazz revivalist trumpeter, leader, arranger; b. Santa Cruz, Calif., Dec. 19, 1911; d. Santa Rosa, Calif., Nov. 5, 1989. His powerful trumpet playing helped spark generations of revival bands dedicated to the sounds of early jazz. He formed his first band as a youth in 1925; worked as a ship's musician during vacations from high school and college; played with various bands in Calif. during the 1930s, including a long spell with Carol Lofner. In the late 1930s he led his own big band at Sweet's Ballroom in Oakland. After becoming dissatisfied with swing he began seeking new sources of inspiration, which he found in the music of King Oliver's Creole Jazz Band and other 1920s recordings. His new small band began in 1939 with a residency at the Big Bear in Berkeley Hills; he later set up a cooperative nightclub of his own, the Dawn Club on Annie Street in San Francisco. The band's 1939 residency there launched the first jazz "revival," recreating the classic New Orleans style. His band was soon called the Yerba Buena Jazz Band, and such stars of the revival genre as Turk Murphy, Bob Scobey, and Clancy Hayes passed through. The Yerba Buena Band first recorded on Watters's 30th birthday in 1941. He led the band until December 1950, except for a period of Navy service during World War II, where he led his own Navy Band. While he was in the service, musicians from the Yerba Buena participated in the Bunk Johnson sessions (1943–44) which were held at a Longshoreman's Hall and sponsored by the Hot Jazz Society of San Francisco. Once he returned from the war, Watters resumed where he had left off and by 1946 was recording the Yerba Buena in venues like the Avalon Ballroom in order to get an authentic dance hall sound. In 1950 he retired from music to study geology and pursue his favorite hobby, the collection and study of gemstones. He later reunited his band for a short while before retiring from music in the late 1950s; though he recorded again in 1964 and played powerfully. He composed the jazz numbers "Big Bear Stomp" and "Emperor Norton's Hunch" and the piano rag "The Villain." His arrangements of vintage New Orleans–style tunes are still extremely popular with repertory groups. Murphy and Scobey went on to form groups of their own, making the Yerba Buena important not only for its own sake but also as an incubator for further developments of the revival sound. Today, bands like the South Frisco Jazz Band, Jacques Gauthe's Creole Rice Yerba Buena Jazz Band, and the High Society Jazz Band of Paris attest to the enduring influence of Watters's contributions.

Disc.: *On the Air* (1941–46); *Complete Good Time Jazz Recordings* (1941); *Dawn Club Favorites* (1946); *San Francisco Style, Vols. 1, 2, 3* (1946); *Lu Watters Jazz* (1951); *Originals and Ragtime* (1954); *Stomps, etc. and the Blues* (1954); *Dixieland Jamboree* (1956); *Together Again* (1963); *Blues over Bodega* (1964).—**JC/MM/LP**

Watts, Andre, brilliant American pianist; b. Nuremberg, June 20, 1946. He was born in a U.S. Army camp to a black American soldier and a Hungarian woman. His mother gave him his earliest piano lessons. After the family moved to the U.S., he studied with Genia Robiner, Doris Bawden, and Clement Petrillo at the Philadelphia Musical Academy. At the age of 9, he made his first public appearance playing the Haydn Concerto in D major at a children's concert of the Philadelphia Orch. His parents were divorced in 1962, but his mother continued to guide his studies. At 14, he played César Franck's *Symphonic Variations* with the Philadelphia Orch.; at 16, he became an instant celebrity when he played Liszt's 1st Piano Concerto at one of the televised Young People's Concerts with the N.Y. Phil., conducted by Leonard Bernstein, on Jan. 15, 1963. His youth and the fact that he was partly black contributed to his success, but it was the grand and poetic manner of his virtuosity that conquered the usually skeptical press. Still, he insisted on completing his academic education. In 1969 he joined the class of Leon Fleisher at the Peabody Cons. of Music in Baltimore, obtaining his Artist's Diploma in 1972. In the meantime, he developed an international career. He made his European debut as soloist with the London Sym. Orch. on June 12, 1966; then played with the Concertgebouw Orch. in Amsterdam. On Oct. 26, 1966, he played his first solo recital in N.Y., inviting comparisons in the press with the great piano virtuosos of the past. In 1967 he was soloist with the Los Angeles Phil. under Zubin Mehta on a tour of Europe and Asia. On his 21st birthday he played the 2nd Piano Concerto of Brahms with the Berlin Phil. In 1970 he revisited his place of birth and played a solo recital with a success that was made all the more sensational because he was a native son, albeit not of the native race. He also became a favorite at important political occasions; he played at President Richard Nixon's inaugural concert at Constitution Hall in Washington, D.C., in 1969, at the coronation of the Shah of Iran, and at a festive celebration of the President of the Congo. In 1973 he toured Russia. On Nov. 28, 1976, he played a solo recital on live network television. He was also the subject of a film documentary. In 1973 he received an honorary doctorate from Yale Univ.; in 1975 he was given another honorary doctorate by Albright Coll. He celebrated the 25th anniversary of his debut with the N.Y. Phil. as soloist under Zubin Mehta in the Liszt 1st Concerto, the Beethoven 2nd Concerto, and the Rachmaninoff 2nd Concerto in a concert telecast live on PBS (Jan. 13, 1988). In 1988 he received the Avery Fisher Prize. In 1995 he marked the 40th anniversary of his debut.—**NS/LK/DM**

Watts, Ernie, American saxophonist; b. Norfolk, Va., Oct. 23, 1945. His first significant employment included a 1966 to 1968 stint with the Buddy Rich band, after which Watts moved to Los Angeles, where he landed a most favorable spot in 1972 as a regular performer in NBC's *Tonight Show* band. He worked with Gerald Wilson and Oliver Nelson and recorded with Bobby Bryant and Jean-Luc Ponty in the 1960s. During the 1970s he played with notables such as Lee Ritenour, Stanley Clarke, and his idol, Cannonball Adderley. In 1982, he received a Grammy Award for his performance on the soundtrack to the film *Chariots of Fire.* His own output in the early 1980s did not reach the heights of making any original, pure statements one would expect from a musician with such a broad musical background. What seems to have changed his course is his affiliation with Charlie Haden's Quartet West in the mid- 1980s. The series of recordings made with this group convey his rich lyrical sense and his integrity and warmth. In the 1990s, he began to make recordings that were compositionally strong and marked by his gift of improvisational playing. While some of the recordings he made in the 1990s attempt to blend various approaches to R&B, World music, pop music, and vocals, and are challenging in their accessibility, the straight-ahead jazz recordings with his own quartet best display his gifts as a performer.

DISC.: *The Ernie Watts Quartet* (1987); *Project Activation Earth* (1989); *Afoxe* (1993); *Reaching Up* (1994); *Unity* (1995); *Now Is the Hour* (1996); *The Long Road Home* (1996).—**GK**

Watts, Helen (Josephine), admired Welsh contralto; b. Milford Haven, Dec. 7, 1927. She was a student of Caroline Hatchard and Frederick Jackson at the Royal Academy of Music in London. She began her career singing in the Glyndebourne Festival Chorus and the BBC Chorus in London. Her first appearance as a soloist was in 1953. In 1955 she made her first appearance at the London Promenade Concerts singing Bach arias under Sargent's direction. Thereafter she distinguished herself as a concert artist, appearing in principal European and North American music centers. She also pursued an operatic career. In 1958 she made her operatic debut as Didymus in *Theodora* with the Handel Opera Soc. at the Camden Festival, and continued to appear with the Soc. until 1964. In 1964 she made her debut at the Salzburg Festival as the 1st Maid in *Elektra* and toured Russia with the English Opera Group as Britten's Lucretia. She made her first appearance at London's Covent Garden as the 1st Norn in *Götterdämmerung* in 1965, and continued to sing there until 1971. In 1966 she made her U.S. debut in Delius' *A Mass of Life* in N.Y. She sang Mistress Quickly at her first appearance with the Welsh National Opera in Cardiff in 1969, where she was a leading member of the company until 1983. In 1978 she was made a Commander of the Order of the British Empire. While she had success in opera, she particularly excelled as a concert artist. Her concert repertoire extended from Bach to the masters of the 20th century.—**NS/LK/DM**

Watts, Jeff "Tain," jazz percussionist; b. Pittsburgh, Jan. 20, 1960. He began playing the drums at ten and from 14 studied percussion in high school. He was the youngest timpanist in the Pittsburgh Youth Symphony; entered Duquesne Univ., worked with Michael Kumer, and at 17 joined the funk group Flavor. He then studied with Joe Hunt at Berklee, where he played funk and fusion with Branford Marsalis, Wallace Roney, Kevin Eubanks, Victor Bailey, Donald Harrison, Greg Osby, and others. He was the rhythm anchor for Wynton Marsalis's group from its beginnings in 1982 until the celebrated departure of Watts, Kenny Kirkland, and Branford Marsalis to tour with British pop star Sting in 1988. He has also worked with Ron Carter, Slide Hampton, David Murray, and recorded with Ellis Marsalis (1990), Sonny Rollins, and McCoy Tyner. He played and acted in *Mo Better Blues*, directed by Spike Lee (1988). In 1992, he played in the *Tonight Show* orchestra alongside Branford and Kirkland, but left the orchestra when Marsalis gave up its leadership. He has since worked actively as a session drummer.

DISC.: WYNTON MARSALIS: *Think of One* (1983). WATTS: *Megawatts* (1991); *Citizen Tain* (1999).—**LP**

Watts, John (Everett), American composer and synthesizer player; b. Cleveland, Tenn., July 16, 1930; d. N.Y., July 1, 1982. He was educated at the Univ. of Tenn. (B.A., 1949), the Univ. of Colo. (M.M., 1953), the Univ. of Ill. (1955–56), Cornell Univ. (1958–60), and the Univ. of Calif. at Los Angeles (1961–62); among his mentors were David Van Vactor, Cecil Effinger, Burrill Phillips, Robert Palmer, and Roy Harris. He was founder-director of the Composers Theatre in N.Y. (1964–82), which presented a vast number of works by American composers; taught at the New School for Social Research in N.Y. (from 1967), where he was founder-director of its electronic music program (from 1969); he made many appearances as a virtuoso on the ARP synthesizer.

WORKS: INSTRUMENTAL AND/OR VOCAL: Piano Sonata (1958; rev. 1960); *Signals* for Soprano and Orch. (1970); *Piano for Te* for Piano, 13 Players, and Tape (1973); *Laugharne* for Soprano, Tape, and Orch. (1974); *Mots d'heures: Gousses, Rames* for Voices and Tape (1974); *Piano for Te Tutti* for Piano and Tape (1975); *Maxi- concerto* (1976); *Canonades* for Strings (1978); *Keepsakes* for Tape and Orch. (1978); *Le Match de Boxe* (1978); *Barbro Variations* for Piano, 4-Hands (1979); *Easy Songs for Lazy Singers* (1981). ELECTRONIC: *WARP* for Brass Quintet, Synthesizer, and Tape (1971); *Elegy to Chimney: in memoriam* for Trumpet, Synthesizer, and Tape (1972); *MAS* (1976); *Entectics* for Tape and Synthesizer (1978); *Processional* for Tape and 10 Trumpets (1978); *A Little Night Music* (1979); *Timespace* for Tape (1979); *Ach!* for Tape and Optional Synthesizer (1980). Dance Scores: *Study for Solo Figure/Film* (1968); *Perimeters* (1969); *Glass and Shadows* (1971); *Laura's Dance* (1971); *Margins* (1972); *Still Life* (1972); *Locrian* (1973); *Songandance* (1973); *BUD (1975)* (1975); *Heirlooms* (1977); *#SS* (1977); *UPS* (1977); *Entries* (1978); *GO* (1978); *Night Remembrance* (1979). OTHER: Film scores; conceptual art.—**NS/LK/DM**

Waxman (real name, **Wachsmann**), **Franz,** German-American composer and conductor; b. Königshütte, Dec. 24, 1906; d. Los Angeles, Feb. 24, 1967. He studied in Dresden and Berlin. He went to the U.S. in 1934 and settled in Hollywood, where he took lessons with Schoenberg. Waxman became a successful composer for films; his musical score for *Sunset Boulevard* won the Academy Award for 1950; also was active as a conductor; was founder-conducter of the Los Angeles Music Festival (1947–67). His other film scores included *Magnificent Obsession* (1935), *Captains Courageous* (1937), *The Philadelphia Story* (1940), *Sunset Boulevard* (1950), *Stalag 17* (1953), *Sayonara* (1957), and *Sunrise at Campobello* (1960). He also composed the orch. works *Athaneal the Trumpeter*, overture (1945), a Trumpet Concerto (1946), *Carmen Fantasy* for Violin and Orch., after Bizet (1947), *Sinfonietta* for Strings and Timpani (1955), *Goyana* for Piano and Strings (1960), and a Cello Concerto as well as some vocal pieces, including *Joshua*, oratorio for Narrator, Solo Voices, Chorus, and Orch. (Dallas, May 23, 1959).—**NS/LK/DM**

Weatherford, Teddy, jazz pianist, arranger (leader); b. Bluefield, W.Va., Oct. 11, 1903; d. Calcutta, India, April 25, 1945. He lived in New Orleans from 1915 until 1920; during this time, he learned to play piano. He moved to Chicago, did extensive gigging, then regular work with Jimmie Wade and Erskine Tate. Weatherford sailed to the Orient with Jack Carter's Orch. in August 1926. He remained to work in the Far East, then led his own band in Singapore, Manila, and Shanghai. He briefly returned to the U.S. in 1934 to recruit Buck Clayton's Big Band for residency at Candidrome, Shanghai. Except for a visit to the Paris International Exposition (summer 1937) and some appearances later that year in Sweden, he worked in Asia for the rest of his life; his band played for a long residency at the Grand Hotel, Calcutta, also appearing in Bombay, Ceylon, and other Indian cities. He made a number of recordings while in India, some under his own name, others as featured accompanist for various popular artists, including American singer Bob Lee, violinist Zarata, and singer Paquita. Weatherford died of cholera in the Presidency General Hospital, Calcutta.

DISC.: **LOUIS ARMSTRONG:** *Portrait of the Artist as a Young Man* (1923); *1923–1926* (1925); *Young Louis The Sideman* (1924–27); "Static Strut"/"Stomp Off, Let's Go" (1926); "Tea for Two"/"Weather Beaten Blues" (1937); "Weather Blues"/ "Maple Leaf Rag" (1937); *Piano and Swing* (1938). **EDDIE SOUTH:** *1923–1937* (1923); "Someday Sweetheart"/"Mobile Blues" (1923).—**JC/LP**

Weather Report, American jazz-rock fusion group. Weather Report was the most successful of the jazz-rock fusion groups of the 1970s, groups that were influenced by Miles Davis's forays into rhythmic, electrified music in the late 1960s. All 15 of their albums reached the pop charts between 1971 and 1986, and they scored a million-selling album with *Heavy Weather*.

Weather Report was formed in December 1970 by keyboard player Josef Zawinul (b. Vienna, Austria, July 7, 1932) and saxophonist Wayne Shorter (b. Newark, N.J., Aug. 25, 1933), both of whom had played in Miles Davis's band. They added a rhythm section consisting of bassist Miroslav (Ladislav) Vitous (b. Prague, Czechoslovakia, Dec. 6, 1947); drummer Alphonse Mouzon (b. Charleston, S. C., Nov. 21, 1948); and percussionist Airto (Guimorva) Moreira (b. Itaipolis, Brazil, Aug. 5, 1941); other than Zawinul and Shorter, the band's personnel would change frequently. Signed to Columbia Records, the group released its first album, *Weather Report*, which reached the pop charts in July 1971.

Moreira left after the release of the first album and was replaced by Dom Um Romão; Mouzon left in 1972 and was replaced by Eric Gravatt. Weather Report then recorded its second album, *I Sing the Body Electric*, half of which came from a concert performed in Tokyo. The LP reached the pop charts in July 1972 and was nominated for a Grammy for Best Jazz Performance by a Group. *Sweetnighter*, the third album, entered the pop charts in May 1973 for a stay of almost four months.

Mouzon left Weather Report and was replaced by drummer Ishmael Wilburn for *Mysterious Traveler*, which entered the pop charts in June 1974 for a run of more than five months. The album also featured bassist Alphonso Johnson (b. Philadelphia, Feb. 2, 1951), who then replaced Vitous. Before the release of the 1975 album *Tale Spinnin'*, Wilburn was replaced by drummer Alyrio Lima, and Um Romão by percussionist Ngudu (real name Leon Chancler); *Tale Spinnin'* was the group's highest-charting album yet. By the time of 1976's *Black Market*, Ngudu had left and Lima had been replaced by drummer Chester Thompson. The album was notable for the appearance on one track of fretless bassist Jaco (John Anthony) Pastorius (III) (b. Norristown, Pa., Dec. 1, 1951; d. Ft. Lauderdale, Fla., Sept. 21, 1987), who then replaced Johnson and became an important influence in the group.

Thompson departed, and Weather Report added two percussionists, Alex (Alejandro Neciosup) Acuña and Manola Badrena, for the seventh album, *Heavy Weather*, which spent five months in the pop charts following its release in March 1977 and sold a million copies. By the release of *Mr. Gone*, which entered the pop charts in October 1978, the group had been reduced to the trio of Zawinul, Shorter, and Pastorius. Drummer Peter Erskine (b. Somers Point, N.J., May 5, 1954) made the band a quartet for the double live album *8:30*, which won the 1979 Grammy for Best Jazz Fusion Performance. The same unit stayed intact for *Night Passages* (1980), but by the time of the second album to be named *Weather Report* (1982), Pastorius had left and been replaced by bassist Victor Bailey; the drummer was Omar Hakim, and percussionist José Rossy had once again made the group a quintet. The album earned another Grammy nomination for Best Jazz Fusion Performance, as did 1983's *Procession*.

In 1984 percussionist Mino Cinélu replaced Rossy, and Peter Erskine replaced his replacement around 1985, when Shorter temporarily left the group to be replaced by guitarist Steve Khan. Shorter returned for the reunion album *This Is This* in 1986, but after that Weather Report consisted of Zawinul, Erskine, and Khan and was renamed Weather Update. Even that group dissolved by 1988, when Zawinul organized a new band, the Zawinul Syndicate.

DISC.: *Weather Report* (1971); *I Sing the Body Electric* (1972); *Sweetnighter* (1973); *Mysterious Traveller* (1974); *Tale Spinnin'*

(1975); *Black Market* (1976); *Heavy Weather* (1977); *Mr. Gone* (1978); *8:30* (1979); *Night Passage* (1980); *Procession* (1983); *Domino Theory* (1984); *Sportin' Life* (1985); *This Is This* (1987). **—WR**

Weathers, Felicia, black American soprano; b. St. Louis, Aug. 13, 1937. She took vocal lessons at the Ind. Univ. School of Music in Bloomington with St. Leger, Kullman, and Manski. She made her operatic debut in Zürich in 1961. In 1963 she sang at the Hamburg State Opera and subsequently was a regular member there (1966–70). In 1965 she made her Metropolitan Opera debut in N.Y.; also sang at Covent Garden in London in 1970.**—NS/LK/DM**

Weaver, James (Merle), American harpsichordist, pianist, fortepianist, and teacher; b. Champaign, Ill., Sept. 25, 1937. He was educated at the Univ. of Ill. (B.A., 1961; M.M., 1963), where he received instruction in harpsichord from George Hunter. He also was a student of Leonhardt at the Sweelinck Cons. in Amsterdam (1957–59). In 1967 he became curator of historic instruments at the Smithsonian Institution in Washington, D.C., where he co-founded the period instrument group the Smithsonian Chamber Players in 1976. He also pursued a solo career as a keyboard artist, taught at Cornell Univ. and the American Univ., and gave master classes in 18th-century performance practice. **—NS/LK/DM**

Weavers, The, American folk-music group. **Membership:** originally, Pete Seeger, ten., bjo., gtr. (b. N.Y., May 3, 1919); Lee Elhardt Hays, bs. (b. Little Rock, Ark., March 14, 1914; d. North Tarrytown [now Sleepy Hollow], N.Y., Aug. 26, 1981); Ronnie Gilbert, contralto (b. N.Y., Sept. 7, 1926); Fred Hellerman, bar. (b. N.Y., May 13, 1927).

The Weavers were the first broadly popular group of contemporary urban folk musicians and singers. Thus, they are a direct influence on such subsequent groups as The Kingston Trio and Peter, Paul and Mary, as well as on the overall folk revival of the late 1950s and early 1960s. They adapted folk songs from many different countries into their own vibrant style, popularizing a wide range of music, as well as performed the songs of such American folk predecessors as Lead Belly and Woody Guthrie; they also wrote their own material. Their most successful recordings were the singles "Goodnight Irene"/"Tzena Tzena Tzena," "On Top of Old Smoky," and "So Long (It's Been Good to Know Yuh)" and their album *The Weavers at Carnegie Hall.*

Seeger and Hays were former members of The Almanac Singers; they became involved with Gilbert and Hellerman through their work with People's Songs, an organization that promoted the performance of topical folk music in support of left-wing causes. They first performed together at a benefit for People's Songs in November 1948. They played at benefits and on local radio during 1949, initially as the No-Name Quartet, then took their name from the 1892 German play *The Weavers* by Gerhart Hauptmann. In September 1949 they made their first recordings for the independent Charter Records label, which released the single "Wasn't That a Time" (music and lyrics by Lee Hays)/"Dig My Grave" (traditional Bahamian folk hymn). In December they recorded a second single, "The Hammer Song" (later known as "If I Had a Hammer"; music by Pete Seeger, lyrics by Lee Hays)/"Banks of Marble" (music and lyrics by Les Rice) for Hootenanny Records.

The Weavers were on the verge of disbanding in December 1949 when they auditioned at the Village Vanguard in N.Y. Booked into the club for two weeks at the end of the year, they were extended for six months. They signed to Decca Records and their single "Tzena Tzena Tzena" (music by Issachor Miron [real name Michrovsky], revised by Julius Grossman, English lyrics by Mitchell Parish)/"Goodnight Irene" (music and lyrics by Lead Belly), credited to Gordon Jenkins and His Orch. and The Weavers, became a massive hit. "Tzena Tzena Tzena" hit the Top Ten in July, while "Goodnight Irene" topped the charts for months, starting in August; the disc reportedly sold about two million copies.

The Weavers were set to become regulars on a summer replacement television program when Seeger was cited in the publication *Red Channels: Communist Influence on Radio and Television* in June and the contract was canceled. This marked the beginning of the blacklisting of the group for its political views. Nevertheless, they resumed performing and recording following a summer layoff. They enjoyed their second chart single in December with "The Roving Kind" (music and lyrics by Jessie Cavanaugh and Arnold Stanton, adapted from a traditional English folk song), the B-side of which was "(The Wreck of the) John B" (music and lyrics by Lee Hays, adapted from a Bahamian folk song collected by Carl Sandburg).

At the start of 1951 The Weavers undertook a six-month tour of the major nightclubs in the U.S. In February they scored their second Top Ten hit with "So Long (It's Been Good to Know Yuh)" (music and lyrics by Woody Guthrie), again credited to Gordon Jenkins and His Orch. and The Weavers. They reached the Top Ten for the third time with their second million-seller, "On Top of Old Smoky," credited to The Weavers and Terry Gilkyson, in April. (Though it was a traditional American folk song, "On Top of Old Smoky" was copyrighted as having new lyrics and arrangement by Seeger. He later denied the credit.)

The campaign against The Weavers' political associations intensified during the summer of 1951, as a television appearance and a scheduled concert at the Ohio State Fair were canceled and other bookings began to diminish. In August, however, they reached the charts with both sides of their single "Kisses Sweeter than Wine" (music by "Joel Newman" [Lead Belly], adapted from the Irish folk song "Drimmer's Cow," lyrics by "Paul Campbell" [The Weavers])/"When the Saints Go Marching In" (music by James M. Black, lyrics by Katharine E. Purvis).

In February 1952 a former People's Song associate falsely testified before the House Committee on Un-American Activities that each of The Weavers was a current or former member of the Communist party.

However, the group managed two more chart entries, "Wimoweh" (music and lyrics by "Paul Campbell" [The Weavers], adapted from "Mbube," music and lyrics by Solomon Linda) in February, and "Around the Corner (Beneath the Berry Tree)" (music and lyrics by Josef Marais, adapted from a South African folk song), both credited to The Weavers and Gordon Jenkins. They continued to perform occasionally through December and recorded for Decca until February 1953, then were forced to disband because of the blacklist.

On Dec. 24, 1955, The Weavers reunited for a performance at Carnegie Hall in N.Y. The concert was so successful that they were able to reestablish the group on a part-time basis, giving more concerts and signing to the independent Vanguard Records label, which released an album of the show, *The Weavers at Carnegie Hall*, in April 1957. But they continued to be blacklisted in the mainstream media, never again, for example, appearing on network television.

Jimmie Rodgers reached the Top Ten in December 1957 with a revival of "Kisses Sweeter than Wine." The Weavers released a second Vanguard album, the live set *The Weavers on Tour*, in 1958. Seeger left the group during the recording of their first studio album for the label, *The Weavers at Home* (released August 1958), and was replaced by Erik Darling (b. Baltimore, Sept. 25, 1933) of the folk group the Tarriers, who was credited on the album as a "guest artist." The Kingston Trio topped the charts in November 1958 with their self-titled debut album, which featured songs recorded earlier by The Weavers. The Weavers' 1959 studio album, *Travelling on with The Weavers*, featured five tracks with Seeger and 11 with Darling. In May 1959 the group embarked on an international tour, performing in Israel and in Europe through September.

On April 1, 1960, they again performed at Carnegie Hall, recording another live album, *The Weavers at Carnegie Hall, Vol. 2*, which became their first charting LP in January 1961, also stimulating sales of their first *Carnegie Hall* album, which belatedly reached the charts in March 1961. In December a new adaptation of "Mbube," "The Lion Sleeps Tonight" (music and lyrics by Hugo Peretti, Luigi Creatore, George David Weiss, and Albert Stanton), drawing heavily on The Weavers' "Wimoweh," became a #1 gold-selling hit for the Tokens. Peter, Paul and Mary's revival of "The Hammer Song," titled "If I Had a Hammer," reached the Top Ten in October 1962.

In 1963 The Weavers released a new studio album, *The Weavers' Almanac*. Though featured on the album, Erik Darling had left the group and been replaced by Frank Hamilton (b. N.Y., Aug. 3, 1934), the cofounder of the Old Town School of Folk Music in Chicago. As The Weavers planned a reunion at Carnegie Hall for the spring, Hamilton announced his departure, and the two shows, May 2 and 3, which featured Hays, Gilbert, Hellerman, Seeger, Darling, and Hamilton, served as an introduction for the newest member, Bernie Krause. The performances were recorded and released on two Vanguard albums, *Reunion at Carnegie Hall, 1963* (released December 1963) and *Reunion at Carnegie Hall, Part 2* (August 1965). Trini Lopez reached the Top Ten in August 1963 with another revival of "If I Had a Hammer."

The Weavers disbanded in early 1964. In April 1966 The Beach Boys scored a Top Ten hit with "Sloop John B," an adaptation of "(The Wreck of the) John B." Robert John revived "The Lion Sleeps Tonight" for a million-selling Top Ten hit in 1972. Fred Hellerman produced Pete Seeger's 1979 album *Circles & Seasons*, and on one track they sang together with Ronnie Gilbert. They agreed to participate in a film documentary about The Weavers with Lee Hays in 1980, and this resulted in two reunion concerts, held on Nov. 28–29, 1980, at Carnegie Hall. The shows were recorded for an album, *Together Again*, released in 1981. The quartet reunited a final time in June 1981 to perform at the Croton Festival. The film, *The Weavers: Wasn't That a Time!*, opened in 1982. Vanguard released a four-CD boxed set of The Weavers' recordings for Decca and Vanguard, also titled *Wasn't That a Time*, in 1993. In 1999, a quartet featuring singer/songwriter Michael Smith and singer Barbara Barrow began to tour as The Weavers, doing faithful renditions fo the group's songs.

WRITINGS: *The W. Songbook* (N.Y., 1960).

DISC.: *At Carnegie Hall* (1956); *At Carnegie Hall No. 2* (1960); *Reunion at Carnegie Hall—1963* (1963); *Reunion at Carnegie Hall No. 2* (1963); *Wasn't That a Time* (rec. 1948–92; rel. 1993); *Best of Pete Seeger* (rec. 1948–52; rel. 1996).—**WR**

Webb, Charles H(aizlip, Jr.), American music educator, pianist, organist, and conductor; b. Dallas, Feb. 14, 1933. He was educated at Southern Methodist Univ. (A.B. and M.Mus., 1955) and at Ind. Univ. (D.Mus., 1964). In 1957–58 he was asst. to the dean of the School of Music at Southern Methodist Univ. In 1958 he joined the faculty of the School of Music at Ind. Univ. as an instructor in piano, becoming an asst. prof. and asst. dean in 1964, assoc. prof. in 1967, assoc. dean in 1969, and dean in 1973. Upon his retirement in 1997, he was named a Distinguished Prof. Under Webb's leadership, the School of Music not only retained but enhanced its position among the world's leading schools of music. From 1961 he served as organist of the First Methodist Church in Bloomington, Ind. He also was conductor of the Indianapolis Symphonic Choir from 1967 to 1981. In addition to his appearances as a concert organist, he also made tours in the U.S. in duo recitals with the pianist Wallace Hornibrook. In 1983 he was named a member of the Ind. Academy.—**NS/LK/DM**

Webb, Jimmy, the hit MOR songwriter who wanted to be a singer and wanted to be hip; b. Elk City, Olka., Aug. 15, 1946. The son of a Baptist Minister, he played the organ in his father's church, where he enjoyed by re-harmonizing the hymns. He started writing religious songs, but when rock and roll hit, he formed a band.

He dissected pop songs and wrote follow-ups to chart hits that often were better than the originals. He moved to Los Angeles and got a job with Motown's publishing company, Jobete, transcribing songs for tunesmiths who couldn't write music. He began to make the rounds with his own songs, landing the romantic ballad "By the Time I Get to Phoenix" with Johnny Rivers.

Glen Campbell heard the song and cut it himself. Campbell's version rose to #26, becoming his first pop hit. As this hit started to break, Rivers had put Webb to work on another project, writing the songs for a new vocal group called the Fifth Dimension on his Soul City label. Webb's "Up, Up and Away" rose to #7 on the pop charts. Between those two songs, they took home five Grammy Awards, including a Song of the Year statuette for Webb. Eventually, "By the Time I Get to Phoenix" became the third most recorded song in the BMI repertoire. "Up, Up and Away" became a major airline's theme song for years. Suddenly, 21-year-old Jimmy Webb was the hottest songwriter in Hollywood.

During 1968, Webb penned tunes for Campbell such as the #39 "Gentle on My Mind," which won two Grammys, and the gold #3 "Wichita Lineman," also a Grammy winner. He wrote a song that bordered on oratorio—a complex, orchestral suite called "MacArthur Park." He persuaded musical stage star Richard Harris to perform it. At over seven minutes in length, radio resisted it, but constant requests forced their hand. The song eventually rose to #2 in the spring of 1968, taking the largely Webb-written album *A Tramp Shining* to #4. Donna Summer took "MacArthur Park" all the way to the top of the charts 10 years later.

Webb and Harris collaborated again on the *The Yard Went on Forever* album the next year. Arguably a better album, it lacked the hit impetus "MacArthur Park" gave the previous effort and only reached #27. By 1969 Webb was still churning out hits and had broadened his scope to include film scores. His work started to take on an edge—how far could he take his creative ambitions before he fell on his face? As a songwriter, he rarely did that, at least in public.

However, Webb had two other goals. He wanted to write a musical and he wanted to be taken seriously as a performer. Several theater projects never came to fruition as the decade turned. However, he did release an album, an elaborately scored opus called *Words and Music*. It sold poorly and eroded his credibility with his pop songwriting peers. His second effort, *And So On*, took a more stripped-down approach, with guest a appearance by jazz guitarist Larry Coryell but with none of the orchestra grandeur. Similarly, *Letters* sported a guest vocal by Joni Mitchell, as did *Land's End*. The biggest problem with Webb as a performer was that his voice was not one of nature's great instruments. However, the albums are worthwhile for the same reason listening to a songwriter sing his compositions is always worthwhile—it offers a special perspective on the songs.

Webb continued to compose prolifically through the 1970s, writing and producing an album for the Supremes and reuniting with both Glen Campbell and the Fifth Dimension. He wrote the bulk of Art Garfunkel's *Watermark*, a gold, #19 hit in 1978. He also wrote for singers ranging from Joe Cocker to Joan Baez to Frank Sinatra. Sinatra felt Webb was the finest songwriter of his generation.

For his own 1977 album, Webb turned to George Martin. Although the album proved of only passing interest and generated few sales, it included a song called "The Highwayman," which became a major vehicle and name for a country supergroup featuring Johnny Cash, Kris Kristofferson, Willie Nelson, and Waylon Jennings.

Intent on writing more serious compositions, and harking back to his earlier church-based inspirations, he created a cantata called *The Animals' Christmas*. He conducted the premiere of the piece at N.Y.'s Cathedral of St. John the Divine, with Art Garfunkel as one of the singers.

By the late 1980s, hits were fewer and further between so Webb hit the road again, accompanied by Coryell on guitar. His small, intimate performances at cabaret spaces earned him high praise, despite the scabrous nature of the shows. He returned to recording, working with Linda Ronstadt on *Suspending Disbelief*. She brought along other singers, including David Crosby, Don Henley, and J. D. Souther. He recorded a sort of "best of" album called *Ten Easy Pieces* on which he did his own versions of his most popular tunes. He also wrote a book about his craft called *Tunesmith: Inside the Art of Songwriting*. Still itching to get on Broadway, he started collaborating with actor Chazz Palminteri on a project. Webb also set up an Internet music site to release an album of Kenny Rankin performing his songs.

DISC.: *Jim Webb Sings Jim Webb* (1968); *Words & Music* (1970); *And So On* (1971); *Letters* (1972); *Land's End* (1974); *El Mirage* (1977); *Angel Heart* (1982); *Suspending Disbelief* (1993); *Ten Easy Pieces* (1996).—**BH**

Webbe, Samuel, foremost English composer of glees; b. probably in London, 1740; d. there, May 15, 1816. He was apprenticed to a carpenter when he was 11, but also studied music on his own; was a music copyist while studying with the organist Barbandt. His canon "O that I had wings" won a prize of the Noblemen's and Gentlemen's Catch Club in 1766, and he subsequently carried off 26 other prizes from then until 1792. He became organist of the Portuguese and Sardinian chapels in 1776, and remained active at the latter until about 1813. He was made librarian of the Glee Club at its foundation in 1787; his glee "Glorious Apollo" was the opening glee at every one of its meetings during its existence; he also served as secretary of the Catch Club from 1794 until his death. Although he was most famous in his day for his glees, he also wrote music for the Roman Catholic liturgy; his antiphon *O salutaris hostia* (1782) is his best-known work today, being the hymn tune "Melcombe," generally used for Keble's hymn *New every morning is the love*; he also wrote music for the Anglican service. His son, also named Samuel Webbe (b. London, c. 1770; d. there, Nov. 25, 1843), was an organist and composer; he studied with his father and then held various posts as an organist. He wrote the music for an operatic farce, *The Speechless Wife* (Covent Garden, London, May 22, 1794), as well as numerous glees, catches, and songs, music for the Roman Catholic liturgy, 4 harp sonatas, and much piano music.

WORKS: VOCAL: Secular: 8 books of catches, canons, and glees for 3 to 6 Voices (London, c. 1764–95); *A Collection* *of Vocal Music* for 2 to 5 Voices (London, 1795; with his son); *6 Original Glees* (London, 1840; ed. by his son); various other works in anthologies of the 18th and 19th centuries. **Latin Sacred:** *An Essay on the Church Plain Chant* (London, 1782); *A Collection of Sacred Music as Used in the Chapel of the King of Sardinia* (London, c. 1785); *A Collection of Masses with Accompaniment for the Organ* (London, 1792); *A Collection of Motetts or Antiphons* (London, 1792). **English Sacred:** *8 Anthems in Score for the Use of Cathedrals and Country Choirs* (London, 1794); *12 Anthems* (London, c. 1798); *A Collection of Original Psalm Tunes* for 3 to 4 Voices (London, c. 1805; with his son). **INSTRUMENTAL:** 6 sonatas for Piano or Harpsichord (London, c. 1780); organ music.—**NS/LK/DM**

Webber, Andrew Lloyd
See **Lloyd Webber, Sir Andrew,**

Webber, Julian Lloyd
See **Lloyd Webber, Julian**

Weber, family of German musicians:

(1) Weber, Fridolin, German singer and violinist, uncle of **Carl Maria (Friedrich Ernst) von Weber;** b. Zell, Wiesental, 1733; d. Vienna, Oct. 23, 1779. He served in the Mannheim electoral chapel. He had 4 daughters.

(2) (Maria) Josepha Weber, soprano; b. Zell, c. 1759; d. Vienna, Dec. 29, 1819. After appearances in provincial music centers, she settled in Vienna in 1788; that same year, she married the violinist Franz de Paula Hofer (1755–96), one of Mozart's friends. Her second husband was the bass and actor (Friedrich) Sebastian Mayer (1773–1835), the creator of the role of Pizarro in Beethoven's *Fidelio*. She was a leading singer in Vienna, being closely associated with Schikaneder's Theater auf der Wieden from 1790; she retired from the stage in 1805. Mozart wrote the aria *Schön lacht der holde Frühling*, K. 580, for her, as well as the role of the Queen of the Night in his opera *Die Zauberflöte*; nevertheless, he disparaged her character in a letter of Dec. 15, 1781.

(3) (Maria) Aloysia (Louise Antonia) Weber, soprano; b. c. 1760; d. Salzburg, June 8, 1839. She studied voice with Mozart while he was in Mannheim (1777–78); he fell in love with her, but she left him. After singing in Munich (1778–79), she went to Vienna as a member of the German opera (1779–82) and the Italian opera (1782–92). She married the court actor and painter Joseph Lange (1751–1831) in 1780; she left him in 1795 to pursue a concert career. Mozart wrote a number of concert arias for her, as well as the role of Madame Herz in his *Der Schauspieldirektor*.

(4) (Maria) Constanze (Constantia) (Caecilia Josepha Johanna Aloisia) Weber, soprano; b. Zell, Jan. 4, 1762; d. Salzburg, March 6, 1842. She was the wife of **Wolfgang Amadeus Mozart**.

(5) (Maria) Sophie Weber, soprano; b. Zell, Oct. 1763; d. Salzburg, Oct. 26, 1846. She married **Jakob Haibel** in 1807. She was with Mozart during the last hours of his life, and related her account of his death to her brother-in-law, Georg Nikolaus Nissen, the Danish statesman and music scholar, who wrote a biography of Mozart.—**NS/LK/DM**

Weber, Alain, French composer and teacher; b. Château- Thierry, Dec. 8, 1930. He studied at the Paris Cons. with Robert Dussault (theory), Jules Gentil (piano), Jean Gallon and Henri Challan (harmony), Tony Aubin (composition), and Olivier Messiaen (analysis). In 1952 he won the Premier Grand Prix de Rome and worked at the Villa Medici there. Upon returning to Paris, he taught at the Cons. He was the author of various pedagogical tomes. His opera *La Rivière Perdue* was awarded the Grand Prix Audiovisuel de l'Europe by the Académie du Disque Français in 1982. He also was made an Officier de l'Ordre National du Mérite.

WORKS: DRAMATIC: Opera: *La Voie Unique* (1957); *La Rivière Perdue* (1981–82); *Le Rusé Petit Jean* (1984). **Ballet:** *Le Petit Jeu* (1951); *Epitome* (1972). **ORCH.:** *Suite Pour une Pièce Vue* (1954); Sym. (1954–55); *Scherzo Burlesque* (1957); *Croquis de Table* for Chamber Orch. (1957); Concerto for Horn and Strings (1958); *Exergues* for Strings (1959); Piano Concertino (1961); *Midjaay*, symphonic poem (1964); Trombone Concerto (1964); *Variantes* for 2 Percussion and Orch. (1964); *Variations* (1965); *Strophes* for Trumpet, Strings, and Percussion (1966); *Commentaires Concertants* for Flute and Orch. (1967); *Gravitations* for Piano, Strings, and Percussion (1968); *Solipsisme* for String Quartet, String Orch., Piano, and Percussion (1968); *D'Après Wols* for Cello and Orch. (1969); *Cercles* for Violin and Orch. (1970); *Linéaire I* for Alto Saxophone and Orch. (1973); *Paraphrases Dialoguées* for Ondes Martenot and Orch. (1975); *Ricordarsi* for Strings (1975); *Cantus* for Harp or Celtic Harp and Strings (1976); *Traces* for 2 Violins and Strings (1978); *Haltia* (1980); *Lied* for Strings (1980); *Concert* for Winds (1983); *Alliages* (1997). **CHAMBER:** Wind Quintet (1955); Clarinet Sextet (1956); Sonata for Oboe and Harp or Piano (1961; also for Clarinet and Harp or Piano, 1992); *Sonate da tre* for Piano, Violin, and Cello (1968); Viola Sonata (1968); *Liminaire* for Wind Quintet (1973); *Epodes* for Saxophone, Oboe, Clarinet, and Bassoon (1974); *Projections* for 5 or More Percussionists (1974); *Linéaire II* for 8 Instruments (1977) and *III* for Ondes Martenot Sextet (1977); *Syllepse* for Piano, Percussion, and Ondes Martenot (1977); *Macles* for 4 Trumpets, 3 Trombones, and Tuba (1978); *Huaco* for Flute, Viola, and Harp (1979); *Assonances* for Oboe, Alto Saxophone, and Cello (1980); *Improvisations Enchainées* for Celtic or Grand Harp and Flute (1980); *Octuor* for 8 Instruments (1981); Saxophone Quartet (1984); *Alternances* for Piano and Violin (1988); *Anamorphoses* for Trombone and Harp Soloists and 3 Trombones (1991); *Versets* for Organ and Trombone Quartet (1992); *Neumes* for Organ and Trombone Quartet (1992); *Constellaire* for Mandolin, Guitar, and Celtic Harp (1994); *Et L'On Vit des Fées Débarquer sur la Plage* for Harp (1994); *Acquatintes* for Baroque Lute (1997); *Cadentiel* for Violin (1997). **Piano:** *Modes enfantines* (1968); *Études acrostiches en forme de variations* (1970); *Climax* (1987). **VOCAL:** *2 Mélodies* for Baritone and Piano (1950); *5 Poèmes* for Mezzo-soprano and Orch. (1953); *Phonènimie* for Chorus and 5 Players (1983); *Le "Chan" du Potager* for Reciter, Soprano, Piano, Violin, and Trumpet (1984); *2 Préludes Rimbaldiens* for Soprano and Piano or Harp or Guitar (1989).—**NS/LK/DM**

Weber, Albert, German-American piano manufacturer; b. Heiligenstadt, July 8, 1828; d. N.Y., June 25, 1879. He went to N.Y. in 1844 and began manufacturing pianos in 1851. In 1869 he opened his first public wareroom at 16th and Fifth Ave. Weber is credited with having coined the term "baby grand" to designate the short grand piano. Unlike other major piano manufacturers, he did not invent or create anything new in piano construction. However, his pianos were known for their superb craftsmanship. After his death, the Weber Piano Co. was continued by his son, Albert Jr., who unsuccessfully attempted to break the Steinway monopoly of artists and orchs. It became the Weber-Wheelock Co. in 1892, and then merged into the Aeolian, Weber Piano & Pianola Co. in 1903.—**LK/DM**

Weber, Ben (actually, **William Jennings Bryan**), American composer; b. St. Louis, July 23, 1916; d. N.Y., May 9, 1979. He received lessons in piano and singing but was autodidact in composition. He also studied medicine briefly at DePaul Univ. in Chicago. In 1945 he settled in N.Y., where he was active as a copyist. He was associated with the ISCM and the American Composers Alliance, becoming president of the latter in 1959. In 1950 and 1953 he held Guggenheim fellowships, in 1960 he received an award and citation from the National Inst. of Arts and Letters, and from 1965 to 1968 he held the 1st Phoebe Ketchum Thorne Music Fund Award. In 1971 he was elected to membership in the National Inst. of Arts and Letters. He left the memoir, *How I Took 63 Years to Commit Suicide* (1979; excerpts in the *Brooklyn Literary Review*, II, 1981). In 1938 Weber embraced 12-tone writing but he retained the firm tonal foundation of his melodic and contrapuntal structures. His chamber and vocal works were particularly notable.

WORKS: ORCH.: *Piece* for Oboe and Orch. (1943–44); 2 sinfonias: No. 1 for Cello and Orch. (1945–46; also for Cello and Piano) and No. 2, *Sinfonia Clarion*, for Small Orch. (1973; N.Y., Feb. 26, 1974); *Symphony on Poems of William Blake* for Baritone and Chamber Orch. (1950; N.Y., Oct. 28, 1952); *2 Pieces* for Strings (1950); Violin Concerto (1954); *Prelude and Passacaglia* (1954; Louisville, Jan. 1, 1955); *Rapsodie concertante* for Viola and Small Orch. (1957); Piano Concerto (N.Y., March 21, 1961); *Dolmen: An Elegy* for Winds and Strings (1964); *Dramatic Piece* for Violin and Orch. (1970). **CHAMBER:** *Intermezzo* for Clarinet and Piano (1935–36); *The Pool of Darkness* for Flute, Trumpet, Bassoon, Violin, Cello, and Piano (1939); 2 pieces for Clarinet and Piano (1939); *Pastorale* for Wind Quintet (1939); *Scherzino* for Wind Quintet (1939); 2 violin sonatas (1939; 1942, rev. 1943); *Fantasie* for Violin and Piano (1939–40); *Lyric Piece* for String Quartet (1940); *Variations* for Clarinet, Violin, Cello, and Piano (1941); 2 concertinos: No. 1 for Clarinet, Violin, and Cello (1941) and No. 2 for Flute, Oboe, Clarinet, and String Quartet (1956); *5 Pieces* for Cello and Piano (1941); *Divertimento* for 2 Cellos (1941); 3 string quartets (1941; 1951; 1959, unfinished); *Rhapsodie* for Cello and Wind Quintet (1942); *Ballade* for Cello and Piano (1943; also for Orch., 1945); Piano Trio (n.d.; unfinished); Oboe Quintet (n.d.; destroyed); *Dance No. 1* (1948) and *No. 2* (1949) for Cello; *Sonata da camera* for Violin and Piano (1950); Concerto for Piano, Cello, and Wind Quintet (1950); 2 serenades: No. 1 for Harpsichord, Flute, Oboe, and Cello (1953) and No. 2 for String Quartet and Double Bass (1956); *Colloquy* for 2 Trumpets, 2 Horns, 2 Trombones, and Tuba (1955); *Chamber Fantasie* for 2 Clarinets, Bass Clarinet, Harp, Violin, 2 Cellos, and Double Bass (1959); Duo for Clarinet and Cello (1960); *Prelude and Nocturne* for Flute, Celesta, and Cello (1965); *Consort of Winds* for Wind Quintet (1974); *Capriccio* for Cello and Piano (1977). **Piano:** *5 Bagatelles* (1939); 3 suites (1940–41; 1948; for 4-Hands, 1964); *Fantasy (Variations)* (1946); *New Adventures* (1956); Sonata (1970; unfinished); *Intermezzo* (1972); *Ciaconna, Capriccio* (1979; unfinished). **VOCAL:** *Song of the Idiot* for Soprano and Orch. (1941); *Concert Aria after Solomon* for Soprano and 8 Instruments (1949); *3 Songs* for Soprano and String Quartet or String Orch. (1958); *The Ways*, song cycle for Soprano or Tenor and Piano (1961); *Fugue and Finale* for Soprano and 7 Instruments (1969); choral pieces; other songs.—**NS/LK/DM**

Weber, Bernhard Anselm, German pianist, conductor, and composer; b. Mannheim, April 18, 1764; d. Berlin, March 23, 1821. He commenced keyboard training with Vogler in 1773, and after studying singing with Holzbauer and theory with Einberger, he returned to Vogler to study composition in 1775. He took courses in theology and law at the Univ. of Heidelberg in 1781; then traveled as a performer on the Xanorphica, a keyboard instrument invented by Rölling. In 1787 he became music director of Grossmann's opera troupe in Hannover, touring with it in 1790 in Holland, Germany, and Scandinavia. After a sojourn in Stockholm, he performed in Hamburg. In 1792 he was named joint music director (with Bernhard Wessely) of Berlin's Nationaltheater; in 1796 became its first music director, and in 1803 was elevated to the post of Kapellmeister; he retained his title when the German and Italian theaters merged in 1811. During his Berlin tenure, he championed the music of Gluck, conducting his *Iphigénie en Tauride* on Feb. 24, 1795. Weber distinguished himself as a pianist and conductor. Although he was a prolific composer, only a few songs from his stage works retained their popularity. His incidental music to Schiller's drama *Wilhelm Tell* (1804), however, was long admired.

BIBL.: H. Fischer, *B.A. W.* (diss., Univ. of Berlin, 1923); K. Hassan, *B.A. W. (1764–1821); Ein Musiker für das Theater* (Frankfurt am Main, 1997).—**NS/LK/DM**

Weber, Carl Maria (Friedrich Ernst) von, celebrated German composer, pianist, and conductor, nephew of **Fridolin Weber** (see **Weber**); b. Eutin, Oldenburg, Nov. 18, 1786; d. London, June 5, 1826. His father, Franz Anton von Weber (1734?–1812), was an army officer and a good musical amateur who played the violin and served as Kapellmeister in Eutin. It was his fondest wish that Carl Maria would follow in the footsteps of Mozart as a child prodigy (Constanze Weber, Mozart's wife, was his niece, thus making Carl Maria a first cousin of Mozart by marriage). Carl Maria's mother was a singer of some ability; she died when he was 11. Franz Anton led a wandering life as music director of his own theater company, taking his family with him on his tours. Although this mode of life interfered with Carl Maria's regular education, it gave him practical knowledge of the stage, and stimulated his imagination as a dramatic composer. His first teachers were his father and his half-brother Fritz, a pupil of Haydn; at Hildburghausen, where he found himself with his father's company in 1796, he also received piano instruction from J. P. Heuschkel. The next year he was in Salzburg, where he attracted the attention of Michael Haydn, who taught him counterpoint; he composed a set of *6 Fughetten* there, which were publ. in

1798. As his peregrinations continued, he was taught singing by Valesi (J. B. Wallishauser) and composition by J. N. Kalcher in Munich (1798–1800). At the age of 12, he wrote an opera, *Die Macht der Liebe und des Weins*; it was never performed and the MS has not survived. Through a meeting with Aloys Senefelder, the inventor of lithography, he became interested in engraving; he became Senefelder's apprentice, acquiring considerable skill in the method, and he engraved his own *6 Variations on an Original Theme* for Piano (Munich, 1800). His father became interested in the business possibilities of lithography, and set up a workshop with him in Freiberg; however, the venture failed, and the young Carl Maria turned again to music. He composed a 2-act comic opera, *Das Waldmädchen*, in 1800; it was premiered in Freiberg on Nov. 24, 1800, 6 days after his 14th birthday; performances followed in Chemnitz (Dec. 5, 1800) and Vienna (Dec. 4, 1804). In 1801 the family was once more in Salzburg, where he studied further with Michael Haydn. Weber wrote another opera, *Peter Schmoll und seine Nachbarn* (1801–02). He gave a concert in Hamburg in Oct. 1802, and the family then proceeded to Augsburg; they remained there from Dec. 1802 until settling in Vienna in Sept. 1803. There, there Weber continued his studies with Abbé Vogler, at whose recommendation he secured the post of conductor of the Breslau Opera in 1804. He resigned this post in 1806 after his attempts at operatic reform caused dissension. In 1806 he became honorary Intendant to Duke Eugen of Württemberg-Öls at Schloss Carlsruhe in Upper Silesia; much of his time was devoted to composition there. In 1807 he was engaged as private secretary to Duke Ludwig in Stuttgart, and also gave music lessons to his children. This employment was abruptly terminated when Weber became innocently involved in a scheme of securing a ducal appointment for a rich man's son in order to exempt him from military service, and accepted a loan of money. This was a common practice at the Stuttgart court, but as a result of the disclosure of Weber's involvement, he was arrested (Feb. 9, 1810) and kept in prison for 16 days. This matter, along with several others, was settled to his advantage, only to find him the target of his many creditors, who had him rearrested on Feb. 17. Finally, agreeing to pay off his debts as swiftly as possible, he was released and then banished by King Friedrich. He then went to Mannheim, where he made appearances as a pianist. He next went to Darmstadt, where he rejoined his former teacher, Vogler, for whom he wrote the introduction to his teacher's ed. of 12 Bach chorales. On Sept. 16, 1810, Weber's opera *Silvana* was successfully premiered in Frankfurt am Main; the title role was sung by Caroline Brandt, who later became a member of the Prague Opera; Weber and Brandt were married in Prague on Nov. 4, 1817. Weber left Darmstadt in Feb. 1811 for Munich, where he composed several important orch. works. Weber's 1-act Singspiel, *Abu Hassan*, was successfully given in Munich on June 4, 1811. From Aug. to Dec. 1811, Weber and Bärmann gave concerts in Switzerland; after appearing in Prague in Dec. 1811, they went to Leipzig in Jan. 1812, and then on to Weimar and Dresden. On March 15, 1812, they gave a concert in Berlin, which was attended by King Friedrich Wilhelm III. On Dec. 17, 1812, Weber was soloist at the premiere of his 2nd Piano Concerto in Gotha. Upon his return to Prague in Jan. 1813, he was informed that he was to be the director of the German Opera there. He was given extensive authority, and traveled to Vienna to engage singers; he also secured the services of Franz Clement as concertmaster. During his tenure, Weber presented a distinguished repertoire, which included Beethoven's *Fidelio*; however, when his reforms encountered determined opposition, he submitted his resignation (1816). On Dec. 14, 1816, he was appointed Musikdirektor of the German Opera in Dresden by King Friedrich August III. He opened his first season on Jan. 30, 1817; that same year, he was named Königlich Kapellmeister and began to make sweeping reforms. About this time he approached Friedrich Kind, a Dresden lawyer and writer, and suggested to him the idea of preparing a libretto on a Romantic German subject for his next opera. They agreed on *Der Freischütz*, a fairy tale from the *Gespensterbuch*, a collection of ghost stories by J. A. Apel and F. Laun. The composition of this work, which was to prove his masterpiece, occupied him for 3 years; the score was completed on May 13, 1820, and 2 weeks later Weber began work on the incidental music to Wolff's *Preciosa*, a play in 4 acts with spoken dialogue; it was produced in Berlin on March 14, 1821. A comic opera, *Die drei Pintos*, which Weber started at about the same time, was left unfinished. After some revisions, *Der Freischütz* was accepted for performance at the opening of Berlin's Neues Schauspielhaus. There arose an undercurrent of rivalry with Spontini, director of the Berlin Opera, a highly influential figure in operatic circles and at court. Spontini considered himself the guardian of the Italian-French tradition in opposition to the new German Romantic movement in music. Weber conducted the triumphant premiere of *Der Freischütz* on June 18, 1821; the work's success surpassed all expectations and the cause of new Romantic art was won. *Der Freischütz* was soon staged by all the major opera houses of Europe. In English, it was given first in London, on July 22, 1824; translations into other languages followed. Weber's next opera was *Euryanthe*, produced in Vienna on Oct. 25, 1823, with only moderate success. Meanwhile, Weber's health was affected by incipient tuberculosis and he was compelled to spend part of 1824 in Marienbad for a cure. He recovered sufficiently to begin the composition of *Oberon*, a commission from London's Covent Garden. The English libretto was prepared by J. R. Planché, based on a translation of C. M. Wieland's verse- romance of the same name. Once more illness interrupted Weber's progress on his work; he spent part of the summer of 1825 in Ems to prepare himself for the journey to England. He set out for London in Feb. 1826, a dying man. On his arrival, he was housed with Sir George Smart, the conductor of the Phil. Soc. of London. Weber threw himself into his work, presiding over 16 rehearsals for *Oberon*. On April 12, 1826, he conducted its premiere at Covent Garden, obtaining a tremendous success. Despite his greatly weakened condition, he conducted 11 more performances of the score and also participated in various London concerts, playing for the last time a week before his death. He was found dead in his room on the morning of June 5, 1826. He was buried in London. His remains were removed to Dresden in 1844. On Dec. 14, 1844, they were taken to the Catholic cemetery in Dresden to the accompaniment of funeral music arranged from motifs from *Euryanthe* for wind instruments as prepared and conducted by Wagner. The next day, Weber's remains were interred as Wagner delivered an oration and conducted a chorus in his specially composed *An Webers Grabe*.

Weber's role in music history is epoch-making. In his operas, particularly in *Der Freischütz*, he opened the era of musical Romanticism, in decisive opposition to the established Italianate style. The highly dramatic and poetic portrayal of a German fairy tale, with its aura of supernatural mystery, appealed to the public, whose imagination had been stirred by the emergent Romantic literature of the period. Weber's melodic genius and mastery of the craft of composition made it possible for him to break with tradition and to start on a new path, at a critical time when individualism and nationalism began to emerge as sources of creative artistry. His instrumental works, too, possessed a new quality that signalized the transition from Classical to Romantic music. For piano he wrote pieces of extraordinary brilliance, introducing some novel elements in chord writing and passage work. He was an excellent pianist; his large hands gave him an unusual command of the keyboard (he could stretch the interval of a twelfth). Weber's influence on the development of German music was very great. The evolutionary link to Wagner's music drama is evident in the coloring of the orch. parts in Weber's operas and in the adumbration of the principle of leading motifs. Finally, he was one of the first outstanding interpretative conducting podium figures.

WORKS: In the list of Weber's works that follows, his compositions are identified by the J. numbers established by F. Jahns in his *Carl Maria von Weber in seinen Werken: Chronologisch-thematisches Verzeichniss seiner sämmtlichen Compositionen* (Berlin, 1871). **DRAMATIC: Opera:** *Die Macht der Liebe und des Weins,* J. Anh. 6, Singspiel (1798; not perf.; not extant); *Das Waldmädchen*, J. Anh. 1, Romantic comic opera (Freiberg, Nov. 24, 1800; only fragments extant); *Peter Schmoll und seine Nachbarn*, J.8 (1801–02; Augsburg, March 1803?; music not extant, dialogue lost); *Rübezahl*, J.44–46 (1804–05; unfinished; only 3 numbers extant); *Silvana*, J.87, Romantic opera (1808–10; Frankfurt am Main, Sept. 16, 1810, composer conducting); *Abu Hassan*, J.106, Singspiel (1810–11; Munich, June 4, 1811, composer conducting); *Der Freischütz*, J.277, Romantic opera (1817–21; Berlin, June 18, 1821, composer conducting); *Die drei Pintos*, J. Anh. 5, comic opera (begun in 1820; unfinished; libretto rev. by the composer's grandson, Carl von Weber, and Gustav Mahler; extant music completed by adding other works by the composer, with scoring by Mahler; Leipzig, Jan. 20, 1888, Mahler conducting); *Euryanthe*, J.291, grand heroic Romantic opera (1822–23; Vienna, Oct. 25, 1823, composer conducting); *Oberon, or The Elf King's Oath*, J.306, Romantic opera (1825–26; London, April 12, 1826, composer conducting). **Other:** Overture and 6 numbers for Schiller's tr. of Gozzi's *Turandot, Prinzessin von China*, J.75 (Stuttgart, Sept. 1809); *Rondo alla polacca* for Tenor for Haydn's pasticchio *Der Freibrief*, J.77 (1809); Duet for Soprano and Tenor for Haydn's *Der Freibrief*, J.78 (1809); 4 songs for Voice and Guitar (one with Men's Chorus) for Kotzebue's *Der arme Minnesinger*, J.110–13 (1811); *Scena ed aria* for Soprano for Méhul's opera *Héléna*, J.178 (1815); 2 songs for Baritone and for Soprano and Bass for Fischer's Singspiel *Der travestirte Aeneas*, J.183–84 (1815); 2 songs for Baritone and for Tenor for Gubitz's festspiel *Lieb' und Versöhnen*, J.186–87 (1815); Ballade for Baritone and Harp for Reinbeck's *Gordon und Montrose*, J.189 (1815); Arietta for Soprano for Huber's and Kauer's *Das Sternenmädchen im Maidlinger Walde*, J.194 (1816; text not extant); Romance for Voice and Guitar for Castelli's *Diana von Poitiers*, J.195 (1816); 10 numbers and 1 song for Unaccompanied Mezzo-soprano for Müllner's *König Yngurd*, J.214 (Dresden, April 14, 1817); 6 numbers for Moreto's *Donna Diana*, J.220 (1817); Song for Solo Voices and Chorus for Kind's *Der Weinberg an der Elbe*, J.222 (1817); Romance for Voice and Guitar for Kind's *Das Nachtlager von Granada*, J.223 (1818); 2-part song for Tenor and Bass for Holbein's *Die drei Wahrzeichen*, J.225 (1818); Dance and song for Tenor and Chorus for Hell's *Das Haus Anglade*, J.227 (1818; may not be by Weber); 8 numbers for Gehe's *Heinrich IV, König von Frankreich*, J.237 (Dresden, June 6, 1818); *Scena ed aria* for Soprano for Cherubini's opera *Lodoïska*, J.239 (1818); Chorus for 2 Sopranos and Bass for Grillparzer's *Sappho*, J.240 (1818); Song for Voice and Piano or Guitar for Kind's *Der Abend am Waldbrunnen*, J.243 (1818); 4 vocal numbers, march, and melodrama for Rublack's *Leib' um Liebe*, J.246 (1818); Agnus Dei for 2 Sopranos, Alto, and Wind Instruments for Blankensee's *Carlo*, J.273 (1820); 4 harp numbers for Houwald's *Der Leuchtturm*, J.276 (Dresden, April 26, 1820); Overture and 11 numbers to Wolff's *Preciosa*, J.279 (Berlin, March 14, 1821); Song for 2 Sopranos, Alto, Chorus, and Guitar for Shakespeare's *The Merchant of Venice*, J.280 (1821); one instrumental number (from the adagio of the Sym. No. 1 in C major, J.50) and 5 choruses for Robert's *Den Sachsensohn vermählet heute*, J.289 (1822); Arioso and recitative for Bass and Soprano for Spontini's opera *Olympie*, J.305 (1825). **ORCH.:** *Romanza Siciliana* in G minor for Flute and Orch., J.47 (1805); Horn Concertino in E minor, J.188 (1806; not extant; 2nd ver., 1815); 6 Variations on "A Schüsserl und a Reind'rl" in C major for Viola and Orch., J.49 (1806); 2 syms.: No. 1 in C major, J.50 (1807) and No. 2 in C major, J.51 (1807); *Grande Ouverture à plusiers instruments*, J.54 (rev. overture to *Peter Schmoll und seine Nachbarn*, J.8; 1807); *Grand Pot-Pourri* for Cello and Orch., J.64 (1808); *Andante e Rondo Ungarese* in C minor for Viola and Orch., J.79 (1809); Variations in F major for Cello and Orch., J.94 (1810); 2 piano concertos: No. 1 in C Major, J.98 (1810) and No. 2 in E-flat major, J.155 (Gotha, Dec. 17, 1812, composer soloist); Clarinet Concertino in E-flat major, J.109 (1811); 2 clarinet concertos: No. 1 in F minor, J.114 (1811) and No. 2 in E-flat major, J.118 (1811) *Adagio und Rondo* in F Major for Harmonichord and Orch., J.115 (1811); Bassoon Concerto in F major, J.127 (1811; 1st confirmed perf., Prague, Feb. 19, 1813; rev. 1822); *Der Beherrscher der Geister*, overture, J.122 (rev. of the lost *Rübezahl* overture; 1811); *Andante e Rondo Ungarese* in C minor for Bassoon and Orch., J.158 (rev. of J.79; 1813); *Deutscher (Original-Walzer)* in D major, J.185 (orch. arr. of a song in Fischer's Singspiel, *Der travestirte Aeneas*, J.183–84; 1815); *Tedesco* in D major, J.191 (1816); *Jubel-Ouvertüre* in E major, J.245 (1818); Konzertstück in F minor for Piano and Orch., J.282 (1821). **Wind Instruments:** *Tusch* for 20 Trumpets, J.47a (1806); *Waltz* for Flute, 2 Clarinets, 2 Horns, Trumpet, and 2 Bassoons, J.149 (1812); *Marcia vivace* for 10 Trumpets, J.288 (1822); *March* for Wind Band, J.307 (also arr. for Soloists, Chorus, and Orch.; rev. of No. 5 of *Six Petites Pièces Faciles*, J.13; 1826). **CHAMBER:** *Neuf variations sur un air norvégien* for Violin and Piano, J.61 (1808); Piano Quartet in B-flat major, J.76 (1809); *Six sonates progressives* for Violin and Piano, J.99–104 (1810); *Melody* in F major for Clarinet, J.119 (1811); *Seven*

Variations on a Theme from Silvana for Clarinet and Piano, J.128 (1811); Clarinet Quintet in B-flat major, J.182 (1815); *Grand Duo Concertant* for Piano and Clarinet, J.204 (1815–16); *Divertimento assai facile* for Guitar and Piano, J.207 (1816); Trio for Flute, Cello, and Piano, J.259 (1819). **Piano Solo:** *Sechs Fughetten*, J.1–6 (1798); *Six Variations on an Original Theme*, J.7 (1800); *Douze Allemandes*, J.15–26 (1801); *Sechs Ecossaisen*, J.29–34 (1802); *Huit Variations Sur L'air De Ballet De Castor Et Pollux* From Vogler's Opera, J.40 (1804); *Six Variations Sur L'air De Naga "Woher Mag Dies Wohl Kommen?"* From Vogler's Opera *Samori*, with Violin and Cello Ad Libitum, J.43 (1804); *Sept Variations Sur L'air "Vien Quà, Dorina Bella"* By Bianchi, J.53 (1807); *Theme Original Varié* (7 Variations), J.55 (1808); *Momento Capriccioso* in B-flat Major, J.56 (1808); *Grande Polonaise* in E-flat Major, J.59 (1808); 4 Sonatas: No. 1 in C Major, J.138 (1812), No. 2 in A-flat Major, J.199 (1816), No. 3 in D Minor, J.206 (1816), and No. 4 in E Minor, J.287 (1822); 7 Variations on "A Peine Au Sortir De L'enfance" From Méhul's Opera *Joseph*, J.141 (1812); *Sechs Favorit-walzer Der Kaiserin Von Frankreich, Marie Louise*, J.143–48 (1812); *Air Russe* ("Schöne Minka") (9 Variations), J.179 (1815); *Sieben Variationen über Ein Zigeunerlied*, J.219 (1817); *Rondo Brillante* ("La Gaité") in E-flat Major, J.252 (1819); *Aufforderung Zum Tanze: Rondo Brillant* in D-flat Major, J.260 (1819); *Polacca Brillante* ("L'hilarité") in E Major, J.268 (1819). **DUET:** *Six petites pièces faciles*, J.9–14 (1801); *Six pièces*, J.81–86 (1809); *Huit pièces*, J.236, 242, 248, 253–54, 264–66 (1818–19). **VOCAL: Concert Arias:** "Il momento s'avvicina," recitative and rondo for Soprano and Orch., J.93 (1810); "Misera me!," scena ed aria for Soprano and Orch. for *Atalia* J.121 (1811); "Qual altro attendi," scena ed aria for Tenor, Chorus, and Orch., J.126 (1812); "Signor, se padre sei," scena ed aria for Tenor, Choruses, and Orch. for *Ines de Castro*, J.142 (1812); "Non paventar mia vita," scena ed aria for Soprano and Orch. for *Ines de Castro*, J.181 (1815). **Masses:** Mass in E-flat major for Soprano, Alto, Tenor, Bass, Chorus, Organ, and Orch., J. Anh. 8 (1802); Mass in E-flat major for Soprano, Alto, Tenor, Bass, Chorus, and Orch., J.224, "Missa Sancta No. 1" (1817–18); Offertory, "Gloria et honore," for Soprano, Chorus, and Orch., for the Missa Sancta No. 1, J.226 (1818); Offertory, "In die solemnitatis," for Soprano, Chorus, and Orch., for the Missa Sancta No. 2, J.250 (1818); Mass in G major for Soloists, Chorus, and Orch., J.251, "Missa Sancta No. 2" or "Jubelmesse" (1818–19). **Cantatas:** *Der erste Ton* for Reciter and Orch., with closing chorus, J.58 (1808; rev. 1810); *In seiner Ordnung schafft der Herr*, hymn for Soloists, Chorus, and Orch., J.154 (1812); *Kampf und Sieg* for Soloists, Chorus, and Orch., J.190 (concerning the battle of Waterloo; 1815); *L'Accoglienza* for 3 Sopranos, Tenor, 2 Basses, Chorus, and Orch., J.221 (1817); *Jubel-Cantate* for Soloists, Chorus, and Orch., J.224 (1818); *Du, bekranzend unsre Laren* for 2 Sopranos, Alto, Tenor, Bass, Chorus, Piano, and Flute, J.283 (1821); *Wo nehm ich Blumen her* for Soprano, Tenor, Bass, and Piano, J.290 (1823). **Other:** Many other choral works and part songs, including *Trauer- Musik* for Baritone, Choir, and 10 Wind Instruments, J.116 (1811); *Das Turnierbankett* for 2 Tenors, Bass, and 2 Men's Choruses, J.132 (1812); *Schwabisches Tanzlied* for Soprano, 2 Tenors, 2 Basses, and Piano, J.135 (1812); *Kriegs-Eid* for Unison Men's Voices and 7 Instruments, J.139 (1812); *Leyer und Schwert*, 6 songs for 4 Men's Voices, J.168–73 (1814); *Natur und Liebe* for 2 Sopranos, 2 Tenors, 2 Basses, and Piano, J.241 (1818); also canons for 3 or 4 Voices; more than 80 songs; 6 vocal duets; *Zehn schottische Nationalgesange*, arrangements for Voice with accompaniments for Flute, Violin, Cello, and Piano, J.295–304 (1825).

WRITINGS: Weber's critical writings on music are valuable. He also left an autobiographical sketch, an unfinished novel, poems, etc. Editions of his writings include T. Hell, ed., *Hinterlassene Schriften von C.M. v.W.* (3 vols., Dresden and Leipzig, 1828; 2nd ed., 1850); G. Kaiser, ed., *Sämtliche Schriften von C.M. v.W.: Kritische Ausgabe* (Berlin and Leipzig, 1908); W. Altmann, ed., *W.s ausgewählte Schriften* (Regensburg, 1928); K. Laux, ed., *C.M. v.W.: Kunstansichten* (Leipzig, 1969; 2nd ed., 1975); J. Warrack, ed., and M. Cooper, tr., *C.M. v.W.: Writings on Music* (Cambridge, 1982).

BIBL.: COLLECTED WORKS, SOURCE MATERIAL: There is no complete ed. of Weber's works. A projected collected ed., *C.M. v.W.: Musikalische Werke: Erste kritische Gesamtausgabe*, under the general editorship of H.J. Moser, was abandoned with the outbreak of World War II; only 3 vols. were publ. (Vol. II/1, Augsburg, 1926; Vol. II/2, Augsburg, 1928; Vol. II/3, Braunschweig, 1939). Previously unpubl. works are found in L. Hirschberg, ed., *Reliquienschrein des Meisters C.M. v.W.* (Berlin, 1927). The standard thematic catalogue was prepared by F. Jähns, *C.M. v.W in seinen Werken: Chronologisch-thematisches Verzeichniss seiner sämmtlichen Compositionen* (Berlin, 1871). See also the vols. by H. Dunnebeil, *C.M. v.W.: Verzeichnis seiner Kompositionen* (Berlin, 1942; 2nd ed., 1947) and *Schrifttum über C.M. v.W.* (Berlin, 1947; 4th ed., 1957), D. and A. Henderson, *C.M. v.W.: A Guide to Research* (N.Y., 1989), and G. Allroggen and J. Veit, eds., *W.-Studien* (Mainz, 1993 et seq.). **CORRESPONDENCE:** C. von Weber (grandson of the composer), ed., *Reise-Briefe von C.M. v.W. an seine Gattin Carolina* (Leipzig, 1886); E. Rudorff, *Briefe von C.M. v.W. an Hinrich Lichtenstein* (Braunschweig, 1900); G. Kaiser, ed., *W.s Briefe an den Grafen Karl von Brühl* (Leipzig, 1911); L. Hirschberg, ed., *Siebenundsiebzig bisher ungedruckte Briefe C.M. v.W.s* (Hildburghausen, 1926); H. Worbs, ed., *C.M. v.W. Briefe* (Frankfurt am Main, 1982). **BIOGRAPHICAL:** W. Neumann, *W.: Eine Biographie* (Kassel, 1855); M. von Weber (son of the composer), *C.M. v.W.: Ein Lebensbild* (3 vols., Leipzig, 1864–66; abr. Eng. tr. by J. Simpson as *W.: The Life of an Artist*, 2 vols., London, 1865; 2nd Ger. ed., abr., by R. Pechel, Berlin, 1912); F. Jähns, *C.M. v.W.: Eine Lebensskizze nach authentischen Quellen* (Leipzig, 1873); J. Benedict, *W.* (London and N.Y., 1881; 5th ed., 1899); L. Nohl, *W.* (Leipzig, 1883); A. Reissmann, *W.: Sein Leben und seine Werke* (Berlin, 1886); H. Gehrmann, *C.M. v.W.* (Berlin, 1899); G. Servières, *W.* (Paris, 1906; new ed., 1925); H. von der Pfordten, *W.* (Leipzig, 1919); A. Cœuroy, *W.* (Paris, 1925; 2nd ed., 1953); E. Kroll, *C.M. v.W.* (Potsdam, 1934); W. Saunders, *W.* (London and N.Y., 1940); L. and R. Stebbins, *Enchanted Wanderer: The Life of C.M. v.W.* (N.Y., 1940); H. Moser, *C.M. v.W.: Leben und Werk* (Leipzig, 1941; 2nd ed., 1955); P. Raabe, *Wege zu W.* (Regensburg, 1942); W. Zentner, *C.M. v.W.: Sein Leben und sein Schaffen* (Olten, 1952); H. Schnoor, *W.: Gestalt und Schöpfung* (Dresden, 1953); F. Gruniger, *C.M. v.W.: Leben und Werk* (Freiburg im Breisgau, 1954); K. Laux, *C.M. v.W.* (Leipzig, 1966; 2nd ed., 1986); J. Warrack, *C.M. v.W.* (N.Y. and London, 1968; 2nd ed., 1976); D. Härtwig, *C.M. v.W.* (Leipzig, 1986); K. Höcker, *Oberons Horn: Das Leben von C.M. v.W.* (Berlin, 1986); H. Hoffmann, *C.M. v.W.: Biographie eines realistichen Romantikers* (Düsseldorf, 1986). **WEBER AND HIS CONTEMPORARIES:** H. Krüger, *Pseudoromantik, Friedrich Kind und der Dresdener Liederkreis* (Leipzig, 1904); H. and C. Cox, eds., *Leaves from the Journals of Sir George Smart* (London, 1907). **CRITICAL, ANALYTICAL:** F. Kind, *Freischütz-Buch* (Leipzig, 1843); R. Wagner: articles on W. in his *Gesammelte Schriften und Dichtungen* (Vol. I, Leipzig, 1871; Eng. tr. by W. Ashton Ellis as *The Prose Works of Richard Wagner*, Vol. VII, London, 1898); A. Jullien, *W. à Paris en 1826* (Paris, 1877); G.

Kaiser, *Beiträge zu einer Charakteristik W.s als Musikschriftsteller* (Leipzig, 1910); W. Georgii, *C.M. v.W. als Klavierkomponist* (diss., Univ. of Halle, 1914); E. Hasselberg, ed., *Der Freischütz: Friedrich Kinds Operndichtung und ihre Quellen* (Berlin, 1921); M. Degen, *Die Lieder von C.M. v.W.* (Freiburg im Breisgau, 1923); E. Reiter, *W.s künstlerische Persönlichkeit aus seinen Schriften* (Leipzig, 1926); A. Sandt, *W.s Opern in ihrer Instrumentation* (Frankfurt am Main, 1932); P. Listl, *C.M. v.W. als Ouverturenkomponist* (diss., Univ. of Würzburg, 1936); H. Schnoor, *W. auf dem Welttheater: Ein Freischützbuch* (Dresden, 1942; 4th ed., 1963); G. Jones, *Backgrounds and Themes of the Operas of C.M. v.W.* (diss., Cornell Univ., 1972); M. Tusa, *Euryanthe and C.M. v.W.'s Dramaturgy of German Opera* (Oxford, 1991); F. Heidlberger, *C.M. v. W. und hector Berlioz: Studien zur französischen W.-Rezeption* (Tutzing, 1994); W. Wagner, *C.M. v. W. und die deutsche Nationalopera* (Mainz, 1994); C. Schneider, *W. (1786–1826)* (Paris, 1998). **Miscellaneous:** F. Rapp, *Ein unbekanntes Bildnis W.s* (Stuttgart, 1937); G. Hausswald, ed., *C.M. v.W.: eine Gedenkschrift* (Dresden, 1951).—**NS/LK/DM**

Weber, Friedrich Dionys (actually, **Bedrich Diviš**), Bohemian pedagogue, writer on music, and composer; b. Velichov, near Carlsbad, Oct. 9, 1766; d. Prague, Dec. 25, 1842. He began his musical studies with F. Beier in Velichov; after studies at the Doupov Gymnasium and courses in theology, philosophy, and law in Prague, he completed his musical training with Abbé Vogler and also met Mozart. Weber devoted himself mainly to pedagogy: he was one of the founders of the Prague Cons., which he served as its first director from 1811 until his death, and was also was director of the Prague Organ School (1839–42). Among his extant works is the opera *König der Genien* (Prague, June 1, 1800), the cantata *Böhmens Errettung* (Prague, April 22, 1797), various dance pieces for Orch., 3 quartets for 4 Horns, 3 Sextets for 6 Horns, and a number of piano pieces.

WRITINGS (all publ. in Prague): *Das Konservatorium der Musik zu Prag* (1817); *Allgemeine theoretisch-praktische Vorschule der Musik* (1828); *Lehrbuch der Harmonielehre und des Generalbasses* (1830–34); *Vollständige Theorie der Musik* (1840); *Allgemeine musikalische Zeichenlehre* (2nd ed., 1841); *Harmonielehre* (2nd ed., 1841); *Notenbeispiele zu F.D. Webers Vorschule der Musik* (1843); *Theoretisch-praktisches Lehrbuch der Tonsetzkunst* (2nd ed., 1843). —**NS/LK/DM**

Weber, (Jacob) Gottfried, eminent German music theorist and composer; b. Freinsheim, near Mannheim, March 1, 1779; d. Kreuznach, Sept. 21, 1839. He studied law at Heidelberg and Göttingen, and filled positions as judge in Mannheim (1802), Mainz (1814), and Darmstadt (1818); was appointed General State Prosecutor of Hesse in 1832. He was an excellent amateur pianist and also played the flute and the cello. In 1806 he founded a musical society called "Conservatorium" in Mannheim, and in 1824 he began the magazine *Caecilia*, which he ed. until his death. He made a thorough study of the theoretical works of Marpurg, Kirnberger, Abbé Vogler, and others, and then brought out his important treatise *Versuch einer geordneten Theorie der Tonsetzkunst* (3 vols., 1817–21; 2nd ed. in 4 vols., 1824; 3rd ed. in 4 vols., 1830–32), in which he introduced the now widely accepted symbols for designating the major keys with capital letters and minor keys with small letters, Roman figures for degrees of the scale, etc. It was publ. in Eng. in Boston (1846) and London (1851). His other writings include *Über chronometrische Tempobezeichnung* (Mainz, 1817), *Allgemeine Musiklehre zum Selbstunterricht für Lehrer und Lernende* (Darmstadt, 1822; 3rd ed., 1831), *Ergebnisse der bisherigen Forschungen über die Echtheit des Mozart'schen Requiems* (Mainz, 1826), *Weitere Ergebnisse der weiteren Forschungen über die Echtheit des Mozart'schen Requiems* (Mainz, 1827), and *Generalbasslehre zum Selbstunterricht* (Mainz, 1833). He composed 2 masses, a requiem mass, a Te Deum, and other sacred works, some chamber music, and songs.—**NS/LK/DM**

Weber, Joe (actually, **Morris Joseph**), American actor, singer, producer, and director; b. N.Y., Aug. 11, 1867; d. Los Angeles, May 10, 1942. At the age of 10, he appeared on stage for the first time with the youthful Lew Fields, and for the next 20 years, they toured regularly as the comedy duo of Weber and Fields. They then opened Weber and Field's Broadway Music Hall in N.Y. in 1896, and subsequently presented highly successful burlesques and variety musicals. They dissolved their partnership in 1904, but in later years made a few appearances together. Weber spent his succeeding years mainly as a producer of musicals.

BIBL.: F. Inman, *W. and Fields* (N.Y., 1924).—**LK/DM**

Weber, Ludwig, eminent Austrian bass; b. Vienna, July 29, 1899; d. there, Dec. 9, 1974. He studied with Alfred Boruttau in Vienna. He made his operatic debut there at the Volksoper as Fiorello in 1920, and then sang in Barmen-Elberfeld (1925–27), Düsseldorf (1927–30), and Cologne (1930–33). After singing at the Bavarian State Opera in Munich (1933–45), he was one of the principal members of the Vienna State Opera (1945–60); also appeared at London's Covent Garden (1936–39; 1947; 1950–51) and at the Bayreuth Festivals (1951–60). He was a prof. at the Salzburg Mozarteum (from 1961). He was one of the foremost Wagnerian bass singers of his time, excelling particularly as Daland, Gurnemanz, and Hagen. He also distinguished himself in such roles as Rocco, Kaspar, Baron Ochs, Méphistophélès, and Wozzeck.—**NS/LK/DM**

Weber, Margrit, Swiss pianist; b. Ebnat-Kappel, Feb. 24, 1924. She studied organ with Heinrich Funk in Zürich; then received training in piano from Max Egger and Walter Lang at the Cons. there. She was employed as an organist at the age of 15, then devoted herself chiefly to the piano. She toured Europe, presenting many new works; also played in the U.S. and Canada. She was the soloist in the first performances of piano concertos by Martinů and Alexander Tcherepnin, and of Stravinsky's *Movements* for Piano and Orch., which she performed under Stravinsky's direction in N.Y. on Jan. 10, 1960.—**NS/LK/DM**

Webern, Anton (Friedrich Wilhelm) von, remarkable Austrian composer (he removed the nobiliary particle "von" in 1918 when such distinctions were outlawed in Austria); b. Vienna, Dec. 3, 1883; d. (accidentally shot and killed by an American soldier) Mittersill, Sept. 15, 1945. He received his first instruction in music from his mother, an amateur pianist, then studied piano, cello, and theory with Edwin Komauer in Klagenfurt; he also played cello in the orch. there. In 1902 he entered the Univ. of Vienna, where he studied harmony with Graedener and counterpoint with Navratil; Webern also attended classes in musicology with Adler, receiving his Ph.D. in 1906 with a diss. on *Heinrich Isaac's Choralis Constantinus II.* In 1904 he began private studies in composition with Schoenberg, whose ardent disciple he became; Berg also studied with Schoenberg. Together, Schoenberg, Berg, and Webern laid the foundations of what became known as the 2nd Viennese School of composition. The unifying element was the adoption of Schoenberg's method of composition with 12 tones related only to one another. Malevolent opponents referred to Schoenberg, Berg, and Webern as a Vienna Trinity, with Schoenberg as God the Father, Berg as God the Son, and Webern as the Holy Ghost; the last appellation was supposed to describe the phantomlike substance of some of Webern's works. From 1908 to 1914 Webern was active as a conductor in Vienna and in Germany. In 1915–16 he served in the army; in 1917–18, was conductor at the Deutsches Theater in Prague. In 1918 he settled in Mödling, near Vienna, where he taught composition privately; from 1918 to 1922 he supervised the programs of the Verein für Musikalische Privataufführungen (Society for Private Musical Performances), organized in Vienna by Schoenberg with the intention of promoting modern music without being exposed to reactionary opposition (music critics were not admitted to these performances). Webern was conductor of the Schubertbund (1921–22) and the Mödling Male Chorus (1921–26); he also led the Vienna Workers' Sym. concerts (1922–34) and the Vienna Workers' Chorus (1923–34), both sponsored by the Social Democratic Party. From 1927 to 1938 he was a conductor on the Austrian Radio; furthermore, he conducted guest engagements in Germany, Switzerland, and Spain; from 1929, he made several visits to England, where he was a guest conductor with the BBC Sym. Orch. For the most part, however, he devoted himself to composition, private teaching, and lecturing. After Hitler came to power in Germany in 1933, Webern's music was banned as a manifestation of "cultural Bolshevism" and "degenerate art." His position became more difficult after the Anschluss in 1938, for his works could no longer be publ.; he eked out an existence by teaching a few private pupils and making piano arrangements of musical scores by others for Universal Edition. After his son was killed in an air bombardment of a train in Feb. 1945, he and his wife fled from Vienna to Mittersill, near Salzburg, to stay with his married daughters and grandchildren. His life ended tragically on the evening of Sept. 15, 1945, when he was shot and killed by an American soldier after stepping outside his son-in-law's residence (for a full account, see H. Moldenhauer, *The Death of Anton Webern: A Drama in Documents*, N.Y., 1961).

Webern left relatively few works, and most of them are of short duration (the 4th of his 5 Pieces for Orch., op.10, scored for clarinet, trumpet, trombone, mandolin, celesta, harp, drum, violin, and viola, takes only 19 seconds to play), but in his music he achieves the utmost subtilization of expressive means. He adopted the 12-tone method of composition almost immediately after its definitive formulation by Schoenberg (1924), and extended the principle of nonrepetition of notes to tone colors, so that in some of his works (e.g., Sym., op.21) solo instruments are rarely allowed to play 2 successive thematic notes. Dynamic marks are similarly diversified. Typically, each 12-tone row is divided into symmetric sections of 2, 4, or 6 members, which enter mutually into intricate but invariably logical canonic imitations. Inversions and augmentations are inherent features; melodically and harmonically, the intervals of the major seventh and minor ninth are stressed. Single motifs are brief, and stand out as individual particles or lyric ejaculations. The impact of these works on the general public and on the critics was disconcerting, and upon occasion led to violent demonstrations; however, the extraordinary skill and novelty of technique made this music endure beyond the fashions of the times; performances of Webern's works multiplied after his death, and began to influence increasingly larger groups of modern musicians. Stravinsky acknowledged the use of Webern's methods in his latest works; jazz composers have professed to follow Webern's ideas of tone color; analytical treatises have been publ. in several languages. The International Webern Festival celebrated the centennial of his birth in Dec. 1983 in Vienna.

WORKS: ORCH.: *Im Sommerwind*, idyll for Large Orch. (1904; Seattle, May 25, 1962, Ormandy conducting); *Passacaglia*, op.1 (1908; Vienna, Nov. 4, 1908, composer conducting); *6 Orchestral Pieces*, op.6 (1909; Vienna, March 31, 1913, Schoenberg conducting; rev. 1928; Berlin, Jan. 27, 1929); *5 Orchestral Pieces*, op.10 (1911–13; Zürich, June 22, 1926, composer conducting); *5 Orchestral Pieces*, op.posthumous (1913; Cologne, Jan. 13, 1969); Sym. for Chamber Ensemble, op.21 (1928; N.Y., Dec. 18, 1929); *5 Movements* for String Quartet, op.5, arr. for String Orch. (1928–29; Philadelphia, March 26, 1930); *Variations*, op.30 (1940; Winterthur, March 3, 1943). **CHAMBER:** String Quartet, in one movement (1905; Seattle, May 26, 1962); Piano Quintet, in one movement (Vienna, Nov. 7, 1907); 5 Movements for String Quartet (1909; Vienna, Feb. 8, 1910); 4 pieces for Violin and Piano, op.7 (1910; rev. 1914); 6 bagatelles for String Quartet, op.9 (1911–13; Donaueschingen, July 19, 1924); *3 Little Pieces* for Cello and Piano, op.11 (1914; Mainz, Dec. 2, 1924); String Trio, op.20 (1926–27; Vienna, Jan. 16, 1928); Quartet for Violin, Clarinet, Tenor Saxophone, and Piano, op.22 (1930; Vienna, April 13, 1931); Concerto for 9 Instruments, op.24 (1934; Prague, Sept. 4, 1935); String Quartet, op.28 (1936–38; Pittsfield, Mass., Sept. 22, 1938). **Piano:** *Variations* (1936; Vienna, Oct. 26, 1937). **VOCAL:** *Entflieht auf leichten Kähnen* for Chorus, op.2 (1908; Furstenfeld, April 10, 1927); 2 songs for Chorus, Celesta, Guitar, Violin, Clarinet, and Bass Clarinet, after Goethe, op.19 (1926); *Das Augenlicht* for Chorus and Orch., op.26 (1935; London, June 17, 1938); *1st Cantata* for Soprano, Chorus, and Orch. (1938–39; London, July 12, 1946); *2nd Cantata* for Soprano, Bass, Chorus, and Orch. (1941–43; Brussels, June 23, 1950); 2 sets of 5 songs for Voice and Piano, after Stefan George, opp. 3 and 4 (1908–09); 2 songs for Voice and Instrumental Ensemble, after Rilke, op.8 (1910; rev. 1921 and 1925); 4 songs for Voice and Piano, op.12 (1915–17); 4 songs for Voice and Orch., op.13 (1914–18); 6 songs for Voice and Instruments, after Georg Trakl, op.14 (1919–21; Donaueschingen, July 20, 1924); *5 Sacred Songs* for Voice and Instruments, op.15 (1917–22; Vienna, Oct. 9, 1924, composer conducting); *5 Canons* on Latin texts for Voice, Clarinet, and Bass Clarinet, op.16 (1923–24; N.Y., May 8, 1951); *3 Traditional Rhymes* for Voice and Instruments, op.17 (1924–25; N.Y., March 16, 1952); 3 songs for Voice, Clarinet, and Guitar, op.18 (1925; Los Angeles, Feb. 8, 1954); 3 songs for Voice and Piano, op.23 (1933–34); 3 songs for Voice and Piano, op.25 (1934). **OTHER:** Arrangements for Chamber Orch. of Schoenberg's Chamber Sym., op.9 (1923), Schubert's *Deutsche Tanze* (1931), and Bach's *Ricercare a 6* from *Das musikalische Opfer* (London, April 25, 1935, composer conducting).

WRITINGS: W. Reich ed. *Der Weg zur neuen Musik* (Vienna, 1933; new ed., 1960; Eng. tr., 1963) and *Anton Webern: Weg und Gestalt: Selbstzeugnisse und Worte der Freunde* (Zürich, 1961).

BIBL.: R. Leibowitz, *Schoenberg et son école* (Paris, 1947; Eng. tr., 1949); W. Kolneder, *A. W.: Einführung in Werk und Stil* (Rodenkirchen, 1961; Eng. tr., 1968); H. Moldenhauer, *The Death of A. W.: A Drama in Documents* (N.Y., 1961); G. Perle, *Serial Composition and Atonality: An Introduction to the Music of Schoenberg, Berg and W.* (Berkeley, 1962; 5th ed., rev., 1982); H. Moldenhauer and D. Irvine, eds., *A. v. W.: Perspectives* (Seattle, 1966); F. Wildgans, *A. W.* (London, 1966); *A. v.W.: Sketches (1926–1945)* (facsimile reproductions from W.'s sketchbooks, with commentary by E. Krenek and foreword by H. Moldenhauer; N.Y., 1968); R. Ringger, *A. W.s Klavierlieder* (Zürich, 1968); L. Somfai, *A. W.* (Budapest, 1968); C. Rostand, *A. W.: L'Homme et son oeuvre* (Paris, 1969); H. Deppert, *Studien zur Kompositionstechnik im instrumentalen Spätwerk A. W.s* (Darmstadt, 1972); W. Stroh, *A. v.W.; Historische Legitimation* (Göppingen, 1973); F. Döhl, *W.s Beitrag zur Stilwende der neuen Musik* (Munich, 1976); H. and R. Moldenhauer, *A. v.W.: Chronicle of His Life and Work* (N.Y., 1978); R. Schulz, *Über das Verhältnis von Konstruktion und Ausdruck in den Werken A. W.s* (Munich, 1982); E. Hilmar, ed., *A. W. 1883–1983: Eine Festschrift zum hundertsten Geburtstag* (Vienna, 1983); Z. Roman, *A. v.W.: An Annotated Bibliography* (Detroit, 1983); K. Bailey, *The Twelve-Note Music of A. W.: Old Forms in a New Language* (Cambridge, 1991); K. Essl, *Das Synthses-Denken bei A. W.: Studien zur Musikauffassung des späten W. unter besonderer Berücksichtigung seiner eigenen Analysen zu op.28 und 30* (Tutzing, 1991); G. Cox, *A. W.s Studienzeit: Seine Entwicklung im Lichte der Sätze und Fragmente für Klavier* (Frankfurt am Main, 1992); M. Hayes, *A. v.W.* (London, 1995); A. Schreffler, *W. and the Lyric Impulse: Songs and Fragments on Poems of Georg Trakl* (Oxford, 1995); B. Zuber, *Gesetz + Gestalt: Studien zum Spätwerk A. W.s* (Munich, 1995); K. Bailey, ed., *W. Studies* (N.Y., 1996); H. Krones and M. Wagner, *A. W. und die Musik des zwanzigsten Jahrhunderts* (Vienna, 1997); G. Pongratz, *A. W.s Variationen für Klavier opus 27: Musikwissenschaftlicher Diskurs mit Ableitung eines interdisziplinären Hörstudienansatzes* (Hildesheim, 1997); K. Bailey, *The Life of W.* (Cambridge, 1998); B. Simms, ed., *Schoenberg, Berg, and W.: A Companion to the Second Viennese School* (Westport, Conn., 1999).—**NS/LK/DM**

Webster, Ben(jamin Francis), important and influential jazz tenor saxophonist best known for his stint with Duke Ellington, also pianist, arranger; b. Kansas City, Mo., March 27, 1909; d. Amsterdam, Holland, Sept. 20, 1973. Webster first studied violin, then piano. He attended Wilberforce Coll.; afterwards, he played piano in a silent-movie house and then worked with several local bands. Around 1929, he joined the family band led by W. H. Young (Lester's father) in Campbell Kirkie, N.Mex. Webster toured with the band for three months and began specializing on the saxophone. He worked with several other bands before joining Bennie Moten from winter 1931–32 until early 1933 (including a visit to N.Y.). In 1933, Webster worked with Andy Kirk at Fairyland Park, Kansas City, and then moved to N.Y. to join Fletcher Henderson in July 1934 (he worked again with Henderson in autumn 1937 in Chicago). Through the 1930s, Webster worked with various leaders, including Benny Carter (autumn 1934), Cab Calloway (spring 1936–summer 1937), Stuff Smith (early 1938), Roy Eldridge (later 1938), and Teddy Wilson's Big Band (April 1939–January 1940). He joined Duke Ellington in Boston (January 1940); Ben had previously worked with Duke for two brief spells in 1935 and 1936. Webster recorded many celebrated solos while with Ellington, especially on "Cottontail"; also on "All Too Soon" and "Sepia Panorama." He was said to have been influenced by Hodges's approach to ballads while in the band. Webster left Duke in 1943. He led his own band on 52nd Street, had a short stay in Sid Catlett's Band (early 1944), was with Raymond Scott on CBS, and two months with John Kirby (June–July 1944). Webster had a brief spell with Stuff Smith early in 1945, but from October 1944 mostly led his own small groups for various club dates in N.Y. and Chicago. He rejoined Duke Ellington from November 1948 until September 1949, then worked with Jay McShann in Kansas City; he also toured with "Jazz at the Philharmonic." Webster returned to Kansas City, worked regularly with Bob Wilson's Band and freelanced. He moved back to N.Y. in late 1952, led his own small groups, did studio work and freelance recordings, then lived for several years in Calif., occasionally returning to N.Y. during the late 1950s to perform. From 1962 he worked mainly in N.Y., until December 1964 when he moved to Europe. He used Holland as a central base for solo tours in Europe, making regular visits to Great Britain. He moved to Copenhagen in the late 1960s.

Saxophonists are still trying to figure out how Webster obtained some of his extraordinarily expressive effects, from a breathy, impassioned style on ballads to a hair-raising, powerful scream on blues and up-tempo numbers. His full-bodied tone, warm vibrato, and bluesy melodies straddled the middle group between Coleman Hawkins's harmonic explorations and Lester Young's lyrical journeys; these players were his only equals during the 1930s and 1940s.

DISC.: *He Played It That Way* (1943); *Alternate and Incomplete Takes* (1944); *Ben and the Boys* (1944); *Complete Ben Webster on Emarcy* (1951); *Soulville* (1957); *At the Nuway Club* (1958); *Ben Webster Meets Oscar Peterson* (1959); *Meets Gerry Mulligan* (1959); *At the Renaissance* (1960); *Rare Live Performance* (1962); *Soulmates* (1963); *Swingin' In London* (1967); *Meets Don Byas (in the Black Forest)* (1968); *At Work in Europe* (1969); *Live in Amsterdam* (1969); *Did You Call* (1972); *Live in Paris, 1972* (1972); *Makin' Whoopee* (1972); *My Man* (1973).

BIBL.: Jan Evensmo, *Tenor Saxophone of Ben Webster* (Hosle, 1978); Peter Langhorn and Thorbjorn Sjogren, *Ben: The Music of Ben Webster: A Discography* (Copenhagen, 1996).—**JC/LP/JE**

Webster, Beveridge, respected American pianist and teacher; b. Pittsburgh, May 13, 1908; d. Hanover, N.H., June 30, 1999. He studied with his father, also named Beveridge Webster, the founder-director of the Pittsburgh Cons. In 1921 he was sent to Europe and pursued his training with Isidor Philipp and Nadia Boulanger at the Paris Cons., where he was the first American to graduate with the premier prix in piano in 1926. While in Paris, he was befriended by Ravel. He also was a student of Schnabel in Berlin. After touring Europe, he made his U.S. debut as soloist in the MacDowell 2nd Piano Concerto with the N.Y. Phil. on Nov. 11, 1934. His Carnegie Hall recital debut in N.Y. followed on Nov. 30, 1934. In subsequent years, Webster appeared as a soloist with many U.S. orchs., gave recitals, and played in chamber music concerts. He taught at the New England Cons. of Music in Boston from 1940 to 1946 and then at the Juilliard School of Music in N.Y. from 1946 to 1990. Webster acquired a notable reputation for his insightful performances of the music of Debussy and Ravel. In 1968 he gave the first complete N.Y. cycle of Debussy's piano music. He played all of Ravel's solo piano music there in 1975. On Nov. 11, 1984, he celebrated the 50th anniversary of his U.S. debut in a N.Y. recital. He also was a champion of Schoenberg, Berg, Bartók, and Stravinsky, and of many American composers, among them Copland, Sessions, Harris, and Carter.—**NS/LK/DM**

Webster, Freddie, bebop-flavored jazz trumpeter; b. Cleveland, c. 1916; d. Chicago, April 1, 1947. He attended Central H.S. in Cleveland. As a teenager he led his own band, which included pianist Tadd Dameron, and also worked in a band led by saxist Marion Sears (brother of Al Sears). During 1938, Webster worked in bands led by Earl Hines and Erskine Tate. In 1939, he led his own band before moving to N.Y. He worked in several bands there, including stints with Benny Carter (early 1940; again autumn 1943), Ed Durham (later 1940), Louis Jordan (early 1941), Earl Hines (mid-1941), Lucky Millinder (autumn 1941 to spring 1942; autumn 1944 to winter 1945), Jimmie Lunceford (summer 1943), Sabby Lewis (spring 1944), and brief spells with Cab Calloway and George Johnson (summer 1945). Played in John Kirby's Sextet for six months (c. August 1945). With Dizzy Gillespie (1946), Webster worked briefly with "Jazz at the Philharmonic" (early 1947). He collapsed and died in a hotel room while preparing to work with saxist Sonny Stitt in Chicago.

Webster is a legendary figure cited as a favorite by Miles Davis and others. On the basis of his recordings he had a magnificent, big sound but was a somewhat awkward bop soloist.

DISC.: *Masters of Jazz, Vol. 5: Female* (1931). **EARL HINES AND HIS ORCHESTRA:** *Harlem Lament* (1933); *1937–1939* (1937). **LOUIS JORDAN:** *Let the Good Times Roll* (1938); *1940–1941* (1940). **JIMMY LUNCEFORD:** *1941–1945* (1941). **LUCKY MILLINDER:** *1941–1942* (1941). **BILLIE HOLIDAY:** *Complete Commodore Recordings* (1939). **BENNY CARTER AND HIS BAND:** *1943–1946* (1943). **DIZZY GILLESPIE:** *Good Jelly Blues* (1944); *Complementary Works, Vol. 5* (1945); *You're Not the Kind* (1946). **SARAH VAUGHAN:** *It's You or No One* (1946); *Tenderly* (1946); *Time and Again* (1946); *Boston Bounce* (1975). **GEORGIE AULD & HIS BAND:** *In the Middle* (1988); *Handicap* (1990). **BENNY CARTER:** *Advanced Swing* (1996); *Jazz Profile* (1997). **BILLY ECKSTINE:** *1944–1945* (1997). **EARL HINES:** *Piano Man!* (1995); *Original Historic Recordings* (1996); *Rosetta* (1996); *1941* (1996); *Piano Man 1928–1955* (1998). **LOUIS JORDAN:** *Louis Jordan and His Tympany Five* (1995); *Let the Good Times Roll: Anthology* (1999). —**JC/LP**

Webster, Paul (Francis), big band jazz trumpeter; b. Kansas City, Mo., Aug. 24, 1909; d. N.Y., May 6, 1966. He initially was taught by his uncle, trumpeter **Sam Ford**. Attended Lincoln H.S. and gigged with band led by Clarence Lover (1925). Went to Fisk Univ. and played with the Memphis band, The Boston Serenaders (1926), returned to Kansas City and worked as an embalmer before becoming a professional musician. He had long associations with Bennie Moten (summer 1927–summer 1928, with brief returns through the early 1930s); Jimmie Lunceford (1931, and then spring 1935–44); Cab Calloway (late 1940s to early 1950s); and Charlie Barnet (1946–47 and again 1952–53). After his last stint with Barnet, he took a day job in the U.S. Immigration Service; later, he worked for the N.Y. subway, and he continued to play and record regularly in the early 1960s. He died of a respiratory ailment. —**JC/LP**

Webster, Sir David (Lumsden), Scottish opera administrator; b. Dundee, July 3, 1903; d. London, May 11, 1971. He was educated at the Univ. of Liverpool, then commenced a commercial career while pursuing his various interests in the arts. From 1940 to 1945 he was chairman of the Liverpool Phil. Soc. In 1945 he became general administrator of the Covent Garden Opera Trust, in which capacity he helped to launch the careers of many famous singers, among them Jon Vickers and Joan Sutherland. He was knighted in 1961 and was made a Knight Commander of the Royal Victorian Order in 1970. An account of his career by M. Haltrecht, under the title *The Reluctant Showman*, was publ. in 1975. —**NS/LK/DM**

Wecker, Georg Kaspar, German organist, teacher, and composer; b. Nuremberg (baptized), April 2, 1632; d. there, April 20, 1695. He studied organ with Erasmus Kindermann, and in 1651 obtained a position as church organist in Nuremberg; his last appointment was at the Sebaldkirche there (1686–95). He also was a respected teacher; Johann Krieger and Pachelbel were among his pupils. His extant works comprise 5 cantatas, 37 sacred and 1 secular song, and a keyboard fugue. —**NS/LK/DM**

Weckerlin, Jean-Baptiste-Théodore, eminent French music scholar and composer; b. Guebwiller, Alsace, Nov. 9, 1821; d. Trottberg, near Guebwiller, May 20, 1910. He ran away from home and settled in Paris in 1843; entered the Paris Cons. in 1844, where he studied with Ponchard (singing) and Halévy (composition). He wrote a heroic sym., *Roland*, for Soloists, Chorus, and Orch. (1847) while still a student; after graduating in 1849, he took part with Seghers in the direction of the Société Sainte-Cécile (1850–55), which brought out some of his works. He achieved his first success with the 1-act comic opera, *L'Organiste dans l'embarras* (Théâtre-Lyrique, 1853). It was followed by 2 comic operas in Alsatian dialect, *Die drifach Hochzitt im Bäsethal* (Colmar, 1863) and *D'r verhäxt' Herbst* (Colmar, 1879), and the 1-act opera *Après Fontenoy* (Théâtre-Lyrique, 1877). In 1863 he became librarian and archivist of the Société des Compositeurs de Musique. He became asst. librarian (1869) and librarian (1876) of the Paris Cons., retiring in 1909. He won distinction as a composer of grand choral works; also wrote 12 stage works, orch. music, chamber music, hundreds of songs, and many piano pieces. He ed. various early French stage works and many folk-song collections.

WRITINGS (all publ. in Paris): *Opuscules sur la chanson populaire et sur la musique* (1874); *Musiciana* (1877); *Bibliothèque du Conservatoire national de musique et de déclamation: Catalogue bibliographique ... de la Reserve* (1885); *La chanson populaire* (1886); *Nouveau musiciana* (1890); *Dernier musiciana* (1899).

BIBL.: H. Expert, *Catalogue de la bibliothèque musicale de M. J.B. W.* (Paris, 1908).—**NS/LK/DM**

Weckmann, Matthias, distinguished German organist and composer; b. Niederdorla, near Muhlhausen, Thuringia, c. 1619; d. Hamburg, Feb. 24, 1674. He was the son of a clergyman and organist. He was a chorister in the Dresden court chapel, where he was a pupil of Heinrich Schütz. In 1633 Weckmann was sent to Hamburg for further study with Reinken, Jakob Praetorius, and H. Scheidemann, by whom he was trained in the organ method of Sweelinck. In 1637 Weckmann became organist at the Dresden electoral chapel, and in 1642 he was made director of the court chapel in Nykøbing, Denmark. He then resumed his Dresden post in 1647, where he became a friend of J. J. Froberger; in 1655 he went to Hamburg as organist at the Jacobikirche, and in 1660 founded, with Christoph Bernhard, the Collegium Musicum, a concert society for the performance of new works (it was discontinued after Weckmann's death). Among his extant works are 13 accompanied vocal compositions, 9 songs, 9 sonatas a 4, 2 sonatas a 3, and a few keyboard pieces. See M. Seiffert, ed., Denkmäler Deutscher Tonkunst, VI (1901), and *Matthias Weckmann: Vierzehn Praeludien, Fugen und Toccaten*, Organum, 4th series, III (Leipzig, 1925); also G. Ilgner, ed., *Matthias Weckmann: Gesammelte Werke*, Das Erbe Deutscher Musik, 2nd series, IV (1942).

BIBL.: G. Ilgner, *M. W. Sein Leben und seine Werke* (Wolfenbüttel and Berlin, 1939); H. Davidson, *M. W.: The Interpretation of His Organ Music* (3 vols., Stockholm, 1991–93).—**NS/LK/DM**

Weede (real name, **Wiedefeld**), **Robert,** American baritone; b. Baltimore, Feb. 11, 1903; d. Walnut Creek, Calif., June 9, 1972. After winning the National Federation of Music Clubs award (1927), he studied at the Eastman School of Music in Rochester, N.Y., and in Milan. In 1933 he became a soloist at N.Y.'s Radio City Music Hall. On May 15, 1937, he made his Metropolitan Opera debut in N.Y. as Tonio, where he was on the roster until 1942, and then again in 1944–45, 1948–50, and 1952–53. He also sang Rigoletto in Chicago (1939), San Francisco (1940), and at the N.Y.C. Opera (1948). In later years he made appearances on Broadway and toured in the musicals *The Most Happy Fella* and *Milk and Honey*. During his operatic career, he sang mainly in operas by Verdi and Puccini.—**NS/LK/DM**

Weelkes, Thomas, important English organist and composer; b. c. 1575; d. London, Nov. 30, 1623. He was organist at Winchester Cathedral (1598–1601?), then organist and informator choristarum at Chichester Cathedral. He held both of these positions until his drunkenness led to his dismissal in 1617; he again served erratically as organist from 1622. In 1602 he was granted the degree of B.Mus. at New Coll., Oxford. Weelkes was one of the great English madrigalists, possessing remarkable power in melodic characterization of text. He occasionally used chromatic progressions in harmony that were well in advance of his time. He wrote a considerable amount of church music and instrumental works.

WORKS: 10 services; many anthems (see D. Brown, W. Collins, and P. le Huray, eds., *Thomas Weelkes: Collected Anthems*, Musica Britannica, XXIII, 1966; 2nd ed., rev., 1975); *Madrigals to 3. 4. 5. & 6. Voyces* (London, 1597; ed. by E. Fellowes; 2nd ed., rev., 1967, by T. Dart, The English Madrigalists, IX); *Balletts and Madrigals to Five Voyces, with One to 6. Voyces* (London, 1598; ed. by E. Fellowes; 2nd ed., rev., 1968, by T. Dart, The English Madrigalists, X); *Madrigals of 5. and 6. Parts, apt for the Viols and Voices* (London, 1600; ed. by E. Fellowes; 2nd ed., rev., 1968, by T. Dart, The English Madrigalists, XI, XII); *Ayeres or Phantasticke Spirites for Three Voices* (London, 1608; ed. by E. Fellowes; 2nd ed., rev., 1965, by T. Dart, The English Madrigalists, XIII); 4 keyboard pieces; several works for Viols.

BIBL.: C. Welch, *Two Cathedral Organists, T. W. (1601–1623) and Thomas Kelway (1720–1744)* (Chichester, 1957); W. Collins, *The Anthems of T. W.* (diss., Univ. of Mich., 1960); D. Morse, *Word-painting and Symbolism in the Secular Choral Works by T. W., Tudor Composer* (diss., N. Y. Univ., 1961).—**NS/LK/DM**

Weerbeke (also **Weerbecke, Werbecke, Werbeke, Werbeck**), **Gaspar van,** significant Netherlandish composer; b. Oudenaarde, c. 1445; d. after 1517. By 1471 he was active at the Sforza court in Milan. He was in Flanders and Burgundy in 1472–73 to recruit singers for the court choir of Duke Galeazzo Maria Sforza, whom he served as vice-abbate of the cantori de camera. After serving as a member of the papal choir (1471–92), he was again active in Milan at the court of Duke Ludovico Sforza, "il Moro." He also held benefices in the Utrecht and Therouanne dioceses and was associated with the court choir of Philip the Fair, Archduke of Austria and Duke of Burgundy. From 1500 to 1509 he was again a member of the papal choir; however, he was referred to as "Cantor capellae papalis" as late as 1514; in 1517 he was listed as canonicus of the church of S. Maria ad Gradus in Mainz. Weerbeke was an outstanding composer of liturgical and non-liturgical sacred music. His extant works include 8 mass ordinaries, 2 credos, 22 motet cycles, and 21 other motets. Five chansons attributed to him remain doubtful. See A. Smijers, ed., *Van Ockeghem tot Sweelinck* (Amsterdam, 1949–56) and G. Tintori, *Gaspar van Weerbeke: Messe e mottetti*, Archivum Musices Metropolitanum Mediolanense, XI (Milan, 1963).

Bibl.: G. Croll, *Das Motettenwerk G. v.W.* (diss., Univ. of Göttingen, 1954).—**NS/LK/DM**

Wegelius, Martin, eminent Finnish composer and pedagogue; b. Helsinki, Nov. 10, 1846; d. there, March 22, 1906. He studied philosophy, taking his master's degree in 1869; studied music with Rudolf Bibl in Vienna (1870–71), with Richter, Reinecke, and Jadassohn in Leipzig (1871–73), and with Rheinberger in Munich (1877–78). In 1882 he was appointed director of the newly founded Helsinki Cons., holding this post until his death. Under his guidance, the institution became one of the finest schools in Europe, with excellent teachers. Sibelius was one of the pupils of Wegelius; others were Jarnefelt, Melartin, and Palmgren. Wegelius emphasized the cultivation of national Finnish music, and thus was mainly responsible for the magnificent development of Finland as a musical nation.

Works: *Daniel Hjort*, overture (1872); *Divertissement a la hongroise* (1880); *Rondo quasi fantasia* for Piano and Orch. (1872); *Mignon*, 6 songs with Orch., after Goethe's *Westöstlicher Diwan* (1875); Christmas Cantata (1877); *The 6th of May*, festival cantata (1878); Violin Sonata; piano pieces; songs.

Writings: *Lärobok i allmän musiklära och analys* (Textbook of General Music Theory and Analysis; 2 vols., Helsinki, 1888–89); *Hufvuddragen af denn västerländska musikens historia* (Outlines of the History of Western Music; 3 vols., Helsinki, 1891–93); *Kurs i homofons sats* (Course in Homophonic Composition; 2 vols., Helsinki, 1897–1905).

Bibl.: K. Flodin, *M. W.* (in Swedish, Stockholm, 1916; in Finnish, Helsinki, 1922); O. Andersson, ed., *M. W.: konstnärsbrev* (M.W.: Letters; 2 vols., Helsinki, 1918–19).—**NS/LK/DM**

Wehle, Karl, Bohemian pianist and composer; b. Prague, March 17, 1825; d. Paris, June 3, 1883. Trained for a mercantile career, he abandoned it for music and studied piano with Moscheles at Leipzig and Kullak in Berlin. He made extended tours to Asia, Africa, America, and Australia, but resided chiefly in Paris. He publ. a number of brilliant compositions for piano, among them *Sérénade napolitaine, Allegro à la hongroise, 3 tarentelles, 2 impromptus, Berceuse javanaise, Marche cosaque, Fête bohémienne,* and *Un Songe à Vaucluse.* —**NS/LK/DM**

Weidemann, Friedrich, German baritone; b. Ratzeburg, Jan. 1, 1871; d. Vienna, Jan. 30, 1919. He studied with Vilmar in Hamburg and Muschler in Berlin, making his debut in 1896 in Brieg; he then sang in Essen (1897–98), Hamburg (1898–1901), and Riga (1901–03). In 1903 he joined the Vienna Court Opera, where he remained until his death. He was highly regarded for his performances in operas by Wagner and Richard Strauss.—**NS/LK/DM**

Weidinger, Anton, Austrian trumpeter; b. Vienna, June 9, 1767; d. there, Sept. 20, 1852. He was trained in Vienna, and after service in regimental bands, he became a member of the Vienna Court Orch. in 1792; later mastered the keyed trumpet and gave many concerts in Vienna. In 1803 he toured Germany, France, and England as a virtuoso. Haydn wrote his Trumpet Concerto for him.—**NS/LK/DM**

Weidinger, Christine, American soprano; b. Springville, N.Y., March 31, 1946. She studied in Phoenix, Wuppertal, and Los Angeles. In 1972 she won the Metropolitan Opera National Auditions and made her operatic debut in Washington, D.C., as Musetta. On Nov. 24, 1972, she made her Metropolitan Opera debut in N.Y. as Ortlinde, remaining on its roster until 1976. From 1981 she made appearances in Europe. In 1989 she sang Amendaide in *Tancredi* in Los Angeles, and then was engaged as Vitellia at Milan's La Scala and as Lucia in Cincinnati in 1990. Following a return to Los Angeles as Elettra and Fiordiligi in 1991, she sang Maria Stuarda in Barcelona in 1992 and in Monte Carlo in 1993. In 1995 she portrayed Donna Anna in Santiago and Elettra at the Welsh National Opera in Cardiff. She sang Elisabeth in *Don Carlos* in Buenos Aires in 1998.—**NS/LK/DM**

Weidt, Lucie, German-born Austrian soprano; b. Troppau, Silesia, c. 1876; d. Vienna, July 28, 1940. She studied with her father, and then with Rosa Papier in Vienna. She made her operatic debut in Leipzig in 1900, and in 1902 she made her first appearance at the Vienna Opera as Elisabeth, remaining on its roster until 1927. She sang in Munich from 1908 to 1910. On Nov. 18, 1910, she made her first American appearance, as Brünnhilde in *Die Walküre*, at the Metropolitan Opera in N.Y.; after a season there, she sang in Italy. In 1909 she married Baron Joseph von Urmenyi. Her voice was of unusual attractiveness and power, enabling her to perform Wagnerian parts with distinction.—**NS/LK/DM**

Weigel, Eugene (Herbert), American composer, violist, organist, and teacher; b. Cleveland, Oct. 11, 1910. He studied composition with Arthur Shepherd at Western Reserve Univ. and violin with Maurice Hewitt at the Cleveland Inst. of Music (1930–32); later had composition lessons with Hindemith at Yale Univ. (B.M., 1946) and viola lessons with Hugo Kortschak. He was active as an organist and choirmaster (1929–41); and also was a founding member of the Walden String Quartet (1930–35). While at Yale Univ., he served as music director of its Thomas More Chapel and played viola in the New Haven (Conn.) Sym. Orch.; appeared in various ensembles, including one in N.Y. with Hindemith on the viola d'amore in a performance of Bach's *St. John Passion*. In 1946–47 he was again a member of the Walden String Quartet during its residency at Cornell Univ. He played in the first performances of Schoenberg's String Trio and Ives's 2nd String Quartet; continued to play with the quartet at the Univ. of Ill. (1947–57), where he also taught composition and experimental theory. In 1954–55 he held a Guggenheim fellowship. In 1955 he became composer-in-residence at Mont. State Univ. in Missoula, which was renamed the Univ. of Mont. that same year; remained there until 1972. He also was a founder-member of the Mont. String Quartet (1957–72). In 1972 he retired to Vancouver Island, Canada; conducted the Malespina Chorus and was prof. emeritus at Malespina Coll. (1974–76). In later years, he devoted much time to writing poetry, preparing his memoirs, and pursuing an avid interest in architecture.

WORKS: DRAMATIC: Opera: *The Lion Makers* (1953); *The Mountain Child* (1959). **ORCH.:** *Sonata* for Strings (1948); *Festival Fanfare* (1948); *Prairie Symphony* (1952); *Concerto festivo* for Flute, Harpsichord, and Strings (Berlin Festival, 1959); *Fantasy and Fugue* for Concert Band (1967). **CHAMBER:** Clarinet Quintet (1946); Woodwind Quintet (1949); Trombone Quartet (1953); *Maine Sketches* for Horn and Piano (1954); Duo for Clarinet and Bassoon (1955); piano pieces. **VOCAL:** *Fall of the Leaf* for Baritone and String Quartet (1938); *Prayer for Peace* for Chorus, Brass, and Percussion (1961); songs.—**NS/LK/DM**

Weigl, family of Austrian musicians:

(1) Joseph (Franz) Weigl, cellist; b. in Bavaria, May 19, 1740; d. Vienna, Jan. 25, 1820. Upon the recommendation of Haydn, he was made a cellist at the Eisenstadt court in 1761; he married (Anna Maria) Josepha Scheffstoss, a former singer at the court, in 1764. In 1769 he was named first cellist of the Italian Opera orch. at the Kärnthnertortheater in Vienna; in 1792 he became a member of the Hofkapelle.

(2) Joseph Weigl, composer and conductor, son of the preceding; b. Eisenstadt, March 28, 1766; d. Vienna, Feb. 3, 1846. He was taken to Vienna in 1769, where he trained with Sebastian Witzig (singing and thoroughbass) in 1775; soon became a pupil of Albrechtsberger, with whom he remained until 1782. At age 16 Weigl wrote his first opera, *Die unnütze Vorsicht*, for a marionette theater, winning the esteem of Gluck and Salieri. At 19 he became a pupil in composition of Salieri, who secured a position for him in the Court Theater; he was deputy Kapellmeister by 1790; in 1792 he was made Kapellmeister and composer. From 1827 to 1838 he was Vice-Kapellmeister at the court, retiring from public life in 1839. His first notable success as a composer for the theater came with his opera *La Principessa d'Amalfi* (Vienna, Jan. 10, 1794), which Haydn described as a masterpiece (in a letter to Weigl after the perf.); it was followed by *Das Waisenhaus* (Vienna, Oct. 4, 1808) and *Die Schweizerfamilie* (Vienna, March 14, 1809; produced in Paris, Feb. 6, 1827, as *Emmeline, ou La Famille suisse*); it was staged in opera houses all over Europe until about 1900, when it disappeared from the repertoire. His ballets also won a wide hearing.

WORKS: DRAMATIC: Opera (all first perf. in Vienna unless otherwise given): *Die unnütze Vorsicht oder Die betrogene Arglist* (Feb. 23, 1783); *Il Pazzo per forza* (Nov. 14, 1788); *La caffettiera bizzarra* (Sept. 15, 1790); *Der Strassensammler (Lumpensammler) oder Ein gutes Herz ziert jeden Stand*, comic opera (Oct. 13, 1792); *La Principessa d'Amalfi*, comic opera (Jan. 10, 1794); *Das Petermännchen* (part 1, April 8, 1794; part 2, April ?, 1794); *Giuletta e Pierotto* (Oct. 16, 1794); *I solitari*, opera seria (March 15, 1797); *L'amor marinaro ossia Il Corsaro* (Oct. 15, 1797); *Das Dorf im Gebirge*, Singspiel (April 17, 1798); *L'accademia del maestro Cisolfaut* (Oct. 14, 1798); *L'uniforme*, heroic-comic opera (1800); *Die Herrenhuterin*, Singspiel (Nov. 26, 1804; in collaboration with I. Umlauf and F. Devienne); *Vestas Feuer*, heroic opera (Aug. 7, 1805); *Il Principe invisibile* (Oct. 4, 1806); *Kaiser Hadrian* (May 21, 1807); *Ostade oder Adrian von Ostade* (Oct. 3, 1807); *Cleopatra* (Milan, Dec. 19, 1807); *Il Rivale di se stesso* (Milan, April 18, 1808); *Das Waisenhaus*, Singspiel (Oct. 4, 1808); *Die Schweizerfamilie*, Singspiel (March 14, 1809); *Die Verwandlungen*, operetta (Berlin, Feb. 1810); *Der Einsiedler auf den Alpen* (June 13, 1810); *Franciska von Foix*, heroic-comic opera (Feb. 7, 1812); *Der Bergsturz*, Singspiel (Dec. 19, 1813); *Die Jugend (Jugendjahre) Peter des Grossen* (Dec. 10, 1814); *L'imboscata* (Milan, Nov. 8, 1815); *Margaritta d'Anjou ossia L'Orfano d'Inghilterra*, melodramma eroi-comico (Milan, July 26, 1816); *Die Nachtigall und der Rabe* (April 20, 1818); *Daniel in der Löwengrube oder Baals Sturz*, heroic opera (April 13, 1820); *König Waldemar oder Die dänischen Fischer*, Singspiel (May 11, 1821); *Edmund und Caroline* (Oct. 21, 1821); *Die eiserne Pforte*, grand opera (Feb. 27, 1823). **Other Dramatic:** Ballets, incidental music used in several plays, and the oratorio *La passione di Gesù Cristo* (1804). **OTHER:** Many cantatas; songs; masses; the oratorio *La passione di Gesù Cristo* (1804); instrumental works.

(3) Thaddäus Weigl, conductor, music publisher, and composer, brother of the preceding; b. April 8, 1776; d. Vienna, Feb. 29, 1844. He studied theory with Albrechtsberger, and then was employed in the Court Theater's music publishing house from 1795. He organized his own publishing concern in 1803; also was Vice-Kapellmeister to his brother, becoming a composer at the Court Theater in 1806. His publishing business ended in bankruptcy in 1831. He wrote 5 operettas and 15 ballets.

BIBL.: F. Grasberger, *J. W. (1766–1846): Leben und Werk mit besonderer Berücksichtingung der Kirchenmusik* (diss., Univ. of Vienna, 1938).—**NS/LK/DM**

Weigl, Karl,

Austrian-born American composer; b. Vienna, Feb. 6, 1881; d. N.Y., Aug. 11, 1949. He studied piano with Door and theory with Fuchs at the Cons. of the Gesellschaft der Musikfreunde in Vienna (graduated, 1902). Weigl then took composition lessons with Zemlinsky, then attended courses in musicology at the Univ. of Vienna with Adler (Ph.D., 1903). From 1918 to 1928 he was on the faculty of the New Vienna Cons., and from 1930 to 1938 he taught theory at the Univ. of Vienna. After the Anschluss in 1938, he emigrated to N.Y., becoming a naturalized American citizen in 1943. He was respected both in Austria and in America as a composer, and a concerted effort was made to promote his music, but with little success. His 5th Sym., *Apocalyptic* (1945), was performed posthumously by Leopold Stokowski with the American Sym. Orch. (N.Y., Oct. 27, 1968). He wrote 6 syms. (1908, 1922, 1931, 1936, 1945, 1947), several overtures, Violin Concerto (1928), 8 string quartets, String Sextet, 2 violin sonatas, numerous choruses, piano pieces, and songs. He was married to **Valery (Vally) Weigl**.—**NS/LK/DM**

Weigl, Valery (Vally),

Austrian-born American composer and music therapist; b. Vienna, Sept. 11, 1894; d. N.Y., Dec. 25, 1982. She studied music in Vienna with her husband, **Karl Weigl**. She taught music in Vienna and Salzburg (1921–38). After the Anschluss in 1938, she and her husband went to the U.S., where she obtained employment as music adviser with the American Theater Wing in N.Y. (1947–58); from 1954 to 1964 she gave courses in music therapy at the N.Y. Medical Coll. and wrote therapy programs for UNESCO. She was an energetic peace activist, and served as a co-founder of the Friends' Arts for World Unity Committee. With equal energy, she promoted her husband's compositions, which were little appreciated and seldom played.

WORKS: *New England Suite* for Clarinet, Cello, and Piano (1955); *Nature Moods* for Soprano, Clarinet, and Violin (1960); *Mood Sketches* for Wind Quintet (1964); *Peace Is a Shelter* for Chorus, Soloist, and Piano (1970); *The People Yes*, cantata (1976). **—NS/LK/DM**

Weikert, Ralf, Austrian conductor; b. St. Florian, Nov. 10, 1940. He studied at the Bruckner Cons. in Linz; then took a course in conducting with Swarowsky at the Vienna Academy of Music. In 1965 he won 1st prize in the Nicolai Malko Conducting Competition in Copenhagen. In 1966 he became conductor of the City Theater in Bonn; then was chief conductor there (1968–77). In 1977 he was appointed deputy Generalmusikdirektor of the Frankfurt am Main Opera; also conducted at the Hamburg State Opera, the Deutsche Oper in Berlin, the Vienna State Opera, and the Zürich Opera. In 1981 he was named chief conductor of the Salzburg Mozarteum Orch. and music director of the Landestheater in Salzburg. He was music director of the Zürich Opera from 1983 to 1992.**—NS/LK/DM**

Weikl, Bernd, esteemed Austrian baritone; b. Vienna, July 29, 1942. He received his training at the Mainz Cons. (1962–65) and the Hannover Hochschule für Musik (1965–67). In 1968 he made his operatic debut as Ottakar in *Der Freischütz* at the Hannover Opera, where he sang until 1970. From 1970 to 1973 he was a member of the Deutsche Oper am Rhein in Düsseldorf. In 1971 he made his first appearance at the Salzburg Easter Festival as Melot in *Tristan und Isolde*. In 1972 he sang for the first time at the Bayreuth Festival as Wolfram. He appeared at the Hamburg State Opera (from 1973) and at the Berlin Deutsche Opera (from 1974). In 1975 he made his debut at London's Covent Garden as Rossini's Figaro. In 1976 he created the role of Ferdinand in Einem's *Kabale und Liebe* in Vienna. On Dec. 22, 1977, he made his Metropolitan Opera debut in N.Y. as Wolfram, where he returned in such roles as Amfortas, Jochanaan, Beethoven's Don Fernando, and Mandryka. He was a soloist in Bach's *St. Matthew Passion* at his Salzburg Festival debut in 1984. His portrayal of Hans Sachs was greatly admired, and he sang that role at Milan's La Scala and at Covent Garden in 1990 and at the Metropolitan Opera and the San Francisco Opera in 1993. In 1995 he was engaged as Amfortas at the Bayreuth Festival. He portrayed Jochanaan at the Metropolitan Opera in 1996 and at the San Francisco Opera in 1997. On March 21, 1999, he sang Wagner's Dutchman at the opening of the new Macau Cultural Centre. As a concert artist, he appeared widely in oratorio and lieder performances.**—NS/LK/DM**

Weil, Bruno, German conductor; b. Hahnstätten, Nov. 24, 1949. He studied with Swarowsky in Vienna and Ferrara in Italy. He conducted opera in Wiesbaden (1975–77) and Braunschweig (1977–81). After winning 2nd prize in the Karajan conducting competition in 1979, he appeared with the Berlin Phil. In 1980 he conducted at the Deutsche Oper in Berlin. He became Generalmusikdirektor in Augsburg in 1981. In 1984 he was a guest conductor of the Yomiuri Nippon Sym. Orch. in Tokyo. In 1985 he made his debut at the Vienna State Opera conducting *Aida*. He conducted *Don Giovanni* at the Salzburg Festival in 1988, the year he also made his U.S. debut at a N.Y. Schubertiade. During the 1990–91 season, he toured Germany with the English Chamber Orch. In 1991 he became music director of the Carmel (Calif.) Bach Festival. He made his Glyndebourne Festival debut conducting *Così fan tutte* in 1992. In 1994 he became Generalmusikdirektor of the Duisburg Sym. Orch.**—NS/LK/DM**

Weil, Hermann, German baritone; b. Karlsruhe, May 29, 1876; d. (of a heart attack while fishing in Blue Mountain Lake, N.Y.) July 6, 1949. He studied voice with Adolf Dippel in Frankfurt am Main. He made his operatic debut as Wolfram in *Tannhäuser* at Freiburg, Baden, on Sept. 6, 1901, then sang in Vienna, Brussels, Amsterdam, Milan, and London; he participated in the Bayreuth Festivals (1909–12). On Nov. 17, 1911, he made a successful debut as Kurvenal in *Tristan und Isolde* at the Metropolitan Opera in N.Y. In 1917 he returned to Germany. He sang at the Vienna State Opera (1920–23), toured the U.S. with the German Opera Co. (1923–24), and appeared at the Bayreuth Festival (1924–25); in 1939 he settled in N.Y. as a vocal teacher. The extensive range of his voice, spanning 3 full octaves, enabled him to undertake bass parts as well as those in the baritone compass. He had about 100 roles in his repertoire, excelling in Wagnerian operas.**—NS/LK/DM**

Weill, Kurt (Julian), remarkable German-born American composer; b. Dessau, March 2, 1900; d. N.Y., April 3, 1950. He was a private pupil of Albert Bing in Dessau (1915–18); in 1918–19 he studied at the Berlin Hochschule für Musik with Humperdinck (composition), Friedrich Koch (counterpoint), and Krasselt (conducting). He was then engaged as an opera coach in Dessau and was also theater conductor at Ludenscheid. In 1920 he moved to Berlin and was a student of Busoni at the Prussian Academy of Arts until 1923; also studied with Jarnach there (1921–23). His first major work, the Sym. No. 1, *Berliner Sinfonie*, was composed in 1921. However, it was not performed in his lifetime; indeed, its MS was not recovered until 1955, and it was finally premiered by the North German Radio Sym. Orch. in Hamburg in 1958. Under the impact of new trends in the musical theater, Weill proceeded to write short satirical operas in a sharp modernistic manner: *Der Protagonist* (1924–25) and *Royal Palace* (1925–26). There followed a striking "songspiel" (a hybrid term of English and German words), *Mahagonny*, to a libretto by Bertolt Brecht, savagely satirizing the American primacy of money (1927); it was remodeled and was presented as the 3-act opera *Aufstieg und Fall der Stadt Mahagonny* (1929). Weill's greatest hit in this genre came with a modernistic version of Gay's *The Beggar's Opera*, to a pungent libretto by Brecht; under the title *Die Dreigroschenoper* (1928), it was staged all over Germany, and was also produced in translation throughout Europe. Marc Blitzstein later made a new libretto for the opera, versified in a modern American style, which was produced as *The Threepenny Opera*, the exact translation of the German title. Its hit number, "Mack the Knife," became tremendously successful.

After the Nazi ascent to power in Germany, Weill and his wife, **Lotte Lenya**, who appeared in many of his musical plays, went to Paris in 1934. They settled in the U.S. in 1935; Weill became a naturalized American citizen in 1943. Quickly absorbing the modes and fashions of American popular music, he recreated, with astonishing facility, and felicity, the typical form and content of American musicals; this stylistic transition was facilitated by the fact that in his European productions he had already absorbed elements of American popular songs and jazz rhythms. His highly developed assimilative faculty enabled him to combine this Americanized idiom with the advanced techniques of modern music (atonality, polytonality, polyrhythms) and present the product in a pleasing, and yet sophisticated and challenging, manner. However, for all of his success in American-produced scores, the great majority of his European works remained to be produced in America only posthumously. The Kurt Weill Edition of his complete works began publ. in 1997 under the auspices of the Kurt Weill Foundation for Music, Inc., and the European American Music Corp.

WORKS: DRAMATIC: *Zaubernacht*, ballet (Berlin, Nov. 18, 1922); *Der Protagonist*, opera (1924–25; Dresden, March 27, 1926); *Royal Palace*, ballet-opera (1925–26; Berlin, March 2, 1927; original orchestration not extant; reconstructed as a ballet by Gunther Schuller and Noam Sheriff, San Francisco, Oct. 5, 1968); *Na und?*, opera (1926–27; not perf.; not extant); *Der Zar lasst sich photographieren*, opera (1927; Leipzig, Feb. 18, 1928); *Mahagonny*, "songspiel" (Baden-Baden, July 17, 1927; remodeled as a 3-act opera, *Aufstieg und Fall der Stadt Mahagonny*, 1927–29; Leipzig, March 9, 1930); *Happy End*, comedy (Berlin, Sept. 2, 1929); *Der Jasager*, school opera (Berlin radio, June 23, 1930); *Die Burgschaft*, opera (1930–31; Berlin, March 10, 1932); *Der Silbersee*, musical play (1932–33; simultaneous premiere in Leipzig, Erfurt, and Magdeburg, Feb. 18, 1933); *Die sieben Todsunden der Kleinburger*, ballet (Paris, June 7, 1933); *Der Kuhnhandel*, operetta (1934; Düsseldorf, March 22, 1990; rev. as a musical comedy, *A Kingdom for a Cow*, London, June 28, 1935); *Der Weg der Verheissung*, biblical drama (1934–35; Chemnitz, June 13, 1999; rev. by L. Lewisohn as *The Eternal Road*, 1935–36; N.Y., Jan. 7, 1937); *Johnny Johnson*, musical fable (N.Y., Nov. 19, 1936); *Davy Crockett*, musical play (1938; unfinished); *Knickerbocker Holiday*, operetta (Hartford, Conn., Sept. 26, 1938; contains the popular "September Song"); *Railroads on Parade*, historical pageant (1938–39; N.Y. World's Fair, April 30, 1939); *The Ballad of Magna Carta*, scenic cantata (1939; CBS, Feb. 4, 1940); *Ulysses Africanus*, musical play (1939; unfinished); *Lady in the Dark*, musical play (1940; N.Y., Jan. 23, 1941); *One Touch of Venus*, musical comedy (N.Y., Oct. 7, 1943); *The Firebrand of Florence*, operetta (1944; N.Y., March 22, 1945); *Down in the Valley*, folk opera (1945–48; Bloomington, Ind., July 15, 1948); *Street Scene*, opera (1946; N.Y., Jan. 9, 1947); *Love Life*, vaudeville (1947; N.Y., Oct. 7, 1948); *Lost in the Stars*, musical tragedy, after Alan Paton's *Cry, the Beloved Country* (N.Y., Oct. 30, 1949); *Huckleberry Finn*, musical (1950; unfinished). **Film:** *You and Me* (1937–38); *The River Is Blue* (1937–38; discarded); *Where Do We Go from Here?* (1943–44); *Salute to France* (1944). **ORCH.:** Symphonic Poem (1920?; not extant); 1 unnumbered sym. (1920; not extant); 2 numbered syms.: No. 1, *Berliner Sinfonie* (1921; Hamburg, Jan. 17, 1958) and No. 2, *Pariser Symphonie* (1933; Amsterdam, Oct. 11, 1934; U.S. premiere as *3 Night Scenes*, N.Y., Dec. 13, 1934); Divertimento (1922); *Sinfonia sacra* or *Fantasia, Passacaglia, und Hymnus* (1922); *Quodlibet*, suite from *Zaubernacht* (1923; Coburg, Feb. 6, 1926); Concerto for Violin, Woodwinds, Double Bass, and Percussion (1924; Paris, June 11, 1925); *Berlin im Licht* for Military Band (1928); *Kleine Dreigroschenmusik* for Winds, concert suite from *Die Dreigroschenoper* (1929). **CHAMBER:** 2 movements for String Quartet: *Allegro deciso* and *Andantino* (n.d.; N.Y., March 7, 1977); 1 unnumbered string quartet (1919); 1 numbered string quartet (1923); Cello Sonata (1920). **VOCAL:** *Sulamith*, cantata for Soprano, Women's Chorus, and Orch. (1920; not extant); *Psalm VIII* for 8 Voices (1921; partly lost); *Recordare* for Chorus and Children's Chorus (1923); *Das Studenbuch*, 6 songs for Tenor or Soprano and Orch. (1924; partly lost); *Der neue Orpheus*, cantata for Soprano, Violin, and Orch. (1925; Berlin, March 2, 1927); *Vom Tod im Wald*, ballad for Bass and 10 Wind Instruments (Berlin, Nov. 23, 1927); *Das Berliner Requiem*, cantata for Tenor, Baritone, Bass, Chorus, and 15 Instruments (1928; Frankfurt am Main Radio, May 22, 1929); *Der Lindberghflug*, cantata after a radio score for Tenor, Baritone, Chorus, and Orch. (with Hindemith; Baden-Baden, July 28, 1929; rescored by Weill as totally his own work, Berlin, Dec. 5, 1929; rev. 1930 as *Der Flug des Lindberghs* and then later retitled *Der Ozeanflug*, without Lindbergh's name, as a gesture of protest against Lindbergh's militant neutrality toward Nazi Germany); *Zu Potsdam unter den Eichen* for Men's Voices (1929); *Song of the Railroads* (1938); *4 American Songs* (1939); *Kiddush* for Tenor, Chorus, and Organ (1946); many songs.

WRITINGS: S. Hinton and J. Schebera, eds., *Musik und Theater: Gesammelte Schriften* (Leipzig, 1990).

BIBL.: H. Kotschenreuther, *K. W.* (Berlin, 1962); K. Kowalke, *K. W. in Europe* (Ann Arbor, 1979); R. Sanders, *The Days Grow Short: The Life and Music of K. W.* (N.Y., 1980); D. Jarman, *K. W.: An Illustrated Biography* (Bloomington, Ind., 1982); J. Schebera, *K. W.: Leben und Werk* (Leipzig, 1983); K. Kowalke, ed., *A New Orpheus: Essays on K. W.* (New Haven, 1986); S. Cook, *Opera During the Weimar Republic: The Zeitopern of Ernst Krenek, K. W., and Paul Hindemith* (Ann Arbor, 1987); D. Drew, *K. W.: A Handbook* (Berkeley, 1987); S. Hinton, ed., *K. W.: The Threepenny Opera* (Cambridge, 1990); J. Schebera, *K. W. 1900–1950: Eine Biographie in Texten, Bildern und Dokumenten* (Leipzig, 1990); R. Taylor, *K. W.: Composer in a Divided World* (London, 1991); K. Kowalke and H. Edler, eds., *A Stranger Here Myself: K. W.-Studien* (Hildesheim, 1993); G. Diehl, *Der junge K. W. und seine Oper "Der Protagonist: " Exemplarische Untersuchungen zur Deutung des frühen kompositorischen Werkes* (2 vols., Kassel, 1994); N. Grosch, J. Lucchesi, and J. Schebera, eds., *K. W.-Studien* (Stuttgart, 1996); H. Geuen, *Von der Zeitoper zur Broadway Opera: K. W. und die Idee des musikalischen Theaters* (Schliengen, 1997); D. Farneth, *K. W.: A Life in Pictures and Documents* (Woodstock and London, 1999).—**NS/LK/DM**

Weinberger, Jaromir, Czech-born American composer; b. Prague, Jan. 8, 1896; d. (suicide) St. Petersburg, Fla., Aug. 8, 1967. He was a student of Křička and Hoffmeister in Prague and of Reger in Leipzig. In 1922 he became a teacher of composition at Ithaca (N.Y.) Coll. Returning to his homeland, he scored a remarkable success with his opera *Švanda dudák* (Schwanda the Bagpiper; Prague, April 27, 1927). It subsequently was performed throughout Europe to critical acclaim. With the dismemberment of his homeland by the Nazis in 1939, Weinberger fled to the U.S. and later became a naturalized citizen. Weinberger's success with *Švanda* *dudák* was a signal one. Even though the opera eventually went unperformed, its "Polka and Fugue" became a popular concert piece. He committed suicide, despondent over the lack of interest in his works.

WORKS: DRAMATIC: Opera: *Kocourkov* (c. 1926); *Švanda dudák* (Schwanda the Bagpiper; Prague, April 27, 1927); *Die geliebte Stimme* (Munich, Feb. 28, 1931); *Lidé z Polkerflatu* (The Outcasts of Polker Flat; Brno, Nov. 19, 1932); *Valdstejn* (Vienna, Nov. 18, 1937). **Operetta:** *Frühlingsstürme* (1933); *Apropo co dela Andula* (n.d.); *Na ruzich ustlano* (Bed of Roses; 1934); *Cisar pan na tresnich* (n.d.). **ORCH.:** *Overture to a Marionette Play* (1916); *Christmas* for Organ and Orch. (1929); *Liebesplauder, Neckerei* for Small Orch. (1929); *Passacaglia* for Organ and Orch. (1931); *Overture to a Knightly Play* (1931); *Neima Ivrit* (Hebrew Song; 1936); Concerto for Timpani, 4 Trumpets, and 4 Trombones (1939); *Under the Spreading Chestnut Tree* for Piano and Orch. (N.Y., Oct. 12, 1939; rev. 1941); *The Legend of Sleepy Hollow* (1940); *Prelude and Fugue on Dixie* (1940); *The Bird's Opera*, overture (1940; Detroit, Nov. 13, 1941); *Song of the High Seas* (N.Y., Nov. 9, 1940); *Mississippi Rhapsody* for Band (1940); Alto Saxophone Concerto (1940); *Czech Rhapsody* (Washington, D.C., Nov. 5, 1941); *The Lincoln Symphony* (Cincinnati, Oct. 17, 1941); *Prelude to the Festival* for Band (1941); *Afternoon in the Village* for Band (1951); *Préludes religieux et profanes* (1953); *Aus Tirol* (1959); *A Waltz Overture* (1960). **CHAMBER:** *Colloque sentimental* for Violin and Piano (1920); *Cowboy's Christmas* for Violin and Piano (1924); *Banjos* for Violin and Piano (1924); *Czech Songs and Dances* for Violin and Piano (1929); sonatinas for Clarinet or Oboe or Bassoon or Piano (1940); *10 Characteristic Solos* for Snare Drum and Piano (1940). **KEYBOARD: Piano:** 2 sonatas (1915; *Spinet Sonata*, 1915); *Gravures* (1924); *Etude on a Polish Chorale* (1924). **Organ:** *Bible Poems* (1939); Sonata (1941); *6 Religious Preludes* (1946); *Dedications* (1954); *Meditations* (1956). **VOCAL:** *Psalm CL* for Soprano or Tenor and Organ (1940); *The Way to Emmaus* for Soprano or Tenor and Organ (1940); *Ecclesiastes* for Soprano, Baritone, Chorus, Organ, and Bells (1945); *Ave* for Chorus and Orch. (1962); *5 Songs from Des Knaben Wunderhorn* (1962); many Czech songs.
—NS/LK/DM

Weiner, Lazar, Russian-American pianist, conductor, and composer, father of **Yehudi Wyner;** b. Cherkassy, near Kiev, Oct. 27, 1897; d. N.Y., Jan. 10, 1982. He emigrated to America in 1914, and became associated with numerous Jewish artistic activities in N.Y.; also took private lessons in composition with Robert Russell Bennett, Frederick Jacobi, and Joseph Schillinger. From 1929 to 1975 he was music director of the Central Synagogue in N.Y.; conducted classes in the Yiddish art song at Hebrew Union Coll., the Jewish Theological Seminary, and the 92nd Street Y; served as music director of the WABC weekly radio program *The Message of Israel* (1934–69). His compositions include an opera, *The Golem* (1956; White Plains, N.Y., Jan. 13, 1957), 5 ballets, 7 cantatas, including *Man of the World* (1939), *To Thee, America* (1943), *The Legend of Toil* (1945), *The Last Judgement* (1966), and *Amos* (1970), over 100 liturgical works, more than 150 songs, many to Yiddish texts, and some orch. and chamber music.**—NS/LK/DM**

Weiner, Leó, eminent Hungarian composer and pedagogue; b. Budapest, April 16, 1885; d. there, Sept. 13, 1960. He was a student of Koessler at the Budapest Academy of Music (1901–06). In 1908 he joined its faculty as a teacher of theory, becoming a prof. of composition in 1912 and of chamber music in 1920. He retired in 1957 but continued to teach there as prof. emeritus until his death. In 1907 he won the Franz-Josef-Jubiläumspreis, and in 1950 and 1960 the Kossuth Prize. In 1953 he was made an Eminent Artist by the Hungarian government. Weiner was particularly influential as a pedagogue. Many outstanding Hungarian composers and performers studied with him, among them Doráti, Foldes, Solti, Starker, and Varga. In his compositions, he generally remained faithful to the precepts of the Austro-German Romantic tradition.

WORKS: DRAMATIC: *A gondolás* (The Gondolier), opera (n.d.; in collaboration with A. Szirmai; not extant); *Csongor és Tünde*, incidental music to M. Vörösmarty's play (1913; Budapest, Dec. 6, 1916; as a ballet, Budapest, Nov. 8, 1930; orch. suite, 1937). **ORCH.:** *Scherzo* (1905); *Serenade* for Small Orch. (Budapest, Oct. 22, 1906); *Farsang* (Carnival) for Small Orch. (1907); Piano Concertino (1923); *Katonásdi* (Toy Soldiers; 1924); Suite (1931); *Divertimento No. 1* for Strings (1934), *No. 2* for Strings (1938), *No. 3: Impressioni ungheresi* (1949), *No. 4* (1951), and *No. 5* (1951); *Pastorale, phantaisie et fugue* for Strings (1934); *Ballata* for Clarinet and Orch. (1949); *Romanze* for Cello, Harp, and Strings (1949); *Változatok egy magyar népdal fölött* (Variations on a Hungarian Folk Song; 1949); *Preludio, notturno e scherzo diabolico* (1950); *Három magyar népi tánc* (3 Hungarian Folk Dances) for Salon Orch. (1951); *Ünnepi hangok* (Festal Sounds; 1951); 2 violin concertos (1950, 1957; both arranged from the 2 violin sonatas, 1911, 1918); *Toldi*, symphonic poem (1952); *Passacaglia* (1955); *Magyar gyermek-és népdalok* (Hungarian Children's Songs and Folk Songs) for Small Orch. (1955). **CHAMBER:** *Scherzo* for String Quintet (1905); *Magyar ábránd* (Hungarian Fantasy) for Tárogató and Cimbalom (1905–06); 3 string quartets (1906; 1921; *Pastorale, phantaisie et fugue*, 1938); String Trio (1908); *Ballade* for Clarinet or Viola and Piano (1911); 2 violin sonatas (1911, 1918; both arranged as violin concertos, 1950, 1957); *Romanze* for Cello and Piano (1921); *Peregi verbunk* (Pereg Recruiting Dance) for Violin or Viola or Clarinet and Piano (1951; also for Wind Quintet and String Quintet, 1957); *Bevezetés és csürdöngölö* (Introduction and Stamping Dance) for Wind Quintet and String Quintet (1957). **Piano:** *Tarantella* for 2 Pianos, 8-Hands (1905); *Változatok* (Variations; 1905); *Caprice* (1908); 2 passacaglias (n.d., 1936); *Präludieum, Nocturne und Scherzo* (1911); *Miniatür-Bilder* (1918); *Magyar parasztdalok* (Hungarian Peasant Songs; 5 sets, 1932–50); *Lakodalmas* (Wedding Dance; 1936); *Három magyar népi tánc* (3 Hungarian Folk Dances; 1941); *Változatok egy magyar népdal fölött* (Variations on a Hungarian Folk Song; 1950); Suite for 2 Pianos (1950); *Farsang* (Carnival) for 2 Pianos (1950); *Magyar népi muzsika* (Hungarian Folk Music; 1953); pieces for young people. **VOCAL:** *Agnus Dei* for Chorus (1906); *Gloria* for Chorus (1906). **OTHER:** Transcriptions for orch. of works by Bach, Schubert, Berlioz, Liszt, Tchaikovsky, and Bartók; cadenzas for Beethoven's piano concertos Nos. 1–4 (Milan, 1950).

WRITINGS (all publ. in Budapest): *Összhangzattanra előkeszitő jegyzetek* (Notes in Preparation for a Harmony Treatise; 1910; 3rd ed., 1917, as *Az összhangzattan előkészitő iskolája* [Preparatory School in Harmony]; 6th ed., 1955); *A zenei formák vázlatos ismertetése* (A General Sketch of Musical Forms; 1911); *Elemző összhanszattan: Funkciótan* (Analytic Harmony: Function; 1944); *A hangszeres zene formái* (The Forms of Instrumental Music; 1955).

BIBL.: G. Gál, *W. L. Életműve* (L. W.'s Lifework; Budapest, 1959).—**NS/LK/DM**

Weingartner, (Paul) Felix, Edler von Münzberg, illustrious Austrian conductor; b. Zara, Dalmatia, June 2, 1863; d. Winterthur, May 7, 1942. After his father's death in 1868, his mother took him to Graz, where he studied music with W.A. Rémy. He publ. some piano pieces when he was 16 years old; Brahms recommended him for a stipend that enabled him to take music courses with Reinecke, Jadassohn, and Paul at the Leipzig Cons. (1881–83). He received the Mozart Prize at his graduation. He was introduced to Liszt, who recommended Weingartner's opera *Sakuntala* for production in Weimar (March 23, 1884), a signal honor for a young man not yet 21 years old. While progressing rapidly as a composer, Weingartner launched a brilliant career as a conductor, which was to become his prime vocation. He conducted in Königsberg (1884–85), Danzig (1885–87), Hamburg (1887–89), and Mannheim (1889–91). In 1891 he was engaged as court conductor in Berlin, where he led the Royal Opera until 1898 and the royal orch. concerts until 1907; he also conducted the Kaim Orch. in Munich (1898–1905). His reputation as a fine musician was enhanced by his appearances as an ensemble player in the Weingartner Trio, with himself as pianist, Rettich as violinist, and Warnke as cellist. In 1908 he succeeded Mahler as music director of the Vienna Court Opera and conducted there until 1911. He also was Mahler's successor as conductor of the Vienna Phil. (1908–27), with which he won great renown. He likewise served as Generalmusikdirektor in Darmstadt (1914–19) and as director of the Vienna Volksoper (1919–24). In 1927 he became director of the Basel Cons. He also conducted sym. concerts in Basel. After serving as a guest conductor of the Vienna State Opera (1934–35), he again was its director (1935–36); then once more was a guest conductor there (1936–38). Throughout the years he had engagements as guest conductor with major European orchs. He made his American debut with the N.Y. Phil. on Feb. 12, 1904 and later conducted the N.Y. Sym. Soc. (Jan.-March 1906). He appeared with the Boston Opera Co. on Feb. 12, 1912, conducting *Tristan und Isolde*; he and his 3rd wife, **Lucille Marcel**, were engaged for a season with the Boston Opera Co. in 1913. (His 1st wife was Marie Juillerat, whom he married in 1891; his 2nd wife was the Baroness Feodora von Dreifus, whom he married in 1903). He made his debut at Covent Garden in London in 1939 conducting *Parsifal*. He eventually settled in Interlaken, where he established a summer conducting school. Although Weingartner was trained in the Austro-German Romantic tradition, his approach to conducting was notable for its eschewing of Romantic excess. Indeed, he acquired a remarkable reputation for his devotion to the composer's intentions, which he conveyed to his musicians via an unostentatious baton technique. His interpretations of the Austro-German repertoire were acclaimed for their authority and integrity. He was the first conductor to record all the Beethoven syms. Weingartner was also a competent music editor; he was on the editorial board for the complete works of Berlioz (1899) and of Haydn (1907). Despite the pressure of his activities as a conductor, he found time for composition. In addition to his first opera, *Sakuntala*, he wrote the operas *Malawika* (Munich, 1886), *Genesius* (Berlin, Nov. 15, 1892), *Orestes*, a trilogy (Leipzig, Feb. 15, 1902), *Kain und Abel* (Darmstadt, May 17, 1914), *Dame Kobold* (Darmstadt, Feb. 23, 1916), *Die Dorfschule* (Vienna, May 13, 1920), *Meister Andrea* (Vienna, May 13, 1920), and *Der Apostat* (not perf.). He also composed 7 syms. (1899–1937); various other orch. works, including pieces for Voice and Orch. and Chorus and Orch.; songs; much chamber music, including 5 string quartets, 2 violin sonatas, and piano pieces. He made arrangements of Beethoven's "Hammerklavier" Sonata, op.106, and of Weber's *Aufforderung zum Tanz*. He was an excellent writer on musical subjects. Among his publs. were: *Die Lehre von der Wiedergeburt und das musikalische Drama* (1895), *Über das Dirigieren* (1896; 5th ed., 1913; a fundamental essay on conducting), *Bayreuth 1876–1896* (1897; 2nd ed., 1904), *Die Symphonie nach Beethoven* (1897; 4th ed., 1901; Eng. tr., 1904; new tr. as *The Symphony since Beethoven*, 1926), *Ratschläge für Aufführung der Sinfonien Beethovens* (1906; 3rd ed., 1928; Eng. tr., London, 1907), *Akkorde: Gesammelte Aufsätze von Felix Weingartner* (1912), a polemical pamphlet, *Erlebnisse eines kgl. Kapellmeisters in Berlin* (1912; an attack upon the Berlin intendancy; a rebuttal was publ. by A. Wolff in *Der Fall Weingartner*, 1912), *Ratschläge für Aufführung der Sinfonien Schuberts und Schumanns* (1918), *Ratschläge für Aufführung der Sinfonien Mozarts* (1923), and *Lebenserinnerungen* (vol. I, 1923; vol. II, 1929; Eng. version, London, 1937, as *Buffets and Rewards: A Musician's Reminiscences*), *Unwirkliches und Wirkliches* (1936).

BIBL.: E. Krause, *F. W. als schaffender Künstler* (Berlin, 1904); P. Riesenfeld, *F. W. Ein kritischer Versuch* (Breslau, 1906); W. Hutschenruyter, *Levensschets en portret van F. W.* (Haarlem, 1906); J. Lustig, *F. W. Persönlichkeiten* (Berlin, 1908); W. Jacob, *F. W.* (Wiesbaden, 1933); *Festschrift für Dr. F. W. zu seinem siebzigsten Geburtstag* (Basel, 1933); C. Dyment, *F. W.: Recollections and Recordings* (Rickmansworth, 1975).—**NS/LK/DM**

Weinlig, Christian Ehregott, German organist and composer, uncle of **(Christian) Theodor Weinlig;** b. Dresden, Sept. 30, 1743; d. there, March 14, 1813. He studied with Homilius at the Dresden Kreuzschule. In 1767 he was organist at the Evangelical Church in Leipzig, in 1773, at Thorn, and, in 1780, organist at the Frauenkirche. In 1785 he succeeded his teacher, Homilius, as Kantor of the Kreuzschule. He publ. sonatas for piano, with flute and cello, and brought out several oratorios as well as also light theater pieces.—**NS/LK/DM**

Weinlig, (Christian) Theodor, noted German music theorist and teacher, nephew of **Christian Ehregott Weinlig;** b. Dresden, July 25, 1780; d. Leipzig, March 7, 1842. After a period of study with his uncle (1804–6), he became a pupil of Stanislao Mattei in Bologna. He was Kantor of the Dresden Kreuzschule (1814–17) and of the Leipzig Thomasschule (from 1823). He enjoyed high repute as a teacher of theory and composition, numbering Richard Wagner among his pupils. His own works include a *Deutsches Magnificat* for Soloists, Chorus, and Orch. and vocalises. He publ. a manual, *Theoretisch-praktische Anleitung zur Fuge, für den Selbstunterricht* (Dresden, 1845; 2nd ed., 1852).

BIBL.: A. Kurz, *Geschichte der Familie W. von 1580 bis 1850* (Bonn, 1912); R. Roch, *C.T. W., der Lehrer Richard Wagners* (diss., Univ. of Leipzig, 1917).—**NS/LK/DM**

Weinmann, Karl, eminent German musicologist; b. Vohenstrauss, Upper Palatinate, Dec. 22, 1873; d. Pielenhofen, near Regensburg, Sept. 26, 1929. He was a pupil of Haberl and Haller at the Kirchenmusikschule in Regensburg, in Berlin, and in Innsbruck; after further study with Peter Wagner at the Univ. of Freiburg im Breisgau, he obtained the degree of Ph.D. there (1905) with the diss. *Das Hymnarium Parisiense;* later obtained a doctorate in theology at the Kirchenmusikschule in Regensburg (1917). After his ordination to the priesthood, he became a prof. at the Kirchenmusikschule in Regensburg; in 1910, succeeded Haberl as its director. He was ed. of the *Kirchenmusikalisches Jahrbuch* (1909–11), *Musica Sacra* (from 1911), and *Cäcilienvereinsorgan* (from 1926). He ed. for Pustet (after the *Editio vaticana*) *Römisches Gradualbuch* (1909; 4th ed., 1928); *Graduale* (1910); *Kyriale* (1911); *Totenoffizium* (1912; 2nd ed., 1928); *Graduale parvum* (1913); *Römisches Vesperbuch mit Psalmenbuch* (1915); *Karwochenbuch* (1924); *Feier der heiligen Karwoche* (1925); *Sonntagsvesper und Komplet* (2nd ed., 1928). He was also ed. of the collection *Kirchenmusik,* for which he wrote *Geschichte der Kirchenmusik* (1906; 4th ed., 1925; Eng. tr., 1910; also tr. into French, Italian, Polish, and Hungarian), and monographs on Leonhard Paminger (1907) and Carl Proske (1909). Other writings included *Palestrinas Geburtsjahr* (Regensburg, 1915), *Stille Nacht, heilige Nacht: Die Geschichte des Liedes zu seinem 100. Geburtstag* (1918; 2nd ed., 1920), and *Das Konzil von Trent und die Kirchenmusik* (1919).—**NS/LK/DM**

Weinrich, Carl, eminent American organist and teacher; b. Paterson, N.J., July 2, 1904; d. Princeton, N.J., May 13, 1991. After graduation from N.Y.U. (B.A., 1927), he studied at the Curtis Inst. of Music in Philadelphia (1927–30); also studied organ privately with Farnam and Dupré, and piano with Chasins. In 1930 he became the successor of Farnam as organist at the Holy Communion Church in N.Y. He taught at Westminster Choir Coll. in Princeton, N.J. (1934–40), Wellesley Coll. (1936–46), and at Columbia Univ. (1942–52); also was director of music at Princeton Univ. Chapel (1943–73). Weinrich toured extensively as a recitalist.—**NS/LK/DM**

Weinstock, Herbert, American writer on music; b. Milwaukee, Nov. 16, 1905; d. N.Y., Oct. 21, 1971. He was educated in his native town, and later took courses at the Univ. of Chicago. He was active in N.Y. as a music ed. for the publisher Alfred A. Knopf.

WRITINGS (all publ. in N.Y.): With W. Brockway, *Men of Music* (1939; 2nd ed., rev. and enl., 1950); with W. Brockway, *The Opera: A History of Its Creation and Performance* (1941; 2nd ed., 1962, as *The World of Opera*); *Tchaikovsky* (1943); *Handel* (1946; 2nd ed., 1959; also in Ger.); *Chopin: The Man and His Music* (1949; 2nd ed., 1959); *Music as an Art* (1953; 2nd ed., 1966, as *What Music Is*); *Donizetti and the World of Opera in Italy, Paris and Vienna in the First Half of the Nineteenth Century* (1963); *Rossini: a Biography* (1968); *Vincenzo Bellini: His Life and Operas* (1971).—**NS/LK/DM**

Weinzweig, John (Jacob), Canadian composer, teacher, and administrator; b. Toronto, March 11, 1913. He learned to play the mandolin, piano, tuba, tenor saxophone, and double bass. He was a student of Willan (counterpoint and fugue), Leo Smith (harmony), and MacMillan (orchestration) at the Univ. of Toronto (B.Mus., 1937), of Reginald Stewart (conducting) at the Toronto Cons. of Music, and of Rogers (orchestration and composition) at the Eastman School of Music in Rochester, N.Y. (M.Mus., 1938). After serving as founder-conductor of the Univ. of Toronto Sym. Orch. (1934–37), he taught at the Toronto Cons. of Music (1939–43; 1945–60) and at the Univ. of Toronto (1952–78). In 1951 he founded the Canadian League of Composers and was its first president until 1957, and then again from 1959 to 1963. He was the author of *John Weinzweig: His Words and His Music* (Grimsby, Ontario, 1986) and *Sounds and Reflections* (Grimsby, 1990). In 1974 he was made an Officer of the Order of Canada and in 1988 he received the Order of Ontario. In his music, Weinzweig began using serial procedures in 1939. His output continued to reflect his interest in advanced compositional means of expression throughout his career.

WORKS: DRAMATIC: Ballet: *The Whirling Dwarf* (1939); *Red Ear of Corn* (Toronto, March 2, 1949). **Other:** 4 film scores; more than 100 radio scores. **ORCH.:** *Legend* (1937); *The Enchanted Hill* (1938); Suite (1938); *Spectre* for Timpani and Strings (1938); *A Tale of Tuamotu* for Bassoon and Orch. (1939); Sym. (1940); *Rhapsody* (1941); *Interlude in an Artist's Life* for Strings (1943); *Our Canada* (1943); *Band- Hut Sketches* for Band (1944); *Edge of the World* (1946); 11 divertimentos: No. 1 for Flute and Strings (1946), No. 2 for Oboe and Strings (1948), No. 3 for Bassoon and Strings (1960), No. 4 for Clarinet and Strings (1968; out of chronological order), No. 5 for Trumpet, Trombone, and Winds (1961), No. 6 for Alto Saxophone and Strings (1972), No. 7 for Horn and Strings (1979), No. 8 for Tuba and Orch. (1980), No. 9 for Full Orch. (1982), No. 10 for Piano and Strings (1988), and No. 11 for English Horn and Strings (1990); *Round Dance* (1950); Violin Concerto (1951–54; Toronto, May 30, 1955); *Symphonic Ode* (1958); Piano Concerto (Toronto, Dec. 15, 1966); Concerto for Harp and Chamber Orch. (Toronto, April 30, 1967); *Dummiyah* (Silence; Toronto, July 4, 1969); *Out of the Blues* for Concert Band (1981). **CHAMBER:** 3 string quartets (1937, 1946, 1962); Violin Sonata (1943); *Fanfare* for 3 Trumpets, 3 Trombones, and Percussion (1943); *Intermissions* for Flute and Oboe (1943); Cello Sonata, *Israel* (1949); Woodwind Quintet (1964); Clarinet Quintet (1965); *Around the Stage in 25 Minutes During Which a Variety of Instruments Are Struck* for Percussionist (1970); *Riffs* for Flute (1974); *Contrasts* for Guitar (1976); *Pieces of 5* for Brass Quintet (1976); *Refrains* for Double Bass and Piano (1977); *18 Pieces* for Guitar (1980); *15 Pieces* for Harp (1983); *Music Centre Serenade* for Flute, Horn, Viola, and Cello (1984); *Conversations* for 3 Guitars (1984); *Cadenza* for Clarinet (1986); *Birthday Notes* for Flute and Piano (1987); *Tremologue* for Viola (1987). **KEYBOARD: Piano:** 2 suites (1939, 1950); *Swing a Fugue* (1949); *Melos* (1949); Sonata (1950); *Impromptus* (1973); *CanOn Stride* (1986); *Tango for 2* (1986; rev. 1987); *Micromotions* (1988); *3 Pieces* (1989); *Duologue* for 2 Pianos (1990). **Organ:** *Improvisations on an Indian Tune* (1942). **VOCAL:** *Wine of Peace* for Soprano and Orch. (1957); *Trialogue* for Soprano, Flute, and Piano (1971); *Private Collection* for Soprano and Piano (1975); *Choral Pieces* (1985–86).

BIBL.: E. Keillor, *J. W. and His Music: The Radical Romantic of Canada* (Metuchen, N.J., 1994).—**NS/LK/DM**

Weir, Dame Gillian (Constance), outstanding New Zealand organist and harpsichordist; b. Martinborough, Jan. 17, 1941. She studied with Ralph Downes at the Royal Coll. of Music in London (1962–65), then pursued private training with Anton Heiller, Marie-Claire Alain, and Boulanger (1965–66). She won the St. Albans International Organ Competition in 1964. In 1965 she made her debut at London's Royal Festival Hall, and subsequently appeared throughout the world as a recitalist on both the organ and the harpsichord. In 1982 she was featured in the television film *Toccata: Two Weeks in the Life of Gillian Weir.* In 1984 she gave a recital at N.Y.'s Alice Tully Hall on an organ designed by her husband. She served as president of the Incorporated Assn. of Organists (1982–83) and of the Incorporated Soc. of Musicians (1992–93). In 1989 she was made a Commander, and in 1996 a Dame Commander, of the Order of the British Empire. Weir maintains a catholic repertory, ranging from early music to contemporary scores. She has given premiere performances of many works written for her, including William Mathias's Organ Concerto (London, Sept. 12, 1984).—**NS/LK/DM**

Weir, Judith, English composer; b. Cambridge (of Scottish parents), May 11, 1954. After studies with Tavener in London, she received training in computer music from Vercoe at the Mass. Inst. of Technology (1973). From 1973 to 1976 she was a student of Holloway at King's Coll., Cambridge. She also studied with Schuller and Messiaen at the Berkshire Music Center in Tanglewood (summer, 1975). From 1979 to 1982 she taught at the Univ. of Glasgow, and then held a creative arts fellowship at Trinity Coll., Cambridge, from 1983 to 1985. She was composer-in-residence of the Royal Scottish Academy of Music and Drama in Glasgow from 1988 to 1991. From 1995 to 1997 she was the Fairbairn composer-in-association of the City of Birmingham Sym. Orch. In her diverse output, Weir has effectively utilized both traditional and contemporary techniques in creating a highly individual means of expression.

WORKS: DRAMATIC: Opera: *The Black Spider* (1984; Canterbury, March 6, 1985); *A Night at the Chinese Opera* (1986–87; Cheltenham, July 8, 1987); *The Vanishing Bridegroom* (Glasgow, Oct. 17, 1990); *Scipio's Dream,* recomposition of Mozart's *Il Sogno di Scipione* (BBC 2 TV, London, Nov. 24, 1991); *Blond Eckbert* (1993; London, April 20, 1994). **ORCH.:** *Wunderhorn* (1978); *Isti Mirant Stella* (Orkney, June 23, 1981); *The Ride Over Lake Constance* (London, March 12, 1984); *Sederunt Principes* for Chamber Orch. (London, Sept. 1, 1987; also for Strings); *Music, Untangled* (Tanglewood, Aug. 3, 1991; rev. 1992); *Heroic Strokes of the Bow (Heroische Bogenstriche)* (Leverkusen, Oct. 26, 1992); *Forest* (Birmingham, Dec. 13, 1995); Piano Concerto (1996–97; London, June 12, 1997); *Certum ex Incertis* (Birmingham, June 9, 1998). **CHAMBER:** *Out of the Air* for Flute, Oboe, Clarinet, Horn, and Bassoon (1975; London, Feb. 8, 1976); *Harmony and Invention* for Harp (1978; rev. 1980); *King Harald Sails to Byzantium* for Flute, Clarinet, Violin, Cello, Piano, and Marimba (Orkney, June 18, 1979); *Pas de Deux* for Violin and Oboe (1980); *Several Concertos* for Flute, Cello, and Piano (1980; Dundee, Jan. 21, 1981); Cello Sonata (1980); *Music for 247 Strings* for Violin and Piano (London, Oct. 5, 1981); *Spij Dobrze (Pleasant Dreams)* for Double Bass and Tape (Kazimierz Dolny, Poland, Sept. 8, 1983); *A Serbian Cabaret* for Violin, Viola, Cello, and Piano (Bath, June 8, 1984); *Sketches from a Bagpiper's Album* for Clarinet and Piano (1984; 1st complete perf., London, March 14, 1985); *The Bagpiper's String Trio* for Violin, Viola, and Cello (Cambridge, May 19, 1985); *Airs from Another Planet* for Flute, Oboe, Clarinet, Bassoon, Horn, and Piano (Fife, Oct. 14, 1986); *Gentle Violence* for Piccolo and Guitar (London, April 10, 1987); *Mountain Airs* for Flute, Oboe, and Clarinet (Tunbridge Wells, Feb. 25, 1988); *Distance and Enchantment* for Piano, Violin, Viola, and Cello (London, Sept. 26, 1989); *Heaven Ablaze in His Breast* for Chorus, 2 Pianos, and 8 Dancers (Basildon, Oct. 5, 1989); String Quartet (Liverpool, Oct. 2, 1990); *I Broke Off a Golden Branch* for Violin, Viola, Cello, Double Bass, and Piano (1991; Cheltenham, July 5, 1992); *El Rey de Francia* for Violin, Viola, Cello, and Piano (London, April 8, 1993); *Musicians Wrestle Everywhere* for 10 Players (1994; Birmingham, March 5, 1995); *Sleep Sound Ida Mornin'* for 2 Violins (Boston, Jan. 28, 1995); *The Story Behind the Song is Forgotten* for Flute, Oboe, Clarinet, Piano, Cello, and Percussion (London, Nov. 18, 1997); Piano Trio (1997–98; N.Y., May 19, 1998); *Free Standing Flexible Structure* for Chamber Ensemble (Birmingham, Nov. 23, 1998); *Unlocked* for Cello (Birmingham, May 28, 1999). **KEYBOARD: Piano:** *An Mein Klavier* (Blacknell, July 20, 1980); *The Art of Touching the Keyboard* (London, May 31, 1983); *Michael's Strathspey* (London, Dec. 17, 1985); *Ardnamurchan Point* for 2 Pianos (London, Oct. 18, 1990); *Roll Off the Ragged Rocks of Sin* (London, Oct. 1, 1992); *The King of France* (1993; London, Jan. 5, 1994). **Organ:** *Wild Mossy Mountains* (Edinburgh, Sept. 10, 1982); *Ettrick Banks* (Edinburgh, Aug. 28, 1985). **VOCAL:** *25 Variations* for Soprano and 6 Players (1976); *Black Birdsong* for Baritone, Flute, Oboe, Violin, and Cello (Oxford, Nov. 5, 1977); *King Harald's Saga* for Soprano (Dumfries, May 17, 1979); *Scotch Minstrelsy* for Tenor or Soprano and Piano (Glasgow, May 14, 1982); *Ascending Into Heaven* for Chorus and Organ (St. Albans, July 5, 1983); *The Consolations of Scholarship* for Soprano and Chamber Ensemble (Durham, May 5, 1985); *Illuminare, Jerusalem (Jerusalem, Rejoice for Joy)* for Chorus and Organ (Cambridge, Dec. 24, 1985); *Songs from the Exotic* for Low Voice and Piano (Cambridge, Oct. 7, 1987); *Lovers, Learners, and Libations* for Mezzo-soprano, Tenor, Baritone, and Early Music Consort (1987; Glasgow, Feb. 12, 1988); *A Spanish Liederbooklet* for Soprano and Piano (Cheltenham, July 6, 1988); *Missa del Cid* for Chorus and Speaker (1988); *The Romance of Count Arnaldos* for Soprano and 5 Players (Brighton, May 13, 1989); *Don't Let That Horse* for Soprano and Horn (Glasgow, Sept. 16, 1990); *Ox Mountain Was Covered by Trees* for Soprano, Countertenor, Baritone, and Orch. (Canterbury, Sept. 30, 1990; also for Soprano, Countertenor, and Piano, London, Sept. 30, 1997); *On Buying a Horse* for Medium Voice and Piano (1991; Edinburgh, Feb. 18, 1992); *The Alps* for Soprano, Clarinet, and Viola (1992; Plymouth, May 28, 1993); *Broken Branches* for Soprano, Piano, and String Bass (N.Y., May 23, 1992); *2 Human Hymns* for Chorus and Organ (1994; Aberdeen, Oct. 1995); *Our Revels Now Are Ended* for Women's Voices and Chamber Ensemble (London, March 21, 1995); *Moon and Star* for Chorus and Orch. (London, Aug. 11, 1995); *Sanctus* for Chorus and Orch. (Stuttgart, Aug. 15, 1995); *Horse d'oeuvres* for Mezzo-soprano and Orch. (London, June 24, 1996); *Ständchen* for Baritone and Piano (1997); *Storm* for Youth Chorus and Chamber Ensemble (1997);

My Guardian Angel for Chorus and Audience (London, Dec. 23, 1997); *Natural History* for Soprano and Orch. (1998; Boston, Jan. 14, 1999); *All the Ends of the Earth* for Chorus, 3 Percussion, and Harp (London, Sept. 28, 1999).—**NS/LK/DM**

Weis, (Carl) Flemming, Danish composer and organist; b. Copenhagen, April 15, 1898; d. there, Sept. 30, 1981. He studied organ and theory with Gustav Helsted at the Copenhagen Cons. (1916–20), then took courses in organ with Karl Straube and in theory and composition with Paul Graener at the Leipzig Hochschule für Musik (graduated, 1923). He served as organist of the St. Anna Church in Copenhagen (1929–68); was a member of the board of the Soc. for Contemporary Music (1926–56; president, 1942–56) and a member of the board of the Danish Soc. of Composers (president, 1963–75). His music followed the traditions of the Danish School. Under the influence of Carl Nielsen, he wrote a number of symphonic pieces imbued with Romantic fervor and gentle humor.

WORKS: ORCH.: *Praeludium og Intermezzo* for Oboe and Strings (1933); Concertino for Clarinet and Strings (1935); *Symphonic Overture* (1938); *Introduction grave* for Piano and Orch. (1941); 2 syms. (1942, 1948); *In temporis vernalis* (1945; Copenhagen, Jan. 14, 1948); *Musikantiski ouverture* (1949); Concertino for Strings (1960); *Femdelt form III* (Quintuple Form III; Randers, Feb. 5, 1963); *Sine nomine* (Copenhagen, March 18, 1973); *Chaconne* (1974). **CHAMBER:** 4 string quartets (1922, 1925, 1937, 1977); *Music* for 3 Woodwinds (1928); Clarinet Sonata (1931); Violin Sonata (1932–41); *Serenade uden reelle hensigter* (Serenade without Serious Intentions) for Wind Quintet (1938); Sonatina for Flute, Violin, and Cello (1942); *Diverterende musik* (Diverting Music) for Flute, Violin, Viola, and Cello (1943); Oboe Sonata (1946); *Variations* for Wind Quintet (1946); Flute Sonata (1956); *Fantasia seria* for String Quartet (1956); *5 Epigrams* for String Quartet (1960); *Femdelt form II* (Quintuple Form II) for String Quintet (1962); *Rhapsodic Suite* for Violin (1966); *Static Situations* for String Quartet (1970); *3 sstre* (3 Sisters) for Cello (1973); *3 Mobiles* for Flute, Violin, Viola, and Cello (1974); *3 Aspects* for Guitar (1975); *Dialogues* for Flute and Guitar (1977). **KEYBOARD: Piano:** Suite (1945–46); Sonatina (1949); *12 Monologues* (1958); *Femdelt form I* (Quintuple Form I; 1961); *Limitations I* (1965) and *II* (1968). **Organ:** Concertino (1957). **VOCAL:** *Det forjoettede land* (The Promised Land) for Chorus and Orch. (Copenhagen, Nov. 8, 1949); *Coeli enarrant* for Soprano and Organ (1955–56); *Sinfonia proverbiorum* for Chorus and Orch. (Copenhagen, June 21, 1959); *3 Japanese Bird Cries* for Soprano, Viola, and Guitar (1976); choruses; anthems; songs.—**NS/LK/DM**

Weis, Karel, Czech writer on music, ethnomusicologist, and composer; b. Prague, Feb. 13, 1862; d. there, April 4, 1944. He studied violin at the Prague Cons., and also organ with Skuherský and composition with Fibich at the Organ School in Prague. He subsequently filled various posts as organist and conductor in Prague and other cities. He devoted much of his time to collecting Bohemian folk songs, and publ. them in 15 vols. (1928–41).

WORKS: DRAMATIC: Opera: *Viola,* after Shakespeare's *Twelfth Night* (Prague, Jan. 17, 1892; rev. version as *Blíženci* [The Twins], Prague, Feb. 28, 1917); *Der polnische Jude* (Prague, March 3, 1901); *Die Dorfmusikanten* (Prague, Jan. 1, 1905); *Der Revisor,* after Gogol (1907); *Utok na mlýn,* after Zola's *L'Attaque du moulin* (Prague, March 29, 1912); *Lešetínský kovář* (The Blacksmith of Lesetin; Prague, June 6, 1920); *Bojarská nevěsta* (The Boyar's Bride; Prague, Feb. 18, 1943). **OTHER:** *Helios a Selene,* symphonic poem; Sym.; choral pieces; songs; piano works.

BIBL.: L. Firkušný, *K. W.* (Prague, 1949).—**NS/LK/DM**

Weisberg, Arthur, American bassoonist and conductor; b. N.Y., April 4, 1931. He attended the Juilliard School of Music in N.Y., where he studied bassoon with Simon Kovar and conducting with Jean Morel. He played bassoon with the Houston, Baltimore, and Cleveland orchs.; from 1956 to 1970, he was bassoonist with the N.Y. Woodwind Quintet. In 1960 he formed the Contemporary Chamber Ensemble, with which he travels widely in Europe and America. He held teaching posts at the Juilliard School of Music (1960–68), at the State Univ. of N.Y. at Stony Brook (1971–89), and at Yale Univ. (1975–89). In 1987–88 he was chief conductor of the Iceland Sym. Orch. in Reykjavík. He publ. *The Art of Wind Playing* (1973) and *Performing Twentieth-Century Music: A Handbook for Conductors and Instrumentalists* (1993).—**NS/LK/DM**

Weisgall, Hugo (David), distinguished Moravian-born American composer and pedagogue; b. Eibenschütz, Oct. 13, 1912. He emigrated with his family to the U.S. and became a naturalized American citizen in 1926. He studied at the Peabody Cons. of Music in Baltimore (1927–32), and subsequently had composition lessons with Sessions at various times between 1932 and 1941. He also was a pupil of Reiner (conducting diploma, 1938) and Scalero (composition diploma, 1939) at the Curtis Inst. of Music in Philadelphia, and pursued academic studies at Johns Hopkins Univ. (Ph.D., 1940, with a diss. on primitivism in 17th-century German poetry). After military service in World War II, he was active as a conductor, singer, teacher, and composer. He was founder-conductor of the Chamber Soc. of Baltimore (1948) and the Hilltop Opera Co. (1952), and was director of the Baltimore Inst. of Musical Arts (1949–51). He taught at Johns Hopkins Univ. (1951–57); also was made chairman of the faculty of the Cantors' Inst. at the Jewish Theological Center in N.Y. in 1952. He taught at the Juilliard School of Music (1957–70) and at Queens Coll. of the City Univ. of N.Y. (from 1961). He served as president of the American Music Center (1963–73). In 1966 he was composer-in-residence at the American Academy in Rome. He held 3 Guggenheim fellowships and received many prizes and commissions; in 1975 he was elected to membership in the National Inst. of Arts and Letters, and in 1990 became president of the American Academy and Inst. of Arts and Letters, which, in 1994, awarded him its Gold Medal for Music. Weisgall's music constitutes the paragon of enlightened but inoffensive modernism; he is a master of all musical idioms, and bungler of none. His intentions in each of his works never fail in the execution; for this reason his music enjoys numerous performances, which are usually accepted with pleasure by the audiences, if not by the majority of important music critics.

Works: Dramatic: Opera: *Night* (1932); *Lillith* (1934); *The Tenor* (1948–50; Baltimore, Feb. 1, 1952); *The Stronger* (Lutherville, Md., Aug. 9, 1952); *6 Characters in Search of an Author* (1953–56; N.Y., April 26, 1959); *Purgatory* (1958; Washington, D.C., Feb. 17, 1961); *The Gardens of Adonis* (1959; rev. 1977–81; Omaha, Sept. 12, 1992); *Athaliah* (1960–63; N.Y., Feb. 17, 1964); *9 Rivers from Jordan* (1964–68; N.Y., Oct. 9, 1968); *Jennie, or The Hundred Nights* (1975–76; N.Y., April 22, 1976); *Esther* (N.Y., Oct. 6, 1993). **Ballet:** *Quest* (Baltimore, May 17, 1938; suite, N.Y., March 21, 1942); *Art Appreciation* (Baltimore, 1938); *One Thing Is Certain* (Baltimore, Feb. 25, 1939); Outpost (1947). **ORCH.:** *Overture in F* (London, July 29, 1943); *Appearances and Entrances* (1960); *Proclamation* (1960); *Prospect* (1983); *Tekiator* (1985). **CHAMBER:** *Graven Images*, chamber pieces for Various Instruments (1964 et seq.); *Arioso and Burlesca* for Cello and Piano (1984); *Tangents* for Flute and Marimba (1985). **KEYBOARD: Piano:** 2 sonatas (1931, 1982); *Variations* (1939). **Organ:** *Chorale Prelude* (1938). **VOCAL:** *Hymn* for Chorus and Orch. (1941); *Soldier Songs* for Baritone and Orch. (1944–46; N.Y., April 26, 1954; rev. 1965; Baltimore, March 30, 1966); *A Garden Eastward*, cantata for High Voice and Orch. (1952; Baltimore, Jan. 31, 1953); solo songs.—**NS/LK/DM**

Weisgarber, Elliot, American-born Canadian composer, clarinetist, and teacher; b. Pittsfield, Mass., Dec. 5, 1919. He received training in clarinet from Rosario Mazzeo, from Gustave Lanzenus in N.Y., and from R. Mont Arey at the Eastman School of Music in Rochester, N.Y., where he also studied composition (B.Mus., 1942; M.Mus., 1943). He later pursued his studies in composition with Boulanger in Paris (1952–53) and with Halsey Stevens in Los Angeles (1958–59). From 1944 to 1958 he taught at the Women's Coll. of the Univ. of N.C. He also played clarinet in orchs. and chamber music groups. After teaching at the Univ. of Calif. at Los Angeles (1958–59), he was on the faculty of the Univ. of British Columbia in Vancouver (1960–84). In 1973 he became a naturalized Canadian citizen. He received Canada Council grants to study music in Japan (1966; 1967; 1968–69), where he learned to play the shakuhachi. In his music, Weisgarber has composed not only scores along traditional Western lines but also pieces utilizing Japanese folk melos and instruments.

Works: Dramatic: Television and radio scores. **ORCH.:** 3 syms. (1961–83); *Sinfonia Concertante* for Oboe, 2 Horns, and Strings (1962); *Kyoto Landscapes: Lyrical Evocations* (1970; rev. 1972); *Illahee Chanties* for Chamber Orch. (1971); *Autumnal Music* for English Horn and Strings (1973); *Musica serena* for Small Orch. (1974); *Netori: A Fantasie* for Alto Saxophone and Orch. (1974); Violin Concerto (1974; rev. 1987); *A Pacific Trilogy* (1974); *A Northumbrian Elegy* (1977). **CHAMBER:** Sonata for Flute, Clarinet, and Piano (1953); *Divertimento* for String Trio (1956) and for Horn, Viola, and Piano (1959); Flute Sonata (1963); Suite for Viola and Piano (1964); Sonata for Solo Cello (1965); *Epigrams* for Flute and Koto or Piano (1970; rev. 1973); *Rokudan Henko-no-shirabe* for 2 Kotos and 2 Shamisen (1971); *6 Miniatures After Hokusai* for Violin and Piano (1972); *Fantasia a Tre* for Violin, Horn, and Piano (1975); Cello Sonata (1980); String Quartet No. 6 (1980); *32 Concert Études* for Clarinet (1986); Clarinet Quintet (1988); *Sonata Piacevole* for Clarinet and Piano (1990); *Music in Memory of Andrei Sakharov* for Flute, Violin, Viola, Cello, and Piano (1990); Trio for Violin, Cello, and Piano (1993); *Amadablam: A Soliloquy* for Piano (1994). **VOCAL:** *Num mortuis resurgent?*, cantata for Chorus (1963; rev. 1973); *Ren-ai-to toki ni tsuite* (Of Love and Time) for Soprano, Flute, Oboe, String Trio, and Harpsichord (1971); *Night* for Baritone, Chorus, and String Quartet or String Orch. (1973; rev. 1982); *As We Stood Then*, song cycle for Mezzo-soprano or Baritone, Viola, and Piano (1975); *Illusions of Mortality*, song cycle for Voice and Piano (1975); *Canticle* for Chorus, Horn, and Strings (1978); *10 Japanese Folk Songs* for Soprano and Piano (1981); *Omnia Exeunt in Misterium*, song cycle for Soprano and Orch. (1994).—**NS/LK/DM**

Weiskopf, Joel, jazz pianist, brother of **Walt Weiskopf;** b. Syracuse, N.Y., March 31, 1962. At age four he started playing piano by ear. He studied formally until 17 when he won top honors at the N.Y. Scholastic Music Association Classical Piano Competition. After high school he attended the New England Cons. of Music in Boston, Mass. He was soon chosen as a member of the New England Cons. Honors Jazz Quintet, which toured throughout the greater Boston area. In 1985 he graduated with "Distinction in Performance" and moved to N.Y.C. Soon thereafter he got the call to join Woody Herman. He played, composed, and arranged for Herman's band for one year and left the band shortly berfore Herman's death in 1987. Weiskopf then moved back to N.Y.C. In 1989 he won first place in the Great American Jazz Piano Competition. Since then he has worked with Gerry Mulligan, Hubert Laws, Clark Terry, Mel Lewis, Quincy Jones, the Buddy Rich Band, Joe Lovano, Dakota Staton, and Julius Hemphill as well as with L. Subramanium, and Salamat Ali Khan. He has also recorded with Larry Coryell, Tom Harrell, Jimmy Cobb, Billy Hart, Richard Stoltzman, Shunzu Ono, Charli Persip, and his brother **Walt Weiskopf.** He performs throughout the N.Y. area with his trio and quintet.

Disc.: WALT WEISKOPF: *Night Lights* (1995); *Songs for My Mother* (1997); *Search* (1999).—**LP**

Weiskopf, Walt(er David), soprano and tenor saxophone, composer, brother of **Joel Weiskopf;** b. Fort Gordon, Ga., July 30, 1959. He was born when his father, a doctor, was a captain in the Army. Soon his family moved to Syracuse, N.Y., where he grew up with his younger brother Joel. They had a piano at home and their father played often, mostly Classical music: Chopin, Grieg, and others. Weiskopf took piano lessons for a few months at age five; he started playing clarinet in fourth grade. Later, became interested in jazz and switched to alto saxophone. At first he was mainly aware of big bands—Woody Herman, Stan Kenton, Basie, Ellington—but then he heard Miles Davis's *My Funny Valentine* and it became his favorite album. Later, he got some Charlie Parker records, as well as Stan Getz, Dexter Gordon, and Coltrane; at about 15 he began transcribing solos. At 16 he landed a gig in a local big band in Syracuse, and was thrilled sitting next to J. R. Monterose, who became a mentor. In 1980 he took a Bachelor's degree from the Eastman School of Music in Rochester, N.Y., where he studied saxophone with Ramon Ricker. He moved to N.Y.C. in fall of 1980. He became friendly with Ralph LaLama and altoist Andy Fusco, both of whom were playing with the Buddy Rich band. When LaLama left the band, Weiskopf was invited to take his place on tenor. He stayed for two years and the tenor became his main instrument. He joined the Toshiko Akiyoshi Jazz Orch. on second tenor in 1983, after the group relocated to N.Y. from Los Angeles; he has recorded four CDs with the Orch. as well as three with Akiyoshi's small group. In the late 1980s, during his tenure with the Akiyoshi Band, he began working with and writing for his own rehearsal quartet that included pianist Joel Weiskopf, bassist Jay Anderson, and drummer Jeff Hirshfield; the first of his CDs as a leader was recorded in 1989. He studied under clarinetist Leon Russianoff in 1988–89 and earned an MA in clarinet performance from Queens Coll. of the City Univ. of N.Y. During his years in N.Y., Weiskopf has been featured with drummer/composer Roland Vazquez, pianist Renee Rosnes, drummer Eliot Zigmund, the Carnegie Hall Jazz Band, and the Andy LaVerne group (1998). He joined drummer Rick Hollander's quartet in 1996. Weiskopf has performed with the American Ballet Theatre Orch., the American Composer's Orch., and the Concordia Chamber Orch.; he performed the Aaron Copland Concerto for clarinet as guest soloist with the Gotham Chamber Orch. in N.Y.C. (1994) and received performance grants from the National Endowment for the Arts in 1989, 1991, and 1994 to fund live performances of his music in N.Y.C. Since 1991 he has been a regular fixture at Jamey Aebersold's Summer Jazz Workshops and is currently is on the faculty at Jersey City State Coll. in N.J. and the New School in N.Y.

DISC.: *Exact Science* (1989); *Mindwalking* (1990); *Simplicity* (1992); *World Away* (1995); *Song for My Mother* (1997).—**LP**

Weismann, Julius, German pianist, conductor, and composer; b. Freiburg im Breisgau, Dec. 26, 1879; d. Singen am Hohentweil, Dec. 22, 1950. He began piano lessons at 9 with Seyffart, and later studied composition with Rheinberger in Munich (1892). He received advanced piano training from Dimmler in Freiburg im Breisgau (1893) and took courses at the Univ. of Lausanne; he also studied composition with Bussmeyer, von Herzogenberg in Berlin (1898–99), and Thuille in Munich (1899–1902). He was active as a pianist and conductor in Freiburg im Breisgau from 1906, where he founded (with E. Doflein) the Musikseminar in 1930, subsequently serving as a teacher of harmony and as director of the piano master class; after retiring in 1939, he devoted himself fully to composition. He received the Beethoven Prize (1930), the Bach Prize of Leipzig (1939), and the Ehrenbürgerrecht of Freiburg im Breisgau (1939); was made an honorary prof. by the government (1936) and by the state of Baden (1950). The Julius Weismann Archive was founded in his memory in Duisburg in 1954.

WORKS: DRAMATIC: Opera: *Schwanenweiss* (1919–20; Duisburg, Sept. 29, 1923); *Ein Traumspiel* (1922–24; Duisburg, 1925); *Leonce und Lena* (Mannheim, 1924); *Regina del lago* (Karlsruhe, 1928); *Die Gespenstersonate* (1929–30; Munich, Dec. 19, 1930); *Die pfiffige Magd* (1937–38; Leipzig, Feb. 11, 1939). **Ballet:** *Tanzphantasie* (1910; orchestrated from the piano piece); *Die Landsknechte: Totentanz* (1936); *Sinfonisches Spiel* (1937). **ORCH.:** 3 piano concertos (1909–10, rev. 1936; 1941–42; 1942–48); 4 violin concertos (1910–11; 1929; 1942; 1943); *Suite* for Piano and Orch. (1927); Concerto for Flute, Clarinet, Bassoon, Trumpet, Timpani, and Strings (1930); Horn Concerto (1935); Cello Concerto (1941–43); 2 syms. (1940, 1940); *Theme, Variations and Fugue* for Trautonium and Orch. (1943; also for Violin and Piano); *Musik* for Bassoon and Orch. (1947). **CHAMBER:** Piano Quintet (1902); 13 string quartets (1905; 1907; 1910; *Fantastischer Reigen*, 1913; 1914; 1918–22; 1922; 1929; *Fugue*, 1931; 1932; 1940; 1943–45; 1947); 3 piano trios (1908–09; 1916; 1921); 4 violin sonatas (1909; 1917; 1917, arranged for Clarinet and Piano, 1941; 1921); Flute Sonata (1941); *Sonatina concertante* for Cello and Piano (1941; also for Cello and Chamber Orch.); Trio for Flute, Clarinet, and Bassoon (1942); *Theme, Variations and Fugue* for Violin and Piano (1943; also for Trautonium and Orch.); Viola Sonata (1945); various other chamber works; piano pieces. **VOCAL:** *Macht hoch die Tür*, Christmas cantata for Soprano, Chorus, and Orch. (1912); *Psalm XC* for Baritone, Chorus, and Orch. (1912); *Der Wächterruf* for Soprano, Baritone, Chorus, and Orch. (1947–50); various men's and women's choruses; solo songs.

BIBL.: F. Herzfeld, *J. W. und seine Generation* (Duisburg, 1965).—**NS/LK/DM**

Weiss, family of German musicians:

(1) Johann Jacob Weiss, lutenist and composer; b. c. 1662; d. Mannheim, Jan. 30, 1754. He was active in Breslau from about 1686. Around 1708 he was made court lutenist of the Palatine chapel in Düsseldorf, following it to Heidelberg in 1718 and to Mannheim in 1720.

(2) Silvius Leopold Weiss, lutenist and composer, son of the preceding; b. Breslau, Oct. 12, 1686; d. Dresden, Oct. 16, 1750. He most likely was a pupil of his father. He was in the service of Count Carl Philipp of the Palatinate in Breslau by 1706, and then was in Italy with Alexander Sobiesky, Prince of Poland (1708–14). In 1715 he entered the service of the Hessen- Kassel court, and shortly thereafter went to Düsseldorf; in 1717 he joined the chapel of the Saxon court in Dresden, where his status was formalized in 1718. He also traveled as a virtuoso, appearing in Prague (1717), London (1718), Vienna (1718–19), Munich (1722), Berlin (1728), and Leipzig (1739), where he visited J.S. Bach. Weiss was one of the foremost performers on and composers for the lute. His extant works number almost 600, the largest corpus of solo lute works by any composer in history. D. Smith ed. his complete works (Frankfurt am Main, 1980 et seq.). His son, Johann Adolf Faustinus Weiss (b. Dresden, April 15, 1741; d. there, Jan. 21, 1814), was also a lutenist and composer who served as chamber lutenist at the Dresden court from 1763 until his death. He traveled widely, and composed a number of lute pieces and some guitar music.

BIBL.: K. Prusik, *Kompositionen des Lautenisten S.L. W.* (diss., Univ. of Vienna, 1924); W. Mason, *The Lute Music of S.L. W.* (diss., Univ. of N.C., 1949); D. Smith, *The Late Sonatas of S.L. W.* (diss., Stanford Univ., 1977); U. Neu, *Harmonik und Affektgestaltung in den Lautenkompositionen von S.L. W.* (Frankfurt am Main, 1995).

(3) Johann Sigismund Weiss, lutenist, viola da gambist, violinist, and composer, brother of the preceding; b. probably in Breslau, c. 1689; d. Mannheim, April 12,

1737. He most likely studied with his father. He became a lutenist at the Palatine chapel in Düsseldorf about 1708, following it to Heidelberg in 1718 and to Mannheim in 1720. In 1732 he was named director of instrumental music there, and later served as Konzertmeister and theorbo player. As a composer, he was one of the finest representatives of the early Mannheim school.—**NS/LK/DM**

Weiss, Adolph, American composer and bassoonist; b. Baltimore, Sept. 12, 1891; d. Van Nuys, Calif., Feb. 21, 1971. He studied piano, violin, and bassoon, and at the age of 16 was engaged as 1st bassoonist of the Russian Sym. Orch. of N.Y.; then joined the N.Y. Phil. (1909) and the N.Y. Sym. Orch. (1910). He also studied composition with Cornelius Rybner at Columbia Univ. In 1916 he joined the Chicago Sym. Orch. as bassoonist, and also studied theory with Adolf Weidig and Theodore Ötterstrom in Chicago; then was bassoonist with the Eastman Theatre Orch. in Rochester, N.Y. (from 1921). In 1926 he went to Berlin and became the first American student of Schoenberg, whose influence was decisive in the formation of his musical style. Returning to the U.S., he played in the San Francisco Sym. Orch. (from 1936), the MGM Studios Orch. (from 1938), and the Los Angeles Phil. (from 1951). He held a Guggenheim fellowship (1931), and received a National Inst. of Arts and Letters award (1955).

WORKS: ORCH.: *I segreti* (1922; Rochester, N.Y., May 1, 1925); Chamber Sym. (1927); *American Life*, "scherzoso jazzoso" (1929; N.Y., Feb. 21, 1930); *Theme and Variations* (1933); Suite (1938); *10 Pieces* for Low Instrument and Orch. (1943); Trumpet Concerto (1952). **CHAMBER:** 3 string quartets (1925, 1926, 1932); *Sonata da camera* for Flute and Viola (1929); Quintet for Flute, Oboe, Clarinet, Bassoon, and Horn (1931); *Petite suite* for Flute, Clarinet, and Bassoon (1939); Violin Sonata (1941); *Passacaglia* for Horn and Viola (1942); Sextet for Flute, Oboe, Clarinet, Bassoon, Horn, and Piano (1947); Trio for Clarinet, Viola, and Cello (1948); Concerto for Bassoon and String Quartet (1949); Trio for Flute, Violin, and Piano (1955); *5 Fantasies* for Violin and Piano (1956); *Tone Poem* for Brass and Percussion (1957); *Rhapsody* for 4 Horns (1957); *Vade mecum* for Wind Instruments (1958). **Piano:** *Fantasie* (1918); *12 Preludes* (1927); Sonata (1932); *Protest* for 2 Pianos (1945); *Pulse of the Sea* (1950). **VOCAL:** *7 Songs* for Soprano and String Quartet (1928); *The Libation Bearers*, choreographic cantata for Soloists, Chorus, and Orch. (1930); *Ode to the West Wind* for Baritone, Viola, and Piano (1945).

BIBL.: W. George, *A. W.* (diss., Univ. of Iowa, 1971); B. Kopp, *The Twelve-tone Techniques of A. W.* (diss., Northwestern Univ., 1981).—**NS/LK/DM**

Weiss, Franz, Austrian violist and composer; b. Silesia, Jan. 18, 1778; d. Vienna, Jan. 25, 1830. When Prince Razumovsky formed his string quartet in Vienna (1808), Weiss was engaged as violist, with Schuppanzigh as 1st violin, Prince Razumovsky as 2nd violin, and Linke as cellist. Weiss composed some orch. pieces and chamber music.—**NS/LK/DM**

Weiss, Sid, jazz bassist; b. Schenectady, N.Y., April 30, 1914; d. Riverside, Calif., March 29, 1994. He started on violin, then played clarinet and tuba; he then switched to string bass while at high school. He first worked professionally at age 17 in N.Y.C. In the mid- to late-1930s, he worked with Wingy Manone (1934–36), Artie Shaw (1936; again September 1937–39 when the band broke up). After a few months in late 1939 with Joe Marsala, he joined Tommy Dorsey (March 1940–November 1941), and then spent three years with Benny Goodman (1943–45). After working with Goodman, he did a USO tour, then returned to the U.S. where, from 1946, he was primarily active as a studio musician. He did work on occasion with several leaders, including Eddie Condon, Joe Bushkin, and Benny Goodman (including appearance with Benny in the film *Make Mine Music*) during the late 1940s. He moved to Los Angeles in August 1954, where he held a day job working in an electronics company; he continued to gig and play sessions through the mid-1960s. In 1968, he was appointed business representative for recording department of Local 47, Musicians' Union, a position he held for three years, and he then worked for the Calif. department of labor until his retirement in 1979.

DISC.: "Swingin' on That Famous Door" (1935); "On the Sunny Side of the Street" (1941); "Limehouse Blues" (1941); "If I Had You" (1941); "The World is Waiting for the Sunrise" (1942); "The Wang Wang Blues" (1942); "Rachel's Dream" (1944); "Only Another Boy and Girl" (1944); *The Complete Commodore Jazz Recordings, Vol.2* (1944); *After You've Gone* (1944); *Concerto for Cozy Cozy Cole 1944* (1970); *Piano After Midnight* (1957); *Concerto for Cozy* (1959); *Chicago Jazz* (1950); *The B.G. Six* (1945); *After Hours with Joe Bushkin* (1952); *The Pied Piper of Jazz* (1982).—**JC/LP**

Weissberg, Yulia (Lazarevna), Russian composer; b. Orenburg, Jan. 6, 1880; d. Leningrad, March 1, 1942. She studied piano with Rimsky- Korsakov and instrumentation with Glazunov at the St. Petersburg Cons. (1903–05) and continued her musical training with Humperdinck and Reger in Germany (1907–12). She was a co-ed. of the journal *Muzykalny Sovremennik* (1915–17) and choral director of the Young Workers' Cons. (1921–23). She married **Andrei Rimsky-Korsakov**.

WORKS: DRAMATIC: Opera: *Rusalochka* (1923); *Gulnara* (1935); *Gusi-lebedi* (Geese Swans; 1937); *Myortvaya tsarevna* (The Dead Princess; 1937). **ORCH.:** *Skazochka* (Tale; 1928); *Nochyu* (At Night), symphonic poem (1929); *Ballade* (1930); *Sailor's Dance* (1936). **VOCAL:** *Rautendelein* for Voice and Orch. (1912); *Poyot pechalniy golos* (A Sad Voice Sings) for Voice and Orch. (1924); *Dvenadsat* (The 12) for Chorus and Orch. (Leningrad, May 12, 1926); *5 Children's Songs* for Voice and Orch. (1929); *Lunnaya skazka* (The Story of the Moon) for Voice, Flute, and String Quartet (1929); *Garafitsa* for Voice, Cello, and Harp or Piano (1938); numerous solo songs; children's choruses; folk song arrangements.—**NS/LK/DM**

Weissenberg, Alexis (Sigismond), noted Bulgarian-born French pianist; b. Sofia, July 26, 1929. He studied piano at a very early age with his mother, and then pursued training with Pantcho Vladigerov. During the German occupation of his homeland, he and his mother were briefly confined in a concentration camp but then were allowed to emigrate to Palestine; in 1945 he made his first appearance as a soloist with an orch. there. In 1946 he went to N.Y. to study at the Juilliard School of Music; his principal mentor was Olga Samaroff, but he also received instruction from Artur Schnabel and Wanda Landowska. In 1947 he won the Leventritt Competition, which led to his U.S. debut that same year with George Szell and the N.Y. Phil.; after touring extensively, he settled in France in 1956, became a naturalized citizen. He withdrew from public appearances for a decade in which he devoted himself to further study and teaching. In 1966 he resumed his career and subsequently toured all over the world. **—NS/LK/DM**

Weissenborn, Günther (Albert Friedrich), German pianist and conductor; b. Coburg, June 2, 1911. He studied at the Hochschule für Musik in Berlin. He was an organist and choir director in Berlin (1934–37). He was then a conductor in Halle (1937–42), Hannover (1944), and Göttingen (1945–47) before returning to Hannover as conductor of the Hausegger Chamber Orch. Apart from his activities as a conductor, Weissenborn earned a fine reputation as a piano accompanist in lieder recitals.**—NS/LK/DM**

Weissensee, Friedrich, distinguished German composer; b. Schwerstedt, Thuringia, c. 1560; d. Altenweddingen, near Magdeburg, 1622. He became Rektor of the grammar school in Gebesee, near Erfurt, in 1590, and about 1596 he was made Kantor at the grammar school in Magdeburg; in 1602 he became a clergyman in Altenweddingen. He was one of the finest German composers of Protestant church music of his era.

WORKS (all publ. in Magdeburg): *Evangelisch Sprüche auf die vornehmsten Fest-Tage* for 5 Voices (1595); *Hochzeit-Lied aus den Sprüchwörten Salomonis am 31. Capitel...dem...Peters Rathmann* for 6 Voices (1599); *Hochzeitlicher Ehren Dantz, auff das adelige Beylager des...Wolffgang Spitznasen zu Magdeburgk Domherrn* for 6 Voices (1600); *Opus melicum methodicum et plane novum, singulis diebus...et festis accomodatas* for 4 to 10 and 12 Voices (1602); *Geistliche Braut und Hochzeit Gesang, zu Ehren...Georgio Schultzen* for 6 Voices (1611); *Sponsis novellis* for 8 Voices (1619); *Geistlich Braut und Hochzeitliedt, ex Cant. Cant. Cantic. Cap. 5 und 7 ad 9* for 6 Voices (n.d.); various other works in contemporary collections.

BIBL.: B. Engelke, *F. W. und sein Opus melicum* (diss., Univ. of Kiel, 1927).**—NS/LK/DM**

Weitzmann, Carl Friedrich, noted German music theorist, writer on music, and composer; b. Berlin, Aug. 10, 1808; d. there, Nov. 7, 1880. He studied violin with Henning and theory with Klein, and later, at Kassel, was a pupil of Spohr and Hauptmann. He was concertmaster in Riga (1832–34), Reval (1834–36), and St. Petersburg (1836–46). After sojourns in Paris and London (1846–48), he settled in Berlin as a teacher of composition. He was an ardent disciple and friend of Wagner and Liszt; among his posthumous papers was found the original MS of a double fugue for piano by Wagner, with corrections in the handwriting of Weinlig (Wagner's teacher). The piece was publ. by E. Istel in *Die Musik* (July 1912). Weitzmann was an original thinker in his harmonic theories; made an investigation of the modulatory functions of the whole-tone scale, and interested Liszt in its use. He composed a 4th variation to Liszt's *Todtentanz.* A full exposition of his theories is found in a book by his American pupil E.M. Bowman, *K.F. Weitzmann's Manual of Musical Theory* (N.Y., 1877). Weitzmann's theoretical works include *Der übermässige Dreiklang* (1853), *Geschichte der Septimen-Akkordes* (1854), *Der verminderte Septimen-Akkord* (1854), *Geschichte der griechischen Musik* (1855), *Harmoniesystem* (1860), *Die neue Harmonielehre im Streit mit der alten* (1861), *Geschichte des Klavierspiels und der Klavierlitteratur* (1863, as Part III of the Lebert- Stark piano method; 2nd ed., 1879, printed separately, with an added *Geschichte des Klaviers;* Eng. tr., N.Y., 1894, with a biographical sketch by Otto Lessmann; 3rd Ger. ed., Leipzig, 1899, as *Geschichte der Klaviermusik,* ed. by Max Seiffert, with a suppl., *Geschichte des Klaviers,* by Otto Fleischer), and *Der letzte der Virtuosen* (on Tausig; 1868). He also wrote many essays for various musical periodicals. As a composer, he followed the fashionable Romantic trends. His works include the operas *Räuberliebe* (1834), *Walpurgisnacht* (1835), and *Lorbeer und Bettelstab* (1836), which he brought out in Reval, as well as 3 books of *Valses nobles* for Piano, and *Preludes and Modulations* for Piano, in 2 parts, "Classic" and "Romantic." He also wrote 2 books of ingenious canonic *Rätsel* for Piano, 4-Hands, and 2 books of *Kontrapunkt-Studien* for Piano.**—NS/LK/DM**

Welcher, Dan, American composer, conductor, and teacher; b. Rochester, N.Y., March 2, 1948. He studied bassoon and composition (with Adler and Benson) at the Eastman School of Music in Rochester (B.Mus., 1969). Following further training in composition with Ulehla and Flagello at the Manhattan School of Music in N.Y. (M.M., 1972), he pursued postgraduate studies in electronic music at the Aspen (Colo.) Music School (summer, 1972). He was a bassoonist in the Rochester Phil. (1968–69) and the U.S. Military Academy Band at West Point, N.Y. (1969–72), and then was 1st bassoonist in the Louisville Orch. (1972–78). From 1972 to 1978 he also taught at the Univ. of Louisville. In 1976 he became a member of the artist faculty at the Aspen Music Festival, where he served each summer until 1993. In 1978 he joined the faculty of the Univ. of Tex. at Austin, where he was made a full prof. in 1989. In 1985–86 he was a visiting assoc. prof. at the Eastman School of Music. From 1980 to 1990 he was asst. conductor of the Austin Sym. Orch. He served as composer-in-residence of the Honolulu Sym. Orch. from 1990 to 1993.

WORKS: DRAMATIC: Opera: *Della's Gift* (1986; Austin, Tex., Feb. 1987). **ORCH.:** *Episodes* (1970; Buffalo, Jan. 1971); Flute Concerto (Louisville, April 1974); *Concerto da camera* for Bassoon and Small Orch. (1975); *Dervishes: Ritual Dance-Scene* (1976; Louisville, April 1977); *The Visions of Merlin* (1980); *Prairie Light: 3 Texas Watercolors of Georgia O'Keeffe* (1985; Sherman, Tex., March 1, 1986); *Arches: An Impression* for Concert Band (1985); *The Yellowstone Fires* for Wind Ensemble (1988); *Castle Creek,* fanfare-overture (Aspen, Colo., July 7, 1989); Clarinet Concerto (Honolulu, Oct. 15, 1989); *Haleakala: How Maui Snared the Sun* for Narrator and Orch. (Honolulu, Sept. 15, 1991); *Bridges,* 5 pieces for Strings (1991); 2 syms.: No. 1 (1992; Honolulu, April 4, 1993) and No. 2, *Night Watchers* (Flagstaff,

Ariz., Nov. 9, 1994); Violin Concerto (Aspen, Colo., July 2, 1993); Piano Concerto, *Shiva's Drum* (1993–94; Round Top Festival, Tex., June 11, 1994); *Zion* for Wind Ensemble (1994; Boulder, Colo., Feb. 24, 1995; also for Orch., 1999); *Bright Wings* (1995); *Spumante* (1997). **CHAMBER:** *Nocturne and Dance* for Trumpet and Piano (1966); *Elizabethan Variations* for 4 Recorders (1968); 3 wind quintets (1972, 1977, 1986); Violin Sonata (1974); Trio for Violin, Cello, and Piano (1976); *Partita* for Horn, Violin, and Piano (1980); *Fantasy: In Memoriam Anwar Sadat* for Carillon (1982); Brass Quintet (1983; N.Y., Feb. 1984); Quintet for Clarinet and Strings (N.Y., April 1984); *Hauntings* for Tuba Ensemble (1986); *Listen Up!* for Wind Quintet (1986); *White Mares of the Moon* for Flute and Harp (1986); 2 string quartets: No. 1 (1987; N.Y., May 11, 1988) and No. 2, *Harbor Music* (Cleveland, Oct. 28, 1992); *Firewing: The Flame and the Moth* for Oboe and Percussion (1987); *Chameleon Music* for 10 Percussionists (San Antonio, Nov. 1988); *Stigma* for Contrabass and Piano (N.Y., June 1989); *Zephyrus* for Flute, Violin, Viola, and Cello (1990); *Tsunami* for Cello, Percussion, and Piano (1991); *Phaedrus* for Clarinet, Violin, and Piano (1995); *Dante Dances* for Clarinet and Piano (1996); *Spirit Realms* for Flute and Percussion (1996); piano pieces. **VOCAL:** *Black Riders* for High Voice and Chamber Ensemble (1971); *Abeja Blanca* for Mezzo-soprano, English Horn, and Piano (1978); *Vox Femina* for Soprano and Ensemble (1984); *Evening Scenes: 3 Poems of James Agee* for Tenor and Ensemble (1985; Dallas, Jan. 1986); *Tickets for a Prayer Wheel* for Baritone and Viola (1997); *JFK: The Voice of Peace*, oratorio (1998); *Canticles of the Sun* for Chorus (2000).—**NS/LK/DM**

Weldon, George, English conductor; b. Chichester, June 5, 1906; d. Cape Town, South Africa, Aug. 16, 1963. He studied at the Royal Coll. of Music in London with Sargent. He conducted various provincial orchs., and traveled as a guest conductor in North Africa, Turkey, and Yugoslavia. He was conductor of the City of Birmingham Sym. Orch. (1943–51) and second conductor of the Halle Orch. in Manchester under Barbirolli (from 1952); he also conducted the Sadler's Wells Royal Ballet in London (1955–56).—**NS/LK/DM**

Weldon, Georgina (née **Thomas**), English soprano; b. London, May 24, 1837; d. Brighton, Jan. 11, 1914. She took up singing after her marriage to Capt. Weldon in 1860, and did not appear in public until 1870. She organized an orphan asylum for the purpose of musical education, and also dabbled in music publishing. Special interest attaches to her because of her romantic friendship with Gounod, who during his London sojourn (1870–75) lived at her residence, and whom she assisted in training the Gounod Choir. She translated his autobiography (which goes only as far as 1859) into English (1875). Their relationship deteriorated, leading to a legal entanglement in connection with her claims regarding the copyright of Gounod's choral works; she wrote acrimonious letters to the press, defending her stand. She also publ. some songs of her own (to French texts) and the didactic manuals *Hints for Pronunciation in Singing* (1872) and *Musical Reform* (1875).—**NS/LK/DM**

Welin, Karl-Erik (Vilhelm), Swedish organist, pianist, and composer; b. Genarp, May 31, 1934; d. Mallorca, May 30, 1992. He studied organ with Alf Linden at the Stockholm Musikhögskolan (graduated, 1961). He also received training in composition from Bucht (1958–60) and Lidholm (1960–64), in piano from Sven Brandel, and at the summer courses in new music in Darmstadt with David Tudor (1960–62). As a performer, he was a proponent of the extreme avant-garde in Sweden. He became well known via many appearances on Swedish TV. In contrast, his compositions followed a more mellow path. While he embraced serial techniques, he did so with Romantic elan.

WORKS: DRAMATIC: *Dummerjöns* (Tom Fool), children's television opera (1966–67); *Copelius*, ballet (1968); *Ondine*, theater music (1968); *Vindarnas grotta* (Cave of the Winds), television ballet (Stockholm TV, March 30, 1969); *Drottning Jag* (Queen Ego), opera (1972; Stockholm, Feb. 17, 1973); *Don Quijote*, scenic oratorio (1990–91). **ORCH.:** *Pereo* for 36 Strings (1964); Sym. (1985–86; Malmö, Oct. 22, 1987); Concertino for Clarinet, Viola, Piano, and Orch. (1987). **CHAMBER:** *Sermo modulatus* for Flute and Clarinet (1959); *Manzit* for Clarinet, Trombone, Violin, Piano, and Percussion (1962); *Esservecchia* for Electric Guitar, Horn, Trombone, and Piano (1963); *Warum nicht?* for Flute, Violin, Cello, Xylophone, Vibraphone, and Tam-tam (1964); 9 string quartets (c. 1964–90); *Etwas für...* for Wind Quintet (1966); *Ben fatto* for Instrument or an infinite number of Instruments (1968); *PC–132* for String Quartet (1970); *Harmonies* for Clarinet, Trombone, Cello, and Piano (1972); *Pagabile* for Chamber Ensemble (1972); *Eurytmi* for Piano Quartet (1979); *Denby-Richard* for Flute and Cello (1981); *Solo* for Bassoon (1983); *EssAEG* for 2 Pianos and Electronics (1988); *Viriditas per Omnibus* for 12 Instruments (1988). **VOCAL:** *4 Chinese Poems* for Chorus (1956); *Renovations* for Soprano, Flute, Violin, Mandolin, Celesta, and Percussion (1960); Cantata for Children's Chorus, Violin, Flute, and Harpsichord (1960); *Glazba* for Soprano, 3 Flutes, and Bassoon (1968); *A New Map of Hell* for Chorus (1971); *Aver la forza di...* for Chorus and String Orch. (1972); *Ett svenskt rekviem* for Soloists, Chorus, and Orch. (1976); *Flying Safe* for Soprano, Flute, and Chorus (1980); *L'aveu* for Soloists, Chorus, and Orch. (1982–83); *Crepusculo* for Chorus (1992).—**NS/LK/DM**

Welitsch (real name, **Veličkova**), **Ljuba,** remarkable Bulgarian-born Austrian soprano; b. Borissovo, July 10, 1913. She studied violin as a child. After attending the Sofia Cons. and the Univ. of Sofia, she studied voice with Lierhammer in Vienna. In 1936 she made her operatic debut at the Sofia Opera, and after singing in Graz (1937–40), Hamburg (1942–43), and Munich (1943–46), she joined the Vienna State Opera, having sung there previously at the 80th birthday celebration for Richard Strauss on June 11, 1944, as Salome, which became her most celebrated role. She made her London debut with the visiting Vienna State Opera as Donna Anna in Don Giovanni on Sept. 20, 1947, a role she repeated in 1948 at the Glyndebourne Festival. On Feb. 4, 1949, she made her Metropolitan Opera debut in N.Y. as Salome, remaining on the company's roster until 1952; she sang at London's Covent Garden in 1953. In subsequent years, she appeared in character roles in Vienna; returned to the Metropolitan Opera in 1972 in a speaking role in *La Fille du régiment*. Among her other notable roles were Aida, Musetta, Minnie, Rosalinde, Jenůfa, and Tosca.

BIBL.: E. Benke, *L. W.* (Vienna, 1994).—**NS/LK/DM**

Welk, Lawrence (LeRoy), American orchestra leader and accordionist; b. near Strasburg, N.Dak., March 11, 1903; d. Santa Monica, Calif., May 17, 1992. When big band music was at its height in the 1930s and 1940s, Welk led a successful territory band in the Midwest. After the Swing Era waned in the late 1940s, Welk prospered, launching a local television show in Los Angeles that joined a national network in the mid-1950s and continued to broadcast into the 1980s, bringing with it substantial recording success. Welk's light, sweet dance style was appropriately dubbed "champagne music," and his ingratiating manner as a master of ceremonies endeared him to millions of faithful viewers long after his contemporaries had disappeared.

Welk's parents, Ludwig and Christina Schwahn Welk, were natives of Alsace-Lorraine who immigrated to the U.S. in 1892, settling on a farm in N.Dak. Due to the family's European background, their isolation on the farm, and Welk's brief schooling, he did not learn to speak English until he was an adult and always spoke with a German accent. Welk's father played the accordion, and Welk took to the instrument as a child, turning to it more seriously at age 11 while recovering from appendicitis. When he was 17 his father bought him an expensive accordion on the understanding that he would work on the farm for four years while turning over his earnings as a musician to the family; he kept the bargain and left home on his 21st birthday.

Welk formed his first band in the summer of 1925. In 1927 he moved to Yankton, S.Dak., where the four-piece Welk's Novelty Orch. appeared on local radio station WNAX and began to build a following. By 1930 he had signed with a national booking agency and toured in many parts of the country. He married nursing student Fern Renner on April 19, 1931; they had three children.

Welk's orchestra remained a moderately successful territory band until 1937, when he began to try to reach a larger audience. He gained residencies at several major hotels, starting with the St. Paul in St. Paul, Minn. At the William Penn Hotel in Pittsburgh, where he opened on New Year's Eve, 1938, and had a national radio hookup, he adopted the band name Lawrence Welk and His Champagne Music to describe his light, danceable sound. He also acquired a theme song, "Bubbles in the Wine" (music by Welk, lyrics by Frank Loesser).

Welk had been recording for many years, starting when he paid for his own session with Gennett in the 1920s and cut the single "Spiked Beer"/"Shanghai Honeymoon." Now signed to Vocalion, he reached the hit parade for the first time in February 1939 with "Annabelle," returning in April with "The Moon Is a Silver Dollar" (music by Sammy Fain, lyrics by Mitchell Parish).

In 1940, Welk moved his base of operations to Chicago and took up a residency at the Trianon ballroom that lasted ten years. He scored his next Top Ten hit in May 1944 with "Don't Sweetheart Me" (music by Cliff Friend, lyrics by Charles Tobias). In 1945 he teamed with Red Foley for "Shame on You" (music and lyrics by Spade Cooley)/"At Mail Call Today" (music and lyrics by Gene Autry and Fred Rose), which topped the country charts in November.

Welk launched his own weekly radio show on the ABC network on June 1, 1949; it ran for two years. Leaving the Trianon in 1950, he toured the West Coast, debuting at the Aragon ballroom in Santa Monica and on a local television station on May 2, 1951. He scored another Top Ten hit with "Oh, Happy Day" (music and lyrics by Don Howard Koplow and Nancy Binns Reed) in February 1953.

The Lawrence Welk Show debuted nationally on the ABC television network on July 2, 1955. Although the Swing Era was a memory and rock 'n' roll was coming to the fore, Welk, with the charm of his heavily accented introductions and pleasant music, became vastly successful. *Lawrence Welk and His Sparkling Strings*, the first of 42 chart albums, became a Top Ten hit in 1956, and before the year was out Welk had returned to the Top Ten with the LPs *Bubbles in the Wine*, *Say It with Music*, and *Merry Christmas*. He also had a second show on ABC, *Lawrence Welk's Top Tunes and New Talent* for three years starting in October 1956.

Welk's records stopped charting after 1957, and he switched record labels, to Dot Records, by 1960, with dramatic results. *Last Date* returned him to the Top Ten of the LP charts by early 1961, and "Calcutta" (music by Heino Gase) became his biggest hit single ever, topping the charts in February 1961 and going gold, as did the accompanying album, *Calcutta!* The LP earned a 1961 Grammy nomination for Best Performance by an Orchestra, for Dancing. Welk's four subsequent LPs, *Yellow Bird* (1961), *Moon River*, *Young World*, and *Baby Elephant Walk and Theme from The Brothers Grimm* (all 1962) also reached the Top Ten, and his albums continued to chart regularly up to 1973, with 1966's *Winchester Cathedral* also going gold.

Although Welk's program was never among the most popular on television (it was rated among the top 25 shows only during the years 1965–68, never ranking higher than 12th), it attracted a steady audience, and when ABC canceled the show after 16 years in 1971, it did so more because of demographics than because of any fall-off in viewership. Welk was able to continue on television by organizing his own syndicated network; in fact, the show ran on more stations than before, and it went on another 11 years, finally concluding in 1982, although reruns still appear. Welk retired from performing after a concert in San Francisco in June 1982. He maintained his business interests, including the Welk Group of record labels, which acquired the classical/folk label Vanguard in 1986. Welk died of pneumonia at the age of 89 in 1992.

Writings (all written with B. McGeehan): *Wunnerful, Wunnerful! The Autobiography of L. W.* (Englewood Cliffs, N.J., 1971); *Ah-One, Ah- Two! Life with My Musical Family* (Englewood Cliffs, N.J., 1974); *My America, Your America* (Englewood Cliffs, N.J., 1976); *L. W.'s Musical Family Album* (Englewood Cliffs, N.J., 1977); *This I Believe* (Englewood Cliffs, N.J., 1979); *You're Never Too Young* (Englewood Cliffs, N.J., 1981).

Bibl.: C. Sanders and G. Weissman, *Champagne Music: The L. W. Show* (N.Y., 1985).—**WR**

Wellek, Albert, eminent Austrian musicologist and psychologist; b. Vienna, Oct. 16, 1904; d. Mainz, Aug. 27, 1972. He studied composition and conducting at the Prague Cons. (graduated, 1926) and music history, literature, and philosophy at the Univ. of Prague; was a student of Adler, Lach, Ficker, and Wellesz at the Univ. of Vienna (Ph.D., 1928, with the diss. *Doppelempfinden und Programmusik*); then studied psychology in Vienna and at the Univ. of Leipzig; in 1938 he completed his Habilitation at the Univ. of Munich with his *Typologie der Musikbegabung im deutschen Volke: Grundlegung einer psychologischen Theorie der Musik und Musikgeschichte* (publ. in Munich, 1939; 2nd ed., 1970). He became an asst. lecturer and then lecturer at the Univ. of Leipzig Inst. of Psychology in 1938; in 1942 he was made acting prof. of psychology at the Univ. of Halle; after serving as prof. of psychology and educational science at the Univ. of Breslau (1943–46), he founded the Univ. of Mainz Inst. of Psychology in 1946, remaining there until his death. Wellek was the foremost music psychologist of his time, being an authority on the theory of hearing.

WRITINGS: *Das absolute Gehör und seine Typen* (Leipzig, 1938; 2nd ed., 1970); *Das Problem des seelischen Seins: Die Strukturtheorie Felix Kruegers: Deutung und Kritik* (Leipzig, 1941; 2nd ed., 1953); *Die Polarität im Aufbau des Charakters: System der konkreten Charakterkunde* (Bern and Munich, 1950; 3rd ed., 1966); *Die Wiederherstellung der Seelenwissenschaft im Lebenswerk Felix Kruegers: Längsschnitt durch ein halbes Jahrhundert der Psychologie* (Hamburg, 1950; 2nd ed., 1968); *Ganzheitpsychologie und Strukturtheorie* (Bern, 1955; 2nd ed., 1969); ed. *20. Kongress der Deutschen Gesellschaft für Psychologie: Berlin 1955* (Berlin, 1955); *Der Rückfall in die Methodenkrise der Psychologie und ihre Überwindung* (Göttingen, 1959; 2nd ed., 1970); *Musikpsychologie und Musikästhetik: Grundriss der systematischen Musikwissenschaft* (Frankfurt am Main, 1963); *Psychologie* (Berlin and Munich, 1963; 3rd ed., 1971); *Melancholie in der Musik* (Hamburg, 1969); *Witz-Lyrik-Sprache* (Bern and Munich, 1970).

BIBL.: *Archiv für die Gesamt Psychologie*, CXVI (1964; includes Festschrift for Wellek's 60th birthday).—**NS/LK/DM**

Weller, Walter, distinguished Austrian conductor; b. Vienna, Nov. 30, 1939. He received training in violin from Moravec and Samohyl at the Vienna Academy of Music. He also studied conducting with Böhm and Stein, and later received guidance from Krips and Szell. In 1956 he became a violinist in the Vienna Phil., subsequently serving as one of its concertmasters (1964–69). He also was 2nd violin in the Wiener Kozerthaus Quartet until founding his own Weller Quartet in 1958, with which he toured with notable success throughout Europe, North America, and Asia. In 1966 he began conducting but it was not until 1968 that he made his professional debut as a conductor of the Vienna Phil. From 1969 he conducted at the Volksoper and State Opera in Vienna. After serving as Generalmusikdirektor in Duisburg (1971–72), he was music director of the Niederösterreichesche Tonkünsterorchester in Vienna (1975–78). He also began to appear as a guest conductor with major European orchs. and opera houses. From 1977 to 1980 he was principal conductor and musical adviser of the Royal Liverpool Phil., and then was principal conductor of the Royal Phil. in London from 1980 to 1985. From 1991 to 1997 he was music director of the Royal Scottish National Orch. in Glasgow, and he concurrently served as music director of the Theater and Sym. Orch. in Basel from 1994. While Weller is esteemed for his unmannered interpretations of the great Austro-German masterworks, he has also demonstrated a capacity to project modern scores with fine results.—**NS/LK/DM**

Wellesz, Egon (Joseph), eminent Austrian-born English composer, musicologist, and pedagogue; b. Vienna, Oct. 21, 1885; d. Oxford, Nov. 9, 1974. He studied harmony with Carl Frühling in Vienna and then was a pupil in musicology with Adler at the Univ. of Vienna (graduated, 1908); he also received private instruction from Schoenberg. From 1911 to 1915 he taught music history at the Neues Cons. in Vienna; in 1913 he was engaged as a lecturer on musicology at the Univ. of Vienna and was a prof. there from 1930 to 1938, when the annexation of Austria by Nazi Germany compelled him to leave. He went to England in 1938; joined the music dept. of the Univ. of Oxford, which in 1932 had conferred upon him the degree of Mus.Doc. (*honoris causa*). In 1943 he became a lecturer in music history at the Univ. of Oxford; in 1946 he was appointed to the editorial board of the *New Oxford History of Music*, to which he then contributed, and was Univ. Reader in Byzantine music at Oxford (1948–56). Wellesz received the Prize of the City of Vienna in 1953. He was president of the Univ. of Oxford Byzantine Soc. (1955–66). In 1957 he was made a Commander of the Order of the British Empire and was awarded the Grande Médaille d'Argent of the City of Paris. In 1961 he was awarded the Austrian Great State prize. A scholar and a musician of extraordinary capacities, Wellesz distinguished himself as a composer of highly complex musical scores and as an authority on Byzantine music.

WORKS: DRAMATIC: Opera: *Die Prinzessin Girnara* (1919–20; Hannover, May 15, 1921; rev. version, Mannheim, Sept. 2, 1928); *Alkestis* (1922–23; Mannheim, March 20, 1924); *Opferung des Gefangenen* (1924–25; Cologne, April 10, 1926); *Scherz, List und Rache* (1926–27; Stuttgart, March 1, 1928); *Die Bakchantinnen* (1929–30; Vienna, June 20, 1931); *Incognita* (Oxford, Dec. 5, 1951). **Ballet:** *Das Wunder der Diana* (1915; Mannheim, March 20, 1924); *Persisches Ballett* (1920; Donaueschingen, 1924); *Achilles auf Skyros* (1921; Stuttgart, March 4, 1926); *Die Nächtlichen* (1923; Berlin, Nov. 20, 1924). **ORCH.:** *Vorfrühling*, symphonic poem (1912); *Suite* for Violin and Chamber Orch. (1924); Piano Concerto (1934); *Prosperos Beschwörungen*, after Shakespeare's *The Tempest* (1936–38; Vienna, Feb. 19, 1938); 9 syms.: No. 1, in C (1945), No. 2, in E- flat (1948), No. 3, in A (1951), No. 4, *Symphonia Austriaca*, in G (1953), No. 5 (1956; Düsseldorf, Feb. 20, 1958), No. 6 (1965; Nuremberg, June 1, 1966), No. 7 (1968), No. 8 (1971), and No. 9 (1971; Vienna, Nov. 22, 1972); Violin Concerto (1961; Vienna, Jan. 19, 1962); *Music* for Strings (1964); *Divertimento* for Chamber Orch. (1969); *Symphonischer Epilog* (1969). **CHAMBER:** 9 string quartets (1912, 1917, 1918, 1920, 1944, 1947, 1948, 1957, 1966); *Geistiges Lied* for Piano Trio (1918); Sonata for Solo Cello (1921); *2 Pieces* for Clarinet and Piano (1922); Sonata for Solo Violin (1924); Suite for Violin and Piano (1937); *Little Suite* for Flute (1937); Octet for Clarinet, Horn, Bassoon, and String Quintet (1948–49); Suite for Wind Quintet (1954); Suite in 3 movements for Bassoon (1956); Clarinet Quintet (1959); 2 string trios (1962, 1969); *5 Miniatures* for Violin and Piano (1965); *Music* for String Quartet (1968); String Quintet (1970). **KEYBOARD: Piano:** *3 Piano Pieces* (1912); *Epigramme* (1913); *5 Dance Pieces* (1927); *Triptych* (1966); *Studies in Grey* (1969). **Organ:** *Partita* (1966). **VOCAL:** *Gebete der Mädchen zur Maria* for Soprano, Chorus, and Orch. (1909); *Mitte des Lebens*, cantata (1932); *Amor timido*, cantata for Soprano and Orch. (1935); *5 Sonnets by Elizabeth Barrett Browning* for Soprano and String Quartet (1935); *Lied der Welt* for Soprano and Orch. (1937); *Leben, Traum und Tod* for Contralto and Orch. (1937); *Short Mass* for Chorus and Small Orch. (1937); *The Leaden Echo and the Golden Echo* for Soprano, Violin, Clarinet, Cello, and Piano, after Hopkins (1944); *4 Songs of Return* for Soprano and Small Orch. (1961); *Duineser Elegie* for Soprano, Chorus, and Chamber Ensemble (1963); *Ode to Music* for Baritone and Chamber Orch. (1964); *Vision* for Soprano and Orch. (1966); *Mirabile Mysterium*, Christmas cantata (1967); *Canticum Sapientiae* for Baritone, Chorus, and Orch. (1968; Graz, Oct. 25, 1969).

WRITINGS: *Arnold Schönberg* (Vienna, 1921; Eng. tr., 1924); *Byzantinische Kirchenmusik* (Breslau, 1927); *Eastern Elements in Western Chant: Studies in the Early History of Ecclesiastical Music*, Monumenta Musicae Byzantinae, subsidia, II (1947; 2nd ed., 1967); *A History of Byzantine Music and Hymnography* (Oxford, 1949; 3rd ed., rev., 1963); *Essays on Opera* (London, 1950); *The Origin of Schoenberg's 12-tone System* (Washington, D.C., 1958); *Byzantinische Musik, Das Musikwerk*, I (1959; Eng. tr., 1959); *Die Hymnen der Ostkirche*, Basiliensis de musica orationes, I (Kassel, 1962); *J.J. Fux* (London, 1965); also ed. *Ancient and Oriental Music*, Vol. I, *The New Oxford History of Music* (Oxford, 1957); ed. with M. Velimirović, *Studies in Eastern Chant*, I-III (London, 1966–71); ed. with F. Sternfeld, *The Age of Enlightenment (1745–1790)*, Vol. VII, *The New Oxford History of Music* (Oxford, 1973).

BIBL.: R. Schollum, *E. W.* (Vienna, 1964); C. Benser, *E. W. (1885–1974): Chronicle of a Twentieth-Century Musician* (N.Y., 1985); L. Wedl, *Die Bakchantinnen von E. W.: Oder Das göttliche Wunder* (Vienna, 1992); H. Vogg, ed., *Am Beispiel E. W.: Sein Briefwechsel mit Doblinger als Zeugnis der Partnerschaft zwischen Komponist und Verlag* (Vienna, 1996).—**NS/LK/DM**

Wells, Dicky (William), jazz trombonist, singer, arranger, composer; b. Centerville, Tenn., June 10, 1907; d. N.Y., Nov. 12, 1985. Family moved to Louisville, Ky., in 1911. (It is said that he first encountered there the music of a player who was a lifelong influence, Jimmy Harrison.) Studied music from the age of ten, played baritone horn in the Booker T. Washington Community Center Band at 13 and trombone from the age of 16. He played locally in Lucius Brown's Band, then went to N.Y. in drummer Lloyd W. Scott's Band (1926). Remained in N.Y. with the band, which was later led by Lloyd's brother Cecil Scott. Worked mainly with Cecil Scott until early 1930, then joined Elmer Snowden's Band (1930–31), appearing with Snowden in the film *Smash Your Baggage*. Through the 1930s, he worked with several leaders, including Benny Carter (1932–33, and again in early 1934) and Teddy Hill, joining Hill in September 1934 and remaining with the band for a trip to Europe (summer 1937), where he recorded with Django Reinhardt. After 1937, Wells regularly led his own recording bands, also appeared on many freelance recordings. He joined Count Basie at The Famous Door in July 1938, and played regularly with Basie until early 1950 (with a brief break from early 1946–47). For Basie he wrote "After Theatre Jump" (1944) and others, but the famous "Dickie's Dream" (1939) was written for him by Lester Young. After leaving Basie, Wells worked in Jimmy Rushing's Band before going to France in October 1952, toured Europe with Bill Coleman's Swing Stars. Returned to N.Y. in February 1953, worked with Lucky Millinder (autumn 1953), worked briefly with Earl Hines in 1954, then freelanced with various leaders, mainly in N.Y. He toured Europe in autumn 1959 and spring 1961 with Buck Clayton's All Stars. He joined Ray Charles's Big Band in November 1961 for 18 months and also worked in the 1960s for B. B. King. During the 1960s, Wells continued to play regularly with various leaders, mainly in N.Y. Wells did freelance recording and touring for the remainder of his career, occasionally playing sessions with various Basie sidemen and alumni under the banner of the Countsmen. In late 1968, Wells toured Europe with Buddy Tate's Band and played at the New Orleans Jazz Fest in June 1969. He left full-time music, but continued to gig. He was seriously injured in a mugging incident during 1976, but recovered and resumed playing. He toured Europe with Earle Warren and Claude Hopkins. Continued to play during the early 1980s, often with Bobby Booker's big band.

His brilliant style was characterized by daring leaps and speech-like quartertones, especially evident in his first recordings and on through the 1940s.

DISC.: *Dickie Wells in Paris* (1937); *Bones for the King* (1958); *Trombone Four in Hand* (1959); *Lonesome Road* (1981); Kansas City Seven: "After Theatre Jump" (1944).—**JC/LP**

Wells, Kitty (originally, **Deason, Ellen Muriel**), American country singer and guitarist; b. Nashville, Tenn., Aug. 30, 1919. Wells was the most successful female country singer of the 1950s and 1960s. She was the first major female singer in country music and one of the few to emerge before the 1960s. Her biggest hit was her first, "It Wasn't God Who Made Honky Tonk Angels," and among the 81 songs she placed on the country singles charts between 1952 and 1979, her other #1 hits were "One by One," a duet with Red Foley, and "Heartbreak U.S.A."

Wells's father, Charles Deason, worked in the lumber business and as a railroad brakeman; he also played guitar and performed locally with his brothers. He gave his daughter her first guitar, which she began to play at 14. At 15 she dropped out of school and went to work at a shirt factory, but she also performed locally with her sisters and a cousin as The Deason Sisters. They made their local radio debut in 1936. On Oct. 31, 1937, she married Johnnie (John Robert) Wright (b. 1914), a cabinetmaker and aspiring musician. They formed a trio with Wright's sister and performed on local radio as Johnnie Wright and the Harmony Girls.

On Oct. 27, 1939, Wells gave birth to a daughter, Ruby Wright, who grew up to perform with her parents and on her own. As Wells took a less active role in the family band, Wright teamed with Jack Anglin to form Johnnie Wright and the Happy Roving Cowboys with Jack Anglin. The group moved to Greensboro, N.C., in

1940 and appeared on radio as The Tennessee Hillbillies. Over the next several years they appeared on several radio stations in the mid-South. They were in Charleston, W. Va., on March 30, 1942, when Wells gave birth to a son, Bobby Wright, who grew up to perform with his parents and act on television. In 1945 she had a second daughter, Carol Sue, who also performed with her parents. After Anglin was drafted, Wells took a more prominent role in the group. Anglin returned from the service in January 1946, and, in 1947, as The Tennessee Mountain Boys, they spent a year on the *Grand Ole Opry*, moving to the *Louisiana Hayride* in February 1948.

Wright and Anglin signed to RCA Victor in 1949, making records as Johnnie and Jack. Wells also recorded for the label without success. Johnnie and Jack scored two Top Ten country hits in 1951 and were invited to become permanent members of the *Grand Ole Opry* at the start of 1952. Wells was all but retired at this point, but Wright arranged for her to record a demo of an answer song to Hank Thompson's hit "The Wild Side of Life," "It Wasn't God Who Made Honky Tonk Angels" (music and lyrics by J. D. Miller). Released by Decca Records, it hit #1 in the country charts in August 1952, the first country chart-topper by a solo female singer. Soon Wells, too, was asked to join the *Grand Ole Opry*. She made her debut with the program on Sept. 13, 1952.

Thereafter, Wells performed on the *Grand Ole Opry*, toured as part of the "Johnnie and Jack Show," and recorded for Decca. Her next Top Ten country hit, which entered the charts in March 1953, was an answer song to Webb Pierce's "Back Street Affair," "Paying for That Back Street Affair." Her third Top Ten country hit, "Hey Joe," which charted in September, was another answer song to an identically titled hit by Carl Smith. Among her three Top Ten country hits in 1954, the most successful was a duet with Red Foley, "One by One" (music and lyrics by Johnnie Wright, Jack Anglin, and Jim Anglin), which hit #1 in July. She and Foley had two more Top Ten country hits in 1955, and she had four more of her own during the year, the most successful of which was "Makin' Believe" (music and lyrics by Jimmy Work), which was held out of #1 only by the long- running success of Webb Pierce's "In the Jailhouse Now." She had another Top Ten country hit with Foley in 1956, "You and Me" (music and lyrics by Johnnie Wright, Jack Anglin, and Jim Anglin), as well as two others on her own. Her four Top Ten country hits in 1957 included "Oh, So Many Years Ago," a duet with Webb Pierce.

Wells was less consistently successful over the next few years, scoring five Top Ten country hits between 1958 and 1960. But the chart-topping success of "Heartbreak U.S.A." (music and lyrics by Harlan Howard) in July 1961 revived her career, and she scored four Top Ten country hits in 1962, three in 1964, and three in 1965. Her recording career cooled thereafter, although she continued to chart consistently through 1972. After Jack Anglin's death in a car accident on March 7, 1963, Wright reorganized their touring package as the "Kitty Wells and Johnnie Wright Family Show." Starting in 1969, the show was broadcast as a syndicated television program for a number of years. Wells left MCA Records, which had taken over Decca, in 1973 and signed to Capricorn, where she recorded the album *Forever Young* (its title song written by Bob Dylan) with members of The Allman Brothers Band. By the late 1970s she was recording on her own Ruboca Records label.

In 1988, Wells sang with Brenda Lee and Loretta Lynn on a "Honky Tonk Angels' Medley" on k.d. lang's *Shadowland* album, resulting in a Grammy nomination for Best Country Vocal Collaboration. Wells also sang on a remake of "It Wasn't God Who Made Honky Tonk Angels" on Dolly Parton, Loretta Lynn, and Tammy Wynette's gold- selling 1993 album *Honky Tonk Angels*. Wells continued to tour regularly with her family show in the late 1990s.

WRITINGS: *Favorite Songs and Recipes* (1973).

DISC.: *Country Music Hall of Fame* (rec. 1952–61; rel. 1991); *The Queen of Country Music* (complete recordings; 1993).

BIBL.: A. Dunkleberger, *Queen of Country Music, The Life Story of K. W.*—**WR**

Wells, Mary, the first artist to score a Top Ten and #1 hit for Motown Records; b. Detroit, Mich., May 13, 1943; d. Los Angeles, July 26, 1992. Wells was born in a fatherless home; her mother was a domestic. By the time Mary turned 10, she had started performing at talent shows around the Detroit area. In her teens, she brought the song "Bye Bye Baby" to Berry Gordy, hoping to land it with Jackie Wilson. Gordy not only liked the song, he liked the singer. "Bye Bye Baby" became her first hit, rising to #8 R&B.

The teen had a great image for Motown, one that created the mold for the label's female roster through the 1960s: she was shy but sexy, demure but with a big voice. She became the mouthpiece for some of Smokey Robinson's best compositions, taking his tune "Two Lovers" to the top of the R&B charts and #7 pop, "You Beat Me to the Punch" to #1 R&B and #9 pop, and "The One Who Really Loves You" to #8 pop. Her biggest hit, "My Guy," topped the charts in the summer of 1964, when she toured England with the Beatles. She was just 21 years old at the time.

She was wooed away from Motown and signed to 20th Century–Fox, who promised her not only to continue her music career but also to expand it into film. As it turned out, they couldn't deliver either. Through the late 1960s and early 1970s, she continued to perform and record, but without Robinson's material, it just didn't work as well. Even her husband Cecil Womack couldn't help, although the songs they recorded together had a very un-Motown funkiness. By the mid-1980s, she was pretty much relegated to the oldies circuit.

In the early 1990s, Wells, a heavy smoker, was diagnosed with cancer. Attempts to treat it left her destitute, unable even to pay the rent. The Rhythm and Blues Foundation came through with $50,000, and artists ranging from Diana Ross to Rod Stewart to Bruce Springsteen donated funds. She died of the illness in 1992.

DISC.: *Bye, Bye Baby, I Don't Want to Take a Chance* (1961); *The One Who Really Loves You* (1962); *Two Lovers* (1962); *Live on*

Stage (1963); *Together* (1964); *My Guy* (1964); *Mary Wells Sings "My Guy"* (1964); *Mary Wells* (1965); *Love Songs of the Beatles* (1965); *Vintage Stock* (1966); *Ooh Movietone* (1966); *My Baby Just Cares for Me* (1966); *Two Sides Of...* (1966); *Servin' Up Some Soul* (1968); *In and Out of Love* (1981); *Keeping My Mind on Love* (1990); *You Beat Me to the Punch* (1995).—**BH**

Welser-Möst (real name, **Möst**), **Franz,** prominent Austrian conductor; b. Linz, Aug. 16, 1960. He began his training in Linz with Balduin Sulzer. He studied at the Munich Hochschule für Musik. After becoming a finalist in the Karajan conducting competition in 1979, he served as principal conductor of the Austrian Youth Orch. In 1985 he was named music director of the Winterthur and Norrköping sym. orchs. He made a successful British debut as a guest conductor with the London Phil. in 1986, and subsequently led it on a tour of Europe. In 1987 he made his debut as an opera conductor in Vienna with *L'Italiana in Algeri*. In 1989 he made his U.S. debut as a guest conductor with the St. Louis Sym. Orch. From 1990 to 1996 he was principal conductor of the London Phil. In 1992 he made his first appearance with the Zürich Opera conducting *Der Rosenkavalier*. He became its music director in 1995, where he programmed a complete *Ring* cycle for the 2000–01 season. In 1998 he made his debut with the Vienna Phil. at the Mozart Festival Week in Salzburg. In 1999 he was appointed music director of the Cleveland Orch., which position he was to assume in 2002. As a guest conductor, he has been engaged by many major European and American orchs. In addition to the classics, Welser-Möst has programmed many 20th century scores, including those of Stravinsky, Bartók, Schmidt, Korngold, Orff, Kodály, Pärt, Kancheli, and H.K. Gruber.—**NS/LK/DM**

Welsh, Thomas, English bass, teacher, and composer; b. Wells, c. 1780; d. Brighton, Jan. 24, 1848. He was a grandson of **Thomas Linley Sr.** He became a chorister at Wells Cathedral, and a pupil of J. B. Cramer and Baumgarten. He made his opera debut in London at the age of 12; after his voice changed, he became a bass, and sang in oratorio. He was particularly distinguished as a vocal teacher; he publ. *Vocal Instructor, or the Art of Singing Exemplified in 15 Lessons leading to 40 Progressive Exercises* (London, 1825). His wife and pupil, Mary Anne (née Wilson; 1802–67), whom he married in 1827, was a noted soprano who made her debut at Drury Lane on Jan. 18, 1821, in Arne's *Artaxerxes*. He composed several theater pieces, including the operatic farce *The Green-eyed Monster, or How to Get your Money* (London, Oct. 14, 1811), piano sonatas, glees, duets, and partsongs.—**NS/LK/DM**

Welte, Michael, German manufacturer of musical instruments; b. Unterkirnach, Black Forest, Sept. 29, 1807; d. Freiburg im Breisgau, Jan. 17, 1880. Having served an apprenticeship with Josef Blessing, a maker of musical clocks, he established himself at Voehrenbach (1832). He exhibited his first "orchestrion" at Karlsruhe in 1849, and later took his sons (Emil, Berthold, and Michael Jr.) into partnership. His instruments obtained first prizes at London (1862), Paris (1867), Munich (1885), Vienna (1892), Chicago (1893), St. Louis (1904), Leipzig (1909), and Turin (1911); in 1872 the factory was removed to Freiburg im Breisgau. His oldest son, Emil Welte (b. Voehrenbach, April 20, 1841; d. Norwich, Conn., Oct. 25, 1923), established a branch in N.Y. (1865); he improved the then newly invented paper roll (taking the place of the earlier wooden cylinders), and was the first to use it, in connection with a pneumatic action, in a large orchestrion built for Theiss's Alhambra Court (N.Y.). A son of Berthold Welte, Edwin (b. Freiburg im Breisgau, 1875; d. there, Jan. 4, 1958), applied the paper roll to the piano, creating in 1904 the "Welte-Mignon Reproducing Piano," which could control pedaling and gradations of touch, a definite improvement on the ordinary player-piano, which could produce only pitches. Josef Hoffmann, Paderewski, and Wanda Landowska made rolls for it. The application of the same principle to the organ resulted in the invention of the "Philharmonic Organ" (1912). The firm ceased to exist in 1954.—**NS/LK/DM**

Welting, Ruth, American soprano; b. Memphis, Tenn., May 11, 1948; d. Ashville, N.C., Dec. 16, 1999. She received training from Daniel Ferro in N.Y., Luigi Ricci in Rome, and Jeanne Reiss in Paris. In 1970 she made her operatic debut as Blondchen at the N.Y.C. Opera. As a guest artist, she sang in Houston, San Antonio, Dallas, Sante Fe, and San Francisco. In 1975 she made her first appearance at London's Covent Garden as Zerbinetta, a role that she also sang at her Metropolitan Opera debut in N.Y. on March 20, 1976. She continued to make appearances at the Metropolitan Opera until 1994. In 1979 she sang the Fairy Godmother in *Cendrillon* in Ottawa and in 1980 in Washington, D.C. In 1982 she made her first appearance at the Salzburg Festival as Zerbinetta. She sang Marie in *La Fille du Régiment* in Barcelona in 1984. In 1990 she appeared as Ophelia in Thomas' *Hamlet* at the Chicago Lyric Opera. Among her other roles were Zerlina, Gilda, Norina, Adele, Sophie, and the Princess in *L'Enfant et les Sortilèges*. She also appeared frequently as a lieder artist.—**NS/LK/DM**

Wendling, family of German musicians of Alsatian descent:

(1) Johann Baptist Wendling, flutist and composer; b. Rappoltsweiler, Alsace, June 17, 1723; d. Munich, Nov. 27, 1797. He was a flutist in Zweibrücken (1747–50), where he gave lessons to Duke Christian IV, then was active in Mannheim as an instructor to the elector, Carl Theodor, and as a member of the Court Orch. In 1752 he married Dorothea Wendling, who often traveled with him on concert tours; among the cities he visited were Paris (played at the Concert Spirituel with Christian IV, 1762, and with Mozart, 1778), London (1771), and Vienna (1776). In 1778 he went with the Mannheim court to Munich, although he spent most of his later years in Mannheim. He composed 9 flute concertos, 9 quartets, 36 trios, and various other works. Mozart orchestrated one of his flute concertos (K. 284e).

(2) Dorothea Wendling (née **Spurni**), singer; b. Stuttgart, March 21, 1736; d. Munich, Aug. 20, 1811. In

1752 she joined the Mannheim court as a singer, and by 1760 was its principal member. When the court moved to Munich in 1778, she elected to remain in Mannheim, where she was active mainly as a teacher from 1790. She was held in great repute by her contemporaries. Mozart composed the role of Ilia in *Idomeneo* and the concert aria K. 486a/295a for her. She was married to Johann Baptist Wendling.

(3) Elisabeth Augusta Wendling, singer, daughter of Johann Baptist Wendling and Dorothea Wendling (née Spurni), b. Mannheim, Oct. 4, 1752; d. Munich, Feb. 18, 1794. She first sang at the Mannheim Court Opera on Nov. 4, 1769, with her mother and her aunt. She appeared in Zweibrücken in 1772, and was a guest artist in Munich (from 1784). Mozart wrote the 2 French ariettas K. 307 and K. 308 for her.

(4) Franz (Anton) Wendling, violinist, brother of Johann Baptist Wendling; b. Rappoltsweiler, Oct. 21, 1729; d. Munich, May 16, 1786. In 1755 he became a violinist and in 1774 first violinist in the Mannheim Court Orch. He went with it to Munich in 1778, where he also appeared as a ballet conductor. In 1764 he married Elisabeth Augusta Wendling (née Sarselli).

(5) Elisabeth Augusta (née **Sarselli**) **Wendling,** singer, wife of Franz (Anton) Wendling; b. Mannheim, Feb. 20, 1746; d. Munich, Jan. 10, 1786. In 1762 she became a court musician in Mannheim, and in 1776 she was named third soprano; in 1778 she went with the court to Munich. She was greatly admired by her contemporaries. Mozart wrote the role of Electra in *Idomeneo* for her.

(6) Dorothea Wendling, singer, daughter of Franz (Anton) Wendling and Elisabeth Augusta Wendling (née **Sarselli**) and niece of Dorothea Wendling (née Spurni); b. Mannheim, Jan. 27, 1767; d. Munich, May 19, 1839. She was a pupil of her in Mannheim. In 1778 she made her debut in Munich. She sang mainly in Mannheim before devoting herself to teaching.

(7) (Johann) Karl Wendling, violinist and conductor, nephew of Johann Baptist Wendling; b. Zweibrücken, March 30, 1750; d. Mannheim, Nov. 10, 1834. He was a violinist in the Mannheim Court Orch. (from 1765). After the Court Orch. moved to Munich in 1778, he remained in Mannheim and was a violinist in the new National Theater there. He was active as a conductor there from about 1782.—**NS/LK/DM**

Wendt, Larry (actually, **Lawrence Frederick**), American composer and writer on music; b. Napa, Calif., April 5, 1946. After training in chemistry at San Jose State Coll. (1964–67) and the Univ. of Mont. (1967–68), he studied with Strang (composition) and took courses in comparative literature at San Jose State Univ. (B.A., 1975). He was active as an electronics technician in the music dept. and recording studios at San Jose State Univ. From 1978 he utilized his own electronic and computer equipment to produce various works, a number of which he recorded on his own Frog Hollow label. With S. Ruppenthal, he publ. the books *Vocable Gestures: A Historical Survey of Sound Poetry* (1977) and *A Sketch of American Text-Sound Composition and the Works of Charles Amirkhanian* (1979). Most of his music is for tape.—**NS/LK/DM**

Wenkel, Ortrun, German mezzo-soprano; b. Buttstadt, Oct. 25, 1942. After training at the Franz Liszt Hochschule für Music in Weimar, she attended the master classes of Paul Lohmann at the Frankfurt am Main Hochschule für Musik; she also studied with Elsa Cavelti. While still a student, she made her concert debut in London in 1964. In 1971 she made her operatic debut as Gluck's Orfeo in Heidelberg, and subsequently appeared in opera at Milan's La Scala, London's Covent Garden, Munich, Hamburg, Salzburg, Berlin, Vienna, and Zürich. She also pursued a highly active career as a concert artist, singing with major orchs. and as a recitalist. Her expansive repertoire ranges from the Baroque era to the contemporary period.—**NS/LK/DM**

Wenkoff, Spas, Bulgarian tenor; b. Tirnovo, Sept. 23, 1928. He received his training from Jossifow in Sofia, Safirowa in Russe, and Kemter in Dresden. In 1954 he made his operatic debut as Kote in Dolidse's *Keto und Kote* in Tirnovo. After singing in Russe (1962–65), Döbeln (1965–68), Magdeburg (1968–71), and Halle (1971–75), he appeared as Tristan at the Dresden State Opera in 1975. From 1976 he sang at the Berlin State Opera. In 1976 he made his debut at the Bayreuth Festival as Tristan, and continued to appear there until 1983. He made his Metropolitan Opera debut in N.Y. as Tristan on Jan. 9, 1981. In 1982 he sang Tannhäuser at the Vienna State Opera. In 1984 he appeared at the Deutsche Oper in Berlin. He sang Tannhäuser in Bern in 1987. In addition to his Heldentenor roles, he also sang roles in operas by Verdi and Puccini.—**NS/LK/DM**

Wennerberg, Gunnar, Swedish writer, politician, and composer, uncle of **Sara (Margarete Eugenia Euphrosyne) Wennerberg-Reuter;** b. Lidköping, Oct. 2, 1817; d. Läckö, Aug. 22, 1901. He studied at the Univ. of Uppsala (Ph.D., 1845), and entered the Swedish Parliament in 1876. Although he was autodidact as a composer, he found a following as a composer of vocal music, becoming best known for his works for men's voices, most notably *Hor oss, Svea!* (1853). He publ. a popular collection of vocal duets for men's voices and piano as *Gluntarne* (1849–51) and 55 of the Psalms for solo voice or voices, chorus, and piano (1861–86). He attempted to write several major works, including a *Stabat mater* and a series of oratorios on the life of Christ, but only 2 of the latter were completed. His literary works were publ. in 4 vols. (1881–85).

Bibl.: S. Almquist, *Om G. W.: Hans tid och hans gärning* (Stockholm, 1917); C. Hennerberg, *Förteckning över G. W.s Tonverk* (Stockholm, 1918); G. Jeanson, *G. W. som Musiker* (Stockholm, 1929).—**NS/LK/DM**

Wennerberg-Reuter, Sara (Margareta Eugenia Euphrosyne), Swedish composer, niece of **Gunnar Wennerberg;** b. Otterstad, Feb. 11, 1875; d. Stockholm, March 29, 1959. She studied organ and harmony in Göteborg with Andrée. After training in organ and choral music at the Stockholm Cons. (1893–95), she was a student of Jadassohn and Reinecke at the Leipzig Cons. (1896–98) and of Bruch at the Berlin Hochschule für Musik (1901–02). She composed instrumental pieces, cantatas, and songs.—**NS/LK/DM**

Wenten, Nyoman, Indonesian musician and dancer; b. Sading, near Denpasar, Bali, June 15, 1945. He studied dance and music from an early age with his grandfather; continued studies at the National Cons. of Music and Dance in Bali, the Traditional Music Cons. in Surakarta (1962–65), and the National Music and Dance Academy in Yogyakarta (B.F.A., 1970); taught at the latter institutions as well as the Dance Cons. in Yogyakarta (1964–70). He received an M.F.A. from the Calif. Inst. of the Arts (1974); taught there (from 1971) and also gave workshops at both the Los Angeles and Berkeley campuses of the Univ. of Calif. He was director of the Music, Dance, and Language Program for the Indonesian consulate in Los Angeles. He toured in Asia, North America, and Europe (from 1964); appeared at the Los Angeles Olympic Arts Festival (1984) and the International Festival of Arts in Mexico (1985). He is a remarkable performer in both Balinese and Javanese dance and music; he frequently performs with his wife, Nanik, and her father, **K. R. T. Wasitodiningrat.—NS/LK/DM**

Wenzinger, August, prominent Swiss cellist, viola da gambist, conductor, teacher, and music editor; b. Basel, Nov. 14, 1905. He received his basic training at the Basel Cons.; then studied cello with Paul Grümmer and theory with Jarnach at the Hochschule für Musik in Cologne; also took private cello lessons with Feuermann in Berlin. He subsequently served as 1st cellist in the Bremen City Orch. (1929–34) and the Basel Allgemeine Musikgesellschaft (1936–70). He became interested in reviving the classical Baroque repertoire on original instruments, and acquired facility on the viola da gamba; conducted early music with the Capella Coloniensis of the West German Radio in Cologne (1954–58) and later led performances of Baroque operas in Hannover (1958–66). He taught at the Schola Cantorum Basiliensis (from 1933); founded its viola da gamba trio in 1968. He ed. Bach's unaccompanied cello suites and several Baroque operas, and also publ. exercises for the viola da gamba, *Gambenübung* (2 vols., 1935, 1938) and *Gambenfibel* (with M. Majer; 1943).—**NS/LK/DM**

Werba, Erik, eminent Austrian pianist, teacher, composer, and writer on music; b. Baden, near Vienna, May 23, 1918; d. Hinterbrühl, April 9, 1992. He studied piano with Oskar Dachs and composition with Joseph Marx at the Vienna Academy of Music and musicology with Lach, Wellesz, and Schenk at the Univ. of Vienna (1936–40). He was active as a music critic for various newspapers (1945–65); also was on the staff of the *Österreichische Musikzeitschrift* (from 1952). In 1949 he commenced touring throughout Europe as an accompanist to leading singers of the day; also was a prof. of song and oratorio at the Vienna Academy of Music (from 1949). In addition to numerous articles, he publ. *Joseph Marx* (Vienna, 1964), *Hugo Wolf oder der zornige Romantiker* (Vienna, 1971), *Erich Marckhl* (Vienna, 1972), and *Hugo Wolf und seine Lieder* (Vienna, 1984). He composed a Singspiel, *Trauben für die Kaiserin* (Vienna, 1949), several song cycles, and chamber music pieces, among them *Sonata notturna* for Bassoon and Piano (1972).—**NS/LK/DM**

Werckmeister, Andreas, eminent German organist, organ examiner, music theorist, and composer; b. Benneckenstein, Thuringia, Nov. 30, 1645; d. Halberstadt, Oct. 26, 1706. He studied organ with his uncle, Christian Werckmeister, organist in Bennungen, near Sangerhausen, and after studies at the Nordhausen Gymnasium (1660–62), continued his training at the Quedlinburg Gymnasium, where another of his uncles, Victor Werckmeister, served as Kantor. He was organist in Hasselfelde, near Blankenburg (1664–74). After serving as organist and notary in Elbingerode (1674–75), he went to Quedlinburg as organist of the collegiate church of St. Servatius and of the court of the abbess and Countess of Palatine, Anna Sophia I. He also was named organist of the Wipertikirche in 1677, and in 1696 settled in Halberstadt as organist of the Martinikirche. Werckmeister was highly influential as a music theorist; his exposition of number symbolism in music and its theological basis remains invaluable. Among his compositions are *Musikalische Privatlust* for Violin and Basso Continuo (Quedlinburg, 1689) and various organ pieces.

Writings: *Orgel-Probe, oder Kurtze Beschreibung, wie und welcher Gestalt man die Orgel-Wercke von den Orgelmachern annehmen, probiren, untersuchen und den Kirchen liefern könne und solle* (Frankfurt am Main and Leipzig, 1681; 2nd ed., 1698, as *Erweiterte und verbesserte Orgel-Probe;* 5th ed., 1783; Eng. tr. by G. Krapf, 1976); *Musicae mathematicae Hodegus curiosus, oder Richtiger musicalischer Weg- Weiser* (Frankfurt am Main and Leipzig, 1686; 2nd ed., 1687); *Musicalische Temperatur, oder Deutlicher und warer mathematischer Unterricht, wie man durch Anweisung des Monochordi ein Clavier, sonderlich die Orgel-Wercke, Positive, Regale, Spinetten und dergleichen wol temperirt stimmen könne* (Frankfurt am Main and Leipzig, c. 1686–87; not extant; 2nd ed., 1691); *Der edlen Music-Kunst Würde, Gebrauch und Missbrauch, so wohl aus der heiligen Schrift als auch aus etlich alten und neubewährten reinen Kirchen-Lehrern* (Frankfurt am Main and Leipzig, 1691); *Hypomnemata musica, oder Musicalisches Memorial, welches bestehet in kurtzer Erinnerung dessen, so bisshero unter guten Freunden discurs-weise, insonderheit von der Composition und Temperatur möchte vorgangen seyn* (Quedlinburg, 1697); *Die nothwendigsten Anmerckungen und Regeln, wie der Bassus continuus oder General-Bass wol könne tractiret werden* (Aschersleben, 1698; 2nd ed., 1715); *Cribrum musicum, oder Musicalisches Sieb, darinnen einige Mängel eines halb gelehrten Componisten vorgestellet und das Böse von dem Guten gleichsam ausgesiebet und abgesondert worden* (Quedlinburg and Leipzig, 1700); *Harmonologia musica, oder Kurtze Anleitung zur musicalischen Composition* (Frankfurt am Main and Leipzig, 1702); *J.N.J. Organum Gruningense redivivum, oder Kurtze Beschreibung des in der Grüningischen Schlos-Kirchen berühmten Orgel-Wercks* (Quedlinburg and Aschersleben, 1705); *Musicalische Paradoxal-Discourse, oder Ungemeine Vorstellungen, wie die Musica einen hohen und göttlichen Uhrsprung habe* (Quedlinburg, 1707).

Bibl.: J. Götzen, *Der Welt-berühmte Musicus und Organista wurde bey trauriger Leich-Bestellung des Weyland edlen und Kunst-Hocherfahrnen Herr Andeae W.s* (Halberstadt, 1707); *W.-Kolloquium* (1985) (in Ger. and Eng., Michaelstein/Blankenburg, 1986).—**NS/LK/DM**

Werder, Felix, German-born Australian composer and music critic; b. Berlin, Feb. 22, 1922. He acquired early music training from his father, a cantor and composer of liturgical music. He also learned to play piano, viola, and clarinet. Among his teachers were Boas Bischofswerder and Arno Nadel. His family went to England in 1934 to escape Nazi persecution and then settled in Australia in 1941. He taught music in Melbourne high schools, and was a music critic for the Melbourne newspaper *Age* (1960–77). He was a prolific composer but discarded many of his scores. Werder's musical idiom was determined by the cross-currents of European modernism, with a gradual increase in the forcefulness of his resources, among them electronics.

WORKS: DRAMATIC: *Kisses for a Quid*, opera (1960); *En passant*, ballet (1964); *The General*, opera (1966); *Agamemnon*, opera (1967); *The Affair*, opera (1969); *Private*, television opera (1969); *The Vicious Square*, opera (1971); *The Conversion*, opera (1973); *Banker*, music theater (1973); *La belle dame sans merci*, ballet (1973); *Quantum*, ballet (1973); *Bellifull*, music theater (1976); *The Director*, music theater (1980); *The Medea*, opera (1984–85; Melbourne, Sept. 17, 1985); *Business Day*, music theater (1988). **ORCH.:** 6 syms.: No. 1 (1948–51; withdrawn), No. 2 (1959), No. 3, *Laocoön* (1965), No. 4 (1970), No. 5 (1971), and No. 6 (1979); Flute Concerto (1954); Piano Concerto (1955); 2 violin concertos (1956, 1966); *Brand*, symphonic poem (1956); *Sinfonia in Italian Style* (1957); *La Primavera*, symphonic poem (1957); *Abstraction* (1958); *Hexastrophe* (1961); *Monostrophe* (1961); Clarinet Concerto (1962); Viola Concerto (1963); *Konzert Musik* for 10 Solo Instruments and Orch. (1964); *Dramaturgie* (1966); *Morgen Rot* for Violin and Chamber Orch. (1968); *Strettophone* (1968); *Tower Concerto* (1968); *After Watteau* for Violin and Orch. (1968); *Sound Canvas* (1969); *Klang Bilder* (1969); *Triple Measure* (1970); *Don Giovanni Retired* (1971); *Prom Gothic* for Organ and Orch. (1972); *Sans souci*, flute concerto (1974); *Brandenburgisches Konzert I* for Strings (1974) and *II* for Saxophone and Orch. (1988); Concerto No. 2 for Piano, Winds, and Percussion (1975); *Cranach's Hunt*, horn concerto (1975); *Strettone* (1978); *Concerto for Orchestra* (1986); *Concert Music* for Bass Clarinet and Orch. (1987); *Renunciation* for Viola and Orch. (1987); *The Wenzel Connection*, clarinet concertino (1990); *Music a While* for Chamber Orch. (1991). **CHAMBER:** 4 violin sonatas: No. 1 (1958; old No. 2; former No. 1 of 1947 withdrawn), No. 2 (1963; old No. 3), No. 3 (1986), and No. 4, *Music Today* (1988); 12 string quartets, including Nos. 1–3 (withdrawn) and Nos. 4–12 (1955, 1956, 1962, 1965, 1966, 1968, 1970, 1972, 1974); 3 violin sonatas (1947, 1958, 1963); 2 piano quartets (1954, 1978); Cello Sonata (1956); 3 piano trios (1958, 1963, 1969); Quintet for Clarinet, Horn, and String Trio (1959); Flute Sonata (1960); Clarinet Sonata (1960); Horn Sonata (1960); Sonata for Wind Quintet (1961); Septet for Flute, Clarinet, Horn, and Strings (1963); Piano Quintet (1963); Sonata for Solo Violin (1965); *Apostrophe* for Wind Quintet (1965); Clarinet Quintet (1965); *Satyricon* for 6 Horns (1967); Sonata for Solo Cello (1968); Trio for Harp, Bass Clarinet, and Percussion (1969); *Activity* for Piano and Percussion (1969); *Triphony* for Flute, Guitar, and Bongos (1969); *Faggotiana* for Bassoon and String Trio (1970); *Tetract* for Viola, Oboe, and 2 Percussion (1970); *Divertimento* for Guitar and String Quartet (1970); Wind Quartet (1971); *Percussion Play* for Percussion (1971); *Index* for Chamber Ensemble (1976); *3* for Piano Trio (1976); *Night Out*, flute quartet (1982); *Aurora Australis* for Chamber Ensemble (1984); *Interconnections* for 2 Violins (1986); *Music at Night*, flute quartet (1986); *Off Beat* for Cello and Piano (1990); *Quadrella*, saxophone quartet (1990); *Taffelmusik* for Clarinet, Cello, and Piano (1991). **KEYBOARD: Piano:** 5 sonatas (1942, 1953, 1968, 1970, 1973); Sonata for 2 Pianos (1960). **Organ:** *Toccata* (1971); *Holy Thursday* (1975); *Epiphanien Weg* (1987). **Harpsichord:** Sonata (1963). **VOCAL:** *Radica Piece*, anti-Vietnam War cantata (1967); *Francis Bacon Essays*, choral oratorio (1971); *Terror Australis*, cantata for Soprano, Percussion, and Strings (1980); *Requiem* for Soprano, Flute, Oboe, Clarinet, Percussion, Organ, and Strings (1980); *Belsazar* for Chorus and Instrumental Ensemble (1988); *Lost Dramas* for Soprano and Chamber Ensemble (1990).
—NS/LK/DM

Werle, Lars Johan, Swedish composer; b. Gavle, June 23, 1926. He studied with Back (composition) and Moberg (musicology) at the Univ. of Uppsala (1948–51). He held positions at the Swedish Radio (1958–70) and as an instructor at the National School of Music Drama in Stockholm (1970–76), and then was resident composer of Göteborg (1976–79). In his music, he employs an amiably modern idiom, stimulating to the untutored ear while retaining the specific gravity of triadic tonal constructions. His theater operas have been received with smiling approbation.

WORKS: DRAMATIC: *Drömmen om Thérèse* (The Dream of Thérèse), opera, after Zola (Stockholm, May 26, 1964); *Zodiak*, ballet (1966; Stockholm, Feb. 12, 1967); *Resan* (The Voyage), opera, after J. P. Jersild (Hamburg, March 2, 1969); *En saga om sinnen*, television opera (Swedish TV, June 21, 1971); *Tintomara*, opera, after C. J. L. Almquist (1972; Stockholm, Jan. 18, 1973); *Medusan och djävulen* (Medusa and the Devil), lyrical mystery play (1973); *Animalen*, musical (Göteborg, May 19, 1979); *Är gryningen redan här*, ballet (Göteborg, Sept. 5, 1980); *En midsommarnattsdröm* (A Midsummer Night's Dream), opera, after Shakespeare (1984; Malmö, Feb. 8, 1985); *Gudars skymning eller När kärleken blev blind...*, cabaret (1985); *Lionardo*, opera (1985–88; Stockholm, March 31, 1988); *Kvinnogräl*, opera (Göteborg, Oct. 18, 1986); *Tavlan eller En eftermiddag på Prado*, chamber opera (1991–93); *Hercules*, opera (1993); *Äppelgriget*, opera (1995–96). **ORCH.:** *Sinfonia da camera* (1960); *Summer Music 1965* for Strings and Piano (1965); *Vaggsång för jorden* (1977); *Animalen* (1986); *Födelse* for Band (1992). **CHAMBER:** *Pentagram* for String Quartet (1959–60); *Attitudes* for Piano (1965); *Variété* for String Quartet (1971); *Tva miniatyrer* for Flute and Marimba (1988–89). **VOCAL:** *Canzone 126 di Francesco Petrarca* for Chorus (1967); *Nautical Preludes* for Chorus (1970); *Chants for Dark Hours* for Mezzo-soprano, Flute, Guitar, and Percussion (1972); *Flower Power* for 6 or More Voices and Instruments (1974); *Trees*, 4 poems for Baritone and Chorus, after e. e. cummings (1979); *Sweet sixties: Dialog* for Solo Voices and Keyboard (1990); *Ännu sjunger valarna*, cantata for Soloists and Chamber Ensemble (1992); *Sonetto 292* for Soprano and Chorus (1993).
—NS/LK/DM

Werner, Eric, Austrian-American musicologist; b. Lundenberg, near Vienna, Aug. 1, 1901; d. N.Y., July 28, 1988. He studied composition with Kornauth in Vienna and with Schrecker and Busoni in Berlin, and also took courses at the univs. of Graz, Vienna, Prague, Berlin, Göttingen, and Strasbourg, receiving his Ph.D. in 1928 from the Univ. of Strasbourg. He held teaching positions at the Saarbrücken Cons. (1926–33) and the Breslau

Jewish Theological Seminary (1935–38). In 1938 he went to the U.S. He was a prof. at the Hebrew Union Coll. (later merged with the Jewish Inst. of Religion in N.Y.) in Cincinnati (1939–67), then chairman of the musicology dept. at the Univ. of Tel Aviv (1967–72). He was an authority on Jewish and early Christian music.

WRITINGS: *In the Choir Loft: A Manual for Organists and Choir Directors in American Synagogues* (N.Y., 1957); *The Sacred Bridge: Liturgical Parallels in Synagogue and Early Church* (2 vols., N.Y., 1959, 1984); *Hebrew Music* (Cologne, 1961); *From Generation to Generation: Studies on Jewish Musical Tradition* (N.Y., 1962); *Mendelssohn: A New Image of the Composer and His Age* (N.Y., 1963); *A Voice Still Heard: The Sacred Songs of the Ashkenazic Jews* (Philadelphia, 1976).

BIBL.: J. Cohen, *Bibliography of the Publications of E. W.* (Tel Aviv, 1968).—**NS/LK/DM**

Werner, Gregor Joseph, Austrian organist and composer; b. Ybbs an der Donau, Jan. 28, 1693; d. Eisenstadt, Burgenland, March 3, 1766. In 1728 he was appointed Kapellmeister to Prince Esterházy at Eisenstadt. In 1761 Haydn was named Vice-Kapellmeister, and succeeded him after his death. Werner wrote a number of works, including 26 masses, 18 oratorios, and many instrumental pieces. Haydn had great respect for him, and arranged his fugues for string quartet.

BIBL.: H. Dopf, *Die Messenkompositionen G.J. W.s* (diss., Univ. of Innsbruck, 1956); C. Warner, *A Study of Selected Works of G.J. W.* (diss., Catholic Univ. of America, 1965).—**NS/LK/DM**

Wernick, Richard, American composer, teacher, and conductor; b. Boston, Jan. 16, 1934. He was a student in theory and composition of Fine, Shapero, and Berger at Brandeis Univ. (B.A., 1955), in composition of Toch, Blacher, and Copland and in conducting of Bernstein and Lipkin at the Berkshire Music Center at Tanglewood (summers, 1954–55), and in composition of Kirchner at Mills Coll. in Oakland, Calif. (M.A., 1957). In 1957–58 he was music director and composer-in-residence of the Royal Winnipeg Ballet in Canada. In 1964–65 he taught at the State Univ. of N.Y. at Buffalo, and in 1965–66 at the Univ. of Chicago, where he conducted its sym. orch. (1965–68). In 1968 he joined the faculty of the Univ. of Pa., where he conducted its sym. orch. (until 1970); he was also chairman of its music dept. (1969–74), served as prof. of music (1977–86), the Irving Fine Prof. of Music (1986–92), and the Magnin Prof. of Humanities (from 1992). From 1968 he also was music director of the Penn Contemporary Players. He held grants from the Ford Founation (1962–64) and the NEA (1975, 1979, 1982). In 1976 he received a Guggenheim fellowship and an award from the National Inst. of Arts and Letters. He won the Pulitzer Prize in Music in 1977 for his *Visions of Terror and Wonder* for Mezzo-soprano and Orch. In 1986 he received a Kennedy Center Friedheim Award for his Violin Concerto. As a composer, Wernick has followed an eclectic course in which he utilizes the most advantageous traditional and modern means of expression.

WORKS: DRAMATIC: Opera: *Maggie* (1959; unfinished; in collaboration with I. Fine). **Ballet:** *The Twisted Heart* (Winnipeg, Nov. 27, 1957); *Fete Brilliante* (Winnipeg, Jan. 13, 1958); *The Emperor's Nightingale* (1958); *The Queen of Ice* (1958); *The Nativity* (1960; CBS-TV, Jan. 1, 1961). **Other:** Incidental music to plays and film scores. **ORCH.:** *Aeva* (Chicago, Dec. 1966); Concerto for Cello and 10 Players (Washington, D.C., Feb. 1980); *Fanfare for a Festive Occasion* (Pittsburgh, Oct. 23, 1981); Violin Concerto (1984; Philadelphia, Jan. 17, 1986); Viola Concerto, *Do not go gentle...* (1986; Annandale-on-Hudson, N.Y., May 8, 1987); 2 syms.: No. 1 (1988; Wilkes-Barre, Pa., Jan. 1989) and No. 2, for Soprano and Orch. (1993; Philadelphia, Jan. 19, 1995); Piano Concerto (1989–90; Washington, D.C., Feb. 1991); Saxophone Quartet Concerto (1991); Cello Concerto (1992); *Musica da Camerata* (1999). **CHAMBER:** *4 Pieces* for String Quartet (1955); *Divertimento* for Viola, Cello, Clarinet, and Bassoon (Oakland, Calif., May 1956); Duo Concertante for Cello and Piano (1960); Trio for Violin, Clarinet, and Cello (1961; Waltham, Mass., Dec. 7, 1962); 6 string quartets: No. 1 (Rochester, N.Y., Dec. 5, 1963), No. 2 (1972–73), No. 3 (1988; N.Y., Jan. 1990), No. 4 (1990; Philadelphia, April 29, 1991), No. 5, with soprano (1995), and No. 6 (1998); *Music* for Viola d'Amore (1964; Buffalo, April 1965); *Stretti* for Clarinet, Violin, Viola, and Guitar (1965); *Cadenzas and Variations II* for Violin (1970) and *III* for Cello (1972); *Introits and Canons* for Chamber Ensemble (1977; N.Y., Jan. 1978); *Partita* for Violin (N.Y., Sept. 1978); *In Praise of Zephyrus* for Oboe and String Trio (1981); *Formula: P———m* for Violin and Cello (1981; Chicago, Jan. 22, 1982); Piano Sonata (1982; Washington, D.C., Jan. 15, 1983); Cello Sonata (1982; N.Y., Dec. 5, 1983); Brass Quintet, *Musica Ptolemeica* (1987); *Cassation* for Horn, Oboe, and Piano (1995); Trio for Violin, Cello, and Piano (1996); Violin Sonata (1997). **VOCAL:** *From Tulips and Chimneys* for Baritone and Orch. (Salt Lake City, June 1956); *Full Fadom 5* for Chorus and Chamber Ensemble (Bay Shore, N.Y., May 1964); *what if a much of a which of a wind* for Chorus and Prepared Piano, 4-Hands (1964); *Lyrics from IXI* for Soprano, Vibraphone-Marimba, and Contrabass (1966); *Haiku of Basho* for Soprano, Flute, Clarinet, Violin, Contrabass, 2 Percussion, Piano, and Tape (Chicago, March 1, 1968); *Moonsongs from the Japanese* for Soprano and Tape (1969); *Beginnings* for Chorus (1970); *A Prayer for Jerusalem* for Mezzo-soprano and Percussion (1971); *Kaddish-Requiem* for Cantor, Mezzo-soprano, and Chamber Ensemble (1971); *Kee el Asher*for Chorus (1972); *Songs for Remembrance* for Mezzo-soprano, Shawm, English Horn, and Oboe (1973); *Visions of Terror and Wonder* for Mezzo-soprano and Orch. (Aspen, Colo., July 19, 1976); *Contemplations of the 10th Muse* for Soprano and Piano (2 books, 1977, 1979); *And on the 7th Day...* for Cantor and Percussionists (Bridgeport, Conn., April 1979); *A Poison Tree* for Soprano, Flute, Clarinet, Violin, Cello, and Piano (1979; Syracuse, N.Y., Jan. 1980); *The Oracle of Shimon bar Yochai* for Soprano, Cello, and Piano (N.Y., Dec. 8, 1983); *I Too* for Voice and Piano (1984); *Oracle II* for Soprano, Oboe, and Piano (1985; Baltimore, Feb. 1987); *V'sham'ru* for Cantor and Unspecified Single Instrument (1985; rev. 1995); *The 11th Commandment, "No, thou shalt not Xerox® music"* for Chorus and Piano and Organ (1987); *Ball of Sun* for Voice and Piano (1989); *Fragments of Prophecy* for Boy's Chorus and Mixed Chorale (1991); *Two for Jan* [De Gaetani] for Soprano, Mezzo-soprano, Oboe/English Horn, Bass Clarinet, and Cello (1991); *...and a time for peace* for Soprano and Orch. (1994). **OTHER:** Numerous educational works, including *A Musical Game of Tag* for 2 Violins, *Peter's March* for 3 Violins, etc.—**NS/LK/DM**

Werrecore (also Vercore, Verecore, Verrechore, Werrekoren), Matthias Hermann, composer; b. probably in Vercore or Warcoing, Hainaut, date unknown; d. after 1574. He most likely was of

Flemish birth; however, the records of Milan Cathedral reveal that his father, Eligio, was from Milan. In 1522 Werrecore became maestro di cappella at Milan Cathedral, and in 1550 Oliviero di Phalansis was named his temporary successor, followed by Simon Boyleau in 1557–58. Werrecore was mistakenly identified with Matthäus Le Maistre by Fétis and Kade; research by Haberl, Elsa Bienenfeld, and Cecie Stainer demonstrated the fallacy of this assumption. He composed the famous *Bataglia taliana* for 4 Voices, which celebrated the defeat of France at the Battle of Pavia in 1525 (publ. with the German title *Die Schlacht vor Pavia* in Schmeltzl's collection *Guter seltzamer...teutscher Gesang*, Nuremberg, 1544; ed. in Denkmäler der Tonkunst in Österreich, XXXVII, Jg. XVIII/2, 1911; reprint as *La bataglia taliana...con alcune villote*, Venice, 1549; 2nd ed., enl., 1552). He also composed *20 Cantum...liber primus* for 5 Voices (Milan, 1555) and a few motets.—**NS/LK/DM**

Werrenrath, Reinald, American baritone; b. Brooklyn, Aug. 7, 1883; d. Plattsburg, N.Y., Sept. 12, 1953. He was a pupil of his father, a tenor, then of David Bispham and Herbert Witherspoon. He began his career as a concert singer he was also in oratorio. He made his operatic debut on Feb. 19, 1919, at the Metropolitan Opera in N.Y., as Silvio in Pagliacci, and remained with the company until 1921; he then devoted himself to teaching and concert singing. He appeared in public for the last time at Carnegie Hall in N.Y. on Oct. 23, 1952. He ed. *Modern Scandinavian Songs* (2 vols., Boston, 1925–26).—**NS/LK/DM**

Wert, Giaches (or **Jaches**) **de,** eminent Flemish composer; b. probably in Weert, near Antwerp, between May 6 and Aug. 18, 1535; d. Mantua, May 6, 1596. He was taken to Italy in childhood to serve as a chorister at the court of Maria di Cordona, Marchese della Padulla, in Avellino, near Naples. By 1558 he was in the service of Count Alfonso Gonzaga in Novellara, and in 1565 he was appointed maestro di cappella at the ducal chapel of S. Barbara in Mantua, which was to remain the center of his activities for the remainder of his life. Wert's early years in Mantua were made difficult by the enmity of his fellow members of the cappella, most especially Agostino Bonvicino, who had hoped to become maestro di cappella; while he failed to attain this post, he did succeed in pursuing an adulterous relationship with Wert's wife. Wert himself later had an affair with Tarquinia Molza, a niece of Francesco Maria Molza, a fine poet and musician in Ferrara. In 1580 Wert received Mantuan citizenship. In 1582–83 and again in 1585 Gastoldi was called upon to serve as maestro di cappella during bouts of ill health by Wert; in 1592 he was formally appointed Wert's successor, although Wert remained active at the court until his death. Wert was greatly esteemed by contemporary musicians; Palestrina praised him, and he was also mentioned favorably by Thomas Morley, Artusi, G.B. Doni, and Monteverdi. Wert was distinguished as both a madrigalist and a composer of sacred works. See C. MacClintock and M. Bernstein, eds., *G. d.W.: Collected Works*, Corpus Mensurabilis Musicae, XXIV (1961–).

WORKS (all 1st publ. in Venice): **VOCAL: Secular:** *Il primo libro de madrigali* for 5 Voices (1558); *Il primo libro de madrigali* for 4 Voices (1561); *Madrigali del fiore, libro primo* for 5 Voices (1561); *Madrigali del fiore, libro secondo* for 5 Voices (1561); *Il terzo libro de madrigali* for 5 Voices (1563); *Il secondo libro de madrigali, nuovamente con nuova giunta ristampati* for 5 Voices (1564); *Il quarto libro de madrigali* for 5 Voices (1567); *Il quinto libro de madrigali* for 5 Voices (1571); *Il sesto libro de madrigali* for 5 Voices (1577); *Il settimo libro de madrigali* for 5 Voices (1581); *L'ottavo libro de madrigali* for 5 Voices (1586); *Il nono libro de madrigali* for 5 Voices (1581); *Il primo libro delle canzonette, villanelle* for 5 Voices (1589); *Il decimo libro de madrigali* for 5 Voices (1591); *L'undecimo libro de madrigali* for 5 Voices (1595); *Il duodecimo libro de madrigali* for 4 to 7 Voices (1608); other works in contemporary collections. **Sacred:** *Motectorum liber primus* for 5 Voices (1566); *Il secondo libro de motetti* for 5 Voices (1581); *Modulationum liber primus* for 6 Voices (1581); other works in contemporary collections. **INSTRUMENTAL:** Fantasias, *a 4*.

BIBL.: C. MacClintock, *The Five-part Madrigals of G. d.W.* (diss., Ind. Univ., 1955); M. Bernstein, *The Sacred Vocal Music of G. d.W.* (diss., Univ. of N.C., 1964); C. MacClintock, *G. d.W. (1535–1596): Life and Works*, Musicological Studies and Documents, XVII (1966).—**NS/LK/DM**

Wesembeek, Léon-Philippe-Marie Burbure de

See **Burbure de Wesembeek, Léon-Philippe Marie**

Wesendonck, Mathilde (née **Luckemeyer**), German poet; b. Elberfeld, Dec. 23, 1828; d. Traunblick, near Altmünster on the Traunsee, Austria, Aug. 31, 1902. Her first meeting with Richard Wagner took place in Zürich, early in 1852, and soon developed into a deep friendship. She wrote the famous *Fünf Gedichte* (*Der Engel, Stehe still, Träume, Schmerzen*, and *Im Treibhaus*), which Wagner set to music as studies for *Tristan und Isolde*. On May 19, 1848, she married Otto Wesendonck (b. March 16, 1815; d. Berlin, Nov. 18, 1896); in 1857 he gave Wagner the use of a beautiful house on his estate on Lake Zürich, where the first act of *Tristan und Isolde* was written and the 2nd act sketched.

BIBL.: A. Heintz, ed., *Briefe Richard Wagners an Otto Wesendonk* (Charlottenburg, 1898; 2nd ed., aug., 1905 by W. Golther; Eng. tr., 1911); idem, ed., *Richard Wagner an M. W.: Tagebuchblätter und Briefe 1853–1871* (Leipzig, 1904; 30th ed., rev., 1906; Eng. tr., 1905); H. Belart, *Richard Wagners Liebestragodie mit M. W.* (Dresden, 1912); J. Kapp, ed., *Richard Wagner an M. und Otto W.* (Leipzig, 1915; 2nd ed., 1936); E. Müller von Asow, ed., *Johannes Brahms und M. W.: Ein Briefwechsel* (Vienna, 1943); J. Bergfeld, *Otto und M. W.s Bedeutung für das Leben und Schaffen Richard Wagners* (Bayreuth, 1968).—**NS/LK/DM**

Wesley, prominent English family:

(1) John Wesley, clergyman and a founder of Methodism, brother of Charles Wesley; b. Epworth, Lincolnshire, June 17, 1703; d. London, March 2, 1791. He was educated at Christ Church, Oxford (graduated, 1724), and in 1728 he became a priest. With his brother Charles and 2 others, he helped to found the Methodist movement; in 1735 he went to the U.S. with his brother to do missionary work, and publ. his first *Collection of Psalms* *and Hymns* (Charlestown, 1737). Returning to England, he spread the doctrine of Methodism and became famous as a preacher and writer. He has been called "the father of Methodist hymnology."

BIBL.: R. Green, *Works of J. and Charles W.* (London, 1896); J. Nuelsen, *J. W. und das deutsche Kirchenlied* (Bremen, 1938); E. Routley, *The Musical W.s* (London, 1968).

(2) Charles Wesley (I), clergyman, a founder of Methodism, and hymn writer, brother of John Wesley; b. Epworth, Lincolnshire, Dec. 18, 1707; d. London, March 29, 1788. He was educated at Christ Church, Oxford. With his brother and 2 others, he helped to organize the Methodist movement. In 1735 he followed his brother to the U.S. as a missionary but soon returned to England, where he later became associated with the Church of England. During his years as a Methodist, he acquired a notable reputation as a hymn writer. Among his most celebrated hymns are "Hark, the Herald Angels Sing, Christ the Lord Is Risen Today," and "Love Divine, All Loves Excelling."

BIBL.: R. Green, *Works of John and C. W.* (London, 1896); E. Routley, *The Musical W.s* (London, 1968).

(3) Charles Wesley (II), organist and composer, nephew of John Wesley and Charles Wesely (I) and brother of Samuel Wesley; b. Bristol, Dec. 11, 1757; d. London, May 23, 1834. He was a pupil of Kelway and Boyce in London, then held various positions as a church organist. He publ. in London 6 string quartets (c. 1776), 6 concertos for Organ or Harpsichord and Orch. (c. 1781), Concerto grosso in 7 parts (c. 1782), Variations on "God Save the King" for Piano (c. 1799), 6 voluntaries for Organ (1812), and a Piano Sonata (c. 1820). His vocal works include the cantata *Caractacus* (1791), 15 anthems, 6 hymns, and various songs.

BIBL.: E. Routley, *The Musical W.s* (London, 1968).

(4) Samuel Wesley, organist and composer, nephew of John Wesley and Charles Wesley (II) and brother of the preceding; b. Bristol, Feb. 24, 1766; d. London, Oct. 11, 1837. When he was 6 he commenced music studies with the Bristol organist David Williams, and he began to compose at the age of 8; learned to play the violin as well as the organ. He composed the oratorio *Ruth* when he was only 8; he publ. 8 sonatas for keyboard at 12. He soon acquired a fine reputation as an organist, while composing prolifically. In 1787 he suffered a skull injury in a fall into a building excavation, which impaired him emotionally for the remainder of his life. He was married to Charlotte Martin in 1793, but they separated in 1795; some years later he became intimate with his housekeeper, Sarah Suter; the burden of supporting his children by both Martin and Suter exacerbated his condition. In order to make ends meet, he played in concerts, appeared as an organist and conductor, gave lectures, and taught. In his last years he wrote a number of hymns. Wesley was a notable composer of Latin church music, and he also wrote for the Anglican church. He composed much instrumental music, his masterpiece being the Sym. in B-flat major (1802). He also wrote an autobiography (c. 1836).

WORKS: 5 masses and about 55 other Latin sacred works; the oratorios *Ruth* (1774) and *The Death of Abel* (1779); services and anthems; hymn tunes; sacred songs; secular choruses, part-songs, glees, duets, and solo songs; 5 overtures (1775, 1778, 1780, 1813, c. 1834); 4 syms. (1784, 1784, c. 1790, 1802); 2 harpsichord concertos (both c. 1774); 4 organ concertos (1787, 1800, c. 1811, c. 1815); 8 violin concertos (1779, 1781, c. 1782, 1782, c. 1782, 1783, 1785, c. 1812); Sinfonia obbligato (1781); 3 string quartets (1779; 1779–80; c. 1800); several trios and sonatas; numerous works for Organ and other Solo Keyboard Instruments.

BIBL.: W. Winters, *An Account of the Remarkable Musical Talents of Several Members of the W. Family* (London, 1874); E. Wesley (his daughter), *Letters of S. W. to Mr. Jacobs Relating to the Introduction into This Country of the Works of Bach* (London, 1875; 2nd ed., 1878); G. Stevenson, *Memorials of the W. Family* (London, 1876); J. Lightwood, *S. W., Musician: The Story of His Life* (London, 1937); E. Routley, *The Musical W.s* (London, 1968); H. Ambrose, *The Anglican Anthems and Roman Catholic Motets of S. W. (1766–1837)* (diss., Boston Univ., 1969); J. Schwarz Jr., *The Orchestral Music of S. W.* (diss., Univ. of Md., 1971); J. Marsh, *The Latin Church Music of S. W.* (diss., Univ. of York, 1975).

(5) Samuel Sebastian Wesley, organist and composer, illegitimate son of the preceding; b. London, Aug. 14, 1810; d. Gloucester, April 19, 1876. When he was 10 he was elected a chorister of the Chapel Royal; also sang at St. Paul's Cathedral. He received training in organ and composition from his father. From the age of 16 he was organist in various London churches, including St. James's Chapel (from 1826), St. Giles (1829–32), St. John (1829–31), and Hampton Parish Church (1831–32), then organist at Hereford Cathedral (1832–35), Exeter Cathedral (1835–41), Leeds Parish Church (1842–49), Winchester Cathedral (1849–65), Winchester Coll. (1850–65), and Gloucester Cathedral (1865–76). He received the degrees of B.Mus. and D.Mus. at Oxford (1839). He won great renown as an organist, excelling at improvisation. As a composer, he became best known for his Anglican cathedral music.

WORKS: 13 pieces of service music; 38 anthems, including such well-known examples as Ascribe unto the Lord, Blessed Be the God and the Father, Let Us Lift Up Our Heart, The Wilderness and the Solitary Place, Thou Wilt Keep Him in Perfect Peace", and "Wash Me Thoroughly"; secular choruses, part-songs, glees, and songs; Sym. (c. 1832); ballet music; Overture in C (c. 1827); organ music; piano pieces. COLLECTIONS AND EDITIONS: "The Psalter...with Chants" (Leeds, 1843);" A Selection of Psalms and Hymns" (London, 1864); "The European Psalmist" (London, 1872); "The Welburn Appendix of Original Hymns and Tunes" (London, 1875).

WRITINGS: *A Few Words on Cathedral Music* (London, 1849); *Reply to the Inquiries of the Cathedral Commissioners Relative to the Improvement in the Music of Divine Worship in Cathedrals* (London, 1854).

BIBL.: G. Stevenson, *Memorials of the W. Family* (London, 1876); E. Routley, *The Musical W.s* (London, 1968); P. Chappell, *Dr. S.S. W.* (Great Wakering, 1977).—**NS/LK/DM**

Wesley-Smith, Martin, Australian composer and teacher; b. Adelaide, June 10, 1945. He was educated at the univs. of Adelaide (B.M., 1969; M.M., 1971) and of York in England (Ph.D., 1974); his mentors in composition were Peter Tahourdin, Peter Maxwell Davies, Sandor Veress, and Jindrich Feld. In 1974 Wesley-Smith became a lecturer in electronic music at the New South Wales State Conservatorium of Music in

Sydney, where he was senior lecturer in composition and electronic music from 1980; he was also a reader in composition at the Univ. of Hong Kong (1994–95). He was founder-director of watt, an electronic music and audio-visual performing group, with which he toured internationally; he was also founder-musical director of T.R.E.E. (Theatre Reaching Environments Everywhere). With Ian Fredericks, he organized the first computer music studio in mainland China in 1986. In 1987 he was the Australia Council's Don Banks Composer Fellow. In his extensive output, Wesley-Smith follows an imaginative, eclectic course. While he has composed in most genres, he has gained particular notice for his effective computer and audio-visual works, finding particular inspiration in the writings of Lewis Carroll. Some of his works are overtly political.

WORKS: DRAMATIC: *Pi in the Sky*, children's opera (1971); *The Wild West Show*, children's music theater (1971); *Machine*, children's music theater (1972); *Boojum!*, music theater (1985–86); *Quito*, audio-visual music theater (1994); *Encountering Sorro (Ch'ü Yüan Laments)*, radiophonic piece (1994). **ORCH.:** *Interval Piece* (1970); *Hansard Music* (1970); *Sh...* for Audience and Orch. (1973); *Beta-Globin DNA 3* (1990). **CHAMBER:** *Improvistions* for Trumpet and Piano (1966); *Tiger, Tiger* for Violin Duet (1970); *Doublets 2(a)* for Saxophone, Tape, and Delay (1974), *2(d)* for Trombone, Tape, and Delay (1987), and *2(e)* for Clarinet, Tape, and Delay (1987); *Dodgson's Dream* for Clarinet, Tape, and Transparencies (1979); *Pat-a-Cake* for Trombone and Tape (1980); *For Marimba and Tape* (1982); *Doodles* for Soloist and Tape (1983); *For (Bass) Clarinet and Tape* (1983); *Snark-Hunting* for Flute, Piano, Percussion, Cello, and Tape (1984); *White Knight* for Trombone, Marimba, and Tape (1984; also various other versions); *Smudge (Malin 2)* for MIDI Keyboard and Apple Macintosh Computer (1989); *hex D2* for Percussion Quartet (1990); *db* for Flute, Clarinet, Piano, and Cello (1991); *Visiting the Queen* for Marimba and Yamaha Disklavier (1992); *Balibo* for Flute and Tape (1992). **VOCAL:** *Gum Tears of an Arabian Tree* for Tenor and Quintet (1966); *2 Shakespearean Songs* for Chorus (1967); *To Noddy-Man* for High Voice and Piano Duet (1969); *Doublets 2(b)* for Countertenor, Tape, and Tape Delay (1974); *Who Killed Cock Robin?* for Chorus (1979); *Lost in Space* for Children's Chorus and Orch. (1982); *Songs for Snark- Hunter* for Chorus and Piano (1985); *Songs of Australia* for Chorus, Piano, Percussion, and Tape (1988); *Tiananmen Square* for Chorus (1989); *Timor et Tremor*, song cycle for Tenor, Flute, Clarinet, Piano, Cello, and Tape (1991); *Flora, Fauna, and LORNA!* for Vocal Sextet (1992). **TAPE:** *Vietnam Image* (1970); *Media Music 1* (1972) and *2* (1973); *Kdadalak (For the Children of Timor)* for Tape and Transparencies (1977); *Japanese Pictures* for Tape and Transparencies (1981); *Echoes and Star Tides* for Tape and Transparencies (1981; in collaboration with I. Fredericks); *Electronic Study 37(b)* (1982); *Dah Dit Dah Dah* (1983; in collaboration with J. Piché and O. Shoji); *Wattamolla Red* for Tape and Transparencies (1983); *VENCEREMOS!* for Tape and Transparencies (1984); *Snark-Hunting 2* for Tape and Transparencies (1986); *Chi'il Yüan, By the Burning River* (1988); *Rabbit-Hole Music 1 and 2* (1990).—**NS/LK/DM**

Wessely, Othmar, Austrian musicologist; b. Linz, Oct. 31, 1922; d. Vienna, April 20, 1998. He was educated at the Bruckner Cons. in Linz, the Vienna Academy of Music, and the Univ. of Vienna (Ph.D., 1947, with the diss. *Anton Bruckner in Linz*; Habilitationsschrift, 1959, with his *Arnold von Bruck: Leben und Umwelt*). From 1950 to 1963 he was a member of the faculty of the Univ. of Vienna. After teaching at the Univ. of Graz (1963–71), he returned to the Univ. of Vienna in 1971 as prof. of musicology, retiring in 1993. From 1974 to 1991 he also was president of the Publishing Soc. for Monuments of Music in Austria.

WRITINGS: *Musik in Oberösterreich* (Linz, 1951); *Die Musikinstrumentsammlung des Oberösterreichischen Landesmuseums* (Linz, 1952); *Johann Joseph Fux und Johann Mattheson* (Graz, 1966); ed. *Ernst Ludwig Gerber: Historisch-biographisches Lexikon der Tonkünstler (1790–1792) und Neues historisch-biographisches Lexikon der Tonkünstler (1812–1814)* (4 vols., Graz, 1966–77); *Johann Joseph Fux und Francesco Antonio Vallotti* (Graz, 1967); *Pietro Pariatis Libretto zu Johann Joseph Fuxens "Costanza e fortezza"* (Graz, 1969); *Johann Joseph Fux: Persönlichkeit, Umwelt, Nachwelt* (Graz, 1979).—**NS/LK/DM**

Wessman, Harri (Kristian), Finnish composer; b. Helsinki, March 29, 1949. He learned to play the cello and double bass in his youth. He took courses in musicology and languages at the Univ. of Helsinki (1967–73) and also studied composition privately with Kokkonen, continuing under his tutelage at the Sibelius Academy in Helsinki (1973–78). His works are lyrical and melodic.

WORKS: DRAMATIC: *Onnen arvoitus* (The Riddle of Happiness), play for Children's Chorus, Recorder, and Percussion (1986); *Päivikki*, ballet (1987). **ORCH.:** *Serenade* for Trumpet and Strings (1976); *Sarja jousiorkesterille musiikista Eha Lättemäen runoihin* (Suite for String Orch. from the Music to Poems by Eha Lättemäe; 1978); *Prinsessa joka nukkui sata vuotta* (The Princess Who Slept a Hundred Years) for Trumpet or Soprano and String Orch. (1981); 2 piano concertinos (1982, 1987); *Loitsunpuhallus* for Wind Orch. (1984); *Koraalialkusoitto* (Choral Overture; 1984); *Serenade* for Piano and Strings (1985); *Tango tan-tan-tan* (1985); *Väinämöinen* (1985); Trumpet Concerto (1987); *Adagio and Andante* for Strings (1988); *Parodioita Parodies* for Strings (1988); *Larghetto Espressivo* for Strings (1990). **CHAMBER:** *Musiikkia uruille* (Music for Organ; 1977); Violin Sonata (1978); 2nd Cello Sonata (1979); *Syksyn sävyinen fantasia* (Autumnal Fantasia) for Cello and Piano (1980); *2 intermezzi* for Piano (1980, 1981); Trio for Accordion, Flute, and Guitar (1981); *Je chante la beauté de la solitude* for Accordion (1982); *Prelude and Sicilienne* for Violin, Cello, and Piano (1983); Piano Quartet (1985); *Es sangen drei Engel* for Oboe and Organ (1986); Accordion Sonata (1986); 2 suites for 2 Violins (1986, 1988); *Teema ja muunnelmia vaskiyhtyeelle* (Theme and Variations for Brass Ensemble; 1986–87); *Dialogos*, 25 pieces for Flute and Piano (1988); Sonata for Solo Violin (1988); Horn Sonata (1989); *Capriccio* for Wind Nonet (1990). **VOCAL:** *Lauluja tuimista linnuista* for Chorus and Piano (1977); *Kolme laulua V.A. Koskenniemen runoihin* (3 Songs to Poems by V.A. Koskenniemi) for Chorus (1979); *Kaksi laulua sekakuorolle Marianna Kalliolan runoihin* (2 Songs for Mixed Chorus to Poems by Marianna Kalliola; 1980); *Vaggvisa, Det viner på fjällen* for Children's Chorus (1982); *Nelja laulua Lauri Pohjanpään runoihin* (4 Songs to Poems by Lauri Pohjanpää) for Children's Chorus (1983); *Ligg ej och dra dig!* for Men's Chorus (1984); *Det blir kyligt* for Men's Chorus (1985); *Ljusa vindar* (Light Winds), cantata for Children's Chorus and Instrumental Ensemble (1989).—**NS/LK/DM**

Westenburg, Richard, American conductor; b. Minneapolis, April 26, 1932. He studied at Lawrence

Univ. (B.Mus., 1954) and at the Univ. of Minn. (M.A., 1956); then went to Paris, where he studied with Boulanger and Cochereau (1959–60); subsequently, he did postgraduate work at the Theological Seminary School of Sacred Music in N.Y. (1960–66). From 1956 to 1960 he taught music at the Univ. of Mont.; then served as director of music at the First Unitarian Church in Worcester, Mass. (1960–62). In 1964 he went to N.Y., where he was engaged as organist and choirmaster of the Central Presbyterian Church, holding this position until 1974. In 1968 he founded Musica Sacra and became its music director; he also served as music director of the Collegiate Chorale (1973–79). He was conductor-in-residence at the Cathedral Church of St. John the Divine (1974–86) and music director there (1976–83). He served as head of the choral dept. of the Juilliard School in N.Y. from 1977 to 1989; he was appointed visiting prof. at Rutgers, the State Univ. of N.J., in 1986; he became music director at the Fifth Avenue Presbyterian Church in N.Y. in 1990.—**NS/LK/DM**

Westenholz or **Westenholtz, Carl August Friedrich,** German tenor, conductor, and composer; b. Lauenburg, July 1736; d. Ludwigslust, Jan. 24, 1789. He entered the choir of the Mecklenburg-Schwerin Hofkapelle in 1749, where he studied voice with A. C. Kunzen and cello with F. X. Woschitka. In 1753 he was made Kammersänger to the court. When the Hofkapelle moved to Ludwigslust in 1767, he was appointed its Konzertmeister and director. From 1770 until his death he was its Kapellmeister, where he raised standards to a high level. He became best known as a composer of sacred vocal music, namely of the cantatas *Die Hirten bey der Krippe zu Bethlehem* (1774), *Die Auferstehung Jesu Christi* (1777), *Das Vertrauen auf Gott* (1787), and *Ist Gott für mich* (n.d.), the oratorio *Golgotha* (n.d.), and various chorales. He also wrote secular vocal music and some instrumental works, including 2 harpsichord concertos, a Cello Concerto, a Sonata for Harpsichord and Violin, and keyboard pieces. In 1770 he married the Italian soprano Barbara Lucietta Fricemelica (née Affabili) Westenholz (b. Venice, 1725; d. Ludwigslust, Sept. 20, 1776). She became a member of the Schwerin Hofkapelle in 1757, and later was much esteemed as a member of the Ludwigslust court. In 1777 he married the German singer, pianist, and composer (Eleonore) Sophia Maria (née Fritscher) Westenholz (b. Neubrandenburg, July 10, 1759; d. Ludwigslust, Oct. 4, 1838). She studied piano and voice with J. W. Hertel, the Schwerin court composer. When she was about 16 she became a singer at the Ludwigslust Hofkapelle. By 1799 she was Kapellmeisterin there, remaining a leading figure until her retirement in 1821. She also toured throughout Germany and won accolades as a pianist. Among her compositions were vocal and keyboard pieces. They had 2 sons: Friedrich Westenholz (b. Ludwigslust, May 28, 1778; d. Berlin, March 12, 1840), was an oboist and composer. He studied with his mother and J. F. Braun. He served as a chamber musician in the Berlin Hofkapelle until his retirement in 1828. Among his works were concertante syms., chamber music, piano pieces, and songs. Carl Ludwig Cornelius Westenholz (b. Ludwigslust, Jan. 12, 1788; d. there, Feb. 4, 1854), was a violinist, pianist, and composer. From 1809 to 1837 he was a violinist in the Ludwigslust Hofkapelle, and then went with it to Schwerin. He composed a *Divertimento* for Harpsichord, Violin, and Bass and some keyboard pieces. Carl August Friedrich also had an illegitimate son, Friedrich Carl Westenholz (b. Cramon, Feb. 12, 1756; d. Ludwigslust, March 15, 1802), who was a cellist and organist. From 1774 to 1781 he was a cellist in the Ludwigslust Hoskapelle. After studies in Lübeck, he returned to the Ludwigslust Hofkapelle in 1783 and became the piano teacher of the duke's children. —**LK/DM**

Westerberg, Stig (Evald Börje), Swedish conductor; b. Malmö, Nov. 26, 1918. He studied at the Stockholm Musikhögskolan (1937–42) and with Kletzki in Paris. He was a répétiteur at Stockholm's Royal Theater (1943–46) and then conducted at the Oscarsteatern; after conducting the Gävleborg Sym. Orch. (1949–53), he returned to Stockholm as a conductor at the Royal Theater; in 1957 he became chief conductor of the Swedish Radio Sym. Orch. He taught conducting at the Musikhögskolan from 1969, becoming a prof. there in 1971. From 1978 to 1985 he was chief conductor of the Malmö Sym. Orch. He became well known for his performances of both traditional and contemporary Swedish scores.—**NS/LK/DM**

Westergaard, Peter (Talbot), American composer, music theorist, and teacher; b. Champaign, Ill., May 28, 1931. He was a student of Piston at Harvard Coll. (A.B., 1953), of Milhaud at the Aspen (Colo.) Music School (summers, 1951–52) and at the Paris Cons. (1953), of Sessions at Princeton Univ. (M.F.A., 1956), and of Fortner in Detmold (1956) and in Freiburg im Breisgau (1957) on a Fulbright fellowship. After serving as a guest lecturer at the Staatliche Hochschule für Musik in Freiburg im Breisgau (1958), he taught at Columbia Univ. (1958–66). In 1966–67 he was a visiting lecturer at Princeton Univ. In 1967–68 he taught at Amherst Coll. He became an assoc. prof. at Princeton Univ. in 1968, and a full prof. in 1971. He served as chairman of its music dept. (1974–78; 1983–86). In 1995 he was named the William Shubael Conant Prof. of Music there. He also held the endowed chair at the Univ. of Ala. School of Music in 1995. In addition to various commissions, he held a Guggenheim fellowship (1964–65) and an NEA grant (1990–91). He wrote various articles for journals and publ. the study *An Introduction to Tonal Theory* (N.Y., 1975). In his compositions, Westergaard explored the potentialities of total organization of tones, rhythms, and other compositional elements.

WORKS: DRAMATIC: *Charivari*, chamber opera (1953); *Mr. and Mrs. Discobbolos*, chamber opera (1966); *The Tempest*, opera (1988–90; Lawrenceville, N.J., July 8, 1994). **ORCH.:** *Symphonic Movement* (1954); *5 Movements* for Small Orch. (1958); *Noises, Sounds, and Sweet Airs* for Chamber Orch. (1968); *Tuckets and Sennets* for Band (1969). **CHAMBER:** *Partita* for Flute, Violin, and Harpsichord (1953; rev. 1956); *Invention* for Flute and Piano (1955); String Quartet (1957); Quartet for Violin, Vibraphone, Clarinet, and Cello (1960); Trio for Flute, Cello, and Piano (1962); *Variations for 6 Players* for Flute, Clarinet, Percussion, Piano, Violin, and Cello (1963); *Divertimento on Discobbolic*

Fragments for Flute and Piano (1967); *Moto perpetuo* for Flute, Oboe, Clarinet, Bassoon, Trumpet, and Horn (1976); *Alonzo's Grief* for Piano (1977); 2 *Fanfares* for 3 Trumpets and 3 Trombones (1988). **VOCAL:** *Cantata I: The Plot Against the Giant* for Women's Chorus, Clarinet, Cello, and Harp (1956), *II: A Refusal to Mourn the Death, by Fire, of a Child in London* for Bass and 10 Instruments (1958), and *III: Leda and the Swan* for Mezzo-soprano, Vibraphone, Marimba, and Viola (1961); *Spring and Fall: To a Young Child* for Voice and Piano (1960; also for Voice and 5 Instruments, 1964); *There Was a Little Man* for Soprano and Violin (1982); *Ariel Music* for High Soprano and Chamber Ensemble (1987); *Ode* for Soprano, Flute, Clarinet, Violin, Viola, and Harp (1989).—**NS/LK/DM**

Westergaard, Svend, Danish composer and pedagogue; b. Copenhagen, Oct. 8, 1922; d. Hillerd, near Copenhagen, June 22, 1988. He studied composition with Hffding, Hjelmborg, and Jersild at the Copenhagen Cons. He began teaching there in 1951, serving as a prof. of theory (from 1967) and also its director (1967–71). He publ. the study *Harmonilaere* (Copenhagen, 1961).

WORKS: ORCH.: *Elegy* for Strings (1949); *Pezzo sinfonico* (1950); Oboe Concerto (1950); 2 syms.: No. 1, *Sinfonia* (1955) and No. 2, *Sinfonia da camera* (1968); *L'Homme arme*, canzona for 16 Instruments (1959; rev. for Orch., 1970); *Capriccio* for Violin and String Orch. (1960); *Variazioni sinfoniche* (Danish Radio, June 12, 1960); Cello Concerto (1961; Århus, Oct. 22, 1962; rev. 1973); *Pezzo concertante* (Danish Radio, Aug. 19, 1965); *Sinfonia da camera* (Copenhagen, March 24, 1969); *Varianti sinfoniche* for Winds and Percussion (1972); *Transformazioni sinfonische* for Piano and Orch. (1976; Danish Radio, Oct. 27, 1977). **CHAMBER:** 2 wind quintets (1948, 1949); *Tema con variazioni* for Clarinet Quintet (1949); String Quartet (1968); Sonata for Solo Flute (1971); Sonata for Solo Cello (1979).—**NS/LK/DM**

Westerhoff, Christian Wilhelm, German violinist, violist, and composer; b. Osnabrück, 1763; d. Bückeburg, Jan. 26, 1806. He was reared in a musical family. After serving as an instrumentalist at the Burgsteinfurt court (1786–90), he toured as a virtuoso. About 1795 he became Konzertmeister at the Schaumburg-Lippe court in Bückeburg. He composed a Simphonie concertante for Clarinet, Bassoon, and Orch. (c. 1793), a Sym. (1800), various concertos, including a Bassoon Concerto (1794), 2 flute concertos (1794, 1799), 3 viola concertos (c. 1795), 3 clarinet concertos (1798, 1799, 1807), a Cello Concerto (1800), and a Double Bass Concerto (1800), and several chamber pieces.—**LK/DM**

Westerhout, Nicolà van
See **Van Westerhout, Nicolà**

Westerlinck, Wilfried, Belgian composer and teacher; b. Louvain, Oct. 3, 1945. He was a student of Legley (harmony) at the Brussels Cons. and of Verbesselt (analysis) and Sternefeld (conducting) at the Royal Flemish Cons. of Music in Antwerp. From 1971 to 1983 he taught at the latter. In 1977 he won the Antwerp composition prize and in 1985 his total output was awarded the Baie Prize.

WORKS: ORCH.: *Metamorfose* (1971); *Elegie van de zee en van de liefde* (1975); *Landschappen II* for Strings (1979). **CHAMBER:** Clarinet Quintet (1966); *Epigrammen* for String Trio (1968); *"S"* for Trumpet and Tape (1972–80); *Maclou* for Horn (1975); *Canto I* for Guitar (1976), *II* for Cello (1982), and *III* for Harp (1982); *Aquarel* for Flute (1977); *Landschappen I* for Wind Quintet (1977) and *IV* for Flute, Harp, and String Trio (1981); String Quartet (1978); *Epitaphe* for String Quartet (1983); Sinfonietta for Chamber Ensemble (1986). **Piano:** 3 sonatas (1983, 1985, 1986); *Variations on a Theme by Paganini* (1985).
—**NS/LK/DM**

Westlake, Nigel, Australian clarinetist and composer; b. Perth, Sept. 6, 1958. He received training in clarinet from his father, Donald Westlake (1970–78), principal clarinetist in the Sydney Sym. Orch. After studying film music at the Australian Film and TV School (1982), he studied clarinet and contemporary music with Harry Sparnaay in Amsterdam (1983). In 1993 he received an Australia Council grant that enabled him to study composition with Richard Meale and composition and conducting with Richard Mills. From 1975 he was active as a freelance clarinetist. In 1987 he served as composer-in-residence for the ABC Radio. From 1987 to 1992 he was a principal member of the Australia Ensemble, a chamber music septet which toured extensively in Australia and abroad. In 1992 he toured Australia and England with John Williams's septet Attacca. Westlake has pursued a highly successful dual career as a clarinetist and composer. As a performer, he has demonstrated his mastery of the clarinet in an expansive repertoire ranging from the classics to popular music. As a composer, he has written both serious and lighter scores, proving himself especially adept at film, radio, and television scores.

WORKS: DRAMATIC: Theater music; film scores, including *Antarctica* (1991) and *Breaking Through* (1993); radio and television music. **ORCH.:** *Cudmirrah Fanfare* (1985); *Antarctica*, suite from the film score for Guitar and Orch. (1992); *Out of the Blue* for Strings (1994). **CHAMBER:** *Omphalo Centric Liecture* for 4 Percussion (1984); *Onomatopoeia* for Bass Clarinet and Digital Delay (1984); *Our Mum Was a Waterfall* for Soprano Saxophone, Percussion, and Electronics (1984); *Fabian Theory* for Percussion and Digital Delay (1987); *Moving Air* for 4 Percussion (1989); *Refractions at Summercloud Bay* for Bass Clarinet, Alto Flute, Violin, Viola, and Cello (1989); *Entomology* for Chamber Group and Tape (1990); *Malachite Glass* for Bass Clarinet and 4 Percussion (1990); *Call of the Wild* for Bass Clarinet, Percussion, and Tape (1992); *Tall Tales But True* for Violin, Double Bass, 2 Guitars, Piano, Clarinet, and Percussion (1992); *Touching Wood* for Violin, Double Bass, 2 Guitars, Piano, Clarinet, and Percussion (1992); *The Devil's Marbles* for Guitar and Digital Delay (1994); *High Tension Wires* for String Quartet (1994); *Songs from the Forest* for 2 Guitars (1994).—**NS/LK/DM**

Westmorland, 11th Earl of
See **Burghersh, Lord John Fane, 11th Earl of Westmorland**

Weston, Randy, American pianist and composer; b. Brooklyn, N.Y., April 6, 1926. He grew up in Brooklyn, where his father had a West Indian restaurant frequented by jazz musicians. It was his father who first taught him about African history and who encouraged his piano studies. He started his professional career later than many, at age 23, and then not in a jazz context but rather as accompanist to blues singer Bull Moose Jackson. Subsequent jobs were with Eddie "Cleanhead" Vinson, trumpeter Kenny Dorham, and drummer Art Blakey, and Weston became friends with Thelonious Monk and studied informally with him. In 1954 he became the first modern musician to record for the fledgling Riverside label, and it was his albums for that company that first gained him a nationwide reputation. In 1960 he recorded an influential album for Roulette, the five-movement suite *Uhuru Afrika*. It used large-group arrangements by trombonist Melba Liston, who had previously arranged for his quintet; they have continued to work together, off and on, ever since. *Uhuru Afrika* had an all-star cast that prominently featured the percussion of Babatunde Olatunji, Candido, and Armando Peraza, plus drummers Max Roach, Charlie Persip, and G. T. Hogan along with 13 all-star horn players. It was the strongest expression yet of his interest in Africa. By this time he was regularly featuring drummer Big Black in his groups, emphasizing the African element even outside of such special projects. The following year he visited Nigeria, returning in 1963. A similar album was recorded that year, *Highlife*, which has been combined with *Uhuru Afrika* on a limited edition CD. He also spent a year touring N.Y.C. elementary schools with his sextet, the group was involved in a History of Jazz program, giving 40 concerts in that time that traced the history of the music from Africa through the Caribbean, the black church, New Orleans jazz, etc. The program was sponsored by Pepsi-Cola, and the players worked for union scale.

He toured North Africa in the beginning of 1967, sponsored by the U.S. State Department, and decided to settle there. He spent most of his time until 1973 in Africa, opening his African Rhythms Club in Tangier. In that period, he had no records released, a drought broken by an atypical 1972 album on CTI, *Blue Moses*, which found him pressured into playing electric piano. He then lived in France and Africa again, though this time around he continued to release records while based abroad. He returned to the United States in the early 1990s and began a fruitful association with Verve. His small group African Rhythms, which works as a sextet or septet, has been his touring group for much of the decade.

DISC.: *Trio and Solo* (1955); *Get Happy* (1955); *Jazz a la Bohemia* (1956); *With These Hands* (1956); *How High the Moon* (1956); *Little Niles* (1958); *Destry Rides Again* (1959); *Live at the Five Spot* (1959); *Uhura Africa/Highlife* (1961); *Berkshire Blues* (1965); *Blue Moses* (1972); *Tanjah* (1973); *Carnival: Live at Montreux '74* (1975); *Blues to Africa* (1975); *The Healers* (1987); *Perspective* (1989); *Portraits of Thelonious Monk: Well You Needn't* (1990); *Self Portraits: The Last Day* (1990); *Portraits of Duke Ellington: Caravan* (1990); *The Spirits of Our Ancestors* (1992); *Volcano Blues* (1993); *Monterey '66* (1994); *Marrakech in the Cool of the Evening* (1994); *Splendid Master Gnawa Musicians of Morocco & Randy Weston* (1994); *Saga* (1995); *The Riverside Records Story* (1997); *Earth Birth* (1997).—**SH**

Westphal, Rudolf (Georg Hermann), notable German music scholar; b. Oberkirchen, July 3, 1826; d. Stadthagen, July 10, 1892. He was a student of classical philology in Marburg. He taught at the Univ. of Breslau (1858–62) and at the Moscow lyceum (1875–80), and subsequently lived in Leipzig, Bückeburg, and Stadthagen. He wrote numerous learned papers on Greek music, and maintained that the Greeks employed polyphony, a theory that he himself eventually abandoned as untenable.

WRITINGS: With A. Rossbach, *Metrik der griechischen Dramatiker und Lyriker* (3 vols., 1854–63; 3rd ed. as *Theorie der musischen Künste der Hellenen*, 1885–89); *Die Fragmente und Lehrsätze der griechischen Rhythmiker* (1861); *System der antiken Rhythmik* (1865); *Geschichte der alten und mittelalterlichen Musik* (1865; unfinished; includes *Plutarch über die Musik*, 1864); *Theorie der neuhochdeutschen Metrik* (1870; 2nd ed., 1877); *Elemente des musikalischen Rhythmus mit besonderer Rücksicht auf unsre Opernmusik* (1872); *Allgemeine Theorie der musikalischen Rhythmik seit J.Seb. Bach* (1880); *Die Musik des griechischen Altertums* (1883); *Allgemeine Metrik der indo-germanischen und semitischen Völker auf Grundlage der vergleichenden Sprachwissenschaft* (1892; with addendum by R. Kruse, *Der griechische Hexameter in der deutschen Nachdichtung*); *Aristoxenos von Tarent: Metrik und Rhythmik des klassischen Hellenentums* (2 vols., 1883–93).—**NS/LK/DM**

Westrup, Sir Jack (Allan), eminent English musicologist; b. London, July 26, 1904; d. Headley, Hampshire, April 21, 1975. He received his education at Dulwich Coll., London (1917–22), and at Balliol Coll., Oxford (B.A. and B.Mus., 1926; M.A., 1929). He was an asst. classics master at Dulwich Coll. (1928–34), then was a music critic for the *Daily Telegraph* (1934–39); he also was ed. of the *Monthly Musical Record* (1933–45). He gave classes at the Royal Academy of Music in London (1938–40), then was lecturer in music at King's Coll., Newcastle upon Tyne (1941–44), the Univ. of Birmingham (1944–47), and Wadham Coll., Oxford (1947–71). In 1946 he received an honorary degree of D.Mus. at the Univ. of Oxford. In 1947 he was named chairman of the editorial board of *The New Oxford History of Music*. In 1959 he succeeded Eric Blom as ed. of *Music & Letters*. From 1958 to 1963 he was president of the Royal Musical Assn. He was also active as a conductor; he conducted the Oxford Opera Club (1947–62), the Oxford Univ. Orch. (1954–63), and the Oxford Bach Choir and Oxford Orch. Soc. (1970–71). He was knighted in 1961. Westrup prepared major revisions of Walker's *A History of Music in England* (Oxford, 3rd ed., 1952) and of Fellowes's *English Cathedral Music* (London, 5th ed., 1969); he also supervised rev. eds. of Blom's *Everyman's Dictionary of Music* (4th ed., 1962; 5th ed., 1971). He was co-ed., with F. Harrison, of the *Collins Music Encyclopedia* (London, 1959; American ed. as *The New Coll. Encyclopedia of Music*, N.Y., 1960).

WRITINGS (all publ. in London unless otherwise given): *Purcell* (1937; 4th ed., rev., 1980); *Handel* (1938); *Liszt* (1940); *Sharps and Flats* (1940); *British Music* (1943; 3rd ed., 1949); *The Meaning of Musical History* (1946); *An Introduction to Musical History* (1955); *Music: Its Past and Its Present* (Washington, D.C., 1964); *Bach Cantatas* (1966); *Schubert Chamber Music* (1969); *Musical Interpretation* (1971).

BIBL.: F. Sternfeld et al., eds., *Essays on Opera and English Music in Honour of Sir J. W.* (Oxford, 1975).—**NS/LK/DM**

Wettergren, Gertrud (née Pålson), Swedish contralto; b. Eslöv, Feb. 17, 1897; d. Stockholm, June

1991. She studied at the Stockholm Cons., and later in London. She made her operatic debut as Cherubino at the Royal Opera in Stockholm in 1922, and remained on its roster for 30 years. On Dec. 20, 1935, she appeared at the Metropolitan Opera in N.Y. as Amneris in *Aida*. She sang there until 1938, and also sang with the Chicago Opera (1936–38) and at London's Covent Garden (1936, 1939). In 1925 she married Erik Wettergren, director of the National Museum of Stockholm. Among her most esteemed roles were Venus, Fricka, Brangäne, Dalila, Carmen, Mignon, Marfa, and Herodias; she also sang in many Swedish operas.—**NS/LK/DM**

Wettling, George (Godfrey), jazz drummer; b. Topeka, Kans., Nov. 28, 1907; d. N.Y., June 6, 1968. His family moved to Chicago when he was young; there he studied drums with Roy Knapp and heard early jazz players like Baby Dodds. Wettling worked in several Chicago bands during the 1920s, then played with Paul Mares in the mid-1930s. He toured with British bandleader Jack Hylton's band in 1935, and played in several cities with Wingy Manone a year later. In late 1936, Wettling settled in N.Y., and joined Artie Shaw's first big band, leaving in March 1937. After working with Bunny Berigan (March–December 1937) and Red Norvo (1938), he joined Paul Whiteman (1939–March 1941), while also working freelance and recording. He worked with various leaders over the next few years, including frequent appearances with Miff Mole's Band (1943–44). From 1943–52, he was a staff musician at the ABC studios; during this period did many jazz gigs including long spells at Eddie Condon's Club. He made numerous recordings in the 1940s and 1950s with Yank Lawson, Dick Cary, Billie Holiday, PeeWee Russell, Jack Teagarden, Hackett, Spanier, Bud Freeman, Joe Sullivan, Sidney Bechet, and Ralph Sutton. Wettling was briefly out of action in the summer 1946 because of a broken arm. From 1953 he led own small groups in N.Y. He played many sessions with Eddie Condon during the 1950s and toured Great Britain with him in January 1957. Wettling played with Muggsy Spanier occasionally in 1959 and 1960 and did a brief tour with Bud Freeman (autumn 1960); he made regular playing trips to Toronto during the 1960s, and toured briefly with the Dukes of Dixieland. During the last years of his life he led his own trio at the Gaslight Club in N.Y., and also worked in Clarence Hutchenrider's Trio. An amateur painter, several of his works graced jazz record album covers; a collection of his paintings is held at the Inst. of Jazz Studies at Rutgers Univ. He died of lung cancer in N.Y. and was buried in Chicago.

DISC.: *George Wettling's Jazz Band* (1951); *Jazz Trios* (1956); *Dixieland in Hi-Fi* (1957).—**JC/LP**

Wetz, Richard, German composer, conductor, and teacher; b. Gleiwitz, Feb. 26, 1875; d. Erfurt, Jan. 16, 1935. He studied with R. Hofmann in Leipzig and Thuille in Munich (1899–1900), and also attended the Univ. of Munich. He was a theater conductor in Straslund and Barmen, and in 1906 settled in Erfurt as conductor of the Musikverein and the Singakademie; also taught at the Weimar Hochschule für Musik (from 1916). His output was greatly influenced by Bruckner. A Richard Wetz-Gesellschaft was founded in Gleiwitz in 1943 to promote his music, which included an opera, *Das ewige Feuer* (Düsseldorf, March 19, 1907), *Kleistouvertüre* for Orch., 2 violin concertos, 3 syms., various choral works, including a *Requiem* for Baritone, Chorus, and Orch. and the *Weihnachtsoratorio* for Soprano, Baritone, Chorus, and Orch., lieder, and some chamber music, including 2 string quartets.

WRITINGS: *Anton Bruckner* (Leipzig, 1922); *Franz Liszt* (Leipzig, 1925); *Beethoven* (Erfurt, 1927; 2nd ed., 1933).

BIBL.: G. Armin, *Die Lieder von R. W.* (Leipzig, 1911); E. Schellenberg, *R. W.* (Leipzig, 1911; 2nd ed., 1914); H. Polack, *R. W. Sein Werk* (Leipzig, 1935).—**NS/LK/DM**

Wetzler, Hermann (Hans), American organist, conductor, and composer; b. Frankfurt am Main (of American parents), Sept. 8, 1870; d. N.Y., May 29, 1943. He was taken to the U.S. as a child but in 1882 returned to Germany, where he studied at the Hoch Cons. in Frankfurt am Main and studied with Clara Schumann (piano), Iwan Knorr (counterpoint), and Humperdinck (instrumentation). In 1892 he went to N.Y., where he was organist at Old Trinity Church (1897–1901); in 1903 he established the Wetzler Sym. Concerts, which had considerable success; Richard Strauss conducted a series of 4 concerts of his own works with the Wetzler group (Feb.-March, 1904), including the premiere of the *Sinfonia domestica*. In 1905 he returned to Germany and conducted in various German cities and throughout Europe. In 1940 he returned to the U.S. He publ. *Wege zur Musik* (Leipzig, 1938).

WORKS: DRAMATIC: Opera: *Die baskische Venus* (Leipzig, Nov. 18, 1928; the *Symphonic Dance in the Basque Style* was extracted from this score as a concert piece). **Incidental Music To:** Shakespeare's *As You Like It* (1917). **ORCH.:** *Symphonic Fantasy* (1922); *Visionen* (1923); *Assisi*, legend (1924); *Symphonie concertante* for Violin and Orch. (1932). **OTHER:** Chamber music, including a String Quartet (1937); much vocal music, including a *Magnificat* for Soprano, Boy's or Women's Chorus, and Organ (1936), choruses, and songs. —**NS/LK/DM**

Weyrauch, August Heinrich von, German composer; b. Riga, April 30, 1788; b. place and date unknown. In 1824 he publ. (under his own name) a song, "Nach Osten" (words by Wetzel). About 1840 an anonymous Paris publisher reprinted it, with Schubert's name on the title page, as "Adieu" (French words by Belanger); a piano transcription of it, also crediting the authorship to Schubert, was publ. by Döhler in Germany (1843); Schlesinger of Berlin reprinted the song, with a German tr. of the French text, as Schubert's in 1845; since then it has been reprinted many times as Schubert's by European and American publishers. —**NS/LK/DM**

Weyse, Christoph Ernst Friedrich, eminent Danish pianist, organist, pedagogue, and composer of German descent; b. Altona, March 5, 1774; d. Copenhagen, Oct. 8, 1842. He studied with his grandfather, a cantor in Altona, and in 1789 went to Copenhagen, where he studied with J. A. P. Schulz; he remained there the rest of his life. After establishing his reputation as a pianist, he devoted himself to the organ. He was deputy organist (1792–94) and principal organist (1794–1805) at the Reformed Church, and then served as principal organist at the Cathedral from 1805 until his death, winning great renown as a master of improvisation. In 1816 he was named titular prof. at the Univ. and was awarded an honorary doctorate in 1842, the year of his death. In 1819 he was appointed court composer. Through the court conductor Kunzen, he became interested in a movement for the establishment of a national school of Danish opera, for which his works (together with those of Kuhlau) effectively prepared the way. He remains best known for his fine songs.

Works: Dramatic: Opera (all 1st perf. in Copenhagen): *Sovedrikken* (The Sleeping Potion; April 21, 1809); *Faruk* (Jan. 30, 1812); *Ludlams hule* (Ludlam's Cave; Jan. 30, 1816); *Floribella* (Jan. 29, 1825); *Et eventyr i Rosenborg Have* (An Adventure in Rosenborg Gardens; May 26, 1827); *Festen påa Kenilworth* (Jan. 6, 1836). **Incidental Music To:** Shakespeare's *Macbeth* (1817); J. Ewald's *Balders død* (The Death of Baldur; 1832). **Orch.:** 7 syms. (1795–99). **Chamber:** Sonata for 2 Bassoons (c. 1798). **Keyboard:** Various piano works, including (6) *Allegri di bravura* (Berlin, 1796), (8) *Études* (1837), and many waltzes, impromptus, and écossaises; 32 organ preludes; the folk- song collection *Halvtresindstyve gamle kaempeviser* (1840–42). **Vocal:** *Miserere* for Double Chorus and Orch. (1818); various cantatas (1818–22); numerous songs, many of which were publ. as *Romancer og sange* (1852–60).

Bibl.: A. Berggreen, *C.E.F. W.s biographie* (Copenhagen, 1876); J. Larsen, *W.s sange* (Copenhagen, 1942); C. Harting, *W.s kantater* (diss., Univ. of Copenhagen, 1955).—**NS/LK/DM**

Whaley, Wade, early jazz clarinetist; b. New Orleans, Feb. 22, 1892; d. Brooklyn, N.Y., Feb. 1968. He originally played string bass and guitar, then clarinet (taught by Lorenzo Tio Jr.). His first work on clarinet was with Armand Piron's Orch. at the Temple Theatre; subsequently, he worked with the Crescent Band, Buddie Petit, Manuel Perez, Kid Ory, and John Robichaux. Whaley formed his own band in 1916, left to join Jelly Roll Morton in Los Angeles (1917), then returned to New Orleans and led his own band in Bucktown. He moved back to the West Coast in November 1919 to join Kid Ory. Whaley led his own band, but worked regularly with Kid Ory from 1922. After Ory moved to Chicago (1925), Whaley formed his own Black and Tan Jazz Hounds and achieved great success during the late 1920s. In the early 1930s, he played in pit orchestra at the Capitol Durlesque Hall in San Francisco. In 1934, he left full-time music to work in the shipyards at San Jose. He began working regularly on the clarinet after appearing with the All-Star New Orleans Band in San Francisco (May 1943). In April 1944 (immediately after the death of Jimmie Noone), Whaley took part a in broadcast with Kid Ory; this served to introduce him to a wider public. During the next few years continued to play regularly, taking part in several recording sessions. He then retired from making music.—**JC/LP**

Whalum, Kirk, American trumpet player; b. Memphis, Tenn., 1958. He grew up in Memphis influenced by church music and playing horn in his father's church choir. As a teenager, Whalum earned a music scholarship to Tex. Southern Univ. in Houston. It was here that he formed his own band. By 1979, he was opening for such artists as Bob James, who invited him to play on his Columbia album, *12*. Whalum soon earned a deal with Columbia Records. Since then he has toured with an array of contemporary pop and jazz artists, including the group Take 6, Marcus Miller, George Benson, Luther Vandross, Larry Carlton, and singers Nancy Wilson and Michael Franks. His 1985 debut, *Floppy Disk*, hinted at the smooth silky sound that would become the hallmark of many 1980s instrumentalists, including George Howard, James Carter, and Najee. A steady stream of successful records helped to cement Whalum's standing in the industry. However, his most important contribution to music came in 1992. Whalum's sax solo on Whitney Houston's "I Will Always Love You," from the mega-platinum soundtrack album *The Bodyguard*, boosted his visibility and appeal. He has toured with Whitney Houston during the past several years, a stint that has included performances in South Africa and a White House reception for Nelson Mandela. Whalum continues to be an in-demand session player in addition to recording his own albums as leader. He is currently based in Los Angles.

Disc.: *Floppy Disk* (1985); *And You Know That* (1988); *The Promise* (1989); *Cache* (1992); *In this Life* (1995); *Colors* (1997). **—DPe**

Whear, Paul William, American composer; b. Auburn, Ind., Nov. 13, 1925. He studied engineering at Marquette Univ. (B.N.S.), DePauw Univ. (B.A.), and Case Western Reserve Univ. (Ph.D.), then made a 180° turn toward the art of music and attended classes of Gardner Read at Boston Univ. and of Wayne Barlow at the Eastman School of Music in Rochester, N.Y. From 1960 to 1969 Whear served as chairman of the music dept. at Doane Coll.; in 1969 he was appointed a prof. of music and chairman of the theory and composition dept. at Marshall Univ. He wrote 4 syms., including No. 2, *The Bridge* (1971), No. 3, *The Galleries* (1975), and No. 4 for Band (1979), as well as overtures, chamber music, and choral works.—**NS/LK/DM**

Wheeler, (E. B.) De Priest, early jazz trombonist; b. Kansas City, Mo., March 1, 1903; d. Jamaica, Queens, N.Y., April 10, 1998. He played trumpet and mellophone in The Knights of Pythias Band while attending Lincoln H.S. in Kansas City, journeyed to St. Louis with the Knights of Pythias Band in 1917. He returned to Kansas City, worked in a local dance hall for a year, then in 1918 played in the resident band at the Chauffeur's Club in St. Louis. He was with Dave Lewis's Jazz Boys in Kansas City, then toured with a circus band until 1922. He joined Wilson Robinson's Syncopators in St. Louis (1923) and toured the Pantages Circuit from Chicago to Calif. with that band. The band settled in N.Y. early in 1925 and were renamed The Cotton Club Orch.; subsequently they worked under the leadership of violinist Andrew Freer until his death in 1927. Later on the group became known as The

Missourians, and from 1930 worked as Cab Calloway's Band. Wheeler remained with Cab Calloway until January 1940 (including a trip to Europe in 1934). He worked for the postal authorities for many years, but continued to play part-time with bands and orchestras through the 1950s.

DISC.: *Harlem in the Twenties, Vol. 1* (1929). **CAB CALLOWAY:** *Cab Calloway and the Missourians* (1929); *1930–1931* (1930); *1931–1932* (1931); *1932* (1932); *On Film (1934–1950)* (1934); *1937–1938* (1937); *1938–1939* (1938). "At the Clam-Bake Carnival" (1938); "Ratamacue" (1939); "Utt da Zay" (The Tailor's Song) (1939); "I'm Now Prepared to Tell the World It's You" (1932); "The Ghost of Smoky Joe: Fox Trot" (1939); "Down Hearted Blues" (1931); "You Can't Stop Me from Lovin' You" (1931); "Riverboat Shuffle" (1925); "Trylon Swing" (1939); "I Ain't Gettin' Nowhere Fast" (1939); "Moon at Sea" (1937); "Mama I Wanna Make Rhythm" (1937); *Cab Calloway and His Orchestra* (1943); *Minnie the Moocher* (1989); *Cab Calloway, Featuring Chuck Berry* (1993); *Jumpin' Jive* (1996); *Original Historic Recordings* (1996); *His Best Recordings* (1996); *1930–1939* (1997); *Keep That Hi- De-Hi in Your Soul* (1999); *Jive formation Please: 1938–141* (1999); *Best of the Big Bands, Vol. 2* (1999); *Masterpieces, Vol. 12- Original* (1999).—**JC/LP**

Whettam, Graham (Dudley), English composer; b. Swindon, Sept. 7, 1927. He received guidance from Eric Fenby but otherwise was an autodidact as a musician. He devoted himself principally to composition and the cause of copyright protection. He served as chairman of the Composers' Guild of Great Britain (1971; 1983–86), and subsequently was its copyright consultant. He withdrew most of his compositions written prior to 1959. Whettam has revealed a fine command of orch. writing. His works have been widely performed in England and on the Continent.

WORKS: ORCH.: 2 clarinet concertos: No. 1 (Bournemouth, Nov. 5, 1959) and No. 2 (1982; Warwick, Jan. 8, 1983); *Introduction and Scherzo impetuoso* (1960); *Variations* for Oboe, Bassoon, and Strings (1961); *Sinfonia contra timore* (1962; Birmingham, Feb. 25, 1965); Cello Concerto (1962; Manchester, Dec. 1981); *Sinfonietta stravagante* (1964); *Sinfonia concertante* (Newcastle upon Tyne, Oct. 1966); *The Masque of the Red Death*, 2 dance scenes (1968); *Sinfonia intrepida* (1976; Liverpool, Jan. 18, 1977); *Sinfonia drammatica* (Jena, March 15, 1978); *Hymnos* for Strings (1978; adapted from the String Quartet No. 2); *Concerto conciso* for Strings (Stratford-upon-Avon, Aug. 21, 1981); *An English Suite* (1984); *Symphonic Prelude* (1985); *Ballade* for Violin and Orch. (1988); *Concerto Ardente* for Horn and Strings (1992; Malvern, June 1993); *Les Roseaux au Vent* for 2 Oboes, English Horn, and Strings (Utrecht, Oct. 1993). **Brass Band:** *Partita* (1975); *Invocation* (1977). **CHAMBER:** *Prelude, Allegro and Postlude* for Flute, Oboe, and Piano (1955); 3 sonatas for Solo Violin (1957, rev. 1987; 1972; 1989); *Fantasy* for 10 Winds (1960; rev. 1979); 2 oboe quartets (1960, 1973); *Music* for Brass for 3 Trumpets and 3 Trombones (1964); 3 string quartets: No. 1 (1967), No. 2, *Hymnos* (1978), and No. 3 (1980); Sextet for Flute, Oboe, Clarinet, Bassoon, Horn, and Piano (1970); *Duo declamando* for Horn and Piano (1972); Trio for Oboe, Clarinet, and Bassoon (1975); Trio for Horn, Violin, and Piano (1976); Concerto for 10 Winds (1979); *Quintetto concertato* for Flute, Oboe, Clarinet, Bassoon, and Horn (1979); *Serenade* for Viola or Clarinet and Guitar (1981); *Suite* for Timpani (1982); *Percussion Partita* for 6 Players (1985); Quartet for 4 Horns (1986); *Canticles* for Horn Quartet and Organ (1987); Clarinet Sonata (1988); Sonata for Solo Cello (1990); *Andromeda* for Percussion Quartet (1990); *Idyll* for Horn and Organ (1992); Concerto for Brass Quintet (1993). **KEYBOARD: Piano:** *Prelude, Scherzo, and Elegy* (1964; rev. 1986); *Prelude and Scherzo impetuoso* (1967); *Night Music* (1969). **Organ:** *Partita* (1962); *Triptych* (1966). **VOCAL:** *The Wounded Surgeon Plies the Steel* for Chorus (1959); *Magnificat and Nunc dimittis* for Chorus and Organ (1961); *Missa brevis* for Chorus and Organ (1963); *Mary Modyr Cum and Se* for Chorus and Organ (1963); *Do Not Go Gentle into That Good Night* for 5 Solo Voices or 5-part Chorus (1965); *Celebration* for Contralto, Chorus, Organ, Orch., Brass Band, and Audience Unisono (1975); *On the Beach at Night* for Chorus (1979); *Consecration* for Chorus, Organ, Brass, and Percussion (1982); *A Mass for Canterbury* for Chorus (1986; Utrecht, June 25, 1988); songs.—**NS/LK/DM**

White (or **Whyte**), **Robert,** English composer; b. c. 1538; d. London, Nov. 1574. He was a chorister and subsequently one of the cantores at Trinity Coll., Cambridge, obtaining his Mus.B. from Cambridge (1560). In 1562 he was made Master of the Choristers at Ely Cathedral, a post formerly held by his father-in-law, **Christopher Tye**. He left his post in 1566 and by 1567 was Master of the Choristers at Chester Cathedral; in 1569 he assumed that post at Westminster Abbey, being formally confirmed in 1570. He died of the plague. While not as gifted a composer as Tye, he was nevertheless highly influential. His finest works are 2 sets of Lamentations. He was also one of the first English composers to write fantasias. See P. Buck et al., eds., *Robert White*, Tudor Church Music, V (1926), and I. Spector, ed., *Robert White: The Instrumental Music*, Recent Researches in the Music of the Renaissance, XII (1972).

BIBL.: D. Mateer, *A Comparative Study and Critical Transcription of the Latin Sacred Music of R. W.* (diss., Queen's Univ., Belfast, 1976).—**NS/LK/DM**

White, Amos (Mordechai), cornetist; b. Kingstree, S.C., Nov. 6, 1889; d. Alameda, Calif., July 1980. Orphaned at the age of nine, he entered Jenkins' Orphanage in Charleston, S.C. He began playing cornet, and later toured with the orphanage band. He studied at the Benedict Coll., S.C., then returned to the orphanage, did some teaching there, and also did more touring. From 1913 until 1918 he worked with circus shows and minstrel bands. He served in the 816th Pioneer Infantry Band in France (1918–), then settled in New Orleans. He worked as a type-setter, but gigged with many leaders: Papa Celestin, Armand Piron, George Moret and with The Excelsior. He led his own band at The Spanish Fort before joining Fate Marable on the S.S. *Capitol.* White worked on and off with Marable until 1924, and worked with The Alabamians (under Ed Howard) in 1925. He then toured with Mamie Smith (1927), led The Georgia Minstrels (1928), then played with Harvey's Radio Minstrels(1928). He settled in Phoenix, Ariz., worked with Bradley's Dublin Orch. (1929), then led his own band and worked with Gregorio Goyer, W, Gills, Felipe Lopez, etc. White moved to Oakland, Calif., in 1934, ran his own part-time band and did local gigs. He owned a print shop for many years, during the 1960s, and continued to play occasional dates with marching bands.—**JC/LP**

White, Andrew (Nathaniel III), jazz tenor saxophonist, bass guitarist; b. Washington, D.C., Sept. 6, 1942. He studied saxophone as a child and later took lessons in oboe and music theory at Howard Univ. in Washington, D.C., graduating in 1964. He played in the JFK Quintet, which existed from 1960 to 1963, with Joe Chambers on drums and Walter Booker on bass. After further study at Dartmouth Coll. in Hanover, N.H., and at the Paris Cons., he was principal oboist in the American Ballet Theatre orchestra in N.Y. (1968–72). He then played bass guitar for Stevie Wonder and other popular musicians (1969–73); during this time he also made hundreds of transcriptions of recorded solos by John Coltrane, Eric Dolphy, and Charlie Parker, which he has sold through the mail. His Coltrane transcriptions are legendary for their meticulous detail and because he has transcribed every commercially issued recording as well as a number of broadcasts. In 1976 he arranged the music for and performed in the big-band tribute to Coltrane at the Newport in N.Y. Jazz Festival. He has since focused on performing jazz, playing alto and soprano saxophone as a sideman to Elvin Jones and Beaver Harris.

DISC.: **JFK QUINTET:** *New Jazz Frontiers from Washington* (1961); *Young Ideas* (1962); *Sun and Moon Have Come Together* (1969); *Passion Flower* (1974); *Seven Giant Steps for Coltrane* (1974); *Marathon* (1975); *Andrew White Live in New York* (1977); *I Love Japan* (1979); *Conversations* (1982).

WRITINGS: *Hey Kid! Wanna Buy a Record? A Treatise on Self Production in the Music Business* (Washington D.C., 1982); *Andrew's X-Rated Band Stories* (Washington, D.C., 1984); *Trane 'n Me: A Treatise on the Music of John Coltrane* (Washington D.C., 1981); *Sideman!: X-Rated Band Stories, Vol. Two* (Washington D.C., 1986).—**NS/LP**

White, Barry, African American soul crooner whose sound became synonymous with seduction; b. Galveston, Tex., Sept. 12, 1944. His voice became so distinctive, his songs so charged with pheremonal energy that he joked about women continually introducing him to children conceived to his records. During the late 1970s and early 1980s, if Barry White was not part of your seduction package, you weren't trying.

Ironically, White initially would have preferred a career behind the scenes. He started singing in church in Galveston, but by 10 he had moved on to church organist and choir director. Soon, his family relocated to Watts. At 16, he started recording with The Upfronts, singing and playing piano. He worked on the sessions that produced Bob and Earl's minor hit, "The Harlem Shuffle" (later a bigger hit for The Rolling Stones).

White's studio prowess impressed Bob Keane, a successful independent record owner who had recorded Sam Cooke and had big hits with Ritchie Valens, the Bobby Fuller Four, and numerous surf bands. Keane took White on as an A&R man. He worked with The Versatiles (who would later morph into the Fifth Dimension). He produced (and surfed with) The Majestics. He produced a Top 20 hit for Viola Wills in the mid-1960s and some late 1960s hits with Felice Taylor.

Eventually, Keane dissolved several of his labels in 1968 and White went independent. He found odd jobs like producing the music for the kid's show *The Banana Splits*. By 1972, he was on welfare. Another former Keane employee contacted White about a girl group with whom he wanted White to work. The process took nearly a year, but the group, Love Unlimited, started off with the #14 pop hit "Walking in the Rain (with the One I Love)." The album *From a Girl's Point of View* sold over a million copies. However, relationships with their record label became bad, forcing White to put Love Unlimited on hold.

He started making demos for another project, a male vocal group. On hearing the demos, friends convinced him that no one else could sing these songs as well as he could. His album *I've Got So Much to Give* came out in 1973, and suddenly the 275-pound White became the sexiest man on vinyl. From being on welfare just a year earlier, in 1973 White paid $1 million in income tax.

Feeling successful, he decided to take a risk. He put together a complete orchestra and recorded what amounted to a small sonata. With swirling strings and a big R&B back beat, the Love Unlimited Orch.'s "Love's Theme" topped the charts and went gold. The vocal group Love Unlimited extricated themselves from their label problems and started recording.

For the next five years, using this three-pronged attack, White ruled the airwaves and record stores. He went Top Ten pop with "Can't Get Enough of Your Love Baby" (#1, 1974), "You're the First, the Last, My Everything" (#2, 1974) and "It's Ecstasy When You Lie Next to Me" (#4, 1977), to name but a few. During that time, his work in its various guises sold nearly 100 million records worldwide.

Despite a slightly waning success, CBS offered him a custom label in 1980, paying him in the neighborhood of $14 million, alleged to be the most money offered for such a project to that date. Unfortunately for all parties concerned, the Unlimited Gold label was not the success they hoped it would be. The tides had started to change from the big, lush productions that had come to typify White's work. Over the course of the deal, White's hits were few and far between. When the deal ran out, White decided to retire.

As musical retirements go, White gave it a good run. However, in 1988 A&M records thought the time was again right for Barry White and signed him up, starting with an album whose title announced *The Man Is Back!* He released three more albums with A&M over the next six years, finishing off with the multi-platinum *The Icon Is Love.*

Although he took another five-year hiatus from recording, his profile remained high. His voice was featured on several episodes of the animated series *The Simpsons*. On the late 1990s hit television series *Ally McBeal*, one character couldn't get in the mood without at least playing White's "You're the First, the Last, My Everything" in his head. This thread climaxed with a live appearance by White on the show.

The appearance coincided with his return to recording on adult-oriented Private Music. His *Staying Power* featured a leaner sound (though not a leaner White), that showed off his voice well. Although he's not likely to have another run like he did in the 1970s, the new record illustrates that his creative success continues to be unlimited.

DISC.: *I've Got So Much to Give* (1973); *Stone Gon'* (1973); *Can't Get Enough* (1974); *Just Another Way to Say I Love You* (1975); *Barry White's Greatest Hits* (1975); *Let the Music Play* (1976); *Is This Whatcha Wont?* (1976); *Barry White Sings for Someone You Love* (1977); *The Man* (1978); *The Message Is Love* (1979); *I Love to Sing the Songs I Sing* (1979); *Barry White's Greatest Hits, Vol. 2* (1980); *Sheet Music* (1980); *Barry & Glodean* (1981); *Beware!* (1981); *Change* (1982); *Dedicated* (1983); *The Right Night and Barry White* (1987); *The Man Is Back!* (1988); *Put Me in Your Mix* (1992); *Just for You* (boxed set; 1992); *The Icon Is Love* (1994); *Barry White's All-Time Greatest Hits* (1994); *Staying Power* (1999). **LOVE UNLIMITED:** *From a Girl's Point of View We Give to You...* (1972); *Under the Influence of...* (1973); *In Heat* (1974); *He's All I've Got* (1976); *Love is Back* (1979); *The Best of Love Unlimited* (1995). **THE LOVE UNLIMITED ORCH.:** *Rhapsody in White* (1974); *Together Brothers* (soundtrack; 1974); *White Gold* (1974); *Music Maestro Please* (1975); *My Sweet Summer Suite* (1976); *My Musical Bouquet* (1978); *Super Movie Themes, Just a Little Bit Different* (1979); *Let 'Em Dance* (1981); *Welcome Aboard (Presents Mr. Webster Lewis)* (1981); *Rise* (1983); *The Best of Love Unlimited Orch.* (1995).—**BH**

White, Chris(topher Wesley), jazz bassist, educator; N.Y., July 6, 1936. He was born in Harlem but grew up in Brooklyn; his mother was a piano teacher. In January 1963 he was with Dizzy Gillespie. In the 1970s he was on recordings by Grandmaster Flash, one of the pioneers of rap. He has become a leading educator and arts administrator, with expertise in computer applications. From 1973–76 he was the director of Rutgers Inst. of Jazz Studies and was co-Director, Jazz Lab, Bennington Summers Bennington Coll. in 1976. From 1984–86 he was the Project Director of Alpines Project (Arts Literacy Project in Elementary Schools), a public school teacher training program held at Newark Community School of the Arts. From 1987–91 he was Director of the Professional Division Newark Community School of the Arts, which provided established professionals with retraining in state-of-the-art technology, and professional level educational experiences for gifted and talented students. From the early 1990s, he was Director, Jazz Opportunities for Youth (JOY), at Montclair State Univ. (MSU). He toured Eastern Europe with MSU Jumpin Jamming Jazz which included college students and six high school JOY students. He created Special Improv Workshop for visiting Buena Vista, Ariz., high school band at MSU (1993), the Newark Jazz Festival Jazz Improv Workshop (1994), and Montclair HS Jazz Improv Workshop (1995). He is a music professor at Bloomfield State Coll.—**LP**

White, Clarence Cameron, African American violinist and composer; b. Clarksville, Tenn., Aug. 10, 1880; d. N.Y., June 30, 1960. He studied at the Oberlin (Ohio) Cons. (1896–1901), with Samuel Coleridge-Taylor in London (1906; 1908–10), and with Raoul Laparra in Paris (1930–32). He taught at various institutions while pursuing a concert career and was director of music at the Hampton (Va.) Inst. (1932–35). In 1919 he helped to organize the National Assn. of Negro Musicians. He won the Bispham Medal for his opera *Ouanga* (1932) and the Benjamin Award for his *Elegy* for Orch. (1954). His major works were written in a neo-Romantic style with occasional infusions of Negro folk melos.

WORKS: DRAMATIC: Opera: *Ouanga* (concert perf., Chicago, Nov. 1932; stage perf., South Bend, Ind., June 10, 1949); *Carnival Romance* (1952). **Ballet:** *A Night in Sans Souci* (1929). **Incidental Music To:** J. Matheus's *Tambour* (1929). **ORCH.:** Sym.; *Kutamba Rhapsody* (1942); *Elegy* (1954); *Dance Rhapsody* (1955); *Poeme* (1955). **CHAMBER:** *Bandana Sketches,* violin suite (1918); *From the Cotton Fields,* violin suite (1920); 2 string quartets (1931, 1931); *Legende d'Afrique* for Cello and Piano (1955); keyboard pieces. **VOCAL:** *Heritage* for Soprano, Tenor, Chorus, and Orch. (1959); songs; numerous arrangements of spirituals, including *40 Negro Spirituals* (1927) and *Traditional Negro Spirituals* (1940).—**NS/LK/DM**

White, Donald H(oward), American composer and pedagogue; b. Narberth, Pa., Feb. 28, 1921. He studied music education at Temple Univ. in Philadelphia (B.S., 1942) and composition with Persichetti at the Philadelphia Cons. (1946) and with Rogers and Hanson at the Eastman School of Music in Rochester, N.Y. (M.M., 1947; Ph.D., 1952). In 1947 he joined the faculty of DePauw Univ. in Greencastle, Ind., where he was chairman of composition and theory studies (1948–81), a prof. (1959–81), and director of the school of music (1974–78); he was chairman of the music dept. at Central Washington Univ. in Ellensburg, Wash. (1981–90).

WORKS: ORCH.: *Sagan,* overture (1946); *Kennebec Suite* (1947); Overture (1951); Cello Concerto (1952); *Divertimento No. 2* for Strings (1968). **Band:** *Ambrosian Hymn Variants* (1963); *Terpsimetrics* (1968); Concertino for Timpani, Winds, and Percussion (1973); *Lyric Suite* for Euphonium and Wind Ensemble (1978); *4 Bagatelles* (1989). **CHAMBER:** Trumpet Sonata (1946); *3 to 5* for Woodwind Quintet (1964); *Serenade No. 3* for Brass Quintet (1965); Trombone Sonata (1966); Tuba Sonata (1978); Quintet for Brass (1980). **VOCAL:** *Song of Mankind* for Soloists, Chorus, and Orch. (1970); *From the Navajo Children* for Chorus and Wind Ensemble (1978); choruses.—**NS/LK/DM**

White, Eric Walter, English writer on music and administrator; b. Bristol, Sept. 10, 1905; d. London, Sept. 13, 1985. He attended Clifton Coll., Bristol, and studied English at Balliol Coll., Oxford (1924–27). After working as a translator for the League of Nations in Geneva (1929–33), he was employed by the National Council for Social Service in London (1935–42); in 1942 he became asst. secretary of the Council for the Encouragement of Music and the Arts, which became the Arts Council of Great Britain in 1946; he retired in 1971. He publ. valuable studies on Stravinsky and an invaluable register of English opera premieres.

WRITINGS (all publ. in London): *Stravinsky's Sacrifice to Apollo* (1930); *Stravinsky: A Critical Survey* (1947); *Benjamin Britten: A Sketch of His Life and Works* (1948; 3rd ed., enl., 1970 as *Benjamin Britten: His Life and Operas*); *The Rise of English Opera* (1951); *Stravinsky: The Composer and His Works* (1966; 2nd ed., rev., 1979); *A History of English Opera* (1983); *A Register of First Performances of English Operas and Semi-Operas from the 16th Century to 1980* (1983).—**NS/LK/DM**

White, Felix Harold, English composer; b. London, April 27, 1884; d. there, Jan. 31, 1945. He studied piano with his mother but otherwise was self-taught in music. He devoted himself mainly to composition but also publ. a *Dictionary of Musical Terms* and some short monographs on musicians.

WORKS: ORCH.: *Shylock*, overture (London, Sept. 1907); *Polonaise* (1908); *Astarte Syriaca*, tone poem (1909; London, Jan. 1911); *Meditation* (1911); Suite (1913); *Impressions of England*, suite (1918); *The Deserted Village*, tone poem (1923); *Nocturne* (1936); Overture (1937). **CHAMBER:** *Romance* for Cello and Piano (1907); Cello Sonata (1910); *Dawn* for 12 Cellos (1922); Trio for Oboe or Violin, Viola, and Piano (1922); *4 Proverbs* for Flute, Oboe, Violin, Viola, and Cello (1925); *Orison* for 4 Cellos (1937); many piano pieces. **VOCAL:** Choral pieces; part songs; numerous solo songs.—**NS/LK/DM**

White, Frances, American composer; b. Philadelphia, Aug. 30, 1960. She studied at the Univ. of Md. (B.Mus., 1981), Brooklyn Coll. (M.A., 1982), and Princeton Univ. (M.A., 1990), where she subsequently began a Ph.D. program in composition. In 1980–81 she was a member of the Univ. of Md.'s 20th-Century Music Ensemble; in 1993 she was composer-in-residence at the Univ. of Mo. in Kansas City. From 1985 to 1987 she served as technical assistant to John Cage in the creation of his works for computer- generated tape, *Essay*, *Stratified Essay*, and *Voiceless Essay*. In 1990 she won first prize in the program music category and 2nd prize in the mixed category in the 18th Bourges International Electro-Acoustic Music Competition; she also received ASCAP awards (1990, 1993, 1994). White's compositions, often of exquisite beauty, have been almost exclusively for instruments and tape, with particular emphasis on the creation of interactive sonic landscapes; her *Winter Aconites* (a species of flowering bulb, *Eranthis hyemalis*) for 6 Instruments and Tape (1993), a commission from ASCAP in memory of John Cage, was created at the Winham Laboratory at Princeton Univ. on a NeXT workstation using Cmix and Csound software. White currently lives in Princeton, N.J., with her husband, the writer James Pritchett, 2 cats, and an ever-expanding collection of species and hybrid orchids.

WORKS: *Ogni pensiero vola* for Tape (1985); *Chiaroscura* for Percussion and Tape (1986); *Design for an Invisible City* for Tape (1987); *Valdrada* for Tape (1988); *Still Life With Piano* for Piano and Tape (1989); *Resonant Landscape*, interactive computer-music installation (1990); *Trees* for 2 Violins, Viola, and Tape (1992); *Nocturne* for Tape (1992); *Walks Through Resonant Landscape 1–5* for Tape (1992; derived from the interactive computer-music installation *Resonant Landscape*, 1990); *Winter Aconites* for Clarinet, Electric Guitar, Cello, Double Bass, Piano, Vibraphone, and Tape (1993).—**NS/LK/DM**

White, John (Reeves), American musicologist and conductor; b. Houston, Miss., May 2, 1924; d. N.Y., July 12, 1984. He studied at the Cincinnati Cons. (1941–43); also took courses at the Paris Cons. (1945). He obtained his M.A. at Colo. Coll. in 1948 and his Ph.D. at Ind. Univ. in 1952; he also received the degree of Dr. of Natural Philosophy at the Inst. of Neurophenomenology in Amherst, Mass. (1975). He held teaching posts at Colo. Coll. (1947–52), the Univ. of Richmond (1953–61), Ind. Univ. (1961–66; 1970–71), and Hunter Coll. of the City Univ. of N.Y. (from 1971). From 1966 to 1970 he conducted the N.Y. Pro Musica. White produced reconstructions of several medieval and Renaissance dramatic works. He ed. *The Keyboard Tablature of Johannes of Lublin* (6 vols., 1964–67), *François Dandrieu: Harpsichord Music* (1965), and *Michelangelo Rossi: Complete Keyboard Works* (1967). With J. Dos Passos and H. Fitzgerald, he ed. *The Arts between the Wars: A Symposium* (1964). —**NS/LK/DM**

White, Maude Valerie, English composer; b. Dieppe, France (of English parents), June 23, 1855; d. London, Nov. 2, 1937. She studied with W. S. Rockstro in Torquay and Oliver May in London, then was a pupil of G. A. Macfarren at the Royal Academy of Music in London (1876–79), where she became the first woman to win the Mendelssohn Scholarship (1879). She continued her studies with R. Fuchs in Vienna (1883). She traveled extensively through Europe and South America, lived in London, and then for some years in Florence. She was best known as a composer of songs. She publ. her memoirs, *Friends and Memories* (London, 1914), and *My Indian Summer* (London, 1932).

WORKS: *The Enchanted Heart*, ballet (1912–13); incidental music; *Agnus Dei* for Chorus and Orch. (1879); about 200 songs to Eng., Ger., Fr., and It. texts; vocal duets; *Naissance d'amour* for Cello and Piano (1893); many piano pieces.—**NS/LK/DM**

White, Michael, American composer and teacher; b. Chicago, March 6, 1931. He studied at the Chicago Musical Coll. and at the Juilliard School of Music in N.Y. with Peter Mennin. In 1963 he received a Guggenheim fellowship. He taught at the Oberlin (Ohio) Coll. Cons. of Music (1964–66), the Philadelphia Coll. of Performing Arts (1966–79), and the Juilliard School in N.Y. (from 1979). Among his works are several operas, including *Metamorphosis* (1968), *Opposites* for Wind Ensemble (1970), *Passion According to a Cynic* (1971), Violin Concerto (1979), Double Concerto for Violin, Viola, and Orch. (1981), *The 3 Muses* for Harpsichord (1984), *Museum Pieces* for Flute and Guitar (1987), Sonata for Solo Viola (1988), other chamber pieces, guitar music, choruses, and song cycles.—**NS/LK/DM**

White, Robert, American tenor; b. N.Y., Oct. 27, 1936. He was the son of Joseph White, the "Silver Masked Tenor" of the early radio era in N.Y. He began his career with appearances on Fred Allen's radio program when he was 9. After studying music at Hunter Coll., he continued his training with Boulanger and Souzay in France; then completed his studies at the Juilliard School of Music in N.Y. (M.S., 1968), where he found a mentor in Beverley Peck Johnson. He sang with the N.Y. Pro Musica and appeared with various American opera companies before becoming successful as a concert singer. His repertoire ranges from the Baroque to Irish ballads. He sang in a "Homage to John McCormack" at N.Y.'s Alice Tully Hall during the 1985–86 season.—**NS/LK/DM**

White, Ruth, American composer; b. Pittsburgh, Sept. 1, 1925. She studied composition with Lopatnikoff (B.F.A., 1948; M.F.A., 1949) and received training in piano at the Mellon Inst. in Pittsburgh. She then studied at the Univ. of Calif. at Los Angeles (1951–54) and had private composition lessons with Antheil (1952–54). She specialized in teaching music to children and wrote much didactic music. Her other music followed along conventional lines until she took up electronic composition in 1964.

WORKS: DRAMATIC: *Pinions*, opera (1967); film and television music. **ORCH.:** Suite (1949); *Shofar Symphony* (1965). **CHAMBER:** Various works; piano pieces. **VOCAL:** *Palestinean Song Cycle* for Voice, Bassoon, Piano, and Percussion (1949); *Songs from the Japanese Poets* for Voice and Piano (1949); *Settings for Lullabies from 'round the World* for Tenor, Soprano, Piano, Cello, and Horn (1955); *Garden of Delights* for Soprano and Electronics (1971); about 150 songs for children. **ELECTRONIC:** *7 Trumps from the Tarot Cards* (1967); *Flowers of Evil* (1969); *Short Circuits* (1970). **OTHER:** Pedagogical pieces. **—NS/LK/DM**

White, Sonny (Ellerton Oswald), pianist; b. Panama, Nov. 11, 1917; d. N.Y., April 28, 1971. He played piano from the age of eight, and became a professional musician at the age of 18. His did early work with Jesse Stone, then with Willie Bryant (1937) and Teddy Hill (1938). He became a regular accompanist for Billie Holiday (1939), and later that year worked with Frankie Newton. He began a long association with Benny Carter in February 1940, worked briefly with Artie Shaw in 1941, then worked regularly with Benny Carter until spending two years in the U.S. Army (1943–45). He rejoined Benny Carter early in 1946, worked with Hot Lips Page in 1947. From 1947 until 1954, he played residency at the Cinderella Club, N.Y., in a band led by trumpeter Harvey Davis. In December 1954 he joined Wilbur de Paris and worked regularly in that band until the early 1960s (including a trip to Africa in 1957). From 1963 until 1967 he worked mainly with Louis Metcalf at the Ali Baba, N.Y. and was with Eddie Barefield's Trio in late 1968. He joined Jonah Jones in April 1969.**—JC/LP**

White, Willard (Wentworth), notable West Indian bass-baritone and actor; b. St. Catherine, Jamaica, Oct. 10, 1946. He studied at the Juilliard School in N.Y., where he attended Callas's master classes. In 1974 he made his operatic debut in Washington, D.C., as Trulove in *The Rake's Progress*, and then appeared as Colline in *La Bohème* at the N.Y.C. Opera. He also made his European operatic debut that year at the Welsh National Opera in Cardiff as Osmin. In 1976 he made his first appearance with the English National Opera in London as Seneca in *L'incoronazione di Poppea*. His debut at the Glyndebourne Festival followed in 1978 as the Speaker in *Die Zauberflöte*, and he also sang Don Diego in *L'Africaine* at his first appearance at London's Covent Garden. After appearing as Plutone in *Orfeo* at the Salzburg Festival in 1980, he returned to the English National Opera as Hunding in 1983 and to the Glyndebourne Festival as Gershwin's Porgy in 1986. In 1989 he sang Wotan at the Scottish Opera in Glasgow and took the title role in Shakespeare's *Othello* at the Royal Shakespeare Co. He returned to Covent Garden as Porgy in 1992, sang Golaud at the San Francisco Opera in 1995, and appeared in Ligeti's *Le Grand Macabre* in Paris and Salzburg in 1997. In 1998 he sang Boris Godunov at the English National Opera. He was made a Commander of the Order of the British Empire in 1995. White has demonstrated a mastery of both vocal and dramatic elements in his varied roles as a singer and an actor. **—NS/LK/DM**

White, William, English composer; b. c. 1585; d. c. 1665. He served as one of the singing-men at Westminster. He is known to have composed fantasies and anthems, although some of the works attributed to him may be by Matthew White or other composers named White.**—NS/LK/DM**

Whitehead, Alfred (Ernest), English-born Canadian organist, choirmaster, teacher, and composer; b. Peterborough, Ont., July 10, 1887; d. Amherst, Nova Scotia, April 1, 1974. He was a pupil of Haydn Keeton and C. C. Francis of Peterborough Cathedral, and then of A. Eaglefield Hull. In 1912 he emigrated to Canada, and in 1913 became the first fellow by examination of the Canadian Guild (later Coll.) of Organists; in 1916 he obtained his B.Mus. at the Univ. of Toronto and in 1922 his D.Mus. at McGill Univ. in Montreal. In 1924 he became a fellow of the Royal Coll. of Organists and winner of the Lafontaine Prize. He was organist and choirmaster at St. Andrew's Presbyterian Church in Truro, Nova Scotia (1912–15). He then was organist and choirmaster at St. Peter's Anglican Church in Sherbrooke, Quebec (1915–22) and at Christ Church Cathedral in Montreal (1922–47); he also taught organ, theory, and composition at the McGill Cons. (1922–30). After serving as head of the music dept. at Mt. Allison Univ. (1947–53), he was organist and choirmaster at Trinity United Church in Amherst (1953–71). He was president of the Canadian Coll. of Organists (1930–31; 1935–37) and was honorary vice-president (1971–73) and honorary president (1973–74) of the Royal Canadian Coll. of Organists. He wrote a number of distinguished sacred works, excelling as a composer of motets and anthems. He was also a painter and philatelist.**—NS/LK/DM**

Whitehill, Clarence (Eugene), American baritone, later bass-baritone; b. Parnell, Iowa, Nov. 5, 1871; d. N.Y., Dec. 18, 1932. He studied with L. A. Phelps in Chicago, earning his living as a clerk in an express office. He also sang in churches. He then went to Paris in 1896, where he studied with Giraudet and Sbriglia. He made his operatic debut on Oct. 31, 1898, at the Théâtre Royal de la Monnaie in Brussels. He was the first American male singer to be engaged at the Opéra-Comique in Paris (1899); he then was a member of Henry Savage's Grand English Opera Co. at the Metropolitan Opera in N.Y. in 1900. He went for further study to Stockhausen in Frankfurt am Main, and from there to Bayreuth, where he studied the entire Wagnerian repertoire with Cosima Wagner; after engagements in Germany, he was a member of the Cologne Opera (1903–08). On Nov. 25, 1909, he made his Metropolitan Opera debut in N.Y. as Amneris with notable success; he sang at the Met for a season. He was then again on its roster from 1914 until his death. He also sang with the Chicago Opera (1911–14; 1915–17). Among his finest roles were Hans Sachs, Gounod's Méphistophélès, and Golaud.—**NS/LK/DM**

Whitehouse, William Edward, esteemed English cellist and pedagogue; b. London, May 20, 1859; d. there, Jan. 12, 1935. He studied at the Royal Academy of Music in London, and joined its faculty after graduation. From 1889 until 1904 he was cellist in the London Trio with Achille Simonetti (violin) and Amina Goodwin (piano), with whom he toured all over Europe. He was greatly esteemed as a teacher; among his pupils were Felix Salmond and Beatrice Harrison. He wrote a number of attractive cello pieces (*Allegro perpetuo, Remembrance, Serenade*, etc.) and ed. several cello works of the 18th century. He publ. a memoir, *Recollections of a Violoncellist* (London, 1930).—**NS/LK/DM**

White Lafitte, José (Silvestre de los Dolores), noted Cuban violinist, teacher, and composer; b. Matanzas, Jan. 17, 1836; d. Paris, March 15, 1918. He went to Paris as a youth and studied violin with Alard at the Paris Cons., obtaining first prize in 1856. After playing first violin in a quintet and giving concerts (1857–58), he was active in Cuba. He was again in Paris (1861–74), where he secured his reputation as a virtuoso and chamber music artist; he also toured in Europe and South America, later becoming court violinist to the emperor Dom Pedro II of Brazil. In 1889 he settled in Paris, where he later taught a master class at the Cons. He composed a Violin Concerto, a String Quartet, pieces for violin and piano, and some church music.
—**NS/LK/DM**

Whiteman, Paul (Samuel), expansive American orchestra conductor, violinist, and violist; b. Denver, Colo., March 28, 1890; d. Doylestown, Pa., Dec. 29, 1967. At a time when jazz was synonymous with popular music, Whiteman was the most successful bandleader of the day, a popularizer who combined a grounding in the European classical tradition with an appreciation of contemporary popular styles, leading to a hybrid he called "symphonic jazz." He was the biggest recording artist of the 1920s and among the biggest of the 1930s; his orchestra toured successfully for 40 years; he hosted a series of radio and television shows (even becoming a network executive); his band was the launching ground for numerous prominent jazz musicians and popular singers; and he commissioned many notable semiclassical works, the best known of which was George Gershwin's *Rhapsody in Blue*, which became his musical signature.

Whiteman was the son of Wilberforce James Whiteman (1857–1939) and Elfrida Dalison Whiteman. His mother was a singer. His father, at the time of his son's birth, was a music teacher in Denver; from 1894 to 1934 he would be the superintendent of music education in the Denver public school system. As a child Whiteman studied violin and viola with his father and with Max Bendix. At the age of 17 he dropped out of the Univ. of Denver and became first violist with the Denver Symphony Orch. He married singer Nellie Stack in 1908, but the marriage was annulled. In 1914 he moved to San Francisco and played in an orchestra at the Panama-Pacific Exposition of 1915. That same year he joined the San Francisco Symphony Orch., also playing in the Minetti String Quartet. He enlisted in the navy in 1918 and led a band at a nearby naval base.

Discharged shortly after the end of World War I in November, he organized a sextet to play at a restaurant, then directed the orchestra at the Fairmont Hotel in early 1919. His nine-piece group opened at the Hotel Alexandria in Los Angeles on Nov. 13, 1919, and became a hit with the film community. At this time he hired Ferde Grofé as pianist/arranger; Grofé would stay with his organization into the 1940s, providing many of his best-received arrangements.

Whiteman moved to the Ambassador Hotel in Atlantic City in the spring of 1920, where he was seen by executives of Victor Records, which was holding a convention in the city, and signed to the label. His first record, pairing "Avalon" and "Dance of the Hours," was not successful, but his second, "Whispering"/"The Japanese Sandman," released in September, sold more than two million copies. "Wang Wang Blues" was another million-seller in early 1921. Meanwhile, Whiteman had moved his band to the Palais Royale nightclub in N.Y., a residency that would last four years. He continued to score big record hits during 1921: "My Mammy" in June, "Cherie" in July, and "Song of India" in September. That month he began appearing at the Palace Theatre in addition to his nightclub stand. Irving Berlin's "Say It with Music" was a big hit for Whiteman in November, and "Do It Again" and "Stumblin" were best-sellers in July 1922. Whiteman and his band were the pit orchestra for *George White's Scandals* (N.Y., Aug. 28, 1922); the score was written by Gershwin and included "I'll Build a Stairway to Paradise," another best-seller for Whiteman. "Hot Lips" was a top record in September, and he had the biggest hit of his career in December with the three-million-selling "Three O'Clock in the Morning."

In 1921, Whiteman had been married briefly to showgirl Alfrica Smith. On Nov. 4, 1922, he married dancer Vanda Hoff (real name Mildred Vanderhoff). The couple had one son. Whiteman undertook a British tour, opening in the revue *Brighter London* on March 28, 1923, and staying in the U.K. until August. While he was away his biggest U.S. hits included "Parade of the Wooden Soldiers" in April and "Bambalina" in June. He again appeared on Broadway in the *Ziegfeld Follies of 1923* (N.Y., Oct. 20, 1923), which ran 333 performances.

In a bid to lend respectability to jazz, Whiteman performed a concert at Aeolian Hall in N.Y. on Feb. 12, 1924, dubbed "An Experiment in Modern Music," for which he commissioned works from such composers as Victor Herbert and Gershwin, who played piano in the premiere performance of *Rhapsody in Blue*. The concert was a watershed in the history of music and a turning point in the careers of both the composer and the conductor. Gershwin accompanied the Whiteman orchestra on the early dates of its first North American tour in the spring of 1924 and recorded the *Rhapsody* with Whiteman; the recording became one of the first inductees of the NARAS Hall of Fame in 1974.

Whiteman toured more extensively in the fall of 1924, beginning a pattern of traveling that would occupy much of the rest of his career. Meanwhile, he continued to score some of the biggest record hits of the time, including his third million-seller, "Linger Awhile" in March, Berlin's "What'll I Do?" in August, Gershwin's "Somebody Loves Me" in December, and Berlin's "All Alone" in February 1925. He spent much of 1925 and the early part of 1926 touring the U.S., then left for a European tour at the end of March, staying on the continent until July. Meanwhile, vocals began to turn up on his records for the first time, including "Valencia," the biggest hit of 1926, which had a chorus sung by Franklyn Baur. At the same time, Whiteman began to play more "hot" jazz in his shows and to expand his performance into more of a variety show than a dance concert as he began to play extended engagements at movie theaters.

In September 1926, while appearing in Los Angeles, Whiteman hired the vocal duo of Bing Crosby and Al Rinker, taking them back to N.Y., where he added Harry Barris and dubbed the trio The Rhythm Boys. It was the vocal team of Jack Fulton, Charles Gaylord, and Austin Young, however, that sang on his next big hit, "The Birth of the Blues," in December, while Fulton was the featured singer on "In a Little Spanish Town," a best-seller in January 1927. In N.Y., Whiteman opened his own Club Whiteman, appeared at the Paramount, and led the pit orchestra in the musical *Lucky* (N.Y., March 22, 1927).

Whiteman's decision to switch record companies from Victor to Columbia in April 1928 led to a flurry of recordings to complete his Victor contract and several big hits, among them "My Blue Heaven" in November, "Among My Souvenirs" in March 1928, "Together" and "Ramona" in April, "Ol' Man River," from the Jerome Kern–Oscar Hammerstein II musical *Show Boat* (vocal by Crosby) in May, and "My Angel" in July. His biggest Columbia hit was "Great Day" in December. On Feb. 5 he had begun hosting a weekly radio series, *The Old Gold–Paul Whiteman Hour*, on CBS. With the coming of sound, Hollywood became interested in him, and he signed to Universal Pictures to star in *The King of Jazz*, a musical revue that was one of the first color films.

The beginning of the Depression in the fall of 1929 was devastating to the entertainment business. *The King of Jazz* was a box office flop, Whiteman's radio show ended, his concert bookings dried up, and he gave up recording for a year after a September 1930 session that produced his next big hit, "Body and Soul." Laying off many of his musicians and cutting the salaries of the rest, he relocated to Chicago, taking up a residency at the Granada Café and then at the Edgewater Beach Hotel in the summer of 1931. During this period he and his third wife divorced, and on Aug. 18, 1931, he married Margaret Livingston, a film actress who in 1933 coauthored with Isabel Leighton a book that chronicled her efforts to help him control his weight, *Whiteman's Burden*. The couple adopted three daughters and a son in the course of their 36-year marriage.

RCA Victor bought out Whiteman's Columbia contract in September 1931 and returned him to the recording studio; his next major hit, in February 1932, was "All of Me" with Mildred Bailey, who had joined the band in 1929, on vocals. Whiteman returned to N.Y. and began an extended appearance at the Biltmore Hotel while also launching a new radio show at the start of 1932.

Whiteman moved to the *Kraft Music Hall* radio series in late 1933, at the same time scored big record hits with Kern and Otto Harbach's "Smoke Gets in Your Eyes" from the Broadway musical *Roberta* and with "Wagon Wheels" from *Hold Your Horses*. He returned to Broadway himself in the circus musical *Jumbo* (N.Y., Nov. 16, 1935), which ran 233 performances, during which he moved from the *Kraft Music Hall* to a new radio show, *Paul Whiteman's Musical Varieties*, which ran for a year. Also in November 1935 he made his second feature-film appearance, in *Thanks a Million*. In the summer of 1936 he followed *Jumbo* producer Billy Rose to Forth Worth to appear at the Frontier Centennial through November. He spent the spring of 1937 at the Drake Hotel in Chicago, returned to Fort Worth in the summer, and was back at the Drake in the fall. In December he moved to the Coconut Grove in Los Angeles and began a new radio show, *Chesterfield Presents*, which ran for two years.

On May 30, 1940, Whiteman temporarily disbanded his orchestra and went to Hollywood, where he appeared in the Mickey Rooney–Judy Garland film *Strike Up the Band*. He reorganized the band in the fall and was back on the road by January 1941. On Oct. 7 he joined the radio show hosted by comedians George Burns and Gracie Allen, staying with it for two years.

Whiteman had recorded briefly for Decca Records in 1938 after his RCA Victor contract ran out; he returned to RCA in February 1942 but made only a few recordings before moving to the newly formed Capitol Records, for which he recorded a handful of sides before the onset of the musicians' union strike on July 31, 1942, the most notable of which were "Trav'llin' Light," featuring a vocal by Billie Holiday (appearing under the pseudonym "Lady Day"), and "The Old Music Master," featuring his former vocalist and Capitol coowner Johnny Mercer.

Whiteman again disbanded in the summer of 1942, largely due to the U.S. entry into World War II, which found many of his band members going into the service. After his second season with Burns and Allen, he became musical director for the Blue radio network (later the American Broadcasting Company, or ABC), in September 1943. In this capacity he originated several radio programs, among them the 1944–45 *Music Out of the Blue* series, for which he commissioned new works by Grofé, Leonard Bernstein, Aaron Copland, Igor Stravinsky, Morton Gould, David Rose, Richard Rodgers, Duke Ellington, Eric Korngold, Victor Young, and others. He made a series of film appearances during this period, in *Atlantic City* (1944), *Rhapsody in Blue* (1945) (a biography of Gershwin, in which he played himself), and *The Fabulous Dorseys* (1947) (again as himself).

In 1947–48 he became a disc jockey, as *The Paul Whiteman Club* was broadcast nationally on weekday afternoons. On April 2, 1949, he moved to television, hosting *Paul Whiteman's Teen-Age Club*, which ran for five years. He also hosted the TV shows *Paul Whiteman's Goodyear Revue* (1951–52), *On the Boardwalk* (spring 1954), and *America's Greatest Bands* (summer 1955).

Even during Whiteman's heyday in the 1920s, the definition of jazz was changing, such that his billing as the King of Jazz was questioned. Nevertheless, his long-running band employed a large number of musicians who gained prominence as jazz players, including Henry Busse, Bix Beiderbecke, Tommy Dorsey, Jimmy Dorsey, Frank Trumbauer, Jack Teagarden, Red Norvo, Eddie Lang, Joe Venuti, Red Nichols, and Bunny Berigan. He also helped launch the singing careers of Morton Downey, as well as Crosby, Bailey, and Mercer. And he regularly recorded the work of the era's top composers, such as Kern and Berlin, while helping to sponsor Gershwin's transition from the musical theatre to the concert hall.

WRITINGS: With M. McBride, *Jazz* (N.Y., 1926); with L. Lieber, *How to Be a Bandleader* (N.Y., 1941); *Records for the Millions* (N.Y., 1948).

BIBL.: C. Johnson, *P. W.: A Chronology* (Williamstown, Mass., 1977); T. DeLong, *Pops: P. W., King of Jazz* (Piscataway, N.J., 1983).—**WR**

Whitfield, Mark, American guitarist; b. Lindenhurst, N.Y., Oct. 6, 1966. He began his musical studies at an early age, playing bass until his family relocated to Seattle, where he landed a spot as guitarist in the school band. Mostly self-taught, his exceptional abilities became apparent in a high school jazz competition sponsored by Berklee, where he subsequently enrolled with a full scholarship. After graduation, he relocated to N.Y. Like many of his contemporaries, he showed promise, and has lived up to that promise. Stylistically he is a hard-bop stylist, though he has flirted with pop-jazz on occasion. His guitar influences include George Benson, Wes Montgomery, Kenny Burrell, and Grant Green. He has established himself as one of the top jazz guitarists of his generation.

DISC.: *The Marksman* (1990); *Patrice* (1991); *Mark Whitfield* (1993); *True Blue* (1994); *7th Avenue Stroll* (1995); *Forever Love* (1997); *Fingerpainting: The Music of Herbie Hancock* (1997). —**PMac**

Whithorne (real name, **Whittern**), **Emerson,** American composer; b. Cleveland, Sept. 6, 1884; d. Lyme, Conn., March 25, 1958. He had his name legally changed in 1918 to Whithorne (the original family name of his paternal grandfather). He studied in Cleveland with J. H. Rogers; embarked on a musical career at the age of 15, and appeared as a pianist on the Chautauqua circuit for 2 seasons. In 1904 he went to Vienna and took piano lessons with Leschetizky and theory and composition lessons with Robert Fuchs; from 1905 to 1907 he was a piano pupil of Artur Schnabel. In 1907 he married Ethel Leginska, acting as her impresario in Germany until 1909; they were separated in 1912, and divorced in 1916. Between 1907 and 1915, Whithorne lived mainly in London; he studied Chinese and Japanese music from materials in the British Museum, and wrote several pieces based on oriental tunes (*Adventures of a Samurai*; settings for *The Yellow Jacket*; *The Typhoon*). Returning to America, he became ed. for the Art Publication Society of St. Louis (1915–20). He then settled in N.Y. and devoted himself entirely to composition; was an active member of the League of Composers in N.Y. In his music, he assumed a militantly modernistic attitude; wrote several pieces in the fashionable "machine music" style.

WORKS: DRAMATIC: Incidental music. **ORCH.:** *The Rain* (Detroit, Feb. 22, 1913); *La nuit* (1917); *Adventures of a Samurai*, suite (1919); *Ranga*, symphonic suite (1920); *The Aeroplane* (1920; Birmingham, England, Jan. 30, 1926; arranged from the piano piece); *N.Y. Days and Nights* (1923; Philadelphia, July 30, 1926; arranged from the piano piece); *Poem* for Piano and Orch. (Chicago, Feb. 4, 1927); *Fata Morgana*, symphonic poem (1927; N.Y., Oct. 11, 1928); Violin Concerto (1928–31; Chicago, Nov. 12, 1931); 2 syms.: No. 1 (1929; Cincinnati, Jan. 12, 1934) and No. 2 (1935; Cincinnati, March 19, 1937); *The Dream Pedlar*, symphonic poem (1930; Los Angeles, Jan. 15, 1931); *Fandango* (1931; N.Y., April 19, 1932); *Moon Trail*, symphonic poem (Boston, Dec. 15, 1933); *Sierra Morena* (N.Y., May 7, 1938); *Serenade* for Strings (1943). **CHAMBER:** 2 string quartets (n.d., 1930); *Quartettino orientale* (1916?); *Greek Impressions* for String Quartet (1917); Piano Quintet (1928); Violin Sonata (1932). **Piano:** *The Aeroplane* (1920?; also arranged for Orch.); *N.Y. Days and Nights* (1922; also arranged for Orch.); *El camino real*, suite (1937). **VOCAL:** 2 *Chinese Poems* for Voice and Piano (1921); 2 *Chinese Nocturnes* for Voice and Piano (1921); *Saturday's Child* for Mezzo-soprano, Tenor, and Chamber Orch. (N.Y., March 13, 1926); *The Grim Troubador* for Medium Voice and String Quartet (1927; also for Medium Voice and Piano).

BIBL.: J. Howard, *E. W.* (N.Y., 1929).—**NS/LK/DM**

Whiting, Arthur Battelle, American pianist, teacher, and composer, nephew of **George E(lbridge) Whiting;** b. Cambridge, Mass., June 20, 1861; d. Beverly, Mass., July 20, 1936. He studied in Boston with Sherwood (piano), Maas (harmony), and Chadwick (composition). In 1883 he went to Munich and took courses at the Cons. with Rheinberger (until 1885). Returning to the U.S., he stayed in Boston until 1895, then settled in N.Y. From 1907 he gave educational chamber music concerts at Yale, Harvard, Princeton, and Columbia Univs., and in 1911 he inaugurated a series of concerts of early music, playing the harpsichord, other artists being Constance Edson (violin), Georges Barrère (flute), and Paul Kefer (viola da gamba).

WORKS: Concert Overture (Boston, Feb. 5, 1886); Piano Concerto (Boston, Nov. 16, 1888, composer soloist); *Fantasie* for Piano and Orch. (Boston, March 5, 1897, composer soloist); *Suite* for Strings and 4 Horns (Boston, March 13, 1891); *The Golden Cage*, dance pageant (1926); Piano Quintet; String Quartet; Piano Trio; Violin Sonata; many piano pieces, including 6 *Bagatelles*, *Suite moderne*, and 3 *Characteristic Waltzes*; also *Melodious Technical Studies*; *Pianoforte Pedal Studies* (with text in Eng. and Ger.); musical settings from the *Rubaiyat* of Omar Khayyam for Baritone; anthems; songs; etc.—**NS/LK/DM**

Whiting, George E(lbridge), American organist, pedagogue, and composer, uncle of **Arthur Battelle Whiting;** b. Holliston, Mass., Sept. 14, 1840; d. Cambridge, Mass., Oct. 14, 1923. He began to study at age 5 with his brother Amos, a church organist, and played in public at the age of 13; at 17 he became organist of the North Congregational Church at Hartford. He studied with George W. Morgan in N.Y., then went to England, where he became a pupil of W. T. Best of Liverpool (1863). Returning to America, he became organist at St. Joseph's in Albany, N.Y., where the famous soprano Emma Albani sang in his choir. He then moved to Boston, where he was organist at King's Chapel (1869–74); in 1874 he went to Berlin and studied harmony with Haupt and orchestration with Radecke. Finally settling in Boston, he taught the organ at the New England Cons. of Music (until 1879, and again from 1883 to 1897). In the interim he was a teacher at the Cincinnati Coll. of Music (1879–83). He was renowned as a teacher. He publ. *The Organist* (Boston, 1870) and *The First 6 Months on the Organ* (1871). He also wrote many sacred works: 2 masses, Vesper Services, a *Te Deum*, the secular cantatas *The Tale of the Viking, Dream Pictures, March of the Monks of Bangor, Midnight*, and *Henry of Navarre*, the one-act opera *Lenora*, to an Italian libretto (1893), a Sym., a Piano Concerto, an overture to Tennyson's *The Princess*, a Suite for Cello and Orch., piano pieces, songs, etc.—**NS/LK/DM**

Whitlock, Percy (William), English organist and composer; b. Chatham, June 1, 1903; d. Bournemouth, May 1, 1946. He received musical instruction as a choirboy at Rochester Cathedral, and then studied in London at the Guildhall School of Music and the Royal Coll. of Music. After serving as assistant organist at Rochester Cathedral (1921–30), he settled in Bournemouth and was director of music at St. Stephen's (1930–35) and borough organist (1932–46). He became well known as a recitalist. He composed a Sym. for Organ and Orch., much organ music, including a Sonata, *Plymouth Suite*, and *5 Short Pieces in Various Styles*, and many vocal works, among them services, anthems, hymn tunes, and motets.—**NS/LK/DM**

Whitmer, T(homas) Carl, American organist, teacher, and composer; b. Altoona, Pa., June 24, 1873; d. Poughkeepsie, N.Y., May 30, 1959. He studied piano with C. Jarvis, organ with S.P. Warren, and composition with W.W. Gilchrist. He was director of the School of Music, Stephens Coll., Columbia, Mo. (1899–1909); director of music at the Pa. Coll. for Women in Pittsburgh (1909–16); organist and choirmaster of the Sixth Presbyterian Church in Pittsburgh (1916–32); then taught privately at Dramamount, his farm near Newburgh, N.Y. He publ. *The Way of My Heart and Mind* (Pittsburgh, 1920) and *The Art of Improvisation: A Handbook of Principles and Methods* (N.Y., 1934; rev. ed., 1941).

WORKS: DRAMATIC: *Oh, Isabel*, opera (1951); sacred music dramas. **ORCH.:** *Poem of Life* for Piano and Orch. (1914); *A Syrian Night*, ballet suite (Pittsburgh, Feb. 17, 1919); *Radiations over a 13th Century Theme* for Strings (1935). **CHAMBER:** Several works, including piano pieces and organ music. **VOCAL:** *Supper at Emmaus*, choral suite (Pittsbirgh, Feb. 21, 1939); *Chant Me the Poem That Comes from the Soul*, cantata, after Walt Whitman (Pittsburgh, Feb. 19, 1942); anthems; songs. —**NS/LK/DM**

Whitney, John, American experimental filmmaker, computer- graphics artist, and Pythagorean-inspired speculative theorist of the analogies between music and the visual arts; b. Pasadena, Calif., April 8, 1917; d. Santa Monica, Calif., Sept. 22, 1995. He was a pioneer in 20th-century motion graphics, having invented cinema techniques in the 1940s that became an established part of the repertoire of special effects later used in film titles and television. His interest in the complementarity of visual and aural arts began with a series of experimental films made with his brother James, including the silent *24 Variations* (1939–40) and the series of *5 Film Exercises* (1943–44), which made use of synthesized pendulum music. With the development of computer graphics, he produced a number of what are now classic pieces, utilizing the music of a variety of composers; these include *Permutations* (1968; re-ed., 1979; with Indian tabla music by Balachandra), *Matrix I* (1971; with music adapted from sonatas by Antonio Soler) and *III* (1972; with music from Terry Riley's *Rainbow in Curved Air*), and Arabesque (1975; with improvised music by Manoocheher Sadeghi). His *Moondrum: Twelve Works for Videodisc* (1989–95) is a poetic response to the arts of Native Americans and was produced using a real- time composing program developed by Whitney and Jerry Reed; the series comprises *Moondrum: Dream Songs* (Memories of prehistory), *Navajo: Weaver's Art, Hopi: Dance Ceremonies, Kwakiutl* (The Northern Pacific tootem sculptors and Dance of the Dream Catcher), *Qxaquitl (Quetzalcoatl): About Time and Deity* (*Introduction, Blood Sacrifice at Pyramids of Copan, Stone Bells: Quetzacotl, Stone Bells: A Marching Procession*, and *A Noisy Festival at the Great Calendar Stone*), *Black Elk Requiem* (a memorial to the exiled Oglala Sioux people), *Chaco* (Fajada Buttle spiral petroglyph wedge of solstice sunlight), *Mimbres Star* (a pottery design marks the supernova event of 1054 A.D.), *Chumash* (rock paintings of the Southern Calif. coastline), *Kachina: A Memory of Bird and Snake Deities-Sand Paintings* (*Introduction to all symbols, Sand paintings*, and *Beatification of the Kachina Deity*), *Chapala* (Snapshots: dream symbols on warrior shields), and *Acoma: For The Infanta. The God King.* (3 cradle songs in 3 colors, With earthquake and Official Royal Seal, and "When the wind blow the cradle will rock"). These and many other computer-generated aural/visual compositions exemplify his ideas about the inherent complementarity of music and visual art, with the harmonic motion evident in tonal music made visible in the charge and release of tensional visual forces. His work has been supported by IBM; he also received NEA grants, a Guggenheim fellowship (1947–48), and a bronze medal from the Academy of Motion Picture Arts and Science for pioneering achievements in film. After retiring from his teaching position in the art dept. of the Univ. of Calif. at Los Angeles in 1986, he devoted himself to composition in his studio in Pacific Palisades, Calif. He publ. *Digital Harmony: On the Complementarity of Music and Visual Art* (Peterborough, N.H., 1980); also the articles "Writing on Water—Action Painting with Music," *Media Arts Journal* (Spring-Summer 1990) and "To Paint on Water: The Audiovisual Duet of Complementarity," *Computer Music Journal* (Fall 1994), and the video documentary, *A Personal Search: For the Complementarity of Music and Visual Art* (Santa Monica, Calif., 1992).—**NS/LK/DM**

Whitney, Myron (William), esteemed American bass; b. Ashby, Mass., Sept. 5, 1836; d. Sandwich, Mass., Sept. 19, 1910. He was a pupil of E. H. Frost in Boston, and made his debut there at the Tremont Temple as a soloist in Handel's *Messiah* (Dec. 25, 1858). He sang throughout New England during the next 10 years and then pursued training with Vannucini in Florence and Randegger in London. He sang regularly in opera as well as oratorio in the U.S. from 1873. He toured with the Theodore Thomas Orch. (1878–82) and appeared frequently with the Boston Ideal Opera Co. (1879–1900); he also was a member of the American Opera Co. (1885–86). He was generally considered the leading American oratorio artist of his day. His son, Myron Whitney Jr. (1872–1954), a baritone, traveled as joint artist with Melba and Nordica. He also taught singing at the New England Cons. of Music in Boston. —**NS/LK/DM**

Whitney, Robert (Sutton), American conductor; b. Newcastle upon Tyne, England (of an American father and an English mother), July 9, 1904; d. Louisville, Ky., Nov. 22, 1986. He studied with Sowerby in Chicago, and took lessons in conducting with Eric De Lamarter there. In 1937 he was engaged as conductor of the Louisville Phil. (later renamed the Louisville Orch.), a post he held until 1967. A munificent grant from the Rockefeller Foundation enabled the Louisville Orch. to commission works from American and foreign composers, each to be paid a set fee of $1,000; the project proved highly successful, and the orch. was able to give first performances of works by Honegger, Milhaud, Malipiero, Petrassi, Krenek, Dallapiccola, Toch, Chávez, Villa-Lobos, Ginastera, Schuman, Virgil Thomson, Cowell, Piston, Sessions, Antheil, Creston, Mennin, and others; it recorded some 200 contemporary symphonic works on Louisville Orch. Records. From 1956 to 1972 he was dean of the Univ. of Louisville School of Music; also taught conducting at the Univ. of Cincinnati Coll.-Cons. of Music (1967–70). He composed a *Concerto Grosso* (1934), Sym. in E minor (1936), *Sospiri di Roma* for Chorus and Orch. (1941), and Concertino (1960). —**NS/LK/DM**

Whittaker, Howard, American composer and music educator; b. Lakewood, Ohio, Dec. 19, 1922. He studied with Herbert Elwell in Cleveland, and in 1948 was appointed director of the Cleveland Music School Settlement. In most of his works he applies modified serial procedures, but refuses to abandon tonality. Among his compositions are a Piano Concerto, 2 Murals for Orch. (Cleveland, March 31, 1960), chamber music, organ pieces, and songs.—**NS/LK/DM**

Whittaker, W(illiam) G(illies), respected English choral conductor, pedagogue, and composer; b. Newcastle upon Tyne, July 23, 1876; d. Orkney Islands, July 5, 1944. He studied science at Armstrong Coll., Univ. of Durham, and also received training in organ and singing before joining its faculty in 1898. He was the 1st Gardiner Prof. of Music at the Univ. of Glasgow (1929–38) and was principal of the Royal Scottish Academy of Music in Glasgow (1929–41); he also was active as a choral conductor, and conducted various choral societies in Newcastle and London. He became well known as a Bach conductor and scholar, and ed. various instrumental works of the 17th and 18th centuries. He composed *A Lykewake Dirge* and *The Celestial Sphere* for Chorus and Orch., *Psalm CXXXIX; Among the Northumbrian Hills*, piano quintet, piano pieces, and songs. He also prepared folk-song arrangements.

WRITINGS: *Fugitive Notes on Certain Cantatas and the Motets of J.S. Bach* (London, 1924); *Class Singing* (London, 1925; 2nd ed., 1930); *Collected Essays* (Oxford, 1940); *The Cantatas of J.S. Bach, Sacred and Secular* (London, 1959).—**NS/LK/DM**

Whittal, Arnold (Morgan), English musicologist; b. Shrewsbury, Nov. 11, 1935. He took courses at Emmanuel Coll., Cambridge (B.A., 1959), completing his training at the Univ. there (Ph.D., 1964, with the diss. *La Querelle des Bouffons*). He then taught at the Univ. of Nottingham (1964–69), Univ. Coll., Cardiff (1969–75), and King's Coll., London (from 1976).

WRITINGS: *Schoenberg Chamber Music* (London, 1972); *Music since the First World War* (London, 1977; 3rd ed., 1988); *Britten and Tippett: Studies in Themes and Techniques* (Cambridge, 1982); *Romantic Music: A Concise History from Schubert to Sibelius* (London, 1987); with J. Dunsby, *Music Analysis in Theory and Practice* (New Haven, Conn., 1988).—**NS/LK/DM**

Whittall, Gertrude Clarke, American patroness of music and literature; b. Bellevue, Nebr., Oct. 7, 1867; d. Washington, D.C., June 29, 1965. Her maiden name was Clarke; she married Matthew John Whittall on June 4, 1906. In 1935 she donated to the Library of Congress in Washington, D.C., a quartet of Stradivari instruments—2 violins (including the famous "Betts"), a viola, and a cello—together with 4 Tourte bows; she added another Stradivari violin (the "Ward") and another Tourte bow in 1937. In 1936 she established an endowment fund in the Library of Congress to provide public concerts at which these instruments would be used, and in 1938 the Whittall Pavilion was built in the library to house them and to serve other purposes in the musical life of the library. In subsequent years, she continued to add to her gifts to the library on behalf of both music and literature; one series enabled the Whittall Foundation to acquire many valuable autograph MSS of composers from Bach to Schoenberg and, in particular, the finest single group of Brahms MSS gathered anywhere in the world.

BIBL.: W. Orcutt, *The Stradivari Memorial at Washington* (Washington, D.C., 1938); E. Waters, *Autograph Musical Scores in the W. Foundation Collection* (Washington, D.C., 1951). —**NS/LK/DM**

Whittenberg, Charles, American composer and teacher; b. St. Louis, July 6, 1927; d. Hartford, Conn., Aug. 22, 1984. He was a student of Phillips and Rogers at the Eastman School of Music in Rochester, N.Y. (B.A., 1948). From 1961 to 1963 he was ed. of the *American Composers Alliance Bulletin*. In 1962 he became associated with the Columbia-Princeton Electronic Music Center and became a teacher at Bennington (Vt.) Coll. After teaching at the Center of Liberal Studies in Washington, D.C. (1965), he served as an assoc. prof. at the Univ. of Conn. in Storrs (1967–77), where he was director of its Contemporary Music Projects. In 1963 and 1964 he held Guggenheim fellowships, and in 1965–66 the prize of the American Academy in Rome. Whittenberg was especially adept at writing brass music.

Works: Orch.: *Event* for Chamber Orch. and Tape (1963; N.Y., April 28, 1964); *Correlatives* (1969); *Serenade* for Strings (1971–73). **Chamber:** *Dialogue and Aria* for Flute and Piano (1956); *Fantasy* for Wind Quintet (1961); *Concert Piece* for Bassoon and Piano (1961; rev. 1971); *Structures* for 2 Pianos (1961); *Triptych* for Brass Quintet (1962); Chamber Concerto for Violin and 7 Instruments (1963); Cello Sonata (1963); *Duo-Divertimento* for Flute and Double Bass (1963); *3 Pieces* for Clarinet (1963; rev. 1969); *Variations* for 9 Players (1964; rev. 1970); 2 string quartets (1965; 1974–75); *4 Forms and an Epilogue* for Harpsichord (1965); *Polyphony* for Trumpet (1965); Sextet for Flute, Clarinet, Bassoon, Violin, Cello, and Double Bass (1967); *Conversations* for Double Bass (1967); *3 Compositions* for Piano (1967; rev. 1969); *Games of 5* for Wind Quintet (1968); *Iambi* for 2 Oboes (1968; rev. 1972); Concerto for Brass Quintet (1968–69); *Winter Music* for Violin (1971); *Sonata- fantasia* for Cello (1973); *5 Feuilletons* for Clarinet (1976); *In Memoriam Benjamin Britten* for Percussion (1977). **Vocal:** *3 Songs on Texts of Rilke* for Soprano and 9 Instruments (1957–62); *Concertante* for Baritone, Viola, Flute, and Vibraphone (1961); *From the Sonnets to Orpheus* for Narrator and Soprano (1962); *Vocalise* for Soprano and Viola (1963); *A Sacred Triptych* for Chorus (1971). **Tape:** *Study I* for Cello and Tape (1961); *Electronic Study II* for Double Bass and Tape (1961); *Study* for Clarinet and Electronic Extensions (1961); *Event II* for Double Bass, Flute, Strings, and Tape (1963). **—NS/LK/DM**

Who, The, extremely popular British rock band who created the first rock opera (*Tommy*) among many other achievements. **Membership:** Pete Townshend, lead and rhythm gtr., voc. (b. Chiswick, London, England, May 19, 1945); Roger Daltrey, lead voc. (b. Hammersmith, London, March 1, 1944); John Entwhistle, bs., French horn, voc. (b. Chiswick, London, Oct. 9, 1944); Keith Moon, drm. (b. Wembley, London, Aug. 23, 1947; d. there, Sept. 7, 1978). Keith Moon was replaced by Kenney Jones (b. Stepney, East London, Sept. 16, 1948).

In 1959, Pete Townshend and classically trained John Entwhistle formed The Confederates while still in grammar school. Three years later, Roger Daltrey invited Entwhistle to join his band, The Detours, soon adding Townshend and drummer Doug Sanden. Daltrey functioned as the leader, lead guitarist, and lead singer with the group but eventually assumed the sole role of lead vocalist. Under manager Peter Meaden, the group adopted a colorful "mod" image, became The High Numbers, and issued their first single, "I'm the Face," in mid-1964. By October 1964, they had replaced Sanden with Keith Moon from the surf band The Beachcombers. The group became The Who under new managers Kit Lambert and Chris Stamp, who encouraged Townshend to develop his songwriting. The two urged the group to display open aggression on stage and cultivated the group's mod image with flashy clothes, including Townshend's renowned Union Jack jacket. In 1965, during a performance at the Railway Tavern, Pete Townshend inadvertently broke the neck of his guitar on a low ceiling. Townshend and Keith Moon subsequently destroyed their equipment, an expensive practice the group reenacted at virtually every performance for the next four years.

Enjoying a highly successful residency at London's Marquee club, The Who signed to American Decca (Brunswick and later Reaction and Track in Great Britain) on the recommendation of American producer Shel Talmy. They scored four consecutive smash hits in Britain through the spring of 1966 with Talmy as producer: "I Can't Explain," the archetypal heavy metal "Anyway, Anyhow, Anywhere," the instant classic "My Generation," and "Substitute." "I Can't Explain" and "My Generation" became minor American hits. Their debut album contained "My Generation," "The Kids Are Alright," and the satiric "A Legal Matter," all by Townshend, plus the manic instrumental "The Ox," but it failed to sell in the U.S. "I'm a Boy" and "Happy Jack" became smash British hits and their second album, *Happy Jack*, yielded their first major American hit with the title song, while including Entwhistle's "Boris the Spider" and "Whiskey Man," and Townshend's first attempt at an extended piece, "A Quick One While He's Away."

Launched in America with their frenetic performance at the Monterey International Pop Festival in June 1967 (later chronicled in the D. A. Pennebaker film) and subsequent late summer tour in support of Herman's Hermits, The Who issued one of the earliest concept albums, *The Who Sell Out*, a tribute to Britain's pirate radio stations, at year's end. Featuring a bizarre album cover and satiric radio station commercials between songs, the album contained the near-smash British and American hit "I Can See for Miles," "Armenia City in the Sky," and the gentle "Rael." The Who quickly became a major concert attraction in the U.S. and next released the anthology set *Magic Bus*, which included Townshend's "Call Me Lightning," "Magic Bus" (a major American hit), and "Pictures of Lily" (a smash British hit in 1967), and a remake of the surf song "Bucket T.," featuring Entwhistle's humorous French horn solo.

The Who's next album was the highly influential "rock opera" *Tommy*. Although not the first work of its kind, the album proved hugely successful, remaining on the album charts for more than two years and yielding a major hit with "Pinball Wizard." An odd and elaborate tale of lost innocence, redemption, and contrition, *Tommy* featured a number of instrumental interludes and Sonny Boy Williamson's "Eyesight to the Blind," as well as the psychedelic "Acid Queen," the inspiring "Sensation," the liberating "I'm Free," and Tommy's final rejection and plea for acceptance, "We're Not Gonna Take It"/"See Me, Feel Me." Performed in its entirety only twice—once in London and once in N.Y.—*Tommy* drew the attention and praise of "serious" drama, opera, and classical music critics as well as fans and rock critics.

Tommy was performed in excerpted form by The Who for nearly two years and inspired both an all-star London stage production and an excessive and frankly unfortunate film by Ken Russell. The stage production, released on album in late 1972, featured the London Symphony Orch. and Chamber Choir and performances by Rod Stewart, Merry Clayton, Steve Winwood, Sandy Denny, Richie Havens, Ringo Starr, and The Who. Director, screenwriter, and coproducer Ken Russell's 1975 film version, an extravagant and bizarre production replete with repulsive, inane, and tedious scenes, featured Roger Daltrey as Tommy and performances by Eric Clapton, Tina Turner, Elton John, and the members of The Who. It also contained the decidedly shallow acting and poor musical performances of Ann-Margret, Oliver Reed, and Jack Nicholson.

Seriously challenging The Rolling Stones' claim to being "the world's greatest rock-and-roll band," particularly after their celebrated appearance at the Woodstock Music and Art Fair (and subsequent film) in August 1969, The Who next recorded *Live at Leeds*, one of the most exciting live albums ever issued. The album produced a major American hit with Eddie Cochran's "Summertime Blues" and contained Johnny Kidd's "Shakin' All Over" and extended versions of both "My Generation" and "Magic Bus." The 1995 CD reissue doubled the length of the original album.

Who's Next, their first studio album in two years, was another milestone in the history of rock, showcasing Townshend's outstanding and innovative use of synthesizers. The album included several finely crafted and brilliantly performed extended pieces such as "Baba O'Riley," "The Song Is Over," and the disillusioned "Won't Get Fooled Again" (a near-smash British and major American hit), as well as the menacing "Behind Blue Eyes" (a moderate American hit) and Entwhistle's "My Wife." The Who soon issued the anthology set *Meaty, Beaty, Big and Bouncy*, which Townshend reviewed in *Rolling Stone*. The album successfully collected the singles of The Who through "Pinball Wizard" and "The Magic Bus," and included Townshend's overlooked "The Seeker." In the summer of 1972, The Who scored a near-smash British and major American hit with "Join Together."

The Who's next album of new material was the double-record set *Quadrophenia*. Although greeted by equivocal reviews, the album was perhaps even more ambitious and personal than *Tommy* and every bit its equal in musical and dramatic terms. Concerned with the early history of The Who and the Mod movement through its protagonist Jimmy, *Quadrophenia*'s title referred to Jimmy's double schizophrenia, the four members of The Who as representatives of the four sides of his personality, and the four recurrent musical themes of the album. Oddly criticized for its lack of unity, the album was heavily orchestrated and lavishly produced. It included "I'm One," "5:15," "Is It in My Head," and "Drowned," plus the minor hits "Love, Reign O'er Me" and "The Real Me." For the first time in two years, The Who toured in support of the album.

In the meantime, the members of The Who had pursued individual projects. Keith Moon appeared in Frank Zappa's film *200 Motels* (1971) and the David Essex films *That'll Be the Day* (1973) and *Stardust* (1974). John Entwhistle recorded three solo albums, including a brilliant debut, through 1973. Pete Townshend supported Eric Clapton's "comeback" at London's Rainbow Theatre in January 1973 and recorded his solo debut for fellow devotees of guru Meher Baba. *Who Came First* proved so popular that it was issued as a regular commercial release. With Townshend handling virtually every musical instrument and engineering chore, the album included "Pure and Easy," "Nothing Is Everything (Let's See Action)," and an adaptation of Meher Baba's Universal Prayer, "Parvardigar." Roger Daltrey's debut solo album proved the most successful of the group member's outside releases. Produced by David Courtney and former pop star Adam Faith, *Daltrey* featured the collaborative compositions of Courtney, Faith, and Leo Sayer. The album yielded a smash British and minor American hit with "Giving It All Away" and contained outstanding existential songs such as "The Way of the World," "You Are Yourself," and "Hard Life," plus "One Man Band."

During 1974, John Entwhistle assembled a remarkable collection of mostly unreleased Who material as *Odds and Sods*. An excellent summation of the career of The Who, the album included their first single release, "I'm the Face," a dynamic and superior version of "Pure and Easy," the menacing and moving "Naked Eye," and the neglected rock anthem, "Long Live Rock." John Entwhistle toured and recorded with the band Ox in 1975, as Keith Moon issued his first solo album and Daltrey his second. Daltrey's *Ride a Rock Horse* included "Oceans Away" and yielded a minor hit with Russ Ballard's "Come and Get Your Love."

The Who's next album, *The Who by Numbers*, was recorded during a relatively inactive period that lasted until 1977, but it was perhaps the group's weakest effort to date, producing a major hit with "Squeeze Box." The Who conducted a major American tour in 1975 and 1976 (including a joint performance with The Grateful Dead in October 1976), but Townshend, suffering permanent hearing loss and desirous of spending more time with his family, withdrew from the public eye. Daltrey appeared in Ken Russell's equivocal *Lisztomania* movie as composer Franz Liszt in 1975 and Moon moved to Los Angeles in 1976. Daltrey recorded his third solo album in 1977 and Townshend reemerged triumphantly with *Rough Mix*, recorded with Ronnie Lane of The Faces.

In 1978, The Who returned with their first album in nearly three years, *Who Are You*. It contained "Had Enough," "Sister Disco," and "Music Must Change" and produced a major hit with the title song. However, on Sept. 7, 1978, Keith Moon was found dead in his London flat at the age of 31, the victim of a drug overdose. By the beginning of 1979, former Small Faces drummer Kenney Jones had replaced Moon. The group toured in the summer of 1979, augmented by keyboardist John "Rabbit" Bundrick, a former member of Free. During the year, The Who released two feature-length films and double-record soundtrack albums, the excellent documentary *The Kids Are Alright* and the fictional *Quadrophenia*, based on their 1973 album. *The Kids Are Alright* included the first offical release from the legendary 1968 television special *The Rolling Stones Rock and Roll Circus* and the soundtrack yielded a minor hit with "Long Live Rock." Perhaps due to American audiences' unfamiliarity with the Mod movement, *Quadrophenia* failed at the box office. The soundtrack album featured remixes from the original album, three new songs, and an entire side of "oldies" such as James Brown's "Night Train" and The Ronettes' "Be My Baby."

The Who toured America again in late 1979, but, at a performance at Cincinnati's Riverfront Stadium on Dec. 3, eleven people were killed in the crush of callous fans outside the stadium, an unfortunate legacy to the career of one of rock music's most talented and exciting acts. By 1980, The Who had switched to Warner Bros. for their American releases, and Townshend had recorded *Empty Glass*, with its near-smash hit "Let My Love Open the Door," as his debut for his new label, Atco. Roger Daltrey starred in the title role of the film *McVicar*, based on the life of bank robber John McVicar, widely known in Great Britain for his repeated escapes from prison. The soundtrack album, credited to Daltrey and Russ Ballard, featured all the members of The Who, producing a major hit with "Without Your Love." In 1981, The Who toured again and released *Face Dances*, which yielded a major hit with "You Better You Bet."

In 1982 and 1983, The Who conducted their "Farewell Tour" of stadiums with The Clash as their opening act, officially disbanding in December 1983. The tour produced the live set *Who's Last*. Atco issued Townshend's *All the Best Cowboys Have Chinese Eyes*, and Townshend joined the prestigious publishing firm Faber and Faber as an editor in 1983. Townshend's *Scoop* compiled his demo recordings, as would *Another Scoop* in 1987. Roger Daltrey appeared in the BBC production of *The Beggar's Opera* as McHeath and later costarred in the BBC-Time-Life production of Shakespeare's *Comedy of Errors*. He switched to Atlantic for *Parting Should Be Painless*, followed in 1985 by *Under the Raging Moon*. During 1985, Pete Townshend published his first book, the collection of poetry and prose *Horse's Neck*, and recorded the ambitious *White City—A Novel* with Pink Floyd guitarist David Gilmour, among others. The album yielded a major hit with "Face the Face."

The Who reunited for the Live Aid concert in July 1985, but immediately went their separate ways. Townshend toured England with Deep End, which included David Gilmour, and the tour produced both a concert video and album released in 1986. John Entwhistle toured on his own in 1988 and Townshend composed and recorded songs for the musical *The Iron Man*, based on a children's story by Ted Hughes. The album included The Who's "Dig" and "Fire" and John Lee Hooker's "Over the Top" and "I Eat Heavy Metal."

Townshend, Daltrey, and Entwhistle reunited for a Who stadium tour in 1989 sponsored by Budweiser and Miller Lite beers. For the tour, the three were augmented by guitarist Steve Bolton, keyboardist John "Rabbit" Bundrick, drummer Simon Phillips, a five-piece horn section, and three backup vocalists. The tour included two full performances of *Tommy*, one in N.Y. and one in Los Angeles. The Los Angeles show, the highlight of the tour, was offered as a pay-per-view cable televison show and featured guest performances by Steve Winwood, Elton John, Billy Idol, Phil Collins, and Patti Labelle. However, the tour was viewed cynically by critics. The Who were inducted into the Rock and Roll Hall of Fame in 1990.

In November 1991, Pete Townshend began working with Des McAnuff, the artistic director of the La Jolla (Calif.) Playhouse to transform *Tommy* into a stage musical. The setting was changed, connecting dialogue was added, and Townshend composed one new song, "I Believe My Own Eyes." The show opened at the La Jolla Playhouse in July 1992, debuted on Broadway in April 1993, and won five Tony Awards. The show went on national tour in October.

In the meantime, Roger Daltrey starred in the 1990 film *Mack the Knife* with Raul Julia and recorded *Rocks in the Head*. In 1994, he conducted a "Daltrey Sings Townshend" tour with a 32-piece orchestra. Pete Townshend composed and recorded the ambitious *PsychoDerelict* and toured the show with three actors and an eight-piece band in 1993. The August performance at the Brooklyn Academy of Music was later broadcast as part of PBS television's *Great Performances* series. In 1995, John Entwhistle toured as a member of Ringo Starr's All-Starr Band.

In June 1996, Pete Townshend, Roger Daltrey, and John Entwhistle reunited to perform *Quadrophenia* at the Prince's Trust benefit show in London's Hyde Park with Billy Idol, Gary Glitter, and drummer Zak Starkey (Ringo's son). They subsequently performed the show five times at N.Y.'s Madison Square Garden in July and toured North America with the show for five weeks in the fall. In 1998, Townshend's keyboardist daughter Emma recorded her debut album *Winterland*. In 1999, the Who once again reunited for a single benefit concert; they then toured into 2000.

DISC.: *The Who Sings My Generation* (1966); *Happy Jack* (1967); *The Who Sell Out* (1967); *Magic Bus* (1968); *Tommy* (1969); *Live at Leeds* (1970); *Who's Next* (1971); *Meaty, Beaty, Big and Bouncy* (1971); *Quadrophenia* (1973); *Odds and Sods* (1974); *The Who by Numbers* (1975); *Who Are You* (1978); *The Kids Are Alright* (soundtrack; 1979); *Face Dances* (1981); *Hooligans* (1981); *It's Hard* (1982); *Who's Last* (1984); *Who's Missing* (rec. 1965–72; rel. 1986); *Two's Missing* (rec. 1964–73; rel. 1987); *Join Together* (1990); *30 Years of Maximum R&B: The Gift Set* (1994); *Live on the BBC* (rec. 1964–73; rel. 2000). **JOHN ENTWHISTLE:** *Smash Your Head against the Wall* (1971); *Whistle Rhymes* (1972); *Rigor Mortis Sets In* (1973); *Mad Dog (with Ox)* (1975); *Too Late the Hero* (1981); *The Rock* (1996); *King Biscuit Flower Hour* (1997). **ROGER DALTREY:** *Daltrey* (1973); *Ride a Rock Horse* (1975); *One of the Boys* (1977); *Best Bits* (1982); *Parting Should Be Painless* (1984); *Under a Raging Moon* (1985); *Rocks in the Head* (1992). **ROGER DALTREY/RICK WAKEMAN:** *Lisztomania* (soundtrack; 1975). **ROGER DALTREY/RUSS BALLARD:** *McVicar* (soundtrack; 1980). **PETE TOWNSHEND:** *Who Came First* (1972); *Empty Glass* (1980); *All the Best Cowboys Have Chinese Eyes* (1982); *Scoop* (1983); *White City: A Novel* (1985); *Another Scoop* (rec. 1964–84; rel. 1986); *Pete Townshend's Deep End Live!* (1986); *The Iron Man (A Musical by Pete Townshend)* (1989); *PsychoDerelict* (1993). **PETE TOWNSHEND AND RONNIE LANE:**

Rough Mix (1977). **EMMA TOWNSHEND:** *Winterland* (1998).

WRITINGS: P. Townshend, *Horse's Neck* (Boston, 1985); S. Clarke (compiler), *The W. in Their Own Words* (N.Y., 1979).

BIBL.: G. Herman, *The W.* (N.Y., 1972); J. Stein and C. Johnston, *The W.* (N.Y., 1973); *Rolling Stone, The W.* (San Francisco, 1975); G. Tremlett, *The W.* (N.Y., 1975); J. Swenson, *The W.: Britain's Greatest Rock Group* (N.Y., 1979); D. Butler, with C. Trengrove and P. Lawrence, *Full Moon: The Amazing Rock and Roll Life of Keith Moon* (N.Y., 1981); R. Barnes, *The W.: Maximum R&B* (London, 1982; N.Y., 1983; London, 1996); D. Marsh, *Before I Get Old: The Story of The W.* (N.Y., 1983); J. Benson, *Uncle Joe's Record Guide: Eric Clapton, Jimi Hendrix, The W.* (Glendale, Calif., 1987); S. Wolter and K. Kimber, *The W. in Print: An Annotated Bibliography, 1965 through 1990* (Jefferson, N.C., 1992); G. Guiliano, *Behind Blue Eyes: The Life of Pete Townshend* (N.Y., 1996); J. Perry, *Meaty Beaty Big and Bouncy* (N.Y., 1998).—**BH**

Whyte, Ian, Scottish conductor, broadcasting administrator, and composer; b. Dunfermline, Aug. 13, 1901; d. Glasgow, March 27, 1960. He was a pupil of David Stephen (composition) and Philip Halstead (piano) at the Carnegie Dunfermline Trust Music School, and later was a student of Stanford and Vaughan Williams at the Royal Coll. of Music in London. Upon his return to Scotland, he was made music director to Lord Glentanar in 1923. From 1931 to 1945 he was head of music for the BBC in Glasgow, and then conductor of its orch. from 1945 until his death. His extensive output, which includes operas, operettas, ballets, 2 syms., symphonic poems, overtures, concertos, chamber music, piano pieces, choruses, hymns, carols, and many songs, reflects his Scottish heritage.—**NS/LK/DM**

Whythorne, Thomas, English lutenist, teacher, and composer; b. Ilminster, 1528; d. London, July 31(?), 1596. He attended Magdalen Coll. School, Oxford, and matriculated at Magdalen Coll., then was a servant and scholar to John Heyward, during which time he took up the virginals and lute and learned to write English verse; subsequently was in the service of the Duchess of Northumberland. After traveling on the Continent (c. 1553–55), he returned to England, where he was in the service of various patrons. In 1571 he was named master of music at the chapel of Archbishop Parker. His *Songes for Three, Fower and Five Voyces* (London, 1571) were the first in that genre to be publ. in England; later brought out *Duos, or Songs* for Two Voices (London, 1590). His autobiography (c. 1576), discovered in 1955, was publ. in Oxford in 1961 in his original phonetic spelling, and reprinted in modern spelling in 1963, ed. by J.M. Osborn.

BIBL.: P. Warlock, *T. W.: An Unknown Elizabethan Composer* (London, 1925); J. Jobling, *A Critical Study and Partial Transcription of the Two Published Collections of T. W.* (diss., Univ. of Sheffield, 1978).—**NS/LK/DM**

Wich, Günther, German conductor; b. Bamberg, May 23, 1928. He studied flute with Gustav Scheck in Freiburg im Breisgau (1948–52). In 1952 he made his conducting debut there, serving as chief conductor of its Opera until 1959. He then was conductor of the Graz Opera (1959–61), and later Generalmusikdirektor in Hannover (1961–65) and at the Deutsche Oper am Rhein in Düsseldorf (1965–80). In 1982 he joined the faculty of the Würzburg Hochschule für Musik.—**NS/LK/DM**

Wickham, Florence, American contralto and composer; b. Beaver, Pa., 1880; d. N.Y., Oct. 20, 1962. She studied in Philadelphia and then was a pupil of Franz Emerich in Berlin; she also studied with Mathilde Mallinger. In 1902 Wickham made her operatic debut as Fidès in Wiesbaden. After appearances in Schwerin and Munich, she sang the role of Kundry in *Parsifal* in Henry W. Savage's touring opera troupe in America (1904–05). In 1908 she appeared in Wagnerian roles at London's Covent Garden. On Nov. 17, 1909, she made her Metropolitan Opera debut in N.Y. as Verdi's Emilia. She remained on its roster until 1912, and then sang in concerts and devoted herself to composition. She wrote the operettas *Rosalynd* (1938) and *The Legend of Hex Mountain* (1957).—**NS/LK/DM**

Wicks, (Edward) Allan, English organist and choirmaster; b. Harden, Yorkshire, June 6, 1923. He studied organ with Thomas Armstrong at Christ Church, Oxford, and also was made a Fellow of the Royal Coll. of Organists. He was asst. organist at York Minster (1947–54). After serving as organist and choirmaster at Manchester Cathedral (1954–61), he distinguished himself in those capacities at Canterbury Cathedral (1961–88); he also toured as a recitalist in England, Europe, and the U.S. In 1974 he was awarded a D.Mus. by the Archbishop of Canterbury and in 1985 was given an honorary D.Mus. by the Univ. of Kent; in 1988 he was made a Commander of the Order of the British Empire. His repertoire is exhaustive, ranging from early music to modern English compositions. —**NS/LK/DM**

Widdop, Walter, English tenor; b. Norland, April 19, 1892; d. London, Sept. 6, 1949. He was a student of Dinh Gilly. In 1923 he made his operatic debut as Radames with the British National Opera Co. in Leeds. In 1924 he sang in *Siegfried* at London's Covent Garden, returning there as Siegmund (1932) and Tristan (1933; 1937–38). He was also a guest artist in Spain, Holland, and Germany. In addition to his operatic roles, he also was admired as an oratorio singer. The night before he died he sang Lohengrin's Farewell at a London Promenade concert.—**NS/LK/DM**

Widerkehr (also **Wiederkehr** or **Viderkehr**), **Jacques (-Christian-Michel),** lsatian composer and cellist; b. Strasbourg, April 18, 1759; d. Paris, April 1823. He studied with F. X. Richter and Dumonchau in Strasbourg, then in about 1783 settled in Paris, where he was active as a cellist. He became well known as a composer of symphonies concertantes for wind instruments. He also wrote an opera, *Oreste*, Revolutionary hymns, and much chamber music, including 2 sonatas for Piano with Violin and Bass Accompaniment, 6 *Duo concertants* for 2 Violins or Cellos (Paris, c. 1794), 3 *quatuors concertants* for String Quartet

(Paris, 1797), 3 *quatuors* (Paris, c. 1803), *1er quintetto* for 2 Violins, 2 Violas, and Cello (Paris, c. 1808), 3 duos for Piano and Violin or Oboe or Clarinet (Paris, c. 1817), 4 *quatuors* (Paris, c. 1819), and 3 trios for Flute, Horn, and Bassoon (Paris, c. 1820). He has often been confused with the trombonist, teacher, and composer Philippe Widerkehr, who was active in Paris (1793–1816) and who may have been his brother.—**NS/LK/DM**

Widmann, Erasmus, distinguished German organist, instrumentalist, teacher, and composer; b. Schwäbisch Hall (baptized), Sept. 15, 1572; d. Rothenburg ob der Tauber, Oct. 31, 1634. While attending the Schwäbisch Hall Lateinschule, he learned to play the organ, harpsichord, lute, viol, flute, trombone, and zither; then pursued his education at the Univ. of Tubingen (B.A., 1590). By 1595 he was organist in Eisenerz, Styria, and then organist in Graz (1596–98). He subsequently returned to Schwäbisch Hall as Kantor. From 1602 to 1613 he was Präzeptor and organist at the Weickersheim court. In 1613 he went to Rothenburg ob der Tauber as Präzeptor and Kantor; in 1614 he also became organist at the Jacobskirche there. His last years were made miserable by the 30 Years' War. His wife and daughter died of the plague, which also claimed him. He was a significant composer of instrumental and vocal music, both sacred and secular. A selected edition of his works was ed. by G. Reichert in Das Erbe Deutscher Musik, Sonderreihe, III (1955).

WRITINGS: *Musicae praecepta latino-germanica in usum studiosae juventutis* (Rothenburg ob der Tauber, 1614).

BIBL.: E. Schmidt, *Zur Geschichte des Gottesdienstes und der Kirchenmusik in Rothenburg ob der Tauber* (Rothenburg ob der Tauber, 1905); Graf zu Eulenberg, *E. W.s Leben und Werke* (Munich, 1907); G. Reichert, *E. W.: Leben, Wirken und Werke eines württembergisch-fränkischen Musikers* (Stuttgart, 1951).
—**NS/LK/DM**

Widor, Charles-Marie (-Jean-Albert), distinguished French organist, pedagogue, and composer; b. Lyons, Feb. 21, 1844; d. Paris, March 12, 1937. His father, an Alsatian of Hungarian descent, was organist at the church of St.-François in Lyons and was active as an organ builder. Widor was a skillful improviser on the organ while still a boy, and became organist at the Lyons lycee when he was 11. After studies with Fétis (composition) and Lemmens (organ) in Brussels, he became organist at St.-François in Lyons (1860), and gained high repute via provincial concerts. In 1870–71 he held a provisional appointment as organist at St.-Sulpice in Paris, where he served as organist from 1871 until 1934. On April 19, 1934, he played his *Pièce mystique* there, composed at age 90. Around 1880 he began writing music criticism under the pen name "Aulétès" for the daily *L'Estafette*. In 1890 he became prof. of organ and in 1896 prof. of composition at the Paris Cons. In 1910 he was elected a member of the Academie des Beaux-Arts, of which he became permanent secretary in 1913. He had many distinguished pupils, including Albert Schweitzer, with whom he collaborated in editing the first 5 vols. of an 8-vol. ed. of J.S. Bach's organ works (N.Y., 1912–14). As a composer, he wrote copiously in many forms but is best known for his organ music, especially his 10 "symphonies" (suites). A master organ virtuoso, he won great renown for his performances of Bach and for his inspired improvisations.

WORKS: **DRAMATIC** (all 1st perf. in Paris): *Maître Ambros*, opera (May 6, 1886); *Les Pêcheurs de Saint- Jean*, opera (Dec. 26, 1905); *Nerto*, opera (Oct. 27, 1924); *La Korrigane*, ballet (Dec. 1, 1880); *Jeanne d'Arc*, ballet-pantomime (1890); also incidental music to *Conte d'avril* (Sept. 22, 1885) and to *Les Jacobites* (Nov. 21, 1885). **ORCH.:** Syms.: No. 1 (c. 1870), No. 2 (1886), and No. 3 for Organ and Orch. (1895); *Sinfonia sacra* for Organ and Orch. (1908); *Symphonie antique* for Organ and Orch. (1911); 2 piano concertos (1876, 1906); Cello Concerto (1882); *La Nuit de Walpurgis*, symphonic poem for Chorus and Orch. (c. 1887; London, April 19, 1888); *Fantasie* for Piano and Orch. (1889); *Ouverture espagnole* (1898); *Choral et variations* for Harp and Orch. (1900). **CHAMBER:** 2 piano quintets (c. 1890, 1896); Piano Quartet (1891); Piano Trio (1875); *Sérénade* for Piano, Flute, Violin, Cello, and Harmonium (c. 1883); *4 pièces* for Piano, Violin, and Cello (1890); *Suite* for Flute and Piano (1898); *Soirs d'Alsace* for Piano, Violin, and Cello (1908); *Introduction et rondo* for Clarinet and Piano (1898); *3 pièces* for Oboe and Piano (1909); *Suite* for Cello and Piano (1912); *Suite florentine* for Piano and Flute or Violin (1920). **KEYBOARD: Piano:** *Variations de concert sur un thème original* (1867); *6 morceaux de salon* (1872); *6 valses caractéristiques* (1877); *12 feuillets d'album* (1877); *La Barque* (1877); *La Corricolo* (1877); *Suite polonaise* (c. 1885); *Suite* (c. 1887); *Conte d'automne* (1904); *Suite écossaise* (c. 1905). **Organ:** 10 syms.: Nos. 1–4 (1876), Nos. 5–8 (c. 1880), *Symphonie gothique* (1895), and *Symphonie romaine* (1900); *Suite latine* (1927); *3 nouvelles pièces* (1934); *Pièce mystique* (c. 1934); 8 sonatas. **VOCAL:** Many works, both sacred and secular, with instrumental and orch. accompaniment.

WRITINGS (all publ. in Paris): *Technique de l'orchestre moderne* (1904; 5th ed., rev. and enl., 1925; Eng. tr., 1906; 2nd ed., rev., 1946); *Notice sur la vie et les oeuvres de Camille Saint-Saëns* (1922); *Initiation musicale* (1923); *Académie des Beaux-Arts: Fondations, portraits de Massenet à Paladilhe* (1927); *L'Orgue moderne: La Décadence dans la facture contemporaine* (1928).

BIBL.: H. Reynaud, *L'Œuvre de C.-M. W.* (Lyons, 1900); J. Rupp, *C.-M. W. und sein Werk* (Bremen, 1912); A. Thomson, *The Life and Times of C.-M. W., 1844–1937* (Oxford, 1988); S. Hiemke, *Die Bach-Rezeption C.-M. W.s* (Frankfurt am Main, 1994); B. van Oosten, *C.-M. W.: Vater der Orgelsymphonie* (Paderborn, 1997).
—**NS/LK/DM**

Wiechowicz, Stanislaw, Polish composer, pedagogue, choral conductor, and writer on music; b. Kroszyce, Nov. 27, 1893; d. Kraków, May 12, 1963. He received his training at the Kraków Cons., the Dalcroze Inst. in Dresden, the St. Petersburg Cons., and the Schola Cantorum in Paris. After teaching theory (1921–30) and composition (1930–39) at the Poznań Cons., he was a prof. of composition at the Kraków Cons. from 1945 until his death. In 1950 he was awarded the Polish State Prize for composition. Wiechowicz excelled as a composer of vocal music.

WORKS: **ORCH.:** *Babie lato* (Martinmas Summer), symphonic poem (1922); *Chmiel* (The Hopvine), symphonic scherzo (1926); *Ruta* (Rue), sumphonic poem (1930); *Ulegalki* (The Wild Pears), symphonic portraits (1944); *Kasia* (Kate), folk suite for 2 Clarinets and Strings (1946); *Suita pastoralna* (1952); *Serenade* *polska* (1953); *Koncert staromiejski* (Old Town Concerto) for Strings (1954). **VOCAL:** *Pastoralki*, Christmas cantata for Voice, Chorus, and Percussion (1929); *Dzień słowiański* (Slav Day), cantata for Chorus and Brass Band (1929); *Kantata romantyczna* for Soprano, Chorus, and Orch. (1930); *3 suity ludowe* (3 Folk Suites) for Solo Voices, Chorus, and Orch. (1942); *Psalmodia* for Chorus and Orch. (1944); *Z Wojtusiowej izbyi* (From Wojtek's Room), children's cantata for Solo Voices, Chorus, and Orch. (1944); *A czemużeś nie przyjechał* (Why Did You Not Come?), rustic scene for Chorus and Orch. (1948); *Na glinianym wazoniku* (On a Little Clay Pot) for Chorus and Orch. (1948); *Kantata żniwna* (Harvest Cantata) for Chorus (1948); *Kantata Mickiewiczowska* for Chorus and Orch. (1950); *List do March Chagalla* (Letter to Marc Chagall), dramatic rhapsody for 2 Solo Voices, Male and Female Speakers, Chorus, and Orch. (1961); *Zstąp, gołębico* (O Dove, Descend), cantata for Soprano, Chorus, and Orch. (1962–63); many other pieces; numerous folk song arrangements.—**NS/LK/DM**

Wieck, family of German musicians:

(1) (Johann Gottlob) Friedrich Wieck, music pedagogue; b. Pretzsch, near Torgau, Aug. 18, 1785; d. Loschwitz, near Dresden, Oct. 6, 1873. After studying music with P.-J. Milchmeyer in Torgau, he pursued training in theology at the Univ. of Wittenberg; he then was active as a private tutor. In 1816 he went to Leipzig as a music teacher. In 1818 he founded a piano factory and a circulating music library, but eventually devoted himself entirely to pedagogy. In 1843 Mendelssohn offered him a professorship in piano at the newly organized Leipzig Cons., which he declined; in 1844 he settled in Dresden. In 1871 he helped to establish the Wieck-Stiftung to assist musically gifted youths. He married Marianne Tromlitz in 1816; after their divorce in 1824, she married his old friend Adolf Bargiel; the product of this marriage was Woldemar Bargiel. In 1828 Wieck married Clementine Fechner. He won great distinction as a pedagogue. Among his pupils were his daughters Clara and Marie, his son Alwin, Hans von Bülow, Fritz Spindler, Isidor Seiss, and Gustav Merkel. He was also Robert Schumann's teacher, but bitterly opposed Schumann's marriage to his daughter Clara. He publ. *Klavier und Gesang* (Leipzig, 1853; 3rd ed., aug., 1878; Eng. tr., 1878) and *Musikalische Bauernspruche* (Dresden, 1871; 2nd ed., 1876); also publ. studies and dances for piano, songs, and singing exercises; ed. piano pieces. For a biography of his daughter Clara, see **Schumann, Clara (Josephine)** (née **Wieck**).

(2) Alwin Wieck, violinist, pianist, and teacher; b. Leipzig, Aug. 27, 1821; d. Dresden, Oct. 21, 1885. He studied piano with his father and violin with David. After playing violin in the St. Petersburg Italian Opera orch. (1849–59), he settled in Dresden as a music teacher. He publ. *Materialen zu Friedrich Wiecks Pianoforte-Methodik* (Berlin, 1875) and *Vademecum perpetuum für den ersten Pianoforte-Unterricht nach Fr. Wiecks Methode* (Leipzig, c. 1875). He also wrote piano music.

(3) Marie Wieck, pianist and teacher; b. Leipzig, Jan. 17, 1832; d. Dresden, Nov. 2, 1916. She studied with her father, and at the age of 11 made her debut at a concert given by her half sister, Clara Schumann. She was appointed court pianist to the Prince of Hohenzollern in 1858. After tours of Germany, England, and Scandinavia, she settled in Dresden as a teacher of piano and singing. Her last public appearance was with the Dresden Phil. in Nov. 1915, playing the Schumann Concerto. She publ. piano pieces and songs, and also ed. her father's *Pianoforte-Studien*. She wrote *Aus dem Kreise Wieck- Schumann* (1912; 2nd ed., aug., 1914).

BIBL.: A. von Meichsner, *F. W. und seine beiden Töchter Clara Schumann, geb. Wieck, und Marie Wieck* (Leipzig, 1875); A. Kohut, *F. W.: Ein Lebens- und Künsterbild* (Dresden, 1888); V. Joss, *F. W. und sein Verhältnis zu Robert Schumann* (Leipzig, 1900); idem, *Der Musikpädagoge F. W. und seine Familie* (Dresden, 1902); M. Wieck, *Aus dem Kreise W.-Schumann* (Dresden, 1912; 2nd ed., 1914); K. Walch- Schumann, *F. W.: Briefe aus den Jahren 1830–1838* (Cologne, 1968).—**NS/LK/DM**

Wiedebein, Gottlob, German organist, conductor, and composer; b. Eilenstadt, July 27, 1779; d. Braunschweig, April 17, 1854. After studying in Braunschweig with his uncle and J. Schwanenberger, he was active as a teacher until being made principal conductor of the court orch. (1816) and opera (1818); he was compelled by ill health to give up his posts in 1832. He enjoyed a great reputation; Schumann sought his advice. He wrote some excellent lieder. Among his other works are an overture, the oratorio *Die Befreiung Deutschlands* (c. 1822), various cantatas and motets, piano pieces, and organ music.—**NS/LK/DM**

Wiedemann, Ernst Johann, German organist, conductor, teacher, and composer; b. Hohengiersdorf, Silesia, March 28, 1797; d. Potsdam, Dec. 7, 1873. From 1818 to 1852 he was organist of the Roman Catholic Church in Berlin, where he founded and conducted 2 singing societies. He composed a Te Deum for Soloists, Chorus, and Orch., masses, motets, and hymns. —**NS/LK/DM**

Wiedemann, Hermann, German baritone; b. 1879; d. Berlin, July 2, 1944. He made his operatic debut in Elberfeld in 1905. After singing in Brünn (1906–10), he was a member of the Hamburg Opera (1910–14), the Berlin Royal Opera (1914–16), and the Vienna Court (later State) Opera (1916–44). He also sang at the Salzburg Festivals (1922–41) and at London's Covent Garden (1933, 1938). Among his best roles were Guglielmo, Beckmesser, Alberich, and Donner. —**NS/LK/DM**

Wiedermann, Bedřich Antonín, Czech organist, pedagogue, and composer; b. Ivanovice na Hané, Nov. 10, 1883; d. Prague, Nov. 5, 1951. He studied theology in Olmütz (1904–08), during which period he deputized as organist and choirmaster at the Cathedral. He then studied with Klička (organ, 1908–09) and Novák (composition, 1909–10) at the Prague Cons. After serving as organist in Brünn (1910–11) and Prague (1911–17), he was choirmaster in Karlín (1917–19) and a violist in the Czech Phil. in Prague. From 1920 to 1932 he gave a series of organ recitals at Prague's Smetana Hall, which featured works of Bach, Handel, Franck, and Czech composers of the Baroque era. He also toured England and the U.S. (1924), Germany (1925), Sweden

(1926), and Belgium (1935). In 1917 he became a teacher at the Prague Cons., where he led a master class from 1944. In 1946 he was made a prof. at the Prague Academy of Arts. Among his compositions were various organ pieces.—**NS/LK/DM**

Wiegand, (Josef Anton) Heinrich, German bass; b. Fränkisch-Crumbach in the Odenwald, Sept. 9, 1842; d. Frankfurt am Main, May 28, 1899. He studied voice privately in Paris, becoming a member of the opera at Zürich in 1870. He then sang in Cologne, and from 1873 to 1877 was the leading bass at the Frankfurt am Main Opera. In 1877 he toured America with the Adams-Pappenheim troupe; was in Leipzig (1878–82), sang at the Vienna Court Opera (1882–84), and then was engaged at Hamburg. He also appeared in the *Ring* cycle in Berlin (1881) and London (1882).—**NS/LK/DM**

Wiel, Taddeo, Italian musicologist and composer; b. Oderzo, Treviso, Sept. 24, 1849; d. Venice, Feb. 17, 1920. He studied in Venice, and was asst. librarian of the Venice Biblioteca Marciana. He composed some vocal music and piano pieces, and prepared librettos, but his importance rests upon his work as a musicologist.

Writings (all publ. in Venice): *I codici musicali contariniani del secolo SVII nella R. Biblioteca di San Marco in Venezia* (1888); *Benedetto Marcello: Un prologo e un sonetto satirico* (1894); *I teatri musicali veneziani del settecento: Catalogo delle opere in musica rappresentate nel secolo XVIII in Venezia* (1897).—**NS/LK/DM**

Wielhorsky, Count Mikhail, Russian arts patron and composer of Polish descent; b. Volhynia, Nov. 11, 1788; d. Moscow, Sept. 9, 1856. His principal mentor in music was Martin y Soler; he learned to play the violin and piano, and began composing at 13. After studying counterpoint in Riga, he completed his studies with Cherubini in Paris (1808). In 1810 he went to St. Petersburg, where his home became the gathering place of many eminent musicians; in 1816 he went to live at his estate in the Kursk province, where he maintained a private orch. After living in Moscow (1823–26) and again in St. Petersburg (1826–56), he spent his last days at his estate near Moscow. His brother, Count Matvei Wielhorsky (b. St. Petersburg, April 26, 1794; d. Nice, March 3, 1866), was also a patron of the arts as well as a cellist; he studied cello with Adolph Meinhardt and Bernard Romberg; toured throughout Russia and in Europe. He lived with his brother in St. Petersburg (1826–56), where he helped to organize the city's branch of the Russian Musical Soc. in 1859. A distant relative, Joseph Wielhorsky (1817–92), was also a musician who composed piano pieces and songs.

Works: *Tsigane* (The Gypsies), opera (1838); 3 syms. (1822, 1822, n.d.); 2 overtures (1822, 1836); *Air varié* for Orch.; *Theme varié*; String Quartet; String Quintet; piano pieces; many choral works and songs.—**NS/LK/DM**

Wiemann, Ernst, German bass; b. Stapelberg, Dec. 21, 1919; d. Hamburg, May 17, 1980. He studied in Hamburg and Munich. After making his operatic debut in Kiel (1938), he sang in provincial German opera houses until joining the Hamburg State Opera in 1955. On Nov. 17, 1961, he made his Metropolitan Opera debut in N.Y. as Heinrich in *Lohengrin*, and remained on its roster until 1969. In 1971 he sang Gurnemanz at London's Covent Garden. He also appeared as a guest artist with opera companies on both sides of the Atlantic. He was best known for his Mozart, Wagner, and Verdi roles.—**NS/LK/DM**

Wiéner, Jean, French pianist and composer of Austrian descent; b. Paris, March 19, 1896; d. there, June 8, 1982. He studied with Gédalge at the Paris Cons. From 1920 to 1924 he presented the Concerts Jean Wiéner, devoted to the energetic propaganda of new music. He presented several premieres of works by modern French composers, and also performed pieces by Schoenberg, Berg, and Webern. He was the first Frenchman to proclaim jazz as a legitimate art form; also teamed with Clément Doucet in duo-piano recitals, in programs stretching from Mozart to jazz. His compositions reflect his ecumenical convictions, as exemplified in such works as *Concerto franco-americain* for Clarinet and Strings (1923) and a desegregationist operetta, *Olive chez les nègres* (1926). He also wrote an Accordion Concerto (1957) and a Concerto for 2 Guitars (1966), but he became famous mainly for his idiosyncratic film music. —**NS/LK/DM**

Wiener, Otto, Austrian baritone; b. Vienna, Feb. 13, 1913. He was a student in Vienna of Küper and Duhan. In 1939 he began his career as a concert singer. In 1952 he appeared for the first time at the Salzburg Festival, and in 1953 made his operatic stage debut as Simon Boccanegra in Graz. He was a member of the Deutsche Oper am Rhein in Düsseldorf (1956–59). From 1957 to 1963 he sang at the Bayreuth Festivals. From 1957 he also sang at the Vienna State Opera and from 1960 to 1970 at the Bavarian State Opera in Munich. On Oct. 18, 1962, he made his Metropolitan Opera debut in N.Y. as Hans Sachs, remaining on its roster for a season. As a guest artist, he appeared in London, Rome, Milan, and other operatic centers. Throughout the years he continued his concert career as well. Following his retirement in 1976, he served as director of the opera school at the Vienna State Opera. Among his other roles were the Dutchman, Gunther, Wotan, La Roche in *Capriccio*, and Pfitzner's Palestrina.—**NS/LK/DM**

Wieniawski, Adam Tadeusz, Polish composer and music educator, nephew of **Henryk Wieniawski** and **Jozef Wieniawski;** b. Warsaw, Nov. 27, 1879; d. Bydgoszcz, April 21, 1950. He studied in Warsaw with Melcer-Szczawiński and Noskowski, then in Berlin with Bargiel, and in Paris with d'Indy, Fauré, and Gédalge. He fought in the French army during World War I. He returned to Warsaw in 1918 as a teacher at the Chopin School of Music, and was appointed its director in 1928.

Works: **Dramatic:** **Opera:** *Megaië* (1910; Warsaw, Dec. 28, 1912); *Zofka*, comic opera (1923); *Wyzwolony* (The Freed Man; Warsaw, July 5, 1928); *Król Kochanek* (The King as Paramour), musical comedy (Warsaw, March 19, 1931). **Ballet:** *Lalita* (1922); *Aktea w Jerozolimie* (Actea in Jerusalem;

Warsaw, June 4, 1927). OTHER: Orch. pieces, including *Bajeczki* (Tittle-tattle), sinfonietta, and 8 symphonic poems; chamber music; piano pieces; folk song arrangements.—**NS/LK/DM**

Wieniawski, Henryk (also known as **Henri**), famous Polish violinist, teacher, and composer, brother of **Jozef Wieniawski** and uncle of **Adam Tadeusz Wieniawski;** b. Lublin, July 10, 1835; d. Moscow, March 31, 1880. His mother, Regina Wolff-Wieniawska, was a talented pianist. He began training with Jan Hornziel and Stanislaw Serwaczynski in Warsaw; upon the advice of his mother's brother, Edouard Wolff, who lived in France, she took Henryk to Paris, where he entered the Cons. at the age of 8, first in Clavel's class and, the following year, in the advanced class of Massart. At the age of 11 he graduated with first prize in violin, an unprecedented event in the annals of the Paris Cons. After further private studies with Massart (1846–48), he made his Paris debut on Jan. 30, 1848, in a concert accompanied by his brother at the piano. He gave his first concert in St. Petersburg on March 31, 1848, and played 4 more concerts there. He then played in Finland and the Baltic provinces; after several successful appearances in Warsaw, he returned in 1849 to Paris, where he studied composition with Hippolyte Collet at the Cons., graduating with an "accessit" prize in 1850. From 1851 to 1853 he gave about 200 concerts in Russia with his brother. He also devoted much time to composition, and by age 18 had composed and publ. his virtuoso 1st Violin Concerto, which he played with extraordinary success in Leipzig that same year. In 1858 he appeared with Anton Rubinstein in Paris and in 1859 in the Beethoven Quartet Society concerts in London, where he appeared as a violist as well as a violinist. In 1860 he went to St. Petersburg and was named solo violinist to the Czar, and also concertmaster of the orch. and 1st violinist of the string quartet of the Russian Musical Soc.; likewise, he served as prof. of violin at the newly founded Cons. (1862–68). He continued to compose and introduced his greatly esteemed 2nd Violin Concerto in St. Petersburg on Nov. 27, 1862, with Rubinstein conducting. In 1872 he went on a tour of the U.S. with Rubinstein; one of the featured works was Beethoven's *Kreutzer Sonata*, which they performed about 70 times. When Rubinstein returned to Europe, Wieniawski continued his American tour, which included Calif. He returned to Europe in 1874, gave several concerts with Rubinstein in Paris and, in the same year, succeeded Vieuxtemps as prof. of violin at the Brussels Cons., resigning in 1877 owing to an increasingly grave heart condition. He suffered an attack during a concert in Berlin on Nov. 11, 1878, but still agreed to play several concerts in Russia; he made his farewell appearance in Odessa in April 1879. His last months were spent in Moscow, where he was taken to the home of Madame von Meck, Tchaikovsky's patroness, in Feb. 1880. He was married to Isobel Hampton, an Englishwoman; their youngest daughter, Irene, wrote music under the pen name Poldowski. Wieniawski was undoubtedly one of the greatest violinists of the 19th century; he possessed a virtuoso technique and an extraordinary range of dynamics. He was equally distinguished as a chamber music player. As a composer, he remains best known today for his 2 violin concertos and an outstanding set of études. He also composed numerous other orch. works as well as pieces for solo or 2 violins. A complete ed. of his works commenced publication in Kraków in 1962.

BIBL.: A. Desfossez, *Henri W.: Esquisse* (The Hague, 1856); J. Reiss, *Henryk W.* (Warsaw, 1931; 2nd ed., 1970); I. Yampolsky, *G. Vinyavsky* (Moscow, 1955); V. Grigoriev, *G. Vinyavsky* (Moscow, 1966); W. Dulęba, *Henryk W.* (Kraków, 1967); W. Grigoriew, *Henryk W.: Zycie i twórczość* (Warsaw, 1986); E. Grabkowski, *H. W.: Anegdoty i ciekawostki* (Kraków, 1991).—**NS/LK/DM**

Wieniawski, Jozef, distinguished Polish pianist, pedagogue, and composer, brother of **Henryk Wieniawski** and uncle of **Adam Tadeusz Wieniawski;** b. Lublin, May 23, 1837; d. Brussels, Nov. 11, 1912. He studied piano with Synek in Lublin, and at age 10 entered the Paris Cons., where he received lessons in piano from Zimmerman, Marmontel, and Alkan and in composition from LeCouppey (graduated, 1850). He toured Russia with his brother (1851–53), then was awarded a scholarship from the Czar for study with Liszt in Weimar (1855–56); he received training in theory from A.B. Marx in Berlin (1856–58). Wieniawski taught piano at the Russian Musical Soc. in Moscow (1864–65), then taught piano for one term at the Moscow Cons. before resuming private teaching. In 1875–76 he was director of the Warsaw Musical Soc., with which he appeared as a chamber music artist and as a choral conductor. He then was prof. of piano at the Brussels Cons. (1878–1912).

WORKS: ORCH.: Sym.; Piano Concerto; Fantasia for 2 Pianos and Orch.; *Suite romantique; Guillaume de Paciturne*, overture. CHAMBER: Violin Sonata; Cello Sonata; String Quartet; Piano Trio. Piano: 5 waltzes; 2 tarantellas; 3 fantasias; 2 barcarolles; 4 polonaises; Sonata; 9 mazurkas; 2 études de concert; 24 études. VOCAL: Various pieces.

BIBL.: J. Delcroix, *Joseph W.: Notices biographiques et anecdotiques* (Brussels, 1908).—**NS/LK/DM**

Wiens, Edith, Canadian soprano; b. Saskatoon, Saskatchewan, June 9, 1950. She studied on scholarship at the Hannover Hochschule für Musik (concert performance dipiloma, 1974), she continued her training at the Oberlin (Ohio) Coll.-Cons. of Music (M.A. in music theater, 1976). In 1979 she went to Munich to complete her vocal training with Ernst Haefliger and Erik Werba, taking the gold medal at the Schumann Competition in Zwickau that same year. In 1981 she made her first appearance as a soloist with the Berlin Phil., and thereafter was engaged to sing with principal orchs. of Europe and North America. As a recitalist, she sang in various Canadian cities as well as in N.Y., Paris, Berlin, Leipzig, Munich, and Vienna. In 1986 she made her operatic debut as Donna Anna with the Glyndebourne Opera; subsequently sang at the Amsterdam Opera, Milan's La Scala, Buenos Aires's Teatro Colón, and the National Arts Centre in Ottawa. Her concert repertoire extends from Bach to Richard Strauss.—**NS/LK/DM**

Wieprecht, Friedrich Wilhelm, German trombonist and inventor; b. Aschersleben, Aug. 8, 1802; d.

Berlin, Aug. 4, 1872. He studied in Dresden and Leipzig, where he was already famous as a trombonist. He invented the bass tuba (1835, with the instrument maker Moritz), the bathyphon, a contrabass clarinet (1839, with Skorra), the "piangendo" on brass instruments with pistons, and an improved contrabass bassoon. His claim of priority over Sax, in the invention of the saxhorns, remains moot.

Bibl.: A. Kalkbrenner, *W. W., Direktor: Sein Leben und Wirken nebst einem Auszug seiner Schriften* (Berlin, 1882). **—NS/LK/DM**

Wierzbillowicz, Alexander, Polish cellist and pedagogue; b. St. Petersburg (of Polish parents), Jan. 8, 1850; d. there, March 15, 1911. He studied in Warsaw and was a student of Davidov at the St. Petersburg Cons. In 1885 he became 1st cellist in the orch. of the Imperial Opera in St. Petersburg. He also made highly successful tours of Europe as a soloist, and also played in various chamber music settings. In 1889 he became prof. of cello at the St. Petersburg Cons.**—LK/DM**

Wieslander, (Axel Otto) Ingvar, Swedish composer and conductor; b. Jönköping, May 19, 1917; d. Malmö, April 29, 1963. He received training in theory from Sven Svensson at the Univ. of Uppsala. He also took some lessons in composition with Lars-Erik Larsson. After training at the Stockholm Musikhögskolan (conducting with Tor Mann; music teacher's diploma, 1945), he completed his studies in Paris on a French scholarship (1947–48) with Tony Aubin (composition) and Eugène Bigot (conducting). From 1949 to 1960 he was director of music at the Malmö City Theater, and then was its chorus master from 1960 to 1963. He was co-founder of the Ars Nova Concert Soc., of which he was chairman (1960–63). In his music, his erstwhile neo-Classical style with infusions of 12-tone writing eventually evolved into a highly personal 12-tone style.

Works: Dramatic: *Nordisk saga*, ballet (1950); *Fröknarna i parken*, radio opera (1953); *Skymningslekar*, ballet (1954); *Skalknallen*, chamber opera (1958; Malmö, Feb. 7, 1959); incidental music. **Orch.:** 6 syms. (1951; *Sinfonia piccola*, 1953; *Sinfonia notturna*, 1954; *Sinfonia seria*, 1956; *Sinfonia da camera*, 1962; *Sinfonia ecloga*, 1962); *Overtura giocosa* (1957); Concerto for Strings (1961); *Forspel (Intrada seria)* (1961); *Mutazioni* for 2 Pianos and Orch. (Malmö, Nov. 27, 1962). **Chamber:** 5 string quartets (1948; 1949, rev. 1954; 1957; 1958; 1961). **Vocal:** Choruses; songs.**—NS/LK/DM**

Wigglesworth, Frank, American composer and teacher; b. Boston, March 3, 1918. He was educated at Columbia Univ. (B.S., 1940) and Converse Coll., Spartanburg, S.C. (M.Mus., 1942), his principal mentors being Ernest White, Luening, and Cowell; Wigglesworth also studied with Varèse (1948–51). He taught at Converse Coll. (1941–42), Greenwich House, N.Y. (1946–47), Columbia Univ. and Barnard Coll. (1947–51), and Queens Coll. of the City Univ. of N.Y. (1955–56). In 1954 he joined the faculty of the New School for Social Research in N.Y., where he was chairman of the music dept. (from 1965); he also taught at the Dalcroze School in N.Y. (from 1959) and at the City Univ. of N.Y. (1970–76). From 1951 to 1954 he was a fellow and in 1969–70 composer-in-residence at the American Academy in Rome; he held MacDowell Colony fellowships in 1965 and 1972. In 1985 he was composer-in- residence at Bennington College's Chamber Music Conference and Composers' Forum of the East. He is a great-nephew of **Elizabeth Sprague Coolidge**. His output reflects a fine command of orch., instrumental, and vocal writing; he makes use of both tonal and atonal techniques.

Works: Dramatic: *Young Goodman Brown*, ballet (1951); *Between the Atoms and the Stars*, musical play (1959); *Hamlet*, incidental music to Shakespeare's play (1960); *Ballet for Esther Brooks*, ballet (1961); *The Willowdale Handcar*, opera (1969). **Orch.:** *New England Concerto* for Violin and Strings (1941); *Music* for Strings (1946); *Fantasia* for Strings (1947); *3 Movements* for Strings (1949); *Summer Scenes* (1951); *Telesis* (1951); Concertino for Piano and Strings (1953); 3 syms. (1953, 1958, 1960); *Concert Piece* (1954); Viola Concertino (1965); *3 Portraits* for Strings (1970); *Music* for Strings (1981); *Aurora* (1983); *Sea Winds* (1984). **Chamber:** Trio for Flute, Banjo, and Harp (1942); *Serenade* for Flute, Viola, and Guitar (1954); Brass Quintet (1958); Harpsichord Sonata (1960); Viola Sonata (1965); String Trio (1972); Woodwind Quintet (1975); *4 Winds* for Horn, 2 Trumpets, and Trombone (1978); Brass Quintet (1980); Viola Sonata (1980); *After Summer Music* for Flute, Viola, and Guitar (1983); *Honeysuckle* for Viola (1984); piano pieces. **Vocal:** *Isaiah* for Chorus and Orch. (1942); *Sleep Becalmed* for Chorus and Orch. (1950); *Super flumina Babilonis* for Chorus (1965); *Psalm CXLVIII* for Chorus, 3 Flutes, and 3 Trombones (1973); *Duets*, song cycle for Mezzo-soprano and Clarinet (1977–78); various masses; anthems; solo songs.**—NS/LK/DM**

Wigglesworth, Mark, English conductor; b. Sussex, July 19, 1964. He was a student of George Hurst at the Royal Academy of Music in London. In 1989 he captured 1st prize in the Kondrashin competition in the Netherlands; that same year, he became music director of the Premiere Ensemble of London. In 1990 he conducted *Don Giovanni* with the Opera Factory in London. He subsequently served as its music director (1991–94) and appeared as a guest conductor with principal British orchs. as well as those on the Continent. From 1991 to 1993 he was assoc. conductor of the BBC Sym. Orch. in London. In 1992 he made his U.S. debut as a guest conductor with the Dallas Sym. Orch., and subsequently appeared with the Philadelphia Orch., the Chicago Sym. Orch., the Minn. Orch. in Minneapolis, the St. Louis Sym. Orch., the Los Angeles Phil., and the N.Y. Phil. In 1996 he became music director of the BBC National Orch. of Wales in Cardiff, which position he retained until 2000.**—NS/LK/DM**

Wihan, Hans (actually, **Hanuš**), noted Czech cellist and pedagogue; b. Politz, near Braunau, Bohemia, June 5, 1855; d. Prague, May 1, 1920. He studied at the Prague Cons. with František Hegenbarth, and while still a young man taught cello at the Salzburg Mozarteum; completed his studies with C. Davidov. He played in orchs. in Nice, Prague, Berlin, Sondershausen, and Munich, and in 1888 succeeded Hegenbarth as prof. of cello and chamber music at the Prague Cons. In 1891 he formed the Bohemian String Quartet, selecting his four most talented pupils (Karel Hoffmann, Josef Suk, Oscar

Nedbal, and Otto Berger). After Berger's retirement in 1897, owing to ill health, Wihan himself took his place as cellist (until 1914); also toured widely as a soloist in Europe. In 1919 he resumed his position at the Prague Cons. Dvořák wrote his Cello Concerto for Wihan; however, the 2 had a falling-out and the first performance was given by Leo Stern. Strauss wrote his E-flat major Sonata for him.—**NS/LK/DM**

Wihtol (Vitols), Joseph (actually, **Jāzeps**), eminent Latvian composer and pedagogue; b. Volmar, July 26, 1863; d. Lübeck, April 24, 1948. He studied at the St. Petersburg Cons. (1880–86) with Rimsky-Korsakov. After graduation, he was engaged as an instructor there. He succeeded Rimsky-Korsakov in 1908 as prof. of composition; among his students were Prokofiev and Miaskovsky. He was also music critic for the German daily *St. Petersburger Zeitung* (1897–1914). In 1918 he left St. Petersburg and was director of the Latvian Opera in Riga (from 1918). In 1919, he founded the National Cons. there, serving as its rector from 1919 to 1935 and again from 1937 to 1944; many Latvian composers were his students. As the Soviet armies approached Riga (1944), Wihtol went to Germany, remaining there until his death. His autobiography and collection of writings appeared in 1944. He composed the first Latvian sym. In his music, he followed the harmonic practices of the Russian school, but often employed Latvian folk-song patterns.

WORKS: ORCH.: Sym. (St. Petersburg, Dec. 17, 1887); *La Fête Ligho*, symphonic tableau (1890); *Spriditis*, Latvian fairy tale (1908). **CHAMBER:** String Quartet (1899); *10 chants populaires lettons*, "miniature paraphrases" for Piano. **VOCAL:** *Beverinas dziedonis* (The Bard of Beverin) for Chorus and Orch. (1891); *Ouverture dramatique* (1895); *Gaismas pils* (The Castle of Light) for Chorus and Orch. (1899); *Upe un cilvka dzive* (River and Human Life) for Chorus (1903); 2 cantatas: *Song* (1908) and *Aurora Borealis* (1914); arrangements of 200 Latvian songs for voice and piano and for piano solo (2 books; 1906, 1919); many Latvian choral ballads; songs.

BIBL.: O. Gravitis, *Jāzeps Vītols un latviešu tautas dziesma* (Jāzeps Vitols and Latvian Folk Song; Riga, 1958).—**NS/LK/DM**

Wijdeveld, Wolfgang, Dutch composer, pianist, music educator, and music critic; b. The Hague, May 9, 1910; d. Laren, Dec. 12, 1985. He was the son of the noted Dutch architect Hendricus Wijdeveld. He studied piano with Willem Andriessen, theory with Sem Dresden, and violin with Kint at the Amsterdam Cons.; also took private lessons in composition with Pijper. After serving as director of the Zwolle Cons. (1940–46), he taught piano at the Utrecht Cons. (1946–76). From 1956 to 1968 he also was music critic of the Amsterdam newspaper *Het Vrije Volk*. He made tours as a pianist at home and abroad.

WORKS: ORCH.: *Concertstuk* (1952); *Intro in Hollandse trant* (1981). **CHAMBER:** Piano Trio (1933); Wind Quintet (1934); *Litanie* for Cello and Piano (1945; rev. 1978); Violin Sonata (1948); Flute Sonatina (1948); *Sarabande du roi* for Oboe and Piano (1950; also for Piano); *Sonatine Simple* for Violin and Piano (1952); *Little Suite* for Violin and Piano (1953); Sonata for 2 Violins and Piano (1954); *Introduction and Caprice* for Violin and Piano (1954); Trio for Flute, Oboe, and Bassoon (1958); *Snarenspel* for Guitar and Piano (1958); Concerto for Guitar and String Trio (1960); Sonatina for Solo Accordion (1963); *Notebook V* for Harpsichord (1968); Trio for Flute, English Horn, and Bassoon (1978). **KEYBOARD: Piano:** *Kermesse* for 2 Pianos (1935); 3 sonatas (1940; 1956; *For Americans*, 1963); *Escapades* (1945); 2 sonatinas (1946, 1953); *Sarabande du roi* (1950; rev. 1979; also for Oboe and Piano); *Notebooks I-IV* (1968–69); *Gregorius in Eden* for Piano, 4-Hands (1977). **Organ:** *Introduction and Gigue* (1949); *12 pezzi diversi* for Organ, 4-Hands (1977). **VOCAL:** *Psalm 150* for Chorus and Orch. (1950); *Matrooslied* for Chorus and Small Orch. (1966); songs. —**NS/LK/DM**

Wiklund, Adolf, Swedish conductor, pianist, and composer; b. Långserud, June 5, 1879; d. Stockholm, April 3, 1950. He was the son of an organist. He entered the Stockholm Cons. in 1896, and graduated in 1901 as an organist and music teacher. After studies with Richard Andersson (piano) and Johan Lindegren (composition and counterpoint), he held a state composer's fellowship (1902–04) and the Jenny Lind fellowship (1905–06). During this period, he studied in Paris, where he was organist of the Swedish Church (1903–04), and in Berlin with Kwast (piano). In 1902 he made his formal debut as a piano soloist in his own *Konsertstycke* for Piano and Orch. From 1906 he was principally active as a conductor and composer. After working at the Karlsruhe Opera and then the Berlin Royal Opera (1908–11), he returned to Stockholm as a conductor at the Royal Theater (from 1911), serving as music director (1923–24). From 1924 to 1938 he held the post of 2nd conductor of the Concert Soc. He also appeared frequently as a guest conductor throughout Europe. In 1915 he became a member of the Royal Academy of Music in Stockholm. His music, marked by fine workmanship, remained faithful to Nordic Romanticism. He composed 2 fine piano concertos, and the popular *Tre stycken* for Harp and Strings.

WORKS: ORCH.: *Konsertstycke* for Piano and Orch. (1902); Concerto Overture (1903); 2 piano concertos (1906, rev. 1935; 1917); *Sommarnatt och soluppgång*, sumphonic poem (1918); Sym. (1922); *Tre stycken* (3 Pieces) for Harp and Strings (1924); *Little Suite* (1928); *Sång till våren*, symphonic poem (1934); *Symfonisk prolog* (1934); suites. **CHAMBER:** Violin Sonata (1906); piano pieces. **VOCAL:** Songs.—**NS/LK/DM**

Wikmanson, Johan, Swedish organist and composer; b. Stockholm, Dec. 28, 1753; d. there, Jan. 10, 1800. He was trained as an engineer, but also had lessons in thoroughbass and piano from H. P. Johnsen; also studied composition with Abbé Vogler and J. M. Kraus. He served as organist at the Dutch Reformed Church (1772–81) and at the Storkyrkan Cathedral (1781–1800); in 1788 he was elected a member of the Royal Academy of Music, where he was made director of education in 1796 and a teacher of harmony and theory in 1797. His output reveals the influence of Kraus, Haydn, and C. P. E. Bach. Among his compositions are music for various stage pieces, *Menuetto allegro* for Orch., 3 string quartets (publ. in Stockholm, 1801; ed. in Monumenta Musicae Svecicae, II, 1970), a Zither Sonata, numerous keyboard works, including 2 piano sonatas, a cantata, *Häckingen*, and some 30 songs.

BIBL.: C.-G. Mörner, *J. W. und de Brüder Silverstolpe* (diss., Univ. of Uppsala, 1952).—**NS/LK/DM**

Wilbye, John, important English composer; b. Diss, Norfolk (baptized), March 7, 1574; d. Colchester, c.Sept. 1638. By 1598 he was a musician at Hengrave Hall, the home of Sir Thomas Kytson, near Bury St. Edmunds. After the death of Lady Kytson (1628), he settled in Colchester, where he spent his last years with her daughter, Lady Rivers. During his years at Hengrave, he acquired considerable wealth. He was a master of the madrigal; his *Second Set of Madrigals* (1609) constitutes the most significant collection of English madrigals.

WORKS: *The First Set of English Madrigals* for 3 to 6 Voices (London, 1598; ed. by E. Fellowes, The English Madrigalists; 2nd ed., rev., 1966, by T. Dart); *The Second Set of Madrigals* for 3 to 6 Voices, *Apt both for Voyals and Voyces* (London, 1609; ed. by E. Fellowes, The English Madrigalists; 2nd ed., rev., 1966, by T. Dart); also a few sacred vocal pieces and instrumental works.

BIBL.: H. Heurich, *J. W. in seinen Madrigalen: Studien zu einem Bilde seiner Persönlichkeit* (Augsburg, 1931); D. Brown, *J. W.* (London, 1974).—**NS/LK/DM**

Wild, Earl, greatly talented American pianist; b. Pittsburgh, Nov. 26, 1915. He was a child prodigy; blessed with absolute pitch, he could read music and play piano by age 6. When he was 12, he became a student of Selmar Jansen; also pursued training at the Carnegie Inst. of Technology (graduated, 1934). While still a teenager, he played on KDKA Radio in Pittsburgh and in the Pittsburgh Sym. Orch. After appearing as a soloist with the NBC Orch. in N.Y. in 1934, he settled there; pursued further training with Egon Petri, and later with Paul Doguereau and Volya Lincoln. In 1937 he became the staff pianist of Toscanini's NBC Sym. Orch. in N.Y. He was the first American pianist to give a recital on U.S. television in 1939. In 1942 he appeared as soloist in Gershwin's *Rhapsody in Blue* with Toscanini and the NBC Sym. Orch. He made his N.Y. recital debut at Town Hall on Oct. 30, 1944. From 1944 to 1968 he worked as a staff pianist, conductor, and composer for ABC while continuing to make occasional appearances as a soloist with orchs. and as a recitalist. After leaving ABC, he pursued a brilliant international career as a virtuoso par excellence; he also served as artistic director of the Concert Soloists of Wolf Trap, a chamber ensemble (1978–81). He devoted part of his time to teaching and was on the faculties of Pa. State Univ. (1965–68), the Juilliard School in N.Y. (1977–87), the Manhattan School of Music (1982–84), and Ohio State Univ. (from 1987). Among his compositions are the Easter oratorio *Revelations* (1962), a ballet, incidental music, orch. pieces, including *Variations on an American Theme*, after Stephen Foster's *Camptown Races*, for Piano and Orch. (Des Moines, Sept. 26, 1992, composer soloist), and a number of transcendentally resonant piano transcriptions of vocal and orch. works. A phenomenal technician of the keyboard, he won particular renown for his brilliant performances of the Romantic repertoire. In addition to works by such masters as Liszt and Chopin, he sought out and performed rarely heard works of the past. He also performed contemporary music, becoming especially esteemed for his idiomatic interpretations of Gershwin. Among the scores he commissioned and introduced to the public were concertos by Paul Creston (1949) and Marvin David Levy (1970).—**NS/LK/DM**

Wildberger, Jacques, Swiss composer and teacher; b. Basel, Jan. 3, 1922. He received training in piano from Eduard Ehrsam, Eduard Henneberger, and Paul Baumgartner and in theory from Gustav Güldenstein at the Basel Cons., and later pursued studies in composition with Vogel in Ascona (1948–52). From 1959 to 1966 he taught composition, analysis, and instrumentation at the Karlsruhe Hochschule für Musik. After living in Berlin on a Deutscher Akademischer Austauschdienst scholarship (1967), he taught composition, analysis, and counterpoint at the Basel Academy of Music until 1987. In 1981 he was awarded the composition prize of the Swiss Musicians Assn. In his music, he developed a sui generis serial system, with a total emancipation of dissonances.

WORKS: DRAMATIC: *Epitaphe pour Evariste Galois*, "documented action" for Narrator, Soprano, Baritone, Speaking Chorus, Tape, and Orch. (1962; Basel, May 20, 1964). **ORCH.:** *Tre mutazioni* for Chamber Orch. (1953); *Intensio-Centrum-Remissio* (1958); *Musik* for 22 Solo Strings (1960); Oboe Concerto (1963); *Mouvements* (1964); *Contratempi* for Flute and 4 Orch. Groups (1970); *Konzertante Szenen* for Saxophone and Orch. (1981); *Canto* (1982); *...und füllet die Erde und machet sie euch untertan...* (1988–89); *Concerto for Orchestra* (1991–92); *Kammerkonzert* for Strings and Synthesizer (1995–96). **CHAMBER:** Quartet for Flute, Clarinet, Violin, and Cello (1952); Trio for Oboe, Clarinet, and Bassoon (1952); *Concentrum* for Harpsichord (1956); *Zeitebenen* for 8 Players (1958); *Musik* for Cello and Piano (1959); *Rondeau* for Oboe (1962); Quartet for Flute, Oboe, Harp, and Piano (1967); *Recontres* for Flute and Piano (1967); *Diario* for Clarinet (1971–75); *Retrospective I* and *II* for Flute (both 1972); *Prismes* for Alto Saxophone (1975); *Portrait* for Alto Saxophone (1983); *Kanons und Interludien* for 4 Clarinets (1984); *Diaphonie* for Viola (1986); *Los pajarillos no cantan* for Guitar (1987); *Notturno* for Viola and Piano (1990); *Tantôt libre, tantôt recherchée* for Cello (1992–93); *Commiato* for String Quartet (1997); piano pieces; organ music. **VOCAL:** *Vom Kommen und Gehen des Menschen*, cantata for Soprano, Baritone, Chorus, and Orch. (1954); *Ihr meint, das Leben sei kurz...*, cantata for Chorus and 10 Instruments (1957); *In My End Is My Beginning*, cantata for Soprano, Tenor, and Small Orch. (1964); *La Notte* for Mezzo-soprano, 5 Instruments, and Tape (1967); *Double Refrain* for Flute, English Horn, Guitar, and Tape (1972); *...die Stimme, die alte schwächer werdende Stimme...* for Soprano, Cello, Orch., and Tape (1973–74); *Tod und Verklärung* for Baritone and Chamber Orch. (1977); *An die Hoffnung* for Soprano, Narrator, and Orch. (1979); *Du holde Kunst* for Narrator, Soprano, and Orch. (1987–88).—**NS/LK/DM**

Wildbrunn (real name, **Wehrenpfennig**), **Helene,** Austrian soprano; b. Vienna, April 8, 1882; d. there, April 10, 1972. She studied with Rosa Papier in Vienna. She made her operatic debut as a contralto at the Vienna Volksoper in 1906, then sang in Dortmund (1907–14). She began singing soprano roles in 1914, when she joined the Stuttgart Opera, where she remained until 1918. She sang in Berlin at the State Opera (1916–25) and the Deutsche Opera (1926–29); she was a principal member of the Vienna State Opera (1919–32), and made guest appearances at Covent Garden in London, La Scala in Milan, and the Teatro Colón in Buenos Aires. After her retirement in 1932, she taught voice at the Vienna Academy of Music (until 1950). Among her finest roles were Kundry, Brünnhilde, Fricka, Isolde, Donna Anna, and Leonore.—**NS/LK/DM**

Wilder, Alec (actually, **Alexander Lafayette Chew**), remarkably gifted American composer, distinguished in both popular and serious music; b. Rochester, N.Y., Feb. 16, 1907; d. Gainesville, Fla., Dec. 22, 1980. He studied composition at the Eastman School of Music in Rochester with Herbert Inch and Edward Royce, then moved to N.Y., where he entered the world of popular music; he also wrote excellent prose. His popular songs were performed by Frank Sinatra, Judy Garland, and other celebrated singers; his band pieces were in the repertoire of Benny Goodman and Jimmy Dorsey. He excelled in the genre of short operas scored for a limited ensemble of singers and instruments and suitable for performance in schools, while most of his serious compositions, especially his chamber music, are set in an affably melodious, hedonistic, and altogether ingratiating manner. He publ. a useful critical compilation, *American Popular Song: The Great Innovators* (N.Y., 1972), which included analyses of the songs of Jerome Kern, Vincent Youmans, George Gershwin, Cole Porter, and others. He also publ. the vol. *Letters I Never Mailed* (1975).

Works: Dramatic: *Juke Box*, ballet (1942); *The Lowland Sea*, folk drama (Montclair, N.J., May 8, 1952); *Cumberland Fair*, a jamboree (Montclair, May 22, 1953); *Sunday Excursion*, musical comedy (Interlochen, Mich., July 18, 1953); *Miss Chicken Little* (CBS-TV, Dec. 27, 1953; stage production, Piermont, N.Y., Aug. 29, 1958); 3 operas: *Kittiwake Island* (Interlochen, Aug. 7, 1954), *The Long Way* (Nyack, N.Y., June 3, 1955), and *The Impossible Forest* (Westport, Conn., July 13, 1958); *The Truth about Windmills*, chamber opera (Rochester, N.Y., Oct. 14, 1973); *The Tattooed Countess*, chamber opera (1974); *The Opening*, comic opera (1975); 3 children's operas: *The Churkendoose, Rachetty Pachetty House*, and *Herman Ermine in Rabbit Town*. **Orch.:** *Symphonic Piece* (Rochester, N.Y., June 3, 1929); Suite for Clarinet and Strings (1947); Concerto for Oboe and Strings (1950); *Beginner's Luck* for Wind Ensemble (1953); 2 concertos for Horn and Chamber Orch. (1954, 1960); 4 works entitled *An Entertainment* (1961–71): No. 1 for Wind Ensemble, No. 2 for Orch., No. 3 for Wind Ensemble, and No. 4 for Horn and Chamber Orch.; 2 concertos for Trumpet and Wind Ensemble; Concerto for Tuba and Wind Ensemble; Suite for Horn and Strings (1965); Suite for Saxophone and Strings (1965); Concerto for Saxophone and Chamber Orch. (1967); *Air* for Horn and Wind Ensemble (1968); Concerto for Euphonium and Wind Ensemble (1971). **Chamber:** 10 wind quintets (1953–72); 3 horn sonatas (1954, 1957, 1965); 2 flute sonatas (1958, 1962); Saxophone Sonata (1960); Clarinet Sonata (1963); 3 bassoon sonatas (1964, 1968, 1973); Nonet for Brass (1969); many other sonatas; numerous pieces for wind and brass instruments; piano music, including a sonata. **Vocal:** *8 Songs* for Voice and Orch. (Rochester, N.Y., June 8, 1928); *Children's Plea for Peace* for Narrator, Chorus, and Orch. (1969); many other songs.

Bibl.: *A. W. and His Friends* (Boston, 1974); *A. W. (1907–1980): An Introduction to the Man and His Music* (Newton Centre, Mass., 1991); D. Demsey and R. Prather, *A. W.: A Bio-Bibliography* (Westport, Conn., 1993); D. Stone, *A. W. in Spite of Himself: A Life of the Composer* (N.Y., 1996).—**NS/LK/DM**

Wilder, Philip van, Flemish-born English lutenist and composer; b. c. 1500; d. London, Feb. 24, 1553. He entered the service of King Henry VIII of England about 1520. He later was placed in charge of the king's private music, and also taught lute to Princess Mary. Wilder was held in high regard at the court. Among his works are both sacred and secular vocal pieces and some instrumental music.—**LK/DM**

Wilderer, Johann Hugo von, German composer; b. in Bavaria, 1670 or 1671; d. Mannheim (buried), June 7, 1724. He studied with Legrenzi in Venice and by 1692 was court organist at the St. Andreas church in Düsseldorf. By 1696 he was vice-Kapellmeister at the court there, being elevated to Kapellmeister in 1703. After a new elector came upon the scene in 1716, the courts of Düsseldorf and Innsbruck were joined in Heidelberg and then in Mannheim (1720), during which time Wilderer remained in his position. His importance rests upon his role in fostering the development of German opera and of what became known as the Mannheim school of composition. He wrote 11 operas, 2 oratorios, 4 cantatas, and some sacred works. —**NS/LK/DM**

Wildgans, Friedrich, Austrian composer and teacher; b. Vienna, June 5, 1913; d. Modling, near Vienna, Nov. 7, 1965. He studied with J. Marx. He taught at the Salzburg Mozarteum (1934–36). In 1936 he became a clarinetist in the Vienna State Opera orch.; owing to his opposition to the Nazis, he lost his position in 1939 and remained suspect until the destruction of the Third Reich. He then was a teacher (1945–47; 1950–57) and a prof. (1957–65) at the Vienna Academy of Music. In 1946 he married **Ilona Steingruber**. He publ. *Entwicklung der Musik in Österreich im 20. Jahrhundert* (Vienna, 1950) and *Anton Webern* (London, 1966). He wrote in all genres, in an ultramodern style, eventually adopting the 12-tone technique.

Works: Dramatic: *Der Baum der Erkenntniss*, opera (1932); *Der Diktator*, operetta (1933); theater, film, and radio scores. **Orch.:** *Griechischer Frühling* (1926–27); *Little Symphony* for Chamber Orch. (1929); *Mondnächte* (1932); Concerto for Trumpet, Strings, and Percussion (1933); 2 concertos for Clarinet and Small Orch. (1933, 1948); Concerto for Horn and Chamber Orch. (1934); Concerto for Organ, Brass, and Percussion (1934); *Sinfonia austriaca* (1934); *Laienmusik* (1941). **Chamber:** Flute Sonata (1926); Horn Sonatine (1927); *Little Trio* for Strings (1929); *Little Trio* for Flute, Clarinet, and Bassoon (1930); *Little Duo* for 2 Violins (1930); Sonatine for Clarinet and Bassoon (1930); Sonatine for 2 Clarinets (1931); *Little Trio* for Oboe, English Horn, and Bassoon (1932); *Capriccio* for 2 Clarinets and Bass Clarinet (1932); *Little Sonatine* for Trumpet and Piano (1933); *3 Inventions* for Clarinet and Horn (1935); *Spielmusik* for Recorders (1935); *Salzburger Hornmusik* (1935); *Kleine Trompetenmusik* (1935); *Kleine Haus- und Spielmusik* for Flute, Violin, and

Viola (1935); Duo-Sonatine for Violin and Cello (1942); Clarinet Sonatine (1950). **KEYBOARD: Piano:** 2 sonatas (1926, 1929). **Organ:** Concerto (1930). **VOCAL:** Choral pieces; lieder.—**NS/LK/DM**

Wilding-White, Raymond, American composer, teacher, and photographer; b. Caterham, Surrey, England, Oct. 9, 1922. He was a student at the Juilliard School of Music in N.Y. (1947–49), the New England Cons. of Music in Boston (B.M., 1951; M.M., 1953), of Copland and Dallapiccola at the Berkshire Music Center in Tanglewood (summers, 1949–51), and of Read at Boston Univ. (D.M.A., 1962). He taught at the Case Inst. of Technology in Cleveland (1961–67) and at De Paul Univ. in Chicago (1967–88). In 1969 he founded the Loop Group for the performance of 20th-century music, which continued to be active through various transformations until its demise in 1989. He also was active on the radio and prepared numerous programs for WFMT-FM in Chicago, including 366 broadcasts of "Our American Music" for the American bicentennial (1976), "Music Chicago Style" for the Chicago sesquicentennial (1987), and a memorial tribute to John Cage (1992). As a photographer, his work has been exhibited in many settings.

WORKS: DRAMATIC: *The Trees*, ballet (1949); *The Tub*, chamber opera (1952); *The Selfish Giant*, television fable (1952); *The Lonesome Valley*, ballet (1960); *Yerma*, opera (1962); *Encounters*, ballet (1967); *Beth*, musical (1989–90; renamed *Trio* in 1994); *Gifts*, liturgical drama (1993); "action pieces" entitled *MY aLBUM*. **ORCH.:** Sym. for Swing Orch. (1947); Piano Concerto (1949); Concertante for Violin, Horns, and Strings (1963); *Bandmusic* for Concert Band (1966); *Whatzit* No. 4 for Orch. and Tape (1969); Violin Concerto (1978); 3 *Symphony of Symphonies* (1995, et seq.). **CHAMBER:** 6 string quartets: No. 1 (1948), No. 2 (1966), No. 3, *The Forrest*, for Tenor and String Quartet (1970), No. 4 (1981), No. 5 (1987–88), and No. 6, *The Song Quartet* (1987–88); Violin Sonata (1956); *Variations* for Chamber Organ and String Trio (1959); *5 Fragments* for Jazz Ensemble (1966); pieces entitled *Whatzit* mostly for Solo Instrument and Tape (1967–75); piano music. **VOCAL:** *Even Now* for Baritone and Orch. (1954); *Paraphernalia* for Chorus and 5 Instruments (1959); *Haiku* for Soprano, Tenor, and Instruments (1967); *The Southern Harmony* for Amateur Chorus and Orch; *De Profundis* for Solo Voices, Chorus, and Orch.; various Psalm settings, etc. —**NS/LK/DM**

Wiley, Lee, jazz singer, composer; b. Fort Gibson, Okla., Oct. 9, 1915; d. N.Y., Dec. 11, 1975. She studied in Tulsa, Okla., and later moved to N.Y. where she sang in the Paramount Show (c. 1930) and joined Leo Reisman at the Central Park Casino (c. 1931). Wiley began regular radio work with Reisman and continued with radio series after leaving Reisman in 1933; later Wiley did radio shows with Paul Whiteman, Willard Robison, and others. Wiley recorded with Johnny Green, The Casa Loma Band, and Victor Young; she co-composed several numbers with Young by writing the lyrics to "Got the South in My Soul," "Anytime, Anyday, Anywhere," and "Eerie Moan." During the late 1930s and early 1940s did a series of recordings (with all-star accompaniment) featuring compositions by George Gershwin, Cole Porter, Rodgers and Hart, and Harold Arlen. In June 1943 married Jess Stacy; their marriage lasted for five years. During the mid-1940s, Lee sang with Stacy's short-lived big band. Subsequently, she worked as a solo artist and made occasional television and radio appearances. One of her early compositions, "Anytime, Anyday, Anywhere," became a hit single through the Joe Morris-Laurie Tate recording; in 1963 a semi-biographical film of Lee's life was given world-wide television showings. Her last public engagement was at Newport Festival in N.Y., 1972.

DISC.: *Complete Young Lee Wiley* (1931–33); *I've Got You Under My Skin* (1931); *On the Air, Vol. 1* (1932); *On the Air, Vol. 2* (1944); *Night in Manhattan* (1950); *Duologue* (1954); *As Time Goes By* (1956); *West of the Moon* (1956); *Touch of the Blues* (1957); *Back Home Again* (1971); *Lee Wiley Sings George Gershwin* (1972).

BIBL.: Claude Schlouch, *Love-Lee, Lee Wiley: A Discography* (Marseille, France, 1983).—**JC/LP**

Wilhelmj, August (Emil Daniel Ferdinand Viktor), famous German violinist; b. Usingen, Sept. 21, 1845; d. London, Jan. 22, 1908. He received his earliest instruction in music from his mother, who was an amateur pianist, then studied violin with Konrad Fischer, court musician at Wiesbaden in 1849, making his first appearance there as a child prodigy on Jan. 8, 1854. In 1861, at the recommendation of Liszt, he was sent to the Leipzig Cons., where he studied with David (violin) and with Hauptmann and Richter (harmony and composition); in 1864 he went to Frankfurt am Main for an additional course with Raff. In 1865 he began his concert career, touring Switzerland. He then played in the Netherlands and England (1866), France and Italy (1867), Russia, Switzerland, France, and Belgium (1869), England, Scotland, and Ireland (1869–70), and then traveled through the Netherlands, Scandinavia, Germany, and Austria (1871–74), to England (1875–77), and to America (1878); he made a tour of the world to South America, Australia, and Asia (1878–82). In 1876 he was concertmaster of the Bayreuth Festival orch. For several years he lived chiefly at Biebrich am Rhein, where he established (with R. Niemann) a master school for violin playing. In 1886 he moved to Blasewitz, near Dresden; in 1894 he was appointed prof. of violin at the Guildhall School of Music in London. His first wife, whom he married in 1866, was Baroness Liphardt, a niece of David; in 1895 he married the pianist Mariella Mausch. He made a famous arrangement of Bach's air from the orch. Suite in D major that became known as the *Air on the G String* (Bach's original bore no such specification). He also arranged Wagner's *Träume* for violin and orch., wrote a cadenza to Beethoven's Violin Concerto, and further composed, for Violin and Orch., 2 *Konzertstücke* (No. 2, *In memoriam*), *Alla polacca*, and *Theme and Variations* (after 2 caprices of Paganini), *Romanze* for Piano, and songs. With James Brown he publ. *A Modern School for the Violin* (6 parts).

BIBL.: E. Frassinesi, *A. W. Violinista. Memorie* (Mirandola, 1913); E. Wagner, *Der Geigerkönig A. W.* (Homburg, 1928). —**NS/LK/DM**

Wilkerson, Don, jazz tenor saxophonist; b. Moreauville, La., 1932; d. Houston, Tex., July 18, 1986.

The family moved to Houston, Tex., when he was a youngster. He taught himself to play and began playing tenor sax on gigs while still in high school. He played with Amos Milburn (1948) and Charles Brown (1948–49), and then returned to Houston for local work (1950–54). Wilkerson toured and recorded with Ray Charles through the balance of the 1950s and was featured on his hits, "I Got a Woman," "Come Back Baby," and "Hallelujah, I Love Her So." He joined Blue Note in the early 1960s during their soul/jazz years, often working with guitarist Grant Green.

DISC.: *Texas Twister* (1960); *Elder Don* (1962); *Preach, Brother!* (1962); *Shoutin'* (1963).—**MM/LP**

Wilkins, Christopher, American conductor; b. Boston, May 28, 1957. After taking his bachelor's degree from Harvard Coll. (1978), he studied conducting with Otto-Werner Mueller at Yale Univ. (M.M., 1981); also held the John Knowles Paine Traveling Fellowship for study at the (West) Berlin Hochschule für Musik. In 1981–82 he was conductor-in-residence at the State Univ. of N.Y. at Purchase. In 1982–83 he was the Exxon Conducting Assistant with the Ore. Sym. Orch. in Portland and a conducting fellow at the Berkshire Music Center at Tanglewood. He was asst. conductor of the Cleveland Orch. (1983–85) and assoc. conductor of the Utah Sym. Orch. in Salt Lake City (1986–89). In 1989 he became music director of the Colo. Springs Sym. Orch.; concurrently held that title with the San Antonio Sym. Orch. from 1991. In 1992 he received the Seaver/NEA award.—**NS/LK/DM**

Wiłkomirski, distinguished family of Polish musicians:

(1) Alfred Wiłkomirski, violinist and teacher; b. Azov, Russia, Jan. 3, 1873; d. Łódź, July 31, 1950. He began training in Tiflis, and then went to Moscow in 1898 to study with Hřímalý (violin) at the Cons. and with Bezekirsky (violin) and Kruglyov and G. Conus (theory) at the Phil. Soc.'s Higher School of Music. In 1919 he settled in Poland. From 1920 to 1926 he was headmaster of a music school in Kalisz, and then was head of the Music Inst. in Lublin in 1926–27. He was a member of the Warsaw String Quartet in 1927–28. From 1929 to 1939 he was a prof. at Helena Kijeńska-Dobkiewicz's Cons. in Łódź, and also was a lecturer at the Open Univ. and at a music school in Pabianice. From 1945 until his death he was a prof. at the State Higher School of Music in Łódź. He had 4 children who became musicians:

(2) Kazimierz Wiłkomirski, cellist, conductor, pedagogue, and composer; b. Moscow, Sept. 1, 1900; d. Warsaw, March 7, 1995. He studied cello with Alfred von Glehn at the Moscow Cons. (1911–17), and also received private training in composition from Bolesław Jaworski. He then studied composition with Roman Statkowski and conducting with Emil Młynarski at the Warsaw Cons. (1919–23), where he received an honors degree. In 1934 he attended Hermann Scherchen's conducting course in Switzerland. From 1926 to 1934 he was first cellist and a conductor with the Warsaw Phil. After serving as director of the Polish Cons. in Gdańsk (1934–39), he was rector of the State Higher School of Music in Łódź (1945–47). From 1947 to 1952 he was director and conductor of the Opera and Phil. in Wrocław. After holding these positions with the Baltic Phil. in Gdańsk (1952–57), he again held them with the Opera and Phil. in Wrocław (1957–62). He also served as a prof. at the conservatories in those cities. In 1963 he was appointed to the chair in chamber music at the State Higher School of Music in Warsaw.

WORKS: ORCH.: Sym. (1922); *Jungfrau,* symphonic poem (1930); *Suita kaszubska* (Cassubian Suite) for Winds (1946); Sinfonia concertante for Cello and Orch. (Kraków, Sept. 8, 1950). **CHAMBER:** 2 Preludes for Cello and Piano (1918); *Scherzo* for Cello and Piano (1918); *Ballada* for Cello and Piano (1918); Violin Sonata (1919); *Poemat* (Poem) for Cello and Piano (1924); *Ballada* for Violin and Piano (1926); String Quartet (Warsaw, March 3, 1942); *Aria* for Cello and Piano (1943); 12 Studies for Cello (1950). **Piano:** Sonata (1920). **VOCAL:** *Requiem* for Solo Voices, Chorus, and Orch. (1923); Mass for Solo Voices, Chorus, and Organ (1937); *Prorok* (Prophet), cantata for Baritone and Orch. (1950); *Kantata wrocławska* (Wrocław Cantata) for Soprano, Chorus, and Orch. (Warsaw, Dec. 1951); *Kantata gdańska* (Gdańsk Cantata) for Solo Voices, Chorus, and Orch. (Gdańsk, March 30, 1955); *Kantata o św. Jacku* (Cantata about St. Jacek) for Solo Voices, Chorus, and Orch. (Kraków, Oct. 20, 1957).

(3) Maria Wiłkomirska, pianist and teacher; b. Moscow, April 3, 1904; d. Warsaw, June 19, 1995. She was a student of Bryusova (theory) and Jaworski (piano) at the Moscow Cons., and then studied with Józef Turczyński in Warsaw (1920). From 1934 to 1939 she was a prof. at the Gdańsk Cons. In 1945 she joined the faculty of the State Higher School of Music in Łódź, where she held the piano chair from 1952. She also was on the faculty of the State Higher School of Music in Warsaw from 1951, where she held its piano chair from 1964. She made tours as both a soloist and as a chamber music player.

(4) Józef Wiłkomirsk,a cellist, conductor, and composer; b. Kalisz, May 15, 1926. He studied with Zdzisław Górzyński and Włodzimierz Ormicki at the State Higher School of Music in Łódź, and then attended the State Higher School of Music in Warsaw. He pursued training in conducting with Walerian Bierdiajew. In 1946 he became a cellist in the State Phil. in Łódź and in the opera orch. in Warsaw. In 1950–51 he was conductor of the State Phil. in Kraków. After serving as conductor of the State Phil. in Poznań (1954–57), he was music director of the Szczecin Phil. (1957–71). In 1978 he founded the Phil. in Wałbrzych (later the Sudetes Phil.), which he subsequently led as music director.

WORKS: DRAMATIC: Ballet-pantomime: *Baśń o królewiczu Jasnym* (Fairy-Tale of the Fair Prince; 1972). **ORCH.:** Concerto for Harp and Chamber Orch. (1969); 2 sinfoniettas (1969, 1970); *Zamek Królewski w Warszawie* (Royal Castle in Warsaw), suite (1971); *Poemat żałobny* (Funeral Poem; 1973); *Concerto for Orchestra* (1973); Cello Concertino (1974). **CHAMBER:** Sonata for Solo Cello (1967); *Mała suita* (Little Suite) for Cello (1970); Violin Sonata (1971); Cello Sonata (1971); Piano Trio (1971); Double Bass Sonata (1972); *Suita taneczna* (Dance Suite) for Percussion Quartet (1972); Concerto for 4 Harps (1972); Viola Sonata (1975); Sonata for Solo Violin (1975); String Quartet (1975). **VOCAL:** *Pieśni miłosne* (Love Songs) for Soprano and Piano (1975; also for Soprano and Orch., 1976);

Wrześniowy alarm (September Alarm) for Soprano, Baritone, Reciter, Chorus, and Orch. (1976).

(5) Wanda Wiłkomirska, violinist and pedagogue; b. Warsaw, Jan. 11, 1929. She was only 5 when she began to study violin with her father, and at age 7 she made her public debut. After studies with Eugenia Umińska and Irena Dubiska, she graduated with honors from the State Higher School of Music in Łódź in 1947. She completed her training with Ede Zathureczky in Budapest, and with Henryk Szeryng in Paris (1960). She won prizes in the Geneva (2nd, 1946), Budapest (2nd, 1948), Leipzig (4th, 1950), and Poznań (2nd, 1953) competitions. In addition to appearances in chamber music settings, she also was a soloist with orchs. in Europe, North and South America, Australia, and Asia. In 1982 she went to Germany and in 1983 became a prof. at the Hochschule für Musik of Heidelberg-Mannheim.

BIBL.: J. Rawik, *Maestra: Opowieść o W. W.* (Warsaw, 1993). **—NS/LK/DM**

Willaert, Adrian, important Flemish composer and pedagogue; b. Bruges or Roulaers, c. 1490; d. Venice, Dec. 7, 1562. He enrolled as a law student at the Univ. of Paris, then devoted himself to music. He studied composition with Jean Mouton, a musician in the Royal Chapel. In 1515 he entered the service of Cardinal Ippolito I d'Este of Ferrara. He accompanied the cardinal, who was Archbishop of Esztergom, to Hungary in 1517; the cardinal died in 1520, and Willaert entered the service of Duke Alfonso I d'Este of Ferrara (1522); subsequently, Willaert was in the service of Cardinal Ippolito II d'Este, the Archbishop of Milan (1525–27). On Dec. 12, 1527, he was appointed maestro di cappella of San Marco in Venice. With the exception of 2 visits to Flanders (1542 and 1556–57), he remained in Venice for the rest of his life, as a composer and teacher. Among his famous pupils were Zarlino, Cipriano de Rore, Andrea Gabrieli, and Costanzo Porta. Willaert was justly regarded as a founder of the great Venetian school of composition; the style of writing for 2 antiphonal choirs (prompted by the twin opposed organs of San Marco) was principally initiated by him. He was one of the greatest masters of the madrigal and of the instrumental ricercare; he also wrote motets, chansons, Psalms, and Masses. For the complete works, see H. Zenck and W. Gerstenberg, eds., *Adrian Willaert: Opera omnia*, in the Corpus Mensurabilis Musicae series, iii/1 (Rome, 1950–77).

WORKS: *Liber quinque missarum* (Venice, 1536); *Hymnorum musica* (Venice, 1542); *I sacri e santi salmi che si cantano a Vespro e Compieta...* for 4 Voices (Venice, 1555; aug. ed., 1571); *Motecta...liber primus* for 4 Voices (Venice, 1539; aug. ed., 1545); *Mottetti...libro secundo* for 4 Voices (Venice, 1539; aug. ed., 1545); *Motecta...liber primus* for 5 Voices (Venice, 1539); *Il primo libro di motetti* for 6 Voices (Venice, 1542); *Musica nova* (Venice, 1559); *Livre de meslanges...26 chansons* (Paris, 1560); *Cincquiesme livre de chansons* for 3 Voices (Paris, 1560); *Musica nova* (Venice, 1559); *Madrigali* for 4 Voices (Venice, 1563); *9 ricercares a 3* (1551; ed. by H. Zenck, Mainz and Leipzig, 1933).

BIBL.: E. Gregoir, *A. W.* (Brussels, 1869); E. Hertzmann, *A. W. in der weltlichen Vokalmusik seiner Zeit* (Leipzig, 1931); I. Bossuyt, *A. W., ca. 1490–1562: Leven en werk: Stijl en genres* (Leuven, 1985); G. Ongaro, *The Chapel of St. Mark's at the Time of A. W. (1527–1562); A Documentary Study* (diss., Univ. of N.C., 1986).**—NS/LK/DM**

Willan, (James) Healey, eminent English-born Canadian composer, organist, choral conductor, and teacher; b. Balham, Oct. 12, 1880; d. Toronto, Feb. 16, 1968. He received training in piano, organ, harmony, and counterpoint at the St. Saviour's Choir School in Eastbourne (1888–95), where he found a mentor in its headmaster and organist-choirmaster Walter Hay Sangster. He then studied organ with William Stevenson Hoyte and piano with Evlyn Howard-Jones in London. Willan began his career as organist of the St. Cecilia Soc. (1895–1900), and then was conductor of the Wanstead Choral Soc. (1904–05) and of the Thalian Operatic Soc. (1906). He also served as organist-choirmaster at St. Saviour's Church, St. Alban's, Herts (1898–1900), Christ Church, Wanstead (1900–03), and St. John the Baptist, Holland Rd., Kensington (1903–13). In 1913 he settled in Toronto as head of theory at the Cons. of Music and as organist at St. Paul's Anglican Church, Bloor Street. In 1914 he also became a lecturer and examiner at the Univ. of Toronto, where he served as music director of its Hart House Theatre (1919–25). From 1920 to 1936 he was vice-principal of the Toronto Cons. of Music. In 1921 he became organist-choirmaster at the Anglican Church of St. Mary Magdalene, a position he retained until his death. From 1932 to 1964 he was the organist of the Univ. of Toronto, where he also taught counterpoint and composition from 1937 to 1950. In 1933 he founded the Tudor Singers, conducting them until 1939. In 1953 he founded the Toronto Diocesan Choir School, which he served as music director. In 1956 the Archbishop of Canterbury conferred upon him the Lambeth Doctorate, the highest honor that can be bestowed upon a musician by the Anglican church. He received the Canada Council Medal in 1961. In 1967 he was made a Companion of the Order of Canada. On July 4, 1980, the Canadian Post Office issued a commemorative stamp bearing his likeness, making Willan the first composer to receive that distinction. As a composer, Willan excelled in music for liturgical use. He was a determined proponent of the Oxford Movement in the Anglican Church, and thus championed the cause of Anglo-Catholicism. Particularly notable in this regard were his 14 settings of the *Missa brevis* (1928–63), the set of 11 *Liturgical Motets* (1928–37), the plainsong-with-fauxbourdons settings of the Canticles, and the *Responsaries for the Offices of Tenebrae* (1956). In 1953 Willan's commissioned homage anthem, *O Lord, Our Governour*, was performed at the coronation of Queen Elizabeth II in London. Willan was thus the first non-resident of Great Britain to receive such an honor. His organ music is also of great distinction. His *Introduction, Passacaglia, and Fugue* (1916) is his masterpiece in that genre. Of his other works, the opera *Deirdre*, the 2 syms., and the Piano Concerto are worthy achievements.

WORKS: DRAMATIC: *The Beggar's Opera*, ballad opera (1927); *The Order of Good Cheer*, ballad opera (1928); *Transit Through Fire: An Odyssey of 1942*, radio opera (1941–42; CBC, March 8, 1942); *Hymn for Those in the Air*, incidental music

(1942); *Deirdre*, radio opera (1943–45; CBC, April 20, 1946; rev. version for the stage, Toronto, April 2, 1965); *Brebeuf*, pageant (CBC, Sept. 26, 1943); 4 other ballad operas; 14 sets of incidental music, etc. **ORCH.:** 2 syms.: No. 1 (Toronto, Oct. 8, 1936) and No. 2 (1941; rev. 1948; Toronto, May 18, 1950); Piano Concerto (Montreal, Aug. 24, 1944; rev. 1949); *Royce Hall Suite* for Concert Band (1949); *Overture to an Unwritten Comedy* (1951); *3 Fanfares* (1959); *Poem* for Strings (1959); 5 marches and other pieces. **CHAMBER:** Trio for Violin, Cello, and Piano (1907); 2 violin sonatas (1916, 1921). **KEYBOARD: Piano:** *Variations and Epilogue on an Original Theme* (1913–15). **Organ:** 2 preludes and fugues (1908, 1909); *Introduction, Passacaglia and Fugue* (1916); *Rondino, Elegy and Chaconne* (1956); *Fugal Trilogy* (1958); *5 Pieces* (1958); *Passacaglia and Fugue* (1959); 97 chorale preludes; many other pieces, including arrangements. **VOCAL:** *An Apostrophe to the Heavenly Hosts* for Chorus (1921); *The Mystery of Bethlehem*, cantata for Soprano, Bass, Chorus, and Organ (1923); *6 Motets* for Chorus (1924); *The 3 Kings* for Chorus (1928); *Rise Up, My Love, My Fair One* for Chorus (1929); *Behold the Tabernacle of God* for Chorus (1933); *Gloria Deo per immensa saecula* for Chorus (1950); *O Lord, Our Governour* for Chorus and Orch. (1952); *Coronation Suite* for Chorus and Orch. (1952); *The Story of Bethlehem* for Chorus and Organ (1955); other choral works include 14 settings of the *Missa brevis* (1928–63), 11 *Liturgical Motets* (1928–37), other motets, 39 fauxbourdons and 15 full settings of the Canticles, more than 40 anthems, over 30 hymn-anthems, 31 hymn tunes, more than 40 fauxbourdons to hymn tunes, many plainsong adaptions, carols, secular vocal pieces, etc.

BIBL.: F. Clarke, *H. W.: Life and Music* (Toronto, 1983). **—NS/LK/DM**

Willcocks, Sir David (Valentine), English organist, conductor, and music educator; b. Newquay, Dec. 30, 1919. He was educated at Clifton Coll., the Royal Coll. of Music, and King's Coll., Cambridge. During World War II, he served in the British army. He was organist at Salisbury Cathedral (1947–50) and Worcester Cathedral (1950–57), then at King's Coll., Cambridge (1957–73); he also held the posts of univ. lecturer (1957–74) and univ. organist (1958–74) at Cambridge. Concurrently, he led the City of Birmingham Choir (1950–57) and was conductor of the Cambridge Univ. Musical Soc. (1958–73). In 1960 he became music director of the Bach Choir; in 1974 he also assumed the post of director of the Royal Coll. of Music in London, remaining there until 1984. He was made a Commander of the Order of the British Empire in 1971 and was knighted in 1977. He served as general ed. of the Church Music series of the Oxford Univ. Press.**—NS/LK/DM**

Willent-Bordogni, Jean-Baptiste-Joseph, French bassoonist, teacher, and composer; b. Douai, Dec. 8, 1809; d. Paris, May 11, 1852. He studied with Delcambre at the Paris Cons. and played the bassoon in the orch. of the Théâtre-Italien in Paris. He married the daughter of the singing teacher Bordogni (1834) and added her name to his. He taught at the Brussels Cons., and in 1848 was appointed to the faculty of the Paris Cons. He wrote a number of works for the bassoon, and publ. a method for it. He also brought out 2 operas in Brussels: *Le Moine* (1844) and *Van Dyck* (1845). **—NS/LK/DM**

Williams, "Buster," American bassist; b. Camden, N.J., April 17, 1942. He gained prominence in the 1960s playing for Gene Ammons, Sonny Stitt, Dakota Staton, Betty Carter, Sarah Vaughan, Nancy Wilson, and Miles Davis. He sat in the Jazz Crusaders' revolving bass chair from 1967 to 1969, then became a member of Herbie Hancock's underrated but groundbreaking groups from 1969 to 1972. After leaving Hancock, he played with Dexter Gordon and Mary Lou Williams before joining the legendary Ron Carter Quartet. He has been primarily a sideman, playing with a wide array of artists, most notably Kenny Barron, with whom he was a member of the Thelonious Monk tribute group Sphere.

DISC.: *Tokudo* (1989).**—PMac**

Williams, Alberto, important Argentine composer and music educator; b. Buenos Aires, Nov. 23, 1862; d. there, June 17, 1952. He was the grandson of an Englishman, and his maternal grandfather, Amancio Alcorta, was one of Argentina's early composers. Williams studied piano with Mathías, harmony with Durand, counterpoint with Godard, and composition with Franck and Bériot on a scholarship at the Paris Cons. He returned to Argentina in 1889 and founded the Alberto Williams Cons. in 1893. He also organized branches of the Cons. in provincial towns of Argentina, numbering more than 100, and founded a music publ. firm, La Quena (also a music magazine of that name). The greatest influence in his music was that of Franck, but modernistic usages are found in Williams's application of whole-tone scales, parallel chord progressions, etc. In many of his works he used characteristic melorhythms of Argentina. He composed a number of piano pieces in Argentine song and dance forms (milongas, gatos, cielitos, etc.). Williams also publ. numerous didactic works and several books of poetry.

WORKS: 9 syms. (all 1st perf. in Buenos Aires): No. 1 (Nov. 25, 1907), No. 2, *La bruja de las montañas* (Sept. 9, 1910), No. 3, *La Selva sagrada* (Dec. 8, 1934), No. 4, *El Ataja-Caminos* (Dec. 15, 1935), No. 5, *El corazón de la muñeca* (Nov. 29, 1936), No. 6, *La muerte del cometa* (Nov. 26, 1937), No. 7, *Eterno reposo* (Nov. 26, 1937), No. 8 (1938), and No. 9 (1939); several suites of Argentine dances; 3 violin sonatas (1905, 1906, 1907); Cello Sonata (1906); Piano Trio (1907); a great number of piano albums, the last of which was *En el parque* (1952).

BIBL.: Z. Lacoigne, *A. W.: Músico argentino* (Buenos Aires, 1942); *Homenajes a A. W.* (Buenos Aires, 1942); V. Risolía, *A. W., Curriculum vitae* (Buenos Aires, 1944).**—NS/LK/DM**

Williams, Camilla, African American soprano and teacher; b. Danville, Va., Oct. 18, 1922. She studied at Va. State Coll. (B.S., 1941) and with Marion Szekely-Freschl, Hubert Giesen, Sergius Kagen, and Leo Taubman in Philadelphia. She won the Marian Anderson Award twice (1943, 1944) as well as the Philadelphia Orch. Youth Award (1944). On May 15, 1946, she made her operatic debut at the N.Y.C. Opera as Cio-Cio-San, remaining on its roster until 1954; also toured widely as a concert artist. She taught at Brooklyn Coll. of the City Univ. of N.Y. (1970–73) and at the Ind. Univ. School of Music in Bloomington (from 1977).**—NS/LK/DM**

Williams, Clarence, important early African American jazz and blues pianist, record producer, composer; b. Plaquemine (Delta), La., Oct. 8, 1893; d. Queens, N.Y., Nov. 6, 1965. He was the son of bass-player **Dennis Williams** and was married to Eva Taylor; their daughter, **Irene**, did professional work as a singer. He was part Creole and part Choctaw; at one time, his birth date was given as 1898; however, further research revealed it as 1893. His childhood included periods of working in a hotel and singing in a street band. His family moved to New Orleans in 1906. At the age of 12 he ran away with Billy Kersand's Minstrel Show, working as a master of ceremonies and singer. He returned to New Orleans and began concentrating on playing the piano, receiving some lessons from Ophelia Gould Smith. By 1913 he had begun composing; he also toured vaudeville circuits as a dancer. Williams did extensive touring in a duo with Armand Piron and they briefly toured with W. C. Handy (c. 1917). With Piron, he started a publishing company and, when it failed, Williams moved to Chicago and opened a music store near the Vendome Theatre. Later he opened other shops in Chicago before moving to N.Y. around 1920, where he organized his own highly successful publishing company. He cut his first records in 1921, singing with a white band. He was a "race-record" judge for the Okeh recording company from 1923–28, and occasionally led his own bands at various venues, usually in and around N.Y. He also appeared regularly on radio programs, sometimes in company with Eva Taylor (they had married in 1921), sometimes as solo vocalist, pianist, or jug-player. During the 1920s and 1930s he organized many recording sessions, playing piano or acting solely as director. Williams played on sessions with Bessie Smith, and she cut several of his songs; he also backed vocalists Butterbeans & Susie, Sara Martin, and Sippie Wallace. He made nearly 300 sides under his own name in the period 1921–38, including the Blue Five sessions of 1924, with Thomas Morris, Charlie Irvis or John Mayfield, Sticky Elliott or Sidney Bechet, and Buddy Christian. Louis Armstrong was a member in 1924 and 1925, as were Buster Bailey, Aaron Thompson, Coleman Hawkins, Don Redman, and Bubber Miley later. They continued recording through 1927. He also made nearly 100 recordings for Okeh, Vocalion, and Victor between 1927 and 1939, with "washboard" bands that included Ed Allen, Bailey or Cecil Scott, and Floyd Casey. He published and promoted the work of Fats Waller, James P. Johnson, Willie "The Lion" Smith, and others.

Williams wrote words and/or music for "Royal Garden Blues," "Cake Walking Babies from Home," "Gulf Coast Blues," "Michigan Water Blues," "Swing Brother Swing," "The Stuff Is Here (And It's Mellow)," "Wild Cat Blues," "West End Blues," "West Indies Blues," "Squeeze Me," "Baby, Won't You Please Come Home," "Tain't Nobody's Business If I Do," and many, many more, often working with Spencer Williams (no relation). After the late 1930s Williams concentrated on writing, but led a final Blue Five session in 1941 with James P. Johnson, Wellman Braud, and Taylor doing the vocals. He sold his publishing catalogue to Decca in 1943 for a reputed $50,000 and lived well on his royalties for the rest of his life. He owned a bargain store in Harlem for many years. In 1956, he lost his sight after being knocked down by a taxi, but continued to work until shortly before his death.

DISC.: "Kansas City Man Blues" (1923); "Cake Walkin' Babies from Home".

BIBL.: Tom Lord, *Clarence Williams* (London, 1976).
—JC/LP/MM

Williams, Claude, American guitarist and string instrumentalist; b. Muskogee, Okla., Feb. 22, 1908. His first recordings were made for the Brunswick label in 1928, playing guitar and violin with the Twelve Clouds of Joy (a band led first by Terrence Holder, then by Andy Kirk) with pianist Mary Lou Williams arranging and composing. The band made their N.Y. debut at the Roseland Ballroom and at Harlem's Savoy. Upon returning to Kansas City, the band became part of the thriving scene where musicians at 50 clubs near 18th and Vine battled it out in jams and cutting contests. After working awhile in Kansas City, he headed for Chicago where he was playing guitar with Eddie Cole's band. When assembling his first band in 1936, Count Basie found him and hired him and put him in a prominent role (playing rhythm guitar) that garnered him brief national fame before he was replaced by Freddie Green. In the 1940s, he freelanced with various bands in the Midwest, and by the 1950s was using amplification on his fiddle. He worked in Los Angeles with Roy Milton's Blues Band (1951–52), and in 1953 moved back to Kansas City to lead his own combo on fiddle and guitar. Saxophonist Eddie "Cleanhead" Vinson was a member of that group. He led his own groups and freelanced around Kansas City throughout the 1960s, toured Europe in the 1970s, and worked and recorded with pianist Jay McShann into the 1980s. His last album to feature his guitar work was his 1980 album *Fiddler's Dream*. Since then, he has focused exclusively on violin. He continued his freelance work and recorded a couple of albums during the 1980s and 1990s and began touring Europe in 1997. He has won numerous awards, including his 1989 induction into the Okla. Jazz Hall of Fame. He celebrated his 89th birthday teaching students at the Smithsonian National Museum of American History, and continued an active schedule with overseas tours, club appearances, an ocean cruise, and other engagements.

DISC.: *Live at J's, Vol. 1, 2* (1993); *Statesmen of Jazz* (1995); *SwingTime in New York* (1995); *King of Kansas City* (1997).**—NAL**

Williams, Clifton, American bandmaster and composer; b. Traskwood, Ark., March 26, 1923; d. South Miami, Fla., Feb. 12, 1976. He studied at La. State Univ. (B.M., 1947) and with Rogers and Hanson at the Eastman School of Music in Rochester, N.Y. (M.M., 1948). He played horn with the sym. orchs. of San Antonio and New Orleans; was on the staff of the music dept. at the Univ. of Tex. in Austin (1949–66); then at the Univ. of Miami (1966–76). He composed band music, including the phenomenally popular *Sinfonians*. His other band pieces include *Trail Scenes, Trilogy Suite,* Concertino for Percussion and Band, 3 symphonic dances, *Fanfare and*

Allegro, Dedicatory Overture, Dramatic Essay: The Ramparts, The Patriots (commissioned by NORAD), *Songs of Heritage, Academic Procession, Castle Gap March,* and *Strategic Air Command.*—**NS/LK/DM**

Williams, Cootie (Charles Melvin), important jazz trumpet, long associated with Duke Ellington, leader; b. Mobile, Ala., July 10, 1911; d. N.Y., Sept. 15, 1985. He said he got his nickname when, as a small child, he heard a live band and later described their playing as "cootie, cootie, cootie" (not from the slang word for head lice). He was raised by an aunt after his mother, a pianist, died when he was eight. He played trombone, tuba, and drums in the school band, taught himself to play trumpet, then took lessons from Charles Lipskin. Williams began to do local gigs with Holman's Jazz Band and Johnny Pope's Band, and at 14 did a summer tour with the Young Family Band (with Lester and Lee). He moved to Pensacola, Fla. (in company of Edmond Hall) and joined a band led by Eagle Eye Shields and subsequently joined Alonzo Ross's De Luxe Syncopators (1926). Except for a brief absence, he worked with Alonzo Ross all through 1927; went with the band to N.Y. in spring of 1928. After gigging around N.Y., he joined Duke Ellington in mid-1929, replacing Bubber Miley, who had become increasingly unreliable due to heavy drinking. Ellington wrote "Concerto for Cootie" (1940) for him, which became "Do Nothing Till You Hear from Me," when words were written for it. From 1937 to 1940, he recorded as the leader of the Gotham Stompers, using Ellington and Webb band personnel plus vocalist Ivie Anderson. He also recorded with Lionel Hampton, Teddy Wilson, and Billie Holiday during this period.

Williams remained with Duke until November 1940, then joined Benny Goodman until October 1941 (he had first appeared with Benny Goodman at Carnegie Hall Concert in January 1938). He was featured on small group versions of "Breakfast Feud," "Wholly Cats," "Royal Garden Blues," and on the big band "Superman" (by Eddie Sauter). He then formed his own big band, which played long residencies at the Savoy Ballroom during the 1940s. He was very sympathetic to the new music of the 1940s; in 1944 Bud Powell was his pianist, and was featured on a number of recordings and broadcasts. Williams's his band was the first to record Thelonious Monk's *Round Midnight* and the Monk-Kenny Clarke piece "Epistrophy" ("Fly Right"). Charlie Parker was in the band briefly and solos on a broadcast of "Floogie Boo" (1944); Eddie Lockjaw Davis and Sam the Man Taylor were also with the band. Williams's band scored its biggest hits in the mid-1940s with "Torch Song," featuring vocalist Pearl Bailey, and "Cherry Red Blues" with singer and saxophonist Eddie Vinson. Williams cut down to a small band in 1948. After the Savoy closed, Cootie toured as a single; later, he formed his own quartet; served as a session musician on various R&B dates in the early 1950s, and teamed with Rex Stewart on some studio dates in 1957 and 1958.

Williams toured Europe with his own small band early in 1959. He returned to Benny Goodman briefly from late July 1962, then rejoined Duke Ellington in autumn of 1962, remaining except for short breaks until Ellington's death (1974); in the 1970s, Ellington featured him primarily as a soloist rather than with the trumpet section. Ellington wrote "New Concerto for Cootie" in the early 1960s. Thereafter he worked in Mercer Ellington's Band until 1975. He was in poor health (1978) but continued to play, including engagements in Europe, until 1983. Williams's sound was incredibly powerful.

DISC.: *Sextet and Orchestra: 1944 Recordings* (1944); *Things Ain't What They Used to Be* (1944); *Big Challenge* (1957); *Cootie and Rex* (1957); *Cootie Williams in Hi Fi* (1958); *Do Nothing Till You Hear from Me* (1959); *Solid Trumpet of Cootie Williams* (1962). —**JC/LP**

Williams, Deniece (originally, **Chandler, Deniece**), R&B chart topper of the mid-1970s and 1980s who has since converted to gospel music; (b. Gary, Ind., June 3, 1951). Like so many performers, Deniece Williams began singing in church but became aware of R&B and pop as a teenager. She took a job working part-time at a local record store during high school. Singing along with records impressed her boss, who invited people from Chicago's Toddlin' Town Records to hear her. They, too, were impressed and recorded "Love Is Tears" with her. The record became a local hit and started the high school student off as a singer.

When Williams graduated from high school she started to pursue a degree in nursing. However, Stevie Wonder had heard her singles and asked her if she would join his band as a backing vocalist. She worked with Wonder from 1972–76, appearing on four of his albums. When Wonder moved from Detroit to Los Angeles, Deniece moved, too. In addition to her work with Wonder, she sang with artists such as Minnie Ripperton and Roberta Flack.

Maurice White co-produced her Columbia debut, *This Is Niecy* and took her on the road with Earth Wind and Fire. The single from the album, "Free," had moderate success in the U.S., reaching #2 on the R&B charts and hitting #25. The song was a huge hit in England. The album did go gold in the U.S., hitting #33. In England, Williams gave a royal command performance for Prince Charles. Two years later, she released *That's What Friends Are For*, an album of duets with Johnny Mathis. It was a good match—it brought the youth and raw soul of Williams together with the class and cachet of Mathis, who had not had a chart single since 1974. "Too Much, Too Little, Too Late" topped the pop and R&B charts and went gold in the spring of 1978. They followed this with a version of Marvin Gaye and Tammy Terrell's Motown classic "You're All I Need to Get By," which missed the pop Top 40 but went #10 R&B. The album rose to #19 and was certified gold just two weeks after it came out.

In 1981, Williams went into the studio with Thom Bell recording *My Melody*. That album garnered the R&B hit "Silly." Continuing to work with Bell on her next album, *Neicy*, she again topped the R&B charts with a version of the Royalettes' hit "It's Gonna Take a Miracle," taking it to #10 pop. *Neicy* peaked at #20. Williams started to take a little more control of her career and music with 1983's *I'm So Proud*, co-producing the record with Bill Neal. She continued to do this with her next album, *Let's Hear It for the Boy*. The title track came from the hit movie *Footloose*, hitting the top of the charts and going platinum. The album topped out at #28. When her impact on the pop charts waned after this, Williams went back to gospel. Her 1986 duet, "They Say" with Sandy Patti, won a Best Gospel Performance by a Duo or Group, Choir or Chorus. Her own "I Surrender All" won Best Soul Gospel Performance, Female. She also won that award in 1987 for "I Believe in You." Since then, she has continued to record both sacred and secular music. She performed for the Pope in both 1991 and 1993.

DISC.: *Untitled* (1972); *This Is Niecy* (1976); *Song Bird* (1977); *That's What Friends Are For* (with Johnny Mathis; 1978); *When Love Comes Calling* (1979); *My Melody* (1981); *Niecy* (1982); *I'm So Proud* (1983); *Let's Hear It for the Boy* (1984); *Hot on the Trail* (1986); *From the Beginning* (1986); *Water under the Bridge* (1987); *As Good as It Gets* (1988); *So Glad I Know* (1988); *Special Love* (1989); *Lullabies to Dreamland* (1991); *Love Solves It All* (1996); *This Is My Song* (1998).—**HB**

Williams, Grace (Mary), Welsh composer; b. Barry, Glamorganshire, Feb. 19, 1906; d. there, Feb. 10, 1977. Her father led the local boy's chorus and played the piano in a home trio, with Grace on the violin and her brother on the cello. In 1923 she entered the music dept. of the Univ. of Wales in Cardiff, in the composition class of David Evans. Upon graduation in 1926, she enrolled at the Royal Coll. of Music in London. There she was accepted as a student of Vaughan Williams, who had the greatest influence on her career as a composer, both in idiom and form; she also took classes with Gordon Jacob. She subsequently received the Octavia Traveling Scholarship and went to Vienna to take lessons with Wellesz (1930–31). She did not espouse the atonal technique of the 2nd Viennese School, but her distinctly diatonic harmony with strong tertian underpinning was artfully embroidered with nicely hung deciduous chromatics of a decidedly nontonal origin. She marked May 10, 1951, in her diary as a "day of destruction," when she burned all her MSS unworthy of preservation. Among her practical occupations were teaching school and writing educational scripts for the BBC. She was particularly active in her advancement of Welsh music.

WORKS: DRAMATIC: *Theseus and Ariadne*, ballet (1935); *The Parlour*, opera (1961). **ORCH.:** *Sinfonia concertante* for Piano and Orch. (1941); 2 syms. (1943; 1956, rev. 1975); *Sea Sketches* for Strings (1944); Violin Concerto (1950); Trumpet Concerto (1963); *Castell Caernarfon*, for the investiture of the Prince of Wales (1969). **CHAMBER:** Sextet for Oboe, Trumpet, Violin, Viola, Cello, and Piano (1931); Suite for 9 Instruments (1934). **VOCAL:** Numerous choruses; songs.

BIBL.: M. Boyd, *G. W.* (Cardiff, 1980).—**NS/LK/DM**

Williams, Hank (Hiram), preeminent American country singer, songwriter, and guitarist; b. Mount Olive West, Ala., Sept. 17, 1923; d. Oak Hill, W. Va., Jan. 1, 1953. Williams was among the most popular recording artists in country music in the late 1940s and early 1950s, numbering among his hits "Lovesick Blues"; as a songwriter he was without peer in country music, penning songs such as "Cold, Cold Heart," "Jambalaya (On the Bayou)," and "Kaw-Liga" that defined the musical genre and set a permanent standard for country songwriting. His work alternated between maudlin and vengeful romantic sentiments such as "Why Don't You Love Me" and "Your Cheatin' Heart" and expressions of giddy and humorous elation such as "Hey, Good Lookin'" and "Baby, We're Really in Love." While these songs and his performances of them determined the form of country music, they also appealed beyond it: many of his compositions were covered as pop hits, and his music influenced the development of rock 'n' roll.

Williams's father, Elonzo Huble Williams, was a farmer at the time of his birth, although he was usually employed as a railroad engineer for a lumber company. After his father was hospitalized in January 1930, Williams was raised by his mother, Jessie Lillybelle Skipper Williams, who worked as a nurse and later ran boardinghouses. He attended a singing school as a child and learned to play the guitar before adolescence, taking lessons from a street musician named Rufus Payne who was known as "Tee-Tot." In 1937 he moved with his family to Montgomery, Ala., where he performed on the street, won amateur contests, and sang on local radio; soon he formed his own band, The Drifting Cowboys, for personal appearances around the area. In 1942 he gave up regular performing and turned to defense work after having been rejected for the service due to a back problem later diagnosed as spina bifida. He left his job and returned to performing full-time in August 1944.

On Dec. 15, 1944, Williams married Audrey Mae Sheppard Guy, a divorcée with a daughter who had worked at a drugstore. In September 1946, Williams went to Nashville to audition songs for publisher Fred Rose of the Acuff-Rose publishing company. Rose accepted several of Williams's songs and, also impressed with him as a performer, arranged for him to make his first recordings for the independent Sterling Records label on Dec. 11, 1946. This resulted in his debut record release, "Calling You"/"Never Again (Will I Knock on Your Door)" in January 1947; both songs were his own compositions. There was a second Sterling recording session on Feb. 13, 1947, then Rose got Williams signed to the larger MGM label, for which he began recording on April 21, resulting in the June single release "Move It on Over"/"(Last Night) I Heard You Crying in Your Sleep"; again, both songs were written by Williams. "Move It on Over" became his first country chart hit in August 1947. His subsequent releases were less successful, but Hawkshaw Hawkins recorded his song "Pan American" for a Top Ten country hit in May 1948. On May 26, 1948, Williams and his wife divorced, though they reconciled shortly after.

Williams's recording of his song "I'm a Long Gone Daddy" reached the country charts in July 1948, on its way to a Top Ten showing in September; on Aug. 7, Williams became a regular performer on the Shreveport, La., radio show the *Louisiana Hayride*. His breakthrough hit came not with one of his own songs, but with his revival of the 1922 song "Lovesick Blues" (music by Cliff Friend, lyrics by Irving Mills), which topped the country charts and reached the pop charts in May 1949, selling a million copies. As a result, he was invited to perform on the *Grand Ole Opry*, the premiere country radio show based in Nashville; he made his debut on June 11, 1949, and quickly becoming a regular. On May 26 he and his ex-wife became the parents of Randall Hank Williams, known as Hank Williams Jr.; their divorce was nullified on Aug. 9.

Williams scored another five Top Ten hits on the country charts during 1949, the most successful being "Wedding Bells" (music and lyrics by Claude Boone) and "My Bucket's Got a Hole in It" (music and lyrics by Clarence Williams). He reached the country Top Ten eight times in 1950, hitting #1 with "Long Gone Lonesome Blues," "Why Don't You Love Me," and "Moanin' the Blues," all his own compositions. He had eight more Top Ten country hits in 1951, including two chart-toppers, the million-selling "Cold, Cold Heart" and "Hey, Good Lookin'," both of which he wrote. Tony Bennett's cover of "Cold, Cold Heart" hit #1 in the pop charts in November, also selling a million copies, and in the same month Jo Stafford and Frankie Laine reached the pop Top Ten with their version of "Hey, Good Lookin'."

Williams hit the Top Ten of the country charts with six recordings in 1952, only one of which, "Jambalaya (On the Bayou)" (music and lyrics by Hank Williams), went to #1 during the year, selling a million copies and crossing over to the pop charts. With three of the others, "Honky Tonk Blues" (music and lyrics by Hank Williams), "Half as Much" (music and lyrics by Curley Williams), and "Settin' the Woods on Fire" (music and lyrics by Fred Rose and Ed G. Nelson), just missing the top of the charts, he ranked as the year's most successful country recording artist. In addition, Jo Stafford reached the pop Top Ten with "Jambalaya." But at the same time Williams's personal life was disastrous. Drinking heavily and taking drugs to ease the pain from his spinal disorder, he frequently missed performances. He and his wife separated in January 1952 and divorced on July 10. On Aug. 11 the *Grand Ole Opry* fired him, and the following month he returned to the *Louisiana Hayride*. On Oct. 15 he agreed to support the child of Bobbie Jett, a woman with whom he had had a liaison; three days later he married Billie Jean Jones Eshliman, a telephone operator. He died at 29 of a severe heart condition and hemorrhage sometime during the night of Dec. 31, 1952–Jan. 1, 1953, while on his way to a concert performance.

Williams's most recent single at the time of his death, "I'll Never Get Out of This World Alive" (music and lyrics by Hank Thompson and Fred Rose), re-entered the country charts and hit #1 in late January. As MGM released his last recordings, he scored five more Top Ten country hits during the year, including three #1s, "Kaw-Liga" (music and lyrics by Hank Williams and Fred Rose), "Your Cheatin' Heart" (music and lyrics by Hank Williams; inducted into the Grammy Hall of Fame in 1983), and "Take These Chains from My Heart" (music and lyrics by Fred Rose and Hy Heath). "Kaw-Liga" was the biggest country hit of the year, and Williams again was the year's most successful country recording artist. "Your Cheatin' Heart" was covered for a million-selling Top Ten pop hit by Joni James. In April 1954, Tony Bennett peaked in the pop Top Ten with a cover of "There'll Be No Teardrops Tonight" (music and lyrics by Hank Williams and Nelson King), a song Williams had used as the B-side of a single in 1949.

After 1953, MGM continued to release archival recordings by Williams, scoring a Top Ten country hit in the spring of 1955 with his 1949 demo "Please Don't Let Me Love You" (music and lyrics by Ralph Jones). His catalogue of songs became a basic repertory for country artists, who frequently revived his songs for hits. Among the most successful of these were Jerry Lee Lewis's country Top Ten rendition of Williams's 1952 song "You Win Again" in 1958 and Charley Pride's country #1 with the same song in 1980; B. J. Thomas's pop Top Ten version of "I'm So Lonesome I Could Cry" in 1966; Charley Pride's "Kaw-Liga," a country Top Ten in 1969; Linda Ronstadt's country Top Ten with "I Can't Help It (If I'm Still in Love with You)" in 1975; and Charley Pride's country chart-topper with "Honky Tonk Blues" in 1980.

Meanwhile, Williams's own recordings proved perennially popular. The album *Hank Williams's Greatest Hits*, released in April 1963, reached the country charts in 1968 and went gold in 1969. In 1966, MGM overdubbed strings on some of his recordings and "I'm So Lonesome I Could Cry" returned to the country charts, followed by the album *The Legend Lives Anew*. The double album *24 of Hank Williams's Greatest Hits*, though it contained overdubbed recordings, was MGM's most elaborate reissue yet when it was released in 1971, and it became the most successful, eventually going platinum. *Hank Williams Sr. Live at the Grand Ole Opry* reached the country charts in 1976, and "Why Don't You Love Me" returned to the country singles charts. His *24 Greatest Hits Vol. 2* was in the country charts in 1977 and, in the 1980s and 1990s, Williams's recordings, now controlled by the PolyGram label and released on its Polydor and Mercury labels, benefited from more care and scholarship. *Rare Takes and Radio Cuts* reached the country charts in 1984. During the later 1980s and 1990s, almost every known recording by the legendary star became available in one form or another.

WRITINGS: With J. Rule, *H. W. Tells How to Write Folk and Western Music to Sell* (Nashville, 1951); D. Cusic, ed., *H. W.: The Complete Lyrics* (N.Y., 1992).

DISC.: *Hank Williams Sings* (1952); *Moanin' the Blues* (1952); *Memorial Album* (1953); *Hank Williams as Luke the Drifter* (1953); *Honky Tonkin* (1954); *I Saw the Light* (1954); *Ramblin' Man* (1954); *36 of Hank Williams's Greatest Hits* (1957); *36 More of Hank Williams's Greatest Hits* (1958); *Sing Me a Blue Song* (1958); *The Immortal Hank Williams* (1958); *The Unforgettable Hank Williams* (1959); *The Lonesome Sound of Hank Williams* (1960); *Wait for the Light to Shine* (1960); *Greatest Hits* (1961); *Hank Williams Lives Again* (1961); *Sing Me a Blue Song* (1961); *Wanderin' Around* (1961); *I'm Blue Inside* (1961); *The Spirit of Hank Williams* (1961); *On Stage! Hank Williams Recorded Live* (1962); *Greatest Hits, Vol. 2* (1962); *14 More Greatest Hits, Vol. 2* (1962); *On Stage, Vol. 2* (1963); *14 More Greatest Hits, Vol. 3* (1963); *Very Best* (1963); *Very Best, Vol. 2* (1964); *Lost Highway (and Other Folk Ballads)* (1964); *The Hank Williams Story* (1965); *Kaw-Liga and Other Humorous Songs* (1965); *The Legend Lives Anew (Hank Williams with Strings)*

(1966); *More Hank Williams and Strings* (1966); *I Won't Be Home No More* (1967); *Hank Williams and Strings, Vol. 3* (1968); *In the Beginning* (1968); *The Essential Hank Williams* (1969); *Life to Legend* (1970); *24 of Hank Williams's Greatest Hits* (1970); *24 Karat Hank Williams* (1970); *Archetypes* (1974); *A Home in Heaven* (1976); *On Stage Recorded Live* (1976); *Live at the Grand Ole Opry* (1976); *24 Greatest His, Vol. 2* (1977); *Hank Williams* (1965); *Mr. and Mrs. Hank Williams (with Audrey)* (1966); *The Immortal Hank Williams* (1966). **LUKE THE DRIFTER:** *Luke the Drifter* (1955); *Movin' On-Luke the Drifter* (1966). **HANK WILLIAMS AND HANK WILLIAMS JR.:** *Hank Williams Sr. and Hank Williams Jr.* (1965); *Hank Williams Sr. and Hank Williams Jr., Again* (1966); *The Legend of Hank Williams in Song and Story* (1973); *Insights into Hank Williams in Story and Song* (1974); *The Best of Hank and Hank Back to Back: Like Father, Like Son* (1992); *40 Greatest Hits* (1984); *Rare Takes and Radio Cuts* (1984); *Hank Williams on the Air* (1985); *I Ain't Got Nothin' but Time, December 1946–August 1947* (1985); *Lovesick Blues, August 1947–December 1948* (1985); *Lost Highway, December 1948–March 1949* (1985); *I'm So Lonesome I Could Cry, March 1949–August 1949* (1986); *Long Gone Lonesome Blues, August 1949–December 1950* (1987); *Hey Good Lookin', December 1950–July 1951* (1987); *Let's Turn Back the Years, July 1951–June 1952* (1987); *I Won't Be Home No More, June 1952–September 1952* (1987); *The Original Singles Collection* (1990); *Health and Happiness Shows* (1993); *The Hits, Vol. 1* (1994); *The Hits, Vol. 2* (1995); *The Collectors' Edition* (1995); *Low Down Blues* (1996); *Lonesome Blues* (1990); *Hank Williams and The Drifting Cowboys on Radio* (1982); *Just Me and My Guitar* (1985); *The First Recordings* (1986); *Rare Demos: First to Last* (1990); *The Legend Lives Anew* (1995); *The Legendary Hank Williams* (2000); *Grand Ole Country Classics* (1987). **HANK WILLIAMS SR./HANK WILLIAMS JR./HANK WILLIAMS III:** *Men with Broken Hearts* (1996).

BIBL.: W. Stone and A. Rankin, *Life Story of Our H. W. "The Drifting Cowboy"* (Montgomery, Ala., 1953); J. Rivers, *H. W.: From Life to Legend* (Denver, 1967); R. Williams, *Sing a Sad Song: The Life of H. W.* (Garden City, N.Y., 1970; rev. ed., 1973); *H. W.: The Legend* (Nashville, 1972); Odom and Burton, *The H. W. Story* (Greenville, Ala., 1974); R. Krishef, *H. W.* (Minneapolis, 1978); J. Caress, *H. W.: Country Music's Tragic King* (Briarcliff Manor, N.Y., 1979); *H. W. as We Knew Him* (Georgiana and Chapman, Ala., 1982); C. Flippo, *Your Cheatin' Heart: A Biography of H. W.* (Garden City, N.Y., 1981); G. Koon, *H. W.: A Bio-Bibliography* (Westport, Conn., 1983); J. Sutton, *The Man Behind the Scenes (Pappy Neal McCormick and H. W.)* (DeFuniak Springs, Fla., 1987); L. Williams (his stepdaughter) and D. Vinicur, *Still in Love with You: The Story of H. and Audrey W.* (Nashville, 1989); J. Williams (his illegitimate daughter) and P. Thomas, *Ain't Nothin' As Sweet as My Baby: The Story of H. W.'s Lost Daughter* (N.Y., 1990); A. Rogers and B. Gidoll, *The Life and Times of H. W.* (Nashville, 1993); C. Escott with G. Merritt and W. MacEwen, *H. W.: The Biography* (Boston, 1994); T. Jones, *The Essential H. W.* (Nashville, 1996); Zwisohn, *H. W.* (N.Y., 1998); J. Arp, *The First Outlaw: H. W.*.—**WR**

Williams, James, American pianist; b. Memphis, Tenn., March 8, 1951. He was influenced by 1960s soul and the gospel music of the African American church. He spent time working and studying in Memphis before heading to Boston in 1972 for a five-year stint as an instructor at the Berklee Coll. of Music. During this period he worked with a number of name artists including Woody Shaw, Joe Henderson, and Clark Terry. His stay with Art Blakey's Jazz Messengers (1977–81) brought him his first taste of public and critical acclaim. During the 1980s and 1990s, he worked extensively as a sideman with players such as Bobby Hutcherson and Tom Harrell. He has fronted some impressive groups of his own and recorded a number of valuable albums in addition to producing the work of other artists (e.g., Harold Mabern, Donald Brown, Billy Pierce). An admitted student and purveyor of the music of Phineas Newborn Jr., he also leads the Contemporary Piano Ensemble, a group that includes his peers Harold Mabern, Geoff Keezer, and Mulgrew Miller, and is dedicated to fostering the legacy of Newborn and others of his ilk. His own style is marked by a prodigious technique, a fluent two-handed attack, and a rich harmonic knowledge that makes his music always sound fresh and engaging.

DISC.: *Alter Ego* (1984); *Progress Report* (1985); *Talkin' Trash* (1993); *Up to the Minute Blues* (1994); *At Maybeck Recital Hall* (1996); *Truth, Justice, and Blues* (1996).—**CH**

Williams, Jessica, highly original jazz pianist, composer; b. Baltimore, Md., March 17, 1948. After studying classical music at the Peabody Cons., she turned to jazz. At 16 she got her first gig in a local club, with Mickey Fields and Buck Hill and continued working locally. In 1968 she worked in Philly Joe Jones's quintet with Tyree Glenn in Philadelphia. Moving to Calif. in 1978, she became house pianist at the Keystone Korner, where she backed up Dexter Gordon, Stan Getz, Charlie Haden, Art Blakey, Pharoah Sanders, Eddie Harris, and others. She began recording her work on her own label, Quanta, wrote for the Bay Area Jazz Composers Orch. and took up abstract painting. In 1979 she formed a trio with John Witala (bass) and Dave Tucker, then Bud Pangler (drums). During the early 1980s, she began overdubbing synthesizer parts to her piano work. During the 1990s, she has made frequent tours of Europe. In 1988, she was given an NEA grant to write and perform "Tutu's Dream," dedicated to Bishop Desmond Tutu, and a year later a second grant to compose and arrange a piece in honor of Thelonious Monk. She won a Guggenheim Fellowship in 1994.

Williams is a dynamic, original, and virtuosic artist. Her quirky often humorous solos have been compared to Thelonious Monk, while she carries forward the classical-jazz fusion of cooler players like Bill Evans.

DISC.: *Orgonomic Music* (1979); *Rivers of Memory* (1980). **E. HARRIS:** *Update* (1982); *Nothin' But the Truth* (1986); *And Then, There's This* (1990); *Live at Maybeck Recital Hall, V* (1992); *Arrival* (1993); *Next Step* (1993); *Momentum* (1994); *Arrival* (1994); *Inventions* (1995); *Encounters* (1995); *Gratittude* (1996); *Standards* (1997); *Jessica's Blues* (1997).—**LP**

Williams, John (Christopher), remarkable Australian guitarist; b. Melbourne, April 24, 1941. He began his training with his father, the guitarist Leonard Williams. In 1952 he settled in London, where he made his first appearance in 1955. He continued his studies with Segovia at the Accademia Musicale Chigiana in Siena (1957–59). In 1958 he made his formal debut at London's Wigmore Hall. From 1960 to 1973 he was prof. of guitar at the Royal Coll. of Music in London. Following successful tours to the Soviet Union in 1962 and the U.S. and Japan in 1963, he performed with outstanding success on regular tours of Europe, North and South America, Australia, and the Far East. In 1980 he was made an Office of the Order of the British Empire. Williams' repertoire is truly egalitarian in its scope. While he is admired for his performances of the standard works for the guitar, he has done much to expand the repertoire by giving the premieres of scores by Brouwer, Dodgson, Previn, Schulthorpe, Takemitsu, and Westlake. In addition, he has found success in jazz and pop genres as well.—**NS/LK/DM**

Williams, John (Towner), enormously successful American composer and conductor; b. N.Y., Feb. 8, 1932. He was a student of Robert van Epps (orchestration) at Los Angeles City Coll., and also studied privately with Mario Castelnuovo-Tedesco (composition) in Los Angeles and with Rosina Lhévinne (piano) in N.Y. He became notably successful as a composer, arranger, and conductor for films and television. Among his numerous successful film scores were *Valley of the Dolls* (1967), *The Reivers* (1969), *Goodbye Mr. Chips* (1969), *Fiddler on the Roof* (1971; Academy Award), *The Poseidon Adventure* (1972), *Images* (1972), *Cinderella Liberty* (1973), *Tom Sawyer* (1974), *The Towering Inferno* (1974), *Jaws* (1975; Academy Award, Grammy Award, and Golden Globe Award), *Star Wars* (1977; Academy Award, 3 Grammy Awards, and Golden Globe Award), *Close Encounters of the Third Kind* (1977; 2 Grammy Awards), *Superman* (1978; 2 Grammy Awards), *The Empire Strikes Back* (1980; 2 Grammy Awards), *Raiders of the Lost Ark* (1981; Grammy Award), *E.T.* (1982; Academy Award, 3 Grammy Awards, and Golden Globe Award), *Return of the Jedi* (1983), *Indiana Jones and the Temple of Doom* (1984), *The Witches of Eastwick* (1987), *J.F.K.* (1991), *Jurassic Park* (1993), *Schindler's List* (1993; Academy Award), *Sabrina* (1995), *Nixon* (1995), *Amistad* (1998), and *Saving Private Ryan* (1998).

In 1980 Williams became conductor of the Boston Pops Orchs., a position he retained until 1993. During his generally successful tenure, he diversified his appeal to Boston Pops audiences by conducting selections from his own extraordinarily popular film scores. Among his other compositional efforts were *Essay* for Strings (1966), Sym. (1966), Sinfonietta for Wind Ensemble (1968), Concerto for Flute, Strings, and Percussion (1969), Violin Concerto (1974–76; St. Louis, Jan. 29, 1981), Tuba Concerto (1985), *Celebration Fanfare* for Orch. (1986), *The 5 Sacred Trees*, concerto for Bassoon and Strings (1992–94; N.Y., April 12, 1995), and Cello Concerto (Tanglewood, July 7, 1994).—**NS/LK/DM**

Williams, Martin, American music critic and writer on music; b. Richmond, Va., Aug. 9, 1924; d. Washington, D.C., April 10, 1992. He studied English literature at the univs. of Va. (B.A., 1948) and Pa. (M.A., 1950), and then was a Ph.D. candidate at Columbia Univ. (1950–56), where he also lectured on English and the humanities at Columbia Coll. (1952–56). Thereafter he lectured on both musical and nonmusical subjects at various institutions of higher learning in the U.S. From 1971 to 1981 he was director of the jazz program division of performing arts at the Smithsonian Institution in Washington, D.C. After serving as ed. of special projects for the Smithsonian Institution Press (1981–91), he was a researcher at the Smithsonian Institution (from 1991). In 1978 he held a Guggenheim fellowship. He won the ASCAP-Deems Taylor Award for his expertise as a music critic in both 1973 and 1986. While his sympathies ranged widely, Williams became especially known for his erudite writings on jazz.

WRITINGS (all publ. in N.Y.): Ed. *The Art of Jazz* (1959); ed. *Jazz Panorama* (1962); *Where's the Melody?: A Listener's Introduction to Jazz* (1966); *Jazz Masters of New Orleans* (1967); *Jazz Masters in Transition: 1957–1969* (1970); *The Jazz Tradition* (1970; 3rd ed., rev., 1993); *Jazz Heritage* (1985); *Jazz in Its Time* (1989); *Jazz Changes* (1992); *Hidden in Plain Sight: An Examination of the American Arts* (1992).—**LK/DM**

Williams, Peter (Fredric), eminent English musicologist, organist, and harpsichordist; b. Wolverhampton, May 14, 1937. He was educated at St. John's Coll., Cambridge (B.A., 1958; Mus.B., 1959; M.A., 1962; Ph.D., 1963). In 1962 he joined the faculty of the Univ. of Edinburgh as a lecturer, subsequently becoming a reader (1972) and a prof. (1982); at the university, he held the first chair in performance practice in the United Kingdon. In 1985 he was made Arts and Sciences Distinguished Prof. at Duke Univ. in Durham, N.C., where he was chairman of the music dept. (1985–88), univ. organist (1985–90), and director of the graduate center for performance practice studies (from 1990). As a performing artist, Williams made appearances as a recitalist from 1965. As a scholar, he ranks among the foremost authorities on the organ. In addition to his learned books and articles, he has served as general ed. of the series Biblioteca Organologica (80 vols., 1966 et seq.) and as founding ed. of *The Organ Yearbook* (from 1969). He is also founder-general ed. of the series Cambridge Studies in Performance Practice and of the Duke Univ. series Sources and Interpretation of Music. He is also general ed. of the New Oxford J.S. Bach Edition.

WRITINGS: *The European Organ 1450–1850* (London, 1966; 2nd ed., 1968); *Figured Bass Accompaniment* (2 vols., Edinburgh, 1970; 2nd ed., 1972); *Bach Organ Music* (London, 1972; 2nd ed., 1974); *A New History of the Organ From the Greeks to the Present Day* (London, 1980); *The Organ Music of J.S. Bach* (3 vols., Cambridge, 1980–84); ed., *Bach, Handel and Scarlatti: Tercentenary Essays* (Cambridge, 1985); *Playing the Works of Bach* (N.Y., 1986); *The Organ* (London and N.Y., 1988); with L. Todd, ed., *Mozart: Perspectives in Performance* (Cambridge, 1991); *The Organ in Western Culture 750–1250* (Cambridge, 1993); *The King of Instruments or, How Do Churches Come to Have Organs?* (London, 1993); *The Chromatic Fourth During Four Centuries of Music* (Oxford, 1997).—**NS/LK/DM**

Williams, Ralph Vaughan
See **Vaughan Williams, Ralph**

Williams, Roger (Louis Weertz), American pianist and arranger; b. Omaha, Nebr., Oct. 1, 1924. Williams was the most successful pianist of the second half of the 1950s, starting with his recording of "Autumn Leaves." He continued to score hits into the early 1970s, including "Till" and "Born Free."

Williams's mother was director of the symphony orchestra at Emporia State Coll. in Kans.; he began playing the piano at age three. After serving in the navy during World War II, he graduated from Idaho State Univ. at Pocatello, later taking his masters degree and Ph.D. at Drake Univ. He attended the Juilliard School of Music and studied privately with jazz pianists Lennie Tristano and Teddy Wilson. He earned a spot on the TV show *Arthur Godfrey's Talent Scouts*, which led to his being signed by Kapp Records. His instrumental recording of "Autumn Leaves" (music by Joseph Kosma, French lyrics by Jacques Prevert, English lyrics by Johnny Mercer) hit #1 in October 1955 and sold a million copies, launching his career.

"Wanting You" (music by Sigmund Romberg, lyrics by Oscar Hammerstein II) peaked in the Top 40 in January 1956, followed by "La Mer (Beyond the Sea)" (music and French lyrics by Charles Trenet, English lyrics by Jack Lawrence) in March, the same month that his album *Roger Williams* (aka *Autumn Leaves*) reached the LP charts. In February 1957, Williams released his fourth Top 40 hit, "Almost Paradise" (music by Norman Petty) and first Top Ten, gold-selling album, *Songs of the Fabulous Fifties*. His fifth Top 40 hit, "Till" (music by Charles Danvers, lyrics by Carl Sigman), appeared in the fall; it was a million-seller. A *Till* LP was released in March 1958, reaching the Top Ten and going gold.

Williams scored his second Top Ten single with a revival of the 1947 song "Near You" (music by Francis Craig, lyrics by Kermit Goell) in September 1958; an identically titled album also hit the Top Ten. Williams's singles were less successful after 1958, but he continued to score with his LPs: *More Songs of the Fabulous Fifties*, released in May 1959, went gold; *With These Hands* reached the Top Ten in 1960; *Temptation* was in the Top Ten in 1961; *Greatest Hits*, released in January 1962, went gold; and *Maria* hit the Top Ten in 1962.

Williams continued to chart with several albums a year in the early 1960s, then made a considerable commercial comeback in 1966, first with the gold-selling album *Somewhere My Love* (aka *I'll Remember You*), which spent more than a year in the charts, and then with a Top Ten recording of the theme from the movie *Born Free* (music by John Barry, lyrics by Don Black), which led to a gold-selling Top Ten album.

Williams's albums continued to reach the charts until 1972, and he continued to record for MCA (which absorbed Kapp Records) and later for Bainbridge Records.—**WR**

Williams, Vanessa, the dethroned Miss America who went on to success as an actress and singer; b. Tarrytown, N.Y., March 18, 1963. Vanessa Williams's career seemed to be over before it began. Crowned the first African-American Miss America, she had to give up her crown when some sexually explicit pictures taken during her rebellious late teens surfaced in *Penthouse* magazine. However, she made the adage that any publicity is good publicity.

Both of Williams's parents taught music in elementary schools. She grew up in comfortable Millwood, N.Y. and won a musical scholarship to Syracuse Univ. By her junior year, the funds had dried up. Although she considered herself a liberal and a feminist, as a lark she entered the beauty pageant circuit leading to the Miss America contest. She won, becoming Miss New York and then Miss America.

Several years before that, she had worked as a receptionist for a N.Y. modeling agency. Her boss asked her to pose for some sexually explicit pictures and she agreed. About midway through her reign as Miss America, the pictures were published in *Penthouse* and the pageant officials asked her to relinquish her crown.

She laid low for a few years, surfacing in Hollywood in 1987 in the film *The Pick-Up Artist*. The following year, she launched a career as a recording artist with *The Right Stuff*. An R&B singer in the classic sense of the word, Williams displayed a well-trained, supple voice. The song "Dreaming" rose to #8, sending the album to #38 and gold.

After another three years, she put out *The Comfort Zone*. The song "Saving the Best for Last" became an even bigger hit, topping the pop chart for five weeks and going gold. The album hit #17 and went double platinum. A year later, "Love Is," her duet with Brian McKnight from the *Beverly Hills 90210* soundtrack album, hit #3.

It was another three years before she put out *Sweetest Days*. In between, she took on several film roles and made her Broadway debut, taking over the title role in the musical *Kiss of the Spider Woman*. The title track from *Sweetest Days* rose to #18, but the album stalled at #57. That year, she had a #4 gold hit with "Color of the Wind," the theme song from the Disney film *Pocahontas*.

Although subsequent albums didn't set the charts on fire, they were full of the same musical exuberance and depth of feeling her hits possessed. Her work as an actress, a balancing act throughout her career, seems to have taken precedent over her musical endeavors.

Disc.: *The Right Stuff* (1988); *The Comfort Zone* (1991); *Sweetest Days* (1995); *Star Bright* (1996); *Next* (1997); *Greatest Hits: The First Ten Years* (1998).—**BH**

Williams, Willie, jazz tenor saxophonist; b.Wilmington, N.C., Nov. 1, 1958. His family moved to Philadelphia when he was just an infant. At age six he picked up a clarinet and within two weeks was playing songs from the radio. Recognizing his gift, Willie's parents, though poor, found teachers for him immediately. He studied classical music and performed in orchestras and ensembles both in and out of school. Upon graduating high school as valedictorian, he attended the Philadelphia Coll. of the Performing Arts by day (B.A. 1980) and pursued his new interest in jazz by night. He began gigging with local organ trios and also recorded more than 50 dates for Philadelphia International Records before he turned 20. While leading his own group, he was discovered by Bobby Watson who encouraged him to come to N.Y. Almost immediately, he was performing and recording with Art Blakey, Jaki Byard, and Sam

Rivers. He also worked in the pit bands of Broadway shows until Art Taylor asked him to join his quintet, "Taylor's Wallers." He began leading his own quintet in 1987, and made his first recording a year later. He has actively freelanced with various leaders, including Charles Fambrough (from 1982), Arthur Taylor (from 1988), and T. S. Monk (from 1991). He has been teaching at CCNY since 1990.

Disc.: *House Calls* (1988); *Armageddon Time* (1992); *Spirit Willie* (1992); *WW3* (1993).—**LP**

Williams (Goreed), Joe (actually, **Joseph**), African American jazz and blues singer; b. Cordele, Ga., Dec. 12, 1918; d. Las Vegas, Nev., March 29, 1999. Though he sang urban and jump blues with a rangy bass- baritone reminiscent of Joe Turner, Williams consistently worked with jazz musicians, notably as the singer in Count Basie's band from 1954 to 1961. That association established the late-blooming singer, especially through their recording of the R&B hit "Every Day," enabling Williams to launch a 35-year solo career as a nightclub entertainer.

Willams was the illegitimate son of Willie Goreed and Anne Beatrice Gilbert. The family lived together briefly in Osilla, Ga., then Williams's mother returned to live with her parents in Cordele before moving to Chicago and earning enough money as a domestic to bring her son, mother, and sister north when Williams was still a small child. His mother sang and played keyboards in church, where he first sang in public. At 16 he dropped out of high school to sing in a club for tips, making his professional debut in 1937 with Jimmie Noone's band. He appeared with Coleman Hawkins's big band in 1941 and toured with Lionel Hampton in 1943, later working with Andy Kirk, Albert Ammons and Pete Johnson, Red Saunders, and King Kolax. In 1943 he married Wilma Cote. They divorced in 1946 and he married Ann Kirksey, from whom he was divorced in 1950. He married Lemma Reid in 1951; they had two children and divorced on Sept. 10, 1964.

In 1950, Williams sang with a septet led by Count Basie during a Chicago engagement. Around this time he made his first recordings with Red Saunders. A session backed by King Kolax for the Chess Records subsidiary Checker included his first recording of "Every Day I Have the Blues" (music and lyrics by Peter Chatman, aka Memphis Slim), which entered the R&B singles charts in October 1952 and became a Top Ten hit. But Williams's big break came at the age of 36, when he joined Count Basie as his permanent singer on Christmas Day 1954. In July 1955 they recorded a session for Norman Granz's Clef Records label that included a remake of "Every Day I Have the Blues." Released as "Every Day," it reached the R&B charts in July and made the Top Ten.

In October 1957, Basie and Williams switched to Roulette Records and Williams recorded his first solo album, *A Man Ain't Supposed to Cry*. The following month they appeared in the film *Jamboree*. They reached the pop singles charts in August 1958 with "Going to Chicago Blues" (music and lyrics by Count Basie and Jimmy Rushing, additional lyrics by Jon Hendricks), on which they were joined by the vocal trio Lambert, Hendricks, and Ross. In December 1960 they appeared in the Jerry Lewis comedy *Cinderfella*.

Williams left Basie for a solo career in January 1961, initially backed by a quintet led by Harry "Sweets" Edison. From the start, he was able to play in the most prestigious nightclubs in the U.S., and by 1962 he was appearing at such notable events as the Newport Jazz Festival and touring overseas. That year, he signed to RCA Victor Records and made a series of albums for the label through 1965. On Jan. 7, 1965, he married Jillean Milne Hughes-D'Aeth, at first living with her in N.Y., then moving to Las Vegas in 1968.

Williams recorded less frequently and for less prominent record labels after the mid-1960s while maintaining his status as a major nightclub performer. In 1968 he returned to a big band format when he recorded the album *Something Old, New and Blue* with the Thad Jones–Mel Lewis Jazz Orch. for United Artists Records. In July 1970 he had a non-singing acting role in the film *The Moonshine War*, and thereafter he made occasional appearances as an actor on television, notably a continuing role on *The Cosby Show* (1984–92). Starting in 1979 he was a frequent Grammy nominee in the Best Jazz Vocal Performance category, first gaining a nomination for the GNP/Crescendo album *Prez and Joe*, on which he was accompanied by the Lester Young tribute band Prez Conference.

He was nominated again in 1982 for his Warner Bros. album *8 to 5 I Lose*, won the award in 1984 for his Delos album *Nothin' but the Blues*, and was nominated in 1986 for the Delos album *I Just Want to Sing* and in 1987 for the Verve album *Every Night*. In 1988 he duetted with Lena Horne on "I Won't Leave You Again" for her album *The Men in My Life*, and they earned a Grammy nomination for Best Jazz Vocal Performance, Duo, or Group; he was nominated alone again in 1989 for his Verve album *In Good Company*.

Williams had periodically appeared with Count Basie during his solo years, and following Basie's death in 1984 he undertook a tour of the U.S. and Europe with the Basie Orch. under the direction of Thad Jones in 1985. In March 1993 Williams initiated a recording contract with Telarc Jazz by releasing *Live at Orchestra Hall, Detroit*, on which he was accompanied by the Basie Orch. His January 1994 Telarc release, *Here's to Life*, found him performing with the even larger backing of the British-based Robert Farnon Orch. In April 1995 he released *Feel the Spirit*, an album of spirituals. In 1996, at age 77, he headlined a concert at the JVC Jazz Festival in N.Y. He died of natural causes at 80 in 1999.

Disc.: *Every Day: Best of the Verve Years* (rec. 1954–89; rel. 1993); *Count Basie Swings/Joe Williams Sings* (1955); *The Greatest!* (1957); *Joe Williams Newport '63* (1963); *Presenting Joe Williams, Thad Jones and Mel Lewis (with) the Jazz Orchestra* (1966); *Live* (1974); *Prez Conference* (1979); *In Good Company* (1989); *Ballad and Blues Master* (1992); *Every Night* (1992); *Live at Orchestra Hall, Detroit* (1993); *Here's the Life* (1994); *Feel the Spirit* (1995).

Bibl.: L. Gourse, *Every Day: The Story of J. W.* (London, 1985).—**WR**

Williamson, John Finley, distinguished American choral conductor and music educator; b. Canton,

Ohio, June 23, 1887; d. Toledo, Ohio, May 28, 1964. He studied at Otterbein Coll. in Westerville, Ohio (graduated, 1911); then studied singing with Herbert Wilbur Greene, Herbert Witherspoon, and David Bispham in N.Y. and organ with Karl Straube in Leipzig. He became minister of music at the Westminster Presbyterian Church in Dayton, Ohio, where he founded a choir in 1920; in 1926 he founded the Westminster Choir School there. In 1929 he moved it to Ithaca, N.Y., and in 1932 to Princeton, N.J., where it later became Westminster Choir Coll.; he was its president until 1958. He led its choir on many tours of the U.S. and took it on 4 world tours. He ed. the Westminster Series of choral music.

Bibl.: D. Wehr, *J.F. W. (1887–1964): His Life and Contribution to Choral Music* (diss., Miami Univ., Oxford, Ohio, 1971).
—NS/LK/DM

Williamson, Malcolm (Benjamin Graham Christopher),

prominent Australian composer, pianist, organist, and conductor; b. Sydney, Nov. 21, 1931. He attended the New South Wales State Conservatorium of Music in Sydney (1944–50), where he received training from Goossens (composition) and Sverjensky (piano). He also studied horn and violin. Settling in London, he pursued his training in composition with Lutyens and Erwin Stein (1953–57). He also studied the organ. As a performing artist, he appeared in his own organ and piano concertos. In 1963 he was awarded the Bax Memorial Prize. In 1970–71 he served as composer-in-residence at Westminster Choir Coll. in Princeton, N.J. Williamson was made Master of the Queen's Musick in 1975. He was named a Commander of the Order of the British Empire in 1976. From 1983 to 1986 he was a visiting prof. at Strathclyde Univ. In his output, Williamson has been influenced by Stravinsky, Britten, and Messiaen along with jazz and popular music. The general accessibility of his works is complemented by fine craftsmanship.

Works: DRAMATIC: Opera: *Our Man in Havana* (1962–63; London, July 2, 1963); *The English Eccentrics*, chamber opera (1963–64; Aldeburgh, June 11, 1964); *The Happy Prince*, children's opera (1964–65; Farnham, May 22, 1965); *Julius Caesar Jones*, children's opera (1965; London, Jan. 4, 1966); *The Violins of St. Jacques* (London, Nov. 29, 1966); *Dunstan and the Devil* (Cookham, May 19, 1967); *The Growing Castle*, chamber opera (Dynevor, Aug. 13, 1968); *Lucky Peter's Journey* (London, Dec. 18, 1969); *The Red Sea* (1971–72; Dartington, April 14, 1972). **Cassations:** *The Moonrakers* (Brighton, April 22, 1967); *Knights in Shining Armour* (Brighton, April 29, 1968); *The Snow Wolf* (Brighton, April 29, 1968); *Genesis* (Black Mountain, N.C., June 1971); *The Stone Wall* (London, Sept. 18, 1971); *The Winter Star* (Holm Cutram, June 19, 1973); *The Glitter Gang* (1973–74; Sydney, Feb. 23, 1974); *La Terre des Rois* (1974); *The Valley and the Hill* (Liverpool, June 21, 1977); *Le Pont du diable* or *The Devil's Bridge* (Angouleme, March 1982). **Ballet:** *The Display* (Adelaide, March 14, 1964); *Spectrum* (1964; Bury St. Edmunds, Sept. 21, 1967); *Sun into Darkness* (1965–66; London, April 13, 1966); *Bigfella TootsSquoodge and Nora* (1967; Manchester, Sept. 25, 1976); *Perisynthyon* (1974); *Heritage* (1985). **Other:** Incidental music and film, radio, and television scores. **ORCH.:** 7 syms.: No. 1, *Elevamini* (1956–57; private perf., London, June 1957; public perf., Melbourne, Nov. 13, 1963), No. 2, *Pilgrim på havet* (1968–69; Bristol, Oct. 29, 1969), No. 3, *The Icy Mirror*, for Soprano, Mezzo-soprano, 2 Baritones, Chorus, and Orch. (Cheltenham, July 9, 1972), No. 4 (1977), No. 5, *Aquerò* (1979–80; London, April 23, 1980), No. 6 (1982; Australian Broadcasting Corp. FM, Sept. 29, 1986), and No. 7 for Strings (1984); *Santiago de Espada*, overture (private perf., London, June 1957; public perf., BBC, Feb. 8, 1958); 4 piano concertos: No. 1 (1957–58; Cheltenham, July 15, 1958), No. 2 for Piano and Strings (1960), No. 3 (1962; Sydney, June 1964), and No. 4 (1993–94); *Sinfonia concertante* for 3 Trumpets, Piano, and Strings (1958–62; Glasgow, May 21, 1964); Organ Concerto (London, Sept. 8, 1961); *Our Man in Havana*, suite from the opera (1963; Glasgow, Jan. 6, 1966); *The Display*, suite from the ballet (1963–64; Adelaide, March 14, 1964); Violin Concerto (1964–65; Bath, June 12, 1965); *Concerto Grosso* (1964–65; London, Aug. 28, 1965); *Symphonic Variations* (Edinburgh, Sept. 9, 1965); *Sinfonietta* (1965–67; *Toccata, Elegy*, and *Tarantella*, BBC, March 21, 1965; *Prelude*, Stratford upon Avon, Feb. 10, 1967); *Epitaphs for Edith Sitwell* for Strings (1966; London, April 1972; arranged from the organ piece); *A Word from Our Founder* (1969); Concerto for 2 Pianos and Strings (1972); Concerto for Harp and Strings, *Au Tombeau du Martyr Juif Inconnu* (1973–76; London, Nov. 17, 1976); 2 *Pieces* for Strings (1975; from the piano pieces *The Bridge That Van Gogh Painted*); *The Bridge That Van Gogh Painted* for Strings (1975; arranged from the piano pieces); *The House of Windsor*, suite (1977); *Fiesta* (Geneva, March 14, 1978); *Ochre* (London, Sept. 2, 1978; also for Organ and Strings); *Fanfarade* (London, May 10, 1979); *Lament (in Memory of Lord Mountbattten of Burma)* for Violin and Strings (1979–80; Edinburgh, May 5, 1980); *Ode for Queen Elizabeth* for Strings (private perf., Edinburgh, July 3, 1980; public perf., Edinburgh, Aug. 25, 1980); *In Thanksgiving—Sir Bernard Heinze* (Sydney, July 1, 1982); *Cortège for a Warrior* (1984); *Lento* for Strings (1985); *Bicentennial Anthem* (1988). **CHAMBER:** 3 string quartets (*Winterset*, 1947–48; 1954; 1993); Nonet for Strings, Wind, and Harp (1949); *Piece* for 7 Winds and Piano (1953); *Variations* for Cello and Piano (London, Nov. 21, 1964); Concerto for Wind Quintet and 2 Pianos, 8- Hands (1964–65; London, April 9, 1965); *Serenade* for Flute, Piano, and String Trio (London, March 8, 1967); *Pas de Quatre* for Flute, Oboe, Clarinet, Bassoon, and Piano (Newport, R.I., Aug. 21, 1967); Piano Quintet (1967–68; Birmingham, March 23, 1968); *Partita on Themes of Walton* for Viola (BBC-TV, March 29, 1972); *Canberra Fanfare* for Brass and Percussion (1973); *Adelaide Fanfare* for Brass and Organ (1973); Piano Trio (1976); *Konstanz Fanfare* for Brass, Percussion, and Organ (1980); *Richmond Fanfare* for Brass, Percussion, and Organ (1980); *Fontainebleu Fanfare* for Brass, Percussion, and Organ (1981); *Ceremony for Oodgeroo* for Brass Quintet (1988); *Fanfares and Chorales* for Brass Quintet (1991); *Day That I Have Loved* for Harp (1993–94). **KEYBOARD: Piano:** 4 sonatas (1955–56; 1957, rev. 1970–71; 1958; 1963); *Travel Diaries* (1960–61); *5 Preludes* (1966); Sonata for 2 Pianos (1967); *Haifa Watercolours* (1974); *The Bridge That Van Gogh Painted and the French Camargue* (1975); *Ritual of Admiration* (1976); *Himna Titu* (1984); *Springtime on the River Moskva* (1987). **Organ:** *Fons Amoris* (1955–56); *Resurgence du Feu (Paques 1959)* (1959); Sym. (1960); *Vision of Christ Phoenix* (1961; rev. 1978); *Elegy-J.F.K.* (1964); *Epitaphs for Edith Sitwell* (Aldeburgh, June 17, 1966; arranged for String Orch.); *Peace Pieces* (2 vol., 1970–71); *Little Carols of the Saints* (1971–72); *Mass of a Medieval Saint* (1973); *Fantasy on This Is May Father's World* (1975); *Fantasy on O Paradise!* (1976); *The Lion of Suffolk (for Benjamin Britten)* (1977). **VOCAL:** *Mass* for Chorus (1957); Concerto for Soprano, Oboe, English Horn, Cello, and Organ (1957); *Adoremus*, Christmas cantata for Alto, Tenor, Chorus, and Organ (1959); *Tu es Petrus*, cantata for Speaker, Chorus, and

Organ (1961); *Agnus Dei* for Soprano, Chorus, and Organ (1961); *Dignus est Agnus* for Soprano, Chorus, and Organ (1961); *Procession of Psalms* for Chorus and Organ or Piano (1961); *Symphony for Voices* for Contralto and Chorus (London, May 2, 1962); *The Morning of the Day of Days*, Easter cantata for Soprano, Tenor, Chorus, and Organ (1962); *Te Deum* for Unison Voices and Piano or Organ (1963); *Celebration of Divine Love*, cantata for Soprano or Tenor and Piano (London, April 8, 1963); *Mass of St. Andrew* for Unison Voices and Piano or Organ (1964); *A Psalm of Praise* for Unison Voices and Organ (1965); *The Brilliant and the Dark* for Women's Voices and Orch. (1966; London, June 3, 1969); *6 English Lyrics* for Alto or Baritone and Piano or String Orch. (1966); *Mowing the Barley* for Chorus and Orch. (London, March 1, 1967); *I Will Lite up Mine Eyes*, anthem for Chorus, Echo Chorus, and Organ (Syndey, May 3, 1970); *Cantate domino* for Chorus and Organ (Princeton, N.J., Oct. 21, 1970); *Te Deum* for Chorus, Organ, and Optional Brass (1971); *The Death of Cuchulain* for 5 Men's Voices and Percussion (London, Nov. 6, 1971); *The Musicians of Bremen* for 6 Men's Voices (1972); *Ode to Music* for Chorus, Echo Chorus, and Orch. (1972–73; London, Feb. 3, 1973); *Pietà* for Soprano, Oboe, Bassoon, and Piano (London, Oct. 31, 1973); *Canticle of Fire* for Chorus and Organ (N.Y., May 20, 1973); *The World at the Manger*, Christmas cantata for Soprano, Baritone, Chorus, and Organ or Piano Duet (Leicester, Dec. 6, 1973); *Hammarskjöld Portrait* for Soprano and String Orch. (London, July 30, 1974); *Mass of St. James* for Unison Voices and Piano or Organ (1975); *Les Olympiques* for Mezzo-soprano and String Orch. (1976; Meyer, Germany, June 19, 1977); *Jubilee Hymn* for Chorus and Orch. or Piano (London, Feb. 6, 1977); *Mass of Christ the King* for 2 Sopranos, Baritone, Echo Chorus, Chorus, and Orch. (1977–78; London, Nov. 3, 1978); *Kerygma*, anthem for Chorus and Organ (London, March 11, 1979); *Little Mass of St. Bernadette* for Unbroken Voices and Organ or Instruments (London, Nov. 26, 1980); *Mass of St. Margaret of Scotland* for Congregation, Optional Chorus, and Organ (1980); *Josip Broz Tito* for Baritone and Orch. (1980–81; Skopje, March 9, 1981; also for Baritone and Piano); *Mass of the People of God* for Voices and Organ (1980–81; Bromsgrove, April 29, 1981); *The Feast of Eurydice* for Mezzo-soprano, Piano, Flute, and Percussion (1983); *A Pilgrim Liturgy*, cantata for Mezzo-soprano, Baritone, Chorus, and Orch. (1984–85); *The True Endeavour* for Speaker, Chorus, and Orch. (1988); *The Dawn Is at Hand*, choral sym. (1989); *Mass of St. Ethelreda (on Themes of Lennox Berkeley)* for Chorus and Organ (1990); *Requiem for a Tribe Brother* for Chorus (1992); numerous other vocal works.—**NS/LK/DM**

Willis, Larry, American pianist, keyboardist; b. N.Y., Dec. 20, 1942. While attending the Manhattan School of Music, he started playing with Jackie McLean and made his recording debut on McLean's 1965 album *Right Now*. Since then, he has been in demand, having played on more than 250 albums and performed with musicians as diverse as Miles Davis, Hugh Masekela, Herb Alpert, Nat and Cannonball Adderley, Carla Bley, and Stan Getz. From 1972 to 1977 he was the keyboardist for Blood, Sweat, & Tears, an erratic period in the band's history. His playing with the group, however, was always solid, and he left BS&T before it became nothing more than a backing band for David Clayton-Thomas. During the past 20 years, he has led some great dates, playing fusion, funk, and straight-ahead with excellent interpretative ability. He is music director of Mapleshade Productions, and though he has only a few domestic albums in print, he appears as sideman on many of Mapleshade's recordings.

Disc.: *Inner Crisis* (1973); *Portraits in Ivory and Brass* (1992); *Solo Spirit* (1993).—**PMac**

Willmers, Rudolf, Danish pianist and composer; b. Copenhagen, Oct. 31, 1821; d. Vienna, Aug. 24, 1878. His father, a Danish agriculturist, sent him to Germany at the age of 13 to study science, but Willmers turned to music. He took lessons with Hummel for 2 years and with Friedrich Schneider for a year, becoming a concert pianist and touring successfully in Germany and Austria; he was much acclaimed in Paris and London (1846–47). In 1866 he settled in Vienna. His technical specialty was the performance of "chains of trills," for which he was famous. He wrote a number of brilliant piano solos: *6 études, Sérénade érotique* (for the left hand), *Sehnsucht am Meere, Un Jour d'été en Norvège, 2 études de concert* (*La pompa di festa* and *La danza delle Baccanti*), *Sonata héroïque, Tarantella giocosa, La Sylphide, Trillerketten, Aus der Geisterwelt*, tremolo-caprice, and *Allegro symphonique*. He also composed some chamber music. —**NS/LK/DM**

Wills, Arthur, English organist, teacher, and composer; b. Coventry, Sept. 19, 1926. He was educated at the Coll. of St. Nicholas, Canterbury, and at the Univ. of Durham (D.Mus.). In 1949 he became asst. organist at Ely Cathedral, and then was organist and director of music there from 1958 to 1990. From 1964 to 1992 he was also a prof. at the Royal Academy of Music in London. As a recitalist, he toured throughout Europe, the U.S., and the Far East. He was the author of the vol. *Organ* (1984; 2nd ed., 1993). In 1990 he was made an Officer of the Order of the British Empire.

Works: DRAMATIC: Opera: *Winston and Julia* (1988). **ORCH.:** Sym. (1957); Concerto for Organ, Timpani, and Strings (1969); *The Fenlands* for Organ and Brass Band (1981); *A Muse of Fire*, overture for Brass Band (1983). **CHAMBER:** Guitar Sonata (1972); *Sonata 1984* for Piano (1984); *Sacrae symphoniae: Veni Creator Spiritus* for Double Wind Quintet (1987); Concerto for Guitar and Organ (1988); *Oration* for Tenor Trombone and Piano (1993). **Organ:** Over 60 pieces, including a Sonata (1963); *Symphonia Eliensis* (1976); Transcription of Mussorgsky's *Pictures at an Exhibition* (1980); *Bhagavad Gita*, sym. (1995–98). **VOCAL:** *An English Requiem* for Soprano, Bass, Chorus, and Orch., after Dylan Thomas, Donne, and Shakespeare (1971); *The Gods of Music* for Chorus, Brass, Percussion, and Organ (1992); *A Toccata of Galuppi's*, scena for Countertenor and String Quartet (1993); *The Shining Sea* for Tenor, Chorus, Strings, Percussion, Piano, and Organ (1994–96); 85 liturgical pieces (1958–96).—**NS/LK/DM**

Wills, Bob (actually, James Robert), versatile American bandleader, fiddler, singer, and songwriter; b. near Kosse, Tex., March 6, 1905; d. Fort Worth, Tex., May 13, 1975. Wills popularized the eclectic style of country music known as Western swing. The most successful country bandleader of the 1940s, he and His Texas Playboys had a million-seller with "San Antonio Rose," which he also wrote. He was a major influence on such successors as Merle Haggard, Willie Nelson, Waylon Jennings, and George Strait.

Wills was the first son of John Thompkins and Emmaline Foley Wills. His father was a migrant farm worker. His father and grandfather were both fiddlers, and he learned mandolin and guitar as a child to accompany them. At ten he began playing the fiddle in public. He left home in 1924 and moved to Amarillo. In 1926 he married Edna Posey and tried to become a farmer, but he had returned to music by 1927 while supporting himself primarily as a barber.

Wills moved to Fort Worth in 1929 and joined a medicine show, where he met Herman Arnspiger, with whom he formed the Wills Fiddle Band; they played on local radio. By the fall of 1930 they had added other members, notably singer Milton Brown, and become the Aladdin Laddies, sponsored on WBAP by the Aladdin Lamp Company. In January 1931 they became the Light Crust Doughboys when the mill that made Light Crust Flour took up their sponsorship. Brown left the band in February 1932 and was replaced by singer Tommy Duncan (1911–67), who would be the primary vocalist in Wills's bands thereafter.

Wills and Duncan left the Light Crust Doughboys in August 1933, moved to Waco, and formed The Playboys. As Bob Wills and His Texas Playboys they first appeared on KVOO in Tulsa on Feb. 9, 1934, after which they established themselves as the major band in the area. They were contracted to the American Record Company (ARC) in 1935 and recorded their first tracks on Sept. 23; the recordings were issued on the Brunswick label. (Later ARC recordings were released on the Vocalion and OKeh labels; after ARC was absorbed by Columbia Records, they were on Columbia.)

Wills and his wife divorced in 1936. That same year he married and divorced his second wife, Ruth McMaster. He married and divorced Mary Helen Brown in 1938; in 1939 they remarried and divorced again. He married his fourth wife, Mary-Louise Parker, in July 1939; they divorced in June 1941. He married his fifth wife, Betty Anderson, in 1942. They remained married until his death 33 years later. Wills fathered six children.

In 1940, Wills appeared in the motion picture *Take Me Back to Oklahoma*, for which he also wrote five songs. It was the first of a series of B-movies he made over the next several years, including *Go West, Young Lady* (November 1941), *Rhythm Round-Up* (1945), *Blazing the Western Trail* (1945), *Lawless Empire* (February 1946), *Frontier Frolic* (1946), *Echo Ranch* (1948), and *Corral Cuties* (1954).

Wills first recorded "San Antonio Rose" as an instrumental in 1938. Reissued in late 1940, it became a pop hit for him in January 1941, selling a million copies. He had also recorded a version with lyrics, titled "New San Antonio Rose"; his version of the song reached the pop charts in May 1941, but a cover record by Bing Crosby had peaked in the Top Ten in April and it also became a million-seller.

Wills disbanded in December 1942 and joined the army at the age of 37. He was discharged as unfit for service on July 27, 1943, and, with Tommy Duncan, went to Calif. in the fall of 1943 and reorganized The Texas Playboys. In the fall of 1944 he scored a double-sided chart hit with "We Might as Well Forget It" (music and lyrics by Johnny Bond)/"You're from Texas." "Smoke on the Water" (music and lyrics by Earl Nunn and Zeke Clements) topped the country charts for Wills in April 1945; he returned to #1 on the country charts with "Stars and Stripes on Iwo Jima" (music and lyrics by Wills and Cliff Johnson) in July and with "Silver Dew on the Blue Grass Tonight" (music and lyrics by Ed Burt) in December. "White Cross on Okinawa" was a #1 country hit in January 1946, followed by "New Spanish Two Step" (which also reached the pop charts) in May. Wills returned to the top of the country charts with "Sugar Moon" (music and lyrics by Wills and Cindy Walker) in June 1947.

Tommy Duncan was the featured vocalist on all of Wills's major hits from 1945 to 1947; in the fall of 1948 he left Wills and formed his own band. Wills was less successful on records thereafter, though he reached the country Top Ten with "Ida Red Likes the Boogie" and "Faded Love" (music and lyrics by Wills and his father, John Wills) in 1950. During the 1950s, Wills performed primarily in Tex. and Okla. and ran dance halls, notably the Bob Wills Ranch House in Dallas. He recorded for MGM (1947–54) and Decca (1955–57). Ray Price scored a #1 country hit with Wills's composition "My Shoes Keep Walking Back to You" (music and lyrics also by Lee Ross) in September 1957.

Wills signed to Liberty Records in 1959 and reunited with Tommy Duncan. Their "Heart to Heart Talk" (music and lyrics by Lee Ross) reached the country Top Ten in 1960; "The Image of Me," co-billed to Wills and Duncan, was Wills's final country singles chart entry in January 1961. Floyd Cramer reached the pop Top Ten with his instrumental revival of "San Antonio Rose" in July.

Wills suffered heart attacks in 1962 and 1964, after which he disbanded, though he continued to front bands and to record, notably reaching the country charts with the Kapp Records LPs *From the Heart of Texas* (1966), *King of Western Swing* (1967), and *Here's That Man Again* (1968). On May 31, 1969, he suffered a paralyzing stroke, but he was able to participate in the first day of recording for The Texas Playboys reunion album *For the Last Time*, supervised by Merle Haggard, on Dec. 3, 1973. Then he had another stroke, which left him in a coma until his death from pneumonia on May 13, 1975.

DISC.: *For the Last Time* (1973); *Historic Edition* (rec. 1935–48; rel. 1982); *The Tiffany Transcriptions, Vols. 1–10* (rec. late 1940s; rel. 1982–91); *Anthology 1935–1973* (1991); *Encore* (rec. 1960–1963; rel. 1994); *The Longhorn Recordings* (1964).

BIBL.: J. Latham, *The Life of B. W.: The King of Western Swing* (Odessa, Tex., 1974; 2nd ed., rev., 1987); A. Stricklin with J. McConal, *My Years with B. W.* (San Antonio, 1976); C. Townsend, *San Antonio Rose: The Life and Music of B. W.* (Urbana, Ill., 1976); R. Sheldon, *B. W.: Hubbin' It* (Nashville, 1995); R. Wills (his daughter), *The King of Western Swing: B. W. Remembered* (N.Y., 1998).—**WR**

Willson, (Robert) Meredith (Reiniger), American songwriter, conductor, and flutist; b. Mason City, Iowa, May 18, 1902; d. Santa Monica, Calif., June 15, 1984. Willson did not produce the work he is known for, the Broadway musical *The Music Man*, until he was

55 years old. Before that he had a varied career that included stints as a flutist and piccolo player, a composer of classical works and film scores, a musical director and performer on radio and television, a memoirist, a novelist, and a hit songwriter. Nevertheless, he is best remembered for his three musicals of the late 1950s and early 1960s, the others being *The Unsinkable Molly Brown* and *Here's Love*, and for being the composer and lyricist of such standards as "It's Beginning to Look a Lot Like Christmas" and "Till There Was You." Willson's work often evoked a sense of turn-of-the-century Americana, although his patriotic themes reflected not just nostalgia but also the exuberance and raffishness of a young country: his most memorable character, Professor Harold Hill of *The Music Man*, was a con man.

Willson's mother, Rosalie Reiniger Willson, was a piano teacher, and he took his first lessons from her; he also learned the flute and piccolo, which he played in the Mason City H.S. Band. After finishing high school in 1919, he moved to N.Y. and attended the Damrosch Inst. of Musical Art (since renamed Juilliard). He undertook private study with Georges Barrère (flute; 1920–29), Julius Gold (1921–23), Henry Hadley (1923–24), Bernard Wagenaar, and Mortimer Wilson. On Aug. 29, 1920, he was married for the first time; he and his wife Elizabeth divorced in 1947. In 1921, at the age of 19, he was hired as first flutist in John Philip Sousa's Band, a position he held until 1923, when he joined the Rialto Theatre Orch. led by Hugo Riesenfeld. In 1924 he moved to the N.Y. Philharmonic–Symphony Orch. under Arturo Toscanini and also played with the N.Y. Chamber Music Society. He had his first song in a motion picture in October 1928, when "My Cavalier" (music by Riesenfeld, lyrics by Willson) was used in *The Cavalier*.

In 1929, Willson moved to San Francisco and became musical director of the Northwest territory for the American Broadcasting Company (not the current ABC) and of local radio station KFRC. In 1932 he became musical director of the Western division of the National Broadcasting Company (NBC).

Willson's Symphony No. 1 in F Minor, titled *San Francisco*, was written to commemorate the 30th anniversary of the San Francisco earthquake. It was premiered by the San Francisco Symphony Orch. with the composer conducting on April 19, 1936.

In 1937, Willson moved to Los Angeles, expanding his duties with NBC to include conducting the music on various radio programs and gradually becoming an on-air personality. The play *The Little Foxes* (N.Y., Feb. 15, 1939) featured a song, "Never Feel Too Weary to Pray," written by Willson, and he was responsible for the score of the motion picture version, which was released in August 1941. He also composed and arranged the music for the Charlie Chaplin film *The Great Dictator*, released in October 1940. Meanwhile, he had written a second symphony, titled *The Missions of California*, which was premiered by the Los Angeles Symphony Orch. with Albert Coates conducting on April 21, 1940.

Willson wrote "You and I" as the theme song for one of his radio programs, *Maxwell House Coffee Time*; when it was recorded by Glenn Miller and His Orch. in 1941 it became his first Top Ten hit in September. (Bing Crosby's version also made the Top Ten.) His second came in December, when Tommy Dorsey and His Orch. with Frank Sinatra on vocals scored with "Two in Love."

Upon the entry of the U.S. into World War II, Willson joined the army and became musical director of the Armed Forces Radio Service, a position he held until he was mustered out in 1945. In 1946 he had his own radio series, *The Meredith Willson Show*, on NBC. He married actress and singer Ralina (Rini) Zarova on March 13, 1948. (She died of cancer Dec. 6, 1966, at age 54.) Having previously published a musical instruction book, he wrote a memoir of his childhood in Iowa, *And There I Stood with My Piccolo*, published in 1948. This led his friend, songwriter Frank Loesser, to suggest a musical based on his reminiscences, which he began to work on a few years later.

The Meredith Willson Show came to television for four weeks in the summer of 1949, although Willson continued to be occupied primarily with radio, appearing in 1950 on the series *The Big Show* with Tallulah Bankhead, for which he wrote the popular closing theme, "May the Good Lord Bless and Keep You." In December 1951 he became a panelist on the TV quiz show *The Name's the Same*, staying with the program for two seasons. That same month his seasonal standard, "It's Beginning to Look a Lot Like Christmas," became a hit for Perry Como. In 1952, Willson published a novel, *Who Did What to Fidalia?*

Willson's "I See the Moon" was introduced by The Mariners on the TV show *Arthur Godfrey and His Friends* and became a hit for them in the fall of 1953. In 1955, Willson published another memoir, *Eggs I Have Laid*. But much of his time in the mid-1950s was taken up writing the libretto, music, and lyrics for *The Music Man*, the story of a con man posing as a band instructor in the fictional town of River City, Iowa, in the summer of 1912. When the show opened on Broadway in 1957 it became one of the biggest hits of the decade, running 1,375 performances and winning the Tony Award for Outstanding Musical.

The impressive score, largely written in the musical styles of the period, such as marches ("Seventy-Six Trombones") and barbershop quartets ("Lida Rose")—and also featuring songs closely integrated into the story, notably the patter song "Ya Got Trouble"—was not conducive to producing outside hits. (The exception, "Till There Was You," which became a Top 40 hit for Anita Bryant a year and a half after the show opened and became a standard recorded even by The Beatles, was the only song Willson did not write specifically for the show; it was a revised version of a song he had written in 1950 called "Till I Met You.")

The cast album, released in early 1958, was a massive hit, reaching #1, staying in the charts for more than four years, selling a million copies, and winning the Grammy Award for Best Original Cast Album. Its success spawned several other recordings of the show's music, including one by Willson and his wife, *...And Then I Wrote the Music Man*, in 1960. (Willson also wrote a book about the creation of the show, *"But He Doesn't Know the Territory."*)

Willson's second musical, *The Unsinkable Molly Brown* (1960), also was set in the early part of the century in the U.S. While not as successful as *The Music Man*, it ran 532 performances; its cast album reached the Top Ten and stayed in the charts almost a year. (Nat "King" Cole had a singles chart entry with the song "If I Knew" from the show.)

The film version of *The Music Man*, released in August 1962, closely followed the stage version. The soundtrack album was a gold-selling Top Ten hit that stayed in the charts for over a year. Willson's final Broadway musical, *Here's Love* (1963), based on the 1947 film *Miracle on 34th Street*, ran 334 performances, and its cast album spent several months in the charts. The film version of *The Unsinkable Molly Brown* was released in July 1964 and its soundtrack album stayed in the charts more than six months.

Willson married for a third time, to Rosemary Sullivan, on Valentine's Day, 1968. Under the auspices of the San Francisco and Los Angeles Civic Light Opera, he wrote the operetta *1491*, "a romantic speculation" based on the life of Christopher Columbus. It was given a tryout in Los Angeles in September and October 1969 but never brought to Broadway. Willson then retired; he died of heart failure at age 82.

WORKS: MUSICALS: *The Music Man* (N.Y., Dec. 19, 1957); *The Unsinkable Molly Brown* (N.Y., Nov. 3, 1960); *Here's Love* (N.Y., Oct. 3, 1963). **FILMS:** *The Great Dictator* (1940); *The Little Foxes* (1941); *The Music Man* (1962); *The Unsinkable Molly Brown* (1964).

WRITINGS: *What Every Young Musician Should Know* (N.Y., 1938); *And There I Stood with My Piccolo* (N.Y., 1948); *Who Did What to Fidalia?* (N.Y., 1952); *Eggs I Have Laid* (N.Y., 1955); *"But He Doesn't Know the Territory"* (N.Y., 1959).—**WR**

Wilm, (Peter) Nicolai von, German pianist, conductor, and composer; b. Riga, March 4, 1834; d. Wiesbaden, Feb. 20, 1911. He studied with Plaidy, Becker, and Richter at the Leipzig Cons. In 1857–58 he was in Riga as a theater conductor, and in 1860 he proceeded to St. Petersburg, where he was an instructor at the Nikolaievsky Inst. until 1875; he subsequently lived in Dresden (1875–78) and then Wiesbaden. A highly prolific composer (more than 250 scores), he is best known through his chamber music. He wrote a String Sextet, String Quartet, Piano Trio, Cello Sonata, 2 violin sonatas, and Sonata for Violin and Harp; also numerous pieces for Piano, including *Kleine Suite, Herbstfrüchte, Im russischen Dorf, Stimmungen, Dorf und Waldidyllen, Musikalisches Dekameron*, etc., for Piano, 4-Hands, *Eine Nordlandfahrt, Reisebilder aus Schlesien, Musikalische Federzeichnungen, Kalendarium*, etc., variations and other pieces for 2 pianos, men's choruses, and songs.—**NS/LK/DM**

Wilms, Jan Willem (actually, **Johann Wilhelm**), German-born Dutch pianist, organist, flutist, teacher, and composer; b. Witzhelden, near Solingen, March 30, 1772; d. Amsterdam, July 19, 1847. He received his early music training from his father and elder brother. In 1791 he settled in Amsterdam as a pianist, flutist, and teacher, and later was organist of the United Baptist Church (1823–46). He composed 2 piano concertos, 2 flute concertos, 2 string quartets, 2 piano trios, 3 violin sonatas, 2 flute sonatas, a Clarinet Concerto, and 3 syms. He was the author of the Dutch national song "Wien Neerlands bloed door d'aderen vloeit" (1815).

BIBL.: E. Klusen, *J.W. W. und das Amsterdamer Musikleben (1772–1847)* (Buren, 1975).—**NS/LK/DM**

Wilson, Cassandra, American vocalist; b. Jackson, Miss., Dec. 5, 1955. She came to N.Y. in 1982, already a professional singer. Besides working with the already established Dave Holland and New Air, she collaborated with the musicians gathered around alto saxophonist Steve Coleman who were inventing a style they called M-Base. At the beginning of her recording career she was also identified with this style, a dense, funky sound, due to her appearances on several Coleman-led albums and her use of that pool of musicians on her first two albums. She started moving away from that sound on her third album, *Blue Skies*, a standards collection. She reverted to electric bands featuring original material plus a few standards reworked in eccentric ways. Though her career lost sales momentum, her reputation as a promising singer continued to grow, leading Blue Note to sign her. Pairing her with producer Craig Street provided the fresh start she needed, and her reworked style and focus—sparse instrumentation, laid-back vocals, and greater variety of cover material—helped her cross over to the more sophisticated segment of the pop audience. She is now one of the most popular and commercially successful young jazz singers on the scene, and her style and choice of material has become a much-copied template for other singers looking to expand beyond the standards audience.

DISC.: *Point of View* (1986); *Air Show No. 1* (1986); *World Expansion (By the M-Base Neophyte)* (1987); *Days Aweigh* (1987); *Sine Die* (1988); *Blue Skies* (1988); *Jump World* (1990); *She Who Weeps* (1991); *Live* (1991); *Dance to the Drums Again* (1992); *After the Beginning Again* (1992); *Blue Light 'Til Dawn* (1993); *New Moon Daughter* (1995); *Rendezvous* (1997); *Steve Turre* (1997); *Traveling Miles* (1999).—**SH**

Wilson, Charles (Mills), Canadian composer, conductor, and teacher; b. Toronto, May 8, 1931. He studied composition with Ridout at the Royal Cons. of Music of Toronto, and also with Foss (summer, 1950) and Chávez (summer, 1951) at the Berkshire Music Center in Tanglewood. Returning to Toronto, he received his B.Mus. (1952) and later was awarded his D.Mus. (1956). From 1954 to 1964 he was organist-choirmaster at Chalmers United Church in Guelph. He also was founder-conductor of the Guelph Light Opera and Oratorio Co. (1955–74) and conductor of the Bach-Elgar Choir of Hamilton (1962–74). In 1979 he became a teacher at the Univ. of Guelph. In his music, Wilson has adopted many of the prevailing stylistic elements of his era.

WORKS: DRAMATIC: *The Strolling Clerk from Paradise*, chamber opera (1952); *Ballet Score* (1969); *Phrases from Orpheus*, piece for Chorus and Dancers (1970; Guelph, May 10, 1971);

Heloise and Abelard, opera (1972; Toronto, Sept. 8, 1973); *The Selfish Giant,* children's opera (1972; Toronto, Dec. 20, 1973); *The Summoning of Everyman,* church opera (1972; Halifax, April 6, 1973); *Kamouraska,* opera (1975); *Psycho Red,* opera (1977); *Tim,* radio opera (1990). **ORCH.:** Sym. (1953); *Sonata da chiesa* for Oboe and Strings (1960); *Theme and Evolutions* (1966); Sinfonia for Double Orch. (1972; Toronto, March 3, 1973); *Symphonic Perspectives: Kingsmere* (Ottawa, Oct. 4, 1974); *Conductus* for Piano and Orch. (1979). **CHAMBER:** 4 string quartets (1950, 1968, 1975, 1983); String Trio (1963); *Concerto 5x4x3* for String Quintet or Woodwind Quartet or Brass Trio (1970). **VOCAL:** *On the Morning of Christ's Nativity,* cantata for Soprano, Tenor, Baritone, Chorus, and Orch. (1963); *The Angels of the Earth,* oratorio for Soprano, Baritone, Narrators, Chorus, and Orch. (1966; Guelph, June 19, 1967); *En Guise d'Orphée* for Baritone and String Orch. (1968); *Christo paremus canticam* for Chorus and Orch. (Hamilton, Dec. 2, 1973); *Image out of Season* for Chorus and Brass Quintet (1973); *Missa brevis* for Chorus and Brass (1975); *Song for St. Cecilia's Day* for Soprano, Tenor, Chorus, and Orch. (1976); *First Book of Madrigals* for Soprano and Instrumental Ensemble (1980); *Un Canadien errant* for Mezzo-soprano, Tenor, Chorus, and Instrumental Ensemble (1981); *Invocation* for 8 Solo Voices and Tape (1982); *2 Voices* for Mezzo-soprano, Clarinet, Cello, Piano, 2 Percussion, and Tape (1983); *The Revelation to St. John* for 3 Choruses, 3 Conductors, and Organ (1984); solo songs. **OTHER:** Tape pieces.—**NS/LK/DM**

Wilson, Ian, Irish composer; b. Belfast, Dec. 26, 1964. He studied composition at the Univ. of Ulster (1983–86), where he was awarded the first doctorate in composition from the new, 7-year-old institution. A member of Aosdána, Ireland's state-sponsored academy of creative artists, Wilson was a part-time instrumental teacher in Northern Ireland until 1998 when he became a full-time composer. His ear for engaging and exhilarating instrumental sonorities is particularly refreshing at the turn of the millennium. He has been especially inspired by pictorial art, most often by the works of Paul Klee.

WORKS: ORCH.: *Running, Thinking, Finding* (1989); *Rise* (1993; Ulster, April 22, 1994); *Rich Harbour,* organ concerto (1994–95; Dublin, June 21, 1996); *Between the Moon and the Deep Blue Sea* (1997); *Who's Afraid of Red, Yellow, and Blue?,* saxophone concerto (1998; Ulster, April 30, 1999); *Shining Forth,* concerto for Cello and Small Orch. (London, June 27, 1998); *Limena,* concerto for Piano and Strings (1998; Limerick, March 4, 1999); *What We Can See of the Sky Has Fallen* (1998–99; Belfast, April 24, 1999); 2 violin concertos: No. 1, *Messenger* (1998–99; Dublin, Jan. 12, 2000) and No. 2, *An Angel Serves a Small Breakfast,* after the Klee painting (1999). **CHAMBER:** *...and flowers fall...,* septet (1990); *Drive* for Soprano Saxophone and Piano (1992; also for Clarinet and Violin); 5 string quartets: No. 1, *Winter's Edge* (1992), No. 2, *The Capsizing Man and Other Stories* (1994), No. 3, *Towards the Far Country,* after Klee (1996), No. 4, *Oil and Temper* (2000), and No. 5 (2000); *Timelessly This* for Flute or Clarinet and String Trio (1992); *so softly* for Saxophone Quartet (1992); 3 piano trios: No. 1, *Mais quand elle sourit* (1993), No. 2, *The Seven Last Words* (1995), and No. 3, *Catalan Tales (after Miró)* (1996); *6 Days at Jericho* for Cello and Piano (1995); *Leaves and Navels* for Flute, Guitar, Viola, and Cello (1996–97); *Phosphorus,* string trio (1997); *Spilliaert's Beach* for Alto Flute and Piano (1999). **Piano:** *BIG* (1991); *A Haunted Heart* (1996). **VOCAL:** *Near the Western Necropolis* for Mezzo-soprano and Chamber Orch. (1998); *Limbo* for Chorus, after Seamus Heaney (1999); *Under the Lark Full Cloud* for Chorus, after Dylan Thomas (1999). **—LK/DM**

Wilson, Jackie, enormously successful and influential R&B singer of the late 1950s and early 1960s; b. Detroit, Mich., June 9, 1934; d. Mount Holly, N.J., Jan. 21, 1984. A Golden Gloves boxing champion in Detroit at the age of 16, Jackie Wilson was "discovered" by Johnny Otis at a talent show in 1951. He sang with The Thrillers, an R&B quartet, and recorded for Dizzy Gillespie's Dee Gee label, eventually replacing Clyde McPhatter in Billy Ward's Dominoes in 1953. The group's first release with Wilson, "You Can't Keep a Good Man Down," became a near-smash R&B hit and was soon followed by the R&B smash "Rags to Riches." Wilson was lead singer on The Dominoes first pop hit, "St. Therese of the Roses" in 1956, but opted for a solo career in late 1957, to be replaced by Eugene Mumford.

Signing with Brunswick Records, Jackie Wilson recorded in N.Y. and soon achieved a minor pop hit with "Reet Petite," co-written by Berry Gordy Jr., who later formed the immensely successful Motown organization. Gordy also co-wrote Wilson's major pop and R&B smash hits "To Be Loved," "That's Why" and "I'll Be Satisfied," and his top R&B and smash pop hit classic "Lonely Teardrops." Wilson also appeared in the 1959 film *Go, Johnny, Go,* singing "You'd Better Know It."

Performing engagements at major Los Angeles, Las Vegas and N.Y. nightclubs and recording a variety of material, including bland pop material and classical adaptations such as "Night," "Alone at Last" and "My Empty Arms," Jackie Wilson suffered through intrusive arrangements and critical neglect in the early 1960s. Nonetheless, he scored four two-sided crossover hits in 1960–61 with "Night"/"Doggin' Around," "(You Were Made for) All My Love"/"A Woman, a Lover, a Friend," "Alone at Last"/"Am I the Man," and "My Empty Arms"/The Tear of the Year." "Night" was a pop smash, while "Alone at Last" and "My Empty Arms" were near-smash pop hits. "Doggin' Around" and "A Woman, a Lover, a Friend" were top R&B hits. Later in 1961 Wilson achieved major pop and R&B hits with "Please Tell Me Why" and "I'm Comin' Back to You," followed by the moderate pop hits "Years from Now" and "The Greatest Hurt." He subsequently formed a songwriting partnership with Alonzo Tucker that yielded a top R&B and smash pop hit with "Baby Workout" in 1963. Later major R&B and moderate pop hits included "Shake a Hand" (with Linda Hopkins) and "Shake! Shake! Shake!" Although he continued to score hits over the next three years, Jackie Wilson didn't achieve another major pop and smash R&B hit until he began recording in Chicago with producer Carl Davis. Under Davis, Wilson staged a dramatic comeback with "Whispers (Gettin' Louder)"; the classic "(Your Love Keeps Lifting Me) Higher and Higher," a top R&B and smash pop hit; and "I Get the Sweetest Feeling." He recorded with Count Basie in 1968 and managed his last near-smash R&B and moderate pop hit with late 1970's "This Love Is Real" He was subsequently relegated to the oldies revival circuit, despite continued R&B hits into 1975. On the night of Sept. 29, 1975, while performing at the Latin Casino near Cherry Hill, N.J., Wilson had a massive heart attack that left him in a coma. He remained hospitalized until his eventual death on Jan. 21, 1984, at the age of 49. Jackie Wilson was inducted into the Rock and Roll Hall of Fame in 1987.

Disc.: **BILLY WARD AND THE DOMINOES:** *Billy Ward and The Dominoes* (1956); *21 Original Greatest Hits Featuring Clyde McPhatter and Jackie Wilson* (1960); *14 Hits (1951–1965)* (1977); *14 Original Greatest Hits* (1978); *21 Hits* (1977); *Sixty Minute Man: The Best of Billy Ward and The Dominoes; Meet Billy Ward and His Dominoes* (1993). **THE DOMINOES:** *Have Mercy Baby* (1985). **JACKIE WILSON AND THE DOMINOES:** *14 Hits* (1977). **JACKIE WILSON:** *He's So Fine* (1958); *Lonely Teardrops* (1959); *So Much* (1960); *Sings the Blues* (1960); *My Golden Favorites* (1960); *A Woman, a Lover, a Friend* (1960); *You Ain't Heard Nothin' Yet* (1961); *By Special Request* (1961); *Body and Soul* (1962); *Sings the World's Greatest Melodies* (1962); *At the Copa* (1962); *Baby Workout* (1963); *Merry Christmas* (1963); *My Golden Favorites, Vol. 2* (1964); *Somethin' Else* (1964); *Soul Time* (1965); *Spotlight on Jackie Wilson* (1965); *Soul Galore* (1966); *Whispers* (1967); *Higher and Higher* (1967); *I Get the Sweetest Feeling* (1968); *Greatest Hits* (1969); *Do Your Thing* (1969); *It's All a Part of Love* (1970); *You Got Me Walking* (1971); *This Love Is Real* (1973); *Beautiful Day* (1973); *Nowstalgia* (1974); *Nobody but You* (1977); *The Jackie Wilson Story* (1983); *The Jackie Wilson Story, Vol. 2* (1985); *The Soul Years* (1966); *Reet Petite* (1985); *Very Best* (1987); *Through the Years: A Collection of Rare Album Tracks and Single Sides* (1987); *Merry Christmas from Jackie Wilson* (1991); *Mr. Excitement* (1992); *Very Best* (1994). **JACKIE WILSON AND LINDA HOPKINS:** *Shake a Hand* (1963). **JACKIE WILSON AND COUNT BASIE:** *Manufacturers of Soul* (1968).—**BH**

Wilson, John, English lutenist, singer, and composer; b. Faversham, Kent, April 5, 1595; d. London, Feb. 22, 1674. He was musically gifted, and at the age of 19 wrote music for *The Maske of Flowers*. According to some indications, he participated as a singer in a production of Shakespeare's *Much Ado about Nothing* (as Jacke Wilson). In 1635 he was made one of the King's Musicians. He was in favor with Charles I, whom he followed to Oxford during the civil war in 1644, and was made a D.Mus. by Oxford Univ. on March 10, 1644; he was "Musick Professor" there from 1656 until 1661. Upon the Restoration he resumed his post at court, and on Oct. 22, 1662, became the successor of Henry Lawes as a Gentleman of the Chapel Royal. He publ. *Psalterium Carolinum: The Devotions of His Sacred Majestie* for 3 Voices and Basso Continuo (London, 1657) and *Cheerfull Ayres or Ballads...* for 3 Voices and Basso Continuo (Oxford, 1660) as well as numerous songs in contemporary collections.

Bibl.: H. Henderson, *The Vocal Music of J. W.* (diss., Univ. of N.C., 1962).—**NS/LK/DM**

Wilson, Nancy, American singer; b. Chillicothe, Ohio, Feb. 20, 1937. She developed musically at an early age, singing in choirs and dance bands as a teenager in Columbus, Ohio. In 1956 she joined Rusty Bryant's Carolyn Club Band and made her first recordings for Dot Records. Her next collaboration was with Cannonball Adderley in 1959. Still hooked on straight-ahead jazz, she recorded her first hit with Adderley, "Save Your Love for Me," in 1962. From there she picked up a more pop-oriented style and a new momentum, putting 33 albums on the charts between 1962 and 1977. Some of the hit songs from that period include "Peace of Mind," "Don't Come Running Back to Me," "Face It Girl, It's Over," and "Now I'm a Woman." Her "How Glad I Am" won a Grammy for Best R&B Song in 1964. In 1983 she won a song festival award in Tokyo and recorded five albums for Japanese labels over the next few years. During that time she also made one pop record in the U.S., *The Two of Us*, with Ramsey Lewis.

Disc.: *Nancy Wilson/Cannonball Adderley* (1961); *Yesterday's Love Songs, Today's Blues* (1963); *Welcome to My Love* (1967); *Lush Life* (1967); *But Beautiful* (1969); *The Two of Us* (1984); *Keep You Satisfied* (1986); *Forbidden Lover* (1987); *Nancy Now!* (1988); *Lady with a Song* (1990); *I Wish You Love* (1992); *Love, Nancy* (1994); *Spotlight on Nancy Wilson* (1995); *Ballads, Blues, and Big Bands: The Best of Nancy Wilson* (1996); *If I Had My Way* (1997); *Greatest Hits* (1999).—**NC**

Wilson, Olly (Woodrow), African American composer, conductor, and teacher; b. St. Louis, Sept. 7, 1937. He taught himself to play the piano and double bass, and gained valuable experience performing in both jazz and classical settings. He studied at Washington Univ. in St. Louis (B.M., 1959), the Univ. of Ill. (M.M., 1960), with Wykes, Kelley, and Bezanson at the Univ. of Iowa (Ph.D., 1964), and at the Ill. Studio for Experimental Music (1967). In 1971–72 he pursued research in indigenous music in West Africa. After teaching at Fla. A.&M. Univ. (1960–62) and the Oberlin (Ohio) Coll. Cons. of Music (1965–70), he was prof. of music at the Univ. of Calif. at Berkeley (from 1970). In 1977–78 he was a visiting artist at the American Academy in Rome. He conducted much contemporary music and contributed important articles on African and African American music to scholarly journals. In 1968 he won the Dartmouth Arts Council Prize for his electronic piece *Cetus*. In 1971 and 1977 he held Guggenheim fellowships. Wilson found inspiration in jazz and West African music to develop his own highly diverse and often complex style of composition. He has also used electronic elements to great effect.

Works: **DRAMATIC:** *Dance Music I* (1963) and *II* (1965), ballets; *The 18 Hands of Jerome Harris*, ballet (1971); incidental music. **ORCH.:** *Structure* (1960); *3 Movements* (1964); *Voices* (1970); *Akwan* for Piano, Electric Piano, and Orch. (1972); *Reflections* (1978); *Trilogy* (1979–80); *Lumina* (1981); Sinfonia (1984); *Houston Fanfare* (1986); *Expansions II* (1990) and *III* (1993); Viola Concerto (1994). **CHAMBER:** *Prelude and Line Study* for Wind Quintet (1959); Trio for Flute, Cello, and Piano (1959); String Quartet (1961); Violin Sonata (1961); *Dance Suite* for Winds (1962); *Soliloquy* for Double Bass (1962); Sextet for Flute, Clarinet, Bassoon, Horn, Trumpet, and Trombone (1963); *Piece for 4* for Flute, Trumpet, Double Bass, and Piano (1966); *Piano Piece* for Piano and Tape (1969); *Echoes* for Clarinet and Tape (1974–75); Trio for Violin, Cello, and Piano (1977); *A City Called Heaven* for Flute, Clarinet, Violin, Cello, Piano, and

Percussion (1989). **VOCAL:** *2 Dutch Poems* for Voice and Piano (1960); *Gloria* for Voice (1961); *Wry Fragments* for Tenor and Percussion (1961); *And Death Shall Have No Dominion* for Tenor and Percussion (1963); *Chanson Innocent* for Alto and 2 Bassoons (1965); *Biography* for Soprano and Ensemble (1966); *In Memoriam Martin Luther King Jr.* for Chorus and Tape (1968); *Spirit Song* for Soprano, Chorus, and Orch. (1973); *Sometimes* for Tenor and Tape (1976); *No More* for Tenor and Chamber Ensemble (1985); *I Shall Not Be Moved* for Soprano and Chamber Ensemble (1992–93). **ELECTRONIC:** *Cetus* (1967); *Black Martyrs* (1972). **—NS/LK/DM**

Wilson, Ransom, American flutist and conductor; b. Tuscaloosa, Ala., Oct. 25, 1951. He studied with Philip Dunigan at the N.C. School of the Arts in Winston-Salem, and also profited from advice given by Jean-Pierre Rampal. He pursued training in conducting from Roger Nierenberg in N.Y. (1980–82), James Dixon in Iowa City (1982), Otto-Werner Mueller in New Haven (1983–85), and Leonard Bernstein (1985–87). Wilson quickly established his reputation as a virtuoso flutist via appearances as a soloist with orchs., as a recitalist, and as a chamber music artist. In 1981 he founded and subsequently served as music director of the Solisti N.Y. Orch. From 1983 he also was artistic director of the OK Mozart International Festival in Bartlesville, Okla. He likewise was music director of the Tuscaloosa Sym. Orch. (1985–92), of Opera Omaha (1994–95), of the San Francisco Chamber Sym. (1994–96), and of the Idyllwild Arts Academy Orch. (from 1997). In 1992 he joined the faculty of the Yale Univ. School of Music as a flute teacher. He was an asst. conductor at the Metropolitan Opera in N.Y. in 1996. In 1997 he was a guest conductor of the Hallé Orch. in Manchester. He conducted *La Cenerentola* at the Teatro Victória Eugénia in San Sebastián in 1998. In addition to his performances of such masters as Mozart, Rossini, Beethoven, Tchaikovsky, Ravel, and Barber, Wilson has also championed the music of such contemporary composers as Kernis and Danielpour.**—NS/LK/DM**

Wilson, Richard (Edward), American composer, pianist, and teacher; b. Cleveland, May 15, 1941. Following lessons in piano, theory, and composition at the Cleveland Music School Settlement (1954–59), he pursued his studies with Moevs (composition) at Harvard Univ. (A.B., 1963), at the American Academy in Rome, and at Rutgers Univ. (M.A. in theory, 1966). He also studied piano with Shure in Aspen, Colo., and N.Y. (1960), and with Wührer in Munich (1963). In 1966 he joined the faculty of Vassar Coll., where he was made a prof. of music in 1976. He also served as chairman of its music dept. (1979–82; 1985–88; 1995–98). In 1992 he became composer-in-residence of the American Sym. Orch. in N.Y. He received annual ASCAP awards from 1970. In 1986 he received the Walter Hinrichsen Award of the American Academy and Inst. of Arts and Letters. In 1992–93 he held a Guggenheim fellowship. He received the Stoeger Prize of the Chamber Music Soc. of Lincoln Center in 1994. He has received commissions from the Chicago Chamber Musicians (String Quartet No. 4, 1997) and the Koussevitzky Foundation (Triple Concerto, 1999). In his output, Wilson has followed a freely atonal course with special attention paid to lyrical expressivity.

WORKS: DRAMATIC: Opera: *Æthelred the Unready* (1993–94). **ORCH.:** *Initiation* (1970); Concerto for Voice and Chamber Orch. (1979; Poughkeepsie, N.Y., Jan. 13, 1980); *11 Sumner Place* for Symphonic Band (1981; N.Y., June 23, 1982); Concerto for Bassoon and Chamber Orch. (1983); 2 syms.: No. 1 (Kingston, N.Y., Oct. 19, 1984) and No. 2 (1986; Annandale-on-Hudson, N.Y., Jan. 30, 1987); *Jubilation* for Wind Ensemble (Poughkeepsie, N.Y., June 7, 1987); *Silhouette* (London, Nov. 12, 1988); Suite for Small Orch. (Great Barrington, Mass., Sept. 10, 1988); *Articulations* (San Francisco, May 11, 1989); Piano Concerto (N.Y., May 5, 1991); *Agitations* (1994); *A Child's London* for Narrator and Orch. (Woodstock, N.Y., March 8, 1997); Triple Concerto for Horn, Bass Clarinet, Marimba, and Orch. (N.Y., March 17, 1999); *Intimations* for Piano and Orch. (Annandale-on-Hudson, N.Y., Feb. 11, 2000). **CHAMBER:** Trio for Oboe, Violin, and Piano (1964); *Fantasy and Variations* for Chamber Ensemble (1965; N.Y., April 27, 1967); *Concert Piece* for Violin and Piano (1967); 4 string quartets: No. 1 (1969), No. 2 (1977), No. 3 (1982), and No. 4 (1997; N.Y., Jan. 17, 1998); Quartet for 2 Flutes, String Bass, and Harpsichord (1969); *Music* for Cello (1971; N.Y., Jan. 24, 1972); *Music* for Flute (1972); Wind Quintet (1974); *Serenade: Variations on a Simple March* for Clarinet, Viola, and Brass (1978); *Deux pas de trois: Pavane and Tango* for Flute, Oboe, and Harpsichord (1979); *Profound Utterances: Music* for Bassoon (1980); *Figuration: Music* for Clarinet, Cello, and Piano (1980); *Short Notice* for Clarinet and Cello (1981); *Gnomics* for Flute, Oboe, and Clarinet (1981); *Character Studies* for Oboe and Piano (1982); *Dithyramb* for Oboe and Clarinet (1982); Suite for Winds (1983); *Line Drawings* for 2 Clarinets (1984); *Flutations* for Flute (1985); *Lord Chesterfield to His Son* for Cello (1987); *Music* for Viola (1988); *Contentions* for Chamber Ensemble (1988); Viola Sonata (1989); *Intonations*, 5 pieces for Horn (1989); *Affirmations* for Flute, Clarinet, Violin, Cello, and Piano (1990; N.Y., March 7, 1991); *Touchstone* for Flute (1991; rev. 1995); *Civilization and Its Discontents* for Tuba (1992); *3 Interludes* for Violin and Piano (1996; Poughkeepsie, N.Y., Nov. 23, 1997). **Piano:** *Eclogue* (Poughkeepsie, N.Y., Dec. 5, 1974); *Sour Flowers: 8 Piano Pieces in the Form of an Herbal* (Poughkeepsie, N.Y., Sept. 19, 1979); *A Child's London*, 6 pieces (1984); *Fixations* (1985; Poughkeepsie, N.Y., Jan. 28, 1986); *Intercalations* (N.Y., Nov. 9, 1986). **VOCAL:** *In Schrafft's* for Men's Chorus and Piano, 4-Hands (1966; also for Chorus, Clarinet, Harpsichord, and Marimba, 1979); *A Dissolve* for Women's Chorus (1968); *Can* for Chorus (1968); *Light in Spring Poplars* for Chorus (1968); *Soaking* for Chorus (1969); *Home from the Range* for Chorus (1970); *Elegy* for Chorus (1971); *Hunter's Moon* for Chorus (1972); *The Ballad of Longwood Glen* for Tenor and Harp (1975); *August 22* for Chorus, Piano, and Percussion (1976); *A Theory* for Soprano and Vibraphone (1980); *3 Painters* for High Voice and Piano (1984); *Tribulations*, 5 songs for Voice and Piano (1988); *Persuasions* for Soprano, Flute, Oboe, Bassoon, and Harpsichord (Washington, D.C., Nov. 30, 1990); *The 2nd Law* for Baritone and Piano (1991); *On the Street* for Baritone and Piano or Strings (1992); *Poor Warren* for Chorus and Piano (Poughkeepsie, N.Y., March 28, 1995); *Pamietam* for Mezzo-soprano and Orch. (Annandale-on-Hudson, N.Y., Oct. 27, 1995); *5 Love Songs on Poems of John Skelton* for High Voice and Piano (1995); *Transfigured Goat* for Soprano, Baritone, Clarinet, and Piano (Poughkeepsie, N.Y., Nov. 8, 1996).**—NS/LK/DM**

Wilson, Robert, notable American theater director, stage designer, and dramatist; b. Waco, Tex., Oct. 4,

1941. After training at the Univ. of Tex. (1959–65), he took his B.F.A. in architecture at the Pratt Inst. in N.Y. In 1969 he began his career as a dramatist. His collaboration with Philip Glass on *Einstein on the Beach* (Avignon Festival and the Metropolitan Opera, N.Y., 1976) brought him wide recognition, and he subsequently collaborated with Gavin Bryars on *Medea* (Lyons, 1984) and with Glass on portions of *The Civil Wars* (1984–87). His later work has been seen to best advantage in *Médée* by Charpentier (Lyons, 1984), *Salome* (Milan, 1987), *Alceste* (Chicago, 1990), *Die Zauberflöte* (Paris, 1991), *Madama Butterfly* (Stuttgart, 1993), and *Prometeo* by Nono (Brussels, 1997). He also created the pop opera trilogy, a "reinvention of H. G. Wells's *The Time Machine*," that includes *The Black Rider* (1993; music by Tom Waits), *Alice* (1995; music by Tom Waits and Kathleen Brennan), and *Time Rocker* (1996; music by Lou Reed). In 1997 he produced Gertrude Stein's *Saints and Singing* at the Hebbel Theater in Berlin, and in 1998 the Berliner Ensemble presented his production of Bertolt Brecht's *Oceanflight*. In 1998 he also mounted his first production, *Lohengrin*, with the Metropolitan Opera in N.Y. On July 7, 1999, his *The Days Before Death Destruction & Detroit III*, to a libretto after Umberto Eco's *The Island of the Day Before*, with music by Ryuichi Sakamoto (founder of the techno-pop group Yellow Magic Orchestra [YMO] and winner of an Academy Award for his film score for *The Last Emperor*), was given its first perf. in N.Y. Wilson has been engaged for the *Ring* cycle at the Bayreuth Festival in 2000. His provocative productions have elicited great interest and much controversy. He is an acknowledged master of mixed-media forms.

BIBL.: L. Shyer, *R. W. and His Collaborators* (N.Y., 1990). **—NS/LK/DM**

Wilson, Roland, distinguished English cornetto player, conductor, and music scholar; b. Leeds, June 26, 1951. He took up the trumpet at the age of 8, and later studied at the Royal Coll. of Music in London (1968–72) and pursued training in cornetto playing with Don Smithers at the Royal Cons. of Music at The Hague (1977–78). In 1976 he founded and became director of Musica Fiata, an ensemble devoted to the performance of music of the 16th and 17th centuries on period instruments. He conducted it at many of the major European music festivals. In 1992 he also founded and became music director of the early music vocal ensemble La Capella Ducale. As a guest conductor, he has appeared with most of the principal early music groups in Europe. He has pursued research in early performance practice and has ed. music from original sources. Wilson has won critical approbation for his historically informed, discerning, and vibrant performances and recordings of such masters as Gabrieli, Praetorius, Monteverdi, Schütz, Frescobaldi, and Schein.**—LK/DM**

Wilson, Steve, jazz soprano and alto saxophonist; b. Hampton, Va., Feb. 9, 1961. He began his formal training at age 12 and played in various R&B and funk bands through his teens. His interest in jazz developed during his last years of high school and continued to grow while attending the Va. Commonwealth Univ. in Richmond. He was lead altoist with the award-winning VCU Jazz Orch. In 1986 Wilson landed a chair in the band O.T.B (Out of the Blue), a sextet of promising young jazz players sponsored by Blue Note records. In the summer of 1987, he moved to N.Y. and continued performing and recording with O.T.B. until 1989. In 1988 drummer Ralph Peterson, another O.T.B. alumnus, asked him to join his quintet and then his "Fo'tet." He also toured the U.S. and Europe for one year with the Lionel Hampton Orch. (1989–90). Since the late 1980s, he has been busy touring and/or recording with a slew of jazz performers, both young and old; notable associations include two years with the American Jazz Orch. (1990–92), Rennee Rosnes (from 1990), and the Smithsonian Jazz Orch. (from 1991). In 1991 he became an adjunct faculty member in the jazz program at William Paterson Coll. He has led his own quintet through the 1990s. In 1998 he was performing regularly at Smalls in N.Y. with the Avishai Cohen group, where Chick Corea heard and hired him at the end of the year. In December 1998 he began touring and recording as part of Chick Corea and Origin.

DISC.: *New York Summit* (1991); *Blues for Marcus* (1993). **—LP**

Wilson, Todd, American organist, choral conductor, and teacher; b. Toledo, Nov. 3, 1954. He began his music studies in Toledo (1963–72), and then was a student of Wayne Fisher (organ) and John Quincy Bass (piano) at the Univ. of Cincinnati Coll.-Cons. of Music (B.M., 1976; M.M., 1978). He later received coaching in organ from Russell Saunders at the Eastman School of Music in Rochester, N.Y. (1990–92). In 1972 he made his recital debut in Toledo, and in 1982 he made his first appearance as a soloist with the Long Island Phil. in N.Y. As a recitalist, he toured extensively in North America. His engagements abroad took him to Notre Dame Cathedral in Paris and to Canterbury Cathedral in 1978, and in 1992 he was soloist with the Slovakian Radio Sym. Orch. in Vienna and in 1996 he appeared with the City of London Sinfonia at St. Alban's. From 1989 to 1993 he was head of the organ dept. at the Baldwin-Wallace Coll. Cons. of Music, and then was director of music and organist at the Presbyterian Church of the Covenant in Cleveland, chairman of the organ dept. of the Cleveland Inst. of Music, and director of the Univ. Circle Chorale and Chamber Choir of Cleveland. His repertoire ranges from the 17th century to the contemporary era. Among his notable recordings are the complete organ works of Maurice Duruflé and Frank Bridge.**—LK/DM**

Wilson-Johnson, David (Robert), English baritone; b. Northampton, Nov. 16, 1950. He studied at the British Inst. in Florence, at St. Catharine's Coll., Cambridge (B.A., 1973), and at the Royal Academy of Music in London (1973–76). In 1976 he made his operatic debut in the premiere of *We Come to the River* at London's Covent Garden, and then appeared as the Speaker in *Die Zauberflöte* at the Welsh National Opera in Cardiff. He made his recital debut at London's Wigmore Hall in 1977. In 1980 he created the role of

Arthur in *The Lighthouse* in Edinburgh, and also appeared with the Glyndebourne Touring Opera. He first sang at the London Promenade Concerts in 1981. In 1988 he created the title role in the British concert premiere of Messiaen's *St. François d'Assise* in London. Following debuts at the Salzburg Festival in Bach's *St. John Passion* and at the Paris Opéra in *Die Meistersinger von Nürnberg* in 1989, he made his U.S. debut with the Cleveland Orch. in 1990. He appeared for the first time at the English National Opera in London in 1991 in *Billy Budd*, and then made his Netherlands Opera debut in Amsterdam in 1993 in Birtwistle's *Punch and Judy*. He returned to the Netherlands Opera in 1995 to sing in Schoenberg's *Die Glückliche Hand* and *Von Heute auf Morgen*. In 1997 he sang in Pfitzner's *Palestrina* at Covent Garden. His expansive concert repertoire includes works by Purcell, Handel, Bach, Haydn, Mozart, Schubert, and Berlioz, as well as much contemporary music. **—NS/LK/DM**

Wilson Phillips, the offspring of two Calif. musical dynasties made second-generation harmony; **Membership:** Chynna Phillips, voc. (b. Los Angeles, Feb. 12, 1968); Carnie Wilson, voc. (b. Los Angeles, April 29, 1968); Wendy Wilson, voc. (b. Los Angeles, Oct. 16, 1969).

If The Beach Boys and the Mamas and the Papas were the preeminent purveyors of Calif. vocal harmony in the 1960s, the daughters of Brian Wilson and John and Michelle Phillips developed the sound into one that worked in the 1990s, at least for a little while. Being well related, they attracted attention just by working together, and it wasn't long before songwriters like Glenn Ballard and producer Richard Perry came aboard. With bright close harmonies and videocentric good looks (although the camera tended to shy away from the more heavy-set Carnie), they were primed to become stars. The group became an early signing by SBK Records, and generated one of the label's chart topping hits, "Hold On." This was followed by two other #1s "Release Me," and "You're in Love." A fourth single from their eponymous debut, "Impulsive," rose to #4. The album hit #2 and went quintuple platinum.

Where the trio's debut was full of bright bonhomie, the follow-up used the signature harmonies to illuminate much darker topics, like growing up with fathers who were notorious for their problems. The album debuted at #4 and went platinum out of the box, but radio couldn't seem to find anything to play from it. The planned tour was scrapped and the group didn't so much break up as dissipate.

Chynna Phillips recorded a solo album, *Naked and Scared*, and appeared on Broadway and on MTV. The Wilson sisters made a Christmas album in 1993 and in 1997 recorded with their father as The Wilsons.

Disc.: *Wilson Phillips* (1990); *Shadows & Light* (1992).**—BH**

Wimberger, Gerhard, Austrian composer, conductor, and pedagogue; b. Vienna, Aug. 30, 1923. He was educated at the Salzburg Mozarteum (1940–41; 1945–47), where he received training in composition from Bresgen and J. N. David and in conducting from Krauss and Paumgartner. From 1948 to 1951 he conducted at the Salzburg Landestheater. In 1953 he joined the faculty of the Salzburg Mozarteum, where he taught conducting until 1968 and composition from 1968 until his retirement in 1991. In 1990 he served as president of the AKM (Staatlich genehmigte Gesellschaft der Autoren, Komponisten, und Musikverleger) of Austria. In 1967 he was awarded the Austrian State Prize for composition. He won the Würdigungspreis for music in 1977, the same year that he was made a corresponding member of the Akademie der Schönen Künste in Munich. In his works, Wimberger makes use of various styles and techniques, including jazz and other popular genres. His dramatic works reveal a penchant for the use of wit and irony.

Works: Dramatic: *König für einem Tag*, ballet (1951); *Schaubudengeschichte*, opera (1952–53; Mannheim, Nov. 25, 1954); *Der Handschuh*, chamber ballet (1955); *La Battaglia oder Der rote Federbusch*, comic opera (1959–60; Schwetzingen, May 12, 1960); *Hero und Leander*, dance drama (1962–63); *Dame Kobold*, musical comedy (1963–64; Frankfurt am Main, Sept. 24, 1964); *Das Opfer Helena*, chamber musical (1967); *Lebensregeln*, catechism with music (1970–72; Munich, Aug. 27, 1972); *Paradou*, opera (1985); *Fürst von Salzburg—Wolf Dietrich*, scenic chronicle (Salzburg, June 11, 1987); other works for the theater, radio, and television. **Orch.:** *Musica brevis* (1950); Chamber Concerto for 4 Winds, Percussion, and Strings (1952); *Divertimento* for Strings (1954); 2 piano concertos: No. 1 for Piano and Chamber Orch. (1955) and No. 2 (1980–81; Munich, June 4, 1984); *Augustin- Variationen* (1956); *Figuren und Phantasien* (1956); *Partita giocosa* for Small Orch. (1960); *Étude dramatique* (1961); *Risonanze* for 3 Orch. Groups (1965–66; Berlin, Jan. 31, 1968); *Chronique* (1968–69); *Multiplay* for 23 Players (1972–73; Salzburg, April 9, 1974); *Motus* (1976; Wuppertal, May 5, 1978); *Programm* (1977–78; Bonn, May 10, 1978); *Ausstrahlungen W.A. Mozart'scher Themen* (1978; Munich, Nov. 25, 1979); Concertino (1981; Lugano, March 25, 1982); *Nachtmusik Trauermusik Finalmusik* (1988); *Vagabondage* for Big Band (1988; Salzburg, Oct. 19, 1989); Synthesizer Concerto (1989); *Tanzkonzert* for Chamber Orch. (1992; Vienna, Feb. 11, 1993); *Ahnungen* (1994). **Chamber:** Trio for Flute, Violin, and Piano (1951); *4 Stücke* for Flute and Piano (1952); *Stories* for Winds and Percussion (1962); *Short Stories* for 11 Winds (1974–75; Frankfurt am Main, Feb. 6, 1977); *Plays* for 12 Cellos, Winds, and Percussion (1975; Salzburg, Aug. 27, 1976); *Concerto a dodici (Viaggi)* for 12 Instruments (1977; Vienna, Feb. 20, 1978); String Quartet (1978; Salzburg, Aug. 23, 1980); *Rufe* for 12 Brass Instruments (1979); *Phantasie* for 6 Players (1982; Salzburg, Aug. 4, 1983); 3 synthesizer sonatas (1990); Quintet for Flute, Oboe, Clarinet, Bassoon, and Horn (1990); *Szenerie* for Violin and Piano (1993; Hannover, Dec. 9, 1994); *Burletta* for Violin and Piano (1993). **Keyboard: Piano:** Sonata for 2 Pianos (1950); *5 Studien* (1952); *Konturen* (1977); *Disegni* (1991; Vienna, April 29, 1992). **Organ:** *Signum* (1969; Salzburg, Jan. 10, 1970). **Vocal:** *Kantate vom Sport* (1952); *Drei lyrische Chanons nach Gedichten von Jacques Prévert* for Voice and Chamber Orch. (1957); *Heiratspostkantate* for Chorus, Harpsichord, and Double Bass (1957); *4 Sätze nach deutschen Volksliedern* for Soprano, Chorus, and Jazz Combo (1966); *Ars amatoria*, cantata for Soprano, Baritone, Chorus, Combo, and Chamber Orch. (1967); *4 Songs* for Voice and 16 Instruments (1969; Gelsenkirchen, Feb. 26, 1975); *Singsang* for Voice and Beat Combo (1970); *Memento Vivere* for Mezzo-soprano, Baritone, 3 Speakers, Chorus, Orch., and Tape (1973–74; Salzburg, Aug. 7, 1975); *Mein Leben mein Tod* for Baritone, Instruments, and Tape (1976; Salzburg, March 30, 1977); *Sonetti in vita e in morte di Madonna Laura* for Chorus (1979; Vienna, May 10, 1983); *Sechs Liebeslieder* for Baritone and Harpsichord (1980); *Wir hören zu atmen nicht auf*, song cycle for Woman's Voice and Piano (1988); *Tagebuch 1942—Jochen Klepper* for Baritone, Chorus, and Orch. (1990–91); *Die Eitelkeit im Leben des Managers* for Soprano, Mezzo-soprano, and Orch. (Gutersloh, July 1, 1991); *Im Namen der Liebe*, song cycle for Man's Voice and Piano (Salzburg, Nov. 16, 1992). **ELECTRONIC:** *Versuch I: Klänge* (1975) and *II: Natur Musik* (1975).

BIBL.: H. Goertz, *G. W.* (Vienna, 1991).—**NS/LK/DM**

Winant, William, American percussionist; b. N.Y., Feb. 11, 1953. His mother was the well-known casting director Ethel Winant; his father, H.M. Wynant, was an actor. He was educated at York Univ. in Toronto (B.F.A., 1977) and Mills Coll. in Oakland, Calif. (M.F.A., 1982). He toured with Steve Reich and Musicians (1973) and the Kronos Quartet (1984). In 1983 he became a visiting lecturer at the Univ. of Calif. at Santa Cruz, and in 1984 joined the percussion faculty at the Univ. of Calif. at Berkeley; also was principal percussionist of the Cabrillo Music Festival (1984–93) and of the San Francisco Contemporary Music Players (from 1988). A leading avant-garde percussionist, Winant has given first performances of works by such composers as John Cage, Frederic Rzewski, Daniel Lentz, John Zorn, Somei Satoh, and Morton Feldman. He appeared as a soloist with the Los Angeles Phil. and Cabrillo Festival Orch., and at the Ravinia Music Festival. In 1984 he formed (with David Abel, violin, and Julie Steinberg, piano) the Abel-Steinberg-Winant Trio, with which he toured widely and recorded; he also performed with Room (with Larry Ochs and Chris Brown) and with the live electroacoustic ensemble Challenge (with Anthony Braxton and David Rosenboom). From 1993 he became active with the rock bands Oingo Boingo and Mr. Bungle.—**NS/LK/DM**

Winbeck, Heinz, German composer and teacher; b. Piflas, near Landshut, Feb. 11, 1946. He received his training in Munich, where he took courses with Magda Rusy (piano) and Fritz Rieger (conducting) at the Richard Strauss Cons. (1964–67), and with Genzmer and Bialas (composition) and Koetsier (conducting) at the Hochschule für Musik (1967–73). From 1974 to 1978 he was active as a conductor and composer in Ingolstadt and Wunsiedel. After teaching at the Munich Hochschule für Musik (1980–88), he was prof. of composition at the Würzburg Hochschule für Musik (from 1988). In 1985 he received the music prize of the Akademie der Schönen Künste in Berlin. In 1988 he was composer-in-residence at the Cabrillo (Calif.) Music Festival. Winbeck's compositions are personal reflections in a modern, expansive style.

WORKS: ORCH.: *Sonosoillent* for Cello and Strings (1971); *Entgegengesang* (1973; Stuttgart, June 16, 1974); *Lenau-Fantasien* for Cello and Chamber Orch. (1979; Munich, Oct. 7, 1980); *Denk ich an Haydn*, 3 fragments (Remscheid, March 31, 1982); 4 syms.: No. 1, *Tu Solus* (1983; Donaueschingen, Oct. 19, 1984; rev. version, Munich, April 19, 1985), No. 2 (1986–87; Saarbrücken, May 31, 1987), No. 3, *Grodek*, for Alto, Speaker, and Orch. (1987–88; Munich, Nov. 25, 1988), and No. 4, *De Profundis*, for Speaker, Alto, Baritone, Chorus, Orch., Electronics, and Tape (1991–93; Bonn, Sept. 13, 1993). **CHAMBER:** *Musik* for Wind Quintet (1971); *Espaces* for 4 Percussionists, Piano, and Flute (1971–72); *Nocturne I* for Chamber Ensemble (1972); *Poco a poco...* for Piano and String Trio (Hitzacker, July 21, 1974); 3 string quartets: No. 1 (1979), No. 2, *Tempi notturni* (1979; Hitzacker, July 27, 1980), and No. 3, *Jagdquartett* (1983–84; Hamburg, Oct. 12, 1984); *Blick in den Strom* for String Quintet (1981; N.Y., Jan. 26, 1993). **VOCAL:** *In Memoriam Paul Celan* for Soprano, Flute, Piano, and Percussion (1970); *Sie Tanzt* for Baritone and Chamber Ensemble (1971); *Nocturne II, Nacht mein Augentrost*, for Chorus, 5 Flutes, 2 Guitars, Bandolon, Organ, and 5 Percussionists (1973); *Chansons a temps* for Women's Voices and 13 Instruments (1976).—**NS/LK/DM**

Winbergh, Gösta, Swedish tenor; b. Stockholm, Dec. 30, 1943. He studied in Stockholm with Erik Saedén at the Musikhögskolan and pursued training at the Royal Opera School. In 1971 he made his operatic debut as Rodolfo in Göteborg; after singing with the Royal Opera in Stockholm (1973–80), he was a member of the Zürich Opera (from 1981). In 1982 he sang for the first time at London's Covent Garden as Titus. He made his debut at the Metropolitan Opera in N.Y. on Nov. 22, 1983, as Don Ottavio. In 1985 he sang at Milan's La Scala for the first time as Tamino. In 1988 he was engaged as Des Grieux in Houston. He made his first appearance at London's Covent Garden in 1993 as Walther von Stolzing, and returned there in 1997 as Lohengrin. He portrayed Parsifal at the Deutsche Oper in Berlin in 1998. As a concert artist, Winbergh sang widely in Europe and abroad. His other roles include Count Almaviva, Ferrando, Mithridates, Nemorino, Lensky, Massenet's Des Grieux, Alfredo, Faust, and Lohengrin. —**NS/LK/DM**

Wincenc, Carol, talented American flutist and teacher; b. Buffalo, June 29, 1949. She studied in Italy with Severino Gazzelloni, taking courses at the Accademia Musicale Chigiana in Siena (1966–67) and at the Accademia di Santa Cecilia in Rome (1967–68); she was a pupil of Robert Willoughby at the Oberlin (Ohio) Coll. Cons. of Music (1967–69), of Harold Bennett at the Manhattan School of Music in N.Y. (B.Mus., 1971), and of Arthur Lora at the Juilliard School in N.Y. (M.M., 1972). She was first flutist in the National Orchestral Assn. in N.Y. (1970–71), the Aspen (Colo.) Festival Chamber Orch. (1970–72), and the St. Paul (Minn.) Chamber Orch. (1972–77). After winning the Concert Artist's Guild Award, she made her recital debut at N.Y.'s Carnegie Recital Hall in 1972. She won first prize at the Naumburg Competition in 1978. In subsequent years, she appeared as a soloist with major world orchs., as a recitalist and as a chamber music player. She was founder-artistic director of the International Flute Festival in St. Paul, Minn. (1985–87). She taught at the Manhattan School of Music (1980–86), the Ind. Univ. School of Music in Bloomington (1986–88), and the Juilliard School (from 1988). She won particular distinction for her promotion of contemporary music; commissioned and premiered various works for flute, including pieces by Lukas Foss, Joan Tower, Giya Kancheli, and Henryk Gorecki.—**NS/LK/DM**

Winchester, Lem(uel Davis), jazz vibraphonist; b. Philadelphia, March 19, 1928; d. Indianapolis, Jan. 13, 1961. His grandfather was a drummer who accompanied vocalist/comedian Bert Williams and other artists in the teens and 1920s. His parents moved to Wilmington, Del., where he studied piccolo, then tenor and baritone saxophones, and later, after having learned to play the piano with two fingers (like Lionel Hampton), took up vibraphone in 1947. From 1950 he worked as a Wilmington police officer but continued performing regularly and appeared at the Newport festival in 1958. In 1960 he quit the police force to play music full-time and soon recorded with Johnny Hammond Smith and Oliver Nelson. He died playing Russian roulette.

DISC.: *Tribute to Clifford Brown* (1958); *Winchester Special* (1959); *Another Opus* (1960); *Lem's Beat* (1960); *With Feeling* (1960).—**LP**

Windgassen, Wolfgang (Fritz Hermann), distinguished German tenor; b. Annemasse, Haute Savoie, June 26, 1914; d. Stuttgart, Sept. 8, 1974. He received his early vocal training from his father, Fritz Windgassen (b. Hamburg, Feb. 9, 1883; d. Murnau, April 17, 1963), who was a leading tenor at the Stuttgart Opera, then continued his studies at the Stuttgart Cons. with Maria Ranzow and Alfons Fischer. He made his operatic debut in Pforzheim in 1941 as Alvaro in *La forza del destino*; after military service in the German army, he joined the Stuttgart Opera in 1945, remaining on its roster until 1972. From 1951 to 1970 he appeared at the Bayreuth Festivals, where he was a leading Heldentenor. He made his Metropolitan Opera debut in N.Y. on Jan. 22, 1957, as Siegmund, but sang there only that season. He sang regularly at Convent Garden in London from 1955 to 1966. He was especially successful in Wagnerian roles, as Tannhäuser, Tristan, Parsifal, Siegfried, and Lohengrin; he also appeared as Radamès and Don José.

BIBL.: B. Wessling, *W. W.* (Bremen, 1967).—**NS/LK/DM**

Winham, Godfrey, English-American composer and computer specialist; b. London, Dec. 11, 1934; d. Princeton, N.J., April 26, 1975. He studied composition and piano at the Royal Academy of Music in London. In 1954 went to the U.S., where he took courses at Princeton Univ. (A.B., 1956; M.F.A., 1958); received his Ph.D. degree there with the diss. *Composition with Arrays* (1965); then joined the staff as a lecturer on electronic music and computer composition. In 1969 he worked on the computerized synthesis of music and speech. Apart from his programmed compositions on a computer, he wrote 2 string quartets, *The Habit of Perfection* for Voice and String Quartet, and several piano pieces. He married **Bethany Beardslee** in 1956.

BIBL.: L. Basius, *The Music Theory of G. W.* (Princeton, 1997).—**NS/LK/DM**

Winkelmann, Hermann, notable German tenor; b. Braunschweig, March 8, 1849; d. Vienna, Jan. 18, 1912. He started out as a piano maker, but became interested in singing. He studied voice in Paris and with Koch in Hannover, making his operatic debut in *Il Trovatore* in Sondershausen (1875), and then sang in Altenburg, Darmstadt, and Leipzig. In 1878 he joined the Hamburg Opera, and appeared with the company during its visit to London in 1882 at Drury Lane; he worked in Wagnerian roles under Richter's direction. His success induced Richter to recommend him to Wagner, who chose him to create the role of Parsifal at Bayreuth (July 26, 1882). From 1883 to 1906, when he retired on a pension, he was one of the brightest stars of the Vienna Court Opera, where one of his most brilliant achievements was the performance of the role of Tristan (with Materna as Isolde) in the Vienna premiere (Oct. 4, 1883). In 1884 he sang in the U.S. at the Wagner festivals given by Theodore Thomas in N.Y., Boston, Philadelphia, Cincinnati, and Chicago.—**NS/LK/DM**

Winkler, Peter (Kenton), American composer, teacher, pianist, and writer on music; b. Los Angeles, Jan. 26, 1943. He was a student of Shifrin, Lewin, and Imbrie at the Univ. of Calif. at Berkeley (B.A., 1964) and of Kim, Babbitt, and Cone at Princeton Univ. (M.F.A., 1967). He taught at the State Univ. of N.Y. at Stony Brook (from 1971) and was ed. of the *Journal of Popular Music Studies* (1992–95). He was a founding member of the U.S. branch of the International Assn. for the Study of Popular Music, serving as its chair in 1990–91. In 1997 he became pianist for Play it By Ear, the N.Y. improvisational opera company. In 1978 he held a MacDowell Colony fellowship.

WORKS: DRAMATIC: *Tingle-Tangle: A Wedekind Cabaret* (N.Y., July 1994; in collaboration with W. Bolcom and A. Black); *Out!*, musical (1997); other theater pieces; incidental music for plays, radio, and television. **ORCH.:** Sym. (1971–78); *Serenade* for Strings (1998). **CHAMBER:** String Quartet (1965–67); *Clarinet Bouquet: 4 Concert Rags* for Clarinet, Piano, and Bass (1976–80); *Recitativo e Terzetto* for Oboe, Clarinet, and Bassoon (1980); *No Condition is Permanent* for Flute, Clarinet, Violin, Cello, Piano, and Percussion (1980–89); *Solitaire* for Clarinet (1989); *Gospel Hymn* for Violin and Piano (1990); *Waterborne* for Violin and Tape (1991); *Saboreando el Gusto Cubano* for Violin, Piano, and Percussion (Havana, Oct. 6, 1994); *9 Waltzes* for Violin, Cello, and Piano (1997); *Returning to the Root* for Horn and Piano (2000). **VOCAL:** *Praise of Silence* for Soprano, Chorus, Renaissance Ensemble, and Tape (1969).—**NS/LK/DM**

Winograd, Arthur, American cellist and conductor; b. N.Y., April 22, 1920. He studied at the New England Cons. of Music in Boston (1937–40) and at the Curtis Inst. of Music in Philadelphia (1940–41). He played the cello in the Boston Sym. Orch. (1940–41) and in the NBC Sym. Orch. in N.Y. (1942–43), then was a member of the Juilliard String Quartet and the faculty of the Juilliard School of Music in N.Y. (1946–55). He was active as a conductor for MGM Records (1954–58) and Audio Fidelity Records (1958–60), then as music director of the Birmingham (Ala.) Sym. Orch. (1960–64) and the Hartford (Conn.) Sym. Orch. (1964–85).—**NS/LK/DM**

Winston, George, the first major "new age" artist; b. Mich., 1949. In what he refers to as "folk piano," the impressionistic, airy melodies of his second album of solo piano *Autumn* helped create the musical parameters of "new age" music and made George Winston the genre's first platinum artist.

Born in Mich., Winston spent most of his formative years in Mont. He became very fond of instrumental music like Booker T. and the MGs and The Ventures, but didn't start playing himself until his late teens. While he started on the electronic organ and electric piano, he started listening to New Orleans stride and latter-day R&B artists ranging from Fats Waller to Professor Longhair. This informed his first recording, *Blues and Ballads*, recorded for Takoma, a label better known for guitarists like John Fahey, who mined a similar musical vein.

Although the album was received decently, Winston didn't record again for nearly eight years. By this time, the bluesy edge had muted into a haunting impressionistic sound, given further depth by the theme of the record: autumn in Mont. He called the record *Autumn*. He signed to Windham Hill Records, a company known for its mellow acoustic records; Windham Hill sold as many copies in stores that specialized in sandalwood incense and wind chimes as it did in more conventional record stores. *Autumn* became a phenomenal success, going platinum. Over the course of the next two years he expanded on the theme with *Winter into Spring* and his holiday album *December*, which also went platinum.

Again, he virtually dropped out of sight, recording only the musical portion of a children's record, over which Meryl Streep read *The Velveteen Rabbit*. He didn't re-appear on the record racks for another nine years, at which point he finished his seasons cycle with the album *Summer*, which went gold.

Changing the focus a bit, Winston started another, less constrained cycle of his musical impression of places. This commenced with the Grammy-winning gold album *Forest*. He ventured into soundtracks with a couple of animated Peanuts cartoons and the music to the film *Sadako and the Thousand Paper Cranes*. This, in turn, revealed another of Winston's burgeoning interests, as it featured him not on the piano but on the Hawaiian slack key guitar. He created Dancing Cat, his own imprint via his long-time record company Windham Hill. Through this label, he started to release albums by the masters of the slack key guitar.

Winston's next album paid tribute to the creator of the music for the early Peanuts animations and one of his major influences, Vince Guaraldi. Perhaps his most coherently lyrical work, as it deals in songs rather than impressions, the album had the impact of seeing an early Picasso portrait—he didn't have to paint both eyes on one side of the face, but he wanted to.

In 1988 Winston signed a long-term agreement with Windham Hill that allowed him to record works for solo guitar and harmonica, albums geared to children, and more Dancing Cat records, as well as his piano solos. His first album under the deal brought him back to his "places" cycle, an impressionistic look at the *Plains*. However, he intimated that his next album would be a disk of dance music. Winston remains one of music's more unpredictable artists.

Disc.: *Ballads & Blues: 1972* (1972); *Autumn* (1980); *Winter into Spring* (1982); *December* (1982); *Summer* (1991); *Forest* (1994); *Sadako and the Thousand Paper Cranes* (1995); *Linus & Lucy: The Music of Vince Guaraldi* (1996); *Plains* (1999).—**BH**

Winter, Johnny and Edgar, blues guitarists/keyboardists, saxophonists. **Membership:** Johnny Winter, gtr., voc. (b. Leland, Miss., Feb. 23, 1944); Edgar Winter, kybd., sax., voc. (b. Beaumont, Tex., Dec. 28, 1946).

Offered a lucrative contract by Columbia Records in 1969, blues guitarist Johnny Winter was initially hailed as rock music's next superstar, yet he failed to live up to his record company's publicity. Nonetheless, he recorded several best-selling albums with producer-guitarist Rick Derringer, including 1973's *Still Alive and Well*. Johnny's keyboardist-saxophonist brother Edgar Winter fared better commercially, first with White Trash, then later with the Edgar Winter Group. That group included guitarists Ronnie Montrose and Rick Derringer for their best-selling *They Only Come Out at Night* album and top hit single "Frankenstein." In the late 1970s Johnny Winter brought blues legend Muddy Waters a modicum of recognition by producing his albums for Blue Sky Records. However, neither Johnny nor Edgar Winter were able to reestablish their 1970s popularity in the 1980s or 1990s.

Johnny and Edgar Winter, born albinos, grew up in Beaumont, Tex., where Johnny took up clarinet at age 6, later graduating to ukelele then guitar by age 11. Edgar learned keyboards and saxophone, and the brothers formed Johnny and the Jammers around 1959. The brothers toured the Southern club circuit in a group called Black Plague in the early 1960s. Johnny briefly traveled to Chicago in 1962, subsequently manning Edgar's band from 1964 to 1966. Johnny ended up in Houston and began backing local bluesmen and recording for regional labels. In April 1968 Johnny formed Winter with bassist Tommy Shannon and drummer John "Red" Turner for various Tex. engagements, and the group was briefly praised in a *Rolling Stone* article about the Tex. music scene in its Dec. 2, 1968, issue, which led to a flurry of interest in the artist.

Johnny Winter was sought out by N.Y. entrepreneur Steve Paul, who booked Winter into his N.Y. club, The Scene. Graduating to the Fillmore East, Winter was signed to Columbia Records for hundreds of thousands of dollars in 1969, an unprecedented amount for an unproved artist. Accompanied by a massive publicity campaign, Winter's debut Columbia album sold quite well without yielding a hit single. He recorded *Second Winter* in Nashville with brother Edgar, who signed with Epic Records and recorded his debut, *Entrance*, virtually by himself. In 1970 Johnny Winter formed Johnny Winter and with former McCoys Rick and Randy Zehringer, but their debut album sold poorly, despite the inclusion of the original version of "Rock and Roll Hoochie Koo," written by Rick Zehringer, now using the last name Derringer. The live follow-up became the best-selling album of Johnny Winter's career, but he soon went into semi-retirement, suffering from exhaustion, depression, and heroin addiction.

By 1971 Edgar Winter had formed White Trash with guitarist Floyd Radford and vocalist Jerry LaCroix, scoring a minor hit with "Keep Playin' That Rock 'n' Roll." Rick Derringer supplanted Radford for the best-selling live set *Roadwork*, which featured Derringer's "Still Alive and Well" and a new version of "Rock and Roll Hoochie Koo." Winter subsequently formed the Edgar Winter Band with guitarist Ronnie Montrose and multi-instrumentalist Dan Hartman. With Derringer producing, *They Only Come Out at Night* became the best-selling album of Edgar's career, yielding a top hit with the instrumental "Frankenstein" and a major hit with "Free Ride." With Derringer replacing Montrose, *Shock Treatment* produced the moderate hit "River's Risin'."

Johnny Winter reemerged in 1973 with *Still Alive and Well*, his most critically successful album. It included Derringer's title song as well as the Winter originals "Rock and Roll" and "Too Much Seconal," and "Silver Train," written for him by Rolling Stones Mick Jagger and Keith Richards. After *Saints and Sinners*, Johnny Winter switched to Steve Paul's Blue Sky label, where he recorded four albums and produced four albums for blues legend Muddy Waters. In 1975 Edgar Winter recorded the solo jazz-style *Jasmine Nightdreams* for Blue Sky and a final album with The Edgar Winter Group. In 1976 Johnny and Edgar Winter recorded the modest-selling album *Together*.

Edgar recorded two final albums for Blue Sky through the early 1980s, reemerging in the late 1980s to tour with Leon Russell. Johnny Winter continued to record into the 1990s, first for the Chicago-based Alligator label, then one album for MCA/Voyager, and three albums for Pointblank and Relix in the 1990s.

DISC.: JOHNNY WINTER: *Raw to the Bone (1967)* (1993); *Early Times* (1970); *The Progressive Blues Experiment* (1969); *J. W.* (1969); *Second Winter* (1969); *J. W. And* (1970); *J. W. And—Live* (1971); *Still Alive and Well* (1973); *Saints and Sinners* (1974); *Scorchin' Blues* (1992); *A Rock 'n' Roll Collection* (1994); *Ready for Winter* (1981); *John Dawson Winter III* (1974); *Captured Live* (1976); *Nothin' but the Blues* (1977); *White, Hot and Blue* (1978); *Raisin' Cain* (1980); *Guitar Slinger* (1984); *Serious Business* (1985); *3rd Degree* (1986); *The Winter of '88* (1988); *Let Me In* (1991); *Hey, Where's Your Brother* (1992); *The Winter Scene* (1990). **JOHNNY AND EDGAR WINTER:** *Together Live* (1976). **JOHNNY WINTER/SONNY TERRY/WILLIE DIXON:** *Whoopin'* (1984). **EDGAR WINTER:** *Entrance* (1970); *Jasmine Nightdreams* (1975); *The E. W. Album* (1979); *Standing on Rock* (1981); *Mission Earth* (1989); *The E. W. Collection* (1989). **EDGAR WINTER'S WHITE TRASH:** *White Trash* (1971); *Road Work* (1972); *Recycled* (1977). **THE EDGAR WINTER GROUP:** *They Only Come Out at Night* (1972); *Shock Treatment* (1974); *The E. W. Group with Rick Derringer* (1975).—**BH**

Winter, Paul, American composer and instrumentalist; b. Altoona, Pa., Aug. 31, 1939. He was in the 3rd generation of a family of professional musicians; his great-aunts and -uncles belonged to the vaudeville troupe that introduced the saxophone to the U.S. He began playing drums at the age of 5, piano at 6, and clarinet at 8; by the time he was 12, he had discovered bebop, chosen the saxophone as his primary instrument, and formed his first band. He studied English composition at Northwestern Univ. (B.A., 1961) while frequenting jazz clubs in Chicago. In 1961 he formed The Paul Winter Sextet with fellow students. They were subsequently sent abroad on a State Dept. cultural exchange program (1962); before disbanding in 1965, the group had released 7 recordings. Winter moved to Conn. and formed the stylistically eclectic Paul Winter Consort in 1967. The Consort released 4 highly successful recordings before disbanding in 1972; the group was re-formed in 1977 with a more consistent style that integrated natural sounds with gentle, improvisatory music. In 1980 Winter founded Living Music Records, whose name suggests his strong environmental and humanistic concerns. Many of his concerts and recordings take place in unusual locations or for the benefit of social causes; he was an artist-in-residence at the Cathedral of St. John the Divine in N.Y. His compositions combine jazz, folk, ethnic, and classical elements in a style that has been a prototype for New Age music. Among his noteworthy recordings are *Icarus* (1972), *Common Ground* (1977), and *Earth: Voices of a Planet* (1990).—**NS/LK/DM**

Winter, Peter (von), German composer; b. Mannheim (baptized), Aug. 28, 1754; d. Munich, Oct. 17, 1825. He was a violinist in the Electoral orch. at the age of 10, and was given permanent employment there in 1776. He studied with Abbé Vogler, then went with the court to Munich in 1778 and became director of the Court Orch.; in 1787 he was named court Vice-Kapellmeister and in 1798 court Kapellmeister. In 1814 he received a title of nobility from the court for his long service. In Munich he brought out a number of operas, of which the most important were *Helena und Paris* (Feb. 5, 1782), *Der Bettelstudent oder Das Donnerwetter* (Feb. 2, 1785), *Der Sturm* (1798), *Marie von Montalban* (Jan. 28, 1800), and *Colmal* (Sept. 15, 1809). Frequent leaves of absence from Munich enabled him to travel; in Venice he produced his operas *Catone in Utica* (1791), *I sacrifizi di Creta ossia Arianna e Teseo* (Feb. 13, 1792), *I Fratelli rivali* (Nov. 1793), and *Belisa ossia La fedelità riconosciuta* (Feb. 5, 1794). In Prague he produced the opera *Ogus ossia Il trionfo del bel sesso* (1795). In Vienna he brought out *Das unterbrochene Opferfest* (June 14, 1796; his most successful opera; produced all over Europe), *Babylons Pyramiden* (Oct. 25, 1797), and *Das Labirint oder Der Kampf mit den Elementen* (June 12, 1798). In Paris he produced his only French opera, *Tamerlan* (Sept. 14, 1802), in London the Italian operas *La grotta di Calipso* (May 31, 1803), *Il trionfo dell'amor fraterno* (March 22, 1804), *Il ratto di Proserpina* (May 3, 1804), and *Zaira* (Jan. 29, 1805), and in Milan *Maometto II* (Jan. 28, 1817), *I due Valdomiri* (Dec. 26, 1817), and *Etelinda* (March 23, 1818). He also wrote several ballets, oratorios and sacred cantatas for the Munich court chapel, 28 masses and a vast amount of other church music, 4 syms. (including the grand choral sym. *Die Schlacht*, 1814), overtures, Violin Concerto, Flute Concerto, Bassoon Concerto, 2 oboe concertos, other concerted works, and much chamber music, including 12 divertimentos for 2 Violins, Viola, and Cello and a Divertimento for 2 Violins, Viola, Cello, and 2 Horns, 6 string quartets, 3 quintets, 2 sextets, a Septet, an Octet, sonatas, etc. He publ. *Vollständige Singschule* (Mainz, 1825; 2nd ed., 1874).

Bibl.: J. Arnold, *P. W.* (Erfurt, 1810); W. Neumann, *P. W.* (Kassel, 1856); V. Frensdorf, *P. W. als Opernkomponist* (diss., Univ. of Munich, 1908); L. Kuckuk, *P. W. als deutscher Opernkomponist* (diss., Univ. of Heidelberg, 1923); E. Loeffler, *P. W. als Kirchenmusiker* (diss., Univ. of Frankfurt am Main, 1929); T. Gebhard, *Studien zum Klarinettensatz und -stil in den konzertanten Werken von Georg-Friedrich Fuchs, P.v. W. und Franz Danzi* (Hildesheim, 1998).—**NS/LK/DM**

Winternitz, Emanuel, Austrian-American musicologist and museum curator; b. Vienna, Aug. 4, 1898; d. N.Y., Aug. 22, 1983. He served in the Austrian army in World War I, and after the Armistice studied jurisprudence at the Univ. of Vienna (LL.D., 1922). He was engaged as a corporate lawyer in Vienna (1929–38). After the Anschluss in 1938, he emigrated to the U.S., where he devoted himself mainly to lecturing on art; served as Peripatetic Professor for the Carnegie Foundation. In 1942 he was appointed keeper of musical instruments at the Metropolitan Museum in N.Y.; in 1949, was named curator of the Crosby Brown Collection of Musical Instruments of All Nations at the Metropolitan. He also administered the Andre Mertens Galleries for Musical Instruments (1971–73). In 1973 he became curator emeritus of the Metropolitan. Among his principal endeavors was musical iconography. He publ. a valuable reference work, *Musical Autographs from Monteverdi to Hindemith* (2 vols., Princeton, N.J., 1955). Other books were *Keyboard Instruments in the Metropolitan Museum of Art* (N.Y., 1961), *Die schönsten Musikinstrumente des Abendlandes* (Munich, 1966; Eng. tr., 1967, as *Musical Instruments of the Western World*), *Gaudenzio Ferrari, his School, and the Early History of the Violin* (Milan, 1967), *Musical Instruments and their Symbolism in Western Art* (N.Y., 1967; 2nd ed., 1979), and *Leonardo da Vinci as a Musician* (New Haven, Conn., 1982).
—**NS/LK/DM**

Winwood, Steve, (a.k.a. Stevie) one of the most distinguished talents in English music; b. Birmingham, England, May 12, 1948. Steve Winwood took to the stage as a teenager, and never let it go. At 15, he and his bass-playing brother Muff were asked to join the Spencer Davis Group. With Steve's preternaturally soulful vocals, they generated hits with "I'm a Man" and the classic "Gimme Some Lovin'." In other words, by 17, he had recorded a couple of songs that remain part of the litany of classic rock. Where that might have been the end for some artists, for Winwood it was just the beginning.

He formed Traffic, a group that reflected his burgeoning interest in jazz, successfully blending it with the SDG's soulful pop. Traffic broke up for a brief time for Winwood to enlist Eric Clapton in arguably the first "supergroup," Blind Faith. He had worked with Clapton several years earlier on the Powerhouse sessions. Blind Faith lasted for one incendiary, chart-topping album, after which Winwood joined another former Cream member, Ginger Baker, in his "supergroup" The Air Force, which featured Winwood's Traffic mate Chris Wood and his old Blind Faith mate Rick Gretch, Denny Laine of the Moody Blues, and many others. The band released an album and then imploded on the weight of its talent.

In 1970 Winwood began working on his solo debut. However, former Traffic bandmakes Jim Capaldi and Chris Wood soon joined him and the album began a revival of Traffic, becoming *John Barleycorn Must Die*. Over the course of the next five years, Traffic put out eight albums. Additionally, Winwood went to Nigeria in 1963 and worked with a couple of local drummers on the album *Aiye- Keta (the Third Word)*, a fusion of African and Western sounds that was 10 years ahead of its time.

By 1976, Winwood was exhausted. He did some informal work recording with Japanese percussionist Stoma Yamashta and his group Go. Then, in 1977, Winwood did something people thought was 10 years overdue: he released a solo record (a 1971 album called *Winwood* compiled his work in various groups). Featuring Capaldi and other former bandmates, the album still had a whiff of Traffic musically. It didn't fly commercially, as 1977 was the height of the punk rock explosion, although the album did manage to reach #22 on the U.S. charts. For the next four years, Winwood bided his time and got up to date with musical technology.

In 1981 Winwood re-emerged from his seclusion with the album *Arc of a Diver*. Recorded using state-of-the-art synthesizers, samplers, and studio equipment allowed Winwood to play every note on the record. The #7 hit "While You See a Chance" propelled the album to #3 and platinum. A year and a half later, he came back with *Talking Back to the Night*, an album that used the same formula as *Arc of a Diver* but lacked some of the spark. The album received a lukewarm reception both critically and commercially.

Retreating for another four years, he came up with *Back in the High Life*. It was the album he had been working on for the last 25 years. Full of soulful songs, real horns, and impassioned performances, the album rose to #3 and spun off the chart-topping hit "Higher Love," the #8 "The Finer Things," and two other Top 40 singles: the title track and "Freedom Overspill." "Higher Love" won both Record of the Year and Best Pop Vocal Performance, Male at the 1986 Grammy Awards.

A greatest hits record came out, featuring a remixed version of an ignored song from *Talking Back to the Night*. In this guise, "Valerie" rose to the Top Ten. In 1988 Winwood returned with *Roll with It*. A more R&B-oriented album, it reunited him with Jim Capaldi for one song. The album spun off three hits. The title track spent four weeks at #1. "Don't You Know What the Night Can Do?" hit #6 and "Holding On" fell just shy of the Top Ten at #11. The album topped the charts and went double platinum.

1990's *Refugees of the Heart* was something of a letdown after the fire of *Roll with It*. Leaning even more toward the sound of Traffic, the album featured Jim Capaldi both on drums and as collaborator on the album's only hit, "One and Only Man," which reached

#18. The album went gold and fizzled at #27. However, on the ensuing tour, Winwood and Capaldi threw in a few Traffic songs and the audiences went wild. In 1994 they put out the first Traffic record in nearly 20 years, *Far from Home*. They toured it, playing at Woodstock '95.

In 1997 they released the disappointing *Junction Seven* as a Steve Winwood album. While the album failed to chart or generate a single, and although the winds of pop music might seem to have blown past Winwood, his history proves that it's never safe to write him off.

DISC.: *Winwood* (1971); *Steve Winwood* (1977); *Arc of a Diver* (1981); *Talking Back to the Night* (1982); *Back in the High Life* (1986); *Roll with It* (1988); *Refugees of the Heart* (1990); *The Finer Things* (boxed set, 1995); *Junction Seven* (1997).

BIBL.: C. Welch, *Roll with It* (a.k.a. *Keep on Running*) (London, 1989).—**BH**

Wiora, Walter, important German musicologist; b. Kattowitz, Dec. 30, 1906; d. Tutzing, Feb. 8, 1997. He studied in Berlin at the Hochschule für Musik (1925–27) and received training in musicology from Abert, Blume, Hornbostel, Sachs, Schering, and Schünemann. He continued his studies with Gurlitt at the Univ. of Freiburg im Breisgau (Ph.D., 1937, with the diss. *Die Variantenbildung im Volkslied: Ein Beitrag zur systematischen Musikwissenschaft*), and completed his Habilitation there in 1941 with his *Die Herkunft der Melodien in Kretschmers und Zuccalmaglios Sammlung* (publ. in an enl. ed. as *Die rheinisch-bergischen Melodien bei Zuccalmaglio und Brahms*, Bad Godesberg, 1953). He was an asst. at the Deutsches Volksliedarchiv in Freiburg im Breisgau (1936–41). After serving as a reader in musicology at the Univ. of Posen, he returned to Freiburg im Breisgau and was archivist at the Deutsches Volksliedarchiv (1946–58), and then was prof. of musicology at the Univ. of Kiel (1958–64) and at the Univ. of Saarbrücken (1964–72). His principal achievement was his advocacy of a system of "essential research" in musicology that utilizes both traditional and contemporary principles.

WRITINGS: *Die deutsche Volksliedweise und der Osten* (Wolfenbüttel and Berlin, 1940); *Zur Frühgeschichte der Musik in den Alpenlandern* (Basel, 1949); *Das echte Volkslied* (Heidelberg, 1950); *Europäische Volksmusik und abendländische Tonkunst* (Kassel, 1957); *Die geschichtliche Sonderstellung der abendländischen Musik* (Mainz, 1959); *Die vier Weltalter der Musik* (Stuttgart, 1961; Eng. tr., 1965, as *The Four Ages of Music*); *Komponist und Mitwelt* (Kassel, 1964); ed. *Die Ausbreitung des Historismus über die Musik* (Regensburg, 1969); *Das deutsche Lied: Zur Geschichte und Ästhetik einer musikalischen Gattung* (Wolfenbüttel and Zürich, 1971); *Historische und systematische Musikwissenschaft* (Tutzing, 1972); *Ergebnisse und Aufgaben vergleichender Musikforschung* (Darmstadt, 1975); *Das musikalische Künstwerk* (Tutzing, 1983).

BIBL.: L. Finscher and C.-H. Mahling, eds., *Festschrift für W. W.* (Kassel, 1967); C.-H. Mahling, ed., *Beiträge zu einer musikalischen Gattung: W. W. zum 70. Geburtstag* (Tutzing, 1979); C.-H. Mahling and R. Seiberts, eds., *Festschrift W. W. zum 90. Geburtstag (30. Dezember 1996)* (Tutzing, 1997).—**NS/LK/DM**

Wirén, Dag (Ivar), prominent Swedish composer; b. Striberg, Oct. 15, 1905; d. Danderyd, April 19, 1986. He studied at the Stockholm Cons. with Oskar Lindberg and Ernest Ellberg (1926–31), then in Paris with Leonid Sabaneyev (1932–34). He returned to Sweden in 1934, and was music critic for the *Svenska Morgonbladet* (1938–46) and then vice-president of the Soc. of Swedish Composers (1947–63). His early music was influenced by Scandinavian Romanticism; later he adopted a more sober and more cosmopolitan neo-Classicism, stressing the symmetry of formal structure; in his thematic procedures he adopted the method of systematic intervallic metamorphosis rather than development and variation. He ceased composing in 1972.

WORKS: DRAMATIC: *Blått, gult, rott* (Blood, Sweat, Tears), radio operetta (1940); *Den glada patiensen*, radio operetta (1941); *Oscarbalen* (Oscarian Ball), ballet (1949); *Den elaka drottningen* (The Wicked Queen), television ballet (1960; Swedish TV, Nov. 22, 1961); incidental music for plays and films. **ORCH.:** 2 overtures (1931, 1940); 5 syms. (1932; 1939; 1943–44; 1951–52; Stockholm, Dec. 5, 1964); Sinfonietta (1933–34); Cello Concerto (1936); *Serenade* for Strings (1937); *Little Suite* (1941); *Romantic Suite* (1945); Violin Concerto (1945–46); Piano Concerto (1947–50); *Divertimento* (1954–57); *Triptyk* (1958); *Music* for Strings (1966–67; Stockholm, Jan. 12, 1968); Flute Concertino (1972). **CHAMBER:** 5 string quartets (1930; 1935; 1941–45; 1952–53; 1969–70); 2 piano trios (1933, 1961); Violin Sonatina (1939); Quartet for Flute, Oboe, Clarinet, and Cello (1956); *Little Serenade* for Guitar (1964); Wind Quintet (1971). **Piano:** *Theme and Variations* (1933); *5 Ironic Miniatures* (1942–45); Sonatina (1950); *5 Improvisations* (1959); *Little Piano Suite* (1971). **VOCAL:** Songs.—**NS/LK/DM**

Wirth, Helmut (Richard Adolf Friedrich Karl), German musicologist and composer; b. Kiel, Oct. 10, 1912. He studied composition with R. Oppel, then took courses in musicology with Fritz Stein and Blume at the Univ. of Kiel (Ph.D., 1937, with the diss. *Joseph Haydn als Dramatiker*; publ. in Wolfenbüttel and Berlin, 1940). From 1936 he was active with the Hamburg Radio; also was lecturer at the Schleswig-Holstein Academy of Music in Lübeck (1952–72). He was a founder-member of the Haydn Inst. of Cologne, and edited works for the complete ed. of Haydn's works. He publ. the study *Max Reger* (Hamburg, 1973). Among his compositions are orch. pieces, chamber music, piano pieces, and songs.—**NS/LK/DM**

Wise, Michael, English organist and composer; b. probably in Salisbury, c. 1647; d. there (killed in a dispute with the night watch), Aug. 24, 1687. He was a chorister at the Chapel Royal (1660–63). After serving as lay clerk at St. George's Chapel in Windsor and at Eton Coll. (1666–68), he was organist and instructor of the choristers at Salisbury Cathedral (from 1668). In 1676 he also was made a Gentleman of the Chapel Royal, and in 1687 he was appointed almoner and master of the choristers at St. Paul's Cathedral. His extant works comprise some 31 anthems, 4 services, songs, and catches.—**NS/LK/DM**

Wise, Patricia, American soprano and teacher; b. Wichita, July 31, 1943. She studied in Kans. and Santa Fe, and with Margaret Harshaw in N.Y. In 1966 she made her operatic debut in Kansas City as Mozart's

Susanna, and then joined the N.Y.C. Opera. She made her first appearance at London's Covent Garden in 1971 as Rossini's Rosina, and then made her debut as Strauss's Zerbinetta at the Glyndebourne Festival in 1972. From 1976 to 1991 she was a member of the Vienna State Opera, where she became well known for her roles in operas by Mozart and Strauss. She also sang in other European operatic centers, including engagements as Verdi's Nannetta at Milan's La Scala in 1980, the Protagonist in the premiere of Berio's *Un re in ascolto* in Salzburg in 1984, Berg's Lulu in Geneva in 1985, and Verdi's Gilda in Madrid in 1989. From 1995 she taught at the Ind. Univ. School of Music in Bloomington. She was honored as a Kammersängerin of the Vienna State Opera in 1996.—**NS/LK/DM**

Wiseman, Mac (Malcolm B.), bluegrass and country vocalist, b. Crimora, Va., May 23, 1925. Unique among country artists, Wiseman has managed to straddle the division between bluegrass and commercial country throughout his career, maintaining a traditional sound in his arrangements and choice of material. His fuzzy-voiced tenor is immediately recognizable in whatever genre of music he records.

Wiseman was born in rural Va. in the Shenandoah Valley, where he was surrounded by old-time country music. He studied classical music at the Shenandoah Cons. in Dayton, and then worked as an announcer at a small radio station out of Harrisburg, Pa. His first break as a singer came performing with Molly O'Day after World War II. In the late 1940s, he hooked up briefly with Lester Flatt and Earl Scruggs, who had just left Bill Monroe's band. In 1950, Wiseman joined Monroe as lead vocalist, working for him for about a year.

A year later, Wiseman was signed as a solo act to Dot Records; six years later, he was hired as a house producer for the company, running their country-music division through the early 1960s. Wiseman's first hit recordings were the sentimental "Tis Sweet to Be Remembered" and "Shackles and Chains," both accompanied by a hybrid country/bluegrass band, featuring two fiddlers playing in harmony (something Wiseman borrowed from the popular Western Swing style). In 1959, he had his biggest hit with the weeper "Jimmy Brown the Newsboy."

In the 1960s, Wiseman continued to record in a traditional country vein, even though the Nashville Sound was beginning to encroach on his (and most other) recordings. He left Dot for Capitol in the early 1960s, followed by a stint with MGM and then RCA. When Lester Flatt split from Earl Scruggs (because Scruggs wanted to record more popular music) in 1969, Wiseman teamed up with his old friend, recording a number of traditional bluegrass albums, first for RCA and then CMH. This return to bluegrass won him new friends on the traditional music circuit.

After Flatt died, Wiseman remained a popular touring attraction, returning to performing straight country, although he recorded only rarely. In 1986, when MCA revived the Dot label, he returned for an album in the style of his late 1950s recordings.

DISC.: *Early Dot Recordings* (rec. 1950s); *Teenage Hangout* (rec. 1950s). Osborne Brothers: *The Essential Bluegrass Album* (1979); *Grassroots to Bluegrass* (1990).—**RC**

Wishart, Peter (Charles Arthur), English composer and teacher; b. Crowborough, June 25, 1921; d. Frome, Aug. 14, 1984. He received training in composition from Hely-Hutchinson at the Univ. of Birmingham (1938–41) and from Boulanger in Paris (1947–48). He taught at the Univ. of Birmingham (1950–59), the Guildhall School of Music in London (from 1961), King's Coll., London (1972–77), and the Univ. of Reading (1977–84). He publ. the books *Harmony* (London, 1956) and *Key to Music* (London, 1971).

WORKS: DRAMATIC: Opera: *2 in the Bush* (1956); *The Captive* (1960); *The Clandestine Marriage* (1971); *Clytemnestra* (1973). **Other:** Ballets; incidental music. **ORCH.:** 2 violin concertos (1951, 1968); 2 syms. (1953, 1973); *Aubade* for Flute and Strings (1955); *Concerto piccolo* (1955); *Concerto for Orchestra* (1957); Concerto for Piano and Small Orch. (1958); *Divisions* (1965); *5 Pieces* for Strings (1967). **CHAMBER:** 2 cassations for Violin and Viola (1948, 1950); Sonata for Piano Duet (1949); 2 string quartets (1951, 1954); *Cantilena* for 4 Cellos (1957); *Profane Concerto* for Flute, Oboe, and Harpsichord (1962); organ music. **VOCAL:** Sacred and secular pieces.—**NS/LK/DM**

Wisłocki, Stanisław, Polish conductor, pianist, pedagogue, and composer; b. Rzeszów, July 7, 1921; d. Warsaw, May 31, 1998. He studied with Seweryn Barbag in Lwów, and then at the Timişoara Academy of Music with George Simonis (composition and conducting) and Emil Michail (piano). In 1945 he founded the Polish Chamber Orch. in Warsaw, and in 1947 he founded the Poznań Phil., which he led as music director until 1958. From 1951 he also taught conducting at the State Higher School of Music in Poznań. In 1955 he became a prof. at the State Higher School of Music in Warsaw, where he held its conducting chair from 1958. From 1961 to 1968 he conducted the National Phil. in Warsaw. He served as music director of the Grand Orch. of the Polish Radio and TV from 1978 to 1982. He also appeared as a guest conductor throughout Europe, North and South America, and Japan.

WORKS: ORCH.: *Na rozstajach* (At the Crossroads), symphonic poem (1942); Sym. (1944); *Taniec zbójnicki* (Highland Robbers' Dance) for Chamber Orch. (1945); Overture for Chamber Orch. (1945); *Nokturn* (1947); Piano Concerto (1949); *Symfonia o tańcu* (Dance Sym.; 1951); *Ballada symfoniczna* (Symphonic Ballad; 1952). **CHAMBER:** Violin Sonata (1942); Piano Quartet (1943). **Piano:** *Sonata na tematy Scarlattigeo* (Sonata on Themes of Scarlatti; 1942); 2 suites (1943).—**NS/LK/DM**

Wissmer, Pierre, Swiss-born French composer and pedagogue; b. Geneva, Oct. 30, 1915; d. Valcros, France, Nov. 4, 1992. He went to Paris to study with Roger-Ducasse (composition) at the Cons., Daniel-Lesur (counterpoint) at the Schola Cantorum, and Munch (conducting) at the École Normale de Musique. Returning to Geneva, he taught composition at the Cons. (1944–48). He was active as a music critic and also served as head of the chamber music dept. of the Geneva Radio. After serving as asst. director of programming of Radio

Luxembourg (1951–57), he was director of programming of Luxembourg Television (1957–63). In 1958 he became a naturalized French citizen. He was director of the Schola Cantorum in Paris (1957–63) and of the École Nationale de Musique in Le Mans (1969–81), and also was prof. of composition and orchestration at the Geneva Cons. (1973–86). In 1983 he was awarded the Grand Prix Musical of Geneva for his creative efforts. His output reveals an adept handling of traditional and contemporary styles.

Works: Dramatic: *Le Beau dimanche*, ballet (1939; Geneva, March 20, 1944); *Marion ou la belle au tricorne*, comic opera (1945; Radio Suisse Romande, Geneva, April 16, 1947); *Capitaine Bruno*, opera (Geneva, Nov. 9, 1952); *Léonidas ou la cruauté mentale*, opéra bouffe (Paris, Sept. 12, 1958); *Alerte, puits 21*, ballet (1963); *Christina et les Chimères*, ballet (1964). **Orch.:** *Mouvement* for Strings (1937); 3 piano concertos (1937, 1948, 1971); 9 syms. (1938; 1951; 1955; 1962; 1969; 1975–77; 1983; 1985–86; 1988–89); *Antoine et Cléopâtre*, symphonic suite (1943); 3 violin concertos (1944, 1954, 1987); *La Mandrellina*, overture (1952); *Divertimento* (1953); *L'Enfant et la rose*, symphonic variations (1957); *Clamavi*, triptych (1957); Clarinet Concerto (1960); Oboe Concerto (1963); *Concerto valcrosiano* (1966); *Concertino-croisiere* for Flute, Piano, and Strings (1966); *Stèle* for Strings (1969); *Triptyque romand* (1972); *Dialogue* for Bassoon or Cello and Orch. (1974); *Variations sur un Noël imaginaire* (1975); *Symphonietta concertante* for Flute, Harp, and Orch. (1982); *Musique à divers temps* for Strings (1988–89). **Chamber:** 3 string quartets (1937, 1949, 1972); *Sérénade* for Oboe, Clarinet, and Horn (1938); *Divertissement sur un choral* for 11 Instruments (1939); Clarinet Sonatina (1941); Violin Sonatina (1946); *Prestilagoyana* for 2 Guitars (1959); *Quadrige* for Flute, Violin, Cello, and Piano (1961); Sonatina for Flute and Guitar (1962); Wind Quintet (1964); *Partita* for Guitar (1971); *Trio Adelfiano* for Flute, Cello, and Piano (1978); *Quattro piccoli quadri Veneziano* for Violin, Viola, and Cello (1984); *Askok* for Flute and Guitar (1984); *Ritratto* for 2 Guitars (1984); *Propos* for Oboe, Clarinet, and Bassoon (1986); *Tre pezzi valcorsiani* for 2 Guitars (1987); *Automne* for Guitar (1988–89); *Primavera* for Guitar (1988–89). **Keyboard: Piano:** Sonata (1949); *Trois Études* (1967); *Trois Silhouettes* (1968); *Bea, Sandrine et Monsieur Pompon (le chat)* (1986); *Cavaliere e cavallo* (1986); *3 Romances* for Piano, 4-Hands (1988–89); *Episodes* (1988–89); *Musique pour jeunes virtuoses* (1988–89). **Organ:** *Réflexions* (1973); *Apôtre Paul* (1985). **Vocal:** *Naïdes* for Narrator, Soloists, Chorus, and Orch. (1941); *Hérétique et Relapse* for Tenor, Chorus, and Orch. (1962); *Un Banquier sans visage* for Soloists, Dancers, and Orch. (1964); *Le Quatrième Mage*, oratorio for Soloists, Chorus, and Orch. (1965); *I Cadieni* for Voices and Orch. (1980); choruses; songs. **—NS/LK/DM**

Wiszniewski, Zbigniew, Polish composer and teacher; b. Lwów, July 30, 1922; d. Warsaw, Oct. 11, 1999. He received training in theory and composition from Kazimierz Sikorski and in viola from Mieczysław Szaleski at the State Higher School of Music (1946–51) in Łódź. In 1954 he became a teacher in a state secondary music school in Warsaw, where he later taught at the Academy of Music from 1979 to 1988 and again from 1993 until his death. He was ed.-in-chief of the periodical *Poradnik Muzyczny* from 1982 to 1984. In 1959 he won the RAI Award in the International Prix Italia Competition in Sorrento, in 1969 1st prize in the Premiere Semaine Chrétienne Internationale de TV competition in Monaco, and in 1972 the Prime Minister's Award of Poland.

Works: Dramatic: *Neffru*, radio opera (1958–59); *Ad hominem*, ballet (1962; Warsaw, Oct. 7, 1964); *Genesis*, television oratorio for Baritone, Actor, Chorus, and Orch. (1967); *Bracia* (The Brothers), television oratorio for Actor, Men's Chorus, and Orch. (1970–72); *Pater Noster*, radio opera (1971–74). **Orch.:** *Triptychon* (1967); Concerto for Clarinet and Strings (1968–70); Concertante for Oboe, Harpsichord, and Strings (1987); Violin Concerto (1987); *Sinfonia da camera* for Strings (1987); Double Concerto for Trumpet, Accordion, and Orch. (1989). **Chamber:** 2 string quartets (1952, 1990); Trio for Oboe, Harp, and Viola (1963); *Tristia* for 8 Instruments (1965); *Kammermusik No. 1* for Oboe, Oboe d'Amore, English Horn, and Bassoon (1965–67), *No. 2* for 10 Instruments (1966), *No. 3* for Percussion (1966; Warsaw, Sept. 1975), and *No. 4* for 10 Instruments (1972–73); Sonata for Solo Cello (1977); Duo for Bass Tuba and Percussion (1981); Quartet for 4 Violins (1982); Duo for Accordion and Guitar (1984); *Ballada* for Mandolin and Celtic Harp (1985; Paris, July 1986); Trio for Alto Saxophone, Accordion, and Percussion (1985); Quartet for Lute, Percussion, Bombarde, and Crumhorn (Warsaw, May 16, 1987); *Trigonos* for 2 Accordions and Organ (Legnica, Oct. 1987); Trio for Viola d'Amore, Accordion, and Organ (1987; Legnica, Sept. 30, 1988); Trio for Flute, Harpsichord, and Cello (1988); Duo for 2 Cellos (1988; Warsaw, May 19, 1989); Sonata for Solo Oboe (1989); Duo for Accordion and Trombone (1990); Sonata for Viola d'Amore (1992). **Keyboard: Harpsichord:** *Für Cembalo* (Kraków, April 23, 1985). **Organ:** *Für Orgel* (Legnica, Oct. 3, 1986). **Vocal:** *Tre pezzi della tradizione* for Chorus and Orch. (Venice, Sept. 16, 1964); *Sichel versäumter Stunden*, cantata for Chorus and Orch. (1971); *Ballade de Villon de la Grosse Margot* for Baritone, Chorus, and 5 Instruments (1988); *Kanon* for Chorus and Instruments (1992).**—NS/LK/DM**

Wit, Antoni, Polish conductor; b. Kraków, Feb. 7, 1944. He was educated in his native city, taking courses in conducting at the State Coll. of Music (graduated, 1967) and in law at the Jagiellonian Univ. (graduated, 1969). He won 2nd prize in the Karajan Competition in Berlin (1971) and completed his conducting studies at the Berkshire Music Center, Tanglewood (summer, 1973). He was asst. conductor of the National Phil. in Warsaw (1967–70), then conducted the Poznań State Phil. (1970–72) and the Pomeranian Phil. in Bydgoszcz (1974–77). After serving as artistic director of the Polish Radio and Television Sym. Orch. in Kraków (1977–83), he held that title with the Polish Radio and Television National Sym. Orch. in Katowice (from 1983); also toured widely as a guest conductor.**—NS/LK/DM**

Witherspoon, Herbert, American bass; b. Buffalo, N.Y., July 21, 1873; d. N.Y., May 10, 1935. He studied composition with Horatio Parker and voice with Gustav Stoeckel at Yale Univ. (graduated, 1895); then was a pupil of MacDowell in N.Y. He then studied singing with Bouhy in Paris, Henry Wood in London, and G.B. Lamperti in Berlin. Returning to America, he made his operatic debut as Ramfis in *Aida* with Savage's Castle Square Opera Co. in N.Y. in 1898. On Nov. 26, 1908, he made his Metropolitan Opera debut in N.Y. as Titurel in *Parsifal*; remained on its roster until 1916, where he distinguished himself in such roles as Sarastro, King Marke, Pogner, the Landgrave, and Gurnemanz. In 1922 he founded the American Academy of Teachers of Singing, subsequently serving as its first president. In 1925 he became president of the Chicago Musical Coll., and in 1931, president of the Cincinnati Cons. of Music; in 1933 he returned to N.Y., and in May 1935, was chosen to succeed Gatti-Casazza as general manager of the Metropolitan Opera, but he died of a heart attack after only a month in his post. He publ. *Singing: A Treatise for Teachers and Students* (N.Y., 1925) and *36 Lessons in Singing for Teacher and Student* (Chicago, 1930).—**NS/LK/DM**

Witt, Friedrich, German violinist and composer; b. Hallenbergstetten, Württemberg, Nov. 8, 1770; d. Würzburg, Jan. 3, 1836. At the age of 19, he was engaged as violinist in the orch. of Prince von Oettingen, and from 1802 he was Kapellmeister at Würzburg, at first to the Prince-Bishop, then to the Grand Duke, and finally to the city. It was Witt who composed the so-called Jena Sym., misattributed to Beethoven (see H.C. Robbins Landon's article in the *Music Review* for May 1957). Other works by Witt include the historical opera *Palma* (Frankfurt am Main, 1804), the comic opera *Das Fischerweib* (Würzburg, 1806), the oratorios *Der leidende Heiland* (Würzburg, 1802) and *Die Auferstehung Jesu*, masses and cantatas, 9 syms., music for wind band, 7 concertos and sinfonie concertanti, Flute Concerto, Quintetto for Piano and Strings or Winds, Septet for String Quartet and Winds, etc.—**NS/LK/DM**

Wittgenstein, Paul, noted Austrian-born American pianist and teacher; b. Vienna, Nov. 5, 1887; d. Manhasset, N.Y., March 3, 1961. He was of a musical family and studied piano with Malvine Brée and Theodor Leschetizky and theory with Josef Labor. He made his first public appearance as a pianist in 1913 in Vienna. He lost his right arm in World War I, at the Russian front; he was a prisoner of war in Omsk, Siberia; was repatriated in 1916. He then developed an extraordinary technique for left hand alone, and performed a concerto specially composed for him by his teacher, Labor. Wittgenstein subsequently commissioned left-hand piano concertos from Richard Strauss, Ravel, Prokofiev, Korngold, Benjamin Britten, and other composers, of which he gave the premieres (except the Prokofiev concerto, which he found unsuitable). He appeared in the major musical centers in Europe; toured America in 1934; in 1938, settled in N.Y.; became a naturalized American citizen in 1946. He taught privately in N.Y. (1938–60); also at the Ralph Wolfe Cons. in New Rochelle (1938–43), and at Manhattanville Coll. of the Sacred Heart (1940–45). John Barchilon's novel *The Crown Prince* (1984) is based on his career. He was a brother of the famous philosopher Ludwig Wittgenstein. —**NS/LK/DM**

Wittich, Marie, German soprano; b. Giessen, May 27, 1868; d. Dresden, Aug. 4, 1931. She studied with Otto-Ubridz in Würzburg, making her debut as Azucena at the age of 14 in Magdeburg in 1882; she then sang in Düsseldorf, Basel, and Schwerin. In 1889 she became a member of the Dresden Court Opera, remaining on its roster until 1914; while there, she was chosen by Richard Strauss to create the role of Salome in 1905. She also made guest appearances at Covent Garden in London (1905–06) and in Bayreuth (1901–10). —**NS/LK/DM**

Wittinger, Robert, Austrian-born German composer; b. Knittelfeld, April 10, 1945. He grew up in Budapest, where he studied with Zsolt Durkó. He then studied in Warsaw (1964), received training in electronic music in Munich (1965), and attended the summer courses in new music in Darmstadt (1965–68). He subsequently was active at the Villa Massimo in Rome on a scholarship (1972–73). His technique of composition is sonoristic, with sound blocks forming thematic groups, while the continuity is achieved by Baroque formulas; the titles of his pieces are often indicative of their construction.

WORKS: ORCH.: 5 syms.: No. 1 (1962–63; rev. 1976), No. 2 for Women's Chorus and Orch. (1978–80), No. 3, *Funèbre* (1982), No. 4 (1993), and No. 5 (1995); *Dissoziazioni* (1964); *Consonante* for English Horn and Orch. (1965); *Espressioni*, ballet music (1966); *Concentrazione* (1966); *Compensazioni* for Small Orch. (1967); *Irreversibilitazione* for Cello and Orch. (1967); *Om* (1968); *Divergenti* (West Berlin, Oct. 4, 1970); *Sinfonia* for Strings (1970); *Costellazioni* (Stuttgart, Sept. 25, 1971); *Montaggio*, concerto No. 1 for Small Orch. (1972); *Relazioni* for 7 Soloists and Orch. (West Berlin, April 11, 1972); Concerto for Oboe, Harp, and Strings (1972); *Concerto Polemica* (1975); *Concerto Lirico* (1977); *Concerto Entusiastico* (1977); Concerto for 2 Pianos and Orch. (1981); *Concerto Grosso* (1983); *Intreccio* (1985); Violin Concerto (1988); *Cronogramme I* for Strings, Harp, Piano, and Percussion (1992–93; Graz, Oct. 8, 1993); *Sinfonietta* (1994); Concerto for String Trio and Orch. (1997). **CHAMBER:** 4 string quartets (1964, 1966, 1970, 1977); *Concentrazioni*, wind quintet (1965); *Itrospezioni* for Bassoon (1967); *Tendenze* for Piano, Cello, and Percussion (1970); *Tensioni*, wind quintet (1970); *Tolleranza* for Oboe, Celesta, and Percussion (1970); *6 Strutture simmetriche*, each for a different Solo Instrument (1970); *Sillogismo* for Violin and Percussion (1974); *Dialoghi e scherzino* for 2 Pianos (1985). **VOCAL:** *Catalizzazioni* for 24 Vocalists and 7 Instrumentalists (1972); *Maldoror-Requiem* for Chorus and Orch. (1984–86).—**NS/LK/DM**

Wittrisch, Marcel, German tenor; b. Antwerp, Oct. 1, 1901; d. Stuttgart, June 3, 1955. He studied at the Munich and Leipzig conservatories. He made his operatic debut as Konrad in *Hans Heiling* in Halle in 1925, then sang in Braunschweig (1927–29). In 1929 he became a member of the Berlin State Opera, where he sang leading roles until 1943; he also made guest appearances at Covent Garden in London (1931) and at Bayreuth (1937). In 1950 he joined the Stuttgart Opera, where he remained until his death. In addition to his operatic career, he gained wide renown as a concert singer.—**NS/LK/DM**

Wixell, Ingvar, Swedish baritone; b. Luleå, May 7, 1931. He received his training at the Stockholm Musikhögskolan. In 1952 he made his concert debut in Gävle and in 1955 his operatic debut as Papageno at the

Royal Theater in Stockholm, where he sang regularly from 1956. In 1960 he sang with the Royal Opera on its visit to London's Covent Garden. He made his first appearance at the Glyndebourne Festival in 1962 as Cuglielmo. In 1966 he made his debut at the Salzburg Festival as Count Almaviva, and continued to sing there until 1969. From 1967 he sang at the Deutsche Oper in Berlin, and made his U.S. debut as Belcore in Chicago that same year. In 1971 he made his first appearance at the Bayreuth Festival as the Herald in *Lohengrin*. In 1972 he made his debut at Covent Garden as Simon Boccanegra, and continued to sing there regularly until 1977. On Jan. 29, 1973, he made his Metropolitan Opera debut in N.Y. as Rigoletto, where he made occasional appearances until 1980. He sang Amonasro in Houston in 1987. From 1987 to 1990 he sang once more at Covent Garden. In 1990 he appeared as Scarpia in Stuttgart, which role he then sang at Earl's Court in London in 1991. Among his other roles were Don Giovanni, Marcello, Germont, and Mandryka.—**NS/LK/DM**

Wlaschiha, Ekkehard, German baritone; b. Pirna, May 28, 1938. He was trained in Leipzig. In 1961 he made his operatic debut as Don Fernando in *Fidelio* in Gera. After singing in Dresden and Weimar (1964–70), he was a member of the Leipzig Opera from 1970. From 1983 he sang at the Berlin State Opera. In 1985 he appeared as Kaspar in *Der Freischütz* in the reopening of the Semper Opera House in Dresden. He made his debut at the Bayreuth Festival as Kurwenal in 1986. For his first appearance at London's Covent Garden in 1990, he sang Alberich in *Siegfried*, a role he also sang at the Lyric Opera in Chicago in 1996 and at the Metropolitan Opera in 1997. He sang in the premiere of Henze's *Venus und Adonis* in Munich in 1997. Among his other roles are Pizzaro, Tonio, Telramund, Scarpia, and Jochanaan.—**NS/LK/DM**

Wohl, Yehuda, German-born Israeli composer; b. Berlin, March 5, 1904; d. Tel Aviv, July 12, 1988. He went to Palestine in 1933 and had private studies with Ben-Haim in Tel Aviv; taught until 1972. Under the pseudonym Yehuda Bentow, he wrote popular songs in the ethnic style.

WORKS: DRAMATIC: Radio Opera: *Hagadér* (1947); *The Circle* (1976). **ORCH.:** 3 syms. (1944, 1946, 1954); *Rondo patetico* for Strings (1950); *Miriam- Danze* (1955); *Discussione* for Piano and Orch. (1956); *Fata morgana* (1960); *Canto capricioso* (1967); *With Mixed Feelings* for Piano, Percussion, and Strings (1970); *Light and Shadow* (1972); *Those Were the Days* (1973); *Festival Overture* (1979). **CHAMBER:** *Quartetto appassionato* for String Quartet (1949); *Duo sensible* for Violin and Piano (1951); *Diary* for Flute, Oboe, Clarinet, and Bassoon (1961); *Associations* for Chamber Ensemble (1966); *Hagashot* (Encounters) for Chamber Ensemble (1968); *Atmosphere* for Organ and Tape (1970); *Trigon* for Piano Trio (1971); *Faces* for Brass Ensemble and Percussion (1973); many piano pieces. **VOCAL:** *Tagore-Songs* for 2 Voices, Piano, and Flute (1955); *An Arch Smile* for Narrator and Orch. (1959).—**NS/LK/DM**

Woldemar, Michel, French violinist and composer; b. Orléans, June 17, 1750; d. Clermont-Ferrand, Dec. 19, 1815. He studied with Lolli and Mestrino. After teaching violin in Paris, he served as music director of a group of strolling players; eventually settled in Clermont-Ferrand as maître de chapelle at the Cathedral. By adding a 5th string (c) to the violin, he obtained an instrument that he called "violon- alto," because it included the viola range, and for which he wrote a concerto. He also publ. 3 violin concertos, a String Quartet, duos for 2 violins and for violin and viola, *Sonates fantomagiques* for Violin *(L'Ombre de Lolli, de Mestrino, de Pugnani, de Tartini)*, 12 grand solos, *6 rêves ou Caprices, Caprices ou Etudes, Le Nouveau Labyrinth pour violon*, followed by studies in double stops, *Le Nouvel Art de l'archet, Etude élémentaire de l'archet moderne*, variations on *Les Folies d'Espagne*, etc., and methods for violin, viola, and clarinet. He also developed a system of musical stenography (*Tableau mélotachigraphique*) and a method of musical correspondence (*Notographie*). —**NS/LK/DM**

Wöldike, Mogens, Danish organist, conductor, and composer; b. Copenhagen, July 5, 1897; d. there, Oct. 20, 1988. He studied with Thomas Laube and Carl Nielsen in Copenhagen, where he also attended the Univ. (1920). From 1919 he was active as an organist and choirmaster in Copenhagen churches; in 1931 he became organist at the Christiansborg Palace Church, a post that he also held at the Copenhagen Cathedral (1959–72); from 1937 to 1977 he also appeared as a conductor with the Danish Radio. With his son-in-law, **Jens Peter Larsen**, he ed. the hymnbook of the Danish Church (1954, 1973); he also publ. 3 vols. of organ music (Copenhagen, 1943, 1960, 1982).—**NS/LK/DM**

Wolf, Ernst Wilhelm, German composer; b. Grossenbehringen, near Gotha (baptized), Feb. 25, 1735; d. Weimar (buried), Dec. 1, 1792. After studies at the Eisenach and Gotha Gymnasien, he entered the Univ. of Jena (1755), where he was made director of the collegium musicum. He was active in Naumburg as a music teacher to the von Ponickau family before becoming music tutor to the sons of Duchess Anna Amalia in Weimar; later was named court Konzertmeister (1761), organist (1763), and Kapellmeister (1772) there. He publ. *Auch eine Reise aber nur eine kleine Musik in den Monaten Junius, Julius und August 1782 zum Vergnügen angestellt und auf Verlangen beschrieben* (Weimar, 1784), *Vorbericht als eine Anleitung zum guten Vortrag beim Klavier-Spielen* (Leipzig, 1785), and *Musikalischer Unterricht für Liebhaber und diejenigen, welche die Musik treiben und lehren wollen* (Dresden, 1788).

WORKS: DRAMATIC (all 1st perf. in Weimar): *Das Gärtnermädchen*, comic opera (1769); *Das Rosenfest*, operetta (1772); *Die Dorfdeputierten*, comic opera (1772); *Die treuen Köhler*, operetta (1772); *Der Abend im Walde*, comic opera (1773); *Das grosse Los*, comic opera (1774); *Ehrlichkeit und Liebe*, Schauspiel (1776); *Le Monde de la lune*, comic opera (n.d.); *Alceste*, opera (1780); 10 others not extant. **ORCH.:** Various syms. (partitas); about 25 concertos for Harpsichord or Piano. **CHAMBER:** 6 string quartets; 2 quintets; 6 sonatas for Piano, Violin, and Cello; over 55 sonatas for Piano or Harpsichord. **VOCAL:** 9 cantatas; 5 oratorios; a sacred concerto; sacred choruses and songs; secular cantatas and songs.

BIBL.: J. Brockt, *E.W. W.: Leben und Werke* (diss., Univ. of Breslau, 1927).—**NS/LK/DM**

Wolf, Hugo (Filipp Jakob), famous Austrian composer, one of the greatest masters of the German lied; b. Windischgraz, Styria, March 13, 1860; d. Vienna, Feb. 22, 1903. His father, Philipp Wolf (1828–87), was a gifted musician from whom Hugo received piano and violin lessons at a very early age; he later played 2nd violin in the family orch. While attending the village primary school (1865–69), he studied piano and theory with Sebastian Weixler. In 1870 he was sent to the Graz regional secondary school, but left after a single semester and in 1871 entered the St. Paul Benedictine Abbey in Carinthia, where he played violin, organ, and piano. In 1873 he was transferred to the Marburg secondary school and remained devoted to musical pursuits. In 1875 he went to Vienna, where he became a pupil at the Cons. He studied piano with Wilhelm Schenner and harmony and composition with Robert Fuchs and later with Franz Krenn. When Wagner visited Vienna in 1875, Wolf went to see him, bringing along some of his compositions; the fact that Wagner received him at all, and even said a few words of encouragement, gave Wolf great impetus toward further composition. But he was incapable of submitting himself to academic discipline, and soon difficulties arose between him and the Cons. authorities. He openly expressed his dissatisfaction with the teaching, which led to his expulsion for lack of discipline in 1877. He then returned to his native town, but after a few months at home decided to go to Vienna again, where he managed to support himself by giving music lessons to children in the homes of friends. By that time he was composing diligently, writing songs to texts by his favorite poets—Goethe, Lenau, Heine. It was also about that time that the first signs of a syphilitic infection became manifest. An unhappy encounter with Brahms in 1879, who advised him to study counterpoint before attempting to compose, embittered him, and he became determined to follow his own musical inclinations without seeking further advice. That same year he met Melanie (née Lang) Köchert, whose husband, Heinrich Köchert, was the Vienna court jeweller. By 1884 she had become Wolf's mistress and a great inspiration in his creative work. After serving a brief and acrimonious tenure as 2nd conductor in Salzburg in 1881, he returned to Vienna in 1882 and in 1883 became music critic of the weekly *Wiener Salonblatt*. He took this opportunity to indulge his professional frustration by attacking those not sympathetic to new trends in music. He poured invective of extraordinary virulence on Brahms, thus antagonizing the influential Hanslick and other admirers of Brahms. But he also formed a coterie of staunch friends, who had faith in his ability. Yet he was singularly unsuccessful in his repeated attempts to secure performances for his works. He submitted a string quartet to the celebrated Rose Quartet, but it was rejected. Finally, Hans Richter accepted for the Vienna Phil. Wolf's symphonic poem *Penthesilea*, but the public performance was a fiasco, and Wolf even accused Richter of deliberately sabotaging the work; later he reorchestrated the score, eliminating certain crudities of the early version. In 1887 he resigned as music critic of the *Wiener Salonblatt* and devoted himself entirely to composition. He became convinced that he was creating the greatest masterpieces of song since Schubert and Schumann, and stated his conviction in plain terms in his letters. In historical perspective, his self-appraisal has proved remarkably accurate, but psychologists may well wonder whether Wolf was not consciously trying to give himself the needed encouragement by what must have seemed to him a wild exaggeration. However, a favorable turn in his fortunes soon came. On March 2, 1888, Rosa Papier became the first artist to sing one of Wolf's songs in public. On March 23, 1888, Wolf himself played and sang several of his songs at a meeting of the Vienna Wagner-Verein; on Dec. 15, 1888, he made his public debut as accompanist in his songs to the tenor Ferdinand Jäger, which proved the first of many highly successful recitals by both artists. Soon Wolf's name became known in Germany, and he presented concerts of his own works in Berlin, Darmstadt, Mannheim, and other musical centers. He completed the first part of his great cycle of 22 songs, *Italienisches Liederbuch*, in 1891, and composed the 2nd part (24 songs) in 5 weeks, in the spring of 1896. While Wolf could compose songs with a facility and degree of excellence that were truly astounding, he labored painfully on his orch. works. His early sym. was never completed, nor was a violin concerto; the work on *Penthesilea* took him a disproportionately long time. In 1895 he undertook the composition of his opera, *Der Corregidor*, to the famous tale by Alarcón, *El sombrero de tres picos*, and, working feverishly, completed the vocal score with piano accompaniment in a few months. The orchestration took him a much longer time. *Der Corregidor* had its premiere in Mannheim on June 7, 1896. While initially a success, however, the opera failed to find wide appeal and was soon dropped from the repertoire. Wolf subsequently revised the score, and in its new version *Der Corregidor* was brought out in Strasbourg on April 29, 1898. He never completed his 2nd opera, *Manuel Venegas* (also after Alarcón); fragments were presented in concert in Mannheim on March 1, 1903. In the meantime, his fame grew. A Hugo Wolf-Verein was organized at Berlin in 1896, and did excellent work in furthering performances of Wolf's songs in Germany. Even more effective was the Hugo Wolf-Verein in Vienna, founded by Michel Haberlandt on April 22, 1897 (disbanded in 1906). As appreciation of Wolf's remarkable gifts as a master of lied began to find recognition abroad, tragedy struck. By early 1897, he was a very ill man, both mentally and physically. According to Wolf, Mahler promised to use his position as director of the Vienna Court Opera to mount a production of *Der Corregidor*. When the production failed to materialize, Wolf's mental condition disintegrated. He declared to friends that Mahler had been relieved of his post, and that he, Wolf, had been appointed in his stead. On Sept. 20, 1897, Wolf was placed in a private mental institution. After a favorable remission, he was discharged (Jan. 24, 1898), and traveled in Italy and Austria. After his return to Vienna, symptoms of mental derangement manifested themselves in even greater degree. In Oct. 1898 he attempted suicide by throwing himself into the Traunsee in Traunkirkchen, but was saved and placed in the Lower Austrian provincial asylum in Vienna. (A parallel with Schumann's case forcibly suggests itself.) He remained in confinement, gradually lapsing into complete irrationality. He died at the age of 42, and was buried near the graves of Schubert and Beethoven in Vienna's Central Cemetery; a monument was unveiled on Oct. 20, 1904. His mistress plunged to her death from the 4th-floor window of her home in Vienna on March 21, 1906.

Wolf's significance in music history rests on his songs, about 300 in number, many of them publ. posthumously. The sobriquet "the Wagner of the lied" may well be justified in regard to involved contrapuntal texture and chromatic harmony, for Wolf accepted the Wagnerian idiom through natural affinity as well as by clear choice. The elaboration of the accompaniment, and the incorporation of the vocal line into the contrapuntal scheme of the whole, are Wagnerian traits. But with these external similarities, Wolf's dependence on Wagner's models ceases. In his intimate penetration of the poetic spirit of the text, Wolf appears a legitimate successor to Schubert and Schumann. Wolf's songs are symphonic poems in miniature, artistically designed and admirably arranged for voice and piano, the combination in which he was a master. A complete ed. of his works, ed. by H. Jancik et al., began publ. in Vienna in 1960.

WORKS: DRAMATIC: Opera: *König Alboin* (1876–77; fragment); *Der Corregidor* (1895; Mannheim, June 7, 1896); *Manuel Venegas* (1897; fragments perf. in concert, Mannheim, March 1, 1903). **Incidental Music To:** Kleist's *Prinz Friedrich von Homburg* (1884; unfinished); Ibsen's *Das Fest auf Solhaug* (Vienna, Nov. 21, 1891). **ORCH.:** Violin Concerto (1875; unfinished); Sym. in B-flat major (1876–77; unfinished; Scherzo and Finale completed; scored by H. Schultz and publ. in Leipzig and Vienna, 1940); Sym. in G Minor (1877; unfinished); Sym. in F minor (1879; not extant); *The Corsair*, overture (1877–78; not extant); *Penthesilea*, symphonic poem (1883–85); *Italienische Serenade* for Small Orch. (1892; arrangement of the *Serenade* for String Quartet); *Dritte Italienische Serenade* (1897; unfinished); *Trantella* on *Funiculi, finiculà* (1897; fragment). **CHAMBER:** String Quartet in D major (1876; unfinished); Piano Quintet (1876; fragment; not extant); Violin Sonata in G minor (1877; fragment); String Quartet in D minor (1878–84); *Intermezzo* in E-flat major for String Quartet (1886); *Serenade* for String Quartet (1887; arr. for Small Orch. as *Italienische Serenade*, 1892); *Serenade* (1889; fragment). **Piano:** Sonata in E-flat major/D major (1875; unfinished); *Variations* in G major (1875); *Variations* in E major/A major (c. 1875; fragment); Sonata in D major (1875; unfinished); Sonata in G major (1876; unfinished); *Fantasia* in B-flat major (1876; unfinished); *March* in E-flat major for 4-Hands (1876); Sonata in G minor (1876; unfinished); *Rondo capriccioso* (1876); *Wellenspiel* in D major (1877; unfinished; not extant); *Verlegenheit* in A minor (1877; fragment); *Humoreske* in G minor (1877); *Schlummerlied* in G major (1878); *Scherz und Spiel* in G major (1878); *Fantasie über Lortzings Zar und Zimmermann* (c. 1878; not extant); *Reiseblätter nach Gedichten von Lenau* (c. 1878–79; not extant); *Paraphrase über Die Meistersinger von Nürnberg von Richard Wagner* in G major (c. 1880); *Paraphrase über Die Walküre von Richard Wagner* in E minor (c. 1880); Canons in C major (c. 1882). **VOCAL: Choral:** *Die Stimme des Kindes* for Voices and Piano (1876); *Im stillen Friedhof* for Voices and Piano (1876); *Im Sommer* for Men's Voices (1876); *Geistesgruss* for Men's Voices (1876); *Mailied* for Men's Voices (1876); *Wanderers Nachtlied* for Men's Voices (1876; not extant); *Die schöne Nacht* for Men's Voices (1876; not extant); *Fröhliche Fahrt* for Voices (1876); *Mailied* for Men's Voices (1876; fragment); *Grablied* for Voices (1876); *An Himmelshohn die Sterne gehn* for Voices (c. 1876); *Die Stunden verrauschen* for Solo Voices, Mixed Voices, and Orch. (1878; unfinished); *Sechs geistliche Lieder* for Voices (all 1881; rev. by E. Thomas, 1903); *Wahlspruch* for Men's Voices (c. 1883; not extant); *Christnacht* for Solo Voices, Mixed Voices, and Orch. (1886–89; rev. by M. Reger and F. Foll, 1903); *Elfenlied* for Soprano, Women's Voices, and Orch. (1889–91). **Songs:** *12 Lieder aus der Jugendzeit* (1888); *Lieder nach verschiedenen Dichtern*, 31 songs (1877–97); *Gedichte von Mörike*, 53 songs (1888); *Gedichte von Eichendorff*, 20 songs (1886–88); *Gedichte von Goethe*, 51 songs (1888–89); *Spanisches Liederbuch*, 44 songs after Geibel and Heyse (1889–90); *Italienisches Liederbuch*, 46 songs after Heyse, in 2 parts: 22 songs (1890–91), 24 songs (1896). 20 of the songs were orchestrated by Wolf; others by Max Reger. 40 previously unpubl. songs, mostly of the earliest period, were publ. in Leipzig in 1936, in 4 vols., as *Nachgelassene Werke*, ed. by R. Haas and H. Schultz.

WRITINGS: R. Batka and H. Werner, eds., *Hugo Wolf: Musikalische Kritiken* (Leipzig, 1911; Eng. tr., 1979).

BIBL.: CORRESPONDENCE: E. Hellmer, ed., *H. W.: Briefe an Emil Kauffmann* (Berlin, 1903); M. Haberlandt, ed., *H. W.: Brief an Hugo Faisst* (Stuttgart, 1904); H. Werner, ed., *H. W.: Briefe an Oskar Grohe* (Berlin, 1905); E. Hellmer, ed., *H. W.: Familienbriefe* (Leipzig, 1912); H. Werner, ed., *H. W.: Briefe an Rosa Mayreder, mit einem Nachwort der Dichtetrin des "Corregidors"* (Vienna, 1921); idem, *H. W.: Briefe an Henriette Lang, nebst den briefen an deren Gatten, Prof. Joseph Freiherr von Schey* (Regensburg, 1922); H. Nonveiller, ed., *H. W.: Briefe an Heinrich Potpeschnigg* (Stuttgart, 1923); F. Grasberger, ed., *H. W.: Briefe an Melanie Kochert* (Tutzing, 1964; Eng. tr., 1991); E. Hilmar and W. Obermaier, eds., *Briefe an Frieda Zerny* (Vienna, 1978); D. Langberg, ed., *H. W.: Vom Sinn der Töne: Briefe und Kritiken* (Leipzig, 1991). **MEMOIRS:** H. Haberlandt, *H. W.: Erinnerungen und Gedanken* (Leipzig, 1903; 2nd ed., enl., 1911); H. Werner, *H. W. in Maierling: Eine Idyll* (Leipzig, 1913); E. Hellmer, *H. W.: Erlebtes und Erlauschtes* (Vienna, 1921); H. Werner, *Der H. W.-Verein in Wien* (Regensburg, 1921); idem, *Gustav Schur: Erinnerungen an H. W., nebst H. W.s Briefen an Gustav Schur* (Regensburg, 1922); idem, *H. W. in Perchtoldsdorf* (Regensburg, 1924); R. Kukula, *Erinnerungen eines Bibliothekars* (Weimar, 1925); H. Werner, *H. W. und der Wiener Akademische Wagner-Verein* (Regensburg, 1927); F. Eckstein, *Alte unnennbare Tage* (Vienna, 1936); M. Klinckerfuss, *Aufklänge aus versunkener Zeit* (Urach, 1947). **BIOGRAPHICAL:** E. Decsey, *H. W.* (Berlin and Leipzig, 1903–06); E. Schmitz, *H. W.* (Leipzig, 1906); E. Newman, *H. W.* (London, 1907); M. Morold, *H. W.* (Leipzig, 1912); E. Decsey, *H. W.: Das Leben und das Lied* (Berlin, 1919; 2nd ed., 1921); K. Grunsky, *H. W.* (Leipzig, 1928); B. Benevisti-Viterbi, *H. W.* (Rome, 1931); H. Hécaen, *Mani et inspiration musicale: Le cas H. W.* (Bourdeaux, 1934); H. Schouten, *H. W.: Mens en componist* (Amsterdam, 1935); A. Ehrmann, *H. W.: Sein Leben in Bildern* (Leipzig, 1937); R. Litterscheid, *H. W.* (Potsdam, 1939); M. Hattingberg-Graedener, *H. W.: Vom Wesen und Werk des grössten Liedschöpfers* (Vienna and Leipzig, 1941; 2nd ed., rev., 1953); K. Eickemeyer, *Der Verlauf der Paralyse H. W.s* (diss., Univ. of Jena, 1945); A. Orel, *H. W.* (Vienna, 1947); F. Walker, *H. W.: A Biography* (London, 1951; 2nd ed., enl., 1968); N. Loeser, *H. W.* (Antwerp, 1955); D. Lindner, *H. W.* (Vienna, 1960); E. Werba, *H. W. oder der zornige Romantiker* (Vienna, 1971); K. Honolka, *H. W.: Sein Leben,* *sein Werk, seine Zeit* (Stuttgart, 1988). CRITICAL, ANALYTICAL: *Gesammelte Aufsätze über H. W.* (Berlin, 1898–1900); P. Müller, *H. W.* (Berlin, 1904); K. Heckel, *H. W. in seinem Verhältnis zu Richard Wagner* (Munich, 1905); K. Grunsky, *H. W.-Fest in Stuttgart: Festschrift* (Gutenberg, 1906); W. Salomon, *H. W. als Liederkomponist* (diss., Univ. of Frankfurt am Main, 1925); K. Varges, *Der Musikkritiker H. W.* (Magdeburg, 1934); G. Bieri, *Die Lieder von H. W.* (Bern, 1935); A. Breitenseher, *Der Gesangstechnik in den Liedern H. W.s* (diss., Univ. of Vienna, 1938); U. Sennhenn, *H. W.s Spanisches und Italienisches Liederbuch* (diss., Univ. of Frankfurt am Main, 1955); E. Sams, *The Songs of H. W.* (London, 1961; 2nd ed., rev. and enl., 1981); R. Egger, *Die Deklamationsrhythmik H. W.s in historischer Sicht* (Tutzing, 1963); M. Shott, *H. W.'s Music Criticism* (diss., Ind. Univ., 1964); C. Rostand, *H. W.* (Paris, 1967); P. Boylan, *The Lieder of H. W.* (diss., Univ. of Mich., 1968); B. Campbell, *The Solo Sacred Lieder of H. W.* (diss., Columbia Univ., 1969); M. Carner, *H. W. Songs* (London, 1982); E. Werba, *H. W. und seine Lieder* (Vienna, 1984); D. Stein, *H. W.'s Lieder and Extensions of Tonality* (Ann Arbor, 1985); J. Haywood, *The Musical Language of H. W.* (Ilfracombe, 1986); D. Ossenkop, *H. W.: A Guide to Research* (Westport, Conn., 1988); H.-H. Geyer, *H. W.s Mörike-Vertonungen: Vermannigfaltigung in lyrischer Konzentration* (Kassel, 1991); S. Youens, *H. W.: The Vocal Music* (Princeton, 1992); A. Glauert, *H. W. and the Wagnerian Inheritance* (Cambridge, 1999).—**NS/LK/DM**

Wolf, Johannes, eminent German musicologist; b. Berlin, April 17, 1869; d. Munich, May 25, 1947. He studied at the Hochschule für Musik in Berlin. He took courses in musicology at the Univ. of Berlin with Philipp Spitta and Heinrich Bellermann, and then with Riemann at the Univ. of Leipzig, where he received his Ph.D. in 1893 with the diss. *Ein anonymer Musiktraktat des 11. bis 12. Jahrhunderts;* he completed his Habilitation at the Univ. of Berlin with his *Florenz in der Musikgeschichte des 14. Jahrhunderts* in 1902, and then taught the history of early music and church music. He also was on the faculty of the Berlin Akademie für Kirchen- und Schulmusik from 1908 to 1927. He was appointed director of the early music collection of the Prussian Library in Berlin in 1915; from 1927 to 1934 he was director of its entire music collection. He was a leading authority on medieval and Renaissance music; his writings on the history of notation are especially important. He ed. a complete edition of the works of Obrecht (Leipzig, 1908–21); for Denkmäler Deutscher Tonkunst, he selected vocal works of J.R. Ahle (vol. V, 1901) and G. Rhau's *Newe deudsche geistliche Gesenge für die gemeinen Schulen* (vol. XXXIV, 1908); for Denkmäler der Tonkunst in Österreich, he ed. H. Isaac's secular works (vols. XXVIII, Jg.XIV/1, 1907, and XXXIII, Jg.XVI/1, 1909); also ed. *Der Squarcialupi-Codex aus dem Nachlass herausgegeben von H. Albrecht* (Lippstadt, 1955).

WRITINGS: *Geschichte der Mensuralnotation von 1250 bis 1460 nach den theoretischen und praktischen Quellen* (Leipzig, 1904); *Handbuch der Notationskunde* (2 parts, Leipzig, 1913, 1919); *Musikalische Schrifttafeln* (Leipzig, 1922–23; 2nd ed., 1927); *Die Tonschriften* (Breslau, 1924); *Geschichte der Musik in allgemeinverstandlicher Form* (3 vols., Leipzig, 1925–29).

BIBL.: W. Lott, H. Osthoff, and W. Wolffheim, eds., *Musikwissenschaftliche Beiträge: Festschrift für J. W. zu seinem 60. Geburtstag* (Berlin, 1929).—**NS/LK/DM**

Wolfe, Paul (Cecil), American conductor, violinist, harpsichordist, and oboist; b. N.Y., May 8, 1926. He commenced music training as a child and made his debut as a violinist at N.Y.'s Barbison Hall in 1938. He studied at Queen's Coll. in N.Y. (1942–45) and received training in violin from Mischakoff, Shumsky, Totenberg, and Varid, in oboe from Anton Maly, and in conducting from Barzin and Fritz Mahler. From 1946 to 1949 he was concertmaster and assistant conductor of the U.S. Air Force Orch. in Washington, D.C. He was assistant conductor of the National Orchestral Assn. (1950–61) and conductor of the Fla. West Coast Sym. Orch. in Sarasota, a position he held for 35 years. He also remained active as an instrumentalist.—**NS/LK/DM**

Wolfe, Stanley, American composer and music educator; b. N.Y., Feb. 7, 1924. He was a student of Bergsma, Persichetti, and Mennin at the Juilliard School of Music in N.Y. (B.S., 1952; M.S., 1955). In 1955 he joined its faculty and taught theory, contemporary music, and composition. From 1956 until his retirement in 1989 he served as director of the Juilliard Extension Division. In 1957 he held a Guggenheim fellowship. He received the Alice M. Ditson/American Sym. Orch. prize in 1961. In 1969, 1970, and 1977 he held NEA grants. In 1990 he received a citation and recording award from the American Academy and Inst. of Arts and Letters. In his music, Wolfe has eschewed avant-garde experimentation and has opted to infuse his well-crafted scores with welcome lyricism and melody.

WORKS: DRAMATIC: *King's Heart,* dance piece (1956). ORCH.: 7 syms.: No. 1 (1952), No. 2 (1955), No. 3 (Albuquerque, Nov. 18, 1959), No. 4 (1965; Albuquerque, Dec. 7, 1966), No. 5 (N.Y., April 2, 1971), No. 6 (1981), and No. 7 (1995); *Canticle* for Strings (1957); *Lincoln Square Overture* (1958); *Variations* (1967); Violin Concerto (1989). CHAMBER: *Adagio* for Woodwind Quintet (1948); String Quartet (1961).—**NS/LK/DM**

Wolff, Albert (Louis), noted French conductor and composer; b. Paris (of Dutch parents), Jan. 19, 1884; d. there, Feb. 20, 1970. He studied with Leroux, Gédalge, and Vidal at the Paris Cons. From 1906 to 1910 he was organist of St. Thomas Aquinas in Paris. In 1908 he became a member of the staff of the Paris Opéra-Comique; after serving as its chorus master, he made his conducting debut there, leading the premiere of Laparra's *La Jota,* on April 26, 1911. From 1919 to 1921 he was conductor of the French repertoire at the Metropolitan Opera in N.Y.; conducted the premiere of his opera *L'Oiseau bleu* there on Dec. 27, 1919. Upon his return to Paris in 1921, he was music director of the Opéra-Comique until 1924; in 1925 he became 2nd conductor of the Concerts Pasdeloup, and then was principal conductor from 1934 to 1940; also was conductor of the Concerts Lamoureux from 1928 to 1934. He toured South America from 1940 to 1945; then returned to Paris, where he was director-general of the Opéra-Comique in 1945–46 and thereafter he continued to conduct occasionally there. At the Paris Opéra from 1949; in addition, he made appearances as a sym. conductor. He particularly distinguished himself as a champion of French music of his era; he conducted the premieres of Debussy's *La Boîte à joujoux,* Ravel's *L'Enfant et les sortilèges,*

Roussel's Sym. No. 4, and Poulenc's *Les Mamelles de Tirésias*.

WORKS: DRAMATIC: Opera: *Soeur Beatrice* (1911; Nice, 1948); *Le marchand de masques* (Nice, 1914); *L'Oiseau bleu* (N.Y., Dec. 27, 1919). **ORCH.:** *La randonnée de l'âme défunte*, symphonic poem (1926); Flute Concerto (1943); Sym. (1951). **OTHER:** *Requiem* for Soloists, Chorus, and Orch. (1939); other vocal music; chamber pieces; film music.—**NS/LK/DM**

Wolff, Beverly, American mezzo-soprano; b. Atlanta, Nov. 6, 1928. She learned to play the trumpet and then played in the Atlanta Sym. Orch.; subsequently, she received vocal training from Sidney Dietch and Vera McIntyre at the Academy of Vocal Arts in Philadelphia. In 1952 she won the Philadelphia Youth Auditions and made her formal debut with Ormandy and the Philadelphia Orch.; also appeared as Dinah in the television premiere of Bernstein's *Trouble in Tahiti*. On April 6, 1958, she made her N.Y.C. Opera debut as Dinah, and subsequently sang there regularly until 1971; she also was a guest artist with various other opera companies in the U.S. and abroad.—**NS/LK/DM**

Wolff, Christian, French-born American composer and teacher; b. Nice, March 8, 1934. He went to the U.S. in 1941 and became a naturalized American citizen in 1946. He studied piano with Grete Sultan (1949–51) and composition with John Cage (1950–51), and then pursued training in classical languages at Harvard Univ. (B.A., 1955). After studying Italian literature and classics at the Univ. of Florence (1955–56), he returned to Harvard (Ph.D. in comparative literature, 1963). From 1962 to 1970 he taught classics at Harvard. In 1971 he joined the faculty of Dartmouth Coll. to teach classics, comparative literature, and music, and was made prof. of music and of classics in 1978. He also was a guest lecturer at various institutions of higher learning, and contributed articles on literature and music to many publications. He evolved a curiously static method of composition, using drastically restricted numbers of pitches. His only structural resources became arithmetical progressions of rhythmic values and the expressive use of rests. He used 3 different pitches in his Duo for Violin and Piano; 4 different pitches in the Trio for Flute, Cello, and Trumpet (1951); 9 in a piano piece called *For Piano I*. Beginning in 1957 he introduced into his works various degrees of free choice; sometimes the players are required to react to the musical activities of their partners according to spontaneous and unanticipated cues.

WORKS: Trio for Flute, Trumpet, and Cello (1951); *Summer* for String Quartet (1961); *For 5 or 10 Players* for Any Instruments (1962); *In Between Pieces* for 3 Players Using Any Sound Sources (1963); *For 1, 2 or 3 People* for Any Sound-producing Means (1964); Septet for Any 7 Players and Conductor (1964); *Pairs* for Any 2, 4, 6, or 8 Players (1968); *Prose Collection* for Variable Numbers of Players, Found and Constructed Materials, Instruments, and Voices (1968–71); *Lines* for String Quartet (1972); *Changing the System* for 8 or More Instruments, Voices, and Percussion (1972–73); *Wobbly Music* for Chorus, Keyboard, Guitars, and at Least 2 Melody Instruments (1975–76); *Braverman Music* for Chamber Ensemble (1978); *Rock About, Instrumental, Starving to Death on a Government Claim* for Violin and Viola (1979–80); *Isn't This a Time* for Any Saxophone or Multiple Reeds (1982); *Peace March 1* for Flute (1983–84), *2* for Flute, Clarinet, Cello, Percussion, and Piano (1984), and *3* for Flute, Cello, and Percussion (1984); *Leaning Forward* for Soprano, Britone, Clarinet, and Cello (1988); *Emma* for Viola, Cello, and Piano (1989); *Rosas* for Piano and Percussion (1990); *For Si* for Chamber Ensemble (1990–91); *Aina Gonna Study War No More* for Timpani and Marimbaphone (1993); *Memory* for Chamber Ensemble (1994); *Spring* for Chamber Orch. (1995); *Bratislava* for Chamber Ensemble (1995).—**NS/LK/DM**

Wolff, Christoph (Johannes), eminent German musicologist; b. Solingen, May 24, 1940. He was educated at the univs. of Berlin (1960–63), Freiburg im Breisgau (1963–65), and Erlangen (Ph.D., 1966, with the diss. *Der stile antico in der Musik Johann Sebastian Bachs: Studien zu Bachs Spätwerk*; publ in Wiesbaden, 1968). After lecturing at the Univ. of Erlangen (1966–69), he was an asst. prof. at the Univ. of Toronto (1968–70). He was assoc. prof. (1970–73) and prof. (1973–76) of musicology at Columbia Univ. In 1973 and 1975 he was a visiting prof. at Princeton Univ. From 1974 he served as ed. of the *Bach-Jahrbuch*. In 1976 he became prof. of musicology at Harvard Univ., where he was chairman of the musicology dept. (1980–88; 1990–91), the William Powell Mason Prof. (from 1985), and dean of the Graduate School of Arts and Sciences (from 1992). In 1990 he was made honorary prof. at the Univ. of Freiburg im Breisgau. In 1978 he was awarded the Dent Medal of the Royal Musical Assn. of London and in 1982 he was elected a fellow of the American Academy of Arts and Sciences. Wolff discovered 31 unknown organ chorales by Bach in the Neumeister Collection of the music library at Yale Univ. in 1984, which were publ. in 1985. He has ed. critical editions of works by Scheidt, Buxtehude, Bach, Mozart, and Hindemith, and has written extensively on the history of music from the 15th century to the present.

WRITINGS: Ed. *The String Quartets of Haydn, Mozart, and Beethoven: Studies of the Autograph Manuscripts* (Cambridge, Mass., 1980); ed. with H.-J. Schulze, *Bach Compendium: Analytisch-bibliographisches Repertorium der Werke Johann Sebastian Bachs* (7 vols., Leipzig and Dresden, 1986–89); *Bach: Essays on His Life and Music* (Cambridge, Mass., 1991); *Mozart's Requiem: Historical and Analytical Studies, Documents, Score* (Berkeley, 1993); ed. *Wereld van de Bach-cantates: The World of the Bach Cantatas* (N.Y., 1997 et seq.); ed. *The New Bach Reader* (N.Y., 1998).—**NS/LK/DM**

Wolff, Edouard, Polish pianist, teacher, and composer; b. Warsaw, Sept. 15, 1816; d. Paris, Oct. 16, 1880. He studied in Warsaw with Zawadski (piano) and Elsner (composition), then was a piano pupil of Würfel in Vienna. In 1835 he settled in Paris, and became an esteemed teacher; he was a friend of Chopin, and imitated him in his piano music. He publ. 350 opus numbers for piano, among them several albums of études, a waltz, *La Favorite*, *Chansons polonaises originales*, *Tarentelle*, *Chansons bacchiques*, and a Piano Concerto; also 30 celebrated duos for piano and violin with Bériot, and 8 more with Vieuxtemps. His sister, Regina Wolff, a pianist, was the mother of the violinist **Henryk Wieniawski**.—**NS/LK/DM**

Wolff, Fritz, German tenor; b. Munich, Oct. 28, 1894; d. there, Jan. 18, 1957. He studied with Heinrich König in Würzburg. He made his operatic debut as Loge in 1925 at the Bayreuth Festival, where he continued to make appearances until 1941; also sang in Hagen and Chemnitz. In 1930 he joined the Berlin State Opera, remaining on its roster until 1943; also made guest appearances at Covent Garden in London (1929–33; 1937–38), and in Vienna, Paris, Chicago, and Cleveland. From 1950 he was a prof. at the Hochschule für Musik in Munich. His finest roles included Parsifal and Lohengrin.—**NS/LK/DM**

Wolff, Hellmuth Christian, German musicologist and composer; b. Zürich, May 23, 1906; d. Leipzig, July 1, 1988. He studied musicology at the Univ. of Berlin with Abert, Schering, Blume, and Sachs (Ph.D., 1932, with the diss. *Die Venezianische Oper in der zweiten Hälfte des 17. Jahrhunderts*; publ. in Berlin, 1937; 2nd ed., 1975). He completed his Habilitation at the Univ. of Kiel in 1942 with his *Die Barockoper in Hamburg 1678–1738* (publ. in Wolfenbuttel, 1957). From 1954 to 1971 he was a prof. of musicology at the Univ. of Leipzig. Beginning in 1956 he devoted a great deal of his time to painting, and exhibited in Leipzig and other German cities.

WORKS: DRAMATIC: Opera: *Der kleine und der grosse Klaus* (1931; rev. 1940); *Die törichten Wünsche* (1942–43); *Der Tod des Orpheus* (1947); *Ich lass' mich scheiden* (1950). **Ballet:** *Moresca* (1969). **Scenic Oratorio:** *Esther* (1945). **Other:** Incidental music. **ORCH.:** *3 Werke* for Chamber Orch. (1932); *Concerto for Orchestra* (1933); Concerto for Oboe and Chamber Orch. (1933); *Heitere Musik über ostinate Rhythmen* (1938); Suite (1940); *Inferno 1944* (1946); *Serenade* for Strings (1946); Concerto for Piano and Strings (1947); Violin Concerto (1948); *Sinfonia da missa* (1949); Double Bass Concerto (1968); *Handel Suite* (1970); *Paul Klee Suite* (1973). **OTHER:** Chamber music; piano pieces; songs.

WRITINGS: *Agrippina, eine italienische Jugendoper von G.Fr. Händel* (Wolfenbüttel and Berlin, 1943); *Die Musik der alten Niederländer (15. und 16. Jahrhundert)* (Leipzig, 1956); *Die Händel-Oper auf der modernen Bühne* (Leipzig, 1957); *Oper: Szene und Darstellung von 1600 bis 1900* (Leipzig, 1968); *Die Oper* (3 vols., Cologne, 1971–72; also in Eng.); *Ordnung und Gestalt: die Musik von 1900 bis 1950* (Bonn, 1977).—**NS/LK/DM**

Wolff, Hugh (MacPherson), American conductor; b. Paris (of American parents), Oct. 21, 1953. He was taken to the U.S. by his family when he was 10. He studied piano with Fleisher and Shure and composition with Crumb, then received instruction in composition from Kirchner at Harvard Univ. (B.A., 1975). After studying composition with Messiaen, piano with Sancan, and conducting with Bruck at the Paris Cons., he completed his training with Fleisher at the Peabody Inst. in Baltimore (M.M. in piano, 1977; M.M. in conducting, 1978). He was Exxon/Arts Endowment Conductor (1979–82) and assoc. conductor (1982–85) of the National Sym. Orch. in Washington, D.C.; also was music director of the Northeastern Pa. Phil. (1981–86); likewise appeared as a guest conductor throughout the U.S.; made his European debut with the London Phil. (1983). In 1985 he became the first co-recipient (with Kent Nagano) of the Affiliated Artists' Seaver Conducting Award. He was music director of the N.J. Sym. Orch. (1985–92), and then its principal guest conductor (1992–93). In 1986 he made his N.Y.C. Opera debut conducting *Le nozze di Figaro*. From 1988 to 1991 he was principal conductor of the St. Paul (Minn.) Chamber Orch., then became its music director in 1991. He also was principal conductor of the Grant Park Sym. Orch. in Chicago from 1994 and chief conductor of the Frankfurt am Main Radio Sym. Orch. from 1995.—**NS/LK/DM**

Wolff, Jean-Claude, French composer; b. Paris, Oct. 1946. He studied in Paris at the École Normale de Musique and at the Cons. (prix de composition, 1974), his principal mentors being Henri Dutilleux, Jean-Marie Guézec, Michael Philippot, and Ivo Malec. He also received training in composition from Franco Donatoni at the Accademia Musicale Chigiana in Siena, and was in residence at the Villa Medici in Rome under the auspices of the Académie de France (1978–80). He was awarded prizes in composition in the Jeunesses Musicales Internationales competition in Belgrade in 1979, the G. B. Viotti competition in Vercelli in 1986, and the Vienna Modern Masters competition in 1990. In 1992 he served as artist-in-residence of the Fondation d'Art Henri Clews in Napoule, Alpes-Maritimes.

WORKS: *Morale I* for English Horn (1973), *II* for Guitar (1981), *III* for Guitar, Violin, and Zarb (1975), and *IV* for Electric Guitar (1984; Angers, Oct. 9, 1986); *Moissons* for Amateur Chamber Orch. (1975); 8 syms.: No. 2 for Violin and Orch. (1978; Rome, July 11, 1979), No. 3 (1982; Paris, Nov. 17, 1983), No. 1 (1983; Nancy, April 25, 1985), No. 4 for 35 Instruments (1985; Paris, March 5, 1988), No. 5 for 38 Instruments (1992; Paris, Jan. 9, 1994), No. 6, *Eléménts d'une traversée*, for 6 Vocal Soloists, Chorus, and Orch. (1994), No. 7 for English Horn and String Orch. (1995), and No. 8 for Flute, Clarinet, and Tape (1997); *Duo* for Guitars (1978); Concerto for String Orch. (Rome, June 29, 1979); *Comme un paysage frôle* for Electroacoustic Instrumental Ensemble (1979); *Tristes* for Chamber Orch. (Rome, Dec. 3, 1979); *Nuit* for Soprano and String Quartet (Rome, June 18, 1980); Octet for Clarinet, Bassoon, Horn, 2 Violins, Viola, Cello, and Double Bass (1980; Boswill, Switzerland, Nov. 25, 1982); *Articulations* for Flute, Clarinet, Percussion, 2 Guitars, Harp, Violin, and Double Bass (1984; Amsterdam, April 6, 1985); *Reflet* for Flute, Harp, Violin, and Cello (1986); *Traces* for Amateur Chamber Ensemble (1987); *Tiercés* for Flute, Harp, Violin, and Cello (1987; Amsterdam, May 8, 1988); Septet for Piano, Oboe, Percussion, Guitar, Electric Guitar, Harp, and Double Bass (1988; Paris, May 23, 1999); Trio for Piano, Violin, and Horn (1989; Paris, Feb. 11, 1991); Trio for Guitars (Orléans, Oct. 28, 1990); Duo for Harps (1990); *Psaume 88* for Chorus and Instrumental Ensemble (1990); *Errances* for Flute, Saxophone, Violin, and Cello (Amsterdam, May 12, 1991); *Mosaïques* for Flute, Viola, and Guitar (1991; Echirolles, Nov. 28, 1995); *Marche lente* for Flute, Harp, and Percussion (Montpellier, May 15, 1992); Suite for Violin and Piano (1993); *Trois solitudes* for Cello and Piano (1993; Echirolles, Nov. 28, 1995); *Incantation* for Harp (Rheims, Aug. 21, 1994); *Chants* for Wind Quintet (1994; Echirolles, May 30, 1995); Sonata for 8 Cellos (1994; Rencontres, May 9, 1996); *L'inquiétude* for Mezzo-soprano and Instrumental Ensemble (1995; Meylan, Nov. 29, 1996); *Crépuscules* for Piano (1996; Paris, Nov. 20, 1997); *Thrène* for Flute, Clarinet, Violin, Cello, and Piano (1997; l'Avray, May 25, 1998); *Paysages d'encres* for Electric Guitar and String Trio (1997); *Onze préludes* for Piano (1997); *Poèmes orientaux* for Contralto and Piano (1998);

Psaumes for 6 Women's Voices, Baritone, and Instrumental Ensemble (1998; Geneva, Aug. 20, 1999); *Sinfonietta* for Orch. (1998; Le Blanc-Mesnil, June 4, 1999); *Une lecture de Marie Noël* for 2 Flutes, 2 Clarinets, Trombone, Percussion, Piano, and Cello (Le Blanc-Mesnil, June 4, 1999); Sonatine for Oboe and Piano (1999); *Le lointain le plus proche* for Soprano and Harp (1999). **—LK/DM**

Wolf-Ferrari (real name, **Wolf**), **Ermanno,** famous Italian opera composer; b. Venice, Jan. 12, 1876; d. there, Jan. 21, 1948. His father was a well-known painter of German descent and his mother was Italian; about 1895 he added his mother's maiden name to his surname. He began piano study as a small child but also evinced a talent for art; after studying at the Accademia di Belle Arti in Rome (1891–92), he went to Munich to continue his training but then turned to music and studied counterpoint with Rheinberger at the Akademie der Tonkunst (1892–95). In 1899 he returned to Venice, where his oratorio *La Sulamite* was successfully performed. This was followed by the production of his first major opera, *Cenerentola* (1900), which initially proved a failure; however, its revised version for Bremen (1902) was well received and established his reputation as a composer for the theater. From 1903 to 1909 he was director of the Liceo Benedetto Marcello in Venice; then devoted himself mainly to composition and later was prof. of composition at the Salzburg Mozarteum (1939–45). He obtained his first unqualified success with the production of the comic opera *Le donne curiose* (Munich, 1903); the next opera, *I quattro rusteghi* (Munich, 1906), was also well received. There followed his little masterpiece, *Il segreto di Susanna* (Munich, 1909), a one-act opera buffa in the style of the Italian verismo (Susanna's secret being not infidelity, as her husband suspected, but indulgence in surreptitious smoking). Turning toward grand opera, he wrote *I gioielli della Madonna*; it was brought out at Berlin in 1911, and soon became a repertoire piece everywhere; he continued to compose, but his later operas failed to match the appeal of his early creations.

WORKS: DRAMATIC: Opera: *Cenerentola* (Venice, Feb. 22, 1900; rev. version as *Aschenbrödel*, Bremen, Jan. 31, 1902); *Le Donne curiose* (1902–03; in Ger. as *Die neugierigen Frauen*, Munich, Nov. 27, 1903; in Italian, N.Y., Jan. 3, 1912); *I quattro rusteghi* (in Ger. as *Die vier Grobiane*, Munich, March 19, 1906); *Il segreto di Susanna* (in Ger. as *Susannens Geheimnis*, Munich, Dec. 4, 1909; in Italian, N.Y., March 14, 1911); *I gioielli della Madonna* (in Ger. as *Der Schmuck der Madonna*, Berlin, Dec. 23, 1911; in Italian, Chicago, Jan. 16, 1912; in Eng. as *The Jewels of the Madonna*, N.Y., Oct. 14, 1913); *L'amore medico* (in Ger. as *Der Liebhaber als Arzt*, Dresden, Dec. 4, 1913; in Italian, N.Y., March 25, 1914); *Gli Amanti sposi* (c. 1916; Venice, Feb. 19, 1925); *Das Himmelskleid* (c. 1917–25; Munich, April 21, 1927; in Italian as *La veste di cielo*); *Sly, ovvero La leggenda del dormiente risvegliato* (Milan, Dec. 29, 1927); *La vedova scaltra* (Rome, March 5, 1931); *Il campiello* (Milan, Feb. 11, 1936); *La dama boba* (Milan, Feb. 1, 1939); *Gli dei a Tebe* (in Ger. as *Der Kuckuck in Theben*, Hannover, June 5, 1943); also an ed. of Mozart's *Idomeneo* (Munich, June 15, 1931). **ORCH.:** *Serenade* for Strings (c. 1893); *Kammersymphonie* (1901); *Idillio-concertino* for Oboe, 2 Horns, and Strings (1933); *Suite-concertino* for Bassoon, 2 Horns, and Strings (Rome, March 26, 1933); *Suite veneziano* for Small Orch. (1936); *Divertimento* (1937); *Arabeschi* (1940); Violin Concerto (1946); *Symphonia brevis* (1947); Cello Concerto (c. 1947). **CHAMBER:** String Quintet (1894); 3 violin sonatas (1895, 1901, c. 1940); 2 piano trios (c. 1897, 1900); Piano Quintet (1900); String Quartet (1940); String Quintet (1942); String Trio (1946); *Introduzione e balletto* for Violin and Cello (1946); piano pieces. **VOCAL:** *La Sulamite*, canto biblico (1889); *Talitha kumi*, oratorio (1900); *La vita nuova*, cantata (1901; Munich, Feb. 21, 1903); *La passione* for Chorus (1939; also for Voice and Piano, 1940); other large and small choral works.

BIBL.: H. Teibler, *E. W.-F.* (Leipzig, 1906); E. Stahl, ed., *E. W.-F.* (Salzburg, 1936); R. de Rensis, *E. W.-F., La sua vita d'artista* (Milan, 1937); A. Grisson, *E. W.-F.: autorisierte Lebensbeschreibung* (Regensburg, 1941; 2nd ed., enl., 1958); R. de Rensis and G. Vannini, *In memoria di E. W.-F.* (Siena, 1948); W. Pfannkuch, *Das Opernschaffen E. W.-F.s* (diss., Univ. of Kiel, 1952); A. Suder, ed., *E. W.-F.* (Tutzing, 1986).**—NS/LK/DM**

Wölfl (Woelfl, Wölffl), Joseph, Austrian pianist and composer; b. Salzburg, Dec. 24, 1773; d. London, May 21, 1812. He was a pupil of Leopold Mozart and Michael Haydn while serving as a chorister at the Salzburg Cathedral (1783–86). He was then in Vienna (1790–92) and Warsaw (1793), and again in Vienna from 1795; he was considered Beethoven's rival as a pianist. In 1798 he married the actress Therese Klemm. Traveling through Germany, he gave numerous concerts as a pianist, reaching Paris in 1801, where he produced 2 French operas and was acclaimed as a piano virtuoso. In 1805 he went to London, and almost immediately established himself in the public's favor as a pianist and teacher. He was, however, of an eccentric disposition, and became involved in all sorts of trouble. He died in obscurity at the age of 38. In his professional life, he emphasized the sensational element and gave fanciful titles to his works; he named one of his piano sonatas *Ne plus ultra* and claimed that it was the most difficult piece ever written. Some of his piano pieces were publ. in monthly issues, under the title *The Harmonic Budget* (London, 1810).

WORKS: DRAMATIC: Opera: *Der Höllenberg* (Vienna, Nov. 21, 1795); *Das schöne Milchmädchen, oder der Guckkasten* (Vienna, Jan. 5, 1797); *Der Kopf ohne Mann* (Vienna, Dec. 3, 1798); *Das trojanische Pferd* (Vienna, 1797); *L'Amour romanesque* (Paris, 1804); *Fernando, ou Les Maures* (Paris, 1805). **Ballet:** *La Surprise de Diane* (London, Sept. 21, 1805); *Alzire* (London, Jan. 27, 1807). **ORCH.:** 7 piano concertos, including *Le Calme* and *Grand concerto;* 2 syms. **CHAMBER:** 12 string quartets; 6 piano trios; 2 trios for 2 Clarinets and Bassoon. **Piano:** Numerous sonatas; many sets of variations; a *Méthode* (with 100 studies); sonatas for Piano, 4-Hands; waltzes, polonaises, rondos, fantasias, etc. **VOCAL:** Songs.

BIBL.: R. Baum, *J. Wölfl: Leben, Klavierwerke, Klavierkammermusik und Klavierkonzerte* (Kassel, 1928).**—NS/LK/DM**

Wolfram, Joseph Maria, Bohemian composer; b. Dobrzan, July 21, 1789; d. Teplitz, Sept. 30, 1839. He studied with J. A. Koželuch in Prague, then moved to Vienna as a music teacher. He then became a government official at Theusing, and mayor of Teplitz (1824). He brought out several successful operas: *Maja und*

Alpino (Prague, May 24, 1826), *Der Bergmonch* (Dresden, March 14, 1830), and *Das Schloss Candra* (Dresden, Dec. 1, 1832). A *Missa nuptialis* and some piano pieces and songs by him were publ.—**NS/LK/DM**

Wolfrum, Philipp, German conductor, musicologist, and composer; b. Schwarzenbach-am-Wald, Dec. 17, 1854; d. Sa maden, May 8, 1919. He was a pupil of Rheinberger and Wullner in Munich, receiving his Ph.D. at Leipzig Univ. in 1890 with the diss. *Die Entstehung und erste Entwickelung des deutschen evangelischen Kirchenliedes in musikalischer Beziehung*. After serving as a music teacher in a Bamberg seminary (1879–84), he was named director of music at Heidelberg Univ., where he was made a prof. in 1898. He was also founder-conductor of the noted Heidelberg Bachverein (from 1885), with which he championed the music of Bach; he also furthered the cause of Bruckner and Reger. In addition to his composition, he also ed. *Der evangelische Kirchenchor* (collection of 44 hymns) and *Pfälzisches Melodienbuch*. His brother, Karl Wolfrum (b. Schwarzenbach-am-Wald, Aug. 14, 1856; d. Neustadt-an-der-Aisch, May 27, 1937), was a pedagogue and composer.

WORKS: *Festliche Ouvertüre; Das grosse Halleluja*, ode for Chorus and Orch. (1886); *Ein Weihnachtsmysterium*, Christmas play, for Chorus and Orch. (1899); Piano Quartet; String Quartet; Piano Trio; Cello Sonata; 3 organ sonatas.

WRITINGS: *Joh. Seb. Bach* (2 vols., 1906; 2nd ed. of vol. 1, 1910); *Die evangelische Kirchenmusik: Ihr Stand und ihre Weiterentwicklung* (1914); *Luther und Bach* (1917); *Luther und die Musik* (1918).—**NS/LK/DM**

Wolkenstein, Oswald von, South Tirolean Minnesänger; b. Schöneck in Pustertal, c. 1377; d. Merano, Aug. 2, 1445. He led an adventurous life, traveling through Russia, Persia, Greece, Spain, France, Italy (with King Ruprecht in 1401), etc. For several years (from 1415) he was in the service of King (later Emperor) Sigismund, whom he accompanied to the Council of Constance. The musical settings that he devised for his poems are notable for their genuine melodic quality; some of them are in 2-part and 3-part counterpoint; there are also examples of canonic imitation. For his output, see J. Schatz and O. Keller, eds., *Oswald von Wolkenstein: Geistliche und weltliche Lieder, ein- und mehrstimmig*, Denkmäler der Tonkunst in Österreich, XVIII, Jg.IX (1902), K. Klein, W. Weiss, N. Wolf, and W. Salmen, eds., *Die Lieder Oswalds von Wolkenstein* (Tübingen, 1962; 2nd ed., rev., 1975 by H. Moser, N.R. Wolf, and N. Wolf), B. Wachinger, ed. and tr., *Oswald von Wolkenstein: Eine Auswahl aus seinen Liedern* (Ebenhausen, 1964), H. Moser and U. Müller, eds., *Oswald von Wolkenstein: Abbildungen zur Überlieferung, I: Die Innsbrucker Wolkenstein-Handschrift* (Göppingen, 1972), and U. Müller and F. Spechter, eds., *Oswald von Wolkenstein: Handschrift A in Abbildung* (Stuttgart, 1974).

BIBL.: W. Marold, *Kommentar zu den Liedern O.s v.W.* (diss., Univ. of Göttingen, 1926); H. Lowenstein, *Wort und Ton bei O. v.W.* (Königsberg, 1932); E. Timm, *Die Überlieferung der Lieder O.s v.W.* (Lübeck and Hamburg, 1972); I. Pelnar, *Die mehrstimmigen Lieder O.s v.W.* (diss., Univ. of Munich, 1977); A. Schwob, *O. v.W.: eine Biographie* (Bolzano, 1977).—**NS/LK/DM**

Wolpe, Stefan, significant German-American composer and pedagogue; b. Berlin, Aug. 25, 1902; d. N.Y., April 4, 1972. He studied theory with Juon and Schreker at the Berlin Hochschule für Musik (1919–24). After graduation, he became associated with choral and theatrical groups in Berlin, promoting social causes; composed songs on revolutionary themes. With the advent of the anti-Semitic Nazi regime in 1933, he went to Vienna, where he took lessons with Webern; then traveled to Palestine in 1934; taught at the Jerusalem Cons. In 1938 he emigrated to the U.S., where he devoted himself mainly to teaching. He was on the faculty of the Settlement Music School in Philadelphia (1939–42), at the Philadelphia Academy of Music (1949–52), at Black Mountain Coll., N.C. (1952–56), and at Long Island Univ. (1957–68). He also taught privately. Among his students were Elmer Bernstein, Ezra Laderman, Ralph Shapey, David Tudor, and Morton Feldman. He was married successively to Ola Okuniewska, a painter, in 1927, to Irma Schoenberg (1902–84), a Romanian pianist, in 1934, and to Hilda Morley, a poet, in 1948. In 1966 he was elected a member of the National Inst. of Arts and Letters. He contributed numerous articles to German and American music magazines. In his style of composition, he attempted to reconcile the contradictions of triadic tonality (which he cultivated during his early period of writing "proletarian" music), atonality without procrustean dodecaphony, and serialism of contrasts obtained by intervallic contraction and expansion, metrical alteration, and dynamic variegation; superadded to these were explorations of Jewish cantillation and infatuation with jazz. Remarkably enough, the very copiousness of these resources contributed to a clearly identifiable idiom.

WORKS: DRAMATIC: Opera: *Schöne Geschichten* (1927–29); *Zeus und Elida* (1928). **Ballet:** *The Man from Midian* (1942). **Incidental Music To:** *De liegt Hund begraben* (1932); Bertolt Brecht's *The Good Woman of Setzuan* (1953) and *The Exception and the Rule* (1961); *Peer Gynt* (1954); *The Tempest* (1960). **ORCH.:** *Passacaglia* (1937); *The Man from Midian*, suite from the ballet (1942); Sym. (1955–56; rev. 1964); Piece for Piano and 16 Players (1961); *Chamber Piece No. 1* for 14 Players (1964) and *No. 2* for 13 Players (1965–66). **CHAMBER:** *Duo in Hexachord* for Oboe and Clarinet (1936); *Lied, Anrede, Hymnus* for Oboe and Piano (1939); Oboe Sonata (1941); Violin Sonata (1949); Quartet for Tenor Saxophone, Trumpet, Percussion, and Piano (1950; rev. 1954); *12 Pieces* for String Quartet (1950); *Piece* for Oboe, Cello, Percussion, and Piano (1955); Quintet for Clarinet, Horn, Cello, Harp, and Piano with Baritone (1957); *Piece in 2 Parts* for Flute and Piano (1960); *In 2 Parts* for Clarinet, Trumpet, Violin, Cello, Harp, and Piano (1962); *Piece for 2 Instrumental Units* for Flute, Oboe, Violin, Cello, Double Bass, Percussion, and Piano (1963); *Trio in 2 Parts* for Flute, Cello, and Piano (1964); *Piece in 2 Parts for Violin Alone* (1964); *Solo Piece* for Trumpet (1966); *Piece for Violin Alone* (1966); *From Here on Farther* for Clarinet, Bass Clarinet, Violin, and Piano (1969); String Quartet (1969); *Piece for Trumpet and 7 Instruments* for Trumpet, Clarinet, Bassoon, Horn, Violin, Viola, Cello, and Double Bass (1971). **Piano:** *March and Variations* for 2 Pianos (1933); *4 Studies on Basic Rows* (1935–36); *Zemach Suite* (1939–41); *Pastorale* (1941); *Toccata* (1941); *Music for Any Instruments: Interval Studies* (1944–49); *Battle Piece* (1947); *2 Studies* (part 2, 1948); *Music for a Dancer* (1950); *7 Pieces* for 3

Pianos (1951); *Waltz for Merle* (1952); *Enactments* for 3 Pianos (1953); *Form* (1959); *Form IV: Broken Sequences* (1969). **VOCAL:** 4 cantatas: *Yigdal* for Baritone, Chorus, and Organ (1945), *Lazy Andy Ant* for Voice and 2 Pianos (1947), *Street Music* for Baritone, Speaker, Flute, Oboe, Clarinet, Cello, and Piano (1962), and Cantata for Mezzo-soprano, 3 Women's Voices, and 9 Instruments (1963); choral songs; solo songs.

BIBL.: H. Sucoff, *Catalogue and Evaluation of the Work of S. W.* (N.Y., 1969).—**NS/LK/DM**

Wolpert, Franz Alfons, German composer and music theorist; b. Wiesentheid, Oct. 11, 1917; d. there, Aug. 7, 1978. He sang in the Cathedral choir in Regensburg, and studied there at a Catholic church music school. He took lessons in composition with Wolf-Ferrari at the Salzburg Mozarteum (1939–41), where he subsequently taught (1941–44); was a teacher in Salem, Lake Constance (from 1950). He publ. the useful vol. *Neue Harmonik: die Lehre von den Akkordtypen* (Regensburg, 1952; 2nd ed., rev. and enl., 1972). His compositions include a comic opera, *Der eingebildete Kranke* (1975), a ballet, *Der goldene Schuh* (1956), *Banchetto musicale No. 1* for Violin and Chamber Orch. (1952) and *No. 2* for Piano and Orch. (1953), chamber music, organ and piano pieces, choral works, and over 50 lieder.—**NS/LK/DM**

Womack, Bobby, underground soul icon; b. Cleveland, Ohio, March 4, 1944. An extremely talented guitarist, when the fortunes of his solo career hit slow points, he reverted to studio and side work. However, as a solo artist, Womack shone. He probably would have been far more successful if his first marriage had been a bit quieter.

He began working professionally with his brothers in a family gospel group, The Womacks. On the gospel circuit, they became friendly with Sam Cooke and the Soul Stirrers. When Cooke went secular, he brought in Womack as his guitarist. He also signed The Womack Brothers to his SAR label. Working gospel, they kept the family name. They took the pop music guise The Valentinos and created a fine body of work highlighted by "It's All Over Now" and "Looking for a Love," which went Top Ten R&B in 1962. The Rolling Stones took the former song to #26, their second American hit in 1964. The latter was The J. Geils Band's first hit, rising to #39 in 1972.

Cooke died and The Valentinos broke up around the same time in 1964. Womack became a first-call soul session man, recording with Aretha Franklin, King Curtis, and Ray Charles. However, two months after Cooke died, Womack married his widow. The upshot in the soul community had a chilling effect on his career, keeping him from recording solo for a number of years. He did write and perform on many sessions. His "I'm a Midnight Mover" rose to #24 pop and "I'm in Love" was a substantial R&B hit for Wilson Pickett. He also wrote and played on "Trust Me" for Janis Joplin.

He started to record solo in the late 1960s with minor R&B success. He finally broke through as a solo artist in 1971 with "That's the Way I Feel about Cha." The song hit #27 pop and #2 R&B. A year later, "Woman's Got to Have It" topped the R&B charts and "Harry Hippie" rose to #31 pop, #8 R&B and went gold. "Nobody Loves You When You're Down and Out" hit #29 pop and #2 R&B in 1973. In 1974, in the wake of the J. Geils Band cover, he remade "Looking for a Love" and topped the R&B charts, taking it to #10 pop and going gold. Over the next couple of years, he had such Top Ten R&B hits as "You're Welcome, Stop on By," "Check It Out," and "Daylight."

The late 1970s saw him falling by the musical wayside, with albums on Columbia and Arista that didn't sell. This was partly because his output lacked the spark of others who followed in his musical footsteps, such as Sly and the Family Stone, and partly because of Womack's drug abuse. He did contribute key parts in the studio, like the wha-wha guitar and popping bass on Sly's "Family Affair." He also wrote the score to the film *Across 110th St.* and George Benson's hit "Breezin'."

In 1981 a small, well-funded label called Beverly Glen (cf. Anita Baker) signed a newly clean and sober Womack. The new album, *The Poet*, topped the R&B charts led by the #3 R&B hit, "If You Think You're Lonely Now." The follow-up, *The Poet II*, included three duets with Patti LaBelle. Two of them, "Love Has Finally Come at Last" and "I Wish He Didn't Trust Me So Much," became top 5 R&B hits.

During the rest of the 1980s and into the 1990s, Womack made several high profile cameo appearances, singing with Todd Rundgren, The Rolling Stones, and Artists United Against Apartheid, as well as doing some work with the reunited Womack Brothers. Shortly after that reunion, one of his brothers was killed and his son committed suicide. His second marriage ended in divorce (as his first one did in 1970).

He finally returned as a solo artist with *Resurrection* on Rolling Stone Ron Wood's custom label Slide. Although it featured heavy friends like Wood, Charlie Watts, Keith Richards, and Stevie Wonder, the album was poorly distributed and promoted and quickly fell of the radar. His output for the rest of the 1990s was been sporadic, with more reissue material than any new music. His 1999 album *Traditions* found him making his first stab at a holiday album with middling success.

DISC.: *The Womack Live* (1967); *Fly Me to the Moon* (1969); *My Prescription* (1970); *Communication* (1971); *Understanding* (1972); *Across 110th Street* (1972); *The Facts of Life* (1973); *Lookin' for a Love Again* (1974); *BW Goes C&W* (1974); *I Don't Know What the World Is Coming To* (1975); *Safety Zone* (1975); *I Can Understand It* (1975); *Home Is Where the Heart Is* (1976); *Pieces* (1977); *Save the Children* (1979); *Roads of Life* (1979); *The Poet* (1981); *The Poet II* (1984); *Bobby Womack & the Valentinos* (1984); *So Many Rivers* (1985); *Someday We'll All Be Free* (1985); *Womagic* (1986); *Last Soul Man* (1987); *I Still Love You* (1993); *I Wanna Make Love to You* (1993); *Soul Seduction Supreme* (1994); *Soul Sensation Live* (1998); *Back to My Roots* (1999); *Traditions* (1999).—**BH**

Wonder, Stevie (originally, **Morris, Steveland**), child prodigy star who matured into one of the greatest pop singer/songwriters of the 1960s–80s; b. Saginaw, Mich., May 13, 1950. Afflicted by blindness as a newborn, Steveland Morris moved with his family to Detroit in 1954. Playing harmonica by the age of five, he started piano lessons at six and took up drums at eight. Writing his first song by the age of ten, Wonder was spotted in 1961 by The Miracles' Ronnie White, who took him to Brian Holland. Holland arranged an audition with Motown Records' Berry Gordy Jr., and Wonder was immediately signed to the Tamla label and assigned the name "Little" Stevie Wonder. Working primarily with songwriter-producer Henry Cosby until 1970, Wonder scored a surprising top pop and rhythm-and-blues hit in 1963 with the raucous harmonica instrumental, "Fingertips—Part 2," recorded live at Chicago's Regal Theater, complete with mistakes, musical puns, and a shouting stage manager. The following year he enrolled in the Mich. School for the Blind, studied classical piano, and managed moderate pop hits with the harmonica-based songs "Workout, Stevie, Workout" and "Harmonica Man." He also appeared in the 1964 films *Bikini Beach* and *Muscle Beach Party*.

Dropping the "Little" appellation in the summer of 1964, Stevie Wonder emerged in 1965 and 1966 with the energetic dance-style smash hit "Uptight (Everything's Alright)" (which he cowrote with Henry Cosby and Sylvia Moy), the major hit "Nothing's Too Good for My Baby," and a near-smash hit version of Bob Dylan's "Blowin' in the Wind" from *Uptight*. While recording a wide variety of material on his albums, Wonder quickly established himself as a popular crossover singles artist with romantic ballads and uptempo pop-style songs such as "A Place in the Sun," "Trav'lin' Man," the top rhythm-and-blues and pop smash "I Was Made to Love Her," and "I'm Wondering," the latter two cowritten with Cosby and Moy. Following an album of Christmas material and an instrumental album released under the name Rednow Eivets (Stevie Wonder backwards), Wonder's *For Once in My Life* yielded five hits, including the top R&B and smash pop hit "Shoo-Be-Doo-Be-Doo-Da-Day" and the crossover smash hit title song. *My Cherie Amour* produced two smash hits with the title song and "Yester-Me, Yester-You, Yesterday."

Stevie Wonder's first self-produced album, *Signed Sealed and Delivered*, contained four hits, including the top R&B and smash pop hit title song and the crossover smash "Heaven Help Us All." Unjustly criticized for the easy-listening nature of his songs (only "My Cherie Amour" proved a smash easy-listening hit), Wonder certainly did record pop-style material, and his flexible vocal style was unlike any other Motown act. He began experimenting with various rhythmic and musical textures and different electric keyboard instruments, including the synthesizer, with *Where I'm Coming From*. The album included the crossover smash "If You Really Love Me" and the neglected ballad "Never Dreamed You'd Leave in Summer," both written by Wonder and then-wife Syreeta Wright.

In 1971, at the age of 21, Stevie Wonder negotiated a new contract with Motown that gave him artistic control over his recordings and provided for the unprecedented formation of his own music publishing company, Black Bull Music, and production company, Taurus Productions. For his first album under the new contract, *Music of My Mind*, he played every instrument, coauthored the songs with Syreeta Wright, and produced. The album sold remarkably well despite yielding only one hit, "Superwoman (Where Were You When I Needed You)." The album began to establish Wonder as an album artist, and, as a consequence of a well-received summer 1972 tour with The Rolling Stones, he attracted a huge following among the white rock audience while retaining his black fans.

Stevie Wonder's growing popularity and recognition was immeasurably bolstered by the exceptional *Talking Book* album, one of the finest albums of the 1970s. In addition to producing two top pop hits with the mellow "You Are the Sunshine of My Life" (a smash R&B hit) and the seminal "Superstition" (a top R&B hit), the album contained three other excellent songs, "You've Got It Bad Girl," "Blame It on the Sun," and "I Believe (When I Fall in Love It Will Be Forever)." For his next album, Wonder performed virtually all the instrumental chores and solely composed all the songs. The monumental *Innervisions* yielded two top rhythm-and-blues and smash pop hits with the socially conscious "Higher Ground" and "Living for the City," and the smash R&B and major pop hit "Don't You Worry 'bout a Thing." The album also included favorites such as "Too High," "Golden Lady," and "All in Love Is Fair."

Working with other artists, Stevie Wonder cowrote The Miracles' 1970 top pop and rhythm-and-blues hit "The Tears of a Clown," wrote and produced The Spinners' 1970 smash R&B and major pop hit "It's a Shame," and wrote Rufus's 1974 smash pop and R&B hit "Tell Me Something Good." He produced Syreeta Wright's first and second albums and Minnie Riperton's *Perfect Angel*, which included her top pop and smash R&B hit "Lovin' You." However, on Aug. 6, 1973, he was involved in a serious auto accident near Durham, N.C., that left him in a coma for four days.

Stevie Wonder staged a remarkable recovery and recorded yet another outstanding album, *Fulfillingness' First Finale*. It debuted at the top of the album charts and produced the top pop and R&B hit "You Haven't Done Nothin'" (ostensibly an indictment of Richard Nixon) and the seminal crossover smash "Boogie On, Reggae Woman," while including the religious "Heaven Is 10 Million Years Away." Following a tour in the winter of 1974, Wonder essentially retired from the road to work on his epic, *Songs in the Key of Life*. Eventually issued in the fall of 1976 accompanied by a four-song EP, the album included two top crossover hits, "I Wish" and the tribute to Duke Ellington, "Sir Duke." The album also contained the moderate crossover hits "Another Star" and "As," as well as "Isn't She Lovely" and other captivating songs. Earlier, in April, Wonder had signed a contract renewal with Motown valued at $13 million, the largest such contract to date.

Film producer Michael Braun subsequently approached Stevie Wonder about composing a song for a documentary on plant life. Wonder ultimately composed and recorded an entire score, later returning to the studio to add more songs and lyrics and overdub the sounds of nature. Eventually issued as *Journey through the Secret Life of Plants*, the album was criticized as esoteric, inaccessible, and tedious, yet it yielded a crossover smash with "Send One Your Love." Wonder toured in 1980 and recorded *Hotter Than July*, which produced a top rhythm-and-blues and smash pop hit with "Master Blaster (Jammin')," inspired by Bob Marley, and the smash R&B and major pop hit "I Ain't Gonna Stand for It." The album also contained his tribute to Martin Luther King Jr., "Happy Birthday," the ballad "Lately," and uptempo songs such as "Let's Get Serious" and "Always."

Stevie Wonder has maintained a relatively low profile since the early 1980s. In 1982, he scored a top rhythm-and-blues and smash pop hit with "That Girl" from his anthology set *Original Musiquarium*, which also provided hits with "Do I Do" and "Ribbon in the Sky." His duet with Paul McCartney on "Ebony and Ivory" also became a top R&B and smash pop hit in 1982. He participated in the campaign to establish Martin Luther King Jr.'s birthday as a national holiday and hosted a 1986 television special marking its first celebration. He provided seven original songs to the soundtrack to the 1984 film *The Woman in Red*, including the maudlin top pop and rhythm-and-blues hit "I Just Called to Say I Love You" and the major crossover hit "Love Light in Flight." The soundtrack album also included the didactic "Don't Drive Drunk," but the song did not appear in the movie.

Touring in 1983 and 1986, Stevie Wonder issued his first album of new material in five years, *In Square Circle*, in 1985. The album yielded four hits, including the top pop and rhythm-and-blues hit "Part-Time Lover" and the crossover smash "Go Home." He participated in the recording of U.S.A. for Africa's "We Are the World" in 1985 and later recorded with Elton John and Gladys Knight as Dionne Warwick's "friends" on the top pop and rhythm-and-blues hit, "That's What Friends Are For." *Characters*, from 1987, produced two top R&B hits with "Skeletons" (a major pop hit) and "You Will Know," and the R&B smash duet with Michael Jackson, "Get It." Stevie Wonder was inducted into the Rock and Roll Hall of Fame in 1989. He composed and recorded 11 songs for the soundtrack to Spike Lee's provocative film *Jungle Fever*, released in 1991. He eventually toured in support of 1995's *Conversation Peace*, recording the live *Natural Wonder* album with the Tokyo Philharmonic Orch.

DISC.: *Tribute to Uncle Ray* (1963); *The Jazz Soul of Little Stevie Wonder* (1963); *The 12-Year-Old Genius* (1963); *Workout, Stevie, Workout* (1963); *With a Song in My Heart* (1964); *Stevie at the Beach* (1964); *Uptight—Everything's Alright* (1966); *Down to Earth* (1966); *I Was Made to Love Her* (1967); *Someday at Christmas* (1967); *Eivets Rednow* (1968); *For Once in My Life* (1969); *My Cherie Amour* (1969); *Live* (1970); *Signed, Sealed and Delivered* (1970); *Where I'm Coming From* (1971); *Music of My Mind* (1972); *Talking Book* (1972); *Innervisions* (1973); *Fulfillingness' First Finale* (1974); *Songs in the Key of Life* (1976); *Journey through the Secret Life of Plants* (1979); *Hotter Than July* (1980); *The Woman in Red* (music from soundtrack; 1984); *In Square Circle* (1985); *Characters* (1987); *Jungle Fever* (music from soundtrack; 1991); *Conversation Peace* (1995); *Natural Wonder* (live; 1995).

BIBL.: C. Dragonwagon, *S. W.* (N.Y., 1977); C. Elsner, *S. W.* (N.Y., 1977); J. Haskins, *The S. W. Scrapbook* (N.Y., 1978).**—BH**

Wong, Francis, American woodwind instrumentalist, composer; b. San Francisco, Calif., April 13, 1957. Starting on violin at the age of 10, he moved on to the sax by the end of junior high. In 1987, he began investigating numerous indigenous instruments of Asia, like the shinobue, yokobue, and erhu. Although the tenor saxophone is his primary axe, Wong's also an expressive composer-improviser on flute, clarinet, and violin.

He founded The Great Wall Quartet (with Jang, Mark Izu, E.W. Wainwright Jr., and Hafez Modirzadeh) in 1990 to perform jazz tunes, original works, pieces by contemporary Asian American composers, and Chinese classical and folk material. After releasing the group's inaugural effort in 1993, he has appeared as a leader or co-leader on six other albums. He has also collaborated on a number of Jon Jang and Glenn Horiuchi recordings, and performed live with such luminaries as James Newton, George Lewis, and Cecil Taylor. In addition to his work as a composer-performer, he heads Asian Improv Arts in San Francisco, an organization which sponsors showcases for Asian American musicians and artists, including the annual Asian American Jazz Festival and Asian Improv Records. He is also a four- time grant recipient from the Calif. Arts Council Artist in Residency program and is on the faculty at San Francisco State Univ. and the New Coll. of Calif. He is currently working on a large ensemble concept with vocalist/writer Genny Lim.

DISC.: *Great Wall* (1993); *Ming* (1995); *Chicago Time Code* (1995); *Duets I* (1996); *Urban Reception* (1996); *Devotee* (1997); *Pilgrimage* (1997).**—SP**

Wood, Haydn, English violinist and composer; b. Slaithwaite, March 25, 1882; d. London, March 11, 1959. He entered the Royal Coll. of Music in London at 15, where he studied with Fernández Arbós (violin) and Stanford (composition); later studied with César Thomson in Brussels. His works include a Piano Concerto, a Violin Concerto, 8 overtures, 8 rhapsodies for band, 18 orch. studies, 31 entr'actes for orch., 12 violin solos, 2 flute pieces, 3 accordion solos, and about 200 songs. **—NS/LK/DM**

Wood, Hugh (Bradshaw), English composer and teacher; b. Parbold, Lancashire, June 27, 1932. After attending the Univ. of Oxford, he studied in London with W. S. Lloyd Webber, Anthony Milner, Iain Hamilton, and Mátyás Seiber. From 1958 to 1967 he taught at Morley Coll., London. He also was a prof. of harmony at the Royal Academy of Music in London from 1962 to 1965. After serving as a research fellow in composition at the Univ. of Glasgow (1966–70), he lectured on music at the univs. of Liverpool (1971–73) and Cambridge (from 1977). His output is reflective of contemporary compositional trends but not without a welcome infusion of lyricism undergirded by fine craftsmanship.

WORKS: ORCH.: Cello Concerto (London, Aug. 26, 1969); Chamber Concerto (London, Nov. 27, 1971; rev. 1978); Violin Concerto (Liverpool, Sept. 19, 1972); Sym. (1979–82; London, July 23, 1982); *Comus Quadrilles* (BBC Radio 3, London, May 3, 1988); Piano Concerto (London, Sept. 10, 1991); *Variations* (1997). **CHAMBER:** 1 unnumbered string quartet (1957; Cheltenham, July 11, 1959); 4 numbered string quartets: No. 1

(Cheltenham, July 5, 1962), No. 2 (Cardiff, Nov. 2, 1970), No. 3 (Bath, May 31, 1978), and No. 4 (1992–93; BBC, Birmingham, May 19, 1993); *Variations* for Viola and Piano (1958; London, July 7, 1959); Trio for Flute, Viola, and Piano (1961); Quintet for Clarinet, Horn, Violin, Cello, and Piano (Cheltenham, July 11, 1967); Piano Trio (Brighton, May 10, 1984); *Paraphrase on "Bird of Paradise"* for Clarinet and Piano (London, March 4, 1985); Horn Trio (1987–89; London, Nov. 27, 1989); *Funeral Music* for Brass Quintet (Three Choirs Festival, Aug. 24, 1992); *Poem* for Violin and Piano (1993; London, Jan. 10, 1994); Clarinet Trio (Cheltenham, July 7, 1997). **KEYBOARD: Piano:** 3 Pieces (1960–63; Cheltenham, July 2, 1963); *50 Chords for David Matthews* for 2 Pianos (1993). **Organ:** *Capriccio* (London, May 17, 1967). **VOCAL:** *Laurie Lee Songs* for High Voice and Piano (1959; Liverpool, May 23, 1971; also for High Voice and Orch., 1986–87); 4 Songs for Contralto, Clarinet, Violin, and Cello (London, March 7, 1961; rev. 1963); *Scenes from Comus* for Soprano, Tenor, and Orch., after Milton (London, Aug. 2, 1965); 3 Choruses (1965–66; London, May 6, 1966); *D. H. Lawrence Songs* for High Voice and Piano (1966–74); *Grave Songs I* (1966–77; Dartington, July 30, 1977), *II* (1977–82; Canterbury, Sept. 29, 1987), and *III* (1966–83) for High Voice and Piano; *The Horses* for High Voice and Piano, after Ted Hughes (London, Nov. 13, 1967; rev. 1968); *The Rider Victory* for High Voice and Piano, after Edwin Muir (Glasgow, Nov. 28, 1968); *To a Child Dancing in the Wind* for Chorus, after Yeats (1973); *Song Cycle to Poems of Pablo Neruda* for High Voice and Orch. (1973–74; London, Feb. 18, 1974); *To a Friend Whose Work has Come to Nothing* for Chorus, after Yeats (1973–89; London, Oct. 29, 1989); *A Christmas Poem* for Chorus (1984; Cambridge, Nov. 27, 1986); *Lines to Mr. Hodgson* for Soprano and Piano, after Byron (Cambridge, April 24, 1988); *Marina* for High Voice, Violin, Alto Flute, Horn, Harp, and Viola, after T.S. Eliot (1988–89); Cantata for Chorus and Orch., after D.H. Lawrence (London, Sept. 4, 1989); *The Kingdom of God* for Chorus, after Francis Thompson (London, July 3, 1994).—**NS/LK/DM**

Wood, Joseph, American composer and teacher; b. Pittsburgh, May 12, 1915. He was a student of Wagenaar at the Juilliard School of Music (graduated, 1949) and of Luening at Columbia Univ. (M.A., 1950) in N.Y. From 1950 to 1985 he was a prof. of composition at the Oberlin (Ohio) Coll. Cons. of Music. He composed in a generally accessible vein with some excursions into serialism.

WORKS: DRAMATIC: *The Mother*, opera (1945); *The Progression*, ballet-cantata (1968); incidental music. **ORCH.:** 4 syms. (1939, 1952, 1958, 1983); *Divertimento* for Piano and Chamber Orch. (1959); Violin Concerto (1961); Concerto for Chamber Orch. (1973–74). **CHAMBER:** Piano Trio (1937); Viola Sonata (1938); 3 string quartets (1942, 1965, 1975); Violin Sonata (1947); Piano Quintet (1956); piano pieces. **VOCAL:** *Te Deum* for Chorus and Orch. (1982); choruses; songs. —**NS/LK/DM**

Wood, Sir Henry J(oseph), eminent English conductor; b. London, March 3, 1869; d. Hitchin, Hertfordshire, Aug. 19, 1944. Of musical parentage, he was taught to play the piano by his mother; he participated in family musicales from the age of 6; he was equally precocious on the organ. At the age of 10 he often acted as a deputy organist, and gave organ recitals at the Fisheries Exhibition (1883) and at the Inventions Exhibition (1885). In 1886 he entered the Royal Academy of Music in London, where his teachers were Prout, Steggall, Macfarren, and Garcia; he won 4 medals. In 1888 he brought out some of his songs, then composed light operas and cantatas. However, soon his ambition crystallized in the direction of conducting; after making his debut in 1888, he was active with various theater companies. On Aug. 10, 1895, he began his first series of Promenade Concerts (the famous "Proms") in Queen's Hall, London, with an orch. of about 80 members. Their success was so conspicuous that a new series of concerts was inaugurated on Jan. 30, 1897, under Wood's direction, and flourished from the beginning. In 1899 he founded the Nottingham Orch.; he also was conductor of the Wolverhampton Festival Choral Soc. (1900), the Sheffield Festival (1902–11), and the Norwich Festival (1908). In 1904 he was a guest conductor of the N.Y. Phil. He was married to Olga Urusova, a Russian noblewoman, and became greatly interested in Russian music, which he performed frequently at his concerts. He adopted a Russian pseudonym, Paul Klenovsky, for his compositions and arrangements, and supplied an imaginary biography of his alter ego for use in program notes. His wife died in 1909, and Wood married Muriel Greatorex in 1911. In 1921 he received the Gold Medal of the Royal Phil. Soc. He was made a Companion of Honour in 1944. In 1918 he was offered the conductorship of the Boston Sym. Orch. as successor to Muck, but declined. In 1923 he was appointed prof. of conducting and orch. playing at the Royal Academy of Music. Wood continued to conduct the Promenade Concerts almost to the end of his life, presenting the last concert on July 28, 1944. Among his popular arrangements were Chopin's *Marche Funèbre*, some works by Bach, and the *Trumpet Voluntary* (mistakenly attributed to Purcell, but actually by Jeremiah Clarke). He publ. *The Gentle Art of Singing* (4 vols.; 1927–28) and *About Conducting* (London, 1945), and ed. the *Handbook of Miniature Orchestral and Chamber Music Scores* (1937). He wrote an autobiography, *My Life and Music* (London, 1938). A commemorative postage stamp with his portrait was issued by the Post Office of Great Britain on Sept. 1, 1980.

BIBL.: R. Newmarch, *H.J. W.* (London, 1904); T. Russell et al., eds., *Homage to Sir H. W.: A World Symposium* (London, 1944); W. Thompson et al., *Sir H. W.: Fifty Years of the Proms* (London, 1944); J. Wood, *The Last Years of H.J. W.* (London, 1954); R. Pound, *Sir H. W.: A Biography* (London, 1969); A. Orga, *The Proms* (London, 1974); D. Cox, *The H. W. Proms* (London, 1980); A. Jacobs, *H.J. W.: Maker of the Proms* (London, 1994). —**NS/LK/DM**

Wood, Thomas, English composer and author; b. Chorley, Lancashire, Nov. 28, 1892; d. Bures, Essex, Nov. 19, 1950. He was educated at Exeter Coll., Oxford, then studied at the Royal Academy of Music in London with Stanford (composition) and Herbert Fryer (piano); subsequently, Wood took his D.Mus. at the Univ. of Oxford (1920). He was music director at Tonbridge School (1920–24), and then lecturer and precentor at Exeter Coll. (1924–28). His extensive travels took him to the Far East and the Arctic; his familiarity with the sea was reflected in many of his compositions for Chorus and Orch., such as *40 Singing Seamen* (1925), *Master Mariners* (1927), and *Merchantmen* (1934), and in *A Seaman's*

Overture for Orch. (1927). He ed. vol. II of the *Oxford Song Book* (1928; 3rd ed., 1937). His books include *Music and Boyhood* (1925) and the autobiographical *True Thomas* (1936); he also publ. *Cobbers* (on his Australian tour of 1930–32), which became highly popular in England, and a sequel to it, *Cobbers Campaigning* (1940). **—NS/LK/DM**

Wood, Vishnu (William Clifford), jazz bass, oud, dil rhuba, tamboura, composer, educator; b. North Wilkesboro, N.C., Nov. 7, 1937. His family moved to Detroit when he was in his early teens. His father played various reed instruments, and a brother, Max, played bass. Vishnu studied harmony, piano, and solfege at the Detroit Inst. of Music and Art (1959–61) and studied bass with Gaston Brohan and John Matthews of the Detroit Symphony. Woods moved to N.Y. in 1961. He worked with Alice Coltrane, Max Roach, S. Rivers, Archie Shepp, Terry Gibbs, Rahsaan Roland Kirk, Pharoah Sanders, and James Moody, as well as with dance troupes and in theater. In 1966–67, he went to Africa with Randy Weston, including an extended stay in Morocco in 1968. He has taught music at various colleges, including directing the music program at Hampshire Coll. (1976–80). Since 1984, he has directed Vishnu & the Safari East Concert Workshop Ensemble, playing instruments and music from various cultures primarily for public school children.**—LP**

Woodard, Rickey, American saxophonist; b. Nashville, Tenn., Aug. 5, 1950. His tenor style draws from both swing era and mainstream, modern jazz players such as Don Byas, Wardell Grey, and Gene Ammons, and his ballad approach displays traces of Dexter Gordon's lyric consciousness. His alto tone is less distinctive and he has de-emphasized the horn in recent years. Raised in Nashville, he did not have much choice but to go into music, joining his five brothers and sisters in the family's R&B band. As part of the children's musical education, his father made them listen to Duke Ellington, Count Basie, Lucky Thompson, and Ray Charles. Woodard joined Charles in 1980 and spent about eight years on the road with his band. He settled in Los Angeles in 1988 and has become a pillar of the Southern Calif. jazz scene, featured in The Clayton–Hamilton Jazz Orch., Jeannie and Jimmy Cheatham's Sweet Baby Blues Band, and The Frank Capp Juggernaut. He toured with Horace Silver in the mid-1990s and Silver showcased his tenor work on his 1994 Columbia album *Pencil Packin' Papa*. He has performed with Benny Carter and Harry "Sweets" Edison, and works around Southern Calif. with his own combo and a popular three-tenor group with revolving personnel, including Plas Johnson, Harold Land, Charles Owens, Pete Christlieb, and Herman Riley.

DISC.: *California Cooking!* (1991); *The Frank Capp Trio Presents Rickey Woodard* (1991); *The Tokyo Express* (1992); *Night Mist* (1992); *Yazoo* (1994); *Quality Time* (1995); *The Silver Strut* (1996); *The Tenor Trio* (1997).**—AG**

Woodbury (real name, **Woodberry**), **Isaac Baker,** American composer, organist, teacher, editor, and writer on music; b. Beverly, Mass., Oct. 23, 1819; d. Columbia, S.C., Oct. 26, 1858. Originally a blacksmith, he began training in music with Lowell Mason in Boston in 1832 and later studied in London and Paris (1838–39); returning to Boston, he pursued a varied career. With his cousin Benjamin F. Baker, he organized the National Musical Convention, a teacher training school. In 1849 he went to N.Y. He was organist at Rutgers Street Church (1850–51) and served as ed. of the *American Monthly Musical Review* (1850–53) and the *New York Musical Pioneer* (1855–58). Woodbury's prolific output includes some 700 compositions and publs., among them 16 collections and eds., 3 oratorios, a musical drama, over 400 hymn tunes, several songs, piano pieces, and 8 pedagogical vols.

BIBL.: R. Copeland, *I.B. W.: The Life and Works of an American Musical Populist* (Lanham, Md., 1995).**—NS/LK/DM**

Woodbury, Arthur N(eum), American composer, bassoonist, saxophonist, and teacher; b. Kimball, Nebr., June 20, 1930. He studied composition with William Billingsley at the Univ. of Idaho (B.S., 1951; M.M., 1955). After private composition lessons with Robert Morton in San Francisco (1956–57), he pursued postgraduate composition studies with Imbrie at the Univ. of Calif. at Berkeley (1957–58). He later studied computer music at Stanford Univ. (1970). He pursued a vigorous career as a performer, both as a member of various orchs. and as a soloist. From 1963 to 1972 he taught at the Univ. of Calif. at Davis. From 1967 to 1972 he served as ed. of the avant-garde journal *Source*. In 1972 he joined the faculty of the Univ. of South Fla. in Tampa, where he was a prof. from 1987 until 1998. In 1999 he joined the Harry James Orch. Woodbury's early works were written in a traditional modern idiom; later he branched out as a composer of experimental music, making use of electronics and aleatory techniques.

WORKS: Woodwind Quartet (1955); Sym. (1958); *Introduction and Allegro* for Band (1965); *Autobiography: Patricia Belle* for Soprano, Live Electronics, and Amplified Instruments (1968); *Recall*, theater piece for Actor, Tape, and Live Electronics (1969); *Remembrances*, trio for Violin, Alto Saxophone, and Vibraphone (1969); *Velox*, computer piece (1970); *WernerVonBraunasaurus Rex* for Electronic Piano, Guitar, and Moog Synthesizer (1979); *Jazz Fugue* for Saxophone Quartet and Accompaniment (1980); *Diversions* for Piano (1980–83); *Passacaglia, Interlude, and Canon* for Organ (1981; also for Concert Band, 1984); *Tocata española* for Marimba or Percussion and Cello (1983); *No More Jim Beam, Please* for Jazz Quartet (1985); *Learnin' the Blues* for Jazz Quintet (1986); *Wild Nights* for Voice and Piano (1988); *Variations on a Cadenza* for Flute and Percussion (1989); *3 Brief Pieces* for Clarinet and Bassoon (1990); *Homage to Erik* for Trumpet and Piano (1993); *When Nod Dreams* for 2 Oboes and English Horn (1994); *Little Serenade* for Guitar (1995); *Recuerdos de Cuba* for Orch. (1997); *Possible Musics II* for Amplified Cello and Tape (1997).**—NS/LK/DM**

Woods, Phil(ip Wells), important jazz alto saxophonist, clarinetist, leader, composer; b. Springfield, Mass., Nov. 2, 1931. He grew up with Joe Morello and Sal Salvador. During his adolescence in Springfield, Mass., in the early 1940s, he went to hear the Duke Ellington Orch. Johnny Hodges played a solo on "Mood to Be Wooed," and shortly afterward, Woods bought his first Charlie Parker record, "Ko-Ko." He studied saxophone at age 12 with Harvey La Rose. When he was 14 years old, Woods heard more of Charlie Parker's music and fell in love with it. After finishing high school, he spent the summer at the Manhattan School of Music, and then proceeded to earn a B.A. in Music from Juilliard in 1953. Despite being a clarinet major, he put himself through Juilliard by giving saxophone lessons. He joined the small combo of Jimmy Raney in 1955. After Charlie Parker died, he and Chan, Parker's widow, with whom he was close, got married, and Woods adopted her daughter Kim, who became a jazz singer. He then spent two years with George Wallington, dividing his time with stints in Dizzy Gillespie's big band (including a tour of the Middle East for the U.S. State Department in 1956) and a two-alto unit with Gene Quill in 1957. He was in the Quincy Jones big band and was stranded with the Free and Easy show in Europe (early February 1960), along with Clark Terry, and Julius Watkins. He was a member of Buddy Rich's big band, staying with him until 1961. He became a prolific studio and session musician in the 1960s, working on film soundtracks, cutting his own records, and working on dates by Benny Carter and others. In 1968, he moved to Europe and formed The European Rhythm Machine (1968–72, named for its European rhythm section). He returned to the U.S. in 1973, settling in eastern Pa. He formed an acoustic quintet there in 1974, featuring pianist Mike Melillo, bassist Steve Gilmore, guitarist Harry Leahy, and drummer Bill Goodwin; with only a few changes in personnel, the group has continued to work with Woods through the 1990s. Leahy left the group in 1978, which was then reduced to a quartet until trumpeter Tom Harrell joined in 1983; Harrell who remained with the group for six years. More recently, trumpeter Hal Crook (1989–92) and Bryan Lynch (1993–present) have worked with the group. While Gilmore and Goodwin have remained steady members, pianist Melillo has been replaced, first by Hal Galper (1980–90), then by Jim McNeely (1990–95), and most recently by Bill Charlap.

Woods was voted best alto saxophonist by *Down Beat* readers from 1975–95. He has served as an educator throughout his career, founded jazz and arts organizations in his home area of eastern Pa., and is IAJE's Interest Co-Chair for Woodwinds. In May of 1994, Woods received an honorary doctorate from East Stroudsburg Univ. of Pa., only the second individual to receive such recognition. An outspoken "purist," he never played fusion—though his Rhythm Machine did use aggresive rock rhythms—and has been among the fiercest critics of free music. Four of his albums have won Grammys.

DISC.: *Early Quintets* (1954); *Phil Woods New Jazz Quintet* (1954); *Pot Pie* (1954); *Phil Woods New Jazz Quartet* (1955); *Woodlore* (1955); *Altology* (1956); *Pairing Off* (1956); *Woods-Quill Sextet* (1956); *Bird's Night* (1957); *Phil Talks with Quill* (1957); *Phil Woods Sextet* (1957); *Phil and Quill with Prestige* (1957); *Warm Woods* (1957); *Rights of Swing* (1960); *Directly from the Half Note* (1966); *Birth of the ERM* (1968); *At the Montreux Jazz Festival* (1969); *Freedom Jazz Dance* (1969); *Round Trip* (1969); *At the Frankfurt Jazz Festival* (1970); *Musique Du Bois* (1974); *Floresta Canto* (1975); *Images* (1975); *New Phil Woods Album* (1975); *Phil Woods/Michel Legrand* (1975); *Phil Woods Six: Live from the Showboat* (1976); *Song for Sisyphus* (1977); Phil Woods Orch.: *I Remember* (1978). **MICHEL LEGRAND & CO.:** *Le Jazz Grand-Gryphon* (1978); *Crazy Horse* (1979). **PHIL WOODS QUARTET:** *More Live-Adelphi* (1979); *Phil Woods/Lew Tabackin* (1980); Phil Woods Quartet: *At the Village Vanguard* (1982); *Ole Dude and the Fundance Kid* (1984); *Live from the Village Vanguard* (1985); *Here's to My Lady* (1988); *Little Big Band* (1988). **BENNY CARTER:** *My Man Benny, My Man Phil* (1989); *All Bird's Children* (1990); *An Affair to Remember* (1995). **BENNY CARTER/PHIL WOODS:** *Another Time, Another Place* (1996). **PHIL WOODS QUINTET:** *Mile High Jazz* (1996). **PHIL WOODS & THE FESTIVAL ORCH.:** *Celebration* (1997).—**LP/NAL**

Woodward, Roger (Robert), Australian pianist; b. Sydney, Dec. 20, 1942. He studied piano with Alexander Sverjensky in Sydney, then obtained a Polish government scholarship and went to Warsaw, where he took lessons with Zbigniew Drzwiecki. He won 1st prize in the Chopin Competition in 1968, an auspicious award that propelled him on an international career. In 1971 he settled in London, where he gained renown among international avant-garde composers by repeatedly performing works by such uncompromising celebrants of quaquaversal modern idioms as Takemitsu, Barraqué, Stockhausen, and Birtwistle; faithful to his antecedents, he also placed on his programs works of Australian composers such as Boyd, Meale, and Sculthorpe. He participated in several American concerts of contemporary music, including a marathon series presented in Los Angeles. In 1985 he played the complete works of Chopin in a series of 16 concerts. In 1986 he was soloist in the first performance of Xenakis's *Keqrops* with Zubin Mehta and the N.Y. Phil. In 1980 he was made an Officer of the Order of the British Empire.—**NS/LK/DM**

Woodworth, G(eorge) Wallace, American choral conductor, organist, and music educator; b. Boston, Nov. 6, 1902; d. Cambridge, Mass., July 18, 1969. He was educated at Harvard Univ. (B.A., 1924; M.A., 1926), then studied conducting with Malcolm Sargent at the Royal Coll. of Music in London (1927–28). In 1924 he joined the staff of the music dept. at Harvard, and was engaged as conductor of the Radcliffe Choral Soc.; also led the Pierian Sodality Orch. of Harvard Univ. (1928–32) and the Harvard Glee Club (1933–38). In 1940 he was appointed organist and choirmaster for the Harvard Univ. Chapel. He was made James Edward Ditson Professor of Music at Harvard in 1954. He conducted the Harvard-Radcliffe Chorus on its transcontinental U.S. tour in 1954, and took the Harvard Glee Club on its European tour in 1956. He retired in 1969. Woodworth publ. *The World of Music* (Cambridge, Mass., 1964).

BIBL.: L. Berman, ed., *Words and Music: The Composer's View: A Medley of Problems and Solutions in Honor of G.W. W.* (Cambridge, 1972).—**NS/LK/DM**

Woodyard, Sam(uel), jazz drummer; b. Elizabeth, N.J., Jan. 7, 1925; d. Paris, Sept. 20, 1988. He was self-taught, playing with various local groups around

Elizabeth and Newark, N.J. He worked in the 1950s for various leaders, including Paul Gayten (1950–51), Joe Holiday (late 1951), Roy Eldridge (1952), and Milt Buckner (1953–55). He is best remembered for his long stint with Duke Ellington, from 1955–66. He was Ellington's favorite drummer (after Sonny Greer). His trademark was a cross stick over the rim of his snare drum, doubling the hi-hat on the backbeats (two and four). In the late 1960s, he moved to Los Angeles and was inactive for a while due to ill health. He returned to performing in the late 1970s, primarily working in Europe for the last decade of his life, often accompanying French jazz-pop pianist Claude Bolling.

Disc.: **Duke Ellington:** *Ellington at Newport* (1956); *D. E. Vol. 7 Studio sessions* (1957/58); *D. E. Vol. 2 California Dance Duke Ellington* (1958). **John Coltrane:** *Coltrane and Ellington* (1962).—**LP**

Woollen, (Charles) Russell, American composer, pianist, and organist; b. Harford, Conn., Jan. 7, 1923; d. Charlottesville, Va., March 16, 1994. He was educated at St. Mary's Univ. in Baltimore (B.A., 1944) and at the Catholic Univ. of America in Washington, D.C. (M.A., in Romance languages, 1948). He also studied for the priesthood and attended the Pius X School of Liturgical Music in N.Y. After being ordained a priest in the Hartford Diocese in 1947, he studied Gregorian chant at the Benedictine Abbey in Solesmes in 1948. He also received private training in piano and organ, and also in composition from Franz Wasner. His other mentors in composition were Nabakov at the Peabody Cons. of Music in Baltimore (1949–51), Boulanger in Paris (1951), and Piston at Harvard Univ. (1953–55). From 1948 to 1962 he taught at the Catholic Univ. of America. He was staff keyboard player with the National Sym. Orch. in Washington, D.C., from 1956 to 1980. After leaving the priesthood in 1964, he taught at Howard Univ. in Washington, D.C. (1969–74). In 1982 he became organist at the Arlington (Va.) Unitarian Church. Although considered a minor composer, with the bulk of his manuscripts remaining unpublished at the time of his death, with Robert Evett and Robert Parris, Wollen contributed to the development of the so-called "Washington School of Composers" that flourished in the 1960s and 1970s.

Works: **Dramatic:** *The Decorator*, television opera (N.Y., May 24, 1959). **Orch.:** *Toccata* (1955); 2 syms.: No. 1 (1957–61) and No. 2 (1977–78; Washington, D.C., April 8, 1979); *Summer Jubilee Overture* (1958); *Modal Offerings* (1960); 2 Pieces for Piano and Orch. (1962–76); *Miranda's Supper* (1964–65); Suite for Flute and Strings (1966; rev. 1979); Suite for Bassoon and Orch. (1988–91); *Prayer and Celebration* (1990). **Chamber:** Piano Quartet (1952); Flute Quartet (1953); Wind Quintet (1955); Piano Trio (1957); *Triptych* for 10 Brasses (1960); Trio for Flute, Oboe, and Harpsichord (1967); Trombone Sonata (1972); Wind Quartet (1975). **Piano:** 2 sonatinas (1954, 1962); Sonata for Piano, 4-Hands (1955). **Vocal:** *Hymn on the Morning of Christ's Nativity* for Soprano, Alto, Chorus, and Orch. (1958); *In martyrum memoriam*, cantata in memory of President John F. Kennedy, Robert F. Kennedy, and Martin Luther King Jr., for Soprano, Baritone, Chorus, and Orch. (1968–69; Washington, D.C., Nov. 16, 1969); *The Pasch*, cantata for Soprano, Bass, Chorus, and Orch. (1974; rev. 1984); *Mass for a Great Space* for Chorus and Orch. (1986); *Alexandria Suite* for Chorus and Small Orch. (1987); other masses; choruses; songs.—**NS/LK/DM**

Worbs, Hans Christoph, German music scholar; b. Guben, Jan. 13, 1927. He studied at the Humboldt Univ. in Berlin (degrees, 1952 and 1958). He subsequently settled in Hamburg, where he was active as a music critic and writer.

Writings: *Der Schlager: Bestandsaufnahme, Analyse, Dokumentation* (Bremen, 1963); *Welterfolge der modernen Oper* (Berlin, 1967); *Felix Mendelssohn-Bartholdy* (Reinbek, 1974); *Modest Mussorgsky* (Reinbek, 1976); *Albert Lortzing* (Reinbek, 1980); *Das Dampkonzert: Musik und Musikleben des 19. Jahrhunderts in der Karikatur* (Wilhelmshaven, 1981).—**NS/LK/DM**

Wordsworth, Barry, English conductor; b. Worcester Park, Surrey, Feb. 20, 1948. He studied conducting with Boult, winning the Tagore Gold Medal at the Royal Coll. of Music in London in 1970. That same year he was co-winner of the Sargent Conductors' Prize. He received training in harpsichord from Leonhardt in Amsterdam. He appeared as a conductor with the Royal Ballet of London (1974–84), and with the Australian Ballet and the Ballet of Canada. From 1982 to 1984 he was music director of the New Sadler's Wells Opera in London. In 1989 he became principal conductor of the Brighton Phil. and the BBC Concert Orch. in London. He also was music director of the Royal Ballet in London and of the Birmingham Royal Ballet from 1990. In 1991 he made his debut at London's Covent Garden conducting *Carmen*. In 1993 he was conductor of the Last Night of the Proms gala with the BBC Sym. Orch. in London.
—**NS/LK/DM**

Wordsworth, William (Brocklesby), English composer; b. London, Dec. 17, 1908; d. Kingussie, Scotland, March 10, 1988. He was descended from the brother of the poet William Wordsworth. He studied with his father, then with George Oldroyd (1921–31), and later with Tovey at the Univ. of Edinburgh (1934–36). In 1950 he won 1st prize in the Edinburgh International Festival Soc. competition with his 2nd Sym. In 1959 he served as president of the Composers' Guild of Great Britain. His music is marked by a certain austerity in the deployment of thematic materials.

Works: **Orch.:** *Sinfonia* for Strings (1936); *3 Pastoral Sketches* (1937); *Theme and Variations* (1941); 8 syms. (1944; 1947–48; 1951; 1953; 1959–60; 1976–77; 1981; 1986); Piano Concerto (1946); *Divertimento* (1954); Violin Concerto (1955); *Sinfonietta* for Small Orch. (1957); *Variations on a Scottish Theme* for Small Orch. (1962); Cello Concerto (1963); *A Highland Overture* (1964); *Jubilation* (1965); *Conflict*, overture (1968); *Sinfonia semplice* for Amateur String Orch. (1969); *Valediction* (1969); *Spring Festival Overture* (1970); *Confluence*, symphonic variations (1975); *Elegy for Frieda* for Strings (1982). **Chamber:** 2 cello sonatas (1937, 1959); 6 string quartets (1941, 1944, 1947, 1950, 1957, 1964); 2 violin sonatas (1944, 1967); String Trio (1945); Piano Quartet (1948); Piano Trio (1949); Oboe Quartet (1949); Clarinet Quintet (1952); Wind Trio (1953); Piano Quintet (1959); Sonata for Solo Cello (1961); *Symposium* for Violin, Strings,

Piano, and Percussion (1972); *Conversation Piece* for Violin and Guitar (1983); solo piano pieces, including a Sonata (1939). **VOCAL:** *The Houseless Dead* for Baritone, Chorus, and Orch., after D.H. Lawrence (1939); *Dies Domini*, oratorio (1942–44); *Lucifer Yields* for Soloists, Chorus, and Orch. (1949); *A Vision* for Women's Chorus and String Orch. (1950); *A Song of Praise* for Chorus and Orch. (1956); *A Pattern of Love* for Low Voice and String Orch. (1969–70); *The 2 Brigs*, dramatic cantata (1971); *The Solitary Reaper* for Soprano, Piano, and Clarinet (1973); solo songs.—**NS/LK/DM**

Workman, William, American baritone; b. Valdosta, Ga., Feb. 4, 1940. He studied with Martial Singher at the Curtis Inst. of Music in Philadelphia and at the Music Academy of the West in Santa Barbara, Calif.; then went to Europe and took voice lessons with Hedwig Schilling in Hamburg. He made his operatic debut with the Hamburg State Opera in 1965. In 1972 he became a member of the Frankfurt am Main Opera; also made guest appearances in Stuttgart, Strasbourg, Paris, and Vienna. In 1984 he appeared at London's Covent Garden.—**NS/LK/DM**

Wörner, Karl(heinz) H(einrich), German musicologist; b. Waldorf, near Heidelberg, Jan. 6, 1910; d. Heiligenkirchen, near Detmold, Aug. 11, 1969. He studied at the Berlin Hochschule für Musik and took courses in musicology with Schünemann, Schering, Blume, Hornbostel, and Sachs at the Univ. of Berlin (Ph.D., 1931, with the diss. *Beiträge zur Geschichte des Leitmotivs in der Oper*). He was music critic of the *Berliner Zeitung am Mittag* (1933–34); then (1935–40) opera conductor at Stettin, Magdeburg, and Frankfurt am Main. He was in the German army during World War II; in 1944, was taken prisoner of war by the U.S. Army and spent 2 years in an American internment camp. After his release, he taught at the Heidelberg Hochschule für Musik (1946–54). From 1954 to 1958 he was on the staff of B. Schotts Söhne (Mainz); in 1958, joined the faculty of the Folkwangschule in Essen; from 1961, taught at the North-West Germany Academy of Music in Detmold.

WRITINGS: *Mendelssohn-Bartholdy* (Wiesbaden, 1947); *Musik der Gegenwart: Geschichte des neuen Musik* (Mainz, 1949); *Robert Schumann* (Zürich, 1949); *Musiker-Worte* (Baden-Baden, 1949); *Geschichte der Musik* (Göttingen, 1954; 6th ed., aug., 1975; Eng. tr., 1973); *Neue Musik in der Entscheidung* (Mainz, 1954); *Gotteswort und Magie: Die Oper "Moses und Aron" von Arnold Schönberg* (Heidelberg, 1959; Eng. tr., aug., 1963); *Karlheinz Stockhausen: Werk und Wollen 1950–1962* (Rodenkirchen, 1963; Eng. tr., aug., 1973); *Das Zeitalter der thematischen Prozesse in der Geschichte der Musik* (Regensburg, 1969); *Die Musik in der Geistesgeschichte: Studien zur Situation der Jahre um 1910* (Bonn, 1970).—**NS/LK/DM**

Woronoff, Wladimir, Russian-born Belgian composer; b. St. Petersburg, Jan. 5, 1903; d. Brussels, April 21, 1980. He studied violin as a child. He left Russia after the Revolution and settled in Belgium in 1922, where he took lessons in composition with Souris in Brussels. In 1954 he destroyed most of his early works, including the ballet *Le Masque de la mort rouge*, *Suite de Bruxelles* for Orch., and *Concert lyrique* for Piano and Orch.; he revised most of his remaining scores. His catalogue of extant works after this self-auto-da-fé includes *La Foule* for Bass, Chorus, and Orch. (1934; rev. 1965), *Annas et le Lépreux* for Low Voice and Piano (1946), *Les 12*, 3 fragments from the poem by Alexander Blok, for Low Voice and Orch. or Piano (1921–63), *Strophes concertantes* for Piano and Orch. (1964), *Lueur tournante* for Narrator and Orch. (1967), *Tripartita* for Viola and Chamber Orch. (1970), and *Vallées* for 2 Pianos (1971).—**NS/LK/DM**

Wořzischek (Voříšek), Johann Hugo (Jan Václav), esteemed Bohemian composer, pianist, and organist; b. Wamberg, May 11, 1791; d. Vienna, Nov. 19, 1825. He began his music studies with his father, and while still a child toured Bohemia as a keyboard prodigy. After training in law and esthetics at the Univ. of Prague (1810–13), he completed his law studies in Vienna, and also studied composition with Tomaschek in Prague. In 1813 he settled in Vienna, where he was employed in the civil service while making appearances as a keyboard artist; also received piano lessons from Hummel. From 1818 until his death he was conductor of the Gesellschaft der Musikfreunde; also served as asst. court organist (1822–23) and as principal court organist (from 1823). He was a friend of Schubert, and also knew Beethoven. He composed a Sym., choral works with Orch., a Piano Concerto, etc., but of more interest are his piano pieces, especially the *Rhapsodies* (1818) and *Impromptus* (1822), because Schubert was strongly influenced by them. A Piano Sonata in B minor (1820) shows kinship with Beethoven.—**NS/LK/DM**

Wöss, Kurt, Austrian conductor; b. Linz, May 2, 1914; d. Dresden (while rehearsing the Dresden Phil.), Dec. 4, 1987. He studied conducting with Weingartner in Vienna, and also pursued musicological studies at the Univ. of Vienna with Haas, Lach, Orel, and Wellesz; taught an orch. class at the Vienna Academy of Music (1938–40). He conducted the Niederösterreichisches Tonkünstler-Orch. in Vienna (1948–51) and the Nippon Phil. in Tokyo (1951–54). From 1956 to 1959 he was principal conductor of the Victoria Sym. Orch. in Melbourne and of the Australian National Opera; in 1961 he returned to Linz, where he was chief conductor of the Bruckner Orch. until 1976; also conducted again in Tokyo. He publ. *Ratschläge zur Aufführung der Symphonien Anton Bruckners* (Linz, 1974).—**NS/LK/DM**

Wotquenne (-Plattel), Alfred (Camille), Belgian musicologist; b. Lobbes, Jan. 25, 1867; d. Antibes, France, Sept. 25, 1939. He studied at the Royal Cons. in Brussels with Brassin (piano), Mailly (organ; premier prix, 1888), and Dupont and Gevaert (theory); from 1894 to 1896 he was deputy secretary and librarian and from 1896 to 1918 secretary and librarian there. He settled in Antibes as a singing teacher and organist, and subsequently was made maitre de chapelle at its cathedral (1921). He prepared a card catalogue of 18,000 Italian "cantate da camera" of the 18th century; ed. *Chansons italiennes de la fin du XVIe siècle* (canzonette *a* 4); continued the collections begun by Gevaert, *Répertoire* *classique du chant français and Répertoire français de l'ancien chant classique*; and ed. a new collection, *Répertoire Wotquenne* (4 vols. publ.); also ed. violin sonatas of Tartini, Veracini, and others and composed much sacred music. The MSS of several important bibliographies in his collection were bought by the Library of Congress in Washington, D.C., in 1929; these comprise *Répertoire des textes publiés par les éditeurs parisiens Ballard, Histoire musicale et chronologique du Théâtre de la Foire depuis 1680 jusqu'à 1762, Histoire du nouveau Théâtre-Italien à Paris (1718–1762)*, etc. A large part of his private music library was also bought by the Library of Congress.

WRITINGS: *Catalogue de la bibliothèque du Conservatoire Royal de Musique de Bruxelles* (vol. I, 1894; with a suppl., *Libretti d'opéras et d'oratorios italiens du XVIIe siècle*, 1901; II, 1902; III, 1908; IV, 1912; V, 1914); *Étude bibliographique sur les oeuvres de Baldassare Galuppi* (1899; 2nd ed., aug., 1902 as *Baldassare Galuppi: Étude bibliographique sur ses oeuvres dramatiques*); *Thematisches Verzeichnis der Werke von Christoph Willibald von Gluck* (1904); *Alphabetisches Verzeichnis der Stücke in Versen aus den dramatischer Werken von Zeno, Metastasio und Goldoni* (1905); *Thematisches Verzeichnis der Werke von Carl Philipp Emanuel Bach* (1905); *Étude bibliographique sur le compositeur napolitain Luigi Rossi* (1909; with thematic catalogue).—**NS/LK/DM**

Woytowicz, Boleslaw, Polish pianist, pedagogue, and composer; b. Dunajowce, Dec. 5, 1899; d. Katowice, July 11, 1980. He began musical training with his grandfather, the organist and composer Mikolaj Woytowicz. After piano lessons with Nowacki and Hanicki (1913–15) and Wielhorski (1916–17), he took his Ph.D. in philology at the Univ. of Kiev and studied mathematics and law at the Univ. of Warsaw. He pursued further piano instruction with Michalowski at the Chopin Music Coll. in Warsaw (1920–24) and received composition training with Wielhorski, Szopski, and Maliszewski, and later with Boulanger in Paris (1929–32). In 1924 he launched his career as a pianist. He also was a prof. of piano and theory at the Chopin Music Coll. (1924–39), a teacher of piano and composition at the Katowice Cons. (from 1945), and a prof. of composition at the Kraków Cons. (from 1963). In 1937 he received the Polish State Prize for music.

WORKS: DRAMATIC: Ballet: *Powrót* (1937). ORCH.: Piano Concerto (1932); *Zalobny poema* (Funeral Poem; 1935); 3 syms.: No. 1 (1938), No. 2 (1945; Kraków, Sept. 27, 1946), and No. 3, *Concertante*, for Piano and Orch. (1963); *Symphonic Sketches* (1949). CHAMBER: 2 string quartets (1932, 1953); Flute Sonata (1952). Piano: *12 Études* (1948); *10 Études* (1960); *Little Piano Sonata* (1974). VOCAL: *Kolysanka* (Cradle Song) for Soprano, Flute, Clarinet, Bassoon, and Harp (1931); *Kantata na pochwale pracy* (Cantata in Praise of Labor; 1948); *Prorok* (The Prophet), cantata (1950); *Lamento* for Soprano, Piano, and Clarinet (1960).—**NS/LK/DM**

Wranitzky, Anton, Bohemian violinist, pedagogue, and composer, brother of **Paul Wranitzky;** b. Neureisch, Moravia, June 13, 1761; d. Vienna, Aug. 6, 1820. He studied violin with his brother, then had composition lessons in Vienna with Albrechtsberger, Haydn, and Mozart. In 1783 he became choirmaster at the chapel of the Theresianisch-Savoyische Akademie in Vienna. In 1790 he entered the service of Prince Lobkowitz, becoming his Kapellmeister in 1797; from 1807 he was also director of the orch. of the Court Theater and from 1814 director of the orch. of the Theater an der Wien. His students included Mayseder and Schuppanzigh. His large output includes 15 syms., overtures, 15 violin concertos, a concerto for 2 violins, 2 concertos for violin and cello, a concerto for 2 violins and cello, a concerto for 2 violas, serenatas, notturnos, dances, marches, etc., much chamber music, including string quartets, sextets, quintets, and trios, as well as various sonatas and keyboard pieces, and vocal works, including Masses and other sacred pieces, various secular choruses, songs, etc.—**NS/LK/DM**

Wranitzky, Paul, distinguished Bohemian violinist, conductor, and composer, brother of **Anton Wranitzky;** b. Neureisch, Moravia, Dec. 30, 1756; d. Vienna, Sept. 26, 1808. After studying in Moravia, he went in 1776 to Vienna, where he was a pupil of Joseph Martin Kraus and Haydn. Around 1785 he was named music director to Count Johann Nepomuk Esterházy; from about 1790 he served as director of the orchs. at the Court Theaters in Vienna. His opera *Oberon, König der Elfen* was given with excellent success in Vienna on Nov. 7, 1789; other operas and Singspiels produced by him in Vienna were *Rudolf von Felseck* (Oct. 6, 1792), *Merkur, der Heurat-Stifter* (Feb. 21, 1793), *Das Fest der Lazzaroni* (Feb. 4, 1794), *Die gute Mutter* (May 11, 1795), *Johanna von Montfaucon* (Jan. 25, 1799), *Der Schreiner* (July 18, 1799), *Das Mitgefühl* (April 21, 1804), and *Die Erkenntlichkeit* (July 22, 1805). He also produced several successful ballets, wrote incidental music to plays, and composed a great deal of instrumental music, including 51 syms., 5 concertos for various instruments with orch., various quintets, over 80 string quartets, quartets for flute and strings, piano quartets, string trios, keyboard sonatas, and vocal works.

BIBL.: J. Pešková, *Vranického Oberon a jeho vliv na rozvoj singspielu* (W.'s Oberon and Its Influence on the Development of the Singspiel; diss., Univ. of Prague, 1955); M. Vysinova, *Ke komorni tvorb Pavla Vranickeho* (P. W.'s Chamber Works; diss., Univ. of Prague, 1969).—**NS/LK/DM**

Wright, Frank, free-jazz tenor saxophonist, leader; b. Grenada, Miss., July 9, 1935; d. Germany, May 17, 1990. He grew up in Memphis and Cleveland, where he played bass guitar with local band leader Little Chickadee and backed R&B artists including Rosco Gordon, Bobby "Blue" Bland, and B.B. King. He switched to tenor saxophone following the influence of Albert Ayler, whom he met in Cleveland. In the early 1960s he moved to N.Y.C. and recorded with H. Grimes (1965), J. Coursil, A. Jones (1967); Wright played with Albert Ayler, Larry Young, Noah Howard, S. Murray, and briefly with Cecil Taylor, and John Coltrane. He moved to Europe in 1969 and lived in Paris, where he led a quartet in which his sidemen were Howard (later replaced by Alan Silva), the pianist Bobby Few, and the drummer Muhammad Ali; with this group, he made recordings in 1969 and 1970 before returning to the U.S. for a brief period in 1971. After moving again to France, he continued to lead the quartet (recording in 1972 and 1974) and toured Europe. In the mid-1980s he performed and recorded with Taylor's big band. Wright was also an ordained minister.

DISC.: *Frank Wright Trio* (1965); *Trio* (1965); *Your Prayer* (1967); *Kevin, My Dear Son* (1978); *Stove Man, Love Is the Word* (1979).—**LP**

Wright, Maurice, American composer and teacher; b. Front Royal, Va., Oct. 17, 1949. He studied with Iain Hamilton at Duke Univ. (B.A., 1972) and Mario Davidovsky at Columbia Univ. (D.M.A., 1988). In 1980 he joined the faculty of Temple Univ., where he is the Laura Carnell Prof. He also taught at the Univ. of Pa. in 1999.

WORKS: DRAMATIC: Opera: *The 5th String* (1980; Des Moines, July 7, 1998); *The Trojan Conflict* (Philadelphia, April 20, 1989); *Dr. Franklin* (Philadelphia, Oct. 15, 1990). **ORCH.:** *Stellae* for Orch. and Tape (Tanglewood, Aug. 10, 1978); *Night Scenes* (N.Y., Jan. 18, 1989); *Concertpiece* for Marimba and Orch. (Boston, April 15, 1994). **CHAMBER:** 7 chamber syms. (1973, 1974, 1977, 1979, 1984, 1985, 1996); 2 string quartets (1983, 1987); *Grand Duo* for Viola and Percussionist (1985); *Movement in Time* for 2 Percussionists and Tape (1985); Brass Quintet (1986); Trio for Violin, Cello, and Piano (1994); *Taylor Series* for Saxophone, Piano, and Videotape (1999). **Piano:** Sonatina (1967); Chamber Sym. for Piano and Tape (1976); 2 sonatas (1982, 1983); Suite (1983); *Eastern Suite* (1998). **VOCAL:** Cantata for Tenor, Percussion, and Tape (1975); Madrigals (1977); *Night Watch* for Soprano and Piano (1978); *Like an Autumn Sky* for Chorus, Piano, and 2 Percussionists (1980); *Earth, Sky, Sea...* for Man's Voice and Piano (1982).—**NS/LK/DM**

Wuensch, Gerhard (Joseph), Austrian-Canadian composer and teacher; b. Vienna, Dec. 23, 1925. He received training in musicology at the Univ. (Ph.D., 1950) and in piano and composition at the Academy of Music (diplomas in both, 1952) in Vienna. As a Fulbright fellow, he pursued studies in theory with Pisk and Kennan at the Univ. of Tex. (1954–56). After teaching at Butler Univ. in Indianapolis (1956–63), he settled in Canada and taught at the univs. of Toronto (1964–69) and Calgary (1969–73). In 1973 he joined the faculty of the Univ. of Western Ontario in London, where he was chairman of the theory and composition dept. (1973–76) and a prof. (1978–91). In 1991 he was made prof. emeritus. As a composer, his works reveal a familiarity with a wide spectrum of styles and genres.

WORKS: DRAMATIC: *Labyrinth*, ballet (1957); *Il Pomo d'Oro*, comedy-ballet (1958); *Nice People: 3 Scenes from Contemporary Life*, chamber opera (1990; London, Ontario, Nov. 28, 1991). **ORCH.:** *Nocturne* (1956); *Variations on a Dorian Hexachord* (1959); 3 syms.: No. 1 (1959), No. 2 for Band (1960), and No. 3 for Brass and Percussion (1967); *Ballad* for Trumpet and Orch. (1962); Concerto for Piano and Chamber Orch. (1971); *Scherzo* for Piano and Winds (1971); Concerto for Bassoon and Chamber Orch. (1976); Concerto for Organ, 3 Trumpets, Timpani, and Strings (1976); *Ad Usum Ligorum*, concerto for 2 Pianos and Orch. (1981); *Serenade for a Summer Evening* (1986); *Variations and Fugue on a Mozartian Theme* (1986). **CHAMBER:** Trio for Clarinet, Bassoon, and Piano (1948); 2 string quartets (1953, 1963); 2 woodwind quintets (1963, 1967); *Music* for 7 Brass Instruments (1966); *4 Mini-Suites* for Accordion (1968); *Polysonics* for Variable Instrumentation (1969); *Cameos* for Flute and Piano (1969); *Music Without Pretensions* for Accordion and String Quartet (1969); Suite for Trumpet and Organ (1970); *Variations* for Clarinet and Piano (1971); 6 Duets for Flute and Clarinet (1971); *Prélude, Aria, and Fugue* for Accordion and Brass Quartet (1971); *Musica Giocosa* for Flute and Piano (1976); *Ménage à Trois* for Violin, Clarinet, and Piano (1987); *Recycling* for Tuba, Horn, and Piano (1989). **Piano:** *Esquisse* (1950; rev. 1970); 2 mini suites (1969, 1976); *12 Glimpses into 20th Century Idioms* (1969); *Valses nostalgiques* for Piano, 4-Hands (1972); Sonata for Piano, 4-Hands (1977); *Ping Pong Anyone?* (1986). **VOCAL:** *Symphonia sacra* for Soprano, Baritone, Chorus, Brass, Percussion, and Organ (1961); *Vexilla regis prodeunt* for Soloists, Chorus, and Organ (1968); 6 Songs for Voice, Flute, and Accordion (1970); *Laus sapientiae* for Soprano, Tenor, Baritone, Chorus, Organ, Brass, and Orch. (1977); *Songs, Lieder, and Melodies* for Voice, Clarinet, and Piano (1982); *4 Episodes from the Gospel of St. John* for Soloists, Chorus, Congregation, and Organ (1988); *Pygmalion* for Baritone and String Quartet (1989; London, Ontario, Jan. 29, 1995).—**NS/LK/DM**

Wüerst, Richard (Ferdinand), German composer, music critic, and teacher; b. Berlin, Feb. 22, 1824; d. there, Oct. 9, 1881. He studied violin with Ferdinand David at the Leipzig Cons., where he also took lessons with Mendelssohn. He then taught at Kullak's Neue Akademie der Tonkunst in Berlin. As music critic for the *Berliner Fremdenblatt*, he exercised considerable influence; publ. *Leitfaden der Elementartheorie der Musik* (1867; Eng. tr. as *Elementary Theory of Music and Treatment of Chords*, Boston, 1893). As a composer, he was a follower of Mendelssohn.

WORKS: DRAMATIC: Opera: *Der Rotmantel* (Berlin, 1848); *Vineta* (Pressburg, Dec. 21, 1862); *Eine Künstlerreise* (with Winterfeld; Berlin, 1868); *Faublas* (Berlin, 1873); *A-ing-fo-hi* (Berlin, Jan. 28, 1878); *Die Offiziere der Kaiserin* (Berlin, 1878). **ORCH.:** 3 syms.; *Ein Märchen*, symphonic fantasy; *Variations sur une chanson nègre de Kentucky* (on Stephen Foster's *My Old Kentucky Home*); *Sous le balcon*, serenade for String Orch. with Cello Obbligato; *Russische Suite* for String Orch. with Violin Obbligato; *Tanz der Mücken, Fliegen und Käfer*, scherzo. **CHAMBER:** Piano Trio; Cello Sonata; 3 string quartets; various violin pieces. **VOCAL:** *Der Wasserneck*, cantata; songs; vocal duets and terzets.—**NS/LK/DM**

Wührer, Friedrich (Anton Franz), distinguished Austrian pianist and pedagogue; b. Vienna, June 29, 1900; d. Mannheim, Dec. 27, 1975. He studied piano with Franz Schmidt, theory and composition with Joseph Marx, and conducting with Ferdinand Löwe at the Vienna Academy of Music (1915–20); also studied law and musicology at the Univ. of Vienna. From 1923 he made regular tours of Europe. He taught at the Vienna Academy of Music (1922–32), at the Hochschule für Musik in Mannheim (1934–36), in Kiel (1936–39), in Vienna (1939–45), at the Salzburg Mozarteum (1948–51), in Mannheim (1952–57), and in Munich (1957–68). He publ. *Meisterwerke der Klaviermusik* (Wilhelmshaven, 1966). His performances of the Classical and Romantic repertoires were highly regarded. He also championed the cause of 20th-century composers, ranging from Schoenberg to Prokofiev.—**NS/LK/DM**

Wüllner, Franz, important German pianist, conductor, and composer, father of **Ludwig Wüllner;** b.

Münster, Jan. 28, 1832; d. Braunfels-an-der-Lahn, Sept. 7, 1902. He studied with Schindler in Münster and Frankfurt am Main (1846–50). From 1850 to 1854 he was active as a concert artist. He was a teacher at the Munich music school (1856–58), then music director in Aachen (1858–64). He returned to Munich in 1864, where he became court music director of the church choir. He then taught at the music school (from 1867), and also conducted at the Court Opera. Under unfavorable conditions (against Wagner's wishes), he prepared and conducted the first perf. of *Das Rheingold* (Sept. 22, 1869) and *Die Walküre* (June 26, 1870), the success of which led to his appointment as principal conductor there in 1871. In 1877 he became court conductor at Dresden, and also director of the Cons. In 1882 Schuch was promoted to take his place; thereafter Wüllner was one of the conductors of the Berlin Phil. for the 1882–1885 seasons. He became conductor of the Gurzenich Concerts in Cologne in 1884 and director of the Cologne Cons., later becoming also municipal music director, posts he held until his death. He was highly regarded as a choral composer. He publ. the valuable book of vocal exercises *Chorübungen der Münchener Musikschule* (3 vols., Munich, 1876; new ed. by R. Stephani, 1953–54; Eng. tr., 1882). He was a friend of Brahms.

WORKS: VOCAL: Voice and Orch.: *Die Flucht der heiligen Familie; Heinrich der Finkler; Deutscher Siegesgesang; Lied und Leben; Psalm 98; Psalm 127.* **Other:** Church music; songs.

BIBL.: E. Prieger, *F. W.: ein Nachruf* (Bonn, 1902); E. Wolff, ed., *Johannes Brahms im Briefwechsel mit F. W.* (Berlin, 1922; with a list of works); D. Kamper, *F. W.: Leben, Wirken und kompositorisches Schaffen* (Cologne, 1963); idem, ed., *Richard Strauss und F. W. im Briefwechsel* (Cologne, 1963).—**NS/LK/DM**

Wüllner, Ludwig, distinguished German singer, son of **Franz Wüllner;** b. Münster, Aug. 19, 1858; d. Kiel, March 19, 1938. He studied Germanic philology at the Univs. of Munich, Berlin, and Strasbourg. He taught Germanic philology at the Akademie in Münster (1884–87), and sang occasionally in concert. His music training began only in 1887, when he took a course of study at the Cologne Cons. A second change of vocation brought him to the Meiningen Court Theater, where he appeared as an actor of heroic parts in the spoken drama (1889–95); he became friendly with Brahms, who commended his singing of German folk songs. In 1895 he gave song recitals in Berlin with such acclaim that he decided to devote himself mainly to lieder. He then made tours of all Europe, arousing tremendous enthusiasm. His first recital in N.Y. (Nov. 15, 1908) was a sensational success, and he followed it by an extensive tour of the U.S. and then another (1909–10). His peculiar distinction was his ability to give an actor's impersonation of the character of each song, introducing an element of drama on the concert stage.

BIBL.: F. Ludwig, *L. W.: Sein Leben und seine Kunst* (Leipzig, 1931).—**NS/LK/DM**

Wunderlich, Fritz (actually, **Friedrich Karl Otto),** outstanding German tenor; b. Kusel, Sept. 26, 1930; d. Heidelberg, Sept. 17, 1966. He was a student of Margarete von Wintenfeld at the Freiburg im Breisgau Hochschule für Musik (1950–55). While still a student, he appeared as a soloist with the Freiburg im Breisgau Choir, and then sang Tamino in a school performance of *Die Zauberflöte* (1954). In 1955 he made his professional operatic debut in Stuttgart as Eislinger in *Die Meistersinger von Nürnberg,* where he sang until 1958. From 1958 to 1960 he was a member of the Frankfurt am Main Opera. In 1958 he sang at the Aix-en-Provence Festival, and then appeared as Henry in *Die schweigsame Frau* at the Salzburg Festival in 1959. In 1960 he became a member of the Bavarian State Opera in Munich and in 1962 was made a Kammersänger. He also was a member of the Vienna State Opera from 1962. In 1965 he made his debut as Don Ottavio at London's Covent Garden. He appeared at the Edinburgh Festival in 1966. Wunderlich was scheduled to make his Metropolitan Opera debut in N.Y. as Don Ottavio on Oct. 8, 1966, but his career of great promise was tragically cut short by his death in a fall at his home. He was acclaimed for the extraordinary beauty of his lyric tenor voice. In addition to his remarkable Mozartian roles, he also was admired for such roles as Alfredo, Lensky, Jeník, Palestrina, and Leukippos. He likewise was noted for his operetta and lieder performances.

BIBL.: W. Pfister, *F. W.: Biographie* (Zürich, 1990).
—**NS/LK/DM**

Wunderlich, Heinz, noted German organist, choral conductor, and pedagogue; b. Leipzig, April 25, 1919. He studied organ with Straube in Leipzig (1935–41), then composition and conducting with J. N. David. He held several organ and choral conducting posts (1943–58); taught at the Halle Staatliche Hochschule für Musik (1947–58); was Kirchenmusikdirektor at St. Jacobi in Hamburg (1958–82), where his concerts of choral music by the German masters and of the organ works of Reger, as well as his restoration of the famous Arp Schnitger organ, received great acclaim; he toured the U.S. with his choir (1978). As prof. of organ at the Hamburg Hochschule für Musik (from 1974), he attracted students from many countries.—**NS/LK/DM**

Wünsch, Walther, Austrian ethnomusicologist; b. Gablonz an der Niesse, July 23, 1908; d. Vienna, Feb. 24, 1991. He studied with Becking at the German Univ. in Prague (Ph.D., 1932, with the diss. *Die Geigentechnik der jugoslawischen Guslaren*; publ. in Brno, 1934) and completed his Habilitation in 1960 at the Univ. of Graz. After working at the musicological inst. of the Pestalozzi Academy in Prague (1932–35), he was active at the Inst. for Acoustics in Berlin (1935–38). From 1945 he was active as a chamber music player and taught at the Steiermarkischen Landeskonservatorium; in 1960 he joined the faculty of the Inst. for Music Ethnology at the Graz Hochschule für Musik, where he became a prof. in 1968. He publ. several important studies on ethnomusicology, including *Heldensänger in Südosteuropa* (Leipzig, 1937).—**NS/LK/DM**

Wuorinen, Charles (Peter), prominent American composer, pedagogue, pianist, and conductor; b.

N.Y., June 9, 1938. He was a student of Beeson, Ussachevsky, and Luening at Columbia Univ. (B.A., 1961; M.A., 1963), where he then taught (1964–71). With Harvey Sollberger, he founded the Group for Contemporary Music in 1962, which became a vital force in the propagation of modern music via concerts and recordings. He was a visiting lecturer at Princeton Univ. (1967–68) and the New England Cons. of Music in Boston (1968–71). After serving as adjunct lecturer at the Univ. of South Fla. (1971–72), he was on the faculty of the Manhattan School of Music in N.Y. (1972–79). From 1973 to 1987 he was artistic director and chairman of the American Composers Orch. in N.Y. In 1984 he became a prof. at Rutgers, the State Univ. of N.J. From 1985 to 1989 he served as composer-in-residence of the San Francisco Sym. He was a visiting prof. at the State Univ. of N.Y. at Buffalo from 1989 to 1994. Wuorinen has received numerous prizes, grants, and commissions, among them the Joseph Bearns Prize (1958, 1959, 1961), a National Inst. of Arts and Letters Award (1967), 2 Guggenheim fellowships (1968, 1972), the Pulitzer Prize in Music for his *Times Encomium* (1970), the Brandeis Univ. Creative Arts Award (1970), NEA grants (1974, 1976), Rockefeller Foundation fellowships (1979, 1980, 1981), and a MacArthur Foundation fellowship (1986–91). He also was elected to membership in the American Academy and Inst. of Arts and Letters. Wuorinen publ. the book *Simple Composition* (N.Y., 1979), which gives insight into his use of 12-tone composition. Wuorinen is one of the most representative of contemporary composers of his generation. His techniques derive from Stravinsky's early period, when stark primitivism gave way to austere linear counterpoint. An even greater affinity in Wuorinen's music is with the agglutinative formations of unrelated thematic statements as practiced by Varèse. A more literal dependence connects Wuorinen's works with the dodecaphonic method of composition as promulgated by Schoenberg. These modalities and relationships coalesce in Wuorinen's writing into a sui generis complex subdivided into melodic, harmonic, and contrapuntal units that build a definitive formal structure. The foundation of his method of composition is serialism, in which pitch, time, and rhythmic divisions relate to one another in a "time point system," which lends itself to unlimited tonal and temporal arrangements, combinations, and permutations. In his prolific output, Wuorinen has explored the entire vocabulary of serial composition.

WORKS: DRAMATIC: *The Politics of Harmony*, masque (1966–67; N.Y., Oct. 28, 1968); *The W. of Babylon (or The Triumph of Love Over Moral Depravity)*, Baroque burlesque (partial perf., N.Y., Dec. 15, 1975; 1st complete perf., San Francisco, Jan 20, 1989); *Delight of the Muses*, ballet (1991; N.Y., Jan. 29, 1992; based on the orch piece). **ORCH.:** Concert-Piece for Piano and Strings (Bennington, Vt., Aug. 18, 1956); *Music* (N.Y., Dec. 1, 1956); *Alternating Currents* for Chamber Orch. (1957); *Concertante I* for Violin and Strings (Middlebury, Vt., July 7, 1957) and *IV* for Violin, Piano, and Chamber Orch. (Bennington, Vt., Aug. 29, 1959); 3 numbered syms.: No. 1 (1957–58; N.Y., March 7, 1958), No. 2 (1958; N.Y., Feb. 27, 1959), and No. 3 (N.Y., Nov. 11, 1959); 2 violin concertos: No. 1 (1958) and No. 2 for Amplified Violin and Orch. (1971–72; Tanglewood, Aug. 4, 1972); *Concertone* for Brass Quintet and Orch. (1960; Iowa City, Feb. 19, 1964); *An Educator's "Wachet Auf"* for Chamber Orch. (1961); *Evolutio Transcripta* for Chamber Orch. (Bennington, Vt., Aug. 19, 1961; transcription of the organ piece); *Orchestral and Electronic Exchanges* for Orch. and Tape (1964–65; N.Y., July 30, 1965); 3 piano concertos: No. 1 (1965–66; Iowa City, May 4, 1966), No. 2 for Amplified Piano and Orch. (1973–74; N.Y., Dec. 6, 1974), and No. 3 (1982–83; Troy, N.Y., May 4, 1984); *Contrafactum* (Iowa City, Nov. 19, 1969); *Grand Bamboula* for Strings (1971; Iowa City, Sept. 30, 1972); *A Reliquary for Igor Stravinsky* (1974–75; Ojai, Calif., June 1, 1975); Percussion Sym. (1976; Somerville, N.J., Jan. 26, 1978); *Tashi* for Clarinet, Violin, Cello, Piano, and Orch. (1975–76; Cleveland, Oct. 13, 1976); *Two-Part Symphony* (1977–78; N.Y., Dec. 11, 1978); *The Magic Art*, instrumental masque, after Purcell (1977–79; St. Paul, Minn., Sept. 26, 1979); *Ancestors* for Chamber Orch. (Portland, Ore., Aug. 10, 1978); *Short Suite* (1981; Purchase, N.Y., Feb. 13, 1983); *Rhapsody* for Violin and Orch. (1983; San Francisco, Jan. 16, 1985); *Bamboula Squared* for Orch. and Tape (1983–84; N.Y., June 4, 1984); Concertino (1984; also for 15 Solo Instruments, N.Y., Feb. 5, 1985); *Movers and Shakers* (Cleveland, Dec. 13, 1984); *Crossfire* (1984; Baltimore, May 9, 1985); *Prelude to Kullervo* for Tuba and Orch. (N.Y., Nov. 21, 1985); *The Golden Dance* (1985–86; San Francisco, Sept. 10, 1986); *Fanfare for the Houston Symphony* (Houston, March 15, 1986); *Galliard* for Chamber Orch. (Cleveland, Sept. 27, 1987); *Five*, concerto for Amplied Cello and Orch. (1987; N.Y., April 28, 1988); *Bamboula Beach*, overture (1987; Miami, Feb. 4, 1988); *Another Happy Birthday* (San Francisco, Sept. 14, 1988); *Machault Mon Chou* (1988; San Francisco, May 24, 1989); *Astra* (1989–90; Copenhagen, Aug. 11, 1990); *Delight of the Muses* (Stony Brook, N.Y., Nov. 9, 1991; as a ballet, N.Y., Jan. 29, 1992); *Microsymphony* (1992); Saxophone Quartet Concerto (1992); *The Mission of Virgil* (1993); *Windfall* (1994). **CHAMBER:** *Prelude and Fugue* for 4 Percussionists (1955; Urbana, Ill., March 1, 1956); Sonatina for Woodwind Quartet (Bennington, Vt., Aug. 15, 1956); *Into the Organ Pipes and Steeples* for 11 Instruments (1956); *Subversion* for String Septet (1956; Bennington, Vt., Aug. 1957); 3 wind quintets: No. 1 (1956; N.Y., Jan. 16, 1957), No. 2 (1958), and No. 3 (1977; N.Y., Feb. 24, 1978); 1 unnumbered string quartet (Bennington, Vt., Aug. 1957); 3 numbered string quartets: No. 1 (1970–71; Chicago, Oct. 11, 1971), No. 2 (1978–79; Jackson, Wy., Aug. 1, 1979), and No. 3 (1986–86; Hanover, N.H., Nov. 6, 1987); *3 Mass Movements* for Violin (East Hampton, N.Y., July 28, 1957); *Triptych* for Violin, Viola, and Percussion (1957; N.Y., Jan. 19, 1958); *Spectrum* for Violin and Brass Quintet (Philadelphia, April 10, 1958); *Movement* for Wind Quintet (1958; 1st movement of his 2nd Wind Quintet); *Concertante II* for Violin and Chamber Ensemble (Middlebury, Vt., July 6, 1958) and *III* for Harpsichord, Oboe, Violin, Viola, and Cello (1959; N.Y., Aug. 2, 1961); *3 Pieces* for String Quartet (Bennington, Vt., Aug. 9, 1958); *Trio Concertante* for Oboe, Violin, and Piano (Troy, N.Y., Oct. 31, 1958); *Musica duarum partium ecclesiastica* for Brass Quartet, Timpani, Piano, and Organ (1959); Flute Sonata (1960; WNYC Radio, N.Y., Nov. 17, 1962); *Consort of 4 Trombones* (N.Y., April 4, 1960); *Turetzky Pieces* for Flute, Clarinet, and Double Bass (Westbrook, Conn., Aug. 7, 1960); *8 Variations* for Violin and Harpsichord (1960; N.Y., June 21, 1961); *Consort from Instruments and Voices* (1960–61; N.Y., Jan. 15, 1961); *Tiento Sobre Cabezón* for Flute, Oboe, Violin, Viola, Cello, Harpsichord, and Piano (N.Y., Aug. 2, 1961); Concert for Double Bass (1961; Southport, Conn., May 11, 1962); 3 trios for Flute, Cello, and Piano: No. 1 (N.Y., Dec. 14, 1961), No. 2 (1962; N.Y., May 6, 1963), and No. 3 (1972–73; N.Y., May 28, 1973); Octet for Oboe, Clarinet, Horn, Trombone, Violin, Cello, Double Bass, and Piano (1961–62; N.Y., Sept. 27,

1962); *Invention* for Percussion Quintet (N.Y., March 6, 1962); *Duuiensela* for Cello and Piano (New Haven, Conn., April 30, 1962); *Bearbeitungen über das Glogauer Liederbuch* for Flute, Clarinet, Violin, and Double Bass (Hartford, Conn., July 17, 1962); chamber concertos for Cello and 10 Players (1963; N.Y., Feb. 17, 1964), for Flute and 10 Players (Tanglewood, Aug. 9, 1964), for Oboe and 10 Players (N.Y., Nov. 8, 1965), and for Tuba, 12 Winds, and 12 Drums (1969–70; N.Y., March 7, 1971); *Flute Variations I* (N.Y., Dec. 18, 1963) and *II* (1968; Jersey City, N.J., April 17, 1969); *Variations à 2* for Flute and Piano (1963–64); Composition for Violin and 10 Instruments (1963–64; N.Y., April 26, 1964); Composition for Oboe and Piano (1964–65; Boston, April 3, 1966); *The Bells* for Percussion (1965–66); *Bicinium* for 2 Oboes (1966; N.Y., May 10, 1967); *Janissary Music* for Percussionist (part 1, Swarthmore, Pa., Oct. 26, 1966; part 2, N.Y., March 12, 1967); *Salve Regina: John Bull* for 14 Instruments (N.Y., Oct. 31, 1966); Duo for Violin and Piano (1966–67; N.Y., April 17, 1968); String Trio (1967–68; Washington, D.C., Oct. 27, 1968); *Adapting to the Times* for Cello and Piano (1968–69; Amherst, Mass., Feb. 25, 1970); *Nature's Concord* for Trumpet and Piano (1969); *The Long and the Short* for Violin (Berkeley, Calif., Aug. 4, 1969); *Ringing Changes* for Percussion Ensemble (1969–70; Wayne, N.J., April 28, 1970); *Cello Variations I* (Philadelphia, Dec. 8, 1970) and *II* (1975; WQXR Radio, N.Y., Dec. 1976); *Canzona* for 12 Instruments (1971; N.Y., Jan. 31, 1972); *Bassoon Variations* for Bassoon, Harp, and Timpani (1971–72; Cambridge, Mass., Oct. 28, 1973); *Harp Variations* for Harp, Violin, Viola, and Cello (1971–72; N.Y., April 17, 1973); *Violin Variations* (N.Y., May 14, 1972); *On Alligators* for 8 Instruments (1972); *Speculum speculi* for 6 Players (1972; Grand Forks, N.Dak., Jan. 14, 1973); *Arabia Felix* for 6 Instruments (1973; N.Y., Feb. 23, 1974); *Grand Union* for Cello and Drums (Chicago, Nov. 5, 1973); *Fantasia* for Violin and Piano (1974; Baltimore, Dec. 14, 1975); *Tashi* for Clarinet, Violin, Cello, and Piano (1975; Colorado Springs, Jan. 15, 1976); *Hyperion* for Chamber Ensemble (1975; Adelaide, March 21, 1976); *Album Leaf* for Violin and Cello (1976); *The Winds* for 8 Winds and Piano (1976–77; N.Y., May 19, 1977); *6 Pieces* for Violin and Piano (1977; N.Y., April 18, 1978); *Fast Fantasy* for Cello and Piano (1977); *Archangel* for Bass Trombone and String Quartet (1977; N.Y., Dec. 18, 1978); *Archaeopteryx* for Bass Trombone and 10 Players (1978; Caramoor, N.Y., July 1, 1982); Percussion Duo for Mallet Instruments and Piano (Iowa City, Oct. 29, 1979); *Fortune* for Clarinet, Violin, Cello, and Piano (1979); *Joan's* for Flute, Clarinet, Violin, Cello, and Piano (1979; N.Y., March 23, 1980); *Beast 708* for Computer-generated Tape or 10 Instruments (1980); Horn Trio (1981; N.Y., April 18, 1983); Trio for Bass Trombone, Tuba, and Contrabass (1981; N.Y., April 14, 1983); *N.Y. Notes* for 6 Instruments (1981–82; Sacramento, Nov. 8, 1982); *Divertimento* for Alto Saxophone and Piano (1982; N.Y., March 6, 1983); *Divertimento* for String Quartet (1982; Glen Falls, N.Y., May 9, 1983); *Spinoff* for Violin, Contrabass, and Conga Drums (N.Y., May 18, 1983); Trio for Violin, Cello, and Piano (Union, N.J., Oct. 1, 1983); Concertino for 15 Instruments (1984); *Horn Trio Continued* (1985; Los Angeles, May 24, 1988); Trombone Trio (1985; N.Y., Nov. 6, 1986); Double Solo for Horn Trio (1985; N.Y., March 16, 1986); *Fanfare for Rutgers University* for 2 Horns, 2 Trumpets, and 2 Trombones (1986); *A Doleful Dompe on Deborah's Departure as well as Borda's Bawdy Badinage* for English Horn, Violin, and Cello (1986); Violin Sonata (Washington, D.C., Nov. 25, 1988); String Sextet (1988–89; Covington, Ga., Nov. 4, 1989); Saxophone Quartet (1992); Percussion Quartet (1994); Piano Quintet (1994; Chicago, Feb. 19, 1995); *Guitar Variations* (1994). **KEYBOARD: Piano:** *Scherzo* (1953; N.Y., May 13, 1956); *Song and Dance* (1955; N.Y., May 13, 1956); *2 Tranquil Pieces* (1956); 1 unnumbered sonata (N.Y., Dec. 16, 1958); 3 numbered sonatas: No. 1 (1969; Washington, D.C., Dec. 14, 1970), No. 2 (Washington, D.C., Oct. 2, 1976), and No. 3 (1986; N.Y., March 29, 1989); *3 Prepositions* (1958); *Piano Variations* (1963; N.Y., Jan. 13, 1964); *Making Ends Meet* for Piano, 4-Hands (1966; Washington, D.C., May 19, 1968); *12 Short Pieces* (1973); *Self-Similar Waltz* (1977; Evanston, Ill., May 11, 1978); *The Blue Bamboula* (1980; Tokyo, May 29, 1981); *Capriccio* (1980–81; N.Y., April 14, 1982); *Album Leaf* (N.Y., May 30, 1984); *Bagatelle* (1987–88; Buffalo, June 12, 1989). **Organ:** *Homage à Bach* (1955; Gardner, Mass., June 30, 1956); *Evolutio: Organ* (1961; Boston, April 8, 1962; also transcribed for Orch.); *Natural Fantasy* (1985; N.Y., Jan. 31, 1988). **Harpsichord:** *Harpsichord Diversions* (1966). **VOCAL:** *O Filii et Filiae* for Chorus (1953; N.Y., May 2, 1954); *Te decet hymnus* for Soloists, Chorus, Timpani, Organ, and Piano (1954; N.Y., May 13, 1956); *Faire, If You Expect Admiring, and Turne Backe, You Wanton Flyer* for Men's Chorus (N.Y., May 13, 1956); *Dr. Faustus Lights the Lights* for Narrator and 7 Players (1956–57; N.Y., April 8, 1957); *Wandering in This Place* for Mezzo-soprano (1957); *Be Merry All That Be Present* for Chorus and Organ (1957; N.Y., Jan. 26, 1958); *The Door in the Wall* for 2 Mezzo-sopranos and Piano (N.Y., April 22, 1960; also for Mezzo-soprano, Soprano, and Piano); *On the Raft* for 2 Mezzo-sopranos and Piano (N.Y., April 22, 1960; also for Mezzo-soprano, Soprano, and Piano); *Madrigale spirituale sopra Salmo Secundo* for Tenor, Bass, and 6 Instruments (Bennington, Vt., Aug. 27, 1960); *Symphonia sacra* for Tenor, Baritone, Bass, and 6 Instruments (N.Y., March 27, 1961); *The Prayer of Jonah* for Chorus and String Quintet (1962; N.Y., March 21, 1963); *Super salutem* for Men's Voices and Instruments (1964); *A Song to the Lute in Musicke* for Soprano and Piano (1969–70; N.Y., Jan. 11, 1971); *A Message to Denmark Hill* for Baritone, Flute, Cello, and Piano (1970); *Mannheim 87.87.87.* for Chorus and Organ (N.Y., May 1, 1973); *An Anthem for Epiphany* for Chorus, Trumpet, and Organ (1974); 6 Songs for Countertenor or Alto, Tenor, and 6 Instruments (1977; Wayne, N.J., Jan. 26, 1978); 3 Songs for Tenor and Piano (1978–79); *Psalm 39* for Baritone and Guitar (1979); *The Celestial Sphere*, oratorio for Chorus and Orch. (1980; Rock Island, Ill., April 25, 1981); Mass for Soprano, Chamber Chorus, Violin, 3 Trombones, and Organ (1982; N.Y., Nov. 23, 1983); *A Solis Ortu* for Chorus (1988–89; N.Y., Dec. 30, 1990); *Twang* for Mezzo-soprano or Soprano and Piano (1988–89); *Genesis* for Chorus and Orch. (1989; San Francisco, Sept. 26, 1991); *Missa Brevis* for Chorus and Organ (1991; N.Y., Feb. 23, 1992); *A Winter's Tale* for Soprano and Piano (Atlanta, Oct. 12, 1992; also for Soprano, Clarinet, Horn, String Trio, and Piano, Houston, Jan. 10, 1995). **ELECTRONIC:** *Time's Encomium* (1968–69).

BIBL.: R. Burbank, *C. W.: A Bio-Bibliography* (Westport, Conn., 1994).—**NS/LK/DM**

Würfel, Wenzel Wilhelm (actually, **Václav Vilem**), Bohemian pianist, conductor, teacher, and composer; b. Pláňany, near Kolín, May 6, 1790; d. Vienna, March 23, 1832. He made tours as a pianist while still a child, then was a pupil of Tomaschek in Prague. In 1815 he went to Warsaw as prof. of organ and thoroughbass at the Cons., numbering Chopin among his students. After conducting at the Kärnthnertortheater in Vienna (1824–26), he toured as a pianist. His opera *Rübezahl* was first performed in Prague on Oct. 7,

1824, with excellent success, and enjoyed popularity for some years. He also wrote the opera *Der Rotmantel* (1826), many piano pieces in a bravura style, and pedagogical pieces for keyboard.—**NS/LK/DM**

Wurlitzer, family of German-American instrument dealers and makers:

(1) (Franz) Rudolph Wurlitzer, (b. Schoneck, Saxony, Jan. 31, 1831; d. Cincinnati, Jan. 14, 1914) emigrated to the U.S. in 1853. After settling in Cincinnati, he became active as an instrument dealer. With his brother Anton, he organized Rudolph Wurlitzer & Bro. in 1872. The business became the Rudolph Wurlitzer Co. in 1890, with Rudolph serving as president (1890–1912) and as chairman (1912–14). The Wurlitzer firm brought out the Wurlitzer Hope-Jones Unit Orch., better known as "the Mighty Wurlitzer," a theater organ, in 1910. Their jukeboxes were manufactured between 1933 and 1974, in 1935 they began making a console upright spinet piano, and from 1947 they manufactured electronic organs. Wurlitzer had 3 sons and 1 grandson who joined the business:

(2) Howard Eugene Wurlitzer; b. Cincinnati, Sept. 5, 1871; d. N.Y., Oct. 30, 1928. Through his efforts, the company became highly successful. He served as its president (1912–27) and chairman (1927–28).

(3) Rudolph Henry Wurlitzer; b. Cincinnati, Dec. 30, 1873; d. there, May 27, 1948. He studied in Cincinnati and then went to Berlin in 1891 to study violin with Emanuel Wirth, the history of musical instruments with Oskar Fleischer, and acoustics with Hermann von Helmholtz; he also studied with the violin authority August Riechers. Upon his return to Cincinnati in 1894, he joined the firm as a director, and then held the posts of secretary and treasurer (1899–1912), vice-president (1912–27), president (1927–32), and chairman (1932–42).

(4) Farny Reginald Wurlitzer; b. Cincinnati, Dec. 7, 1883; d. North Tonawanda, N.Y., May 6, 1972. He studied at the Cincinnati Technical School before pursuing his education in Germany as an apprentice to various instrument makers (1901–04). He then returned to Cincinnati to join the firm and became head of the automatic musical instrument dept. in 1907; in 1909 he became head of the Rudolph Wurlitzer Manufacturing Co. in North Tonawanda, which commenced making coin-operated phonographs in 1933; he was president (1932–41) and chairman (1941–66) of the firm.

(5) Rembert Wurlitzer, son of Rudolph Henry Wurlitzer; b. Cincinnati, March 27, 1904; d. N.Y., Oct. 21, 1963. He studied at Princeton Univ., then received training in violin-making from Amedee Dieudonne in Mirecourt and worked with Alfred Hill in London. After returning to Cincinnati, he was made a vice-president of the company. In 1937 he became head of the company's violin dept. in N.Y., which he made an independent firm in 1949; the company won great distinction and remained active until 1974.

BIBL.: J. Fairfield, *W. World of Music: 100 Years of Musical Achievement* (Chicago, 1956); J. Landon, *Behold the Mighty W.* (Westport, Conn., 1983).—**NS/LK/DM**

Wurm, Marie, noted English pianist; b. Southampton, May 18, 1860; d. Munich, Jan. 21, 1938. She studied piano with Raff and Clara Schumann in Germany. Returning to England, she took theory lessons with Stanford and Arthur Sullivan. She was quite successful as a concert pianist in England and Germany; in 1925 she settled in Munich. Her avocation was conducting; she organized a women's orch. in Berlin, and conducted its inaugural concert on Oct. 10, 1899, arousing considerable curiosity. She was an ambitious composer and also publ. *Das ABC der Musik and Praktische Vorschule zur Caland- Lehre*. Her sisters, Adela Wurm and Mathilda Wurm, who made their careers in England, changed their last name to Verne in order to exorcise the vermicular sound of the original German family name, as pronounced in English.

WORKS: *Die Mitschuldigen*, opera (Leipzig, 1923); Piano Concerto; String Quartet; Violin Sonata; Cello Sonata; Piano Sonata; numerous piano pieces (*Valse de concert, Barcarolle, Sylph Dance, Suite*, gavottes, mazurkas, etc.).—**NS/LK/DM**

Würtzler, Aristid von, Hungarian-born American harpist and composer; b. Budapest, Sept. 20, 1930. He attended the Franz Liszt Academy of Music in Budapest (1951–56), where he studied harp with Miklós Rékai and composition with Kodály. He left Hungary during the 1956 uprising and emigrated to the U.S., where he was 1st harpist with the Detroit Sym. Orch. (1957) and the N.Y. Phil. (1958–62). He subsequently served as head of the harp dept. of the Hartt Coll. of Music in Hartford, Conn. (1963–70). In 1970 he accepted teaching positions at N.Y.U. and Hofstra Univ. He founded the N.Y. Harp Ensemble, for which he commissioned works from contemporary composers, including Ligeti, Stockhausen, Hovhaness, Bernstein, Serly, Saygun, and Takemitsu. In 1981 he gave master classes in China, the first of their kind.—**NS/LK/DM**

Wu-Tang Clan, one of the most successful rap music posses of the 1990s. **MEMBERSHIP:** RZA (real name, Robert Diggs); Genius/GZA (real name, Gary Grice); Ol' Dirty Bastard (real name, Russell Jones); Method Man (real name, Clifford Smith); Raekwon the Chef (real name, Corey Woods); Ghostface Killah (real name, Denis Coles); U-God (real name, Lamont Hawkins); Inspectah Deck (real name, Jason Hunter); Masta Killa (real name, E. Turner).

Using the same business plan as George Clinton did nearly two decades earlier, the Wu-Tang Clan signed a contract that would allow the individual members of the collective to record for whomever they pleased. This allowed the group exposure on nearly every major label and many of the larger independents, with the diverse financial results and security of a wide distribution base.

The collective started coming together under aegis of DJ RZA, GZA Genius, and Ol' Dirty Bastard (most frequently known by his initials, ODB). Both ODB and GZA had recorded with little success. They brought in RZA as the collective's beatmaster general and producer. RZA took off from the P-Funk inspired beats of West Coast producers like Dr. Dre, creating something more stripped down and ominous. Bringing in a half a dozen more homiez, the collective took the name Wu-

Tang from a piece of martial arts mysticism about an invincible sword and the warriors who wield it.

They self-released their debut single "Protect Ya Neck." It quickly rose to the top of the underground, becoming a substantial hit, introducing RZA's musical style as well as the group's bantering cross-talk between eight intelligent, wise-ass MCs. They received many offers, but their demand for individual artists to record where they wanted caused many labels to withdraw. BMG-distributed Loud records finally proved amenable to their demands, and the Wu-Tang Clan released *Enter the Wu-Tang (36 Chambers)* in 1993. The album received considerable critical acclaim and slowly built a following. "Method Man" rose into the pop charts. "C.R.E.A.M. (Cash Rules Everything Around Me)" broke them even further, rising to #60 and topping the maxi-single chart. The album went platinum and the Clan was on its way.

Over the course of the next four years, GZA, RZA, Method Man, Raekwon, and ODB all recorded solo albums. RZAs recorded with the hip-hop supergroup the Gravediggaz, which included De La Soul's Prince Paul and Statsasonic's Fruitkwan. Their debut album went gold. Raekwan recorded a track with Ghostface Killa for the *Fresh* soundtrack. Method Man's *Tical* in 1994 became a huge hit, with his duet with Mary K. Blige on "You're All I Need (To Get By)" leading the way. ODB followed with *Return to the 36 Chambers,* which went gold. In 1995 Genius and Raekwon released critically acclaimed albums. Raekwon's disc was almost a duo project with Ghostface Killah. Ghostface Killah dropped his solo debut in 1996. ODB recorded the bizarre single "Fantasy" with Mariah Carey. As with P-Funk before them, every solo album was treated like a group project, with different pieces of the group on them.

Additionally, the group created their own line of clothing, Wu-Wear. Image Comics put out a book based on their actual characters and their mythical roots.

In 1997 the group reunited as the Wu-Tang Clan for *Wu-Tang Forever*. Going gold out of the box and debuting at #1, the album lived up to its build-up as the most anticipated hip-hop album of the year. By year's end, it went quadruple platinum. Another spate of solo albums followed, with U-God's *Redemption* debuting the group's own imprint, ODB came out with another album, *N***a, Please,* and became involved in several drug cases. Inspectah Deck put out *Uncontrollable Substance,* featuring most of the group; it sounded like a continuation of the Wu-Tang albums. Method Man recorded a duet with Redman called *Blackout* that went platinum, as did his *Tical 2000.*

With a mixture of business smarts and street smarts, the Wu-Tang clan has the right stuff to make hip-hop legends long into the new millennium.

DISC.: *Enter the Wu-Tang (36 Chambers)* (1993); *Wu-Tang Forever* (1997).—**BH**

Wyk, Arnold(us Christian Vlok) van, South African composer, pianist, and teacher; b. Calvinia, Cape Province, April 26, 1916; d. Cape Town, May 27, 1983. He studied at Stellenbosch Univ., near Cape Town (1936–38), then went to London, where he studied with Theodore Holland (composition) and Harold Craxton (piano) at the Royal Academy of Music (1938–43). From 1939 to 1944 he worked for the BBC. In 1946 he returned to South Africa and taught at the Univ. of Cape Town (1949–61) and the Stellenbosch Univ. (1961–78). He also was active as a pianist.

WORKS: ORCH.: 2 syms.: No. 1 (1941–43) and No. 2, *Sinfonia ricercata* (Cape Town, March 13, 1952); *Southern Cross* (1943); *Rhapsody* (Cape Town, March 4, 1952); *Aubade* for Small Orch. (1955); *Primavera* (1960); *Maskerade* (1962–64); *Gebede by jaargetye in die Boland* (1966). **CHAMBER:** *5 Elegies* for String Quartet (1940–41); String Quartet No. 1 (1946); *Duo concertante* for Viola and Piano (1962); *Music for 13 Players* (1969); various piano pieces. **VOCAL:** Choral pieces; songs.—**NS/LK/DM**

Wykes, Robert (Arthur), American flutist, teacher, and composer; b. Aliquippa, Pa., May 19, 1926. He studied composition with Phillips and Barlow at the Eastman School of Music in Rochester, N.Y. (B.M. and M.M., 1949). He played flute in the Toledo Sym. Orch. while teaching at Bowling Green State Univ. (1950–52), and then taught at the Univ. of Ill. (1952–55). In 1955 he joined the faculty of Washington Univ. in St. Louis, where he was a prof. (1965–88). He also was a flutist with the St. Louis Sym. Orch. (1963–67) and the Studio for New Music in St. Louis (1966–69). In 1950 and 1951 he held MacDowell Colony fellowships. He was composer-in-residence with the Djerassi Resident Artist Program in 1989. In 1990–91 he was a visiting scholar at Stanford Univ. His *Lyric Symphony* received honorable mention for the Friedheim Award in 1980 and his *3 Facets of Friendship* for Flute and Clarinet won the National Flute Assn. Newly Published Music Award in 1992.

WORKS: DRAMATIC: Chamber Opera: *The Prankster* (1951; Bowling Green, Ohio, Jan. 12, 1952). **Other:** Scores for documentary films, including *Robert Kennedy Remembered* (Academy Award, 1969), *Monument to the Dream, John F. Kennedy 1917–1963,* and *The Eye of Jefferson.* **ORCH.:** *Divertimento* for Small Orch. (1949); *Density III* (1959; St. Louis, Jan. 8, 1960); Concertino for Flute, Oboe, Piano, and Strings (1963); *Wave Forms and Pulses* (University City, Mo., May 2, 1964); *Horizons* (1964); *The Shape of Time* (St. Louis, April 1, 1965); *Toward Time's Receding* (St. Louis, April 7, 1972); *A Shadow of Silence I* (1972); *Western Wyndes* for Symphonic Band (Barrington, Ill., May 21, 1974); *A Lyric Symphony* (St. Louis, May 10, 1980); *Paris: 2nd Symphony* (St. Louis, Sept. 27, 1981). **Concert Band:** *A Summer Day* (St. Louis, April 9, 1988). **CHAMBER:** Flute Sonata (1955); String Sextet (1958); Piano Quintet (1959); *Points and Excursions* for Brass Quintet (1962); *Cheirality* for String Quartet (1970); Duo for Violin and Harp (St. Louis, March 1982); *3 Concert Etudes* for Flute (1989); *For Cello* (1989); *3 Facets of Friendship* for Flute and Clarinet (1990); *In Memoriam Oliver Nelson* for Flute and Piano (1990); *9 Miniatures: 3 Sets of 3* for Violin, Cello, and Piano (1993); piano and organ pieces. **VOCAL:** *Letter to an Alto Man* for Chorus, Harp, Piano, Percussion, Soloist, and Orch. (1966–67; St. Louis, May 19, 1967); *Adequate Earth* for 2 Male Narrators, Baritone, 3 Choruses, and Orch., after Donald Finkel (1975–76; St. Louis, Feb. 5, 1976); *For You Shall Go Out With Joy,* anthem for Chorus, 2 Trumpets, Harp, and Organ (1992).—**NS/LK/DM**

Wylde, Henry, English conductor, composer, and music educator; b. Bushey, Hertfordshire, May 22, 1822; d. London, March 13, 1890. He was the son of Henry Wylde, a London organist and composer of glees. He studied piano with Moscheles, then with Cipriani Potter at the Royal Academy of Music in London. In 1852 he founded in London the New Phil. Society, and conducted its concerts in cooperation with Spohr until 1858, when he took complete charge of its concerts (until 1879). In 1861 he founded the London Academy of Music and later supervised the building of St. George's Hall (1867) to house it. In 1863 he became a prof. of music there, retaining this post until his death. He publ. *The Science of Music* (1865), *Music in Its Art-Mysteries* (1867), *Modern Counterpoint in Major Keys* (1873), *Occult Principles of Music* (1881), *Music as an Educator* (1882), and *The Evolution of the Beautiful in Sound* (1888). Among his works are *Paradise Lost*, oratorio after Milton (London, May 11, 1853), a Piano Concerto (London, April 14, 1852), songs, and piano pieces.—**NS/LK/DM**

Wyner, Susan Davenny, American soprano and conductor; b. New Haven, Conn., Oct. 17, 1943. She was educated at Cornell Univ., graduating summa cum laude in music and English literature in 1965, and then pursued vocal studies with Herta Glaz (1969–75). She received a Fulbright scholarship and a grant from the Ford Foundation. She also won the Walter W. Naumberg Prize. In 1972 she made her Carnegie Recital Hall debut in N.Y., and in 1974 she made her orch. debut as a soloist with the Boston Sym. Orch. On Oct. 23, 1977, she made her first appearance at the N.Y.C. Opera as Monteverdi's Poppaea. On Oct. 8, 1981, she made her Metropolitan Opera debut in N.Y. as Woglinde in *Das Rheingold*. An exceptionally intelligent singer, she became equally successful as a performer of music in all historic idioms, from early Renaissance works to the most intransigent ultramodern scores. In later years, she pursued a conducting career. She married **Yehudi Wyner** in 1967.—**NS/LK/DM**

Wyner, Yehudi, Canadian-born American composer, pianist, conductor, and teacher, son of **Lazar Weiner;** b. Calgary, June 1, 1929. He studied at the Juilliard School of Music in N.Y. (graduated, 1946), with Donovan and Hindemith at Yale Univ. (A.B., 1950; B.Mus., 1951; M.Mus., 1953), and with Piston at Harvard Univ. (M.A., 1952). After working at the American Academy in Rome (1953–56), he was active in N.Y. as a pianist and conductor. He served as music director of the Turnau Opera, a repertory company, from 1961 to 1964, and of the New Haven Opera from 1968 to 1977. He joined the faculty of the Yale Univ. School of Music in 1963 and taught there until 1977, and also was chairman of its composition faculty for several years. In 1968 he was appointed keyboard artist for the Bach Aria Group. From 1975 to 1997 he was on the piano and chamber music faculty of the Tanglewood Music Center. He also was prof. of music at the State Univ. of N.Y. at Purchase from 1978 to 1989, where he was dean of its music division from 1978 to 1982. In 1982 he was composer-in-residence at the Santa Fe Chamber Music Festival. In 1987 he was a visiting prof. of composition at Cornell Univ. In 1987–88 he was a visiting prof. at Brandeis Univ., and then served as the Walter W. Naumburg Prof. of Composition there from 1989. He also was director of the Brandeis Contemporary Chamber Players. In 1991 he was composer-in-residence at the American Academy in Rome. He was a visiting prof. at Harvard Univ. from 1991 to 1993, and from 1996 to 1998. In 1998 he was a resident fellow at the Rockefeller Foundation at Bellagio. In 1958–59 and 1977–78 he held Guggenheim fellowships. He received the Rome Prize, a grant from the American Inst. of Arts and Letters (1961), the Brandeis Creative Arts Award (1963), and the Elise Stoeger Prize for lifetime contribution to chamber music from the Chamber Music Soc. of Lincoln Center (1998). In 1999 he was elected to the American Academy of Arts and Letters. His first marriage ended in divorce in 1966, and in 1967 he married **Susan Davenny Wyner** in 1967. In his music, Wyner often seeks to synthesize and reconcile disparate elements of past and present, and of high and low art. Classical, chromatic, and serial elements coexist. In some of his output, melodic, rhythmic, and gestural inflections from his Jewish heritage are absorbed into the musical texture. The result is an eclectic but personal style, poetic and lyrical in its essence.

WORKS: DRAMATIC: Incidental Music: *The Old Glory* (1964); *The Mirror* (1972–73). **ORCH.:** *Da camera* for Piano and Orch. (1967); *Prologue and Narrative* for Cello and Orch. (BBC, Manchester, April 29, 1994); *Lyric Harmony* (1995); *Epilogue* (1996). **CHAMBER:** *Short Sonata* for Clarinet and Piano (1950); *Dance Variations* for Wind Quintet, Trumpet, Trombone, and Cello (1953; rev. 1959); Concert Duo for Violin and Piano (1955–57); *Serenade* for Flute, Trumpet, Horn, Trombone, Viola, Cello, and Piano (1958); *Passover Offering* for Flute, Clarinet, Trombone, and Cello (1959); *3 Informal Pieces* for Violin and Piano (1961; rev. 1969); *Cadenza!* for Clarinet and Piano or Harpsichord (1969); *De novo* for Cello and Ensemble (1971); *Dances of Atonement* for Violin and Piano (1976); *All the Rage* for Flute and Piano (1980); *Romances* for Piano Quartet (1980); *Tanz and Maissele* for Clarinet, Violin, Cello, and Piano (1981); *Passage I* for 7 Instruments (1983); Wind Quintet (1984); String Quartet (1985); *Verzagen* for Violin and Piano (1986); *Sweet Consort* for Flute and Piano (1988); *Sweet is the Work* for Winds, Brass, and Piano (1990); *Trapunto Junction* for Horn, Trumpet, Trombone, and Percussion (1991); *Changing Time* for Violin, Clarinet, Cello, and Piano (1991); *Amadeus' Billiard* for Violin, Viola, Double Bass, Bassoon, and 2 Horns, after Mozart, K.205 (1991); *Il Cane Minore* for 2 Clarinets and Bassoon (1992); *Brandeis Sunday* for String Quartet (1996); Horn Trio (1997); *Madrigal* for String Quartet (1999); Quartet for Oboe and String Trio (1999). **KEYBOARD: Piano:** *Easy Suite* (1949); *Partita* (1952); Sonata (1954); *3 Short Fantasies* (1963–71); *Wedding Dances from the Notebook of Suzanne da Venné* (1964–94); *New Fantasies* (1991); *Post- Fantasies* (1993–94). **Organ:** *2 Chorale Preludes* (1951). **VOCAL:** *Psalm CXLIII* for Chorus (1952); *Dedication Anthem* for Chorus and Organ (1957); *Friday Evening Service* for Cantor, Chorus, and Organ (1963); *Torah Service* for Chorus and Instruments (1966); *Liturgical Fragments for the High Holidays* for Chorus (1970); *Memorial Music* for Soprano and 3 Flutes (1971–73); *Canto cantabile* for Soprano and Band (1972); *Intermedio* for Soprano and Strings (1974); *Fragments from Antiquity* for Soprano and Orch. (1978–81); *On This Most Voluptuous Night* for Soprano and 7 Instruments (1982); *Leonardo Vincitore* for 2

Sopranos, Double Bass, and Piano (1988); *O to Be a Dragon* for Women's Voices and Piano (1989); *Restaurants, Wines, Bistros, Shrines*, song cycle for Soprano, Baritone, and Piano (1994); *Torah Service Responses* for Chorus and Mixed Ensemble (1994); *A Mad Tea Party* for Soprano, 2 Baritones, Flute, Violin, Cello, and Piano (1996); *Praise Ye the Lord* for Soprano and Ensemble (1996); *The Second Madrigal* for Soprano and 11 Players (1999); various songs (1950–98).—**NS/LK/DM**

Wynette, Tammy (originally, **Pugh, Virginia Wynette**), 1960s country crooner, b. near Tupelo, Miss., May 5, 1942; d. Nashville, Tenn., April 6, 1998. Raised by her grandparents in rural Miss., Wynette showed early musical talent, learning to play several instruments as well as singing. She joined her mother in Birmingham, Ala., during her teen years, and was married for the first time at age 17; the marriage ended by the time she was 20. Wynette worked as a beautician during the day and club singer at night, to support her three children. Local success led to a regular featured slot on the Country Boy Eddy Show, and then on Porter Wagonner's popular syndicated country program.

Wynette came to Nashville in the mid-1960s in search of a career, auditioning for several labels while working as a singer and song-plugger. Ace producer Billy Sherrill recognized her potential and signed her to Epic, where she had an immediate hit with 1966's "Apartment Number 9," followed by the racy (for the time) "Your Good Girl's Gonna Go Bad." Wynette's good-girl-on-the-edge-of-going-bad image was underscored in a series of hits, including "I Don't Wanna Play House" from 1967 (about a woman reluctant to participate in an affair with a married man) and "D-I-V-O-R-C-E" from 1968 (where a battling husband and wife try to hide "the facts" about their deteriorating marriage from the kids who apparently were not too swift as spellers). Oddly enough, the same year brought "Stand by Your Man," the ultimate beat-me-whip-me-but-I'll-still-be-true-to-you saga, with Wynette's powerful delivery subtly changing the song's message (it's hard to believe that the big-lunged Wynette would stay home and bake cookies while her husband slept around!). 1969 brought more hits with "Singing My Song" and "The Ways to Love a Man."

In 1968, Wynette began a seven-year stormy relationship with hard-drinkin' country star George Jones, making for excellent tabloid headlines. The duo often recorded together, including an album of duets from 1972 (with a hit in 1973 with "We're Gonna Hold On") and again in 1976, hitting it big with "Golden Ring" and "Near You" (even though they divorced in 1975); they re-teamed in 1980, scoring a hit with "Two-Story House." Meanwhile, Tammy continued to record through the 1970s, scoring major hits through the middle of the decade, including 1972's "Bedtime Story" (which sounded like a combination of the instrumental part of "Stand by Your Man" and the gooey children's theme of "I Don't Wanna Play House") and "My Man (Understands)" (which clones the sentiments of "Stand by Your Man"); 1973's "Kids Say the Darndest Things" (perhaps the only country song to take its title from Art Linkletter); 1974's "Another Lonely Song" (which brought Wynette to tears because of the line "I shouldn't give a damn" which she felt was sinful); and her last solo #1 country hit, "You and Me," from 1976. Many of these songs were cowritten by producer Sherrill, and were carefully crafted to fit Wynette's image.

By the early to mid-1980s, Wynette's career was in the doldrums. The increasingly pop orientation of Sherrill's production was ill-suited to her basically honky-tonk style, and she was reduced to singing warmed-over pop songs like "Sometimes When We Touch" (a duet with Mark Grey). An attempt to remake her for the new country generation in 1987 on her album *Higher Ground*, produced by Steve Buckingham and featuring a duet with Ricky Skaggs, was a critical, if not financial, success. Wynette even dipped to self-parody, recording with the English-based techno-rock group KLF, scoring a British hit in 1992 with "Justified and Ancient."

At the end of 1993, Wynette was hospitalized suffering from a serious infection; she recovered, but was in a weakened condition. In 1994, she reunited with George Jones for an album and tour, but then died of a blood clot on April 9, 1998.

Disc.: *Your Good Girl's Gonna Go Bad* (1967); *Stand by Your Man* (1969); *Higher Ground* (1987); *Anniversary* (rec. 1967–87; rel. 1987); *Heart Over Mind* (1990); *Tears of Fire* (rec. 1967–92; rel. 1992). George Jones: *We Love to Sing about Jesus* (1972); *Golden Ring* (1976); *Together Again* (1980; *One* (with George Jones; 1994). Dolly Parton and Loretta Lynn: *Honky Tonk Angels*.—**RC**

Wyschnegradsky, Ivan (Alexandrovich), Russian composer, master of microtonal music; b. St. Petersburg, May 16, 1893; d. Paris, Sept. 29, 1979. He studied composition with Nikolai Sokoloff at the St. Petersburg Cons., and in 1920 settled in Paris. He devoted virtually his entire musical career to the exploration and creative realization of music in quarter tones and other microtonal intervals. He had a quarter tone piano constructed for him, and also publ. a guide, *Manuel d'harmonie à quarts de ton* (Paris, 1932). On Nov. 10, 1945, he presented in Paris a concert of his music, at which he conducted the first performance of his *Cosmos* for 4 Pianos, with each pair tuned at quarter tones. Bruce Mather took interest in Wyschnegradsky's music and gave a concert of his works at McGill Univ. in Montreal that included 3 premieres (Feb. 10, 1977). With the exception of these rare concerts, Wyschnegradsky remains a figure of legend; few performances of his music are ever given in Europe or North America. He regarded his *La Journée de l'existence* for Narrator, Orch., and Chorus ad libitum (to his own text; 1916–17; rev. 1927 and 1940) as his germinal work, opening the path to microtonal harmony; he dated this "awakening to ultrachromaticism" as having occurred on Nov. 7, 1918. At his death, he left sketches for a short opera in 5 scenes, *L'Éternel Étranger*, begun in 1939 but never completed. Also unfinished was the ambitious *Polyphonie spatiale*.

Works (all in quarter tones unless otherwise given): *La Journée de l'existence* for Narrator, Orch., and Chorus ad libitum (1916–17; rev. 1927 and 1940); *Chant douloureux et étude* for Violin and Piano (1918); *7 Variations on the Note C* for 2 Pianos

(1918–20; perf. in 1945 as *5 Variations*; then 2 more were added); *Chant funèbre* for Strings and 2 Harps (1922); *Chant nocturne* for Violin and 2 Pianos (1923; rev. 1972); 2 string quartets (1924; 1931–32); *2 Choruses* for Voices and 4 Pianos (1926); *Prélude et fugue sur un chant de l'Evangile rouge* for String Quartet (1927); *Prélude et Danse* for 2 Pianos (1928); *Ainsi parlait Zarathoustra* for Orch. (1929–30; arr. for 4 Pianos, 1936); *2 études de concert* for Piano (1931; arr. for 2 Pianos, 1936); *Étude en forme de scherzo* for 2 Pianos (1932); *Prélude et Fugue* for 2 Pianos (1933); *24 préludes* for 2 Pianos (1934; rev. 1958–60); *4 Fragments symphoniques* for 4 Pianos (1934, final version, 1968; 1937; 1946; 1956); *Le Mot* for Soprano and Piano (1935; half-tones); *Linnite*, pantomime for 3 Women's Voices and 4 Pianos (1937); *Acte chorégraphique* for Bass-baritone, Chorus, and 4 Pianos (1938–40; rev. 1958–59); *Cosmos* for 4 Pianos (1940; suppressed); *Prélude et Fugue* for 3 Pianos (1945); *2 Fugues* for 2 Pianos (1951); *5 variations sans thème et conclusion* for Orch. (1951–52); *Sonate en un mouvement* for Viola and 2 Pianos (1956; suppressed); *Transparences I* and *II* for Ondes Martenot and 2 Pianos (1956, 1963); *Arc-en-ciel* for 6 Pianos (1956); *Étude sur le carré magique sonore* for Piano (1956; based on the "magic square" principle of cyclical structure, written in a tempered scale without quarter tones); *Étude tricesimoprimal* for Fokker-organ (1959; for the Dutch physicist Adriaan Fokker's 31-tone organ); *Composition* for String Quartet (1960); *2 pièces* for Microtonal Piano (1960); *Étude sur les mouvements rotatoires* for 4 Pianos (1961; orchestrated 1964); *2 Compositions*: No. 1 for 3 Pianos and No. 2 for 2 Pianos (1962); *Prélude et étude* for Microtonal Piano (1966); *Intégrations* for 2 Pianos (1967); *Symphonie en un mouvement* for Orch. (1969); *Dialogues à trois* for 3 Pianos (1973–74; sixth tones). **—NS/LK/DM**

Wyttenbach, Jürg, Swiss pianist, conductor, teacher, and composer; b. Bern, Dec. 2, 1935. He studied piano and theory with Fischer and Veress at the Bern Cons. After further studies with Lefébure and Calvet at the Paris Cons. (1955–57), he completed his training in piano with Karl Engel (1958–59). In 1959 he became a teacher at the Biel Music School. In 1962 he became a teacher at the Bern Cons. From 1967 he taught at the Basel Academy of Music. He also appeared frequently as a pianist and conductor, championing particularly the cause of contemporary music. His own music utilizes both aleatory and serialism.

WORKS: DRAMATIC: *Beethoven: Sacré? Sacré Beethoven!* for Singer, Speaker, Musician, and Projection (1977); *Patchwork an der Wäscheleine*, scenic collage (1979); *Chansons ricochets*, madrigal comedy for 5 Singers (1980); *Hors jeux*, "sport-opera" (1981–82); *ENCORE! Tics and Tricks* for Actor and Cello (1987). **ORCH.:** Piano Concerto (1959; rev. 1973); *Conteste* for Chamber Orch. (1969). **CHAMBER:** *Serenade* for Flute and Piano (1959–79); Oboe Sonata (1962–72); *3 Movements* for Oboe, Harp, and Piano (1963); *Divisions* for Piano and 9 Solo Strings (1964); *Anrufungen und Ausbruch* for Woodwinds and Brass (1966); *Ad libitum* for 1 or 2 Flutes (1969); *Exécution ajournée* for 13 Players (1969–70) and for String Quartet (1970); *Kunststücke, die Zeit totzuschlagen* for Player (1972); *Noch weisst du nicht, wess Kind du bist* for Piano, Violin, and Singer ad libitum (1977); *Claustrophonie* for Violin (1979); *Tarantella* for Violin (1983); *schlagZEITschlag* for 4 Percussionists (1990–92); *Flûte Alors!* for Flute and Clarinet (1996); piano pieces. **VOCAL:** *Sutil und Laar* for Chorus and Piano, 4-Hands (1964); *Vier Kanzonen* for Soprano and Cello (1964); *2 Nonsense Verses, and Epigram and a Madrigal* for Soprano and Cello or Bassoon (1964); *De Matalli* for Baritone and Orch. (1964–65); *Lamentoroso* for Voice and 6 Clarinets (1984); *Harmonie mit schräger Dämpfung*, 7 songs for Singing Violinist, after Paul Klee (1990); *Laut Käfig*, 17 haikus for Soprano and Harp or Guitar (1995–97).**—NS/LK/DM**

Wyzewa (Wyzewski), Théodore (Teodor) de, noted Polish-born French musicologist; b. Kalushin, Russian Poland, Sept. 12, 1862; d. Paris, April 7, 1917. In 1869 his parents settled in France. He was educated in Beauvais, Paris, and at the Univ. of Nancy (licence-ès-lettres, 1882). In 1884 he founded in Paris, with Edouard Dujardin, the *Revue Wagnérienne*, which, until it ceased publication in 1888, did much to advance the cause of Wagner in France. Wyzewa's importance as a musicologist rests upon his research concerning the life and work of Mozart, about whom he publ. new facts in "Recherches sur la jeunesse de Mozart," in the *Revue des Deux Mondes* (1904–5), and in *Wolfgang Amédée Mozart. Sa vie musicale et son oeuvre, de l'enfance à la pleine maturité* (with G. de Saint-Foix; 2 vols., Paris, 1912; 3 more vols. added by Saint-Foix in 1937, 1940, and 1946). Wyzewa also wrote *Beethoven et Wagner* (Paris, 1898; new ed., 1914). He also ed. 20 piano sonatas of Clementi with a biographical notice (vol. I, Paris, 1917; vol. II, by H. Expert).

BIBL.: P. Delsemme, *Teodor de Wyzewa et le cosmopolitisme littéraire en France à l'époque du symbolisme* (Brussels, 1967); N. di Girolamo, *Teodor de Wyzewa: dal symbolismo ad tradizionalismo 1885–87* (Bologna, 1969).**—NS/LK/DM**

X

X, one of the most challenging groups to emerge from the Los Angeles punk scene of the late 1970s. **Membership:** John Doe (John Nommensen), bs., voc. (b. Decatur, Ill., Feb. 25, 1954); Exene Cervenka (Christine Cervenka), voc. (b. Chicago, Feb. 1, 1956); Billy Zoom, lead gtr. (b. Feb. 20, ca. 1949); D(on) J. Bonebrake, drm. (b. Burbank, Calif., Dec. 8, 1955). Billy Zoom departed in 1985, to be replaced by guitarists Dave Alvin (b. Los Angeles, Nov. 11, 1955) and Tony Gilkyson (b. Los Angeles, Aug. 6, 1952). Alvin left in 1987, and the band ended in 1988; Doe, Cervenka, Gilkyson, and Bonebrake reunited in 1993.

X garnered critical adulation for their stunning debut album *Los Angeles*, on Slash Records. Featuring the ragged, oblique harmonies and demanding, pessimistic songwriting of John Doe and Exene Cervenka, X's first four albums were produced by former Doors keyboardist Ray Manzarek. Retaining artistic control over their recordings with their switch to the major label Elektra in 1982, X achieved their biggest-seller with 1983's *More Fun in the New World*. However, X never achieved the commercial success envisioned by critics. Recording and performing in an acoustic folk and country style in the mid-1980s with the Knitters, augmented by Dave Alvin, X endured until 1988, and reunited in 1993.

John Doe grew up in Baltimore and manned local rock bands until moving to Los Angeles in 1976. In 1977 he met guitarist Billy Zoom, ostensibly a veteran of the bands of Gene Vincent and Ray Campi, and met Exene Cervenka at a poetry workshop in Venice, Calif. They played at Hollywood's seminal punk club the Masque, and added drummer D. J. Bonebrake, who debuted with X in February 1978. They began winning a rabid following by regularly playing at underground Los Angeles clubs, and released their debut single, "Adult Books "Slash," We're Desperate," on the Dangerous label in April 1978.

Spotted by former Doors keyboardist Ray Manzarek in 1979, X eventually signed with the independent label Slash. With Manzarek producing, their debut album, *Los Angeles*, depicted the seamy underside of the city and its punk subculture in such songs as "Johnny Hit and Run Paulene," "Sex and Dying in High Society," and the classic title song. The album drew praise from critics on both coasts. Doe and Cervenka married, and X appeared in the classic punk documentary film *The Decline of Western Civilization*, and later *Urgh! A Music War*. Their second album, *Wild Gift*, was also critically lauded and included "In This House That I Call a Home," "When Our Love Passed Out on the Couch," and "It's Who You Know."

Switching to the major label Elektra, retaining producer Ray Manzarek and winning artistic control over their recordings, X scored their first significant success with 1983's *Under the Big Black Sun*. The album contained favorites such as "Motel Room in My Bed," "Riding with Mary," and the haunting "Come Back to Me," but it failed to produce a hit single. *More Fun in the New World*, their final album with producer Manzarek, became their best-selling album, featuring the explosive "Devil Doll," the countrified "New World," and the funky "True Love." In 1985 X employed heavy-metal producer Michael Wagener for the equivocal *Ain't Love Grand*, which includes "Burning House of Love," "Around My Heart," and "Little Honey," cowritten by Doe and the Blasters' Dave Alvin. At the end of 1985 John Doe and Exene Cervenka divorced, and Doe left the band.

Beginning in 1984, various members of X and the Blasters assembled to play local benefit concerts. The loosely assembled aggregation became known as the Knitters and played acoustic-based folk and country–style music. In 1986 the Knitters, with John Doe, Exene Cervenka, Dave Alvin, D. J. Bonebrake, and stand-up bassist Johnny Ray Bartel, toured and recorded *Poor Little Critter on the Road*. The album includes Alvin's "4th of July," "Cryin' But My Tears Are Far Away," and a remake of X's "The New World."

After Zoom left X, guitarists Dave Alvin and Tony Gilkyson from the band Lone Justice took his place.

Alvin stayed on for one album, *See How We Are*, which included his "4th of July" as well as "In the Time It Takes" and and the ballad "When It Rains," before leaving for a solo career. X maintained through 1988 with Doe, Cervenka, Gilkyson, and Bonebrake.

Following X's breakup, Exene Cervenka retreated to Idaho, taught herself guitar, and recorded two solo albums produced by Tony Gilkyson, while Doe recorded a single solo album and appeared in the movies *Roadside Prophets* and *Pure Country*. In 1993 John Doe, Exene Cervenka, Tony Gilkyson, and D. J. Bonebrake reunited as X for *Hey Zeus* on Mercury Records; they issued the live acoustic set *Unclogged* on their own independent label, Infidelity, two years later.

DISC.: **X:** *Los Angeles* (1980); *Wild Gift* (1981); *Los Angeles/Wild Gift* (1988); *Under the Big Black Sun* (1982); *More Fun in the New World* (1983); *Ain't Love Grand* (1985); *See How We Are* (1987); *Live at the Whisky a-Go-Go on the Fabulous Sunset Strip* (1988); *Hey Zeus* (1993); *Unclogged* (1995). **THE KNITTERS:** *Poor Little Critter on the Road* (1986). **EXENE CERVENKA:** *Old Wives' Tales* (1989); *Running Sacred* (1990). **JOHN DOE:** *Meet John Doe* (1990).—**BH**

Xenakis, Iannis, eminent Greek-born French composer, music theorist, and teacher; b. Brăila, Romania (of Greek parents), May 29, 1922. At the age of 10, he was taken to Greece by his parents, where he began his music studies at 12 with Aristotle Koundourov. In 1938 he enrolled in a preparatory course in engineering at the Athens Polytechnic but then abandoned his studies when he became active in the Greek resistance movement against the Nazi occupation forces. He was severely wounded in a skirmish, and lost an eye. Shortly after, he was captured but managed to escape a death sentence by fleeing the country. He settled in France in 1947 and in 1965 became a naturalized French citizen. From 1947 to 1960 he worked as an architect in collaboration with Le Corbusier. In the meantime, he studied composition in Paris with Honegger and Milhaud at the École Normale de Musique, and with Messiaen at the Cons. (1950–52). He then pursued studies with Scherchen in Gravesano, Switzerland. While working with Le Corbusier on the Philips Pavillion at the 1958 World's Fair in Brussels, he met Varèse, who was then working on his *Poème electronique* for the exhibit; Xenakis received from him some stimulating advice on the creative potentialities of the electronic medium. In 1966 he founded and became director of the Centre d'Études Mathématics et Automatiques Musicales in Paris. He also was founder-director of the Center for Mathematical and Automated Music at Ind. Univ. in Bloomington, where he served on its faculty from 1967 to 1972. From 1972 to 1974 he was associated with the Centre National de la Recherche Scientifique in Paris. He was a prof. at the Univ. of Paris from 1972 to 1989. He publ. the book *Musiques formelles* (Paris, 1963; Eng. tr., 1971, as *Formalized Music*; 2nd ed., rev. 1992). For his doctorat es lettres from the Sorbonne in Paris in 1976, he wrote the thesis *Art/Sciences: Alliages* (Paris, 1979; Eng. tr., N.Y., 1985). Among his subsequent writings were *Kéleütha: Écrits* (Paris, 1994) and *Il faut être constamment un immigré* (Paris, 1997). In 1974 he received the Ravel Medal of France. In 1975 he was elected an honorary member of the American Academy of Arts and Letters. He received the Grand Prix National de la Musique of France in 1976. Xenakis was made a member of the Académie des Beaux-arts of France in 1983. In 1987 he received the Grand Prix for music of Paris, and in 1999 he was awarded the Polar Music Prize. His hardships and sufferings during his participation in the Greek resistance movement, and his pursuit of a career in engineering and architecture, profoundly influenced him as a composer. Early in his career he moved beyond dogmatic serialism by connecting mathematical concepts to the organization of a musical composition, particularly set theory, symbolic logic, and probabalistic calculus. He promulgated the stochastic method, which is teleologically directed and deterministic. His use of the computer led him to develop the computer drawing board UPIC, which he used for both compositional and educational purposes.

WORKS: **DRAMATIC:** *Oresteïa*, incidental music (1965–66; Ypsilanti, Mich., June 14, 1966); *Medea*, theater music (Paris, March 29, 1967); *Kraanerg*, ballet (1968–69; Ottawa, June 2, 1969); *Antikhthon*, ballet (1971; Bonn, Sept. 21, 1974); *Les Bacchantes*, theater music (1992–93). **ORCH.:** *Metastasis* (1953–54; Donaueschingen, Oct. 15, 1955); *Pithoprakta* (1955–56; Munich, March 8, 1957); *Achorripsis* (1956–57; Brussels, July 20, 1958); *Syrmos* for 18 or 36 Strings (1959); *Duel*, game for 2 "antagonistic" Orchs., mathematically based on game theory, with the audience determining the winning orch. (1959; Radio Hilversum, Oct. 18, 1971); *ST/48-1,240162* (ST = stochastic; 48 = number of players; 1 = 1st work for this contingent; 240162 = 24 January 1962, date of the work) (1959–62; Paris, 1968); *Stratégie*, game for 2 Orchs. (1959–62; Venice, April 25, 1963); *Akrata* (Pure) for 16 Winds (1964–65; Oxford, June 28, 1966); *Terrêtektorh* for 88 Players scattered among the audience (1965–66; Royan, April 3, 1966); *Polytope de Montréal*, light- and-sound spectacle for 4 Small (identical) Orchs. (1967); *Nomos gamma* for 98 Players scattered among the audience (1967–68; Royan, April 4, 1969); *Synaphaï* for Piano and Orch. (1969; Royan, April 6, 1971); *Eriadnos* for 8 Brasses and 10 String Instruments or their multiples (1973); *Erikhthon* for Piano and Orch. (Paris, May 21, 1974); *Noomena* (Paris, Oct. 16, 1974); *Empreintes* (La Rochelle, June 29, 1975); *Jonchaies* (Paris, Dec. 21, 1977); *Pour les Baleines* for Strings (1982; Orléans, Dec. 2, 1983); *Shaar* for Strings (Tel Aviv, Feb. 3, 1983); *Lichens* (1983; Liège, April 16, 1984); *Alax* (Cologne, Sept. 15, 1985); *Horos* (Tokyo, Oct. 24, 1986); *Kegrops* for Piano and Orch. (N.Y., Nov. 13, 1986); *Tracées* (Paris, Sept. 17, 1987); *Ata* (1987; Donaueschingen, May 3, 1988); *Tuorakemsu* (Tokyo, Oct. 9, 1990); *Kyania* (Montpellier, Dec. 7, 1990); *Krinoïdi* (1991; Parma, May 1992); *Dox-Orkh* for Violin and Orch. (Strasbourg, Oct. 6, 1991); *Roáï* (1991; Berlin, March 24, 1992); *Trookh* for Trombone and Orch. (1991; Stockholm, March 26, 1993); *Dämmerschein* (1993–94; Lisbon, June 9, 1994); *Koïranoï* (1994; Hamburg, March 1, 1996); *Voile* for Strings (Munich, Nov. 16, 1995); *Ioolkos* (1995; Donaueschingen, Oct. 20, 1996); *Sea-Change* (London, July 23, 1997). **CHAMBER:** *Achorripsis* for 21 Players (1956–57; Buenos Aires, July 20, 1958); *ST/4* for String Quartet (1956–62); *ST/10-1,080262* (ST = stochastic; 10 = number of players; 1 = 1st work of this contingent; 080262 = 8 February 1962, date of the work) for Clarinet, Bass Clarinet, 2 Horns, Harp, Percussion, and String Quartet (1956–62; Paris, May 1962); *Morsima- Amorsima* for Piano, Violin, Cello, and Double Bass (1956–62; Athens, Dec. 6, 1962); *Analogiques* for 9 Strings and Tape (Gravesano,1959); *Atrées* for 11 Players (1960; Paris, June 28, 1962); *Amorisma- Morsiama* for Clarinet, Bass Clarinet,

2 Horns, Trumpet, Harps, Trombone, 2 Percussion, Violin, and Cello (1962); *Eonta* for 2 Trumpets, 3 Trombones, and Piano (1963–64; Paris, Dec. 16, 1964); *Hiketides Les Suppliantes d'Eschyle* for Brass and Strings (Epidarus, 1964); *Akrata* for 16 Wind Instruments (1964–65; Oxford, June 28, 1966); *Nomos Alpha* for Cello (Bremen, May 5, 1966); *Anaktoria* for Clarinet, Bassoon, Horn, String Quintet, and Double Bass (Avignon, July 3, 1969); *Persephassa* for 6 Percussionists (Persepolis, Sept. 9, 1969); *Charisma* for Clarinet and Cello (Royan, April 6, 1971); *Aroura* for 12 Strings (Lucerne, Aug. 24, 1971); *Mikka* for Violin (1971; Paris, Oct. 27, 1972); *Linaia-Agon* for Horn, Trombone, and Tuba (London, April 26, 1972); *Phlegra* for 11 Instruments (1975; London, Jan. 26, 1976); *Psappha* for Percussion (1975; London, May 5, 1976); *Theraps* for Double Bass (1975–76; Royan, March 26, 1976); *Retours-Windungen* for 12 Cellos (Bonn, Feb. 20, 1976); *Epeï* for English Horn, Clarinet, Trumpet, 2 Trombones, and Double Bass (Montreal, Dec. 9, 1976); *Mikka "S"* for Violin (Orléans, March 11, 1976); *Dmaathen* for Oboe and Percussion (1976; N.Y., May 1977); *Kottos* for Cello (La Rochelle, June 28, 1977); *Ikhoor* for String Trio (Paris, April 2, 1978); *Pleiades* for 6 Percussion (1978; Strasbourg, May 17, 1979); *Palimpsest* for Piano and Percussion (Aquila, March 3, 1979); *Dikhthas* for Violin and Piano (1979; Bonn, June 4, 1980); *Komboï* for Harpsichord and Percussion (Metz, Nov. 22, 1981); *Embellie* for Viola (Paris, March 30, 1981); *Khal Perr* for Brass Quintet and Percussion (Beaune, July 15, 1983); *Tetras* for String Quartet (Lisbon, June 8, 1983); *Thalleïn* for 14 Players (London, Feb. 4, 1984); *A l'île de Gorée* for Amplified Harpsichord and 12 Players (Amsterdam, July 4, 1986); *Akea* for Piano and String Quartet (Paris, Dec. 14, 1986); *Keren* for Trombone (Strasbourg, Sept. 19, 1986); *Jalons* for 15 Players (1986; Paris, Jan. 26, 1987); *XAS* for Saxophone Quartet (Lille, Nov. 17, 1987); *Rebonds A* (1987–88; Rome, July 1, 1988) and *B* (Avignon, July 24, 1989) for Percussion; *Waarg* for 13 Players (London, May 6, 1988); *Echange* for Bass Clarinet and 13 Players (Amsterdam, April 26, 1989); *Oophaa* for Harpsichord and Percussion (Warsaw, Sept. 17, 1989); *Okho* for 3 Djembes (Paris, Oct. 20, 1989); *Epicycle* for Cello and 12 Players (London, May 18, 1989); *Tetora* for String Quartet (1990; Witten, April 27, 1992); *Paille in the Wind* for Cello and Piano (Milan, Dec. 14, 1992); *Plektó (Flechte)* for 6 Players (1993; Witten, April 24, 1994); *Mnamas Xapin Witoldwi Lutoslavskiemu* (In Memory of Witold Lutosławski) for 2 Horns and 2 Trumpets (Warsaw, Sept. 21, 1994); *Ergma* for String Quartet (The Hague, Dec. 17, 1994); *Kaï* for 9 Players (Oldenburg, Nov. 12, 1995); *Kuïlenn* for 9 Winds (1995; Amsterdam, June 10, 1996); *Ittidra* for String Sextet (Frankfurt am Main, Oct. 4, 1996); *Hunem-Iduhey* for Violin and Cello (N.Y., Aug. 9, 1996); *Roscobeck* for Cello and Double Bass (Cologne, Dec. 6, 1996); *Zythos* for Trombone and 6 Percussion (1996; Birmingham, April 4, 1997). **KEYBOARD: Piano:** *Herma* (1960–61; Tokyo, Feb. 2, 1962); *Evryali* (N.Y., Oct. 23, 1973); *Mists* (Edinburgh, 1981); *À r. (Hommage à Ravel)* (Montpellier, Aug. 2, 1987). **Organ:** *Gmeeoorh* (Hartford, 1974). **Harpsichord:** *Khoaï* (Cologne, May 5, 1976); *Naama* (Luxembourg, May 20, 1984). **VOCAL:** *Zyia* for Soprano, Men's Chorus, Flute, and Piano (1952; Evreux, April 5, 1994); *Polla ta dhina* (Many Are the Wonders) for Children's Chorus, Winds, and Percussion (Stuttgart, Oct. 25, 1962); *Hiketides* for Women's Chorus and 10 Instruments or Orch. (1964); *Nuits* for 12 Voices (1967; Royan, April 7, 1968); *Cendrées* for Chorus and Orch. (1973–74; Lisbon, June 20, 1974); *N'Shima* for 2 Mezzo-sopranos, Horns, 2 Trombones, and Cello (1975; Jerusalem, Feb. 1976); *Akanthos* for Soprano, Flute, Clarinet, 2 Violins, Viola, Cello, Double Bass, and Piano (Strasbourg, June 17, 1977); *À Colone* for Men's Chorus, Horn, Trombone, and Double Bass (Metz, Nov. 19, 1977; also for Men's or Women's Chorus, 3 Horns, 3 Trombones, 3 Cellos, and 3 Double Basses); *À Hélène* for Mezzo- soprano, Women's Chorus, and 2 Clarinets (Epidarus, July 1977); *Anemoessa* for Chorus and Orch. (Amsterdam, June 21, 1979); *Aïs* for Baritone, Percussion Soloist, and Orch. (1980; Munich, Feb. 13, 1981); *Nekuïa* for Chorus and Orch. (Cologne, March 26, 1981); *Serment-Orkos* for Chorus (Athens, Sept. 6, 1981); *Pour la Paix* for Chorus and Tape (1981; Paris, April 23, 1982); *Pour Maurice* for Baritone and Piano (Brussels, Oct. 18, 1982); *Chant des Soleils* for Chorus, Children's Chorus, Brass, and Percussion (1983); *Idmen A* for Chorus and 4 Percussion and *B* for Chorus and 6 Percussion (Strasbourg, July 24, 1985); *Nyuyo (Soleil couchant)* for Voice, Skakuhachi, and 2 Kotos (Angers, June 30, 1985); *Kassandra* for Amplified Baritone and Percussion (Gibellina, Italy, Aug. 21, 1987); *Knephas* for Chorus (London, June 24, 1990); *La Deesse Athena* for Baritone and Instruments (Athens, May 3, 1992); *Pu wijnuej we fyp* for Children's Chorus (Paris, Dec. 5, 1992); *Bakxai Evrvpidov* for Baritone, Women's Chorus, and 9 Instruments (London, Sept. 1, 1993); *Sea Nymphs* for Chorus (London, Oct. 23, 1994). **Tape:** *Diamorphoses* (1957; Brussels, Oct. 5, 1978); *Concret PH* (Brussels, 1958); *Analogique B* (1958–59; Gravesano, 1959); *Orient-Occident* (Cannes, May 1960); *The Thessaloniki World Fair* (1961); *Bohor I* (Paris, Dec. 15, 1962) and *II* (1975); *Hibiki Hana Ma* (1969–70; Osaka, 1970; in versions for 12 or 4 channels); *Persepolis* (Persepolis, Aug. 26, 1971); *Polytope de Cluny* (Paris, Oct. 13, 1972); *Polytope II* (1974); *La Légende d'Er* (1977; Paris, Feb. 11, 1978); *Mycènes Alpha* (Mycènes, Aug. 2, 1978); *Pour la Paix* (1981); *Taurtriphanie* (Arles, July 13, 1987); *Voyage absolu des Unari vers Andromède* (Osaka, Jan. 4, 1989); *Gendy3* (Metz, Nov. 17, 1991).

BIBL.: M. Bois, *I. X.: The Man and His Music: A Conversation with the Composer and a Description of His Works* (Westport, Conn., 1980); *Regards sur I. X.* (Paris, 1981); N. Matossian, *I. X.* (Paris, 1981; Eng. tr., 1986; 2nd ed., 1990); E. Restagno, ed., *X.* (Turin, 1988); A. Baltensperger, *I. X. und die stochastische Musik: Komposition im Spannungsfeld von Architektur und Mathematik* (Bern, 1996); M. Solomos, *I. X.* (Mercuès, 1996).—**NS/LK/DM**

Xyndas, Spyridon, Greek composer; b. Corfu, June 8, 1812; d. Athens, Nov. 12, 1896. He studied in Italy. He composed many attractive popular Greek songs, several operas to Italian librettos (*Il Conte Giuliano, I due pretendenti*, etc.), and *The Parliamentary Candidate* (Athens, March 1888), which was probably the first opera with a Greek text. He became blind toward the end of his life.—**NS/LK/DM**

Y

Yakovlev, Leonid, Russian baritone; b. Kherson government, April 12, 1858; d. Petrograd, June 2, 1919. After training with Ryadnov in Kiev, he completed his studies in Italy. He commenced his career in Tiflis. In 1887 he joined the Maryinsky Theater in St. Petersburg, where he sang in the premiere of Tchaikovsky's *The Queen of Spades* (Dec. 19, 1890). In 1906 he retired from the operatic stage to teach voice. He also was active as an opera producer at the Maryinsky Theater. His most famous role was Onegin, but he also scored success as Escamillo, Nevers, and Wolfram.—**NS/LK/DM**

Yamada, Kōsaku (Kōsçak), eminent Japanese conductor and composer; b. Tokyo, June 9, 1886; d. there, Dec. 29, 1965. He studied vocal music with Tamaki Shibata and cello and theory with Werkmeister at the Tokyo Imperial Academy of Music (1904–08), then composition with Bruch and Karl Leopold Wolf at the Berlin Hochschule für Musik (1908–13). He founded the Tokyo Phil. in 1915, and also appeared as a guest conductor with the N.Y. Phil. in 1918 in a program of Japanese music, including some of his own works; conducted in Russia in 1930 and 1933, and then throughout Europe in 1937. His compositions follow in the German Romantic tradition of Wagner and Strauss, with impressionistic overtones. Although most of his MSS were destroyed during the Allied air raid on Tokyo on May 25, 1945, several works have been restored from extant orch. parts.

WORKS: DRAMATIC: Opera: *Ochitaru tennyo* (The Depraved Heavenly Maiden; 1912; Tokyo, Dec. 3, 1929); *Alladine et Palomides* (1913); *Ayame* (The Sweet Flag; Paris, 1931); *Kurofune* (The Black Ships; 1939); *Yoake* (The Dawn; 1939; Tokyo, Nov. 28, 1940); *Hsiang Fei* (1946–47; Tokyo, May 1954). **ORCH.:** Sym., *Kachidoki to heiwa* (The Shout of Victory and Peace; 1912; Tokyo, Dec. 6, 1914); *Shōwa sanka* (Homage to Shōwa), symphonic poem (1938; Tokyo, May 13, 1939); *Kamikaze*, symphonic poem (1944). **CHAMBER:** Several pieces. **VOCAL:** *Meiji shōka* (Ode to the Meiji) for Chorus and Orch. (1921; Tokyo, April 26, 1925); 2 cantatas: *Bonno-Koru* (Tokyo, Oct. 9, 1932) and *Tairiku no reimei* (The Dawn of the Orient; Tokyo, July 7, 1941); nearly 1,000 choral pieces and songs.—**NS/LK/DM**

Yamaguchi, Motohumi, Japanese instrumentalist and composer; b. Tokyo, Nov. 7, 1954. After cello studies at Masashino Music Univ., he became the main flute and shamisen player for Kodo in 1980, a highly disciplined performing ensemble founded in 1971 by Tagayasu Den, a scholar of traditional Japanese arts, under the name Ondekoza ("demon drummers"); under the direction of a new leader, Kawauchi, the group was renamed Kodo (translating to both "heartbeat" and "children of the drum," referring to the taiko that is so central to its performances). Kodo has given choreographed performances throughout Asia, the Americas, and Europe; in 1988 the ensemble held its first annual Earth Celebration on Sado Island, attracting performers from all over the world. Among his compositions for the group are *Hae* for Koto, Japanese drum, and Caribbean drum (1982), *Tjanang Sari* for Percussion, after Balinese gamelan (1987), and *Kariuta* for 2 Shinobue (Japanese flutes) (1989). Other members of the ensemble include Leonard Eto (b. N.Y., March 5, 1963) and Yoshiaki Oi (b. Tokyo, March 28, 1951). Among Kodo's many celebrated recordings are *Kodo* (1981), *Kodo, Heartbeat Drummers of Japan* (1985), and *Blessing of the Earth* (1989). —**NS/LK/DM**

Yamashita, Yosuke, jazz pianist, composer; b. Tokyo, Feb. 26, 1942. In 1962, he entered the conservatory at Kunitachi, where for five years he specialized in composition. During this time he became part of a group with Terumasa Hino and Masabumi Kikuchi that played at the club Gin-Paris. In 1969 he formed his own free-jazz trio with Seiichi Nakamura (tenor saxophone; replaced in 1972 by Akira Sakata on alto; then Kazunori

Takeda on tenor in 1980) and Takeo Moriyama (drums; replaced in 1976 by Shota Koyama). He made his first tour of Europe in 1974; in 1976 played at Montreux, where he met bassist Adelhard Roidinger, with whom he toured Japan as a duo in 1977; in 1979 he appeared at the Newport (in N.Y.) Festival and recorded with members of the Art Ensemble of Chicago. His trio toured Japan along with the Globe Unity Orch., and then worked as a quartet with the addition of bassist Katsuo Kuninaka. In 1981 Yamashita's group worked with altoist Eiichi Hayashi. Yamashita was voted Jazzman of the Year in 1982 by readers of *Swing Journal*. In 1983 he disbanded his small group and formed a big band, the Panja Swing Orch., also composed for classical orchestra, and played with Korean and Japanese percussionists. In 1984 he performed as a soloist and gave duo concerts with Japanese players of traditional music such as Eitetsu Hayahi (wadaiko), Suiho Tousya (nohkan), and Hozan Yamamoto (shakuhachi), with whom he played in Europe in 1985. At the Centre Georges-Pompidou in Paris in 1987 he played in duet with Takeo Moriyama. He has also played with Elvin Jones, Mal Waldron (a favorite of his), Bennie Wallace, Pheeroan akLaff (1990), Cecil McBee, and Bill Laswell's group Last Exit. In the 1990s he reinterpreted Ravel's *Boléro* and Gershwin's *Rhapsody in Blue*.

DISC.: *Concert in Jazz* (1969); *Clay* (1974); *Ghosts by Albert Ayler* (1974); *Breath Take* (1975); *Inner Space* (1977); *First Time* (1979); *Live and Then Picasso* (1981); *In Europe* (1983); *Sakura* (Cherry) (1990); *Kurdish Dance* (1993); *Tribute to Mal Waldron* (1994).—**LP**

Yamash'ta, Stomu (real name, **Tsutomu Yamashita**), Japanese percussionist and composer; b. Kyoto, March 10, 1947. He was trained in music by his father. He played piano in his infancy, drums at puberty, and in early adolescence he became a timpanist for the Kyoto Phil. and Osaka Phil.; also worked in several film studios in Tokyo. At 16, he went to London for further study, and later went to the U.S. as a scholarship student at the Interlochen (Mich.) Arts Academy; continued his musical education in Boston, N.Y., and Chicago. Returning to Japan, he gave solo performances as a percussionist. Yamash'ta developed a phenomenal degree of equilibristic prestidigitation, synchronously manipulating a plethora of drums and a congregation of oriental bells and gongs while rotating 360 from the center of a circle to reach the prescribed percussionable objects. As a composer, he cultivates a manner of controlled improvisation marked by constantly shifting meters. In 1970 he formed the Red Buddha Theater (an ensemble of actors, musicians, and dancers), for which he composed 2 musical pageants, *Man from the East* (1971) and *Rain Mountain* (1973). Other works include a ballet, *Fox* (1968); *Hito* for any 3 instruments (1970); *Prisms* for percussion (1970); *Red Buddha* for chamber ensemble (1971); percussion scores for many Japanese films, as well as for Ken Russell's *The Devils* (with Peter Maxwell Davies, 1971) and Robert Altman's *Images* (1972). —**NS/LK/DM**

Yampolsky, Abram (Ilyich), distinguished Russian violin pedagogue, uncle of **Izrail (Markovich) Yampolsky;** b. Ekaterinoslav, Oct. 11, 1890; d. Moscow, Aug. 17, 1956. He studied violin with Korguyev at the St. Petersburg Cons. (graduated, 1913), and also received instruction in composition from Sokolov, Wihtol, and Steinberg. After teaching at the Ekaterinoslav music school (1913–20), he settled in Moscow, where he was concertmaster of the conductorless ensemble Persymfans (1922–32); was also prof. (1926–56) and chairman of the violin dept. (1936–56) at the Cons. Yampolsky was made a Doctor of Arts (1940). He was teacher and adviser to a number of prominent Soviet violinists, among them Kogan, Elizaveta Gilels, Grach, Zhuk, and Sitkovetsky.—**NS/LK/DM**

Yampolsky, Izrail (Markovich), Russian musicologist and lexicographer, nephew of **Abram (Ilyich) Yampolsky;** b. Kiev, Nov. 21, 1905; d. Moscow, Sept. 20, 1976. He studied violin with his uncle, then entered the Moscow Cons., where he took courses in advanced theory with Miaskovsky and Gliere; he subsequently taught violin at the Music Academy in Moscow (1931–58); gave lectures in music history there; also taught at the Cons. (1934–49). A fine and diligent research scholar, he publ. a number of excellent monographs dealing mainly with violin and violinists: on the foundations of violin fingering (Moscow, 1933; 3rd expanded ed., 1955; Eng. tr., London, 1967); *Henryk Wieniawski* (Moscow, 1955); *Enescu* (Moscow, 1956; also in Romanian, Bucharest, 1959); on the music of Yugoslavia (Moscow, 1958); *Paganini* (Moscow, 1961; 2nd ed., 1968); *David Oistrakh* (Moscow, 1964); *Fritz Kreisler* (1975).—**NS/LK/DM**

Yancey, Jimmy (actually, **James Edwards**), jazz pianist; b. Chicago, Feb. 20, 1898; d. there, Sept. 17, 1951. He was a singer and dancer in a Vaudeville act as a child; then taught himself to play the piano and appeared in Chicago clubs. In 1925 he gave up his stage career and worked as a groundskeeper at Comiskey Park. With the revival of boogie-woogie in the mid-1930s, he returned to playing jazz piano and garnered praise in jazz circles. He sometimes worked with his wife, blues singer Estella "Mama" Yancey (1896–1986). —**JC/LP**

Yang, Liqing, Chinese composer and writer on music; b. Sichuan, April 30, 1942. After taking degrees at the Shenyang Cons. of Music (B.A., 1970) and Shanghai Cons. of Music (M.A., 1980), he pursued postgraduate studies with Kurt Bauer (piano diploma, 1983) and Alfredo Koerppen (Ph.D. in composition, 1983) at the Hannover Hochschule für Musik. He was an asst. prof. of composition at Shenyang Cons. (1970–78); then was a lecturer (1983–86), assoc. prof. (1986–90), and prof. (from 1991) at the Shanghai Cons., where he also served as dean of its composition and conducting dept. (from 1991). In 1990 he was a guest prof. at the Salzburg Mozarteum. Yang has spoken throughout Germany, Austria, and Switzerland on new music in China; in 1995 he conducted research in the U.S. on a grant from the Asian Cultural Council. His articles on such wide-ranging topics as new notation, neoromanticism,

Charles Ives, and postmodernism have appeared in various Chinese publications; he also publ. *The Compositional Techniques of Olivier Messiaen* (1989).

Works: Dramatic: *The Night of a Festival* for Dancer and Small Orch. (1973); *The Seedling* for Dancer and Small Orch. (1973); *Mister O*, incidental music (1977); *The Monument without Inscription*, dance/drama for Chorus and Orch. (1989; in collaboration with Lu Pei); *Red Cherry*, film music for Soprano, Liu Qin, Zhong Ran, and Orch. (1995). **Orch.:** *Set Sail*, concerto for Piano and Chinese Orch. (1975); *Festival by Hailan River*, rondo (1978); *Yi* (1982–83); *Suicide by the Wujiang River* for Pipa and Orch. (1986); *Festival Overture* (1987); *Ode to Apollo* (1991); *Elegy—Jian He Shui* for Erhu and Chinese Orch. (1991; also for Erhu and Traditional Orch., 1995); *Two Folksongs* for Piano and Orch. (1993; also for Violin and Orch.); *The Chess Game* for Shun, Pipa, and Orch. (1994); *Concerto for Zheng* for Zheng and Orch. (1995); *Costs of Peace* (1995). **Chamber:** *Violin Concerto* for Violin and Piano (1970); *Chamber Music for Ten* for Flute, Oboe, Clarinet, Bassoon, Horn, and Strings (1982–83). **Keyboard: Piano:** *Two Preludes* (1962); *Nine Pieces on the Shanxi Folksongs* (1962–63); *Sonatina* (1964); *Mountain Song & Work Song* for Piano, 4-Hands (1980). **Vocal:** *Dujuan Mountain Suite* for Soprano, Baritone, Piano, Jinghu, Erhu, and Percussion (1974); *The Sun*, ballet music for Soprano, Chorus, and Orch. (1976); *Four Poems from Tang-Dynasty* for Mezzo-soprano, Piano, and 2 Percussion (1981); *Three F.G. Lorca Songs* for Mezzo-soprano, Flute, Cello, and Piano (1982); *The Story About the Birth of Tao* for Chorus, to a text by Brecht (1982); *Prelude, Interludes, and Postlude* for Chorus and Orch. (1990).—**NS/LK/DM**

Yankelevich, Yuri, Russian violinist and pedagogue; b. Basel, March 7, 1909; d. Moscow, Sept. 12, 1973. He studied with Anisim Berlin in Omsk, Johannes Nalbandian at the Petrograd Cons., and A. Yampolsky at the Moscow Cons. (graduated, 1932), where he subsequently taught, becoming a prof. in 1961. Among his outstanding students were Spivakov and Tretyakov. **—NS/LK/DM**

Yannatos, James, American composer, conductor, and teacher; b. N.Y., March 13, 1929. He was a student of Hindemith and Porter at Yale Univ. (B.M., 1951; M.M., 1952) and of Bezanson at the Univ. of Iowa (Ph.D., 1960). He also studied with Bernstein, Steinberg, Boulanger, Milhaud, and Dallapiccola. From 1964 he taught at Yale Univ. He also was active as a conductor of youth orchs. and choral groups, and conducted various chamber orchs. He was the author of *Explorations in Musical Materials* (1978).

Works: Dramatic: Theater pieces. **Orch.:** *Ritual Images* for Orch. and Tape (1974); 4 syms.: No. 1 (1984), No. 2, *Touch the Earth*, for Soprano, Mezzo-soprano, and Orch. (1986), No. 3, *Prisms* (1988), and No. 4, *Tiananmen Square* (1989–90); Contrabass Concerto (1986); Piano Concerto (1992–93); Concerto for String Quartet and Orch. (1997); Concerto for Percussion Ensemble (1997). **Chamber:** *Rites* for Horn (1987); *Quo Libet* for Brass Trio and Percussion (1987); *Bagatelles* for Violin and Cello (1989). **Vocal:** *Trinity Mass* for Narrator, Voices, Chorus, and Orch. (1983–84); choruses.—**NS/LK/DM**

Yannay, Yehuda, Romanian-born Israeli-American composer, conductor, and teacher; b. Timişoara, May 26, 1937. He went with his family to Israel in 1951 and studied composition with Boscovich. After graduating from the Rubin Academy of Music in Tel Aviv (1964), he went to the U.S. on a Fulbright grant and pursued training with Berger, Shapero, and Krenek at Brandeis Univ. (M.F.A., 1966). He also studied with Schuller at the Berkshire Music Center at Tanglewood (summer, 1965) before completing his training at the Univ. of Ill. in Urbana (1968–70; D.M.A., 1974). From 1970 he taught theory and composition at the Univ. of Wisc. in Milwaukee. In 1971 he organized the "Music from Almost Yesterday" concert series, with which he programmed numerous contemporary scores. In his own extensive and varied output, Yannay has experimented with live electronics, synthesizers, and environmental resources. His experimentation with the synthesizer led to his creation of the genre he described as "synthesizer theater."

Works: *The Chain of Proverbs*, youth cantata (1962); *Spheres* for Soprano and 10 Instruments (1963); *Incantations* for Voice, Keyboard, and Interior Piano (1964); *2 Fragments* for Violin and Piano (1966); *Wraphap*, theater piece for Actress, Amplified Aluminum Sheet, and Yannaychord (1969); *Coloring Book for the Harpist* (1969); Concerto for Audience and Orch. (1971); *The Hidden Melody* for Cello and Horn (1977); Concertino for Violin and Chamber Orch. (1980); *Celan Ensembles: Augentanz* and *Galgenlied* for Tenor and Instruments (1986–), *In Madness There is Order* for Voice, Projections, and Synthesizers (1988), and *Spiegeltanz* for Voice, Horn, and 2 Marimbas (1989); Duo for Flute and Cello (1991); *The Oranur Experiment*, music video (part 1, *Journey to Orgonon*, 1991; in collaboration with J. Fortier); *Tableau One:"...in sleep one often finds solutions..."* (from *Journey to Orgonon*) for Actor, Projections, and Synthesizers (1992; in collaboration with J. Fortier and M. Mellott); *In Madness There is Order*, music video (1992); *Cello Solo for "I can't fathom it"* for Projection Theater (1993); *5 Pieces for 3 Players* for Soprano Saxophone, Clarinet, and Marimba (1994); *Piano Portfolio* (1994–); *Exit Music at Century's End* for Chamber Orch. (1995); *Tangoul Mortii (Tango of Death)* for Double Bass or Cello (1995–97); *Radiant, Inner Light* for Narrator, Custom Percussion Instruments, and Projections (1999).—**NS/LK/DM**

Yansons, Arvid, Latvian conductor, father of **Mariss Jansons**; b. Leipaja, Oct. 24, 1914; d. Manchester, England, Nov. 21, 1984. He studied violin at the Leipaja Cons. (1929–35), then took courses in violin, conducting, and composition at the Riga Cons. (1940–44). In 1944 he made his conducting debut in Riga; in 1948 he was made assoc. conductor of the Leningrad Phil.; also appeared as a guest conductor throughout the Soviet Union, Europe, Australia, and Japan. From 1965 he made regular guest conducting appearances with the Halle Orch. in Manchester; also served as head of the conducting class at the Leningrad Cons. (from 1972). **—NS/LK/DM**

Yardbirds, The, famed blues-rock band that introduced three guitarists (Eric Clapton, Jeff Beck, and Jimmy Page) to the rock world. **Membership:** Keith Relf, voc., har. (b. Richmond, Surrey, England, March 22, 1943; d. West London, May 14, 1976); Chris Dreja, rhythm gtr. (b. Surbiton, Surrey, Nov. 11, 1946); Paul Samwell-Smith, bs. (b. London, May 8, 1943); Jim Mc-

Carty, drm. (b. Liverpool, Lancashire, England, July 25, 1943); Anthony "Top" Topham, lead gtr (b. England, 1947). Topham was replaced by Eric Clapton (real name, Clapp) (b. Ripley, Surrey, March 30, 1945) in October 1963. Clapton was replaced by Jeff Beck (b. Wallington, Surrey, June 24, 1944) in March 1965. Samwell-Smith was replaced by Jimmy Page (b. Jan. 9, 1944, in London) in June 1966.

Keith Relf, Chris Dreja, Paul Samwell-Smith, and Jim McCarty, formed the Metropolitan Blues Quartet in the spring of 1963, adding lead guitarist Tony "Top" Topham in June. They played engagements in Richmond-area clubs and took over residency of the Crawdaddy Club from the Rolling Stones. Topham was replaced by Eric Clapton, a former member of The Roosters and Casey Jones and The Engineers, in October. Developing a devoted following with their dynamic "rave-ups" (extended instrumental passages) of blues material, The Yardbirds first recorded behind bluesman Sonny Boy Williamson and later moved to London's Marquee club, where they recorded their debut album, *Five Live Yardbirds*, for Britain's Columbia Records. Their debut American album for Epic Records, *For Your Love*, produced a smash hit with Graham Gouldman's title song, already a smash British hit. However, disillusioned by the seemingly commercial and pop direction the group was taking, Clapton had already left in March 1965 in favor of John Mayall's Bluesbreakers, to be replaced by Jeff Beck of the Tridents.

The Yardbirds enjoyed their most creative and successful period during the tenure of Jeff Beck. Their second American album, *Having a Rave Up with The Yardbirds*, contained one live side of blues material, such as Howlin' Wolf's "Smokestack Lightning" and Bo Diddley's "I'm a Man," recorded with Eric Clapton, and a studio side featuring Jeff Beck. The studio side comprised two Graham Gouldman songs, "Heart Full of Soul" and "Evil-Hearted You," the socially conscious "You're a Better Man than I," the Gregorian chant-like "Still I'm Sad," Johnny Burnette and The Rock 'n' Roll Trio's "The Train Kept A-Rollin,'" recorded at the Sun Studios in Memphis, and "I'm a Man." "Heart Full of Soul" and "Evil Hearted You"/"Still I'm Sad" were smash British hits, while "Heart Full of Soul" and the studio version of "I'm a Man" proved major American hits. Garnering an enhanced reputation for Beck's creative use of feedback and their experimentation with unusual musical scales and instrumentation, The Yardbirds next recorded the British-only *Roger the Engineer*. Many of the cuts were contained on the American album *Over Under Sideways Down*, which yielded the major American hits "Over Under Sideways Down" and "Shapes of Things" (smash British hits), and included the exotic-sounding "Hot-House of Omagarashid" and "Ever Since the World Began," as well as the favorites "Lost Woman" and "Jeff's Boogie."

In 1966, Chris Dreja recorded two unsuccessful solo singles, and that June, Paul Samwell-Smith departed The Yardbirds to become a producer, most notably for Cat Stevens. Sessions guitarist Jimmy Page was recruited to take up bass, but switched to lead guitar when Jeff Beck became ill in September. With Dreja moving to bass and Beck's return, Beck and Page played twin lead guitars until November, when Beck quit the group. This lineup recorded only two songs, "Happenings Ten Years Time Ago" (a moderate American hit) and "Stroll On," performed in the movie *Blow Up*. With Beck's departure, the remaining four continued to perform and record as The Yardbirds under producer Mickie Most. Achieving minor American hits with "Little Games," "Ha Ha Said the Clown," and Nilsson's "Ten Little Indians," the aggregation recorded one American album, *Little Games*.

In the summer of 1968, Keith Relf and Jim McCarty dropped out of The Yardbirds to form the short-lived duo Together, and Page and Dreja unsuccessfully attempted to recruit guitarist Terry Reid and drummer B. J. Wilson for The New Yardbirds. With Dreja's departure to become a photographer, Page enlisted three new members to meet the group's contractual obligations that fall and, in October, the group changed its name to Led Zeppelin. The Yardbirds were inducted into the Rock and Roll Hall of Fame in 1992. Keith Relf and Jim McCarty subsequently formed the progressive group Renaissance with Relf's vocalist sister Jane in 1969, but after one album produced by Paul Samwell-Smith, Relf and McCarty left. Entirely reconstituted with vocalist Annie Haslam, Renaissance enjoyed considerable album success in the 1970s. Relf later played with Medicine Head, featuring vocalist John Fiddler, and eventually formed Armageddon around 1975. The group recorded one album for A&M Records, but on May 14, 1976, Relf was found dead in his West London home at the age of 33, apparently electrocuted while playing guitar. McCarty formed Shoot in 1970 and later joined Illusion with Jane Relf. Chris Dreja, Paul Samwell-Smith, and McCarty reunited for live engagements in 1983 and later formed Box of Frogs with former Medicine Head vocalist John Fiddler for two albums for Epic. In 1989, McCarty formed the British Invasion All-Stars.

DISC.: THE YARDBIRDS: *Five Live Yardbirds* (1964); *For Your Love* (1965); *Having a Rave Up* (1965); *Over Under Sideways Down* (1966); *Live with Sonny Boy Williamson* (1966); *Little Games* (1967); *Live at the BBC* (rec. 1965–68; rel. 1997). **ERIC CLAPTON, JEFF BECK, AND JIMMY PAGE:** *Guitar Boogie* (1972).—**BH**

Yardumian, Richard, American composer; b. Philadelphia (of Armenian parents), April 5, 1917; d. Bryn Athyn, Pa., Aug. 15, 1985. He studied harmony with William Happich, counterpoint with H. Alexander Matthews, piano with George Boyle (1939–41), and later attended Monteux's conducting school in Hancock, Maine (summer, 1947); received additional musical training from Thomson in N.Y. (1953). His compositions reflect the spirit of Armenian folk songs and religious melodies. A number of his works were first performed by the Philadelphia Orch.

WORKS: ORCH.: *Armenian Suite* (1937–54; Philadelphia, March 5, 1954); *Symphonic Suite* (1939); *3 Pictographs of an Ancient Kingdom* (1941); *Desolate City* (1943–44; Philadelphia, April 6, 1945); Violin Concerto (1949; Philadelphia, March 30, 1950; rev. 1960); 2 syms.: No. 1 (1950; rev., Philadelphia, Dec. 1, 1961) and No. 2, *Psalms*, for Mezzo-soprano or Baritone and Orch. (1947–64; Philadelphia, Nov. 13, 1964); *Epigram: William*

M. Kincaid for Flute and Strings (1951; also for Flute and String Quartet); *Passacaglia, Recitatives and Fugue*, piano concerto (1957; Philadelphia, Jan. 3, 1958); *Veni sancte Spiritus*, chorale prelude for Chamber Orch. (1958); *Num komm der heiden Heiland*, chorale prelude (1978; arranged from an organ piece). **CHAMBER:** Flute Quintet (1951; arranged for Flute and Strings); *Cantus animae et cordis* for String Quartet (1955; arranged for Strings, 1955). **KEYBOARD: Piano:** *3 Preludes: Wind* (1938), *Sea* (1936), and *Sky* (1944; orchestrated 1945); *Dance* (1942); *Chromatic Sonata* (1946); *Prelude and Chorale* (1946). **Organ:** Various pieces. **VOCAL:** *Create in Me a Clean Heart* for Mezzo-soprano or Baritone and Chorus (1962); *Magnificat* for Women's Voices (1965); *Come Creator Spirit*, mass for Mezzo-soprano or Baritone, Chorus, Congregation, and Orch. or Organ (1965–66; N.Y., March 31, 1967); *The Story of Abraham*, oratorio for Soloists, Chorus, Orch., and Film (1968–71; rev. 1973); *Narek: Der Asdvadz* for Mezzo-soprano, Horn, and Harp (1983); *Hrashapar* for Chorus, Organ, and Orch. (1984); about 100 chorales for Chorus (1944–85).—**NS/LK/DM**

Yashirō, Akio, Japanese composer and teacher; b. Tokyo, Sept. 10, 1929; d. Yokohama, April 9, 1976. He studied piano with Leonid Kreutzer and composition with Hashimoto, Ifukube, and Ikenouchi at the Tokyo Geijutsu Daigaku, graduating in 1949. He then went to Paris, where he studied composition with Noël Gallon at the Cons. (1951–54), and took private lessons with Boulanger and Messiaen. Returning to Japan, he joined the faculty of the Tokyo Geijutsu Daigaku (1956) and the Toho Gakuen School of Music (1958).

WORKS: String Quartet (1954–55); Sonata for 2 Flutes and Piano (1957–58); Sym. (Tokyo, June 9, 1958); Cello Concerto (Tokyo, June 24, 1960); Piano Sonata (1960); Piano Concerto (Tokyo, Nov. 5, 1967); *Ouverture de fête* for Brass Ensemble (Sapporo, Feb. 3, 1972).—**NS/LK/DM**

Yasser, Joseph, Polish-born Russian-American organist, conductor, and musicologist; b. Łódź, April 16, 1893; d. N.Y., Sept. 6, 1981. He studied at the Moscow Cons., graduating in 1917 as an organist. After several years of teaching organ in Moscow and Siberia, he reached Shanghai in 1921, and conducted a choral society there; subsequently emigrated to the U.S. (1923); served as organist at Temple Rodeph Sholom in N.Y. (1929–60); held various positions in American musicological groups. His most important contribution to music theory was *A Theory of Evolving Tonality* (N.Y., 1932), in which he proffered an ingenious hypothesis as to the origin of the pentatonic and heptatonic scales, and, operating by inductive reasoning, suggested that the ultimate Western scale would contain 19 degrees. He contributed several articles to *Musical Quarterly* (April and July 1937 and July 1938) dealing with quartal harmony, which were publ. in a separate ed. (N.Y., 1938).—**NS/LK/DM**

Yates, Peter B., Canadian-American writer on music; b. Toronto, Nov. 30, 1909; d. N.Y., Feb. 25, 1976. He studied at Princeton Univ. (B.A., 1931). He married the pianist Frances Mullen in 1933. From 1937 to 1962 he was a functionary at the Calif. Dept. of Employment in Los Angeles, but this bureaucratic occupation did not preclude his activities as a musical catalyst. In 1939 he inaugurated on the rooftop of his house in the Silver Lake district of Los Angeles a chamber concert series which was to become an important cultural enterprise in subcultural Calif., under the name "Evenings on the Roof," he served as coordinator of these concerts from 1939 to 1954, when they were moved to a larger auditorium in downtown Los Angeles and became known as the "Monday Evening Concerts." In 1968 he was appointed chairman of the music dept. at the State Univ. of N.Y. at Buffalo. He publ. *An Amateur at the Keyboard* (N.Y., 1964), *Twentieth-Century Music* (N.Y., 1967), and a collection of poems.—**NS/LK/DM**

Yellin, Pete, jazz alto saxophonist, educator, flutist; b. N.Y., July 18, 1941. His father was a pianist and NBC staffer. Pete studied saxophone with Joe Alldard and flute with Harold Bennett. He earned a degree from Juilliard (even though he had had an athletic scholarship to the Univ. of Denver as freshman and for a time considered a basketball career). He played with Lionel Hampton in the early 1960s, and then with Buddy Rich and Tito Puente. He joined Joe Henderson's band in 1970 and remained until 1973; formed his own band the next year, and played at the Newport Jazz Festival in N.Y.; returned to play with Puente in 1974. He worked in the horn sections of Rich and Bob Mintzer during the 1980s. He's a solid, sometimes exuberant player with extensive range, as well as a decent flutist. He has been director of the jazz program at Long Island Univ.—Brooklyn campus since 1981.

DISC.: *It's the Right Thing* (1973); *Dance of Allegra* (1973). —**LP**

Yepes, Narciso, noted Spanish guitarist and lutenist; b. Lorca, Nov. 14, 1927. He took up the guitar at the age of 6. At 12, he entered the Valencia Cons. He was 15 when he became a student of the pianist Vicente Ascencio. In 1947 he made his formal debut as a soloist in Rodrigo's *Concierto de Aranjuez* with Argenta and the Orquesta Nacional de España in Madrid. In 1950 he went to Paris for further training with Enesco and Gieseking. He subsequently pursued an international career as a virtuoso. From 1964 he played a 10-string guitar of his own design. Yepes's repertoire is remarkably expansive, extending from the 15th century to the present day. He has won particular distinction for his performances of the lute music of Bach on both lute and guitar. Among composers who have written works for him are Bacarisse, Balada, Ernesto Halffter, Moreno-Torroba, Ohana, and Françaix. He also has written film music and prepared transcriptions for the guitar. —**NS/LK/DM**

Yes, a seminal British band of the 1970s **MEMBERSHIP:** Jon Anderson, voc. (b. Accrington, Lancashire, England, Oct. 25, 1944); Tony Kaye, kybd. (b. Leicester, England, Jan. 11, 1946); Peter Banks, gtr. (b. Barnet, Hereford, England, April 8, 1947); Chris Squire, bs. (b. London, England, March 4, 1948); Bill Bruford, drm. (b. Sevenoaks, Kent, England, May 17, 1949). Peter Banks departed in 1970, to be replaced by Steve Howe (b.

London, England, April 8, 1947). Tony Kaye left in 1971, to be replaced by Rick Wakeman (b. West London, England, May 18, 1949). Bill Bruford left in 1972, to be replaced by Alan White (b. Pelton, County Durham, England, June 14, 1949). Wakeman left in 1974, to be replaced by Patrick Moraz (b. Morges, Switzerland, June 24, 1948). Wakeman returned when Moraz left in 1976. Jon Anderson and Wakeman left in 1980, to be replaced by vocalist Trevor Horn (b. Hertfordshire, England, July 15, 1949) and keyboardist Geoff Downes. Yes disbanded later in 1980, regrouping in 1983 with Anderson, Kaye, Squire, and White, adding guitarist Trevor Rabin (b. Johannesburg, South Africa, Jan. 13, 1954). Anderson left in 1988, and then Anderson, Kaye, Squire, White, Rabin, Bruford, Wakeman, and Howe reunited in 1991 as Yes; the band returned to its 1983–1987 lineup in 1994.

Yes, along with the Moody Blues and the Nice/ Emerson, Lake and Palmer, was an early progressive-rock band, prominently featuring keyboards, orchestral-style arrangements, and classical-style music. Gaining their first recognition as the opening act for Cream's farewell London performance in late 1968, Yes's success was based largely on thick vocal harmonies, astounding but uninspired instrumental technique, and regular use of sophisticated electronic gear. Propelled into American popularity with *The Yes Album*, which featured all original material and introduced the synthesizer to the group sound, Yes was fronted by songwriter-vocalist Jon Anderson, whose work was frequently criticized as obtuse, pretentious, and inaccessible. After scoring their first album and singles success under classically trained keyboardist Rick Wakeman, Yes recorded *Fragile* and *Close to the Edge*, hailed as classics for their textural and melodic richness. Wakeman left in 1974 and quickly established himself as a purveyor of orchestrated rock-instrumental versions of classic tales. In the mid-1970s the various members began recording albums on their own, and Wakeman returned to Yes in 1976. He left again in 1980 and the group disbanded for a time, reuniting for the biggest hit of their career, "Owner of a Lonely Heart," in late 1983. Enduring a protracted period of legal disputes in the late 1980s, Yes reunited again in 1991.

Yes was formed in 1968 after the meeting of vocalist Jon Anderson and bassist Chris Squire. Anderson had been touring and performing with bands such as the Warriors for a decade, whereas the classically trained Squire had formed his own band at 16 and joined Syn (whose guitarist was Peter Banks) in 1965 for two years of engagements. Seeking to form a group that emphasized vocal harmonies backed by dense, structured music, Anderson and Squire recruited Banks, keyboardist Tony Kaye, and drummer Bill Bruford. After substituting for an absent Sly and the Family Stone at the Speakeasy Club in October 1968, Yes secured a residency at the Marquee Club and subsequently opened for Cream's farewell concerts at the Royal Albert Hall in December.

Signed to Atlantic Records, Yes released the classically influenced debut album *Time and a Word*, recorded with full orchestra, which began to establish the group's British reputation as a technically proficient progressive-rock band. In 1970 Banks departed to form his own band, Flash, and was replaced by classically trained guitarist Steve Howe, a veteran of bands such as the Syndicate, Bodast, and Tomorrow. Howe's instrumental talents extended from guitar to pedal steel guitar and, later, guitar synthesizer.

With Anderson providing most of the group's material and Kaye introducing the synthesizer to the group sound, Yes broke through in the United States with *The Yes Album* and its moderate hit "Your Move." Containing six pieces, three of which were nine minutes in length, the instrumentally complex album was hailed as an early example of symphonic rock. Yes first toured America in a support role in 1971, but soon suffered the departure of Tony Kaye for his own group Badger. He was replaced by Rick Wakeman, a former member of the Strawbs. Wakeman had entered the prestigious Royal Academy of Music at 16 for more than a year's study of piano and clarinet before leaving to teach music and record with T. Rex, Cat Stevens, and David Bowie. Wakeman introduced multiple keyboards, such as the mellotron, clavinet, and harpsichord, to Yes and became the group's focal point in concert. The next Yes album, *Fragile*, with cover art by Roger Dean, featured four group pieces and five individual works, yielding a major hit with an editied version of "Roundabout."

After touring the United States as a headline act in 1972, Yes recorded *Close to the Edge*, which contained only three songs, the side-long title track, the moderate hit "And You and I," and "Siberian Khatru." However, shortly after the album was recorded, Bill Bruford left to join King Crimson and was replaced by classically trained drummer Alan White, a session player for Gary Wright, George Harrison, and Joe Cocker and a former member of John Lennon's Plastic Ono Band. Following the live three-record set *Yessongs*, Jon Anderson and Steve Howe composed the lyrics to *Tales from Topographic Oceans*, based on guru Paramhansa Yoganada's Shastic Scriptures. An elaborately experimental work, the album explored a variety of musical textures, themes, and instrumentation and received mixed reviews.

In June 1974 Rick Wakeman departed Yes to pursue a solo career already initiated on A&M Records with the instrumental *Six Wives of Henry VIII* album. His *Journey to the Centre of the Earth*, based on the Jules Verne story and narrated by actor David Hemmings, was recorded live with 45-piece orchestra and 48-person choir at the London Royal Festival Hall in January 1974. Wakeman soon became recognized as a purveyor of contemporary light orchestral music, and he next recorded the ambitious *Myths and Legends of King Arthur and the Knights of the Round Table*. The work was premiered as a pageant on ice at the London Empire Pool in May 1975 with massive orchestral and choral support. Wakeman toured America with a hundred-person-plus entourage of singers and musicians in early 1975, and returned late in the year with a trimmed-down English Rock Ensemble. He also wrote the score to the Ken Russell film *Lisztomania*, recorded *No Earthly Connection* with the English Rock Ensemble, and performed the soundtrack to the movie *White Rock*.

In the meantime, classically trained Swiss keyboardist Patrick Moraz, a former member of Refugee and the composer of numerous film scores, joined Yes in August 1974. His debut with Yes, *Relayer*, contained only three pieces, including the side-long "Gates of Delirium." The various members of Yes began recording solo albums in 1975. Yes mounted its most massive tour of America in summer 1976, and Wakeman rejoined the group late in the year following the departure of Moraz, who joined the Moody Blues, staying for 14 years. Yes embarked on a massive world tour in 1977 in support of *Going for the One*, then moved toward shorter songs for 1978's *Tormato*.

In the summer of 1980 Jon Anderson and Rick Wakeman left Yes to pursue solo projects. They were replaced by vocalist Trevor Horn and keyboardist Geoff Downes, who had scored a moderate hit in 1979–1980 with "Video Killed the Radio Star" as the Buggles. By fall the new edition of Yes was touring in support of *Drama*, but the group subsequently broke up. Jon Anderson collaborated with Greek keyboardist Vangelis (Evangelos Papathanassiou), achieving minor hits with "I Hear You Now" and "I'll Find My Way Home." He also recorded three solo albums for three different labels during the 1980s. Steve Howe and Geoff Downes formed Asia with vocalist-bassist John Wetton and drummer Carl Palmer. Asia scored a smash hit with "Heat of the Moment" and a near-smash with "Don't Cry," but Howe left in 1985 to form the short-lived GTR with vocalist Max Bacon and guitarist Steve Hackett, achieving a major hit with "When the Heart Rules the Mind."

In 1983 Yes regrouped with original members Jon Anderson, Tony Kaye, Chris Squire, and Alan White, adding South African guitarist Trevor Rabin. *90125* yielded a top hit with Rabin's "Owner of a Lonely Heart" and a major hit with "Leave It." *Big Generator*, from 1987, produced two moderate hits, "Love Will Find a Way" and "Rhythm of Love." Anderson left again in 1988, recording *Anderson, Bruford, Wakeman, Howe*, as Squire and Rabin laid claim to the Yes name. Trevor Rabin recorded a solo album in 1989, and Yes ultimately reunited with Anderson, Kaye, Squire, White, Rabin, Bruford, Wakeman, and Howe for 1991's dismal *Union* album and a new round of touring. In the 1990s Wakeman also recorded for Relativity Records.

By 1994 Howe, Wakeman, and Bruford had left Yes again, with Rabin taking over control of the group. Yes recorded *Talk* for Victory Records, while Howe recorded for Relativity and Herald and Anderson recorded for Windham Hill and Angel.

DISC.: **YES:** *Y.* (1969); *Time and a Word* (1970); *Yesterdays (songs from above two albums)* (1975); *The Y. Album* (1971); *Fragile* (1972); *Close to the Edge* (1972); *Yessongs* (1973); *Tales from Topographic Oceans* (1974); *Relayer* (1974); *Going for the One* (1977); *Tormato* (1978); *Drama* (1980); *Yesshows* (1980); *Classic Y.* (1981); *"90125"* (1983); *90125 Live: The Solos* (1985); *Big Generator* (1987); *Yesyears* (1991); *Yestory* (1992); *Union* (1991); *An Evening of Y. Music Plus* (1994); *Talk* (1994). **ANDERSON, BRUFORD, WAKEMAN, HOWE:** *Anderson, Bruford, Wakeman, Howe* (1989). **FLASH (WITH PETER BANKS):** *Flash* (1972); *Flash in the Can* (1972); *Out of Our Heads* (1973). **PETER BANKS:** *The Two Sides of Peter Banks* (1973). **BADGER (WITH TONY KAYE):** *One Live Badger* (1973); *White Lady* (1974). **RICK WAKEMAN:** *The Six Wives of Henry VIII* (1973); *Journey to the Centre of the Earth* (1974); *The Myths and Legends of King Arthur* (1975); *No Earthly Connection* (1976); *White Rock* (soundtrack; 1977); *Criminal Record* (1977); *Rhapsodies* (1979); *Greatest Hits* (1994). **RICK WAKEMAN/ROGER DALTREY:** *Lisztomania* (soundtrack; 1975). **REFUGEE (WITH PATRICK MORAZ):** *Refugee* (1974). **PATRICK MORAZ:** *i* (1976). **PATRICK MORAZ AND BILL BRUFORD:** *Flags* (1990). **STEVE HOWE:** *Beginnings* (1975); *The Steve Howe Album* (1980); *Not Necessarily Acoustic* (1994). **ASIA:** *Asia* (1982); *Alpha* (1983); *Astra* (1985). **GTR:** *GTR* (1986). **CHRIS SQUIRE:** *Fish Out of Water* (1975). **CINEMA (WITH ALAN WHITE):** *Wrong House* (1988). **JON ANDERSON:** *Olias of Sunhollow* (1976); *Song of Seven* (1980); *Animation* (1982); *3 Ships* (1985); *In the City of Angels* (1988); *Deseo* (1994): *Change We Must* (1994). **JON AND VANGELIS:** *Short Stories* (1980); *Friends of Mr. Cairo* (1981); *Private Collection* (1983); *Best* (1984). **TREVOR RABIN:** *Trevor Rabin* (1978); *Can't Look Away* (1989).—**BH**

Yeston, Maury, American composer and music theorist; b. Jersey City, N.J., Oct. 23, 1945. He studied at Yale Univ. with Waite and Forte (B.A., 1967; Ph.D., 1974), subsequently joining the composition faculty there and becoming director of the BMI Musical Theater Workshop in N.Y. His first major stage work was the Broadway musical *Nine* (1982), based on Fellini's movie *8 1/2*, which won Tony and Drama Desk awards; it includes opulent recollections of Baroque and Romantic styles, continuing the operatic trend in musical theater established by Stephen Sondheim and Andrew Lloyd Webber. He also wrote incidental music for Caryl Churchill's play *Cloud Nine* and for *Nukata*, a musical written in Japanese and premiered in Tokyo. His theoretical writings are sophisticated; his *Stratification of Musical Rhythm* (New Haven, 1975), elucidates one of the only plausible theories on rhythmic structure yet proposed. He also ed. *Readings in Schenker Analysis* (New Haven, 1977). Among his compositions are a cello concerto (1977), *Goya, a Life in Song* (1987), and another musical, *Grand Hotel* (1989).—**NS/LK/DM**

Yim, Jay Alan, American composer and teacher; b. St. Louis, April 24, 1958. He studied composition with Peter Racine Fricker and Gordon Crosse at the Univ. of Calif. at Santa Barbara (1976–80), with Justin Connolly at the Royal Coll. of Music in London (1980; M.Mus., 1981), and with Earl Kim, Donald Martino, and Peter Maxwell Davies at Harvard Univ. (1982–84; Ph.D., 1989). From 1984 to 1988 he held a teaching fellowship at Harvard Univ., and then joined the faculty of Northwestern Univ. in 1989. He led composition seminars in Amsterdam, Berlin, and San Diego in 1996, and at the Peabody Cons. of Music in Baltimore in 1998. In 1995–96 he was a Composer-Fellow for the Chicago Sym. Orch.

Yim's music creates highly energetic sound worlds with touches of advanced impressionism.

WORKS: ORCH.: *Askesis* (1980–81; rev. 1987; Amsterdam, Sept. 11, 1988); *Karénas* for Double String Orch., Harp, and Antique Cymbals (1986; Tanglewood, Aug. 5, 1987); *Geometry and Delirium* for Amplified Small Chamber Orch. and Electronics (1987–89; London, March 18, 1989); *Pictures from the Water Trade* for Oboe and Orch. (Cambridge, Mass., May 6, 1989); *Rain Palace* for Oboe, English Horn, and Orch. (1993); *Rough Magic* (1996–97; Chicago, Jan. 30, 1997). **CHAMBER:** *Pìak* for 2 Oboes, 2 English Horns, 2 Bassoons, and Contrabassoon (1981); *Autumn Rhythm* for String Quartet (1984–85); *Moments of Rising Mist* for 7 Players (1984–86); *Sea Urchin Harakiri* for 5 Players (1986; rev. 1990); *Becalmed on Strange Waters* for Clarinet and 9 Strings (1989); *Zazanza* for 10 Players (1989); *Radiant Shadows* for Percussion Ensemble (1991); *Song in Memory of a Circle* for Flute and Electronics (1992); *Broken Prisms* for 7 Players (1995); *Escape Velocity*, series of pieces for Different Wind Instruments (1995); *Orenda* for Cello, 2 Bows, and Live Electronics (1995–97); *Twine (Escape Velocity 2.1)* for Quarter-tone Flute and Prepared Marimba (1997–98; rev. 1999); *Circle Song* for Alto Flute, Oboe, and Clarinet (1997–98). **KEYBOARD: Piano:** *Timescreen 1* and *2* (1983–84); *:[ten]dril* (1999). **VOCAL:** *Eastern Windows* for Soprano, Harp, and Strings (1981; rev. 1985); *LHOOQ* for Soprano and 7 Players (1990).—**LK/DM**

Yoffe, Shlomo, Polish-born Israeli composer and teacher; b. Warsaw, May 19, 1909; d. Dec. 29, 1995. After training in Poland and Czechoslovakia, he emigrated to Palestine and pursued studies with Partos and Boscovich in Jerusalem and Tel Aviv. From 1953 to 1973 he was director of the Studio for Music Education for Gilboa and Bet-Shean.

WORKS: ORCH.: *Ruth*, symphonic suite (1954); 3 syms. (1955, 1957, 1958); Violin Concerto (1956); *Views of the Emek*, symphonic suite (1958); *Symphonic Poem on Jewish Themes* (1959); *Divertimento* (1959); Cello Concertino (1959); Oboe Concerto (1960); Concerto for Strings (1961); *3 Pieces* for Horn and Strings (1966); *Fantasia concertante* for Brass Quartet and Orch. (1968); *Beit- Alfa*, symphonic poem (1972); *Introduction, Dance and Finale* for Chamber Orch. (1972); *Sobu Zion*, overture (1973); *5 Sketches of Old Jerusalem* for Chamber Orch. (1973); *Fantasy* for Oboe and Chamber Orch. (1975); Sinfonietta (1977); *The Beautiful City* (1978); Concerto for Vibraphone and Strings (1979); *Variations on "Eshkolit"* for Chamber Orch. (1979); *Landscapes* (1981); *Israel Sketches* (1984). **CHAMBER:** Quartet for 2 Flutes, Cello, and Piano (1957); 2 string quartets (1961, 1969); *Fantasy* for String Quartet (1966); Chamber Concerto for Violin and 10 Players (1966); *Affettuoso* for 2 Flutes (1966); Brass Quartet (1967); *Musica concertante* for Clarinet and 3 Percussionists (1973); *Etude* for 13 Players (1974); *Serenata* for Wind Quintet (1975); *Nonetto* for Strings (1976); *Depressed Story* for Clarinet and String Quartet (1983); Quintet for Horn and String Quartet (1986); *Monologue* for Violin (1987). **VOCAL:** *What Name Shall I Call?* for Soprano and Chamber Orch. (1975); *Psalm 125* for Narrator and Orch. (1978); *Shake Thyself from the Dust* for Voice, Clarinet, and Strings (1988); various cantatas; songs. —**NS/LK/DM**

Yon, Pietro Alessandro, Italian-born American organist, composer, and teacher; b. Settimo Vittone, Aug. 8, 1886; d. Huntington, N.Y., Nov. 22, 1943. He studied with Fumagalli at the Milan Cons., then at the Turin Cons. (1901–04), and at the Accademia di Santa Cecilia in Rome with Remigio Renzi (organ) and Sgambati (piano), graduating in 1905. He subsequently served as organist at St. Peter's in Rome (1905–07). In 1907 he emigrated to the U.S.; from 1907 to 1919, and again from 1921 to 1926, was organist at St. Francis-Xavier's in N.Y.; then was appointed organist of St. Patrick's Cathedral in N.Y., a post he held until his death. He became a naturalized American citizen in 1921. He was greatly esteemed as an organist and teacher; composed numerous organ pieces, of which *Gesu Bambino* (1917) became popular and was publ. in various instrumental and vocal arrangements; he also wrote an oratorio, *The Triumph of St. Patrick* (N.Y., April 29, 1934); several masses and other religious services. A novel based on his life, *The Heavens Heard Him*, written by V.B. Hammann and M.C. Yon, was publ. in N.Y. in 1963.—**NS/LK/DM**

Yonge (also **Young, Younge**), **Nicholas,** English singer and music editor; b. Lewes; d. London (buried), Oct. 23, 1619. He was a chorister at St. Paul's Cathedral. He translated and arranged a number of Italian madrigals, which he publ. in 2 books under the general title *Musica transalpina* (1588, 1597).

BIBL.: D. Scott, *A Transcription and Detailed Study of "Musica transalpina"* (diss., Univ. of London, 1968).—**NS/LK/DM**

York, Wes(ley), American composer; b. Portland, Maine, May 27, 1949. He studied theory privately with John Heiss, electronic music at the Mass. Inst. of Technology, and composition with Robert Cogan and Thomas DeLio at the New England Cons. of Music (B.M., 1981; M.M., 1984). York has composed works for theater, film, television, and dance, as well as for the concert hall and is also a respected writer on contemporary American music, especially Philip Glass and Morton Feldman. He moved to N.Y. in 1992, becoming closely affiliated with the American Music Center.

WORKS: DRAMATIC: Incidental Music To: *Much Ado About Nothing* (1970); *A Full Moon in March* (1973); *At the Hawk's Well* (1973). **Film:** *Hearing Voices* (1989); *Resilient Spirits* (2000). **CHAMBER:** *Two spirits, one inside the other, both of them singing* for Chamber Orch. (1984); *Reminiscence 2* for Flute, Clarinet, and Piano (1986); *Muscle Music* for Chamber Orch. (1991); *For Cello and Piano* (2000). **Piano:** *Music for Strings* (1989); *Bartlett's Rhapsody* (1989); *Reminiscence* (1989); *Right at the Center of the Sky* (1992); *For the day the time changes* (1998). **VOCAL:** *Alleluia* for Chorus (1983); *Three Native Songs* for Soprano, Baritone, Piano, Percussion, and 2 Flutes (1985); *Two Songs on a Poem of Su Tung* for Tenor, Bass, and Piano (1985); *For the Sleepwalkers* for Baritone, Piano, Cello, Bass, and Chorus (1986); *Songs from the Levertov Scores* for Soprano, Violin, and Marimba (1986); *My Heart is Different* for Soprano and Piano (1988); *Solitary Songs* for Baritone (1992); *Protest Song* for Soprano, Piano, and Double Bass (1993); *Songs from the Lakota* for Soprano and Piano (1996); *Journey* for Tenor, 2 Percussion, Piano, Violin, Cello, and Double Bass (1997); *Wedding Song* for Soprano and Piano (2000). **COMPUTER:** *Microtonal Musicbox* (1983).—**NS/LK/DM**

Yoshida, Tsunezō, Japanese ethnomusicologist; b. Kohama, Fukui prefecture, Feb. 3, 1872; d. Kyoto, May

16, 1957. After graduating from the Tokyo School of Music (1897), he taught at training colleges in Fukui (1897–1903) and Kyoto (1903–35). In 1920 he began studying Buddhist music in collaboration with Dōnin Taki (1890–1943), a priest of the Tendai sect and a performer of Buddhist chant, with whom he produced several books and transcription anthologies on Buddhist chant, beginning with *Kada ongaku ron* (On the Music of Gāthā; 1934). Yoshida founded a research inst. on Buddhist music at Enryaku-ji (the headquarters of the Tendai sect) in 1950. He received a number of honors during his lifetime, including the Medal of Honor with Purple Ribbon (1955).—**NS/LK/DM**

Yost, Michel, famous French clarinetist and composer; b. Paris, 1754; d. there, July 5, 1786. He studied with Beer. He wrote 14 clarinet concertos, 30 quartets for clarinet and strings, 8 books of duos for clarinets, and *Airs variés* for clarinet, with viola and bass.—**NS/LK/DM**

Youll, Henry, English composer who flourished c. 1600. He publ. *Canzonets to three voyces* (London, 1608; ed. in The English Madrigalists, XXVIII, 1968).
—**NS/LK/DM**

Youmans, Vincent (Millie), American composer and theatrical producer; b. N.Y., Sept. 27, 1898; d. Denver, April 5, 1946. Youmans wrote some of the defining songs of the 1920s, including "Tea for Two," "I Want to Be Happy," and "More than You Know." Despite a career shortened by illness, he was the primary composer of 11 Broadway musicals, including *No, No, Nanette*, and he worked with many of the major lyricists of his day, including Ira Gershwin, Otto Harbach, Oscar Hammerstein II, and B. G. De Sylva.

Youmans was the son of Vincent Miller and Lucy Gibson Millie Youmans. His family owned a chain of N.Y. hat stores, and he grew up in the wealthy N.Y. suburb of Larchmont, attending private schools and beginning college at Yale's engineering school. His interest in becoming an engineer quickly waned, however, and after briefly working in the family business, he took a job making piano rolls and selling pianos for the Aeolian Company. With the U.S. entry into World War I in April 1917, he enlisted in the navy and was sent to the Great Lakes Training Station near Chicago, where he played piano in a band and wrote music, including a march that was adopted by John Philip Sousa and that Youmans later adapted into the song "Hallelujah!" for his 1927 musical *Hit the Deck!* Youmans went to Tin Pan Alley after the war, working as a song plugger at Jerome H. Remick, music publisher. Remick gave him his first song publication, "The Country Cousin" (lyrics by Alfred Bryan) in 1920, and the same year two of his songs were used in the revue *Piccadilly to Broadway*, which closed out of town but launched his association with Ira Gershwin. They teamed up again for *Two Little Girls in Blue* (which also had music by Paul Lannin); it was a moderate success, running 135 performances and featuring "Oh Me! Oh My!," which became a hit for Frank Crumit and the Paul Biese Trio in November 1921, after the show had closed in N.Y. and embarked on a successful road tour.

Youmans collaborated with composer Herbert Stothart and lyricist-librettists Otto Harbach and Oscar Hammerstein II on the operetta *Wildflower*, the longest-running show of the 1922–23 season at 477 performances. It produced two big hits, "Bambalina," which became a best-seller for Paul Whiteman and His Orch. in June 1923, and the title song, recorded by Ben Bernie and His Orch. Youmans, Stothart, and Hammerstein then teamed with lyricist-librettist William Cary Duncan for *Mary Jane McKane*, a modestly successful musical that opened on Broadway in December 1923, beating by a month the Youmans–Zelda Sears musical *Lollipop*, also a modest success. Youmans next wrote the music for *No, No, Nanette*, which had lyrics by Otto Harbach, who co-wrote the libretto with Frank Mandel. After the show's tryouts in Detroit and Cincinnati, two new songs with lyrics by Irving Caesar were inserted: "Tea for Two" and "I Want to Be Happy." The show then became such a success in Chicago that it stayed there for the 1924–25 season while spawning other touring versions and a London production that ran 665 performances. Meanwhile, recording artists began to discover the score: among the many versions of "I Want to Be Happy," the most popular was the one by Vincent Lopez and His Orch., while Marion Harris had the best-selling record of "Tea for Two" in February 1925. Thus, when *No, No, Nanette* finally reached N.Y. in September it was already an international success. It conquered Broadway too, running 321 performances. Youmans's next Broadway show, *Oh, Please!*, a vehicle for Beatrice Lillie, was a failure in N.Y. (it eventually made money on the road), but "I Know that You Know" (lyrics by Anne Caldwell) from the score became a hit for Nat Shilkret and the Victor Orch. in April 1927. The show is also notable for its chorus, which contained both of the women Youmans would marry. The first was dancer Anne Varley, whom Youmans married on Feb. 7, 1927, while she was still appearing in *Oh, Please!* They became the parents of twins, but the marriage foundered in its first year, and they divorced in 1933. Youmans formed a longer lasting liaison with dancer Mildred Antoinette Boots, who was his companion for years prior to their marriage on Oct. 21, 1935. Youmans scored the third and final Broadway hit of his career with *Hit the Deck!*, which had a naval theme and which he co-produced. The show ran 352 performances and featured two hit songs, the most popular recordings of which appeared on either side of a single disc, Victor 20599: on one side was Nat Shilkret's recording of Youmans's World War I march, "Hallelujah!" (lyrics by Leo Robin and Clifford Grey); on the other, Roger Wolfe Kahn and His Orch.'s version of "Sometimes I'm Happy." The latter song had a history too. As "Come On and Pet Me" (lyrics by William Cary Duncan and Oscar Hammerstein II), it was written for *Mary Jane McKane* but cut before that show opened. With a new lyric by Irving Caesar, it was put into Youmans's failed 1925 musical *A Night Out*—which never reached N.Y.—before finally finding favor two years later in *Hit the Deck!* Youmans's tendency to reuse melodies from earlier shows was not unique among composers, but the extent of his cannibalization was unusual.

Rainbow, which Youmans wrote with Hammerstein, was seen as something of a sequel to Hammerstein's ambitious 1927 musical *Show Boat*, but a disastrous opening night doomed it. Youmans then determined to better control his works: he leased the Cosmopolitan Theatre and produced his next musical, *Great Day*, himself. Unfortunately, it was another flop, but after it closed three of its songs became hits: the title song was a best-seller for Paul Whiteman with Bing Crosby on vocals in December 1929; Whiteman and Crosby also had a hit with "Without a Song;" and Ruth Etting scored with "More than You Know" (all lyrics by Billy Rose and Edward Eliscu). The introduction of sound films in 1928 led to a slew of movie musicals, and several of Youmans's shows were adapted for the screen in 1930, beginning with *No, No, Nanette*. In the wake of the film's release, the Ipana Troubadors had a revival hit with "Tea for Two," and Red Nichols and His Five Pennies brought back "I Want to Be Happy." (Those were the only songs in the movie retained from the stage version.) Then came *Song of the West*, a film version of *Rainbow*, and *Hit the Deck* (sans exclamation mark). Youmans wrote a new song for each. He also wrote three songs for *What a Widow!*, his first original score for a motion picture. Youmans's next stage musical was the Florenz Ziegfeld production *Smiles*, which featured Fred and Adele Astaire. It was a failure, but a year after it opened on Broadway, there were two hit recordings of one of its songs, "Time on My Hands" (lyrics by Harold Adamson and Mack Gordon), the first by Smith Ballew and His Piping Rock Orch., the second by Leo Reisman and His Orch. with a vocal by Lee Wiley. Youmans again acted as his own producer for *Through the Years*, which flopped, although Reisman made a hit out of "Drums in My Heart" (lyrics by Edward Heyman) in March 1932. Nacio Herb Brown and Richard A. Whiting were the credited composers of the successful musical *Take a Chance* (N.Y., Nov. 26, 1932), for which B. G. De Sylva served as co-producer, co-librettist, and lyricist, but Youmans contributed five tunes, his last for Broadway, including "Rise 'n Shine," which became a hit for Paul Whiteman in January 1933. Youmans spent May to August 1933 in Hollywood writing songs for *Flying Down to Rio*. The film is remembered for establishing the dancing team of Fred Astaire and Ginger Rogers. In his four songs, all of which became hits, Youmans demonstrated an affinity for Latin rhythms. The dance tune "The Carioca" was recorded by several artists; the most popular version was by Enric Madriguera and His Orch., a best-seller in March 1934. (It was also nominated for an Academy Award.) Astaire and Rudy Vallée divided the other songs between them, with Vallée having the most successful version of the tango "Orchids in the Moonlight" and Astaire the biggest hit with "Music Makes Me," while the two had equally popular recordings of the title song. (All lyrics were by Gus Kahn and Edward Eliscu.)

Unfortunately, *Flying Down to Rio* marked the end of Youmans's career as a composer. He contracted tuberculosis in 1934 and retired to Colo. for his health. Aspiring to write serious music, he studied with various teachers and spurned offers to write for Hollywood or Broadway. He produced but did not write music for *Vincent Youmans' Revue* (Baltimore, Jan. 27, 1944), which closed out of town. He and his second wife divorced in January 1946. He died of tuberculosis in April at the age of 47. Four months later, Perry Como had a chart revival of "More than You Know." Les Paul made the charts in 1952 with an instrumental treatment of "The Carioca," and in 1955 MGM released an all-star remake of *Hit the Deck* that contained a previously unused Youmans melody. But by far the most frequently revived Youmans work was *No, No, Nanette*, along with its songs "Tea for Two" and "I Want to Be Happy." In 1958 the Tommy Dorsey Orch. Starring Warren Covington had a Top Ten, gold-selling record of "Tea for Two Cha Cha," following with a chart record of "I Want to Be Happy Cha Cha" that was also recorded by Enoch Light and the Light Brigade. A more conventional revival of "Tea for Two" was a chart record for Nino Tempo and April Stevens in 1964. A Broadway revival of *No, No, Nanette* (N.Y., Jan. 19, 1971) became the biggest hit of the 1970–71 season, running 861 performances, and its cast album reached the charts.

WORKS (only works for which Youmans was a primary, credited composer are listed): **MUSICALS/REVUES** (dates refer to N.Y. openings unless otherwise indicated): *Two Little Girls in Blue* (May 3, 1921); *Wildflower* (Feb. 7, 1923); *Mary Jane McKane* (Dec. 25, 1923); *Lollipop* (Jan. 21, 1924); *No, No, Nanette* (Chicago, May 5, 1924; London, March 11, 1925; N.Y., Sept. 16, 1925); *Oh, Please!* (Dec. 17, 1926); *Hit the Deck!* (April 25, 1927); *Rainbow* (Nov. 21, 1928); *Great Day* (Oct. 17, 1929); *Smiles* (Nov. 18, 1930); *Through the Years* (Jan. 28, 1932). **FILMS:** *Song of the West* (1930); *Hit the Deck* (1930); *What a Widow!* (1930); *Flying Down to Rio* (1933); *No, No, Nanette* (1940); *Hit the Deck* (1955).

BIBL.: G. Bordman, *Days to Be Happy, Years to Be Sad: The Life and Music of V. Y.* (N.Y., 1982).—**WR**

Young, family of English singers:

(1) Cecilia Young, soprano; b. London (baptized), Feb. 7, 1712; d. there, Oct. 6, 1789. She was a student of Geminiani. On March 4, 1730, she made her first public appearance at a benefit concert at London's Drury Lane Theatre. In 1732–33 she began singing in English operas by Lampe and Smith, and in 1735 Handel engaged her for the premieres of his *Ariodante* and *Alcina*. In 1737 she married **Thomas Augustine Arne**, and subsequently sang in his works in London. In 1742 she and her husband visited Dublin, where she sang in the first performances of his oratorio *The Death of Abel* on Feb. 18, 1744. They returned to Dublin in 1755, being accompanied by Arne's gifted student, Charlotte Brent. By then Young and Arne's marriage had become tempestuous, and Arne and Brent returned to London, leaving his wife in the company of her young niece, Polly Young. In 1762 Young and her niece returned to London. Young and her husband were reconciled shortly before his death in 1778.

(2) Isabella Young, soprano, sister of the preceding; b. London, date unknown; d. there, 1795. After singing minor roles at London's Drury Lane Theatre in 1733–34, she appeared in concerts. On May 10, 1737, she created the role of Margery in John Frederick Lampe's *The Dragon of Wantley* in London, and soon became his wife. Thereafter she appeared in all of his operas. In 1748 they went to Dublin, where Young sang at the Smock Alley Theatre. In 1750 they proceeded to Edinburgh. After her husband's death in 1751, she returned to London and sang at Covent Garden.

(3) Esther Young, contralto, sister of the two preceding; b. London, Feb. 14, 1717; d. there (buried), June 6, 1795. She began her career as a concert singer in 1736. On May 10, 1737, she created the role of Mauxalinda in Lampe's *The Dragon of Wantley* in London, and subsequently sang in other operas by him. In 1744 she sang Juno and Ino in the first performance of Handel's *Semele* in London. She appeared frequently at Covent Garden until 1776. Her best known role was Lucy in *The Beggar's Opera*.

(4) Isabella Young, mezzo-soprano, niece of **(1) Cecilia Young;** b. probably in London, date unknown; d. there, Aug. 17, 1791. She was a student of Waltz. In March 1751 she made her debut in a concert with Waltz in London. Arne engaged her to sing in his operas in 1754. From 1755 to 1777 she appeared frequently at London's Drury Lane Theater. She also sang in Handel's works from 1756 until his death in 1759. Young was best known as a concert and oratorio artist.

(5) Elizabeth Young, contralto, sister of the preceding; b. probably in London, date unknown; d. there, April 12, 1773. She sang in Arne's works in Dublin and in London in 1756. In 1758 she appeared as Lucy in *The Beggar's Opera* in London. She sang frequently at London's Drury Lane Theatre until 1772.

(6) Polly Young, soprano, sister of the two preceding; b. London, c. 1749; d. there, Sept. 20, 1799. She was taken to Dublin as a child by the Arnes, and began singing in public when she was 6. After appearing as both an actress and a singer, she returned to London and sang at Covent Garden from 1762 to 1764. She appeared in minor roles at the King's Theatre from 1764 until her marriage to **François-Hippolyte Barthélémon** in 1766. Thereafter they appeared in concerts in London, Ireland, and on the Continent.—**NS/LK/DM**

Young (real name, **Youngs**), **(Basil) Alexander,** English tenor; b. London, Oct. 18, 1920; d. Macclesfield, March 5, 2000. He was a pupil of Steffan Pollmann at the Royal Coll. of Music in London. He sang with the BBC and Glyndebourne choruses (1948–49); in 1950 he made his operatic debut as Scaramuccio in *Ariadne auf Naxos* at the Edinburgh Festival. He sang regularly at London's Covent Garden (1955–70), appeared with other English opera companies and in the U.S., and toured widely as a concert artist. From 1973 to 1986 he was head of the school of vocal studies at the Royal Northern Coll. of Music in Manchester; was also founder-conductor of the Jubilate Choir of Manchester (1977). His operatic repertory ranged from Monteverdi to Stravinsky; he was particularly admired for his performances of Handel's music. —**NS/LK/DM**

Young, Douglas, English composer and pianist; b. London, July 18, 1947. He studied at the Royal Coll. of Music in London with Anthony Milner (composition) and Anthony Hopkins (piano), obtaining his B.M. in 1969. In 1970 he made his debut as a pianist at the Royal Festival Hall in London. He was founder-director of the Dreamtiger ensemble (from 1975).

WORKS: DRAMATIC: Ballet: *Pasiphae* (1969); *Charlotte Bronte-Portrait* (1973–74); *Ludwig, Fragmente eines Ratsels* (Munich, June 14, 1986). **ORCH.:** *Sinfonietta* (1968–70); Piano Concertino (1972–74); *3 Regions from Terrain* (1974); *Sea Change* (1976); *Circus Band Et al (after Ives)* (1977); *Virages-Region I*, cello concerto (1978); *William Booth Enters Heaven (after Ives)* (1980); *Rain, Steam, and Speed* (1981); *Lament on the Destruction of Forests* (1986). **CHAMBER:** *Essay* for String Quartet (1971); *Compasses* for Clarinet and String Trio (1972–77); *Croquis et Agaceries (after Satie)* for Flute, Cello, and Piano (1976); *10 preludes de la porte heroique du Ciel* for Cello and Piano (1977); *Trajet/inter/lignes* for Flute (1978–80); *Fantomes* for String Trio (1980–81); *Arabesque breve* for Cello (1982); String Trio 1985 for Violin, Viola, and Cello (1983–85); piano pieces. **VOCAL:** *The Listeners*, cantata for Narrator, Soprano, Women's Voices, and Chamber Orch. (1967); *Vers d'un voyage vers l'hiver* for 12 Solo Voices (1975–77); *Journey between 2 Worlds* for Chorus, Rock Group, Steel Band, and Orch. (1979); *Sports et Divertissement (after Satie)* for Narrator, Clarinet, String Trio, and Piano (1981); *Songs of Exile* for Countertenor or Contralto and Lute (1984). —**NS/LK/DM**

Young, Faron, a 1950s-era honky-tonker who became a 1960s-era country music mainstay, b. Shreveport, La., Feb. 25, 1932; d. Nashville, Tenn., Dec. 10, 1996. Born in Shreveport, Young was raised on a small farm outside of town. He began playing guitar from an early age, and was already a competent country performer when he entered high school. After a brief stab at college in the early 1950s, Young's musical career interrupted his education. He was signed to the popular La. Hayride radio program, where he met another future crooner, Webb Pierce, and the duo were soon touring Southern honky-tonks and clubs.

In 1951 Young was signed to Capitol, having hits with the barroom tear- jerkers "Tattle Tale Tears" and "Have I Waited Too Long." Young spent two years in the army from 1952–54, but in the middle of his army service (primarily as an entertainer for the troops) he was invited to join The Grand Ole Opry. After his service, he scored his biggest hits, including 1955's country anthem, "Live Fast, Love Hard and Die Young." More honky-tonk standards followed, including 1956's "I've Got Five Dollars and It's Saturday Night," 1958's "That's the Way I Feel," and 1959's "Country Girl." In 1958, Young made his big-screen debut with Ferlin Husky and Zsa Zsa Gabor in *Country Music Holiday*, as well as appearing in the film biopic of *Daniel Boone*.

In the 1960s, Young entered the mainstream Nashville music-business world with a vengeance. While his recordings continued, they tended to be conventional middle-of-the-road country crooning (1967's "I Guess I Had Too Much to Dream Last Night" being an example of the excesses of this period). Meanwhile, he founded the influential trade-music paper, *Music City News*, opened his own music publishing company, and developed his own Nashville-based racetrack. The 1970s saw Young's activities trailing off as a performer, as his importance as a businessperson grew. While he still had hits in the first half of the decade, later his music-making dropped off. By the 1980s, he was recording only rarely, while still maintaining a regular presence on the Opry, starring on country music TV specials, and continuing to make personal appearances.

In the 1990s, Young's career slowed, although he did continue to perform in country hot spots like Branson, Mo., where he cut a live album in 1993. In 1996, suffering from emphysema and prostrate problems, Young took his own life by a self-inflicted gunshot wound.

Disc.: *Live Fast, Live Hard, 1952–62* (1995).—**RC**

Young, La Monte (Thornton), American composer of the extreme avant-garde; b. Bern, Idaho, Oct. 14, 1935. He studied clarinet and saxophone with William Green in Los Angeles (1951–54); also attended Los Angeles City Coll. (1953–56) and studied counterpoint and composition privately with Leonard Stein (1955–56); was a pupil of Robert Stevenson at the Univ. of Calif. at Los Angeles (B.A., 1958); pursued further training with Seymour Shifrin and Andrew Imbrie at the Univ. of Calif. at Berkeley (1958–60) and attended the summer courses in new music in Darmstadt; subsequently studied electronic music with Richard Maxfield at the New School for Social Research in N.Y. (1960–61). In 1963 he married the artist and illustrator Marian Zazeela with whom he subsequently gave audio-visual performances in a series of "Sound/Light Environments" in Europe and America. In 1970 he visited India to study Eastern philosophy and train himself physically, mentally, and vocally for cosmic awareness, gradually arriving at the realization that any human, subhuman, or inhuman activity constitutes art; in his *Composition 1990* he starts a fire on the stage while releasing captive butterflies in the hall. In his attempt to overcome terrestrial limitations, he has decreed for himself a circadian period of 26 hours. He achieves timelessness by declaring, "This piece of music may play without stopping for thousands of years." Several of his works consist solely of imperious commands: "Push the piano to the wall; push it through the wall; keep pushing," or, more succinctly, "Urinate." He ed. *An Anthology of Chance Operations, Concept Art, Anti-Art*, etc. (N.Y., 1963; 2nd ed., rev., 1970), which, with his own *Compositions 1960*, had primary influence on concept art and the Fluxus movement; his own contribution to it was a line drawn in India ink on a 3 x 5 filing card. He has contributed extensively to the study of just intonation and to the development of tuning systems based on the set of rational numbers which make up the components of his periodic composite sound waveform environments. He received a Guggenheim fellowship and a grant from the NEA. Among his ascertainable works are *5 Little Pieces* for string quartet (1956); *For Brass* (1957); *For Guitar* (1958); trio for strings (1958); *Poem* for tables, chairs, and benches (moving furniture about; Univ. of Calif., Berkeley, Jan. 5, 1960); *Arabic Numeral* (any Integer) for gong or piano (1960); *Studies in the Bowed Disc* for gong (1963); *The Well-Tuned Piano* (1964); *The Tortoise Droning Selected Pitches from the Holy Numbers of the 2 Black Tigers, the Green Tiger, and the Hermit* (N.Y., Oct. 30, 1964); *The Tortoise Recalling the Drone of the Holy Numbers as They Were Revealed in the Dreams of the Whirlwind and the Obsidian Gong, Illuminated by the Sawmill, the Green Sawtooth Ocelot, and the High-Tension Line Stepdown Transformer* (N.Y., Dec. 12, 1964); *Map of 49's Dream of Two Systems of 11 Sets of Galactic Intervals Ornamental Lightyears Tracery* for voices, various instruments, and sine wave drones (Pasadena, Calif., Jan. 28, 1968); and *The Subsequent Dreams of China* (1980). Also an arbitrary number of pieces of "conceptual" music and tape recordings of his own monophonous vocalizing achieved by both inspiration and expiration so that the vocal line is maintained indefinitely; various physical exercises with or without audible sounds. His *Selected Writings* were publ. in Munich in 1969.

Bibl.: W. Mertens, *American Minimal Music: L. Y., Terry Riley, Steve Reich, Philip Glass* (London, 1991).—**NS/LK/DM**

Young, Larry (aka **Aziz, Khalid Yasin Abdul**), jazz organist; b. Newark, N.J., Oct. 7, 1940; d. N.Y., March 30, 1978. His father was an organist, and he had classical training as a pianist. His "Unity" is a favorite of many musicians. He knew Coltrane, and the two may have recorded together in private. He was in Tony Williams's Lifetime (1969–71) and early 1970s and also worked with Miles Davis.

Disc.: *Testifying* (1960); *Young Blues* (1960); *Groove Street* (1962); *Complete Blue Note Recordings* (1964); *Into Somethin'* (1964); *Unity* (1965); *Of Love and Peace* (1966); *Contrasts* (1967); *Heaven on Earth* (1968); *Mother Ship* (1969); *Lawrence of Newark* (1973); *Fuel* (1975); *Spaceball* (1975).—**LP**

Young, Lee (actually, **Leonidas Raymond**), jazz drummer; b. New Orleans, March 7, 1917. The younger brother of **Lester Young**, he was raised in the Young family band. Because of the age difference, he was not personally very close to Lester and often would not see him for years at a time. He led a group in Hollywood featuring Lester (1941–42); played with Lester and Charlie Parker at JATP (1946), Nat Cole, Benny Goodman, and did studio work. He stopped performing in the mid-1960s and devoted himself to producing new pop acts.

Disc.: *Jazz at the Philharmonic 1944–1946* (1946); *Jazz at the Philharmonic 1946* (1946).—**LP/JC**

Young, Lester (Willis), ("Pres" or "Prez"; in early years "Red," or as Jo Jones said, "Mississippi Red"), highly influential and important jazz tenor saxophonist; brother of **Lee Young;** b. Woodville, M.S., Aug. 27, 1909; d. N.Y., March 15, 1959. Only four years younger than Coleman Hawkins, with whom he is often contrasted, Young first recorded 15 years after Hawkins's debut and was perceived as the leading tenor stylist of the next generation. A prime influence on bebop players, his style later served as the basis for cool jazz as well. Thus he is one of the key figures in the history of jazz.

He was born among his mother's family in Woodville, on the La. border, but his immediate family was based in nearby Algiers and New Orleans, and this had a tremendous musical impact on him. He studied violin, trumpet, and drums with his father, and then alto saxophone. He performed in the touring family band, with residencies in Memphis (1919, upon his parents' separation), and Minneapolis (by 1920). He credited the influences of Frankie Trumbauer and, to a lesser extent, Jimmy Dorsey, and was probably influenced by Louis Armstrong, thus escaping the Hawkins hegemony. He began to specialize on the tenor sax and toured with other bands, beginning with Art Bronson (for the entire year 1928) and including Walter Page's Blue Devils (1930), Bronson again (second half of 1930), and various groups in Minneapolis (1931). There he fathered a daughter, Beverly, with a white woman named Bess Cooper who died shortly after; Young then wed a woman named Beatrice. He joined the Blue Devils, a descendant of Page's band (1932–May 1933), then King Oliver (c. May–November 1933), and subsequently played with various bands around Kansas City. He first worked with Count Basie in early 1934, transferred to Fletcher Henderson in late March, but left in July after band members criticized his style. For the next year and a half he again shuttled between Kansas City and Minneapolis; in 1936 he returned to Basie in Kansas City, making his first recordings on Nov. 9 and remaining in the band until December 1940. During this period Young created a sensation among such musicians as Charlie Parker and Dexter Gordon for his light, beautiful tone, his perfect phrasing, and his seemingly endless flow of melodic invention. He also guested on a now-celebrated series of recordings with Billie Holiday, who dubbed him the "Pres" ("President") of the saxophone. Their relationship was platonic; however, as Young had been involved with a white woman named Mary since coming to N.Y. with Basie in December 1936 (Beatrice stayed behind), and their relationship later became a common-law marriage.

Young left Basie to become a leader, but had little success. In early 1941 he freelanced around N.Y., leading his own band at Kelly's Stables (February 27–March 17), then joined his brother, drummer Lee Young, in L.A. (through the summer of 1942). They appeared at Cafe Society Downtown in N.Y. from Sept. 1 until the death of their father on Feb. 6, 1943, when Lee returned to L.A. He appeared with the Al Sears band (March to late September 1943), mostly on a U.S.O. tour to military bases across the states. He filled in for a week with Basie at N.Y.'s Apollo Theater in October and then rejoined Basie full-time around Dec. 1. He became famous, and won first place in a *Down Beat* poll at the end of 1944, but by this time he was in the army, having been inducted on Sept. 30. His Army file indicates that he had a criminal record, but research by Evan Spring shows that Young had never faced a judge in Manhattan anytime between 1937 and 1944; his record must have been from another location. His tour of duty was a disaster. He was made an ordinary soldier with little opportunity to make music, and on Feb. 16, 1945, was court-martialed for possession of marijuana and barbiturates and sent to detention barracks. Shortly after his dishonorable discharge on Dec. 1, he memorialized his experience in "D. B. Blues," one of the first blues pieces with an eight-bar bridge. Contrary to popular opinion, Young was anything but broken by his experience, at least not musically. This is evidenced by his post-war recordings, which are exuberant, extroverted, honking affairs. His style had been changing gradually: by late 1943 there was a definite thickening of tone and a more overtly bluesy, wailing approach, which led to a new set of followers, including the young Sonny Rollins. Meanwhile, many young players went back to Young's 1930s work for inspiration in what became known as cool jazz.

In the late 1940s, Young was a celebrity and at his peak financially. Producer Norman Granz booked him regularly for JATP tours and recordings (from 1946) and also recorded him as a leader (from 1949). He toured widely with his own quartet or quintet, and from 1956 often traveled as a single, guesting with local rhythm sections. He married a final time, wedding a black woman, also named Mary, with whom he had two children: Yvette (1947) and Lester Jr. (1948). Young's health gradually deteriorated, primarily due to his alcoholism; he died just hours after returning from a foreshortened Paris engagement and projected European tour.

There has been some speculation that Young died from advanced stages of syphilis. The initial suspicion came from this author's noting that his army file indicated he was "syphilitic at present" and Young's own report that he had had to take a spinal tap. A spinal was only given if one had a positive blood test for syphilis. The test would be positive even for latent syphilis, which is not serious. The spinal would determine the stage of the disease. If it was serious, one would not be drafted, so Young must have had latent syphilis when he entered the army. However, syphilis could only have killed him had he lived considerably longer. And had it been advanced enough to kill him he would have been too paralyzed to play, but even on his last recordings just two weeks before his death his playing is solid. He could have had encephalitis, as has also been claimed, but this a direct result of syphilis and would not be what killed him. Likely, he died from cirrhosis, which is more deadly than syphilis. There is general agreement that he had cirrhosis by the time he was hospitalized in 1955; and on his last night he was spitting up blood, which is a dangerous sign of liver failure.

Young's influential and witty slang is preserved on two audio interviews, one of about 10 minutes with Chris Albertson (1958) and one running about 45 minutes with François Postif (Paris, Feb. 6, 1959). He also appears in silent footage from 1938, in a 1944 Academy Award–winning short, *Jammin' the Blues* (sound dubbed), a 1950 JATP film (sound dubbed), and briefly as a soloist in "The Sound of Jazz" (TV broadcast, 1957). He played clarinet in a lovely, wistful style on recordings in 1938, and also, though he was out of practice, in 1958.

DISC.: **78S:** Jones-Smith Inc.: *(Oh) Lady Be Good* and *Shoe Shine Boy* (2 takes; 1936). Basie: *Honeysuckle Rose* and *One O'Clock Jump* (both 1937); *Jumpin' at the Woodside* (1938); *Jive at Five, Clap Hands Here Comes Charlie,* and *Lester Leaps In* (2 takes; all 1939); *Tickle Toe* (1940). Holiday: *Back in Your Own Backyard* and *I Can't Get Started* (2 takes each; 1938). Kansas City Seven: *After Theatre Jump* (2 takes; 1944); L.Y.: *D. B. Blues* and *These Foolish Things* (1945); *Lester Young–Buddy Rich Trio* (with Nat Cole, piano; 1946). JATP: *Embraceable You* (1949); *Complete Lester Young on Keynote* (1943); *Pres: The Complete Savoy Recordings* (1944); *Aladdin Sessions* (1945); *Prez Conferences 1946–1958* (1946); *Live at the Royal Roost 1948* (1948); *Jammin' with Lester*

(1950); *Pres Is Blue* (1950); *With the Oscar Peterson Trio* (1952); *In Washington D.C. 1956, Vols. 1–4* (1956); *Jazz Giants '56* (1956); *Prez in Europe* (1956); *Pres and Teddy* (Wilson; 1956); *Laughin' to Keep from Cryin'* (1958). **LP:** *Historical Prez* (live; 1940–44).

BIBL.: D. Gelly, *L.Y.* (Tunbridge Wells, England, and N.Y., 1984); L. Porter, *L.Y.* (Boston, 1985); F. Büchmann-M ller, *You Just Fight for Your Life: The Story of L.Y.* (biography) and *You Got to Be Original, Man!: The Music of L.Y.* (annotated discography with transcriptions; both Westport, Conn., 1990); L. Porter, *A L.Y. Reader* (Washington, D.C., 1991; includes all Young interviews previously published or newly transcribed from tape); Luc Delannoy, *Pres: The Story of L.Y.* (in French 1987; Eng. tr., Fayetteville, Ark., 1993); Bernard Cash, *An Analysis of the Improvisation Technique of Lester Willis Young, 1936–1942* (thesis, Univ. of Hull, 1982); Luc Delannoy, *Lester Young, Profession: Président* (Paris, 1987); Robert August Luckey, *A Study of Lester Young and His Influence upon His Contemporaries* (diss., U. of Pittsburgh, 1981).—**LP**

Young, Neil, exceptional songwriter and author of lyrically beautiful love songs, hard-edged rockers, potent sociopolitical pieces, and evocative songs, sometimes reflectively melancholic, sometimes brooding and desperate; b. Toronto, Ontario, Canada, Nov. 12, 1945. **Crazy Horse,** backup band. **MEMBERSHIP:** Danny Whitten, gtr., voc. (d. Los Angeles, Nov. 29, 1972); Billy Talbot, bs.; Ralph Molina, drm. After the tenures of Nils Lofgren, voc., gtr. (b. Chicago, June 21, 1951) and Greg Leroy, voc., gtr., Frank Sampedro became the group's permanent guitarist, in 1975.

Neil Young scored his biggest early success with *After the Goldrush* and *Harvest*. Recognized as a potent lead guitarist, Young subsequently embarked on an erratic solo career that gained him the reputation as one of the most enigmatic and elusive artists to emerge from the 1960s. He has often worked with the backup band Crazy Horse, who have inspired him to some of his best work on album and on stage. Often changing styles, Young has continued to record with Crazy Horse while also rejoining Crosby, Stills, and Nash from time to time, as well as working with other accompanists, including a 1995 collaboration with Pearl Jam.

Neil Young grew up in Winnipeg, Manitoba, where he formed Neil Young and the Squires while in high school. He later returned to his birthplace, Toronto, to play folk music at clubs in the city's Yorkville district, where he met Stephen Stills, Richie Furay, and Joni Mitchell. After joining the Mynah Birds, which included bassist Bruce Palmer and later funk star Rick James, Young traveled with Palmer to Los Angeles, where he again encountered Furay and Stills and subsequently formed the Buffalo Springfield in March 1966 with them. The group became known for the exciting lead guitar duels between Stills and Young in concert, and for their involvement in the developing folk-rock movement. Although the group disbanded in May 1968, Young contributed some of their best- remembered songs, including "Flying on the Ground Is Wrong," the psychedelic "Mr. Soul," the major production effort "Broken Arrow," and the lyrical "On the Way Home" and "I Am a Child."

Subsequently pursuing a solo career, Young released his debut album, largely overlooked, which included two of his typical, brooding songs, "The Loner" and "I've Been Waiting for You," as well as the poignant "Old Laughing Lady" and the bizarre "Last Trip to Tulsa." His second album, *Everybody Knows This Is Nowhere*, was recorded with Crazy Horse, whom Young had met in 1968. Previously known as the Rockets, Crazy Horse was comprised of Danny Whitten, Billy Talbot, and Ralph Molina. During the mid-1960s the three had been members of the vocal group Danny and the Memories in the Los Angeles area before they moved to San Francisco in 1966 and took up instruments. They returned to Los Angeles and added violinist Bobby Notkoff and guitarists Leon and George Whitsell, becoming the Rockets for local engagements and one album on White Whale Records. Young's *Everybody Knows This Is Nowhere*, often regarded as one of his finest albums, yielded the minor hit "Cinnamon Girl" and included the title song as well as "The Losing End" and the classics "Cowgirl in the Sand" and "Down by the River."

In June 1969 Neil Young joined David Crosby, Stephen Stills, and Graham Nash for touring, including their celebrated appearance at the Woodstock Festival, and the recording of *DéjàVu.* Adding cohesion and instrumental vitality to the otherwise remarkably subdued group, Young contributed "Helpless" and the three-part "Country Girl" to the best-selling album.

Having fired Crazy Horse because of Danny Whitten's increasing dependence on heroin, Young reluctantly rehired the band for his next solo album, *After the Goldrush*, which featured Crazy Horse's newest member, guitarist Nils Lofgren, and keyboardist-producer Jack Nitzsche. The album produced a moderate hit with "Only Love Can Break Your Heart" and contained the potent classic "Southern Man" as well as "Tell Me Why," "When You Dance I Can Really Love," and Young obscurities "Birds" and "I Believe in You."

Between May and August 1970 Young rejoined Crosby, Stills and Nash on tour. His response to the murder of four students at Kent State Univ. by National Guardsmen, "Ohio," became a major hit at the end of June. The tour's subsequent live album, *Four Way Street*, included a number of Young favorites. Young then embarked on a solo tour, but retreated into inactivity soon after to recover from a slipped disc.

Crazy Horse, comprised of Whitten, Talbot, Molina, Lofgren, and Jack Nitzsche, recorded their debut album for Reprise. Released in 1971, the album included Lofgren's "Beggar's Day," Young's "Dance, Dance, Dance," and Whitten's "I Don't Want to Talk About It" and "Come On Baby, Let's Go Downtown." However, by the end of 1971 Lofgren had left the group and Whitten had become useless. With Talbot and Molina as mainstays, neither *Loose* nor *At Crooked Lake* fared well for Crazy Horse. Danny Whitten died of a heroin overdose on Nov. 29, 1972, in Los Angeles. That, coupled with the overdose death of road crew member Bruce Berry, severely affected Neil Young.

Neil Young's next album, 1972's *Harvest*, featured a new backup group, the Stray Gators, with pedal steel guitarist Ben Keith, pianist Nitzsche, bassist Tim Drummond, and drummer Kenneth Buttrey. It became

Young's best-selling album, yielding a top hit with "Heart of Gold" and a moderate hit with the reflective "Old Man" while containing the resigned "Out on the Weekend," "A Man Needs a Maid" (recorded with the London Symphony Orch.), and the ironically prophetic "The Needle and the Damage Done." After touring again in fall 1972 with the Stray Gators, Young issued *Journey Through the Past* as the soundtrack to the retrospective film premiered five months later. The album, an odd collection of performances by Young, the Buffalo Springfield, and Crosby, Stills, Nash and Young, and the frankly incoherent movie were not well received.

Mounting a massive American tour in early 1973, Neil Young recorded his next album, *Time Fades Away*, on tour. The album featured "Journey Through the Past," "Last Dance," and "Don't Be Denied," and sold modestly. Young reassembled Crazy Horse with Ralph Molina, Billy Talbot, Nils Lofgren, and Ben Keith for extensive touring in 1973–1974, with recordings from the tour eventually issued in 1975 as *Tonight's the Night*. Dedicated to Danny Whitten and Bruce Berry, the album was a highly personal, starkly harrowing, and decidedly anti-music business album. It included Whitten's "Come On Baby, Let's Go Downtown" and Young's own antidrug title song as the album's opening and closing tracks. The rather somber and restrained studio album *On the Beach* had intervened. It contained several surreal songs, such as "Vampire Blues" and "Ambulance Blues," as well as "See the Sky About to Rain" and the minor hit "Walk On By."

Neil Young toured extensively with Crosby, Stills and Nash in 1974–1975, subsequently recording *Zuma* with Crazy Horse, now comprised of Ralph Molina, Billy Talbot, and new guitarist Frank Sampedro. Without yielding a hit single, the album marked the beginning of Young's return to public favor. It contained the seven-minute "Cortez the Killer" and "Pardon My Heart." Young and Stephen Stills reunited for *Long May You Run*, which included Young's title song and "Midnight on the Bay," but the concurrent tour was aborted when Young developed throat problems. Young next planned to release the three record–set anthology *Decade*, but it was deferred in favor of *American Stars 'n' Bars*, which featured Crazy Horse on one side and the vocal assistance of Linda Ronstadt, Emmylou Harris, and Nicolette Larson. The album contained the potent "Like a Hurricane" and the humorous "Homegrown." *Decade* followed in 1978, compiling material from Young's days with both the Buffalo Springfield and Crosby, Stills and Nash, as well as Young solo material and five previously unreleased songs, including "Love Is a Rose," later popularized by Linda Ronstadt.

Neil Young mounted his first major tour in nearly two years with Crazy Horse in fall 1978 in support of *Comes a Time*, his most accessible album since *Harvest*, and Crazy Horse's *Crazy Moon* on RCA Records. The tour, filmed and recorded, yielded the flawed 1979 movie *Rust Never Sleeps* and the double-record set *Live Rust*, which includes Young's "Lotta Love," a near-smash hit for Nicolette Larson in 1978–1979. The studio album *Rust Never Sleeps* contains one acoustic side and one side recorded with Crazy Horse. It yielded a minor hit with the anthemic "Hey Hey, My My (Into the Black)," reprised in "My My, Hey Hey (Out of the Blue)" as a tribute to the Sex Pistols' Johnny Rotten, while containing "Thrasher," "Powderfinger," and the unusual social commentary "Welfare Mothers." *Hawks and Doves*, recorded with session musicians, was followed by Neil Young and Crazy Horse's *re-ac-tor* in late 1981.

Neil Young subsequently switched to Geffen Records for the strange, synthesizer-dominated *Trans* and rockabilly-style *Everybody's Rockin'*, recorded with a band called the Shocking Pinks. Touring regularly in the 1980s, he next recorded the country-style *Old Ways* with Bela Fleck and Nashville studio veterans Ralph Mooney and Hargus "Pig" Robbins. He co-founded the Farm Aid benefit concert in 1985 with Willie Nelson, and he performed at it. Young mounted the most ambitious tour of his career with Crazy Horse in support of 1986's *Landing on Water*. In 1987 Young began hosting annual benefits in the San Francisco Bay Area for the Bridge School, a program for physically disabled, nonspeaking children that regularly drew top-name performers.

After *Life*, Neil Young returned to Reprise Records for the big-band, blues-style *This Note's for You* in 1987, which featured the satirical title song, a parody of the Budweiser beer commercial. The video for the song was at first rejected by MTV because it attacked the increasing commercialism in rock music. Two years later, his *Freedom* album, with "Wrecking Ball" and the anthemic "Rockin' in the Free World," became his best-selling album in years. In 1990 Crazy Horse recorded their first album in more than 10 years, *Left for Dead*, and accompanied Young on *Ragged Glory*, which includes "F9*!#in' Up," "Mansion on the Hill," and "Love and Only Love."

Freedom and *Ragged Glory* helped reestablish Young as a contemporary recording artist, drawing comparisons to his finest previous work. Dubbed the Godfather of Grunge, he demonstrated his interest in current music by booking SonicYouth as his opening act during his 1991 tour with Crazy Horse. Late that year Young issued *Weld*, recorded on tour, and *Arc*, a 35-minute set comprised of feedback and electronic shrieks. The two sets were released simultaneously with a third set, *ArcWeld*, that combined both albums.

Neil Young enjoyed his greatest acclaim in years during the 1990s. He returned to the acoustic sound of folk rock with 1992's *Harvest Moon*, inappropriately labeled the follow-up to 1972's *Harvest*. Recorded with the Stray Gators, the band who helped record *Harvest*, the album failed to produce a hit single, although the video for the title track received wide play on both MTV and VH-1, and the album proved to be his most popular since 1979's *Live Rust*. Young's performance on the MTV show *Unplugged* was recorded and issued in 1993, followed a year later by *Sleeps with Angels*, recorded with Crazy Horse, which included his title song lament to Kurt Cobain. Young substituted for an ill Eddie Vedder at a Pearl Jam concert in San Francisco in June 1995. Only days later, Reprise issued *Mirror Ball*, recorded with Pearl Jam as his backing band. The album featured Vedder sharing vocals with Young on the title song, "Peace and Love," cowritten by Vedder, and "Throw Your Hatred Down," "Act of Love," and "I'm the Ocean."

Disc.: **NEIL YOUNG:** *N. Y.* (1969); *After the Goldrush* (1970); *Harvest* (1972); *Journey Through the Past* (soundtrack; 1972); *Time Fades Away* (1973); *On the Beach* (1974); *Tonight's the Night* (1975); *Decade* (1977); *Comes a Time* (1978); *Hawks and Doves* (1980); *Trans* (1983); *Old Ways* (1985); *Landing on Water* (1986); *Lucky Thirteen* (1993); *Freedom* (1989); *Arc* (1991); *Harvest Moon* (1992); *Unplugged* (1993); *Mirror Ball* (1995). **THE ROCKETS:** *The Rockets* (1968). **NEIL YOUNG AND CRAZY HORSE:** *Everybody Knows This Is Nowhere* (1969); *Zuma* (1975); *Rust Never Sleeps* (1979); *Live Rust* (1979); *re-ac-tor* (1981); *Life* (1987); *Ragged Glory* (1990); *Weld* (1991); *Arc Weld* (1991); *Sleeps with Angels* (1994); *Broken Arrow* (1996). **NEIL YOUNG, CRAZY HORSE, AND THE BULLETS:** *American Stars 'n' Bars* (1977). **CRAZY HORSE:** *Crazy Horse* (1971); *Loose* (1972); *At Crooked Lake* (1972); *Crazy Moon* (1978); *Left for Dead* (1990). **THE STILLS-YOUNG BAND:** *Long May You Run* (1976). **NEIL YOUNG AND THE SHOCKING PINKS:** *Everybody's Rockin'* (1983). **NEIL YOUNG AND THE BLUENOTES:** *This Note's for You* (1988).

Bibl.: C. Dufrechou, *N. Y.* (N.Y., 1978); J. Rogan, *N. Y.: The Definitive Story of His Musical Career* (London, 1982).—**BH**

Young, Percy M(arshall), English writer on music; b. Northwich, Cheshire, May 17, 1912. He studied English, music, and history as an organ scholar at Selwyn Coll., Cambridge (B.A., 1933; Mus.B., 1934), then went to Dublin, where he graduated from Trinity Coll. (Mus.D., 1937); upon his return to England, he took courses with C.B. Rootham and E.J. Dent in Cambridge. He subsequently occupied various teaching posts; from 1944 to 1966, was director of music at the Coll. of Technology in Wolverhampton. He publ. a number of arrangements of early English songs, and also composed some vocal pieces and a *Fugal Concerto* for 2 pianos and strings (1954). However, he is known principally for his scholarly biographical studies and essays.

Writings (all publ. in London unless otherwise given): *Samuel Pepys' Music Book* (1942); *Handel* (1947; 3rd ed., rev., 1979); *The Oratorios of Handel* (1953); *Messiah: A Study in Interpretation* (1951); *A Critical Dictionary of Composers and Their Music* (1954; U.S. ed. as *Biographical Dictionary of Composers*); *Elgar, O.M.: A Study of a Musician* (1955; 2nd ed., 1973); ed. *Letters of Edward Elgar and Other Writings* (1956); *Tragic Muse: The Life and Works of Robert Schumann* (1957; 2nd ed., rev., 1961); *The Choral Tradition: An Historical and Analytical Survey from the 16th Century to the Present Day* (1962; 2nd ed., rev., 1982); *Zoltán Kodály* (1964); ed. *Letters to Nimrod from Edward Elgar* (1965); *A History of British Music* (1967); *Keyboard Musicians of the World* (1967); ed. *Elgar: A Future for English Music and Other Lectures* (1968); *Debussy* (1969); *The Bachs, 1500–1850* (1970); *Sir Arthur Sullivan* (1971); *A Concise History of Music* (1974); *Beethoven: A Victorian Tribute* (1976); *Alice Elgar: Enigma of a Victorian Lady* (1977); *George Grove* (1980); *Mozart* (1987); *Elgar, Newman and the Dream of Gerontius: In the Tradition of English Catholicism* (Brookfield, Vt., 1995).—**NS/LK/DM**

Young, Victor, American pianist and composer; b. Bristol, Tenn., April 9, 1889; d. Ossining, N.Y., Sept. 2, 1968. He studied piano with Isidor Philipp in Paris. He toured in England and the U.S. as accompanist to prominent singers; held various teaching positions; was music director in Thomas A. Edison's Experimental Laboratory in West Orange, N.J., conducting tonal tests and making piano recordings under Edison's personal supervision (1919–27). He wrote the musical score for one of the earliest sound films, *In Old California*; composed some 300 film scores altogether; also wrote, for orch., *Scherzetto, Jeep, In the Great Smokies, Charm Assembly Line Ballet*, etc.; piano pieces.—**NS/LK/DM**

Young, William, English viol player and composer; b. place and date unknown; d. Innsbruck, April 23, 1662. By at least 1652 he was in the service of the Archduke Ferdinand Karl in Innsbruck, and accompanied him on sojourns to Italy. Another William Young, who was a violinist in the royal music of Charles II in London (1660–71), may have been his son. The elder Young was a distinguished composer of music for the viol. His publ. works comprise *Almain and Sarabande* for Lyra-viol (1651), and 11 *Sonate à 3, 4, 5 voci con alcune allemand, correnti e balletti à 3* (Innsbruck, 1653; 11 sonatas and 4 suites ed. in 1930); various other instrumental works remain in MS.

Bibl.: W. Whittaker, *The Concerted Music of W. Y.* (Oxford, 1931).—**NS/LK/DM**

Youngbloods, The, West Coast hippie-rock band of the late 1960s. **Membership:** Jesse Colin Young, voc., gtr., bs. (b. Perry Miller on Nov. 11, 1944, N.Y.C.); Jerry Corbitt, gtr., bs., voc. (b. 1946, Tifton, Ga.); Lowell "Banana" Levinger, kybd., gtr., bjo., mdln., pno. (b. 1946, Cambridge, Mass.); and Joe Bauer, drm. (b. Sept. 26, 1941, Memphis, Tenn.; d. 1988).

Jesse Colin Young dropped out of college and assumed his stage name in 1963 to play East Coast folk clubs. He recorded one album for Capitol before switching to Mercury, where he recorded *Jesse Colin Young and The Youngbloods* with Peter Childs and John Sebastian. During 1965, he formed a duet with Jerry Corbitt, adding Lowell "Banana" Levinger and Joe Bauer by year's end. As The Youngbloods, the group performed as the house band at N.Y.'s Cafe A-Go-Go and signed with RCA Records, achieving their first minor hit with the silly dance ditty "Grizzly Bear" by Corbitt. Their RCA debut album included "Get Together" by Chester Powers (a.k.a. Dino Valenti), a minor hit in 1967 and a smash hit upon re- release in 1969. *Earth Music*, recorded in N.Y.C., contained Young's "All My Dreams Blue" and "The Wine Song," the ditty "Euphoria," and an excellent version of Tim Hardin's "Reason to Believe." In late 1967, Corbitt left The Youngbloods for a solo career, and the others continued as a trio, moving to the San Francisco Bay area. *Elephant Mountain*, recorded in Hollywood with Charlie Daniels as principal producer, came to be regarded as their finest album. It included "Rain Song," several gentle Young songs such as "Sunlight," "Beautiful," and "Ride the Wind," and two rather ominous Young songs, "Darkness, Darkness" and "Quicksand." In 1970, The Youngbloods signed with Warner Brothers Records and formed their own label, Raccoon. However, none of the albums for the label by

The Youngbloods, Bauer, Young, and two spinoff groups featuring Bauer and Banana sold particularly well, and by 1972 the group had broken up.

Jesse Colin Young's first solo album for Warner Brothers, *Song for Juli*, contained idyllic songs such as "Morning Sun," "High on a Ridgetop," and "Country Home," as well as the title song, written for his daughter. The album became the best-selling album of his solo career, although he continued to record for Warner Brothers through 1977. He switched to Elektra for *American Dreams* and eventually recorded *The Highway Is for Heroes* for Cypress Records. In the 1990s, he re-emerged with *Swept Away* on his own Ridgetop label.

DISC.: JESSE COLIN YOUNG: *The Soul of a City Boy* (1964); *Jesse Colin Young and The Youngbloods* (1965); *Two Trips with Jesse Colin Young* (1970); *Together* (1972); *Song for Juli* (1973); *Light Shine* (1974); *Songbird* (1975); *On the Road* (1976); *Love on the Wing* (1977); *American Dreams* (1978); *The Highway Is for Heroes* (1987); *Swept Away* (1994). **THE YOUNGBLOODS:** *The Youngbloods* (1967); *Earth Music* (1967); *Elephant Mountain* (1969); *Rock Festival* (1970); *Ride the Wind* (1971); *Sunlight* (1971); *Good and Dusty* (1971); *High on a Ridgetop* (1972). **JERRY CORBITT:** *Corbitt* (1969); *Jerry Corbitt* (1971). **JOE BAUER:** *Moonset* (1971). **BANANA AND THE BUNCH:** *Mid-Mountain Ranch* (1972).—**BH**

(Young) Rascals, The, white R&B popsters of the 1960s; **MEMBERSHIP:** Felix Cavaliere, org., voc. (b. Pelham, N.Y., Nov. 29, 1943); Eddie Brigati, perc., voc. (b. Garfield, N.J., Oct. 22, 1946); Gene Cornish, gtr. (b. Ottawa, Ontario, Canada, May 14, 1945); Dino Danelli, drm. (b. Jersey City, N.J., July 23, 1945).

The Young Rascals were formed in Garfield, N.J., in 1964 by Dino Danelli and three former members of Joey Dee's Starliters, Felix Cavaliere, Gene Cornish, and Eddie Brigati. Cavaliere had performed with the high school group The Stereos and led Felix and The Escorts while attending Syracuse Univ. The Young Rascals debuted at the local Choo Choo Club in February 1965 and developed a reputation as an exciting live act. Playing R&B–style music centered around the vocals and organ playing of Cavaliere, the group graduated to Manhattan clubs by the fall of 1965.

Signed to Atlantic Records by Ahment Ertegun, The Young Rascals' second single, "Good Lovin," a cover version of The Olympics' minor 1965 hit, became a top pop hit in early 1966 and was followed by the major hits "You Better Run" (written by Cavaliere and Brigati) and "I've Been Lonely Too Long" (by Cavaliere). Their first two R&B–styled albums became best-sellers, yet they adopted a lighter sound for *Groovin'*. The album yielded a top pop and smash R&B hit with the title song and smash pop hits with "A Girl Like You" and "How Can I Be Sure," all three written by Cavaliere and Brigati.

After another major hit with "It's Wonderful," The Young Rascals became simply The Rascals for the smash pop hit "A Beautiful Morning," by Cavaliere and Brigati. *Freedom Suite*, a double-record set that included an entire instrumental record entitled "Music Music," yielded the top pop and major rhythm-and-blues hit "People Got to Be Free" and the major hit "A Ray of Hope," both by Cavaliere and Brigati. "See" and "Carry Me" became major hits for The Rascals, but, by the time the group had switched to Columbia Records in 1971, only Cavaliere and Danelli remained. The group disbanded in 1972 after two poor-selling albums for the label. The Rascals were inducted into the Rock and Roll Hall of Fame in 1997.

In late 1972, Gene Cornish and Dino Danelli formed Bulldog, managing a moderate hit with "No." Later in the decade, they formed Fotomaker with Wally Bryson, former lead guitarist for The Raspberries. Felix Cavaliere surfaced as a solo artist on Bearsville Records in 1974 and manned the group Treasure in 1977. He eventually scored a moderate solo hit with "Only a Lonely Heart Sees" on Epic in 1980. Eddie Brigati joined his brother David, another former member of Joey Dee's Starliters, for a neglected album on Elektra Records in 1976.

In 1988, Felix Cavaliere, Gene Cornish, and Dino Danelli reunited as The Rascals for the 40th anniversary concert of Atlantic Records and subsequently conducted a national tour. Danelli and Cornish began touring as The New Rascals in 1989. In 1994, Felix Cavaliere returned to recording with *Dreams in Motion* for producer Don Was's new Karambolage label.

DISC.: THE YOUNG RASCALS: *The Young Rascals* (1966); *Collections* (1967); *Groovin'* (1967). **THE RASCALS:** *Once upon a Dream* (1968); *Freedom Suite* (1969); *See* (1970); *Search and Nearness* (1971); *Peaceful World* (1971); *The Island of Real* (1972); *Searching for Ecstasy: The Rest of The Rascals, 1969–72* (1986). **BULLDOG (WITH GENE CORNISH AND DINO DANELLI):** *Bulldog* (1972); *Smasher* (1974). **FOTOMAKER (WITH GENE CORNISH AND DINO DANELLI):** *Fotomaker* (1978); *Vis-a-vis* (1978); *Transfer Station* (1979). **FELIX CAVALIERE:** *Felix Cavaliere* (1974); *Destiny* (1975); *Castles in the Air* (1980); *Dreams in Motion* (1994). **TREASURE (WITH FELIX CAVALIERE):** *Treasure* (1977). **BRIGATI:** *Lost in the Wilderness* (1976).—**BH**

Youssoupoff, Prince Nikolai Borisovich, Russian musical dilettante and writer on music; b. St. Petersburg, 1827; d. Baden-Baden, Aug. 3, 1891. He studied violin with Vieuxtemps, and was an eager collector of violin literature; had a private orch. in his palace in St. Petersburg, but lived abroad for many years. He composed a programmatic sym., *Gonzalvo de Córdova*, with violin obbligato, *Concerto symphonique* for violin and orch., and several pieces for violin and piano (*Féeries de la scène, Hallucination, Chant d'amour, Plainte, Saltimbanques*, etc.). He also publ. an interesting book on violin making, *Luthomonographie, historique et raisonnée: Essai sur l'histoire du violon et sur les ouvrages des anciens luthiers célèbres du temps de la Renaissance, par un amateur* (Frankfurt am Main, 1862), and *Musique sacrée suivie d'un choix de morceaux de chants d'église* (Paris, 1862, as Vol. I of a projected *Histoire de la musique en Russie*; contains a valuable study of Russian neumes and examples of traditional chants). Themes from Youssoupoff's *Ballet d'Espagne* were used by Bériot for a group of 6 violin duets.—**NS/LK/DM**

Yo-Yo, Ma
See **Ma, Yo-Yo**

Yradier (Iradier), Sebastian de, Spanish song composer; b. Sauciego, Álava, Jan. 20, 1809; d. Vitoria, Dec. 6, 1865. He composed theater music. After 1851, he became singing master to the Empress Eugénie in Paris; for some time he lived in Cuba. He publ. a number of melodious songs in a Spanish manner; one of them, *El arreglito*, subtitled *Chanson havanaise*, was used by Bizet for the famous *Habanera* in *Carmen*; Bizet retained the key and the pattern of the accompaniment, making minor changes in the melody to adjust it to French words. Yradier's other songs that became famous are *La paloma* and *Ay Chiquita!* In Paris he publ. 2 collections, *Echo d'Espagne* (8 songs) and *Fleurs d'Espagne* (25 songs). **—NS/LK/DM**

Yriarte (Iriarte), Tomás de, Spanish poet and musician; b. Puerto de la Cruz de Orotava, Tenerife, Canary Islands, Sept. 18, 1750; d. Santa Maria, near Cádiz, Sept. 17, 1791. He studied in Madrid. He was secretary at the Chancellery of State in Madrid and chief archivist at the Ministry of War. His literary works include a long didactic poem, *La música* (Madrid, 1779; Eng. tr., 1807). He composed tonadillas and some vocal and instrumental music.

BIBL.: E. Cotarelo y Mori, *I. y su época* (Madrid, 1897); J. Subira, *El compositor I. y el cultivo español del melólogo* (2 vols., Madrid, 1949–50); R. Cox, *T. d.I.* (N.Y., 1972).**—NS/LK/DM**

Ysaÿe, Eugène (-Auguste), famous Belgian violinist, conductor, and composer, brother of **Théophile Ysaÿe;** b. Liège, July 16, 1858; d. Brussels, May 12, 1931. At the age of 4, he began to study violin with his father, a theater conductor, and at the age of 7 he was enrolled at the Liège Cons. as a pupil of Désiré Heynberg, winning 2nd prize in 1867. In 1869 he left the Cons. in a dispute with his mentor, but was readmitted in 1872 as a pupil of Rodolphe Massart, winning 1st prize in 1873 and the silver medal in 1874; then continued his training on a scholarship at the Brussels Cons. with Wieniawski; later completed his studies with Vieuxtemps in Paris (1876–79). In 1879 he became concertmaster of Bilse's orch. in Berlin; appeared as a soloist at Pauline Lucca's concerts in Cologne and Aachen; in Germany he met Anton Rubinstein, who took him to Russia, where he spent 2 winters; he also toured in Norway. In 1883 he settled in Paris, where he met Franck, d'Indy et al., and gave successful concerts; he formed a duo with the pianist Raoul Pugno, and started a long series of concerts with him, establishing a new standard of excellence. On Sept. 26, 1886, he married Louise Bourdeau; Franck dedicated his violin sonata to them as a wedding present; Ysaÿe's interpretation of this work made it famous. In 1886 he was named a prof. at the Brussels Cons. (resigned in 1898); in 1886 he also organized the Ysaÿe Quartet (with Crickboom, Léon Van Hout, and Joseph Jacob); Debussy dedicated his string quartet to Ysaÿe's group, which gave its first performance at the Société Nationale in Paris on Dec. 29, 1893. In 1889 Ysaÿe made successful appearances in England. On Nov. 16, 1894, he made his American debut playing the Beethoven Violin Concerto with the N.Y. Phil., and creating a sensation by his virtuosity. He revisited America many times, with undiminished acclaim. He began his career as a conductor in 1894, and established in Brussels his own orch., the Société des Concerts Ysaÿe. When the Germans invaded Belgium in 1914, he fled to London, where he remained during World War I. On April 5, 1918, he made his American debut as a conductor with the Cincinnati Sym. Orch., and also led the Cincinnati May Festival in that year. His success was so great that he was offered a permanent position as conductor of the Cincinnati Sym. Orch., which he held from 1918 to 1922. He then returned to Belgium and resumed leadership of the Société des Concerts Ysaÿe. After the death of his first wife, he married, on July 9, 1927, an American pupil, Jeannette Dincin.

Ysaÿe's style of playing is best described as heroic, but his art was equally convincing in the expression of moods of exquisite delicacy and tenderness; his frequent employment of "tempo rubato" produced an effect of elasticity without distorting the melodic line. His works include 8 violin concertos; 6 sonatas for solo violin; *Poème nocturne* for violin, cello, and strings; *Les Harmonies du soir* for string quartet and string orch.; *Divertimento* for violin and orch.; *Méditation* for cello and string orch.; *Chant d'hiver* for violin and chamber orch.; *Trio de concert* for 2 violins, viola, and orch.; *Amitié* for 2 violins and orch. At the age of 70, he began the composition of an opera in the Walloon language, *Piér li Houïeu* (Peter the Miner), which was premiered in Liège on March 4, 1931, in the presence of the composer, who was brought to the theater in an invalid's chair, suffering from the extreme ravages of diabetes, which had necessitated the amputation of his left foot. He began the composition of a 2nd Walloon opera, *L'Avierge di Piér* (La Vierge de Pierre), but had no time to complete it. In 1937 Queen Elisabeth of Belgium inaugurated the annual Prix International Eugene Ysaÿe in Brussels; the first winner was David Oistrakh.

BIBL.: E. Christen, *Y.* (Geneva, 1946; 2nd ed., 1947); A. Ysaÿe and B. Ratcliffe, *Y.: His Life, Work and Influence* (London, 1947); A. Ysaÿe, *E. Y.: Sa vie d'après les documents receuillis par son fils* (Brussels, 1948; a considerably altered version of the preceding; Eng. tr., 1980, as *Y., By His Son Antoine*); A. Ysaÿe, *E. Y., 1858–1931* (Brussels, 1972); M. Benoît-Jeannin, *E. Y.: Le dernier romantique ou le sacre du violon* (Brussels, 1989); M. Stockhem, *E. Y. et la musique de chambre* (Liège, 1990).**—NS/LK/DM**

Ysaÿe, Théophile, Belgian pianist and composer, brother of **Eugène (-Auguste) Ysaÿe;** b. Verviers, March 22, 1865; d. Nice, March 24, 1918. He was a pupil at the Liège Cons. (1876–80), then studied at the Kullak Academy in Berlin (from 1881), and took lessons from Franck in Paris (1885). Returning to Belgium, he became director of the Académie de Musique in Brussels. He was noted as a fine ensemble player, and gave sonata recitals with his brother; during the latter's absence on tours, he also conducted the Société des Concerts Ysaÿe in Brussels. After the invasion of Belgium in 1914, he went with his brother to London; fearful of the Zeppelin air raids on London, he went to Nice, where he remained until his death. He was a prolific composer; his brother conducted a concert of Théophile's works in Brussels, on Nov. 6, 1904, including the premieres of his Sym. in

F major and the symphonic poem *Le Cygne*. Other works were a piano concerto, symphonic poems, *Fantaisie sur un thème populaire wallon* for orch., piano Quintet, piano pieces, and a requiem.—**NS/LK/DM**

Yttrehus, Rolv (Berger), American composer and teacher; b. Duluth, March 12, 1926. He was educated at the Univ. of Minn. in Duluth (B.S. in music, 1950), the Univ. of Mich. (M.M., 1953), and the Accademia di Santa Cecilia in Rome (diploma, 1962). His mentors in composition were Ross Lee Finney (1950–53), Roger Sessions (1957–60), Aaron Copland (1958), and Goffredo Petrassi (1960–62). He also received instruction in harmony from Nadia Boulanger (1954–55). He taught at the Univ. of Mo. (1963–68), Purdue Univ. (1968–69), the Univ. of Wisc. in Oshkosh (1969–77), and Rutgers, the State Univ. of N.J. (1977–96), where he subsequently was prof. emeritus. Yttrehus's music has been performed on both sides of the Atlantic, and frequently in N.Y. by various ensembles. Schoenberg and Sessions have been principal influences on his works, which may be characterized as dramatic and rhythmically energetic. He uses the 12 tone system in his explorations of what he refers to as the two energies of music: the rhythmic energy of upbeat-downbeat and shifted accents, and the harmonic-melodic energy of dissonance.

WORKS: ORCH.: Overture (1952); *Fantasy* (1953); *Espressioni* (1962); Sym. No. 1 (1995; rev. version, Warsaw, Sept. 1998). **Band:** *Prelude, 1950* (1950). **CHAMBER:** *Cosmophography* for 4 Clarinets (1948); Violin Sonata (1951); Duo for Violin and Viola (1954); Quartet for Flute and Strings (1955); *2 Movements* for String Quartet (1960); *Music* for Winds, Percussion, and Viola (1961); Sextet for Horn, Trumpet, Violin, Double Bass, Piano, and Percussion (1964–70; rev. 1974); *Music* for Winds, Percussion, Cello, Voices, and Tape (1969); Quintet for Flute, Clarinet, Violin, Cello, and Piano (1973); Percussion Sonata (1983; rev. 1988); Cello Sonata (1988); *Plectrum Spectrum* for Chamber Group (2000). **KEYBOARD: Piano:** *6 Pieces* (1957); *Explorations* (1985); *Raritan Variation* (1989). **VOCAL:** *6 Haiku* for Soprano, Flute, Cello, and Harp (1959); *Angstwagen* for Soprano and Percussion (1971; rev. 1981); *Gradus ad Parnassum* for Soprano, Chamber Orch., and Tape, after Nietzsche and J.J. Fux (1974–79).—**NS/LK/DM**

Yuasa, Jōji, Japanese composer and teacher; b. Koriyama, Aug. 12, 1929. He was a premed student at Keio Univ. As a composer, he was autodidact. In 1952 he became active with the Jikkenkobo (Experimental Workshop) in Tokyo. In 1968–69 he held a Japan Soc. fellowship. He served as composer-in-residence at the Univ. of Calif. at San Diego in 1976, and then was in Berlin under the auspices of the Deutscher Akademischer Austauschdienst in 1976–77. From 1981 to 1984 he was on the faculty of the Univ. of Calif. at San Diego, and then was a teacher in the art dept. of the graduate school at Nihon Univ. and at the Tokyo Coll. of Music. Yuasa has received numerous commissions and honors. In 1966 and 1967 he won the Prix Italia. He received the Otaka Prize in 1972, 1988, and 1997. In 1973 and 1983 he took the Grand Prize at the Japan Arts Festival. He won the Hida-Furukawa Music Grand Prize in 1995, the same year that he received the Kyoto Music Grand Prize. In 1996 he won the Suntory Music Prize. In his output, Yuasa has found inspiration in both the Western and non-Western traditions.

WORKS: DRAMATIC: Film scores. **ORCH.:** *Projection—Flower, Bird, Wind, Moon* for 8 Kotos and Orch. (Bunka Hoso, Nov. 24, 1967); *Chronoplastic—Between Stasis and Kinesis* (NHK, Tokyo, Nov. 15, 1972); *TIME of Orchestral Time* (1975–76; Tokyo, April 23, 1977); *Requiem* (1980); *Suite SCENES from Bashô* (1980–89; 1st complete perf., N.Y., Feb. 23, 1990); *A Perspective for Orchestra* (NHK, Tokyo, Nov. 1983); *Revealed Time* for Viola and Orch. (Tokyo, Oct. 3, 1986); *Hommage à Sibelius—The Midnight Sun* (Helsinki, May 3, 1991); *Eye on Genesis II* (Tokyo, May 1, 1992); Piano Concertino (Nagoya, Sept. 24, 1994); *The Narrow Road into the Deep North: Bashô* (Koriyama, April 8, 1995); Violin Concerto, *In Memory of Toru Takemitsu* (Tokyo, Oct. 28, 1996); *Tokugawa Yoshinobu* (1998). **CHAMBER:** *Projection* for 7 Players (Tokyo, July 12, 1955); *Interpenetration I* for 2 Flutes (Tokyo, July 1, 1963) and *II* for 2 Percussionists (Tokyo, June 4, 1983); *Projection* for Cello and Piano (Tokyo, Oct. 11, 1967); *Projection—Arrogance of the Dead* for Electric Guitar(s) (NHK, Tokyo, June 7, 1968); *Triplicity* for Double Bass (Honolulu, July 1970); *Projection I* (Honolulu, July 1970) and *II* (Tokyo, Nov. 27, 1996) for String Quartet; *Inter-posi-play-tion I* for Flute, Piano, and 2 Percussion (Tokyo, Nov. 5, 1971) and *II* for Flute, Harp, and Percussion (Tokyo, Dec. 19, 1973); *Territory* for Marimba, Flute, Clarinet, Percussion, and Double Bas (1974); *Not I, but the Wind...* for Amplified Alto Saxophone (1976); *My Blue Sky No. 3* for Violin (Berlin, May 1977); *Domain* for Flute (Tokyo, Feb. 17, 1978); *Clarinet Solitude* for Clarinet (Tokyo, Sept. 19, 1980); *A Winter Day—Hommage to Bashô* for Flute, Clarinet, Percussion, Harp, and Piano (Toronto, Feb. 14, 1981); *Mai-Bataraki II* for Alto Flute or Noh Flute (Los Angeles, March 20, 1987); *Nine Levels by Ze Ami* for Chamber Ensemble and Quadraphonic Computer-generated Tape (1987–88; Paris, April 11, 1988); *Terms of Temporal Detailing* for Bass Flute (San Diego, June 1989); *Viola Locus* for Viola (Yono, Nov. 25, 1995); *JO HA KYU* for 5 Players (1995–96; 1st complete perf., Yono, April 13, 1996); *Solitude in Memoriam T. T.* for Violin, Cello, and Piano (N.Y., Feb. 8, 1997); *Reigaku* for Alto Flute (Berlin, Sept. 17, 1997); *Cosmos Haptic IV* for Cello and Piano (Tokyo, Oct. 31, 1997). **KEYBOARD: Piano:** *2 Pastorals* (Tokyo, Aug. 9, 1952); *Three Score Set* (Tokyo, Sept. 1953); *Serenade: Chant pour "Do"* (1954); *Cosmos Haptic I* (Tokyo, June 22, 1957) and *II—Transfiguration* (Yokohama, Feb. 21, 1986); *Projection Topologic* (Karuisawa, Aug. 19, 1959); *Projection Esemplastic* (1961; Tokyo, Feb. 23, 1962); *On the Keyboard* (Tokyo, Feb. 15, 1972); *Melodies* (Tokyo, July 11, 1997). **VOCAL:** *Kansoku* for Voices (1964); *Questions* for Chorus (Tokyo, March 9, 1971); *Utterance* for Chorus (Tokyo, Dec. 5, 1971); *"Calling Together"* for Chorus (1973; Tokyo, Feb. 6, 1974); *Projection on Bashô's Haiku* for Chorus and Vibraphone (Tokyo, Nov. 11, 1974); *Projection Onomatopoetic* for Chorus (Tokyo, April 19, 1979); *Asakano Eishô* for Women's Chorus (Koriyama, Aug. 7, 1982); *Observations on Weather Forecasts* for Baritone and Trumpet (Tokyo, June 1, 1983); *Composition on Ze-Ami's Nine Grades* for Men's Chorus (1983–84; Tokyo, Oct. 1984); *Shin Kiyari Kanda Sanka* for Men's Chorus and 5 or More Shakuhachi (Tokyo, Oct. 1, 1984); *Uta Asobi* (Play Songs) *on Onomatopoeia* for Children's Chorus (Tokyo, Nov. 30, 1985); *Mutterings* for Soprano or Mezzo-soprano and 7 Players (Lerchenborg, July 31, 1988); *Phonomatopoeia* for Chorus (Tokyo, Oct. 25, 1991); *Responsorium* for the *Requiem for Reconciliation* for Soprano, Alto, Tenor, Baritone, Chorus, and Orch. (Stuttgart, Aug. 16, 1995); *Cosmic Solitude* for

Baritone, Chorus, and Orch. (Stuttgart, Sept. 11, 1997). **ELECTRONIC:** *Aoi no Ue* (1961; N.Y., Dec. 1968); *Icon on the Source of White Noise* (NHK, Tokyo, March 1967); *Voices Coming* (NHK, Tokyo, Sept. 1969); *Music for Space Projection* (Osaka, Sept. 1970); *My Blue Sky No. 1* (NHK, Tokyo, Oct. 1975) and *No. 2—In Southern California* (1976); *Towards "The Midnight Sun"* (N.Y., June 3, 1984); *A Study in White* (San Francisco, May 1987); *Eye on Genesis for UPIC* (Fukushima, Aug. 21, 1991). **OTHER:** *Koto Uta Bashô's Five Haiku* for Koto and 17-gen Koto (Tokyo, Nov. 6, 1978); *Mai-Bataraki from Ritual for Delphi* for Shakuhachi and Percussion (Delphi, Oct. 16, 1979); *Ishibutai Kô* for Ryuteki, 3 Shakuhachis, 17-gen Koto, and 2 Percussion (NHK, Tokyo, Nov. 1981); *To the Genesis* for Sho (Tokyo, March 18, 1988); *Fûshi Gyô-Un* for Alto, Tenor, and Traditional Japanese Instruments (Tokyo, June 29, 1988); *Cosmos Haptic—Kokuh* for 20-gen Koto and Shakuhachi (Tokyo, Dec. 10, 1990).—**NS/LK/DM**

Yudina, Maria, eminent Russian pianist and pedagogue; b. Nevel, near Vitebsk, Sept. 9, 1899; d. Moscow, Nov. 19, 1970. She took piano lessons in Vitebsk with Frieda Teitelbaum-Levinson, then enrolled at the Petrograd Cons., where she studied piano with Anna Essipova, Vladimir Drozdov, and Leonid Nikolayev, theory with Maximilian Steinberg and J. Wihtol, and score reading with N. Tcherepnin and Emil Cooper. In 1921 she joined the piano faculty of the Petrograd Cons., holding this position until 1930. From 1932 to 1934 she taught at the Tiflis Cons. From 1936 to 1951 she was a prof. at the Moscow Cons., and from 1944 to 1960 taught piano and chamber music performance at the Gnessin Inst. in Moscow. Among her students was Andrei Balanchivadze. Yudina began her career as a pianist in 1921, and gave her last concert in Moscow on May 18, 1969. She also was a guest artist in East Germany (1950) and in Poland (1954). She publ. memoirs and reminiscences of famous composers she had met in Russia. Yudina enjoyed great renown as an intellectual musician capable of presenting the works she performed with a grand line, both didactic and inspired. But rather than accepting the traditional interpretation of classical music, she introduced a strong personal element differing from accepted norms, so that her performances of works by Bach, Mozart, Beethoven, and Brahms were revelations to some listeners, and abominations to the old school of pianism. Yudina was also an ardent champion of modern music, placing on her programs compositions by such masters of new techniques as Stravinsky, Schoenberg, Berg, Webern, and Bartók at a time when their works were not acceptable in Russia. She also played piano pieces by Soviet composers, particularly Prokofiev and Shostakovich. She gave numerous concerts of chamber music. A vol. of her articles, reminiscences, and materials was publ. in Moscow in 1978.—**NS/LK/DM**

Yun, Isang, important Korean-born German composer and teacher; b. Tongyong, Sept. 17, 1917; d. Berlin, Nov. 3, 1995. He studied Western music in Korea (1935–37) and in Japan (1941–43). During World War II, he was active in the anti-Japanese underground; in 1943 he was imprisoned, and then spent the rest of the war in hiding until the liberation in 1945. He became a music teacher in Tongyong in 1946, and later taught in Pusan; in 1953 he became a prof. of composition at the Univ. of Seoul; then studied with Revel at the Paris Cons. (1956–57) and with Blacher, Rufer, and Schwarz-Schilling at the Berlin Hochschule für Musik (1958–59); also attended the summer courses in new music in Darmstadt. He settled permanently in Berlin, where he produced several successful theatrical works, marked by a fine expressionistic and coloristic quality, and written in an idiom of euphonious dissonance. His career was dramatically interrupted when, on June 17, 1967, he and his wife were brutally abducted from West Berlin by secret police agents of South Korea, and forced to board a plane for Seoul, where they were brought to trial for sedition; he was sentenced to life imprisonment; his wife was given 3 years in jail. This act of lawlessness perpetrated on the territory of another country prompted an indignant protest by the government of West Germany, which threatened to cut off its substantial economic aid to South Korea; 23 celebrated musicians, including Stravinsky, issued a vigorous letter of protest. As a result of this moral and material pressure, South Korea released Yun and his wife after nearly 2 years of detention, and they returned to Germany. In 1969–70 he taught at the Hannover Hochschue für Musik. In 1970 he was appointed lecturer in composition at the Berlin Hochschule für Musik, where he was a prof. from 1973 to 1985. In 1971 he became a naturalized German citizen.

WORKS: DRAMATIC: Opera: *Der Traum des Liu-Tung* (Berlin, Sept. 25, 1965); *Träume* (1965–68; Nuremberg, Feb. 23, 1969; an amalgam of the preceding opera and the following one); *Die Witwe des Schmetterlings* (Bonn, Dec. 9, 1967; Eng. version as *Butterfly Widow*, Evanston, Ill., Feb. 27, 1970); *Geisterliebe* (1969–70; Kiel, June 20, 1971); *Sim Tjong* (1971–72; Munich, Aug. 1, 1972). **ORCH.:** *Symphonische Szenen* (1960; Darmstadt, Sept. 7, 1961); *Bara* (1960; Berlin, Jan. 19, 1962); *Colloides sonores* for Strings (Hamburg, Dec. 12, 1961); *Fluktuationen* (1964; Berlin, Feb. 10, 1965); *Réak* (Donaueschingen, Oct. 23, 1966); *Dimension* (Nuremberg, Oct. 22, 1971); *Konzertante Figuren* for Small Orch. (1972; Hamburg, Nov. 30, 1973); *Ouvertüre* (Berlin, Oct. 4, 1973; rev. 1974); *Harmonia* for Winds, Harp, and Percussion (1974; Herford, Jan. 22, 1975); Cello Concerto (Royan, March 25, 1976); Concerto for Flute and Small Orch. (Hitzacker, July 30, 1977); Double Concerto for Oboe, Harp, and Small Orch. (Berlin, Sept. 26, 1977); *Muak* (Mönchengladbach, Nov. 9, 1978); *Fanfare and Memorial* (Münster, Sept. 18, 1979); *Exemplum:im memoriam Kwangju* (Cologne, May 8, 1981); Clarinet Concerto (1981; Munich, Jan. 29, 1982); 3 violin concertos: No. 1 (1981), No. 2 (1983–86; Stuttgart, Jan. 20, 1987), and No. 3 (1992); 5 syms.: No. 1 (1983; Berlin, May 14, 1984), No. 2 (Berlin, Dec. 9, 1984), No. 3 (Saarbrücken, Sept. 22, 1985), No. 4 (Tokyo, Nov. 13, 1986), and No. 5 for Baritone and Orch. (Berlin, Sept. 17, 1987); *Gong-Hu* for Harp and Strings (1984; Lucerne, Aug. 22, 1985); *Mugung-Dong* for Winds, Percussion, and Double Bass (Hamburg, June 22, 1986); *Impression* for Small Orch. (1986; Frankfurt am Main, Feb. 9, 1987); *Duetto concertante* for Oboe or English Horn, Cello, and Strings (Rottweil, Nov. 8, 1987); 2 chamber syms. (1987, 1989); Oboe Concerto (1990); *Silia* (1992). **CHAMBER:** 6 string quartets (Nos. 1 and 2 withdrawn; 1959; 1988; 1990; 1992); *Musik* for 7 Instruments (Darmstadt, Sept. 4, 1959); *Loyang* for Chamber Ensemble (1962; Hannover, Jan. 23, 1964); *Gasa* for Violin and Piano (Prague, Oct. 2, 1963); *Garak* for Flute and Piano (1963; Berlin,

Sept. 11, 1964); *Nore* for Cello and Piano (1964; Bremen, May 3, 1968); *Riul* for Clarinet and Piano (Erlangen, July 26, 1968); *Images* for Flute, Oboe, Piano, and Cello (1968; Oakland, Calif., March 24, 1969); *Glissés* for Cello (1970; Zagreb, May 8, 1971); *Piri* for Oboe or Clarinet (Bamberg, Oct. 25, 1971); Trio for Flute, Oboe, and Violin (1972–73; Mannheim, Oct. 18, 1973); Trio for Violin or Viola, Cello, and Piano (1972–73; Berlin, Feb. 23, 1973); *Étüden* for 1 or More Flutes (Kyoto, July 16, 1974); *Rondell* for Oboe, Clarinet, and Bassoon (Bayreuth, Sept. 30, 1975); *Pièce concertante* for Chamber Ensemble (Hamburg, June 15, 1976); Duo for Viola and Piano (1976; Rome, May 3, 1977); *Königliches Thema* for Violin (1976; Düsseldorf, April 1, 1977); Octet for Clarinet, Bassoon, Horn, and String Quintet (Paris, April 10, 1978); Sonata for Oboe, Harp, and Viola or Cello (Saarbrücken, July 6, 1979); *Novellette* for Flute, Violin, and Cello or Viola (1980; Bremen, Feb. 5, 1981); Concertino for Accordion and String Quartet (Trossingen, Nov. 6, 1983); Sonatina for 2 Violins (Tokyo, Dec. 15, 1983); *Monolog* for Bass Clarinet (Melbourne, April 9, 1983); *Inventionen* for 2 Oboes or 2 Flutes (1983; Witten, April 29, 1984); *Monolog* for Bassoon (1983–84; Nice, Feb. 3, 1985); Duo for Cello and Harp or Piano (Ingleheim, May 27, 1984); Quintet for Clarinet and String Quartet (Kusatsu, Japan, Aug. 24, 1984); *Li-Na im Garten* for Violin (1984–85; Berlin, Nov. 28, 1985); *Recontre* for Clarinet, Harp or Piano, and Cello (Hitzacker, Aug. 2, 1986); Quartet for 2 Piccolos, 4 Flutes, 2 Alto Flutes, and 2 Bass Flutes (Berlin, Aug. 27, 1986); Quintet for Flute and String Quartet (1986; Paris, Jan. 17, 1987); *Tapis* for String Quintet (Mannheim, Nov. 20, 1987); *In Balance* for Harp (Hamburg, April 8, 1987); *Kontraste* for Violin (Hamburg, April 10, 1987); *Pezzo fantasioso* for Chamber Ensemble (Chiusi, July 10, 1988); Quartet for Flute, Violin, Cello, and Piano (1988); *Distanzen* for Flute, Oboe, Clarinet, Bassoon, Horn, and String Quintet (Berlin, Oct. 9, 1988); *Intermezzo* for Cello and Accordion (1988); *Contemplation* for 2 Violas (Berlin, Oct. 9, 1988); *Sori* for Flute (N.Y., Nov. 7, 1988); *Together* for Violin and Double Bass (1989; Århus, April 28, 1990); *Rufe* for Oboe and Harp (Ravensburg, Nov. 10, 1989); *Kammerkonzert I* (Amsterdam, June 16, 1990) and *II* (Berlin, Oct. 21, 1990); Wind Quintet (1991); Violin Sonata (1991); Trio for Clarinet, Bassoon, and Horn (1992); Quartet for Trumpet, Horn, Trombone, and Piano (1992); *Espace I* for Cello and Piano (1992) and *II* for Cello, Harp, and Oboe ad libitum (1992); *7 Études* for Cello (1993); Wind Octet (1994); *Ostwestiche Miniaturen* for Oboe and Cello (1994). **KEYBOARD: Piano:** *Fünf Klavierstücke* (1958; Bilthoven, Sept. 6, 1959); *Interludium A* (Tokyo, May 6, 1982). **Harpsichord:** *Shao Yang Yin* (1966; Freiburg im Breisgau, Jan. 12, 1968). **Organ:** *Tuyaux sonores* (Hamburg, March 11, 1967); *Fragment* (Hamburg, May 17, 1975). **VOCAL:** *Om mani padme hum* for Soprano, Baritone, Chorus, and Orch. (1964; Hannover, Jan. 30, 1965); *Ein Schmetterlingstraum* for Chorus and Percussion ad libitum (1968; Hamburg, May 8, 1969); *Schamanengesange aus Geisterliebe* for Alto and Chamber Orch. (1969–70; orchestrated by E. Koch-Raphael; Berlin, Dec. 16, 1977); *Namo* for 3 Sopranos and Orch. (Berlin, May 4, 1971; also for Soprano and Orch., 1975; Münster, May 10, 1976); *Gagok* for Voice, Guitar, and Percussion (Barcelona, Oct. 25, 1972; also for Voice and Harp, 1985); *Vom Tao* for Chorus, Organ, and Percussion (1972; Hamburg, May 21, 1976; rev. 1982; Vienna, Nov. 6, 1986); *Memory* for 3 Voices and Percussion (Rome, May 3, 1974); *An der Schwelle* for Baritone, Women's Chorus, Organ, Flute, Oboe, Trumpet, Trombone, and 2 Percussion (Kassel, April 5, 1975); *Der weise Mann*, cantata for Baritone, Chorus, and Orch. (Berlin, June 9, 1977); *Teile dich Nacht* for Soprano and Chamber Ensemble (1980; Witten, April 26, 1981); *O Licht...* for Chorus, Violin, and Percussion (Nuremberg, June 21, 1981); *Der Herr ist mein Hirte* for Chorus and Trombone (1981; Stuttgart, Nov. 14, 1982).

BIBL.: H.-W. Heister and W.-W. Sparrer, eds., *Der Komponist I. Y.* (Munich, 1987); H. Bergmeier, ed., *I. Y.: Festschrift zum 75. Geburtstag 1992* (Berlin, 1992).—**NS/LK/DM**

Z

Z, Pamela (née **Pamela Ruth Brooks**), lively American composer, performer, and audio artist; b. Buffalo, July 13, 1956. Her mother was a singer and her father played German blockflutes and choreographed musicals for local high schools. She sang as a child, making her first public appearance at the Smedley Elementary School in 1961 at the age of 5 in a duet with her older sister; also played viola and guitar. She began formal vocal training with Barbara Eanes; also composed songs for voice and guitar. She studied at the Univ. of Colo. at Boulder (B.M., 1978) and had vocal training with John Paton. After teaching in public schools (1978–80), she pursued a full-time music career, performing in clubs, coffee houses, and restaurants (1980–84). She began composing experimental performance works for voice and electronic processing in 1983, as well as a score for a short film by Elena-María Bey, *Diese Jugend*. She moved to San Francisco in 1984, where she continued performing works for voice and electronics and also began composing works for dance; she also studied *bel canto* technique with John McLain (from 1990). In 1987 she began producing a bi-annual performance event presenting integrated evenings of works by experimental artists of various disciplines called "Z Programs." In 1989 she began touring throughout the U.S., and, from 1996, internationally. From 1988 she began collaborating regularly with such artists as Donal Swearingen, The Qube Chix, Miya Masaoka, and the choreographer Jo Kreiter. In 1999 she studied Butoh dance with Kazuo Ohno and Yoshito Ohno in Yokohama, Noh theater with Richard Emmert, and Japanese singing with Etsuko Takezawa. Pamela Z works primarily with voice, live electronic processing, and sampling technology, and her compositions, imaginatively scored, often make use of found texts and such found objects as cellular phones and boomboxes. In her performances, she creates layered works combining operatic *bel canto* and experimental extended vocal techniques with a battery of digital delays, spoken word, and sampled concrete sounds triggered with a MIDI controller called The BodySynth, which allows her to manipulate sound with physical gestures. Her performances range in scale from small concerts to large-scale multimedia works appropriate for proscenium or flexible black-box venues. Her numerous awards include grants from the Calif. Arts Council (1993–97), an ASCAP Music Award (1998), and an NEA/Japan U.S. Friendship Commission fellowship (1998).

WORKS: *City* (1984); *Modern World* (1985); *Broken Glass* (1985); *Pearls (the Gem of the Sea)* (1985); *Giant Faces* (1985); *2 Black Rubber Raincoats* (1985); *Badagada* (1986); *Pop Titles "You"* (1986); *In the Other World* (1986); *Mad* (1987); *Ciao Fun* (1987); *Echolocation* (1988); *Z Songs* (1989); *Zunddadit* (1989); *What Will It Be* (1989); *Unaccompanied Melody for Minor Ninths and Octaves* (1989); *Harmonized Whisper* (1989); *In Tymes of Olde* (1991); *Sali Sali* (1991); *Smleheessege* (1991; in collaboration with Richard Zvonar); *Obsession, Addiction, and the Aristotelian Curve* (1991; in collaboration with Barbara Imhoff); *If You Want To* (1991); *Bald Boyfriend* (1991); *Heh Zahno* (1992); *Bone Music* (1992); *Stch-tch-na-ko* (1992); *Circle of Bone* (1992–93); *Plastic Orchestra* (1993); *Dream Encoding* (1993); *Trip* (1994); *Parts of Speech* (1994–96); *Correspondence* (1995); *Typewriter* (1995); *Soudscore for Wind Water Wings* (1995); *ReSounding (a Portrait of Downtown San Francisco)* (1995); *The MUNI Section*, from *Metrodaemonium* (1996); *Mona Lisa* (1996; in collaboration with Donald Swearingen and Laetitia Sonami); *Hoist* (1996); *The This* (1997); *Layers* (1997; in collab. with Lukas Ligeti); *Carpark* (1997); *Sustain II* (1997); *Shifting Conditions in the Southland* (1998); *The Schmetterling* (1998); *Parts of Speech* (1998); *Keitai* (1999); *Nihongo de Nanashoo (for "Gaijin")* (1999); *Excerpts from Gaijin* (1999); *Hitobashira for Voice, Processing, Samples, and Text* (1999); *Copra Dock Dances* (1999); *...and on your left...* (2000).—**LK/DM**

Zabaleta (Zala), Nicanor, eminent Spanish harpist; b. San Sebastián, Jan. 7, 1907; d. San Juan, Puerto Rico, March 31, 1993. He studied harp with Vicenta Tormo de Calvo at the Madrid Cons. (graduated, 1920) and with Luisa Menárguez, then went to Paris and studied harp with Marcel Tournier and harmony, counterpoint, and fugue with Marcel Rousseau and

Eugène Cools. In 1926 he made his Paris debut. On July 5, 1934, he made his N.Y. debut at the Lewisohn Stadium. In subsequent years, Zabaleta pursued a far-ranging concert career, appearing as a soloist with the world's principal orchs., giving numerous recitals, and being active as a chamber music player. In 1956 he was awarded the Henriette Cohen Prize of England, in 1982 he received the Premio Nacional de Música of Spain, and in 1988 he became a member of the Real Academia de Bellas Artes de San Fernando in Madrid. Zabaleta was one of the foremost harpists of the 20th century. His repertoire embraced works from the Baroque era to his own day. He brought to light various early MSS and ed. the vol. *Spanische Meister des 16. und 17. Jahrhunderts* (Mainz, 1985). His virtuoso performances of the harp literature of the 18th and 19th centuries were highly esteemed. He also did much to further the cause of contemporary harp music by commissioning works from many notable composers, among them Villa-Lobos, Rodrigo, Montsalvatge, Milhaud, Krenek, Piston, Hovhaness, and Farkas.—**NS/LK/DM**

Zaccaria, Nicola (Angelo), Greek bass; b. Piraeus, March 9, 1923. He received training at the Royal Cons. in Athens. In 1949 he made his operatic debut as Raimondo in *Lucia di Lammermoor* at the Athens Opera. In 1953 he won the La Scala singing competition in Milan, where he made his first appearance as Sparafucile that same year; from then until 1974 he was a member of the company, singing many leading bass roles. He made his first appearance at the Vienna State Opera in 1956. In 1957 he made his debut at the Salzburg Festival as Don Fernando and at London's Covent Garden as Oroveso, where he sang again in 1959. In 1976 he appeared as King Marke in Dallas. He sang Colline in Macerata in 1982. His guest engagements also took him to such operatic centers as Cologne, Geneva, Moscow, Berlin, Edinburgh, Brussels, and Monte Carlo. In addition, he also appeared as a concert artist. Among his other roles were Sarastro, the Commendatore, Creon, Silva, Zaccaria, and Bellini's Rodolfo.—**NS/LK/DM**

Zacconi, Lodovico (Giulio Cesare), Italian music theorist; b. Pesaro, June 11, 1555; d. Fiorenzuola di Focara, near Pesaro, March 23, 1627. He became an Augustinian novice in Pesaro in 1568, where he was a subdeacon by 1573 and received training in organ; in 1575 he became a priest. In 1577 he entered the Augustinian convent of S. Stefano in Venice, where he sang in the convent choir under I. Baccusi; also studied counterpoint with A. Gabrieli. He pursued literary studies in Pavia, where he became cursorato in 1583; then studied theology in Padua. In 1585 he began preaching in Boara Polesine, near Rovigo, but later that year became a singer to Archduke Karl of Austria in Graz. In 1590 he entered the service of Duke Wilhelm V of Bavaria. In 1596 he resumed his service in the Augustinian order as a preacher and administrator in Italy and Crete, and as a prior in Pesaro; he retired in 1612. His chief work, *Prattica di musica utile et necessaria si al compositore per comporre i canti suoi regolatamente, si anco al cantore* (Venice, 1592) and *Prattica di musica seconda parte* (Venice, 1622), contains treatises on mensural theory and counterpoint, detailed descriptions of contemporary musical instruments, and explanations for executing the ornaments in vocal polyphonic music. He also wrote 4 books of *Canoni musicali*, with comments and solutions (publ. by F. Vatielli, Pesaro, 1905). Most of his other music is lost. He also prepared a MS autobiography (1626).

Bibl.: F. Vatielli, *Di L. Z.: Notizie su la vita e le opere* (Pesaro, 1912); G. Singer, *L. Z.'s Treatment of the "Suitability and Classification of All Musical Instruments" in the "Prattica di musica" of 1592* (diss., Univ. of Southern Calif., 1968); G. Gruber, *L. Z. als Musiktheoretiker* (Habilitationsschrift, Univ. of Vienna, 1972).
—**NS/LK/DM**

Zach, Jan, Czech composer and organist; b. Czellakowitz, Nov. 13, 1699; d. Ellwangen, May 24, 1773. He went to Prague in 1724, and became a violinist at St. Gallus and St. Martin; also studied organ and composition with B. Czernohorsky. He served as organist at St. Martin and later at the monastic church of the Merciful Brethren and the Minorite chapel of St. Ann. After serving as court Kapellmeister in Mainz (1745–56), he traveled widely as a performer. He composed both sacred and instrumental works, including a fine Requiem in C minor, a *Stabat Mater*, a *Missa solemnis*, sinfonias, partitas, concertos, and keyboard works.

Bibl.: K. Komma, *Johann Z. und die tschechischen Musiker im deutschen Umbruch des 18. Jahrhundert* (Kassel, 1938); A. Ollig, *Die Orgelmusik Johann Z.s* (diss., Univ. of Mainz, 1954).
—**NS/LK/DM**

Zacharias, Christian, German pianist and conductor; b. Tamshedpur, India (of German parents), April 27, 1950. He was taken to Germany as an infant and began piano lessons at an early age. He was a student of Irène Slavin at the Karlsruhe Hochschule für Musik (1960–69), and then of Perlemuter in Paris. In 1969 he took 2nd prize in the Geneva Competition, in 1973 2nd prize in the Van Cliburn Competition, and in 1975 the Ravel Prize in the European Broadcasting Union Competition. In 1976 he made his London debut. He made his U.S. debut as a soloist with the Boston Sym. Orch. in 1979. In 1981 he made his Salzburg Festival debut as soloist in the Mozart Concerto, K.453. In subsequent years, he toured throughout the world in a repertoire extending from Mozart to the moderns. He also pursued a career as a conductor. In 2000 he became artistic director and principal conductor of the Lausanne Chamber Orch.—**NS/LK/DM**

Zachow (Zachau), Friedrich Wilhelm, distinguished German organist, pedagogue, and composer; b. Leipzig, probably on Nov. 13, 1663; d. Halle, Aug. 7, 1712. His maternal grandfather and father were Stadtpfeifer, and he received training in organ and as a Stadtpfeifer. In 1676 he went with his family to Eilenburg, where he most likely studied with Johann Hildebrand. From 1684 until his death he was organist at the Marienkirche in Halle, where he also led the noted musical performances every third Sunday. Zachow was one of the leading composers of church cantatas and keyboard works of his day. He also was a noted teacher, numbering Handel among his pupils. For his works, see G. Körner, ed., *F.W. Z.: Gesammtausgabe seiner sämmtlichen Orgelcompositionen* (Erfurt and Leipzig, c. 1850), M. Seiffert, ed., *F.W. Z: Gesammelte Werke*, Denkmäler Deutscher Tonkunst, XXI-XXII (1905), A. Adrio, ed., *F.W. Z.: Choralvorspiele für Orgel* (Berlin, 1952), and H. Lohmann, ed., *F.W. Z: Gesammelte Werke für Tasteninstrumente* (Wiesbaden, 1966).

Bibl.: A. Wicke, *Die Kantaten F.W. Z.s in ihrer geschichtlichen Stellung* (diss., Humboldt Univ., Berlin, 1956); G. Thomas, *F.W. Z.* (Regensburg, 1966).—**NS/LK/DM**

Zádor, Dezső, Hungarian baritone; b. Horna Krupa, March 8, 1873; d. Berlin, April 24, 1931. He studied in Budapest and Vienna. He made his debut as Almaviva in 1898 in Czernowitz; then sang in Elberfeld (1898–1901); was subsequently a member of the Komische Oper in Berlin (1906–11). In 1911 he joined the Dresden Court Opera, singing there until 1916; then went to the Budapest Opera (1916–19); was later a member of the Berlin Städtische Oper (1920–24). He made guest appearances at Covent Garden in London and in Paris, Milan, and Chicago. During the last years of his career, he sang bass roles.—**NS/LK/DM**

Zador, Eugene (real name, **Jenő Zádor**), Hungarian-American composer; b. Bátaszék, Nov. 5, 1894; d. Los Angeles, April 4, 1977. He studied music with a local teacher. In 1911 he enrolled in the Vienna Cons., and studied composition with Heuberger. From 1912 to 1914 he was in Leipzig, where he took a course with Reger; also attended classes in musicology with Abert and Schering; continued musicological studies with Volbach at the Univ. of Münster (Ph.D., 1921, with the diss. *Wesen und Form der symphonischen Dichtung von Liszt bis Strauss*). He settled in Vienna, and taught at the Neues Konservatorium there. Following the Anschluss of Austria by the Nazi regime in 1938, Zador emigrated to the U.S.; he settled in Hollywood, where he became successful and prosperous as an orchestrator of film scores; made some 120 orchestrations in all; at the same time, he continued to compose music in every conceivable genre. Zador was a master of musical sciences, excelling in euphonious modern harmonies, and an expert weaver of contrapuntal voices; his colorful writing for instruments was exemplary. He possessed a special skill in handling Hungarian folk motifs in variation form; in this, he followed the tradition of Liszt. During his European period, he composed some fashionable "machine music," as demonstrated with particular effect in his *Sinfonia tecnica*.

Works: DRAMATIC: Opera: *Diana* (Budapest, Dec. 22, 1923); *A holtak szigete* (The Island of the Dead; Budapest, March 29, 1928); *Revisor* (The Inspector General; 1928; rev. and reorchestrated, Los Angeles, June 11, 1971); *X-mal Rembrandt* (referring to the multiple copies of Rembrandt's self-portraits; Gera, May 24, 1930); *Asra* (Budapest, Feb. 15, 1936); *Christoph Columbus* (N.Y., Oct. 8, 1939); *The Virgin and the Fawn* (Los Angeles, Oct. 24, 1964); *The Magic Chair* (Baton Rouge, La., May 14, 1966); *The Scarlet Mill* (N.Y., Oct. 26, 1968); *Yehu, a Christmas Legend* (1974). Ballet: *Maschinenmensch* (1934). ORCH.: *Bánk bán*, symphonic poem (1918); 4 syms.: No. 1, *Romantische Symphonie* (1922), No. 2, *Sinfonia tecnica* (Paris, May 26, 1932), No. 3, *Tanzsymphonie* (Budapest, Feb. 8, 1937), and No. 4, *Children's Symphony* (1941); *Variations on a Hungarian Folk Song* (Vienna, Feb. 9, 1927); *Rondo* (1934); *Hungarian Caprice* (Budapest, Feb. 1, 1935); *Pastorale and Tarantella* (Chicago, Feb. 5, 1942); *Biblical Triptych* (Chicago, Dec. 9, 1943); *Elegie and Dance* (Philadelphia, March 12, 1954); *Divertimento* for Strings (1955); *Fugue-Fantasia* (1958); *Rhapsody* (Los Angeles, Feb. 5, 1961); *Christmas Overture* (1961); *Variations on a Merry Theme* (1963; Birmingham, Ala., Jan. 12, 1965); *5 Contrasts* (Philadelphia, Jan. 8, 1965); Trombone Concerto (Rochester, Mich., July 20, 1967); *Rhapsody* for Cimbalom and Orch. (Los Angeles, Nov. 2, 1969); *Studies* (Detroit, Nov. 12, 1970); *Fantasia hungarica* for Double Bass and Orch. (1970); Accordion Concerto (1971); *Hungarian Scherzo* (1975); Concerto for Oboe and Strings (1975). CHAMBER: Chamber Concerto for Strings, 2 Horns, and Piano (1930); Piano Quintet (1933); Suite for Brass (1961); Suite for 8 Cellos (1966); Suite for Woodwind Quintet (1972); Brass Quintet (1973); piano pieces. VOCAL: *Cantata tecnica* (1961); *Scherzo domestico* for Chorus (1961); *The Remarkable Adventure of Henry Bold* for Narrator and Orch. (Beverly Hills, Calif., Oct. 24, 1963); *The Judgement*, oratorio (1974); *Cain*, melodrama for Baritone, Chorus, and Orch. (1976); songs.

Bibl.: L. Zador, *E. Z.: A Catalogue of His Works* (San Diego, Calif., 1978).—**NS/LK/DM**

Zafred, Mario, Italian conductor, music critic, and composer; b. Trieste, Feb. 21, 1922; d. Rome, May 22, 1987. He was a pupil of Pizzetti at the Accademia di Santa Cecilia in Rome. After serving as music critic of *Unità* (1949–56) and *Giustizia* (1956–63), he was active as a conductor. From 1968 to 1974 he was artistic director of the Rome Opera. In conformity with his Communist convictions, he composed in an accessible style.

Works: DRAMATIC: Opera: *Amleto* (1961); *Wallenstein* (1965). ORCH.: 7 syms. (1943, 1944, 1949, 1950, 1954, 1958, 1970); Flute Concerto (1951); Violin Concerto (1953); Triple Concerto for Violin, Cello, Piano, and Orch. (1954); *Sinfonia breve* for Strings (1955); Harp Concerto (1956); Viola Concerto (1957); Cello Concerto (1958); Piano Concerto (1960); Concerto for 2 Pianos and Orch. (1961); *Metamorfosi* (1964); Concerto for Strings (1969). CHAMBER: 4 string quartets (1941, 1947, 1948, 1953); 3 piano trios (1942, 1945, 1954); Wind Quintet (1952); String Sextet (1967). Piano: 4 sonatas (1941, 1943, 1950, 1960). VOCAL: Numerous choruses and solo songs. —**NS/LK/DM**

Zagiba, Franz, eminent Austrian musicologist; b. Rosenau, Oct. 20, 1912; d. Vienna, Aug. 12,1977. He studied musicology with Dobroslav Orel and received training in Hungarian and Slavonic studies at the Univ. of Bratislava (Ph.D., 1937, with the diss. *Denkmäler der Musik in den Franziskanerklöstern in der Ostslovakei*; publ. in Prague, 1940, as *Hudobné pamiatky františkánskych kláštorov na východnom Slovensku*); completed his Habilitation in 1944 at the Univ. of Vienna with his *Geschichte der slowakischen Musik* (publ. in Bratislava, 1943, as *Dejiny slovenskj hudby od najstarších čias až do reformácie*). After serving as director of the musicological inst. of the Bratislava Academy of Sciences, he joined the faculty of the Univ. of Vienna in 1944, where he became a full prof. in 1972. In 1952 he founded the International Chopin Soc. His learned writings ranged from pre-medieval to 20th-century music.

Writings: *Literárny a hudobný život v Rožňave v 18. a 19. storoči* (Literary and Musical Life in Roznava in the 18th and 19th Centuries; Košice, 1947); *Tvorba sovietskych komponistov* (The Music of Soviet Composers; Bratislava, 1947); *Chopin und Wien* (Vienna, 1951); *Tschaikowskij: Leben und Werk* (Vienna, 1953); *Die ältesten musikalischen Denkmäler zu Ehren des hl. Leopold: Ein Beitrag zur Choralpflege in Österreich am Ausgang des Mittelalters* (Vienna, 1954); *Johann L. Bella (1843–1936) und das Wiener Musikleben* (Vienna, 1955); *Das Geistesleben der Slaven im frühen Mittelalter: Die Anfänge des slavischen Schrifttums aus dem Gebiete des östlichen Mitteleuropa vom 8. bis 10. Jahrhundert* (Vienna, 1971); *Musikgeschichte Mitteleuropas von den Anfängen bis zum Ende des 10. Jahrhunderts* (Vienna, 1976).—**NS/LK/DM**

Zagortsev, Vladimir, Russian composer; b. Kiev, Oct. 27, 1944. He was a student of Liatoshinsky and Shtogarenko at the Kiev Cons. While he adopted total serial procedures, he also utilized Ukrainian folk melos in many of his works.

Works: **DRAMATIC:** **Opera:** *Dolores* (1981–85). **ORCH.:** *Gradations* (1966); *Games* (1967–68); 3 syms.: No. 1 (1968), No. 2 for Mezzo-soprano, Tenor, and Orch. (1976–78), and No. 3, *Symphony of Anxiety* (1986–87). **CHAMBER:** Violin Sonata (1964); Sextet (1964); String Quartet (1965); Volumes for Clarinet, Tenor Saxophone, Trumpet, Piano, and Violin (1965); Sonata for Piano, Percussion, and Strings (1969); Oboe Sonata (1978); Viola Sonata (1979); 5 chamber concertos (1991–96). **Piano:** *Rhythms* (1969); Sonata (1980–81); *3 Epitaphs* (1998); *Game of Refrains* (1999). **VOCAL:** *Sayings* for Mezzo-soprano and Piano or Chamber Orch. (1963); *A Day in Pereyaslavl* for Chorus and Orch. (1979); 2 chamber cantatas (1980, 1981). —**NS/LK/DM**

Zagrosek, Lothar, German conductor; b. Waging, Nov. 13, 1942. After training in Munich and at the Essen Folkwangschule, he studied conducting with Swarowsky in Vienna, and also received guidance from Karajan, Kertesz, and Maderna. In 1967 he began his career, conducting opera in Salzburg, Kiel, and Darmstadt. In 1972 he became conductor in Solingen. He made his first appearance at the Salzburg Festival in 1973 conducting the Mozarteum Orch. In 1977 he became Generalmusikdirektor in Mönchengladbach. From 1978 he made frequent guest conducting appearances with the London Sinfonietta, establishing a fine reputation as an interpretor of contemporary music. From 1982 to 1987 he was chief conductor of the Austrian Radio Sym. Orch. in Vienna. He made appearances as a guest conductor in the U.S. from 1984. From 1986 to 1989 he was music director of the Paris Opéra. In 1987 he conducted *Così fan tutti* at the Glyndebourne Festival. He appeared with the English National Opera in London in 1989 conducting *Die Zauberflöte.* From 1990 to 1993 he was Generalmusikdirektor of the Leipzig Opera. He was Generalmusikdirektor of the Stuttgart Opera from 1998.—**NS/LK/DM**

Zagwijn, Henri, Dutch composer and teacher; b. Nieuwer-Amstel, July 17, 1878; d. The Hague, Oct. 23, 1954. He was basically autodidact as a composer. In 1916 he became a teacher at the Rotterdam School of Music. With Sem Dresden, he founded the Soc. of Modern Composers of the Netherlands in 1918. From 1931 he taught at the Rotterdam Cons. He was a follower of Rudolf Steiner's anthroposophic movement and publ. *De muziek in het licht der anthroposophie* (Rotterdam, 1925). He also publ. a biography of Debussy (The Hague, 1940). In his music, Zagwijn was particularly influenced by the French school.

Works: **ORCH.:** *Auferstehung,* prelude (1918); *Weihe-Nacht,* prelude (1918); 2 piano concertantes (1939, 1941); Flute Concertante (1940); Harp Concerto (1948); *Concertstuk* (1950); *Elegia e capriccio* for Harp and Orch. (1950); *Tema con variazione* for Strings (1951); *Entrata* for Band (1951); *Marcia* for Band (1951); *Pastorale et hymne* (1952); *Scènes de ballet* (1952); *Suite symphonique* (1953). **CHAMBER:** Suite for Wind Sextet (1915); Piano Trio (1915); 2 string quartets (1918, 1949); *Nocturne* for Flute, English Horn, Clarinet, Bassoon, Horn, Harp, and Celesta (1918); String Sextet (1932); Quintet for Flute, Violin, Viola, Cello, and Harp (1937); *Pastorale* for Flute, Oboe, and Piano (1937); *Introduzione e scherzetto* for Flute, Viola, and Harp (1940); *Mystère* for Harp and Piano (1941); 2 trios for Flute, Oboe, and Clarinet (1944, 1949); *Scherzo* for Wind Sextet (1946); String Trio (1946); *Andante* for Flute and Organ (1946); *Esquisse* for Trombone and Piano (1947); Wind Quintet (1948); *Cortège* for Brass Ensemble (1948); Sonata for Flute and Harpsichord (1949); *Entrata e fuga* for Flute, Oboe, Violin, Viola, Cello, and Harpsichord (1950); Sonata for Flute, Clarinet, and Harpsichord (1950); *Elegia e ditirambo* for 2 Violins and Piano (1951); *Preludio* for 2 Violins (1951); Suite for 2 Oboes (1951); *Entrata giocosa* for Horn, 2 Trumpets, and Trombone (1952); Trio for Oboe, Clarinet, and Piano (1952); *Canzone e riddone* for Flute and Piano (1952); *Capriccio* for Violin and Harpsichord or Piano (1953); *Elegia e visione* for Cello and Piano (1953); *Suite lyrique* for 4 Recorders (1954); *Sarabande e fandango* for Guitar and Harpsichord or Piano (1954). **KEYBOARD:** **Piano:** *Suite sinfonica* (1943); *Petite suite (in stile antico)* for 2 Pianos (1944); Suite (1945); *Triade* (1954). **Organ:** *Fantasia e fuga* (1952). —**NS/LK/DM**

Zaidel-Rudolph, Jeanne, prominent South African composer; b. Pretoria, July 9, 1948. She began piano instruction at the age of 5 with her aunt, and in her youth began to appear publicly. In 1966 she entered the Univ. of Pretoria, where she studied composition with Johann Potgieter and Arthur Wegelin (B.Mus., 1969; M.Mus., 1972); in 1973 she studied in London with John Lambert (composition), John Lill (piano), and Tristam Carey (electronic music) at the Royal Coll. of Music, where she won the R.O. Morris and Cobbett composition prizes. After further training in composition with Ligeti at the Hamburg Hochschule für Musik (1974), she returned to South Africa and was a lecturer in the music dept. at the Univ. of the Witwatersand in Johannesburg from 1975 to 1977. She then studied for her D.Mus. degree under Stefans Grove at the Univ. of Pretoria, becoming the first woman in South African history to receive such a degree in composition in 1979. From 1978 to 1982 she again was a lecturer at the Univ. of the Witwatersand; after serving as head of music for the Performing Arts Workshop in Johannesburg (1983–84), she was senior lecturer at the Univ. of the Witwatersand (from 1985). She was also active as a pianist and organist, serving in the latter capacity at the Sydenham/Highlands North Synagogue in Johannesburg. While her compositions utilize various contemporary techniques, she has succeeded in finding a highly personal style, frequently melding Western and African elements. Her Jewish heritage is affirmed in many of her works as well, most notably in the inspiration she has found in the Bible and Jewish mysticism.

WORKS: DRAMATIC: *Animal Farm*, opera (1978); *A Rage in a Cage*, rock opera (1983); *The River People— Abantubomlambo*, ballet (Durban, July 1987); *African Dream*, film score (1988). **ORCH.:** Concert Overture (1979); *5 Chassidic Melodies* for Small Orch. (1981); 2 syms.: No. 1, *Construction Symphony* (1985) and No. 2, *Sefirot Symphony*, for Wind, Brass, Percussion, and Harp (1990); *Fanfare Festival Overture* (1985; Johannesburg, Aug. 1986); *Tempus fugit* (Johannesburg, Oct. 1986); *At the End of the Rainbow*, symphonic poem (Johannesburg, Aug. 1988); Piano Concerto (1995). **CHAMBER:** *Kaleidoscope* for Winds and Percussion (1971); *Canonetta for 4* for Trumpet, Bassoon, Viola, and Vibraphone (1973); *Reaction* for Piano, Cello, and Percussion (1973); *Tango for Tim* for Guitar (1973); Chamber Concertino for 11 Instruments (1979); *The Fugue That Flew Away* for Flute and Piano (1979); *3 Chassidic Pieces* for Flute, Violin, and Cello (1982); *4 "Minim"* for Cello and Piano (1982); *Brass Quintet—and All That Jazz* for 2 Trumpets, Horn, Trombone, and Tuba (1983); *Margana* for Flute, Violin, Cello, and 2 Percussionists (1985); *Masada* for String Quartet and Bassoon (1989); Sextet (1990); *5 African Sketches* for Guitar (1991); *Suite Afrique* for Cello and Piano (1993). **Piano:** Sonata (1969); *7 Variations on an Original Theme* (1971); *3 Dimensions* (1974); *Virtuoso I* (1987); *Mixed Feelings: For Sara* (1988); *Mosaic* (1989); *Awaiting Game* (1993). **VOCAL:** *Settings of a Selection of Afrikaans Poems* for Soprano and Piano (1968); *Dialogue of Self and Soul* for 8 Soloists and Speaking Chorus (1971); *Setting of the Swaziland National Anthem* for Chorus and Piano (1974); *5 Pieces* for Soprano and Wind Quartet (1976); *Boy on a Swing* for Women's Chorus, Piano, and Percussion (1983; also for Soprano and Piano, 1992); *Back to Basics* for Narrator, Piano, and Prepared Piano (1983); *It's a Woman's World* for Chorus and Piano (1985); *Peace* for Chorus and Guitar (1991); *Hell, Well Heavens* for Soprano and Piano (1993); *Ukuthula* for Soprano, Mezzo-soprano, and Orch. (1993; Johannesburg, Feb. 25, 1994).—**NS/LK/DM**

Zajick (real name, **Zajic**), **Dolora,** American mezzo-soprano; b. Reno, Nev., 1960. She took premed courses at the Univ. of Nev. and received some vocal instruction. After joining the Nev. Opera chorus, she studied voice with its artistic director, Ted Puffer. She began her career singing comprimario roles with the Nev. Opera before pursuing training at the Manhattan School of Music in N.Y. In 1982 she took the Bronze Medal at the Tchaikovsky Competition in Moscow. Following further studies with the San Francisco Opera Merola Program, she made her formal operatic debut as Azucena with the San Francisco Opera in 1985. In 1986 she won the Richard Tucker Award, and then sang at the Houston Grand Opera in 1987. She made her Metropolitan Opera debut in N.Y. on Oct. 8, 1988, as Azucena. In 1989 she portrayed that role again at the Vienna State Opera and sang Amneris at the San Francisco Opera. She returned to San Francisco as Marfa in 1990, the same year she appeared as Amneris at the Lyric Opera of Chicago and as Azucena in Florence. In 1993 she sang Azucena in Barcelona. After singing Ulrica at the Metropolitan Opera in 1995, she returned there as Santuzza in 1997, the same year she appeared as Lady Macbeth in Hamburg. In 1999 she returned to the Metropolitan Opera as Amneris. She also appeared as a soloist with many orchs. and as a recitalist.—**NS/LK/DM**

Zak, Yakov (Izrailevich), Russian pianist and teacher; b. Odessa, Nov. 20, 1913; d. Moscow, June 28, 1976. He studied with Starkova at the Odessa Cons., graduating in 1932, and then was a student of Neuhaus at the Moscow Cons., graduating in 1935. At the International Competition for pianists in Warsaw in 1937, he received 1st prize and a special award of a posthumous mask of Chopin for his performance of a Chopin mazurka. He joined the faculty of the Moscow Cons. in 1935; became head of the piano dept. there in 1965. As a concert pianist, Zak toured all over Europe. He played in the U.S. in 1965 and 1967, and was acclaimed for his Soviet-like virtuosity. In 1966 he was made a People's Artist of the U.S.S.R.—**NS/LK/DM**

Zallinger, Meinhard von, Austrian conductor; b. Vienna, Feb. 25, 1897; d. Salzburg, Sept. 24, 1990. He studied piano and conducting at the Salzburg Mozarteum, and also took music courses at the Univ. of Innsbruck. He conducted at the Mozarteum (1920–22), then was on the staff of the Bavarian State Opera in Munich (1926–29) and the Cologne Opera (1929–35). He returned to the Bavarian State Opera in 1935, conducting there until 1944; was then made Generalmusikdirektor in Duisburg. In 1947 he became director of the Mozarteum Orch., and also held the same office at the Salzburg Landestheater. He was music director in Graz (1949–50), of the Vienna Volksoper (1950–53), and the Komische Oper in East Berlin (1953–56). He served again as a conductor at the Bavarian State Opera (1956–73); was concurrently director of the summer academy at the Mozarteum (1956–68).—**NS/LK/DM**

Zamara, Antonio, Italian harpist, pedagogue, and composer; b. Milan, June 13, 1829; d. Hietzing, near Vienna, Nov. 11, 1901. He studied with Sechter at the Vienna Cons. He was solo harpist in the orch. of the Vienna Court Opera (from 1842), and also prof. of harp at the Vienna Cons. He publ. *Harfenschule* (4 books); a number of pieces for Harp Solo (*Barcarolle, La Rêveuse, Chant du berceau, L'Absence, Marche des Croates*, etc.), pieces for Harp and Cello (*Elégie, L'addio*, etc.), and transcriptions of operatic airs for 2 harps.—**NS/LK/DM**

Zambello, Francesca, American opera producer; b. N.Y., Aug. 24, 1956. She was educated at Colgate Univ. (B.A., 1978) and received training in opera production from Jean-Pierre Ponnelle. After serving as asst. director at the Lyric Opera in Chicago (1981–82) and the San Francisco Opera (1983–84), she was co-artistic director of the Skylight Opera Theater in Milwaukee from 1985 to 1990. With Ponnelle, she collaborated on a staging of Rossini's *L'occasione fa il ladro* in Pesaro in 1987, a production later mounted at Milan's La Scala in 1989. Her *Beatrice di Tenda* was produced in Venice in 1987. She staged the U.S. premiere of Stephen Oliver's *Mario and the Magician* in Milwaukee in 1989. In 1990 she secured her reputation as one of the leading opera producers of her era with a staging of *War and Peace* in Seattle. In 1991 she produced *Les Troyens* in Los Angeles, and, that same year, became the first American producer to work at the Bolshoi Theater in Moscow where she staged *Turandot*. In 1992 she produced *Lucia di Lammermoor* at the Metropolitan Opera in N.Y. She was engaged to stage the premiere of Goehr's *Arianna* at the English National Opera in London in 1995. After producing *Iphigénie en Tauride* at the Glimmerglass Opera in N.Y. in 1997, she mounted *Tristan und Isolde* in Seattle in 1998. **—NS/LK/DM**

Zamboni, Luigi, noted Italian bass; b. Bologna, 1767; d. Florence, Feb. 28, 1837. He made his debut in 1791 in Ravenna in *Fanatico in Berlina* by Cimarosa, then sang throughout Italy, establishing himself as one of the finest interpreters of buffo roles of his time; 1816 he created the role of Figaro in Rossini's *Il Barbiere di Siviglia*. He retired from the stage in 1825.**—NS/LK/DM**

Zandonai, Riccardo, Italian composer; b. Sacco di Rovereto, Trentino, May 30, 1883; d. Pesaro, June 5, 1944. He was a pupil of Gianferrari at Rovereto (1893–98), then studied with Mascagni at the Liceo Rossini in Pesaro. He graduated in 1902; for his final examination he composed a symphonic poem for Solo Voices, Chorus, and Orch., *Il ritorno di Odisseo*. He then turned to opera, which remained his favored genre throughout his career. His first opera was *La coppa del re* (c. 1906), which was never performed. After writing the children's opera *L'uccelino d'oro* (Sacco di Rovereto, 1907), he won notable success with his third opera, *Il grillo del focolare*, after Dickens's *The Cricket on the Hearth* (Turin, Nov. 28, 1908). With his next opera, *Conchita*, after the novel *La Femme et le pantin* by Pierre Louÿs (Milan, Oct. 14, 1911), he established himself as an important Italian composer; the title role was created by the soprano Tarquinia Tarquini, whom Zandonai married in 1917. *Conchita* received its American premiere in San Francisco on Sept. 28, 1912; as *La Femme et le pantin* it was given at the Opéra-Comique in Paris on March 11, 1929. Zandonai's reputation was enhanced by subsequent works, notably *Francesca da Rimini*, after Gabriele d'Annunzio (Turin, Feb. 19, 1914; Metropolitan Opera, N.Y., Dec. 22, 1916), but a previous opera, *Melenis* (Milan, Nov. 13, 1912), was unsuccessful. During World War I, Zandonai participated in the political agitation for the return of former Italian provinces; he wrote a student hymn calling for the redemption of Trieste (1915). His other operas were *La via della finestra* (Pesaro, July 27, 1919; rev. version, Trieste, Jan. 18, 1923), *Giulietta e Romeo* (Rome, Feb. 14, 1922), *I Cavalieri di Ekebù* (Milan, March 7, 1925), *Giuliano* (Naples, Feb. 4, 1928), *Una partita* (Milan, Jan. 19, 1933), *La farsa amorosa*, after Alarcón's *El sombrero de tres picos* (Rome, Feb. 22, 1933), and *Il bacio* (1940–44; unfinished). Among his orch. works were *Serenata medioevale* for Cello, Harp, 2 Horns, and Strings (1909), *Terra nativa*, 2 suites, *Primavera in Val di Sole* (1914–15) and *Autonno fra i monti* (Patria lontana) (1917–18), *Concerto romantico* for Violin and Orch. (1919), *Ballata eroica* (1929), *Fra gli alberghi delle Dolomiti* (1929), *Quadri di Segantini* (1930–31), *Il flauto notturno* for Flute and Small Orch. (1934), *Concerto andaluso* for Cello and Small Orch. (1934), *Colombina overture* (1935), *Rapsodia trentina* (1936), and *Biancaneve* (1940). Other compositions included works for band, *Messa da Requiem* for Chorus (1915) and various other choral works, several vocal works with orch., and some chamber music. In 1939 he was appointed director of the Liceo Rossini in Pesaro, remaining there for the rest of his life.

BIBL.: V. Bonajuti Tarquini, *R. Z. nel ricordo dei suoi intimi* (Milan, 1951); G. Barblan, *R. Mariani, et al., A R. Z.* (Trento, 1952); B. Cagnoli, *R. Z.* (Trento, 1978); R. Chiesa, ed., *R. Z.* (Milan, 1984); A. Bassi, *R. Z.* (Milan, 1989).**—NS/LK/DM**

Zandt, Marie Van
See **Van Zandt, Marie**

Zanella, Amilcare, Italian composer, pianist, conductor, and pedagogue; b. Monticelli d'Ongina, Piacenza, Sept. 26, 1873; d. Pesaro, Jan. 9, 1949. He studied with Andreotti in Cremona, then with Bottesini at the Parma Cons., graduating in 1891. In 1892 he went to South America as a pianist and opera conductor; returning to Italy in 1901, he organized his own orch., giving sym. concerts in the principal Italian cities and introducing his own works. He then was director of the Parma Cons. (1903–05) and the Liceo Rossini in Pesaro (1905–39); also served as pianist of the Trio di Pesaro (1927–49).

WORKS: DRAMATIC: Opera: *Aura* (Pesaro, Aug. 27, 1910); *La Sulamita* (Piacenza, Feb. 11, 1926); *Il Revisore*, after Gogol (1938; Trieste, Feb. 20, 1940). **ORCH.:** *Concerto sinfonico* for Piano and Orch. (1897–98); *Fede*, symphonic poem (1901); 2 syms.: No. 1 (1901) and No. 2, *Sinfonia fantastica* (1919); *Fantasia e grande fugato sinfonico* for Piano and Orch. (1902); *Vita*, symphonic poem (1907); *Fantasia sinfonica* (1918); *Edgar Poe*, symphonic impression (c. 1921); *Poemetto* for Violin and Orch. (1922); *Elegia e momento frenetico* for Keyed Xylophone and Strings (1923). **CHAMBER:** 2 piano trios (1899, 1928); Brass Quintet (n.d.); Nonet (1906); 2 string quartets (1918, 1924); Piano Quintet (1917); Violin Sonata (1917); Cello Sonata (1917); various piano pieces. **VOCAL:** *Messa di Requiem* for 3 Men's Voices and Organ (1915); pieces for Solo Voice and Orch.; many choral works.

BIBL.: *A. Z., artista, uomo, educatore* (Ferrara, 1932); A. Dioli and M. Nobili, *La vita e l'arte di A. Z.* (Bergamo, 1941). **—NS/LK/DM**

Zanelli (Morales), Renato, esteemed Chilean baritone, later tenor; b. Valparaiso, April 1, 1892; d. Santiago, March 25, 1935. After studies in Neuchâtel and Turin, he pursued a business career in his homeland. His voice was discovered by Angelo Querez, who became his mentor in Santiago, where he made his debut as a baritone as Valentine in 1916. On Nov. 19, 1919, he appeared for the first time with the Metropolitan Opera in N.Y. as Amonasro. He remained on its roster until 1923, and then went to Milan, where he resumed vocal studies. He made his debut as a tenor in the role of Raoul at the Teatro San Carlo in Naples in 1924, and subsequently appeared in Rome, in London (Covent Garden, 1928–30), at La Scala in Milan (1920–32), and at the Teatro Colón in Buenos Aires. He won great distinction with his portrayals of Otello, Lohengrin, and Tristan.**—NS/LK/DM**

Zanettini, Antonio
See **Gianettini, Antonio**

Zangius (Zange), Nikolaus, German organist and composer; b. c. 1570; d. Berlin, c. 1618. He was a chamber musician in Braunschweig (1597). He went to Danzig as deputy Kapellmeister (1599), and soon became Kapellmeister at the Marienkirche. Zangius left at the outbreak of the plague in 1602, and was active in the imperial court in Prague until 1605. He returned to Danzig in 1607, but soon went to Stettin, finally returning to his court post in Prague in 1610. He was active in Berlin as Kapellmeister to the Elector of Brandenburg from 1612. He was a distinguished composer of secular and sacred ensemble songs. For his works, see H. Sachs and A. Pfalz, *Nikolaus Zangius: Geistliche und weltliche Gesange*, Denkmäler der Tonkunst in Österreich, LXXXVII (1951).

BIBL.: J. Sachs, *N. Zanges weltliche Lieder* (diss., Univ. of Vienna, 1934).—**NS/LK/DM**

Zanten, Cornelie Van
See **Van Zanten, Cornelie**

Zappa, Frank (actually, **Francis Vincent**), seeded American rock artist; b. Baltimore, Dec. 21, 1940; d. Los Angeles, Dec. 4, 1993. The family moved to Calif. From his school days, he played guitar and organized groups with weird names such as The Omens and Captain Glasspack and His Magic Mufflers. In 1960 he composed the sound track for the film *The World's Greatest Sinner*, and in 1963 he wrote another sound track, *Run Home Slow*. In 1965 he joined the rhythm-and-blues band The Soul Giants; he soon took it under his own aegis and thought up for it the surrealist logo The Mothers of Invention. His recording of it, and another album, *Freak Out!*, became underground hits; along with *We're Only in It for the Money* and *Cruising with Ruben and The Jets*, these works constituted the earliest "concept" albums, touching every nerve in a gradually decivilized Calif. life-style—rebellious, anarchistic, incomprehensible, and yet tantalizing. The band became a mixed-media celebration of total artistic, political, and social opposition to the Establishment, the ingredients of their final album, *Mothermania*. Moving farther afield, Zappa produced a video-movie, *200 Motels*, glorifying itinerant sex activities. He became a cult figure, and as such suffered the penalty of violent adulation. Playing in London in 1971, he was painfully injured when a besotted fan pushed him off the stage. Similar assaults forced Zappa to hire an athletic bodyguard for protection. In 1982 his planned appearance in Palermo, Sicily, the birthplace of his parents, had to be cancelled because the mob rioted in anticipation of the event. He deliberately confronted the most cherished social and emotional sentiments by putting on such songs as *Broken Hearts Are for Assholes*, and his release *Jewish Princess* offended, mistakenly, the sensitivity of American Jews. His production *Joe's Garage* contained Zappa's favorite scatological materials, and he went on analyzing and ridiculing urinary functions in such numbers as *Why Does It Hurt When I Pee*. He managed to upset the members of his own faith in the number titled *Catholic Girls*. His *Hot Rats*, a jazz-rock release, included the famous *Willie the Pimp*, and exploited the natural revulsion to unclean animals. In 1980 he produced the film *Baby Snakes*, which shocked even the most impervious senses. He declared in an interview that classical music is only "for old ladies and faggots," but he astounded the musical community when he proclaimed his total adoration of the music of Edgar Varèse and gave a lecture on Varèse in N.Y. Somehow, without formal study, he managed to absorb the essence of Varèse's difficult music. This process led Zappa to produce truly astonishing full orch. scores reveling in artful dissonant counterpoint, *Bob in Dacron and Sad Jane* and *Mo' 'n Herb's Vacation*, and the cataclysmic *Penis Dimension* for chorus, soloists, and orch., with a text so anatomically precise that it could not be performed for any English-speaking audience.

An accounting of Zappa's scatological and sexological proclivities stands in remarkable contrast to his unimpeachable private life and total abstention from alcohol and narcotic drugs. An unexpected reflection of Zappa's own popularity was the emergence of his adolescent daughter, curiously named Moon Unit, as a voice-over speaker on his hit *Valley Girls*, in which she used the vocabulary of growing womanhood of the San Fernando Valley near Los Angeles, with such locutions as "Grody to the Max" (repellent) and "Barfs Me Out" (disgusting). His son, Dweezil Zappa, is also a musician; his first album, *Havin' a Bad Day*, was modestly successful. In 1985 Zappa became an outspoken opponent of the activities of the PMRC (Parents Music Resource Center), an organization comprised largely of wives of U.S. Senators who accused the recording industry of exposing the youth of America to "sex, violence, and the glorification of drugs and alcohol." Their demands to the RIAA (Recording Industry Assn. of America) included the labeling of record albums to indicate lyric content. Zappa voiced his opinions in no uncertain terms, first in an open letter published in Cashbox, and then in one direct to President Reagan; finally, on Sept. 19, 1985, he appeared at the first of a series of highly publicized hearings involving the Senate Commerce, Technology and Transporation Committee, the PMRC, and the RIAA, where he delivered a statement to Congress which began "The PMRC proposal is an ill-conceived piece of nonsense which fails to deliver any real benefits to children, infringes the civil liberties of people who are not children and promises to keep the courts busy for years, dealing with the interpretational and enforcemental problems inherent in the proposal's design." Audio excerpts from these hearings can be heard, in original and Synclavier-manipulated forms, on his album *Zappa Meets The Mothers of Prevention*. Later recordings that made extensive use of the Synclavier included *Francesco Zappa* and *Jazz From Hell*. With P. Occhiogrosso, he publ. an unrestrained autobiographical vol., *The Real Frank Zappa Book* (N.Y., London, Toronto, Sydney, and Tokyo, 1988), rich in undeleted scatological expletives.

BIBL.: N. Obermanns, *Z.log* (Los Angeles, 1981); B. Watson, *Z.: The Dialectics of Negative Poodle Play* (N.Y., 1994).
—**NS/LK/DM**

Zaręebski (Zarembski), Juliusz, Polish pianist and composer; b. Zhitomir, Feb. 28, 1854; d. there, Sept. 15, 1885. He studied piano with Dachs and composition with Krenn at the Vienna Cons., graduating with gold medals in both in 1872, attended classes at the St. Petersburg Cons. (1873), and completed his training with Liszt in Rome (1874). He toured as a virtuoso from 1874, and was prof. of piano at the Brussels Cons. (from 1880). He wrote a distinguished Piano Quintet and several effective piano pieces.

BIBL.: T. Strumillo, *J. Z.* (Kraków, 1954).—**NS/LK/DM**

Zaremba, Nikolai (Ivanovich), Russian composer and pedagogue; b. near Vitebsk, June 15, 1821; d. St. Petersburg, April 8, 1879. He studied piano and cello, then went to Berlin, where he took lessons with Adolf Marx; also attended the Univ. of St. Petersburg. In 1854 he became director of the choral society at the Lutheran church of St. Peter and St. Paul in St. Petersburg, and in 1859 he became a teacher of harmony and composition at the St. Petersburg branch of the Russian Musical Soc. When the St. Petersburg Cons. was founded in 1862, he was engaged as a teacher of composition, and from 1867 to 1871 served as its director. He was the first to teach music theory using Russian terminology rather than the prevalent German nomenclature; among his students was Tchaikovsky. In his musical views Zaremba was extremely conservative. He was also apt to connect harmony rules with religious notions (such as piety being expressed by major keys, and sin and corruption by minor keys). Mussorgsky ridiculed Zaremba in his satirical piece *Rayok*, in which he illustrated Zaremba's Classical tastes by a mock quotation from Handel. —**NS/LK/DM**

Zarinš, Margeris, Latvian composer; b. Jaunpiebalga, May 24, 1910. He studied composition in Riga with Wihtol at the Latvian Cons. (1929–33), and also took lessons in piano and organ. From 1940 to 1950 he was director of music of the Latvian Art Theater. From 1956 to 1968 he was secretary-general of the Union of Latvian Composers. In his works, he stylized the elements of Latvian folk songs. He was particularly successful in his operas on contemporary subjects, often with a satirical tilt. In his *Opera uz lankuma* (Opera in the Town Square; 1970), he attempted to revive the early Soviet attempts to bring theatrical spectacles into the streets.

WORKS: DRAMATIC: Opera: *Kungs un spēlmanitis* (The King and the Little Musician; 1939); *Uz jauno krastu* (To New Shores; 1955); *Zalās dzirnavas* (The Green Mill; 1958); *Nabaqu opera* (Beggar's Opera; 1964); *Sveta Mauricija brinumdarbs* (Miracle of St. Mauritius; 1964); *Opera uz lankuma* (Opera in the Town Square; 1970). **ORCH.:** Piano Concerto (1937); *Greek Vases* for Piano and Orch. (1946; rev. 1960). **VOCAL:** Oratorios, including *Valmieras varoni* (The Heroes of Valmiera; 1950) and *Mahagoni* (Mahagonny), a propaganda work denouncing the Western colonial policies in Africa (1965); numerous choruses based on Latvian folk songs.

BIBL.: L. Krasinska, *M. Z.* (Riga, 1960).—**NS/LK/DM**

Zarlino, Gioseffo, important Italian music theorist and composer; b. Chioggia, probably Jan. 31, 1517; d. Venice, Feb. 4, 1590. He received his academic training from the Franciscans, his teacher in music being Francesco Maria Delfico. In 1532 he received the 1st tonsure, in 1537 took minor orders, and in 1539 was made a deacon. He was active as a singer (1536) and organist (1539–40) at Chioggia Cathedral. After his ordination, he was elected capellano and mansionario of the Scuola di S. Francesco in Chioggia in 1540. In 1541 he went to Venice to continue his musical training with Willaert. On July 5, 1565, he succeeded his fellow pupil Cipriano de Rore as maestro di cappella at San Marco, holding this position until his death. He also was chaplain of S. Severo (from 1565) and a canon of the Chioggia Cathedral chapter (from 1583). His students included G.M. Artusi, Girolamo Diruta, Vincenzo Galilei, and Claudio Merulo. Zarlino's historical significance rests upon his theoretical works, particularly his *Le istitutioni harmoniche* (1558), in which he treats the major and minor thirds as inversions within a fifth, and consequently, the major and minor triads as mutual mirror reflections of component intervals, thus anticipating the modern dualism of Rameau, Tartini, Hauptmann, and Riemann. He also gives lucid and practical demonstrations of double counterpoint and canon, illustrated by numerous musical examples. While adhering to the system of 12 modes, he places the Ionian rather than the Dorian mode at the head of the list, thus pointing toward the emergence of the major scale as the preponderant mode; he gives 10 rules for proper syllabification of the text in musical settings. His *Dimostrationi harmoniche* (1571) was publ. in the form of 5 dialogues between Willaert and his disciples and friends. Zarlino's theories were attacked, with a violence uncommon even for the polemical spirit of the age, by Vincenzo Galilei, his former pupil, in *Dialogo della musica antica e della moderna* (Florence, 1581) and *Discorso intorno alle opere di Gioseffo Zarlino* (Florence, 1589). In reply to the first of Galilei's books, Zarlino publ. *Sopplimenti musicali* (1588). In the latter, he suggests equal temperament for the tuning of the lute. As a composer, Zarlino was an accomplished craftsman who wrote both sacred and secular works.

WRITINGS: *Le istitutioni harmoniche* (Venice, 1558; 3rd ed., rev., 1573; Eng. tr. of part 3 by G. Marco and C. Palisca, 1968, as *The Art of Counterpoint*); *Dimostrationi harmoniche* (Venice, 1571; 2nd ed., 1573); *Sopplimenti musicali* (Venice, 1588); also *De tutte l'opere del r.m.G. Zarlino* (4 vols., 1588–89; contains the 3 preceding vols. with a 4th vol. of non-musical writings).

BIBL.: G. Artusi, *Impresa del molto Rev. M.G. Z. da Chioggia...dichiarata* (Bologna, 1604); G. Ravagnan, *Elogio di G. Z. e di Cristoforo Sabbadino* (Venice, 1819); F. Caffi, *Della vita e delle opere del prete G. Z.* (Venice, 1836); V. Bellemo, *G. Z.: Memoria* (Chioggia, 1884); R. Flury, *G. Z. als Komponist* (Winterthur, 1962); K. Berger, *Musica Ficta: Theories of Accidental Inflections in Vocal Polyphony from Marchetto da Padova to G. Z.* (Cambridge, 1987); R. Airoldi, *La teoria del temperamento nell'eta di G. Z.* (Cremona, 1989); L. Tiozzo, *G. Z., teorico musicale* (Conselve, 1992).—**NS/LK/DM**

Zarotus, Antonio, Italian music printer, active in Milan. He printed a *Missale Romanum* dated April 26, 1476, in which he used for the first time movable type for the music (the type is in Gothic style). This incunabulum was publ. 6 months earlier than the *Missale* of Ulrich Han, at one time considered the earliest specimen of music printed from movable type.—**NS/LK/DM**

Zarth (also **Czard, Czarth, Szarth, Tzarth, Zardt**), **Georg,** Bohemian violinist and composer; b. Hochtann, near Deutschbrod, April 8, 1708; d. probably in Mannheim, after 1778. He first studied with Lukas Lorenz in Deutschbrod, then received training in violin from F. Trimmer and J. Rosetter and in flute from Biarelli in Vienna, where he became a friend of Franz Benda, with whom he remained professionally associated for some 20 years. In 1729 he went to Poland, and about 1731 he entered the service of the royal chapel in Warsaw. In 1733 he became a musician in the Dresden Court Orch., entering the service of the crown prince (later Friedrich II the Great of Prussia) in Ruppin in 1734. He moved with his patron to Rheinsberg in 1736, and then to Berlin in 1740 when Friedrich became king. Zarth went in 1757–58 to Mannheim, where he was a member of the Court Orch. until 1778. He publ. *6 sonates* for Violin and Basso Continuo, op.2 (Paris, c. 1750; not extant). Several sonatas and trios are in MS.—**NS/LK/DM**

Zarzycki, Alexander, Polish pianist and composer; b. Lemberg, Feb. 21, 1834; d. Warsaw, Nov. 1, 1895. He studied piano with Rudolf Viole in Berlin and composition with N. Reber and K. Reinecke in Paris. He began his career in his homeland in 1856 and subsequently gave brilliant concerts in Germany, Austria, and England. He was director of the Warsaw Music Soc. (1871–75). From 1879 to 1888 he was director of the Warsaw Music Inst. He wrote effective piano pieces (*nocturnes, mazurkas, waltzes*, etc.) as well as a Piano Concerto, *Grande Polonaise* for Piano with Orch., *Introduction et Cracovienne* for Violin and Orch., *Suite polonaise* for Orch., *Mazourka* in G major for Violin, with Orch. (very popular), and 2 albums of songs.
—**NS/LK/DM**

Zaslaw, Neal (Alexander), American musicologist; b. N.Y., June 28, 1939. He studied at Harvard Univ. (B.A., 1961), and then took flute lessons at the Juilliard School of Music in N.Y. (M.S., 1963). He subsequently studied musicology with Paul Henry Lang at Columbia Univ. (M.A., 1965; Ph.D., 1970, with the diss. *Materials for the Life and Works of Jean-Marie Leclair l'Aine*). He taught at City Coll. of the City Univ. of N.Y. (1968–70), and in 1970 he joined the faculty of Cornell Univ. He was ed.-in-chief of *Current Musicology* (1967–70). Zaslaw publ. the vols. *Edward A. MacDowell* (N.Y., 1964) and *Mozart's Symphonies: Context, Performance Practice, Reception* (Oxford, 1990). With W. Cowdery, he ed. *The Complete Mozart: A Guide to the Musical Works of Wolfgang Amadeus Mozart* (N.Y., 1991). He also ed. *Mozart's Piano Concertos: Text, Context, Interpretation* (Ann Arbor, 1996). In 1995 he became editor of the 7th ed. of the Mozart Köchel catalog.—**NS/LK/DM**

Zavertal, Ladislaw (Joseph Philip Paul; actually, Josef Filip Pavel), Czech-born English conductor and composer; b. Milan, Sept. 29, 1849; d. Cadenabbia, Jan. 29, 1942. He was the son of the conductor and composer Wenceslaw (Václav) Hugo Zavrtal (b. Polepy, Aug. 31, 1821; d. Leitmeritz, Sept. 8, 1899) and nephew of the conductor and composer Josef Rudolf Zavrtal (b. Polepy, Nov. 5, 1819; d. Leitmeritz, May 3, 1893). He began his musical training with his father and his mother, the soprano Carlotta Maironi da Ponte, then studied violin with Tosti at the Naples Cons. His first opera, *Tita*, was orchestrated by his father and premiered in Treviso (May 29, 1870); in 1871 he went to Milan as music director of the Teatro Milanese. That same year he went to Glasgow, where he conducted various orch. groups; in 1881 he became bandmaster of the Royal Artillery Band at Woolwich; then was active in London, where he conducted concerts at St. James's Hall and Queen's Hall (1889–95) and Sunday concerts at the Royal Albert Hall (1895–1905); in 1896 he became a British subject; in 1906 he retired to Italy.

WORKS: DRAMATIC: Opera: *Tita* (Treviso, May 29, 1870; orchestrated by his father; rev. 1880 as *Adriana, ovvero Il burratinaro di Venezia*); *I tre perucchi* (Milan, 1871); *La sura palmira sposa* (Milan, 1872); *Una notte à Firenze* (1872–73; in Czech as *Noc ve Florence*, Prague, March 20, 1880); *A Lesson in Magic* (1880; Woolwich, April 27, 1883; rev. as *Love's Magic*, 1889; Woolwich, Feb. 18, 1890); *Mirra* (1882–83; in Czech, Prague, Nov. 7, 1886). **ORCH.:** 2 syms. (1878–84; 1884); 3 overtures: *Garibaldi* (1882; not extant; reconstructed as *Sinfonia patriottica*, 1918), *Loyal Hearts* (1897), and *Slavonic Overture* (1898); *Chanson arabe* (1882); *Al fresco* for Strings (1884); *Virtute et valore*, march. **OTHER:** Band pieces; Piano Quintet (1877); Piano Quartet (c. 1877); choral works.

BIBL.: "Un ambrosiano" (pseudonym of G. Bampo), *Del maestro di musica milanese Ladislao Z.* (Milan, 1904); A. Faraone, *Il Commendatore Ladislao Z.* (Treviso, 1929); H. Farmer, *Ladislao Z.: His Life and Work* (London, 1949); idem, *Cavaliere Z. and the Royal Artillery Band* (London, 1951).—**NS/LK/DM**

Zawinul, Joe, Austrian keyboardist; b. Vienna, Austria, July 7, 1932. He started on accordion at age six, then studied classical piano and composition at the Vienna Cons. He worked with Austrian saxophonist Hans Koller in 1952 and began to gig with his own trio in Germany and France. In 1958, he won a scholarship to Berklee Coll. of Music. He left after only one week to go with Maynard Ferguson's band. He then worked briefly with Slide Hampton and served as Dinah Washington's accompanist from 1959 to 1961. After a one-month gig with Harry "Sweets" Edison, he joined Cannonball Adderley. These gigs were conventional and mainstream, and took Zawinul away somewhat from his timbral experimentations. However, they did allow him the opportunity to more fully absorb the jazz language.

He evolved from a mainstream, hard-bop pianist to a soul/jazz pianist to a jazz/rock pioneer. With Adderley, he was able to further develop his compositional skills, writing "Walk Tall," "Country Preacher," and the hit "Mercy, Mercy, Mercy." His affinity for unusual sounds also brought him to the attention of Miles Davis. He wrote "In a Silent Way," "Pharoah's Dance," and "Double Image" for Davis. These compositions helped establish the electric piano as a viable jazz instrument and not merely a cheap substitute for a grand piano.

He formed Weather Report with Shorter in 1971, which allowed him to pursue more sophisticated synthesized timbres. He graduated from the electric piano to more sophisticated and expressive synthesizers and developed reed-like and string-like timbres that enhanced, reinforced, and strengthened Wayne Shorter's saxophone. The group's first albums were primarily improvised, later becoming more structured. He also incorporated unique keyboard configurations and techniques. After more than a decade of success Weather Report broke up in 1985.

He immediately formed Weather Update, which, because of legal issues regarding the name similarities, quickly became Zawinul Syndicate. His music became more synthesizer-heavy and groove-oriented without becoming ponderous or heavy-handed. Ethnic, jazz, and electric music were artfully combined. His method of composing became more expansive. He would compose by recording hours and hours of improvisations, then transcribing them for band. Because of recent acoustic dogma, his importance has been marginalized. Undaunted, he continues to grow and explore as a composer and improviser. His music continues to inspire and uplift. The pendulum will swing back, and he will be appreciated for his tremendous contribution to jazz and fusion.

DISC.: *The Rise & Fall of the Third Stream* (1965); *Money in the Pocket* (1966); *Zawinul* (1970); *Dialects* (1986); *Immigrants* (1988); *Black Water* (1989); *Beginning* (1990); *Lost Tribes* (1992); *Stories of the Danube* (1995); *My People* (1996).—**JE**

Zaytz, Giovanni von (real name, **Ivan Zajc**), Croatian composer; b. Fiume, Aug. 3, 1831; d. Zagreb, Dec. 16, 1914. He was trained by his father, a bandmaster in the Austrian army, then at the Milan Cons. with Stefano Ronchetti-Monteviti, Lauro Rossi, and Alberto Mazzucato (1850–55). Returning to Fiume, he conducted the municipal band; then was a theater conductor in Vienna (1862–70). Upon entering professional life, he changed his name to Giovanni von Zaytz. In 1870 he settled in Zagreb; was conductor of the Zagreb Opera (1870–89) and director of the Cons. there (until 1908). He composed about 1,200 works of all descriptions (among them 20 operas), and was the author of the first Croatian national opera, *Nikola Šubrič Zrinski* (Zagreb, Nov. 4, 1876). He also wrote several Italian operas, of which *Amelia, ossia Il Bandito* (Fiume, April 14, 1860) enjoyed considerable popularity. Other operas and operettas (all first perf. in Vienna) were *Mannschaft an Bord* (Dec. 15, 1863), *Fitzliputzli* (Nov. 5, 1864), *Die Lazzaroni vom Stanzel* (May 4, 1865), *Die Hexe von Boissy* (April 24, 1866), *Nachtschwärmer* (Nov. 10, 1866), *Das Rendezvous in der Schweiz* (April 3, 1867), *Das Gaugericht* (Sept. 14, 1867), *Nach Mekka* (Jan. 11, 1868), *Somnambula* (Jan. 21, 1868), *Schützen von Einst und Jetzt* (July 25, 1868), *Meister Puff* (May 22, 1869), and *Der gefangene Amor* (Sept. 12, 1874). In addition, he wrote incidental music for 22 plays, 60 cantatas, 250 choral works, sacred and secular, 40 overtures, symphonic poems, more than 200 songs, chamber music, and numerous piano pieces.

BIBL.: A. Goglia, *I. Z.* (Zagreb, 1932); H. Pettan, *I. Z.* (Zagreb, 1971).—**NS/LK/DM**

Zbinden, Julien-François, Swiss composer, pianist, and administrator; b. Rolle, Nov. 11, 1917. He began piano lessons at the age of 8 and later attended the Lausanne Cons. He also studied at the teacher's training college in the canton of Vaud (1934–38; graduated, 1938), and then was active as a pianist. After teaching himself harmony, form, and composition, he pursued training in counterpoint and orchestration with Gerber. In 1947 he joined Radio Lausanne as a pianist and music producer, becoming head of the music dept. in 1956. From 1965 to 1982 he was deputy director of musical broadcasts of the Radio-Télévision Suisse Romande. He served as president of the Swiss Musicians Assn. (1973–79) and of SUISA (the Swiss music copyright society; 1987–91). In 1978 the French government made him an Officier de l'ordre des Arts et des Lettres. His early love of jazz, as well as the influence of Ravel, Stravinsky, and Honegger, were important factors in the development of his own musical style. Among his works were *La Pantoufle*, farce-ballet (1958), *Fait divers*, opera (1960), radiophonic scores, Piano Concerto (1944), *Concerto da camera* for piano and strings (1950–51), 4 syms., *Suite française* for strings (1954), *Rhapsodie* for violin and orch. (1956), *Jazzific 59–16* for jazz group and strings (1958), *Concerto breve* for cello and orch. (1962), Violin Concerto (1962–64), *Concerto for Orchestra* (1977), much chamber music, *Terra Dei*, oratorio for soloists, chorus, and orch. (1966–67), and other vocal works.

BIBL.: C. Tappolet, *J.-F. Z.: Compositeur* (Geneva, 1995). —**NS/LK/DM**

Zeani (real name, **Zahan**), **Virginia,** Romanian soprano; b. Solovastru, Oct. 21, 1928. She studied in Bucharest with Lipkowska and with Pertile in Milan. She made her operatic debut as Violetta in Bologna in 1948; then sang in London (1953), in Rome, at La Scala in Milan (1956), and at Covent Garden in London (1959). She made her Metropolitan Opera debut in N.Y. as Violetta on Nov. 12, 1966, where she sang for only one season. In 1980 she joined the faculty of the Ind. Univ. School of Music in Bloomington, where she was made a Distinguished Prof. in 1994 and Prof. Emeritus in 1995. She married **Nicola Rossi-Lemeni** in 1958. Among her finest roles were Lucia, Elvira, Maria di Rohan, Desdemona, Aida, Leonora, and Tosca.—**NS/LK/DM**

Zecchi, Adone, Italian composer and conductor; b. Bologna, July 23, 1904. He studied composition with Franco Alfano at the Liceo Musicale in Bologna, graduating in 1926. In 1927 he founded the choral group Corale Euridice, which he led until 1943. In 1930 he founded the Orch. Bolognese de Camera. In 1942 he was appointed to the faculty of the Bologna Cons.; he became its director in 1961. In his compositions he follows the path of Italian neo-Classicism, but applies dodecaphonic formulas in some of his music. He publ. a number of manuals on choral conducting, including the reference work *Il coro nella storia e dizionario dei nomi e dei termini* (Bologna, 1960) and *Il direttore di coro* (Milan, 1965). In collaboration with R. Allorto, he brought out *Educazione musicale* (Milan, 1962); *Canti natalizi di altri paesi* (Milan, 1965); *Canti natalizi italiani* (Milan, 1965);

Canti della vecchia America (Milan, 1966); and *Il mondo della musica* (Milan, 1969).

WORKS: *Partita* for Orch. (1933); *Toccata, Ricercare e Finale* for Orch. (1941); *2 astrazioni in forma di fuga* for Small Ensemble (Copenhagen, June 2, 1947); *Requiem* for Chorus and Orch. (1946); *Caleidofonia* for Violin, Piano, and Orch. (1963); *Trattenimento musicale* for 11 groups of String Instruments (1969). **—NS/LK/DM**

Zecchi, Carlo, Italian pianist and conductor; b. Rome, July 8, 1903; d. Salzburg, Aug. 31, 1984. He studied at the Liceo and Cons. in Rome, where he received instruction in piano from Bajardi and in composition from Bustini, Refice, and Setaccioli; continued his training with Schnabel and Busoni in Berlin, where he made his debut as a pianist at the age of 17. He subsequently toured throughout Europe and the U.S. until giving up his solo career in 1939 to tour in duo recitals with the cellist Enrico Mainardi; also studied conducting with H. Munch and Guarnieri; from 1947 he pursued a successful career as a guest conductor; taught at the Accademia di Santa Cecilia in Rome and also gave summer master classes in Salzburg.**—NS/LK/DM**

Zechberger, Günther, Austrian conductor, teacher, and composer; b. Zams, Tirol, April 24, 1951. He studied composition and guitar at the Cons. (1968–74) and musicology at the Univ. (1974–80) in Innsbruck. He received training in conducting from Eric Ericson and Witold Rowicki, and in composition from Boguslaw Schaeffer. From 1970 to 1991 he taught guitar in Tirolean schools. In 1984 he founded the Tiroler Ensemble für Neue Musik, which he conducted in many performances of contemporary scores. He also taught at the Univ. of Innsbruck. In his music, structural complexities predominate but not without special regard for sonoristic effects.

WORKS: Septet for Flute, Oboe, Clarinet, and String Quartet (1972–73); Trio for Clarinet, Horn, and Bassoon (1972–73); Trio for Violins (1975); *o crux ave*, 7 pieces for Good Friday for Chorus (1978); *Schlusstück* for Chorus and Orch. (1979); *Mass* for Chorus and Orch. (1979); Trombone Quartet (1980); *stabat mater I* for Speaker's Chorus (1981) and *II* for Vocal Ensemble and 8 Players (1985–94); *Im Nebel* for Mezzo-soprano and Orch., after Hermann Hesse (1982); *Studie* for 14 Instruments (1982–83); Sextet for 3 Guitars and 3 Metronomes (1982–83); *Neunzehn* for 8 Instruments (1983); *Kanon* for 2 Tape Recorders and Audience (1983); *Hendekagon* for 26 Instruments (1983–84); *Tieferschüttert* for Mezzo-soprano, Alto Trombone, and Guitar (1984); String Quartet (1984–85); *Choros* for 5 Players (1985); *Kammermusik* for Conductor and 5 Players (1986); *Dear Mr. J.*, action music (1987); *Interview* for Tape (1987); *Stiegenhausmusik*, installation for Voice and 8 Instruments (1986); *Asambari* for 2 Guitars (1988–89); Concerto for Guitar, Live Electronics, and Orch. (1988); *Sakralcollage* for Flute, Bass Flute, Zither, Guitar, and Synthesizer (1989); *...with one limit...* for Cello, Computer, and Live Electronics (1990); *toucher* for Guitar and Live Electronics (1990); String Sextet (1990); *Partita* for Mezzo-soprano and 5 Instruments (1990); *upstairs* for Voice and 7 Instruments (1991); *Scopello* for Baritone Saxophone, Trombone, Live Electronics, and Computer (1991); *Bacchacaglia* for Soprano, Instruments, Computer, Live Electronics, and Broadcasting Equipment (1992); *stills* for Saxophone, Bass Flute, and Trombone (1992); *R.E.P.04* for Bass Flute, Trombone, Computer, and Live Electronics (1992–93); *...und teilen die grune Insel mit ihren Blicken...* for Trombone (1993); *die farbe der nacht* for Alto Saxophone, Trombone, Percussion, and UPIC (1993); *Tangenten* for Voice and Instrumental Ensemble (Turkish Radio, Istanbul, Oct. 22, 1994); *horizontal radio*, collage in collaboration with composers from all over the world (broadcast, June 22–23, 1995).**—NS/LK/DM**

Zechlin, Ruth, German composer, pedagogue, organist, and harpsichordist; b. Grosshartmannsdorf, near Freiberg, Saxony, June 22, 1926. She studied at the Leipzig Hochschule für Musik (1943–45; 1946–49), where her mentors included J.N. David and Wilhelm Weismann (composition), Anton Rohden and Rudolf Fischer (piano), and Karl Straube and Günther Ramin (organ). In 1950 she went to East Berlin as a teacher at the Hochschule für Musik, and then was a prof. of composition at that city's Hanns Eisler Hochschule für Musik from 1969 to 1986. In 1970 she was made a member of the Akademie der Künste of the German Democratic Republic. From 1990 to 1993 she was vice-president of the Akademie der Künste in Berlin. Among her honors were the Goethe Prize of the City of Berlin (1962), as well as the Arts Prize (1965) and 2 National Prizes (1975, 1982) of the German Democratic Republic, and the Cross of Merit, 1st Class, of the Federal Republic of Germany (1997).

WORKS: DRAMATIC: *Reineke Fuchs*, opera (1967; Berlin, April 1968); *La Vita*, ballet (1983; Berlin, Feb. 2, 1985); *Sommernachtsträume* or *Die Salamandrin und die Bildsäule* (1990); *Die Reise*, chamber opera (1992; Saarbrücken, Feb. 28, 1998); *Un baiser pour le Roi*, dance piece (Passau, June 16, 1995). **ORCH.:** *Violin Concerto 1963* (1963; Gera, Feb. 28, 1964); 3 syms.: No. 1 (Leipzig, Sept. 12, 1965), No. 2 (Potsdam, Nov. 16, 1966), and No. 3 (1971; Berlin, Jan. 7, 1972); 2 chamber syms.: No. 1 (1967; Leoben, Nov. 18, 1968) and No. 2 (1973; Stralsund, Feb. 25, 1974); Piano Concerto (1974; Berlin, Feb. 17, 1975); 2 organ concertos: No. 1 (1974; Leipzig, Sept. 20, 1975) and No. 2 (Frankfurt an der Oder, Oct. 2, 1975); *Kristalle* for Harpsichord and Strings (1975; Freiberg, Saxony, Nov. 2, 1976); *Briefe* (1978; Halle, Jan. 28, 1980); *Situationen* (1980; Berlin, Feb. 19, 1981); *Musik* (1980; Berlin, Oct. 2, 1981); *Metamorphosen* (1982; Berlin, Feb. 24, 1983); *Musik zu Bach* (1983; Berlin, Feb. 28, 1985); *Linien* for Harpsichord and Orch. (1986; Schwerin, June 22, 1988); *Kristallisation* (1987; Cologne, Jan. 27, 1989); Violin Concerto: *Hommage à György Kurtág* (1990; Chemnitz, June 6, 1994); *Stufen* (Hamburg, Dec. 12, 1993); *Venezianisches*, concerto for Harpsichord and Strings (1994; Flensburg, Nov. 7, 1995); *Varianten zu Goethes Märchen* for Chamber Orch. (1998; Passau, July 8, 1999); *Triptychon 2000* (Passau, July 28, 2000). **CHAMBER:** 7 string quartets: No. 1 (Leipzig, Oct. 4, 1959), No. 2 (Berlin, July 5, 1965), No. 3 (1970; Berlin, Nov. 22, 1971), No. 4 (Berlin, Oct. 27, 1971), No. 5 (1971; Frankfurt an der Oder, March 9, 1972), No. 6 (1977; Berlin, Jan. 28, 1978), and No. 7 (1995; Chemnitz, Oct. 28, 1996); *Amor und Psyché*, chamber music with Harpsichord (1966; Berlin, Feb. 4, 1967); *Hommage à PHL* for String Quintet and Percussion (Berlin, Dec. 6, 1973); *pour la flûte* (1973; Berlin, Sept. 22, 1975); *Begegnungen*, chamber music (1977; Berlin, Feb. 4, 1978); *Hommage à Shakespeare*, scene for Chamber Ensemble (1978; Schwerin, March 9, 1980); *Reflexionen* for 14 Strings (Berlin, Nov. 5, 1979); *Beschwörungen* for Percussionist (1980; Dresden, May 25, 1981); *Katharsis* for Oboe, Cello, and Percussion (1981; Leipzig, Feb. 5, 1982); *da capo* for Violin (1982; Berlin, Nov. 3, 1986); *Musik* for Cello (1983; Berlin, March 22, 1986);

Konstellationen for 10 Brass Instruments (1985; Eisenach, June 14, 1986); *Synthese* for Organ and Percussion (1986; Vienna, July 24, 1987); *7 Versuche und 1 Ergebnis* for Saxophone Quartet (1988; Berlin, Feb. 20, 1989); *5 Mobiles* for Harp (1988); *Szenische Kammermusik nach Heiner Müllers Hamletmaschine* for 5 Instrumentalists (Berlin, Dec. 1, 1991); *Musik zu Kafka II* for Percussionist (Heidelberg, Sept. 25, 1992); *3 Briefe an HWH* for Oboe (1992; Stuttgart, Nov. 24, 1993); *Alternativer Baukasten* for Chamber Ensemble (Nuremberg, Nov. 12, 1993); *Akzente und Flächen* for 5 Percussionists (1993; Berlin, Feb. 22, 1994); *Circulation* for 8 Percussion (1994); *Musik* for 3 Percussionists (1995; Saarbrücken, May 8, 1996); *In memoriam Witold Lutosławski* for Viola (1995; Flensburg, April 14, 1996); *5 Studien and 1 Collage* for Chamber Ensemble (1996; Potsdam, April 20, 1997); *Epigramme* for Cello and Contrabass (1997; Rheinsberg, March 7, 1998); *An Aphrodite* for Oboe (1998; Passau, June 18, 1999); *Aphorismen zu Goethes Urworte Orphisch* for Oboe and Harpsichord (1998; Passau, June 18, 1999); *Musikalische Antworten auf Johann Sebastian Bach* for Flute and Organ (1999; Rheinsberg, June 17, 2000). **KEYBOARD: Harpsichord:** 11 pieces (1957–94). **Organ:** 12 pieces (1969–93). **VOCAL:** Mass for Chorus (1945–93; Berlin, Nov. 10, 1996); *Keunergeschichten* for Speaker and Chamber Ensemble, after Bertolt Brecht (Berlin, Nov. 16, 1966); *Ode an die Luft* for Mezzo-soprano and Orch., after Pablo Neruda (1974); *Canzoni alla notte* for Baritone and Orch., after Quasimodo (1974; Leipzig, Oct. 15, 1976); *An Aphrodite* for Alto, Baritone, Pantomime, and 7 Musicians (Berlin, Feb. 25, 1977); *Das Hohelied* for Tenor and Orch. (1979; Leipzig, Nov. 5, 1980); *Angelus-Silesius-Sprüche* for Chorus (1983); *Hommage à Bach* for Chorus (1985); *Prometheus* for Speaker, Piano, and Percussion (1986; Berlin, May 8, 1987); *Das A und das O* for Alto (1990; Kassel, June 26, 1991); *Frühe Kafka-Texte* for Mezzo-soprano and Instruments (1990; Heidelberg, Sept. 25, 1991); *Geistliche Kreise* for 3 Choruses (1995; Passau, June 21, 1996); *3 Lieder nach Texten der Hildegard von Bingen* for Mezzo-soprano and Flute (1996; Weimar, Aug. 8, 1998); *2 Gesänge nach Friederike Mayröcker* for Mezzo-soprano (1997); *Stabat Mater* for Tenor and Organ (1999); *Dies irae* for Mezzo-soprano and Organ (1999).—**NS/LK/DM**

Zedda, Alberto, Italian conductor and musicologist; b. Milan, Jan. 2, 1928. He studied organ with Galliera, conducting with Votto and Giulini, and composition with Fait at the Milan Cons. In 1956 he made his debut as a conductor in Milan. He subsequently went to the U.S., where he taught at the Cincinnati Coll. of Music (1957–59). Returning to Europe, he conducted at the Deutsche Oper in West Berlin (1961–63); then conducted at the N.Y.C. Opera. With Philip Gossett, he served as co-ed. of the complete works of Rossini. Zedda was artistic director of the Teatro Comunale in Genoa in 1992 and of Milan's La Scala in 1992–93. —**NS/LK/DM**

Zednik, Heinz, Austrian tenor; b. Vienna, Feb. 21, 1940. He was a student of Marga Wissmann at the Vienna Cons. In 1963 he made his operatic debut as Trabuco in *La forza del destino* in Graz. In 1965 he became a member of the Vienna State Opera, where he created the role of Kalb in Einem's *Kabale und Liebe* in 1976. His guest engagements took him to such operatic centers as Munich, Paris, Nice, Moscow, and Montreal. In 1970 he made his first appearance at the Bayreuth Festival as David in *Die Meistersinger von Nürnberg*, and he returned there to sing Loge and Mime in the centenary *Ring* cycle in 1976. In 1980 he was made an Austrian Kammersänger. For his first appearance at the Salzburg Festival (1981), he sang Bardolfo in *Falstaff*. On Sept. 22, 1981, he made his Metropolitan Opera debut in N.Y. as Mime in *Das Rheingold*. He returned to Salzburg to create the roles of the Regisseur in Berio's *Un re in ascolto* (1984) and Hadank in Penderecki's *Die schwarze Maske* (1986). In 1987 he appeared as Pedrillo at the Metropolitan Opera, and returned there during the 1989–90 season as Mime. In 1996 he sang Baron Laur in Weill's *Silbersee* at the London Promenade Concerts. —**NS/LK/DM**

Zeffirelli, Franco (real name, **Gian Franco Corsi**), prominent Italian opera director and designer; b. Florence, Feb. 12, 1923. He began his career as an actor, and then became an assistant to Visconti. His first operatic production was *La Cenerentola* at Milan's La Scala (1953). In 1958 he mounted *La Traviata* in Dallas, and in 1959 *Lucia di Lammermoor* at London's Covent Garden, where he later produced *Falstaff* (1961), *Alcina* and *Don Giovanni* (1962), and *Tosca*. He also worked at the Metropolitan Opera in N.Y., where he was chosen to produce Barber's *Antony and Cleopatra* as the opening work at the new house at Lincoln Center in 1966. In later years, he devoted himself to operatic film productions, winning particular acclaim for his filming of *La Traviata* (1983) and *Otello* (1986); he also brought out the film biography *The Young Toscanini* (1988). —**NS/LK/DM**

Zehetmair, Thomas, Austrian violinist; b. Salzburg, Nov. 23, 1961. His parents were violinists. After demonstrating prodigious talent, he studied with his father, Helmut Zehetmair, and with Franz Samohyl at the Salzburg Mozarteum. He was still a small child when he began to appear in public; later pursued advanced training with Max Rostal and Nathan Milstein. After winning 1st prize in the Mozart competition in 1978, he scored a major success with his first appearance at Vienna's Musikverein. He subsequently was engaged as a soloist with leading European and U.S. orchs.; also appeared as a recitalist and chamber music player in a catholic repertoire ranging from early music to contemporary scores.—**NS/LK/DM**

Zehnder, Max, Swiss composer; b. Turgi, Nov. 17, 1901; d. St. Gallen, July 16, 1972. He studied with Wenz, Lang, Andreae, Vogler, and Laquai at the Zürich Cons. (1923–26). He was on the faculty of the Rorschach Training Coll. in Canton St. Gallen (1931–68), where he also conducted its orch. His compositions developed from a late-Romantic to a neo-Classical style and include a String Quartet (1928), *Praludium und Chaconne* for Strings (1941), 2 cantatas (1947, 1960), *In memoriam* for Strings and Organ (1965), *Mouvements* for Strings (1970), various choruses, and songs.—**NS/LK/DM**

Zeidman, Boris, Russian composer and pedagogue; b. St. Petersburg, Feb. 10, 1908; d. Tashkent, Dec. 30, 1981. He studied composition at the Leningrad

Cons. with Maximilian Steinberg, graduating in 1931, and then taught music in various schools in Russia, Azerbaijan, and Uzbekistan.

WORKS: DRAMATIC: Opera: *The People's Wrath* (Baku, Dec. 28, 1941); *Son of the Regiment* (Baku, Feb. 23, 1955); *Zainab and Omon* (1958); *The Russians* (1970). **Ballet:** *The Gold Key* (1955); *The Dragon and the Sun* (1964). **ORCH.:** 2 piano concertos (1931, 1935); Viola Concerto (1938); Bassoon Concerto (1938); Cello Concerto (1948); *Songs of Struggle* (1966); Violin Concerto (1968); *Days of Spring* (1971). **OTHER:** Chamber music; songs; teaching collections.—**NS/LK/DM**

Zeinally, Assaf, Azerbaijani composer; b. Derbent, April 5, 1909; d. Baku, Oct. 27, 1932. He studied cello and trumpet at the Baku Cons., graduating in 1931, but died a year later, at the age of 23. He was a highly promising musician; his particular merit was the attempt to compose music in classical forms on folk themes; in this manner he wrote several violin pieces, a *Children's Suite* for Piano, and many songs to words by native poets.

BIBL.: Kh. Melikov, *A. Z.* (Baku, 1956; 2nd ed., 1969). —**NS/LK/DM**

Zeisl, Eric(h), Austrian-born American composer; b. Vienna, May 18, 1905; d. Los Angeles, Feb. 18, 1959. A son of prosperous parents who owned a coffeehouse, he entered the Vienna Academy of Music at 14. He was a pupil of Richard Stöhr, Joseph Marx, and Hugo Kauder, and publ. his first songs at the age of 16. In 1934 he won the Austrian State Prize for his *Requiem concertante*. After the seizure of Austria by the Nazis in 1938, he fled to Paris, and at the outbreak of World War II in 1939, went to the U.S.: in 1941 he settled in Los Angeles; in 1945 he became a naturalized American citizen. He taught at the Southern Calif. School of Music; from 1949 until his death he was on the staff at Los Angeles City Coll. Increasingly conscious in exile of his Jewish heritage, he selected biblical themes for his stage works; death interrupted the composition of his major work, the music drama *Job*; Hebraic cantillation is basic to this period. His style of composition reflects the late Romantic school of Vienna, imbued with poetic melancholy, with relief provided by eruptions of dancing optimism. He was at his best in his song cycles.

WORKS: DRAMATIC: *Die Fahrt ins Wunderland*, children's opera (Vienna, 1934); *Leonce und Lena*, Singspiel (1937; Los Angeles, 1952); *Job*, opera (1939–41; 1957–59; unfinished); *Pierrot in der Flasche*, ballet (Vienna Radio, 1935); *Uranium 235*, ballet (1946); *Naboth's Vineyard*, ballet (1953); *Jacob und Rachel*, ballet (1954). **ORCH.:** *Kleine Symphonie* (Vienna Radio, May 30, 1937); *Passacaglia-Fantasie* (Vienna, Nov. 4, 1937); *November*, suite for Chamber Orch. (N.Y., Jan. 25, 1941); *Cossack Dance* (from the unfinished opera *Job*, Los Angeles, Aug. 18, 1946); *Return of Ulysses*, suite for Chamber Orch. (Chicago, Nov. 17, 1948); *Variations and Fugue on Christmas Carols* (1950); Piano Concerto (1951); *Concerto grosso* for Cello and Orch. (1956). **CHAMBER:** Violin Sonata (1950); Viola Sonata (1950); Cello Sonata (1951); Trio for Flute, Viola, and Harp (1956). **VOCAL:** *Mondbilder* for Baritone and Orch. (1928); *Requiem ebraico* (1945); *Kinderlieder* for Soprano; *6 Lieder* for Baritone.

BIBL.: M. Cole and B. Barclay, *Armseelchen: The Life and Music of E. Z.* (Westport, Conn., 1984).—**NS/LK/DM**

Zeisler, Fannie Bloomfield (née **Blumenfeld**), noted Austrian-American pianist; b. Bielitz, Austrian Silesia, July 16, 1863; d. Chicago, Aug. 20, 1927. Her original name was changed when the family settled in Chicago in 1868. Her first teachers there were Carl Wolfsohn and Bernhard Ziehn. She made her concert debut in Chicago on Feb. 26, 1875, then went to Vienna, where she studied with Leschetizky (1878–83). From 1883 until 1893 she played annually in the U.S. In 1893 she made a tour of Germany and Austria, which established her reputation as one of the best women pianists; other European tours followed in 1894–95, 1898, 1902–03, 1911–12, and 1914. She then returned to Chicago, making her farewell appearance there on Feb. 25, 1925, in a special concert to mark her golden jubilee. On Oct. 18, 1885, she married Sigmund Zeisler, a Chicago lawyer.—**NS/LK/DM**

Zeitlin, Denny, American pianist; b. Chicago, Ill., April 10, 1938. He began recording in the early 1960s while still studying medicine at Johns Hopkins Univ. Often teamed with bassist Charlie Haden, he made a series of well-regarded albums for Columbia. Over the next two decades he devoted more time to psychiatry practice but continued to perform occasional gigs on the West Coast. In the 1970s, he dabbled with electronic keyboards and worked on the soundtrack to the film *Invasion of the Body Snatchers*. Since the 1980s, he has returned to the acoustic piano, continuing to perform and record with some regularity.

DISC.: *Time Remembers One Time Once* (1983); *Homecoming* (1986); *Trio* (1988); *In the Moment* (1989); *Live at Maybeck, Vol. 27* (1993); *Concord Duo Series, Vol. Eight* (1995).—**WB**

Zeitlin, Zvi, Yugoslav-American violinist and pedagogue; b. Dubrovnik, Feb. 21, 1923. He studied at the Hebrew Univ. in Jerusalem, then was a violin student of Sascha Jacobson, Louis Persinger, and Ivan Galamian at the Juilliard School of Music in N.Y. In 1940 he made his professional debut as soloist with the Palestine Orch.; in 1951 he made his N.Y. debut. He subsequently appeared as a soloist with many orchs., and also gave recitals. In 1967 he joined the faculty of the Eastman School of Music in Rochester, N.Y. He was noted for his intelligent performances of modern violin works.—**NS/LK/DM**

Zelenka, István, Hungarian-born Austrian, later Swiss composer; b. Budapest, July 30, 1936. After training in Budapest, he pursued studies at the Vienna Academy of Music, where he received 1st prize in composition in 1962. In 1960 he became a naturalized Austrian citizen. He later settled in Switzerland and became a naturalized Swiss citizen in 1976. In addition to working as a producer and programmer of music for the Radio Suisse Romande (from 1978), he lectured on contemporary music at the Geneva Cons. (from 1980). In 1982 he was a co-founder of the group DIGITALISMUS, and in 1983 of the collective private publishing venture EDITION ZWACHEN. In his music, Zelenka has followed an experimental course, utilizing various contemporary techniques.

WORKS: DRAMATIC: Music Theater: *Dove, dove, Signore, Signori?* (1971); *Un Faust-digest agréménte* (1979);

C'est avec reconnaissance et émotion qud j'ai appris très sincèrement dévoué à tous! (1980); *Estouffade de volailles* (1984). **ORCH.:** *A propos FAFNER* (1971); *Le très Saint Empire de Rome, comment tient-il encore debout?* for Viola d'Amore and Orch. (1981); *Credo* for Orch. and Video (1983); *Médaille, pile ET face* (1984); *La Traque* for Cello and Orch. (1985); *Etat de siège(s)* (1989). **CHAMBER:** *Ritournelles* for Flute, Oboe, Bassoon, and 2 Harpsichords (1975); *Vivat Nucleus'* for Wind Quintet and Tape (1978); *Progression/Regression?* for Violin and Piano (1979); *Deus ex laminae* for 2 Pianos and 2 Cymbals (1979); *...The permanent variations produced by confined breeding and changing circumstances are continued and...* for Alto Flute and String Trio (1979); *Fünf Analysen eines Farbbildes* for Violin and Piano (1981); *Due(tt) (Il) o* for Clarinet, Violin, Cello, and Piano (1983); *Souvenir d'enfance/mémoire d'adulte* for Cello and Synthesizer (1984); *Gebeetstunde* for 2 Cellists, 3 Pianists, and 8 Cymbalists (1986); *Musique des sphères* for Clarinet, Violin, Horn, Bassoon, Viola, Cello, Double Bass, and 2 Cassettophones (1990). **OTHER:** Vocal works; electroacoustic scores.—**NS/LK/DM**

Zelenka, Jan Dismas, notable Bohemian composer; b. Launowitz, Oct. 16, 1679; d. Dresden, Dec. 22, 1745. He was the son of an organist and it is most probable that he received his early music training from his father. About 1710 he went to Prague, where he attended the Jesuit Clementinum. He also learned to play the double bass and was a member of the orch. of Count Hartog. Upon Hartog's recommendation in 1710, Zelenka was accepted as a member of the Dresden court orch. In 1715 he went to Venice to study with Lotti and, between 1716 and 1719, he spent considerable time in Vienna studying with Fux. With his training completed, Zelenka remained at the Dresden court for the rest of his life. In 1721 he became vice-Kapellmeister there, but was passed over as Kapellmeister in 1731 when Hasse accepted the court's appointment. In 1735 he was named Kirchen-compositeur to the court. Zelenka was particularly known during his lifetime as a composer of sacred music, winning the admiration of Bach and Telemann. His extensive output of such music included the oratorios *Il serpente di bronzo* (1730), *Gesù al Calvario* (1735), and *I Penitenti al sepolchro del Redentore* (1736), about 20 masses, 2 Magnificats, over 35 cantatas, and various motets, Psalms, antiphons, hymns, and other pieces. For the coronation of the Holy Roman Emperor Karl VI as King of Bohemia, Zelenka composed the *Melodrama de Sancto Wenceslao ("Sub olea pacis et palma virtutis conspicua orbi Regia Bohemiae Corona")*, which was first performed in Frankfurt am Main on Nov. 12, 1723. Almost all of the MSS of Zelenka's sacred music were lost in 1945. Since several of his instrumental works were publ. in his lifetime, copies have survived and today Zelenka is known as a distinguished and refreshing composer of instrumental music. Among his extant works for orch. are 5 capriccios (1–4, 1717–18; 5, 1729), a *Simphonie a 8 Concertante* (1723), a *Concerto a 8 Concertante* (1723), and the *Hipocondrie a 7 Concercante* (1723). Also extant are 6 Trio or Quadro Sonatas for 2 Oboes, Bassoon, and Basso Continuo (c. 1720).

BIBL.: W. Reich, *Zwei Z.-Stücken* (Dresden, 1987). —**NS/LK/DM**

Zelenski, Wladislaw, Polish composer and pedagogue; b. Grodkowice, near Kraków, July 6, 1837; d. Kraków, Jan. 23, 1921. He studied violin with Wojciechowski, then received training in piano from Germasz and in composition from Mirecki in Krakow (1854–59); in 1859 he entered the Jagiellonian Univ. in Prague as a philosophy student (Ph.D., 1862), and pursued training in piano with Dreyschock and in organ and counterpoint with J. Kreiči. After further studies with N.H. Reber at the Paris Cons. (1866), he completed his musical training with Damcke (1868–70). He taught at the Warsaw Music Inst. (1872–81), where he also was music director of the music society. In 1881 he organized the Kraków Cons., and remained its director until his death; he also taught piano and theory there. As a pedagogue, he enjoyed a very high reputation; among his pupils were Stojowski, Opieński, and Szopski.

WORKS: DRAMATIC: Opera: *Konrad Wallenrod* (Lemberg, Feb. 26, 1885); *Goplana* (Kraków, July 23, 1896); *Janek* (Lemberg, Oct. 4, 1900); *Stara baśń* (Lemberg, March 14, 1907). **ORCH.:** 2 syms. (1871, 1913); 3 overtures (1857; *W Tatrach* [In the Tatras], 1871–72; *Echa lesne* [Echoes of the Woods], n.d.); Piano Concerto (n.d.). **CHAMBER:** 4 string quartets; String Sextet; Piano Trio; 2 violin sonatas; Piano Quartet; numerous piano pieces, including 3 sonatas. **VOCAL:** Sacred and secular choral works; about 100 solo songs.

BIBL.: F. Szopski, *W. Z.* (Warsaw, 1928); Z. Jachimecki, *W. Z.: Zycie i twórczość, 1837–1921* (Kraków, 1952).—**NS/LK/DM**

Železný, Lubomír, Czech composer; b. Ostrava, March 16, 1925; d. Prague, Sept. 27, 1979. He studied composition with Karel Janeček at the Prague Cons. (1945–48) and with Bočkovec at the Prague Academy of Musical Arts (1948–50). He worked in the music dept. of Prague Radio and was chairman of the Union of Czech Composers and Concert Artists (1972–79).

WORKS: ORCH.: 2 *Gavottes* (1954); 2 violin concertos (1958–59; 1974–75); 2 syms. (1961–62; 1970); Concerto for Flute, Strings, and Piano (1966); Cello Concerto (1968); *Concertant Music* for Viola, Strings, and Piano (1969); *Festive March* (1971). **CHAMBER:** Flute Sonata (1943); Trio for Flute, Viola, and Cello (1946); 2 violin sonatas (1948, 1971); Quartet for Flute, Violin, Viola, and Cello (1948); 2 string quartets (1959–60; 1968); Piano Trio (1966); Quintet for 2 Violins, Clarinet, Viola, and Cello (1969); Wind Quintet (1970). **VOCAL:** *Brigand Songs* for Tenor and Orch. (1958); choruses; solo songs.—**NS/LK/DM**

Zelinka, Jan Evangelista, Czech composer; b. Prague, Jan. 13, 1893; d. there, June 30, 1969. He studied music with his father, the organist and composer, Jan Evangelista Zelinka (1856–1935), and later with J.B. Foerster, Suk, Novák, and Ostrčil.

WORKS: DRAMATIC: Opera: *Dceruška hostinského* (The Tavernkeeper's Little Daughter; 1921; Prague, Feb. 24, 1925); *Devátá louka* (The 9th Meadow; 1929; Prague, Sept. 19, 1931); *Odchod dona Quijota* (Departure of Don Quixote; 1936); *Paličatý švec* (The Stubborn Cobbler; 1940; Prague, March 28, 1944); *Meluzína* (The Wailing Wind; 1947; Plzeň, April 15, 1950); *Námluvy bez konce* (Endless Wooing), radio opera (Czech Radio, Jan. 27, 1950); *Masopustní noc* (Shrovetide Night; 1956); *Lásky žal i smích* (Love's Woe and Laughter), after Goldoni (1958); *Škola pro ženy* (School for Wives), after Molière (1959); *Blouznivé jaro* (A Fanciful Spring; 1960); *Dčevěný kůň* (The Wooden Horse; 1962–63). **Ballet-pantomime:** *Skleněná panna* (The

Glass Doll; 1927; Prague, July 2, 1928). **Scenic Melodrama:** *Srdce na prázdninách* (Heart on a Fishhook; 1932; Brno, Jan. 28, 1938). Also incidental music. **ORCH.:** *Overture to a Renaissance Comedy* (1919); *Pariz—Glotton*, overture burlesque (1931); *Weekend*, suite (1939); *Sinfonia rustica* (1956); *A Slovak Summer* (1959); *Musichetta primaverale* for Chamber Orch. (1962); *Satiricon*, suite (1964). **CHAMBER:** 2 nonets: *Capriccio* (1937) and *Cassation* (1943); *Late Summer*, piano trio (1949); *Sonata leggera* for Saxophone and Piano (1962); Piano Sonata (1926); organ pieces. **VOCAL:** Cantatas; songs.—**NS/LK/DM**

Zeljenka, Ilja, Slovak composer; b. Bratislava, Dec. 21, 1932. Following private training with Zimmer (harmony and counterpoint) and Macudzinski (piano), he studied with Cikker (composition) at the Bratislava Academy of Music and Drama (1951–56). He was a dramaturg with the Slovak Phil. (1957–61) and the Czechoslovak Radio (1961–68) in Bratislava, and later served as chairman of the Slovak Music Union (1990–91). Zeljenka has followed a varied course as a composer and has utilized various contemporary means of expression, ranging from post-Webern serialism to electronics.

WORKS: ORCH.: 5 syms.: No. 1 (1954–55), No. 2 for Strings (1961), No. 3 (1972), No. 4, *Ballet Symphony* (1978), and No. 5 (1984); *Dramatic Overture* (1955); *Revolution Overture* (1962); *Structures* (1964); 2 piano concertos (1966, n.d.); *Meditation* (1969); *Variations* (1971); Concerto for Violin and Strings (1974); *Music* for Piano and Strings (1976); *Epilogue to the Memory of E. Spitz* (1979); *Ouvertura giocosa* (1982); Concerto for Clarinet, Strings, Xylophone, and Kettledrum (1984); *Dialogues* for Cello and Chamber String Orch. (1984); *Music* (1987); Concertino for Chamber String Orch., Clarinet, Piano, and Percussion (1988); *Enchanted Movement* (1989); Violin Concerto (1989). **CHAMBER:** 2 piano quintets (1953, 1959); 5 string quartets (1965, 1976, 1979, 1986, 1988); *Polymetric Music* for 4 String Quintets (1969); *Elegy* for Strings (1973); *Musica slovaca* for Strings (1975; also for String Quartet, 1986); Piano Trio (1975); Quintet for Winds and Percussion (1977); *Monologues* for Cello (1982); *3 Pieces* for Flute (1984); Trio for Flute, Oboe, and Bassoon (1985); *Music* for Cello and Piano (1986); *Sonata-Ballad* for Viola and Piano (1988). **KEYBOARD: Piano:** *Bagatelles* (1955); 4 sonatas (1958, 1974, 1985, 1989); *Capriccio* (1982); *Little Suite* (1987); *5 Etudes* (1988); *3 Preludes and Fugues* (1988). **Organ:** *Ligatures* (1972); *6 Studies* (1976); *Reliefs* (1979); *Letters to Friends* (1984). **VOCAL:** *Plays* for 13 Singers and Percussion (1968); *Metamorphoses XV* for Narrator and Chamber Ensemble (1969); *Caela Hebe* for Chorus and 13 Instruments (1970); *Galgenlieder* for Soprano, String Quartet, Clarinet, Flute, and Piano (1975); *Mutations* for Soprano, Bass, Wind Quintet, and Percussion (1979); *Music* for Voices, Wind Quintet, and Percussion (1980); *Musik für Morgenstern* for Bass, Clarinet, and Chamber String Orch. (1983); *Songs of Youth* for Chorus, Trumpet, and Kettledrums (1985); *Aztecian Songs* for Soprano, Piano, and Percussion (1986); *Magic Formulas* for Alto and String Quartet (1988).—**NS/LK/DM**

Zeller, Carl (Johann Adam), Austrian composer; b. St. Peter-in-der-Au, June 19, 1842; d. Baden, near Vienna, Aug. 17, 1898. He learned to sing and play various instruments in his youth, and at age 11 became a member of the boy's choir at the Vienna court chapel; pursued training in law at the Univ. of Vienna and the Univ. of Graz (Dr.Jur., 1869) and in composition from Simon Sechter in Vienna. After practicing law, he was an official in the Austrian Ministry of Education and Culture (from 1873). Although following music only as an avocation, he became one of the most popular operetta composers of the day, winning extraordinary success with his *Der Vogelhändler* (Vienna, Jan. 10, 1891) and *Der Obersteiger* (Vienna, Jan. 5, 1894). Other successful operettas (all produced in Vienna) were *Joconda* (March 18, 1876), *Die Carbonari* (Nov. 27, 1880), *Der Vagabund* (Oct. 30, 1886), and *Der Kellermeister* (Dec. 21, 1901).

BIBL.: C.W. Zeller, *Mein Vater C. Z.* (St. Pölten, 1942).—**NS/LK/DM**

Zelter, Carl Friedrich, eminent German composer and teacher; b. Berlin, Dec. 11, 1758; d. there, May 15, 1832. The son of a mason, he was brought up in the same trade, but his musical inclinations soon asserted themselves. He began training in piano and violin at 17, and from 1779 he was a part-time violinist in the Doebbelin Theater orch. in Berlin; was a pupil of C.F.C. Fasch (1784–86). In 1786 he brought out a funeral cantata on the death of Frederick the Great. In 1791 he joined the Singverein (later Singakademie) conducted by Fasch, often acting as his deputy, and succeeding him in 1800. He was elected associate ("Assessor") of the Royal Academy of the Arts in Berlin in 1806, becoming a prof. in 1809. In 1807 he organized a Ripienschule for orch. practice, and in 1809 he founded in Berlin the Liedertafel, a pioneer men's choral society that became famous; similar organizations were subsequently formed throughout Germany, and later in America. Zelter composed about 100 men's choruses for the Liedertafel. In 1822 he founded the Royal Inst. for Church Music in Berlin, of which he was director until his death (the Inst. was later reorganized as the Akademie für Kirchen- und Schulmusik). His students included Mendelssohn, Meyerbeer, Loewe, and Nicolai. Goethe greatly admired Zelter's musical settings of his poems, preferring them to Schubert's and Beethoven's; this predilection led to their friendship, which was reflected in a voluminous correspondence, *Briefwechsel zwischen Goethe und Zelter* (ed. in 6 vols. by F.W. Riemer, Berlin, 1833–34; ed. in 3 vols. by L. Geiger, Leipzig, 1906; ed. in 4 vols. by M. Hecker, Leipzig, 1913; Eng. tr. by A.D. Coleridge, London, 1887). His songs are historically important, since they form a link between old ballad types and the new art of the lied, which found its flowering in Schubert and Schumann. Zelter's settings of Goethe's *König von Thule* and of *Es ist ein Schuss gefallen* became extremely popular. He publ. a biography of Fasch (Berlin, 1801). Zelter's autobiography was first publ. under the title *C.F. Zelter. Eine Lebensbeschreibung nach autobiographischen Manuscripten*, ed. by W. Rintel, then as *C.F. Zelter. Darstellungen seines Lebens* (Weimar, 1931).

WORKS: VOCAL: Lieder: *12 Lieder am Klavier zu singen* (Berlin and Leipzig, 1796); *12 Lieder am Klavier zu singen* (Berlin, 1801); *Sammlung kleiner Balladen und Lieder* (Hamburg, c. 1802); *Sämmtliche Lieder, Balladen und Romanzen* (4 vols., Berlin, 1810–13); *Neue Liedersammlung* (Zürich and Berlin, 1821); *6 deutsche Lieder* for Bass and Piano (Berlin, c. 1826); *6 deutsche Lieder* for Alto and Piano (Berlin, c. 1827); *Täfellieder für 4*

Männerstimmen (Berlin, n.d.); *10 Lieder für Männerstimmen* (Berlin, c. 1831); *Liedertafel-Gesänge* (6 vols.); etc. **OTHER VOCAL:** Many other works, including sacred and secular choral pieces. **OTHER:** Viola Concerto (1779); various keyboard pieces.

BIBL.: W. Bornemann, *Die Z.sche Liedertafel in Berlin* (Berlin, 1851); L. Sieber, *C.F. Z. und der deutsche Männergesang* (Basel, 1862); G. Kruse, Z. (Leipzig, 1915; 2nd ed., 1921); A. Morgenroth, *C.F. Z.* (diss., Univ. of Berlin, 1922); G. Schünemann, *C.F. Z., der Begründer der preussischen Musikpflege* (Berlin, 1932); G. Wittmann, *Das klavierbegleitete Sololied K.F. Z.s* (diss., Univ. of Giessen, 1936); G. Schünemann, *C.F. Z.: Der Mensch und sein Werk* (Berlin, 1937); S. Holtzmann, ed., *C.F. Z. im Spiegel seines Briefwechsel mit Goethe* (Weimar, 1957); W. Reich, ed., *C.F. Z., Selbstdarstellung* (Zürich, 1958); K. Taubert, *C.F. Z.: Ein Leben durch das Handwerk für die Musik* (Berlin, 1958); M. Victor, *C.F. Z. und seine Freundschaft mit Goethe* (Berlin and Weimar, 1958); R. Barr, *C.F. Z.: A Study of the Lied in Berlin during the Late 18th and Early 19th Centuries* (diss., Univ. of Wisc., 1968); D. Fischer-Dieskau, *C.F. Z. und das Berliner Musikleben seiner Zeit: Eine Biographie* (Berlin, 1997).—**NS/LK/DM**

Zeltser, Mark, Russian-born American pianist; b. Kishinev, April 8, 1947. He began piano lessons as a child under his mother's tutelage and made his debut as a soloist with the Kishinev Phil. when he was 9. He pursued training with Flier at the Moscow Cons., graduating in 1971. In the meantime, he captured 3rd prize in the Long-Thibaud Competition in Paris in 1967 and 2nd prize in the Busoni Competition in Bolzano in 1968. In 1976 he played at the Spoleto Festival. He made his first appearance at the Salzburg Festival in 1977. In 1978 he made his N.Y. debut. In subsequent seasons, he appeared as a soloist with many of the world's major orchs. and as a recitalist.—**NS/LK/DM**

Zemlinsky, Alexander von, important Austrian composer and conductor of partly Jewish descent (he removed the nobiliary particle "von" in 1918 when such distinctions were outlawed in Austria); b. Vienna, Oct. 14, 1871; d. Larchmont, N.Y., March 15, 1942. At the Vienna Cons. he studied piano with Door (1887–90) and composition with Krenn, Robert Fuchs, and J.N. Fuchs (1890–92). In 1893 he joined the Vienna Tonkünstlerverein. In 1895 he became connected with the orch. society Polyhymnia, and met Schoenberg, whom he advised on the technical aspects of chamber music; Schoenberg always had the highest regard for Zemlinsky as a composer and lamented the lack of appreciation for Zemlinsky's music. There was also a personal bond between them; in 1901 Schoenberg married Zemlinsky's sister Mathilde. Zemlinsky's first opera, *Sarema*, to a libretto by his own father, was premiered in Munich on Oct. 10, 1897; Schoenberg made a Klavierauszug of it. Zemlinsky also entered into contact with Mahler, music director of the Vienna Court Opera, who accepted Zemlinsky's opera *Es war einmal* for performance; Mahler conducted its premiere at the Court Opera on Jan. 22, 1900, and it became Zemlinsky's most popular production. From 1900 to 1906 Zemlinsky served as conductor of the Karlstheater in Vienna; in 1903 he conducted at the Theater an der Wien; in 1904 he was named chief conductor of the Volksoper; in 1910 he orchestrated and conducted the ballet *Der Schneemann* by the greatly talented 11-year-old wunderkind Erich Korngold. About that time, he and Schoenberg organized in Vienna the Union of Creative Musicians, which performed his tone poem *Die Seejungfrau*. In 1911 Zemlinsky moved to Prague, where he became conductor at the German Opera, and also taught conducting and composition at the German Academy of Music (from 1920). In 1927 he moved to Berlin, where he obtained the appointment of asst. conductor at the Kroll Opera, with Otto Klemperer as chief conductor and music director. When the Nazis came to power in Germany in 1933, he returned to Vienna, and also filled engagements as a guest conductor in Russia and elsewhere. After the Anschluss of 1938, he emigrated to America. As a composer, Zemlinsky followed the post-Romantic trends of Mahler and Richard Strauss. He was greatly admired but his works were seldom performed, despite the efforts of Schoenberg and his associates to revive his music. How strongly he influenced his younger contemporaries is illustrated by the fact that Alban Berg quoted some of Zemlinsky's music from the *Lyric Symphony* in his own *Lyrische Suite*.

WORKS: DRAMATIC: Opera: *Sarema* (1894–95; Munich, Oct. 10, 1897); *Es war einmal* (1897–99; Vienna, Jan. 22, 1900); *Der Traumgörge* (1903–06; Nuremberg, Oct. 11, 1980); *Kleider machen Leute* (1907–10; Vienna, Dec. 2, 1910; rev. 1921); *Eine florentinische Tragödie* (1915–16; Stuttgart, Jan. 30, 1917); *Der Zwerg*, after Oscar Wilde's *The Birthday of the Infanta* (1920–21; Cologne, May 28, 1922); *Der Kreidekreis* (1930–32; Zürich, Oct. 14, 1933); *Der König Kandaules* (1935–36; left in short score; completed by A. Beaumont, 1989); also 5 unfinished operas: *Malwa* (1902; 1912–13), *Herrn Arnes Schatz* (1917), *Raphael* (1918), *Vitalis* (1926), and *Circe* (1939–41). **Mimodrama:** *Ein Lichtstrahl* (1903). **Ballet:** *Das gläsende Herz*, after Hofmannsthal (1901). **Incidental Music To:** Shakespeare's *Cymbeline* (1914). **ORCH.:** 3 syms.: No. 1 (1892), No. 2 (1897; Vienna, March 5, 1899), and No. 3, *Lyrische Symphonie*, for Soprano, Baritone, and Orch., after Rabindranath Tagore (1922–23; Prague, June 4, 1924); Suite (c. 1894); *Der Ring des Ofterdingen*, overture (1894–95); *Die Seejungfrau*, tone poem after Andersen (1902–03); Sinfonietta (1934). **CHAMBER:** *Serenade* for Violin and Piano (1892); Suite for Violin and Piano (c. 1893); String Quintet (c. 1895); Trio for Clarinet or Viola, Cello, and Piano (1895); 4 string quartets: No. 1 (c. 1895; Vienna, Dec. 2, 1896), No. 2 (1913–15), No. 3 (1924), and No. 4, Suite (1936). **Piano:** *Ländliche Tanze* (1891); *Fantasien über Gedichte von Richard Dehmel* (1898). **VOCAL:** *Lieder* for Voice and Piano (2 books, 1894–96); *Der alte Garten* for Voice and Orch. (1895); *Die Reisen* for Voice and Orch., after Eichendorff (1895); *Orientalisches Sonett* for Voice and Piano (1895); *Waldgespräch* for Soprano, 2 Horns, Harp, and Strings (1895–96); *Nun schwillt der See so bang* for Voice and Piano (1896); *Süsse Sommernacht* for Voice and Piano (1896); *Frühlingsglaube* for Voices and Strings (1896); *Frühlingsbegräbnis* for Soprano, Alto, Tenor, Bass, Chorus, and Orch. (1896; Vienna, Feb. 11, 1900); *Gesänge* for Voice and Piano (2 books, c. 1896); *Walzer-Gesänge nach toskanischen Volksliedern* for Voice and Piano (1898); *Irmelin Rose und andere Gesänge* for Voice and Piano (1898); *Turmwächterlied und andere Gesänge* for Voice and Piano (1898–99); *Ehetanzlied und andere Gesänge* for Voice and Piano (c. 1900); *Psalm No. 83* for Chorus and Orch. (1900); *Es war ein alter König* for Voice and Piano (1903); *Schmetterlinge* for Voice and Piano (1904); *Ansturm* for Voice and Piano (1907); *Auf See* for Voice and Piano (1907); *Jane Grey* for

Voice and Piano (1907); *Psalm No. 23* for Voices and Orch. (1910); *6 Gesänge* for Mezzo-soprano or Baritone and Piano or Orch. (1910–13); *Symphonische Gesänge* for Voice and Orch. (1929); *6 Lieder* for Voice and Piano (1934); *Psalm No. 13* for Voices and Orch. (1935); *12 Lieder* for Voice and Piano (1937).

BIBL.: H. Weber, *A. Z.: Eine Studie* (Vienna, 1977); W. Loll, *Zwischen Tradition und Avantgarde: Die Kammermusik A. Z.s* (Kassel, 1990); O. Biba, *A. Z.: Bin ich ein Wiener? Ausstellung im Archiv der Gesellschaft der Musikfreunde in Wien: Katalog* (Vienna, 1992); U. Rademacher, *Vokales Schaffen an der Schwelle zur neuen Musik: Studien zur Klavierlied A. Z.s* (Kassel, 1996).—**NS/LK/DM**

Zenatello, Giovanni, Italian tenor; b. Verona, Feb. 22, 1876; d. N.Y., Feb. 11, 1949. He was originally trained as a baritone by Zannoni and Moretti in Verona. He made his official operatic debut as such in Belluno in 1898 as Silvio in Pagliacci; sang in minor opera companies in Italy; then went to Naples, where he sang the tenor role of Canio in 1899. He sang the role of Pinkerton in the first performance of Puccini's *Madama Butterfly* (La Scala, Milan, Feb. 17, 1904). In 1905 he sang at Covent Garden, London. On Nov. 4, 1907, he made his American debut in N.Y. as Enzo Grimaldo in Ponchielli's *La Gioconda.* From 1909 to 1912, and again in 1913–14, he was the leading tenor of the Boston Opera Co.; during the season of 1912–13, he sang with the Chicago Opera Co; also traveled with various touring opera companies in South America, Spain, and Russia. He eventually settled in N.Y. as a singing teacher, maintaining a studio with his wife, **Maria Gay**, whom he married in 1913. Together, they trained many famous singers, among them Lily Pons and Nino Martini. He retired from the stage in 1928.—**NS/LK/DM**

Zender, (Johannes Wolfgang) Hans, distinguished German conductor, composer, and pedagogue; b. Wiesbaden, Nov. 22, 1936. He studied with August Leopolder (piano) and Kurt Hessenberg (composition) at the Frankfurt am Main Hochschule für Musik (1956–59), received private instruction in choral conducting from Kurt Thomas, and was a student of Edith Picht-Axenfeld (piano), Carl Ueter (conducting), and Wolfgang Fortner (composition) at the Freiburg im Breisgau Hochschule für Musik (1959–63). In 1963–64 he held a fellowship at the Villa Massimo in Rome, where he worked with Bernd Alois Zimmermann. After serving as chief conductor of the Bonn City Theater (1964–68), he held another fellowship at the Villa Massimo in Rome in 1968–69. From 1969 to 1972 he was Generalmusikdirektor of Kiel. He was chief conductor of the Saarland Radio Sym. Orch. in Saarbrücken from 1971 to 1984. He served as Generalmusikdirektor of Hamburg from 1984 to 1987, where he was in charge of the State Opera and the Phil. State Orch. He was chief conductor of the Netherlands Radio Chamber Orch. in Hilversum from 1987 to 1991, and concurrently was principal guest conductor of the Opera National in Brussels. In 1988 he became a prof. of composition at the Frankfurt am Main Hochschule für Musik, and in 1999 he also became permanent guest conductor of the SWR (South West Radio) Sym. Orch. of Baden-Baden and Freiburg im Breisgau. In 1978 he was awarded the Saarland Arts Prize and in 1997 the Music Prize and the Goethe Prize of Frankfurt am Main. He was made a member of the Freie Akademie der Künste in Hamburg in 1985, of the Akademie der Künste in Berlin in 1989, and of the Bayerische (Bavarian) Akademie der Schönen Künste in Munich in 1994. To mark his 60th birthday, a "Hans Zender Edition" of 17 CDs featuring his conductorship appeared in 1997. In 1999 he was the guest of honor at the Villa Massimo in Rome. As a guest conductor, Zender has appeared throughout Germany and widely abroad. He is the author of the vols. *Happy New Ears: Das Abenteuer, Musik zu hören* (Freiburg im Breisgau, 1991) and *Wir steigen niemals in denselben Fluss* (Freiburg im Breisgau, 1996). After composing along strict serial lines, he developed an intriguing individual voice in which time and space became crucial elements.

WORKS: DRAMATIC: *Stephen Climax*, opera after James Joyce (1979–84; Frankfurt am Main, June 15, 1986; 2 suites, 1984); *Don Quijote de la Mancha*, theatrical adventure after Cervantes (1989–91; Stuttgart, Oct. 3, 1993; rev. 1994; Heidelberg, Jan. 1999); *Nanzen und die Katze*, radio play (1995). **ORCH.:** *Schachspiel* for 2 Orch. Groups (1969); *Modelle* (1971–73); *Zeitströme* (1974); *Dialog mit Haydn* for 2 Pianos and 3 Orch. Groups (1982); *5 Haiku* for Flute and Strings (1982); *Lo-Shu V* for Flute and Orch. (1987); *Koan* (Freiburg im Breisgau, Nov. 19, 1996); *Schumann-Fantasie* (1997; Cologne, Sept. 1, 1998); *Kalligraphie I-X* (1998 et seq.). **CHAMBER:** Concerto for Flute and Solo Instrument (1959); *Tre Pezzi* for Oboe (1963); Quartet for Flute, Cello, Piano, and Percussion (1964); *Trifolium* for Flute, Cello, and Piano (1966); *Litanei* for 3 Cellos (1976); *Lo-Shu I* for 1 to 3 Flutes, 1 to 3 Cellos, and 1 to 3 Percussion (1977), *II* for Flute (1979), *VI* for Flute and Cello (1989; Stuttgart, March 10, 1990), and *VII, 4 Enso* for 2 Instrumental Groups (Witten, April 27, 1997); *Hölderlin lesen I* for String Quartet and Speaking Voice (1980), *II* for Speaking Voice, Viola, and Live Electronics (Stuttgart, Nov. 15, 1987), and *III, "denn wiederkommen"* for String Quartet and Speaking Voice (1991; Hombroich, May 31, 1992). **KEYBOARD:** *3 Nocturnes* for Harpsichord (1963); *Chiffren* for Harpsichord (1976); *Memorial*, 3 studies for Piano (1989; Hamburg, June 14, 1990); *Spazierwege und Spiele*, 14 piano pieces for Children (Detmold, Nov. 4, 1990). **VOCAL:** 3 *Rondels nach Mallarmé* for Alto, Flute, and Viola (1961); *3 Lieder* for Soprano and Orch., after Eichendorff (1963–64); *Vexilla regis*, concerto for Soprano, Flute, Trumpet, and Instrument (1964); *Canto I* for Chorus, Flute, Piano, Strings, and Percussion (1965), *II* for Soprano, Chorus, and Orch., after Ezra Pound (1967), *III* for Soprano, Tenor, Baritone, 10 Instruments, and Live Electronics, after Cervantes (1968), *IV* for 16 Voices and 16 Instruments (1969–72), *V* for Voices and Percussion ad libitum (1972–74), *VI* for Bass-baritone, Chorus, and Tape ad libitum (1988; Stuttgart, May 23, 1990), *VII: Nanzen No Kyô* for 4 Choruses and 4 Instrumental Groups (1992; Cologne, June 11, 1993), and *VIII: Shir Hashirim-Lied der Lieder* for Soloists, Chorus, Live Electronics, and Orch. (1992–96; first complete perf., Saarbrücken, March 29, 1998); *Les Sirénes chantent quand la raison s'endort* for Soprano, Flute, Clarinet, Cello, Vibraphone, and Piano (1966); *Muji No Kyô* for Voice, Flute, Violin or Cello, Piano, Synthesizer, and Tutti Instrument (1975); *Kantate nach Meister Eckhart* for Alto, Alto Flute, Cello, and Harpsichord (1980); *Die Wüste hat zwölf Ding'* for Alto and Small Orch. (1985); *Schubert-Chöre*, adaptation of 4 pieces for Tenor, Chorus, and Orch. (Bonn, Nov. 19, 1986); *Jours de Silence* for Baritone and Orch. (1987–88); *Fūrin No Kyō* for Soprano, Clarinet, and Ensemble (1988; Graz, Oct. 20, 1989); *Animula* for Women's Chorus, Chamber Orch., and Tape (1988–96); *Winterreise*, "composed interpretation" of Schubert's song cycle for Tenor and Small Orch. (Frankfurt am Main, Sept. 21, 1993); *Römer VIII, 26* for Soprano, Alto, Organ, and Live Electronics ad libitum (Kassel, April 1, 1994); *Johannes III, 1–5* for Chorus (1997; Cologne, June 19, 1998); *Music to hear* for Soprano, 2 Flutes, and Chamber Ensemble, after Shakespeare (1998; Vienna, Nov. 1999). **ELECTRONIC:** *Bremen Wood* (1967); *Elemente* (1976). **OTHER:** Orchestration of 5 *Préludes* by Debussy for Small Orch. (Frankfurt am Main, Nov. 24, 1991). —**NS/LK/DM**

Zeno, Apostolo, famous Italian opera librettist; b. Venice, Dec. 11, 1668; d. there, Nov. 11, 1750. In 1710 he founded the Giornale dei Letterati d'Italia, and in 1718 he was appointed court poet at Vienna; returned to Venice in 1729. The total number of librettos written by him (some in collaboration with Pietro Pariati) is 71; they were collected and ed. by Gasparo Gozzi as *Poesie drammatiche di Apostolo Zeno* (10 vols., Venice, 1744; reprinted in 11 vols., Orléans, 1785–86). A man of great knowledge and culture, he was also an ardent numismatist; his large collection of coins was exhibited at Vienna in 1955.

BIBL.: M. Fehr, *A. Z. und seine Reform des Operntexts* (diss., Univ. of Zürich, 1912); R. Freeman, *Opera Without Drama: Currents of Change in Italian Opera, 1675–1725, and the Roles Played therein by Z., Caldara, and Others* (diss., Princeton Univ., 1967).—**NS/LK/DM**

Zeuner, Charles (actually, **Heinrich Christoph**), German-American organist; b. Eisleben, Saxony, Sept. 20, 1795; d. (suicide) Philadelphia, Nov. 7, 1857. He studied in Weimar with Hummel and with Michael Gottard Fischer in Erfurt. About 1830 he settled in Boston, where he became organist at the Park St. Church; was also organist of the Handel and Haydn Soc. (1830–37), and briefly its president (1838–39). He then went to Philadelphia, where he served as a church organist. He composed one of the earliest American oratorios, *The Feast of Tabernacles* (1832; Boston, May 3, 1837). He publ. *Church Music, Consisting of New and Original Anthems, Motets and Chants* (1831), The American Harp (1832), The Ancient Lyre, a book of hymn tunes (1833 and several later eds.), and Organ Voluntaries (1840), and contributed to Lowell Mason's *Lyra Sacra* (1832). Some of his compositions are also included in *The Psaltery*, ed. by Mason and Webb (1845).

BIBL.: W. Biggers, *The Choral Music of C. Z. (1795–1857), German-American Composer, with a Performance Edition of Representative Works* (diss., Univ. of Iowa, 1976).—**NS/LK/DM**

Žganec, Vinko, Croatian ethnomusicologist; b. Vratišinci, Jan. 22, 1890; d. Zagreb, Dec. 12, 1976. He studied law at the Univ. of Zagreb (doctorate, 1919). He then became interested in song collecting; traveled in the countryside gathering native melodies. He publ. several albums of harmonizations of these songs and numerous articles in Croatian, German, and American music journals dealing with specific aspects of Croatian songs; in his analyses of their structure, he applied modern methods of ethnomusicology. He was a lecturer on folk music at the Zagreb Academy of Music (1949–68).—**NS/LK/DM**

Zhelobinsky, Valeri (Viktorovich), Russian composer, pianist, and teacher; b. Tambov, Jan. 27, 1913; d. Leningrad, Aug. 13, 1946. He studied in Tambov and with Shcherbachev at the Leningrad Cons. (1928–32). He taught at the Tambov Music School. As a pianist, he performed mainly his own compositions. His operas were written in a fine Romantic manner.

WORKS: DRAMATIC: *Kamarinsky muzhik*, opera (Leningrad, Sept. 15, 1933); *Her Saint's Day*, opera (1934; Leningrad, Feb. 22, 1935); *Mother*, opera, after Maxim Gorky (Leningrad, Dec. 30, 1938); *The Last Ball*, operetta (Leningrad, March 30, 1939); film scores. **ORCH.:** 6 syms.: No. 1 (1930), No. 2, *To the Memory of Revolutionary Victims* (1932), No. 3, *Dramatic* (Moscow, Dec. 17, 1939), No. 4 (Moscow, May 30, 1943), No. 5 (1944), and No. 6 (1946); 3 piano concertos (1933, 1934, 1939); Violin Concerto (1934); *Romantic Poem* for Violin and Orch. (1939). **Piano:** *24 Preludes*; 2 children's albums.—**NS/LK/DM**

Zhiganov, Nazib, Russian composer and music educator of Tatar heritage; b. Uralsk, Jan. 15, 1911; d. Kazan, June 2, 1988. He was reared in an orphan asylum and first studied music in Kazan. He went to Moscow, where he studied at a technological school and then pursued musical training with Litinsky at the Cons. (graduated, 1938). In 1945 he became director and a prof. of the newly founded Kazan Cons. In his music, he attempted to create a new national Tatar school of composition, following the harmonic and instrumental precepts of the Russian national school.

WORKS: DRAMATIC: Opera (all 1st perf. in Kazan): *Katchkyn* (June 17, 1939); *Irek* (Liberty; Feb. 24, 1940); *Altyntchetch* (The Golden Haired; July 12, 1941); *Ildar* (Nov. 7, 1942); *Tulyak* (July 27, 1945); *Namus* (Honor; June 25, 1950); *Dzhalil*, operatic monologue (1950). **Ballet:** *Zugra* (Kazan, May 17, 1946). **Other:** Film music. **ORCH.:** 4 syms. (1937, 1968, 1971, 1973); overtures; suites; marches. **OTHER:** Chamber music; piano pieces; vocal music.

BIBL.: Y. Girshman, *N. Z.* (Moscow, 1957).—**NS/LK/DM**

Zhitomirsky, Alexander, Russian composer and pedagogue; b. Kherson, May 23, 1881; d. Leningrad, Dec. 16, 1937. He took violin lessons in Odessa and in Vienna, and also studied piano. Returning to Russia, he entered the St. Petersburg Cons. as a student of Rimsky-Korsakov, Liadov, and Glazunov, graduating in 1910; from 1915 to 1937 he was on its faculty as an instructor in composition and orchestration. In his compositions, he followed the style and manner of the Russian national school; he wrote a Violin Concerto (1937), String Quartet (1923), and a number of songs and choruses. —**NS/LK/DM**

Zhivotov, Alexei, Russian composer; b. Kazan, Nov. 14, 1904; d. Leningrad, Aug. 27, 1964. He studied at the Leningrad Cons. with Shcherbachev, graduating in 1930. During the siege of Leningrad by the Nazis (1941–42), he remained in the city and was awarded a medal for valor. Among his works were film music, several orch. pieces, and much vocal music, including patriotic choruses and songs.—**NS/LK/DM**

Zhuk, Isaak, Russian violinist; b. Poltava, Dec. 16, 1902; d. Moscow, April 4, 1973. He studied with I.

Goldberg in Poltava, where he made his debut (1917), then with S. Korguyev at the Leningrad Cons. (1924) and A. Yampolsky at the Moscow Cons. (1925–30). He organized the Bolshoi Quartet and was one of its members (1931–68); was concertmaster of the U.S.S.R. Sym. Orch. (1952–69). His son, Valentin Zhuk (b. Moscow, June 28, 1934), is a talented violinist. He studied with Yampolsky, and received prizes in various international competitions, including the Tchaikovsky (Moscow, 6th, 1958), Paganini (Genoa, 2nd, 1963), and Long-Thibaud (Paris, 2nd, 1960). He was concertmaster of the Moscow Phil. (from 1970).—**NS/LK/DM**

Zhukovsky, Herman, Ukrainian composer; b. Radzivilovo, Volynya, Nov. 13, 1913; d. Kiev, March 15, 1976. He studied piano and composition at the Kiev Cons., graduating in 1941. From 1951 to 1958 he taught theory there. He wrote various works in the approved style of socialist realism, using authentic Ukrainian song patterns for his materials, but a crisis supervened in his steady progress when his opera *From the Bottom of My Heart* (Moscow, Jan. 16, 1951) was viciously attacked by the cultural authorities of the Soviet government for alleged ideological and musical aberrations; he revised the score, and the new version was approved. His other operas were *Marina* (Kiev, March 12, 1939), *The First Spring* (1960), *Contrasts of Centuries*, operatic trilogy (1967), *A Soldier's Wife*, monodrama for Baritone (1968), and *One Step to Love* (1970). He also wrote the ballets *Rostislava* (1955), *Forest Song* (Moscow, May 1, 1961), and *Death and the Maiden* (1970), as well as film scores, Piano Concerto (1938), Violin Concerto (1953), chamber music, etc.—**NS/LK/DM**

Ziani, Marco Antonio, Italian composer, nephew of **Pietro Andrea Ziani;** b. Venice, c. 1653; d. Vienna, Jan. 22, 1715. In 1686 he was named maestro di cappella at S. Barbara in Mantua. In 1700 he became Vice-Hofkapellmeister at the Vienna court, and in 1712 he was elevated to Hofkapellmeister. He composed 45 operas and serenades, of which the following were produced in Vienna: *Il Giordano pio* (July 26, 1700), *Gli ossequi della notte* (July 22, 1701), *Il Temistocle* (June 9, 1701), *La fuga dell'invidia* (Nov. 15, 1701), *Il Romolo* (June 9, 1702), *Cajo Popilio* (June 9, 1704), *L'Ercole vincitore dell'invidia* (March 19, 1706), *Il Meleagro* (Aug. 16, 1706), *Chilonida* (April 21, 1709), *Il Campidoglio ricuperato* (July 26, 1709), and *L'Atenaide* (with Negri, Caldara, and F. Conti; Nov. 19, 1714). He also composed church music. —**NS/LK/DM**

Ziani, Pietro Andrea, Italian organist and composer, uncle of **Marco Antonio Ziani;** b. Venice, c. 1616; d. Naples, Feb. 12, 1684. He took holy orders in 1640, then was a canon regular and organist at S. Salvatore in Venice. From 1657 to 1659 he served as maestro di cappella at S. Maria Maggiore in Bergamo; in 1662 he became Vice-Kapellmeister to the Dowager Empress Eleonora in Vienna. In 1669 he succeeded Cavalli as 1st organist at San Marco in Venice; went to Naples in 1677, where he was named a teacher at the Cons. S. Onofrio. He also became honorary organist at the Naples court, where he was made maestro di cappella in 1680; was pensioned in 1684. He wrote 23 operas, including *Le fortune di Rodope, e di Damira* (Venice, Carnival 1657), *L'Antigona delusa da Alceste* (Venice, Jan. 15, 1660), *La congiura del vizio contra la virtù* (Vienna, Nov. 15, 1663), and *La Circe* (Vienna, June 9, 1665). He also composed sonatas for 3, 4, 5, or 6 instruments (1691), church music, etc.—**NS/LK/DM**

Zich, Jaroslav, Czech composer and teacher, son of **Otakar Zich;** b. Prague, Jan. 17, 1912. He studied with his father, at the Prague Cons. (1928–31) with Foerster, and at the Charles Univ. in Prague. From 1952 to 1977 he taught at the Prague Academy of Music.

WORKS: DRAMATIC: Melodrama: *Romance helgolandská* (1934). **ORCH.:** *Rhapsody* for Cello and Orch. (1956). **CHAMBER:** Duo for Violin and Cello (1930); String Quartet (1931); *Ekloga, nokturno a pastorale* for Piano (1932); *Matenik* for Cello and Piano (1935); *U muziky* for Octet (1940); *Malá serenáda* for Wind Quintet (1974). **VOCAL:** *Letmý host* for Voice and Orch. (1932); solo songs.—**NS/LK/DM**

Zich, Otakar, Czech composer and musicologist, father of **Jaroslav Zich:;** b Králové Městec, March 25, 1879; d. Ouběnice, near Benešov, July 9, 1934. He studied mathematics at the Univ. of Prague (Ph.D., 1901), and also received training in musicology from Hostinský and in composition from Stecker (1897–1901); completed his Habilitation at the Univ. of Prague in 1911. After teaching in a secondary school in Domažlice (from 1901), he was made prof. of philosophy at the Univ. of Brno in 1919. From 1924 he was prof. of aesthetics at the Univ. of Prague.

WRITINGS (all publ. in Prague): *Smetanova Hubička* (Smetana's The Kiss; 1911); *Hector Berlioz a jeho Episoda ze života umělcova* (Hector Berlioz and His Episode from the Life of an Artist; 1914); *Česke lidové tance s proměnlivým taktem* (Czech Folkdances with a Changing Beat; 1917); *Symfonické básně Smetanovy* (Smetana's Symphonic Poems; 1924; 2nd ed., 1949); *Estetika dramatického uměni* (Aesthetics of Dramatic Art; 1931).

WORKS: DRAMATIC: Opera: *Marlíčský nápad* (Painter's Whim; 1908; Prague, March 11, 1910); *Vina* (Guilt; 1911–15; Prague, March 14, 1922); *Preciézky*, after Molière's *Les Précieuses ridicules* (1924; Prague, May 11, 1926). **VOCAL:** Cantatas, song cycles, part-songs, etc.

BIBL.: J. Hutter, *O. Z. a jeho "Vina"* (Prague, 1922); J. Burjanek, *O. Z.: Studie k vývoji českého muzikologického myšleni v prvni tčetine našeho stoleti* (O.Z.: A Study of the Development of Czech Musicological Thought in the First Third of This Century; Prague, 1966).—**NS/LK/DM**

Zichy, Géza, Count Vasony-Keö, Hungarian left-hand pianist and composer; b. Sztára Castle, July 22, 1849; d. Budapest, Jan. 14, 1924. He studied with Volkmann and Liszt. At the age of 14 he lost his right arm in a hunting accident, and, refusing to give up music, developed his left-hand technique to the point of virtuosity; also made arrangements for left hand. On several occasions he played in public with Liszt an arrangement of the *Rákóczy March* for 3 hands. From 1875 to 1918 he was president of the National Cons. in Budapest; was also Intendant of the National Theater and Opera there (1890–94). He composed operas, produced at Budapest: *A vár története* (Castle Story; May 16, 1888), *Alár* (April 11, 1896), and *Roland mester* (Jan. 10, 1899). Other works include a dramatic trilogy on the life of Rákóczi, *Nemo* (March 30, 1905), *Rákóczi Ferenz* (Jan. 30, 1909), and *Rodostó* (March 20, 1912), *Gemma*, ballet (Prague, 1903), *Dolores*, cantata (1889), Piano Concerto (1902), Piano Sonata, studies and piano pieces for the left hand alone, songs, etc. He publ. an autobiography, *Aus meinem Leben* (Ger. ed., 3 vols., 1911–20). **—NS/LK/DM**

Ziegler, Delores, American mezzo-soprano; b. Atlanta, Sept. 4, 1951. She studied at the Univ. of Tenn. After beginning her career with concert engagements, she made her operatic stage debut in Knoxville in 1978 as Verdi's Flora. In 1978–79 she was a member of the Santa Fe Opera apprenticeship program; in 1979, appeared as Verdi's Maddalena in St. Louis. She made her European operatic debut in Bonn in 1981 as Dorabella. In 1982 she sang for the first time at the Cologne Opera. In 1984 she appeared as Dorabella at her Glyndebourne debut and as Bellini's Romeo at her La Scala debut in Milan. She sang for the first time at the Salzburg Festival in 1985 as Minerva in Henze's setting of *Il Ritorno d'Ulisse*. In 1990 she made her Metropolitan Opera debut as Gounod's Siebel. In 1996 she portrayed Dorabella at the Washington (D.C.) Opera. She sang Bellini's Romeo in Atlanta in 1999. As a guest artist, she also sang in Munich, Florence, Hamburg, San Diego, Toronto, and elsewhere; also was widely engaged as a concert artist. **—NS/LK/DM**

Ziehn, Bernhard, noted German-American music theorist and teacher; b. Erfurt, Jan. 20, 1845; d. Chicago, Sept. 8, 1912. He studied in Erfurt, and was a schoolteacher in Mühlhausen. In 1868 he emigrated to the U.S., and taught German, mathematics, and music theory at the German Lutheran School in Chicago (1868–71). Subsequently he became a private music teacher, and established himself as a theorist. His "enharmonic law," built on the principle of functional equality of chords, is an original contribution to the theory of harmony.

WRITINGS: *System der Übungen für Clavierspieler* (1881); *Ein Lehrgang für den ersten Clavierunterricht* (1881); *Harmonie- und Modulationslehre* (1887; 2nd ed., 1909; completely recast and publ. in Eng. as *Manual of Harmony: Theoretical and Practical*, 1907); *Five- and Six-Part Harmonies* (1911); *Canonical Studies: A New Technic in Composition* (1912; in both Eng. and Ger.); *Gesammelte Aufsätze zur Geschichte und Theorie der Musik* (Chicago, 1927).

BIBL.: H.J. Moser, *B. Z.: Der deutsch-amerikanische Musiktheoretiker* (Bayreuth, 1950).**—NS/LK/DM**

Ziehrer, Carl Michael, Austrian bandleader and composer; b. Vienna, May 2, 1843; d. there, Nov. 14, 1922. Entirely self-taught in music, he organized in 1863 a dance orch., with which he made tours of Austria and Germany, introducing his own pieces. With an enlarged orch. (50 players), he established a regular series of popular concerts in Vienna, which met with great success; in 1908 he was appointed music director of the court balls. He wrote nearly 600 marches and dances for orch. (some very popular: *Meeresleuchten, Evatöchter, Donauwalzer, Alt-Wien, Ziehrereien*, etc.), and produced in Vienna a number of operettas: *Wiener Kinder* (Feb. 19, 1881), *Mahomeds Paradies* (Feb. 26, 1866), *König Jerôme* (Nov. 28, 1878), *Ein Deutschmeister* (Nov. 30, 1888), *Der schöne Rigo* (May 24, 1898), *Die Landstreicher*, his best work (July 29, 1899), *Die drei Wünsche* (March 9, 1901), *Der Fremdenführer* (Oct. 11, 1902), *Der Schätzmeister* (Dec. 10, 1904), *Fesche Geister* (July 7, 1905), *Am Lido* (Aug. 31, 1907), *Ein tolles Mädel* (Nov. 8, 1907), *Der Liebeswalzer* (Oct. 24, 1908), *Die Gaukler* (Sept. 6, 1909), *Herr und Frau Biedermeier* (Oct. 5, 1910), *In 50 Jahren* (Jan. 7, 1911), *Furst Casimir* (Sept. 13, 1913), *Der Husarengeneral* (Oct. 3, 1913), *Das dumme Herz* (Feb. 27, 1914), and *Die verliebte Eskadron* (July 11, 1920).

BIBL.: M. Schönherr, *C.M. Z.* (Vienna, 1973); idem, *C.M. Z.: Sein Werk, sein Leben, seine Zeit* (Vienna, 1975).**—NS/LK/DM**

Zilcher, (Karl) Hermann (Josef), German composer, pianist, and pedagogue; b. Frankfurt am Main, Aug. 18, 1881; d. Würzburg, Jan. 1, 1948. He studied piano with his father, Paul Zilcher, and then continued his training at the Hoch Cons. in Frankfurt am Main (1897–1901) with Kwast (piano) and Knorr and Scholz (composition). After serving on its faculty (1905–08), he was a prof. at the Akademie der Tonkunst in Munich (1908–20). From 1920 to 1944 he was director of the Würzburg Cons. He also made tours as a pianist. His music represents an amalgam of late Romantic and Impressionist elements.

WORKS: DRAMATIC: *Fitzebutze*, Traumspiel (1903); *Doktor Eisenbart* (1922); incidental music. **ORCH.:** 4 syms.; 2 violin concertos; *Bayerische Suite* for Accordion Orch.; Accordion Concerto. **OTHER:** Many piano pieces, including a Sym. for 2 Pianos; numerous songs.

BIBL.: W. Altmann, *H. Z.* (Leipzig, 1907); H. Oppenheim, *H. Z.* (Munich, 1921).**—NS/LK/DM**

Zillig, Winfried (Petrus Ignatius), German conductor and composer; b. Würzburg, April 1, 1905; d. Hamburg, Dec. 17, 1963. He studied at the Würzburg Cons. and with Schoenberg in Vienna (1925–26) and in his master classes at the Prussian Academy of Arts in Berlin (1926–28). After working as répétiteur in Oldenburg (1928–32), he conducted in Düsseldorf (1932–37); was music director of the Essen Opera (1937–40), the Poznań Opera (1940–43), and the Düsseldorf Opera (1946–47); then was chief conductor of the Hesse Radio in Frankfurt am Main (1947–51). He was director of the music division of the North German Radio in Hamburg from 1959 to 1963.

WORKS: DRAMATIC: Opera: *Rosse* (Düsseldorf, Feb. 11, 1933); *Das Opfer* (Hamburg, Nov. 12, 1937); *Die Windsbraut* (Leipzig, May 12, 1941); *Troilus und Cressida* (1949; rev. 1963); *Bauernpassion*, television opera (1955); *Die Verlobung in St. Domingo*, radio opera (1956); *Das Verlöbnis* (1962; Linz, Nov. 23, 1963). **Other:** Incidental music. **ORCH.:** *Choralkonzert* (1924); Overture (1928); *Concerto for Orchestra* (1930); Concerto for Cello and Wind Orch. (1934; rev. 1952); *Tansymphonie* (1938); Concerto in One Movement (1948); Violin Concerto (1955); *Fantasia, Passacaglia, and Fugue on the Meistersinger Chorale*

(1963). **OTHER:** Chamber music; choral pieces; solo vocal works.

WRITINGS: *Variationen über neue Musik* (Munich, 1959; 2nd ed., 1963, as *Die neue Musik: Linien und Porträts; Von Wagner bis Strauss*).

BIBL.: S. Hilger, *Autonom oder angewandt?: Ze den Hörspielmusiken von W. Z. und Bernd Alois Zimmermann* (Mainz, 1996). **—NS/LK/DM**

Zimbalist, Efrem (Alexandrovich), eminent Russian-born American violinist and pedagogue; b. Rostov-na-Donu, April 21, 1889; d. Reno, Nev., Feb. 22, 1985. He studied violin with his father, an orch. musician, and from 1901 to 1907 was a pupil of Leopold Auer at the St. Petersburg Cons., graduating with the gold medal. He made a highly successful European appearance as a soloist in the Brahms Concerto in Berlin, Nov. 7, 1907. In 1911 he emigrated to the U.S.; made his American debut with the Boston Sym. Orch. on Oct. 27, 1911, playing the first American performance of Glazunov's Violin Concerto. In 1914 he married **Alma Gluck**, who died in 1938; his 2nd wife, whom he married in 1943, was **Mary Louise Curtis Bok**, founder of the Curtis Inst. Of Music in Philadelphia; in 1928 he joined its faculty; was its director from 1941 to 1968. After Mrs. Zimbalist's death in 1970, he moved to Reno, Nev., to live with his daughter. His son, Efrem Zimbalist Jr., was a well-known actor. Zimbalist was also a composer: he wrote the opera *Landara* (Philadelphia, April 6, 1956), a musical comedy, *Honeydew* (N.Y., 1920), *Slavonic Dances* for Violin and Orch. (1911), *American Rhapsody* for Orch. (Chicago, March 3, 1936; rev. version, Philadelphia, Feb. 5, 1943), *Portrait of an Artist*, symphonic poem (Philadelphia, Dec. 7, 1945), Violin Concerto (1947), Cello Concerto (1969), String Quartet, Violin Sonata, *Concert Phantasy on Le Coq d'or* for Violin and Piano, *Sarasateana* for Violin and Piano, songs, etc. He publ. *One Hour's Daily Exercise* for the violin.
—NS/LK/DM

Zimerman, Krystian, outstanding Polish pianist; b. Zabrze, Dec. 5, 1956. He commenced piano lessons at age 5 with his father; when he was 7 he became a pupil of Andrzej Jasiński, with whom he later studied at the Katowice Cons. In 1975 he won 1st prize in the Chopin Competition in Warsaw; then played with great success in Munich, Paris, London, and Vienna. In 1976 he was a soloist with the Berlin Phil. He made his first American appearance in 1978, and subsequently toured throughout the world to great critical acclaim. His performances of the Romantic repertory are remarkable for their discerning spontaneity. He has also played contemporary works, including Lutosławski's Piano Concerto (1988), which is dedicated to him.**—NS/LK/DM**

Zimmer, Ján, significant Slovak composer and pianist; b. Ružomberok, May 16, 1926; Bratislava, Jan. 21, 1993. He studied with Suchoň at the Bratislava Cons. (graduated, 1948), with Farkas at the Budapest Academy of Music (1948–49), and in Salzburg (1949). After working for the Czech Radio in Bratislava (1945–48), he taught at the Bratislava Cons. from 1948 until losing his post in 1952 under the Communist regime. In subsequent years, Zimmer devoted himself to composition and made occasional appearances as a pianist, principally in programs of his own works. His music was marked by a mastery of form, technique, and expression. While he sometimes utilized 12-tone and other modern techniques, he generally forged his own course as a worthy representative of the Slovak tradition.

WORKS (all 1st perf. in Bratislava unless otherwise given): **DRAMATIC:** *Oedipus Rex*, opera (1963–64); *Héraklés*, opera-ballet (1972); *The Broken Line*, opera (1974); film music. **ORCH.:** 7 piano concertos: No. 1 (1949; March 14, 1950), No. 2 (1952), No. 3 (1958; Jan. 14, 1960), No. 4 (1960; Oct. 11, 1962), No. 5 for Piano, Left-hand, and Orch. (1964; June 3, 1965), No. 6 (1972), and No. 7 (1985); Concerto grosso for 2 Pianos, 2 String Orchs., and Percussion (1950–51); *The Tratas*, 2 suites (1952, 1956; also for Piano); Violin Concerto (1953; May 4, 1957); *Rhapsody* for Piano and Orch. (1954); Concertino for Piano and Strings (1955; Prague, Feb. 17, 1957); 12 syms.: No. 1 (1955; Dec. 2, 1956), No. 2 (1957–58), No. 3 (1959), No. 4 for Soprano, Tenor, Chorus, and Orch. (1959; Feb. 2, 1961), No. 5 (1961; March 3, 1963), No. 6, *Improvisata* (1964–65), No. 7 (1966; March 4, 1967), No. 8 (1971), No. 9 (1973), No. 10 for Chamber Orch. (1976), No. 11 (1981), and No. 12 for Orch. and Tape (1986); Concerto for Organ, Strings, and Percussion (Dec. 5, 1957); *Strečno*, symphonic poem (1959); *Small Fantasy* for Piano and Orch. (1960); *Concerto da camera* for Oboe and Strings (1961); Concerto for 2 Pianos and Orch. (1967; Nov. 3, 1968); *French Suite* for Chamber Orch. (1968); *Songs Without Words* for Strings (1970); *Music from Old Bratislava* (1975); *Concerto Prelude* (1981); Chamber Concerto for Organ and Strings (1984); *Concerto Poliphonico* (1987); *3 Dancing Pieces* for Piano and Orch. (1988); Concertino for Viola and Chamber Orch. (1989). **CHAMBER:** Suite for Violin and Piano (1958); Viola Sonata (1958); *2 Slovak Dances* for Violin and Piano (1959); 3 string quartets (1960, 1982, 1987); Wind Quintet (1968); *Ballade and Burlesque* for Viola (1976); *Poetical Sonata* for Violin and Piano (1976); *Variations* for 2 Violins and Viola (1977); Flute Sonata (1978); Trio for Flute, Violin, and Piano (1979). **KEYBOARD: Piano:** 7 sonatas (1948, 1961, 1966, 1971, 1978, 1979, 1987); 4 sonatas for 2 Pianos (1954, 1958, 1965, 1972); *Concerto for Piano Without Orchestra* (1956); *2 Romantic Pieces* (1975); *Bagatelles* (1983); *Introduction and Toccata* (1986); *4 Pieces* for Piano, 4-Hands (1988). **Organ:** *Prelude and Fugue* (1952); *Phantasy and Toccata* (1958); Concerto (1960); 2 sonatas (1970, 1981); *3 Small Preludes* (1977). **VOCAL:** *Magnificat* for Chorus and Orch. (1952); *Peace* for Chorus and Orch. (1954); *Death Shall Have No Dominion*, oratorio for Soloists, Chorus, and Orch. (1968); *Phantasy* for Men's Chorus, Piano, and Orch. (1975); choral pieces; song cycles.**—NS/LK/DM**

Zimmerman, Franklin B(ershir), American musicologist; b. Wauneta, Kans., June 20, 1923. He was educated at the Univ. of Southern Calif. in Los Angeles (B.A., 1949; M.A., 1952; Ph.D., 1958, with the diss. *Purcell's Musical Heritage: A Study of Musical Styles in 17th-century England*) and at Oxford Univ. (B.Litt., 1956). He taught at the State Univ. of N.Y. in Potsdam (1958–59) and at the Univ. of Southern Calif. (1959–64), and then was prof. of music at Dartmouth Coll. (1964–67), the Univ. of Ky. (1967–68), and the Univ. of Pa. (from 1968). In 1996 he developed a new musical notation called "Visible Music Soundscapes," which is designed to help children learn to read music and sight sing more easily. The new notation is copyrighted, trademarked, and has a patent pending. He devoted much time to the study of English Baroque music, particularly the life and works of Purcell.

WRITINGS: *Henry Purcell, 1659–1695: An Analytical Catalogue of His Music* (London, 1963); *Henry Purcell, 1659–1695: His Life and Times* (London, 1967; 2nd ed., rev., 1983); *Henry Purcell, 1659–1694: Melodic and Intervallic Indexes to His Complete Works* (Philadelphia, 1975); *Henry Purcell: A Guide to Research* (N.Y., 1988).—**NS/LK/DM**

Zimmerman, Pierre-Joseph-Guillaume, famous French piano teacher and composer; b. Paris, March 19, 1785; d. there, Oct. 29, 1853. The son of a Paris piano maker, he entered the Paris Cons. in 1798, studying under Boieldieu, Rey, Catel, and Cherubini; won the premier prix for piano in 1800, and for harmony in 1802. He became a prof. of piano there in 1816, and was pensioned in 1848. Among his many pupils were Alkan, Marmontel, Lacombe, Ambroise Thomas, and César Franck. His chief work is the *Encyclopédie du pianiste*, a complete method for piano, part III of which is a treatise on harmony and counterpoint. Among his compositions was the opera *L'Enlèvement* (Paris, Oct. 26, 1830), 2 piano concertos, a Piano Sonata, 24 études, etc. —**NS/LK/DM**

Zimmermann, Agnes (Marie Jacobina), German-English pianist and composer; b. Cologne, July 5, 1845; d. London, Nov. 14, 1925. As a young girl she went to England, and at 9 became a student of Cipriani Potter and Charles Steggall at the Royal Academy of Music in London, where she later studied with Ernst Pauer (piano) and G. Macfarren (composition). She made her debut at the Crystal Palace on Dec. 5, 1863, then toured England with excellent success, being praised for her fine renditions of classical works. She ed. the sonatas of Mozart and Beethoven and the complete piano works of Schumann (for Novello). She was also a competent composer, numbering among her works a piano trio, 3 violin sonatas, cello sonata, and many playable piano pieces.—**NS/LK/DM**

Zimmermann, Anton, Austrian composer; b. Pressburg, 1741; d. there, Oct. 16, 1781. He was organist at St. Martin's Church in Pressburg, and in 1776 he was named Kapellmeister and court composer to Count Joseph Batthyany, the Archibishop (later cardinal) of Hungary. His works include *Narcisse et Pierre*, Singspiel (Pressburg, 1772; not extant), *Andromeda und Perseus*, melodrama (Vienna, April 23, 1781), and *Zelmor und Ermide*, melodrama (n.d.); also about 25 syms. (serenatas), concertos, much chamber music, including various nocturnes, cassations, 12 string quintets, 6 string quartets, sonatas, etc., and much sacred music.—**NS/LK/DM**

Zimmermann, Bernd (actually, **Bernhard**) **Alois,** remarkable German composer; b. Bliesheim, March 20, 1918; d. (suicide) Königsdorf, Aug. 10, 1970. He commenced training as a music teacher at the Cologne Hochschule für Musik in 1937. In 1939 he was drafted into the German Army. After being discharged due to ill health in 1942, he returned to Cologne and studied musicology. In 1945 he resumed his training as a music teacher, taking his examination in 1947. He concurrently studied music theory with Heinrich Lemacher and composition with Philipp Jarnach. In 1948 he attended the summer course in new music in Darmstadt given by René Leibowitz. Zimmermann served as president of the German section of the ISCM in 1956–57. In 1957 he received a scholarship to the Villa Massimo in Rome, where he was in residence again in 1963. He was appointed prof. of composition at the Cologne Hochschule für Musik in 1957. In 1960 he was awarded the Grosser Kunstpreis of North Rhine-Wesphalia, and in 1966 the Kunstpreis of the City of Cologne. In spite of his talent, Zimmermann was haunted by self doubt and increasing despair. At the age of 52 he took his own life. His works reveal a mastery of various techniques, ranging from serialism to electronics, and including what he described as collage. Whatever means he utilized, he created works of notable individuality and merit. C. Bitter ed. a vol. of his writings as *Intervall und Zeit: Aufsätze und Schriften* (Mainz, 1974).

WORKS: DRAMATIC: *Alagoana*, ballet (1950–55; Essen, Dec. 17, 1955); *Des Menschen Unterhaltsprozess gegen Gott*, radio opera after Calderón de la Barca (WDR, Cologne, June 12, 1952; concert perf., Cologne, July 13, 1987); *Kontraste*, ballet (1953; Bielefeld, April 24, 1954); *Perspektiven*, ballet for 2 Pianos (1955–56; 1st complete perf., Darmstadt, July 10, 1956; stage perf., Düsseldorf, June 2, 1957); *Die Soldaten*, opera after J.M.R. Lenz (1957–65; Cologne, Feb. 15, 1965); *Présence*, ballet for Violin, Cello, and Piano (concert perf., Darmstadt, Sept. 8, 1961; stage perf., Stuttgart, May 16, 1968); *Musique pour les soupers du Roi Ubu*, ballet (1962–66; concert perf., Berlin, Jan. 31, 1968; stage perf., Düsseldorf, April 25, 1968); Cello Concerto in the form of a "pas des trois" (1965–66; concert perf., Strasbourg, April 8, 1968; stage perf., Wuppertal, May 12, 1968). **ORCH.:** *Sinfonia prosodica* (1945; 1st complete perf., Mönchengladbach, Sept. 9, 1947); Sym. (1947; rev. version, Brussels, Nov. 20, 1953); *Concerto for Orchestra* (1948; Darmstadt, July 10, 1949); Concerto for Strings (1948; Schloss Brühl, July 25, 1949; after the Trio for Violin, Viola, and Cello, Cologne, June 23, 1944); *Symphonische Variationen und Fuge über "In dulci jubilo"* (Koblenz, Dec. 10, 1949); Violin Concerto (Baden-Baden, Dec. 10, 1950); *Alagoana*, suite after the ballet (1950–55; Baden-Baden, Nov. 24, 1956); Concerto for Oboe and Small Orch. (Donaueschingen, Oct. 11, 1952); Suite (Hamburg, Oct. 31, 1952); Concerto for Cello and Small Orch. (1953; rev. version as *Canto di speranza* for Cello and Small Orch., 1957; Südwestfunk, Baden-Baden, July 28, 1958; concert perf., Darmstadt, Sept. 12, 1958); *Metamorphose* for Small Orch. (Hamburg, March 13, 1954); *Nobody knows de trouble I see*, trumpet concerto (1954; Hamburg, Oct. 11, 1955); *Impromptu* (Cologne, June 24, 1958); *Dialoge*, concerto for 2 Pianos and Orch. (WDR, Cologne, Dec. 5, 1960; concert perf., Mannheim, March 10, 1968; also as *Monologe* for 2 Pianos, 1964; Cologne, Jan. 7, 1965); *Giostra Genovese* for Small Orch. (Bonn, Nov. 30. 1962); *Cinque Capricci*, after Frescobaldi (partial perf., Cologne, Dec. 17, 1962); *Antiphonen* for Viola and Orch. (1962; Berlin, Oct. 8, 1965); *Un "petit rien"* for Small Orch. (1964; Berlin, Sept. 24, 1989); Cello Concerto in the form of a "pas de trois" (1965–66; concert perf., Strasbourg, April 8, 1968; stage perf., Wuppertal,

May 12, 1968); *Photoptosis* (1968; Gelsenkichen, Feb. 14, 1969); *Stille und Umkehr* (1970; Nuremberg, March 19, 1971). **Wind Ensemble:** *Söbensprung* (1950); *Rheinische Kirmenstänze* (1950–62; WDR, Cologne, Aug. 2, 1963). **CHAMBER:** *Kleine Suite* for Violin and Piano (1942; Cologne, Jan. 22, 1944); Trio for Violin, Viola, and Cello (Cologne, June 23, 1944; also utilized in the Concerto for Strings, 1948; Schloss Brühl, July 25, 1949); Violin Sonata (1949; Cologne, Feb. 15, 1950); Sonata for Solo Violin (Darmstadt, July 8, 1951); Sonata for Solo Viola (Donaueschingen, Oct. 15, 1955); Sonata for Solo Cello (Stuttgart, April 23, 1960); *Présence*, ballet for Violin, Cello, and Piano (concert perf., Darmstadt, Sept. 8, 1961; stage perf., Stuttgart, May 16, 1968); *Tempus loquendi* for 3 Flutes, 1 Player (1963; Darmstadt, July 18, 1964); *Die Befristeten* for Jazz Quintet (1967); *Intercomunicazione* for Cello and Piano (WDR, Cologne, April 26, 1967); *Vier kurze Studien* for Cello (1970; Frankfurt am Main, March 1, 1971). **Piano:** *Extemporale*, 5 pieces (1939–46; Cologne, April 12, 1946); *Capriccio* (Horrem, July 12, 1946); *Enchridion* for Piano, 4-Hands (1949); *Perspektiven*, ballet for 2 Pianos (1955–56; 1st complete perf., Darmstadt, July 10, 1956; stage perf., Düsseldorf, June 2, 1957); *Konfigurationen*, 8 pieces (Basel, Nov. 25, 1956); *Monologe* for 2 Pianos (1964; Cologne, Jan. 7, 1965; also as *Dialoge*, concerto for 2 Pianos and Orch., WDR, Cologne, Dec. 5, 1960; concert perf., Mannheim, March 10, 1968). **VOCAL:** *Fünf Lieder* for Middle Voice and Piano (1942–46); *Drei Geistliche Lieder* for Middle Voice and Piano (1946; Cologne, June 18, 1952); *Die Brünnlein, die da fliessen* for Alto, Baritone, Chorus, and Orch. (1947); *Lob der Torheit*, burlesque cantata for Soprano, Tenor, Bass, Chorus, and Orch., after Goethe (Cologne, May 25, 1948); *Omnia tempus habent*, cantata for Soprano and 17 Instruments (1957; WDR, Cologne, Nov. 27, 1958); *Die Soldaten*, vocal sym. for Soprano, Mezzo-soprano, Alto, Tenor, Baritone, Bass, and Orch., after the opera (1957–63; WDR, Cologne, May 20, 1963); *Requiem für einem jungen Dichter* for Speaker, Soprano, Baritone, 3 Choruses, Tape, Orch., Jazz Combo, and Organ (1967–69; Düsseldorf, Dec. 11, 1969); *Ich wandte mich und sah an alles Unrecht, das geschah unter der Sonne*, ecclesiastical action for 2 Speakers, Bass, and Orch. (1970; Kiel, Sept. 2, 1972). **ELECTRONIC:** *Tratto* (1965–67; Cologne, Nov. 29, 1967); *Tratto II* (1970).

BIBL.: W. Konold, ed., *B.A. Z.: Dokumente und Interpretationen* (Cologne, 1986); idem, *B.A. Z.: Der Komponist und sein Werk* (Cologne, 1986); J. Hiekel, *B.A. Z.s Requiem für einen jungen Dichter* (Stuttgart, 1995); S. Hilger, *Autonom oder angewandt?: Zu den Hörspielmusiken von Winfried Zillig und B.A. Z.* (Mainz, 1996). **—NS/LK/DM**

Zimmermann, Frank Peter, German violinist; b. Duisburg, Feb. 27, 1965. As a child he took violin lessons with his mother, making his public debut with the Duisburg Sym. Orch. at 10. He then studied with W. Gradow at the Essen Folkwang-Musikhochschule and with H. Krebbers at the Robert-Schumann-Institut of the Düsseldorf Hochschule für Musik. In 1979 he appeared at the Lucerne Festival; made his British debut as soloist with the Royal Phil. at the Portsmouth Festival in 1981 and his U.S. debut as soloist with the Pittsburgh Sym. Orch. in 1984; also toured the Soviet Union in 1984. In subsequent years, he appeared as a soloist with principal orchs. and toured widely as a recitalist. His repertoire ranges from Bach to Prokofiev.**—NS/LK/DM**

Zimmermann, Udo, noted German composer, conductor, pedagogue, and Intendant; b. Dresden, Oct. 6, 1943. He was a student of Johannes Thilman (composition) and took courses in conducting and voice at the Dresden Hochschule für Musik (1962–68). In 1967 and 1968 he held the Felix-Mendelssohn-Bartholdy-Stipendium. From 1968 to 1970 he attended Kochan's master classes in composition at the Akademie der Künste in East Berlin. In 1970 he became a dramaturg for contemporary music theater at the Dresden State Opera, where he was active until 1984. He became founder-director of Dresden's Studio Neue Musik in 1974. In 1976 he began teaching at the Dresden Hochschule für Musik, where he was made a prof. of composition in 1978 and a prof. of experimental music theater and composition in 1982. He was active as a conductor from 1984, making guest appearances in Europe and abroad. In 1986 he became director of Dresden's Center for Contemporary Music. He became artistic director of Dresden's musica-viva-ensemble in 1988. In 1990 he was made Intendant of the Leipzig Opera. He became Generalintendant of the Deutsche Oper in Berlin in 2001. In 1983 he was made a member of the Akademie der Künste in Berlin and of the Freien Akademie der Künste in Hamburg. He served as president of the Freien Akademie der Künste in Leipzig from 1992. Zimmermann's music owes much to the so-called "new simplicity" style. In his operatic scores, he has brought new life to the genre of Literaturoper.

WORKS: DRAMATIC: Opera: *Die weisse Rose* (1966; Dresden, June 17, 1967); *Die zweite Entscheidung* (1969; Magdeburg, March 10, 1970); *Levins Mühle* (Dresden, March 27, 1973); *Der Schuhu und die fliegende Prinzessin* (Dresden, Dec. 30, 1976); *Die wundersame Schustersfrau* (1981; Schwetzingen, April 25, 1982); *Weisse Rose* (Hamburg, Feb. 27, 1986); *Die Sündflut* (1991); *Gantenbein* (1998). **ORCH.:** Violin Concerto (1964); *Dramatische Impression* (Chemnitz, May 5, 1966; also for Cello and Piano, 1963); Kettledrum Concerto (1966); *Musik* for Strings (1968; Leipzig, Jan. 28, 1969); *Mutazioni* (1969; Dresden, Oct. 26, 1973); *L'homme: Meditationen* (1970; Dresden, Sept. 22, 1972); *Sieh, meine Augen: Reflexionen* for Chamber Orch. (1970; Dresden, Jan. 27, 1972); *Sinfonia come un grande lamento*, in memory of García Lorca (1977; Dresden, May 25, 1978); *Songerie* for Chamber Orch., in memory of Karl Böhm (Salzburg, Aug. 12, 1982); *Mein Gott, wer trommelt denn da?: Reflexionen* (1985; Hannover 16, 1986); Viola Concerto (1986); *Nouveaux divertissements—d'après Rameau* for Horn and Chamber Orch. (1987; Dresden, June 1, 1988); *Dans la marche: Hommage à Witold Lutosawski* (L'Aquila, Oct. 16, 1994). **CHAMBER:** *Dramatische Impression* for Cello and Piano (1963; also for Orch., 1966); Violin Sonatina (1964); *Movimenti caratteristici* for Cello (1965); *Episoden* for Wind Quintet (1971); *Tänzerinnen* for Chamber Ensemble (1973); *Canticum Marianum* for 12 Cellos (1983). **KEYBOARD: Piano:** Sonata (1967). **Harpsichord:** *Die Spieldose*, étude (1981). **VOCAL:** *Vaterunserlied*, motet for 4 Voices (1959); *Wort ward Fleisch*, motet for 8 Voices (1961); *Grab und Kreuz*, motet for 8 Voices (1962); 5 Songs for Baritone and Chamber Orch., after Borchert (1964); *Neruda-Lieder* for Voice, Clarinet, and Piano (1965); *Sonetti amorosi* for Alto, Flute, and String Quartet (1966; Dresden, Oct. 28, 1967); *Der Mensch*, cantata for Soprano and 13 Players (Görlitz, Oct. 8, 1970); *Ein Zeuge der Liebe, die besiegt den Tod* for Soprano and Chamber Orch. (Frankfurt am Main, March 11, 1973); *Ode an das Leben* for Mezzo-soprano, 3 Choruses, and Orch., after Neruda and Carus (1974; Dresden, Jan. 23, 1975); *Psalm der Nacht* for Women's

Chorus, Men's Voices, Percussion, and Organ, after Sachs (1976; Kassel, Sept. 17, 1977); *Hymnus an die Sonne* for Soprano, Flute, and Harpsichord, after Kleist (Frankfurt an der Oder, Oct. 23, 1977); *Pax questuosa* for 5 Solo Voices, 3 Choruses, and Orch. (1981; Berlin, Dec. 14, 1982); *Wenn ich an Hiroshima denke* for Soprano, Flute, and Piano (Nordhausen, Nov. 22, 1981; also for Soprano and Chamber Orch., Tokyo, Dec. 23, 1982); *Gib Licht meinen Augen, oder ich entschlafe des Todes* for Soprano, Baritone, and Chamber Orch. (1986; Berlin, Feb. 17, 1987); *Wenn ein Wintervogel das Herz...*, song cycle for Baritone and Piano (Bonn, Dec. 14, 1990).

BIBL.: F. Hennenberg, *U. Z.: Leidenschaft Musik, Abenteuer Theater: Komponist-Intendant-Dirigent* (Bonn, 1992). —**NS/LK/DM**

Zimmermann, Walter, German composer; b. Schwabach, April 15, 1949. He studied piano, violin, and oboe. While serving as pianist in the "ars-nova-ensemble" of Nuremberg (1968–70), he pursued training in composition with Werner Heider. He then studied with Otto Laske at the Institut voor Sonologie at the Univ. of Utrecht and at the Jaap Kunst Ethnological Center at the Univ. of Amsterdam (1970–73). In 1974 he studied computer music in Hamilton, N.J. In 1977 he founded the Beginner Studio in Cologne, which specialized in concerts of novel music. In 1988 he lectured at the Univ. of The Hague. In 1993 he became a teacher of composition at the Berlin Hochschule für Musik. He publ. the books *Desert Plants* (Vancouver, 1976) and *Insel Musik* (Cologne, 1977), and ed. a vol. of Morton Feldman's essays (Kerpen, 1985). Among his compositions are a number of short works of varied ensembles.

WORKS: *Akkordarbeit* for Orch. (1971); *Lokale Musik*, a series of pieces for Various Forces (1977–81); *Die Blinden*, static drama for 12 Singers and 9 Instruments (1984); *Über die Dörfer*, music theater for Soloists, 3 Choruses, and Organ (1986); *Ataraxia* for Piano and Orch. (1988); *Hyperion*, short opera (1989–90); *Diastasis/Diastema* for 2 Orchs. and 1 Conductor (1991–92); *Oedipus Coloneus*, music theater (1995).—**NS/LK/DM**

Zinck, Bendix (actually, Benedikt) Friedrich, German instrumentalist and composer, brother of **Hardenack Otto Conrad Zinck;** b. Husum, Holstein (baptized), March 8, 1743; d. Ludwigslust, Mecklenburg, June 23, 1801. He studied violin, harpsichord, and organ with his father, the town musician Bendix Friedrich Zinck. He was a violinist in the Ludwigslust Hofkapelle (1767–1801), and also toured as a violinist and keyboard artist in Europe. In 1781 he married the court singer Charlotte Nussbaum (1760–1817). Among his works are 15 syms., vocal pieces, and chamber music.—**NS/LK/DM**

Zinck, Hardenack Otto Conrad, German instrumentalist, singer, teacher, and composer, brother of **Bendix (Benedikt) Friedrich Zinck;** b. Husum, Holstein, July 2, 1746; d. Copenhagen, Feb. 15, 1832. He began his training with his father, the town musician Bendix Friedrich Zinck, and later studied with C.P.E. Bach in Hamburg. In 1777 he became 1st flutist and chamber musician in the Ludwigslust Hofkapelle, and in 1787 he was named Singmeister (1st accompanist) in the Copenhagen Hofkapelle. He also was active as a church organist and teacher in Copenhagen, where he founded a Singakademie (1800). He produced an opera to a Danish text, *Selim og Mirza* (Copenhagen, Feb. 1, 1790), and also composed several oratorios and cantatas, lieder, instrumental music, etc. He publ. *Die nördliche Harfe, ein Versuch in Fragmenten und Skizzen über Musik und ihre Anwendung im Norden* (Copenhagen, 1801; on Scandinavian music) and *Vorlesungen über Musik und ihre nützlichste Anwendung* (Copenhagen, 1813).—**NS/LK/DM**

Zingarelli, Nicola Antonio, Italian composer and pedagogue; b. Naples, April 4, 1752; d. Torre del Greco, near Naples, May 5, 1837. He studied at the Cons. S. Maria di Loreto in Naples with Fenaroli, Speranza, Anfossi, and Sacchini. His first stage work, *I quattro pazzi*, was performed at the Cons. in 1768. After finishing school in 1772, he earned his living as a violin teacher. He spent much time traveling throughout Italy, supervising the production of his operas. In 1793 he was appointed maestro di cappella at the Cathedral of Milan, in 1794, at the Santa Casa in Loreto, and in 1804, at the Sistine Chapel in the Vatican. In 1811, for refusing to conduct a Te Deum to celebrate the birthday of Napoleon's son, the "King of Rome," he was imprisoned at Civitavecchia, and later transported to Paris by order of Napoleon, who set him at liberty and liberally paid him for a Mass written in Paris. As Fioravanti had meanwhile become maestro di cappella at St. Peter's, Zingarelli went to Naples, and in 1813 became director of the royal Collegio di Musica; in 1816 he succeeded Paisiello as maestro di cappella at the Naples Cathedral. He was renowned as a teacher, numbering Bellini, Mercadante, Carlo Conti, Lauro Rossi, Morlacchi, and Michael Costa among his students. His operas, interpreted by the finest singers of the time (Catalani, Crescentini, Grassini, Marchesi, and Rubinelli), were highly successful. His facility was such that he was able to write an opera in a week. He wrote 37 operas in all.

WORKS: DRAMATIC: Opera (all 1st perf. at La Scala in Milan): *Alsinda* (Feb. 22, 1785); *Ifigenia in Aulide* (Jan. 27, 1787); *La morte de Cesare* (Dec. 26, 1790); *Pirro, re d'Epiro* (Dec. 26, 1791); *Il mercato di Monfregoso* (Sept. 22, 1792); *La secchia rapita* (Sept. 7, 1793); *Artaserse* (Dec. 26, 1793); *Giulietta e Romeo*, after Shakespeare (Jan. 30, 1796); *Meleagro* (Jan. 1798); *Il ritratto* (Oct. 12, 1799); *Clitennestra* (Dec. 26, 1800); *Il bevitore fortunato* (Nov. 1803). Other Opera: *I quattro pazzi* (Naples, 1768); *Montezuma* (Naples, Aug. 13, 1781); *Ricimero* (Venice, May 5, 1785); *Armida* (Rome, Carnival 1786); *Antigono* (Mantua, April 13, 1786); *Artaserse* (Trieste, March 19, 1789); *Antigone* (Paris, April 30, 1790); *Pharamond* (1790); *Annibale in Torino* (Turin, Carnival 1792); *Atalanta* (Turin, Carnival 1792); *L'oracolo sannita* (Turin, Carnival 1792); *La Rossana* (Genoa, Carnival 1793); *Apelle* (Venice, Nov. 18, 1793; rev. as *Apelle e Campaspe*, Bologna, 1795); *Gerusalemme distrutta* (Florence, 1794); *Alzira* (Florence, Sept. 7, 1794); *Quinto Fabio* (Livorno, 1794); *Il conte di Saldagna* (Venice, Dec. 26, 1794); *Gli Orazi e i Curiazi* (Naples, Nov. 4, 1795); *Andromeda* (Venice, 1796); *La morte di Mitridate* (Venice, May 27, 1797); *Ines de Castro* (Milan, Oct. 11, 1798); *Carolina e Mexicow* (Venice, Carnival 1798); *I veri amici repubblicani* (Turin, Dec. 26, 1798); *Il ratto delle Sabine* (Venice, Dec. 26, 1799); *Edipo a Colono* (Venice, Dec. 26, 1802); *La notte dell'amicizia* (Venice, Carnival

1802); *Il ritorno di Serse* (Modena, July 16, 1808); *Baldovino* (Rome, Feb. 11, 1811); *Berenice, regina d'Armenia* (Rome, Nov. 12, 1811); *Malvina* (Naples, Carnival 1829; in collaboration with M. Costa). **Oratorios:** *Pimmalione* (Naples, 1779); *Ero* (Milan, 1786); *Telemaco* (Milan, 1787); *Il trionfo di David* (Naples, 1788); *Francesca da Rimini* (Rome, 1804); *Tancredi al sepolcro di Clorinda* (Naples, 1805); *La fuga in Egitto* (Naples, 1837). **OTHER:** A vast amount of church music; the Cons. di Loreto contains 541 MSS by Zingarelli, in a collection known as "Annuale di Zingarelli" (or "Annuale di Loreto"), including a series of masses for every day in the year; a 4-part Miserere "alla Palestrina" (1827); 73 Magnificats, 28 Stabat Maters, 21 Credos, many Te Deums, motets, hymns, etc.; also syms., solfeggi, arias, organ sonatas, some chamber music.

BIBL.: R. Liberatore, *Necrologia di N. Z.* (Naples, 1837); A. Schmid, *Joseph Haydn und N. Z.* (Vienna, 1847).—**NS/LK/DM**

Zinkeisen, Konrad Ludwig Dietrich, German violinist and composer; b. Hannover, June 3, 1779; d. Braunschweig, Nov. 28, 1838. He was trained by his father, and by Rode at Wolfenbüttel. He played first violin under Forkel at the Academic Concerts in Göttingen, and in 1819 he was appointed a chamber musician in the Braunschweig court orch. He wrote 6 violin concertos, 4 orch. overtures, 3 string quartets; concertos for oboe, for clarinet, for basset horn, and for bassoon, various other pieces for solo instruments with orch., music for military band, and choral works.—**NS/LK/DM**

Zinman, David (Joel), talented American conductor; b. N.Y., July 9, 1936. He studied violin at the Oberlin (Ohio) Coll. Cons. of Music (B.M., 1958), and composition at the Univ. of Minn. (M.A., 1963). He took lessons in conducting at the Berkshire Music Center at Tanglewood, and with Monteux at his summer school in Maine; from 1961 to 1964 he was Monteux's assistant. After a successful engagement as guest conductor with the Nederlands Kamerorkest, he served as its conductor from 1965 to 1977. In 1972 he was appointed music adviser to the Rochester (N.Y.) Phil.; then was its music director (1974–85); also served as chief conductor of the Rotterdam Phil. (1979–82). He was principal guest conductor (1983–85) and then music director (from 1985) of the Baltimore Sym. Orch. While retaining his latter post, he also served as artistic director of the Minn. Orch.'s Viennese Sommerfest (1994–96) and as music director of the Zürich Tonhalle Orch. (from 1995). He appeared as a guest conductor with various orchs. in North America and Europe, becoming well known for his performances of the Classical and Romantic repertory.—**NS/LK/DM**

Zipoli, Domenico, Italian composer and organist; b. Prato, Oct. 16, 1688; d. Santa Catalina, near Cordoba, Argentina, Jan. 2, 1726. He studied in Florence, then with A. Scarlatti in Naples, L.F. Vannucci in Bologna, and B. Pasquini in Rome, where he became organist at the Jesuit Church in 1715. His oratorios *Sant' Antonio di Padova* (1712) and *Santa Caterina, vergine, e martire* (1714) were presented in Rome. In 1716 he publ. *Sonate d'intavolatura per organo e cimbalo*. He joined the Jesuit order at Seville in 1716, and in 1717 went to South America, where he became organist of the Jesuit church in Cordoba, Argentina. Walsh of London reprinted parts of the *Sonate d'intavolatura* under the titles *Six Suits of Italian Lessons for the Harpsichord* and *Third Collection of Toccatas, Vollentarys and Fugues*.

BIBL.: L. Ayestaran, *D. Z., el gran compositor y organista romano del 1700 en el Rio de La Plata* (Montevideo, 1941; radically rev. and amplified, Montevideo, 1962); S. Erickson-Bloch, *The Keyboard Music of D. Z.* (diss., Cornell Univ., 1975); M. De Santis, ed., *D. Z.: Itinerari iberoamericani delle musica italiana nel Settecento: Atti del convegno internaxionale, Prato, 30 settembre-2 ottobre 1988* (Florence, 1994).—**NS/LK/DM**

Ziporyn, Evan (Averill), American composer, clarinetist/bass clarinetist, and conductor; b. Chicago, Dec. 14, 1959. His father is a forensic psychiatrist who has concertized as a violinist and his mother is an attorney. Evan studied violin, piano, and clarinet in his early childhood, and by the age of 15 was proficient on all single-reed instruments. He began composing at the age of 14 under the tutelage of Betty Jacobsen and Don Owens. After attending the Eastman School of Music (1977–78), he studied at Yale Univ. (B.A. in music, 1981) and the Univ. of Calif. at Berkeley (M.A. in composition, 1986; Ph.D. in composition, 1990), where his principal mentors were Martin Bresnick, Andrew Imbrie, Michael Senturia, and John Blacking. Upon completion of a Fulbright fellowship in Indonesia, he became musical coordinator of San Francisco's Gamelan Sekar Jaya in 1988. In 1990 he joined the faculty at the Mass. Inst. of Technology as an asst. prof., becoming a full prof. in 1999. In 1993 he founded in Boston the Gamelan Galak Tika. Ziporyn's work is greatly influenced by his 20-year involvement with Balinese Gamelan. His innovative compositions frequently commingle Western and Gamelan instruments, such as in his collaboration with the noted Balinese composer I Nyoman Windha on *Kekembagan* (1990), a border-crossing work for Balinese Gamelan and Saxophone Quartet. Ziporyn is also a notable clarinetist/bass clarinetist who has enjoyed a long association with N.Y.'s Bang On A Can since its founding in 1987; he is currently a member of its select Bang On A Can All-Stars and also regularly performs and records as a featured soloist with Steve Reich and Musicians. His distinctive set of extended performance techniques are put to fine use in his own compositions as well as in new works by Bresnick, Michael Gordon, and David Lang. As a conductor, he has toured Europe with Germany's Ensemble Modern and also recorded Gordon's *Weather* with Ensemble Resonanz. He has received grants and awards from ASCAP (1990–92; 1993), the Rockefeller Foundation (1991–92; 1995–96; 1997–98), the New England Foundation for the Arts (1992), NEA/Arts International (1993), and Meet the Composer (1994, 2000).

WORKS: ORCH.: *Pleasureville, Pain City* (1985); *Filling Station* (1986); *Houtman's Men in Buleleng* for 17-piece Wind Ensemble (1994); *Kebyar Maya* for Cello and Orch. of Cellos (1995); *Tsmindao Ghmerto* for Bass Clarinet and Wind Ensemble (1998). **GAMELAN:** *Night Bus* for Sundanese Gamelan (1990); *Kekembangan* for Balinese Gamelan and Saxophone Quartet (1990; in collaboration with I Nyoman Windha); *Tire Fire* for Guitar Quartet and Balinese Gamelan (1993); *Amok!* for Balinese Gamelan, Processed Double Bass, and Sampler (1996).

CHAMBER ENSEMBLE: *Luv Time* for Chamber Ensemble (1984); *Twine* for Chamber Ensemble (1985); *Tree Frog* for Chamber Ensemble (1990); *Dog Dream* for Chamber Ensemble (1990); *Bossa Nova* for Brass Quintet (1991); *Aneh Tapi Nyata* for Chamber Ensemble and Balinese Percussion (1992); *Eel Bone* for String Quartet (1996); *Dreams of a Dominant Culture* for Flute, Clarinet, Percussion, Electric Piano, Violin, and Cello (1997); *Serenity Now* for Wind Nonet (1998); *Melody Competition* for Percussion Sextet (1999). **SOLO INSTRUMENTS:** Clarinet: *33 Vortices* for 5 Clarinets (1980); *Waiting By The Phone* for Clarinet (1986); *What She Saw There* for Bass Clarinet or Cello and 2 Marimbas (1988); *Walk the Dog* for Bass Clarinet and Tape (1991); *Tsmindao Ghmerto* for Bass Clarinet (1992); *Partial Truths* for Bass Clarinet (1997); *Four Impersonations* for Clarinet (1999). **OTHER:** *China Spring* for Oboe and Piano (1991); *The Motions* for Viola with Optional Chamber Accompaniment (1991); *Studies in Normative Behaviour, Vol. I* for Percussionist (1991); *Current Rate* for Pipa Duo (1998). Piano: *Weltscenen* (1981); *The Water's Fine* (1983); *Some Coal* (1985); *Fractal Head* (1987).—**LK/DM**

Zipp, Friedrich, German composer, organist, and pedagogue; b. Frankfurt am Main, June 20, 1914. He studied at the Hoch Cons. in Frankfurt am Main (1933–34) and in Berlin at the Univ. and at the Staatliche Hochschule für Musik, where his composition teacher was Knab. In 1947 he became a teacher and in 1962 a prof. at the Staatliche Hochschule für Musik in Frankfurt am Main; also was active as an organist. He composed *Musik* for Orch. (1936), *Sinfonietta* for Youth Orch. (1958), *Kirchensuite* for String Orch. (1962), String Quartet (1943), *Au clair de la lune* for Oboe and Piano (1963), and numerous choral pieces and songs. He publ. *Vom Wesen der Musik* (Heidelberg, 1974).—**NS/LK/DM**

Zítek, Otakar, Czech music critic and composer; b. Prague, Nov. 5, 1892; d. Bratislava, April 28, 1955. He studied composition with Novák at the Prague Cons. and musicology with Guido Adler and Grädener at the Univ. of Vienna. Upon graduation, he wrote music criticism for the *Hudební Revue* and the *Lidové Noviny* in Prague; gave lectures on opera at the Prague Cons.; then was administrator at the National Theater in Brno (1921–29); taught at the Brno Cons. (1931–39). From 1939 to 1941 he was in the Buchenwald concentration camp, but was released, and worked as a theater director in Plzeň (1941–43); supervised opera theaters in Prague and Brno (1946–49). He composed the operas *Vznesene srdce* (The Exalted Heart; 1918) and *Pád Petra Králence* (The Downfall of Peter Kralence; Brno, March 23, 1923), a ballet after Wilde's *Birthday of the Infanta* (Plzeň [Pilsen], 1942), *Město*, symphonic poem (1925), songs, etc. He publ. *O novou zpevohru* (On New Opera; Prague, 1920).—**NS/LK/DM**

Ziv, Mikhail, Russian composer; b. Moscow, May 25, 1921. He studied at the Moscow Cons. with Kabalevsky; graduated in 1947. As a composer, Ziv devoted himself mainly to the musical theater. He wrote the comic operas *Son of a King's Minister* (1973) and *Gentlemen Artists* (1980), several fairy tales for children, 3 syms. (1946, 1960, 1968), 2 sinfoniettas (1958, 1962), 2 string quartets (1945, 1955), Piano Quintet (1947), many choruses, piano pieces, and songs, and film music. —**NS/LK/DM**

Živković, Milenko, Serbian composer and pedagogue; b. Belgrade, May 25, 1901; d. there, June 29, 1964. He studied at the Stanković Music School in Belgrade and graduated in law from the Univ. of Belgrade (1924). He then studied composition with Grabner at the Leipzig Cons. (1925–29) and d'Indy at the Paris Schola Cantorum (1929–31). Returning to Belgrade, he was director of the Stanković Music School (1937–47); taught at the Academy of Music (1945–64); was rector and prof. of composition there (1952–60). A follower of the national school of composition, he wrote music permeated with ethnic Balkan melorhythms. His works include *Symphonic Prologue* (Belgrade, April 16, 1935), *Zelena godina* (Green Year), folk ballet scenes for Orch. (Belgrade, April 27, 1937), several suites of Serbian dances for piano, and numerous choruses.—**NS/LK/DM**

Zmeskall, Nikolaus (Paul), Edler von Domanovecz, Hungarian diplomat and musical amateur; b. Lestine (baptized, Nov. 20), 1759; d. Vienna, June 23, 1833. He served as secretary of the Hungarian Chancellery in Vienna (1784–1825), and was a close friend of Beethoven, who dedicated to him the String Quartet, op.95. Zmeskall was also a composer in his own right, numbering 16 string quartets and other instrumental music among his works.

BIBL.: A. Sandberger, *Beethovens Freund Z. als Komponist* (Munich, 1924); C. Pidoll, *Verklungenes Spiel: Erinnerungen des Herrn N. Z.* (Innsbruck, 1949).—**NS/LK/DM**

Znosko-Borovsky, Alexander, Russian composer; b. Kiev, Feb. 27, 1908; d. there, March 8, 1983. He studied violin and composition at the Kiev Cons. In the face of a threatened Nazi invasion in 1941, he went to Ashkhabad, Turkmenia, where he was instrumental in promoting indigenous music. Several of his works were based on Turkmenian themes.

WORKS: DRAMATIC: *Akpamyk*, ballet (Ashkhabad, April 14, 1945); film music. **ORCH.:** 2 violin concertos: No. 1 (1932) and No. 2 (Kiev, Dec. 17, 1955); *Kiev*, symphonic poem (Kiev, March 9, 1949); 3 syms. (1958, 1960, 1967); *At the Mausoleum*, symphonic poem (1960); Cello Concerto (1968); Oboe Concerto (1971); Flute Concerto (1972); Trombone Concerto (1975); Horn Concerto (1976). **CHAMBER:** 2 string quartets (1937, 1942); *Scherzo* for 3 Trombones (1938); 2 sonatas for Solo Violin (1951, 1965). **VOCAL:** *Our Victory*, cantata (Kiev, May 8, 1946).—**NS/LK/DM**

Zoghby, Linda, American soprano; b. Mobile, Ala., Aug. 17, 1949. She studied voice with Elena Nikolaidi at Fla. State Univ. She made her professional debut at the Grant Park Festival in Chicago in 1973, and subsequently sang opera in N.Y., Washington, D.C., Dallas, Santa Fe, Houston, and New Orleans. She received a critical accolade on Jan. 19, 1982, when she substituted on short notice for Teresa Stratas and sang the role of Mimi in the Zeffirelli production of *La Bohème* at the Metropolitan Opera in N.Y. Her other roles include Pamina, Donna Elvira, and Marguerite in *Faust*. —NS/LK/DM

Zoilo, Annibale, Italian composer; b. Rome, c. 1537; d. Loreto, 1592. He was maestro di cappella at San Luigi dei Francesi from 1561 to 1566 and at San Giovanni in Laterano from Jan. 1568 to June 1570. In 1570 he became a singer in the Papal Choir in Rome, remaining there until he left due to ill health in 1577; then was in the service of Cardinal Sirleto. After serving as maestro di cappella at Todi Cathedral (1581–84), he held that post at the Santa Casa in Loreto (from 1584). In 1577 he and Palestrina were entrusted with the revision of the Roman Gradual (Editio Medicaea). He composed both sacred and secular vocal works. He publ. *Libro secondo de madrigali* for 4 to 5 Voices (Rome, 1563). Other madrigals were publ. in contemporary collections.

BIBL.: H. Lincoln, *A. Z.: The Life and Works of a Sixteenth-century Italian Composer* (diss., Northwestern Univ., 1951). —NS/LK/DM

Zöller, Karlheinz, German flutist; b. Höhr-Grenzhausen, Aug. 24, 1928. He was educated at the Frankfurt am Main Hochschule für Musik and the Northwest German Music Academy in Detmold. In 1947 he won 1st prize in the German radio competition in Frankfurt am Main; then was active as a recitalist and chamber player. Zöller was 1st flutist with the Berlin Phil. (1960–69). After a series of concert appearances in Europe and America, he rejoined the Berlin Phil. in 1977. —NS/LK/DM

Zöllner, Carl Friedrich, German choral conductor and composer, father of **Heinrich Zöllner;** b. Mittelhausen, March 17, 1800; d. Leipzig, Sept. 25, 1860. He studied at the Thomasschule in Leipzig. He became a vocal instructor, and began writing men's choruses. In 1833 he founded in Leipzig a "Liedertafel" known as the Zöllner-Verein, a men's choral society modeled after Zelter's Berlin organization. After Zöllner's death, several choral societies were united to form the Zöllner-Bund. Zöllner was one of the most successful German composers of part-songs for men's choruses. He also wrote for mixed chorus, and songs with piano accompaniment.

BIBL.: R. Hansch, *Der Liedermeister C.F. Z.* (Dresden, 1927). —NS/LK/DM

Zöllner, Heinrich, German composer and conductor, son of **Carl Friedrich Zöllner;** b. Leipzig, July 4, 1854; d. Freiburg im Breisgau, May 4, 1941. He studied at the Leipzig Cons., where his teachers were Reinecke, Jadassohn, Richter, and Wenzel (1875–77), then went to Tartu, where he was music director at the Univ. In 1885 he went to Cologne, where he taught at the Cons. and conducted choruses. In 1890 he was engaged to lead the Deutscher Liederkranz in N.Y.; in 1898 he returned to Germany. From 1902 to 1907 he taught composition at the Leipzig Cons., and from 1907 to 1914 he was conductor at the Flemish Opera in Antwerp; subsequently settled in Freiburg im Breisgau. He wrote 10 operas, of which the following were produced: *Frithjof* (Cologne, 1884), *Die lustigen Chinesinnen* (Cologne, 1886), *Faust* (Munich, Oct. 19, 1887), *Matteo Falcone* (N.Y., 1894), *Der Überfall* (Dresden, Sept. 7, 1895), *Die versunkene Glocke* (Berlin, July 8, 1899), *Der Schützenkönig* (Leipzig, 1903), and *Zigeuner* (Stuttgart, 1912). Other works include the musical comedy *Das hölzerne Schwert* (Kassel, 1897), a great number of choral works with orch., 5 syms., and some chamber music.—NS/LK/DM

Zolotarev, Vasili (Andreievich), eminent Russian composer and pedagogue; b. Taganrog, March 7, 1872; d. Moscow, May 25, 1964. He studied violin and theory at the Imperial Court Chapel in St. Petersburg, and from 1893 to 1897 took composition lessons with Balakirev. He then entered the St. Petersburg Cons. in the class of Rimsky-Korsakov, graduating in 1900, then received the Rubinstein Prize for his cantata *Paradise and Peri*. He was instructor of violin at the Court Chapel (1897–1900), and then teacher of composition at the Rostov Music School (1906–08), the Moscow Cons. (1908–18), the Ekaterinodar Cons. (1918–24), the Odessa Cons. (1924–26), the Kiev Musico-Dramatic Inst. (1926–31), the Sverdlovsk Music School (1931–33), and the Minsk Cons. (1933–41). In 1955 he was awarded the Order of Lenin. Several well-known Soviet composers were his pupils, among them Polovinkin, Dankevich, and Vainberg. In his music, Zolotarev continued the line of the Russian national school of composition, based on broad diatonic melos, mellifluous euphonious harmonies, and, in his operas, a resonant flow of choral singing. He publ. a manual on the fugue (Moscow, 1932; 3rd ed., 1965) and a vol. of reminiscences (Moscow, 1957).

WORKS: **DRAMATIC:** **Opera:** *The Decembrists* (Moscow, Dec. 27, 1925); *Ak-Gul* (1942). **Ballet:** *Lake Prince* (1948; Minsk, Jan. 15, 1949). **ORCH.:** 7 syms. (1902, 1905, 1935, 1936, 1942, 1943, 1962); *Moldavian Suite* (1926); *Uzbek Suite* (1931); *Tadzhik Suite* (1932); *Belorussian Suite* (1936); Cello Concerto (1943); *Rhapsodie hébraïque* (n.d.). **CHAMBER:** 6 string quartets (1899, 1902, 1907, 1912, 1916, 1945); 2 piano sonatas (1903, 1919); Piano Quintet (1904); String Quintet (1904); Piano Trio (1905); Violin Sonata (1922). **VOCAL:** Many songs.

BIBL.: S. Nisievich, *V.A. Z.* (Moscow, 1964).—NS/LK/DM

Zoltán, Aladár, Romanian composer and administrator; b. Mărtinis-Harghita, May 31, 1929; d. Tîrgu-Mureş, July 9, 1978. He was a student of Jodal and Demian at the Cluj Cons. (1946–53). In 1965 he became director of the Tîrgu-Mure Phil.

WORKS: **DRAMATIC:** *Poarta de sur* (The Marriage; 1962). **ORCH.:** *Divertisment* for 2 Clarinets and Strings (1952); *Dansuri din Corund*, suite (Tîrgu-Mure, June 15, 1960); 2 syms.: No. 1 (Tîrgu-Mure, May 5, 1961; rev. 1963) and No. 2 (Tîrgu-Mure, June 24, 1972); *Dansuri de pe Mures*, suite (1968); *Suita piccola* (1970); *Introduction and Allegro* (1974–77; Tîrgu-Mure, Oct. 30, 1977). **CHAMBER:** Nonet (1952–53); Bassoon Sonata (1954–55); String Quartet (1965); piano music. **VOCAL:** 4 cantatas (1953–65); songs.—NS/LK/DM

Zombies, The, one of the most under-rated and under-appreciated bands of the British Invasion.

Membership: Rod Argent, kybd. (b. St. Albans, England, June 14, 1945); Paul Atkinson, gtr. (b. Cuffley, England, March 19, 1946); Colin Blunstone, voc. (b. Hatfield, England, June 24, 1945); Hugh Grundy, drm. (b. Winchester, England, March 6, 1945); Chris White, bs. (b. Barnet, England, March 7, 1943).

The group came together when Argent, Blunstone, and Grundy were studying at St. Albans. Their original bassist left the band for medical school and was replaced by White, whose father let them rehearse in a store attic. Early in 1964, the quartet won a contest organized by the *London Evening News*. The prize was an audition with Decca records. Decca signed them and their first single, "She's Not There," rose to #2 in the U.S. pop charts. With its uncharacteristic minor key and keyboard solo (this was the era when the Beatles made the guitar king), it stood out among the pop music of the time.

After a couple of singles that didn't chart, they hit the Top Ten again with "Tell Her No." They toured supporting the Searchers and Herman's Hermits, recorded a soundtrack for the film *Bunny Lake Is Missing*, and several singles that went nowhere. They left Decca and signed with Columbia. Feeling like they had nothing left to lose, they recorded one of the first concept records, *Odessey and Oracle* (the title misspelled by a Columbia art director). The album was so unusual it nearly didn't get released. It probably wouldn't have mattered to the band at that point, because as soon as they left the studio, they broke up. However, Al Kooper prevailed on Columbia, and the album came out.

Argent and White formed Argent. Atkinson went on to success as an A&R man. Blunstone became a successful solo artist. Ironically, in 1969, after the *Odessey and Oracle* album has slipped out of print, the single "Time of the Season" became their third top-10 single, going gold. The group, however, resisted invitations to reform. In fact, they didn't play together for another 30 years, when *Odessey and Oracle* was re-released and they got on stage, impromptu. Ironically, having never played "Time of the Season" live, it was a struggle getting through it. With this late 1990s re-release and several other reconsiderations of their music in the 1990s, they enter the new millennium perhaps more popular than at any time since the early 1960s.

Disc.: *The Zombies* (1964); *Begin Here* (1965); *Bunny Lake Is Missing* (1965); *Odessey and Oracle* (1968).—**BH**

Zoras, Leonidas, Greek composer and conductor; b. Sparta, March 8, 1905; d. Athens, Dec. 22, 1987. He studied law at the Univ. of Athens, and at the same time took conducting lessons with Mitropoulos, and studied composition with Kalomiris, Lavrangas, and Riadis. From 1926 to 1938 he taught theory at the Odeon Music School in Athens; then studied conducting with Gmeindl, Schmalstich, and F. Stein and composition with Blacher, Grabner, and Hoffer at the Berlin Hochschule für Musik (1938–40). After conducting at the Greek National Opera in Athens (1948–58), he returned to Berlin as a conductor at the Deutsche Opera and RIAS (1958–68). He was director of the Athens National Cons. from 1968. He wrote an opera, *Elektra* (1969), the ballet *Violanto* (1931), *Night Song* for Cello and Chamber Orch. (1927), *Legend* for Orch. (1936), Sym. (1947), *Concertino* for Violin and 11 Woodwind Instruments (1950), Violin Sonata (1950), String Quartet (1969), numerous piano pieces, choruses, and songs.—**NS/LK/DM**

Zorn, John, innovative American composer and instrumentalist; b. N.Y., Sept. 2, 1953. After a brief college "stint" in St. Louis and world travels, he became an active contributor to the downtown music scene in N.Y.; performed with various avant-garde and rock musicians, including pianist Wayne Horvitz, drummer David Moss, and the Kronos Quartet. His *The Big Gundown* (1986) uses the music of film composer Ennio Morricone (b. 1928) as material to be freely distorted and reworked. His major works include *Archery* (1981), *Cobra* (group improvisation; 1986), *A Classic Guide to Strategy*, Vol. I (solo with tape), *News for Lulu* for Trio (1987), and *Spillane* (1988). He also composed *Roadrunner* for Accordion (1986), *Cat O'Nine Tails* for String Quartet (1988), and, *For Your Eyes Only* for Orch. (1989; rev. version, N.Y., Oct. 14, 1994), and *The Deadman* for String Quartet (1990). He plays saxophone, keyboards, duck calls, and other semi-demi-musical instruments in dense, loud aural canvases that have been compared to the works of Jackson Pollock (and also to an elephant trapped in barbed wire).—**NS/LK/DM**

Zorzor, Stefan, Romanian composer; b. Oradea, April 4, 1932. After training at the Bucharest Cons. (1951–52; 1956–61), he was active as a composer and teacher.

Works: Orch.: *Concerto for Orchestra* (1965; Bucharest, June 1967); *Nocturne* (Cluj-Napoca, Feb. 12, 1966); *Muzică festivă* (1967; Cluj-Napoca, Feb. 12, 1968). **Chamber:** 4 string quartets (1960; 1962; 1967–68; *Il ritorno*, 1977); Violin Sonata (1963); Wind Quintet (1967); *Heteroquintet* for Flute, Violin, Cello, Piano, and Percussion (1968); *Circulara*, quintet for 5 Different Instruments (1969); *Reprize* for Cello and Piano (1975); *Deformanţi*, concertino for Violin, Viola, Cello, Piano, and Harpsichord (1978). **Piano:** *5 Pieces* (1965–74); *4 Pieces* (1970); *Acuta* (1970). **Vocal:** *Ţara mea* (My Country), cantata for Women's Chorus and Small Orch. (1956); choruses.—**NS/LK/DM**

Zottmayr, Georg, distinguished German bass; b. Munich, Jan. 24, 1869; d. Dresden, Dec. 11, 1941. He studied in Munich, and began his career primarily as a concert singer. In 1906 he made his operatic debut with the Vienna Court Opera; later was a member of the German Theater in Prague (1908–10). In 1910 he joined the Dresden Court (later State) Opera, where he enjoyed a career of great distinction. He was considered one of the outstanding Wagnerians of his time, numbering among his finest roles King Marke, Hunding, Gurnemanz, Pogner, and Daland.—**NS/LK/DM**

Zouhar, Zdeněk, Czech composer and teacher; b. Kotvrdovice, Feb. 8, 1927. He was a pupil in Bratislava (1946–51) of Blažek and Kunz before settling in Brno, where he studied with Schaefer at the Janáček Academy of Music (1965–67) and pursued his education at the Univ. (Ph.D., 1962). After serving as head of the music dept. of the Univ. library (1953–61), he taught at the Janáček Academy of Music (from 1962). His music makes multifarious use of modern techniques, including a fairly orthodox dodecaphony.

WORKS: DRAMATIC: *Metamorphosis*, chamber radio opera (1971); *A Great Love*, comic opera (1986); ballets. **ORCH.:** *Sports Pages*, suite (1959); *Music* for Strings (1966); *Symphonic Triptych* (Brno Radio, Nov. 29, 1967); Triple Concerto for Clarinet, Trumpet, Trombone, and Orch. (1970); *Variations on a Theme by Bohuslav Martinů* (1979); *Musica giocosa* (1981); *Blanenská*, suite (1981); *Divertimento No. 3* for Brass Band (1993). **CHAMBER:** *Epilogue* for Cello (1949); *Spring Suite* for 3 Violins (1949); *Aulularia* for Chamber Ensemble (1956); *151* for Wind Quintet (1958); Trio for Flute, Clarinet, and Bass Clarinet (1962); *Études* for 4 Horns (1963); *Divertimento No. 1* for 4 Winds and Percussion (1965); *Variations* for Oboe and Piano (1965); 2 string quartets (1966, 1983); Brass Quintet (1985); Trio for Piccolo, Flute, and Alto Flute (1988); *Music Between Verses* for Flute, Oboe, Cello, Piano, and Reciter (1991); *Like Water* for Clarinet, Bassoon, and Piano (1994); piano pieces; organ music. **VOCAL:** *Midnight Mass* for Soloists, Chorus, Orch., and Organ (1957); *The Flames of Constance*, oratorio (1988); *3 Melodramas* for Narrator and Piano (1995); choral works; songs. **ELECTROACOUSTIC:** *Widecrossing* (1994).—**NS/LK/DM**

Zschau, Marilyn, American soprano; b. Chicago, Feb. 9, 1944. She studied at the Juilliard School of Music in N.Y. (1961–65) and in Mont. with John Lester. In 1965–66 she toured as a member of the Met National Co. In 1967 she made her debut as Marietta in *Die Tote Stadt* at the Vienna Volksoper, and in 1971 appeared for the first time at the Vienna State Opera as the Composer in *Ariadne auf Naxos*. She made her N.Y.C. Opera debut in 1978 as Minnie in *La Fanciulla del West*, returning there as Cio-Cio-San, Odabella in *Attila*, and Maddalena in *Andrea Chenier*. On Feb. 4, 1985, she made her Metropolitan Opera debut in N.Y. as Musetta. She sang for the first time at Milan's La Scala in 1986 as the Dyer's Wife in *Die Frau ohne Schatten*; thereafter sang with major opera houses on both sides of the Atlantic. In 1993 she electrified audiences with her debut at the London Promenade Concerts in a concert performance as Elektra with Andrew Davis conducting the BBC Sym. Orch. She was engaged as Brünnhilde in the *Ring* cycle at the Seattle Opera in 1995. In 1996 she portrayed Elektra in Buenos Aires. Among her many admired roles are Mozart's Countess, Fiordiligi, Aida, Desdemona, Leonora, Tosca, Octavian, the Marschallin, Salome, and Shostakovich's Katerina.—**NS/LK/DM**

Zubiaurre (y Urionabarrenechea), Valentí, Spanish composer; b. Villa de Garay, Feb. 13, 1837; d. Madrid, Jan. 13, 1914. He was a chorister at Bilbao, and at the age of 16 undertook a voyage to South America. He returned to Spain in 1866, and took music lessons with Hilarión Eslava at the Madrid Cons. He wrote a considerable number of sacred works, then turned to opera, receiving 1st national prize with his *Fernando el Emplazado* (Madrid, May 12, 1871). In 1875 he was named 2nd maestro at the Royal Chapel in Madrid, and in 1878 succeeded Eslava as 1st maestro; in the same year, he was appointed a prof. at the Madrid Cons. His 2nd opera, *Ledia*, was produced with considerable success in Madrid on April 22, 1877. He also composed several zarzuelas. a sym., a potpourri of Basque folksongs, and choruses.—**NS/LK/DM**

Zucca, Mana
See **Mana-Zucca**

Zuccalmaglio, Anton Wilhelm Florentin von, German collector of folk songs and writer on music; b. Waldbrol, April 12, 1803; d. Nachrodt, near Gruna, Westphalia, March 23, 1869. The son of a physician who was a musical amateur, he learned music at home, then pursued academic studies in Mulheim am Rhein, Cologne, and the Univ. of Heidelberg. He contributed to the *Neue Zeitschrift für Musik* during Schumann's editorship, under the pseudonyms Wilhelm von Waldbrühl and Dorfküster Wedel. He publ. 2 collections of folk songs, in 1829 and 1836 (with E. Baumstark), then brought out (with A. Kretzschmer) the important compilation *Deutsche Volkslieder mit ihren Originalweisen* (2 vols., 1838, 1840; reprint, Hildesheim, 1969). However, these songs are only partly authentic; a few melodies were composed by Zuccalmaglio himself; others were combined from various sources; the texts were frequently rearranged. Brahms made use of the collection for his arrangements of German folk songs. —**NS/LK/DM**

Zuckerkandl, Victor, Austrian musicologist and aesthetician; b. Vienna, July 2, 1896; d. Locarno, April 25, 1965. He studied at the Univ. of Vienna (Ph.D., 1927). He conducted in Vienna and in other cities; also was a music critic for Berlin newspapers (1927–33) and taught theory and appreciation courses in Vienna (1934–38). He went to the U.S. to teach at Wellesley Coll. (1940–42); during World War II, he worked as a machinist in a Boston defense plant (1942–44). He then taught theory at the New School for Social Research in N.Y. (1946–48). A grant from the American Philosophical Soc. enabled him to develop a course for non-musicians on the nature and significance of tonal music; after he joined the faculty of St. John's Coll. in 1948, this course was adopted as a general requirement. He retired to Ascona in 1964, lecturing at the Jung Inst. and the Eranos Conference in Zürich before his death. His books represent a synthesis of theory (mostly following Schenker's analytic theories; music cognition; and intellectual metaphysics); they include *Sound and Symbol: Music and the External World* (1956), *The Sense of Music* (1959), and *Man the Musician* (1973).—**NS/LK/DM**

Zuckert, Leon, Ukrainian-born Canadian violinist, violist, conductor, and composer; b. Poltava, May 4, 1904; d. Toronto, May 29, 1992. He studied violin with Boris Brodsky in Poltava (1916–18). Following sojourns in Poland and Argentina, he settled in Canada in 1929. In 1937 he took a conducting course with Reginald Stewart at the Toronto Cons. of Music. He was active as a performer, composer, and arranger for Canadian radio programs. He also played in various orchs., including the Winnipeg Sym. Orch. (1932–34), the Toronto Sym.

Orch. (1951–56; 1961–63), and the Halifax Sym. Orch. (1963–65; 1967–69). His works generally followed in the tonal tradition. His wife was the poet Ella Bobrow, who collaborated with him on many songs.

WORKS: DRAMATIC: Ballet: *Preciosa y el Viento* (1986). **ORCH.:** *My Canadian Travels* (1938); 2 syms. (1949, 1962); *Quetico* (1957); *Divertimento Orientale* for Oboe and Strings (1965); *2 Moods in 1* for Strings (1967); *My Paintings* for Strings (1969); *Impressions of Tenerife* (1970); *Fantasia on Ukrainian Themes* (1973); *2 Spanish Meditations* (1974); Concerto for Bassoon and Strings (1976); *Elegía: Elegy* (1977); *A Homage* (1980); *Escenas Granadinas: Spanish Ballet Suite* (1980); *Symphonic Sketch* (1982); *Evening in a Russian Village* for Mandolin Orch. (1985). **CHAMBER:** *N'ila* for Violin or Cello and Piano or String Quartet (1916; rev. 1953); *Gypsy Memories* for Violin and Piano (1938); *2 Hebrew Pieces* for String Quartet (1947; rev. 1982); *Preludio en Modo Antiquo* for Brass (1964); String Quartet (1965); *Psychedelic Suite* for Brass Quintet (1968); *Little Spanish Dance* for Flute and Piano (1970); *Sonata Amorfa* for Violin and Piano (1970); *Elegiac Improvisation* for Flute and Piano (1972); *Sue Le Lac Baptiste, Ontario* for Saxophone and Piano (1972); *Short Suite* for Trumpet or Clarinet or Viola and Piano (1974); Suite for Bassoon (1975); Concerto for 2 Cellos and Piano (1979; also for Cello, Bassoon, and Piano); *Melancholic Piece* for Trombone or Bassoon or Cello and Piano (1980); *For Ofra: 2 Contrasting Moods* for Cello and Piano (1982); Sonata for Solo Viola (1984); piano pieces. **VOCAL:** *Prayer* for Voice and String Quartet (1960); *Dnieper* for Chorus and Orch. (1961); *Song in Brass* for Voice, Viola, Brass, Timpani, and Percussion (1964); *Quinteto de la Luna y del Mar y Oceánida* for Medium Voice, String Quartet, and Piano (1972); *In the Gleam of Northern Lights* for Chorus, Dancers, and Orch. (1974; also for Chorus, 2 Pianos, Strings, and Percussion); *Longing for Peace* for Baritone, Chorus or Men's Chorus, and Piano or Orch. (1978); *Sholem-yeh! Milhome-nein!* for Chorus and Piano (1985); other choruses and songs. **—NS/LK/DM**

Zukerman, Eugenia (née **Rich**), American flutist; b. Cambridge, Mass., Sept. 25, 1944. She studied flute with Julius Baker at the Juilliard School of Music in N.Y. (1964–66). In 1970 she won the Young Concert Artists Audition, which resulted in her formal recital debut at Town Hall in N.Y. in 1971; subsequently appeared as a soloist with orchs., as a recitalist, and as a chamber music player. From 1968 to 1985 she was married to **Pinchas Zukerman**, with whom she often appeared in concerts. She contributed various articles on music to newspapers and journals and appeared as a commentator on music on television; authored a novel deceptively titled *Deceptive Cadence* (1980).**—NS/LK/DM**

Zukerman, Pinchas, outstanding Israeli violinist, violist, and conductor; b. Tel Aviv, July 16, 1948. He began to study music with his father, taking up the violin at age 6; he then enrolled at the Tel Aviv Academy of Music, where he studied with Ilona Feher. With the encouragement of Isaac Stern and Pablo Casals, he became a scholarship student at the Juilliard School of Music in N.Y., where he studied with Ivan Galamian (1961–67). In 1967 he shared 1st prize in the Leventritt Competition in N.Y. with Kyung-Wha Chung, and then launched a brilliant career as a soloist with the major American and European orchs. He also appeared as both violinist and violist in recitals with Isaac Stern and Itzhak Perlman. He subsequently devoted part of his time to conducting, appearing as a guest conductor with the N.Y. Phil., Philadelphia Orch., Boston Sym. Orch., Los Angeles Phil., and many others. From 1980 to 1987 he was music director of the St. Paul (Minn.) Chamber Orch. He was principal guest conductor of the Dallas Sym. Orch. summer music festival (1990–92). In 1993 he became a teacher at the Manhattan School of Music in N.Y. During the 1994–95 season, he made a world tour as a conductor with the English Chamber Orch. He was married to **Eugenia Zukerman** from 1968 to 1985, then to the American actress Tuesday Weld. His performances as a violinist are distinguished by their innate emotional élan and modern virtuoso technique. **—NS/LK/DM**

Zukofsky, Paul, remarkable American violinist, conductor, and teacher; b. N.Y., Oct. 22, 1943. He was born into an intellectual family. His father was the poet and writer Louis Zukofsky, who late in life penned the novel *Little* (1970), which relates the life of a violin prodigy. Paul Zukofsky began music lessons at the age of 3 and violin instruction at 4. He was 7 when he became a student of Galamian in N.Y. At 8, he made his debut as a soloist with the New Haven (Conn.) Sym. Orch. His recital debut at N.Y.'s Carnegie Hall came when he was 13. At 16, he entered the Juilliard School of Music in N.Y., where he earned his B.M. and M.S. (1964). In 1964–65 he was a Creative Assn. at the Center for Creative and Performing Arts at the State Univ. of N.Y. at Buffalo. He then taught at the New England Cons. of Music in Boston and at the Berkshire Music Center at Tanglewood. In 1969 he became a teacher at the State Univ. of N.Y. at Stony Brook. In 1983–84 he held a Guggenheim fellowship. In 1984 he became conductor of the Contemporary Chamber Ensemble at the Juilliard School. He also taught violin there. From 1987 to 1989 he was director of chamber music activities there. From 1989 to 1995 he served as director of the Arnold Schoenberg Inst. at the Univ. of Southern Calif. in Los Angeles; then taught violin briefly there. From his earliest years he was fascinated by ultramodern music and developed maximal celerity, dexterity, and alacrity in manipulating special techniques, in effect transforming the violin into a multimedia instrument beyond its normal capacities. As both a violinist and conductor, Zukofsky has been a determined proponent of contemporary music. His astounding repertoire includes works by Ives, Schnabel, Rudhyar, Schuman, Cage, Carter, Sessions, Feldman, Babbitt, Penderecki, Wuorinen, Glass, and a host of others.**—NS/LK/DM**

Zumpe, Herman, German conductor and composer; b. Oppach, April 9, 1850; d. Munich, Sept. 4, 1903. He studied in Bautzen and Leipzig. In 1872 he joined Wagner at Bayreuth, aiding in the preparation of the performances of *Der Ring des Nibelungen*; then conducted opera in Salzburg, Wurzburg, Madgeburg, Frankfurt am Main, and Hamburg. After some years spent in teaching and composing, he was appointed court conductor in Stuttgart in 1891. In 1895 he was called to Munich to become conductor of the Kaim

Orch. He then was court conductor in Schwerin (1897–1900), at which time he returned to Munich as Generalmusikdirektor.

WORKS: **DRAMATIC:** Opera: *Anahna* (Berlin, 1881); *Sawitri* (completed by Rössler; Schwerin, Sept. 8, 1907; perf. simultaneously with *Das Gespenst von Horodin*); *Das Gespenst von Horodin* (Hamburg, 1910; perf. simultaneously with *Sawitri*). Operetta: Farinelli (Hamburg, 1886); Karin (Hamburg, 1888); Polnische Wirtschaft (Hamburg, 1889). **OTHER:** Sym. (1868), overtures, 2 string quartets (1871, 1891), piano pieces, and many vocal works, including songs.

BIBL.: E. von Possart et al., *H. Z.: Persönliche Erinnerungen nebst Mitteilungen aus seinen Tagebuchblättern und Briefen* (Munich, 1905).—**NS/LK/DM**

Zumsteeg, Johann Rudolf, German composer and conductor; b. Sachsenflur, Odenwald, Jan. 10, 1760; d. Stuttgart, Jan. 27, 1802. As a pupil at the Carlsschule (near Stuttgart), he was a classmate of Schiller. He studied cello with Eberhard Malterre and cello and composition with Agostino Poli in Stuttgart, and in 1781 became solo cellist in the Court Orch. there. He served as music master at the Carlsschule (1785–94), and in 1791 was made director of German music at the Stuttgart Court Theater. In 1793 he succeeded Poli as court Konzertmeister, where he championed the works of Mozart. He produced 8 operas at Stuttgart, of which the best was *Die Geisterinsel*, after Shakespeare's *The Tempest* (Nov. 7, 1798). His other stage works included *Zalaor* (March 2, 1787), *Tamira* (June 13, 1788), *Das Pfauenfest* (Feb. 24, 1801), and *Ebondocani* (Dec. 8, 1803). He also wrote a Sym., 2 overtures, 10 cello concertos, 2 flute concertos, a Concerto for 2 Flutes, chamber music, and choral works, including some 30 cantatas. However, it is chiefly as the precursor of Loewe and Schubert in the composition of art songs that he is historically important. Zumsteeg wrote 20 ballades for Voice and Piano, including settings for Schiller's *Maria Stuart*, Bürger's *Lenore*, Goethe's *Colma*, etc.

BIBL.: I. Arnold, *J.R. Z.: Seine kurze Biographie* (Erfurt, 1810; with a list of works); L. Landshoff, *J.R. Z. (1760–1802): Ein Beitrag zur Geschichte des Liedes und der Ballade* (diss., Univ. of Berlin, 1902); F. Szymichowski, *J.R. Z. als Komponist von Balladen und Monodien* (Stuttgart, 1932); G. Maier, *Die Lieder J.R. Z.s und ihr Verhältnis zu Schubert* (Göppingen, 1971).—**NS/LK/DM**

Zundel, John, German organist and hymn writer; b. Hochdorf, Dec. 10, 1815; d. Cannstadt, July 1882. He was an organist and bandmaster in St. Petersburg; in 1847, went to America, where he became organist at the Central Methodist Episcopal Church in N.Y. He returned to Germany in 1877. In America he ed. the *Monthly Choir and Organ Journal*, and was also one of the compilers, in association with Henry Ward Beecher, of the *Plymouth Collection* (1855). He wrote the celebrated hymn *Love Divine*, also known as *Beecher* or *Zundel*, which is included in *Zundel's Christian Heart Songs* (1870).—**NS/LK/DM**

Zupko, Ramon, American composer and teacher; b. Pittsburgh, Nov. 14, 1932. He was a student of Persichetti at the Juilliard School of Music in N.Y. (B.S., 1956; M.S., 1957). Following further studies with Schiske at the Vienna Academy of Music on a Fulbright fellowship (1958–59), he pursued training in electronic music at Columbia Univ. and with Koenig at the Univ. of Utrecht. He taught theory and was director of the electronic music studio at the Chicago Musical Coll. of Roosevelt Univ. (1967–71). In 1971 he joined the faculty of Western Mich. Univ. in Kalamazoo, where he served as a prof. of composition and director of the electronic and computer music there. He received NEA grants (1978, 1980, 1985), a Koussevitzky Foundation Award (1981), a Guggenheim fellowship (1981–82), an American Academy and Inst. of Arts and Letters award (1982), and a Gilmore Foundation Commission (1990). In his music, Zupko has pursued his interest in contemporary compositional modes of expression while attempting to synthesize them with both music of the past and with non-Western traditions. His Violin Concerto (1962) won 1st prize in the 1965 City of Trieste International Composition Contest.

WORKS: **DRAMATIC:** *Proud Music of the Storm*, multimedia theater-dance piece (1975–76; Kalamazoo, Mich., Dec. 1976); *Rituals*, musical dance-theater piece (1981). **ORCH.:** *Prologoe, Aria, and Dance* for Horn and Strings (1961); *Prelude and Bagatelle* for Strings (1961); *Variations* (1961); Violin Concerto (1962); *Translucents* for Strings (1967); *Tangents* for 18 Brass Instruments (1967); *Radiants* (1971); *Windsongs*, piano concerto (1979; Kalamazoo, Mich., Feb. 1980); *Life Dances* (Tanglewood, Aug. 1981); *Canti Terrae* (1982; N.Y., Feb. 1989); 2 syms.: No. 1, *Earth and Sky*, for Symphonic Band (Kalamazoo, Mich., Nov. 1984) and No. 2, *Blue Roots* (1986; Kalamazoo, Mich., March 1989); *Vox Naturae*, concerto for Brass Quintet and Orch. (1991–92; Kalamazoo, Mich., Nov. 1992). **CHAMBER:** Violin Sonata (1958); Trio for Piano, Violin, and Cello (1958); *Reflexions* for 8 Instruments (1964); *Emulations* for Piano and Tape (1969); *Trichromes* for Wind Ensemble and Tape (1973); *Masques* for Amplified Piano and Brass Quintet (1973); *Fixations* for Piano, Violin, Cello, and Tape (1974); *Fluxus I* for Tape (1977), *II* for Piano (1978), *III* for Amplified Violin, Percussion, and Tape (1978), *IV* for Guitar (1987), *V* for Clarinet and Tape (1987), *VI* for Trumpet and Tape (1988), *VII* for Trombone and Tape (1988), *VIII* for Alto Saxophone and Tape (1988), *IX* for Piano and Tape (1990), *X* for Horn and Tape (1993), *XI* for Flute and Tape (1994), and *XII* for Mallet Instruments and Tape (1994); *Nocturnes* for 2 Pianos (1977); *Fantasies* for Woodwind Quintet (1979); *Noosphere* for String Quartet (1980); *Te Deum Trilogy* for Organ (1984); *Solo Passages* for Horn, Flute, Harp, and String Trio (1985); *Pro and Contra Dances* for Brass Quintet (1986); *Chorale* for Brass Quintet (1989); *Folksody* for Piano Trio (1990); *Chaconne* for Piano (1995). **VOCAL:** *All the Pretty Horses* for Choruses and Chamber Orch. (1962); *This is the Garden* for Chorus, Solo Instruments, and Strings (1962); *La Guerre* for Soprano and Chamber Ensemble (1965); *Voices* for Soprano and Tape (1972); *Where the Mountain Crosses*, song cycle for Mezzo-soprano and Piano (1982).—**NS/LK/DM**

Zur Mühlen, Raimund von, German tenor and pedagogue; b. Livonia, Nov. 10, 1854; d. Steyning, Sussex, Dec. 9, 1931. He began his training at the Berlin Hochschule für Musik, then studied with Stockhausen in Frankfurt am Main and Bussine in Paris; he also took a special course with Clara Schumann, who instructed him in the interpretation of songs by Schumann and Schubert, which gave him the foundation of his career.

He had his greatest success in England, where he lived from 1905 until his death. It was he who introduced into London the "song recital" (Liederabend; programs devoted exclusively to songs). He was also a fine teacher.

Bibl.: D. von Zur Mühlen, *Der Sänger R. v.Z.M.* (Hannover, 1969).—**NS/LK/DM**

Zverev, Nikolai, noted Russian piano pedagogue; b. Volokalamsk, 1832; d. Moscow, Oct. 12, 1893. He was a student of Alexander Dubuc in Moscow and Henselt in St. Petersburg, and also took harmony lessons with Tchaikovsky. He established in Moscow a music boarding school for young pianists; among these inmates were Rachmaninoff and Siloti. Scriabin also took piano lessons with Zverev, although he did not lodge in his music school. From 1870 to his death, Zverev taught piano at the Moscow Cons. Zverev was highly esteemed as a pedagogue, and was one of the most prominent representatives of the Russian pianistic method, which emphasized songful melody and freedom of hand movement.—**NS/LK/DM**

Zweers, Bernard, Dutch composer; b. Amsterdam, May 18, 1854; d. there, Dec. 9, 1924. He studied at the Amsterdam Cons., and later in Leipzig with Jadassohn. Returning to the Netherlands, he became a prof. of theory at the Amsterdam Cons. (1895). He wrote 3 syms., *Kroningscantate* for Soprano, Tenor, Chorus, and Orch., *St. Nicolasfeest*, children's cantata, *Kosmos* (Psalm 104) for Chorus and Orch., *Ons Hollandsch* for Men's Chorus and Orch., church music, and songs. —**NS/LK/DM**

Zweig, Fritz, Bohemian-born American conductor and teacher; b. Olmütz, Sept. 8, 1893; d. Los Angeles, Feb. 28, 1984. He received training in theory from Schoenberg in Vienna. After serving on the staff of the Mannheim National Theater (1912–14; 1919–21), he was asst. conductor at the Barmen-Elberfeld Opera (1921–23). In 1923 he went to Berlin as a conductor at the Volksoper, and then was a conductor at the Städtische Oper from 1927. When the Nazis came to power in 1933, Zweig was banned from the Städtische Oper. In 1934 he became a conductor at the German Theater in Prague. In 1938 he fled Prague in the face of the Nazi dismemberment of Czechoslovakia and lived in Paris. With the defeat of France by the Nazis in 1940, he once more fled and made his way to the U.S. He subsequently was active as a music teacher in Los Angeles. His most notable student was Lawrence Foster.—**NS/LK/DM**

Zwilich, Ellen Taaffe, remarkable American composer; b. Miami, April 30, 1939. She learned to play the piano, trumpet, and violin. During her high school studies, she was active as a conductor, arranger, and composer with the band and orch. Following training in violin and composition at Fla. State Univ. in Tallahassee (B.M., 1960; M.M., 1962), she settled in N.Y. and pursued studies in violin with Galamian. From 1965 to 1972 she was a violinist in the American Sym. Orch. She continued her training in composition at the Juilliard School with Carter and Sessions, taking the first doctorate in composition ever granted there to a woman in 1975. While still at Juilliard, her compositions began to attract notice. In 1974 she received the Elizabeth Sprague Coolidge Chamber Music Medal. In 1975 she was awarded the gold medal at the G.B. Viotti composition competition in Vercelli, Italy. She received grants from the Martha Baird Rockefeller Fund in 1977, 1979, and 1982. In 1980–81 she held a Guggenheim fellowship. In 1983 she became the first woman to win the Pulitzer Prize in Music for her 1st Sym. In 1984 she received an award from the American Academy and Inst. of Arts and Letters, and in 1992 she was elected to its membership. From 1995 to 1999 she held the first Composer's Chair at Carnegie Hall. In her music, Zwilich has succeeded in combining technical expertise with a distinct power of communication. Her idiomatic writing is ably complemented by a poetic element found in her handling of melody, harmony, and counterpoint.

Works: **Dramatic:** **Ballet:** *Tanzspiel* (1987; N.Y., April 27, 1988). **Orch.:** *Symposium* (1973; N.Y., Jan. 31, 1975); 4 syms.: No. 1, originally titled *3 Movements for Orchestra* (N.Y., May 5, 1982), No. 2, *Cello Symphony* (San Francisco, Nov. 13, 1985), No. 3 (1992; N.Y., Feb. 25, 1993), and No. 4, *The Gardens*, for Chorus, Children's Chorus, Handbells, and Orch. (1999; East Lansing, Feb. 5, 2000); *Prologue and Variations* for Strings (1983; Chattanooga, April 10, 1984); *Celebration* (Indianapolis, Oct. 12, 1984); *Concerto grosso* (1985; Washington, D.C., May 9, 1986); Piano Concerto (Detroit, June 26, 1986); *Images* for 2 Pianos and Orch. (1986; Washington, D.C., March 28, 1987); *Symbolon* (Leningrad, June 1, 1988); Trombone Concerto (1988; Chicago, Feb. 2, 1989); Flute Concerto (1989; Boston, April 26, 1990); Concerto for Bass Trombone, Strings, Timpani, and Cymbals (1989; Chicago, April 30, 1991); Oboe Concerto (1990; Cleveland, Jan. 17, 1991); Concerto for Violin, Cello, and Orch. (Louisville, Dec. 5, 1991); Bassoon Concerto (1992; Pittsburgh, May 13, 1993); Concerto for Horn and Strings (Rochester, N.Y., Aug. 1, 1993); *Fantasy* (1993; Long Beach, Calif., Jan. 14, 1994); Trumpet Concerto, *American* (San Diego, Sept. 24, 1994); Triple Concerto for Piano, Violin, Cello, and Orch. (1995; Minneapolis, Feb. 7, 1996); *Jubilation* (Athens, Ga., April 14, 1996); *Peanuts Gallery* for Piano and Orch. (1996; N.Y., March 22, 1997); Violin Concerto (1997; N.Y., March 26, 1998). **Band:** *Ceremonies* (1988; Tallahassee, Fla., March 3, 1989). **Chamber:** *Sonata in 3 Movements* for Violin and Piano (1973–74); 2 string quartets: No. 1 (1974; Boston, Oct. 31, 1975) and No. 2 (N.Y., Dec. 1, 1998); *Clarino Quartet* for 4 Trumpets or 4 Clarinets (1977); Chamber Sym. for Flute, Clarinet, Violin, Viola, Cello, and Piano (Boston, Nov. 30, 1979); String Trio (1982); *Divertimento* for Flute, Clarinet, Violin, and Cello (1983); *Fantasy* for Harpsichord (1983; N.Y., April 10, 1984); *Intrada* for Flute, Clarinet, Violin, Cello, and Piano (1983); Double Quartet for Strings (N.Y., Oct. 21, 1984); Concerto for Trumpet and 5 Players (1984; Pittsburgh, May 6, 1985); Trio for Piano, Violin, and Cello (1987); *Praeludium* for Organ (1987; Philadelphia, May 1, 1988); Quintet for Clarinet and String Quartet (1990). **Vocal:** *Einsame Nacht*, song cycle for Baritone and Piano, after Hesse (1971); *Im Nebel* for Contralto and Piano, after Hesse (1972); *Trompeten* for Soprano and Piano, after Georg Trakl (1974); *Emlékezet* for Soprano and Piano, after Sandor Petofi (1978); *Passages* for Soprano, Flute, Clarinet, Violin, Viola, Cello, Piano, and Percussion (1981; Boston, Jan. 29, 1982; also for Soprano and Chamber Orch., 1982; St. Paul, Minn., Nov. 17, 1983); *Thanksgiving Song* for

Chorus and Piano (1986); *Immigrant Voices* for Chorus, Brass, Timpani, and Strings (N.Y., June 10, 1991); *A Simple Magnificat* for Chorus and Organ (New Haven, Conn., Dec. 6, 1994). **—NS/LK/DM**

Zwyssig, Alberich (actually, **Joseph**), Swiss composer; b. Bauen, Nov. 17, 1808; d. Mehrerau, Nov. 18, 1854. He entered the order of the Cistercians in 1826, giving up his real name, Joseph, for the monastic name Alberich. He was Kapellmeister in the monasteries of Wettingen, Zug, Wurmbach, and (shortly before his death) Mehrerau. His *Schweizer Psalm* for Men's Chorus (1841) attained great popularity, and in 1961 it was named as a pro tempore national anthem of Switzerland. He further composed many sacred and secular choruses, and church music with organ accompaniment.

Bibl.: B. Widmann, *A. Z. als Komponist* (Bregenz, 1905); H. Meng, *A. Z., 1808–1854: Gedenkschrift* (Wettingen, 1954). **—NS/LK/DM**

Zykan, Otto M., Austrian composer; b. Vienna, April 29, 1935. He received training in piano and composition (with Schiske) at the Vienna Academy of Music. In 1965 he founded the "Salonkonzerte" in Vienna, and appeared as a pianist in many contemporary scores. He also worked in contemporary music theater circles. From 1975 he devoted most of his time to film projects, for which he composed, wrote screen plays, and directed.

Works: Dramatic: *Sings Nähmaschine ist die beste*, theater piece (1966); *Schön der Reihe nach*, ballet (1966); *Lehrstück am Beispiel Schönbergs*, music theater-action (1974); *Kunst kommt von Gönnen*, opera (1980); *Auszählreim*, opera (1986; rev. 1987); *Wahr ist, dass der Tiger frisst*, choral opera (1994); *Mesmer*, film music (1994). **Orch.:** Piano Concerto (1958); *Kurze Anweisung* (1969); *Symphonie der heilen Welt*, scenic concerto (1977); *Ausgesucht Freundliches*, concerto for 2 Soloists, Chorus, and Orch. (1979); Cello Concerto (1982). **Chamber:** Cello Sonata (1958); 4 string quartets (1958, n.d., 1990, 1990); *Kryptomnemie* for Winds, Percussion, and Piano (1963); *6 Chansons, die keine sind* for Piano (1965); *Kammermusik* for 12 Instruments (1965); *4 Nachtstück* for Piano (1968); *Miles Smiles*, chamber music (1970); Trio for Solo Violin (1977). **Vocal:** *Inscene* for 1 to 5 Voices (1967); *Rondo: Alles ist Musik was nicht Gymnastik ist* for Speaker and Tape (1971); *Die Orgel der Barbarei* for 4 Singers, Soloist, and Tuba (1984); *Engels Engel* for 3 Vocalists or Chorus and Tape (1988).**—NS/LK/DM**

Zylis-Gara, Teresa, Polish soprano; b. Landvarov, Jan. 23, 1935. She was a student of Olga Ogina at the Łódź Academy of Music. After taking 1st prize in the Warsaw Competition in 1954, she sang on the radio and with the Phil. in Kraków. In 1956 she made her operatic debut as Halka in Katowice, and then sang in various Polish music centers. In 1960 she won 1st prize in the Munich Competition, which led to an engagement in Oberhausen. In 1962 she sang in Dortmund and in 1965 in Düsseldorf. In 1965 she made her debut at the Glyndebourne Festival as Octavian. She sang in Paris in 1966. In 1968 she appeared as Donna Elvira at the Salzburg Festival and made her Covent Garden debut in London as Violetta. On Dec. 17, 1968, she made her Metropolitan Opera debut in N.Y. as Donna Elvira, and continued on its roster until 1984. From 1972 she also sang at the Vienna State Opera. In 1973 she appeared in Barcelona. She sang Liù at the Orange Festival in 1979. In 1988 she appeared as Desdemona at the Hamburg State Opera. Throughout the years, she also pursued an active concert career. Among her other operatic roles were Fiordiligi, Tatiana, Manon Lescaut, Elisabeth, Elsa, Anna Bolena, and the Marschallin.**—NS/LK/DM**

Genre

INDEX

CLASSICAL

Early Music

Renaissance

Agostini, Lodovico
Agostini, Paolo
Agricola, Alexander
Agricola (real name, Sore), Martin
Aguilera de Heredia, Sebastián
Ahle, Johann Rudolf
Aichinger, Gregor
A Kempis, Nicolaus
Albani, Mattia (real name, Mathias Alban)
Albert, Heinrich
Alberti, Gasparo
Albrici, Vincenzo
Aleotti, Raffaella
Alison (or Allison, Allysonn, etc.), Richard
Allegri, Domenico
Allegri, Gregorio
Allegri, Lorenzo
Almeida, Fernando d'
Altenburg, Michael
Ammerbach, Elias Nicolaus
Ammon, Blasius
Amner, John
Ana, Francesco d'
Anchieta, Juan de
Ancina, (Giovanni) Giovenale
Andreini, Virginia (née Rampnoni)
Anerio, Felice
Anerio, Giovanni Francesco
Anglesi, Domenico
Animuccia, Giovanni
Animuccia, Paolo
Annibale Il Padovano
Antegnati, Costanzo
Antico, Andrea
Antonelli, Abundio
Appenzeller, Benedictus
Appleby, Thomas
Arbeau, Thoinot (real name, Jean Tabourot)
Arcadelt, Jacob or Jacques
Archilei, Vittoria (née Concarini)
Aretino, Paolo
Arresti, Giulio Cesare
Artusi, Giovanni Maria
Ashwell (also Ashewell, Hashewell), Thomas
Asola or Asula, Giammateo or Giovanni Matteo
Aston, Hugh
Attaignant, Pierre
Auxcousteaux (also Aux-Cousteaux, Hautcousteaux), Artus
Ayleward, Richard
Baccusi, Ippolito
Bach Family
  Bach, Christoph
  Bach, Heinrich
  Bach, Johann(es Hans)
Bacilly, Bénigne de
Baïf, Jean-Antoine de
Bakfark, Valentin (or Bálint)
Balbi, Lodovico or Ludivico
Baldwin, John
Ballard Family
Baltzar, Thomas
Ban, Joan Albert
Banchieri, Adriano (actually, Tomaso)
Banestre, Gilbert
Banister, John
Banwart, Jakob
Barbarino, Bartolomeo
Barberiis, Melchiore de
Barbetta, Giulio Cesare
Bardi, Giovanni de'
Baroni, Leonora
Bartei, Girolamo
Bartolomeo degli Organi (Baccio Fiorentino)
Baryphonus, Henricus (real name, Heinrich Pipegrop)
Basile, Andreana
Bassano (also Bassani), Giovanni
Baston, Josquin
Bateson, Thomas
Bathe, William
Batten, Adrian
Bauldewijn (also Bauldeweyn, Bauldoin, Baudoin, etc.), Noël
Becker, Dietrich
Beheim, Michel
Bellasio, Paolo
Bell'Haver, Vincenzo
Belli, Domenico
Belli, Girolamo
Belli, Giulio
Bendinelli, Agostino
Bendinelli, Cesare
Benet, John
Benevoli, Orazio
Bennet, John
Berchem, Jacquet or Jachet de
Berger, Andreas
Bermudo, Juan
Bernard der Deutsche
Bernardi, Stefano
Bernhard, Christoph
Bertali, Antonio
Bertani, Lelio
Berti, Carlo
Berti, Giovanni Pietro
Bertin de la Doué, Thomas
Bertoldo, Sperindio (Sper'in Dio)
Bertrand, Antoine de
Besard, Jean-Baptiste
Besler, Samuel
Beurhaus, Friedrich
Bevin, Elway
Bianchini, Domenico
Bianco, Pietro Antonio
Bildstein, Hieronymus
Bilhon (Billhon, Billon), Jhan (Jean, Jan, Jehan, Joannes) de (du)
Binchois (Binch, Binche), Gilles (de)
Blackhall, Andrew
Bleyer, Nicolaus
Blitheman, John
Böddecker, Philipp Friedrich
Bodenschatz, Erhard
Boësset, Antoine (Sieur de Villedieu)
Bollius, Daniel
Bona (or Buona), Valerio
Bona, Giovanni
Bonhomme, Pierre
Boni, Guillaume
Bonini, Severo
Bontempi (real name, Angelini), Giovanni Andrea
Bottrigari, Ercole
Bourgeois, Loys
Bournonville, Jean de
Bournonville, Valentin de
Bouzignac, Guillaume
Bovicelli, Giovanni Battista
Brade, William
Brandt, Jobst vom (or Jodocus de Brant)
Brant, Jan
Brätel, Ulrich
Breitengraser, Wilhelm
Briegel, Wolfgang Carl
Bruck (or Brouck), Arnold von (known also as Arnold de Bruges and Arnoldo Flamengo)
Brudieu, Joan
Brumel, Antoine
Brunelli, Antonio
Brunetti, Domenico
Bryne, Albert or Albertus
Bucenus, Paulus
Buchner, Hans
Buchner, Philipp Friedrich
Bull, John
Buonamente, Giovanni Battista
Burck (real name, Moller), Joachim á
Burmeister, Joachim
Burtius (also known as Burci or Burzio), Nicolaus
Busnois, Antoine
Buus, Jacques (Jachet de or van Paus; Jacobus Bohusius; Jacob Buus)
Byrd, William
Cabezón (Cabeçon), Antonio de
Caccini, Francesca (nicknamed "La Cecchina")
Caccini, Giulio
Calvisius, Sethus (real name, Seth Kallwitz)
Cambefort, Jean de
Campion (Campian), Thomas
Canis, Cornelius or Corneille
Caproli or Caprioli, Carlo
Cara, Marchetto
Cardoso, Manuel
Carissimi, Giacomo
Caron, Philippe
Carpentras (real name, Elzéar Genet)
Carver, Robert
Castello, Dario
Castro, Jean de
Caustun, Thomas
Cavalieri, Emilio de'
Cavalli (real name, Caletti), Pier Francesco
Cavazzoni (also called da Bologna and d'Urbino), Marco Antonio
Cavazzoni, Girolamo
Cavendish, Michael
Cazzati, Maurizio
Cecchino, Tomaso
Cellarius, Simon
Cerone, Domenico Pietro
Certon, Pierre
Cesti, Antonio (baptismal name, Pietro)
Chambonnières, Jacques Champion, Sieur de

Waissel (Waisselius), Matthäus
Walliser, Christoph Thomas
Walter or Walther (real name, Blankenmüller), Johann(es)
Walther, Johann Jacob
Wanless, John
Wannenmacher (Latinized as Vannius), Johannes
Ward, John
Wecker, Georg Kaspar
Weckmann, Matthias
Weelkes, Thomas
Weerbeke (also Weerbecke, Werbecke, Werbeke, Werbeck), Gaspar van
Weissensee, Friedrich
Werrecore (also Vercore, Verecore, Verrechore, Werrekoren), Matthias Hermann
Wert, Giaches (or Jaches) de
White (or Whyte), Robert
White, William
Whythorne, Thomas
Widmann, Erasmus
Wilbye, John
Wilder, Philip van
Willaert, Adrian
Wilson, John
Yonge (also Young, Younge), Nicholas
Youll, Henry
Zangius (Zange), Nikolaus
Zarlino, Gioseffo
Ziani, Pietro Andrea
Zoilo, Annibale

Baroque

Abbatini, Antonio Maria
Abell, John
Abos, Girolamo
Adami da Bolsena, Andrea
Agostini, Pietro Simone
Agrell, Johan Joachim
Ahle, Johann Georg
Ahle, Johann Rudolf
A Kempis, Nicolaus
Akeroyde, Samuel
Albani, Mattia (real name, Mathias Alban)
Albergati (Capacelli), Pirro
Alberti, Giuseppe Matteo
Alberti, Johann Friedrich
Albicastro, Henricus (real name, Heinrich Weissenburg)
Albinoni, Tomaso Giovanni
Albrici, Vincenzo
Aldrich, Henry
Aldrovandini, Giuseppe (Antonio Vincenzo)
Alghisi, Paris Francesco
Almeida, Fernando d'
Amadei, Filippo
Amalia, Catharina
Anet, (Jean-Jacques-) Baptiste
Anet, Jean-Baptiste
Araujo, Juan de
Ariosti, Attilio (Malachia)
Arresti, Giulio Cesare
Aschenbrenner, Christian Heinrich
d'Astorga, Baron Emanuele (Gioacchino Cesare Rincón)
Aubert Family
  Aubert, Jacques
Aufschnaiter, Benedict Anton
Ayleward, Richard
Babell, William
Bach Family
  Bach, Christoph
  Bach, Georg Christoph
  Bach, Heinrich
  Bach, Johann Aegidius
  Bach, Johann Ambrosius
  Bach, Johann Bernhard
  Bach, Johann Christoph
  Bach, Johann Christoph
  Bach, Johann Christoph
  Bach, Johann(es Hans)
  Bach [I], Johann Jacob
  Bach [II], Johann Jacob
  Bach, Johann Ludwig
  Bach, Johann Michael
  Bach, Johann Nicolaus
  Bach, Johann Sebastian
Bachofen, Johann Caspar
Bacilly, Bénigne de
Badia, Carlo Agostino
Bai (also Baj), Tommaso
Baltzar, Thomas
Banister, John
Banister, John, Jr.
Banwart, Jakob
Baroni, Leonora
Barsanti, Francesco
Bassani (Bassano, Bassiani), Giovanni Battista
Bâton, Charles, le jeune
Battistini, Giacomo
Becker, Dietrich
Beer, Johann
Bellinzani, Paolo Benedetto
Bembo, Antonia
Bendeler, Johann Philipp
Bendinelli, Agostino
Bendler, Salomon
Benevoli, Orazio
Berardi, Angelo
Berenstadt, Gaetano
Bergiron de Briou, Nicolas-Antoine, Seigneur du Fort Michon
Bernabei, Ercole
Bernabei, Giuseppe Antonio
Bernacchi, Antonio Maria
Bernardi, Bartolomeo
Bernhard, Christoph
Bernier, Nicolas
Bertali, Antonio
Bertalotti, Angelo Michele
Bertin de la Doué, Thomas
Bertouch, George von
Biber, Heinrich Ignaz Franz von
Bioni, Antonio
Biordi, Giovanni
Birkenstock, Johann Adam
Blamont, François Colin de
Blanchard, Esprit Joseph Antoine
Blankenburg, Quirin van (full name, Quirinus Gerbrandszoon van Blankenburg)
Bleyer, Georg
Blow, John
Böhm, Georg
Bokemeyer, Heinrich
Bona, Giovanni
Bononcini, Antonio Maria
Bononcini, Giovanni
Bononcini, Giovanni Maria
Bonporti, Francesco Antonio
Bontempi (real name, Angelini), Giovanni Andrea
Borosini, Francesco
Boschi, Giuseppe Maria
Bourgeois, Thomas-Louis (-Joseph)
Bournonville, Jacques de
Bournonville, Valentin de
Bousset, Jean-Baptiste
Boutmy Family
  Boutmy, Jacques-Adrien
Boxberg, Christian Ludwig
Boyvin, Jacques
Bréhy, Hercule
Briegel, Wolfgang Carl
Brixi, Šimon
Bronner, Georg
Brossard, Sébastien de
Bruhns, Nicolaus
Bryne, Albert or Albertus
Buffardin, Pierre-Gabriel
Bullis, Thomas
Buttstett, Johann Heinrich
Buxtehude, Dietrich
Cabanilles, Juan Bautista José
Caesar, Johann Melchior
Caldara, Antonio
Calegari, Francesco Antonio
Cambefort, Jean de
Cambert, Robert
Campion, François
Campra, André
Cannabich Family
  Cannabich, Martin Friedrich
Capricornus, Samuel Friedrich
Caproli or Caprioli, Carlo
Carey, Henry
Carissimi, Giacomo
Casini, Giovanni Maria
Castrucci, Pietro
Cavalli (real name, Caletti), Pier Francesco
Cazzati, Maurizio
Cesti, Antonio (baptismal name, Pietro)
Cesti, Remigio
Chambonnières, Jacques Champion, Sieur de
Chancy, François de
Charpentier, Marc-Antoine
Chaumont, Lambert
Child, William
Clari, Giovanni Carlo Maria
Clarke, Jeremiah
Colasse, Pascal
Colista, Lelio
Collin (Colin) de Blamont, François
Colonna, Giovanni Paolo
Conradi, Johann Georg
Conti, Francesco Bartolomeo
Cooke, Henry
Corbett, William
Corbetta, Francesco
Corelli, Arcangelo

Löwe von Eisenach, Johann Jakob
Lubeck, Vincent
Lulier, Giovanni Lorenzo
Lully, Jean-Baptiste (originally, Giovanni Battista Lulli)
Mace, Thomas
Majo, Giuseppe de
Mancini, Francesco
Manfredini, Francesco Onofrio
Mannelli, Carlo
Marais, Marin
Marazzoli, Marco
Marcello, Alessandro
Marcello, Benedetto
Marchand, Louis
Marini, Biagio
Mascitti, Michele
Mathieu Family
    Mathieu, Michel
Matho, Jean-Baptiste
Matteis, Nicola
Mattheson, Johann
Maupin
Meck, Joseph
Meder, Johann Valentin
Melani Family
    Melani, Jacopo
    Melani, Atto
    Melani, Alessandro
Mell, Davis
Merighi, Antonia Margherita
Merula, Tarquinio
Míča, František Antonín (Václav)
Michna, Adam Václav
Monferrato, Natale
Montéclair, Michel Pignolet de (real name, Michel Pignolet)
Monti Family
    Monti, Anna Maria
    Monti, Laura
Moreau, Jean-Baptiste
Moulinié, Etienne
Mouret, Jean-Joseph
Muffat, Georg
Muffat, Gottlieb (Theophil)
Murschhauser, Franz Xaver Anton
Mylius, Wolfgang Michael
Naudot, Jacques-Christophe
Navas, Juan (Francisco) de
Neri, Massimiliano
Neumark, Georg
Nicolini (real name, Nicolo Grimaldi)
Nivers, Guillaume Gabriel
Noordt, Anthoni van
North, Roger
Notari, Angelo
Orefice, Antonio
Orejón y Aparicio, José de
Orlandini, Giuseppe Maria
Ouvrard, René
Pacchioni, Antonio Maria
Pace, Pietro
Pachelbel, Johann
Pachelbel, Wilhelm Hieronymus
Pacini, Andrea
Pagliardi, Giovanni Maria
Paisible, James
Palella, Antonio
Pallavicino, Carlo
Pari, Claudio
Partenio, Gian Domenico
Pasquini, Bernardo
Patiño, Carlos
Pederzuoli, Giovanni Battista
Pekiel, Bartlomiej
Pellegrin, Claude Mathieu
Pellegrini, Valeriano
Penna, Lorenzo
Pepusch, John Christopher (actually Johann Christoph)
Peranda, Marco Gioseppe
Perti, Giacomo or Jacopo Antonio
Petit
Pez or Petz, Johann Christoph
Pezel (Petzold, Petzel, Pezelius, etc.), Johann Christoph
Pezold or Petzold, Christian
Pfleger, Augustin
Philidor (real name, Danican) Family
    Danican, Jean
    Danican Philidor (le cadet), André
    Danican Philidor, Jacques
    Danican Philidor, Anne
    Danican Philidor, Pierre
Philip de Bourbon
Piani, Giovanni Antonio
Pietkin, Lambert
Pigott, Francis
Piroye, Charles
Pisendel, Johann Georg
Pistocchi, Francesco Antonio Mamiliano
Pitoni, Giuseppe Ottavio
Playford, Henry
Playford, John
Poglietti, Alessandro
Pohle, David
Poitevin, Guillaume
Pollarolo, Carlo Francesco
Pollarolo, (Giovanni) Antonio
Pontac, Diego de
Porpora, Nicola (Antonio)
Porsile, Giuseppe
Porta, Giovanni
Porter, Walter
Pradas Gallen, José
Praelisauer Family
Predieri Family
    Predieri, Giacomo (Maria)
    Predieri, Antonio
    Predieri, Giacomo Cesare
    Predieri, Luca Antonio
Prendcourt, "Captain" de
Prin, Jean-Baptiste
Prinner, Johann Jacob
Printz, Wolfgang Caspar
Profe, Ambrosius
Prota Family
    Prota, Ignazio
    Prota, Tommaso
Provenzale, Francesco
Purcell, Daniel
Purcell, Henry
Quantz, Johann Joachim
Quinault, Jean-Baptiste-Maurice
Quintavalle, Antonio
Racquet, Charles
Raison, André
Rameau, Jean-Philippe
Rascarini, Francesco Maria
Reading, John
Rebel Family
    Rebel, Anne-Renée
    Rebel (le père), Jean-Féry
    Rebel (le fils), François
Reinken (Reincken), Jan Adams
Reusner (or Reussner), Esaias
Reutter, Georg (von)
Ricciotti, Carlo
Richter, Ferdinand Tobias
Rist, Johann
Ritter, Christian
Robinson, Anastasia
Rodriguez, Vicente
Römhild or Römhildt, Johann Theodor
Roseingrave Family
    Roseingrave, Daniel
    Roseingrave, Thomas
    Roseingrave, Ralph
Rosier, Carl
Sainte-Colombe, Sieur de or Monsieur de (real name, August Dautrecourt)
Sammartini, Giuseppe (Francesco Gaspare Melchiorre Baldassare)
Sances, Giovanni Felice
Sanz, Gaspar
Sarro (or Sarri), Domenico Natale
Sartorio, Antonio
Sauveur, Joseph
Scalzi, Carlo
Scarabelli, Diamante Maria
Scarlatti, (Giuseppe) Domenico
Scarlatti, (Pietro) Alessandro (Gaspare)
Schacht, Matthias Henriksen
Scheidemann, Heinrich
Schelle, Johann
Schemelli, Georg Christian
Schenck, Johannes
Schieferdecker, Johann Christian
Schmelzer, Johann Heinrich
Schmidt, Johann Christoph
Schröter, Christoph Gottlieb
Schulze, Christian Andreas
Schürmann, Georg Caspar
Schütz, Gabriel
Schütz, Heinrich (also Henrich)
Schwemmer, Heinrich
Sebastiani, Johann
Seedo (Sidow or Sydow)
Seixas (real name, Vas), (José Antonio) Carlos de
Selle, Thomas
Senaillé (also Senaillié, Senallié, etc.), Jean Baptiste
Senesino (real name, Francesco Bernardi)
Seyfert, Johann Caspar
Shore, John
Siface (real name, Giovanni Francesco Grossi)
Simonelli, Matteo
Simpson (Sympson), Christopher
Siret, Nicholas
Somis, Giovanni Battista
Somis, Lorenzo Giovanni
Sorge, Georg Andreas
Speer, Daniel

Classical

Bernasconi, Andrea
Bernasconi, Antonia
Bernier, Nicolas
Bertalotti, Angelo Michele
Berteau, Martin
Bertheaume, Isidore
Bertini, Giuseppe
Bertini, Salvatore
Bertolli, Francesca
Berton, Pierre-Montan
Bertoni, Ferdinando (Gioseffo)
Bertouch, George von
Besozzi, Alessandro
Bianchi, Antonio
Bianchi, Francesco
Billings, William
Binder, Christlieb Siegmund
Bini, Pasquale
Bioni, Antonio
Biordi, Giovanni
Birkenstock, Johann Adam
Blainville, Charles-Henri de
Blamont, François Colin de
Blanchard, Esprit Joseph Antoine
Blankenburg, Quirin van (full name, Quirinus Gerbrandszoon van Blankenburg)
Blavet, Michel
Boccherini, (Ridolfo) Luigi
Bode, Johann Joachim Christoph
Bodinus, Sebastian
Böhm, Georg
Boismortier, Joseph Bodin de
Bokemeyer, Heinrich
Bond, Chapel
Bonno, Giuseppe
Bononcini, Giovanni
Bonporti, Francesco Antonio
Borghi, Giovanni Battista
Boroni, Antonio
Borosini, Francesco
Bortniansky, Dimitri (Stepanovich)
Bosch, Pieter Joseph van den
Boschi, Giuseppe Maria
Bourgeois, Thomas-Louis (-Joseph)
Bournonville, Jacques de
Bousset, Jean-Baptiste
Boutmy Family
    Boutmy, Josse (actually, Charles Joseph)
    Boutmy, Guillaume
    Boutmy, Jean-Joseph
Boyce, William
Brant, Per
Braun Family
    Braun, Anton
    Braun, Johann
    Braun, Johann Friedrich
    Braun, Maria Louise
    Braun, Moriz
Bréhy, Hercule
Brent, Charlotte
Breval, Jean-Baptiste Sebastien
Brioschi, Antonio
Brixi, Franz (actually, František) Xaver
Brixi, Šimon
Brixi, Viktorin (Ignać)
Broche, Charles
Broschi, Riccardo
Brosmann (a Sancto Hieronymo), Damasus
Brossard, Sébastien de
Brown, John
Brunetti Family
    Brunetti, Giovan Gualberto
    Brunetti, Antonio
    Brunetti, Giuseppe
Brunetti, Gaetano
Bullant, Antoine
Burton, John
Bury, Bernard de
Busby, Thomas
Cafaro, Pasquale
Caffarelli (real name, Gaetano Majorano)
Caldara, Antonio
Calegari, Francesco Antonio
Calzabigi, Ranieri (Simone Francesco Maria) di
Cambini, Giuseppe Maria (Gioacchino)
Camerloher, Placidus Cajetan von
Campagnoli, Bartolommeo
Campion, François
Campra, André
Candeille, Pierre Joseph
Cannabich Family
    Cannabich, Martin Friedrich
    Cannabich, (Johann) Christian (Innocenz Bonaventura)
Carestini, Giovanni
Carey, Henry
Carr Family
    Carr, Thomas
Carvalho, João de Sousa
Castrucci, Pietro
Cavalieri, Catarina (real name, Franziska Cavalier)
Cherubini, (Maria) Luigi (Carlo Zenobio Salvatore)
Chilcot, Thomas
Ciampi, Vincenzo (Legrenzio)
Cibber, Susanne Maria
Cimarosa, Domenico
Cirri, Giovanni Battista
Clari, Giovanni Carlo Maria
Clementi, Muzio (baptized Mutius Philippus Vincentius Franciscus Xaverius)
Clérambault, Louis Nicolas
Clive, Kitty (actually, Catherine née Raftor)
Cocchi, Gioacchino
Colla, Giuseppe
Collin (Colin) de Blamont, François
Conti, Francesco Bartolomeo
Conti, Gioacchino
Cooke, Benjamin
Corbett, William
Cornelys, T(h)eresa (née Imer)
Corradini, Francesco
Corrette, Michel
Corri, Domenico
Corselli (real name, Courcelle), Francesco
Couperin
Couperin, Armand-Louis
Couperin, François
Couperin, Gervais-François
Couperin, Nicolas
Couperin, Pierre-Louis
Cramer, Wilhelm
Crotch, William
Cuzzoni, Francesca
Czernohorsky (Černohorský), Bohuslav Matj
Dagincour, François
Dal Barba, Daniel
Dall'Abaco, Evaristo Felice
Dall'Abaco, Joseph-Marie-Clément
Dandrieu, Jean François
Da Ponte, Lorenzo (real name, Emanuele Conegliano)
Daquin, Louis-Claude
Dauvergne, Antoine
David, Giacomo
Davies, Cecilia
De Amicis, Anna Lucia
De Fesch (also Defesch, du Feche, de Feghe, de Veg), Willem
Della Ciaia, Azzolino Bernardino
Deller, Florian Johann
Dencke, Jeremiah
Desmarets, Henri
Desmazures, Laurent
Dezède, Nicolas
Dibdin, Charles
Dittersdorf, Karl Ditters von (original name, Karl Ditters)
Döbricht, Johanna Elisabeth
Doles, Johann Friedrich
Duni, Egidio (Romualdo)
Duport, Jean-Louis
Duport, Jean-Pierre
Durante, Francesco
Duschek, Franz Xaver (real name, František Xaver Dušek)
Eberlin (Eberle), Johann Ernst
Eccles Family
    Eccles, Henry
    Eccles, John
Eck, Friedrich Johann (Gerhard)
Eckard (Eckardt, Eckart), Johann Gottfried
Edelmann, Jean-Frédéric
Egli, Johann Heinrich
Eichner, Ernst (Dieterich Adolph)
Ertmann, (Catharina) Dorothea von (née Grautmann)
Esteve (Estebe) y Grimau, Pablo
Exaudet, André-Joseph
Eybler, Joseph Leopold, Edler von
Fabri, Annibale Pio
Falckenhagen, Adam
Fasch, Karl Friedrich Christian (baptized Christian Friedrich Carl)
Favart, Charles-Simon
Favart, Marie (née -Justine-Benoîte Duronceray)
Fedeli Family
    Fedeli, Giuseppe
Fel, Marie
Felton, William
Ferraresi del Bene, Adriana (née Gabrieli)
Ferrari, Domenico
Festing, Michael (Christian)
Fiala, Joseph

Lalouette, Jean Francois
Lampe, John Frederick (actually, Johann Friedrich)
Lampugnani, Giovanni Battista
Lang, Johann Georg
Langdon, Richard
Langlé, Honoré (François Marie)
Lanzetti, Salvatore
La Pouplinière, Alexandre-Jean-Joseph Le Riche de
Larrivée, Henri
Laruette, Jean-Louis
Laschi, Luisa
Lates, James
Latilla, Gaetano
Lauffensteiner, Wolff Jacob
Law, Andrew
Leach, James
Lebrun, Franziska (Dorothea née Danzi)
Lebrun, Jean
Lebrun, Louis-Sébastien
Lebrun, Ludwig August (actually, Ludwig Karl Maria)
Leclair Family
    Leclair, Jean-Marie
    Leclair, Jean-Marie (le second or le cadet)
    Leclair, Pierre
    Leclair, Jean-Benoît
Leduc, Pierre (le jeune)
Leduc (Le Duc), Simon (l'aîné)
Legros, Joseph
Lemaire, Louis
Lemoyne, Jean-Baptiste
Leo, Leonardo (Lionardo Ortensio Salvatore de)
L'Épine, (Francesca) Margherita de
Le Sueur or Lesueur, Jean François
Leutgeb, Joseph (Ignaz)
Levasseur, Rosalie (Marie-Rose-Claude-Josèphe)
Leveridge, Richard
Lidarti, Christian Joseph
Lidón, José
Lima, Jeronymo Francisco de
Lindeman Family
    Lindeman, Ole Andreas
Linike Family
    Linike, Christian Bernhard
    Linike, Johann Georg
Linley Family
    Linley, Thomas, Sr.
    Linley, Elizabeth Ann
    Linley, Thomas, Jr.
    Linley, Mary
Lipawsky or Lipavský, Joseph
Literes Carrión, Antonio
Lobkowitz Family
    Lobkowitz, Philipp Hyacinth (Filipp Hyacint)
    Lobkowitz, Ferdinand Philipp Joseph (Ferdinand Filipp Josef)
Locatelli, Pietro Antonio
Loeillet Family (also spelled L'Oeillet, Luly, Lulli, Lullie, Lully)
    Loeillet, Jean Baptiste
    Loeillet, Jacques (Jacob)
Logroscino, Nicola Bonifacio
Löhlein, Georg Simon
Lolli, Antonio
Lotti, Antonio
Louis Ferdinand (actually, Friedrich Christian Ludwig)
Lucchesi, Andrea
Lyon, James
Mahaut, Antoine
Majo, Gian Francesco (de)
Majo, Giuseppe de
Maldere, Pierre van
Mancini, Francesco
Mandini, Stefano
Manfredini, Francesco Onofrio
Manfredini, Vincenzo
Manna, Gennaro
Manzuoli, Giovanni
Mara, Gertrud (Elisabeth née Schmeling)
Marais, Marin
Marcello, Alessandro
Marcello, Benedetto
Marchand, Louis
Marchand, (Simon-) Luc
Marchesi, Luigi (Lodovico)
Maresch, Johann Anton (real name, Jan Antonín Mareš)
Maria Antonia Walpurgis
Marpurg, Friedrich Wilhelm
Marsh, John
Martin, François
Martínez, Marianne (actually, Anna Katharina) von
Martini, Giovanni Battista
Martini, Jean Paul Egide (real name, Johann Paul Ágid Schwarzendorf)
Martín y Soler, (Atanasio Martín Ignacio) Vicente (Tadeo Francisco Pellegrin)
Mascitti, Michele
Mašek, Vincenz
Mathieu Family
    Mathieu, Michel
    Mathieu, Julien-Amable
    Mathieu, Michel-Julien
Matho, Jean-Baptiste
Mattei, Stanislao
Mattheson, Johann
Mayr, (Johannes) Simon (actually, Giovanni Simone)
Mazzinghi, Joseph
McGibbon, William
Meck, Joseph
Méhul, Etienne-Nicolas
Mei, Orazio
Méreaux Family
    Méreaux, Nicolas-Jean Le Froid de
Merighi, Antonia Margherita
Meyer, Philippe-Jacques
Míča, František Adam
Míča, František Antonín (Václav)
Michl, Joseph (Christian) Willibald
Millico, (Vito) Giuseppe
Mingotti, Pietro
Mingotti, Regina (née Valentini)
Misón, Luis
Moller, John Christopher (real name, Johann Christoph Möller)
Molter, Johann Melchior
Momigny, Jérôme-Joseph de
Mondonville, Jean-Joseph Cassanéa de
Monn (originally Mann), Johann Christoph
Monn, Matthias Georg or Georg Matthias (born Johann Georg Mann)
Monsigny, Pierre-Alexandre
Montagnana, Antonio
Montéclair, Michel Pignolet de (real name, Michel Pignolet)
Monti Family
    Monti, Anna Maria
    Monti, Laura
    Monti, Marianna
    Monti, Gaetano
Monticelli, Angelo Maria
Monza, Carlo
Mooser, (Jean Pierre Joseph) Aloys
Moreira, António Leal
Mornington, Garret Wesley, First Earl of
Mouret, Jean-Joseph
Mozart, (Johann Georg) Leopold
Mozart, Maria Anna (Walburga Ignatia)
Mozart, Wolfgang Amadeus (baptismal names, Johannes Chrysostomus Wolfgangus Theophilus)
Muffat, Gottlieb (Theophil)
Müller, August Eberhard
Murschhauser, Franz Xaver Anton
Müthel, Johann Gottfried
Mysliveček (Mysliweczek; Misliveček), Josef
Nardini, Pietro
Nares, James
Naudot, Jacques-Christophe
Naumann, Johann Gottlieb
Nebra (Blasco), José (Melchor de)
Neefe, Christian Gottlob
Negri, Maria Rosa
Neruda, Johann Baptist Georg (actually, Jan Křtitel Jiří)
Nichelmann, Christoph
Nicolai, David Traugott
Nicolini (real name, Nicolo Grimaldi)
Niemtschek (Niemetschek, Němeček), Franz Xaver
Oginski, Prince Michal Kleofas
Ordonez or Ordoñez, Carlos d'
Orejón y Aparicio, José de
Orgitano Family
    Orgitano, Vincenzo
    Orgitano, Paolo
Orlandini, Giuseppe Maria
Oswald, James
Ottani, Bernardo
Ottani, Gaetano
Oxinaga, Joaquin de
Pacchiarotti, Gasparo
Pacchioni, Antonio Maria
Pachelbel, Charles Theodore (actually, Carl Theodor)
Pachelbel, Wilhelm Hieronymus
Pacini, Andrea
Paganelli, Giuseppe Antonio
Paisible, Louis Henri
Paisiello, Giovanni
Palella, Antonio
Palomino, José

Romantic

Badini, Ernesto
Baermann, Carl (actually, Karl Bärmann)
Bähr, (Franz) Josef
Baillot, Pierre (-Marie-François de Sales)
Baini, Giuseppe (also known as Abbate Baini)
Bairstow, Sir Edward (Cuthbert)
Baker, Benjamin Franklin
Baker, Theodore
Balakirev, Mily (Alexeievich)
Balanchivadze, Meliton (Antonovich)
Balart, Gabriel
Balatka, Hans
Balbi, Melchiore
Baldi, João José
Balfe, Michael William
Balling, Michael
Bandrowski-Sas, Alexander
Banister, Henry Charles
Bannister, Henry (-Marriott)
Banti, Brigida (née Giorgi)
Bantock, Sir Granville (Ransome)
Barbaia or Barbaja, Domenico
Barbieri, Carlo Emanuele
Barbieri, Francisco Asenjo
Barbieri-Nini, Marianna
Barblan, Otto
Bargiel, Woldemar
Barili, Alfredo
Barrére, Georges
Bárta, Josef
Bartay, Andreas
Bartay, Ede
Barthélémon, François-Hippolyte
Bartlett, Homer Newton
Bartók, Béla (Viktor János)
Basili, Francesco
Bassi, Amedeo (Vittorio)
Bassi, Carolina Manna
Bassi, Luigi
Bastiaans, Johannes Gijsbertus
Battaille, Charles-Amable
Battistini, Gaudenzio
Battistini, Mattia
Bauer, Harold
Baumbach, Friedrich August
Baumgarten, Karl Friedrich
Bausznern, Waldemar von
Bazelaire, Paul
Beach, Mrs. H.H.A. (née Amy Marcy Cheney)
Beaulieu (real name, Martin-Beaulieu), Marie-Désiré
Beauvarlet-Charpentier, Jean-Jacques
Becher, Alfred Julius
Bechstein, (Friedrich Wilhelm) Carl
Beck, Franz Ignaz
Beck, Johann H(einrich)
Becker, Carl Ferdinand
Becker, Constantin Julius
Becker, Gustave Louis
Becker, Jean
Becker, (Jean Otto Eric) Hugo
Beckman, Bror
Bečvařovský, Anton Felix (Antonín František)
Beddoe, Dan
Beecham, Sir Thomas
Beecke, (Notger) Ignaz (Franz) von
Beer, (Johann) Joseph
Beer-Walbrunn, Anton
Beethoven, Ludwig van
Beffara, Louis-François
Beffroy de Reigny, Louis-Abel
Begnis, Giuseppe de
Belcher, Supply
Belcke, Friedrich August
Beliczay, Julius (Gyula) von
Bell, W(illiam) H(enry)
Bella, Johann Leopold (Ján Levoslav)
Bellaigue, Camille
Bellermann, Johann Friedrich
Bellermann, (Johann Gottfried) Heinrich
Belletti, Giovanni Battista
Bellincioni, Gemma (Cesira Matilda)
Bellini, Vincenzo
Belloc-Giorgi, Teresa (née Maria Teresa Ottavia Faustina Trombetta)
Bendel, Franz
Bendix, Otto
Bendix, Victor Emanuel
Bendl, Karl (Karel)
Benedetti, Michele
Benedict, Sir Julius
Benelli, Antonio Peregrino (Pellegrino)
Benincori, Angelo Maria
Bennard, George
Bennett, Joseph
Bennett, Sir William Sterndale
Bennewitz (real name, Benevic), Anton(ín)
Benoît, Camille
Benoit, Peter (Léopold Léonard)
Benucci, Francesco
Benvenuti, Tommaso
Berbiguier, Antoine (Benoît-) Tranquille
Berens, (Johann) Hermann
Berger, Francesco
Berger, Ludwig
Berger, Rudolf
Berggreen, Andreas Peter
Bergmann, Carl
Bergmans, Paul (Jean Étienne Charles Marie)
Beringer, Oscar
Bériot, Charles (-Auguste) de
Berlijn, Anton (real name, Aron Wolf)
Berlioz, (Louis-) Hector
Bernasconi, Antonia
Bernuth, Julius von
Berr (original name, Beer), Friedrich
Berté, Heinrich
Bertheaume, Isidore
Bertin, Louise (-Angélique)
Bertini, (Benoît-) Auguste
Bertini, Domenico
Bertini, Giuseppe
Bertini, Henri (-Jérôme)
Bertini, Salvatore
Bertinotti (-Radicati), Teresa
Berton, Henri-Montan
Bertoni, Ferdinando (Gioseffo)
Bertram, Theodor
Bertrand, Aline
Berutti (originally, Beruti), Arturo
Berwald, Johan Fredrik (Johann Friedrich)
Best, W(illiam) T(homas)
Bethune, (Green) Thomas
Betz, Franz
Bezekirsky, Vasili
Bianchi, Antonio
Bianchi, Francesco
Bianchi, Valentina
Bierey, Gottlob Benedikt
Bignami, Carlo
Bigot (de Morogues), Marie (née Kiéné)
Billings, William
Billington, Elizabeth (née Weichsel)
Billroth, Theodor
Bilse, Benjamin
Bird, Arthur
Birnbach, Heinrich
Birnbach, Karl Joseph
Bishop, Anna (née Ann Riviere)
Bishop, Sir Henry (Rowley)
Bispham, David (Scull)
Bitter, Carl Hermann
Bittner, Julius
Bizet, Georges (baptismal names, Alexandre-César-Léopold)
Black, Andrew
Blaes, Arnold Joseph
Blagrove, Henry Gamble
Blahetka, Marie Léopoldine
Blangini, (Giuseppe Marco Maria) Felice
Blaramberg, Pavel (Ivanovich)
Blass, Robert
Blatt, František Tadeáš
Blauvelt, Lillian Evans
Blaze (called Castil-Blaze), François-Henri-Joseph
Blaze, Henri, Baron de Bury
Blech, Leo
Blewitt, Jonathan
Bliss, Philip P(aul)
Bloch, Ernest
Blockx, Jan
Blodek, Wilhelm (actually, Vilém)
Blondeau, Pierre-Auguste-Louis
Blume, (Ferdinand Anton) Clemens
Blumenfeld, Felix (Mikhailovich)
Blüthner, Julius (Ferdinand)
Boccherini, (Ridolfo) Luigi
Bochsa, (Robert-) Nicolas-Charles
Bode, Johann Joachim Christoph
Boeck, August de
Boehm, Theobald
Boëllmann, Léon
Boëly, Alexandre Pierre François
Böhm, Joseph
Böhner, (Johann) Ludwig
Boieldieu, François-Adrien
Boise, Otis Bardwell
Boito, Arrigo (baptismal name, Enrico)
Bolzoni, Giovanni
Bomtempo, João Domingos
Bonavia, Ferruccio
Bonci, Alessandro
Bond, Chapel
Bonfichi, Paolo
Boninsegna, Celestina
Bonnet, Joseph (Élie Georges Marie)

Heinemeyer, Ernst Wilhelm
Heinrich, Anthony Philip (actually, Anton Philipp)
Heinroth, Johann August Gunther
Heintze, Gustaf (Hjalmar)
Heinze, Gustav Adolf
Heise, Peter (Arnold)
Hekking, André
Hekking, Anton
Hekking, Gérard
Hellendaal, Pieter
Heller, Stephen
Hellmesberger Family
Hellmesberger, Sr., Georg
Hellmesberger, Sr., Joseph
Hellmesberger, Jr., Georg
Hellmesberger, Jr., Joseph
Hellmesberger, Ferdinand
Hellwig, Karl (Friedrich) Ludwig
Helsted, Gustaf
Henkel, Heinrich
Henkel, (Johann) Michael
Henneberg, Johann Baptist
Henneberg, Richard
Hennerberg, Carl Fredrik
Hennessy, Swan
Hennig, Carl
Hennig, Carl Rafael
Henning, Carl Wilhelm
Henriques, Fini (Valdemar)
Henschel, Lillian June (née Bailey)
Henschel, Sir (Isidor) George (actually, Georg)
Hensel, Fanny (Cäcilie) (née Mendelssohn-Bartholdy)
Hensel, Heinrich
Henselt, (Georg Marin) Adolf von
Hentschel, Franz
Hentschel, Theodor
Herbeck, Johann (Franz), Ritter von
Herbert, Victor (August)
Herbst, Johannes
Hering, Karl Gottlieb
Héritte-Viardot, Louise-Pauline-Marie
Hermann, Hans
Hermesdorff, Michael
Hermstedt, (Johann) Simon
Hernández Sales, Pablo
Hernándo (y Palomar), Rafael (José María)
Hérold, (Louis-Joseph) Ferdinand
Herold, Vilhelm (Kristoffer)
Herrmann, Gottfried
Herschel, Sir (Frederick) William (Friedrich Wilhelm)
Hertz, Alfred
Hervé (real name, Florimond Ronger)
Herz, Henri (actually, Heinrich)
Herzog, Emilie
Herzog, Johann Georg
Herzogenberg, (Leopold) Heinrich (Picot de Peccaduc), Freiherr von
Hesch, Wilhelm (real name, Vilém Heš)
Hess, Joachim
Hesse, Adolph (Friedrich)
Hesselberg, Edouard Gregory
Hetsch, (Karl) Ludwig Friedrich
Heuberger, Richard (Franz Joseph)
Hewitt, James
Heyman, Katherine Ruth Willoughby
Hignard, (Jean-Louis) Aristide
Hiles, Henry
Hill, Alfred (Francis)
Hill, Edward Burlingame
Hill, Ureli Corelli
Hillemacher
Hiller, Ferdinand (von)
Hiller, Friedrich Adam
Hiller, Johann Adam
Himmel, Friedrich Heinrich
Hinrichs, Gustav
Hinshaw, William Wade
Hinton, Arthur
Hochberg, Hans Heinrich, XIV, Bolko Graf von
Hodges, Edward
Höeberg, Georg
Hoffman, Richard
Hoffmann, E(rnst) T(heodor) A(madeus)
Hoffmann, Heinrich August
Hoffmeister, Franz Anton
Hoffmeister, Karel
Hoffstetter, Roman
Hofmann, Casimir (actually, Kazimierz)
Hofmann, Heinrich (Karl Johann)
Hofmann, Josef (Casimir) (actually, Józef Kazimierz)
Hofmann, Leopold
Hol, Richard
Holbrooke, Joseph (actually, Josef Charles)
Holden, Oliver
Hollaender, Alexis
Hollaender, Gustav
Hollaender, Viktor
Holland, Justin
Holmès (real name, Holmes), Augusta (Mary Anne)
Holmes, Alfred
Holst, Gustav(us Theodore von)
Holstein, Franz (Friedrich) von
Holter, Iver (Paul Fredrik)
Holý, Alfred
Holyoke, Samuel (Adams)
Homer, Louise (Dilworth née Beatty)
Homer, Sidney
Hood, George
Hook, James
Hopekirk, Helen
Hopkins, (Charles) Jerome
Hopkins, Edward (John)
Hopkins, John Henry
Hopkinson, Francis
Horák, Adolph
Horák, Antonin
Horák, Eduard
Horak, Wenzel (Vaclav) Emanuel
Horn, Charles Edward
Horn, Karl Friedrich
Horneman, Christian Frederik Emil
Horneman, Johan Ole Emil
Hornstein, Robert von
Horsley, Charles Edward
Horsley, William
Horszowski, Mieczyslaw
Hoschna (Hoschner), Karl
Houseley, Henry
Hřimalý, Adalbert (Vojtěch)
Hřimalý, Johann (Jan)
Hubay, Jenő
Huber, Hans
Huberman, Bronislaw
Hubert, Nikolai
Huberti, Gustave (-Léon)
Hüe, Georges (Adolphe)
Hueffer, Francis (real name, Franz Hüffer)
Hughes, Rupert
Hullah, John (Pyke)
Hüllmandel, Nicolas-Joseph
Hummel, Ferdinand
Hummel, Johann Nepomuk
Humperdinck, Engelbert
Hünten, Franz
Huntington, Jonathan
Huré, Jean
Hurlstone, William (Yeates)
Hus-Desforges, Pierre Louis
Huss, Henry Holden
Huszka, Jenő
Hutcheson, Ernest
Hutschenruyter (Hutschenruijter) Family
Hutschenruyter, Wouter
Hutschenruyter, Willem Jacob
Hutschenruyter, Wouter
Hüttenbrenner, Anselm
Hyde, Walter
Igumnov, Konstantin (Nikolaievich)
Ilyinsky, Alexander Alexandrovich
Incledon, Charles
d'Indy, (Paul-Marie-Théodore-Vincent)
Ingalls, Jeremiah
Innes (real name, Iniss), Frederick Neil
Insanguine, Giacomo (Antonio Francesco Paolo Michele)
Inzenga (y Castellanos), José
Iparraguirre y Balerdí, José María de
Ipavec, Benjamin
Ippolitov-Ivanov (real name, Ivanov), Mikhail (Mikhailovich)
Ireland, John (Nicholson)
Isaac, Adèle
Isler, Ernst
Isouard, Nicolò
Ivanov, Mikhail Mikhailovich
Ivanov, Nikolai (Kuzmich)
Ivanov-Boretzky, Mikhail Vladimirovich
Ivanovici, Ion
Ives, Charles (Edward)
Ives, Elam, Jr.
Ivry, Paul Xavier Désiré, Marquis d'
Jacchia, Agide
Jackson, George K(nowil)
Jackson, Samuel P.
Jackson, William
Jacob, Benjamin
Jacobi, Georg
Jadassohn, Salomon
Jadin, Hyacinthe
Jadin, Louis Emmanuel
Jadlowker, Hermann
Jaëll, Alfred
Jaëll, Marie (née Trautmann)

Kraus, Joseph Martin
Krauss, (Marie) Gabrielle
Krebs (real name, Miedcke), Carl August
Krebs Family
  Krebs, Johann Gottfried
Kreisler, Fritz (actually, Friedrich)
Krejči, Josef
Krenn, Franz
Kretschmer, Edmund
Kreubé, Charles Frédéric
Kreusser, Georg Anton
Kreutzer, Conradin (originally, Conrad)
Kreutzer, Jean Nicolas Auguste
Kreutzer, Léon Charles François
Kreutzer, Rodolphe
Křížkovsyký, Pavel (baptized Karel)
Krommer (Kramář), Franz Vincez (František Vincenc)
Kronold, Hans
Kronold, Selma
Krow, Josef Theodor
Krückl, Franz
Krug, (Wenzel) Joseph
Krüger, Wilhelm
Krull, Annie (actually, Marie Anna)
Krumpholtz, Anne-Marie (née Steckler)
Krumpholtz, Jean-Baptiste (Johann Baptist or Jan Křtitel)
Krushelnitskaya, Salomea (Ambrosivna)
Kubelík, Jan
Kucharz, Johann Baptist (real name, Jan Křtitel Kucha)
Kücken, Friedrich Wilhelm
Kufferath, Hubert Ferdinand
Kufferath, Johann Hermann
Kufferath, Louis
Kufferath, Maurice
Küffner, Joseph
Kuhlau, (Daniel) Friedrich (Rudolph)
Kühnau, Johann Christoph
Kullak, Adolf
Kullak, Franz
Kullak, Theodor
Kummer, Friedrich August
Kunits, Luigi von (actually, Ludwig Paul Maria)
Kunkel, Charles
Kunkel, Jacob
Kunwald, Ernst
Kunzen Family
  Kunzen, Friedrich Ludwig Aemilius
  Kunzen, Louise Friederica Ulrica
Kurpiński, Karol (Kazimierz)
Kurt, Melanie
Kurz, Selma
Kurz, Vilém
Kuula, Toivo (Timoteus)
Kwast, James
Labarre, Théodore (François-Joseph)
Labatt, Leonard
Labia, Fausta
Labinsky, Andrei (Markovich)
Labitzky Family
  Labitzky, Joseph
  Labitzky, Wilhelm
  Labitzky, August
Lablache, Luigi
Labor, Josef
Labroca, Mario
Labunski, Wiktor
Laburda, Jiří
Lacépède, Bernard Germaine Etiènne Médard de la Villesur-Illon, Count of
Lacerda, Francisco (Inácio da Silveira de Sousa Pereira Forjaz) de
Lach, Robert
Lachenmann, Helmut Friedrich
Lachner Family
  Lachner, Theodor
  Lachner, Franz Paul
  Lachner, Ignaz
  Lachner, Vincenz
Lachnith, Ludwig Wenzel
Lacombe, Louis (Trouillon)
Lacombe, Paul
Lacome (actually, Lacôme d'Estalenx), Paul (-Jean-Jacques)
Lacroix, Antoine
Ladmirault, Paul (-Émile)
Ladurner, Ignace Antoine (François Xavier) (Ignaz Anton Franz Xaver Joseph)
Ladurner, Josef Aloix
La Fage, (Juste-) Adrien (-Lenoir) de
Lafont, Charles-Philippe
Lagoanère, Oscar de
La Houssaye, Pierre (-Nicolas)
Laidlaw, Anna Robena
Lajarte, Théodore (-Édouard Dufaure de)
Lalo, Édouard (-Victoire-Antoine)
La Marre (Lamare), Jacques-Michel-Hurel de
Lambert, Lucien
Lambillotte, Louis
Lamond, Frederic(k Archibald)
Lamote de Grignon, Juan
Lamoureux, Charles
Lamperti, Francesco
Lamperti, Giovanni Battista
Landowska, Wanda (Alexandra)
Landré, Willem (actually, Guillaume Louis Frédéric)
Lang, Benjamin (Johnson)
Lang, Johann Georg
Lang, Josephine (Caroline)
Lang, Margaret Ruthven
Langdon, Richard
Lange Family
  Lange, Samuel de
  Lange, Samuel de
  Lange, Daniël de
Lange, Gustav
Lange-Müller, Peter Erasmus
Langer, Victor
Langhans, (Friedrich) Wilhelm
Langlé, Honoré (François Marie)
Lanier, Sidney (Clopton)
Lankow, Anna
Lanner, August (Joseph)
Lanner, Joseph (Franz Karl)
Lanza, Francesco
Laparra, Raoul
Laserna, Blas de
Láska, Gustav
Laskovsky, Ivan Fyodorovich
Lassalle, Jean (-Louis)
Lassen, Eduard
La Tombelle, (Antoine Louis Joseph Gueyrand) Fernand (Fouant) de
Latrobe, Christian Ignatius
Laub, Ferdinand
Laub, Thomas (Linnemann)
Lauska, Franz (Seraphinus Ignatius)
Lavallée, Calixa
Lavignac, (Alexandre Jean) Albert
Lavotta, János
Lavrangas, Dionyssios
Lavrovskaya, Elizaveta Andreievna
Law, Andrew
Lays, François
Lazzari, (Joseph) Sylvio
Leach, James
Lebert (real name, Levi), Sigmund
Leborne, Aimé-Ambroise-Simon
Leborne, Fernand
Lebrun, Franziska (Dorothea née Danzi)
Lebrun, Jean
Lebrun, Louis-Sébastien
Lebrun, Ludwig August (actually, Ludwig Karl Maria)
Lecoq, (Alexandre) Charles
Leduc, Alphonse
Leduc, Pierre (le jeune)
Lefébure-Wély, Louis James Alfred
Lefebvre, Charles Éduoard
Lefèvre, (Jean) Xavier
Leffler-Burckhard, Martha
Le Flem, Paul
Legnani, (Rinaldo) Luigi
Legros, Joseph
Lehár, Franz (actually, Ferenc)
Lehmann, Lilli
Lehmann, Liza (actually, Elizabeth Nina Mary Frederica)
Lehmann, Marie
Lekeu, Guillaume (Jean Joseph Nicolas)
Lemare, Edwin (Henry)
Lemière de Corvey, Jean Frédéric Auguste
Lemmens, Jacques Nicolas (Jaak Nikolaas)
Lemmens-Sherrington (originally, Sherrington), Helen
Lemoyne, Jean-Baptiste
Lenepveu, Charles (Ferdinand)
Lenormand, René
Léonard, Hubert
Leoncavallo, Ruggero
Leoni, Franco
Leonova, Darya (Mikhailovna)
Leroux, Xavier (Henry Napoléon)
Leschetizky, Theodor (Teodor)
Leslie, Henry (David)
Lessel, Franz (actually, Franciszek)
Le Sueur or Lesueur, Jean François
Leutgeb, Joseph (Ignaz)
Levadé, Charles (Gaston)
Levasseur, Jean-Henri
Levasseur, Nicolas (-Prosper)
Levasseur, Rosalie (Marie-Rose-Claude-Josèphe)
Levey, Richard C.

Parry, John
Parry, Joseph
Parry, Sir C(harles) Hubert H(astings)
Pasdeloup, Jules-Étienne
Pashkevich, Vasily (Alexeievich)
Pasini (-Vitale), Lina
Passy, (Ludvig Anton) Edvard
Pasta, Giuditta (Maria Costanza née Negri)
Pasterwitz, Georg (actually Robert) von
Patey, Janet (Monach née Whytock)
Paton, Mary Ann
Patti Family
Patti, Salvatore
Patti, Amalia
Patti, Carolotta
Patti, Adelina (actually, Adela Juana Maria)
Pauer, Ernst
Pauer, Max von
Paul, Oskar
Paulli, Holger Simon
Paulus, Olaf
Paur, Emil
Pauwels, Jean-Englebert
Pavesi, Stefano
Peabody, George
Pearsall, Robert Lucas
Pecháček, Franz Xaver
Pedrell, Carlos
Pedrell, Felipe
Pedrollo, Arrigo
Pedrotti, Carlo
Peelaert, Augustin-Philippe (-Marie-Ghislain)
Pelissier, Victor
Peralta, Angela
Pérez Martínez, Vicente
Perfall, Karl Freiherr von
Perger, Richard von
Peri, Achille
Périer, Jean (Alexis)
Perne, François Louis
Perosi, Don Lorenzo
Perotti, Giovanni Agostino
Perotti, Giovanni Domenico
Perron (real name, Pergamenter), Karl
Persiani, Fanny (née Tacchinardi)
Persiani, Giuseppe
Persuis, Louis-Luc Loiseau de
Pessard, Émile (-Louis-Fortuné)
Peter, John Frederick (actually, Johann Friedrich)
Peter, Simon
Peterson-Berger, (Olof) Wilhelm
Petrella, Errico
Petrelli, Eleanora (née Wigstorm)
Petri, Johann Samuel
Petrini Family
Petrini, (Marie) Therese
Petrini, Francesco
Petrov, Osip (Afanasievich)
Petrova-Vorobieva, Anna
Petrucci, Brizio
Pfeiffer, (Johann) Michael Traugott
Pfitzner, Hans (Erich)
Pflughaupt, Robert
Pfundt, Ernst (Gotthold Benjamin)
Phile (Fyles, Pfeil, Phyla, etc), Philip
Philidor (real name, Danican) Family
Danican Philidor, François-André
Philipp, Isidor
Phillipps, Adelaide
Phillips, Henry
Phillips, Philip
Piatti, Alfredo (Carlo)
Piccinni, (Vito) Niccolò (Marcello Antonio Giacomo)
Pichl, Wenzel (actually Václav)
Pieltain, Dieudonné-Pascal
Pierné, (Henri-Constant-) Gabriel
Pierpont, James
Pierson (real name, Pearson), Henry Hugo (Hugh)
Pilinski, Stanislaw
Pinelli, Ettore
Pini-Corsi, Antonio
Pinsuti, Ciro
Pinto, George Frederick
Pirro, André (Gabriel Edme)
Pisaroni, Benedetta (Rosmunda)
Pischek, Johann Baptist (Jan Křtitel Pišek)
Pischna, Josef
Piticchio, Francesco
Pitt, Percy
Pixis, Friedrich Wilhelm
Pixis, Johann Peter
Pizzetti, Ildebrando
Plaichinger, Thila
Plaidy, Louis
Plancken, Corneille Vander
Plançon, Pol (-Henri)
Planquette, (Jean-) Robert
Plantade, Charles-Henri
Planté, Francis
Platania, Pietro
Platel, Nicolas-Josef
Pleyel, Ignace Joseph (actually, Ignaz Josef)
Pleyel, (Joseph Stephen) Camille
Pocci, Franz, Graf von
Poelchau, Georg Johann David
Pohl, Carl Ferdinand
Pohlig, Karl
Poise, (Jean Alexandre) Ferdinand
Poissl, Johann Nepomuk, Freiherr von
Pokorny, Franz (actually František Xaver Jan)
Polacco, Giorgio
Polledro, Giovanni Battista
Pollet Family
Pollet, Charles-François-Alexandre
Pollet, Joseph
Pollini, Bernhard (real name, Baruch Pohl)
Pollini, Francesco (Giuseppe)
Ponchielli, Amilcare
Pond, Sylvanus Billings
Poniatowski, Józef (Michal Xsawery Franciszek Jan), Prince of Monte Rotondo
Pons, José
Pontelibero, Ferdinando
Poole, Elizabeth
Popper, David
Porro, Pierre-Jean
Porta, Bernardo
Porter, Samuel
Portugal (Portogallo; real name, Ascenção orAssumpção), Marcos Antônio (da Fonseca)
Porumbescu, Ciprian
Posse, Wilhelm
Pothier, Dom Joseph
Pott, August Friedrich
Potter, (Philip) Cipriani (Hambley)
Pougin (Paroisse-Pougin), François-Auguste-)Arthur
Pouteau, Joseph
Powell, Maud
Pownall, Mary Ann
Pozzoli, Ettore
Praeger, Ferdinand (Christian Wilhelm)
Prati, Alessio
Pratt, Silas Gamaliel
Pratt, Waldo Selden
Praupner, Jan (Josef)
Praupner, Václav (Josef Bartoloměj)
Preindl, Josef
Presser, Theodore
Preumayr Family
Preumayr, Johan Conrad
Preumayr, Carl Josef
Preumayr, Frans Carl
Prévost, Eugène-Prosper
Prianishnikov, Ippolit (Petrovich)
Proch, Heinrich
Prod'homme, J(acques)-G(abriel)
Propiac, (Catherine Joseph Ferdinand) Girard de
Proske, Carl
Prot, Félix-Jean
Prota Family
Prota, Giuseppe
Prota, Gabriele
Prota, Givoanni
Prout, Ebenezer
Prudent, Emile (Racine Gauthier)
Prumier, Antoine
Prüwer, Julius
Pryor, Arthur (Willard)
Puccini Family
Puccini, Antonio
Puccini, Domenico
Puccini, Michele
Puccini, Giacomo (Antonio Domenico Michele Secondo Maria)
Pucitta, Vincenzo
Puente, Giuseppe Del
Puget, Loïsa (actually, Louise-Françoise)
Pugnani, (Giulio) Gaetano (Gerolamo)
Pugni, Cesare
Pugno, (Stéphane) Raoul
Puig, Bernardo Calvo
Puppo, Giuseppe
Puzzi, Giovanni
Pyne, Louisa (Fanny)
Quaile, Elizabeth
Quattrini, Jan Ludwik
Queralt, Francisco
Quesne, (Louis) Joseph (Marie)
Rachmaninoff, Sergei (Vassilievich)
Radicati, Felice Alessandro

Modern

GENRE INDEX

Ackley, Alfred H(enry)
Ackté (real name, Achté), Aino
Adam, Claus
Ádám, Jeno
Adam, Theo
Adamis, Michael
Adamowski, Joseph (actually, Josef)
Adamowski, Timothée
Adams, John (Coolidge)
Adams, John Luther
Adams, Suzanne
Adaskin, Murray
Addinsell, Richard (Stewart)
Addison, Adele
Addison, John (Mervyn)
Adès, Thomas (Joseph Edmund)
Adkins, Cecil (Dale)
Adler, Clarence
Adler, F. Charles
Adler, Kurt
Adler, Kurt Herbert
Adler, Peter Herman
Adler, Samuel (Hans)
Adni, Daniel
Adolphus, Milton
Adomián, Lan
Adorno (real name, Wiesengrund), Theodor
Affré, Agustarello
Agghházy, Károly
Agnew, Roy (Ewing)
Agosti, Guido
Agostini, Mezio
Aguirre, Julían
Ahern, David (Anthony)
Ahlersmeyer, Mathieu
Ahlgrimm, Isolde
Ahlin, Čvetka
Ahlstrom, David
Ahna, Pauline de
Ahnsjö, Claes-H(åkan)
Aho, Kalevi
Ahrens, Joseph (Johannes Clemens)
Ahronovich, Yuri (Mikhailovich)
Ainsley, John Mark
Aitken, Hugh
Aitken, Robert (Morris)
Aitken, Webster
Ajmone-Marsan, Guido
Akimenko (real name, Yakimenko), Fyodor (Stepanovich)
Akiyama, Kazuyoshi
Akses, Necil Kâzim
Akutagawa, Yasushi
Alagna, Roberto
Alain, Jehan (Ariste)
Alain, Marie-Claire
Alain, Olivier
Alaleona, Domenico
Alarie, Pierrette (Marguerite)
Albanese, Licia
Albani (real name, Lajeunesse), Dame (Marie Louise Cécile) Emma
Albéniz, Isaac (Manuel Francisco)
d'Albert, Eugen (actually, Eugène Francis Charles)
Albert, Karel
Albert, Stephen (Joel)
Albertsen, Per Hjort
Albrecht, Alexander
Albrecht, George Alexander
Albrecht, Gerd
Albrecht, Hans
Albright, William (Hugh)
Alcaide, Tomáz (de Aquino Carmelo)
Alcántara, Theo
Alda (real name, Davies), Frances (Jeanne)
Aldenhoff, Bernd
Aldrich, Putnam (Calder)
Alemshah, Kourkene
Aler, John
Alessandrescu, Alfred
d'Alessandro, Raffaele
Alessandro, Victor (Nicholas)
Alexander, Haim
Alexander, John
Alexander, Josef
Alexander, Roberta
Alexandra, Liana
Alexandrov, Alexander
Alexandrov, Anatoli
Alexanian, Diran
Alexeev, Dmitri
Alfano, Franco
Alferaki, Achilles
Alfvén, Hugo (Emil)
Ali-Sade, Frangis
Allanbrook, Douglas (Phillips)
Alldahl, Per-Gunnar
Alldis, John
Allen, Betty
Allen, Paul Hastings
Allen, Sir Hugh (Percy)
Allen, Sir Thomas (Boaz)
Allende (-Saron), (Pedro) Humberto
Allers, Franz
Allgén, Claude Loyola (actually, Klas Thure)
Allin, Norman
Almeida, Antonio (Jacques) de
Almeida, Laurindo
Alnaes, Eyvind
Alnar, Hasan Ferid
Alpaerts, Flor
Alpaerts, Jef
Alpenheim, Ilse von
Alsina, Carlos Roqué
Alsop, Marin
Altani, Ippolit (Karlovich)
Altenburg, Detlef
Altenburger, Christian
Althouse, Paul (Shearer)
Altman, Ludwig
Altmeyer, Jeannine (Theresa)
Altmeyer, Theo(dor David)
Altschuler, Modest
Alva, Luigi (real name, Luis Ernesto Alva Talledo)
Alvarez (real name, Gourron), Albert (Raymond)
Álvarez, Javier
Alvarez (de Rocafuerte), Marguerite d'
Alvary, Lorenzo
Alwin, Karl (real name, Alwin Oskar Pinkus)
Alwyn, Kenneth (in full, Kenneth Alwyn Wetherall)
Alwyn, William
Åm, Magnar
Amacher, Maryanne
Amaducci, Bruno
Amar, Licco (actually, Liko)
Amara (real name, Armaganian), Lucine
Amato, Pasquale
Ambros, Vladimír
d'Ambrosio, Alfredo
Ambrosius, Hermann
Ameling, Elly (actually, Elisabeth Sara)
Ameller, André (Charles Gabriel)
Ameln, Konrad
Amengual (-Astaburuaga), René
Amfitheatrof, Daniele (Alexandrovich)
Amirkhanian, Charles (Benjamin)
Amirov, Fikret (Meshadi Jamil)
Ammann, Benno
Amoyal, Pierre
Amram, David (Werner III)
Amy, Gilbert
Ančerl, Karel
Ancona, Mario
Anda, Géza
Anday, Rosette
Anderberg, Carl-Olof
Anders, Peter
Andersen, Karl August
Andersen, Karsten
Anderson, Beth (actually, Barbara Elizabeth)
Anderson, (Evelyn) Ruth
Anderson, June
Anderson, Laurie
Anderson, Leroy
Anderson, Marian
Anderson, T(homas) J(efferson Jr.)
d'Andrade, Francesco
Andrašovan, Tibor
André, Franz
André, Maurice
Andreae, Marc (Edouard)
Andreae, Volkmar
Andreis, Josip
Andreoli, Carlo
Andreoli, Guglielmo
Andrésen, Ivar
Andricu, Mihail (Gheorghe)
Andriessen, Hendrik (Franciscus)
Andriessen, Jurriaan
Andriessen, Louis (Joseph)
Andriessen, Willem (Christiaan Nicolaas)
Andsnes, Leif Ove
Angel, Marie
Angerer, Paul
Angermüller, Rudolph (Kurt)
Anglés, Higini
Anhalt, István
Anievas, Agustin
Anitúa, Fanny
Anosov, Nikolai
Anrooy (actually, Anrooij), Peter van
Anselmi, Giuseppe
Ansermet, Ernest (Alexandre)
Ansorge, Conrad (Eduard Reinhold)
Ansseau, Fernand

Balassa, Sándor
Bales, Richard (Henry Horner)
Balfoort, Dirk Jacobus
Balkwill, Bryan (Havell)
Ball, Michael
Ballantine, Edward
Ballard, Louis W(ayne)
Ballif, Claude, (André François)
Balling, Michael
Ballista, Antonio
Ballou, Esther (Williamson)
Balmer, Luc
Balogh, Ernö
Baloković, Zlatko
Balsam, Artur
Balsys, Eduardas
Baltsa, Agnes
Bal y Gay, Jesús
Bamberger, Carl
Bamboschek, Giuseppe
Bamert, Matthias
Bampton, Rose (Elizabeth)
Bandrowska-Turska, Eva
Bandrowski-Sas, Alexander
Bank, Jacques
Banks, Don(ald Oscar)
Bannister, Henry (-Marriott)
Bantock, Sir Granville (Ransome)
Bär, Olaf
Barab, Seymour
Baranović, Krešimir
Barati, George (real name, György Baráti)
Barbe, Helmut
Barbeau, (Charles) Marius
Barber, Samuel
Barbier, René (Auguste-Ernest)
Barbieri, Fedora
Barbirolli, Sir John (actually, Giovanni Battista)
Barblan, Guglielmo
Barblan, Otto
Barbosa-Lima, Carlos
Barbour, J(ames) Murray
Barce, Ramón
Bárdos, Lajos
Barenboim, Daniel
Barere, Simon
Bargielski, Zbigniew
Barié, Augustin
Barili, Alfredo
Bar-Illan, David (Jacob)
Barilli, Bruno
Barjansky, Alexander
Barkauskas, Vytautas (Pranas Marius)
Barkel, Charles
Barkin, Elaine R(adoff)
Barlow, Fred
Barlow, Harold
Barlow, Howard
Barlow, Samuel L(atham) M(itchell)
Barlow, Stephen
Barlow, Wayne (Brewster)
Barnes, Milton
Barnett, Bonnie
Barnett, John (Manley)
Barolsky, Michael
Baron, Samuel
Barraqué, Jean
Barraud, Henry
Barrére, Georges
Barrientos, Maria
Barroso Neto, Joaquim Antonio
Barrueco, Manuel
Barry, Gerald (Anthony)
Barry, Jerome
Barshai, Rudolf (Borisovich)
Barsova (real name, Vladimirova), Valeria
Barstow, Dame Josephine (Clare)
Bárta, Lubor
Bartha, Dénes
Bartholomée, Pierre
Bartlett, Homer Newton
Barto, Tzimon, (real name, John Barto Smith, Jr.)
Bartók, Béla (Viktor János)
Bartoletti, Bruno
Bartoli, Cecilia
Bartolozzi, Bruno
Bartoš, Jan Zdeněk
Barzin, Leon (Eugene)
Barzun, Jacques (Martin)
Bashkirov, Dmitri (Alexandrovich)
Bashmet, Yuri
Basilides, Mária
Basiola, Mario
Bassett, Leslie (Raymond)
Bassi, Amedeo (Vittorio)
Bastianelli, Giannotto
Bastianini, Ettore
Bastin, Jules
Bate, Jennifer (Lucy)
Bate, Stanley (Richard)
Bates, Leon
Bath, Hubert
Báthy, Anna
Bátiz (Campbell), Enrique
Battistini, Mattia
Battle, Kathleen (Deanna)
Baud-Bovy, Samuel
Baudo, Serge (Paul)
Baudrier, Yves (Marie)
Bauer, Harold
Bauer, Marion (Eugenie)
Bauer, Ross
Bauld, Alison (Margaret)
Baum, Kurt
Baumann, Hermann (Rudolf Konrad)
Baumann, Max (Georg)
Baumgartner, Rudolf
Baur, Jürg
Bausznern, Waldemar von
Bautista, Julián
Bavicchi, John (Alexander)
Bax, Sir Arnold (Edward Trevor)
Bay, Emmanuel
Bayle, François
Bazelaire, Paul
Bazelon, Irwin (Allen)
Bázlik, Miro
Beach, Mrs. H.H.A. (née Amy Marcy Cheney)
Beardslee, Bethany
Beattie, Herbert (Wilson)
Becerra (-Schmidt), Gustavo
Bechi, Gino
Beck, Conrad
Beck, Jean-Baptiste
Beck, Johann H(einrich)
Beck, Sydney
Beck, Thomas Ludvigsen
Becker, Frank
Becker, Günther (Hugo)
Becker, Gustave Louis
Becker, Heinz
Becker, (Jean Otto Eric) Hugo
Becker, John J(oseph)
Beckman, Bror
Beckwith, John
Beddoe, Dan
Bedford, David (Vickerman)
Bedford, Steuart (John Rudolf)
Beecham, Sir Thomas
Beecroft, Norma (Marian)
Beer-Walbrunn, Anton
Beglarian, Eve
Beglarian, Grant
Béhague, Gerard H(enri)
Behrend, (Gustav) Fritz
Behrend, Siegfried
Behrens, Hildegard
Behrens, Jack
Bekker, (Max) Paul (Eugen)
Bekku, Sadao
Belkin, Boris
Bell, Donald (Munro)
Bell, Joshua
Bell, W(illiam) H(enry)
Bella, Johann Leopold (Ján Levoslav)
Bellaigue, Camille
Bellezza, Vincenzo
Bellincioni, Gemma (Cesira Matilda)
Bělohlávek, Jiří
Benary, Barbara
Benatzky, Ralph (actually, Rudolf Josef František)
Benda, Hans von
Bendix, Otto
Bendix, Victor Emanuel
Ben-Dor, Gisèle (née Buka)
Benestad, Finn
Bengtsson, Gustaf Adolf Tiburt(ius)
Bengtsson, (Lars) Ingmar (Olof)
Ben-Haim (real name, Frankenburger), Paul
Benjamin, Arthur
Benjamin, George (William John)
Benjamin, William E(mmanuel)
Bennard, George
Bennet, Sir Richard Rodney
Bennett, Joseph
Bennett, Robert Russell
Bennewitz (real name, Benevic), Anton(ín)
Benoît, Camille
Benson, Joan
Benson, Warren (Frank)
Bent, Margaret (Hilda)
Bentoiu, Pascal
Bentonelli (real name, Benton), Joseph (Horace)
Bentzon, Jørgen
Bentzon, Niels Viggo
Ben-Yohanan, Asher
Benzell, Mimi
Benzi, Roberto

Boronat, Olimpia
Borowski, Felix
Borris, Siegfried
Borroff, Edith
Bortkiewicz, Sergei (Eduardovich)
Börtz, Daniel
Borup-Jørgensen, (Jens) Axel
Borwick, Leonard
Bos, Coenraad Valentyn
Boscovich, Alexander Uriah
Bose, Hans-Jürgen von
Boskovsky, Willi
Bosmans, Henriëtte (Hilda)
Bosseur, Jean-Yves
Bossi, (Marco) Enrico
Bossi, (Rinaldo) Renzo
Bostridge, Ian (Charles)
Botstein, Leon
Botstiber, Hugo
Bottenberg, Wolfgang (Heinz Otto)
Bottje, Will Gay
Boucourechliev, André
Boudreau, Robert (Austin)
Boughton, Rutland
Boughton, William (Paul)
Bouhy, Jacques (-Joseph André)
Boulanger, Lili (Juliette Marie Olga)
Boulanger, Nadia (Juliette)
Boulez, Pierre
Boulnois, Joseph
Boult, Sir Adrian (Cedric)
Bour, Ernest
Bourdin, Roger
Bourgault-Ducoudray, Louis-Albert
Bourguignon, Francis de
Bouvet, Charles (René Clement)
Bovet, Joseph
Bovy, Vina (real name, Malvina Johanna Pauline Félicité Bovi van Overberghe)
Bowen, (Edwin) York
Bowles, Paul (Frederic)
Bowman, James (Thomas)
Boyd, Anne (Elizabeth)
Boydell, Brian (Patrick)
Boykan, Martin
Boyle, George Frederick
Bozay, Attila
Božič, Darijan
Bozza, Eugène
Bradley, Gwendolyn
Bradshaw, Merrill (Kay)
Braein, Edvard Fliflet
Brailowsky, Alexander
Brain, Alfred (Edwin)
Brain, Aubrey (Harold)
Brain, Dennis
Braithwaite, (Henry) Warwick
Braithwaite, Nicholas (Paul Dallon)
Brancour, René
Brand, Max(imilian)
Brandts-Buys, Jan (Willem Frans)
Brandukov, Anatol (Andreievich)
Brannigan, Owen
Brant, Henry
Branzell, Karin Maria
Braslau, Sophie
Braun, Carl
Braun, Peter Michael
Braunfels, Walter
Bravničar, Matija
Bream, Julian (Alexander)
Brecknock, John
Bredemeyer, Reiner
Brediceanu, Tiberiu
Brehm, Alvin
Brehme, Hans (Ludwig Wilhelm)
Breil, Joseph Carl
Brelet, Gisèle (Jeanne Marie Noémie)
Brema, Marie (real name, Minny Fehrmann)
Brémond, François
Brendel, Alfred
Brendel, Wolfgang
Brennan, John Wolf
Brenta, Gaston
Bresgen, Cesar
Bresnick, Martin
Bressler, Charles
Bressler-Gianoli, Clotilde
Bretan, Nicolae
Bretón y Hernández, Tomás
Brett, Charles (Michael)
Breuer, Hans (real name, Johann Peter Joseph)
Bréval, Lucienne (real name, Berthe Agnes Lisette Schilling)
Brevik, Tor
Bréville, Pierre (-Onfroy de)
Brewer, Sir (Alfred) Herbert
Brewster, W(illiam) Herbert, Sr.
Brey, Carter
Brian, (William) Havergal
Briccetti, Thomas (Bernard)
Brice, Carol (Lovette Hawkins)
Bricken, Carl Ernest
Brico, Antonia
Bridge, Frank
Bridge, Joseph (Cox)
Bridge, Sir (John) Frederick
Brilioth, Helge
Brînduš, Nicolae
Britain, Radie
Britten, (Edward) Benjamin, Lord Britten of Aldeburgh
Brkanović, Ivan
Broadstock, Brenton (Thomas)
Brockway, Howard A.
Brod, Max
Brodie, Paul (Zion)
Brogi, Renato
Brogue, Roslyn
Broman, Natanael
Broman, Sten
Bronfman, Yefim
Brons, Carel
Bronsart (von Schellendorf), Hans
Bronsart (von Schellendorf), Ingeborg (née Starck)
Bronskaya, Evgenya (Adolfovna)
Brooks, Patricia
Broome, (William) Edward
Broqua, Alfonso
Brosa, Antonio
Brott, Alexander
Brott, Boris
Brott, Denis
Brouwenstijn, Gré (actually, Gerarda Demphina Van Swol)
Brouwer, Leo
Brouwer, Margaret
Brown, Chris
Brown, Earle (Appleton, Jr.)
Brown, Eddy
Brown, Iona
Brown, Merton (Luther)
Brown, Newel Kay
Brown, Rayner
Browning, John
Brownlee, John (Donald Mackensie)
Bruce, (Frank) Neely
Bruch, Max (Christian Friedrich)
Bruck, Charles
Brückner-Rüggeberg, Wilhelm
Bruggen, Frans
Brumby, Colin (James)
Brun, Fritz
Brün, Herbert
Bruneau, (Louis-Charles-Bonaventure-) Alfred
Brunelle, Philip
Brunner, Adolf
Brunold, Paul
Brunswick, Mark
Bruscantini, Sesto
Brusilovsky, Evgeni (Grigorievich)
Brusilow, Anshel
Bruson, Renato
Brusselmans, Michel
Brustad, Bjarne
Bruynèl, Ton
Bruzdowicz, Joanna
Bryars, (Richard) Gavin
Brymer, Jack
Bryn-Julson, Phyllis (Mae)
Bubalo, Rudolph
Bucchi, Valentino
Bucci, Mark
Buchanan, Isobel
Buchbinder, Rudolf
Buchla, Donald (Frederick)
Bucht, Gunnar
Büchtger, Fritz
Buck, Sir Percy Carter
Buckley, Emerson
Buckley, John
Buckner, Thomas
Buczek, Barbara
Buczynski, Walter (Joseph)
Budd, Harold (Montgomery)
Bughici, Dumitru
Buhlig, Richard
Bujarski, Zbigniew
Buketoff, Igor
Buller, John
Bullock, Sir Ernest
Bumbry, Grace (Melzia Ann)
Bungert, (Friedrich) August
Bunin, Revol
Burchuladze, Paata
Burganger, Judith
Burge, David (Russell)
Burgess, Anthony (real name, John Anthony Burgess Wilson)
Burgess, Sally
Burghauser, Jarmil

Donalda (real name, Lightstone), Pauline
Donath, Helen (née Erwin)
Donati, Pino
Donato, Anthony
Donatoni, Franco
Donaudy, Stefano
Dönch, Karl
Dong, Kui
Donohoe, Peter (Howard)
Donostia, José Antonio de (real name, José Gonzalo Zulaica y Arregui)
Donovan, Richard Frank
Dooley, William (Edward)
Dopper, Cornelis
Doran, Matt (Higgins)
Doráti, Antal
Doret, Gustave
Dorfmann, Ania
Dostal, Nico(laus Josef Michäel)
Doubrava, Jaroslav
Dougherty, Celius (Hudson)
Douglas, Barry
Douglas, Clive (Martin)
Dounias, Minos
Dounis, Demetrius Constantine
Downes, Ralph (William)
Downes, Sir Edward (Thomas)
Downey, John (Wilham)
Doyen, Albert
Draeseke, Felix (August Bernhard)
Drăgoi, Sabin V(asile)
Dragon, Carmen
Drake, Alfred (real name, Alfredo Capurro)
Drake, Earl R(oss)
Dranishnikov, Vladimir
Draper, Charles
Drdla, Franz (actually, František Alois)
Dreier, Per
Drejsl, Radim
Dresden, Sem
Dresher, Paul (Joseph)
Dressel, Erwin
Drew, James
Dreyfus, George (actually, Georg)
Dreyfus, Huguett (Pauline)
Driessler, Johannes
Drigo, Riccardo
Dring, Madeleine
Drogin, Barry (Jay)
Druckman, Jacob (Raphael)
Drummond, Dean
Drury, Stephen
Drysdale, (George John) Learmont
Drzewiecki, Zbigniew
Dubensky, Arcady
Dubois, (François-Clément) Théodore
Dubois, Léon
Dubois, Pierre-Max
Dubrovay, László
Duchâble, François-René
Duckworth, William (Ervin)
Ducloux, Walter (Ernest)
Dudarova, Veronika
Duesing, Dale
Dufallo, Richard (John)
Duffy, John
Dufourcq, Norbert
Dufourt, Hugues
Dufranne, Hector (Robert)
Dugan, Franjo
Duhamel, Antoine
Dukas, Paul
Duke, John (Woods)
Dukelsky, Vladimir (Alexandrovich)
Dumitrescu, Gheorghe
Dumitrescu, Ion
Dunbar, W. Rudolph
Duncan, (Robert) Todd
Dunhill, Thomas (Frederick)
Dunlap, Arlene
Dunlap, Richard
Dunn, James Philip
Dunn, Mignon
Dunn, Susan
Dunn, Thomas (Burt)
Dupin, Paul
Dupont, Gabriel
DuPré, Jacqueline
Dupré, Marcel
Dupuis, Albert
Dupuis, Sylvain
Durey, Louis (Edmond)
Durkó, Zsolt
Durlet, Emmanuel
Duruflé, Marie-Madeleine (née Chevalier)
Duruflé, Maurice
Dusapin, Pascal
Dushkin, Samuel
Dutilleux, Henri
Dutoit, Charles (Edouard)
Duval, Denise
Duvosel, Lieven
Dux, Claire
Dvarionas, Balis
Dvořáček, Jiří
Dvořáková, Ludmila
Dvorský, Peter (actually, Petr)
Dyer-Bennet, Richard
Dyson, Sir George
Dzegelenok, Alexander (Mikhailovich)
Dzerzhinsky, Ivan (Ivanovich)
Eaglen, Jane
Eames, Emma (Hayden)
Easdale, Brian
Easton, Florence (Gertrude)
Eaton, John (Charles)
Ebel, Arnold
Eben, Petr
Eberhard, Dennis
Eckerberg, (Axel) Sixten (Lennart)
Eckert, Rinde
Eckhardt-Gramatté, S(ophie)-C(armen) "Sonia"
Eda-Pierre, Christiane
Eddy, (Hiram) Clarence
Edel, Yitzhak
Edelmann, Otto (Karl)
Edelmann, Sergei
Eder, Helmut
Edlund, Lars
Edmunds, John (actually, Charles Sterling)
Edvaldsdóttir, Sigrún
Edwards, Julian
Edwards, Ross
Edwards, Sian
Eeden, Jean-Baptiste van den
Effinger, Cecil
Egge, Klaus
Eggen, Arne
Eggen, Erik
Eggerth, Martha (real name, Márta Eggert)
Egk (real name, Mayer), Werner
Egmond, Max (Rudolf) van
Egorov, Youri
Ehlers, Alice (Pauly)
Ehrenberg, Carl (Emil Theodor)
Ehrlich, Abel
Ehrling, (Evert) Sixten
Eichheim, Henry
Eichhorn, Kurt (Peter)
Eimert, (Eugen Otto) Herbert
Einem, Gottfried von
Eiríksdóttir, Karólína
Eisenberg, Maurice
Eisler, Hanns (Johannes)
Eisler, Paul
Eisma, Will (Leendert)
Eitler, Esteban
Ek, (Fritz) Gunnar (Rudolf)
Ekier, Jan (Stanisław)
Eklund, Hans
Ekman, Karl
El-Dabh, Halim (Abdul Messieh)
Elder, Mark (Philip)
Elgar, Sir Edward (William)
Elías, Alfonso de
Elías, Manuel Jorge de
Elias, Rosalind
Elizalde, Federico
Elizza, Elise (real name, Elisabeth Letztergroschen)
Elkus, Albert (Israel)
Elkus, Jonathan (Britton)
Ellberg, Ernst (Henrik)
Eller, Heino
Elling, Catharinus
Elliott, Paul
Ellis, Brent
Ellis, Osian (Gwynn)
Elman, Mischa (actually, Mikhail Saulovich)
Elmendorff, Karl (Eduard Maria)
Elming, Poul
Elmo, Cloe
Elmore, Robert Hall
Eloy, Jean-Claude
Elston, Arnold
El-tour, Anna
Elvira, Pablo
Elwell, Herbert
Elwes, Gervase (Cary)
Emery, Walter (Henry James)
Emmanuel, (Marie François) Maurice
Enacovici, George
Enesco, Georges (real name, George Enescu)
Engel, Joel
Engel, Karl (Rudolf)
Engel, Lehman
Engelmann, Hans Ulrich
Engerer, Brigitte
Engländer, Ludwig

Frith, Fred
Froidebise, Pierre (Jean Marie)
Fromm, Herbert
Frugoni, Orazio
Frumerie, (Per) Gunnar (Fredrik) de
Fryer, George Herbert
Fryklöf, Harald (Leonard)
Fuchs, Carl (Dorius Johannes)
Fuchs, Joseph (Philip)
Fuchs, Lillian
Fuchs, Marta
Fuerstner, Carl
Fuga, Sandro
Fugère, Lucien
Fujikawa, Mayumi
Fuleihan, Anis
Fulkerson, Gregory (Locke)
Fulkerson, James (Orville)
Fuller, Albert
Fumet, Dynam-Victor
Furlanetto, Ferruccio
Gabriel, Charles H(utchinson)
Gabrilowitsch, Ossip (Salomonovich)
Gaburo, Kenneth (Louis)
Gade, Axel Willy
Gade, Jacob
Gadski, Johanna (Emilia Agnes)
Gadzhibekov, Sultan
Gadzhibekov, Uzeir
Gadzhiev, (Akhmed) Jevdet
Gage, Irwin
Gagnebin, Henri
Gaigerova, Varvara
Gailhard, Pierre
Gaillard, Marius-François
Gaito, Constantino
Gál, Hans
Galajikian, Florence Grandland
Galamian, Ivan (Alexander)
Galas, Diamanda (Dimitria Angeliki Elena)
Galeffi, Carlo
Galeotti, Cesare
Gales, Weston
Galimir, Felix
Galindo (Dimas), Blas
Galkin, Elliott W(ashington)
Gall (real name, Galle), Yvonne
Gall, Jeffrey (Charles)
Galla-Rini, Anthony
Galli, Amintore
Gallico, Paolo
Galli-Curci, Amelita
Galliera, Alceo
Gallignani, Giuseppe
Galli-Marié, Célestine (Laurence née Marié de l'Isle)
Gallo, Fortune
Gallois-Montbrun, Raymond
Gallon, Jean
Gallon, Noël
Galston, Gottfried
Galway, James
Gamba, Piero (actually, Pierino)
Gandini, Gerardo
Gandolfi, Riccardo (Cristoforo Daniele Diomede)
Ganelin, Viacheslav
Gange, Fraser
Gann, Kyle (Eugene)
Ganne, (Gustave) Louis
Ganz, Rudolph
Ganz, Wilhelm
Ganzarolli, Wladimiro
Garaguly, Carl von
Garant, (Albert Antonio) Serge
Garbin, Edoardo
Garbousova, Raya
García Mansilla, Eduardo
Gardelli, Lamberto
Garden, Mary
Gardiner, H(enry) Balfour
Gardiner, Sir John Eliot
Gardner, John (Linton)
Gardner, Samuel
Garland, Peter
Garreta, Julio
Garrett, Lesley
Garrido, Pablo
Garrison, Jon
Garrison, Mabel
Gasdia, Cecilia
Gastaldon, Stanislas
Gastoué, Amédée(-Henri-Gustave-Noël)
Gatti, Daniele
Gatty, Nicholas Comyn
Gaubert, Philippe
Gauk, Alexander
Gaul, Alfred (Robert)
Gaul, Harvey B(artlett)
Gauthier, (Ida Joséphine Phoebe) Eva
Gavazzeni, Gianandrea
Gavoty, Bernard (Georges Marie)
Gavrilov, Andrei
Gawrónski, Wojciech
Gay, Maria (née Pitchot)
Gayer (Ashkenasi), Catherine
Gazzelloni, Severino
Gebhard, Heinrich
Gédalge, André
Gedda (real name, Ustinov), Nicolai (Harry Gustav)
Gedda, Giulio Cesare
Gefors, Hans
Gehlhaar, Rolf (Rainer)
Geiser, Walther
Geisler, Paul
Geissler, Fritz
Gelber, Bruno-Leonardo
Gelbrun, Artur
Gellman, Steven (David)
Gelmetti, Gianluigi
Gencer, Leyla
Gendron, Maurice
Genzmer, Harald
George, Earl
Georges, Alexandre
Georgescu, Dan Corneliu
Georgescu, George
Georgiadis, Georges
Georgii, Walter
Gérardy, Jean
Gerber, René
Gerelli, Ennio
Gergiev, Valery (Abissalovich)
Gerhard, Roberto
Gerhardt, Elena
Gericke, Wilhelm
Gerlach, Theodor
Gerle, Robert
German, Sir Edward (real name, German Edward Jones)
Germani, Fernando
Gernsheim, Friedrich
Gerschefski, Edwin
Gerster, Etelka
Gerster, Ottmar
Gerstman, Blanche
Gertler, André
Gerville-Réache, Jeanne
Gesensway, Louis
Geszty (real name, Witkowsky), Sylvia
Getty, Gordon
Gevaert, François Auguste
Geyer, Stefi
Ghedini, Giorgio Federico
Gheluwe, Leon van
Ghent, Emmanuel (Robert)
Gheorghiu, Angela
Gheorghiu, Valentin
Ghezzo, Dinu
Ghiaurov, Nicolai
Ghiglia, Oscar
Ghis, Henri
Ghisi, Federico
Ghitalla, Armando
Giacomini, Giuseppe
Gialdini, Gialdino
Gianneo, Luis
Giannetti, Giovanni
Giannini, Dusolina
Giannini, Ferruccio
Giannini, Vittorio
Gibbs, Cecil Armstrong
Gibson, Sir Alexander (Drummond)
Gideon, Miriam
Giebel, Agnes
Gielen, Michael (Andreas)
Gieseking, Walter (Wilhelm)
Gifford, Helen (Margaret)
Gigli, Beniamino
Gigout, Eugène
Gilardi, Gilardo
Gilbert, Anthony (John)
Gilbert, Henry F(ranklin Belknap)
Gilbert, Jean (real name, Max Winterfeld)
Gilbert, Kenneth
Gilbert, Pia
Gilbert, Sir W(illiam) S(chwenck)
Gilboa, Jacob
Gilchrist, William Wallace
Gilels, Elizabeta
Gilels, Emil (Grigorievich)
Gilibert, Charles
Gillis, Don
Gilly, Dinh
Gil-Marchex, Henri
Gilse, Jan van
Gilson, Paul
Giltay, Berend
Gimenez, Raul
Giménez (Jiménez) (y Bellido), Jerónimo
Gimpel, Bronislav
Gimpel, Jakob

Groves, Sir Charles (Barnard)
Grovlez, Gabriel (Marie)
Grozăvescu, Trajan
Gruber, H(einz) K(arl) "Nali"
Gruberová, Edita
Gruenberg, Erich
Gruenberg, Louis
Gruhn (originally, Grunebaum), Nora
Grumiaux, Arthur
Grümmer, Elisabeth
Grümmer, Paul
Grün, Jakob
Grundheber, Franz
Grunenwald, Jean-Jacques
Grüner-Hegge, Odd
Grünfeld, Alfred
Guadagno, Anton
Guarino, Carmine
Guarino, Piero
Guarnieri, Antonio
Guarnieri, (Mozart) Camargo
Guarrera, Frank
Gubaidulina, Sofia (Asgatovna)
Gubrud, Irene (Ann)
Gudmundsen-Holmgreen, Pelle
Gueden, Hilde
Guelfi, Giangiacomo
Guerra-Peixe, César
Guerrini, Guido
Guest, George (Hywel)
Guézec, Jean-Pierre
Gui, Vittorio
Guilfoyle, Ronan
Guillou, Jean
Guion, David (Wendell Fentress)
Gulbranson, Ellen (née Norgren)
Gulda, Friedrich
Guleghina, Maria
Gülke, Peter
Gulli, Franco
Gundry, Inglis
Gunn, Glenn Dillard
Gunsbourg, Raoul
Günther, Mizzi
Gunzenhauser, Stephen (Charles)
Gura, Eugen
Gura, Hermann
Guridi (Bidaola), Jésus
Gurlitt, Manfred
Gurney, Ivor (Bertie)
Guschlbauer, Theodor
Gusikoff, Michel
Gustafson, Nancy
Gutchë, Gene (real name, Romeo Maximilian Eugene Ludwig Gutsche)
Gutheil-Schoder, Marie
Gutiérrez, Horacio
Gutiérrez Heras, Joaquín
Gutman, Natalia
Güttler, Ludwig
Guy, Barry (John)
Guyonnet, Jacques
Haarklou, Johannes
Haas, Joseph
Haas, Monique
Haas, Pavel
Haas, Werner
Hába, Alois
Hába, Karel
Habich, Eduard
Hacker, Alan (Ray)
Hackett, Charles
Hadley, Henry (Kimball)
Hadley, Jerry
Hadley, Patrick (Arthur Sheldon)
Hadow, Sir W(illiam) H(enry)
Hadzidakis, Manos
Haebler, Ingrid
Haefliger, Ernst
Haenchen, Hartmut
Haendel, Ida
Hafez (Shabana), Abdel Halim
Hafgren, Lily (Johana Maria)
Hagegård, Håkan
Hageman, Richard
Hager, Leopold
Hagerup Bull, Edvard
Hägg (Peterson), Gustaf Wilhelm
Hahn, Reynaldo
Haieff, Alexei (Vasilievich)
Haile, Eugen
Hailstork, Adolphus (Cunningham)
Haimovitz, Matt
Haitink, Bernard (Johann Herman)
Hajdu, André
Hajdu, Mihály
Håkanson, Knut (Algot)
Hakim, Talib Rasul (real name, Stephen Alexander Chambers)
Halász, László
Hale, Robert
Halffter (Escriche), Ernesto
Halffter (Escriche), Rodolfo
Halffter (Jiménez-Encina), Cristóbal
Hall, Frederick Douglass
Hall, Marie (actually, Mary Paulina)
Hall, Pauline (Margarete)
Hallberg, Björn Wilho
Hallén, (Johannes) Andreas
Hallgrímsson, Haflidi (Magnus)
Hallnäs, (Johan) Hilding
Halm, August Otto
Halpern, Steven (Barry)
Halstead, Anthony (George)
Halvorsen, Johan
Halvorsen, Leif
Hamari, Julia
Hambourg Family
    Hambourg, Michael (Mikhail)
    Hambourg, Mark
    Hambourg, Jan
    Hambourg, Boris
Hambraeus, Bengt
Hameenniemi, Eero (Olavi)
Hamelin, Marc-André
Hamerik (real name, Hammerich), Ebbe
Hamilton, Iain (Ellis)
Hammerschlag, János
Hammerstein, Oscar II (Greeley Clendenning)
Hammerstein, Oscar
Hammond, Dame Joan (Hood)
Hammond, Frederick (Fisher)
Hammond-Stroud, Derek
Hampson, Thomas
Hampton, Calvin
Handford, Maurice
Handley, Vernon (George)
Handschin, Jacques (Samuel)
Handt, Herbert
Hanfstängel, Marie (née Schröder)
Hann, Georg
Hannan, Michael (Francis)
Hannay, Roger D(urham)
Hannikainen Family
    Hannikainen, Pekka (or Pietari) (Juhani)
    Hannikainen, (Toivo) Ilmari
    Hannikainen, Tauno (Heikki)
    Hannikainen, Arvo (Sakari)
    Hannikainen, Väinö (Aatos)
Hansen, (Emil) Robert
Hanson, Howard (Harold)
Hanuš, Jan
Haquinius, (Johan) Algot
Harasiewicz, Adam
Harasowski, Adam
Harašta, Milan
Harbison, John (Harris)
d'Harcourt, Eugène
d'Harcourt, Marguerite (née Béclard)
d'Hardelot, Guy (actually, Mrs. W.I. Rhodes, née Helen Guy)
Hardenberger, Håkan
Harding, A(lbert) A(ustin)
Harich-Schneider, Eta (Margarete)
Harline, Leigh
Harling, William Franke
Harmat, Artur
Harmati, Sándor
Harnoncourt, Nikolaus (in full, Johann Nikolaus de la Fontaine und d'Harnoncourt-Unverzagt)
Harnoy, Ofra
Harper, Edward (James)
Harper, Heather (Mary)
Harrell, Lynn (Morris)
Harrell, Mack
Harrhy, Eiddwen (Mair)
Harries, Kathryn
Harris, (William) Victor
Harris, Donald
Harris, Roy (actually, Leroy Ellsworth)
Harrison, Beatrice
Harrison, Guy Fraser
Harrison, Julius (Allan Greenway)
Harrison, Lou (Silver)
Harrison, May
Harriss, Charles A(lbert) E(dwin)
Harsanyi, Janice (née Morris)
Harsanyi, Nicholas
Harsányi, Tibor
Harshaw, Margaret
Hart, Frederic Patton
Hart, Fritz (Bennicke)
Hart, Weldon
Harth, Sidney
Hartig, Heinz (Friedrich)
Hartke, Stephen (Paul)
Hartley, Walter S(inclair)
Hartmann, Arthur (Martinus)
Hartmann, Carl
Hartmann, Karl Amadeus
Hartmann, Pater (real name, Paul Eugen Josef von An der Lan-Hochbrunn)

Jürgens, Jürgen
Jurinac, Sena (actually, Srebrenka)
Jurjäns, Andrejs
Jurovský, Šimon
Juzeliūnas, Julius
Jyrkiäinen, Reijo (Einari)
Kàan-Albest, Heinrich (originally, Jindřich z Albestů Kàan)
Kabaivanska, Raina (Yakimova)
Kabalevsky, Dmitri (Borisovich)
Kabasta, Oswald
Kabeláč, Miloslav
Kabos, Ilona
Kačinskas, Jerome
Kacsóh, Pongrác
Kadosa, Pál
Kafenda, Frico
Kagan, Oleg
Kagel, Mauricio (Raúl)
Kagen, Sergius
Kahane, Jeffrey (Alan)
Kahn, Erich Itor
Kahn, Gus(tave)
Kahn, Otto Hermann
Kahn, Robert
Kahowez, Günter
Kaipainen, Jouni (Ilarí)
Kaiser, Alfred
Kajanus, Robert
Kalabis, Viktor
Kalafati, Vasili (Pavlovich)
Kalaš, Julius
Kalenberg, Josef
Kalichstein, Joseph
Kálik, Václav
Kalish, Gilbert
Kallenberg, Siegfried Garibaldi
Kallir, Lilian
Kallstenius, Edvin
Kálmán, Emmerich (actually, Imre)
Kálmán, Oszkár
Kalmár, László
Kalninš, Alfreds
Kalninš, Imants
Kalninš, Janis
Kalomiris, Manolis
Kalter (real name, Aufrichtig), Sabine
Kamensky, Alexander
Kamieński, Lucian
Kaminski, Heinrich
Kaminski, Joseph
Kamionsky, Oscar (Isaievich)
Kamu, Okko (Tapani)
Kancheli, Giya (Alexandrovich)
Kander, John (Harold), and Fred Ebb
Kang, Sukhi
Kanitz, Ernest (actually, Ernst)
Kann, Hans
Kannen, Günter von
Kanner-Rosenthal, Hedwig
Kantorow, Jean-Jacques
Kapell, William
Kaplan, Mark
Kapp, Artur
Kapp, Eugen (Arturovich)
Kapp, Richard
Kapp, Villem
Kappel, Gertrude
Kapr, Jan
Kaprál, Václav
Kaprálová, Vitězslava
Karabtchewsky, Isaac
Karajan, Herbert (actually, Heribert) von
Karastoyanov, Assen
Karayev, Kara (Abulfazogli)
Kardoš, Dezider
Kardos, István
Karel, Rudolf
Karetnikov, Nikolai
Karg-Elert (real name, Karg), Sigfrid
Karjalainen, Ahti
Karkoff, Maurice (Ingvar)
Karkoschka, Erhard
Karlins, M(artin) William
Karlowicz, Mieczyslaw
Karpath, Ludwig
Karpman, Laura
Karr, Gary (Michael)
Kars, Jean-Rodolphe
Kartsev, Alexander
Karyotakis, Theodore
Kasarova, Vesselina (Ivanova)
Kaschmann (Kašman), Giuseppe
Kasemets, Udo
Kashkashian, Kim
Kasianov, Alexander
Kašlík, Václav
Kasparov, Yuri
Kaspszyk, Jacek
Kassern, Tadeusz (Zygfrid)
Kastalsky, Alexander (Dmitrievich)
Kastle, Leonard (Gregory)
Kastner, Alfred
Kastner, (Macario) Santiago
Kastorsky, Vladimir (Ivanovich)
Katchen, Julius
Kates, Stephen (Edward)
Katims, Milton
Katin, Peter (Roy)
Katsaris, Cyprien
Kats-Chernin, Elena
Kattnigg, Rudolf
Katulskaya, Elena
Katwijk, Paul van
Katz, Martin
Katz, Mindru
Katzer, Georg
Kauder, Hugo
Kauffmann, Leo Justinus
Kaufman, Harry
Kaufman, Louis
Kaufmann, Armin
Kaufmann, Julie
Kaufmann, Walter
Kaun, Hugo
Kavafian, Ani
Kavafian, Ida
Kavrakos, Dimitri
Kay, Hershy
Kay, Ulysses Simpson
Kayser, Leif
Kazandjiev, Vasil
Kazarnovskaya, Ljuba
Kazuro, Stanislaw
Keats, Donald (Howard)
Kee, Cornelis
Kee, Piet(er Willem)
Keene, Christopher
Keene, Constance
Keenlyside, Simon
Kegel, Herbert
Kehr, Günter
Keilberth, Joseph
Kelberine, Alexander
Keldorfer, Robert
Keldorfer, Viktor (Josef)
Kelemen, Milko
Kelemen, Zoltán
Kell, Reginald (Clifford)
Keller, Hermann
Keller, Homer
Kelley, Edgar Stillman
Kelley, Jessie Stillman
Kelly, Bryan
Kelly, Robert
Kelterborn, Rudolf
Kemp, Barbara
Kempe, Rudolf
Kempen, Paul van
Kempff, Wilhelm (Walter Friedrich)
Keneman, Feodor
Kenessey, Jenö
Kenins, Talivaldis
Kennan, Kent Wheeler
Kennedy, John
Kennedy, Nigel (Paul)
Kennedy-Fraser, Marjorie (née Kennedy)
Kenny, Yvonne
Kentner, Louis (actually, Lajos Philip)
Kenton (real name, Kornstein), Egon
Kern, Adele
Kern, Jerome (David)
Kern, Patricia
Kernis, Aaron Jay
Kerr, Harrison
Kersjes, Anton (Frans Jan)
Kersters, Willem
Kertész, István
Kes, Willem
Kessler, Thomas
Kessner, Daniel (Aaron)
Ketèlbey, Albert (William)
Ketting, Otto
Ketting, Piet
Keuris, Tristan
Keussler, Gerhard von
Khachaturian, Aram (Ilich)
Khachaturian, Karen (Surenovich)
Khadzhiev, Parashkev
Khaikin, Boris (Emmanuilovich)
Kharitonov, Dimitri
Khessin, Alexander (Borisovich)
Khodzha-Einatov, Leon
Khrennikov, Tikhon (Nikolaievich)
Khristov, Dobri
Kiberg, Tina
Kielland, Olav
Kienzl, Wilhelm
Kiepura, Jan
Kiesewetter, Tomasz
Kijima, Kiyohiko
Kiladze, Grigori
Kilar, Wojciech
Kilenyi, Edward, Jr.
Kilenyi, Edward, Sr.

Kovařovic, Karel
Kowalski, Jochen
Kowalski, Július
Kowalski, Max
Kox, Hans
Koyama, Kiyoshige
Kozina, Marjan
Kozlovsky, Ivan (Semyonovich)
Kozma, Matei
Kozolupov, Semyon Matveievich
Kraemer, (Thomas Wilhelm) Nicholas
Kraft, Leo (Abraham)
Kraft, Walter
Kraft, William
Krainev, Vladimir (Vsevolodovich)
Kramer, A(rthur) Walter
Krapf, Gerhard
Krapp, Edgar
Krása, Hans (actually, Johann)
Krasner, Louis
Krásová, Marta
Kraus, Detlef
Kraus, Ernst
Kraus, Felix von
Kraus, Lili
Kraus, Otakar
Kraus, (Wolfgang Ernst) Richard
Krause, Tom
Krauss, Clemens (Heinrich)
Kraus (Trujillo), Alfredo
Krauze, Zygmunt
Krebs, Helmut
Krein, Alexander (Abramovich)
Krein, Grigori (Abramovich)
Krein, Julian (Grigorievich)
Kreisler, Fritz (actually, Friedrich)
Kreizberg, Yakov
Krejčí, Iša (František)
Krejčí, Miroslav
Krek, Uroš
Kremenliev, Boris
Kremer, Gidon
Kremlev, Yuli (Anatolyevich)
Krenek (originally, Křenek), Ernst
Krenn, Fritz
Krenn, Werner
Krenz, Jan
Kresánek, Jozef
Kretschmer, Edmund
Kreuder, Peter Paul
Kreutz, Arthur
Křička, Jaroslav
Krieger, Armando
Krieger, Edino
Krips, Henry (Joseph)
Krips, Josef
Krivine, Emmanuel
Křivinka, Gustav
Kroeger, Karl
Krohn, Felix (Julius Theofil)
Kroll, William
Krombholc, Jaroslav
Kromolicki, Joseph
Kronold, Selma
Krstič, Petar
Krueger, Karl (Adalbert)
Krull, Annie (actually, Marie Anna)
Krushelnitskaya, Salomea (Ambrosivna)
Kruyf, Ton de
Kubelík, Jan
Kubelík, (Jeroným) Rafael
Kubiak, Teresa (originally, Tersa Wojtaszek)
Kubik, Gail (Thompson)
Kubín, Rudolf
Kučera, Václav
Kuebler, David
Kuerti, Anton (Emil)
Kufferath, Maurice
Kuhlmann, Kathleen
Kuhn, Gustav
Kuhn, Laura (Diane née Shipcott)
Kuhse, Hanne-Lore
Kuijken Family
  Kuijken, Wieland
  Kuijken, Sigiswald
  Kuijken, Barthold
Kuivila, Ron
Kulenkampff, Georg
Kulenty, Hanna
Kulesha, Gary
Kulka, János
Kullman, Charles
Kunad, Rainer
Kunc, Božidar
Kunc, Jan
Kundera, Ludvík
Kunits, Luigi von (actually, Ludwig Paul Maria)
Künneke, Eduard
Kunst, Jos
Kunwald, Ernst
Kunz, Alfred (Leopold)
Kunz, Erich
Kunz, Ernst
Kunzel, Erich
Kupferberg, Herbert
Kupferman, Meyer
Kupkovič, Ladislav
Kupper, Annelies (Gabriele)
Kuri-Aldana, Mario
Kurka, Robert (Frank)
Kurt, Melanie
Kurtág, György
Kurtz, Efrem
Kurz, Selma
Kurz, Siegfried
Kurz, Vilém
Kusche, Benno
Kutavičius, Bronislovas
Kutev, Filip
Kuula, Toivo (Timoteus)
Kuusisto, Ilkka Taneli
Kuusisto, Taneli
Kuyper, Elisabeth
Kuznetsova, Maria (Nikolaievna)
Kvam, Oddvar S(chirmer)
Kvandal (real name, Johansen), (David) Johan
Kvapil, Jaroslav
Kvernadze, Bidzina (actually, Alexander Alexandrovich)
Kwast, James
Kwella, Patrizia
Kwiatkowski, Ryszard
Kyllönen, Timo-Juhani
Kyriakou, Rena
La Barbara, Joan (Linda née Lotz)
Labbette, Dora
Labèque, Katia and Marielle
Labey, Marcel
Labia, Fausta
Labia, Maria
Labinsky, Andrei (Markovich)
Labor, Josef
Labroca, Mario
Labunski, Felix (actually, Feliks Roderyk)
Labunski, Wiktor
Laburda, Jiří
La Casinière, Yves de
Lacerda, Francisco (Inácio da Silveira de Sousa Pereira Forjaz) de
Lach, Robert
Lachenmann, Helmut Friedrich
Lachmann, Robert
Laderman, Ezra
Ladmirault, Paul (-Émile)
La Forge, Frank
Lagger, Peter
Lagoanère, Oscar de
Lagoya, Alexandre
Lajovic, Anton
Lajtai, Lajos
Lajtha, László
Lakes, Gary
Lakner, Yehoshua
Laks, Simon (actually, Szymon)
La Liberté, (Joseph-François) Alfred
Lalo, Charles
Lamb, Joseph F(rancis)
Lambert, (Leonard) Constant
Lambert, Lucien
Lambro, Phillip
Lammers, Gerda
Lamond, Frederic(k Archibald)
La Montaine, John
Lamote de Grignon, Juan
Lamote de Grignon y Ribas, Ricardo
Lamperti, Giovanni Battista
Lamy, Fernand
Lancen, Serge (Jean Mathieu)
Lanchbery, John (Arthur)
Landau, Siegfried
Landowska, Wanda (Alexandra)
Landowski, Marcel (François Paul)
Landré, Guillaume (Louis Frédéric)
Landré, Willem (actually, Guillaume Louis Frédéric)
Lane, Eastwood
Lane, Louis
Lang, David
Láng, István
Lang, Margaret Ruthven
Lang, Walter
Langdon, Michael (real name, Frank Birtles)
Lange Family
  Lange, Samuel de
  Lange, Daniël de
Langendorff, Frieda
Langgaard, Rued (Immanuel)
Langlais, Jean (François-Hyacinthe)
Langridge, Philip (Gordon)
Lankester, Michael (John)
Lansky, Paul

Mureşianu, Iacob
Muro, Bernardo de
Murphy, Suzanne
Murray, Ann
Murray, Bain
Murray, Michael
Murray, Thomas (Mantle)
Murray, William
Murrill, Herbert (Henry John)
Musgrave, Thea
Mushel, Georgi
Musin, Ilya (Alexandrovich)
Musin, Ovide
Mustonen, Olli
Muti, Riccardo
Mutter, Anne-Sophie
Muzio, Claudia (real name, Claudina Muzzio)
Mycielski, Zygmunt
Mykietyn, Paweł
Mysz-Gmeiner, Lula (née Gmeiner)
Nabokov, Nicolas (actually, Nikolai)
Nagano, Kent (George)
Nagel, Wilibald
Naginski, Charles
Nancarrow, Conlon
Naoumoff, Émile
Napoli, Gennaro
Napoli, Jacopo
Nápravnik, Eduard (Francevič)
Nash, Heddle
Nasidze, Sulkhan
Nastasijević, Svetomir
Nat, Yves
Natanson, Tadeusz
Natra, Sergiu
Naumann, (Karl) Ernst
Naumann, Siegfried
Navarra, André (-Nicolas)
Navarrini, Francesco
Navarro, (Luis Antonio) García
Naylor, Bernard (James)
Naylor, Edward (Woodall)
Nazareth, Daniel
Nazareth (Nazaré), Ernesto (Júlio de)
Neary, Martin (Gerard James)
Neblett, Carol
Nedbal, Oskar
Neel, (Louis) Boyd
Nees, Staf (Gustaaf Frans)
Nef, Albert
Nef, Isabelle (Lander)
Nef, Karl
Neglia, Francesco Paolo
Negrea, Marţian
Negri, Gino
Negri, Vittorio
Neidlinger, Gustav
Neikrug, Marc (Edward)
Nejedlý, Vít
Nelhybel, Vaclav
Nelson, John (Wilton)
Nelson, Judith (Anne née Manes)
Nelson, Ron(ald Jack)
Nelsova (real name, Katznelson), Zara
Nelsson, Woldemar
Nemescu, Octavian
Németh, Mária
Némethy, Ella
Nemiroff, Isaac
Nemtin, Alexander
Nenov, Dimiter
Nepomuceno, Alberto
Neri, Giulio
Neruda Family
Neruda, Wilma Maria Francisca (Vilemína Maria Franziška)
Neruda, Marie (Arlbergová)
Neruda, Franz (František Xaver Viktor)
Nessi, Giuseppe
Nesterenko, Evgeni (Evgenievich)
Nešvera, Josef
Neuhaus, Heinrich (Gustavovich)
Neuhaus, Rudolf
Neuhold, Günter
Neumann, Angelo
Neumann, Franz (František)
Neumann, Frederick (actually, Fritz)
Neumann, Václav
Neumann, Věroslav
Neumann, Wolfgang
Nevada (real name, Wixom), Emma
Nevada, Mignon (Mathilde Marie)
Neveu, Ginette
Nevin, Arthur (Finley)
Nevin, Ethelbert (Woodbridge)
Neway, Patricia
Newlin, Dika
Newman, Alfred
Newman, Anthony
Newman, Ernest (originally, William Roberts)
Newman, Randy
Newman, William S(tein)
Newmarch, Rosa (Harriet née Jeaffreson)
Newmark, John (originally, Hans Joseph Neumark)
Newton, Ivor
Ney, Elly
Nezhdanova, Antonina (Vasilievna)
Niblock, Phill
Nicholls, Agnes
Nicholson, George (Thomas Frederick)
Nicholson, Sir Sydney (Hugo)
Nicodé, Jean-Louis
Nicolescu, Marianna
Nicolet, Aurele
Niculescu, Ştefan
Niecks, Frederick (actually, Friedrich)
Nielsen, Alice
Nielsen, Carl (August)
Nielson, (Carl Henrik) Ludolf
Nielsen, Inga
Nielsen, Ludvig
Nielsen, Riccardo
Nielsen, Svend
Nielsen, Tage
Niemann, Walter
Nigg, Serge
Niimi, Tokuhide
Nikiprowetzky, Tolia
Nikisch, Arthur
Nikolais, Alwin (Theodore)
Nikolayeva, Tatiana (Petrovna)
Nikolov, Lazar
Nikolovski, Vlastimir
Nilsson, (family surname Svensson), (Märta) Birgit
Nilsson, Bo
Nilsson, Leo
Nilsson, Sven
Nilsson, Torsten
Nimsgern, Siegmund
Nin-Culmell, Joaquín (María)
Nin (y Castellanos), Joaquín
Nishimura, Akira
Nishizaki, Takako
Nissen, Hans Hermann
Nissman, Barbara
Nixon, Marni (née Margaret Nixon McEathron)
Nixon, Roger
Niyazi (real name, Taghi-zade-Khadzhibekov)
Nobel, Felix de
Noble, Dennis (William)
Noble, Ray(mond Stanley)
Noble, (Thomas) Tertius
Nobre, Marlos
Noda, Ken
Noda, Teruyuki
Noehren, Robert
Noetel, Konrad Friedrich
Nolte, Ewald V(alentin)
Noni, Alda
Nono, Luigi
Norberg-Schulz, Elizabeth
Norby, Erik
Nordal, Jón
Nordgren, Pehr Henrik
Nordheim, Arne
Nordica (real name, Norton), Lillian
Nordin, Lena
Nordoff, Paul
Nordqvist, Gustaf (Lazarus)
Nordqvist, (Johan) Conrad
Noren, Heinrich (real name, Heinrich Suso Johannes Gottlieb)
Norena, Eidé (real name, Kaja Andrea Karoline Hansen-Eidé)
Nørgård, Per
Nørholm, Ib
Norman, Jessye
Norrington, Sir Roger (Arthur Carver)
Norris, David Owen
North, Alex
Norup, Bent
Noskowski, Zygmunt
Noté, Jean
Nottara, Constantin
Nouguès, Jean
Novães, Guiomar
Novák, Jan
Novák, Milan
Novák, Vitězslav (actually, Augustín Rudolf)
Novello-Davies (real name, Davies), Clara
Novotná, Jarmila
Novotný, Václav Juda
Nowak, Lionel (Henry)
Nowowiejski, Felix
Nucci, Leo
Nummi, Seppo (Antero Yrjönpoika)
Nunes, Emmanuel

Parsch, Arnošt
Parsons, Geoffrey (Penwill)
Pärt, Arvo
Partch, Harry
Partos, Oedoen (actually, Ödön)
Partridge, Ian (Harold)
Pasatieri, Thomas
Pasero, Tancredi
Pashchenko, Andrei (Filippovich)
Pasini, Laura
Pasini (-Vitale), Lina
Paskalis, Kostas
Pasquotti, Corrado
Pásztory, Ditta
Patachich, Iván
Pataky, Kálmán
Patanè, Giuseppe
Patinkin, Mandy
Patorzhinsky, Ivan (Sergeievich)
Patterson, Paul (Leslie)
Patti Family
Patti, Amalia
Patti, Adelina (actually, Adela Juana Maria)
Pattiera, Tino
Pattison, Lee
Patzak, Julius
Pauer, Jíří
Pauer, Max von
Pauk, György
Paul, Thomas (Warburton)
Paull, Barberi
Paulson, Gustaf
Paulus, Olaf
Paulus, Stephen (Harrison)
Pauly, Rosa (actually, Rose née Pollak)
Paunović, Milenko
Paur, Emil
Pavarotti, Luciano
Payne, Anthony (Edward)
Payne, Maggi (actually, Margaret Ducé)
Paz, Juan Carlos
Pazovsky, Ariy (Moiseievich)
Pearlman, Martin
Pears, Sir Peter (Neville Luard)
Pease, James
Pechner, Gerhard
Pederzini, Gianna
Pedrell, Carlos
Pedrell, Felipe
Pedrollo, Arrigo
Peerce, Jan (real name, Jacob Pincus Perelmuth)
Peeters, Flor
Peiko, Nikolai
Peinemann, Edith
Peixinho, Jorge (Manuel Rosada Marques)
Pekinel, Güher and Süher
Pelemans, Willem
Pelletier, (Louis) Wilfred
Penderecki, Krzysztof
Penherski, Zbigniew
Pennario, Leonard
Pentland, Barbara (Lally)
Pépin, (Jean-Josephat) Clermont
Pepöck, August
Pepping, Ernst
Peragallo, Mario
Perahia, Murray
Perera, Ronald (Christopher)
Peress, Maurice
Pergament, Moses
Perger, Richard von
Peričić, Vlastimir
Perick (real name, Prick), Christof
Périer, Jean (Alexis)
Perkins, John MacIvor
Perkowski, Piotr
Perle, George
Perlea, Jonel
Perlemuter, Vlado
Perlis, Vivian
Perlman, Itzhak
Perlongo, Daniel
Pernerstorfer, Alois
Pernet, André
Perosi, Don Lorenzo
Perrachio, Luigi
Perrault, Michel (Brunet)
Perron (real name, Pergamenter), Karl
Perry, Janet
Perry, Julia (Amanda)
Persen, John
Persichetti, Vincent (Ludwig)
Persinger, Louis
Pertile, Aureliano
Pešek, Libor
Peskanov, Mark
Peskó, Zoltán
Pesonen, Olavi
Pessard, Émile (-Louis-Fortuné)
Pestalozzi, Heinrich
Peters (real name, Petermann), Roberta
Petersen, Wilhelm
Peters (Lazzara), Bernadette
Peterson, Wayne
Peterson-Berger, (Olof) Wilhelm
Petkov, Dimiter
Petra-Basacopol, Carmen
Petrassi, Goffredo
Petrauskas, Kipras
Petrauskas, Mikas
Petrella, Clara
Petri, Egon
Petri, Michala
Petrić, Ivo
Petridis, Petros (John)
Petrobelli, Pierluigi
Petrov, Andrei (Pavlovich)
Petrov, Ivan (Ivanovich)
Petrov, Nikolai (Arnoldovich)
Petrovics, Emil
Petrushka, Shabtai (Arieh)
Petrželka, Vilém
Pettersson, Gustaf Allan
Petyrek, Felix
Petzold, Rudolf
Petzoldt, Richard (Johannes)
Peyser, Joan (née Gilbert)
Pfister, Hugo
Pfitzner, Hans (Erich)
Philipp, Franz
Philipp, Isidor
Philippot, Michel
Phillips, Burrill
Phillips, Harvey (Gene)
Phillips, Peter (Sayer)
Piaf, Edith (real name, Giovanna Gassion)
Piatigorsky, Gregor
Piazzolla, Astor
Piccaver (real name, Peckover), Alfred
Picchi, Mirto
Picchi, Silvano
Picka, František
Picken, Laurence (Ernest Rowland)
Picker, Tobias
Pickett, Philip
Pick-Mangiagalli, Riccardo
Pierce, Webb
Pierné, (Henri-Constant-) Gabriel
Pierné, Paul
Pijper, Willem
Pilarczyk, Helga (Käthe)
Pimsleur, Solomon
Pingoud, Ernest
Pini-Corsi, Antonio
Pinkham, Daniel (Rogers, Jr.)
Pinnock, Trevor (David)
Piňos, Alois Simandl
Pinto, Alfredo
Pinto, Francisco António Norberto dos Santos
Pinto, Octavio
Pinza, Ezio (baptized Fortunio)
Pipkov, Lubomir
Pipkov, Panayot
Pires, (Luis) Filipe
Pires, Maria-João
Pirogov, Alexander (Stepanovich)
Pironkoff, Simeon
Pirro, André (Gabriel Edme)
Pirrotta, Nino (actually, Antonino)
Pirumov, Alexander
Pisk, Paul A(madeus)
Piston, Walter (Hamor, Jr.)
Pistor, Gotthelf
Pitfield, Thomas B(aron)
Pitt, Percy
Pittaluga, Gustavo
Pittel, Harvey
Pittman-Jennings, David
Pitzinger, Gertrude
Pizzetti, Ildebrando
Pizzi, Pier Luigi
Pizzini, Carlo Alberto
Plaichinger, Thila
Plakidis, Peteris
Plamenac, Dragan
Plançon, Pol (-Henri)
Planté, Francis
Plaschke, Friedrich (real name, Bedřich Plaške)
Plasson, Michel
Platania, Pietro
Pleasants, Henry
Plé-Caussade, Simone
Pleeth, William
Pleshakov, Vladimir
Pleskow, Raoul
Plessis, Hubert (Lawrence) du
Pletnev, Mikhail
Plishka, Paul (Peter)
Plowright, Rosalind (Anne)
Plush, Vincent
Podéšt, Ludvík

Renz, Frederick
Repin, Vadim
Rescigno, Nicola
Resnik, Regina
Rethberg, Elisabeth (real name, Lisbeth Sattler)
Réti, Rudolph (Richard)
Reuss-Belce, Luise
Rey, Cemal Reshid
Reynolds, Anna
Rhodes, Jane (Marie Andrée)
Ribaupierre, André de
Ricci, Ruggiero
Richter, Hans (Johann Baptist Isidor)
Richter, Karl
Richter, Sviatoslav (Teofilovich)
Richter-Haaser, Hans
Rickards, Steven
Ridder, Anton de
Ridderbusch, Karl
Rider-Kelsey, Corinne (née Rider)
Riegel, Kenneth
Riemenschneider, (Charles) Albert
Ries, Franz
Rifkin, Joshua
Riley, Terry (Mitchell)
Rilling, Helmuth
Rimini, Giacomo
Rimmer, John (Francis)
Rimsky-Korsakov, Nikolai (Andreievich)
Ringbom, Nils-Eric
Rios, Waldo de los
Risler, Edouard
Ritchie, Margaret (Willard)
Ritchie, Stanley (John)
Ritter, Hermann
Rivé-King, Julie
Robbin, Catherine
Robertson, Rae
Robertson, Stewart (John)
Robin, Mado
Robinson, Faye
Robinson, (Peter) Forbes
Robinson, Sharon
Robles, Marisa
Robson, Christopher
Rocherolle, Eugénie
Rockefeller, Martha Baird
Rockmore, Clara
Rode, Wilhelm
Rodgers, Joan
Roesgen-Champion, Marguerite
Rogé, Pascal
Rogers, Clara Kathleen (née Bartnett)
Rogers, Nigel (David)
Roget, Henriette
Rogg, Lionel
Rogister, Jean (François Toussaint)
Rögner, Heinz
Rojo Olalla, Casiano
Rolandi, Gianna
Roldán, Amadeo
Rolfe Johnson, Anthony
Roll, Michael
Roman, Stella (real name, Florica Vierica Alma Stela Blasu)
Romberg, Sigmund
Romero Family
  Romero, Celedonio
  Romero, Celin
  Romero, Pepe
  Romero, Angel
Ronald, Sir Landon (real name, Landon Ronald Russell)
Röntgen, Julius
Roocroft, Amanda
Rooley, Anthony
Roosevelt, J(oseph) Willard
Rootering, Jan-Hendrik
Rootham, Cyril (Bradley)
Rorem, Ned
Rosand, Aaron
Rosé, Arnold (Josef)
Rose, Bernard (William George)
Rose, Jerome
Rose, Leonard (Joseph)
Rösel, Peter
Rosell, Lars-Erik
Rosen, Charles (Welles)
Rosen, Jerome (William)
Rosen, Nathaniel (Kent)
Rosenboom, David (Charles)
Rosenman, Leonard
Rosenshein, Neil
Rosenthal, Moriz
Rosing, Vladimir
Rösler, Endre
Ross, Hugh (Cuthbert, Melville)
Ross, Scott
Rosseau, Norbert (Oscar Claude)
Rossellini, Renzo
Rossi, Giulio
Rossi, Tino
Rossi-Lemeni, Nicola
Rössl-Majdan, Hildegard
Rostal, Max
Rostropovich, Leopold
Rostropovich, Mstislav (Leopoldovich)
Rosvaenge (real name, Rosenving-Hansen), Helge
Roth, Daniel
Roth, Feri
Rothenberger, Anneliese
Rothier, Léon
Rothmüller, (Aron) Marko
Rothwell, Evelyn
Röttger, Heinz
Rotzsch, Hans-Joachim
Rouleau, Joseph (Alfred Pierre)
Rousseau, Eugene
Roussel, Albert (Charles Paul Marie)
Rousselière, Charles
Rousset, Christophe
Routh, Francis (John)
Routley, Erik (Reginald)
Rowley, Alec
Roxburgh, Edwin
Rozanov, Sergei (Vasilievich)
Rozkošný, Josef Richard
Rubinstein, Arthur (actually, Artur)
Rubinstein, Beryl
Rübsam, Wolfgang
Rudnytsky, Antin
Rudorff, Ernst (Friedrich Karl)
Rudy, Mikhail
Ruffo, Titta (real name, Ruffo Cafiero Titta)
Ruiter, Wim de
Rummel Family
  Rummel, Walter Morse
Rúnólfsson, Karl Ottó
Rupp, Franz
Russell, (George) Alexander
Russell, Lillian (real name, Helen Louise Leonard)
Rutkowski, Bronislaw
Rütti, Carl
Ružiková, Zuzana
Rybner, (real name, Růbner), (Peter Martin) Cornelius
Rydl, Kurt
Rypdal, Terje
Rysanek, Leonie
Ryterband, Roman
Rzewski, Frederic (Anthony)
Saar, Mart
Saariaho, Kaija (Anneli)
Sabaneyev, Leonid (Leonidovich)
Sabbatini, Giuseppe
Sacco, P(atrick) Peter
Sacher, Paul
Sachs, Joel
Sachse, Leopold
Sack (real name, Weber), Erna
Sadie, Julie Anne (née McCormack)
Sadie, Stanley (John)
Sadra, I Wayan
Saenz, Pedro
Saeverud, Harald (Sigurd Johan)
Safonov, Vasili (Ilich)
Sagaev, Dimiter
Sahl, Michael
Saikkola, Lauri
Saint-George, Henry
Saint-Marcoux, Micheline Coulombe
Saint-Saëns, (Charles-) Camille
Saito, Hideo
Sakač, Branimir
Salazar, Manuel
Salerno-Sonnenberg, Nadja
Saléza, Albert
Salignac, Thomas (real name, Eustace Thomas)
Sallinen, Aulis
Salmanov, Vadim (Nikolaievich)
Salmenhaara, Erkki (Olavi)
Salmhofer, Franz
Salminen, Matti
Salmond, Felix (Adrian Norman)
Salomon, (Naphtali) Siegfried
Salonen, Esa-Pekka
Salonen, Sulo (Nikolai)
Salter, Lionel (Paul)
Saltzmann-Stevens, Minnie
Salva, Tadeáš
Salvayre, Gaston (actually, Gervais-Bernard)
Salviucci, Giovanni
Salzedo (actually, Salzédo), (Léon) Carlos
Salzman, Eric
Samara, Spiro (Spyridon Filiskos)
Samaroff, Olga (née Hickenlooper)
Samazeuilh, Gustave (Marie Victor Fernand)

Stanford, Sir Charles Villiers
Stanislav, Josef
Stanley, Frank (originally, Grinsted, William Stanley)
Stapp, Olivia
Starek, Jiří
Starer, Robert
Stark, Robert
Starker, János
Staryk, Steven
Statkowski, Roman
Staudigl (II), Joseph
St. Clair, Carl
St. Clair, Cyrus
Steber, Eleanor
Stecker, Karel
Štědroň, Miloš
Štědroň, Vladimír
Steel, Christopher (Charles)
Stefánsson, Fjölnir
Steffek, Hanny (actually, Hannelore)
Steffen, Wolfgang
Stehle, Adelina
Stehman, Jacques
Steiger, Anna
Steiger, Rand
Stein, Horst (Walter)
Stein, Leon
Stein, Leonard
Stein, Peter
Stein, Richard Heinrich
Steinbach, Fritz
Steinberg, Maximilian (Osseievich)
Steinberg, (Carl) Michael (Alfred)
Steinberg, Pinchas
Steinberg, William (actually, Hans Wilhelm)
Steinberg, Ze'ev (Wolfgang)
Steiner, Emma
Steiner, Max(imilian Raoul Walter)
Steinert, Alexander Lang
Steingruber, Ilona
Steinitz, (Charles) Paul (Joseph)
Stella, Antonietta
Stemper, Frank
Stenberg, Jordan
Stenhammar, (Karl) Wilhelm (Eugen)
Stenz, Markus
Štěpan, Václav
Stepanian, Aro (Levoni)
Stephan, Rudi
Stephănescu, George
Stephens, John (Elliott)
Steptoe, Roger (Guy)
Stern, Isaac
Sternberg, Constantin
Sternberg, Erich Walter
Sternberg, Jonathan
Sternefeld, Daniël
Steuermann, Edward (actually, Eduard)
Stevens, Bernard (George)
Stevens, Delores (Elaine)
Stevens, Denis (William)
Stevens, Halsey
Stevens, Horace (Ernest)
Stevens, Risë
Stevenson, Robert (Murrell)
Stevenson, Ronald
Stewart, Reginald (Drysdale)
Stewart, Thomas (James)
Stibilj, Milan
Stich-Randall, Teresa
Stiedry, Fritz
Stiehl Family
Stiehl, Carl (Karl) Johann Christian
Stignani, Ebe
Still, William Grant
Stilwell, Richard (Dale)
Stock, David (Frederick)
Stock, Frederick (actually, Friedrich August)
Stockhausen Family
Stockhausen, Julius (Christian)
Stockhausen, Franz
Stockhausen, Karlheinz
Stockhoff, Walter William
Stoeckel, Gustave J(acob)
Stoessel, Albert (Frederic)
Stöhr, Richard
Stojanović, Peter Lazar
Stojowski, Sigismund (actually, Zygmunt Denis Antoni)
Stoker, Richard
Stokes, Eric (Norman)
Stokowski, Leopold (Anthony)
Stoliarsky, Piotr (Solomonovich)
Stoltzman, Richard (Leslie)
Stolz, Robert (Elisabeth)
Stolze, Gerhard
Stone, Carl
Storchio, Rosina
Story, Liz
Stott, Kathryn (Linda)
Stout, Alan (Burrage)
Stoutz, Edmond de
Stoyanov, Pencho
Stoyanov, Veselin
Stracciari, Riccardo
Stradal, August
Straesser, Joep
Strang, Gerald
Stransky, Josef
Straram, Walther
Strassburg, Robert
Stratas, Teresa (real name, Anastasia Stratakis)
Strategier, Herman
Straube, (Montgomery Rufus) Karl (Siegfried)
Straus, Oscar (Nathan)
Strauss Family
Strauss, Eduard
Strauss, Richard (Georg)
Stravinsky, Igor (Feodorovich)
Stravinsky, (Sviatoslav) Soulima
Street, Tison
Streich, Rita
Strens, Jules
Stresemann, Wolfgang
Strickland, Lily (Teresa)
Strickland, William
Stringfield, Lamar (Edwin)
Stroe, Aurel
Strong, George Templeton
Strong, Susan
Strouse, Charles (Louis)
Strube, Gustav
Stückgold, Grete (née Schneidt)
Stückgold, Jacques
Stucky, Steven (Edward)
Studer, Cheryl
Stürmer, Bruno
Sturzenegger, (Hans) Richard
Stutschewsky, Joachim
Stutzmann, Nathalie
Styne, Jule (originally, Stein, Julius Kerwin)
Subono, Blacius
Subotnick, Morton
Subowo, Yohanes
Sucher, Rosa (née Hasselbeck)
Suchoň, Eugen
Suchý, František
Suckling, Norman
Suda, Stanislav
Sugár, Rezső
Suggia, Guilhermina
Suitner, Otmar
Suk (I), Josef
Suk (II), Josef
Suk, Váša (Václav; Viacheslav Ivanovich)
Sukegawa, Toshiya
Sukerta, Pande Made
Šulek, Stjepan
Sultan, Grete
Sumac, Yma (real name, Emperatriz Chavarri)
Sumera, Lepo
Summerly, Jeremy
Summers, Jonathan
Summers, Patrick
Sundgrén-Schnéevoigt, Sigrid Ingeborg
Sunnegårdh, Thomas
Suñol (y Baulenas), Gregoria María
Suolahti, Heikki
Supervia, Conchita
Suratno, Nano
Surdin, Morris
Surinach, Carlos
Surzyćnski, Józef
Susa, Conrad
Susskind (originally, Süsskind), (Jan) Walter
Sutanto
Suter, Hermann
Suter, Robert
Sutermeister, Heinrich
Suthaus, (Heinrich) Ludwig
Sutherland, Dame Joan
Sutherland, Margaret (Ada)
Sutro, Rose Laura
Suwardi (Soewardi), Aloysius
Suzuki, Shin'ichi
Suzuki, Yukikazu
Svanholm, Set (Karl Viktor)
Švara, Danilo
Svéd, Sándor
Sveinbjörnsson, Sveinbjörn
Sveinsson, Atli Heimer
Svenden, Birgitta
Svendsen, Johan (Severin)
Svetlanov, Evgeny (Feodorovich)
Sviridov, Georgi (Vasilevich)
Svoboda, Josef
Svoboda, Tomáš
Swann, Frederick (Lewis)

Tijardović, Ivo
Tikka, Kari (Juhani)
Tikotsky, Evgeni (Karlovich)
Tilles, Nurit
Tilney, Colin
Timmermans, Ferdinand
Tinel, Edgar (Pierre Joseph)
Tinsley, Pauline (Cecilia)
Tintner, Georg (Bernhard)
Tiomkin, Dimitri
Tipo, Maria (Luisa)
Tippett, Sir Michael (Kemp)
Tischhauser, Franz
Tishchenko, Boris (Ivanovich)
Tisné, Antoine
Titus, Alan (Wilkowski)
Titus, Hiram
Tjeknavorian, Loris
Tobias, Rudolf
Tocchi, Gian Luca
Tocco, James
Toch, Ernst
Toczyska, Stefania
Toda, Kunio (actually, Morikuni)
Toduţă, Sigismund
Toebosch, Louis
Tofft, Alfred
Togi, Suenobu
Togni, Camillo
Tokatyan, Armand
Tolbecque Family
  Tolbecque, Auguste
Toldrá, Eduardo
Tolonen, Jouko (Paavo Kalervo)
Tolstoy, Dmitri
Tomášek, Jaroslav
Tomasi, Henri (Frédien)
Tómasson, Jónas
Tomlinson, John (Rowland)
Tommasini, Vincenzo
Tomotani, Kōji
Tomowa-Sintow, Anna
Tone, Yasunao
Töpper, Hertha
Toradze, Alexander (David)
Toradze, David (Alexandrovich)
Torkanowsky, Werner
Torke, Michael
Tormis, Veljo
Törne, Bengt (Axel) von
Torres-Santos, Raymond
Tortelier, Paul
Tortelier, Yan Pascal
Tosatti, Vieri
Toscanini, Arturo
Toselli, Enrico
Tosti, Sir (Francesco) Paolo
Totenberg, Roman
Touma, Habib Hassan
Tourangeau, (Marie Jeannine) Huguette
Tourel (real name, Davidovich), Jennie
Tournemire, Charles (Arnould)
Tours, Frank E(dward)
Tovey, Sir Donald (Francis)
Tower, Joan (Peabody)
Townsend, Douglas
Toyama, Yuzo
Tozzi, Giorgio (actually, George)
Trampler, Walter
Tranchell, Peter (Andrew)
Trapp, (Hermann Emil Alfred) Max
Traubel, Helen (Francesca)
Travis, Roy (Elihu)
Traxel, Josef
Treger, Charles
Treigle, Norman
Tremblay, George (Amedée)
Tremblay, Gilles (Léonce)
Treptow, Günther (Otto Walther)
Tretyakov, Viktor (Viktorovich)
Tréville, Yvonne de (real name, Edyth La Gierse)
Trifunović, Vitomir
Trimble, Lester (Albert)
Trneček, Hanuš
Trojahn, Manfred
Trojan, Václav
Trombly, Preston (Andrew)
Trotter, Thomas (Andrew)
Troyanos, Tatiana
Truax, Barry (Douglas)
Trythall, (Harry) Gil(bert)
Trythall, Richard
Tsontakis, George
Tsoupaki, Calliope
Tsouyopoulos, Georges
Tsukatani, Akihirô
Tsvetanov, Tsvetan
Tua, Teresina (actually, Maria Felicità)
Tubb, Carrie (actually, Caroline Elizabeth)
Tubin, Eduard
Tucci, Gabriella
Tucker, Richard (real name, Reuben Ticker)
Tuckwell, Barry (Emmanuel)
Tudor, David (Eugene)
Tudoran, Ionel
Tully, Alice
Tunley, David (Evatt)
Tupkov, Dimiter
Turchi, Guido
Tureck, Rosalyn
Turetzky, Bertram (Jay)
Turini, Ronald
Turnage, Mark-Anthony
Turner, Dame Eva
Turner, Robert (Comrie)
Turnovský, Martin
Turok, Paul (Harris)
Turovsky, Yuli
Turski, Zbigniew
Tutev, Georgi
Tuthill, Burnet Corwin
Tuukkanen, Kalervo
Tüür, Erkki-Sven
Tuxen, Erik (Oluf)
Tveitt, (Nils) Geirr
Twardowski, Romuald
Tweedy, Donald (Nichols)
Tyler, James (Henry)
Tyranny, Blue Gene (real name, Robert Nathan Sheff)
Tzipine, Georges
Uchida, Mitsuko
Ugarte, Floro M(anuel)
Ughi, Uto
Uhde, Hermann
Uhl, Alfred
Uhl, Fritz
Ujj, Béla
Ulanowsky, Paul
Ulfrstad, Marius Moaritz
Ulfung, Ragnar (Sigurd)
Ullmann, Viktor
Um Kalthoum (actually, Fatma el-Zahraa Ibrahim)
Underwood, James
Ung, Chinary
Unger, (Ernst) Max
Unger, Gerhard
Uppman, Theodor
Upshaw, Dawn
Urbanner, Erich
Uribe-Holguín, Guillermo
Urlus, Jacques (Jacobus)
Urner, Catherine Murphy
Urrutia-Blondel, Jorge
Ursuleac, Viorica
Usandizaga, José Maria
Usmanbaş, Ilhan
Ussachevsky, Vladimir (Alexis)
Ustvolskaya, Galina (Ivanovna)
Vacek, Miloš
Vačkář Family
  Vačkář, Václav
  Vačkář, Dalibor Cyril
  Vačkář, Tomas
Vaduva, Leontina
Vainberg, Moisei
Vajda, János
Valcárcel, Edgar
Valcárcel, Teodoro
Valdengo, Giuseppe
Valdes, Maximiano
Válek, Jiří
Valen, (Olav) Fartein
Valente, Benita
Valente, Vincenzo
Valenti, Fernando
Valentini-Terrani, Lucia
Valkare, Gunnar
Vallée, Rudy (Hubert Prior)
Vallerand, Jean (d'Auray)
Valleria (real name, Schoening), Alwina
Valletti, Cesare
Vallin, Ninon
Valverde, Joaquín
Van Allan, Richard (real name, Alan Philip Jones)
van Appledorn, Mary Jeanne
Van Asperen, Bob
Vancea, Zeno (Octavian)
Van Dam, José (real name, Joseph Van Damme)
Van de Moortel, Arie
Van den Boorn-Coclet, Henriette
Vandermaesbrugge, Max
Vandernoot, André
Van der Stucken, Frank (Valentin)
Van der Velden, Renier
Van de Vate, Nancy
Van de Woestijne, David
Van Durme, Jef
Van Dyck, Ernest (Marie Hubert)
Vaness, Carol (Theresa)

Warren, Leonard
Warren, Raymond (Henry Charles)
Washburn, Robert
Wasitodiningrat, K.R.T. (Kanjeng Raden Tumengung, a title of honorary royal status)
Watanabe, Akeo
Watkinson, Carolyn
Watson (real name, McLamore), Claire
Watson, Lillian
Watts, André
Watts, Helen (Josephine)
Watts, John (Everett)
Waxman (real name, Wachsmann), Franz
Weathers, Felicia
Weaver, James (Merle)
Webb, Charles H(aizlip, Jr.)
Weber, Alain
Weber, Ben (actually, William Jennings Bryan)
Weber, Ludwig
Weber, Margrit
Webern, Anton (Friedrich Wilhelm) von
Webster, Beveridge
Webster, Sir David (Lumsden)
Weckerlin, Jean-Baptiste-Théodore
Weede (real name, Wiedefeld), Robert
Weidemann, Friedrich
Weidinger, Christine
Weidt, Lucie
Weigel, Eugene (Herbert)
Weigl, Karl
Weigl, Valery (Vally)
Weikert, Ralf
Weikl, Bernd
Weil, Bruno
Weil, Hermann
Weill, Kurt (Julian)
Weinberger, Jaromir
Weiner, Lazar
Weiner, Leó
Weingartner, (Paul) Felix, Edler von Münzberg
Weinrich, Carl
Weinzweig, John (Jacob)
Weir, Dame Gillian (Constance)
Weir, Judith
Weis, (Carl) Flemming
Weis, Karel
Weisberg, Arthur
Weisgall, Hugo (David)
Weisgarber, Elliot
Weismann, Julius
Weiss, Adolph
Weissberg, Yulia (Lazarevna)
Weissenberg, Alexis (Sigismond)
Weissenborn, Günther (Albert Friedrich)
Welcher, Dan
Weldon, George
Welin, Karl-Erik (Vilhelm)
Welitsch (real name, Veličkova), Ljuba
Weller, Walter
Wellesz, Egon (Joseph)
Welser-Möst (real name, Möst), Franz
Welting, Ruth
Wendt, Larry (actually, Lawrence Frederick)
Wenkel, Ortrun
Wenkoff, Spas
Wennerberg-Reuter, Sara (Margareta Eugenia Euphrosyne)
Wenten, Nyoman
Wenzinger, August
Werba, Erik
Werder, Felix
Werle, Lars Johan
Wernick, Richard
Werrenrath, Reinald
Wesley-Smith, Martin
Wessman, Harri (Kristian)
Westenburg, Richard
Westerberg, Stig (Evald Börje)
Westergaard, Peter (Talbot)
Westergaard, Svend
Westerlinck, Wilfried
Westlake, Nigel
Weston, Randy
Wettergren, Gertrud (née Pålson)
Wetz, Richard
Wetzler, Hermann (Hans)
Whear, Paul William
Whettam, Graham (Dudley)
White, Amos (Mordechai)
White, Andrew (Nathanial III)
White, Chris(topher) Wesley
White, Clarence Cameron
White, Donald H(oward)
White, Felix Harold
White, Frances
White, Maude Valérie
White, Michael
White, Robert
White, Ruth
White, Willard (Wentworth)
Whitehead, Alfred (Ernest)
Whitehill, Clarence (Eugene)
Whitehouse, William Edward
White Lafitte, José (Silvestre de los Dolores)
Whithorne (real name, Whittern), Emerson
Whiting, Arthur Battelle
Whitlock, Percy (William)
Whitmer, T(homas) Carl
Whitney, John
Whitney, Robert (Sutton)
Whittaker, Howard
Whittaker, W(illiam) G(illies)
Whittenberg, Charles
Whyte, Ian
Wich, Günther
Wickham, Florence
Wicks, (Edward) Allan
Widdop, Walter
Widor, Charles-Marie (-Jean-Albert)
Wiechowicz, Stanislaw
Wieck Family
 Wieck, Marie
Wiedemann, Hermann
Wiedermann, Bedřich Antonín
Wiemann, Ernst
Wiéner, Jean
Wiener, Otto
Wieniawski, Adam Tadeusz
Wieniawski, Jozef
Wiens, Edith
Wieslander, (Axel Otto) Ingvar
Wigglesworth, Frank
Wigglesworth, Mark
Wihan, Hans (actually, Hanuš)
Wihtol (Vitols), Joseph (actually, Jāzeps)
Wijdeveld, Wolfgang
Wiklund, Adolf
Wild, Earl
Wildberger, Jacques
Wildbrunn (real name, Wehrenpfennig), Helene
Wilder, Alec (actually, Alexander Lafayette Chew)
Wildgans, Friedrich
Wilding-White, Raymond
Wilkins, Christopher
Wilkomirski Family
 Wilkomirski, Alfred
 Wilkomirski, Kazimierz
 Wilkomirski, Maria
 Wilkomirski, Józef
 Wilkomirski, Wanda
Willan, (James) Healey
Willcocks, Sir David (Valentine)
Williams, Alberto
Williams, Camilla
Williams, Clifton
Williams, Grace (Mary)
Williams, John (Christopher)
Williams, John (Towner)
Williams, Peter (Fredric)
Williamson, John Finley
Williamson, Malcolm (Benjamin Graham Christopher)
Wills, Arthur
Willson, (Robert) Meredith (Reiniger)
Wilson, Charles (Mills)
Wilson, Ian
Wilson, Olly (Woodrow)
Wilson, Ransom
Wilson, Richard (Edward)
Wilson, Roland
Wilson, Todd
Wilson-Johnson, David (Robert)
Wimberger, Gerhard
Winant, William
Winbeck, Heinz
Winbergh, Gösta
Wincenc, Carol
Windgassen, Wolfgang (Fritz Hermann)
Winham, Godfrey
Winkler, Peter (Kenton)
Winograd, Arthur
Winternitz, Emanuel
Wirén, Dag (Ivar)
Wirth, Helmut (Richard Adolf Friedrich Karl)
Wise, Patricia
Wishart, Peter (Charles Arthur)
Wislocki, Stanislaw
Wissmer, Pierre
Wiszniewski, Zbigniew
Wit, Antoni
Witherspoon, Herbert
Wittgenstein, Paul
Wittich, Marie
Wittinger, Robert
Wittrisch, Marcel

JAZZ

Early

Brown, Steve (Theodore)
Brown, Tom (Red)
Brunis, (originally Brunies), Georg(e Clarence)
Bushell, Garvin (Payne)
Busse, Henry
Caldwell, Happy (actually, Albert W.)
Carey, Mutt (actually, Thomas; aka Papa)
Carr, Mancy (Peck)
Carver, Wayman (Alexander)
Casey, Bob (actually, Robert Hanley)
Casey, Floyd
Catlett, Sid(ney) (aka "Big Sid")
Celestin, Papa (actually, Oscar Phillip)
Chittison, Herman ("Ivory")
Christensen, Axel (Waldemar)
Christian, Emile (Joseph; aka "Bootmouth")
Clark, June (actually, Algeria Junius)
Clay, Sonny (actually, William Rogers Campbell)
Cless, (George) Rod(erick)
Cobb, Junie (actually, Junius C.)
Cole, June (Lawrence)
Collins, Lee(ds)
Condon, Eddie (actually, Albert Edwin)
Cook, Doc (originally, Cooke, Charles L.)
Coon, Carleton (A. Sr.)
Cottrell, Louis (Albert), Jr.
Cox, Ida (née Prather)
Creath, Charlie (actually, Charles Cyril)
Crosby, Bob (actually, George Robert)
Cuffee, Ed(ward Emerson)
Davenport, "Cow Cow" (actually, Charles Edward)
DeParis, Wilbur
Dodds, Baby (actually, Warren)
Dodds, Johnny (actually, John M.)
Dunn, Johnny
Dutrey, Honore
Edwards, Bass (Henry)
Edwards, Eddie (actually Edwin Branford; aka Daddy)
Europe, James Reese
Feather, Leonard (Geoffrey Feder)
Fitzgerald, Ella (Jane)
Foster, Pops (actually, George Murphy)
Garland, Ed Montudi(e) (actually, Edward Bertram)
Goldkette, Jean
Green, Charlie (aka Big Green; Long Boy)
Hall, Minor (Ram)
Hall, Tubby (Alfred)
Hardy, Emmett (Louis)
Haughton, Chauncey
Hayes, Edgar (Junius)
Hazel, Monk (Arthur)
Higginbotham, J. C. (aka Jack; Jay C.; and "Higgy")
Hill, Chippie (Bertha)
Hill, Tiny (actually, Thomas)
Hodes, Art(hur W.)
Howard, Darnell
Howard, Kid (Avery)
Humphrey, Percy
Hunt, Pee Wee (Walter)
Hunter, Alberta (aka Beatty, Josephine)
Hutchenrider, Clarence (Behrens)
Irvis, Charlie (actually, Charles)
Irwin, Cecil
Jackson, Cliff (actually, Clifton Luther)
Jackson, Dewey
Jackson, Preston (originally, McDonald, James Preston)
Jackson, Rudy (actually, Rudolph)
Jackson, Tony (actually, Anthony)
Jefferson, Hilton (W.)
Jefferson, Maceo B.
Jenkins, Freddie
Johnson, Bill (actually, William K.)
Johnson, Bill (actually, William Manuel)
Johnson, Bunk (William Geary)
Johnson, Charlie (actually, Charles Wright)
Johnson, Dink (Oliver)
Johnson, Freddy
Johnson, James P(rice)
Johnson, Lonnie (Alonzo)
Johnson, Pete(r)
Jones, Claude B.
Jones, Isham
Jones, Snags (actually, Clifford)
Kelley, Peck (John Dickson)
Kelly, (Edgar) Guy
Kemp, Hal (actually, James Harold)
Keppard, Freddie
Kirkeby, "Ed" Wallace Theodore
Ladnier, Tommy (originally, Ladner, Thomas)
Laine, Papa Jack (actually, George Vitelle)
Lang, Eddie (originally, Massaro, Salvatore)
Lang, Walter
Lateiner, Jacob
Lecuna, Juan Vicente
Lees, Benjamin
Lehmann, (Ludwig) Fritz
Lewis, George (originally, Zeno, George Louis Francis)
Lindsey, John
Lingle, Paul,
Lofton, Cripple Clarence
Lunceford, Jimmie (actually, James Melvin)
Lund, Signe
Lytell, Jimmy (originally, Sarrapede, James)
McCord, Castor,
McKenzie, Red (William)
McKinney, William
McPartland, Jimmy (actually, James Dougald/Douglas)
Melrose, Frank(lyn Taft)
Mezzrow, Mezz (originally, Mesirow, Milton)
Miley, Bubber (James Wesley)
Mitchell, Louis (A.)
Morand, Herb
Morton, Jelly Roll (actually, Lamothe, Ferdinand Joseph)
Napoleon, Phil (actually, Filippo Napoli)
Naylor, Oliver
Nelson, Big Eye Louis (actually DeLisle, Louis Nelson)
Nelson, "Dave" Davidson C.
Nicholas, Albert (Nick)
Nichols, Red (actually, Ernest Loring)
Noone, Jimmie
Norvo, Red (actually, Norville, Kenneth)
Nunez, Alcide "Yellow"
Oliver, King (actually, Joe)
Ory, Kid (actually Edward)
Ossman, Vess L. (actually, Sylvester Louis)
Page, Hot Lips (actually, Oran Thaddeus)
Pavageau, Alcide "Slow Drag"
Picou, Alphonse
Pinkett, (William) Ward
Piron, A(rmand) J(ohn)
Pollack, Ben,
Randolph, Zilner T(renton)
Reinhardt, Django (Jean Baptiste)
Reuss, Allan
Rey, Alvino
Rhodes, Todd (Washington)
Rich, Buddy (Bernard)
Roach, Max(well Lemuel)
Robertson, Zue (actually, C. Alvin)
Robinson, J(oseph) Russel
Robinson, Prince
Rollini, Adrian
Roppolo, Leon (Joseph)
Sanders, Joe (actually, Joseph L.),
Saunders, Red (Theodore)
Sayles, Emanuel (Rene; aka Manny)
Schoebel, Elmer
Scobey, Bob (actually, Robert Alexander Jr.)
Scott, Bud (Arthur Jr.)
Scott, Cecil (Xavier) Jr.
Scott, James (Sylvester)
Scott, Leon
Shaw, Lige (Elijah W.)
Shoffner, Bob (actually, Robert Lee)
Signorelli, Frank
Simeon, Omer (Victor)
Singleton, Zutty (actually, Arthur James)
Sissle, Noble (Lee)
Smith, Joe (actually, Joseph C.)
Smith, Pine Top (Clarence)
Smith, Russell (T.; aka "Pops")
Smith, Warren (Doyle; aka Smitty)
Smith, Willie "The Lion" (originally Bertholoff, William Henry Joseph Bonaparte)
Snow, Valaida
Snowden, Elmer (Chester; aka "Pops")
Souchon, Edmond (II; aka "Doc")
Spanier, "Muggsy" (Francis Joseph)
Spargo, Tony (originally, Sbarbaro, Antonio)
Spivey, Victoria (Regina; aka "Queen Victoria")
St. Cyr, Johnny (actually, John Alexander)
Sweatman, Wilbur (C.)
Tate, Erskine
Teschemacher, Frank (aka Tesch)

Tio, Lorenzo, Jr.
Tough, Dave (actually, David Jarvis)
Towles, Nat
Trumbauer, Frankie (also, Trombar, Frank)
Venuti, Joe (Giuseppe)
Waller, "Fats" (Thomas Wright)
Weatherford, Teddy
Weber, Joe (actually, Morris Joseph)
Wettling, George
Whaley, Wade
Wheeler, (E. B.) De Priest
White, Amos (Mordechai)
Williams, Clarence
Yancey, Jimmy (actually, James Edwards)

Swing

Abrams (Abramovitch), Max
Addison, Bernard (S.; Bunky)
Alemán, Oscar (Marcelo)
Allard, Joe (Joseph A.)
Ammons, Albert (C.)
Anderson, "Buddy" (Bernard Hartwell)
Anderson, "Cat" (William Alonzo)
Anderson, Ed(ward) ("Andy")
Anderson, Ivie (Marie; "Ivy")
Anthony (Antonini), Ray(mond)
Arbello, Fernando
Auld, Georgie (born John Altwerger)
Barbarin, Paul (Adolphe)
Barker, Danny (actually Daniel Moses)
Barnet, Charlie (actually, Charles Daly)
Basie, Count (real name, William)
Bauer, Billy (actually, William Henry)
Bauzá, Mario
Bechet, Sidney (Joseph)
Berigan, Bunny (Rowland Bernard)
Berry, Chu (actually, Leon Brown)
Bigard, Barney (Alban Leon)
Blanton, Jimmy (actually, James)
Bose, Sterling (Belmont) (Boze, Bozo)
Bostic, Earl
Boswell Sisters, The
Bowlly, Al
Bradley, Will (originally, Schwichtenberg, Wilbur)
Bradshaw, Tiny (Myron)
Braud (Breaux), Wellman
Bregman, Buddy
Briggs, Pete
Brown, Cleo(patra)
Brown, Lawrence
Brown, Les(ter Raymond)
Brown, Pete (James Ostend)
Brown, Pud (Albert)
Brown, Ray(mond Matthews)
Bryant, Clora
Bryant, Willie (actually, William Steven)
Buckner, Milt(on Brent)
Bullock, Chick (Charles)
Bunch, John
Bunn, Teddy (actually, Theodore Leroy)
Burroughs, Alvin ("Mouse")
Bushell, Garvin (Payne)
Bushkin, Joe (Joseph)
Busse, Henry
Butterfield, Billy (actually, Charles William)
Butterfield, Erskine
Byas, Don (Carlos Wesley)
Caceres, Ernie (actually, Ernesto)
Caiazza, Nick (actually, Nicholas)
Calloway, Blanche
Calloway, Cab(ell III)
Capp, Frank
Carhart, George
Carlisle, Una Mae
Carney, Harry (Howell)
Carpenter, Wingie (actually, Theodore)
Carter, Benny (actually, Bennett Lester; aka "The King")
Carver, Wayman (Alexander)
Cary, Dick (actually, Richard Durant)
Casey, Al(bert Aloysius)
Castle, Lee
Challis, Bill (actually, William H.)
Chambers, Henderson (Charles)
Cheatham, Doc (actually, Adolphus Anthony)
Chilton, John (James)
Christensen, Axel (Waldemar)
Christian, Charlie (actually, Charles)
Clark, Spencer W.
Clarke, George F.
Claxton, Rozelle
Clay, Shirley
Clayton, Buck (actually, Wilbur Dorsey)
Clinton, Larry
Clooney, Rosemary
Coker, Henry (L.)
Cole, Cozy (actually, William Randolph)
Cole, June (Lawrence)
Coleman, Bill (actually, William Johnson)
Collins, Shad (actually, Lester Rallingston)
Columbus, Chris(topher) (originally, Morris, Joseph Christopher Columbus)
Connor, Chris
Cooper, Bob (actually, Robert William)
Cooper, Harry (R.)
Costa, Johnny
Crawford, Jimmy (actually, James Strickland; aka Jimmie)
Crumbley, Elmer (E.)
Cruz, Celia
Davison, Wild Bill (actually, William Edward)
DeFranco, Buddy (actually, Boniface Ferdinand Leonardo)
Dickerson, Carroll
Disley, Diz (actually, William Charles)
Donahue, Sam(uel Koontz)
Dorsey, Jimmy (actually, James Francis)
Dorsey, Tommy (actually, Thomas Francis Jr.)
Douglass, Bill
Duke, Doug(las) (originally, Ovidio Fernandez)
Durham, Eddie
Edison, Harry Sweets
Eldridge, (David) Roy (aka Little Jazz)
Ellington, Duke (actually, Edward Kennedy)
Elman, Ziggy (originally, Finkelman, Harry)
Erwin, Pee Wee (actually, George)
Evans, Herschel
Ferguson, Maynard
Florence, Bob
Francis, Panama (actually, David Albert)
Freeman, Bud (Lawrence)
Gaillard, Slim (Bulee)
Glenn, (Evans) Tyree
Grappelli (Grappelly), Stephane
Gray (Knoblaugh), Glen
Greer, Sonny (William Alexander)
Grimes, Tiny (Lloyd)
Guy, Fred
Hardee, John
Harding, Buster (Lavere)
Hardwick(e), Otto (Toby)
Harris, Bill (Willard Palmer)
Harris, Joe
Hawkins, Coleman (Randolph)
Hawkins, Erskine (Ramsey)
Haymes, Joe
Haynes, Cyril
Haywood, Cedric
Heard, J(ames) C(harles)
Henderson, Fletcher (Hamilton Jr.; aka Smack)
Henderson, Horace (W.)
Henry, (Frank) Haywood
Herman, Woody (actually, Woodrow Charles)
Heywood, Eddie (actually, Edward Jr.)
Hill, Ernest ("Bass")
Hines, Earl (Kenneth; aka Fatha)
Hinton, Milt(on John; aka the Judge)
Hite, Les
Hodeir, André
Hodges, Johnny
Holiday, Billie (Elinore Harris)
Hopkins, Claude (Driskett)
Howard, Paul (Leroy)
Humes, Helen
Hutton, Ina Ray
Hyman, Dick (actually, Richard Roven)
Inge, Edward (Frederick)
Ingham, Keith
Jackson, "Bull Moose" Benjamin Clarence
Jackson, Chubby (Greig Stewart)
Jackson, Cliff (actually, Clifton Luther)
Jackson, Dewey
Jackson, Franz (R.)
Jackson, Milt(on; aka "Bags")
Jackson, Preston (originally, McDonald, James Preston)
Jackson, Quentin (Leonard; aka Butter)
James, Elmer (Taylor)
James, Harry (Haag)
Jefferson, Hilton (W.)
Jefferson, Maceo B.
Jenkins, Freddie
Jenkins, George
Johnson, Bill (actually, William)
Johnson, Bill (actually, William K.)
Johnson, Budd (Albert J.)
Johnson, Buddy (Woodrow Wilson)

Johnson, Charlie (actually, Charles Wright)
Johnson, Floyd "Candy"
Johnson, Freddy
Johnson, Gus (Jr.)
Johnson, James P(rice)
Johnson, J. J. (James Louis)
Johnson, Keg (Frederic H.)
Johnson, Lem(uel Charles)
Johnson, Manzie (Isham)
Johnson, Money (Harold)
Johnson, Pete(r)
Johnson, Walter
Jones, Claude B.
Jones, Etta
Jones, Isham
Jones, Jimmy (actually, James Henry)
Jones, Jo(nathan)
Jones, Slick (actually, Wilmore)
Jones, Snags (actually, Clifford)
Jones, Wallace (Leon)
Jordan, Steve (actually, Stephen Philip)
Kahn, Tiny (Norman)
Kaminsky, Max
Kelley, Peck (John Dickson)
Kelly, (Edgar) Guy
Kemp, Hal (actually, James Harold)
Kenton, Stan(ley Newcomb)
Keyes, Joe
Kirby, John
Kirk, Andy (actually, Andrew Dewey)
Kirkpatrick, Don(ald E.)
Konitz, Lee
Krupa, Gene
Kühn, Rolf
Kyser, Kay (actually, James King Kern)
Laine, Cleo (originally, Campbell, Clementina Dinah)
LaPorta, John (D.)
LaVere, Charlie (Johnson, Charles LaVere)
Lawson, Yank (actually John Rhea)
Leeman, Cliff(ord); aka Mr.Time, the Sheriff)
Leitham, John
Leonard, Harlan
Lewis, (Big) Ed (actually, Edward)
Lewis, Sabby (William Sebastian)
Light, Enoch (Henry)
Livingston, Fud (Joseph Anthony)
Livingston, Jay (originally, Levison, Jacob Harold), and Ray(mond Bernard) Evans
Lombardo, Guy (actually, Gaetano Alberto)
Lucie, Lawrence (Larry)
Lundy, Carmen
Lyttleton, Humphrey "Humph" (Richard Adeane)
Marsh, Warne (Marion)
Martin, Freddy
McConnell, Rob
McCorkle, Susannah
McDonough, Dick (actually, Richard)
McKendrick, "Big Mike" (actually, Reuben Michael)
McKendrick, Little Mike (actually, Gilbert Michael)
McKinley, Ray(mond Frederick)
McKinney, Nina Mae
McRae, Teddy (actually, Theodore; aka Mr. Bear)
McShann, Jay (James Columbus; aka Hootie)
Mehegan, John
Metcalf, Louis (Jr.)
Middleton, Velma
Miller, (Alton) Glenn
Miller, Eddie (originally, Muller, Edward Raymond)
Millinder, Lucky (actually, Lucius Venable)
Mince, Johnny (originally, Muenzenberger, John Henry)
Mitchell, George (Little Mitch)
Moncur, Grachan (Jr.)
Moore, Dudley (Stuart John)
Morgan, Al(bert)
Mosley, Snub (Lawrence Leo)
Nance, Ray (Willis)
Nanton, Tricky Sam
Napoleon, Phil (actually, Filippo Napoli)
Napoleon, Teddy (actually, Napoli, Edward George)
Navarro, Fats (actually, Theodore)
Neville Brothers, The
Newton, Frankie (actually, William Frank)
Nichols, Herbie (actually, Herbert Horatio)
Nichols, Red (actually, Ernest Loring)
Noone, Jimmie
Norvo, Red (actually, Norville, Kenneth)
O'Day, Anita (originally, Colton, Anita Belle)
O'Hara, Betty
Oliver, Sy (Melvin James)
Page, Walter
Parenti, Tony (actually, Anthony)
Parrish, Avery
Pastor, Tony (originally, Pestritto, Anthony/Antonio)
Payne, Bennie (actually, Benjamin E.)
Person, Eric
Prima, Louis
Procope, Russell
Quealey, Chelsea
Ramirez, Ram (Roger)
Randolph, Irving "Mouse"
Redman, Don(ald Matthew)
Rosolino, Frank
Royal, Marshal (Walton)
Russell, Luis (Carl)
Salvador, Sal (Sergio)
Sampson, Edgar (Melvin; aka The Lamb)
Sandole, Dennis
Saury, Maxim
Sauter, Eddie (actually, Edward Ernest)
Schoenberg, Loren
Scott, Cecil (Xavier) Jr.
Scott, Hazel (Dorothy)
Scott, Raymond (originally, Warnow, Harry)
Scott, Ronnie
Scott, Tony (originally, Sciacca, Anthony)
Sears, Al(bert Omega)
Sedric, Gene (actually, Eugene Hall; aka "Honey Bear")
Shaughnessy, Ed(win Thomas)
Shavers, Charlie (actually, Charles James)
Shaw, Artie (originally, Arshawsky, Arthur Jacob)
Shaw, Lige (Elijah W.)
Shearing, George (Albert)
Sherman, Jimmy (actually, James Benjamin)
Sherock, Shorty (originally, Cherock, Clarence Francis)
Shirley, Jimmy (actually, James Arthur)
Shu, Eddie (originally, Shulman, Edward)
Sims, Zoot (John Haley)
Singer, Hal (actually, Harold; aka Cornbread)
Sissle, Noble (Lee)
Smalls, Cliff (actually, Clifton Arnold)
Smith, Buster (Henry)
Smith, Floyd (Wonderful)
Smith, Jabbo (Cladys)
Smith, Joe (actually, Joseph C.)
Smith, Pine Top (Clarence)
Smith, Russell (T.; aka "Pops")
Smith, Stuff (Hezekiah Leroy Gordon)
Smith, Tab (Talmadge)
Smith, Warren (Doyle; aka Smitty)
Smith, Willie (actually, William McLeish)
Smith, Willie "The Lion" (originally Bertholoff, William Henry Joseph Bonaparte)
Snow, Valaida
Snowden, Elmer (Chester; aka "Pops")
Socarras, Alberto
South, Eddie (actually, Edward Otha)
Spivak, Charlie (actually, Charles)
Stacy, Jess (Alexandria)
Stark, Bobby (actually, Robert Victor)
Stepton, Rick
Stevenson, George (Edward)
Stewart, Rex (William Jr.)
Stewart, Slam (Leroy Elliott)
Stone, Jesse
Strayhorn, Billy (actually, William Thomas)
Sudhalter, Dick (actually, Richard M.)
Sullivan, Joe (actually, Joseph Michael)
Sullivan, Maxine
Syms, Sylvia
Tate, Buddy (George Holmes)
Tatum, Art(hur, Jr.)
Teagarden, Charlie (actually, Charles; aka Little T)
Teagarden, Jack (Weldon Leo; aka Big T)
Texier, Henri
Tharpe, Sister Rosetta (originally, Nubin, Rosetta)
Thornhill, Claude
Tiberi, Frank
Tizol, Juan (Vincente Martinez)
Trent, Alphonso (also Alphonse)

Bebop

Jones, Thad(deus Joseph)
Jones, Willie (actually, William)
Kahn, Tiny (Norman)
Kaminsky, Max
Kawaguchi, George
Kenton, Stan(ley Newcomb)
Kitamura, Eiji
Klemmer, John
Konitz, Lee
Kühn, Rolf
Kuhn, Steve (actually, Stephen Lewis)
LaFaro, Scott
Laine, Frankie (originally, Lo Vecchio, Francesco Paolo)
Lambert, Dave
LaRoca, Pete (Sims, Peter)
Lawrence, Arnie (Finkelstein, Arnold Lawrence)
Lawrence, Doug(las Marshall)
Laws, Hubert
Lee, Bill (actually, William James Edwards)
Leitch, Peter
Lellis, Tom (actually, Thomas Richard)
Lewis, John (Aaron)
Lewis, Ramsey
Lightsey, Kirk
Lincoln, Abbey (Woolridge, Anna Marie) (Aminata Moseka)
Lovano, Joe
Lytle, Johnny
McCann, Les(lie Coleman; aka Maxie)
McClure, Ron(ald Dix)
McGhee, Howard (B. aka Maggie)
McKee, Andy
McKibbon, Al(fred Benjamin)
McKusick, Hal
McLean, Jackie (aka John Lenwood Jr.; Abdul Kareem; Omar Ahmed)
McNeely, Jim (actually, James Harry)
McNeil, John
McPartland, Marian (originally, Turner, Margaret)
McVea, Jack
Monk, Thelonious (Sphere)
Montgomery, Buddy (Charles F.)
Montgomery, Wes (John Leslie)
Moody, James
Morris, Byron
Mossman, Michael
Mraz, George (Jiri)
Mulligan, Gerry (actually, Gerald Joseph Mulligan)
Murphy, Mark
Navarro, Fats (actually, Theodore)
Nelson, Oliver (Edward)
Nicholas, Albert (Nick)
Nichols, Herbie (actually, Herbert Horatio)
Nichols, Red (actually, Ernest Loring)
Nordine, Ken
Norvo, Red (actually, Norville, Kenneth)
Otis, Johnny (John Veliotes)
Paich, Marty
Parker, Charlie (actually, Charles Jr.)
Parker, Kim
Parlan, Horace (Louis)
Pass, Joe (originally, Passalaqua, Joseph Anthony Jacobi)
Pepper, Art(hur Edward Jr.)
Person, Houston
Peterson, Oscar
Petrucciani, Michel
Pettiford, Oscar
Piket, Roberta
Ponomarev, Valery
Potter, Chris
Powell, Sheldon
Prysock, Arthur "Red"
Puente, Tito
Purdie, Bernard (Pretty)
Quebec, Ike (Abrams)
Reid, Rufus (L.)
Rice, Charlie
Rollins, Sonny (Theodore Walter)
Rosenthal, Ted
Rosnes, Renee (Irene Louise)
Rouse, Charlie
Rudolph, Steve
Ruff, Willie (Henry, Jr.)
Ruiz, Hilton
Sandoval, Arturo
Schnitter, David (Bertram)
Schuller, George
Schuur, Diane ("Deedles")
Scott, Bobby
Scott, Ronnie
Scott, Shirley
Scott, Tony (originally, Sciacca, Anthony)
Sears, Al(bert Omega)
Shank, Bud (Clifford Everett Jr.)
Shavers, Charlie (actually, Charles James)
Shaw, Lige (Elijah W.)
Shaw, Woody (Herman II)
Shearing, George (Albert)
Shorter, Wayne
Shu, Eddie (originally, Shulman, Edward)
Sims, Zoot (John Haley)
Singer, Hal (actually, Harold; aka Cornbread)
Smalls, Cliff (actually, Clifton Arnold)
Smith, Jimmy (actually, James Oscar Jr.)
Smith, Russell (T.; aka "Pops")
Smith, Stuff (Hezekiah Leroy Gordon)
Smith, Tab (Talmadge)
Smith, Warren (Doyle; aka Smitty)
Smith, Willie "The Lion" (originally Bertholoff, William Henry Joseph Bonaparte)
Stamm, Marvin
Staton, Dakota (Aliyah Rabia)
Stepton, Rick
Stitt, Sonny (Edward)
Strozier, Frank
Stubblefield, John(ny IV)
Sullivan, Ira (Brevard Jr.)
Tabnik, Richard
Talbert, Thomas
Tana, Akira
Taylor, Art(hur S., Jr.)
Taylor, Billy (actually, William Edward Jr.)
Terry, Clark (Mumbles)
Thielemans, Toots
Thomas, Leon (actually, Amos Leone, Jr.)
Thomas, Rene
Thompson, "Sir" Charles
Tjader, Cal(len Radcliffe, Jr.)
Torff, Brian (Quade)
Treadwell, George (McKinley)
Tucker, Mickey
Turrentine, Stanley (William)
Tyner, (Alfred) McCoy
Vaughan, Sarah (Lois)
Vignola, Frank
Vinnegar, Leroy
Vinson, Eddie "Cleanhead"
Vitro, Roseanna
Waits, Tom
Wallington, George
Washington, Grover, Jr.
Watanabe, Sadao
Watkins, Julius
Watts, Ernie
Weiskopf, Joel
Weiskopf, Walt(er David)
Weston, Randy
Wilkerson, Don
Williams, "Buster"
Williams (Goreed), Joe (actually, Joseph)
Willis, Larry
Wilson, Nancy
Wilson, Steve
Winchester, Lem(uel Davis)
Winter, Paul
Wood, Vishnu (William Crawford)
Woodard, Rickey
Woods, Phil(ip Wells)
Yellin, Pete
Young, Lee (actually, Leonidas Raymond)

Avant-garde

Abdullah, Ahmed
Abe, Kaoru
Adams, Pepper (Park III)
Adderley, Cannonball (Julian Edwin)
Adderley, Nat(haniel Sr.)
Ade, Sunny (Prince Sunday Adeniyi Adegeye)
Aebersold, Jamey
Akagi, Kei
Alcorn, Alvin (Elmore)
Ali, Rashied (originally Patterson, Robert)
Allen, Geri
Almeida, Laurindo
Altschul, Barry
Amirkhanian, Charles (Benjamin)
Ammons, Gene (Eugene; "Jug")
Amsallem, Franck
Anderson, Ray (Robert)
Ayler, Albert
Bark, Jan (Helge Guttorm)
Barker, Danny (actually Daniel Moses)
Bauer, Billy (actually, William Henry)
Benson, George
Berardi, Sangeeta Michael
Berne, Tim
Blackman, Cindy

Young, La Monte (Thornton)
Young, Larry (aka Aziz, Khalid Yasin Abdul)
Zawinul, Joe
Zeitlin, Denny

Revivalist

Alexander, Monty (Montgomery Bernard)
Allen, Carl
Allison, Ben
Anderson, Wessell ("Warmdaddy")
Aula, Giacomo
Azzolina, Jay
Bargad, Rob
Berger, Dave
Berger, Kenny
Bilk, (Mr.) Acker (Bernard Stanley)
Bowen, Ralph (Michael)
Brown, Steve (Theodore)
Brunis, (originally Brunies), Georg(e Clarence)
Bryson, Jeanie
Bunnett, Jane
Burno, Dwayne
Burton, Gary
Butterfield, Paul
Campbell, John (Elwood II)
Carmichael, Judy
Carrington, Terri Lyne
Carroll, Barbara (actually, Coppersmith, Barbara Carole)
Carter, James
Charlap, Bill
Chestnut, Cyrus
Clarke, Stanley (M.)
Colley, Scott
Coltrane, Ravi (John)
Connick, Harry Jr.
Copeland, Keith (Lamont)
Daniels, Eddie (actually, Edward Kenneth)
De Francesco, Joey
DeRose, Dena
Dyson, Willard
Eubanks, Robin
Fagan, Chris
Feather, (Billie Jane Lee) Lorraine
Ferrell, Rachelle
Ford, Ricky (actually, Richard Allen)
Fountain, Pete
Fox, Donal
Freelon, Nnenna
Garrett, Kenny
Handy, Craig (Mitchell)
Hara (Tsukahara), Nobuo
Hargrove, Roy (Anthony Jr.)
Harrison, Donald
Hart, Antonio
Jackson, Javon
Johnston, Randy
Juris, Vic
Klugh, Earl
Kohlman, (Louis) Freddie
Krall, Diana (Jean)
Lyttleton, Humphrey "Humph" (Richard Adeane)
McBride, Christian
McFerrin, Bobby (actually, Robert)
McGarity, (Robert) Lou(is)
Moore, Ralph
Murphy, Turk (Melvin Edward Alton)
Narell, Andy
Nascimento, Milton
Neumeister, Ed (actually, Edward Paul)
Neville, Chris
Parker, Leon
Pine, Courtney
Pizzarelli, John (Paul Jr.)
Porter, Art
Redman, Joshua
Reeves, Diane
Roberts, Marcus (Marthaniel)
Roney, Wallace
Rubalcaba, Gonzalo
Rubin, Vanessa
Sanabria, Bobby (actually, Robert D.)
Sanborn, David
Sidran, Ben
Siegel, Janis
Stryker, Dave (actually, David Michael)
Vache, Warren (Webster Jr.),
Watters, Lu(cious)
Watts, Jeff "Tain"
Whalum, Kirk
White, Barry
Whitfield, Mark
Williams, James
Williams, Jessica
Williams, Willie

POPULAR

Country

Acuff, Roy (Clayton)
Arnold, Eddy (originally, Richard Edward)
Atkins, Chet (originally, Chester Burton)
Autry, Gene (originally Orvin Gene Autry)
Brooks, Garth
Bryant, Boudleaux (Diadorius) and Felice (Matilda Genevieve Scaduto)
Buffett, Jimmy
Byrds, The
Campbell, Glen (G. Travis C.)
Carter Family, The
Cash, Johnny
Cash, Rosanne
Cline, Patsy (originally, Hensley, Virginia Patterson)
Crowell, Rodney
Denver, John (originally, Deutschendorf, Henry John)
Exile
Fender, Freddy (originally, Huerta, Baldemar)
Flatt and Scruggs
Foley, Red (Clyde Julian)
Ford, Tennessee Ernie (actually, Ernest Jennings)
Haggard, Merle (M. Ronald)
Harris, Emmylou
Hill, Faith
Husky, Ferlin
Ives, Burl (Icle Ivanhoe)
Jackson, Wanda
Jennings, Waylon
Jones, George
Judds, The
Kristofferson, Kris
Lee, Brenda (originally, Tarpley, Brenda May)
Lynn, Loretta (née Webb)
Macon, "Uncle" Dave (actually, David Harrison)
Mandrell, Barbara (Ann)
McEntire, Reba
Monroe, Bill (actually, William Smith)
Murray, Anne
Nelson, Willie (actually, William Hugh)
Page, Patti (originally, Fowler, Clara Ann)
Parton, Dolly (Rebecca)
Pride, Charley
Reeves, Jim (actually, James Travis)
Robbins, Marty (originally, Robinson, Martin David)
Rodgers, Jimmie (actually, James Charles)
Seeger, Mike
Seeger, Pete(r) R.
Skaggs, Ricky
Smith, Carl (M.)
Snow, Hank (Clarence Eugene)
Stanley Brothers, The
Thompson, Hank (Henry William)
Tubb, Ernest (Dale)
Twain, Shania (originally, Eileen Evans)
Wagoner, Porter (Wayne)
Walker, Jerry Jeff (originally, Crosby, Ronald Clyde)
Watson, Doc (Arthel Lane)
Wells, Kitty (originally, Deason, Ellen Muriel)
Williams, Hank (Hiram)
Wills, Bob (actually, James Robert)
Wiseman, Mac (Malcolm B.)
Wynette, Tammy (real name, Pugh, Virginia Wynette)
Young, Faron

Pop

ABBA
Adler, Richard
Almanac Singers, The
Alpert, Herb
American Quartet, The
Andrews, Julie (originally Julia Elizabeth Wells)
Andrews Sisters, The
Anka, Paul
Arlen, Harold (Hyman Arluck)
Ashman, Howard
Association, The
Astaire, Fred (originally Frederick E. Austerlitz Jr.)
Austin, Gene
Bacharach, Burt
Baez, Joan
Bailey, Mildred (Eleanor Rinker)
Barenaked Ladies
Barry, Jeff and Ellie Greenwich
Bassey, Shirley
Belafonte, Harry (actually, Harold George Jr.)

Lisa Lisa and Cult Jam
Lloyd Webber, Sir Andrew
Loggins and Messina
Luboff, Norman
Macdonough, Harry (John S. MacDonald)
Maltby, Richard Jr., and David Shire
Mancini, Henry (Enrico Nicola)
Manhattan Transfer, The
Mann, Barry, and Cynthia Weil
Martin, Dean (originally, Crocetti, Dino Paul)
Martin, Hugh, and Ralph Blane (Uriah Hunsecker)
Martin, Mary (Virginia)
Martino, Al(fred Cini)
Marx, Richard
Mathis, Johnny
McDonald, Michael
McGuire Sisters, The
McHugh, Jimmy (actually, James Francis)
Mercer, Johnny (actually, John Herndon)
Merman, Ethel (originally, Zimmermann, Ethel Agnes)
Merrill, Bob (originally, Lavan, Henry Robert Merrill)
Michael, George (originally, Panayiotous, Georgios Kryiacos)
Midler, Bette
Miller, (Alton) Glenn
Mills Brothers, The
Minnelli, Liza
Mitchell, Joni (originally, Anderson, Roberta Joan)
Monaco, James V.
Monroe, Vaughn
Morgan, Russ
Morgan (Riggins), Helen
Murray, Billy (actually, William Thomas)
New Christy Minstrels, The
Niles, John Jacob
Ocean, Billy (originally, Charles, Leslie Sebastian)
Ochs, Phil
O'Day, Anita (originally, Colton, Anita Belle)
Ohio Players
Osmond, Donny and Marie
Page, Patti (originally, Fowler, Clara Ann)
Palmer, Robert (Alan)
Partridge Family, The
Paul, Les (originally, Polfuss, Lester William)
Paul Revere and The Raiders
Peerless Quartet, The
Peter, Paul & Mary
Pomus, Doc (originally, Felder, Jerome E.)
Rawls, Lou
Ray, Johnnie (actually, John Alvin)
Reddy, Helen
REO Speedwagon
Richie, Lionel
Rivers, Johnny (originally, Ramistella, John)
Robeson, Paul (Leroy Bustill)
Sade (actually, Helen Folsade Audu)
Sainte-Marie, Buffy
Seal (originally, Samuel, Sealhenry)
Seals and Crofts
Searchers, The
Sedaka, Neil
Selena (Quintanilla Perez)
Sheila E(scovedo)
Shirelles, The
Shore, Dinah (Frances Rose)
Simon, Carly
Simon and Garfunkel
Simply Red
Sinatra, Frank (actually, Francis Albert)
Sinatra, Nancy
Sly & The Family Stone
Smith, Kate (actually, Kathryn Elizabeth)
Smiths, The
Southern, Jeri (actually, Genevieve Hering)
Spice Girls
Streisand, Barbra
Tiffany (Renee Darwish)
Tiny Tim (originally, Khaury, Herbert Buckingham)
Tony Orlando and Dawn
Tormé (Torme), Mel(vin Howard)
Toto
UB40
Van Heusen, James "Jimmy" (originally, Babcock, Edward Chester)
Vega, Suzanne
Ventures, The
Vinton, Bobby (actually, Stanley Robert)
Waller, "Fats" (Thomas Wright)
Waring, Fred(eric Malcolm)
Warren, Diane
Warren, Harry (originally, Guaragna, Salvatore)
Warwick, Dionne
Washington, Dinah
Waters, Muddy (real name, McKinley Morganfield)
Weavers, The
Webb, Jimmy
Whiteman, Paul (Samuel)
Williams, Vanessa
Willson, (Robert) Meredith (Reiniger)
Wilson, Cassandra
Wilson, Nancy
Winston, George
Wonder, Stevie (originally, Morris, Steveland)
Youmans, Vincent (Millie)
Young, Neil
(Young) Rascals, The

R&B/Rap

Baker, Anita
Baker, Lavern (Dolores Williams)
Ballard, Hank
Beastie Boys
Benton, Brook (Benjamin Peay)
Bland, Bobby "Blue" (originally Robert Calvin)
Bofill, Angela
Booker T & the MGs
Bostic, Earl
Brandy, (actually, Norwood Brandy)
Brown, Bobby
Brown, James
Brown, Ruth (née Alston Weston)
Bryson, Peabo (Pepo Bryson)
Burke, Solomon
Butler, Jerry
Butterfield, Paul
Calloway, Cab(ell III)
Cameo
Carey, Mariah
Charles, Ray (originally, Robinson, Ray Charles)
Cliff, Jimmy (Chambers, James)
Clinton, George
Clovers, The
Coasters, The
Cole, Nat "King" (originally, Coles, Nathaniel Adams)
Cole, Natalie
Coleman, George (Edward)
Combs, Sean "Puffy" (aka "Puff Daddy")
Commodores, The
Cooke, Sam
Coolio (originally, Ivey, Artis)
Cray, Robert
Davis, Reverend Gary D.
DeBarge
Dixon, Willie (James)
DJ Jazzy Jeff and the Fresh Prince
Dr. Dre (originally, Young, Andre)
Earth, Wind and Fire
Edmonds, Kenneth ("Babyface")
Elliott, Missy "Misdemeanor" (actually, Melissa Arnette)
En Vogue
Fifth Dimension, The
Four Tops, The
Franklin, Aretha
Gaye, Marvin (originally, Marvin Gay Jr.)
Gladys Knight and The Pips
Gordy, Berry Jr.
Grandmaster Flash (originally, Saddler, Joseph)
Green, Al (originally, Greene)
Handy, W(illiam) C(hristopher)
Havens, Richie
Hayes, Isaac
Hill, Lauryn
Hooker, John Lee
Howlin' Wolf (originally, Burnett, Chester Arthur)
Impressions, The
Ingram, James
Isley Brothers, The
Jackson, Janet
Jackson, Mahalia
Jackson, Michael
James, Elmore (originally, Brooks, Elmore)
James, Etta (originally, Hawkins, Jamesetta)
James, Rick (originally, Johnson, James Jr.)
John, Little Willie (actually, William)

Johnson, Henry
Johnson, Robert (Leroy)
Jordan, Louis (Thomas)
Junior Walker and The All Stars
Kelly, R(obert)
Khan, Chaka (Yvette Marie Stevens)
King, B. B. (Riley B.)
King, Ben(jamin) E(arl Nelson)
King (Ousley), Curtis
Kool and the Gang
LaBelle
Lead Belly (originally, Ledbetter, Huddie)
Leiber, Jerry (Jerome), and Mike (Michael Endore) Stoller
Lisa Lisa and Cult Jam
Little Anthony and the Imperials
Lynne, Gloria
Marie, Teena (originally, Brockert, Mary Christine)
Marley, Bob (actually, Robert Nesta)
Martha and the Vandellas
Marvelettes, The
MC Lyte (originally, Moorer, Lana)
McPhatter, Clyde
Moonglows, The
New Edition
Notorious B.I.G. (originally, Wallace, Christopher)
N.W.A.
Ohio Players
Otis, Johnny (John Veliotes)
Pickett, Wilson
Platters, The
Pointer Sisters, The
Pomus, Doc (originally, Felder, Jerome E.)
Price, Lloyd
Prince (Roger Nelson)
Public Enemy
Queen Latifah (originally, Owens, Dana Elaine)
Redding, Otis
Reed, Jimmy
Richie, Lionel
Righteous Brothers, The
Rufus
Run-DMC
Salt-N-Pepa
Sam and Dave
Scott, Shirley
Sheila E(scovedo)
Sledge, Percy
Sly & The Family Stone
Smith, Bessie (Elizabeth)
Smith, Clara
Smith, Mamie (Robinson)
Smith, Tab (Talmadge)
Snoop Dogg (originally, Broadus, Calvin; aka Snoop Doggy Dogg)
Spinners, The
Stylistics, The
Sugarhill Gang, The
Summer, Donna (originally, Gaines, LaDonna)
Supremes, The
Temptations, The
Terrell, Tammi (Thomasina Montgomery)
TLC
Turner, (Big) Joe (actually, Joseph Vernon Turner Jr.)
Turner, Ike and Tina
Vandross, Luther
Vinson, Eddie "Cleanhead"
Warwick, Dionne
Washington, Dinah
Waters, Ethel
Waters, Muddy (real name, McKinley Morganfield)
Watley, Jody
Williams, Deniece
Williams, Vanessa
Wilson, Jackie
Wilson, Steve
Womack, Bobby
Wonder, Stevie (originally, Morris, Steveland)
Wu-Tang Clan
(Young) Rascals, The

Rock

AC/DC
Adams, Bryan
Aerosmith
Allman Brothers Band, The
Animals, The
Band, The
Bangles, The
Barenaked Ladies
Beach Boys, The
Beastie Boys
Beatles, The
Beck (David Campbell)
Beck, Jeff
Berry, Chuck (actually, Charles Edward Anderson)
Blasters, The
Blondie
Blood, Sweat and Tears
Blue Öyster Cult
Blues Traveler
Bon Jovi
Boston
Bowie, David (originally, Jones, David)
Box Tops, The
Bread
Browne, Jackson
Buffalo Springfield
Buffett, Jimmy
Burnette, Johnny, and Dorsey Burnette
Bush, Kate (Catherine)
Buzzcocks, The
Byrds, The
Canned Heat
Cannon, Freddie "Boom Boom" (Freddy Picariello)
Captain Beefheart (Don Van Vliet)
Carnes, Kim
Cars, The
Chad and Jeremy
Chicago
Clapton, Eric (originally, Clapp, Eric Patrick)
Clash, The
Clinton, George
Cochran, Eddie
Cockburn, Bruce
Cocker, Joe (John)
Cohen, Leonard
Cole, Paula
Cooder, Ry
Cooper, Alice
Costello, Elvis (originally, McManus, Declan)
Cranberries, The
Cream
Creedence Clearwater Revival
Crosby, Stills, Nash (and Young)
Crow, Sheryl
Culture Club
Dave Matthews Band
Def Leppard
Depeche Mode
Devo
Diddley, Bo (originally, McDaniel, Ellas)
Dion (DiMucci) and The Belmonts
Domino, Fats (actually, Antoine)
Donovan (Leitch)
Doors, The
Duran Duran
Dylan, Bob (originally, Zimmerman, Robert)
Eagles
Eddy, Duane
Electric Light Orchestra (ELO)
Emerson, Lake and Palmer
Etheridge, Melissa
Eurythmics
Everly Brothers, The
Exile
Fairport Convention
Faithfull, Marianne
Fame, Georgie (originally, Powell, Clive)
Fleetwood Mac
Flying Burrito Brothers, The
Fogelberg, Dan
Frampton, Peter
Fugs, The
Gary Puckett and The Union Gap
Geldof, Bob
Genesis
Go-Go's, The
Goo Goo Dolls
Grass Roots, The
Grateful Dead, The
Green Day
Guess Who, The
Guns N' Roses
Hall and Oates
Harrison, George
Heart
Hendrix, Jimi (actually, James Marshall)
Henley, Don
Herman's Hermits
Hiatt, John
Hicks, Dan
Hollies, The
Holly, Buddy (actually, Charles Hardin)
Hooters, The
Huey Lewis and the News
Hüsker Dü
Idol, Billy (originally, Broad, William Michael Albert)

Indigo Girls, The
INXS
Iron Butterfly
Iron Maiden
Jackson, Joe
Jam, The
Jane's Addiction
Jefferson Airplane
Jethro Tull
Jett (Larkin), Joan
J. Geils Band, The
Joel, Billy
John, Elton (originally, Dwight, Reginald)
John, Little Willie (actually, William)
Jones, Rickie Lee
Joplin, Janis
Journey
Joy Division
Judas Priest
Kansas
Kingsmen, The
Kinks, The
Kiss
Kooper, Al
Lauper, Cyndi (actually, Cynthia Ann Stephanie)
Led Zeppelin
Lennon, John
Lewis, Jerry Lee
Little Feat
Little Richard (originally, Penniman, Richard)
Living Colour
Los Lobos
Love
Lovin' Spoonful, The
Lynyrd Skynyrd
Madonna (Louise Ciccone)
Mamas and the Papas, The
Manfred Mann
Manson, Marilyn (originally, Warner, Brian)
Marshall Tucker Band, The
Mayall, John
McCartney, Paul
MC5
McLachlan, Sarah
Meat Loaf (originally, Aday, Marvin Lee)
Mellencamp, John
Metallica
Miller, Steve
Mitch Ryder and the Detroit Wheels
Moby Grape
Monkees, The
Moody Blues, The
Morrison, Van (actually, George Ivan)
Mötley Crüe
Mott the Hoople
Nelson, Rick (Eric)
New York Dolls
Nilsson, Harry
Nirvana
Nugent, Ted
Nyro, Laura
Orbison, Roy
Osbourne, Ozzy (actually, John Michael)
Palmer, Robert (Alan)
Parker, Graham
Parsons, Alan
Paul Revere and The Raiders
Pearl Jam
Perkins, Carl
Pink Floyd
Pitney, Gene
Poco
Police, The
Pop, Iggy (originally, Osterberg, James Jewel)
Presley, Elvis
Pretenders, The
Procol Harum
Queen
Quicksilver Messenger Service
Raitt, Bonnie
Ramones, The
Raspberries
Red Hot Chili Peppers
Reed, Lou(is Alan)
R.E.M.
Rockpile
Rolling Stones, The
Ronettes, The
Ronstadt, Linda
Roxy Music
Rundgren, Todd
Rush
Russell, Leon (Hank Wilson)
Sahm, Doug
Sam the Sham & the Pharaohs
Santana
Sayer, Leo (Gerard Hugh)
Scaggs, Boz (actually, Scaggs, William Royce)
Seal (originally, Samuel, Sealhenry)
Seeger, Pete(r) R.
Seger, Bob
Sex Pistols, The
Sha Na Na
Shannon, Del (originally, Westover, Charles)
Simon, Carly
Simple Minds
Slade
Small Faces
Smashing Pumpkins
Smith, Chas
Smith, Patti
Sonny and Cher
Soundgarden
Specials, The
Spector, Phil
Spirit
Spooky Tooth
Springfield, Dusty (originally, O'Brien, Mary Isabel Catherine Bernadette)
Springfield, Rick (originally, Springthorpe, Richard)
Springsteen, Bruce
Squeeze
Starr, Ringo (originally, Starkey, Richard)
Steely Dan
Steppenwolf
Stevens, Cat (originally, Georgiou, Steven)
Stewart, Rod
Styx
Talking Heads
Taylor, James
10cc
Tom Petty and the Heartbreakers
T. Rex
Turtles, The
U2
Valens, Ritchie (originally, Valenzuela, Richard)
Van Halen
Vaughan Brothers, The
Velvet Underground, The
Vincent, Gene (originally, Craddock, Vincent Eugene)
Walsh, Joe
War
Wells, Mary
Who, The
Wilson, Jackie
Wilson Phillips
Winter, Johnny and Edgar
Winwood, Steve (also known as Stevie)
X
Yardbirds, The
Yes
Young, Neil
Youngbloods, The
Zappa, Frank (actually, Francis Vincent)
Zombies, The

Nationality INDEX

Anderson, "Cat" (William Alonzo)
Anderson, Chris
Anderson, Ed(ward) ("Andy")
Anderson, (Evelyn) Ruth
Anderson, Ivie (Marie; "Ivy")
Anderson, June
Anderson, Laurie
Anderson, Leroy
Anderson, Marian
Anderson, Ray (Robert)
Anderson, T(homas) J(efferson Jr.)
Anderson, Wessell ("Warmdaddy")
Andrews Sisters, The
Anievas, Agustin
Antes, John
Antheil, George (actually, Georg Carl Johann)
Anthony, Charles (real name, Carlogero Antonio Caruso)
Anthony, James R(aymond)
Anthony (Antonini), Ray(mond)
Antokoletz, Elliott (Maxim)
Applebaum, Edward
Appleman, Rich
Appleton, Jon (Howard)
Apthorp, William Foster
Arel, Bülent
Argento, Dominick
Arlen, Harold (Hyman Arluck)
Armstrong, Karan
Armstrong (born Hardin), Lil(ian)
Armstrong, Louis
Arnold, Byron
Arnold, Eddy (originally, Richard Edward)
Arodin (Arnondrin), Sidney (J.)
Arrau, Claudio
Arroyo, Martina
Artzt, Alice (Josephine)
Asawa, Brian
Aschaffenburg, Walter
Ashforth, Alden (Banning)
Ashley, Robert (Reynolds)
Ashman, Howard
Asia, Daniel
Association, The
Astaire, Fred (originally Frederick E. Austerlitz Jr.)
Atchley, Kenneth
Atkins, Chet (originally, Chester Burton)
Atlas, Allan W(arren)
Auer, Edward
Auger, Arleen (Joyce)
Augustus, Janice G.
Auld, Georgie (born John Altwerger)
Austin, Gene
Austin, Larry (Don)
Austin, Lovie (born Cora Calhoun)
Austin, William W(eaver)
Autori, Franco
Autry, Gene (originally Orvin Gene Autry)
Avshalomov, Aaron
Ax, Emanuel
Ayler, Albert
Ayres, Frederic (real name, Frederick Ayres Johnson)
Azzolina, Jay
Babbitt, Milton (Byron)
Babin, Victor
Babitz, Sol
Bach, Jan (Morris)
Bacharach, Burt
Bacon, Ernst
Badea, Christian
Baez, Joan
Bailey, Buster (William C.)
Bailey, Mildred (Eleanor Rinker)
Bain, Wilfred
Baird, Julianne
Baird, Martha
Baker, Anita
Baker, Benjamin Franklin
Baker, Chet (actually, Chesney Henry)
Baker, Claude
Baker, David (Nathaniel)
Baker, Julius
Baker, Lavern (Dolores Williams)
Baker, Theodore
Baldwin
Bales, Richard (Henry Horner)
Ballantine, Edward
Ballard, Hank
Ballard, Louis W(ayne)
Ballou, Esther (Williamson)
Balsam, Artur
Bamberger, Carl
Bampton, Rose (Elizabeth)
Band, The
Bangles, The
Barab, Seymour
Barati, George (real name, György Baráti)
Barbarin, Paul (Adolphe)
Barber, Samuel
Barbour, J(ames) Murray
Bargad, Rob
Barker, Danny (actually Daniel Moses)
Barkin, Elaine R(adoff)
Barlow, Harold
Barlow, Howard
Barlow, Samuel L(atham) M(itchell)
Barlow, Wayne (Brewster)
Barnet, Charlie (actually, Charles Daly)
Barnett, Bonnie
Barnett, John (Manley)
Baron, Samuel
Barrére, Georges
Barron, Bill (actually, William Jr.)
Barron, Kenny (actually, Kenneth)
Barrueco, Manuel
Barry, Jeff and Ellie Greenwich
Barry, Jerome
Bartlett, Homer Newton
Barto, Tzimon, (real name, John Barto Smith, Jr.)
Barzun, Jacques (Martin)
Basie, Count (real name, William)
Bassett, Leslie (Raymond)
Bassey, Shirley
Bates, Leon
Battle, Kathleen (Deanna)
Bauer, Billy (actually, William Henry)
Bauer, Harold
Bauer, Marion (Eugenie)
Bauer, Ross
Baum, Kurt
Bavicchi, John (Alexander)
Bazelon, Irwin (Allen)
Beach, Mrs. H.H.A. (née Amy Marcy Cheney)
Beach Boys, The
Beardslee, Bethany
Beastie Boys
Beattie, Herbert (Wilson)
Bechet, Sidney (Joseph)
Beck (David Campbell)
Beck, Johann H(einrich)
Beck, Sydney
Becker, Frank
Becker, Gustave Louis
Becker, John J(oseph)
Beglarian, Eve
Beglarian, Grant
Béhague, Gerard H(enri)
Behrens, Jack
Beiderbecke, Bix (actually Leon Bix)
Belafonte, Harry (actually, Harold George Jr.)
Belcher, Supply
Bell, Joshua
Benary, Barbara
Bennard, George
Bennett, Robert Russell
Bennett, Tony (originally, Anthony Dominick Benedetto)
Benson, George
Benson, Joan
Benson, Warren (Frank)
Benton, Brook (Benjamin Peay)
Benton, Rita
Bentonelli (real name, Benton), Joseph (Horace)
Benzell, Mimi
Berardi, Sangeeta Michael
Berberian, Cathy (actually, Catherine)
Berezowsky, Nicolai
Berg, Bob (actually, Robert)
Berger, Arthur (Victor)
Berger, Dave
Berger, Jean
Berger, Kenny
Bergman, Alan and Marilyn (Keith)
Bergsma, William (Laurence)
Berigan, Bunny (Rowland Bernard)
Berlin, Irving (originally, Baline, Israel)
Berlinski, Herman
Berne, Tim
Bernheimer, Martin
Bernstein, Lawrence F.
Bernstein, Leonard (actually, Louis)
Bernstein, Martin
Berry, Chu (actually, Leon Brown)
Berry, Chuck (actually, Charles Edward Anderson)
Berry, Wallace (Taft)
Bessaraboff, Nicholas (actually, Nikolai)
Bethune (Green), Thomas
Beversdorf, (Samuel) Thomas
Bible, Frances
Bielawa, Herbert
Bigard, Barney (Alban Leon)
Biggs, E(dward George) Power
Billings, William
Bilson, Malcolm

Diemer, Emma Lou
Dietz, Howard
Di Giuseppe, Enrico
Diller, Angela
Dilling, Mildred
Di Meola, Al
Dinerstein, Norman (Myron)
Dion (DiMucci) and The Belmonts
Ditson, Oliver
Dixon, Bill (actually, William Robert)
Dixon, (Charles) Dean
Dixon, James
Dixon, Willie (James)
DJ Jazzy Jeff and the Fresh Prince
Dlugoszewski, Lucia
Doane, William H(oward)
Dobbs, Mattiwilda
Dodds, Baby (actually, Warren)
Dodds, Johnny (actually, John M.)
Dodge, Charles (Malcolm)
Doggett, Bill (actually, William Ballard)
Doktor, Paul (Karl)
Dolphy, Eric (Allan)
Domino, Fats (actually, Antoine)
Donahue, Sam(uel Koontz)
Donaldson, Walter J.
Donath, Helen (née Erwin)
Donato, Anthony
Donovan, Richard Frank
Dooley, William (Edward)
Doors, The
Doran, Matt (Higgins)
Doráti, Antal
Dorian, Frederick (real name, Friedrich Deutsch)
Dorough, Bob (actually, Robert)
Dorsey, Jimmy (actually, James Francis)
Dorsey, Tommy (actually, Thomas Francis Jr.)
Dougherty, Celius (Hudson)
Douglas, Dave (actually, David Dewel)
Douglass, Bill
Downes, Edward O(lin) D(avenport)
Downes, (Edwin) Olin
Downey, John (Wilham)
Doyle, Arthur
Dräger, Hans-Heinz
Dragon, Carmen
Drake, Alfred (real name, Alfredo Capurro)
Drake, Earl R(oss)
Dr. Dre (originally, Young, Andre)
Dresher, Paul (Joseph)
Drew, James
Drew, Kenny (actually, Kenneth Sidney)
Drinker, Henry S(andwith, Jr.)
Drogin, Barry (Jay)
Druckman, Jacob (Raphael)
Drummond, Billy
Drummond, Dean
Drummond, Ray
Drury, Stephen
Dubin, Al(exander)
Duckles, Vincent H(arris)
Duckworth, William (Ervin)
Ducloux, Walter (Ernest)
Duesing, Dale
Dufallo, Richard (John)
Duffy, John
Duke, Doug(las) (originally, Ovidio Fernandez)
Duke, John (Woods)
Duke, Vernon (originally, Dukelsky, Vladimir)
Dukelsky, Vladimir (Alexandrovich)
Dunbar, Ted (actually, Earl Theodore Dunbar Jr.)
Duncan, (Robert) Todd
Dunlap, Arlene
Dunlap, Richard
Dunn, James Philip
Dunn, Johnny
Dunn, Mignon
Dunn, Susan
Dunn, Thomas (Burt)
Durham, Eddie
Dutrey, Honore
Dwight, John Sullivan
Dyer-Bennet, Richard
Dykema, Peter (William)
Dylan, Bob (originally, Zimmerman, Robert)
Dyson, Willard
Eagles
Eames, Emma (Hayden)
Earhart, Will
Earth, Wind and Fire
Eastman, George
Eaton, John (Charles)
Eberhard, Dennis
Eckert, Rinde
Eckstine, Billy (actually, William Clarence Eckstein)
Eddy, Duane
Eddy, (Hiram) Clarence
Edison, Harry Sweets
Edmonds, Kenneth ("Babyface")
Edmunds, John (actually, Charles Sterling)
Edson, Lewis
Edwards, Bass (Henry)
Edwards, Cliff (actually, Clifton A.; aka Ukulele Ike)
Edwards, Eddie (actually Edwin Branford; aka Daddy)
Edwards, Julian
Effinger, Cecil
Ehlers, Alice (Pauly)
Ehrlich, Marty
Eichheim, Henry
Einstein, Alfred
Eisenberg, Maurice
El-Dabh, Halim (Abdul Messieh)
Eldridge, (David) Roy (aka Little Jazz)
Elf, Mark
Elfman, Danny
Elias, Rosalind
Elkus, Albert (Israel)
Elkus, Jonathan (Britton)
Ellington, Duke (actually, Edward Kennedy)
Ellinwood, Leonard (Webster)
Elliott, Missy "Misdemeanor" (actually, Melissa Arnette)
Ellis, Brent
Ellis, Don(ald Johnson)
Elman, Mischa (actually, Mikhail Saulovich)
Elman, Ziggy (originally, Finkelman, Harry)
Elmore, Robert Hall
Elson, Arthur
Elson, Louis (Charles)
Elston, Arnold
Elwell, Herbert
Emerson, Luther Orlando
Emery, Stephen Albert
Emmett, Daniel Decatur
Engel, Carl
Engel, Lehman
English, Granville
En Vogue
Eppert, Carl
Epstein, David M(ayer)
Erb, Donald (James)
Erickson, Robert
Erwin, Pee Wee (actually, George)
Escot, Pozzi
Escovedo, Pete
Esham, Faith
Estefan, Gloria (Maria née Fajardo)
Estes, Simon (Lamont)
Etheridge, Melissa
Etler, Alvin (Derald)
Eubanks, Robin
Europe, James Reese
Evans, Gil (originally, Green, Ian Ernest Gilmore)
Evans, Herschel
Evans, Richard (Joseph) Bunger
Everly Brothers, The
Evett, Robert
Ewen, David
Ewing, Maria (Louise)
Exile
Fabian (actually, Forte, Fabiano)
Fagan, Chris
Fain, Sammy (originally, Samuel Feinberg)
Fairchild, Blair
Fairlamb, James Remington
Faith, Percy
Falcon, Ruth
Falletta, JoAnn
Farberman, Harold
Farkas, Philip (Francis)
Farley, Carole Ann
Farrar, Geraldine
Farrell, Eileen
Farrell, Joe
Farwell, Arthur (George)
Faulk, Dan
Faull, Ellen
Fay, Amy (Amelia Muller)
Fay, Maude
Feather, (Billie Jane Lee) Lorraine
Feather, Leonard (Geoffrey Feder)
Feinstein, Michael
Felciano, Richard
Feldman, Jill
Feldman, Morton
Feliciano, José
Fender, Freddy (originally, Huerta, Baldemar)
Fennell, Frederick

Mentzner, Susanne
Menuhin, Hephzibah
Mercer, Johnny (actually, John Herndon)
Merman, Ethel (originally, Zimmermann, Ethel Agnes)
Merriam, Alan P(arkhurst)
Merrill, Bob (originally, Lavan, Henry Robert Merrill)
Merrill, Robert
Merriman, Nan (actually, Katherine-Ann)
Merritt, A(rthur) Tillman
Merritt, Chris (Allan)
Metallica
Metcalf, Louis (Jr.)
Metheny, Pat(rick Bruce)
Meyer, Leonard B(unce)
Meyerowitz, Jan (actually, Hans-Hermann)
Meyers, Anne Akiko
Mezzrow, Mezz (originally, Mesirow, Milton)
Michalsky, Donal
Middleton, Robert (Earl)
Middleton, Velma
Midler, Bette
Migenes-Johnson, Julia
Mikhashoff, Yvar (real name, Ronald Mackay)
Milburn, Ellsworth
Miley, Bubber (James Wesley)
Miller, (Alton) Glenn
Miller, Dayton C(larence)
Miller, Eddie (originally, Muller, Edward Raymond)
Miller, Marcus
Miller, Mildred
Miller, Mitch(ell William)
Miller, Robert
Miller, Steve
Millinder, Lucky (actually, Lucius Venable)
Millo, Aprile (Elizabeth)
Mills, Charles (Borromeo)
Mills, Erie
Mills, Kerry (real name, Frederick Allen)
Mills Brothers, The
Milnes, Sherrill (Eustace)
Milstein, Nathan (Mironovich)
Mince, Johnny (originally, Muenzenberger, John Henry)
Mingus, Charles (Jr.)
Minnelli, Liza
Minter, Drew
Mischakoff (real name, Fischberg), Mischa
Mitchell, George (Little Mitch)
Mitchell, Howard
Mitchell, Leona
Mitchell, Louis (A.)
Mitchell, Roscoe (Edward Jr.)
Mitchell, William J(ohn)
Mitch Ryder and the Detroit Wheels
Mitropoulos, Dimitri
Mizelle, (Dary) John
Moby Grape
Moevs, Robert W(alter)
Moffett, Charles (Mack Sr.)
Moffo, Anna
Mollenhauer, Emil
Monaco, James V.
Moncur, Grachan (Jr.)
Monk, Meredith (Jane)
Monk, Thelonious (Sphere)
Monkees, The
Monroe, Bill (actually, William Smith)
Monroe, Vaughn
Montague, Stephen (Rowley)
Montecino, Alfonso
Monteux, Pierre
Montgomery, Buddy (Charles F.)
Montgomery, Wes (John Leslie)
Moody, James
Moog, Robert (Arthur)
Moonglows, The
Moore, Carman (Leroy)
Moore, Dorothy Rudd
Moore, Douglas (Stuart)
Moore, Grace
Moore, Jerrold Northrop
Moore, John W(eeks)
Moore, Mary (Louise) Carr
Moorman, Joyce Solomon
Moorman, (Madeline) Charlotte
Moran, Robert (Leonard)
Morand, Herb
Mordden, Ethan
Morell, Barry
Morgan, Al(bert)
Morgan, (Edward) Lee
Morgan, Justin
Morgan, Russ
Morgan (Riggins), Helen
Morini (real name, Siracusano), Erica
Moross, Jerome
Morris, Byron
Morris, Harold
Morris, James (Peppler)
Morris, Joan (Clair)
Morris, Lawrence
Morris, Robert (Daniel)
Morton, Jelly Roll (actually, Lamothe, Ferdinand Joseph)
Morton, Lawrence
Moser, Thomas
Mosko, Lucky (actually, Stephen L.)
Mosley, Snub (Lawrence Leo)
Moss, David (Michael)
Moss, Lawrence (Kenneth)
Mossman, Michael
Motian, (Stephen) Paul
Mötley Crüe
Muczynski, Robert
Mulligan, Gerry (actually, Gerald Joseph Mulligan)
Mumma, Gordon
Munn, Zae
Munsel, Patrice (Beverly)
Murphy, Mark
Murphy, Paul
Murphy, Turk (Melvin Edward Alton)
Murray, Bain
Murray, Billy (actually, William Thomas)
Murray, David (Keith)
Murray, Michael
Murray, Sunny (James Marcellus Arthur)
Murray, Thomas (Mantle)
Murray, William
Mursell, James L(ockhart)
Nabokov, Nicolas (actually, Nikolai)
Nagano, Kent (George)
Naginski, Charles
Nance, Ray (Willis)
Nanton, Tricky Sam
Napoleon, Phil (actually, Filippo Napoli)
Napoleon, Teddy (actually, Napoli, Edward George)
Narell, Andy
Narmour, Eugene
Nathan, Hans
Naumburg, Walter W(ehle)
Navarro, Fats (actually, Theodore)
Naylor, Oliver
Neblett, Carol
Neidlinger, Buell
Neikrug, Marc (Edward)
Nelhybel, Vaclav
Nelson, Big Eye Louis (actually DeLisle, Louis Nelson)
Nelson, "Dave" Davidson C.
Nelson, John (Wilton)
Nelson, Judith (Anne née Manes)
Nelson, Oliver (Edward)
Nelson, Rick (Eric)
Nelson, Robert U(riel)
Nelson, Ron(ald Jack)
Nelson, Willie (actually, William Hugh)
Nelsova (real name, Katznelson), Zara
Nemiroff, Isaac
Nettl, Bruno
Nettl, Paul
Neumann, Frederick (actually, Fritz)
Neumeister, Ed (actually, Edward Paul)
Nevada (real name, Wixom), Emma
Nevada, Mignon (Mathilde Marie)
Neville, Chris
Neville Brothers, The
Nevin, Arthur (Finley)
Nevin, Ethelbert (Woodbridge)
Neway, Patricia
New Christy Minstrels, The
New Edition
Newlin, Dika
Newman, Alfred
Newman, Anthony
Newman, Randy
Newman, William S(tein)
Newton, Frankie (actually, William Frank)
New York Dolls
Niblock, Phill
Nicholas, Albert (Nick)
Nichols, Herbie (actually, Herbert Horatio)
Nichols, Red (actually, Ernest Loring)
Nielsen, Alice
Nikolais, Alwin (Theodore)
Niles, John Jacob
Nilsson, Harry
Nirvana
Nissman, Barbara

Powell, Mel (real name, Melvin Epstein)
Powell, Sheldon
Powers, Harold S(tone)
Pratt, Awadagin
Pratt, Silas Gamaliel
Pratt, Waldo Selden
Prausnitz, Frederik (actually, Frederick William)
Premru, Raymond (Eugene)
Presley, Elvis
Presser, Theodore
Pressler, Menahem
Pretenders, The
Previn, André (George) (real name, Andreas Ludwig Priwin)
Previte, Bobby
Price, Florence B(eatrice née Smith)
Price, Lloyd
Price, (Mary Violet) Leontyne
Price, Ray (Noble)
Pride, Charley
Prima, Louis
Primosch, James
Primrose, William
Prince (Roger Nelson)
Procope, Russell
Pruett, James W(orrell)
Pruslin, Stephen (Lawrence)
Pryor, Arthur (Willard)
Prysock, Arthur "Red"
Public Enemy
Puente, Tito
Pugliese, Michael (Gabriel)
Pullen, Don (Gabriel)
Purdie, Bernard (Pretty)
Putnam, Ashley (Elizabeth)
Quealey, Chelsea
Quebec, Ike (Abrams)
Queen Latifah (originally, Owens, Dana Elaine)
Queler, Eve (née Rabin)
Quicksilver Messenger Service
Quittmeyer, Susan
Quivar, Florence
Rabin, Michael
Rabinof, Benno
Racette, Patricia
Rachmaninoff, Sergei (Vassilievich)
Ragin, Derek Lee
Rahn, John
Rains, Leon
Raitt, Bonnie
Raksin, David
Ramey, Phillip
Ramey, Samuel (Edward)
Ramirez, Ram (Roger)
Ramones, The
Randall, J(ames) K(irtland)
Randle, Thomas
Randolph, David
Randolph, Irving "Mouse"
Randolph, Zilner T(renton)
Rands, Bernard
Rankin, Nell
Rapchak, Lawrence
Rascher, Sigurd (Manfred)
Raskin, Judith
Raspberries
Rathaus, Karol
Ratner, Leonard G(ilbert)
Raver, Leonard
Rawls, Lou
Ray, Don Brandon
Ray, Johnnie (actually, John Alvin)
Razaf, Andy (originally, Razafinkeriefo, Andreamenentania Paul)
Read, Daniel
Read, Gardner
Reale, Paul
Reardon, John
Redding, Otis
Red Hot Chili Peppers
Redman, Don(ald Matthew)
Redman, Joshua
Redman, (Walter) Dewey
Reed, H(erbert) Owen
Reed, Jimmy
Reed, Lou(is Alan)
Reese, Gustave
Reeves, David Wallis
Reeves, Diane
Reeves, Jim (actually, James Travis)
Rehfuss, Heinz (Julius)
Reich, Steve (actually, Stephen Michael)
Reid, Cornelius L.
Reid, Rufus (L.)
Reinagle, Alexander
Reiner, Fritz (actually, Frigyes)
Reise, Jay
R.E.M.
Remington, Emory
Renz, Frederick
REO Speedwagon
Rescigno, Nicola
Resnik, Regina
Return to Forever
Reuss, Allan
Revelli, William D(onald)
Rey, Alvino
Reynolds, Roger (Lee)
Reynolds, Verne (Becker)
Rhodes, Phillip (Carl)
Rhodes, Todd (Washington)
Rhodes, Willard
Ribot, Marc
Ricci, Ruggiero
Rice, Charlie
Rich, Alan
Rich, Buddy (Bernard)
Richie, Lionel
Richings (originally, Reynoldson), (Mary) Caroline
Richter, Marga
Rickards, Steven
Riddle (Jr.), Nelson (Smock)
Rider-Kelsey, Corinne (née Rider)
Riegel, Kenneth
Riegger, Wallingford (Constantin)
Riemenschneider, (Charles) Albert
Rieti, Vittorio
Rifkin, Joshua
Righteous Brothers, The
Riley, John
Riley, Terry (Mitchell)
Ringer, Alexander L(othar)
Rivé-King, Julie
Rivers, Johnny (originally, Ramistella, John)
Rivers, Sam(uel Carthorne)
Roach, Max(well Lemuel)
Robbins, Marty (originally, Robinson, Martin David)
Roberts, Marcus (Marthaniel)
Roberts, Megan
Robertson, David
Robertson, Herb
Robertson, Leroy
Robertson, Zue (actually, C. Alvin)
Robeson, Paul (Leroy Bustill)
Robinson, Earl (Hawley)
Robinson, Faye
Robinson, J(oseph) Russel
Robinson, Michael
Robinson, Perry (Morris)
Robinson, Prince
Robinson, Ray
Robinson, Sharon
Robison, Paula (Judith)
Rochberg, George
Rocherolle, Eugénie
Rockefeller, Martha Baird
Rockmore, Clara
Rodeheaver, Homer A(lvan)
Rodgers, Jimmie (actually, James Charles)
Rodgers, Richard (Charles)
Rodriguez, Robert Xavier
Rodwin, David
Rodzinski, Artur
Rogers, Bernard
Rogers, Clara Kathleen (née Bartnett)
Rolandi, Gianna
Rollini, Adrian
Rollins, Sonny (Theodore Walter)
Rolnick, Neil (Burton)
Romberg, Sigmund
Rome, Harold (Jacob)
Ronettes, The
Roney, Wallace
Ronstadt, Linda
Roosevelt, J(oseph) Willard
Root, Frederick W(oodman)
Root, George Frederick
Roppolo, Leon (Joseph)
Rorem, Ned
Rosand, Aaron
Rose, Jerome
Rose, Leonard (Joseph)
Rosen, Charles (Welles)
Rosen, Jerome (William)
Rosen, Nathaniel (Kent)
Rosenblum, Mathew
Rosenboom, David (Charles)
Rosenfeld, Paul (Leopold)
Rosenman, Leonard
Rosenshein, Neil
Rosenstock, Joseph
Rosenthal, Ted
Rosewoman, Michele
Rosner, Arnold
Rosolino, Frank
Ross, Hugh (Cuthbert, Melville)
Ross, Scott
Ross, Walter (Beghtol)
Rothenberg, Ned

Sherock, Shorty (originally, Cherock, Clarence Francis)
Sherry, Fred (Richard)
Shicoff, Neil
Shifrin, David
Shifrin, Seymour
Shilkret, Nat(haniel)
Shirelles, The
Shirley, George (Irving)
Shirley, Jimmy (actually, James Arthur)
Shoemaker, Carolie J.
Shoffner, Bob (actually, Robert Lee)
Shore, Dinah (Frances Rose)
Shorter, Wayne
Shu, Eddie (originally, Shulman, Edward)
Shulman, Alan
Shumsky, Oscar
Shure, Leonard
Sidlin, Murray
Sidran, Ben
Siegel, Janis
Siegel, Jeffrey
Siegmeister, Elie
Signorelli, Frank
Sills, Beverly (real name, Belle Miriam Silverman)
Silva, Alan (Treadwell)
Silver, Sheila
Silverstein, Joseph
Simeon, Omer (Victor)
Simmons, Calvin (Eugene)
Simon, Abbey
Simon, Carly
Simon, Stephen (Anthony)
Simon and Garfunkel
Sims, Ezra
Sims, Jon Reed
Sims, Zoot (John Haley)
Sinatra, Frank (actually, Francis Albert)
Sinatra, Nancy
Singer, Hal (actually, Harold; aka Cornbread)
Singleton, Alvin (Elliot)
Singleton, Zutty (actually, Arthur James)
Sirota, Robert
Sissle, Noble (Lee)
Sitkovetsky, Dmitry
Skaggs, Ricky
Skilton, Charles Sanford
Skinner, Ernest M(artin)
Skrowaczewski, Stanislaw
Slatkin, Felix
Slatkin, Leonard (Edward)
Slawson, Wayne
Sledge, Percy
Slenczynska, Ruth
Slonimsky, Nicolas (actually, Nikolai Leonidovich)
Sly & The Family Stone
Smallens, Alexander
Smalls, Cliff (actually, Clifton Arnold)
Smashing Pumpkins
Smit, Leo
Smith, Bessie (Elizabeth)
Smith, Buster (Henry)
Smith, Carleton Sprague
Smith, Carl (M.)
Smith, Chas
Smith, Clara
Smith, David Stanley
Smith, Floyd (Wonderful)
Smith, Gregg
Smith, Hale
Smith, Howie
Smith, Jabbo (Cladys)
Smith, Jimmy (actually, James Oscar Jr.)
Smith, Joe (actually, Joseph C.)
Smith (real name, Vielehr), Julia (Frances)
Smith, Kate (actually, Kathryn Elizabeth)
Smith, Lawrence Leighton
Smith, Leland (Clayton)
Smith, Leonard B(ingley)
Smith, Mamie (Robinson)
Smith, Patrick J(ohn)
Smith, Patti
Smith, Pine Top (Clarence)
Smith, Russell (T.; aka "Pops")
Smith, Stuff (Hezekiah Leroy Gordon)
Smith, Tab (Talmadge)
Smith, Warren (Doyle; aka Smitty)
Smith, Warren (Jr.)
Smith, William O(verton)
Smith, Willie (actually, William McLeish)
Smith, Willie "The Lion" (originally Bertholoff, William Henry Joseph Bonaparte)
Smither, Howard E(lbert)
Smithers, Don (LeRoy)
Smoker, Paul (Alva)
Snoop Dogg (originally, Broadus, Calvin; aka Snoop Doggy Dogg)
Snow, Hank (Clarence Eugene)
Snow, Valaida
Snowden, Elmer (Chester; aka "Pops")
Sobolewski, Edward (actually, Johann Friedrich Eduard)
Sokoloff, Nicolai
Sollberger, Harvey (Dene)
Solomon, Izler
Solomon, Maynard (Elliott)
Solum, John (Henry)
Solzhenitsyn, Ignat
Somary, Johannes (Felix)
Somer, (Ruth) Hilde
Somogi, Judith
Sondheim, Stephen (Joshua)
Sonneck, Oscar G(eorge) T(heodore)
Sonny and Cher
Sopkin, Henry
Souchon, Edmond (II; aka "Doc")
Soundgarden
Sousa, John Philip
South, Eddie (actually, Edward Otha)
Southern, Eileen
Southern, Jeri (actually, Genevieve Hering)
Sowerby, Leo
Spaeth, Sigmund
Spalding, Albert
Spanier, "Muggsy" (Francis Joseph)
Spano, Robert
Spargo, Tony (originally, Sbarbaro, Antonio)
Speach, Bernadette (Marie)
Speaks, Oley
Spector, Phil
Spelman, Timothy (Mather)
Sperry, Paul
Spiegel, Laurie
Spiegelman, Joel (Warren)
Spies, Claudio
Spinner, Bob (actually, Robert Channing)
Spinners, The
Spirit
Spivacke, Harold
Spivak, Charlie (actually, Charles)
Spivey, Victoria (Regina; aka "Queen Victoria")
Spratlan, Lewis
Springfield, Rick (originally, Springthorpe, Richard)
Springsteen, Bruce
Stacy, Jess (Alexandria)
Stacy, Thomas
Stafford, Jo (Elizabeth)
Stahlman, Sylvia
Stalvey, Dorrance
Stamm, Marvin
Stanley, Frank (originally, Grinsted, William Stanley)
Stanley Brothers, The
Stapp, Olivia
Starer, Robert
Stark, Bobby (actually, Robert Victor)
Starker, János
Staton, Dakota (Aliyah Rabia)
St. Clair, Carl
St. Clair, Cyrus
St. Cyr, Johnny (actually, John Alexander)
Stebbins, George C(oles)
Steber, Eleanor
Steely Dan
Steiger, Anna
Steiger, Rand
Stein, Leon
Stein, Leonard
Steinberg, (Carl) Michael (Alfred)
Steinberg, Pinchas
Steinberg, William (actually, Hans Wilhelm)
Steiner, Emma
Steiner, Max(imilian Raoul Walter)
Steinert, Alexander Lang
Stemper, Frank
Stenberg, Jordan
Stephens, John (Elliott)
Steppenwolf
Stepton, Rick
Sterling, Antoinette
Stern, Isaac
Stern, Mike (actually, Michael)
Sternberg, Jonathan
Stevens, Delores (Elaine)
Stevens, Halsey
Stevens, Risë
Stevenson, George (Edward)
Stevenson, Robert (Murrell)
Stewart, Rex (William Jr.)
Stewart, Slam (Leroy Elliott)
Stewart, Thomas (James)

Turner, (Big) Joe (actually, Joseph Vernon Turner Jr.)
Turner, Ike and Tina
Turner, Joe (actually, Joseph H.)
Turner, Mark
Turok, Paul (Harris)
Turré, Steve
Turrentine, Stanley (William)
Turtles, The
Tusler, Robert Leon
Tuthill, Burnet Corwin
Tweedy, Donald (Nichols)
Tyler, Charlie (Lacy)
Tyler, James (Henry)
Tyner, (Alfred) McCoy
Tyranny, Blue Gene (real name, Robert Nathan Sheff)
Ulanowsky, Paul
Ulmer, James Blood
Underwood, James
Ung, Chinary
Uppman, Theodor
Upshaw, Dawn
Upton, George P(utnam)
Urner, Catherine Murphy
Ussachevsky, Vladimir (Alexis)
Uttal, Jai
Vache, Warren (Webster Jr.),
Valens, Ritchie (originally, Valenzuela, Richard)
Valente, Benita
Valenti, Fernando
Vallée, Rudy (Hubert Prior)
Valleria (real name, Schoening), Alwina
van Appledorn, Mary Jeanne
Van der Slice, John
Van der Stucken, Frank (Valentin)
Van de Vate, Nancy
Vandross, Luther
Van Eps, George (Abel)
Vaness, Carol (Theresa)
Van Halen
Van Heusen, James "Jimmy" (originally, Babcock, Edward Chester)
Van Slyck, Nicholas
Van Tieghem, David
Van Vactor, David
Van Zandt, Marie
Varèse, Edgard (Victor Achille Charles)
Varnay, Astrid (Ibolyka Maria)
Varner, Tom
Vaughan, Sarah (Lois)
Vaughan Brothers, The
Vaughn, Billy
Vázsonyi, Bálint
Vazzana, Anthony
Vega, Aurelio de la
Vega, Ray
Vega, Suzanne
Veinus, Abraham
Velvet Underground, The
Vengerova, Isabelle (actually, Isabella Afanasievna)
Ventures, The
Venuti, Joe (Giuseppe)
Vercoe, Barry
Vercoe, Elizabeth
Verrall, John (Weedon)
Verrett, Shirley
Vierk, Lois V
Vignola, Frank
Vincent, Gene (originally, Craddock, Vincent Eugene)
Vincent, John
Vinnegar, Leroy
Vinson, Eddie "Cleanhead"
Vinton, Bobby (actually, Stanley Robert)
Virizlay, Mihály
Vitro, Roseanna
Voigt, Deborah
Voisin, Roger (Louis)
Von Stade, Frederica
Voorhees, Donald
Votapek, Ralph
Vronsky, Vitya
Wadsworth, Charles (William)
Wadsworth, Stephen
Wagenaar, Bernard
Wagner, Joseph (Frederick)
Wagner, Roger (Francis)
Wagoner, Porter (Wayne)
Waits, Tom
Waldman, Frederic
Waldrop, Gideon W(illiam)
Walker, Edyth
Walker, George (Theophilus)
Walker, Jerry Jeff (originally, Crosby, Ronald Clyde)
Wallace, Stewart (Farrell)
Wallenstein, Alfred
Waller, "Fats" (Thomas Wright)
Walsh, Joe
Walter, Bruno (full name, Bruno Walter Schlesinger)
Walter, David Edgar
Walter, Thomas
War
Ward, Helen
Ward, John M(ilton)
Ward, Robert (Eugene)
Ward, Samuel Augustus
Ward-Steinman, David
Warfield, Sandra
Warfield, William (Caesar)
Waring, Fred(eric Malcolm)
Warland, Dale
Warren, Diane
Warren, Elinor Remick
Warren, Harry (originally, Guaragna, Salvatore)
Warren, Leonard
Warwick, Dionne
Washburn, Robert
Washington, Dinah
Washington, Grover, Jr.
Waters, Ethel
Waters, Muddy (real name, McKinley Morganfield)
Watkins, Julius
Watley, Jody
Watson (real name, McLamore), Claire
Watson, Doc (Arthel Lane)
Watters, Lu(cious)
Watts, André
Watts, Ernie
Watts, Jeff "Tain"
Watts, John (Everett)
Weatherford, Teddy
Weather Report
Weathers, Felicia
Weaver, James (Merle)
Weavers, The
Webb, Charles H(aizlip, Jr.)
Webb, Jimmy
Weber, Ben (actually, William Jennings Bryan)
Weber, Joe (actually, Morris Joseph)
Webster, Ben(jamin Francis)
Webster, Beveridge
Webster, Freddie
Webster, Paul
Weede (real name, Wiedefeld), Robert
Weidinger, Christine
Weigel, Eugene (Herbert)
Weigl, Karl
Weigl, Valery (Vally)
Weill, Kurt (Julian)
Weinrich, Carl
Weinstock, Herbert
Weisberg, Arthur
Weisgall, Hugo (David)
Weisgarber, Elliot
Weiskopf, Joel
Weiskopf, Walt(er David)
Weiss, Adolph
Weiss, Sid
Welcher, Dan
Welk, Lawrence (real name LeRoy)
Wells, Kitty (originally, Deason, Ellen Muriel)
Wells, Mary
Welting, Ruth
Wendt, Larry (actually, Lawrence Frederick)
Wernick, Richard
Werrenrath, Reinald
Westenburg, Richard
Westergaard, Peter (Talbot)
Weston, Randy
Wettling, George
Wetzler, Hermann (Hans)
Whaley, Wade
Whalum, Kirk
Whear, Paul William
Wheeler, (E. B.) De Priest
White, Amos (Mordechai)
White, Andrew (Nathanial III)
White, Barry
White, Chris(topher) Wesley
White, Clarence Cameron
White, Frances
White, John (Reeves)
White, Michael
White, Robert
White, Ruth
White, Sonny (Ellerton Oswald)
Whitehill, Clarence (Eugene)
Whiteman, Paul (Samuel)
Whitfield, Mark
Whithorne (real name, Whittern), Emerson
Whiting, Arthur Battelle
Whiting, George E(lbridge)
Whitmer, T(homas) Carl
Whitney, John
Whitney, Myron (William)

AMERICAN-ITALIAN

AMERICAN-MORAVIAN

ARABIAN

ARGENTINE

ARGENTINE-AMERICAN

ARGENTINE-GERMAN

ARMENIAN

Komitas (real name, Sogomonian)
Lisitsyan, Pavel (Gerasimovich) (actually, Pogos Karapetovich)
Mansurian, Tigran
Melikyan, Romanos Hovakimi
Mirzoyan, Edvard (Mikaeli)
Saradzhev, Konstantin
Spendiarov, Alexander (Afanasii)
Stepanian, Aro (Levoni)
Tavrizian, Mikhail (Arsenievich)
Tigranian, Armen (Tigran)

AUSTRALIAN

Agnew, Roy (Ewing)
Ahern, David (Anthony)
Angel, Marie
Antill, John (Henry)
Austral, Florence (real name, Mary Wilson)
Banks, Don(ald Oscar)
Bauld, Alison (Margaret)
Benjamin, Arthur
Bonynge, Richard (Alan)
Boyd, Anne (Elizabeth)
Broadstock, Brenton (Thomas)
Brownlee, John (Donald Mackensie)
Brumby, Colin (James)
Butterley, Nigel (Henry)
Charteris, Richard
Collier, Marie
Cowie, Edward
Douglas, Clive (Martin)
Dreyfus, George (actually, Georg)
Edwards, Ross
Fisher, Sylvia (Gwendoline Victoria)
Fowler, Jennifer
Freeman, David
Gifford, Helen (Margaret)
Grandi, Margherita (née Margaret Garde)
Grant, Clifford (Scantlebury)
Hannan, Michael (Francis)
Heinze, Sir Bernard (Thomas)
Hill, Alfred (Francis)
Holland, Dulcie (Sybil)
Howard, Leslie (John)
Hughes, Robert Watson
Humble, (Leslie) Keith
Hungerford, Bruce
Hutcheson, Ernest
INXS
Kats-Chernin, Elena
Kenny, Yvonne
Krips, Henry (Joseph)
Lawrence, Marjorie (Florence)
Le Gallienne, Dorian (Leon Marlois)
Lumsdaine, David (Newton)
Mackerras, Sir (Alan) Charles (MacLaurin)
Madge, Geoffrey Douglas
Marshall-Hall, George W(illiam) L(ouis)
Meale, Richard (Graham)
Melba, Dame Nellie (actually, Helen Porter née Mitchell Armstrong)
Mewton-Wood, Noel
Mills, Richard (John)
Minton, Yvonne (Fay)
Moodie, Alma
Morison, Elsie (Jean)
Moshinsky, Elijah
Nathan, Isaac
Parsons, Geoffrey (Penwill)
Plush, Vincent
Reddy, Helen
Ritchie, Stanley (John)
Sculthorpe, Peter (Joshua)
Simon, Geoffrey
Sitsky, Larry
Stevens, Horace (Ernest)
Summers, Jonathan
Sutherland, Dame Joan
Sutherland, Margaret (Ada)
Tibbits, George (Richard)
Tunley, David (Evatt)
Vaughan, Denis (Edward)
Vine, Carl
Werder, Felix
Wesley-Smith, Martin
Westlake, Nigel
Williams, John (Christopher)
Williamson, Malcolm (Benjamin Graham Christopher)
Woodward, Roger (Robert)

AUSTRIAN

Adelburg, August, Ritter von
Adler, Guido
Ahlgrimm, Isolde
Albrechtsberger, Johann Georg
Alpenheim, Ilse von
Ambros, August Wilhelm
Ammon, Blasius
Angerer, Paul
Apostel, Hans Erich (Heinrich)
Artaria
Ascher, Leo
Asplmayr, Franz
Asriel, André
Assmayer, Ignaz
Auer, Max
Aufschnaiter, Benedict Anton
Badura-Skoda (real name, Badura), Paul
Bähr, (Franz) Josef
Berg, Alban (Maria Johannes)
Berger, Theodor
Bernet, Dietfried
Berry, Walter
Bildstein, Hieronymus
Bischof, Rainer
Bittner, Julius
Blahetka, Marie Léopoldine
Blaukopf, Kurt
Bodanzky, Artur
Boesch, Christian
Böhm, Karl
Bonno, Giuseppe
Boskovsky, Willi
Botstiber, Hugo
Brandt, Marianne (real name, Marie Bischoff)
Brendel, Alfred
Bresgen, Cesar
Bruckner, (Josef) Anton
Brüll, Ignaz
Buchbinder, Rudolf
Bussani, Dorothea
Cavalieri, Catarina (real name, Franziska Cavalier)
Cerha, Friedrich
Chorzempa, Daniel (Walter)
Clemencic, René
Clement, Franz
Czerny, Carl
Czerwenka, Oskar
Dachs, Joseph
Dallapozza, Adolf
D'Angeri, Anna (real name, Anna von Angermayer de Redernburg)
David, Johann Nepomuk
David, Thomas Christian
Decsey, Ernst (Heinrich Franz)
Deller, Florian Johann
Demus, Jörg (Wolfgang)
Demuth (real name, Pokorný), Leopold
Dermota, Anton
Dernesch, Helga
Dessoff, Margarethe
Deutsch, Otto Erich
Diabelli, Anton
Dittersdorf, Karl Ditters von (original name, Karl Ditters)
Döhler, Theodor (von)
Dont, Jakob
Door, Anton
Doppler, (Albert) Franz (Ferenc)
Doppler, Árpád
Doppler, Karl (Károly)
Dostal, Nico(laus Josef Michäel)
Draghi, Antonio
Drechsler, Joseph
Eberl, Anton (Franz Josef)
Edelmann, Otto (Karl)
Eder, Helmut
Ehrlich, (Karl) Heinrich (Alfred)
Einem, Gottfried von
Eisler, Paul
Elizza, Elise (real name, Elisabeth Letztergroschen)
Eller, Louis
Epstein, Julius
Epstein, Richard
Equiluz, Kurt
Erbse, Heimo
Eybler, Joseph Leopold, Edler von
Eysler (actually, Eisler), Edmund
Fahrbach, Philipp
Fall, Leo(pold)
Federhofer, Hellmut
Felix, Hugo
Felsenstein, Walter
Fischer, Betty
Fischer, György
Fischer, Wilhelm (Robert)
Fischhof, Joseph
Forti, Anton
Fricci (real name, Frietsche), Antonietta
Fricsay, Ferenc
Friebert, (Johann) Joseph
Frimmel, Theodor von
Frischenschlager, Friedrich
Fuchs, Johann Nepomuk
Fuchs, Robert
Furrer, Beat
Füssl, Karl Heinz
Fux, Johann Joseph

Mosel, Ignaz Franz von
Mottl, Felix (Josef)
Mozart, Franz Xaver Wolfgang
Mozart, (Johann Georg) Leopold
Mozart, Maria Anna (Walburga Ignatia)
Mozart, Wolfgang Amadeus (baptismal names, Johannes Chrysostomus Wolfgangus Theophilus)
Müller, Adolf, Jr.
Müller, Adolf, Sr. (real name, Matthias Schmid)
Müller, Maria
Müller, Wenzel
Müller-Hermann, Johanna
Neuhold, Günter
Neukomm, Sigismund, Ritter von
Neumann, Angelo
Neumann, Wolfgang
Nikisch, Arthur
Noren, Heinrich (real name, Heinrich Suso Johannes Gottlieb)
Nowak, Leopold
Ordonez or Ordoñez, Carlos d'
Orel, Alfred
Pachler-Koschak, Marie Leopoldine
Paminger, Leonhard
Papier, Rosa
Paradis, Maria Theresia von
Pasterwitz, Georg (actually Robert) von
Patzak, Julius
Pauer, Ernst
Pauer, Max von
Paumgartner, Bernhard
Paur, Emil
Pecháček, Franz Xaver
Pepöck, August
Perger, Richard von
Pernerstorfer, Alois
Pirck, Wenzel Raimund (Johann)
Plaichinger, Thila
Pollak, Egon
Popp, Lucia
Posch, Isaac
Preindl, Josef
Prenner, Georg
Prinner, Johann Jacob
Proch, Heinrich
Prohaska, Carl
Prohaska, Felix
Prohaska, Jaro(slav)
Prüwer, Julius
Rahbari, Alexander (actually, Ali)
Rapf, Kurt
Rappoldi, Eduard
Rats, Erwin
Reining, Maria
Reinmar (real name, Wochinz), Hans
Reuss-Belce, Luise
Reutter, Georg (von)
Reutter, (Johann Adam Joseph Karl) Georg von
Rezniek, Emil Nikolaus von
Richter, Ferdinand Tobias
Riepel, Joseph
Rokitansky, Hans, Freiherr von
Roller, Alfred
Rosbaud, Hans
Rosé, Arnold (Josef)
Rosenthal, Moriz
Rössl-Majdan, Hildegard
Rott, Hans (actually, Johann Carl Maria)
Rottenberg, Ludwig
Rubin, Marcel
Rufer, Josef (Leopold)
Rydl, Kurt
Rysanek, Leonie
Salmhofer, Franz
Satter, Gustav
Scaria, Emil
Schack, Benedikt (Emanuel)
Schalk, Franz
Schalk, Josef
Scheff, Fritzi
Scheidl, Theodor
Schenk, Erich
Schenk, Johann Baptist
Schenk, Otto
Schenker, Heinrich
Schiff, András
Schiff, Heinrich
Schikaneder, Emanuel (actually, Johannes Joseph)
Schimon, Adolf
Schipper, Emil (Zacharias)
Schiske, Karl (Hubert Rudolf)
Schmelzer, Johann Heinrich
Schmelzl, Wolfgang
Schmid, Anton
Schmidt, Franz
Schneider, Peter
Schneiderhan, Wolfgang (Eduard)
Schoberlechner, Franz
Schollum, Robert
Schönherr, Max
Schrammel, Johann
Schreker, Franz
Schubert, Ferdinand (Lukas)
Schubert, Franz (Peter)
Schuch, Ernst von
Schuppanzigh, Ignaz
Schwarz, Paul
Schwarz, Vera
Schwertsik, Kurt
Sechter, Simon
Seyfried, Ignaz (Xaver), Ritter von
Siegl, Otto
Singer, Peter (Alkantara) (actually, Josef Anton)
Slezak, Leo
Soldat, Marie
Soltesz, Stefan
Sonnleithner Family
  Sonnleithner, Christoph
  Sonnleithner, Joseph
  Sonnleithner, Ignaz (von)
Spinner, Leopold
Spitzmüller (-Harmersbach), Alexander, Freiherr von
Sprongl, Norbert
Stadler, Abbé Maximilian (actually, Johann Karl Dominik)
Stadler, Anton (Paul)
Stadlmair, Hans
Stainer, Jacob (or Jakob)
Starzer, Josef
Staudigl (I), Joseph
Staudigl (II), Joseph
Steffek, Hanny (actually, Hannelore)
Stegmayer, Ferdinand
Stegmayer, Matthäus
Stehle, Adelina
Steingruber, Ilona
Stolz, Robert (Elisabeth)
Strauss Family
  Strauss, Johann (Baptist) (I)
  Strauss, Johann (Baptist) (II)
  Strauss, Josef
  Strauss, Eduard
Strauss, Christoph
Streicher, Johann Andreas
Suitner, Otmar
Sulzer, Julius Salomon
Sulzer, Salomon
Suppan, Wolfgang
Suppé, Franz (von) (real name, Francesco Ezechiele Ermenegildo, Cavaliere Suppé-Demelli)
Süssmayr, Franz Xaver
Swarowsky, Hans
Swieten, Gottfried (Bernhard), Baron van
Tachezi, Herbert
Tenschert, Roland
Teyber Family
  Teyber, Matthäus
  Teyber, Elisabeth
  Teyber, Anton
  Teyber, Franz
  Teyber, Therese
Thuille, Ludwig (Wilhelm Andreas Maria)
Töpper, Hertha
Tritonius, Petrus (real name, Peter Treybenreif)
Uhl, Alfred
Uhl, Fritz
Ullmann, Viktor
Umlauf, Carl Ignaz Franz
Umlauf, Ignaz
Umlauf, Michael
Urbanner, Erich
Vesque von Püttlingen, Johann
Vogl, Johann Michael
Volkert, Franz (Joseph)
Waechter, Eberhard
Wagenseil, Georg Christoph
Wagner, Sieglinde
Waldmann, Maria
Weber, Ludwig
Webern, Anton (Friedrich Wilhelm) von
Weidinger, Anton
Weidt, Lucie
Weigl Family
  Weigl, Joseph (Franz)
  Weigl, Joseph
  Weigl, Thaddäus
Weikert, Ralf
Weikl, Bernd
Weingartner, (Paul) Felix, Edler von Münzberg
Weiss, Franz
Welitsch (real name, Veličkova), Ljuba
Wellek, Albert
Weller, Walter
Welser-Möst (real name, Möst), Franz
Werba, Erik

AUSTRIAN-AMERICAN

AUSTRIAN-CANADIAN

AUSTRIAN-CHILEAN

AUSTRIAN-FRENCH

AUSTRIAN-GERMAN

AUSTRIAN-HUNGARIAN

AZERBAIJANI

BAVARIAN

BELGIAN

Kuijken Family
Kuijken, Wieland
Kuijken, Sigiswald
Kuijken, Barthold
Laporte, André
Leduc, Jacques
Legley, Victor
Lekeu, Guillaume (Jean Joseph Nicolas)
Lemmens, Jacques Nicolas (Jaak Nikolaas)
Lenaerts, René Bernard (Maria)
Léonard, Hubert
Limnander de Nieuwenhove, Armand Marie Ghislain
Lonque, Georges
Louël, Jean (Hippolyte Oscar)
Lunssens, Martin
Maes, Jef
Mahillon, Charles (-Borromée)
Maison, René
Maldeghem, Robert Julien van
Maréchal, Adolphe
Marsick, Armand (Louis Joseph)
Marsick, Martin (-Pierre-Joseph)
Massart, (Joseph) Lambert
Massart, Nestor-Henri-Joseph
Mathieu, Émile (-Louis-Victor)
Meester, Louis de
Meulemans, Arthur
Michel, Paul-Baudouin
Miry, Karel
Monte, Philippe de (Filippo di Monte or Philippus de Monte)
Mortelmans, Ivo (Oscar)
Mortelmans, Lodewijk
Mortier, Gérard
Moulaert, Pierre
Moulaert, Raymond (Auguste Marie)
Munck, (Pierre Joseph) Ernest, Chevalier de
Musin, Ovide
Nees, Staf (Gustaaf Frans)
Nisard, Théodore (pen name of Abbé Théodule-Eléazar-Xavier Normand)
Noté, Jean
Peeters, Flor
Pelemans, Willem
Plancken, Corneille Vander
Poot, Marcel
Pousseur, Henri (Léon MarieThérèse)
Quinet, Fernand
Quinet, Marcel
Radoux, Jean-Théodore
Radoux-Rogier (real name, Radoux), Charles
Rasse, François (Adolphe Jean Jules)
Remoortel, Edouard van
Rogister, Jean (François Toussaint)
Roland, Claude-Robert
Rosseau, Norbert (Oscar Claude)
Rossum, Frederik (Leon Hendrik) van
Ryelandt, Joseph
Samuel, Adolphe (-Abraham)
Samuel Léopold
Samuel-Holeman, Eugène
Sarly, Henry
Sass, Marie Constance
Sax, Adolphe (actually, Antoine-Joseph)
Sax, Charles-Joseph
Schmitt, Camille
Schoemaker, Maurice
Servais, (Adrien-) François
Servais, Joseph
Simonis, Jean-Marie
Snel, Joseph-François
Souris, André
Stehman, Jacques
Sternefeld, Daniël
Strens, Jules
Swert, Jules de
Thielemans, Toots
Thomas, Rene
Thomson, César
Tinel, Edgar (Pierre Joseph)
Van Dam, José (real name, Joseph Van Damme)
Van de Moortel, Arie
Van den Boorn-Coclet, Henriette
Van den Borren, Charles (-Jean-Eugène)
Vandermaesbrugge, Max
Vandernoot, André
Van der Straeten, Edmond
Van der Velden, Renier
Van de Woestijne, David
Van Doorslaer, Georges
Van Durme, Jef
Van Dyck, Ernest (Marie Hubert)
Van Immerseel, Jos
Van Nevel, Paul
Verbesselt, August
Veremans, Renaat
Vieuxtemps, Henri
Vreuls, Victor (Jean Léonard)
Waelput, Hendrik
Wangermée, Robert
Westerlinck, Wilfried
Woronoff, Wladimir
Wotquenne (-Plattel), Alfred (Camille)
Ysaÿe, Eugène (-Auguste)
Ysaÿe, Théophile

BELGIAN-AMERICAN

Barzin, Leon (Eugene)

BELGIAN-FRENCH

Fétis, Adolphe (-Louis-Eugène)
Franck, Joseph
Momigny, Jérôme-Joseph de
Tolbecque Family
Tolbecque, Jean-Baptiste-Joseph
Tolbecque, Isidore-Joseph
Tolbecque, August-Joseph
Tolbecque, Charles-Joseph
Tolbecque, Auguste

BOHEMIAN

Bárta, Josef
Bečvařovský, Anton Felix (Antonín František)
Beer, (Johann) Joseph
Benda, Franz (actually, František)
Benda, Georg Anton (Jiří Antonín)
Biber, Heinrich Ignaz Franz von
Blatt, František Tadeáš
Brixi, Franz (actually, František) Xaver
Cervený, Wenzel Franz (Václav František)
Czernohorsky (Černohorský), Bohuslav Matj
Dessauer, Josef
Dlabacž, Gottfried Johann (actually, Bohumír Jan Dlabač)
Drdla, Franz (actually, František Alois)
Dreyschock, Alexander
Dreyschock, Raimund
Duschek, Franz Xaver (real name, František Xaver Dušek)
Dussek, Johann Ladislaus (real name, Jan Ladislav Dusík)
Fassbender, Zdenka
Fiala, Joseph
Förster, Josef
Fučik, Julius (Arnošt Vilém)
Führer, Robert (Johann Nepomuk)
Gassmann, Florian Leopold
Gelinek (also Jelinek), Josef (Joseph)
Gläser, Franz (Joseph)
Gregora, František
Gyrowetz, Adalbert (Mathias) (original name, Vojtěch Matyáš Jirovec)
Habermann, Franz (actually, František Václav)
Habert, Johannes Evangelista
Halir, Karl (original name, Karel Hali)
Hammerschmidt, Andreas
Hampel, Anton Joseph
Hampel, Hans
Hauschka, Vincenz
Hauser, Franz (actually, František)
Hensel, Walther (real name, Julius Janiczek)
Hesch, Wilhelm (real name, Vilém Heš)
Horák, Adolph
Horák, Eduard
Horak, Wenzel (Vaclav) Emanuel
Jacob, Gunther (Wenceslaus)
Janowka (Janovka), Thomas Balthasar (Tomáš Baltazar)
Jansa, Leopold
Kàan-Albest, Heinrich (originally, Jindřich z Albestů Kàan)
Kalliwoda (Kalivoda), Johann Wenzel (Jan Křtitel Václav)
Kammel, Antonín
Kittl, Johann Friedrich (Jan Bedřich)
Klička, Josef
Knittl, Karel
Kocžwara, František
Komzák, Karel
Koželuh (Kozeluch, Koscheluch), Johann Antonín (Jan Evangelista Antonin Tomáš)
Koželuh (Kozeluch, Kotzeluch), Leopold (Jan Antonín)
Krejči, Josef
Křížkovsyký, Pavel (baptized Karel)
Krow, Josef Theodor
Krumpholtz, Jean-Baptiste (Johann Baptist or Jan Křtitel)
Kucharz, Johann Baptist (real name, Jan Křtitel Kucha)
Lachnith, Ludwig Wenzel
Láska, Gustav
Lauska, Franz (Seraphinus Ignatius)
Lipawsky or Lipavský, Joseph
Lobkowitz Family
Lobkowitz, Philipp Hyacinth (Filipp Hyacint)

BOHEMIAN-AMERICAN

BOLIVIAN

BRAZILIAN

BRAZILIAN-AMERICAN

BULGARIAN

BULGARIAN-AMERICAN

BULGARIAN-FRENCH

BURGUNDIAN

BYZANTINE

CANADIAN

Applebaum, Louis
Archer (originally, Balestreri), Violet
Argenta (real name, Herbison), Nancy
Baker, Michael Conway
Barbeau, (Charles) Marius
Barenaked Ladies
Barnes, Milton
Beckwith, John
Beecroft, Norma (Marian)
Bell, Donald (Munro)
Benjamin, William E(mmanuel)
Bernardi, Mario (Egidio)
Betts, Lorne
Bissell, Keith (Warren)
Bley, Paul
Bottenberg, Wolfgang (Heinz Otto)
Bowen, Ralph (Michael)
Brady, Tim
Brodie, Paul (Zion)
Broome, (William) Edward
Brott, Alexander
Brott, Boris
Brott, Denis
Buczynski, Walter (Joseph)
Bunnett, Jane
Burr, Henry (Henry H. McClaskey)
Burritt, Lloyd (Edmund)
Champagne (actually, Desparois dit Champagne), Claude (Adonaï)
Cherney, Brian (Irwin)
Ciamaga, Gustav
Cockburn, Bruce
Cohen, Leonard
Collier, Ron(ald William)
Coulthard, Jean
Crew Cuts, The
Culver, (David) Andrew
Dawson, Ted
Dela, Maurice (real name, Albert Phaneuf)
Delamont, Gordon (Arthur)
Dion, Celine
Dolin, Samuel (Joseph)
Donalda (real name, Lightstone), Pauline
Eckhardt-Gramatté, S(ophie)-C(armen) "Sonia"
Farnam, (Walter) Lynnwood
Farrow, Norman D.
Feldbrill, Victor
Ferguson, Maynard
Fiala, George (Joseph)
Fialkowska, Janina
Fleming, Robert (James Berkeley)
Fodi, John
Forrester, Maureen (Kathleen Stewart)
Forsyth, Malcolm (Denis)
Freedman, Harry
Frey, Paul
Garant, (Albert Antonio) Serge
Gauthier, (Ida Joséphine Phoebe) Eva
Gellman, Steven (David)
Gilbert, Kenneth
Glick, Srul Irving
Gold, Arthur
Goldberg, Theo
Gould, Glenn (Herbert)
Guess Who, The
Hamelin, Marc-André
Harnoy, Ofra
Harriss, Charles A(lbert) E(dwin)
Hawkins, John
Heppner, Ben
Hétu, Jacques (Joseph Robert)
Iseler, Elmer (Walter)
James, (Mary) Frances
Jehin-Prume (originally Jehin), Frantz (Franccois)
Joachim, Otto
Jones, (Herbert) Kelsey
Jones, Oliver
Kallmann, Helmut (Max)
Kalninš, Janis
Kasemets, Udo
Katin, Peter (Roy)
Kenins, Talivaldis
Klein, Lothar
Kolinski, Mieczyslaw
Komorous, Rudolf
Krall, Diana (Jean)
Kulesha, Gary
Kunz, Alfred (Leopold)
La Liberté, (Joseph-François) Alfred
lang, k.d.
Lanza, Alcides (Emigdio)
Laplante, (Joseph) André (Roger)
Lavallée, Calixa
Le Caine, Hugh
Leitch, Peter
Lightfoot, Gordon
Lortie, Louis
Lucas, Clarence (Reynolds)
Macdonough, Harry (John S. MacDonald)
MacMillan, Sir Ernest (Alexander Campbell)
Mann, Leslie (Douglas)
Margison, Richard (Charles)
Marshall, Lois (Catherine)
Mather, (James) Bruce
Mathieu, (Joseph) Rodolphe
Mathieu, (René) André (Rodolphe)
Matthews, Michael (Bass)
Matton, Roger
Mauro, Ermanno
Mazzoleni, Ettore
McCauley, William (Alexander)
McConnell, Rob
McLachlan, Sarah
Mercure, Pierre
Mills-Cockell, John
Mitchell, Joni (originally, Anderson, Roberta Joan)
Morawetz, Oskar
Morel, (Joseph Raoul) François (d'Assise)
Murray, Anne
Nattiez, Jean-Jacques
Naylor, Bernard (James)
Neel, (Louis) Boyd
Newmark, John (originally, Hans Joseph Neumark)
Oswald, John
Oundjian, Peter
Papineau-Couture, Jean
Parker, Jamie (real name, James Edward Kimura)
Parker, Jon Kimura (real name, John David Kimura)
Parlow, Kathleen
Pelletier, (Louis) Wilfred
Pentland, Barbara (Lally)
Pépin, (Jean-Josephat) Clermont
Perrault, Michel (Brunet)
Peterson, Oscar
Polgar, Tibor
Prévost, (Joseph Gaston Charles) André
Quesne, (Louis) Joseph (Marie)
Quilico, Gino
Quilico, Louis
Rae, Allan
Rathburn, Eldon (Davis)
Rea, John (Rocco)
Reid, John (Charles)
Ridout, Godfrey
Robbin, Catherine
Rosnes, Renee (Irene Louise)
Rouleau, Joseph (Alfred Pierre)
Rush
Saint-Marcoux, Micheline Coulombe
Schafer, R(aymond) Murray
Schudel, Thomas (Michael)
Simoneau, Léopold
Smith, (Joseph) Leo(pold)
Somers, Harry (Stewart)
Staryk, Steven
Stratas, Teresa (real name, Anastasia Stratakis)
Surdin, Morris
Symonds, Norman
Taylor, Janis (actually, Janice Kathleen née Schuster)
Tourangeau, (Marie Jeannine) Huguette
Tremblay, Gilles (Léonce)
Truax, Barry (Douglas)
Turini, Ronald
Turner, Robert (Comrie)
Turovsky, Yuli
Twain, Shania (originally, Eileen Evans)
Vallerand, Jean (d'Auray)
Vickers, Jon(athan Stewart)
Vivier, Claude
Walter, Arnold (Maria)
Weinzweig, John (Jacob)
Whitehead, Alfred (Ernest)
Wiens, Edith
Willan, (James) Healey
Wilson, Charles (Mills)
Zuckert, Leon

CANADIAN-AMERICAN

Yates, Peter B.

CATALAN

Anglés, Higini
Esteve (Estebe) y Grimau, Pablo
Gallès, José
Garreta, Julio
Homs (Oller), Joaquín
Lamote de Grignon, Juan
Lamote de Grignon y Ribas, Ricardo
Llobet, Miguel
Llongueras y Badia, Juan
Manén, Juan
Millet, Luis

Jedlička, Dalibor
Jeremiáš, Bohuslav
Jeremiáš, Jaroslav
Jeremiáš, Otakar
Ježek, Jaroslav
Jílek, František
Jirák, K(arel) B(oleslav)
Jirásek, Ivo
Jirko, Ivan
Jonák, Zdeněk
Juchelka, Miroslav
Kabeláč, Miloslav
Kalabis, Viktor
Kalaš, Julius
Kálik, Václav
Kapr, Jan
Kaprál, Václav
Kaprálová, Vitězslava
Karel, Rudolf
Kašlík, Václav
Klein, Gideon
Klička, Václav
Klima, Alois
Klusák, Jan
Kocián, Jaroslav
Kohoutek, Ctirad
Kopecký, Pavel
Kopelent, Marek
Korte, Oldřich František
Košler, Zdeněk
Kout, Jiří
Kovaříček, František
Kovařovic, Karel
Krása, Hans (actually, Johann)
Krásová, Marta
Krejčí, Iša (František)
Krejčí, Miroslav
Křička, Jaroslav
Křivinka, Gustav
Krombholc, Jaroslav
Kubín, Rudolf
Kučera, Václav
Kunc, Jan
Kundera, Ludvík
Kurz, Vilém
Kvapil, Jaroslav
Laburda, Jiří
Laub, Ferdinand
Lídl, Václav
Liška, Zdeněk
Loudová, Ivana
Lucký, Štěpán
Ludikar (real name, Vyskočil), Pavel
Lukáš, Zdeněk
Mácha, Otmar
Mařák, Otakar
Matěj, Josef
Matys, Jiří
Medek, Ivo
Míča, František Antonín (Václav)
Michna, Adam Václav
Moor (real name, Mohr), Karel
Moravec, Ivan
Moscheles, Ignaz
Mraczek (actually, Mraček), Joseph Gustav
Mraz, George (Jiri)
Munclinger, Milan
Nedbal, Oskar
Nejedlý, Vít
Nejedlý, Zdeněk
Neruda, Johann Baptist Georg (actually, Jan Křtitel Jiří)
Nešvera, Josef
Neubauer, Franz Christoph
Neumann, Franz (František)
Neumann, Václav
Neumann, Věroslav
Niemtschek (Niemetschek, Němeček), Franz Xaver
Novák, Jan
Novák, Vitězslav (actually, Augustín Rudolf)
Novotná, Jarmila
Novotný, Václav Juda
Ondříček Family
  Ondříček, Ignac
  Ondříček, Jan
  Ondříček, František
  Ondříček, Emanuel
Orel, Dobroslav
Ostrčil, Otakar
Páleníček, Josef
Palkovsk, Oldřich
Palkovský, Pavel
Panenka, Jan
Parsch, Arnošt
Pauer, Jíří
Pešek, Libor
Petrželka, Vilém
Petyrek, Felix
Picka, František
Piňos, Alois Simandl
Plaschke, Friedrich (real name, Bedřich Plaške)
Podéšt, Ludvík
Podešva, Jaromír
Polívka, Vladimír
Pololáník, Zdeněk
Ponc, Miroslav
Popper, David
Poštolka, Milan
Pražák, Přemysl
Přibyl, Vilém
Přihoda, Váša
Puschmann, Josef
Racek, Jan
Raichl, Miroslav
Rambousek, Joseph
Ranczak, Hildegard
Reinberger, Jiří
Reiner, Karel
Reisserová, Julie
Rezá, Ivan
Rídký, Jaroslav
Ríhovský, Vojtch
Rozkošný, Josef Richard
Ružika, Rudolf
Ružiková, Zuzana
Ryba, Jakub (Šimon) Jan
Rychlík, Jan
Schaefer, Theodor
Schulhoff, Ervín
Seger (also Seeger, Seegr, Segert, Zeckert, etc.), Josef (Ferdinand Norbert)
Seidel, Jan
Šejna, Karel
Šesták, Zdenk
Ševik, Otakar
Simai, Pavol
Šín, Otakar
Slavický, Klement
Smetáček, Václav
Sokola, Miloš
Sommer, Vladimír
Soukupová, Věra
Šourek, Otakar
Spilka, František
Šrámek, Vladimír
Srnka, Jiří
Šrom, Karel
Stanislav, Josef
Starek, Jiří
Stecker, Karel
Štědroň, Bohumír
Štědroň, Miloš
Štědroň, Vladimír
Steffan, Joseph Anton (Josef Antonín Štepán)
Štěpan, Václav
Suchý, František
Suda, Stanislav
Suk (I), Josef
Suk (II), Josef
Svoboda, Josef
Sychra, Antonín
Talich, Václav
Tattermuschová, Helena
Tausinger, Jan
Tomášek, Jaroslav
Trojan, Václav
Tuma, Franz (actually, František Ignác Antonin Tůma)
Turnovský, Martin
Vacek, Miloš
Vačkář Family
  Vačkář, Václav
  Vačkář, Dalibor Cyril
  Vačkář, Tomas
Válek, Jiří
Vanhal (also van Hal, Vanhall, Wanhal, etc.), Johan Baptist (actually, Jan Křtitel)
Vogel, Jaroslav
Volek, Jaroslav
Vomáčka, Boleslav
Vorlová, Sláva (actually, Miroslava Johnova)
Vostřák, Zbyněk
Vycpálek, Ladislav
Vysloužil, Jiří
Weinberger, Jaromir
Weis, Karel
Wiedermann, Bedřich Antonín
Wihan, Hans (actually, Hanuš)
Zach, Jan
Železný, Lubomír
Zelinka, Jan Evangelista
Zich, Jaroslav
Zich, Otakar
Zítek, Otakar
Zouhar, Zdeněk

CZECH-AMERICAN

Adler, Kurt
Adler, Peter Herman
Reif, Paul

DANISH

DANISH-AMERICAN

DUTCH

Delden, Lex van
Deutekom, Cristina (real name, Stientje Engel)
Diepenbrock, Alphons (Johannes Maria)
Dijk, Jan van
Dopper, Cornelis
Dresden, Sem
Egmond, Max (Rudolf) van
Eisma, Will (Leendert)
Enthoven, (Henri) Emile
Escher, Rudolf (George)
Eyck, Jacob van
Eyken (Eijken), Jan Albert van
Felderhof, Jan (Reindert Adriaan)
Flipse, Eduard
Flothuis, Marius (Hendrikus)
Foch (real name, Fock), Dirk
Frid, Géza
Giebel, Agnes
Gilse, Jan van
Giltay, Berend
Godron, Hugo
Griend, Koos van de
Groot, Cor de
Hacquart, Carolus
Hageman, Maurits (Leonard)
Haitink, Bernard (Johann Herman)
Hartog, Eduard de
Havingha, Gerhardus
Hekking, Anton
Hekster, Walter
Helmont, Charles-Joseph van
Hemel, Oscar van
Hengeveld, Gerard
Henkemans, Hans
Heppener, Robert
Herpol, Homer (Latinized as Homerus Herpolitanus)
Hertog, Johannes den
Hess, Joachim
Hijman, Julius
Hoboken, Anthony van
Hodemont, Leonard (Collet) de
Holl, Robert
Holt, Simeon ten
Hoogstraten, Willem van
Horst, Anthon van der
Hove, Joachim van den
Hoyoul, Balduin
Hupperts, Paul (Henri Franciscus Marie)
Hutschenruyter (Hutschenruijter) Family
Hutschenruyter, Wouter
Hutschenruyter, Willem Jacob
Hutschenruyter, Wouter
Ingenhoven, Jan
Kee, Cornelis
Kee, Piet(er Willem)
Kersjes, Anton (Frans Jan)
Kes, Willem
Ketting, Otto
Ketting, Piet
Keuris, Tristan
King, Harold Charles
Klerk, Albert de
Knap, Rolf
Koeberg, Frits Ehrhardt Adriaan
Koenen, Tilly (actually, Mathilde Caroline)
Koetsier, Jan
Konink, Servaas de
Koole, Arend (Johannes Christiaan)
Koopman, Ton (actually, Antonius Gerhardus Michael)
Kox, Hans
Kruyf, Ton de
Kunst, Jaap (Jakob)
Kunst, Jos
Kuyper, Elisabeth
La Hèle, George de
Landré, Guillaume (Louis Frédéric)
Landré, Willem (actually, Guillaume Louis Frédéric)
Lange Family
Lange, Samuel de
Lange, Samuel de
Lange, Daniël de
Leeuw, Reinbert de
Leeuw, Ton (Antonius Wilhelmus Adrianus) de
Le Maîstre, Mattheus
Leonhardt, Gustav (Maria)
Lichtveld, Lou (actually, Lodewijk Alphonsus Maria)
Loevendie, Theo
Lübeck, Ernst
Lübeck, Johann Heinrich
Lübeck, Louis
Mahaut, Antoine
Malbecque, Guillaume
Manneke, Daan
Marez Oyens, Tera de
Masséus, Jan
Mengelberg, (Josef) Willem
Mengelberg, Karel (Willem Joseph)
Messchaert, Johannes (Martinus)
Monnikendam, Marius
Mul, Jan
Mulder, Ernest Willem
Mulder, Herman
Ninot le Petit (real name, Johannes Baltazar)
Nobel, Felix de
Noordt, Anthoni van
Noske, Frits (Rudolf)
Obrecht (Obreht, Hobrecht, Obertus, Hobertus), Jacob
Ohms, Elisabeth
Orthel, Léon
Otterloo, (Jan) Willem van
Paap, Wouter
Padbrué, Cornelis Thymanszoon
Padbrué, David Janszoon
Pijper, Willem
Ponse, Luctor
Porcelijn, David
Prioris, Johannes
Raalte, Albert van
Raxach, Enrique
Reeser, (Hendrik) Eduard
Regis, Johannes
Regt, Hendrik de
Reinken (Reincken), Jan Adams
Rettich, Wilhelm
Richter, Nico (Max)
Ridder, Anton de
Röntgen, Julius
Roos, Robert de
Ruiter, Wim de
Ruyneman, Daniel
Sales, Franz
Sandt, Maximilian van de
Schäfer, Dirk
Schat, Peter
Schlegel, Leander
Schouwman, Hans
Schröder, Jaap
Schurmann (Schürmann), (Eduard) Gerard
Schuyt (Schuijt), Cornelis (Floriszoon)
Schuyt, Nico(laas)
Seroen, Berthe
Sigtenhorst-Meyer, Bernhard van den
Smijers, Albert(us Antonius)
Smits van Waesberghe, Jos(eph Maria Antonius Franciscus)
Soudant, Hubert
Sparnaay, Harry
Speuy, Henderick (Joostzoon)
Spoorenberg, Erna
Stam, Henk (actually, Hendrikus Gerardus)
Straesser, Joep
Strategier, Herman
Sweelinck (real name, Swybbertszoon), Jan Pieterszoon
Timmermans, Ferdinand
Toebosch, Louis
Urlus, Jacques (Jacobus)
Utendal, Alexander
Valerius, Adrianus (Adriaan, Adriaen)
Vallet or Valet, Nicolas
Van Asperen, Bob
Van Lier, Bertus
Van Lier, Jacques
Van Nes, Jard
Van Rooy, Anton(ius Maria Josephus)
Van't Hof, Jasper
Van Zanten, Cornelie
Verhulst, Johannes (actually, Josephus Hermanus)
Vermeulen, Matthijs
Vlijmen, Jan van
Vonk, Hans
Voormolen, Alexander (Nicolas)
Voorn, Joop
Vossius, Isaac
Vranken, Jaap
Vredenburg, Max
Vriend, Jan
Vroons, Frans (actually, Franciscus)
Waart, Edo (actually, Eduard) de
Wagemans, Peter-Jan
Wagenaar, Johan
Wassenaer, Count Unico Wilhelm van
Weerbeke (also Weerbecke, Werbecke, Werbeke, Werbeck), Gaspar van
Wijdeveld, Wolfgang
Wilms, Jan Willem (actually, Johann Wilhelm)
Zagwijn, Henri
Zweers, Bernard

DUTCH-AMERICAN

Brico, Antonia

DUTCH-ENGLISH

ECUADORIAN

EGYPTIAN

ENGLISH

Cairns, David (Adam)
Callcott, John Wall
Camden, Archie (actually, Archibald Leslie)
Cameron, (George) Basil
Campion (Campian), Thomas
Campoli, Alfredo
Cannon, (Jack) Philip
Cantelo, April (Rosemary)
Cardew, Cornelius
Cardus, Sir (John Frederick) Neville
Carewe, John (Maurice Foxall)
Carey, Henry
Carner, Mosco
Carron (real name, Cox), Arthur
Carse, Adam (von Ahn)
Carte, Richard D'Oyly
Casken, John (Arthur)
Caustun, Thomas
Cavendish, Michael
Cellier, Alfred
Chad and Jeremy
Chance, Michael
Chappell & Co.
Chilcot, Thomas
Child, William
Chilton, John (James)
Chorley, Henry F(othergill)
Christophers, Harry
Cibber, Susanne Maria
Clapton, Eric (originally, Clapp, Eric Patrick)
Clark, Frederick Scotson
Clark, Graham
Clark, Petula (originally, Owen, Sally)
Clarke, Jeremiah
Clash, The
Clay, Frederic (Emes)
Cleobury, Nicholas (Randall)
Cleobury, Stephen (John)
Clive, Kitty (actually, Catherine née Raftor)
Coates, Albert
Coates, Edith (Mary)
Coates, Eric
Coates, John
Cobbett, Walter Willson
Cocker, Joe (John)
Cohen, Harriet
Coleridge-Taylor, Samuel
Colles, H(enry) C(ope)
Collingwood, Lawrance (Arthur)
Collins, Anthony (Vincent Benedictus)
Collins, Michael
Collins, Phil
Connolly, Justin (Riveagh)
Cook, Thomas (Aynsley)
Cooke, Arnold (Atkinson)
Cooke, Benjamin
Cooke, Deryck (Victor)
Cooke, Henry
Cooper, Imogen
Cooper, Martin (Du Pré)
Copley, John (Michael)
Coprario or Coperario, Giovanni (real name, John Cooper)
Corbett, William
Corder, Frederick
Corder, Paul
Cornysh or Cornyshe, William
Costa, Sir Michael (Andrew Agnus) (actually, Michele Andrea Agniello)
Costello, Elvis (originally, McManus, Declan)
Cosyn, Benjamin
Coward, Sir Noël (Peirce)
Cowen, Sir Frederic (Hymen)
Cox, John
Cream
Cross, Joan
Crosse, Gordon
Crossley, Paul (Christopher Richard)
Crossley-Holland, Peter
Crotch, William
Culshaw, John (Royds)
Culture Club
Cummings, David (Michael)
Cummings, W(illiam) H(ayman)
Cure, The
Curzon, Sir Clifford (Michael)
Cusins, Sir William (George)
Dale, Benjamin (James)
Daniel, Paul (Wilson)
Dannreuther, Edward (George)
Darke, Harold (Edwin)
Darnton, (Philip) Christian
Dart, (Robert) Thurston
Dave Clark Five
Davenport, Francis William
Davies, (Albert) Meredith
Davies, Cecilia
Davies, Fanny
Davies, Hugh (Seymour)
Davies, Sir Peter Maxwell
Davis, Sir Andrew (Frank)
Davis, Sir Colin (Rex)
Davison, J(ames) W(illiam)
Davy, John
Davy, Richard
Dawson, Frederick
Dawson, Lynne
Dean, Stafford (Roderick)
Dean, Winton (Basil)
Deering (or Dering), Richard
Def Leppard
De Lara (real name, Cohen), Isidore
Delius, Frederick (actually, Fritz Theodor Albert)
Deller, Alfred (George)
Del Mar, Jonathan (Rene)
Del Mar, Norman (René)
Demuth, Norman
Dent, Edward J(oseph)
Depeche Mode
De Peyer, Gervase (Alan)
Desmond, Astra
Dew, John
Dexter, John
Dibdin, Charles
Dickinson, Meriel
Dickinson, Peter
Disley, Diz (actually, William Charles)
Dodgson, Stephen (Cuthbert Vivian)
Dolmetsch, (Eugène) Arnold
Donington, Robert
Donohoe, Peter (Howard)
Dowland, John
Dowland, Robert
Downes, Ralph (William)
Downes, Sir Edward (Thomas)
Draper, Charles
Dring, Madeleine
Dunbar, W. Rudolph
Dunhill, Thomas (Frederick)
Dunstable or Dunstaple, John
DuPré, Jacqueline
Duran Duran
Dykes, John Bacchus
Dyson, Sir George
Eaglen, Jane
Easdale, Brian
East, Michael
East, Thomas
Easton, Florence (Gertrude)
Eccles Family
- Eccles (Eagles), Solomon
- Eccles (Eagles), Solomon
- Eccles (Eagles), Henry
- Eccles, Henry
- Eccles, John

Edwards, Richard
Edwards, Sian
Elder, Mark (Philip)
Electric Light Orchestra (ELO)
Elgar, Sir Edward (William)
Ella, John
Ellerton, John Lodge (real name, John Lodge)
Elliott, Paul
Ellis (real name, Sharpe), Alexander J(ohn)
Elvey, Sir George (Job)
Elvey, Stephen
Elwes, Gervase (Cary)
Emerson, Lake and Palmer
Emery, Walter (Henry James)
Eno, Brian (Peter George St. John le Baptiste de la Salle)
d'Erlanger, Baron Frédéric
Esswood, Paul (Lawrence Vincent)
Eurythmics
Evans, Anne
Evans, Edwin, Jr.
Evans, Edwin Sr.
Excestre, William
Fairport Convention
Faithfull, Marianne
Falkner, Sir (Donald) Keith
Fallows, David (Nicholas)
Fame, Georgie (originally, Powell, Clive)
Farjeon, Harry
Farmer, John
Farnaby, Giles
Farncombe, Charles (Frederick)
Farrant, John
Farrant, Richard
Farrar, Ernest (Bristow)
Fayrfax, Robert
Fellowes, E(dmund) H(orace)
Felton, William
Fenby, Eric (William)
Ferneyhough, Brian (John Peter)
Ferrier, Kathleen (Mary)
Festing, Michael (Christian)
Finnissy, Michael (Peter)
Finzi, Gerald (Raphael)

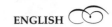

Howard, Ann (real name, Pauline Swadling)
Howarth, Elgar
Howarth, Judith
Howell, Dorothy
Howells, Anne (Elizabeth)
Howells, Herbert (Norman)
Howes, Frank (Stewart)
Hoyland, Vic(tor)
Hudson, Frederick
Hudson, George
Hueffer, Francis (real name, Franz Hüffer)
Huggett, Monica
Hughes, Dom Anselm
Hull, Arthur Eaglefield
Hullah, John (Pyke)
Human League, The
Humfrey, Pelham
Hunter, Rita (Nellie)
Hurd, Michael (John)
Hurford, Peter (John)
Hurlstone, William (Yeates)
Hurst, George
Hurwitz, Emanuel (Henry)
Hutchings, Arthur (James Bramwell)
Hyde, Walter
Hytner, Nicholas
Idol, Billy (originally, Broad, William Michael Albert)
Incledon, Charles
Ingham, Keith
Ireland, John (Nicholson)
Iron Maiden
Irving, Robert (Augustine)
Isserlis, Steven
Ives, Simon
Jackson, Francis (Alan)
Jackson, William
Jacob, Benjamin
Jacob, Gordon (Percival Septimus)
Jacobs, Arthur (David)
Jacobson, Maurice
Jacques, (Thomas) Reginald
Jairazbhoy, Nazir (Ali)
Jam, The
Jeffreys, George
Jenkins, Graeme (James Ewers)
Jenkins, John
Jethro Tull
John, Elton (originally, Dwight, Reginald)
Johnson, Graham (Rhodes)
Johnson, John
Johnson, Robert Sherlaw
Jonas, Peter
Jones, Ada
Jones, (James) Sidney
Jones, Philip (Mark)
Jones, Richard
Jones, Robert
Jones, William
Josephs, Wilfred
Joubert, John (Pierre Herman)
Joy Division
Judd, James
Kaiser, Alfred
Karpeles, Maud
Kastner, (Macario) Santiago
Keenlyside, Simon
Kell, Reginald (Clifford)
Keller, Hans (Heinrich)
Kelly, Bryan
Kemble, Adelaide
Kemp, Joseph
Kennedy, (George) Michael (Sinclair)
Kennedy, Nigel (Paul)
Kent, James
Kentner, Louis (actually, Lajos Philip)
Ketèlbey, Albert (William)
Kidson, Frank
King, Alec (actually, Alexander) Hyatt
King, Matthew Peter
King, Robert (John Stephen)
King, Thea
King Crimson
Kinks, The
Kirbye, George
Kirckman (also Kirchmann or Kirkman), Jacob
Kirkby, (Carolyn) Emma
Kirkby-Lunn, Louise
Knight, Joseph Philip
Knussen, (Stuart) Oliver
Knyvett, Charles, Jr.
Knyvett, Charles, Sr.
Knyvett, William
Kollmann, Augustus Frederic Christopher (actually, August Friedrich Christoph)
Korchinska, Maria
Kraus, Lili
Kraus, Otakar
Kwella, Patrizia
Labbette, Dora
Laidlaw, Anna Robena
Laine, Cleo (originally, Campbell, Clementina Dinah)
Lambe, Walter
Lambert, (Leonard) Constant
Lampadarios (real name, Klada), Joannes
Lampe, John Frederick (actually, Johann Friedrich)
Lanchbery, John (Arthur)
Langdon, Michael (real name, Frank Birtles)
Langdon, Richard
Langridge, Philip (Gordon)
Lanier, Nicholas
Lankester, Michael (John)
Lates, James
Latham-Koenig, Jan
Latrobe, Christian Ignatius
Laurence, Elizabeth
Lawes, Henry
Lawes, William
Lawrence, Gertrude (real name, Gertrud Alexandra Dagmar Lawrence Klasen)
Lawton, Jeffrey
Layton, Robert
Leach, James
Ledger, Philip (Stevens)
Led Zeppelin
LeFanu, Nicola (Frances)
Le Fleming, Christopher (Kaye)
Legge, Walter
Leginska (real name, Liggins), Ethel
Lehmann, Liza (actually, Elizabeth Nina Mary Frederica)
Leigh, Walter
Leighton, Kenneth
Leighton, Sir William
Lemmens-Sherrington (originally, Sherrington), Helen
Lennon, John
Leppard, Raymond (John)
Leslie, Henry (David)
Leveridge, Richard
Levin, Tony
Lewis, Sir Anthony (Carey)
Lewis, Richard (real name, Thomas Thomas)
Licette, Miriam
Lill, John (Richard)
Lindley, Robert
Linley Family
  Linley, Thomas, Sr.
  Linley, Elizabeth Ann
  Linley, Thomas, Jr.
  Linley, Mary
  Linley, Ozias Thurston
  Linley, William
Lipkin, Malcolm (Leyland)
Lloyd, A(lbert) L(ancaster)
Lloyd, Charles Harford
Lloyd, Edward
Lloyd, George (Walter Selwyn)
Lloyd, John
Lloyd, Jonathan
Lloyd, Robert (Andrew)
Lloyd-Jones, David (Mathias)
Lloyd Webber, Sir Andrew
Lloyd Webber, Julian
Locke (also Lock), Matthew
Lockspeiser, Edward
Loder, Edward (James)
Loder, George
Loewenberg, Alfred
Long, Kathleen
Loosemore, Henry
Lott, Dame Felicity (Ann)
Lowe, Edward
Lubbock, John
Lucas, Leighton
Lucas, Mary Anderson
Ludford, Nicholas
Lugge, John
Lumsden, Sir David (James)
Lutyens, (Agnes) Elisabeth
Lutz, (Wilhelm) Meyer
Luxon, Benjamin
Lympany, Dame Moura (real name, Mary Johnstone)
Lyttleton, Humphrey "Humph" (Richard Adeane)
Lytton, Paul
Maas, Joseph
Macdonald, Hugh (John)
Mace, Thomas
Macfarren, Sir George (Alexander)
Macfarren, Walter (Cecil)
Macintyre, Margaret
Maconchy, Dame Elizabeth
Mainwaring, John
Malcolm, George (John)

Manfred Mann
Mann, William (Somervell)
Manning, Jane (Marian)
Manns, Sir August (Friedrich)
Mantovani, (Annunzio Paolo)
Mapleson, James Henry
Marbeck or Marbecke, John
Marlow, Richard (Kenneth)
Marriner, Sir Neville
Marsh, John
Marsh, Roger (Michael)
Martland, Steve
Maryon (-d'Aulby), (John) Edward
Massey, Andrew (John)
Masterson, Valerie
Matthay, Tobias (Augustus)
Matthews, Colin
Matthews, David (John)
Matthews, Denis (James)
Matthews, Michael Gough
Maw, (John) Nicholas
May, Edward Collett
May, Florence
Mayall, John
Maybrick, Michael (pseudonym, Stephen Adams)
Mayer, Sir Robert
Maynard, John
Mazzinghi, Joseph
McCabe, John
McCartney, Paul
McCreesh, Paul
McGegan, Nicholas
McLaughlin, John
McPartland, Marian (originally, Turner, Margaret)
Medlam, Charles
Mell, Davis
Mellers, Wilfrid (Howard)
Menges, Isolde (Marie)
Menges, (Siegfried Frederick) Herbert
Menuhin, Yehudi, Lord Menuhin of Stoke d'Abernon
Merrick, Frank
Michael, George (originally, Panayiotous, Georgios Kryiacos)
Michaels-Moore, Anthony
Mico, Richard
Middleton, Hubert Stanley
Mildmay, (Grace) Audrey (Louise St. John)
Miles, Philip Napier
Milford, Robin (Humphrey)
Miller, Jonathan (Wolfe)
Mills, S(ebastian) B(ach)
Milner, Anthony (Francis Dominic)
Milton, John
Mitchell, Donald (Charles Peter)
Mitchinson, John (Leslie)
Moeran, E(rnest) J(ohn)
Moiseiwitsch, Benno
Monckton, (John) Lionel (Alexander)
Monk, William Henry
Montagu-Nathan, M(ontagu) (real name, Montagu Nathan)
Moody, Fanny
Moody Blues, The
Moore, Dudley (Stuart John)
Moore, Gerald
Moore, Ralph
Mori, Frank (Francis)
Mori, Nicolas
Morley, Thomas
Morris, R(eginald) O(wen)
Morton, Robert
Mott the Hoople
Mount-Edgcumbe, Richard, Second Earl of
Muldowney, Dominic (John)
Mulliner, Thomas
Mullings, Frank (Coningsby)
Mundy, John
Mundy, William
Munrow, David (John)
Murrill, Herbert (Henry John)
Myers, Rollo (Hugh)
Nares, James
Nash, Heddle
Naylor, Edward (Woodall)
Naylor, John
Neary, Martin (Gerard James)
Neate, Charles
Neighbour, O(liver) W(ray)
Newbould, Brian (Raby)
Newman, Ernest (originally, William Roberts)
Newmarch, Rosa (Harriet née Jeaffreson)
Newton, Ivor
Nicholls, Agnes
Nicholson or Nicolson, Richard
Nicholson, George (Thomas Frederick)
Nicholson, Sir Sydney (Hugo)
Noble, Dennis (William)
Noble, Ray(mond Stanley)
Noble, (Thomas) Tertius
Norrington, Sir Roger (Arthur Carver)
Norris, David Owen
North, Roger
Novello, Clara (Anastasia)
Novello, (Joseph) Alfred
Novello, Vincent
Nyman, Michael (Laurence)
Oakeley, Sir Herbert (Stanley)
Ocean, Billy (originally, Charles, Leslie Sebastian)
Odington, Walter
Ogdon, John (Andrew Howard)
Oldham, Arthur (William)
Oldman, C(ecil) B(ernard)
Oliver, Stephen (Michael Harding)
Opie, Alan (John)
Ord, Boris
Orr, C(harles) W(ilfred)
Ortiz, Cristina
Osborne, Nigel
Osbourne, Ozzy (actually, John Michael)
Oury, Antonio James
Ouseley, Sir Frederick (Arthur) Gore
Oxley, Tony
Packe, Thomas
Page, Christopher (Howard)
Paisible, James
Palmer, Felicity (Joan)
Palmer, Robert (Alan)
Panufnik, Sir Andrzej
Parikian, Manoug
Parish-Alvars, Elias
Parke Family
  Parke, William Thomas
  Parke, John
  Park(e), Maria Hester
Parker, Graham
Parratt, Sir Walter
Parrott, Andrew (Haden)
Parrott, (Horace) Ian
Parry, Sir C(harles) Hubert H(astings)
Parsley, Osbert
Parsons, Alan
Parsons, Robert
Parsons, William
Partridge, Ian (Harold)
Patterson, Paul (Leslie)
Pauk, György
Paxton, Stephen
Payne, Anthony (Edward)
Pears, Sir Peter (Neville Luard)
Pearsall, Robert Lucas
Peerson, Martin
Pepusch, John Christopher (actually Johann Christoph)
Pet Shop Boys
Petzold, Rudolf
Philips, Peter
Phillipps, Adelaide
Phillips, Henry
Phillips, Peter (Sayer)
Piccaver (real name, Peckover), Alfred
Picken, Laurence (Ernest Rowland)
Pickett, Philip
Pierson (real name, Pearson), Henry Hugo (Hugh)
Pigott, Francis
Pilkington, Francis
Pine, Courtney
Pink Floyd
Pinnock, Trevor (David)
Pinto, George Frederick
Pitfield, Thomas B(aron)
Pitt, Percy
Playford, Henry
Playford, John
Pleeth, William
Plowright, Rosalind (Anne)
Plummer, John
Police, The
Pollak, Anna
Poole, Elizabeth
Porter, Andrew (Brian)
Porter, Samuel
Porter, Walter
Poston, Elizabeth
Potter, (Philip) Cipriani (Hambley)
Pouishnov, Lev
Pountney, David (Willoughby)
Power (Powero, Polbero, etc.), Leonel (Lionel, Leonell, Leonelle, Leonellus, Lyonel, etc.)
Pownall, Mary Ann
Prelleur, Peter
Prendcourt, "Captain" de
Preston, Simon (John)
Preston, Thomas
Priestman, Brian
Pritchard, Sir John (Michael)
Procol Harum

ENGLISH-AMERICAN

ENGLISH-CANADIAN

ESTONIAN

FILIPINO

FINNISH

Flodin, Karl (Theodor)
Fordell, Erik
Fougstedt, Nils-Eric
Furuhjelm, Erik Gustaf
Hameenniemi, Eero (Olavi)
Hannikainen Family
  Hannikainen, Pekka (or Pietari) (Juhani)
  Hannikainen, (Toivo) Ilmari
  Hannikainen, Tauno (Heikki)
  Hannikainen, Arvo (Sakari)
  Hannikainen, Väinö (Aatos)
Heininen, Paavo (Johannes)
Heiniö, Mikko
Hynninen, Jorma
Ikonen, Lauri
Jalas (real name, Blomstedt), Jussi
Johansson, Bengt (Viktor)
Jokinen, Erkki
Jyrkiäinen, Reijo (Einari)
Kaipainen, Jouni (Ilarí)
Kajanus, Robert
Kamu, Okko (Tapani)
Karjalainen, Ahti
Kilpinen, Yrjö (Henrik)
Klami, Uuno (Kalervo)
Klemetti, Heikki
Kokkonen, Joonas
Kortekangas, Olli
Krause, Tom
Krohn, Felix (Julius Theofil)
Krohn, Ilmari (Henrik Reinhold)
Kuula, Toivo (Timoteus)
Kuusisto, Ilkka Taneli
Kuusisto, Taneli
Kyllönen, Timo-Juhani
Launis (real name, Lindberg), Armas (Emanuel)
Leiviskä, Helvi (Lemmikki)
Liljeblad, Ingeborg
Lindberg, Magnus (Gustaf Adolf)
Lindeman, Osmo (Uolevi)
Linjama, Jouko (Sakari)
Linko, Ernst
Linnala, Eino (Mauno Aleksanteri)
Maasalo, Armas (Toivo Valdemar)
Madetoja, Leevi (Antti)
Marttinen, Tauno (Olavi)
Mattila, Karita (Marjatta)
Melartin, Erkki (Gustaf)
Merikanto, Aarre
Merikanto, (Frans) Oskar
Meriläinen, Usko
Mielck, Ernst
Mononen, Sakari (Tuomo)
Mustonen, Olli
Nordgren, Pehr Henrik
Nummi, Seppo (Antero Yrjönpoika)
Pacius, Fredrik (actually, Friedrich)
Palmgren, Selim
Panula, Jorma
Pesonen, Olavi
Pingoud, Ernest
Pylkkänen, Tauno Kullervo
Raitio, Pentti
Raitio Väinö (Eerikki)
Ranta, Sulho
Rautavaara, Einojuhani (actually, Eino Juhani)
Rautio, Matti
Rechberger, Herman(n)
Ringbom, Nils-Eric
Rydman, Kari
Saariaho, Kaija (Anneli)
Saikkola, Lauri
Sallinen, Aulis
Salmenhaara, Erkki (Olavi)
Salminen, Matti
Salonen, Esa-Pekka
Salonen, Sulo (Nikolai)
Saraste, Jukka-Pekka
Schnéevoigt, Georg (Lennart)
Segerstam, Leif (Selim)
Sermilä, Jarmo (Kalevi)
Sibelius, Jean (actually, Johan Julius Christian)
Similä, Martti
Sipilä, Eero (Aukusti)
Söderblom, Ulf
Sonninen, Ahti
Sundgrén-Schnéevoigt, Sigrid Ingeborg
Suolahti, Heikki
Talvela, Martti (Olavi)
Tawaststjerna, Erik (Werner)
Tervani, Irma
Tiensuu, Jukka
Tikka, Kari (Juhani)
Tolonen, Jouko (Paavo Kalervo)
Törne, Bengt (Axel) von
Tulindberg, Erik (Eriksson)
Tuukkanen, Kalervo
Wegelius, Martin
Wessman, Harri (Kristian)

FLEMISH

A Kempis, Nicolaus
Arcadelt, Jacob or Jacques
Baston, Josquin
Bauldewijn (also Bauldeweyn, Bauldoin, Baudoin, etc.), Noël
Benoit, Peter (Léopold Léonard)
Berchem, Jacquet or Jachet de
Blockx, Jan
Bruck (or Brouck), Arnold von (known also as Arnold de Bruges and Arnoldo Flamengo)
Buus, Jacques (Jachet de or van Paus; Jacobus Bohusius; Jacob Buus)
Canis, Cornelius or Corneille
Coclico, Adrianus Petit
Cornet, Peeter
Danckerts, Ghiselin
Divitis (de Ryche, le Riche), Antonius (Antoine)
Faignient, Noë
Gallus, Johannes (Jean le Cocq, Maître Jean, Mestre Jhan)
Gerarde, Derick
Gero, Jhan (Jehan)
Gheyn, Matthias van den
Ghiselin, Johannes
Gombert, Nicolas
Hèle, George de la
Hellinck, Lupus (Wulfaert)
Hucbald, (Hugbaldus, Ubaldus, Uchubaldus)
Isaac (Isaak, Izak, Yzac, Ysack), Heinrich or Henricus
Kerckhoven, Abraham van den
La Rue, Pierre de (Petrus Platensis, Pierchon, Pierson, Pierzon, Perisone, Pierazon de la Ruellien)
Loeillet Family (also spelled L'Oeillet, Luly, Lulli, Lullie, Lully)
  Loeillet, Jean Baptiste
  Loeillet, Jacques (Jacob)
  Loeillet, Jean Baptiste
Luython, Charles
Macque, Giovanni (Jean) de
Maessens, Pieter
Martini, Johannes
Mel, Rinaldo del
Nasco, Jan
Ockeghem (Okeghem, Okengheim, Ockenheim, etc.), Johannes (Jean, Jehan de)
Pevernage, Andries
Phalèse, Pierre
Piéton, Loyset
Pipelare, Matthaeus
Pullaer, Louis van
Pullois, Jean or Johannes
Richafort, Jean
Rogier, Philippe
Rore, Cipriano de
Rosier, Carl
Ruckers Family
  Ruckers, Hans
  Ruckers, Johannes
  Ruckers, Andreas or Andries "the elder"
  Ruckers, Andreas or Andries "the younger"
Sayve, Lambert de
Turnhout, Gérard de (van)
Urreda, Johannes
Vaet, Jacobus
Verdonck, Cornelis
Waelrant, Hubert
Wert, Giaches (or Jaches) de
Willaert, Adrian

FRANCO-FLEMISH

Appenzeller, Benedictus
Binchois (Binch, Binche), Gilles (de)
Clemens non Papa (real name, Jacob Clement)
Courtois, Jean
Crecquillon, Thomas
Des Prez, Josquin
Ghersem, Géry (de)
Lantins, Arnold de
Lantins, Hugo de
Lasso, Orlando di
Lupi, Johannes
Maillart, Pierre
Manchicourt, Pierre de
Orto (real name, Dujardin), Marbrianus de
Phinot, Dominique
Tinctoris, Johannes

FRENCH

Adam, Adolphe (Charles)
Adam de la Halle
Adam de St. Victor
Affré, Agustarello

Aimon, (Pamphile Léopold), François
Alain, Jehan (Ariste)
Alain, Marie-Claire
Alain, Olivier
Alard, (Jean-) Delphin
Alary, Jules (Eugène Abraham)
d'Alembert, Jean-le-Rond
Alexandre, Charles-Guillaume
Alkan (real name, Morhange), Charles-Valentin
Almeida, Antonio (Jacques) de
Altès, Ernest-Eugène
Altès, Joseph-Henri
Alvarez (real name, Gourron), Albert (Raymond)
Ameller, André (Charles Gabriel)
Amiot, Jean Joseph Marie
Amoyal, Pierre
Amy, Gilbert
André, Maurice
Anet, (Jean-Jacques-) Baptiste
Anet, Jean-Baptiste
Arban, (Joseph) Jean-Baptiste (Laurent)
Arbeau, Thoinot (real name, Jean Tabourot)
Arma, Paul (real name, Imre Weisshaus)
Arnould, (Madeleine) Sophie
Arrieu, Claude
Attaignant, Pierre
Auber, Daniel-François-Esprit
Aubert Family
- Aubert, Jacques
- Aubert, Louis
- Aubert, Jean-Louis

Aubert, Louis (François Marie)
Aubéry du Boulley, Prudent-Louis
Aubin, Tony (Louis Alexandre)
Aubry, Pierre
Auda, Antoine
Audran, (Achille) Edmond
Audran, Marius-Pierre
Aurelianus Reomensis
Auriacombe, Louis
Auric, Georges
Auxcousteaux (also Aux-Cousteaux, Hautcousteaux), Artus
Azaïs, Hyacinthe
Aznavour, Charles (originally Varenagh Aznavourian)
Bachelet, Alfred
Bacilly, Bénigne de
Bacquier, Gabriel(-Augustin-Raymond-Théodore-Louis)
Baïf, Jean-Antoine de
Baillot, Pierre (-Marie-François de Sales)
Balbastre (or Balbâtre), Claude(-Bénigne)
Ballard Family
- Ballard, Robert
- Ballard, Pierre
- Ballard, Robert
- Ballard, Robert
- Ballard, Christophe

Ballif, Claude, (André François)
Barié, Augustin
Barlow, Fred
Barraqué, Jean
Barraud, Henry
Barthélémon, François-Hippolyte
Bâton, Charles, le jeune
Battaille, Charles-Amable
Baudo, Serge (Paul)
Baudrier, Yves (Marie)
Bayle, François
Bazelaire, Paul
Beaulieu (real name, Martin-Beaulieu), Marie-Désiré
Beauvarlet-Charpentier, Jean-Jacques
Bedos de Celles, Dom François
Beffara, Louis-François
Beffroy de Reigny, Louis-Abel
Bellaigue, Camille
Bembo, Antonia
Benoît, Camille
Benzi, Roberto
Berbiguier, Antoine (Benoît-) Tranquille
Bergiron de Briou, Nicolas-Antoine, Seigneur du Fort Michon
Berlioz, (Louis-) Hector
Bernac (real name, Bertin), Pierre
Bernier, Nicolas
Béroff, Michel
Berteau, Martin
Bertheaume, Isidore
Bertin, Louise (-Angélique)
Bertin de la Doué, Thomas
Bertini, (Benoît-) Auguste
Bertini, Henri (-Jérôme)
Berton, Henri-Montan
Berton, Pierre-Montan
Bertrand, Aline
Bertrand, Antoine de
Besard, Jean-Baptiste
Bigot, Eugène
Bigot (de Morogues), Marie (née Kiéné)
Bilhon (Billhon, Billon), Jhan (Jean, Jan, Jehan, Joannes) de (du)
Bizet, Georges (baptismal names, Alexandre-César-Léopold)
Blainville, Charles-Henri de
Blamont, François Colin de
Blanchard, Esprit Joseph Antoine
Blavet, Michel
Blaze (called Castil-Blaze), François-Henri-Joseph
Blaze, Henri, Baron de Bury
Blondeau, Pierre-Auguste-Louis
Bochsa, (Robert-) Nicolas-Charles
Boëllmann, Léon
Boëly, Alexandre Pierre François
Boësset, Antoine (Sieur de Villedieu)
Boieldieu, François-Adrien
Boismortier, Joseph Bodin de
Bolling, Claude
Bondeville, Emmanuel (Pierre Georges) de
Bondon, Jacques (Lauret Jules Désiré)
Boni, Guillaume
Bonnet, Joseph (Élie Georges Marie)
Bordes, Charles (Marie Anne)
Boschot, Adolphe
Bosseur, Jean-Yves
Boucher, Alexandre-Jean
Boucourechliev, André
Bouhy, Jacques (-Joseph André)
Boulanger, Lili (Juliette Marie Olga)
Boulanger, Nadia (Juliette)
Boulez, Pierre
Boulnois, Joseph
Bour, Ernest
Bourdin, Roger
Bourgault-Ducoudray, Louis-Albert
Bourgeois, Loys
Bourgeois, Thomas-Louis (-Joseph)
Bournonville, Jacques de
Bournonville, Jean de
Bournonville, Valentin de
Bousset, Jean-Baptiste
Bouvet, Charles (René Clement)
Bouzignac, Guillaume
Boyvin, Jacques
Bozza, Eugène
Brăiloiu, Constantin
Brailowsky, Alexander
Branchu, Alexandrine Caroline (née Chevalier de Lavit)
Brancour, René
Brassin, Louis
Brelet, Gisèle (Jeanne Marie Noémie)
Brémond, François
Breval, Jean-Baptiste Sebastien
Bréval, Lucienne (real name, Berthe Agnes Lisette Schilling)
Bréville, Pierre (-Onfroy de)
Broche, Charles
Brossard, Sébastien de
Bruck, Charles
Brumel, Antoine
Bruneau, (Louis-Charles-Bonaventure-) Alfred
Brunold, Paul
Bruzdowicz, Joanna
Buffardin, Pierre-Gabriel
Bullant, Antoine
Bury, Bernard de
Busnois, Antoine
Büsser, (Paul-) Henri
Calvé (real name, Calvet de Roquer), (Rosa-Noémie) Emma
Cambefort, Jean de
Cambert, Robert
Cambreling, Sylvain
Campion, François
Campra, André
Candeille, (Amélie) Julie
Candeille, Pierre Joseph
Canteloube (de Malaret), (Marie-) Joseph
Capet, Lucien
Caplet, André
Capoul, (Joseph-Amédée-) Victor
Cardon, Jean-Baptiste
Caron, Rose (Lucille) (née Meuniez)
Carpentras (real name, Elzéar Genet)
Cartan, Jean
Carvalho (real name, Carvaille), Léon
Carvalho, Caroline (née Caroline-Marie Félix-Miolan)
Casadesus, François Louis
Casadesus, Gaby (née Gabrielle L'Hôte)
Casadesus, Henri
Casadesus, Jean-Claude
Casadesus, Jean (Claude Michel)
Casadesus, Marius
Casadesus, Robert (Marcel)

Casanova, André
Castelmary, Armand (real name, Comte Armand de Castan)
Catel, Charles-Simon
Cavaillé-Coll, Aristide
Cellier, Alexandre (-Eugène)
Certon, Pierre
Chabrier, (Alexis-) Emmanuel
Chailley, Jacques
Chambonnières, Jacques Champion, Sieur de
Chaminade, Cécile (Louise Stéphanie)
Chancy, François de
Charpentier, Gustave
Charpentier, Jacques
Charpentier, Marc-Antoine
Charton-Demeur, Anne
Chausson, (Amédée-) Ernest
Chaynes, Charles
Chéreau, Patrice
Chevalier, Maurice
Chevillard, (Paul Alexandre) Camille
Chollet, Jean Baptiste (Marie)
Choron, Alexandre (Étienne)
Christie, William (Lincoln)
Cigna, Gina (real name, Ginetta Sens)
Clapisson, (Antoine-) Louis
Clément, Edmond (Frédéric-Jean)
Clérambault, Louis Nicolas
Clérice, Justin
Clicquot Family
 Clicquot, Robert
 Clicquot, Jean Baptiste
 Clicquot, Louis-Alexandre
 Clicquot, François-Henri
Cluytens, André
Cochereau, Pierre
Colasse, Pascal
Colin, Pierre
Collard, Jean-Philippe
Collin (Colin) de Blamont, François
Colonne, Édouard (actually, Judas)
Combarieu, Jules (-Léon-Jean)
Comet, Catherine
Compère, Loyset
Constant, Marius
Coquard, Arthur (-Joseph)
Corrette, Michel
Cortot, Alfred (Denis)
Cossira (real name, Coussival), Emil
Coste, Napoléon
Costeley, Guillaume
Couperin
Couperin, Armand-Louis
Couperin, Charles
Couperin, François
Couperin, François, Sieur de Crouilly
Couperin, Gervais-François
Couperin, Louis
Couperin, Nicolas
Couperin, Pierre-Louis
Coussemaker, (Charles-) Edmond (-Henri) de
Crespin, Régine
Cristiani, Lisa (Barbier)
Cziffra, György
Dabadie, Henri-Bernard
Dagincour, François
Dalayrac, Nicolas(-Marie)
Dalberto, Michel (Jean Jacques)
Dalmorès, Charles (real name, Henry Alphonse Boin)
Dalvimare (real name, d'Alvimare), (Martin-) Pierre
Damase, Jean-Michael
Dancla, Arnaud Phillipe
Dancla, (Jean Baptiste) Charles
Dancla, (Jean Pierre) Léopold
Dandelot, Georges (Edouard)
Dandrieu, Jean François
D'Anglebert, Jean-Henri
Danhauser, Adolphe-Léopold
Daniel, Salvador (real name, Francisco Daniel; also known as Salvador-Daniel)
Daniel-Lesur, Jean Yves (real name, Daniel Jean Yves Lesur)
Daniélou, Alain
Danjou, Jean-Louis-Félix
Daquin, Louis-Claude
Darasse, Xavier
Darré, Jeanne-Marie
D'Ascoli, Bernard
Dauprat, Louis-François
Daussoigne-Méhul, Louis-Joseph
Dauvergne, Antoine
Davaux, Jean-Baptiste
David, Félicien (-César)
David, José
David, Léon
David, Samuel
Debain, Alexandre-François
Debussy, (Achille-)Claude
Decaux, Abel
Decoust, Michel
Degeyter, Pierre
Delaborde, Elie (Miriam) (née Elie Miriam)
Delacôte, Jacques
Delage, Maurice (Charles)
Delalande (also de La Lande, Lalande, etc.), Michel-Richard
Delannoy, Marcel
Deldevez, Edouard (-Marie-Ernest)
Delibes, (Clément-Philibert-)Léo
Della Maria, (Pierre-Antoine-) Dominique
Delmas, Jean-François
Delmas, Marc-Jean-Baptiste
Delmotte, Roger
Delna (real name, Ledan), Marie
Delsart, Jules
Delvincourt, Claude
Demarquez, Suzanne
Demessieux, Jeanne
Demougeot, (Jeanne Marguerite) Marcelle (Decorne)
Denis, Didier
Déré, Jean
Dérivis, Henri Etienne
Dérivis, Prosper
Dervaux, Pierre
Deschamps-Jehin, (Marie-)Blanche
Deslandres, Adolphe-Edouard-Marie
Desmarets, Henri
Desmazures, Laurent
Désormière, Roger
Dessay, Natalie
Destouches, André-Cardinal
Deutsch, Max
Devienne, François
Dezède, Nicolas
Dhomont, Francis
Diaz (de la Peña), Eugène (-Emile)
Diderot, Denis
Diemer, Louis (-Joseph)
Diet, Edmond-Marie
Dietsch, (Pierre-)Louis(-Philippe)
Dieupart, Charles François
Dillon, Henri
Dizi, François-Joseph
Doche, Joseph-Denis
Doire, René
Dolmetsch, Carl Frederick
Dourlen, Victor(-Charles-Paul)
Doyen, Albert
Dreyfus, Huguett (Pauline)
Drouet, Louis François-Philippe
Dubois, (François-Clément) Théodore
Dubois, Pierre-Max
Du Cange, Charles Du Fresne, Sieur
Du Caurroy, François-Eustache, Sieur de St.-Frémin
Duchâble, François-René
Du Fay, Guillaume (real name, Willem Du Fayt)
Dufourcq, Norbert
Dufourt, Hugues
Duhamel, Antoine
Duiffoprugcar (real name, Tieffenbrucker), Gaspar
Dukas, Paul
Du Mont or Dumont (real name, de Thier), Henri or Henry
Duparc (real name, Fouques-Duparc), (Marie-Eugène-) Henri
Dupin, Paul
Dupont, Gabriel
Dupont, Pierre
Duport, Jean-Louis
Duport, Jean-Pierre
Duprato, Jules-Laurent
Dupré, Marcel
Duprez, Gilbert(-Louis)
Durand, Emile
Durand, Marie-Auguste
Durey, Louis (Edmond)
Duruflé, Marie-Madeleine (née Chevalier)
Duruflé, Maurice
Dusapin, Pascal
Dutilleux, Henri
Duval, Denise
Duvernoy, Charles
Duvernoy, Frédéric Nicolas
Duvernoy, Henri-Louis-Charles
Duvernoy, Victor-Alphonse
Écorcheville, Jules (Armand Joseph)
Eda-Pierre, Christiane
Eler, André-Frédéric
Elias Salomon or Salomonis
Elleviou, (Pierre-) Jean (-Baptiste-François)
Eloy, Jean-Claude
Elwart, Antoine (-Amable-Élie)
Emmanuel, (Marie François) Maurice
Engerer, Brigitte

Isouard, Nicolò
Ivry, Paul Xavier Désiré, Marquis d'
Jacob, Maxime
Jacquet de la Guerre, Elisabeth-Claude
Jacquillat, Jean-Pierre
Jadin, Hyacinthe
Jadin, Louis Emmanuel
Jaëll, Marie (née Trautmann)
Jambe de Fer, Philibert
Jancourt, (Louis Marie) Eugène
Janequin (Jannequin), Clément
Jankélévitch, Vladimir
Janson, Jean-Baptitste-Aimé Joseph ("l'aîné")
Jarre, Maurice (Alexis)
Jaubert, Maurice
Jausions, Dom Paul
Jeannin, Dom Jules Cécilien
Jehannot de l'Escurel or Jehan de Lescurel
Jélyotte, Pierre de
Jolivet, André
Jonas, Émile
Joncières, Victorin de (real name, Felix Ludger Rossignol)
Journet, Marcel
Joy, Geneviéve
Juhan, James
Jullien, Gilles
Jullien, (Jean-Lucien-) Adolphe
Jullien, Louis
Kalkbrenner, Frédéric (Friedrich Wilhelm Michael)
Kantorow, Jean-Jacques
Katsaris, Cyprien
Klosé, Hyacinthe-Eléonore
Koechlin, Charles (Louis Eugène)
Koering, René
Kreubé, Charles Frédéric
Kreutzer, Jean Nicolas Auguste
Kreutzer, Léon Charles François
Kreutzer, Rodolphe
Krivine, Emmanuel
La Barre Family (original name probably Chabanceau)
  La Barre, Pierre de
  La Barre, Anne de
  La Barre, Joseph de
  La Barre, Pierre de
La Barre, Michel de
Labarre, Théodore (François-Joseph)
L'Abbé Family (real name, Saint-Sévin)
  Saint-Sévin, Pierre-Philippe
  Saint-Sévin, Pierre
  Saint-Sévin, Joseph-Barnabé
Labèque, Katia and Marielle
Labey, Marcel
La Borde or Laborde, Jean-Benjamin (-François) de
La Casinière, Yves de
Lacépède, Bernard Germaine Etiènne Médard de la Villesur-Illon, Count of
Lacombe, Louis (Trouillon)
Lacombe, Paul
Lacome (actually, Lacôme d'Estalenx), Paul (-Jean-Jacques)
Lacroix, Antoine
Ladmirault, Paul (-Émile)
La Fage, (Juste-) Adrien (-Lenoir) de
L'Affilard, Michel
Lafont, Charles-Philippe
La Garde, Pierre de
Lagoanère, Oscar de
Lagoya, Alexandre
La Grange, Henry-Louis de
La Guerre, Élisabeth Jacquet de
La Guerre, Michel de
La Houssaye, Pierre (-Nicolas)
Lajarte, Théodore (-Édouard Dufaure de)
Laks, Simon (actually, Szymon)
La Laurencie, (Marie Bertrand) Lionel (Jules), Comte de
Lalo, Charles
Lalo, Édouard (-Victoire-Antoine)
Lalo, Pierre
Lalouette, Jean Francois
Laloy, Louis
La Marre (Lamare), Jacques-Michel-Hurel de
Lambert, Lucien
Lambert, Michel
Lambillotte, Louis
Lamoureux, Charles
Lamy, Fernand
Lancen, Serge (Jean Mathieu)
Landormy, Paul (Charles-René)
Landowska, Wanda (Alexandra)
Landowski, Marcel (François Paul)
Langlais, Jean (François-Hyacinthe)
Langlé, Honoré (François Marie)
Laparra, Raoul
Laporte, Joseph de
La Pouplinière, Alexandre-Jean-Joseph Le Riche de
La Presle, Jacques de
Larrivée, Henri
Laruette, Jean-Louis
Laskine, Lily
Lassalle, Jean (-Louis)
La Tombelle, (Antoine Louis Joseph Gueyrand) Fernand (Fouant) de
Lavagne, André
Lavignac, (Alexandre Jean) Albert
Lays, François
Lazarus, Daniel
Lazzari, (Joseph) Sylvio
Le Bé, Guillaume
Lebègue, Nicolas-Antoine
Leborne, Aimé-Ambroise-Simon
Leborne, Fernand
Lebrun, Jean
Lebrun, Louis-Sébastien
Leclair Family
  Leclair, Jean-Marie
  Leclair, Jean-Marie (le second or le cadet)
  Leclair, Pierre
  Leclair, Jean-Benoît
Lecoq, (Alexandre) Charles
Leduc, Alphonse
Leduc, Pierre (le jeune)
Leduc (Le Duc), Simon (l'aîné)
Lefébure, Yvonne
Lefébure-Wély, Louis James Alfred
Lefebvre, Charles Éduoard
Lefèvre, (Jean) Xavier
Le Flem, Paul
Legrand, Michel (Jean)
Legrense, Johannes
Legros, Joseph
Le Heurteur, Guillaume
Leibowitz, René
Le Jeune, Claude (or Claudin)
Lemaire (or Le Maire), Jean
Lemaire, Louis
Lemière de Corvey, Jean Frédéric Auguste
Lemoyne, Jean-Baptiste
Lenepveu, Charles (Ferdinand)
Lenormand, René
Leoninus (Magister Leoninus, Magister Leonini, Magister Leo, Magister Leonis)
Le Rochois, Marthe
Le Roux, François
Le Roux, Gaspard
Le Roux, Maurice
Leroux, Xavier (Henry Napoléon)
Le Roy, Adrien
Le Roy, René
L'Estocart, Paschal de
Le Sueur or Lesueur, Jean François
Lesure, François (-Marie)
Levadé, Charles (Gaston)
Levasseur, Jean-Henri
Levasseur, Nicolas (-Prosper)
Levasseur, Rosalie (Marie-Rose-Claude-Josèphe)
Levidis, Dimitri
Lévy, Lazare
Lévy, Michel-Maurice
Lhérie (real name, Lévy), Paul
Lhéritier, Jean
Libert, Henri
Libon, Philippe
Lioncourt, Guy de
Lirou, Jean François Espic, Chevalier de
Litaize, Gaston
Litolff, Henry Charles
Lombard, Alain
Long, Marguerite (Marie-Charlotte)
Longy, (Gustave-) Georges (-Léopold)
Lopez, Francis(co)
Loqueville, Richard
Loriod, Yvonne
Loucheur, Raymond
Louis XIII
Loulié, Étienne
Lubin, Germaine (Léontine Angélique)
Luigini, Alexandre (-Clément-Léon-Joseph)
Lully, Jean-Baptiste (originally, Giovanni Battista Lulli)
Lupi Second, Didier
Machabey, Armand
Machaut (also Machault, Machau, Mauchault), Guillaume de (Guillelmus de Mascaudio)
Mâche, François-Bernard
Magnard, (Lucien-Denis-Gabriel-), Albéric
Magne, Michel
Maistre, Jhan
Malec, Ivo
Malgoire, Jean-Claude
Malherbe, Charles (-Théodore)

Prod'homme, J(acques)-G(abriel)
Propiac, (Catherine Joseph Ferdinand) Girard de
Prot, Félix-Jean
Prudent, Emile (Racine Gauthier)
Prumier, Antoine
Prunières, Henry
Puget, Loïsa (actually, Louise-Françoise)
Pugno, (Stéphane) Raoul
Puig-Roget, Henriette
Quatremère de Quincy, Antoine-Chrysostome
Queffélec, Anne (Tita)
Quentin, Jean-Baptiste
Quinault, Jean-Baptiste-Maurice
Quinault, Philippe
Rabaud, Henri (Benjamin)
Racquet, Charles
Ragué, Louis-Charles
Raimbaut de Vaqueiras
Raimon de Miraval
Raison, André
Rameau, Jean-Philippe
Rampal, Jean-Pierre (Louis)
Raoul de Beavais
Raoul de Ferrières
Raoul de Soissons
Rault, Félix
Ravel, (Joseph) Maurice
Rebel Family
Rebel, Jean
Rebel, Anne-Renée
Rebel (le père), Jean-Féry
Rebel (le fils), François
Reber, (Napoléon-) Henri
Reicha (Rejcha), Antoine (-Joseph) (Antonin or Anton)
Reinhardt, Django (Jean Baptiste)
Renaud (real name, Cronean), Maurice (Arnold)
Renié, Henriette
Rey, Jean-Baptiste
Rey, Louis-Charles-Joseph
Reyer (real name, Rey), (Louis-Etienne-) Ernest
Rhené-Baton (real name, René Baton)
Rhodes, Jane (Marie Andrée)
Riegel (later changed to Rigel), Henri (Heinrich) Joseph
Rigel, Henri-Jean
Rivier, Jean
Robert, Pierre
Robin, Mado
Rode, (Jacques-) Pierre (Joseph)
Rogé, Pascal
Roger, Gustave-Hippolyte
Roger, Victor
Roger-Ducasse, Jean (-Jules Aimable)
Roget, Henriette
Rokseth, Yvonne (née Rihouët)
Roland-Manuel (real name, Roland Alexis Manuel Lévy)
Rolland, Romain
Rollin, Jean
Ropartz, (Joseph) Guy (Marie)
Rosenthal, Manuel
Rossi, Tino
Roth, Daniel
Rothier, Léon
Rouget, Gilbert
Rouget de l'Isle or Lisle, Claude-Joseph
Rousseau, Jean-Jacques
Rousseau, Marcel (-Auguste-Louis)
Rousseau, Samuel-Alexandre
Roussel, Albert (Charles Paul Marie)
Rousselière, Charles
Rousset, Christophe
Roussier, Abbé Pierre-Joseph
Royer, Joseph-Nicolas-Pancrace
Rôze, Marie (real name, Hippolyte Ponsin)
Rudy, Mikhail
Ruwet, Nicolas
Sainte-Colombe, Sieur de or Monsieur de (real name, August Dautrecourt)
Saint-Foix, (Marie-Olivier-) Georges (du Parc Poulain), Comte de
Saint-Huberty, Mme. de (real name, Antoinette Cécile Clavel)
Sainton, Prosper (Philippe Cathérine)
Saint-Saëns, (Charles-) Camille
Salabert, Francis
Saléza, Albert
Salignac, Thomas (real name, Eustace Thomas)
Salvayre, Gaston (actually, Gervais-Bernard)
Samazeuilh, Gustave (Marie Victor Fernand)
Sarrette, Bernard
Satie, Erik (Alfred-Leslie)
Sauguet, Henri (real name, Jean Pierre Poupard)
Sauret, Emile
Saury, Maxim
Sauveur, Joseph
Schaeffer, Pierre
Schaeffner, André
Scherchen, Tona
Schmitt, Florent
Schmitz, Elie Robert
Schneider, Hortense (Caroline-Jeanne)
Schneitzhoeffer, Jean
Schoelcher, Victor
Schöne, Lotte (real name, Charlotte Bodenstein)
Scio, Julie-Angélique
Scribe, (Augustin) Euègene
Scudo, P(ietro)
Séjan, Nicolas
Selva, Blanche
Semet, Théophile (-Aimé-Emile)
Senaillé (also Senaillié, Senallié, etc.), Jean Baptiste
Sénéchal, Michel
Sérieyx, Auguste (Jean Maria Charles)
Sermisy, Claudin or Claude de
Servais, François (Franz Matheiu)
Séverac, (Marie-Joseph-Alexandre) Déodat de
Simon, Prosper-Charles
Simon-Girard, Juliette
Singher, Martial (Jean-Paul)
Siohan, Robert (-Lucien)
Siret, Nicholas
Solié, Jean-Pierre
Sonami, Laetitia
Soubies, Albert
Souhaitty, Jean-Jacques
Soustrot, Marc
Souzay, Gérard (real name, Gérard Marcel Tisserand)
Soyer, Roger (Julien Jacques)
Spencer, Émile-Alexis-Xavier
Stendhal (real name, Marie-Henri Beyle)
Stoltz, Rosine (real name, Victoire Noël)
Straram, Walther
Straus, Oscar (Nathan)
Strauss, Isaac
Stuck, Jean-Baptiste
Stutzmann, Nathalie
Szalowski, Antoni
Tabuteau, Marcel
Tacchino, Gabriel
Taffanel, (Claude-) Paul
Tagliaferro, Magda
Tagliafico, (Dieudonné) Joseph
Tailleferre (real name, Taillefesse), (Marcelle) Germaine
Tansman, Alexandre
Tariol-Baugé, Anne
Taskin, (Emile-) Alexandre
Taskin, Pascal (-Joseph)
Terrasse, Claude (Antoine)
Tessier, André
Tessier, Charles
Texier, Henri
Thévenard, Gabriel-Vincent
Thibaud, Jacques
Thibaudet, Jean-Yves
Thibault, Geneviève (La Comtesse Hubert de Chambure)
Thibaut IV
Thienen, Marcel van
Thill, Georges
Thiriet, Maurice
Thomas, (Charles Louis) Ambroise
Thomé, Francis (baptized François Luc Joseph)
Tiersot, (Jean-Baptiste-Elisée-) Julien
Tilmant, Théophile (Alexandre)
Tisné, Antoine
Titelouze, Jean or Jehan
Tomasi, Henri (Frédien)
Tortelier, Paul
Tortelier, Yan Pascal
Tournemire, Charles (Arnould)
Tourte, François (Xavier)
Trebelli, Zélia (real name, Gloria Caroline Gillebert)
Trial Family
Trial, Jean-Claude
Trial, Antoine
Tulou, Jean-Louis
Tzipine, Georges
Ugalde, Delphine (née Beaucé)
Urhan, Chrétien
Vachon, Pierre
Vadé, Jean-Joseph
Vallas, Léon
Vallin, Ninon
Varney, Louis
Varney, Pierre Joseph Alphonse
Vasseur, Léon (Félix Augustin Joseph)
Végh, Sándor (Alexandre)

FRENCH-AMERICAN

FRENCH-ARGENTINE

FRENCH-CATALAN

FRENCH-ITALIAN

GEORGIAN

GERMAN

Graunke, Kurt (Karl Wilhelm)
Graupner, (Johann) Christoph
Greber, Jakob
Greindl, Josef
Greiter, Matthaeus or Matthias
Grell, (August) Eduard
Griepenkerl, Friedrich (Conrad)
Griesbacher, Peter
Grimm, Friedrich Melchior, Baron von
Grimm, Heinrich
Grimm, Julius Otto
Grimm, Karl
Grimm, (Karl Konstantin) Louis (Ludwig)
Grishkat, Hans (Adolf Karl Willy)
Groh, Johann
Grosheim, Georg Christoph
Grosskopf, Erhard
Grua, Franz Paul (Francesco da Paula or Paolo)
Grümmer, Elisabeth
Grümmer, Paul
Grund, Friedrich Wilhelm
Grundheber, Franz
Grützmacher, Friedrich (Wilhelm Ludwig)
Gudehus, Heinrich
Guhr, Karl (Wilhelm Ferdinand)
Gülke, Peter
Gumbert, Ferdinand
Gumpelzhaimer, Adam
Gura, Eugen
Gura, Hermann
Gurlitt, Cornelius
Gurlitt, Manfred
Gurlitt, Wilibald
Gutheil-Schoder, Marie
Gutmann, Adolph
Güttler, Ludwig
Haas, Joseph
Haas, Karl (Wilhelm Jacob)
Haas, Werner
Haase, Hans
Haberbier, Ernst
Haberl, Franz Xaver
Habich, Eduard
Haeffner, Johann Christian Friedrich
Haenchen, Hartmut
Hagen, Friedrich Heinrich von der
Hagen-Groll, Walter
Hakenberger, Andreas
Halm, August Otto
Hampe, Michael (Hermann)
Hampel, Gunter
Han (Hahn), Ulrich (known as Udalricus Gallus)
Hanff, Johann Nikolaus
Hanfstängel, Marie (née Schröder)
Hanisch, Joseph
Hanke, Karl
Harich-Schneider, Eta (Margarete)
Harnisch, Otto Siegfried
Harrer, (Johann) Gottlob
Hartig, Heinz (Friedrich)
Hartmann, Carl
Hartmann, Karl Amadeus
Hartmann, Pater (real name, Paul Eugen Josef von An der Lan-Hochbrunn)
Hartmann, Rudolf
Härtwig, Dieter
Häser, August Ferdinand
Häser, Charlotte (Henriette)
Hass, Sabine
Hasse, Johann Adolf
Hasse, Karl
Hassler Family
    Hassler, Isaak
    Hassler, Caspar
    Hassler, Hans (Johann) Leo
    Hassler, Jakob
Hassler, Johann Wilhelm
Haupt, Karl August
Hauptmann, Cornelius
Hauptmann, Moritz
Hauschild, Wolf-Dieter
Hausmann, Robert
Haussmann, Valentin
Hausswald, Günter
Havemann, Gustav
Hebenstreit, Pantaleon
Heckel, Johann Adam
Heermann, Hugo
Heger, Robert
Heinefetter Family
    Heinefetter, Sabine
    Heinefetter, Clara
    Heinefetter, Kathinka
Heinemann, Alfred
Heinemeyer, Ernst Wilhelm
Heinichen, Johann David
Heinitz, Wilhelm
Heinroth, Johann August Gunther
Heinze, Gustav Adolf
Heiss, Hermann
Heitmann, Fritz
Helder, Bartholomäus
Helfritz, Hans
Hellwig, Karl (Friedrich) Ludwig
Helmholtz, Hermann (Ludwig Ferdinand) von
Hemmel, Sigmund
Hempel, Frieda
Henkel, Heinrich
Henkel, (Johann) Michael
Henneberg, Richard
Hennig, Carl
Hennig, Carl Rafael
Henning, Carl Wilhelm
Hensel, Fanny (Cäcilie) (née Mendelssohn-Bartholdy)
Hensel, Heinrich
Henselt, (Georg Marin) Adolf von
Hentschel, Franz
Hentschel, Theodor
Henze, Hans Werner
Herbart, Johann Friedrich
Herbig, Günther
Herbst, Johann Andreas
Hering, Karl Gottlieb
Herman, Nicolaus
Hermann, Hans
Hermann, Roland
Hermesdorff, Michael
Hermstedt, (Johann) Simon
Herold, Johannes
Herrmann, Gottfried
Herrmann, Hugo
Hertel, Johann Wilhelm
Herz, Joachim
Herzog, Johann Georg
Hess, Ludwig
Hesse, Adolph (Friedrich)
Hesse, Ernst Christian
Hesse, Ludwig Christian
Hesse, Max
Hessenberg, Kurt
Hetsch, (Karl) Ludwig Friedrich
Heugel, Johannes
Heuss, Alfred (Valentin)
Hey, Julius
Heyden (Heiden, Haiden), Hans
Heyden (Heiden, Haiden), Sebald
Heyer, Wilhelm (Ferdinand)
Hickmann, Hans (Robert Hermann)
Hildegard von Bingen
Hillebrecht, Hildegard
Hiller, Ferdinand (von)
Hiller, Friedrich Adam
Hiller, Johann Adam
Himmel, Friedrich Heinrich
Hitzler, Daniel
Hochberg, Hans Heinrich, XIV, Bolko Graf von
Hockh, Carl
Hoelscher, Ludwig
Hoelscher, Ulf
Hoerburger, Felix
Hoesslin, Franz von
Höffer, Paul
Höffgen, Marga
Hoffmann, Bruno
Hoffmann, E(rnst) T(heodor) A(madeus)
Hoffmann, Hans
Hoffmann, Heinrich August
Hoffmeister, Franz Anton
Hoffstetter, Roman
Hofmann, Heinrich (Karl Johann)
Hofmann, Peter
Höll, Hartmut
Hollaender, Alexis
Hollaender, Gustav
Hollaender, Viktor
Hölle, Matthias
Höller, Karl
Höller, York (Georg)
Hollreiser, Heinrich
Hollweg, Ilse
Hollweg, Werner (Friedrich)
Holm, Renate
Holm, Richard
Holstein, Franz (Friedrich) von
Holtzner, Anton
Homilius, Gottfried August
Höngen, Elisabeth
Hopf, Hans
Horn, Karl Friedrich
Hornstein, Robert von
Hotter, Hans
Huber, Kurt
Hübler, Klaus K(arl)
Hummel, Ferdinand
Humperdinck, Engelbert
Humpert, Hans
Hünten, Franz
Hurlebusch, Conrad Friedrich

Kulenkampff, Georg
Kullak, Adolf
Kullak, Franz
Kullak, Theodor
Kummer, Friedrich August
Kümmerle, Salomon
Kunad, Rainer
Künneke, Eduard
Kunzen Family
  Kunzen, Johann Paul
  Kunzen, Adolph Carl
  Kunzen, Friedrich Ludwig Aemilius
  Kunzen, Louise Friederica Ulrica
Kupfer, Harry
Kupper, Annelies (Gabriele)
Kurz, Siegfried
Kürzinger, Ignaz Franz Xaver
Kusche, Benno
Kusser (or Cousser), Johann Sigismund
Kwast, James
Labitzky Family
  Labitzky, Joseph
  Labitzky, Wilhelm
  Labitzky, August
Lachenmann, Helmut Friedrich
Lachmann, Robert
Lachner Family
  Lachner, Theodor
  Lachner, Franz Paul
  Lachner, Ignaz
  Lachner, Vincenz
Lammers, Gerda
Lang, Johann Georg
Lang, Josephine (Caroline)
Lange, Francisco Curt (actually, Franz Curt)
Lange, Gustav
Langendorff, Frieda
Langhans, (Friedrich) Wilhelm
Lankow, Anna
Lassus, Ferdinand de
Lassus, Rudolph de
Laubenthal (real name, Neumann), Horst (Rüdiger)
Laubenthal, Rudolf
Lautenbacher, Susanne
Lebert (real name, Levi), Sigmund
Lebrun, Franziska (Dorothea née Danzi)
Lebrun, Ludwig August (actually, Ludwig Karl Maria)
Lechner, Leonhard (Leonardus Lechner Atheses or Athesinus)
Leffler-Burckhard, Martha
Lehmann, Lilli
Lehmann, (Ludwig) Fritz
Lehmann, Marie
Lehnhoff, Nikolaus
Leider, Frida
Leisentrit, Johannes
Leitner, Ferdinand
Lemacher, Heinrich
Lemnitz, Tiana (Luise)
Le Sage de Richée, Philipp Franz
Levi, Hermann
Lewandowski, Louis
Lichtenstein, Karl August, Freiherr von
Liebig, Karl
Liliencron, Rochus (Traugott Ferdinand), Freiherr von
Lincke, (Carl Emil) Paul
Lindpaintner, Peter Joseph von
Linike Family
  Linike, Ephraim
  Linike, Christian Bernhard
  Linike, Johann Georg
Lipphardt, Walther
Lipsius, Marie (pen name, La Mara)
Lobe, Johann Christian
Loewe, (Johann) Carl (Gottfried)
Loewe, Sophie (Johanna)
Logier, Johann Bernhard
Löhlein, Georg Simon
Löhner, Johann
Löhse, Otto
Lorenz, Max
Lortzing, (Gustav) Albert
Löschhorn, (Carl) Albert
Lothar, Mark
Louis, Rudolf
Louis Ferdinand (actually, Friedrich Christian Ludwig)
Löwe von Eisenach, Johann Jakob
Lubeck, Vincent
Ludecus, Matthäus
Ludwig, Christa
Ludwig, Friedrich
Ludwig, Walther
Luther, Martin
Mach, Ernst
Maderna, Bruno
Maelzel, Johannes Nepomuk
Mager, Jörg
Mahrenholz, Christhard (actually, Christian Reinhard)
Mainzer, Joseph
Malten (real name, Müller), Therese
Mancinus (real name, Mencken), Thomas
Mangold, Carl (Ludwig Amand)
Mangold, (Johann) Wilhelm
Mara, Gertrud (Elisabeth née Schmeling)
Marchesi de Castrone, Mathilde (née Graumann)
Maria Antonia Walpurgis
Märkl, Jun
Markull, Friedrich Wilhelm
Markwort, Johann Christian
Marpurg, Friedrich
Marpurg, Friedrich Wilhelm
Marschner, Heinrich (August)
Martienssen, Carl Adolf
Martini, Jean Paul Egide (real name, Johann Paul Ágid Schwarzendorf)
Marx, Adolf Bernhard
Marx, Karl
Marxsen, Eduard
Massonneau, Louis
Masur, Kurt
Mattheson, Johann
Matthus, Siegfried
Mauersberger, Rudolf
Maurer, Ludwig (Wilhelm)
Mayer, Charles
Mayr, (Johannes) Simon (actually, Giovanni Simone)
Meck, Joseph
Medek, Tilo
Meder, Johann Valentin
Mehlig, Anna
Meier, Waltraud
Meiland, Jakob
Meinardus, Ludwig (Siegfried)
Mendel, Hermann
Mendelssohn, Arnold (Ludwig)
Mendelssohn (-Bartholdy), (Jacob Ludwig) Felix
Mengelberg, Kurt Rudolf
Menter, Joseph
Menter, Sophie
Merkel, Gustav Adolf
Merklin, Joseph
Merrem-Nikisch, Grete
Mersmann, Hans
Mettenleiter, Dominicus
Mettenleiter, Johann Georg
Metternich, Josef
Metzger, Heinz-Klaus
Metzger-Latterman, Ottilie
Metzmacher, Ingo
Meyer, Ernst Hermann
Meyer, Sabine
Meyerbeer, Giacomo (real name, Jakob Liebmann Beer)
Meyrowitz, Selmar
Michael Family
  Michael, Rogier
  Michael, Tobias
  Michael, Christian
  Michael, Samuel
Michael, David Moritz
Michl, Joseph (Christian) Willibald
Middelschulte, Wilhelm
Miedél, Rainer
Mielke, Antonia
Mies, Paul
Milder-Hauptmann, (Pauline) Anna
Mizler, Lorenz Christoph
Mödl, Martha
Moeck, Hermann
Mohaupt, Richard
Molique, (Wilhelm) Bernhard
Molitor, Raphael
Moll, Kurt
Möllendorff, Willi von
Molter, Johann Melchior
Moralt Family
  Moralt, Joseph
  Moralt, Johann Baptist
  Moralt, Philipp
  Moralt, Georg
Moralt, Rudolf
Moran-Olden (real name, Tappenhorn), Fanny
Morena (real name, Meyer), Berta
Mörike, Eduard
Moritz, Landgrave of Hessen-Kassel
Moser, Andreas
Moser, Edda (Elisabeth)
Moser, Hans Joachim
Moszkowski, Moritz
Muck, Karl
Mueller (actually, Müller) von Asow, Erich H(ermann)
Muffat, Georg

NATIONALITY INDEX

Türk, Daniel Gottlob
Türrschmidt, Carl
Uber Family
Uber, Christian Benjamin
Uber, Christian Friedrich Hermann
Uber, Alexander
Uhde, Hermann
Unger, (Ernst) Max
Unger, Georg
Unger, Gerhard
Urban, Heinrich
Ursprung, Otto
Valentin, Erich
Valesi, Giovanni (real name, Johann Evangelist Walleshauser)
Varady, Julia
Vento, Ivo de
Vetter, Michael
Vetter, Walther
Vierdanck, Johann
Viole, Rudolf
Virdung, Sebastian
Vogel, Johann Christoph
Vogelweide, Walther von der
Vogl, Adolf
Vogl, Heinrich
Vogler, Georg Joseph
Vogt, Hans
Volbach, Fritz
Volckmar, Wilhelm (Adam Valentin)
Völker, Franz
Volkmann, (Friedrich) Robert
Vopelius, Gottfried
Voss, Charles
Voss, Friedrich
Vrieslander, Otto
Vulpius (real name, Fuchs), Melchior
Wachsmann, Klaus P(hilipp)
Wachtel, Theodor
Wagenseil, Johann Christoph
Wagner, (Adolf) Wieland (Gottfried)
Wagner, Cosima
Wagner, Georg Gottfried
Wagner, Johanna
Wagner, Karl Jakob
Wagner, Peter (Joseph)
Wagner, Siegfried (Helferich Richard)
Wagner, (Wilhelm) Richard
Wagner, Wolfgang (Manfred Martin)
Wagner-Régeny, Rudolf
Waissel (Waisselius), Matthäus
Walcha, (Arthur Emil) Helmut
Walcker, Eberhard Friedrich
Wallat, Hans
Wallberg, Heinz
Walter or Walther (real name, Blankenmüller), Johann(es)
Walter, Georg A.
Waltershausen, H(ermann) W(olfgang Sartorious), Freiherr von
Walther, Johann Gottfried
Walther, Johann Jacob
Waltz, Gustavus
Wand, Günter
Wangenheim, Volker
Wannenmacher (Latinized as Vannius), Johannes
Warlich, Reinhold von
Wasielewski, Wilhelm Joseph von
Weber Family
Weber, Fridolin
Weber, (Maria) Josepha
Weber, (Maria) Aloysia (Louise Antonia)
Weber, (Maria) Constanze (Constantia) (Caecilia Josepha Johanna Aloisia)
Weber, (Maria) Sophie
Weber, Bernhard Anselm
Weber, Carl Maria (Friedrich Ernst) von
Weber, (Jacob) Gottfried
Wecker, Georg Kaspar
Weckmann, Matthias
Weidemann, Friedrich
Weil, Bruno
Weil, Hermann
Weinlig, Christian Ehregott
Weinlig, (Christian) Theodor
Weinmann, Karl
Weismann, Julius
Weiss Family
Weiss, John Jacob
Weiss, Silvius Leopold
Weiss, Johann Sigismund
Weissenborn, Günther (Albert Friedrich)
Weissensee, Friedrich
Weitzmann, Carl Friedrich
Welte, Michael
Wendling Family
Wendling, Johann Baptist
Wendling, Dorothea (née Spurni)
Wendling, Elisabeth Augusta
Wendling, Franz (Anton)
Wendling, Elisabeth Augusta (née Sarselli)
Wendling, Dorothea
Wendling, (Johann) Karl
Wenkel, Ortrun
Werckmeister, Andreas
Wesendonck, Mathilde (née Luckemeyer)
Westenholz or Westenholtz, Carl August Friedrich)
Westerhoff, Christian Wilhelm
Westphal, Rudolf (Georg Hermann)
Wetz, Richard
Weyrauch, August Heinrich von
Wich, Günther
Widmann, Erasmus
Wieck Family
Wieck, (Johann Gottlob) Friedrick Wieck
Wieck, Alwin
Wieck, Marie
Wiedebein, Gottlob
Wiedemann, Ernst Johann
Wiedemann, Hermann
Wiegand, (Josef Anton) Heinrich
Wiemann, Ernst
Wieprecht, Friedrich Wilhelm
Wilderer, Johann Hugo von
Wilhelmj, August (Emil Daniel Ferdinand Viktor)
Wilm, (Peter) Nicolai von
Winbeck, Heinz
Windgassen, Wolfgang (Fritz Hermann)
Winkelmann, Hermann
Winter, Peter (von)
Wiora, Walter
Wirth, Helmut (Richard Adolf Friedrich Karl)
Witt, Friedrich
Wittich, Marie
Wittinger, Robert
Wittrisch, Marcel
Wlaschiha, Ekkehard
Wolf, Ernst Wilhelm
Wolf, Johannes
Wolff, Christoph (Johannes)
Wolff, Fritz
Wolff, Hellmuth Christian
Wolfrum, Philipp
Wolpert, Franz Alfons
Worbs, Hans Christoph
Wörner, Karl(heinz) H(einrich)
Wüerst, Richard (Ferdinand)
Wüllner, Franz
Wüllner, Ludwig
Wunderlich, Fritz (actually, Friedrich Karl Otto)
Wunderlich, Heinz
Yun, Isang
Zacharias, Christian
Zachow (Zachau), Friedrich Wilhelm
Zagrosek, Lothar
Zangius (Zange), Nikolaus
Zechlin, Ruth
Zelter, Carl Friedrich
Zender, (Johannes Wolfgang) Hans
Zilcher, (Karl) Hermann (Josef)
Zillig, Winfried (Petrus Ignatius)
Zimmermann, Bernd (actually, Bernhard) Alois
Zimmermann, Frank Peter
Zimmermann, Udo
Zimmermann, Walter
Zinck, Bendix (actually, Benedikt) Friedrich
Zinck, Hardenack Otto Conrad
Zinkeisen, Konrad Ludwig Dietrich
Zipp, Friedrich
Zöller, Karlheinz
Zöllner, Carl Friedrich
Zöllner, Heinrich
Zottmayr, Georg
Zuccalmaglio, Anton Wilhelm Florentin von
Zumpe, Herman
Zumsteeg, Johann Rudolf
Zundel, John
Zur Mühlen, Raimund von

GERMAN-AMERICAN

Altman, Ludwig
Apel, Willi
Baermann, Carl (actually, Karl Bärmann)
Beissel, Johann Conrad
Beyer, Johanna Magdalena
Bodky, Erwin
Damrosch, Frank (Heino)
Damrosch, Leopold
Damrosch, Walter (Johannes)
David, Hans T(heodor)
Dippel, (Johann) Andreas

Dux, Claire
Eckhard, Jacob
Eichberg, Julius
Fischer, Carl
Fries, Wulf (Christian Julius)
Gebhard, Heinrich
Goldbeck, Robert
Goodman (real name, Guttmann), Alfred
Grobe, Charles
Kahn, Erich Itor
Kahn, Otto Hermann
Klemm, Johann Gottlob
Koch, Caspar (Petrus)
Krapf, Gerhard
Kunkel, Charles
Kunkel, Jacob
Leichtentritt, Hugo
Lewisohn, Adolph
Liebling, Emil
Liebling, Georg
Listemann, Bernhard
Luders, Gustav (Carl)
Manski, Dorothée
Marx, Josef
Misch, Ludwig
Moldenhauer, Hans
Mollenhauer, Eduard
Moller, John Christopher (real name, Johann Christoph Möller)
Mueller, Otto-Werner
Müller, George Godfrey (actually, Georg Gottfried)
Neuendorff, Adolph (Heinrich Anton Magnus)
Olitzka, Rosa
Olitzki, Walter
Pachelbel, Charles Theodore (actually, Carl Theodor)
Pechner, Gerhard
Phile (Fyles, Pfeil, Phyla, etc), Philip
Reimers, Paul
Remy, Alfred
Rethberg, Elisabeth (real name, Lisbeth Sattler)
Rupp, Franz
Sachse, Leopold
Schirmer Family
- Schirmer, Johann Georg
- Schirmer, Ernst Ludwig Rudolf
- Schirmer, (Friedrich) Gustav (Emil)
- Schirmer, Gustave
- Schirmer, Rudolph Edward
- Schirmer, third, Gustave
- Schirmer, Rudolph Edward

Schmidt, John Henry (actually, Johann Heinrich)
Schnabel, Karl Ulrich
Schoen-René, Anna
Steinway & Sons
Steinweg
Stoeckel, Gustave J(acob)
Stone, Kurt
Strube, Gustav
Tannenberg, David
Thomas, Theodore (Christian Friedrich)
Trampler, Walter
Waxman (real name, Wachsmann), Franz
Weber, Albert
Wolpe, Stefan
Wurlitzer Family
- Wurlitzer, (Franz) Rudolph
- Wurlitzer, Howard Eugene
- Wurlitzer, Rudolph Henry
- Wurlitzer, Farny Reginald
- Wurlitzer, Rembert

Zeuner, Charles (actually, Heinrich Christoph)
Ziehn, Bernhard

GERMAN-BOHEMIAN

Waldstein, Ferdinand Ernst Joseph Gabriel, Count von Waldstein und Wartenberg zu Dux

GERMAN-ENGLISH

Benedict, Sir Julius
Engel, Carl
Niecks, Frederick (actually, Friedrich)
Zimmermann, Agnes (Marie Jacobina)

GERMAN-ISRAELI

Barolsky, Michael

GERMAN-RUSSIAN

Albrecht Family
- Albrecht, Karl (Franz)
- Albrecht, Konstantin (Karl)
- Albrecht, Eugen (Maria)
- Albrecht, Ludwig (Karl)

GERMAN-SWISS

Pfeiffer, (Johann) Michael Traugott

GHANAIAN

Nketia, J(oseph) H(ansen) Kwabena

GREEK

Adamis, Michael
Alypius
Aperghis, Georges
Argiris, Spiros
Aristides Quintilianus
Aristotle
Aristoxenus
Baltsa, Agnes
Calvocoressi, Michel Dimitri
Caridis, Miltiades
Christou, Jani
Ctesibius or Ktesibios, known as Ctesibius of Alexandria
Didymus, Chalcenterus (of the Brazen Guts)
Dounias, Minos
Eratosthenes
Euclid
Floros, Constantin
Georgiades, Thrasybulos
Georgiadis, Georges
Hadzidakis, Manos
Ioannidis, Yannis
Kalomiris, Manolis
Karrer, Paul (real name, Paulos Karrerēs
Karyotakis, Theodore
Kavrakos, Dimitri
Kounadis, Arghyris
Kyriakou, Rena
Lavrangas, Dionyssios
Mamangakis, Nikos
Mantzaros, Nicolaos
Michaelides, Solon
Moscona, Nicola
Pallandios, Menelaos
Papaioannou, Yannis (Andreou)
Paskalis, Kostas
Petridis, Petros (John)
Plato
Plutarch
Poniridis, Georges
Ptolemy (in Latin Claudius Ptolemaeus)
Pythagoras
Riadis (real name, Khu), Emilios
Samara, Spiro (Spyridon Filiskos)
Sgouros, Dimitris
Sicilianos, Yorgos
Skalkottas, Nikos (actually, Nikolaos)
Sklavos, George
Souliotis, Elena
Terzakis, Dimitri
Theodorakis, Mikis (actually, Michael George)
Tsoupaki, Calliope
Tsouyopoulos, Georges
Varvoglis, Mario
Vitalis, George
Xyndas, Spyridon
Zaccaria, Nicola (Angelo)
Zoras, Leonidas

GREEK-AMERICAN

Antoniou, Theodore
Dounis, Demetrius Constantine

GREEK-FRENCH

Stamaty, Camille (-Marie)

GUATEMALAN

Ley, Salvador

HAWAIIAN

Lee, Dai-Keong
Lili'uokalani (Lydia Kamaka'eha Paki)

HUNGARIAN

Abraham, Paul (originally, Pál Ábrahám)
Ábrányi, Emil
Ábrányi, Kornél
Ádám, Jeno
Aggházy, Károly
Amar, Licco (actually, Liko)
Anday, Rosette
Auer, Leopold
Bachrich, Sigmund (real name, Sigismund)
Bakfark, Valentin (or Bálint)
Balassa, Sándor
Balogh, Ernö
Bárdos, Lajos
Bartay, Andreas
Bartay, Ede
Bartha, Dénes

Bartók, Béla (Viktor János)
Basilides, Mária
Báthy, Anna
Beliczay, Julius (Gyula) von
Berté, Heinrich
Bokor, Margit
Bónis, Ferenc
Bozay, Attila
Buttykay (real name, Gálszécsy és Butykai), Ákos
Czibulka, Alphons
Darvos, Gábor
Dávid, Gyula
Decsényi, János
Demény, Desiderius
Dobos, Kálmán
Dohnányi, Ernst (Ernő) von
Dubrovay, László
Durkó, Zsolt
Eggerth, Martha (real name, Márta Eggert)
Eötvös, Peter
Erdélyi, Miklós
Erkel, Franz (actually, Ferenc)
Ernster, Desz
Fachiri, Adila
Farkas, Edmund (Ödön)
Farkas, Ferenc
Farnadi, Edith
Ferand, Ernst (Thomas)
Ferencsik, János
Filtsch, Karl (actually, Károly)
Fischer, Ádám
Fischer, Annie (actually, Anny)
Fischer, Iván
Flesch, Carl (actually, Károly)
Fürst, Janos
Fusz, János
Gerster, Etelka
Gertler, André
Geszty (real name, Witkowsky), Sylvia
Goldmark, Karl (actually, Károly)
Gombosi, Otto (János)
Gungl, Joseph (József)
Hajdu, Mihály
Hamari, Julia
Hammerschlag, János
Harászti, Emil
Harmat, Artur
Harsányi, Tibor
Hegedüs, Ferenc
Hegyesi (real name, Spitzer), Louis
Heller, Stephen
Hidas, Frigyes
Hubay, Jenő
Hüni-Mihacsek, Felice
Huszka, Jenő
Isoz, Kálmán
Ivogün, Maria (real name, Ilse Kempner)
Jandó, Jenő
Jankó, Paul von
Járdányi, Pál
Jemnitz, Sándor (Alexander)
Jeney, Zoltán
Joachim, Joseph
Kabos, Ilona
Kacsóh, Pongrác
Kadosa, Pál
Kálmán, Emmerich (actually, Imre)
Kálmán, Oszkár
Kalmár, László
Kalter (real name, Aufrichtig), Sabine
Kardos, István
Kárpáti, János
Kelemen, Zoltán
Kéler-Béla (real name, Adalbert Paul [Albrecht Pál] von Kéler)
Kenessey, Jenö
Kenton (real name, Kornstein), Egon
Király, Ernö
Klafsky, Katharina (Katalin)
Kocsár, Miklós
Kocsis, Zoltan (György)
Kodály, Zoltán
Kókai, Rezső
Komjáti, Károly
Konti, József
Konya, Sándor
Koréh, Endre
Kórodi, Andras
Kósa, György
Kraft, Nikolaus
Kroó, György
Kubelík, Jan
Kulka, János
Kurtág, György
Lajtai, Lajos
Lajtha, László
Láng, István
Langer, Victor
Lászlò, Magda
Lavotta, János
Lehel, György
Lendvai, Ernő
Lendvai, (Peter) Erwin
Lendvay, Kamilló
Léner, Jenö
Liszt, Franz (Ferenc; baptized Franciscus)
Lukács, Miklós
Major (real name, Mayer), (Jakab) Gyula
Major, Ervin
Maros, Rudolf
Marton, Eva
Martzy, Johanna
Mátray (real name, Róthkrepf), Gábor
Matzenauer, Margarete
Melles, Carl
Mihalovich, Edmund von (Ödön Péter József de)
Mihály, András
Molnár, Antal
Moór, Emanuel
Mosonyi, Mihály (real name, Michael Brand)
Mysz-Gmeiner, Lula (née Gmeiner)
Németh, Mária
Némethy, Ella
Orbán, György
Orgeni, Aglaja (real name, Anna Maria von Görger St. Jorgen)
Pásztory, Ditta
Patachich, Iván
Pataky, Kálmán
Pauly, Rosa (actually, Rose née Pollak)
Petrovics, Emil
Poldini, Ede (Eduard)
Pongrácz, Zoltán
Radnai, Miklós
Radó, Aladár
Ránki, Dezső
Ránki, György
Reményi (real name, Hoffmann), Ede (Eduard)
Ribáry, Antal
Rösler, Endre
Rozsnyai, Zoltán
Sárai, Tibor
Sárközy, István
Sárosi, Bálint
Sáry, László
Sass, Sylvia
Sébastian, Georges (real name, György Sebestyén)
Sebestyén, János
Seidl, Anton
Siki, Béla
Siklós (real name, Schönwald), Albert
Simándy, József
Somfai, László
Somogyi, László
Soproni, József
Sucher, Josef
Sugár, Rezső
Svéd, Sándor
Szabados, Béla Antal
Szabó, Ferenc
Szabolcsi, Bence
Szántó, Theodor
Székely, Endre
Székely, Mihály
Szekelyhidy, Ferenc
Szelényi, István
Szendy, Árpád
Szenkar, Eugen (actually, Jenő)
Szervánszky, Endre
Szokolay, Sándor
Szőllősy, András
Szönyi, Erzsébet
Takács, Jenő
Tardos, Béla
Thern, Károly
Thomán, István
Tóth, Aladár
Ujfalussy, József
Ujj, Béla
Unger, Caroline
Vajda, János
Varkonyi, Béla
Várnai, Péter P(ál)
Vécsey, Jenö
Vincze, Imre
Viski, János
Weiner, Leó
Zádor, Dezsö
Zichy, Géza, Count Vasony-Keö
Zmeskall, Nikolaus (Paul), Edler von Domanovecz

HUNGARIAN-AMERICAN

Delmar, Dezso
Dick, Marcel
Joseffy, Rafael
Kanner-Rosenthal, Hedwig
Kilenyi, Edward, Sr.

HUNGARIAN-DANISH

HUNGARIAN-FRENCH

ICELANDIC

INDIAN

INDONESIAN

IRISH

IRISH-AMERICAN

IRISH-SWISS

ISRAELI

Shiloah, Amnon
Shmueli, Herzl
Singer, George
Steinberg, Ze'ev (Wolfgang)
Sternberg, Erich Walter
Stutschewsky, Joachim
Tal, Josef (real name, Joseph Gruenthal)
Talmi, Yoav
Taube, Michael
Vered, Ilana
Wohl, Yehuda
Yoffe, Shlomo
Zukerman, Pinchas

ISRAELI-AMERICAN

Kalichstein, Joseph
Perlman, Itzhak
Vardi, Emanuel
Yannay, Yehuda

ISRAELI-ENGLISH

Inbal, Eliahu

ITALIAN

Aaron or Aron, Pietro
Abbà-Cornaglia, Pietro
Abbadia, Natale
Abbado, Claudio
Abbado, Marcello
Abbado, Roberto
Abbatini, Antonio Maria
Accardo, Salvatore
Accorimboni, Agostino
Adami da Bolsena, Andrea
Adolfati, Andrea
Afranio de Pavia (family name, Albonese)
Agazzari, Agostino
Agnelli, Salvatore
Agnesi-Pinottini, Maria Teresa
Agosti, Guido
Agostini, Lodovico
Agostini, Mezio
Agostini, Paolo
Agostini, Pietro Simone
Agricola, Benedetta Emilia (née Molteni)
Aguiari or Agujari, Lucrezia
Agus, Giuseppe
Agus, Joseph
Alagna, Roberto
Alaleona, Domenico
Albergati (Capacelli), Pirro
Alberghi, Paolo Tommaso
Alberti, Domenico
Alberti, Gasparo
Alberti, Giuseppe Matteo
Albinoni, Tomaso Giovanni
Alboni, Marietta (actually, Maria Anna Marzia)
Albrici, Vincenzo
Aldrovandini, Giuseppe (Antonio Vincenzo)
Aleotti, Raffaella
Alessandri, Felice
Alfano, Franco
Alfieri, Pietro
Algarotti, Francesco
Alghisi, Paris Francesco
Aliprandi, Bernardo
Allegranti, (Teresa) Maddalena
Allegri, Domenico
Allegri, Gregorio
Allegri, Lorenzo
Amadei, Filippo
Amati Family
  Amati, Andrea
  Amati, Antonio
  Amati, Girolamo
  Amati, Niccolo
  Amati, Girolamo
Amato, Pasquale
Ambrose (Ambrosius), Saint
d'Ambrosio, Alfredo
Amendola, Giuseppe
Amicis, Anna Lucia de
Amorevoli, Angelo (Maria)
Ana, Francesco d'
Ancina, (Giovanni) Giovenale
Ancona, Mario
Andreas de Florentia
Andreini, Virginia (née Rampnoni)
Andreoli, Carlo
Andreoli, Guglielmo
Andreozzi, Gaetano
Anerio, Felice
Anerio, Giovanni Francesco
Anfossi, Pasquale
Angeloni, Carlo
Anglesi, Domenico
Animuccia, Giovanni
Animuccia, Paolo
Annibale, Domenico
Annibale Il Padovano
Ansani, Giovanni
Anselmi, Giuseppe
Antegnati, Costanzo
Anthonello de Caserta
Antico, Andrea
Antonacci, Anna Caterina
Antonelli, Abundio
Antoni, Antonio d'
Antonicelli, Giuseppe
Anzaghi, Davide
Aprile, Giuseppe
Araia or Araja, Francesco
Arangi-Lombardi, Giannina
Archilei, Vittoria (née Concarini)
Arditi, Luigi
Aretino, Paolo
d'Arienzo, Nicola
Ariosti, Attilio (Malachia)
Arresti, Giulio Cesare
Arrigo, Girolamo
Arrigoni, Carlo
Artusi, Giovanni Maria
Asioli, Bonifazio
Asola or Asula, Giammateo or Giovanni Matteo
Aspa, Mario
Astarita, Gennaro
d'Astorga, Baron Emanuele (Gioacchino Cesare Rincón)
Astrua, Giovanna
Aula, Giacomo
Auletta, Pietro
Aurisicchio, Antonio
Auteri Manzocchi, Salvatore
Avoglio, Christina Maria
d'Avossa, Giuseppe
Ayo, Félix
Babbi, Gregorio (Lorenzo)
Babbi, (Pietro Giovanni) Cristoforo (Bartolomeo Gasparre)
Babini, Matteo
Baccaloni, Salvatore
Baccusi, Ippolito
Badia, Carlo Agostino
Badini, Ernesto
Baggiani, Guido
Bai (also Baj), Tommaso
Baini, Giuseppe (also known as Abbate Baini)
Balbi, Lodovico or Ludivico
Balbi, Melchiore
Ballista, Antonio
Banchieri, Adriano (actually, Tomaso)
Banti, Brigida (née Giorgi)
Barbaia or Barbaja, Domenico
Barbarino, Bartolomeo
Barbella, Emanuele
Barberiis, Melchiore de
Barbetta, Giulio Cesare
Barbieri, Carlo Emanuele
Barbieri, Fedora
Barbieri-Nini, Marianna
Barblan, Guglielmo
Bardi, Giovanni de'
Barilli, Bruno
Baroni, Leonora
Barsanti, Francesco
Bartei, Girolamo
Bartoletti, Bruno
Bartoli, Cecilia
Bartolino da Padova (Magister Frater Bartolinus de Padua; Frater carmelitus)
Bartolomeo degli Organi (Baccio Fiorentino)
Bartolozzi, Bruno
Basile, Andreana
Basili, Francesco
Basiola, Mario
Bassani (Bassano, Bassiani), Giovanni Battista
Bassano (also Bassani), Giovanni
Bassi, Amedeo (Vittorio)
Bassi, Carolina Manna
Bassi, Luigi
Bastianelli, Giannotto
Bastianini, Ettore
Battistini, Gaudenzio
Battistini, Giacomo
Battistini, Mattia
Bechi, Gino
Begnis, Giuseppe de
Bellasio, Paolo
Belletti, Giovanni Battista
Bellezza, Vincenzo
Bell'Haver, Vincenzo
Belli, Domenico
Belli, Girolamo
Belli, Giulio
Bellincioni, Gemma (Cesira Matilda)
Bellini, Vincenzo
Bellinzani, Paolo Benedetto

Colista, Lelio
Colla, Giuseppe
Colonna, Giovanni Paolo
Coltellini, Celeste
Conforti (Conforto), Giovanni Luca
Conti, Carlo
Conti, Francesco Bartolomeo
Conti, Gioacchino
Coppini, Alessandro
Coppola, Piero
Coppola, Pietro Antonio (Pierantonio)
Corbetta, Francesco
Corelli, Arcangelo
Corelli, Franco
Cornelys, T(h)eresa (née Imer)
Coronaro Family
  Coronaro, Antonio
  Coronaro, Gaetano
  Coronaro, Gellio (Benevenuto)
Corradini, Francesco
Corri, Domenico
Corselli (real name, Courcelle), Francesco
Corsi (Corso), Giuseppe (called Celano after his birthplace)
Corsi, Jacopo
Corteccia, (Pier) Francesco
Cortellini, Camillo
Cossotto, Fiorenza
Cossutta, Carlo
Cotogni, Antonio
Crescentini, Girolamo
Cristofori, Bartolomeo
Crivelli, Gaetano
Crivelli, Giovanni Battista
Croce, Giovanni
Cupido, Alberto
Cuzzoni, Francesca
Dal Barba, Daniel
Dall'Abaco, Evaristo Felice
Dall'Abaco, Joseph-Marie-Clément
Dallapiccola, Luigi
Dalla Rizza, Gilda
Dalla Viola, Alfonso
Dalla Viola, Francesco
Dal Monte, Toti (real name, Antonietta Meneghelli)
Dal Pane, Domenico
Da Ponte, Lorenzo (real name, Emanuele Conegliano)
d'Avalos, Francesco
Davico, Vincenzo
David, Giacomo
David, Giovanni
De Amicis, Anna Lucia
De Angelis, Nazzareno
De Bassini (real name, Bassi), Achille
DeFabritiis, Oliviero (Carlo)
De Ferrari, Serafino (Amedeo)
De Giosa, Nicola
Degli Antoni, Pietro
Degrada, Francesco
Della Ciaia, Azzolino Bernardino
Della Corte, Andrea
Della Valle, Pietro
Delle Sedie, Enrico
Dell'Orefice, Giuseppe
Del Monaco, Giancarlo
Del Monaco, Mario
Delogu, Gaetano
De Luca, Giuseppe
De Lucia, Fernando
Denza, Luigi
De Sabata, Victor (actually, Vittorio)
De Santi, Angelo
Desderi, Ettore
De Vito, Gioconda
Di Capua, Eduardo
Diruta, Girolamo
Di Stefano, Giuseppe
Dominiceti, Cesare
Donati or Donato, Baldassare
Donati, Ignazio
Donati, Pino
Donatoni, Franco
Donaudy, Stefano
Doni, Antonio Francesco or Antonfrancesco
Doni, Giovanni Battista
Donizetti, (Domenico) Gaetano (Maria)
Donizetti, Giuseppe
Donzelli, Domenico
Draghi, Giovanni Battista
Dragonetti, Domenico (Carlo Maria)
Drigo, Riccardo
Duni, Egidio (Romualdo)
Durante, Francesco
Elmo, Cloe
Ephrikian, Angelo
Erede, Alberto
Errani, Achille
Esposito, Michele
Evangelisti, Franco
Fabri, Annibale Pio
Fabrizi, Vincenzo
Faccio, Franco (Francesco Antonio)
Fago, (Francesco) Nicola
Failoni, Sergio
Falchi, Stanislao
Falco, Michele
Falcone, Achille
Falconieri, Andrea
Fancelli, Giuseppe
Fano, (Aronne) Guido Alberto
Farina, Carlo
Farinelli (real name, Finco), Giuseppe (Francesco)
Fasano, Renato
Fattorini, Gabriele
Favero, Mafalda
Fedeli Family
  Fedeli, Carlo
  Fedeli, Ruggiero
  Fedeli, Giuseppe
Fedeli, Vito
Federici, Vincenzo
Fellegara, Vittorio
Fenaroli, Fedele
Feo, Francesco
Ferni-Giraldoni, Carolina
Ferrabosco, Alfonso, the Elder
Ferrabosco, Domenico Maria
Ferrandini, Giovanni Battista (actually, Zaneto)
Ferrani (real name, Zanaggio), Cesira
Ferrara, Franco
Ferraresi del Bene, Adriana (née Gabrieli)
Ferrari, Benedetto
Ferrari, Carlotta
Ferrari, Domenico
Ferrari, Giacomo Gotifredo
Ferrari-Fontana, Edoardo
Ferrari-Trecate, Luigi
Ferrero, Lorenzo
Ferrero, Willy
Ferretti, Dom Paolo
Ferretti, Giovanni
Ferri, Baldassare
Ferro, Gabriele
Festa, Costanzo
Filiasi, Lorenzo
Filippi, Filippo
Finazzi, Filippo
Fioravanti, Valentino
Fioravanti, Vincenzo
Fiorè, Andrea Stefano
Fiorillo, Federigo
Fiorillo, Ignazio
Fioroni, Giovanni Andrea
Fischietti, Domenico
Fiume, Orazio
Floridia, Pietro
Florimo, Francesco
Foggia, Francesco
Fogliani (Fogliano), Giacomo
Fogliani (Fogliano), Ludovico
Fontana, Giovanni Battista
Fontanelli, Alfonso
Fontei, Nicolò
Formichi, Cesare
Foroni, Jacopo
Franceschini, Petronio
Francesco Canova de Milano
Franchetti, Alberto
Franci, Benvenuto
Franci, Carlo
Fraschini, Gaetano
Frazzi, Vito
Freccia, Massimo
Freni (real name, Fregni), Mirella
Freschi, (Giovanni) Domenico
Frescobaldi, Girolamo
Frezzolini, Erminia
Frontini, Francesco Paolo
Frugoni, Orazio
Fuga, Sandro
Fumagalli Family
  Fumagalli, Disma
  Fumagalli, Adolfo
  Fumagalli, Polibio
  Fumagalli, Luca
Furlanetto, Bonaventura
Furlanetto, Ferruccio
Furno, Giovanni
Gabrieli, Andrea (also known as Andrea di Cannaregio)
Gabrieli, Giovanni
Gabrielli, Caterina
Gabrielli, Domenico
Gabrielli, Nicolò
Gabussi, Giulio Cesare
Gaffurius (also Gafurius, Gaffurio, etc.), Franchinus (also Franchino)
Gagliano Family
Gagliano, Giovanni Battista da
Gagliano, Marco da

Lucchesi, Andrea
Lucchesini, Andrea
Luchetti, Veriano
Luisi, Fabio
Lulier, Giovanni Lorenzo
Lunelli, Renato
Lurano, Filippo de
Luzzaschi, Luzzasco
Mabellini, Teodulo
Maggini, Gio(vanni) Paolo
Magini-Coletti, Antonio
Mainardi, Enrico
Majo, Gian Francesco (de)
Majo, Giuseppe de
Majone or Mayone, Ascanio
Malanotte (-Montresor), Adelaide
Malipiero, Francesco
Malipiero, Gian Francesco
Malipiero, Riccardo
Maliponte (real name, Macciaïoli), Adriana
Malvezzi, Cristofano
Mancinelli, Luigi
Mancini, Francesco
Mandini, Stefano
Manelli, Francesco
Manfredini, Francesco Onofrio
Manfredini, Vincenzo
Manna, Gennaro
Mannelli, Carlo
Mannino, Franco
Mantelli, Eugenia
Manzoni, Giacomo
Manzuoli, Giovanni
Marazzoli, Marco
Marcello, Alessandro
Marcello, Benedetto
Marchesi, Luigi (Lodovico)
Marchesi de Castrone, Salvatore (full name and title, Salvatore Marchesi, Cavaliere de Castrone, Marchese della Rajata)
Marchetti, Filippo
Marchetto da Padova
Marchisio, Barbara
Marcolini, Marietta
Marenzio, Luca
Margola, Franco
Mariani, Angelo (Maurizio Gaspare)
Mariani, Luciano
Marini, Biagio
Marini, Ignazio
Marinuzzi, Gino (I)
Marinuzzi, Gino (II)
Mario, Giovanni Matteo, Cavaliere de Candia
Marliani, Count Marco Aurelio
Martinelli, Caterina
Martinelli, Giovanni
Martini, Giovanni Battista
Martucci, Giuseppe
Mascagni, Pietro
Maschera, Florentio or Florenzo
Mascheroni, Edoardo
Masini, Angelo
Masini, Galliano
Massaino (Massaini), Tiburtio
Mattei, Stanislao
Mattei, Tito
Matteis, Nicola
Matteo da Perugia
Mayone, Ascanio
Mazzocchi, Domenico
Mazzocchi, Virgilio
Mazzoleni, Ester
Mei, Girolamo
Mei, Orazio
Melani Family
Melani, Jacopo
Melani, Atto
Melani, Alessandro
Melis, Carmen
Meluzzi, Salvatore
Menotti, Gian Carlo
Mercadante, (Giuseppe) Saverio (Raffaele)
Merighi, Antonia Margherita
Merli, Francesco
Merlo, Alessandro
Merula, Tarquinio
Merulo (real name, Merlotti), Claudio
Mestrino, Nicola
Metastasio, Pietro (real name, Antonio Domenico Bonaventura Trapassi)
Michelangeli, Arturo Benedetti
Micheli, Domenico
Micheli, Romano
Michi, Orazio
Mila, Massimo
Milanollo, (Domenica Maria) Teresa
Milanuzzi, Carlo
Millico, (Vito) Giuseppe
Minghetti, Angelo
Mingotti, Pietro
Mingotti, Regina (née Valentini)
Minoja, Ambrogio
Molinari, Bernardino
Molinari-Pradelli, Francesco
Molinaro, Simone
Mombelli, Domenico
Monferrato, Natale
Mongini, Pietro
Monleone, Domenico
Montagnana, Antonio
Montella, Giovanni Domenico
Montemezzi, Italo
Monteverdi, Claudio (Giovanni Antonio)
Monteverdi, Giulio Cesare
Monti Family
Monti, Anna Maria
Monti, Laura
Monti, Marianna
Monti, Gaetano
Monticelli, Angelo Maria
Monza, Carlo
Moreschi, Alessandro
Moriani, Napoleone
Morlacchi, Francesco (Giuseppe Baldassare)
Mortari, Virgilio
Mortaro, Antonio
Mosca, Giuseppe
Mosca, Luigi
Mugnone, Leopoldo
Mulè, Giuseppe
Murio-Celli, Adelina
Muro, Bernardo de
Mustafà, Domenico
Muti, Riccardo
Muzio, Claudia (real name, Claudina Muzzio)
Muzio, (Donnino) Emanuele
Naldi, Giuseppe
Nanino (Nanini), Giovanni Bernardino
Nanino (Nanini), Giovanni Maria
Napoli, Gennaro
Napoli, Jacopo
Nardini, Pietro
Nasolini, Sebastiano
Nataletti, Giorgio
Navarrini, Francesco
Neglia, Francesco Paolo
Negri, Gino
Negri, Maria Rosa
Negri, Vittorio
Nenna, Pomponio
Neri, Giulio
Neri, Massimiliano
Neri, Saint Donna Filippo
Nessi, Giuseppe
Niccolò da Perugia
Nicolini (real name, Nicolo Grimaldi)
Nicolini, Giuseppe
Nielsen, Riccardo
Nini, Alessandro
Nola, Giovanni Domenico del Giovane da
Noni, Alda
Nono, Luigi
Notari, Angelo
Nozzari, Andrea
Nucci, Leo
Olivero, Magda (actually, Maria Maddalena)
Orefice, Antonio
Orefice, Giacomo
Orgitano Family
Orgitano, Vincenzo
Orgitano, Paolo
Orgitano, Raffaele
Orlandi, Ferdinando
Orlandini, Giuseppe Maria
Orologio, Alessandro
Ottani, Bernardo
Ottani, Gaetano
Pacchiarotti, Gasparo
Pacchioni, Antonio Maria
Pace, Pietro
Pacelli, Asprilio
Pachmann, Vladimir de
Pacini, Andrea
Pacini, Giovanni
Padovano, Annibale
Paër, Ferdinando
Paganelli, Giuseppe Antonio
Paganini, Niccolò
Pagliardi, Giovanni Maria
Pagliughi, Lina
Paisiello, Giovanni
Palazzesi, Matilde
Palazzotto e Tagliavia, Giuseppe
Palella, Antonio
Palestrina, Giovanni Pierluigi da
Pallavicino, Benedetto
Pallavicino, Carlo
Palma, Silvestro

Ronconi Family
  Ronconi, Domenico
  Ronconi, Giorgio
  Ronconi, Felice
  Ronconi, Sebastiano
Ronga, Luigi
Ronzi de Begnis (originally, Ronzi), Giuseppina
Rosa, Salvator(e)
Rossellini, Renzo
Rossi, Abbate Francesco
Rossi, Giovanni (Gaetano)
Rossi, Giulio
Rossi, Lauro
Rossi, Luigi
Rossi, Mario
Rossi, Michel Angelo
Rossi, Salamone (also Salomone, Salamon dé, or Shlomo)
Rossi-Lemeni, Nicola
Rossini, Gioachino (Antonio)
Rota (real name, Rinaldi), Nino
Rovelli, Pietro
Rovere, Agostino
Rovetta, Giovanni
Rubini, Giovanni Battista
Ruffo, Titta (real name, Ruffo Cafiero Titta)
Ruffo, Vincenzo
Ruggi, Francesco
Rusca, Francesco
Rusconi, Gerardo
Russolo, Luigi
Rust, Giacomo
Rutini, Ferdinando
Rutini, Giovanni Marco
Sabbatini, Galeazzo
Sabbatini, Giuseppe
Sabbatini, Luigi Antonio
Sacchini, Antonio (Maria Gasparo Gioacchino)
Sacrati, Francesco
Sala, Nicola
Sales (de Sala), Pietro Pompeo
Salieri, Antonio
Salimbeni, Felice
Salvi, Lorenzo
Salvini-Donatelli, Fanny (real name, Francesca Lucchi)
Salviucci, Giovanni
Sammarco, (Giuseppe) Mario
Sammartini, Giovanni Battista
Sammartini, Giuseppe (Francesco Gaspare Melchiorre Baldassare)
Sances, Giovanni Felice
Sangiovanni, Antonio
Sanjust, Filippo
Santi, Nello
Santini, Abbate Fortunato
Santini, Gabriele
Santoliquido, Francesco
Santucci, Marco
Sanzogno, Nino
Saporiti (real name, Codecasa), Teresa
Saracini, Claudio
Sarro (or Sarri), Domenico Natale
Sarti, Giuseppe
Sartori, Claudio
Sartorio, Antonio
Sbriglia, Giovanni
Scacchi, Marco
Scacciati, Bianca
Scalchi, Sofia
Scalero, Rosario
Scalzi, Carlo
Scandello, Antonio
Scarabelli, Diamante Maria
Scarlatti, (Giuseppe) Domenico
Scarlatti, (Pietro) Alessandro (Gaspare)
Scarpini, Pietro
Scelsi, Giacinto (actually, Conte Giacinto Scelsi di Valva)
Schipa, Tito (actually, Raffaele Attilio Amadeo)
Schmidl, Carlo
Sciarrino, Salvatore
Scimone, Claudio
Sciutti, Graziella
Scontrino, Antonio
Scotti, Antonio
Scotto, Renata
Segni, Julio
Senesino (real name, Francesco Bernardi)
Serafin, Tullio
Seraphin (also Serafin, Serafino), Sanctus (Santo)
Serassi, Giuseppe
Sereni, Mario
Serini, Giovanni Battista
Serra, Luciana
Serrao, Paolo
Sgambati, Giovanni
Sgrizzi, Luciano
Shira, Francesco
Siboni, Giuseppe (Vincenzo Antonio)
Siciliani, Alessandro
Siepi, Cesare
Siface (real name, Giovanni Francesco Grossi)
Sigismondi, Giuseppe
Silveri, Paolo
Simionato, Giulietta
Simonelli, Matteo
Sinico, Francesco
Sinigaglia, Leone
Sinopoli, Giuseppe
Sirmen, Maddalena Laura (née Lombardini)
Sivori, (Ernesto) Camillo
Smareglia, Antonio
Soderini, Agostin
Soffredini, Alfredo
Solera, Temistocle
Solerti, Angelo
Somis, Giovanni Battista
Somis, Lorenzo Giovanni
Sonzogno, Edoardo
Soresina, Alberto
Soriano, Francesco
Spataro, Giovanni
Spinelli, Nicola
Spontini, Gaspare (Luigi Pacifico)
Squarcialupi, Antonio
Stabile, Mariano
Stagno, Roberto (real name, Vincenzo Andriolo)
Steffani, Agostino
Stella, Antonietta
Stignani, Ebe
Stivori, Francesco
Storchio, Rosina
Stracciari, Riccardo
Strada, Anna Maria
Stradella, Alessandro
Stradivari (Latinized as Stradivarius), Antonio
Strehler, Giorgio
Strepponi, Giuseppina (Clelia Maria Josepha)
Striggio, Alessandro
Strozzi, Barbara
Strozzi, Giulio
Strozzi, Piero
Tacchinardi, Nicola
Taddei, Giuseppe
Tadolini, Eugenia (née Savonari)
Tadolini, Giovanni
Tagliabue, Carlo
Tagliapietra, Gino
Tagliapietra, Giovanni
Tagliavini, Ferruccio
Tagliavini, Luigi Ferdinando
Taglietti, Giulio
Taglietti, Luigi
Tajo, Italo
Tamagno, Francesco
Tamberlik, Enrico
Tamburini, Antonio
Tango, Egisto
Tarchi, Angelo
Tarditi, Paolo
Tarisio, Luigi
Tartini, Giuseppe
Tassinari, Pia
Tebaldi, Renata
Tebaldini, Giovanni
Tenaglia, Antonio Francesco
Tenducci, Giusto Ferdinando
Terrabugio, Giuseppe
Terziani, Eugenio
Tesi-Tramontini, Vittoria
Tess (real name, Tesscorolo), Giulia
Tessarini, Carlo
Testore, Carlo Giuseppe
Testori, Carlo Giovanni
Tetrazzini, Eva
Tetrazzini, Luisa (actually, Luigia)
Thomas Aquinas, Saint
Tibaldi, Giuseppe (Luigi)
Tiby, Ottavio
Tipo, Maria (Luisa)
Tocchi, Gian Luca
Togni, Camillo
Tomadini, Jacopo
Tomasi, Biagio
Tomasini, Alois Luigi
Tommasini, Vincenzo
Torchi, Luigi
Torelli, Gasparo
Torelli, Giuseppe
Torrefranca, Fausto (Acanfora Sansone dei duchi di Porta e)
Torri, Pietro
Tosatti, Vieri
Toscanini, Arturo
Toselli, Enrico

ITALIAN-AMERICAN

ITALIAN-ARGENTINE

ITALIAN-ENGLISH

ITALIAN-GERMAN

ITALIAN-RUSSIAN

JAMAICAN

JAPANESE

Satoh, Toyohiko
Shibata, Minao
Shimizu, Osamu
Shimoyama, Hifumi
Shinohara, Makota
Shirai, Mitsuko
Sukegawa, Toshiya
Suzuki, Shin'ichi
Suzuki, Yukikazu
Takahashi, Aki
Takahashi, Yuji
Takase, Aki
Takata, Saburô
Takeda, Yoshimi
Takemitsu, Tōru
Tanabe, Hisao
Tanaka, Karen
Tanaka, Toshimitsu
Toda, Kunio (actually, Morikuni)
Togi, Suenobu
Tomotani, Kōji
Tone, Yasunao
Toyama, Yuzo
Tsuji, Shōichi
Tsukatani, Akihirô
Uchida, Mitsuko
Wakasugi, Hiroshi
Watanabe, Akeo
Watanabe, Sadao
Yamada, Kōsaku (Kōsçak)
Yamaguchi, Motohumi
Yamashita, Yosuke
Yamash'ta, Stomu (real name, Tsutomu Yamashita)
Yashirō, Akio
Yoshida, Tsunezō
Yuasa, Jōji

JAPANESE-AMERICAN
Araki, James (Jimmy)

KOREAN
Chin, Unsuk
Chung, Kyung-Wha
Hwang, Byung-Ki
Jo, Sumi
Kang, Sukhi
Paik, Byung-Dong
Paik, Kun-Woo
Shim, Kunsu

KOREAN-AMERICAN
Paik, Nam June

LATVIAN
Baklanov (real name, Bakkis), Georgy (Andreievich)
Idelsohn, Abraham Zevi
Ivanovs, Janis
Jadlowker, Hermann
Jansons, Mariss
Jörn, Karl
Jurjäns, Andrejs
Kalninš, Alfreds
Kalninš, Imants
Kremer, Gidon
Mediņš Family
  Mediņš, Jāzeps
  Mediņš, Jēkabs
  Mediņš, Jānis
Plakidis, Peteris
Rosowsky, Solomon
Vasks, Pēteris
Wihtol (Vitols), Joseph (actually, Jāzeps)
Yansons, Arvid
Zarinš, Margeris

LATVIAN-AMERICAN
Gesensway, Louis

LIEGEOIS
Ciconia, Johannes

LITHUANIAN
Bajoras, Feliksas
Balakauskas, Osvaldus
Balsys, Eduardas
Barkauskas, Vytautas (Pranas Marius)
Dvarionas, Balis
Grad, Gabriel
Juozapaitis, Jurgis
Juzeliūnas, Julius
Kutavičius, Bronislovas
Petrauskas, Kipras
Petrauskas, Mikas
Raciunas, Antanas
Rekašius, Antanas
Tallat-Kelpša, Juozas

MACEDONIAN
Makedonski, Kiril
Nikolovski, Vlastimir

MALTESE
Abos, Girolamo

MEXICAN
Adomián, Lan
Álvarez, Javier
Anitúa, Fanny
Araiza, (José) Francisco
Ayala Pérez, Daniel
Bátiz (Campbell), Enrique
Bernal Jiménez, Miguel
Carrillo (-Trujillo), Julián (Antonio)
Catán, Daniel
Chávez (y Ramírez), Carlos (Antonio de Padua)
Cruz-Romo, Gilda
Dominguez, Oralia
Elías, Alfonso de
Elías, Manuel Jorge de
Enríquez, Manuel
Estrada, Julio
Galindo (Dimas), Blas
Gomezanda, Antonio
González-Avila, Jorge
Gutiérrez Heras, Joaquín
Halffter (Escriche), Rodolfo
Hernández, Hermilio
Herrera de la Fuente, Luis
Huízar (García de la Cadena), Candelario
Ibarra (Groth), Federico
Jiménez-Mabarak, Carlos
Kuri-Aldana, Mario
Lara, Augustín
Lavalle-García, Armando
Lavista, Mario
López Capillas, Francesco
Mata, Eduardo
Moncayo García, José Pablo
Morales, Melesio
Muench, Gerhart
Nancarrow, Conlon
Navarro, Juan
Padilla, Juan Gutiérrez de
Peralta, Angela
Ponce, Manuel (Maria)
Quintanar, Héctor
Revueltas, Silvestre
Rolón, José
Sandi, Luis
Sarabia, Guillermo
Savín, Francisco
Szeryng, Henryk
Vargas, Ramón (Arturo)

MOLDAVIAN
Cebotari (real name, Cebutaru), Maria

MORAVIAN
Brosmann (a Sancto Hieronymo), Damasus
Ernst, Heinrich Wilhelm
Finger, Gottfried
Herbst, Johannes
Krommer (Kramář), Franz Vincez (František Vincenc)
Krückl, Franz
Míča, František Adam
Neruda Family
  Neruda, Josef
  Nerudova, Amálie
  Neruda, Viktor
  Neruda, Wilma Maria Francisca (Vilemína Maria Franziška)
  Neruda, Marie (Arlbergová)
  Neruda, Franz (František Xaver Viktor)
Schindler, Anton Felix
Van Vleck, Jacob
Vejvanovský, Pavel Josef

NEW ZEALANDER
Birnie, Tessa (Daphne)
Body, Jack (actually, John Stanley)
Braithwaite, (Henry) Warwick
Cresswell, Lyell (Richard)
Farquhar, David (Andross)
Hammond, Dame Joan (Hood)
Hutchens, Frank
Lewis, Keith
Lilburn, Douglas (Gordon)
Lockwood, Annea (actually, Anna Ferguson)
Maconie, Robin (John)
McIntyre, Sir Donald (Conroy)
Rimmer, John (Francis)
Te Kanawa, Dame Kiri
Tintner, Georg (Bernhard)
Weir, Dame Gillian (Constance)

NICARAGUAN
Delgadillo, Luis (Abraham)

NIGERIAN

NORWEGIAN

PANAMANIAN

PERUVIAN

POLISH

Koczalski, Raoul (actually, Raul Armand Georg)
Koffler, Józef
Kolberg, (Henryk) Oskar
Kontski, Antoine de
Kontski, Apollinaire de
Kontski, Charles de
Kord, Kazimierz
Kotoński, Włodzimierz
Krauze, Zygmunt
Krenz, Jan
Kubiak, Teresa (originally, Tersa Wojtaszek)
Kulenty, Hanna
Kurpiński, Karol (Kazimierz)
Kwiatkowski, Ryszard
Laso, Aleksander
Lefeld, Jerzy Albert
Leschetizky, Theodor (Teodor)
Lessel, Franz (actually, Franciszek)
Lipińsky, Carl (Karol Józef)
Lissa, Zofia
Lobaczewska (Gerard de Festenburg), Stephania
Luciuk, Juliusz (Mieczyslaw)
Ludkewycz, Stanislaus
Lukomska, Halina
Luria, Juan (real name Johannes Lorie)
Lutoslawski, Witold
Machl, Tadeusz
Madey, Bogusław
Maklakiewicz, Jan Adam
Maksymiuk, Jerzy
Malawski, Artur
Maliszewski, Witold
Markowski, Andrzej
Maszyński, Piotr
Melcer (-Szczawiński), Henryk
Meyer, Krzysztof
Mielczewski, Marcin
Mikuli, Karl (Karol)
Mirecki, Franz (actually, Franciszek Wincenty)
Mlynarski, Emil (Simon)
Moniuszko, Stanislaw
Morawski-Dąbrowa, Eugeniusz
Moss, Piotr
Moszumańska-Nazar, Krystyna
Mycielski, Zygmunt
Mykietyn, Paweł
Natanson, Tadeusz
Nidecki, Tomasz Napoleon
Noskowski, Zygmunt
Nowakowski, Józef
Nowowiejski, Felix
Ochman, Wieslaw
Oginski, Prince Michal Kleofas
Opieński, Henryk
Orlowski, Antoni
Paciorkiewicz, Tadeusz
Paderewski, Ignacy (Jan)
Padlewski, Roman
Palester, Roman
Pankiewicz, Eugeniusz
Pekiel, Bartlomiej
Penderecki, Krzysztof
Penherski, Zbigniew
Perkowski, Piotr
Poniatowski, Józef (Michal Xsawery Franciszek Jan), Prince of Monte Rotondo
Poradowski, Stefan (Boleslaw)
Przybylski, Bronislaw Kazimierz
Ptaszyńska, Marta
Radziwill, Prince Anton Heinrich (Antoni Henryk)
Radziwill, Prince Maciej
Raisa, Rosa (real name, Raisa or Rose Burschstein)
Reiss, Józef (Wladyslaw)
Rogowski, Ludomir (Michal)
Roguski, Gustav
Rowicki, Witold
Rózycki, Ludomir
Rudziski, Witold
Rudziski, Zbigniew
Rutkowski, Bronislaw
Rychlik, Józef
Rytel, Piotr
Sari, Ada (real name, Jadwiga Szajerowa)
Schaeffer, Boguslaw (Julien)
Schulz-Evler, Andrei
Semkow, Jerzy
Serocki, Kazimierz
Sikorski, Kazimierz
Sikorski, Tomasz
Smendzianka, Regina
Soltys, Adam
Soltys, Mieczyslaw
Sowinski, Wojciech (Albert)
Spisak, Michal
Stachowski, Marek
Statkowski, Roman
Stefani, Jan
Stefani, Józef
Stolpe, Antoni
Stückgold, Jacques
Surzycński, Józef
Synowiec, Ewa (Krystyna)
Szabelski, Boleslaw
Szalonek, Witold (Jósef)
Szamotul, Waclaw z
Szeligowski, Tadeusz
Sztompka, Henryk
Szulc, Józef Zygmunt
Szweykowski, Zygmunt M(arian)
Szymanowska, Maria Agate (née Wolowska)
Szymanowski, Karol (Maciej)
Szymánski, Paweł
Tausig, Carl (actually, Karol)
Tchaikowsky, André
Toczyska, Stefania
Turski, Zbigniew
Twardowski, Romuald
Urbaniak, Michal
Walaciński, Adam
Wallek-Walewski, Boleslaw
Wiechowicz, Stanislaw
Wieniawski, Adam Tadeusz
Wieniawski, Henryk (also known as Henri)
Wieniawski, Jozef
Wierzbillowicz, Alexander
Wilkomirski Family
 Wilkomirski, Alfred
 Wilkomirski, Kazimierz
 Wilkomirski, Maria
 Wilkomirski, Józef
 Wilkomirski, Wanda
Wislocki, Stanislaw
Wiszniewski, Zbigniew
Wit, Antoni
Wolff, Edouard
Woytowicz, Boleslaw
Zarębski (Zarembski), Juliusz
Zarzycki, Alexander
Zelenski, Wladislaw
Zimerman, Krystian
Zylis-Gara, Teresa

POLISH-AMERICAN

Adamowski, Joseph (actually, Josef)
Adamowski, Timothée
Dushkin, Samuel
Kiepura, Jan
Kronold, Hans
Kronold, Selma
Lévy, Heniot
Maciejewski, Roman
Munz, Mieczyslaw
Rudnytsky, Antin
Sembrich, Marcella (real name, Prakseda Marcelina Kochańska)
Steuermann, Edward (actually, Eduard)
Szumowska, Antoinette

POLISH-ENGLISH

Poldowski (pen name of Irene Regine Wieniawska; by marriage, Lady Dean Paul)

POLISH-GERMAN

Scharwenka, (Franz) Xaver
Scharwenka, (Ludwig) Philipp

POLISH-SWISS

Bronarski, Ludwik (Ryszard Marian)

PORTUGUESE

Alcaide, Tomáz (de Aquino Carmelo)
Almeida, Fernando d'
Almeida, Francisco António de
d'Andrade, Francesco
d'Arneiro, (José Augusto) Ferreira Veiga
Arroyo, João Marcellino
Avondano, Pedro Antonio
Baldi, João José
Bomtempo, João Domingos
Cardoso, Manuel
Carvalho, João de Sousa
Cassuto, Álvaro (Leon)
Coelho, Rui
Dimas de Melo Pimenta, Emanuel
Fernándes, Armando José
Freitas (Branco), Frederico (Guedes) de
Freitas Branco, Luís de
Holý, Alfred
João IV
Keil, Alfredo
Lacerda, Francisco (Inácio da Silveira de Sousa Pereira Forjaz) de
Leça, Armando Lopes
Lésbio, António Marques

PRUSSIAN

PUERTO RICAN

ROMAN

ROMANIAN

ROMANIAN-AMERICAN

ROMANIAN-FRENCH

RUSSIAN

Blaramberg, Pavel (Ivanovich)
Blumenfeld, Felix (Mikhailovich)
Bolshakov, Nikolai
Borodin, Alexander (Porfirievich)
Borodina, Olga (Vladimirovna)
Bortkiewicz, Sergei (Eduardovich)
Bortniansky, Dimitri (Stepanovich)
Brandukov, Anatol (Andreievich)
Brodsky, Adolf
Bronskaya, Evgenya (Adolfovna)
Brusilovsky, Evgeni (Grigorievich)
Bunin, Revol
Burchuladze, Paata
Chaliapin, Feodor (Ivanovich)
Chernov, Vladimir
Conus, Georgi (Eduardovich)
Conus, Julius
Cooper, Emil (Albertovich)
Cui, César (Antonovich)
Dargomyzhsky, Alexander (Sergeievich)
Davidenko, Alexander
Davidov, Carl
Davidov, Stepan Ivanovich
Demidenko, Nikolai
Denisov, Edison
Derzhinskaya, Xenia (Georgievna)
Diaghilev, Sergei (Pavlovich)
Dobrowen, Issay (Alexandrovich) (real name, Ishok Israelevich Barabeichik)
Dokshitcher, Timofei
Dolukhanova, Zara
Dranishnikov, Vladimir
Dubuque, Alexander
Dudarova, Veronika
Dzegelenok, Alexander (Mikhailovich)
Dzerzhinsky, Ivan (Ivanovich)
Edelmann, Sergei
Egorov, Youri
El-tour, Anna
Engel, Joel
Ermler, Mark
Ershov, Ivan (Vasilievich)
Eshpai, Andrei (Yakovlevich)
Eshpai, Yakov
Essipoff (Essipova), Anna
Evseyev, Sergei
Falik, Yuri
Famintsyn, Alexander (Sergeievich)
Fayer, Yuri
Fedoseyev, Vladimir (Ivanovich)
Feinberg, Samuel
Feltsman, Vladimir
Fere, Vladimir
Figner, Nikolai (Nikolaievich)
Findeisen, Nikolai (Fyodorovich)
Firsova, Elena (Olegovna)
Flier, Yakov (Vladimirovich)
Fomin, Evstignei
Fried, Oskar
Gaigerova, Varvara
Ganelin, Viacheslav
Gauk, Alexander
Gavrilov, Andrei
Gergiev, Valery (Abissalovich)
Gilels, Elizabeta
Gilels, Emil (Grigorievich)
Ginsburg, Lev (Solomonovich)
Glazunov, Alexander (Konstantinovich)
Glière, Reinhold (Moritsovich)
Glinka, Mikhail (Ivanovich)
Gnessin, Mikhail (Fabianovich)
Goedike, Alexander
Goldenweiser, Alexander (Borisovich)
Goldstein, Mikhail
Golitzin, Nikolai (Borisovich)
Golitzin, Yuri (Nikolaievich)
Golovanov, Nikolai (Semyonovich)
Golubev, Evgeny
Golyscheff, Jefim
Gorchakov (real name, Zweifel), Sergei
Gorchakova, Galina
Gordeli, Otar
Gubaidulina, Sofia (Asgatovna)
Gulak-Artemovsky, Semyon Stepanovich
Guleghina, Maria
Gussakovsky, Apollon
Gutman, Natalia
Hambourg Family
Hambourg, Michael (Mikhail)
Hambourg, Mark
Hambourg, Jan
Hambourg, Boris
Hartmann, Thomas (Alexandrovich de)
Hubert, Nikolai
Hvorostovsky, Dmitri
Igumnov, Konstantin (Nikolaievich)
Ilyinsky, Alexander Alexandrovich
Iokeles, Alexander
Ippolitov-Ivanov (real name, Ivanov), Mikhail (Mikhailovich)
Isserlis, Julius
Ivanov, Konstantin
Ivanov, Mikhail Mikhailovich
Ivanov, Nikolai (Kuzmich)
Ivanov-Boretzky, Mikhail Vladimirovich
Ivanov-Radkevitch, Nikolai
Jaroff, Sergei
Juon, Paul (actually, Pavel Fedorovich)
Jurgenson, Pyotr (Ivanovich)
Kabalevsky, Dmitri (Borisovich)
Kagan, Oleg
Kalafati, Vasili (Pavlovich)
Kalinnikov, Vasili (Sergeievich)
Kamensky, Alexander
Kamionsky, Oscar (Isaievich)
Karatygin, Viacheslav (Gavrilovich)
Karayev, Kara (Abulfazogli)
Karetnikov, Nikolai
Kartsev, Alexander
Kashin, Daniil Nikitich
Kashkin, Nikolai Dmitrievich
Kashperov, Vladimir (Nikitich)
Kasianov, Alexander
Kastalsky, Alexander (Dmitrievich)
Kastorsky, Vladimir (Ivanovich)
Katulskaya, Elena
Kazarnovskaya, Ljuba
Keldysh, Yuri (Vsevolodovich)
Keneman, Feodor
Khachaturian, Aram (Ilich)
Khachaturian, Karen (Surenovich)
Khaikin, Boris (Emmanuilovich)
Khandoshkin, Ivan (Yevstafievich)
Kharitonov, Dimitri
Khessin, Alexander (Borisovich)
Khodzha-Einatov, Leon
Khokhlov, Pavel (Akinfievich)
Khrennikov, Tikhon (Nikolaievich)
Kiladze, Grigori
Kissin, Evgeny (Igorevich)
Kitaenko, Dmitri
Klementyev, Lev (Mikhailovich)
Klenovsky, Nikolai (Semyonovich)
Klimov, Valery (Alexandrovich)
Knaifel, Alexander (Aronovich)
Knipper, Lev (Konstantinovich)
Knushevitsky, Sviatoslav (Nikolaievich)
Kogan, Leonid (Borisovich)
Kogan, Pavel
Kondrashin, Kirill (Petrovich)
Kopylov, Alexander (Alexandrovich)
Korchmarev, Klimenti (Arkadievich)
Korndorf, Nikolai
Kotek, (Eduard) Joseph (actually, Yosif Yosifovich)
Koval, Marian (Viktorovich)
Kovalev, Pavel
Kozlovsky, Ivan (Semyonovich)
Kozolupov, Semyon Matveievich
Krainev, Vladimir (Vsevolodovich)
Krein, Alexander (Abramovich)
Krein, Grigori (Abramovich)
Krein, Julian (Grigorievich)
Kreizberg, Yakov
Kremlev, Yuli (Anatolyevich)
Krushelnitskaya, Salomea (Ambrosivna)
Kuznetsova, Maria (Nikolaievna)
Kvernadze, Bidzina (actually, Alexander Alexandrovich)
Labinsky, Andrei (Markovich)
Laskovsky, Ivan Fyodorovich
Lavrovskaya, Elizaveta Andreievna
Lazarev, Alexander
Ledenev, Roman (Semyonovich)
Leiferkus, Sergei (Petrovich)
Lemeshev, Sergei (Yakovlevich)
Lenz, Wilhelm von
Leonova, Darya (Mikhailovna)
Lhévinne, Josef
Lhévinne, Rosina (née Bessie)
Liadov, Anatoli (Konstantinovich)
Liadov, Konstantin (Nikolaievich)
Liapunov, Sergei (Mikhailovich)
Lipkovska, Lydia (Yakovlevna)
Listov, Konstantin
Litinsky, Genrik
Litvinenko-Wohlgemut, Maria (Ivanova)
Litvinne, Félia (real name, Françoise-JeanneSchütz)
Lobanov, Vassily
Lokshin, Alexander
Lomakin, Gavriil Yakimovich
Lubimov, Alexei
Lubotsky, Mark (Davidovich)
Lvov, Alexei Feodorovich
Machavariani, Alexei (Davidovich)
Maizel, Boris
Makarova, Nina
Maruzin, Yuri
Masurok, Yuri (Antonovich)
Maxakova, Mariya (Petrovna)

RUSSIAN-AMERICAN

Dubensky, Arcady
Gabrilowitsch, Ossip (Salomonovich)
Gardner, Samuel
Goldovsky, Boris
Gordon, Jacques
Kelberine, Alexander
Koshetz, Nina (Pavlovna)
Kouguell, Arkadie
Koutzen, Boris
Lev, Ray
Luboshutz (real name, Luboshitz), Pierre
Malkin, Jacques
Malkin, Joseph
Malkin, Manfred
Parris, Herman
Pleshakov, Vladimir
Reisenberg, Nadia
Rosing, Vladimir
Saminsky, Lazare
Spivakovsky, Tossy
Sternberg, Constantin
Stravinsky, (Sviatoslav) Soulima
Toradze, Alexander (David)
Weiner, Lazar
Yasser, Joseph

RUSSIAN-ARGENTINE
Ficher, Jacobo

RUSSIAN-FRENCH
Schloezer, Boris de
Scriabine, Marina

RUSSIAN-POLISH
Szeluto, Apolinary

SCOTTISH
Abell, John
Baillie, Dame Isobel (Isabella)
Blackhall, Andrew
Buchanan, Isobel
Carver, Robert
Chisholm, Erik
Dalby, (John) Martin
Dickie, Murray
Dillon, James
Donegan, Lonnie (actually, Anthony James)
Donovan (Leitch)
Drysdale, (George John) Learmont
Easton, Sheena (originally, Orr, S. Shirley)
Finnie, Linda
Garden, Mary
Gibson, Sir Alexander (Drummond)
Glen, John
Glennie, Evelyn (Elizabeth Ann)
Gow, Nathaniel
Gow, Niel
Gray, Cecil
Gray, Linda Esther
Gunn, John
Hamilton, Iain (Ellis)
Henderson, Roy (Galbraith)
Hislop, Joseph
Hogarth, George
Johnson, Robert
Kennedy-Fraser, Marjorie (née Kennedy)
Kraemer, (Thomas Wilhelm) Nicholas
Lamond, Frederic(k Archibald)
Lockhart, James (Lawrence)
Loughran, James
MacCunn, Hamish (James)
Mackenzie, Sir Alexander (Campbell)
MacMillan, James
Marshall, Margaret (Anne)
Mathieson, Muir
Maxwell, Donald
McEwen, Sir John (Blackwood)
McGibbon, William
McKellar, Kenneth
McLaughlin, Marie
Musgrave, Thea
Orr, Robin (actually, Robert Kemsley)
Oswald, James
Parepa-Rosa, Euphrosyne (née Parepa de Boyescu)
Patey, Janet (Monach née Whytock)
Paton, Mary Ann
Peebles, David
Reid, (real name, Robertson), General John
Robertson, Rae
Robertson, Stewart (John)
Robson, Christopher
Runnicles, Donald
Scott, Francis George
Stewart, Reginald (Drysdale)
Templeton, John
Thomson, Bryden
Thomson, George
Thomson, John
Thorpe Davie, Cedric
Tyson, Alan (Walker)
Wallace, John
Wallace, William
Ward, David
Warrack, Guy (Douglas Hamilton)
Webster, Sir David (Lumsden)
Weir, Judith
Whyte, Ian

SCOTTISH-AMERICAN
Arbuckle, Matthew
Friskin, James
Gange, Fraser

SERBIAN
Binički, Stanislav
Danon, Oskar
Erić, Zoran
Gostuški, Dragutin
Hristič, Stevan
Ilitsch, Daniza
Josif, Enriko
Konjović, Petar
Kostić, Vojislav
Krstič, Petar
Maksimović, Rajko
Manojlović, Kosta
Marić, Ljubica
Marinkoví, Josef
Milojević, Miloje
Mokranjac, Stevan (Stojanović)
Mokranjac, Vasilije
Nastasijević, Svetomir
Paunović, Milenko
Peričić, Vlastimir
Radíc, Dušan
Radovanovic, Vladan
Rajičič, Stanojlo
Ristić, Milan
Rupnik, Ivan
Tajčević, Marko
Trifunović, Vitomir
Vučković, Vojislav
Vukdragović, Mihailo
Živković, Milenko

SERBIAN-AMERICAN
Velimirović, Miloš

SILESIAN
Gregor, Christian Friedrich
Janitsch, Johann Gottlieb
Lincke, Joseph

SINGAPOREAN
Tan, Melvyn

SINGAPOREAN-AMERICAN
Tan, Margaret Leng

SLOVAK
Albrecht, Alexander
Andrašovan, Tibor
Bázlik, Miro
Bella, Johann Leopold (Ján Levoslav)
Berger, Roman
Burlas, Ladislav
Cikker, Jan
Domanský, Hanuš
Elschek, Oskár
Ferenczy, Oto
Figuš-Bystrý, Viliam
Frešo, Tibor
Grešák, Jozef
Hatrík, Juraj
Holoubek, Ladislav
Hrušovský, Ivan
Jurovský, Šimon
Kafenda, Frico
Kardoš, Dezider
Klega, Miroslav
Kořínek, Miloslav
Kowalski, Július
Kresánek, Jozef
Kupkovič, Ladislav
Macák, Ivan
Malovec, Jozef
Moyzes, Alexander
Moyzes, Mikuláš
Novák, Milan
Očenáš, Andrej
Parík, Ivan
Pospíšil, Juraj
Rajter, L'udovít
Salva, Tadeáš
Schneider-Trnavský, Mikuláš
Sixta, Jozef
Slovák, Ladislav
Suchoň, Eugen
Zeljenka, Ilja
Zimmer, Ján

Los Angeles (real name, Gómez Cima), Victoria de
Malibran, María (Felicità née García)
Manrique de Lara (y Berry), Manuel
Marco, Tomás
Marqués y García, Pedro Miguel
Martín y Soler, (Atanasio Martín Ignacio) Vicente (Tadeo Francisco Pellegrin)
Mayer-Serra, Otto
Mestres-Quadreny, Josep (Maria)
Milán, Luis de
Misón, Luis
Mitjana y Gordón, Rafael
Mompou (Semblança), Federico
Monasterio, Jesús de
Montsalvatge, (Bassols) Xavier
Morales, Cristóbal de
Morera, Enrique (Enric)
Mudarra, Alonso de
Narváez, Luis de
Navarro, (Luis Antonio) García
Navas, Juan (Francisco) de
Nebra (Blasco), José (Melchor de)
Oncina, Juan
Orozco, Rafael
Ortiz, Diego
Oudrid (y Segura), Cristóbal
Oxinaga, Joaquin de
Pablo (Costales), Luís (Alfonso) de
Padilla, Lola Artôt de
Padilla y Ramos, Mariano
Palau Boix, Manuel
Palomino, José
Pareto, Graziella (actually, Graciela)
Pastrana, Pedro de
Patiño, Carlos
Pedrell, Felipe
Peñalosa, Francisco de
Pérez Martínez, Vicente
Pisador, Diego
Pittaluga, Gustavo
Pons, José
Pons, Juan
Pontac, Diego de
Pradas Gallen, José
Puig, Bernardo Calvo
Queralt, Francisco
Querol (Gavaldá), Miguel
Ramos de Pareia, Bartolomé
Raval, Sebastián
Ribera (y Tarragó), Julián
Ripa (y Blanque), Antonio
Robles, Marisa
Rodrigo, Joaquín
Rodrígues de Ledesma, Mariano
Rodriguez, Felipe
Rodriguez, Vicente
Rodriguez de Hita
Rogel, Jose
Rojo Olalla, Casiano
Romero, Mateo (real name, Mathieu Rosmarin)
Ros-Marbá, Antoni
Rubio (Calzón), Samuel
Salazar, Adolfo
Saldoni, Baltasar
Salinas, Francisco de
Santa María, Fray Tomás de
Sanz, Gaspar
Sarasate (y Navascuéz), Pablo (Martín Melitón) de
Savall, Jordi
Segovia, Andrés, Marquis of Salobreia
Sopeña, (Ibáñez), Federico
Soriano, Gonzalo
Soto de Langa, Francisco
Subirá (Puig), José
Suñol (y Baulenas), Gregoria María
Supervia, Conchita
Tárrega (y Eixea), Francisco
Terradellas, Domingo (Miguel Bernabe)
Thomas (Sabater), Juan María
Usandizaga, José Maria
Valls, Francisco
Valverde, Joaquín
Vasquez (Vázquez), Juan
Venegas de Henestrosa, Luis
Victoria, Tomás Luis de
Vignas, Francisco
Vila, Pedro Alberto
Villalba Muñoz, Padre Luis
Viñes, Ricardo
Vives, Amadeo
Yepes, Narciso
Yradier (Iradier), Sebastián de
Yriarte (Iriarte), Tomás de
Zabaleta (Zala), Nicanor
Zubiaurre (y Urionabarrenechea), Valentí

SPANISH-AMERICAN

Jonás, Alberto
Orbón (de Soto), Julián
Romero Family
- Romero, Celedonio
- Romero, Celin
- Romero, Pepe
- Romero, Angel

SWABIAN

Hermannus

SWEDISH

ABBA
Agrell, Johan Joachim
Åhlström, Olof
Ahnsjö, Claes-H(åkan)
Alfvén, Hugo (Emil)
Alldahl, Per-Gunnar
Allgén, Claude Loyola (actually, Klas Thure)
Almqvist, Carl Jonas Love
Anderberg, Carl-Olof
Andrée, Elfrida
Arnoldson, Sigrid
Åstrand, (Karl) Hans (Vilhelm)
Atterberg, Kurt (Magnus)
Aulin, Tor (Bernhard Vilhelm)
Bäck, Sven-Erik
Bark, Jan (Helge Guttorm)
Barkel, Charles
Beckman, Bror
Bengtsson, Gustaf Adolf Tiburt(ius)
Bengtsson, (Lars) Ingmar (Olof)
Berg, (Carl) Natanael
Berglund, Joel (Ingemar)
Berwald, Johan Fredrik (Johann Friedrich)
Björkander, Nils (Frank Frederik)
Björling, Jussi (actually, Johan Jonatan)
Björling, Sigurd
Blomberg, Erik
Blomdahl, Karl-Birger
Blomstedt, Herbert (Thorson)
Bodin, Lars-Gunnar
Boldemann, Laci
Börtz, Daniel
Brant, Per
Branzell, Karin Maria
Brendler, (Frans Fredric) Eduard
Brilioth, Helge
Broman, Natanael
Broman, Sten
Bucht, Gunnar
Byström, Oscar (Fredrik Bernadotte)
Carlid, Göte
Carlstedt, Jan
Claussen, Julia (née Ohlson)
Deák, Csaba
Doese, Helena
Eckerberg, (Axel) Sixten (Lennart)
Edlund, Lars
Ehrling, (Evert) Sixten
Ek, (Fritz) Gunnar (Rudolf)
Eklund, Hans
Ellberg, Ernst (Henrik)
Emsheimer, Ernst
Ericson, Eric
Fernström, John (Axel)
Finnilä, Birgit
Forsell, John (actually, Carl Johan Jacob)
Frigel, Pehr
Frumerie, (Per) Gunnar (Fredrik) de
Fryklöf, Harald (Leonard)
Fryklund, (Lars Axel) Daniel
Garaguly, Carl von
Gedda (real name, Ustinov), Nicolai (Harry Gustav)
Gefors, Hans
Gentele, Goeran
Gille, Jacob Edvard
Glaser, Werner Wolf
Grahn, Ulf
Grandert, Johnny
Grevillius, Nils
Gulbranson, Ellen (née Norgren)
Hafgren, Lily (Johana Maria)
Hagegård, Håkan
Hägg, Jakob Adolf
Hägg (Peterson), Gustaf Wilhelm
Håkanson, Knut (Algot)
Hallberg, Björn Wilho
Hallén, (Johannes) Andreas
Hallnäs, (Johan) Hilding
Hallström, Ivar (Christian)
Hambraeus, Bengt
Haquinius, (Johan) Algot
Hardenberger, Håkan
Hedwall, Lennart
Heintze, Gustaf (Hjalmar)
Hemberg, (Bengt Sven) Eskil
Henneberg, (Carl) Albert (Theodor)
Hennerberg, Carl Fredrik
Hermanson, Åke (Oscar Werner)

SWEDISH-AMERICAN

SWISS

Kletzki, Paul (originally, Pawel Klecki)
Klose, Friedrich (Karl Wilhelm)
Kubelík, (Jeroným) Rafael
Kunz, Ernst
Kurth, Ernst
Lagger, Peter
Lakner, Yehoshua
Lang, Walter
Laquai, Reinhold
Lehmann, Hans Ulrich
Lévy, Ernst
Liebermann, Rolf
Linde, Hans-Martin
Looser, Rolf
Maag, (Ernst) Peter (Johannes)
Magaloff, Nikita
Marek, Czeslaw (Josef)
Mareschall, Samuel
Marescotti, André-François
Martin, Frank (Théodore)
Mathis, Edith
Matthaei, Karl
Meier, Jost
Meili, Max
Merian, Wilhelm
Mieg, Peter
Moeschinger, Albert
Mooser, (Jean Pierre Joseph) Aloys
Mooser, R(obert) Aloys
Moret, Norbert
Moser, Rudolf
Müller von Kulm, Walter
Müller-Zürich (real name, Müller), Paul
Münch, Hans
Munzinger, Karl
Nägeli, Hans Georg
Nef, Albert
Nef, Isabelle (Lander)
Nef, Karl
Nicolet, Aurele
Niedermeyer, (Abraham) Louis
Oboussier, Robert
Pahud, Emmanuel
Pestalozzi, Heinrich
Pfister, Hugo
Raff, (Joseph) Joachim
Refardt, Edgar
Regamey, Constantin
Reich, Willi
Ribaupierre, André de
Rickenbacher, Karl Anton
Roesgen-Champion, Marguerite
Rogg, Lionel
Rütti, Carl
Sacher, Paul
Schibler, Armin
Schmid, Erich
Schnyder von Wartensee, (Franz) Xaver
Schoeck, Othmar
Schuh, Willi
Schulthess, Walter
Senfl, Ludwig
Senn, Kurt Wolfgang
Snetzler (Schnetzler), Johann
Solothurnmann, Juerg
Stader (originally, Molnár), Maria
Staempfli, Edward
Stenzl, Jürg (Thomas)
Stoutz, Edmond de
Stuntz, Joseph Hartmann
Sturzenegger, (Hans) Richard
Suter, Hermann
Suter, Robert
Sutermeister, Heinrich
Tabachnik, Michel
Tappy, Eric
Thalberg, Sigismond (Fortuné François)
Tischhauser, Franz
Varviso, Silvio
Vásáry, Tamás
Veress, Sándor
Vogel, Wladimir (Rudolfovich)
Vogler, Carl
Vollenweider, Andreas
Vuataz, Roger
Weber, Margrit
Wenzinger, August
Wildberger, Jacques
Wyttenbach, Jürg
Zbinden, Julien-François
Zehnder, Max
Zelenka, István
Zwyssig, Alberich (actually Joseph)

SWISS-AMERICAN
Bloch, Suzanne
Bonvin, Ludwig
Ganz, Rudolph
Levy (originally, Lévy), Frank

SWISS-FRENCH
Noverre, Jean-Georges

TADZHIK
Balasanian, Sergei

TRINIDADIAN
Scott, Hazel (Dorothy)

TURKISH
Akses, Necil Kâzim
Alnar, Hasan Ferid
Biret, Idil
Erkin, Ulvi Cemal
Gencer, Leyla
Ilerici, Kemal
Kodalli, Nevit
Mimaroglu, Ilhan Kemaleddin
Rey, Cemal Reshid
Saygun, Ahmed Adnan
Usmanbaş, Ilhan

TURKISH-SPANISH
Pekinel, Güher and Süher

UKRAINIAN
Arkas, Nikolai (Nikolaievich)
Dankevich, Konstantin
Degtiarev, Stepan (Anikievich)
Grabovsky, Leonid
Kalachevsky, Mikhail
Klebanov, Dmitri
Kolessa, Filaret (Mikhailovich)
Leontovich, Mikola (Dmitrovich)
Liatoshinsky, Boris (Nikolaievich)
Lissenko, Nikolai (Vitalievich)
Maiboroda, Georgi
Maisenberg, Oleg
Meitus, Yuli (Sergievich)
Patorzhinsky, Ivan (Sergeievich)
Revutsky, Lev(ko Mikolaievich)
Shamo, Igor
Shtogarenko, Andrei (Yakovlevich)
Simovich, Roman
Taranov, Gleb (Pavlovich)
Verikovsky, Mikhail (Ivanovich)
Zhukovsky, Herman

URUGUAYAN
Ascone, Vicente
Ben-Dor, Gisèle (née Buka)
Broqua, Alfonso
Estrada, Carlos
Fabini, (Felix) Eduardo
Francesch, Homero
Iturriberry, Juan José
Pedrell, Carlos
Soriano, Alberto

URUGUAYAN-AMERICAN
Serebrier, José

VENEZUELAN
Aretz (de Ramón y Rivera), Isabel
Carreño, (Maria) Teresa
Estévez, Antonio
Lauro, Antonio
Lecuna, Juan Vicente
Ramón y Rivera, Luis Felipe
Sojo, Vicente Emilio

VIETNAMESE
Dang Thai Son (actually, Son Thai Dang)
Trån, Van Khê

WALLOON
Pietkin, Lambert

WELSH
Bevin, Elway
Burrowes, Norma (Elizabeth)
Burrows, (James) Stuart
Davies, Arthur
Davies, Ben(jamin) Grey
Davies, Ryland
Davies, Sir (Henry) Walford
Davies, Tudor
Ellis, Osian (Gwynn)
Evans, David (Emlyn)
Evans, Sir Geraint (Llewellyn)
Ffrangcon-Davies, David (Thomas) (real name, David Thomas Davis)
Field, Helen
Glynne, Howell
Greenaway, Peter
Guest, George (Hywel)
Harrhy, Eiddwen (Mair)
Hoddinott, Alun
Howell, Gwynne (Richard)
Hughes, Arwel
Hughes, Owain Arwel
Jenkins, David
Joll, Philip
Jones, Dame Gwyneth
Jones, Daniel (Jenkyn)
Jones, Della

WELSH-AMERICAN

WEST INDIAN

YUGOSLAV

YUGOSLAV-AMERICAN

Women Composers and Musicians
INDEX

Beach, Mrs. H.H.A. (née Amy Marcy Cheney)
Beardslee, Bethany
Beecroft, Norma (Marian)
Beglarian, Eve
Behrens, Hildegard
Bellincioni, Gemma (Cesira Matilda)
Belloc-Giorgi, Teresa (née Maria Teresa Ottavia Faustina Trombetta)
Bembo, Antonia
Benary, Barbara
Ben-Dor, Gisèle (née Buka)
Benson, Joan
Bent, Margaret (Hilda)
Benton, Rita
Benzell, Mimi
Berberian, Cathy (actually, Catherine)
Berganza (Vargas), Teresa
Berger, Erna
Berghaus, Ruth
Bernasconi, Antonia
Bertin, Louise (-Angélique)
Bertinotti (-Radicati), Teresa
Bertolli, Francesca
Bertrand, Aline
Besanzoni, Gabriella
Beyer, Johanna Magdalena
Bianchi, Valentina
Bible, Frances
Bigot (de Morogues), Marie (née Kiéné)
Billington, Elizabeth (née Weichsel)
Biret, Idil
Birnie, Tessa (Daphne)
Bishop, Anna (née Ann Riviere)
Bjoner, Ingrid
Blackburn, Bonnie J.
Blackman, Cindy
Blahetka, Marie Léopoldine
Blauvelt, Lillian Evans
Blegen, Judith
Bloch, Suzanne
Bloom, Jane Ira
Blumental, Felicja
Boatwright, Helen (née Strassburger)
Bofill, Angela
Bok, Mary Louise Curtis
Bokor, Margit
Bond, Victoria
Bonds, Margaret (Allison)
Boninsegna, Celestina
Bonney, Barbara
Borca, Karen
Borgatti, Renata
Borghi, Adelaide
Bori, Lucrezia (real name, Lucrecia Borja y Gonzalez de Riancho)
Borkh, Inge (real name, Ingeborg Simon)
Borodina, Olga (Vladimirovna)
Boronat, Olimpia
Borroff, Edith
Bosmans, Henriëtte (Hilda)
Boswell, Connee (actually, Constance Foore)
Boswell Sisters, The
Boulanger, Lili (Juliette Marie Olga)
Boulanger, Nadia (Juliette)
Bovy, Vina (real name, Malvina Johanna Pauline Félicité Bovi van Overberghe)
Boyd, Anne (Elizabeth)
Brackeen, JoAnne (née Grogan)
Bradley, Gwendolyn
Brambilla, Marietta
Brambilla, Teresa
Branchu, Alexandrine Caroline (née Chevalier de Lavit)
Brandt, Marianne (real name, Marie Bischoff)
Brandy, (actually, Norwood Brandy)
Branzell, Karin Maria
Braslau, Sophie
Braun Family
  Braun, Maria Louise
Brelet, Gisèle (Jeanne Marie Noémie)
Brema, Marie (real name, Minny Fehrmann)
Brent, Charlotte
Bressler-Gianoli, Clotilde
Bréval, Lucienne (real name, Berthe Agnes Lisette Schilling)
Brewer, Teresa (originally Theresa Breuer)
Brice, Carol (Lovette Hawkins)
Brico, Antonia
Britain, Radie
Brogue, Roslyn
Bronsart (von Schellendorf), Ingeborg (née Starck)
Bronskaya, Evgenya (Adolfovna)
Brooks, Patricia
Brouwenstijn, Gré (actually, Gerarda Demphina Van Swol)
Brouwer, Margaret
Brown, Cleo(patra)
Brown, Iona
Brown, Ruth (née Alston Weston)
Bruzdowicz, Joanna
Bryant, Clora
Bryn-Julson, Phyllis (Mae)
Bryson, Jeanie
Buchanan, Isobel
Buczek, Barbara
Bumbry, Grace (Melzia Ann)
Bunnett, Jane
Burganger, Judith
Burgess, Sally
Burrowes, Norma (Elizabeth)
Burzio, Eugenia
Bush, Kate (Catherine)
Bussani, Dorothea
Butt, Dame Clara (Ellen)
Caballé, Montserrat
Cabel, Marie (-Josèphe)
Caccini, Francesca (nicknamed "La Cecchina")
Caduff, Sylvia
Cahill, Teresa (Mary)
Cain, Jackie (actually, Jacqueline Ruth)
Caldwell, Sarah
Callas, Maria (real name, Maria Anna Sofia Cecilia Kalogeropoulos)
Calloway, Blanche
Calvé (real name, Calvet de Roquer), (Rosa-Noémie) Emma
Camporese, Violante
Candeille, (Amélie) Julie
Caniglia, Maria
Cantelo, April (Rosemary)
Capers, Valerie
Caradori-Allan, Maria (Caterina Rosalbina née de Munck)
Carelli, Emma
Carena, Maria
Carey, Mariah
Carlisle, Una Mae
Carlson, Claudine
Carmichael, Judy
Carmirelli, Pina (actually, Giuseppina)
Carnes, Kim
Caron, Rose (Lucille) (née Meuniez)
Carreño, (Maria) Teresa
Carrington, Terri Lyne
Carroll, Barbara (actually, Coppersmith, Barbara Carole)
Carter, Betty (originally, Jones, Lillie Mae; aka Lorene Carter and "Bette Bebop")
Carvalho, Caroline (née Caroline-Marie Félix-Miolan)
Cary, Annie Louise
Casadesus, Gaby (née Gabrielle L'Hôte)
Cash, Rosanne
Castagna, Bruna
Catalani, Angelica
Cavalieri, Catarina (real name, Franziska Cavalier)
Cavalieri, Lina (actually, Natalina)
Cavallo, Enrica
Cebotari (real name, Cebutaru), Maria
Cerquetti, Anita
Chaminade, Cécile (Louise Stéphanie)
Chang, Sarah
Charton-Demeur, Anne
Chen Yi
Cher (originally, Sarkisian, Cherilyn)
Chiara, Maria(-Rita)
Chin, Unsuk
Chookasian, Lili
Chung, Kyung-Wha
Chung, Myung-Wha
Cibber, Susanne Maria
Ciesinski, Katherine
Ciesinski, Kristine
Cigna, Gina (real name, Ginetta Sens)
Clarey, Cynthia
Clark, Petula (originally, Owen, Sally)
Clarke, Rebecca (Thacher)
Claussen, Julia (née Ohlson)
Clercx, Suzanne
Cline, Patsy (originally, Hensley, Virginia Patterson)
Clive, Kitty (actually, Catherine née Raftor)
Clooney, Rosemary
Coates, Edith (Mary)
Coates, Gloria
Cobelli, Giuseppina
Coertse, Mimi
Cohen, Harriet
Colbran, Isabella (Isabel Angela)
Cole, Natalie
Cole, Paula
Collier, Marie
Collins, Judy

Foerstrová-Lautererová, Berta
Folville, Eugénie-Émilie Juliette
Fontyn, Jacqueline
Fornia-Labey, Rita (née Regina Newman)
Forrester, Maureen (Kathleen Stewart)
Fortunato, D'Anna
Fowler, Jennifer
Francis, Connie (actually, Concetta Franconero)
Frank, Pamela
Franklin, Aretha
Franks, Rebecca Coupe
Freelon, Nnenna
Freeman, Betty (née Wishnick)
Freer, Eleanor (née Everest)
Frege, Livia (née Gerhard)
Fremstad, Olive
Freni (real name, Fregni), Mirella
Freund, Marya
Frezzolini, Erminia
Fricci (real name, Frietsche), Antonietta
Friderici-Jakowicka, Teodozja
Fried, Miriam
Frijsh, Povla (real name, Paula Frisch)
Fuchs, Lillian
Fuchs, Marta
Fujiie, Keiko
Fujikawa, Mayumi
Fürsch-Madi(er), Emma or Emmy
Gabriel, Mary Ann Virginia
Gabrielli, Caterina
Gadski, Johanna (Emilia Agnes)
Gaigerova, Varvara
Galajikian, Florence Grandland
Galas, Diamanda (Dimitria Angeliki Elena)
Gall (real name, Galle), Yvonne
Galli, Caterina
Galli-Curci, Amelita
Galli-Marié, Célestine (Laurence née Marié de l'Isle)
Gallmeyer, Josefine, (real name, Josefina Tomaselli)
Garbousova, Raya
García, Eugénie
Garden, Mary
Garland, Judy (originally, Frances Ethel Gumm)
Garrett, Lesley
Garrison, Lucy McKim
Garrison, Mabel
Gasdia, Cecilia
Gauthier, (Ida Joséphine Phoebe) Eva
Gay, Maria (née Pitchot)
Gayer (Ashkenasi), Catherine
Geistinger, Marie (Maria Charlotte Cäcilia)
Gencer, Leyla
Gerhardt, Elena
Gerson-Kiwi, (Esther) Edith
Gerster, Etelka
Gerstman, Blanche
Gerville-Réache, Jeanne
Geszty (real name, Witkowsky), Sylvia
Geyer, Stefi
Gheorghiu, Angela
Giannini, Dusolina
Gibbs, Georgia (originally, Fredda Gibbons)
Gibson, Debbie
Gideon, Miriam
Giebel, Agnes
Gifford, Helen (Margaret)
Gilbert, Pia
Gilberto, Astrud
Gilels, Elizabeta
Gipps, Ruth (Dorothy Louisa)
Giteck, Janice
Glanville-Hicks, Peggy
Glaz, Herta
Glenn, Carroll
Glennie, Evelyn (Elizabeth Ann)
Glover, Jane (Alison)
Glover, Sarah Anna
Gluck, Alma (née Reba Fiersohn)
Glyn, Margaret H(enrietta)
Goddard, Arabella
Go Gos, The
Goltz, Christel
Gomez, Jill
Gondek, Juliana (Kathleen)
Goodson, Katharine
Goossens Family
  Goossens, Marie (Henriette)
  Goossens, Sidonie
Gorchakova, Galina
Gorr, Rita (real name, Marguerite Geirnaert)
Gosfield, Annie (actually, Anne)
Gottlieb, (Maria) Anna
Graham, Susan
Grandi, Margherita (née Margaret Garde)
Grandval, Marie Félicie Clémence de Reiset
Grant, Amy
Grassini, Giuseppina (Maria Camilla)
Graupner, Catherine Comerford
Gray, Anne
Gray, Linda Esther
Green, Elizabeth A(dine) H(erkimer)
Greenawald, Sheri (Kay)
Greenfield, Elizabeth Taylor
Grey, Madeleine, (real name, Madeleine Nathalie Grumberg)
Griebling, Karen (Jean)
Grieg, Nina (née Hagerup)
Grimaud, Hélène
Grisi, Giuditta
Grisi, Giulia
Grist, Reri
Grob-Prandl, Gertrud
Gruberová, Edita
Gruhn (originally, Grunebaum), Nora
Grümmer, Elisabeth
Grünbaum (originally, Müller), Therese
Gubaidulina, Sofia (Asgatovna)
Gubrud, Irene (Ann)
Gueden, Hilde
Gulbranson, Ellen (née Norgren)
Guleghina, Maria
Günther, Mizzi
Gustafson, Nancy
Gutheil-Schoder, Marie
Gutman, Natalia
Haas, Monique
Haebler, Ingrid
Haendel, Ida
Hafgren, Lily (Johana Maria)
Hall, Marie (actually, Mary Paulina)
Hall, Pauline (Margarete)
Hamari, Julia
Hammond, Dame Joan (Hood)
Hanfstängel, Marie (née Schröder)
Hanuszewska-Schaeffer, Mieczyslawa Janina
d'Harcourt, Marguerite (née Béclard)
d'Hardelot, Guy (actually, Mrs. W.I. Rhodes, née Helen Guy)
Harich-Schneider, Eta (Margarete)
Harnoy, Ofra
Harper, Heather (Mary)
Harrhy, Eiddwen (Mair)
Harries, Kathryn
Harris, Emmylou
Harrison, Beatrice
Harrison, May
Harsanyi, Janice (née Morris)
Harshaw, Margaret
Harwood, Elizabeth (Jean)
Häser, Charlotte (Henriette)
Haskil, Clara
Hass, Sabine
Hasse, Faustina (née Bordoni)
Hauk, Minnie (real name, Amalia Mignon Hauck)
Hayasaka, Sachi
Hayes, Catherine
Haymon, Cynthia
Hays, Sorrel (actually, Doris Ernestine)
Heckscher, Céleste de Longpré (née Massey)
Heinefetter Family
  Heinefetter, Sabine
  Heinefetter, Clara
  Heinefetter, Kathinka
Heldy, Fanny (real name, Marguerite Virginia Emma Clémentine Deceuninck)
Helm, Anny
Hempel, Frieda
Hendricks, Barbara
Henriot-Schweitzer, Nicole
Henschel, Lillian June (née Bailey)
Hensel, Fanny (Cäcilie) (née Mendelssohn-Bartholdy)
Héritte-Viardot, Louise-Pauline-Marie
Herzog, Emilie
Hess, Dame Myra
Hesse-Bukowska, Barbara
Hewitt, Helen (Margaret)
Heyman, Katherine Ruth Willoughby
Hidalgo, Elvira de
Hier, Ethel Glenn
Hildegard von Bingen
Hill, Chippie (Bertha)
Hill, Faith
Hill, Lauryn
Hillebrecht, Hildegard
Hillis, Margaret (Eleanor)
Hinderas (real name, Henderson), Natalie
Hoch, Beverly
Hodgson, Alfreda (Rose)
Höffgen, Marga

ISBN 0-02-865571-0
90000
9 780028 655710